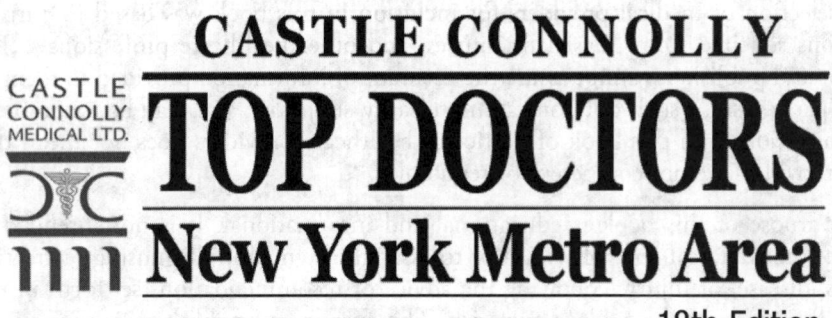

CASTLE CONNOLLY
TOP DOCTORS
New York Metro Area

18th Edition

Top Doctors Make A Difference

America's Trusted Source For
Identifying Top Doctors

For more information, please contact:

Castle Connolly Medical Ltd., 42 West 24th St, New York, New York 10010
212-367-8400x110
E-mail: info@castleconnolly.com
Web site: www.castleconnolly.com.

Library of Congress Control Number: 2014952102
ISBN   1-935036-02-5   978-1-935036-02-9   (paperback)
Printed in the United States of America

Table of Contents

Table of Contents

Table of Contents

Table of Contents

Table of Contents

Hippocratic Oath

I swear by Apollo the physician, and Asklepios, and health, and All-Heal and all the gods and goddesses, that, according to my ability and judgement, I will keep this Oath and this stipulation — to reckon him who taught me this Art equally dear to me as my parents, to share my substance with him, and relieve his necessities if required; to look upon his offspring in the same footing as my own brothers, and to teach them this Art, if they should wish to learn it, without fee or stipulation; and that by precept, lecture and every other mode of instruction, I will impart a knowledge of the Art to my own sons, and those of my teachers, and to disciples bound by a stipulation and oath according to the law of medicine, but to none others.

I will follow that system of regimen which, according to my ability and judgement, I consider for the benefit of my patients, and abstain from whatever is deleterious and mischievous. I will give no deadly medicine to anyone if asked nor suggest any such counsel; and in like manner I will not give to a woman a pessary to produce abortion. With purity and wholeness I will pass my life and practice my Art.

I will not cut persons labouring under the stone, but will leave this to be done by men who are practitioners of this work. Into whatever houses I enter, I will go into them for the benefit of the sick, and will abstain from every voluntary act of mischief and corruption; and, further, from the seduction of females or males, of freemen and slaves. Whatever, in connection with my professional practice, or not in connection with it, I see or hear, in the life of men, which ought not to be spoken of abroad, I will not divulge, as reckoning that all such should be kept secret. While I continue to keep this Oath unviolated, may it be granted to me to enjoy life and the practice of the art, respected by all men, in all times! But should I trespass and violate this Oath, may the reverse be my lot!

From Dorland's Illustrated Medical Dictionary. 27th ed. (Philadelphia) W.B. Saunders Co., 1988. Hippocratic Oath. [Hippocrates. Greek physician, 460-377 B.C.]

About the Publishers

John K. Castle, the Chairman of Castle Connolly Medical Ltd., has spent much of the last three decades involved with healthcare institutions and issues. Mr. Castle served as Chairman of the Board of New York Medical College for eleven years, an institution where he served on the Board of Trustees for twenty-two years.

Mr. Castle has been extensively involved in other healthcare and voluntary activities as well. He served for five years as a commissioner and officer of the Joint Commission formerly known as (JCAHO), the body which accredits most public and private hospitals throughout the United States. Mr. Castle has also served as a trustee of five different hospitals in the metropolitan New York region, including NewYork Presbyterian Hospital, where he continues to serve.

Mr. Castle has also served as the Chairman of the Columbia Presbyterian Science Advisory Council and as a Director of the Whitehead Institute for Biomedical Research. He is a Fellow of New York Academy of Medicine and has served as a Trustee of the Academy. He was Chairman of the United Hospital Fund of New York's Capital Campaign and continues as Director Emeritus of the United Hospital Fund. He is a Life Member of the MIT Corporation, the governing body of the Massachusetts Institute of Technology.

Mr. Castle received his bachelor's degree from the Massachusetts Institute of Technology, his MBA as a Baker Scholar with High Distinction from Harvard, and two Honorary Doctorate degrees.

Mr. Castle's goal, as is the goal of Dr. John Connolly and all the Castle Connolly team, is to publish *America's Top Doctors*, *America's Top Doctors for Cancer*, *Top Doctors: New York Metro Area*, and other materials as well as build websites to help the public identify the very best in healthcare resources.

John J. Connolly, Ed.D., - the nation's foremost expert on identifying top physicians, is the President & CEO of Castle Connolly Medical Ltd. publisher of *America's Top Doctors®* and other consumer guides to help people find the best healthcare. He is also Vice-Chairman of Castle Connolly Graduate Medical Ltd., which publishes review manuals to assist resident physicians and fellows in preparing for their board exams.

Dr. Connolly served as President of New York Medical College, the nation's second largest private medical college, for more than ten years. He is a Fellow of the New York Academy of Medicine, a Fellow of the New York Academy of Sciences, a Director of the Northeast Business Group on Health, a member of the President's Council of the United Hospital Fund, and a member of the Board of the American Swiss Foundation.

Dr. Connolly has served as trustee of two hospitals and as Chairman of the Board of one. He is extensively involved in healthcare and community activities and has served on a number of voluntary and corporate boards including the Board of the American Lyme Disease Foundation, of which he is a founder and past chairman, and the Culinary Institute of America for over 20 years where he is now Chairman Emeritus. He also served as a director and Chairman of the Professional Examination Service and is presently on the board of the American Swiss Foundation. His current corporate board service includes: Baker and Taylor; Air Methods Corporation; Dearborn Risk Management and the Advisory Board of the Hudson Group. He holds a Bachelor of Science degree from Worcester State College, a Master's degree from the University of Connecticut, and a Doctor of Education degree in College and University Administration from Teacher's College, Columbia University, honorary doctorates (LHD) from Mercy College and Worcester State University.

Over the years, Dr. Connolly has served on the boards of, and as an officer of, numerous not-for-profit organizations including: President, Sullivan County Association for Retarded Children; Director and Chairman United Way of Dutchess County; Director and Founding Chairman Dutchess County Industrial Development Agency; Director and Founder Dutchess County Economic Development Association, President, Westchester County Historical Society.

Medical Advisory Board

Castle Connolly Medical Ltd. is pleased to be associated with a distinguished group of medical leaders who offer invaluable advice and wisdom in its efforts to assist consumers in making good healthcare choices. We thank each member of the Medical Advisory Board for their valuable contributions.

Foreword

Dear Reader:

Choosing a doctor is one of the most important choices in your life. However, most of us put little effort into this selection. We simply pick a name from a list or get a recommendation from a friend.

Most of us have very little information about our doctors, and/or don't know where to get it. With the publication of this Castle Connolly Guide—Top Doctors: New York Metro Area, you can learn about doctors' medical school education, residency, training, fellowships, board certifications, hospital appointments and much more. The Guide also describes in simple terms what information you should ascertain about each doctor and how to evaluate it. This information gathering is essential for anyone who wants to find a good doctor to truly meet his or her healthcare needs.

As an administrator and nurse who deals with the problems of health on a daily basis, I know well the importance of getting the best healthcare. Our center assists medical malpractice victims. The human tragedy we often encounter is heartbreaking.

In many cases, had the patient taken a few minutes to make a modest effort to learn more about his or her doctor's background, a serious incident may have been avoided.

That is why *Top Doctors: New York Metro Area* is so important to consumers. In this new and rapidly changing healthcare environment, patients must be well informed. Many do not trust the healthcare system. They are not confident that their health plan, their hospital, or even their doctor, is motivated to protect them and to ensure that they get excellent care.

The Castle Connolly Guide is a comprehensive guide chock full of valuable information. It is completely consumer-friendly, giving readers all that they need to know to make intelligent, informed choices.

Use it well and in good health!

Sincerely,

Sandra Gainer, R.N.
Associate Director
National Center for Patient Rights

Foreword

The Best in American Medicine
www.CastleConnolly.com

Why Top Doctors Make A Difference:
A Message for Employers and Families

Most people would agree that gambling with their health is a dangerous idea. When it comes to medical care, excellence and expertise are crucially important. Yet Americans receive top-quality care from their doctors and hospitals only about half of the time. From inadequate screening during routine checkups to subpar treatment of critical illnesses, inferior care can have costly and tragic results. Too often, patients simply don't know how to find the best doctor to deliver the best care.

Castle Connolly takes this challenge seriously. Since the company's founding in 1991, our "Top Doctors" guides have been identifying the nation's best doctors and hospitals in every part of the country and in every medical specialty. Our lists are based on peer nominations and professional assessments by our physician-led research team – not on hype, advertising, or third parties that have something to gain by recommending a particular provider. Castle Connolly's Top Doctors are rigorously selected from among hundreds of thousands of physicians. Our intensive research methodology is designed to identify doctors that will speed patients' healing, minimize pain and discomfort, shorten recovery periods and enhance and lengthen lives – in other words, achieve the best possible health outcomes.

Today, such independent assessment of medical care is more important than ever. Anyone can draw up a "best of" list – and many organizations do. Pharmaceutical companies favor those physicians who are high prescribers of their drugs. To many health insurers a physician's fees are often a more important factor than quality. Many publications and websites recommend health care providers who pay to get their names mentioned. But Castle Connolly has no such conflicts of interest. Our sole purpose is to help patients, their families and their employers find health care providers who deliver superior results.

Some people believe that patient ratings are the best source of information on doctors. Unfortunately, that is a misguided assumption. Patients may be able to rate a doctor's "bedside manner," but they know little about the complexity of medical care. In fact, an article in Forbes magazine pointed out - "The current system might just kill you. Many doctors, in order to get high ratings (and a higher salary), over-prescribe and over-test, just to "satisfy" patients, who probably aren't qualified to judge their care. And there's a financial cost, as flawed survey methods and the decisions they induce, produce billions more in waste."

After a physician's name is submitted by colleagues as part of our nomination process for consideration as a Top Doctor, our physician-led research team delves into the professional records of top nominated physicians in order to ascertain those that have exceptional training, experience and are highly regarded by their peers. In addition, disciplinary histories and malpractice actions, when available, are also carefully scrutinized.

Why Top Doctors Make A Difference

Top Doctors can have an enormous impact. For patients and their families, the value of receiving first-class medical care is great but unquantifiable – it's measured in quality and even length of life. Employers, however, can see the results in their bottom line. Faulty diagnoses and improper treatment take a toll in productivity and ripple out into higher workplace costs. No company should have to make do for weeks or months without a key employee or executive, when a Top Doctor may have solved the patient's problem efficiently and simply.

Castle Connolly has dozens of examples, some dramatic and lifesaving, that demonstrate the point that finding the best doctor or hospital can make a significant difference in patients' lives. The few that follow clearly demonstrate this point.

- Kay was examined by her local physician, who advised her that lumps in her breast were very likely malignant and recommended an immediate mastectomy. Closer investigation by a Castle Connolly specialist showed that the lumps were in fact benign and Kay avoided the cost, trauma and pain of a radical mastectomy.

- June was a 92 year old woman diagnosed with rectal cancer. A local surgeon recommended an operation that would leave her incontinent or, he suggested, she would be dead in 3-6 months. Castle Connolly recommended a top doctor in one of the nation's top cancer centers. After eight chemo sessions and radiation, she is now cancer free!

- Jim was scheduled for surgery to amputate his foot. A relative contacted Castle Connolly to check out his doctor. The research team quickly identified the surgeon as one who had lost his license in one state and was disciplined in another. The surgery was rescheduled with a different surgeon.

- Rose and Liz, both in their 60's and carrying a few extra pounds, needed knee surgery. Rose chose a physician who practiced near her home, while Liz picked a Castle Connolly Top Doctor. Two years after her operation, Rose still uses a cane much of the time. Six months following surgery, Liz was back to her old self and feeling terrific. No doubt, a Top Doctor had a major impact on Liz's favorable outcome.

- Karl, the manager of a horse farm, suddenly had a problem with one of his eyes. A local ophthalmologist diagnosed glaucoma and told Karl he needed immediate surgery. Castle Connolly referred him to a Top Doctor, who has been successfully treating Karl with eye drops ever since.

Expertise and leading-edge technology are especially important in diagnosing and treating cancer, stroke and cardiovascular patients. Administered by a Top Doctor, sophisticated techniques may keep pancreatic and brain cancer sufferers alive for years, compared with the few months that conventional chemotherapy normally achieves. Top Doctors often have higher cure rates for prostate and breast cancer, thanks in part to early detection, but also due to more advanced treatment options.

Patients with cardiac disease can frequently avoid open-heart or multiple-bypass surgery with stents and other less-invasive technologies. And although many physicians will counsel elderly patients to avoid surgery under any circumstances, a Top Doctor may be able to operate on people 90 years of age or older and still achieve excellent outcomes. Stroke victims, in the hands of a Top Doctor, can recover to a degree unheard of just a few years ago. World-class neurosurgeons can deal with bleeding strokes that were formerly inoperable. Early detection through imaging and swift treatment with drugs can dissolve clots blocking critical blood flow to the brain before permanent damage is done – and without invasive procedures. Men operated on at hospitals and by surgeons with high volumes of particular procedures, specifically radical prostatectomy, had a 7.7 percent risk of recurrence of prostate cancer as compared to 10.9 percent for surgeries done by physicians with lower surgical volumes.

As further evidence of this principle, consider the following statistics, all reported in a recent Newsweek article and based on professional journal reports.

At one leading specialty hospital, the five year <u>survival rate</u> for Stage IV prostate cancer is 71 percent vs. 38 percent nationally.

At a major academic health center for Stage IV cervical cancer the <u>survival rate</u> is 33 percent vs. 16 percent nationally. For breast cancer, after a mastectomy, 81 percent of women treated at top centers are still alive after five years compared to 77 percent nationally.

In addition, a recent study in the *Journal of the National Cancer Institute* found that treatment variation from surgeon to surgeon is significant and may account for up to 30% of recurrences of the cancer. Also, in late 2011, "The Annals of Surgery" published a study that demonstrated that patients with an uneventful course of surgery and recovery had a mean cost per case of $27,946.00 versus $159,345.00 for those patients with complications.

A significant study was recently published in the *New England Journal of Medicine*. It reviewed the actual surgery results of gastric bypass surgery on 10,343 patients by the same 20 surgeons, between 2006 and 2012.

The differences between the most skilled and least skilled surgeons were remarkable. Comparing the top 25% to the bottom 25%, the researchers found:

- The least-skilled surgeons had nearly triple the rate of complications, 14.5% versus 5.2%.

- The least-skilled surgeons required longer operations, 137 minutes versus 98 minutes.

- Although death is a very rare outcome for gastric bypass surgery, patients had a higher risk of dying if their operations were done by the least-skilled doctors, 0.26% versus 0.05%.

Why Top Doctors Make A Difference

Across the board, the most skilled surgeons had better results. Atul Gawande, M.D. in his best-selling book Better, recounted the following concerning the expected outcomes of surgery and how the expectation was a fairly even distribution of outcomes:

"But the evidence indicated otherwise. What you tend to find instead is a bell curve, with a handful of teams showing disturbingly poor outcomes for their patients, a handful obtaining remarkably good results, and a great undistinguished middle. After an ordinary hernia operation, for example, the chances a patient will have a recurrent hernia are one in ten with surgeons at the unhappy end of the spectrum, one in twenty with those in the middle majority, and under one in five hundred with an elite handful."

The bottom line: Top Doctors can help patients in ways not generally available in the medical community. But while people intuitively know this to be true, most lack the resources to make the best choices when they fall ill. Many people rely on referrals from the family physician, yet even a trusted and competent physician may not be the best source of information. Doctors are busy with their practices, and their referral contacts are usually limited to their plan network or hospital. Few have time to research who, wherever in the nation, is really the best for a particular procedure or problem. That often leaves patients who need a top specialist at the mercy of advertising and hearsay. They may even pick a name at random from their insurer's directory or website, or even respond to advertising.

Knowledgeable employers realize that providing employees and their families with access to the best medical care, as well as avoiding the worst, impacts a company's bottom line in a positive way. Money saved on the wrong treatment, unnecessary surgery, days lost from work, or the focus on the illness of a loved one or oneself instead of work, are worth the effort to identify the best doctors.

Castle Connolly is committed to helping such patients get the care they need and deserve. Our professional staff, with years of experience, has earned us the trust and respect of the medical and lay communities alike. We are in a unique position to assist individuals and companies in accessing the best and most efficient healthcare available today. Castle Connolly Guides and our website are comprehensive, user-friendly resources that let consumers find a doctor by name, specialty, and geographic location – or even by special expertise in a particular disease or procedure. Hospital affiliations and contact information are presented clearly and concisely. The guides and website also include helpful tools for choosing a Top Doctor, with tips on how to evaluate a physician's education, experience, and personal suitability.

When it comes to healthcare, cutting corners rarely pays off. Unlike its imitators, Castle Connolly provides thorough and unbiased research by trained professionals. We believe that choosing a Top Doctor is the most important decision a patient can make and we work tirelessly to facilitate that decision.

Introduction

A savvy consumer, searching for a car, restaurant, house or even a spouse, can easily find a guidebook to help. Yet, when it comes to choosing healthcare providers, the bookshelves are nearly bare.

Top Doctors: New York Metro Area has been written to fill that void. It will guide you in making critical —even lifesaving—choices.

This Guide Has Two Goals:

- To provide you with a base of information and a framework of understanding so that you can participate in the important healthcare choices that will maximize your own health, your family's health and the quality of your life.

- To provide detailed information on more than 6,500 well-trained, highly competent physicians from which you may confidently choose your personal best doctors for your own healthcare needs and those of your family.

Medicine is often described as a combination of art and science. This description holds true for the process of selecting the best medical care. This book describes the "science" of making that selection. It is not magical or even difficult. It is simply a matter of knowing what information you should have and where to find it.

The "art" is what you will bring to the selection process. It is based upon your feelings, your needs and the chemistry that develops between you and those who provide your healthcare. Castle Connolly's *Top Doctors: New York Metro Area* will help you prepare for that interaction and will guide you in getting the most from it.

Most importantly, Castle Connolly's *Top Doctors: New York Metro Area* will tell you how to combine the art and science so that you can make the best choices.

How to Use This Guide

This book has been written as a basic, "how to" guide for selecting the best healthcare. Section One provides important information on how to choose the best doctors. Doctors are the most important providers of healthcare and regardless of the type of medical insurance you have, you want the very best doctors to attend to your healthcare needs. Section Three contains listings of doctors as well as information on hospitals invited to participate in the Guide's Partnership for Excellence program. Section Four includes information on "Centers of Excellence"—special programs and services—offered by a number of the hospitals participating in the Partnership for Excellence program. Section Five contains six appendices with important and interesting information.

Introduction

There Are Two Effective Ways to Use This Guide:

- Start at the beginning. This method will give you a broad understanding of the healthcare field and a clearer perspective of where you, the patient, fit in it. This method will arm you with necessary information for making informed choices and will help you find the best doctors.

- Study the doctor listings. While at least a brief reading of some or all of the introductory chapters is recommended so that, in the end, you will make well-informed choices, it is understandable that you may wish to go straight to the physician listings. The organization of these listings is outlined on pages 71 to 79. You will find guidelines for effectively using the listings on these pages.

Each chapter begins with explanations of terms that may be new to you. Reviewing these terms will help you read the section more easily.

In preparing this book, we've left little to chance or question. We hope to inspire you to assume a curious and insistent attitude as you make the healthcare choices that will take you and your family through life.

The Doctor of Choice

Primary Care Physicians

Quick Tips

- The time to establish a relationship with a doctor is while you are healthy. The top doctor to establish your relationship with is the one who is most likely to keep you healthy: A primary care doctor.

- Primary means first, so a primary care doctor is the first one you see for most health problems.

- It is difficult for any doctor, however skilled, to make judgements based on only one visit or a single test.

- Your primary care doctor can educate you about the "hows" and "whys" of health maintenance and disease prevention and follow up to help you stay faithful to the course the two of you have agreed upon.

- Any doctor with a license can practice in any specialty he/she chooses. Board certification is your assurance that the doctor has appropriate training in the specialty.

- When considering recommendations, use the old navigational technique of triangulation: focus on doctors whose names are mentioned by three or more people.

- Hospital telephone referral lines are not designed to distinguish among hundreds of doctors who may be more or less well regarded by other doctors, or who may be better suited to a particular caller when factors other than location, insurance coverage and office hours are taken into consideration.

- Many local medical societies publish directories, some of which are intended primarily for doctor-to-doctor referrals, while others are distributed to the public. They provide information but do not address quality.

- The internet provides many websites that provide lists of doctors: some are of questionable quality. Be careful that the information is from a trusted source.

Quick Take

... Primary care physician. That's a hot term in healthcare today. Who is this physician? How do you find one?...

Key Terms

Lupus Erythematosus - An autoimmune disorder, also referred to as SLE, or simply "lupus". It can cause inflammation and possible damage to a number of vital organs and is commonly marked by joint pain, facial and other rashes, abnormally high antibody levels, and diminished red blood cell levels.

Lyme Disease - An infectious disease, transmitted through the bite of a deer tick, which may or may not produce a distinctive bull's-eye rash at the site of the tick bite. First identified in Lyme, Connecticut, the infection may also produce other symptoms, including flu-like aches, arthritic joint pain, and, in complicated cases, cardiac abnormalities.

Managed Care - The process of integrating the finance and delivery of healthcare to control costs and improve quality. A managed care plan typically involves a group of practitioners who "manage" care for a specified population.

Osteopath - A healthcare professional who has earned a degree in osteopathic medicine, a D.O. Osteopathic medicine emphasizes massage and bone manipulation while traditional western allopathic medicine emphasizes treatment with drugs and surgery.

Preventive Medicine/Care - Health services that are aimed at maintaining good health and preventing illness. These services include routine physical examinations, immunizations, certain screening tests such as mammograms or Pap tests, as well as the practice of good health habits.

Primary Care Physician - The first doctor consulted for any health problem, a Primary Care Physician is a specialist who offers basic, including preventive, medical care. It is important to maintain an ongoing relationship with your primary care physician.

Specialist - A physician who practices in one or more of the 25 specialties defined by the American Board of Medical Specialties (ABMS). The term is also used to denote a physician's area of practice, such as pediatrics, geriatrics, surgery, etc.

Subspecialist - A specialist who obtains further training and certification in one or more of the 70 subspecialties approved by the American Board of Medical Specialties. The physician must first be certified in a specialty. For example, a board certified internist may become certified in cardiology or gastroenterology.

Primary Care Physicians

When it comes to choosing a doctor, too many people let the decision slide until they are sick or hurt and need immediate medical attention. That's unfortunate if an illness that could have been managed successfully develops to a stage where it becomes difficult to control or cure. It's even more unfortunate if the illness could have been prevented in the first place.

The time to establish a relationship with a doctor is while you are healthy, and the best one to establish your relationship with is the one who is most likely to keep you healthy: a primary care doctor.

Primary means first, so a primary care doctor is the first one you see for any health problem. Primary also means basic, so a primary care doctor offers the kind of fundamental care that can keep you healthy.

Yes, You Do Need a Doctor When You're Healthy.

Here are four good reasons why you should start your search for a primary care doctor now:

Reason One

A primary care doctor can put your current medical condition into a context that consists of your medical history, current condition as compared with past medical status, and changes in your body and environment over time. It is difficult for any doctor, however skilled, to make informed medical judgments based on only one visit or a single test. Conditions well out of normal range are easy to pick up, but extreme variations do not always occur and a serious illness may develop slowly with only a gradual increase in symptoms. The operative word is continuity: ideally, your medical care should not be interrupted by changes in providers.

Reason Two

A primary care doctor is better able to treat you as a whole person. Medicine has become very specialized and procedure-oriented, but the human body is not a loose collection of unrelated parts. It is a "whole" with strong interrelationships among all biological systems. Some of the poorest medical care results from people jumping from subspecialist to subspecialist. Despite talent, skill and training, no specialist knows the patient well enough, or for long enough, to be able to take the whole person into consideration and track the normal patterns of evolution and change. We end up with a specialist for every organ and system instead of a doctor who will care for the whole person.

Reason Three

A primary care doctor can establish preventive programs. Our healthcare system does not place enough emphasis on preventing illness; most healthcare dollars are spent on curative, rather than preventive, medicine. However, the status quo is slowly changing, and it is within primary care that the change is most evident. Your primary care doctor can educate you about the hows and whys of health maintenance and disease prevention and can follow up to help you stay faithful to the course the two of you have agreed upon. Only an ongoing relationship makes this possible.

Reason Four

A primary care doctor can save you money. Managed care advocates, among others, have long deplored the waste inherent in a system in which patients can simply call any specialist any time they have an ache or pain or are not feeling well. Primary care doctors can monitor referrals to specialists, following the patient closely to put together a variety of observations, opinions, and test results in order to treat each person on an individual basis. This improves the quality of care and also controls costs.

Patients who visit specialists without some guidance from a primary care doctor may choose the wrong specialist based on a general observation and self-diagnosis about the problem or illness they're experiencing. While in some cases the problem may be obvious (for example, an eye injury), in others it may be more subtle. Diseases such as lupus erythematosus and Lyme disease, for example, often have a myriad of symptoms that are easily misinterpreted by laypersons; in fact, they are often difficult even for doctors to diagnose accurately. While certain problems may require the collaboration of several specialists, it is important to have a primary care doctor navigating the course.

Finally, it is estimated that almost half of all emergency room visits in some areas are for non-emergencies; it's the most expensive place to receive primary care. When people have primary care doctors, they tend to turn to them rather than to hospital emergency departments.

If you are enrolled in any kind of managed care program, health maintenance organization (HMO) or other program, you will almost always be required to select a primary care doctor from its roster. Managed care executives recognize the necessity of a primary care doctor, not only for delivering quality healthcare, but also for controlling costs.

How to Find a Doctor

Unless you already have a primary care doctor you are satisfied with, you will have to find one. How? Here are five possible avenues to begin the process of finding the doctor that best suits your needs; each has limits, however.

Doctor Referrals

If you are moving and are leaving a trusted doctor behind, get a recommendation or two before you go. Furthermore, ask in what context and how well your doctor knows the new doctor—they may not have met since medical school.

Friends and Relatives

Always keep in mind that such recommendations are based largely on what may be "simpatico," or a personal affinity. Ask why your friend likes the doctor. It might be because the fees are low or the doctor makes house calls or is warm and sociable—all valid considerations, but certainly not principal determinants. So be wary of the generalized recommendation that "Dr. Jones is just wonderful." When considering recommendations, use the old navigational technique of triangulation: focus on doctors whose names are mentioned by three or more people.

Hospital Referral Services

Hospital telephone referral lines are not designed to distinguish among hundreds of doctors who may be more or less well regarded by other doctors, or who may be better suited to a particular caller when factors other than location, insurance coverage and office hours are taken into consideration. It would be impolitic for hospital referral services to rate their doctors. Their recommendations are based on specialty and geographic proximity, usually by way of a computer that rotates through the lists to "recommend" the next three names in line, and all members of the medical staff are eligible to participate.

Medical Society Directories

Many local medical societies publish directories, some of which are intended primarily for doctor-to-doctor referrals, while others are distributed to the public. These directories usually provide names, addresses, phone numbers and specialties and can be useful sources. However, they do not distinguish among doctors in any way. All members of the medical society, usually a countywide organization, are eligible for inclusion. This also applies to the referral lines offered by many medical societies.

The Internet

There are many websites that provide information on doctors. Some are directories or internet phone books. These can be helpful. Some claim to be based on quality measures. Many of these require physicians to pay, others are of questionable quality. Be sure the site sponsor or source is a trusted one.

Many Ways to Say Doctor

In this guide, the term "doctor" is used to describe only medical doctors who have received a Doctor of Medicine degree (MD) and osteopaths who have received a Doctor of Osteopathic Medicine degree (DO). Doctors who have been trained in the British system may hold a degree of Bachelor of Medicine (MB), Bachelor of Surgery (BS), or Bachelor of Chirurgia (BCh), which is based on the ancient Greek term that refers to surgery.

The more formal term for any of these practitioners is "physician." However, most people use the more popular term "doctor," which is the one generally used in this book. Our discussions do not include other kinds of doctors such as dentists, podiatrists, psychologists or chiropractors, who also deliver healthcare.

Primary Care: The Fundamental Four

There is not complete agreement in medicine on which specialties are practiced by the group of doctors known as primary care specialists. For the purposes of this book, we have included the following specialties: Internal Medicine, Pediatrics, Family Practice and Obstetrics and Gynecology. Most adults choose general internists as their primary care doctors and select pediatricians for their children. There is also another type of specialist, the family practitioner, who cares for both children and adults. In addition to such generalists, many women also select an obstetrician/gynecologist as their primary care providers.

- A **general internist**, specializing in internal medicine, is trained to treat all internal organs and systems of the body. Many internists also are board certified in a subspecialty such as cardiology, gastroenterology or geriatric medicine. Therefore, if you have a history of heart disease, you may wish to select an internist who has additional training in cardiology, but who primarily practices general internal medicine. On the other hand, your primary care doctor may refer you to a cardiologist when necessary, and both may treat you over a period of years. In fact, it is not unusual for a patient with a serious or complex illness to be followed by two or three doctors, with the primary care doctor "quarterbacking" the team.

- A **family practitioner** is very broadly trained. Such doctors come closest to the general practitioner of the past. They are qualified to treat all family members, including children.

- A **pediatrician** is the doctor you would choose for the care of your children. As with doctors in internal medicine, pediatricians often have a subspecialty such as cardiology, rheumatology or endocrinology.

- **Obstetricians and Gynecologists** are the subject of significant debate in terms of their appropriateness as primary care doctors. The American Board of Obstetrics and Gynecology states that these doctors are specialists and are not generally trained for primary care. However, the reality is that many, particularly those who solely practice gynecology, often serve as a woman's primary care doctor. Gynecologists are divided on the issue. One recent study showed that 95 percent of visits to ob-gyns are self-referred and that about 60 percent of visits to these specialists are for diagnostic services and preventive services. Another study, by the American College of Obstetricians and Gynecologists, showed that 54 percent of women who see a gynecologist use these doctors for primary care. Reflecting the reality of current medical practice, we have included these specialists in the primary care category.

A *businessman in his late fifties, a long-time competitive*
runner, had surgery in one of New York's top hospitals to
repair a badly torn Achilles tendon. At his first follow-up
visit to the orthopaedic surgeon, he was assured that "everything was
healing perfectly," that he had nothing to be concerned about, and
that he would soon be up and running again. Shortly thereafter, just
before a summer camping trip, he decided to have his yearly physical
examination. The primary care doctor examined the site of the
surgery, probing up and down the whole length of the leg. Explaining
that he was concerned about certain swelling and discoloration, the
doctor arranged for a further examination with ultrasound imaging.
This sophisticated test showed that a blood clot had formed in the
upper part of the leg, which could have caused severe disability and
even death had it gotten into the bloodstream and traveled to the
heart or brain. It was the primary care doctor, who knew the patient
well, who discovered the potentially fatal condition while carefully
conducting a full physical exam.

What Makes A "Top" Doctor

Quick Tips

- If in doubt about a doctor's training, ask the doctor if the residency completed was in the specialty of his/her practice. If not, ask why not.

- Board certification and recertification are the best ways to measure competence and training.

- The easiest way you can assess the quality of a doctor's residency program is to see if it took place in a large medical center with a name you recognize.

- If a doctor does not have admitting privileges or is not on the attending staff of a hospital, you might consider choosing another doctor.

- There are many excellent, well-trained doctors at community hospitals and they should be as carefully evaluated and considered in your search as a doctor at a teaching hospital.

- Doctors who are full-time academicians may be in the forefront of new techniques and research, but they are not necessarily better doctors.

- The best care is provided by a combination of primary care doctors and other specialists and subspecialists.

- Do not hesitate to ask how frequently your doctor has performed a procedure and with what degree of success. Practice may not lead to perfection, but it improves skills and enhances the probability of success.

- Check the date of graduation from medical school or completion of residency if you want to know precisely how long a doctor has been in practice.

Quick Take

... If a doctor does not have admitting privileges or is not on the attending staff of a hospital, you might consider choosing another doctor. ...

Key Terms

Academic Medical Center - A large medical complex that centers around a teaching hospital in which residency and fellowship programs are offered, where the medical school faculty practices full time and where major clinical research activities occur.

Board Certified - Term signifying that a doctor is qualified for specialization by one of the American Board of Medical Specialties (ABMS) boards. Qualification includes completing an approved residency and passing a rigid exam.

Board Eligible - Term signifying that a doctor has completed an approved residency but has not yet taken the exam given by one of the ABMS recognized boards. The term conveys no official status in the eyes of the ABMS.

Clinical - Medical care that involves direct contact with patients.

Credentialing - A process of screening conducted by hospitals wherein they review the training and licenses of doctors applying to practice on their medical staffs.

Indemnity - A form of health insurance coverage that pays for healthcare but permits the patients to select their provider. Until 1990, indemnity insurance covered most insured people in the United States.

Licensure - Official credentials by individual states that permit a doctor to practice medicine in that state. In some states, doctors may be licensed with no more than one year of post-graduate training.

Residency - A training period spent in a hospital by a graduate of a medical school before going into practice. Residents have earned a medical degree and, therefore, are doctors, but must complete an approved residency and pass an exam to become board certified.

Tertiary Care - Medical services provided by a hospital or medical center that include complex treatments and procedures such as open heart surgery, organ transplants and burn care.

What Makes A "Top" Doctor

Castle Connolly's Top Doctors™ selection process begins with surveys of physicians and healthcare professionals. Each year, Castle Connolly surveys thousands of physicians and other healthcare professionals and asks them to identify excellent doctors in every specialty in their region and throughout the nation. When we began the research for the first edition of America's Top Doctors®, we surveyed over 230,000 of the nation's leading medical specialists, department chairs, residency program directors, vice presidents of medical affairs and presidents of the nation's leading medical centers and specialty hospitals.

In addition to mail and online surveys, the Castle Connolly physician-led research team makes thousands of phone calls each year, talking with leading specialists, chairs of clinical departments and vice presidents of medical affairs, seeking to identify top specialists for most diseases and procedures.

The Castle Connolly physician-led research team carefully reviews the credentials of every physician being considered for inclusion in Castle Connolly Guides, magazine articles and website. The review includes, among other factors, scrutiny of medical education, training, hospital appointments, administrative posts, professional achievements, and malpractice and disciplinary history.

Information on outcomes, procedure volume and malpractice is becoming increasingly available, but the public disclosure varies from state to state. Castle Connolly uses its best efforts to gather the information that is available and use it effectively. Ultimately, however, it is the professional judgment of the Castle Connolly editors, the Chief Medical and Research Officer and the research staff, which determines Castle Connolly Top Doctor™ selection.

Physicians may also be removed from the Castle Connolly lists if, in the judgment of the selection team, that is warranted. Some of the reasons physicians are removed include retirement, change in practice (taking a full time administrative post, for example), unavailability to patients, malpractice or disciplinary issues, negative physician or patient feedback, professional demeanor or a change in the "mix" of specialists Castle Connolly will present for a given community. Being removed from a Castle Connolly list does not necessarily indicate something negative about the physician. At the same time, Castle Connolly does not claim to identify every excellent physician in the nation or a region. The physicians identified through the Castle Connolly research process are clearly among the very best, but there are always other very good physicians not identified by Castle Connolly and that is why our guides, websites and other distribution channels for this critical information describe a process whereby consumers can identify excellent physicians using their own efforts.

There are four basic criteria for selecting your own best doctor: professional preparation, professional reputation, office and practice arrangements and personal or bedside manner. The first three of these assessments can be made prior to your first visit, which is when you can make your fourth evaluation.

Professional Preparation

Education

Your review of your prospective doctor's education and training should begin with medical school. While you may feel that the institution where someone earned a bachelor's degree could be an indication of the quality of the doctor, most people in the medical field do not believe it plays a major role. A degree from a highly selective undergraduate college or university will help an aspiring doctor gain admission to a medical school, but once there, all students are peers. However, the information on undergraduate colleges, if important to you, is available in the American Board of Medical Specialties (ABMS) Compendium of Certified Medical Specialists and other medical directories.

American medical schools are highly standardized, at least in terms of minimum quality. All U.S. medical schools that grant medical degrees (MDs) and osteopathic degrees (DOs) are accredited by a group known as the LCME (Liaison Committee for Medical Education). Most are also accredited by the appropriate state agency, if one exists, and by regional accrediting agencies that accredit colleges and universities of all kinds.

Furthermore, U.S. medical schools have universally high standards for admission, including success on the undergraduate level and on the Medical College Admissions Tests (MCATs). Although frequently criticized for being slow to change and for training too many specialists, the system of medical education in the United States has insured high quality in medical practice. One recent positive change is a strong effort in most medical schools to diversify the composition of the student body. While these schools have been less successful in enrolling racial minorities, the number of women in U.S. medical schools has increased to the point where they now make up about 50 percent of most classes. In certain specialties preferred by female medical graduates (pediatrics, for example), it is possible that, in coming years, the majority of specialists will be female.

Most doctors practicing in the United States are graduates of U.S. medical schools. There are two other groups of doctors in practice who make up a substantial proportion of the total doctor population. They are: (1) foreign nationals who graduated from foreign schools; and (2) U.S. nationals who graduated from foreign schools (Canadian medical schools are not considered foreign). About one out of three physicians currently practicing in the U.S. represent these groups.

Foreign Medical Graduates

Foreign medical schools vary greatly in quality. Even some of the oldest and finest European schools have become virtually "open door institutions," with huge numbers of unscreened students who make teaching and learning difficult. Others are excellent and provided the model for our own system of medical education.

The fact that someone graduated from a foreign school does not mean that he or she is a poor doctor. Foreign schools, like U.S. schools, produce good doctors and poor doctors. Foreign medical graduates must pass the same exam taken by U.S. graduates for licensure, but the failure rate for foreign graduates is significantly higher. In the first year of using the new United States Medical Licensing Exam (USMLE), 93 percent of U.S. medical school graduates passed Step II, the clinical exam, as compared with 39 percent of foreign graduates. It is clear that the quality of foreign schools, if not individual doctors, is not the same as U.S. medical schools, at least as measured by our standards. Nonetheless, many communities and patients have been well served by foreign medical graduates practicing in this country—often in areas where it has been difficult to attract graduates of American schools.

Residency

Most doctors practicing today have at least three years of postgraduate training (following the MD or DO) in an approved residency program. This is not only an important step in the process of becoming a competent doctor, but it is also a requirement for board (specialty) certification. Most people assume that a prospective doctor needs to complete a three-year residency program to obtain a medical license. This is not true in some states. New York State, for example, requires only one postgraduate year. However, since all approved residencies last at least three years, and some, such as neurosurgery, general surgery, orthopaedic surgery and urology, may extend for five or more years, it is important to know the details of a doctor's training. Licensure alone is not enough of a basis on which to make a good choice.

Without undertaking extensive and detailed research on every residency program, the best assessment you can make of a doctor's residency program is to see if it took place in a large medical center whose name you recognize. The more prestigious institutions tend to attract the best medical students, sometimes regardless of the quality of the individual residency program. If in doubt about a doctor's training, ask the doctor if the residency completed was in the specialty of his/her practice. If not, ask why.

It is also important to be certain that a doctor completed a residency that has been approved by the appropriate governing board of the specialty such as the American Board of Surgery, the American Board of Radiology or the American Osteopathic Board of Pediatrics. These board groups are listed in Appendix A. If you are really concerned about a doctor's training, you should first call the hospital that offered the residency and ask if the residency was approved by the appropriate specialty group. If still in doubt, review the publication Directory of Graduate Medical Education Programs, often called the "green book," found in medical school or hospital libraries, which lists all approved residencies.

Board Certification

With an MD or DO degree and a license, an individual may practice any kind of medicine—with or without additional special training. For example, doctors with a license but no special training may call themselves cardiologists or pediatricians. This is why board certification is such an important factor. Twenty-five specialties are recognized by the American Board of Medical Specialties (ABMS). (Visit www.abms.org or call (312) 436-2600 for more information.) Eighteen boards certify in 106 specialties under the aegis of the American Osteopathic Association (AOA). (Visit www.osteopathic.org or call 800-621-1773 for more information.) Doctors who have qualified for such specialization are called board certified; they have completed an approved residency and passed the board's exam. (See Appendix A for an approved ABMS and AOA list; see pages 81-87 for a description of each specialty and subspecialty.) While many doctors who are not board certified do call themselves specialists, board certification is the best standard by which to measure competence and training.

You can be confident that doctors who are board certified have at a minimum the proper training in their specialty and have demonstrated their proficiency through supervision and testing. While there are many non-board certified doctors who are highly competent, it is more difficult to assess the level of their training. Board certification alone does not guarantee competence, but it is a standard that reflects successful completion of an appropriate training program.

Recertification

A relatively new focus of the specialty boards is the area of recertification. Until recently, board certification lasted for an unlimited time period. Now, almost all of the boards have put time limits on the certification period. For example, in internal medicine, it is ten years; in family practice seven years. In osteopathic medicine, some of the boards need to set a recertification period within 10 years. Many have done so already. These more stringent standards reflect an increasing emphasis, by both the medical boards and state agencies responsible for licensing doctors, on recertification.

Since the policies of the boards vary widely, it is good procedure to ask a doctor if certification was awarded and when. If the date was seven to ten years ago, ask if he/she has been recertified. Note: The most recent date of board certification or recertification is indicated in each physician's listing in this guide.

Unfortunately, many boards permit "grandfathering," whereby already certified doctors do not have to be recertified, and recertification demands apply only to newly certified doctors. Appendix A contains a list of the names and addresses of the boards and the certification period for each board specialty. Even if recertification is not required, it is good professional practice for doctors to undertake the process. It assures you, the patient, that they are attempting to stay current.

Many states have a continuing medical education (CME) requirement for doctors. These states typically require a minimum number of CME credits for a doctor to maintain a medical license. Seven states require 150 CME credits over a three-year period. Osteopathic doctors are required to take 120 hours of CME credits within three years to maintain certification.

Board Eligibility

Many doctors who have been recently trained are waiting to take the boards. They are sometimes described as "board eligible," a common term that the ABMS advocates abandoning because of its ambiguity. Board eligible means that the doctor has completed an approved residency and is qualified to sit for the related board's exam.

Each member board of the ABMS has its own policy regarding the use and recognition of the board eligible term. Therefore, the description "board eligible" should not be viewed as a genuine qualification, especially if a doctor has been out of medical school long enough to have taken the certification exam. To the boards, a doctor is either board certified or not. Furthermore, most of the specialty boards permit unlimited attempts to pass the exam and, in some cases, doctors who have failed the exam twice or even ten times continue to call themselves board eligible. In osteopathic medicine, the board eligible status is recognized only for the first six years after completion of a residency.

Self-Designated Medical Specialties

In addition to the ABMS and AOA-approved list of specialties and subspecialties, there is a wide variety of other doctors, and groups of doctors, who may call themselves "specialists". There are, at present, at least 100 such groups called self-designated medical specialties. They range from doctors who are working to create a recognized body of knowledge and subspecialty training to less formal groups interested in a particular approach to the practice of medicine. These groups may or may not have standards for membership. There is no way of determining the true extent of their members' training, and they are not recognized by the ABMS* or the AOA. While you should be cautious of doctors who claim they are specialists in these areas, many do have advanced training and the groups at least offer a listing of people interested in a particular approach to medical care. Rely on board certification to assure yourself of basic competence and use membership in one of these groups to indicate strong interest and possible additional training in a particular aspect of medicine. A list of these self-designated medical specialties may be found in Appendix B.

Fellowships

The purpose of a fellowship is to provide advanced training in the clinical techniques and research of a particular subspecialty. In the U.S. there are a variety of fellowship programs available to doctors, and they fall into two broad categories: approved and unapproved. Approved fellowships are those approved by the appropriate medical specialty board (e.g., the American Board of Radiology) and that lead to a subspecialty certificate. Fellowship programs that are not approved are often in the same areas of training as those that are, but they do not lead to a subspecialty

---

* One subspecialty, not yet recognized by the ABMS - Pediatric Neurosurgery - has been included because the retaining and certification process is rigorous and meaningful.

certificate. Unfortunately, all too often, unapproved fellowships exist only to provide relatively inexpensive labor for the research and/or patient care activities of a clinical department in a medical school or hospital. In such cases, the learning that takes place is secondary and may be a good deal less than in an approved fellowship. On the other hand, any fellowship is better than none at all and some unapproved fellowships have that status for a valid reason, which should not reflect negatively on the program. For example, the fellowship may have been recently created with approval being sought. To check that a fellowship is an approved one, call the hospital where the training took place or the medical board for that specialty.

Professional Reputation

There are doctors who meet every professional standard on paper, but who are simply not good doctors. In all probability, the medical community has ascertained that while the individual may still practice medicine, his or her reputation will reflect that collective assessment. There are also doctors who are outstanding leaders in their fields because of research or professional activities, but who are not particularly strong or perhaps even active in patient care. It is important to distinguish that kind of professional reputation from a reputation as a competent, caring doctor in delivering patient care. In a consumer survey conducted by the management consulting firm Towers Perrin, the chief criterion by which the respondents selected doctors was reputation. This was the most important factor for those enrolled in either managed care or indemnity plans.

Hospital Appointment

Most doctors are on the medical staff of one or more hospitals and are known as attendings. If a doctor does not have admitting privileges or is not on the attending staff of a hospital, you may wish to consider choosing another doctor. It can be very difficult to ascertain whether the lack of hospital appointment is for a good reason or not. For example, it is understandable that some doctors who are raising families or heading toward retirement choose not to meet the demands (meetings, committees, etc.) of being an attending. However, if you need care in a hospital, the lack of such an appointment means that another doctor will have to oversee that care. In some specialties such as dermatology and psychiatry, doctors may conduct their entire practices in the office, and a hospital appointment is not as essential, or as good a criterion for assessment, as in other specialties.

While mistakes are made, most hospitals are quite careful about admissions to their medical staffs. The best hospitals are highly selective, so a degree of screening (or "credentialing") has been done for you. In other words, the best doctors practice at the best hospitals. Since caring for a patient in the hospital is often a team effort involving a number of specialists, the reputation of the hospital where the doctor admits patients carries special weight. Hospital medical staffs also review their colleagues credentials before authorizing them to perform specific procedures. In addition, they typically reappoint their medical staffs—and review them—every two or three years. In effect, this is an additional screening to protect patients. It is especially true of hospitals that have what are known as closed staffs, where it is impossible to obtain admitting privileges unless there is a vacancy that the administration and medical staff deem necessary to fill. If you are having some type of surgical procedure and are concerned about the doctor's skill or experience with it, it may be worthwhile to call the Medical Affairs office at the doctor's hospital to see if he or she is authorized to perform that procedure in the hospital.

The reasons for a hospital's selectivity are easy to understand: every hospital wants to have the best reputation possible in order to attract patients, and no hospital, excellent or not, wishes to expose itself to liability. Obviously, the quality of the medical staff is immensely important in creating that reputation. Unfortunately, some hospitals are less diligent when a major group practice of doctors, all of whom have previously been affiliated with the institution, adds new members. In such cases, the hospital may almost automatically grant privileges without conducting the same intensive review given to individual doctors who are not members of a group practice. Also, some hospitals are less selective in granting privileges when beds are empty than when beds are full, since additional attendings provide additional patients.

A last and very important reason why a hospital appointment is an essential requirement in your choice of a doctor is that many states permit doctors to practice without malpractice insurance. If you are injured as a result of the doctor's poor care, you could be without recourse. However, few hospitals permit doctors to practice in them unless they carry malpractice insurance. This not only protects the hospital, but the patient as well.

Many people believe that they should choose a doctor with an appointment at a major medical center as opposed to a community hospital. This assumption is incorrect on two counts. For one thing, there are many excellent, well-trained doctors at community hospitals and they should be as carefully evaluated and considered in your search as a doctor at a large institution. What's more, the term "medical center" has less significance today than it did years ago when the term was used to describe only the major university hospitals of medical schools. A true medical center is a teaching hospital that offers multiple residency programs and at which the medical school faculty practices full-time, with fellowship programs and major clinical research activities an integral part of the teaching of medical students. These large centers also are involved in tertiary care, offering services such as organ transplants, burn care and cardiovascular surgery.

Today many community hospitals have added the term medical center to their name. They do this for two purposes: to indicate that they, too, offer advanced and sophisticated medical programs, and to compete for patients with the academic medical centers. With academic medical centers turning out many well-trained specialists and subspecialists who establish practices in nearby communities and then want to continue the highly specialized techniques they have learned, many community hospitals have initiated tertiary care programs of their own, further blurring the distinction between medical centers and hospitals.

In any case, most of our healthcare today is delivered outside of the hospital in ambulatory outpatient settings. Those who are hospitalized for acute illness (e.g., surgery, serious infection) will find that community hospitals and their staffs are well-suited to the task.

When extremely difficult and complex problems develop, or when tertiary care is needed, many communities have excellent academic medical centers. Of course, they offer primary care as well, especially to those who live nearby. This illustrates the point, once again, that medical care is a local issue.

Medical School Faculty Appointment

Many doctors have appointments on the faculties of medical schools. There is a range of categories from "straight" appointments—meaning full-time appointment as professor, associate professor, assistant professor or instructor—to clinical ranks that may reflect lesser degrees of involvement in teaching or research. If someone carries what is known as a straight academic rank (i.e., professor of surgery, without "clinical" in the title), this usually means that the individual is engaged full-time in medical school research and/or teaching activities. The title "professor of clinical surgery" usually describes a doctor who has a full-time appointment in a medical school, but who puts a greater emphasis on clinical practice (patient care) than on research or teaching. The title "clinical professor of surgery" usually specifies a part-time or adjunct appointment and less direct involvement in medical school activities.

Doctors who are full-time academicians may be in the forefront of new techniques and research, but they are not necessarily better doctors. Nonetheless, you can be assured that they have the support of other faculty, residents and medical students.

When you are seeking a subspecialist, a doctor's relationship to a medical school becomes more meaningful since medical school faculties tend to be made up of subspecialists. You are less likely to find large numbers of general or primary care practitioners engaged full-time on a medical school faculty. The newest approaches and techniques in medicine, for the most part, are explored and developed by medical school faculties in their laboratories and clinical practice settings. This is where they practice their subspecialties, as well as teach and perform research. Such leading specialists are not necessarily better doctors than community doctors—they are trained to provide a different kind of medical care. The best care is provided by a combination of primary care doctors and other specialists and subspecialists.

Medical Society Membership

Most medical society memberships sound very prestigious and some are; however, there are many societies that are not selective and which virtually any doctor can join. In addition, membership in many of the more prestigious societies is based on research and publication, or on leadership in the field, and may have little to do with direct patient care. While it is clearly an honor to be invited to join these groups, membership may be less than helpful in discerning whether a doctor can meet your needs.

Board certified doctors are referred to as Diplomates of the Board. Some of the colleges of medical specialties (e.g., the American College of Radiology and the American College of Surgeons) have multiple levels of recognition. The first is basic membership and the second, more prestigious and difficult to obtain, is status as a Fellow. Fellowship status in the colleges is meaningful and is based on experience, professional achievement and recognition by one's peers, including extensive experience in patient care. It should be viewed as a significant professional qualification.

Experience

Experience is difficult to assess. Obviously, in most cases, an older doctor has more experience; on the other hand, a younger doctor has been more recently immersed in residency, the challenge of medical school, or even a fellowship, and may be the most up-to-date. If a doctor is board certified, you may assume that assures at least a minimal amount of experience, but it could be as little as a year. In this guide the board certification date may reflect a doctor's most recent recertification, so check the date of graduation from medical school or completion of residency if you want to know precisely how long a doctor has been in practice.

There is a good deal of evidence that there is a positive relationship between quantity of experience and quality of care. That is, the more often a doctor performs a procedure, the better he/she becomes at it. That is why it is important to ask a doctor about his or her experience with the procedure that you need. Does the doctor see and treat similar cases every day, every week or only rarely? Of course, with some rare conditions, rarely is the only possible answer, but it is relative frequency that is critical. Major metropolitan areas, especially New York and San Francisco, became leaders in the treatment of AIDS because of the large number of patients seen in those metropolitan areas. Doctors in the suburbs of New York City (especially in New York's Westchester, Nassau and Suffolk counties) and in Fairfield County, Connecticut became leaders in the research and treatment of Lyme disease because that region is the epicenter of the disease.

In some states, data is available on volume or numbers of certain procedures performed at hospitals. Likewise, The Leapfrog Group (www.leapfroggroup.org) compares hospitals' performance on the national standards of safety, quality and efficiency - areas of healthcare that are most relevant to consumers and this information is later used to improve hospital quality, save healthcare spending and assist hospital employees with purchasing strategies. The federal government has posted outcome data for hospitals, but for a limited number of procedures, on a website www.medicare.gov/hospitalcompare. There is a good deal of controversy, however, on the validity and usefulness of such data. Opponents cite the fact that some of the data is produced from Medicare patient records only and, thus, is based solely on an elderly population that does not represent the total activity of a hospital or doctor. Proponents of the use of such volume data agree that it is not perfect, but suggest that it can be one useful criterion in selecting the best places to receive care for these specific problems. Recognizing the limitations of such data, the healthcare consumer may, nonetheless, find it of interest and use.

Office and Practice Arrangements

Although clearly not as important as training or reputation, office and practice arrangements are usually of great significance to patients. Practice arrangements include office hours, office location, billing procedures and office testing among the many factors that result in how well the office is run.

Many years ago most doctors practiced independently in private offices. They were called solo practitioners and usually had agreements with other doctors to respond to their patients' calls when they were unavailable. In recent decades, most doctors have entered group practices; indeed, this is becoming the most common way for young doctors to begin to practice. Two or more doctors in the same specialty, or in different specialties (a multi-specialty group), share offices and staff to lower their costs of operations. They also cover for each other on rotation for weekends, evenings and vacations. As a patient you may prefer one of the following: a solo practitioner who is covered occasionally; a group where you usually, but not always, see the same doctor; or a multi-specialty group where, if a consultation or referral is necessary, the specialist is at the same location. The choice is really one of personal preference.

There are other factors relating to practice arrangements that may or may not be important to an individual when choosing a doctor. One is the location of the office. A consumer poll conducted for the Robert Wood Johnson Foundation identified office location as one of the two most important factors in the selection of a doctor (the other was a recommendation by a relative or friend). Actually, the site of the office can be very important in choosing a doctor you may visit on a regular basis. If the location is inconvenient, you may be discouraged from making needed visits.

Another important factor concerns the use of nurse practitioners and physician's assistants in the office. Licensed nurse practitioners are advanced practice nurses in primary care. They have additional training beyond the basic requirements for nursing licensure, usually a master's degree or special certificate. They perform a broad range of nursing functions as well as functions that, historically, have been performed by doctors, including assessing and diagnosing, conducting physical examinations, ordering diagnostic tests, implementing treatment plans and monitoring patient status. Physician's assistants are licensed to provide medical care in many states. However, unlike nurses, they may practice only under a doctor's direction and supervision. According to an article in the professional journal Family Practice Management, these "midlevel providers," as they are called, "can handle 80 to 90 percent of the problems that occasion office visits." These providers have become more of a presence in healthcare in recent years, especially in medical groups and HMOs. If you don't think you will be satisfied having your office visit and examination conducted by anyone but the doctor, you should determine up front how many midlevel providers are on staff and how extensive their responsibilities are.

Narrowing the Choice

Here are 10 additional questions that will guide you in assessing if the practice patterns or arrangements of a doctor meet your needs. If there are other items not listed that are important to you, add them to the list before you make your initial appointment. You should try to obtain as much of the information as possible from the staff.

- Are you currently accepting new patients and, if so, is a referral required?
- On average, how long does a patient have to wait for an appointment?
- Are you open on weekends? In the evening?
- If lab work and X-rays are performed in the office what are the qualifications of the people doing the tests?
- Are full payment, deductibles or co-payments required at the time of the appointment?
- Do you accept my insurance plan? Medicare? Medicaid? Workers' compensation? No-fault insurance?
- Do you accept credit cards and, if so, which do you accept?
- Do you accept patient phone calls?
- Do you use electronic medical records?
- Is your office handicapped-accessible?

If you have a chronic illness or disease, there may be certain additional aspects of a doctor's practice that could be particularly important to you. You should discuss any chronic problems when first establishing a relationship with a doctor. In fact, you may want to find a doctor with special interest or training in that problem.

House calls also continue to be important to some people. Yes, some doctors still do make house calls! In fact, a recent American Medical News article suggested that 43 percent of internal medicine specialists and 65 percent of family practice specialists made one or more house calls a year. However, it is important to point out that the number of doctors making house calls has declined because of technology, liability risks and time pressures. Important diagnostic equipment often cannot be carried around in a doctor's little black bag and is only available in the office or hospital. Also, the time required to visit one patient at home markedly reduces the time available to see other patients.

Personal or Bedside Manner

To many patients, once they have determined that a doctor is competent, the doctor's professional manner—also known as bedside manner—is the most important part of their choice. The Towers Perrin report cited earlier indicated that after reputation, skill in communicating was the most important factor sought in doctors. Patients prefer sensitive and caring doctors who listen carefully and demonstrate their concern. Studies show that such doctors are sued less often than others!

What characteristics make up a doctor's personal manner? The four described below may, when considered together, give you a clear idea of whether a particular doctor will be your personal "top" doctor.

- **Listening**. Professional manner includes the doctor's willingness to listen to patients, be supportive and understanding, explain procedures and exhibit concern and respect. These skills are expressed at the bedside, in the office, or in any setting where there is doctor/patient contact. Listening is also a valuable diagnostic tool. Unfortunately, these skills often have not been taught well in medical schools and the lack of them forms the primary basis for complaints from patients. However, there is growing emphasis on these vital interpersonal and communications skills in medical schools today and with good reason. They are critically important to most patients.

- **Cultural Sensitivity.** Some patients may prefer doctors who speak their language or are familiar with their cultural background. The term "culturally competent physician" is a relatively new one describing doctors who have the needed skills and attitudes to effectively treat patients from minority cultures.

- **Ethical, Religious and Philosophical Views.** Religion, or at least views on issues such as abortion, utilization of life-sustaining measures, natural childbirth, breast-feeding and other such matters can also be important. It is perfectly appropriate to ask doctors their views on sensitive issues.

- **Decision-making Procedures.** Years ago patients took the words of the doctor as law, not to be questioned or perhaps even discussed. That is not the case today. Consumers are better informed about health issues and may want to be actively involved in the decision making that affects their health. Some patients do not feel this way and are comfortable accepting a doctor's diagnosis or course of treatment without question. Some doctors—in diminishing numbers, thankfully—feel uncomfortable with patients who want everything explained to them or want to be involved in decision-making. Consider how you feel about this issue and discuss it with your doctor to be certain you are on compatible wavelengths.

Of course, what ultimately makes a "top" doctor are the results, the "outcomes," of care. Unfortunately, there is relatively little information available to consumers on the outcomes of physicians and hospitals. Some states, New York for example, have produced studies on outcomes for cardiac surgery. Also, some HMOs are talking about producing report cards for doctors. Generally, however, consumers will have difficulty finding outcome studies for individual doctors.

On the other hand, there is a growing movement to track and publish outcomes data on hospitals. The federal government has taken the lead by releasing outcomes data by hospitals for selected procedures. Visit www.hospitalcompare.hhs.gov.

*O*ne woman—a long-time City resident who moved to the suburbs to be near her children—found out the hard way about advice when she selected a doctor on the basis of her neighbor's glowing praise. During the initial visit, the patient's numerous questions about her chronic arthritis condition went unanswered while the doctor merely patted her on the shoulder and assured her that he would "take care of everything." While the paternalistic attitude might have suited the neighbor's needs, it fell far short for this senior patient, who was used to a good give-and-take with her former internist. She resumed her search for a doctor—this time with the assistance of the Castle Connolly guide, a more reliable source than a friend's recommendation.

The Best in American Medicine
www.CastleConnolly.com

You And Your Doctor: A Team

Quick Tips

- Always obtain copies of all medical records and tests for your files.

- When selecting a doctor, especially a primary care doctor, it is appropriate to request an interview to get acquainted.

- Good doctors listen, good patients talk.

- Always bring a pad and pencil with you to medical appointments. When the doctor gives you instructions, take notes.

- The Physician's Desk Reference, commonly known as the PDR, is available in most libraries and is an excellent resource for learning more about medications. (The PDR web page is at http://www.pdr.net)

- Do not hesitate to ask your pharmacist about side effects, generic substitutions and other questions related to your medications.

Quick Take

... The best doctor-patient relationship is based on a two-way dialogue. Be open and honest and seek a doctor who is the same. ...

Key Terms

American Medical Association - A membership organization of physicians and their professional associations dedicated to promoting the art and science of medicine and the betterment of public health through establishing and promoting ethical, educational, and clinical standards for the medical profession. It represents the interests of physicians on the national level.

Baseline Tests - A series of basic, routine medical tests—such as electrocardiogram, complete blood count, blood pressure measurement, weight measurement, and chest X-ray—that are usually completed by a physician upon a patient's initial visit in order to provide a standard for comparison during subsequent health examinations.

Generic Drugs - Prescription medications that have been marketed by one company under a proprietary or brand name and which may be sold, after the original exclusive patent expires, under a generic name or the name assigned to it during an early stage of development. Most generic drugs are less expensive than proprietary versions and are just as effective except in cases when, because of different manufacturing processes, they are not bioequivalent or handled by the body in an identical manner.

Third Party Payer - An organization such as indemnity insurance company or managed care organization that provides individual and group health insurance, or a governmental department which assumes responsibility for the payment of an individual's healthcare, either directly to the healthcare provider or by means of reimbursement to the individual (Medicare and Medicaid are such government programs).

You And Your Doctor: A Team

Trust and respect between doctors and patients have reached a low point in modern American society. A recent poll of consumers sponsored by the American Medical Association (AMA) concluded that approximately 70 percent of those who responded agreed with the statement that "people are beginning to lose faith in their doctors." (Despite concerns about doctors in general, much research has shown that patients tend to rate their own doctors well.)

Trust between doctors and patients has declined for many reasons, including unrealistic expectations on the part of some patients and the patronizing attitudes of some doctors, which clash with the higher education level and medical sophistication of many patients. This has been further complicated by changing financial arrangements, particularly those involving the government and third-party payers, and the perception that some doctors seem to be motivated not by the values of the Hippocratic Oath (See page xi), but by those of the marketplace. The AMA poll cited earlier found that 69 percent of respondents agreed that doctors "are too interested in making money." Perhaps a significant factor in creating this atmosphere is that in many cases the relationship between doctor and patient now has another dimension, the managed care organization. Another significant contributor is the huge amount of paperwork required from doctors. Generated by quality-assurance efforts, regulation, complex billing and managed care procedures, this burden reduces the time doctors are able to spend with patients.

Given the formidable obstacles, it might seem impossible to find a primary care doctor who is well suited to your needs. If you have carefully read the preceding chapters, your work is half done. What remains is to find that special individual who fits the criteria.

The Initial Interview

When selecting a doctor, especially a primary care doctor, it is appropriate to request an exploratory interview. Frequently, doctors will engage in such brief interviews at no charge, at a reduced fee or by telephone. It is preferable to find out about a doctor's credentials, office hours and billing procedures from the staff beforehand so you don't waste time asking about basic facts. This leaves time to ask the doctor questions that will allow you to determine what kind of relationship could develop. It is interesting that many parents will insist on interviewing a pediatrician for their child but wouldn't think of interviewing a physician for themselves.

Ask the Right Questions

The most important aspect of this session is to see if you can develop a positive doctor/patient relationship. Are you comfortable with the doctor's manner, style and general personality? Do you feel a strong sense of trust in the doctor? Here are five questions to ask the doctor plus two questions to ask yourself that may lead you closer to a selection.

- What is your experience in treating _____ (if you are seeking care for a particular illness or condition)?

- Are you open to treatments and therapies that do not rely heavily on medication?

- What preventive programs do you suggest for someone of my age, sex and health status?

- How do you feel about involving patients in decision-making?

- What are your views on_____(ethical and moral issues of importance to you as a patient)?

Even when the doctor is responding to your questions, you should ask yourself:

- Is the doctor paying attention to me and really considering my questions or do the impersonal "stock" answers indicate that the doctor's thoughts are elsewhere?

- Does this doctor speak about good health and prevention with the personal knowledge of someone who seems to practice it?

If your prospective doctor seems to measure up to your standards, get the relationship off to a good start by making an appointment for a complete check-up. During this appointment, you will have an opportunity to share your medical and family history and baseline tests will be performed to serve as a standard in the years ahead.

Talking with Your Doctor

After you have selected your doctor, your first appointment should include an extensive review of your medical history. Your doctor should spend time with you, ask questions and listen to your responses carefully.

Medical students are often told, "Listen to your patients. They'll tell you what's wrong with them." This conveys an important lesson not only for doctors, but for patients: Good doctors listen; good patients talk.

Analysis of doctor/patient conversations has revealed that many patients wait until the end of a conversation, even until they are saying goodbye, to tell their doctors what is really bothering them. This is just a small example of the dynamics of doctor/patient relationships. It is also a good example of a waste of valuable time— the doctor's and the patient's. One reason doctors need to be trained to be good listeners is that they frequently must ascertain what is troubling the patient not by what is said directly, but by what is said indirectly, not at all or through body language and other signs. However, it is always easier, less time-consuming and certainly more effective if a patient can describe problems completely and accurately.

Before you even see a doctor, you should prepare thoroughly. You should have a complete record of your medical history, including a record of X-rays and any other diagnostic tests, as well as blood workups. You need information about childhood diseases, chronic conditions, hospitalizations, past and present medications, doses and drug reactions, if any, and, if possible, something about the health history of your parents and even their siblings. Except for the last item, these are available to patients from their previous doctors or hospitals. That is why it is useful to obtain copies of all medical records and tests for your own files. Not only will this save you time and effort, but may avoid additional testing and expense. Your doctor will also ask many seemingly personal questions about your work, education, sex life and even drug and alcohol use. These are all part of a complete medical history and will help your doctor better understand you and your state of health.

If you have a particular problem or concern, describe all your symptoms. Try not to minimize or exaggerate and, most of all, don't deny.

If you have questions to ask your doctor, make a list. Always bring a pad and pencil with you to medical appointments. When the doctor gives you instructions, take notes or ask the doctor to write them down for you. If a prescription is written, ask about doses, side effects, efficacy and alternative medications as well as generic substitutes. The Physician's Desk Reference (www.pdr.net), commonly known as the PDR, is available in most libraries and is an excellent resource for learning more about medications. You can also get a great deal of information on medications from another health professional, your pharmacist. Do not hesitate to ask your pharmacist about side effects, generic substitutions and other questions related to your medications. However, if the information you receive conflicts with that given by your doctor, consult with the doctor and follow his or her directions.

A Matter of Time

Patients want and expect doctors who listen, express concern, explain conditions and procedures in a clear and understandable manner, discuss medications and their effects and side effects thoroughly, return calls, are available when needed and, perhaps most importantly, spend sufficient time with them. With increasing demands on their time, many doctors are left with an uneasy feeling of "running to stay in place." The end result may be a tendency, unintended for the most part, to rush through a patient visit. This situation contributes to the erosion of the doctor/patient relationship.

Also contributing to this problem is pervasive lateness on the part of doctors. Patients frequently complain that they spend hours in a doctor's waiting room, long past the appointed hour (research has shown the average wait is 20 minutes). Unfortunately, the duration of a patient visit is not always predictable and unexpected delays may occur if the diagnosis is complicated or if a patient needs to discuss what is on his or her mind. The doctor who spends extra time with another patient is probably the doctor you want for yourself. If the lateness is excessive, persistent and without apparent good reason, discuss it with your doctor and, if it is interfering with your relationship, consider changing doctors.

Today many primary care physicians are changing their practices to a new model known as concierge or "private medicine." In this model, physicians reduce their practice patient load from, say, 2,200 patients to 600. Each patient who remains in, or enters, a concierge practice is required to pay an annual fee typically ranging from $1,500 to $5,000, or even more. As a function of the reduced patient load, the physicians have far greater time to spend with each patient and can offer faster appointments or better access sometimes even around the clock. The physician can also focus more on preventive medicine and other aspects of sound patient care, a luxury and benefit to the patient that many physicians in a primary care practice cannot enjoy.

A fter a delay of two hours in his doctor's office, one patient, a self-employed marketing consultant, made sure that it would never happen again. Did he have a showdown with the doctor? Did he decide never to return? Not at all. He simply made it a point to call the doctor's office two hours before his scheduled appointment to see how the schedule was running. He then adjusted his own schedule to coincide with the doctor's.

Strengthening Your Team

Quick Tips

- The more complex and difficult the problem, the more important reputation is. In fact, you might well narrow your focus to doctors on the staffs of certain medical centers noted for excellence with specific problems.

- Doctors typically refer patients to doctors on the staffs of the same hospitals where they practice.

- If the lateness of your doctor is excessive, persistent and without apparent good reason, discuss it with him or her.

- If you are not comfortable with your primary care doctor's referral, ask for a number of options. If necessary, you may consider going "out of network" even if you have to pay some or all of the fee.

- In many cases, insurance companies will pay for second opinions, but check ahead of time to make sure your insurance plan does cover them.

- One way HMOs control costs is by limiting second opinions.

- Doctors may have different solutions to the same problem — and any one or more could work.

Quick Take

... The old adage, two heads are better than one, often applies in healthcare, too. Expanded options include referrals, second opinions, alternative therapies and clinical trials. ...

Key Terms

Alternative Therapy - Non-traditional forms of healthcare — including acupuncture, homeopathy, naturopathy, massage, reflexology, biofeedback, hypnotherapy, herbology, therapeutic touc, and prayer — that are often based on ancient healing methods and have not been tested in a conventional scientific manner.

Clinical Trial - An experimental trial of a new drug or therapy in a selected group of human volunteers who suffer from the condition for which the experimental drug or treatment is to be used.

Double Blind Study - One form of a clinical trial in which two groups of volunteers — one group receiving the real drug or treatment and the other receiving a placebo or dummy — are followed for a specific period of time by researchers who do not know themselves who is receiving which therapy.

Protocol - A rigid set of rules set up for a clinical trial by the Food and Drug Administration (FDA) which must be followed strictly by all researchers and volunteers participating in the trial.

Strengthening Your Team

When You Need a Specialist

For the most part, selecting a specialist is similar to choosing a primary care doctor. There is one major difference, however; typically you will be referred to a specialist by your primary care doctor. Suggesting a consultation does not show a weakness on the part of the doctor. On the contrary, the real weakness lies in a doctor's reluctance to suggest consultations when advisable. Your primary care doctor will receive a written report from any consultation or referral. You should request a copy as well.

Ask your doctor why this particular specialist is being recommended. Find out about the specialist's training and experience. If your doctor has sent many patients to the same doctor for the same treatment, you should find out how successful the treatment was and if the patients were satisfied. You might also ask if the specialist would be the one selected for your doctor's own personal care. You should feel comfortable about seeing the specialist and, if you are not, ask for another recommendation or find a different one on your own.

Frequently, patients do seek out specialists on their own. If you are attempting to find a specialist or subspecialist without the guidance of your primary care doctor, use the various selection procedures described in Chapters One, Two and Three. When selecting a physician on your own, even greater emphasis should be placed on board certification in the relevant specialty. If you are trying to find someone to treat a very specific problem, make certain that the individual is well trained in that area. You may check to see if a doctor is board certified by calling the American Board of Medical Specialties at (312) 436-2600 or visiting their web site at www.abms.org.

You will also want to know if the specialist you select is well respected. The more complex and difficult the problem, the more important reputation is. In fact, you might narrow your focus to doctors on the staffs of certain medical centers noted for excellence in treating your specific problem. There are a number of books and magazine articles such as the annual U.S. News & World Report issue on America's best hospitals that offer views on the best medical centers for specific problems.

Finally, make certain your doctor and the specialist communicate easily about your case. If you should have a problem with a specialist, or if you are not pleased with the care given, let your primary care doctor know about it right away.

Doctors typically refer patients to doctors on the staffs of the same hospitals at which they practice. There are good and poor reasons for this, as explained below.

Why Doctors Usually Refer to Doctors in the Same Hospitals

Good Reasons:
- They know the doctors better.

- They continue to be involved in the case.

- Coordination of multiple specialists may be easier.

Poor Reasons:
- It is easier.

- They will get referrals back.

- It reduces the chance of losing the patient to another doctor.

- It may help build social or professional relationships.

- The hospital may pressure doctors to refer within the institution.

In today's managed care environment doctor referrals usually are restricted to other doctors in the managed care organization's network. Sometimes the referring doctor may not even be familiar with the other doctor's qualifications. If you are not comfortable with your primary care doctor's referral, ask for a number of options. If necessary, you may consider going "out of network" even if you have to pay some or all of the fee.

Second Opinions

Second opinions are a valuable medical tool, infrequently used in many instances, overused in others. Clearly, you do not want to get another doctor's opinion on every ailment or problem, but there are definitely times you should seek out a second opinion:

- Before major surgery.

- When the diagnosis is serious or life-threatening.

- If a rare disease is diagnosed.

- If the diagnosis is uncertain.

- If you think the number of tests or procedures recommended is excessive.

- If a test result has serious implications—a positive Pap smear for example—have the test re-done immediately before taking further action.

- If the treatment suggested is risky or expensive.

- If you are uncomfortable with the diagnosis and treatment recommended.

- If a course of treatment is not working.

- If you question your doctor's competence.

- If your insurance company requires it.

Most doctors will be supportive if you request a second opinion and many will even recommend it. In many cases, insurance companies will pay for second opinions, but check ahead of time to make sure your insurance plan does indeed cover them. In an HMO, you may have to be more assertive because one way that HMOs control costs is by limiting second opinions. This is especially true if you want an opinion outside the plan's network.

Often, the opinion of a second doctor will affirm the opinion of the first, but the reassurance may be worth the time and extra cost. On the other hand, if the second opinion differs from the first, you have two remaining alternatives: seek the opinion of a third doctor, or educate yourself as much as possible by talking with both doctors and reading up on the problem (trusting your instincts about which diagnosis is correct). If the diagnosis is the same but the recommended treatments differ, remember that doctors may have different solutions to the same problem—and any one or more could be efficient. For example, an orthopaedic surgeon may recommend surgery to correct a knee injury while a physiatrist (a doctor certified in physical medicine and rehabilitation) may recommend rehabilitation. One might work better than the other or they could both work equally well. The choice may be based on your preference. Remember, however, that surgical solutions can rarely be reversed. It usually is best to try a non-surgical solution first, if possible.

Complementary Medicine: Exploring Your Options

A recent study conducted by the University of Florida estimated that 86 percent of households in the U.S. use some type of complementary therapies (a term that implies that these therapies are used along with conventional medical treatment rather than in place of them). Total out-of-pocket expenditures for complementary/alternative medicine approach $30 billion annually, estimates David Eisenberg, MD and colleagues at the Harvard/Beth Israel Center for the Study of Alternative Medicine Research. They further point out that total visits to complementary/alternative providers numbered 629 million in 1997 as compared to 386 million visits to primary care physicians.

One of the reasons conventional medical therapies are conventional is that most have been proven to be effective in a rigorous scientific manner, while many complementary/alternative therapies have not been tested under accepted scientific conditions. You should always consider the possibility that some alternative therapies, since they are unproven, may do more harm than good. The alternative approaches in use today range from legitimate searches for new therapies to outright quackery and fraud. Without the guidance of the scientific and medical community, it is sometimes impossible for doctors, let alone consumers, to tell the difference.

Nonetheless, doctors are becoming more open to the use of complementary/alternative approaches. One study reported that about 30 percent of doctors questioned in the Los Angeles area said that they were open to complementary/alternative practices in one form or another and that acceptance is growing. Medical scientists are also indicating a new interest in studying approaches to health that may complement the strengths of Western medicine. Some of the therapies being explored include mind-body medicine, hypnotherapy, biofeedback, chiropractic, vital energy, metabolic therapy, naturopathy, homeopathy, therapeutic touch, acupuncture, prayer and the use of herbs.

Alternative healthcare often complements rather than replaces Western medicine. As such, the terms complementary or integrative, which accurately describe the relationship between Western and alternative healthcare, are used with increased frequency as this type of approach towards medicine becomes more commonplace.

In a New England Journal of Medicine study, 72 percent of the respondents who used unconventional therapies did not inform their medical doctor that they had done so. That is unfortunate, because such treatments could be greatly enhanced with the support and advice of a primary care doctor. More worrisome is the great danger that some people may use alternative treatments in lieu of, rather than as a supplement to, more conventional and proven medical therapies. A classic and tragic example of this was the surge of patients who traveled to Mexico to seek a "magic bullet" cure for cancer promised by the drug Laetrile (made from apricot pits). There was no magic; indeed, patients lost money, hope and, in some cases, the opportunity for timely use of proven treatment. If you do explore alternative therapies, be certain to let your doctor know about it. Some may be harmful, especially if you are undergoing another treatment under your doctor's direction.

To learn more about complementary/alternative medicine, contact the National Center for Complementary and Alternative Medicine Clearinghouse to locate a source of reliable information on the practice you are considering (see Appendix E).

How to Use Complementary/Alternative Medicine Wisely and Well

- Try to learn everything you can about the particular therapy that interests you. Your local library and the Internet both have substantial materials on complementary/alternative medicine.

- Discuss your plans with your doctor. You might gain some insight into the therapy in terms of its possible risks. Furthermore, if you are currently under medical treatment, you should make certain that the two approaches will not conflict in some way.

- If you start an alternative therapy and it does not appear to be providing relief, or seems to be worsening the condition, contact your doctor immediately.

Clinical Trials: Should You Participate?

Each year, more than half a million Americans, some of them sick, but even more of them healthy, volunteer to take part in experimental trials of new drugs and therapies. Before drugs, vaccines, biological agents and medical devices are made available for general use by doctors and their patients, they must go through extensive testing on animals and humans called "clinical trials." There is probably at least one clinical trial in process at some medical center for almost every serious disease.

On the plus side, a clinical trial offers the opportunity for prompt use of a drug or other treatment that seems promising, and comes with the bonus of regular and thorough medical examinations at no cost to you (some trials even make allowances for participants' travel and other expenses). Moreover, patients are encouraged to discuss all of their experiences regarding the trial. You will probably learn more about your condition and feel more in control, which can have a very positive effect. On the downside, you may be giving up standard treatment for something that may or may not be better. There is even the possibility that you will not get a drug at all, because most trials are conducted by the double-blind method, in which half of the participants get the drug and half get a placebo, or "dummy" medicine. Even the doctors conducting the trials do not know who is getting which drug.

What to Know Before You Get Involved

If you are considering participating in a clinical trial, you will want to know:

- Who is the sponsor? Look for a federal government, major health organization, drug company or university-sponsored trial.

- Do any impartial authorities monitor the trial? Every hospital conducting research has an institutional review board (IRB) consisting of medical professionals and community leaders who approve that hospital's participation. There are also data and safety monitoring boards that oversee trials.

- What is the financial relationship, if any, between the doctor, hospital and the company or agency sponsoring the trial?

- Will there be pain or discomfort? Will diagnostic tests be involved? Get detailed answers to these concerns before you sign any form.

- How often will I be examined? This depends on the guidelines of the trial (called the protocol). You should make every effort to keep your appointments.

- Does my own doctor get a record of my participation in the trial? Routine health information is sent to your doctor, but details relevant to a "blinded" trial are not disclosed until the trial is over.

- Is the drug in this trial approved for treatment of any other disorder? If the answer is yes, you then know that the drug has a prior safety record.

- After the study has ended, if I have responded well to the drug, will I be able to continue using it, even before it is approved?

- Can I drop out?

If you are interested in participating in a clinical trial, make your desire known to your doctor, who can track down openings in trials being conducted by medical centers, private foundations, drug companies, physician groups and the federal government. You can also access information on clinical trials by visiting the CenterWatch Clinical Trials Listing Service at www.centerwatch.com or the web site of the National Cancer Institute at www.cancer.gov/clinicaltrials.

Easy Access to specialists and subspecialists, especially in large metropolitan areas, presents certain problems in coordination of care that a patient should be aware of. This difficulty is probably epitomized by one woman who was treated by a dermatologist, an ophthalmologist, a rheumatologist, a psychiatrist and an allergist, all of whom had office space in her very large apartment complex on Manhattan's upper west side-thus eliminating her need to even put on her coat. Fortunately, all were quite competent and had all the necessary qualifications. Unfortunately, each was affiliated with a different medical center, which made coordinating her care with her primary care doctor very complex.

Changing Your Doctor

Quick Tips

- Surgical solutions can rarely be reversed. It usually is best to try a non-surgical solution first, if possible.

- You should always consider the possibility that alternative therapies - simply because they are unproven - may do more harm than good.

- If you do explore alternative therapies, be certain to let your doctor know about it. Some may be harmful, especially if you are undergoing another treatment under your doctor's direction.

- Before you decide to part company with your doctor, ask yourself if you've been a responsible patient.

- A doctor-patient relationship is like a marriage — both sides have to work to make it successful.

- Expressing your dissatisfaction may open the communication lines between you and your doctor; you might even end up in a better relationship with your present doctor

- Unless the situation is intolerable or the doctor is impaired, stay with your current doctor until you have found another one that you like

- When changing doctors, you may have to sign a release with your new doctor approving the transfer of all your medical records to the new office. These records cannot be withheld for any reason, even if you have not yet paid your last bill.

Quick Take

... There's a big difference between doctor-hopping and changing doctors for a good reason. Most failed doctor-patient relationships can be attributed to some common complaints but sometimes are a matter of self-defense...

Key Terms

National Practitioner Data Bank - A computerized listing, created by an Act of Congress, to track health professionals who are disciplined for unprofessional behavior and to deter them from simply moving their practicies from one state to another.

Public Citizen Health Research Group - A Washington, D.C. based consumer advocacy group that has been publicly critical of many medical practices that the group considers detrimental to public healthcare.

Changing Your Doctor

Obviously, at times there are good reasons for changing doctors. Some are very simple and straightforward, such as a doctor's retirement, illness or death, your own relocation or a change in your health plan. About 40 percent of people enrolling in managed care plans have to change their doctor to one who is affiliated with their plan.

The onset of a chronic condition may also prompt a change to a different medical specialist, such as a rheumatologist or cardiologist, if a condition needs to be managed by a specialist other than a primary care doctor.

If you have continuing symptoms that your doctor has been unable to diagnose or if, after a diagnosis, your problems continue to linger without improvement, you should at least consider getting a second opinion and, depending on that opinion, possibly change doctors. Doctors often have different approaches to the same problem. A different doctor may offer a different perspective and, perhaps, a solution.

You might also change doctors in order to find one who includes complementary/alternative medicine in the treatment or to find one who can help you enroll in a clinical trial.

People who have hostile feelings toward organized medicine tend to change doctors frequently; their complaints then become a self-fulfilling prophecy. They don't get continuous, quality care because it's impossible for anyone to deliver it. On the other hand, negative feelings may be prompted by unfortunate encounters with incompetent doctors or by the patronizing or otherwise inappropriate attitudes expressed by some doctors toward patients. Patients on the receiving end of such a relationship should continue their search for a doctor who better meets their needs.

Eight Reasons to Say Goodbye

Here are the eight most common complaints about "doctors I don't go to anymore."

Poor Bedside Manner

Good medical care is more than diagnosis and treatment; it's also an attitude on the part of the doctor that sparks a sense of trust in the patient. Being under the care of a doctor who is impersonal, abrupt, bored, arrogant, condescending or sarcastic may, in the end, be counterproductive.

The doctor's aloofness could have a more serious explanation: substance abuse or psychological impairment, which, according to a recent American Medical Association report, affect 30,000 to 40,000 physicians. Mood swings and detachment are signs to watch for.

Too Vague and Evasive

A doctor who dismisses problems with "it's nothing to worry about" or "let me take care of it" or who uses medical jargon isn't interested in having you as a partner in your healthcare. The effect of this evasiveness can be anger, fear and confusion, leading to failure to follow directions and failure of treatment.

Never on Schedule

Medical emergencies can make appointment scheduling an inexact science, but when snafus become chronic, it's a sign of trouble. An explanation can ease the frustration, but make-up time should not be at your expense.

Couldn't Diagnose the Problem

Some conditions can't be diagnosed on-the-spot. Others aren't attributable to one specific cause. That doesn't excuse an incomplete workup, however, which may leave you with a condition that could have been treated earlier.

Ordered too Many Tests

Sophisticated technology is available and doctors tend to use it, although some testing may not be necessary. The number of tests performed for diagnosis seems to be reduced in patient-doctor relationships where communication is strong.

Discouraged Second Opinions

A doctor who dissuades you from talking to another doctor may perceive it as questioning his or her professional abilities.

Didn't Protect My Medical Privacy

No patient should have to discuss the reason for a visit, payment or payment problems within earshot of other patients or staff.

Under certain conditions, medical records can be requested by and turned over to insurance companies, lawyers, employers and certain others without your consent, but you can certainly see them, too, to make sure they contain the proper information. In all 50 states and the District of Columbia, federal law grants patients access to their medical records.

Unpleasant Office Staff

Repeated incidents such as rudeness over the telephone, a brusque physician's assistant or being kept waiting in an examining room for a long time before the doctor shows up are all annoying indications that a staff could do better.

The staff takes its cues from the chief. A doctor who doesn't demand the highest level of performance from a staff may be sending a message about his or her own laxity in diagnosis and treatment.

Should You Switch?

If these conditions exist in your doctor-patient relationship, it may be time to consider finding a new doctor. But before you decide to part company with your doctor, ask yourself if you've been a responsible patient. Often problems arise when patients don't reveal their full medical history or if they forget to alert their doctor about other drugs they are taking. A doctor-patient relationship is like a marriage—both sides have to work to make it successful.

If you're sure the problem isn't on your side, however, confront your doctor with your grievances. Or, if it's easier for you, you may want to write them in a letter. Expressing your dissatisfaction may open the communication lines between you and your doctor. You might even end up in a better relationship with your present doctor. Sometimes doctors aren't aware that they are in the midst of a deteriorating relationship until a patient wants to leave.

But if you are still unhappy with your doctor and you've decided a change is necessary, you can make a clean break by simply going to another doctor. Keep in mind, however, that your most important concern should be continuity of care. So, unless the situation is intolerable or the doctor is impaired, stay with your current doctor until you have found another one that you like.

Generally, medical records are kept by your doctor until you have found a new one. You will then have to sign a release with your new doctor approving the transfer of all your medical records to the new office. These records cannot be withheld for any reason, even if you have not yet paid your last bill.

Finally, don't feel embarrassed or guilty if you decide to change doctors. Remember, good quality medical care is your right!

Self Defense: Avoiding Questionable Doctors

In addition to finding good doctors, you also want to be able to identify and avoid doctors who have a history of professional problems. One way to do this is to make certain a doctor has not been disciplined by your state or, in fact, any state. You can call the appropriate state agency (listed in Appendix E) or check the web sites of those state agencies that make this information available. These sites list the names of doctors who have been disciplined by their state or by the federal government. The disciplinary actions were taken for a variety of reasons, including overprescribing or misprescribing medications, criminal convictions, alcohol or drug abuse and patient sexual abuse.

You also may visit the 'Doctor Disciplinary Search' section of the Castle Connolly Medical Ltd. web site (www.CastleConnolly.com) for links to those states with discipline information on their sites. You may also visit the American Medical Association (AMA) at www.ama-assn.org and American Board of Medical Specialities (ABMS) at www.abms.org. For the websites for biographical information about doctors, including board certification see Appendix D.

The Public Citizen Health Research Group, which publishes a report on the number of physicians disciplined in each state, believes that many states are not aggressive enough in monitoring doctors. They have been leading the call for public access to the National Practitioner Data Bank. The Data Bank was created in 1986 by an Act of Congress to track professionals who are disciplined for unprofessional behavior and to deter them from simply moving their practices from one state to another. The Data Bank became operational in 1990 and contains a record of adverse actions such as license removal, loss of clinical privileges and professional society membership actions taken against doctors and other licensed health professionals such as dentists. It contains the names of more than 170,000 health practitioners who have either a licensing action or malpractice judgment or settlement against them. There is strong pressure from some medical groups either to do away with the Data Bank or to place even stricter controls on access to it. They support their position with examples of errors in the handling of sensitive information. It is unlikely that Congress would permit the elimination of the Data Bank. In fact, it is possible that at some time in the future, access may be made more available to the public. However, at the present time there is no public general access to this information. After intense pressure a restricted data bank can now be accessed by research and journalism groups, provided they agree to newly imposed restrictions, which may be found unworkable.

A data service used by lawyers to check on a doctor's or hospital's malpractice history is LEXIS/NEXIS, the computerized legal information service. Some libraries will do a LEXIS/NEXIS search for a fee. Public access to the listing of malpractice payments is one issue on which doctors are very sensitive, and rightfully so. Many malpractice payments are made by insurance companies over the objections of doctors because the insurers feel it's cheaper to settle than to fight. Yet, doctors who feel they are blameless contend that these settlements reflect negatively on them. Also, since so many specialists, such as those in obstetrics and gynecology, are subject to more frequent lawsuits because of the nature of their practices, doctors are concerned about how patients will interpret a malpractice settlement. A few states, for example Massachussetts, make this information available on the State Health Department website. Check to see if it is available in your state. (See Doctor Disciplinary Search section on the Castle Connolly Medical Ltd website (www.CastleConnolly.com.)

People who believe they have a problem with a doctor, whether in regard to fees, treatment or ethics, may contact the appropriate local medical society in the county in which the doctor practices or the state medical society. State health departments are also places consumers may turn to for assistance or information on disciplinary actions taken against doctors. The health department, typically, will only divulge that an action has been taken but will not give you any specific information about it (See Appendix E for phone numbers and addresses).

Changing your doctor should not be considered a setback in your search for the best doctor to meet your needs. As you may have come to understand throughout preceding chapters in this book, the personal and treatment styles doctors bring to their practices vary greatly. What is important for you, as a patient, to realize is that these subtle and immeasurable characteristics can be as important as clinical skills. There is, in fact, substantial empirical and anecdotal evidence demonstrating that confidence in the healer and the healing process plays a major role in many cures. Your main objective is to find the therapy—in combination with the professional who is providing the therapy—that works best for you.

In one case involving a woman in her mid-thirties, the doctor-patient relationship was severed over what was basically a conflict in personalities: the woman wished to have more control over her healthcare, and the doctor was reluctant to give it. The impasse was reached before the two could attempt any kind of a compromise, and the woman went off in search of a doctor who would better suit her personal needs. A year later, after a fruitless search for a doctor whose medical expertise she respected, she returned to her original doctor.

The Best in American Medicine
www.CastleConnolly.com

Choosing a Doctor in a Health Plan

Quick Tips

- A data service used by lawyers to check on a doctor's or hospital's malpractice history is Lexis/Nexis, the computerized legal information service. Lexis will do a search and issue a report on any malpractice awards or settlements ordered by a court.

- State health departments are also places consumers may turn to for assistance or information on disciplinary actions taken against doctors.

- There is substantial empirical and anecdotal evidence demonstrating that confidence in the healer and the healing process plays a major role in many cures.

- People who belive they have a problem with a doctor in regard to fees, treatment, or ethics, may contact the appropriate local medical society in the county in which the doctor practices, or the state medical society.

- When choosing a doctor in a health plan, use the same criteria you would apply to selecting a doctor in a fee-for-service practice.

- Typically, you will be sent a list with little information other than the doctor's name, specialty and address. Find out more about those doctors you may be considering.

- In some cases, a health plan will agree to pay at least a consultation fee if you feel strongly that you need to discuss your problem with another doctor outside of the health plan network

- If method of health plan payment to physicians is an issue of concern to you, it may be wise to ask your doctor about the method of compensation in the health plan in which you are enrolled.

Quick Take

... The rules are different but they are not difficult to play by. The first step is to sort out the alphabet soup of models. The model of health plan usually determines how your care will be delivered and often your satisfaction with it ...

Key Terms

Capitation - A method of payment to physicians and other healthcare providers whereby a fixed amount of money is allotted for each patient served.

EPO - An Exclusive Provider Organization is similar to a PPO except the patients must use only providers in the EPO.

Group Model HMO - A model of an HMO in which the HMO contracts with large multi-specialty groups of doctors to provide care, usually from a number of central locations.

Health Maintenance Organization (HMO) - One type of managed care organization that provides for a wide range of comprehensive healthcare services for its members in return for a fixed, predetermined fee. The care is provided by a network or group of physicians affiliated with the organization and possibly other healthcare professionals. The term "health plan" is a more common name in use today, which applies to all of the various health insurance organizations described in this list.

IPA - An Independent Practice Association is one model of health maintenance organization (HMO) in which the organization contracts with individual doctors, or groups of doctors, to provide care for the enrolled patients in the doctors' own offices.

PHO - A Physician Hospital Organization is an organization of a hospital and its physicians that may contract with managed care organizations (MCO) or may become licensed as an MCO itself.

PPO - A Preferred Provider Organization is a managed care model that offers healthcare provided by a group of doctors and/or hospitals that have negotiated discounted rates, either capitated or fee-for-service, for enrollees while continuing to provide care for other patients. Patients typically pay less if they use the PPO provider.

PSO - A Provider Service Organization, sometimes called a provider service network (PSN), is a group of doctors that are organized to provide care to a large number of patients, typically under contract to managed care organizations.

Staff Model HMO - A managed care model where the HMO employs the doctors, usally on salary. Care is provided out of a number of centralized locations.

Choosing a Doctor in a Health Plan

At one time only doctors looking for new patients joined HMOs. Today, there is a new reality. Although HMO's still exist, a more common name is health plan. Almost all doctors—more than 80 percent—participate in some kind of managed care arrangement. So it is likely that you will find the best for your own care if you know how to work the system.

When managed care achieves a significant market penetration and begins to control the flow of large numbers of patients, more doctors sign on. Also, many hospitals encourage their doctors to sign on with as many different plans as possible in order to ensure that the hospital does not lose any potential patients. Managed care now enrolls more than one out of every three people in the country, and more than 80 percent of workers who get health insurance through their employer are in some form of managed care. Today, more people are enrolled in PPOs (Preferred Provider Organization), which tend to be more flexible in choices of physicians, than are enrolled in HMOs. However, we will use health plan as "shorthand" for both.

The main factors to focus on in assessing a health plan or a PPO are its resources, primarily doctors and hospitals. First, is there an ample selection of primary care doctors near where you live and work? Second, are the doctors well qualified? This can be answered by following the approach outlined in this book for finding the best doctors. When choosing doctors, it is usually a good idea to call their offices to confirm they are still affiliated with the particular plan. Doctors frequently change affiliations with managed care plans. Also, it is a good idea to check on the procedure for using the doctor listed.

Health plans may list hundreds of doctors but not all of them are necessarily accessible to all members. A large health plan, for example, may restrict the number of specialists that primary care doctors can refer to for various reasons, including location, hospital capacity and general resource allocation. So although you may see the name of an ophthalmologist, gynecologist or other specialist you want to use, and indeed that doctor may be affiliated with the health plan, it does not necessarily follow that your primary care doctor is free to refer you to them. Those specialists may see health plan patients only on a certain basis—for specific procedures, for example, or in a certain geographic region—and then possibly only after a rigorous screening process. These possibilities illustrate the varying styles of operation you will find in managed care plans.

Doctors in health plans are bound by the same professional ethics that guide all doctors. However, there is a major difference; in a health plan, the plan is responsible for providing you with care as well as with a doctor. If your doctor leaves the plan, you don't follow him or her. The plan provides a new doctor for you.

Selecting Doctors in a Health Plan

Selecting a doctor in a health plan can be a greater challenge than selecting one when you have indemnity insurance that leaves you free to select a doctor without the restrictions of the plan. Obviously, in a health plan arrangement you need to select a doctor who belongs to that plan. Studies have shown that about 40 percent of enrollees in managed care plans have to choose a new doctor when they join. However, even in a plan of small size, you will usually have the option of choosing among a number of primary care doctors as well as other specialists and subspecialists. In doing so, utilize the same criteria you would apply to selecting a doctor in a fee-for-service practice.

The first doctor you select in a health plan is your primary care doctor. Typically, you will be sent a list with little information other than the doctor's name, specialty and address. Find out more about those doctors you may be considering. Use the process described earlier in this book. If you make a selection and are not satisfied, request a change. Ask about the procedure for changing doctors before you join the plan.

When you need a specialist, it is your primary care doctor who will refer you, as in traditional indemnity plans. But, unlike indemnity plans in which you can find a specialist on your own if you choose, in managed care plans you must be referred to see a specialist. Again, your choices will be limited in selecting specialists, but be assertive. Ask for a choice of doctors and ask why your primary care doctor recommends a particular specialist. One disadvantage to the IPA model and the network referral process is that primary care doctors can end up making referrals to specialists and/or subspecialists that they do not know. This may result in poor communication between the primary care doctor and the specialist, which is not in the patient's best interest. If you are not satisfied with the choices offered, ask to go outside the plan. Choice of providers outside a plan is built into certain managed care plans (PPOs or POS, Point of Service) and is permitted in many others under certain conditions.

However, if you do not have a choice, or if the choices are not ones with which you agree, consider going outside the health plan. Although you are likely to have to pay more, it may be worth it if you get a correct diagnosis and appropriate treatment for your problem. In some cases, the health plan will agree to pay at least a consultation fee if you feel strongly that you need to discuss your problem with another doctor outside the health plan network. After the consultation, if you still feel the need for a different doctor, at least your choice will be based on more complete information.

One of the most popular options offered by health plans permits going outside of the network of doctors and hospitals—but at an added cost. The point of service, or POS plan, one of the fastest growing offerings of many health plans, permits the health plan member to use doctors, hospitals, and other services that are not part of the health plan network. Typically, the member will pay an additional fee for this choice—for example, 20 percent or 30 percent of the cost—whereas if the member stays "in-network" the health plan will pay all or close to all of the cost.

When leaving the network of a POS, however, patients should find out exactly how much it will cost to do so. Some health plans will pay a percentage of "usual and customary fees" while others will pay a percentage of their own fee schedule, which is usually lower.

HMO Models

Although a large alphabet soup of health plan models has appeared since the big move toward managed care began in the late 1980s, and we now have PPOs, PSOs, and EPOs, two models are most important to the healthcare consumer. One is the staff or group model where patients visit their doctors in a single, or perhaps in a few, locations and where all the doctors and most, if not all, diagnostic and treatment facilities are located. The second is the independent practice association or IPA model where doctors see patients in their private offices. Organizations such as PPOs, EPOs and PSOs tend to be organized on the IPA model.

Whether a group/staff model or an IPA, all health plans require a primary care physician and all have certain protocols, usually involving referral by the primary care physician, to access a specialist.

Doctor Compensation

There is virtually no difference in the types of doctors who practice in the two plan models and each should be evaluated in terms of benefits to the individual patient. There is, however, a separate matter of how doctors in HMOs are compensated, and this issue has become a major concern to both patients and doctors.

Health plans compensate doctors in a number of ways. Doctors who are employed by staff model health plans are usually on salary, perhaps with a quality bonus based on patient satisfaction. In group model health plans, the physician group has a contract with the health plan and the doctors are employed by the group, usually on salary and, again, often with a quality bonus.

In the IPA model, or in PPOs, EPOs, PSOs and other types of managed care organizations the doctors are usually paid in one of two ways. In the past, the predominant payment method was a negotiated fee schedule, typically designed at some discount to the doctor's normal fee. Doctors simply traded the promise of higher volume for a reduced fee. Today, a major method of payment in an IPA is capitation. While this is fast becoming the most common method of payment in IPAs it is also the one generating the most controversy.

Under a capitated or capitation system doctors are paid a set amount per month or per year to provide care to a patient during that time period. So, for example, a primary care physician may be paid $25 per member per month.

Health plans have moved toward capitation as a method of payment because they found that discounted fee-for-service payment methods did not reduce costs as much as had been hoped, if at all. To make up for discounted fees of 20 percent, for instance, some doctors simply scheduled 20 percent more patient visits so that their incomes would not decrease. Doctors openly comment that discounted fees translate to discounted time with patients!

Capitation has helped to control costs. However, it also has introduced a number of important ethical issues for doctors, other healthcare providers, and for patients. Many are troubled by the notion that a doctor could be placed in a situation that appears to promise rewards for not providing care. It is generally recognized that under a fee-for-service system doctors have an incentive to provide more care, even if it is not necessary, because they are paid by the amount of care they deliver. But the reverse is not accepted in such a benign fashion: the concept of a doctor being rewarded to provide less care is of major concern to many people, including many doctors.

Another technique involved in payment systems utilized by managed care companies is called "withholds" or "set-asides." This method is also used to motivate doctors to control costs and, as in capitation, raises similar ethical concerns. Under this method, for example, a group of pediatricians is contracted to care for 1,000 children. That contract is based on a budget of $15,000 a month. A certain amount of that budget, say 20 percent, is reserved for referrals to subspecialists and another 20 percent is set aside or withheld. If the group of doctors uses fewer subspecialist referrals than budgeted they receive the 20 percent that was set aside. If they use more subspecialist referrals than were budgeted the extra amount comes out of the set-aside. The more set-aside that is used for referrals, the less doctors will be able to receive from it.

A great deal of controversy has ensued over these payment mechanisms. Some states, in fact, are legislating to prohibit or restrict these practices. Individual "horror stories" of patients who have been denied appropriate care, such as not being referred to a subspecialist in a timely manner, have been used to demonstrate the issue in human terms.

Some studies demonstrate that when physician-run health plans are paid by capitation and are in control they reduce costs more substantially than other plans. Some doctors strongly support capitation. They believe it makes them, rather than managers, responsible for allocating resources and making medical decisions.

And, despite the outcry, most of the studies of health plan patients versus non-plan patients demonstrate no differences in their health status.

In fact, there is a substantial body of research suggesting that health plan members receive more in the way of preventive services than do non-health plan populations.

If method of payment is an issue of concern to you, it may be wise to ask your doctor about the method of compensation in the health plan in which you are enrolled. If you believe the method would work against you as a patient you should discuss it with your doctor and ask if and how it influences the manner of care for patients. If you are not satisfied by the answer you may want to change doctors or, better yet, change health plans, if possible.

While the wisest course of action is to ask about this issue before joining a health plan, rather than after you have become a member, most plan members have not done this. If you believe you are not receiving appropriate care because of a health plan policy, you can contact your state health insurance department (see Appendix E).

How Doctors and Patients Feel about Managed Care

People enrolled in health plans tend to be satisfied by their plans. However, most doctors do not like managed care—and understandably so! Managed care organizations negotiate deep discounts in fees for doctors. There is no reason doctors should prefer this process, but when managed care controls so many patients there is little choice but to join managed care and negotiate.

Managed care organizations also require doctors to do a substantial amount of paperwork and to follow policies and procedures that control costs and monitor quality. All of this creates a level of business management most doctors resent.

At least a portion of these negative attitudes toward managed care can be ascribed to differences in the organization of medical practices in different parts of the country.

The northeast, south, and southwest regions have been the slowest to accept managed care because doctors generally resisted it more strongly than those in other parts of the country. Doctors in large group practices, which are more common in the far west and midwest than in the east, adapted to managed care more readily. In the northeast, where doctors practice solo or in small groups, the change has been greater and the adjustment more difficult.

Most doctors have adapted and learned to practice successfully in this new medical environment. According to a survey conducted by the American Medical Association, just over a third (210,811) of physicians in this country are now members of group practices. In 1995 group practices numbered 19,788, an increase of 361 percent since 1965. From 1991 to 1995, the number of groups increased by 16.4 percent and the number of group physicians by 14.3 percent.

The survey shows that, in an environment that is organizationally complex, medical groups have changed how they are organized legally, with partnerships declining to 13.8 percent and professional corporations increasing to 77.9 percent. In the latter group, control of decision making remains largely in the physician's hands. This ability to retain decision making power has dramatically altered physicians' attitudes towards managed care.

The view of patients and the public, however, is decidedly more positive about managed care.

A study sponsored by the Medstat Group, J.D. Power and Associates and the New England Medical Center reported that in 20 markets across the United States, health plans received more top scores than PPOs and fee-for-service plans.

The study asked plan members to assess their health plans on choice of providers, physician care, premiums and deductibles and access to care. Health plans topped fee-for-service and point-of-service plans in more than half of the markets.

One of the findings uncovered in a Louis Harris Associates poll of consumers was that of the majority surveyed, 59 percent, believed the trend toward managed care was a good thing as compared to 28 percent who viewed it as a bad thing. Also, 48 percent as compared to 39 percent believed managed care would improve quality, and 59 percent versus 30 percent believed it would help contain the costs of care. Of note was that the response of those people in communities with a high penetration by managed care tended to be the most positive!

There are many studies that have examined the quality of care and the satisfaction of patients in managed care settings. Most show that members of health plans and other managed care organizations are at least as satisfied or more satisfied with their care than people covered by indemnity insurance. Some studies have shown indemnity-covered people are more satisfied, particularly when it relates to choice of doctors. In fact, the issue of greatest concern to health plan enrollees is usually access, particularly to specialists. Advocates of either view can point to studies to support managed care or to criticize it. The key may lay in the studies that have demonstrated that when individuals have a choice, and select a managed care plan, they tend to be more satisfied than those who have no choice.

In terms of quality, the conclusion is similar. While critics may contend that the care delivered by managed care organizations is not adequate, and a study of Medicaid patients is frequently cited to support this view, the overwhelming majority of studies demonstrate no difference in the health status and quality of care of those people covered by managed care plans or by indemnity insurance.

The variability in the results of all of the studies on quality and satisfaction in managed care reinforces the important premise that, as there are good doctors and poor doctors, there are good health plans and poor health plans. It is important for consumers to know how to discern the difference and to put some effort, however modest, into finding the best.

Points to Remember

- To summarize, there is basically no difference in quality between doctors who participate in health plans and those who do not accept insurance. You can find excellent doctors if you're a member of a health plan and you can find poor ones, just as you can find excellent and poor doctors if you carry indemnity insurance. The key is making sure that you find the best available for your own needs and the needs of your family.

Some simple guidelines to remember:

- Review the credentials and training of any doctor who cares for you.

- Make certain that a doctor you select is taking new patients and the waiting period for an appointment is not unreasonable.

- Be sure the health plan has a sufficient number of specialists and subspecialists you may need to see and that they are of high quality. For example, if you have diabetes, you will want to make sure that the plan has endocrinologists on staff or as part of its network. If you have coronary heart disease, you will want to make sure that the plan has first rate cardiologists and an arrangement with an outstanding center where the doctors perform invasive and non-invasive diagnostic techniques and which has a good record for open heart surgery.

- Determine beforehand the health plan's policy for patient referral to subspecialists, especially whether or not you will have a choice and how it may be exercised.

- Inquire about the rules for changing doctors in the plan if you are not satisfied with your initial choice. You will want to know not only the procedure but how often such change is allowed.

- Ask about your options to go out of network and what your additional percentage of payment will be if you exercise this option. In determining what percentage the health plan pays, try to find out whether their payment is based on the health plan fee scale or "usual and customary" fees.

- Ask your doctor about the health plan's compensation system. You want to be sure that the system for paying your doctor will not have a negative influence on your care.

The Best in American Medicine
www.CastleConnolly.com

Directory of Doctors

Includes
Partnership for Excellence
Program

The Best in American Medicine
www.CastleConnolly.com

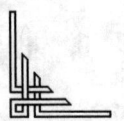

How to use the Directory of Doctors

Castle Connolly Medical Ltd. provides healthcare consumers with an invaluable source of information to identify leading physicians in their own community. This eighteenth edition of the Castle Connolly Guide, *Top Doctors: New York Metro Area*, contains vital information on more than 6,500 of the finest doctors in the region. Our guides are the result of a methodical process requiring a complete credential, licensing and disciplinary review of all doctors nominated for inclusion in the guide.

Why This Book Is Your Best Guide

Top Doctors: New York Metro Area is unique in a number of ways. The first edition of the Guide, published in 1994, was the first selective directory of doctors who practice in the New York metropolitan region. Castle Connolly recognizes that most healthcare is provided locally and people generally obtain their healthcare where they live or work. Therefore, by identifying excellent, caring physicians in every community and in every hospital, we apprise consumers of the best healthcare available to them within their own communities. Healthcare consumers in the New York metropolitan region are very fortunate with the abundance of doctors—approximately 90,000—who practice in the area. On the other hand, making a selection of one out of such a multitude can be a daunting task; it's hard even to know where to start. With *Top Doctors: New York Metro Area* in hand, you are already well on your way to finding the very best doctor for your individual needs and the needs of your family members.

With the profusion of outstanding academic medical centers, tertiary care teaching hospitals and fine regional hospitals in the New York metropolitan area, virtually any medical procedure or treatment can be found close to home. By virtue of this fact, it would be a simple matter to compile a book identifying the outstanding leaders in medical research and academic medicine in the region. Although many of these doctors are included in the listings, their names are to be found among the many excellent and caring doctors who deliver outstanding patient care in every community in the area. The goal—first and foremost—is to help you find the best doctors to meet your healthcare needs where you live and work. Again, a good reason why the Castle Connolly Guide is exceptional.

Further, the Castle Connolly Guide is different from most other listings of doctors in its selection process. Our selection is predicated on an extensive nomination procedure and a set of exacting standards which each nominated doctor was required to meet. To you, this means that the basis for inclusion of every one of the doctors in the listings was twofold: respect of their peers and medical excellence. Doctors do not pay to be listed. Our goal is to serve consumers, not doctors, hospitals or health plans.

How Castle Connolly Selects the Top Doctors

The basis of the Castle Connolly selection process is peer nomination. In some ways, this resembles an enhancement of the process in which a personal physician provides a patient with a referral to another physician for a particular problem. However, if the recommendation of one doctor is good, the recommendation of many doctors is even better.

How do we accomplish this enormous task? Castle Connolly holds an annual nationwide nomination process open to all MDs and DOs with an active medical license. Hospital Presidents, CEOs and Vice Presidents of Medicine are also eligible to participate.

Over the years this enabled the Castle Connolly physician-led research team to select those physicians most highly recommended by their peers. The selection process also considers information on medical training; clinical teaching and research status, and medical discipline checks.

This cumulative database is systematically maintained and continuously updated, and augmented by periodic telephone, mail and internet contact with physicians. The following counties are the focus of this guide:

New York State: New York, Bronx, Kings, Queens, Richmond, Nassau, Rockland, Suffolk, Westchester

New Jersey: Bergen, Essex, Hudson, Mercer, Middlesex, Monmouth, Morris, Passaic, Somerset, Union

Connecticut: Fairfield

Considerations for Inclusion Among the Top Doctors

Castle Connolly considers the following among the varied criteria used to determine physician eligibility for inclusion in our guides.

Professional Qualifications

- Education
- Residency
- Board certification
- Fellowships
- Professional reputation
- Hospital appointment
- Medical school faculty appointment
- Experience
- Disciplinary history

Personal Characteristics/Qualities

Not only do we seek nominations of physicians who excel in academic medicine and research, but most importantly, those who exhibit excellence in patient care. We ask physicians in our survey to consider not only the training and clinical skills of the physicians they nominate, but also interpersonal skills such as the following:

- Listening and communicating effectively
- Demonstrating empathy
- Educating and informing
- Instilling trust and confidence

Verification/Credential Review

The Castle Connolly research staff reviews and refines the pool of nominated physicians in a region, validates nominations and verifies credentials. This results in the development of a preliminary list of physicians. Each provisionally selected physician is then required to complete a comprehensive professional biographical form including their special practice interests (see the "SPECIALTY & SPECIAL EXPERTISE INDEX"). The information contained in the biographical form becomes an integral part of each selected physician's listing in the guide.

The last phase of the process refines the list of provisionally selected doctors by cross-referencing their names against a variety of databases providing confirmation of:

- Board certification and recertification
- Licensing
- Disciplinary history

In some regions, we include a small number of highly peer-reviewed physicians who do not have American board certifications. These physicians have trained and attained equivalent board certification in countries outside the United States.

Physicians ultimately selected for inclusion in *Top Doctors: New York Metro Area* receive formal notification of their nomination for listing upon completion of the final confirmation of their professional credentials.

How You Can Select the Top Doctors

How can you begin to make a choice from such a compilation of names? There is, in fact, a basic step-by-step process which varies somewhat depending on your individual needs as you approach the list. Here are the possibilities:

ONE: **If You are Looking for a Doctor in a Particular County**

The key: Physicians listed in the following pages are organized under the county in which their office is located so that you can go directly to the section listing doctors in your county of residence.

Key fact: Like most healthcare consumers, you probably receive your healthcare locally. If you think about it, you usually have been treated by doctors close to where you live and in community hospitals. If necessary, you may be referred to regional specialists and nearby medical centers.

TWO: **If You are Looking for a Primary Care Physician — a Generalist**

The key: The doctors who practice predominantly primary care, in the specialties of internal medicine, family practice, pediatrics, and obstetrics/gynecology, are designated by the notation a in the listing.

Key fact: Every board certified physician is a specialist. The term "having boards" signifies that a physician has completed an approved residency in a given specialty and has passed a rigorous examination given by that particular board. Therefore, doctors who practice primary care—internists, family practitioners, pediatricians, and Ob/Gyns—are specialists in their respective fields, as are urologists, otolaryngologists and radiologists. These specialists are considered primary care physicians.

THREE: **If You are Looking for a Physician in a Particular Specialty**

The key: Each entry contains the specialty practiced by the doctor and, in most cases, the most recent year of board certification.

Key fact: Many physicians specialize in fields of medicine that are not primary care. These specialists have completed an approved residency in a given specialty and have passed a rigorous exam given by that specialty board. For example, some physicians are board certified in psychiatry, surgery, allergy and immunology or dermatology.

Many doctors choose to specialize further. They choose an additional training program called a fellowship and upon completion of the program, they are required to take another exam in order to be certified as a subspecialist. An example of such subspecialization is an internist (initially board certified in internal medicine) who subspecialize in nephrology or cardiology. This doctor would be termed "double boarded" and would very likely practice nephrology or cardiology rather than internal medicine as a primary care physician.

FOUR: **If You are Looking for a Doctor with Expertise in a Particular Disease or Technique**

The key: Particular skills and interests of the doctors are found under the heading "SPECIALTY & SPECIAL EXPERTISE INDEX."

Key fact: A physician may have a special expertise interest in a particular field of medicine without actually being board certified in that area. Special expertise interests should not be confused with a board certified medical specialty. For example, cosmetic surgery is not an American Board of Medical Specialties recognized specialty, but it may constitute a major practice activity for many plastic surgeons. Certain doctors may develop a reputation as "specialists" in AIDS, diabetes or arthroscopic surgery. None of these are recognized medical specialties, yet they are indications of a doctor's expertise in a disease or medical or surgical procedure which may be helpful if you have the disease or need the procedure.

Many doctors who have a strong interest in, or consider themselves "specializing in," a particular health problem or medical technique form special interest groups referred to as "self-designated medical specialties." These groups are often confused with recognized medical specialties, which they are not. Some of the groups would like to be recognized by the ABMS and may even work toward that goal. For example, adolescent medicine was a special interest and self-designated specialty that is now an ABMS recognized subspecialty.

Choosing a doctor with a special practice interest is an additional step to be considered after you have already narrowed your choices to particular specialists and/or subspecialists. The "SPECIALTY & SPECIAL EXPERTISE INDEX" lists the doctors' special area or areas of expertise and can be particularly useful in identifying physicians who embrace alternative or complementary practices. Self-designated medical specialties are listed in Appendix B.

FIVE: **If You are Looking for a Doctor by Name**

The key: The "ALPHABETICAL LISTING OF DOCTORS" indicates the page on which information on the doctor's credentials can be found. The listing is arranged in last name, first name order.

Key fact: Most people start their search for a doctor through recommendation by family and friends. As a savvy healthcare consumer you realize that such recommendations are often based on personal "chemistry" and may be made by someone who actually knows very little about doctors or healthcare. Therefore, you will want to check the credentials of any recommended doctor and follow the additional recommendations that we have outlined in Sections one and two.

SIX: **If You want Detailed Information on a Particular Doctor**

The key: Each doctor's listing includes a substantial amount of information about the doctor.

Key fact: Wise choices in healthcare are made by consumers who have gathered as much information as possible about a particular doctor. If a professional information form was not returned by a doctor in time for inclusion in the book, our research staff verified certain major points of information (name, address, telephone, hospital affiliation, and specialty) from public sources and we have included this limited information. Even if a doctor's full credentials are included in this book, it is possible that, since the time of publication, the doctor has moved his or her office(s), changed telephone number(s), joined new medical groups, resigned from or joined hospital staffs, and, especially, changed relationships with HMOs and PPOs. Nonetheless, you can, in most cases, track down the doctor by using the following sources:

- Doctor's office—call the office number listed in the directory and ask for a new number.

- Hospitals—call the hospital listed in the directory and ask for help in locating a particular doctor.

- State Health Department—all state health department numbers are listed in Appendix E.

- American Board of Medical Specialties—a complete listing of ABMS Specialty Boards is found in Appendix A.

- American Osteopathic Association—a complete listing of AOA Specialty Boards is found in Appendix A.

Conclusion

You are now ready to work with our directory of more than 6,500 of the finest doctors in the New York metropolitan area. Although you may be well-informed as a result of reading Sections one and two of this book, it is possible that choosing the doctor will seem to be a complex endeavor. The tendency might be to try to get the job done as quickly as possible by choosing a doctor based solely on the convenience of the office's location. To do so would be a big mistake. You want the best healthcare. You deserve it. A little effort will help you to get the best.

There are many excellent doctors in the region not listed in this book. You can identify them by using the process we have described in Sections one and two or, if a doctor in this book is unable to meet your needs, ask about other physicians highly regarded by that doctor.

We believe that this book will educate and enlighten you throughout its pages and that it will prove its value in the end—when you decide on the doctor with whom you plan to have a lasting relationship.

Obtaining Additional Doctor Information

You may wish to call a doctor's office to make an appointment or to help determine if the doctor is the one you want to care for you. Here are some questions you may want to ask:

1. Is a referral required?

2. Are you accepting new patients?

3. Which health plans/insurance do you accept?

4. Do you accept Medicare? Medicaid? Workers' compensation? No-fault insurance?

5. Are payments of deductible and co-payments required at the time of appointment?

6. Do you accept credit cards?

7. Do you see patients in the evening? On weekends?

8. Is the office handicapped-accessible?

9. Do you accept phone calls from patients?

10 Do you communicate with patients via the internet?

11. If you are not comfortable addressing the doctor in English, ask if your native language is spoken by the doctor or by someone else in the office.

Sample Physician Listing

Smith, John MD [Ped] - **Spec Exp:** Asthma Allergy; **Hospital:** Children's Hosp (page 120);
Name [Specialty]   Special Expertise(s)   Admitting Hospital & Hospital
                                                      Information Page

Address: 300 Ridge Road Boston, MA 12345; **Phone:** (617) 555-2343; **Board Cert:** Ped 75;
          Office Address   Office Phone   Board Certification(s)

Med School: Harvard Med Sch 70; **Resid:** Ped, Children's Hosp 73;
        Medical School   Residency(ies)

Fellow: AM, Children's Hosp 74; **Fac Appt:** Assoc Prof Ped, The Med Sch
        Fellowship(s)   Faculty Appointment

* Indicates the most recent date of board certification or recertification.

In our listings of the professional information on doctors, we have abbreviated hospitals and medical schools. The abbreviations are designed to be self-explanatory, but if you need assistance, refer to Appendix C: Hospitals Listings.

Note on Special Expertise(s):

These are not medical specialties as described on pages 81-87, but the areas of expertise or practice interests indicated by the doctor.

The information reported in each doctor's listing is, for the most part, provided by the doctor or his/her office staff. Castle Connolly attempts to verify the data through other sources but cannot guarantee that in all cases all data have been so verified or are accurate. All such information is subject to change from time to time due to changes in physician practices. Many doctors participate in several health plans and/or switch plans frequently. Therefore, you should verify with the doctor's office whether your health plan is currently accepted.

The Best in American Medicine
www.CastleConnolly.com

Medical Specialties
and Subspecialties

In the pages that follow, each list of doctors in a medical specialty or subspecialty is preceded by a brief description of that specialty (or subspecialty) and the training required for board certification.

The following descriptions of medical specialties and subspecialties were provided by the American Board of Medical Specialties (ABMS), an organization comprised of the 24 medical specialty boards that provide certification in 25 medical specialties. A complete listing of all specialists certified by the ABMS can be found in The Official ABMS Directory of Board Certified Medical Specialists, is published by Marquis Who's Who. It is available (either in a multi-volume directory or on CD-ROM) in most public libraries, hospital libraries, university libraries and medical libraries. The ABMS also operates a toll-free phone line at 1-866-275-2267 and a website at www.abms.org to verify the certification status of individual doctors.

The following important policy statement, approved by the ABMS Assembly on March 19, 1987, remains valid.

The Purpose Of Certification
The intent of the certification process, as defined by the member boards of the American Board of Medical Specialties, is to provide assurance to the public that a certified medical specialist has successfully completed an approved educational program and an evaluation, including an examination process designed to assess the knowledge, experience and skills requisite to the provision of high quality patient care in that specialty.

Medical Specialties and Subspecialties

Medical Specialty and Subspecialty Descriptions and Abbreviations

The following medical specialties and subspecialties are indicated in the doctors' listings by their abbreviations. Specialties are indicated in bold, subspecialties in italics, and the four primary care specialties in bold capitals. To review the official American Board of Medical Specialties (ABMS) organization of specialties, refer to Appendix A.

Addiction Psychiatry   *AdP*

Deals with habitual psychological and physiological dependence on a substance or practice which is beyond voluntary control.

Adolescent Medicine   *AM*

Involves the primary care treatment of adolescents and young adults.

Allergy & Immunology   **A&I**

Diagnosis and treatment of allergies, asthma and skin problems such as hives and contact dermatitis.

Cardiac Electrophysiology (Clinical)   *CE*

Involves complicated technical procedures to evaluate heart rhythms and determine appropriate treatment for them.

Cardiovascular Disease   *Cv*

Involves the diagnosis and treatment of disorders of the heart, lungs and blood vessels.

Child & Adolescent Psychiatry   *ChAP*

Deals with the diagnosis and treatment of mental diseases in children and adolescents.

Child Neurology   *ChiN*

Diagnosis and medical treatment of disorders of the brain, spinal cord and nervous system in children.

Clinical Genetics   **CG**

Deals with identifying the genetic causes of inherited diseases and ailments and preventing, when possible, their occurrence.

Colon and Rectal Surgery   **CRS**

Surgical treatment of diseases of the intestinal tract, colon and rectum, anal canal and perianal area.

Critical Care Medicine   *CCM*

Involves diagnosing and taking immediate action to prevent death or further injury of a patient. Examples of critical injuries include shock, heart attack, drug overdose and massive bleeding.

Dermatology D
Diagnosis and treatment of benign and malignant disorders of the skin, mouth, external genitalia, hair and nails, as well as a number of sexually transmitted diseases.

Diagnostic Radiology DR
Involves the study of all modalities of radiant energy in medical diagnoses and therapeutic procedures utilizing radiologic guidance.

Endocrinology, Diabetes & Metabolism EDM
Involves the study and treatment of patients suffering from hormonal and chemical disorders.

FAMILY MEDICINE FMed
Deals with and oversees the total healthcare of individual patients and their family members. Family practitioners are more common in rural areas and may perform procedures more commonly performed by specialists (e.g., minor surgery).

Gastroenterology Ge
The study, diagnosis and treatment of diseases of the digestive organs including the stomach, bowels, liver and gallbladder.

Geriatric Medicine Ger
Deals with diseases of the elderly and the problems associated with aging.

Geriatric Psychiatry GerPsy
Involves the diagnosis, prevention and treatment of mental illness in the elderly.

Gynecologic Oncology GO
Deals with cancers of the female genital tract and reproductive systems.

Hematology Hem
Involves the diagnosis and treatment of diseases and disorders of the blood, bone marrow, spleen and lymph glands.

Hospice and Palliative Medicine H&PM
Palliative care relieves the suffering and provides the best quality of life to people suffering from serious and severe chronic illness. Hospice care focuses on the palliation of a terminally ill patient's symptoms and also provides passionate support to both the patient and their surrounding loved ones.

Infectious Disease Inf
The study and treatment of diseases caused by a bacterium, virus, fungus or animal parasite.

Medical Specialties and Subspecialties

INTERNAL MEDICINE   **IM**

Diagnosis and nonsurgical treatment of diseases, especially those of adults. Internists may act as primary care specialists, highly trained family doctors or they may subspecialize in specialties such as cardiology or nephrology.

Interventional Cardiology   *IC*

A cardiologist with special training who uses minimally invasive and non-surgical procedures to treat cardiovascular diseases.

Maternal & Fetal Medicine   *MF*

Involves the care of women with high-risk pregnancies and their unborn fetuses.

Medical Oncology   *Onc*

Refers to the study and treatment of tumors and other cancers.

Neonatal-Perinatal Medicine   *NP*

Involves the diagnosis and treatments of infants prior to, during and one month beyond birth.

Nephrology   *Nep*

Concerned with disorders of the kidneys, high blood pressure, fluid and mineral balance, dialysis of body wastes when the kidneys do not function and consultation with surgeons about kidney transplantation.

Neurological Surgery   **NS**

Involves surgery of the brain, spinal cord and nervous system.

Neurology   **N**

Diagnosis and medical treatment of disorders of the brain, spinal cord and nervous system.

Neuroradiology   *NRad*

Involves the utilization of imaging procedures during diagnosis as they relate to the brain, spine and spinal cord, head, neck and organs of special sense in adults and children.

Nuclear Medicine   **NuM**

Evaluation of the functions of all the organs in the body and treatment of thyroid disease, benign and malignant tumors and radiation exposure through the use of radioactive substances.

OBSTETRICS & GYNECOLOGY   **ObG**

Deals with the medical aspects of and intervention in pregnancy and labor and the overall health of the female reproductive system.

Occupational Medicine   *OM*
Concentrates on the effect of the work environment on the health of employees.

Ophthalmology   **Oph**
Diagnosis and treatment of diseases of and injuries to the eye.

Orthopaedic Surgery   **OrS**
Involves operations to correct injuries which interfere with the form and function of the extremities, spine and associated structures.

Otolaryngology   **Oto**
Explores and treats diseases in the interrelated areas of the ears, nose and throat.

Pain Medicine   *PM*
Involves providing a high level of care for patients experiencing problems with acute or chronic pain in both hospital and ambulatory settings.

Pathology   **Path**
A doctor trained to examine tissue specimens microscopically and in clinical laboratory tests, to diagnose and monitor diseases.

Pediatric Allergy & Immunology   *PA&I*
A doctor trained in evaluation, physical and laboratory diagnosis and management of disorders involving the immune system in children.

Pediatric Cardiology   *PCd*
Involves the diagnosis and treatment of heart disease in children.

Pediatric Critical Care Medicine   *PCCM*
Involves the care of children who are victims of life threatening disorders such as severe accidents, shock and diabetes acidosis.

Pediatric Endocrinology   *PEn*
Involves the study and treatment of children with hormonal and chemical disorders.

Pediatric Gastroenterology   *PGe*
The study, diagnosis and treatment of diseases of the digestive tract in children.

Pediatric Hematology-Oncology   *PHO*
The study and treatment of cancers of the blood and blood-forming parts of the body in children.

Pediatric Infectious Disease   *PInf*
The study and treatment of diseases caused by a virus, bacterium, fungus or animal parasite in children.

Medical Specialties and Subspecialties

Pediatric Nephrology   *PNep*
Deals with the diagnosis and treatment of disorders of the kidneys in children.

Pediatric Otolaryngology   *PO*
Involves the diagnosis and treatment of disorders of the ear, nose and throat which affect children.

Pediatric Pulmonology   *PPul*
Involves the diagnosis and treatment of diseases of the chest, lungs, and chest tissue in children.

Pediatric Rheumatology   *PRhu*
Involves the treatment of diseases of the joints and connective tissues in children.

Pediatric Surgery   *PS*
Treatment of disease, injury or deformity in children through surgical techniques.

Pediatric Urology   *Ped Uro*
Treatment of urologic congenital anomilies, and childhood and adolescent acquired urologic problems such as disease and trauma.

PEDIATRICS   **Ped**
Diagnosis and treatment of diseases of childhood and monitoring of the growth, development and well-being of preadolescent.

Physical Medicine & Rehabilitation   **PMR**
The use of physical therapy and physical agents such as water, heat, light electricity and mechanical manipulations in the diagnosis, treatment and prevention of disease and body disorders.

Plastic Surgery   **PlS**
Involves reconstructive and cosmetic surgery of the face and other body parts.

Preventive Medicine   **PrM**
A specialty focusing on the prevention of illness and on the health of groups rather than individuals.

Psychiatry   **Psyc**
Examination, treatment and prevention of mental illness through the use of psychoanalysis and/or drugs.

Pulmonary Disease   *Pul*
Involves the diagnosis and treatment of diseases of the chest, lungs and airways.

Radiation Oncology   *RadRO*
Involves the use of radiant energy and isotopes in the study and treatment of disease, especially malignant cancer.

Reproductive Endocrinology   *RE*
Deals with the endocrine system (including the pituitary, thyroid, parathyroid, adrenal glands, placenta, ovaries and testes) and how its failure relates to infertility.

Rheumatology   *Rhu*
Involves the treatment of diseases of the joints, muscles, bones and associated structures.

Sports Medicine   *SM*
Refers to the practice of an orthopedist or other physician who specializes in injuries to the bone or other soft tissues (muscles, tendons, ligaments) caused by participation in athletic active.

Surgery   **S**
Treatment of disease, injury and deformity by surgical procedures.

Surgery of the Hand   *HS*
Involves providing appropriate care for all structures in the upper extremity directly affecting the hand and wrist function.

Thoracic & Cardiac Surgery   **T&CS**
Involves surgery on the heart, lungs and chest area.

Urology   **U**
Diagnosis and treatment of diseases of the genitals in men and disorders of the urinary tract and bladder in both men and women.

Vascular & Interventional Radiology   *VIR*
Involves diagnosing and treating diseases by percutaneous methods guided by various radiologic imaging modalities.

Vascular Surgery   *VascS*
Involves the operative treatment of disorders of the blood vessels excluding those to the heart, lungs or brain.

The Best in American Medicine
www.CastleConnolly.com

The Partnership for Excellence

There are more than 200 acute care and specialty hospitals in the New York metropolitan area, many of which have extraordinary capabilities for superior patient care. Castle Connolly Medical Ltd. has received many requests from book buyers to provide information about hospitals. In response, we have invited a select group of outstanding hospitals to profile their services in this guide through the medium of paid advertorials. This program, called the Partnership for Excellence is totally separate from the physician selection process, which is based upon a completely independent review system. Hospitals that sponsored pages in the Hospital Information Program are organized into three groups: Major Medical Centers, Specialty Hospitals and Regional Medical Centers.

Major Medical Centers begin on the next page and are followed by the Specialty Hospital pages. This section is followed by the listings of doctors. Regional Medical Centers and Hospitals are found at the beginning of each county section - within the doctor listings. The information gives you an overview of programs and services offered by these hospitals, as well as vital information related to their accreditation and sponsorship. Each hospital profile also contains a physician referral number, should you wish to ask the hospitals for recommendations of physicians not listed in the Castle Connolly Guide.

The Centers of Excellence section was also developed in response to requests from our readers who want to know which hospitals have special programs or services focusing on a particular illness or health need. The Centers of Excellence described here are also offered by hospitals participating in the Partnership for Excellence section of this guide. They reflect the depth of commitment of these hospitals, which provides the staff, resources and financial support necessary to develop these special programs. We believe you will find this information helpful in your search for the best healthcare — from both physicians and hospitals— for you and your family.

We are pleased to have these distinguished institutions as partners in our effort to help you meet your healthcare needs.

The following pages contain vital information on seven of the region's Major Medical Centers. A Major Medical Center is an acute care hospital with tertiary care services, residency programs, a major affiliation with a medical school and clinical research programs. A major medical center draws its patients from a broad geographic region, even nationally and internationally and, in many instances, is the center of a network or consortium of hospitals.

The New York metropolitan region is nationally and internationally known for its major medical centers and their excellent programs and services. Some of the nation's leading academic centers are in this region and, in addition to superior patient care and cutting edge patient research, they produce thousands of talented, well trained physicians and other health professionals each year. Castle Connolly Medical Ltd. has invited a number of major medical centers in the region to sponsor the profiles and information that follows.

Major Medical Centers

Atlantic Health System

Barnabas Health

Hackensack University Medical Center

Maimonides Medical Center

Montefiore Medical Center

NewYork-Presbyterian Hospital

NYU Langone Medical Center

The Best in American Medicine
www.CastleConnolly.com

ATLANTIC HEALTH SYSTEM

Atlantic Health System

Atlantic Neuroscience Institute • Carol G. Simon Cancer Center • Gagnon Cardiovascular Institute • Atlantic Rehabilitation • Atlantic Sports Health

Atlantic Health System, 475 South Street, P.O. Box 1905, Morristown, NJ 07962
www.atlantichealth.org

To find a doctor, call 1-800-247-9580 or visit us online

Sponsorship: Voluntary Not–for–Profit • Beds: 1,599 • Accreditation: The Joint Commission

Atlantic Health System is at the forefront of medicine, setting standards for quality health care in New Jersey and beyond. The nationally recognized physicians, experienced nurses and skilled staff provide outstanding and compassionate care. Through our vision, we empower our communities to be the healthiest in the nation. Atlantic Health System includes Morristown Medical Center in Morristown, NJ; Overlook Medical Center in Summit, NJ; Newton Medical Center in Newton, NJ; Chilton Medical Center in Pompton Plains, NJ; and Goryeb Children's Hospital in Morristown, NJ — all of which are accredited by The Joint Commission. Specialty service areas include advanced cardiovascular care, pediatric medical and surgical specialties, neurology, orthopedics and sports medicine. Each of these programs has earned top ratings and recognitions in their respective fields. Atlantic Health System is the official health care partner of the New York Jets and an official health provider of the New Jersey Devils. Atlantic Health System is a clinical and academic affiliate of The Mount Sinai Hospital and the Icahn School of Medicine at Mount Sinai; a Major Clinical Affiliate of Rutgers Cancer Institute of New Jersey; part of Atlantic Accountable Care Organization, one of the largest ACOs in the nation, and is a member of AllSpire Health Partners.

Awards & Recognition:
- Chosen for the past six years by FORTUNE® as one of the magazine's "100 Best Companies to Work For®"
- Recognized six times by AARP as one of the "Best Employers for Workers over 50"
- Named for a fifth consecutive year as one of Health Care's Most Wired organizations in 2014 by Hospitals & Health Networks magazine, the journal of the American Hospital Association
- Recognized for five consecutive years by InformationWeek Magazine on its InformationWeek 500 list, and as one of its "Elite 100" organizations
- Morristown Medical Center, Overlook Medical Center and Newton Medical Center recognized in 2014 as "Leaders in LGBT Healthcare Equality," by the Human Rights Campaign (HRC) Foundation
- Named by Becker's Healthcare as one of the "150 Great Places to Work in Healthcare"

Morristown Medical Center – 100 Madison Avenue, Morristown, NJ 07960
Morristown Medical Center is a nationally recognized provider of high quality health care. The hospital is home to Gagnon Cardiovascular Institute, which performs more cardiac surgeries than any other hospital in NJ (more than 1,500 in 2014) placing its cardiac program in the top two percent in the country. Carol G. Simon Cancer Center offers advanced methods to diagnose, treat and manage all types of cancers. Designated a Regional Perinatal Center, the hospital treats the most complicated obstetrical cases and provides specialized care to sick or premature infants. Goryeb Children's Hospital offers more than 100 board-certified physicians in 20 pediatric specialties. The medical center is verified as a Level I Regional Trauma Center by the American College of Surgeons and designated a Level II by the state of NJ. Morristown Medical Center was re-designated a Magnet Hospital for Excellence in Nursing Service, the highest level of recognition by American Nurses Credentialing Center for facilities that provide acute care services, a distinction awarded to less than five percent of U.S. hospitals.

Awards & Recognition:
U.S. News & World Report 2014: Morristown Medical Center was ranked one of the top five New York metro area hospitals and one of the best hospitals in the nation for 2014-15 in Cardiology & Heart Surgery, Geriatrics, Gynecology, Orthopedics and Pulmonology; "Best Regional Hospital" for cancer, diabetes & endocrinology, gastroenterology & GI surgery, nephrology, neurology & neurosurgery and urology

Inside Jersey/Castle Connolly 2014: Morristown Medical Center: Top N.J. hospital (with 350 beds or more) for fourth consecutive year

Overlook Medical Center – 99 Beauvoir Avenue, Summit, NJ 07901

Overlook Medical Center is a nationally recognized regional medical center in Summit, New Jersey. Within its doors, patients find the nation's top doctors, compassionate care and the most advanced technology and treatments. Atlantic Neuroscience Institute includes the state's first designated Comprehensive Stroke Center. The medical center treats more aneurysm cases than any other institution in New Jersey and is a Level IV Epilepsy Center and the only hospital in the state, and one of 10 in the United States to be designated a "Tourette Syndrome Association Centers of Excellence." Overlook Medical Center is the only NY/NJ hospital with specialists trained in MEG for functional brain mapping, introduced CyberKnife radiation therapy for brain tumors to the tri-state region and continues to lead the way in treating prostate cancer.

Awards & Recognition:
U.S. News & World Report 2014: Overlook Medical Center: recognized as a "Best Regional Hospital" for neurology & neurosurgery, gastroenterology & GI surgery, geriatrics and urology

Newton Medical Center – 175 High Street, Newton, NJ 07860

Newton Medical Center has been providing care to the community since 1932 and serves the people of Sussex and Warren counties in New Jersey, Pike County in Pennsylvania and southern Orange County in New York. Newton Medical Center is a trusted regional resource and a community-focused health care provider dedicated to quality and innovative service.

It is the recipient of the American Heart Association/American Stroke Association's Get With The Guidelines®-Stroke Silver-Plus Quality Achievement Award. Newton Medical is one of a select few health care facilities in New Jersey to be accredited by the Intersocietal Accreditation Commission (IAC) in all three of the following echocardiography procedures: adult transthoracic, adult transesophogeal and adult stress.

Newton Medical Center also operates Milford Health & Wellness and Urgent Care, Sparta Health & Wellness, and Vernon Health & Wellness and Urgent Care.

Awards & Recognition:
Inside Jersey/Castle Connolly 2014: Newton Medical Center: For hospitals with 350 beds or fewer, Top N.J. hospital for third consecutive year, and No. 1 for treatment of breast cancer

Received the Outstanding Achievement Award and Three-Year Approval with Commendation from the American College of Surgeons Commission on Cancer

Chilton Medical Center – 97 West Parkway, Pompton Plains, NJ 07444

Chilton Medical Center is an award-winning community hospital providing innovative, personalized patient care to people of all ages in a compassionate and healing environment. It is recognized by The Joint Commission as a Primary Stroke Center and a Top Performer on Key Quality Measures for heart attack, heart failure, pneumonia and surgical care. It is designated a Breast Imaging Center of Excellence by the American College of Radiology. A recent modernization and enhancement project has transformed the delivery of care throughout the medical center. Among the many enhancements, Chilton has tripled the number of its private rooms, exceeding the standard of any other area hospital.

Awards & Recognition:
Healthgrades: Chilton Medical Center has been five star rated, the highest possible, for Total Knee Replacement in 2012, 2013 and 2014

Goryeb Children's Hospital – 100 Madison Avenue, Morristown, NJ 07960

Upon opening its doors in 2002, Goryeb Children's Hospital quickly became the hospital of choice for families throughout the area, and today treats more than 50,000 pediatric patients annually across 20 different areas of medical and surgical care, including 750 patients annually in the Foley Pediatric Intensive Care Unit and more than 2,500 inpatients. Goryeb Children's Hospital is a state-designated children's hospital. More than 100 board-certified pediatric specialists at Goryeb provide care to patients at multiple locations throughout the state. In addition, Goryeb has more than 250 community pediatricians on staff. The physicians and staff at Goryeb subscribe to a patient- and family-centered philosophy of care, partnering together with families to generate the best possible outcomes. Families and caregivers are educated, supported and empowered to make informed decisions about their child's care and to cope confidently with their child's condition or illness.

Sponsored Page

Honors and Awards

Our hospitals are ranked among the Best New Jersey and Metro Area Hospitals and recognized in a wide range of specialties by U.S. News & World Report, and continually receive high excellence, quality and safety scores from top nationally respected organizations. Our programs and services have earned countless awards in their fields. As a system, Becker's Hospital Review and Modern Healthcare recognized Barnabas Health as a best place to work in health care. The prestigious Joint Commission identified Barnabas Health as a Top Performer for national quality measures and awarded the Acute Coronary Syndrome Disease Specific Care Certification. The system received the CEO Cancer Gold Standard from the American Cancer Society CEO Roundtable on Cancer, and the Voice of the Customer Award from Nuance Healthcare.

Nationally Renowned Services:

- New Jersey's only certified burn treatment facility
- World-class cardiac surgery services for adults, including three cardiac surgery programs
- Pediatric cardiac surgery program in affiliation with NYU School of Medicine
- Third largest adult heart transplant program in the nation with more than 700 transplants and the largest adult heart transplant program on the East Coast
- Only lung transplant program in New Jersey
- One of the country's most comprehensive robotic surgery services
- Accredited certified comprehensive and primary stroke centers
- Fourth largest living donor kidney transplant program in the U.S.
- Renowned neurology and neurosurgery programs
- Trauma center
- Comprehensive cancer services for adults and children (three Valerie Fund Children Centers)
- Leading neonatal intensive care units
- Nationally recognized geriatric services
- Renowned women's and children's services.

HackensackUMC

30 Prospect Avenue, Hackensack, NJ 07601 • 551-996-2000
www.HackensackUMC.org

Number of beds: 775
Number of employees: 7,587
2013 Admissions: 44,760
Sponsorship: A not-for-profit, teaching and research hospital affiliated with Georgetown University School of Medicine, Rutgers Medical School, St. George's University School of Medicine, and Stevens Institute of Technology.
Beds: A 775-bed, Level II Trauma Center, providing tertiary and regional services for the New York/New Jersey metropolitan area.
Accreditation: Joint Commission
HackensackUMC is the recipient of 23 Gold Seals of Approval™ for healthcare quality from the Joint Commission — more than any hospital in the country.
HackensackUMC currently holds Joint Commission Disease-Specific Care Certifications in: Abdominal Aortic Aneurysm, Acute Myocardial Infarction, Asthma, Asthma (Pediatrics), Bone Marrow Transplant, Breast Cancer, Carotid Stenosis, Chronic Obstructive Pulmonary Disease, Colorectal Cancer, Coronary Artery Bypass Graft, Depression, Geriatrics Delirium, Heart Failure, Inpatient Diabetes, Joint Replacement – Hip, Joint Replacement – Knee, Multi-System Trauma, Palliative Care, Peripheral Vascular Disease, Pneumonia, Prostate Cancer, Stroke (Primary Stroke Center), and Uterine-Ovarian Cancer.

BACKGROUND

HackensackUMC, a nonprofit teaching and research hospital located in Bergen County, NJ, is the largest provider of inpatient and outpatient services in the state. Founded in 1888 as the county's first hospital, it is the flagship hospital of Hackensack University Health Network, one of the largest health networks in the state comprised of more than 11,300 employees, 3,100 credentialed medical staff members and 1,697 hospital and nursing home beds. HackensackUMC was listed as the number one hospital in New Jersey in the *U.S. News & World Report's* Best Hospital rankings for 2014-15. It is one of the top 30 hospitals in the nation by receiving 11 national specialty rankings, including a national ranking for the Joseph M. Sanzari Children's Hospital in Neurology and Neurosurgery in the 2014-15 Best Children's Hospitals. The children's hospital is housed with the Donna A. Sanzari Women's Hospital in the Sarkis and Siran Gabrellian Women's and Children's Pavilion, which was designed with The Deirdre Imus Environmental Health Center, and was included on the Green Guide's list of Top 10 Green Hospitals in the U.S. HackensackUMC is among Healthgrades® America's Best 100 Hospitals in five different areas — more than any hospital in the state. It is the only hospital in NJ, NY and New England to be named one of Healthgrades America's 50 Best Hospitals™ for eight years in a row, and receive the Healthgrades Distinguished Hospital Award for Clinical Excellence™ 12 years in a row. The medical center has also been named a Leapfrog Top Hospital, and earned 23 Gold Seals of Approval™ by the Joint Commission — more than any other hospital in the country. It was the first hospital in New Jersey and second in the nation to become a Magnet® recognized hospital for nursing excellence; receiving its fifth consecutive designation in 2014. HackensackUMC earned Practice Greenhealth's highest honor as a 2014 Environmental Excellence Award winner. HackensackUMC is the Hometown Hospital of the New York Giants and the New York Red Bulls and was Official Medical Services Provider to The Barclays PGA Golf Tournament and the NY/NJ Super Bowl XLV111 Host Committee. It remains committed to its community through fundraising and community events.

MEDICAL AND DENTAL STAFF

Since HackensackUMC is one of the region's most comprehensive and progressive medical centers, it easily attracts many of the area's leading physicians — nearly 1,670 of them. These doctors, many of whom are on the cutting-edge in their fields and have received their training at our nation's most prominent institutions, have selected HackensackUMC as their place to practice their best medicine.

NURSING EXCELLENCE

HackensackUMC's 1,918 nurses are renowned for achieving Magnet® recognition for Nursing Excellence, the highest honor that can be bestowed by the American Nurses Credentialing Center. The medical center was the first in New Jersey and the second in the country to receive this designation — a true testament to the quality of care delivered at HackensackUMC.
In January 2014, HackensackUMC received its fifth Magnet® designation by the American Nurses Credentialing Center — making the medical center just one of two hospitals in the entire nation to achieve this feat.

WORLD-CLASS CARDIAC CARE

HackensackUMC is home to one of America's most comprehensive cardiac and vascular hospitals: its Heart & Vascular Hospital, a "hospital within a hospital," integrates preventive, diagnostic and treatment services, with a special focus on cardiovascular disease management and breakthrough research. Inpatients and outpatients are treated for all types of cardiac and vascular diseases, including heart problems, such as: blocked arteries and irregular heartbeats; peripheral vascular disease; and neurovascular diseases, such as stroke and aneurysm. Housing all of these services within one specialized location allows for more efficient, effective patient care.

U.S. News & World Report ranked HackensackUMC #32 out of more than 700 hospitals in the nation for Cardiology & Heart Surgery in their 2014-15 Best Hospitals rankings. HackensackUMC was also named among one of *Becker's Hospital Review's* 100 Hospitals With Great Heart Programs.

ONE OF THE NATION'S LARGEST AND MOST COMPREHENSIVE CANCER CENTERS

At John Theurer Cancer Center, we believe cancer is hard enough for patients and their loved ones. It is this belief that drives our passion to deliver extraordinary care every day, helping us to become one of the nation's top 50 cancer centers, ranked #37 out of more than 900 hospitals by *U.S. News & World Report* – the highest-ranked cancer center in New Jersey with this recognition. It was also listed among the 100 Hospitals and Health Systems With Great Oncology Programs by *Becker's Hospital Review.*

In January 2011, we opened a new building that houses 14 specialty divisions, research and support services. This state-of-the-art facility offers a wide range of free resources to help patients become active participants in their treatment and support their fight against cancer. These resources include yoga, fitness, interactive nutrition classes in the Cooking Studio, art workshops, a patient resource librarian to help patients find credible health information online, and more.

During the past 25 years, we have become one of the largest cancer centers in the United States, but we have kept our focus on the unique needs of our patients. Prevention, treatment, and research advances have grown exponentially during this time. We are not only keeping up with the change of pace, we are at the forefront of providing tomorrow's treatment today by:

• Taking multidisciplinary care to a new level with teams of disease-specific experts under one roof;
• Delivering personalized medicine focused on novel therapies, participatory treatment, predictive measures, and preventive care;
• Advancing research through biomarker-driven clinical trials and translational research;
• Providing holistic care that includes a wide range of complementary services important to the well-being of our patients that can be easily integrated into their care; and
• Creating a comforting environment in a new high-tech, high-touch building.

We believe our model is the next step towards the future of patient care, changing the cancer care experience one patient at a time. To receive information on John Theurer Cancer Center's services, call 551-996-5900 or visit jtcancercenter.org.

ONE OF THE NATION'S RENOWNED PEDIATRIC PROGRAMS

The Joseph M. Sanzari Children's Hospital at HackensackUMC is a state-designated children's hospital and an award-winning facility that has been recognized as one of the top-ranked children's hospitals in New Jersey and in the country. It ranked 44th among the Best Children's Hospitals for Neurology and Neurosurgery in the 2014-15 Best Children's Hospitals rankings by *U.S. News & World Report* — the first hospital in New Jersey to be ranked in any Best Children's Hospitals specialty, and the only hospital in the state to be ranked in Neurology and Neurosurgery.

The Joseph M. Sanzari Children's Hospital was one of the first hospitals in New Jersey to have a separate, dedicated pediatric emergency department (PED) and is an American College of Surgeons designated Level II Trauma Center that cares for pediatric patients. The PER is staffed 24 hours a day, seven days a week with physicians and nurses who are specialized in the care of children requiring emergency medical services. It houses more than 30 specialties in a patient- and family-centered environment that includes children's play and family kitchen areas, and private inpatient rooms with computers, Internet access, and flat-screen plasma televisions.

The cutting-edge technologies facilities, expert staff, dedicated PER and specialty units that distinguish the Joseph M. Sanzari Children's Hospital are second to none.

For more information on any of the services offered at HackensackUMC, please call 551-996-2000, or visit www.HackensackUMC.org.

4802 Tenth Avenue
Brooklyn, New York 11219
Phone: 718.283.6000
For Referral to a Physician:
888.MMC.DOCS (662.3627)

Sponsorship:	Voluntary, Not-for-Profit
Beds:	711 acute, 70 psychiatric
Accreditation:	The Joint Commission
	American College of Surgeons
	American Council of Graduate Medical Education (ACGME)

www.maimonidesmed.org

Maimonides Medical Center is among the largest independent teaching hospitals in the U.S., training more than 450 medical and surgical residents each year. Widely recognized for major achievements in medical technology and patient safety, Maimonides conducts clinical trials for new treatments and therapies, and is cited for overall clinical excellence by numerous health care evaluation services.

Significant Accomplishments

Maimonides' excellence in cardiac care is historic: the first successful human heart transplant in the U.S. was performed at here in 1967, and Maimonides is ranked by the Centers for Medicare & Medicaid Services as one of only 26 hospitals in the U.S. that consistently achieve excellent ratings in heart attack, heart failure and pneumonia patient outcomes.

Physicians at Maimonides were among the first in the U.S. to use computers to enter patient orders, thereby reducing the risk of errors, increasing efficiency, and speeding the healing process.

More babies are born at Maimonides than at any other single-campus hospital in the state of New York – due in no small part to its designation as a Regional Perinatal Center with Obstetric and Pediatric services which are unrivaled in this area.

Centers of Excellence

Cancer Center

The Maimonides Cancer Center, comprised of the Lena Cymbrowitz and Gilbert Rivera Pavilions, offers a fully integrated approach to cancer care that includes prevention, screening, diagnostics, treatment, palliative care and clinical research. Staffed by leading oncologists, radiologists, surgeons, nurses and social workers, the Center provides compassionate, patient-centered, state-of-the-art care. The newly built Breast Center features a spa-like decor in which our dedicated team of breast cancer specialists treat patients.

Heart & Vascular Center

Renowned for its Catheterization Lab and pioneering new surgical procedures, the Maimonides Heart & Vascular Center includes an electrophysiology (EP) lab, hybrid OR, two ICUs, Chest Pain Observation Unit, Advanced Cardiac Care Unit, Congestive Heart Failure program and Atrial Fibrillation Center. The first successful heart transplant in America was performed at Maimonides in 1967. Today, cardiology and cardiothoracic surgery continue to innovate. Maimonides has been ranked by the Centers for Medicare & Medicaid Services as one of the few hospitals in the nation to achieve excellent ratings in both heart attack and heart failure patient outcomes. Its Left Ventricular Assist Device Program, the first in Brooklyn, recently received advanced certification from the Joint Commission.

The Center also offers comprehensive diagnostic, clinical and surgical services for patients with vascular disease and associated conditions. In addition to traditional open surgery, the Center utilizes minimally invasive, endovascular and catheter-directed techniques whenever possible. Our physicians are board-certified, highly-experienced and make use of innovative technologies, such as our accredited Vascular Diagnostics Laboratory and new hybrid OR.

Jaffe Stroke Center

The Jaffe Stroke Center at Maimonides is ranked among the best in the nation. It is currently the site of clinical trials for new stroke medications, medical devices and stroke protocols. The Center offers interventional neuroradiology techniques and telemedicine.

Infants & Children's Hospital

The Maimonides Infants & Children's Hospital, one of only four accredited children's hospitals in NYC, includes comprehensive inpatient services and over 30 pediatric subspecialties. With a Child Life & Creative Arts Therapies Program fully integrated with family-centered care, the Maimonides Infants & Children's Hospital also provides a Pediatric ICU, Neonatal ICU, Outpatient Services and Pediatric ER.

Stella & Joseph Payson Birthing Center

More babies are delivered at Maimonides than at any other single-campus hospital in New York State. The Payson Birthing Center offers a home-like setting with physicians, nurses, midwives and doulas, combined with advanced technology which includes a perinatal testing center with 3-D ultrasound and 24/7 neonatology.

Geriatrics Program

Maimonides serves one of the oldest inpatient populations in New York City, with one quarter of inpatients over the age of 75. The Geriatrics Program is fully equipped to meet the special needs of these seniors, including the assessment of memory loss and expertise in geriatric syndromes such as incontinence, falls and frailty. The Program encompasses inpatient and outpatient services, features the Acute Care for Elderly (ACE) Unit, the Safe at Home program and home-visiting service.

Montefiore

Inspired Medicine

111 East 210th Street
Bronx, New York 10467
1-800-MD-MONTE
www.montefiore.org

Montefiore combines nationally-recognized clinical excellence with a population health perspective that focuses on the health needs of communities, delivering coordinated, compassionate, science-driven care where, when and how patients need it most.

As the University Hospital and academic medical center for Albert Einstein College of Medicine, Montefiore is recognized by *U.S. News & World Report* as a national and regional leader in specialty and primary care for adults and children. Children's Hospital at Montefiore is consistently ranked as one of the nation's best by *U.S. News & World Report*.

Montefiore has more than 150 locations throughout the Bronx and Westchester County, including six hospitals and an extended care facility, with a total of 2,080 beds, as well as New York State's first free-standing emergency department, the nation's largest school health program, and a home health program. Our partnership with Albert Einstein College of Medicine advances clinical and translational research to accelerate the pace at which new discoveries become the treatments and therapies that benefit patients. This long-standing collaboration has resulted in the creation of the Montefiore Einstein Centers of Excellence in cancer care, cardiovascular services, transplantation and children's health, where nationally recognized investigators and multidisciplinary clinical teams collaborate to develop and deliver advanced, innovative care.

Montefiore is a national leader in the research and treatment of acute and chronic diseases and is known and respected for its model of care emphasizing accountability and interdisciplinary programs. A pioneer in the accountable care model of healthcare delivery, in 2011, Montefiore was one of 31 organizations nationally to receive the federal Pioneer Accountable Care Organization designation. After its first year of participation, Montefiore outperformed all other participants nationwide, and was lauded as an exemplar for other health systems to follow.

Montefiore Hospital, Moses Campus
111 East 210th Street
Bronx, New York 10467

Montefiore Mount Vernon Hospital
12 North 7th Avenue
Mount Vernon, New York 10550

Weiler Hospital
1825 Eastchester Road
Bronx, New York 10461

Montefiore Hospital, Wakefield Campus
600 East 233rd Street
Bronx, New York 10466

Montefiore New Rochelle Hospital
16 Guion Place
New Rochelle, New York 10801

Children's Hospital at Montefiore
3415 Bainbridge Avenue
Bronx, New York 10467

Children's Hospital at Montefiore

Since opening its doors to the Bronx, Westchester and surrounding communities in 2001, Children's Hospital at Montefiore (CHAM) has garnered significant attention for its clinical innovation, state-of-the-art care and exceptional outcomes. CHAM's specialty services are consistently recognized by *U.S. News & World Report* and organizations such as the American Diabetes Association and the Muscular Dystrophy Association, to name just two. Backed by more than $20 million in active National Institutes of Health (NIH) research grants, CHAM investigators are working to advance treatments for childhood diseases and disabilities.

Montefiore Einstein Center for Cancer Care

Montefiore Einstein Center for Cancer Care skillfully blends advanced cancer treatment with a compassionate, patient-centered environment to achieve exceptional outcomes for adults and children. At Montefiore, specialists from medical, surgical and radiation oncology draw upon the latest treatments and research to develop personalized care plans for patients with both common and rare forms of cancer. Their efforts are supported by a multidisciplinary team that includes a dedicated psychiatrist and psychological social worker. The Center is a national leader in the use of targeted immunotherapies and is involved in NIH-funded research studying the use of inhaled chemotherapy for lung cancer, the benefits of high-intensity focused ultrasound guided by magnetic resonance imaging in the treatment of bone cancer, and nanomedicines.

Montefiore Einstein Center for Heart & Vascular Care

Offering novel treatments and intricate, lifesaving procedures, the Center for Heart & Vascular Care is a nationally-respected leader in its field. The Center's specialists in adult and pediatric cardiology and cardiovascular surgery provide care for patients with the full spectrum of cardiovascular conditions, including complex valve conditions and advanced heart failure. The Center is a four-time recipient of the Society of Thoracic Surgeons' prestigious "three-star" ranking for its commitment to surgical excellence, and it has been funded through the NIH/National Heart, Lung, and Blood Institute's Cardiothoracic Surgical Trials Network for 10 consecutive years.

Montefiore Einstein Center for Transplantation

The Center for Transplantation is one of the most established transplant programs in the United States. It provides comprehensive organ failure management and performs heart, liver, kidney and pancreas transplants for adults and children. In all areas of transplant, the Center achieves one-year survival rates that are equal to or better than national benchmarks. To ensure the well-being of its patients, the Center consistently works to overcome social, economic and linguistic barriers to transplant. In partnership with the Marion Bessin Liver Research Center at Albert Einstein College of Medicine, the Center is conducting pioneering work in the area of liver disease.

Neurosciences at Montefiore

The Neurosciences Program at Montefiore brings together state-of-the-art technology and nationally-respected specialists to improve outcomes and quality of life for children and adults with neurological disorders. Its services range from endovascular coiling, stereotactic-guided radiosurgery and complex craniofacial reconstructions to specialized programs in neuro-oncology, epilepsy, neuroimmunology and sleep-wake disorders. The program is bolstered by a robust research enterprise that includes NIH- and foundation-sponsored studies.

Surgery at Montefiore

High volumes and exceptional patient outcomes have made the Department of Surgery a magnet for referral. The Department is recognized by the American College of Surgeons' National Surgical Quality Improvement Program for exemplary outcomes in several categories and is a leader in the use of novel, minimally-invasive surgical approaches. Each of its five Divisions—breast, general, pediatric, transplant, and plastic and reconstructive surgery—is led by renowned surgeons who possess unparalleled experience and expertise.

⊣ NewYork-Presbyterian

Affiliated with Columbia University College of Physicians and Surgeons and Weill Cornell Medical College

NewYork-Presbyterian Hospital
Columbia University Medical Center
622 West 168th Street
New York, NY 10032

NewYork-Presbyterian Hospital
Weill Cornell Medical Center
525 East 68th Street
New York, NY 10065

1-877-NYP-WELL (1-877-697-9355)   www.nyp.org

Sponsorship:	Voluntary Not-for-Profit
Beds:	2,613
Accreditation:	Joint Commission on Accreditation of Healthcare Organizations (JCAHO), Commission on Accreditation of Rehabilitation Facilities (CARF) and College of American Pathologists (CAP)

The #1 hospital in New York. 14 years running. Once again, we are proud to be named the top-ranked hospital in the New York metro area. NewYork-Presbyterian placed higher on the Honor Roll of 'America's Best Hospitals' than any other hospital in the region. This is the 14th consecutive year that we've been recognized to the Honor Roll by *U.S. News & World Report*. NewYork-Presbyterian has the most physicians listed in *New York Magazine's* "Best Doctors" issue and is recognized for having more top doctors than any other hospital in the nation.

Overview

NewYork-Presbyterian Hospital, based in New York City, is the nation's largest not-for-profit, non-sectarian hospital, with 2,613 beds. The Hospital has over 2 million inpatient and outpatient visits in a year, including about 13,000 deliveries and over 300,000 visits to its emergency departments. NewYork-Presbyterian's 6,519 affiliated physicians and 21,747 staff provide state-of-the-art inpatient, ambulatory and preventive care in all areas of medicine. The Hospital enjoys a unique affiliation with two of the nation's leading Ivy League medical schools—Columbia University College of Physicians and Surgeons and the Joan and Sanford I. Weill Medical College of Cornell University.

NewYork-Presbyterian Hospital Features Renowned CENTERS OF EXCELLENCE Including:

Morgan Stanley Children's Hospital and the Komansky Center for Children's Health— One of the largest, most comprehensive children's hospitals in the world, providing highly sophisticated pediatric medical, surgical, and intensive care services in a family-friendly, compassionate environment.

NewYork-Presbyterian Cancer Centers—Through a multidisciplinary team approach, we deliver seamless care and offer the latest therapeutic options and clinical trials for all cancer types.

NewYork-Presbyterian Digestive Disease Services—Our collaborative team manages and treats patients with digestive cancers and nonmalignant digestive diseases, such as inflammatory bowel disease, pancreatic and biliary disorders, and colorectal cancer with compassionate care.

NewYork-Presbyterian Heart—Advances in cardiac care—from clinical cardiology, to interventional procedures, to surgical solutions—offer outstanding outcomes to adult and pediatric heart patients.

NewYork-Presbyterian Neuroscience Centers—Expert teams provide the most sophisticated diagnostic and treatment services for Alzheimer's disease, multiple sclerosis, Parkinson's disease, aneurysms, epilepsy, brain tumors, strokes, and other neurological disorders.

NewYork-Presbyterian Psychiatry—NewYork-Presbyterian Hospital's behavioral health and psychiatric services for adults, children, and adolescents offer a full continuum of programs at all levels of care.

NewYork-Presbyterian Transplant Institute—Our experts are internationally known for performing adult and pediatric heart, liver, kidney, pancreas, lung, bone marrow/stem cell, and intestinal and ex vivo transplantation.

NewYork-Presbyterian Vascular Care Center—We provide comprehensive, multidisciplinary preventive, diagnostic, and treatment services for aortic aneurysm, carotid artery disease, blood clots, and peripheral vascular diseases.

William Randolph Hearst Burn Center—NewYork-Presbyterian Hospital is home to the largest and busiest burn center in the nation, caring for more than 5,000 patients annually.

In addition, we offer extraordinary expertise, comprehensive programs, and specialized resources in the fields of AIDS, reproductive medicine and infertility, trauma care, and women's health.

NewYork-Presbyterian Heart—The optimal care of patients with heart disease is achieved by combining an experienced team of clinicians with the latest advances in technology. Basic science and clinical research efforts are aimed at developing more effective, less invasive ways to prevent, diagnose, and treat the full spectrum of cardiac disorders.

NewYork-Presbyterian Neuroscience Centers—Our team provides the most sophisticated diagnostic and treatment services for Alzheimer's disease, multiple sclerosis, Parkinson's disease, aneurysms, epilepsy, brain tumors, strokes, and other neurological disorders. Our scientific investigators are conducting research aimed at better understanding these diseases and further improving patient care.

NewYork-Presbyterian Psychiatry—NewYork-Presbyterian Hospital's behavioral health and psychiatric services for adults, children, and adolescents offer a full continuum of programs at all levels of care—including inpatient, outpatient, partial hospital, day treatment, and residential services. Specialized services are available in neuropsychiatry, chemical dependency, and eating disorders.

NewYork-Presbyterian Transplant Institute—NewYork-Presbyterian Hospital features the largest transplant program in the country. Our experts are internationally known for performing adult and pediatric heart, liver, kidney, pancreas, lung, bone marrow/stem cell, and intestinal and ex vivo transplantation.

NewYork-Presbyterian Vascular Care Center—We provide comprehensive, multidisciplinary preventive, diagnostic, and treatment services for aortic aneurysm, carotid artery disease, blood clots, peripheral vascular diseases, venous insufficiency, and venous ulcers. We take a minimally invasive approach to these diseases whenever possible.

William Randolph Hearst Burn Center—NewYork-Presbyterian Hospital is home to the largest and busiest burn center in the nation, caring for more than 5,000 outpatients annually. Our investigators also conduct research to improve survival and enhance the quality of life of burn victims.

In addition, the Hospital offers extraordinary expertise, comprehensive programs, and specialized resources in the fields of:

AIDS—The Center for Special Studies at NewYork-Presbyterian/Weill Cornell and the AIDS Care Program at NewYork-Presbyterian/Columbia provide comprehensive care for men, women, and children with HIV/AIDS. Both sites are designated as AIDS centers by New York State and by the National Institutes of Health.

Reproductive Medicine and Infertility—Our leading physicians and scientists in reproductive medicine use innovative technology for the comprehensive treatment of infertility in women and men. Our prestigious program is renowned for achieving success rates that are among the best in the world.

Trauma Center—Level 1 designations as an Adult Trauma Unit and a Pediatric Trauma Unit ensure the Hospital upholds the highest standards of 24-hour preparedness and treatment.

Women's Health Care—One of the first hospitals dedicated to women's health, NewYork-Presbyterian has established comprehensive programs which provide health care to women through all stages of their lives. The Hospital offers outstanding services in maternal-fetal health, gynecologic oncology, and a full range of preventive, primary, and specialty care.

NewYork-Presbyterian Healthcare System

NewYork-Presbyterian provides a comprehensive network of healthcare providers throughout the New York metropolitan area, including northern New Jersey, Westchester County, and Fairfield, Connecticut. The full-service system includes 15 acute-care, community hospitals, specialty institutions, 4 long-term facilities, and over 100 outpatient care centers.

NYU Langone
MEDICAL CENTER

NYU LANGONE MEDICAL CENTER

There are good reasons why patients choose NYU Langone:

- Named one of the best hospitals according to *U.S.News & World Report* 2014-2015 Best Hospitals and and nationally ranked in 13 specialties.

- Awarded a Gold Seal of Approval by The Joint Commission for a commitment to high quality care

- Earned an "A" Hospital Safety Score by The Leapfrog Group

- Ranked number one in the nation in overall patient safety and quality among leading academic medical centers participating in the University HealthSystem Consortium (UHC) 2013 Quality and Accountability Study.

- Placed on the Honor Roll and on the list of "America's Safest Hospitals" by the Niagara Health Quality Coalition

- Granted American Nurses Credentialing Center Magnet Recognition® for quality patient care, nursing excellence, and innovations in professional nursing practice

Looking for information on our expert physicians?
Call 1.888.7.NYU.MED (1.888.769.8633).

NYU Langone Medical Center—a world-class, patient-centered, integrated, academic medical center—is one of the nation's premier destinations for excellence in patient care, biomedical research, and medical education.

Located in the heart of Manhattan, NYU Langone is composed of **Tisch Hospital**, its flagship acute care facility; the **Hospital for Joint Diseases**, a dedicated inpatient orthopaedic hospital; **Hassenfeld Children's Hospital**, a comprehensive pediatric hospital supporting a full array of children's health services; **Rusk Rehabilitation**, the #1 rehab program in New York since *U.S. News & World Report* began its hospital rankings in 1989; and a growing ambulatory care network with locations throughout Manhattan, the outer boroughs, and the tri-state area, bringing services directly to where its patients live and work.

Areas of Expertise:

Airway, Breathing & Lung Conditions	Heart & Vascular Conditions
Bone, Joint & Muscle Disorders	Immune System Disorders
Brain & Nervous System Disorders	Infectious Diseases
Cancers, Tumors & Blood Disorders	Kidney, Liver & Urinary Conditions
Diabetes & Other Endocrine Conditions	Mental & Behavioral Health
Digestive & Gastrointestinal Conditions	Nutrition & Weight Management
Ear, Nose, Throat & Mouth Conditions	Pediatric Conditions
Eye Conditions	Reproductive & Sexual Health
Genetic & Chromosomal Disorders	Skin & Cosmetic Conditions

For more information, go to www.nyulangone.org, www.facebook.com/nyulangone, www.twitter.com/nyulmc, and www.youtube.com/nyulmc.

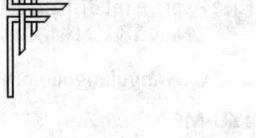

The Best in American Medicine
www.CastleConnolly.com

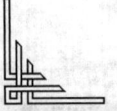
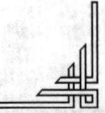

Specialty Hospitals

The New York metropolitan region is unique in its concentration of excellent Specialty Hospitals. Specialty Hospitals include those with a specific patient and disease focus such as cardiac care, psychiatric care and care of diseases and problems of eyes and ears. Many of these hospitals are nationally and internationally known for their outstanding care in these specialty areas and draw patients from the region and beyond who seek their excellent specialized care.

Castle Connolly Medical Ltd. has invited the following outstanding Specialty Hospitals to present important facts and information on their hospitals by sponsoring the profiles that follow.

Specialty Hospitals

Calvary Hospital

Hospital for Special Surgery

Memorial Sloan-Kettering Cancer Center

St Francis Hospital - The Heart Center

CALVARY HOSPITAL

Where Life Continues

1740 Eastchester Road
Bronx, NY 10461
Tel: (718) 518-2000
Fax: (718) 518-2674

150 55th Street
Brooklyn, NY 11220
Tel: (718) 518-2000
Fax: (718) 518-2670

The Dawn Greene Hospice
Mary Manning Walsh Home
1339 York Avenue
New York, NY 10021

www.calvaryhospital.org

Beds:	225 (200 in Bronx, 25 at Brooklyn Satellite located at Lutheran Medical Center)
Accreditation:	The Joint Commission, College of American Pathologists (CAP)

SETTING THE STANDARD FOR PALLIATIVE CARE

Founded in 1899, Calvary Hospital is the nation's only fully accredited acute care specialty hospital dedicated to providing palliative care to adult patients with advanced cancer and life-limiting illnesses. We care for patients at a 200-bed Bronx facility and a 25-bed satellite at Lutheran Medical Center in Brooklyn. Calvary's family-centric approach helps more than 6,000 patients and families each year with inpatient care, outpatient care, Calvary Home Care and Hospice, and the Center for Curative and Palliative Wound Care. The Joint Commission gave Calvary Hospital and our Home Care/Hospice program the Gold Seal of Approval™ in 2013. Press Ganey consistently ranks Calvary in the top one percent of its peers in patient satisfaction. Calvary received a 2012 Circle of Life Award® for innovative palliative and end-of-life care. To learn more or sign up for the e-newsletter, *Calvary Life*, please go to www.calvaryhospital.org.

Acute Inpatient Care

One-page form expedites admissions process. Adults with advanced cancer are assigned a primary physician and a care team: nurse, social worker, dietitian, and case manager. Goal is to maximize physical, spiritual, and emotional comfort. Pastoral care and bereavement support are integral to Calvary care.

Calvary@Home: Home Care, Hospice

Certified Home Health Agency

We provide a full range of home care services, not limited to patients with advanced cancer, in all five boroughs as well as Westchester, Rockland, Putnam, and Nassau counties. Care is coordinated by patient's community physician or Calvary doctor. Nurse is available 24/7 for telephone consults.

Hospice

For people with all terminal diagnoses who are primarily cared for at home or in select nursing facilities. Emphasis on quality of life, control of pain and symptoms, and support for family. Serves patients in Bronx, Brooklyn, Manhattan, Queens, Westchester, Nassau, and Rockland. Care may be coordinated by community physician or Calvary doctor. Nurse is available 24/7 by telephone. Bereavement support. Short-term hospitalization is available for acute symptom management. Goal is to promote quality of life. Through The Dawn Greene Hospice at Mary Manning Walsh Home in Manhattan, Calvary provides short-term inpatient care for a select number of patients.

Family Care

Focuses on the impact of cancer on the family. Family Care Center at the Bronx campus. Extensive bereavement support for adults, teens, and children, including bereavement camp for children and teens who participate in our support groups.

Pastoral Care

Calvary's Clinical Pastoral Education (CPE) program achieved certification by the Association for Clinical Pastoral Education – less than 2 years after the program was re-established. The 20-week, 400-hour program is the country's only CPE program exclusively focused on giving students hands-on experience solely with terminally ill patients in a hospital and home hospice setting.

Palliative Care Institute

Calvary's research and education arm, offers a curriculum for medical students, residents, postdoctoral fellows, and senior health practitioners, as well as health lectures for the community.

Outpatient and Wound Care

Outpatient clinic for cancer patients undergoing active treatment or who do not require acute inpatient care. The Center for Curative and Palliative Wound Care treats complex wounds related to cancer, diabetes, vascular disease, and other illnesses.

Sponsored Page

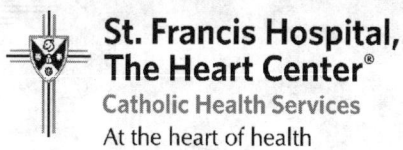

St. Francis Hospital, The Heart Center®

Catholic Health Services
At the heart of health

100 Port Washington Blvd.
Roslyn, New York 11576
www.stfrancisheartcenter.com
(516) 562-6000
1-888-HEARTNY

St. Francis Hospital, The Heart Center® is New York State's only specialty designated cardiac center and a nationally recognized leader in cardiac care. Founded in 1922 by the Franciscan Missionaries of Mary, the Hospital is an innovator in the delivery of specialized cardiovascular services in an environment where excellence and compassion are emphasized. St. Francis also offers a nationally recognized program in non-cardiac surgery, including some of the most advanced technology and minimally invasive techniques available for vascular, prostate, ear-nose-throat (ENT), abdominal, oncologic, gastrointestinal, and orthopedic surgery and procedures.

Cardiac Diagnostics and Treatment

St. Francis Hospital performs one of the highest volumes of cardiac surgical, interventional and arrhythmia procedures in the nation and has been consistently recognized for its outstanding quality of care. In 2014-15, St. Francis Hospital was ranked one of America's top 10 hospitals in cardiology and heart surgery by *U.S. News & World Report*.

Cardiac surgery: In 2013, 1,398 open-heart surgeries were performed at St. Francis Hospital. The Hospital's cardiothoracic surgical staff has the combined experience of over 15,000 open-heart procedures in the last 10 years alone and are experts in all types of heart surgery, from conventional, open-heart bypass to off-pump coronary artery bypass (OPCAB) to the newest, minimally invasive valve procedures, including surgical techniques designed to treat certain cardiac arrhythmias or irregular heart rhythms.

Cardiac catheterization: In 2013, St. Francis interventional cardiologists performed 10,276 cardiac catheterizations and 2,879 percutaneous coronary interventions (angioplasty with stents) and other advanced cardiac and peripheral vascular interventions. The Hospital is also recognized as one of the East Coast's highest volume centers for catheter-based techniques to repair congenital heart defects.

Arrhythmia and Pacemaker Center: Arrhythmia and Pacemaker Center: St. Francis has a leading national program for pacemaker implantation and the diagnosis and treatment of cardiac rhythm abnormalities. The Center has unparalleled expertise in radiofrequency cardiac ablation, including treatment of atrial fibrillation.

Research and Technology: At the St. Francis Cardiac Research Institute, a team of world-renowned researchers is working with the latest noninvasive imaging technology, including advanced techniques and world-class expertise in cardiac CT angiography, cardiac magnetic resonance imaging (MRI), cardiac PET/CT and three-dimensional echocardiography. This multimodality approach to investigating the heart's function and disease processes is aimed at improving methods of diagnosing heart disease. St. Francis is also a pioneer in transaortic valve replacement (TAVR), a new, minimally invasive procedure that channels a tube called a catheter containing a prosthetic valve through the femoral artery to reach the heart. The procedure is typically used for patients who are too elderly or ill for open-heart surgery.

Broad-Based Excellence

St. Francis Hospital is also ranked one of America's best hospitals in gastroenterology and GI surgery; geriatrics; orthopedics; and neurology and neurosurgery by *U.S. News & World Report*. In 2012, the Hospital opened a new Cancer Institute, which brings together all of the essential elements for an integrated approach to treating cancer with the Hospital's signature commitment to quality and compassionate care.

Physician referral: **1-888-HEARTNY**   Sponsorship: Voluntary not-for-profit   Beds: 306
Accreditation: Awarded accreditation from the Joint Commission

The Best in American Medicine
www.CastleConnolly.com

Regional Medical Centers and Hospitals

The New York metropolitan region is fortunate to have a large number of truly excellent Regional Medical Centers and Hospitals. Many of these institutions offer sophisticated services that in years past were offered only at academic medical centers. However, with advancements in medical technology, Regional Medical Centers and Hospitals have access to the equipment, and by virtue of the medical schools and teaching hospitals in the region, the well-trained physicians and staff, to offer these programs.

Regional Medical Centers and Hospitals range in size from the small (100 beds) to the very large (800 beds) but they share a common theme: a primary focus on patient care.

We have invited a select number of excellent Regional Medical Centers and Hospitals to provide readers of the Castle Connolly Guide with information on their institutions and services by sponsoring profiles, which are included at the end of individual county sections in the physician listings that follow.

Regional Medical Centers and Hospitals

Greenwich Hospital

Hackensack University Health Network

Hackensack UMC at Pascack Valley

Hackensack UMC Mountainside

Holy Name Medical Center

New York Hospital Queens

New York Methodist Hospital

Stamford Hospital

SUNY Downstate Medical Center (Univ Hosp of Brooklyn)

Trinitas Regional Medical Center

Valley Hospital

White Plains Hospital Center

Winthrop-University Hospital

SECTION THREE

Physician Listings

The State of New York

The Best in American Medicine
www.CastleConnolly.com

New York (Manhattan)

New York (Manhattan)

Addiction Psychiatry

Frances, Richard J MD (AdP) - **Spec Exp:** Addiction/Substance Abuse; Anxiety & Mood Disorders; Forensic Psychiatry; **Hospital:** Silver Hill Hosp, NYU Langone Med Ctr (page 104); **Address:** 510 E 86th St, Ste 1D, New York, NY 10028; **Phone:** 212-861-0570; **Board Cert:** Psychiatry 1976; Addiction Psychiatry 2012; **Med School:** NYU Sch Med 1971; **Resid:** Psychiatry, Jacobi Med Ctr 1974; **Fellow:** Psychoanalysis, NY Psychoanalytic Inst 1983; **Fac Appt:** Clin Prof Psyc, NYU Sch Med

Galanter, I Marc MD (AdP) - **Spec Exp:** Alcohol Abuse; Drug Abuse; Anxiety & Depression; **Hospital:** NYU Langone Med Ctr (page 104); **Address:** 285 Central Park West, New York, NY 10024-3006; **Phone:** 212-877-4093; **Board Cert:** Psychiatry 1974; Addiction Psychiatry 2011; **Med School:** Albert Einstein Coll Med 1967; **Resid:** Psychiatry, Bronx Muni Hosp 1971; **Fac Appt:** Prof Psyc, NYU Sch Med

Kleber, Herbert D MD (AdP) - **Spec Exp:** Opiate Addiction; Cocaine Addiction; Drug Abuse; **Hospital:** NY-Presby/Columbia Univ Med Ctr, NY (page 102), NY State Psychiatric Inst; **Address:** NY State Psychiatric Inst, 1051 Riverside Drive, Rm 3713, Unit 66, New York, NY 10032-1007; **Phone:** 646-774-6121; **Med School:** Jefferson Med Coll 1960; **Resid:** Psychiatry, Yale-New Haven Hosp 1964; **Fac Appt:** Prof Psyc, Columbia P&S

Levin, Frances R MD (AdP) - **Spec Exp:** Addiction/Substance Abuse; Dual Diagnosis; Substance Abuse in ADHD Patients; Alcohol Abuse; **Hospital:** NY State Psychiatric Inst, NY-Presby/Columbia Univ Med Ctr, NY (page 102); **Address:** NYS Psychiatric Inst, 1051 Riverside Drive, rm 3625, Box 66, New York, NY 10032; **Phone:** 646-774-6137; **Board Cert:** Psychiatry 1990; Addiction Psychiatry 2013; **Med School:** Cornell Univ-Weill Med Coll 1985; **Resid:** Psychiatry, Payne Whitney Clin 1989; **Fellow:** Substance Abuse, Univ MD Med Ctr/NIDA 1990; **Fac Appt:** Prof Psyc, Columbia P&S

Paul, Edward MD (AdP) - **Spec Exp:** Opiate Addiction; Alcohol Abuse; Smoking Cessation; Cocaine Addiction; **Hospital:** NYU Langone Med Ctr (page 104); **Address:** 155 E 31st St, Ste 25J, New York, NY 10016; **Phone:** 212-447-5712; **Board Cert:** Psychiatry 1987; Addiction Psychiatry 2013; **Med School:** Columbia P&S 1982; **Resid:** Psychiatry, Payne Whitney Clin 1987; Psychoanalysis, NYU Med Ctr 1993; **Fellow:** Substance Abuse, NY-Presby/Weill Cornell Med Ctr 1987; **Fac Appt:** Asst Clin Prof Psyc, NYU Sch Med

Perkel, Charles A MD (AdP) - **Spec Exp:** Addiction/Substance Abuse; Alcohol Abuse; Drug Abuse; **Hospital:** Mt Sinai Beth Israel; **Address:** Mt Sinai-Beth Israel, dept Psychiatry, First Ave at 16th St, New York, NY 10003; **Phone:** 212-420-2008; **Board Cert:** Psychiatry 2009; Addiction Psychiatry 2008; **Med School:** South Africa 1985; **Resid:** Psychiatry, Beth Israel Med Ctr 1997; Addiction Psychiatry, Beth Israel Med Ctr 1998

Rosenberg, Kenneth P MD (AdP) - **Spec Exp:** Addiction/Substance Abuse; Sexual Dysfunction; **Hospital:** NY-Presby/Weill Cornell Med Ctr, NY (page 102); **Address:** 49 E 78th St, Ste 2A, New York, NY 10075; **Phone:** 212-861-8807; **Board Cert:** Psychiatry 1992; Addiction Psychiatry 2009; **Med School:** Albert Einstein Coll Med 1983; **Resid:** Psychiatry, NY-Presby/Weill Cornell Med Ctr 1988; **Fellow:** Substance Abuse, NY-Presby/Weill Cornell Med Ctr 1991; Public Health, NY-Presby/Weill Cornell Med Ctr 1992; **Fac Appt:** Assoc Clin Prof Psyc, Cornell Univ-Weill Med Coll

Scimeca, Michael M MD (AdP) - **Spec Exp:** Addiction/Substance Abuse; Alcohol Abuse; **Hospital:** Mt Sinai Hosp, James J. Peters VA Med Ctr-Bronx; **Address:** 200 W 90th St, Ste 11H, New York, NY 10024; **Phone:** 212-580-9605; **Board Cert:** Psychiatry 2007; Addiction Psychiatry 2007; **Med School:** Univ Tex, San Antonio 1978; **Resid:** Psychiatry, Montefiore Med Ctr 1981; **Fac Appt:** Assoc Clin Prof Psyc, Mount Sinai Sch Med

Stelwagon, Jennifer Cooper MD (AdP) - **Spec Exp:** Addiction/Substance Abuse; Psychopharmacology; Psychotherapy; **Hospital:** NY-Presby/Weill Cornell Med Ctr, NY (page 102); **Address:** 420 E 51st St, New York, NY 10022; **Phone:** 212-879-1970; **Board Cert:** Psychiatry 2005; Addiction Psychiatry 2006; **Med School:** Johns Hopkins Univ 1999; **Resid:** Psychiatry, Weill-Cornell Med Ctr 2003; **Fellow:** Addiction Psychiatry, Weill-Cornell Med Ctr 2004

Weiss, Carol J MD (AdP) - **Spec Exp:** Drug Abuse; Alcohol Abuse; **Hospital:** NY-Presby/Weill Cornell Med Ctr, NY (page 102); **Address:** 1044 Madison Ave, Ste PH1, New York, NY 10075; **Phone:** 212-988-1209; **Board Cert:** Psychiatry 1989; Addiction Psychiatry 2013; Addiction Medicine 2009; **Med School:** Johns Hopkins Univ 1983; **Resid:** Psychiatry, New York Hosp-Cornell 1987; **Fellow:** Addiction Psychiatry, New York Hosp-Cornell 1989; **Fac Appt:** Asst Clin Prof Psyc, Cornell Univ-Weill Med Coll

Adolescent Medicine

Bell, David L MD (AM) - **Spec Exp:** Men's Health; **Hospital:** Morgan Stanley Chldns Hosp of NY-Presby, NY (page 102); **Address:** Audubon Primary Care, 21 Audubon Ave, New York, NY 10032; **Phone:** 212-342-4710; **Board Cert:** Pediatrics 2010; **Med School:** Univ Tex SW, Dallas 1989; **Resid:** Pediatrics, Bellevue Hosp 1993; **Fellow:** Adolescent Medicine, UCSF Med Ctr 1996; **Fac Appt:** Asst Prof Ped, Columbia P&S

Catallozzi, Marina MD (AM) - **Spec Exp:** AIDS/HIV in Adolescents; Adolescent Gynecology; Sexually Transmitted Diseases; **Hospital:** Morgan Stanley Chldns Hosp of NY-Presby, NY (page 102); **Address:** 21 Audubon Ave, New York, NY 10032; **Phone:** 212-342-3233; **Board Cert:** Pediatrics 2007; Adolescent Medicine 2013; **Med School:** Brown Univ 1996; **Resid:** Pediatrics, CHOP 2000; **Fellow:** Adolescent Medicine, CHOP 2004; **Fac Appt:** Asst Prof Ped, Columbia P&S

Cohall, Alwyn T MD (AM) - **Spec Exp:** AIDS/HIV in Adolescents; Adolescent Behavior-High Risk; **Hospital:** Morgan Stanley Chldns Hosp of NY-Presby, NY (page 102), NY-Presby/Columbia Univ Med Ctr, NY (page 102); **Address:** 3959 Broadway, Ste 106, New York, NY 10032; **Phone:** 646-284-9725; **Board Cert:** Pediatrics 1986; Adolescent Medicine 2010; **Med School:** UMDNJ-NJ Med Sch, Newark 1980; **Resid:** Pediatrics, Montefiore Med Ctr 1983; **Fellow:** Adolescent Medicine, Mount Sinai Med Ctr 1984; **Fac Appt:** Clin Prof Ped, Columbia P&S

Ipp, Lisa S MD (AM) - **Spec Exp:** Adolescent Gynecology; **Hospital:** NY-Presby/Weill Cornell Med Ctr, NY (page 102), Hosp For Special Surgery (page 109); **Address:** NY Presby Hosp-Pediatrics, 505 E 70th St, Helmsley Tower Fl 5, New York, NY 10021; **Phone:** 212-746-3303; **Board Cert:** Pediatrics 2007; Adolescent Medicine 2011; **Med School:** Cornell Univ-Weill Med Coll 1996; **Resid:** Pediatrics, Hasbro Children's Hosp 1999; **Fellow:** Adolescent Medicine, Mt Sinai Med Ctr 2002; **Fac Appt:** Assoc Clin Prof Ped, Cornell Univ-Weill Med Coll

Lopez, Ralph I MD (AM) - **Spec Exp:** Growth/Development Disorders; Eating Disorders; Learning Disorders; Parenting Issues; **Hospital:** NY-Presby/Weill Cornell Med Ctr, NY (page 102); **Address:** 418 E 71st St, New York, NY 10021-4894; **Phone:** 212-772-8989; **Board Cert:** Pediatrics 1972; **Med School:** NYU Sch Med 1967; **Resid:** Pediatrics, Bellevue Hosp 1969; Pediatrics, Chldns Hosp 1970; **Fellow:** Adolescent Medicine, Chldns Hosp 1971; **Fac Appt:** Clin Prof Ped, Cornell Univ-Weill Med Coll

Marks, Andrea M MD (AM) - **Spec Exp:** Eating Disorders; Adolescent Gynecology; Psychosomatic Disorders; Parenting Issues; **Hospital:** Mt Sinai Hosp; **Address:** Adolescent Young Adult Medicine, 14 E 90th St, Ste 1B, New York, NY 10128; **Phone:** 212-987-1414; **Board Cert:** Pediatrics 1977; **Med School:** Univ Pennsylvania 1972; **Resid:** Pediatrics, Chldns Hosp 1974; **Fellow:** Adolescent Medicine, Chldns Hosp 1975; **Fac Appt:** Assoc Clin Prof Ped, Mount Sinai Sch Med

Nucci-Sack, Anne T MD (AM) - **Spec Exp:** Adolescent Gynecology; Vaccines; **Hospital:** Mt Sinai Hosp; **Address:** Mt Sinai, Adolescent Hlth Ctr, 312 E 94th St, New York, NY 10128; **Phone:** 212-423-3000; **Board Cert:** Pediatrics 1986; Adolescent Medicine 2008; **Med School:** NY Med Coll 1981; **Resid:** Pediatrics, Bronx Municipal Hosp 1984; **Fellow:** Adolescent Medicine, Montefiore Med Ctr 1990; **Fac Appt:** Asst Prof Ped, Mount Sinai-Icahn Sch of Med

Pastore, Doris R MD (AM) - **Spec Exp:** Nutrition; Eating Disorders; **Hospital:** Mt Sinai Hosp; **Address:** Adolescent Young Adult Medicine, 14 E 90 St, Ste 1B, New York, NY 10128; **Phone:** 212-987-1414; **Board Cert:** Pediatrics 2012; Adolescent Medicine 2009; **Med School:** NY Med Coll 1985; **Resid:** Pediatrics, Montefiore Med Ctr 1988; **Fellow:** Adolescent Medicine, N Shore Univ Hosp/Cornell 1990

Pegler, Cynthia R MD (AM) - **Spec Exp:** Adolescent Gynecology; Eating Disorders; **Hospital:** NY-Presby/Weill Cornell Med Ctr, NY (page 102); **Address:** 992 5th Ave, New York, NY 10028; **Phone:** 212-517-5313; **Board Cert:** Pediatrics 2010; Adolescent Medicine 2009; **Med School:** Albany Med Coll 1984; **Resid:** Pediatrics, N Shore Univ Hosp 1987; **Fellow:** Adolescent Medicine, N Shore Univ Hosp 1990

Rosewater, Karen M MD (AM) - **Spec Exp:** Eating Disorders; **Hospital:** Mt Sinai Hosp; **Address:** Adolescent Young Adult Medicine, 14 E 90th St, Ste 1B, New York, NY 10128; **Phone:** 212-987-1414; **Board Cert:** Adolescent Medicine 2009; **Med School:** Yale Univ 1994; **Resid:** Pediatrics, Chldns Hosp 1997; **Fellow:** Adolescent Medicine, Chldns Natl Med Ctr 2000

Rudy, Bret J MD (AM) - **Spec Exp:** HIV in Adolescents; AIDS/HIV; **Hospital:** NYU Langone Med Ctr (page 104), Bellevue Hosp Ctr; **Address:** 145 E 32nd St, rm 1408, 14th Fl Penthouse, New York, NY 10016; **Phone:** 212-263-6425; **Board Cert:** Adolescent Medicine 2008; **Med School:** Univ Pittsburgh 1985; **Resid:** Pediatrics, Chldns Hosp 1988; **Fellow:** Hematology & Oncology, Chldns Hosp 1989; Internal Medicine, Chldns Hosp 1994

Soren, Karen MD (AM) - **Spec Exp:** Adolescent Gynecology; Behavioral Disorders; Chronic Illness; **Hospital:** Morgan Stanley Chldns Hosp of NY-Presby, NY (page 102), NY-Presby/Columbia Univ Med Ctr, NY (page 102); **Address:** Columbia Doctors Adolescent Medicine, 51 W 51st St, New York, NY 10019; **Phone:** 212-326-3350; **Board Cert:** Pediatrics 1987; Adolescent Medicine 2009; **Med School:** NYU Sch Med 1982; **Resid:** Pediatrics, Chldn's Hosp Natl Med Ctr 1985; **Fellow:** Adolescent Medicine, Univ Chicago Med Ctr 1987; **Fac Appt:** Assoc Prof Ped, Columbia P&S

Steever, John B MD (AM) - **Spec Exp:** Adolescent Gynecology; Adolescent Behavior-High Risk; Abuse/Neglect; **Hospital:** Mt Sinai Hosp; **Address:** Mt Sinai Adolescent Hlth Ctr, 312 E 94 St Fl 2, New York, NY 10128; **Phone:** 212-423-2900; **Board Cert:** Pediatrics 2013; Adolescent Medicine 2008; **Med School:** Geo Wash Univ 1993; **Resid:** Pediatrics, Chldn's Hosp 1996; **Fellow:** Adolescent Medicine, Chldn's Hosp 1999; **Fac Appt:** Asst Prof Ped, Mount Sinai Sch Med

Allergy & Immunology

Bassett, Clifford Wayne MD (A&I) - **Spec Exp:** Skin Allergies; Food Allergy; Sinus Disorders; Allergic Rhinitis; **Hospital:** NYU Langone Med Ctr (page 104), NY-Presby/Lower Manhattan Hosp (page 102); **Address:** Allergy & Asthma Care NY, 381 Park Ave S, Ste 1020, New York, NY 10016; **Phone:** 212-260-6078; **Board Cert:** Allergy & Immunology 2006; **Med School:** NY Med Coll 1985; **Resid:** Internal Medicine, Hackensack Univ Med Ctr 1989; **Fellow:** Allergy & Immunology, LI Coll Hosp 1993; **Fac Appt:** Asst Clin Prof Med, NYU Sch Med

Buchbinder, Ellen M MD (A&I) - **Spec Exp:** Asthma & Allergy; Rhinitis; Hives; Food & Drug Allergy; **Hospital:** Mt Sinai Hosp; **Address:** 111 E 88th St, Ste 1-B, New York, NY 10128; **Phone:** 212-410-3246; **Board Cert:** Internal Medicine 1981; Allergy & Immunology 1983; **Med School:** Tulane Univ 1978; **Resid:** Internal Medicine, New England Deaconess Hosp 1981; **Fellow:** Allergy & Immunology, Mass Genl Hosp 1983; **Fac Appt:** Asst Clin Prof Med, Mount Sinai Sch Med

Burton, Daniel A MD (A&I) - **Spec Exp:** Rhinitis; Asthma; Food & Drug Allergy; Urticaria; **Hospital:** NY-Presby/Weill Cornell Med Ctr, NY (page 102), Hosp For Special Surgery (page 109); **Address:** 235 E 67th St, Ste 203, New York, NY 10065; **Phone:** 212-288-9300; **Board Cert:** Internal Medicine 1989; Allergy & Immunology 2013; **Med School:** Wright State Univ 1984; **Resid:** Internal Medicine, St Lukes-Roosevelt Hosp Ctr 1987; **Fellow:** Allergy & Immunology, NY Hosp 1989; **Fac Appt:** Asst Prof Med, Cornell Univ-Weill Med Coll

Canfield, Stephen M MD/PhD (A&I) - **Spec Exp:** Immunotherapy; Asthma & Allergy; Allergic Rhinitis; **Hospital:** NY-Presby/Columbia Univ Med Ctr, NY (page 102); **Address:** Columbia Pulmonary Assocs, 161 Ft Washington Ave, Irving Pav-Rm 310, New York, NY 10032; **Phone:** 212-305-1544; **Board Cert:** Allergy & Immunology 2012; **Med School:** Columbia P&S 1992; **Resid:** Internal Medicine, NY Presby-Columbia Med Ctr 1996; **Fellow:** Allergy & Immunology, Ny Presby-Columbia Med Ctr 2001; **Fac Appt:** Asst Prof Med, Columbia P&S

Chandler, Michael J MD (A&I) - **Spec Exp:** Asthma; Sinus Disorders; Airway Disorders; **Hospital:** Mt Sinai Hosp; **Address:** City Allergy, 115 E 61st St Fl 12, New York, NY 10065; **Phone:** 212-486-6715; **Board Cert:** Internal Medicine 1984; Allergy & Immunology 1987; **Med School:** Wayne State Univ 1981; **Resid:** Internal Medicine, Northwestern Meml Hosp 1984; **Fellow:** Allergy & Immunology, Northwestern Meml Hosp 1986; **Fac Appt:** Asst Clin Prof Med, Mount Sinai Sch Med

Corn, Beth E MD (A&I) - **Spec Exp:** Asthma; Rhinitis; Food Allergy; **Hospital:** Mt Sinai Hosp; **Address:** Mt Sinai, Allergy & Immunology Dept, 5 E 98th St Fl 11, New York, NY 10029; **Phone:** 212-241-0764; **Board Cert:** Allergy & Immunology 2005; **Med School:** Albert Einstein Coll Med 1989; **Resid:** Internal Medicine, St Lukes-Roosevelt Hosp 1992; **Fellow:** Clinical Immunology, Mount Sinai Med Ctr 1994; **Fac Appt:** Asst Prof Med, Mount Sinai Sch Med

Cunningham-Rundles, Charlotte MD/PhD (A&I) - **Spec Exp:** Immunotherapy; Immunodeficiency Disorders; **Hospital:** Mt Sinai Hosp; **Address:** Mt Sinai Hosp, Dept of Med-Allergy & Immunology, 5 E 98th St, Fl 11, New York, NY 10029; **Phone:** 212-659-9268; **Board Cert:** Internal Medicine 1972; **Med School:** Columbia P&S 1969; **Resid:** Internal Medicine, Bellevue Hosp Ctr 1972; **Fellow:** Allergy & Immunology, NYU Med Ctr 1974; **Fac Appt:** Prof Med, Mount Sinai Sch Med

Grubman, Samuel MD (A&I) - **Spec Exp:** Asthma & Allergy; Food Allergy; Immunodeficiency Disorders; Pediatric Allergy & Immunology; **Hospital:** NYU Langone Med Ctr (page 104); **Address:** NY Downtown Allergy, 154 W 14th St Fl 4, New York, NY 10011; **Phone:** 212-616-4122; **Board Cert:** Pediatrics 1987; Allergy & Immunology 2009; **Med School:** Mount Sinai Sch Med 1983; **Resid:** Pediatrics, NYU Med Ctr 1986; **Fellow:** Allergy & Immunology, Montefiore Med Ctr 1988; **Fac Appt:** Assoc Clin Prof Ped, NYU Sch Med

Lubitz, Arthur M MD (A&I) - **Spec Exp:** Allergy; Asthma; Immunotherapy; **Hospital:** Lenox Hill Hosp, NYU Langone Med Ctr (page 104); **Address:** 315 W 57th St, Ste 309, New York, NY 10019; **Phone:** 212-247-7447; **Board Cert:** Internal Medicine 1984; Allergy & Immunology 2013; **Med School:** SUNY Downstate 1980; **Resid:** Internal Medicine, Coney Island Hosp 1983; **Fellow:** Allergy & Immunology, LI Coll Hosp 1985

Mazza, David S MD (A&I) - **Spec Exp:** Asthma; Sinus Disorders; Eczema; **Hospital:** Mt Sinai Roosevelt; **Address:** 7 Lexington Ave, Ste P3, New York, NY 10010-5517; **Phone:** 212-677-7170; **Board Cert:** Pediatrics 1983; Allergy & Immunology 2008; **Med School:** Univ VT Coll Med 1977; **Resid:** Pediatrics, NYU-Bellevue Hosp 1980; **Fellow:** Pediatric Allergy & Immunology, Bellevue Hosp 1982; **Fac Appt:** Asst Prof Ped, Columbia P&S

Shepherd, Gillian M MD (A&I) - **Spec Exp:** Food & Drug Allergy; Rhinosinusitis & Asthma; Urticaria; Insect Allergies; **Hospital:** NY-Presby/Weill Cornell Med Ctr, NY (page 102); **Address:** 235 E 67th St, Ste 203, New York, NY 10065; **Phone:** 212-288-9300; **Board Cert:** Internal Medicine 1979; Allergy & Immunology 1981; **Med School:** NY Med Coll 1976; **Resid:** Internal Medicine, Lenox Hill Hosp 1979; **Fellow:** Allergy & Immunology, New York Hosp-Cornell 1981; **Fac Appt:** Assoc Clin Prof Med, Cornell Univ-Weill Med Coll

Slankard, Marjorie L MD (A&I) - **Spec Exp:** Sinus Disorders; Asthma; Food Allergy; **Hospital:** NY-Presby/Columbia Univ Med Ctr, NY (page 102), Valley Hosp (page 739); **Address:** 51 W 51st St, Ste 360, New York, NY 10019; **Phone:** 212-326-8410; **Board Cert:** Internal Medicine 1974; Allergy & Immunology 1977; **Med School:** Univ MO-Columbia Sch Med 1971; **Resid:** Internal Medicine, New York Hosp 1974; **Fellow:** Allergy & Immunology, New York Hosp-Cornell 1976; Neoplastic Diseases, Mount Sinai Med Ctr 1980; **Fac Appt:** Clin Prof Med, Columbia P&S

Tolston, Evelyn MD (A&I) - **Spec Exp:** Rhinitis; Asthma; Allergy; Sinusitis; **Hospital:** NYU Langone Med Ctr (page 104), Mt Sinai Beth Israel; **Address:** 161 Madison Ave, Ste 3A, New York, NY 10016; **Phone:** 646-424-0400; **Board Cert:** Allergy & Immunology 2005; **Med School:** Ukraine 1982; **Resid:** Internal Medicine, Cabrini Med Ctr 1993; Allergy & Immunology, Montefiore Med Ctr 1995

Cardiac Electrophysiology

Bernstein, Neil E MD (CE) - **Spec Exp:** Arrhythmias; Atrial Fibrillation; Pacemakers; **Hospital:** NYU Langone Med Ctr (page 104); **Address:** NYU Heart Rhythm Ctr, 403 E 34 St, Fl 4, New York, NY 10016; **Phone:** 212-263-3600; **Board Cert:** Internal Medicine 1989; Cardiovascular Disease 2004; Cardiac Electrophysiology 2005; **Med School:** NYU Sch Med 1986; **Resid:** Internal Medicine, NYU/Bellevue Med Ctr 1990; **Fellow:** Cardiovascular Disease, NYU/Bellevue Med Ctr 1994; **Fac Appt:** Asst Prof Med, NYU Sch Med

Biviano, Angelo MD (CE) - **Spec Exp:** Catheter Ablation; Defibrillators; Pacemakers; Atrial Fibrillation; **Hospital:** NY-Presby/Columbia Univ Med Ctr, NY (page 102); **Address:** 161 Fort Washington Ave, Ste 648, New York, NY 10032; **Phone:** 212-305-8559; **Board Cert:** Cardiovascular Disease 2004; Cardiac Electrophysiology 2006; **Med School:** Harvard Med Sch 1997; **Resid:** Internal Medicine, NewYork-Presby Hosp/Columbia Univ Med Ctr 2001; Cardiovascular Disease, NewYork-Presby Hosp/Columbia Univ Med Ctr 2004; **Fellow:** Cardiac Electrophysiology, NewYork-Presby Hosp/Columbia Univ Med Ctr 2005; **Fac Appt:** Asst Prof Med, Columbia P&S

Chinitz, Larry A MD (CE) - **Spec Exp:** Arrhythmias; Pacemakers; Defibrillators; Atrial Fibrillation; **Hospital:** NYU Langone Med Ctr (page 104); **Address:** Heart Rhythm Ctr, 403 E 34th St Fl 4, New York, NY 10016-6402; **Phone:** 212-263-7149; **Board Cert:** Internal Medicine 1982; Cardiovascular Disease 1985; Cardiac Electrophysiology 2013; **Med School:** NYU Sch Med 1979; **Resid:** Internal Medicine, Bellevue Hosp Ctr 1983; **Fellow:** Cardiovascular Disease, NYU Med Ctr/Bellevue Hosp Ctr 1985; Cardiac Electrophysiology, Montefiore Hosp 1986; **Fac Appt:** Assoc Prof Med, NYU Sch Med

Garan, Hasan MD (CE) - **Spec Exp:** Arrhythmias; Cardiac Catheterization; Pacemakers/Defibrillators; **Hospital:** NY-Presby/Columbia Univ Med Ctr, NY (page 102); **Address:** 161 Fort Washington Ave, Ste 648, New York, NY 10032; **Phone:** 212-305-7646; **Board Cert:** Internal Medicine 1977; Cardiovascular Disease 1979; **Med School:** Harvard Med Sch 1974; **Resid:** Internal Medicine, Hosp Univ Penn 1976; **Fellow:** Cardiovascular Disease, Mass Genl Hosp 1978; Cardiac Electrophysiology, Mass Genl Hosp 1979; **Fac Appt:** Prof Med, Columbia P&S

Gomes, Joseph Anthony MD (CE) - **Spec Exp:** Arrhythmias; Heart Attack; Atrial Fibrillation; Pacemakers; **Hospital:** Mt Sinai Hosp; **Address:** Cardiovascular Medicine Assocs, 1190 Fifth Ave, 1-South, Guggenheim Pavilion, New York, NY 10029-6500; **Phone:** 212-241-7272; **Board Cert:** Internal Medicine 1974; Cardiovascular Disease 1975; **Med School:** India 1969; **Resid:** Internal Medicine, Mt Sinai Med Ctr 1973; **Fellow:** Cardiovascular Disease, Bronx VA Med Ctr 1975; **Fac Appt:** Prof Med, Mount Sinai Sch Med

Hanon, Samuel MD (CE) - **Spec Exp:** Arrhythmias; Defibrillators; Heart Failure; Atrial Fibrillation; **Hospital:** Mt Sinai Beth Israel, Mt Sinai Roosevelt; **Address:** Beth Israel Med Ctr, 16th at 1st Ave, 5 Baird Hall, New York, NY 10003; **Phone:** 212-844-1266; **Board Cert:** Cardiovascular Disease 2005; Cardiac Electrophysiology 2006; **Med School:** Albert Einstein Coll Med 1998; **Resid:** Internal Medicine, Beth Israel Med Ctr 2001; **Fellow:** Cardiovascular Disease, Beth Israel Med Ctr 2005; Cardiac Electrophysiology, NY Presby-Columbia Med Ctr 2006

Harnick, David J MD (CE) - **Spec Exp:** Arrhythmias; **Hospital:** Mt Sinai Hosp; **Address:** 148 E 38 St, New York, NY 10003; **Phone:** 212-679-4488; **Board Cert:** Cardiovascular Disease 2012; **Med School:** Mount Sinai Sch Med 1996; **Resid:** Internal Medicine, NY Presby-Columbia Med Ctr 1999; **Fellow:** Cardiovascular Disease, Mount Sinai Med Ctr 2002; Cardiac Electrophysiology, Mount Sinai Med Ctr 2003

Lerman, Bruce MD (CE) - **Spec Exp:** Catheter Ablation; Atrial Fibrillation; Defibrillators; Arrhythmias; **Hospital:** NY-Presby/Weill Cornell Med Ctr, NY (page 102); **Address:** NY Presby/Weill Cornell Med Ctr, 520 E 70th St, Starr 4, New York, NY 10021-9800; **Phone:** 212-746-2169; **Board Cert:** Internal Medicine 1980; Cardiovascular Disease 1985; Cardiac Electrophysiology 2012; **Med School:** Loyola Univ-Stritch Sch Med 1977; **Resid:** Internal Medicine, Northwestern Univ Hosp 1980; Internal Medicine, Univ Michigan Med Ctr 1981; **Fellow:** Cardiovascular Disease, Hosp Univ Penn 1982; Cardiovascular Disease, Johns Hopkins Hosp 1983; **Fac Appt:** Prof Med, Cornell Univ-Weill Med Coll

Love, Charles J MD (CE) - **Spec Exp:** Defibrillator Cable Extraction; Pacemakers; **Hospital:** NYU Langone Med Ctr (page 104), Bellevue Hosp Ctr; **Address:** NYU Heart Rhythmn Center, 403 E 34th St Fl 4, New York, NY 10016; **Phone:** 212-263-7149; **Board Cert:** Internal Medicine 1986; Cardiovascular Disease 1989; Cardiac Electrophysiology 2004; **Med School:** Univ Pittsburgh 1983; **Resid:** Internal Medicine, Ohio State Univ Hosp 1986; **Fellow:** Cardiovascular Disease, Ohio State Univ Hosp 1988; **Fac Appt:** Clin Prof Med, NYU Sch Med

Markowitz, Steven M MD (CE) - **Spec Exp:** Arrhythmias; Atrial Fibrillation; Pacemakers/Defibrillators; Catheter Ablation; **Hospital:** NY-Presby/Weill Cornell Med Ctr, NY (page 102); **Address:** NY-Presby, Cardiac Electrophysiology, 520 E 70th St, Starr Bldg - Fl 4, New York, NY 10021; **Phone:** 212-746-2158; **Board Cert:** Cardiovascular Disease 2005; Cardiac Electrophysiology 2006; **Med School:** Harvard Med Sch 1988; **Resid:** Internal Medicine, NY-Presby/Weill Cornell Med Ctr 1991; **Fellow:** Cardiovascular Disease, NY-Presby/Weill Cornell Med Ctr 1995; Cardiac Electrophysiology, NY-Presby/Weill Cornell Med Ctr 1996; **Fac Appt:** Prof Med, Cornell Univ-Weill Med Coll

Matos, Jeffrey A MD (CE) - **Spec Exp:** Arrhythmias; Pacemakers; Defibrillators; **Hospital:** Lenox Hill Hosp; **Address:** Arrhythmia Assocs NY, 1421 3rd Ave Fl 5, New York, NY 10028; **Phone:** 212-772-6384; **Board Cert:** Internal Medicine 1980; Cardiovascular Disease 1983; **Med School:** Harvard Med Sch 1975; **Resid:** Internal Medicine, Beth Israel Med Ctr 1978; **Fellow:** Cardiovascular Disease, Brigham & Womens Hosp 1980; **Fac Appt:** Assoc Clin Prof Med, NYU Sch Med

Mehta, Davendra MD/PhD (CE) - **Spec Exp:** Arrhythmias; Congenital Heart Disease-Adult; Atrial Fibrillation; Heart Failure; **Hospital:** Mt Sinai St. Luke's; **Address:** 1090 Amsterdam Ave Fl 8, New York, NY 10025; **Phone:** 212-523-5200; **Board Cert:** Cardiovascular Disease 2009; Cardiac Electrophysiology 2009; **Med School:** India 1976; **Resid:** Internal Medicine, Leicester Royal Infirmary 1983; **Fellow:** Cardiovascular Disease, Groby Road Hosp 1986; Electrocardiography, St George's Hosp 1989; **Fac Appt:** Prof Med, Mount Sinai Sch Med

Suri, Ranjit MD (CE) - **Spec Exp:** Arrhythmias; Atrial Fibrillation; Pacemakers; Sudden Death Prevention; **Hospital:** Lenox Hill Hosp; **Address:** Heart Rhythm Assocs of New York, 1421 3rd Ave, Fl 5, New York, NY 10028; **Phone:** 212-390-1020; **Board Cert:** Internal Medicine 2007; Cardiovascular Disease 2006; Cardiac Electrophysiology 2011; **Med School:** India 1982; **Resid:** Internal Medicine, Univ Conn Affil Hosp 1994; **Fellow:** Cardiovascular Disease, Univ Conn Sch Med 1993; Cardiac Electrophysiology, Mass Genl Hosp 2000; **Fac Appt:** Clin Prof Med, Cornell Univ-Weill Med Coll

Whang, William MD (CE) - **Spec Exp:** Catheter Ablation; Arrhythmias; Atrial Fibrillation; Pacemakers/Defibrillators; **Hospital:** NY-Presby/Columbia Univ Med Ctr, NY (page 102); **Address:** 161 Fort Washingon Ave, Ste 648, New York, NY 10032; **Phone:** 212-305-8559; **Board Cert:** Cardiovascular Disease 2004; Cardiac Electrophysiology 2005; **Med School:** Columbia P&S 1998; **Resid:** Internal Medicine, NY-Presby Hosp/Columbia Univ Med Ctr 2001; **Fellow:** Cardiovascular Disease, Mass Genl Hosp 2004; Cardiac Electrophysiology, Mass Genl Hosp 2006; **Fac Appt:** Asst Clin Prof Med, Columbia P&S

Cardiovascular Disease

Andersen, Holly S MD (Cv) - **Spec Exp:** Preventive Cardiology; Women's Health; Mitral Valve Prolapse; **Hospital:** NY-Presby/Weill Cornell Med Ctr, NY (page 102); **Address:** 425 E 61st St Fl 6, New York, NY 10065; **Phone:** 212-752-2000; **Board Cert:** Internal Medicine 2012; Cardiovascular Disease 2005; **Med School:** Univ Rochester 1989; **Resid:** Internal Medicine, NY Presby-Cornell Med Ctr 1992; **Fellow:** Cardiovascular Disease, NY Presby-Cornell Med Ctr 1995; **Fac Appt:** Assoc Clin Prof Med, Cornell Univ-Weill Med Coll

Berdoff, Russell L MD (Cv) - **Spec Exp:** Coronary Artery Disease; Heart Valve Disease; Preventive Cardiology; **Hospital:** Mt Sinai Beth Israel; **Address:** 67 Irving Pl, Fl 7, New York, NY 10003; **Phone:** 212-979-9224; **Board Cert:** Internal Medicine 1978; Cardiovascular Disease 1981; **Med School:** NY Med Coll 1975; **Resid:** Internal Medicine, DC Genl Hosp 1978; **Fellow:** Cardiovascular Disease, Johns Hopkins Hosp 1980; **Fac Appt:** Assoc Clin Prof Med, Albert Einstein Coll Med

Blake, James A MD (Cv) - **Spec Exp:** Congestive Heart Failure; Nuclear Cardiology; Echocardiography; Hypertension; **Hospital:** NY-Presby/Weill Cornell Med Ctr, NY (page 102), Hosp For Special Surgery (page 109); **Address:** 133 E 58th St, Ste 301, New York, NY 10022; **Phone:** 212-755-8700; **Board Cert:** Internal Medicine 1984; Cardiovascular Disease 1987; Echocardiography 2009; Nuclear Cardiology 2009; **Med School:** Albert Einstein Coll Med 1981; **Resid:** Internal Medicine, NY-Presby/Weill Cornell Med Ctr 1984; **Fellow:** Cardiovascular Disease, NY-Presby/Weill Cornell Med Ctr 1987; **Fac Appt:** Assoc Clin Prof Med, Cornell Univ-Weill Med Coll

Blumenthal, David S MD (Cv) - **Spec Exp:** Heart Valve Disease; Preventive Cardiology; Coronary Artery Disease; **Hospital:** NY-Presby/Weill Cornell Med Ctr, NY (page 102); **Address:** 407 E 70th St, Fl 1, New York, NY 10021-5302; **Phone:** 212-861-3222; **Board Cert:** Internal Medicine 1978; Cardiovascular Disease 1981; **Med School:** Cornell Univ-Weill Med Coll 1975; **Resid:** Internal Medicine, NY Hosp 1978; Internal Medicine, NY Hosp 1981; **Fellow:** Cardiovascular Disease, Johns Hopkins Hosp 1980; **Fac Appt:** Clin Prof Med, Cornell Univ-Weill Med Coll

Campagna, Robert MD (Cv) - **Spec Exp:** Coronary Artery Disease; **Hospital:** NY-Presby/Weill Cornell Med Ctr, NY (page 102); **Address:** New York Cardio Assocs, 425 E 61st St Fl 6, New York, NY 10021; **Phone:** 212-752-2000; **Board Cert:** Cardiovascular Disease 2005; **Med School:** Cornell Univ-Weill Med Coll 1989; **Resid:** Internal Medicine, NY Presby-Cornell Med Ctr 1992; **Fellow:** Cardiovascular Disease, NY Presby-Cornell Med Ctr 1995; **Fac Appt:** Assoc Clin Prof Med, Cornell Univ-Weill Med Coll

Carabello, Blase A MD (Cv) - **Spec Exp:** Heart Valve Disease; **Hospital:** Mt Sinai Beth Israel; **Address:** 10 Union Square E, Ste 2A, New York, NY 10003; **Phone:** 212-420-4681; **Board Cert:** Internal Medicine 1977; Cardiovascular Disease 1979; **Med School:** Temple Univ 1973; **Resid:** Internal Medicine, Mass Genl Hosp 1976; **Fellow:** Cardiovascular Disease, Peter Bent Brigham Hosp 1978

Cemaletin, Nevber S MD (Cv) - **Hospital:** Lenox Hill Hosp; **Address:** 110 E 59th St, Ste 9B, New York, NY 10022; **Phone:** 212-583-2899; **Board Cert:** Internal Medicine 1988; Cardiovascular Disease 1989; **Med School:** NY Med Coll 1984; **Resid:** Internal Medicine, Lenox Hill Hosp 1987; **Fellow:** Cardiovascular Disease, Lenox Hill Hosp 1989

Cohen, Michael H MD (Cv) - **Spec Exp:** Congestive Heart Failure; Coronary Artery Disease; Hypertension; Cholesterol/Lipid Disorders; **Hospital:** NY-Presby/Columbia Univ Med Ctr, NY (page 102); **Address:** 161 Fort Washington Ave, rm 328, New York, NY 10032-3713; **Phone:** 212-305-5440; **Board Cert:** Internal Medicine 1971; **Med School:** Johns Hopkins Univ 1965; **Resid:** Internal Medicine, NY-Presby Hosp/Columbia Univ 1971; **Fellow:** Cardiovascular Disease, NY-Presby Hosp/Columbia Univ 1970; **Fac Appt:** Clin Prof Med, Johns Hopkins Univ

Cole, William J MD (Cv) - **Spec Exp:** Coronary Artery Disease; Hypertension; Cholesterol/Lipid Disorders; **Hospital:** NYU Langone Med Ctr (page 104); **Address:** 530 First Ave, Ste 3-D, New York, NY 10016; **Phone:** 212-263-7071; **Board Cert:** Internal Medicine 1983; Cardiovascular Disease 1987; **Med School:** NYU Sch Med 1980; **Resid:** Internal Medicine, Bellevue Hosp-NYU Med Ctr 1984; **Fellow:** Cardiovascular Disease, Bellevue Hosp-NYU Med Ctr 1986; **Fac Appt:** Asst Clin Prof Med, NYU Sch Med

Coppola, John T MD (Cv) - **Spec Exp:** Cardiac Catheterization; Angioplasty; **Hospital:** NYU Langone Med Ctr (page 104), Bellevue Hosp Ctr; **Address:** 275 7th Ave Fl 3, New York, NY 10001; **Phone:** 646-660-9999; **Board Cert:** Internal Medicine 1981; Cardiovascular Disease 1983; Interventional Cardiology 2009; **Med School:** NY Med Coll 1978; **Resid:** Internal Medicine, St Vincent Catholic Med Ctr 1981; **Fellow:** Cardiovascular Disease, St Vincent Catholic Med Ctr 1983

Dangas, George MD/PhD (Cv) - **Spec Exp:** Acute Coronary Syndromes; Angioplasty & Stent Placement; Endovascular Therapy; Percutaneous Vascular Interventions; **Hospital:** Mt Sinai Hosp, Mt Sinai Hosp of Queens; **Address:** Cardiovascular Med Assocs, 1190 5th Ave, rm GP1 South, New York, NY 10029; **Phone:** 212-241-7014; **Board Cert:** Interventional Cardiology 2009; Cardiovascular Disease 2007; Vascular Medicine 2006; Endovascular Medicine 2005; **Med School:** Greece 1989; **Resid:** Internal Medicine, Miriam Hosp 1994; **Fellow:** Cardiovascular Disease, Mount Sinai Hosp 1997; Interventional Cardiology, Mount Sinai Hosp 1998; **Fac Appt:** Prof Med, Mount Sinai Sch Med

Deutsch, Adam MD (Cv) - **Spec Exp:** Hypertension; Cholesterol/Lipid Disorders; Echocardiography; Congestive Heart Failure; **Hospital:** NY-Presby/Weill Cornell Med Ctr, NY (page 102), Lenox Hill Hosp; **Address:** Park Avenue Cardiology, 1036 Park Ave, Ste 1A, New York, NY 10028; **Phone:** 212-879-9000; **Board Cert:** Internal Medicine 2006; Cardiovascular Disease 2009; **Med School:** Albert Einstein Coll Med 1992; **Resid:** Internal Medicine, NY-Presby/Columbia Univ Med Ctr 1995; **Fellow:** Cardiovascular Disease, NY-Presby/Columbia Univ Med Ctr 1998

Devereux, Richard B MD (Cv) - **Spec Exp:** Marfan's Syndrome; **Hospital:** NY-Presby/Weill Cornell Med Ctr, NY (page 102); **Address:** 525 E 68th St, rm K-415, New York, NY 10065; **Phone:** 646-962-4733; **Board Cert:** Internal Medicine 1974; Cardiovascular Disease 1977; **Med School:** Univ Pennsylvania 1971; **Resid:** Internal Medicine, New York Hosp 1974; **Fellow:** Cardiovascular Disease, Hosp Univ Penn - UPHS 1976; **Fac Appt:** Prof Med, Cornell Univ-Weill Med Coll

Drusin, Ronald MD (Cv) - **Spec Exp:** Cholesterol/Lipid Disorders; Coronary Artery Disease; Heart Valve Disease; Transplant Medicine-Heart; **Hospital:** NY-Presby/Columbia Univ Med Ctr, NY (page 102); **Address:** NY-Presby, Cardiology Dept, 161 Fort Washington Ave, Ste 647, New York, NY 10032; **Phone:** 212-305-5371; **Board Cert:** Internal Medicine 1973; Cardiovascular Disease 1975; **Med School:** Columbia P&S 1966; **Resid:** Internal Medicine, NY-Presby/Columbia Univ Med Ctr 1969; **Fellow:** Cardiovascular Disease, NY-Presby/Columbia Univ Med Ctr 1973; **Fac Appt:** Clin Prof Med, Columbia P&S

Dubois, Nicholas B MD (Cv) - **Spec Exp:** Hypertension; Coronary Artery Disease; Nuclear Cardiology; Echocardiography; **Hospital:** Mt Sinai Hosp, Lenox Hill Hosp; **Address:** Mt Sinai Manhattan Heart, 177 E 87th St, Ste 507, New York, NY 10128; **Phone:** 212-828-3200; **Board Cert:** Cardiovascular Disease 2005; Nuclear Cardiology 2005; **Med School:** Cornell Univ 1999; **Resid:** Internal Medicine, Montefiore Med Ctr 2002; **Fellow:** Cardiovascular Disease, Cleveland Clinic 2005; **Fac Appt:** Assoc Prof Med, Mount Sinai Sch Med

Dutta, Timothy C MD (Cv) - **Spec Exp:** Coronary Artery Disease; Cholesterol/Lipid Disorders; **Hospital:** NY-Presby/Weill Cornell Med Ctr, NY (page 102); **Address:** 72nd Street Medical Assocs, 310 E 72nd St, C Level, New York, NY 10021; **Phone:** 212-249-3725; **Board Cert:** Internal Medicine 2012; Cardiovascular Disease 2005; **Med School:** Cornell Univ-Weill Med Coll 1999; **Resid:** Internal Medicine, NY Presby-Cornell Med Ctr 2002; **Fellow:** Cardiovascular Disease, NY Presby-Cornell Med Ctr 2004

Engel, David J MD (Cv) - **Spec Exp:** Cholesterol/Lipid Disorders; Hypertension; Echocardiography; Heart Valve Disease; **Hospital:** NY-Presby/Columbia Univ Med Ctr, NY (page 102); **Address:** Columbia Doctors Midtown, 51 W 51st St, Ste 330, New York, NY 10019; **Phone:** 212-326-8920; **Board Cert:** Cardiovascular Disease 2004; **Med School:** Cornell Univ-Weill Med Coll 1996; **Resid:** Internal Medicine, NY Presby-Columbia Med Ctr 2000; **Fellow:** Cardiovascular Disease, NY Presby-Columbia Med Ctr 2004; **Fac Appt:** Asst Prof Med, Columbia P&S

Franklin, Kenneth W MD (Cv) - **Spec Exp:** Preventive Cardiology; Diagnostic Problems; Coronary Artery Disease; Arrhythmias; **Hospital:** NY-Presby/Weill Cornell Med Ctr, NY (page 102); **Address:** 72nd St Med Assocs, 310 E 72nd St, New York, NY 10021; **Phone:** 212-717-7993; **Board Cert:** Internal Medicine 1981; Cardiovascular Disease 1983; **Med School:** Harvard Med Sch 1978; **Resid:** Internal Medicine, New York Hosp 1981; **Fellow:** Cardiovascular Disease, Univ Penn 1983; Interventional Cardiology, Univ Penn 1984; **Fac Appt:** Clin Prof Med, Cornell Univ-Weill Med Coll

Friedman, Sanford J MD (Cv) - **Spec Exp:** Preventive Cardiology; **Hospital:** Mt Sinai Hosp; **Address:** 941 Park Ave, New York, NY 10028; **Phone:** 212-988-3772; **Board Cert:** Internal Medicine 1980; Cardiovascular Disease 1977; **Med School:** Tufts Univ 1971; **Resid:** Internal Medicine, Mt Sinai Hosp 1974; **Fellow:** Cardiovascular Disease, Mt Sinai Hosp 1976; **Fac Appt:** Assoc Clin Prof Med, Mount Sinai Sch Med

Fuchs, Richard M MD (Cv) - **Spec Exp:** Coronary Artery Disease; Heart Valve Disease; Preventive Cardiology; **Hospital:** NY-Presby/Weill Cornell Med Ctr, NY (page 102); **Address:** 310 E 72nd St, New York, NY 10021; **Phone:** 212-717-2254; **Board Cert:** Internal Medicine 1979; Cardiovascular Disease 1981; **Med School:** Harvard Med Sch 1976; **Resid:** Internal Medicine, New York Hosp 1979; **Fellow:** Cardiovascular Disease, Johns Hopkins Hosp 1982; **Fac Appt:** Clin Prof Med, Cornell Univ-Weill Med Coll

Fuster, Valentin MD/PhD (Cv) - **Spec Exp:** Coronary Artery Disease; Heart Valve Disease; Congenital Heart Disease; Preventive Cardiology; **Hospital:** Mt Sinai Hosp; **Address:** Cardiovascular Med Assocs, 1190 Fifth Ave Fl 1, New York, NY 10029-6500; **Phone:** 212-241-7911; **Board Cert:** Internal Medicine 1976; Cardiovascular Disease 1977; **Med School:** Spain 1967; **Resid:** Internal Medicine, Mayo Clin 1972; Cardiovascular Disease, Mayo Clin 1974; **Fellow:** Cardiovascular Disease, Univ Edinburgh 1971; **Fac Appt:** Prof Med, Mount Sinai Sch Med

Gliklich, Jerry MD (Cv) - **Spec Exp:** Heart Valve Disease; Arrhythmias; **Hospital:** NY-Presby/Columbia Univ Med Ctr, NY (page 102); **Address:** NY-Presby, Heart Ctr, 173 Fort Washington Ave, Ste 606, New York, NY 10032; **Phone:** 212-305-5588; **Board Cert:** Internal Medicine 1978; Cardiovascular Disease 1981; **Med School:** Columbia P&S 1975; **Resid:** Internal Medicine, NY-Presby/Weill Cornell Med Ctr 1978; **Fellow:** Cardiovascular Disease, NY-Presby/Columbia Univ Med Ctr 1981; **Fac Appt:** Clin Prof Med, Columbia P&S

Goldberg, Harvey L MD (Cv) - **Spec Exp:** Coronary Artery Disease; **Hospital:** NY-Presby/Weill Cornell Med Ctr, NY (page 102), Lenox Hill Hosp; **Address:** New York Cardio Assocs, 425 E 61st St, Fl 6, New York, NY 10021-8795; **Phone:** 212-752-2000; **Board Cert:** Internal Medicine 1979; Cardiovascular Disease 1981; **Med School:** Cornell Univ 1976; **Resid:** Internal Medicine, New York Hosp 1979; **Fellow:** Cardiovascular Disease, New York Hosp-Cornell 1981; **Fac Appt:** Assoc Clin Prof Med, Cornell Univ-Weill Med Coll

Goldberg, Nieca MD (Cv) - **Spec Exp:** Women's Health; Preventive Cardiology; Heart Disease in Women; **Hospital:** NYU Langone Med Ctr (page 104), Lenox Hill Hosp; **Address:** Joan H. Tisch Ctr for Women's Health, 207 E 84th St, New York, NY 10128; **Phone:** 212-289-2045; **Board Cert:** Internal Medicine 1987; Cardiovascular Disease 2005; **Med School:** SUNY Downstate 1984; **Resid:** Internal Medicine, St. Luke's - Roosevelt Hosp Ctr - Roosevelt Div 1987; **Fellow:** Cardiovascular Disease, SUNY Downstate Affil Hosp 1990; **Fac Appt:** Assoc Clin Prof Med, NYU Sch Med

Goldman, Martin E MD (Cv) - **Spec Exp:** Heart Valve Disease; Echocardiography; Diagnostic Problems; **Hospital:** Mt Sinai Hosp; **Address:** Mt Sinai, Cardiology Dept, 1190 5th Ave, New York, NY 10029; **Phone:** 212-241-3078; **Board Cert:** Internal Medicine 1979; Cardiovascular Disease 1981; **Med School:** Albert Einstein Coll Med 1976; **Resid:** Internal Medicine, Brigham & Womens Hosp 1978; **Fellow:** Cardiovascular Disease, Mount Sinai Med Ctr 1980; **Fac Appt:** Prof Med, Mount Sinai Sch Med

Goodman, Dennis A MD (Cv) - **Spec Exp:** Preventive Cardiology; Cholesterol/Lipid Disorders; Complementary Medicine; **Hospital:** NYU Langone Med Ctr (page 104), Lenox Hill Hosp; **Address:** Preston Robert Tisch Ctr Men's Hlth, 555 Madison Ave Fl 3, New York, NY 10022; **Phone:** 646-754-2000; **Board Cert:** Internal Medicine 1984; Cardiovascular Disease 1989; **Med School:** South Africa 1979; **Resid:** Internal Medicine, Montefiore Hosp 1984; **Fellow:** Cardiovascular Disease, Baylor Coll Med Affil Hosp 1987; **Fac Appt:** Assoc Clin Prof Med, NYU Sch Med

Halperin, Jonathan L MD (Cv) - **Spec Exp:** Vascular Disease; Atrial Fibrillation; **Hospital:** Mt Sinai Hosp; **Address:** Cardiology Associates, 1190 Fifth Ave, New York, NY 10029; **Phone:** 212-241-7243; **Board Cert:** Internal Medicine 1980; Cardiovascular Disease 1981; **Med School:** Boston Univ 1975; **Resid:** Internal Medicine, Boston Univ Med Ctr 1977; **Fellow:** Vascular Medicine, Boston Univ Med Ctr 1978; Cardiovascular Disease, Boston Univ Med Ctr 1980; **Fac Appt:** Prof Med, Mount Sinai Sch Med

Hecht, Alan MD (Cv) - **Spec Exp:** Heart Valve Disease; Coronary Artery Disease; Arrhythmias; **Hospital:** Mt Sinai Hosp; **Address:** 1075 Park Ave, New York, NY 10128; **Phone:** 212-876-0845; **Board Cert:** Internal Medicine 1984; Cardiovascular Disease 1987; **Med School:** Northwestern Univ 1981; **Resid:** Internal Medicine, Mt Sinai Hosp 1984; **Fellow:** Cardiovascular Disease, Mt Sinai Hosp 1986; **Fac Appt:** Assoc Clin Prof Med, Mount Sinai Sch Med

Horn, Evelyn M MD (Cv) - **Spec Exp:** Pulmonary Hypertension; Heart Failure; Ventricular Assist Device (LVAD); **Hospital:** NY-Presby/Weill Cornell Med Ctr, NY (page 102); **Address:** 520 E 70th St Starr Bldg Fl 4 - Ste 443, New York, NY 10021; **Phone:** 212-746-2381; **Board Cert:** Internal Medicine 1983; Cardiovascular Disease 1985; Advanced Heart Failure & Transplant Cardiology 2010; **Med School:** Mount Sinai Sch Med 1980; **Resid:** Internal Medicine, Mt Sinai Hosp 1983; **Fellow:** Cardiovascular Disease, Cedars-Sinai Med Ctr 1985; **Fac Appt:** Clin Prof Med, Cornell Univ-Weill Med Coll

Inra, Lawrence A MD (Cv) - **Spec Exp:** Coronary Artery Disease; Preventive Cardiology; Cholesterol/Lipid Disorders; Hypertension; **Hospital:** NY-Presby/Weill Cornell Med Ctr, NY (page 102), Hosp For Special Surgery (page 109); **Address:** 407 E 70th St, New York, NY 10021; **Phone:** 212-249-1011; **Board Cert:** Internal Medicine 1979; Cardiovascular Disease 1981; **Med School:** Johns Hopkins Univ 1976; **Resid:** Internal Medicine, Presby/Weill Cornell Med Ctr 1979; **Fellow:** Cardiovascular Disease, Mt Sinai Med Ctr 1981; **Fac Appt:** Clin Prof Med, Cornell Univ-Weill Med Coll

Kamen, Mazen O MD (Cv) - **Spec Exp:** Heart Valve Disease; Cholesterol/Lipid Disorders; Hypertension; Coronary Artery Disease; **Hospital:** NY-Presby/Weill Cornell Med Ctr, NY (page 102); **Address:** 1021 Park Ave, Ste 101, New York, NY 10028; **Phone:** 212-427-5800; **Board Cert:** Cardiovascular Disease 2006; **Med School:** NYU Sch Med 1983; **Resid:** Surgery, NYU Med Ctr 1984; Internal Medicine, NYU Med Ctr 1986; **Fellow:** Cardiovascular Disease, NY-Presby/Weill Cornell Med Ctr 1990; **Fac Appt:** Asst Clin Prof Med, Cornell Univ-Weill Med Coll

Katz, Edward S MD (Cv) - **Spec Exp:** Echocardiography; Cholesterol/Lipid Disorders; Coronary Artery Disease; **Hospital:** NYU Langone Med Ctr (page 104), NYU Hosp For Joint Dis (page 104); **Address:** NYU Cardiology Associates, 530 1st Ave, Ste 9U, New York, NY 10016; **Phone:** 212-263-7751; **Board Cert:** Cardiovascular Disease 2011; Internal Medicine 1988; Echocardiography 2005; **Med School:** NYU Sch Med 1985; **Resid:** Internal Medicine, NYU Med Ctr 1988; **Fellow:** Cardiovascular Disease, NYU Med Ctr 1991; **Fac Appt:** Assoc Prof Med, NYU Sch Med

Katz, Stuart D MD (Cv) - **Spec Exp:** Heart Failure; Transplant Medicine-Heart; **Hospital:** NYU Langone Med Ctr (page 104); **Address:** NYU Cardiology Assocs, 530 First Ave Skirball Bldg - Ste 9U, New York, NY 10016; **Phone:** 212-263-7751; **Board Cert:** Internal Medicine 1986; Cardiovascular Disease 1989; Advanced Heart Failure & Transplant Cardiology 2010; **Med School:** SUNY Downstate 1983; **Resid:** Internal Medicine, Francis Scott Key Med Ctr 1986; **Fellow:** Cardiovascular Disease, Montefiore Med Ctr 1989; **Fac Appt:** Prof Med, NYU Sch Med

Kligfield, Paul MD (Cv) - **Hospital:** NY-Presby/Weill Cornell Med Ctr, NY (page 102); **Address:** NY-Presby, Cardiology Dept, 525 E 68th St, Ste L195, New York, NY 10021; **Phone:** 212-746-4686; **Board Cert:** Internal Medicine 1973; Cardiovascular Disease 1975; **Med School:** Harvard Med Sch 1970; **Resid:** Internal Medicine, Beth Israel Deaconess Med Ctr 1972; **Fellow:** Cardiovascular Research, St Georges Hosp 1973; Cardiovascular Disease, NY-Presby/Weill Cornell Med Ctr 1975; **Fac Appt:** Prof Med, Cornell Univ-Weill Med Coll

Kronzon, Itzhak MD (Cv) - **Spec Exp:** Heart Valve Disease; Echocardiography; Cardiac Imaging; Pericardial Disease; **Hospital:** Lenox Hill Hosp; **Address:** Lenox Hill Hosp, Cardiology Dept, 100 E 77th St Fl 2, New York, NY 10075; **Phone:** 212-434-6119; **Board Cert:** Internal Medicine 1979; Cardiovascular Disease 1981; Echocardiography 2013; **Med School:** Israel 1964; **Resid:** Internal Medicine, Hadassah Hosp 1969; **Fellow:** Cardiovascular Disease, Montefiore Med Ctr 1973; Cardiovascular Disease, NYU Med Ctr 1974; **Fac Appt:** Prof Med, NYU Sch Med

Kutnick, Richard T MD (Cv) - **Spec Exp:** Echocardiography; **Hospital:** Lenox Hill Hosp; **Address:** 1421 3rd Ave, Fl 6, New York, NY 10028; **Phone:** 212-879-2628; **Board Cert:** Internal Medicine 1979; Cardiovascular Disease 1981; **Med School:** Tufts Univ 1976; **Resid:** Internal Medicine, Lenox Hill Hosp 1979; **Fellow:** Cardiovascular Disease, Lenox Hill Hosp 1981; **Fac Appt:** Asst Prof Med, NYU Sch Med

Latif, Farhana MD (Cv) - **Spec Exp:** Cardiomyopathy; Heart Failure; Transplant Medicine-Heart; Transesophageal Echocardiogram (TEE); **Hospital:** NY-Presby/Columbia Univ Med Ctr, NY (page 102); **Address:** Columbia Ctr for Advanced Cardiac Care, 622 W 168th St, New York, NY 10032; **Phone:** 212-305-0200; **Board Cert:** Cardiovascular Disease 2008; Advanced Heart Failure & Transplant Cardiology 2012; **Med School:** Albany Med Coll 1998; **Resid:** Internal Medicine, Mon-tefiore Med Ctr 2001; **Fellow:** Cardiovascular Disease, Montefiore Med Ctr 2005; Heart Failure & Transplant, Montefiore Med Ctr 2007

Lewis, Benjamin H MD (Cv) - **Spec Exp:** Cardiac Stress Testing; Heart Disease & Gender; Echocardiography; Preventive Cardiology; **Hospital:** NY-Presby/Columbia Univ Med Ctr, NY (page 102), Lenox Hill Hosp; **Address:** 51 W 51st St, Fl 3, Ste 365, New York, NY 10019; **Phone:** 212-326-8425; **Board Cert:** Internal Medicine 1980; Cardiovascular Disease 1983; **Med School:** UCSF 1977; **Resid:** Internal Medicine, Columbia-Presby Hosp 1980; **Fellow:** Cardiovascular Disease, Brigham Womens Hosp 1982; **Fac Appt:** Assoc Prof Med, Columbia P&S

Mancini, Donna M MD (Cv) - **Spec Exp:** Congestive Heart Failure; Transplant Medicine-Heart; **Hospital:** NY-Presby/Columbia Univ Med Ctr, NY (page 102); **Address:** NY-Presby, Ctr Advanced Cardiac Care, 622 W 168th St Fl 12 - rm 134, New York, NY 10032; **Phone:** 212-305-4600; **Board Cert:** Internal Medicine 1983; Cardiovascular Disease 1987; Advanced Heart Failure & Transplant Cardiology 2010; **Med School:** Albert Einstein Coll Med 1980; **Resid:** Internal Medicine, Jacobi Med Ctr 1983; **Fellow:** Cardiovascular Disease, Jacobi Med Ctr 1986; **Fac Appt:** Prof Med, Columbia P&S

Masri, Bassem M MD (Cv) - **Spec Exp:** Cholesterol/Lipid Disorders; Coronary Artery Disease; Preventive Cardiology; Hypertension; **Hospital:** NY-Presby/Weill Cornell Med Ctr, NY (page 102); **Address:** NY-Presby, Cardiac Prevention Ctr, 1305 York Ave Fl 8, New York, NY 10021; **Phone:** 646-962-6004; **Med School:** Lebanon 1988; **Resid:** Internal Medicine, Ameri Univ Beirut 1991; **Fellow:** Cardiovascular Disease, Baylor Med Ctr 1991; **Fac Appt:** Asst Prof Med, Cornell Univ-Weill Med Coll

Matta, Raymond J MD (Cv) - **Hospital:** Mt Sinai Hosp; **Address:** 1120 Park Ave, Ste 1C, New York, NY 10128; **Phone:** 212-410-5800; **Board Cert:** Internal Medicine 1973; Cardiovascular Disease 1975; **Med School:** Univ Pittsburgh 1969; **Resid:** Internal Medicine, Mass Genl Hosp 1971; **Fellow:** Cardiovascular Disease, Brigham & Womens Hosp 1975; **Fac Appt:** Assoc Clin Prof Med, Mount Sinai Sch Med

Mattes, Leonard MD (Cv) - **Hospital:** Mt Sinai Hosp; **Address:** 1199 Park Ave, Ste 1F, New York, NY 10128; **Phone:** 212-876-7045; **Board Cert:** Internal Medicine 1972; Cardiovascular Disease 1975; **Med School:** Tulane Univ 1962; **Resid:** Internal Medicine, Mount Sinai Med Ctr 1967; Cardiovascular Disease, Mount Sinai Med Ctr 1969; **Fellow:** Cardiovascular Disease, Mount Sinai Med Ctr 1968; **Fac Appt:** Asst Clin Prof Med, Mount Sinai Sch Med

Maurer, Mathew S MD (Cv) - **Spec Exp:** Heart Failure; Cardiomyopathy; Hypertrophic Cardiomyopathy; Transplant Medicine-Heart; **Hospital:** NY-Presby/Columbia Univ Med Ctr, NY (page 102); **Address:** Columbia Ctr for Advanced Cardiac Care, 622 W 168th St, New York, NY 10032; **Phone:** 212-305-9808; **Board Cert:** Internal Medicine 2005; Cardiovascular Disease 2009; Advanced Heart Failure & Transplant Cardiology 2010; **Med School:** Mount Sinai Sch Med 1992; **Resid:** Internal Medicine, NY-Presby/Columbia Univ Med Ctr 1996; **Fellow:** Cardiovascular Disease, NY-Presby/Columbia Univ Med Ctr 1999; **Fac Appt:** Assoc Prof Med, Columbia P&S

Meller, Jose MD (Cv) - **Spec Exp:** Preventive Cardiology; Coronary Artery Disease; Heart Disease in Pregnancy; Heart Valve Disease; **Hospital:** Mt Sinai Hosp; **Address:** 941 Park Ave, New York, NY 10028; **Phone:** 212-988-3772; **Board Cert:** Internal Medicine 1973; Cardiovascular Disease 1975; **Med School:** Chile 1969; **Resid:** Internal Medicine, Elmhurst Hosp 1971; Internal Medicine, Mt Sinai Med Ctr 1972; **Fellow:** Cardiovascular Disease, Mt Sinai Med Ctr 1974; **Fac Appt:** Clin Prof Med, Mount Sinai Sch Med

Mellow, Ellen MD (Cv) - **Spec Exp:** Women's Health; Critical Care; Hypertension; **Hospital:** NY-Presby/Weill Cornell Med Ctr, NY (page 102); **Address:** 110 E 59th St, Ste 10B, New York, NY 10022; **Phone:** 212-838-0099; **Board Cert:** Internal Medicine 1983; Cardiovascular Disease 1989; **Med School:** Cornell Univ-Weill Med Coll 1980; **Resid:** Internal Medicine, NY-Presby/Weill Cornell Med Ctr 1983; **Fellow:** Cardiovascular Disease, Hosp Univ Penn 1986; Critical Care Medicine, Natl Inst Hlth 1986; **Fac Appt:** Asst Prof Med, Cornell Univ-Weill Med Coll

Miller, David H MD (Cv) - **Spec Exp:** Hypertension; Coronary Artery Disease; **Hospital:** NY-Presby/Weill Cornell Med Ctr, NY (page 102); **Address:** NY-Presby, Cardiology Dept, 520 E 70th St, Ste 443, New York, NY 10021; **Phone:** 212-746-2144; **Board Cert:** Internal Medicine 1980; Cardiovascular Disease 1981; **Med School:** Univ VA Sch Med 1976; **Resid:** Internal Medicine, NY-Presby/Weill Cornell Med Ctr 1979; **Fellow:** Cardiovascular Disease, NY-Presby/Weill Cornell Med Ctr 1981; **Fac Appt:** Assoc Prof Med, Cornell Univ-Weill Med Coll

Mueller, Richard L MD (Cv) - **Spec Exp:** Vein Disorders; Stress Echocardiography; Hypertension; Echocardiography; **Hospital:** NY-Presby/Weill Cornell Med Ctr, NY (page 102), Mt Sinai St. Luke's; **Address:** Cardiovascular Diagnostics, PC, 401 E 55th St, New York, NY 10022-6158; **Phone:** 212-593-9800; **Board Cert:** Internal Medicine 2010; Cardiovascular Disease 2000; Echocardiography 2009; Vascular Medicine 2006; **Med School:** UCSF 1987; **Resid:** Internal Medicine, North Shore Univ Hosp 1991; Internal Medicine, Meml Sloan Kettering Cancer Ctr 1990; **Fellow:** Cardiovascular Disease, New York Hosp 1994; **Fac Appt:** Asst Clin Prof Med, Cornell Univ-Weill Med Coll

Nash, Ira S MD (Cv) - **Spec Exp:** Preventive Cardiology; Coronary Artery Disease; **Hospital:** Lenox Hill Hosp, NS-LIJ Hlth Sys; **Address:** Park East Cardiovascular, 158 E 84th St, New York, NY 10028; **Phone:** 212-535-6340 x204; **Board Cert:** Internal Medicine 1987; Cardiovascular Disease 1989; **Med School:** Harvard Med Sch 1984; **Resid:** Internal Medicine, Beth Israel Hosp 1987; **Fellow:** Cardiovascular Disease, Beth Israel Hosp 1990

O'Brien, Francis J MD (Cv) - **Spec Exp:** Preventive Cardiology; **Hospital:** NYU Langone Med Ctr (page 104), Bellevue Hosp Ctr; **Address:** Murray Hill Medical Group, 347 E 37th St Fl 2, New York, NY 10016; **Phone:** 212-726-7457; **Board Cert:** Internal Medicine 1985; Cardiovascular Disease 1989; **Med School:** Harvard Med Sch 1982; **Resid:** Internal Medicine, NYU Med Ctr 1986; **Fellow:** Cardiovascular Disease, Bellevue-NYU Hosp 1988; **Fac Appt:** Assoc Clin Prof Med, NYU Sch Med

Olin, Jeffrey W DO (Cv) - **Spec Exp:** Peripheral Vascular Disease; Renal Artery Stenosis; Carotid Artery Disease; Vascular Disease; **Hospital:** Mt Sinai Hosp; **Address:** Cardiovascular Medicine Associates, 5 E 98th St Fl 3, New York, NY 10029; **Phone:** 212-241-9454; **Board Cert:** Internal Medicine 1981; Nephrology 1984; Vascular Medicine ; **Med School:** Univ Hlth Sci, Coll Osteo Med 1977; **Resid:** Internal Medicine, Cleveland Clinic 1981; **Fellow:** Nephrology, Cleveland Clinic 1983; **Fac Appt:** Prof Med, Mount Sinai-Icahn Sch of Med

Pinney, Sean MD (Cv) - **Spec Exp:** Transplant Medicine-Heart; Heart Failure; Pulmonary Hypertension; Congenital Heart Disease; **Hospital:** Mt Sinai Hosp; **Address:** Mt Sinai, Cardiovascular Med Assocs, 5 E 98th St Fl 3, New York, NY 10029; **Phone:** 212-241-7300; **Board Cert:** Cardiovascular Disease 2011; Advanced Heart Failure & Transplant Cardiology 2012; **Med School:** Georgetown Univ 1994; **Resid:** Internal Medicine, Bet Israel Deaconess Med Ctr 1999; **Fellow:** Cardiovascular Disease, NY-Presby/Columbia Univ Med Ctr 2001; Transplant Medicine, NY-Presby/Columbia Univ Med Ctr 2002; **Fac Appt:** Assoc Prof Med, Mount Sinai Sch Med

Poon, Michael MD (Cv) - **Spec Exp:** Coronary Artery Disease; Pulmonary Hypertension; Cardiac CT Angiography; Cardiac Imaging; **Hospital:** Stony Brook Univ Hosp, Mt Sinai Hosp; **Address:** 70 Bowery, Ste 303, New York, NY 10013; **Phone:** 212-925-4088; **Board Cert:** Cardiovascular Disease 2007; Cardiovascular Computed Tomography 2008; **Med School:** Mount Sinai Sch Med 1987; **Resid:** Internal Medicine, Mount Sinai Med Ctr 1991; **Fellow:** Cardiovascular Disease, Mount Sinai Med Ctr 1993; **Fac Appt:** Prof Med, SUNY Stony Brook

Post, Martin R MD (Cv) - **Spec Exp:** Coronary Artery Disease; Cholesterol/Lipid Disorders; **Hospital:** NY-Presby/Weill Cornell Med Ctr, NY (page 102); **Address:** 425 E 61st St Fl 6, New York, NY 10021-8722; **Phone:** 212-752-2000; **Board Cert:** Internal Medicine 1974; Cardiovascular Disease 1974; **Med School:** SUNY Upstate Med Univ 1967; **Resid:** Internal Medicine, Ohio State Univ Hosp 1970; **Fellow:** Cardiovascular Disease, New York Hosp 1972

Radwaner, Bradley A MD (Cv) - **Spec Exp:** Preventive Cardiology; Cholesterol/Lipid Disorders; Interventional Cardiology; **Hospital:** Lenox Hill Hosp; **Address:** NY Ctr for The Prevention of Heart Dis., 136 E 57th St, Ste 1001, New York, NY 10022; **Phone:** 212-717-0666; **Board Cert:** Internal Medicine 1983; Cardiovascular Disease 1985; **Med School:** Cornell Univ-Weill Med Coll 1980; **Resid:** Internal Medicine, Lenox Hill Hosp 1983; **Fellow:** Cardiovascular Disease, St Lukes Hosp 1985; Interventional Cardiology, NYU Med Ctr 1986; **Fac Appt:** Asst Clin Prof Med, Cornell Univ-Weill Med Coll

Reichstein, Robert P MD (Cv) - **Spec Exp:** Preventive Cardiology; Atrial Fibrillation; Hypertension; **Hospital:** Mt Sinai Hosp; **Address:** 1185 Park Ave, Ste 1L, New York, NY 10128; **Phone:** 212-996-2900; **Board Cert:** Internal Medicine 1980; Cardiovascular Disease 1983; **Med School:** Ros Franklin Univ/Chicago Med Sch 1977; **Resid:** Internal Medicine, Mt Sinai Hosp 1981; **Fellow:** Cardiovascular Disease, Mt Sinai Hosp 1984; **Fac Appt:** Asst Clin Prof Med, Finch/Chicago Med Sch

Rentrop, K. Peter MD (Cv) - **Spec Exp:** Nuclear Cardiology; **Hospital:** NYU Langone Med Ctr (page 104); **Address:** 920 Broadway, Ste 600, New York, NY 10010; **Phone:** 212-475-8066; **Board Cert:** Internal Medicine 1973; Nuclear Cardiology 2013; **Med School:** Germany 1966; **Resid:** Internal Medicine, Detroit Med Ctr 1970; Internal Medicine, Cleveland Clin 1971; **Fellow:** Cardiovascular Disease, Cleveland Clin 1973; **Fac Appt:** Prof Med, NY Med Coll

Romanello, Paul P MD (Cv) - **Spec Exp:** Cholesterol/Lipid Disorders; Coronary Artery Disease; Hypertension; Nuclear Cardiology; **Hospital:** Lenox Hill Hosp; **Address:** Park East Cardiovascular, 158 E 84th St, New York, NY 10028; **Phone:** 212-535-6340; **Board Cert:** Internal Medicine 1987; Cardiovascular Disease 1989; Nuclear Cardiology 2008; **Med School:** SUNY Upstate Med Univ 1983; **Resid:** Internal Medicine, Lenox Hill Hosp 1987; **Fellow:** Cardiovascular Disease, Lenox Hill Hosp 1989

Rosenbaum, Marlon S MD (Cv) - **Spec Exp:** Congenital Heart Disease-Adult; Heart Valve Disease; **Hospital:** NY-Presby/Columbia Univ Med Ctr, NY (page 102); **Address:** NY-Presby, Adult Congential Heart Ctr, 161 Fort Washington Ave, rm 627, New York, NY 10032; **Phone:** 212-305-6936; **Board Cert:** Internal Medicine 1983; Cardiovascular Disease 1985; **Med School:** NYU Sch Med 1980; **Resid:** Internal Medicine, NY-Presby/Columbia Univ Med Ctr 1983; **Fellow:** Cardiovascular Disease, Westchester Med Ctr 1985; Cardiovascular Disease, Mass Genl Hosp 1986; **Fac Appt:** Assoc Clin Prof Med, Columbia P&S

Rozanski, Alan MD (Cv) - **Spec Exp:** Nuclear Cardiology; Stress Management; **Hospital:** Mt Sinai Roosevelt; **Address:** 1111 Amsterdam Ave, New York, NY 10025; **Phone:** 212-523-4011; **Board Cert:** Internal Medicine 1978; Cardiovascular Disease 1983; Nuclear Medicine 1983; **Med School:** Tufts Univ 1975; **Resid:** Internal Medicine, Mt Sinai Hosp 1978; **Fellow:** Cardiovascular Disease, Mt Sinai Hosp 1980; Nuclear Medicine, Cedars-Sinai Med Ctr 1982; **Fac Appt:** Prof Med, Columbia P&S

Ruiz, Carlos E MD/PhD (Cv) - **Spec Exp:** Interventional Cardiology; Transplant Medicine-Heart; Cardiac Catheterization; **Hospital:** Lenox Hill Hosp; **Address:** Lenox Hill Hosp, Cardiac & Vascular, 130 E 77th St Fl 4, New York, NY 10075; **Phone:** 212-434-2606; **Board Cert:** Internal Medicine 1982; **Med School:** Spain 1972; **Resid:** Pediatrics, Univ Barcelona 1973; Internal Medicine, LAC & USC Med Ctr 1978; **Fellow:** Cardiovascular Disease, Univ Barcelona 1975; Critical Care Medicine, LAC & USC Med Ctr 1977

Schiffer, Mark B MD (Cv) - **Spec Exp:** Preventive Cardiology; Cholesterol/Lipid Disorders; Coronary Artery Disease; **Hospital:** Lenox Hill Hosp; **Address:** Park East Cardiovascular, 158 E 84th St, New York, NY 10028; **Phone:** 212-535-6340; **Board Cert:** Internal Medicine 1980; Cardiovascular Disease 1983; **Med School:** Northwestern Univ 1977; **Resid:** Internal Medicine, Lenox Hill Hosp 1981; **Fellow:** Cardiovascular Disease, Lenox Hill Hosp 1983

Schulman, Ira C MD (Cv) - **Spec Exp:** Angina; Heart Failure; Cholesterol/Lipid Disorders; **Hospital:** NYU Langone Med Ctr (page 104), NY-Presby/Lower Manhattan Hosp (page 102); **Address:** 111 Broadway, Fl 2, New York, NY 10006; **Phone:** 212-263-9700; **Board Cert:** Internal Medicine 1977; Cardiovascular Disease 1979; **Med School:** NYU Sch Med 1974; **Resid:** Internal Medicine, Bellevue Hosp 1977; **Fellow:** Cardiovascular Disease, Montefiore Med Ctr 1979; **Fac Appt:** Assoc Prof Med, NYU Sch Med

Schulze, Paul Christian MD/PhD (Cv) - **Spec Exp:** Heart Failure; Vascular Disease; Vasculitis; **Hospital:** NY-Presby/Columbia Univ Med Ctr, NY (page 102); **Address:** NY-Presby, Ctr Advanced Cardiac Care, 622 W 168th St, PH 10 rm 203, New York, NY 10032; **Phone:** 212-305-6916; **Board Cert:** Advanced Heart Failure & Transplant Cardiology 2012; Cardiovascular Disease 2009; Echocardiography 2009; Nuclear Cardiology 2009; **Med School:** Germany 1998; **Resid:** Internal Medicine, Boston Med Ctr 2007; **Fellow:** Cardiovascular Disease, NY-Presby/Columbia Univ Med Ctr 2009; **Fac Appt:** Prof Med, Columbia P&S

Schwartz, Allan MD (Cv) - **Hospital:** NY-Presby/Columbia Univ Med Ctr, NY (page 102); **Address:** 173 Fort Washington Ave, Ste 4-600C, New York, NY 10032; **Phone:** 212-305-5367; **Board Cert:** Internal Medicine 1977; Cardiovascular Disease 1979; **Med School:** Columbia P&S 1974; **Resid:** Internal Medicine, Columbia-Presby Med Ctr 1976; **Fellow:** Cardiovascular Disease, Mass Genl Hosp 1978; **Fac Appt:** Clin Prof Med, Columbia P&S

Schwartz, William J MD (Cv) - **Spec Exp:** Coronary Artery Disease; Cardiac Catheterization; Congestive Heart Failure; **Hospital:** Mt Sinai Hosp; **Address:** Mt Sinai Multispecialty Physicians, 150 E 77th St, Ste 1E, New York, NY 10075; **Phone:** 212-439-6000; **Board Cert:** Internal Medicine 1978; Cardiovascular Disease 1981; **Med School:** Albert Einstein Coll Med 1975; **Resid:** Internal Medicine, Bronx Municipal Hosp 1978; **Fellow:** Cardiovascular Disease, Bronx Municipal Hosp 1981; **Fac Appt:** Asst Prof Med, Mount Sinai Sch Med

Segal, Robert R MD (Cv) - **Spec Exp:** Echocardiography; Vascular Disease; **Hospital:** NYU Langone Med Ctr (page 104); **Address:** Manhattan Cardiology, 211 E 51st St, New York, NY 10022; **Phone:** 646-863-5517; **Board Cert:** Internal Medicine 2011; Cardiovascular Disease 2013; **Med School:** Grenada 1996; **Resid:** Internal Medicine, LIJ Med Ctr 2000; **Fellow:** Cardiovascular Disease, Maimonides Med Ctr 2003

Seinfeld, David MD (Cv) - **Spec Exp:** Preventive Cardiology; **Hospital:** Lenox Hill Hosp; **Address:** 20 E 68th St, Ste 214, New York, NY 10065; **Phone:** 212-288-1538; **Board Cert:** Internal Medicine 1976; Cardiovascular Disease 1979; **Med School:** Albert Einstein Coll Med 1973; **Resid:** Internal Medicine, Montefiore Med Ctr 1976; **Fellow:** Cardiovascular Disease, Montefiore Med Ctr 1978; **Fac Appt:** Assoc Clin Prof Med, Albert Einstein Coll Med

Sherman, Warren MD (Cv) - **Spec Exp:** Angioplasty; Interventional Cardiology; **Hospital:** NY-Presby/Columbia Univ Med Ctr, NY (page 102); **Address:** NY-Presby, Cardiology Dept, 161 Fort Washington Ave Fl 6, New York, NY 10032; **Phone:** 212-304-5697; **Board Cert:** Internal Medicine 1980; Cardiovascular Disease 1983; **Med School:** SUNY Upstate Med Univ 1977; **Resid:** Internal Medicine, Rochester Genl Hosp 1980; **Fellow:** Cardiovascular Disease, OR Hlth Sci Univ 1982; **Fac Appt:** Assoc Prof Med, Columbia P&S

Shimony, Rony MD (Cv) - **Spec Exp:** Coronary Artery Disease; Arrhythmias; Heart Failure; Non-Invasive Cardiology; **Hospital:** Mt Sinai Hosp; **Address:** 485 Madison Ave Fl 17, New York, NY 10022; **Phone:** 212-752-2700; **Board Cert:** Internal Medicine 1987; Cardiovascular Disease 1989; **Med School:** SUNY Buffalo 1984; **Resid:** Internal Medicine, Lenox Hill Hosp 1987; **Fellow:** Cardiovascular Disease, Lenox Hill Hosp 1989; Cardiac Electrophysiology, Lenox Hill Hosp 1992; **Fac Appt:** Asst Prof Med, Mount Sinai Sch Med

Siegal, Michael S MD (Cv) - **Spec Exp:** Coronary Artery Disease; **Hospital:** Mt Sinai Roosevelt; **Address:** 30 Central Park S, Ste 13A, New York, NY 10019; **Phone:** 212-319-1700; **Board Cert:** Internal Medicine 1980; Cardiovascular Disease 1983; **Med School:** Columbia P&S 1977; **Resid:** Internal Medicine, Bellevue/NYU Med Ctr 1980; **Fellow:** Cardiovascular Disease, Mt Sinai Hosp 1982

Siegel, Stephen A MD (Cv) - **Spec Exp:** Sports Medicine-Cardiology; Preventive Cardiology; Cholesterol/Lipid Disorders; Hypertension; **Hospital:** NYU Langone Med Ctr (page 104); **Address:** 245 E 35th St, New York, NY 10016; **Phone:** 212-684-1108; **Board Cert:** Internal Medicine 1981; Cardiovascular Disease 1983; **Med School:** Med Coll VA 1978; **Resid:** Internal Medicine, NYU Med Ctr/Bellevue Hosp Ctr 1981; **Fellow:** Cardiovascular Disease, NYU Med Ctr/Bellevue Hosp Ctr 1983; **Fac Appt:** Asst Clin Prof Med, NYU Sch Med

Sklaroff, Herschel J MD (Cv) - **Spec Exp:** Angina; Syncope; Hypertension; Diagnostic Problems; **Hospital:** Mt Sinai Hosp; **Address:** 1175 Park Ave, New York, NY 10128; **Phone:** 212-289-6500; **Board Cert:** Internal Medicine 1969; Cardiovascular Disease 1977; **Med School:** Univ Pennsylvania 1961; **Resid:** Internal Medicine, Mount Sinai Med Ctr 1965; Cardiovascular Disease, Mount Sinai Med Ctr 1966; **Fac Appt:** Clin Prof Med, Mount Sinai Sch Med

Slater, William R MD (Cv) - **Spec Exp:** Arrhythmias; Heart Valve Disease; Cardiac Electrophysiology; **Hospital:** NYU Langone Med Ctr (page 104); **Address:** NYU Medical Ctr, Div Cardiology, 530 First Ave Skirball Bldg - Ste 9U, New York, NY 10016; **Phone:** 212-263-7463; **Board Cert:** Internal Medicine 1981; Cardiovascular Disease 1985; **Med School:** Harvard Med Sch 1978; **Resid:** Internal Medicine, Bellevue Hosp Ctr 1981; **Fellow:** Cardiovascular Disease, Mt Sinai Hosp 1984; Cardiovascular Disease, Mass Genl Hosp/Brigham & Womens Hosp 1986; **Fac Appt:** Assoc Prof Med, NYU Sch Med

Spiegel, Alan MD (Cv) - **Spec Exp:** Arrhythmias; Heart Valve Disease; Cholesterol/Lipid Disorders; Preventive Cardiology; **Hospital:** NYU Langone Med Ctr (page 104); **Address:** Concorde Medical Grp-Cardiology Division, 38 E 32nd St, Ste 801, New York, NY 10016; **Phone:** 212-684-7172; **Board Cert:** Internal Medicine 1981; Cardiovascular Disease 1987; **Med School:** Albert Einstein Coll Med 1978; **Resid:** Internal Medicine, Bellevue Hosp Ctr 1982; **Fellow:** Cardiovascular Disease, Univ of Penn 1984; **Fac Appt:** Asst Clin Prof Med, NYU Sch Med

Stein, Richard A MD (Cv) - **Spec Exp:** Preventive Cardiology; Coronary Artery Disease; Cardiac Rehabilitation; **Hospital:** NYU Langone Med Ctr (page 104); **Address:** NYU Cardiology Associates, 530 First Ave, Ste 9U, New York, NY 10016; **Phone:** 212-263-7751; **Board Cert:** Internal Medicine 1973; Cardiovascular Disease 1975; Sports Medicine 2007; **Med School:** NYU Sch Med 1967; **Resid:** Internal Medicine, Univ Hosp 1969; **Fellow:** Cardiovascular Disease, Univ Hosp 1974; **Fac Appt:** Prof Med, NYU Sch Med

Steinbaum, Suzanne R DO (Cv) - **Spec Exp:** Heart Disease in Women; Cholesterol/Lipid Disorders; Preventive Cardiology; Heart Disease in African Americans; **Hospital:** Lenox Hill Hosp; **Address:** Lenox Hill Heart & Vascular Inst, 110 E 59th St, Ste 8A, New York, NY 10022; **Phone:** 212-434-6902; **Board Cert:** Cardiovascular Disease 2005; **Med School:** Kirksville Coll Osteo Med 1994; **Resid:** Internal Medicine, Beth Israel Med Ctr 1998; **Fellow:** Preventive Medicine, Beth Israel Med Ctr 1999; Cardiovascular Disease, Beth Israel Med Ctr 2002

Steingart, Richard M MD (Cv) - **Spec Exp:** Heart Failure; Heart Disease in Cancer Patients; Cardiac Effects of Cancer/Cancer Therapy; Amyloid Heart Disease; **Hospital:** Meml Sloan Kettering Canc Ctr (page 110); **Address:** 1275 York Ave Fl 3, New York, NY 10065; **Phone:** 212-639-8488; **Board Cert:** Internal Medicine 1977; Cardiovascular Disease 1979; **Med School:** Mount Sinai Sch Med 1974; **Resid:** Internal Medicine, Yale-New Haven Hosp 1977; **Fellow:** Cardiovascular Disease, Mt Sinai Med Ctr 1979; **Fac Appt:** Prof Med, Cornell Univ-Weill Med Coll

Tenenbaum, Joseph MD (Cv) - **Spec Exp:** Heart Valve Disease; Coronary Artery Disease; Atrial Fibrillation; Critical Care; **Hospital:** NY-Presby/Columbia Univ Med Ctr, NY (page 102); **Address:** 173 Ft Washington Ave, MHC Bldg - Fl 4 - Ste 606, New York, NY 10032; **Phone:** 212-305-5288; **Board Cert:** Internal Medicine 1977; Cardiovascular Disease 1979; **Med School:** Harvard Med Sch 1974; **Resid:** Internal Medicine, Columbia-Presby Med Ctr 1977; **Fellow:** Cardiovascular Disease, Mt Sinai Hosp 1979; **Fac Appt:** Prof Med, Columbia P&S

Tyberg, Theodore MD (Cv) - **Spec Exp:** Coronary Artery Disease; Cholesterol/Lipid Disorders; **Hospital:** NY-Presby/Weill Cornell Med Ctr, NY (page 102); **Address:** 425 E 61st St, Fl 6, New York, NY 10065; **Phone:** 212-752-2000; **Board Cert:** Internal Medicine 1978; Cardiovascular Disease 1981; **Med School:** Rush Med Coll 1975; **Resid:** Internal Medicine, New York Hosp 1978; **Fellow:** Cardiovascular Disease, Yale-New Haven Hosp 1980; **Fac Appt:** Assoc Clin Prof Med, Cornell Univ-Weill Med Coll

Unger, Allen MD (Cv) - **Spec Exp:** Cholesterol/Lipid Disorders; Hypertension; Preventive Cardiology; Coronary Artery Disease; **Hospital:** Mt Sinai Hosp; **Address:** 12 E 86th St, New York, NY 10028; **Phone:** 212-734-6000; **Board Cert:** Internal Medicine 1968; Cardiovascular Disease 1977; **Med School:** SUNY Upstate Med Univ 1960; **Resid:** Internal Medicine, Mount Sinai Med Ctr 1967; **Fellow:** Cardiovascular Disease, Mount Sinai Med Ctr 1966; **Fac Appt:** Asst Clin Prof Med, Mount Sinai Sch Med

Varriale, Philip MD (Cv) - **Spec Exp:** Coronary Artery Disease; Arrhythmias; Congestive Heart Failure; Pacemakers; **Hospital:** Mt Sinai Beth Israel; **Address:** 222 E 19th St, Ste 2D, New York, NY 10003; **Phone:** 212-777-3219; **Board Cert:** Internal Medicine 1966; Cardiovascular Disease 1970; **Med School:** SUNY Hlth Sci Ctr 1959; **Resid:** Internal Medicine, Brooklyn VA Hosp 1962; Internal Medicine, St Vincents Hosp 1963; **Fellow:** Cardiovascular Disease, St Vincents Hosp 1964; **Fac Appt:** Assoc Clin Prof Med, Mount Sinai Sch Med

Weintraub, Howard S MD (Cv) - **Spec Exp:** Cholesterol/Lipid Disorders; Hypertension; Preventive Cardiology; Metabolic Syndrome; **Hospital:** NYU Langone Med Ctr (page 104); **Address:** 530 First Ave, Ste 4F, New York, NY 10016; **Phone:** 212-263-0855; **Board Cert:** Internal Medicine 1979; Cardiovascular Disease 1985; **Med School:** NYU Sch Med 1976; **Resid:** Internal Medicine, NYU Med Ctr 1979; **Fellow:** Pulmonary Disease, NYU Med Ctr 1980; Cardiovascular Disease, NYU Med Ctr 1982; **Fac Appt:** Clin Prof Med, NYU Sch Med

Weisenseel Jr, Arthur C MD (Cv) - **Spec Exp:** Coronary Artery Disease; Cholesterol/Lipid Disorders; Congestive Heart Failure; Preventive Cardiology; **Hospital:** Mt Sinai Hosp; **Address:** 12 E 86th St, New York, NY 10028; **Phone:** 212-734-6000; **Board Cert:** Internal Medicine 1969; Cardiovascular Disease 1973; **Med School:** Georgetown Univ 1963; **Resid:** Internal Medicine, Mount Sinai Med Ctr 1966; **Fellow:** Cardiovascular Disease, Mount Sinai Med Ctr 1967; **Fac Appt:** Assoc Clin Prof Med, Mount Sinai Sch Med

Wolk, Michael Jay MD (Cv) - **Spec Exp:** Coronary Artery Disease; Heart Failure; Hypertension; **Hospital:** NY-Presby/Weill Cornell Med Ctr, NY (page 102); **Address:** 425 E 61st St, Fl 6, New York, NY 10021; **Phone:** 212-752-2000; **Board Cert:** Internal Medicine 1971; Cardiovascular Disease 1973; **Med School:** Columbia P&S 1964; **Resid:** Internal Medicine, Univ Hosp 1967; **Fellow:** Cardiovascular Disease, New England Med Ctr 1969; Cardiovascular Disease, New York Hosp-Cornell 1970; **Fac Appt:** Clin Prof Med, Cornell Univ-Weill Med Coll

Yadegar, Daniel MD (Cv) - **Hospital:** Lenox Hill Hosp, Mt Sinai Hosp; **Address:** Goldberg & Yadegar, 121 E 60th St, Ste 3, New York, NY 10022; **Phone:** 212-980-7070; **Board Cert:** Internal Medicine 2007; Cardiovascular Disease 2010; **Med School:** Cornell Univ-Weill Med Coll 2004; **Resid:** Internal Medicine, Lenox Hill Hosp 2007; **Fellow:** Cardiovascular Disease, Lenox Hill Hosp 2010

Child & Adolescent Psychiatry

Abright, A. Reese MD (ChAP) - **Spec Exp:** Mood Disorders; ADD/ADHD; Anxiety Disorders; **Hospital:** Elmhurst Hosp Ctr; **Address:** 140 E 40th St, Ste 1B, New York, NY 10016; **Phone:** 212-867-3131; **Board Cert:** Psychiatry 1978; Child & Adolescent Psychiatry 1981; **Med School:** Univ Tex SW, Dallas 1973; **Resid:** Psychiatry, NY Hosp/Payne-Whitney Clin 1977; **Fellow:** Child & Adolescent Psychiatry, NY Hosp/Payne Whitney Clin 1979; **Fac Appt:** Clin Prof Psyc, NY Med Coll

Bartell, Abraham MD (ChAP) - **Spec Exp:** Psychiatry in Cancer; Psychiatry in Physical Illness; **Hospital:** Meml Sloan Kettering Canc Ctr (page 110); **Address:** 1275 York Ave Fl 9, New York, NY 10065; **Phone:** 646-888-0060; **Board Cert:** Psychiatry 2010; Child & Adolescent Psychiatry 2012; **Med School:** SUNY Downstate 1993; **Resid:** Psychiatry, Emma P Bradley Hosp 1996; **Fellow:** Child & Adolescent Psychiatry, Emma P Bradley Hosp 1998

Becker, Ina MD (ChAP) - **Spec Exp:** Anxiety Disorders; Mood Disorders; ADD/ADHD; **Hospital:** NY-Presby/Columbia Univ Med Ctr, NY (page 102); **Address:** 49 W 24th St, Ste 1010, New York, NY 10010; **Phone:** 917-441-0880; **Board Cert:** Psychiatry 2005; Psychosomatic Medicine 2008; **Med School:** Germany 1987; **Resid:** Psychiatry, Montefiore Med Ctr 1993; **Fac Appt:** Asst Clin Prof Psyc, Columbia P&S

Boorady, Roy Joseph MD (ChAP) - **Spec Exp:** Psychopharmacology; ADD/ADHD; Anxiety Disorders; **Hospital:** NYU Langone Med Ctr (page 104); **Address:** Child Mind Institute, 445 Park Ave at 56th St, New York, NY 10022; **Phone:** 646-625-4294; **Board Cert:** Psychiatry 1993; Child & Adolescent Psychiatry 1994; **Med School:** SUNY Buffalo 1987; **Resid:** Psychiatry, Mass Mental Hlth Ctr 1991; **Fellow:** Child & Adolescent Psychiatry, Mass Genl Hosp 1993

Burkes, Lynn MD (ChAP) - **Spec Exp:** Diagnostic Problems; ADD/ADHD; Divorce/Family Issues; Developmental Disorders; **Hospital:** NYU Langone Med Ctr (page 104); **Address:** 185 West End Ave, Ste 1E, New York, NY 10023-5539; **Phone:** 212-362-5920; **Board Cert:** Psychiatry 1977; Child & Adolescent Psychiatry 1978; **Med School:** Med Coll PA 1970; **Resid:** Psychiatry, Albert Einstein Affil Hosp 1973; **Fellow:** Psychiatry, Bellevue Hosp 1975; **Fac Appt:** Assoc Clin Prof Psyc, NYU Sch Med

Coffey, Barbara J MD (ChAP) - **Spec Exp:** Tourette's Syndrome; ADD/ADHD; Obsessive-Compulsive Disorder; Psychopharmacology; **Hospital:** Mt Sinai Hosp; **Address:** Tics & Tourette's Clin & Rsch Program, 1240 Park Ave, New York, NY 10029; **Phone:** 212-659-1660; **Board Cert:** Psychiatry 1981; Child & Adolescent Psychiatry 1986; **Med School:** Tufts Univ 1975; **Resid:** Psychiatry, Boston Med Ctr 1978; **Fellow:** Child & Adolescent Psychiatry, Tufts Med Ctr 1980; **Fac Appt:** Prof Psyc, Mount Sinai Sch Med

Fox, Sarah J MD (ChAP) - **Spec Exp:** Anxiety & Mood Disorders; Eating Disorders; Psychoanalysis; **Hospital:** NY-Presby/Columbia Univ Med Ctr, NY (page 102); **Address:** 210 W 89th St, New York, NY 10024; **Phone:** 212-874-4558; **Board Cert:** Psychiatry 1991; Child & Adolescent Psychiatry 1994; **Med School:** Tufts Univ 1982; **Resid:** Psychiatry, Bronx Psych Ctr 1984; Psychiatry, Montefiore Med Ctr 1985; **Fellow:** Child & Adolescent Psychiatry, Columbia-Presby Med Ctr 1987

Gabbay, Vilma MD (ChAP) - **Spec Exp:** Depression; Mood Disorders; Tourette's Syndrome; **Hospital:** Mt Sinai Hosp; **Address:** Pediatric Mood & Anxiety Disorders Prog, 1240 Park Ave, New York, NY 10029; **Phone:** 212-659-1660; **Board Cert:** Psychiatry 2005; Child & Adolescent Psychiatry 2007; **Med School:** Israel 1994; **Resid:** Psychiatry, Montefiore Med Ctr 2001; **Fellow:** Child & Adolescent Psychiatry, NYU Med Ctr 2003; **Fac Appt:** Assoc Prof Psyc, Mount Sinai Sch Med

Grice, Dorothy MD (ChAP) - **Spec Exp:** Obsessive-Compulsive Disorder; Tourette's Syndrome; Autism; **Hospital:** Mt Sinai Hosp; **Address:** 1425 Madison Ave Fl 4, New York, NY 10029; **Phone:** 212-659-1675; **Board Cert:** Psychiatry 1993; Child & Adolescent Psychiatry 2007; **Med School:** Med Univ SC 1988; **Resid:** Psychiatry, Med Univ SC Med Ctr 1992; **Fellow:** Child & Adolescent Psychiatry, Yale Child Study Ctr 1996

Havens, Jennifer MD (ChAP) - **Spec Exp:** Bereavement/Traumatic Grief; **Hospital:** Bellevue Hosp Ctr, NYU Langone Med Ctr (page 104); **Address:** NYU Child Study Ctr, One Park Ave, Fl 7th, New York, NY 10016; **Phone:** 212-263-6622; **Board Cert:** Psychiatry 1991; Child & Adolescent Psychiatry 1993; **Med School:** Tufts Univ 1986; **Resid:** Psychiatry, NY Presby Hosp 1988; **Fellow:** Child & Adolescent Psychiatry, NY Presby Hosp 1991; **Fac Appt:** Assoc Prof ChAP, NYU Sch Med

Hirsch, Glenn S MD (ChAP) - **Spec Exp:** Anxiety & Mood Disorders; Tourette's Syndrome; Bipolar/Mood Disorders; ADD/ADHD; **Hospital:** NYU Langone Med Ctr (page 104), Bellevue Hosp Ctr; **Address:** NYU Child Study Center, 1 Park Ave, Fl 7, New York, NY 10016; **Phone:** 646-754-5187; **Board Cert:** Psychiatry 1984; Child & Adolescent Psychiatry 1985; **Med School:** Albert Einstein Coll Med 1979; **Resid:** Psychiatry, New York Hosp-Cornell 1982; **Fellow:** Child & Adolescent Psychiatry, Columbia-Presby Med Ctr 1984; **Fac Appt:** Asst Prof ChAP, NYU Sch Med

Koplewicz, Harold S MD (ChAP) - **Spec Exp:** Anxiety & Mood Disorders; Psychopharmacology; ADD/ADHD; **Address:** Child Mind Inst, 445 Park Ave at 56th St, New York, NY 10022; **Phone:** 212-308-3118; **Board Cert:** Psychiatry 1983; Child & Adolescent Psychiatry 1984; **Med School:** Albert Einstein Coll Med 1978; **Resid:** Psychiatry, Presby/Westchester Div 1981; Psychiatry, NY State Psych Inst 1983; **Fellow:** Psychiatric Research, NY State Psych Inst 1985

Kron, Leo L MD (ChAP) - **Spec Exp:** Psychopharmacology; Psychotherapy; **Hospital:** Mt Sinai Roosevelt; **Address:** 30 E 76th St, Ste 3A, New York, NY 10021; **Phone:** 212-861-7001; **Board Cert:** Psychiatry 1977; Child & Adolescent Psychiatry 1986; **Med School:** Univ British Columbia Fac Med 1971; **Resid:** Psychiatry, Montefiore Med Ctr 1976; **Fellow:** Child & Adolescent Psychiatry, St Lukes Hosp 1978; **Fac Appt:** Asst Clin Prof Psyc, Columbia P&S

Lewis, Owen MD (ChAP) - **Spec Exp:** Psychotherapy; Psychopharmacology; **Hospital:** NY-Presby/Columbia Univ Med Ctr, NY (page 102); **Address:** 11 E 87th St, New York, NY 10128; **Phone:** 212-996-8196; **Board Cert:** Psychiatry 1982; Child & Adolescent Psychiatry 1986; **Med School:** Mount Sinai Sch Med 1976; **Resid:** Psychiatry, NY-Presby/Weill Cornell Med Ctr 1980; **Fellow:** Child & Adolescent Psychiatry, NY-Presby/Weill Cornell Med Ctr 1982; **Fac Appt:** Clin Prof Psyc, Columbia P&S

Liaw, Karen Ron-Li MD (ChAP) - **Spec Exp:** ADD/ADHD; Anxiety & Mood Disorders; Post Traumatic Stress Disorder; Bereavement/Traumatic Grief; **Hospital:** NYU Langone Med Ctr (page 104); **Address:** NYU Child Study Ctr, 1 Park Ave Fl 7, New York, NY 10016; **Phone:** 212-263-6622; **Board Cert:** Psychiatry 2008; Child & Adolescent Psychiatry 2012; **Med School:** Baylor Coll Med 2003; **Resid:** Psychiatry, Massachusetts Genl Hosp 2007; **Fellow:** Child & Adolescent Psychiatry, NYU Med Ctr 2009; **Fac Appt:** Asst Clin Prof ChAP, NYU Sch Med

Moreau, Donna L MD (ChAP) - **Spec Exp:** Psychotherapy & Psychopharmacology; Anxiety & Mood Disorders; **Hospital:** Morgan Stanley Chldns Hosp of NY-Presby, NY (page 102); **Address:** 110 East End Ave, New York, NY 10028-7412; **Phone:** 212-772-9205; **Board Cert:** Psychiatry 1985; Child & Adolescent Psychiatry 1991; **Med School:** SUNY Hlth Sci Ctr 1980; **Resid:** Psychiatry, NY Hosp/Payne Whitney Clin 1983; **Fellow:** Child & Adolescent Psychiatry, NY Hosp/Payne Whitney Clin 1985; **Fac Appt:** Assoc Clin Prof Psyc, Columbia P&S

Newcorn, Jeffrey H MD (ChAP) - **Spec Exp:** Psychopharmacology; ADD/ADHD; Developmental Disorders; Behavioral Disorders; **Hospital:** Mt Sinai Hosp; **Address:** Mount Sinai Hosp, Dept Psychiatry, One Gustave L Levy Pl, Box 1230, New York, NY 10029; **Phone:** 212-659-8705; **Board Cert:** Psychiatry 1982; Child & Adolescent Psychiatry 1984; **Med School:** Univ Rochester 1977; **Resid:** Psychiatry, Tufts-New England Med Ctr 1980; **Fellow:** Child & Adolescent Psychiatry, Tufts-New England Med Ctr 1982; **Fac Appt:** Assoc Prof Psyc, Mount Sinai Sch Med

Perry, Richard MD (ChAP) - **Spec Exp:** Pervasive Development Disorders; Behavioral Disorders; Psychopharmacology; **Hospital:** Bellevue Hosp Ctr, NYU Langone Med Ctr (page 104); **Address:** 55 W 74th St, Ste A, New York, NY 10023-2429; **Phone:** 212-595-0116; **Board Cert:** Psychiatry 1976; Child & Adolescent Psychiatry 1985; **Med School:** Belgium 1970; **Resid:** Psychiatry, Bellevue Hosp 1972; **Fellow:** Child & Adolescent Psychiatry, Bellevue Hosp 1974; **Fac Appt:** Clin Prof Psyc, NYU Sch Med

Ravitz, Alan J MD (ChAP) - **Spec Exp:** Psychopharmacology; Anxiety Disorders; **Address:** 57 W 57th St, Ste 1207, New York, NY 10019; **Phone:** 971-639-5764; **Board Cert:** Psychiatry 1984; Child & Adolescent Psychiatry 1986; Forensic Psychiatry 2007; **Med School:** Mich State Univ 1978; **Resid:** Psychiatry, Univ Chicago Med Ctr 1982; **Fellow:** Child & Adolescent Psychiatry, Univ Chicago Med Ctr 1984; **Fac Appt:** Assoc Prof Psyc, NYU Sch Med

Rynn, Moira A MD (ChAP) - **Spec Exp:** Anxiety Disorders; Mood Disorders; Clinical Trials; **Hospital:** NY State Psychiatric Inst, Morgan Stanley Chldns Hosp of NY-Presby, NY (page 102); **Address:** 1051 Riverside Drive, Child & Adolescent Psych, Kolb Annex, Fl 2, New York, NY 10032; **Phone:** 646-774-5805; **Board Cert:** Psychiatry 2006; Child & Adolescent Psychiatry 2007; **Med School:** UMDNJ-NJ Med Sch, Newark 1991; **Resid:** Psychiatry, Hosp U Penn 1995; Child Psychiatry, Children's Hosp 1997; **Fellow:** Research, Hosp U Penn 1998; **Fac Appt:** Prof Psyc, Columbia P&S

Shatkin, Jess P MD (ChAP) - **Spec Exp:** Behavioral Disorders; Anxiety & Mood Disorders; ADD/ADHD; Autism; **Hospital:** NYU Langone Med Ctr (page 104), Bellevue Hosp Ctr; **Address:** One Park Ave, 7th Fl, New York, NY 10016; **Phone:** 646-754-4900; **Board Cert:** Psychiatry 2011; Child & Adolescent Psychiatry 2013; **Med School:** SUNY Hlth Sci Ctr 1996; **Resid:** Psychiatry, UCLA NPI 1999; **Fellow:** Child & Adolescent Psychiatry, UCLA NPI 2001; **Fac Appt:** Assoc Clin Prof ChAP, NYU Sch Med

Spencer, Elizabeth Kay MD (ChAP) - **Hospital:** NYU Langone Med Ctr (page 104); **Address:** 121 E 31st St, Ste 1B, New York, NY 10016-6835; **Phone:** 212-684-3810; **Board Cert:** Psychiatry 1990; Child & Adolescent Psychiatry 1992; **Med School:** Geo Wash Univ 1979; **Resid:** Pediatrics, Univ Maryland Hosp 1982; Psychiatry, NYU Med Ctr 1986; **Fellow:** Behavioral Pediatrics, Univ Maryland Hosp 1984; Child & Adolescent Psychiatry, NYU Med Ctr 1988

Turecki, Stanley K MD (ChAP) - **Spec Exp:** Temperamentally Difficult Child; ADD/ADHD; Parenting Issues; Anxiety & Mood Disorders; **Hospital:** Lenox Hill Hosp; **Address:** 136 E 64th St, Ste 1B, New York, NY 10065; **Phone:** 212-355-2535; **Board Cert:** Psychiatry 1978; Child & Adolescent Psychiatry 1981; **Med School:** South Africa 1961; **Resid:** Psychiatry, Tara Hospital 1969; Psychiatry, Mt Sinai Hosp 1971

Walkup, John T MD (ChAP) - **Spec Exp:** Anxiety Disorders; **Hospital:** NY-Presby/Weill Cornell Med Ctr, NY (page 102); **Address:** NY Presby/Weill Cornell Med Ctr, Div Child and Adolescent Psychiatry, 525 E 68th St, rm F-1109, New York, NY 10065; **Phone:** 212-746-1891; **Board Cert:** Psychiatry 1987; Child & Adolescent Psychiatry 1992; **Med School:** Univ Minn 1982; **Resid:** Psychiatry, Yale-New Haven Hosp 1985; **Fellow:** Child Psychiatry, Yale Chld Study Ctr 1988; **Fac Appt:** Prof Psyc, Cornell Univ-Weill Med Coll

Walsh, Peter MD (ChAP) - **Hospital:** NY-Presby/Columbia Univ Med Ctr, NY (page 102); **Address:** 115 Central Park W, Ste 5, New York, NY 10023; **Phone:** 212-579-5552; **Med School:** Georgetown Univ 1991; **Resid:** Psychiatry, NY Presby-Columbia Med Ctr 1994; **Fellow:** Child & Adolescent Psychiatry, NY Presby-Columbia Med Ctr 1996

Child Neurology

Akman, Cigdem I MD (ChiN) - **Spec Exp:** Epilepsy; **Hospital:** NY-Presby/Columbia Univ Med Ctr, NY (page 102); **Address:** Harkness Pavilion, 180 Fort Washington Ave, Fl 5, New York, NY 10032; **Phone:** 212-305-7549; **Board Cert:** Child Neurology 2014; Clinical Neurophysiology 2005; **Med School:** Turkey 1988; **Resid:** Pediatrics, Maimonides Med Ctr 1996; Neurology, SUNY Hlth Sci Ctr 1999; **Fellow:** Child Neurology, Columbia-Presy Med Ctr 2000; Epilepsy, Chldren's Hosp 2002; **Fac Appt:** Assoc Clin Prof N, Columbia P&S

Allen, Jeffrey C MD (ChiN) - **Spec Exp:** Neuro-Oncology; Brain Tumors; Neurofibromatosis; **Hospital:** NYU Langone Med Ctr (page 104); **Address:** Hassenfeld Childrens Ctr, 160 E 32nd St Fl 2 - Ste L3, New York, NY 10016; **Phone:** 212-263-9907; **Board Cert:** Child Neurology 1977; **Med School:** Harvard Med Sch 1969; **Resid:** Pediatric Neurology, Montreal Chldns Hosp 1976; **Fac Appt:** Prof Ped, NYU Sch Med

Aron, Alan Milford MD (ChiN) - **Spec Exp:** Neurofibromatosis; Movement Disorders; Developmental Delay; Seizure Disorders; **Hospital:** Mt Sinai Hosp; **Address:** Mt Sinai Hosp, Child Neurology, 5 E 98th St, Fl 10, Box 1206, New York, NY 10029; **Phone:** 212-831-4393; **Board Cert:** Pediatrics 1963; Neurology 1967; Child Neurology 1969; **Med School:** Columbia P&S 1958; **Resid:** Pediatrics, Babies Hosp-Columbia-Presby Hosp 1961; **Fellow:** Pediatric Neurology, Babies Hosp-Columbia Presby Hosp 1964; **Fac Appt:** Prof N, Mount Sinai Sch Med

Chiriboga-Klein, Claudia MD (ChiN) - **Spec Exp:** Developmental Disorders; Movement Disorders; Spasticity Management; **Hospital:** NY-Presby/Columbia Univ Med Ctr, NY (page 102); **Address:** 180 Fort Washington Ave Fl 5, Harkness Pavilion, New York, NY 10032; **Phone:** 212-305-8549; **Board Cert:** Child Neurology 1989; **Med School:** Argentina 1982; **Resid:** Pediatrics, St Lukes-Roosevelt Med Ctr 1985; Neurology, Columbia-Presby Med Ctr 1988; **Fac Appt:** Assoc Clin Prof N, Columbia P&S

De Vivo, Darryl C MD (ChiN) - **Spec Exp:** Metabolic Disorders; Neuromuscular Disorders; Spinal Muscular Atrophy (SMA); Muscular Dystrophy; **Hospital:** NY-Presby/Columbia Univ Med Ctr, NY (page 102); **Address:** Neurological Inst, 710 W 168th St, Ste NI 201, New York, NY 10032; **Phone:** 212-305-5244; **Board Cert:** Child Neurology 1972; **Med School:** Univ VA Sch Med 1964; **Resid:** Pediatrics, Mass Genl Hosp 1966; Neurology, Mass Genl Hosp 1967; **Fellow:** Neurology, Natl Inst Hlth 1969; Child Neurology, Chldns Hosp 1970; **Fac Appt:** Prof N, Columbia P&S

Engel, Murray MD (ChiN) - **Spec Exp:** Neurophysiology; Neurodevelopmental Disabilities; Epilepsy; **Hospital:** NY-Presby/Weill Cornell Med Ctr, NY (page 102), Stamford Hosp (page 971); **Address:** 525 E 68th St, New York, NY 10021; **Phone:** 212-746-3278; **Board Cert:** Pediatrics 1979; Neurology 1980; Clinical Neurophysiology 2005; **Med School:** Univ Chicago-Pritzker Sch Med 1972; **Resid:** Pediatrics, Yale-New Haven Hosp 1974; Child Neurology, NY-Presby/Columbia Univ Med Ctr 1977; **Fac Appt:** Prof Ped, Cornell Univ-Weill Med Coll

Fryer, Robert H MD (ChiN) - **Spec Exp:** Concussion; Headache; **Hospital:** NY-Presby/Columbia Univ Med Ctr, NY (page 102), Stamford Hosp (page 971); **Address:** ColumbiaDoctors Midtown, Neurology, 51 W 51st St, Ste 310, New York, NY 10019; **Phone:** 646-426-3876; **Board Cert:** Child Neurology 2014; **Med School:** Georgetown Univ 1996; **Resid:** Pediatrics, Georgetown Univ Hosp 1998; Child Neurology, NY-Presby/Columbia Univ Med Ctr 2001; **Fac Appt:** Asst Clin Prof N, Columbia P&S

Kairam, Ram MD (ChiN) - **Spec Exp:** Autism; Behavioral Disorders; **Hospital:** NY-Presby/Columbia Univ Med Ctr, NY (page 102); **Address:** 945 West End Ave, Ste 1D, New York, NY 10025; **Phone:** 212-865-7443; **Board Cert:** Pediatrics 1981; Child Neurology 1989; Neonatal-Perinatal Medicine 1981; **Med School:** India 1970; **Resid:** Pediatrics, Harlem Hosp Ctr 1977; Neonatal-Perinatal Medicine, NY-Presby/Columbia Univ Med Ctr 1979; **Fellow:** Pediatric Neurology, NY-Presby/Columbia Univ Med Ctr 1982; **Fac Appt:** Asst Prof Ped, Columbia P&S

Kaufman, David M MD (ChiN) - **Spec Exp:** Epilepsy/Seizure Disorders; Headache; Learning Disorders; Autism; **Hospital:** Mt Sinai Hosp, Lenox Hill Hosp; **Address:** 3 E 83rd St, New York, NY 10028-0459; **Phone:** 212-737-4911; **Board Cert:** Pediatrics 1980; **Med School:** Boston Univ 1975; **Resid:** Pediatrics, New York Hosp 1977; Neurology, Mount Sinai Hosp 1978; **Fellow:** Child Neurology, Mount Sinai Hosp 1980; **Fac Appt:** Assoc Clin Prof N, Mount Sinai Sch Med

Khakoo, Yasmin MD (ChiN) - **Spec Exp:** Neuro-Oncology; Brain Tumors-Pediatric; **Hospital:** Meml Sloan Kettering Canc Ctr (page 110); **Address:** Meml Sloan-Kettering, Ped Neuro-Onc, 1275 York Ave, New York, NY 10065; **Phone:** 212-639-8292; **Board Cert:** Pediatrics 2008; Child Neurology 2007; **Med School:** Columbia P&S 1990; **Resid:** Pediatrics, UCSF Med Ctr 1993; **Fellow:** Child Neurology, UCSF Med Ctr 1996; Neuro-Oncology, Meml Sloan-Kettering Cancer Ctr 1999

Kosofsky, Barry E MD/PhD (ChiN) - **Spec Exp:** Developmental Disorders; Autism; Stroke; **Hospital:** NY-Presby/Weill Cornell Med Ctr, NY (page 102); **Address:** Cornell Med Ctr, Dept Pediatrics, 505 E 70th St, Helmsley Tower Fl 3, New York, NY 10021; **Phone:** 212-746-3321; **Board Cert:** Child Neurology 1993; **Med School:** Johns Hopkins Univ 1985; **Resid:** Pediatrics, Chldns Hosp 1987; Child Neurology, Mass Genl Hosp 1990; **Fellow:** Neurological Biology, Mass Genl Hosp 1992; **Fac Appt:** Prof Ped, Cornell Univ-Weill Med Coll

Miles, Daniel K MD (ChiN) - **Spec Exp:** Tuberous Sclerosis; Epilepsy; **Hospital:** NYU Langone Med Ctr (page 104); **Address:** New York Epilepsy & Neurology, 223 E 34th St Fl 1, New York, NY 10016; **Phone:** 646-558-0808; **Board Cert:** Child Neurology 1994; **Med School:** UMDNJ-NJ Med Sch, Newark 1983; **Resid:** Pediatrics, St Christopher's Hosp 1986; **Fellow:** Pediatric Neurology, Chlds Meml Hosp 1989; Epilepsy, Boston Chlds Hosp 1990

Molofsky, Walter J MD (ChiN) - **Spec Exp:** Seizure Disorders; Headache; ADD/ADHD; Stroke; **Hospital:** Mt Sinai Beth Israel, Mt Sinai Hosp; **Address:** BIMC, Child Neurology, 10 Union Square E, Ste 5G, New York, NY 10003; **Phone:** 212-844-6944; **Board Cert:** Pediatrics 1982; Child Neurology 1986; **Med School:** NYU Sch Med 1976; **Resid:** Pediatrics, NY-Presby/Columbia Univ Med Ctr 1978; **Fellow:** Child Neurology, NY-Presby/Columbia Univ Med Ctr 1981; **Fac Appt:** Assoc Prof N, Mount Sinai-Icahn Sch of Med

Riviello Jr, James J MD (ChiN) - **Spec Exp:** Epilepsy/Seizure Disorders; Epilepsy in Tuberous Sclerosis; Electrical Status Epilepticus Of Sleep; **Hospital:** Morgan Stanley Chldns Hosp of NY-Presby, NY (page 102); **Address:** NY-Presby, Child Neurology, 180 Fort Washington Ave, rm 542, New York, NY 10032; **Phone:** 646-426-3876; **Board Cert:** Pediatrics 1984; Child Neurology 1985; Clinical Neurophysiology 2006; Epilepsy 2013; **Med School:** Tufts Univ 1978; **Resid:** Pediatrics, St Christopher Hosp Chldn 1980; Neurology, Temple Univ Hosp 1982; **Fellow:** Pediatric Neurology, St Christopher's Hosp Chldn 1981; Pediatric Neurology, St Christopher's Hosp Chldn 1984; **Fac Appt:** Prof N, Columbia P&S

Wells, John T MD (ChiN) - **Spec Exp:** Pediatric Neurology; Concussion; Cerebral Palsy; Learning Disorders; **Hospital:** NYU Langone Med Ctr (page 104); **Address:** NYU Neurology Assocs Faculty Practice, 240 E 38th St Fl 20, New York, NY 10016; **Phone:** 212-263-7744; **Board Cert:** Child Neurology 2006; **Med School:** SUNY Stony Brook 1988; **Resid:** Pediatrics, Long Island Jewish Med Ctr 1991; Child Neurology, NYU Med Ctr 1994; **Fac Appt:** Assoc Clin Prof N, NYU Sch Med

Wolf, Steven M MD (ChiN) - **Spec Exp:** Epilepsy; Headache; Migraine; **Hospital:** Mt Sinai Beth Israel, Mt Sinai Roosevelt; **Address:** Beth Israel Med Ctr, Dept Ped Neurology, 10 Union Square East, Ste 5J, New York, NY 10003; **Phone:** 212-844-6944; **Board Cert:** Child Neurology 2006; Epilepsy 2013; Clinical Neurophysiology 2008; **Med School:** Albany Med Coll 1989; **Resid:** Pediatrics, Montefiore Med Ctr 1991; **Fellow:** Child Neurology, Montefiore Med Ctr 1994; Epilepsy, Montefiore Med Ctr 1995; **Fac Appt:** Assoc Prof N, Albert Einstein Coll Med

Clinical Genetics

Anyane-Yeboa, Kwame MD (CG) - **Spec Exp:** Dysmorphology; Prenatal Diagnosis; **Hospital:** Morgan Stanley Chldns Hosp of NY-Presby, NY (page 102); **Address:** Morgan Stanley Chldn's Hosp NY, 3959 Broadway, rm 718N, New York, NY 10032; **Phone:** 212-305-6731; **Board Cert:** Pediatrics 1979; Clinical Genetics 1982; **Med School:** Ghana 1972; **Resid:** Pediatrics, Harlem Hosp Ctr 1977; **Fellow:** Clinical Genetics, Babies Hosp-Columbia P&S 1980; **Fac Appt:** Assoc Prof Ped, Columbia P&S

Chung, Wendy Kay MD (CG) - **Spec Exp:** Cancer Genetics; Metabolic Genetic Disorders; **Hospital:** NY-Presby/Columbia Univ Med Ctr, NY (page 102); **Address:** 3959 Broadway Ave, Ste 718, New York, NY 10032; **Phone:** 212-305-6731; **Board Cert:** Clinical Genetics 2012; Clinical Molecular Genetics 2005; **Med School:** Cornell Univ 1998; **Resid:** Clinical Genetics, NY-Presby/Columbia Univ Med Ctr 2002; **Fellow:** Genetics, NY-Presby/Columbia Univ Med Ctr 2003; **Fac Appt:** Asst Prof Ped, Columbia P&S

Cunniff, Christopher M MD (CG) - **Spec Exp:** Genetic Disorders; Chromosome Disorders; Fetal Alcohol Syndrome; Developmental Disorders; **Hospital:** NY-Presby/Weill Cornell Med Ctr, NY (page 102); **Address:** 505 E 70th St, Helmsley Tower Fl 3, New York, NY 10021; **Phone:** 646-962-2205; **Board Cert:** Pediatrics 2010; Clinical Genetics 1990; **Med School:** UAB Sch Med 1984; **Resid:** Pediatrics, Med Ctr Hosp of VT 1987; **Fellow:** Clinical Genetics, UCSD Med Ctr 1989; **Fac Appt:** Prof Ped, Cornell Univ-Weill Med Coll

Davis, Jessica G MD (CG) - **Spec Exp:** Marfan's Syndrome; Mental Retardation; Neurofibromatosis; Ehlers-Danlos Syndrome; **Hospital:** NY-Presby/Weill Cornell Med Ctr, NY (page 102), Hosp For Special Surgery (page 109); **Address:** 505 E 70th St, Box 128, New York, NY 10065; **Phone:** 646-962-2205; **Board Cert:** Clinical Genetics 1984; **Med School:** Columbia P&S 1959; **Resid:** Pediatrics, St Luke's Hosp 1962; Clinical Genetics, Albert Einstein Coll Med Affil Hosp 1965; **Fellow:** Cytogenetics, Albert Einstein Coll Med Affil Hosp 1966; Pediatrics, Albert Einstein Col Med Affil Hosp 1968; **Fac Appt:** Assoc Clin Prof Ped, Cornell Univ-Weill Med Coll

Desnick, Robert J MD/PhD (CG) - **Spec Exp:** Inherited Metabolic Disorders; Lysosomal Diseases; Gaucher Disease; Porphyria; **Hospital:** Mt Sinai Hosp; **Address:** Mount Sinai Med Ctr, Icahn Med Inst, 1425 Madison Ave, Fl 14, rm 14-34, Box 1498, New York, NY 10029; **Phone:** 212-659-6700; **Board Cert:** Clinical Genetics 1982; Clinical Biochemical Genetics 1982; Clinical Molecular Genetics 2010; **Med School:** Univ Minn 1971; **Resid:** Pediatrics, Univ Minn Hosps 1973; **Fac Appt:** Prof Emeritus CG, Mount Sinai Sch Med

Lichter-Konecki, Uta MD/PhD (CG) - **Spec Exp:** Inborn Errors of Metabolism; Inherited Metabolic Disorders; Lysosomal Diseases; **Hospital:** NY-Presby/Columbia Univ Med Ctr, NY (page 102); **Address:** 3959 Broadway Fl 7 - rm 718, New York, NY 10032; **Phone:** 212-305-6731; **Board Cert:** Clinical Biochemical Genetics 2005; Clinical Genetics 2013; **Med School:** Germany 1984; **Resid:** Pediatrics, Univ Heidelberg Affil Hosp 1992; **Fellow:** Clinical Biochemical Genetics, Univ Heidelberg Affil Hosp 1995; Clinical Genetics, Natl Inst Health 2003; **Fac Appt:** Asst Prof Ped, Columbia P&S

Mehta, Lakshmi MD (CG) - **Spec Exp:** Birth Defects; Endocrine Disorders; **Hospital:** Mt Sinai Hosp; **Address:** Mount Sinai Med Ctr, Div Human Genetics, 1428 Madison Ave Fl 1, New York, NY 10029; **Phone:** 212-241-6947; **Board Cert:** Clinical Genetics 2010; **Med School:** India 1977; **Resid:** Pediatrics, Postgrad Inst 1981; **Fellow:** Pediatrics, Leicester Royal Infirm 1986; Clinical Genetics, Mount Sinai Med Ctr 1988; **Fac Appt:** Assoc Prof Ped, Mount Sinai Sch Med

Pappas, John Georgios MD (CG) - **Spec Exp:** Genetic Disorders; Growth Disorders; **Hospital:** NYU Langone Med Ctr (page 104), NYU Hosp For Joint Dis (page 104); **Address:** 301 E 17th St Fl 3, New York, NY 10003; **Phone:** 212-598-6205; **Board Cert:** Pediatrics 2007; Clinical Genetics 2010; **Med School:** Greece 1985; **Resid:** Pediatrics, Beth Israel Med Ctr 1991; **Fellow:** Clinical Genetics, Mt Sinai Med Ctr 1995; **Fac Appt:** Asst Prof Ped, NYU Sch Med

Wasserstein, Melissa MD (CG) - **Spec Exp:** Phenylketonuria (PKU); Fabry's Disease; Metabolic Genetic Disorders; **Hospital:** Mt Sinai Hosp; **Address:** Mt Sinai Med Ctr, Clin Genetics, 1428 Madison Ave, rm AB1-12, New York, NY 10029; **Phone:** 212-241-6947; **Board Cert:** Pediatrics 2010; Clinical Biochemical Genetics 2010; **Med School:** NYU Sch Med 1992; **Resid:** Pediatrics, Mt Sinai Med Ctr 1995; **Fellow:** Clinical Genetics, Mt Sinai Med Ctr 1997; **Fac Appt:** Assoc Prof CG, Mount Sinai Sch Med

Colon & Rectal Surgery

Arnell, Tracey D MD (CRS) - **Spec Exp:** Laparoscopic Surgery; Diverticulitis; Inflammatory Bowel Disease; Anorectal Disorders; **Hospital:** NY-Presby/Columbia Univ Med Ctr, NY (page 102); **Address:** 161 Fort Washington Ave Fl 5, New York, NY 10032; **Phone:** 212-342-1734; **Board Cert:** Surgery 2009; Colon & Rectal Surgery 2010; **Med School:** Univ Wash 1992; **Resid:** Surgery, Harbor-UCLA Med Ctr 1998; **Fellow:** Colon & Rectal Surgery, Lahey Clinic 1999; **Fac Appt:** Asst Prof S, Columbia P&S

Bernstein, Mitchell A MD (CRS) - **Spec Exp:** Colon & Rectal Cancer & Surgery; Inflammatory Bowel Disease; Anorectal Disorders; Hemorrhoids; **Hospital:** NYU Langone Med Ctr (page 104); **Address:** NYU dept Surgery, 530 First Ave, Ste 7V, New York, NY 10016; **Phone:** 646-501-0584; **Board Cert:** Surgery 2004; Colon & Rectal Surgery 2007; **Med School:** Univ Miami Sch Med 1989; **Resid:** Surgery, Univ Mass Med Ctr 1994; **Fellow:** Colon & Rectal Surgery, Cleveland Clinic 1995; **Fac Appt:** Assoc Prof S, Columbia P&S

Brandeis, Steven Z MD (CRS) - **Spec Exp:** Hemorrhoids; Anal Disorders & Reconstruction; Colon & Rectal Cancer; Anorectal Disorders; **Hospital:** NYU Langone Med Ctr (page 104); **Address:** 251 E 33rd St Fl 2 - Ste 2N, New York, NY 10016; **Phone:** 212-696-5411; **Board Cert:** Colon & Rectal Surgery 1982; **Med School:** NYU Sch Med 1975; **Resid:** Surgery, NYU Med Ctr-Bellevue Hosp 1980; **Fellow:** Colon & Rectal Surgery, RWJ Univ Hosp 1981; **Fac Appt:** Asst Prof S, NYU Sch Med

Chessin, David B MD (CRS) - **Spec Exp:** Laparoscopic Surgery; Colon & Rectal Cancer & Surgery; Inflammatory Bowel Disease; Anorectal Disorders; **Hospital:** Mt Sinai Hosp; **Address:** Manhattan Surgical Assocs, 25 E 98th St, Ste 1, New York, NY 10021; **Phone:** 212-517-8600; **Board Cert:** Surgery 2008; Colon & Rectal Surgery 2010; **Med School:** Rutgers R W Johnson Med Sch 2000; **Resid:** Surgery, Mt Sinai Hosp 2003; Surgery, Mt Sinai Hosp 2007; **Fellow:** Research, Meml Sloan Kettering Cancer Ctr 2005; Colon & Rectal Surgery, Mt Sinai Hosp 2008; **Fac Appt:** Asst Clin Prof S, Mount Sinai Sch Med

Feingold, Daniel L MD (CRS) - **Spec Exp:** Colon & Rectal Cancer; Minimally Invasive Surgery; Diverticulitis; Colostomy Avoidance; **Hospital:** NY-Presby/Columbia Univ Med Ctr, NY (page 102); **Address:** NY Presby Hosp-Columbia, 161 Fort Washington Ave, New York, NY 10032; **Phone:** 212-342-1155; **Board Cert:** Surgery 2012; Colon & Rectal Surgery 2014; **Med School:** Ros Franklin Univ/Chicago Med Sch 1996; **Resid:** Surgery, Barnes-Jewish Hosp 1998; Surgery, NY-Presby/Columbia Univ Med Ctr 2003; **Fellow:** Surgical Oncology, NIH Natl Cancer Inst 2000; Colon & Rectal Surgery, Robert Wood Johnson Affil Hosp 2004; **Fac Appt:** Assoc Clin Prof S, Columbia P&S

Gorfine, Stephen R MD (CRS) - **Spec Exp:** Anal Disorders & Reconstruction; Hemorrhoids; Rectal Cancer; Anal Cancer; **Hospital:** Mt Sinai Hosp; **Address:** Manhattan Surgical Associates, 25 E 69th St, New York, NY 10021-4925; **Phone:** 212-517-8600; **Board Cert:** Internal Medicine 1981; Surgery 2007; Colon & Rectal Surgery 1988; **Med School:** Univ Mass Sch Med 1978; **Resid:** Internal Medicine, Mt Sinai Hosp 1981; Surgery, Mt Sinai Hosp 1985; **Fellow:** Colon & Rectal Surgery, Ferguson Hosp 1987; **Fac Appt:** Clin Prof S, Mount Sinai Sch Med

Guillem, Jose G MD (CRS) - **Spec Exp:** Colon & Rectal Cancer; Rectal Cancer/Sphincter Preservation; Colon & Rectal Cancer-Hereditary; Peritoneal Mucinous Carcinomatosis; **Hospital:** Meml Sloan Kettering Canc Ctr (page 110); **Address:** MSKCC, Colon & Rectal Surgery, 1275 York Ave, Ste C1077, New York, NY 10065; **Phone:** 212-639-8278; **Board Cert:** Surgery 2004; Colon & Rectal Surgery 2005; **Med School:** Yale Univ 1983; **Resid:** Surgery, NY-Presby/Columbia Univ Med Ctr 1990; **Fellow:** Colon & Rectal Surgery, Lahey Clin 1991; **Fac Appt:** Prof CRS, Cornell Univ-Weill Med Coll

Khaitov, Sergey MD (CRS) - **Spec Exp:** Colon & Rectal Cancer; Inflammatory Bowel Disease/Crohn's; Hemorrhoids; Anorectal Disorders; **Hospital:** Mt Sinai Hosp; **Address:** 98th St Fl 14 - Ste D, New York, NY 10029; **Phone:** 212-241-1763; **Board Cert:** Surgery 2008; Colon & Rectal Surgery 2010; **Med School:** Ukraine 1995; **Resid:** Surgery, Hadassah Univ Hosp; Surgery, Mt Sinai Med Ctr; **Fellow:** Colon & Rectal Surgery, Mt Sinai Med Ctr 2008; **Fac Appt:** Asst Prof S, Mount Sinai Sch Med

Ky, Alex Jenny MD (CRS) - **Spec Exp:** Incontinence-Fecal; Robotic Surgery; Rectal Cancer/Sphincter Preservation; Colostomy Avoidance; **Hospital:** Mt Sinai Hosp; **Address:** 5 E 98th St, Fl 14, Ste D, New York, NY 10029; **Phone:** 212-241-3547; **Board Cert:** Surgery 2010; Colon & Rectal Surgery 2011; **Med School:** SUNY Stony Brook 1994; **Resid:** Surgery, Lenox Hill Hosp 1999; **Fellow:** Colon & Rectal Surgery, Mt Sinai Hosp 2000; **Fac Appt:** Assoc Prof S, Mount Sinai Sch Med

Lee, Sang Won MD (CRS) - **Spec Exp:** Inflammatory Bowel Disease; Diverticulitis; Anorectal Disorders; Colon & Rectal Cancer & Surgery; **Hospital:** NY-Presby/Weill Cornell Med Ctr, NY (page 102); **Address:** NY-Presby/Weill Cornell Med Ctr, 1315 York Ave, Fl 2, New York, NY 10021; **Phone:** 212-746-6030; **Board Cert:** Surgery 2012; Colon & Rectal Surgery 2013; **Med School:** NYU Sch Med 1993; **Resid:** Surgery, Beth Israel Deaconess Med Ctr 2001; **Fellow:** Laparoscopic Surgery, NY-Presby/Weill Cornell Med Ctr 2002; Colon & Rectal Surgery, NY-Presby/Weill Cornell Med Ctr 2003; **Fac Appt:** Assoc Prof S, Cornell Univ-Weill Med Coll

Martz, Joseph E MD (CRS) - **Spec Exp:** Laparoscopic Surgery; Gastrointestinal Surgery; Colon & Rectal Cancer; Minimally Invasive Surgery; **Hospital:** Mt Sinai Beth Israel; **Address:** 10 Union Square E, New York, NY 10003; **Phone:** 212-420-3960; **Board Cert:** Surgery 2010; Colon & Rectal Surgery 2011; **Med School:** NYU Sch Med 1995; **Resid:** Surgery, Beth Israel Med Ctr 2000; **Fellow:** Colon & Rectal Surgery, Lahey Clinic 2001

Milsom, Jeffrey W MD (CRS) - **Spec Exp:** Laparoscopic Surgery; Inflammatory Bowel Disease/Crohn's; Colon & Rectal Cancer & Surgery; **Hospital:** NY-Presby/Weill Cornell Med Ctr, NY (page 102); **Address:** Weill Cornell Physicians, Colon & Rectal Surgery, 520 E 70th St Fl 8, New York, NY 10021; **Phone:** 646-962-2993; **Board Cert:** Colon & Rectal Surgery 1986; **Med School:** Univ Pittsburgh 1979; **Resid:** Surgery, St Lukes-Roosevelt Hosp 1981; Surgery, Univ Virginia Med Ctr 1984; **Fellow:** Colon & Rectal Surgery, Ferguson Hosp 1985; **Fac Appt:** Prof S, Cornell Univ-Weill Med Coll

Penzer, Jason MD (CRS) - **Spec Exp:** Hemorrhoids; Colon & Rectal Cancer; Diverticulitis; Inflammatory Bowel Disease; **Hospital:** Lenox Hill Hosp, Mt Sinai Beth Israel; **Address:** Manhattan Colorectal, 515 Madison Ave, Ste 705, New York, NY 10022; **Phone:** 212-675-2997; **Board Cert:** Surgery 2010; Colon & Rectal Surgery 2011; **Med School:** Yale Univ 1996; **Resid:** Surgery, St Vincent's Hosp 2001; **Fellow:** Colon & Rectal Surgery, UMDNJ Med Ctr 2002; **Fac Appt:** Asst Clin Prof S, NY Med Coll

Sonoda, Toyooki MD (CRS) - **Spec Exp:** Inflammatory Bowel Disease; Laparoscopic Surgery; Colon & Rectal Cancer & Surgery; Crohn's Disease; **Hospital:** NY-Presby/Weill Cornell Med Ctr, NY (page 102); **Address:** Weill Cornell-Colon & Rectal Surgery, 1315 York Ave Fl 2, New York, NY 10021; **Phone:** 212-746-6030; **Board Cert:** Surgery 2010; Colon & Rectal Surgery 2011; **Med School:** Yale Univ 1993; **Resid:** Surgery, UCSF Med Ctr 1995; Surgery, Cleveland Clinic 1998; **Fellow:** Laparoscopic Surgery, Mt Sinai Med Ctr 1999; Colon & Rectal Surgery, Cleveland Clinic 2000; **Fac Appt:** Assoc Clin Prof S, Cornell Univ-Weill Med Coll

Steinhagen, Randolph M MD (CRS) - **Spec Exp:** Colon & Rectal Cancer & Surgery; Crohn's Disease; Diverticulitis; Ulcerative Colitis; **Hospital:** Mt Sinai Hosp, St. John's Riverside Hosp-Andrus Pavil; **Address:** Div Colon & Rectal Surgery, 5 E 98th St, Fl 14, Ste D, Box 1259, New York, NY 10029-6501; **Phone:** 212-241-3547; **Board Cert:** Surgery 2012; Colon & Rectal Surgery 1985; **Med School:** Wayne State Univ 1977; **Resid:** Surgery, Mount Sinai Hosp 1982; **Fellow:** Colon & Rectal Surgery, Cleveland Clinic 1983; **Fac Appt:** Prof S, Mount Sinai Sch Med

Temple, Larissa MD (CRS) - **Spec Exp:** Colon & Rectal Cancer; Anal Cancer; Laparoscopic Surgery; **Hospital:** Meml Sloan Kettering Canc Ctr (page 110); **Address:** 1275 York Ave Fl 10, New York, NY 10065; **Phone:** 212-639-6081; **Board Cert:** Surgery 2011; Colon & Rectal Surgery 2014; **Med School:** Univ Calgary 1994; **Resid:** Surgery, Univ Toronto 2000; **Fellow:** Surgical Oncology, Meml Sloan Kettering Cancer Ctr 2002

Weiser, Martin R MD (CRS) - **Spec Exp:** Colon & Rectal Cancer; Laparoscopic Surgery; Cancer Surgery; **Hospital:** Meml Sloan Kettering Canc Ctr (page 110); **Address:** MSKCC, Colon & Rectal Surgery, 1275 York Ave, Ste C1075, New York, NY 10065; **Phone:** 212-639-6698; **Board Cert:** Surgery 2009; Colon & Rectal Surgery 2012; **Med School:** Univ Chicago-Pritzker Sch Med 1991; **Resid:** Surgery, Brigham & Womens Hosp 1998; Colon & Rectal Surgery, Mt Sinai Hosp 2002; **Fellow:** Research, Harvard Med Sch 1995; Surgical Oncology, Meml Sloan-Kettering Cancer Ctr 2000; **Fac Appt:** Assoc Prof S, Cornell Univ-Weill Med Coll

Whelan, Richard L MD (CRS) - **Spec Exp:** Laparoscopic Surgery; Colon & Rectal Cancer; Diverticulitis; **Hospital:** Mt Sinai Roosevelt; **Address:** Mt Sinai, Colon & Rectal Surgery, 425 W 59th St, Ste 7B, New York, NY 10019; **Phone:** 212-523-8172; **Board Cert:** Colon & Rectal Surgery 1989; **Med School:** Columbia P&S 1982; **Resid:** Surgery, NY-Presby/Columbia Univ Med Ctr 1987; **Fellow:** Colon & Rectal Surgery, Univ Minn Med Ctr 1988; **Fac Appt:** Prof S, Columbia P&S

Critical Care Medicine

Halpern, Neil A MD (CCM) - **Hospital:** Meml Sloan Kettering Canc Ctr (page 110), Mt Sinai Hosp; **Address:** 1275 York Ave, Ste C-1179H, New York, NY 10065; **Phone:** 212-639-6731; **Board Cert:** Internal Medicine 1984; Critical Care Medicine 2009; **Med School:** Mount Sinai Sch Med 1981; **Resid:** Internal Medicine, Mount Sinai Hosp 1984; **Fellow:** Critical Care Medicine, Univ Pittsburgh Med Ctr 1985; **Fac Appt:** Prof Med, Cornell Univ-Weill Med Coll

Wagner, Ira J MD (CCM) - **Hospital:** Lenox Hill Hosp; **Address:** Lenox Hill Hospital, East Bldg, 100 E 77th St Fl 4, New York, NY 10021; **Phone:** 212-434-4130; **Board Cert:** Internal Medicine 1980; Critical Care Medicine 2009; **Med School:** SUNY Downstate 1976; **Resid:** Internal Medicine, St Vincent's Hosp 1979; **Fellow:** Critical Care Medicine, Univ Pittsburgh 1980

Dermatology

Albom, Michael J MD (D) - **Spec Exp:** Mohs Surgery; Reconstructive Surgery; Skin Cancer; **Hospital:** NYU Langone Med Ctr (page 104), Lenox Hill Hosp (Manh Eye, Ear & Throat Hosp); **Address:** 33 E 70th St, New York, NY 10021; **Phone:** 212-517-2121; **Board Cert:** Dermatology 1976; **Med School:** Boston Univ 1970; **Resid:** Dermatology, Boston Univ Med Ctr 1974; **Fellow:** Mohs Surgery, NYU Med Ctr 1975; **Fac Appt:** Clin Prof D, NYU Sch Med

Alexiades-Armenakas, Macrene R MD/PhD (D) - **Spec Exp:** Skin Laser Surgery; Cosmetic Dermatology; Photodynamic Therapy; **Address:** 955 Park Ave, New York, NY 10028; **Phone:** 212-570-2067; **Board Cert:** Dermatology 2011; **Med School:** Harvard Med Sch 1997; **Resid:** Dermatology, NYU Med Ctr 2001; **Fac Appt:** Assoc Clin Prof D, Yale Univ

Alexis, Andrew F MD (D) - **Spec Exp:** Ethnic Skin Disorders; Black/Asian Skin Care; Acne; Psoriasis; **Hospital:** Mt Sinai Roosevelt; **Address:** 425 W 59th St, Fl 5, rm C, New York, NY 10019; **Phone:** 212-523-6003; **Board Cert:** Dermatology 2003; **Med School:** Columbia P&S 1999; **Resid:** Dermatology, NY Presby-Cornell Med Ctr 2003; **Fellow:** Dermatologic Pharmacology, NYU Med Ctr 2004; **Fac Appt:** Assoc Prof D, Mount Sinai Sch Med

Amin, Snehal P MD (D) - **Spec Exp:** Skin Laser Surgery; Mohs Surgery; Skin Cancer; **Hospital:** NY-Presby/Weill Cornell Med Ctr, NY (page 102); **Address:** Manhattan Dermatology & Cosmetic Surgery, 820 Second Ave, Ste 3A, New York, NY 10017; **Phone:** 212-661-3376; **Board Cert:** Dermatology 2013; **Med School:** Albert Einstein Coll Med 2000; **Resid:** Dermatology, NY Presby-Weill Cornell Med Ctr 2004; **Fellow:** Mohs Surgery, Skin Laser Surgery Spec-NY/NJ 2005; **Fac Appt:** Asst Prof D, Cornell Univ-Weill Med Coll

Aranoff, Shera M MD (D) - **Spec Exp:** Skin Cancer; Cosmetic Dermatology; Acne; Dermatologic Surgery; **Hospital:** Lenox Hill Hosp; **Address:** 975 Park Ave, Ste 1-A, New York, NY 10028; **Phone:** 212-772-9305; **Board Cert:** Dermatology 1980; **Med School:** NY Med Coll 1973; **Resid:** Dermatology, Westchester Co Med Ctr 1980

Avram, Marc R MD (D) - **Spec Exp:** Hair Restoration/Transplant; Skin Laser Surgery; Cosmetic Dermatology; Botox Therapy; **Hospital:** NY-Presby/Weill Cornell Med Ctr, NY (page 102); **Address:** 905 5th Ave, MS 10021, New York, NY 10021-2650; **Phone:** 212-734-4007; **Board Cert:** Dermatology 2012; Hair Restoration Surgery 2007; **Med School:** SUNY Downstate 1989; **Resid:** Dermatology, Mass Genl Hosp 1994; **Fac Appt:** Clin Prof D, Cornell Univ-Weill Med Coll

Becker, David S MD (D) - **Spec Exp:** Mohs Surgery; Dermatologic Surgery; Skin Cancer; **Hospital:** NY-Presby/Weill Cornell Med Ctr, NY (page 102); **Address:** The Dermatologic Society of Greater NY, 205 E 69th St, Ste 1C, New York, NY 10021; **Phone:** 212-772-3600; **Board Cert:** Dermatology 2002; **Med School:** UCSF 1989; **Resid:** Dermatology, UCSF Med Ctr 1993; **Fellow:** Dermatologic Surgery, Mass Genl Hosp 1994

Belsito, Donald V MD (D) - **Spec Exp:** Contact Dermatitis; Cutaneous Lymphoma; Psoriasis; Atopic Dermatitis; **Hospital:** NY-Presby/Columbia Univ Med Ctr, NY (page 102); **Address:** Columbia Dermatology Associates, 51 W 51st St, Fl 3, Ste 390, New York, NY 10019; **Phone:** 212-305-5293; **Board Cert:** Internal Medicine 1979; Dermatology 1983; Clinical & Laboratory Dermatologic Immunology 1985; **Med School:** Cornell Univ-Weill Med Coll 1976; **Resid:** Internal Medicine, Case West Res Univ Hosps 1979; Dermatology, NYU Med Ctr 1982; **Fellow:** Dermatologic Research, NYU Med Ctr 1983; **Fac Appt:** Prof D, Columbia P&S

Berkowitz, Eric Z MD (D) - **Spec Exp:** Skin Cancer; Mohs Surgery; Cosmetic Dermatology; **Hospital:** Mt Sinai Hosp; **Address:** 390 West End Ave, Ste 1G, New York, NY 10024; **Phone:** 212-877-0171; **Board Cert:** Dermatology 2014; **Med School:** Albert Einstein Coll Med 2001; **Resid:** Dermatology, Mount Sinai Med Ctr 2005; **Fellow:** Dermatologic Surgery, Mount Sinai Med Ctr 2006

Bernstein, Robert M MD (D) - **Spec Exp:** Hair Transplant-Robotic Surgery; Hair Restoration/Transplant; Hair Loss; Hair Loss in Women; **Hospital:** NY-Presby/Columbia Univ Med Ctr, NY (page 102); **Address:** Bernstein Med - Ctr for Hair Restoration, 110 E 55th St, Fl 11, New York, NY 10022; **Phone:** 212-826-2400; **Board Cert:** Dermatology 1982; Hair Restoration Surgery 1995; **Med School:** UMDNJ-NJ Med Sch, Newark 1978; **Resid:** Dermatology, Einstein Affil Hosp 1982; **Fac Appt:** Clin Prof D, Columbia P&S

Berson, Diane S MD (D) - **Spec Exp:** Aging Skin; Acne; Skin Cancer; **Hospital:** NY-Presby/Weill Cornell Med Ctr, NY (page 102); **Address:** 211 E 53rd St, Ste 3, New York, NY 10022-4803; **Phone:** 212-355-3511; **Board Cert:** Dermatology 2009; **Med School:** NYU Sch Med 1984; **Resid:** Dermatology, SUNY Hlth Sci Ctr 1988; **Fac Appt:** Assoc Prof D, Cornell Univ-Weill Med Coll

Brademas, Mary Ellen MD (D) - **Spec Exp:** Cosmetic Dermatology; Nail Diseases; **Hospital:** NYU Langone Med Ctr (page 104), Bellevue Hosp Ctr; **Address:** 11 5th Ave, Ste F, New York, NY 10003; **Phone:** 212-477-1515; **Board Cert:** Dermatology 1983; **Med School:** Georgetown Univ 1979; **Resid:** Dermatology, Johns Hopkins Hosp 1981; Dermatology, NYU Med Ctr 1983; **Fac Appt:** Assoc Clin Prof D, NYU Sch Med

Brandt, Fredric S MD (D) - **Spec Exp:** Botox Therapy; Cosmetic Dermatology; **Address:** Laser & Skin Surgery Ctr, 323 E 34th St Fl 2, New York, NY 10016; **Phone:** 212-889-7096; **Board Cert:** Internal Medicine 1978; Dermatology 1981; **Med School:** Hahnemann Univ 1975; **Resid:** Internal Medicine, NYU-VA Hosp 1978; Dermatology, Jackson Meml Hosp 1981

Buchness, Mary Ruth MD (D) - **Spec Exp:** Skin Infections; Skin Cancer; Cosmetic Dermatology; Psoriasis; **Hospital:** NY-Presby Hosp/The Allen Hosp (page 102); **Address:** 560 Broadway, Ste 406, New York, NY 10012; **Phone:** 212-822-3515; **Board Cert:** Dermatology 1986; **Med School:** Columbia P&S 1982; **Resid:** Dermatology, Columbia Univ Med Ctr 1986; **Fac Appt:** Assoc Prof Med, NY Med Coll

Burke, Karen E MD/PhD (D) - **Spec Exp:** Skin Cancer; Cosmetic Dermatology; Aging Skin; **Hospital:** Mt Sinai Hosp; **Address:** 429 E 52nd St, New York, NY 10022; **Phone:** 212-754-1100; **Board Cert:** Dermatology 1985; **Med School:** NYU Sch Med 1978; **Resid:** Dermatology, NYU Med Ctr 1983; **Fac Appt:** Asst Clin Prof D, Mount Sinai Sch Med

Carucci, John A MD/PhD (D) - **Spec Exp:** Mohs Surgery; **Hospital:** NYU Langone Med Ctr (page 104); **Address:** 240 E 38th St Fl 12, New York, NY 10016; **Phone:** 212-263-7019; **Board Cert:** Dermatology 2007; **Med School:** SUNY Downstate 1994; **Resid:** Dermatology, NYU Med Ctr 1998; **Fellow:** Mohs Surgery, Yale-New Haven Hosp 2000; **Fac Appt:** Assoc Prof D, NYU Sch Med

Clark, Sheryl MD (D) - **Spec Exp:** Melanoma; Skin Cancer; Skin Laser Surgery; Cosmetic Dermatology; **Hospital:** NY-Presby/Weill Cornell Med Ctr, NY (page 102); **Address:** 109 E 61st St, New York, NY 10065; **Phone:** 212-750-2905; **Board Cert:** Dermatology 1988; **Med School:** Case West Res Univ 1982; **Resid:** Dermatology, Barnes Hosp-Wash Univ 1988; **Fac Appt:** Asst Clin Prof D, Cornell Univ-Weill Med Coll

Cohen, David E MD (D) - **Spec Exp:** Occupational Dermatology; Contact Dermatitis; **Hospital:** NYU Langone Med Ctr (page 104); **Address:** NYU Dermatologic Assocs, 530 1st Ave, Ste 7R, New York, NY 10016; **Phone:** 212-263-5889; **Board Cert:** Dermatology 2012; Occupational Medicine 1996; **Med School:** SUNY Stony Brook 1989; **Resid:** Dermatology, NYU Med Ctr 1993; **Fellow:** Occupational Medicine, Columbia Univ Sch of Public Hlth 1994; **Fac Appt:** Assoc Prof D, NYU Sch Med

Colbert, David A MD (D) - **Spec Exp:** Cosmetic Dermatology; Facial Rejuvenation; **Address:** 119 Fifth Ave Fl 5, New York, NY 10003; **Phone:** 212-352-3333; **Board Cert:** Dermatology 2007; **Med School:** NY Med Coll 1987; **Resid:** Internal Medicine, Cabrini Med Ctr 1990; **Fellow:** Dermatology, NY Presby-Columbia Med Ctr 1995

Cook-Bolden, Fran Elesha MD (D) - **Spec Exp:** Black/Asian Skin Care; **Hospital:** Mt Sinai Roosevelt; **Address:** 150 E 58th St Fl 3rd Annex, New York, NY 10155; **Phone:** 212-223-6599; **Board Cert:** Dermatology 2008; **Med School:** Howard Univ 1987; **Resid:** Internal Medicine, Univ Hosp-SUNY Hlth Ctr 1990; **Fellow:** Dermatology, NYU Med Ctr 1996; **Fac Appt:** Asst Clin Prof D, Columbia P&S

Davis, Joyce MD (D) - **Spec Exp:** Acne; Hair loss; Cosmetic Dermatology; **Hospital:** Mt Sinai Beth Israel, Mt Sinai Hosp; **Address:** 69 Fifth Ave, New York, NY 10003; **Phone:** 212-242-3066; **Board Cert:** Dermatology 1983; **Med School:** Albert Einstein Coll Med 1979; **Resid:** Dermatology, Mount Sinai Med Ctr 1983

DeLeo, Vincent A MD (D) - **Spec Exp:** Contact Dermatitis; **Hospital:** Mt Sinai Roosevelt, Mt Sinai Beth Israel; **Address:** 1090 Amsterdam Ave, Fl 11, New York, NY 10025; **Phone:** 212-523-5898; **Board Cert:** Dermatology 2009; **Med School:** Louisiana State U, New Orleans 1969; **Resid:** Dermatology, USPHS Hosp 1974; Dermatology, NY-Presby/Columbia Univ Med Ctr 1975; **Fac Appt:** Clin Prof D, Columbia P&S

Demar, Leon K MD (D) - **Spec Exp:** Skin Cancer; Acne; Cosmetic Dermatology; Pediatric Dermatology; **Hospital:** Lenox Hill Hosp, NY-Presby/Columbia Univ Med Ctr, NY (page 102); **Address:** 985 5th Ave, New York, NY 10075; **Phone:** 212-988-9010; **Board Cert:** Dermatology 1977; **Med School:** NYU Sch Med 1973; **Resid:** Dermatology, Stanford Med Ctr 1975; Dermatology, Columbia-Presby Med Ctr 1977; **Fac Appt:** Asst Clin Prof D, Columbia P&S

Felderman, Lenora MD (D) - **Spec Exp:** Cosmetic Dermatology; Facial Rejuvenation; Acne & Rosacea; Skin Cancer; **Hospital:** NY-Presby/Weill Cornell Med Ctr, NY (page 102); **Address:** 1317 3rd Ave, Fl 8, New York, NY 10021-2995; **Phone:** 212-734-0091; **Board Cert:** Dermatology 2009; **Med School:** NY Med Coll 1981; **Resid:** Dermatology, Montefiore Med Ctr 1985; **Fac Appt:** Asst Clin Prof D, Cornell Univ-Weill Med Coll

Foitl, Daniel R MD (D) - **Spec Exp:** Cosmetic Dermatology; Laser Surgery; Skin Cancer; Facial Rejuvenation; **Hospital:** NY-Presby/Weill Cornell Med Ctr, NY (page 102); **Address:** Sutton Place Dermatology, 445 E 58th St Fl 1, New York, NY 10022; **Phone:** 212-838-0270; **Board Cert:** Dermatology 2004; Dermatopathology 1998; Anatomic Pathology 1991; **Med School:** NYU Sch Med 1986; **Resid:** Anatomic Pathology, Columbia-Presby Med Ctr 1990; Internal Medicine, Columbia-Presby Med Ctr 1992; **Fellow:** Dermatology, New York Hosp 1994; Dermatopathology, New York Hosp 1995

Franks Jr, Andrew G MD (D) - **Spec Exp:** Lupus/SLE; Raynaud's Disease; Scleroderma; Dermatomyositis; **Hospital:** NYU Langone Med Ctr (page 104); **Address:** NYU Dermatologic Assocs, 240 E 38th St, New York, NY 10016; **Phone:** 212-263-5015; **Board Cert:** Internal Medicine 1975; Dermatology 1977; Rheumatology 1978; **Med School:** NY Med Coll 1971; **Resid:** Internal Medicine, Beth Israel Med Ctr 1974; Dermatology, Columbia-Presby Med Ctr 1975; **Fellow:** Rheumatology, Columbia-Presby Med Ctr 1977; **Fac Appt:** Prof D, NYU Sch Med

Garzon, Maria C MD (D) - **Spec Exp:** Pediatric Dermatology; Vascular Malformations/Birthmarks; Mycosis Fungoides; **Hospital:** NY-Presby/Columbia Univ Med Ctr, NY (page 102); **Address:** Columbia Univ, Dept Dermatology, 161 Ft Washington Ave Fl 12, New York, NY 10032; **Phone:** 212-305-5293; **Board Cert:** Dermatology 2013; Pediatric Dermatology 2015; Pediatrics 2009; **Med School:** Columbia P&S 1988; **Resid:** Pediatrics, Columbia Presby-Babies Hosp 1991; **Fellow:** Dermatology, Columbia Presby Med Ctr 1995; **Fac Appt:** Assoc Clin Prof D, Columbia P&S

Gendler, Ellen C MD (D) - **Spec Exp:** Cosmetic Dermatology; Contact Dermatitis; Botox Therapy; Facial Rejuvenation; **Hospital:** NYU Langone Med Ctr (page 104); **Address:** 1035 Fifth Ave, New York, NY 10028; **Phone:** 212-288-8222; **Board Cert:** Dermatology 1985; **Med School:** Columbia P&S 1981; **Resid:** Dermatology, NYU Med Ctr 1985; **Fac Appt:** Assoc Clin Prof D, NYU Sch Med

Geronemus, Roy G MD (D) - **Spec Exp:** Skin Cancer; Mohs Surgery; Cosmetic Dermatology; **Hospital:** New York Eye & Ear Infirm of Mt Sinai, NYU Langone Med Ctr (page 104); **Address:** Laser Skin Surgical Ctr of NY, 317 E 34th St, Ste 11, New York, NY 10016; **Phone:** 212-686-7306; **Board Cert:** Dermatology 1983; **Med School:** Univ Miami Sch Med 1979; **Resid:** Dermatology, NYU-Skin Cancer Unit 1983; **Fellow:** Mohs Surgery, NYU-Skin Cancer Unit 1984; **Fac Appt:** Clin Prof D, NYU Sch Med

Gmyrek, Robyn S MD (D) - **Spec Exp:** Cosmetic Dermatology; Photodynamic Therapy; Skin Laser Surgery-Resurfacing; Varicose Veins; **Hospital:** NY-Presby/Columbia Univ Med Ctr, NY (page 102); **Address:** Columbia Univ Skin & Laser Ctr, 51 W 51st St, Ste 390, New York, NY 10020; **Phone:** 212-326-8889; **Board Cert:** Dermatology 2009; **Med School:** Columbia P&S 1996; **Resid:** Dermatology, NY-Presby/Columbia Univ Med Ctr 2000; **Fac Appt:** Asst Clin Prof D, Columbia P&S

Goldberg, David J MD (D) - **Spec Exp:** Mohs Surgery; Skin Cancer; Cosmetic Dermatology; Laser Surgery; **Hospital:** Mt Sinai Hosp, Hackensack Univ Med Ctr (page 96); **Address:** Skin Laser & Surg Specialsits of NY & NJ, 115 E 57th St, Ste 400, New York, NY 10022; **Phone:** 212-750-8900; **Board Cert:** Dermatology 1984; Clinical & Laboratory Dematologic Immunology 1987; **Med School:** Yale Univ 1980; **Resid:** Dermatology, NYU Med Ctr 1984; **Fellow:** Mohs Surgery, NYU Med Ctr 1985; **Fac Appt:** Clin Prof D, Mount Sinai Sch Med

Goldenberg, Gary MD (D) - **Spec Exp:** Skin Cancer; Psoriasis; Eczema; Cosmetic Dermatology; **Hospital:** Mt Sinai Hosp; **Address:** Mount Sinai Dermatology, 5 E 98th St Fl 5, New York, NY 10029; **Phone:** 212-241-9728; **Board Cert:** Dermatology 2006; Dermatopathology 2007; **Med School:** Temple Univ 2002; **Resid:** Dermatology, Wake Forest Univ Baptist Med Ctr 2006; **Fellow:** Dermatopathology, Univ Colorado 2007; **Fac Appt:** Asst Prof D, Mount Sinai Sch Med

Gordon, Marsha L MD (D) - **Spec Exp:** Cosmetic Dermatology; Botox Therapy; Facial Rejuvenation; **Hospital:** Mt Sinai Hosp; **Address:** 5 E 98th St Fl 5, New York, NY 10029-6574; **Phone:** 212-241-9728; **Board Cert:** Dermatology 1988; **Med School:** Univ Pennsylvania 1984; **Resid:** Dermatology, Mt Sinai Med Ctr 1988; **Fac Appt:** Clin Prof D, Mount Sinai Sch Med

Green, Michele S MD (D) - **Spec Exp:** Cosmetic Dermatology; Skin Laser Surgery; Facial Rejuvenation; Botox Therapy; **Hospital:** Lenox Hill Hosp; **Address:** 156 E 79th St, Ste 1B, New York, NY 10075; **Phone:** 212-535-3088; **Board Cert:** Dermatology 2013; **Med School:** Mount Sinai Sch Med 1991; **Resid:** Dermatology, Mt Sinai Hosp 1995

Greenspan, Alan H MD (D) - **Spec Exp:** Skin Cancer; Dermatologic Surgery; Phototherapy; **Hospital:** NYU Langone Med Ctr (page 104); **Address:** 39 Broadway, Ste 3005, New York, NY 10006; **Phone:** 212-509-5200; **Board Cert:** Dermatology 2009; **Med School:** Northwestern Univ 1979; **Resid:** Internal Medicine, Northwestern Meml Hosp 1981; Dermatology, NYU Med Ctr 1984; **Fac Appt:** Asst Clin Prof D, NYU Sch Med

Gribetz, Carin H MD (D) - **Spec Exp:** Cosmetic Dermatology; Acne & Rosacea; **Hospital:** Mt Sinai Hosp; **Address:** 108 E 86th St, Ste 1N, New York, NY 10028; **Phone:** 212-289-3300; **Board Cert:** Dermatology 2006; **Med School:** Cornell Univ 2000; **Resid:** Dermatology, Mount Sinai Med Ctr 2004; **Fac Appt:** Asst Clin Prof D, Mount Sinai Sch Med

Gross, Dennis F MD (D) - **Spec Exp:** Cosmetic Dermatology; **Hospital:** NYU Langone Med Ctr (page 104); **Address:** 900 Fifth Ave, New York, NY 10021; **Phone:** 212-725-4555; **Board Cert:** Dermatology 1990; **Med School:** SUNY Stony Brook 1986; **Resid:** Dermatology, NYU Med Ctr 1990; **Fac Appt:** Asst Clin Prof D, NYU Sch Med

Grossman, Melanie MD (D) - **Spec Exp:** Skin Laser Surgery; Facial Rejuvenation; Cosmetic Dermatology; Botox Therapy; **Hospital:** NY-Presby/Columbia Univ Med Ctr, NY (page 102); **Address:** 161 Madison Ave, Ste 4NW, New York, NY 10016-5405; **Phone:** 212-725-8600; **Board Cert:** Dermatology 2010; **Med School:** NYU Sch Med 1988; **Resid:** Internal Medicine, Yale-New Haven Hosp 1989; Dermatology, Columbia-Presby Med Ctr 1992; **Fellow:** Laser Surgery, Mass Genl Hosp 1995; **Fac Appt:** Asst Clin Prof D, Columbia P&S

Hale, Elizabeth K MD (D) - **Spec Exp:** Skin Cancer; Mohs Surgery; Laser Surgery; Facial Rejuvenation; **Hospital:** NYU Langone Med Ctr (page 104); **Address:** Complete Skin MD, 225 E 64th St, Fl 2, New York, NY 10065; **Phone:** 212-759-4900; **Board Cert:** Dermatology 2012; **Med School:** NYU Sch Med 1998; **Resid:** Dermatology, NYU Med Ctr 2002; **Fellow:** Mohs Surgery, NYU Med Ctr 2003; **Fac Appt:** Assoc Clin Prof D, NYU Sch Med

Halpern, Allan C MD (D) - **Spec Exp:** Skin Cancer; Melanoma; Melanoma Early Detection/Prevention; **Hospital:** Meml Sloan Kettering Canc Ctr (page 110); **Address:** Memorial Sloan-Kettering Cancer Ctr, 16 E 60th St Fl 3 - Ste 302, New York, NY 10022; **Phone:** 646-888-6013; **Board Cert:** Internal Medicine 1984; Dermatology 1988; **Med School:** Albert Einstein Coll Med 1981; **Resid:** Internal Medicine, Montefiore Hosp 1985; Dermatology, Hosp Univ Penn 1989; **Fellow:** Epidemiology, Hosp Univ Penn 1989; **Fac Appt:** Assoc Prof Med, Cornell Univ-Weill Med Coll

Hatcher, Virgil MD (D) - **Spec Exp:** Cosmetic Dermatology; Psoriasis; Viral Infections; **Hospital:** Mt Sinai Beth Israel; **Address:** 309 W 23rd St Fl 3, New York, NY 10011-2172; **Phone:** 212-675-4244; **Board Cert:** Dermatology 2009; **Med School:** UCSF 1978; **Resid:** Dermatology, NYU Med Ctr 1982; **Fellow:** Virology, NYU Med Ctr 1983; **Fac Appt:** Asst Clin Prof D, NYU Sch Med

Hochman, Herbert A MD (D) - **Spec Exp:** Cosmetic Dermatology; Skin Laser Surgery; Skin Cancer; **Hospital:** Lenox Hill Hosp; **Address:** 1020 Park Ave, New York, NY 10028-0913; **Phone:** 212-861-1656; **Board Cert:** Dermatology 1977; **Med School:** Tulane Univ 1970; **Resid:** Dermatology, Montefiore Med Ctr 1976

Jacobs, Michael Ira MD (D) - **Spec Exp:** Skin Cancer; Melanoma; Cosmetic Dermatology; **Hospital:** NY-Presby/Weill Cornell Med Ctr, NY (page 102); **Address:** 407 E 70th St Fl 2, New York, NY 10021-5302; **Phone:** 212-772-7190; **Board Cert:** Dermatology 1981; **Med School:** Cornell Univ-Weill Med Coll 1977; **Resid:** Dermatology, New York Hosp 1981; **Fac Appt:** Assoc Clin Prof D, Cornell Univ-Weill Med Coll

Karen, Julie K MD (D) - **Spec Exp:** Mohs Surgery; Skin Cancer; Laser Surgery; Facial Rejuvenation; **Hospital:** NYU Langone Med Ctr (page 104); **Address:** Complete Skin MD, 225 E 64th St Fl 2, New York, NY 10065; **Phone:** 212-759-4900; **Board Cert:** Dermatology 2007; **Med School:** Cornell Univ 2003; **Resid:** Dermatology, NYU Med Ctr 2007; **Fellow:** Dermatologic Surgery, NYU& MSK Cancer Ctr 2008; **Fac Appt:** Asst Clin Prof D, NYU Sch Med

Katz, Bruce MD (D) - **Spec Exp:** Laser Surgery; Cosmetic Surgery; Facial Rejuvenation; Cosmetic Dermatology; **Hospital:** Mt Sinai Hosp; **Address:** Juva Skin, Laser & Body Contouring Center, 60 E 56th St, Fl 2, New York, NY 10022-3350; **Phone:** 212-688-5882; **Board Cert:** Dermatology 1983; **Med School:** McGill Univ 1977; **Resid:** Internal Medicine, Columbia Presby Med Ctr 1979; Dermatology, Columbia Presby Med Ctr 1982; **Fac Appt:** Clin Prof D, Mount Sinai Sch Med

Katz, Susan MD (D) - **Spec Exp:** Psoriasis; Skin Cancer & Moles; Cutaneous Lymphoma; Cosmetic Dermatology; **Hospital:** NYU Langone Med Ctr (page 104); **Address:** 111 Broadway Fl 2, New York, NY 10006; **Phone:** 212-263-9700; **Board Cert:** Dermatology 2009; **Med School:** NYU Sch Med 1977; **Resid:** Internal Medicine, Roosevelt Hosp 1979; Dermatology, Montefiore Med Ctr 1983; **Fac Appt:** Asst Clin Prof D, NYU Sch Med

Kauvar, Arielle B MD (D) - **Spec Exp:** Laser Surgery; Cosmetic Dermatology; Mohs Surgery; Botox Therapy; **Hospital:** NYU Langone Med Ctr (page 104), New York Eye & Ear Infirm of Mt Sinai; **Address:** 1044 Fifth Ave, New York, NY 10028; **Phone:** 212-249-9440; **Board Cert:** Dermatology 2011; **Med School:** Harvard Med Sch 1989; **Resid:** Dermatology, NYU Med Ctr 1993; **Fellow:** Mohs Surgery, Laser & Skin Surgery Ctr 1994; **Fac Appt:** Assoc Clin Prof D, NYU Sch Med

Kenet, Barney J MD (D) - **Spec Exp:** Dermatologic Surgery; Cosmetic Dermatology; Liposuction; **Hospital:** NY-Presby/Weill Cornell Med Ctr, NY (page 102); **Address:** 25 E 86th St, Lobby A, New York, NY 10028; **Phone:** 212-535-9753; **Board Cert:** Dermatology 2012; **Med School:** Brown Univ 1988; **Resid:** Dermatology, New York Hosp 1992

Khorasani, Hooman MD (D) - **Spec Exp:** Mohs Surgery; Skin Cancer; Reconstructive Surgery; Clinical Trials; **Hospital:** Mt Sinai Hosp; **Address:** 5 E 98th St, Dept Dermatology, Fl 5, New York, NY 10029; **Phone:** 212-241-9728; **Board Cert:** Dermatology 2010; **Med School:** Univ SC Sch Med 2005; **Resid:** Plastic/Reconstructive Surgery, USC Med Ctr 2007; Dermatology, Metropolitan Hosp 2010; **Fellow:** Dermatologic Surgery, Mount Sinai Med Ctr 2011; **Fac Appt:** Asst Prof D, Mount Sinai Sch Med

Kline, Mitchell A MD (D) - **Spec Exp:** Melanoma; Skin Cancer; Mohs Surgery; Cosmetic Dermatology; **Hospital:** NY-Presby/Weill Cornell Med Ctr, NY (page 102); **Address:** 700 Park Ave, New York, NY 10021; **Phone:** 212-517-6555; **Board Cert:** Dermatology 2009; **Med School:** Univ Pennsylvania 1985; **Resid:** Internal Medicine, Graduate Hosp 1987; Dermatology, New York Hosp 1990

Krant, Jessica J MD (D) - **Spec Exp:** Cosmetic Dermatology; Skin Cancer & Moles; Mohs Surgery; **Hospital:** SUNY Downstate Med Ctr (Univ Hosp Brooklyn) (page 449); **Address:** Art of Dermatology, 860 5th Ave, New York, NY 10065; **Phone:** 212-488-5599; **Board Cert:** Dermatology 2011; **Med School:** Columbia P&S 1998; **Resid:** Dermatology, SUNY Dowstate Med Ctr 2002

Kriegel, David A MD (D) - **Spec Exp:** Mohs Surgery; Skin Cancer; **Hospital:** Mt Sinai Hosp; **Address:** Manhattan Ctr for Dermatology, 250 W 57th St, Ste 825, New York, NY 10107; **Phone:** 212-489-6669; **Med School:** Boston Univ 1987; **Resid:** Dermatology, Tufts Med Ctr 1991; **Fellow:** Mohs Surgery, Stony Brook Univ Hosp 1993; **Fac Appt:** Assoc Prof D, Mount Sinai Sch Med

Lacouture, Mario E MD (D) - **Spec Exp:** Skin Problems in Cancer Therapy; Hair Problems in Cancer Therapy; Nail Problems in Cancer Therapy; **Hospital:** Meml Sloan Kettering Canc Ctr (page 110); **Address:** Memorial Sloan Kettering, Dermatology, 16 E 60th St Fl 3 - Ste 302, New York, NY 10022; **Phone:** 646-888-6014; **Board Cert:** Dermatology 2013; **Med School:** Colombia 1997; **Resid:** Surgery, Cleveland Clinic 2002; Dermatology, Univ Chicago Hosp 2005; **Fellow:** Dermatology, Brigham & Women's Hosp 2006

Lebwohl, Mark G MD (D) - **Spec Exp:** Skin Cancer; Psoriasis; Eczema; **Hospital:** Mt Sinai Hosp; **Address:** Dermatology Assocs, 5 E 98th St, Fl 5, New York, NY 10029-6501; **Phone:** 212-241-9728; **Board Cert:** Internal Medicine 1981; Dermatology 1983; **Med School:** Harvard Med Sch 1978; **Resid:** Internal Medicine, Mt Sinai Hosp 1981; Dermatology, Mt Sinai Hosp 1983; **Fellow:** Dermatology, Mt Sinai Hosp 1983; **Fac Appt:** Prof D, Mount Sinai Sch Med

Levitt, Jacob O MD (D) - **Hospital:** Mt Sinai Hosp; **Address:** 5 E 98th St, Dept Dermatology Fl 5, New York, NY 10029; **Phone:** 212-241-9728; **Board Cert:** Dermatology 2013; **Med School:** Albert Einstein Coll Med 2000; **Resid:** Dermatology, Mt Sinai Med Ctr 2004

Lombardo, Peter C MD (D) - **Spec Exp:** Skin Cancer; Cosmetic Dermatology; **Hospital:** Mt Sinai Roosevelt, NY-Presby/Columbia Univ Med Ctr, NY (page 102); **Address:** Sutton Place Dermatology, 445 E 58th St, New York, NY 10022-2302; **Phone:** 212-838-0270; **Board Cert:** Dermatology 2009; **Med School:** Albany Med Coll 1959; **Resid:** Dermatology, Columbia-Presby 1965; Internal Medicine, St Luke's-Roosevelt Hosp Ctr 1966; **Fac Appt:** Assoc Clin Prof D, Columbia P&S

Marmur, Ellen S MD (D) - **Spec Exp:** Cosmetic Dermatology; Mohs Surgery; Laser Surgery; Skin Cancer; **Hospital:** Mt Sinai Hosp; **Address:** 12 E 87th St, Ste 1-A, New York, NY 10128; **Phone:** 212-996-6900; **Board Cert:** Dermatology 2013; **Med School:** Albert Einstein Coll Med 1999; **Resid:** Dermatology, New York Hosp 2003; **Fellow:** Mohs Surgery, Hackensack Hosp 2004; Cosmetic Dermatology, Hackensack Hosp 2004; **Fac Appt:** Assoc Clin Prof D, Mount Sinai Sch Med

Morel, Kimberly D MD (D) - **Spec Exp:** Pediatric Dermatology; Vascular Birthmarks; Atopic Dermatitis; Psoriasis; **Hospital:** NY-Presby/Columbia Univ Med Ctr, NY (page 102), Morgan Stanley Chldns Hosp of NY-Presby, NY (page 102); **Address:** Columbia Univ, Dept Dermatology, 161 Fort Washington Ave Fl 12, New York, NY 10032; **Phone:** 212-305-5293; **Board Cert:** Pediatrics 2014; Dermatology 2013; Pediatric Dermatology 2008; **Med School:** SUNY Downstate 1996; **Resid:** Pediatrics, NY Presby Hosp/Columbia 1999; Dermatology, NY Presby Hosp/Columbia 2003; **Fellow:** Pediatric & Adolescent Dermatology, Chldn's Hosp 2003; **Fac Appt:** Assoc Clin Prof D, Columbia P&S

Myskowski, Patricia L MD (D) - **Spec Exp:** Cutaneous Lymphoma; AIDS-Kaposi's Sarcoma; Skin Cancer; **Hospital:** Meml Sloan Kettering Canc Ctr (page 110); **Address:** Memorial Sloan Kettering, Dermatology, 16 E 60th St Fl 3 - Ste 302, New York, NY 10022; **Phone:** 646-888-6018; **Board Cert:** Dermatology 1980; Clinical & Laboratory Dematologic Immunology 1985; **Med School:** Brown Univ 1975; **Resid:** Internal Medicine, Bronx VA Hosp 1977; Dermatology, NY Hosp-Cornell Med Ctr 1980; **Fellow:** Dermatology, Meml Sloan Kettering Cancer Ctr 1981; **Fac Appt:** Assoc Prof D, Cornell Univ-Weill Med Coll

Nehal, Kishwer S MD (D) - **Spec Exp:** Skin Cancer; Melanoma; Mohs Surgery; Dermatologic Surgery; **Hospital:** Meml Sloan Kettering Canc Ctr (page 110); **Address:** Memorial Sloan Kettering, Dermatology, 16 E 60th St Fl 3 - Ste 302, New York, NY 10021; **Phone:** 646-888-6019; **Board Cert:** Dermatology 2005; **Med School:** Boston Univ 1992; **Resid:** Dermatology, NYU Med Ctr 1996; **Fellow:** Dermatologic Surgery, NYU Med Ctr 1998

Orbuch, Philip MD (D) - **Spec Exp:** Pediatric Dermatology; Skin Cancer; **Hospital:** NYU Langone Med Ctr (page 104), Bellevue Hosp Ctr; **Address:** 345 E 37th St, Ste 307, New York, NY 10016; **Phone:** 212-532-5355; **Board Cert:** Dermatology 2009; **Med School:** Israel 1981; **Resid:** Dermatology, NYU Med Ctr 1985; **Fellow:** Dermatology, NYU Med Ctr 1986; **Fac Appt:** Assoc Clin Prof D, NYU Sch Med

Orentreich, David S MD (D) - **Spec Exp:** Dermatologic Surgery; Liposuction; Hair Restoration/Transplant; Laser Surgery; **Hospital:** Mt Sinai Hosp; **Address:** 909 5th Ave, New York, NY 10021; **Phone:** 212-794-0800; **Board Cert:** Dermatology 1984; **Med School:** Columbia P&S 1980; **Resid:** Dermatology, Mt Sinai Med Ctr 1984; **Fac Appt:** Asst Clin Prof D, Mount Sinai Sch Med

Orlow, Seth J MD/PhD (D) - **Spec Exp:** Pediatric Dermatology; Birthmarks/Hemangiomas; Psoriasis/Eczema; **Hospital:** NYU Langone Med Ctr (page 104); **Address:** NYU Dermatologic Assocs, Faculty Practice Twr, 530 First Ave Fl 7 - Ste 7R, New York, NY 10016-6402; **Phone:** 212-263-5889; **Board Cert:** Dermatology 2014; Pediatric Dermatology 2014; **Med School:** Albert Einstein Coll Med 1986; **Resid:** Dermatology, Yale-New Haven Hosp 1989; **Fellow:** Pediatric Dermatology, Yale-New Haven Hosp 1990; **Fac Appt:** Prof D, NYU Sch Med

Ostad, Ariel MD (D) - **Spec Exp:** Skin Cancer; Mohs Surgery; Skin Laser Surgery; Cosmetic Dermatology; **Hospital:** NYU Langone Med Ctr (page 104), Lenox Hill Hosp; **Address:** 897 Lexington Ave, New York, NY 10065; **Phone:** 212-517-7900; **Board Cert:** Dermatology 2014; **Med School:** NYU Sch Med 1991; **Resid:** Dermatology, NYU Med Ctr 1995; **Fellow:** Dermatologic Surgery, UCLA Med Ctr 1996; **Fac Appt:** Asst Prof D, NYU Sch Med

Podwal, Mark H MD (D) - **Spec Exp:** Skin Cancer; **Hospital:** NYU Langone Med Ctr (page 104); **Address:** 55 E 73rd St, New York, NY 10021; **Phone:** 212-288-7488; **Board Cert:** Dermatology 1975; **Med School:** NYU Sch Med 1970; **Resid:** Dermatology, Kings Co Hosp Ctr 1972; Dermatology, Bellevue Hosp 1974; **Fac Appt:** Assoc Clin Prof D, NYU Sch Med

Polis, Laurie J MD (D) - **Spec Exp:** Cosmetic Dermatology; Skin Laser Surgery; Facial Rejuvenation; **Hospital:** Mt Sinai Hosp; **Address:** 197 Grand St, Ste 3E, New York, NY 10013; **Phone:** 212-431-1600; **Board Cert:** Dermatology 1989; **Med School:** Mount Sinai Sch Med 1983; **Resid:** Dermatology, Montefiore Med Ctr 1989; **Fac Appt:** Asst Prof D, Mount Sinai Sch Med

Prioleau, Philip G MD (D) - **Spec Exp:** Melanoma; Skin Cancer; Mohs Surgery; **Hospital:** NY-Presby/Weill Cornell Med Ctr, NY (page 102); **Address:** 1035 5th Ave, Ste C, New York, NY 10028; **Phone:** 212-794-3548; **Board Cert:** Surgery 1973; Anatomic Pathology 1979; Dermatopathology 1980; Dermatology 1983; **Med School:** Med Univ SC 1967; **Resid:** Surgery, Univ Virginia Hlth Sys 1972; Plastic Surgery, Duke Univ Hosp 1975; **Fellow:** Dermatopathology, Barnes-Jewish Hosp 1980; Dermatology, NYU Med Ctr 1981; **Fac Appt:** Assoc Clin Prof D, Cornell Univ-Weill Med Coll

Prystowsky, Janet MD (D) - **Spec Exp:** Mohs Surgery; Cosmetic Dermatology; Skin Cancer; Laser Surgery; **Hospital:** Mt Sinai Roosevelt; **Address:** 110 E 55th St Fl 7, New York, NY 10022; **Phone:** 212-230-1212; **Board Cert:** Dermatology 1987; **Med School:** Univ Chicago-Pritzker Sch Med 1983; **Resid:** Dermatology, Hosp Univ Penn 1987; **Fellow:** Mohs Surgery, SUNY Stony Brook Med Ctr 1998

Ramsay, David L MD (D) - **Spec Exp:** Cutaneous Lymphoma; Skin Cancer; Mycosis Fungoides; **Hospital:** NYU Langone Med Ctr (page 104); **Address:** NYU Med Ctr, Dermatology, 530 1st Ave, Ste 7G, New York, NY 10016; **Phone:** 212-683-6283; **Board Cert:** Dermatology 1974; **Med School:** Indiana Univ 1969; **Resid:** Dermatology, NYU Med Ctr 1973; **Fellow:** Dermatology, Univ IL Med Ctr 1974; **Fac Appt:** Clin Prof D, NYU Sch Med

Ratner, Desiree MD (D) - **Spec Exp:** Mohs Surgery; Skin Cancer; **Hospital:** Mt Sinai Beth Israel; **Address:** Continuum Cancer Ctr, Dermatology, 325 W 15th St, Ste J, New York, NY 10011; **Phone:** 212-367-0145; **Board Cert:** Dermatology 2012; **Med School:** Johns Hopkins Univ 1989; **Resid:** Internal Medicine, Beth Israel Deaconess Med Ctr 1990; Dermatology, Univ Michigan Med Ctr 1993; **Fellow:** Mohs Surgery, New England Med Ctr 1994; Mohs Surgery, Lahey Clin 1995; **Fac Appt:** Prof D, Columbia P&S

Rigel, Darrell S MD (D) - **Spec Exp:** Melanoma; Skin Cancer; Cosmetic Dermatology; **Hospital:** NYU Langone Med Ctr (page 104); **Address:** 35 E 35th Street, Ste 208, New York, NY 10016; **Phone:** 212-684-5964; **Board Cert:** Dermatology 1983; **Med School:** Geo Wash Univ 1978; **Resid:** Dermatology, NYU Med Ctr 1982; **Fellow:** Dermatologic Surgery, NYU Med Ctr 1983; **Fac Appt:** Clin Prof D, NYU Sch Med

Rokhsar, Cameron K MD (D) - **Spec Exp:** Skin Laser Surgery; Skin Cancer; Mohs Surgery; Facial Rejuvenation; **Hospital:** Mt Sinai Hosp, Winthrop Univ Hosp (page 536); **Address:** NY Cosmetic, Skin & Laser Surgery Ctr, 328 E 75th St, Ste A, New York, NY 10021; **Phone:** 212-285-1110; **Board Cert:** Dermatology 2012; **Med School:** NYU Sch Med 1998; **Resid:** Dermatology, Albert Einstein Affil Hosp 2002; **Fellow:** Dermatologic Surgery, Laser & Skin Surgery Ctr of La Jolla 2004; **Fac Appt:** Asst Prof D, Albert Einstein Coll Med

Romano, John F MD (D) - **Spec Exp:** Cosmetic Dermatology; **Hospital:** NY-Presby/Weill Cornell Med Ctr, NY (page 102); **Address:** 58 A W 15 St, New York, NY 10011; **Phone:** 212-242-5815; **Board Cert:** Dermatology 1980; **Med School:** Cornell Univ 1973; **Resid:** Internal Medicine, St Vincents Hosp 1976; Dermatology, New York Hosp 1978; **Fac Appt:** Asst Clin Prof D, Cornell Univ-Weill Med Coll

Roth, Jeffrey S MD/PhD (D) - **Spec Exp:** Melanoma; Skin Cancer; HIV-Related Skin Disorders; Cosmetic Dermatology; **Hospital:** Mt Sinai Hosp; **Address:** Park Avenue Dermatology Assocs, 580 Park Ave, New York, NY 10065-7313; **Phone:** 212-752-3692; **Board Cert:** Dermatology 2013; **Med School:** Columbia P&S 1989; **Resid:** Dermatology, Columbia-Presby Hosp 1993; **Fac Appt:** Asst Clin Prof D, Mount Sinai Sch Med

Safai, Bijan MD (D) - **Spec Exp:** Dermatologic Surgery; Skin Cancer; Skin Laser Surgery; Cosmetic Dermatology; **Hospital:** Metropolitan Hosp Ctr - NY; **Address:** 625 Park Ave, New York, NY 10065; **Phone:** 212-988-8918; **Board Cert:** Dermatology 1974; **Med School:** Iran 1965; **Resid:** Internal Medicine, VA Med Ctr 1970; Dermatology, NYU Med Ctr 1973; **Fellow:** Immunology, Meml Sloan-Kettering Cancer Ctr 1974; **Fac Appt:** Prof D, NY Med Coll

Schultz, Neal B MD (D) - **Spec Exp:** Cosmetic Dermatology; Melanoma Early Detection/Prevention; Skin Laser Surgery; Facial Rejuvenation; **Hospital:** Mt Sinai Hosp; **Address:** Park Avenue Skin Care, 1130 Park Ave, New York, NY 10128; **Phone:** 212-369-9600; **Board Cert:** Dermatology 1978; **Med School:** Columbia P&S 1973; **Resid:** Internal Medicine, Mt Sinai Hosp 1975; Dermatology, Mt Sinai Hosp 1978; **Fac Appt:** Clin Prof D, Mount Sinai Sch Med

Schweiger, Eric S MD (D) - **Spec Exp:** Cosmetic Dermatology; Acne; Facial Rejuvenation; Skin Laser Surgery-Resurfacing; **Hospital:** Mt Sinai Hosp; **Address:** Schweiger Dermatology, 110 E 55th St, Fl 19, New York, NY 10022; **Phone:** 212-283-3000; **Board Cert:** Dermatology 2008; **Med School:** Albert Einstein Coll Med 2003; **Resid:** Dermatology, Univ Kansas Med Ctr 2008; **Fac Appt:** Asst Clin Prof D, Mount Sinai Sch Med

Seidenberg, Roy Stern MD (D) - **Spec Exp:** Cosmetic Dermatology; Acne; **Hospital:** NYU Langone Med Ctr (page 104); **Address:** 317 E 34th St Fl 5, New York, NY 10016; **Phone:** 212-421-7546; **Board Cert:** Dermatology 2008; **Med School:** NY Med Coll 1991; **Resid:** Internal Medicine, Montefiore Med Ctr 1994; Dermatology, Cooper Hosp 1998; **Fellow:** Dermatologic Surgery, Boston Univ Med Ctr 1995; **Fac Appt:** Asst Clin Prof D, NYU Sch Med

Shelton, Ronald M MD (D) - **Spec Exp:** Cosmetic Dermatology; Mohs Surgery; Skin Laser Surgery; Skin Cancer; **Hospital:** Mt Sinai Hosp; **Address:** The NY Aesthetic Consultants, 260 E 66th St, New York, NY 10065; **Phone:** 212-593-1818; **Board Cert:** Dermatology 1990; **Med School:** SUNY Upstate Med Univ 1984; **Resid:** Dermatology, Brooke Army Med Ctr 1990; **Fellow:** Mohs Surgery, UCSF Med Ctr 1993; **Fac Appt:** Assoc Clin Prof D, Mount Sinai Sch Med

Shieh, Sherry MD (D) - **Spec Exp:** Skin Cancer; Ethnic Skin Disorders; Black/Asian Skin Care; Laser Surgery; **Hospital:** Mt Sinai Roosevelt, Mt Sinai Beth Israel; **Address:** 928 Broadway, Ste 204, New York, NY 10010; **Phone:** 212-982-8229; **Board Cert:** Dermatology 2004; **Med School:** Med Coll VA 1999; **Resid:** Dermatology, SUNY-Buffalo Affil Hosp 2004; **Fellow:** Cutaneous Oncology, Roswell Park Cancer Inst 2001; **Fac Appt:** Asst Clin Prof D, Columbia P&S

Shim-Chang, Helen MD (D) - **Spec Exp:** Dermatopathology; **Hospital:** Mt Sinai Hosp; **Address:** Dermatology Assocs, 5 E 98th St Fl 5, New York, NY 10029; **Phone:** 212-241-9728; **Board Cert:** Anatomic Pathology 1997; Dermatopathology 1998; Dermatology 2008; **Med School:** Hahnemann Univ 1991; **Resid:** Internal Medicine, Mt Sinai Sch Med 1993; Dermatology, Mt Sinai Sch Med 1997; **Fellow:** Dermatopathology, Mt Sinai Hosp 1998

Shupack, Jerome L MD (D) - **Spec Exp:** Rare Skin Disorders; Psoriasis; Eczema; Blistering Diseases; **Hospital:** NYU Langone Med Ctr (page 104); **Address:** 530 1st Ave, Ste 7F, New York, NY 10016-6402; **Phone:** 212-263-7344; **Board Cert:** Dermatology 1970; **Med School:** Columbia P&S 1963; **Resid:** Internal Medicine, Mt Sinai Hosp 1965; Dermatology, NYU Med Ctr 1970; **Fac Appt:** Prof D, NYU Sch Med

Silverberg, Nanette B MD (D) - **Spec Exp:** Pediatric Dermatology; Vitiligo; Atopic Dermatitis; Viral Infections; **Hospital:** Mt Sinai Beth Israel, Mt Sinai St. Luke's; **Address:** 10 Union Square E, Ste 3C, New York, NY 10003; **Phone:** 212-844-8800; **Board Cert:** Dermatology 2014; Pediatric Dermatology 2004; **Med School:** SUNY Downstate 1994; **Resid:** Dermatology, SUNY Downstate Med Ctr 1998; **Fellow:** Pediatric Dermatology, Chldn's Meml Hosp 1999; **Fac Appt:** Clin Prof D, Columbia P&S

Sobel, Howard MD (D) - **Spec Exp:** Cosmetic Dermatology; Botox Therapy; Skin Laser Surgery; Liposuction; **Hospital:** Lenox Hill Hosp, Mt Sinai Beth Israel; **Address:** NY Inst of Aesthetic Derm and Laser Surg, 960A Park Ave, New York, NY 10028-0325; **Phone:** 212-288-0060; **Med School:** Albert Einstein Coll Med 1975; **Resid:** Dermatology, Emory Univ Hosp 1979

Soter, Nicholas A MD (D) - **Spec Exp:** Urticaria; Psoriasis; Vasculitis; Phototherapy; **Hospital:** NYU Langone Med Ctr (page 104); **Address:** 240 E 38th St, Fl 12, New York, NY 10016-6402; **Phone:** 212-263-5015; **Board Cert:** Dermatology 1970; Clinical & Laboratory Dematologic Immunology 1985; **Med School:** Univ Tex SW, Dallas 1965; **Resid:** Dermatology, Baylor Affil Hosps 1968; Dermatology, Mass Genl Hosp 1969; **Fellow:** Immunology, Mass Genl Hosp 1973; **Fac Appt:** Prof D, NYU Sch Med

Tanenbaum, Diane G MD (D) - **Spec Exp:** Skin Cancer; **Hospital:** Lenox Hill Hosp, NYU Langone Med Ctr (page 104); **Address:** 16 E 79th St, Ste 22, New York, NY 10075-0150; **Phone:** 212-249-6122; **Board Cert:** Dermatology 1971; **Med School:** SUNY Downstate 1964; **Resid:** Dermatology, NYU Med Ctr 1970; **Fac Appt:** Assoc Clin Prof D, NYU Sch Med

Unger, Walter P MD (D) - **Spec Exp:** Hair Restoration/Transplant; **Hospital:** Mt Sinai Hosp; **Address:** 710 Park Ave, New York, NY 10021-6591; **Phone:** 212-249-9393; **Board Cert:** Dermatology 1968; Hair Restoration Surgery 2008; **Med School:** Univ Toronto 1963; **Resid:** Dermatology, Philadelphia Skin-Cancer Hosp 1967; Internal Medicine, Sunny Brook Hosp 1968; **Fac Appt:** Clin Prof D, Mount Sinai Sch Med

Vogel, Louis N MD (D) - **Spec Exp:** Cosmetic Dermatology; Botox Therapy; Hair Removal-Laser; **Hospital:** NYU Langone Med Ctr (page 104); **Address:** 16 Park Ave, Ste 1D, New York, NY 10016-4329; **Phone:** 212-447-5443; **Board Cert:** Internal Medicine 1980; Dermatology 1983; **Med School:** Boston Univ 1977; **Resid:** Internal Medicine, NYU Med Ctr 1980; Dermatology, NYU Med Ctr 1983; **Fac Appt:** Asst Clin Prof D, NYU Sch Med

Walther, Robert MD (D) - **Spec Exp:** Acne; Skin Cancer; Psoriasis; **Hospital:** NY-Presby/Columbia Univ Med Ctr, NY (page 102); **Address:** 161 Ft Wahington Ave Fl 12, New York, NY 10032; **Phone:** 212-326-8465; **Board Cert:** Dermatology 2009; Internal Medicine 1977; **Med School:** Univ NC Sch Med 1973; **Resid:** Internal Medicine, Univ Miami Hosps 1975; Dermatology, Columbia-Presby Hosp 1978; **Fellow:** Dermatology, Rockefeller Univ Hosp 1980; **Fac Appt:** Clin Prof D, Columbia P&S

Warner, Robert MD (D) - **Spec Exp:** Laser Surgery; Laser Hair Removal; Cosmetic Dermatology; Botox Therapy; **Hospital:** Mt Sinai Hosp; **Address:** 580 Park Ave, New York, NY 10065; **Phone:** 212-752-3692; **Board Cert:** Dermatology 1981; **Med School:** SUNY Hlth Sci Ctr 1977; **Resid:** Dermatology, Mount Sinai Hosp 1981; **Fac Appt:** Asst Clin Prof D, Mount Sinai Sch Med

Wattenberg, Debra J MD (D) - **Spec Exp:** Cosmetic Dermatology; Botox Therapy; Skin Laser Surgery; Acne; **Hospital:** Mt Sinai Hosp; **Address:** Wattenberg Dermatology, 875 Fifth Ave, New York, NY 10065; **Phone:** 212-288-3200; **Board Cert:** Dermatology 2011; **Med School:** Mount Sinai Sch Med 1988; **Resid:** Dermatology, Mount Sinai Hosp 1992; **Fac Appt:** Assoc Clin Prof D, Mount Sinai Sch Med

Wechsler, Amy B MD (D) - **Spec Exp:** Cosmetic Dermatology; Acne; Skin Laser Surgery; **Address:** 3 E 69th St, New York, NY 10021; **Phone:** 212-396-2500; **Board Cert:** Psychiatry 2010; Dermatology 2005; **Med School:** Cornell Univ 1995; **Resid:** Psychiatry, Payne Whitney Clinic 1999; Dermatology, SUNY Downstate Med Ctr 2005; **Fellow:** Child & Adolescent Psychiatry, Payne Whitney Clinic 2001

Wexler, Patricia MD (D) - **Spec Exp:** Facial Rejuvenation; Liposuction; Botox Therapy; Acne; **Hospital:** Mt Sinai Hosp; **Address:** 145 E 32nd St Fl 7, New York, NY 10016; **Phone:** 212-684-2626; **Board Cert:** Internal Medicine 1983; Dermatology 1986; **Med School:** Belgium 1979; **Resid:** Internal Medicine, Beth Israel Med Ctr 1982; Dermatology, Mt Sinai Hosp 1986; **Fellow:** Infectious Disease, Beth Israel Med Ctr 1983; **Fac Appt:** Assoc Clin Prof D, Mount Sinai Sch Med

Zeichner, Joshua MD (D) - **Spec Exp:** Acne & Rosacea; Cosmetic Dermatology; **Hospital:** Mt Sinai Hosp; **Address:** Mount Sinai Dermatology, 5 E 98th St, Fl 5, New York, NY 10029; **Phone:** 212-241-9728; **Board Cert:** Dermatology 2009; **Med School:** Johns Hopkins Univ 2003; **Resid:** Dermatology, Mount Sinai Hosp 2008; **Fellow:** Dermatologic Pharmacology, Mount Sinai Hosp 2009; **Fac Appt:** Asst Prof D, Mount Sinai-Icahn Sch of Med

Diagnostic Radiology

Abramson, Sara J MD (DR) - **Spec Exp:** Pediatric Radiology; **Hospital:** Meml Sloan Kettering Canc Ctr (page 110); **Address:** 444 E 68th St, New York, NY 10065; **Phone:** 212-639-2184; **Board Cert:** Diagnostic Radiology 1976; **Med School:** Mount Sinai Sch Med 1971; **Resid:** Pediatrics, Mt Sinai Hosp 1973; Diagnostic Radiology, Chldns Mercy Hosp 1976; **Fellow:** Pediatric Radiology, Chldns Hosp 1981

Adler, Ronald S MD/PhD (DR) - **Spec Exp:** Musculoskeletal Imaging; Ultrasound; Power Doppler Imaging; **Hospital:** NYU Langone Med Ctr (page 104), NYU Hosp For Joint Dis (page 104); **Address:** Ctr for Musculoskeletal Care-Radiology Dept, 333 E 38th St Fl 6, New York, NY 10016; **Phone:** 646-501-7440; **Board Cert:** Diagnostic Radiology 1988; **Med School:** Wayne State Univ 1984; **Resid:** Diagnostic Radiology, Univ Mich Hosps 1988; **Fellow:** Ultrasound/CT/MRI, Univ Mich Hosps 1989; **Fac Appt:** Prof Rad, Cornell Univ-Weill Med Coll

Akin, Oguz MD (DR) - **Spec Exp:** Prostate Cancer; Kidney Cancer; Genitourinary Cancer; MRI; **Hospital:** Meml Sloan Kettering Canc Ctr (page 110); **Address:** Meml Sloan-Kettering Cancer Ctr, 1275 York Ave, rm C276H, New York, NY 10065; **Phone:** 212-639-3458; **Board Cert:** Diagnostic Radiology 2007; **Med School:** Turkey 1996; **Resid:** Diagnostic Radiology, Baskent Univ Sch Med 2001; **Fellow:** Body Imaging, Meml Sloan Kettering Cancer Ctr 2004

Austin, John H. M. MD (DR) - **Spec Exp:** Lung Cancer; Thoracic Radiology; **Hospital:** NY-Presby/Columbia Univ Med Ctr, NY (page 102); **Address:** NY-Presby, Radiology, 177 Fort Washington Ave, Ste 3-202C, New York, NY 10032; **Phone:** 212-305-2639; **Board Cert:** Diagnostic Radiology 1970; **Med School:** Yale Univ 1965; **Resid:** Diagnostic Radiology, UCSF Med Ctr 1968; **Fellow:** Diagnostic Radiology, UCSF Med Ctr 1970; **Fac Appt:** Prof Emeritus Rad, Columbia P&S

Barone, Clement M MD (DR) - **Spec Exp:** Women's Imaging; Mammography; Bone Densitometry; **Hospital:** Mt Sinai Hosp; **Address:** 1440 York Ave, Ste P-1, New York, NY 10075; **Phone:** 212-988-1303; **Board Cert:** Diagnostic Radiology 1974; **Med School:** NY Med Coll 1968; **Resid:** Diagnostic Radiology, Mt Sinai Hosp 1970; Diagnostic Radiology, Mt Sinai Hosp 1974; **Fac Appt:** Asst Clin Prof, Mount Sinai Sch Med

Berson, Barry MD (DR) - **Spec Exp:** Mammography; Breast Imaging; Bone Densitometry; **Hospital:** Mt Sinai Hosp; **Address:** NY Medical Imaging Associates, 165 E 84th St, New York, NY 10028-0302; **Phone:** 212-535-9770; **Board Cert:** Diagnostic Radiology 1990; **Med School:** Mount Sinai Sch Med 1984; **Resid:** Diagnostic Radiology, Mount Sinai Hosp 1990; **Fellow:** Neuroradiology, NYU Med Ctr 1992

Brill, Paula W MD (DR) - **Spec Exp:** Pediatric Radiology; Ultrasound; **Hospital:** NY-Presby/Weill Cornell Med Ctr, NY (page 102); **Address:** 525 E 68th St, New York, NY 10065; **Phone:** 212-746-2554; **Board Cert:** Pediatrics 1970; Diagnostic Radiology 1971; Pediatric Radiology 2005; **Med School:** Cornell Univ-Weill Med Coll 1962; **Resid:** Pediatrics, New York Hosp 1968; Diagnostic Radiology, New York Hosp 1971; **Fellow:** Diagnostic Radiology, Cornell Univ 1971; **Fac Appt:** Prof Rad, Cornell Univ-Weill Med Coll

Brown, Marc MD (DR) - **Hospital:** NY-Presby/Columbia Univ Med Ctr, NY (page 102); **Address:** ColumbiaDoctors Midtown Radiology, 51 W 51st St, Ste 300, New York, NY 10019; **Phone:** 212-326-8517; **Board Cert:** Diagnostic Radiology 1996; **Med School:** Columbia P&S 1992; **Resid:** Diagnostic Radiology, NY-Presby/Columbia Univ Med Ctr 1996; **Fellow:** Breast Imaging, NY-Presby/Columbia Univ Med Ctr 1997; **Fac Appt:** Assoc Prof Rad, Columbia P&S

Chaim, Joshua L DO (DR) - **Spec Exp:** CT Scan; Ultrasound; MRI; **Hospital:** Meml Sloan Kettering Canc Ctr (page 110); **Address:** Meml Sloan Kettering Cancer Ctr, Dept of Radiology, 1275 York Ave Fl 2nd, New York, NY 10065; **Phone:** 646-888-4530; **Board Cert:** Diagnostic Radiology 2007; **Med School:** NY Coll Osteo Med 2002; **Resid:** Diagnostic Radiology, St Barnabas Hosp 2007; **Fellow:** Body Imaging, Meml Sloan Kettering Cancer Ctr 2008

Cohen, Burton A MD (DR) - **Spec Exp:** CT Scan; MRI; PET Imaging; **Hospital:** Mt Sinai Hosp; **Address:** New York Medical Imaging Associates, 165 E 84th St, New York, NY 10028; **Phone:** 212-535-9770; **Board Cert:** Diagnostic Radiology 1979; **Med School:** NY Med Coll 1975; **Resid:** Diagnostic Radiology, Mt Sinai Hosp 1979; **Fac Appt:** Assoc Clin Prof Rad, Mount Sinai Sch Med

Dershaw, D. David MD (DR) - **Spec Exp:** Breast Imaging; Breast Cancer; Mammography; **Hospital:** Meml Sloan Kettering Canc Ctr (page 110); **Address:** 300 E 66th St, rm 727, New York, NY 10065; **Phone:** 646-888-4505; **Board Cert:** Diagnostic Radiology 1978; Radiology 1974; **Med School:** Jefferson Med Coll 1974; **Resid:** Diagnostic Radiology, NY-Presby/Weill Cornell Med Ctr 1978; **Fellow:** Ultrasound, Thomas Jefferson Univ Hosp 1979; **Fac Appt:** Prof Rad, Cornell Univ-Weill Med Coll

Edelstein, Barbara A MD (DR) - **Spec Exp:** Breast Cancer; Women's Imaging; **Address:** 1045 Park Ave, New York, NY 10028; **Phone:** 212-860-7700; **Board Cert:** Diagnostic Radiology 1983; **Med School:** NY Med Coll 1977; **Resid:** Diagnostic Radiology, Montefiore Med Ctr 1982

Fefferman, Nancy R MD (DR) - **Spec Exp:** Pediatric Radiology; **Hospital:** NYU Langone Med Ctr (page 104); **Address:** 660 1st Ave Fl 3, New York, NY 10016; **Phone:** 212-263-5362; **Board Cert:** Radiology 1996; Pediatric Radiology 2009; **Med School:** NYU Sch Med 1991; **Resid:** Radiology, NYU Langone Med Ctr 1996; **Fellow:** Pediatric Radiology, NYU Langone Med Ctr 1997; **Fac Appt:** Asst Prof Rad, NYU Sch Med

Feigin, Kimberly N MD (DR) - **Spec Exp:** Breast Imaging; Mammography; **Hospital:** Meml Sloan Kettering Canc Ctr (page 110); **Address:** MSK Breast Imaging Ctr, 300 E 66th St, Fl 5, New York, NY 10065; **Phone:** 646-888-5219; **Board Cert:** Diagnostic Radiology 2012; **Med School:** Univ Rochester 1997; **Resid:** Diagnostic Radiology, NY Presby Hosp 2001; **Fellow:** Diagnostic Radiology, Meml Sloan Kettering Cancer Ctr 2002

Fried, Karen O MD (DR) - **Spec Exp:** Ultrasound; Thyroid Ultrasound; Vascular Ultrasound; **Address:** Lenox Hill Radiology, 61 E 77th St, New York, NY 10075; **Phone:** 212-772-3111; **Board Cert:** Diagnostic Radiology 1990; **Med School:** Albany Med Coll 1985; **Resid:** Diagnostic Radiology, LIJ Med Ctr 1990; **Fellow:** Cross Sectional Imaging, LIJ Med Ctr 1991

Fuqua III, James L MD (DR) - **Spec Exp:** CT Scan; Gastrointestinal Imaging; MRI; Ultrasound; **Hospital:** Meml Sloan Kettering Canc Ctr (page 110); **Address:** Meml Sloan Kettering Cancer Ctr, Dept of Radiology, 1275 York Ave Fl 2nd, New York, NY 10065; **Phone:** 646-888-4529; **Board Cert:** Diagnostic Radiology 2007; **Med School:** Univ Tenn Coll Med 2002; **Resid:** Diagnostic Radiology, Methodist Hosp 2007; **Fellow:** Body Imaging, Meml Sloan Kettering Cancer Ctr 2008

Ginsberg, Michelle S MD (DR) - **Spec Exp:** Lung Cancer; Thoracic Radiology; Pulmonary Embolism; Gastrointestinal Imaging; **Hospital:** Meml Sloan Kettering Canc Ctr (page 110); **Address:** Meml Sloan Kettering Cancer Ctr, 1275 York Ave, Dept Radiology, New York, NY 10021; **Phone:** 212-639-7292; **Board Cert:** Diagnostic Radiology 1995; **Med School:** Brown Univ 1990; **Resid:** Radiology, Montefiore Med Ctr- Weiler Div 1995; **Fellow:** Diagnostic Radiology, Meml Sloan Kettering Cancer Ctr 1996; **Fac Appt:** Assoc Prof Rad, Cornell Univ-Weill Med Coll

Henschke, Claudia L MD/PhD (DR) - **Spec Exp:** Lung Cancer; Lung Disease; Thoracic Radiology; **Hospital:** Mt Sinai Hosp; **Address:** Mt Sinai, Radiology, 1 Gustave Levy Pl, Box 1234, New York, NY 10029; **Phone:** 212-241-2420; **Board Cert:** Diagnostic Radiology 1981; **Med School:** Howard Univ 1977; **Resid:** Diagnostic Radiology, Brigham & Womens Hosp 1982; **Fac Appt:** Prof Rad, Mount Sinai Sch Med

Herman, Zeva W MD (DR) - **Spec Exp:** Breast Imaging; Ultrasound; MRI; **Hospital:** Mt Sinai Hosp; **Address:** NY Medical Imaging Associates, 165 E 84th St, New York, NY 10065; **Phone:** 212-535-9770; **Board Cert:** Diagnostic Radiology 1993; **Med School:** Mount Sinai Sch Med 1988; **Resid:** Diagnostic Radiology, Lenox Hill Hosp 1992; **Fellow:** Body Imaging, Meml Sloan Kettering Cancer Ctr 1993

Holliday, Roy A MD (DR) - **Spec Exp:** Head & Neck Imaging; **Hospital:** New York Eye & Ear Infirm of Mt Sinai, Mt Sinai Beth Israel; **Address:** New York Eye & Ear Infirmary, Dept Radiology, 310 E 14th St, North Bldg - Ground Fl, New York, NY 10003; **Phone:** 212-979-4397; **Board Cert:** Diagnostic Radiology 1986; **Med School:** NYU Sch Med 1982; **Resid:** Diagnostic Radiology, NYU Med Ctr 1986; **Fellow:** Neuroradiology, NYU Med Ctr 1987; **Fac Appt:** Prof Rad, Albert Einstein Coll Med

Hricak, Hedvig MD/PhD (DR) - **Spec Exp:** Prostate Cancer-MR Spectroscopy (MRSI); Gynecologic Cancer; **Hospital:** Meml Sloan Kettering Canc Ctr (page 110); **Address:** 1275 York Ave, Ste C278, New York, NY 10065; **Phone:** 800-525-2225; **Board Cert:** Diagnostic Radiology 1978; **Med School:** Yugoslavia 1970; **Resid:** Diagnostic Radiology, St Joseph Mercy Hosp 1977; **Fellow:** Ultrasound/CT, Henry Ford Hosp 1978; **Fac Appt:** Prof Rad, Cornell Univ-Weill Med Coll

Jacobs, Morton MD (DR) - **Spec Exp:** Neuroradiology; Head & Neck Imaging; Musculoskeletal Imaging; **Address:** Manhattan Diagnostic Radiology, 340 E 64th St, New York, NY 10065; **Phone:** 212-508-8890; **Board Cert:** Diagnostic Radiology 1976; Neuroradiology 2006; **Med School:** Ros Franklin Univ/Chicago Med Sch 1972; **Resid:** Diagnostic Radiology, New York Hosp 1976; **Fellow:** Neuroradiology, New York Hosp 1979

Levy, Miriam MD (DR) - **Spec Exp:** Breast Imaging; Mammography; Women's Imaging; **Address:** Medical Imaging of Manhattan, LLC, 635 Madison Ave, Fl 16, New York, NY 10065; **Phone:** 212-794-2500; **Board Cert:** Diagnostic Radiology 1983; **Med School:** Albert Einstein Coll Med 1979; **Resid:** Diagnostic Radiology, George Wash Univ Hosp 1982; Diagnostic Radiology, St Vincents Hosp 1983; **Fellow:** Ultrasound/CT/MRI, New York Hosp 1984; **Fac Appt:** Asst Clin Prof Path, Mount Sinai Sch Med

Math, Kevin R MD (DR) - **Spec Exp:** Musculoskeletal Imaging; MRI; **Hospital:** Mt Sinai Beth Israel; **Address:** East Manhattan Diagnostic Imaging, 424 E 89th St, New York, NY 10128; **Phone:** 212-410-5100; **Board Cert:** Diagnostic Radiology 1993; **Med School:** SUNY Upstate Med Univ 1988; **Resid:** Diagnostic Radiology, SUNY Hlth Sci Ctr 1993; **Fellow:** Musculoskeletal Imaging, Hosp Special Surgery/Weill Cornell Med Ctr 1994; **Fac Appt:** Assoc Clin Prof Rad, Albert Einstein Coll Med

Megibow, Alec J MD (DR) - **Spec Exp:** Abdominal Imaging; Gastrointestinal Imaging; CT Body Scan; **Hospital:** NYU Langone Med Ctr (page 104), Bellevue Hosp Ctr; **Address:** NYU Radiology dept, 550 1st Ave, HCC 232, New York, NY 10016; **Phone:** 212-263-5222; **Board Cert:** Diagnostic Radiology 1978; **Med School:** SUNY Upstate Med Univ 1974; **Resid:** Diagnostic Radiology, Bellevue/NYU Langone Med Ctr 1978; **Fellow:** Abdominal Imaging, NYU Langone Med Ctr 1978; **Fac Appt:** Prof Rad, NYU Sch Med

Miller, Theodore T MD (DR) - **Spec Exp:** Interventional Radiology; Ultrasound; CT Scan; **Hospital:** Hosp For Special Surgery (page 109); **Address:** Dept Radiology, 535 E 70th St, New York, NY 10021; **Phone:** 212-606-1127; **Board Cert:** Diagnostic Radiology 1993; **Med School:** Vanderbilt Univ 1987; **Resid:** Radiology, Mt Sinai Hosp 1992; **Fellow:** Radiology, Hosp for Special Surgery 1993; **Fac Appt:** Prof Rad, Cornell Univ-Weill Med Coll

Mintz, Douglas N MD (DR) - **Spec Exp:** Musculoskeletal Imaging; Bone Tumors; Trauma Radiology; **Hospital:** Hosp For Special Surgery (page 109); **Address:** Hospital for Special Surgery, Rediology & Imaging Dept, 535 E 70th St, Fl 3, New York, NY 10021; **Phone:** 212-606-1828; **Board Cert:** Diagnostic Radiology 1997; **Med School:** Columbia P&S 1988; **Resid:** Radiology, Lenox Hill Hosp 1997; **Fellow:** Musculoskeletal Imaging, Hosp for Special Surgery 1998

Mitnick, Julie S MD (DR) - **Spec Exp:** Mammography; Breast Cancer; **Address:** Murray Hill Radiology & Mammography, 650 1st Ave Fl 2, New York, NY 10016; **Phone:** 212-686-4440; **Board Cert:** Diagnostic Radiology 1977; **Med School:** NYU Sch Med 1972; **Resid:** Diagnostic Radiology, NYU Med Ctr 1977; **Fellow:** Pediatric Radiology, NYU Med Ctr 1978; **Fac Appt:** Assoc Clin Prof Rad, NYU Sch Med

Morris, Elizabeth A MD (DR) - **Spec Exp:** Breast Imaging; Breast MRI; Breast Cancer; **Hospital:** Meml Sloan Kettering Canc Ctr (page 110); **Address:** MSKCC, Radiology, 300 E 66th St, Fl 7, New York, NY 10065; **Phone:** 646-888-4510; **Board Cert:** Diagnostic Radiology 1994; **Med School:** UCSF 1989; **Resid:** Diagnostic Radiology, NY-Cornell Med Ctr 1994; **Fellow:** Breast Imaging, Meml Sloan-Kettering Cancer Ctr 1995; **Fac Appt:** Prof Rad, Cornell Univ-Weill Med Coll

Naidich, David P MD (DR) - **Spec Exp:** Chest Radiology; Chronic Lung Disease; Lung Cancer; Pulmonary Embolism; **Hospital:** NYU Langone Med Ctr (page 104), Bellevue Hosp Ctr; **Address:** NYU Medical Center, Dept Radiology, 660 1st Ave Fl 7, New York, NY 10016; **Phone:** 212-263-5229; **Board Cert:** Diagnostic Radiology 1980; **Med School:** NYU Sch Med 1975; **Resid:** Diagnostic Radiology, Johns Hopkins Hosp 1979; **Fellow:** Cross Sectional Imaging, Johns Hopkins Hosp 1980; **Fac Appt:** Prof Rad, NYU Sch Med

Neistadt, L Daniel MD (DR) - **Spec Exp:** CT Body Scan; Gastrointestinal Imaging; Ultrasound; PET Imaging; **Address:** Manhattan Diagnostic Radiology, 400 E 66th St, New York, NY 10065; **Phone:** 212-838-4243; **Board Cert:** Internal Medicine 1975; Nuclear Medicine 1977; Diagnostic Radiology 1980; **Med School:** Stanford Univ 1972; **Resid:** Nuclear Medicine, New York Hosp 1977; Diagnostic Radiology, New York Hosp 1980; **Fellow:** Ultrasound/CT, New York Hosp 1981

Newhouse, Jeffrey H MD (DR) - **Spec Exp:** Abdominal Imaging; **Hospital:** NY-Presby/Columbia Univ Med Ctr, NY (page 102); **Address:** 622 W 168th St, New York, NY 10032; **Phone:** 212-305-7898; **Board Cert:** Diagnostic Radiology 1972; **Med School:** Harvard Med Sch 1967; **Resid:** Diagnostic Radiology, Mass Genl Hosp 1972; **Fac Appt:** Prof Rad, Columbia P&S

Novick, Mark D MD (DR) - **Spec Exp:** Mammography; Breast Imaging; MRI; Women's Imaging; **Address:** Lenox Hill Radiology, 61 E 77th St, New York, NY 10075; **Phone:** 212-772-3111; **Board Cert:** Diagnostic Radiology 1983; **Med School:** Univ Tenn Coll Med 1978; **Resid:** Diagnostic Radiology, Univ Tenn Med Ctr 1982

Panicek, David M MD (DR) - **Spec Exp:** Bone Cancer; Soft Tissue Tumors; Musculoskeletal Tumors; **Hospital:** Meml Sloan Kettering Canc Ctr (page 110); **Address:** MSKCC, Radiology, 1275 York Ave, Ste C276G, New York, NY 10065; **Phone:** 212-639-5825; **Board Cert:** Diagnostic Radiology 1984; **Med School:** Cornell Univ-Weill Med Coll 1980; **Resid:** Diagnostic Radiology, NY-Presby/Weill Cornell Med Ctr 1984; **Fac Appt:** Prof Rad, Cornell Univ-Weill Med Coll

Pavlov, Helene MD (DR) - **Spec Exp:** Sports Medicine Radiology; Musculoskeletal Imaging; Orthopaedic Imaging; **Hospital:** Hosp For Special Surgery (page 109), NY-Presby/Weill Cornell Med Ctr, NY (page 102); **Address:** Hosp for Special Surgery, 535 E 70th St Fl 3, New York, NY 10021-4892; **Phone:** 212-606-1132; **Board Cert:** Diagnostic Radiology 1976; **Med School:** Temple Univ 1972; **Resid:** Diagnostic Radiology, Germantown Hosp 1976; **Fellow:** Musculoskeletal Imaging, Hosp For Special Surg 1977; **Fac Appt:** Prof Rad, Cornell Univ-Weill Med Coll

Pfaff, H Charles MD (DR) - **Spec Exp:** Musculoskeletal Imaging; Neuroradiology; **Hospital:** Mt Sinai Beth Israel, New York Eye & Ear Infirm of Mt Sinai; **Address:** New York Radiology Partners, 147 W 15th St, New York, NY 10011; **Phone:** 212-473-5323; **Board Cert:** Diagnostic Radiology 1992; **Med School:** Univ NC Sch Med 1987; **Resid:** Diagnostic Radiology, NY Presby/Columbia Med Ctr 1992; **Fellow:** Neuroradiology, NY Presby/Columbia Med Ctr 1993; **Fac Appt:** Asst Prof Rad, Albert Einstein Coll Med

Potter, Hollis G MD (DR) - **Spec Exp:** Musculoskeletal Imaging; Cartilage Damage; Arthroplasty Imaging; **Hospital:** Hosp For Special Surgery (page 109); **Address:** Hosp for Special Surgery, MRI-basement, 535 E 70th St, Ste MRI, New York, NY 10021-4892; **Phone:** 212-606-1023; **Board Cert:** Diagnostic Radiology 1990; **Med School:** NY Med Coll 1985; **Resid:** Diagnostic Radiology, N Shore Univ Hosp 1990; **Fellow:** Musculoskeletal Imaging, Hosp for Special Surgery 1991; **Fac Appt:** Prof Rad, Cornell Univ-Weill Med Coll

Prince, Martin R MD/PhD (DR) - **Spec Exp:** MRI Angiography; Abdominal Imaging; Body Imaging; Interventional Radiology; **Hospital:** NY-Presby/Weill Cornell Med Ctr, NY (page 102), NY-Presby/Columbia Univ Med Ctr, NY (page 102); **Address:** 416 E 55th St, New York, NY 10022; **Phone:** 212-746-6000; **Board Cert:** Diagnostic Radiology 1993; **Med School:** Harvard Med Sch 1985; **Resid:** Internal Medicine, UCSF Med Ctr 1987; Radiology, Mass Genl Hosp 1993; **Fellow:** Angiography, Mass Genl Hosp 1988; Magnetic Resonance Imaging, Mass Genl Hosp 1993; **Fac Appt:** Prof Rad, Cornell Univ-Weill Med Coll

Recht, Michael MD (DR) - **Spec Exp:** Musculoskeletal Imaging; **Hospital:** NYU Langone Med Ctr (page 104); **Address:** NYU Sch Med, Dept Radiology, 660 First Ave Fl 3, New York, NY 10016; **Phone:** 212-263-9530; **Board Cert:** Diagnostic Radiology 1987; **Med School:** Univ Pennsylvania 1983; **Resid:** Radiology, Hosp Univ Penn 1987; **Fellow:** Interventional Radiology, Hosp Univ Penn 1988; Musculoskeletal Imaging, UCSD Med Ctr 1992; **Fac Appt:** Prof Rad, NYU Sch Med

Rosenberg, Zehava S MD (DR) - **Spec Exp:** Musculoskeletal Imaging; **Hospital:** NYU Langone Med Ctr (page 104), NYU Hosp For Joint Dis (page 104); **Address:** NYU Hosp for Joint Diseases, 301 E 17th St, rm 600, New York, NY 10003; **Phone:** 212-598-6373; **Board Cert:** Diagnostic Radiology 1985; **Med School:** Univ Conn 1980; **Resid:** Diagnostic Radiology, Einstein Affil Hosp 1984; **Fellow:** Musculoskeletal Imaging, NY Columbia-Presby Hosp 1986; **Fac Appt:** Prof Rad, NYU Sch Med

Rosenfeld, Stanley MD (DR) - **Spec Exp:** Mammography; Ultrasound; Breast MRI; **Hospital:** Mt Sinai Hosp; **Address:** Rosetta Radiology, 1421 3rd Ave, New York, NY 10028; **Phone:** 212-744-5538; **Board Cert:** Diagnostic Radiology 1978; **Med School:** Albert Einstein Coll Med 1974; **Resid:** Diagnostic Radiology, Montefiore Hosp Med Ctr 1978; **Fac Appt:** Asst Prof Rad, Mount Sinai Sch Med

Ruzal-Shapiro, Carrie MD (DR) - **Spec Exp:** Pediatric Radiology; **Hospital:** NY-Presby/Columbia Univ Med Ctr, NY (page 102); **Address:** NY Presby/Columbia-Dept Radiology, 3959 Broadway, Chony 3 North, New York, NY 10032; **Phone:** 212-305-9665; **Board Cert:** Diagnostic Radiology 1988; Pediatric Radiology 2004; **Med School:** Columbia P&S 1982; **Resid:** Radiology, NY-Presby/Columbia Univ Med Ctr 1988; **Fellow:** Pediatric Radiology, NY-Presby/Columbia Univ Med Ctr 1989; **Fac Appt:** Clin Prof Rad, Columbia P&S

Schwartz, Lawrence H MD (DR) - **Hospital:** NY-Presby/Columbia Univ Med Ctr, NY (page 102); **Address:** NY-Presby, Radiology, 622 W 168th St Fl 1 - rm 336, New York, NY 10032; **Phone:** 212-305-8994; **Board Cert:** Diagnostic Radiology 1991; **Med School:** Boston Univ 1986; **Resid:** Diagnostic Radiology, NY-Presby/Weill Cornell Med Ctr 1991; **Fellow:** Ultrasound/CT/MRI, Brigham & Womens Hosp 1991; **Fac Appt:** Prof Rad, Columbia P&S

Som, Peter MD (DR) - **Spec Exp:** Head & Neck Imaging; CT Scan; MRI; Cancer Imaging; **Hospital:** Mt Sinai Hosp; **Address:** Radiology Associates, 1176 Fifth Ave, New York, NY 10029; **Phone:** 212-241-8333; **Board Cert:** Diagnostic Radiology 1972; **Med School:** NYU Sch Med 1967; **Resid:** Diagnostic Radiology, Mt Sinai Hosp 1971; **Fac Appt:** Prof Rad, Mount Sinai Sch Med

Sonnenblick, Emily B MD (DR) - **Spec Exp:** Breast Imaging; Breast MRI; **Hospital:** Mt Sinai Hosp; **Address:** Dubin Breast Ctr, 1176 Fifth Ave, Box 1160, New York, NY 10029; **Phone:** 212-241-3300; **Board Cert:** Diagnostic Radiology 1987; **Med School:** Cornell Univ-Weill Med Coll 1982; **Resid:** Diagnostic Radiology, Hosp Univ Penn 1984; Diagnostic Radiology, Columbia-Presby Med Ctr 1986; **Fellow:** Ultrasound, Mt Sinai Med Ctr 1987

Wolff, Steven D MD/PhD (DR) - **Spec Exp:** Cardiovascular Imaging; Cardiac MRI; **Hospital:** Lenox Hill Hosp, NY-Presby/Columbia Univ Med Ctr, NY (page 102); **Address:** 170 E 77th St, New York, NY 10075; **Phone:** 212-369-9200; **Board Cert:** Diagnostic Radiology 1994; **Med School:** Duke Univ 1989; **Resid:** Diagnostic Radiology, Johns Hopkins Hosp 1994

Yankelevitz, David F MD (DR) - **Spec Exp:** Lung Cancer; Thoracic Radiology; **Hospital:** Mt Sinai Hosp; **Address:** Mt Sinai, Radiology, 1 Gustave Levy Pl, Box 1234, New York, NY 10029; **Phone:** 212-241-2420; **Board Cert:** Diagnostic Radiology 1987; Nuclear Medicine 1987; **Med School:** SUNY Hlth Sci Ctr 1981; **Resid:** Diagnostic Radiology, Long Island Coll Hosp 1984; Nuclear Medicine, NY-Presby/Weill Cornell Med Ctr 1986; **Fellow:** Diagnostic Radiology, NY-Presby/Weill Cornell Med Ctr 1987; **Fac Appt:** Prof Rad, Cornell Univ-Weill Med Coll

Endocrinology, Diabetes & Metabolism

Bergman, Donald MD (EDM) - **Spec Exp:** Osteoporosis; Thyroid Disorders; Calcium Disorders; Bone Disorders-Metabolic; **Hospital:** Mt Sinai Hosp; **Address:** 1199 Park Ave, Ste 1F, New York, NY 10128; **Phone:** 212-876-7333; **Board Cert:** Internal Medicine 1975; Endocrinology, Diabetes & Metabolism 1977; **Med School:** Jefferson Med Coll 1971; **Resid:** Obstetrics & Gynecology, Mt Sinai Hosp 1972; Internal Medicine, Mt Sinai Hosp 1975; **Fellow:** Endocrinology, Diabetes & Metabolism, Mt Sinai Hosp 1977; **Fac Appt:** Clin Prof Med, Mount Sinai Sch Med

Bilezikian, John P MD (EDM) - **Spec Exp:** Osteoporosis; Bone Disorders-Metabolic; **Hospital:** NY-Presby/Columbia Univ Med Ctr, NY (page 102); **Address:** Columbia Metabolic Bone Disease Program, Harkness Pavilion, 180 Ft Washington Ave Fl 9 - Ste 904, New York, NY 10032; **Phone:** 212-305-2663; **Board Cert:** Internal Medicine 1975; Endocrinology, Diabetes & Metabolism 1977; **Med School:** Columbia P&S 1969; **Resid:** Internal Medicine, NY-Presby/Columbia Univ Med Ctr 1975; **Fellow:** Endocrinology, Diabetes & Metabolism, Natl Inst Health 1977; **Fac Appt:** Prof Med, Columbia P&S

Bloomgarden, Zachary T MD (EDM) - **Spec Exp:** Diabetes; Diabetic Kidney Disease; Diabetic Leg/Foot; Cholesterol/Lipid Disorders; **Hospital:** Mt Sinai Hosp; **Address:** 35 E 85th St, New York, NY 10028-0954; **Phone:** 212-879-5933; **Board Cert:** Internal Medicine 1977; Endocrinology, Diabetes & Metabolism 1979; **Med School:** Albert Einstein Coll Med 1974; **Resid:** Internal Medicine, Montefiore Med Ctr 1977; **Fellow:** Endocrinology, Diabetes & Metabolism, Vanderbilt Univ Med Ctr 1979; **Fac Appt:** Clin Prof Med, Mount Sinai Sch Med

Blum, Conrad B MD (EDM) - **Spec Exp:** Cholesterol/Lipid Disorders; Thyroid Disorders; Diabetes; **Hospital:** NY-Presby/Columbia Univ Med Ctr, NY (page 102); **Address:** 51 W 51 St, rm 360, New York, NY 10022-1002; **Phone:** 212-326-8421; **Board Cert:** Internal Medicine 1976; Endocrinology, Diabetes & Metabolism 1977; **Med School:** Northwestern Univ 1971; **Resid:** Internal Medicine, Brigham & Women's Hosp 1976; **Fellow:** Endocrinology, Diabetes & Metabolism, Northwestern Meml Hosp 1977; **Fac Appt:** Clin Prof Med, Columbia P&S

Bockman, Richard S MD/PhD (EDM) - **Spec Exp:** Bone Disorders-Metabolic; Osteoporosis; Parathyroid Disorders; Paget's Disease of Bone; **Hospital:** Hosp For Special Surgery (page 109), NY-Presby/Weill Cornell Med Ctr, NY (page 102); **Address:** 519 E 72nd St, Ste 206, New York, NY 10021; **Phone:** 212-606-1458; **Board Cert:** Internal Medicine 1975; **Med School:** Yale Univ 1967; **Resid:** Internal Medicine, NYU Langone Med Ctr 1973; **Fellow:** Endocrinology, Diabetes & Metabolism, NY-Presby/Weill Cornell Med Ctr 1975; **Fac Appt:** Prof Med, Cornell Univ-Weill Med Coll

Brett, Elise M MD (EDM) - **Spec Exp:** Diabetes; Osteoporosis; **Hospital:** Mt Sinai Hosp; **Address:** 1192 Park Ave, New York, NY 10128; **Phone:** 212-831-2100; **Board Cert:** Internal Medicine 2007; Endocrinology, Diabetes & Metabolism 2009; **Med School:** Mount Sinai Sch Med 1994; **Resid:** Internal Medicine, Mt Sinai Hosp 1997; **Fellow:** Endocrinology, Diabetes & Metabolism, Mt Sinai Hosp 1999; **Fac Appt:** Assoc Clin Prof Med, Mount Sinai Sch Med

Brillon, David J MD (EDM) - **Spec Exp:** Diabetes; Thyroid Disorders; Clinical Trials; **Hospital:** NY-Presby/Weill Cornell Med Ctr, NY (page 102); **Address:** Cornell-Weill Physicians-Endocrinology, 525 E 68th St Fl 20, Baker Pavilion, New York, NY 10065; **Phone:** 212-746-6290; **Board Cert:** Internal Medicine 1983; Endocrinology, Diabetes & Metabolism 1987; **Med School:** Brown Univ 1980; **Resid:** Internal Medicine, Rochester Genl Hosp 1983; **Fellow:** Endocrinology, Strong Meml Hosp 1986; Endocrinology, Diabetes & Metabolism, UCSD Med Ctr 1988; **Fac Appt:** Clin Prof Med, Cornell Univ-Weill Med Coll

Bukberg, Phillip MD (EDM) - **Spec Exp:** Diabetes; Cholesterol/Lipid Disorders; **Hospital:** Mt Sinai Beth Israel; **Address:** 317 E 17th St Fl 7, Fierman Hall, New York, NY 10003; **Phone:** 212-420-2777; **Board Cert:** Internal Medicine 1977; Endocrinology, Diabetes & Metabolism 1979; **Med School:** SUNY Downstate 1973; **Resid:** Internal Medicine, St Vincent's Hosp & Med Ctr 1977; **Fellow:** Endocrinology, Meml Sloan Kettering Cancer Ctr 1979; Endocrinology, Mt Sinai Hosp 1982

Davies, Terry F MD (EDM) - **Spec Exp:** Thyroid Disorders in Pregnancy; Graves' Disease; Hashimoto's Disease; Thyroid Cancer; **Hospital:** Mt Sinai Hosp, VA Hudson Valley-FDR/Montrose; **Address:** 5 E 98th St, Box 1055, New York, NY 10029-6500; **Phone:** 212-241-7975; **Med School:** England, UK 1971; **Resid:** Internal Medicine, Univ Newcastle Affil Hosp 1975; **Fellow:** Endocrinology, Diabetes & Metabolism, Univ Newcastle Affil Hosp 1977; Endocrinology, Diabetes & Metabolism, Natl Inst Hlth 1979; **Fac Appt:** Prof Med, Mount Sinai Sch Med

Fagin, James A MD (EDM) - **Spec Exp:** Thyroid Cancer; **Hospital:** Meml Sloan Kettering Canc Ctr (page 110); **Address:** Meml Sloan-Kettering Cancer Ctr, 1275 York Ave, New York, NY 10065; **Phone:** 646-888-2718; **Board Cert:** Internal Medicine 1987; Endocrinology, Diabetes & Metabolism 2010; **Med School:** Argentina 1973; **Resid:** Internal Medicine, Hammersmith/W Middlesex Hosp 1981; Endocrinology, Diabetes & Metabolism, Hosp Italiano 1983; **Fellow:** Endocrinology, Diabetes & Metabolism, VA Wadsworth Hosp/Cedars-Sinai Med Ctr 1985

Fish, Stephanie A MD (EDM) - **Spec Exp:** Thyroid Cancer; **Hospital:** Meml Sloan Kettering Canc Ctr (page 110); **Address:** Maml Sloan Kettering Cancer Ctr, Dept Endocrinology, 1275 York Ave, New York, NY 10065; **Phone:** 646-888-3274; **Board Cert:** Internal Medicine ; Endocrinology, Diabetes & Metabolism 2012; **Med School:** NYU Sch Med 1997; **Resid:** Internal Medicine, Hosp U Penn 2000; **Fellow:** Endocrinology, Diabetes & Metabolism, Hosp U Penn 2002

Goland, Robin S MD (EDM) - **Spec Exp:** Diabetes; **Hospital:** NY-Presby/Columbia Univ Med Ctr, NY (page 102); **Address:** Naomi Berrie Diabetes Ctr, 1150 St Nicolas Ave Fl 2, New York, NY 10032; **Phone:** 212-851-5494; **Board Cert:** Internal Medicine 1983; Endocrinology 1989; **Med School:** Columbia P&S 1980; **Resid:** Internal Medicine, Columbia-Presby Med Ctr 1984; **Fellow:** Endocrinology, Diabetes & Metabolism, Columbia-Presby Med Ctr 1987; **Fac Appt:** Prof Med, Columbia P&S

Greene, Loren Wissner MD (EDM) - **Spec Exp:** Thyroid Disorders; Osteoporosis; Ethics; **Hospital:** NYU Langone Med Ctr (page 104), NY-Presby/Lower Manhattan Hosp (page 102); **Address:** 650 First Ave, Fl 7, New York, NY 10016-6402; **Phone:** 212-263-7449; **Board Cert:** Internal Medicine 1978; Endocrinology, Diabetes & Metabolism 1981; **Med School:** NYU Sch Med 1975; **Resid:** Internal Medicine, Bellevue Hosp Ctr-NYU 1978; **Fellow:** Endocrinology, Bellevue Hosp Ctr-NYU 1980; Medical Ethics, NYU 2012

Haber, Richard S MD (EDM) - **Spec Exp:** Thyroid Disorders; Thyroid Cancer; Parathyroid Disorders; Parathyroid Cancer; **Hospital:** Mt Sinai Hosp; **Address:** Mt Sinai, Endocrinology, 5 E 98th St Fl 11, New York, NY 10029; **Phone:** 212-241-7975; **Board Cert:** Endocrinology, Diabetes & Metabolism 1983; Internal Medicine 1980; **Med School:** NYU Sch Med 1977; **Resid:** Internal Medicine, SUNY Hlth Sci Ctr 1980; **Fellow:** Endocrinology, Diabetes & Metabolism, NY-Presby/Columbia Univ Med Ctr 1983; **Fac Appt:** Prof Med, Mount Sinai Sch Med

Hodak, Steven P MD (EDM) - **Spec Exp:** Thyroid Cancer; Metabolic Disorders; Neuroendocrinology; **Hospital:** NYU Langone Med Ctr (page 104); **Address:** NYU Langone Diabetes & Endocrine Assos, 530 First Ave, Schwartz East, Ste 5E-5F, New York, NY 10016; **Phone:** 212-481-1350; **Board Cert:** Internal Medicine 2004; Endocrinology, Diabetes & Metabolism 2005; **Med School:** Georgetown Univ 1999; **Resid:** Internal Medicine, George Washington U Hosp 2003; **Fellow:** Endocrinology, George Washington U Hosp 2005; **Fac Appt:** Assoc Clin Prof Med, Univ Pittsburgh

Jacobs Jr, Thomas P MD (EDM) - **Spec Exp:** Adrenal Disorders; Pituitary Disorders; Calcium Disorders; Thyroid Disorders; **Hospital:** NY-Presby/Columbia Univ Med Ctr, NY (page 102); **Address:** 161 Fort Washington Ave, rm 210, MS 10032, New York, NY 10032-3713; **Phone:** 212-305-5578; **Board Cert:** Internal Medicine 1973; Endocrinology, Diabetes & Metabolism 1975; **Med School:** Johns Hopkins Univ 1968; **Resid:** Internal Medicine, Columbia Presby Hosp 1973; **Fellow:** Endocrinology, Diabetes & Metabolism, Univ Wash Med Ctr 1975; **Fac Appt:** Clin Prof Med, Columbia P&S

Kleinberg, David L MD (EDM) - **Spec Exp:** Pituitary Disorders; Neuroendocrinology; **Hospital:** NYU Langone Med Ctr (page 104); **Address:** 650 First Ave Fl 4, New York, NY 10016; **Phone:** 212-263-6772; **Board Cert:** Internal Medicine 1972; Endocrinology 1975; **Med School:** Univ Miami Sch Med 1966; **Resid:** Internal Medicine, Maimonides Med Ctr 1968; Internal Medicine, NY-Presby/Columbia Univ Med Ctr 1971; **Fellow:** Endocrinology, Diabetes & Metabolism, NY-Presby/Columbia Univ Med Ctr 1970; **Fac Appt:** Prof Med, NYU Sch Med

Klyde, Barry J MD (EDM) - **Spec Exp:** Thyroid Disorders; Adrenal Disorders; Reproductive Endocrinology; Bone Disorders-Metabolic; **Hospital:** NY-Presby/Weill Cornell Med Ctr, NY (page 102); **Address:** 520 E 72nd St, Ste L0, New York, NY 10021-4840; **Phone:** 212-772-3333; **Board Cert:** Internal Medicine 1977; Endocrinology, Diabetes & Metabolism 1981; **Med School:** Stanford Univ 1974; **Resid:** Internal Medicine, New York Hosp 1977; **Fellow:** Endocrinology, Diabetes & Metabolism, New York Hosp & Rockefeller Univ 1979; **Fac Appt:** Asst Clin Prof Med, Cornell Univ-Weill Med Coll

Levine, Alice C MD (EDM) - **Spec Exp:** Adrenal Disorders; Pituitary Disorders; Reproductive Endocrinology; **Hospital:** Mt Sinai Hosp; **Address:** Mt Sinai School of Med, Dept of Medicine - Endocrinology, 5 E 98th St Fl 11, New York, NY 10029; **Phone:** 212-241-7975; **Board Cert:** Internal Medicine 1984; Endocrinology, Diabetes & Metabolism 1987; **Med School:** Columbia P&S 1981; **Resid:** Internal Medicine, NYU/Manhattan VA Hosp 1984; **Fellow:** Endocrinology, Diabetes & Metabolism, Mt Sinai Med Ctr 1986; **Fac Appt:** Prof Med, Mount Sinai Sch Med

Levy, Carol J MD (EDM) - **Spec Exp:** Diabetes; Diabetes in Pregnancy; Thyroid Disorders; **Hospital:** Mt Sinai Hosp; **Address:** Mt Sinai Diabetes Ctr, 10 E 102nd St Fl 5, New York, NY 10029; **Phone:** 212-241-3422; **Board Cert:** Endocrinology, Diabetes & Metabolism 2005; **Med School:** Northwestern Univ 1988; **Resid:** Internal Medicine, Beth Israel Deaconess Medical Ctr 1991; **Fellow:** Endocrinology, Diabetes & Metabolism, Joslin Diabetes Ctr 1993; **Fac Appt:** Assoc Prof Med, Mount Sinai Sch Med

Maclaren, Noel Keith MD (EDM) - **Spec Exp:** Diabetes; Obesity; Thyroid Disorders; Addison's Disease; **Hospital:** Lenox Hill Hosp, NY-Presby/Weill Cornell Med Ctr, NY (page 102); **Address:** Bioseek Endocrine Clinic, 200 W 57th St, Ste 605, New York, NY 10019; **Phone:** 212-371-0658; **Board Cert:** Pediatrics 1977; Pediatric Endocrinology 1978; **Med School:** New Zealand 1963; **Resid:** Internal Medicine, Wellington Public Hosp 1967; **Fellow:** Pediatric Endocrinology, Johns Hopkins Hosp 1973; Pediatric Endocrinology, Univ MD Hosp 1974; **Fac Appt:** Prof Ped, Cornell Univ-Weill Med Coll

Martorella, Andrew J MD (EDM) - **Spec Exp:** Diabetes; Thyroid Disorders; Adrenal Disorders; Pituitary Disorders; **Hospital:** NY-Presby/Weill Cornell Med Ctr, NY (page 102), Hosp For Special Surgery (page 109); **Address:** 215 E 68th St, Ste 8, New York, NY 10065; **Phone:** 212-288-2869; **Board Cert:** Internal Medicine 2004; Endocrinology, Diabetes & Metabolism 2008; **Med School:** Georgetown Univ 2000; **Resid:** Internal Medicine, Boston Univ Med Ctr 2003; **Fellow:** Endocrinology, Diabetes & Metabolism, Weill-Cornell Med Ctr/MSK Cancer Ctr 2005; **Fac Appt:** Asst Clin Prof Med, Cornell Univ-Weill Med Coll

McConnell, Robert J MD (EDM) - **Spec Exp:** Thyroid Disorders; Thyroid Ultrasound; **Hospital:** NY-Presby/Columbia Univ Med Ctr, NY (page 102); **Address:** 161 Fort Washington Ave, rm 210, New York, NY 10032-3713; **Phone:** 212-305-5579; **Board Cert:** Internal Medicine 1978; Endocrinology, Diabetes & Metabolism 1981; **Med School:** Columbia P&S 1973; **Resid:** Internal Medicine, Barnes Hosp 1975; **Fellow:** Endocrinology, Diabetes & Metabolism, Columbia-Presby Hosp 1978; **Fac Appt:** Clin Prof Med, Columbia P&S

Mechanick, Jeffrey I MD (EDM) - **Spec Exp:** Nutrition; Thyroid Disorders; Thyroid Cancer; Bone Disorders-Metabolic; **Hospital:** Mt Sinai Hosp; **Address:** 1192 Park Ave, New York, NY 10128; **Phone:** 212-831-2100; **Board Cert:** Internal Medicine 1988; Endocrinology, Diabetes & Metabolism 2013; **Med School:** Mount Sinai Sch Med 1985; **Resid:** Internal Medicine, Baylor Affil Hosp 1988; **Fellow:** Endocrinology, Diabetes & Metabolism, Mt Sinai Hosp 1990; **Fac Appt:** Clin Prof Med, Mount Sinai Sch Med

Peck, Valerie H MD (EDM) - **Spec Exp:** Osteoporosis; Thyroid Disorders; Menopause Problems; Weight Management; **Hospital:** NYU Langone Med Ctr (page 104); **Address:** 135 E 37th St, New York, NY 10016; **Phone:** 212-213-3233; **Board Cert:** Internal Medicine 1977; Endocrinology, Diabetes & Metabolism 1979; **Med School:** NYU Sch Med 1974; **Resid:** Internal Medicine, Bellevue Hosp Ctr 1977; **Fellow:** Endocrinology, Bellevue Hosp Ctr 1978; **Fac Appt:** Assoc Clin Prof Med, NYU Sch Med

Poretsky, Leonid MD (EDM) - **Spec Exp:** Diabetes; Thyroid Disorders; **Hospital:** Mt Sinai Beth Israel; **Address:** 317 E 17th St Fl 7, Fierman Hall, New York, NY 10003; **Phone:** 212-420-2226; **Board Cert:** Internal Medicine 1983; Endocrinology, Diabetes & Metabolism 1985; **Med School:** Russia 1977; **Resid:** Internal Medicine, Coney Island Hosp 1983; **Fellow:** Endocrinology, Beth Israel Hosp 1985; **Fac Appt:** Prof Med, Albert Einstein Coll Med

Rayfield, Elliot J MD (EDM) - **Spec Exp:** Diabetes; Hypoglycemia; **Hospital:** Mt Sinai Hosp; **Address:** Park Avenue Diabetes Care, 1150 Park Ave, Fl 1, New York, NY 10128; **Phone:** 212-427-9191; **Board Cert:** Internal Medicine 1971; Endocrinology, Diabetes & Metabolism 1973; **Med School:** Jefferson Med Coll 1967; **Resid:** Internal Medicine, Univ Mich Hosp 1970; **Fellow:** Endocrinology, Diabetes & Metabolism, Peter Bent Brigham Hosp 1971; **Fac Appt:** Clin Prof Med, Mount Sinai Sch Med

Sabra, Mona M MD (EDM) - **Spec Exp:** Thyroid Cancer; **Hospital:** Meml Sloan Kettering Canc Ctr (page 110); **Address:** Meml Sloan Kettering Cancer Inst, Dept Endocrinology, 1275 York Ave, New York, NY 10065; **Phone:** 646-888-3275; **Board Cert:** Internal Medicine 2010; Endocrinology, Diabetes & Metabolism 2012; **Med School:** Lebanon 1996; **Resid:** Internal Medicine, Good Samaritan Hosp 2000; **Fellow:** Endocrinology, Diabetes & Metabolism, Univ Maryland Hosp 2002

Seltzer, Terry F MD (EDM) - **Spec Exp:** Diabetes; Thyroid Disorders; Calcium Disorders; Adrenal Disorders; **Hospital:** NYU Langone Med Ctr (page 104); **Address:** 530 1st Ave, Schwartz Ctr, Ste 5E-5F, New York, NY 10016-6402; **Phone:** 212-263-8717; **Board Cert:** Internal Medicine 1980; Endocrinology 1983; **Med School:** Harvard Med Sch 1977; **Resid:** Internal Medicine, NYU-Bellevue Hosp 1980; **Fellow:** Endocrinology, Diabetes & Metabolism, NYU-Bellevue Hosp 1982; **Fac Appt:** Asst Prof Med, NYU Sch Med

Seplowitz, Alan H MD (EDM) - **Spec Exp:** Thyroid Disorders; Diabetes; Cholesterol/Lipid Disorders; **Hospital:** NY-Presby/Columbia Univ Med Ctr, NY (page 102); **Address:** 161 Fort Washington Ave, Ste 4-422, New York, NY 10032-3729; **Phone:** 212-305-5503; **Board Cert:** Internal Medicine 1975; Endocrinology 1977; **Med School:** Columbia P&S 1972; **Resid:** Internal Medicine, Columbia-Presby Med Ctr 1974; **Fellow:** Lipid Metabolism, Natl Inst Hlth 1976; Endocrinology, Diabetes & Metabolism, Columbia-Presby Med Ctr 1978; **Fac Appt:** Assoc Prof Med, Columbia P&S

Shane, Elizabeth J MD (EDM) - **Spec Exp:** Bone Disorders-Metabolic; Osteoporosis; Parathyroid Disorders; **Hospital:** NY-Presby/Columbia Univ Med Ctr, NY (page 102); **Address:** 180 Ft Washington Ave, rm 910, New York, NY 10032; **Phone:** 212-305-2042; **Board Cert:** Internal Medicine 1978; Endocrinology 1981; **Med School:** Univ Toronto 1975; **Resid:** Internal Medicine, Columbia-Presby Hosp 1978; **Fellow:** Endocrinology, Columbia-Presby Hosp 1981; **Fac Appt:** Clin Prof Med, Columbia P&S

Silverberg, Shonni J MD (EDM) - **Spec Exp:** Parathyroid Disorders; Osteoporosis; Calcium Disorders; **Hospital:** NY-Presby/Columbia Univ Med Ctr, NY (page 102); **Address:** 180 Fort Washington Ave Fl 9, New York, NY 10032; **Phone:** 212-305-2663 x1; **Board Cert:** Internal Medicine 1983; Endocrinology, Diabetes & Metabolism 1985; **Med School:** Cornell Univ-Weill Med Coll 1980; **Resid:** Internal Medicine, NY Hosp 1983; **Fellow:** Endocrinology, Diabetes & Metabolism, Columbia-Presby Med Ctr 1986; **Fac Appt:** Prof Med, Columbia P&S

Siris, Ethel S MD (EDM) - **Spec Exp:** Osteoporosis; Paget's Disease of Bone; Bone Disorders-Metabolic; **Hospital:** NY-Presby/Columbia Univ Med Ctr, NY (page 102); **Address:** 180 Ft Washington Ave, HP Bldg Fl 9 - Ste 903, New York, NY 10032-3710; **Phone:** 212-305-9531; **Board Cert:** Internal Medicine 1974; Endocrinology, Diabetes & Metabolism 1977; **Med School:** Columbia P&S 1971; **Resid:** Internal Medicine, NY-Presby/Columbia Univ Med Ctr 1974; **Fellow:** Research, Natl Inst of Hlt 1976; Endocrinology, Diabetes & Metabolism, NY-Presby/Columbia Univ Med Ctr 1977; **Fac Appt:** Prof Med, Columbia P&S

Tamler, Ronald MD/PhD (EDM) - **Spec Exp:** Diabetes; Hypogonadism; **Hospital:** Mt Sinai Hosp; **Address:** Mt Sinai Diabetes Ctr St, 10 E 102nd St Fl 5, New York, NY 10029; **Phone:** 212-241-3422; **Board Cert:** Internal Medicine 2004; Endocrinology, Diabetes & Metabolism 2006; **Med School:** Germany 1999; **Resid:** Internal Medicine, Newton-Wellesley Hosp 2002; Internal Medicine, Boston Med Ctr 2004; **Fellow:** Endocrinology, Diabetes & Metabolism, Mt Sinai Med Ctr 2006; **Fac Appt:** Assoc Prof Med, Mount Sinai Sch Med

Tuttle, R. Michael MD (EDM) - **Spec Exp:** Thyroid Cancer; **Hospital:** Meml Sloan Kettering Canc Ctr (page 110); **Address:** MSKCC, Endocrinology, 1275 York Ave, New York, NY 10065; **Phone:** 646-888-2716; **Board Cert:** Endocrinology, Diabetes & Metabolism 2004; **Med School:** Univ Louisville Sch Med 1987; **Resid:** Internal Medicine, DD Eisenhower Army Med Ctr 1990; **Fellow:** Endocrinology, Diabetes & Metabolism, Madigan Army Med Ctr 1993; **Fac Appt:** Prof Med, Cornell Univ-Weill Med Coll

Wardlaw, Sharon L MD (EDM) - **Spec Exp:** Neuroendocrinology; Pituitary Disorders; **Hospital:** NY-Presby/Columbia Univ Med Ctr, NY (page 102); **Address:** 180 Fort Washington Ave, rm 970, New York, NY 10032; **Phone:** 212-305-2254; **Board Cert:** Internal Medicine 1978; Endocrinology, Diabetes & Metabolism 1979; **Med School:** Cornell Univ-Weill Med Coll 1975; **Resid:** Internal Medicine, Case Western Univ Hosp 1977; **Fellow:** Endocrinology, Diabetes & Metabolism, Columbia Presby Hosp 1980; **Fac Appt:** Prof Med, Columbia P&S

Zweig, Susan B MD (EDM) - **Spec Exp:** Thyroid Disorders; Diabetes; Polycystic Ovarian Syndrome; Osteoporosis; **Hospital:** NYU Langone Med Ctr (page 104), Bellevue Hosp Ctr; **Address:** 135 E 37th St, New York, NY 10016; **Phone:** 212-725-7841; **Board Cert:** Internal Medicine 2010; Endocrinology, Diabetes & Metabolism 2012; **Med School:** Israel 1997; **Resid:** Internal Medicine, St Lukes Roosevelt Hosp Ctr 2000; **Fellow:** Endocrinology, Beth Israel Med Ctr 2002; **Fac Appt:** Asst Clin Prof Med, NYU Sch Med

Family Medicine

Bauchman, Gail Beth MD (FMed) - **Spec Exp:** Women's Health; Adolescent Medicine; **Address:** Charles B. Wang Community Health Ctr, 268 Canal St Fl 1, New York, NY 10013; **Phone:** 212-966-0228; **Board Cert:** Family Medicine 2013; **Med School:** SUNY Stony Brook 1985; **Resid:** Family Medicine, Bronx-Lebanon Med Ctr 1989; **Fellow:** Adolescent Medicine, Mt Sinai Hosp 1990

Calman, Neil S MD (FMed) *PCP* - **Hospital:** Mt Sinai Hosp, Mt Sinai Beth Israel; **Address:** Institute for Family Health, 16 E 16th St, New York, NY 10003-3105; **Phone:** 212-924-7744; **Board Cert:** Family Medicine 2013; **Med School:** Rush Med Coll 1975; **Resid:** Family Medicine, Montefiore Hosp Med Ctr 1978; **Fac Appt:** Prof FMed, Mount Sinai Sch Med

Elmaleh, Rebecca MD (FMed) *PCP* - ; **Address:** 70 E 10th St, Ste 1T, New York, NY 10003; **Phone:** 212-253-2488; **Med School:** Univ MD Sch Med 1982; **Resid:** Family Medicine, Montefiore Med Ctr 1985

Firshein, Richard N DO (FMed) - **Spec Exp:** Nutrition & Disease Prevention/Control; Integrative Medicine; Asthma; **Address:** 1226 Park Ave, Ste 1B, New York, NY 10128; **Phone:** 212-860-0282; **Med School:** NY Coll Osteo Med 1984

Guardarramas, Gabriel MD (FMed) *PCP* - **Spec Exp:** Travel Medicine; **Hospital:** Mt Sinai Beth Israel, Mt Sinai St. Luke's; **Address:** 600 W 111th St, Ste 1E, New York, NY 10025; **Phone:** 212-222-1142; **Board Cert:** Family Medicine 2004; **Med School:** Mexico 1975; **Resid:** Family Medicine, Lutheran Med Ctr 1978; Family Medicine, Glen Cove Comm Hosp 1980

Horowitz, Mark Emil MD (FMed) *PCP* - **Spec Exp:** Adolescent Medicine; **Hospital:** Mt Sinai Beth Israel; **Address:** Downtown Family Med, 42 Broadway, Ste 1530, New York, NY 10004; **Phone:** 212-482-2400; **Board Cert:** Family Medicine 2012; **Med School:** SUNY Stony Brook 1983; **Resid:** Family Medicine, Somerset Med Ctr 1986; **Fellow:** Adolescent Medicine, Metropolitan Hosp Ctr 1987; Ambulatory Pediatrics, Metropolitan Hosp Ctr 1987

Kessler, George J DO (FMed) *PCP* - **Spec Exp:** Osteopathic Manipulation; Nutrition; **Hospital:** NY-Presby/Weill Cornell Med Ctr, NY (page 102); **Address:** 165 West End Ave, Ste 1K, New York, NY 10023; **Phone:** 212-877-7043; **Med School:** Kirksville Coll Osteo Med 1973

Kligler, Benjamin E MD (FMed) *PCP* - **Spec Exp:** Complementary Medicine; **Hospital:** Mt Sinai Beth Israel; **Address:** Continuum Ctr for Health & Healing, 245 Fifth Ave, Fl 2, New York, NY 10016; **Phone:** 646-935-2257; **Board Cert:** Family Medicine 2008; **Med School:** Boston Univ 1990; **Resid:** Family Medicine, Albert Einstein Affil Hosps 1994; **Fac Appt:** Asst Prof FMed, Albert Einstein Coll Med

Levy, Albert MD (FMed) *PCP* - **Spec Exp:** Hypertension; Diabetes; Sexual Dysfunction; Anxiety & Depression; **Hospital:** Mt Sinai Hosp, Lenox Hill Hosp; **Address:** 911 Park Ave, New York, NY 10075; **Phone:** 212-288-7193; **Board Cert:** Family Medicine 2006; **Med School:** Brazil 1973; **Resid:** Surgery, Maimonides Hosp 1978; Family Medicine, Kings County Hosp 1980; **Fac Appt:** Asst Prof FMed, Mount Sinai-Icahn Sch of Med

Liakeas, George P MD (FMed) *PCP* - **Hospital:** Mt Sinai Beth Israel; **Address:** Lexington Medical Assocs, 686 Lexington Ave, Ste 3N, New York, NY 10022; **Phone:** 212-750-5088; **Board Cert:** Family Medicine 2006; **Med School:** Albert Einstein Coll Med 1997; **Resid:** Family Medicine, Mt Sinai Beth Israel Med Ctr 2000

Lyon, Valerie K MD (FMed) *PCP* - **Spec Exp:** Preventive Medicine; **Hospital:** NYU Langone Med Ctr (page 104), Lenox Hill Hosp; **Address:** 59 E 54th St Fl 2, New York, NY 10022; **Phone:** 212-750-8330; **Board Cert:** Family Medicine 2006; **Med School:** Temple Univ 1986; **Resid:** Family Medicine, South Nassau Comm Hosp 1989

Prine, Linda W MD (FMed) *PCP* - **Hospital:** Mt Sinai Beth Israel; **Address:** The Institute for Family Health, 16 E 16th St, New York, NY 10003-3105; **Phone:** 212-924-7744; **Board Cert:** Family Medicine 2014; **Med School:** Cornell Univ-Weill Med Coll 1987; **Resid:** Family Medicine, Montefiore Med Ctr 1990; **Fac Appt:** Assoc Clin Prof FMed, Albert Einstein Coll Med

Schiller, Robert M MD (FMed) *PCP* - **Spec Exp:** Complementary Medicine; **Hospital:** Mt Sinai Beth Israel; **Address:** The Institute for Family Health, 16 E 16th St, New York, NY 10003-3105; **Phone:** 212-924-7744; **Board Cert:** Family Medicine 2006; **Med School:** NYU Sch Med 1982; **Resid:** Family Medicine, Montefiore Med Ctr 1985; **Fac Appt:** Asst Prof FMed, Albert Einstein Coll Med

Shepard, Richard DO (FMed) *PCP* - **Hospital:** Mt Sinai Roosevelt; **Address:** Manhattan Medical Care, 140 W 69th St, New York, NY 10023; **Phone:** 212-496-9620; **Board Cert:** Family Medicine 2008; Pediatrics 1980; **Med School:** Univ Osteo Med & Hlth Sci, Des Moines 1974; **Resid:** Pediatrics, St Vincent Hosp Med Ctr 1977; Family Medicine, Stony Brook Univ Med Ctr 1985

Stancliff, Sharon MD (FMed) - **Spec Exp:** Addiction Medicine; AIDS/HIV; **Address:** Harm Reduction Coalition, 22 W 27th St Fl 5, New York, NY 10001; **Phone:** 212-213-6376; **Board Cert:** Family Medicine 2005; **Med School:** UC Davis 1987; **Resid:** Family Medicine, Univ AZ Med Ctr 1990

Gastroenterology

Ackert, John J MD (Ge) - **Spec Exp:** Endoscopy; Colonoscopy; Gastroesophageal Reflux Disease (GERD); **Hospital:** NYU Langone Med Ctr (page 104); **Address:** Concorde Med Grp, 232 E 30th St Fl Ground, New York, NY 10016; **Phone:** 212-889-5544 x169; **Board Cert:** Internal Medicine 1975; Gastroenterology 1977; **Med School:** NYU Sch Med 1972; **Resid:** Internal Medicine, Bellevue Hosp Ctr 1975; **Fellow:** Gastroenterology, Bellevue Hosp Ctr 1977

Baiocco, Peter J MD (Ge) - **Spec Exp:** Inflammatory Bowel Disease; Colon Cancer Screening; Gastroesophageal Reflux Disease (GERD); Endoscopy; **Hospital:** Lenox Hill Hosp; **Address:** 1317 3rd Ave Fl 5, New York, NY 10021-2995; **Phone:** 212-734-8811; **Board Cert:** Internal Medicine 1981; Gastroenterology 1983; **Med School:** Mount Sinai Sch Med 1978; **Resid:** Internal Medicine, Lenox Hill Hosp 1981; **Fellow:** Gastroenterology, Lenox Hill Hosp 1983; **Fac Appt:** Asst Clin Prof Med, NYU Sch Med

Basuk, Paul M MD (Ge) - **Spec Exp:** Colonoscopy; Pancreatic/Biliary Endoscopy (ERCP); Barrett's Esophagus; Pancreatic & Biliary Disease; **Hospital:** NY-Presby/Weill Cornell Med Ctr, NY (page 102); **Address:** 210 E 86th St, Ste 201, New York, NY 10028; **Phone:** 212-861-9715; **Board Cert:** Internal Medicine 1983; Gastroenterology 1987; **Med School:** Northwestern Univ 1980; **Resid:** Internal Medicine, UCSF Med Ctr 1983; **Fellow:** Gastroenterology, UCSF Med Ctr 1987; **Fac Appt:** Asst Clin Prof Med, Cornell Univ-Weill Med Coll

Bednarek, Karl T MD (Ge) - **Spec Exp:** Colon & Rectal Cancer Detection; **Hospital:** Mt Sinai Beth Israel; **Address:** Mt Sinai Beth Israel Med Ctr, 10 Union Square E, Ste 2G, New York, NY 10003; **Phone:** 212-844-6335; **Board Cert:** Internal Medicine 1985; **Med School:** Mount Sinai Sch Med 1982; **Resid:** Internal Medicine, Beth Israel Med Ctr 1986; **Fellow:** Gastroenterology, Beth Israel Med Ctr 1988; **Fac Appt:** Asst Prof Med, Albert Einstein Coll Med

Bernstein, Brett B MD (Ge) - **Spec Exp:** Gastroesophageal Reflux Disease (GERD); Capsule Endoscopy; Colon Cancer Screening; **Hospital:** Mt Sinai Beth Israel; **Address:** Mt Sinai Beth Israel Med Ctr, 10 Union Square E, Ste 2G, New York, NY 10003; **Phone:** 212-844-6330; **Board Cert:** Gastroenterology 2005; **Med School:** Mount Sinai Sch Med 1988; **Resid:** Internal Medicine, Beth Israel Med Ctr 1992; **Fellow:** Gastroenterology, Beth Israel Med Ctr 1994; **Fac Appt:** Asst Prof Med, Albert Einstein Coll Med

Borcich, Anthony S MD (Ge) - **Spec Exp:** Liver Disease; Hepatitis C; HIV & Hepatitis Co-Infection; **Hospital:** Mt Sinai Hosp, Lenox Hill Hosp; **Address:** 800A 5th Ave, New York, NY 10065; **Phone:** 212-722-8400; **Board Cert:** Internal Medicine 1987; Gastroenterology 1989; **Med School:** Northwestern Univ-Feinberg Sch Med 1984; **Resid:** Internal Medicine; St Lukes-Roosevelt Hosp 1987; **Fellow:** Gastroenterology, St Lukes-Roosevelt Hosp 1989; **Fac Appt:** Asst Clin Prof Med, Mount Sinai Sch Med

Brown Jr, Robert S MD (Ge) - **Spec Exp:** Hepatitis; Liver Disease; Transplant Medicine-Liver; Autoimmune Liver Disease; **Hospital:** NY-Presby/Columbia Univ Med Ctr, NY (page 102), NY-Presby/Weill Cornell Med Ctr, NY (page 102); **Address:** Ctr for Liver Disease & Transplantation, 622 W 168th St PH Bldg Fl 14 - rm 105, New York, NY 10032; **Phone:** 212-305-1305; **Board Cert:** Internal Medicine 2012; Gastroenterology 2005; Transplant Hepatology 2010; **Med School:** NYU Sch Med 1989; **Resid:** Internal Medicine, Beth Israel Deaconess Med Ctr 1992; **Fellow:** Gastroenterology, UCSF Med Ctr 1994; Hepatology, UCSF Med Ctr 1995; **Fac Appt:** Prof Med, Columbia P&S

Cantor, Michael C MD (Ge) - **Spec Exp:** Colon Cancer; Hepatitis; Liver Disease; **Hospital:** NY-Presby/Weill Cornell Med Ctr, NY (page 102); **Address:** 310 E 72nd St Fl Level C, New York, NY 10021-4703; **Phone:** 212-472-3333; **Board Cert:** Internal Medicine 1985; Gastroenterology 1989; **Med School:** Columbia P&S 1982; **Resid:** Internal Medicine, New York Hosp 1985; **Fellow:** Gastroenterology, New York Hosp 1988; **Fac Appt:** Asst Clin Prof Med, Cornell Univ-Weill Med Coll

Carr-Locke, David L MD (Ge) - **Spec Exp:** Pancreatic/Biliary Endoscopy (ERCP); Pancreatic & Biliary Disease; Endoscopic Therapies; **Hospital:** Mt Sinai Beth Israel; **Address:** Mt Sinai Beth Israel, Gastroenterology, 10 Union Sq E, Ste 2G, New York, NY 10003; **Phone:** 212-420-4605; **Board Cert:** Internal Medicine 1974; **Med School:** England, UK 1972; **Resid:** Obstetrics & Gynecology, Orsett Hosp 1974; Internal Medicine, Leicester Hosp 1976; **Fellow:** Gastroenterology, Leicester Hosp 1978; Research, New Eng Baptist Hosp 1979; **Fac Appt:** Prof Med, Mount Sinai-Icahn Sch of Med

Chang, Peter K MD (Ge) - **Spec Exp:** Endoscopy; **Hospital:** Mt Sinai Hosp; **Address:** 1049 Park Ave, Ste 1C, New York, NY 10028; **Phone:** 212-427-9888; **Board Cert:** Internal Medicine 2013; Gastroenterology 2013; **Med School:** Mount Sinai Sch Med 1996; **Resid:** Internal Medicine, Mt Sinai Hosp 2000; **Fellow:** Gastroenterology, Mt Sinai Hosp 2003

Chapman, Mark L MD (Ge) - **Spec Exp:** Inflammatory Bowel Disease/Crohn's; Peptic Ulcer Disease; Gastrointestinal Motility Disorders; **Hospital:** Mt Sinai Hosp; **Address:** 12 E 86th St, Ste 4, New York, NY 10028; **Phone:** 212-861-2000; **Board Cert:** Internal Medicine 1968; Gastroenterology 1970; **Med School:** SUNY Downstate 1961; **Resid:** Internal Medicine, Montefiore Med Ctr 1963; Internal Medicine, Mt Sinai Hosp 1964; **Fellow:** Gastroenterology, Mt Sinai Hosp 1966; **Fac Appt:** Assoc Clin Prof Med, Mount Sinai Sch Med

Cohen, Jonathan MD (Ge) - **Spec Exp:** Pancreatic/Biliary Endoscopy (ERCP); Colonoscopy; Barrett's Esophagus; Gastrointestinal Cancer; **Hospital:** NYU Langone Med Ctr (page 104); **Address:** Concorde Med Grp, 232 E 30th St, New York, NY 10016; **Phone:** 212-889-5544; **Board Cert:** Gastroenterology 2005; **Med School:** Harvard Med Sch 1990; **Resid:** Internal Medicine, Beth Israel Deaconess Med Ctr 1993; **Fellow:** Gastroenterology, UCLA Med Ctr 1995; Endoscopy, Wellesley Hosp 1995; **Fac Appt:** Clin Prof Med, NYU Sch Med

Cohen, Seth A MD (Ge) - **Spec Exp:** Pancreatic/Biliary Endoscopy (ERCP); Colonoscopy; Endoscopy; **Hospital:** Mt Sinai Beth Israel, Lenox Hill Hosp; **Address:** 305 Second Ave, Lower Level Suite #3, New York, NY 10003; **Phone:** 212-734-8874; **Board Cert:** Internal Medicine 1989; Gastroenterology 2004; **Med School:** Columbia P&S 1986; **Resid:** Internal Medicine, Mount Sinai Med Ctr 1989; **Fellow:** Gastroenterology, St Luke's-Roosevelt Hosp Ctr 1991; Gastroenterology, Beth Israel Hosp 1992

Connor, Bradley A MD (Ge) - **Spec Exp:** Travel Medicine; Parasitic Infections; Diarrheal Diseases; Tropical Diseases; **Hospital:** NY-Presby/Weill Cornell Med Ctr, NY (page 102); **Address:** 50 E 69th St, New York, NY 10021; **Phone:** 212-988-2800; **Board Cert:** Internal Medicine 1982; Gastroenterology 1985; **Med School:** Univ Tex SW, Dallas 1978; **Resid:** Internal Medicine, UT Hlth Sci Ctr-Bexar Co/A Murphy VA Hosps 1981; **Fellow:** Gastroenterology, NY-Presby/Weill Cornell Med Ctr 1984; **Fac Appt:** Clin Prof Med, Cornell Univ-Weill Med Coll

Cooper, Robert B MD (Ge) - **Spec Exp:** Colon Cancer Screening; Gastroesophageal Reflux Disease (GERD); Celiac Disease; Gallbladder Disease; **Hospital:** NY-Presby/Weill Cornell Med Ctr, NY (page 102); **Address:** 635 Madison Ave Fl 17, New York, NY 10022; **Phone:** 212-717-4967; **Board Cert:** Internal Medicine 1984; Gastroenterology 1989; **Med School:** Cornell Univ-Weill Med Coll 1981; **Resid:** Internal Medicine, NY Hosp/Weill Cornell Med Ctr 1984; **Fellow:** Gastroenterology, NY Hosp/Weill Cornell Med Ctr 1987; **Fac Appt:** Asst Clin Prof Med, Cornell Univ-Weill Med Coll

Dieterich, Douglas T MD (Ge) - **Spec Exp:** Hepatitis; AIDS/HIV-Gastrointestinal Complications; Liver Disease; Endoscopy; **Hospital:** Mt Sinai Hosp; **Address:** 5 E 98th St Fl 11, New York, NY 10029; **Phone:** 212-241-7270; **Board Cert:** Internal Medicine 1981; Gastroenterology 1987; **Med School:** NYU Sch Med 1978; **Resid:** Internal Medicine, Bellevue Hosp Ctr 1981; **Fellow:** Gastroenterology, Bellevue Hosp Ctr 1983; **Fac Appt:** Prof Med, Mount Sinai Sch Med

Faust, Michael J MD (Ge) - **Spec Exp:** Gastrointestinal Disorders; **Hospital:** NYU Langone Med Ctr (page 104); **Address:** 345 E 37th St, Ste 207, New York, NY 10016-3256; **Phone:** 212-986-3330; **Board Cert:** Internal Medicine 1981; Gastroenterology 1983; **Med School:** NYU Sch Med 1978; **Resid:** Internal Medicine, Bellevue Hosp/NYU Med Ctr 1981; **Fellow:** Gastroenterology, Bellevue Hosp 1983; **Fac Appt:** Asst Clin Prof Med, NYU Sch Med

Ferran, Elena N MD (Ge) - **Spec Exp:** Colonoscopy; Endoscopy; Irritable Bowel Syndrome; Liver Disease; **Hospital:** NYU Langone Med Ctr (page 104); **Address:** NYU-Tisch Ctr for Womens Hlth, 207 E 84th St Fl 2, New York, NY 10128; **Phone:** 646-754-3300; **Board Cert:** Gastroenterology 2008; **Med School:** Italy 1988; **Resid:** Internal Medicine, St Vincent's Hosp 1995; **Fellow:** Gastroenterology, St Vincent's Hosp 1997; Hepatology, Mt Sinai Hosp 1998

Fochios, Steven E MD (Ge) - **Spec Exp:** Endoscopy; **Hospital:** Lenox Hill Hosp; **Address:** 117 E 65th St, New York, NY 10065; **Phone:** 212-861-4278; **Board Cert:** Internal Medicine 1980; Gastroenterology 1985; **Med School:** Geo Wash Univ 1976; **Resid:** Internal Medicine, Lenox Hill Hosp 1979; **Fellow:** Gastroenterology, Lenox Hill Hosp 1981

Foong, Anthony MD (Ge) - **Spec Exp:** Endoscopy; Colonoscopy; Gastrointestinal Disorders; Hemorrhoids; **Hospital:** Mt Sinai Beth Israel; **Address:** 210 Canal St, Ste 601, New York, NY 10013; **Phone:** 212-693-2100; **Board Cert:** Internal Medicine 1984; Gastroenterology 1987; **Med School:** Tufts Univ 1981; **Resid:** Internal Medicine, Univ MD Hosp 1984; **Fellow:** Gastroenterology, St Luke's-Roosevelt Hosp Ctr 1986

Frank, Michael S MD (Ge) - **Spec Exp:** Inflammatory Bowel Disease/Crohn's; Colonoscopy; Endoscopy; **Hospital:** Lenox Hill Hosp; **Address:** 9 E 63rd St, New York, NY 10065; **Phone:** 212-593-7170; **Board Cert:** Internal Medicine 1977; Gastroenterology 1979; **Med School:** Albert Einstein Coll Med 1974; **Resid:** Internal Medicine, Bronx Municipal Hosps 1977; **Fellow:** Gastroenterology, Montefiore Med Ctr 1979; **Fac Appt:** Assoc Clin Prof Med, NYU Sch Med

Freiman, Hal MD (Ge) - **Spec Exp:** Gastroesophageal Reflux Disease (GERD); Colon Cancer Screening; Irritable Bowel Syndrome; Hepatitis; **Hospital:** Mt Sinai Beth Israel, NYU Langone Med Ctr (page 104); **Address:** 59 W 12th St, Ste 1D, New York, NY 10011-8520; **Phone:** 212-206-0074; **Board Cert:** Internal Medicine 1981; Gastroenterology 1983; **Med School:** Albany Med Coll 1978; **Resid:** Internal Medicine, St Vincent's Hosp 1981; **Fellow:** Gastroenterology, Westchester Co Med Ctr 1983

Friedlander, Charles N MD (Ge) - **Spec Exp:** Colonoscopy; Irritable Bowel Syndrome; **Hospital:** NYU Langone Med Ctr (page 104); **Address:** Concorde Med Grp, 232 E 30th St, New York, NY 10016-8202; **Phone:** 212-889-5544 x169; **Board Cert:** Internal Medicine 1974; Gastroenterology 1977; **Med School:** SUNY Downstate 1968; **Resid:** Internal Medicine, Bellevue Hosp 1974; **Fellow:** Gastroenterology, NYU Med Ctr 1976; **Fac Appt:** Assoc Prof Med, NYU Sch Med

Gerdes, Hans MD (Ge) - **Spec Exp:** Endoscopy; Endoscopic Ultrasound; Barrett's Esophagus; Gastrointestinal Cancer; **Hospital:** Meml Sloan Kettering Canc Ctr (page 110); **Address:** MSKCC, Gastroenterology, 1275 York Ave, New York, NY 10065; **Phone:** 212-639-7108; **Board Cert:** Internal Medicine 1987; Gastroenterology 1989; **Med School:** Cornell Univ-Weill Med Coll 1983; **Resid:** Internal Medicine, NY-Presby/Weill Cornell Med Ctr 1986; **Fellow:** Gastroenterology, Meml Sloan-Kettering Cancer Ctr 1989; **Fac Appt:** Prof Med, Cornell Univ-Weill Med Coll

Gerson, Charles MD (Ge) - **Spec Exp:** Irritable Bowel Syndrome; Diarrheal Diseases; **Hospital:** Mt Sinai Hosp; **Address:** 80 Central Park West, Ste B, New York, NY 10023-5204; **Phone:** 212-496-6161; **Board Cert:** Internal Medicine 1970; Gastroenterology 1972; **Med School:** SUNY Downstate 1962; **Resid:** Internal Medicine, Bellevue Hosp 1964; Internal Medicine, Mount Sinai Hosp 1965; **Fellow:** Gastroenterology, Bellevue Hosp 1968; Gastroenterology, Mount Sinai Hosp 1969; **Fac Appt:** Clin Prof Med, Mount Sinai Sch Med

Goldberg, Myron D MD (Ge) - **Spec Exp:** Colon Cancer Screening; Colonoscopy; Endoscopy; Hepatitis B & C; **Hospital:** Lenox Hill Hosp, NYU Langone Med Ctr (page 104); **Address:** 110 E 59th St, Ste 10C, New York, NY 10022-1304; **Phone:** 212-583-2900; **Board Cert:** Internal Medicine 1977; Gastroenterology 1979; **Med School:** Albert Einstein Coll Med 1971; **Resid:** Internal Medicine, Montefiore Med Ctr 1973; Internal Medicine, Lenox Hill Hosp 1974; **Fellow:** Gastroenterology, Columbia-Presby Hosp 1977; Gastroenterology, Lenox Hill Hosp 1978; **Fac Appt:** Asst Clin Prof Med, NYU Sch Med

Goldin, Howard MD (Ge) - **Spec Exp:** Inflammatory Bowel Disease/Crohn's; Endoscopy; Liver Disease; **Hospital:** NY-Presby/Weill Cornell Med Ctr, NY (page 102), Rockefeller Univ Hosp; **Address:** 646 Park Ave, New York, NY 10065; **Phone:** 212-249-0404; **Board Cert:** Internal Medicine 1968; Gastroenterology 1973; **Med School:** Cornell Univ-Weill Med Coll 1961; **Resid:** Internal Medicine, New York Hosp 1964; **Fellow:** Gastroenterology, New York Hosp 1966; **Fac Appt:** Clin Prof Med, Cornell Univ-Weill Med Coll

Green, Peter MD (Ge) - **Spec Exp:** Celiac Disease; Endoscopy; Colonoscopy; Malabsorption Syndrome; **Hospital:** NY-Presby/Columbia Univ Med Ctr, NY (page 102); **Address:** NY-Presby, Celiac Disease Ctr, 180 Fort Washington Ave, Ste 936, New York, NY 10032; **Phone:** 212-305-5590; **Med School:** Australia 1970; **Resid:** Internal Medicine, Royal Northshore Med Ctr 1974; **Fellow:** Gastroenterology, Beth Israel Deaconess Med Ctr 1976; Gastroenterology, NY-Presby/Columbia Univ Med Ctr 1977; **Fac Appt:** Prof Med, Columbia P&S

Gress, Frank G MD (Ge) - **Spec Exp:** Pancreatic/Biliary Endoscopy (ERCP); Pancreatic & Biliary Disease; Barrett's Esophagus; Endoscopic Ultrasound; **Hospital:** NY-Presby/Columbia Univ Med Ctr, NY (page 102); **Address:** CUMC, Digestive & Liver Diseases, 161 Fort Washington Ave, Ste 852A, New York, NY 10032; **Phone:** 212-305-1909; **Board Cert:** Gastroenterology 2012; **Med School:** Mount Sinai Sch Med 1988; **Resid:** Internal Medicine, Montefiore Med Ctr 1991; **Fellow:** Gastroenterology, Brooklyn Hosp Ctr 1993; Advanced Endoscopy, Indiana Univ Med Ctr 1994

Haber, Gregory B MD (Ge) - **Spec Exp:** Endoscopy; Pancreatic/Biliary Endoscopy (ERCP); Endoscopic Ultrasound; Barrett's Esophagus; **Hospital:** Lenox Hill Hosp; **Address:** Lenox Hill Hosp, Gastroenterology, 100 E 77th St Fl 2, New York, NY 10075; **Phone:** 212-434-6279; **Med School:** Univ Toronto 1970; **Resid:** Internal Medicine, Univ Toronto Med Ctr 1975; **Fellow:** Gastroenterology, Univ Toronto Med Ctr 1978

Hammerman, Hillel S MD (Ge) - **Spec Exp:** Swallowing Disorders; Liver Disease; Colonoscopy; **Hospital:** Lenox Hill Hosp; **Address:** 210 E 73rd St, Ste 1C, New York, NY 10021; **Phone:** 212-288-1030; **Board Cert:** Internal Medicine 1981; Gastroenterology 1983; **Med School:** Cornell Univ-Weill Med Coll 1978; **Resid:** Internal Medicine, Baltimore City Hosps 1981; **Fellow:** Gastroenterology, Lahey Clinic 1983

Harary, Albert M MD (Ge) - **Spec Exp:** Endoscopy & Colonoscopy; Gastroesophageal Reflux Disease (GERD); Swallowing Disorders; **Hospital:** Lenox Hill Hosp, NYU Langone Med Ctr (page 104); **Address:** 110 E 55th St, Fl 17, New York, NY 10022; **Phone:** 212-702-0123; **Board Cert:** Internal Medicine 1982; Gastroenterology 1985; **Med School:** Columbia P&S 1979; **Resid:** Internal Medicine, Univ Miami Affil Hosp 1982; **Fellow:** Gastroenterology, Univ Miami Affil Hosp 1984; **Fac Appt:** Asst Clin Prof Med, NYU Sch Med

Itzkowitz, Steven H MD (Ge) - **Spec Exp:** Colon & Rectal Cancer; Colon & Rectal Cancer Detection; Inflammatory Bowel Disease; Hereditary Cancer; **Hospital:** Mt Sinai Hosp; **Address:** Gastroenterology Faculty Practice Assocs, 5 E 98th St, Fl 11, New York, NY 10029; **Phone:** 212-241-4299; **Board Cert:** Internal Medicine 1982; Gastroenterology 1985; **Med School:** Mount Sinai Sch Med 1979; **Resid:** Internal Medicine, Bellevue Hosp/NYU Med Ctr 1982; **Fellow:** Gastroenterology, UCSF Med Ctr 1984; **Fac Appt:** Prof Med, Mount Sinai-Icahn Sch of Med

Jacobson, Ira M MD (Ge) - **Spec Exp:** Pancreatic/Biliary Endoscopy (ERCP); Hepatitis C; Inflammatory Bowel Disease; Liver Disease; **Hospital:** NY-Presby/Weill Cornell Med Ctr, NY (page 102); **Address:** Center for the Study of Hepatitis C, 1305 York Ave Fl 4, New York, NY 10021; **Phone:** 646-962-4040; **Board Cert:** Internal Medicine 1982; Gastroenterology 2009; Transplant Hepatology 2006; **Med School:** Columbia P&S 1979; **Resid:** Internal Medicine, UCSF Med Ctr 1982; **Fellow:** Gastroenterology, Mass Genl Hosp 1984; **Fac Appt:** Prof Med, Cornell Univ-Weill Med Coll

Jaffin, Barry W MD (Ge) - **Spec Exp:** Gastrointestinal Motility Disorders; Inflammatory Bowel Disease; **Hospital:** Mt Sinai Hosp; **Address:** 620 Columbus Ave, New York, NY 10024; **Phone:** 212-721-2600; **Board Cert:** Internal Medicine 1984; Gastroenterology 1987; **Med School:** Mount Sinai Sch Med 1981; **Resid:** Internal Medicine, Med Ctr Hosp 1984; **Fellow:** Gastroenterology, Boston Univ Med Ctr 1986; **Fac Appt:** Asst Clin Prof Med, Mount Sinai Sch Med

Janec, Eileen MD (Ge) - **Spec Exp:** Rectal Cancer; Gallbladder Disease; Irritable Bowel Syndrome; Endoscopy; **Hospital:** NYU Langone Med Ctr (page 104); **Address:** NYU, Gastroenterology, 160 E 34th St Fl 9, New York, NY 10016; **Phone:** 212-731-5678; **Board Cert:** Gastroenterology 2004; **Med School:** Dominica 1998; **Resid:** Internal Medicine, SUNY Hlth Sci Ctr 2001; **Fellow:** Gastroenterology, Univ Hosp-UMDNJ 2004; Advanced Endoscopy, Washington Univ Phys 2005; **Fac Appt:** Asst Prof Med, NYU Sch Med

Kahaleh, Michel MD (Ge) - **Spec Exp:** Pancreatic Disease; Pancreatic Cancer; **Hospital:** NY-Presby/Weill Cornell Med Ctr, NY (page 102); **Address:** 1305 York Ave Fl 4, New York, NY 10065; **Phone:** 646-962-4000; **Board Cert:** Internal Medicine 2009; Gastroenterology 2009; **Med School:** Belgium 1994; **Resid:** Internal Medicine, Univ Chicago Med Ctr 1999; **Fellow:** Gastroenterology, Esrasme Hosp/Univ Brussels; **Fac Appt:** Clin Prof Med, Cornell Univ-Weill Med Coll

Kairam, Indira R MD (Ge) - **Spec Exp:** Colon Cancer; Peptic Ulcer Disease; Hepatitis C; **Hospital:** Mt Sinai St. Luke's, Mt Sinai Roosevelt; **Address:** 945 West End Ave, Ste 1D, New York, NY 10025-3573; **Phone:** 212-865-7355; **Board Cert:** Internal Medicine 1978; **Med School:** India 1973; **Resid:** Internal Medicine, St Clare's Hosp 1978; **Fellow:** Gastroenterology, Lahey Clinic 1980

Kavaler, Leon MD (Ge) - **Hospital:** Mt Sinai Hosp; **Address:** 68 E 86th St, New York, NY 10028-1012; **Phone:** 212-535-1845; **Board Cert:** Gastroenterology 2007; **Med School:** SUNY Upstate Med Univ 1989; **Resid:** Internal Medicine, Mt Sinai Med Ctr 1993; **Fellow:** Gastroenterology, Mt Sinai Med Ctr 1995

Khodadadian, Shawn MD (Ge) - **Hospital:** Lenox Hill Hosp, NYU Langone Med Ctr (page 104); **Address:** Manhattan Gastroenterology, 170 E 78th St, New York, NY 10075; **Phone:** 212-427-8761; **Board Cert:** Internal Medicine 2007; Gastroenterology 2010; **Med School:** SUNY Stony Brook 2003; **Resid:** Internal Medicine, Lenox Hill Hosp 2007; **Fellow:** Gastroenterology, Lenox Hill Hosp 2010

Kim, Michelle K MD (Ge) - **Spec Exp:** Endoscopic Ultrasound; Endoscopy; Gastrointestinal Cancer; **Hospital:** Mt Sinai Hosp; **Address:** Mt Sinai Faculty Practice, 5 E 98th St Fl 11, Box 1069, New York, NY 10029; **Phone:** 212-241-4299; **Board Cert:** Gastroenterology 2005; **Med School:** Stanford Univ 1999; **Resid:** Internal Medicine, NY-Presby/Weill Cornell Med Ctr 2002; **Fellow:** Gastroenterology, NY-Presby/Weill Cornell Med Ctr 2005; **Fac Appt:** Asst Prof Med, Mount Sinai Sch Med

Kim-Schluger, Hyung Leona MD (Ge) - **Spec Exp:** Transplant Medicine-Liver; Liver Disease; Hepatitis C; **Hospital:** Mt Sinai Hosp; **Address:** 5 E 98 St, Fl 12, New York, NY 10029; **Phone:** 212-659-8031; **Board Cert:** Transplant Hepatology 2008; **Med School:** Columbia P&S 1988; **Resid:** Internal Medicine, NY-Presby/Columbia Univ Med Ctr 1991; **Fellow:** Gastroenterology, NY-Presby/Columbia Univ Med Ctr 1993; Transplant Hepatology, Mount Sinai Med Ctr 2008

Kimball, Annetta J MD (Ge) - **Spec Exp:** Hepatitis; Inflammatory Bowel Disease/Crohn's; Irritable Bowel Syndrome; **Hospital:** Mt Sinai Roosevelt; **Address:** 315 W 57th St, Ste 301, New York, NY 10019; **Phone:** 212-371-8900; **Board Cert:** Internal Medicine 1972; Gastroenterology 1973; **Med School:** Boston Univ 1968; **Resid:** Internal Medicine, Roosevelt Hosp 1970; Internal Medicine, Mount Sinai Hosp 1971; **Fellow:** Gastroenterology, Mount Sinai Hosp 1973; **Fac Appt:** Assoc Clin Prof Med, Columbia P&S

Knapp, Albert B MD (Ge) - **Spec Exp:** Colonoscopy/Polypectomy; Endoscopy; Liver Disease; Transplant Medicine-Liver; **Hospital:** NYU Langone Med Ctr (page 104), Lenox Hill Hosp; **Address:** 760 Park Ave, New York, NY 10021; **Phone:** 212-737-3446; **Board Cert:** Internal Medicine 1982; Gastroenterology 1987; **Med School:** Columbia P&S 1979; **Resid:** Internal Medicine, Montefiore Med Ctr 1982; **Fellow:** Gastroenterology, Brigham & Womens Hosp 1985; Virology, Pasteur Inst 1975; **Fac Appt:** Clin Prof Med, NYU Sch Med

Kornbluth, Arthur Asher MD (Ge) - **Spec Exp:** Ulcerative Colitis; Crohn's Disease; Colonoscopy; Inflammatory Bowel Disease; **Hospital:** Mt Sinai Hosp, Mt Sinai Beth Israel; **Address:** 1751 York Ave, New York, NY 10128; **Phone:** 212-369-2490; **Board Cert:** Internal Medicine 1987; Gastroenterology 2012; **Med School:** SUNY Hlth Sci Ctr 1984; **Resid:** Internal Medicine, Montefiore-Einstein Div Med Ctr 1988; **Fellow:** Gastroenterology, Mt Sinai Hosp 1990; **Fac Appt:** Clin Prof Med, SUNY Downstate

Kotler, Donald P MD (Ge) - **Spec Exp:** Esophageal Disorders; Nutrition & AIDS; Hepatitis; **Hospital:** Mt Sinai St. Luke's; **Address:** 1090 Amsterdam Ave Fl 4, New York, NY 10025; **Phone:** 212-961-5530; **Board Cert:** Internal Medicine 1976; Gastroenterology 1979; **Med School:** Albert Einstein Coll Med 1973; **Resid:** Internal Medicine, Bronx Muni Hosp 1976; **Fellow:** Gastroenterology, Hosp Univ Penn - UPHS 1978; **Fac Appt:** Prof Med, Columbia P&S

Krumholz, Michael MD (Ge) - **Spec Exp:** Colonoscopy; Colon Cancer Screening; **Hospital:** Lenox Hill Hosp, Mt Sinai Hosp; **Address:** 111 E 80th St, Ste 1C, New York, NY 10075; **Phone:** 212-734-5533; **Board Cert:** Internal Medicine 1983; Gastroenterology 1987; **Med School:** Mount Sinai Sch Med 1980; **Resid:** Internal Medicine, Beth Israel Hosp 1984; **Fellow:** Gastroenterology, Lenox Hill Hosp 1986

Kummer, Bart A MD (Ge) - **Spec Exp:** Colonoscopy; Endoscopy; **Hospital:** NYU Langone Med Ctr (page 104), NY-Presby/Lower Manhattan Hosp (page 102); **Address:** NYU Langone Trinity Ctr, 111 Broadway, Fl 2, New York, NY 10006; **Phone:** 212-263-9700; **Board Cert:** Internal Medicine 1982; Gastroenterology 1985; **Med School:** Cornell Univ-Weill Med Coll 1979; **Resid:** Internal Medicine, Harlem Hosp 1982; **Fellow:** Gastroenterology, St Luke's-Roosevelt Hosp Ctr 1985; **Fac Appt:** Asst Prof Med, NYU Sch Med

Kurtz, Robert C MD (Ge) - **Spec Exp:** Pancreatic Cancer (Familial); Gastrointestinal Cancer; Endoscopy; Biliary Disease; **Hospital:** Meml Sloan Kettering Canc Ctr (page 110); **Address:** MSKCC, Gastroenterology, 1275 York Ave, New York, NY 10065; **Phone:** 212-639-7620; **Board Cert:** Internal Medicine 1971; Gastroenterology 1977; **Med School:** Jefferson Med Coll 1968; **Resid:** Internal Medicine, Meml Sloan-Kettering Cancer Ctr 1971; **Fellow:** Gastroenterology, Meml Sloan-Kettering Cancer Ctr 1973; **Fac Appt:** Prof Med, Cornell Univ-Weill Med Coll

Lambroza, Arnon MD (Ge) - **Spec Exp:** Achalasia; Gastroesophageal Reflux Disease (GERD); Barrett's Esophagus; Swallowing Disorders; **Hospital:** NY-Presby/Weill Cornell Med Ctr, NY (page 102), Lenox Hill Hosp; **Address:** 1085 Park Ave, New York, NY 10128-0320; **Phone:** 212-517-7570; **Board Cert:** Internal Medicine 1987; Gastroenterology 2011; **Med School:** Albert Einstein Coll Med 1984; **Resid:** Internal Medicine, Hosp Univ Penn 1987; **Fellow:** Gastroenterology, New York Hosp 1990; **Fac Appt:** Assoc Clin Prof Med, Cornell Univ-Weill Med Coll

Lax, James D MD (Ge) - **Spec Exp:** Liver Disease; Gastroesophageal Reflux Disease (GERD); Barrett's Esophagus; Eosinophilic Esophagitis; **Hospital:** Mt Sinai Roosevelt, NY-Presby/Weill Cornell Med Ctr, NY (page 102); **Address:** 160 E 72nd St Fl Ground, New York, NY 10021-4364; **Phone:** 212-988-5740; **Board Cert:** Internal Medicine 1984; Gastroenterology 1987; **Med School:** NYU Sch Med 1981; **Resid:** Internal Medicine, St Luke's-Roosevelt Hosp Ctr 1984; **Fellow:** Gastroenterology, St Luke's-Roosevelt Hosp Ctr 1986; **Fac Appt:** Asst Clin Prof Med, Cornell Univ-Weill Med Coll

Lebwohl, Oscar MD (Ge) - **Spec Exp:** Endoscopy; Colonoscopy; Ulcerative Colitis; Gastrointestinal Cancer; **Hospital:** NY-Presby/Columbia Univ Med Ctr, NY (page 102); **Address:** NY-Presby, Gastroenterology, 161 Fort Washington Ave, rm 420, New York, NY 10032; **Phone:** 212-305-5363; **Board Cert:** Internal Medicine 1975; Gastroenterology 1977; **Med School:** Harvard Med Sch 1972; **Resid:** Internal Medicine, Mt Sinai Hosp 1975; **Fellow:** Gastroenterology, NY-Presby/Columbia Univ Med Ctr 1976; Hepatology, Mt Sinai Hosp 1977; **Fac Appt:** Prof Med, Columbia P&S

Lewis, Blair MD (Ge) - **Spec Exp:** Endoscopy; Capsule Endoscopy; **Hospital:** Mt Sinai Hosp; **Address:** 1067 5th Ave, New York, NY 10128-0101; **Phone:** 212-369-6600; **Board Cert:** Internal Medicine 1985; Gastroenterology 1987; **Med School:** Albert Einstein Coll Med 1982; **Resid:** Internal Medicine, Montefiore Med Ctr 1985; **Fellow:** Gastroenterology, Mt Sinai Med Ctr 1987; **Fac Appt:** Clin Prof Med, Mount Sinai Sch Med

Lightdale, Charles J MD (Ge) - **Spec Exp:** Barrett's Esophagus; Gastrointestinal Cancer; Endoscopic Ultrasound; **Hospital:** NY-Presby/Columbia Univ Med Ctr, NY (page 102); **Address:** NY-Presby, Gastroenterology, 161 Fort Washington Ave, rm 812, New York, NY 10032; **Phone:** 212-305-3423; **Board Cert:** Internal Medicine 1972; Gastroenterology 1973; **Med School:** Columbia P&S 1966; **Resid:** Internal Medicine, Yale-New Haven Hosp 1968; Internal Medicine, NY-Presby/Weill Cornell Med Ctr 1969; **Fellow:** Gastroenterology, NY-Presby/Weill Cornell Med Ctr 1973; Gastroenterology & Nutrition, Meml Sloan-Kettering Cancer Ctr 1973; **Fac Appt:** Prof Med, Columbia P&S

Loria, Jeffrey Michael MD (Ge) - **Hospital:** Lenox Hill Hosp; **Address:** 178 E 85th St, Fl 4, New York, NY 10028; **Phone:** 212-288-2278; **Board Cert:** Internal Medicine 2012; Gastroenterology 2005; **Med School:** NY Med Coll 1987; **Resid:** Internal Medicine, Lenox Hill Hosp 1991; **Fellow:** Gastroenterology, Elmhurst Hosp Ctr 1994

Lucak, Susan L MD (Ge) - **Spec Exp:** Irritable Bowel Syndrome; Liver Disease; **Hospital:** Lenox Hill Hosp; **Address:** 903 Park Ave, New York, NY 10075; **Phone:** 212-861-0481; **Board Cert:** Internal Medicine 1984; Gastroenterology 2011; **Med School:** Albert Einstein Coll Med 1981; **Resid:** Internal Medicine, Montefiore Med Ctr 1985; **Fellow:** Gastroenterology, Montefiore Med Ctr 1987; Research, Columbia Presby Med Ctr 1991

Lustbader, Ian J MD (Ge) - **Spec Exp:** Hepatitis C; Colonoscopy; Crohn's Disease; **Hospital:** NYU Langone Med Ctr (page 104); **Address:** 245 E 35th St Fl 1, New York, NY 10016-4283; **Phone:** 212-685-5252; **Board Cert:** Internal Medicine 1985; Gastroenterology 1987; **Med School:** Columbia P&S 1982; **Resid:** Internal Medicine, St Luke's-Roosevelt Hosp Ctr 1985; **Fellow:** Gastroenterology, Bellevue Hosp 1987; **Fac Appt:** Asst Prof Med, NYU Sch Med

Magun, Arthur M MD (Ge) - **Spec Exp:** Hepatitis; Ulcerative Colitis; Endoscopy; Crohn's Disease; **Hospital:** NY-Presby/Columbia Univ Med Ctr, NY (page 102); **Address:** NY-Presby, Gastroenterology, 161 Fort Washington Ave, New York, NY 10032; **Phone:** 212-305-5287; **Board Cert:** Internal Medicine 1980; Gastroenterology 1983; **Med School:** Mount Sinai Sch Med 1977; **Resid:** Internal Medicine, NY-Presby/Columbia Univ Med Ctr 1980; **Fellow:** Gastroenterology, NY-Presby/Columbia Univ Med Ctr 1983; **Fac Appt:** Prof Med, Columbia P&S

Marion, James F MD (Ge) - **Spec Exp:** Colonoscopy; Colitis; Crohn's Disease; **Hospital:** Mt Sinai Hosp; **Address:** 12 E 86th St, Ste 1, New York, NY 10028; **Phone:** 212-861-2000; **Board Cert:** Gastroenterology 2005; **Med School:** Columbia P&S 1989; **Resid:** Internal Medicine, NY Presby/Columbia Univ Med Ctr 1992; **Fellow:** Gastroenterology, Mt Sinai Hosp 1995; **Fac Appt:** Assoc Clin Prof Med, Mount Sinai Sch Med

Markowitz, Arnold J MD (Ge) - **Spec Exp:** Hereditary Cancer; Colon Cancer Screening; Gastrointestinal Cancer; **Hospital:** Meml Sloan Kettering Canc Ctr (page 110); **Address:** 1275 York Avenue, New York, NY 10065; **Phone:** 212-639-2901; **Board Cert:** Gastroenterology 2013; **Med School:** NYU Sch Med 1987; **Resid:** Internal Medicine, NYU Med Ctr 1990; **Fellow:** Gastroenterology, Univ MI Hosp 1992; Gastroenterology, Hosp Univ Penn 1994; **Fac Appt:** Clin Prof Med, Cornell Univ-Weill Med Coll

Markowitz, David D MD (Ge) - **Spec Exp:** Gastroesophageal Reflux Disease (GERD); Esophageal Disorders; **Hospital:** NY-Presby/Columbia Univ Med Ctr, NY (page 102); **Address:** 161 Ft Washington Ave, Ste 853, New York, NY 10032; **Phone:** 212-305-1024; **Board Cert:** Internal Medicine 1988; Gastroenterology 2011; **Med School:** Columbia P&S 1985; **Resid:** Internal Medicine, Presby/Columbia Univ Med Ctr 1988; **Fellow:** Gastroenterology, Presby/Columbia Univ Med Ctr 1991; **Fac Appt:** Assoc Prof Med, Columbia P&S

Marsh Jr, Franklin MD (Ge) - **Spec Exp:** Liver Disease; Endoscopy; Gastrointestinal Motility Disorders; Colon & Rectal Cancer; **Hospital:** NY-Presby/Weill Cornell Med Ctr, NY (page 102); **Address:** 342 E 67th St, Ste 1D, New York, NY 10065-6238; **Phone:** 212-288-8820; **Board Cert:** Internal Medicine 1981; Gastroenterology 1985; **Med School:** SUNY Buffalo 1978; **Resid:** Internal Medicine, Harlem Hosp 1982; **Fellow:** Gastroenterology, NY-Presby/Weill Cornell Med Ctr 1985

Milano, Andrew MD (Ge) - **Spec Exp:** Endoscopy; Inflammatory Bowel Disease/Crohn's; Esophageal Disorders; **Hospital:** NYU Langone Med Ctr (page 104); **Address:** NYU, Gastroenterology Dept, 530 1st Ave, Ste 4D, New York, NY 10016; **Phone:** 212-263-7483; **Board Cert:** Internal Medicine 1977; Gastroenterology 1972; **Med School:** NYU Sch Med 1964; **Resid:** Internal Medicine, Bellevue Hosp 1967; **Fellow:** Gastroenterology, Bellevue Hosp 1968; **Fac Appt:** Clin Prof Med, NYU Sch Med

Min, Albert D MD (Ge) - **Spec Exp:** Hepatitis B & C; Liver Disease; **Hospital:** Mt Sinai Beth Israel; **Address:** Mt Sinai Beth Israel Med Ctr, 10 Union Square E, Ste 2G, New York, NY 10003; **Phone:** 212-420-4751; **Board Cert:** Internal Medicine 1988; **Med School:** Univ Rochester 1985; **Resid:** Gastroenterology, SUNY Stony Brook 1988; **Fellow:** Hepatology, Montefiore Med Ctr 1991; **Fac Appt:** Assoc Clin Prof Med, Albert Einstein Coll Med

Miskovitz, Paul F MD (Ge) - **Spec Exp:** Endoscopy; Liver & Biliary Disease; Hepatitis; **Hospital:** NY-Presby/Weill Cornell Med Ctr, NY (page 102); **Address:** 635 Madison Ave, Fl 17, New York, NY 10022; **Phone:** 212-717-4966; **Board Cert:** Internal Medicine 1978; Gastroenterology 1981; **Med School:** Cornell Univ-Weill Med Coll 1975; **Resid:** Internal Medicine, NY-Presby/Columbia Univ Med Ctr 1978; **Fellow:** Gastroenterology, NY-Presby/Columbia Univ Med Ctr 1980; **Fac Appt:** Clin Prof Med, Cornell Univ-Weill Med Coll

Nagler, Jerry MD (Ge) - **Spec Exp:** Inflammatory Bowel Disease; Irritable Bowel Syndrome; **Hospital:** NY-Presby/Weill Cornell Med Ctr, NY (page 102); **Address:** 407 E 70th St Fl 5, New York, NY 10021-5302; **Phone:** 212-628-7777; **Board Cert:** Internal Medicine 1976; Gastroenterology 1983; **Med School:** Yale Univ 1973; **Resid:** Internal Medicine, NY-Presby/Columbia Univ Med Ctr 1976; **Fellow:** Gastroenterology, NY-Presby/Weill Cornell Med Ctr 1978; **Fac Appt:** Assoc Clin Prof Med, Cornell Univ-Weill Med Coll

Ottaviano, Lawrence MD (Ge) - **Spec Exp:** Peptic Ulcer Disease; Colitis; **Address:** 60 Gramercy Park N, Ste 1B, New York, NY 10010; **Phone:** 212-254-1220; **Board Cert:** Internal Medicine 1988; Gastroenterology 2006; **Med School:** Grenada 1984; **Resid:** Internal Medicine, Cabrini Med Ctr 1987; **Fellow:** Gastroenterology, Cabrini Med Ctr 1989; **Fac Appt:** Asst Clin Prof Med, NY Med Coll

Pochapin, Mark B MD (Ge) - **Spec Exp:** Pancreatic Cancer; Endoscopic Ultrasound; Colon & Rectal Cancer Detection; **Hospital:** NYU Langone Med Ctr (page 104); **Address:** NYU Med Ctr, Gastroenterology, 240 E 38th St Fl 23, New York, NY 10016; **Phone:** 212-263-3095; **Board Cert:** Gastroenterology 2004; **Med School:** Cornell Univ-Weill Med Coll 1988; **Resid:** Internal Medicine, NY-Presby/Weill Cornell Med Ctr 1991; **Fellow:** Gastroenterology, Montefiore Med Ctr 1993; **Fac Appt:** Prof Med, NYU Sch Med

Poneros, John M MD (Ge) - **Spec Exp:** Malabsorption Syndrome; Barrett's Esophagus; Pancreatic & Biliary Disease; **Hospital:** NY-Presby/Columbia Univ Med Ctr, NY (page 102); **Address:** Gastroenterology Assocs, 161 Fort Washington Ave, Ste 862, New York, NY 10032; **Phone:** 212-305-1021; **Board Cert:** Gastroenterology 2011; **Med School:** Columbia P&S 1995; **Resid:** Internal Medicine, NY-Presby/Columbia Univ Med Ctr 1998; **Fellow:** Gastroenterology, Mass Genl Hosp 2001; Advanced Endoscopy, Brigham & Womens Hosp 2002

Rieber, Jonathan M MD (Ge) - **Spec Exp:** Gastroesophageal Reflux Disease (GERD); Inflammatory Bowel Disease; Colonoscopy; **Hospital:** NY-Presby Hosp/The Allen Hosp (page 102), Lawrence Hosp Ctr (page 102); **Address:** 5030 Broadway, Ste 707, New York, NY 10034; **Phone:** 718-412-3445; **Board Cert:** Internal Medicine 2008; Gastroenterology 2010; **Med School:** NY Med Coll 1994; **Resid:** Internal Medicine, NY-Presby/Columbia Med Ctr 1997; **Fellow:** Gastroenterology, NYU Med Ctr 2000; **Fac Appt:** Asst Clin Prof Med, Columbia P&S

Robbins, David H MD (Ge) - **Spec Exp:** Endoscopy; Gastrointestinal Cancer; Colon Cancer Screening; Therapeutic Endoscopy; **Hospital:** Lenox Hill Hosp, Mt Sinai Beth Israel; **Address:** Lenox Hill Hosp, Div Gastroenterology, 100 E 77th St, Lachman, rm 2, New York, NY 10075; **Phone:** 212-434-3427; **Board Cert:** Internal Medicine 2003; Gastroenterology 2005; **Med School:** Mount Sinai Sch Med 1999; **Resid:** Internal Medicine, Hosp Univ Penn 2001; **Fellow:** Gastroenterology, Med Univ S Caroline 2004; **Fac Appt:** Asst Prof Med, Mount Sinai Sch Med

Robilotti Jr, James G MD (Ge) - **Spec Exp:** Irritable Bowel Syndrome; Peptic Ulcer Disease; Gastroesophageal Reflux Disease (GERD); Colon Cancer Screening; **Hospital:** Mt Sinai Beth Israel; **Address:** 29 Washington Sq West, New York, NY 10011-9180; **Phone:** 212-475-4030; **Board Cert:** Internal Medicine 1972; Gastroenterology 1981; **Med School:** UMDNJ-NJ Med Sch, Newark 1965; **Resid:** Internal Medicine, St Vincent's Hosp 1968; **Fellow:** Gastroenterology, St Vincent's Hosp 1970; **Fac Appt:** Assoc Clin Prof Med, NY Med Coll

Romeu, Jose N MD (Ge) - **Spec Exp:** Colonoscopy/Polypectomy; Colonoscopy; Gastrointestinal Cancer; Gastroesophageal Reflux Disease (GERD); **Hospital:** Mt Sinai Hosp, Lenox Hill Hosp; **Address:** 65 E 96th St, New York, NY 10128-0145; **Phone:** 212-534-6747; **Board Cert:** Internal Medicine 1973; Gastroenterology 1975; **Med School:** NYU Sch Med 1970; **Resid:** Internal Medicine, Mt Sinai Hosp 1973; **Fellow:** Gastroenterology, Mt Sinai Hosp 1976; **Fac Appt:** Asst Prof Med, Mount Sinai Sch Med

Rubin, Moshe MD (Ge) - **Spec Exp:** Enteroscopy-Small Bowel; Colonoscopy; Celiac Disease; Inflammatory Bowel Disease; **Hospital:** NY-Presby/Weill Cornell Med Ctr, NY (page 102), NY Hosp Queens (page 498); **Address:** 1020 Park Ave, Fl 1, New York, NY 10028; **Phone:** 212-772-1012; **Board Cert:** Internal Medicine 1986; Gastroenterology 1989; **Med School:** Yale Univ 1983; **Resid:** Internal Medicine, New York Hosp 1986; **Fellow:** Gastroenterology, Columbia-Presby Hosp 1988; **Fac Appt:** Assoc Prof Med, Cornell Univ-Weill Med Coll

Ruoff, Michael MD (Ge) - **Spec Exp:** Esophageal Disorders; Malabsorption; **Hospital:** NYU Langone Med Ctr (page 104); **Address:** Concorde Med Grp, 232 E 30th St Fl 1, New York, NY 10016-8202; **Phone:** 212-889-5544 x145; **Board Cert:** Internal Medicine 1980; Gastroenterology 1972; **Med School:** NYU Sch Med 1963; **Resid:** Internal Medicine, Bellevue Hosp 1966; **Fellow:** Gastroenterology, NYU Med Ctr 1967; **Fac Appt:** Clin Prof Med, NYU Sch Med

Salik, James M MD (Ge) - **Spec Exp:** Colonoscopy; Liver Disease; Inflammatory Bowel Disease; **Hospital:** NYU Langone Med Ctr (page 104); **Address:** Concorde Med Grp, 232 E 30th St, New York, NY 10016; **Phone:** 212-889-5544 x145; **Board Cert:** Internal Medicine 1983; Gastroenterology 1985; **Med School:** NYU Sch Med 1980; **Resid:** Internal Medicine, Bellevue Hosp 1983; **Fellow:** Gastroenterology, Bellevue Hosp 1985; **Fac Appt:** Asst Prof Med, NYU Sch Med

Scherl, Ellen MD (Ge) - **Spec Exp:** Inflammatory Bowel Disease; Crohn's Disease; Ulcerative Colitis; **Hospital:** NY-Presby/Weill Cornell Med Ctr, NY (page 102); **Address:** NY-Presby, IBD Ctr, 1315 York Ave, New York, NY 10021; **Phone:** 212-746-5077; **Board Cert:** Internal Medicine 1983; **Med School:** NY Med Coll 1977; **Resid:** Internal Medicine, Beth Israel Med Ctr 1981; **Fellow:** Gastroenterology, Mt Sinai Hosp 1983; **Fac Appt:** Prof Med, Cornell Univ-Weill Med Coll

Schiano, Thomas D MD (Ge) - **Spec Exp:** Liver Disease; Transplant Medicine-Bowel; Hepatitis; Portal Hypertension; **Hospital:** Mt Sinai Hosp; **Address:** Mt Sinai Med Ctr, Liver Diseases, 5 E 98th St, Fl 12, New York, NY 10029; **Phone:** 212-241-8035; **Board Cert:** Transplant Hepatology 2006; Gastroenterology 2005; **Med School:** Mexico 1987; **Resid:** Internal Medicine, Maimonides Med Ctr 1992; Gastroenterology, Temple Univ Hosp 1995; **Fellow:** Nutrition, Meml Sloan-Kettering Cancer Ctr 1993; Hepatology, Mt Sinai Med Ctr 1996; **Fac Appt:** Prof Med, Mount Sinai-Icahn Sch of Med

Schmerin, Michael J MD (Ge) - **Spec Exp:** Colonoscopy; Gastroscopy; Gastroesophageal Reflux Disease (GERD); **Hospital:** NY-Presby/Weill Cornell Med Ctr, NY (page 102), Lenox Hill Hosp; **Address:** 1060 Park Ave, Ste 1G, New York, NY 10128-1095; **Phone:** 212-348-3166; **Board Cert:** Internal Medicine 1976; Gastroenterology 1977; **Med School:** Jefferson Med Coll 1973; **Resid:** Internal Medicine, NY-Presby/Weill Cornell Med Ctr 1976; **Fellow:** Gastroenterology, NY-Presby/Weill Cornell Med Ctr 1977; **Fac Appt:** Asst Clin Prof Med, Cornell Univ-Weill Med Coll

Schneebaum, Cary MD (Ge) - **Spec Exp:** Colon Cancer Screening; Endoscopy; **Hospital:** Mt Sinai Beth Israel; **Address:** 155 5th Ave, Fl 2, New York, NY 10010; **Phone:** 212-741-6100; **Board Cert:** Internal Medicine 1984; **Med School:** SUNY Hlth Sci Ctr 1981; **Resid:** Internal Medicine, Beth Israel Med Ctr 1984; **Fellow:** Gastroenterology, Beth Israel Med Ctr 1986

Schneider, Lewis P MD (Ge) - **Spec Exp:** Colon Cancer; Gastroesophageal Reflux Disease (GERD); Colon & Rectal Cancer; Capsule Endoscopy; **Hospital:** NY-Presby/Columbia Univ Med Ctr, NY (page 102); **Address:** 51 W 51 St, Ste 360, New York, NY 10019; **Phone:** 212-326-8426; **Board Cert:** Internal Medicine 1981; **Med School:** SUNY Downstate 1978; **Resid:** Internal Medicine, Columbia-Presby Hosp 1981; **Fellow:** Gastroenterology, Columbia-Presby Hosp 1983; **Fac Appt:** Asst Clin Prof Med, Columbia P&S

Sherman, Alex MD (Ge) - **Spec Exp:** Liver Disease; Hepatitis; Endoscopy; Pancreatic/Biliary Endoscopy (ERCP); **Hospital:** NYU Langone Med Ctr (page 104); **Address:** Concorde Medical Group, 232 E 30th St, New York, NY 10016-8202; **Phone:** 212-889-5544; **Board Cert:** Internal Medicine 1986; Gastroenterology 1989; **Med School:** NYU Sch Med 1983; **Resid:** Internal Medicine, Bronx Municipal Hosp 1986; **Fellow:** Gastroenterology, NYU Med Ctr 1989; **Fac Appt:** Assoc Clin Prof Med, NYU Sch Med

Shike, Moshe MD (Ge) - **Spec Exp:** Gastrointestinal Cancer; Nutrition & Cancer Prevention; Endoscopy; **Hospital:** Meml Sloan Kettering Canc Ctr (page 110); **Address:** MSKCC, Gastroenterology, 1275 York Ave, Ste 6, New York, NY 10065; **Phone:** 212-639-7230; **Board Cert:** Internal Medicine 1977; Gastroenterology 1981; **Med School:** Israel 1974; **Resid:** Internal Medicine, Mt Auburn Hosp 1977; **Fellow:** Gastroenterology, Toronto Genl Hosp 1981; **Fac Appt:** Prof Med, Cornell Univ-Weill Med Coll

Solny, Meyer N MD (Ge) - **Spec Exp:** Endoscopy; Colonoscopy; Gastroesophageal Reflux Disease (GERD); **Hospital:** NY-Presby/Weill Cornell Med Ctr, NY (page 102), Lenox Hill Hosp; **Address:** 1 E 68th St, Ste 1E, New York, NY 10065; **Phone:** 212-570-6945; **Board Cert:** Internal Medicine 1977; Gastroenterology 1979; **Med School:** Columbia P&S 1974; **Resid:** Internal Medicine, NY Presby Hosp/Cornell 1977; **Fellow:** Gastroenterology, NY Presby Hosp/Cornell 1979

Starpoli, Anthony A MD (Ge) - **Spec Exp:** Gastroesophageal Reflux Disease (GERD); **Hospital:** Lenox Hill Hosp, NYU Langone Med Ctr (page 104); **Address:** 80 5th Ave, Ste 1605, New York, NY 10011; **Phone:** 212-673-2721; **Board Cert:** Internal Medicine 1989; **Med School:** Univ IL Coll Med 1986; **Resid:** Internal Medicine, Sound Shore Med Ctr 1989; **Fellow:** Gastroenterology, St Vincents Hosp 1991; **Fac Appt:** Asst Clin Prof Med, NY Med Coll

Stein, Jeffrey A MD (Ge) - **Spec Exp:** Gallbladder Disease; Pancreatic Disease; Liver Disease; **Hospital:** NY-Presby/Columbia Univ Med Ctr, NY (page 102); **Address:** 161 Ft Washington Ave, Ste 937, New York, NY 10032; **Phone:** 212-305-5444; **Board Cert:** Internal Medicine 1971; Gastroenterology 1973; **Med School:** Harvard Med Sch 1965; **Resid:** Internal Medicine, Presbyterian Hosp 1968; **Fellow:** Gastroenterology, Presbyterian Hosp 1971; **Fac Appt:** Clin Prof Med, Columbia P&S

Tobias, Hillel MD (Ge) - **Spec Exp:** Liver Disease; Hepatitis B & C; Liver & Biliary Disease; **Hospital:** NYU Langone Med Ctr (page 104); **Address:** 232 E 30th St, New York, NY 10016-8202; **Phone:** 212-889-5544; **Board Cert:** Internal Medicine 1967; Gastroenterology 1979; Transplant Hepatology 2006; **Med School:** Washington Univ, St Louis 1960; **Resid:** Internal Medicine, Bellevue Hosp Ctr 1963; Hepatology, Royal Free Hosp 1965; **Fellow:** Hepatology, Mt Sinai Hosp 1967; **Fac Appt:** Prof Med, NYU Sch Med

Traube, Morris MD (Ge) - **Spec Exp:** Esophageal Disorders; Swallowing Disorders; Gastroesophageal Reflux Disease (GERD); Endoscopy & Colonoscopy; **Hospital:** NYU Langone Med Ctr (page 104); **Address:** Ambulatory Care Ctr-West Side, 355 W 52nd St Fl 6, New York, NY 10019; **Phone:** 646-754-2100; **Board Cert:** Internal Medicine 1981; Gastroenterology 1983; **Med School:** SUNY Downstate 1978; **Resid:** Internal Medicine, Maimonides Med Ctr 1981; **Fellow:** Gastroenterology, Yale-New Haven Hosp 1984; **Fac Appt:** Prof Med, Yale Univ

Ullman, Thomas A MD (Ge) - **Spec Exp:** Irritable Bowel Syndrome; Ulcerative Colitis; Inflammatory Bowel Disease/Crohn's; Colon & Rectal Cancer; **Hospital:** Mt Sinai Hosp; **Address:** Mt Sinai Hosp, Gastroenterology, 5 E 98th St Fl 11, New York, NY 10028; **Phone:** 212-241-4299; **Board Cert:** Gastroenterology 2009; **Med School:** Cornell Univ-Weill Med Coll 1992; **Resid:** Internal Medicine, NY-Presby/Weill Cornell Med Ctr 1995; **Fellow:** Gastroenterology, Yale-New Haven Hosp 1999; **Fac Appt:** Assoc Prof Med, Mount Sinai-Icahn Sch of Med

Wang, Timothy C MD (Ge) - **Spec Exp:** Gastrointestinal Cancer; **Hospital:** NY-Presby/Columbia Univ Med Ctr, NY (page 102); **Address:** Gastroenterology Assocs, 161 Fort Washington Ave, Ste 862, New York, NY 10032; **Phone:** 212-305-1021; **Board Cert:** Internal Medicine 1986; Gastroenterology 1989; **Med School:** Columbia P&S 1983; **Resid:** Internal Medicine, Barnes Jewish Hosp 1986; **Fellow:** Gastroenterology, Mass General Hosp 1989; Research, Harvard Medical School 1989; **Fac Appt:** Prof Med, Columbia P&S

Waye, Jerome D MD (Ge) - **Spec Exp:** Endoscopy; Colon Cancer; Colonoscopy; **Hospital:** Mt Sinai Hosp, Lenox Hill Hosp; **Address:** 650 Park Ave, New York, NY 10065; **Phone:** 212-439-7779; **Board Cert:** Internal Medicine 1965; Gastroenterology 1970; **Med School:** Boston Univ 1958; **Resid:** Internal Medicine, Mt Sinai Hosp 1961; **Fellow:** Gastroenterology, Mt Sinai Hosp 1962; **Fac Appt:** Clin Prof Med, Mount Sinai-Icahn Sch of Med

Weiss, Robert A MD (Ge) - **Spec Exp:** Colon Cancer; Gastroesophageal Reflux Disease (GERD); Endoscopy; **Hospital:** Mt Sinai Beth Israel; **Address:** 380 2nd Ave, Ste 1004, New York, NY 10010; **Phone:** 212-473-4100; **Board Cert:** Internal Medicine 1987; Gastroenterology 1989; **Med School:** Mount Sinai Sch Med 1983; **Resid:** Internal Medicine, Beth Israel Med Ctr 1986; **Fellow:** Gastroenterology, Elmhurst Hosp Ctr-Mt Sinai 1988; **Fac Appt:** Asst Clin Prof Med, Albert Einstein Coll Med

Zlatanic, Jusuf MD (Ge) - **Spec Exp:** Endoscopy; **Hospital:** Lenox Hill Hosp; **Address:** The Endoscopy Suite, 132 E 76th St, Ste 2G, New York, NY 10021; **Phone:** 212-794-0833; **Board Cert:** Internal Medicine 2004; Gastroenterology 2007; **Med School:** Serbia 1989; **Resid:** Internal Medicine, Lenox Hill Hosp 1994; **Fellow:** Gastroenterology, Lenox Hill Hosp 1997

Geriatric Medicine

Adelman, Ronald D MD (Ger) - **Spec Exp:** Geriatric Care; Palliative Care; Preventive Medicine; **Hospital:** NY-Presby/Weill Cornell Med Ctr, NY (page 102); **Address:** Irving Sherwood Wright Ctr on Aging, 1484-1486 1st Ave, New York, NY 10075; **Phone:** 212-746-7000; **Board Cert:** Internal Medicine 1982; Geriatric Medicine 2009; Hospice & Palliative Medicine 2012; **Med School:** Albert Einstein Coll Med 1978; **Resid:** Internal Medicine, Montefiore Med Ctr 1982; **Fac Appt:** Prof Med, Cornell Univ

Babitz, Lisa E MD (Ger) *PCP* - **Spec Exp:** Geriatric Medicine; **Hospital:** Mt Sinai Roosevelt; **Address:** 457 W 57th St, New York, NY 10019; **Phone:** 212-265-1471; **Board Cert:** Internal Medicine 1984; **Med School:** Yale Univ 1981; **Resid:** Internal Medicine, Yale-New Haven Hosp 1984; **Fellow:** Geriatric Medicine, NYU Med Ctr 1986; **Fac Appt:** Assoc Clin Prof Med, Columbia P&S

Bradley, Sara MD (Ger) *PCP* - **Spec Exp:** Alzheimer's Disease; Dementia; Frail Elderly; Depression; **Hospital:** Mt Sinai Hosp; **Address:** Martha Stewart Center for Living, 1440 Madison Ave, New York, NY 10029; **Phone:** 212-659-8552; **Board Cert:** Internal Medicine 2005; Geriatric Medicine 2008; **Med School:** Univ Pittsburgh 2002; **Resid:** Internal Medicine, Mt Sinai Hosp 2005; **Fellow:** Geriatric Medicine, Mt Sinai Hosp 2008; **Fac Appt:** Asst Prof Med, Mount Sinai-Icahn Sch of Med

Callahan, Eileen H MD (Ger) - **Spec Exp:** Frail Elderly; Preventive Medicine; Dementia; Alzheimer's Disease; **Hospital:** Mt Sinai Hosp; **Address:** Martha Stewart Center for Living, 1440 Madison Ave, New York, NY 10029; **Phone:** 212-659-8552; **Board Cert:** Internal Medicine 2004; Geriatric Medicine 2008; **Med School:** UMDNJ-NJ Med Sch, Newark 1991; **Resid:** Internal Medicine, St Vincents Hosp 1995; **Fellow:** Geriatric Medicine, Mt Sinai Med Ctr 1997; **Fac Appt:** Assoc Prof Med, Mount Sinai-Icahn Sch of Med

Chang, Christine MD (Ger) *PCP* - **Spec Exp:** Alzheimer's Disease; Dementia; **Hospital:** Mt Sinai Hosp; **Address:** Martha Stewart Ctr for Living Mt Sinai, 1440 Madison Ave Fl 1, New York, NY 10029; **Phone:** 212-659-8552; **Board Cert:** Internal Medicine 2008; Geriatric Medicine 2010; **Med School:** Duke Univ 1995; **Resid:** Internal Medicine, Univ Pitt Hlth Sys 1998; **Fellow:** Geriatric Medicine, Johns Hopkins Hosp 2000; **Fac Appt:** Asst Prof Med, Mount Sinai Sch Med

Chun, Audrey K MD (Ger) *PCP* - **Spec Exp:** Dementia; Depression; Preventive Medicine; **Hospital:** Mt Sinai Hosp; **Address:** Martha Stewart Ctr for Living at Mt Sinai, 1440 Madison Ave, New York, NY 10029; **Phone:** 212-659-8552; **Board Cert:** Geriatric Medicine 2012; Internal Medicine 2013; **Med School:** Baylor Coll Med 1998; **Resid:** Internal Medicine, Baylor Med Ctr 2001; **Fellow:** Geriatric Medicine, Mt Sinai Med Ctr 2003; **Fac Appt:** Asst Prof Med, Mount Sinai-Icahn Sch of Med

Feher, Laszlo A DO (Ger) *PCP* - **Spec Exp:** Preventive Medicine; **Hospital:** NYU Langone Med Ctr (page 104); **Address:** 251 E 33rd St, Ste 2S, New York, NY 10016; **Phone:** 212-686-4212; **Board Cert:** Internal Medicine 2007; Geriatric Medicine 2008; **Med School:** NY Coll Osteo Med 1993; **Resid:** Internal Medicine, St Lukes Roosevelt Hosp 1996; **Fellow:** Geriatric Medicine, Bellevue Hosp Ctr 1998

Finkelstein, Martin S MD (Ger) - **Spec Exp:** Geriatric Care; Preventive Medicine; **Hospital:** NYU Langone Med Ctr (page 104); **Address:** 314 E 30th St, New York, NY 10016-6402; **Phone:** 646-370-2000; **Board Cert:** Internal Medicine 1970; **Med School:** NYU Sch Med 1964; **Resid:** Internal Medicine, Bellevue Hosp 1966; Internal Medicine, Stanford Univ Med Ctr 1967; **Fellow:** Infectious Disease, Stanford Univ Med Ctr 1968; **Fac Appt:** Assoc Clin Prof Med, NYU Sch Med

Fogel, Joyce F MD (Ger) *PCP* - **Spec Exp:** Memory Disorders; Geriatric Functional Assessment; Preventive Medicine; **Hospital:** Mt Sinai Beth Israel-BK; **Address:** 275 8th Ave, New York, NY 10011-8305; **Phone:** 212-463-0101; **Board Cert:** Internal Medicine 1985; Geriatric Medicine 2011; **Med School:** SUNY Downstate 1982; **Resid:** Internal Medicine, Kings Co Hosp 1985; **Fellow:** Geriatric Medicine, Bellevue/NYU Med Ctr 1989; **Fac Appt:** Assoc Clin Prof Med, NY Med Coll

Karp, Adam H MD (Ger) *PCP* - **Spec Exp:** Falls in the Elderly; Geriatric Care; Preventive Medicine; **Hospital:** NYU Hosp For Joint Dis (page 104), NYU Langone Med Ctr (page 104); **Address:** 301 E 17th St, rm 208A, New York, NY 10003; **Phone:** 212-598-6738; **Board Cert:** Internal Medicine 2010; Geriatric Medicine 2012; **Med School:** Albert Einstein Coll Med 1987; **Resid:** Internal Medicine, Maimonides Med Ctr 1990; **Fellow:** Geriatric Medicine, Bellevue Hosp/NYU 1992; **Fac Appt:** Asst Clin Prof Med, NYU Sch Med

Korc-Grodzicki, Beatriz MD/PhD (Ger) - **Spec Exp:** Alzheimer's Disease; Preventive Medicine; Cancer in the Elderly; **Hospital:** Meml Sloan Kettering Canc Ctr (page 110); **Address:** Meml Sloan Kettering Cancer Ctr, 1275 York Ave, New York, NY 10065; **Phone:** 646-888-3154; **Board Cert:** Internal Medicine 2007; Geriatric Medicine 2012; **Med School:** Uruguay 1983; **Resid:** Internal Medicine, Univ Rochester Med Ctr 1997; **Fellow:** Geriatric Medicine, Univ Rochester Med Ctr 2002; **Fac Appt:** Assoc Prof Med, Mount Sinai Sch Med

Lachs, Mark S MD (Ger) - **Spec Exp:** Abuse/Neglect; **Hospital:** NY-Presby/Weill Cornell Med Ctr, NY (page 102); **Address:** Irving Sherwood Wright Med Ctr on Aging, 1484 First Ave, New York, NY 10075; **Phone:** 212-746-7000; **Board Cert:** Internal Medicine 1988; Geriatric Medicine 2012; **Med School:** NYU Sch Med 1985; **Resid:** Internal Medicine, Hosp Univ Penn - UPHS 1988; **Fellow:** Geriatric Medicine, Yale-New Haven Hosp 1990; **Fac Appt:** Prof Med, Cornell Univ-Weill Med Coll

Leipzig, Rosanne M MD (Ger) *PCP* - **Spec Exp:** Medications in the Elderly; Alzheimer's Disease; Dementia; **Hospital:** Mt Sinai Hosp; **Address:** Martha Stewart Center for Living, 1440 Madison Ave, New York, NY 10029; **Phone:** 212-689-8552; **Board Cert:** Internal Medicine 1982; Geriatric Medicine 2008; Hospice & Palliative Medicine 2012; **Med School:** Univ Mich Med Sch 1978; **Resid:** Internal Medicine, Strong Meml Hosp 1982; **Fellow:** Clinical Pharmacology, New York Hosp 1985; **Fac Appt:** Prof Med, Mount Sinai Sch Med

Morrison, R. Sean MD (Ger) - **Spec Exp:** Palliative Care; Alzheimer's Disease; Dementia; Frail Elderly; **Hospital:** Mt Sinai Hosp; **Address:** Martha Stewart Center for Living, 1440 Madison Ave, New York, NY 10029; **Phone:** 212-659-8552; **Board Cert:** Internal Medicine 2014; Geriatric Medicine 2006; Hospice & Palliative Medicine 2008; **Med School:** Univ Chicago-Pritzker Sch Med 1990; **Resid:** Internal Medicine, NY-Presby/Weill Cornell Med Ctr 1993; **Fellow:** Geriatric Medicine, Mt Sinai Med Ctr 1996; **Fac Appt:** Prof Med, Mount Sinai-Icahn Sch of Med

Peterson, Monte H MD (Ger) *PCP* - **Spec Exp:** Geriatric Functional Assessment; Dementia; Frail Elderly; **Hospital:** Mt Sinai Beth Israel; **Address:** Beth Israel Senior Health Ctr, 275 8th Ave, New York, NY 10011; **Phone:** 212-463-0101; **Board Cert:** Internal Medicine 1982; Geriatric Medicine 2009; **Med School:** Univ Iowa Coll Med 1979; **Resid:** Internal Medicine, UCSF/San Joaquin Vly Hosp 1982; **Fellow:** Geriatric Medicine, NY Presby-Cornell Med Ctr 1983; Geriatric Medicine, Mt Sinai Med Ctr 1984; **Fac Appt:** Asst Prof Med, Albert Einstein Coll Med

Raman, Bharathi MD (Ger) - **Spec Exp:** Long Term Care; Palliative Care; **Hospital:** NY-Presby/Weill Cornell Med Ctr, NY (page 102); **Address:** Irving Sherwood Wright Ctr on Aging, 1484-1486 1st Ave, New York, NY 10075; **Phone:** 212-746-7000; **Board Cert:** Internal Medicine 1988; Geriatric Medicine 2011; Hospice & Palliative Medicine 2012; **Med School:** India 1977; **Resid:** Internal Medicine, Woodhull Med & Mental Hlth Ctr 1988; **Fellow:** Geriatric Medicine, Mt Sinai Med Ctr 1990; **Fac Appt:** Asst Prof Med, Cornell Univ-Weill Med Coll

Siegler, Eugenia L MD (Ger) *PCP* - **Spec Exp:** Dementia; Geriatric Care; **Hospital:** NY-Presby/Weill Cornell Med Ctr, NY (page 102); **Address:** Irving Sherwood Wright Ctr on Aging, 1484-1486 First Ave, New York, NY 10075; **Phone:** 212-746-7000; **Board Cert:** Internal Medicine 1986; Geriatric Medicine 2010; **Med School:** Johns Hopkins Univ 1983; **Resid:** Internal Medicine, Bellevue Hosp 1986; **Fellow:** Geriatric Medicine, Hosp Univ Penn 1989; **Fac Appt:** Assoc Prof Med, Cornell Univ-Weill Med Coll

Geriatric Psychiatry

Devanand, Davangere P MD (GerPsy) - **Spec Exp:** Memory Disorders; Alzheimer's Disease; Depression; Cognitive Loss in Aging; **Hospital:** NY State Psychiatric Inst, NY-Presby/Columbia Univ Med Ctr, NY (page 102); **Address:** NYS Psychiatric Inst, 1051 Riverside Dr, Unit 126, New York, NY 10032; **Phone:** 646-774-8658; **Board Cert:** Psychiatry 1985; Geriatric Psychiatry 2010; **Med School:** India 1979; **Resid:** Psychiatry, SUNY Upstate Med Ctr 1982; Psychiatry, Yale-New Haven Hosp 1984; **Fellow:** Biological Psychiatry, NY-Presby/Columbia Univ Med Ctr 1985; **Fac Appt:** Prof Psyc, Columbia P&S

Lantz, Melinda S MD (GerPsy) - **Spec Exp:** Dementia; Anxiety & Depression; Complementary Medicine; Palliative Care; **Hospital:** Mt Sinai Beth Israel; **Address:** Beth Israel Med Ctr, 1st Ave at 16th St, Bernstein Pavilion, rm 6K40, New York, NY 10003; **Phone:** 212-420-2457; **Board Cert:** Psychiatry 1991; Addiction Psychiatry 2003; Geriatric Psychiatry 2004; **Med School:** Rutgers R W Johnson Med Sch 1986; **Resid:** Psychiatry, Long Island Jewish Med Ctr 1989; **Fac Appt:** Assoc Prof Psyc, Albert Einstein Coll Med

Reisberg, Barry MD (GerPsy) - **Spec Exp:** Alzheimer's Disease; Behavioral Problems & Dementia; Cognitive Loss in Aging; Depression; **Hospital:** NYU Langone Med Ctr (page 104); **Address:** NYU Med Ctr, Psychiatry, 145 E 32nd St, Ste 508, New York, NY 10016; **Phone:** 212-263-8550; **Board Cert:** Psychiatry 1976; Geriatric Psychiatry 2012; **Med School:** NY Med Coll 1972; **Resid:** Psychiatry, Metropolitan Hosp 1975; **Fellow:** Psychiatric Research, Univ London 1975; **Fac Appt:** Prof Psyc, NYU Sch Med

Serby, Michael J MD (GerPsy) - **Spec Exp:** Alzheimer's Disease; Depression; Parkinson's Disease; **Hospital:** Mt Sinai Beth Israel; **Address:** 317 E 17th St, Fl 9, New York, NY 10003; **Phone:** 212-420-2421; **Board Cert:** Psychiatry 1979; Geriatric Psychiatry 2010; **Med School:** Emory Univ 1969; **Resid:** Psychiatry, Bellevue Hosp-NYU 1976; **Fac Appt:** Clin Prof Psyc, Albert Einstein Coll Med

Gynecologic Oncology

Abu-Rustum, Nadeem R MD (GO) - **Spec Exp:** Ovarian Cancer; Uterine Cancer; Cervical Cancer; Vulvar Disease/Cancer; **Hospital:** Meml Sloan Kettering Canc Ctr (page 110); **Address:** MSKCC, Gyn Oncology, 160 E 53rd St, New York, NY 10019; **Phone:** 646-497-9055; **Board Cert:** Obstetrics & Gynecology 2013; Gynecologic Oncology 2013; **Med School:** Lebanon 1990; **Resid:** Obstetrics & Gynecology, Greater Baltimore Med Ctr 1994; **Fellow:** Gynecologic Oncology, Meml Sloan-Kettering Cancer Ctr 1997; **Fac Appt:** Prof ObG, Cornell Univ-Weill Med Coll

Anderson, Lisa L MD (GO) - **Spec Exp:** Gynecologic Cancer; Trophoblastic Tumors; Cervical Dysplasia in HIV-Positive; Gynecologic Surgery-Complex; **Hospital:** Mt Sinai Roosevelt; **Address:** 425 W 59th St, Ste 9B, New York, NY 10019; **Phone:** 212-523-7752; **Board Cert:** Obstetrics & Gynecology 2013; Gynecologic Oncology 2013; **Med School:** Italy 1980; **Resid:** Obstetrics & Gynecology, Montefiore/JacobiMed Ctrs 1986; **Fellow:** Gynecologic Oncology, Brigham & Women's Hosp 1991; **Fac Appt:** Asst Clin Prof ObG, Columbia P&S

Barakat, Richard R MD (GO) - **Spec Exp:** Robotic Surgery; Ovarian Cancer; Uterine Cancer; Cervical Cancer; **Hospital:** Meml Sloan Kettering Canc Ctr (page 110); **Address:** MSKCC, Gyn Oncology, 160 E 53rd St, New York, NY 10019; **Phone:** 646-497-9055; **Board Cert:** Obstetrics & Gynecology 2013; Gynecologic Oncology 2013; **Med School:** SUNY Hlth Sci Ctr 1985; **Resid:** Obstetrics & Gynecology, Bellevue Hosp 1989; **Fellow:** Gynecologic Oncology, Meml Sloan-Kettering Cancer Ctr 1991; **Fac Appt:** Prof ObG, Cornell Univ-Weill Med Coll

Blank, Stephanie V MD (GO) - **Spec Exp:** Gynecologic Cancer; **Hospital:** NYU Langone Med Ctr (page 104); **Address:** NYU, Clin Cancer Ctr, 240 E 38th St Fl 19, New York, NY 10016; **Phone:** 212-731-5705; **Board Cert:** Obstetrics & Gynecology 2013; Gynecologic Oncology 2013; **Med School:** UCSD 1994; **Resid:** Obstetrics & Gynecology, NY-Presby/Weill Cornell Med Ctr 1998; **Fellow:** Gynecologic Oncology, Hosp Univ Penn 2001; **Fac Appt:** Assoc Prof NuM, NYU Sch Med

Brown, Carol L MD (GO) - **Spec Exp:** Ovarian Cancer; Cervical Cancer; Uterine Cancer; Laparoscopic Surgery; **Hospital:** Meml Sloan Kettering Canc Ctr (page 110); **Address:** 1275 York Ave, rm H1311, New York, NY 10065; **Phone:** 212-639-7659; **Board Cert:** Obstetrics & Gynecology 2013; Gynecologic Oncology 2013; **Med School:** Columbia P&S 1986; **Resid:** Obstetrics & Gynecology, Hosp Univ Penn 1990; **Fellow:** Gynecologic Oncology, Meml Sloan Kettering Cancer Ctr 1992; Research, Meml Sloan Kettering Cancer Ctr 1994; **Fac Appt:** Asst Prof ObG, Cornell Univ-Weill Med Coll

Burke, William M MD (GO) - **Spec Exp:** Gynecologic Cancer; Minimally Invasive Surgery; Robotic Surgery; Ovarian Cancer-Advanced; **Hospital:** NY-Presby/Columbia Univ Med Ctr, NY (page 102); **Address:** Columbia Ob/Gyn, 161 Fort Washington Ave, Ste 837, New York, NY 10032; **Phone:** 212-305-3410; **Board Cert:** Obstetrics & Gynecology 2013; Gynecologic Oncology 2013; **Med School:** Columbia P&S 1996; **Resid:** Obstetrics & Gynecology, Columbia-Presby Med Ctr 2000; **Fellow:** Gynecologic Oncology, Univ Michigan 2003; **Fac Appt:** Asst Clin Prof ObG, Columbia P&S

Caputo, Thomas A MD (GO) - **Spec Exp:** Cervical Cancer; Ovarian Cancer; Uterine Cancer; Vulvar Disease/Cancer; **Hospital:** NY-Presby/Weill Cornell Med Ctr, NY (page 102); **Address:** NY-Presby, Gyn Oncology, 525 E 68th St, Ste J130, New York, NY 10021; **Phone:** 212-746-3179; **Board Cert:** Obstetrics & Gynecology 1993; Gynecologic Oncology 1977; **Med School:** UMDNJ-NJ Med Sch, Newark 1965; **Resid:** Obstetrics & Gynecology, Martland Hosp 1969; **Fellow:** Gynecologic Oncology, Emory Univ Hosp 1975; **Fac Appt:** Prof ObG, Cornell Univ-Weill Med Coll

Chi, Dennis S MD (GO) - **Spec Exp:** Ovarian Cancer; Uterine Cancer; Cervical Cancer; Gynecologic Surgery-Complex; **Hospital:** Meml Sloan Kettering Canc Ctr (page 110); **Address:** MSKCC, Gyn Oncology, 1275 York Ave, New York, NY 10065; **Phone:** 212-639-5016; **Board Cert:** Obstetrics & Gynecology 2013; Gynecologic Oncology 2013; **Med School:** NYU Sch Med 1990; **Resid:** Obstetrics & Gynecology, NYU Med Ctr 1994; **Fellow:** Gynecologic Oncology, Meml Sloan Kettering Cancer Ctr 1997; **Fac Appt:** Prof ObG, Cornell Univ-Weill Med Coll

Curtin, John P MD (GO) - **Spec Exp:** Uterine Cancer; Ovarian Cancer; Laparoscopic Surgery; Gestational Trophoblastic Disease; **Hospital:** NYU Langone Med Ctr (page 104); **Address:** NYU, Clin Cancer Ctr, 240 E 38th St, Fl 19, New York, NY 10016; **Phone:** 212-731-5345; **Board Cert:** Obstetrics & Gynecology 2013; Gynecologic Oncology 2013; **Med School:** Creighton Univ 1979; **Resid:** Obstetrics & Gynecology, Univ Minn Med Ctr 1984; **Fellow:** Gynecologic Oncology, Meml Sloan-Kettering Cancer Ctr 1988; **Fac Appt:** Prof ObG, NYU Sch Med

Dottino, Peter R MD (GO) - **Spec Exp:** Laparoscopic Surgery; Gynecologic Cancer; Uterine Cancer; Ovarian Cancer; **Hospital:** Mt Sinai Hosp, Maimonides Med Ctr (page 98); **Address:** 800A 5th Ave, Ste 405, New York, NY 10065; **Phone:** 212-888-8439; **Board Cert:** Obstetrics & Gynecology 2013; Gynecologic Oncology 2013; **Med School:** Georgetown Univ 1979; **Resid:** Obstetrics & Gynecology, SUNY Downstate Med Ctr 1983; **Fellow:** Gynecologic Oncology, Mt Sinai Hosp 1986; **Fac Appt:** Assoc Clin Prof ObG, Mount Sinai-Icahn Sch of Med

Fishman, David A MD (GO) - **Spec Exp:** Gynecologic Cancer; Ovarian Cancer-Early Detection; Minimally Invasive Surgery; **Hospital:** Mt Sinai Hosp; **Address:** Ruttenberg Treatment Ctr, 1470 Madison Ave Fl 3, New York, NY 10029; **Phone:** 212-241-1111; **Board Cert:** Obstetrics & Gynecology 2013; Gynecologic Oncology 2013; **Med School:** Texas Tech Univ 1988; **Resid:** Obstetrics & Gynecology, Yale-New Haven Hosp 1992; **Fellow:** Gynecologic Oncology, Yale-New Haven Hosp 1994; **Fac Appt:** Prof ObG, Mount Sinai-Icahn Sch of Med

Holcomb, Kevin M MD (GO) - **Spec Exp:** Robotic Surgery; Laparoscopic Surgery; Ovarian Cancer; **Hospital:** NY-Presby/Weill Cornell Med Ctr, NY (page 102); **Address:** Weill Cornell Med Ctr, Div Gyn Oncology, 525 E 68th St, Ste J 130, New York, NY 10065; **Phone:** 212-746-7553; **Board Cert:** Obstetrics & Gynecology 2013; Gynecologic Oncology 2013; **Med School:** NY Med Coll 1992; **Resid:** Obstetrics & Gynecology, NY-Presby/Weill Cornell Med Ctr 1996; **Fellow:** Gynecologic Oncology, SUNY Downstate Med Ctr 1999; **Fac Appt:** Assoc Clin Prof ObG, Cornell Univ-Weill Med Coll

Koulos, John P MD (GO) - **Spec Exp:** Uterine Cancer; Ovarian Cancer; Cervical Cancer; Vulvar & Vaginal Cancer; **Hospital:** Mt Sinai Beth Israel; **Address:** BIMC, Cancer Ctr, 10 Union Square E, Ste 4C, New York, NY 10003; **Phone:** 212-844-5729; **Board Cert:** Obstetrics & Gynecology 2013; Gynecologic Oncology 2013; **Med School:** Northwestern Univ 1978; **Resid:** Obstetrics & Gynecology, Northwestern Meml Hosp 1982; **Fellow:** Gynecologic Oncology, Meml Sloan-Kettering Cancer Ctr 1984

Lallas, Thomas A MD (GO) - **Spec Exp:** Gynecologic Cancers; **Hospital:** Lenox Hill Hosp, NY-Presby/Weill Cornell Med Ctr, NY (page 102); **Address:** 877 Park Ave, New York, NY 10075; **Phone:** 212-838-0886; **Board Cert:** Obstetrics & Gynecology 2013; Gynecologic Oncology 2013; **Med School:** Univ VA Sch Med 1992; **Resid:** Obstetrics & Gynecology, Lenox Hill Hosp 1996; **Fellow:** Gynecologic Oncology, Univ Iowa Hosps 1999; **Fac Appt:** Asst Clin Prof ObG, Cornell Univ-Weill Med Coll

Nagarsheth, Nimesh MD (GO) - **Spec Exp:** Cervical Cancer; Ovarian Cancer; Uterine Cancer; Vaginal Cancer; **Hospital:** Mt Sinai Hosp, Englewood Hosp & Med Ctr; **Address:** Ruttenberg Treatment Ctr, 1470 Madison Ave Fl 3, New York, NY 10029; **Phone:** 212-241-1111; **Board Cert:** Obstetrics & Gynecology 2013; Gynecologic Oncology 2013; **Med School:** Mount Sinai Sch Med 1997; **Resid:** Obstetrics & Gynecology, Duke Univ Hosp 1997; **Fellow:** Gynecologic Oncology, Mt Sinai Hosp 2004; **Fac Appt:** Assoc Prof ObG, Mount Sinai-Icahn Sch of Med

Pothuri, Bhavana MD (GO) - **Spec Exp:** Gynecologic Cancers; Minimally Invasive Gynecologic Surgery; Fertility Preservation in Cancer; **Hospital:** NYU Langone Med Ctr (page 104); **Address:** 240 E 38th St Fl 19, New York, NY 10016; **Phone:** 212-731-6455; **Board Cert:** Obstetrics & Gynecology 2013; Gynecologic Oncology 2013; **Med School:** Jefferson Med Coll 1995; **Resid:** Obstetrics & Gynecology, Lankenau Hosp 1999; **Fellow:** Gynecologic Oncology, Meml Sloan Kettering Cancer Ctr 2003; **Fac Appt:** Assoc Prof ObG, NYU Sch Med

Poynor, Elizabeth A MD/PhD (GO) - **Spec Exp:** Gynecologic Cancer; Gynecologic Surgery-Complex; Laparoscopic Surgery; Breast Cancer; **Hospital:** Lenox Hill Hosp, Meml Sloan Kettering Canc Ctr (page 110); **Address:** 1050 5th Ave, New York, NY 10028; **Phone:** 212-426-2700; **Board Cert:** Obstetrics & Gynecology 2013; Gynecologic Oncology 2013; **Med School:** Columbia P&S 1988; **Resid:** Obstetrics & Gynecology, Hosp Univ Penn 1992; **Fellow:** Gynecologic Oncology, Meml Sloan-Kettering Cancer Ctr 1995

Rahaman, Jamal MD (GO) - **Spec Exp:** Robotic Surgery; Minimally Invasive Gynecologic Surgery; Gynecologic Cancer-Rare; Gynecologic Surgery-Complex; **Hospital:** Mt Sinai Hosp; **Address:** 1136 5th Ave, Ste 1B, New York, NY 10128; **Phone:** 212-427-1415; **Board Cert:** Obstetrics & Gynecology 2013; Gynecologic Oncology 2013; **Med School:** Jamaica 1984; **Resid:** Obstetrics & Gynecology, Lincoln Med Ctr 1991; Obstetrics & Gynecology, Mt Sinai Hosp 1993; **Fellow:** Cardiovascular Surgery, Texas Heart Inst 1990; Gynecologic Oncology, Mt Sinai Hosp 1995; **Fac Appt:** Assoc Clin Prof ObG, Mount Sinai-Icahn Sch of Med

Sonoda, Yukio MD (GO) - **Spec Exp:** Laparoscopic Surgery; Fertility Preservation in Cancer; Uterine Cancer; **Hospital:** Meml Sloan Kettering Canc Ctr (page 110); **Address:** 1275 York Ave, Ste H1307, New York, NY 10065; **Phone:** 212-639-6450; **Board Cert:** Obstetrics & Gynecology 2013; Gynecologic Oncology 2013; **Med School:** Geo Wash Univ 1992; **Resid:** Obstetrics & Gynecology, SUNY Buffalo 1997; **Fellow:** Gynecologic Oncology, Meml Sloan Kettering Cancer Ctr 2000; Laparoscopic Surgery, Hosp Edouard Herriot 2001

Wallach, Robert C MD (GO) - **Spec Exp:** Vulvar & Vaginal Cancer; Ovarian Cancer; Cervical Cancer; Peritoneal Carcinomatosis; **Hospital:** NYU Langone Med Ctr (page 104), Bellevue Hosp Ctr; **Address:** 240 E 38th St Fl 19th, New York, NY 10016; **Phone:** 212-731-6450; **Board Cert:** Obstetrics & Gynecology 1967; Gynecologic Oncology 1974; **Med School:** Yale Univ 1960; **Resid:** Obstetrics & Gynecology, Beth Israel Med Ctr 1965; **Fellow:** Gynecologic Oncology, SUNY Downstate Med Ctr 1966; **Fac Appt:** Prof ObG, NYU Sch Med

Wright, Jason MD (GO) - **Spec Exp:** Gynecologic Cancer; Gynecologic Surgery; Ovarian Cancer; Uterine Cancer; **Hospital:** NY-Presby/Columbia Univ Med Ctr, NY (page 102); **Address:** Herbert Irving Pav, Gynecologic Oncology, 161 Fort Washington Ave Fl 8 - rm 837, New York, NY 10032; **Phone:** 212-305-3410; **Board Cert:** Obstetrics & Gynecology 2012; Gynecologic Oncology 2012; **Med School:** Univ MO-Kansas City 1999; **Resid:** Obstetrics & Gynecology, Barnes-Jewish Hosp 2003; **Fellow:** Gynecologic Oncology, Barnes-Jewish Hosp 2006

Zakashansky, Konstantin MD (GO) - **Spec Exp:** HPV-Human Papilloma Virus; Hysterectomy Alternatives; Robotic Surgery; **Hospital:** Mt Sinai Hosp, Lutheran Med Ctr - Brooklyn; **Address:** Ruttenberg Treatment Ctr, 1470 Madison Ave, New York, NY 10029; **Phone:** 212-241-1111; **Board Cert:** Obstetrics & Gynecology 2013; Gynecologic Oncology 2013; **Med School:** SUNY Stony Brook 2000; **Resid:** Obstetrics & Gynecology, Beth Israel Med Ctr 2004; **Fellow:** Gynecologic Oncology, Mt Sinai Med Ctr 2007; **Fac Appt:** Assoc Prof ObG, Mount Sinai Sch Med

Hand Surgery

Athanasian, Edward A MD (HS) - **Spec Exp:** Bone & Soft Tissue Tumors; Hand & Upper Extremity Tumors; Limb Surgery/Reconstruction; **Hospital:** Hosp For Special Surgery (page 109), Meml Sloan Kettering Canc Ctr (page 110); **Address:** 523 E 72nd St Fl 4, New York, NY 10021; **Phone:** 212-606-1962; **Board Cert:** Orthopaedic Surgery 2008; Hand Surgery 2008; **Med School:** Columbia P&S 1988; **Resid:** Surgery, Beth Israel Deaconess Med Ctr 1989; Orthopaedic Surgery, Hosp Special Surgery 1993; **Fellow:** Hand Surgery, Mayo Clin 1994; Orthopaedic Oncology, Meml Sloan-Kettering Cancer Ctr 1995; **Fac Appt:** Assoc Clin Prof OrS, Cornell Univ-Weill Med Coll

Barron Jr, Otis A MD (HS) - **Spec Exp:** Carpal Tunnel Syndrome; Elbow Surgery; Nerve & Tendon Reconstruction; **Hospital:** Mt Sinai Roosevelt; **Address:** CV Starr Hand Surgery Ctr, 1000 10th Ave Fl 3rd, New York, NY 10019; **Phone:** 212-523-7590; **Board Cert:** Orthopaedic Surgery 2009; Hand Surgery 2009; **Med School:** Tulane Univ 1989; **Resid:** Surgery, Tulane Univ Affil Hosps 1994; **Fellow:** Shoulder Surgery, Columbia Presby Hosp 1995; Hand Surgery, St Lukes Roosevelt Hosp 1996; **Fac Appt:** Asst Clin Prof S, Columbia P&S

Beldner, Steven MD (HS) - **Spec Exp:** Elbow Surgery; Hand & Wrist Surgery; **Hospital:** Mt Sinai Beth Israel, Mt Sinai St. Luke's; **Address:** Hand Surgery Ctr, 321 E 34th St, New York, NY 10016; **Phone:** 212-340-0000; **Board Cert:** Orthopaedic Surgery 2010; Hand Surgery 2010; **Med School:** UMDNJ-NJ Med Sch, Newark 1991; **Resid:** Orthopaedic Surgery, NYU-Bellevue Hosp 1996; **Fellow:** Hand Surgery, NYU Med Ctr 1997; **Fac Appt:** Asst Prof OrS, Albert Einstein Coll Med

Botwinick, Nelson G MD (HS) - **Spec Exp:** Trauma; Carpal Tunnel Syndrome; Arthritis Hand Surgery; **Hospital:** NY-Presby/Lower Manhattan Hosp (page 102); **Address:** NY Downtown Ortho Assocs, 170 William St Fl 8, New York, NY 10038; **Phone:** 212-312-5598; **Board Cert:** Orthopaedic Surgery 2009; Hand Surgery 2009; **Med School:** NYU Sch Med 1980; **Resid:** Orthopaedic Surgery, NYU Med Ctr 1985; **Fellow:** Orthopaedic Surgery, NYU Med Ctr 1986; **Fac Appt:** Assoc Clin Prof OrS, NYU Sch Med

Carlson, Michelle G MD (HS) - **Spec Exp:** Sports Injuries; Hand & Upper Extremity Surgery; Arthritis; Pediatric Hand Surgery; **Hospital:** Hosp For Special Surgery (page 109), NY-Presby/Weill Cornell Med Ctr, NY (page 102); **Address:** 523 E 72nd St Fl 4 - rm 408, New York, NY 10021; **Phone:** 212-606-1546; **Board Cert:** Orthopaedic Surgery 2007; Hand Surgery 2007; **Med School:** Cornell Univ 1987; **Resid:** Orthopaedic Surgery, Hosp Special Surg 1992; **Fellow:** Hand Surgery, Hosp Special Surg 1993; **Fac Appt:** Assoc Clin Prof OrS, Cornell Univ-Weill Med Coll

Catalano III, Louis W MD (HS) - **Spec Exp:** Hand & Upper Extremity Surgery; Wrist Surgery; Rotator Cuff Surgery; **Hospital:** Mt Sinai Roosevelt; **Address:** 1000 10th Ave, Fl 3rd, New York, NY 10019; **Phone:** 212-523-7590; **Board Cert:** Orthopaedic Surgery 2014; Hand Surgery 2014; **Med School:** NYU Sch Med 1994; **Resid:** Surgery, Barnes Jewish Hosp 1995; Orthopaedic Surgery, Barnes Jewish Hosp 1999; **Fellow:** Hand Surgery, St. Lukes Roosevelt Hosp 2000; **Fac Appt:** Asst Clin Prof OrS, Columbia P&S

Daluiski, Aaron MD (HS) - **Spec Exp:** Pediatric Hand Surgery; Elbow Surgery; Fractures; **Hospital:** Hosp For Special Surgery (page 109), NY-Presby/Weill Cornell Med Ctr, NY (page 102); **Address:** 523 E 72nd St Fl 4, New York, NY 10021; **Phone:** 212-606-1284; **Board Cert:** Orthopaedic Surgery 2005; Hand Surgery 2006; **Med School:** UCLA 1994; **Resid:** Orthopaedic Surgery, UCLA Med Ctr 2000; **Fellow:** Orthopaedic Research, UCLA School of Med 2001; Hand & Microvascular Surgery, Hosp Special Surgery 2006; **Fac Appt:** Asst Prof OrS, Cornell Univ-Weill Med Coll

Gilbert, Richard S MD (HS) - **Spec Exp:** Hand & Wrist Surgery; Elbow Surgery; Arthroscopic Surgery; **Hospital:** Mt Sinai Hosp; **Address:** Manhattan Orthopedic & Sports Medicine Grp, 1065 Park Ave Fl 2, New York, NY 10128; **Phone:** 212-289-0700; **Board Cert:** Orthopaedic Surgery 2013; Hand Surgery 2013; **Med School:** Mount Sinai Sch Med 1993; **Resid:** Orthopaedic Surgery, Mt Sinai Med Ctr 1999; **Fellow:** Hand Surgery, Yale-New Haven Hosp 2000; **Fac Appt:** Asst Clin Prof OrS, Mount Sinai Sch Med

Glickel, Steven Z MD (HS) - **Spec Exp:** Hand & Wrist Surgery; Elbow Surgery; Peripheral Nerve Surgery; **Hospital:** Mt Sinai Roosevelt; **Address:** CV Starr Hand Surgery Ctr, 1000 10th Ave Fl 3, New York, NY 10019; **Phone:** 212-523-7590; **Board Cert:** Orthopaedic Surgery 1985; Hand Surgery 2010; **Med School:** Harvard Med Sch 1976; **Resid:** Surgery, NY-Presby/Columbia Univ Med Ctr 1978; Orthopaedic Surgery, Brigham & Womens Hosp 1981; **Fellow:** Research, NY-Presby/Columbia Univ Med Ctr 1982; Hand Surgery, St Lukes-Roosevelt Hosp 1983; **Fac Appt:** Clin Prof OrS, Columbia P&S

Hotchkiss, Robert N MD (HS) - **Spec Exp:** Wrist Surgery; Elbow Reconstruction; Dupuytren's Contracture; Hand & Upper Extremity Surgery; **Hospital:** Hosp For Special Surgery (page 109); **Address:** 523 E 72nd St Fl 4, New York, NY 10021; **Phone:** 212-606-1964; **Board Cert:** Orthopaedic Surgery 2010; Hand Surgery 2010; **Med School:** Johns Hopkins Univ 1980; **Resid:** Surgery, Johns Hopkins Hosp 1982; Orthopaedic Surgery, Johns Hopkins Hosp 1985; **Fellow:** Hand & Microvascular Surgery, Union Meml Hosp 1987; **Fac Appt:** Assoc Prof OrS, Cornell Univ-Weill Med Coll

King, William L MD (HS) - **Spec Exp:** Carpal Tunnel Syndrome; Hand Reconstruction; Microvascular Surgery; Fractures; **Hospital:** NYU Hosp For Joint Dis (page 104), Lenox Hill Hosp; **Address:** 424 Madison Ave, Fl 9, New York, NY 10017; **Phone:** 212-813-2104; **Board Cert:** Orthopaedic Surgery 2009; **Med School:** Columbia P&S 1974; **Resid:** Surgery, St Lukes-Roosevelt Hosp Ctr 1976; Orthopaedic Surgery, Columbia-Presby Med Ctr 1979; **Fellow:** Hand & Microvascular Surgery, Univ Colorado Hosp 1980; **Fac Appt:** Asst Prof OrS, NYU Sch Med

Lee, Steve K MD (HS) - **Spec Exp:** Peripheral Nerve Surgery; Tendon Surgery; Wrist/Hand Injuries; Ligament Reconstruction; **Hospital:** Hosp For Special Surgery (page 109); **Address:** HSS, Div Hand Surgery, 523 E 72nd St Fl 4, Esat River Professional Bldg, New York, NY 10021; **Phone:** 212-606-1730; **Board Cert:** Orthopaedic Surgery 2011; Hand Surgery 2011; **Med School:** Duke Univ 1993; **Resid:** Orthopaedic Surgery, Yale-New Haven Hosp 1998; **Fellow:** Hand Surgery, NYU Hosp Joint Diseases 2003; **Fac Appt:** Assoc Prof OrS, Cornell Univ-Weill Med Coll

Lenzo, Salvatore R MD (HS) - **Spec Exp:** Carpal Tunnel Syndrome; Arthritis; Hand Injuries; Congenital Hand Deformities; **Hospital:** NYU Hosp For Joint Dis (page 104), NYU Langone Med Ctr (page 104); **Address:** 955 5th Ave, New York, NY 10075; **Phone:** 212-734-9949; **Board Cert:** Orthopaedic Surgery 2010; Hand Surgery 2010; **Med School:** NYU Sch Med 1981; **Resid:** Orthopaedic Surgery, Bellevue Hosp 1986; **Fellow:** Hand Surgery, Bellevue Hosp 1987; **Fac Appt:** Asst Clin Prof OrS, NYU Sch Med

Melone Jr, Charles P MD (HS) - **Spec Exp:** Wrist Surgery; Fractures; Sports Injuries; **Hospital:** Mt Sinai Beth Israel; **Address:** Hand Surgery Ctr, 321 E 34th St, New York, NY 10016; **Phone:** 212-340-0000; **Board Cert:** Orthopaedic Surgery 1976; **Med School:** Georgetown Univ 1969; **Resid:** Surgery, Nassau Univ Med Ctr 1971; Orthopaedic Surgery, Nassau Univ Med Ctr 1974; **Fellow:** Hand Surgery, NYU Med Ctr 1975; **Fac Appt:** Prof OrS, Albert Einstein Coll Med

Polatsch, Daniel B MD (HS) - **Spec Exp:** Wrist Surgery; Carpal Tunnel Syndrome; Wrist/Hand Injuries; Fractures; **Hospital:** Mt Sinai Beth Israel; **Address:** The Hand Surgery Ctr, 321 E 34th St Fl 1, New York, NY 10016; **Phone:** 212-340-0000; **Board Cert:** Orthopaedic Surgery 2005; Hand Surgery 2008; **Med School:** NYU Sch Med 1997; **Resid:** Orthopaedic Surgery, NYU Hosp Joint Diseases 2002; **Fellow:** Hand Surgery, Harvard/Brigham & Womens Hosp 2003; **Fac Appt:** Asst Prof OrS, Mount Sinai-Icahn Sch of Med

Pruzansky, Mark E MD (HS) - **Spec Exp:** Arthritis Hand Surgery; Carpal Tunnel Syndrome; Sports Injuries; Wrist Surgery; **Hospital:** Mt Sinai Hosp, Lenox Hill Hosp; **Address:** HandSport Surgery Inst, 975 Park Ave, Ste 1B, MS 10028, New York, NY 10028; **Phone:** 212-249-8700; **Board Cert:** Orthopaedic Surgery 1980; Hand Surgery 2013; Orthopaedic Sports Medicine 2007; **Med School:** Mount Sinai Sch Med 1974; **Resid:** Orthopaedic Surgery, Mount Sinai Med Ctr 1978; **Fellow:** Hand Surgery, South Baptist Hosp 1978; Hand Surgery, Pacific Presby Hosp 1979; **Fac Appt:** Asst Prof OrS, Mount Sinai Sch Med

Raskin, Keith B MD (HS) - **Spec Exp:** Wrist/Hand Injuries; Arthritis; Carpal Tunnel Syndrome; Elbow Surgery; **Hospital:** NYU Langone Med Ctr (page 104); **Address:** 317 E 34th St, Fl 3, New York, NY 10016; **Phone:** 212-263-4263; **Board Cert:** Orthopaedic Surgery 2013; Hand Surgery 2013; **Med School:** Geo Wash Univ 1983; **Resid:** Orthopaedic Surgery, NYU Med Ctr 1988; **Fellow:** Hand Surgery, Union Meml Hosp 1989; **Fac Appt:** Assoc Clin Prof OrS, NYU Sch Med

Rettig, Michael E MD (HS) - **Spec Exp:** Fractures; Arthritis; Nerve Disorders/Surgery; **Hospital:** NYU Langone Med Ctr (page 104); **Address:** 317 E 34th St Fl 3, New York, NY 10016; **Phone:** 212-889-8600; **Board Cert:** Orthopaedic Surgery 2005; Hand Surgery 2005; **Med School:** SUNY Upstate Med Univ 1986; **Resid:** Orthopaedic Surgery, NYU Med Ctr 1991; **Fellow:** Hand Surgery, Mayo Clin 1992; **Fac Appt:** Asst Prof OrS, NYU Sch Med

Rosenwasser, Melvin P MD (HS) - **Spec Exp:** Carpal Tunnel Syndrome; Sports Injuries; Elbow Surgery; Trauma; **Hospital:** NY-Presby/Columbia Univ Med Ctr, NY (page 102); **Address:** New York Orthopedic Hosp Assocs, 622 W 168th St, PH 11, rm 1150, New York, NY 10032; **Phone:** 212-305-8036; **Board Cert:** Orthopaedic Surgery 1999; Hand Surgery 2011; **Med School:** Columbia P&S 1976; **Resid:** Surgery, St. Luke's - Roosevelt Hosp Ctr - Roosevelt Div 1979; Orthopaedic Surgery, NY-Presby/Columbia Univ Med Ctr 1982; **Fellow:** Hand Surgery, NY-Presby/Columbia Univ Med Ctr 1983; **Fac Appt:** Prof OrS, Columbia P&S

Strauch, Robert J MD (HS) - **Spec Exp:** Hand & Upper Extremity Surgery; Carpal Tunnel Syndrome; Pediatric Hand Surgery; Congential Hand Deformities; **Hospital:** NY-Presby/Columbia Univ Med Ctr, NY (page 102); **Address:** NY Orthopedic Hosp Assocs, 622 W 168th St, rm 1119, New York, NY 10032; **Phone:** 212-305-4272; **Board Cert:** Orthopaedic Surgery 2005; Hand Surgery 2005; **Med School:** Columbia P&S 1986; **Resid:** Orthopaedic Surgery, NY-Presby/Columbia Univ Med Ctr 1991; **Fellow:** Hand Surgery, Indiana Hand Ctr 1992; **Fac Appt:** Prof OrS, Columbia P&S

Wolfe, Scott W MD (HS) - **Spec Exp:** Wrist Surgery; Nerve Disorders/Surgery; Fractures; Hand & Upper Extremity Surgery; **Hospital:** Hosp For Special Surgery (page 109); **Address:** HSS, Hand Surgery, 535 E 70th St, New York, NY 10021; **Phone:** 212-606-1529; **Board Cert:** Orthopaedic Surgery 2013; Hand Surgery 2013; **Med School:** Cornell Univ-Weill Med Coll 1984; **Resid:** Surgery, St Lukes-Roosevelt Hosp Ctr 1986; Orthopaedic Surgery, Hosp Special Surgery 1989; **Fellow:** Hand & Microvascular Surgery, NY-Presby/Columbia Univ Med Ctr 1990; **Fac Appt:** Prof OrS, Cornell Univ-Weill Med Coll

Yang, S Steven MD (HS) - **Spec Exp:** Congenital Hand Deformities; Dupuytren's Contracture; Reconstructive Surgery; Microvascular Surgery; **Hospital:** NYU Langone Med Ctr (page 104), NYU Hosp For Joint Dis (page 104); **Address:** NYU Hand Center, 530 First Ave, Ste 8U, New York, NY 10016; **Phone:** 646-501-0740; **Board Cert:** Orthopaedic Surgery 2009; Hand Surgery 2009; **Med School:** Duke Univ 1988; **Resid:** Orthopaedic Surgery, Lenox Hill Hosp 1994; **Fellow:** Hand Surgery, Hosp for Special Surgery 1995; **Fac Appt:** Assoc Clin Prof OrS, NYU Sch Med

Hematology

Aledort, Louis M MD (Hem) - **Spec Exp:** Bleeding/Coagulation Disorders; Platelet Disorders; Paroxysmal Nocturnal Hemoglobinuria; **Hospital:** Mt Sinai Hosp; **Address:** 1470 Madison Ave Fl 3rd, New York, NY 10029; **Phone:** 212-860-0205; **Board Cert:** Internal Medicine 1966; Hematology 1972; **Med School:** Albert Einstein Coll Med 1959; **Resid:** Internal Medicine, Univ Va Med Ctr 1961; Internal Medicine, U Rochester Med Ctr 1964; **Fellow:** Hematology, Strong Meml Hosp 1965; **Fac Appt:** Prof Med, Mount Sinai Sch Med

Amorosi, Edward L MD (Hem) - **Spec Exp:** Leukemia & Lymphoma; Bleeding/Coagulation Disorders; **Hospital:** NYU Langone Med Ctr (page 104); **Address:** 240 E 38th St Fl 19th, New York, NY 10016; **Phone:** 212-731-5187; **Board Cert:** Internal Medicine 1966; Hematology 1972; Medical Oncology 1977; **Med School:** NYU Sch Med 1959; **Resid:** Internal Medicine, Georgetown Univ Hosp 1961; Internal Medicine, NYU Med Ctr 1962; **Fellow:** Hematology, Bellevue Hosp Ctr 1965; **Fac Appt:** Assoc Prof Med, NYU Sch Med

Araten, David MD (Hem) - **Spec Exp:** Anemia-Aplastic; Hematologic Malignancies; Paroxysmal Nocturnal Hemoglobinuria; **Hospital:** NYU Langone Med Ctr (page 104); **Address:** NYU Clin Cancer Ctr, 240 E 38th St Fl 19, New York, NY 10016; **Phone:** 212-731-5186; **Board Cert:** Internal Medicine 2004; Hematology 2009; Medical Oncology 2009; **Med School:** Harvard Med Sch 1991; **Resid:** Internal Medicine, NY-Presby/Columbia Univ Med Ctr 1994; **Fellow:** Hematology & Oncology, Meml Sloan-Kettering Cancer Ctr 1999; **Fac Appt:** Asst Prof Onc, NYU Sch Med

Castro-Malaspina, Hugo R MD (Hem) - **Spec Exp:** Myelodysplastic Syndromes; Bone Marrow Failure Disorders; Bone Marrow Transplant; Anemia-Aplastic; **Hospital:** Meml Sloan Kettering Canc Ctr (page 110); **Address:** 1275 York Ave, New York, NY 10065; **Phone:** 800-525-2225; **Med School:** Peru 1971; **Resid:** Internal Medicine, St Louis Hosp 1974; **Fellow:** Hematology & Oncology, Andean Biology Inst 1976; Pediatric Hematology-Oncology, St Louis Hosp 1977

Diaz, Michael MD (Hem) - **Spec Exp:** Anemia; Bleeding/Coagulation Disorders; Lymphoma; **Hospital:** Mt Sinai Hosp; **Address:** 108 E 96th St, New York, NY 10128; **Phone:** 212-876-4500; **Board Cert:** Internal Medicine 1979; Hematology 1986; **Med School:** St Louis Univ 1971; **Resid:** Internal Medicine, Lenox Hill Hosp 1974; **Fellow:** Hematology, Elmhurst Hosp 1976; **Fac Appt:** Asst Clin Prof Med, Mount Sinai Sch Med

Diuguid, David L MD (Hem) - **Spec Exp:** Bleeding/Coagulation Disorders; Leukemia & Lymphoma; **Hospital:** NY-Presby/Columbia Univ Med Ctr, NY (page 102); **Address:** NY-Presby, Hematology, 161 Fort Washington Ave Fl 10, New York, NY 10032; **Phone:** 212-305-5098; **Board Cert:** Internal Medicine 1982; Hematology 1986; Medical Oncology 1985; **Med School:** Cornell Univ-Weill Med Coll 1979; **Resid:** Internal Medicine, Boston Med Ctr 1983; **Fellow:** Hematology & Oncology, Beth Israel Deaconess Med Ctr 1986; **Fac Appt:** Assoc Prof Med, Columbia P&S

Fruchtman, Steven M MD (Hem) - **Spec Exp:** Myeloproliferative Disorders; Polycythemia Rubra Vera; **Address:** 1150 Park Ave, Ste Medical, New York, NY 10128; **Phone:** 212-427-7700; **Board Cert:** Internal Medicine 1980; Hematology 1984; **Med School:** NY Med Coll 1977; **Resid:** Internal Medicine, Kings Co Hosp Ctr 1981; **Fellow:** Hematology, Mount Sinai Med Ctr 1984; Hematology, Meml Sloan Kettering Cancer Ctr 1985; **Fac Appt:** Assoc Prof Hem & Onc, NY Med Coll

Goldenberg, Alec S MD (Hem) - **Spec Exp:** Breast Cancer; Lymphoma; Bleeding/Coagulation Disorders; **Hospital:** NYU Langone Med Ctr (page 104), Bellevue Hosp Ctr; **Address:** 157 E 32nd St Fl 2, New York, NY 10016; **Phone:** 212-689-6791; **Board Cert:** Internal Medicine 1986; Medical Oncology 1987; **Med School:** Johns Hopkins Univ 1980; **Resid:** Internal Medicine, Bellevue Hosp 1984; **Fellow:** Hematology & Oncology, Meml Sloan-Kettering Canc Ctr 1988; **Fac Appt:** Assoc Clin Prof Med, NYU Sch Med

Green, David L MD/PhD (Hem) - **Spec Exp:** Hematologic Malignancies; Platelet Disorders; Anemia; **Hospital:** NYU Langone Med Ctr (page 104); **Address:** NYU Clin Cancer Ctr, Hem/Onc, 240 E 38th St Fl 19, New York, NY 10016; **Phone:** 212-263-5466; **Board Cert:** Internal Medicine 2004; Hematology 2013; **Med School:** NYU Sch Med 1991; **Resid:** Internal Medicine, Mount Sinai Hosp 1993; **Fellow:** Hematology, Johns Hopkins Hosp 1994; Medical Oncology, Meml Sloan-Kettering Cancer Ctr 1997; **Fac Appt:** Asst Prof Onc, NYU Sch Med

Gruenstein, Steven MD (Hem) - **Spec Exp:** Hematologic Malignancies; Gastrointestinal Cancer; Lung Cancer; **Hospital:** Mt Sinai Hosp; **Address:** Central Park Hematology & Oncology, 12 E 86th St, New York, NY 10028; **Phone:** 212-861-6660; **Board Cert:** Internal Medicine 1988; Medical Oncology 2013; **Med School:** Italy 1984; **Resid:** Internal Medicine, Metropolitan Hosp Ctr 1987; **Fellow:** Hematology & Oncology, Beth Israel Med Ctr 1990; **Fac Appt:** Assoc Clin Prof Med, Mount Sinai-Icahn Sch of Med

Hymes, Kenneth B MD (Hem) - **Spec Exp:** Bleeding/Coagulation Disorders; Leukemia & Lymphoma; Cutaneous T-cell Lymphoma; Mycosis Fungoides; **Hospital:** NYU Langone Med Ctr (page 104); **Address:** NYU Clinical Cancer Center, 240 E 38th St, Fl 19, New York, NY 10016-6402; **Phone:** 212-731-5189; **Board Cert:** Internal Medicine 1978; Hematology 1980; Medical Oncology 1981; **Med School:** SUNY Upstate Med Univ 1975; **Resid:** Internal Medicine, Barnes Hosp 1978; **Fellow:** Hematology, NYU Med Ctr 1980; Medical Oncology, NYU Med Ctr 1981; **Fac Appt:** Assoc Prof Hem & Onc, NYU Sch Med

Isola, Luis M MD (Hem) - **Spec Exp:** Anemia-Aplastic; Hodgkin's Lymphoma; Multiple Myeloma; **Hospital:** Mt Sinai Hosp; **Address:** Ruttenberg Treatment Ctr, 1470 Madison Ave Fl 3, New York, NY 10029; **Phone:** 212-241-6021; **Board Cert:** Internal Medicine 1986; Hematology 1988; **Med School:** Argentina 1979; **Resid:** Internal Medicine, Ctr Med Edu 1983; **Fellow:** Hematology, Mt Sinai Hosp 1985; **Fac Appt:** Prof Med, Mount Sinai-Icahn Sch of Med

Jakubowski, Ann MD/PhD (Hem) - **Spec Exp:** Leukemia; Bone Marrow Transplant; Stem Cell Transplant; **Hospital:** Meml Sloan Kettering Canc Ctr (page 110); **Address:** MSKCC, Hematology, 1275 York Ave, New York, NY 10065; **Phone:** 212-639-5013; **Board Cert:** Internal Medicine 1984; Medical Oncology 1987; Hematology 1986; **Med School:** Univ Conn 1981; **Resid:** Internal Medicine, Mt Sinai Hosp 1984; **Fellow:** Hematology, Montefiore Hosp 1985; Medical Oncology, Meml Sloan-Kettering Cancer Ctr 1988

Jurcic, Joseph G MD (Hem) - **Spec Exp:** Leukemia; Myelodysplastic Syndromes; Clinical Trials; **Hospital:** NY-Presby/Columbia Univ Med Ctr, NY (page 102); **Address:** 161 Fort Washington Ave, Garden Level, New York, NY 10032; **Phone:** 646-317-5077; **Board Cert:** Medical Oncology 2005; Hematology 2008; **Med School:** Univ Pennsylvania 1988; **Resid:** Internal Medicine, Barnes Hosp 1991; **Fellow:** Hematology & Oncology, Meml Sloan Kettering Cancer Ctr 1994; **Fac Appt:** Clin Prof Med, Columbia P&S

Lamanna, Nicole MD (Hem) - **Spec Exp:** Leukemia-Chronic Lymphocytic; Leukemia-Acute Lymphoblastic; Leukemia-Myeloid; Hematologic Malignancies; **Hospital:** NY-Presby/Columbia Univ Med Ctr, NY (page 102); **Address:** 161 Fort Washington Ave, Herbert Irving Pavilion, Garden Level, New York, NY 10032; **Phone:** 646-317-5077; **Board Cert:** Medical Oncology 2004; **Med School:** Albert Einstein Coll Med 1997; **Resid:** Internal Medicine, NYU Langone Med Ctr 2000; **Fellow:** Hematology & Oncology, Meml Sloan-Kettering Cancer Ctr 2004; **Fac Appt:** Assoc Clin Prof Med, Columbia P&S

Leonard, John P MD (Hem) - **Spec Exp:** Lymphoma; Hematologic Malignancies; **Hospital:** NY-Presby/Weill Cornell Med Ctr, NY (page 102); **Address:** NY-Presby/Weill Cornell Med Ctr, 520 E 70th St, Star Pavilion 3, New York, NY 10021; **Phone:** 646-962-2068; **Board Cert:** Hematology 2006; Medical Oncology 2007; **Med School:** Univ VA Sch Med 1990; **Resid:** Internal Medicine, NY Hosp-Cornell Med Ctr 1993; **Fellow:** Hematology & Oncology, NY Hosp-Cornell Med Ctr 1996; **Fac Appt:** Prof Med, Cornell Univ-Weill Med Coll

Levine, Randy L MD (Hem) - **Spec Exp:** Hematologic Malignancies; Bleeding/Coagulation Disorders; **Hospital:** Lenox Hill Hosp, Mt Sinai Roosevelt; **Address:** 4 E 76th St, New York, NY 10021; **Phone:** 212-717-1020; **Board Cert:** Internal Medicine 1982; Hematology 1984; Blood Banking 1985; **Med School:** SUNY Buffalo 1979; **Resid:** Internal Medicine, Montefiore Med Ctr 1982; **Fellow:** Hematology, Montefiore Med Ctr 1983; Blood Banking, Mt Sinai Med Ctr 1984; **Fac Appt:** Assoc Clin Prof Med, NYU Sch Med

Mears, John Gregory MD (Hem) - **Spec Exp:** Lymphoma; Leukemia; Multiple Myeloma; **Hospital:** NY-Presby/Columbia Univ Med Ctr, NY (page 102); **Address:** NY-Presby, Hematology, 161 Fort Washington Ave, Ste 923, New York, NY 10032; **Phone:** 212-305-3506; **Board Cert:** Internal Medicine 1976; Hematology 1978; **Med School:** Columbia P&S 1973; **Resid:** Internal Medicine, Boston Med Ctr 1975; **Fellow:** Hematology & Oncology, NY-Presby/Columbia Univ Med Ctr 1978; **Fac Appt:** Clin Prof Hem & Onc, Columbia P&S

Meyer, Richard J MD (Hem) - **Spec Exp:** Lymphoma; Leukemia; Anemia; **Hospital:** Mt Sinai Hosp; **Address:** 1150 Park Ave, Ste 1D, New York, NY 10128-1234; **Phone:** 212-427-7700; **Board Cert:** Internal Medicine 1975; Hematology 1978; Medical Oncology 1979; **Med School:** Mount Sinai Sch Med 1972; **Resid:** Internal Medicine, Mt Sinai Hosp 1975; **Fellow:** Hematology, Mt Sinai Hosp 1977; Medical Oncology, Mt Sinai Hosp 1977; **Fac Appt:** Assoc Clin Prof Hem, Mount Sinai Sch Med

Moskovits, Tibor MD (Hem) - **Spec Exp:** Lymphoma; Breast Cancer; Lung Cancer; **Hospital:** NYU Langone Med Ctr (page 104); **Address:** 240 E 38th St Fl 19th, New York, NY 10016; **Phone:** 212-731-5191; **Board Cert:** Internal Medicine 1988; Medical Oncology 2004; **Med School:** SUNY Downstate 1985; **Resid:** Internal Medicine, Beth Israel Med Ctr 1988; **Fellow:** Hematology, Bellevue Hosp Ctr 1992; Medical Oncology, Bellevue Hosp Ctr 1993; **Fac Appt:** Asst Clin Prof Med, NYU Sch Med

Niesvizky, Ruben MD (Hem) - **Spec Exp:** Multiple Myeloma; Leukemia; Lymphoma; Waldenstrom's Macroglobulinemia; **Hospital:** NY-Presby/Weill Cornell Med Ctr, NY (page 102); **Address:** Myeloma Ctr, 428 E 72nd St, New York, NY 10021; **Phone:** 212-746-3964; **Med School:** Mexico 1985; **Resid:** Internal Medicine, Natl Univ/Inst of Nutrition 1988; **Fellow:** Hematology, Mount Sinai Med Ctr 1990; Hematology & Oncology, Meml Sloan Kettering Cancer Ctr 1994; **Fac Appt:** Assoc Prof Med, Cornell Univ-Weill Med Coll

Ossias, A Lawrence MD (Hem) - **Spec Exp:** Lymphoma; Leukemia; Coagulation/Bleeding Disorders; **Hospital:** Mt Sinai Hosp; **Address:** 1112 Park Ave, New York, NY 10128; **Phone:** 212-427-9333; **Board Cert:** Internal Medicine 1972; Hematology 1972; Medical Oncology 1979; **Med School:** Yale Univ 1965; **Resid:** Internal Medicine, Bronx Municipal Hosp 1970; **Fellow:** Hematology, Mt Sinai Med Ctr 1972; **Fac Appt:** Asst Clin Prof Hem, Mount Sinai-Icahn Sch of Med

Raphael, Bruce Gordon MD (Hem) - **Spec Exp:** Leukemia & Lymphoma; Multiple Myeloma; Anemia; **Hospital:** NYU Langone Med Ctr (page 104); **Address:** NYU Clin Cancer Ctr, 240 E 38th St, Fl 19, New York, NY 10016; **Phone:** 212-731-5185; **Board Cert:** Internal Medicine 1978; Hematology 1980; Medical Oncology 1981; **Med School:** McGill Univ 1975; **Resid:** Internal Medicine, Jewish Genl Hosp 1977; **Fellow:** Hematology & Oncology, Meml Sloan-Kettering Cancer Ctr 1978; Hematology & Oncology, NYU Med Ctr 1980; **Fac Appt:** Clin Prof Med, NYU Sch Med

Savage, David G MD (Hem) - **Spec Exp:** Stem Cell Transplant; Bone Marrow Transplant; Leukemia & Lymphoma; **Hospital:** NY-Presby/Columbia Univ Med Ctr, NY (page 102); **Address:** NY-Presby, Hematology, 161 Fort Washington Ave Fl 10, New York, NY 10032; **Phone:** 212-305-5098; **Board Cert:** Internal Medicine 1977; Hematology 1982; Medical Oncology 1985; **Med School:** Columbia P&S 1974; **Resid:** Internal Medicine, Harlem Hosp Ctr 1977; **Fellow:** Hematology & Oncology, NY-Presby/Columbia Univ Med Ctr 1982; **Fac Appt:** Prof Med, Columbia P&S

Scigliano, Eileen MD (Hem) - **Spec Exp:** Bone Marrow Transplant; **Hospital:** Mt Sinai Hosp; **Address:** 1470 Madison Ave, New York, NY 10029; **Phone:** 212-241-6021; **Board Cert:** Internal Medicine 1984; Hematology 1988; **Med School:** Israel 1981; **Resid:** Internal Medicine, Kings County Hosp 1984; **Fellow:** Medical Oncology, VA Med Ctr 1985; Hematology, Mount Sinai Hosp 1988; **Fac Appt:** Assoc Prof Med, Mount Sinai Sch Med

Soff, Gerald A MD (Hem) - **Spec Exp:** Bleeding/Coagulation Disorders; Thrombotic Disorders; Hematologic Disorders in Cancer Patients; Anemia; **Hospital:** Meml Sloan Kettering Canc Ctr (page 110); **Address:** MSKCC, Hematology, 1275 York Ave, Fl 4, Ste 1, New York, NY 10065; **Phone:** 212-639-2335; **Board Cert:** Internal Medicine 1984; Hematology 1988; **Med School:** Johns Hopkins Univ 1981; **Resid:** Internal Medicine, Med Coll Virginia Hosp 1984; **Fellow:** Hematology & Oncology, Beth Israel Deaconess Med Ctr 1988

Tallman, Martin S MD (Hem) - **Spec Exp:** Leukemia; **Hospital:** Meml Sloan Kettering Canc Ctr (page 110); **Address:** MSKCC, Leukemia Svc, 1275 York Ave, Ste H-719, Box 380, New York, NY 10065; **Phone:** 212-639-3842; **Board Cert:** Internal Medicine 1983; Medical Oncology 1987; Hematology 1988; **Med School:** Ros Franklin Univ/Chicago Med Sch 1980; **Resid:** Internal Medicine, Evanston Hosp 1983; **Fellow:** Medical Oncology, Fred Hutchinson Cancer Ctr 1987; **Fac Appt:** Prof Med, Cornell Univ-Weill Med Coll

Troy, Kevin M MD (Hem) - **Spec Exp:** Leukemia; Lymphoma; Multiple Myeloma; **Hospital:** Mt Sinai Hosp; **Address:** 1470 Madison Ave Fl 3, Box 1079, New York, NY 10029; **Phone:** 212-824-8858; **Board Cert:** Internal Medicine 1982; Hematology 1984; **Med School:** Univ Conn 1979; **Resid:** Internal Medicine, Lenox Hill Hosp 1982; **Fellow:** Hematology, Mount Sinai Hosp 1984; **Fac Appt:** Assoc Clin Prof Med, Mount Sinai Sch Med

Van Besien, Koen W MD/PhD (Hem) - **Spec Exp:** Lymphoma; Stem Cell Transplant; **Hospital:** NY-Presby/Weill Cornell Med Ctr, NY (page 102); **Address:** NY-Presby, Hem/Onc, 520 E 70th St, Starr Bldg, Ste 303, New York, NY 10021; **Phone:** 212-746-2048; **Board Cert:** Internal Medicine 2005; Medical Oncology 2005; Hematology 2006; **Med School:** Belgium 1984; **Resid:** Internal Medicine, Univ Leuven Med Ctr 1987; **Fellow:** Hematology & Oncology, IU Hlth Hosp 1990; **Fac Appt:** Prof Hem & Onc, Cornell Univ-Weill Med Coll

Vogel, James M MD (Hem) - **Spec Exp:** Breast Cancer; Colon Cancer; Leukemia & Lymphoma; Platelet Disorders; **Hospital:** Mt Sinai Hosp, Mt Sinai Hosp of Queens; **Address:** 111 E 88th St, Ste 1A, New York, NY 10128-1243; **Phone:** 212-369-4250; **Board Cert:** Internal Medicine 1969; Hematology 1972; Medical Oncology 1973; **Med School:** Columbia P&S 1962; **Resid:** Internal Medicine, Mount Sinai Med Ctr 1965; **Fellow:** Medical Oncology, Natl Cancer Inst 1968; Hematology, Mount Sinai Hosp 1969; **Fac Appt:** Assoc Clin Prof Med, Mount Sinai Sch Med

Wisch, Nathaniel MD (Hem) - **Spec Exp:** Lymphoma; Gastrointestinal Cancer; Leukemia; Anemia-Cancer Related; **Hospital:** Mt Sinai Hosp, Lenox Hill Hosp; **Address:** Central Park Hematology & Oncology, 12 E 86th St, New York, NY 10028; **Phone:** 212-861-6660; **Board Cert:** Internal Medicine 1965; Hematology 1972; Medical Oncology 1977; **Med School:** Northwestern Univ 1958; **Resid:** Internal Medicine, VA Hosp 1960; Internal Medicine, Montefiore Hosp 1961; **Fellow:** Hematology & Oncology, Mount Sinai Hosp 1964; **Fac Appt:** Clin Prof Hem, Mount Sinai-Icahn Sch of Med

Wolf, David J MD (Hem) - **Spec Exp:** Hematologic Malignancies; Hematology-Benign; Solid Tumors; **Hospital:** NY-Presby/Weill Cornell Med Ctr, NY (page 102); **Address:** 115 E 61st St Fl 11, New York, NY 10065; **Phone:** 212-688-7100; **Board Cert:** Internal Medicine 1976; Hematology 1978; Medical Oncology 1979; **Med School:** SUNY Hlth Sci Ctr 1973; **Resid:** Internal Medicine, NY Hosp/Meml Hosp 1976; **Fellow:** Hematology, NY Hosp 1978; **Fac Appt:** Asst Clin Prof Med, Cornell Univ-Weill Med Coll

Hospice & Palliative Medicine

Chai, Emily J MD (H & PM) - **Spec Exp:** Palliative Care; Geriatric Care; **Hospital:** Mt Sinai Hosp; **Address:** Mt Sinai Med Ctr, Palliative Care Div, 1 Gustave L Levy Pl, Box 1070, New York, NY 10029; **Phone:** 212-659-8552; **Board Cert:** Internal Medicine 2011; Geriatric Medicine 2012; Hospice & Palliative Medicine 2008; **Med School:** NYU Sch Med 1998; **Resid:** Internal Medicine, Mt Sinai Med Ctr 2001; **Fellow:** Geriatric Medicine, Mt Sinai Med Ctr 2002; **Fac Appt:** Assoc Prof Med, Mount Sinai-Icahn Sch of Med

Edwards, Wendy S A MD (H & PM) - **Spec Exp:** Palliative Care; Pain Management; **Hospital:** Lenox Hill Hosp; **Address:** 100 E 77th St, 6 Black Hall, New York, NY 10075; **Phone:** 212-434-2140; **Board Cert:** Internal Medicine 1980; Hospice & Palliative Medicine 2010; **Med School:** Med Coll PA 1976; **Resid:** Internal Medicine, Metrowest Med Ctr 1978; Internal Medicine, Boston Univ Hosp 1979

Glare, Paul Andrew MD (H & PM) - **Spec Exp:** Palliative Care; Pain-Cancer; **Hospital:** Meml Sloan Kettering Canc Ctr (page 110); **Address:** Meml Sloan Kettering Cancer Ctr, 1275 York Ave, Box 496, New York, NY 10065; **Phone:** 646-888-3065; **Med School:** Australia 1981; **Resid:** Internal Medicine, Syndey Hosp; Pain Medicine, Royal Prince Alfred Hosp; **Fellow:** Pain & Palliative Care, Eversleigh Hosp; Hospice & Palliative Medicine, Cleveland Clinic

Tickoo, Roma MD (H & PM) - **Spec Exp:** Palliative Care; Pain-Cancer; Geriatric Care; **Hospital:** Meml Sloan Kettering Canc Ctr (page 110); **Address:** Meml Sloan Kettering Cancer Ctr, 1275 York Ave, New York, NY 10065; **Phone:** 646-888-2694; **Board Cert:** Internal Medicine 2004; Geriatric Medicine 2007; Hospice & Palliative Medicine 2008; Pain Medicine 2008; **Med School:** India 1985; **Resid:** Internal Medicine, Flushing Med Ctr 2004; **Fellow:** Geriatric Medicine, NYU Med Ctr 2005

Infectious Disease

Brause, Barry MD (Inf) - **Spec Exp:** Bone/Joint Infections; Skin/Soft Tissue Infections; Infections in Prosthetic Devices; **Hospital:** Hosp For Special Surgery (page 109), NY-Presby/Weill Cornell Med Ctr, NY (page 102); **Address:** 535 E 70th St, Ste 657W, New York, NY 10021; **Phone:** 212-774-7411; **Board Cert:** Internal Medicine 1973; Infectious Disease 1976; **Med School:** Univ Pittsburgh 1970; **Resid:** Internal Medicine, NY-Presby/Weill Cornell Med Ctr 1973; **Fellow:** Infectious Disease, NY-Presby/Weill Cornell Med Ctr 1975; **Fac Appt:** Prof Med, Cornell Univ-Weill Med Coll

Brown, Arthur E MD (Inf) - **Spec Exp:** Infections in Cancer Patients; Fungal Infections; Infections in Immunocompromised Patients; **Hospital:** Meml Sloan Kettering Canc Ctr (page 110); **Address:** 1275 York Ave, New York, NY 10065; **Phone:** 212-639-8475; **Med School:** Jefferson Med Coll 1971; **Resid:** Internal Medicine, Roosevelt Hosp 1972; Internal Medicine, USPHS Hosp-Staten Island NY & USPHS Hosp 1974; **Fellow:** Internal Medicine, Roosevelt Hosp 1976; Infectious Disease, Mem Sloan Kettering Cancer Ctr 1978; **Fac Appt:** Clin Prof Med, Cornell Univ-Weill Med Coll

Busillo, Christopher P MD (Inf) - **Spec Exp:** AIDS/HIV; Travel Medicine; Lyme Disease; **Hospital:** NYU Langone Med Ctr (page 104); **Address:** 111 Broadway Fl 4, New York, NY 10006; **Phone:** 212-263-9700; **Board Cert:** Internal Medicine 2011; Infectious Disease 2012; **Med School:** Italy 1986; **Resid:** Internal Medicine, Cabrini Med Ctr 1989; **Fellow:** Infectious Disease, Cabrini Med Ctr 1991

Caplivski, Daniel Simon MD (Inf) - **Spec Exp:** Travel Medicine; Tropical Diseases; Malaria; AIDS/HIV; **Hospital:** Mt Sinai Hosp; **Address:** 5 E 98th St Fl 8, New York, NY 10029; **Phone:** 212-241-7468; **Board Cert:** Infectious Disease 2005; **Med School:** Yale Univ 2000; **Resid:** Internal Medicine, Mt Sinai Med Ctr 2003; **Fellow:** Infectious Disease, Mt Sinai Med Ctr 2005; **Fac Appt:** Assoc Prof Med, Mount Sinai Sch Med

El-Sadr, Wafaa M MD (Inf) - **Spec Exp:** AIDS/HIV; Tuberculosis; **Hospital:** Harlem Hosp Ctr; **Address:** Harlem Hosp, Div of Infectious Dis, 506 Lenox Ave MLK Bldg - rm 3101A, New York, NY 10037; **Phone:** 212-939-2936; **Board Cert:** Internal Medicine 1979; Infectious Disease 1982; **Med School:** Egypt 1975; **Resid:** Internal Medicine, Our Lady of Mercy Med Ctr 1977; Internal Medicine, Cabrini Med Ctr 1979; **Fellow:** Infectious Disease, VA Medical Ctr 1982; **Fac Appt:** Prof Epidemiol, Columbia P&S

Flood, Mary T MD/PhD (Inf) - **Spec Exp:** HIV; Hepatitis; Sexually Transmitted Diseases; **Hospital:** NY-Presby/Columbia Univ Med Ctr, NY (page 102); **Address:** NY Presbyterian Hosp, Infectious Dis, 180 Fort Washington Ave, Ste 242, Harkness Pavilion, New York, NY 10032-3702; **Phone:** 212-305-8039; **Board Cert:** Internal Medicine 2012; Infectious Disease 2004; **Med School:** Columbia P&S 1987; **Resid:** Internal Medicine, NY-Presby Hosp 1991; **Fellow:** Infectious Disease, NY-Presby Hosp 1993; **Fac Appt:** Assoc Prof Med, Columbia P&S

Glesby, Marshall J MD/PhD (Inf) - **Spec Exp:** HIV/AIDS; **Hospital:** NY-Presby/Weill Cornell Med Ctr, NY (page 102); **Address:** 525 E 68th St, Baker Bldg - Fl 24, MS 97, New York, NY 10065; **Phone:** 212-746-4177; **Board Cert:** Internal Medicine 2014; Infectious Disease 2004; **Med School:** Johns Hopkins Univ 1989; **Resid:** Internal Medicine, Johns Hopkins Hosp 1992; **Fellow:** Infectious Disease, Johns Hopkins Hosp 1994; **Fac Appt:** Assoc Prof Med, Cornell Univ-Weill Med Coll

Greene, Jeffrey B MD (Inf) - **Spec Exp:** AIDS/HIV; Fungal Infections; Bone/Joint Infections; Epstein-Barr Virus; **Hospital:** NYU Langone Med Ctr (page 104); **Address:** 530 First Ave HCC Bldg - Ste 7J, New York, NY 10016; **Phone:** 212-375-2940; **Board Cert:** Internal Medicine 1979; Infectious Disease 1982; **Med School:** NYU Sch Med 1976; **Resid:** Internal Medicine, Bellevue Hosp 1979; **Fellow:** Infectious Disease, Bellevue Hosp 1982; **Fac Appt:** Clin Prof Med, NYU Sch Med

Gumprecht, Jeffrey P MD (Inf) - **Spec Exp:** AIDS/HIV; Travel Medicine; Infections-Surgical; **Hospital:** Mt Sinai Hosp; **Address:** 1100 Park Ave, Ste 1C, New York, NY 10128; **Phone:** 212-427-9550; **Board Cert:** Internal Medicine 1987; **Med School:** Albany Med Coll 1983; **Resid:** Internal Medicine, Mt Sinai Med Ctr 1987; **Fellow:** Infectious Disease, Montefiore Med Ctr 1990; **Fac Appt:** Asst Clin Prof Med, Iceland

Hammer, Glenn S MD (Inf) - **Spec Exp:** AIDS/HIV; Hospital Acquired Infections; Infections-Surgical; **Hospital:** Mt Sinai Hosp; **Address:** 1100 Park Ave, Ste 1C, New York, NY 10128; **Phone:** 212-427-9550; **Board Cert:** Infectious Disease 1974; Internal Medicine 1973; **Med School:** NYU Sch Med 1969; **Resid:** Internal Medicine, Mt Sinai Hosp 1972; **Fellow:** Infectious Disease, Mt Sinai Hosp 1974; **Fac Appt:** Asst Clin Prof Med, Mount Sinai-Icahn Sch of Med

Hammer, Scott M MD (Inf) - **Spec Exp:** AIDS/HIV; **Hospital:** NY-Presby/Columbia Univ Med Ctr, NY (page 102); **Address:** 630 W 168th St Fl 8, New York, NY 10032; **Phone:** 212-305-8039; **Board Cert:** Internal Medicine 1975; Infectious Disease 1980; **Med School:** Columbia P&S 1972; **Resid:** Internal Medicine, Columbia-Presby Hosp 1974; Internal Medicine, Stanford Univ Hosp 1975; **Fellow:** Infectious Disease, Mass Genl Hosp 1981; **Fac Appt:** Prof Med, Columbia P&S

Hartman, Barry J MD (Inf) - **Spec Exp:** Endocarditis; Infections-Surgical; Parasitic Infections; Lyme Disease; **Hospital:** NY-Presby/Weill Cornell Med Ctr, NY (page 102); **Address:** 407 E 70th St, Fl 4, New York, NY 10021; **Phone:** 212-744-4882; **Board Cert:** Internal Medicine 1976; Infectious Disease 1980; **Med School:** Penn State Coll Med 1973; **Resid:** Internal Medicine, NY-Presby/Weill Cornell Med Ctr 1976; **Fellow:** Infectious Disease, NY-Presby/Weill Cornell Med Ctr 1981; **Fac Appt:** Clin Prof Med, Cornell Univ-Weill Med Coll

Helfgott, David C MD (Inf) - **Spec Exp:** Infections in Immunocompromised Patients; **Hospital:** NY-Presby/Weill Cornell Med Ctr, NY (page 102); **Address:** The Travel Med Ctr of Manhattan, 212 E 68th St, New York, NY 10065; **Phone:** 212-879-6004; **Board Cert:** Internal Medicine 1986; Infectious Disease 1988; **Med School:** Yale Univ 1983; **Resid:** Internal Medicine, NY Hosp/Cornell Med Ctr 1986; **Fellow:** Infectious Disease, NY Hosp/Cornell Med Ctr 1988; **Fac Appt:** Asst Clin Prof Med, Cornell Univ-Weill Med Coll

Horowitz, Harold W MD (Inf) - **Spec Exp:** AIDS/HIV; Tick-borne Diseases; Clinical Trials; Fevers of Unknown Origin; **Hospital:** Bellevue Hosp Ctr, NYU Langone Med Ctr (page 104); **Address:** NYU Schl Med, Div of Infectious Dis, 550 First Ave, NBV 16 S 5, New York, NY 10016; **Phone:** 212-263-2115; **Board Cert:** Internal Medicine 1983; Infectious Disease 1988; **Med School:** NYU Sch Med 1979; **Resid:** Internal Medicine, Univ Wisconsin Hosp 1983; **Fellow:** Infectious Disease, Tufts-New England Med Ctr 1986; **Fac Appt:** Prof Med, NYU Sch Med

Jacobs, Jonathan L MD (Inf) - **Spec Exp:** AIDS/HIV; **Hospital:** NY-Presby/Weill Cornell Med Ctr, NY (page 102); **Address:** 449 E 68th St, Ground Fl, New York, NY 10065; **Phone:** 212-734-1365; **Board Cert:** Internal Medicine 1983; Infectious Disease 1986; **Med School:** Yale Univ 1980; **Resid:** Internal Medicine, NY Hosp/Cornell Med Ctr 1983; **Fellow:** Infectious Disease, NY Hosp/Cornell Med Ctr 1986; **Fac Appt:** Assoc Clin Prof Med, Cornell Univ-Weill Med Coll

Lerner, Chester W MD (Inf) - **Spec Exp:** AIDS/HIV; Travel Medicine; Sexually Transmitted Diseases; **Hospital:** NY-Presby/Lower Manhattan Hosp (page 102), NY-Presby/Weill Cornell Med Ctr, NY (page 102); **Address:** Weill Cornell Physician Organization, 156 William St Fl 7, New York, NY 10038-2612; **Phone:** 212-312-5920; **Board Cert:** Internal Medicine 1981; Infectious Disease 1984; **Med School:** Univ Pittsburgh 1978; **Resid:** Internal Medicine, Lenox Hill Hosp 1981; **Fellow:** Infectious Disease, Lenox Hill Hosp 1983; **Fac Appt:** Asst Clin Prof Med, Cornell Univ-Weill Med Coll

Louie, Eddie MD (Inf) - **Spec Exp:** Lyme Disease; AIDS/HIV; Hospital Acquired Infections; Travel Medicine; **Hospital:** NYU Langone Med Ctr (page 104); **Address:** 530 1st Ave, Ste 7J, New York, NY 10016; **Phone:** 212-682-9202; **Board Cert:** Internal Medicine 1982; Infectious Disease 1986; **Med School:** NYU Sch Med 1979; **Resid:** Internal Medicine, Kings Co Hosp Ctr 1983; **Fellow:** Infectious Disease, NYU Med Ctr 1985; **Fac Appt:** Assoc Clin Prof Med, NYU Sch Med

McMeeking, Alexander A MD (Inf) - **Spec Exp:** AIDS/HIV; Hepatitis; Lyme Disease; Travel Medicine; **Hospital:** NYU Langone Med Ctr (page 104); **Address:** Chelsea Village Medical, 155 W 19th St Fl 4th, New York, NY 10011; **Phone:** 212-929-2629; **Board Cert:** Internal Medicine 1985; Infectious Disease 1988; **Med School:** UMDNJ-NJ Med Sch, Newark 1982; **Resid:** Internal Medicine, St Luke's-Roosevelt Hosp 1985; **Fellow:** Infectious Disease, Bellvue Hosp/NYU Med Ctr 1987; **Fac Appt:** Assoc Clin Prof Med, NYU Sch Med

Miller, Dennis K MD (Inf) - **Spec Exp:** Lyme Disease; AIDS/HIV; Travel Medicine; Tropical Diseases; **Hospital:** Lenox Hill Hosp; **Address:** 4 E 76th St, New York, NY 10021-1811; **Phone:** 212-472-1237; **Board Cert:** Internal Medicine 1985; Infectious Disease 1988; **Med School:** Rush Med Coll 1982; **Resid:** Internal Medicine, Lenox Hill Hosp 1985; **Fellow:** Infectious Disease, Lenox Hill Hosp 1987

Mullen, Michael P MD (Inf) - **Spec Exp:** Osteomyelitis; AIDS/HIV; Hospital Acquired Infections; Tuberculosis; **Hospital:** Mt Sinai Hosp; **Address:** Mt Sinai Hosp, Infectious Disease, 5 E 98th St, Fl 8 & 11, New York, NY 10029; **Phone:** 212-241-3150; **Board Cert:** Internal Medicine 1985; Infectious Disease 1986; **Med School:** Spain 1981; **Resid:** Internal Medicine, Kingsbrook Jewish Med Ctr 1984; **Fellow:** Infectious Disease, Cabrini Med Ctr 1986; **Fac Appt:** Prof Med, Mount Sinai-Icahn Sch of Med

Murray, Henry W MD (Inf) - **Spec Exp:** Parasitic Infections; Travel Medicine; Tropical Diseases; **Hospital:** NY-Presby/Weill Cornell Med Ctr, NY (page 102); **Address:** NY Presby-Cornell Med Ctr, 525 E 68th St, Box 125, New York, NY 10065; **Phone:** 212-746-6330; **Board Cert:** Internal Medicine 1975; Infectious Disease 1978; **Med School:** Cornell Univ-Weill Med Coll 1972; **Resid:** Internal Medicine, New York Hosp 1974; Internal Medicine, Johns Hopkins Hosp 1975; **Fellow:** Infectious Disease, G Washington Univ Hosp 1978; **Fac Appt:** Prof Med, Cornell Univ-Weill Med Coll

Neibart, Eric P MD (Inf) - **Spec Exp:** Travel Medicine; AIDS/HIV; Fungal Infections; **Hospital:** Mt Sinai Hosp; **Address:** 1100 Park Ave, Ste 1C, New York, NY 10128-1202; **Phone:** 212-427-9550; **Board Cert:** Internal Medicine 1983; Infectious Disease 1986; **Med School:** UMDNJ-NJ Med Sch, Newark 1980; **Resid:** Internal Medicine, Mt Sinai Med Ctr 1983; **Fellow:** Infectious Disease, Mt Sinai Med Ctr 1986; **Fac Appt:** Asst Clin Prof Med, Mount Sinai Sch Med

Perlman, David C MD (Inf) - **Spec Exp:** AIDS/HIV; Lyme Disease; Travel Medicine; Tuberculosis; **Hospital:** Mt Sinai Beth Israel, Lenox Hill Hosp; **Address:** BIMC, Infectious Disease, 10 Union Square E, rm 3F, New York, NY 10003; **Phone:** 212-844-8549; **Board Cert:** Internal Medicine 1986; Infectious Disease 1988; **Med School:** Albert Einstein Coll Med 1983; **Resid:** Internal Medicine, Meml Sloan-Kettering Cancer Ctr 1986; **Fellow:** Infectious Disease, Montefiore Med Ctr 1988; **Fac Appt:** Prof Med, Albert Einstein Coll Med

Pollock, Alan A MD (Inf) - **Spec Exp:** Lyme Disease; Viral Infections; **Hospital:** Lenox Hill Hosp; **Address:** 184 E 70th St, Ste B1, New York, NY 10021-5110; **Phone:** 212-988-2702; **Board Cert:** Internal Medicine 1975; Infectious Disease 1978; **Med School:** NY Med Coll 1972; **Resid:** Internal Medicine, Lenox Hill Hosp 1975; **Fellow:** Infectious Disease, Manhattan VA Hosp 1977; **Fac Appt:** Asst Clin Prof Med, NYU Sch Med

Polsky, Bruce W MD (Inf) - **Spec Exp:** AIDS/HIV; Viral Infections; Infections in Cancer Patients; AIDS Related Cancers; **Hospital:** Mt Sinai Roosevelt, Mt Sinai St. Luke's; **Address:** UMPA, Infectious Disease, 36 W 60th St, New York, NY 10023; **Phone:** 212-523-2525; **Board Cert:** Internal Medicine 1983; Infectious Disease 1986; **Med School:** Wayne State Univ 1980; **Resid:** Internal Medicine, Montefiore Hosp 1983; **Fellow:** Infectious Disease, Meml Sloan-Kettering Cancer Ctr 1986; **Fac Appt:** Prof Med, Mount Sinai-Icahn Sch of Med

Press, Robert A MD/PhD (Inf) - **Spec Exp:** Infections-Surgical; Hospital Acquired Infections; **Hospital:** NYU Langone Med Ctr (page 104); **Address:** 530 1st Ave, Ste 7G, New York, NY 10016-6402; **Phone:** 212-263-7229; **Board Cert:** Internal Medicine 1976; **Med School:** NYU Sch Med 1973; **Resid:** Internal Medicine, Beth Israel Hosp 1975; Internal Medicine, Bellevue Hosp 1976; **Fellow:** Infectious Disease, Montefiore Hosp Med Ctr 1978; **Fac Appt:** Clin Prof Med, NYU Sch Med

Romagnoli, Mario MD (Inf) - **Spec Exp:** AIDS/HIV; Bone/Joint Infections; **Hospital:** Lenox Hill Hosp; **Address:** 903 Park Ave, New York, NY 10075; **Phone:** 212-396-3390; **Board Cert:** Internal Medicine 1979; Infectious Disease 1982; **Med School:** Columbia P&S 1976; **Resid:** Internal Medicine, NY-Presby/Columbia Univ Med Ctr 1979; **Fellow:** Infectious Disease, Beth Israel Deaconess Med Ctr 1981; **Fac Appt:** Assoc Prof Med, Columbia P&S

Rosenberg, Howard E MD (Inf) - **Spec Exp:** Travel Medicine; **Hospital:** NY-Presby/Weill Cornell Med Ctr, NY (page 102); **Address:** 235 E 67th St, Ste 205, New York, NY 10065; **Phone:** 212-744-1170; **Board Cert:** Internal Medicine 2005; Infectious Disease 2008; **Med School:** SUNY Downstate 1992; **Resid:** Internal Medicine, NY-Presby/Weill Cornell Med Ctr 1995; Internal Medicine, Meml Sloan-Kettering Cancer Ctr 1996; **Fellow:** Infectious Disease, NY-Presby/Weill Cornell Med Ctr 1998; **Fac Appt:** Assoc Prof Med, Cornell Univ-Weill Med Coll

Scully, Brian E MD (Inf) - **Spec Exp:** Lyme Disease; Infections in Transplant Patients; Hospital Acquired Infections; Infections in Immunocompromised Patients; **Hospital:** NY-Presby/Columbia Univ Med Ctr, NY (page 102); **Address:** NY-Presby, Infectious Disease, 180 Fort Washington Ave Fl 2 - rm 242, Harkness Pavilion, New York, NY 10032; **Phone:** 212-305-8039; **Board Cert:** Internal Medicine 1975; Infectious Disease 1982; **Med School:** Ireland 1971; **Resid:** Internal Medicine, St Lukes-Roosevelt Hosp 1975; **Fellow:** Infectious Disease, NY-Presby/Columbia Univ Med Ctr 1982; **Fac Appt:** Assoc Prof Med, Columbia P&S

Simberkoff, Michael S MD (Inf) - **Spec Exp:** AIDS/HIV; Infections-Respiratory; Hospital Acquired Infections; Tuberculosis; **Hospital:** VA NY Harbor Hlthcare Sys-Manhattan Campus; **Address:** 423 E 23rd St, 3 West Executive Office, New York, NY 10010; **Phone:** 212-951-3417; **Board Cert:** Internal Medicine 1980; Infectious Disease 1972; **Med School:** NYU Sch Med 1962; **Resid:** Internal Medicine, Bellevue Hosp Ctr 1964; Internal Medicine, NYU Med Ctr 1967; **Fellow:** Infectious Disease, Bellevue Hosp Ctr 1969; **Fac Appt:** Prof Med, NYU Sch Med

Smith, Paul T MD (Inf) - **Spec Exp:** AIDS/HIV; Skin/Soft Tissue Infections; Infections in Transplant Patients; Travel Medicine; **Hospital:** NY-Presby/Weill Cornell Med Ctr, NY (page 102), Hosp For Special Surgery (page 109); **Address:** 943 Lexington Ave, New York, NY 10021; **Phone:** 212-396-4077; **Board Cert:** Internal Medicine 2005; Infectious Disease 2007; **Med School:** Hahnemann Univ 1992; **Resid:** Internal Medicine, NY-Presby/Weill Cornell Med Ctr 1995; **Fellow:** Infectious Disease, Yale-New Haven Hosp 1997; **Fac Appt:** Asst Clin Prof Med, Cornell Univ-Weill Med Coll

Soave, Rosemary MD (Inf) - **Spec Exp:** Infections in Transplant Patients; **Hospital:** NY-Presby/Weill Cornell Med Ctr, NY (page 102); **Address:** I D Assocs, 1305 York Ave Fl 4, New York, NY 10021; **Phone:** 646-962-4800; **Board Cert:** Internal Medicine 1979; Infectious Disease 1984; **Med School:** Cornell Univ-Weill Med Coll 1976; **Resid:** Internal Medicine, New York Hosp/Cornell Med Ctr 1979; Internal Medicine, Meml Sloan Kettering Cancer Ctr 1980; **Fellow:** Infectious Disease, New York Hosp/Cornell Med Ctr 1982; **Fac Appt:** Assoc Prof Med, Cornell Univ-Weill Med Coll

New York (Manhattan) *Infectious Disease*

Vielemeyer, Ole MD (Inf) - **Spec Exp:** Staphylococcal Infections; Diagnostic Problems; Hospital Acquired Infections; Travel Medicine; **Hospital:** NY-Presby/Weill Cornell Med Ctr, NY (page 102); **Address:** Infectious Disease Assocs, 1305 York Ave Fl 4, New York, NY 10021; **Phone:** 646-962-4800; **Board Cert:** Internal Medicine 2010; Infectious Disease 2003; Medical Microbiology 2003; **Med School:** Germany 1993; **Resid:** Internal Medicine, Rochester Genl Hosp 2000; **Fellow:** Infectious Disease, Yale-New Haven Hosp 2002; Medical Microbiology, Yale-New Haven Hosp 2003; **Fac Appt:** Asst Prof Med, Cornell Univ-Weill Med Coll

Wallach, Frances MD (Inf) - **Spec Exp:** AIDS/HIV; Infection Control; HIV & Blood Transfusions; **Hospital:** Mt Sinai Hosp; **Address:** 17 E 102nd St Fl 3rd, New York, NY 10029; **Phone:** 212-241-7968; **Board Cert:** Internal Medicine 1989; Infectious Disease 2012; **Med School:** Albany Med Coll 1985; **Resid:** Internal Medicine, Montefiore Med Ctr 1989; **Fellow:** Infectious Disease, NY Hosp-Cornell Med Ctr 1992; **Fac Appt:** Asst Prof Med, Mount Sinai Sch Med

Yancovitz, Stanley R MD (Inf) - **Spec Exp:** Lyme Disease; Endocarditis; Bone/Joint Infections; Tuberculosis; **Hospital:** Mt Sinai Beth Israel; **Address:** 10 Union Sq, Ste 3F, New York, NY 10003; **Phone:** 212-420-2600; **Board Cert:** Internal Medicine 1973; Infectious Disease 1976; **Med School:** SUNY Downstate 1967; **Resid:** Internal Medicine, Metropolitan Hosp Ctr 1969; Internal Medicine, Beth Israel Med Ctr 1973; **Fellow:** Infectious Disease, Mt Sinai Hosp 1975; **Fac Appt:** Prof Med, Albert Einstein Coll Med

Internal Medicine

Amsterdam, Alison D MD (IM) *PCP* - **Spec Exp:** Women's Health; **Hospital:** Mt Sinai Hosp; **Address:** Manhattan Internal Medicine, 108 E 96th St, New York, NY 10128; **Phone:** 646-745-2888; **Board Cert:** Internal Medicine 2003; **Med School:** Geo Wash Univ 2000; **Resid:** Internal Medicine, NYU Med Ctr 2003; **Fellow:** Women's Health, Meml Sloan Kettering Cancer Ctr 2005

Aronne, Louis J MD (IM) - **Spec Exp:** Weight Management; Obesity; Diabetes; **Hospital:** NY-Presby/Weill Cornell Med Ctr, NY (page 102); **Address:** Weill Med Ctr for Weight Mgmt, 1165 York Ave, New York, NY 10065; **Phone:** 646-962-2111; **Board Cert:** Internal Medicine 1984; **Med School:** Johns Hopkins Univ 1981; **Resid:** Internal Medicine, Jacobi Med Ctr 1984; Internal Medicine, NY-Presby/Weill Cornell Med Ctr 1986; **Fac Appt:** Clin Prof Med, Cornell Univ-Weill Med Coll

Babbar, Rajeev MD (IM) *PCP* - **Spec Exp:** Osteoporosis; Geriatric Medicine; **Hospital:** NYU Langone Med Ctr (page 104); **Address:** NYU Trinity Ctr, 111 Broadway Fl 2, New York, NY 10006; **Phone:** 212-263-9700; **Board Cert:** Internal Medicine 2004; **Med School:** Mount Sinai Sch Med 1991; **Resid:** Internal Medicine, Mt Sinai Hosp 1994; **Fac Appt:** Asst Clin Prof Med, NYU Sch Med

Barley, Christopher L MD (IM) *PCP* - **Hospital:** NY-Presby/Weill Cornell Med Ctr, NY (page 102); **Address:** 110 E 55th St Fl 9, New York, NY 10022; **Phone:** 212-758-3590; **Board Cert:** Internal Medicine 2006; **Med School:** Geo Wash Univ 1993; **Resid:** Internal Medicine, NY-Presby/Weill Cornell Med Ctr 1996; **Fac Appt:** Asst Clin Prof Med, Cornell Univ-Weill Med Coll

Baskin, David H MD (IM) *PCP* - **Spec Exp:** Preventive Medicine; Cholesterol/Lipid Disorders; **Hospital:** Mt Sinai Roosevelt; **Address:** 185 West End Ave, Ste 1M, New York, NY 10023; **Phone:** 212-595-7701; **Board Cert:** Internal Medicine 1985; **Med School:** Boston Univ 1982; **Resid:** Internal Medicine, St Lukes-Roosevelt Hosp 1985; **Fac Appt:** Asst Clin Prof Med, Columbia P&S

Boxer, William P MD (IM) *PCP* - **Spec Exp:** Osteoporosis; **Hospital:** Lenox Hill Hosp; **Address:** Medical Associates East, 220 E 69th St, New York, NY 10021; **Phone:** 212-570-1800; **Board Cert:** Internal Medicine 2010; **Med School:** SUNY Upstate Med Univ 1997; **Resid:** Internal Medicine, Boston Med Ctr 2000

Bregman, Zachary MD (IM) *PCP* - **Spec Exp:** Pulmonary Disease; Complex Diagnosis; **Hospital:** NS-LIJ Hlth Sys; **Address:** 247 3rd Ave, Ste 304, New York, NY 10010; **Phone:** 212-505-6663; **Board Cert:** Internal Medicine 1986; **Med School:** Univ Pennsylvania 1981; **Resid:** Internal Medicine, Beth Israel Med Ctr 1984; **Fellow:** Pulmonary Disease, Beth Israel Med Ctr 1986

Bruno, Peter J MD (IM) *PCP* - **Spec Exp:** Sports Medicine; **Hospital:** Lenox Hill Hosp; **Address:** 110 E 59th St, Ste 9A, New York, NY 10022; **Phone:** 212-583-2898; **Board Cert:** Internal Medicine 1979; **Med School:** Hahnemann Univ 1975; **Resid:** Internal Medicine, Lenox Hill Hosp 1979; **Fac Appt:** Assoc Prof Med, NYU Sch Med

Bush, Michael N MD (IM) *PCP* - **Spec Exp:** Preventive Medicine; Travel Medicine; **Hospital:** Lenox Hill Hosp, NYU Langone Med Ctr (page 104); **Address:** 115 E 57th St, Ste 630, New York, NY 10022; **Phone:** 212-583-2990; **Board Cert:** Internal Medicine 1981; **Med School:** SUNY Downstate 1978; **Resid:** Internal Medicine, Lenox Hill Hosp 1981; **Fac Appt:** Assoc Clin Prof Med, NYU Sch Med

Case, David B MD (IM) *PCP* - **Spec Exp:** Hypertension; Preventive Cardiology; **Hospital:** NY-Presby/Columbia Univ Med Ctr, NY (page 102); **Address:** 635 Madison Ave Fl 7, New York, NY 10022; **Phone:** 212-857-4660; **Board Cert:** Internal Medicine 1974; **Med School:** Columbia P&S 1968; **Resid:** Internal Medicine, Johns Hopkins Hosp 1970; **Fellow:** Cardiovascular Disease, NY-Presby/Columbia Univ Med Ctr 1972; **Fac Appt:** Assoc Clin Prof Med, Cornell Univ-Weill Med Coll

Charap, Mitchell MD (IM) *PCP* - **Hospital:** NYU Langone Med Ctr (page 104); **Address:** NYU, Internal Med, 530 1st Ave, Ste 7B, New York, NY 10016; **Phone:** 212-263-7442; **Board Cert:** Internal Medicine 2012; **Med School:** NYU Sch Med 1977; **Resid:** Internal Medicine, NYU Med Ctr 1981; **Fac Appt:** Prof Med, NYU Sch Med

Charap, Peter MD (IM) *PCP* - **Spec Exp:** Preventive Medicine; **Hospital:** Mt Sinai Hosp; **Address:** Assocs in Internal Med, 234 Central Park West, New York, NY 10024; **Phone:** 212-579-2200; **Board Cert:** Internal Medicine 1987; **Med School:** Mount Sinai Sch Med 1984; **Resid:** Internal Medicine, Mt Sinai Hosp 1987; **Fellow:** Public Health & Genl Preventive Med, Mt Sinai Hosp 1988; **Fac Appt:** Asst Clin Prof Med, Mount Sinai-Icahn Sch of Med

Cohen, Richard P MD (IM) *PCP* - **Spec Exp:** Complex Diagnosis; Preventive Medicine; **Hospital:** NY-Presby/Weill Cornell Med Ctr, NY (page 102); **Address:** 235 E 67th St, New York, NY 10021; **Phone:** 212-734-6464; **Board Cert:** Internal Medicine 1978; **Med School:** Cornell Univ-Weill Med Coll 1975; **Resid:** Internal Medicine, NY-Presby/Weill Cornell Med Ctr 1978; **Fellow:** Infectious Disease, NY-Presby/Weill Cornell Med Ctr 1979; **Fac Appt:** Clin Prof Med, Cornell Univ-Weill Med Coll

Cohen, Robert L MD (IM) *PCP* - **Spec Exp:** Preventive Medicine; **Hospital:** NYU Langone Med Ctr (page 104); **Address:** 314 W 14th St Fl 5, New York, NY 10014; **Phone:** 212-620-0144; **Board Cert:** Internal Medicine 1978; **Med School:** Rush Med Coll 1975; **Resid:** Internal Medicine, Cook Co Hosp 1978; **Fac Appt:** Asst Clin Prof Med, NYU Sch Med

Cohn, Symra A MD (IM) *PCP* - **Spec Exp:** Women's Health; **Hospital:** NY-Presby/Weill Cornell Med Ctr, NY (page 102); **Address:** 3 E 71st St, New York, NY 10021; **Phone:** 212-288-1302; **Board Cert:** Internal Medicine 2005; **Med School:** NY Med Coll 1991; **Resid:** Internal Medicine, NY-Presby/Weill Cornell Med Ctr 1994; **Fac Appt:** Asst Clin Prof Med, Cornell Univ-Weill Med Coll

Constantiner, Arturo MD (IM) *PCP* - **Spec Exp:** Hypertension; Kidney Disease; Kidney Stones; Dialysis Care; **Hospital:** NY-Presby/Lower Manhattan Hosp (page 102); **Address:** 145 Chambers St, New York, NY 10007; **Phone:** 212-349-8455; **Board Cert:** Internal Medicine 1979; Nephrology 2006; **Med School:** Mexico 1975; **Resid:** Internal Medicine, Elmhurst Hosp 1979; **Fellow:** Nephrology, Mt Sinai Hosp 1981; **Fac Appt:** Asst Clin Prof Med, NYU Sch Med

Cunningham-Rundles, Ward MD (IM) *PCP* - **Spec Exp:** Allergy & Immunology; **Hospital:** NY-Presby/Weill Cornell Med Ctr, NY (page 102), Mt Sinai Hosp; **Address:** 240 E 68th St, New York, NY 10065; **Phone:** 212-737-8973; **Board Cert:** Internal Medicine 1976; **Med School:** NYU Sch Med 1971; **Resid:** Internal Medicine, NYU-Bellevue Hosp 1973; **Fellow:** Immunology, Meml Sloan-Kettering Cancer Ctr 1975; Medical Oncology, Meml Sloan-Kettering Cancer Ctr 1976; **Fac Appt:** Asst Clin Prof Med, Cornell Univ-Weill Med Coll

Dechiario, Alan A MD (IM) *PCP* - **Spec Exp:** Preventive Medicine; **Hospital:** NY-Presby/Columbia Univ Med Ctr, NY (page 102); **Address:** New York Physicians, 635 Madison Ave Fl 8, New York, NY 10022; **Phone:** 212-857-4511; **Board Cert:** Internal Medicine 2013; **Med School:** SUNY Stony Brook 1990; **Resid:** Internal Medicine, Columbia-Presby Med Ctr 1993; **Fac Appt:** Asst Clin Prof Med, Columbia P&S

Dhalla, Satish MD (IM) *PCP* - **Spec Exp:** Hypertension; Diabetes; Travel Medicine; Preventive Medicine; **Hospital:** NYU Langone Med Ctr (page 104); **Address:** NYU Trinity Ctr, 111 Broadway, Fl 2, New York, NY 10006; **Phone:** 212-263-9700; **Board Cert:** Internal Medicine 1976; **Med School:** India 1972; **Resid:** Internal Medicine, Beekman Downtown Hosp 1976; **Fac Appt:** Assoc Clin Prof Med, NYU Sch Med

Dolinsky, Jason H MD (IM) *PCP* - **Spec Exp:** Preventive Medicine; **Hospital:** Mt Sinai Hosp, Mt Sinai Beth Israel; **Address:** 899 Lexington Ave, New York, NY 10065; **Phone:** 212-737-1102; **Board Cert:** Internal Medicine 2007; **Med School:** NYU Sch Med 1994; **Resid:** Internal Medicine, Hosp Univ Penn 1997

Ehrlich, Martin Harvey MD (IM) *PCP* - **Spec Exp:** Complementary Medicine; Preventive Medicine; Acupuncture; **Hospital:** Mt Sinai Beth Israel; **Address:** Ctr for Health & Healing, 245 5th Ave Fl 2, New York, NY 10016; **Phone:** 646-935-2265; **Board Cert:** Internal Medicine 1988; **Med School:** Columbia P&S 1985; **Resid:** Internal Medicine, Harlem Hosp 1989; **Fac Appt:** Asst Prof Med, Albert Einstein Coll Med

Etingin, Orli MD (IM) *PCP* - **Spec Exp:** Preventive Medicine; Bleeding/Coagulation Disorders; Women's Health; **Hospital:** NY-Presby/Weill Cornell Med Ctr, NY (page 102); **Address:** 425 E 61st St, Fl 11, New York, NY 10065; **Phone:** 212-821-0926; **Board Cert:** Internal Medicine 1984; Hematology 1988; **Med School:** Albert Einstein Coll Med 1980; **Resid:** Internal Medicine, NY-Presby/Weill Cornell Med Ctr 1983; **Fellow:** Hematology & Oncology, NY-Presby/Weill Cornell Med Ctr 1986; **Fac Appt:** Clin Prof Med, Cornell Univ-Weill Med Coll

Fafalak, Robert G MD (IM) *PCP* - **Spec Exp:** Rheumatology; **Hospital:** NYU Langone Med Ctr (page 104); **Address:** 36 W 9th St, Ste 1A, New York, NY 10011; **Phone:** 212-933-0072; **Board Cert:** Internal Medicine 2008; **Med School:** NY Med Coll 1987; **Resid:** Internal Medicine, New York Hosp 1990; **Fellow:** Rheumatology, Hosp for Special Surgery 1992

Federman, Alex D MD (IM) *PCP* - **Spec Exp:** Preventive Medicine; Hypertension; **Hospital:** Mt Sinai Hosp; **Address:** Internal Med Assocs, 17 E 102nd St Fl 7, New York, NY 10029; **Phone:** 212-659-8551; **Board Cert:** Internal Medicine 2009; **Med School:** SUNY Downstate 1996; **Resid:** Internal Medicine, Montefiore Med Ctr 1999; **Fac Appt:** Assoc Prof Med, Mount Sinai-Icahn Sch of Med

Feltheimer, Seth D MD (IM) *PCP* - **Spec Exp:** Preventive Medicine; Perioperative Medical Care; **Hospital:** NY-Presby/Columbia Univ Med Ctr, NY (page 102); **Address:** NY-Presby, Primary Care, 180 Fort Washington Ave, Ste 248, New York, NY 10032; **Phone:** 212-305-8669; **Board Cert:** Internal Medicine 1984; **Med School:** Spain 1981; **Resid:** Internal Medicine, Kingsbrook Jewish Med Ctr 1984; **Fellow:** Internal Medicine, NY-Presby/Columbia Univ Med Ctr 1985; **Fac Appt:** Assoc Prof Med, Columbia P&S

Feuer, Martin M MD (IM) *PCP* - **Spec Exp:** Bronchitis; Asthma; Emphysema; Chronic Obstructive Lung Disease (COPD); **Hospital:** Mt Sinai Beth Israel, Mt Sinai Hosp; **Address:** 899 Lexington Ave, New York, NY 10065; **Phone:** 212-744-5433; **Board Cert:** Internal Medicine 1966; Pulmonary Disease 1972; **Med School:** NYU Sch Med 1959; **Resid:** Internal Medicine, Mt Sinai Hosp 1963; **Fellow:** Pulmonary Disease, Montefiore Med Ctr 1965; **Fac Appt:** Asst Prof Med, Mount Sinai-Icahn Sch of Med

Fiedler, Robert P MD (IM) *PCP* - **Spec Exp:** Thyroid Disorders; Diabetes; **Hospital:** Mt Sinai Hosp; **Address:** 1175 Park Ave, New York, NY 10128; **Phone:** 212-289-6500 x114; **Board Cert:** Internal Medicine 1970; Endocrinology, Diabetes & Metabolism 1972; **Med School:** Albert Einstein Coll Med 1964; **Resid:** Internal Medicine, DC Gen Hosp 1966; Internal Medicine, VA Med Ctr 1967; **Fellow:** Endocrinology, Mt Sinai Hosp 1969; **Fac Appt:** Assoc Clin Prof Med, Mount Sinai-Icahn Sch of Med

Fisher, Laura Lani MD (IM) *PCP* - **Spec Exp:** Preventive Medicine; Lyme Disease; Women's Health; **Hospital:** NY-Presby/Weill Cornell Med Ctr, NY (page 102); **Address:** 1385 York Ave, New York, NY 10021; **Phone:** 212-717-5920; **Board Cert:** Internal Medicine 1987; **Med School:** Brown Univ 1984; **Resid:** Internal Medicine, NY Hosp-Cornell Med Ctr 1987; **Fellow:** Infectious Disease, Mass Genl Hosp 1989; **Fac Appt:** Asst Clin Prof Med, Cornell Univ-Weill Med Coll

Fried, Richard P MD (IM) *PCP* - **Spec Exp:** Lyme Disease; Fevers of Unknown Origin; AIDS/HIV; **Hospital:** Mt Sinai Roosevelt; **Address:** 15 W 72nd St, Ste 1N, New York, NY 10023; **Phone:** 212-580-4840; **Board Cert:** Internal Medicine 1972; Infectious Disease 1974; **Med School:** Columbia P&S 1968; **Resid:** Internal Medicine, St Lukes-Roosevelt Hosp 1972; **Fellow:** Infectious Disease, Stanford Univ Hosp & Clins 1974; **Fac Appt:** Assoc Clin Prof Med, Columbia P&S

Friedman, Jeffrey P MD (IM) *PCP* - **Spec Exp:** Preventive Medicine; Travel Medicine; **Hospital:** NYU Langone Med Ctr (page 104); **Address:** MHMG, Primary Care, 317 E 34th St Fl 10, New York, NY 10016; **Phone:** 212-726-7440; **Board Cert:** Internal Medicine 1986; **Med School:** NYU Sch Med 1983; **Resid:** Internal Medicine, Bellevue Hosp 1987; **Fac Appt:** Assoc Clin Prof Med, NYU Sch Med

Gafanovich, Marina MD (IM) *PCP* - **Hospital:** NY-Presby/Weill Cornell Med Ctr, NY (page 102); **Address:** 1550 York Ave, New York, NY 10028; **Phone:** 212-249-6218; **Board Cert:** Internal Medicine 2006; **Med School:** Israel 2002; **Resid:** Internal Medicine, N Shore Univ Hosp 2005

Galland, Leo MD (IM) - **Spec Exp:** Nutrition; Chronic Illness; Complementary Medicine; **Address:** Foundation for Integrated Medicine, 20 Fifth Ave, Ste 1E, New York, NY 10011; **Phone:** 212-989-6733; **Board Cert:** Internal Medicine 1972; **Med School:** NYU Sch Med 1968; **Resid:** Internal Medicine, Bellevue Hosp 1972; **Fellow:** Behavioral Medicine, Univ Conn Hlth Ctr 1981

Gelbard, Sandra N MD (IM) *PCP* - **Spec Exp:** Preventive Medicine; **Hospital:** Lenox Hill Hosp; **Address:** 993 Park Ave, New York, NY 10028; **Phone:** 212-988-5303; **Board Cert:** Internal Medicine 2014; **Med School:** SUNY Stony Brook 1999; **Resid:** Internal Medicine, NYU Med Ctr 2003

Golden, Flavia A MD (IM) *PCP* - **Spec Exp:** Women's Health; **Hospital:** NY-Presby/Weill Cornell Med Ctr, NY (page 102); **Address:** 310 E 72nd St, New York, NY 10021; **Phone:** 212-396-3016; **Board Cert:** Internal Medicine 2013; **Med School:** NYU Sch Med 1990; **Resid:** Internal Medicine, NY-Presby/Weill Cornell Med Ctr 1993; **Fac Appt:** Asst Prof Med, Cornell Univ-Weill Med Coll

Goldin, Daniel MD (IM) *PCP* - **Hospital:** NY-Presby/Weill Cornell Med Ctr, NY (page 102); **Address:** 646 Park Ave, New York, NY 10065; **Phone:** 212-717-4884; **Board Cert:** Internal Medicine 2004; **Med School:** Cornell Univ-Weill Med Coll 2001; **Resid:** Internal Medicine, Weill Cornell Med Ctr 2004

Goldstein, Paul H MD (IM) *PCP* - **Spec Exp:** Preventive Medicine; **Hospital:** NYU Langone Med Ctr (page 104); **Address:** 80 5th Ave, Ste 1601, New York, NY 10011; **Phone:** 212-645-8500; **Board Cert:** Internal Medicine 1985; **Med School:** NY Med Coll 1982; **Resid:** Internal Medicine, St Vincents Hosp 1985

Greaney, Edward J MD (IM) *PCP* - **Spec Exp:** Preventive Medicine; Nutrition; Hypertension; **Hospital:** NYU Langone Med Ctr (page 104); **Address:** MHMG, Primary Care, 317 E 34th St Fl 4, New York, NY 10016; **Phone:** 212-726-7488; **Board Cert:** Internal Medicine 2010; **Med School:** NYU Sch Med 1995; **Resid:** Internal Medicine, NYU Med Ctr 1999; **Fac Appt:** Asst Clin Prof Med, NYU Sch Med

Haber, Stuart W MD (IM) *PCP* - **Spec Exp:** AIDS/HIV; Travel Medicine; Infectious Disease; **Hospital:** Mt Sinai Roosevelt; **Address:** 12-A Sheridan Square, New York, NY 10014; **Phone:** 212-929-2370; **Board Cert:** Internal Medicine 1986; **Med School:** NYU Sch Med 1983; **Resid:** Internal Medicine, Emory Univ Hosp 1986; **Fellow:** Infectious Disease, Emory Univ Hosp 1989

Halperin, Ira C MD (IM) - **Spec Exp:** Leukemia; Myeloproliferative Disorders; **Hospital:** Mt Sinai Beth Israel; **Address:** 2 Fifth Ave, Ste 9, New York, NY 10011-8855; **Phone:** 212-254-5940; **Board Cert:** Internal Medicine 1970; Hematology 1976; Medical Oncology 1979; **Med School:** NYU Sch Med 1962; **Resid:** Internal Medicine, St Vincents Hosp 1966; **Fellow:** Hematology, Mt Sinai Hosp 1969

Hart, Catherine C MD (IM) *PCP* - **Spec Exp:** Infectious Disease; **Hospital:** NY-Presby/Weill Cornell Med Ctr, NY (page 102); **Address:** 310 E 72nd St, Fl 2, New York, NY 10021; **Phone:** 212-396-3272; **Board Cert:** Internal Medicine 1984; Infectious Disease 1986; **Med School:** Univ Pennsylvania 1980; **Resid:** Internal Medicine, NY-Presby/Weill Cornell Med Ctr 1983; **Fellow:** Infectious Disease, NY-Presby/Weill Cornell Med Ctr 1985; **Fac Appt:** Asst Clin Prof Med, Cornell Univ-Weill Med Coll

Hauptman, Allen S MD (IM) *PCP* - **Spec Exp:** Preventive Medicine; **Hospital:** NYU Langone Med Ctr (page 104); **Address:** MHMG, Primary Care, 317 E 34th St Fl 7, New York, NY 10016; **Phone:** 212-726-7494; **Board Cert:** Internal Medicine 1981; **Med School:** NYU Sch Med 1978; **Resid:** Internal Medicine, NYU-Bellevue Hosp 1981; **Fac Appt:** Asst Clin Prof Med, NYU Sch Med

Hoffman, Eileen M MD (IM) *PCP* - **Spec Exp:** Women's Health; **Hospital:** NYU Langone Med Ctr (page 104); **Address:** 35 E 35th St, Ste 1J, New York, NY 10016; **Phone:** 646-424-1530; **Board Cert:** Internal Medicine 1982; **Med School:** SUNY Stony Brook 1979; **Resid:** Internal Medicine, NYU-Bellevue Hosp Ctr 1982; **Fellow:** Immunology, Rockefeller Univ 1983; **Fac Appt:** Asst Clin Prof Med, NYU Sch Med

Horbar, Gary M MD (IM) *PCP* - **Spec Exp:** Preventive Medicine; **Hospital:** Lenox Hill Hosp; **Address:** 6 E 85th St, New York, NY 10028; **Phone:** 212-570-9119; **Board Cert:** Internal Medicine 1979; **Med School:** NY Med Coll 1976; **Resid:** Internal Medicine, Lenox Hill Hosp 1980; **Fac Appt:** Asst Clin Prof Med, NYU Sch Med

Horovitz, Len H MD (IM) *PCP* - **Spec Exp:** Bronchoscopy; Asthma; Emphysema; **Hospital:** Lenox Hill Hosp; **Address:** 47 E 77th St, Ste 201, New York, NY 10075; **Phone:** 212-744-3001; **Board Cert:** Internal Medicine 1980; Pulmonary Disease 1984; **Med School:** NYU Sch Med 1976; **Resid:** Internal Medicine, Lenox Hill Hosp 1980; **Fellow:** Pulmonary Disease, Lenox Hill Hosp 1982

Kaminsky, Donald L MD (IM) *PCP* - **Spec Exp:** AIDS/HIV; Tropical Diseases; Travel Medicine; **Hospital:** Mt Sinai Beth Israel; **Address:** Gramercy Park Physicians, 10 Union Square East, Ste 5M, New York, NY 10003; **Phone:** 212-253-6800; **Board Cert:** Internal Medicine 1982; **Med School:** Geo Wash Univ 1979; **Resid:** Internal Medicine, Beth Israel Med Ctr 1982; **Fellow:** Infectious Disease, Beth Israel Med Ctr 1984

Kennedy, James T MD (IM) *PCP* - **Spec Exp:** Preventive Medicine; **Hospital:** NYU Langone Med Ctr (page 104); **Address:** 650 1st Ave Fl 3, New York, NY 10016; **Phone:** 212-689-7768; **Board Cert:** Internal Medicine 1978; **Med School:** NYU Sch Med 1972; **Resid:** Internal Medicine, Bellevue Hosp 1977; **Fac Appt:** Clin Prof Med, NYU Sch Med

Kennish, Arthur J MD (IM) *PCP* - **Spec Exp:** Mitral Valve Disease; Coronary Artery Disease; Cardiovascular Disease; Preventive Cardiology; **Hospital:** Mt Sinai Hosp; **Address:** 108 E 96th St, New York, NY 10128; **Phone:** 212-410-6610; **Board Cert:** Internal Medicine 1980; Cardiovascular Disease 1983; **Med School:** Albert Einstein Coll Med 1977; **Resid:** Internal Medicine, Mt Sinai Hosp 1980; **Fellow:** Cardiovascular Disease, Mt Sinai Hosp 1982; **Fac Appt:** Asst Clin Prof Med, Mount Sinai-Icahn Sch of Med

Kent, Jennifer MD (IM) *PCP* - **Hospital:** Mt Sinai Hosp; **Address:** Primary Care Assocs, 10 E 102nd St Fl 6, New York, NY 10029; **Phone:** 212-241-6585; **Board Cert:** Internal Medicine 2013; **Med School:** Israel 2000; **Resid:** Internal Medicine, Mt Sinai Hosp 2003; **Fac Appt:** Asst Prof Med, Mount Sinai-Icahn Sch of Med

Knoepflmacher, Paul MD (IM) *PCP* - **Hospital:** Mt Sinai Hosp; **Address:** Manhattan Internal Medicine, 108 E 96th St, New York, NY 10128; **Phone:** 646-745-2888; **Board Cert:** Internal Medicine 2009; **Med School:** UMDNJ-NJ Med Sch, Newark 1996; **Resid:** Internal Medicine, Mt Sinai Hosp 1999

Kurth, Rebecca J MD (IM) *PCP* - **Spec Exp:** Preventive Medicine; **Hospital:** NY-Presby/Columbia Univ Med Ctr, NY (page 102); **Address:** 800A Fifth Ave, Ste 502A, New York, NY 10065; **Phone:** 212-230-1081; **Board Cert:** Internal Medicine 2011; **Med School:** Columbia P&S 1987; **Resid:** Internal Medicine, NY Presby-Columbia Med Ctr 1990; **Fac Appt:** Asst Clin Prof Med, Columbia P&S

Lamm, Steven MD (IM) *PCP* - **Spec Exp:** Obesity; Sexual Dysfunction; Preventive Medicine; Men's Health; **Hospital:** NYU Langone Med Ctr (page 104); **Address:** Ctr for Men's Hlth, 555 Madison Ave Fl 2, New York, NY 10022; **Phone:** 212-988-1146; **Board Cert:** Internal Medicine 1977; **Med School:** NYU Sch Med 1974; **Resid:** Internal Medicine, NYU Med Ctr 1979; **Fellow:** Rheumatology, NYU Med Ctr 1978; **Fac Appt:** Asst Clin Prof Med, NYU Sch Med

Legato, Marianne J MD (IM) *PCP* - **Spec Exp:** Cardiovascular Disease; Gender Specific Medicine; **Hospital:** NY-Presby/Columbia Univ Med Ctr, NY (page 102), Lenox Hill Hosp; **Address:** 903 Park Ave, Ste 2A, New York, NY 10075; **Phone:** 212-737-5663; **Board Cert:** Internal Medicine 2013; **Med School:** NYU Sch Med 1962; **Resid:** Internal Medicine, NY-Presby/Columbia Univ Med Ctr 1965; **Fellow:** Cardiovascular Disease, NY-Presby/Columbia Univ Med Ctr 1968; **Fac Appt:** Prof Emeritus Med, Columbia P&S

Leonard, Michael R MD (IM) *PCP* - **Hospital:** NY-Presby/Weill Cornell Med Ctr, NY (page 102); **Address:** 1550 York Ave, New York, NY 10028; **Phone:** 212-249-8056; **Board Cert:** Internal Medicine 2006; **Med School:** Mount Sinai Sch Med 1992; **Resid:** Internal Medicine, New York Hosp 1995

Lewin, Margaret MD (IM) *PCP* - **Spec Exp:** Preventive Medicine; Women's Health; Travel Medicine; **Hospital:** NY-Presby/Weill Cornell Med Ctr, NY (page 102), Hosp For Special Surgery (page 109); **Address:** 635 Madison Ave, Fl 8, New York, NY 10022; **Phone:** 212-857-4505; **Board Cert:** Internal Medicine 1980; Hematology 1982; Medical Oncology 1983; **Med School:** Case West Res Univ 1977; **Resid:** Internal Medicine, NY-Presby/Weill Cornell Med Ctr 1980; **Fellow:** Hematology & Oncology, NY-Presby/Weill Cornell Med Ctr 1983; **Fac Appt:** Assoc Clin Prof Med, Cornell Univ-Weill Med Coll

Lewin, Neal A MD (IM) *PCP* - **Spec Exp:** Preventive Medicine; Headache; Migraine; Complex Diagnosis; **Hospital:** NYU Langone Med Ctr (page 104); **Address:** 120 E 36th St, Ste 1B, New York, NY 10016; **Phone:** 212-889-2813; **Board Cert:** Internal Medicine 1977; Emergency Medicine 2012; **Med School:** SUNY Downstate 1974; **Resid:** Internal Medicine, NYU-Bellevue Hosp 1977; **Fac Appt:** Prof Med, NYU Sch Med

Lewin, Sharon MD (IM) *PCP* - **Spec Exp:** AIDS/HIV; Travel Medicine; Women's Health; Fevers of Unknown Origin; **Hospital:** Mt Sinai Roosevelt; **Address:** 139 W 82nd St, New York, NY 10024; **Phone:** 212-496-7200; **Board Cert:** Internal Medicine 1978; Infectious Disease 1980; **Med School:** Univ Toronto 1975; **Resid:** Internal Medicine, Wadsworth VA Hosp 1978; **Fellow:** Infectious Disease, NYU-Bellevue Hosp 1980; **Fac Appt:** Asst Clin Prof Med, Columbia P&S

Liguori, Michael MD (IM) *PCP* - **Spec Exp:** Geriatric Rehabilitation; AIDS/HIV; Geriatric Care; **Hospital:** NYU Langone Med Ctr (page 104); **Address:** 80 5th Ave, Ste 1601, New York, NY 10011; **Phone:** 212-645-8500; **Board Cert:** Internal Medicine 1985; **Med School:** Mount Sinai Sch Med 1981; **Resid:** Internal Medicine, St Vincents Hosp 1984

Lipton, Mark S MD (IM) *PCP* - **Spec Exp:** Preventive Cardiology; Coronary Artery Disease; Non-Invasive Cardiology; Cholesterol/Lipid Disorders; **Hospital:** NYU Langone Med Ctr (page 104); **Address:** 635 Madison Ave, Fl 3, New York, NY 10022; **Phone:** 212-570-2077; **Board Cert:** Internal Medicine 1981; Cardiovascular Disease 1985; **Med School:** NYU Sch Med 1978; **Resid:** Internal Medicine, NYU-Bellevue Hosp 1981; **Fellow:** Cardiovascular Disease, NYU Med Ctr 1985; **Fac Appt:** Assoc Clin Prof Med, NYU Sch Med

Liu, George MD (IM) *PCP* - **Spec Exp:** Endocrinology; Chinese Community Health; Diabetes; **Hospital:** NY-Presby/Weill Cornell Med Ctr, NY (page 102), NYU Langone Med Ctr (page 104); **Address:** 185 Canal St Fl 6, New York, NY 10013; **Phone:** 212-343-7323; **Board Cert:** Internal Medicine 1983; **Med School:** Cornell Univ-Weill Med Coll 1978; **Resid:** Internal Medicine, NYU Med Ctr-Manhattan VA Hosp 1981; **Fellow:** Endocrinology, Stanford Univ Hosp & Clins 1983; **Fac Appt:** Asst Clin Prof Med, NYU Sch Med

Lodge Jr, Henry S MD (IM) *PCP* - **Spec Exp:** Preventive Medicine; **Hospital:** NY-Presby/Columbia Univ Med Ctr, NY (page 102); **Address:** New York Physicians, 635 Madison Ave, Fl 8, New York, NY 10022-1009; **Phone:** 212-857-4555; **Board Cert:** Internal Medicine 1988; **Med School:** Columbia P&S 1985; **Resid:** Internal Medicine, NY-Presby/Columbia Univ Med Ctr 1988; **Fac Appt:** Prof Med, Columbia P&S

Logan, Bruce D MD (IM) *PCP* - **Spec Exp:** Preventive Medicine; Hypertension; Diabetes; Cholesterol/Lipid Disorders; **Hospital:** NY-Presby/Lower Manhattan Hosp (page 102), NY-Presby/Weill Cornell Med Ctr, NY (page 102); **Address:** 170 William St, New York, NY 10038; **Phone:** 212-608-6634; **Board Cert:** Internal Medicine 1978; **Med School:** Columbia P&S 1972; **Resid:** Internal Medicine, Harlem Hosp Ctr 1978; **Fac Appt:** Assoc Clin Prof Med, Cornell Univ-Weill Med Coll

Mann, Samuel J MD (IM) - **Spec Exp:** Hypertension; **Hospital:** NY-Presby/Weill Cornell Med Ctr, NY (page 102); **Address:** Hypertension Center, Weill Cornell Med Ctr, 424 E 70th St, New York, NY 10021; **Phone:** 646-962-2606; **Board Cert:** Internal Medicine 1975; **Med School:** SUNY Downstate 1972; **Resid:** Internal Medicine, St Lukes Roosevelt Hosp 1975; **Fellow:** Hypertension, Mt Sinai Hosp 1983; **Fac Appt:** Clin Prof Med, Cornell Univ-Weill Med Coll

Meller, Jennifer MD (IM) *PCP* - **Hospital:** NY-Presby/Weill Cornell Med Ctr, NY (page 102); **Address:** Park Avenue Medicine, 1020 Park Ave Fl 1, New York, NY 10028; **Phone:** 646-403-9685; **Board Cert:** Internal Medicine 2009; **Med School:** NYU Sch Med 1996; **Resid:** Internal Medicine, NYU Bellevue Hosp 1999; **Fac Appt:** Asst Clin Prof Med, Cornell Univ-Weill Med Coll

Merrell, Woodson Charles MD (IM) *PCP* - **Spec Exp:** Integrative Medicine; Complementary Medicine; Preventive Medicine; Acupuncture; **Hospital:** Mt Sinai Beth Israel; **Address:** 44 E 67th St, New York, NY 10065; **Phone:** 212-535-1012; **Med School:** Columbia P&S 1976; **Resid:** Internal Medicine, St Lukes-Roosevelt Med Ctr 1979; **Fac Appt:** Asst Prof Med, Mount Sinai-Icahn Sch of Med

Minkowitz, Susan MD (IM) *PCP* - **Spec Exp:** Asthma; Emphysema; Hypertension; Chronic Obstructive Lung Disease (COPD); **Hospital:** NYU Langone Med Ctr (page 104); **Address:** 355 W 52nd St, Fl 7, New York, NY 10019; **Phone:** 646-778-5555; **Board Cert:** Internal Medicine 1988; **Med School:** NY Med Coll 1984; **Resid:** Internal Medicine, Metropolitan Hosp Ctr 1987; **Fellow:** Pulmonary Disease, Montefiore Med Ctr 1989; **Fac Appt:** Asst Prof Med, NYU Sch Med

Morledge, Louis J MD (IM) *PCP* - **Spec Exp:** Travel Medicine; **Hospital:** NYU Langone Med Ctr (page 104), Lenox Hill Hosp; **Address:** 150 E 58th St, Fl 18, New York, NY 10155; **Phone:** 212-583-2830; **Board Cert:** Internal Medicine 2007; **Med School:** NY Med Coll 1990; **Resid:** Internal Medicine, Lenox Hill Hosp 1993; **Fellow:** Community Medicine, St Vincent Hosp 1994; **Fac Appt:** Asst Clin Prof Med, NYU Sch Med

Mulvehill, Joseph MD (IM) *PCP* - **Spec Exp:** Concierge Medicine; House Calls; **Hospital:** Lenox Hill Hosp, Mt Sinai Hosp; **Address:** Park Avenue Concierge Med, 10 E 78th St, Ste 1B, New York, NY 10075; **Phone:** 212-737-3136; **Board Cert:** Internal Medicine 2014; **Med School:** SUNY Stony Brook 1997; **Resid:** Internal Medicine, A Einstein Coll Med Affil Hosp 2000

Nelson, Deena J MD (IM) *PCP* - **Spec Exp:** Cancer Survivors-Late Effects of Therapy; Cancer Prevention; **Hospital:** NY-Presby/Weill Cornell Med Ctr, NY (page 102); **Address:** 635 Madison Ave Fl 8, New York, NY 10022; **Phone:** 212-857-4670; **Board Cert:** Internal Medicine 1980; **Med School:** Albert Einstein Coll Med 1977; **Resid:** Internal Medicine, NY-Presby/Weill Cornell Med Ctr 1979; Internal Medicine, Jewish-Barnes Hosp 1980; **Fac Appt:** Asst Clin Prof Med, Cornell Univ-Weill Med Coll

Olichney, John J MD (IM) *PCP* - **Hospital:** Mt Sinai Roosevelt; **Address:** 350 W 58th St, New York, NY 10019; **Phone:** 212-246-9101; **Board Cert:** Internal Medicine 1974; **Med School:** Albany Med Coll 1969; **Resid:** Internal Medicine, St Lukes-Roosevelt Hosp 1972; **Fellow:** Hematology, St Lukes-Roosevelt Hosp Ctr 1973; **Fac Appt:** Clin Prof Med, Columbia P&S

Orsher, Stuart I MD (IM) *PCP* - **Spec Exp:** Preventive Medicine; **Hospital:** Lenox Hill Hosp; **Address:** 9 E 79th St, New York, NY 10075; **Phone:** 212-535-7763; **Board Cert:** Internal Medicine 1983; **Med School:** Hahnemann Univ 1975; **Resid:** Internal Medicine, Lenox Hill Hosp 1978

Pecker, Mark S MD (IM) - **Spec Exp:** Hypertension; **Hospital:** NY-Presby/Weill Cornell Med Ctr, NY (page 102); **Address:** NY-Presby, Hypertension Ctr, 424 E 70th St, New York, NY 10021; **Phone:** 646-962-2605; **Board Cert:** Internal Medicine 1980; **Med School:** NYU Sch Med 1977; **Resid:** Internal Medicine, UT Southwestern Hosp 1980; **Fac Appt:** Clin Prof Med, Cornell Univ-Weill Med Coll

Porder, Joseph B MD (IM) *PCP* - **Spec Exp:** Preventive Cardiology; Nutrition; Echocardiography; Preventive Medicine; **Hospital:** Mt Sinai Hosp; **Address:** 1160 5th Ave, Ste 102, New York, NY 10029; **Phone:** 212-860-5500; **Board Cert:** Internal Medicine 1985; Cardiovascular Disease 1987; **Med School:** Columbia P&S 1982; **Resid:** Internal Medicine, Mt Sinai Hosp 1985; **Fellow:** Cardiovascular Disease, Mt Sinai Hosp 1987

Primas, Ronald Alan MD (IM) *PCP* - **Spec Exp:** Preventive Medicine; Travel Medicine; House Calls; Concierge Medicine; **Hospital:** Mt Sinai Hosp; **Address:** 952 5th Ave, Ste 1D, New York, NY 10075; **Phone:** 212-737-1212; **Board Cert:** Internal Medicine 2010; **Med School:** Amer Univ Caribbean 1986; **Resid:** Internal Medicine, Methodist Hosp 1990; **Fellow:** Preventive Medicine, UCSD Med Ctr 1991

Rieger, Jill M MD (IM) *PCP* - **Hospital:** NY-Presby/Weill Cornell Med Ctr, NY (page 102); **Address:** Weill-Cornell Medical Assocs, 425 E 61st St Fl 11, New York, NY 10065; **Phone:** 646-962-2399; **Board Cert:** Internal Medicine 2011; **Med School:** Cornell Univ 1998; **Resid:** Internal Medicine, New York Hosp 2001

Rosen, Nedra J MD (IM) *PCP* - **Spec Exp:** Preventive Medicine; **Hospital:** Lenox Hill Hosp, NYU Langone Med Ctr (page 104); **Address:** 115 E 57th St, Ste 630, New York, NY 10022; **Phone:** 212-583-2990; **Board Cert:** Internal Medicine 1983; **Med School:** NY Med Coll 1980; **Resid:** Internal Medicine, Lenox Hill Hosp 1983

Salsitz, Edwin A MD (IM) - **Spec Exp:** Addiction/Substance Abuse; Opiate Addiction; **Hospital:** Mt Sinai Beth Israel; **Address:** Mt Sinai, Chemical Dependency, 1st Ave at 16th St, Bernstein Pavilion, Rm 10B45, New York, NY 10003; **Phone:** 212-420-4400; **Board Cert:** Internal Medicine 1977; Pulmonary Disease 1980; **Med School:** SUNY Buffalo 1972; **Resid:** Obstetrics & Gynecology, Beth Israel Med Ctr 1974; Internal Medicine, Beth Israel Med Ctr 1977; **Fellow:** Pulmonary Disease, Beth Israel Med Ctr 1979; **Fac Appt:** Asst Clin Prof Med, Albert Einstein Coll Med

Schneider, Steven J MD (IM) *PCP* - **Spec Exp:** Travel Medicine; Occupational Medicine; Lyme Disease; **Hospital:** NYU Langone Med Ctr (page 104), Lenox Hill Hosp; **Address:** 115 E 57th St, Ste 630, New York, NY 10022; **Phone:** 212-583-2880; **Board Cert:** Internal Medicine 1979; **Med School:** Johns Hopkins Univ 1976; **Resid:** Internal Medicine, Presby Med Ctr 1979

Sherman, Iris K MD (IM) *PCP* - **Spec Exp:** Diabetes; Hypertension; Preventive Cardiology; **Hospital:** Mt Sinai Hosp; **Address:** Westside Internal Med, 620 Columbus Ave, New York, NY 10024; **Phone:** 212-874-6600; **Board Cert:** Internal Medicine 2006; **Med School:** SUNY Downstate 1993; **Resid:** Internal Medicine, Mt Sinai Hosp 1996

Siegel, Marc K MD (IM) *PCP* - **Hospital:** NYU Langone Med Ctr (page 104); **Address:** 650 1st Ave Fl 7, New York, NY 10016; **Phone:** 212-532-1214; **Board Cert:** Internal Medicine 2011; **Med School:** SUNY Buffalo 1985; **Resid:** Internal Medicine, NYU/Bellevue Hosp 1988; **Fac Appt:** Assoc Prof Med, NYU Sch Med

Silverman, David MD (IM) *PCP* - **Spec Exp:** Infectious Disease; Preventive Medicine; **Hospital:** NYU Langone Med Ctr (page 104); **Address:** 239 Central Park West, Ste 1A-N, New York, NY 10024; **Phone:** 212-496-1929; **Board Cert:** Internal Medicine 1979; **Med School:** Columbia P&S 1976; **Resid:** Internal Medicine, NYU-Bellevue Hosp 1980; **Fellow:** Infectious Disease, NYU-Bellevue Hosp 1981; **Fac Appt:** Assoc Clin Prof Med, NYU Sch Med

Silvershein, Daniel I MD (IM) *PCP* - **Hospital:** NYU Langone Med Ctr (page 104); **Address:** Concorde Medical Group, 235 E 38th St, New York, NY 10016; **Phone:** 212-599-7101; **Board Cert:** Internal Medicine 2006; **Med School:** Boston Univ 1993; **Resid:** Internal Medicine, NYU Med Ctr 1996

Smith, Sharon E MD (IM) *PCP* - **Spec Exp:** Preventive Medicine; **Hospital:** Lenox Hill Hosp; **Address:** Manhattan Physician Grp, 215 E 95th St, New York, NY 10128; **Phone:** 212-491-2400; **Board Cert:** Internal Medicine 2009; **Med School:** Howard Univ 1996; **Resid:** Internal Medicine, St Vincents Hosp 1999

Solomon, Gregory W MD (IM) *PCP* - **Spec Exp:** Preventive Medicine; Hypertension; Cholesterol/Lipid Disorders; Concierge Medicine; **Hospital:** Mt Sinai Hosp; **Address:** 899 Lexington Ave, New York, NY 10065; **Phone:** 212-717-9205; **Board Cert:** Internal Medicine 2005; **Med School:** NYU Sch Med 1991; **Resid:** Internal Medicine, Montefiore Med Ctr 1994; **Fac Appt:** Assoc Clin Prof Med, Mount Sinai-Icahn Sch of Med

Spero, Marc MD (IM) - **Spec Exp:** Diving Medicine; Asthma; Emphysema; Sarcoidosis; **Hospital:** NYU Langone Med Ctr (page 104), Lenox Hill Hosp; **Address:** 110 E 55th St Fl 17, New York, NY 10022; **Phone:** 212-355-8315; **Board Cert:** Internal Medicine 1977; Pulmonary Disease 1980; **Med School:** Albert Einstein Coll Med 1973; **Resid:** Internal Medicine, St Luke's Hosp 1977; **Fellow:** Pulmonary Disease, St Luke's Hosp 1979

Tay, Steven I MD (IM) *PCP* - **Spec Exp:** Geriatric Care; Preventive Medicine; **Hospital:** Mt Sinai Beth Israel; **Address:** Gramercy Park Physicians, 10 Union Square East, Ste 5M-1, New York, NY 10003; **Phone:** 212-253-9322; **Board Cert:** Internal Medicine 1977; Geriatric Medicine 2004; **Med School:** SUNY Downstate 1974; **Resid:** Internal Medicine, Kings Co Hosp 1977

Underberg, James MD (IM) - **Spec Exp:** Cholesterol/Lipid Disorders; Hypertension; Preventive Cardiology; **Hospital:** NYU Langone Med Ctr (page 104); **Address:** MHMG, Lipid Disorders, 317 E 34th St Fl 7, New York, NY 10016; **Phone:** 212-726-7430; **Board Cert:** Internal Medicine 1989; **Med School:** Univ Pennsylvania 1986; **Resid:** Internal Medicine, NYU Med Ctr/Bellevue Hosp Ctr 1989; **Fac Appt:** Asst Clin Prof Med, NYU Sch Med

Vega, Aida MD (IM) *PCP* - **Hospital:** Mt Sinai Hosp; **Address:** Primary Care Assocs, 10 E 102nd St Fl 5E, New York, NY 10029; **Phone:** 212-241-6585; **Board Cert:** Internal Medicine 1983; **Med School:** Boston Univ 1980; **Resid:** Internal Medicine, Univ Conn Hlth Ctr 1983

Weinstein, Jay S MD (IM) *PCP* - **Spec Exp:** Preventive Medicine; **Hospital:** NS-LIJ Hlth Sys; **Address:** 927 Park Ave, New York, NY 10028; **Phone:** 212-584-2619; **Board Cert:** Internal Medicine 2011; **Med School:** Hahnemann Univ 1987; **Resid:** Internal Medicine, St Vincents Hosp 1991

Witt III, Marvin MD (IM) *PCP* - **Spec Exp:** Diabetes; Hypertension; Preventive Medicine; **Hospital:** Lenox Hill Hosp; **Address:** Advantage Care Physicians, 590 5th Ave, New York, NY 10036; **Phone:** 212-582-7117; **Board Cert:** Internal Medicine 1986; **Med School:** Germany 1983; **Resid:** Internal Medicine, Bridgeport Hosp 1986

Yaffe, Bruce H MD (IM) *PCP* - **Spec Exp:** Colonoscopy; Endoscopy; Preventive Medicine; **Hospital:** Lenox Hill Hosp; **Address:** Yaffe Ruden & Assocs, 201 E 65th St, New York, NY 10065; **Phone:** 212-879-4700; **Board Cert:** Internal Medicine 1979; Gastroenterology 1981; **Med School:** Geo Wash Univ 1976; **Resid:** Internal Medicine, Mount Sinai Hosp 1979; Hepatology, Mount Sinai Hosp 1980; **Fellow:** Gastroenterology, Lenox Hill Hosp 1982

Zaremski, Benjamin MD (IM) *PCP* - **Spec Exp:** Cardiovascular Disease; Preventive Cardiology; Preventive Medicine; **Hospital:** Mt Sinai Beth Israel, Lenox Hill Hosp; **Address:** 510 E 80th St, New York, NY 10075; **Phone:** 212-517-0022; **Board Cert:** Internal Medicine 1986; **Med School:** Dominican Republic 1981; **Resid:** Internal Medicine, Metropolitan Hosp 1984; **Fellow:** Cardiovascular Disease, St Francis Hosp/Metropolitan Hosp 1986

Zeale, Peter J MD (IM) *PCP* - **Spec Exp:** Hypertension; Cholesterol/Lipid Disorders; Concierge Medicine; **Hospital:** NYU Langone Med Ctr (page 104); **Address:** 275 7th Ave Fl 3, New York, NY 10011; **Phone:** 646-660-9998; **Board Cert:** Internal Medicine 1982; **Med School:** Georgetown Univ 1979; **Resid:** Internal Medicine, St Vincents Hosp 1983

Ziecheck, Wendy S MD (IM) *PCP* - **Spec Exp:** Preventive Medicine; Women's Health; Weight Management; **Hospital:** NY-Presby/Weill Cornell Med Ctr, NY (page 102); **Address:** 110 E 55th St Fl 9, New York, NY 10022; **Phone:** 212-758-3590; **Board Cert:** Internal Medicine 2008; **Med School:** Cornell Univ-Weill Med Coll 1995; **Resid:** Internal Medicine, NY Presby Hosp/Cornell 1998

Interventional Cardiology

Attubato, Michael J MD (IC) - **Spec Exp:** Coronary Angioplasty/Stents; Peripheral Vascular Disease; Heart Valve Disease; **Hospital:** NYU Langone Med Ctr (page 104), Bellevue Hosp Ctr; **Address:** NYU Langone Medical Center, 530 First Ave, HCC Bldg - Fl 14, New York, NY 10016; **Phone:** 212-263-5656; **Board Cert:** Internal Medicine 1984; Cardiovascular Disease 1987; Interventional Cardiology 2010; **Med School:** NYU Sch Med 1981; **Resid:** Internal Medicine, NYU Med Ctr 1985; **Fellow:** Cardiovascular Disease, NYU Med Ctr 1987; **Fac Appt:** Assoc Prof Med, NYU Sch Med

Feit, Frederick MD (IC) - **Spec Exp:** Cardiac Catheterization; Angioplasty & Restenosis; **Hospital:** NYU Langone Med Ctr (page 104); **Address:** NYU Cardiac Catheterization Lab, 530 1st Ave HTC Bldg Fl 14, New York, NY 10016; **Phone:** 212-263-5656; **Board Cert:** Internal Medicine 1976; Cardiovascular Disease 1979; Interventional Cardiology 2010; **Med School:** NYU Sch Med 1972; **Resid:** Internal Medicine, NYU Med Ctr 1976; **Fellow:** Cardiovascular Disease, NYU Med Ctr 1978; **Fac Appt:** Assoc Prof Onc, NYU Sch Med

Gray, William A MD (IC) - **Spec Exp:** Peripheral Vascular Disease; Percutaneous Valve Repair; Coronary Artery Disease; Mitral Valve Surgery; **Hospital:** NY-Presby/Columbia Univ Med Ctr, NY (page 102); **Address:** NY-Presby, Interventional Cardiology, 161 Fort Washington Ave Fl 6, New York, NY 10032; **Phone:** 212-305-7060; **Board Cert:** Internal Medicine 1987; Interventional Cardiology 2011; Vascular Medicine 2004; **Med School:** Temple Univ 1984; **Resid:** Internal Medicine, Rhode Island Hosp 1988; **Fellow:** Cardiovascular Disease, Rhode Island Hosp 1992; **Fac Appt:** Asst Prof Med, Columbia P&S

Kodali, Susheel K MD (IC) - **Spec Exp:** Cardiac Catheterization; Angioplasty & Stent Placement; Heart Valve Disease; **Hospital:** NY-Presby/Columbia Univ Med Ctr, NY (page 102); **Address:** NY-Presby, Interventional Cardiology, 177 Fort Washington Ave, Ste 5C-501, New York, NY 10032; **Phone:** 212-342-0444; **Board Cert:** Interventional Cardiology 2006; Cardiovascular Disease 2005; **Med School:** UCLA-David Geffen Sch Med 1998; **Resid:** Internal Medicine, UCSF Med Ctr 2001; **Fellow:** Cardiovascular Disease, NY-Presby/Columbia Univ Med Ctr 2004; Interventional Cardiology, UCSF Med Ctr 2005; **Fac Appt:** Asst Prof Med, Columbia P&S

Krishnan, Prakash MD (IC) - **Spec Exp:** Acute Coronary Syndromes; Peripheral Vascular Disease; Cardiac Catheterization; Endovascular Disease; **Hospital:** Mt Sinai Hosp; **Address:** Mt Sinai, Cardiology, 1190 5th Ave, 1 South, New York, NY 10029; **Phone:** 212-427-1540; **Board Cert:** Cardiovascular Disease 2005; Interventional Cardiology 2007; **Med School:** India 1997; **Resid:** Internal Medicine, St Vincents Hosp 2000; **Fellow:** Cardiovascular Disease, Ochsner Clin Fdn 2003; Interventional Cardiology, Mt Sinai Hosp 2004; **Fac Appt:** Asst Prof Med, Mount Sinai-Icahn Sch of Med

Leon, Martin B MD (IC) - **Hospital:** NY-Presby/Columbia Univ Med Ctr, NY (page 102); **Address:** 161 Ft Washington Ave, Irving Pavillion Fl 6 - Ste 607, New York, NY 10032; **Phone:** 212-305-7060; **Board Cert:** Internal Medicine 1979; Cardiovascular Disease 1983; **Med School:** Yale Univ 1975; **Resid:** Internal Medicine, Yale-New Haven Hosp 1978; **Fellow:** Cardiovascular Disease, Yale-New Haven Hosp 1980

Mehran, Roxana MD (IC) - **Spec Exp:** Cardiac Catheterization; Acute Coronary Syndromes; Arrhythmias; **Hospital:** Mt Sinai Hosp; **Address:** Cardiocascular Medicine Associates, 1190 5th Ave S, rm GP1-S, Guggenheim Pavilion, New York, NY 10029; **Phone:** 212-659-9691; **Board Cert:** Cardiovascular Disease 2011; Interventional Cardiology 2011; **Med School:** Grenada 1987; **Resid:** Internal Medicine, Univ Conn Hlth Ctr 1991; **Fellow:** Cardiovascular Disease, Mount Sinai Med Ctr 1994; Interventional Cardiology, Mount Sinai Med Ctr 1995; **Fac Appt:** Prof Med, Mount Sinai Sch Med

Moreno, Pedro R MD (IC) - **Spec Exp:** Angioplasty & Stent Placement; Cardiac Catheterization; **Hospital:** Mt Sinai Hosp; **Address:** Mt Sinai, Cardiology, 1190 5th Ave, GP1-W, New York, NY 10029; **Phone:** 212-241-3497; **Board Cert:** Cardiovascular Disease 2011; Interventional Cardiology 2011; **Med School:** Colombia 1984; **Resid:** Internal Medicine, Universidad Javeriana Affil Hosp; Internal Medicine, Brigham & Womens Hosp 1997; **Fellow:** Cardiovascular Disease, Brigham & Womens Hosp 2000; Interventional Cardiology, Mass Genl Hosp 2001; **Fac Appt:** Prof Med, Mount Sinai-Icahn Sch of Med

Moses, Jeffrey W MD (IC) - **Spec Exp:** Angiography-Coronary; Angioplasty & Stent Placement; Heart Valve Disease; **Hospital:** NY-Presby/Columbia Univ Med Ctr, NY (page 102); **Address:** 161 Ft Washington Ave, Herbert Irving Pavillion Fl 6th, New York, NY 10032; **Phone:** 212-305-7060; **Board Cert:** Internal Medicine 1977; Cardiovascular Disease 1981; Interventional Cardiology 2009; **Med School:** Univ Pennsylvania 1974; **Resid:** Internal Medicine, Penn Presby Med Ctr 1977; **Fellow:** Cardiovascular Disease, Penn Presby Med Ctr 1980

Parikh, Manish A MD (IC) - **Spec Exp:** Coronary Angioplasty/Stents; **Hospital:** Lenox Hill Hosp; **Address:** 51 W 51st St, Ste 330, New York, NY 10019; **Phone:** 212-326-8532; **Board Cert:** Cardiovascular Disease 2010; Interventional Cardiology 2010; **Med School:** UMDNJ-NJ Med Sch, Newark 1990; **Resid:** Internal Medicine, NY Presby Hosp 1993; **Fellow:** Cardiovascular Disease, NY Presby Hosp 1997; **Fac Appt:** Asst Prof Med, Cornell Univ-Weill Med Coll

Sharma, Samin K MD (IC) - **Spec Exp:** Angioplasty & Stent Placement; Heart Valve Disease; **Hospital:** Mt Sinai Hosp; **Address:** Mt Sinai Hosp, Cardiology, 1190 5th Ave, New York, NY 10029; **Phone:** 212-427-1540; **Board Cert:** Internal Medicine 1986; Cardiovascular Disease 1989; Interventional Cardiology 2011; **Med School:** India 1978; **Resid:** Internal Medicine, SMS Hosp 1982; Internal Medicine, NYU Downtown Hosp 1986; **Fellow:** Cardiovascular Disease, Elmhurst Hosp Ctr 1988; Interventional Cardiology, Mt Sinai Hosp 1990; **Fac Appt:** Prof Med, Mount Sinai-Icahn Sch of Med

Slater, James N MD (IC) - **Spec Exp:** Coronary Angioplasty/Stents; Heart Valve Disease; Cardiac Catheterization; **Hospital:** NYU Langone Med Ctr (page 104), Mt Sinai St. Luke's; **Address:** 426 W 58th St, New York, NY 10019; **Phone:** 212-247-0790; **Board Cert:** Internal Medicine 1980; Cardiovascular Disease 1985; Interventional Cardiology 2010; **Med School:** Univ Rochester 1977; **Resid:** Internal Medicine, NYU-Bellevue Hosp 1981; **Fellow:** Cardiovascular Disease, NYU-Bellevue Hosp 1983; **Fac Appt:** Prof Med, NYU Sch Med

Stone, Gregg W MD (IC) - **Spec Exp:** Angioplasty & Stent Placement; Coronary Artery Disease; **Hospital:** NY-Presby/Columbia Univ Med Ctr, NY (page 102); **Address:** 161 Fort Washington Ave, Irving Pavillion Fl 6 - Ste 607, New York, NY 10032; **Phone:** 212-305-7060; **Board Cert:** Internal Medicine 1985; Cardiovascular Disease 1987; **Med School:** Johns Hopkins Univ 1982; **Resid:** Internal Medicine, NY Hosp-Cornell Medical Ctr 1985; **Fellow:** Cardiovascular Disease, Cedars-Sinai Medical Ctr 1988; Coronary Angioplasty, Mid-America Heart Inst 1989; **Fac Appt:** Prof Med, Columbia P&S

Weinberger, Judah Z MD/PhD (IC) - **Spec Exp:** Cardiac Catheterization; Peripheral Vascular Disease; Coronary Artery Disease; Heart Valve Disease; **Hospital:** NY-Presby/Columbia Univ Med Ctr, NY (page 102), NYU Langone Med Ctr (page 104); **Address:** Heart Ctr, 173 Fort Washington Ave, Ste 4-602, New York, NY 10032; **Phone:** 212-305-1581; **Board Cert:** Internal Medicine 1984; Cardiovascular Disease 1985; Interventional Cardiology 2009; **Med School:** Harvard Med Sch 1980; **Resid:** Internal Medicine, Brigham & Womens Hosp 1982; **Fellow:** Cardiovascular Disease, Brigham & Womens Hosp 1985; **Fac Appt:** Assoc Prof Med, Columbia P&S

Wilentz, James Robert MD (IC) - **Spec Exp:** Angiography & Stent Placement; Carotid Artery Disease; Peripheral Vascular Disease; Coronary Artery Disease-Complex; **Hospital:** NY-Presby/Weill Cornell Med Ctr, NY (page 102); **Address:** 428 E 72nd St, Ste 600, New York, NY 10021; **Phone:** 646-962-4448; **Board Cert:** Internal Medicine 1979; Cardiovascular Disease 1985; Interventional Cardiology 2013; **Med School:** NYU Sch Med 1976; **Resid:** Internal Medicine, Brigham & Womens Hosp 1979; **Fellow:** Cardiovascular Disease, Boston Med Ctr 1984; Interventional Cardiology, Emory Univ Hosp 1986; **Fac Appt:** Asst Prof Med, Cornell Univ-Weill Med Coll

Maternal & Fetal Medicine

Berkowitz, Richard L MD (MF) - **Spec Exp:** Fetal Therapy; Multiple Gestation; Pregnancy & Hematologic Abnormalities; **Hospital:** NY-Presby/Columbia Univ Med Ctr, NY (page 102); **Address:** 5939 Broadway, New York, NY 10032; **Phone:** 212-326-8951; **Board Cert:** Obstetrics & Gynecology 2005; Maternal & Fetal Medicine 2005; **Med School:** NYU Sch Med 1965; **Resid:** Obstetrics & Gynecology, NY Hosp-Cornell Med Ctr 1972; **Fac Appt:** Prof ObG, Columbia P&S

Bianco, Angela MD (MF) - **Spec Exp:** Pregnancy-High Risk; Fetal Diagnosis & Therapy; **Hospital:** Mt Sinai Hosp; **Address:** Mt Sinai, Maternal Fetal Med, 5 E 98th St, rm 256, New York, NY 10029; **Phone:** 212-241-5681; **Board Cert:** Obstetrics & Gynecology 2013; Maternal & Fetal Medicine 2013; **Med School:** Penn State Coll Med 1989; **Resid:** Obstetrics & Gynecology, NYU Med Ctr 1993; **Fellow:** Maternal & Fetal Medicine, Mt Sinai Hosp 1995; **Fac Appt:** Assoc Prof ObG, Mount Sinai-Icahn Sch of Med

Brustman, Lois E MD (MF) - **Spec Exp:** Prematurity/Low Birth Weight Infants; Diabetes in Pregnancy; Hypertension in Pregnancy; **Hospital:** Mt Sinai Roosevelt; **Address:** St Lukes-Roosevelt Hosp, Ob/Gyn, Perinatal Assocs, 1000 10th Ave, Fl 11, New York, NY 10019; **Phone:** 212-523-7579; **Board Cert:** Obstetrics & Gynecology 2013; Maternal & Fetal Medicine 2013; **Med School:** NY Med Coll 1979; **Resid:** Obstetrics & Gynecology, Montefiore Med Ctr 1984; **Fellow:** Maternal & Fetal Medicine, Montefiore Med Ctr 1988; **Fac Appt:** Assoc Prof ObG, Columbia P&S

Cole, David S MD (MF) - **Spec Exp:** Pregnancy-High Risk; **Hospital:** Mt Sinai St. Luke's; **Address:** St Lukes-Roosevelt Perinatal Assocs, 1000 10th Ave Fl 11 - Ste 11A61, New York, NY 10019; **Phone:** 212-523-7579; **Board Cert:** Obstetrics & Gynecology 2012; Maternal & Fetal Medicine 2012; **Med School:** Univ Miami Sch Med 1995; **Resid:** Obstetrics & Gynecology, Montefiore Med Ctr 2000; **Fellow:** Maternal & Fetal Medicine, Montefiore Med Ctr 2003

D'Alton, Mary E MD (MF) - **Spec Exp:** Pregnancy-High Risk; Multiple Gestation; Prenatal Diagnosis; **Hospital:** NY-Presby/Columbia Univ Med Ctr, NY (page 102); **Address:** Columbia Ob/Gyn, 51 W 51st St, Ste 320, New York, NY 10019; **Phone:** 212-326-8951; **Board Cert:** Obstetrics & Gynecology 2014; Maternal & Fetal Medicine 2014; **Med School:** Ireland 1976; **Resid:** Obstetrics & Gynecology, Ottowa Genl Hosp 1982; **Fellow:** Maternal & Fetal Medicine, Tufts-New Eng Med Ctr 1984; **Fac Appt:** Prof ObG, Columbia P&S

Eddleman, Keith A MD (MF) - **Spec Exp:** Obstetric Ultrasound; Pregnancy-High Risk; Fetal Therapy; Reproductive Genetics; **Hospital:** Mt Sinai Hosp; **Address:** Mt Sinai Hosp, Maternal-Fetal Med, 5 E 98th St, rm 256, New York, NY 10029; **Phone:** 212-241-5681; **Board Cert:** Obstetrics & Gynecology 2013; Maternal & Fetal Medicine 2013; Clinical Genetics 2010; **Med School:** Wake Forest Univ 1985; **Resid:** Obstetrics & Gynecology, G Washington Univ Med Ctr 1989; **Fellow:** Maternal & Fetal Medicine, Mt Sinai Hosp 1991; Genetics, NY-Presby Hosp/Weill Cornell Med Ctr 1996; **Fac Appt:** Prof ObG, Mount Sinai-Icahn Sch of Med

Grunebaum, Amos MD (MF) - **Spec Exp:** Pregnancy-High Risk; Amniocentesis; **Hospital:** NY-Presby/Weill Cornell Med Ctr, NY (page 102); **Address:** Dept Obstetrics & Gynecology, 525 E 68th St, Ste J-130, New York, NY 10065; **Phone:** 212-746-0714; **Board Cert:** Obstetrics & Gynecology 2013; Maternal & Fetal Medicine 2013; **Med School:** Germany 1974; **Resid:** Anesthesiology, Maimonides Med Ctr 1978; Obstetrics & Gynecology, Downstate Med Ctr 1982; **Fellow:** Maternal & Fetal Medicine, Downstate Med Ctr 1984; **Fac Appt:** Assoc Prof ObG, Columbia P&S

Hutson, J. Milton MD (MF) - **Spec Exp:** Multiple Gestation; Pregnancy After Age 35; Amniocentesis; **Hospital:** NY-Presby/Weill Cornell Med Ctr, NY (page 102); **Address:** 523 E 72nd St Fl 9, New York, NY 10021; **Phone:** 212-472-5340; **Board Cert:** Obstetrics & Gynecology 1997; Maternal & Fetal Medicine 1997; **Med School:** UAB Sch Med 1975; **Resid:** Obstetrics & Gynecology, Univ Hosp 1979; **Fellow:** Maternal & Fetal Medicine, NY-Presby/Columbia Univ Med Ctr 1982; **Fac Appt:** Asst Clin Prof ObG, Cornell Univ-Weill Med Coll

Kalish, Robin MD (MF) - **Spec Exp:** Pregnancy-High Risk; Diabetes in Pregnancy; Hypertension in Pregnancy; Lupus/SLE in Pregnancy; **Hospital:** NY-Presby/Weill Cornell Med Ctr, NY (page 102); **Address:** NY-Presby, Maternal-Fetal Med, 525 E 68th St, Ste J130, New York, NY 10065; **Phone:** 212-746-3146; **Board Cert:** Obstetrics & Gynecology 2013; Maternal & Fetal Medicine 2013; **Med School:** Univ Tenn Coll Med 1996; **Resid:** Obstetrics & Gynecology, Winthrop Univ Hosp 2000; **Fellow:** Maternal & Fetal Medicine, NY-Presby/Weill Cornell Med Ctr 2003; **Fac Appt:** Assoc Prof ObG, Cornell Univ-Weill Med Coll

Patrick, Sharon MD (MF) - **Spec Exp:** Pregnancy-High Risk; Premature Labor; **Hospital:** Mt Sinai Roosevelt; **Address:** 800A 5th Ave, Ste 503, New York, NY 10065; **Phone:** 212-230-1785; **Board Cert:** Obstetrics & Gynecology 2013; Maternal & Fetal Medicine 2013; **Med School:** Case West Res Univ 1986; **Resid:** Obstetrics & Gynecology, NY-Presby/Columbia Univ Med Ctr 1990; **Fellow:** Maternal & Fetal Medicine, NY-Presby/Columbia Univ Med Ctr 1992

Rebarber, Andrei MD (MF) - **Spec Exp:** Multiple Gestation; Obstetric Ultrasound; Amniocentesis; Fetal Therapy; **Hospital:** Mt Sinai Hosp; **Address:** Maternal Fetal Med Assocs, 70 E 90th St, Ste 2, New York, NY 10128; **Phone:** 212-722-7409; **Board Cert:** Obstetrics & Gynecology 2013; Maternal & Fetal Medicine 2013; **Med School:** SUNY Upstate Med Univ 1991; **Resid:** Obstetrics & Gynecology, Beth Israel Med Ctr 1995; **Fellow:** Maternal & Fetal Medicine, Yale-New Haven Hosp 1997; **Fac Appt:** Clin Prof ObG, Mount Sinai-Icahn Sch of Med

Roman, Ashley S MD (MF) - **Spec Exp:** Pregnancy-High Risk; Fetal Diagnosis & Therapy; Obstetric Ultrasound; Prenatal Diagnosis; **Hospital:** NYU Langone Med Ctr (page 104); **Address:** NYU Maternal Fetal Care Ctr, 150 E 32nd St, Ste 101, New York, NY 10016; **Phone:** 212-263-7021; **Board Cert:** Obstetrics & Gynecology 2013; Maternal & Fetal Medicine 2013; **Med School:** Tulane Univ 1998; **Resid:** Obstetrics & Gynecology, UCLA Med Ctr 2002; **Fellow:** Maternal & Fetal Medicine, NYU Med Ctr 2005; **Fac Appt:** Asst Clin Prof ObG, NYU Sch Med

Rosenn, Barak MD (MF) - **Spec Exp:** Diabetes in Pregnancy; Obstetric Ultrasound; **Hospital:** Mt Sinai Roosevelt; **Address:** St Lukes-Roosevelt Perinatal Assocs, 1000 10th Ave, Ste 11A61, New York, NY 10019; **Phone:** 212-523-7579; **Board Cert:** Maternal & Fetal Medicine 2013; Obstetrics & Gynecology 2013; **Med School:** Israel 1983; **Resid:** Obstetrics & Gynecology, Hadassah Israel 1989; Obstetrics & Gynecology, Univ Cincinnati Hosp 1997; **Fellow:** Maternal & Fetal Medicine, Univ Cincinnati Hosp 2000; **Fac Appt:** Prof ObG, Columbia P&S

Saltzman, Daniel MD (MF) - **Spec Exp:** Pregnancy-High Risk; Prenatal Diagnosis; Ultrasound; Pregnancy After Age 35; **Hospital:** Mt Sinai Hosp; **Address:** Maternal Fetal Med Assocs, 70 E 90th St, New York, NY 10128; **Phone:** 212-722-7409; **Board Cert:** Obstetrics & Gynecology 2013; Maternal & Fetal Medicine 2013; **Med School:** SUNY Buffalo 1979; **Resid:** Obstetrics & Gynecology, G Washington Univ Hosp 1983; **Fellow:** Maternal & Fetal Medicine, Brigham & Womens Hosp 1985; **Fac Appt:** Clin Prof ObG, Mount Sinai-Icahn Sch of Med

Simpson, Lynn L MD (MF) - **Spec Exp:** Pregnancy-High Risk; Prenatal Diagnosis; Fetal Echocardiography; Multiple Gestation; **Hospital:** Morgan Stanley Chldns Hosp of NY-Presby, NY (page 102), NY-Presby/Columbia Univ Med Ctr, NY (page 102); **Address:** Ctr for Prenatal Pediatrics, 3959 Broadway Fl 12, New York, NY 10032; **Phone:** 212-305-3151; **Board Cert:** Obstetrics & Gynecology 2013; Maternal & Fetal Medicine 2013; **Med School:** Queens Univ 1988; **Resid:** Obstetrics & Gynecology, Kingston Genl Hosp 1993; **Fellow:** Maternal & Fetal Medicine, Beth Israel Deaconess Med Ctr 1995; **Fac Appt:** Prof ObG, Columbia P&S

Stone, Joanne L MD (MF) - **Spec Exp:** Prenatal Ultrasound; Twin to Twin Transfusion Syndrome (TTTS); Diabetes in Pregnancy; Genetic Disorders; **Hospital:** Mt Sinai Hosp; **Address:** Mt Sinai, Maternal-Fetal Med, 5 E 98th St, rm 256, New York, NY 10029; **Phone:** 212-241-5681; **Board Cert:** Obstetrics & Gynecology 2013; Maternal & Fetal Medicine 2013; **Med School:** Columbia P&S 1987; **Resid:** Obstetrics & Gynecology, Mt Sinai Hosp 1991; **Fellow:** Maternal & Fetal Medicine, Mt Sinai Hosp 1993; **Fac Appt:** Prof ObG, Mount Sinai-Icahn Sch of Med

Wapner, Ronald J MD (MF) - **Spec Exp:** Perinatal Medicine; Genetic Disorders; Multiple Gestation; Vomiting-Cyclic; **Hospital:** NY-Presby/Columbia Univ Med Ctr, NY (page 102); **Address:** 51 W 51st St, Ste 320, New York, NY 10019; **Phone:** 212-326-8951; **Board Cert:** Obstetrics & Gynecology 2000; Maternal & Fetal Medicine 2000; Clinical Genetics 2010; **Med School:** Jefferson Med Coll 1972; **Resid:** Obstetrics & Gynecology, Thomas Jefferson Univ Hosp 1976; **Fellow:** Maternal & Fetal Medicine, Thomas Jefferson Univ Hosp 1978; Medical Genetics, Thomas Jefferson Univ Hosp 1992; **Fac Appt:** Prof ObG, Columbia P&S

Medical Oncology

Aghajanian, Carol A MD (Onc) - **Spec Exp:** Ovarian Cancer; Gynecologic Cancer; Trophoblastic Tumors; **Hospital:** Meml Sloan Kettering Canc Ctr (page 110); **Address:** MSKCC, Gyn Oncology Svc, 300 E 66th St, New York, NY 10065; **Phone:** 646-888-4217; **Board Cert:** Internal Medicine 2012; Medical Oncology 2005; **Med School:** SUNY Downstate 1989; **Resid:** Internal Medicine, Mt Sinai Hosp 1992; **Fellow:** Medical Oncology, Meml Sloan-Kettering Cancer Ctr 1995; **Fac Appt:** Prof Med, Cornell Univ-Weill Med Coll

Bajorin, Dean F MD (Onc) - **Spec Exp:** Bladder Cancer; Testicular Cancer; Genitourinary Cancer; Clinical Trials; **Hospital:** Meml Sloan Kettering Canc Ctr (page 110); **Address:** MSKCC, Genitourinary Onc Svc, 1275 York Ave, New York, NY 10065; **Phone:** 646-422-4333; **Board Cert:** Internal Medicine 1981; Medical Oncology 1985; **Med School:** NY Med Coll 1978; **Resid:** Internal Medicine, Hartford Hosp 1981; **Fellow:** Medical Oncology, Meml Sloan-Kettering Cancer Ctr 1985; **Fac Appt:** Prof Med, Cornell Univ-Weill Med Coll

Baselga, Jose T MD/PhD (Onc) - **Spec Exp:** Breast Cancer; Drug Development; **Hospital:** Meml Sloan Kettering Canc Ctr (page 110); **Address:** MSKCC, Breast Cancer, 300 E 66th St, New York, NY 10021; **Phone:** 646-497-9064; **Board Cert:** Internal Medicine 1989; Medical Oncology 2011; **Med School:** Spain 1983; **Resid:** Internal Medicine, SUNY Hlth Sci Ctr 1989; **Fellow:** Medical Oncology, Meml Sloan-Kettering Cancer Ctr 1992

Belenkov, Elliot Michael MD (Onc) - **Spec Exp:** Solid Tumors; **Hospital:** Mt Sinai Hosp, Lenox Hill Hosp; **Address:** 178 E 85th St, Fl 4, New York, NY 10028; **Phone:** 212-472-5500; **Board Cert:** Internal Medicine 1987; Medical Oncology 2011; **Med School:** Russia 1976; **Resid:** Psychiatry, Metro Hospital 1983; Internal Medicine, Metro Hospital 1986; **Fellow:** Hematology, Lenox Hill Hosp 1988; **Fac Appt:** Asst Clin Prof Onc, Mount Sinai-Icahn Sch of Med

Beltran, Himisha MD (Onc) - **Spec Exp:** Prostate Cancer (advanced); Urologic Cancer; Clinical Trials; **Hospital:** NY-Presby/Weill Cornell Med Ctr, NY (page 102); **Address:** NY Presby-Weill Cornell Med Ctr, 525 E 68th St, Starr Pavilion, Fl 3, New York, NY 10065; **Phone:** 646-962-2072; **Board Cert:** Internal Medicine 2007; Hematology 2011; Medical Oncology 2011; **Med School:** NY Med Coll 2004; **Resid:** Internal Medicine, Hosp U Penn 2007; **Fellow:** Hematology & Oncology, NY Presby-Weill Cornell Med Ctr 2010; **Fac Appt:** Asst Prof Onc, Cornell Univ-Weill Med Coll

Berman, Ellin MD (Onc) - **Spec Exp:** Leukemia; Lymphoma; **Hospital:** Meml Sloan Kettering Canc Ctr (page 110); **Address:** MSKCC, Leukemia Svc, 1275 York Ave, New York, NY 10065; **Phone:** 212-639-7762; **Board Cert:** Internal Medicine 1980; Medical Oncology 1985; Hematology 1984; **Med School:** Harvard Med Sch 1977; **Resid:** Internal Medicine, Boston Med Ctr 1980; **Fellow:** Medical Oncology, Meml Sloan-Kettering Cancer Ctr 1983; **Fac Appt:** Prof Med, Cornell Univ-Weill Med Coll

Bosl, George J MD (Onc) - **Spec Exp:** Testicular Cancer; Genitourinary Cancer; **Hospital:** Meml Sloan Kettering Canc Ctr (page 110); **Address:** MSKCC, Genitourinary Onc Svc, 1275 York Ave, Ste 1289, New York, NY 10065; **Phone:** 212-639-8473; **Board Cert:** Internal Medicine 1976; Medical Oncology 1979; **Med School:** Creighton Univ 1973; **Resid:** Internal Medicine, NY-Presby/Weill Cornell Med Ctr 1975; Internal Medicine, Meml Sloan-Kettering Cancer Ctr 1977; **Fellow:** Medical Oncology, Univ Minn Med Ctr 1979; **Fac Appt:** Prof Med, Cornell Univ-Weill Med Coll

Brentjens, Renier J MD (Onc) - **Spec Exp:** Leukemia; Leukemia-Chronic Lymphocytic; T cell Immune Therapy; Cancer Immune Therapy; **Hospital:** Meml Sloan Kettering Canc Ctr (page 110); **Address:** Meml Sloan Kettering Cancer Ctr, 1275 York Ave Fl 4 - Ste 3, New York, NY 10021; **Phone:** 212-639-7053; **Board Cert:** Medical Oncology 2002; **Med School:** SUNY Buffalo 1996; **Resid:** Internal Medicine, Yale-New Haven Hosp 1999; **Fellow:** Medical Oncology, Meml Sloan Kettering Cancer Ctr 2001; **Fac Appt:** Assoc Prof Med, Cornell Univ-Weill Med Coll

Brunckhorst, Keith R MD (Onc) - **Hospital:** Lenox Hill Hosp; **Address:** 110 E 59th St, Ste 2B, New York, NY 10022; **Phone:** 212-583-2858; **Board Cert:** Internal Medicine 1979; Hematology 1982; Medical Oncology 1983; **Med School:** NY Med Coll 1976; **Resid:** Internal Medicine, Stamford Hosp 1979; **Fellow:** Hematology & Oncology, Lenox Hill Hosp 1983

Chachoua, Abraham MD (Onc) - **Spec Exp:** Lung Cancer; Thoracic Cancers; Bladder Cancer; Kidney Cancer; **Hospital:** NYU Langone Med Ctr (page 104); **Address:** NYU Clin Cancer Ctr, 160 E 34th St Fl 8, New York, NY 10016; **Phone:** 212-731-5388; **Med School:** Australia 1978; **Resid:** Internal Medicine, Alfred Hosp 1982; **Fellow:** Hematology & Oncology, Alfred Hosp 1985; Hematology & Oncology, NYU Med Ctr 1988; **Fac Appt:** Assoc Prof Med, NYU Sch Med

Chapman, Paul B MD (Onc) - **Spec Exp:** Melanoma; Immunotherapy; Clinical Trials; Vaccine Therapy; **Hospital:** Meml Sloan Kettering Canc Ctr (page 110); **Address:** MSKCC, Melanoma Svc, 160 E 53rd St Fl 5, New York, NY 10022; **Phone:** 646-497-9067; **Board Cert:** Internal Medicine 1984; Medical Oncology 1987; **Med School:** Cornell Univ-Weill Med Coll 1981; **Resid:** Internal Medicine, Univ Chicago Hosps 1984; **Fellow:** Medical Oncology, Meml Sloan-Kettering Cancer Ctr 1987; **Fac Appt:** Prof Med, Cornell Univ-Weill Med Coll

Cohen, Seymour M MD (Onc) - **Spec Exp:** Breast Cancer; Melanoma; Lung Cancer; Lymphoma; **Hospital:** Mt Sinai Hosp; **Address:** 535 E 86th St, New York, NY 10028; **Phone:** 917-783-5195; **Board Cert:** Internal Medicine 1971; Medical Oncology 1973; **Med School:** Univ Pittsburgh 1962; **Resid:** Internal Medicine, Montefiore Med Ctr 1964; Internal Medicine, Mount Sinai Med Ctr 1965; **Fellow:** Hematology, Mount Sinai Med Ctr 1966; Hematology & Oncology, LI Jewish Hosp 1969; **Fac Appt:** Assoc Clin Prof Onc, Mount Sinai Sch Med

Coleman, Morton MD (Onc) - **Spec Exp:** Leukemia & Lymphoma; Hodgkin's Lymphoma; Multiple Myeloma; **Hospital:** NY-Presby/Weill Cornell Med Ctr, NY (page 102); **Address:** 407 E 70th St, Fl 3, New York, NY 10021; **Phone:** 212-517-5900; **Board Cert:** Internal Medicine 1971; Hematology 1972; Medical Oncology 1973; **Med School:** Med Coll VA 1963; **Resid:** Internal Medicine, Grady Meml Hosp 1965; Internal Medicine, NY-Presby/Weill Cornell Med Ctr 1968; **Fellow:** Hematology & Oncology, NY-Presby/Weill Cornell Med Ctr 1970; **Fac Appt:** Clin Prof Hem & Onc, Cornell Univ-Weill Med Coll

Decter, Julian A MD (Onc) - **Spec Exp:** Leukemia & Lymphoma; Multiple Myeloma; Myelodysplastic Syndromes; Hodgkin's Lymphoma; **Hospital:** NY-Presby/Weill Cornell Med Ctr, NY (page 102); **Address:** NY-Presby, Hem/Onc, 407 E 70th St Fl 4, New York, NY 10021; **Phone:** 212-517-5900; **Board Cert:** Internal Medicine 1972; Hematology 1974; Medical Oncology 1975; **Med School:** NYU Sch Med 1966; **Resid:** Internal Medicine, OSU Med Ctr 1968; **Fellow:** Hematology, NYU Med Ctr 1970; Medical Oncology, Natl Cancer Inst 1974; **Fac Appt:** Assoc Clin Prof Onc, Cornell Univ-Weill Med Coll

Dickler, Maura N MD (Onc) - **Spec Exp:** Breast Cancer; Clinical Trials; **Hospital:** Meml Sloan Kettering Canc Ctr (page 110); **Address:** 300 E 66th St, New York, NY 10065; **Phone:** 646-888-5456; **Board Cert:** Medical Oncology 2008; **Med School:** Univ Chicago-Pritzker Sch Med 1991; **Resid:** Internal Medicine, Univ Chicago Hosps 1994; **Fellow:** Medical Oncology, Meml Sloan Kettering Cancer Ctr 1998; **Fac Appt:** Assoc Prof Onc, Cornell Univ-Weill Med Coll

Feldman, Darren R MD (Onc) - **Spec Exp:** Genitourinary Cancer; Testicular Cancer; Kidney Cancer; **Hospital:** Meml Sloan Kettering Canc Ctr (page 110); **Address:** MSKCC, Genitourinary Oncology Svc, 1275 York Ave, New York, NY 10065; **Phone:** 646-422-4491; **Board Cert:** Internal Medicine 2004; Medical Oncology 2008; Hematology 2009; **Med School:** Univ MD Sch Med 2001; **Resid:** Internal Medicine, NYU Med Ctr 2004; **Fellow:** Hematology & Oncology, Meml Sloan-Kettering Cancer Ctr 2008

Fine, Howard A MD (Onc) - **Spec Exp:** Brain Tumors; Neuro-Oncology; **Hospital:** NYU Langone Med Ctr (page 104); **Address:** NYU Clin Cancer Ctr, 160 E 34th St, New York, NY 10016; **Phone:** 212-731-5089; **Board Cert:** Internal Medicine 1987; Medical Oncology 1989; **Med School:** Mount Sinai Sch Med 1984; **Resid:** Internal Medicine, Hosp Univ Penn 1987; **Fellow:** Medical Oncology, Dana-Farber Cancer Ctr 1989; **Fac Appt:** Prof Onc, NYU Sch Med

Fine, Robert Lance MD (Onc) - **Spec Exp:** Pancreatic Cancer; Drug Development; Pituitary Tumors; Gastrointestinal Cancer; **Hospital:** NY-Presby/Columbia Univ Med Ctr, NY (page 102); **Address:** NY-Presby, Pancreas Ctr, 161 Fort Washington Ave Fl 8, New York, NY 10032; **Phone:** 212-305-1168; **Board Cert:** Internal Medicine 1983; Medical Oncology 1985; **Med School:** Univ Chicago-Pritzker Sch Med 1979; **Resid:** Internal Medicine, Stanford Univ Hosp & Clins 1982; **Fellow:** Medical Oncology, Natl Cancer Inst 1985; **Fac Appt:** Assoc Prof Med, Columbia P&S

Fornier, Monica N MD (Onc) - **Spec Exp:** Breast Cancer; **Hospital:** Meml Sloan Kettering Canc Ctr (page 110); **Address:** MSKCC, Breast Cancer, 300 E 66th St, New York, NY 10065; **Phone:** 646-888-5240; **Med School:** Italy 1992; **Resid:** Internal Medicine, Univ Hosp; **Fellow:** Medical Oncology, Natl Cancer Inst; Medical Oncology, Meml Sloan-Kettering Cancer Ctr 2002

Gabrilove, Janice L MD (Onc) - **Spec Exp:** Myelodysplastic Syndromes; Leukemia; Hematologic Malignancies; Myeloproliferative Disorders; **Hospital:** Mt Sinai Hosp; **Address:** Mt Sinai, Hem/Onc, 1 Gustave L Levy Pl, Box 1079, New York, NY 10029; **Phone:** 212-241-9650; **Board Cert:** Internal Medicine 1980; Medical Oncology 1983; **Med School:** Mount Sinai Sch Med 1977; **Resid:** Internal Medicine, NY-Presby/Columbia Univ Med Ctr 1980; **Fellow:** Hematology & Oncology, Meml Sloan-Kettering Cancer Ctr 1983; **Fac Appt:** Prof Hem & Onc, Mount Sinai-Icahn Sch of Med

Gaynor, Mitchell MD (Onc) - **Spec Exp:** Breast Cancer; Lung Cancer; Nutrition & Cancer; Complementary Medicine; **Hospital:** NY-Presby/Weill Cornell Med Ctr, NY (page 102); **Address:** 215 E 72nd St, New York, NY 10021; **Phone:** 212-472-2828; **Board Cert:** Internal Medicine 1985; Medical Oncology 1987; Hematology 1988; **Med School:** Univ Tex SW, Dallas 1982; **Resid:** Internal Medicine, NY-Presby/Weill Cornell Med Ctr 1985; **Fellow:** Hematology & Oncology, NY-Presby/Weill Cornell Med Ctr 1988; **Fac Appt:** Asst Clin Prof Med, Cornell Univ-Weill Med Coll

Gelmann, Edward P MD (Onc) - **Spec Exp:** Prostate Cancer; Bladder Cancer; Kidney Cancer; **Hospital:** NY-Presby/Columbia Univ Med Ctr, NY (page 102); **Address:** NY-Presby, Hem/Onc, 161 Fort Washington Ave Fl 9, New York, NY 10032; **Phone:** 212-305-5098; **Board Cert:** Internal Medicine 1979; Medical Oncology 1981; **Med School:** Stanford Univ 1976; **Resid:** Internal Medicine, Univ Chicago Hosps 1979; **Fellow:** Medical Oncology, Natl Cancer Inst 1981; **Fac Appt:** Prof Med, Columbia P&S

Goldberg, Arthur I MD (Onc) - **Spec Exp:** Breast Cancer; Prostate Cancer; Colon & Rectal Cancer; Anal Cancer; **Hospital:** Lenox Hill Hosp, Mt Sinai Hosp; **Address:** 121 E 79th St, New York, NY 10075; **Phone:** 212-249-0030; **Board Cert:** Internal Medicine 1974; Medical Oncology 1975; **Med School:** SUNY Hlth Sci Ctr 1969; **Resid:** Internal Medicine, NY-Presby/Weill Cornell Med Ctr 1970; Internal Medicine, NYU-Bellevue Hosp 1973; **Fellow:** Cancer Immunology, Natl Cancer Inst 1972; Medical Oncology, Meml Sloan-Kettering Cancer Ctr 1975

Grace, William MD (Onc) - **Spec Exp:** Breast Cancer; Liver Cancer; Pancreatic Cancer; Lung Cancer; **Hospital:** Lenox Hill Hosp; **Address:** 945 5th Ave, New York, NY 10021; **Phone:** 212-675-6826 x201; **Board Cert:** Internal Medicine 1976; Medical Oncology 1977; **Med School:** Boston Univ 1969; **Resid:** Internal Medicine, St Vincents Hosp 1971; **Fellow:** Hematology & Oncology, Dartmouth-Hitchcock Med Ctr 1976; **Fac Appt:** Assoc Clin Prof Med, NY Med Coll

Grossbard, Michael L MD (Onc) - **Spec Exp:** Leukemia & Lymphoma; Gastrointestinal Cancer; Colon & Rectal Cancer; Multiple Myeloma; **Hospital:** Mt Sinai Roosevelt; **Address:** Laura and Isaac Perlmutter Cancer Center, 240 E 38th St, Fl 19th, New York, NY 10016; **Phone:** 646-501-9305; **Board Cert:** Internal Medicine 1989; Medical Oncology 2011; **Med School:** Yale Univ 1986; **Resid:** Internal Medicine, Mass Genl Hosp 1989; **Fellow:** Medical Oncology, Dana Farber Cancer Inst 1991; **Fac Appt:** Clin Prof Hem & Onc, Columbia P&S

Hassoun, Hani MD (Onc) - **Spec Exp:** Hematologic Malignancies; Multiple Myeloma; Lymphoma; Stem Cell Transplant; **Hospital:** Meml Sloan Kettering Canc Ctr (page 110); **Address:** MSKCC, Hem/Onc, 1275 York Ave, New York, NY 10065; **Phone:** 212-639-3228; **Board Cert:** Internal Medicine 1986; Medical Oncology 1989; **Med School:** France 1983; **Resid:** Internal Medicine, Brigham & Womens Hosp 1986; **Fellow:** Hematology & Oncology, Tufts-St Elizabeth Hosp 1989; **Fac Appt:** Assoc Prof Med, Cornell Univ-Weill Med Coll

Hershman, Dawn L MD (Onc) - **Spec Exp:** Breast Cancer; Cancer Survivors-Late Effects of Therapy; Clinical Trials; **Hospital:** NY-Presby/Columbia Univ Med Ctr, NY (page 102); **Address:** NY-Presby, Hem/Onc, 161 Fort Washington Ave Fl 10, New York, NY 10032; **Phone:** 212-305-5098; **Board Cert:** Internal Medicine 2007; Medical Oncology 2011; **Med School:** Albert Einstein Coll Med 1994; **Resid:** Internal Medicine, NY-Presby/Columbia Univ Med Ctr 1998; **Fellow:** Medical Oncology, NY-Presby/Columbia Univ Med Ctr 2001; **Fac Appt:** Asst Prof Med, Columbia P&S

Hirschman, Richard J MD (Onc) - **Spec Exp:** Breast Cancer; Colon Cancer; Lung Cancer; **Hospital:** Mt Sinai Beth Israel; **Address:** 247 3rd Ave, Ste 401, New York, NY 10010; **Phone:** 212-228-0471; **Board Cert:** Internal Medicine 1971; Hematology 1972; Medical Oncology 1973; **Med School:** Johns Hopkins Univ 1965; **Resid:** Internal Medicine, Bellevue Hosp Ctr 1967; Internal Medicine, NY-Presby/Columbia Univ Med Ctr 1970; **Fellow:** Hematology & Oncology, NY-Presby/Columbia Univ Med Ctr 1971; **Fac Appt:** Assoc Clin Prof Med, Mount Sinai-Icahn Sch of Med

Hirshaut, Yashar MD (Onc) - **Spec Exp:** Breast Cancer; Lung Cancer; Colon Cancer; **Hospital:** Lenox Hill Hosp, NY-Presby/Weill Cornell Med Ctr, NY (page 102); **Address:** 860 5th Ave, New York, NY 10065; **Phone:** 212-861-1799; **Board Cert:** Internal Medicine 1972; Medical Oncology 1975; **Med School:** Albert Einstein Coll Med 1963; **Resid:** Internal Medicine, Montefiore Med Ctr 1965; **Fellow:** Medical Oncology, Natl Cancer Inst 1968; Medical Oncology, Meml Sloan-Kettering Cancer Ctr 1970; **Fac Appt:** Assoc Clin Prof Med, Cornell Univ-Weill Med Coll

Holcombe, Randall F MD (Onc) - **Spec Exp:** Gastrointestinal Cancer; Liver Cancer; Clinical Trials; Pancreatic Cancer; **Hospital:** Mt Sinai Hosp; **Address:** Ruttenberg Treatment Ctr, 1470 Madison Ave, Fl 3, New York, NY 10029; **Phone:** 212-241-6756; **Board Cert:** Internal Medicine 1986; Medical Oncology 2013; Hematology 2012; **Med School:** UMDNJ-NJ Med Sch, Newark 1983; **Resid:** Internal Medicine, Brigham & Womens Hosp 1986; **Fellow:** Hematology & Oncology, Brigham & Womens Hosp 1989; **Fac Appt:** Prof Med, Mount Sinai-Icahn Sch of Med

Holland, James F MD (Onc) - **Spec Exp:** Breast Cancer; Pancreatic Cancer; **Hospital:** Mt Sinai Hosp; **Address:** Mt Sinai, Med Oncology, 1 Gustave L Levy Pl, Box 1079, New York, NY 10029; **Phone:** 212-241-4495; **Board Cert:** Internal Medicine 1955; **Med School:** Columbia P&S 1947; **Resid:** Internal Medicine, NY-Presby/Columbia Univ Med Ctr 1949; Internal Medicine, Francis Delafield Hosp 1952; **Fellow:** Medical Oncology, Francis Delafield Hosp 1953; **Fac Appt:** Prof Med, Mount Sinai Sch Med

Horwitz, Steven M MD (Onc) - **Spec Exp:** Cutaneous T-cell Lymphoma; Hodgkin's Lymphoma; Lymphoma, Non-Hodgkin's; Clinical Trials; **Hospital:** Meml Sloan Kettering Canc Ctr (page 110); **Address:** MSKCC, Med Oncology, 1275 York Ave, New York, NY 10065; **Phone:** 212-639-3045; **Board Cert:** Medical Oncology 2011; **Med School:** Case West Res Univ 1993; **Resid:** Internal Medicine, Univ Richester Strong Meml Hosp 1996; **Fellow:** Medical Oncology, Stanford Univ Hosp & Clins 1999

Hudis, Clifford A MD (Onc) - **Spec Exp:** Breast Cancer; **Hospital:** Meml Sloan Kettering Canc Ctr (page 110); **Address:** MSKCC, Breast Cancer, 300 E 66th St Fl 3, New York, NY 10065; **Phone:** 646-888-5449; **Board Cert:** Internal Medicine 1986; Medical Oncology 2011; **Med School:** Med Coll PA Hahnemann 1983; **Resid:** Internal Medicine, Hosp Univ Penn 1987; **Fellow:** Medical Oncology, Meml Sloan-Kettering Cancer Ctr 1991; **Fac Appt:** Prof Med, Cornell Univ-Weill Med Coll

Ilson, David H MD/PhD (Onc) - **Spec Exp:** Esophageal Cancer; Colon & Rectal Cancer; Mesothelioma; Unknown Primary Cancer; **Hospital:** Meml Sloan Kettering Canc Ctr (page 110); **Address:** MSKCC, Gastrointestinal Oncology Svc, 300 E 66th St Fl 10, New York, NY 10065; **Phone:** 646-497-9053; **Board Cert:** Internal Medicine 1989; Medical Oncology 2012; **Med School:** NYU Sch Med 1986; **Resid:** Internal Medicine, Bellevue Hosp 1989; **Fellow:** Medical Oncology, Meml Sloan-Kettering Cancer Ctr 1992; **Fac Appt:** Assoc Prof Med, Cornell Univ-Weill Med Coll

Jagannath, Sundar MD (Onc) - **Spec Exp:** Multiple Myeloma; **Hospital:** Mt Sinai Hosp; **Address:** Ruttenberg Treatment Ctr, 1470 Madison Ave Fl 3, New York, NY 10029; **Phone:** 212-241-7873; **Board Cert:** Internal Medicine 1980; Medical Oncology 1985; **Med School:** India 1976; **Resid:** Internal Medicine, Bronx Lebanon Hosp 1979; Internal Medicine, Harper-Grace Hosp 1980; **Fellow:** Medical Oncology, Univ Tex-MD Anderson Cancer Ctr 1982; **Fac Appt:** Prof Onc, Mount Sinai-Icahn Sch of Med

Kelsen, David Paul MD (Onc) - **Spec Exp:** Gastrointestinal Cancer; Neuroendocrine Tumors; Colon & Rectal Cancer; Pancreatic Cancer; **Hospital:** Meml Sloan Kettering Canc Ctr (page 110); **Address:** MSKCC, Gastrointestinal Onc Svc, 300 E 66th St Fl 10, New York, NY 10065; **Phone:** 646-888-4179; **Board Cert:** Internal Medicine 1976; Medical Oncology 1979; **Med School:** Hahnemann Univ 1972; **Resid:** Internal Medicine, Temple Univ Hosp 1976; **Fellow:** Medical Oncology, Meml Sloan-Kettering Cancer Ctr 1978; **Fac Appt:** Prof Med, Cornell Univ-Weill Med Coll

Kemeny, Nancy E MD (Onc) - **Spec Exp:** Colon Cancer; Rectal Cancer; Liver Cancer; **Hospital:** Meml Sloan Kettering Canc Ctr (page 110); **Address:** MSKCC, Gastrointestinal Oncology Svc, 300 E 66th St Fl 10, New York, NY 10065; **Phone:** 646-888-4180; **Board Cert:** Internal Medicine 1974; Medical Oncology 1981; **Med School:** UMDNJ-NJ Med Sch, Newark 1971; **Resid:** Internal Medicine, St Lukes Hosp 1974; **Fellow:** Medical Oncology, Mem Sloan-Kettering Cancer Ctr 1976; **Fac Appt:** Prof Med, Cornell Univ-Weill Med Coll

Klafter, Robert MD (Onc) - **Spec Exp:** Leukemia; Breast Cancer; **Hospital:** Mt Sinai Hosp, Lenox Hill Hosp; **Address:** Central Park Hematology & Oncology, 12 E 86th St, New York, NY 10028; **Phone:** 212-861-6660; **Board Cert:** Hematology 2011; Medical Oncology 2011; **Med School:** NYU Sch Med 1994; **Resid:** Internal Medicine, NYU Med Ctr 1997; **Fellow:** Hematology & Oncology, Emory Univ Hosp 2001; **Fac Appt:** Assoc Clin Prof Med, Mount Sinai Sch Med

Klein, Paula MD (Onc) - **Spec Exp:** Breast Cancer; **Hospital:** Mt Sinai Beth Israel; **Address:** Mt Sinai BIMC, Cancer Ctr, 325 W 15th St, Ste J, New York, NY 10011; **Phone:** 212-604-6021; **Board Cert:** Internal Medicine 1989; Medical Oncology 2009; **Med School:** SUNY Downstate 1986; **Resid:** Internal Medicine, NYU-Bellevue Hosp 1989; **Fellow:** Hematology & Oncology, NYU-Bellevue Hosp 1998; **Fac Appt:** Asst Prof Med, NY Med Coll

Kozuch, Peter S MD (Onc) - **Spec Exp:** Gastrointestinal Cancer; Esophageal Cancer; Pancreatic Cancer; **Hospital:** Mt Sinai Beth Israel, Mt Sinai St. Luke's; **Address:** Mt Sinai BIMC, Cancer Ctr, 10 Union Square E, Ste 4C, New York, NY 10003; **Phone:** 212-844-8070; **Board Cert:** Medical Oncology 2010; Hematology 2004; **Med School:** Hahnemann Univ 1994; **Resid:** Internal Medicine, Boston Med Ctr 1997; **Fellow:** Medical Oncology, UT MD Anderson Cancer Ctr 2000; **Fac Appt:** Assoc Clin Prof Med, Albert Einstein Coll Med

Kris, Mark G MD (Onc) - **Spec Exp:** Lung Cancer; Mediastinal Tumors; Thymoma; Thoracic Cancers; **Hospital:** Meml Sloan Kettering Canc Ctr (page 110); **Address:** MSKCC, Thoracic Oncology Svc, 160 E 53rd St, Fl 9, New York, NY 10022; **Phone:** 646-497-9163; **Board Cert:** Internal Medicine 1980; Medical Oncology 1983; **Med School:** Cornell Univ-Weill Med Coll 1977; **Resid:** Internal Medicine, NY-Presby/Weill Cornell Med Ctr 1980; **Fellow:** Medical Oncology, Meml Sloan-Kettering Cancer Ctr 1983; **Fac Appt:** Prof Med, Cornell Univ-Weill Med Coll

Krug, Lee M MD (Onc) - **Spec Exp:** Small Cell Lung Cancer; Mesothelioma; Clinical Trials; **Hospital:** Meml Sloan Kettering Canc Ctr (page 110); **Address:** MSKCC, Thoracic Surgery, 300 E 66th St, New York, NY 10065; **Phone:** 646-888-4201; **Board Cert:** Internal Medicine 2007; Medical Oncology 2009; **Med School:** Washington Univ, St Louis 1994; **Resid:** Internal Medicine, Johns Hopkins Hosp 1997; **Fellow:** Medical Oncology, Meml Sloan-Kettering Cancer Ctr 1999

Kruger, Bernard M MD (Onc) - **Spec Exp:** Breast Cancer; **Hospital:** Lenox Hill Hosp; **Address:** 170 E 78th St, New York, NY 10075; **Phone:** 212-772-9222; **Board Cert:** Internal Medicine 1974; Medical Oncology 1979; **Med School:** Univ Colorado 1968; **Resid:** Internal Medicine, Boston Med Ctr 1972; Internal Medicine, Georgetown Univ Hosp 1974; **Fellow:** Medical Oncology, Mt Sinai Hosp 1976

Maki, Robert G MD/PhD (Onc) - **Spec Exp:** Sarcoma-Soft Tissue; Gastrointestinal Stromal Tumors; Desmoid Tumors; Bone Tumors; **Hospital:** Mt Sinai Hosp; **Address:** Ruttenberg Treatment Ctr, 1470 Madison Ave Fl 3, New York, NY 10029; **Phone:** 212-241-6756; **Board Cert:** Internal Medicine 2005; Medical Oncology 2007; **Med School:** Cornell Univ-Weill Med Coll 1992; **Resid:** Internal Medicine, Brigham & Womens Hosp 1995; **Fellow:** Medical Oncology, Dana-Farber Cancer Inst 1998; **Fac Appt:** Prof Onc, Mount Sinai-Icahn Sch of Med

Malamud, Stephen C MD (Onc) - **Spec Exp:** Breast Cancer; Gastrointestinal Cancer; Lung Cancer; **Hospital:** Mt Sinai Beth Israel; **Address:** Mt Sinai BIMC, Cancer Ctr, 325 W 15th St W, Ste J, New York, NY 10011; **Phone:** 212-604-6011; **Board Cert:** Internal Medicine 1981; Medical Oncology 1983; **Med School:** Albert Einstein Coll Med 1978; **Resid:** Internal Medicine, Beth Israel Med Ctr 1981; **Fellow:** Medical Oncology, Mt Sinai Hosp 1983; **Fac Appt:** Assoc Clin Prof Onc, Mount Sinai-Icahn Sch of Med

Mazumder, Amitabha MD (Onc) - **Spec Exp:** Stem Cell Transplant; Bone Marrow Transplant; Multiple Myeloma; **Hospital:** NYU Langone Med Ctr (page 104); **Address:** NYU Clin Cancer Ctr, 240 E 38th St Fl 19, New York, NY 10016; **Phone:** 212-731-5757; **Board Cert:** Medical Oncology 2009; **Med School:** Johns Hopkins Univ 1977; **Resid:** Internal Medicine, Baylor Med Ctr 1979; **Fellow:** Medical Oncology, Natl Inst Hlth 1983; **Fac Appt:** Prof Onc, NYU Sch Med

Meyers, Marleen MD (Onc) - **Spec Exp:** Breast Cancer; **Hospital:** NYU Langone Med Ctr (page 104); **Address:** NYU, Med Oncology, 160 E 34th St Fl 3, New York, NY 10016; **Phone:** 212-731-5348; **Board Cert:** Internal Medicine 1982; Medical Oncology 1985; **Med School:** NYU Sch Med 1979; **Resid:** Internal Medicine, NYU Med Ctr 1983; **Fellow:** Medical Oncology, Meml Sloan-Kettering Cancer Ctr 1985; **Fac Appt:** Asst Prof Med, NYU Sch Med

Moore, Anne MD (Onc) - **Spec Exp:** Breast Cancer; **Hospital:** NY-Presby/Weill Cornell Med Ctr, NY (page 102); **Address:** Weill Cornell Breast Ctr, 425 E 61st St Fl 8, New York, NY 10065; **Phone:** 212-821-0550; **Board Cert:** Internal Medicine 1973; Hematology 1976; Medical Oncology 2008; **Med School:** Columbia P&S 1969; **Resid:** Internal Medicine, NY-Presby/Weill Cornell Med Ctr 1973; **Fellow:** Medical Oncology, Rockefeller Univ Hosp 1976; **Fac Appt:** Prof Med, Cornell Univ-Weill Med Coll

Morris, Michael J MD (Onc) - **Spec Exp:** Prostate Cancer; Genitourinary Cancer; **Hospital:** Meml Sloan Kettering Canc Ctr (page 110); **Address:** MSKCC, Genitourinary Oncology Svc, 1275 York Ave, New York, NY 10065; **Phone:** 646-422-4469; **Board Cert:** Medical Oncology 2009; **Med School:** Mount Sinai Sch Med 1994; **Resid:** Internal Medicine, NY-Presby/Columbia Univ Med Ctr 1997; **Fellow:** Hematology & Oncology, Meml Sloan-Kettering Cancer Ctr 1999

Moskowitz, Craig H MD (Onc) - **Spec Exp:** Hodgkin's Lymphoma; Lymphoma, Non-Hodgkin's; **Hospital:** Meml Sloan Kettering Canc Ctr (page 110); **Address:** MSKCC, Hem/Onc, 1275 York Ave, New York, NY 10065; **Phone:** 212-639-2696; **Board Cert:** Medical Oncology 2005; **Med School:** Wayne State Univ 1988; **Resid:** Internal Medicine, Bronx Muni Hosp 1992; **Fellow:** Hematology & Oncology, Meml Sloan-Kettering Cancer Ctr 1994

Motzer, Robert J MD (Onc) - **Spec Exp:** Kidney Cancer; Testicular Cancer; Genitourinary Cancer; **Hospital:** Meml Sloan Kettering Canc Ctr (page 110); **Address:** MSKCC, Med Oncology, 1275 York Ave, New York, NY 10065; **Phone:** 646-422-4312; **Board Cert:** Internal Medicine 1984; Medical Oncology 1987; **Med School:** Univ Mich Med Sch 1981; **Resid:** Internal Medicine, Meml Sloan-Kettering Cancer Ctr 1984; **Fellow:** Medical Oncology, Meml Sloan-Kettering Cancer Ctr 1987; **Fac Appt:** Assoc Prof Med, Cornell Univ-Weill Med Coll

Muggia, Franco M MD (Onc) - **Spec Exp:** Gynecologic Cancer; **Hospital:** NYU Langone Med Ctr (page 104); **Address:** NYU Clin Cancer Ctr, 160 E 34th St Fl 4, New York, NY 10016; **Phone:** 212-731-5433; **Board Cert:** Internal Medicine 1968; Medical Oncology 1973; Hematology 1974; **Med School:** Cornell Univ-Weill Med Coll 1961; **Resid:** Internal Medicine, Hartford Hosp 1964; **Fellow:** Hematology & Oncology, Francis A Delafield Hosp 1967; **Fac Appt:** Prof Med, NYU Sch Med

Nanus, David M MD (Onc) - **Spec Exp:** Prostate Cancer; Bladder Cancer; Testicular Cancer; Genitourinary Cancer; **Hospital:** NY-Presby/Weill Cornell Med Ctr, NY (page 102); **Address:** NY Presby-Cornell Med Ctr, Payson Pav, 525 E 68th St, Fl 3, Ste 341, New York, NY 10021; **Phone:** 646-962-2072; **Board Cert:** Internal Medicine 1985; Medical Oncology 1987; **Med School:** Univ Hlth Scis, Chicago Med Sch 1982; **Resid:** Internal Medicine, Bronx Muni Hosp 1985; **Fellow:** Medical Oncology, Meml Sloan Kettering Canc Ctr 1989; **Fac Appt:** Prof Onc, Cornell Univ-Weill Med Coll

Norton, Larry MD (Onc) - **Spec Exp:** Breast Cancer; **Hospital:** Meml Sloan Kettering Canc Ctr (page 110); **Address:** MSKCC, 300 E 66th St BAIC Bldg Fl 9 - Ste 933, New York, NY 10065; **Phone:** 646-888-5438; **Board Cert:** Internal Medicine 1975; Medical Oncology 1977; **Med School:** Columbia P&S 1972; **Resid:** Internal Medicine, Bronx Muni Hosp 1975; **Fellow:** Medical Oncology, Natl Cancer Inst 1977; **Fac Appt:** Prof Onc, Cornell Univ-Weill Med Coll

O'Connor, Owen A MD/PhD (Onc) - **Spec Exp:** Hodgkin's Lymphoma; Lymphoma, Non-Hodgkin's; Drug Development; Clinical Trials; **Hospital:** NY-Presby/Columbia Univ Med Ctr, NY (page 102); **Address:** Columbia Doctors Midtown, 51 W 51st St, Ste 200, New York, NY 10019; **Phone:** 212-326-5720; **Board Cert:** Internal Medicine 2004; Medical Oncology 2005; **Med School:** Rutgers R W Johnson Med Sch 1994; **Resid:** Internal Medicine, NY-Presby/Weill Cornell Univ Med Ctr 1996; **Fellow:** Medical Oncology, Memorial Sloan-Kettering Cancer Ctr 2000; **Fac Appt:** Asst Clin Prof Med, Columbia P&S

O'Reilly, Eileen M MD (Onc) - **Spec Exp:** Pancreatic Cancer; Esophageal Cancer; Colon & Rectal Cancer; Liver Cancer; **Hospital:** Meml Sloan Kettering Canc Ctr (page 110); **Address:** MSKCC, Gastrointestinal Oncology Svc, 160 E 53rd St, New York, NY 10019; **Phone:** 646-888-4182; **Med School:** Ireland 1990; **Resid:** Internal Medicine, St Vincents Hosp 1994; **Fellow:** Hematology & Oncology, St Vincents Hosp 1995; Medical Oncology, Meml Sloan-Kettering Cancer Ctr 1997; **Fac Appt:** Assoc Prof Onc, Cornell Univ-Weill Med Coll

Offit, Kenneth MD (Onc) - **Spec Exp:** Cancer Genetics; Breast Cancer; Lymphoma; Hodgkin's Disease Consultation; **Hospital:** Meml Sloan Kettering Canc Ctr (page 110); **Address:** MSKCC, Clin Genetics, 1275 York Ave, Box 295, New York, NY 10065; **Phone:** 646-888-4050; **Board Cert:** Internal Medicine 1985; Medical Oncology 1987; **Med School:** Harvard Med Sch 1982; **Resid:** Internal Medicine, Lenox Hill Hosp 1985; **Fellow:** Medical Oncology, Meml Sloan-Kettering Cancer Ctr 1987; Hematology, Meml Sloan-Kettering Cancer Ctr 1988; **Fac Appt:** Prof Med, Cornell Univ-Weill Med Coll

Oh, William K MD (Onc) - **Spec Exp:** Genitourinary Cancer; Prostate Cancer; Testicular Cancer; Adrenal Cancer; **Hospital:** Mt Sinai Hosp; **Address:** Ruttenberg Treatment Ctr, 1470 Madison Ave Fl 3, New York, NY 10029; **Phone:** 212-659-5429; **Board Cert:** Medical Oncology 2009; **Med School:** NYU Sch Med 1992; **Resid:** Internal Medicine, Brigham & Womens Hosp 1995; **Fellow:** Medical Oncology, Dana-Farber Cancer Inst 1997; **Fac Appt:** Prof Onc, Mount Sinai-Icahn Sch of Med

Oratz, Ruth MD (Onc) - **Spec Exp:** Breast Cancer; **Hospital:** NYU Langone Med Ctr (page 104), Lenox Hill Hosp; **Address:** Women's Oncology & Wellness, 345 E 37th St, Ste 202, New York, NY 10016; **Phone:** 212-400-4904; **Board Cert:** Internal Medicine 1985; Medical Oncology 1989; **Med School:** Albert Einstein Coll Med 1982; **Resid:** Internal Medicine, NYU-Bellevue Hosp 1985; **Fellow:** Medical Oncology, NYU-Bellevue Hosp 1988; **Fac Appt:** Assoc Clin Prof Med, NYU Sch Med

Oster, Martin W MD (Onc) - **Spec Exp:** Breast Cancer; Gastrointestinal Cancer; Head & Neck Cancer; Lung Cancer; **Hospital:** NY-Presby/Columbia Univ Med Ctr, NY (page 102); **Address:** NY Presby Hosp-Columbia Univ Med Ctr, 161 Fort Washington Ave, New York, NY 10032-3713; **Phone:** 212-305-8231; **Board Cert:** Internal Medicine 1974; Medical Oncology 1975; **Med School:** Columbia P&S 1971; **Resid:** Internal Medicine, Mass Genl Hosp 1973; **Fellow:** Medical Oncology, Natl Cancer Inst/NIH 1976; **Fac Appt:** Assoc Prof Onc, Columbia P&S

Pasmantier, Mark W MD (Onc) - **Spec Exp:** Lung Cancer; Breast Cancer; Ovarian Cancer; Lymphoma; **Hospital:** NY-Presby/Weill Cornell Med Ctr, NY (page 102); **Address:** 407 E 70th St, Fl 3, New York, NY 10021; **Phone:** 212-517-5900; **Board Cert:** Internal Medicine 1972; Hematology 1974; Medical Oncology 1975; **Med School:** NYU Sch Med 1966; **Resid:** Internal Medicine, Harlem Hosp Ctr 1970; **Fellow:** Hematology, Montefiore Med Ctr 1971; Medical Oncology, NY-Presby/Weill Cornell Med Ctr 1972; **Fac Appt:** Clin Prof Med, Cornell Univ-Weill Med Coll

Pavlick, Anna C DO (Onc) - **Spec Exp:** Melanoma; Skin Cancer; Sarcoma; **Hospital:** NYU Langone Med Ctr (page 104); **Address:** NYU Clin Cancer Ctr, 160 E 34th St Fl 9, New York, NY 10016; **Phone:** 212-731-5431; **Board Cert:** Medical Oncology 2008; **Med School:** UMDNJ Sch Osteo Med 1990; **Resid:** Internal Medicine, Hackensack Univ Med Ctr 1993; **Fellow:** Hematology & Oncology, Meml Sloan-Kettering Cancer Ctr 1996; **Fac Appt:** Assoc Prof Med, NYU Sch Med

Pfister, David G MD (Onc) - **Spec Exp:** Head & Neck Cancer; Laryngeal Cancer; Thyroid Cancer; Immunotherapy; **Hospital:** Meml Sloan Kettering Canc Ctr (page 110); **Address:** MSKCC, Head & Neck Oncology Svc, 205 E 64th St, New York, NY 10065; **Phone:** 646-888-4232; **Board Cert:** Internal Medicine 1985; Medical Oncology 1989; **Med School:** Univ Pennsylvania 1982; **Resid:** Internal Medicine, Hosp Univ Penn 1985; **Fellow:** Epidemiology, Yale-New Haven Hosp 1987; Hematology & Oncology, Meml Sloan-Kettering Cancer Ctr 1989; **Fac Appt:** Assoc Prof Med, Cornell Univ-Weill Med Coll

Pietanza, Maria Catherine MD (Onc) - **Spec Exp:** Lung Cancer; Carcinoid Tumors; Neuroendocrine Tumors; Thoracic Cancers; **Hospital:** Meml Sloan Kettering Canc Ctr (page 110); **Address:** MSKCC, Thoracic Oncology Svc, 300 E 66th St, New York, NY 10065; **Phone:** 646-888-4203; **Board Cert:** Internal Medicine 2004; Medical Oncology 2007; **Med School:** SUNY Downstate 2001; **Resid:** Internal Medicine, NY-Presby/Weill Cornell Med Ctr 2004; **Fellow:** Hematology & Oncology, Mt Sinai Med Ctr 2007

Portlock, Carol S MD (Onc) - **Spec Exp:** Lymphoma; Hodgkin's Lymphoma; **Hospital:** Meml Sloan Kettering Canc Ctr (page 110); **Address:** MSKCC, Lymphoma Svc, 1275 York Ave, New York, NY 10065; **Phone:** 212-639-8109; **Board Cert:** Internal Medicine 1976; Medical Oncology 1977; **Med School:** Stanford Univ 1971; **Resid:** Internal Medicine, Stanford Univ Hosp & Clins 1974; **Fellow:** Medical Oncology, Stanford Univ Hosp & Clins 1976; **Fac Appt:** Clin Prof Med, Cornell Univ-Weill Med Coll

Posner, Marshall R MD (Onc) - **Spec Exp:** Head & Neck Cancer; Skin Cancer-Head & Neck; Thyroid Cancer; **Hospital:** Mt Sinai Hosp; **Address:** Ruttenberg Treatment Ctr, 1470 Madison Ave Fl 3, New York, NY 10029; **Phone:** 212-659-6756; **Board Cert:** Internal Medicine 1978; Medical Oncology 1981; **Med School:** Tufts Univ 1975; **Resid:** Internal Medicine, Boston Med Ctr 1978; **Fellow:** Oncology, Dana-Farber Cancer Inst 1981; **Fac Appt:** Prof Onc, Mount Sinai-Icahn Sch of Med

Ratner, Lynn H MD (Onc) - **Spec Exp:** Breast Cancer; Carcinoid Tumors; Neuroendocrine Tumors; Gliomas; **Hospital:** Mt Sinai Hosp, Lenox Hill Hosp; **Address:** 112 E 83rd St, New York, NY 10028; **Phone:** 212-396-0400; **Board Cert:** Internal Medicine 1977; Medical Oncology 1973; **Med School:** Albert Einstein Coll Med 1964; **Resid:** Internal Medicine, NYU-Bellevue Hosp 1966; Internal Medicine, NYU-Bellevue Hosp 1970; **Fellow:** Medical Oncology, Meml Sloan-Kettering Cancer Ctr 1970

Raza, Azra MD (Onc) - **Spec Exp:** Myelodysplastic Syndromes; Leukemia; Clinical Trials; **Hospital:** NY-Presby/Columbia Univ Med Ctr, NY (page 102); **Address:** NY-Presby, Hem/Onc, 161 Fort Washington Ave Fl 10, New York, NY 10032; **Phone:** 212-305-5098; **Board Cert:** Internal Medicine 1980; Medical Oncology 1985; **Med School:** Pakistan 1976; **Resid:** Internal Medicine, Franklin Sq Hosp 1979; Internal Medicine, Georgetown Univ/VA Med Ctr 1980; **Fellow:** Medical Oncology, Roswell Park Cancer Inst 1982

Reichman, Bonnie S MD (Onc) - **Spec Exp:** Breast Cancer; **Hospital:** NY-Presby/Weill Cornell Med Ctr, NY (page 102); **Address:** 30 E 60th St, Ste 701, New York, NY 10021-4601; **Phone:** 212-688-7715; **Board Cert:** Internal Medicine 1983; Medical Oncology 1985; **Med School:** St Louis Univ 1980; **Resid:** Internal Medicine, N Shore Univ Hosp 1983; **Fellow:** Medical Oncology, Meml Sloan Kettering Cancer Ctr 1987; **Fac Appt:** Assoc Clin Prof Onc, St Louis Univ

Rizvi, Naiyer A MD (Onc) - **Spec Exp:** Thoracic Cancers; Thymoma; Lung Cancer; Clinical Trials; **Hospital:** Meml Sloan Kettering Canc Ctr (page 110); **Address:** MSKCC, Thoracic Oncology Svc, 300 E 66th St, New York, NY 10065; **Phone:** 646-888-4204; **Med School:** Canada 1987; **Resid:** Internal Medicine, University of Manitoba Med Ctr 1992; **Fellow:** Medical Oncology, Beth Israel Med Ctr 1994

Roboz, Gail J MD (Onc) - **Spec Exp:** Leukemia; Myelodysplastic Syndromes; Myeloproliferative Disorders; **Hospital:** NY-Presby/Weill Cornell Med Ctr, NY (page 102); **Address:** 520 E 70th St, New York, NY 10021; **Phone:** 646-962-2700; **Board Cert:** Medical Oncology 2010; Hematology 2010; **Med School:** Mount Sinai Sch Med 1994; **Resid:** Internal Medicine, NY-Presby/Weill Cornell Med Ctr 1997; **Fellow:** Hematology & Oncology, NY-Presby/Weill Cornell Med Ctr 2000; **Fac Appt:** Assoc Prof Med, Cornell Univ-Weill Med Coll

Robson, Mark Emerson MD (Onc) - **Spec Exp:** Breast Cancer; Cancer Genetics; **Hospital:** Meml Sloan Kettering Canc Ctr (page 110); **Address:** MSKCC, Breast Cancer, 300 E 66th St, New York, NY 10065; **Phone:** 646-888-5434; **Board Cert:** Internal Medicine 1989; Medical Oncology 2012; **Med School:** Univ VA Sch Med 1986; **Resid:** Internal Medicine, Walter Reed Army Med Ctr 1989; **Fellow:** Hematology & Oncology, Walter Reed Army Med Ctr 1991

Ruggiero, Joseph T MD (Onc) - **Spec Exp:** Gastrointestinal Cancer; Solid Tumors; **Hospital:** NY-Presby/Weill Cornell Med Ctr, NY (page 102); **Address:** NY-Presby, Solid Tumor Oncology, 1305 York Ave Fl 12, New York, NY 10021; **Phone:** 646-962-6200; **Board Cert:** Internal Medicine 1980; Hematology 1982; Medical Oncology 1983; **Med School:** NYU Sch Med 1977; **Resid:** Internal Medicine, New York Hosp 1980; **Fellow:** Hematology & Oncology, New York Hosp 1983; **Fac Appt:** Assoc Prof Med, Cornell Univ-Weill Med Coll

Sabbatini, Paul J MD (Onc) - **Spec Exp:** Gynecologic Cancer; Uterine Cancer; Ovarian Cancer; **Hospital:** Meml Sloan Kettering Canc Ctr (page 110); **Address:** MSKCC, Gynecologic Oncology, 300 E 66th St, New York, NY 10065; **Phone:** 646-888-4218; **Board Cert:** Internal Medicine 2012; Medical Oncology 2008; **Med School:** Univ Miss 1989; **Resid:** Internal Medicine, Vanderbilt Univ Med Ctr 1992; **Fellow:** Medical Oncology, Meml Sloan-Kettering Cancer Ctr 1996; **Fac Appt:** Asst Prof Med, Cornell Univ-Weill Med Coll

Saltz, Leonard B MD (Onc) - **Spec Exp:** Colon & Rectal Cancer; Gastrointestinal Cancer & Rare Tumors; Neuroendocrine Tumors; Unknown Primary Cancer; **Hospital:** Meml Sloan Kettering Canc Ctr (page 110); **Address:** MSKCC, Gastrointestinal Oncology Svc, 160 E 53rd St, New York, NY 10019; **Phone:** 646-497-9053; **Board Cert:** Internal Medicine 1986; Hematology 1988; Medical Oncology 1989; **Med School:** Yale Univ 1983; **Resid:** Internal Medicine, NY-Presby/Weill Cornell Med Ctr 1986; **Fellow:** Hematology, NY-Presby/Weill Cornell Med Ctr 1988; Oncology, NY-Presby/Weill Cornell Med Ctr 1989; **Fac Appt:** Assoc Prof Med, Cornell Univ-Weill Med Coll

Sara, Gabriel MD (Onc) - **Spec Exp:** Breast Cancer; Lung Cancer; Lymphoma; Gastrointestinal Cancer; **Hospital:** Mt Sinai Roosevelt; **Address:** Mt Sinai Roosevelt, Cancer Ctr, 1000 10th Ave Fl 11, New York, NY 10019; **Phone:** 212-523-7580; **Board Cert:** Internal Medicine 1984; Hematology 1986; Medical Oncology 1987; **Med School:** Lebanon 1980; **Resid:** Internal Medicine, SUNY Downstate Med Ctr 1984; **Fellow:** Hematology & Oncology, St Lukes-Roosevelt Hosp 1986; Hematology & Oncology, NY-Presby/Columbia Univ Med Ctr 1987; **Fac Appt:** Asst Clin Prof Med, Columbia P&S

Scher, Howard I MD (Onc) - **Spec Exp:** Prostate Cancer; Bladder Cancer; Immunotherapy; Clinical Trials; **Hospital:** Meml Sloan Kettering Canc Ctr (page 110); **Address:** MSKCC, Genitourinary Oncology Svc, 1275 York Ave, New York, NY 10065; **Phone:** 646-497-9068; **Board Cert:** Internal Medicine 1979; Medical Oncology 1985; **Med School:** NYU Sch Med 1976; **Resid:** Internal Medicine, NYU-Bellevue Hosp 1980; **Fellow:** Medical Oncology, Meml Sloan-Kettering Cancer Ctr 1983; **Fac Appt:** Prof Med, Cornell Univ-Weill Med Coll

Siegel, Abby B MD (Onc) - **Spec Exp:** Liver Cancer; Biliary Cancer; Colon Cancer; Gastrointestinal Cancer; **Hospital:** NY-Presby/Columbia Univ Med Ctr, NY (page 102); **Address:** Herbert Irving Pavilion, Garden Level, 161 Fort Washington Ave at W 165th St, New York, NY 10032; **Phone:** 212-305-9781; **Board Cert:** Hematology 2004; Medical Oncology 2004; **Med School:** Univ Mass Sch Med 1997; **Resid:** Internal Medicine, NY Presby-Columbia Med Ctr 2000; **Fellow:** Hematology & Oncology, BRigham & Women's Hosp 2002; Hematology & Oncology, NY Presby-Columbia Med Ctr 2004; **Fac Appt:** Asst Prof Med, Columbia P&S

Silverman, Lewis R MD (Onc) - **Spec Exp:** Myelodysplastic Syndromes; Leukemia & Lymphoma; Multiple Myeloma; **Hospital:** Mt Sinai Hosp; **Address:** Ruttenberg Treatment Ctr, 1470 Madison Ave Fl 3, New York, NY 10029; **Phone:** 212-241-6756; **Board Cert:** Internal Medicine 1981; Hematology 1986; Medical Oncology 1987; **Med School:** Belgium 1978; **Resid:** Internal Medicine, Metropolitan Hosp Ctr 1980; Internal Medicine, Montefiore Med Ctr 1981; **Fellow:** Hematology, Montefiore Med Ctr 1982; Medical Oncology, Mt Sinai Hosp 1984; **Fac Appt:** Assoc Prof Med, Mount Sinai-Icahn Sch of Med

Sklarin, Nancy T MD (Onc) - **Spec Exp:** Breast Cancer; **Hospital:** Meml Sloan Kettering Canc Ctr (page 110); **Address:** MSKCC, Breast Cancer, 300 E 66th St, New York, NY 10065; **Phone:** 646-888-5488; **Board Cert:** Internal Medicine 1984; Medical Oncology 1987; Hematology 1988; **Med School:** Albert Einstein Coll Med 1981; **Resid:** Internal Medicine, LI Jewish Med Ctr 1984; **Fellow:** Hematology & Oncology, Mount Sinai Med Ctr 1987; **Fac Appt:** Assoc Prof Med, Cornell Univ-Weill Med Coll

Slovin, Susan F MD/PhD (Onc) - **Spec Exp:** Prostate Cancer; Genitourinary Cancer; Immunotherapy; **Hospital:** Meml Sloan Kettering Canc Ctr (page 110); **Address:** MSKCC, Genitourinary Oncology, 1275 York Ave, New York, NY 10065; **Phone:** 646-422-4470; **Board Cert:** Internal Medicine 2005; Medical Oncology 2009; **Med School:** Jefferson Med Coll 1990; **Resid:** Internal Medicine, Mt Sinai Hosp 1993; **Fellow:** Medical Oncology, Meml Sloan-Kettering Cancer Ctr 1996; **Fac Appt:** Assoc Prof Med, Cornell Univ-Weill Med Coll

Smith, Julia A MD/PhD (Onc) - **Spec Exp:** Breast Cancer; Cancer Risk Assessment; **Hospital:** NYU Langone Med Ctr (page 104), Bellevue Hosp Ctr; **Address:** 221 Lexington Ave, Fl 1, New York, NY 10016; **Phone:** 212-731-5452; **Board Cert:** Internal Medicine 1985; Medical Oncology 1989; **Med School:** NYU Sch Med 1980; **Resid:** Internal Medicine, Brigham & Womens Hosp 1983; **Fellow:** Hematology & Oncology, Meml Sloan-Kettering Cancer Ctr 1986; **Fac Appt:** Asst Clin Prof Med, NYU Sch Med

Speyer, James L MD (Onc) - **Spec Exp:** Ovarian Cancer; Breast Cancer; Graft vs Host Disease; **Hospital:** NYU Langone Med Ctr (page 104), Bellevue Hosp Ctr; **Address:** NYU, Clin Cancer Ctr, 160 E 34th St Fl 4, New York, NY 10016; **Phone:** 212-731-5432; **Board Cert:** Internal Medicine 1977; Hematology 1978; Medical Oncology 1979; **Med School:** Johns Hopkins Univ 1974; **Resid:** Internal Medicine, NY-Presby/Columbia Univ Med Ctr 1976; Hematology, NY-Presby/Columbia Univ Med Ctr 1977; **Fellow:** Medical Oncology, Natl Cancer Inst 1979; **Fac Appt:** Prof Med, NYU Sch Med

Spriggs, David R MD (Onc) - **Spec Exp:** Ovarian Cancer; Drug Development; Uterine Cancer; Gynecologic Cancer; **Hospital:** Meml Sloan Kettering Canc Ctr (page 110); **Address:** MSKCC, Gyn Oncology Svc, 300 E 66th St, New York, NY 10021; **Phone:** 646-888-4223; **Board Cert:** Internal Medicine 1981; Medical Oncology 2006; **Med School:** Univ Wisc 1977; **Resid:** Internal Medicine, NY-Presby/Columbia Univ Med Ctr 1981; **Fellow:** Medical Oncology, Dana-Farber Cancer Inst 1985; **Fac Appt:** Prof Med, Cornell Univ-Weill Med Coll

Stoopler, Mark Benjamin MD (Onc) - **Spec Exp:** Lung Cancer; Esophageal Cancer; Gastrointestinal Cancer; Thoracic Cancers; **Hospital:** NY-Presby/Columbia Univ Med Ctr, NY (page 102); **Address:** NY-Presby, Med Oncology, 161 Fort Washington Ave, Ste 936, New York, NY 10032; **Phone:** 212-305-8230; **Board Cert:** Internal Medicine 1978; Medical Oncology 1981; **Med School:** Cornell Univ-Weill Med Coll 1975; **Resid:** Internal Medicine, N Shore Univ Hosp 1978; **Fellow:** Medical Oncology, Meml Sloan-Kettering Cancer Ctr 1980; **Fac Appt:** Assoc Clin Prof Onc, Columbia P&S

Straus, David J MD (Onc) - **Spec Exp:** Lymphoma; Multiple Myeloma; Hodgkin's Lymphoma; **Hospital:** Meml Sloan Kettering Canc Ctr (page 110); **Address:** 1275 York Ave, Box 406, New York, NY 10065; **Phone:** 212-639-8365; **Board Cert:** Internal Medicine 1972; Hematology 1976; Medical Oncology 1977; **Med School:** Marquette Sch Med 1969; **Resid:** Internal Medicine, Montefiore Med Ctr 1972; **Fellow:** Hematology, Beth Israel Hosp/Brigham Hosp 1974; Medical Oncology, Meml Sloan Kettering Cancer Ctr 1976; **Fac Appt:** Prof Onc, Cornell Univ-Weill Med Coll

Tagawa, Scott T MD (Onc) - **Spec Exp:** Prostate Cancer; Bladder Cancer; Kidney Cancer; Urologic Cancer; **Hospital:** NY-Presby/Weill Cornell Med Ctr, NY (page 102); **Address:** NY Presby-Weill Cornell Med Ctr, 525 E 68th St, Box 403, New York, NY 10065; **Phone:** 646-962-2072; **Board Cert:** Medical Oncology 2005; Hematology 2006; **Med School:** USC-Keck Sch Med 1998; **Resid:** Internal Medicine, USC Med Ctr 2002; **Fellow:** Hematology & Oncology, USC Med Ctr 2005; **Fac Appt:** Assoc Clin Prof Onc, Cornell Univ-Weill Med Coll

Tap, William D MD (Onc) - **Spec Exp:** Sarcoma; Sarcoma-Soft Tissue; Ewing's Sarcoma; Bone Tumors; **Hospital:** Meml Sloan Kettering Canc Ctr (page 110); **Address:** MSKCC, Sarcoma Svc, 300 E 66th St Fl 10, New York, NY 10065; **Phone:** 646-888-4163; **Board Cert:** Medical Oncology 2006; Hematology 2006; **Med School:** Thomas Jefferson Univ 2000; **Resid:** Internal Medicine, Vanderbilt Univ Med Ctr 2003; **Fellow:** Hematology & Oncology, UCLA Med Ctr 2006

Vahdat, Linda T MD (Onc) - **Spec Exp:** Breast Cancer; Breast Cancer-Novel Therapies; Clinical Trials; **Hospital:** NY-Presby/Weill Cornell Med Ctr, NY (page 102); **Address:** 425 E 61st St Fl 8, New York, NY 10065; **Phone:** 212-821-0644; **Board Cert:** Medical Oncology 2005; **Med School:** Mount Sinai Sch Med 1987; **Resid:** Internal Medicine, Mt Sinai Hosp 1990; **Fellow:** Hematology & Oncology, Meml Sloan-Kettering Cancer Ctr 1994; **Fac Appt:** Prof Med, Cornell Univ-Weill Med Coll

Wolchok, Jedd D MD/PhD (Onc) - **Spec Exp:** Melanoma; Immunotherapy; Clinical Trials; Vaccine Therapy; **Hospital:** Meml Sloan Kettering Canc Ctr (page 110); **Address:** MSKCC, Melanoma Svc, 160 E 53rd St Fl 5, New York, NY 10019; **Phone:** 646-497-9067; **Board Cert:** Medical Oncology 2011; **Med School:** NYU Sch Med 1994; **Resid:** Internal Medicine, NYU Med Ctr 1997; **Fellow:** Medical Oncology, Meml Sloan-Kettering Canc Ctr 2000

Zelenetz, Andrew D MD/PhD (Onc) - **Spec Exp:** Lymphoma; Lymphoma, Non-Hodgkin's; **Hospital:** Meml Sloan Kettering Canc Ctr (page 110); **Address:** MSKCC, Lymphoma Svc, 205 E 64th St, New York, NY 10065; **Phone:** 212-639-2656; **Board Cert:** Medical Oncology 2009; **Med School:** Harvard Med Sch 1984; **Resid:** Internal Medicine, Stanford Univ Hosp & Clins 1988; **Fellow:** Medical Oncology, Stanford Univ Hosp & Clins 1991; **Fac Appt:** Asst Prof Med, Cornell Univ-Weill Med Coll

Neonatal-Perinatal Medicine

Caprio, Martha C MD (NP) - **Spec Exp:** Prematurity/Low Birth Weight Infants; **Hospital:** NYU Langone Med Ctr (page 104); **Address:** NYU Neonatology Assocs, 530 1st Ave, rm 7A, New York, NY 10016; **Phone:** 212-263-7950; **Board Cert:** Pediatrics 2010; Neonatal-Perinatal Medicine 2012; **Med School:** Mexico 1985; **Resid:** Pediatrics, NYU Med Ctr 1992; **Fellow:** Neonatal-Perinatal Medicine, NYU Med Ctr 1993; **Fac Appt:** Assoc Prof Med, NYU Sch Med

Holzman, Ian R MD (NP) - **Spec Exp:** Neonatal Nutrition; Necrotizing Enterocolitis; Ethics; Prematurity/Low Birth Weight Infants; **Hospital:** Mt Sinai Hosp; **Address:** Mt Sinai Hosp, Newborn Med, 1 Gustave L Levy Pl, Box 1508, New York, NY 10029; **Phone:** 212-241-5446; **Board Cert:** Pediatrics 1974; Neonatal-Perinatal Medicine 1977; **Med School:** Univ Pittsburgh 1971; **Resid:** Pediatrics, Chldns Hosp 1975; **Fellow:** Neonatal-Perinatal Medicine, Univ CO Hosp 1977; **Fac Appt:** Prof Ped, Mount Sinai-Icahn Sch of Med

Klein, Janice F MD (NP) - **Hospital:** Mt Sinai Roosevelt; **Address:** Mt Sinai Roosevelt, Neonatology, 1000 10th Ave, New York, NY 10019; **Phone:** 212-523-5710; **Board Cert:** Pediatrics 1985; Neonatal-Perinatal Medicine 1985; **Med School:** Albert Einstein Coll Med 1980; **Resid:** Pediatrics, Montefiore Med Ctr 1983; **Fellow:** Neonatal-Perinatal Medicine, Montefiore Med Ctr 1985; **Fac Appt:** Asst Clin Prof Ped, Columbia P&S

Mally, Pradeep MD (NP) - **Hospital:** NYU Langone Med Ctr (page 104); **Address:** NYU Neonatology Assocs, 530 1st Ave, rm 7A, New York, NY 10016; **Phone:** 212-263-7950; **Board Cert:** Neonatal-Perinatal Medicine 2011; **Med School:** India 1988; **Resid:** Pediatrics, Maimonides Med Ctr 1999; **Fellow:** Neonatal-Perinatal Medicine, Westchester Co Med Ctr 2002; **Fac Appt:** Asst Prof Ped, NYU Sch Med

Marron-Corwin, Mary MD (NP) - **Spec Exp:** Neonatal Critical Care; Neonatal Respiratory Care; Substance Abuse Effects in Newborn; Prematurity/Low Birth Weight Infants; **Hospital:** Harlem Hosp Ctr; **Address:** 506 Lenox Ave, MLK Pavilion, Ste 4417, New York, NY 10037; **Phone:** 212-939-8457; **Board Cert:** Neonatal-Perinatal Medicine 2006; **Med School:** Philippines 1985; **Resid:** Pediatrics, St Vincents Hosp Med Ctr 1988; **Fellow:** Neonatal-Perinatal Medicine, Babies Hosp/Colum-Presby Med Ctr 1990; **Fac Appt:** Prof Ped, Columbia P&S

Perlman, Jeffrey M MD (NP) - **Spec Exp:** Neonatal Critical Care; Prematurity/Low Birth Weight Infants; Neonatal Neurology; Lung Disease in Newborns; **Hospital:** NY-Presby/Weill Cornell Med Ctr, NY (page 102); **Address:** NY-Presby, Newborn Med, 525 E 68th St, Ste N-506, New York, NY 10065; **Phone:** 212-746-0318; **Board Cert:** Pediatrics 1983; Neonatal-Perinatal Medicine 1983; **Med School:** South Africa 1974; **Resid:** Pediatrics, Johannesburg Chldns Hosp 1979; Pediatrics, St Louis Chldns Hosp 1981; **Fellow:** Neonatology, St Louis Chldns Hosp 1983; **Fac Appt:** Prof Ped, Cornell Univ-Weill Med Coll

Polin, Richard A MD (NP) - **Spec Exp:** Neonatal Critical Care; Neonatal Care; Jaundice & Bilirubin Metabolism; Lung Disease in Newborns; **Hospital:** Morgan Stanley Chldns Hosp of NY-Presby, NY (page 102); **Address:** NY-Presby, Neonatology, 3959 Broadway, Ste CHN-1201, New York, NY 10032; **Phone:** 212-305-5827; **Board Cert:** Pediatrics 1975; Neonatal-Perinatal Medicine 2010; **Med School:** Temple Univ 1970; **Resid:** Pediatrics, Chldns Meml Hosp 1972; Pediatrics, NY-Presby/Babies & Chldns Hosp 1973; **Fellow:** Neonatal-Perinatal Medicine, NY-Presby/Babies & Chldns Hosp 1976; **Fac Appt:** Prof Ped, Columbia P&S

Nephrology

Ames, Richard P MD (Nep) - **Spec Exp:** Hypertension; Kidney Disease; Dialysis Care; **Hospital:** Mt Sinai Roosevelt; **Address:** 200 W 57th St Fl 15, New York, NY 10019; **Phone:** 917-224-4270; **Board Cert:** Internal Medicine 1974; Nephrology 1972; Medical Oncology 1973; Hematology 1974; **Med School:** Columbia P&S 1958; **Resid:** Internal Medicine, Boston Med Ctr 1961; **Fellow:** Nephrology, Columbia-Presby Hosp 1963; **Fac Appt:** Clin Prof Med, Columbia P&S

Appel, Gerald B MD/PhD (Nep) - **Spec Exp:** Glomerulonephritis; Lupus Nephritis; Nephrotic Syndrome; **Hospital:** NY-Presby/Columbia Univ Med Ctr, NY (page 102); **Address:** NY-Presby, Nephrology, 161 Fort Washington Ave, Ste 202, New York, NY 10032; **Phone:** 212-305-0320; **Board Cert:** Internal Medicine 1975; Nephrology 1978; **Med School:** Albert Einstein Coll Med 1972; **Resid:** Internal Medicine, NY-Presby/Columbia Univ Med Ctr 1975; **Fellow:** Nephrology, NY-Presby/Columbia Univ Med Ctr 1976; Nephrology, Yale-New Haven Hosp 1978; **Fac Appt:** Prof Med, Columbia P&S

August, Phyllis MD (Nep) - **Spec Exp:** Hypertension; Hypertension in Pregnancy; Kidney Disease; **Hospital:** NY-Presby/Weill Cornell Med Ctr, NY (page 102); **Address:** NY-Presby, Hypertension Ctr, 424 E 70th St, New York, NY 10021; **Phone:** 646-962-2605; **Board Cert:** Internal Medicine 1980; Nephrology 1982; **Med School:** Yale Univ 1977; **Resid:** Internal Medicine, NY-Presby/Weill Cornell Med Ctr 1980; **Fellow:** Nephrology, NY-Presby/Weill Cornell Med Ctr 1983; **Fac Appt:** Prof Med, Cornell Univ-Weill Med Coll

Blumenfeld, Jon D MD (Nep) - **Spec Exp:** Polycystic Kidney Disease; Hypertension; Adrenal Disorders; **Hospital:** NY-Presby/Weill Cornell Med Ctr, NY (page 102), Rockefeller Univ Hosp; **Address:** Rogosin Inst, 505 E 70th St, Fl 2, New York, NY 10021; **Phone:** 212-746-1495; **Board Cert:** Internal Medicine 1984; Nephrology 1986; **Med School:** Yale Univ 1981; **Resid:** Internal Medicine, NY-Presby/Weill Cornell Med Ctr 1984; **Fellow:** Nephrology, Brigham & Womens Hosp 1988; **Fac Appt:** Prof Med, Cornell Univ-Weill Med Coll

Cohen, David J MD (Nep) - **Spec Exp:** Transplant Medicine-Kidney; Glomerulonephritis; **Hospital:** NY-Presby/Columbia Univ Med Ctr, NY (page 102); **Address:** Columbia Univ Med Ctr, 622 W 168th St, rm PH 4-124, New York, NY 10032-3720; **Phone:** 212-305-0320 x4; **Board Cert:** Internal Medicine 1980; Nephrology 1984; **Med School:** Albert Einstein Coll Med 1977; **Resid:** Internal Medicine, Mount Sinai Hosp 1980; **Fellow:** Nephrology, Columbia-Presby Hosp 1981; Research, Brigham & Womens Hosp 1983; **Fac Appt:** Clin Prof Med, Columbia P&S

DeFabritus, Albert Michael MD (Nep) - **Spec Exp:** Kidney Disease-Chronic; Hypertension; Anemia in Chronic Kidney Disease; Kidney Stones; **Hospital:** Mt Sinai Beth Israel; **Address:** 352 7th Ave, Ste 1003, New York, NY 10001; **Phone:** 212-807-8817; **Board Cert:** Internal Medicine 1976; Nephrology 1978; **Med School:** NY Med Coll 1973; **Resid:** Internal Medicine, St Vincents Hosp 1976; **Fellow:** Nephrology, NY-Presby/Weill Cornell Med Ctr 1978

DeVita, Maria V MD (Nep) - **Spec Exp:** Glomerulonephritis; Dialysis Care; Hypertension; Kidney Disease-Chronic; **Hospital:** Lenox Hill Hosp; **Address:** Kidney & Hypertension Specialists, 130 E 77th St Fl 5, New York, NY 10075; **Phone:** 212-439-9251; **Board Cert:** Internal Medicine 1988; Nephrology 2012; **Med School:** Georgetown Univ 1984; **Resid:** Internal Medicine, Lenox Hill Hosp 1987; **Fellow:** Nephrology, Lenox Hill Hosp 1989; **Fac Appt:** Clin Prof Med, NYU Sch Med

Gardenswartz, Mark MD (Nep) - **Spec Exp:** Hypertension; Hypertension in Pregnancy; Polycystic Kidney Disease; **Hospital:** Lenox Hill Hosp; **Address:** 110 E 59th St, Ste 10B, New York, NY 10022; **Phone:** 212-583-2930; **Board Cert:** Internal Medicine 1978; Nephrology 1980; **Med School:** Univ Colorado 1975; **Resid:** Internal Medicine, NY-Presby/Columbia Univ Med Ctr 1978; **Fellow:** Nephrology, Univ CO Hosp 1980; **Fac Appt:** Assoc Clin Prof Med, NYU Sch Med

Garvey, Michael MD (Nep) - **Spec Exp:** Dialysis Care; **Hospital:** Mt Sinai Beth Israel; **Address:** 222 W 14th St, New York, NY 10011; **Phone:** 212-807-7920; **Board Cert:** Internal Medicine 1979; Nephrology 1982; **Med School:** NY Med Coll 1975; **Resid:** Internal Medicine, St Vincents Hosp 1979; **Fellow:** Nephrology, NYU Med Ctr 1981

Kim, Tonia Kang-Hae MD (Nep) - **Spec Exp:** Kidney Failure-Acute; Kidney Failure-Chronic; Hypertension; Nephrotic Syndrome; **Hospital:** Mt Sinai Hosp; **Address:** Mt Sinai Medical Ctr, Renal Medicine, 5 E 98th St Fl 11, New York, NY 10029; **Phone:** 212-241-2060; **Board Cert:** Internal Medicine 2000; Nephrology 2012; **Med School:** Albany Med Coll 1997; **Resid:** Internal Medicine, Mt Sinai Med Ctr 2000; **Fellow:** Nephrology, Mt Sinai Med Ctr 2002; **Fac Appt:** Asst Prof Med, Mount Sinai Sch Med

Liu, David T MD (Nep) - **Spec Exp:** Glomerulonephritis; Nephrotic Syndrome; Kidney Failure; Hypertension; **Hospital:** NYU Langone Med Ctr (page 104); **Address:** NYU, Nephrology, 530 1st Ave, Ste 4B, New York, NY 10016; **Phone:** 212-263-0705; **Board Cert:** Internal Medicine 1980; Nephrology 1984; **Med School:** SUNY Buffalo 1977; **Resid:** Internal Medicine, Univ Miami Hosp 1980; **Fellow:** Nephrology, NYU Med Ctr 1984; **Fac Appt:** Asst Clin Prof Med, NYU Sch Med

Matalon, Robert MD (Nep) - **Spec Exp:** Dialysis Care; Kidney Failure; **Hospital:** NYU Langone Med Ctr (page 104), NY-Presby/Lower Manhattan Hosp (page 102); **Address:** NYU, Nephrology, 530 1st Ave, Ste 4A, New York, NY 10016; **Phone:** 212-263-7239; **Board Cert:** Internal Medicine 1970; Nephrology 1974; **Med School:** NYU Sch Med 1964; **Resid:** Internal Medicine, NYU-Bellevue Hosp 1967; **Fellow:** Nephrology, NYU Med Ctr 1969; **Fac Appt:** Assoc Prof Med, NYU Sch Med

Michelis, Michael F MD (Nep) - **Spec Exp:** Kidney Disease; Hypertension; Dialysis Care; **Hospital:** Lenox Hill Hosp; **Address:** 130 E 77th St Fl 5, New York, NY 10075; **Phone:** 212-988-3506; **Board Cert:** Internal Medicine 1969; **Med School:** Geo Wash Univ 1963; **Resid:** Internal Medicine, Lenox Hill Hosp 1965; Internal Medicine, Hosp Univ Penn 1967; **Fellow:** Renal Disease, UPMC 1970

Radhakrishnan, Jai MD (Nep) - **Spec Exp:** Kidney Disease-Chronic; Glomerulonephritis; Lupus Nephritis; **Hospital:** NY-Presby/Columbia Univ Med Ctr, NY (page 102); **Address:** NY-Presby, Nephrology, 622 W 168 St, Ste 476, New York, NY 10032; **Phone:** 212-305-5020; **Board Cert:** Internal Medicine 2013; Nephrology 2013; **Med School:** India 1984; **Resid:** Internal Medicine, Jawaharal Inst 1987; Internal Medicine, Lincoln Hosp 1990; **Fellow:** Nephrology, Mass Genl Hosp 1991; Nephrology, NY-Presby/Columbia Univ Med Ctr 1993; **Fac Appt:** Prof Med, Columbia P&S

Saal, Stuart MD (Nep) - **Spec Exp:** Transplant Medicine-Kidney; **Hospital:** NY-Presby/Weill Cornell Med Ctr, NY (page 102); **Address:** 505 E 70th St, Ste 230, New York, NY 10021-4872; **Phone:** 212-746-1553; **Board Cert:** Internal Medicine 1974; Nephrology 1978; **Med School:** NY Med Coll 1971; **Resid:** Internal Medicine, St Luke's-Roosevelt Hosp Ctr 1974; **Fellow:** Nephrology, NY Hosp 1976; **Fac Appt:** Assoc Clin Prof Med, Cornell Univ-Weill Med Coll

Stern, Leonard MD (Nep) - **Spec Exp:** Kidney Failure-Chronic; Transplant Medicine-Kidney; Bone Disorders-Metabolic; Dialysis Care; **Hospital:** NY-Presby/Columbia Univ Med Ctr, NY (page 102); **Address:** 622 W 168th St, Room PH4-4124, New York, NY 10032-3702; **Phone:** 212-305-3273; **Board Cert:** Internal Medicine 1978; Nephrology 1980; **Med School:** NY Med Coll 1975; **Resid:** Internal Medicine, Jacobi Med Ctr 1978; **Fellow:** Nephrology, Montefiore Med Ctr 1979; Nephrology, Yale-New Haven Hosp 1981; **Fac Appt:** Assoc Prof Med, Columbia P&S

Swidler, Mark A MD (Nep) - **Spec Exp:** Kidney Disease-Geriatric; Dialysis Care; **Hospital:** Mt Sinai Hosp; **Address:** 5 E 98th St Fl 11, Mt Sinai, Renal Care, New York, NY 10029; **Phone:** 212-241-4060; **Board Cert:** Internal Medicine 1981; Nephrology 2010; Geriatric Medicine 2013; **Med School:** Albert Einstein Coll Med 1978; **Resid:** Internal Medicine, Saint Vincent's Hosp 1982; **Fellow:** Nephrology, Mass Genl Hosp 1986; Geriatric Medicine, Mt Sinai Sch Med 2004; **Fac Appt:** Asst Prof Med, Mount Sinai Sch Med

Uribarri, Jaime V MD (Nep) - **Spec Exp:** Nephrotic Syndrome; Kidney Stones; Hypertension; Dialysis Care; **Hospital:** Mt Sinai Hosp; **Address:** 5 E 98th St Fl 11, Mt Sinai, Renal Care, New York, NY 10029; **Phone:** 212-241-4060; **Board Cert:** Internal Medicine 1977; Nephrology 1980; **Med School:** Chile 1973; **Resid:** Internal Medicine, Brooklyn Cumberland Med Ctr 1978; **Fellow:** Nephrology, SUNY Downstate Med Ctr 1980; **Fac Appt:** Prof Med, Mount Sinai Sch Med

Wang, John C MD/PhD (Nep) - **Spec Exp:** Hypertension; **Hospital:** NY-Presby/Weill Cornell Med Ctr, NY (page 102); **Address:** 505 E 70th St, rm 213, New York, NY 10021; **Phone:** 212-746-3097; **Board Cert:** Internal Medicine 1985; Nephrology 1986; **Med School:** Cornell Univ-Weill Med Coll 1979; **Resid:** Internal Medicine, LaGuardia Hosp 1982; **Fellow:** Nephrology, NY-Presby/Weill Cornell Med Ctr 1984; **Fac Appt:** Assoc Clin Prof Med, Cornell Univ-Weill Med Coll

Weisstuch, Joseph M MD (Nep) - **Spec Exp:** Diabetic Kidney Disease; Electrolyte Disorders; Hypertension; **Hospital:** NYU Langone Med Ctr (page 104); **Address:** NYU, Nephrology, 530 1st Ave, Ste 4B, New York, NY 10016; **Phone:** 212-263-0705; **Board Cert:** Internal Medicine 1988; Nephrology 2012; **Med School:** NYU Sch Med 1985; **Resid:** Internal Medicine, NYU Med Ctr 1989; **Fellow:** Nephrology, NYU-Bellevue Hosp 1991; **Fac Appt:** Asst Clin Prof Med, NYU Sch Med

Williams, Gail S MD (Nep) - **Spec Exp:** Kidney Failure-Chronic; Transplant Medicine-Kidney; Hypertension; **Hospital:** NY-Presby/Columbia Univ Med Ctr, NY (page 102); **Address:** NY-Presby, Neurology Dept, 161 Fort Washington Ave, Ste 351, New York, NY 10032; **Phone:** 212-305-5376; **Board Cert:** Internal Medicine 1972; Nephrology 1974; **Med School:** Columbia P&S 1968; **Resid:** Internal Medicine, NY-Presby/Columbia Univ Med Ctr 1972; **Fellow:** Nephrology, NY-Presby/Columbia Univ Med Ctr 1974; **Fac Appt:** Assoc Clin Prof Med, Columbia P&S

Winchester, James F MD (Nep) - **Spec Exp:** Dialysis Care; Polycystic Kidney Disease; Toxicology; Hypertension; **Hospital:** Mt Sinai Beth Israel; **Address:** Mt Sinai BIMC, Nephrology, 10 Union Square E, Ste 2F, New York, NY 10003; **Phone:** 212-420-4070; **Board Cert:** Internal Medicine 2007; **Med School:** Scotland, UK 1969; **Resid:** Internal Medicine, Royal Infirmiry 1972; **Fellow:** Nephrology, Royal Infirmiry 1974; **Fac Appt:** Prof Med, Albert Einstein Coll Med

Winston, Jonathan MD (Nep) - **Spec Exp:** Kidney Disease-Chronic; Kidney Failure; HIV Related Kidney Disease; Glomerulonephritis; **Hospital:** Mt Sinai Hosp; **Address:** Mt Sinai Medical Ctr, Renal Medicine, 5 E 98th St, Fl 11, New York, NY 10029; **Phone:** 212-241-4060; **Board Cert:** Internal Medicine 1980; Nephrology 1984; **Med School:** Geo Wash Univ 1977; **Resid:** Internal Medicine, LIJ Med Ctr 1980; **Fellow:** Nephrology, Mt Sinai Hosp 1982; **Fac Appt:** Prof Med, Mount Sinai-Icahn Sch of Med

Neurological Surgery

Anderson, Richard C.E MD (NS) - **Spec Exp:** Spinal Surgery-Pediatric; Brain & Spinal Tumors-Pediatric; Craniofacial Surgery; Pediatric Neurosurgery; **Hospital:** Morgan Stanley Chldns Hosp of NY-Presby, NY (page 102), St. Joseph's Regl Med Ctr - Paterson; **Address:** Columbia Neurosurgery, 710 W 168th St, rm 213, New York, NY 10032; **Phone:** 212-305-0219; **Board Cert:** Neurological Surgery 2007; Pediatric Neurological Surgery 2008; **Med School:** Johns Hopkins Univ 1997; **Resid:** Neurological Surgery, Columbia Neuro Inst 2004; **Fellow:** Pediatric Neurological Surgery, Univ Utah Hlth Care 2005; **Fac Appt:** Asst Prof NS, Columbia P&S

Angevine, Peter D MD (NS) - **Spec Exp:** Spinal Surgery; Scoliosis; Spinal Deformity; **Hospital:** NY-Presby/Columbia Univ Med Ctr, NY (page 102); **Address:** Columbia Neurosurgery, 710 W 168th St, rm 502, New York, NY 10032; **Phone:** 212-305-1550; **Board Cert:** Neurological Surgery 2008; **Med School:** Columbia P&S 1998; **Resid:** Neurological Surgery, Columbia Presby Med Ctr 2004; **Fellow:** Spine Surgery, Barnes Jewish Hosp 2005; **Fac Appt:** Asst Prof NS, Columbia P&S

Bederson, Joshua B MD (NS) - **Spec Exp:** Brain & Spinal Cord Tumors; Aneurysm-Cerebral; Meningioma; Cerebrovascular Surgery; **Hospital:** Mt Sinai Hosp; **Address:** Mt Sinai Hosp, Neurosurgery, 1 Gustave L Levy Pl, rm 28, Box 1136, New York, NY 10029; **Phone:** 212-241-2377; **Board Cert:** Neurological Surgery 1993; **Med School:** UCSF 1984; **Resid:** Neurological Surgery, UCSF Med Ctr 1990; **Fellow:** Neurovascular Surgery, Barrow Neuro Inst 1990; Microsurgery, Univ Hosp Zurich 1990; **Fac Appt:** Prof NS, Mount Sinai-Icahn Sch of Med

Bilsky, Mark H MD (NS) - **Spec Exp:** Brain & Spinal Cord Tumors; Skull Base Tumors; Spinal Cord Tumors; Spinal Surgery; **Hospital:** Meml Sloan Kettering Canc Ctr (page 110), NY-Presby/Weill Cornell Med Ctr, NY (page 102); **Address:** MSKCC, Neurosurgery, 1275 York Ave, Ste C703, New York, NY 10065; **Phone:** 212-639-8556; **Board Cert:** Neurological Surgery 2010; **Med School:** Emory Univ 1988; **Resid:** Neurological Surgery, NY-Presby/Weill Cornell Med Ctr 1994; **Fellow:** Spine Surgery, Univ Louisville Hosp 1995; **Fac Appt:** Prof NS, Cornell Univ-Weill Med Coll

Boockvar, John A MD (NS) - **Spec Exp:** Brain & Spinal Surgery; Meningioma; Metastatic Cancer; Minimally Invasive Surgery; **Hospital:** Lenox Hill Hosp, Lenox Hill Hosp (Manh Eye, Ear & Throat Hosp); **Address:** Lenox Hill Hosp, Brain Tumor Ctr, 130 E 77th St, New York, NY 10075; **Phone:** 212-434-3900; **Board Cert:** Neurological Surgery 2007; **Med School:** SUNY Downstate 1997; **Resid:** Neurological Surgery, Hosp Univ Penn 2003; **Fellow:** Neuro-Oncology, Hosp Univ Penn 2004; **Fac Appt:** Prof NS, Hofstra N Shore-LIJ Sch Med

Bruce, Jeffrey N MD (NS) - **Spec Exp:** Brain Tumors-Complex; Pituitary Tumors; Skull Base Surgery; Meningioma; **Hospital:** NY-Presby/Columbia Univ Med Ctr, NY (page 102); **Address:** Columbia Neurosurgery, 710 W 168th St, rm 434, New York, NY 10032; **Phone:** 212-305-7346; **Board Cert:** Neurological Surgery 1993; **Med School:** Rutgers R W Johnson Med Sch 1983; **Resid:** Neurological Surgery, NY-Presby/Columbia Univ Med Ctr 1990; **Fellow:** Neurological Surgery, Natl Inst Hlth 1985; **Fac Appt:** Prof NS, Columbia P&S

Choudhri, Tanvir F MD (NS) - **Spec Exp:** Spinal Surgery; Minimally Invasive Surgery; Spinal Tumors; Spinal Disorders-Degenerative; **Hospital:** Mt Sinai Hosp; **Address:** Mt Sinai Hosp, Neurosurgery, 5 E 98th St Fl 7, Box 1136, New York, NY 10029; **Phone:** 212-241-8560; **Board Cert:** Neurological Surgery 2007; **Med School:** Columbia P&S 1994; **Resid:** Neurological Surgery, NY-Presby/Columbia Univ Med Ctr 2001; **Fellow:** Spine Surgery, Barrow Neuro Inst 2002; **Fac Appt:** Asst Prof NS, Mount Sinai-Icahn Sch of Med

Di Giacinto, George V MD (NS) - **Spec Exp:** Spinal Surgery; Pain Management; **Hospital:** Mt Sinai Roosevelt; **Address:** 1000 10th Ave, Ste 5G80, New York, NY 10019; **Phone:** 212-523-8500; **Board Cert:** Neurological Surgery 1981; **Med School:** Harvard Med Sch 1970; **Resid:** Surgery, St Luke's-Roosevelt Hosp Ctr 1972; Neurological Surgery, Columbia-Presby Hosp 1978

Doyle, Werner K MD (NS) - **Spec Exp:** Epilepsy; **Hospital:** NYU Langone Med Ctr (page 104); **Address:** NYU Comprehensive Epilepsy Ctr, 223 E 34th St, New York, NY 10016; **Phone:** 646-558-0804; **Board Cert:** Neurological Surgery 1995; **Med School:** Columbia P&S 1982; **Resid:** Surgery, Roosevelt Hosp Ctr 1985; Neurological Surgery, NYU Med Ctr 1991; **Fellow:** Epilepsy, Yale-New Haven Hosp 1992; **Fac Appt:** Assoc Prof NS, NYU Sch Med

Elowitz, Eric H MD (NS) - **Spec Exp:** Spinal Surgery; Minimally Invasive Spinal Surgery; Spinal Disorders-Degenerative; Spinal Disc Replacement; **Hospital:** NY-Presby/Weill Cornell Med Ctr, NY (page 102); **Address:** Brain & Spine Ctr, 1305 York Ave Fl 9, (at 70th St), New York, NY 10065; **Phone:** 212-746-2870; **Board Cert:** Neurological Surgery 1997; **Med School:** SUNY Downstate 1986; **Resid:** Neurological Surgery, SUNY Downstate Med Ctr 1993; **Fac Appt:** Assoc Prof NS, Cornell Univ-Weill Med Coll

Feldstein, Neil A MD (NS) - **Spec Exp:** Brain & Spinal Tumors-Pediatric; MoyaMoya Disease; Chiari's Deformity; Hydrocephalus; **Hospital:** Morgan Stanley Chldns Hosp of NY-Presby, NY (page 102), NY-Presby/Columbia Univ Med Ctr, NY (page 102); **Address:** Columbia Neurosurgery, 710 W 168th St, Ste 213, New York, NY 10032; **Phone:** 212-305-1396; **Board Cert:** Neurological Surgery 1995; **Med School:** NYU Sch Med 1984; **Resid:** Neurological Surgery, Baylor Med Ctr 1990; **Fellow:** Pediatric Neurological Surgery, NYU Med Ctr 1991; **Fac Appt:** Assoc Prof NS, Columbia P&S

Frempong-Boadu, Anthony K MD (NS) - **Spec Exp:** Minimally Invasive Spinal Surgery; Spinal Reconstructive Surgery; Spinal Cord Tumors; Spinal Reconstructive Surgery; **Hospital:** NYU Langone Med Ctr (page 104); **Address:** NYU, Neurosurgery, 530 1st Ave, Ste 8R, New York, NY 10016; **Phone:** 212-263-6514; **Board Cert:** Neurological Surgery 2004; **Med School:** Temple Univ 1992; **Resid:** Neurological Surgery, NYU Med Ctr 1999; **Fellow:** Spine Surgery, NYU Med Ctr 1997; Minimally Invasive Surgery, UF Hlth Shands Hosp 2000; **Fac Appt:** Assoc Prof NS, NYU Sch Med

Ghatan, Saadi MD (NS) - **Spec Exp:** Pediatric Neurosurgery; Epilepsy; Neuro-Endoscopy; Cerebrovascular Disease; **Hospital:** Mt Sinai Beth Israel; **Address:** Mt Sinai BIMC, Neurosurgery, 1000 10th Ave, Ste 5G-80, New York, NY 10019; **Phone:** 212-636-3232; **Board Cert:** Neurological Surgery 2007; **Med School:** Univ Wash 1993; **Resid:** Surgery, Univ Washington Med Ctr 1994; Neurological Surgery, Univ Washington Med Ctr 2001; **Fellow:** Pediatric Neurological Surgery, Chldns Hosp 2002; Pediatric Neurological Surgery, Great Ormond Street Hosp 2003

Golfinos, John G MD (NS) - **Spec Exp:** Brain Tumors; Skull Base Tumors; **Hospital:** NYU Langone Med Ctr (page 104); **Address:** NYU Med Ctr, Neurosurgery, 530 1st Ave, Ste 8R, New York, NY 10016; **Phone:** 212-263-2950; **Board Cert:** Neurological Surgery 1998; **Med School:** Columbia P&S 1988; **Resid:** Neurological Surgery, Barrow Neuro Inst 1995; **Fac Appt:** Assoc Prof NS, NYU Sch Med

Goodman, Robert R MD/PhD (NS) - **Spec Exp:** Parkinson's Disease/Movement Disorders; Epilepsy; Trigeminal Neuralgia; Hydrocephalus-Adult; **Hospital:** Mt Sinai Roosevelt, Mt Sinai Beth Israel; **Address:** 1 W 85th St, New York, NY 10024; **Phone:** 212-600-4879; **Board Cert:** Neurological Surgery 1993; **Med School:** Johns Hopkins Univ 1982; **Resid:** Neurological Surgery, NY-Presby/Columbia Univ Med Ctr 1989; **Fac Appt:** Assoc Prof NS, Columbia P&S

Gutin, Philip H MD (NS) - **Spec Exp:** Brain Tumors; Meningioma; Acoustic Neuroma; Stereotactic Radiosurgery; **Hospital:** Meml Sloan Kettering Canc Ctr (page 110), NY-Presby/Weill Cornell Med Ctr, NY (page 102); **Address:** MSKCC, Neurosurgery, 1275 York Ave, rm C703, New York, NY 10065; **Phone:** 212-639-8556; **Board Cert:** Neurological Surgery 1981; **Med School:** Univ Pennsylvania 1971; **Resid:** Neurological Surgery, UCSF Med Ctr 1979; **Fellow:** Neuro-Oncology, Natl Cancer Inst 1976; **Fac Appt:** Prof NS, Cornell Univ-Weill Med Coll

Harter, David H MD (NS) - **Spec Exp:** Pediatric Neurosurgery; Arteriovenous Malformations; Vascular Disorders; Spina Bifida; **Hospital:** NYU Langone Med Ctr (page 104); **Address:** NYU, Pediatric Neurosurgery, 317 E 34th St, Ste 1002, New York, NY 10016; **Phone:** 212-263-6419; **Board Cert:** Neurological Surgery 2014; Pediatric Neurological Surgery 2004; **Med School:** Georgetown Univ 1994; **Resid:** Neurological Surgery, Univ MD Med Ctr 1998; **Fellow:** Pediatric Neurological Surgery, Chldns Meml Hosp 2000; **Fac Appt:** Asst Prof NS, NYU Sch Med

Hartl, Roger MD (NS) - **Spec Exp:** Spinal Surgery-Complex; Minimally Invasive Spinal Surgery; Spinal Disc Replacement; Spinal Trauma; **Hospital:** NY-Presby/Weill Cornell Med Ctr, NY (page 102); **Address:** NY-Presby, Neurosurgery, 520 E 70th St, rm 651, New York, NY 10065; **Phone:** 212-746-2152; **Board Cert:** Neurological Surgery 2008; **Med School:** Germany 1993; **Resid:** Neurological Surgery, NY-Presby/Weill Cornell Med Ctr 2003; **Fellow:** Spine Surgery, Barrow Neuro Inst 2004; **Fac Appt:** Assoc Prof NS, Cornell Univ-Weill Med Coll

Jafar, Jafar J MD (NS) - **Spec Exp:** Aneurysm-Cerebral; Brain Tumors; Skull Base Tumors; Acoustic Neuroma; **Hospital:** NYU Langone Med Ctr (page 104), Lenox Hill Hosp; **Address:** NYU, Neurosurgery, 530 1st Ave, Ste 7W, New York, NY 10016; **Phone:** 212-263-6312; **Board Cert:** Neurological Surgery 1984; **Med School:** Iran 1976; **Resid:** Neurological Surgery, Univ Chicago Hosp 1981; Neurological Surgery, Natl Hosp for Nervous Disease 1982; **Fellow:** Neurosurgical Oncology, Univ Hosp 1991; **Fac Appt:** Prof NS, NYU Sch Med

Jenkins III, Arthur L MD (NS) - **Spec Exp:** Spinal Surgery; Minimally Invasive Spinal Surgery; Scoliosis; Spinal Tumors; **Hospital:** Mt Sinai Hosp; **Address:** Faculty Practice Assocs, 5 E 98th St, Fl 7, Box 1136, New York, NY 10029; **Phone:** 212-241-8175; **Board Cert:** Neurological Surgery 2005; **Med School:** Univ Pennsylvania 1993; **Resid:** Neurological Surgery, Mtount Sinai Med Ctr 2000; **Fellow:** Spine Surgery, Brigham & Women's Hosp 2001; **Fac Appt:** Assoc Prof NS, Mount Sinai Sch Med

Kaiser, Michael G MD (NS) - **Spec Exp:** Spinal Surgery-Complex; Minimally Invasive Spinal Surgery; Spinal Disc Replacement; Spinal Cord Tumors; **Hospital:** NY-Presby/Columbia Univ Med Ctr, NY (page 102); **Address:** Neurological Institute, Dept Neurological Surgery, 710 W 168th St, New York, NY 10032; **Phone:** 212-305-0378; **Board Cert:** Neurological Surgery 2004; **Med School:** Yale Univ 1994; **Resid:** Neurological Surgery, Columbia Neuro Inst 2000; **Fellow:** Spine Surgery, Emory Univ Hosp 2001; **Fac Appt:** Assoc Prof NS, Columbia P&S

Kondziolka, Douglas MD (NS) - **Spec Exp:** Brain Tumors-Adult & Pediatric; Brain Tumors-Metastatic; Stereotactic Radiosurgery; Movement Disorders; **Hospital:** NYU Langone Med Ctr (page 104); **Address:** 530 First Ave, Ste 8R, New York, NY 10016; **Phone:** 646-501-2360; **Board Cert:** Neurological Surgery 1994; **Med School:** Univ Toronto 1985; **Resid:** Neurological Surgery, Univ Toronto Affil Hosp 1989; **Fellow:** Stereotactic Neurological Surgery, Univ Pittsburgh Med Ctr 1991

Langer, David J MD (NS) - **Spec Exp:** Neurovascular Surgery; Arteriovenous Malformations; Aneurysm-Cerebral; Carotid Artery Surgery; **Hospital:** Lenox Hill Hosp, N Shore Univ Hosp; **Address:** Lenox Hill Hosp, Brain Tumor Ctr, 130 E 77th St, New York, NY 10075; **Phone:** 212-434-3900; **Board Cert:** Neurological Surgery 2014; **Med School:** Univ Pennsylvania 1991; **Resid:** Neurological Surgery, Hosp Univ Penn 1998; **Fellow:** Neurovascular Surgery, Beth Israel Med Ctr 1999; **Fac Appt:** Asst Prof NS, Hofstra N Shore-LIJ Sch Med

McCormick, Paul C MD (NS) - **Spec Exp:** Spinal Surgery; Spinal Tumors; **Hospital:** NY-Presby/Columbia Univ Med Ctr, NY (page 102); **Address:** Columbia Neurosurgery, 710 W 168th St, Ste 506, New York, NY 10032; **Phone:** 212-305-7976; **Board Cert:** Neurological Surgery 1993; **Med School:** Columbia P&S 1982; **Resid:** Neurology, NY-Presby Hosp 1984; Neurological Surgery, NY-Presby Hosp 1989; **Fellow:** Spine Surgery, John Doyne Hosp 1990; **Fac Appt:** Prof NS, Columbia P&S

McKhann II, Guy M MD (NS) - **Spec Exp:** Brain Tumors; Epilepsy; Hydrocephalus; **Hospital:** NY-Presby/Columbia Univ Med Ctr, NY (page 102); **Address:** Columbia Neurosurgery, 710 W 168th St, Ste 411, New York, NY 10032; **Phone:** 212-305-0052; **Board Cert:** Neurological Surgery 2004; **Med School:** Yale Univ 1990; **Resid:** Neurological Surgery, Univ Washington Med Ctr 1998; **Fellow:** Epilepsy, Univ Washington Med Ctr 1999; **Fac Appt:** Assoc Prof NS, Columbia P&S

Perin, Noel I MD (NS) - **Spec Exp:** Spinal Surgery-Minimally Invasive; Spinal Tumors; **Hospital:** NYU Langone Med Ctr (page 104); **Address:** NYU, Neurosurgery, 530 1st Ave, Ste 8R, New York, NY 10016; **Phone:** 212-263-5732; **Board Cert:** Neurological Surgery 1995; **Med School:** Sri Lanka 1973; **Resid:** Neurological Surgery, NYU Med Ctr 1990; **Fellow:** Spine Surgery, NYU Med Ctr 1991; **Fac Appt:** Asst Prof NS, NYU Sch Med

Post, Kalmon D MD (NS) - **Spec Exp:** Pituitary Tumors; Acoustic Neuroma; Meningioma; **Hospital:** Mt Sinai Hosp; **Address:** Mt Sinai, Neurosurgery, 5 E 98th St Fl 7, New York, NY 10029; **Phone:** 212-241-0933; **Board Cert:** Neurological Surgery 1978; **Med School:** NYU Sch Med 1967; **Resid:** Surgery, NYU-Bellevue Hosp 1969; Neurological Surgery, NYU-Bellevue Hosp 1975; **Fac Appt:** Prof NS, Mount Sinai-Icahn Sch of Med

Quest, Donald O MD (NS) - **Spec Exp:** Spinal Surgery; Neurovascular Surgery; Carotid Artery Surgery; **Hospital:** NY-Presby/Columbia Univ Med Ctr, NY (page 102), Valley Hosp (page 739); **Address:** Neurosurgical Assocs, 710 W 168th, Ste 440, New York, NY 10032; **Phone:** 212-305-5582; **Board Cert:** Neurological Surgery 1978; **Med School:** Columbia P&S 1970; **Resid:** Surgery, Mass Genl Hosp 1972; Neurological Surgery, NY-Presby/Columbia Univ Med Ctr 1976; **Fac Appt:** Clin Prof NS, Columbia P&S

Riina, Howard A MD (NS) - **Spec Exp:** Neuroradiology; Aneurysm-Cerebral; Cerebrovascular Malformations; Stroke; **Hospital:** NYU Langone Med Ctr (page 104); **Address:** NYU Med Ctr, Neurosurgery, 530 1st Ave, Ste 8R, New York, NY 10016; **Phone:** 212-263-5382; **Board Cert:** Neurological Surgery 2004; **Med School:** Temple Univ 1993; **Resid:** Neurological Surgery, Hosp Univ Penn 2000; **Fellow:** Interventional Neuroradiology, Beth Israel Med Ctr 1997; Skull Base Surgery, Barrow Neuro Inst 2001; **Fac Appt:** Prof NS, NYU Sch Med

Schwartz, Theodore H MD (NS) - **Spec Exp:** Brain Tumors; Pituitary Tumors; Minimally Invasive Surgery; Neuro-Endoscopy; **Hospital:** NY-Presby/Weill Cornell Med Ctr, NY (page 102); **Address:** Weill Cornell Med Ctr-Neurosurgery Dept, 525 E 68th St, rm 651, Starr Pavilion, Box 99, New York, NY 10065; **Phone:** 212-746-5620; **Board Cert:** Neurological Surgery 2013; **Med School:** Harvard Med Sch 1993; **Resid:** Neurological Surgery, Columbia-Presby Med Ctr 1999; **Fellow:** Neurological Surgery, Yale-New Haven Med Ctr 2000; **Fac Appt:** Prof NS, Cornell Univ-Weill Med Coll

Sen, Chandranath MD (NS) - **Spec Exp:** Brain Tumors; Skull Base Tumors; Meningioma; **Hospital:** NYU Langone Med Ctr (page 104); **Address:** NYU Med Ctr, Neurosurgery, 530 1st Ave, Ste 8R, New York, NY 10016; **Phone:** 212-263-5333; **Board Cert:** Neurological Surgery 1989; **Med School:** India 1976; **Resid:** Surgery, Univ WI Hosp & Clins 1980; Neurological Surgery, Univ WI Hosp & Clins 1985; **Fellow:** Neurological Surgery, UPMC 1986; **Fac Appt:** Prof NS, NYU Sch Med

Sisti, Michael B MD (NS) - **Spec Exp:** Brain Tumors-Complex; Meningioma; Arteriovenous Malformations; **Hospital:** NY-Presby/Columbia Univ Med Ctr, NY (page 102); **Address:** Columbia Neurosurgery, 710 W 168th St, Ste 413, New York, NY 10032; **Phone:** 212-305-1728; **Board Cert:** Neurological Surgery 1991; **Med School:** Columbia P&S 1981; **Resid:** Neurological Surgery, Neur Inst/Columbia Med Ctr 1988; **Fellow:** Neurological Surgery, Natl Inst Hlth 1983; **Fac Appt:** Assoc Prof NS, Columbia P&S

Snow, Robert B MD (NS) - **Spec Exp:** Spinal Surgery; Spinal Cord Tumors; Minimally Invasive Surgery; **Hospital:** NY-Presby/Weill Cornell Med Ctr, NY (page 102); **Address:** 55 E 72nd St Fl 1st, New York, NY 10021; **Phone:** 212-717-0256; **Board Cert:** Neurological Surgery 1989; **Med School:** Stanford Univ 1981; **Resid:** Neurological Surgery, NY-Presby/Weill Cornell Med Ctr 1986; **Fac Appt:** Prof NS, Cornell Univ-Weill Med Coll

Solomon, Robert A MD (NS) - **Spec Exp:** Aneurysm-Cerebral; Arteriovenous Malformations; Stereotactic Radiosurgery; Carotid Artery Stent Placement; **Hospital:** NY-Presby/Columbia Univ Med Ctr, NY (page 102); **Address:** Columbia Neurosurgery, 710 W 168th St, Ste 439, New York, NY 10032; **Phone:** 212-305-4118; **Board Cert:** Neurological Surgery 1988; **Med School:** Johns Hopkins Univ 1980; **Resid:** Neurological Surgery, NY-Presby/Columbia Univ Med Ctr 1986; **Fac Appt:** Prof NS, Columbia P&S

Souweidane, Mark M MD (NS) - **Spec Exp:** Pediatric Neurosurgery; Minimally Invasive Surgery; Endoscopic Surgery; Brain Tumors-Pediatric; **Hospital:** NY-Presby/Weill Cornell Med Ctr, NY (page 102), Meml Sloan Kettering Canc Ctr (page 110); **Address:** NY-Presby, Neurosurgery, 1305 York Ave Fl 9, New York, NY 10021; **Phone:** 212-746-2363; **Board Cert:** Neurological Surgery 2010; **Med School:** Wayne State Univ 1988; **Resid:** Neurological Surgery, NYU Med Ctr 1994; **Fellow:** Pediatric Neurological Surgery, Hosp Sick Chldn 1995; **Fac Appt:** Prof NS, Cornell Univ-Weill Med Coll

Stieg, Philip E MD/PhD (NS) - **Spec Exp:** Aneurysm-Cerebral; Stroke; Meningioma; Arteriovenous Malformations; **Hospital:** NY-Presby/Weill Cornell Med Ctr, NY (page 102); **Address:** NY-Presby, Neurosurgery, 525 E 68th St, Ste 651, New York, NY 10065; **Phone:** 212-746-4684; **Board Cert:** Neurological Surgery 1992; **Med School:** Med Coll Wisc 1983; **Resid:** Neurological Surgery, Parkland Meml Hosp 1988; **Fac Appt:** Prof NS, Cornell Univ-Weill Med Coll

Sundaresan, Narayan MD (NS) - **Spec Exp:** Spinal Surgery; Brain Tumors; Neuro-Oncology; **Hospital:** Mt Sinai Hosp, Bronx Lebanon Hosp Ctr; **Address:** Central Park Neurosurgery, 1148 5th Ave, New York, NY 10128; **Phone:** 212-876-7575; **Board Cert:** Neurological Surgery 1980; **Med School:** India 1969; **Resid:** Neurological Surgery, Northwestern Meml Hosp 1976; **Fellow:** Neuro-Oncology, Meml Sloan Kettering Cancer Ctr 1977; **Fac Appt:** Prof NS, Mount Sinai Sch Med

Tabar, Viviane MD (NS) - **Spec Exp:** Brain Tumors; Brain Tumors-Metastatic; Brain Mapping; Skull Base Tumors; **Hospital:** Meml Sloan Kettering Canc Ctr (page 110); **Address:** MSKCC, Neurosurgery, 1275 York Ave, rm C711, New York, NY 10065; **Phone:** 212-639-3006; **Board Cert:** Neurological Surgery 2006; **Med School:** Amer Univ Beirut 1989; **Resid:** Neurological Surgery, UMass Genl Hosp 1998

Weiner, Howard L MD (NS) - **Spec Exp:** Pediatric Neurosurgery; Epilepsy; Tuberous Sclerosis; **Hospital:** NYU Langone Med Ctr (page 104); **Address:** NYU Med Ctr, Pediatric Neurosurgery, 317 E 34th St, Ste 1002, New York, NY 10016; **Phone:** 212-263-6419; **Board Cert:** Neurological Surgery 2012; **Med School:** Cornell Univ 1989; **Resid:** Neurological Surgery, NYU Med Ctr 1996; **Fellow:** Pediatric Neurological Surgery, NYU Med Ctr 1997; **Fac Appt:** Prof NS, NYU Sch Med

Winfree, Christopher J MD (NS) - **Spec Exp:** Peripheral Nerve Surgery; Pain-Chronic; Microsurgery; **Hospital:** NY-Presby/Columbia Univ Med Ctr, NY (page 102); **Address:** Columbia Neurosurgery, 710 W 168th St Fl 4, New York, NY 10032; **Phone:** 212-342-2776; **Board Cert:** Neurological Surgery 2007; **Med School:** Columbia P&S 1996; **Resid:** Neurological Surgery, Columbia Neuro Inst 2003; **Fellow:** Peripheral Nerve Surgery, LSU Med Ctr 2004; Stereotactic Neurological Surgery, OR Hlth & Sci Univ Hosp 2005; **Fac Appt:** Asst Prof NS, Columbia P&S

Wisoff, Jeffrey H MD (NS) - **Spec Exp:** Pediatric Neurosurgery; Brain Tumors-Pediatric; Arteriovenous Malformations; **Hospital:** NYU Langone Med Ctr (page 104), Maimonides Med Ctr (page 98); **Address:** NYU Med Ctr, Div Pediatric Neurosurgery, 317 E 34th St, Ste 1002, New York, NY 10016; **Phone:** 212-263-6419; **Board Cert:** Neurological Surgery 1990; Pediatric Neurological Surgery 2008; **Med School:** Geo Wash Univ 1978; **Resid:** Neurological Surgery, NYU-Bellevue Hosp 1984; **Fellow:** Pediatric Neurological Surgery, NYU Med Ctr 1985; **Fac Appt:** Prof NS, NYU Sch Med

Neurology

Apatoff, Brian R MD/PhD (N) - **Spec Exp:** Multiple Sclerosis; Neuro-Immunology; **Hospital:** NY-Presby/Weill Cornell Med Ctr, NY (page 102); **Address:** Multiple Sclerosis Inst, 401 E 55th St, New York, NY 10022; **Phone:** 212-593-6262; **Board Cert:** Neurology 1991; **Med School:** Univ Chicago-Pritzker Sch Med 1984; **Resid:** Neurology, NY-Presby/Columbia Univ Med Ctr 1990; **Fellow:** Multiple Sclerosis, NY-Presby/Columbia Univ Med Ctr 1992; **Fac Appt:** Assoc Prof N, Cornell Univ-Weill Med Coll

Balcer, Laura J MD (N) - **Spec Exp:** Neuro-Ophthalmology; Multiple Sclerosis/Visual Disorders; Parkinson's Disease/Visual Disorders; **Hospital:** NYU Langone Med Ctr (page 104); **Address:** NYU Dept Neurology, 240 E 38th St Fl 200, New York, NY 10016; **Phone:** 646-501-7681; **Board Cert:** Neurology 2006; **Med School:** Johns Hopkins Univ 1991; **Resid:** Neurology, Hosp Univ Penn 1995; **Fellow:** Neuro-Ophthalmology, Hosp Univ Penn/Scheie Inst 1996; **Fac Appt:** Prof N, NYU Sch Med

Bazil, Carl W MD/PhD (N) - **Spec Exp:** Epilepsy; **Hospital:** NY-Presby/Columbia Univ Med Ctr, NY (page 102); **Address:** Columbia Comprehensive Epilepsy Ctr, 710 W 168th St Fl 7, New York, NY 10032; **Phone:** 212-305-1742; **Board Cert:** Neurology 2005; Clinical Neurophysiology 2011; Sleep Medicine 2009; **Med School:** Emory Univ 1989; **Resid:** Neurology, NYU Med Ctr 1993; **Fellow:** Epilepsy, Columbia Presby Med Ctr 1995; **Fac Appt:** Clin Prof N, Columbia P&S

Belok, Lennart C MD (N) - **Spec Exp:** Carpal Tunnel Syndrome; **Hospital:** Mt Sinai Beth Israel; **Address:** 410 E 20th St, Ste MG, New York, NY 10009; **Phone:** 212-254-9716; **Board Cert:** Internal Medicine 1977; Neurology 1983; **Med School:** NY Med Coll 1973; **Resid:** Internal Medicine, Beth Israel Med Ctr 1976; Neurology, NYU Med Ctr 1979

Boniece, Irene R MD (N) - **Spec Exp:** Stroke; Neurologic Critical Care; Stroke/Cerebrovascular Disease; Vascular Neurology; **Hospital:** Mt Sinai Beth Israel, New York Eye & Ear Infirm of Mt Sinai; **Address:** Hyman-Newman Inst Neurology & Neurosurg, 10 Union Square E, Ste 5D, New York, NY 10003; **Phone:** 212-844-1037; **Board Cert:** Neurology 2009; Vascular Neurology 2008; Neurocritical Care 2007; **Med School:** Albany Med Coll 1989; **Resid:** Internal Medicine, NYU/New York VA Med Ctrs 1991; Neurology, Montefiore Med Ctr 1996; **Fellow:** Neurological Science, NY Hosp/Cornell Univ 1993; Neurocritical Care, Beth Israel Med Ctr 1997; **Fac Appt:** Assoc Prof N, Albert Einstein Coll Med

Brannagan III, Thomas H MD (N) - **Spec Exp:** Peripheral Neuropathy; Diabetic Neuropathy; **Hospital:** NY-Presby/Columbia Univ Med Ctr, NY (page 102); **Address:** Columbia Neurology, 710 W 168th St, New York, NY 10032; **Phone:** 212-305-0405; **Board Cert:** Neurology 2005; Clinical Neurophysiology 2009; Neuromuscular Medicine 2012; **Med School:** Univ VA Sch Med 1990; **Resid:** Neurology, NY-Presby/Columbia Univ Med Ctr 1994; **Fac Appt:** Prof N, Columbia P&S

Bressman, Susan MD (N) - **Spec Exp:** Parkinson's Disease; Movement Disorders; Dystonia; Neurodegenerative Disorders; **Hospital:** Mt Sinai Beth Israel; **Address:** 10 Union Square East, Ste 5H, New York, NY 10003; **Phone:** 212-844-8379; **Board Cert:** Neurology 1983; **Med School:** Columbia P&S 1977; **Resid:** Neurology, NY-Presby/Columbia Univ Med Ctr 1981; **Fellow:** Movement Disorders, NY-Presby/Columbia Univ Med Ctr 1983; **Fac Appt:** Prof N, Albert Einstein Coll Med

Britton, Carolyn B MD (N) - Spec Exp: Neurologic Complications-HIV/Infections; Lyme Disease; Multiple Sclerosis; **Hospital:** NY-Presby/Columbia Univ Med Ctr, NY (page 102); **Address:** Columbia Neurology, 710 W 168th St, Ste 232, New York, NY 10032; **Phone:** 212-305-6876; **Board Cert:** Internal Medicine 1979; Neurology 1982; **Med School:** NYU Sch Med 1975; **Resid:** Internal Medicine, Harlem Hosp 1977; Neurology, NY-Presby/Columbia Univ Med Ctr 1980; **Fellow:** Neurology, NY-Presby/Columbia Univ Med Ctr 1983; **Fac Appt:** Assoc Prof N, Columbia P&S

Bronster, David J MD (N) - Spec Exp: Headache; Dizziness; Seizure Disorders; **Hospital:** Mt Sinai Hosp; **Address:** 3 E 83rd St, New York, NY 10028; **Phone:** 212-772-0008; **Board Cert:** Neurology 1984; **Med School:** Mount Sinai Sch Med 1979; **Resid:** Neurology, Mt Sinai Hosp 1983; **Fac Appt:** Assoc Clin Prof N, Mount Sinai-Icahn Sch of Med

Carver, Alan C MD (N) - Spec Exp: Palliative Care; Pain-Cancer; Headache; Pain Management; **Hospital:** Meml Sloan Kettering Canc Ctr (page 110); **Address:** MSKCC, Neurology, 1275 York Ave, New York, NY 10065; **Phone:** 212-639-4851; **Board Cert:** Neurology 2011; Hospice & Palliative Medicine 2012; **Med School:** Boston Univ 1995; **Resid:** Neurology, NY-Presby/Weill Cornell Med Ctr 1999; **Fellow:** Pain & Palliative Care, Meml Sloan-Kettering Cancer Ctr 2000

Charney, Jonathan Z MD (N) - Spec Exp: Headache; Stroke; **Hospital:** Mt Sinai Hosp; **Address:** 1111 Park Ave, Ste 1H, New York, NY 10128; **Phone:** 212-831-2886; **Board Cert:** Neurology 1977; **Med School:** NY Med Coll 1969; **Resid:** Internal Medicine, Methodist Hosp 1971; Neurology, NY-Presby/Columbia Univ Med Ctr 1973; **Fac Appt:** Asst Clin Prof N, Mount Sinai-Icahn Sch of Med

Cohen, Jeffrey MD/PhD (N) - Spec Exp: Epilepsy/Seizure Disorders; Trigeminal Neuralgia; **Hospital:** Mt Sinai Beth Israel; **Address:** Phillips Ambulatory Care Ctr, 10 Union Square E, Ste 5D, New York, NY 10003; **Phone:** 212-844-6111; **Board Cert:** Neurology 1992; Clinical Neurophysiology 2004; **Med School:** SUNY Downstate 1987; **Resid:** Neurology, NY-Presby/Columbia Univ Med Ctr 1991; **Fellow:** Clinical Neurophysiology, NY-Presby/Columbia Univ Med Ctr 1992; **Fac Appt:** Asst Prof N, Mount Sinai Sch Med

Coll, Raymond MD (N) - Spec Exp: Multiple Sclerosis; Headache; Stroke; **Hospital:** NY-Presby/Weill Cornell Med Ctr, NY (page 102); **Address:** 1365 York Ave, New York, NY 10021; **Phone:** 212-249-0840; **Board Cert:** Neurology 1974; **Med School:** South Africa 1961; **Resid:** Neurology, NY-Presby/Weill Cornell Med Ctr 1971; **Fac Appt:** Assoc Clin Prof N, Cornell Univ-Weill Med Coll

Daras, Michael MD (N) - Spec Exp: Neuromuscular Disorders; **Hospital:** NY-Presby/Columbia Univ Med Ctr, NY (page 102); **Address:** Columbia Neurology, 710 W 168th St, Ste 246, New York, NY 10032; **Phone:** 212-305-6876; **Board Cert:** Neurology 1980; **Med School:** Greece 1969; **Resid:** Psychiatry, Elmhurst City Hosp 1976; Neurology, Metropolitan Hosp 1979; **Fellow:** Clinical Neurophysiology, Albert Einstein Affil Hosp 1980; **Fac Appt:** Prof N, Columbia P&S

DeAngelis, Lisa M MD (N) - Spec Exp: Neuro-Oncology; Brain Tumors; Clinical Trials; **Hospital:** Meml Sloan Kettering Canc Ctr (page 110); **Address:** MSKCC, Neurology, 1275 York Ave, New York, NY 10065; **Phone:** 212-639-7123; **Board Cert:** Neurology 1986; **Med School:** Columbia P&S 1980; **Resid:** Neurology, NY-Presby/Columbia Univ Med Ctr 1984; **Fellow:** Neuro-Oncology, Neur Inst/Presby Hosp 1985; Neuro-Oncology, Meml Sloan-Kettering Cancer Ctr 1986; **Fac Appt:** Prof N, Cornell Univ-Weill Med Coll

Devinsky, Orrin MD (N) - **Spec Exp:** Epilepsy/Seizure Disorders; Tuberous Sclerosis; Behavioral Neurology; **Hospital:** NYU Langone Med Ctr (page 104), St. Barnabas Med Ctr (page 94); **Address:** NYU Med Ctr, Epilepsy Ctr, 223 E 34th St, New York, NY 10016; **Phone:** 646-558-0803; **Board Cert:** Neurology 1987; **Med School:** Harvard Med Sch 1982; **Resid:** Neurology, NY-Presby/Weill Cornell Med Ctr 1986; **Fellow:** Epilepsy, Natl Inst Hlth 1988; **Fac Appt:** Prof N, NYU Sch Med

Dinkin, Marc J MD (N) - **Spec Exp:** Neuro-Ophthalmology; Optic Nerve Disorders; Neuromyelitis Optica; **Hospital:** NY-Presby/Weill Cornell Med Ctr, NY (page 102); **Address:** Weill Cornell Eye Assocs, 1305 York Ave Fl 11, Nw York, NY 10021; **Phone:** 646-962-2020; **Board Cert:** Neurology 2007; **Med School:** Cornell Univ-Weill Med Coll 2002; **Resid:** Ophthalmology, NY-Presby/Weill Cornell Med Ctr 2006; **Fellow:** Neuro-Ophthalmology, Mass Eye & Ear Infirm 2007; **Fac Appt:** Asst Prof Oph, Cornell Univ-Weill Med Coll

Elkind, Mitchell MD (N) - **Spec Exp:** Stroke; Cerebrovascular Disease; Dizziness/Vertigo; **Hospital:** NY-Presby/Columbia Univ Med Ctr, NY (page 102); **Address:** Columbia Neurosurgery, 710 W 168th St Fl 2, New York, NY 10032; **Phone:** 212-305-1710; **Board Cert:** Neurology 2007; Vascular Neurology 2008; **Med School:** Harvard Med Sch 1992; **Resid:** Neurology, Mass Genl Hosp 1996; **Fellow:** Stroke, NY-Presby/Columbia Univ Med Ctr 1997; **Fac Appt:** Assoc Prof N, Columbia P&S

Fahn, Stanley MD (N) - **Spec Exp:** Movement Disorders; Parkinson's Disease; **Hospital:** NY-Presby/Columbia Univ Med Ctr, NY (page 102); **Address:** Neurological Institute, 710 W 168th St Fl 3 - rm 350, New York, NY 10032; **Phone:** 212-305-1303; **Board Cert:** Neurology 1968; **Med School:** UCSF 1958; **Resid:** Neurology, Neuro Inst-Columbia 1962; **Fac Appt:** Prof N, Columbia P&S

Fink, Matthew E MD (N) - **Spec Exp:** Cerebrovascular Disease; Stroke; Critical Care; **Hospital:** NY-Presby/Weill Cornell Med Ctr, NY (page 102); **Address:** NY-Presby, Multiple Sclerosis Ctr, 1305 York Ave, New York, NY 10021; **Phone:** 212-746-4564; **Board Cert:** Internal Medicine 1980; Neurology 1983; Vascular Neurology 2005; Neurocritical Care 2010; **Med School:** Univ Pittsburgh 1976; **Resid:** Internal Medicine, Boston Med Ctr 1978; Neurology, NY-Presby/Columbia Univ Med Ctr 1982; **Fac Appt:** Prof N, Cornell Univ-Weill Med Coll

Foo, Sun-Hoo MD (N) - **Spec Exp:** Stroke; Headache; Parkinson's Disease; Dementia; **Hospital:** NYU Langone Med Ctr (page 104), NY-Presby/Lower Manhattan Hosp (page 102); **Address:** 650 1st Ave Fl 4, New York, NY 10016-3240; **Phone:** 212-213-0270; **Board Cert:** Internal Medicine 1976; Neurology 1980; **Med School:** Taiwan 1972; **Resid:** Internal Medicine, St Vincent's Hosp 1976; Neurology, NYU Med Ctr 1979; **Fac Appt:** Prof N, NYU Sch Med

French, Jacqueline MD (N) - **Spec Exp:** Epilepsy/Seizure Disorders; Electrodiagnosis; **Hospital:** NYU Langone Med Ctr (page 104); **Address:** NYU Med Ctr, Epilepsy, 223 E 34th St, New York, NY 10016; **Phone:** 646-558-0868; **Board Cert:** Neurology 1987; **Med School:** Brown Univ 1982; **Resid:** Neurology, Mt Sinai Hosp 1986; **Fellow:** Electroencephalography, Mt Sinai Hosp 1988; Epilepsy, Yale-New Haven Hosp 1989; **Fac Appt:** Prof N, NYU Sch Med

Galetta, Steven MD (N) - **Spec Exp:** Neuro-Ophthalmology; Optic Nerve Disorders; Multiple Sclerosis; **Hospital:** NYU Langone Med Ctr (page 104); **Address:** NYU Med Ctr, Neurology, 240 E 38th St, Fl 20, New York, NY 10016; **Phone:** 212-263-7744; **Board Cert:** Neurology 1988; **Med School:** Cornell Univ-Weill Med Coll 1983; **Resid:** Neurology, Hosp Univ Penn 1987; **Fellow:** Neuro-Ophthalmology, Bascom Palmer Eye Inst 1988; **Fac Appt:** Prof N, NYU Sch Med

Galvin Jr, James MD (N) - **Spec Exp:** Alzheimer's Disease; Memory Disorders; Dementia; Cognitive Impairment/Mild; **Hospital:** NYU Langone Med Ctr (page 104); **Address:** Barlow Memory Ctr, 145 E 32nd St Fl 2, New York, NY 10016; **Phone:** 212-263-3210; **Board Cert:** Neurology 2007; **Med School:** Rutgers-NJ Med Sch 1992; **Resid:** Neurology, Hahnemann Univ Hosp 1996; **Fellow:** Pathology, Hosp Univ Penn 1997; **Fac Appt:** Prof N, NYU Sch Med

Gendelman, Seymour MD (N) - **Spec Exp:** Parkinson's Disease; Dementia; Headache; **Hospital:** Mt Sinai Hosp; **Address:** 5 E 98th St, Fl 7, Box 1139, New York, NY 10029-6501; **Phone:** 212-241-8172; **Board Cert:** Neurology 1971; **Med School:** Geo Wash Univ 1964; **Resid:** Neurology, Mt Sinai Hosp 1968; **Fac Appt:** Clin Prof N, Mount Sinai Sch Med

Goldstein, Jonathan M MD (N) - **Spec Exp:** Myasthenia Gravis; Peripheral Neuropathy; Parkinson's Disease; **Hospital:** Hosp For Special Surgery (page 109); **Address:** HSS, Neurology, 525 E 71st St Fl 5, New York, NY 10021; **Phone:** 646-714-6053; **Board Cert:** Neurology 1991; Neuromuscular Medicine 2011; **Med School:** Brown Univ 1986; **Resid:** Neurology, Yale-New Haven Hosp 1990; **Fellow:** Clinical Neurophysiology, Yale-New Haven Hosp 1991; Neurological Immunology, Yale-New Haven Hosp 1992

Green, Mark W MD (N) - **Spec Exp:** Headache; Pain-Facial; **Hospital:** Mt Sinai Hosp; **Address:** Mt Sinai, Neurology, 5 E 98th St Fl 7, New York, NY 10029; **Phone:** 212-241-7076; **Board Cert:** Neurology 1979; **Med School:** Albert Einstein Coll Med 1974; **Resid:** Neurology, Jacobi Med Ctr 1979; **Fac Appt:** Prof N, Mount Sinai-Icahn Sch of Med

Gruber, Michael L MD (N) - **Spec Exp:** Neuro-Oncology; Headache; Pain-Back & Neck; **Hospital:** NYU Langone Med Ctr (page 104), Overlook Med Ctr (page 92); **Address:** NYU Ambulatory Care Ctr, 240 E 38th St, Fl 19, New York, NY 10016; **Phone:** 212-731-5577; **Board Cert:** Neurology 1975; **Med School:** Temple Univ 1966; **Resid:** Pediatrics, NY-Presby/Columbia Univ Med Ctr 1968; Neurology, NY-Presby/Columbia Univ Med Ctr 1973; **Fellow:** Neuro-Oncology, Mass Genl Hosp 1990; **Fac Appt:** Prof N, NYU Sch Med

Herbstein, Diego J MD (N) - **Spec Exp:** Parkinson's Disease; Cerebrovascular Disease; **Hospital:** Lenox Hill Hosp, NY Hosp Queens (page 498); **Address:** NY Neurological Assocs, 162 E 78th St, New York, NY 10075; **Phone:** 212-794-2281; **Board Cert:** Neurology 1976; **Med School:** Argentina 1968; **Resid:** Internal Medicine, Fernandez 1970; Neurology, Jacobi Med Ctr 1974; **Fac Appt:** Asst Clin Prof N, Cornell Univ-Weill Med Coll

Heublum, Michael MD (N) - **Spec Exp:** Neuromuscular Disorders; Electrodiagnosis; **Hospital:** Mt Sinai Hosp, Mt Sinai Beth Israel; **Address:** 247 3rd Ave, Ste 203, New York, NY 10010; **Phone:** 212-505-9800; **Board Cert:** Internal Medicine 1989; Neurology 1993; **Med School:** SUNY Downstate 1986; **Resid:** Internal Medicine, Staten Island Univ Hosp 1989; Neurology, Mt Sinai Hosp 1992; **Fellow:** Neuromuscular Disease, Univ Michigan Med Ctr 1993

Hiesiger, Emile M MD (N) - **Spec Exp:** Pain-Spine; Pain-Cancer, Spine; Pain-Back; **Hospital:** NYU Langone Med Ctr (page 104), VA NY Harbor Hlthcare Sys-Manhattan Campus; **Address:** 345 E 37th St, Ste 320, New York, NY 10016; **Phone:** 212-263-6123; **Board Cert:** Neurology 1983; **Med School:** NY Med Coll 1978; **Resid:** Neurology, Meml Sloan-Kettering Canc Ctr 1984; **Fac Appt:** Assoc Clin Prof N, NYU Sch Med

Jamieson, Dara G MD (N) - **Spec Exp:** Stroke/Cerebrovascular Disease; Headache; Neurological Imaging; Migraine; **Hospital:** NY-Presby/Weill Cornell Med Ctr, NY (page 102); **Address:** The Headache Center, 428 E 72nd St, Ste 400, New York, NY 10021; **Phone:** 212-746-4249; **Board Cert:** Neurology 1987; Vascular Neurology 2005; **Med School:** Univ Pennsylvania 1982; **Resid:** Internal Medicine, Presby Hosp/Univ Penn 1983; Neurology, Hosp Univ Penn 1986; **Fellow:** Cerebrovascular Disease, Hosp Univ Penn 1989; **Fac Appt:** Assoc Clin Prof N, Cornell Univ-Weill Med Coll

Klebanoff, Louise M MD (N) - **Spec Exp:** Headache; Migraine; Dizziness/Vertigo; Back & Neck Pain; **Hospital:** NY-Presby/Weill Cornell Med Ctr, NY (page 102); **Address:** Weill Cornell General Neurology, 520 E 70th St, Starr Pavilion, Ste 607, New York, NY 10065; **Phone:** 212-746-2271; **Board Cert:** Neurology 1989; **Med School:** Georgetown Univ 1984; **Resid:** Neurology, Columbia Presby Med Ctr 1988; **Fellow:** Critical Care Neurology, Columbia Presby Med Ctr 1990; **Fac Appt:** Asst Prof N, Cornell Univ-Weill Med Coll

Koppel, Barbara Sue MD (N) - **Spec Exp:** Epilepsy; Headache; Stroke; AIDS/HIV; **Hospital:** Metropolitan Hosp Ctr - NY; **Address:** Metropolitan Hosp, Neurology, 1901 First Ave, rm 7C5, New York, NY 10029; **Phone:** 212-423-6676; **Board Cert:** Neurology 1983; **Med School:** Columbia P&S 1978; **Resid:** Internal Medicine, Montefiore Med Ctr 1979; Neurology, NY-Presby/Columbia Univ Med Ctr 1982; **Fac Appt:** Prof N, NY Med Coll

Kuzniecky, Ruben MD (N) - **Spec Exp:** Epilepsy/Seizure Disorders; MRI; Developmental Disorders; Brain Malformations; **Hospital:** NYU Langone Med Ctr (page 104); **Address:** 223 E 34th St Fl Ground, New York, NY 10016; **Phone:** 646-558-0806; **Board Cert:** Neurology 1990; **Med School:** Argentina 1980; **Resid:** Neurology, Montreal Neurological Inst 1986; **Fellow:** Epilepsy, Montreal Neurological Inst 1988; **Fac Appt:** Prof N, NYU Sch Med

Labar, Douglas R MD/PhD (N) - **Spec Exp:** Epilepsy/Seizure Disorders; **Hospital:** NY-Presby/Weill Cornell Med Ctr, NY (page 102); **Address:** Weill Cornell Epilepsy Center, 525 E 68th St, rm K-619, New York, NY 10065; **Phone:** 212-746-2359; **Board Cert:** Neurology 1987; **Med School:** Med Coll PA 1982; **Resid:** Neurology, Columbia Presby Med Ctr 1986; **Fellow:** Neurophysiology, Columbia Presby Med Ctr 1988; **Fac Appt:** Prof N, Cornell Univ-Weill Med Coll

Lange, Dale J MD (N) - **Spec Exp:** Neuromuscular Disorders; Amyotrophic Lateral Sclerosis (ALS); Electromyography; **Hospital:** Hosp For Special Surgery (page 109), NY-Presby/Weill Cornell Med Ctr, NY (page 102); **Address:** HSS, Neurology, 535 E 70th St, Belair 5, New York, NY 10021; **Phone:** 646-797-8917; **Board Cert:** Neurology 1985; Neuromuscular Medicine 2008; **Med School:** NY Med Coll 1978; **Resid:** Neurology, New England Med Ctr 1982; **Fellow:** Neuromuscular Medicine, NY-Presby/Columbia Univ Med Ctr 1983; **Fac Appt:** Prof N, Cornell Univ-Weill Med Coll

Lassman, Andrew B MD (N) - **Spec Exp:** Neuro-Oncology; Gliomas; Brain Tumors; Brain Tumors-Metastatic; **Hospital:** NY-Presby/Columbia Univ Med Ctr, NY (page 102); **Address:** Columbia Neurosurgery, Neuro-Oncology, 710 W 168th St Fl 2, New York, NY 10032; **Phone:** 212-342-0571; **Board Cert:** Neurology 2012; **Med School:** Columbia P&S 1997; **Resid:** Neurology, NY-Presby/Columbia Univ Med Ctr 2001; **Fellow:** Neuro-Oncology, Meml Sloan-Kettering Cancer Ctr 2001; **Fac Appt:** Assoc Prof N, Columbia P&S

Latov, Norman MD/PhD (N) - **Spec Exp:** Peripheral Neuropathy; Neuro-Immunology; **Hospital:** NY-Presby/Weill Cornell Med Ctr, NY (page 102); **Address:** 1305 York Ave Fl 2 - Ste 217, New York, NY 10021; **Phone:** 646-962-3320; **Board Cert:** Neurology 1989; **Med School:** Univ Pennsylvania 1975; **Resid:** Neurology, Columbia-Presby Med Ctr 1979; **Fellow:** Immunology, Columbia-Presby Med Ctr 1981; **Fac Appt:** Prof N, Cornell Univ-Weill Med Coll

Levine, David N MD (N) - **Spec Exp:** Dementia; Stroke; Spinal Cord Disorders; **Hospital:** NYU Langone Med Ctr (page 104); **Address:** 240 E 38th St, Fl 15th, New York, NY 10016-4901; **Phone:** 212-263-7744; **Board Cert:** Neurology 1976; **Med School:** Harvard Med Sch 1968; **Resid:** Neurology, Mass Genl Hosp 1974; **Fellow:** Neurology, Mass Genl Hosp 1976; **Fac Appt:** Prof N, NYU Sch Med

Louis, Elan D MD (N) - **Spec Exp:** Tremor & Dystonia; Huntington's Disease; Parkinson's Disease/Movement Disorders; **Hospital:** NY-Presby/Columbia Univ Med Ctr, NY (page 102); **Address:** Neurological Inst of New York, 710 W 168th St, Ste 350, New York, NY 10032; **Phone:** 212-305-1303; **Board Cert:** Neurology 2014; **Med School:** Yale Univ 1989; **Resid:** Neurology, NY-Presby/Columbia Univ Med Ctr 1993; **Fellow:** Movement Disorders, Neurol Inst of New York 1995; Epidemiology, Neurol Inst of New York 1995; **Fac Appt:** Prof N, Columbia P&S

Lublin, Fred D MD (N) - **Spec Exp:** Multiple Sclerosis; **Hospital:** Mt Sinai Hosp; **Address:** Mount Sinai Med Ctr, Corinne Goldsmith Dickinson Ctr for MS, 5 E 98th St, Box 1138, New York, NY 10029-6574; **Phone:** 212-241-6854; **Board Cert:** Neurology 1977; **Med School:** Jefferson Med Coll 1972; **Resid:** Neurology, NY Hosp/Cornell Med Ctr 1976; **Fac Appt:** Prof N, Mount Sinai Sch Med

Luciano, Daniel J MD (N) - **Spec Exp:** Epilepsy/Seizure Disorders; **Hospital:** NYU Langone Med Ctr (page 104); **Address:** NYU Comprehensive Epilepsy Ctr, 223 E 34th St, New York, NY 10016; **Phone:** 646-558-0805; **Board Cert:** Neurology 1992; Clinical Neurophysiology 2014; **Med School:** UMDNJ-NJ Med Sch, Newark 1984; **Resid:** Neurology, Mt Sinai Hosp 1988; **Fellow:** Epilepsy, Mt Sinai Hosp 1990; **Fac Appt:** Asst Prof N, NYU Sch Med

MacGowan, Daniel J MD (N) - **Spec Exp:** Amyotrophic Lateral Sclerosis (ALS); Electromyography; Neuromuscular Disorders; Peripheral Nerve Disorders; **Hospital:** Mt Sinai Beth Israel; **Address:** Beth Israel/Phillips Amb Care Ctr, 10 Union Square E, Ste 5D, New York, NY 10003; **Phone:** 212-844-8497; **Board Cert:** Neurology 2007; **Med School:** Ireland 1989; **Resid:** Neurology, NY Presby-Weill Cornell Med Ctr 1994; **Fellow:** Cerebrovascular Disease, NY Presby-Columbia Med Ctr 1996; Electromyography, Mount Sinai Med Ctr 1997; **Fac Appt:** Assoc Prof N, Albert Einstein Coll Med

Mandel, Steven MD (N) - **Spec Exp:** Concussion; Voice Disorders; Laryngeal Disorders; Vocal Cord Disorders; **Hospital:** Lenox Hill Hosp; **Address:** 1049 Park Ave, New York, NY 10028; **Phone:** 212-348-3009; **Board Cert:** Neurology 1980; **Med School:** Albert Einstein Coll Med 1975; **Resid:** Neurology, Montefiore Med Ctr 1979; **Fellow:** Neuromuscular Medicine, Washington Univ Med Ctr 1980; **Fac Appt:** Clin Prof N, Hofstra N Shore-LIJ Sch Med

Marder, Karen S MD (N) - **Spec Exp:** Huntington's Disease; Alzheimer's Disease; Dementia; **Hospital:** NY-Presby/Columbia Univ Med Ctr, NY (page 102); **Address:** Columbia Neurosurgery, 710 W 168th St, Ste 104, New York, NY 10032; **Phone:** 212-305-6939; **Board Cert:** Neurology 1989; **Med School:** Cornell Univ-Weill Med Coll 1983; **Resid:** Neurology, NY-Presby/Columbia Univ Med Ctr 1987; **Fellow:** Behavioral Neurology, NY-Presby/Columbia Univ Med Ctr 1989; **Fac Appt:** Prof N, Columbia P&S

Marshall, Randolph S MD (N) - **Spec Exp:** Stroke; Cerebrovascular Disease; Dizziness/Vertigo; Behavioral Neurology; **Hospital:** NY-Presby/Columbia Univ Med Ctr, NY (page 102); **Address:** CUMC/Neurological Inst-Stroke Div, 710 W 168th St Neurologic Bldg, Fl 2nd - rm 640, New York, NY 10032; **Phone:** 212-305-8389; **Board Cert:** Neurology 2014; Vascular Neurology 2008; **Med School:** UCSF 1988; **Resid:** Neurology, NY Presby-Cornell Med Ctr 1992; **Fellow:** Cerebrovascular Disease, Neurological Inst/Columbia Med Ctr 1994; **Fac Appt:** Prof N, Columbia P&S

Mauskop, Alexander MD (N) - **Spec Exp:** Headache; Migraine; Botox Therapy; Pain Management; **Hospital:** Mt Sinai Beth Israel; **Address:** New York Headache Ctr, 30 E 76th St, New York, NY 10021; **Phone:** 212-794-3550; **Board Cert:** Neurology 1987; Headache Medicine 2006; **Med School:** Ukraine 1979; **Resid:** Internal Medicine, Brookdale Hosp 1981; Neurology, Univ Hosp 1984; **Fellow:** Pain Management, Meml Sloan Kettering Cancer Ctr 1986; **Fac Appt:** Assoc Clin Prof N, SUNY Downstate

Mayeux, Richard MD (N) - **Spec Exp:** Alzheimer's Disease; Dementia; **Hospital:** NY-Presby/Columbia Univ Med Ctr, NY (page 102); **Address:** 630 W 168th St, PH 19, New York, NY 10032; **Phone:** 212-305-6939; **Board Cert:** Neurology 1978; **Med School:** Univ Okla Coll Med 1972; **Resid:** Internal Medicine, Boston Med Ctr 1974; Neurology, NY Presby Hosp 1977; **Fellow:** Neurology, Boston Med Ctr 1978; **Fac Appt:** Prof N, Columbia P&S

Miller, Aaron E MD (N) - **Spec Exp:** Multiple Sclerosis; Autoimmune Disease; Optic Nerve Disorders; **Hospital:** Mt Sinai Hosp; **Address:** 5 E 98th St, Fl 1st, Box 1138, New York, NY 10029; **Phone:** 212-241-6854; **Board Cert:** Internal Medicine 1972; Neurology 1977; **Med School:** NYU Sch Med 1968; **Resid:** Internal Medicine, Jacobi Med Ctr 1970; Neurology, Montefiore Med Ctr 1975; **Fellow:** Neurovirology, Johns Hopkins Hosp 1977; **Fac Appt:** Prof N, Mount Sinai Sch Med

Mitsumoto, Hiroshi MD (N) - **Spec Exp:** Amyotrophic Lateral Sclerosis (ALS); Neuromuscular Disorders; Clinical Trials; **Hospital:** NY-Presby/Columbia Univ Med Ctr, NY (page 102); **Address:** Neurological Institute, 710 W 168th St Fl 9, New York, NY 10032; **Phone:** 212-305-1319; **Board Cert:** Neurology 1978; **Med School:** Japan 1968; **Resid:** Internal Medicine, Toho Univ Hosps 1972; Neurology, Univ Hosps 1976; **Fellow:** Neurological Pathology, Cleveland Clinic 1978; Neuromuscular Medicine, New England Med Ctr 1981; **Fac Appt:** Prof N, Columbia P&S

Mohr, JP MD (N) - **Spec Exp:** Stroke; Arteriovenous Malformations; Aphasia; MoyaMoya Disease; **Hospital:** NY-Presby/Columbia Univ Med Ctr, NY (page 102); **Address:** 710 W 168th St, Fl 6, rm 616, New York, NY 10032-2603; **Phone:** 212-305-8033; **Board Cert:** Neurology 1971; Vascular Neurology 2005; **Med School:** Univ VA Sch Med 1963; **Resid:** Neurology, Columbia Presby Med Ctr 1966; **Fellow:** Neurology, Mass Genl Hosp 1969; **Fac Appt:** Prof N, Columbia P&S

Motiwala, Rajeev S MD (N) - **Hospital:** Mt Sinai Hosp; **Address:** Mt Sinai, Neurology, 5 E 98th St Fl 7, New York, NY 10029; **Phone:** 212-241-7076; **Board Cert:** Neurology 1990; **Med School:** India 1979; **Resid:** Neurology, UMDMNJ Med Ctr 1988; **Fac Appt:** Asst Prof N, Mount Sinai-Icahn Sch of Med

Nealon, Nancy M MD (N) - **Spec Exp:** Multiple Sclerosis; **Hospital:** NY-Presby/Weill Cornell Med Ctr, NY (page 102); **Address:** Weill Cornell MS Ctr, 1305 York Ave Fl 2, New York, NY 10021; **Phone:** 646-962-9800; **Board Cert:** Internal Medicine 1978; Neurology 1984; **Med School:** Penn State Coll Med 1975; **Resid:** Neurology, NY-Presby/Weill Cornell Med Ctr 1981; **Fellow:** Neuromuscular Disease, NY-Presby/Weill Cornell Med Ctr 1982; Neuromuscular Medicine, Meml Sloan-Kettering Cancer Ctr 1983; **Fac Appt:** Asst Prof N, Cornell Univ-Weill Med Coll

Neophytides, Andreas MD (N) - **Spec Exp:** Spinal Disorders; Stroke; **Hospital:** NYU Langone Med Ctr (page 104); **Address:** Neurology Consultants, 650 1st Ave Fl 4, New York, NY 10016; **Phone:** 212-213-9580; **Board Cert:** Neurology 1978; **Med School:** Greece 1970; **Resid:** Surgery, LIJ Med Ctr 1973; Neurology, NYU Med Ctr 1976; **Fellow:** Neurological Pharmacology, Natl Inst Hlth 1978; **Fac Appt:** Clin Prof N, NYU Sch Med

Newman, Lawrence C MD (N) - **Spec Exp:** Headache; Pain-Facial; **Hospital:** Mt Sinai Roosevelt; **Address:** St Lukes-Roosevelt Hosp, Headache Inst, 425 W 59th St, Ste 4A, New York, NY 10019; **Phone:** 212-523-5869; **Board Cert:** Neurology 2005; Headache Medicine 2006; **Med School:** Mexico 1983; **Resid:** Neurology, Montefiore Med Ctr 1989; **Fellow:** Headache, Montefiore Med Ctr 1990; **Fac Appt:** Prof N, Albert Einstein Coll Med

Olanow, C Warren MD (N) - **Spec Exp:** Parkinson's Disease; Movement Disorders; **Hospital:** Mt Sinai Hosp; **Address:** 5 E 98 St Fl 1, New York, NY 10029; **Phone:** 212-241-8435; **Med School:** Univ Toronto 1965; **Resid:** Internal Medicine, Queen's Med Ctr 1968; Neurology, Columbia Presby Hosp 1970; **Fellow:** Neurological Anatomy, Columbia Presby Hosp 1971; **Fac Appt:** Prof N, Mount Sinai Sch Med

Olarte, Marcelo R MD (N) - **Spec Exp:** Myasthenia Gravis; Electrodiagnosis; Headache; Neuromuscular Disorders; **Hospital:** Mt Sinai Roosevelt, Lenox Hill Hosp; **Address:** 903 Park Ave, New York, NY 10075; **Phone:** 212-988-9100; **Board Cert:** Neurology 1976; **Med School:** Argentina 1970; **Resid:** Neurology, St Vincents Hosp 1974; **Fellow:** Neuromuscular Medicine, NY-Presby/Columbia Univ Med Ctr 1975

Pacia, Steven V MD (N) - **Spec Exp:** Epilepsy/Seizure Disorders; **Hospital:** NYU Langone Med Ctr (page 104), Lenox Hill Hosp; **Address:** NYU Comprehensive Epilepsy Ctr, 223 E 34th St, New York, NY 10016; **Phone:** 646-558-0867; **Board Cert:** Neurology 1992; Clinical Neurophysiology 2007; **Med School:** Yale Univ 1987; **Resid:** Neurology, Yale-New Haven Hosp 1991; **Fellow:** Epilepsy, Yale-New Haven Hosp 1992; **Fac Appt:** Assoc Prof N, NYU Sch Med

Petito, Frank A MD (N) - **Spec Exp:** Multiple Sclerosis; Headache; Lyme Disease; **Hospital:** NY-Presby/Weill Cornell Med Ctr, NY (page 102); **Address:** 525 E 68th St, Ste 607, New York, NY 10065; **Phone:** 212-746-2309; **Board Cert:** Neurology 1974; **Med School:** Columbia P&S 1967; **Resid:** Neurology, New York Hosp 1971; **Fac Appt:** Prof N, Cornell Univ-Weill Med Coll

Posner, Jerome B MD (N) - **Spec Exp:** Neuro-Oncology; Brain Tumors; Paraneoplastic Syndromes; **Hospital:** Meml Sloan Kettering Canc Ctr (page 110); **Address:** 1275 York Ave, rm C725, New York, NY 10065; **Phone:** 212-639-7047; **Board Cert:** Neurology 1962; **Med School:** Univ Wash 1955; **Resid:** Neurology, Univ WA Affil Hosp 1959; **Fellow:** Biochemistry, Univ WA Affil Hosp 1963; **Fac Appt:** Prof N, Cornell Univ-Weill Med Coll

Rapoport, Samuel MD/PhD (N) - **Spec Exp:** Peripheral Neuropathy; Pain-Back & Neck; Electromyography; **Hospital:** NY-Presby/Weill Cornell Med Ctr, NY (page 102), Lenox Hill Hosp; **Address:** 354 E 76th St, New York, NY 10021; **Phone:** 212-570-0642; **Board Cert:** Neurology 1986; **Med School:** Cornell Univ-Weill Med Coll 1976; **Resid:** Neurology, NY-Presby/Weill Cornell Med Ctr 1982; **Fac Appt:** Assoc Prof N, Cornell Univ-Weill Med Coll

Relkin, Norman R MD/PhD (N) - **Spec Exp:** Alzheimer's Disease; Dementia; Memory Disorders; **Hospital:** NY-Presby/Weill Cornell Med Ctr, NY (page 102); **Address:** Weill Cornell Memory Disorders Program, 428 E 72nd St, Ste 500, New York, NY 10021; **Phone:** 212-746-2441; **Board Cert:** Neurology 1992; **Med School:** Albert Einstein Coll Med 1987; **Resid:** Neurology, New York Hosp 1991; **Fellow:** Behavioral Neurology, New York Hosp-Cornell 1992; **Fac Appt:** Asst Prof N, Cornell Univ-Weill Med Coll

Roberts, J Kirk MD (N) - **Spec Exp:** Dizziness/Vertigo; Balance Disorders; Neuro-Otology; Stroke/Cerebrovascular Disease; **Hospital:** NY-Presby/Columbia Univ Med Ctr, NY (page 102); **Address:** NY Presbyterian/Columbia Med Ctr, Dept Neurology, 710 W 168th St Fl 2 - Ste 246, New York, NY 10032; **Phone:** 212-305-6876; **Board Cert:** Neurology 2006; Vascular Neurology 2008; **Med School:** Cornell Univ-Weill Med Coll 1989; **Resid:** Internal Medicine, Columbia-Presby Med Ctr 1992; Neurology, Columbia-Presby Med Ctr 1995; **Fellow:** Stroke, Columbia-Presby Med Ctr 1997; **Fac Appt:** Assoc Prof N, Columbia P&S

Sadiq, Saud MD (N) - **Spec Exp:** Multiple Sclerosis; **Hospital:** Mt Sinai Roosevelt; **Address:** IMSMP, 521 W 57th St Fl 4, New York, NY 10019; **Phone:** 212-265-8070; **Board Cert:** Neurology 2009; **Med School:** Africa 1979; **Resid:** Neurology, Univ Genl Hosp 1988; **Fellow:** Neurological Immunology, NY-Presby/Columbia Univ Med Ctr 1991

Safdieh, Joseph E MD (N) - **Spec Exp:** Headache; Migraine; Stroke; Dizziness; **Hospital:** NY-Presby/Weill Cornell Med Ctr, NY (page 102); **Address:** NY-Presby, Neurology, 520 70th St, Starr 607, New York, NY 10021; **Phone:** 212-746-3113; **Board Cert:** Neurology 2007; **Med School:** NYU Sch Med 2002; **Resid:** Neurology, NY-Presby/Weill Cornell Med Ctr 2006; **Fac Appt:** Assoc Prof N, Cornell Univ-Weill Med Coll

Sander, Howard W MD (N) - **Spec Exp:** Electromyography; Peripheral Neuropathy; Neuromuscular Disorders; Nerve Conduction Studies; **Hospital:** NYU Langone Med Ctr (page 104); **Address:** NYU Neurology Assocs, 240 E 38th St, Fl 20, New York, NY 10016; **Phone:** 212-263-7744; **Board Cert:** Neuromuscular Medicine 2009; Clinical Neurophysiology 2005; Pain Medicine 2010; Vascular Neurology 2008; **Med School:** SUNY Downstate 1988; **Resid:** Neurology, Albert Einstein Coll Med Affil Hosp 1992; **Fellow:** Electromyography, Mass Genl Hosp 1993; **Fac Appt:** Prof N, NYU Sch Med

Sheinart, Kara F MD (N) - **Spec Exp:** Cerebrovascular Disease; Stroke; **Hospital:** Mt Sinai Hosp; **Address:** 5 E 98th St, Fl 7th, New York, NY 10029; **Phone:** 212-241-7076; **Board Cert:** Neurology 2005; **Med School:** SUNY Downstate 1989; **Resid:** Internal Medicine, Mt Sinai Med Ctr 1990; Neurology, Mt Sinai Med Ctr 1993; **Fellow:** Cerebrovascular Disease, Mt Sinai Med Ctr 1995; **Fac Appt:** Asst Clin Prof N, Mount Sinai Sch Med

Shulman, Melanie MD (N) - **Spec Exp:** Memory Disorders; Epilepsy; **Hospital:** NYU Langone Med Ctr (page 104); **Address:** Barlow Ctr for Memory Eval, 145 E 32nd St Fl 2, New York, NY 10016; **Phone:** 212-263-3210; **Board Cert:** Neurology 2007; **Med School:** Univ Pennsylvania 1991; **Resid:** Neurology, Brigham & Womens Hosp 1995; **Fac Appt:** Asst Clin Prof N, NYU Sch Med

Simpson, David M MD (N) - **Spec Exp:** Infections-CNS; AIDS-Neurologic Complications; Peripheral Neuropathy; Neuromuscular Disorders; **Hospital:** Mt Sinai Hosp; **Address:** Mt Sinai Med Ctr, Dept Neurology, 1 Gustave L Levy Pl, Box 1052, Annenberg, 2nd Flr, New York, NY 10029; **Phone:** 212-241-8748; **Board Cert:** Neurology 1984; Clinical Neurophysiology 2005; Neuromuscular Medicine 2008; **Med School:** SUNY Buffalo 1979; **Resid:** Neurology, NY Hosp-Cornell Med Ctr 1983; **Fellow:** Clinical Neurophysiology, Mass Genl Hosp 1984; **Fac Appt:** Prof N, Mount Sinai Sch Med

Sivak, Mark A MD (N) - **Spec Exp:** Myasthenia Gravis; Amyotrophic Lateral Sclerosis (ALS); Neuromuscular Disorders; **Hospital:** Mt Sinai Hosp; **Address:** Mt Sinai, Neurology, 1468 Madison Ave Annenberg Bldg Fl 2, New York, NY 10029; **Phone:** 212-241-8747; **Board Cert:** Neurology 1978; Neuromuscular Medicine 2008; **Med School:** Univ Louisville Sch Med 1971; **Resid:** Neurology, Mt Sinai Hosp 1975; **Fellow:** Electromyography, Mt Sinai Hosp 1976; Clinical Neurophysiology, Uppsala Univ 1986; **Fac Appt:** Asst Prof N, Mount Sinai-Icahn Sch of Med

Smallberg, Gerald J MD (N) - **Spec Exp:** Spinal Disorders; **Hospital:** Lenox Hill Hosp, Hosp For Special Surgery (page 109); **Address:** 1010 5th Ave, New York, NY 10028; **Phone:** 212-535-5348; **Board Cert:** Neurology 1977; **Med School:** Yale Univ 1969; **Resid:** Internal Medicine, Univ Michigan Med Ctr 1971; Neurology, Hosp Univ Penn 1975; **Fellow:** Neurology, NY-Presby/Columbia Univ Med Ctr 1976

Snyder, David H MD (N) - **Spec Exp:** Multiple Sclerosis; **Hospital:** NY Hosp Queens (page 498), Lenox Hill Hosp; **Address:** NY Neuro Assocs, 162 E 78th St, New York, NY 10075; **Phone:** 212-794-2281; **Board Cert:** Neurology 1975; **Med School:** Univ MD Sch Med 1969; **Resid:** Neurology, Univ MD Med Ctr 1973; **Fellow:** Neuropathology, Albert Einstein Affil Hosp 1975; **Fac Appt:** Asst Clin Prof N, Cornell Univ-Weill Med Coll

Stuebgen, Joerg-Patrick MD (N) - **Spec Exp:** Amyotrophic Lateral Sclerosis (ALS); Peripheral Neuropathy; Neuromuscular Disorders; **Hospital:** NY-Presby/Weill Cornell Med Ctr, NY (page 102), Hosp For Special Surgery (page 109); **Address:** NY-Presby, Neurology, 520 E 70th St, Starr 607, New York, NY 10021; **Phone:** 212-746-2334; **Board Cert:** Neurology 2006; Clinical Neurophysiology 2009; **Med School:** South Africa 1983; **Resid:** Neurology, Univ Pretoria Med Ctr 1989; Neurology, NY-Presby/Weill Cornell Med Ctr 1995; **Fellow:** Clinical Neurophysiology, Menl Sloan-Kettering Cancer Ctr 1995; **Fac Appt:** Prof N, Cornell Univ-Weill Med Coll

Tuchman, Alan J MD (N) - **Spec Exp:** Epilepsy; Multiple Sclerosis; **Hospital:** Montefiore Med Ctr-Wakefield Campus (page 100); **Address:** 975 Park Ave, Ste 1A, New York, NY 10028; **Phone:** 212-772-9305; **Board Cert:** Neurology 1979; **Med School:** Univ Cincinnati 1972; **Resid:** Neurology, Mt Sinai Hosp 1976; **Fellow:** Multiple Sclerosis, Albert Einstein Affil Hosp 1979; **Fac Appt:** Clin Prof N, NY Med Coll

Tuhrim, Stanley MD (N) - **Spec Exp:** Stroke; Cerebrovascular Disease; Fibromuscular Dysplasia; **Hospital:** Mt Sinai Hosp; **Address:** Mt Sinai, Neurology, 5 E 98th St Fl 7, Box 1139, New York, NY 10029; **Phone:** 212-241-7076; **Board Cert:** Neurology 1984; Vascular Neurology 2005; **Med School:** Mount Sinai Sch Med 1979; **Resid:** Neurology, Mt Sinai Hosp 1983; **Fellow:** Cerebrovascular Disease, Univ MD Med Ctr 1984; **Fac Appt:** Prof N, Mount Sinai-Icahn Sch of Med

Waters, Cheryl H MD (N) - **Spec Exp:** Parkinson's Disease; Movement Disorders; **Hospital:** NY-Presby/Columbia Univ Med Ctr, NY (page 102); **Address:** NY-Presby, Neurological Inst, 710 W 168th St Fl 3, New York, NY 10032; **Phone:** 212-305-1303; **Board Cert:** Neurology 1986; **Med School:** Univ Toronto 1980; **Resid:** Internal Medicine, Univ Toronto Med Ctr 1982; Neurology, Univ Toronto Med Ctr 1985; **Fellow:** Neurological Pharmacology, Univ Toronto Med Ctr 1987; **Fac Appt:** Prof N, Columbia P&S

Weinberg, Harold J MD (N) - **Spec Exp:** Headache; Spinal Disorders; Neuromuscular Disorders; Memory Disorders; **Hospital:** NYU Langone Med Ctr (page 104); **Address:** NYU Med Ctr, Neurology, 650 1st Ave, Fl 4, New York, NY 10016; **Phone:** 212-213-9339; **Board Cert:** Neurology 1983; Electrodiagnostic Medicine 1989; **Med School:** Albert Einstein Coll Med 1978; **Resid:** Neurology, NY-Presby/Columbia Univ Med Ctr 1982; **Fellow:** Neuromuscular Medicine, NY-Presby/Columbia Univ Med Ctr 1982; **Fac Appt:** Clin Prof N, NYU Sch Med

Weinberger, Jesse MD (N) - **Spec Exp:** Stroke; **Hospital:** Mt Sinai Hosp; **Address:** Mt Sinai, Neurology, 1468 Madison Ave Annenberg Bldg Fl 2, New York, NY 10029; **Phone:** 212-241-5621; **Board Cert:** Neurology 1976; Vascular Neurology 2005; **Med School:** Johns Hopkins Univ 1971; **Resid:** Neurology, Mt Sinai Hosp 1975; **Fellow:** Cerebrovascular Disease, Univ Hosp Penn 1978; **Fac Appt:** Prof N, Mount Sinai-Icahn Sch of Med

Neuroradiology

Berenstein, Alejandro MD (NRad) - **Spec Exp:** Interventional Neuroradiology; Aneurysm-Cerebral; Endovascular Surgery; Vascular Malformations; **Hospital:** Mt Sinai Roosevelt; **Address:** Ctr Endovascular Surgery, 1000 10th Ave, Ste 10G, New York, NY 10019; **Phone:** 212-636-3400; **Board Cert:** Diagnostic Radiology 1976; **Med School:** Mexico 1970; **Resid:** Diagnostic Radiology, Mt Sinai Hosp 1976; **Fellow:** Neuroradiology, NYU Med Ctr 1978; **Fac Appt:** Prof Rad, Albert Einstein Coll Med

Gobin, Y. Pierre MD (NRad) - **Spec Exp:** Aneurysm-Cerebral; Cerebrovascular Disease; Endovascular Surgery; Interventional Neuroradiology; **Hospital:** NY-Presby/Weill Cornell Med Ctr, NY (page 102); **Address:** NY-Presby, Neuroradiology, 525 E 68th St, Starr 651, New York, NY 10065; **Phone:** 212-746-4998; **Med School:** France 1988; **Resid:** Diagnostic Radiology, Univ Paris Affil Hosp; **Fellow:** Interventional Neuroradiology, Hosp Lariboisiere; **Fac Appt:** Prof Rad, Cornell Univ-Weill Med Coll

Holodny, Andrei I MD (NRad) - **Spec Exp:** MRI; Brain Tumors; **Hospital:** Meml Sloan Kettering Canc Ctr (page 110); **Address:** MSKCC, Neuroradiology, 1275 York Ave, Box 29, New York, NY 10065; **Phone:** 212-639-3182; **Board Cert:** Diagnostic Radiology 1996; Neuroradiology 2009; **Med School:** UMDNJ-NJ Med Sch, Newark 1989; **Resid:** Diagnostic Radiology, NYU-Bellevue Hosp 1994; **Fellow:** Neurological Radiology, NYU Med Ctr 1995

Jahre, Caren MD (NRad) - **Spec Exp:** Cardiac CT Angiography; **Address:** Lenox Hill Radiology & Med Assocs, 61 E 77th St, New York, NY 10075; **Phone:** 212-772-3111; **Board Cert:** Diagnostic Radiology 1988; Neuroradiology 2005; **Med School:** Cornell Univ-Weill Med Coll 1982; **Resid:** Pathology, New York Hosp 1984; Diagnostic Radiology, New York Hosp 1988; **Fellow:** Neuroradiology, New York Hosp 1990

Kelly, Anna B MD (NRad) - **Hospital:** NY-Presby/Columbia Univ Med Ctr, NY (page 102); **Address:** Neuroradiology Inst, 51 W 51st St, Ste 300, New York, NY 10019; **Phone:** 212-326-8518; **Board Cert:** Diagnostic Radiology 1986; Neuroradiology 2005; **Med School:** Univ Cincinnati 1982; **Resid:** Diagnostic Radiology, NY-Presby/Weill Cornell Med Ctr 1986; **Fellow:** Neurological Radiology, NY-Presby/Weill Cornell Med Ctr 1989; **Fac Appt:** Asst Prof Rad, Columbia P&S

Khandji, Alexander G MD (NRad) - **Spec Exp:** Pituitary Disorders; Spine Imaging & Intervention; MRI; Headache; **Hospital:** NY-Presby/Columbia Univ Med Ctr, NY (page 102); **Address:** NY-Presby, Neuroradiology, 177 Fort Washington Ave, Ste 3-113, New York, NY 10032; **Phone:** 212-305-7669; **Board Cert:** Diagnostic Radiology 1985; Neuroradiology 2006; **Med School:** SUNY Downstate 1980; **Resid:** Surgery, Penn State Hershey Med Ctr 1982; Diagnostic Radiology, NY-Presby/Columbia Univ Med Ctr 1985; **Fellow:** Neuroradiology, NY-Presby/Columbia Univ Med Ctr 1987; **Fac Appt:** Prof Rad, Columbia P&S

Knopp, Edmond A MD (NRad) - **Spec Exp:** MRI; Brain Imaging; Spinal Imaging & Intervention; Brain Tumors; **Address:** Zwanger-Pesiri Radiology Grp, 150 E Sunrise Hwy Fl 2, Lindenhurst, NY 11757; **Phone:** 631-225-7200; **Board Cert:** Diagnostic Radiology 1992; Neuroradiology 2005; **Med School:** SUNY Downstate 1986; **Resid:** Surgery, Maimonides Med Ctr 1988; Diagnostic Radiology, St Lukes/Roosevelt Hosp 1992; **Fellow:** Neuroradiology, NYU Med Ctr 1994

Lefton, Daniel R MD (NRad) - **Spec Exp:** Pediatric Neuroradiology; MRI; **Hospital:** Mt Sinai Beth Israel, Mt Sinai Roosevelt; **Address:** Mt Sinai BIMC, Radiology, 1000 10th Ave Fl 4, New York, NY 10019; **Phone:** 212-523-8320; **Board Cert:** Diagnostic Radiology 1993; Neuroradiology 2005; **Med School:** Boston Univ 1988; **Resid:** Diagnostic Radiology, SUNY Downstate Med Ctr 1993; **Fellow:** Neurological Radiology, NYU Med Ctr 1995; Pediatric Neuroradiology, Chldns Hosp 1996; **Fac Appt:** Assoc Prof Rad, Albert Einstein Coll Med

Lis, Eric MD (NRad) - **Spec Exp:** MRI; Brain Tumors; Spinal Tumor Imaging; Pediatric Neuroradiology; **Hospital:** Meml Sloan Kettering Canc Ctr (page 110); **Address:** MSKCC, Neuroradiology, 1275 York Ave, Ste MRI 1158, New York, NY 10065; **Phone:** 212-639-8330; **Board Cert:** Diagnostic Radiology 1995; Neuroradiology 2008; **Med School:** UMDNJ-NJ Med Sch, Newark 1990; **Resid:** Diagnostic Radiology, RWJ Univ Hosp 1995; **Fellow:** Neuroradiology, NY-Presby/Weill Cornell Med Ctr 1997

Meyers, Philip M MD (NRad) - **Spec Exp:** Interventional Neuroradiology; Endovascular Surgery; Aneurysm-Cerebral; Arteriovenous Malformations; **Hospital:** NY-Presby/Columbia Univ Med Ctr, NY (page 102), Valley Hosp (page 739); **Address:** Columbia Neurosurgery, 710 W 168th St, Ste NI-428, New York, NY 10032; **Phone:** 212-305-6384; **Board Cert:** Diagnostic Radiology 1997; Neuroradiology 2012; **Med School:** Case West Res Univ 1989; **Resid:** Neurological Surgery, Univ Cincinnati Med Ctr 1990; Diagnostic Radiology, Univ Cincinnati Med Ctr 1997; **Fellow:** Neurological Radiology, Univ Cincinnati Med Ctr 1998; Neurovascular Surgery, UCSF Med Ctr 2001; **Fac Appt:** Assoc Prof Rad, Columbia P&S

Naidich, Thomas MD (NRad) - **Spec Exp:** Brain Tumors; Stroke; **Hospital:** Mt Sinai Hosp; **Address:** Mt Sinai, Radiology, 1176 5th Ave, New York, NY 10029; **Phone:** 212-241-3423; **Board Cert:** Diagnostic Radiology 1974; Neuroradiology 2005; **Med School:** NYU Sch Med 1969; **Resid:** Diagnostic Radiology, Montefiore Med Ctr 1973; **Fellow:** Neuroradiology, NYU Med Ctr 1975; **Fac Appt:** Prof Rad, Mount Sinai Sch Med

Stambuk, Hilda MD (NRad) - **Spec Exp:** Head & Neck Cancer; Head & Neck Imaging; **Hospital:** Meml Sloan Kettering Canc Ctr (page 110); **Address:** MSKCC, Neuroradiology, 1275 York Ave, Box 29, New York, NY 10065; **Phone:** 212-639-2728; **Board Cert:** Diagnostic Radiology 1994; Neuroradiology 2010; **Med School:** Med Coll GA 1990; **Resid:** Diagnostic Radiology, Univ FL Coll Of Med 1994; **Fellow:** Neuroradiology, Univ FL Coll of Med 1996

Zimmerman, Robert D MD (NRad) - **Spec Exp:** Brain Tumors; Stroke; Brain & Spinal Imaging; Brain Injury-Traumatic; **Hospital:** NY-Presby/Weill Cornell Med Ctr, NY (page 102); **Address:** Neurologic & Head & Neck Imaging, 525 E 68th St, New York, NY 10065; **Phone:** 212-746-2574; **Board Cert:** Diagnostic Radiology 1976; Neuroradiology 2005; **Med School:** Albert Einstein Coll Med 1972; **Resid:** Diagnostic Radiology, Montefiore Med Ctr 1976; **Fellow:** Neurological Radiology, George Washington Univ Hosp 1977

Nuclear Medicine

Carrasquillo, Jorge A MD (NuM) - **Spec Exp:** Radioimmunotherapy of Cancer; PET Imaging; Nuclear Endocrinology; **Hospital:** Meml Sloan Kettering Canc Ctr (page 110); **Address:** 1275 York Ave, Nuclear Medicine Svc, Box 77, New York, NY 10065; **Phone:** 212-639-2459; **Board Cert:** Internal Medicine 1977; Nuclear Medicine 1982; **Med School:** Univ Puerto Rico 1974; **Resid:** Internal Medicine, Univ Dist Hosp 1977; Nuclear Medicine, Univ Wash Hosp 1982; **Fac Appt:** Prof NuM, SUNY Upstate Med Univ

Divgi, Chaitanya R MD (NuM) - **Spec Exp:** Nuclear Oncology; **Hospital:** NY-Presby/Columbia Univ Med Ctr, NY (page 102); **Address:** 622 W 168th St PH Bldg Fl 1 - Ste 333, New York, NY 10032; **Phone:** 212-305-8032; **Board Cert:** Nuclear Medicine 1988; **Med School:** India 1976; **Resid:** Nuclear Medicine, Meml Sloan Kettering Cancer Ctr 1987; **Fellow:** Immunology, Meml Sloan Kettering Cancer Ctr 1988; **Fac Appt:** Prof Rad, Columbia P&S

Friedman, Kent P MD (NuM) - **Spec Exp:** PET Imaging; Cancer Detection & Staging; **Hospital:** NYU Langone Med Ctr (page 104); **Address:** NYU Med Ctr, Radiology Dept, 560 1 Ave Fl 2, New York, NY 10016; **Phone:** 212-263-7410; **Board Cert:** Nuclear Medicine 2004; **Med School:** Univ Conn 2001; **Resid:** Nuclear Medicine, Johns Hopkins Hosp 2004; **Fellow:** Nuclear Medicine, Johns Hopkins Hosp 2005; **Fac Appt:** Asst Prof NuM, NYU Sch Med

Ghesani, Munir MD (NuM) - **Spec Exp:** PET Imaging; Nuclear Cardiology; **Hospital:** NYU Langone Med Ctr (page 104); **Address:** NYU Med Ctr, Radiology Dept, 560 1st Ave Fl 2, New York, NY 10016; **Phone:** 212-263-7410; **Board Cert:** Nuclear Medicine 2011; Diagnostic Radiology 2010; **Med School:** India 1986; **Resid:** Internal Medicine, Jersey City Med Ctr 1993; **Fellow:** Nuclear Medicine, St Lukes-Roosevelt Hosp Ctr 1996; **Fac Appt:** Asst Prof Rad, Columbia P&S

Goldfarb, C. Richard MD (NuM) - **Spec Exp:** Thyroid Cancer; Thyroid Disorders; **Hospital:** Mt Sinai Beth Israel; **Address:** Beth Israel Med Ctr, Dept Radiology, 1st Ave at 16th St, New York, NY 10003; **Phone:** 212-252-6070; **Board Cert:** Nuclear Medicine 1974; Diagnostic Radiology 1975; **Med School:** NY Med Coll 1970; **Resid:** Diagnostic Radiology, St Lukes Hosp 1974; **Fellow:** Nuclear Medicine, St Lukes Hosp 1975; **Fac Appt:** Assoc Prof NuM, Albert Einstein Coll Med

Goldsmith, Stanley J MD (NuM) - **Spec Exp:** Thyroid Cancer; Thyroid Disorders; Nuclear Cardiology; PET Imaging; **Hospital:** NY-Presby/Weill Cornell Med Ctr, NY (page 102); **Address:** 520 E 70th St Starr Bldg - rm 2-21, New York, NY 10021-9800; **Phone:** 212-746-4588; **Board Cert:** Internal Medicine 1969; Nuclear Medicine 1972; Endocrinology, Diabetes & Metabolism 1972; **Med School:** SUNY Downstate 1962; **Resid:** Internal Medicine, Kings Co Hosp 1967; **Fellow:** Endocrinology, Diabetes & Metabolism, Mt Sinai Hosp 1968; **Fac Appt:** Prof Rad, Cornell Univ-Weill Med Coll

New York (Manhattan)

Pandit-Taskar, Neeta MD (NuM) - **Spec Exp:** Radioimmunotherapy of Cancer; Thyroid Cancer; PET Imaging; **Hospital:** Meml Sloan Kettering Canc Ctr (page 110); **Address:** MSKCC, Nuclear Med, 1275 York Ave, rm 223, Box 77, New York, NY 10065; **Phone:** 212-639-7372; **Board Cert:** Nuclear Medicine 2008; **Med School:** India 1990; **Resid:** Nuclear Medicine, Mt Sinai Hosp 1995; **Fellow:** Nuclear Medicine, Meml Sloan-Kettering Cancer Ctr 2001

Sanger, Joseph J MD (NuM) - **Spec Exp:** Nuclear Cardiology; Nuclear Oncology; **Hospital:** NYU Langone Med Ctr (page 104), Bellevue Hosp Ctr; **Address:** NYU Med Ctr, Radiology, 560 1st Ave Tisch Bldg Fl 2, New York, NY 10016; **Phone:** 212-263-7410; **Board Cert:** Nuclear Medicine 1981; **Med School:** NYU Sch Med 1977; **Resid:** Diagnostic Radiology, NYU Med Ctr 1979; **Fellow:** Nuclear Medicine, NYU Med Ctr 1981; **Fac Appt:** Assoc Prof Rad, NYU Sch Med

Scharf, Stephen MD (NuM) - **Spec Exp:** Thyroid & Parathyroid Imaging; Bone Imaging; CT Scan; **Hospital:** Lenox Hill Hosp; **Address:** Lenox Hill Hosp, Nuclear Med, 100 E 77th St, Fl 3, New York, NY 10075; **Phone:** 212-434-2630; **Board Cert:** Internal Medicine 1977; Nuclear Medicine 1979; **Med School:** Albert Einstein Coll Med 1974; **Resid:** Internal Medicine, Bronx Muni Hosp 1976; Nuclear Medicine, Montefiore Med Ctr 1978; **Fellow:** Nephrology, Montefiore Med Ctr 1979; **Fac Appt:** Asst Clin Prof NuM, Albert Einstein Coll Med

Obstetrics & Gynecology

Advincula, Arnold MD (ObG) - **Spec Exp:** Minimally Invasive Gynecologic Surgery; Gynecology Only; Endometriosis; Hysteroscopic Surgery; **Hospital:** NY-Presby/Columbia Univ Med Ctr, NY (page 102); **Address:** 51 W 51st St Fl 3, New York, NY 10019; **Phone:** 212-305-1107; **Board Cert:** Obstetrics & Gynecology 2013; **Med School:** Temple Univ 1994; **Resid:** Obstetrics & Gynecology, Univ NC Hosp 1999; **Fellow:** Minimally Invasive Gynecologic Surgery, Univ NC Hosp 2001; **Fac Appt:** Clin Prof ObG, Columbia P&S

Ascher-Walsh, Charles J MD (ObG) - **Spec Exp:** Uro-Gynecology; Gynecologic Surgery; Pelvic Surgery; Robotic Surgery; **Hospital:** Mt Sinai Hosp; **Address:** 5 E 98th St Fl 2, New York, NY 10029; **Phone:** 212-241-7952; **Board Cert:** Obstetrics & Gynecology 2013; **Med School:** SUNY Hlth Sci Ctr 1995; **Resid:** Obstetrics & Gynecology, Columbia Univ Med Ctr 1999; **Fellow:** Uro-Gynecology, Columbia Univ 2000; **Fac Appt:** Assoc Prof ObG, Mount Sinai Sch Med

Bacall, Charles J MD (ObG) - **Hospital:** Mt Sinai Hosp; **Address:** 1126 Park Ave, New York, NY 10128; **Phone:** 212-289-4500; **Board Cert:** Obstetrics & Gynecology 1981; **Med School:** NY Med Coll 1975; **Resid:** Obstetrics & Gynecology, Mt Sinai Hosp 1979; **Fac Appt:** Asst Clin Prof ObG, Mount Sinai Sch Med

Benedetto-Anzai, Maria T MD (ObG) - **Spec Exp:** Reproductive Endocrinology; Colposcopy; Adolescent Gynecology; **Hospital:** NYU Langone Med Ctr (page 104); **Address:** NY Midtown Ob/Gyn, 800 2nd Ave, Ste 815, New York, NY 10017; **Phone:** 212-263-8682; **Board Cert:** Obstetrics & Gynecology 2013; **Med School:** Italy 1981; **Resid:** Obstetrics & Gynecology, NYU Med Ctr 1999; **Fellow:** Reproductive Endocrinology, Mt Sinai Hosp 1988; Molecular Biology, Mt Sinai Hosp 1991; **Fac Appt:** Asst Prof ObG, NYU Sch Med

Berman, Alvin MD (ObG) - **Spec Exp:** Menopause Problems; Osteoporosis; Sexual Dysfunction; Women's Health over age 40; **Hospital:** Mt Sinai Hosp; **Address:** 111B E 88th St, New York, NY 10128; **Phone:** 212-722-5757; **Board Cert:** Obstetrics & Gynecology 1978; **Med School:** South Africa 1969; **Resid:** Obstetrics & Gynecology, Mount Sinai Hosp 1976; **Fellow:** Neonatal-Perinatal Medicine, Mount Sinai Hosp 1977; **Fac Appt:** Asst Clin Prof ObG, Mount Sinai Sch Med

Blumberg, Isabel S MD (ObG) - **Spec Exp:** Pregnancy; **Hospital:** Mt Sinai Hosp; **Address:** 1123 Park Ave, New York, NY 10028; **Phone:** 917-492-9200; **Board Cert:** Obstetrics & Gynecology 2013; **Med School:** Mount Sinai Sch Med 1998; **Resid:** Obstetrics & Gynecology, Mount Sinai Med Ctr 2002

Brightman, Rebecca C MD (ObG) - **Spec Exp:** Preconception Planning; Menopause Problems; Pregnancy-High Risk; **Hospital:** Mt Sinai Hosp; **Address:** 134 E 93rd St Fl 2nd, New York, NY 10128; **Phone:** 212-348-7800; **Board Cert:** Obstetrics & Gynecology 2012; **Med School:** Mount Sinai Sch Med 1986; **Resid:** Obstetrics & Gynecology, Mt Sinai Med Ctr 1990

Buterman, Irving MD (ObG) - **Spec Exp:** Women's Health; Pregnancy-High Risk; **Hospital:** Lenox Hill Hosp, Mt Sinai Beth Israel; **Address:** 950 Park Ave, New York, NY 10028-0320; **Phone:** 212-472-8200; **Board Cert:** Obstetrics & Gynecology 1983; **Med School:** Netherlands 1971; **Resid:** Obstetrics & Gynecology, Lenox Hill Hosp 1976; **Fellow:** Gynecologic Oncology, Lenox Hill Hosp 1977; **Fac Appt:** Asst Clin Prof ObG, NY Med Coll

Chin, Jean M MD (ObG) *PCP* - **Spec Exp:** Menopause Problems; **Hospital:** Mt Sinai Hosp; **Address:** 785 Park Ave, New York, NY 10021; **Phone:** 212-249-7800; **Board Cert:** Obstetrics & Gynecology 1982; **Med School:** Columbia P&S 1976; **Resid:** Obstetrics & Gynecology, Mt Sinai Hosp 1980; **Fac Appt:** Asst Clin Prof ObG, Columbia P&S

Cox, Kathryn A MD (ObG) - **Spec Exp:** Gynecology Only; Menopause Problems; Gynecologic Surgery; **Hospital:** NY-Presby/Weill Cornell Med Ctr, NY (page 102); **Address:** 330 E 63rd St, Ste 1J, New York, NY 10065; **Phone:** 212-535-2600; **Board Cert:** Obstetrics & Gynecology 1981; **Med School:** Univ Mich Med Sch 1975; **Resid:** Obstetrics & Gynecology, NY-Presby/Weill Cornell Med Ctr 1979

Dabney, Lisa MD (ObG) - **Spec Exp:** Uro-Gynecology; Minimally Invasive Surgery; Incontinence; Menopause Problems; **Hospital:** Mt Sinai St. Luke's; **Address:** 425 W 59th St Fl 5 - Ste 5D, New York, NY 10019; **Phone:** 212-523-7570; **Board Cert:** Obstetrics & Gynecology 2013; **Med School:** UCLA 1995; **Resid:** Obstetrics & Gynecology, Beth Israel Deaconess Med Ctr 1999; **Fellow:** Uro-Gynecology, Bellevue Med Ctr 2000

Diamond, Sharon MD (ObG) *PCP* - **Spec Exp:** Menopause Problems; Pap Smear Abnormalities; Gynecology Only; **Hospital:** Mt Sinai Hosp; **Address:** 61 E 86th St, Ste 1, New York, NY 10028-1003; **Phone:** 212-876-2200; **Board Cert:** Obstetrics & Gynecology 2012; **Med School:** Mount Sinai Sch Med 1979; **Resid:** Obstetrics & Gynecology, Mt Sinai Med Ctr 1983; **Fac Appt:** Asst Clin Prof ObG, Mount Sinai Sch Med

Dobrenis, Andrea M MD (ObG) - **Spec Exp:** Pregnancy; Women's Health; **Hospital:** NY-Presby/Weill Cornell Med Ctr, NY (page 102); **Address:** 425 E 61st St Fl 11, New York, NY 10065; **Phone:** 212-821-0907; **Board Cert:** Obstetrics & Gynecology 2013; **Med School:** Cornell Univ-Weill Med Coll 1988; **Resid:** Obstetrics & Gynecology, New York Hosp 1993; **Fac Appt:** Asst Clin Prof ObG, Cornell Univ-Weill Med Coll

Evans, Mark I MD (ObG) - **Spec Exp:** Reproductive Genetics; Fetal Diagnosis & Therapy; Multiple Gestation; Ultrasound; **Hospital:** Mt Sinai Hosp; **Address:** Comprehensive Genetics, 131 E 65th St, New York, NY 10065; **Phone:** 212-288-1422; **Board Cert:** Obstetrics & Gynecology 2013; Clinical Genetics 1984; **Med School:** SUNY Downstate 1978; **Resid:** Obstetrics & Gynecology, Lying-In Hosp 1982; **Fellow:** Clinical Genetics, Natl Inst Hlth 1984; **Fac Appt:** Prof ObG, Mount Sinai Sch Med

Fishbane-Mayer, Jill MD (ObG) - **Spec Exp:** Gynecology Only; **Hospital:** Mt Sinai Hosp; **Address:** 4 E 95th St, Ste 1A, New York, NY 10128-0705; **Phone:** 212-348-1111; **Board Cert:** Obstetrics & Gynecology 1982; **Med School:** Mount Sinai Sch Med 1976; **Resid:** Obstetrics & Gynecology, Mount Sinai Med Ctr 1980; **Fac Appt:** Assoc Clin Prof ObG, Mount Sinai Sch Med

Francis, Michelle MD (ObG) - **Hospital:** Mt Sinai St. Luke's; **Address:** 425 W 59th St, Ste 5D, New York, NY 10019; **Phone:** 212-523-6333; **Board Cert:** Obstetrics & Gynecology 2013; **Med School:** SUNY Downstate 1999; **Resid:** Obstetrics & Gynecology, SUNY Hlth Sci Ctr 2003

Friedman Jr, Frederick MD (ObG) *PCP* - **Spec Exp:** Women's Health; Pap Smear Abnormalities; **Hospital:** Mt Sinai Hosp; **Address:** 47 E 88th St, Ground Fl, New York, NY 10128; **Phone:** 212-534-0200; **Board Cert:** Obstetrics & Gynecology 2013; **Med School:** SUNY Downstate 1985; **Resid:** Obstetrics & Gynecology, Mount Sinai Hosp 1989; **Fac Appt:** Assoc Prof ObG, Mount Sinai Sch Med

Friedman, Lynn S MD (ObG) - **Spec Exp:** Miscarriage-Recurrent; Infertility; Pregnancy After Age 35; Pap Smear Abnormalities; **Hospital:** Mt Sinai Hosp; **Address:** 885 Park Ave, Ste 1D, New York, NY 10021; **Phone:** 212-737-3282; **Board Cert:** Obstetrics & Gynecology 2013; **Med School:** NYU Sch Med 1984; **Resid:** Obstetrics & Gynecology, Mt Sinai Hosp 1988; **Fac Appt:** Asst Prof ObG, Mount Sinai-Icahn Sch of Med

Goldman, Gary MD (ObG) - **Spec Exp:** Endometriosis; Laparoscopic Surgery-Complex; Hysterectomy Alternatives; **Hospital:** NY-Presby/Weill Cornell Med Ctr, NY (page 102); **Address:** 715 Park Ave, New York, NY 10021; **Phone:** 212-535-6100; **Board Cert:** Obstetrics & Gynecology 2013; **Med School:** SUNY Stony Brook 1986; **Resid:** Obstetrics & Gynecology, NY-Presby/Weill Cornell Med Ctr 1990; **Fac Appt:** Asst Clin Prof ObG, Cornell Univ-Weill Med Coll

Goldstein, Steven R MD (ObG) - **Spec Exp:** Gynecologic Ultrasound; Menopause Problems; Uterine Fibroids; **Hospital:** NYU Langone Med Ctr (page 104); **Address:** 530 1st Av, Ste 10N, New York, NY 10016-6402; **Phone:** 212-263-7416; **Board Cert:** Obstetrics & Gynecology 2011; **Med School:** NYU Sch Med 1975; **Resid:** Obstetrics & Gynecology, NYU Affil Hosps 1980; **Fac Appt:** Prof ObG, NYU Sch Med

Greene, Miriam MD (ObG) - **Spec Exp:** Pregnancy; **Hospital:** NYU Langone Med Ctr (page 104); **Address:** 340 E 34th St, New York, NY 10013; **Phone:** 212-725-3966; **Board Cert:** Obstetrics & Gynecology 2013; **Med School:** NYU Sch Med 1985; **Resid:** Obstetrics & Gynecology, St Lukes Roosevelt Hosp 1989; **Fac Appt:** Asst Clin Prof ObG, NYU Sch Med

Gruss, Leslie MD (ObG) *PCP* - **Spec Exp:** HPV-Human Papilloma Virus; Pap Smear Abnormalities; **Hospital:** NYU Langone Med Ctr (page 104); **Address:** Downtown Women Ob-Gyn Assocs, 568 Broadway, Ste 304, New York, NY 10012; **Phone:** 212-966-7600; **Board Cert:** Obstetrics & Gynecology 2013; **Med School:** Med Coll PA 1983; **Resid:** Obstetrics & Gynecology, Montefiore Med Ctr 1987

Gubernick, Martin MD (ObG) - **Spec Exp:** Pregnancy-High Risk; **Hospital:** NY-Presby/Weill Cornell Med Ctr, NY (page 102); **Address:** 131 E 65th St, New York, NY 10065; **Phone:** 212-288-1422; **Board Cert:** Obstetrics & Gynecology 2013; **Med School:** Northwestern Univ 1982; **Resid:** Obstetrics & Gynecology, New York Hosp 1986

Hardart, Anne MD (ObG) *PCP* - **Spec Exp:** Uro-Gynecology; Incontinence; Laparoscopic Surgery; **Hospital:** Mt Sinai St. Luke's; **Address:** 425 W 59th St Fl 5 - Ste 5D, New York, NY 10019; **Phone:** 212-523-7570; **Board Cert:** Obstetrics & Gynecology 2013; Female Pelvic Medicine & Reconstuctive Surgery 2013; **Med School:** SUNY Stony Brook 1995; **Resid:** Obstetrics & Gynecology, Stony Brook Univ Med Ctr 1999; **Fellow:** Uro-Gynecology, USC Univ Hosp 2002; **Fac Appt:** Asst Clin Prof ObG, Columbia P&S

Harris, Dena E MD (ObG) *PCP* - **Spec Exp:** Gynecology Only; Menopause Problems; Vulvar Disease; **Hospital:** NYU Langone Med Ctr (page 104); **Address:** 430 W Broadway, Ste 2A, New York, NY 10012; **Phone:** 212-941-0011; **Board Cert:** Obstetrics & Gynecology 2012; **Med School:** Hahnemann Univ 1976; **Resid:** Obstetrics & Gynecology, NYU Med Ctr 1980; **Fac Appt:** Asst Clin Prof ObG, NYU Sch Med

Hirsch, Lissa B MD (ObG) - **Spec Exp:** Gynecology Only; Menopause Problems; **Hospital:** Lenox Hill Hosp; **Address:** 755 Park Ave, New York, NY 10021-4255; **Phone:** 212-570-2222; **Board Cert:** Obstetrics & Gynecology 1985; **Med School:** UMDNJ-Rutgers Med Sch 1979; **Resid:** Obstetrics & Gynecology, NYU Med Ctr 1984

Hockstein, Steven MD (ObG) - **Spec Exp:** Pregnancy; **Hospital:** NY-Presby/Weill Cornell Med Ctr, NY (page 102); **Address:** 425 E 61st St Fl 11, New York, NY 10021; **Phone:** 212-821-0810; **Board Cert:** Obstetrics & Gynecology 2013; **Med School:** Univ MD Sch Med 1993; **Resid:** Obstetrics & Gynecology, McGaw Med Ctr 1997; **Fac Appt:** Asst Clin Prof ObG, Cornell Univ-Weill Med Coll

Holland, Claudia MD (ObG) *PCP* - **Hospital:** Mt Sinai Roosevelt; **Address:** 800A 5th Ave, Ste 503, New York, NY 10065; **Phone:** 212-230-1760; **Board Cert:** Obstetrics & Gynecology 2013; **Med School:** Mount Sinai Sch Med 1981; **Resid:** Obstetrics & Gynecology, NYU Med Ctr 1985

Karamitsos, Harry MD (ObG) - **Hospital:** Lenox Hill Hosp; **Address:** Advantage Care Physicians, 215 E 95th St, New York, NY 10128; **Phone:** 212-996-8000; **Board Cert:** Obstetrics & Gynecology 2013; **Med School:** NY Med Coll 1993; **Resid:** Obstetrics & Gynecology, Montefiore Med Ctr 1997

Kent, Joan L MD (ObG) - **Spec Exp:** Gynecology Only; **Hospital:** NY-Presby/Weill Cornell Med Ctr, NY (page 102); **Address:** 235 E 67th St, Ste 204, New York, NY 10065; **Phone:** 212-772-2900; **Board Cert:** Obstetrics & Gynecology 2013; **Med School:** Cornell Univ-Weill Med Coll 1984; **Resid:** Obstetrics & Gynecology, NY-Presby/Weill Cornell Med Ctr 1988; **Fac Appt:** Assoc Prof ObG, Cornell Univ-Weill Med Coll

Kessler, Alan A MD (ObG) - **Spec Exp:** Multiple Gestation; Pregnancy-High Risk; **Hospital:** NY-Presby/Weill Cornell Med Ctr, NY (page 102); **Address:** 131 E 65th St, New York, NY 10065; **Phone:** 212-288-1422; **Board Cert:** Obstetrics & Gynecology 2014; **Med School:** Mexico 1978; **Resid:** Obstetrics & Gynecology, New York Hosp 1983; **Fac Appt:** Assoc Prof ObG, Cornell Univ-Weill Med Coll

Kim, Joyce M MD (ObG) *PCP* - **Spec Exp:** Pregnancy-High Risk; **Hospital:** Mt Sinai Hosp; **Address:** 885 Park Ave St, Ste 1D, New York, NY 10021; **Phone:** 212-737-3282; **Board Cert:** Obstetrics & Gynecology 2013; **Med School:** Mount Sinai Sch Med 1986; **Resid:** Obstetrics & Gynecology, Mount Sinai Hosp 1990; **Fac Appt:** Asst Clin Prof ObG, Mount Sinai Sch Med

Krause, Cynthia L MD (ObG) *PCP* - **Spec Exp:** Menopause Problems; Pap Smear Abnormalities; Ovarian Cancer Genetics; Breast Cancer Genetics; **Hospital:** Mt Sinai Hosp; **Address:** 1185 Park Ave, Ste 1L, New York, NY 10128; **Phone:** 212-369-0602; **Board Cert:** Obstetrics & Gynecology 2012; **Med School:** Duke Univ 1980; **Resid:** Internal Medicine, Baltimore City Hosp 1982; Obstetrics & Gynecology, Mount Sinai Med Ctr 1986; **Fac Appt:** Asst Clin Prof ObG, Mount Sinai Sch Med

Leiter, Gila MD (ObG) - **Spec Exp:** Osteoporosis; Multiple Gestation; Menopause Problems; Uterine Fibroids; **Hospital:** Mt Sinai Hosp, Mt Sinai Beth Israel; **Address:** Park Ave Womens Center, 1160 Park Ave, New York, NY 10028; **Phone:** 212-860-2600; **Board Cert:** Obstetrics & Gynecology 2013; **Med School:** Albert Einstein Coll Med 1983; **Resid:** Obstetrics & Gynecology, Mt Sinai Hosp 1987; **Fac Appt:** Assoc Clin Prof ObG, Mount Sinai Sch Med

Levey, Kenneth A MD (ObG) - **Spec Exp:** Pain-Chronic Pelvic; Endometriosis; Uterine Fibroids; Robotic Surgery; **Hospital:** NYU Langone Med Ctr (page 104); **Address:** NY Pelvic Pain & Minimally Inv Gyn Surg, 90 Maiden Lane, Ste 300, New York, NY 10038; **Phone:** 646-290-9560; **Board Cert:** Obstetrics & Gynecology 2013; **Med School:** SUNY Buffalo 1997; **Resid:** Obstetrics & Gynecology, G Washington Univ Hosp 2001; **Fac Appt:** Asst Clin Prof ObG, NYU Sch Med

Levine, Richard U MD (ObG) - **Spec Exp:** HPV-Human Papilloma Virus; Pap Smear Abnormalities; Gynecology Only; **Hospital:** NY-Presby/Columbia Univ Med Ctr, NY (page 102); **Address:** 51 W 51st St, Fl 3, New York, NY 10019; **Phone:** 212-326-8491; **Board Cert:** Obstetrics & Gynecology 1994; **Med School:** Cornell Univ-Weill Med Coll 1966; **Resid:** Obstetrics & Gynecology, Columbia-Presby Med Ctr 1972; **Fellow:** Gynecologic Oncology, Karolinska Inst 1970; Minimally Invasive Gynecologic Surgery, Bronx Lebanon Hosp 1972; **Fac Appt:** Prof ObG, Columbia P&S

Melnick, Hugh D MD (ObG) - **Spec Exp:** Infertility-IVF; Infertility-Male; Impotence; **Hospital:** Lenox Hill Hosp; **Address:** Advanced Fertility Services, 1625 Third Ave, Ground Fl, New York, NY 10128-3603; **Phone:** 212-369-8700; **Board Cert:** Obstetrics & Gynecology 1978; **Med School:** Temple Univ 1972; **Resid:** Obstetrics & Gynecology, Lenox Hill Hosp 1976

Michel, Ketly MD (ObG) - **Hospital:** Lenox Hill Hosp; **Address:** 261 E 78th St, New York, NY 10075; **Phone:** 212-249-4501; **Board Cert:** Obstetrics & Gynecology 2013; **Med School:** SUNY Upstate Med Univ 1984; **Resid:** Obstetrics & Gynecology, Metropolitan Hosp 1988

Moritz, Jacques MD (ObG) - **Spec Exp:** Hysteroscopic Surgery; Uterine Fibroids; **Hospital:** Mt Sinai Roosevelt; **Address:** 200 W 57th, Ste 1300, New York, NY 10106; **Phone:** 212-603-4160; **Board Cert:** Obstetrics & Gynecology 2013; **Med School:** Univ Miami Sch Med 1988; **Resid:** Obstetrics & Gynecology, NY-Presby/Columbia Univ Med Ctr 1992; **Fac Appt:** Asst Clin Prof ObG, Columbia P&S

Ordorica, Steven A MD (ObG) - **Spec Exp:** Pregnancy-High Risk; Maternal & Fetal Medicine; Pregnancy After Age 35; Preconception Planning; **Hospital:** NYU Langone Med Ctr (page 104); **Address:** NYU Langone Med Ctr, Ob/Gyn, 530 1st Ave, Ste 10Q, New York, NY 10016; **Phone:** 212-263-5982; **Board Cert:** Obstetrics & Gynecology 2013; Maternal & Fetal Medicine 2013; **Med School:** SUNY Stony Brook 1983; **Resid:** Obstetrics & Gynecology, NYU Med Ctr 1987; **Fellow:** Maternal & Fetal Medicine, NYU Med Ctr 1989; **Fac Appt:** Assoc Clin Prof ObG, NYU Sch Med

Phillips, Robin N MD (ObG) *PCP* - **Spec Exp:** Gynecology Only; Menopause Problems; Women's Health over age 40; **Hospital:** Mt Sinai Hosp; **Address:** 1126 Park Ave, New York, NY 10128; **Phone:** 212-534-5300; **Board Cert:** Obstetrics & Gynecology 2000; **Med School:** Mount Sinai Sch Med 1977; **Resid:** Obstetrics & Gynecology, Mount Sinai Med Ctr 1982; **Fac Appt:** Asst Clin Prof ObG, Mount Sinai Sch Med

Rodke, Gae MD (ObG) *PCP* - **Spec Exp:** Vulvar Disease; Gynecologic Surgery; **Hospital:** Mt Sinai Roosevelt; **Address:** 185 West End Ave, Ste 1D, New York, NY 10023-2005; **Phone:** 212-496-9800; **Board Cert:** Obstetrics & Gynecology 2011; **Med School:** Albert Einstein Coll Med 1981; **Resid:** Family Medicine, Univ Hosp 1982; Obstetrics & Gynecology, Univ Hosp 1986; **Fac Appt:** Asst Clin Prof ObG, Columbia P&S

Rothenberg, Susan D MD (ObG) - **Hospital:** Mt Sinai Beth Israel; **Address:** Beth Israel Ob/Gyn Assocs, Phillips Ambulatory Care Ctr, 10 Union Square East, Ste 2B, New York, NY 10003; **Phone:** 212-844-8590; **Board Cert:** Obstetrics & Gynecology 2013; **Med School:** SUNY Upstate Med Univ 1992; **Resid:** Obstetrics & Gynecology, Maimonides Med Ctr 1996

Russell, Shereen H MD (ObG) - **Spec Exp:** Pregnancy-High Risk; **Hospital:** Lenox Hill Hosp; **Address:** 755 Park Ave, New York, NY 10021; **Phone:** 212-570-2222; **Board Cert:** Obstetrics & Gynecology 2012; **Med School:** Univ Conn 1997; **Resid:** Obstetrics & Gynecology, Lenox Hill Hosp 2001

Rutenberg, Kathryn MD (ObG) - **Hospital:** Mt Sinai St. Luke's; **Address:** 30 W 60th St, Ste 1S, New York, NY 10023; **Phone:** 212-636-8900; **Board Cert:** Obstetrics & Gynecology 2013; **Med School:** SUNY Stony Brook 1998; **Resid:** Obstetrics & Gynecology, NYU Med Ctr 2002; **Fac Appt:** Asst Clin Prof ObG, Columbia P&S

Sadarangani, Balvinder Roy MD (ObG) - **Spec Exp:** Infertility; Menopause Problems; Ultrasound; **Hospital:** Mt Sinai Beth Israel; **Address:** 247 3rd Ave, Ste 401, New York, NY 10010; **Phone:** 212-982-4100; **Board Cert:** Obstetrics & Gynecology 1980; **Med School:** India 1968; **Resid:** Obstetrics & Gynecology, St Vincents Hosp 1978

Sandler, Benjamin MD (ObG) - **Spec Exp:** Infertility-IVF; Reproductive Endocrinology; **Hospital:** Mt Sinai Hosp; **Address:** Reproductive Medicine Associates of NY, 635 Madison Ave, Fl 10, New York, NY 10022-1009; **Phone:** 212-756-5777; **Board Cert:** Obstetrics & Gynecology 2012; **Med School:** Mexico 1982; **Resid:** Obstetrics & Gynecology, Michael Reese Hosp 1987; **Fellow:** Reproductive Endocrinology, Mt Sinai Hosp 1989; **Fac Appt:** Asst Clin Prof ObG, Mount Sinai-Icahn Sch of Med

Sassoon, Robert I MD (ObG) - **Spec Exp:** Laparoscopic Surgery; Pregnancy-High Risk; Gynecologic Surgery; **Hospital:** NY-Presby/Weill Cornell Med Ctr, NY (page 102); **Address:** 131 E 65th St, New York, NY 10065; **Phone:** 212-628-1500; **Board Cert:** Obstetrics & Gynecology 2013; **Med School:** Cornell Univ-Weill Med Coll 1981; **Resid:** Obstetrics & Gynecology, NY-Presby/Weill Cornell Med Ctr 1985; **Fac Appt:** Clin Prof ObG, Cornell Univ-Weill Med Coll

Scher, Jonathan MD (ObG) - **Spec Exp:** Gynecology Only; **Hospital:** Mt Sinai Hosp; **Address:** 1126 Park Ave, New York, NY 10128-1203; **Phone:** 212-427-7400; **Board Cert:** Obstetrics & Gynecology 1981; **Med School:** South Africa 1964; **Resid:** Obstetrics & Gynecology, Groote Schuur Hosp 1970; Obstetrics & Gynecology, Kings College Hosp 1972; **Fac Appt:** Asst Clin Prof ObG, Mount Sinai Sch Med

Schwartz, Judith W MD (ObG) - **Spec Exp:** Gynecologic Surgery; Menopause Problems; **Hospital:** Mt Sinai Hosp; **Address:** 45 E 82nd St Fl 1, New York, NY 10028; **Phone:** 212-879-5959; **Board Cert:** Obstetrics & Gynecology 2013; **Med School:** Mount Sinai Sch Med 1982; **Resid:** Obstetrics & Gynecology, Mount Sinai Hosp 1986; **Fac Appt:** Asst Clin Prof ObG, Mount Sinai Sch Med

Schweizer III, William E MD (ObG) - **Spec Exp:** Minimally Invasive Surgery; Gynecologic Surgery; **Hospital:** NYU Langone Med Ctr (page 104); **Address:** NYU Langone Kips Bay Gynecology, 419 Park Ave S, Ste 1305, New York, NY 10016; **Phone:** 212-545-5400; **Board Cert:** Obstetrics & Gynecology 2013; **Med School:** SUNY Stony Brook 1983; **Resid:** Obstetrics & Gynecology, NYU Med Ctr 1987; **Fac Appt:** Assoc Clin Prof ObG, NYU Sch Med

Silverman, Frank MD (ObG) - **Hospital:** NYU Langone Med Ctr (page 104); **Address:** NYU Med Ctr Ob/Gyn, 530 1st Ave, Ste 10N, Skirball Bldg, New York, NY 10016; **Phone:** 212-263-5858; **Board Cert:** Obstetrics & Gynecology 1983; **Med School:** Tulane Univ 1975; **Resid:** Obstetrics & Gynecology, Bellevue Hosp 1979; **Fellow:** Maternal & Fetal Medicine, Bellevue Hosp 1982; **Fac Appt:** Assoc Clin Prof ObG, NYU Sch Med

Smilen, Scott W MD (ObG) - **Spec Exp:** Uro-Gynecology; Pelvic Organ Prolapse Repair; Minimally Invasive Surgery; Incontinence; **Hospital:** NYU Langone Med Ctr (page 104), Valley Hosp (page 739); **Address:** NYU Med Ctr, Urogynecology, 150 E 32nd St Fl 2, New York, NY 10016-6497; **Phone:** 212-263-0395; **Board Cert:** Obstetrics & Gynecology 2013; **Med School:** NYU Sch Med 1988; **Resid:** Obstetrics & Gynecology, NYU Med Ctr 1992; **Fellow:** Uro-Gynecology, NYU Med Ctr 1993; **Fac Appt:** Assoc Prof ObG, NYU Sch Med

Sullum, Stanford N MD (ObG) *PCP* - **Spec Exp:** Gynecology Only; **Hospital:** Mt Sinai Hosp; **Address:** 1136 5th Ave, New York, NY 10128-0122; **Phone:** 212-876-4630; **Board Cert:** Obstetrics & Gynecology 1979; **Med School:** Jefferson Med Coll 1973; **Resid:** Obstetrics & Gynecology, Mount Sinai Hosp 1977; **Fac Appt:** Asst Clin Prof ObG, Mount Sinai Sch Med

Tyagi, Renuka MD (ObG) - **Spec Exp:** Uro-Gynecology; Urology-Female; Incontinence; Interstitial Cystitis; **Hospital:** NY-Presby/Weill Cornell Med Ctr, NY (page 102); **Address:** Iris Cantor Women's Ctr, 425 E 61st St Fl 11, New York, NY 10065; **Phone:** 212-821-0710; **Board Cert:** Obstetrics & Gynecology 2013; **Med School:** Wayne State Univ 2000; **Resid:** Obstetrics & Gynecology, NY-Presby/Weill Cornell Med Ctr 2004; **Fellow:** Female Urology, NY-Presby/Weill Cornell Med Ctr 2005; **Fac Appt:** Asst Prof U, Cornell Univ-Weill Med Coll

Waterstone, Melissa B MD (ObG) - **Spec Exp:** Pregnancy; **Hospital:** NY-Presby/Weill Cornell Med Ctr, NY (page 102); **Address:** Weill Cornell Med Assocs-East Side, 211 E 80th St Fl 2, New York, NY 10021; **Phone:** 646-962-7300; **Board Cert:** Obstetrics & Gynecology 2013; **Med School:** Cornell Univ-Weill Med Coll 1998; **Resid:** Obstetrics & Gynecology, G Washington Univ Hosp 2002

Yale, Suzanne I MD (ObG) - **Hospital:** Lenox Hill Hosp; **Address:** 16 E 82nd St, New York, NY 10028; **Phone:** 212-744-9300; **Board Cert:** Obstetrics & Gynecology 1984; **Med School:** Rutgers R W Johnson Med Sch 1977; **Resid:** Obstetrics & Gynecology, Lenox Hill Hosp 1981

Yarberry-Allen, Patricia MD (ObG) - **Spec Exp:** Gynecology Only; Menopause Problems; Women's Health; Vulvar & Vaginal Disorders; **Hospital:** NY-Presby/Weill Cornell Med Ctr, NY (page 102); **Address:** 509 Madison Ave, Ste 1212, New York, NY 10022; **Phone:** 212-410-4280; **Board Cert:** Obstetrics & Gynecology 1985; **Med School:** Univ Louisville Sch Med 1976; **Resid:** Obstetrics & Gynecology, New York Hosp 1982; **Fellow:** Infectious Disease, New York Hosp 1980; Gynecology, New York Hosp 1980

Young, Bruce K MD (ObG) - **Spec Exp:** Infertility; Minimally Invasive Surgery; Miscarriage-Recurrent; Pelvic Reconstruction; **Hospital:** NYU Langone Med Ctr (page 104), Bellevue Hosp Ctr; **Address:** 530 1st Ave, HCC-5th Fl, Ste 5G, NYU-Langone Medical Center, New York, NY 10016; **Phone:** 212-263-6359; **Board Cert:** Obstetrics & Gynecology 1970; Maternal & Fetal Medicine 1975; **Med School:** NYU Sch Med 1963; **Resid:** Obstetrics & Gynecology, NYU Med Ctr 1968; **Fellow:** Reproductive Endocrinology, NYU Med Ctr 1968; **Fac Appt:** Prof ObG, NYU Sch Med

Occupational Medicine

Landrigan, Philip John MD (OM) - **Spec Exp:** Environmental Health in Children; **Hospital:** Mt Sinai Hosp; **Address:** Mt Sinai, Dept Preventive Med, 17 E 102nd St CAM Bldg Fl 3W - rm D3-145, Box 1057, New York, NY 10029-6500; **Phone:** 212-824-7018; **Board Cert:** Pediatrics 1973; Public Health & Genl Preventive Med 1979; Occupational Medicine 1983; **Med School:** Harvard Med Sch 1967; **Resid:** Internal Medicine, Metro Genl Hosp 1968; Pediatrics, Chldns Hosp 1970; **Fellow:** Epidemiology, Ctrs for Disease Control 1973; Occupational Medicine, Univ London 1977; **Fac Appt:** Prof Ped, Mount Sinai Sch Med

Ophthalmology

Abramson, David H MD (Oph) - **Spec Exp:** Eye Tumors/Cancer; Orbital Tumors/Cancer; Retinoblastoma; Choroidal Melanoma; **Hospital:** Meml Sloan Kettering Canc Ctr (page 110), NY-Presby/Weill Cornell Med Ctr, NY (page 102); **Address:** MSKCC, Ophthalmology, 1275 York Ave, Ste A330, New York, NY 10065; **Phone:** 212-639-7232; **Board Cert:** Ophthalmology 1975; **Med School:** Albert Einstein Coll Med 1969; **Resid:** Ophthalmology, Harkness Eye Inst 1974; **Fellow:** Ocular Oncology, NY-Presby/Columbia Univ Med Ctr 1975; **Fac Appt:** Prof Oph, Cornell Univ-Weill Med Coll

Accardi, Frank E MD (Oph) - **Spec Exp:** Cataract Surgery; Refractive Surgery; **Hospital:** New York Eye & Ear Infirm of Mt Sinai; **Address:** 114 E 27th St, New York, NY 10016; **Phone:** 212-481-4000; **Board Cert:** Ophthalmology 1987; **Med School:** Italy 1979; **Resid:** Internal Medicine, Cabrini Med Ctr 1982; Ophthalmology, SUNY Downstate Med Ctr 1985; **Fellow:** Cornea, SUNY Downstate Med Ctr 1986; **Fac Appt:** Asst Clin Prof Oph, NY Med Coll

Al-Aswad, Lama A MD (Oph) - **Spec Exp:** Glaucoma; **Hospital:** NY-Presby/Columbia Univ Med Ctr, NY (page 102); **Address:** Columbia Ophthalmology Consultants, 635 W 165th St Fl 1, New York, NY 10032; **Phone:** 212-305-9535; **Board Cert:** Ophthalmology 2005; **Med School:** Syria 1993; **Resid:** Ophthalmology, SUNY Downstate Med Ctr 2001; **Fellow:** Research, Mass E&E Infirmary 1998; Glaucoma, Univ Tennessee Hlth Sci Ctr 2003; **Fac Appt:** Assoc Prof Oph, Columbia P&S

Angioletti Jr, Louis V MD (Oph) - **Spec Exp:** Retinal Disorders; Diabetic Eye Disease/Retinopathy; Macular Degeneration; **Hospital:** New York Eye & Ear Infirm of Mt Sinai; **Address:** Angioletti Retina Assocs, 7 Gramercy Park, New York, NY 10003-1759; **Phone:** 212-505-8510; **Board Cert:** Ophthalmology 1975; **Med School:** NY Med Coll 1966; **Resid:** Internal Medicine, St Vincents Hosp 1967; Ophthalmology, NY Eye & Ear Infirm 1973; **Fellow:** Retina, NY Eye & Ear Infirm 1974; **Fac Appt:** Clin Prof Oph, NY Med Coll

Asbell, Penny A MD (Oph) - **Spec Exp:** Corneal Disease & Transplant; LASIK-Refractive Surgery; Cataract Surgery; Keratoconus; **Hospital:** Mt Sinai Hosp; **Address:** 17 E 102nd St, Fl 8, New York, NY 10029; **Phone:** 212-241-0939; **Board Cert:** Ophthalmology 1980; **Med School:** SUNY Buffalo 1975; **Resid:** Ophthalmology, NYU Med Ctr 1979; **Fellow:** Immunology, NYU Med Ctr 1980; Cornea & Ext Eye Disease, LSU Eye Ctr 1982; **Fac Appt:** Prof Oph, Mount Sinai Sch Med

Auran, James D MD (Oph) - **Spec Exp:** Cataract Surgery; Cornea & External Eye Disease; Acanthamoeba Keratitis; Dry Eye Syndrome; **Hospital:** NY-Presby/Columbia Univ Med Ctr, NY (page 102); **Address:** Columbia Ophthalmology Consultants, Edward S Harkness Eye Inst, 635 W 165th St Fl 5th, New York, NY 10032-3701; **Phone:** 212-305-9535; **Board Cert:** Ophthalmology 1989; **Med School:** Cornell Univ-Weill Med Coll 1983; **Resid:** Ophthalmology, Manhattan EET Hosp 1987; **Fellow:** Ophthalmology, Manhattan EET Hosp 1988; **Fac Appt:** Assoc Clin Prof Oph, Columbia P&S

Bansal, Rajendra K MD (Oph) - **Spec Exp:** Glaucoma; Cataract Surgery; **Hospital:** NY-Presby/Columbia Univ Med Ctr, NY (page 102); **Address:** Harkness Eye Inst, 635 W 165th St, New York, NY 10032; **Phone:** 212-568-2600; **Board Cert:** Ophthalmology 1977; **Med School:** India 1967; **Resid:** Ophthalmology, Univ Delhi Hosp 1973; **Fellow:** Glaucoma, Columbia Presby Med Ctr 1979; **Fac Appt:** Assoc Clin Prof Oph, Columbia P&S

Barile, Gaetano R MD (Oph) - **Spec Exp:** Macular Disease/Degeneration; Retinal Disorders; Diabetic Eye Disease/Retinopathy; Retina/Vitreous Consultation; **Hospital:** Lenox Hill Hosp (Manh Eye, Ear & Throat Hosp); **Address:** 210 E 64 St, Fl 7, New York, NY 10065; **Phone:** 212-702-7400; **Board Cert:** Ophthalmology 2008; **Med School:** Cornell Univ 1991; **Resid:** Ophthalmology, Manhattan EET Hosp 1995; **Fellow:** Retina/Vitreous Surgery, Roosevelt Hosp/Harkness Eye Inst 1997; Retina, Moorfields Eye Hosp 1997; **Fac Appt:** Prof Oph, Hofstra N Shore-LIJ Sch Med

Barker, Barbara Ann MD (Oph) - **Spec Exp:** Glaucoma; Corneal Disease; Laser Surgery; **Hospital:** New York Eye & Ear Infirm of Mt Sinai, Mt Sinai Hosp; **Address:** 70 E 96th St, Ste 1B, New York, NY 10128; **Phone:** 212-289-2244; **Board Cert:** Ophthalmology 1981; **Med School:** Mount Sinai Sch Med 1976; **Resid:** Ophthalmology, Mt Sinai Med Ctr 1980; **Fellow:** Glaucoma, Beth Israel Med Ctr 1981; Cornea, Beth Israel Med Ctr 1983; **Fac Appt:** Assoc Clin Prof Oph, Mount Sinai Sch Med

Braunstein, Richard E MD (Oph) - **Spec Exp:** LASIK-Refractive Surgery; Corneal Disease & Transplant; Cataract Surgery; **Hospital:** Lenox Hill Hosp (Manh Eye, Ear & Throat Hosp); **Address:** MEETH, Ophthalmology, 210 E 64th St Fl 7, New York, NY 10065; **Phone:** 212-702-7300; **Board Cert:** Ophthalmology 2006; **Med School:** Columbia P&S 1989; **Resid:** Ophthalmology, Harkness Eye Inst 1993; **Fellow:** Cornea & Ext Eye Disease, Wilmer Eye Inst 1994; **Fac Appt:** Prof Oph, Hofstra N Shore-LIJ Sch Med

Buxton, Douglas F MD (Oph) - **Spec Exp:** Corneal Disease & Transplant; LASIK-Refractive Surgery; Cataract Surgery-Lens Implant; Glaucoma-Pediatric; **Hospital:** New York Eye & Ear Infirm of Mt Sinai; **Address:** 310 E 14th St, Ste 403, New York, NY 10003-4201; **Phone:** 212-979-4410; **Board Cert:** Ophthalmology 2008; Penetrating Keratoplasty 2007; Cataract/Implant Surgery 2002; Refractive Surgery(LASIK) 2002; **Med School:** Cornell Univ-Weill Med Coll 1982; **Resid:** Ophthalmology, NY Eye & Ear Infirm 1986; **Fellow:** Cornea & Ext Eye Disease, NY Eye & Ear Infirm 1988; **Fac Appt:** Assoc Clin Prof Oph, NY Med Coll

Campolattaro, Brian N MD (Oph) - **Spec Exp:** Pediatric Ophthalmology; Strabismus; Tear Duct Problems; Eye Muscle Disorders; **Hospital:** New York Eye & Ear Infirm of Mt Sinai, Lenox Hill Hosp (Manh Eye, Ear & Throat Hosp); **Address:** Ped Ophthalmology of NY, 30 E 40th St, Ste 405, New York, NY 10016-3507; **Phone:** 212-684-3980; **Board Cert:** Ophthalmology 2006; **Med School:** UMDNJ-NJ Med Sch, Newark 1990; **Resid:** Ophthalmology, New York Eye & Ear Infirm 1994; **Fellow:** Pediatric Ophthalmology, St Louis Chldns Hosp 1995; **Fac Appt:** Asst Clin Prof Oph, NY Med Coll

Casper, Daniel S MD/PhD (Oph) - **Spec Exp:** Diabetic Eye Disease; Diabetic Eye Disease/Retinopathy; **Hospital:** NY-Presby/Columbia Univ Med Ctr, NY (page 102); **Address:** Columbia Ophthalmology Consultants, 635 W 165th St, Flanzer Suite, New York, NY 10032-3822; **Phone:** 212-305-9535; **Board Cert:** Ophthalmology 1991; **Med School:** Albany Med Coll 1985; **Resid:** Ophthalmology, Harkness Eye Inst-Columbia 1989; **Fellow:** Oculoplastic Surgery, Harkness Eye Inst-Columbia 1990; **Fac Appt:** Asst Clin Prof Oph, Columbia P&S

Ceisler, Emily J MD (Oph) - **Spec Exp:** Pediatric Ophthalmology; Strabismus; Eye Muscle Disorders-Child & Adult; **Hospital:** NYU Langone Med Ctr (page 104), New York Eye & Ear Infirm of Mt Sinai; **Address:** Pediatric Ophthalmic Consultants, 40 W 72nd St, New York, NY 10023; **Phone:** 212-981-9800; **Board Cert:** Ophthalmology 2008; **Med School:** Harvard Med Sch 1991; **Resid:** Ophthalmology, Mass Eye & Ear Infirmary 1995; **Fellow:** Pediatric Ophthalmology, Manhattan Eye & Ear Infirmary 1996; **Fac Appt:** Asst Clin Prof Oph, NYU Sch Med

Chaiken, Barry G MD (Oph) - **Spec Exp:** Cataract Surgery; LASIK-Refractive Surgery; **Hospital:** New York Eye & Ear Infirm of Mt Sinai, Mt Sinai Roosevelt; **Address:** 625 Park Ave, New York, NY 10065; **Phone:** 212-249-1976; **Board Cert:** Ophthalmology 1981; **Med School:** Columbia P&S 1976; **Resid:** Ophthalmology, Mt Sinai Hosp 1980

Chang, Stanley MD (Oph) - **Spec Exp:** Retina/Vitreous Surgery; Diabetic Eye Disease/Retinopathy; Macular Disease/Degeneration; Retinal Disorders; **Hospital:** NY-Presby/Columbia Univ Med Ctr, NY (page 102); **Address:** 635 W 165th St, Box 92, New York, NY 10032; **Phone:** 212-305-9535; **Board Cert:** Ophthalmology 1979; **Med School:** Columbia P&S 1974; **Resid:** Ophthalmology, Mass Eye & Ear Infirm 1978; **Fellow:** Vitreoretinal Surgery, Bascom Palmer Eye Inst 1979; **Fac Appt:** Prof Oph, Columbia P&S

Charles, Norman C MD (Oph) - **Spec Exp:** Contact Lenses; Cornea & External Eye Disease; Ophthalmic Pathology; Cataract Surgery; **Hospital:** NYU Langone Med Ctr (page 104); **Address:** 620 Park Ave, New York, NY 10065-6561; **Phone:** 212-772-6920; **Board Cert:** Ophthalmology 1971; **Med School:** NYU Sch Med 1963; **Resid:** Ophthalmology, NYU Med Ctr 1970; **Fellow:** Ophthalmic Pathology, NYU Med Ctr 1971; **Fac Appt:** Clin Prof Oph, NYU Sch Med

Chern, Relly D MD (Oph) - **Spec Exp:** Cataract Surgery; Ophthalmic Plastic Surgery; **Hospital:** Lenox Hill Hosp (Manh Eye, Ear & Throat Hosp), New York Eye & Ear Infirm of Mt Sinai; **Address:** 923 5th Ave, Ste 1B, New York, NY 10021; **Phone:** 212-628-0160; **Board Cert:** Ophthalmology 1983; **Med School:** Albert Einstein Coll Med 1976; **Resid:** Ophthalmology, Montefiore Hosp Med Ctr 1980; **Fac Appt:** Asst Clin Prof Oph, Albert Einstein Coll Med

Cioffi, George MD (Oph) - **Spec Exp:** Glaucoma; Cataract Surgery; Anterior Segment Surgery; **Hospital:** NY-Presby/Columbia Univ Med Ctr, NY (page 102); **Address:** 635 W 165th St, New York, NY 10032; **Phone:** 212-305-9535; **Board Cert:** Ophthalmology 2014; **Med School:** Univ SC Sch Med 1987; **Resid:** Ophthalmology, Univ Maryland Affil Hosp 1991; **Fellow:** Glaucoma, Devers Eye Inst 1992; **Fac Appt:** Prof Oph, Columbia P&S

Cohen, Ben Z MD (Oph) - **Spec Exp:** Retina/Vitreous Surgery; Macular Degeneration; Diabetic Eye Disease/Retinopathy; **Hospital:** New York Eye & Ear Infirm of Mt Sinai, Mt Sinai Hosp; **Address:** Retina Assocs of NY, 140 E 80th St, New York, NY 10075; **Phone:** 212-772-0600; **Board Cert:** Ophthalmology 1981; **Med School:** NY Med Coll 1976; **Resid:** Ophthalmology, Univ Chicago Hosps 1980; **Fellow:** Macular Disease, Manhattan Eye & Ear Infirmary 1981; Retina/Vitreous Surgery, Mass Eye & Ear Infirmary 1983; **Fac Appt:** Asst Prof Oph, Mount Sinai Sch Med

Cohen, Leeber MD (Oph) - **Spec Exp:** Cataract Surgery; AIDS Related Eye Diseases; Botox Therapy; **Hospital:** New York Eye & Ear Infirm of Mt Sinai; **Address:** 11 5th Ave, Ste B, New York, NY 10003-4342; **Phone:** 212-777-1644; **Board Cert:** Ophthalmology 1989; **Med School:** SUNY Hlth Sci Ctr 1983; **Resid:** Ophthalmology, Kings Co Hosp/SUNY Downstate 1987; **Fac Appt:** Asst Clin Prof Med, SUNY Downstate

Coleman, Donald Jackson MD (Oph) - **Spec Exp:** Retina/Vitreous Surgery; Ultrasound-Eye; Melanoma-Choroidal (eye); **Hospital:** NY-Presby/Columbia Univ Med Ctr, NY (page 102); **Address:** Columbia Ophthalmology Consultants, Edward S Harkness Eye Inst, 635 W 165th St Fl 1st, Box 92, New York, NY 10032; **Phone:** 212-305-9535; **Board Cert:** Ophthalmology 1969; **Med School:** SUNY Buffalo 1960; **Resid:** Ophthalmology, Columbia-Presby Med Ctr 1967; **Fellow:** Research, Natl Inst Hlth 1968; **Fac Appt:** Prof Oph, Cornell Univ-Weill Med Coll

Cykiert, Robert MD (Oph) - **Spec Exp:** LASIK-Refractive Surgery; Cataract Surgery; Corneal Disease & Transplant; Keratoconus; **Hospital:** NYU Langone Med Ctr (page 104), New York Eye & Ear Infirm of Mt Sinai; **Address:** 345 E 37th St, Ste 210, New York, NY 10016; **Phone:** 212-922-1430; **Board Cert:** Ophthalmology 1981; **Med School:** NY Med Coll 1976; **Resid:** Ophthalmology, Montefiore Med Ctr 1980; **Fellow:** Cornea & Ext Eye Disease, Wills Eye Hosp 1981; **Fac Appt:** Assoc Clin Prof Oph, NYU Sch Med

D'Amico, Donald J MD (Oph) - **Spec Exp:** Diabetic Eye Disease/Retinopathy; Retinal Detachment; Retinal Disorders; **Hospital:** NY-Presby/Weill Cornell Med Ctr, NY (page 102); **Address:** Weill Cornell Eye Associates, Dept of Ophthalmology, 1305 York Ave, Fl 11th, New York, NY 10021; **Phone:** 646-962-2020; **Board Cert:** Ophthalmology 1982; **Med School:** Univ IL Coll Med 1977; **Resid:** Ophthalmology, Mass Eye & Ear Infirm 1981; **Fellow:** Vitreoretinal Surgery, Bascom Palmer Eye Inst 1982; **Fac Appt:** Prof Oph, Cornell Univ-Weill Med Coll

Dayan, Alan R MD (Oph) - **Spec Exp:** Retinal Disorders; Retina/Vitreous Surgery; Macular Degeneration; Retinal Detachment; **Hospital:** New York Eye & Ear Infirm of Mt Sinai; **Address:** NY Vision Grp, 310 E 14th St, Ste 419, New York, NY 10003; **Phone:** 212-677-2000; **Board Cert:** Ophthalmology 2009; **Med School:** Mount Sinai Sch Med 1992; **Resid:** Ophthalmology, NY Eye & Ear Infirm 1996; **Fellow:** Vitreoretinal Disease, Vitreoretinal Fdn 1998

Delerme, Milton MD (Oph) - **Spec Exp:** Anterior Segment Surgery; **Hospital:** Harlem Hosp Ctr; **Address:** 75 E 116th St, New York, NY 10029; **Phone:** 212-828-7700; **Board Cert:** Ophthalmology 1987; **Med School:** UMDNJ-NJ Med Sch, Newark 1978; **Resid:** Surgery, UMDNJ-Univ Hosp 1980; Ophthalmology, Harlem Hosp 1984; **Fellow:** Anterior Segment - External Disease, St Francis Hosp 1985

Della Rocca, Robert C MD (Oph) - **Spec Exp:** Orbital Tumors/Cancer; Eyelid Tumors/Cancer; Oculoplastic Surgery; Eyelid Cancer & Reconstruction; **Hospital:** New York Eye & Ear Infirm of Mt Sinai, Mt Sinai St. Luke's; **Address:** 310 E 14th St, South Bldg, rm 319, New York, NY 10003; **Phone:** 212-979-4575; **Board Cert:** Ophthalmology 1975; **Med School:** Creighton Univ 1967; **Resid:** Ophthalmology, NY Eye & Ear Infirm 1973; **Fellow:** Oculoplastic Surgery, Albany Med Coll/NY Eye & Ear Infirm 1975; **Fac Appt:** Clin Prof Oph, NY Med Coll

Dodick, Jack M MD (Oph) - **Spec Exp:** Cataract Surgery-Lens Implant; Laser Vision Surgery; Anterior Segment Surgery; **Hospital:** NYU Langone Med Ctr (page 104), Lenox Hill Hosp (Manh Eye, Ear & Throat Hosp); **Address:** 535 Park Ave, New York, NY 10065; **Phone:** 212-288-7638; **Board Cert:** Ophthalmology 1969; **Med School:** Univ Toronto 1963; **Resid:** Ophthalmology, Manhattan EE&T Hosp 1967; **Fellow:** Anterior Segment - External Disease, Westchester Co Med Ctr 1968; **Fac Appt:** Prof Oph, NYU Sch Med

Eichenbaum, Joseph W MD (Oph) - **Spec Exp:** Uveitis; Glaucoma; Toxicology; Eye Infections; **Hospital:** Mt Sinai Hosp; **Address:** 1050 Park Ave, New York, NY 10028; **Phone:** 212-289-7200; **Board Cert:** Ophthalmology 1980; **Med School:** Yale Univ 1973; **Resid:** Ophthalmology, NYU Med Ctr 1977; **Fellow:** Oculoplastic & Reconstructive Surgery, Mount Sinai Hosp 1980; **Fac Appt:** Assoc Clin Prof Oph, Mount Sinai Sch Med

Elahi, Ebrahim MD (Oph) - **Spec Exp:** Cosmetic & Reconstructive Surgery; Oculoplastic & Orbital Surgery; Eyelid Tumors/Cancer; Facial Plastic Surgery; **Hospital:** Mt Sinai Hosp, Mt Sinai Beth Israel; **Address:** Fifth Avenue Eye Assocs, 1034 5th Ave, New York, NY 10028; **Phone:** 212-570-0707; **Board Cert:** Ophthalmology 2012; **Med School:** Mount Sinai Sch Med 1996; **Resid:** Ophthalmology, Mt Sinai Hosp 2000; **Fellow:** Ophthalmic Plastic & Reconstructive Surgery, Mt Sinai Hosp 2001; **Fac Appt:** Assoc Clin Prof Oph, Mount Sinai-Icahn Sch of Med

Engel, Harry M MD (Oph) - **Spec Exp:** Retinal Disorders; **Hospital:** Montefiore Med Ctr-Moses Campus (page 100), New York Eye & Ear Infirm of Mt Sinai; **Address:** West Side Retina, 40 W 72nd St, New York, NY 10023; **Phone:** 212-724-2555; **Board Cert:** Ophthalmology 1981; **Med School:** NY Med Coll 1976; **Resid:** Ophthalmology, U Michigan Med Ctr 1980; **Fellow:** Eye Pathology, Wilmer Inst 1981; Retina/Vitreous Surgery, Barnes Jewish Hosp 1982; **Fac Appt:** Clin Prof Oph, Albert Einstein Coll Med

Esposito, Donna A MD (Oph) - **Spec Exp:** Glaucoma; Cataract Surgery; **Hospital:** New York Eye & Ear Infirm of Mt Sinai; **Address:** 49 W 23rd St Fl 12, New York, NY 10010; **Phone:** 212-255-4373; **Board Cert:** Ophthalmology 1991; **Med School:** NY Med Coll 1983; **Resid:** Surgery, St Vincent's Hosp 1985; Ophthalmology, St Vincent's Hosp 1989; **Fellow:** Glaucoma, NY Hosp 1990

Finger, Paul T MD (Oph) - **Spec Exp:** Eye Tumors/Cancer; Choroidal Melanoma; Retinoblastoma; Orbital Tumors/Cancer; **Hospital:** New York Eye & Ear Infirm of Mt Sinai, Lenox Hill Hosp (Manh Eye, Ear & Throat Hosp); **Address:** New York Eye Cancer Center, 115 E 61st St, Fl 5, Ste B, New York, NY 10065; **Phone:** 212-832-8170; **Board Cert:** Ophthalmology 1990; **Med School:** Tulane Univ 1982; **Resid:** Ophthalmology, Manhattan EET Hosp 1986; **Fellow:** Ocular Oncology, N Shore Univ Hosp 1987; **Fac Appt:** Clin Prof Oph, NYU Sch Med

Fisher, Yale L MD (Oph) - **Spec Exp:** Retina/Vitreous Consultation; Diabetic Eye Disease; Ocular Ultrasound; **Hospital:** Lenox Hill Hosp (Manh Eye, Ear & Throat Hosp), NY-Presby/Weill Cornell Med Ctr, NY (page 102); **Address:** Vitreous-Retina-Macula Consults of NY, 460 Park Ave Fl 5, New York, NY 10022; **Phone:** 212-861-9797; **Board Cert:** Ophthalmology 1973; **Med School:** Cornell Univ-Weill Med Coll 1967; **Resid:** Internal Medicine, Cornell Med Ctr 1968; Ophthalmology, Manhattan EE&T Hosp 1971; **Fac Appt:** Clin Prof Oph, Cornell Univ-Weill Med Coll

Florakis, George J MD (Oph) - **Spec Exp:** Cornea Transplant; Corneal Disease; Keratoconus; Anterior Segment Trauma/Reconstruction; **Hospital:** NY-Presby/Columbia Univ Med Ctr, NY (page 102), White Plains Hosp (page 652); **Address:** Edward S Harkness Eye Inst, Columbia Univ Med Ctr/NY Presby Hosp, 635 W 165th St, Ste 303, New York, NY 10032; **Phone:** 212-927-2394; **Board Cert:** Ophthalmology 1989; **Med School:** Columbia P&S 1983; **Resid:** Ophthalmology, Harkness Eye Inst 1987; **Fellow:** Cornea & Ext Eye Disease, Univ Iowa Hosps & Clins 1988; **Fac Appt:** Clin Prof Oph, Columbia P&S

Fong, Raymond MD (Oph) - **Spec Exp:** Cataract Surgery; LASIK-Refractive Surgery; Glaucoma; **Hospital:** Lenox Hill Hosp (Manh Eye, Ear & Throat Hosp), NY-Presby/Lower Manhattan Hosp (page 102); **Address:** 109 Lafayette St Fl 4, New York, NY 10013-4154; **Phone:** 212-274-1900; **Board Cert:** Ophthalmology 1987; **Med School:** Cornell Univ 1981; **Resid:** Internal Medicine, Beth Israel Med Ctr 1982; Ophthalmology, Manhattan EE&T Hosp 1985

Fox, Martin L MD (Oph) - **Spec Exp:** LASIK-Refractive Surgery; Cornea Transplant; Corneal Ring Implants; **Hospital:** New York Eye & Ear Infirm of Mt Sinai; **Address:** 425 Madison Ave, Ste 1501, New York, NY 10017; **Phone:** 212-838-1053; **Board Cert:** Ophthalmology 1981; **Med School:** Hahnemann Univ 1976; **Resid:** Ophthalmology, Boston Univ Med Ctr 1980; **Fellow:** Cornea, NY Eye & Ear Infirmary 1981

Friedman, Alan H MD (Oph) - **Spec Exp:** Uveitis; Eye Tumors/Cancer; Retinal Disorders; Ophthalmic Pathology; **Hospital:** Mt Sinai Hosp, Lenox Hill Hosp; **Address:** 888 Park Ave, Ste 1A, New York, NY 10075; **Phone:** 212-794-2277; **Board Cert:** Ophthalmology 1971; **Med School:** NYU Sch Med 1963; **Resid:** Ophthalmology, NYU Med Ctr 1969; **Fellow:** Ocular Pathology, NYU Langone Med Ctr 1970; Pathology, Hammersmith Hosp 1972; **Fac Appt:** Clin Prof Oph, Mount Sinai Sch Med

Friedman, Robert MD (Oph) - **Spec Exp:** Laser-Refractive Surgery; Cataract Surgery; Retina/Vitreous Surgery; Macular Disease/Degeneration; **Hospital:** Lenox Hill Hosp, Mt Sinai Hosp; **Address:** 1001 Park Ave, New York, NY 10028-0935; **Phone:** 212-772-6202; **Board Cert:** Ophthalmology 1989; **Med School:** Albert Einstein Coll Med 1983; **Resid:** Internal Medicine, St Lukes-Roosevelt Hosp 1984; Ophthalmology, Lenox Hill Hosp 1987; **Fellow:** Vitreoretinal Surgery, Manhattan EE&T Hosp 1988; **Fac Appt:** Asst Clin Prof Oph, Mount Sinai Sch Med

Fromer, Mark D MD (Oph) - **Spec Exp:** Retinal Disorders; Laser Vision Surgery; Cataract Surgery; Diabetic Eye Disease/Retinopathy; **Hospital:** New York Eye & Ear Infirm of Mt Sinai, Lenox Hill Hosp (Manh Eye, Ear & Throat Hosp); **Address:** 550 Park Ave, New York, NY 10065; **Phone:** 212-832-9228; **Board Cert:** Ophthalmology 1989; **Med School:** UMDNJ-Rutgers Med Sch 1984; **Resid:** Ophthalmology, St Vincents Hosp 1988; **Fellow:** Vitreoretinal Surgery, Manhattan EE&T Hosp 1989; **Fac Appt:** Asst Clin Prof Oph, NY Med Coll

Fuchs, Wayne MD (Oph) - **Spec Exp:** Diabetic Eye Disease/Retinopathy; Macular Disease/Degeneration; Retinal Disorders; Pseudoxanthoma Elasticum; **Hospital:** Mt Sinai Hosp; **Address:** 121 E 60th St, Ste 5B, New York, NY 10022; **Phone:** 212-319-8205; **Board Cert:** Ophthalmology 1985; **Med School:** Mount Sinai Sch Med 1979; **Resid:** Ophthalmology, Mt Sinai Hosp 1983; **Fellow:** Vitreoretinal Surgery & Disease, NY-Presby/Weill Cornell Med Ctr 1984; **Fac Appt:** Clin Prof Oph, Mount Sinai-Icahn Sch of Med

Gallin, Pamela F MD (Oph) - **Spec Exp:** Pediatric Ophthalmology; Amblyopia; Strabismus; Lacrimal Gland Disorders; **Hospital:** NY-Presby/Columbia Univ Med Ctr, NY (page 102), Lenox Hill Hosp (Manh Eye, Ear & Throat Hosp); **Address:** NY Presbyterian-Columbia, Harkness Eye Institute/Children's Hosp, 635 W 165 St, Ste 224, New York, NY 10032; **Phone:** 212-305-5407; **Board Cert:** Ophthalmology 1983; **Med School:** Washington Univ, St Louis 1978; **Resid:** Ophthalmology, Mt Sinai Hosp 1982; **Fellow:** Pediatric Ophthalmology, Natl Chldn's Med Ctr 1983; Strabismus, NY-Presby/Columbia Univ Med Ctr 1983; **Fac Appt:** Prof Oph, Columbia P&S

Gentile, Ronald C MD (Oph) - **Spec Exp:** Retina/Vitreous Surgery; Diabetic Eye Disease/Retinopathy; Macular Degeneration; Retinal Disorders; **Hospital:** New York Eye & Ear Infirm of Mt Sinai, Winthrop Univ Hosp (page 536); **Address:** NY Eye & Ear Infirm, 310 E 14th St, Ste 319S, New York, NY 10003; **Phone:** 212-979-4120; **Board Cert:** Ophthalmology 2008; **Med School:** SUNY Downstate 1991; **Resid:** Ophthalmology, NY Eye & Ear Infirm 1995; **Fellow:** Ocular Pathology, NY Eye & Ear Infirm 1996; Retina/Vitreous Surgery, Kresge Eye Inst 1998; **Fac Appt:** Prof Oph, NY Med Coll

Gibralter, Richard P MD (Oph) - **Spec Exp:** Cataract Surgery; Laser Vision Surgery; Cornea Transplant; Corneal Disease & Surgery; **Hospital:** Lenox Hill Hosp (Manh Eye, Ear & Throat Hosp), New York Eye & Ear Infirm of Mt Sinai; **Address:** Cataract and Corneal Associates, 154 E 71st St, New York, NY 10021-5123; **Phone:** 212-628-2202; **Board Cert:** Ophthalmology 1981; **Med School:** Mount Sinai Sch Med 1976; **Resid:** Ophthalmology, Manhattan EE&T Hosp 1980; **Fellow:** Cornea, Manhattan EE&T Hosp 1981; **Fac Appt:** Assoc Clin Prof Oph, NYU Sch Med

Goldstein, Michael T MD (Oph) - **Spec Exp:** Corneal Disease; Keratoconus; Corneal Ring Implants; LASIK-Refractive Surgery; **Hospital:** New York Eye & Ear Infirm of Mt Sinai, Lenox Hill Hosp (Manh Eye, Ear & Throat Hosp); **Address:** 115 E 61st St, Ste 3A, New York, NY 10065; **Phone:** 212-371-6209; **Board Cert:** Ophthalmology 1980; **Med School:** SUNY Downstate 1974; **Resid:** Ophthalmology, Brookdale Hosp Med Ctr 1979; **Fellow:** Cornea, Manhattan Eye, Ear & Throat Hosp 1980

Grayson, Douglas K MD (Oph) - **Spec Exp:** Cataract Surgery; Glaucoma; **Hospital:** New York Eye & Ear Infirm of Mt Sinai; **Address:** Omni Eye Services, 20 E 46th St Fl 15, New York, NY 10017; **Phone:** 212-353-0030; **Board Cert:** Ophthalmology 2006; **Med School:** Brown Univ 1989; **Resid:** Ophthalmology, NY Eye & Ear Infirm 1993; **Fellow:** Glaucoma, NY Eye & Ear Infirm 1994; **Fac Appt:** Asst Prof Oph, NY Med Coll

Guillory, Samuel L MD (Oph) - **Spec Exp:** LASIK-Refractive Surgery; PRK-Refractive Surgery; Pediatric Ophthalmology; Cataract Surgery; **Hospital:** Mt Sinai Hosp; **Address:** 1103 Park Ave, New York, NY 10128; **Phone:** 212-860-5400; **Board Cert:** Ophthalmology 1980; **Med School:** Mount Sinai Sch Med 1975; **Resid:** Ophthalmology, Mt Sinai Hosp 1979; **Fellow:** Ocular Ultrasound, NY-Presby/Weill Cornell Med Ctr 1981; **Fac Appt:** Assoc Clin Prof Oph, Mount Sinai-Icahn Sch of Med

Haight, David H MD (Oph) - **Spec Exp:** Laser Vision Surgery; Cornea Transplant; Cataract Surgery; **Hospital:** Lenox Hill Hosp, NY-Presby/Weill Cornell Med Ctr, NY (page 102); **Address:** 155 E 72nd St, New York, NY 10021-4371; **Phone:** 212-772-9474; **Board Cert:** Ophthalmology 1985; **Med School:** Johns Hopkins Univ 1980; **Resid:** Internal Medicine, Hartford Hosp 1981; Ophthalmology, Manhattan EE&T Hosp 1984; **Fellow:** Cornea, Manhattan EE&T Hosp 1985; **Fac Appt:** Clin Prof Oph, NYU Sch Med

Hall, Lisabeth S MD (Oph) - **Spec Exp:** Pediatric Ophthalmology; Strabismus-Adult & Pediatric; Eye Muscle Disorders; Cataract-Pediatric; **Hospital:** New York Eye & Ear Infirm of Mt Sinai; **Address:** Pediatric Ophthalmic Consultants, 40 W 72nd St, New York, NY 10023; **Phone:** 212-981-9800; **Board Cert:** Ophthalmology 2009; **Med School:** SUNY Stony Brook 1992; **Resid:** Ophthalmology, Manhattan EET Infirm 1996; **Fellow:** Pediatric Ophthalmology, Jules Stein Eye Inst 1997; **Fac Appt:** Assoc Prof Oph, NY Med Coll

Harmon, Gregory K MD (Oph) - **Spec Exp:** Cataract Surgery; Glaucoma; **Hospital:** NY-Presby/Weill Cornell Med Ctr, NY (page 102); **Address:** 205 E 64th St, Ste 101, New York, NY 10065; **Phone:** 212-888-4100; **Board Cert:** Ophthalmology 1991; **Med School:** Mount Sinai Sch Med 1982; **Resid:** Ophthalmology, NY-Presby/Weill Cornell Med Ctr 1986; **Fellow:** Glaucoma, NY-Presby/Weill Cornell Med Ctr 1987; **Fac Appt:** Assoc Prof Oph, Cornell Univ-Weill Med Coll

Heinemann, Murk Hein MD (Oph) - **Spec Exp:** Ocular Ultrasound; Diagnostic Problems; Eye Tumors/Cancer; **Hospital:** Meml Sloan Kettering Canc Ctr (page 110), NY-Presby/Weill Cornell Med Ctr, NY (page 102); **Address:** 1275 York Ave, rm A330, New York, NY 10065; **Phone:** 212-639-7237; **Board Cert:** Ophthalmology 1982; **Med School:** Cornell Univ-Weill Med Coll 1976; **Resid:** Internal Medicine, New York Hosp/Cornell Med Ctr 1977; Ophthalmology, Yale New Haven Hosp 1980; **Fellow:** Ophthalmology, New York Hosp/Cornell Med Ctr 1982; **Fac Appt:** Assoc Prof Oph, Cornell Univ-Weill Med Coll

Horowitz, Jason MD (Oph) - **Spec Exp:** Retinal Disease; Diabetic Eye Disease/Retinopathy; Macular Degeneration; Retina/Vitreous Surgery; **Hospital:** NY-Presby/Columbia Univ Med Ctr, NY (page 102); **Address:** NY-Presby, Harkness Eye Inst, 635 W 165th St, New York, NY 10032; **Phone:** 212-305-9535; **Board Cert:** Ophthalmology 1987; **Med School:** Yale Univ 1981; **Resid:** Ophthalmology, Yale-New Haven Hosp 1985; **Fellow:** Retina/Vitreous Surgery, NY-Presby/Weill Cornell Med Ctr 1986

Jabs, Douglas A MD (Oph) - **Spec Exp:** Uveitis; **Hospital:** Mt Sinai Hosp; **Address:** 17 E 102nd St, New York, NY 10029; **Phone:** 212-241-0939; **Board Cert:** Ophthalmology 1982; Internal Medicine 1983; **Med School:** Johns Hopkins Univ 1977; **Resid:** Ophthalmology, Wilmer Eye Inst 1981; Internal Medicine, Johns Hopkins Hosp 1983; **Fellow:** Rheumatology, Johns Hopkins Hosp 1984; **Fac Appt:** Prof Oph, Mount Sinai Sch Med

Kazim, Michael MD (Oph) - **Spec Exp:** Thyroid Eye Disease; Oculoplastic Surgery; Orbital Tumors/Cancer; Eyelid Tumors/Cancer; **Hospital:** NY-Presby/Columbia Univ Med Ctr, NY (page 102), New York Eye & Ear Infirm of Mt Sinai; **Address:** NY-Presby, Harkness Eye Inst, 635 W 165th St, Ste 207, New York, NY 10032; **Phone:** 212-305-5477; **Board Cert:** Ophthalmology 1989; **Med School:** Columbia P&S 1984; **Resid:** Ophthalmology, Harkness Eye Inst 1988; **Fellow:** Oculoplastic Surgery, Chldns Hosp 1989; Orbital Surgery, Allegheny Genl Hosp 1990; **Fac Appt:** Clin Prof Oph, Columbia P&S

Kelly, Stephen E MD (Oph) - **Spec Exp:** LASIK-Refractive Surgery; Cataract Surgery; Corneal Disease; Glaucoma; **Hospital:** New York Eye & Ear Infirm of Mt Sinai, Lenox Hill Hosp (Manh Eye, Ear & Throat Hosp); **Address:** Cataract & Corneal Associates, 154 E 71st St, New York, NY 10021-5125; **Phone:** 212-628-2202; **Board Cert:** Ophthalmology 1976; **Med School:** Washington Univ, St Louis 1970; **Resid:** Ophthalmology, NY Eye & Ear Infirmary 1975; **Fellow:** Cornea, Manhattan EET Hosp 1976

Klapper, Daniel MD (Oph) - **Spec Exp:** Laser-Refractive Surgery; Glaucoma; Cataract Surgery; **Hospital:** Lenox Hill Hosp (Manh Eye, Ear & Throat Hosp), Montefiore Med Ctr-Einstein Campus (page 100); **Address:** 7 W 81st St, Ste 1A, New York, NY 10024; **Phone:** 212-874-2726; **Board Cert:** Ophthalmology 1991; **Med School:** Albert Einstein Coll Med 1984; **Resid:** Ophthalmology, Brookdale Univ Hosp 1988

Koplin, Richard Steven MD (Oph) - **Spec Exp:** Cataract Surgery; Laser-Refractive Surgery; Eye Trauma; Eye Infections; **Hospital:** New York Eye & Ear Infirm of Mt Sinai; **Address:** Ophthalmic Consultants, 310 E 14th St, South Bldg Fl 2, New York, NY 10003-4201; **Phone:** 212-505-6550; **Board Cert:** Ophthalmology 1975; **Med School:** NY Med Coll 1969; **Resid:** Ophthalmology, NY Eye & Ear Infirm 1973; **Fac Appt:** Assoc Clin Prof Oph, NY Med Coll

Kupersmith, Mark J MD (Oph) - **Spec Exp:** Neuro-Ophthalmology; **Hospital:** Mt Sinai Roosevelt; **Address:** St Lukes-Roosevelt, Ophthalmology, 1000 10th Ave, rm 10 INN, New York, NY 10019; **Phone:** 212-636-3200; **Board Cert:** Ophthalmology 1981; Neurology 1981; **Med School:** Northwestern Univ 1974; **Resid:** Neurology, NYU Med Ctr 1978; Ophthalmology, NYU Med Ctr 1980; **Fac Appt:** Prof Oph, Albert Einstein Coll Med

Lauer, Simeon A MD (Oph) - **Spec Exp:** Oculoplastic Surgery; Ophthalmic Plastic Surgery; Lacrimal Gland Disorders; Orbital Surgery; **Hospital:** Hackensack Univ Med Ctr (page 96), New York Eye & Ear Infirm of Mt Sinai; **Address:** 130 E 67th St, New York, NY 10065; **Phone:** 212-879-6824; **Board Cert:** Ophthalmology 1991; **Med School:** SUNY Downstate 1984; **Resid:** Internal Medicine, Montefiore Med Ctr 1986; Ophthalmology, Montefiore Med Ctr 1989; **Fellow:** Oculoplastic & Reconstructive Surgery, LSU Eye Ctr 1990; **Fac Appt:** Assoc Clin Prof Oph, Albert Einstein Coll Med

Lee, Carol M MD (Oph) - **Spec Exp:** Retina/Vitreous Surgery; Diabetic Eye Disease/Retinopathy; Macular Disease/Degeneration; **Hospital:** NYU Langone Med Ctr (page 104); **Address:** 161 Madison Ave, Ste 5NE, New York, NY 10016; **Phone:** 212-684-2424; **Board Cert:** Ophthalmology 1991; **Med School:** SUNY Downstate 1984; **Resid:** Ophthalmology, NYU Med Ctr 1989; **Fellow:** Retina, Univ IL Eye & Ear Inst 1986; Vitreoretinal Surgery, Barnes-Jewish Hosp 1991; **Fac Appt:** Clin Prof Oph, NYU Sch Med

Leib, Martin L MD (Oph) - **Spec Exp:** Cataract Surgery; Laser Refractive Surgery; Oculoplastic & Orbital Surgery; Laser Surgery; **Hospital:** NY-Presby/Columbia Univ Med Ctr, NY (page 102), Mt Sinai Roosevelt; **Address:** 635 W 165th St, Ste 230, New York, NY 10032; **Phone:** 212-305-2303; **Board Cert:** Ophthalmology 1982; **Med School:** NY Med Coll 1974; **Resid:** Surgery, Mount Sinai Med Ctr 1976; Ophthalmology, McGill Univ Affil Hosp 1979; **Fellow:** Ophthalmic Plastic Surgery, Columbia-Presby Med Ctr 1980; Orbital Surgery, Columbia-Presby Med Ctr 1980; **Fac Appt:** Clin Prof Oph, Columbia P&S

Liebmann, Jeffrey M MD (Oph) - **Spec Exp:** Glaucoma; Cataract Surgery; **Hospital:** New York Eye & Ear Infirm of Mt Sinai; **Address:** Glaucoma Assocs of NY, 121 E 60th St Fl 8, New York, NY 10022; **Phone:** 212-477-7540; **Board Cert:** Ophthalmology 1989; **Med School:** Boston Univ 1983; **Resid:** Ophthalmology, SUNY Downstate Med Ctr 1987; **Fellow:** Glaucoma, NY Eye & Ear Infirm 1988; **Fac Appt:** Clin Prof Oph, NYU Sch Med

Lisman, Richard D MD (Oph) - **Spec Exp:** Oculoplastic Surgery; Eyelid/Tear Duct Reconstruction; Eyelid Cosmetic & Reconstructive Surgery; Orbital & Eyelid Tumors/Cancer; **Hospital:** NYU Langone Med Ctr (page 104), Lenox Hill Hosp (Manh Eye, Ear & Throat Hosp); **Address:** 635 Park Ave, New York, NY 10065; **Phone:** 212-585-1405; **Board Cert:** Ophthalmology 1981; **Med School:** NYU Sch Med 1976; **Resid:** Ophthalmology, Manhattan EET Hosp 1980; **Fellow:** Ophthalmic Plastic Surgery, NY Eye & Ear Infirm 1981; Ophthalmic Plastic Surgery, Manhattan EETT Hosp 1982; **Fac Appt:** Prof Oph, NYU Sch Med

MacKay, Cynthia J MD (Oph) - **Spec Exp:** Diabetic Eye Disease/Retinopathy; Macular Degeneration; Laser Surgery; Retinitis Pigmentosa; **Hospital:** NY-Presby/Columbia Univ Med Ctr, NY (page 102), Lenox Hill Hosp (Manh Eye, Ear & Throat Hosp); **Address:** 315 Central Park West, Ste 1B, New York, NY 10025; **Phone:** 212-772-6050; **Board Cert:** Ophthalmology 1982; **Med School:** SUNY Hlth Sci Ctr 1977; **Resid:** Ophthalmology, Columbia-Presby Med Ctr 1981; **Fellow:** Retina, NYU Med Ctr 1982; **Fac Appt:** Clin Prof Oph, Columbia P&S

Magramm, Irene MD (Oph) - **Spec Exp:** Pediatric Ophthalmology; Strabismus; Cataract Surgery; Diplopia; **Hospital:** Lenox Hill Hosp (Manh Eye, Ear & Throat Hosp); **Address:** 220 E 63rd St, Ste LM, New York, NY 10055; **Phone:** 212-644-5100; **Board Cert:** Ophthalmology 1987; **Med School:** Cornell Univ-Weill Med Coll 1981; **Resid:** Ophthalmology, North Shore Univ Hosp 1985; **Fellow:** Pediatric Ophthalmology, Manhattan EE&T Hosp 1986; **Fac Appt:** Asst Clin Prof Oph, Cornell Univ-Weill Med Coll

Maher, Elizabeth A MD (Oph) - **Spec Exp:** Orbital Surgery; Oculoplastic Surgery; **Hospital:** New York Eye & Ear Infirm of Mt Sinai; **Address:** Omni Eye Services, 20 E 46th St Fl 15, New York, NY 10017; **Phone:** 212-353-0030; **Board Cert:** Ophthalmology 1989; **Med School:** Harvard Med Sch 1984; **Resid:** Internal Medicine, St Lukes-Roosevelt Hosp 1985; Ophthalmology, Manhattan EE&T Hosp 1988; **Fellow:** Ophthalmic Plastic & Reconstructive Surgery, Manhattan EE&T Hosp 1989

Mandel, Eric R MD (Oph) - **Spec Exp:** LASIK-Refractive Surgery; PRK-Refractive Surgery; Corneal Disease; **Hospital:** Lenox Hill Hosp; **Address:** 211 E 70th St, New York, NY 10021; **Phone:** 212-734-0111; **Board Cert:** Ophthalmology 1988; **Med School:** SUNY Stony Brook 1982; **Resid:** Ophthalmology, Lenox Hill Hosp 1986; **Fellow:** Cornea & Ext Eye Disease, Mass Eye & Ear Infirm 1987

Mandelbaum, Sidney H MD (Oph) - **Spec Exp:** Cataract Surgery; Cornea Transplant; Corneal Disease & Surgery; **Hospital:** New York Eye & Ear Infirm of Mt Sinai, Lenox Hill Hosp (Manh Eye, Ear & Throat Hosp); **Address:** East Side Eye Surgeons, 178 E 71st St, New York, NY 10021; **Phone:** 212-650-0400; **Board Cert:** Ophthalmology 1982; **Med School:** Yale Univ 1976; **Resid:** Internal Medicine, NY Hosp 1978; Ophthalmology, LAC-USC Med Ctr 1981; **Fellow:** Cornea, Bascom Palmer Eye Inst 1982; **Fac Appt:** Assoc Clin Prof Oph, Albert Einstein Coll Med

Marr, Brian MD (Oph) - **Spec Exp:** Eye Tumors/Cancer; **Hospital:** Meml Sloan Kettering Canc Ctr (page 110); **Address:** 16 E 60th St, rm 408, New York, NY 10022; **Phone:** 212-744-1700; **Board Cert:** Ophthalmology 2012; **Med School:** Temple Univ 1995; **Resid:** Ophthalmology, NY Eye & Ear Infirmary 1999; **Fellow:** Ophthalmic Oncology, Wills Eye Hosp 2001

Melton, Roberta Christine MD (Oph) - **Spec Exp:** Glaucoma; Diabetic Eye Disease; **Hospital:** NY-Presby/Weill Cornell Med Ctr, NY (page 102); **Address:** 247 3rd Ave, Ste 202, New York, NY 10010-7454; **Phone:** 212-475-3791; **Board Cert:** Ophthalmology 1982; **Med School:** Canada 1977; **Resid:** Ophthalmology, St Vincent's Hosp & Med Ctr 1981; **Fac Appt:** Asst Clin Prof Oph, Cornell Univ-Weill Med Coll

Merhige, Kenneth E MD (Oph) - **Spec Exp:** Cataract Surgery; **Hospital:** Mt Sinai Roosevelt; **Address:** Mt Sinai-St Luke's Hosp Ctr, 1111 Amsterdam Ave, New York, NY 10025; **Phone:** 212-523-2562; **Board Cert:** Ophthalmology 1985; **Med School:** Cornell Univ-Weill Med Coll 1980; **Resid:** Ophthalmology, St Luke's Hosp 1984; **Fellow:** Vitreoretinal Surgery, NY Hosp-Cornell 1985

Merriam, John C MD (Oph) - **Spec Exp:** Cataract Surgery; Reconstructive Surgery; Ophthalmic Plastic Surgery; **Hospital:** NY-Presby/Columbia Univ Med Ctr, NY (page 102); **Address:** Edward S Harkness Eye Inst, 635 W 165th St, Ste 3-305, New York, NY 10032-3724; **Phone:** 212-305-5402; **Board Cert:** Ophthalmology 1983; **Med School:** Harvard Med Sch 1977; **Resid:** Plastic Surgery, Brigham-Boston Chldns Hosp 1979; Ophthalmology, Mass Eye & Ear Infirm 1982; **Fellow:** Ophthalmology, UCSF Med Ctr 1983; **Fac Appt:** Clin Prof Oph, Columbia P&S

Mindel, Joel S MD/PhD (Oph) - **Spec Exp:** Neuro-Ophthalmology; Myasthenia Gravis; Temporal Arteritis; **Hospital:** Mt Sinai Hosp; **Address:** 17 E 102nd St Fl 8, New York, NY 10029; **Phone:** 212-241-0939; **Board Cert:** Ophthalmology 1970; **Med School:** Univ MD Sch Med 1964; **Resid:** Ophthalmology, Univ Michigan Med Ctr 1969; **Fellow:** Neuro-Ophthalmology, Columbia-Presby Med Ctr 1966; Ocular Pharmacology, Mount Sinai Med Ctr 1973; **Fac Appt:** Prof Oph, Mount Sinai Sch Med

Mitchell, John P MD (Oph) - **Spec Exp:** Neuro-Ophthalmology; Cataract Surgery; Glaucoma; **Hospital:** NY-Presby/Columbia Univ Med Ctr, NY (page 102); **Address:** Macula Care, 147 W 142 St, New York, NY 10030; **Phone:** 212-281-8400; **Board Cert:** Ophthalmology 1978; **Med School:** Cornell Univ-Weill Med Coll 1973; **Resid:** Ophthalmology, Harlem Hosp 1977; **Fellow:** Neuro-Ophthalmology, Columbia-Presby Med Ctr 1978

Moazed, Kambiz T MD (Oph) - **Spec Exp:** Cataract Surgery; Eyelid/Tear Duct Reconstruction; Ophthalmic Plastic Surgery; **Hospital:** Mt Sinai Roosevelt; **Address:** Advantage Care Physicians, 4337 Broadway, New York, NY 10033; **Phone:** 212-568-6300; **Board Cert:** Ophthalmology 1983; **Med School:** Iran 1973; **Resid:** Ophthalmology, Mass EE Infirm 1982; **Fellow:** Eye Pathology, Stanford Univ Med Ctr 1977; Oculoplastic Surgery, Edward Harkness Eye Inst 1983; **Fac Appt:** Asst Clin Prof Oph, Columbia P&S

Moskowitz, Bruce K MD (Oph) - **Spec Exp:** Oculoplastic Surgery; Reconstructive Surgery; **Hospital:** New York Eye & Ear Infirm of Mt Sinai; **Address:** 310 E 14th St, Ste 401, New York, NY 10003; **Phone:** 212-979-4586; **Board Cert:** Ophthalmology 2013; **Med School:** SUNY Downstate 1987; **Resid:** Ophthalmology, SUNY Downstate Med Ctr 1991; **Fellow:** Ophthalmology, Kingsbrook Jewish Med Ctr 1992; **Fac Appt:** Asst Clin Prof Oph, NY Med Coll

Moskowitz, Craig J MD (Oph) - **Spec Exp:** Cataract Surgery; Refractive Surgery; Corneal Disease & Surgery; Dry Eye Syndrome; **Hospital:** New York Eye & Ear Infirm of Mt Sinai; **Address:** 1115 5th Ave, New York, NY 10128; **Phone:** 212-517-4500; **Board Cert:** Ophthalmology 2007; **Med School:** NE Ohio Univ 2000; **Resid:** Ophthalmology, McGill Univ 2004; **Fellow:** Cornea & Refractive Surgery, OSU Med Ctr 2007

Muchnick, Richard S MD (Oph) - **Spec Exp:** Pediatric Ophthalmology; Strabismus; **Hospital:** NY-Presby/Weill Cornell Med Ctr, NY (page 102), Lenox Hill Hosp; **Address:** 69 E 71st St, New York, NY 10021-4213; **Phone:** 212-744-1726; **Board Cert:** Ophthalmology 1975; **Med School:** Cornell Univ-Weill Med Coll 1967; **Resid:** Ophthalmology, New York Hosp 1973; **Fellow:** Ophthalmic Plastic Surgery, UCSF Med Ctr 1974; Pediatric Ophthalmology, Manhattan EE&T Hosp 1975; **Fac Appt:** Clin Prof Oph, Cornell Univ-Weill Med Coll

Muldoon, Thomas O MD (Oph) - **Spec Exp:** Retina/Vitreous Surgery; Macular Disease/Degeneration; Diabetic Eye Disease/Retinopathy; **Hospital:** New York Eye & Ear Infirm of Mt Sinai; **Address:** 310 E 14th St, Ste 402, New York, NY 10003-4201; **Phone:** 212-979-4595; **Board Cert:** Ophthalmology 1971; **Med School:** Univ Rochester 1962; **Resid:** Surgery, St Lukes Hosp 1966; Ophthalmology, NY EE Infirm 1969; **Fellow:** Retinal Surgery, NY EE Infirm 1970; **Fac Appt:** Assoc Clin Prof Oph, NY Med Coll

Newton, Michael J MD (Oph) - **Spec Exp:** Cataract Surgery; Refractive Surgery; Eye Infections; Corneal Disease & Surgery; **Hospital:** New York Eye & Ear Infirm of Mt Sinai, Mt Sinai Hosp; **Address:** 799 Park Ave, New York, NY 10021-3275; **Phone:** 212-861-0146; **Board Cert:** Ophthalmology 1978; **Med School:** Tufts Univ 1971; **Resid:** Ophthalmology, Mount Sinai Hosp 1977; **Fellow:** Cornea & Ext Eye Disease, AB Nesburn MD/Doheny Eye Inst 1978; **Fac Appt:** Assoc Clin Prof Oph, Mount Sinai Sch Med

Nightingale, Jeffrey D MD (Oph) - **Spec Exp:** LASIK-Refractive Surgery; Cataract Surgery; **Hospital:** New York Eye & Ear Infirm of Mt Sinai; **Address:** 211 Central Park West, New York, NY 10024-6020; **Phone:** 212-877-7188; **Board Cert:** Ophthalmology 1977; **Med School:** SUNY Hlth Sci Ctr 1972; **Resid:** Ophthalmology, Bronx Lebanon Hosp 1976; **Fellow:** Oculoplastic Surgery, NY Eye & Ear Infirmary 1977

Obstbaum, Stephen A MD (Oph) - **Spec Exp:** Cataract Surgery; Glaucoma; **Hospital:** Lenox Hill Hosp, Lenox Hill Hosp (Manh Eye, Ear & Throat Hosp); **Address:** 210 E 64th St Fl 7th, New York, NY 10065; **Phone:** 212-702-7620; **Board Cert:** Ophthalmology 1974; **Med School:** NY Med Coll 1967; **Resid:** Ophthalmology, Flower Fifth Ave Hosp 1972; **Fellow:** Glaucoma, Washington Univ Affil Hosp 1973; **Fac Appt:** Prof Oph, NYU Sch Med

Odel, Jeffrey G MD (Oph) - **Spec Exp:** Neuro-Ophthalmology; **Hospital:** NY-Presby/Columbia Univ Med Ctr, NY (page 102); **Address:** Harkness Eye Institute, 635 W 165th St, rm 316, New York, NY 10032-3701; **Phone:** 212-305-5415; **Board Cert:** Ophthalmology 1981; **Med School:** Univ Rochester 1975; **Resid:** Ophthalmology, Mt Sinai Hosp 1981; **Fellow:** Ophthalmology, Bascom-Palmer Eye Inst 1977; Ophthalmology, Columbia Presby Med Ctr 1982; **Fac Appt:** Assoc Clin Prof Oph, Columbia P&S

Paccione, Jeffrey C MD (Oph) - **Spec Exp:** Retinal Disorders; Macular Degeneration; **Hospital:** Lenox Hill Hosp (Manh Eye, Ear & Throat Hosp), New York Eye & Ear Infirm of Mt Sinai; **Address:** Retina Assocs of New York, 140 E 80th St, New York, NY 10075; **Phone:** 212-772-0600; **Board Cert:** Ophthalmology 2010; **Med School:** Columbia P&S 1989; **Resid:** Ophthalmology, Manhattan EE&T Hosp 1994; **Fellow:** Vitreoretinal Disease, Mt Sinai Med Ctr 1998; **Fac Appt:** Assoc Clin Prof Oph, Mount Sinai Sch Med

Palu, Richard N MD (Oph) - **Spec Exp:** Oculoplastic & Reconstructive Surgery; **Hospital:** NYU Langone Med Ctr (page 104), Valley Hosp (page 739); **Address:** 161 Madison Ave Fl 6, New York, NY 10016; **Phone:** 212-213-9783; **Board Cert:** Ophthalmology 1990; **Med School:** NYU Sch Med 1984; **Resid:** Ophthalmology, NYU Med Ctr 1988; **Fellow:** Ophthalmic Plastic & Reconstructive Surgery, Mass EE Infirm 1989; **Fac Appt:** Assoc Clin Prof Oph, NYU Sch Med

Prince, Andrew M MD (Oph) - **Spec Exp:** Glaucoma; Cataract Surgery; **Hospital:** New York Eye & Ear Infirm of Mt Sinai, Lenox Hill Hosp (Manh Eye, Ear & Throat Hosp); **Address:** Glaucoma Consultants of Greater NY & NJ, 178 E 71st St, New York, NY 10021-5119; **Phone:** 212-717-2200; **Board Cert:** Ophthalmology 1987; **Med School:** SUNY Downstate 1981; **Resid:** Internal Medicine, Kings Co Hosp Ctr 1982; Ophthalmology, SUNY Downstate Med Ctr 1985; **Fellow:** Glaucoma, NY Eye & Ear Infirmary 1986; **Fac Appt:** Assoc Prof Oph, NYU Sch Med

Raab, Edward L MD (Oph) - **Spec Exp:** Pediatric Ophthalmology; Strabismus; Glaucoma-Pediatric; **Hospital:** Mt Sinai Hosp; **Address:** 17 E 102nd St Fl 8th, New York, NY 10029-6501; **Phone:** 212-369-0988; **Board Cert:** Ophthalmology 1966; **Med School:** NYU Sch Med 1958; **Resid:** Ophthalmology, Mount Sinai 1964; **Fellow:** Pediatric Ophthalmology, Chldns Natl Med Ctr 1967; **Fac Appt:** Prof Oph, Mount Sinai Sch Med

Relland, Maureen A MD (Oph) - **Spec Exp:** Botox Therapy; **Hospital:** New York Eye & Ear Infirm of Mt Sinai, Richmond Univ Med Ctr; **Address:** 352 7th Ave, Ste 805, New York, NY 10001; **Phone:** 212-645-7771; **Board Cert:** Ophthalmology 1971; **Med School:** NY Med Coll 1964; **Resid:** Ophthalmology, St Vincent's Hosp Med Ctr 1968; **Fac Appt:** Asst Clin Prof Oph, NY Med Coll

Ritch, Robert MD (Oph) - **Spec Exp:** Glaucoma; Complementary Medicine; **Hospital:** New York Eye & Ear Infirm of Mt Sinai; **Address:** 310 E 14th St, South Bldg - Fl 3, New York, NY 10003-4201; **Phone:** 212-477-7540; **Board Cert:** Ophthalmology 1977; **Med School:** Albert Einstein Coll Med 1972; **Resid:** Ophthalmology, Mt Sinai Med Ctr 1976; **Fellow:** Glaucoma, Mt Sinai Med Ctr 1978; **Fac Appt:** Prof Oph, Mount Sinai-Icahn Sch of Med

Ritterband, David MD (Oph) - **Spec Exp:** Cataract Surgery; Cornea Transplant; Refractive Surgery; Corneal Disease; **Hospital:** New York Eye & Ear Infirm of Mt Sinai; **Address:** Ophthalmic Consultants, 310 E 14th St, South Bldg - Fl 2, The New York Eye & Ear Infirmary, New York, NY 10003-4201; **Phone:** 212-505-6550; **Board Cert:** Ophthalmology 2006; **Med School:** NY Med Coll 1990; **Resid:** Ophthalmology, NY Med Coll 1994; **Fellow:** Cornea & Ext Eye Disease, Eye & Ear Inst 1995; **Fac Appt:** Clin Prof Oph, NY Med Coll

Rodgers, I. Rand MD (Oph) - **Spec Exp:** Oculoplastic Surgery; Eyelid Cosmetic & Reconstructive Surgery; Eyelid/Tear Duct Disorders; **Hospital:** Mt Sinai Hosp, N Shore Univ Hosp; **Address:** 229 E 79 St, New York, NY 10075; **Phone:** 212-249-7600; **Board Cert:** Ophthalmology 1989; **Med School:** Mount Sinai Sch Med 1983; **Resid:** Surgery, Mt Sinai Med Ctr 1984; Ophthalmology, Mt Sinai Med Ctr 1987; **Fellow:** Ocular Oncology, Manhattan EE&T Hosp 1988; Ophthalmic Plastic Surgery, Mass E&E Infirm 1990; **Fac Appt:** Asst Clin Prof Oph, Mount Sinai Sch Med

Rodriguez-Sains, Rene S MD (Oph) - **Spec Exp:** Eyelid Cosmetic & Reconstructive Surgery; Eyelid Tumors/Cancer; Melanoma; Eye Tumors/Cancer; **Hospital:** New York Eye & Ear Infirm of Mt Sinai, NYU Langone Med Ctr (page 104); **Address:** 799 Park Ave, New York, NY 10021-3275; **Phone:** 212-535-0315; **Board Cert:** Ophthalmology 1982; **Med School:** NYU Sch Med 1977; **Resid:** Internal Medicine, NYU Med Ctr 1988; Ophthalmology, Manhattan EET Hosp 1981; **Fellow:** Ophthalmic Plastic Surgery, Manhattan EET Hosp 1982; **Fac Appt:** Asst Clin Prof Oph, NYU Sch Med

Rosenthal, Jeanne L MD (Oph) - **Spec Exp:** Retina/Vitreous Surgery; Macular Degeneration; Diabetic Eye Disease/Retinopathy; **Hospital:** New York Eye & Ear Infirm of Mt Sinai; **Address:** 20 E 9th St, New York, NY 10003-5944; **Phone:** 212-674-2970; **Board Cert:** Ophthalmology 1985; **Med School:** SUNY Downstate 1979; **Resid:** Ophthalmology, NY Eye & Ear Infirm 1983; **Fellow:** Retina/Vitreous Surgery, NY Eye & Ear Infirm 1985; **Fac Appt:** Clin Prof Oph, NY Med Coll

Rudick Jr, Albert Joseph MD (Oph) - **Spec Exp:** LASIK-Refractive Surgery; Glaucoma; **Hospital:** New York Eye & Ear Infirm of Mt Sinai, NY-Presby/Lower Manhattan Hosp (page 102); **Address:** Assoc Ophthalmologists of NY, 150 Broadway Fl 14 - Ste 1401, New York, NY 10038; **Phone:** 212-233-2344; **Board Cert:** Ophthalmology 1989; **Med School:** Univ Pennsylvania 1983; **Resid:** Ophthalmology, Manhattan EE&T Hosp 1989

Samson, C. Michael MD (Oph) - **Spec Exp:** Uveitis; Immunotherapy; Eye Infections; **Hospital:** New York Eye & Ear Infirm of Mt Sinai; **Address:** 310 E 14th St, Ste 319 S, New York, NY 10003; **Phone:** 212-979-4515; **Board Cert:** Ophthalmology 2011; **Med School:** SUNY Downstate 1994; **Resid:** Ophthalmology, NY Eye & Ear Infirm 1998; **Fellow:** Ophthalmology, Mass Eye & Ear Infirm 2000; **Fac Appt:** Assoc Prof Oph, NY Med Coll

Schiff, William M MD (Oph) - **Spec Exp:** Macular Disease/Degeneration; Diabetic Eye Disease/Retinopathy; Retinal Detachment; Retina/Vitreous Surgery; **Hospital:** Lenox Hill Hosp (Manh Eye, Ear & Throat Hosp); **Address:** MEETH, Ophthalmology, 210 E 64th St, Fl 7, New York, NY 10065; **Phone:** 212-702-7400; **Board Cert:** Ophthalmology 2006; **Med School:** NYU Sch Med 1988; **Resid:** Ophthalmology, NY Eye & Ear Infirm 1994; **Fellow:** Retina/Vitreous Surgery, Harkness Eye Inst/New York Hosp/Roosevelt Hosp 1996; **Fac Appt:** Prof Oph, Hofstra N Shore-LIJ Sch Med

Schrier, Amilia MD (Oph) - **Spec Exp:** Corneal Disease & Surgery; Cornea & External Eye Disease; Cataract Surgery; **Hospital:** Lenox Hill Hosp (Manh Eye, Ear & Throat Hosp), NY-Presby/Columbia Univ Med Ctr, NY (page 102); **Address:** 210 E 64th St, Fl 7, New York, NY 10065; **Phone:** 212-702-7300; **Board Cert:** Ophthalmology 2013; **Med School:** SUNY Downstate 1987; **Resid:** Ophthalmology, SUNY Downstate 1991; **Fellow:** Cornea & Ext Eye Disease, North Shore Univ Hosp 1992; **Fac Appt:** Prof Oph, Hofstra N Shore-LIJ Sch Med

Schubert, Hermann D MD (Oph) - **Spec Exp:** Diabetic Eye Disease/Retinopathy; Macular Degeneration; Retinal Disorders; Retinal Detachment; **Hospital:** NY-Presby/Columbia Univ Med Ctr, NY (page 102); **Address:** 635 W 165th St, Rm 206, New York, NY 10032-3701; **Phone:** 212-305-6534; **Board Cert:** Ophthalmology 1987; Anatomic Pathology 1981; **Med School:** Germany 1974; **Resid:** Pathology, Columbia-Presby Hosp 1979; Ophthalmology, Columbia-Presby Hosp 1985; **Fellow:** Retina/Vitreous Surgery, Wills Eye Hosp 1987; **Fac Appt:** Prof Oph, Columbia P&S

Schwarcz, Robert M MD (Oph) - **Spec Exp:** Oculoplastic Surgery; Cosmetic Surgery-Face; Reconstructive Surgery-Face; Eyelid Surgery; **Hospital:** Montefiore Med Ctr-Wakefield Campus (page 100), New York Eye & Ear Infirm of Mt Sinai; **Address:** 135 E 71st St, Ste 1A, New York, NY 10021; **Phone:** 212-396-4400; **Board Cert:** Ophthalmology 2006; **Med School:** Howard Univ 1999; **Resid:** Internal Medicine, St Lukes-Roosevelt Hosp Ctr 2000; Ophthalmology, SUNY Downstate Med Ctr 2003; **Fellow:** Oculoplastic & Reconstructive Surgery, Jules Stein Eye Inst 2005; Facial Plastic Surgery, UCLA Med Ctr 2006; **Fac Appt:** Assoc Prof Oph, Albert Einstein Coll Med

Seedor, John A MD (Oph) - **Spec Exp:** Cornea & External Eye Disease; Laser Vision Surgery; Laser Refractive Surgery; Cataract Surgery; **Hospital:** New York Eye & Ear Infirm of Mt Sinai; **Address:** Ophthalmic Consultants, 310 E 14th St, Ste 219, New York, NY 10003-4201; **Phone:** 212-505-6550; **Board Cert:** Ophthalmology 1987; **Med School:** Hahnemann Univ 1981; **Resid:** Ophthalmology, NY Eye & Ear Infirm 1985; **Fellow:** Cornea, Emory Univ Hosp 1987; **Fac Appt:** Assoc Clin Prof Oph, NY Med Coll

Serle, Janet B MD (Oph) - **Spec Exp:** Glaucoma; **Hospital:** Mt Sinai Hosp, New York Eye & Ear Infirm of Mt Sinai; **Address:** 17 E 102 St, Fl 8, Box 1183, New York, NY 10029; **Phone:** 212-241-0939; **Board Cert:** Ophthalmology 1987; **Med School:** Harvard Med Sch 1980; **Resid:** Ophthalmology, Mount Sinai Hosp 1985; **Fellow:** Glaucoma, Mount Sinai Hosp 1986; **Fac Appt:** Prof Oph, Mount Sinai-Icahn Sch of Med

Shabto, Uri MD (Oph) - **Spec Exp:** Retinopathy of Prematurity; Macular Disease/Degeneration; Diabetic Eye Disease/Retinopathy; Retinal Detachment; **Hospital:** New York Eye & Ear Infirm of Mt Sinai; **Address:** Retina Consultants of NY, 310 E 14th St, Ste 419, New York, NY 10003; **Phone:** 212-677-2000; **Board Cert:** Ophthalmology 1991; **Med School:** Harvard Med Sch 1986; **Resid:** Ophthalmology, NY Eye & Ear Infirm 1990; **Fellow:** Vitreoretinal Surgery, Montefiore Hosp 1991; **Fac Appt:** Asst Clin Prof Oph, Mount Sinai-Icahn Sch of Med

Sherman, Spencer E MD (Oph) - **Spec Exp:** Cataract Surgery; Glaucoma; Contact Lenses; Refractive Surgery; **Hospital:** Lenox Hill Hosp (Manh Eye, Ear & Throat Hosp), Mt Sinai Hosp; **Address:** 166 E 63rd St, New York, NY 10065; **Phone:** 212-753-8300; **Board Cert:** Ophthalmology 1970; **Med School:** Columbia P&S 1962; **Resid:** Ophthalmology, Mt Sinai Hosp 1968; **Fac Appt:** Asst Clin Prof Oph, Mount Sinai Sch Med

Shulman, Julius MD (Oph) - **Spec Exp:** Cataract Surgery; LASIK-Refractive Surgery; Contact Lenses; Glaucoma; **Hospital:** Mt Sinai Hosp; **Address:** Eastside Eye Assocs, 229 E 79th St, New York, NY 10075; **Phone:** 212-861-6200; **Board Cert:** Ophthalmology 2006; **Med School:** SUNY Downstate 1969; **Resid:** Ophthalmology, Mt Sinai Med Ctr 1975; **Fac Appt:** Asst Clin Prof Oph, Mount Sinai Sch Med

Sidoti, Paul A MD (Oph) - **Spec Exp:** Glaucoma; **Hospital:** New York Eye & Ear Infirm of Mt Sinai, Mt Sinai Beth Israel; **Address:** 310 E 14th St, Ste 319, New York, NY 10003-4201; **Phone:** 212-979-4590; **Board Cert:** Ophthalmology 2005; **Med School:** Albert Einstein Coll Med 1988; **Resid:** Ophthalmology, NY Eye & Ear Infirm 1992; **Fellow:** Glaucoma, Doheny Eye Inst-USC 1994; **Fac Appt:** Prof Oph, NY Med Coll

Sippel, Kimberly MD (Oph) - **Spec Exp:** Corneal Disease; Laser Vision Surgery; Refractive Surgery; **Hospital:** NY-Presby/Weill Cornell Med Ctr, NY (page 102); **Address:** Laser Vision Ctr, 1305 York Ave Fl 12, New York, NY 10021; **Phone:** 646-962-2020; **Board Cert:** Ophthalmology 2012; **Med School:** Columbia P&S 1993; **Resid:** Surgery, Mass Genl Hosp 1995; Ophthalmology, Mass Eye & Ear 2000; **Fellow:** Cornea & Ext Eye Disease, Mass Eye & Ear 2001; **Fac Appt:** Assoc Prof Oph, Cornell Univ-Weill Med Coll

Slakter, Jason S MD (Oph) - **Spec Exp:** Retinal Disorders; Macular Degeneration; **Hospital:** Lenox Hill Hosp (Manh Eye, Ear & Throat Hosp); **Address:** Vitreous-Retina-Macula Consults of NY, 460 Park Ave Fl 5, New York, NY 10022; **Phone:** 212-861-9797; **Board Cert:** Ophthalmology 1989; **Med School:** Albert Einstein Coll Med 1983; **Resid:** Internal Medicine, Winthrop Univ Hosp 1984; Ophthalmology, Manhattan Eye & Ear Infirm 1987; **Fellow:** Retina/Vitreous Surgery, Manhattan Eye & Ear Infirm 1988; **Fac Appt:** Clin Prof Oph, NYU Sch Med

Solomon, Joel M MD (Oph) - **Spec Exp:** Cataract Surgery; Refractive Surgery; Glaucoma; **Hospital:** NYU Langone Med Ctr (page 104); **Address:** 614 2nd Ave, Ste C, New York, NY 10016; **Phone:** 212-689-5080; **Board Cert:** Ophthalmology 1987; **Med School:** Cornell Univ-Weill Med Coll 1981; **Resid:** Internal Medicine, Albany Med Ctr 1983; Ophthalmology, NYU Med Ctr 1986; **Fellow:** Cornea & Ext Eye Disease, Med Coll Wisc/Eye Inst 1987; **Fac Appt:** Clin Prof Oph, NYU Sch Med

Spaide, Richard F MD (Oph) - **Spec Exp:** Retinal Disorders; Macular Degeneration; Diabetic Eye Disease/Retinopathy; Retina/Vitreous Surgery; **Hospital:** Lenox Hill Hosp (Manh Eye, Ear & Throat Hosp); **Address:** VYMNY, 460 Park Ave Fl 5, New York, NY 10022; **Phone:** 212-861-9797; **Board Cert:** Ophthalmology 1987; **Med School:** Jefferson Med Coll 1981; **Resid:** Ophthalmology, St Vincents Hosp 1985; **Fellow:** Vitreoretinal Surgery & Disease, Manhattan EET Hosp 1990; **Fac Appt:** Assoc Clin Prof Oph, NY Med Coll

Sperber, Laurence TD MD (Oph) - **Spec Exp:** LASIK-Refractive Surgery; Cornea Transplant; Corneal Ring Implants; Cataract Surgery; **Hospital:** Lenox Hill Hosp (Manh Eye, Ear & Throat Hosp); **Address:** Refractive Laser Specialists of NY, 166 E 63rd St, New York, NY 10021; **Phone:** 212-753-8300; **Board Cert:** Ophthalmology 2013; **Med School:** Boston Univ 1987; **Resid:** Ophthalmology, Manhattan EET Hosp 1991; **Fellow:** Cornea & Ext Eye Disease, Wills Eye Hosp 1992; **Fac Appt:** Clin Prof Oph, NYU Sch Med

Starr, Christopher E MD (Oph) - **Spec Exp:** LASIK-Refractive Surgery; Cataract Surgery-Lens Implant; Cornea & External Eye Disease; Dry Eye Syndrome; **Hospital:** NY-Presby/Weill Cornell Med Ctr, NY (page 102); **Address:** 1305 York Ave, Fl 12, New York, NY 10028; **Phone:** 646-962-2020; **Board Cert:** Ophthalmology 2014; **Med School:** Cornell Univ-Weill Med Coll 1998; **Resid:** Ophthalmology, Mass Eye & Ear Infirm 2002; **Fellow:** Cornea & Refractive Surgery, Wilmer Eye Inst 2003; **Fac Appt:** Assoc Prof Oph, Cornell Univ-Weill Med Coll

Starr, Michael B MD (Oph) - **Spec Exp:** Cataract Surgery; Corneal Disease & Surgery; Eye Infections; **Hospital:** Lenox Hill Hosp (Manh Eye, Ear & Throat Hosp); **Address:** 67 E 78th St, New York, NY 10075; **Phone:** 212-717-0222; **Board Cert:** Ophthalmology 1978; **Med School:** Mount Sinai Sch Med 1972; **Resid:** Neurology, Mount Sinai 1974; Ophthalmology, Lenox Hill Hosp 1977; **Fellow:** Cornea, UCSF Med Ctr/Francis Proctor Fdn 1979; **Fac Appt:** Assoc Clin Prof Oph, Mount Sinai Sch Med

Steele, Mark MD (Oph) - **Spec Exp:** Pediatric Ophthalmology; Strabismus; Eye Muscle Disorders; **Hospital:** NYU Langone Med Ctr (page 104), New York Eye & Ear Infirm of Mt Sinai; **Address:** Pediatric Ophthalmic Consultants, 40 W 72nd St, New York, NY 10023; **Phone:** 212-981-9800; **Board Cert:** Ophthalmology 1991; **Med School:** NYU Sch Med 1986; **Resid:** Ophthalmology, NYU Med Ctr 1990; **Fellow:** Pediatric Ophthalmology, Wills Eye Hosp 1991; **Fac Appt:** Assoc Clin Prof Oph, NYU Sch Med

Suh, Leejee H MD (Oph) - **Spec Exp:** Cornea Transplant; Laser Vision Surgery; Cataract Surgery; **Hospital:** NY-Presby/Columbia Univ Med Ctr, NY (page 102); **Address:** Columbia Ophthalmology Consultants, Edward S Harkness Eye Inst, 635 W 165th St, New York, NY 10032; **Phone:** 212-305-9535; **Board Cert:** Ophthalmology 2009; **Med School:** NYU Sch Med 2002; **Resid:** Ophthalmology, Johns Hopkins Hosp 2006; **Fellow:** Cornea & Refractive Surgery, Bascom Palmer Eye Inst 2007; **Fac Appt:** Assoc Prof Oph, Columbia P&S

Tello, Celso MD (Oph) - **Spec Exp:** Glaucoma; Cataract Surgery; **Hospital:** New York Eye & Ear Infirm of Mt Sinai; **Address:** Glaucoma Assocs of NY, 310 E 14th St, South Bldg - Ste 304, New York, NY 10003; **Phone:** 212-477-7540; **Board Cert:** Ophthalmology 2011; **Med School:** Ecuador 1988; **Resid:** Ophthalmology, NY Eye & Ear Infirm 1998; **Fellow:** Glaucoma, NY Eye & Ear Infirm 2000; **Fac Appt:** Asst Prof Oph, NYU Sch Med

Walsh, Joseph B MD (Oph) - **Spec Exp:** Diabetic Eye Disease/Retinopathy; Macular Degeneration; Retinal Disorders; **Hospital:** New York Eye & Ear Infirm of Mt Sinai; **Address:** 310 E 14th St, S Bldg Fl 3 - Ste 319, New York, NY 10003-4201; **Phone:** 212-979-4282; **Board Cert:** Ophthalmology 2005; **Med School:** Georgetown Univ 1966; **Resid:** Internal Medicine, Univ Hosp 1968; Ophthalmology, NY Eye & Ear Infirmary 1973; **Fellow:** Retina/Vitreous Surgery, Montefiore Med Ctr 1974; **Fac Appt:** Prof Oph, NY Med Coll

Wang, Frederick M MD (Oph) - **Spec Exp:** Pediatric Ophthalmology; Strabismus; Eye Muscle Disorders; **Hospital:** Lenox Hill Hosp (Manh Eye, Ear & Throat Hosp), Montefiore Med Ctr-Moses Campus (page 100); **Address:** 30 E 40th St, Ste 405, New York, NY 10016-1201; **Phone:** 212-684-3980; **Board Cert:** Pediatrics 1978; Ophthalmology 1980; **Med School:** Albert Einstein Coll Med 1972; **Resid:** Pediatrics, Jacobi Med Ctr 1974; Ophthalmology, Jacobi Med Ctr 1979; **Fellow:** Pediatric Ophthalmology, Chldns Hosp Natl Med Ctr 1980; **Fac Appt:** Clin Prof Oph, Albert Einstein Coll Med

Warren, Floyd A MD (Oph) - **Spec Exp:** Neuro-Ophthalmology; Optic Nerve Disorders; Orbital Diseases; Diplopia; **Hospital:** NYU Langone Med Ctr (page 104), Lenox Hill Hosp (Manh Eye, Ear & Throat Hosp); **Address:** NYU Langone Med Ctr-Dept of Ophthalmology, 530 First Ave, Ste 3B, New York, NY 10016; **Phone:** 212-263-7030; **Board Cert:** Ophthalmology 1985; **Med School:** NYU Sch Med 1979; **Resid:** Ophthalmology, St Vincents Hosp 1983; **Fellow:** Neuro-Ophthalmology, NYU Med Ctr 1984; Neuro-Ophthalmology, Eye & Ear Hosp 1985; **Fac Appt:** Clin Prof Oph, NYU Sch Med

Weiss, Michael J MD/PhD (Oph) - **Spec Exp:** Uveitis; Retinal Disorders; Cataract Surgery; Diabetic Eye Disease; **Hospital:** NY-Presby/Columbia Univ Med Ctr, NY (page 102); **Address:** 635 W 165th St, Ste 101, New York, NY 10032-3701; **Phone:** 212-305-9925; **Board Cert:** Ophthalmology 1987; **Med School:** Columbia P&S 1981; **Resid:** Ophthalmology, Columbia-Presby Med Ctr 1985; **Fac Appt:** Clin Prof Oph, Columbia P&S

Weseley, Peter E MD (Oph) - **Spec Exp:** Retina/Vitreous Surgery; Macular Degeneration; Diabetic Eye Disease/Retinopathy; **Hospital:** New York Eye & Ear Infirm of Mt Sinai; **Address:** 310 E 14th St, Ste 419, New York, NY 10003; **Phone:** 212-979-4286; **Board Cert:** Ophthalmology 2013; **Med School:** Tulane Univ 1987; **Resid:** Ophthalmology, NY E&E Infirm 1991; **Fellow:** Retina/Vitreous Surgery, Devers Eye Inst 1993

Whitmore, Wayne G MD (Oph) - **Spec Exp:** Cataract Surgery; Glaucoma; Corneal Disease; **Hospital:** NY-Presby/Weill Cornell Med Ctr, NY (page 102), Lenox Hill Hosp (Manh Eye, Ear & Throat Hosp); **Address:** 116 E 68th St, New York, NY 10065; **Phone:** 212-249-3030; **Board Cert:** Ophthalmology 1982; **Med School:** Dartmouth Med Sch 1977; **Resid:** Surgery, Baystate Med Ctr 1978; Ophthalmology, NY-Presby/Weill Cornell Med Ctr 1981; **Fellow:** Ophthalmic Oncology, NY-Presby/Weill Cornell Med Ctr 1982; **Fac Appt:** Asst Clin Prof Oph, Cornell Univ-Weill Med Coll

Wisnicki, H. Jay MD (Oph) - **Spec Exp:** Strabismus; Eye Muscle Disorders; Pediatric Ophthalmology; **Hospital:** New York Eye & Ear Infirm of Mt Sinai; **Address:** Union Square Eye Care, 235 Park Ave S Fl 2, New York, NY 10003; **Phone:** 212-844-2020; **Board Cert:** Ophthalmology 1987; **Med School:** SUNY Hlth Sci Ctr 1981; **Resid:** Ophthalmology, Mt Sinai Hosp 1985; **Fellow:** Strabismus, Johns Hopkins Hosp 1986; **Fac Appt:** Clin Prof Oph, Albert Einstein Coll Med

Wong, Raymond F MD (Oph) - **Spec Exp:** Diabetic Eye Disease/Retinopathy; Retinal Detachment; Macular Disease/Degeneration; **Hospital:** New York Eye & Ear Infirm of Mt Sinai; **Address:** 139 Centre St, Ste PH 105, New York, NY 10013; **Phone:** 212-227-5451; **Board Cert:** Ophthalmology 1990; **Med School:** SUNY Hlth Sci Ctr 1984; **Resid:** Ophthalmology, Yale-New Haven Hosp 1988; **Fellow:** Retina/Vitreous Surgery, USC-Doheny Eye Inst 1990; **Fac Appt:** Asst Prof Oph, NY Med Coll

Yagoda, Arnold D MD (Oph) - **Spec Exp:** Macular Degeneration; Laser Vision Surgery; Diabetic Eye Disease/Retinopathy; Retinal Disorders; **Hospital:** New York Eye & Ear Infirm of Mt Sinai; **Address:** 67 E 78th St, New York, NY 10075; **Phone:** 212-744-2513; **Board Cert:** Ophthalmology 1980; **Med School:** Cornell Univ-Weill Med Coll 1975; **Resid:** Ophthalmology, Lenox Hill Hosp 1979; **Fellow:** Vitreoretinal Disease, Montefiore Hosp Med Ctr 1980; **Fac Appt:** Asst Clin Prof Oph, Albert Einstein Coll Med

Yannuzzi, Lawrence A MD (Oph) - **Spec Exp:** Retina/Vitreous Surgery; Macular Disease/Degeneration; Diabetic Eye Disease/Retinopathy; **Hospital:** NY-Presby/Columbia Univ Med Ctr, NY (page 102), Lenox Hill Hosp (Manh Eye, Ear & Throat Hosp); **Address:** Vitreous-Retina-Macula Consultants of NY, 460 Park Ave Fl 5, New York, NY 10022; **Phone:** 212-861-9797; **Board Cert:** Ophthalmology 1970; **Med School:** Boston Univ 1964; **Resid:** Ophthalmology, Manhattan EE&T Hosp 1968; **Fellow:** Ophthalmology, Manhattan EE&T Hosp 1971; **Fac Appt:** Clin Prof Oph, Columbia P&S

Young, Joshua A MD (Oph) - **Spec Exp:** Glaucoma; Corneal Disease; **Hospital:** NYU Langone Med Ctr (page 104), Lenox Hill Hosp (Manh Eye, Ear & Throat Hosp); **Address:** Madison Ophthalmology, 161 Madison Ave, Ste 5 SE, New York, NY 10016; **Phone:** 212-448-0101; **Board Cert:** Ophthalmology 2008; **Med School:** NYU Sch Med 1990; **Resid:** Ophthalmology, NYU Med Ctr 1994; **Fellow:** Cornea & Ext Eye Disease, Mass Eye & Ear Infirm/Harvard 1996; **Fac Appt:** Clin Prof Oph, NYU Sch Med

Zweifach, Philip H MD (Oph) - **Spec Exp:** Cataract Surgery; Neuro-Ophthalmology; **Hospital:** NY-Presby/Weill Cornell Med Ctr, NY (page 102); **Address:** 131 E 69th St, New York, NY 10021-5158; **Phone:** 212-535-1508; **Board Cert:** Ophthalmology 1968; **Med School:** Cornell Univ-Weill Med Coll 1961; **Resid:** Neurology, Boston City Hosp 1963; Ophthalmology, New York Hosp 1966; **Fellow:** Neuro-Ophthalmology, Mass Eye & Ear Infirmary 1967; **Fac Appt:** Clin Prof Oph, Cornell Univ-Weill Med Coll

Orthopaedic Surgery

Adler, Edward M MD (OrS) - **Spec Exp:** Hip Surgery; Knee Surgery; Joint Replacement; Shoulder Surgery; **Hospital:** NYU Hosp For Joint Dis (page 104), NYU Langone Med Ctr (page 104); **Address:** Madison Ave Ortho Assocs, 145 E 32nd St Fl 4th, New York, NY 10016; **Phone:** 212-427-3986; **Board Cert:** Orthopaedic Surgery 2013; **Med School:** UMDNJ-NJ Med Sch, Newark 1984; **Resid:** Orthopaedic Surgery, University Hosp 1989; **Fellow:** Joint Replacement Surgery, Hosp for Joint Diseases 1990; **Fac Appt:** Assoc Clin Prof OrS, NYU Sch Med

Ahmad, Christopher S MD (OrS) - **Spec Exp:** Sports Medicine; Knee Injuries/ACL; Pediatric Orthopaedic Surgery; Shoulder & Elbow Surgery; **Hospital:** NY-Presby/Columbia Univ Med Ctr, NY (page 102); **Address:** NY-Presby, Orthopaedic Surgery, 161 Fort Washington Ave Fl 2, New York, NY 10032; **Phone:** 212-305-4565; **Board Cert:** Orthopaedic Surgery 2014; Orthopaedic Sports Medicine 2014; **Med School:** NYU Sch Med 1994; **Resid:** Orthopaedic Surgery, NY-Presby/Columbia Univ Med Ctr 2000; **Fellow:** Sports Medicine, Kerlan-Jobe Ortho Clin 2001; **Fac Appt:** Assoc Prof OrS, Columbia P&S

Alexiades, Michael M MD (OrS) - **Spec Exp:** Hip Replacement; Knee Replacement; Arthroscopic Surgery; Minimally Invasive Surgery; **Hospital:** Hosp For Special Surgery (page 109), Lenox Hill Hosp; **Address:** 523 E 72nd St Fl 7, East River Profl Bldg, New York, NY 10021; **Phone:** 212-774-7557; **Board Cert:** Orthopaedic Surgery 2012; **Med School:** Cornell Univ-Weill Med Coll 1983; **Resid:** Surgery, Lenox Hill Hosp 1984; Orthopaedic Surgery, Lenox Hill Hosp 1988; **Fellow:** Arthritis Surgery, Hosp for Special Surgery 1989; **Fac Appt:** Asst Clin Prof OrS, Cornell Univ-Weill Med Coll

Allen, Answorth A MD (OrS) - **Spec Exp:** Shoulder & Elbow Surgery; Knee Surgery; Shoulder & Knee Reconstruction; Sports Medicine; **Hospital:** Hosp For Special Surgery (page 109); **Address:** HSS, Orthopaedic Surgery, 525 E 71st St, New York, NY 10021; **Phone:** 212-606-1447; **Board Cert:** Orthopaedic Surgery 2007; Orthopaedic Sports Medicine 2009; **Med School:** Cornell Univ 1988; **Resid:** Orthopaedic Surgery, NY-Presby/Columbia Univ Med Ctr 1993; **Fellow:** Orthopaedic Sports Medicine, Univ Pittsburgh Hosp 1994; **Fac Appt:** Assoc Prof OrS, Cornell Univ-Weill Med Coll

Bauman, Phillip A MD (OrS) - **Spec Exp:** Foot & Ankle Surgery; Knee Surgery; Dance/Sports Medicine; Arthroscopic Surgery; **Hospital:** Mt Sinai Roosevelt; **Address:** 343 W 58th St, New York, NY 10019; **Phone:** 212-506-0228; **Board Cert:** Orthopaedic Surgery 2011; **Med School:** Columbia P&S 1981; **Resid:** Surgery, St Lukes-Roosevelt Hosp Ctr 1984; Orthopaedic Surgery, NY-Presby/Columbia Univ Med Ctr 1987; **Fac Appt:** Asst Prof OrS, Columbia P&S

Bendo, John A MD (OrS) - **Spec Exp:** Spinal Surgery-Minimally Invasive; Scoliosis; Spinal Disc Replacement; Spinal Reconstructive Surgery; **Hospital:** NYU Hosp For Joint Dis (page 104), NYU Langone Med Ctr (page 104); **Address:** NYU, Musculoskeletal Care, 333 E 38th St, Fl 6, New York, NY 10016; **Phone:** 212-598-6625; **Board Cert:** Orthopaedic Surgery 2008; **Med School:** Mount Sinai Sch Med 1989; **Resid:** Orthopaedic Surgery, Mt Sinai Hosp 1994; **Fellow:** Spine Surgery, NYU Hosp Joint Diseases 1995; **Fac Appt:** Assoc Prof OrS, NYU Sch Med

Bharam, Srino MD (OrS) - **Spec Exp:** Hip Surgery; Arthroscopic Surgery-Hip; Hip Resurfacing; Sports Medicine; **Hospital:** Lenox Hill Hosp, Mt Sinai St. Luke's; **Address:** Lenox Hill Hospital, 130 E 77th St Fl 8, New York, NY 10075; **Phone:** 212-691-3535; **Board Cert:** Orthopaedic Surgery 2015; Orthopaedic Sports Medicine 2015; **Med School:** UMDNJ-NJ Med Sch, Newark 1994; **Resid:** Orthopaedic Surgery, Lenox Hill Hosp 2000; **Fellow:** Trauma, Mass General Hosp 2001; Hip Sports Injuries/Arthroscopy, UPMC Ctr for Sports Med 2002

Bitan, Fabien D MD (OrS) - **Spec Exp:** Spinal Surgery-Pediatric & Adult; Spinal Deformity; Spinal Disorders-Degenerative; **Hospital:** Lenox Hill Hosp, Mt Sinai Beth Israel; **Address:** 215 E 77th St, New York, NY 10075; **Phone:** 212-717-7463; **Med School:** France 1985; **Resid:** Orthopaedic Surgery, Clinique Saint Leonard 1996; **Fellow:** Pediatric Orthopaedic Surgery, Hosp Special Surgery 1997; Spine Surgery, Beth Israel Med Ctr 1998

Boland, Patrick MD (OrS) - **Spec Exp:** Bone Cancer; Spinal Tumors; Bone & Soft Tissue Tumors; Limb Sparing Surgery; **Hospital:** Meml Sloan Kettering Canc Ctr (page 110); **Address:** Meml Sloan-Kettering Cancer Ctr, 1275 York Avenue, New York, NY 10065; **Phone:** 212-639-8684; **Board Cert:** Orthopaedic Surgery 2009; **Med School:** Ireland 1967; **Resid:** Surgery, Brigham & Women's Hosp 1973; Orthopaedic Surgery, Middlesex/Hammersmith Hosp 1981; **Fellow:** Orthopaedic Oncology, Meml Sloan-Kettering Cancer Ctr 1982

Bosco III, Joseph A MD (OrS) - **Spec Exp:** Sports Medicine; Knee Surgery; Shoulder Surgery; **Hospital:** NYU Hosp For Joint Dis (page 104), Jamaica Hosp Med Ctr; **Address:** Ctr for Musculoskeletal Care, 333 E 38th St, New York, NY 10016; **Phone:** 646-501-7223; **Board Cert:** Orthopaedic Surgery 2006; **Med School:** Univ VT Coll Med 1986; **Resid:** Orthopaedic Surgery, Univ NC Med Ctr 1991; **Fellow:** Reconstructive Surgery, Univ Ariz Coll Med Affil Hosp 1992; **Fac Appt:** Asst Clin Prof OrS, NYU Sch Med

Bostrom, Mathias P MD (OrS) - **Spec Exp:** Knee Replacement & Revision; Hip Replacement & Revision; Hip & Knee Reconstruction; Musculoskeletal Infections; **Hospital:** Hosp For Special Surgery (page 109), NY-Presby/Weill Cornell Med Ctr, NY (page 102); **Address:** HSS, Orthopaedic Surgery, 535 E 70th St, New York, NY 10021; **Phone:** 212-606-1674; **Board Cert:** Orthopaedic Surgery 2009; **Med School:** Johns Hopkins Univ 1989; **Resid:** Orthopaedic Surgery, Hosp Special Surgery 1995; **Fellow:** Adult Reconstructive Surgery, Hosp Special Surgery 1996; **Fac Appt:** Prof OrS, Cornell Univ-Weill Med Coll

Brisson, Paul M MD (OrS) - **Spec Exp:** Spinal Surgery; **Hospital:** NY-Presby/Lower Manhattan Hosp (page 102), NY-Presby/Weill Cornell Med Ctr, NY (page 102); **Address:** NY Spine Care, 51 E 25th St Fl 6, New York, NY 10010; **Phone:** 212-813-3632; **Board Cert:** Orthopaedic Surgery 2014; **Med School:** Univ Montreal 1979; **Resid:** Orthopaedic Surgery, McGill Med Ctr 1987; **Fellow:** Spine Surgery, Hosp Joint Diseases 1988; Spine Surgery, Buffalo Genl Hosp 1989

Bronson, Michael J MD (OrS) - **Spec Exp:** Knee Replacement; Hip Replacement; Arthritis; **Hospital:** Mt Sinai Hosp; **Address:** Mt Sinai Med Ctr, Dept Orthopedic Surg, 5 E 98th St, Box 1188, New York, NY 10029; **Phone:** 212-241-1640; **Board Cert:** Orthopaedic Surgery 1984; **Med School:** NY Med Coll 1976; **Resid:** Orthopaedic Surgery, Lenox Hill Hosp 1980; **Fellow:** Joint Replacement Surgery, NY Presby/Columbia Med Ctr 1981; **Fac Appt:** Assoc Prof OrS, Mount Sinai Sch Med

Buly, Robert L MD (OrS) - **Spec Exp:** Hip Replacement & Revision; Arthroscopic Surgery-Hip; Knee Replacement; Arthritis; **Hospital:** Hosp For Special Surgery (page 109), NY-Presby/Weill Cornell Med Ctr, NY (page 102); **Address:** Hospital for Special Surgery, 535 E 70th St, New York, NY 10021; **Phone:** 212-606-1971; **Board Cert:** Orthopaedic Surgery 2014; **Med School:** Cornell Univ-Weill Med Coll 1985; **Resid:** Orthopaedic Surgery, Hosp for Special Surg 1990; **Fellow:** Hip Surgery, Mueller Fdn 1991; Joint Reconstruction, Case Western Res/Univ Hosp 1991; **Fac Appt:** Assoc Clin Prof OrS, Cornell Univ-Weill Med Coll

Cammisa Jr, Frank P MD (OrS) - **Spec Exp:** Spinal Surgery; Spinal Disc Replacement; Minimally Invasive Spinal Surgery; Scoliosis; **Hospital:** Hosp For Special Surgery (page 109); **Address:** HSS, Spine Svc, 523 E 72nd St Fl 3, New York, NY 10021; **Phone:** 212-606-1946; **Board Cert:** Orthopaedic Surgery 2011; **Med School:** Columbia P&S 1982; **Resid:** Orthopaedic Surgery, Hosp Special Surgery 1987; **Fellow:** Spine Surgery, Jackson Meml Hosp 1988; **Fac Appt:** Assoc Prof OrS, Cornell Univ-Weill Med Coll

Casden, Andrew M MD (OrS) - **Spec Exp:** Spinal Surgery; Spinal Disc Replacement; Minimally Invasive Spinal Surgery; Scoliosis; **Hospital:** Mt Sinai Hosp, Mt Sinai Beth Israel; **Address:** Mount Sinai Med Ctr, Dept Orth Surg, 5 E 98th St, Fl 9, Box 1188, New York, NY 10029; **Phone:** 212-241-8947; **Board Cert:** Orthopaedic Surgery 2012; **Med School:** Cornell Univ-Weill Med Coll 1983; **Resid:** Orthopaedic Surgery, Hosp Joint Diseases 1988; **Fellow:** Spine Surgery, Rush-Presby Med Ctr 1989; **Fac Appt:** Assoc Prof OrS, Mount Sinai Sch Med

Chapman, Cary B MD (OrS) - **Spec Exp:** Sports Medicine; Arthroscopic Surgery; Foot & Ankle Surgery-Complex; Cartilage Damage & Transplant; **Hospital:** NYU Hosp For Joint Dis (page 104), Staten Island Univ Hosp - North; **Address:** Ortho & Sports Med Consultants of NY, 860 Fifth Ave, Fl Ground, New York, NY 10065; **Phone:** 212-877-3338; **Board Cert:** Orthopaedic Surgery 2007; Orthopaedic Sports Medicine 2011; **Med School:** Columbia P&S 1998; **Resid:** Surgery, NY-Presby/Columbia Univ Med Ctr 2000; Orthopaedic Surgery, NY-Presby/Columbia Univ Med Ctr 2004; **Fellow:** Orthopaedic Research, NY-Presby/Columbia Univ Med Ctr 1999; Foot & Ankle Surgery, Roger Mann MD 2004; **Fac Appt:** Asst Clin Prof OrS, NYU Sch Med

Compito, Catherine A MD (OrS) - **Spec Exp:** Shoulder Surgery; Elbow Surgery; Sports Medicine; Arthroscopic Surgery; **Hospital:** Mt Sinai Beth Israel; **Address:** Beth Israel Orthopedics and Sports Med, 10 Union Square E, Ste 3K, New York, NY 10003; **Phone:** 212-844-8544; **Board Cert:** Orthopaedic Surgery 2009; Orthopaedic Sports Medicine 2011; **Med School:** Albert Einstein Coll Med 1986; **Resid:** Orthopaedic Surgery, Montefiore Med Ctr 1991; **Fellow:** Sports Medicine & Arthroscopic Surgery, Staten Island Univ Hosp 1993; Elbow & Shoulder Surgery, NY-Presby/Columbia Univ Med Ctr 1993

Cordasco, Frank A MD (OrS) - **Spec Exp:** Sports Medicine; Arthroscopic Surgery-Shoulder; Rotator Cuff Surgery; Shoulder Replacement; **Hospital:** Hosp For Special Surgery (page 109); **Address:** Hosp for Special Surgery, 525 E 71 St Fl 2nd, Belaire Bldg, New York, NY 10021; **Phone:** 212-606-1636; **Board Cert:** Orthopaedic Surgery 2013; Orthopaedic Sports Medicine 2009; **Med School:** UMDNJ-NJ Med Sch, Newark 1985; **Resid:** Surgery, NY Univ Med Ctr 1996; Orthopaedic Surgery, Columbia-Presby Hosp 1990; **Fellow:** Elbow & Shoulder Surgery, Columbia-Presby Hosp 1991; **Fac Appt:** Assoc Prof OrS, Cornell Univ-Weill Med Coll

Cornell, Charles N MD (OrS) - **Spec Exp:** Hip Replacement; Knee Replacement; **Hospital:** Hosp For Special Surgery (page 109); **Address:** HSS, Hip & Knee Surgery, 535 E 70th St Fl 3, New York, NY 10021; **Phone:** 212-606-1414; **Board Cert:** Orthopaedic Surgery 2009; **Med School:** Cornell Univ-Weill Med Coll 1980; **Resid:** Surgery, NY-Presby/Weill Cornell Med Ctr 1982; Orthopaedic Surgery, Hosp Special Surgery 1985; **Fellow:** Orthopaedic Trauma, Univ Washington Med Ctr 1985; **Fac Appt:** Prof OrS, Cornell Univ-Weill Med Coll

Craig, Edward V MD (OrS) - **Spec Exp:** Shoulder Arthroscopic Surgery; Shoulder Replacement; Sports Medicine; Elbow Surgery; **Hospital:** Hosp For Special Surgery (page 109), NY-Presby/Weill Cornell Med Ctr, NY (page 102); **Address:** Hosp for Special Surgery, 535 E 70th St, New York, NY 10021; **Phone:** 212-606-1966; **Board Cert:** Orthopaedic Surgery 1984; **Med School:** Columbia P&S 1972; **Resid:** Surgery, St Lukes-Roosevelt Hosp 1976; Orthopaedic Surgery, Columbia-Presby Hosp 1980; **Fellow:** Shoulder Surgery, Columbia-Presby Hosp 1981; Hand Surgery, Columbia-Presby Hosp 1982; **Fac Appt:** Clin Prof OrS, Cornell Univ-Weill Med Coll

Cuomo, Frances MD (OrS) - **Spec Exp:** Shoulder Surgery; Elbow Surgery; Arthroscopic Surgery; **Hospital:** Mt Sinai Beth Israel; **Address:** Beth Israel Orthpaedics & Sports Med, 10 Union Square E, Ste 3M, New York, NY 10003; **Phone:** 212-844-6938; **Board Cert:** Orthopaedic Surgery 2012; **Med School:** NYU Sch Med 1983; **Resid:** Orthopaedic Surgery, Lenox Hill Hosp 1988; **Fellow:** Shoulder Surgery, Columbia-Presby Med Ctr 1989; **Fac Appt:** Asst Prof OrS, Albert Einstein Coll Med

Cushner, Fred D MD (OrS) - **Spec Exp:** Knee Reconstruction; Knee Injuries/Ligament Surgery; Cartilage Damage; Sports Medicine; **Hospital:** Lenox Hill Hosp, Southside Hosp; **Address:** ISK-Inst for Ortho & Sports Med, 210 E 64th St Fl 4, New York, NY 10065; **Phone:** 212-434-4312; **Board Cert:** Orthopaedic Surgery 2007; **Med School:** Med Univ SC 1988; **Resid:** Orthopaedic Surgery, Univ SC Med Ctr 1993; **Fellow:** Knee Reconstruction, Beth Israel Med Ctr 1994; Orthopaedic Sports Medicine, ISK-Inst for Ortho & Sports Med 1995

Deland, Jonathan T MD (OrS) - **Spec Exp:** Foot & Ankle Surgery; Sports Medicine; Arthritis; **Hospital:** Hosp For Special Surgery (page 109); **Address:** HSS, Foot & Ankle, 523 E 72nd St Fl 5, New York, NY 10021; **Phone:** 212-606-1665; **Board Cert:** Orthopaedic Surgery 2013; **Med School:** Columbia P&S 1980; **Resid:** Surgery, St Lukes-Roosevelt Hosp Ctr 1982; Orthopaedic Surgery, Mass Genl Hosp 1987; **Fellow:** Foot & Ankle Surgery, St Lukes-Roosevelt Hosp Ctr 1988; Trauma, Mass Genl Hosp 1989; **Fac Appt:** Prof OrS, Cornell Univ-Weill Med Coll

Egol, Kenneth A MD (OrS) - **Spec Exp:** Trauma; Reconstructive Surgery; Limb Lengthening; Fractures-Non Union; **Hospital:** NYU Hosp For Joint Dis (page 104), Jamaica Hosp Med Ctr; **Address:** 303 2nd Ave, Ste 21, New York, NY 10003; **Phone:** 212-598-3889; **Board Cert:** Orthopaedic Surgery 2012; **Med School:** SUNY Upstate Med Univ 1993; **Resid:** Orthopaedic Surgery, NYU Hosp Joint Diseases 1998; **Fellow:** Trauma, Carolinas Med Ctr 1999; **Fac Appt:** Prof OrS, NYU Sch Med

Elliott, Andrew J MD (OrS) - **Spec Exp:** Foot & Ankle Surgery; Arthroscopic Surgery; Sports Injuries; **Hospital:** Hosp For Special Surgery (page 109); **Address:** Hosp for Special Surgery, Dept Orthopaedic Surg, 420 E 72nd St, Ste 1B, New York, NY 10021; **Phone:** 212-203-0740; **Board Cert:** Orthopaedic Surgery 2010; **Med School:** Harvard Med Sch 1991; **Resid:** Surgery, Yale-New Haven Hosp 1996; **Fellow:** Orthopaedic Surgery, Hosp Special Surgery 1997; **Fac Appt:** Asst Clin Prof OrS, Cornell Univ-Weill Med Coll

Ellis, Scott J MD (OrS) - **Spec Exp:** Foot & Ankle Surgery; Fractures; Arthritis; Ankle Replacement & Revision; **Hospital:** Hosp For Special Surgery (page 109); **Address:** Hospital for Special Surgery, 523 E 72nd St Fl 5, New York, NY 10021; **Phone:** 646-797-8305; **Board Cert:** Orthopaedic Surgery 2010; **Med School:** Johns Hopkins Univ 2002; **Resid:** Orthopaedic Surgery, Hosp Special Surgery 2007; **Fellow:** Foot & Ankle Surgery, Hosp Special Surgery 2008; **Fac Appt:** Asst Prof OrS, Cornell Univ-Weill Med Coll

Errico, Thomas J MD (OrS) - **Spec Exp:** Spinal Surgery; Pediatric Orthopaedic Surgery; Scoliosis; **Hospital:** NYU Hosp For Joint Dis (page 104), NYU Langone Med Ctr (page 104); **Address:** NYU, Musculoskeletal Care, 333 E 38th St, Fl 6, New York, NY 10016; **Phone:** 646-501-7200; **Board Cert:** Orthopaedic Surgery 2007; **Med School:** UMDNJ-NJ Med Sch, Newark 1978; **Resid:** Orthopaedic Surgery, NYU Med Ctr 1983; **Fellow:** Spine Surgery, Toronto Genl Hosp 1984; **Fac Appt:** Prof OrS, NYU Sch Med

Farmer, James C MD (OrS) - **Spec Exp:** Spinal Disorders-Degenerative; Trauma; Spinal Surgery; **Hospital:** Hosp For Special Surgery (page 109); **Address:** Hosp for Special Surgery, 523 E 72nd St Fl 3, East River Professional Bldg, New York, NY 10021; **Phone:** 212-606-1591; **Board Cert:** Orthopaedic Surgery 2007; **Med School:** Georgetown Univ 1988; **Resid:** Orthopaedic Surgery, Hosp Univ Penn 1993; **Fellow:** Spine Surgery, Thos Jefferson Univ Hosp 1994; **Fac Appt:** Assoc Prof OrS, Cornell Univ-Weill Med Coll

Fealy, Stephen MD (OrS) - **Spec Exp:** Sports Medicine; Shoulder Arthroscopic Surgery; Shoulder Replacement; Knee Replacement; **Hospital:** Hosp For Special Surgery (page 109); **Address:** Hosp for Special Surgery, 523 E 72nd St Fl 2nd, New York, NY 10021; **Phone:** 212-606-1894; **Board Cert:** Orthopaedic Surgery 2004; **Med School:** Columbia P&S 1995; **Resid:** Orthopaedic Surgery, Hosp for Special Surg 2000; **Fellow:** Sports Medicine, Hosp for Special Surg 2001; **Fac Appt:** Asst Prof OrS, Cornell Univ-Weill Med Coll

Feldman, David S MD (OrS) - **Spec Exp:** Limb Deformities; Spinal Surgery; Pediatric Orthopaedic Surgery; Scoliosis; **Hospital:** NYU Hosp For Joint Dis (page 104), NYU Langone Med Ctr (page 104); **Address:** 67 Irving Pl Fl 8, New York, NY 10003; **Phone:** 212-533-5310; **Board Cert:** Orthopaedic Surgery 2007; **Med School:** Albert Einstein Coll Med 1988; **Resid:** Surgery, NYU Med Ctr 1989; Orthopaedic Surgery, NYU Hosp Joint Diseases 1993; **Fellow:** Pediatric Surgery, Hosp Sick Chldn 1994; **Fac Appt:** Prof OrS, NYU Sch Med

Figgie, Mark P MD (OrS) - **Spec Exp:** Joint Replacement; Minimally Invasive Surgery; Hip Surgery; Knee Surgery; **Hospital:** Hosp For Special Surgery (page 109); **Address:** 535 E 70th St Fl 3, New York, NY 10021; **Phone:** 212-606-1932; **Board Cert:** Orthopaedic Surgery 2011; **Med School:** Case West Res Univ 1981; **Resid:** Orthopaedic Surgery, Univ Hosps Case Med Ctr 1986; **Fellow:** Biomedical Engineering, Hosp for Special Surg 1987; Arthritis Surgery, Hosp for Special Surg 1988; **Fac Appt:** Clin Prof OrS, Cornell Univ-Weill Med Coll

Flatow, Evan L MD (OrS) - **Spec Exp:** Rotator Cuff Surgery; Shoulder Injuries; Shoulder Replacement; Shoulder Arthroscopic Surgery; **Hospital:** Mt Sinai Hosp, Mt Sinai Roosevelt; **Address:** Mt Sinai Hosp, Orthopaedic Surgery, 5 E 98th St, Fl 9, Box 1188, New York, NY 10029; **Phone:** 212-523-7100; **Board Cert:** Orthopaedic Surgery 2010; **Med School:** Columbia P&S 1981; **Resid:** Surgery, St Lukes-Roosevelt Hosp Ctr 1983; Orthopaedic Surgery, NY-Presby/Columbia Univ Med Ctr 1986; **Fellow:** Shoulder Surgery, NY-Presby/Columbia Univ Med Ctr 1987; **Fac Appt:** Prof OrS, Mount Sinai-Icahn Sch of Med

Fragomen, Austin T MD (OrS) - **Spec Exp:** Limb Deformities; Limb Lengthening; Bone Infections; Blount's Disease; **Hospital:** Hosp For Special Surgery (page 109); **Address:** HSS, Limb Lengthening, 519 E 72nd St, Ste 204, New York, NY 10021; **Phone:** 212-606-1550; **Board Cert:** Orthopaedic Surgery 2007; **Med School:** SUNY Downstate 1997; **Resid:** Surgery, Montefiore Med Ctr 1998; Orthopaedic Surgery, Westchester Med Ctr 2003; **Fellow:** Limb Lengthening, Hosp Special Surgery 2005; **Fac Appt:** Assoc Prof OrS, Cornell Univ-Weill Med Coll

Girardi, Federico P MD (OrS) - **Spec Exp:** Spinal Surgery; Spinal Deformity; Minimally Invasive Spinal Surgery; Spinal Disc Replacement; **Hospital:** Hosp For Special Surgery (page 109); **Address:** HSS Spine Service, 523 E 72nd St Fl 3, New York, NY 10021; **Phone:** 212-606-1946; **Board Cert:** Orthopaedic Surgery 2012; **Med School:** Argentina 1991; **Resid:** Orthopaedic Surgery, Buenos Aires University 1996; **Fellow:** Spine Surgery, Hosp Special Surgery 1999; **Fac Appt:** Asst Prof OrS, Cornell Univ-Weill Med Coll

Gladstone, James N MD (OrS) - **Spec Exp:** Shoulder & Knee Surgery; Cartilage Damage; Knee-Patella Problems; Arthritis; **Hospital:** Mt Sinai Hosp; **Address:** Mt Sinai Med Ctr, 5 E 98th St Fl 9, Box 1188, New York, NY 10029; **Phone:** 212-241-1645; **Board Cert:** Orthopaedic Surgery 2009; Orthopaedic Sports Medicine 2007; **Med School:** Tufts Univ 1990; **Resid:** Orthopaedic Surgery, Columbia-Presby Med Ctr 1995; **Fellow:** Sports Medicine, American Sports Med Inst 1996; **Fac Appt:** Assoc Prof OrS, Mount Sinai Sch Med

Glashow, Jonathan L MD (OrS) - **Spec Exp:** Sports Medicine; Shoulder Surgery; Knee Surgery; Arthroscopic Surgery; **Hospital:** Mt Sinai Hosp; **Address:** 737 Park Ave, Ste 1C, New York, NY 10021; **Phone:** 212-794-5096; **Board Cert:** Orthopaedic Surgery 2014; **Med School:** Cornell Univ-Weill Med Coll 1984; **Resid:** Orthopaedic Surgery, Lenox Hill Hosp 1989; **Fellow:** Arthroscopic Surgery, S CA Ortho Inst 1990; Shoulder Surgery, Univ TX Med Ctr 1990; **Fac Appt:** Assoc Clin Prof OrS, Mount Sinai-Icahn Sch of Med

Goldstein, Jeffrey A MD (OrS) - **Spec Exp:** Spinal Surgery; Minimally Invasive Spinal Surgery; Spinal Disc Replacement; Scoliosis; **Hospital:** NYU Hosp For Joint Dis (page 104), NYU Langone Med Ctr (page 104); **Address:** NYU Hospital for Joint Diseases, 233 Broadway, Ste 640, Woolworth Bldg, New York, NY 10279; **Phone:** 212-513-7711; **Board Cert:** Orthopaedic Surgery 2009; **Med School:** SUNY Downstate 1990; **Resid:** Orthopaedic Surgery, Case West Univ Med Ctr 1995; **Fellow:** Spine Surgery, Maryland Spine Ctr 1996; **Fac Appt:** Clin Prof OrS, NYU Sch Med

Green, Steven M MD (OrS) - **Spec Exp:** Hand & Wrist Surgery; Carpal Tunnel Syndrome; Hand Surgery; **Hospital:** Mt Sinai Hosp, NYU Hosp For Joint Dis (page 104); **Address:** 2 E 88th St, New York, NY 10128-0555; **Phone:** 212-348-6644; **Board Cert:** Orthopaedic Surgery 1977; **Med School:** Albert Einstein Coll Med 1970; **Resid:** Surgery, Georgia Bapt Hosp 1972; Orthopaedic Surgery, Mt Sinai Hosp 1975; **Fellow:** Hand Surgery, Thomas Jefferson Univ Hosp 1978; **Fac Appt:** Assoc Clin Prof OrS, NYU Sch Med

Greisberg, Justin K MD (OrS) - **Spec Exp:** Foot & Ankle Surgery-Complex; Ankle Replacement & Revision; Reconstructive Surgery; Trauma; **Hospital:** NY-Presby/Columbia Univ Med Ctr, NY (page 102); **Address:** Presby/Columbia Univ Med Ctr, Dept Orthopaedic Surgery, 622 W 168 St, Fl PH 11, rm 1153, New York, NY 10032; **Phone:** 212-305-5604; **Board Cert:** Orthopaedic Surgery 2004; **Med School:** Albert Einstein Coll Med 1995; **Resid:** Surgery, Brown Univ Affil Hosp 1996; Orthopaedic Surgery, Rhode Island Hosp 2000; **Fellow:** Orthopaedic Trauma, Rhode Island Hosp 2001; Foot & Ankle Surgery, Harborview Med Ctr 2002; **Fac Appt:** Assoc Clin Prof OrS, Columbia P&S

Grelsamer, Ronald P MD (OrS) - **Spec Exp:** Knee-Patella Problems Consult; Arthritis-Hip & Knee; Sports Medicine; **Hospital:** Mt Sinai Hosp; **Address:** 303 2nd Ave, Ste 19, New York, NY 10003; **Phone:** 646-704-4158; **Board Cert:** Orthopaedic Surgery 2008; **Med School:** Columbia P&S 1979; **Resid:** Orthopaedic Surgery, NY-Presby/Columbia Univ Med Ctr 1984; **Fellow:** Hip & Knee Surgery, NY-Presby/Columbia Univ Med Ctr 1985; **Fac Appt:** Assoc Clin Prof OrS, Mount Sinai Sch Med

Haas, Steven B MD (OrS) - **Spec Exp:** Knee Surgery; Knee Replacement; Minimally Invasive Knee Replacement; **Hospital:** Hosp For Special Surgery (page 109); **Address:** HSS, Knee Surgery, 535 E 70th St, Fl 3, New York, NY 10021; **Phone:** 212-606-1852; **Board Cert:** Orthopaedic Surgery 2014; **Med School:** Univ Rochester 1985; **Resid:** Orthopaedic Surgery, Hosp Special Surgery 1990; **Fellow:** Knee Surgery, Hosp Special Surgery 1991; **Fac Appt:** Clin Prof OrS, Cornell Univ-Weill Med Coll

Hamilton, William G MD (OrS) - **Spec Exp:** Dance Medicine; Sports Medicine; **Hospital:** Mt Sinai Roosevelt, Hosp For Special Surgery (page 109); **Address:** 343 W 58th St, New York, NY 10019-1173; **Phone:** 212-765-2260; **Board Cert:** Orthopaedic Surgery 1971; **Med School:** Columbia P&S 1964; **Resid:** Surgery, St Luke's-Roosevelt Hosp Ctr 1966; Orthopaedic Surgery, Columbia-Presby Hosp 1969; **Fellow:** Pediatric Orthopaedic Surgery, Newington Chldrn's Hosp 1970; **Fac Appt:** Clin Prof OrS, Columbia P&S

Hannafin, Jo Ann MD/PhD (OrS) - **Spec Exp:** Sports Medicine-Women; Shoulder Arthroscopic Surgery; Knee Injuries/Ligament Surgery; Ligament Reconstruction; **Hospital:** Hosp For Special Surgery (page 109); **Address:** HSS, Womens Sports Med, 523 E 72nd St, Fl 6, New York, NY 10021; **Phone:** 212-606-1469; **Board Cert:** Orthopaedic Surgery 2005; Orthopaedic Sports Medicine 2009; **Med School:** Albert Einstein Coll Med 1985; **Resid:** Orthopaedic Surgery, Montefiore Med Ctr 1990; **Fellow:** Orthopaedic Sports Medicine, Hosp Special Surgery 1992; **Fac Appt:** Prof OrS, Cornell Univ-Weill Med Coll

Harwin, Steven F MD (OrS) - **Spec Exp:** Hip & Knee Replacement; Minimally Invasive Surgery; Transfusion Free Surgery; Osteonecrosis; **Hospital:** Mt Sinai Beth Israel; **Address:** Ctr for Reconstructive Joint Surgery, 910 Park Ave, New York, NY 10075; **Phone:** 212-861-9800; **Board Cert:** Orthopaedic Surgery 1976; **Med School:** SUNY Upstate Med Univ 1971; **Resid:** Orthopaedic Surgery, Montefiore Med Ctr 1975; **Fellow:** Joint Replacement Surgery, Traveling Fellowship 1977; **Fac Appt:** Assoc Prof OrS, Albert Einstein Coll Med

Hausman, Michael R MD (OrS) - **Spec Exp:** Hand Reconstruction; Elbow Reconstruction; Reconstructive Microvascular Surgery; Arthroscopic Surgery; **Hospital:** Mt Sinai Hosp; **Address:** Mt Sinai Hosp, Orthopaedic Surgery, 5 E 98th St Fl 9, Box 1188, New York, NY 10029; **Phone:** 212-241-1658; **Board Cert:** Orthopaedic Surgery 2010; Hand Surgery 2010; **Med School:** Yale Univ 1979; **Resid:** Orthopaedic Surgery, Yale-New Haven Hosp 1985; **Fellow:** Hand Surgery, St Lukes-Roosevelt Hosp Ctr 1987; **Fac Appt:** Prof OrS, Mount Sinai-Icahn Sch of Med

Healey, John H MD (OrS) - **Spec Exp:** Bone Tumors; Hip & Knee Replacement in Bone Tumors; Sarcoma; Sarcoma-Soft Tissue; **Hospital:** Meml Sloan Kettering Canc Ctr (page 110), Hosp For Special Surgery (page 109); **Address:** MSKCC, Orthopaedic Surgery, 1275 York Ave, Ste A342, New York, NY 10065; **Phone:** 212-639-7610; **Board Cert:** Orthopaedic Surgery 2007; **Med School:** Univ VT Coll Med 1978; **Resid:** Orthopaedic Surgery, Hosp Special Surgery 1983; **Fellow:** Musculoskeletal Oncology, Meml Sloan-Kettering Cancer Ctr 1984; **Fac Appt:** Prof OrS, Cornell Univ-Weill Med Coll

Hecht, Andrew MD (OrS) - **Spec Exp:** Spinal Surgery; Minimally Invasive Spinal Surgery; Spinal Surgery-Neck; Spinal Cord Injury; **Hospital:** Mt Sinai Hosp; **Address:** Mt Sinai Hosp, Orthopaedic Surgery, 5 E 98th St Fl 4, Box 1188, New York, NY 10029; **Phone:** 212-241-0735; **Board Cert:** Orthopaedic Surgery 2014; **Med School:** Harvard Med Sch 1994; **Resid:** Orthopaedic Surgery, Mass Genl Hosp 1999; **Fellow:** Spine Surgery, Emory Univ Spine Ctr 2001; **Fac Appt:** Asst Prof OrS, Mount Sinai-Icahn Sch of Med

Helfet, David L MD (OrS) - **Spec Exp:** Fractures-Complex & Non Union; Deformity Reconstruction; Pelvic & Acetabular Fractures; Fractures-Stress; **Hospital:** Hosp For Special Surgery (page 109), NY-Presby/Weill Cornell Med Ctr, NY (page 102); **Address:** HSS, Orthopaedic Trauma, 525 E 71st St Fl 2, New York, NY 10021; **Phone:** 212-606-1888; **Board Cert:** Orthopaedic Surgery 1984; **Med School:** South Africa 1975; **Resid:** Surgery, Edendale Hosp 1977; Orthopaedic Surgery, Johns Hopkins Hosp 1981; **Fellow:** Orthopaedic Surgery, Insel Hosp 1981; Orthopaedic Sports Medicine, UCLA Med Ctr 1982; **Fac Appt:** Prof OrS, Cornell Univ-Weill Med Coll

Huang, Russel C MD (OrS) - **Spec Exp:** Minimally Invasive Spinal Surgery; Spinal Disc Replacement; Spinal Cord Injury; Scoliosis; **Hospital:** Hosp For Special Surgery (page 109); **Address:** Hosp for Special Surgery, East River Profl Bldg Fl 3, 523 E 72nd St, New York, NY 10021; **Phone:** 212-606-1634; **Board Cert:** Orthopaedic Surgery 2006; **Med School:** Yale Univ 1998; **Resid:** Orthopaedic Surgery, Hosp Special Surg 2003; **Fellow:** Spine Surgery, Univ Hosps Case Med Ctr 2004; **Fac Appt:** Asst Prof OrS, Cornell Univ-Weill Med Coll

Hubbard, Christopher E MD (OrS) - **Spec Exp:** Foot & Ankle Surgery; Sports Medicine; Arthroscopic Surgery; Ligament Reconstruction; **Hospital:** Mt Sinai Beth Israel; **Address:** BIMC, Orthopaedics & Sports Med, 10 Union Square E, Ste 3M, New York, NY 10003; **Phone:** 212-844-6940; **Board Cert:** Orthopaedic Surgery 2013; **Med School:** UMDNJ-NJ Med Sch, Newark 1994; **Resid:** Orthopaedic Surgery, NY-Presby/Columbia Univ Med Ctr 1999; **Fellow:** Foot & Ankle Surgery, Hosp Special Surgery 2000; **Fac Appt:** Asst Prof OrS, Albert Einstein Coll Med

Hyman, Joshua E MD (OrS) - **Spec Exp:** Pediatric Orthopaedic Surgery; Fractures-Pediatric; Scoliosis; Clubfoot/Foot Deformities in Children; **Hospital:** Morgan Stanley Chldns Hosp of NY-Presby, NY (page 102); **Address:** Columbia Orthopedics, 3959 Broadway, Ste 800N, New York, NY 10032; **Phone:** 212-305-5475; **Board Cert:** Orthopaedic Surgery 2013; **Med School:** Columbia P&S 1990; **Resid:** Surgery, Beth Israel Deaconess Med Ctr 1993; Orthopaedic Surgery, Mass Genl Hosp 1998; **Fellow:** Pediatric Orthopaedic Surgery, Hosp Sick Chldn 1999; **Fac Appt:** Assoc Prof OrS, Columbia P&S

Iorio, Richard MD (OrS) - **Spec Exp:** Joint Replacement; **Hospital:** NYU Langone Med Ctr (page 104); **Address:** NYU Langone Med Ctr, 333 E 38th St, New York, NY 10016; **Phone:** 646-501-7300; **Board Cert:** Orthopaedic Surgery 2015; **Med School:** Boston Univ 1986; **Resid:** Orthopaedic Surgery, Hahnemann Univ Hosp 1991; **Fellow:** Joint Reconstruction, Columbia-Presby Med Ctr 1992; **Fac Appt:** Prof OrS, NYU Sch Med

Kelly, Bryan T MD (OrS) - **Spec Exp:** Hip Surgery; Arthroscopic Surgery; Sports Medicine; **Hospital:** Hosp For Special Surgery (page 109); **Address:** HSS, Hip Preservation, 541 E 71st St, New York, NY 10021; **Phone:** 212-606-1159; **Board Cert:** Orthopaedic Surgery 2006; Orthopaedic Sports Medicine 2013; **Med School:** Duke Univ 1996; **Resid:** Orthopaedic Surgery, Hosp Special Surgery 2001; **Fellow:** Orthopaedic Sports Medicine, Hosp Special Surgery 2003; Hip Sports Injuries/Arthroscopy, UPMC 2004; **Fac Appt:** Assoc Prof OrS, Cornell Univ-Weill Med Coll

Kiernan, Howard A MD (OrS) - **Spec Exp:** Hip Disorders & Dysplasia; Knee Injuries; **Hospital:** NY-Presby/Columbia Univ Med Ctr, NY (page 102); **Address:** 903 Park Ave Fl 1st, New York, NY 10075; **Phone:** 212-602-1800; **Board Cert:** Orthopaedic Surgery 1975; **Med School:** NYU Sch Med 1966; **Resid:** Surgery, Bellevue Hosp Ctr-NYU 1970; Orthopaedic Surgery, Columbia-Presby Med Ctr/NY Ortho Hosp 1973; **Fellow:** Hip Surgery, NY Ortho Hosp 1974; **Fac Appt:** Clin Prof OrS, Columbia P&S

Kim, Yongjung MD (OrS) - **Spec Exp:** Spinal Surgery; Spinal Deformity; Minimally Invasive Spinal Surgery; Spinal Surgery-Pediatric & Adult; **Hospital:** NY-Presby/Columbia Univ Med Ctr, NY (page 102); **Address:** Columbia Orthopaedics, 161 Fort Washington Ave Fl 2, New York, NY 10032; **Phone:** 212-305-4565; **Med School:** Korea 1985; **Resid:** Surgery, Seoul Natl Univ Hosp 1986; Orthopaedic Surgery, Kumkang Genl Hosp 1990; **Fellow:** Spine Surgery, Asian Med Ctr 1994; Spinal Reconstructive Surgery, Hosp Special Surgery 2008; **Fac Appt:** Assoc Prof OrS, Columbia P&S

Klion, Mark J MD (OrS) - **Spec Exp:** Sports Medicine; Arthroscopic Surgery; Rotator Cuff Surgery; **Hospital:** Mt Sinai Hosp; **Address:** Manhattan Orthopedic & Sports Medicine Grp, 1065 Park Ave Fl 2, New York, NY 10128; **Phone:** 212-289-0700; **Board Cert:** Orthopaedic Surgery 2008; **Med School:** Mount Sinai Sch Med 1989; **Resid:** Orthopaedic Surgery, Mt Sinai Medv Ctr 1994; **Fellow:** Sports Medicine & Arthroscopic Surgery, Univ of Chicago Hosps 1995

Kuflik, Paul L MD (OrS) - **Spec Exp:** Spinal Surgery; Minimally Invasive Spinal Surgery; Spinal Deformity; Spinal Disc Replacement; **Hospital:** Mt Sinai Hosp; **Address:** Mt Sinai Med Ctr, Orthopaedics, 5 E 98th St Fl 4, New York, NY 10029; **Phone:** 212-241-8947; **Board Cert:** Orthopaedic Surgery 2010; **Med School:** SUNY Hlth Sci Ctr 1981; **Resid:** Orthopaedic Surgery, NYU Hosp For Joint Diseases 1986; **Fellow:** Spine Surgery, Toronto Genl Hosp 1986; **Fac Appt:** Assoc Prof OrS, Albert Einstein Coll Med

Lane, Joseph M MD (OrS) - **Spec Exp:** Bone Tumors-Benign; Bone Tumors-Metastatic; Bone Tumors; Bone Disorders-Metabolic; **Hospital:** Hosp For Special Surgery (page 109), NY-Presby/Weill Cornell Med Ctr, NY (page 102); **Address:** Hosp for Special Surgery-Ortho Surg Dept, 535 E 70th St, New York, NY 10021; **Phone:** 212-606-1172; **Board Cert:** Orthopaedic Surgery 1998; **Med School:** Harvard Med Sch 1965; **Resid:** Surgery, Hosp Univ Penn 1967; Orthopaedic Surgery, Hosp Univ Penn 1973; **Fellow:** Research, NIH 1969; **Fac Appt:** Prof OrS, Cornell Univ-Weill Med Coll

Lee, Francis Y MD/PhD (OrS) - **Spec Exp:** Bone & Soft Tissue Tumors; Pediatric Orthopaedic Surgery; Bone Tumors-Metastatic; Bone Tumors-Benign; **Hospital:** Morgan Stanley Chldns Hosp of NY-Presby, NY (page 102), NY-Presby/Columbia Univ Med Ctr, NY (page 102); **Address:** Columbia Univ Med Ctr, 3959 Broadway, Ste 800 N, New York, NY 10032; **Phone:** 212-305-3293; **Board Cert:** Orthopaedic Surgery 2012; **Med School:** South Korea 1986; **Resid:** Orthopaedic Surgery, NJ Med Ctr 1997; **Fellow:** Orthopaedic Oncology, Mass Genl Hosp/Chldns Hosp 1998; Pediatric Orthopaedic Surgery, Hosp for Sick Chldn/Univ Toronto 1999; **Fac Appt:** Prof OrS, Columbia P&S

Lee, Steven J MD (OrS) - **Spec Exp:** Hand & Upper Extremity Surgery; Shoulder & Elbow Surgery; Sports Medicine; Arthroscopic Surgery; **Hospital:** Lenox Hill Hosp; **Address:** New York Orthopedics, 159 E 74th St, Fl 2, New York, NY 10021; **Phone:** 212-737-3301; **Board Cert:** Orthopaedic Surgery 2014; **Med School:** Med Coll PA 1993; **Resid:** Surgery, SUNY Stony Brook Univ Hosp 1994; Orthopaedic Surgery, SUNY Stony Brook Univ Hosp 1998; **Fellow:** Hand Surgery, NYU/Hosp for Joint Diseases 1999; Orthopaedic Sports Medicine, Lenox Hill Hosp 2000

Levine, David S MD (OrS) - **Spec Exp:** Foot & Ankle Surgery; Ankle Reconstruction; **Hospital:** Hosp For Special Surgery (page 109); **Address:** Hospital for Special Surgery, 523 E 72 St Fl 5, East River Professional Bldg, New York, NY 10021; **Phone:** 212-606-1940; **Board Cert:** Orthopaedic Surgery 2011; **Med School:** Cornell Univ-Weill Med Coll 1992; **Resid:** Orthopaedic Surgery, Hosp for Special Surgery 1997; **Fellow:** Foot & Ankle Surgery, Harborview Med Ctr 1998; **Fac Appt:** Asst Prof OrS, Cornell Univ-Weill Med Coll

Lonner, Baron S MD (OrS) - **Spec Exp:** Scoliosis; Minimally Invasive Surgery; Spinal Deformity; Spinal Surgery; **Hospital:** NYU Hosp For Joint Dis (page 104), NYU Langone Med Ctr (page 104); **Address:** Scoliosis & Spine Ctr, 820 2nd Ave, Ste 7A, New York, NY 10017; **Phone:** 212-986-0140; **Board Cert:** Orthopaedic Surgery 2008; **Med School:** Boston Univ 1989; **Resid:** Orthopaedic Surgery, Montefiore Med Ctr 1994; **Fellow:** Orthopaedic Surgery, Hosp Special Surgery 1995; **Fac Appt:** Clin Prof OrS, NYU Sch Med

Lorich, Dean G MD (OrS) - **Spec Exp:** Trauma; Fractures-Complex & Non Union; **Hospital:** Hosp For Special Surgery (page 109), NY-Presby/Weill Cornell Med Ctr, NY (page 102); **Address:** Hosp for Special Surg, 520 E 70th St Fl 2, New York, NY 10021; **Phone:** 212-746-4509; **Board Cert:** Orthopaedic Surgery 2010; **Med School:** Univ Pennsylvania 1990; **Resid:** Orthopaedic Surgery, Hosp Univ Penn 1995; **Fellow:** Orthopaedic Surgery, Hosp Special Surg 1996; **Fac Appt:** Assoc Prof OrS, Cornell Univ-Weill Med Coll

Lubliner, Jerry A MD (OrS) - **Spec Exp:** Arthroscopic Surgery; Shoulder Surgery; Knee Surgery; Rotator Cuff Surgery; **Hospital:** Mt Sinai Beth Israel, NYU Hosp For Joint Dis (page 104); **Address:** New York Orthopaedics and Sports Med, 215 E 73rd St, Ste 1C, New York, NY 10021-3653; **Phone:** 212-249-8200; **Board Cert:** Orthopaedic Surgery 2009; Orthopaedic Sports Medicine 2008; **Med School:** SUNY Hlth Sci Ctr 1980; **Resid:** Orthopaedic Surgery, Hosp Joint Diseases 1985; **Fellow:** Sports Medicine, Univ West Ontario Affil Hosps 1986; **Fac Appt:** Assoc Clin Prof S, NYU Sch Med

Lyden, John P MD (OrS) - **Spec Exp:** Joint Replacement; Trauma; Arthroscopic Surgery; Fractures; **Hospital:** Hosp For Special Surgery (page 109), NY-Presby/Weill Cornell Med Ctr, NY (page 102); **Address:** 535 E 70th St Fl 3, New York, NY 10021-4872; **Phone:** 212-606-1126; **Board Cert:** Orthopaedic Surgery 1973; **Med School:** Columbia P&S 1965; **Resid:** Surgery, Roosevelt Hosp 1967; Orthopaedic Surgery, Hosp Special Surg 1972; **Fellow:** Hand Surgery, Hosp Special Surg 1973; **Fac Appt:** Clin Prof OrS, Cornell Univ-Weill Med Coll

Macaulay, William B MD (OrS) - **Spec Exp:** Hip Replacement; Knee Replacement; Minimally Invasive Surgery; Reconstructive Surgery; **Hospital:** NY-Presby/Columbia Univ Med Ctr, NY (page 102); **Address:** NY-Presby, Orthopaedic Surgery, 161 Fort Washington Ave Fl 2, New York, NY 10032; **Phone:** 212-305-6959; **Board Cert:** Orthopaedic Surgery 2012; **Med School:** Columbia P&S 1992; **Resid:** Orthopaedic Surgery, UPMC 1997; **Fellow:** Adult Reconstructive Surgery, Hosp Special Surgery 1999; **Fac Appt:** Prof OrS, Columbia P&S

Marx, Robert G MD (OrS) - **Spec Exp:** Shoulder Surgery; Knee Injuries/Ligament Surgery; Knee Replacement; Sports Medicine; **Hospital:** Hosp For Special Surgery (page 109); **Address:** HSS, Orthopaedic Surgery, 519 E 72nd St, Ste 206, New York, NY 10021; **Phone:** 212-606-1645; **Board Cert:** Orthopaedic Surgery 2014; **Med School:** Canada 1991; **Resid:** Orthopaedic Surgery, Univ Toronto Affil Hosp 1998; **Fellow:** Sports Medicine, Hosp Special Surgery 2000; **Fac Appt:** Prof OrS, Cornell Univ-Weill Med Coll

Mayman, David J MD (OrS) - **Spec Exp:** Hip Replacement & Revision; Knee Replacement & Revision; Hip Replacement-Young Adults; Arthritis-Hip & Knee; **Hospital:** Hosp For Special Surgery (page 109); **Address:** 523 E 72nd St Fl 2, East River Professional Bldg, New York, NY 10021; **Phone:** 212-774-2024; **Board Cert:** Orthopaedic Surgery 2007; **Med School:** Queens Univ 1998; **Resid:** Orthopaedic Surgery, Queen's Univ Affil Hosp 2003; **Fellow:** Adult Reconstructive Surgery, Hosp Special Surgery 2004; Orthopaedic Sports Medicine, Mass General Hosp 2005; **Fac Appt:** Asst Prof OrS, Cornell Univ-Weill Med Coll

McCance, Sean E MD (OrS) - **Spec Exp:** Spinal Surgery; Scoliosis; **Hospital:** Mt Sinai Hosp, Lenox Hill Hosp; **Address:** Spine Assocs, 1155 Park Ave, Ste E, New York, NY 10128; **Phone:** 212-360-6500; **Board Cert:** Orthopaedic Surgery 2010; **Med School:** Columbia P&S 1991; **Resid:** Orthopaedic Surgery, Strong Meml Hosp 1996; **Fellow:** Spine Surgery, Twin Cities Spine Ctr 1997; **Fac Appt:** Assoc Clin Prof OrS, Mount Sinai-Icahn Sch of Med

McCann, Peter D MD (OrS) - **Spec Exp:** Shoulder Surgery; Elbow Surgery; **Hospital:** Mt Sinai Beth Israel; **Address:** Beth Israel Orthopedics & Sports Med, 10 Union Square E, Ste 3M, New York, NY 10003; **Phone:** 212-844-6735; **Board Cert:** Orthopaedic Surgery 2009; **Med School:** Columbia P&S 1980; **Resid:** Surgery, St Vincents Hosp 1982; Orthopaedic Surgery, NY-Presby/Columbia Med Ctr 1985; **Fellow:** Shoulder Surgery, NY-Presby/Columbia Med Ctr 1986; **Fac Appt:** Prof OrS, Mount Sinai-Icahn Sch of Med

McClelland, Shearwood J MD (OrS) - **Spec Exp:** Musculoskeletal Injuries; Joint Replacement; **Hospital:** Harlem Hosp Ctr; **Address:** Harlem Hosp Ctr, Dept Ortho Surgery, 506 Lenox Ave, MLK Bldg Fl 9 - rm 9122, New York, NY 10037-1889; **Phone:** 212-939-3510; **Board Cert:** Orthopaedic Surgery 2007; **Med School:** Columbia P&S 1974; **Resid:** Surgery, St. Lukes Hosp 1976; Orthopaedic Surgery, NY Ortho Hosp-Columbia 1979; **Fellow:** Joint Arthroplasty, Ohio State Univ Med Ctr 1982; **Fac Appt:** Assoc Prof OrS, Columbia P&S

Meere, Patrick Andreas MD (OrS) - **Spec Exp:** Hip Replacement & Revision; Knee Replacement & Revision; Knee Injuries/Ligament Surgery; Robotic Surgery; **Hospital:** NYU Hosp For Joint Dis (page 104), NYU Langone Med Ctr (page 104); **Address:** NYU, Orthopaedic Surgery, 530 First Ave, Ste 5J, New York, NY 10016; **Phone:** 212-263-2366; **Board Cert:** Orthopaedic Surgery 2008; **Med School:** McGill Univ 1988; **Resid:** Orthopaedic Surgery, McGill Univ Affil Hosp 1993; **Fellow:** Reconstructive Surgery, NYU-Hosp Joint Diseases 1995; **Fac Appt:** Assoc Prof OrS, NYU Sch Med

Meislin, Robert J MD (OrS) - **Spec Exp:** Sports Medicine; Hip & Knee Reconstruction; Elbow Reconstruction; Shoulder & Knee Injuries; **Hospital:** NYU Langone Med Ctr (page 104); **Address:** NYU Langone Ctr for Musculoskeletal Care, Sports div, 333 E 8th St Fl 4, New York, NY 10016; **Phone:** 646-501-7223; **Board Cert:** Orthopaedic Surgery 2005; Orthopaedic Sports Medicine 2007; **Med School:** NYU Sch Med 1985; **Resid:** Orthopaedic Surgery, Hosp for Joint Diseases 1991; **Fellow:** Biomedical Engineering, Hosp for Joint Diseases 1987; Sports Medicine, Ortho Specialty Hosp 1992; **Fac Appt:** Asst Prof OrS, NYU Sch Med

Mendoza, Francis X MD (OrS) - **Spec Exp:** Shoulder & Elbow Surgery; Sports Medicine; **Hospital:** Lenox Hill Hosp; **Address:** FXM Shoulders, 333 E 56th St, New York, NY 10022; **Phone:** 212-628-9600; **Board Cert:** Orthopaedic Surgery 1984; **Med School:** Columbia P&S 1976; **Resid:** Surgery, Roosevelt Hosp 1978; Orthopaedic Surgery, NY-Presby/Columbia Univ Med Ctr 1981; **Fellow:** Elbow & Shoulder Surgery, NY-Presby/Columbia Univ Med Ctr 1982

Miyasaka, Kenji C MD (OrS) - **Spec Exp:** Hand Surgery; Hip & Knee Replacement; Fractures; **Hospital:** Mt Sinai Beth Israel, Mt Sinai Hosp; **Address:** Beth Israel Orthopedics, 10 Union Sq E, Philips Ambulatory Care Ctr, New York, NY 10003; **Phone:** 212-844-6750; **Board Cert:** Orthopaedic Surgery 2012; **Med School:** UCSD 1990; **Resid:** Orthopaedic Surgery, SUNY Stony Brook-Univ Hosp 1996; **Fellow:** Joint Reconstruction, Lenox Hill Hosp 1997; Hand Surgery, NY-Presby/Columbia Univ Med Ctr 1998

Moucha, Calin S MD (OrS) - **Spec Exp:** Hip Replacement & Revision; Knee Reconstruction & Revision; Knee Replacement & Revision; Infections in Prosthetic Devices; **Hospital:** Mt Sinai Hosp; **Address:** Mt Sinai Hosp, Orthopaedic Surgery, 5 E 98th St, Fl 7, New York, NY 10029; **Phone:** 212-241-1461; **Board Cert:** Orthopaedic Surgery 2005; **Med School:** Mount Sinai Sch Med 1997; **Resid:** Orthopaedic Surgery, St Lukes-Roosevelt Hosp Ctr 2002; **Fellow:** Hip/Knee Reconstruction, Rush Univ Med Ctr 2003; **Fac Appt:** Asst Prof OrS, Mount Sinai-Icahn Sch of Med

Nercessian, Ohannes A MD (OrS) - **Spec Exp:** Hip & Knee Surgery; Trauma; Arthritis; Hip Replacement & Revision; **Hospital:** NY-Presby/Columbia Univ Med Ctr, NY (page 102); **Address:** 161 Fort Washington Ave, Herbert Irving Pavilion, Fl 2, New York, NY 10032; **Phone:** 212-305-4565; **Board Cert:** Orthopaedic Surgery 2013; **Med School:** Columbia P&S 1981; **Resid:** Surgery, Barnes Jewish Hosp 1983; Orthopaedic Surgery, Columbia Presby Med Ctr 1986; **Fellow:** Hip & Knee Surgery, Columbia Presby Med Ctr 1987; **Fac Appt:** Assoc Clin Prof OrS, Columbia P&S

Neuwirth, Michael G MD (OrS) - **Spec Exp:** Scoliosis; Spinal Deformity; Spinal Surgery; **Hospital:** Mt Sinai Hosp; **Address:** 5 E 98th St Fl 4, New York, NY 10029; **Phone:** 212-241-1071; **Board Cert:** Orthopaedic Surgery 1980; **Med School:** SUNY Downstate 1974; **Resid:** Orthopaedic Surgery, Hosp for Joint Diseases 1978; **Fellow:** Spine Surgery, Rush-Presby Med Ctr 1979; **Fac Appt:** Prof OrS, Mount Sinai Sch Med

Nicholas, Stephen J MD (OrS) - **Spec Exp:** Sports Medicine; Shoulder & Knee Surgery; Arthroscopic Surgery; **Hospital:** Lenox Hill Hosp; **Address:** Lenox Hill Hosp, Orthopaedic Surgery, 130 E 77th St Fl 5, New York, NY 10075; **Phone:** 212-737-3301; **Board Cert:** Orthopaedic Surgery 2015; **Med School:** NY Med Coll 1986; **Resid:** Orthopaedic Surgery, Hosp Special Surgery 1991; **Fellow:** Sports Medicine, Lenox Hill Hosp 1992

O'Leary, Patrick F MD (OrS) - **Spec Exp:** Spinal Surgery; **Hospital:** Hosp For Special Surgery (page 109); **Address:** 1015 Madison Ave, Fl 4, New York, NY 10075; **Phone:** 212-249-8100; **Board Cert:** Orthopaedic Surgery 1983; **Med School:** Ireland 1968; **Resid:** Surgery, Roosevelt Hosp 1972; Orthopaedic Surgery, Hosp Spec Surg 1975; **Fellow:** Spine Surgery, Univ Toronto Genl Ortho Hosp 1976; **Fac Appt:** Assoc Clin Prof OrS, Cornell Univ-Weill Med Coll

O'Malley, Martin J MD (OrS) - **Spec Exp:** Foot & Ankle Surgery; Sports Medicine; Ankle Replacement & Revision; Arthroscopic Surgery; **Hospital:** Hosp For Special Surgery (page 109), NY-Presby/Weill Cornell Med Ctr, NY (page 102); **Address:** Foot & Ankle Orthopedic Surgery, 420 E 72nd St, Ste 1B, New York, NY 10021; **Phone:** 212-203-0740; **Board Cert:** Orthopaedic Surgery 2006; **Med School:** Case West Res Univ 1986; **Resid:** Orthopaedic Surgery, Tufts-New Eng Med Ctr 1992; **Fellow:** Foot & Ankle Surgery, Hosp for Special Surg 1993; **Fac Appt:** Asst Prof OrS, Cornell Univ-Weill Med Coll

Otsuka, Norman Y MD (OrS) - **Spec Exp:** Pediatric Orthopaedic Surgery; Cerebral Palsy; Trauma-Pediatric; Lower Limb Surgery in Children; **Hospital:** NYU Hosp For Joint Dis (page 104); **Address:** NYU Hosp for Joint Diseases, Center for Children, 301 E 17th St, Ste 301/303, New York, NY 10003; **Phone:** 212-598-6286; **Board Cert:** Orthopaedic Surgery 2009; **Med School:** McMaster Univ 1988; **Resid:** Orthopaedic Surgery, Univ Toronto Affil Hosps 1994; **Fellow:** Pediatric Orthopaedic Surgery, Childrens Hosp 1995; **Fac Appt:** Prof OrS, NYU Sch Med

Padgett, Douglas E MD (OrS) - **Spec Exp:** Hip & Knee Replacement; Arthroscopic Surgery-Hip; Arthroscopic Surgery-Knee; Dance Medicine; **Hospital:** Hosp For Special Surgery (page 109); **Address:** Hosp for Special Surgery, 535 E 70 St Fl 3, New York, NY 10021; **Phone:** 212-606-1642; **Board Cert:** Orthopaedic Surgery 2013; **Med School:** NY Med Coll 1982; **Resid:** Orthopaedic Surgery, Hosp Spec Surg 1989; **Fellow:** Hip & Knee Surgery, Rush Presby Med Ctr 1990; **Fac Appt:** Assoc Prof OrS, Cornell Univ-Weill Med Coll

Parks, Michael MD (OrS) - **Spec Exp:** Hip & Knee Replacement; Joint Replacement; Reconstructive Surgery; Arthritis; **Hospital:** Hosp For Special Surgery (page 109); **Address:** 535 E 70th St Fl 6, New York, NY 10021; **Phone:** 646-797-8995; **Board Cert:** Orthopaedic Surgery 2010; **Med School:** Med Univ SC 1990; **Resid:** Orthopaedic Surgery, Duke Univ Med Ctr 1997; **Fellow:** Hip & Knee Surgery, Hosp for Spec Surgery 1998; **Fac Appt:** Asst Prof OrS, Cornell Univ-Weill Med Coll

Pearle, Andrew D MD (OrS) - **Spec Exp:** Knee Replacement; Robotic Surgery; Knee Injuries/ACL; Sports Medicine; **Hospital:** Hosp For Special Surgery (page 109); **Address:** HSS, Sports Med, 523 E 72nd St Fl 6, New York, NY 10021; **Phone:** 212-774-2878; **Board Cert:** Orthopaedic Surgery 2009; **Med School:** Stanford Univ 1998; **Resid:** Orthopaedic Surgery, Hosp Special Surgery 2004; **Fellow:** Sports Medicine, Hosp Special Surgery 2005; **Fac Appt:** Assoc Prof OrS, Columbia P&S

Pellicci, Paul M MD (OrS) - **Spec Exp:** Hip Replacement-Young Adults; Knee Replacement; Joint Replacement; Hip Replacement; **Hospital:** Hosp For Special Surgery (page 109), NY-Presby/Weill Cornell Med Ctr, NY (page 102); **Address:** Hosp for Spec Surgery, 535 E 70th St, New York, NY 10021-4872; **Phone:** 212-606-1010; **Board Cert:** Orthopaedic Surgery 1982; **Med School:** Cornell Univ-Weill Med Coll 1975; **Resid:** Surgery, NY Hosp 1977; Orthopaedic Surgery, Hosp Spec Surg 1980; **Fellow:** Adult Reconstructive Surgery, Brigham & Womens Hosp 1980; **Fac Appt:** Clin Prof OrS, Cornell Univ-Weill Med Coll

Plancher, Kevin D MD (OrS) - **Spec Exp:** Knee Injuries/Ligament Surgery; Shoulder & Elbow Surgery; Rotator Cuff Surgery; Sports Medicine; **Hospital:** Mt Sinai Beth Israel, Lenox Hill Hosp; **Address:** Plancher Orthopaedics & Sports Medicine, 1160 Park Ave, New York, NY 10128; **Phone:** 212-876-5200; **Board Cert:** Orthopaedic Surgery 2007; Hand Surgery 2008; Orthopaedic Sports Medicine 2009; **Med School:** Georgetown Univ 1986; **Resid:** Orthopaedic Surgery, Mass Genl Hosp/Brigham & Womens Hosp 1991; **Fellow:** Hand Surgery, Indiana Hand Ctr 1993; Sports Medicine, Steadman-Hawkins Clinic 1994; **Fac Appt:** Assoc Clin Prof OrS, Albert Einstein Coll Med

Price, Andrew E MD (OrS) - **Spec Exp:** Erbs Palsy/Brachial Plexus Injuries; Fractures-Pediatric; Trauma-Pediatric; **Hospital:** NYU Langone Med Ctr (page 104), Mt Sinai Roosevelt; **Address:** 129A W 20th St, New York, NY 10011; **Phone:** 212-974-7242; **Board Cert:** Orthopaedic Surgery 2011; **Med School:** NYU Sch Med 1980; **Resid:** Orthopaedic Surgery, NYU Med Ctr 1985; **Fellow:** Pediatric Orthopaedic Surgery, Newington Chldns Hosp 1986; **Fac Appt:** Assoc Clin Prof OrS, NYU Sch Med

Qureshi, Sheeraz A MD (OrS) - **Spec Exp:** Spinal Surgery; Spinal Disc Replacement; Spinal Tumors; Minimally Invasive Spinal Surgery; **Hospital:** Mt Sinai Hosp; **Address:** 5 E 98th St, Fl 4, Box 1188, New York, NY 10029; **Phone:** 212-241-3909; **Board Cert:** Orthopaedic Surgery 2010; **Med School:** Tufts Univ 2002; **Resid:** Orthopaedic Surgery, Mt Siani Med Ctr 2007; **Fellow:** Spine Surgery, Case Western Reserve Univ Med Ctr 2009; **Fac Appt:** Assoc Prof OrS, Mount Sinai Sch Med

Ranawat, Amar S MD (OrS) - **Spec Exp:** Knee Replacement & Revision; Hip Replacement & Revision; **Hospital:** Hosp For Special Surgery (page 109); **Address:** Hosp for Special Surgery, 535 E 70th St Fl 6, New York, NY 10021; **Phone:** 646-797-8700; **Board Cert:** Orthopaedic Surgery 2004; **Med School:** Cornell Univ-Weill Med Coll 1996; **Resid:** Orthopaedic Surgery, Hosp Special Surgery 2001; **Fellow:** Orthopaedic Surgery, Lenox Hill Hosp 2002

Rapp, Timothy B MD (OrS) - **Spec Exp:** Sarcoma; Bone Tumors; Musculoskeletal Cancer; **Hospital:** NYU Langone Med Ctr (page 104), NYU Hosp For Joint Dis (page 104); **Address:** NYU Langone Med Ctr, Orthopaedic Surg Dept, 160 E 34th St, New York, NY 10016; **Phone:** 212-731-6558; **Board Cert:** Orthopaedic Surgery 2016; **Med School:** Univ Iowa Coll Med 1997; **Resid:** Orthopaedic Surgery, Univ Washington Med Ctr 2002; **Fellow:** Musculoskeletal Oncology, Univ Washington Med Ctr 2003; **Fac Appt:** Assoc Prof OrS, NYU Sch Med

Rawlins, Bernard A MD (OrS) - **Spec Exp:** Scoliosis; Spinal Surgery; Minimally Invasive Spinal Surgery; Spinal Surgery-Low Back; **Hospital:** Hosp For Special Surgery (page 109); **Address:** HSS, Spine Surgery, 523 E 72nd St Fl 2, New York, NY 10021; **Phone:** 212-606-1632; **Board Cert:** Orthopaedic Surgery 2006; **Med School:** Cornell Univ 1987; **Resid:** Orthopaedic Surgery, NY-Presby/Columbia Univ Med Ctr 1992; **Fellow:** Spine Surgery, Minnesota Spine Ctr 1993; **Fac Appt:** Prof OrS, Cornell Univ-Weill Med Coll

Roberts, Matthew M MD (OrS) - **Spec Exp:** Foot & Ankle Surgery; Trauma; Foot Deformities; Sports Injuries; **Hospital:** Hosp For Special Surgery (page 109); **Address:** HSS Foot & Ankle Surgery, 523 E 72nd St Fl 5, New York, NY 10021; **Phone:** 212-606-1181; **Board Cert:** Orthopaedic Surgery 2014; **Med School:** Univ Tex, Houston 1997; **Resid:** Orthopaedic Surgery, Hosp Special Surgery 2003; **Fellow:** Foot & Ankle Surgery, Univ Washington 2004; **Fac Appt:** Assoc Prof OrS, Cornell Univ-Weill Med Coll

Rodriguez, Jose A MD (OrS) - **Spec Exp:** Hip & Knee Replacement; Arthroscopic Surgery-Hip; Arthroscopic Surgery-Knee; Fractures-Complex; **Hospital:** Lenox Hill Hosp; **Address:** Lenox Hill Hosp, Hip & Knee Surgery, 130 E 77th St Fl 11, New York, NY 10075; **Phone:** 212-434-4799; **Board Cert:** Orthopaedic Surgery 2009; **Med School:** Columbia P&S 1989; **Resid:** Orthopaedic Surgery, Hosp Special Surgery 1994; **Fellow:** Arthritis Surgery, Lenox Hill Hosp 1995

Rose, Donald J MD (OrS) - **Spec Exp:** Dance/Ballet Injuries; Arthroscopic Surgery; Sports Injuries; Hip Surgery; **Hospital:** NYU Hosp For Joint Dis (page 104), NYU Langone Med Ctr (page 104); **Address:** 1095 Park Ave, New York, NY 10128-1154; **Phone:** 212-427-7750; **Board Cert:** Orthopaedic Surgery 2009; **Med School:** Rutgers R W Johnson Med Sch 1980; **Resid:** Orthopaedic Surgery, Hosp for Joint Diseases 1985; **Fellow:** Sports Medicine, Temple Univ Hosp 1986; **Fac Appt:** Assoc Clin Prof OrS, NYU Sch Med

Rose, Howard A MD (OrS) - **Spec Exp:** Sports Medicine; Joint Replacement; Arthroscopic Surgery; **Hospital:** Hosp For Special Surgery (page 109), NY-Presby/Weill Cornell Med Ctr, NY (page 102); **Address:** 535 E 70th St, New York, NY 10021; **Phone:** 212-606-1278; **Board Cert:** Orthopaedic Surgery 1985; **Med School:** Geo Wash Univ 1977; **Resid:** Orthopaedic Surgery, Hosp Special Surg 1982; **Fellow:** Sports Medicine, Brigham & Womens Hosp 1983; Joint Replacement Surgery, Brigham & Womens Hosp 1983; **Fac Appt:** Asst Prof OrS, Cornell Univ-Weill Med Coll

Roye Jr, David P MD (OrS) - **Spec Exp:** Pediatric Orthopaedic Surgery; Scoliosis; Hip Disorders-Pediatric; Neuromuscular Disorders; **Hospital:** Morgan Stanley Chldns Hosp of NY-Presby, NY (page 102), NY-Presby/Columbia Univ Med Ctr, NY (page 102); **Address:** Columbia Orthopaedics, 3959 Broadway, rm 800-North, New York, NY 10032-1559; **Phone:** 212-305-5475; **Board Cert:** Orthopaedic Surgery 1981; **Med School:** Columbia P&S 1975; **Resid:** Orthopaedic Surgery, Columbia-Presby Med Ctr 1989; **Fellow:** Pediatric Orthopaedic Surgery, Hosp for Sick Chldn 1980; **Fac Appt:** Prof OrS, Columbia P&S

Rozbruch, Jacob D MD (OrS) - **Spec Exp:** Spinal Surgery; Shoulder Surgery; Knee Surgery; **Hospital:** Mt Sinai Beth Israel; **Address:** 420 E 72nd St, Ste 1J, New York, NY 10021; **Phone:** 212-744-9857; **Board Cert:** Orthopaedic Surgery 1980; Pediatrics 1979; **Med School:** SUNY Buffalo 1973; **Resid:** Surgery, NY Hosp 1976; Orthopaedic Surgery, Hosp Special Surg 1979; **Fac Appt:** Asst Clin Prof OrS, Albert Einstein Coll Med

Rozbruch, S. Robert MD (OrS) - **Spec Exp:** Limb Lengthening; Limb Deformities; Limb Surgery/Reconstruction; Fractures-Complex & Non Union; **Hospital:** Hosp For Special Surgery (page 109), NY-Presby/Weill Cornell Med Ctr, NY (page 102); **Address:** HSS, Limb Lengthening, 519 E 72nd St, Ste 204, New York, NY 10021; **Phone:** 212-606-1415; **Board Cert:** Orthopaedic Surgery 2009; **Med School:** Cornell Univ-Weill Med Coll 1990; **Resid:** Orthopaedic Surgery, Hosp Special Surgery 1995; **Fellow:** Trauma, Univ Bern Hosp 1997; Limb Lengthening, MD Ctr Limb Lengthening & Recon 1999; **Fac Appt:** Prof OrS, Cornell Univ-Weill Med Coll

Salvati, Eduardo A MD (OrS) - **Spec Exp:** Hip Replacement; Knee Replacement; **Hospital:** Hosp For Special Surgery (page 109); **Address:** 535 E 71st St Belaire Bldg, New York, NY 10021; **Phone:** 212-606-1472; **Board Cert:** Orthopaedic Surgery 1972; **Med School:** Argentina 1963; **Resid:** Orthopaedic Surgery, Univ Florence Ortho Clinic 1965; Orthopaedic Surgery, Hosp Buenos Aires 1969; **Fellow:** Hip & Knee Surgery, Hosp For Spec Surg 1972; **Fac Appt:** Clin Prof OrS, Cornell Univ-Weill Med Coll

Sama, Andrew A MD (OrS) - **Spec Exp:** Spinal Surgery; Spinal Trauma; Spinal Disorders-Degenerative; Spinal Deformity; **Hospital:** Hosp For Special Surgery (page 109), NY-Presby/Weill Cornell Med Ctr, NY (page 102); **Address:** Hosp for Special Surgery, East River Profl Bldg, 523 E 72nd St, New York, NY 10021; **Phone:** 212-606-1946; **Board Cert:** Orthopaedic Surgery 2014; **Med School:** Univ Miami Sch Med 1995; **Resid:** Surgery, Jackson Meml Hosp 2000; **Fellow:** Spine Surgery, Hosp Special Surg 2001; **Fac Appt:** Assoc Prof OrS, Cornell Univ-Weill Med Coll

Sandhu, Harvinder S MD (OrS) - **Spec Exp:** Minimally Invasive Spinal Surgery; Spinal Surgery; **Hospital:** Hosp For Special Surgery (page 109); **Address:** Hosp for Special Surgery, 523 E 72nd St, East River Professional Bldg, New York, NY 10021; **Phone:** 212-606-1798; **Board Cert:** Orthopaedic Surgery 2007; **Med School:** Northwestern Univ 1987; **Resid:** Orthopaedic Surgery, Univ Hosp-SUNY Hlth Sci Ctr 1992; **Fellow:** Spine Surgery, UCLA Med Ctr 1993; **Fac Appt:** Assoc Prof OrS, Cornell Univ-Weill Med Coll

Sands, Andrew K MD (OrS) - **Spec Exp:** Foot & Ankle Surgery; Ankle Replacement & Revision; Arthroscopic Surgery; Sports Medicine; **Hospital:** Mt Sinai Beth Israel, Kingsbrook Jewish Med Ctr; **Address:** NY Downtown Ortho Assocs, 170 William St Fl 8, New York, NY 10038; **Phone:** 212-312-5966; **Board Cert:** Orthopaedic Surgery 2013; **Med School:** NY Med Coll 1985; **Resid:** Orthopaedic Surgery, Lenox Hill Hosp 1990; **Fellow:** Foot & Ankle Surgery, Harborview Med Ctr 1994

Scher, David M MD (OrS) - **Spec Exp:** Pediatric Orthopaedic Surgery; Musculoskeletal Disorders; Trauma; Gait Disorders; **Hospital:** Hosp For Special Surgery (page 109); **Address:** Hosp for Special Surgery, 535 E 70th St Fl 5, New York, NY 10021; **Phone:** 212-606-1253; **Board Cert:** Orthopaedic Surgery 2013; **Med School:** Duke Univ 1993; **Resid:** Orthopaedic Surgery, Hosp Joint Diseases 1999; **Fellow:** Pediatric Orthopaedic Surgery, Childrens Hosp 2000; **Fac Appt:** Assoc Prof OrS, Cornell Univ-Weill Med Coll

Schwab, Frank J MD (OrS) - **Spec Exp:** Spinal Surgery; Pain-Back; Spinal Deformity; Scoliosis; **Hospital:** NYU Hosp For Joint Dis (page 104), New York Methodist Hosp (page 448); **Address:** Ctr for Musculoskeletal Care, 333 E 38th St Fl 6, New York, NY 10016; **Phone:** 646-501-7200; **Board Cert:** Orthopaedic Surgery 2010; **Med School:** Columbia P&S 1990; **Resid:** Surgery, NY Presby-Columbia Med Ctr 1992; Orthopaedic Surgery, NY Presby-Columbia Med Ctr 1996; **Fellow:** Orthopaedic Surgery, Hospital Lariboisiere 1991; Spine Surgery, Maimonides Med Ctr 1997; **Fac Appt:** Clin Prof OrS, NYU Sch Med

Schwartz, Jeffrey M MD (OrS) - **Spec Exp:** Arthroscopic Surgery; Fractures; **Hospital:** Lenox Hill Hosp, NS-LIJ Hlth Sys; **Address:** 73 E 71st St, New York, NY 10021; **Phone:** 212-535-6600; **Board Cert:** Orthopaedic Surgery 1978; **Med School:** NY Med Coll 1972; **Resid:** Orthopaedic Surgery, Lenox Hill Hosp 1976; **Fac Appt:** Asst Clin Prof OrS, Mount Sinai Sch Med

Scott, W Norman MD (OrS) - **Spec Exp:** Knee Injuries; Knee Replacement; Sports Medicine; Knee Surgery; **Hospital:** Lenox Hill Hosp; **Address:** ISK-Inst Ortho & Sports Med, 210 E 64th St Fl 4, New York, NY 10065; **Phone:** 646-293-7501; **Board Cert:** Orthopaedic Surgery 1978; **Med School:** Cornell Univ-Weill Med Coll 1972; **Resid:** Surgery, St Lukes-Roosevelt Hosp Ctr 1974; Orthopaedic Surgery, Hosp Special Surgery 1977; **Fac Appt:** Clin Prof OrS, Cornell Univ-Weill Med Coll

Scuderi, Giles R MD (OrS) - **Spec Exp:** Knee Replacement; Knee Reconstruction; Knee Injuries/Ligament Surgery; Sports Medicine; **Hospital:** Lenox Hill Hosp, Franklin Hosp; **Address:** 210 E 64th St, Fl 4, New York, NY 10065; **Phone:** 212-434-4310; **Board Cert:** Orthopaedic Surgery 2011; **Med School:** SUNY Downstate 1982; **Resid:** Orthopaedic Surgery, Lenox Hill Hosp 1987; **Fellow:** Knee Surgery, Hosp Special Surgery 1988; **Fac Appt:** Asst Clin Prof OrS, Albert Einstein Coll Med

Sculco, Thomas P MD (OrS) - **Spec Exp:** Hip Replacement; Knee Replacement; Minimally Invasive Surgery; Joint Replacement; **Hospital:** Hosp For Special Surgery (page 109); **Address:** HSS, Orthopaedic Surgery, 525 E 71st St Fl 2, New York, NY 10021; **Phone:** 212-606-1475; **Board Cert:** Orthopaedic Surgery 1976; **Med School:** Columbia P&S 1969; **Resid:** Surgery, St Lukes-Roosevelt Hosp Ctr 1971; Orthopaedic Surgery, Hosp Special Surgery 1974; **Fellow:** Research, London Hosp 1975; **Fac Appt:** Prof OrS, Cornell Univ-Weill Med Coll

Simon, Sheldon R MD (OrS) - **Spec Exp:** Foot & Ankle Surgery; Pediatric Orthopaedic Surgery; **Hospital:** Mt Sinai Beth Israel; **Address:** Beth Israel Orthopedics and Sports Med, 10 Union Square E, Ste 3K, New York, NY 10003; **Phone:** 212-844-6756; **Board Cert:** Orthopaedic Surgery 1976; **Med School:** NYU Sch Med 1966; **Resid:** Surgery, NYU Med Ctr 1968; Orthopaedic Surgery, Mass Genl Hosp 1973; **Fac Appt:** Clin Prof OrS, Albert Einstein Coll Med

Sink, Ernest L MD (OrS) - **Spec Exp:** Hip Surgery; Pediatric Orthopaedic Surgery; Trauma; **Hospital:** Hosp For Special Surgery (page 109), NY-Presby/Weill Cornell Med Ctr, NY (page 102); **Address:** 541 E 71st St, Ground Fl, New York, NY 10021; **Phone:** 212-606-1268; **Board Cert:** Orthopaedic Surgery 2013; **Med School:** Univ Tex SW, Dallas 1994; **Resid:** Orthopaedic Surgery, Univ Tex SW Med Ctr 1999; **Fellow:** Pediatric Orthopaedic Surgery, Rady Chldn's Hosp 2000

Spivak, Jeffrey M MD (OrS) - **Spec Exp:** Spinal Surgery; Scoliosis; Sports Medicine Back Injuries; **Hospital:** NYU Hosp For Joint Dis (page 104), NYU Langone Med Ctr (page 104); **Address:** NYU, Spine Surgery, 333 E 38th St Fl 6, New York, NY 10016; **Phone:** 646-501-7200; **Board Cert:** Orthopaedic Surgery 2006; **Med School:** Cornell Univ-Weill Med Coll 1986; **Resid:** Orthopaedic Surgery, NYU Hosp Joint Diseases 1992; **Fellow:** Spine Surgery, Thomas Jefferson Univ Hosp 1993; **Fac Appt:** Asst Prof OrS, NYU Sch Med

Stuchin, Steven A MD (OrS) - **Spec Exp:** Hand Surgery; Arthritis; Hip & Knee Replacement; Hip Resurfacing; **Hospital:** NYU Hosp For Joint Dis (page 104); **Address:** NYU, Musculoskeletal Care, 333 E 38th St Fl 4, New York, NY 10016; **Phone:** 646-501-7300; **Board Cert:** Orthopaedic Surgery 1984; **Med School:** Columbia P&S 1976; **Resid:** Surgery, St Lukes-Roosevelt Hosp Ctr 1978; Orthopaedic Surgery, Hosp Special Surgery 1982; **Fellow:** Hand Surgery, Thomas Jefferson Univ Hosp 1983; **Fac Appt:** Assoc Prof OrS, NYU Sch Med

Su, Edwin P MD (OrS) - **Spec Exp:** Hip Resurfacing; Hip Replacement; Reconstructive Surgery; **Hospital:** Hosp For Special Surgery (page 109); **Address:** HSS, Hip & Knee Surgery, 541 E 71st St, New York, NY 10021; **Phone:** 212-606-1128; **Board Cert:** Orthopaedic Surgery 2006; **Med School:** Cornell Univ-Weill Med Coll 1997; **Resid:** Orthopaedic Surgery, Hosp Special Surgery 2002; **Fellow:** Reconstructive Surgery, Hosp Special Surgery 2003; **Fac Appt:** Assoc Prof OrS, Cornell Univ-Weill Med Coll

Tehrany, Armin MD (OrS) - **Spec Exp:** Arthroscopic Surgery; Sports Medicine; Shoulder Injuries; Knee Injuries/ACL/Meniscus Tears; **Hospital:** Mt Sinai Hosp; **Address:** Manhattan Orthopedic Care, 515 Madison Ave, New York, NY 10022; **Phone:** 212-729-9200; **Board Cert:** Orthopaedic Surgery 2014; **Med School:** NYU Sch Med 1994; **Resid:** Orthopaedic Surgery, Lenox Hill Hosp 1999; **Fellow:** Sports Medicine & Arthroscopic Surgery, Baylor Coll of Med Affil Hosp 2000; **Fac Appt:** Asst Clin Prof OrS, Mount Sinai Sch Med

Tindel, Nathaniel L MD (OrS) - **Spec Exp:** Spinal Surgery; Scoliosis; Minimally Invasive Surgery; Spinal Reconstructive Surgery; **Hospital:** Lenox Hill Hosp; **Address:** NY Ctr for Spinal Disorders, 425 E 79th St, Ste 1H, New York, NY 10075; **Phone:** 212-249-3840; **Board Cert:** Orthopaedic Surgery 2009; **Med School:** Univ Pennsylvania 1989; **Resid:** Orthopaedic Surgery, Lenox Hill Hosp 1994; **Fellow:** Spine Surgery, Univ Miami Hosp 1996; **Fac Appt:** Asst Prof OrS, Albert Einstein Coll Med

Turtel, Andrew H MD (OrS) - **Spec Exp:** Knee Surgery; Shoulder Surgery; Sports Medicine; Arthroscopic Surgery; **Hospital:** Lenox Hill Hosp, Mt Sinai Beth Israel; **Address:** 333 E 56th St, Ground Floor, New York, NY 10022; **Phone:** 212-319-6500; **Board Cert:** Orthopaedic Surgery 2015; **Med School:** SUNY Upstate Med Univ 1985; **Resid:** Orthopaedic Surgery, LI Jewish Med Ctr 1991; **Fellow:** Sports Medicine, NYU Med Ctr 1992; **Fac Appt:** Assoc Clin Prof OrS, Mount Sinai Sch Med

Unis, George L MD (OrS) - **Spec Exp:** Sports Medicine; **Hospital:** Mt Sinai Roosevelt, Mt Sinai St. Luke's; **Address:** 115 E 61st St Fl 8, New York, NY 10065; **Phone:** 212-688-3710; **Board Cert:** Orthopaedic Surgery 1973; **Med School:** UMDNJ-NJ Med Sch, Newark 1965; **Resid:** Surgery, St Lukes Roosevelt Hosp 1967; Orthopaedic Surgery, St Lukes Roosevelt Hosp 1970; **Fac Appt:** Asst Clin Prof OrS, Columbia P&S

Vitale, Michael Guy MD (OrS) - **Spec Exp:** Spinal Surgery-Pediatric; Scoliosis; Limb Lengthening (Ilizarov Procedure); Clubfoot/Foot Deformities in Children; **Hospital:** Morgan Stanley Chldns Hosp of NY-Presby, NY (page 102), NY-Presby/Columbia Univ Med Ctr, NY (page 102); **Address:** Columbia Orthopedics, 3959 Broadway, Ste 800N, New York, NY 10032; **Phone:** 212-305-5475; **Board Cert:** Orthopaedic Surgery 2014; **Med School:** Columbia P&S 1995; **Resid:** Orthopaedic Surgery, NY-Presby/Columbia Univ Med Ctr 2000; **Fellow:** Pediatric Orthopaedic Surgery, Chldns Hosp 2001; **Fac Appt:** Prof OrS, Columbia P&S

Warren, Russell MD (OrS) - **Spec Exp:** Knee Injuries/Ligament Surgery; Shoulder Surgery; Shoulder Replacement; Rotator Cuff Surgery; **Hospital:** Hosp For Special Surgery (page 109); **Address:** HSS, Orthopaedic Surgery, 525 E 71st St, New York, NY 10021; **Phone:** 212-606-1178; **Board Cert:** Orthopaedic Surgery 1974; **Med School:** SUNY Upstate Med Univ 1966; **Resid:** Surgery, St Lukes-Roosevelt Hosp Ctr 1968; Orthopaedic Surgery, Hosp Special Surgery 1973; **Fellow:** Shoulder Surgery, NY-Presby/Columbia Univ Med Ctr 1977; **Fac Appt:** Prof OrS, Cornell Univ-Weill Med Coll

Weiner, Lon S MD (OrS) - **Spec Exp:** Trauma; Fractures; Fractures-Complex & Non Union; **Hospital:** Lenox Hill Hosp, Riverview Med Ctr; **Address:** Lenox Hill Hosp, Orthopaedic Surgery, 130 E 77th St Fl 12, New York, NY 10075; **Phone:** 212-434-4880; **Board Cert:** Orthopaedic Surgery 2011; **Med School:** Mount Sinai Sch Med 1982; **Resid:** Orthopaedic Surgery, Mt Sinai Hosp 1987; **Fellow:** Pediatric Orthopaedic Surgery, Hosp Special Surgery 1988

Weinfeld, Steven B MD (OrS) - **Spec Exp:** Foot & Ankle Surgery; Diabetic Leg/Foot; Foot Deformities; **Hospital:** Mt Sinai Hosp, Hackensack Univ Med Ctr (page 96); **Address:** Mt Sinai Hosp-Dept Ortho Surgery, 5 E 98th St Fl 9, Box 1188, New York, NY 10029; **Phone:** 212-241-1634; **Board Cert:** Orthopaedic Surgery 2009; **Med School:** Albany Med Coll 1990; **Resid:** Orthopaedic Surgery, Albany Med Ctr 1995; **Fellow:** Ankle and Foot Surgery, Union Meml Hosp 1996; **Fac Appt:** Assoc Prof OrS, Mount Sinai Sch Med

Westrich, Geoffrey H MD (OrS) - **Spec Exp:** Hip Replacement & Revision; Knee Replacement & Revision; Arthroscopic Surgery-Hip; Arthroscopic Surgery-Knee; **Hospital:** Hosp For Special Surgery (page 109), NY-Presby/Weill Cornell Med Ctr, NY (page 102); **Address:** Hospital for Special Surgery, 535 E 70th St Fl 3, New York, NY 10021; **Phone:** 212-606-1510; **Board Cert:** Orthopaedic Surgery 2009; **Med School:** Tufts Univ 1990; **Resid:** Orthopaedic Surgery, Hosp for Spec Surg 1995; **Fellow:** Orthopaedic Trauma, Inselspital 1996; Hip/Knee Reconstruction, Hosp for Special Surg 1998; **Fac Appt:** Assoc Prof OrS, Cornell Univ-Weill Med Coll

Widmann, Roger F MD (OrS) - **Spec Exp:** Pediatric Orthopaedic Surgery; Scoliosis; Limb Lengthening; Limb Deformities; **Hospital:** Hosp For Special Surgery (page 109); **Address:** 535 E 70th St, New York, NY 10021; **Phone:** 212-606-1325; **Board Cert:** Orthopaedic Surgery 2008; **Med School:** Yale Univ 1989; **Resid:** Orthopaedic Surgery, Mass General Hosp 1994; **Fellow:** Pediatric Orthopaedic Surgery, Children's Hosp 1995; **Fac Appt:** Clin Prof OrS, Cornell Univ-Weill Med Coll

Windsor, Russell E MD (OrS) - **Spec Exp:** Knee Replacement; Hip Replacement; Knee Injuries/Ligament Surgery; **Hospital:** Hosp For Special Surgery (page 109), NY-Presby/Weill Cornell Med Ctr, NY (page 102); **Address:** Hosp for Special Surgery, 535 E 70th St, New York, NY 10021; **Phone:** 212-606-1166; **Board Cert:** Orthopaedic Surgery 2007; **Med School:** Georgetown Univ 1978; **Resid:** Orthopaedic Surgery, Hosp Univ Penn 1983; **Fellow:** Knee Surgery, Hosp For Special Surg 1984; **Fac Appt:** Prof OrS, Cornell Univ-Weill Med Coll

Youm, Thomas MD (OrS) - **Spec Exp:** Sports Medicine; Arthroscopic Surgery; Knee Injuries/Ligament Surgery; Shoulder Injuries; **Hospital:** NYU Hosp For Joint Dis (page 104); **Address:** 1056 5th Ave, RYC Orthopaedics, New York, NY 10028; **Phone:** 212-348-3636; **Board Cert:** Orthopaedic Surgery 2007; **Med School:** NYU Sch Med 1999; **Resid:** Orthopaedic Surgery, NYU Med Ctr 2004; **Fellow:** Orthopaedic Sports Medicine, Kerlan-Jobe Orthopaedic Clin 2005; **Fac Appt:** Asst Clin Prof OrS, NYU Sch Med

Zambetti Jr, George J MD (OrS) - **Spec Exp:** Knee Reconstruction; Shoulder Surgery; Sports Medicine; Arthroscopic Surgery; **Hospital:** Mt Sinai Roosevelt; **Address:** Columbus Circle Orthopaedics, 343 W 58th St, Ste 7, New York, NY 10019-1173; **Phone:** 212-506-0236; **Board Cert:** Orthopaedic Surgery 1983; **Med School:** Albany Med Coll 1976; **Resid:** Surgery, St Luke's-Roosevelt Hosp 1978; Orthopaedic Surgery, Columbia-Presby Med Ctr 1981

Zuckerman, Joseph D MD (OrS) - **Spec Exp:** Shoulder Replacement; **Hospital:** NYU Hosp For Joint Dis (page 104), NYU Langone Med Ctr (page 104); **Address:** NYU, Musculoskeletal Care, 333 E 38th St, Fl 4, New York, NY 10016; **Phone:** 212-598-6674; **Board Cert:** Orthopaedic Surgery 2007; **Med School:** Med Coll Wisc 1978; **Resid:** Orthopaedic Surgery, Univ Washington Med Ctr 1983; **Fellow:** Arthritis Surgery, Brigham & Womens Hosp 1984; Shoulder Surgery, Mayo Clin 1984; **Fac Appt:** Prof OrS, NYU Sch Med

Otolaryngology

Amin, Milan R MD (Oto) - **Spec Exp:** Swallowing Disorders; Voice Disorders; Vocal Cord Disorders; Laryngeal Cancer; **Hospital:** NYU Langone Med Ctr (page 104); **Address:** NYU Voice Center, 345 E 37th St, Ste 306, New York, NY 10016; **Phone:** 646-754-1207; **Board Cert:** Otolaryngology 2000; **Med School:** Northwestern Univ 1994; **Resid:** Otolaryngology, Temple Univ Med Ctr 1999; **Fellow:** Laryngeal Surgery & Voice Disorders, Wake Forest Univ Med Ctr 2000; **Fac Appt:** Assoc Prof Oto, NYU Sch Med

Aviv, Jonathan MD (Oto) - **Spec Exp:** Voice Disorders; Swallowing Disorders; Cough; Endoscopy; **Hospital:** Mt Sinai Hosp; **Address:** ENT & Allergy Assocs, 210 E 86th St, Fl 9, New York, NY 10028; **Phone:** 212-722-5570; **Board Cert:** Otolaryngology 1990; **Med School:** Columbia P&S 1985; **Resid:** Surgery, Mt Sinai Hosp 1987; Otolaryngology, Mt Sinai Hosp 1990; **Fellow:** Head and Neck Surgery, Mt Sinai Hosp 1991; **Fac Appt:** Prof Oto, Mount Sinai-Icahn Sch of Med

Bennett, Garrett H MD (Oto) - **Spec Exp:** Endoscopic Sinus Surgery; Sinusitis; Sinus Surgery-Revision; Sinus Surgery; **Hospital:** Lenox Hill Hosp; **Address:** 115 E 61st St, Ste 7C, New York, NY 10065; **Phone:** 212-980-2600; **Board Cert:** Otolaryngology 2005; Facial Plastic & Reconstr Surgery 2010; **Med School:** Univ Rochester 1999; **Resid:** Otolaryngology, NYU Med Ctr 2004; **Fellow:** Facial Plastic & Reconstr Surgery, Rousso Facial Plastic Surgery Clin 2005

Blitzer, Andrew MD/DDS (Oto) - **Spec Exp:** Voice Disorders; Swallowing Disorders; Nasal & Sinus Surgery; Botox Therapy; **Hospital:** Mt Sinai Roosevelt; **Address:** Head & Neck Surgical Grp, 425 W 59th St Fl 10, New York, NY 10019; **Phone:** 212-262-9500; **Board Cert:** Otolaryngology 1977; **Med School:** Mount Sinai Sch Med 1973; **Resid:** Surgery, Beth Israel Med Ctr 1974; Otolaryngology, Mt Sinai Hosp 1977; **Fac Appt:** Prof Oto, Columbia P&S

Boyle, Jay O MD (Oto) - **Spec Exp:** Oral Cancers; Melanoma-Head & Neck; Thyroid Cancer; **Hospital:** Meml Sloan Kettering Canc Ctr (page 110); **Address:** Memorial Sloan Kettering Cancer Ctr, 1275 York Ave, New York, NY 10065; **Phone:** 212-639-2906; **Board Cert:** Otolaryngology 1997; **Med School:** Univ Ariz Coll Med 1990; **Resid:** Surgery, Johns Hopkins Hosp 1992; Otolaryngology, Johns Hopkins Bayview Med Ctr 1996; **Fellow:** Head and Neck Surgery, Meml Sloan Kettering Cancer Ctr 1998; **Fac Appt:** Assoc Prof Oto, Cornell Univ-Weill Med Coll

Carew, John F MD (Oto) - **Spec Exp:** Head & Neck Surgery; Head & Neck Cancer; Salivary Gland Tumors & Surgery; Thyroid Surgery; **Hospital:** Lenox Hill Hosp, Mt Sinai Hosp; **Address:** 785 Park Ave, Ste 1A, New York, NY 10021; **Phone:** 212-744-1941; **Board Cert:** Otolaryngology 1998; **Med School:** Cornell Univ-Weill Med Coll 1991; **Resid:** Otolaryngology, Manhattan EE&T Hosp 1997; **Fellow:** Head & Neck Oncology, Meml Sloan Kettering Cancer Ctr 1998; **Fac Appt:** Assoc Clin Prof Oto, Mount Sinai-Icahn Sch of Med

Caruana, Salvatore M MD (Oto) - **Spec Exp:** Head & Neck Cancer; Thyroid & Parathyroid Cancer & Surgery; Robotic Surgery; **Hospital:** NY-Presby/Columbia Univ Med Ctr, NY (page 102); **Address:** NY-Presby, Otolaryngology, 180 Fort Washington Ave Fl 7, New York, NY 10032; **Phone:** 212-305-5335; **Board Cert:** Otolaryngology 1996; **Med School:** Mount Sinai Sch Med 1989; **Resid:** Otolaryngology, NY Eye & Ear Infirm 1995; **Fellow:** Head & Neck Surgical Oncology, Meml Sloan-Kettering Cancer Ctr 1997; **Fac Appt:** Asst Prof Oto, Columbia P&S

Chandrasekhar, Sujana S MD (Oto) - **Spec Exp:** Hearing & Balance Disorders; Cochlear Implants; Acoustic Neuroma; Meniere's Disease; **Hospital:** Mt Sinai Hosp, New York Eye & Ear Infirm of Mt Sinai; **Address:** 210 E 64th St Fl 3, New York, NY 10021; **Phone:** 212-249-3232; **Board Cert:** Otolaryngology 1993; Neurotology 2011; **Med School:** Mount Sinai Sch Med 1986; **Resid:** Surgery, NYU Med Ctr 1988; Otolaryngology, NYU Med Ctr 1992; **Fellow:** Neurotology, House Ear Clin 1993; **Fac Appt:** Assoc Clin Prof Oto, Mount Sinai-Icahn Sch of Med

Close, Lanny G MD (Oto) - **Spec Exp:** Sinus Disorders/Surgery; Endoscopic Sinus Surgery; **Hospital:** NY-Presby/Columbia Univ Med Ctr, NY (page 102); **Address:** Columbia Doctors Midtown, 51 W 51st St Fl 3rd - Ste 385, New York, NY 10022; **Phone:** 212-326-8475; **Board Cert:** Otolaryngology 1977; **Med School:** Baylor Coll Med 1972; **Resid:** Surgery, Johns Hopkins Hosp 1974; Otolaryngology, Baylor Affil Hosps 1977; **Fellow:** Head and Neck Surgery, MD Anderson Cancer Ctr 1979; **Fac Appt:** Prof Oto, Columbia P&S

Constantinides, Minas MD (Oto) - **Spec Exp:** Rhinoplasty; Rhinoplasty Revision; Facial Rejuvenation; Facial Plastic & Reconstructive Surgery; **Hospital:** Lenox Hill Hosp (Manh Eye, Ear & Throat Hosp), NYU Langone Med Ctr (page 104); **Address:** 74 E 79th St, Ste 1B, New York, NY 10075; **Phone:** 212-861-0200; **Board Cert:** Otolaryngology 1994; Facial Plastic & Reconstr Surgery 1997; **Med School:** Columbia P&S 1987; **Resid:** Surgery, Harvard Surg Svcs 1989; Otolaryngology, NYU Medical Center 1993; **Fellow:** Facial Plastic Surgery, Univ Toronto 1994; **Fac Appt:** Asst Prof Oto, NYU Sch Med

Costantino, Peter D MD (Oto) - **Spec Exp:** Skull Base Tumors; Head & Neck Surgery; Craniofacial Surgery/Reconstruction; Facial Paralysis; **Hospital:** Lenox Hill Hosp, NS-LIJ Hlth Sys; **Address:** NY Head & Neck Inst, 130 E 77th St, Fl 10, New York, NY 10075; **Phone:** 212-434-4500; **Board Cert:** Otolaryngology 1990; Facial Plastic & Reconstr Surgery 2000; **Med School:** Northwestern Univ 1984; **Resid:** Surgery, Northwestern Meml Hosp 1986; Otolaryngology, Northwestern Meml Hosp 1989; **Fellow:** Head and Neck Surgery, Northwestern Meml Hosp 1990; Skull Base Surgery, UPMC 1991; **Fac Appt:** Assoc Prof Oto, Hofstra N Shore-LIJ Sch Med

DeLacure, Mark D MD (Oto) - **Spec Exp:** Head & Neck Cancer; Head & Neck Cancer Reconstruction; Reconstructive Microsurgery; **Hospital:** NYU Langone Med Ctr (page 104), VA NY Harbor Hlthcare Sys-Manhattan Campus; **Address:** 160 E 34th St Fl 7, New York, NY 10016; **Phone:** 212-731-5329; **Board Cert:** Otolaryngology 1992; Plastic Surgery 2012; **Med School:** Univ Fla Coll Med 1986; **Resid:** Otolaryngology, Yale Univ Sch Med 1991; Plastic/Reconstructive Surgery, UCLA Med Ctr 1994; **Fellow:** Head & Neck Surgical Oncology, Meml Sloan-Kettering Cancer Ctr 1992; **Fac Appt:** Assoc Clin Prof Oto, NYU Sch Med

Edelstein, David R MD (Oto) - **Spec Exp:** Endoscopic Sinus Surgery; Nasal Reconstruction; Sleep Disorders/Apnea; Rhinoplasty; **Hospital:** Lenox Hill Hosp (Manh Eye, Ear & Throat Hosp), Mt Sinai Hosp; **Address:** Manhattan Otolaryngology Head & Neck Surg, 1421 3rd Ave Fl 4, New York, NY 10028; **Phone:** 212-452-1500; **Board Cert:** Otolaryngology 1985; **Med School:** Boston Univ 1980; **Resid:** Surgery, Mt Sinai Hosp 1981; Otolaryngology, Mt Sinai Hosp 1984; **Fac Appt:** Clin Prof Oto, Cornell Univ-Weill Med Coll

Genden Sr, Eric M MD (Oto) - **Spec Exp:** Head & Neck Cancer & Surgery; Head & Neck Cancer Reconstruction; Airway Reconstruction; Thyroid & Parathyroid Cancer & Surgery; **Hospital:** Mt Sinai Hosp; **Address:** Mt Sinai, Otolaryngology, 10 E 102nd St Fl 3, New York, NY 10029; **Phone:** 212-241-9410; **Board Cert:** Otolaryngology 1999; **Med School:** Mount Sinai Sch Med 1992; **Resid:** Otolaryngology, Barnes-Jewish Hosp 1998; **Fellow:** Head and Neck Surgery, Mt Sinai Hosp 1999; **Fac Appt:** Prof Oto, Mount Sinai-Icahn Sch of Med

Godin, David A MD (Oto) - **Spec Exp:** Laryngeal & Voice Disorders; Sinus Disorders/Surgery; Pediatric Otolaryngology; Thyroid & Parathyroid Surgery; **Hospital:** New York Eye & Ear Infirm of Mt Sinai, Mt Sinai Beth Israel; **Address:** ENT & Allergy Assocs, 261 5th Ave, Fl 9, New York, NY 10016; **Phone:** 212-679-3499; **Board Cert:** Otolaryngology 2001; **Med School:** SUNY Upstate Med Univ 1995; **Resid:** Surgery, Tulane Univ 1996; Otolaryngology, Tulane Univ 2000; **Fac Appt:** Asst Prof Oto, NY Med Coll

Gold, Scott D MD (Oto) - **Spec Exp:** Endoscopic Sinus Surgery; Sinus Disorders/Surgery; **Hospital:** Mt Sinai Beth Israel, Mt Sinai Hosp; **Address:** NY Otolaryngology Group, 36A E 36th St, Ste 200, New York, NY 10016-3401; **Phone:** 212-889-8575; **Board Cert:** Otolaryngology 1983; **Med School:** Mount Sinai Sch Med 1979; **Resid:** Surgery, Mt Sinai Med Ctr 1980; Otolaryngology, Mt Sinai Med Ctr 1983; **Fac Appt:** Asst Clin Prof Oto, Mount Sinai Sch Med

Green, Robert P MD (Oto) - **Spec Exp:** Sinus Disorders; Hearing Loss/Tinnitus; Throat Disorders; **Hospital:** Mt Sinai Hosp; **Address:** 210 E 86th St Fl 9, New York, NY 10028; **Phone:** 212-722-5570; **Board Cert:** Otolaryngology 1981; **Med School:** Harvard Med Sch 1977; **Resid:** Otolaryngology, Mount Sinai Hosp 1981

Guida, Robert A MD (Oto) - **Spec Exp:** Rhinoplasty; Nasal Surgery; Cosmetic Surgery-Face; Skin Laser Surgery; **Hospital:** NY-Presby/Weill Cornell Med Ctr, NY (page 102), Lenox Hill Hosp (Manh Eye, Ear & Throat Hosp); **Address:** 1175 Park Ave, Ste 1B, New York, NY 10128; **Phone:** 212-871-0900; **Board Cert:** Otolaryngology 1989; Facial Plastic & Reconstr Surgery 1994; **Med School:** Hahnemann Univ 1983; **Resid:** Surgery, Graduate Hosp 1985; Otolaryngology, NY Eye & Ear Infirm 1989; **Fellow:** Facial Plastic Surgery, Oregon Hlth Sci Ctr 1990; **Fac Appt:** Assoc Prof Oto, Cornell Univ-Weill Med Coll

Hammerschlag, Paul E MD (Oto) - **Spec Exp:** Cochlear Implants; Hearing Loss; Meniere's Disease; Balance Disorders; **Hospital:** NYU Langone Med Ctr (page 104), New York Eye & Ear Infirm of Mt Sinai; **Address:** 650 First Ave Fl 6, New York, NY 10016-3240; **Phone:** 212-889-2600; **Board Cert:** Otolaryngology 1978; **Med School:** Albert Einstein Coll Med 1972; **Resid:** Surgery, Virginia Mason Hosp 1974; Otolaryngology, Mass Eye & Ear Infirm 1978; **Fellow:** Otolaryngology, Mass Eye & Ear Infirm 1978; **Fac Appt:** Assoc Clin Prof Oto, NYU Sch Med

Har-El, Gady MD (Oto) - **Spec Exp:** Head & Neck Cancer; Thyroid & Parathyroid Surgery; Sinus Tumors; Skull Base Tumors; **Hospital:** Lenox Hill Hosp, Lenox Hill Hosp (Manh Eye, Ear & Throat Hosp); **Address:** Lenox Hill Hosp, Head & Neck Surgery, 186 E 76th St, Fl 2, New York, NY 10021; **Phone:** 212-434-2323; **Board Cert:** Otolaryngology 1992; **Med School:** Israel 1982; **Resid:** Otolaryngology, SUNY Downstate Med Ctr 1991; **Fellow:** Head and Neck Surgery, Long Island Coll Hosp 1987; **Fac Appt:** Prof Oto, SUNY Downstate

Hoffman, Ronald A MD (Oto) - **Spec Exp:** Cochlear Implants; Balance Disorders; Ear Disorders/Surgery; **Hospital:** New York Eye & Ear Infirm of Mt Sinai, Mt Sinai Beth Israel; **Address:** 380 2nd Ave Fl 9, New York, NY 10010; **Phone:** 212-614-8388; **Board Cert:** Otolaryngology 1976; **Med School:** Jefferson Med Coll 1971; **Resid:** Surgery, Lenox Hill Hosp 1973; Otolaryngology, NYU Med Ctr 1976; **Fac Appt:** Prof Oto, Albert Einstein Coll Med

Horn, Corinne E MD (Oto) - **Spec Exp:** Cosmetic Surgery-Face & Neck; Facial Plastic & Reconstructive Surgery; **Hospital:** Mt Sinai Beth Israel, New York Eye & Ear Infirm of Mt Sinai; **Address:** NY Otolaryngology Grp, 36A E 36th St, Ste 200, New York, NY 10016; **Phone:** 212-889-8575; **Board Cert:** Otolaryngology 2006; Facial Plastic & Reconstr Surgery 2009; **Med School:** Columbia P&S 2000; **Resid:** Otolaryngology, Columbia-Presby Hosp 2005; **Fellow:** Facial Plastic & Reconstr Surgery, Univ Illinois Med Ctr 2006

Jacobs, Joseph B MD (Oto) - **Spec Exp:** Endoscopic Sinus Surgery; Sinus Disorders/Surgery; Sinus Surgery-Revision; Allergic Fungal Sinusitis; **Hospital:** NYU Langone Med Ctr (page 104); **Address:** 345 E 37 St, Ste 306, MS 10016, New York, NY 10016-6402; **Phone:** 646-754-1203; **Board Cert:** Otolaryngology 1978; **Med School:** Albert Einstein Coll Med 1974; **Resid:** Surgery, Montefiore Med Ctr 1975; Otolaryngology, NYU Med Ctr 1978; **Fellow:** Plastic/Reconstructive Surgery, UCLA Med Ctr 1979; **Fac Appt:** Prof Oto, NYU Sch Med

Jacobson, Adam S MD (Oto) - **Spec Exp:** Minimally Invasive Surgery; Head & Neck Cancer; Microsurgery; Salivary Gland Tumors & Surgery; **Hospital:** Mt Sinai Beth Israel; **Address:** NY Ctr for Head & Neck, 10 Union Square E, Ste 5B, New York, NY 10003; **Phone:** 212-844-8775; **Board Cert:** Otolaryngology 2007; **Med School:** Rutgers R W Johnson Med Sch 2001; **Resid:** Surgery, Mt Sinai Hosp 2002; Otolaryngology, Mt Sinai Hosp 2006; **Fellow:** Head & Neck Oncology, Mt Sinai Hosp 2007; Microvascular Surgery, Mt Sinai Hosp 2007; **Fac Appt:** Asst Prof Oto, Albert Einstein Coll Med

Jahn, Anthony F MD (Oto) - **Spec Exp:** Voice Disorders/Professional Voice Care; Hearing Loss; Otology & Neuro-Otology; **Hospital:** Mt Sinai Roosevelt; **Address:** Head & Neck Surgical Group, 425 W 59th St Fl 10, New York, NY 10019; **Phone:** 212-262-4400; **Board Cert:** Otolaryngology 1979; **Med School:** Canada 1974; **Resid:** Otolaryngology, Toronto Genl Hosp 1979

Jones, Jacqueline E MD (Oto) - **Spec Exp:** Pediatric Otolaryngology; Sinus Disorders/Surgery; Ear Infections; **Hospital:** NY-Presby/Weill Cornell Med Ctr, NY (page 102), Lenox Hill Hosp; **Address:** 1175 Park Ave, Ste 1A, New York, NY 10128; **Phone:** 212-996-2559; **Board Cert:** Otolaryngology 1989; **Med School:** Cornell Univ 1984; **Resid:** Otolaryngology, Hosp Univ Penn 1989; **Fellow:** Pediatric Otolaryngology, Chldns Hosp 1990; **Fac Appt:** Assoc Prof Oto, Cornell Univ-Weill Med Coll

Josephson, Jordan S MD (Oto) - **Spec Exp:** Rhinoplasty Revision; Endoscopic Sinus Surgery; Nasal & Sinus Disorders; Sleep Apnea; **Hospital:** Lenox Hill Hosp (Manh Eye, Ear & Throat Hosp); **Address:** 205 E 76th St, Ste M1, New York, NY 10021; **Phone:** 212-717-1773; **Board Cert:** Otolaryngology 1988; **Med School:** SUNY Downstate 1983; **Resid:** Surgery, LIJ Med Ctr 1984; Otolaryngology, LIJ Med Ctr 1988; **Fellow:** Sinus Surgery, Johns Hopkins Hosp 1989

Kacker, Ashutosh MD (Oto) - **Spec Exp:** Sinus Surgery; **Hospital:** NY-Presby/Weill Cornell Med Ctr, NY (page 102); **Address:** 1305 York Ave Fl 5, New York, NY 10021; **Phone:** 646-962-5097; **Board Cert:** Otolaryngology 2012; **Med School:** India 1989; **Resid:** Surgery, Lenox Hill Hosp 1997; Otolaryngology, NY Presby Hosp 2001; **Fac Appt:** Assoc Prof Oto, Cornell Univ

Khosh, Maurice M MD (Oto) - **Spec Exp:** Cosmetic Surgery-Face; Reconstructive Surgery-Face; Rhinoplasty; **Hospital:** Mt Sinai Roosevelt; **Address:** 580 Park Ave, Ste 1BE, New York, NY 10065; **Phone:** 212-339-9988; **Board Cert:** Otolaryngology 1997; **Med School:** Albert Einstein Coll Med 1990; **Resid:** Surgery, Columbia Presby Hosp 1992; Otolaryngology, Columbia Presby Hosp 1996; **Fellow:** Facial Plastic Surgery, Univ Washington Med Ctr 1997; **Fac Appt:** Asst Prof Oto, Columbia P&S

Kohan, Darius MD (Oto) - **Spec Exp:** Cochlear Implants; Acoustic Neuroma; Hearing Disorders; Ear Tumors; **Hospital:** Lenox Hill Hosp (Manh Eye, Ear & Throat Hosp), New York Eye & Ear Infirm of Mt Sinai; **Address:** 863 Park Ave, Ste 1E, New York, NY 10021; **Phone:** 212-472-1300; **Board Cert:** Otolaryngology 1990; Neurotology 2012; **Med School:** NYU Sch Med 1984; **Resid:** Surgery, Beth Israel Med Ctr 1986; Otolaryngology, NYU Med Ctr 1990; **Fellow:** Otology, NYU Med Ctr 1991; **Fac Appt:** Assoc Prof Oto, NYU Sch Med

Komisar, Arnold MD/DDS (Oto) - **Spec Exp:** Thyroid & Parathyroid Surgery; Salivary Gland Tumors; Nasal & Sinus Surgery; **Hospital:** Lenox Hill Hosp, NS-LIJ Hlth Sys; **Address:** NY Head & Neck Inst, 130 E 77th St, Fl 10, New York, NY 10075; **Phone:** 212-861-8888; **Board Cert:** Otolaryngology 1979; **Med School:** Hahnemann Univ 1975; **Resid:** Otolaryngology, Mt Sinai Med Ctr 1979; **Fac Appt:** Clin Prof Oto, NYU Sch Med

Koufman, Jamie A MD (Oto) - **Spec Exp:** Voice Disorders; Laryngeal Disorders; **Hospital:** New York Eye & Ear Infirm of Mt Sinai; **Address:** Voice Institute of New York, 200 W 57th St, Ste 1203, New York, NY 10019; **Phone:** 212-463-8014; **Board Cert:** Otolaryngology 1978; **Med School:** Boston Univ 1973; **Resid:** Surgery, Hartford Hosp 1975; Otolaryngology, Boston Univ Med Ctr 1978

Kraus, Dennis H MD (Oto) - **Spec Exp:** Head & Neck Cancer; Skull Base Tumors; Thyroid & Parathyroid Surgery; Sarcoma; **Hospital:** Lenox Hill Hosp, NS-LIJ Hlth Sys; **Address:** NY Head & Neck Inst, 130 E 77th St Fl 10, New York, NY 10075; **Phone:** 212-434-4500; **Board Cert:** Otolaryngology 1990; **Med School:** Univ Rochester 1985; **Resid:** Surgery, Cleveland Clin 1987; Otolaryngology, Cleveland Clin 1990; **Fellow:** Head and Neck Surgery, Meml Sloan-Kettering Cancer Ctr 1991

Krespi, Yosef P MD (Oto) - **Spec Exp:** Sleep Disorders/Apnea/Snoring; Nasal & Sinus Surgery; Head & Neck Cancer & Surgery; Thyroid Cancer; **Hospital:** Lenox Hill Hosp (Manh Eye, Ear & Throat Hosp); **Address:** 110 E 59th St, Ste 10A, New York, NY 10022; **Phone:** 212-434-4500; **Board Cert:** Otolaryngology 1981; **Med School:** Israel 1973; **Resid:** Surgery, Mt Sinai Hosp 1977; Otolaryngology, Mt Sinai Hosp 1980; **Fellow:** Head and Neck Surgery, Mt Sinai Hosp 1980; **Fac Appt:** Clin Prof Oto, Columbia P&S

Krevitt, Lane David MD (Oto) - **Spec Exp:** Thyroid & Parathyroid Surgery; Endoscopic Sinus Surgery; Head & Neck Cancer & Surgery; Sleep Apnea; **Hospital:** Mt Sinai Beth Israel; **Address:** NY Otolaryngology Grp, 36A E 36th St, Ste 200, New York, NY 10016; **Phone:** 212-889-8575; **Board Cert:** Otolaryngology 1999; **Med School:** Hahnemann Univ 1993; **Resid:** Surgery, Montefiore Med Ctr 1994; Otolaryngology, Montefiore Med Ctr 1998; **Fellow:** Head & Neck Surgical Oncology, Montefiore Med Ctr 1999

Kuhel, William I MD (Oto) - **Spec Exp:** Head & Neck Cancer & Surgery; Thyroid Cancer; Parathyroid Cancer; **Hospital:** NY-Presby/Weill Cornell Med Ctr, NY (page 102); **Address:** Weill Greenberg Ctr, 1305 York Ave Fl 5, New York, NY 10021; **Phone:** 646-962-6325; **Board Cert:** Otolaryngology 1988; **Med School:** Univ Mich Med Sch 1983; **Resid:** Surgery, St Vincents Hosp 1985; Otolaryngology, IU Hlth Univ Hosp 1988; **Fellow:** Head and Neck Surgery, MD Anderson Cancer Ctr 1989; **Fac Appt:** Assoc Clin Prof Oto, Cornell Univ-Weill Med Coll

Kuriloff, Daniel B MD (Oto) - **Spec Exp:** Thyroid Disorders; Thyroid Cancer & Surgery; Minimally Invasive Surgery; **Hospital:** Lenox Hill Hosp; **Address:** NY Head & Neck Inst, 110 E 59th St, Ste 10A, New York, NY 10022; **Phone:** 212-262-5555; **Board Cert:** Otolaryngology 1988; **Med School:** Mount Sinai Sch Med 1982; **Resid:** Surgery, Beth Israel Hosp 1984; Otolaryngology, NY Eye & Ear Infirmary 1988; **Fellow:** Head & Neck Surgical Oncology, Univ Mich Med Ctr 1990; **Fac Appt:** Assoc Clin Prof Oto, Columbia P&S

Lalwani, Anil K MD (Oto) - **Spec Exp:** Ear Disorders/Surgery; Facial Nerve Disorders; Cochlear Implants; Skull Base Surgery; **Hospital:** NY-Presby/Columbia Univ Med Ctr, NY (page 102); **Address:** NY-Presby, Otolaryngology, 180 Fort Washington Ave Fl 7, New York, NY 10032; **Phone:** 212-305-1696; **Board Cert:** Otolaryngology 1992; Neurotology 2010; **Med School:** Univ Mich Med Sch 1985; **Resid:** Surgery, Duke Univ Hosp 1987; Otolaryngology, UCSF Med Ctr 1991; **Fellow:** Skull Base Surgery, UCSF Med Ctr 1992; Molecular Genetics, Natl Inst Hlth 1994; **Fac Appt:** Prof Oto, Columbia P&S

Lawson, William MD (Oto) - **Spec Exp:** Sinus Disorders/Surgery; Endoscopic Sinus Surgery; **Hospital:** Mt Sinai Hosp; **Address:** 5 E 98th St Fl 8, Box 1191, New York, NY 10029-6501; **Phone:** 212-241-9410; **Board Cert:** Otolaryngology 1974; **Med School:** NYU Sch Med 1965; **Resid:** Surgery, Bronx VA Hosp 1967; Otolaryngology, Mt Sinai Hosp 1974; **Fac Appt:** Prof Oto, Mount Sinai Sch Med

Lebovics, Robert S MD (Oto) - **Spec Exp:** Head & Neck Inflammatory Disorders; Head & Neck Autoimmune Disease; Head & Neck Infectious Disease; Wegener's Granulomatosis; **Hospital:** Mt Sinai Roosevelt; **Address:** 425 W 59th St, Fl 10, New York, NY 10019; **Phone:** 212-262-2002; **Board Cert:** Otolaryngology 1988; **Med School:** SUNY Downstate 1982; **Resid:** Surgery, Montefiore-Weiler Einstein Div 1983; Otolaryngology, Montefiore-Weiler Einstein Div 1987

Li, Chun-Lun James MD (Oto) - **Spec Exp:** Laryngeal Disorders; Facial Nerve Disorders; Head & Neck Surgery; **Hospital:** New York Eye & Ear Infirm of Mt Sinai; **Address:** 128 Mott St, Ste 608, New York, NY 10013; **Phone:** 212-343-8399; **Board Cert:** Otolaryngology 2012; **Med School:** Mount Sinai Sch Med 1996; **Resid:** Surgery, Beth Israel Med Ctr 1997; Otolaryngology, NY Eye & Ear Infirmary 2001; **Fac Appt:** Asst Prof Oto, NY Med Coll

Lim, Jessica W MD (Oto) - **Spec Exp:** Head & Neck Cancer; Sinus Disorders; Sleep Disorders; Swallowing Disorders; **Hospital:** Lenox Hill Hosp, Lenox Hill Hosp (Manh Eye, Ear & Throat Hosp); **Address:** Lenox Otolaryngology Head & Neck Surgery, 186 E 76th St Fl 2, New York, NY 10021; **Phone:** 212-434-2323; **Board Cert:** Otolaryngology 1998; **Med School:** W VA Univ 1991; **Resid:** Surgery, NYU Med Ctr 1993; Otolaryngology, NYU Med Ctr 1997; **Fellow:** Head and Neck Surgery, Rush Univ Med Ctr 1998; **Fac Appt:** Asst Prof Oto, SUNY Downstate

Linstrom, Christopher James MD (Oto) - **Spec Exp:** Cochlear Implants; Acoustic Neuroma; Otology & Neuro-Otology; Cholesteatoma; **Hospital:** New York Eye & Ear Infirm of Mt Sinai, Westchester Med Ctr; **Address:** NY Eye & Ear Infirm, Otolaryngology, 310 E 14th St, Fl 6, New York, NY 10003; **Phone:** 212-979-4200; **Board Cert:** Otolaryngology 1987; Neurotology 2004; **Med School:** McGill Univ 1982; **Resid:** Surgery, G Washington Univ Hosp 1984; Otolaryngology, NY-Presby/Weill Cornell Med Ctr 1987; **Fellow:** Otology & Neurotology, Michigan Ear Inst 1989; **Fac Appt:** Prof Oto, Mount Sinai-Icahn Sch of Med

Lustig, Lawrence R MD (Oto) - **Spec Exp:** Ear Disorders/Surgery; Hearing Loss; **Hospital:** NY-Presby/Columbia Univ Med Ctr, NY (page 102); **Address:** 51 W 51st St, New York, NY 10019; **Phone:** 212-326-8475; **Board Cert:** Otolaryngology 1998; Neurotology 2006; **Med School:** UCSF 1992; **Resid:** Otolaryngology, UCSF Med Ctr 1997; **Fellow:** Neurotology, John Hopkins Hosp 1999; **Fac Appt:** Prof Oto, Columbia P&S

Markowitz, Arlene H MD (Oto) - **Spec Exp:** Sinus Disorders/Surgery; Endoscopic Sinus Surgery; **Hospital:** NY-Presby/Columbia Univ Med Ctr, NY (page 102), Lenox Hill Hosp; **Address:** 903 Park Ave, New York, NY 10075; **Phone:** 212-794-3999; **Board Cert:** Otolaryngology 1990; **Med School:** Columbia P&S 1984; **Resid:** Otolaryngology, NY-Presby/Columbia Univ Med Ctr 1990; **Fac Appt:** Asst Clin Prof Oto, Columbia P&S

McMenomey, Sean O MD (Oto) - **Spec Exp:** Otology & Neuro-Otology; Hearing Loss; Dizziness/Vertigo; Cochlear Implants; **Hospital:** NYU Langone Med Ctr (page 104), Bellevue Hosp Ctr; **Address:** NYU Otology Assocs, 550 First Ave, Ste 7Q, New York, NY 10016; **Phone:** 212-263-5565; **Board Cert:** Otolaryngology 1993; Neurotology 2014; **Med School:** St Louis Univ 1987; **Resid:** Otolaryngology, Oregon Hlth Sci Ctr 1992; **Fellow:** Otology & Neurotology, Vanderbilt Univ Hosp 1993; **Fac Appt:** Prof Oto, NYU Sch Med

Miller, Philip J MD (Oto) - **Spec Exp:** Rhinoplasty; Cosmetic Surgery-Face; Facial Nerve Disorders; **Hospital:** Lenox Hill Hosp (Manh Eye, Ear & Throat Hosp), NYU Langone Med Ctr (page 104); **Address:** 60 E 56th St Fl 3, New York, NY 10022; **Phone:** 212-750-7100; **Board Cert:** Otolaryngology 1996; Facial Plastic & Reconstr Surgery 1999; **Med School:** Univ Mass Sch Med 1989; **Resid:** Surgery, NYU Med Ctr 1991; Otolaryngology, NYU Med Ctr 1995; **Fellow:** Facial Plastic Surgery, Oregon Hlth Sci Ctr 1996; **Fac Appt:** Asst Prof Oto, NYU Sch Med

Myssiorek, David MD (Oto) - **Spec Exp:** Thyroid & Parathyroid Surgery; Head & Neck Cancer; Salivary Gland Surgery; Paragangliomas; **Hospital:** NYU Langone Med Ctr (page 104), Bellevue Hosp Ctr; **Address:** 160 E 34th St Fl 7, New York, NY 10016; **Phone:** 212-731-6085; **Board Cert:** Otolaryngology 1985; **Med School:** NYU Sch Med 1980; **Resid:** Otolaryngology, Bellevue/NYU/VA Med Ctr 1984; **Fellow:** Head & Neck Oncology, Montefiore Med Ctr 1985; **Fac Appt:** Prof Oto, NYU Sch Med

Nass, Richard L MD (Oto) - **Spec Exp:** Allergy; Sinus Disorders/Surgery; Nasal Surgery; **Hospital:** NYU Langone Med Ctr (page 104), Lenox Hill Hosp; **Address:** 1430 2nd Ave, Ste 108, New York, NY 10021; **Phone:** 212-734-4515; **Board Cert:** Otolaryngology 1979; **Med School:** NYU Sch Med 1975; **Resid:** Otolaryngology, NYU-Bellevue Hosp 1979; **Fac Appt:** Assoc Clin Prof Oto, NYU Sch Med

Pastorek, Norman MD (Oto) - **Spec Exp:** Rhinoplasty; Eyelid Surgery; Cosmetic Surgery-Face; **Hospital:** Lenox Hill Hosp (Manh Eye, Ear & Throat Hosp), NY-Presby/Weill Cornell Med Ctr, NY (page 102); **Address:** 1127 Park Ave, New York, NY 10128; **Phone:** 212-987-4700; **Board Cert:** Otolaryngology 1970; Facial Plastic & Reconstr Surgery 2008; **Med School:** Univ IL Coll Med 1964; **Resid:** Surgery, Hines VA Hosp 1966; Otolaryngology, Univ IL Med Ctr 1969; **Fac Appt:** Clin Prof Oto, Cornell Univ-Weill Med Coll

Persky, Mark S MD (Oto) - **Spec Exp:** Head & Neck Cancer; Skull Base Tumors; Thyroid Cancer; Vascular Lesions-Head & Neck; **Hospital:** NYU Langone Med Ctr (page 104), New York Eye & Ear Infirm of Mt Sinai; **Address:** NYU Langone Med Ctr, Otolaryngology Dept, 160 E 34th St Fl 7, New York, NY 10016; **Phone:** 212-731-6161; **Board Cert:** Otolaryngology 1976; **Med School:** SUNY Upstate Med Univ 1972; **Resid:** Otolaryngology, NYU Bellevue Hosp 1976; **Fellow:** Head and Neck Surgery, Beth Israel Med Ctr 1977; **Fac Appt:** Prof Oto, NYU Sch Med

Pincus, Robert L MD (Oto) - **Spec Exp:** Sinus Disorders; Voice Disorders; Endoscopic Sinus Surgery; Facial Plastic & Reconstructive Surgery; **Hospital:** Mt Sinai Beth Israel, Lenox Hill Hosp; **Address:** NY Otolaryngology Grp, 36A E 36th St, Ste 200, New York, NY 10016-3401; **Phone:** 212-889-8575; **Board Cert:** Otolaryngology 1983; **Med School:** Univ Mich Med Sch 1978; **Resid:** Otolaryngology, Mt Sinai Med Ctr 1983; **Fac Appt:** Assoc Prof Oto, NY Med Coll

Pitman, Michael J MD (Oto) - **Spec Exp:** Laryngeal & Voice Disorders; Voice Disorders/Professional Voice Care; Swallowing Disorders; Airway Disorders; **Hospital:** New York Eye & Ear Infirm of Mt Sinai; **Address:** NY Eye & Ear Infirmary of Mount Sinai, Department of Otolaryngology, 310 E 14th St, Fl 6th, New York, NY 10003; **Phone:** 212-979-4119; **Board Cert:** Otolaryngology 2004; **Med School:** Albert Einstein Coll Med 1998; **Resid:** Surgery, Beth Israel Med Ctr 1999; Otolaryngology, NY Eye & Ear Infirm 2003; **Fellow:** Laryngology, Vanderbilt Univ Med Ctr 2004; **Fac Appt:** Assoc Prof Oto, NY Med Coll

Pollack, Geoffrey MD (Oto) - **Spec Exp:** Head & Neck Surgery; **Hospital:** Mt Sinai St. Luke's; **Address:** 211 Central Park West, New York, NY 10024; **Phone:** 212-873-6175; **Board Cert:** Otolaryngology 1984; **Med School:** Columbia P&S 1979; **Resid:** Otolaryngology, Columbia-Presby Med Ctr 1984

Portnoy, William M MD (Oto) - **Spec Exp:** Facial Plastic & Reconstructive Surgery; Head & Neck Cancer Reconstruction; Rhinoplasty; Rhinoplasty Revision; **Hospital:** Mt Sinai Beth Israel, New York Eye & Ear Infirm of Mt Sinai; **Address:** Chelsea Otolaryngology, 160 W 18th St Fl Ground, New York, NY 10011; **Phone:** 212-366-0848 x201; **Board Cert:** Otolaryngology 1993; Facial Plastic & Reconstr Surgery 1996; **Med School:** Geo Wash Univ 1987; **Resid:** Otolaryngology, NY E&E Infirmary 1992; **Fellow:** Microvascular Surgery, UPMC Mercy Hosp 1993

Rizk, Samieh S MD (Oto) - **Spec Exp:** Facial Plastic & Reconstructive Surgery; Rhinoplasty Revision; Nasal Surgery; **Hospital:** Lenox Hill Hosp; **Address:** 1040 Park Ave, New York, NY 10028; **Phone:** 212-452-3362; **Board Cert:** Otolaryngology 2000; Facial Plastic & Reconstr Surgery 2014; **Med School:** Univ Mich Med Sch 1993; **Resid:** Surgery, Lenox Hill Hosp 1995; Otolaryngology, Manhattan EE&T Hosp 1998; **Fellow:** Facial Plastic & Reconstr Surgery, Facial Surgery Ctr 1999

Roland Jr, J. Thomas MD (Oto) - **Spec Exp:** Acoustic Neuroma; Cochlear Implants; Neuro-Otology; Facial Nerve Disorders; **Hospital:** NYU Langone Med Ctr (page 104); **Address:** NYU Otology Assocs, 550 1st Ave, Ste 7Q, New York, NY 10016; **Phone:** 212-263-5565; **Board Cert:** Otolaryngology 1993; Neurotology 2014; **Med School:** Temple Univ 1983; **Resid:** Otolaryngology, NYU Med Ctr 1992; **Fellow:** Neurotology, NYU Med Ctr 1993; **Fac Appt:** Prof Oto, NYU Sch Med

Rosenberg, David B MD (Oto) - **Spec Exp:** Rhinoplasty Revision; Cosmetic Surgery-Face; Reconstructive Plastic Surgery; **Hospital:** Lenox Hill Hosp (Manh Eye, Ear & Throat Hosp); **Address:** 115 E 61st St Fl 1, New York, NY 10065; **Phone:** 212-832-8595; **Board Cert:** Otolaryngology 2000; Facial Plastic & Reconstr Surgery 2012; **Med School:** Cornell Univ-Weill Med Coll 1993; **Resid:** Surgery, Lenox Hill 1995; Otolaryngology, Manhattan EE&T Hosp 1999; **Fellow:** Facial Plastic Surgery, RWJohnson Univ Hosp 2000

Rothstein, Stephen G MD (Oto) - **Spec Exp:** Voice Disorders; Swallowing Disorders; Laser Surgery; **Hospital:** NYU Langone Med Ctr (page 104); **Address:** 240 E 38th St Fl 14, New York, NY 10016; **Phone:** 212-263-7165; **Board Cert:** Otolaryngology 1988; **Med School:** Ros Franklin Univ/Chicago Med Sch 1982; **Resid:** Surgery, NYU Med Ctr 1984; Otolaryngology, NYU Med Ctr 1987; **Fellow:** Head and Neck Surgery, NYU Med Ctr 1988; **Fac Appt:** Assoc Clin Prof Oto, NYU Sch Med

Sacks, Steven H MD (Oto) - **Spec Exp:** Sinus Disorders/Surgery; Thyroid & Parathyroid Surgery; Salivary Gland Tumors & Surgery; **Hospital:** Mt Sinai Hosp; **Address:** 210 E 86th St, Fl 9th, New York, NY 10028; **Phone:** 212-722-5570; **Board Cert:** Otolaryngology 1981; **Med School:** Washington Univ, St Louis 1977; **Resid:** Otolaryngology, Mt Sinai Hosp 1981; **Fac Appt:** Asst Clin Prof Oto, Mount Sinai Sch Med

Schaefer, Steven D MD (Oto) - **Spec Exp:** Sinus Disorders/Surgery; Head & Neck Surgery; Endoscopic Sinus Surgery; Sinus Tumors; **Hospital:** Lenox Hill Hosp, NS-LIJ Hlth Sys; **Address:** NY Head & Neck Inst, 110 W 59th St, Ste 10A, New York, NY 10022; **Phone:** 212-434-4500 x3; **Board Cert:** Otolaryngology 1978; **Med School:** UC Irvine 1972; **Resid:** Surgery, UCLA Med Ctr 1974; Otolaryngology, Stanford Univ Hosp & Clins 1977; **Fellow:** Neurophysiology, Univ CA Affil Hosp 1972; **Fac Appt:** Prof Oto, NY Med Coll

Schantz, Stimson P MD (Oto) - **Spec Exp:** Head & Neck Surgery; Head & Neck Cancer; Thyroid Cancer; **Hospital:** New York Eye & Ear Infirm of Mt Sinai, Mt Sinai Beth Israel; **Address:** 310 E 14th St Fl 6, New York, NY 10003; **Phone:** 646-943-7935; **Board Cert:** Surgery 2005; **Med School:** Univ Cincinnati 1975; **Resid:** Surgery, Georgetown Univ Med Ctr 1982; Otolaryngology, Univ Illinois Eye & Ear Infirm 1980; **Fellow:** Surgical Oncology, MD Anderson Cancer Ctr 1984; **Fac Appt:** Prof Oto, NY Med Coll

Schneider, Kenneth L MD (Oto) - **Spec Exp:** Snoring/Sleep Apnea; Nasal & Sinus Disorders; Sleep Disorders/Apnea; **Hospital:** NYU Langone Med Ctr (page 104); **Address:** NYU, Otolaryngology, 240 E 38th St Fl 14, New York, NY 10016; **Phone:** 212-263-7165; **Board Cert:** Otolaryngology 1982; **Med School:** SUNY Downstate 1978; **Resid:** Otolaryngology, NYU Med Ctr 1982; **Fellow:** Head and Neck Surgery, Montefiore Med Ctr 1983; **Fac Appt:** Assoc Prof Oto, NYU Sch Med

Sclafani, Anthony P MD (Oto) - **Spec Exp:** Cosmetic Surgery-Face; Rhinoplasty; Botox Therapy; Facial Rejuvenation; **Hospital:** New York Eye & Ear Infirm of Mt Sinai, Northern Westchester Hosp; **Address:** NY Eye & Ear Infirm, Otolaryngology, 310 E 14th St, Fl 6, New York, NY 10003; **Phone:** 646-943-7935; **Board Cert:** Otolaryngology 1996; Facial Plastic & Reconstr Surgery 1999; **Med School:** Univ Pennsylvania 1989; **Resid:** Surgery, Beth Israel Med Ctr 1991; Otolaryngology, NY Eye & Ear Infirm 1995; **Fellow:** Facial Plastic & Reconstr Surgery, St Louis Univ Hosp 1996; **Fac Appt:** Prof Oto, Mount Sinai Sch Med

Selesnick, Samuel H MD (Oto) - **Spec Exp:** Acoustic Neuroma; Cholesteatoma; Hearing Disorders; Cochlear Implant; **Hospital:** NY-Presby/Weill Cornell Med Ctr, NY (page 102), Meml Sloan Kettering Canc Ctr (page 110); **Address:** 1305 York Ave, Fl 5, New York, NY 10021; **Phone:** 646-962-3277; **Board Cert:** Otolaryngology 1990; Neurotology 2008; **Med School:** NYU Sch Med 1985; **Resid:** Surgery, St Vincent's Med Ctr 1987; Otolaryngology, Manhattan EE&T Hosp 1990; **Fellow:** Skull Base Surgery, UCSF Med Ctr 1991; **Fac Appt:** Prof Oto, Cornell Univ-Weill Med Coll

Shemen, Larry J MD (Oto) - **Spec Exp:** Head & Neck Cancer; Thyroid Cancer; Parathyroid Cancer; Snoring/Sleep Apnea; **Hospital:** NY Hosp Queens (page 498), Lenox Hill Hosp; **Address:** 233 E 69th St, Ste 1D, New York, NY 10021; **Phone:** 212-472-8882; **Board Cert:** Otolaryngology 1983; **Med School:** Univ Toronto 1978; **Resid:** Surgery, Cedar-Sinai Med Ctr 1982; Otolaryngology, Weilesley Hosps 1983; **Fellow:** Head and Neck Surgery, Meml Sloan-Kettering Cancer Ctr 1984; **Fac Appt:** Assoc Clin Prof Oto, Cornell Univ-Weill Med Coll

Shin, Edward J MD (Oto) - **Spec Exp:** Head & Neck Surgery; Rhinosinusitis; Clinical Trials; Thyroid Surgery; **Hospital:** New York Eye & Ear Infirm of Mt Sinai, Mt Sinai Beth Israel; **Address:** NY Ear, Nose & Throat Ctr, 310 E 14th St Fl 6, New York, NY 10003; **Phone:** 646-943-7985; **Board Cert:** Otolaryngology 2013; **Med School:** Stanford Univ 1997; **Resid:** Surgery, UCSF Med Ctr 1998; Otolaryngology, UCSF Med Ctr 2002; **Fac Appt:** Assoc Prof Oto, Mount Sinai Sch Med

Shohet, Michael R MD (Oto) - **Spec Exp:** Craniofacial Surgery; Sinus Disorders/Surgery; Facial Plastic & Reconstructive Surgery; **Hospital:** Mt Sinai Hosp; **Address:** ENT & Allergy Assocs, 620 Columbus Ave Fl 2, New York, NY 10024; **Phone:** 212-600-9411; **Board Cert:** Otolaryngology 2001; Facial Plastic & Reconstr Surgery 2014; **Med School:** Univ Cincinnati 1994; **Resid:** Surgery, Loyola Univ Med Ctr 1995; Otolaryngology, Mayo Clin 2000; **Fellow:** Craniofacial Surgery, Univ Bern Affil Hosp 2001; **Fac Appt:** Asst Prof Oto, Mount Sinai Sch Med

Shugar, Joel MD (Oto) - **Spec Exp:** Facial Plastic Surgery; Head & Neck Surgery; Nasal & Sinus Disorders; **Hospital:** Mt Sinai Hosp; **Address:** 55 E 87th St, Ste 1K, New York, NY 10128-1043; **Phone:** 212-289-1731; **Board Cert:** Otolaryngology 1978; **Med School:** McGill Univ 1972; **Resid:** Otolaryngology, Mount Sinai Med Ctr 1978; **Fac Appt:** Assoc Clin Prof Oto, Mount Sinai Sch Med

Singh, Bhuvanesh MD/PhD (Oto) - **Spec Exp:** Head & Neck Cancer & Surgery; Thyroid Cancer; **Hospital:** Meml Sloan Kettering Canc Ctr (page 110); **Address:** MSKCC, Head & Neck Cancer, 1275 York Ave, Ste 5, New York, NY 10065; **Phone:** 212-639-2024; **Board Cert:** Otolaryngology 1998; **Med School:** SUNY Downstate 1991; **Resid:** Otolaryngology, SUNY Downstate Med Ctr 1997; **Fellow:** Head and Neck Surgery, Meml Sloan-Kettering Cancer Ctr 1999; **Fac Appt:** Assoc Prof Oto, Cornell Univ-Weill Med Coll

Slavit, David H MD (Oto) - **Spec Exp:** Voice Disorders; Nasal & Sinus Disorders; Head & Neck Surgery; Thyroid Surgery; **Hospital:** Lenox Hill Hosp, Lenox Hill Hosp (Manh Eye, Ear & Throat Hosp); **Address:** 787 Park Ave, New York, NY 10021-3552; **Phone:** 212-517-9177; **Board Cert:** Otolaryngology 1992; **Med School:** Mount Sinai Sch Med 1986; **Resid:** Otolaryngology, Mayo Clinic 1991; **Fac Appt:** Asst Prof Oto, SUNY Hlth Sci Ctr

Slupchynskyj, Oleh S MD (Oto) - **Spec Exp:** Facial Plastic & Reconstructive Surgery; Eyelid Surgery/Blepharoplasty; Facial Surgery-Chin & Lip; Rhinoplasty; **Hospital:** New York Eye & Ear Infirm of Mt Sinai, Lenox Hill Hosp (Manh Eye, Ear & Throat Hosp); **Address:** 44 E 65th St, Ste 1A, New York, NY 10065; **Phone:** 212-628-6464; **Board Cert:** Otolaryngology 1998; Facial Plastic & Reconstr Surgery 2012; **Med School:** NY Med Coll 1991; **Resid:** Otolaryngology, NY Eye & Ear Infirm 1997; **Fellow:** Facial Plastic Surgery, Univ Rochester Strong Meml Hosp 1998

Stewart, Michael G MD (Oto) - **Spec Exp:** Nasal & Sinus Disorders; Sleep Disorders/Apnea; Head & Neck Surgery; Vocal Cord Disorders; **Hospital:** NY-Presby/Weill Cornell Med Ctr, NY (page 102); **Address:** Weill Greenberg Ctr, 1305 York Ave Fl 5, New York, NY 10021; **Phone:** 646-962-6673; **Board Cert:** Otolaryngology 1995; **Med School:** Johns Hopkins Univ 1988; **Resid:** Surgery, Baylor Med Ctr 1990; Otolaryngology, Baylor Med Ctr 1994; **Fac Appt:** Prof Oto, Cornell Univ-Weill Med Coll

Storper, Ian S MD (Oto) - **Spec Exp:** Cochlear Implants; Acoustic Neuroma; Meniere's Disease; Balance Disorders; **Hospital:** Lenox Hill Hosp (Manh Eye, Ear & Throat Hosp), Lenox Hill Hosp; **Address:** NY Head & Neck Inst, 110 E 59th St, Ste 10A, New York, NY 10022; **Phone:** 212-434-4500 x3; **Board Cert:** Otolaryngology 1995; **Med School:** Univ Pennsylvania 1988; **Resid:** Otolaryngology, UCLA Med Ctr 1994; **Fellow:** Otology & Neurotology, Ear Fdn 1995

Strome, Marshall MD (Oto) - **Spec Exp:** Voice Disorders; Swallowing Disorders; Head & Neck Cancer Reconstruction; Head & Neck Cancer & Surgery; **Hospital:** Mt Sinai St. Luke's, Mt Sinai Hosp; **Address:** 425 W 59th St, Fl 10, New York, NY 10019; **Phone:** 212-262-4444; **Board Cert:** Otolaryngology 1970; **Med School:** Univ Mich Med Sch 1964; **Resid:** Surgery, Harper Hosp 1966; Otolaryngology, Univ Michigan Hosp 1970; **Fac Appt:** Prof Oto, Univ Mich Med Sch

Sulica, Radu Lucian MD (Oto) - **Spec Exp:** Laryngeal Disorders; Voice Disorders; Vocal Cord Disorders; Botox Therapy; **Hospital:** NY-Presby/Weill Cornell Med Ctr, NY (page 102); **Address:** Weill Greenberg Ctr, 1305 York Ave, Fl 5, New York, NY 10021; **Phone:** 646-962-4734; **Board Cert:** Otolaryngology 2000; **Med School:** Georgetown Univ 1993; **Resid:** Surgery, Georgetown Univ Hosp 1995; Otolaryngology, Georgetown Univ Hosp 1999; **Fellow:** Laryngology, St Lukes-Roosevelt Hosp 2000; **Fac Appt:** Assoc Prof Oto, Cornell Univ-Weill Med Coll

Teng, Marita S MD (Oto) - **Spec Exp:** Throat Cancer; Tongue Cancer; Thyroid Disorders; Laryngeal Cancer; **Hospital:** Mt Sinai Hosp; **Address:** 10 E 102nd St, Fl 3, New York, NY 10029; **Phone:** 212-241-9410; **Board Cert:** Otolaryngology 2005; **Med School:** Baylor Coll Med 1999; **Resid:** Surgery, Mt Sinai Med Ctr 2000; Otolaryngology, Mt Sinai Med Ctr 2004; **Fellow:** Head and Neck Surgery, Univ Washington Med Ctr 2005; **Fac Appt:** Assoc Prof Oto, Mount Sinai Sch Med

Urken, Mark MD (Oto) - **Spec Exp:** Head & Neck Cancer & Surgery; Head & Neck Cancer Reconstruction; Thyroid & Parathyroid Cancer & Surgery; Salivary Gland Tumors; **Hospital:** Mt Sinai Beth Israel; **Address:** Inst Head, Neck & Thyroid Cancer, 10 Union Square E, Ste 5B, New York, NY 10003; **Phone:** 212-844-8775; **Board Cert:** Otolaryngology 1986; **Med School:** Univ VA Sch Med 1981; **Resid:** Otolaryngology, Mt Sinai Hosp 1986; **Fellow:** Head and Neck Surgery, Mercy Hosp 1987; **Fac Appt:** Prof Oto, Albert Einstein Coll Med

Volpi, David O MD (Oto) - **Spec Exp:** Sinus Disorders; Sleep Disorders; Snoring/Sleep Apnea; **Hospital:** Lenox Hill Hosp, New York Eye & Ear Infirm of Mt Sinai; **Address:** eOs Sleep, 262 Central Park West, Ste 1H, New York, NY 10024; **Phone:** 212-873-6036; **Board Cert:** Otolaryngology 1988; **Med School:** Hahnemann Univ 1982; **Resid:** Otolaryngology, NY Eye & Ear Infirm 1988

Waner, Milton MD (Oto) - **Spec Exp:** Pediatric Facial Plastic Surgery; Birthmarks/Hemangiomas; Vascular Malformations; **Hospital:** Lenox Hill Hosp (Manh Eye, Ear & Throat Hosp); **Address:** Ctr Vascular Birthmarks, 210 E 64th St Fl 7, New York, NY 10065; **Phone:** 212-434-4050; **Med School:** South Africa 1977; **Resid:** Surgery, Univ Witwatersrand 1980; Otolaryngology, Univ Witwatersrand 1984; **Fellow:** Otolaryngology, Univ Cincinnatti Med Ctr 1985

Westreich, Richard W MD (Oto) - **Spec Exp:** Rhinoplasty; Facial Plastic & Reconstructive Surgery; Cosmetic Surgery-Face; Nasal & Sinus Surgery; **Hospital:** Mt Sinai Hosp, Lenox Hill Hosp; **Address:** 969 Park Ave, Ste 1C, New York, NY 10028; **Phone:** 212-595-1922; **Board Cert:** Otolaryngology 2005; Facial Plastic & Reconstr Surgery 2007; **Med School:** NYU Sch Med 1999; **Resid:** Otolaryngology, Mt Sinai Hosp 2004; **Fellow:** Facial Plastic Surgery, Mt Sinai Hosp 2005; **Fac Appt:** Asst Prof Oto, SUNY Downstate

White, William Matthew MD (Oto) - **Spec Exp:** Cosmetic Surgery-Face; Facial Plastic & Reconstructive Surgery; Skin Cancer-Head & Neck; **Hospital:** NYU Langone Med Ctr (page 104); **Address:** 240 E 38th St Fl 14, New York, NY 10016; **Phone:** 646-501-7906; **Board Cert:** Otolaryngology 2010; Facial Plastic & Reconstr Surgery 2011; **Med School:** Univ Toledo, Med Univ OH 2001; **Resid:** Surgery, Mass Genl Hosp 2002; Otolaryngology, Mass Eye & Ear Infirm 2008; **Fellow:** Facial Plastic & Reconstr Surgery, NYU Sch Med Affil Hosp 2009; **Fac Appt:** Asst Prof Oto, NYU Sch Med

Wong, Richard J MD (Oto) - **Spec Exp:** Head & Neck Cancer; Thyroid Cancer; **Hospital:** Meml Sloan Kettering Canc Ctr (page 110); **Address:** MSKCC, Head & Neck Cancer, 1275 York Ave, New York, NY 10065; **Phone:** 212-639-7638; **Board Cert:** Otolaryngology 2000; **Med School:** Harvard Med Sch 1994; **Resid:** Otolaryngology, Mass Genl Hosp 1999; **Fellow:** Head & Neck Surgical Oncology, Meml Sloan-Kettering Cancer Ctr 2000

Woo, Peak MD (Oto) - **Spec Exp:** Voice Disorders; Laryngeal Disorders; Laryngeal Cancer; **Hospital:** Mt Sinai Hosp; **Address:** 300 Central Park West, Ste 1-H, New York, NY 10024; **Phone:** 212-580-1004; **Board Cert:** Otolaryngology 1983; **Med School:** Boston Univ 1978; **Resid:** Otolaryngology, Boston Univ Med Ctr 1983; **Fac Appt:** Clin Prof Oto, Mount Sinai Sch Med

Zimbler, Marc S MD (Oto) - **Spec Exp:** Cosmetic Surgery-Face; Blepharoplasty; Rhinoplasty; Reconstructive Surgery-Face; **Hospital:** Mt Sinai Beth Israel, Lenox Hill Hosp (Manh Eye, Ear & Throat Hosp); **Address:** 990 5th Ave, New York, NY 10075; **Phone:** 212-570-9900; **Board Cert:** Otolaryngology 2001; Facial Plastic & Reconstr Surgery 2012; **Med School:** Mount Sinai Sch Med 1993; **Resid:** Surgery, NYU Med Ctr 1995; Otolaryngology, NYU Med Ctr 1999; **Fac Appt:** Asst Prof Oto, Albert Einstein Coll Med

Pain Medicine

Ahmed Hosny, M Amr MD (PM) - **Spec Exp:** Pain-Spine; Pain-Neuropathic; Pain-Chronic; **Address:** NY Pain Care, 95 University Pl Fl 8, New York, NY 10003; **Phone:** 212-604-1300; **Board Cert:** Anesthesiology 2014; Pain Medicine 2004; Hospice & Palliative Medicine 2008; **Med School:** Egypt 1995; **Resid:** Anesthesiology, St Lukes-Roosevelt Hosp Ctr 2002; **Fellow:** Pain Management, Beth Israel Deaconess Med Ctr 2003; **Fac Appt:** Assoc Prof Anes, NY Med Coll

Bakshi, Sanjay MD (PM) - **Spec Exp:** Pain-Spine; Pain-Back & Neck; **Hospital:** Lenox Hill Hosp, Bayshore Community Hosp; **Address:** Manhattan Spine & Pain Med, 115 E 57th St, Ste 610, New York, NY 10022; **Phone:** 212-535-3505; **Board Cert:** Anesthesiology 1995; Pain Medicine 2007; **Med School:** India 1989; **Resid:** Anesthesiology, Brookdale Hosp Med Ctr 1994; **Fellow:** Pain Medicine, Johns Hopkins Hosp 1995

Chapman, Kenneth B MD (PM) - **Spec Exp:** Pain-Spine; Pain-Back & Neck; Pain-Interventional Techniques; **Hospital:** NYU Langone Med Ctr (page 104), Staten Island Univ Hosp - North; **Address:** The Spine & Pain Institute of NY, 860 5th Ave, Ste 1B, New York, NY 10065; **Phone:** 212-724-7246; **Board Cert:** Anesthesiology 2006; Pain Medicine 2007; **Med School:** Grenada 2001; **Resid:** Anesthesiology, NY Presby-Columia ed Ctr 2005; **Fellow:** Pain Medicine, Cleveland Clinic 2006

Diwan, Sudhir A MD (PM) - **Spec Exp:** Pain-After Spinal Intervention; Pain-Musculoskeletal; Pain-Neuropathic; Pain-Cancer; **Hospital:** Lenox Hill Hosp; **Address:** Manhattan Spine & Pain Med, 115 E 57th St, Ste 610, New York, NY 10022; **Phone:** 212-535-3505; **Board Cert:** Anesthesiology 2012; Pain Medicine 2013; **Med School:** India 1983; **Resid:** Surgery, St Lukes-Roosevelt Hosp Ctr 1994; Anesthesiology, St Lukes-Roosevelt Hosp Ctr 1997; **Fellow:** Pain Medicine, NY-Presby/Weill Cornell Med Ctr 1998

Epstein, Lawrence J MD (PM) - **Spec Exp:** Pain-Spine; Pain-Neck; Sciatica; **Hospital:** Mt Sinai Hosp; **Address:** Mount Sinai Medical Ctr, Pain Management, 5 E 98th St Fl 6, Box 1192, New York, NY 10029; **Phone:** 212-241-6372; **Board Cert:** Anesthesiology 1987; Pain Medicine 2014; **Med School:** Israel 1983; **Resid:** Anesthesiology, SUNY Brooklyn Med Ctr 1986; **Fellow:** Obstetrics & Anesthesiology, SUNY Brooklyn Med Ctr 1987; **Fac Appt:** Asst Prof Anes, Mount Sinai Sch Med

Freedman, Gordon MD (PM) - **Spec Exp:** Pain-Back & Neck; Reflex Sympathetic Dystrophy (RSD); Pain-Neuropathic; Pain-Cancer; **Hospital:** Mt Sinai Hosp, Mt Sinai Hosp of Queens; **Address:** 1540 York Ave, New York, NY 10028; **Phone:** 212-288-2180; **Board Cert:** Anesthesiology 1992; Pain Medicine 2014; **Med School:** Israel 1985; **Resid:** Anesthesiology, Mt Sinai Hosp 1991; **Fellow:** Pain Medicine, Mt Sinai Hosp 1991; **Fac Appt:** Assoc Prof Anes, Mount Sinai-Icahn Sch of Med

Gharibo, Christopher G MD (PM) - **Spec Exp:** Pain-Back & Neck; Pain-Neuropathic; Pain-Chronic; Complex Regional Pain Syndromes; **Hospital:** NYU Langone Med Ctr (page 104), NYU Hosp For Joint Dis (page 104); **Address:** NYU, Ctr Musculoskeletal Care, 333 E 38th St, Fl 6, New York, NY 10016; **Phone:** 646-501-7246; **Board Cert:** Anesthesiology 1997; Pain Medicine 2009; **Med School:** UMDNJ-NJ Med Sch, Newark 1992; **Resid:** Internal Medicine, UMDNJ-RW Johnson Univ Hosp 1993; Anesthesiology, NYU Med Ctr 1996; **Fellow:** Pain Medicine, Jefferson Univ Hosp 1997; **Fac Appt:** Assoc Prof Anes, NYU Sch Med

Gusmorino, Paul MD (PM) - **Spec Exp:** Pain-Chronic; Pain Rehabilitation & Psychiatry; **Hospital:** NYU Hosp For Joint Dis (page 104); **Address:** 246 E 20th St, New York, NY 10003; **Phone:** 212-598-6606; **Board Cert:** Psychiatry 1980; Child & Adolescent Psychiatry 1982; Pain Medicine 2006; **Med School:** Italy 1974; **Resid:** Psychiatry, Kings County Hosp 1978; **Fellow:** Child & Adolescent Psychiatry, NY-Presby/Westchester Div 1980; **Fac Appt:** Asst Clin Prof Psyc, NYU Sch Med

Jain, Subhash MD (PM) - **Spec Exp:** Pain-Cancer; Pain-Pelvic; Reflex Sympathetic Dystrophy (RSD); Complex Regional Pain Syndromes; **Hospital:** Mt Sinai Beth Israel; **Address:** 360 E 72nd St, Ste C, New York, NY 10021; **Phone:** 212-439-6100; **Board Cert:** Anesthesiology 1994; **Med School:** India 1970; **Resid:** Surgery, St Vincent Med Ctr 1977; Anesthesiology, NY-Presby/Weill Cornell Med Ctr 1979; **Fellow:** Pain Medicine, Meml Sloan-Kettering Cancer Ctr 1980; **Fac Appt:** Assoc Prof Anes, Cornell Univ-Weill Med Coll

Kahn, Stuart B MD (PM) - **Spec Exp:** Pain-Spine; Acupuncture; Pain-Interventional Techniques; **Hospital:** Mt Sinai Hosp; **Address:** 5 E 98th St Fl 4, New York, NY 10029; **Phone:** 212-241-1075; **Board Cert:** Physical Medicine & Rehabilitation 2013; Pain Medicine 2011; **Med School:** SUNY Stony Brook 1988; **Resid:** Physical Medicine & Rehabilitation, NY-Presby/Columbia Univ Med Ctr 1992; **Fellow:** Medical Acupuncture, UCLA Med Ctr 1995; **Fac Appt:** Assoc Prof PMR, Mount Sinai-Icahn Sch of Med

Kaplan, Ronald MD (PM) - **Spec Exp:** Pain-Chronic; **Hospital:** Mt Sinai Beth Israel; **Address:** Pain Medicine & Palliative Care, 10 Union Square E, Ste 2R, New York, NY 10003; **Phone:** 212-844-8930; **Board Cert:** Anesthesiology 2009; Pain Medicine 2014; **Med School:** Univ MD Sch Med 1974; **Resid:** Anesthesiology, Univ Maryland Hosp 1978; **Fellow:** Pediatric Anesthesiology, Chldns Hosp 1979; **Fac Appt:** Clin Prof Anes, Albert Einstein Coll Med

Kotkes, Herschel MD (PM) - **Spec Exp:** Pain-Interventional Techniques; Pain-Back & Neck; Pain-Neuropathic; Reflex Sympathetic Dystrophy (RSD); **Hospital:** Mt Sinai Beth Israel; **Address:** Manhattan Spine & Sports Medicine, 305 E 55th St, Ste 206, New York, NY 10022; **Phone:** 212-319-1339; **Board Cert:** Anesthesiology 2004; Pain Medicine 2005; **Med School:** Israel 1998; **Resid:** Anesthesiology, Hosp Univ Penn 2002; **Fellow:** Pain Medicine, Hosp Univ Penn 2005

Kreitzer, Joel M MD (PM) - **Spec Exp:** Pain-Back; Pain-Cancer; Pain-Neuropathic; **Hospital:** Mt Sinai Hosp, Mt Sinai Hosp of Queens; **Address:** Upper East Side Pain Medicine, 1540 York Ave, New York, NY 10028; **Phone:** 212-288-2180; **Board Cert:** Anesthesiology 1990; Pain Medicine 2014; **Med School:** Albert Einstein Coll Med 1985; **Resid:** Anesthesiology, Mt Sinai Hosp 1988; **Fellow:** Pain Medicine, Mt Sinai Hosp 1989; **Fac Appt:** Assoc Clin Prof Anes, Mount Sinai-Icahn Sch of Med

Kuo, Jonathann MD (PM) - **Spec Exp:** Pain-Spine; Pain-Back & Neck; Pain-Interventional Techniques; **Address:** Hudson Spine & Pain Medicine, 281 Broadway Fl 2, New York, NY 10007; **Phone:** 646-596-7386; **Board Cert:** Anesthesiology 2009; Pain Medicine 2009; **Med School:** Boston Univ 2004; **Resid:** Anesthesiology, NY Presby-Cornell Med Ctr 2007; **Fellow:** Pain Medicine, Cornell Med Ctr/Hosp Special Surgery 2008

Marcus, Norman J MD (PM) - **Spec Exp:** Pain-Back & Neck; Headache; Pain-Musculoskeletal; Reflex Sympathetic Dystrophy (RSD); **Hospital:** NYU Langone Med Ctr (page 104), Lenox Hill Hosp; **Address:** 30 E 40th St, Ste 1100, New York, NY 10016; **Phone:** 212-532-7999; **Board Cert:** Pain Medicine 1993; **Med School:** SUNY Upstate Med Univ 1967; **Resid:** Psychiatry, Montefiore Med Ctr 1971; **Fellow:** Psychosomatic Medicine, Montefiore Med Ctr 1973; Pain Medicine, Lenox Hill Hosp 1995; **Fac Appt:** Assoc Clin Prof Anes, NYU Sch Med

Moqtaderi, Farideh MD (PM) - **Spec Exp:** Acupuncture; Pain-Musculoskeletal; Herpetic Neuralgia (Shingles); Fibromyalgia; **Hospital:** Mt Sinai Hosp; **Address:** One Belmont Drive, Ste 1, Irvington, NY 10533-4850; **Phone:** 917-916-6869; **Board Cert:** Anesthesiology 1973; **Med School:** Iran 1966; **Resid:** Anesthesiology, Mount Sinai Hosp 1969; Anesthesiology, Meml Sloan Kettering Hosp 1971; **Fellow:** Anesthesiology, Westchester Co Med Ctr 1973; **Fac Appt:** Asst Clin Prof Anes, Mount Sinai Sch Med

Ngeow, Jeffrey Y MD (PM) - **Spec Exp:** Pain-Musculoskeletal-Spine & Neck; Reflex Sympathetic Dystrophy (RSD); Acupuncture; Pain-Neuropathic; **Hospital:** Hosp For Special Surgery (page 109); **Address:** HSS, Integrative Care Ctr, 635 Madison Ave Fl 5, New York, NY 10022; **Phone:** 212-224-7918; **Board Cert:** Anesthesiology 1980; Pain Medicine 2005; **Med School:** England, UK 1971; **Resid:** Anesthesiology, Brigham & Womens Hosp 1977; **Fellow:** Pain Medicine, Tufts Med Ctr 1978; **Fac Appt:** Assoc Clin Prof Anes, Cornell Univ-Weill Med Coll

Richman, Daniel I MD (PM) - **Spec Exp:** Pain-Back & Neck; Complex Regional Pain Syndromes; Reflex Sympathetic Dystrophy (RSD); Pain-Neuropathic; **Hospital:** Hosp For Special Surgery (page 109); **Address:** HSS, Pain Mgmt, 429 E 75th St Fl 5, New York, NY 10021; **Phone:** 212-606-1768; **Board Cert:** Anesthesiology 1991; Pain Medicine 2015; **Med School:** UMDNJ-NJ Med Sch, Newark 1986; **Resid:** Anesthesiology, Hartford Hosp 1990; **Fellow:** Pain Medicine, Hosp Special Surgery 1991; **Fac Appt:** Asst Clin Prof Anes, Cornell Univ-Weill Med Coll

Schottenstein, Douglas C MD (PM) - **Spec Exp:** Pain-Spine; Pain-Musculoskeletal; Arthritis; Regenokine Therapy (PRP); **Hospital:** NY-Presby/Columbia Univ Med Ctr, NY (page 102); **Address:** 18 E 48th St, Ste 901, New York, NY 10017; **Phone:** 212-750-1155; **Board Cert:** Neurology 2014; Pain Medicine 2006; **Med School:** Ohio State Univ 2000; **Resid:** Neurology, Emory Univ Hosp 2004; **Fellow:** Pain Medicine, NY-Presby/Columbia Univ Med Ctr 2005

Thomas, Vinoo S MD (PM) - **Spec Exp:** Pain-Low Back; Pain-Neck; Complex Regional Pain Syndromes; Pain-Cancer; **Hospital:** Mt Sinai Hosp; **Address:** Upper East Side Pain Medicine, 1540 York Ave, New York, NY 10029; **Phone:** 212-288-2180; **Board Cert:** Anesthesiology 2007; Pain Medicine 2007; **Med School:** SUNY Upstate Med Univ 2002; **Resid:** Anesthesiology, Mount Sinai Med Ctr 2006; **Fellow:** Pain Medicine, Univ of Virginia Med ctr 2007; **Fac Appt:** Asst Clin Prof Anes, Mount Sinai Sch Med

Waldman, Seth MD (PM) - **Spec Exp:** Pain-Spine; Pain-Neuropathic; Sciatica; Pain-Interventional Techniques; **Hospital:** Hosp For Special Surgery (page 109), Burke Rehab Hosp; **Address:** HSS, Pain Mgmt, 429 E 75th St Fl 5, New York, NY 10021; **Phone:** 212-606-1686; **Board Cert:** Anesthesiology 1994; Pain Medicine 2005; **Med School:** Albany Med Coll 1988; **Resid:** Internal Medicine, Beth Israel Med Ctr 1990; Anesthesiology, Beth Israel Deaconess Hosp 1993; **Fellow:** Pain Medicine, Mass Genl Hosp 1994; **Fac Appt:** Asst Clin Prof Anes, Cornell Univ-Weill Med Coll

Weinberger, Michael L MD (PM) - **Spec Exp:** Pain-Cancer; Pain-Back; Palliative Care; Headache; **Hospital:** NY-Presby/Columbia Univ Med Ctr, NY (page 102); **Address:** Columbia Doctors, Pain Medicine, 1790 Broadway Fl 15 - Ste 1500, New York, NY 10019; **Phone:** 212-305-7114; **Board Cert:** Internal Medicine 1986; Anesthesiology 1990; Hospice & Palliative Medicine 2012; **Med School:** Columbia P&S 1983; **Resid:** Internal Medicine, St Vincents Hosp 1986; Anesthesiology, NY-Presby/Columbia Univ Med Ctr 1989; **Fellow:** Pain Medicine, Meml Sloan-Kettering Cancer Ctr 1990; **Fac Appt:** Assoc Clin Prof Anes, Columbia P&S

Zou, Shengping MD (PM) - **Spec Exp:** Pain-Chronic; Pain-Back; Pain-Neuropathic; Pain-Cancer; **Hospital:** NYU Langone Med Ctr (page 104); **Address:** NYU, Pain Med, 240 E 38th St Fl 14, New York, NY 10016; **Phone:** 212-201-1004; **Board Cert:** Anesthesiology 1999; Pain Medicine 2012; **Med School:** China 1986; **Resid:** Anesthesiology, UMDNJ Med Ctr 1998; **Fellow:** Pain Medicine, UMDNJ Med Ctr 1999; **Fac Appt:** Asst Clin Prof Anes, NYU Sch Med

Pathology

Antonescu, Cristina R MD (Path) - **Spec Exp:** Bone Pathology; Sarcoma-Soft Tissue; Ewing's Sarcoma; **Hospital:** Meml Sloan Kettering Canc Ctr (page 110); **Address:** MSKCC, Pathology, 1275 York Ave Fl 5, New York, NY 10065; **Phone:** 212-639-5905; **Board Cert:** Anatomic Pathology 1998; **Med School:** Romania 1992; **Resid:** Anatomic Pathology, Lenox Hill Hosp 1996; **Fellow:** Pathology-Oncology, Meml Sloan-Kettering Canc Ctr 1997; **Fac Appt:** Assoc Prof Path, Cornell Univ-Weill Med Coll

Bleiweiss, Ira J MD (Path) - **Spec Exp:** Breast Pathology; Breast Cancer; **Hospital:** Mt Sinai Hosp; **Address:** Mt Sinai Med Ctr, Pathology, 1 Gustave Levy Pl, Box 1194, New York, NY 10029; **Phone:** 212-241-9159; **Board Cert:** Anatomic & Clinical Pathology 1988; **Med School:** West Indies 1984; **Resid:** Pathology, Mt Sinai Hosp 1988; **Fellow:** Surgical Pathology, Mt Sinai Hosp 1989; Surgical Pathology, Meml Sloan-Kettering Cancer Ctr 1990; **Fac Appt:** Prof Path, Mount Sinai Sch Med

Borczuk, Alain C MD (Path) - **Spec Exp:** Pulmonary Pathology; Lung Cancer; Mesothelioma; **Hospital:** NY-Presby/Columbia Univ Med Ctr, NY (page 102); **Address:** Columbia Presbyterian, Dept Pathology, 630 W 168th St, VC 14, New York, NY 10032; **Phone:** 212-305-6719; **Board Cert:** Anatomic Pathology 1996; **Med School:** Cornell Univ-Weill Med Coll 1991; **Resid:** Anatomic Pathology, Albert Einstein Coll Med Affil Hosp 1995; **Fac Appt:** Prof Path, Columbia P&S

Cohen, Jean-Marc MD (Path) - **Spec Exp:** Breast Pathology; Thyroid Disorders; **Hospital:** Mt Sinai Beth Israel; **Address:** 10 Union Square E, PACC Bldg, Ste 4H, rm 137, MS 10003, New York, NY 10003; **Phone:** 212-844-8962; **Board Cert:** Anatomic Pathology 2014; Cytopathology 1997; **Med School:** France 1985; **Resid:** Pathology, Mount Sinai Med Ctr 1991; **Fellow:** Cytopathology, Montefiore Med Ctr-Moses Campus 1992

Ellenson, Lora Hendrick MD (Path) - **Spec Exp:** Gynecologic Pathology; Endometrial Cancer; Cervical Cancer; Ovarian Cancer; **Hospital:** NY-Presby/Weill Cornell Med Ctr, NY (page 102); **Address:** NY-Presby/Weill Cornell, Pathology Dept, 525 E 68th St, Starr Pavilion, 10th Fl, New York, NY 10021; **Phone:** 212-746-2700; **Board Cert:** Anatomic Pathology 1990; **Med School:** Stanford Univ 1986; **Resid:** Anatomic Pathology, Johns Hopkins Univ 1990; **Fac Appt:** Prof Path, Cornell Univ-Weill Med Coll

Harpaz, Noam MD/PhD (Path) - **Spec Exp:** Gastrointestinal Pathology; **Hospital:** Mt Sinai Hosp; **Address:** 1468 Madison Ave, Annenberg Bldg Fl 15 - rm 38, New York, NY 10029; **Phone:** 212-241-9115; **Board Cert:** Anatomic & Clinical Pathology 1986; **Med School:** Univ Miami Sch Med 1981; **Resid:** Anatomic & Clinical Pathology, Mt Sinai Med Ctr 1985; **Fac Appt:** Prof Path, Mount Sinai Sch Med

Hoda, Syed A MD (Path) - **Spec Exp:** Breast Cancer; Surgical Pathology; Cytopathology; **Hospital:** NY-Presby/Weill Cornell Med Ctr, NY (page 102); **Address:** NY-Presby, Breast Pathology, 525 E 68th St, Ste 1028 Starr, New York, NY 10021; **Phone:** 212-746-2700; **Board Cert:** Anatomic & Clinical Pathology 1990; Pathology 2012; Cytopathology 1991; **Med School:** Pakistan 1983; **Resid:** Anatomic & Clinical Pathology, Tulane Med Ctr 1990; **Fellow:** Cytopathology, Meml Sloan-Kettering Cancer Ctr 1993; Blood Banking Transfusion Medicine, Meml Sloan-Kettering Cancer Ctr 1994; **Fac Appt:** Clin Prof Path, Cornell Univ-Weill Med Coll

Jessurun, Jose MD (Path) - **Spec Exp:** Gastrointestinal Pathology; **Hospital:** NY-Presby/Weill Cornell Med Ctr, NY (page 102); **Address:** 525 E 68th St, New York, NY 10065; **Phone:** 212-746-2700; **Board Cert:** Anatomic Pathology 1985; **Med School:** Mexico 1978; **Resid:** Pathology, Genl Hosp 1982; Pathology, Jackson Meml Hosp 1983; **Fellow:** Pathology, Mass Genl Hosp 1984; Pathology, Johns Hopkins Hosp 1986; **Fac Appt:** Prof Path, Univ Minn

Klimstra, David MD (Path) - **Spec Exp:** Gastrointestinal Pathology; Colon Cancer; **Hospital:** Meml Sloan Kettering Canc Ctr (page 110); **Address:** Meml Sloan Kettering Canc Ctr, Dept Pathology, 1275 York Ave, New York, NY 10065; **Phone:** 212-639-5905; **Board Cert:** Anatomic Pathology 1992; **Med School:** Yale Univ 1988; **Resid:** Pathology, Yale New Haven Hosp 1991; **Fellow:** Pathology, Meml Sloan Kettering Canc Ctr 1992; **Fac Appt:** Asst Prof Path, Cornell Univ

Magro, Cynthia M MD (Path) - **Spec Exp:** Cutaneous Lymphoma; **Hospital:** NY-Presby/Weill Cornell Med Ctr, NY (page 102); **Address:** 1300 York Ave, Ste F310, New York, NY 10065; **Phone:** 212-746-6434; **Board Cert:** Anatomic Pathology 1988; Dermatopathology 1990; Cytopathology 1991; Pathology 2014; **Med School:** Univ Manitoba 1984; **Resid:** Anatomic Pathology, Mass Genl Hosp 1988; **Fellow:** Cytopathology, Mass Genl Hosp 1989; Dermatology, Mass Genl Hosp 1991

Melamed, Jonathan MD (Path) - **Spec Exp:** Prostate Cancer; Tumor Banking-Prostate; **Hospital:** NYU Langone Med Ctr (page 104); **Address:** NYU Med Ctr, Dept Pathology, 560 First Ave, rm TH412, New York, NY 10016; **Phone:** 212-263-6449; **Board Cert:** Anatomic & Clinical Pathology 1992; **Med School:** South Africa 1985; **Resid:** Pathology, Lenox Hill Hosp 1991; **Fellow:** Pathology, Meml Sloan Kettering Cancer Ctr 1992; Urologic Pathology, Meml Sloan Kettering Cancer Ctr 1993; **Fac Appt:** Prof Path, NYU Sch Med

Orazi, Attilio MD (Path) - **Spec Exp:** Hematopathology; Bone Marrow Pathology; Lymph Node Pathology; Spleen Pathology; **Hospital:** NY-Presby/Weill Cornell Med Ctr, NY (page 102); **Address:** NY-Presby, Pathology, 525 E 68th St, Ste 715 Starr, New York, NY 10065; **Phone:** 212-746-2050; **Board Cert:** Anatomic Pathology 1997; Hematology 1998; **Med School:** Italy 1979; **Resid:** Hematology, Leicester Royal Infirm 1982; Hematopathology, Northampton Genl Hosp 1983; **Fellow:** Anatomic Pathology, Natl Cancer Inst 1985; **Fac Appt:** Prof Path, Cornell Univ-Weill Med Coll

Reuter, Victor E MD (Path) - **Spec Exp:** Prostate Cancer; Genitourinary Pathology; Bladder Cancer; Testicular Cancer; **Hospital:** Meml Sloan Kettering Canc Ctr (page 110); **Address:** MSKCC, Pathology, 1275 York Ave, New York, NY 10021; **Phone:** 212-639-5905; **Board Cert:** Anatomic & Clinical Pathology 1983; **Med School:** Dominican Republic 1978; **Resid:** Anatomic Pathology, Thomas Jefferson Univ Hosp 1981; Clinical Pathology, Thomas Jefferson Univ Hosp 1983; **Fellow:** Surgical Pathology, Meml Sloan-Kettering Cancer Ctr 1985; **Fac Appt:** Prof Path, Cornell Univ-Weill Med Coll

Rosenblum, Marc K MD (Path) - **Spec Exp:** Neuro-Pathology; Brain Tumors; **Hospital:** Meml Sloan Kettering Canc Ctr (page 110); **Address:** MSKCC, Pathology, 1275 York Ave, New York, NY 10065; **Phone:** 212-639-3844; **Board Cert:** Anatomic Pathology 1984; Neuropathology 1988; **Med School:** Univ Miami Sch Med 1979; **Resid:** Anatomic Pathology, Mt Sinai Hosp 1984; **Fellow:** Pathology, Meml Sloan-Kettering Cancer Ctr 1985; Neuropathology, NYU-Bellevue Med Ctr 1987; **Fac Appt:** Prof Path, Cornell Univ-Weill Med Coll

Soslow, Robert A MD (Path) - **Spec Exp:** Gynecologic Pathology; Gynecologic Cancer; Uterine Cancer; **Hospital:** Meml Sloan Kettering Canc Ctr (page 110); **Address:** MSKCC, Pathology, 1275 York Ave, New York, NY 10065; **Phone:** 212-639-5905; **Board Cert:** Anatomic Pathology 1995; **Med School:** Univ Pennsylvania 1991; **Resid:** Anatomic Pathology, Stanford Univ Hosp & Clins 1994; **Fellow:** Immunopathology, Stanford Univ Hosp & Clins 1995; **Fac Appt:** Assoc Prof Path, Cornell Univ-Weill Med Coll

Thung, Swan N MD (Path) - **Spec Exp:** Liver Pathology; Immunopathology; Liver Tumors; **Hospital:** Mt Sinai Hosp; **Address:** Mt Sinai Med Ctr, Pathology, 1 Gustave L Levy Plaza, New York, NY 10029; **Phone:** 212-241-9139; **Board Cert:** Anatomic & Clinical Pathology 1977; Immunopathology 1983; **Med School:** Indonesia 1970; **Resid:** Anatomic & Clinical Pathology, VA Med Ctr 1977; **Fac Appt:** Prof Path, Mount Sinai-Icahn Sch of Med

Travis, William D MD (Path) - **Spec Exp:** Pulmonary Pathology; Lung Cancer; **Hospital:** Meml Sloan Kettering Canc Ctr (page 110); **Address:** Meml Sloan Kettering Cancer Ctr-Dept Path, 1275 York Ave, New York, NY 10065; **Phone:** 212-639-6364; **Board Cert:** Anatomic & Clinical Pathology 1985; **Med School:** Univ Fla Coll Med 1981; **Resid:** Anatomic Pathology, New England Deaconess Hosp 1983; Clinical Pathology, Mayo Clinic 1985; **Fellow:** Surgical Pathology, Mayo Clinic 1986

Wang, Beverly Y MD (Path) - **Spec Exp:** Head & Neck Pathology; **Hospital:** Mt Sinai Beth Israel; **Address:** Beth Israel Medical Ctr, Dept Pathology, First Avenue at 16th St, Silver Bldg Fl 11, New York, NY 10003; **Phone:** 212-844-1959; **Board Cert:** Anatomic Pathology 1998; Cytopathology 1999; Pathology 2014; **Med School:** China 1982; **Resid:** Pathology, Mount Sinai Med Ctr 1998; **Fellow:** Cytopathology, Mount Sinai Med Ctr 1999; **Fac Appt:** Prof Path, Albert Einstein Coll Med

Wenig, Bruce M MD (Path) - **Spec Exp:** Head & Neck Pathology; **Hospital:** Mt Sinai Beth Israel, Mt Sinai St. Luke's; **Address:** Beth Israel Med Ctr, Dept Pathology, First Ave at 16th St, 11 Silver, Rm 34, New York, NY 10003; **Phone:** 212-420-4031; **Board Cert:** Anatomic & Clinical Pathology 1985; Pathology 2014; **Med School:** Israel 1981; **Resid:** Pathology, Mt Sinai Med Ctr 1985; Surgical Pathology, Cedars-Sinai Med Ctr 1986; **Fellow:** Head and Neck Pathology, AFIP 1987; **Fac Appt:** Prof Path, Albert Einstein Coll Med

Zagzag, David MD/PhD (Path) - **Spec Exp:** Neuro-Pathology; Brain Tumors; Tumor Banking-Brain; **Hospital:** NYU Langone Med Ctr (page 104), Bellevue Hosp Ctr; **Address:** NYU Med Ctr, Dept Pathology, 560 First Ave, rm TH412, New York, NY 10016; **Phone:** 212-263-6449; **Board Cert:** Anatomic Pathology 1993; Neuropathology 1993; Pathology 2014; **Med School:** France 1984; **Resid:** Anatomic & Clinical Pathology, NYU Med Ctr 1990; **Fellow:** Neurological Pathology, NYU Med Ctr 1992; **Fac Appt:** Assoc Prof Path, NYU Sch Med

Pediatric Allergy & Immunology

Ehrlich, Paul M MD (PA&I) - **Spec Exp:** Asthma; Food Allergy; **Hospital:** NYU Langone Med Ctr (page 104), New York Eye & Ear Infirm of Mt Sinai; **Address:** Allergy & Asthma Assocs Murray Hill, 35 E 35th St, Ste 202, New York, NY 10016; **Phone:** 212-685-4225; **Board Cert:** Pediatrics 1975; Allergy & Immunology 1977; **Med School:** NYU Sch Med 1970; **Resid:** Pediatrics, NYU-Bellevue Hosp Ctr 1973; **Fellow:** Allergy & Immunology, Walter Reed Army Med Ctr 1976; **Fac Appt:** Asst Clin Prof Ped, NYU Sch Med

Herzog, Ronit MD (PA&I) - **Spec Exp:** Asthma & Allergy; Sinusitis; Food Allergy; Allergic Rhinitis; **Hospital:** NY-Presby/Weill Cornell Med Ctr, NY (page 102); **Address:** NY-Presby, Ped Allergy & Immunology, 505 E 70th St, Fl 3, New York, NY 10021; **Phone:** 646-962-3410; **Board Cert:** Pediatrics 2013; Allergy & Immunology 2006; **Med School:** Israel 1991; **Resid:** Pediatrics, LIJ-Schneider Chldns Hosp 1998; **Fellow:** Pediatric Pulmonology, Mt Sinai Hosp 2004; Allergy & Immunology, Montefiore Med Ctr 2006; **Fac Appt:** Assoc Prof A&I, Cornell Univ-Weill Med Coll

Nowak-Wegrzyn, Anna MD (PA&I) - **Hospital:** Mt Sinai Hosp; **Address:** Mount Sinai, Ped Allergy & Immun, 5 E 98 St Fl 10, New York, NY 10029; **Phone:** 212-241-5548; **Board Cert:** Pediatrics 2012; Allergy & Immunology 2012; **Med School:** Poland 1990; **Resid:** Pediatrics, Univ MD Med Ctr 1997; **Fellow:** Allergy & Immunology, Johns Hopkins Hosp 2000; **Fac Appt:** Assoc Prof Ped, Mount Sinai Sch Med

Sampson Jr, Hugh A MD (PA&I) - **Spec Exp:** Food Allergy; **Hospital:** Mt Sinai Hosp; **Address:** Faculty Practice Assocs, 5 E 98th St Fl 10, New York, NY 10029; **Phone:** 212-241-5548; **Board Cert:** Pediatrics 1980; Allergy & Immunology 1981; **Med School:** SUNY Buffalo 1975; **Resid:** Pediatrics, Chldns Meml Hosp 1979; **Fellow:** Allergy & Immunology, Duke Univ Hosp 1980; **Fac Appt:** Prof Ped, Mount Sinai-Icahn Sch of Med

Sicherer, Scott H MD (PA&I) - **Spec Exp:** Food Allergy; Drug Sensitivity; Eczema; **Hospital:** Mt Sinai Hosp; **Address:** Faculty Practice Assocs, 5 E 98th St, Fl 10, New York, NY 10029; **Phone:** 212-241-5548; **Board Cert:** Pediatrics 2008; Allergy & Immunology 2007; **Med School:** Johns Hopkins Univ 1990; **Resid:** Pediatrics, Mt Sinai Hosp 1994; **Fellow:** Allergy & Immunology, Johns Hopkins Hosp 1997; **Fac Appt:** Prof Ped, Mount Sinai-Icahn Sch of Med

Wang, Julie MD (PA&I) - **Spec Exp:** Food Allergy; Anaphylaxis; Immunotherapy; **Hospital:** Mt Sinai Hosp; **Address:** Mount Sinai, Ped Allergy & Immun, 5 E 98 St Fl 10, New York, NY 10029; **Phone:** 212-241-5548; **Board Cert:** Pediatrics 2011; Allergy & Immunology 2005; **Med School:** Cornell Univ-Weill Med Coll 2000; **Resid:** Pediatrics, NY-Presby/Weill Cornell Med Ctr 2003; **Fellow:** Allergy & Immunology, Mount Sinai Med Ctr 2005; **Fac Appt:** Asst Prof Ped, Mount Sinai Sch Med

Pediatric Cardiology

Addonizio, Linda J MD (PCd) - **Spec Exp:** Transplant Medicine-Heart; Heart Failure; Hypertrophic Cardiomyopathy; **Hospital:** Morgan Stanley Chldns Hosp of NY-Presby, NY (page 102); **Address:** NY-Presby, Ped Cardiology, 3959 Broadway, Ste 229, New York, NY 10032; **Phone:** 212-305-6575; **Board Cert:** Pediatrics 1983; Pediatric Cardiology 1985; **Med School:** Columbia P&S 1978; **Resid:** Pediatrics, NY-Presby/Columbia Univ Med Ctr 1981; **Fellow:** Pediatric Cardiology, NY-Presby/Columbia Univ Med Ctr 1984; **Fac Appt:** Prof Ped, Columbia P&S

Altmann, Karen MD (PCd) - **Spec Exp:** Congenital Heart Disease; Echocardiography; **Hospital:** Morgan Stanley Chldns Hosp of NY-Presby, NY (page 102); **Address:** 3959 Broadway, 2 North, rm 255, New York, NY 10032; **Phone:** 212-305-8509; **Board Cert:** Pediatrics 2014; Pediatric Cardiology 2011; **Med School:** Univ Pennsylvania 1988; **Resid:** Pediatrics, Morgan Stanley Chldn's Hosp 1991; **Fellow:** Pediatric Cardiology, Morgan Stanley Chldn's Hosp 1996; Pediatric Cardiology, Chldn's Hosp 1997; **Fac Appt:** Assoc Prof Ped, Columbia P&S

Argilla, Michael MD (PCd) - **Spec Exp:** Cardiac Catheterization; Critical Care; Congestive Heart Failure; **Hospital:** NYU Langone Med Ctr (page 104); **Address:** NYU Pediatric Cardiology Assocs, 160 East 32 Street, Second Floor, New York, NY 10016; **Phone:** 212-263-5940; **Board Cert:** Pediatrics 2011; Pediatric Cardiology 2008; **Med School:** Univ Colorado 1992; **Resid:** Pediatrics, NYU Med Ctr 1997; **Fellow:** Pediatric Cardiology, NYU Med Ctr 2002; **Fac Appt:** Asst Prof Ped, NYU Sch Med

Arnon, Rica G MD (PCd) - **Spec Exp:** Congenital Heart Disease; **Hospital:** Mt Sinai Hosp, Elmhurst Hosp Ctr; **Address:** 1468 Madison Ave, Ste 3-50, New York, NY 10029-6504; **Phone:** 212-241-7672; **Board Cert:** Pediatrics 1970; Pediatric Cardiology 1973; **Med School:** SUNY Hlth Sci Ctr 1967; **Resid:** Pediatrics, Kings County Hosp 1971; **Fellow:** Pediatric Cardiology, Kings County Hosp 1973; **Fac Appt:** Assoc Prof Ped, Mount Sinai Sch Med

Borg, Morton D MD (PCd) - **Spec Exp:** Fetal Echocardiography; **Hospital:** Mt Sinai Beth Israel, Mt Sinai Hosp; **Address:** Phillips Amb Care Ctr, Dept Peds, 10 Union Square E, Ste 2J, New York, NY 10003-3314; **Phone:** 212-844-8300; **Board Cert:** Pediatrics 1986; Pediatric Cardiology 2010; **Med School:** Albert Einstein Coll Med 1981; **Resid:** Pediatrics, Brookdale Hosp 1984; **Fellow:** Pediatric Cardiology, New York Hosp 1986; **Fac Appt:** Asst Prof Ped, Albert Einstein Coll Med

Brick, David H MD (PCd) - **Spec Exp:** Fetal Echocardiography; Echocardiography; Congenital Heart Disease; Complex Diagnosis; **Hospital:** NYU Langone Med Ctr (page 104); **Address:** Village Pediatric Cardiology, 154 W 14th St, Fl 4, New York, NY 10011; **Phone:** 212-604-7880; **Board Cert:** Pediatric Cardiology 2007; **Med School:** Ohio State Univ 1993; **Resid:** Pediatrics, Univ Hosp Cleveland 1996; **Fellow:** Pediatric Cardiology, NY-Presby Hosp 2000; **Fac Appt:** Asst Clin Prof Ped, NYU Sch Med

Flynn, Patrick A MD (PCd) - **Spec Exp:** Congenital Heart Disease; Echocardiography; Kawasaki Disease; Marfan's Syndrome; **Hospital:** NY-Presby/Weill Cornell Med Ctr, NY (page 102); **Address:** NY-Presby, Ped Cardiology, 525 E 68th St, Ste F695B, New York, NY 10065; **Phone:** 212-746-3561; **Board Cert:** Pediatric Cardiology 2014; **Med School:** Univ MD Sch Med 1986; **Resid:** Pediatrics, NY-Presby/Weill Cornell Med Ctr 1990; **Fellow:** Pediatric Cardiology, NY-Presby/Weill Cornell Med Ctr 1993; **Fac Appt:** Assoc Prof Ped, Cornell Univ-Weill Med Coll

Gelb, Bruce D MD (PCd) - **Spec Exp:** Noonan Syndrome; Marfan's Syndrome; **Hospital:** Mt Sinai Hosp; **Address:** Mt Sinai, Ped Cardiology, 1 Gustave Levy Pl Fl 3, Box 1201, New York, NY 10029; **Phone:** 212-241-8592; **Board Cert:** Pediatric Cardiology 2013; **Med School:** Univ Rochester 1984; **Resid:** Pediatrics, NY-Presby/Columbia Univ Med Ctr 1987; **Fellow:** Pediatric Cardiology, Baylor Med Ctr 1991; **Fac Appt:** Prof Ped, Mount Sinai-Icahn Sch of Med

Glickstein, Julie MD (PCd) - **Spec Exp:** Fetal Echocardiography; **Hospital:** Morgan Stanley Chldns Hosp of NY-Presby, NY (page 102); **Address:** 3959 Broadway, 2 North, rm 255, New York, NY 10032; **Phone:** 212-305-8509; **Board Cert:** Pediatrics 2013; Pediatric Cardiology 2009; **Med School:** Ros Franklin Univ/Chicago Med Sch 1986; **Resid:** Pediatrics, NYU Langone Med Ctr 1989; **Fellow:** Pediatric Cardiology, NYU Langone Med Ctr 1992

Krishnan, Usha MD (PCd) - **Spec Exp:** Pulmonary Hypertension; **Hospital:** NY-Presby/Columbia Univ Med Ctr, NY (page 102); **Address:** 3959 Broadway, 2 North, rm 255, New York, NY 10032; **Phone:** 212-305-8509; **Board Cert:** Pediatric Cardiology 2011; **Med School:** India 1984; **Resid:** Pediatrics, Westchester Med Ctr 1994; **Fellow:** Pediatric Cardiology, NY-Presby/Columbia Med Ctr 1996; **Fac Appt:** Assoc Prof Ped, Columbia P&S

Langsner, Alan M MD (PCd) - **Spec Exp:** Fetal Echocardiography; Congenital Heart Disease-Adult & Child; Preventive Cardiology; **Hospital:** NYU Langone Med Ctr (page 104); **Address:** NYU Pediatric Cardiology Associates, 160 E 32nd St Fl 3, New York, NY 10016; **Phone:** 212-263-5940; **Board Cert:** Pediatrics 1983; **Med School:** Mexico 1977; **Resid:** Pediatrics, Metropolitan Hosp Ctr 1981; **Fellow:** Pediatric Cardiology, NYU Med Ctr 1983; **Fac Appt:** Asst Prof Ped, NYU Sch Med

Love, Barry A MD (PCd) - **Spec Exp:** Patent Foramen Ovale(PFO) Closure; Cardiac Catheterization; Interventional Cardiology; Atrial Septal Defect; **Hospital:** Mt Sinai Hosp; **Address:** Mt Sinai Med Ctr, Div Ped Cardiology, 1468 Madison Ave, Ste 3-50, New York, NY 10029; **Phone:** 212-241-9516; **Board Cert:** Pediatrics 2011; Pediatric Cardiology 2007; **Med School:** Univ Western Ontario 1993; **Resid:** Pediatrics, Chldns Hosp Montreal 1996; **Fellow:** Pediatric Cardiology, Chldns Hosp 2000; **Fac Appt:** Asst Prof Ped, Mount Sinai Sch Med

Martinez, Matthew N MD (PCd) - **Spec Exp:** Fetal Echocardiography; Congenital Heart Disease; **Hospital:** NYU Langone Med Ctr (page 104); **Address:** Village Pediatric Cardiology, 154 W 14th St Fl 4, New York, NY 10011; **Phone:** 212-604-7880; **Board Cert:** Pediatrics 2014; Pediatric Cardiology 2010; **Med School:** Univ Nevada 2001; **Resid:** Pediatrics, Dartmouth-Hitchcock Med Ctr 2004; **Fellow:** Pediatric Cardiology, NY Presby-Columbia Med Ctr 2007

Parness, Ira A MD (PCd) - **Spec Exp:** Echocardiography; Congenital Heart Disease; Fetal Echocardiography; **Hospital:** Mt Sinai Hosp, Englewood Hosp & Med Ctr; **Address:** Mt Sinai, Ped Cardiology, 1 Gustave Levy Pl, Box 1201, New York, NY 10029; **Phone:** 212-241-6640; **Board Cert:** Pediatrics 1984; Pediatric Cardiology 1985; **Med School:** SUNY Downstate 1979; **Resid:** Pediatrics, Brookdale Hosp 1982; **Fellow:** Pediatric Cardiology, Chldns Hosp 1985; **Fac Appt:** Prof Ped, Mount Sinai-Icahn Sch of Med

Presti, Salvatore MD (PCd) - **Spec Exp:** Fetal Echocardiography; Congenital Heart Disease; Kawasaki Disease; **Hospital:** NYU Langone Med Ctr (page 104); **Address:** 110 E 59th St, rm 9B, New York, NY 10022; **Phone:** 212-838-9880; **Board Cert:** Pediatrics 1984; Pediatric Cardiology 2010; **Med School:** Italy 1978; **Resid:** Pediatrics, Lenox Hill Hosp 1982; **Fellow:** Pediatric Cardiology, NYU Med Ctr 1984; **Fac Appt:** Assoc Clin Prof Ped, NYU Sch Med

Seiden, Howard S MD (PCd) - **Spec Exp:** Congenital Heart Disease; Heart Failure; Critical Care; **Hospital:** Mt Sinai Hosp; **Address:** Pediatric Cardiology Assoc, 1 Gustave L Levy Pl, Annenberg-3, Box 1201, New York, NY 10029; **Phone:** 212-241-9516; **Board Cert:** Pediatric Cardiology 2011; **Med School:** Mount Sinai Sch Med 1990; **Resid:** Pediatrics, Mount Sinai Med Ctr 1993; **Fellow:** Pediatric Cardiology, Mount Sinai Med Ctr 1996; Pediatric Critical Care Medicine, Children's Hosp of Philadelphia 1997; **Fac Appt:** Assoc Prof Ped, Mount Sinai Sch Med

Sommer, Robert J MD (PCd) - **Spec Exp:** Congenital Heart Disease; Atrial Septal Defect; Cardiac Catheterization; **Hospital:** NY-Presby/Columbia Univ Med Ctr, NY (page 102), St. Joseph's Regl Med Ctr - Paterson; **Address:** 161 Fort Washington Ave Fl 6, Herbert Irving Pavilion, New York, NY 10032; **Phone:** 212-342-0886; **Board Cert:** Pediatric Cardiology 2013; **Med School:** NYU Sch Med 1985; **Resid:** Pediatrics, Mt Sinai Med Ctr 1988; **Fellow:** Pediatric Cardiology, Mt Sinai Med Ctr 1991; Interventional Cardiology, Childrens Hosp 1991; **Fac Appt:** Asst Clin Prof Ped, Columbia P&S

Starc, Thomas J MD (PCd) - **Spec Exp:** Cholesterol/Lipid Disorders; **Hospital:** Morgan Stanley Chldns Hosp of NY-Presby, NY (page 102); **Address:** NY-Presby, Ped Cardiology, 3959 Broadway, Ste 255, New York, NY 10032; **Phone:** 212-305-4293; **Board Cert:** Pediatrics 1981; Pediatric Cardiology 1983; **Med School:** Mount Sinai Sch Med 1976; **Resid:** Pediatrics, UCSD Med Ctr 1980; **Fellow:** Pediatric Cardiology, NY-Presby/Columbia Univ Med Ctr 1984; **Fac Appt:** Clin Prof Ped, Columbia P&S

Steinberg, L Gary MD (PCd) - **Spec Exp:** Echocardiography; Congenital Heart Disease; **Hospital:** NY-Presby/Weill Cornell Med Ctr, NY (page 102); **Address:** Pediatric Cardiovascular Services, NY Presby Hosp/ Weill Cornell, 525 E 68 St, Ste F666, New York, NY 10065; **Phone:** 212-746-3561; **Board Cert:** Pediatrics 2013; Pediatric Cardiology 2013; **Med School:** Philippines 1985; **Resid:** Pediatrics, Elmhurst Hosp 1989; **Fellow:** Pediatric Cardiology, Mount Sinai Hosp 1992; **Fac Appt:** Asst Prof Ped, Cornell Univ-Weill Med Coll

Steinherz, Laurel J MD (PCd) - **Spec Exp:** Cardiac Effects of Cancer/Cancer Therapy; **Hospital:** Meml Sloan Kettering Canc Ctr (page 110), NY-Presby/Weill Cornell Med Ctr, NY (page 102); **Address:** 1275 York Ave, New York, NY 10021; **Phone:** 212-639-8103; **Board Cert:** Pediatrics 1976; Pediatric Cardiology 1978; **Med School:** Albert Einstein Coll Med 1970; **Resid:** Pediatrics, St Louis Chldns Hosp 1972; **Fellow:** Pediatric Cardiology, NY Hosp-Cornell Med Ctr 1975; **Fac Appt:** Prof Ped, Cornell Univ-Weill Med Coll

Vincent, Julie A MD (PCd) - **Spec Exp:** Interventional Cardiology; Congenital Heart Disease; Cardiac Catheterization; **Hospital:** Morgan Stanley Chldns Hosp of NY-Presby, NY (page 102); **Address:** 3959 Broadway, 2 North, rm 255, New York, NY 10032; **Phone:** 212-342-0610; **Board Cert:** Pediatrics 2013; Pediatric Cardiology 2011; **Med School:** Wayne State Univ 1988; **Resid:** Pediatrics, Chldn's Hosp of MI 1991; **Fellow:** Pediatric Cardiology, Chldn's Hosp of MI 1994; Pediatric Cardiology, TX Chldns Hosp 1995; **Fac Appt:** Assoc Prof Ped, Columbia P&S

Pediatric Critical Care Medicine

Conway Jr, Edward E MD (PCCM) - **Spec Exp:** Neurologic Critical Care; Respiratory Failure; Head Injury; **Hospital:** Mt Sinai Beth Israel; **Address:** Beth Israel Med Ctr, Dept Peds, 350 E 17th St, New York, NY 10003; **Phone:** 212-420-4018; **Board Cert:** Pediatrics 2007; Pediatric Critical Care Medicine 2010; **Med School:** SUNY Hlth Sci Ctr 1984; **Resid:** Pediatrics, Montefiore Med Ctr 1988; **Fellow:** Pediatric Critical Care Medicine, Montefiore Med Ctr-Albert Einstein 1990; **Fac Appt:** Prof Ped, Albert Einstein Coll Med

Greenwald, Bruce M MD (PCCM) - **Spec Exp:** Respiratory Failure; Sepsis & Septic Shock; Asthma; Diabetes Ketoacidosis; **Hospital:** NY-Presby/Weill Cornell Med Ctr, NY (page 102), Meml Sloan Kettering Canc Ctr (page 110); **Address:** Div Pediatric Critical Care Med, 525 E 68th St, Ste M-508, New York, NY 10065; **Phone:** 212-746-3056; **Board Cert:** Pediatrics 1987; Pediatric Critical Care Medicine 2012; **Med School:** NYU Sch Med 1982; **Resid:** Pediatrics, NYU-Bellevue Hosp Ctr 1986; **Fellow:** Pediatric Critical Care Medicine, NY Hosp-Cornell 1988; **Fac Appt:** Clin Prof Ped, Cornell Univ-Weill Med Coll

Pediatric Endocrinology

Fennoy, Ilene MD (PEn) - **Spec Exp:** Growth/Development Disorders; Diabetes; Klinefelter's Syndrome; Obesity; **Hospital:** Morgan Stanley Chldns Hosp of NY-Presby, NY (page 102), Harlem Hosp Ctr; **Address:** 3959 Broadway, rm 106, New York, NY 10032; **Phone:** 212-305-6559; **Board Cert:** Pediatrics 1979; Pediatric Endocrinology 1980; **Med School:** UCSF 1973; **Resid:** Pediatrics, Montefiore Med Ctr 1975; **Fellow:** Nutrition, Columbia-Presby Med Ctr 1977; Endocrinology, Natl Inst Hlth 1979; **Fac Appt:** Assoc Clin Prof Ped, Columbia P&S

Gallagher, Mary P MD (PEn) - **Spec Exp:** Diabetes; **Hospital:** Morgan Stanley Chldns Hosp of NY-Presby, NY (page 102); **Address:** Naomi Berrie Diabetes Ctr, 1150 St Nicholas Ave Fl 2, New York, NY 10032; **Phone:** 212-851-5494; **Board Cert:** Pediatrics 2013; Pediatric Endocrinology 2011; **Med School:** UMDNJ-NJ Med Sch, Newark 1995; **Resid:** Pediatrics, NY-Presby/Columbia Univ Med Ctr 1998; **Fellow:** Pediatric Endocrinology, NY-Presby/Columbia Univ Med Ctr 2002; **Fac Appt:** Asst Prof Ped, Columbia P&S

Kohn, Brenda MD (PEn) - **Spec Exp:** Growth Disorders; Pituitary Disorders; Thyroid Disorders; Adrenal Disorders; **Hospital:** NYU Langone Med Ctr (page 104); **Address:** NYU Fink Ctr, Ped Endocrinology, 160 E 32nd St, Ste L3, New York, NY 10016; **Phone:** 212-263-5940 x5; **Board Cert:** Pediatrics 1981; Pediatric Endocrinology 1983; **Med School:** Albert Einstein Coll Med 1976; **Resid:** Pediatrics, NYU Med Ctr 1979; **Fellow:** Endocrinology, Diabetes & Metabolism, NY-Presby/Weill Cornell Med Ctr 1983; **Fac Appt:** Assoc Prof Ped, NYU Sch Med

New, Maria I MD (PEn) - **Spec Exp:** Adrenal Disorders; Growth/Development Disorders; **Hospital:** Mt Sinai Hosp; **Address:** Mount Sinai Medical Ctr, Ped Adrenal Steroid Disorders Program, 5 E 98th St Fl 10, New York, NY 10029; **Phone:** 212-241-8210; **Board Cert:** Pediatrics 1960; **Med School:** Univ Pennsylvania 1954; **Resid:** Pediatrics, New York Hosp 1957; **Fellow:** Pediatric Endocrinology, New York Hosp 1958; Endocrinology, Diabetes & Metabolism, New York Hosp 1964; **Fac Appt:** Prof Ped, Cornell Univ-Weill Med Coll

Oberfield, Sharon E MD (PEn) - **Spec Exp:** Adrenal Disorders; Neuroendocrine Disorders; Growth Disorders; **Hospital:** Morgan Stanley Chldns Hosp of NY-Presby, NY (page 102); **Address:** Columbia Doctors Midtown, 51 W 51st St Fl 3 - Ste 310, New York, NY 10032; **Phone:** 212-305-6559; **Board Cert:** Pediatrics 1979; Pediatric Endocrinology 2000; **Med School:** Cornell Univ 1974; **Resid:** Pediatrics, NY-Presby/Weill Cornell Med Ctr 1976; **Fellow:** Pediatric Endocrinology, NY-Presby/Weill Cornell Med Ctr 1979; **Fac Appt:** Prof Ped, Columbia P&S

Rapaport, Robert MD (PEn) - **Spec Exp:** Growth Disorders; Thyroid Disorders; Diabetes; **Hospital:** Mt Sinai Hosp; **Address:** Mt Sinai, Ped Endocrinology, 1468 Madison Ave, Ste 4-81, New York, NY 10029; **Phone:** 212-241-8487; **Board Cert:** Pediatrics 1980; Pediatric Endocrinology 1983; **Med School:** SUNY Downstate 1974; **Resid:** Pediatrics, LIJ-Hillside Med Ctr 1977; **Fellow:** Pediatric Endocrinology, St Christopher's Hosp 1978; Pediatric Endocrinology, New York Hosp 1980; **Fac Appt:** Prof Ped, Mount Sinai-Icahn Sch of Med

Sklar, Charles A MD (PEn) - **Spec Exp:** Cancer Survivors-Late Effects of Therapy; Growth Disorders in Childhood Cancer; **Hospital:** Meml Sloan Kettering Canc Ctr (page 110); **Address:** MSKCC, Pediatric Endocrinology, 1275 York Ave, New York, NY 10065; **Phone:** 212-639-8138; **Board Cert:** Pediatrics 1979; Pediatric Endocrinology 2010; **Med School:** USC Sch Med 1974; **Resid:** Pediatrics, Chldns Hosp 1976; **Fellow:** Pediatric Endocrinology, UCSF Med Ctr 1979; **Fac Appt:** Assoc Prof Ped, Cornell Univ-Weill Med Coll

Vargas-Rodriguez, Ileana MD (PEn) - **Spec Exp:** Diabetes; **Hospital:** NY-Presby/Columbia Univ Med Ctr, NY (page 102); **Address:** 1150 St Nicholas Ave, Fl 2, New York, NY 10032; **Phone:** 212-851-5494; **Board Cert:** Pediatric Endocrinology 2010; **Med School:** Albert Einstein Coll Med 1986; **Resid:** Pediatrics, Babies Hosp 1989; **Fellow:** Pediatric Endocrinology, Mt Sinai Hosp 1990

Vogiatzi, Maria G MD (PEn) - **Spec Exp:** Growth Disorders; Pubertal Disorders; Adrenal Disorders; Bone Disorders-Metabolic; **Hospital:** NY-Presby/Weill Cornell Med Ctr, NY (page 102); **Address:** 505 E 70th St, Helmsley Tower Fl 3, New York, NY 10065; **Phone:** 646-962-3442; **Board Cert:** Pediatrics 2014; Pediatric Endocrinology 2012; **Med School:** Greece 1987; **Resid:** Pediatrics, Univ Hosp 1991; **Fellow:** Pediatric Endocrinology, New York Hosp 1993; Pediatric Endocrinology, Baylor Coll Med 1995; **Fac Appt:** Assoc Clin Prof Ped, Cornell Univ-Weill Med Coll

Wallach, Elizabeth MD (PEn) - **Spec Exp:** Diabetes; **Hospital:** Mt Sinai Hosp; **Address:** Mount Sinai,Pediatric Endocrinology, 1468 Madison Ave Fl 4 - Ste 4-81, New York, NY 10029; **Phone:** 212-241-6936; **Board Cert:** Pediatric Endocrinology 2012; **Med School:** SUNY Downstate 1986; **Resid:** Pediatrics, NY-Presby/Columbia Univ Med Ctr 1990; **Fellow:** Pediatric Endocrinology, Mount Sinai Med Ctr 1993; **Fac Appt:** Asst Prof Ped, Mount Sinai Sch Med

Pediatric Gastroenterology

Bangaru, Babu S MD (PGe) - **Spec Exp:** Ulcerative Colitis/Crohn's; Liver Disease; Nutrition; Endoscopy; **Hospital:** NYU Langone Med Ctr (page 104), Flushing Hosp Med Ctr; **Address:** NYU Langone Med Ctr, Div Ped Gastroenterology, 317 E 34th St, Ste 902, New York, NY 10016; **Phone:** 718-592-7797; **Board Cert:** Pediatrics 1978; Pediatric Gastroenterology 2013; **Med School:** India 1970; **Resid:** Pediatrics, St Lukes Hosp 1976; **Fellow:** Hepatology, Albert Einstein Coll Med Affil Hosp 1978; Gastroenterology & Nutrition, Emory Univ Sch Med Affil Hosp 1979; **Fac Appt:** Assoc Clin Prof Ped, NYU Sch Med

Benkov, Keith J MD (PGe) - **Spec Exp:** Inflammatory Bowel Disease/Crohn's; Liver Disease; Celiac Disease; Gastroesophageal Reflux Disease (GERD); **Hospital:** Mt Sinai Hosp, Englewood Hosp & Med Ctr; **Address:** Mt Sinai, Ped Gastroenterology, 5 E 98th St, Fl 10, New York, NY 10029; **Phone:** 212-241-5415; **Board Cert:** Pediatrics 1984; Pediatric Gastroenterology 2012; **Med School:** Mount Sinai Sch Med 1979; **Resid:** Pediatrics, Mt Sinai Hosp 1982; **Fellow:** Pediatric Gastroenterology, Mt Sinai Hosp 1984; **Fac Appt:** Assoc Prof Ped, Mount Sinai-Icahn Sch of Med

Chehade, Mirna A MD (PGe) - **Spec Exp:** Eosinophilic Esophagitis; Food Allergy; Esophageal Disorders; **Hospital:** Mt Sinai Hosp; **Address:** Mount Sinai, Ped Gastroenterology, 5 E 98 St Fl 10, New York, NY 10029; **Phone:** 212-241-4880; **Board Cert:** Pediatric Gastroenterology 2011; **Med School:** Amer Univ Beirut 1996; **Resid:** Pediatrics, Chldns Hosp 2000; **Fellow:** Pediatric Gastroenterology, Mount Sinai Med Ctr 2003; **Fac Appt:** Assoc Prof Ped, Mount Sinai Sch Med

Kazlow, Philip G MD (PGe) - **Spec Exp:** Inflammatory Bowel Disease; Celiac Disease; Nutrition; **Hospital:** Morgan Stanley Chldns Hosp of NY-Presby, NY (page 102), Valley Hosp (page 739); **Address:** NY-Presby, Ped Gastroenterology, 3959 Broadway Fl 7-701C, New York, NY 10032; **Phone:** 212-305-5903; **Board Cert:** Pediatrics 1985; Pediatric Gastroenterology 2012; **Med School:** Mount Sinai Sch Med 1980; **Resid:** Pediatrics, Mt Sinai Hosp 1984; **Fellow:** Pediatric Gastroenterology, Mt Sinai Hosp 1986; **Fac Appt:** Prof Ped, Columbia P&S

Lavine, Joel E MD/PhD (PGe) - **Spec Exp:** Liver Disease; Transplant Medicine-Liver; Pancreatic Disease; Celiac Disease; **Hospital:** Morgan Stanley Chldns Hosp of NY-Presby, NY (page 102); **Address:** Morgan Stanley Childns Hosp, Pediatric Gastroenterology Dept, 21 W 86th St, New York, NY 10024; **Phone:** 212-305-5903; **Board Cert:** Pediatric Gastroenterology 2012; Pediatric Transplant Hepatology 2008; **Med School:** UCSD 1984; **Resid:** Pediatrics, UCSF Med Ctr 1986; **Fellow:** Pediatric Gastroenterology, UCSF Med Ctr 1989; **Fac Appt:** Prof Ped, Columbia P&S

Levine, Jeremiah J MD (PGe) - **Spec Exp:** Inflammatory Bowel Disease; Crohn's Disease; Liver Disease; **Hospital:** NYU Langone Med Ctr (page 104); **Address:** NYU Fink Ctr, Ped Gastroenterology, 160 E 32nd St, L3 Medical, New York, NY 10016; **Phone:** 212-263-5407; **Board Cert:** Pediatrics 1985; Pediatric Gastroenterology 2012; **Med School:** Harvard Med Sch 1980; **Resid:** Pediatrics, Montefiore Med Ctr 1983; **Fellow:** Pediatric Gastroenterology, Chldns Hosp/Mass Genl Hosp 1985; **Fac Appt:** Prof Ped, Albert Einstein Coll Med

Levy, Joseph MD (PGe) - **Spec Exp:** Celiac Disease; Gastroesophageal Reflux Disease (GERD); Nutrition in Autism; Inflammatory Bowel Disease/Crohn's; **Hospital:** NYU Langone Med Ctr (page 104); **Address:** NYU Fink Ctr, Ped Gastroenterology, 160 E 32nd St, L3, New York, NY 10016; **Phone:** 212-263-5407; **Board Cert:** Pediatrics 1981; Pediatric Gastroenterology 2012; **Med School:** Israel 1973; **Resid:** Pediatrics, Beth Israel Med Ctr 1977; **Fellow:** Hematology Research, NY-Presby/Columbia Univ Med Ctr 1975; Pediatric Gastroenterology, NY-Presby/Columbia Univ Med Ctr 1979; **Fac Appt:** Prof Ped, NYU Sch Med

Lobritto, Steven J MD (PGe) - **Spec Exp:** Hepatitis; Liver Disease; Transplant Medicine-Liver; **Hospital:** Morgan Stanley Chldns Hosp of NY-Presby, NY (page 102); **Address:** NY-Presby, Liver Ctr, 3959 Broadway, rm 7-702, New York, NY 10032; **Phone:** 212-305-3000; **Board Cert:** Pediatric Gastroenterology 2014; Pediatric Transplant Hepatology 2008; **Med School:** NY Med Coll 1988; **Resid:** Internal Medicine & Pediatrics, NY-Presby/Weill Cornell Med Ctr 1992; **Fellow:** Pediatric Gastroenterology, NY-Presby/Columbia Univ Med Ctr 1996; **Fac Appt:** Assoc Clin Prof Ped, Columbia P&S

Mencin, Ali A MD (PGe) - **Spec Exp:** Endoscopy; Liver Disease; Eosinophilic Esophagitis; Inflammatory Bowel Disease; **Hospital:** Morgan Stanley Chldns Hosp of NY-Presby, NY (page 102); **Address:** Morgan Stanley Chldns Hosp of NY-Presby, Dept Ped Gastroenterology, 3959 Broadway, Ste 702, New York, NY 10032; **Phone:** 212-305-5903; **Board Cert:** Pediatrics 2010; Pediatric Gastroenterology 2007; **Med School:** Mount Sinai Sch Med 1999; **Resid:** Pediatrics, Montefiore Med Ctr 2003; **Fellow:** Pediatric Gastroenterology, NY Presby-Columbia Med Ctr 2005; **Fac Appt:** Asst Prof Med, Columbia P&S

Sockolow, Robbyn E MD (PGe) - **Spec Exp:** Celiac Disease; Crohn's Disease; Capsule Endoscopy; **Hospital:** NY-Presby/Weill Cornell Med Ctr, NY (page 102); **Address:** NY-Presby, Ped Gastroenterology, 505 E 70th St Fl 3, Helmsley Tower, New York, NY 10021; **Phone:** 646-962-3869; **Board Cert:** Pediatrics 2012; Pediatric Gastroenterology 2010; **Med School:** NY Med Coll 1986; **Resid:** Pediatrics, Montefiore Med Ctr 1989; **Fellow:** Pediatric Gastroenterology, Mt Sinai Hosp 1990; Pediatric Gastroenterology, Montefiore Med Ctr 1992; **Fac Appt:** Assoc Clin Prof Ped, Cornell Univ-Weill Med Coll

Spivak, William MD (PGe) - **Spec Exp:** Ulcerative Colitis; Crohn's Disease; Nutrition; Esophageal Disorders; **Hospital:** NY-Presby/Weill Cornell Med Ctr, NY (page 102), Lenox Hill Hosp; **Address:** 177 E 87th St, Ste 305, New York, NY 10128; **Phone:** 212-369-7700; **Board Cert:** Pediatrics 1981; Pediatric Gastroenterology 2012; **Med School:** Albert Einstein Coll Med 1976; **Resid:** Pediatrics, Jacobi Med Ctr 1979; **Fellow:** Gastroenterology, Chldns Hosp 1982; Research, Brigham & Womens Hosp 1982; **Fac Appt:** Clin Prof Ped, Cornell Univ-Weill Med Coll

Pediatric Hematology-Oncology

Aledo, Alexander MD (PHO) - **Spec Exp:** Leukemia & Lymphoma; Bone Tumors; **Hospital:** NY-Presby/Weill Cornell Med Ctr, NY (page 102), NY Hosp Queens (page 498); **Address:** NY-Presby, Pediatric Hem/Onc, 525 E 68th St, rm P695, New York, NY 10065; **Phone:** 212-746-3400; **Board Cert:** Pediatric Hematology-Oncology 2011; **Med School:** NYU Sch Med 1984; **Resid:** Pediatrics, NY-Presby/Weill Cornell Med Ctr 1987; **Fellow:** Pediatric Hematology-Oncology, Meml Sloan-Kettering Cancer Ctr 1990; **Fac Appt:** Assoc Prof Ped, Cornell Univ-Weill Med Coll

Blei, Francine MD (PHO) - **Spec Exp:** Vascular Malformations/Birthmarks; Hemangiomas; Lymphedema; **Hospital:** Lenox Hill Hosp; **Address:** Vascular Anomalies Program of Lenox Hill, 210 E 64th St Fl 7, New York, NY 10065; **Phone:** 212-702-7795; **Board Cert:** Pediatrics 1987; Pediatric Hematology-Oncology 1987; **Med School:** Israel 1982; **Resid:** Pediatrics, NYU-Bellevue 1985; **Fellow:** Pediatric Hematology-Oncology, Babies Hosp-Columbia Presby 1987

Bussel, James MD (PHO) - **Spec Exp:** Bleeding/Coagulation Disorders; Platelet Disorders; Wiskott-Aldrich Syndrome; **Hospital:** NY-Presby/Weill Cornell Med Ctr, NY (page 102), Lenox Hill Hosp; **Address:** NY-Presby, Pediatric Hem/Onc, 525 E 68th St, rm P695, New York, NY 10065; **Phone:** 212-746-3400; **Board Cert:** Pediatrics 1979; Pediatric Hematology-Oncology 1980; **Med School:** Columbia P&S 1975; **Resid:** Pediatrics, Chldns Hosp 1978; **Fellow:** Pediatric Hematology-Oncology, Meml Sloan-Kettering Cancer Ctr 1981; **Fac Appt:** Prof Ped, Cornell Univ-Weill Med Coll

Carroll, William L MD (PHO) - **Spec Exp:** Leukemia & Lymphoma; Hematologic Malignancies; Stem Cell Transplant; Lymphoma, Non-Hodgkin's; **Hospital:** NYU Langone Med Ctr (page 104); **Address:** NYU, Pediatric Hem/Onc, 160 E 32nd St Fl 2, New York, NY 10016; **Phone:** 212-263-8400; **Board Cert:** Pediatrics 1984; Pediatric Hematology-Oncology 1987; **Med School:** UC Irvine 1978; **Resid:** Pediatrics, Chldns Hosp 1982; **Fellow:** Pediatric Hematology-Oncology, Stanford Univ Hosp & Clins 1987; **Fac Appt:** Prof Ped, NYU Sch Med

Cheung, Nai-Kong V MD/PhD (PHO) - **Spec Exp:** Neuroblastoma; Pediatric Cancers; Clinical Trials; **Hospital:** Meml Sloan Kettering Canc Ctr (page 110); **Address:** 1275 York Ave, New York, NY 10065; **Phone:** 646-888-2313; **Board Cert:** Pediatrics 1987; Pediatric Hematology-Oncology 2012; **Med School:** Harvard Med Sch 1978; **Resid:** Pediatrics, Stanford Univ Hosp 1980; **Fellow:** Pediatric Hematology-Oncology, Stanford Univ Hosp 1982; **Fac Appt:** Assoc Prof Ped, Cornell Univ-Weill Med Coll

Dunkel, Ira J MD (PHO) - **Spec Exp:** Retinoblastoma; Brain & Spinal Cord Tumors; Brain Tumors; Pediatric Cancers; **Hospital:** Meml Sloan Kettering Canc Ctr (page 110); **Address:** MSKCC, Pediatric Hem/Onc, 1275 York Ave, Ste H1102, New York, NY 10065; **Phone:** 212-639-2153; **Board Cert:** Pediatric Hematology-Oncology 2014; **Med School:** Duke Univ 1985; **Resid:** Pediatrics, Duke Univ Hosp 1988; **Fellow:** Pediatric Infectious Disease, Duke Univ Hosp 1989; Pediatric Hematology-Oncology, Meml Sloan-Kettering Cancer Ctr 1992; **Fac Appt:** Assoc Prof Ped, Cornell Univ-Weill Med Coll

Gardner, Sharon L MD (PHO) - **Spec Exp:** Bone Marrow Transplant; Stem Cell Transplant; Neuro-Oncology; Neuroblastoma; **Hospital:** NYU Langone Med Ctr (page 104); **Address:** Steven B Hassenfeld Chldns Ctr, 160 E 32nd St Fl 2, New York, NY 10016; **Phone:** 212-263-8400; **Board Cert:** Pediatric Hematology-Oncology 2014; **Med School:** Hahnemann Univ 1986; **Resid:** Pediatrics, St Christophers Hosp Chldn 1989; **Fellow:** Pediatric Hematology-Oncology, Meml Sloan Kettering Cancer Ctr 1992; **Fac Appt:** Assoc Prof Ped, NYU Sch Med

Garvin Jr, James H MD/PhD (PHO) - **Spec Exp:** Brain Tumors; Pediatric Cancers; Bone Marrow Transplant; Leukemia; **Hospital:** Morgan Stanley Chldns Hosp of NY-Presby, NY (page 102); **Address:** NY-Presby, Pediatric Hem/Onc, 161 Fort Washington Ave, Fl 7, New York, NY 10032; **Phone:** 212-305-8685; **Board Cert:** Pediatrics 1982; Pediatric Hematology-Oncology 1984; **Med School:** Jefferson Med Coll 1976; **Resid:** Pediatrics, Chldns Hosp 1978; Pediatrics, Middlesex Hosp 1979; **Fellow:** Pediatric Hematology-Oncology, Boston Chldn's Hosp/Dana Farber Cancer Inst 1982; **Fac Appt:** Prof Ped, Columbia P&S

Giardina, Patricia J MD (PHO) - **Spec Exp:** Thalassemia; Sickle Cell Disease; Hemophilia; **Hospital:** NY-Presby/Weill Cornell Med Ctr, NY (page 102); **Address:** NY-Presby, Pediatric Hem/Onc, 525 E 68th St, rm P695, New York, NY 10065; **Phone:** 212-746-3446; **Board Cert:** Pediatrics 1973; Pediatric Hematology-Oncology 1974; **Med School:** NY Med Coll 1968; **Resid:** Pediatrics, NY-Presby/Weill Cornell Med Ctr 1971; **Fellow:** Pediatric Hematology-Oncology, NY-Presby/Weill Cornell Med Ctr 1974; **Fac Appt:** Clin Prof Ped, Cornell Univ-Weill Med Coll

Glade Bender, Julia MD (PHO) - **Spec Exp:** Sarcoma; Neuroblastoma; Germ Cell Tumors; Clinical Trials; **Hospital:** Morgan Stanley Chldns Hosp of NY-Presby, NY (page 102); **Address:** Columbia Presbyterian Ped Hem/Oncology, 161 Fort Washington Ave, Herbert Irving Pavilion, IP7, Fl 7, New York, NY 10032; **Phone:** 212-305-9770; **Board Cert:** Pediatric Hematology-Oncology 2013; Pediatrics 2010; **Med School:** Univ Pennsylvania 1992; **Resid:** Pediatrics, Mount Sinai Med Ctr 1995; **Fellow:** Pediatric Hematology-Oncology, Meml Sloan-Kettering Cancer Ctr 1999; **Fac Appt:** Assoc Prof Ped, Columbia P&S

Granowetter, Linda MD (PHO) - **Spec Exp:** Bone Tumors; Lymphoma; Sarcoma-Soft Tissue; Ewing's Sarcoma; **Hospital:** NYU Langone Med Ctr (page 104); **Address:** Steven B Hassenfeld Chldn's Ctr, 160 E 32nd St, New York, NY 10016; **Phone:** 212-263-9660; **Board Cert:** Pediatric Hematology-Oncology 1984; Pediatrics 1983; Hospice & Palliative Medicine 2012; **Med School:** SUNY Stony Brook 1978; **Resid:** Pediatrics, St Christophers Chldns Hosp 1981; **Fellow:** Pediatric Hematology-Oncology, Chldns Hosp 1984; **Fac Appt:** Prof Ped, NYU Sch Med

Kernan, Nancy A MD (PHO) - **Spec Exp:** Bone Marrow Transplant; Stem Cell Transplant; Leukemia; Immune Deficiency; **Hospital:** Meml Sloan Kettering Canc Ctr (page 110); **Address:** 1275 York Ave, New York, NY 10065; **Phone:** 212-639-7250; **Board Cert:** Pediatrics 1983; Pediatric Hematology-Oncology 1984; **Med School:** Cornell Univ-Weill Med Coll 1978; **Resid:** Pediatrics, Chldns Natl Med Ctr 1981; **Fellow:** Pediatric Hematology-Oncology, Meml Sloan Kettering Cancer Ctr 1984; **Fac Appt:** Assoc Prof Ped, Cornell Univ-Weill Med Coll

Kramer, Kim MD (PHO) - **Spec Exp:** Neuroblastoma; Brain & Spinal Cord Tumors; **Hospital:** Meml Sloan Kettering Canc Ctr (page 110); **Address:** MSKCC, Pediatric Hem/Onc, 1275 York Ave, New York, NY 10021; **Phone:** 212-639-6410; **Board Cert:** Pediatric Hematology-Oncology 2011; **Med School:** SUNY Upstate Med Univ 1989; **Resid:** Pediatrics, Strong Meml Hosp 1992; **Fellow:** Pediatric Hematology-Oncology, Strong Meml Hosp 1993; Pediatric Hematology-Oncology, Meml Sloan-Kettering Cancer Ctr 1996

Kushner, Brian H MD (PHO) - **Spec Exp:** Neuroblastoma; Bone Marrow Transplant; Immunotherapy; **Hospital:** Meml Sloan Kettering Canc Ctr (page 110); **Address:** 1275 York Avenue, New York, NY 10065; **Phone:** 212-639-6793; **Board Cert:** Pediatrics 1983; Pediatric Hematology-Oncology 1987; **Med School:** Johns Hopkins Univ 1976; **Resid:** Pediatrics, Columbia-Presby Med Ctr 1978; Pediatrics, NY Hosp 1979; **Fellow:** Pediatric Hematology-Oncology, Boston Chldns Hosp 1980; Pediatric Hematology-Oncology, Meml Sloan Kettering Cancer Ctr 1986; **Fac Appt:** Prof Ped, Cornell Univ-Weill Med Coll

Marcus, Judith R MD (PHO) - **Spec Exp:** Leukemia; Lymphoma; Bleeding/Coagulation Disorders; Solid Tumors; **Hospital:** Morgan Stanley Chldns Hosp of NY-Presby, NY (page 102), White Plains Hosp (page 652); **Address:** 161 Ft Washington Ave, Ste 7I, New York, NY 10032; **Phone:** 212-305-5808; **Board Cert:** Pediatrics 1997; Pediatric Hematology-Oncology 1997; **Med School:** NYU Sch Med 1971; **Resid:** Pediatrics, Bronx Muni Hosp-Albert Einstein 1974; **Fellow:** Pediatric Hematology-Oncology, Meml Sloan Kettering Cancer Ctr 1979; **Fac Appt:** Clin Prof Ped, Columbia P&S

Meyers, Paul A MD (PHO) - **Spec Exp:** Pediatric Cancers; Bone Tumors; Sarcoma; **Hospital:** Meml Sloan Kettering Canc Ctr (page 110); **Address:** MSKCC, Pediatric Hem/Onc, 1275 York Ave, New York, NY 10065; **Phone:** 212-639-5952; **Board Cert:** Pediatrics 1978; Pediatric Hematology-Oncology 1978; **Med School:** Mount Sinai Sch Med 1973; **Resid:** Pediatrics, Mt Sinai Hosp 1976; **Fellow:** Pediatric Hematology-Oncology, NY-Presby/Weill Cornell Med Ctr 1979; **Fac Appt:** Prof Ped, Cornell Univ-Weill Med Coll

Modak, Shakeel MD (PHO) - **Spec Exp:** Neuroblastoma; Solid Tumors; **Hospital:** Meml Sloan Kettering Canc Ctr (page 110); **Address:** 1275 York Ave, Pediatric Day Hospital Fl 9, New York, NY 10021; **Phone:** 212-639-7623; **Board Cert:** Pediatric Hematology-Oncology 2010; **Med School:** India 1988; **Resid:** Pediatrics, Nair Children's Hosp 1991; Pediatrics, Methodist Children's Hosp 1995; **Fellow:** Pediatric Hematology-Oncology, Meml Sloan Kettering Cancer Ctr 1996

O'Reilly, Richard MD (PHO) - **Spec Exp:** Bone Marrow Transplant; Stem Cell Transplant; Hematologic Disorders in Cancer Patients; Hematologic Malignancies; **Hospital:** Meml Sloan Kettering Canc Ctr (page 110); **Address:** MSKCC, Pediatric Hem/Onc, 1275 York Ave, Ste H1409, New York, NY 10065; **Phone:** 212-639-5957; **Board Cert:** Pediatrics 1974; **Med School:** Univ Rochester 1968; **Resid:** Pediatrics, Chldns Hosp 1972; **Fellow:** Hematology, Chldns Hosp 1973; **Fac Appt:** Prof Ped, Cornell Univ-Weill Med Coll

Prockop, Susan E MD (PHO) - **Spec Exp:** Bone Marrow & Stem Cell Transplant; Leukemia; Myelodysplastic Syndromes; Graft vs Host Disease; **Hospital:** Meml Sloan Kettering Canc Ctr (page 110); **Address:** 1275 York Ave, Pediatric Day Hospital Fl 9, New York, NY 10021; **Phone:** 212-639-6715; **Board Cert:** Pediatrics 2011; Pediatric Hematology-Oncology 2008; **Med School:** Columbia P&S 1993; **Resid:** Pediatrics, Columbia Presby/Babies & Children's Hosp 1996; **Fellow:** Pediatric Hematology-Oncology, Meml Sloan Kettering Cancer Ctr 2000

Sheth, Sujit S MD (PHO) - **Spec Exp:** Sickle Cell Disease; Thalassemia; **Hospital:** NY-Presby/Weill Cornell Med Ctr, NY (page 102); **Address:** 525 E 68th St Fl 6 - Ste 695, New York, NY 10065; **Phone:** 212-746-3400; **Board Cert:** Pediatric Hematology-Oncology 2010; **Med School:** India 1988; **Resid:** Pediatrics, NY-Presby/Columbia Univ Med Ctr 1996; **Fellow:** Pediatric Hematology-Oncology, NY-Presby/Columbia Univ Med Ctr 1995; **Fac Appt:** Assoc Clin Prof Ped, Columbia P&S

Steinherz, Peter G MD (PHO) - **Spec Exp:** Leukemia & Lymphoma; Pediatric Cancers; Wilms' Tumor; Kidney Cancer; **Hospital:** Meml Sloan Kettering Canc Ctr (page 110); **Address:** 1275 York Avenue, New York, NY 10065; **Phone:** 212-639-7951; **Board Cert:** Pediatrics 1973; Pediatric Hematology-Oncology 1978; **Med School:** Albert Einstein Coll Med 1968; **Resid:** Pediatrics, NY Presby/Weill Cornell Med Ctr 1971; **Fellow:** Pediatric Hematology-Oncology, NY Presby/Weill Cornell Med Ctr 1975; **Fac Appt:** Prof Ped, Cornell Univ-Weill Med Coll

Trippett, Tanya M MD (PHO) - **Spec Exp:** Hodgkin's Lymphoma; Lymphoma, Non-Hodgkin's; Leukemia; **Hospital:** Meml Sloan Kettering Canc Ctr (page 110); **Address:** MSKCC, Div Pediatric Hem/Onc, 1275 York Ave, New York, NY 10065; **Phone:** 212-639-8267; **Board Cert:** Pediatric Hematology-Oncology 2008; **Med School:** Duke Univ 1985; **Resid:** Pediatrics, Duke Univ Hosp 1988; **Fellow:** Pediatric Hematology-Oncology, Meml Sloan-Kettering Cancer Ctr 1991

Weiner, Michael A MD (PHO) - **Spec Exp:** Lymphoma; Lymphoma, Non-Hodgkin's; Leukemia; **Hospital:** Morgan Stanley Chldns Hosp of NY-Presby, NY (page 102); **Address:** 161 Ft Washington Ave, Ste 7I, New York, NY 10032-3710; **Phone:** 212-305-5808; **Board Cert:** Pediatrics 1980; Pediatric Hematology-Oncology 1980; **Med School:** SUNY Hlth Sci Ctr 1972; **Resid:** Pediatrics, Montefiore Med Ctr 1974; **Fellow:** Pediatric Hematology-Oncology, NYU Med Ctr 1976; Pediatric Hematology-Oncology, Johns Hopkins Hosp 1977; **Fac Appt:** Prof Ped, Columbia P&S

Wexler, Leonard MD (PHO) - **Spec Exp:** Rhabdomyosarcoma; Bone Cancer; Gastrointestinal Stromal Tumors; Sarcoma-Soft Tissue; **Hospital:** Meml Sloan Kettering Canc Ctr (page 110); **Address:** 1275 York Ave, New York, NY 10065; **Phone:** 212-639-7990; **Board Cert:** Pediatrics 2014; Pediatric Hematology-Oncology 2014; **Med School:** Boston Univ 1985; **Resid:** Pediatrics, Montefiore Med Ctr 1988; **Fellow:** Pediatric Hematology-Oncology, Natl Cancer Inst 1992; **Fac Appt:** Assoc Prof Ped, Columbia P&S

Wistinghausen, Birte MD (PHO) - **Spec Exp:** Sarcoma; Leukemia & Lymphoma; Wilms' Tumor; **Hospital:** Mt Sinai Hosp; **Address:** Mt Sinai, Pediatric Hem/Onc, 1468 Madison Ave Fl 4, Annenberg Bldg, New York, NY 10029; **Phone:** 212-241-7022; **Board Cert:** Pediatrics 2014; Pediatric Hematology-Oncology 2010; **Med School:** Germany 1993; **Resid:** Pediatrics, NYU Med Ctr 1999; **Fellow:** Pediatric Hematology-Oncology, NYU Med Ctr 2001; **Fac Appt:** Asst Prof Ped, Mount Sinai-Icahn Sch of Med

Pediatric Infectious Disease

Borkowsky, William MD (PInf) - **Spec Exp:** AIDS/HIV; Congenital Infections; Immune Deficiency; **Hospital:** NYU Langone Med Ctr (page 104), Bellevue Hosp Ctr; **Address:** NYU Langone Med Ctr, Dept Peds, 550 First Ave, Ste NB8 West51, New York, NY 10016; **Phone:** 212-263-5680; **Board Cert:** Pediatrics 1979; Pediatric Infectious Disease 2008; **Med School:** NYU Sch Med 1972; **Resid:** Pediatrics, Bellevue Hosp Ctr 1975; **Fellow:** Infectious Disease, Bellevue Hosp Ctr-NYU 1978; **Fac Appt:** Prof Ped, NYU Sch Med

Foca, Marc D MD (PInf) - **Spec Exp:** Tuberculosis; AIDS/HIV; **Hospital:** Morgan Stanley Chldns Hosp of NY-Presby, NY (page 102); **Address:** Columbia Ped Infectious Disease, 622 W 168th St, VC4-East, New York, NY 10032; **Phone:** 212-305-0739; **Board Cert:** Pediatrics ; Pediatric Infectious Disease 2008; **Med School:** UMDNJ-Rutgers Med Sch 1995; **Resid:** Pediatrics, NY Presbyterian Hosp 1998; **Fellow:** Pediatric Infectious Disease, NY Presbyterian Hosp 1999; **Fac Appt:** Asst Prof Ped, Columbia P&S

Gershon, Anne A MD (PInf) - **Spec Exp:** Vaccines; Hepatitis; Viral Infections; **Hospital:** Morgan Stanley Chldns Hosp of NY-Presby, NY (page 102); **Address:** Columbia Univ Med Ctr, 622 W 168th St PH 17-110 Bldg, New York, NY 10032; **Phone:** 212-305-0635; **Board Cert:** Pediatrics 1992; Pediatric Infectious Disease 2010; **Med School:** Cornell Univ-Weill Med Coll 1964; **Resid:** Pediatrics, New York Hosp 1968; **Fellow:** Infectious Disease, NYU Langone Med Ctr 1971; Infectious Disease, Oxford Univ 1972; **Fac Appt:** Prof Ped, Columbia P&S

Larsen, John G MD (PInf) - **Spec Exp:** Tuberculosis; Viral Infections; Fevers of Unknown Origin; **Hospital:** Mt Sinai Hosp, Elmhurst Hosp Ctr; **Address:** Uptown Pediatrics, 1245 Park Ave, New York, NY 10128-1211; **Phone:** 212-427-0540; **Board Cert:** Pediatrics 1979; Pediatric Infectious Disease 2012; **Med School:** SUNY Hlth Sci Ctr 1974; **Resid:** Pediatrics, Mount Sinai Med Ctr 1977; **Fellow:** Pediatric Infectious Disease, Mount Sinai Med Ctr 1980; **Fac Appt:** Assoc Clin Prof Ped, Mount Sinai Sch Med

Neu, Natalie M MD (PInf) - **Spec Exp:** AIDS/HIV; Sexually Transmitted Diseases; Clinical Trials; **Hospital:** Morgan Stanley Chldns Hosp of NY-Presby, NY (page 102); **Address:** 3959 Broadway, rm 106, New York, NY 10032; **Phone:** 212-305-0635; **Board Cert:** Pediatrics 2008; Pediatric Infectious Disease 2012; **Med School:** Columbia P&S 1991; **Resid:** Pediatrics, Michigan State Med Ctr 1994; **Fellow:** Pediatric Infectious Disease, NY-Presby/Columbia Univ Med Ctr 1997; **Fac Appt:** Assoc Clin Prof Ped, Columbia P&S

Posada, Roberto MD (PInf) - **Spec Exp:** AIDS/HIV; Lyme Disease; Immune Deficiency; Tuberculosis; **Hospital:** Mt Sinai Hosp; **Address:** Mt Sinai, Ped Infectious Disease, 5 E 98th St Fl 3, New York, NY 10029; **Phone:** 212-241-7968; **Board Cert:** Pediatrics 2012; Pediatric Infectious Disease 2008; **Med School:** Colombia 1993; **Resid:** Pediatrics, Montefiore Med Ctr 1997; **Fellow:** Pediatric Infectious Disease, Montefiore Med Ctr 2000; **Fac Appt:** Assoc Prof Ped, Mount Sinai-Icahn Sch of Med

Prince, Alice S MD (PInf) - **Spec Exp:** Pneumococcal Infections; Infections-Respiratory; **Hospital:** Morgan Stanley Chldns Hosp of NY-Presby, NY (page 102); **Address:** 650 W 168th St, Black Bldg - Ste 416, New York, NY 10032-3702; **Phone:** 212-305-8254; **Board Cert:** Pediatrics 1979; Pediatric Infectious Disease 2008; **Med School:** Columbia P&S 1975; **Resid:** Pediatrics, NY Presby-Columbia Med Ctr 1978; **Fellow:** Infectious Disease, NY Presby-Columbia Med Ctr 1981; **Fac Appt:** Prof Ped, Columbia P&S

Saiman, Lisa R MD (PInf) - **Spec Exp:** Cystic Fibrosis Infection; Fungal Infections; Tick-borne Diseases; Tuberculosis; **Hospital:** Morgan Stanley Chldns Hosp of NY-Presby, NY (page 102); **Address:** NY-Presby, Ped Infectious Disease, 650 W 168 St, Ste PH4W-470, New York, NY 10032; **Phone:** 212-305-9446; **Board Cert:** Pediatrics 1987; Pediatric Infectious Disease 2008; **Med School:** Albert Einstein Coll Med 1983; **Resid:** Pediatrics, Babies & Chldns Hosp 1986; **Fellow:** Infectious Disease, Babies & Chldns Hosp 1989; **Fac Appt:** Prof Ped, Columbia P&S

Pediatric Nephrology

Benchimol, Corinne DO (PNep) - **Spec Exp:** Dialysis Care; Hemolytic Uremic Syndrome; Glomerulonephritis; **Hospital:** Mt Sinai Hosp; **Address:** 5 E 98 St Fl 10, New York, NY 10029; **Phone:** 212-241-6187; **Board Cert:** Pediatric Nephrology 2008; **Med School:** Southeastern Univ Coll Osteo Med 1990; **Resid:** Pediatrics, Miami Chldns Hosp 1993; **Fellow:** Pediatric Nephrology, Jacobi Med Ctr 1996; **Fac Appt:** Asst Prof Ped, Mount Sinai Sch Med

Hotchkiss, Hilary M MD (PNep) - **Spec Exp:** Glomerulonephritis; Hypertension in Children; Kidney Disease-Chronic; Transplant Medicine-Kidney; **Hospital:** Mt Sinai Hosp; **Address:** Mt Sinai, Ped Nephrology Div, 5 E 98th St Fl 10, New York, NY 10029; **Phone:** 212-241-6187; **Board Cert:** Pediatrics 2009; Pediatric Nephrology 2013; **Med School:** Albert Einstein Coll Med 1998; **Resid:** Pediatrics, Albert Einstein Affil Hosp 2002; **Fellow:** Pediatric Nephrology, Mt Sinai Hosp 2005; **Fac Appt:** Asst Prof Ped, Mount Sinai-Icahn Sch of Med

Lin, Fangming MD/PhD (PNep) - **Spec Exp:** Kidney Disease-Chronic; Hypertension in Children; Glomerulonephritis; **Hospital:** Morgan Stanley Chldns Hosp of NY-Presby, NY (page 102), NY-Presby/Columbia Univ Med Ctr, NY (page 102); **Address:** Columbia Univ Med Ctr-Div Ped Nephrology, 622 W 168th St, Ste CHN-1102, New York, NY 10032; **Phone:** 212-305-5825; **Board Cert:** Pediatrics 2013; Pediatric Nephrology 2014; **Med School:** China 1984; **Resid:** Pediatrics, NYU Langone Med Ctr 1998; **Fellow:** Pediatric Nephrology, Univ Washington Med Ctr 2001; **Fac Appt:** Assoc Prof Ped, Columbia P&S

Perelstein, Eduardo M MD (PNep) - **Spec Exp:** Kidney Failure; Glomerulonephritis; Hypertension; Transplant Medicine-Kidney; **Hospital:** NY-Presby/Weill Cornell Med Ctr, NY (page 102), NY Hosp Queens (page 498); **Address:** 505 E 70th St, Fl 3, Helmsley Tower, New York, NY 10021; **Phone:** 646-962-4324; **Board Cert:** Pediatrics 2011; Pediatric Nephrology 2012; **Med School:** Argentina 1974; **Resid:** Pediatrics, Chldns Hosp 1978; **Fellow:** Pediatric Nephrology, St Christopher's Hosp for Chldn 1985; Pediatric Nephrology, NY Hosp-Cornell Med Ctr 1987; **Fac Appt:** Assoc Clin Prof Ped, Cornell Univ-Weill Med Coll

Saland, Jeffrey M MD (PNep) - **Spec Exp:** Transplant Medicine-Kidney; Kidney Disease; Hypertension in Children; Hemolytic Uremic Syndrome; **Hospital:** Mt Sinai Hosp; **Address:** Mt Sinai, Ped Nephrology, 5 E 98th St, Fl 10, New York, NY 10029; **Phone:** 212-241-6187; **Board Cert:** Pediatric Nephrology 2011; **Med School:** Univ New Mexico 1995; **Resid:** Pediatrics, Chldns Natl Med Ctr 1998; **Fellow:** Pediatric Nephrology, Univ TX-SW Med Ctr 2000; Pediatric Nephrology, Mt Sinai Hosp 2002; **Fac Appt:** Assoc Prof Ped, Mount Sinai-Icahn Sch of Med

Trachtman, Howard MD (PNep) - **Spec Exp:** Electrolyte Disorders; Hypertension; Hemolytic Uremic Syndrome; Nephrotic Syndrome; **Hospital:** NYU Langone Med Ctr (page 104), Bellevue Hosp Ctr; **Address:** NYU Langone Med Ctr, Ped Nephrology Div, 160 E 32nd St Fl 2, New York, NY 10016; **Phone:** 212-263-5940; **Board Cert:** Pediatrics 1983; Nephrology 2003; **Med School:** Univ Pennsylvania 1978; **Resid:** Pediatrics, Tufts Med Ctr 1980; Pediatrics, Montefiore Med Ctr 1981; **Fellow:** Pediatric Nephrology, Montefiore Med Ctr 1983; **Fac Appt:** Prof Ped, NYU Sch Med

Pediatric Otolaryngology

April, Max M MD (PO) - **Spec Exp:** Sinus Disorders; Neck Masses; Laryngeal Disorders; Sleep Apnea; **Hospital:** NYU Langone Med Ctr (page 104); **Address:** NYU, Otolaryngology, 240 E 38th St, Fl 14, New York, NY 10016; **Phone:** 646-501-7890; **Board Cert:** Otolaryngology 1990; **Med School:** Boston Univ 1985; **Resid:** Otolaryngology, Boston Med Ctr 1990; **Fellow:** Pediatric Otolaryngology, Johns Hopkins Hosp 1991; **Fac Appt:** Prof Oto, NYU Sch Med

Dolitsky, Jay N MD (PO) - **Spec Exp:** Ear Infections; Neck Masses; Tonsil/Adenoid Disorders; Sleep Disorders; **Hospital:** New York Eye & Ear Infirm of Mt Sinai; **Address:** ENT & Allergy Assocs, 261 5th Ave Fl 9, New York, NY 10016; **Phone:** 212-679-3499; **Board Cert:** Otolaryngology 1990; **Med School:** SUNY Downstate 1984; **Resid:** Surgery, NYU-Bellevue Hosp 1987; Otolaryngology, Manhattan EET Hosp 1990; **Fellow:** Pediatric Otolaryngology, Chldns Hosp 1992; **Fac Appt:** Assoc Clin Prof Oto, NY Med Coll

Grunstein, Eli MD (PO) - **Spec Exp:** Cholesteatoma; Cochlear Implants; Hearing Loss; Cleft Palate/Lip; **Hospital:** Morgan Stanley Chldns Hosp of NY-Presby, NY (page 102); **Address:** Morgan Stanley Chldns Hosp of NY, 3959 Broadway, rm 510N, New York, NY 10032; **Phone:** 212-305-8933; **Board Cert:** Otolaryngology 2006; **Med School:** Albert Einstein Coll Med 2000; **Resid:** Surgery, NY Presby Hosp 2001; Otolaryngology, NY Presby Hosp 2005

Haddad Jr, Joseph MD (PO) - **Spec Exp:** Ear Infections; Sinus Disorders; Cleft Palate/Lip; **Hospital:** Morgan Stanley Chldns Hosp of NY-Presby, NY (page 102); **Address:** NY-Presby, Ped Otolaryngology, 3959 Broadway, Ste 501N, New York, NY 10032; **Phone:** 212-305-8933; **Board Cert:** Otolaryngology 1988; **Med School:** NYU Sch Med 1983; **Resid:** Surgery, NY-Presby/Columbia Univ Med Ctr 1985; Otolaryngology, NY-Presby/Columbia Univ Med Ctr 1988; **Fellow:** Pediatric Otolaryngology, Chldns Hosp 1990; **Fac Appt:** Prof Oto, Columbia P&S

Modi, Vikash K MD (PO) - **Spec Exp:** Airway Disorders; Airway Reconstruction; Tonsil/Adenoid Disorders; Cleft Palate/Lip; **Hospital:** NY-Presby/Weill Cornell Med Ctr, NY (page 102); **Address:** 428 E 72nd St, Oxford Bldg, Ste 100, New York, NY 10021; **Phone:** 646-962-3017; **Board Cert:** Otolaryngology 2008; **Med School:** UMDNJ-Rutgers Med Sch 2002; **Resid:** Otolaryngology, USC Univ Hosp 2007; **Fellow:** Pediatric Otolaryngology, Northwestern Univ/Chldns Meml Hosp 2008; **Fac Appt:** Asst Prof Oto, Cornell Univ-Weill Med Coll

Rothschild, Michael A MD (PO) - **Spec Exp:** Sinus Disorders; Swallowing Disorders; Ear Disorders; **Hospital:** Mt Sinai Hosp; **Address:** Park Avenue ENT, 1175 Park Ave, Ste 1A, New York, NY 10128; **Phone:** 212-996-2995; **Board Cert:** Otolaryngology 1994; **Med School:** Yale Univ 1988; **Resid:** Surgery, Mt Sinai Hosp 1990; Otolaryngology, Mt Sinai Hosp 1993; **Fellow:** Pediatric Otolaryngology, Chldns Hosp 1994; **Fac Appt:** Clin Prof Oto, Mount Sinai-Icahn Sch of Med

Ward, Robert F MD (PO) - **Spec Exp:** Airway Disorders; Sinus Disorders/Surgery; Choanal Atresia; Cleft Palate/Lip; **Hospital:** NYU Langone Med Ctr (page 104); **Address:** NYU, Otolaryngology, 240 E 38th St Fl 14, New York, NY 10016; **Phone:** 646-501-7890; **Board Cert:** Otolaryngology 1986; **Med School:** Cornell Univ-Weill Med Coll 1981; **Resid:** Surgery, NY-Presby/Weill Cornell Med Ctr 1983; Otolaryngology, NY-Presby/Weill Cornell Med Ctr 1986; **Fellow:** Pediatric Otolaryngology, Chldns Hosp 1987; **Fac Appt:** Prof Ped, NYU Sch Med

Pediatric Pulmonology

Constantinescu, Andrei E MD/PhD (PPul) - **Spec Exp:** Cystic Fibrosis; Respiratory Failure; Asthma; Ventilation Management-Long Term; **Hospital:** Morgan Stanley Chldns Hosp of NY-Presby, NY (page 102); **Address:** NY-Presby Morgan Stanley, Ped Pulmonology Div, 3959 Broadway, Chony Hosp Central, Fl 7, New York, NY 10032; **Phone:** 212-305-5122; **Board Cert:** Pediatrics 2010; Pediatric Pulmonology 2014; **Med School:** Johns Hopkins Univ 1997; **Resid:** Pediatrics, NY-Presby/Weill Cornell Med Ctr 2002; **Fellow:** Pediatric Pulmonology, Morgan Stanley Chldns Hosp NY-Presby 2005; **Fac Appt:** Asst Prof Ped, Columbia P&S

Dimaio, Mary F MD (PPul) - **Spec Exp:** Cystic Fibrosis; Asthma; Allergy; **Hospital:** NY-Presby/Weill Cornell Med Ctr, NY (page 102), Hosp For Special Surgery (page 109); **Address:** 1440 York Ave, Ste P5, New York, NY 10075; **Phone:** 212-988-5008; **Board Cert:** Pediatrics 1987; Pediatric Pulmonology 2014; Allergy & Immunology 2009; **Med School:** SUNY Hlth Sci Ctr 1981; **Resid:** Pediatrics, Kings Co Hosp/Downstate 1983; Pediatrics, N Shore Univ Hosp 1985; **Fellow:** Pediatric Pulmonology, Mt Sinai Hosp 1988

Kattan, Meyer MD (PPul) - **Spec Exp:** Asthma; Cystic Fibrosis; Chronic Lung Disease; **Hospital:** Morgan Stanley Chldns Hosp of NY-Presby, NY (page 102), Englewood Hosp & Med Ctr; **Address:** NY-Presby, Ped Pulmonology, 3959 Broadway, Ste BHS-701, New York, NY 10032; **Phone:** 212-305-5122; **Board Cert:** Pediatrics 1980; Pediatric Pulmonology 2010; **Med School:** McGill Univ 1973; **Resid:** Pediatrics, Chldns Hosp 1975; Pediatrics, Hosp for Sick Chldn 1976; **Fellow:** Pulmonary Disease, Hosp for Sick Chldn 1978; **Fac Appt:** Prof Ped, Columbia P&S

Lamm, Carin I MD (PPul) - **Spec Exp:** Sleep Disorders/Apnea; Asthma; Cystic Fibrosis; **Hospital:** Morgan Stanley Chldns Hosp of NY-Presby, NY (page 102); **Address:** NY-Presby Morgan Stanley, Div Ped Pulmo, 3959 Broadway, Chony Hosp Central, Fl 7, New York, NY 10032; **Phone:** 212-305-5122; **Board Cert:** Pediatrics 1980; Pediatric Pulmonology 2010; Sleep Medicine 2011; **Med School:** NYU Sch Med 1975; **Resid:** Pediatrics, Mount Sinai Med Ctr 1979; **Fellow:** Pediatric Pulmonology, Mount Sinai Med Ctr 1981; **Fac Appt:** Assoc Prof Ped, Columbia P&S

Loughlin, Gerald M MD (PPul) - **Spec Exp:** Sleep Disorders/Apnea; Swallowing Disorders; Asthma & Chronic Lung Disease; Breathing Disorders; **Hospital:** NY-Presby/Weill Cornell Med Ctr, NY (page 102); **Address:** Weill-Cornell Pediatric Pulmonology, 505 E 70th St, Helmsley Tower Fl 3, New York, NY 10021-4870; **Phone:** 646-962-3410; **Board Cert:** Pediatrics 1993; Pediatric Pulmonology 2010; **Med School:** Univ Rochester 1973; **Resid:** Pediatrics, Univ Ariz Med Ctr 1976; **Fellow:** Pediatric Pulmonology, Univ Ariz Med Ctr 1979; **Fac Appt:** Prof Ped, Cornell Univ-Weill Med Coll

Ting, Andrew S MD (PPul) - **Spec Exp:** Asthma; Cystic Fibrosis; Bronchoscopy; Cough; **Hospital:** Mt Sinai Hosp; **Address:** Pediatric Pulmonary Assocs, 5 E 98th St Fl 10, New York, NY 10029; **Phone:** 212-241-7788; **Board Cert:** Pediatric Pulmonology 2008; **Med School:** NYU Sch Med 1987; **Resid:** Pediatrics, Mt Sinai Med Ctr 1990; **Fellow:** Pediatric Pulmonology, Mt Sinai Med Ctr 1994; **Fac Appt:** Asst Prof Ped, Mount Sinai Sch Med

Vicencio IV, Alfin G MD (PPul) - **Spec Exp:** Asthma; Bronchoscopy; Interventional Pulmonology; **Hospital:** Mt Sinai Hosp; **Address:** Pediatric Pulmonary Assocs, 5 E 98th St Fl 10, New York, NY 10029; **Phone:** 212-241-7788; **Board Cert:** Pediatric Pulmonology 2012; **Med School:** Univ Toledo, Med Univ OH 1996; **Resid:** Pediatrics, Columbia Presby Med Ctr 1999; **Fellow:** Pediatric Pulmonology, Yale-New Haven Hosp 2002; **Fac Appt:** Assoc Prof Ped, Mount Sinai Sch Med

Pediatric Rheumatology

Adams, Alexa B MD (PRhu) - **Spec Exp:** Juvenile Arthritis; Rhematoid Arthritis; Lupus/SLE; Vas-culitis; **Hospital:** Hosp For Special Surgery (page 109); **Address:** HSS Ambulatory Care Ctr, 5535 E 70th St, New York, NY 10021; **Phone:** 212-606-1267; **Board Cert:** Pediatrics 2010; Pediatric Rheumatology 2009; **Med School:** Med Univ SC 1999; **Resid:** Pediatrics, NY Presby Hosp 2003; **Fellow:** Pediatric Rheumatology, NY Presby Hosp 2006; **Fac Appt:** Asst Prof Ped, Cornell Univ-Weill Med Coll

Eichenfield, Andrew H MD (PRhu) - **Spec Exp:** Juvenile Arthritis; Vasculitis; Lupus/SLE; **Hospital:** Morgan Stanley Chldns Hosp of NY-Presby, NY (page 102), Nyack Hosp; **Address:** NY-Presby,Div Ped Rheumatology, 3959 Broadway, rm 106, New York, NY 10032; **Phone:** 212-305-9304; **Board Cert:** Pediatrics 1983; Pediatric Rheumatology 2014; **Med School:** Ros Franklin Univ/Chicago Med Sch 1978; **Resid:** Pediatrics, Mt Sinai Hosp 1981; **Fellow:** Pediatric Rheumatology, Chldns Hosp 1984; **Fac Appt:** Asst Prof Ped, Columbia P&S

Imundo, Lisa F MD (PRhu) - **Spec Exp:** Lupus/SLE; Juvenile Arthritis; Autoimmune Disease; Kawasaki Disease; **Hospital:** Morgan Stanley Chldns Hosp of NY-Presby, NY (page 102), Greenwich Hosp (page 970); **Address:** Columbia Univ Med Ctr, Ped Rheumatology Div, 161 Fort Washington Ave, Fl 2, Herbert Irving Pavilion, New York, NY 10032; **Phone:** 212-305-4308; **Board Cert:** Pediatric Rheumatology 2011; **Med School:** SUNY Downstate 1988; **Resid:** Pediatrics, NY-Presby Columbia Univ Med Ctr 1991; **Fellow:** Pediatric Rheumatology, NY-Presby Columbia Univ Med Ctr 1995; **Fac Appt:** Asst Clin Prof Ped, Columbia P&S

Lazarus, Herbert M MD (PRhu) - **Spec Exp:** Juvenile Arthritis; Lyme Disease; Pain-Muscu-loskeletal; Lupus/SLE; **Hospital:** NYU Langone Med Ctr (page 104), Lenox Hill Hosp; **Address:** Pediatric & Adolescent Med, 390 West End Ave, Ste 1E, New York, NY 10024; **Phone:** 212-787-1444; **Board Cert:** Pediatrics 1987; Pediatric Rheumatology 2014; **Med School:** UMDNJ-NJ Med Sch, Newark 1983; **Resid:** Pediatrics, NYU Med Ctr 1986; **Fellow:** Pediatric Rheumatology, Hosp Joint Diseases 1988; **Fac Appt:** Assoc Clin Prof Ped, NYU Sch Med

Lehman, Thomas MD (PRhu) - **Spec Exp:** Arthritis; Scleroderma; Lupus/SLE; Rheumatoid Arthritis; **Hospital:** Hosp For Special Surgery (page 109), NY-Presby/Weill Cornell Med Ctr, NY (page 102); **Address:** HSS, Ped Rheumatology, 535 E 70th St, Ste 714, New York, NY 10021; **Phone:** 212-606-1151; **Board Cert:** Pediatrics 1979; Pediatric Rheumatology 2014; **Med School:** Jefferson Med Coll 1974; **Resid:** Pediatrics, Chldns Hosp 1976; Pediatrics, UCSF Med Ctr 1977; **Fellow:** Pediatric Rheumatology, Chldns Hosp 1979; Rheumatology, Natl Inst Hlth 1983; **Fac Appt:** Prof Ped, Cornell Univ-Weill Med Coll

Starr, Amy J MD (PRhu) - **Spec Exp:** Juvenile Arthritis; Autoimmune Disease; **Hospital:** Morgan Stanley Chldns Hosp of NY-Presby, NY (page 102); **Address:** NY-Presby, Div Ped Rheumatology, 3959 Broadway, CHN 106, New York, NY 10032; **Phone:** 212-305-9304; **Board Cert:** Pediatrics 1979; Pediatric Rheumatology 2010; **Med School:** Yale Univ 1974; **Resid:** Pediatrics, Albany Med Coll Affil Hosp 1978; **Fac Appt:** Asst Prof Ped, Columbia P&S

Pediatric Surgery

Bodenstein, Lawrence E MD/PhD (PS) - **Spec Exp:** Neonatal Surgery; Tumor Surgery; Colon & Rectal Surgery; Congenital Anomalies; **Hospital:** Morgan Stanley Chldns Hosp of NY-Presby, NY (page 102); **Address:** 3959 Broadway, CHN-215 Fl 2 North, New York, NY 10032; **Phone:** 212-342-8586; **Board Cert:** Surgery 2012; Pediatric Surgery 2005; **Med School:** Harvard Med Sch 1986; **Resid:** Surgery, Beth Israel Deaconess Hosp 1991; **Fellow:** Critical Care Medicine, Beth Israel Deaconess Hosp 1992; Pediatric Surgery, Chldns Hosp-Presbyterian Hosp 1994; **Fac Appt:** Asst Prof S, Columbia P&S

Cooper, Arthur MD (PS) - **Spec Exp:** Trauma; Disaster Preparedness; Child Abuse; **Hospital:** Metropolitan Hosp Ctr - NY; **Address:** Metropolitan Hospital, Dept Surgery, 1901 2nd Ave Fl 5, New York, NY 10029; **Phone:** 212-423-6056; **Board Cert:** Surgery 2012; Pediatric Surgery 2013; Surgical Critical Care 2004; **Med School:** Univ Pennsylvania 1975; **Resid:** Surgery, Hosp Univ Penn 1981; Pediatric Surgery, Childrens Hosp 1984; **Fellow:** Pediatric Nutrition, Columbia P&S-Inst Human Nutrition 1982; **Fac Appt:** Assoc Clin Prof S, Columbia P&S

Ginsburg, Howard B MD (PS) - **Spec Exp:** Neonatal Surgery; Tumor Surgery; Pediatric Urology; Gastrointestinal Surgery; **Hospital:** NYU Langone Med Ctr (page 104), Bellevue Hosp Ctr; **Address:** NYU, Pediatric Surgery, 530 1st Ave, Ste 10W, New York, NY 10016; **Phone:** 212-263-7391; **Board Cert:** Pediatric Surgery 2012; **Med School:** Univ Cincinnati 1972; **Resid:** Surgery, NYU-Bellvue Hosp 1977; Pediatric Surgery, Columbia Presby Med Ctr 1979; **Fellow:** Pediatric Urology, Mass Genl Hosp 1980; **Fac Appt:** Assoc Prof PS, NYU Sch Med

La Quaglia, Michael MD (PS) - **Spec Exp:** Cancer Surgery; Neuroblastoma; Liver Cancer; Wilms' Tumor; **Hospital:** Meml Sloan Kettering Canc Ctr (page 110), NY-Presby/Weill Cornell Med Ctr, NY (page 102); **Address:** MSKCC, Pediatric Surgery, 1275 York Ave, Ste H1315, New York, NY 10065; **Phone:** 212-639-7002; **Board Cert:** Surgery 2003; Pediatric Surgery 2007; **Med School:** UMDNJ-NJ Med Sch, Newark 1976; **Resid:** Surgery, Mass Genl Hosp 1983; **Fellow:** Cardiothoracic Surgery, Broadgreen Ctr 1984; Pediatric Surgery, Chldns Hosp 1985; **Fac Appt:** Prof S, Cornell Univ-Weill Med Coll

Middlesworth, William MD (PS) - **Spec Exp:** Neonatal Surgery; **Hospital:** Morgan Stanley Chldns Hosp of NY-Presby, NY (page 102), White Plains Hosp (page 652); **Address:** Morgan Stanley Children's Hospital, Div Pediatric Surgery, 3959 Broadway Fl 2 - Ste 216B, New York, NY 10032-1537; **Phone:** 212-342-8585; **Board Cert:** Surgery 2007; Pediatric Surgery 2007; **Med School:** Rutgers R W Johnson Med Sch 1989; **Resid:** Surgery, Univ Maryland Hosps 1995; **Fellow:** Pediatric Surgery, Columbia Presby Med Ctr 1997; **Fac Appt:** Asst Prof S, Columbia P&S

Midulla, Peter MD (PS) - **Spec Exp:** Hernia; Gastrointestinal Surgery; Minimally Invasive Surgery; Neonatal Surgery; **Hospital:** Mt Sinai Hosp; **Address:** Mt Sinai, Pediatric Surgery, 5 E 98th St Fl 10, New York, NY 10029; **Phone:** 212-241-1608; **Board Cert:** Surgery 2007; Pediatric Surgery 2009; **Med School:** Albert Einstein Coll Med 1990; **Resid:** Surgery, Mt Sinai Hosp 1997; **Fellow:** Pediatric Surgery, Chldns Natl Med Ctr 1999; **Fac Appt:** Asst Prof Ped, Mount Sinai-Icahn Sch of Med

Quaegebeur, Jan M MD/PhD (PS) - **Spec Exp:** Arterial Switch; Heart Valve Surgery; Pediatric Cardiac Surgery; Congenital Heart Surgery; **Hospital:** Morgan Stanley Chldns Hosp of NY-Presby, NY (page 102); **Address:** NY-Presby, Pediatric Surgery, 3959 Broadway, rm 276, New York, NY 10032; **Phone:** 212-305-5975; **Med School:** Belgium 1969; **Resid:** Surgery, St Michel Clin 1973; **Fellow:** Thoracic Surgery, Baylor Med Ctr 1974; Cardiothoracic Surgery, Univ Hosp 1978; **Fac Appt:** Prof S, Columbia P&S

Spigland, Nitsana A MD (PS) - **Spec Exp:** Pediatric Cancers; Minimally Invasive Surgery; Pediatric Thoracic Surgery; Neonatal Surgery; **Hospital:** NY-Presby/Weill Cornell Med Ctr, NY (page 102); **Address:** NY-Presby, Pediatric Surgery, 520 E 70th St, Ste L-718, New York, NY 10065; **Phone:** 212-746-5648; **Board Cert:** Pediatric Surgery 2013; **Med School:** NY Med Coll 1982; **Resid:** Surgery, Lenox Hill Hosp 1987; **Fellow:** Pediatric Surgery, St Justine Chldns Hosp 1989; **Fac Appt:** Prof S, Cornell Univ-Weill Med Coll

Stylianos, Steven MD (PS) - **Spec Exp:** Trauma; Neonatal Surgery; Chest Wall Deformities; Congenital Anomalies; **Hospital:** Morgan Stanley Chldns Hosp of NY-Presby, NY (page 102); **Address:** Morgan Stanley Chldn's Hosp, 3959 Broadway Fl 205-N, New York, NY 10032; **Phone:** 212-342-8586; **Board Cert:** Surgery 2002; Pediatric Surgery 2013; **Med School:** NYU Sch Med 1983; **Resid:** Surgery, Columbia-Presby Med Ctr 1988; Pediatric Surgery, Chldns Hosp 1992; **Fellow:** Pediatric Surgical Critical Care, New England Med Ctr 1990; **Fac Appt:** Prof S, Columbia P&S

Tomita, Sandra S MD (PS) - **Spec Exp:** Minimally Invasive Surgery; **Hospital:** NYU Langone Med Ctr (page 104); **Address:** 530 1st Ave, Ste 10W, New York, NY 10016; **Phone:** 212-263-7391; **Board Cert:** Surgery 2001; Pediatric Surgery 2007; **Med School:** Northwestern Univ 1988; **Resid:** Surgery, Naval Med Ctr 1989; Surgery, Vanderbilt Univ Hosp 1993; **Fellow:** Pediatric Surgery, St Louis Univ Hosp 1998; **Fac Appt:** Asst Prof S, NYU Sch Med

Velcek, Francisca T MD (PS) - **Spec Exp:** Anorectal Malformations; Pediatric Gynecology; Neonatal Surgery; Hernia; **Hospital:** Lenox Hill Hosp; **Address:** Ped Surg, 965 5th Ave, New York, NY 10075; **Phone:** 212-744-9396; **Board Cert:** Surgery 1974; Pediatric Surgery 2007; **Med School:** Philippines 1966; **Resid:** Surgery, St Clares Hosp 1971; Pediatric Surgery, SUNY Downstate Med Ctr 1975; **Fac Appt:** Clin Prof S, SUNY Hlth Sci Ctr

Pediatric Urology

Casale, Pasquale MD (Ped Uro) - **Spec Exp:** Genitourinary Reconstruction; Minimally Invasive Surgery-Pediatric; Genital Reconstruction-Pediatric; Robotic Surgery-Pediatric; **Hospital:** Morgan Stanley Chldns Hosp of NY-Presby, NY (page 102), NY-Presby/Columbia Univ Med Ctr, NY (page 102); **Address:** Columbia Pediatric Urology, 3959 Broadway Fl 11N, New York, NY 10032; **Phone:** 212-305-9918; **Board Cert:** Urology 2008; Pediatric Urology 2008; **Med School:** Albert Einstein Coll Med 1996; **Resid:** Surgery, Beth israel Med Ctr 1998; Urology, Thos Jefferson Univ Hosp 2002; **Fellow:** Pediatric Urology, Seattle Chldn's Hosp 2004; **Fac Appt:** Prof U, Columbia P&S

Hyun, Grace S MD (Ped Uro) - **Spec Exp:** Hypospadias; Varicocele; Undescended Testis; Minimally Invasive Surgery; **Hospital:** Mt Sinai Hosp; **Address:** Mt Sinai, Pediatric Urology, 5 E 98th St Fl 6, New York, NY 10029; **Phone:** 212-241-4812; **Board Cert:** Urology 2009; Pediatric Urology 2009; **Med School:** Cornell Univ-Weill Med Coll 1997; **Resid:** Urology, NY-Presby/Columbia Univ Med Ctr 2002; **Fellow:** Pediatric Urology, Chldns Hosp 2005; **Fac Appt:** Asst Prof U, Mount Sinai-Icahn Sch of Med

Poppas, Dix P MD (Ped Uro) - **Spec Exp:** Genital Reconstruction-Pediatric; Robotic Surgery-Pediatric; Minimally Invasive Surgery-Pediatric; Congenital Anomalies-Genitourinary; **Hospital:** NY-Presby/Weill Cornell Med Ctr, NY (page 102); **Address:** NY-Presby, Pediatric Urology, 525 E 68th St, Ste F-935, New York, NY 10065; **Phone:** 212-746-5337; **Board Cert:** Urology 2008; Pediatric Urology 2008; **Med School:** Eastern VA Med Sch 1988; **Resid:** Surgery, Eastern VA Med Schl Affil Hosp 1990; Urology, NY-Presby/Weill Cornell Med Ctr 1994; **Fellow:** Pediatric Urology, Chldns Hosp 1996; **Fac Appt:** Prof U, Cornell Univ-Weill Med Coll

Schlussel, Richard N MD (Ped Uro) - **Spec Exp:** Hypospadias; Robotic Surgery; Reconstructive Surgery; Pyeloplasty; **Hospital:** NY-Presby/Weill Cornell Med Ctr, NY (page 102), Englewood Hosp & Med Ctr; **Address:** Pediatric Urology Assocs, 65 E 96th St, Ste 1B, New York, NY 10128; **Phone:** 212-987-9500; **Board Cert:** Urology 2010; Pediatric Urology 2010; **Med School:** Albert Einstein Coll Med 1986; **Resid:** Urology, Mt Sinai Med Ctr 1992; **Fellow:** Pediatric Urology, Boston Children's Hosp 1994

Shapiro, Ellen MD (Ped Uro) - **Spec Exp:** Genitourinary Congenital Anomalies; Fetal Urology; Genital Reconstruction-Pediatric; Hypospadias; **Hospital:** NYU Langone Med Ctr (page 104); **Address:** NYU, Pediatric Urology, 150 E 32nd St Fl 2, New York, NY 10016; **Phone:** 646-825-6326; **Board Cert:** Urology 2008; Pediatric Urology 2008; **Med School:** Univ Nebr Coll Med 1978; **Resid:** Surgery, Johns Hopkins Hosp 1980; Urology, Johns Hopkins Hosp 1986; **Fellow:** Pediatric Urology, Chldns Hosp Michigan 1987; **Fac Appt:** Prof U, NYU Sch Med

Pediatrics

Allendorf, Dennis J MD (Ped) *PCP* - **Spec Exp:** Preventive Medicine; **Hospital:** Morgan Stanley Chldns Hosp of NY-Presby, NY (page 102), Mt Sinai Roosevelt; **Address:** Allendorf & Moise, 401 W 118th St, Ste 2, New York, NY 10027-7216; **Phone:** 212-666-4610; **Board Cert:** Pediatrics 1987; **Med School:** NY Med Coll 1970; **Resid:** Pediatrics, St Luke's-Roosevelt Hosp Ctr 1972; Pediatrics, NY-Presby/Columbia Univ Med Ctr 1973

Arpadi, Stephen M MD (Ped) *PCP* - **Spec Exp:** AIDS/HIV; **Hospital:** Morgan Stanley Chldns Hosp of NY-Presby, NY (page 102), NY-Presby/Columbia Univ Med Ctr, NY (page 102); **Address:** 622 W 168th St, Fl 19, Sergiesky Ctr, Rm 116, New York, NY 10032; **Phone:** 212-342-3200; **Board Cert:** Pediatrics 2009; **Med School:** Geo Wash Univ 1982; **Resid:** Pediatrics, Chldns Hosp Natl Med Ctr 1985; **Fac Appt:** Prof Ped, Columbia P&S

Bodner, Staci M MD/PhD (Ped) *PCP* - **Spec Exp:** Preventive Medicine; **Hospital:** NY-Presby/Weill Cornell Med Ctr, NY (page 102), Morgan Stanley Chldns Hosp of NY-Presby, NY (page 102); **Address:** Manhattan Pediatrics, 125 E 72nd St, Ste 1A, New York, NY 10021; **Phone:** 212-988-6500; **Board Cert:** Pediatrics 2011; **Med School:** Albert Einstein Coll Med 2000; **Resid:** Pediatrics, Mount Sinai Med Ctr 2003

Brovender, Bruce J MD (Ped) *PCP* - **Spec Exp:** Preventive Medicine; **Hospital:** NY-Presby/Weill Cornell Med Ctr, NY (page 102), Lenox Hill Hosp; **Address:** Global Pediatrics, 1559 York Ave, New York, NY 10028; **Phone:** 212-585-3329; **Board Cert:** Pediatrics 2011; **Med School:** Italy 1984; **Resid:** Pediatrics, Lenox Hill Hosp 1987; **Fellow:** Pediatric Hematology-Oncology, NYU/Bellevue Hosp 1988; **Fac Appt:** Asst Clin Prof Ped, Cornell Univ-Weill Med Coll

Brown, Jocelyn M MD (Ped) - **Spec Exp:** Child Abuse; **Hospital:** Morgan Stanley Chldns Hosp of NY-Presby, NY (page 102); **Address:** Child Advocacy Center, 722 W 168th St Fl 8 - Ste 820, New York, NY 10032; **Phone:** 212-305-6474; **Board Cert:** Pediatrics 1987; Child Abuse Pediatrics 2013; **Med School:** France 1981; **Resid:** Pediatrics, St Luke's-Roosevelt Hosp 1984; **Fellow:** Ambulatory Pediatrics, NY-Presby Hosp/Columbia Univ Med Ctr 1986; **Fac Appt:** Prof Ped, Columbia P&S

Burstin, Harris E MD (Ped) *PCP* - **Spec Exp:** Preventive Medicine; **Hospital:** NYU Langone Med Ctr (page 104); **Address:** Pediatric Assocs of NYC, 317 E 34th St Fl 3, New York, NY 10016-4974; **Phone:** 212-725-6300; **Board Cert:** Pediatrics 1983; **Med School:** Mexico 1977; **Resid:** Pediatrics, Bellevue Hosp Ctr 1982; **Fac Appt:** Clin Prof Ped, NYU Sch Med

Cohen, Michel A MD (Ped) *PCP* - **Spec Exp:** Child Development; Sleep Disorders; Preventive Medicine; **Hospital:** NY-Presby/Weill Cornell Med Ctr, NY (page 102); **Address:** Tribeca Pediatrics, 46 Warren St, New York, NY 10007; **Phone:** 212-226-7666; **Board Cert:** Pediatrics 2010; **Med School:** France 1989; **Resid:** Pediatrics, Bellevue Hosp 1991; Pediatrics, Long Island Coll Hosp 1993

Cross, Jennifer MD (Ped) *PCP* - **Spec Exp:** Learning Disorders; Child Development; Behavioral Disorders; Autism; **Hospital:** NY-Presby/Weill Cornell Med Ctr, NY (page 102); **Address:** 505 E 70th St, Fl 3, New York, NY 10065; **Phone:** 646-962-4303; **Board Cert:** Pediatrics 2012; Developmental-Behavioral Pediatrics 2010; **Med School:** England, UK 1983; **Resid:** Pediatrics, Lenox Hill Hosp 1988; **Fellow:** Neonatal-Perinatal Medicine, NY Hosp 1991; Developmental-Behavioral Pediatrics, Westchester Co Med Ctr 1994; **Fac Appt:** Asst Prof Ped, Cornell Univ-Weill Med Coll

Edelstein, Gary S MD (Ped) *PCP* - **Hospital:** Morgan Stanley Chldns Hosp of NY-Presby, NY (page 102), NY-Presby/Weill Cornell Med Ctr, NY (page 102); **Address:** Manhattan Pediatrics, 125 E 72nd St, Ste 1A, New York, NY 10021; **Phone:** 212-988-6500; **Board Cert:** Pediatrics 2007; **Med School:** NYU Sch Med 1990; **Resid:** Pediatrics, Babies & Chldns Hosp 1993; **Fellow:** Ambulatory Pediatrics, Babies & Chldns Hosp 1995; **Fac Appt:** Asst Clin Prof Ped, Columbia P&S

Ferrier, Genevieve E MD (Ped) *PCP* - **Spec Exp:** Preventive Medicine; **Hospital:** NYU Langone Med Ctr (page 104); **Address:** West 11th St Pediatric Assocs, 46 W 11th St, New York, NY 10011-8602; **Phone:** 212-529-4330; **Board Cert:** Pediatrics 2013; **Med School:** Mount Sinai Sch Med 1988; **Resid:** Pediatrics, Chldn's Hosp of Los Angeles 1991

Frank, Maura D MD (Ped) *PCP* - **Spec Exp:** Obesity; Adolescent Medicine; **Hospital:** NY-Presby/Weill Cornell Med Ctr, NY (page 102); **Address:** NY-Presby,Dept Pediatrics, 505 E 70th St Fl 5, Helmsley Tower, New York, NY 10021; **Phone:** 212-746-3303; **Board Cert:** Pediatrics 2007; **Med School:** Cornell Univ-Weill Med Coll 1988; **Resid:** Pediatrics, NY-Presby/Weill Cornell Med Ctr 1991; **Fellow:** Ambulatory Pediatrics, NY-Presby/Weill Cornell Med Ctr 1992; **Fac Appt:** Assoc Clin Prof Ped, Cornell Univ-Weill Med Coll

Freilich, Stephanie B MD (Ped) *PCP* - **Hospital:** Mt Sinai Hosp; **Address:** Carnegie Hill Pediatrics, 1125 Park Ave, Ste A, New York, NY 10128; **Phone:** 212-289-1400; **Board Cert:** Pediatrics 2008; **Med School:** Mount Sinai Sch Med 1991; **Resid:** Pediatrics, Mt Sinai Hosp 1994; **Fac Appt:** Asst Clin Prof Ped, Mount Sinai-Icahn Sch of Med

Goldstein, Judith MD (Ped) *PCP* - **Spec Exp:** Preventive Medicine; **Hospital:** NY-Presby/Weill Cornell Med Ctr, NY (page 102), Lenox Hill Hosp; **Address:** Global Pediatrics, 1559 York Ave, New York, NY 10028; **Phone:** 212-585-3329; **Board Cert:** Pediatrics 1977; **Med School:** SUNY Downstate 1972; **Resid:** Pediatrics, Lenox Hill Hosp 1975; **Fac Appt:** Asst Clin Prof Ped, Cornell Univ-Weill Med Coll

Hes, Dyan S MD (Ped) *PCP* - **Spec Exp:** Obesity; Weight Management; Preventive Medicine; **Hospital:** NY-Presby/Weill Cornell Med Ctr, NY (page 102); **Address:** Gramercy Pediatrics, 67 Irving Pl Fl 3 South, New York, NY 10003; **Phone:** 212-473-4200; **Board Cert:** Pediatrics 2008; **Med School:** Israel 1997; **Resid:** Pediatrics, Montefiore Med Ctr 2000; **Fac Appt:** Asst Clin Prof Ped, Cornell Univ-Weill Med Coll

Hiltebeitel, Carolyn B MD (Ped) *PCP* - **Spec Exp:** Neonatology; Preventive Medicine; **Hospital:** NY-Presby/Weill Cornell Med Ctr, NY (page 102); **Address:** Weill Cornell Medical Assocs, 12 W 72nd St, New York, NY 10023; **Phone:** 646-962-7800; **Board Cert:** Pediatrics 2012; **Med School:** Albert Einstein Coll Med 1994; **Resid:** Pediatrics, Mt Sinai Med Ctr 1997; **Fac Appt:** Asst Prof Ped, Cornell Univ-Weill Med Coll

Ho, Sharon H MD (Ped) *PCP* - **Spec Exp:** Preventive Medicine; **Hospital:** NY-Presby/Columbia Univ Med Ctr, NY (page 102); **Address:** Manhattan Pediatrics, 125 E 72nd St, Ste 1A, New York, NY 10021; **Phone:** 212-988-6500; **Board Cert:** Pediatrics 2010; **Med School:** SUNY Upstate Med Univ 1999; **Resid:** Pediatrics, Wash Univ/St Louis Chldn's Hosp 2002; **Fac Appt:** Asst Clin Prof Ped, Cornell Univ-Weill Med Coll

Inamdar, Sarla N MD (Ped) *PCP* - **Spec Exp:** Rheumatology; Preventive Medicine; **Hospital:** Metropolitan Hosp Ctr - NY; **Address:** 1901 1st Ave, rm 523, New York, NY 10029-7404; **Phone:** 212-423-6056; **Board Cert:** Pediatrics 1974; **Med School:** India 1969; **Resid:** Pediatrics, Metropolitan Hosp Ctr 1973; **Fac Appt:** Clin Prof Ped, NY Med Coll

Kahn, Max A MD (Ped) *PCP -* **Spec Exp:** Preventive Medicine; **Hospital:** NYU Langone Med Ctr (page 104), Lenox Hill Hosp; **Address:** Pediatric & Adolescent Med, 390 West End Ave, Ste 1E, New York, NY 10024; **Phone:** 212-787-1444; **Board Cert:** Pediatrics 1980; **Med School:** Columbia P&S 1975; **Resid:** Pediatrics, Jacobi Med Ctr 1978; **Fac Appt:** Assoc Clin Prof Ped, NYU Sch Med

Karlsrud, Katherine J MD (Ped) *PCP -* **Spec Exp:** Adolescent Medicine; **Hospital:** NY-Presby/Columbia Univ Med Ctr, NY (page 102); **Address:** 56 E 76th St, New York, NY 10021; **Phone:** 212-249-5544; **Board Cert:** Pediatrics 2012; **Med School:** Albany Med Coll 1980; **Resid:** Pediatrics, New York Hosp 1983

Keith, Marie B MD (Ped) *PCP -* **Spec Exp:** Preventive Medicine; **Hospital:** NYU Langone Med Ctr (page 104); **Address:** Soho Pediatric Grp, 552 Broadway Fl 5, New York, NY 10012; **Phone:** 212-334-3366; **Board Cert:** Pediatrics 1979; **Med School:** Mount Sinai Sch Med 1974; **Resid:** Pediatrics, NY-Presby/Columbia Univ Med Ctr 1977

Kon, Shulamite MD (Ped) *PCP -* **Spec Exp:** Preventive Medicine; **Hospital:** Mt Sinai Hosp; **Address:** 240 W 98th St, Ste 1C, New York, NY 10025; **Phone:** 212-662-1212; **Board Cert:** Pediatrics 2007; **Med School:** SUNY Downstate 1985; **Resid:** Pediatrics, Mt Sinai Med Ctr 1988; **Fac Appt:** Asst Clin Prof Ped, Mount Sinai Sch Med

Kotin, Neal M MD (Ped) *PCP -* **Spec Exp:** Asthma; Bronchitis; Sleep Disorders; Pulmonary Disease; **Hospital:** Mt Sinai Hosp, Lenox Hill Hosp; **Address:** Carnegie Hill Pediatrics, 1125 Park Ave, New York, NY 10128-1243; **Phone:** 212-289-1400; **Board Cert:** Pediatrics 2010; Pediatric Pulmonology 2011; **Med School:** Albany Med Coll 1982; **Resid:** Pediatrics, Johns Hopkins Hosp 1985; **Fellow:** Pediatric Pulmonology, Mt Sinai Med Ctr 1988; **Fac Appt:** Asst Clin Prof Ped, Mount Sinai Sch Med

Landreth, Barbara H MD (Ped) *PCP -* **Hospital:** NY-Presby/Weill Cornell Med Ctr, NY (page 102), Lenox Hill Hosp; **Address:** 115 E 67th St, Ste 1C, New York, NY 10021; **Phone:** 212-772-7569; **Board Cert:** Pediatrics 2012; **Med School:** NYU Sch Med 1987; **Resid:** Pediatrics, NY Hosp-Cornell Med Ctr 1991

Lazarus, George M MD (Ped) *PCP -* **Spec Exp:** Preventive Medicine; **Hospital:** Morgan Stanley Chldns Hosp of NY-Presby, NY (page 102), NY-Presby/Weill Cornell Med Ctr, NY (page 102); **Address:** 106 E 78th St, New York, NY 10075-0302; **Phone:** 212-744-0840; **Board Cert:** Pediatrics 1976; **Med School:** Columbia P&S 1971; **Resid:** Pediatrics, NY-Presby/Columbia Univ Med Ctr 1974; **Fac Appt:** Assoc Clin Prof Ped, Columbia P&S

Levitzky, Susan E MD (Ped) *PCP -* **Spec Exp:** Asthma; Child Development; Adoption & Foster Care; Preventive Medicine; **Hospital:** NYU Langone Med Ctr (page 104), Mt Sinai Beth Israel; **Address:** 161 Madison Ave, Ste 6W, New York, NY 10016-5405; **Phone:** 212-213-1960; **Board Cert:** Pediatrics 1972; **Med School:** Univ IL Coll Med 1967; **Resid:** Pediatrics, Bellevue Hosp Ctr 1968; Pediatrics, Beth Israel Hosp 1970; **Fac Appt:** Asst Clin Prof Ped, NYU Sch Med

Licata, Joseph C MD (Ped) *PCP -* **Spec Exp:** Preventive Medicine; **Hospital:** Lenox Hill Hosp, NY-Presby/Weill Cornell Med Ctr, NY (page 102); **Address:** Global Pediatrics, 1559 York Ave, New York, NY 10028; **Phone:** 212-585-3329; **Board Cert:** Pediatrics 1984; **Med School:** Italy 1978; **Resid:** Pediatrics, Lenox Hill Hosp 1984

McCarton, Cecelia M MD (Ped) - **Spec Exp:** Autism; Learning Disorders; ADD/ADHD; Developmental Disorders; **Address:** McCarton Ctr for Developmental Peds, 350 E 82nd St, New York, NY 10028; **Phone:** 212-996-9019; **Board Cert:** Pediatrics 1988; **Med School:** Albert Einstein Coll Med 1970; **Resid:** Pediatrics, Bronx Muni Hosp 1974; **Fellow:** Developmental-Behavioral Pediatrics, Montefiore Med Ctr-Weiler Einstein Div 1977; **Fac Appt:** Clin Prof Ped, Albert Einstein Coll Med

McHugh, Margaret T MD (Ped) *PCP* - **Spec Exp:** Child Abuse; Adolescent Medicine; **Hospital:** Bellevue Hosp Ctr, NYU Langone Med Ctr (page 104); **Address:** Bellevue Hosp, Child Protection Ctr, 462 First Ave, rm GC65, New York, NY 10016; **Phone:** 212-562-6073; **Board Cert:** Pediatrics 1975; Child Abuse Pediatrics 2009; **Med School:** Georgetown Univ 1970; **Resid:** Pediatrics, Metropolitan Hosp 1973; **Fellow:** Ambulatory Pediatrics, Columbia-Presby Med Ctr 1975; **Fac Appt:** Assoc Prof Ped, NYU Sch Med

Meyer, Dodi D MD (Ped) *PCP* - **Spec Exp:** Preventive Medicine; **Hospital:** NY-Presby/Columbia Univ Med Ctr, NY (page 102); **Address:** Washington Heights Family Ctr, 575 W 181st St, New York, NY 10033; **Phone:** 212-342-3060; **Board Cert:** Pediatrics 2013; **Med School:** Argentina 1986; **Resid:** Pediatrics, Bronx-Lebanon Hosp 1991; **Fac Appt:** Assoc Prof Ped, Columbia P&S

Mirante, Rosanna MD (Ped) *PCP* - **Hospital:** Mt Sinai Hosp; **Address:** BSM Pediatrics, 55 E 87th St, Ste 1G, New York, NY 10128; **Phone:** 212-722-0707; **Board Cert:** Pediatrics 2009; **Med School:** NYU Sch Med 1990; **Resid:** Pediatrics, Mount Sinai Hosp 1993

Monti, Louis G MD (Ped) *PCP* - **Spec Exp:** Infectious Disease; Preventive Medicine; **Hospital:** Mt Sinai Hosp; **Address:** BSM Pediatrics, 55 E 87th St, Ste 1G, New York, NY 10128-1049; **Phone:** 212-722-0707; **Board Cert:** Pediatrics 2009; **Med School:** Mount Sinai Sch Med 1980; **Resid:** Pediatrics, Mount Sinai Hosp 1983; **Fellow:** Infectious Disease, Children's Hosp 1985; **Fac Appt:** Asst Clin Prof Ped, Mount Sinai Sch Med

Murphy, Ramon J MD (Ped) *PCP* - **Spec Exp:** Adolescent Medicine; Preventive Medicine; **Hospital:** Mt Sinai Hosp; **Address:** Uptown Pediatrics, 1245 Park Ave, New York, NY 10128; **Phone:** 212-427-0540; **Board Cert:** Pediatrics 2009; **Med School:** Northwestern Univ 1969; **Resid:** Internal Medicine, Cook Co Hosp 1970; Pediatrics, Chldns Meml Hosp 1971; **Fellow:** Pediatrics, Babies & Chldns Hosp 1973; Community Medicine, Mt Sinai Hosp 1974; **Fac Appt:** Clin Prof Ped, Mount Sinai-Icahn Sch of Med

Newman-Cedar, Meryl F MD (Ped) *PCP* - **Spec Exp:** Developmental & Behavioral Disorders; Preventive Medicine; **Hospital:** NY-Presby/Weill Cornell Med Ctr, NY (page 102), Lenox Hill Hosp; **Address:** Upper East Side Pediatrics, 215 E 79th St, Ste 1C, New York, NY 10075; **Phone:** 212-737-7800; **Board Cert:** Pediatrics 1987; **Med School:** SUNY Downstate 1981; **Resid:** Pediatrics, NY Hosp 1985; **Fellow:** Developmental-Behavioral Pediatrics, NY Hosp 1987

Oeffinger, Kevin C MD (Ped) - **Spec Exp:** Cancer Survivors-Late Effects of Therapy; **Hospital:** Meml Sloan Kettering Canc Ctr (page 110); **Address:** 300 E 66th St, New York, NY 10065; **Phone:** 646-888-4730; **Board Cert:** Family Medicine 2013; **Med School:** Univ Tex, San Antonio 1984; **Resid:** Family Medicine, McLennan Co Fam Prac Res 1987; **Fellow:** Research, Fam Practice Faculty Dev Ctr 1988; Cancer Epidemiology, Natl Cancer Inst 2000

Orbe, Jessica M MD (Ped) *PCP* - **Spec Exp:** Preventive Medicine; **Hospital:** Mt Sinai St. Luke's, Mt Sinai Roosevelt; **Address:** West Care Medical, 50 W 77th St, New York, NY 10024; **Phone:** 212-579-5001; **Board Cert:** Pediatrics 2011; **Med School:** SUNY Downstate 1993; **Resid:** Pediatrics, NY-Presby/Columbia Univ Med Ctr 1996

Pasquariello, Palmo J MD (Ped) *PCP* - **Spec Exp:** Preventive Medicine; **Hospital:** Lenox Hill Hosp, NY-Presby/Weill Cornell Med Ctr, NY (page 102); **Address:** Global Pediatrics, 1559 York Ave, New York, NY 10028; **Phone:** 212-585-3329; **Board Cert:** Pediatrics 2010; **Med School:** NY Med Coll 1985; **Resid:** Pediatrics, Lenox Hill Hosp 1988

Poon, Eric Sin-Kam MD (Ped) *PCP* - **Spec Exp:** Asthma; Pediatric Cardiology; Developmental Disorders; Preventive Medicine; **Hospital:** NY-Presby/Weill Cornell Med Ctr, NY (page 102), Mt Sinai Beth Israel; **Address:** 28 E Broadway St Fl 4, New York, NY 10038; **Phone:** 212-941-8108; **Board Cert:** Pediatrics 1988; **Med School:** Mexico 1982; **Resid:** Pediatrics, LI Coll Hosp 1986; **Fellow:** Pediatric Cardiology, NY-Presby/Weill Cornell Med Ctr 1988; **Fac Appt:** Asst Clin Prof Ped, Cornell Univ-Weill Med Coll

Popper, Laura MD (Ped) *PCP* - **Spec Exp:** Preventive Medicine; **Hospital:** Mt Sinai Hosp; **Address:** 116 E 66th St, Ste 1C, New York, NY 10065; **Phone:** 212-794-2136; **Board Cert:** Pediatrics 1981; **Med School:** Columbia P&S 1974; **Resid:** Pediatrics, Babies Hosp 1977; **Fac Appt:** Asst Clin Prof Ped, Mount Sinai Sch Med

Prezioso, Paula J MD (Ped) *PCP* - **Spec Exp:** Adolescent Medicine; Eating Disorders; **Hospital:** NYU Langone Med Ctr (page 104); **Address:** Pediatric Assocs of NYC, 317 E 34th St, Fl 3, New York, NY 10016; **Phone:** 212-725-6300; **Board Cert:** Pediatrics 2013; **Med School:** SUNY Downstate 1987; **Resid:** Pediatrics, NYU Med Ctr/Bellevue Hosp 1991; **Fac Appt:** Assoc Clin Prof Ped, NYU Sch Med

Raucher, Harold S MD (Ped) *PCP* - **Spec Exp:** Infectious Disease; Travel Medicine; **Hospital:** Mt Sinai Hosp, Lenox Hill Hosp; **Address:** Carnegie Hill Pediatrics, 1125 Park Ave, Ste A, New York, NY 10128; **Phone:** 212-289-1400; **Board Cert:** Pediatrics 2009; Pediatric Infectious Disease 2008; **Med School:** Mount Sinai Sch Med 1978; **Resid:** Pediatrics, Mt Sinai Hosp 1981; **Fellow:** Pediatric Infectious Disease, Mt Sinai Hosp 1984; **Fac Appt:** Assoc Clin Prof Ped, Mount Sinai-Icahn Sch of Med

Rosello, Lori J MD (Ped) *PCP* - **Hospital:** NYU Langone Med Ctr (page 104); **Address:** West 11th Street Pediatric Assocs, 46 W 11th St, New York, NY 10011-8602; **Phone:** 212-529-4330; **Board Cert:** Pediatrics 2012; **Med School:** Albert Einstein Coll Med 1987; **Resid:** Pediatrics, Babies Hosp/Columbia 1990; **Fac Appt:** Asst Clin Prof Ped, NYU Sch Med

Rosenbaum, Michael MD (Ped) *PCP* - **Spec Exp:** Nutrition; Growth Disorders; Preventive Medicine; **Hospital:** NY-Presby/Weill Cornell Med Ctr, NY (page 102), Lenox Hill Hosp; **Address:** West End Pediatrics, 450 West End Ave, Ste 1E, New York, NY 10024; **Phone:** 212-769-3070; **Board Cert:** Pediatrics 1988; **Med School:** Cornell Univ-Weill Med Coll 1982; **Resid:** Pediatrics, NY-Presby/Columbia Univ Med Ctr 1985; **Fellow:** Pediatric Endocrinology, NY-Presby/Weill Cornell Med Ctr 1988; **Fac Appt:** Clin Prof Ped, Columbia P&S

Rosenfeld, Suzanne MD (Ped) *PCP* - **Spec Exp:** Adolescent Medicine; Preventive Medicine; **Hospital:** NY-Presby/Weill Cornell Med Ctr, NY (page 102), Lenox Hill Hosp; **Address:** West End Pediatrics, 450 West End Ave, New York, NY 10024; **Phone:** 212-769-3070; **Board Cert:** Pediatrics 1986; **Med School:** Columbia P&S 1980; **Resid:** Pediatrics, Columbia Presby Hosp 1983; **Fellow:** Ambulatory Pediatrics, NY Hosp 1986

Sacker, Ira M MD (Ped) - **Spec Exp:** Eating Disorders; Obesity; **Hospital:** NYU Langone Med Ctr (page 104); **Address:** The Sacker Ctr, 19 W 34th St Fl PH, New York, NY 10001; **Phone:** 212-268-4440; **Board Cert:** Pediatrics 1982; **Med School:** UCLA 1968; **Resid:** Pediatrics, Bellevue Hosp/NYU Med Ctr 1971; **Fellow:** Adolescent Medicine, Chldns Hosp 1972; **Fac Appt:** Asst Clin Prof Ped, NYU Sch Med

Saha, Prantik MD (Ped) *PCP* - **Spec Exp:** Preventive Medicine; **Hospital:** Mt Sinai Roosevelt; **Address:** West Care Pediatrics, 2 W 86th St, Ste 3B, New York, NY 10024; **Phone:** 212-787-1788; **Board Cert:** Pediatrics 2011; **Med School:** Case West Res Univ 1993; **Resid:** Pediatrics, Johns Hopkins Hosp 1996; **Fac Appt:** Asst Clin Prof Ped, Columbia P&S

Sanford, Marie V MD (Ped) *PCP* - **Spec Exp:** Preventive Medicine; **Hospital:** NY-Presby/Weill Cornell Med Ctr, NY (page 102); **Address:** Weill Cornell Medical Assocs-West Side, 12 W 72nd St, New York, NY 10023; **Phone:** 646-962-7800; **Board Cert:** Pediatrics 2008; **Med School:** Mount Sinai Sch Med 1991; **Resid:** Pediatrics, Mount Sinai Med Ctr 1995; **Fac Appt:** Asst Prof Ped, Mount Sinai Sch Med

Similon, Philippe L MD/PhD (Ped) *PCP* - **Spec Exp:** Preventive Medicine; **Hospital:** Lenox Hill Hosp, NY-Presby/Columbia Univ Med Ctr, NY (page 102); **Address:** Park Avenue Pediatrics, 1111 Park Ave, New York, NY 10128; **Phone:** 212-534-3000; **Board Cert:** Pediatrics 2008; **Med School:** Columbia P&S 1997; **Resid:** Pediatrics, NY-Presby Hosp/Columbia Univ Med Ctr 2001

Softness, Barney MD (Ped) *PCP* - **Spec Exp:** Diabetes; Preventive Medicine; **Hospital:** NY-Presby/Weill Cornell Med Ctr, NY (page 102), Lenox Hill Hosp; **Address:** West End Pediatrics, 450 West End Ave, New York, NY 10024; **Phone:** 212-769-3070; **Board Cert:** Pediatrics 1986; Pediatric Endocrinology 1986; **Med School:** Columbia P&S 1980; **Resid:** Pediatrics, Babies Hosp/Columbia Presby Med Ctr 1983; **Fellow:** Pediatric Endocrinology, NY Hosp/Cornell Med Ctr 1985; **Fac Appt:** Assoc Prof Ped, Columbia P&S

Stein, Barry B MD (Ped) *PCP* - **Spec Exp:** Developmental & Behavioral Disorders; Preventive Medicine; **Hospital:** Mt Sinai Hosp, Lenox Hill Hosp; **Address:** Carnegie Hill Pediatrics, 1125 Park Ave, Ste A, New York, NY 10128; **Phone:** 212-289-1400; **Board Cert:** Pediatrics 2010; **Med School:** South Africa 1980; **Resid:** Pediatrics, Mt Sinai Hosp 1986; **Fac Appt:** Asst Clin Prof Ped, Mount Sinai-Icahn Sch of Med

Stern, Marla T MD (Ped) *PCP* - **Hospital:** Mt Sinai Hosp; **Address:** BSM Pediatrics, 55 E 87th St, Ste 1G, New York, NY 10128; **Phone:** 212-722-0707; **Board Cert:** Pediatrics 2015; **Med School:** Mount Sinai Sch Med 1986; **Resid:** Pediatrics, Mt Sinai Med Ctr 1990; **Fac Appt:** Asst Clin Prof Ped, Mount Sinai Sch Med

Trachtenberg, Jennifer B MD (Ped) *PCP* - **Spec Exp:** Parenting Issues; Weight Management; Preventive Medicine; **Hospital:** Mt Sinai Hosp, Lenox Hill Hosp; **Address:** Carnegie Hill Pediatrics, 1125 Park Ave, New York, NY 10128; **Phone:** 212-289-1400; **Board Cert:** Pediatrics 2011; **Med School:** Mount Sinai Sch Med 1993; **Resid:** Pediatrics, Mount Sinai Med Ctr 1996; **Fac Appt:** Asst Clin Prof Ped, Mount Sinai Sch Med

Traister, Michael R MD (Ped) *PCP* - **Spec Exp:** Preventive Medicine; Adolescent Medicine; **Hospital:** NYU Langone Med Ctr (page 104), Lenox Hill Hosp; **Address:** Pediatric & Adolescent Med, 390 West End Ave, Ste 1E, New York, NY 10024; **Phone:** 212-787-1444; **Board Cert:** Pediatrics 1980; **Med School:** NY Med Coll 1975; **Resid:** Pediatrics, Bronx Muni Hosp 1978; **Fellow:** Ambulatory Pediatrics, NYU-Bellevue Hosp 1979; **Fac Appt:** Assoc Clin Prof Ped, NYU Sch Med

van Gilder, Max F MD (Ped) *PCP* - **Spec Exp:** Preventive Medicine; **Hospital:** Mt Sinai Roosevelt; **Address:** West Care Pediatrics, 2 W 86th St, Ste 3B, New York, NY 10024; **Phone:** 212-787-1788; **Board Cert:** Pediatrics 1976; **Med School:** Tulane Univ 1971; **Resid:** Pediatrics, Montefiore Med Ctr 1974; **Fac Appt:** Asst Clin Prof Ped, Columbia P&S

Weinberger, Sylvain M MD (Ped) *PCP* - **Spec Exp:** Prematurity/Low Birth Weight Infants; Preventive Medicine; **Hospital:** NYU Langone Med Ctr (page 104), Mt Sinai Beth Israel; **Address:** Premier Pediatrics, 51 E 25 St Fl 3, New York, NY 10010; **Phone:** 212-598-0331; **Board Cert:** Pediatrics 1982; Neonatal-Perinatal Medicine 1983; **Med School:** Belgium 1977; **Resid:** Pediatrics, LI Jewish Med Ctr 1979; **Fellow:** Neonatology, LI Jewish Med Ctr 1981

Weiss, Jona D MD (Ped) *PCP* - **Spec Exp:** Adolescent Medicine; Preventive Medicine; **Hospital:** NY-Presby/Weill Cornell Med Ctr, NY (page 102), Lenox Hill Hosp; **Address:** 114 E 72nd St, New York, NY 10021; **Phone:** 212-988-6060; **Board Cert:** Pediatrics 2010; **Med School:** SUNY Downstate 1986; **Resid:** Pediatrics, Bellevue Hosp Ctr 1989; **Fac Appt:** Asst Clin Prof Ped, Cornell Univ-Weill Med Coll

Yaker, Michael MD (Ped) *PCP* - **Hospital:** Mt Sinai Hosp; **Address:** Westside Pediatrics, 620 Columbus Ave, Ste 1, New York, NY 10024; **Phone:** 212-874-4500; **Board Cert:** Pediatrics 2010; **Med School:** Mount Sinai Sch Med 1992; **Resid:** Pediatrics, Mt Sinai Hosp 1995; **Fac Appt:** Asst Clin Prof Ped, Mount Sinai-Icahn Sch of Med

Zimmerman, Sol S MD (Ped) *PCP* - **Spec Exp:** Growth/Development Disorders; Behavioral Disorders; Cough-Tic Syndrome; **Hospital:** NYU Langone Med Ctr (page 104); **Address:** Pediatric Assocs of NYC, 317 E 34th St, Fl 3, New York, NY 10016; **Phone:** 212-725-6300; **Board Cert:** Pediatrics 1977; **Med School:** NYU Sch Med 1972; **Resid:** Pediatrics, NYU-Bellevue Hosp 1975; Pediatrics, NYU-Bellevue Hosp 1978; **Fac Appt:** Assoc Prof Ped, NYU Sch Med

Physical Medicine & Rehabilitation

Ahn, Jung H MD (PMR) - **Spec Exp:** Spinal Cord Injury; Stroke Rehabilitation; Neurologic Rehabilitation; **Hospital:** NYU Langone Med Ctr (page 104); **Address:** Ambulatory Care Ctr, 240 E 38th St, Fl 15, New York, NY 10016; **Phone:** 212-263-6122; **Board Cert:** Physical Medicine & Rehabilitation 1980; Spinal Cord Injury Medicine 2008; **Med School:** South Korea 1970; **Resid:** Obstetrics & Gynecology, Elmhurst City Hosp 1976; Physical Medicine & Rehabilitation, NYU Med Ctr 1979; **Fellow:** Spinal Cord Injury Medicine, NYU Med Ctr 1980; **Fac Appt:** Clin Prof PMR, NYU Sch Med

Birnbaum, Henry P MD (PMR) - **Spec Exp:** Pain-Chronic; Sports Medicine; **Hospital:** NYU Langone Med Ctr (page 104); **Address:** 55 W 39th St Fl 12, New York, NY 10018; **Phone:** 212-627-0593; **Board Cert:** Physical Medicine & Rehabilitation 2006; **Med School:** NYU Sch Med 1991; **Resid:** Physical Medicine & Rehabilitation, NYU-Rusk Inst 1995

Brown, Andrew MD (PMR) - **Spec Exp:** Electromyography; **Hospital:** NY-Presby/Lower Manhattan Hosp (page 102); **Address:** 233 Broadway, Ste 640, New York, NY 10279; **Phone:** 212-513-7711; **Board Cert:** Physical Medicine & Rehabilitation 1988; **Med School:** Grenada 1982; **Resid:** Pediatrics, Univ MD Hosp 1984; Physical Medicine & Rehabilitation, Mt Sinai Med Ctr 1987

Bryce, Thomas MD (PMR) - **Spec Exp:** Spinal Cord Injury; Pain-Neuropathic; **Hospital:** Mt Sinai Hosp; **Address:** Rehabilitation Medicine Assocs, 5 E 98th St, Box 1240B, New York, NY 10029; **Phone:** 212-241-6321; **Board Cert:** Physical Medicine & Rehabilitation 2008; Spinal Cord Injury Medicine 2010; Pain Medicine 2013; **Med School:** Albany Med Coll 1993; **Resid:** Physical Medicine & Rehabilitation, Thomas Jefferson Univ Hosp 1997; **Fac Appt:** Assoc Prof PMR, Mount Sinai Sch Med

Dillard, James N MD (PMR) - **Spec Exp:** Pain Management; Acupuncture; Complementary Medicine; Nutrition; **Address:** 161 Madison Ave, Ste 11E, New York, NY 10016; **Phone:** 212-265-4038; **Board Cert:** Physical Medicine & Rehabilitation 2005; **Med School:** Rush Med Coll 1990; **Resid:** Physical Medicine & Rehabilitation, Columbia-Presby Med Ctr 1994; **Fac Appt:** Asst Clin Prof PMR, Columbia P&S

Feinberg, Joseph H MD (PMR) - **Spec Exp:** Peripheral Neuropathy; Spinal Rehabilitation; Electrodiagnosis; Sports Medicine; **Hospital:** Hosp For Special Surgery (page 109); **Address:** HSS, Physical Med & Rehab, 429 E 75th St Fl 3, New York, NY 10021; **Phone:** 212-606-1568; **Board Cert:** Physical Medicine & Rehabilitation 1991; Sports Medicine 2009; **Med School:** Albany Med Coll 1983; **Resid:** Surgery, Mt Sinai Hosp 1985; Physical Medicine & Rehabilitation, Rusk Inst Rehab 1990; **Fellow:** Orthopaedic Pathology, Hosp Special Surgery 1986; Orthopaedic Biomechanics, Univ Iowa Hosp & Clins 1987; **Fac Appt:** Assoc Prof PMR, Cornell Univ-Weill Med Coll

Flanagan, Steven R MD (PMR) - **Spec Exp:** Brain Injury Rehabilitation; Concussion; **Hospital:** NYU Langone Med Ctr (page 104), NYU Rusk Inst (page 104); **Address:** NYU Ambulatory Care Ctr, 240 E 38th St Fl 15, New York, NY 10016; **Phone:** 212-263-6037; **Board Cert:** Physical Medicine & Rehabilitation 2013; **Med School:** UMDNJ-NJ Med Sch, Newark 1988; **Resid:** Physical Medicine & Rehabilitation, Mt Sinai Hosp 1992; **Fac Appt:** Prof PMR, NYU Sch Med

Frieden, Richard A MD (PMR) - **Spec Exp:** Amputee Rehabilitation; Stroke; **Hospital:** Mt Sinai Hosp; **Address:** Mount Sinai, Rehab Med Assocs, 5 E 98th St, Fl 6, New York, NY 10029; **Phone:** 212-241-6335; **Board Cert:** Physical Medicine & Rehabilitation 1988; **Med School:** NY Med Coll 1984; **Resid:** Physical Medicine & Rehabilitation, Rusk Inst Rehab Med 1987; **Fac Appt:** Asst Prof PMR, Mount Sinai Sch Med

Gold, Joan T MD (PMR) - **Spec Exp:** Cerebral Palsy; Spina Bifida; Pediatric Rehabilitation; **Hospital:** NYU Langone Med Ctr (page 104), NYU Hosp For Joint Dis (page 104); **Address:** NYU Hosp for Joint Diseases, 301 E 17th St, Ste 452, New York, NY 10003; **Phone:** 212-598-7671; **Board Cert:** Pediatrics 1979; Physical Medicine & Rehabilitation 1981; Pediatric Rehabilitation Medicine 2008; **Med School:** SUNY Downstate 1974; **Resid:** Pediatrics, Beth Israel Med Ctr 1977; Physical Medicine & Rehabilitation, NYU Rusk Inst 1979; **Fac Appt:** Clin Prof PMR, NYU Sch Med

Gotlin, Robert S DO (PMR) - **Spec Exp:** Sports Medicine; Running Injuries; Pain-Coccyx; Pain-Knee & Shoulder; **Hospital:** Mt Sinai Beth Israel; **Address:** Ctr for Hlth & Healing, 245 5th Ave, Fl 3, New York, NY 10016; **Phone:** 646-935-2255; **Board Cert:** Physical Medicine & Rehabilitation 1992; **Med School:** Southeastern Univ Coll Osteo Med 1987; **Resid:** Physical Medicine & Rehabilitation, Mt Sinai Hosp 1991; **Fac Appt:** Assoc Prof PMR, Albert Einstein Coll Med

Herrera, Joseph E DO (PMR) - **Spec Exp:** Sports Injuries; Pain-Chronic; **Hospital:** Mt Sinai Hosp; **Address:** Mt Sinai Physical Medicine & Rehab, 5 E 98th St Fl 6, New York, NY 10029; **Phone:** 212-241-6321; **Board Cert:** Physical Medicine & Rehabilitation 2005; Sports Medicine 2011; **Med School:** UMDNJ Sch Osteo Med 2000; **Resid:** Physical Medicine & Rehabilitation, Columbia-Presby Hosp 2004; **Fellow:** Sports Medicine, Beth Israel Med Ctr 2005; **Fac Appt:** Asst Prof PMR, Mount Sinai Sch Med

Kim, Heakyung MD (PMR) - **Spec Exp:** Pediatric Rehabilitation; Neuromuscular Disorders; Stroke Rehabilitation; Musculoskeletal Disorders; **Hospital:** Morgan Stanley Chldns Hosp of NY-Presby, NY (page 102), NY-Presby/Columbia Univ Med Ctr, NY (page 102); **Address:** NY-Presby, Physical Med, 180 Fort Washington Ave, Ste 199, New York, NY 10032; **Phone:** 212-305-3535; **Board Cert:** Physical Medicine & Rehabilitation 2009; Pediatric Rehabilitation Medicine 2009; **Med School:** South Korea 1984; **Resid:** Physical Medicine & Rehabilitation, Kessler Inst Rehab 1993; **Fellow:** Pediatric Rehabilitation Medicine, Kessler Inst Rehab 1998; **Fac Appt:** Prof PMR, Columbia P&S

Lachmann, Elisabeth A MD (PMR) - **Spec Exp:** Pain-Back; Sports Medicine; Cancer Rehabilitation; **Hospital:** NY-Presby/Weill Cornell Med Ctr, NY (page 102); **Address:** 117 1/2 E 62nd St, New York, NY 10065; **Phone:** 212-535-3005; **Board Cert:** Physical Medicine & Rehabilitation 1992; **Med School:** Med Coll PA Hahnemann 1987; **Resid:** Physical Medicine & Rehabilitation, NY-Cornell Med Ctr 1991; **Fac Appt:** Assoc Prof PMR, Cornell Univ-Weill Med Coll

Lee, Alexander J MD (PMR) - **Spec Exp:** Pain Management; Pain-Neck; Pain-Low Back; Spinal Rehabilitation; **Hospital:** Mt Sinai Hosp; **Address:** Mt Sinai Dept Orthopaedics, 5 E 98th St Fl 4, New York, NY 10029; **Phone:** 212-241-8947; **Board Cert:** Physical Medicine & Rehabilitation 2009; Pain Medicine 2014; **Med School:** Wayne State Univ 1994; **Resid:** Physical Medicine & Rehabilitation, Kessler Inst 1998; **Fellow:** Pain Medicine, Beth Israel Med Ctr 1999; **Fac Appt:** Asst Prof PMR, Mount Sinai-Icahn Sch of Med

Lutz, Christopher MD (PMR) - **Spec Exp:** Pain-Spine; Pain-Low Back; Sports Medicine; **Hospital:** Hosp For Special Surgery (page 109); **Address:** Hosp for Special Surgery, 75th Street Campus, 429 E 75th St Fl 3, New York, NY 10021; **Phone:** 212-606-1494; **Board Cert:** Physical Medicine & Rehabilitation 2012; **Med School:** Georgetown Univ 1996; **Resid:** Physical Medicine & Rehabilitation, UMDNJ-Kessler Inst for Rehab 2000; **Fellow:** Sports Medicine, Hosp for Special Surgery 2001

Lutz, Gregory MD (PMR) - **Spec Exp:** Spinal Rehabilitation; Sports Medicine; Pain-Low Back; **Hospital:** Hosp For Special Surgery (page 109); **Address:** HSS, Physical Med & Rehab, 429 E 75th St Fl 3, New York, NY 10021; **Phone:** 212-606-1648; **Board Cert:** Physical Medicine & Rehabilitation 2013; **Med School:** Georgetown Univ 1988; **Resid:** Physical Medicine & Rehabilitation, Mayo Clin 1992; **Fellow:** Sports Medicine, Hosp Special Surgery 1993; **Fac Appt:** Assoc Prof PMR, Cornell Univ-Weill Med Coll

Ma, Dong M MD (PMR) - **Spec Exp:** Electromyography; Musculoskeletal Disorders; Acupuncture; **Hospital:** NYU Rusk Inst (page 104), NYU Langone Med Ctr (page 104); **Address:** NYU Ctr for Musculoskeletal Care, 333 E 38th St Fl 5, New York, NY 10016; **Phone:** 646-501-7277; **Board Cert:** Physical Medicine & Rehabilitation 1979; **Med School:** South Korea 1968; **Resid:** Physical Medicine & Rehabilitation, NYU Med Ctr 1976; **Fellow:** Neuromuscular Disease, NYU Med Ctr 1977; **Fac Appt:** Clin Prof PMR, NYU Sch Med

Moldover, Jonathan MD (PMR) - **Spec Exp:** Spinal Rehabilitation; Pain-Chronic; Post Polio Syndrome/Rehabilitation; **Hospital:** Mt Sinai Beth Israel; **Address:** 200 W 57th St, Ste 608, New York, NY 10019-3211; **Phone:** 212-581-4488; **Board Cert:** Physical Medicine & Rehabilitation 1979; Pain Medicine 2013; **Med School:** Columbia P&S 1974; **Resid:** Internal Medicine, Strong Meml Hosp 1976; Physical Medicine & Rehabilitation, NY-Presby/Columbia Univ Med Ctr 1978; **Fac Appt:** Assoc Clin Prof PMR, Albert Einstein Coll Med

Neely, Michael J DO (PMR) - **Spec Exp:** Sports Medicine; Spinal Rehabilitation; Pain-Knee & Shoulder; Osteoarthritis; **Hospital:** NYU Langone Med Ctr (page 104); **Address:** NY Sports Med & Physical Therapy, 18 E 48th St, Ste 802, New York, NY 10017; **Phone:** 212-750-1110; **Board Cert:** Physical Medicine & Rehabilitation 2012; Sports Medicine 2010; **Med School:** Ohio Univ, Coll Osteo Med 1997; **Resid:** Physical Medicine & Rehabilitation, Metro Hlth Med Ctr 2001

O'Dell, Michael Wayne MD (PMR) - **Spec Exp:** Brain Injury Rehabilitation; Stroke Rehabilitation; Multiple Sclerosis; **Hospital:** NY-Presby/Weill Cornell Med Ctr, NY (page 102); **Address:** NY-Presby, Physical Med & Rehab, 525 E 68th St Fl 16, New York, NY 10065; **Phone:** 212-746-1504; **Board Cert:** Physical Medicine & Rehabilitation 1990; **Med School:** Indiana Univ 1985; **Resid:** Physical Medicine & Rehabilitation, Univ Hosp Penn 1989; **Fellow:** Brain Injury, Mediplex-Rehab 1991; **Fac Appt:** Prof PMR, Cornell Univ-Weill Med Coll

Pak, Kevin MD (PMR) - **Spec Exp:** Sports Injuries; **Address:** Hudson Spine & Pain Medicine, 281 Broadway Fl 2, New York, NY 10007; **Phone:** 646-596-7386; **Board Cert:** Physical Medicine & Rehabilitation 2009; Sports Medicine 2010; **Med School:** SUNY Downstate 2004; **Resid:** Physical Medicine & Rehabilitation, Hosp U Penn 2008; **Fellow:** Physical Medicine & Rehabilitation, Hosp Special Surgery 2009

Ragnarsson, Kristjan T MD (PMR) - **Spec Exp:** Spinal Cord Injury; Brain Injury Rehabilitation; Pain-Back & Neck; **Hospital:** Mt Sinai Hosp; **Address:** Mt Sinai, Physical Med & Rehab, 5 E 98th St Fl 6, New York, NY 10029; **Phone:** 212-824-8380; **Board Cert:** Physical Medicine & Rehabilitation 1976; **Med School:** Iceland 1969; **Resid:** Physical Medicine & Rehabilitation, NYU Med Ctr 1974; **Fellow:** Spinal Cord & Brain Injury Rehab, NYU Med Ctr 1975; **Fac Appt:** Prof PMR, Mount Sinai-Icahn Sch of Med

Rashbaum, Ira G MD (PMR) - **Spec Exp:** Stroke Rehabilitation; Pain-Back; **Hospital:** NYU Langone Med Ctr (page 104), NYU Rusk Inst (page 104); **Address:** NYU Med Ctr, Phys Rehab Ctr, 240 E 38 St Fl 15, New York, NY 10016; **Phone:** 212-263-6477; **Board Cert:** Physical Medicine & Rehabilitation 2014; **Med School:** SUNY Upstate Med Univ 1989; **Resid:** Physical Medicine & Rehabilitation, NYU Rusk Inst 1993; **Fac Appt:** Clin Prof PMR, NYU Sch Med

Reid, Malcolm D MD (PMR) - **Hospital:** Mt Sinai Roosevelt; **Address:** 1000 Tenth Ave, Ste 3B-20, New York, NY 10019; **Phone:** 212-523-6595; **Board Cert:** Physical Medicine & Rehabilitation 1992; **Med School:** Harvard Med Sch 1987; **Resid:** Internal Medicine, Winthrop Univ Hosp 1988; **Fellow:** Physical Medicine & Rehabilitation, NY-Presby/Columbia Univ Med Ctr 1991; **Fac Appt:** Asst Clin Prof PMR, Columbia P&S

Rho, Dae Sik MD (PMR) - **Spec Exp:** Sports Medicine; Pain Management; **Hospital:** Lenox Hill Hosp; **Address:** 162 E 78th St Fl 4, New York, NY 10075; **Phone:** 212-439-0008; **Board Cert:** Physical Medicine & Rehabilitation 1980; **Med School:** South Korea 1962; **Resid:** Physical Medicine & Rehabilitation, NYU Med Ctr 1975; **Fac Appt:** Asst Clin Prof PMR, Cornell Univ-Weill Med Coll

Sheth, Parag MD (PMR) - **Spec Exp:** Musculoskeletal Disorders; **Hospital:** Mt Sinai Hosp; **Address:** Mt Sinai Dept Rehabilitation Med, 5 E 98th St Fl 6, Box 1240B, New York, NY 10029; **Phone:** 212-241-6321; **Board Cert:** Physical Medicine & Rehabilitation 2014; **Med School:** SUNY Stony Brook 1987; **Resid:** Physical Medicine & Rehabilitation, St Vincent Hosp Med Ctr 1993; **Fellow:** Physical Medicine & Rehabilitation, Mayo Clin 1994; **Fac Appt:** Asst Prof PMR, Mount Sinai Sch Med

Simotas, Alexander C MD (PMR) - **Spec Exp:** Spinal Rehabilitation; **Hospital:** Hosp For Special Surgery (page 109); **Address:** 429 E 75th St Fl 4, New York, NY 10021; **Phone:** 212-606-1879; **Board Cert:** Physical Medicine & Rehabilitation 2013; **Med School:** Columbia P&S 1986; **Resid:** Physical Medicine & Rehabilitation, NYU-Rusk Inst 1991; **Fellow:** Sports Medicine & Spine Care, Hosp Special Surg 1992

Solomon, Jennifer L MD (PMR) - **Spec Exp:** Spinal Rehabilitation; Sports Injuries; **Hospital:** Hosp For Special Surgery (page 109); **Address:** 429 E 75th St Fl 4, New York, NY 10021; **Phone:** 212-606-1720; **Board Cert:** Physical Medicine & Rehabilitation 2014; Sports Medicine 2012; **Med School:** SUNY Downstate 1999; **Resid:** Physical Medicine & Rehabilitation, UMDNJ/Kessler Rehab Inst 2003; **Fellow:** Sports Medicine, Hosp Special Surg 2004

Stein, Joel MD (PMR) - **Spec Exp:** Stroke Rehabilitation; Neurologic Rehabilitation; Spasticity Management; **Hospital:** NY-Presby/Columbia Univ Med Ctr, NY (page 102); **Address:** NY-Presby, Physical Med & Rehab, 180 Fort Washington Ave, Ste 199, New York, NY 10032; **Phone:** 212-305-3535; **Board Cert:** Internal Medicine 1989; Physical Medicine & Rehabilitation 2013; **Med School:** Albert Einstein Coll Med 1986; **Resid:** Internal Medicine, Montefiore Med Ctr 1989; Physical Medicine & Rehabilitation, NY-Presby/Columbia Univ Med Ctr 1992

Stubblefield, Michael D MD (PMR) - **Spec Exp:** Cancer Rehabilitation; Pain-Cancer; Pain-Neuropathic; Spasticity Management; **Hospital:** Meml Sloan Kettering Canc Ctr (page 110); **Address:** MSKCC, Physical Med & Rehab, 515 Madison Ave Fl 5, New York, NY 10022; **Phone:** 646-888-1936; **Board Cert:** Internal Medicine 2011; Physical Medicine & Rehabilitation 2012; Electrodiagnostic Medicine 2003; **Med School:** Columbia P&S 1996; **Resid:** Internal Medicine, NY-Presby/Columbia Univ Med Ctr 1999; **Fellow:** Physical Medicine & Rehabilitation, NY-Presby/Columbia Univ Med Ctr 2002; **Fac Appt:** Assoc Prof PMR, Cornell Univ-Weill Med Coll

Thomas, David C MD (PMR) - **Hospital:** Mt Sinai Hosp; **Address:** Mount Sinai Med Ctr, 17 E 102nd St Fl 7, New York, NY 10029; **Phone:** 212-824-7210; **Board Cert:** Internal Medicine 2007; Physical Medicine & Rehabilitation 2008; **Med School:** Hahnemann Univ 1991; **Resid:** Internal Medicine, St Vincent Hosp Med Ctr 1994; Physical Medicine & Rehabilitation, Mt Sinai Med Ctr 1998; **Fac Appt:** Prof Med, Mount Sinai Sch Med

Vad, Vijay B MD (PMR) - **Spec Exp:** Pain-Back; Pain-Knee & Shoulder; Sports Medicine-Golf & Tennis Injuries; Joint Pain-Minimally Invasive Therapy; **Hospital:** Hosp For Special Surgery (page 109); **Address:** 519 E 72 St, Ste 203, New York, NY 10021; **Phone:** 212-606-1306; **Board Cert:** Physical Medicine & Rehabilitation 2007; Sports Medicine 2007; **Med School:** Univ Okla Coll Med 1992; **Resid:** Physical Medicine & Rehabilitation, NY-Presby/Weill Cornell Med Ctr 1996; **Fellow:** Sports Medicine, Hosp Special Surg 1997; **Fac Appt:** Asst Prof PMR, Cornell Univ-Weill Med Coll

Varlotta, Gerard P DO (PMR) - **Spec Exp:** Sports Medicine; Pain-Musculoskeletal; Spinal Rehabilitation; Pain-Spine; **Hospital:** NYU Langone Med Ctr (page 104), NYU Hosp For Joint Dis (page 104); **Address:** 820 2nd Ave Fl 7, New York, NY 10017; **Phone:** 212-725-1800; **Board Cert:** Physical Medicine & Rehabilitation 1992; **Med School:** NY Coll Osteo Med 1983; **Resid:** Orthopaedic Surgery, Maimonides Med Ctr 1988; Physical Medicine & Rehabilitation, NYU Rusk Inst 1991; **Fac Appt:** Assoc Clin Prof PMR, NYU Sch Med

Whiteson, Jonathan H MD (PMR) - **Spec Exp:** Cardiac Rehabilitation; Pulmonary Rehabilitation; Geriatric Rehabilitation; Neuro-Rehabilitation; **Hospital:** NYU Rusk Inst (page 104); **Address:** NYU Rusk Inst, 240 E 38th St Fl 15, New York, NY 10016; **Phone:** 212-263-6125; **Board Cert:** Physical Medicine & Rehabilitation 2009; **Med School:** England, UK 1989; **Resid:** Rehabilitation, NYU Rusk Inst 1998; **Fellow:** Cardiac Rehabilitation, NYU Rusk Inst 1999; **Fac Appt:** Asst Prof PMR, NYU Sch Med

Plastic Surgery

Ahn, Christina Y MD (PlS) - **Spec Exp:** Breast Reconstruction; Cosmetic Surgery-Face & Body; Cosmetic Surgery-Breast; **Hospital:** NYU Langone Med Ctr (page 104); **Address:** 630 Third Ave Fl 6 - Ste 601, New York, NY 10017; **Phone:** 212-717-8860; **Board Cert:** Plastic Surgery 1994; **Med School:** NYU Sch Med 1983; **Resid:** Surgery, Mt Sinai Med Ctr 1988; Plastic Surgery, Univ Pittsburgh Med Ctr 1990; **Fellow:** Microvascular Surgery, UCLA Med Ctr 1991; **Fac Appt:** Assoc Prof S, NYU Sch Med

Allen, Robert J MD (PlS) - **Spec Exp:** Breast Reconstruction; Microsurgery; **Hospital:** NYU Langone Med Ctr (page 104), New York Eye & Ear Infirm of Mt Sinai; **Address:** The Ctr for Microsurgucal Breast Recon, 630 3rd Ave, Ste 601, New York, NY 10017; **Phone:** 888-890-3437; **Board Cert:** Plastic Surgery 1985; **Med School:** Med Univ SC 1976; **Resid:** Surgery, LSU Med Ctr 1980; Plastic Surgery, LSU Med Ctr 1981; **Fellow:** Microsurgery, NYU Med Ctr 1983

Ascherman, Jeffrey MD (PlS) - **Spec Exp:** Breast Cosmetic & Reconstructive Surgery; Craniofacial Surgery; Cleft Palate/Lip; **Hospital:** NY-Presby/Columbia Univ Med Ctr, NY (page 102); **Address:** NY-Presby, Plastic Surgery, 161 Fort Washington Ave, Ste 509, New York, NY 10032; **Phone:** 212-305-9612; **Board Cert:** Plastic Surgery 2007; **Med School:** Columbia P&S 1988; **Resid:** Surgery, NY-Presby/Columbia Univ Med Ctr 1991; Plastic Surgery, NY-Presby/Columbia Univ Med Ctr 1994; **Fellow:** Craniofacial Surgery, Hosp Necke-Enfants Malades 1995; **Fac Appt:** Prof S, Columbia P&S

Aston, Sherrell J MD (PlS) - **Spec Exp:** Cosmetic Surgery-Face & Body; Rhinoplasty; Cosmetic Surgery-Breast; Liposuction & Body Contouring; **Hospital:** Lenox Hill Hosp, NYU Langone Med Ctr (page 104); **Address:** 728 Park Ave Fl Ground, New York, NY 10021; **Phone:** 212-249-6000; **Board Cert:** Surgery 1974; Plastic Surgery 1978; **Med School:** Univ VA Sch Med 1968; **Resid:** Surgery, UCLA Med Ctr 1973; Plastic Surgery, NY Hosp 1975; **Fellow:** Surgery, Johns Hopkins Hosp 1970; **Fac Appt:** Prof PlS, NYU Sch Med

Baker III, Daniel C MD (PlS) - **Spec Exp:** Cosmetic Surgery-Face; Reconstructive Surgery-Face; Cancer Reconstruction; Facial Paralysis Reconstruction; **Hospital:** Lenox Hill Hosp (Manh Eye, Ear & Throat Hosp); **Address:** 65 E 66th St, New York, NY 10065; **Phone:** 212-734-9695; **Board Cert:** Plastic Surgery 1978; **Med School:** Columbia P&S 1968; **Resid:** Surgery, UCSF Med Ctr 1975; Plastic Surgery, NYU Med Ctr 1977; **Fellow:** Head and Neck Surgery, Columbia Presby Med Ctr 1978; **Fac Appt:** Prof PlS, NYU Sch Med

Bromley, Gary S MD (PlS) - **Spec Exp:** Cosmetic Surgery; Hand Surgery; Skin Cancer Reconstruction; Skin Cancer; **Hospital:** NY-Presby/Weill Cornell Med Ctr, NY (page 102), Jamaica Hosp Med Ctr; **Address:** 5 E 84th St, New York, NY 10028-0407; **Phone:** 212-570-5443; **Board Cert:** Plastic Surgery 1986; **Med School:** Cornell Univ-Weill Med Coll 1978; **Resid:** Surgery, New York Hosp 1981; Plastic Surgery, New York Hosp 1983; **Fellow:** Hand Surgery, NYU Med Ctr 1984

Broumand, Stafford MD (PlS) - **Spec Exp:** Eyelid Surgery; Breast Surgery; Liposuction & Body Contouring; Craniofacial Surgery/Reconstruction; **Hospital:** Mt Sinai Hosp; **Address:** 740 Park Ave, New York, NY 10021-4251; **Phone:** 212-879-7900; **Board Cert:** Plastic Surgery 2006; **Med School:** Yale Univ 1985; **Resid:** Surgery, Mt Sinai Med Ctr 1990; **Fellow:** Plastic Surgery, Mass Genl Hosp 1992; Cosmetic Plastic Surgery, Cran Hosp Necker 1993; **Fac Appt:** Assoc Clin Prof PlS, Mount Sinai Sch Med

Chen, Constance MD (PlS) - **Spec Exp:** Breast Cosmetic & Reconstructive Surgery; Microsurgery; Breast Cancer & Surgery; **Hospital:** Lenox Hill Hosp, New York Eye & Ear Infirm of Mt Sinai; **Address:** 875 Park Ave, Ste 1F, New York, NY 10075; **Phone:** 212-792-6378; **Board Cert:** Plastic Surgery 2010; **Med School:** Stanford Univ 2001; **Resid:** Surgery, Univ WA Med Ctr 2004; Plastic Surgery, Univ WA Med Ctr 2005; **Fellow:** Plastic/Reconstructive Surgery, NY Presby-Columbia Med Ctr 2008

Chiu, David T.W. MD (PlS) - **Spec Exp:** Hand & Microvascular Surgery; Reconstructive Surgery; Peripheral Nerve Surgery; **Hospital:** NYU Langone Med Ctr (page 104), Lenox Hill Hosp; **Address:** 900 Park Ave, New York, NY 10075; **Phone:** 212-879-8880; **Board Cert:** Plastic Surgery 1982; Hand Surgery 2010; **Med School:** Columbia P&S 1973; **Resid:** Surgery, Barnes-Jewish Hosp 1977; Plastic Surgery, NY-Presby/Columbia Univ Med Ctr 1979; **Fellow:** Hand Surgery, NYU Med Ctr 1980; **Fac Appt:** Prof PlS, NYU Sch Med

Choi, Mihye MD (PlS) - **Spec Exp:** Breast Reconstruction; Liposuction & Body Contouring; Cosmetic Surgery-Breast; Cosmetic Surgery-Face; **Hospital:** NYU Langone Med Ctr (page 104); **Address:** KCNY Plastic Surgery, 305 E 47th St, Ste 1A, New York, NY 10017; **Phone:** 212-355-5779; **Board Cert:** Plastic Surgery 2008; Hand Surgery 2010; **Med School:** Univ Rochester 1987; **Resid:** Surgery, Beth Israel Deaconess Med Ctr 1990; Plastic Surgery, Mt Sinai Hosp 1995; **Fellow:** Hand Surgery, NYU Med Ctr 1996; Research, Mass Genl Hosp 1992; **Fac Appt:** Asst Prof S, NYU Sch Med

Colen, Helen S MD (PlS) - **Spec Exp:** Cosmetic Surgery-Face & Breast; Liposuction & Body Contouring; Vaginal Reconstruction; Tuberous Breasts; **Hospital:** NYU Langone Med Ctr (page 104), Lenox Hill Hosp (Manh Eye, Ear & Throat Hosp); **Address:** 742 Park Ave, New York, NY 10021-4251; **Phone:** 212-772-1300; **Board Cert:** Plastic Surgery 1983; **Med School:** NYU Sch Med 1972; **Resid:** Surgery, Univ Colorado Med Ctr 1979; Plastic Surgery, St Lukes Hosp 1981; **Fellow:** Microsurgery, NYU Med Ctr 1982; **Fac Appt:** Assoc Clin Prof PlS, NYU Sch Med

Cordeiro, Peter G MD (PlS) - **Spec Exp:** Microsurgery; Breast Reconstruction; Facial Plastic & Reconstructive Surgery; Cancer Reconstruction; **Hospital:** Meml Sloan Kettering Canc Ctr (page 110); **Address:** MSKCC, Plastic Surgery, 1275 York Ave, New York, NY 10065; **Phone:** 212-639-2521; **Board Cert:** Surgery 2008; Plastic Surgery 2007; **Med School:** Harvard Med Sch 1983; **Resid:** Surgery, Beth Israel Deaconess Hosp 1989; Plastic Surgery, NYU Med Ctr 1991; **Fellow:** Microsurgery, Meml Sloan-Kettering Cancer Ctr 1992; Craniofacial Surgery, Univ Miami Hosp 1992; **Fac Appt:** Prof S, Cornell Univ-Weill Med Coll

Dayan, Joseph H MD (PlS) - **Spec Exp:** Breast Reconstruction; Cosmetic Surgery-Breast; Lymphedema; **Hospital:** Mt Sinai Beth Israel; **Address:** 10 Union Square E, Ste 2L, New York, NY 10003; **Phone:** 212-844-6171; **Board Cert:** Plastic Surgery 2010; **Med School:** Univ VT Coll Med 2002; **Resid:** Plastic Surgery, Georgetown Univ Hosp 2008; **Fellow:** Plastic/Reconstructive Surgery, Chang Gung Meml Hosp 2009

Diktaban, Theodore MD (PlS) - **Spec Exp:** Liposuction & Body Contouring; Rhinoplasty; Breast Augmentation; Facial Rejuvenation; **Hospital:** Lenox Hill Hosp, Lenox Hill Hosp (Manh Eye, Ear & Throat Hosp); **Address:** 635 Madison Ave, Fl 4th, New York, NY 10022; **Phone:** 212-206-0023; **Board Cert:** Otolaryngology 1981; Plastic Surgery 1988; **Med School:** NY Med Coll 1976; **Resid:** Otolaryngology, Mt Sinai Hosp 1981; Plastic Surgery, Lenox Hill Hosp 1983; **Fellow:** Reconstructive Microsurgery, Univ Louisville Hosp 1984

Disa, Joseph J MD (PlS) - **Spec Exp:** Cancer Reconstruction; Breast Reconstruction; Head & Neck Reconstruction; Microsurgery; **Hospital:** Meml Sloan Kettering Canc Ctr (page 110); **Address:** MSKCC, Plastic Surgery, 1275 York Ave, New York, NY 10065; **Phone:** 212-639-5022; **Board Cert:** Surgery 2005; Plastic Surgery 2009; **Med School:** Univ Mass Sch Med 1988; **Resid:** Surgery, Univ MD Med Ctr 1994; Plastic Surgery, Johns Hopkins Hosp 1996; **Fellow:** Reconstructive Microsurgery, Meml Sloan-Kettering Cancer Ctr 1999; **Fac Appt:** Prof PlS, Cornell Univ-Weill Med Coll

Forley, Bryan G MD (PlS) - **Spec Exp:** Cosmetic Surgery; Reconstructive Surgery; Facial Rejuvenation; Blepharoplasty; **Hospital:** Mt Sinai Beth Israel, New York Eye & Ear Infirm of Mt Sinai; **Address:** 5 E 82nd St, New York, NY 10028-0342; **Phone:** 212-861-3757; **Board Cert:** Plastic Surgery 2008; **Med School:** Mount Sinai Sch Med 1984; **Resid:** Surgery, NYU Med Ctr & Mt Sinai Med Ctr 1989; Plastic Surgery, Saint Francis Meml Hosp 1992; **Fellow:** Craniofacial Surgery, Hosp for Sick Children, Great Ormond St 1993

Foster, Craig A MD (PlS) - **Spec Exp:** Cosmetic Surgery-Face & Nose; Cosmetic Surgery-Breast; Rhinoplasty Revision; Head & Neck Surgery; **Hospital:** Lenox Hill Hosp, Lenox Hill Hosp (Manh Eye, Ear & Throat Hosp); **Address:** 850 Park Ave, Ste 1A, New York, NY 10075; **Phone:** 212-744-5746; **Board Cert:** Otolaryngology 1980; Plastic Surgery 1984; **Med School:** Univ Minn 1974; **Resid:** Otolaryngology, Univ Minn Hosp 1980; Plastic Surgery, NYU Med Ctr 1982

Freund, Robert M MD (PlS) - **Spec Exp:** Cosmetic Surgery-Face & Neck; Cosmetic Surgery-Breast; Rhinoplasty Revision; **Hospital:** Lenox Hill Hosp, Long Is Jewish Med Ctr; **Address:** 170 East End Ave, Ste CS, New York, NY 10128; **Phone:** 212-583-1200; **Board Cert:** Plastic Surgery 2008; **Med School:** Cornell Univ 1987; **Resid:** Surgery, NYU Med Ctr 1993; Plastic Surgery, NYU Med Ctr 1995; **Fellow:** Microvascular Surgery, NYU Med Ctr 1991

Friedman, David J MD (PlS) - **Spec Exp:** Cosmetic Surgery-Face; Liposuction & Body Contouring; Abdominoplasty; Breast Reconstruction; **Hospital:** Mt Sinai Beth Israel, Lenox Hill Hosp; **Address:** 630 Park Ave, New York, NY 10065; **Phone:** 212-439-1600; **Board Cert:** Plastic Surgery 2008; **Med School:** Albany Med Coll 1988; **Resid:** Surgery, Beth Israel Med Ctr 1993; Plastic Surgery, Mt Sinai Med Ctr 1994

Gayle, Lloyd MD (PlS) - **Spec Exp:** Breast Reconstruction & Augmentation; Cosmetic Surgery-Face & Body; Liposuction & Body Contouring; Microsurgery; **Hospital:** NY-Presby/Weill Cornell Med Ctr, NY (page 102), Maimonides Med Ctr (page 98); **Address:** 50 E 69th St, New York, NY 10021; **Phone:** 212-452-5121; **Board Cert:** Plastic Surgery 1993; **Med School:** NYU Sch Med 1983; **Resid:** Surgery, NY Hosp Queens 1988; Plastic Surgery, NY-Presby/Weill Cornell Med Ctr 1990; **Fellow:** Hand & Microvascular Surgery, Davies Med Ctr 1991; **Fac Appt:** Assoc Prof S, Cornell Univ-Weill Med Coll

Glasberg, Scot Bradley MD (PlS) - **Spec Exp:** Cosmetic Surgery-Face & Body; Breast Cosmetic & Reconstructive Surgery; Reconstructive Surgery; Liposuction & Body Contouring; **Hospital:** Lenox Hill Hosp, Englewood Hosp & Med Ctr; **Address:** 42A E 74th St, New York, NY 10021; **Phone:** 212-717-8550; **Board Cert:** Surgery 2008; Plastic Surgery 2010; **Med School:** NYU Sch Med 1990; **Resid:** Surgery, Univ Conn Hlth Ctr 1996; Plastic Surgery, SUNY Downstate Med Ctr 1998; **Fellow:** Craniofacial Surgery, NYU Med Ctr 1993

Godfrey, Norman V MD (PlS) - **Spec Exp:** Rhinoplasty; Nasal Reconstruction; Nasal Surgery; **Hospital:** NY-Presby/Weill Cornell Med Ctr, NY (page 102), NY Hosp Queens (page 498); **Address:** 1158 5th Ave, New York, NY 10029; **Phone:** 212-628-6600; **Board Cert:** Plastic Surgery 1984; **Med School:** Harvard Med Sch 1973; **Resid:** Surgery, NYU-Bellevue Hosp 1978; Plastic Surgery, NYU-Bellevue Hosp 1980; **Fellow:** Microvascular Surgery, NYU-Bellevue Hosp 1981; **Fac Appt:** Asst Clin Prof S, Cornell Univ-Weill Med Coll

Godfrey, Philip M MD/DMD (PlS) - **Spec Exp:** Breast Cosmetic & Reconstructive Surgery; Liposuction & Body Contouring; Abdominoplasty; Congenital Breast Anomalies; **Hospital:** NY-Presby/Weill Cornell Med Ctr, NY (page 102), NY Hosp Queens (page 498); **Address:** 1158 5th Ave, New York, NY 10029; **Phone:** 212-628-6600; **Board Cert:** Plastic Surgery 1988; **Med School:** Med Coll PA 1981; **Resid:** Surgery, Hartford Hosp 1984; Plastic Surgery, NY-Presby/Weill Cornell Med Ctr 1986; **Fellow:** Reconstructive Surgery, Meml Sloan-Kettering Cancer Ctr 1987; **Fac Appt:** Asst Clin Prof S, Cornell Univ-Weill Med Coll

Gotkin, Robert Harold MD (PlS) - **Spec Exp:** Abdominoplasty; Liposuction & Body Contouring; Cosmetic Surgery-Face & Neck; Laser Surgery; **Hospital:** Lenox Hill Hosp (Manh Eye, Ear & Throat Hosp); **Address:** Cosmetique Derm., Laser & Plastic Surg, 625 Park Ave, New York, NY 10065; **Phone:** 212-794-4000; **Board Cert:** Plastic Surgery 1990; **Med School:** Howard Univ 1980; **Resid:** Surgery, SUNY Stony Brook 1985; Plastic Surgery, Georgetown Univ 1988; **Fellow:** Surgical Critical Care, SUNY Stony Brook 1986

Grant, Robert T MD (PlS) - **Spec Exp:** Cosmetic Surgery-Face & Eyes; Cosmetic Surgery-Breast; Breast Reconstruction; Reconstructive Plastic Surgery; **Hospital:** NY-Presby/Columbia Univ Med Ctr, NY (page 102), NY-Presby/Weill Cornell Med Ctr, NY (page 102); **Address:** NY-Presby, Plastic Surgery, 161 Fort Washington Ave, Ste 601, New York, NY 10032; **Phone:** 212-305-3103; **Board Cert:** Surgery 2011; Plastic Surgery 2013; **Med School:** Albany Med Coll 1983; **Resid:** Surgery, NY-Presby/Weill Cornell Med Ctr 1988; Plastic Surgery, NY-Presby/Weill Cornell Med Ctr 1990; **Fellow:** Microvascular Surgery, NYU-Bellevue Hosp 1991; **Fac Appt:** Prof PlS, Columbia P&S

Hidalgo, David A MD (PlS) - **Spec Exp:** Cosmetic Surgery-Face; Cosmetic Surgery-Breast; Rhinoplasty; **Hospital:** NY-Presby/Weill Cornell Med Ctr, NY (page 102), Lenox Hill Hosp (Manh Eye, Ear & Throat Hosp); **Address:** 655 Park Ave, New York, NY 10065; **Phone:** 212-517-9777; **Board Cert:** Plastic Surgery 1987; **Med School:** Georgetown Univ 1978; **Resid:** Surgery, NYU Med Ctr 1983; Plastic Surgery, NYU Med Ctr 1985; **Fellow:** Microsurgery, NYU Med Ctr 1986; **Fac Appt:** Clin Prof S, Cornell Univ-Weill Med Coll

Hirmand, Haideh MD (PlS) - **Spec Exp:** Eyelid Surgery/Blepharoplasty; Facial Rejuvenation; Cosmetic Surgery-Face & Eyes; Breast Cosmetic & Reconstructive Surgery; **Hospital:** NY-Presby/Weill Cornell Med Ctr, NY (page 102), Lenox Hill Hosp (Manh Eye, Ear & Throat Hosp); **Address:** 1040 Park Ave, Ground Fl, New York, NY 10026; **Phone:** 212-744-4400; **Board Cert:** Plastic Surgery 2010; **Med School:** Harvard Med Sch 1990; **Resid:** Plastic Surgery, NY-Presby/Weill-Cornell Med Ctr 1997; **Fellow:** Oculoplastic Surgery, Paces Plastic Surgery/Emory Univ 1998; Craniofacial Surgery, Necker Children's Hosp 1999; **Fac Appt:** Asst Clin Prof S, Cornell Univ-Weill Med Coll

Hoffman, Lloyd A MD (PlS) - **Spec Exp:** Cosmetic Surgery-Face; Liposuction & Body Contouring; Breast Reconstruction; Facial Rejuvenation; **Hospital:** NY-Presby/Weill Cornell Med Ctr, NY (page 102), Lenox Hill Hosp; **Address:** 12A E 68th St, New York, NY 10065; **Phone:** 212-861-1640; **Board Cert:** Plastic Surgery 1989; **Med School:** Northwestern Univ 1978; **Resid:** Surgery, NY-Presby/Weill Cornell Med Ctr 1983; Plastic Surgery, NYU Med Ctr 1986; **Fellow:** Hand Surgery, NYU Med Ctr 1987; **Fac Appt:** Assoc Prof PlS, Cornell Univ-Weill Med Coll

Hunter, John G MD (PlS) - **Spec Exp:** Female Genital Cosmetic Surgery; Cosmetic Surgery-Breast; Cosmetic Surgery-Body; **Hospital:** NY-Presby/Weill Cornell Med Ctr, NY (page 102), New York Methodist Hosp (page 448); **Address:** 47 E 63rd St, Fl Ground, New York, NY 10065; **Phone:** 212-751-4444; **Board Cert:** Plastic Surgery 1991; **Med School:** SUNY Downstate 1983; **Resid:** Surgery, Mount Sinai Hosp 1986; **Fellow:** Plastic Surgery, SUNY Downstate Med Ctr 1988; **Fac Appt:** Assoc Clin Prof S, Cornell Univ-Weill Med Coll

Imber, Gerald MD (PlS) - **Spec Exp:** Cosmetic Surgery-Breast; Eyelid Surgery; Mohs Surgery; Cosmetic Surgery-Face; **Hospital:** NY-Presby/Weill Cornell Med Ctr, NY (page 102); **Address:** 121A E 83rd St, New York, NY 10028; **Phone:** 212-472-1800; **Board Cert:** Plastic Surgery 1976; **Med School:** SUNY Downstate 1966; **Resid:** Surgery, LIJ Med Ctr 1972; Plastic Surgery, NY Hosp 1974; **Fac Appt:** Asst Clin Prof S, Cornell Univ-Weill Med Coll

Jacobs, Elliot W MD (PlS) - **Spec Exp:** Cosmetic Surgery-Face & Breast; Gynecomastia; Body Contouring; Rhinoplasty; **Hospital:** New York Eye & Ear Infirm of Mt Sinai, Mt Sinai Beth Israel; **Address:** 815 Park Ave, New York, NY 10021-3276; **Phone:** 212-570-6080; **Board Cert:** Plastic Surgery 1982; **Med School:** Mount Sinai Sch Med 1970; **Resid:** Surgery, Mt Sinai Med Ctr 1974; Plastic Surgery, Mt Sinai Med Ctr 1977

Karp, Nolan MD (PlS) - **Spec Exp:** Breast Cosmetic & Reconstructive Surgery; Liposuction & Body Contouring; Skin Cancer; **Hospital:** NYU Langone Med Ctr (page 104); **Address:** KCNY Plastic Surgery, 305 E 47th St, Ste 1A, New York, NY 10017; **Phone:** 212-355-5779; **Board Cert:** Plastic Surgery 1994; **Med School:** Northwestern Univ 1983; **Resid:** Surgery, NYU Med Ctr 1988; **Fellow:** Plastic Surgery, NYU Med Ctr 1991

Kim, Tae Ho MD (PlS) - **Spec Exp:** Pediatric Plastic Surgery; Pediatric Craniofacial Surgery; **Hospital:** New York Eye & Ear Infirm of Mt Sinai, Mt Sinai Beth Israel; **Address:** West Village Plastic Surgery, 115 Washington Pl, Unit B, New York, NY 10014; **Phone:** 646-725-8447; **Board Cert:** Plastic Surgery 2013; **Med School:** Univ Pittsburgh 1991; **Resid:** Surgery, UC Irvine Med Ctr 1997; Plastic/Reconstructive Surgery, UMass Meml Med Ctr 1999; **Fellow:** Surgical Research, Chldns Hosp 1996; Pediatric Craniofacial Surgery, Chldns Hosp 2000

Kolker, Adam R MD (PlS) - **Spec Exp:** Cosmetic Surgery-Breast; Breast Reconstruction; Abdominoplasty; Body Contouring After Weight Loss; **Hospital:** Mt Sinai Hosp, Lenox Hill Hosp; **Address:** 710 Park Ave, New York, NY 10021; **Phone:** 212-744-6500; **Board Cert:** Plastic Surgery 2011; Surgery 2005; **Med School:** Albany Med Coll 1990; **Resid:** Surgery, St Vincents Hosp 1995; Plastic/Reconstructive Surgery, Beth Israel Deaconess Med Ctr 1998; **Fellow:** Microsurgery, NYU Med Ctr 1996; Craniofacial Surgery, Royal Chldns Hosp 2000; **Fac Appt:** Assoc Clin Prof S, Mount Sinai-Icahn Sch of Med

LaBruna, Anthony N MD (PlS) - **Spec Exp:** Cosmetic Surgery-Face; Facial Plastic & Reconstructive Surgery; Rhinoplasty Revision; Facial Deformities/Reconstruction; **Hospital:** NY-Presby/Weill Cornell Med Ctr, NY (page 102), Lenox Hill Hosp; **Address:** 45 E 85th St, rm 1A, New York, NY 10028; **Phone:** 212-584-7001; **Board Cert:** Otolaryngology 1997; Plastic Surgery 2012; **Med School:** Cornell Univ-Weill Med Coll 1990; **Resid:** Surgery, Lenox Hill Hosp 1992; Otolaryngology, Manhattan EE&T Hosp 1996; **Fellow:** Plastic Surgery, Mt Sinai Med Ctr 2000; **Fac Appt:** Assoc Clin Prof PlS, Cornell Univ-Weill Med Coll

Lesesne, Carroll B MD (PlS) - **Spec Exp:** Cosmetic Surgery-Face; Rhinoplasty; Abdominoplasty; Skin Cancer; **Hospital:** Lenox Hill Hosp (Manh Eye, Ear & Throat Hosp), Northern Westchester Hosp; **Address:** 620 Park Ave, New York, NY 10065; **Phone:** 212-570-6318; **Board Cert:** Plastic Surgery 1987; **Med School:** Duke Univ 1980; **Resid:** Surgery, Stanford Univ Med Ctr 1983; Plastic Surgery, New York Hosp 1985; **Fellow:** Plastic Surgery, Meml Sloan Kettering Cancer Ctr 1985; **Fac Appt:** Clin Prof PlS, NYU Sch Med

Levine, Jamie P MD (PlS) - **Spec Exp:** Microsurgery; Head & Neck Reconstruction; Facial Plastic & Reconstructive Surgery; Breast Cosmetic & Reconstructive Surgery; **Hospital:** NYU Langone Med Ctr (page 104); **Address:** Plastic Surgery, 305 E 33rd St, Ground FL, New York, NY 10016; **Phone:** 212-263-8452; **Board Cert:** Plastic Surgery 2012; **Med School:** Albany Med Coll 1992; **Resid:** Surgery, Maimonides Med Ctr 1994; Plastic Surgery, NYU Med Ctr 1998; **Fellow:** Microsurgery, NYU Med Ctr 2000; **Fac Appt:** Asst Prof S, NYU Sch Med

Levine, Joshua L MD (PlS) - **Spec Exp:** Breast Cancer & Surgery; Microsurgery; **Hospital:** New York Eye & Ear Infirm of Mt Sinai, Montefiore Med Ctr-Einstein Campus (page 100); **Address:** 3 Columbus Cir, Ste 1410, New York, NY 10019; **Phone:** 212-245-8140; **Board Cert:** Plastic Surgery 2005; **Med School:** Med Coll GA 1994; **Resid:** Plastic Surgery, Montefiore Med Ctr 2001; Plastic Surgery, Montefiore Med Ctr 2003; **Fellow:** Cosmetic Plastic Surgery, NY Eye & Ear Infirm 2003; Reconstructive Microsurgery, Louisiana State Univ Affil Hosp 2004

Matarasso, Alan MD (PlS) - **Spec Exp:** Cosmetic Surgery-Face & Eyes; Rhinoplasty; Liposuction; Abdominoplasty; **Hospital:** Lenox Hill Hosp (Manh Eye, Ear & Throat Hosp); **Address:** 1009 Park Ave, New York, NY 10028; **Phone:** 212-249-7500; **Board Cert:** Plastic Surgery 1986; **Med School:** Univ Miami Sch Med 1979; **Resid:** Surgery, Montefiore Med Ctr 1983; Plastic Surgery, Montefiore Med Ctr 1985; **Fellow:** Cosmetic Surgery, Manhattan EET Hosp 1985; **Fac Appt:** Clin Prof PlS, Albert Einstein Coll Med

Mehrara, Babak J MD (PlS) - **Spec Exp:** Breast Reconstruction; Cancer Reconstruction; Microsurgery; Reconstructive Surgery-Face; **Hospital:** Meml Sloan Kettering Canc Ctr (page 110); **Address:** MSKCC, Plastic Surgery, 160 E 53rd St Fl 10, New York, NY 10022; **Phone:** 212-639-8639; **Board Cert:** Plastic Surgery 2013; **Med School:** Columbia P&S 1993; **Resid:** Surgery, NYU Med Ctr 1998; Plastic Surgery, NYU Med Ctr 2001; **Fellow:** Microsurgery, UCLA Med Ctr 2002; **Fac Appt:** Assoc Prof S, Cornell Univ-Weill Med Coll

Monasebian, Douglas M MD/DMD (PlS) - **Spec Exp:** Cosmetic Surgery-Face; Facial Plastic & Reconstructive Surgery; **Hospital:** Mt Sinai Hosp, Mt Sinai St. Luke's; **Address:** 784 Park Ave, New York, NY 10021; **Phone:** 212-472-8700; **Board Cert:** Plastic Surgery 2009; **Med School:** Univ Nebr Coll Med 1992; **Resid:** Surgery, Univ Nebraska Med Ctr 1995; **Fellow:** Plastic Surgery, Montefiore Med Ctr 1997; **Fac Appt:** Asst Clin Prof PlS, Mount Sinai Sch Med

Otterburn, David M MD (PlS) - **Spec Exp:** Reconstructive Microsurgery; Breast Cosmetic & Reconstructive Surgery; Facial Plastic & Reconstructive Surgery; Oculoplastic Surgery; **Hospital:** NY-Presby/Weill Cornell Med Ctr, NY (page 102); **Address:** 425 E 61st St Fl 10, New York, NY 10065; **Phone:** 212-821-0634; **Board Cert:** Plastic Surgery 2012; Surgery 2007; **Med School:** Rutgers R W Johnson Med Sch 2000; **Resid:** Surgery, Thos Jefferson Univ Hosp 2007; **Fellow:** Plastic Surgery, Emory Univ Hosp 2010; Microsurgery, NYU Med Ctr 2011; **Fac Appt:** Asst Prof S, Cornell Univ

Perrotti, John A MD (PlS) - **Spec Exp:** Liposuction & Body Contouring; Cosmetic Surgery-Face & Breast; Abdominoplasty; Facial Plastic Surgery; **Hospital:** Lenox Hill Hosp (Manh Eye, Ear & Throat Hosp), Lenox Hill Hosp; **Address:** 330 E 63rd St, Ste 1H, New York, NY 10065; **Phone:** 212-861-6363; **Board Cert:** Plastic Surgery 2010; **Med School:** NY Med Coll 1991; **Resid:** Surgery, NY Med Coll/St Vincents Hosp 1996; Plastic Surgery, Cleveland Clin 1998; **Fac Appt:** Asst Clin Prof S, NY Med Coll

Pfeifer, Tracy M MD (PlS) - **Spec Exp:** Cosmetic Surgery-Breast; Body Contouring; Cosmetic Surgery-Face; **Hospital:** Lenox Hill Hosp, Lenox Hill Hosp (Manh Eye, Ear & Throat Hosp); **Address:** 969 Park Ave, New York, NY 10028; **Phone:** 212-860-0670; **Board Cert:** Surgery 2008; Plastic Surgery 2011; **Med School:** Rutgers R W Johnson Med Sch 1991; **Resid:** Surgery, NY-Presby/Weill Cornell Med Ctr 1996; Plastic Surgery, NYU Med Ctr 1998; **Fellow:** Breast Surgery, Inst Reconstructive Breast Surgery 1999

Razaboni, Rosa M MD (PlS) - **Spec Exp:** Cosmetic Surgery; Breast Reconstruction; Cosmetic Surgery-Breast; Body Contouring After Weight Loss; **Hospital:** Lenox Hill Hosp, Mt Sinai Hosp; **Address:** 14-A E 68th St, New York, NY 10065; **Phone:** 212-772-0200; **Board Cert:** Plastic Surgery 1993; **Med School:** Brazil 1975; **Resid:** Surgery, St Vincent Hosp 1985; Plastic Surgery, NYU Med Ctr 1988; **Fellow:** Microsurgery, Hosp Trousseau 1986; **Fac Appt:** Asst Clin Prof S, Mount Sinai Sch Med

Rodriguez, Eduardo De Jesus MD/DDS (PlS) - **Spec Exp:** Facial Plastic & Reconstructive Surgery; Transplant-Face; Craniofacial Surgery/Reconstruction; Maxillofacial Surgery; **Hospital:** NYU Langone Med Ctr (page 104); **Address:** NYU Plastic Surgery Assocs, 305 E 33rd St, Ground FL, New York, NY 10016; **Phone:** 646-501-4481; **Board Cert:** Plastic Surgery 2005; Maxillofacial Surgery 1998; **Med School:** Va Commonwealth Univ Sch Med 1999; **Resid:** Plastic Surgery, Johns Hopkins Hosp 2003; **Fellow:** Reconstructive Microsurgery, Chang Gung Meml Hosp 2004; **Fac Appt:** Prof PlS, NY Med Coll

Romita, Mauro C MD (PlS) - **Spec Exp:** Cosmetic Surgery-Face; Liposuction & Body Contouring; Reconstructive Plastic Surgery; **Hospital:** Lenox Hill Hosp; **Address:** 853 5th Ave, New York, NY 10065; **Phone:** 212-772-3220; **Board Cert:** Plastic Surgery 1983; **Med School:** Univ Miami Sch Med 1973; **Resid:** Surgery, NYU Med Ctr 1978; Plastic Surgery, NYU Med Ctr 1980; **Fellow:** Craniofacial Surgery, NYU Med Ctr 1981; Microsurgery, NYU Med Ctr 1982

Rose, Elliott H MD (PlS) - **Spec Exp:** Facial Paralysis Reconstruction; Cosmetic Surgery-Face & Body; Burns-Reconstructive Plastic Surgery; Microsurgery; **Hospital:** Mt Sinai Hosp; **Address:** The Aesthetic Surgery Center, 895 Park Ave, New York, NY 10075; **Phone:** 212-639-1346; **Board Cert:** Plastic Surgery 1979; **Med School:** Univ Tex Med Br, Galveston 1970; **Resid:** Surgery, UCLA Med Ctr 1973; Plastic Surgery, Stanford Univ Hosp & Clins 1977; **Fellow:** Hand & Microvascular Surgery, UCSF Med Ctr 1978; **Fac Appt:** Assoc Clin Prof PlS, Mount Sinai-Icahn Sch of Med

Rosenblatt, William B MD (PlS) - **Spec Exp:** Nasal Surgery; Cosmetic Surgery-Face & Body; Cosmetic Surgery-Breast; Rhinoplasty; **Hospital:** Lenox Hill Hosp, Lenox Hill Hosp (Manh Eye, Ear & Throat Hosp); **Address:** 308 E 79th St, Ste 1D, New York, NY 10075; **Phone:** 212-570-6100; **Board Cert:** Otolaryngology 1977; Plastic Surgery 1980; **Med School:** NY Med Coll 1973; **Resid:** Otolaryngology, Metropolitan Hosp 1977; Plastic Surgery, Lenox Hill Hosp 1979; **Fac Appt:** Asst Clin Prof PlS, Touro Coll Osteopathic Med-NY

Sabry, M. Zakir MD (PlS) - **Spec Exp:** Cosmetic Surgery; Breast Reconstruction; Craniofacial Surgery; Cleft Palate/Lip; **Hospital:** Lenox Hill Hosp; **Address:** 20 5th Ave, Ste 1D, New York, NY 10011; **Phone:** 212-737-1308; **Board Cert:** Plastic Surgery 2004; **Med School:** NY Med Coll 1993; **Resid:** Surgery, St Vincent Hosp 1999; Plastic Surgery, VA Commonwealth Univ Med Ctr 2001; **Fellow:** Craniofacial Surgery, Barnes-Jewish Hosp 2002; **Fac Appt:** Asst Prof S, NY Med Coll

Schaffner, Adam D MD (PlS) - **Spec Exp:** Cosmetic Surgery-Face & Breast; Breast Reconstruction & Augmentation; Cosmetic Surgery-Body; Facial Plastic Surgery; **Hospital:** Lenox Hill Hosp (Manh Eye, Ear & Throat Hosp), New York Eye & Ear Infirm of Mt Sinai; **Address:** 461 Park Ave S, Ste 7A, New York, NY 10016-6822; **Phone:** 212-481-6696; **Board Cert:** Plastic Surgery 2013; Facial Plastic & Reconstr Surgery 2007; Otolaryngology 2014; **Med School:** Rush Med Coll 1998; **Resid:** Otolaryngology, Stony Brook Univ Hosp 2003; Plastic Surgery, Detroit Med Ctr/Wayne State Univ 2009; **Fellow:** Facial Plastic & Reconstr Surgery, Stanford Affil Hosp/Mittelman FPS 2004; Cosmetic Plastic Surgery, Georgetown Univ Hosp 2010

Schulman, Matthew R MD (PlS) - **Spec Exp:** Cosmetic Surgery-Face; Cosmetic Surgery-Breast; Liposuction; Body Contouring; **Hospital:** Mt Sinai Hosp, Westchester Med Ctr; **Address:** 950 Park Ave, New York, NY 10028; **Phone:** 212-289-1851; **Board Cert:** Plastic Surgery 2007; **Med School:** Jefferson Med Coll 2000; **Resid:** Surgery, Mt Sinai Med Ctr 2003; **Fellow:** Plastic Surgery, Mt Sinai Med Ctr 2006; **Fac Appt:** Assoc Prof PlS, Mount Sinai Sch Med

Schulman, Norman H MD (PlS) - **Spec Exp:** Cosmetic Surgery-Face & Body; Breast Cosmetic & Reconstructive Surgery; Nasal Surgery; Tuberous Breasts; **Hospital:** Lenox Hill Hosp, Lenox Hill Hosp (Manh Eye, Ear & Throat Hosp); **Address:** 308 E 79th St, New York, NY 10075; **Phone:** 212-861-5004; **Board Cert:** Surgery 1973; Plastic Surgery 1976; **Med School:** Tufts Univ 1965; **Resid:** Surgery, Bronx Muni Hosp 1972; Plastic Surgery, Lenox Hill Hosp 1974; **Fellow:** Head and Neck Surgery, Roswell Park Cancer Inst 1975; **Fac Appt:** Clin Prof PlS, Cornell Univ-Weill Med Coll

Schwartz, Mark H MD (PlS) - **Spec Exp:** Cosmetic Surgery-Face & Body; Breast Cosmetic & Reconstructive Surgery; Liposuction & Body Contouring; Body Contouring After Weight Loss; **Hospital:** NY-Presby/Weill Cornell Med Ctr, NY (page 102); **Address:** 79 E 79th St, New York, NY 10075; **Phone:** 212-737-9090; **Board Cert:** Plastic Surgery 2009; **Med School:** Mount Sinai Sch Med 1989; **Resid:** Surgery, Montefiore Med Ctr 1994; Plastic Surgery, NY Presby-Cornell Med Ctr 1996; **Fellow:** Hand & Microvascular Surgery, California Pacific Med Ctr 1997; **Fac Appt:** Asst Clin Prof PlS, Cornell Univ-Weill Med Coll

Shafer, David M MD (PlS) - **Spec Exp:** Facial Plastic & Reconstructive Surgery; Cosmetic & Reconstructive Surgery; Liposuction & Body Contouring; Breast Reconstruction & Augmentation; **Hospital:** Lenox Hill Hosp (Manh Eye, Ear & Throat Hosp); **Address:** 10 E 53rd St Fl 25, New York, NY 10022; **Phone:** 212-888-7770; **Board Cert:** Surgery 2006; Plastic Surgery 2009; **Med School:** Mich State Univ 2000; **Resid:** Surgery, Maricopa Med Ctr 2005; **Fellow:** Plastic Surgery, Mayo Clin 2007

Sharma, Sheel MD (PlS) - **Spec Exp:** Hand Surgery; Peripheral Nerve Surgery; Microsurgery; Cosmetic & Reconstructive Surgery; **Hospital:** NYU Langone Med Ctr (page 104); **Address:** NYU Plastic Surgery Assocs, 305 E 33rd St, New York, NY 10016; **Phone:** 212-263-3707; **Board Cert:** Plastic Surgery 2007; Hand Surgery 2008; **Med School:** India 1986; **Resid:** Surgery, NYU Med Ctr 2002; Plastic Surgery, NYU Med Ctr 2005; **Fellow:** Hand & Microvascular Surgery, Meml Sloan Kettering Cancer Ctr 2006; **Fac Appt:** Asst Prof PlS, NYU Sch Med

Sherman, John E MD (PlS) - **Spec Exp:** Cosmetic Surgery-Face; Liposuction & Body Contouring; Facial Plastic & Reconstructive Surgery; Breast Cosmetic & Reconstructive Surgery; **Hospital:** NY-Presby/Weill Cornell Med Ctr, NY (page 102), Lenox Hill Hosp; **Address:** 1016 5th Ave, New York, NY 10028; **Phone:** 212-535-2300; **Board Cert:** Plastic Surgery 1984; **Med School:** NY Med Coll 1975; **Resid:** Surgery, Montefiore Med Ctr 1978; Plastic Surgery, Meml Sloan-Kettering Cancer Ctr 1980; **Fac Appt:** Asst Clin Prof S, Cornell Univ-Weill Med Coll

Silich, Robert C MD (PlS) - **Spec Exp:** Cosmetic Surgery-Face & Eyes; Cosmetic Surgery-Face & Neck; Cosmetic Surgery-Body; **Hospital:** NY-Presby/Weill Cornell Med Ctr, NY (page 102), Lenox Hill Hosp; **Address:** 121 E 83rd St, Ste A, New York, NY 10028; **Phone:** 212-628-6800; **Board Cert:** Plastic Surgery 2011; **Med School:** Georgetown Univ 1993; **Resid:** Surgery, NY-Presby/Weill Cornell Med Ctr 1997; Plastic Surgery, NY-Presby/Weill Cornell Med Ctr 1999; **Fac Appt:** Asst Clin Prof PlS, Cornell Univ-Weill Med Coll

Silver, Lester MD (PlS) - **Spec Exp:** Cleft Palate/Lip; Pediatric Plastic Surgery; Reconstructive Surgery; **Hospital:** Mt Sinai Hosp; **Address:** 5 E 98th St, Box 1259, New York, NY 10029-6574; **Phone:** 212-241-1968; **Board Cert:** Plastic Surgery 1978; **Med School:** Ros Franklin Univ/Chicago Med Sch 1960; **Resid:** Surgery, Montefiore Med Ctr 1966; Plastic Surgery, Mt Sinai Med Ctr 1969; **Fac Appt:** Prof PlS, Mount Sinai Sch Med

Skolnik, Richard A MD (PlS) - **Spec Exp:** Cosmetic Surgery-Face; Cosmetic Surgery-Breast; Liposuction & Body Contouring; **Hospital:** Mt Sinai Hosp; **Address:** 21 E 87th St, Ste 1A, New York, NY 10128-0506; **Phone:** 212-722-1977; **Board Cert:** Plastic Surgery 1983; **Med School:** Cornell Univ-Weill Med Coll 1976; **Resid:** Surgery, Mt Sinai Hosp 1979; Plastic Surgery, Mt Sinai Hosp 1982; **Fac Appt:** Assoc Clin Prof PlS, Mount Sinai Sch Med

Smith, Mark L MD (PlS) - **Spec Exp:** Breast Reconstruction; Craniofacial Surgery-Pediatric; Cleft Palate/Lip; Lymphedema; **Hospital:** Mt Sinai Beth Israel; **Address:** BIMC, Plastic Surgery, 10 Union Square E, Ste 2L, New York, NY 10003; **Phone:** 212-844-8796; **Board Cert:** Plastic Surgery 2010; **Med School:** Albert Einstein Coll Med 1991; **Resid:** Surgery, NY-Presby/Columbia Univ Med Ctr 1994; Plastic Surgery, NY-Presby/Columbia Univ Med Ctr 1996; **Fellow:** Microsurgery, UT MD Anderson Cancer Ctr 1997; Craniofacial Surgery, Univ Washington Med Ctr 1998; **Fac Appt:** Asst Prof PlS, Albert Einstein Coll Med

Spector, Jason A MD (PlS) - **Spec Exp:** Reconstructive Surgery-Complex; Breast Cosmetic & Reconstructive Surgery; Cosmetic Surgery-Face & Body; Abdominal Wall Reconstruction; **Hospital:** NY-Presby/Weill Cornell Med Ctr, NY (page 102); **Address:** NY-Presby/Weill Cornell Med Ctr, 520 E 70th St, Star Pavilion, Fl 8, New York, NY 10065-4870; **Phone:** 212-746-4532; **Board Cert:** Plastic Surgery 2007; **Med School:** NYU Sch Med 1996; **Resid:** Surgery, NYU Med Ctr 2002; Plastic Surgery, NYU Med Ctr 2005; **Fellow:** Plastic Surgery, NYU Med Ctr 2006; Microsurgery, NYU Med Ctr 2006; **Fac Appt:** Assoc Prof PlS, Cornell Univ-Weill Med Coll

Spinelli, Henry M MD (PlS) - **Spec Exp:** Cosmetic Surgery-Face; Craniofacial Surgery/Reconstruction; Oculoplastic & Orbital Surgery; Eyelid Surgery/Blepharoplasty; **Hospital:** NY-Presby/Weill Cornell Med Ctr, NY (page 102), Lenox Hill Hosp (Manh Eye, Ear & Throat Hosp); **Address:** 875 5th Ave, New York, NY 10021; **Phone:** 212-570-6235; **Board Cert:** Ophthalmology 1987; Plastic Surgery 1993; **Med School:** NYU Sch Med 1981; **Resid:** Ophthalmology, Manhattan EE&T Hosp 1985; Plastic/Reconstructive Surgery, NYU Med Ctr 1990; **Fellow:** Craniofacial Surgery, NYU Med Ctr 1991; **Fac Appt:** Clin Prof S, Cornell Univ-Weill Med Coll

Staffenberg, David A MD (PlS) - **Spec Exp:** Maxillofacial & Craniofacial Surgery; Pediatric Plastic Surgery; Cleft Palate/Lip; Cosmetic & Reconstructive Surgery; **Hospital:** NYU Langone Med Ctr (page 104); **Address:** NYU, Plastic Surgery, 305 E 33rd St, New York, NY 10016; **Phone:** 212-263-8065; **Board Cert:** Plastic Surgery 2009; **Med School:** NY Med Coll 1989; **Resid:** Surgery, Maimonides Med Ctr 1995; Plastic Surgery, Emory Univ Hosp 1997; **Fellow:** Craniofacial & Maxillofacial Surgery, UCLA Med Ctr 1998; **Fac Appt:** Prof PlS, NYU Sch Med

Sultan, Mark R MD (PlS) - **Spec Exp:** Cosmetic Surgery-Face; Cosmetic Surgery-Breast; Breast Reconstruction; Liposuction & Body Contouring; **Hospital:** Mt Sinai Roosevelt, Mt Sinai Beth Israel; **Address:** 1100 Park Ave, New York, NY 10128; **Phone:** 212-360-0700; **Board Cert:** Plastic Surgery 1992; **Med School:** Columbia P&S 1982; **Resid:** Surgery, NY-Presby/Columbia Univ Med Ctr 1987; Plastic Surgery, NY-Presby/Columbia Univ Med Ctr 1990; **Fellow:** Head and Neck Surgery, Emory Univ Hosp 1989; **Fac Appt:** Prof S, Columbia P&S

Swift Jr, Richard W MD (PlS) - **Spec Exp:** Cosmetic Surgery-Face; Cosmetic Surgery-Breast; Liposuction & Body Contouring; **Hospital:** Lenox Hill Hosp (Manh Eye, Ear & Throat Hosp); **Address:** 110 E 87th St, Ste 1C, New York, NY 10128; **Phone:** 212-828-9906; **Board Cert:** Plastic Surgery 2009; **Med School:** Brown Univ 1988; **Resid:** Surgery, SUNY Hlth Sci Ctr 1992; Surgery, St Barnabas Med Ctr 1994; **Fellow:** Plastic Surgery, Oregon Hlth Sci Ctr 1996

Tabbal, Nicolas MD (PlS) - **Spec Exp:** Rhinoplasty; Cosmetic Surgery-Face; Eyelid Surgery; **Hospital:** Lenox Hill Hosp (Manh Eye, Ear & Throat Hosp), NYU Langone Med Ctr (page 104); **Address:** 521 Park Ave, New York, NY 10065; **Phone:** 212-644-5800; **Board Cert:** Plastic Surgery 1980; **Med School:** Lebanon 1972; **Resid:** Surgery, Ameri Univ Med Ctr 1976; Plastic Surgery, Akron City Hosp 1979; **Fellow:** Surgery, SUNY Upstate Med Univ Hosp 1977; Plastic/Reconstructive Surgery, NYU Med Ctr 1980; **Fac Appt:** Assoc Clin Prof PlS, NYU Sch Med

Talmor, Mia MD (PlS) - **Spec Exp:** Breast Reconstruction; Reconstructive Surgery; Cosmetic Surgery-Breast; Nipple Sparing Mastectomy; **Hospital:** NY-Presby/Weill Cornell Med Ctr, NY (page 102); **Address:** 425 E 61st St, Fl 10, New York, NY 10065; **Phone:** 212-821-0933; **Board Cert:** Plastic Surgery 2012; Surgery 2011; **Med School:** Cornell Univ 1993; **Resid:** Surgery, NY-Presby/Weill Cornell Med Ctr 1999; Plastic Surgery, NY-Presby/Weill Cornell Med Ctr 2001; **Fac Appt:** Assoc Clin Prof PlS, Cornell Univ-Weill Med Coll

Taub, Peter J MD (PlS) - **Spec Exp:** Pediatric Plastic Surgery; Craniofacial Surgery; Maxillofacial Surgery; Cleft Palate/Lip; **Hospital:** Mt Sinai Hosp; **Address:** Mt Sinai, Plastic Surgery, 5 E 98th St Fl 14 - Ste B, New York, NY 10029; **Phone:** 212-241-4178; **Board Cert:** Surgery 2009; Plastic Surgery 2013; **Med School:** Albert Einstein Coll Med 1993; **Resid:** Surgery, Mt Sinai Hosp 1999; Plastic Surgery, UCLA Med Ctr 2001; **Fellow:** Craniofacial Surgery, UCLA Med Ctr 2002; **Fac Appt:** Prof S, Mount Sinai-Icahn Sch of Med

Thorne, Charles H MD (PlS) - **Spec Exp:** Cosmetic Surgery-Face; Ear Reconstruction/Microtia; Ear Reshaping (Otoplasty); Craniofacial Surgery; **Hospital:** NYU Langone Med Ctr (page 104); **Address:** 812 Park Ave, New York, NY 10021; **Phone:** 212-794-0044; **Board Cert:** Plastic Surgery 2007; **Med School:** UCLA-David Geffen Sch Med 1981; **Resid:** Surgery, Mass Genl Hosp 1986; Plastic Surgery, NYU Med Ctr 1988; **Fellow:** Craniofacial Surgery, NYU Med Ctr 1989; **Fac Appt:** Assoc Prof PlS, NYU Sch Med

Ting, Jess MD (PlS) - **Spec Exp:** Breast Reconstruction; Cosmetic Surgery; Hand Surgery; **Hospital:** Mt Sinai Hosp; **Address:** Mt Sinai, Plastic Surgery, 5 E 98th St Fl 14 - Ste B, New York, NY 10029; **Phone:** 212-241-4178; **Board Cert:** Plastic Surgery 2012; Hand Surgery 2012; **Med School:** Columbia P&S 1995; **Resid:** Surgery, NY-Presby/Columbia Univ Med Ctr 1998; Plastic Surgery, UPMC 2000; **Fellow:** Hand Surgery, Hosp Special Surgery 2001; **Fac Appt:** Asst Prof S, Mount Sinai-Icahn Sch of Med

Verga, Michele MD (PlS) - **Spec Exp:** Cosmetic Surgery-Face; Liposuction & Body Contouring; Reconstructive Surgery; Hair Restoration/Transplant; **Hospital:** Mt Sinai Hosp; **Address:** 1010 5th Ave, New York, NY 10028-0130; **Phone:** 212-535-0470; **Board Cert:** Plastic Surgery 1984; **Med School:** Italy 1974; **Resid:** Surgery, Mt Sinai Hosp 1978; Surgery, Lutheran Med Ctr 1980; **Fellow:** Plastic Surgery, Mt Sinai Hosp 1983; **Fac Appt:** Asst Clin Prof S, Mount Sinai Sch Med

Vickery, Carlin MD (PlS) - **Spec Exp:** Breast Cosmetic & Reconstructive Surgery; Cosmetic Surgery-Body; Cosmetic Surgery-Face; **Hospital:** Mt Sinai Hosp; **Address:** 1125 5th Ave, New York, NY 10128; **Phone:** 212-288-9800; **Board Cert:** Plastic Surgery 1987; **Med School:** NYU Sch Med 1977; **Resid:** Surgery, NYU Med Ctr 1982; Plastic Surgery, NYU Med Ctr 1984; **Fellow:** Microsurgery, NYU Med Ctr 1985; **Fac Appt:** Assoc Clin Prof S, Mount Sinai Sch Med

Weiss, Paul R MD (PlS) - **Spec Exp:** Breast Cosmetic & Reconstructive Surgery; Cosmetic Surgery-Face; Cosmetic Surgery-Body; **Hospital:** Montefiore Med Ctr-Moses Campus (page 100), Lawrence Hosp Ctr (page 102); **Address:** 1049 5th Ave, Ste 2D, New York, NY 10028-0115; **Phone:** 212-861-8000; **Board Cert:** Surgery 1975; Plastic Surgery 2010; **Med School:** Tulane Univ 1969; **Resid:** Surgery, Montefiore Med Ctr/Bronx Muni Hosp 1974; Plastic Surgery, Montefiore Med Ctr 1976; **Fac Appt:** Clin Prof S, Albert Einstein Coll Med

Wells, Scott B MD (PlS) - **Spec Exp:** Cosmetic Surgery-Face; Cosmetic Surgery-Breast; Liposuction & Body Contouring; **Hospital:** Winthrop Univ Hosp (page 536); **Address:** 655 Park Ave, New York, NY 10065; **Phone:** 212-794-3900; **Board Cert:** Plastic Surgery 2005; **Med School:** NY Med Coll 1985; **Resid:** Surgery, Beth Israel Med Ctr 1990; Plastic/Reconstructive Surgery, SUNY Hlth Sci Ctr 1992

Zevon, Scott J MD (PlS) - **Spec Exp:** Breast Augmentation; Breast Cosmetic & Reconstructive Surgery; Cosmetic Surgery-Face & Body; Liposuction & Body Contouring; **Hospital:** Mt Sinai Roosevelt; **Address:** 75 Central Park W, Ste 1AB, New York, NY 10023; **Phone:** 212-496-6600; **Board Cert:** Plastic Surgery 1989; **Med School:** Boston Univ 1979; **Resid:** Surgery, St Luke's-Roosevelt Hosp Ctr 1984; Plastic Surgery, Nassau Co Med Ctr 1986; **Fellow:** Craniofacial Surgery, Mayo Clinic 1987

Zide, Barry M MD/DMD (PlS) - **Spec Exp:** Facial Surgery-Chin & Lip; Birthmarks/Hemangiomas; Reconstructive Plastic Surgery; Melanoma; **Hospital:** NYU Langone Med Ctr (page 104), Lenox Hill Hosp; **Address:** 420 E 55th St, Ste 1D, New York, NY 10022; **Phone:** 212-421-2424; **Board Cert:** Plastic Surgery 1981; **Med School:** Tufts Univ 1973; **Resid:** Surgery, Stanford Univ Hosp & Clins 1976; Plastic Surgery, Univ NC Hosp 1978; **Fellow:** Head & Neck Oncology, Roswell Park Cancer Inst 1979; Craniofacial Surgery, NYU Med Ctr 1980; **Fac Appt:** Prof PlS, NYU Sch Med

Preventive Medicine

Cahill, John MD (PrM) - **Spec Exp:** Tropical Diseases; Travel Medicine; Parasitic Infections; International Health; **Hospital:** Mt Sinai Roosevelt; **Address:** Univ Med Practice Assocs, 36 W 60th St, New York, NY 10023; **Phone:** 212-523-8672; **Board Cert:** Emergency Medicine 2011; **Med School:** Mount Sinai Sch Med 1996; **Resid:** Emergency Medicine, Rhode Island Hosp 2000; **Fellow:** Tropical Medicine, Rhode Island Hosp 2003; **Fac Appt:** Asst Clin Prof Med, Columbia P&S

Crane, Michael MD (PrM) - **Spec Exp:** Poison Control; **Hospital:** Mt Sinai Hosp; **Address:** Selikoff Ctrs for Occupational Hlth, 1468 Madison Ave Fl 3, New York, NY 10029; **Phone:** 212-241-0659; **Board Cert:** Internal Medicine 1980; Occupational Medicine 1989; **Med School:** Univ Rochester 1977; **Resid:** Internal Medicine, Montefiore Med Ctr 1980; **Fellow:** Preventive Medicine, NY-Presby/Columbia Univ Med Ctr 1986; **Fac Appt:** Asst Prof PrM, Mount Sinai Sch Med

Hoffman, Robert S MD (PrM) - **Spec Exp:** Poison Control; Disaster Preparedness; **Hospital:** NYU Langone Med Ctr (page 104), Bellevue Hosp Ctr; **Address:** NY Poison Control Ctr, 455 1st Ave, rm 123, New York, NY 10016; **Phone:** 212-340-4494; **Board Cert:** Internal Medicine 1987; Emergency Medicine 2005; Medical Toxicology 2008; **Med School:** NYU Sch Med 1984; **Resid:** Internal Medicine, NYU Med Ctr 1987; **Fellow:** Medical Toxicology, NYU Med Ctr 1989; **Fac Appt:** Prof EM, NYU Sch Med

Psychiatry

Adler, Lenard A MD (Psyc) - **Spec Exp:** ADD/ADHD; Psychopharmacology; **Hospital:** NYU Langone Med Ctr (page 104); **Address:** NYU Psychiatry-Behavioral Health, 1 Park Ave, Fl 8, New York, NY 10016; **Phone:** 212-263-3580; **Board Cert:** Psychiatry 1987; **Med School:** Emory Univ 1982; **Resid:** Psychiatry, NYU Med Ctr 1986; **Fac Appt:** Prof Psyc, NYU Sch Med

Alper, Kenneth R MD (Psyc) - **Spec Exp:** Psychopharmacology; **Hospital:** NYU Langone Med Ctr (page 104); **Address:** 150 E 58th St, Fl 25, New York, NY 10155; **Phone:** 212-966-3506; **Board Cert:** Psychiatry 1989; **Med School:** Univ Tex, San Antonio 1984; **Resid:** Psychiatry, NYU Med Ctr 1988; **Fellow:** Clinical Neurophysiology, NYU Med Ctr 1990; **Fac Appt:** Assoc Prof Psyc, NYU Sch Med

Appelbaum, Paul S MD (Psyc) - **Spec Exp:** Forensic Psychiatry; Depression; Anxiety & Mood Disorders; **Hospital:** NY-Presby/Columbia Univ Med Ctr, NY (page 102); **Address:** Columbia University Medical Center, 1051 Riverside Drive, Unit 122, New York, NY 10032; **Phone:** 646-774-8630; **Board Cert:** Psychiatry 1981; Forensic Psychiatry 2013; **Med School:** Harvard Med Sch 1976; **Resid:** Psychiatry, Mass Mental Health Ctr 1980; **Fac Appt:** Prof Psyc, Columbia P&S

Arkow, Stan D MD (Psyc) - **Spec Exp:** Psychotherapy; Psychopharmacology; **Hospital:** NY-Presby/Columbia Univ Med Ctr, NY (page 102); **Address:** 740 W End Ave, Ste 5A, New York, NY 10025; **Phone:** 212-663-5185; **Board Cert:** Psychiatry 1985; **Med School:** Columbia P&S 1977; **Resid:** Psychiatry, NY State Psych Inst 1981; **Fac Appt:** Assoc Clin Prof Psyc, Columbia P&S

Aronoff, Michael S MD (Psyc) - **Spec Exp:** Stress Management; Anxiety & Depression; Sleep Disorders; Family & Couples Therapy; **Hospital:** Lenox Hill Hosp, NYU Langone Med Ctr (page 104); **Address:** 60 Riverside Drive, Ste 16E, New York, NY 10024-6171; **Phone:** 212-799-8257; **Board Cert:** Psychiatry 1977; **Med School:** Univ Pennsylvania 1966; **Resid:** Psychiatry, NY State Psych Inst/Columbia Univ 1972; **Fellow:** Psychoanalysis, Columbia-Presby Hosp 1976; **Fac Appt:** Clin Prof Psyc, NYU Sch Med

Attia, Evelyn MD (Psyc) - **Spec Exp:** Eating Disorders; Obesity; Mood Disorders; **Hospital:** NY-Presby/Columbia Univ Med Ctr, NY (page 102), NY-Presby/Weill Cornell Med Ctr, NY (page 102); **Address:** NYS Psychiatric Inst, 1051 Riverside Drive, Box 98, New York, NY 10032; **Phone:** 646-774-8085; **Board Cert:** Psychiatry 1992; **Med School:** Columbia P&S 1986; **Resid:** Psychiatry, Hosp Univ Penn 1987; Psychiatry, NYS Psychiatric Inst 1990; **Fac Appt:** Clin Prof Psyc, Columbia P&S

Barbuto, Joseph MD (Psyc) - **Spec Exp:** Psychiatry in Cancer; Anxiety & Mood Disorders; Personality Disorders; **Hospital:** NY-Presby/Weill Cornell Med Ctr, NY (page 102), Meml Sloan Kettering Canc Ctr (page 110); **Address:** 945 Fifth Ave Ave, Ste 5, New York, NY 10021; **Phone:** 212-724-7366; **Board Cert:** Psychiatry 1983; **Med School:** Albert Einstein Coll Med 1978; **Resid:** Psychiatry, NY Hosp 1982; **Fellow:** Psychiatric Oncology, Meml Sloan-Kettering Cancer Ctr 1986; **Fac Appt:** Assoc Clin Prof Psyc, Cornell Univ-Weill Med Coll

Basch, Samuel H MD (Psyc) - **Spec Exp:** Psychotherapy; Psychopharmacology; Psychoanalysis; Psychiatry in Physical Illness; **Hospital:** Mt Sinai Hosp; **Address:** 10 E 85th St, Ste 1B, New York, NY 10028; **Phone:** 212-427-0344; **Board Cert:** Psychiatry 1970; **Med School:** Hahnemann Univ 1961; **Resid:** Psychiatry, Mount Sinai Hosp 1965; **Fellow:** Psychoanalysis, Columbia Presby Hosp 1976; **Fac Appt:** Prof Psyc, Mount Sinai Sch Med

Bialer, Philip MD (Psyc) - **Spec Exp:** Psychiatry in Physical Illness; Psychiatry in Head & Neck Cancer; **Hospital:** Meml Sloan Kettering Canc Ctr (page 110); **Address:** MSKCC, Psychiatry, 641 Lexington Ave, Fl 7, New York, NY 10022; **Phone:** 646-888-0009; **Board Cert:** Psychiatry 1989; Psychosomatic Medicine 2005; **Med School:** Ohio State Univ 1977; **Resid:** Internal Medicine, Mt Sinai Hosp 1978; Psychiatry, SUNY Hlth Sci Ctr 1988; **Fellow:** Psychosomatic Medicine, Beth Israel Med Ctr 1989; **Fac Appt:** Assoc Clin Prof Psyc, Cornell Univ-Weill Med Coll

Blatter, Brett L MD (Psyc) - **Spec Exp:** Mood Disorders; Forensic Psychiatry; Psychopharmacology; **Hospital:** NY-Presby/Columbia Univ Med Ctr, NY (page 102), NY State Psychiatric Inst; **Address:** 160 W 73rd St, Ste 1B, New York, NY 10023; **Phone:** 212-769-4128; **Board Cert:** Psychiatry 2013; **Med School:** Johns Hopkins Univ 1997; **Resid:** Psychiatry, NY State Psychiatric Inst 2001; Forensic Psychiatry, NY State Psychiatric Inst 2002; **Fellow:** Emergency Psychiatry, Columbia Univ Med Ctr 2003; **Fac Appt:** Asst Clin Prof Psyc, Columbia P&S

Bone, Stanley MD (Psyc) - **Spec Exp:** Psychotherapy; Psychoanalysis; **Hospital:** NY-Presby/Columbia Univ Med Ctr, NY (page 102); **Address:** 1155 Park Ave, New York, NY 10128; **Phone:** 212-831-0917; **Board Cert:** Psychiatry 1979; **Med School:** Mount Sinai Sch Med 1974; **Resid:** Psychiatry, NY-Presby/Columbia Univ Med Ctr 1978; **Fellow:** Psychoanalysis, NY-Presby/Columbia Univ Med Ctr 1983; **Fac Appt:** Clin Prof Psyc, Columbia P&S

Borbely, Antal MD (Psyc) - **Spec Exp:** Career Related Problems; Relationship Problems; Creativity Enhancement; Psychopharmacology; **Address:** 675 W End Ave, Ste 1A, New York, NY 10025; **Phone:** 212-222-1678; **Board Cert:** Psychiatry 1976; **Med School:** Switzerland 1968; **Resid:** Psychiatry, NY State Psyc Inst 1972; Psychiatry, A Einstein Coll Med Affil Hosps 1973; **Fellow:** Community Psychiatry, A Einstein Coll Med Affil Hosps 1975

Breitbart, William S MD (Psyc) - **Spec Exp:** Psychiatry in Cancer; AIDS Related Cancers; Pain-Cancer; Palliative Care; **Hospital:** Meml Sloan Kettering Canc Ctr (page 110); **Address:** MSKCC, Psychiatry, 641 Lexington Ave, Fl 7, New York, NY 10065; **Phone:** 646-888-0020; **Board Cert:** Internal Medicine 1982; Psychiatry 1986; Psychosomatic Medicine 2005; **Med School:** Albert Einstein Coll Med 1978; **Resid:** Internal Medicine, Bronx Muni Hosp Ctr 1982; Internal Medicine, Bronx Muni Hosp Ctr 1984; **Fellow:** Psychiatric Oncology, Meml Sloan-Kettering Cancer Ctr 1986; **Fac Appt:** Prof Psyc, Cornell Univ-Weill Med Coll

Brodie, Jonathan D MD (Psyc) - **Spec Exp:** Psychopharmacology; Anxiety & Depression; Neuro-Psychiatry; **Hospital:** NYU Langone Med Ctr (page 104); **Address:** 155 E 38th St, Ste 3L, New York, NY 10016; **Phone:** 212-986-6693; **Board Cert:** Psychiatry 1979; **Med School:** NYU Sch Med 1975; **Resid:** Psychiatry, NYU Med Ctr/Bellevue Hosp 1978; **Fac Appt:** Prof Psyc, NYU Sch Med

Bronheim, Harold E MD (Psyc) - **Spec Exp:** Body Image Issues; Relationship Problems; Psychiatry in Physical Illness; Anxiety & Depression; **Hospital:** Mt Sinai Hosp; **Address:** 1155 Park Ave, New York, NY 10128; **Phone:** 212-996-5777; **Board Cert:** Psychiatry 1985; Internal Medicine 1986; Psychosomatic Medicine 2005; Geriatric Psychiatry 2011; **Med School:** SUNY Downstate 1980; **Resid:** Psychiatry, Mt Sinai Hosp 1986; Internal Medicine, Beth Israel Med Ctr 1985; **Fac Appt:** Clin Prof Psyc, Mount Sinai-Icahn Sch of Med

Brown, Richard P MD (Psyc) - **Spec Exp:** Psychopharmacology; Complementary Medicine; **Hospital:** NY-Presby/Columbia Univ Med Ctr, NY (page 102); **Address:** 30 East End Ave, Ste 1C, New York, NY 10028-7053; **Phone:** 212-737-0821; **Board Cert:** Psychiatry 1983; **Med School:** Columbia P&S 1977; **Resid:** Psychiatry, NY Hosp 1982; **Fellow:** Psychopharmacology, NY Hosp 1984; **Fac Appt:** Assoc Prof Psyc, Columbia P&S

Bukberg, Judith MD (Psyc) - **Spec Exp:** Psychotherapy; Psychoanalysis; **Address:** 88 University Pl, Ste 701A, New York, NY 10003; **Phone:** 212-614-0312; **Board Cert:** Psychiatry 1979; **Med School:** Mount Sinai Sch Med 1974; **Resid:** Psychiatry, Mt Sinai Hosp 1978; **Fellow:** Liaison Psychiatry, Meml Sloan-Kettering Cancer Ctr 1980; Psychoanalysis, NY Psychoanalytic Inst 1990; **Fac Appt:** Assoc Clin Prof Psyc, NY Med Coll

Bulgarelli, Christopher G MD (Psyc) - **Spec Exp:** Psychoanalysis; Depression; Anxiety Disorders; **Hospital:** Lenox Hill Hosp; **Address:** 455 W 23rd St, Ste 1BB, New York, NY 10011-2148; **Phone:** 212-807-1054; **Board Cert:** Psychiatry 1991; **Med School:** Tufts Univ 1986; **Resid:** Psychiatry, NYU/Bellevue Hosp 1990; **Fac Appt:** Asst Clin Prof Psyc, NYU Sch Med

Cabaniss, Deborah L MD (Psyc) - **Spec Exp:** Psychoanalysis; Psychodynamic Psychotherapy; **Hospital:** NY State Psychiatric Inst; **Address:** NYS Psychiatric Inst, 1051 Riverside Dr, Unit 63 rm 1300E, New York, NY 10032; **Phone:** 646-774-6335; **Board Cert:** Psychiatry 1993; **Med School:** Columbia P&S 1988; **Resid:** Psychiatry, NYS Psychiatric Inst 1992; **Fellow:** Psychoanalysis, NYS Psychiatric Inst 1996; **Fac Appt:** Clin Prof Psyc, Columbia P&S

Caligor, Eve MD (Psyc) - **Spec Exp:** Psychodynamic Psychotherapy; Personality Disorders; Psychoanalysis; Personality Disorders; **Hospital:** NY-Presby/Columbia Univ Med Ctr, NY (page 102); **Address:** 19 E 88th St, Ste 1D, MS 10128, New York, NY 10128; **Phone:** 212-996-5285; **Board Cert:** Psychiatry 1987; **Med School:** Harvard Med Sch 1982; **Resid:** Psychiatry, NY Presby/Columbia Univ Med Ctr 1986; **Fellow:** Psychiatry, NY Presby/Columbia Univ Med Ctr 1987; **Fac Appt:** Clin Prof Psyc, Columbia P&S

Cherry, Sabrina MD (Psyc) - **Spec Exp:** Psychoanalysis; Psychotherapy; **Hospital:** NY State Psychiatric Inst; **Address:** 285 Central Park W, New York, NY 10024; **Phone:** 212-721-2869; **Board Cert:** Psychiatry 1992; **Med School:** Harvard Med Sch 1987; **Resid:** Psychiatry, NY State Psychiatric Inst 1991; **Fellow:** Psychoanalysis, Columbia Univ-Ctr Psychoanalytic Training 1998; **Fac Appt:** Assoc Clin Prof Psyc, Columbia P&S

Chung, Henry MD (Psyc) - **Spec Exp:** Anxiety & Depression; **Hospital:** Montefiore Med Ctr-Moses Campus (page 100); **Address:** 85 5th Ave, Ste 907, New York, NY 10003; **Phone:** 917-533-6908; **Board Cert:** Psychiatry 2013; **Med School:** SUNY Buffalo 1989; **Resid:** Psychiatry, NY-Presby/Weschester Div 1994; **Fac Appt:** Assoc Clin Prof Psyc, Albert Einstein Coll Med

Cohen, Arnold R MD (Psyc) - **Spec Exp:** Psychotherapy; ADD/ADHD; Autism; **Hospital:** Mt Sinai Hosp; **Address:** 64 E 94th St, Ste 1A, New York, NY 10128; **Phone:** 212-289-6800; **Board Cert:** Psychiatry 1969; **Med School:** SUNY Hlth Sci Ctr 1963; **Resid:** Psychiatry, Mount Sinai Med Ctr 1966; **Fellow:** Child & Adolescent Psychiatry, Mount Sinai Med Ctr 1970; **Fac Appt:** Asst Clin Prof Psyc, Mount Sinai Sch Med

Douglas, Carolyn Jory MD (Psyc) - **Spec Exp:** Depression; Anxiety Disorders; Relationship Problems; **Hospital:** NY-Presby/Columbia Univ Med Ctr, NY (page 102), NY-Presby/Weill Cornell Med Ctr, NY (page 102); **Address:** 345 E 84th St, New York, NY 10028-4434; **Phone:** 212-396-9808; **Board Cert:** Psychiatry 1985; **Med School:** Harvard Med Sch 1980; **Resid:** Psychiatry, Payne Whitney Clin 1984; **Fac Appt:** Assoc Clin Prof Psyc, Columbia P&S

Drooker, Martin A MD (Psyc) - **Spec Exp:** Anxiety & Depression; Bipolar/Mood Disorders; Memory Disorders; Psychopharmacology; **Hospital:** Mt Sinai Hosp; **Address:** 1158 5th Ave, New York, NY 10029; **Phone:** 212-876-6820; **Board Cert:** Psychiatry 1993; Psychosomatic Medicine 2005; Geriatric Psychiatry 2005; **Med School:** SUNY Downstate 1988; **Resid:** Psychiatry, Yale-New Haven Hosp 1992; **Fellow:** Psychosomatic Medicine, Yale-New Haven Hosp 1993; **Fac Appt:** Assoc Clin Prof Psyc, Mount Sinai-Icahn Sch of Med

Fallon, Brian A MD (Psyc) - **Spec Exp:** Lyme Disease-Neuro Complications; Psychosomatic Disorders; Obsessive-Compulsive Disorder; Psychiatry in Physical Illness; **Hospital:** NY State Psychiatric Inst, NY-Presby/Columbia Univ Med Ctr, NY (page 102); **Address:** NY State Psychiatric Inst, 1051 Riverside Drive, rm 3724, Box 69, New York, NY 10032; **Phone:** 646-774-8052; **Board Cert:** Psychiatry 1991; **Med School:** Columbia P&S 1985; **Resid:** Psychiatry, NYS Psychiatric Inst 1989; **Fellow:** Psychiatric Research, NYS Psychiatric Inst 1991; Psychodynamic Psychotherapy, NYS Psychiatric Inst 1990; **Fac Appt:** Prof Psyc, Columbia P&S

Feinberg, Todd E MD (Psyc) - **Spec Exp:** Alzheimer's Disease; Dementia; **Hospital:** Mt Sinai Beth Israel; **Address:** Yarmon Neurobehavior Ctr, 1st Ave at 16th St, Bernstein Pavilion Fl 10th, New York, NY 10003; **Phone:** 212-420-4111; **Board Cert:** Psychiatry 1984; Neurology 1987; **Med School:** Mount Sinai Sch Med 1978; **Resid:** Psychiatry, Mt Sinai Med Ctr 1982; Neurology, Mt Sinai Med Ctr 1984; **Fellow:** Behavioral Neurology, Shands Hosp 1986; **Fac Appt:** Clin Prof N, Albert Einstein Coll Med

Ferran Jr, Ernesto MD (Psyc) - **Spec Exp:** Cultural Psychiatry; Child & Adolescent Psychiatry; Mood Disorders; Divorce/Family Issues; **Hospital:** NYU Langone Med Ctr (page 104); **Address:** 15 Charles St, Ste 6H, New York, NY 10014-3011; **Phone:** 212-924-2673; **Board Cert:** Psychiatry 1983; Child & Adolescent Psychiatry 1986; **Med School:** Albert Einstein Coll Med 1976; **Resid:** Psychiatry, Bellevue Hosp/NYU Med Ctr 1979; **Fellow:** Child & Adolescent Psychiatry, Bellevue Hosp/NYU Med Ctr 1981; **Fac Appt:** Clin Prof ChAP, NYU Sch Med

Finkel, Jay MD (Psyc) - **Spec Exp:** Anxiety Disorders; Mood Disorders; **Address:** 108 E 91st St, Ste 1B, New York, NY 10128-1657; **Phone:** 212-289-2077; **Board Cert:** Psychiatry 1985; **Med School:** NY Med Coll 1980; **Resid:** Psychiatry, Mount Sinai Hosp 1984; **Fac Appt:** Asst Clin Prof Psyc, Mount Sinai Sch Med

First, Michael B MD (Psyc) - **Spec Exp:** Psychotherapy; Psychopharmacology; Sexual Addiction; Sexual Behavior-Compulsive; **Hospital:** NY State Psychiatric Inst, NY-Presby/Columbia Univ Med Ctr, NY (page 102); **Address:** NYS Psychiatric Inst, 1051 Riverside Drive, Box 60, New York, NY 10032; **Phone:** 646-774-7935; **Board Cert:** Psychiatry 1989; **Med School:** Univ Pittsburgh 1983; **Resid:** Psychiatry, NYS Psychiatric Inst 1986; **Fellow:** Psychiatric Research, NYS Psychiatric Inst 1988; **Fac Appt:** Prof Psyc, Columbia P&S

Fox, Herbert A MD (Psyc) - **Spec Exp:** Electroconvulsive Therapy (ECT); Psychotherapy; Psychopharmacology; **Hospital:** Lenox Hill Hosp, Gracie Square Hosp; **Address:** 416 E 76th St, New York, NY 10021-4032; **Phone:** 212-674-8622; **Board Cert:** Psychiatry 1976; **Med School:** Albert Einstein Coll Med 1969; **Resid:** Psychiatry, Montefiore Med Ctr 1973; **Fac Appt:** Assoc Prof Psyc, Cornell Univ-Weill Med Coll

Friedman, Richard Alan MD (Psyc) - **Spec Exp:** Psychopharmacology; Anxiety & Mood Disorders; Depression; **Hospital:** NY-Presby/Weill Cornell Med Ctr, NY (page 102); **Address:** 525 E 68th St, Box 140, New York, NY 10065; **Phone:** 212-746-5775; **Board Cert:** Psychiatry 1989; **Med School:** Rutgers R W Johnson Med Sch 1982; **Resid:** Psychiatry, Mt Sinai Med Ctr 1987; **Fellow:** Psychiatry, Baylor Coll Med Affil Hosps 1989; **Fac Appt:** Clin Prof Psyc, Cornell Univ-Weill Med Coll

Fyer, Minna R MD (Psyc) - **Spec Exp:** Anxiety Disorders; Mood Disorders; Menopause Problems; **Hospital:** NY-Presby/Weill Cornell Med Ctr, NY (page 102); **Address:** 242 E 72nd St, New York, NY 10021-4574; **Phone:** 212-861-2586; **Board Cert:** Psychiatry 1985; **Med School:** SUNY Hlth Sci Ctr 1980; **Resid:** Psychiatry, NY Hosp/Payne Whitney Clin 1984; **Fellow:** Psychopharmacology, NY State Psych Inst 1986; **Fac Appt:** Asst Clin Prof Psyc, Cornell Univ-Weill Med Coll

Ginsberg, David Lloyd MD (Psyc) - **Spec Exp:** Depression; Bipolar/Mood Disorders; Anxiety Disorders; Psychopharmacology; **Hospital:** NYU Langone Med Ctr (page 104); **Address:** NYU, Behavioral Hlth, 1 Park Ave Fl 8, New York, NY 10016; **Phone:** 212-263-7419; **Board Cert:** Psychiatry 2005; Psychosomatic Medicine 2009; **Med School:** Brown Univ 1990; **Resid:** Psychiatry, NYU Med Ctr 1994; **Fac Appt:** Assoc Clin Prof Psyc, NYU Sch Med

Goff, Donald C MD (Psyc) - **Spec Exp:** Schizophrenia; Psychopharmacology; **Hospital:** NYU Langone Med Ctr (page 104); **Address:** 1 Park Ave Fl 8 - rm 8-212, New York, NY 10016; **Phone:** 646-754-4843; **Board Cert:** Psychiatry 1986; **Med School:** UCLA-David Geffen Sch Med 1980; **Resid:** Psychiatry, Mass Genl Hosp 1984; **Fellow:** Psychopharmacology, Tufts-New England Med Ctr 1985; **Fac Appt:** Prof Psyc, NYU Sch Med

Goldenberg, David B MD (Psyc) - **Spec Exp:** HIV Psychiatry; Psychoanalysis; Gender Issues; Psychiatry in Cancer; **Hospital:** NY-Presby/Weill Cornell Med Ctr, NY (page 102); **Address:** 35 E 85th St, New York, NY 10028; **Phone:** 212-717-4834; **Board Cert:** Psychiatry 2007; Psychosomatic Medicine 2005; **Med School:** Univ MD Sch Med 1991; **Resid:** Psychiatry, Yale-New Haven Hosp 1996; **Fellow:** Psychiatry, Meml Sloan-Kettering Cancer Ctr 1997

Goldman, Neil S MD (Psyc) - **Spec Exp:** Mood Disorders; Anxiety Disorders; Addiction/Substance Abuse; **Hospital:** N Shore Univ Hosp; **Address:** 235 W 48th St, Apt 26-H, New York, NY 10036; **Phone:** 212-929-4395; **Board Cert:** Psychiatry 1981; **Med School:** Ros Franklin Univ/Chicago Med Sch 1970; **Resid:** Psychiatry, Brookdale Hosp 1974; **Fellow:** Addiction Psychiatry, St Vincents Hosp 1979; **Fac Appt:** Asst Prof Psyc, NY Med Coll

Goldstein, Susanna K MD (Psyc) - **Spec Exp:** Psychopharmacology; Anxiety & Depression; Clinical Trials; **Hospital:** Lenox Hill Hosp; **Address:** 65 Central Park West, Ste 1BR, New York, NY 10023; **Phone:** 212-362-6657; **Board Cert:** Psychiatry 1985; **Med School:** Israel 1975; **Resid:** Psychiatry, Rambam Med Ctr 1980; Neurology, Rambam Med Ctr 1981; **Fellow:** Biological Psychiatry, Montefiore Med Ctr 1983; **Fac Appt:** Asst Clin Prof Psyc, NYU Sch Med

Goodman, Wayne K MD (Psyc) - **Spec Exp:** Obsessive-Compulsive Disorder; Tourette's Syndrome; Anxiety Disorders; **Hospital:** Mt Sinai Hosp; **Address:** Mount Sinai Hosp, 1 Gustave Levy Pl, Box 1230, New York, NY 10029; **Phone:** 212-659-8860; **Board Cert:** Psychiatry 1988; **Med School:** Boston Univ 1981; **Resid:** Psychiatry, Yale-New Haven Hosp 1985; **Fellow:** Psychiatric Research, Yale-New Haven Hosp 1986; **Fac Appt:** Prof Psyc, Mount Sinai Sch Med

Gorman, Lauren K MD (Psyc) - **Spec Exp:** Psychopharmacology; Anxiety & Mood Disorders; **Hospital:** Mt Sinai Hosp; **Address:** 685 West End Ave, Ste 1AF, New York, NY 10025; **Phone:** 212-580-7713; **Board Cert:** Psychiatry 1983; **Med School:** Columbia P&S 1977; **Resid:** Ophthalmology, Bellevue Hosp 1979; Psychiatry, Mt Sinai Hosp 1982; **Fellow:** Biological Psychiatry, Montefiore Med Ctr 1984; **Fac Appt:** Asst Clin Prof Psyc, Mount Sinai Sch Med

Heller, Stanley S MD (Psyc) - **Spec Exp:** Panic Disorder; Depression; Psychiatry in Physical Illness; **Address:** 1136 Fifth Ave, New York, NY 10128; **Phone:** 212-831-5919; **Board Cert:** Psychiatry 1975; **Med School:** Columbia P&S 1960; **Resid:** Psychiatry, NY State Psychiatric Inst 1966; **Fac Appt:** Assoc Clin Prof Psyc, Columbia P&S

Hoffman, Joel MD (Psyc) - **Spec Exp:** Psychopharmacology; Depression; Treatment Resistant Mental Illness; **Hospital:** Lenox Hill Hosp, NY-Presby/Weill Cornell Med Ctr, NY (page 102); **Address:** 1236 Park Ave, New York, NY 10128-1717; **Phone:** 212-722-3004; **Board Cert:** Psychiatry 1977; **Med School:** Columbia P&S 1963; **Resid:** Internal Medicine, Univ Michigan Med Ctr 1967; Psychiatry, NY State Psychiatric Inst 1972; **Fac Appt:** Asst Clin Prof Psyc, Columbia P&S

Hollander, Eric MD (Psyc) - **Spec Exp:** Obsessive-Compulsive Disorder; Anxiety Disorders; Autism; Body Dysmorphic Disorder (BDD); **Hospital:** Montefiore Med Ctr-Moses Campus (page 100), Lenox Hill Hosp; **Address:** 901 5th Ave, New York, NY 10021; **Phone:** 212-873-4051; **Board Cert:** Psychiatry 1987; **Med School:** SUNY Downstate 1982; **Resid:** Psychiatry, Mt Sinai Hosp 1986; **Fellow:** Psychopharmacology, Columbia Univ-Psych Inst 1988; **Fac Appt:** Prof Psyc, Albert Einstein Coll Med

Kahn, David Alan MD (Psyc) - **Spec Exp:** Anxiety & Mood Disorders; Psychopharmacology; Psychotherapy; Schizophrenia; **Hospital:** NY-Presby/Columbia Univ Med Ctr, NY (page 102); **Address:** 35 E 85th St, New York, NY 10028; **Phone:** 212-472-0100; **Board Cert:** Psychiatry 1984; **Med School:** Columbia P&S 1979; **Resid:** Psychiatry, NYS Psychiatric Inst 1983; **Fellow:** Biological Psychiatry, NYS Psychiatric Inst 1984; **Fac Appt:** Prof Emeritus Psyc, Columbia P&S

Kalinich, Lila J MD (Psyc) - **Spec Exp:** Psychoanalysis; Psychotherapy; **Hospital:** NY-Presby/Columbia Univ Med Ctr, NY (page 102), NY State Psychiatric Inst; **Address:** 333 Central Park W, Ste 12, New York, NY 10025; **Phone:** 212-866-0200; **Board Cert:** Psychiatry 1975; **Med School:** Northwestern Univ 1969; **Resid:** Psychiatry, NY-Presby/Columbia Univ Med Ctr 1973; **Fac Appt:** Clin Prof Psyc, Columbia P&S

Karasu, Sylvia R MD (Psyc) - **Spec Exp:** Weight Management; Depression; Relationship Problems; **Hospital:** NY-Presby/Weill Cornell Med Ctr, NY (page 102); **Address:** 2 E 88th St, New York, NY 10128; **Phone:** 212-534-7822; **Board Cert:** Psychiatry 1981; Child & Adolescent Psychiatry 1982; **Med School:** Albert Einstein Coll Med 1976; **Resid:** Psychiatry, Payne Whitney Clin 1979; **Fellow:** Child Psychiatry, Payne Whitney Clin 1981; **Fac Appt:** Clin Prof Psyc, Cornell Univ-Weill Med Coll

Karasu, T Byram MD (Psyc) - **Spec Exp:** Depression; Personality Disorders; Psychotherapy; **Hospital:** Montefiore Med Ctr-Moses Campus (page 100), Montefiore Med Ctr-Einstein Campus (page 100); **Address:** 2 E 88th St, New York, NY 10128-0555; **Phone:** 212-426-5208; **Board Cert:** Psychiatry 1972; **Med School:** Turkey 1959; **Resid:** Psychiatry, Yale Univ Affil Hosp 1969; **Fac Appt:** Prof Psyc, Albert Einstein Coll Med

Kellner, Charles H MD (Psyc) - **Spec Exp:** Electroconvulsive Therapy (ECT); Depression; Geriatric Psychiatry; **Hospital:** Mt Sinai Hosp; **Address:** 1425 Madison Ave, Box 1230, New York, NY 10029; **Phone:** 212-659-8285; **Board Cert:** Psychiatry 1984; Geriatric Psychiatry 2011; **Med School:** Cornell Univ-Weill Med Coll 1978; **Resid:** Psychiatry, Cedars-Sinai Med Ctr 1981; **Fellow:** Biological Psychiatry, NIH Clinical Ctr 1984; **Fac Appt:** Prof Psyc, Mount Sinai Sch Med

Kocsis, James MD (Psyc) - **Spec Exp:** Psychopharmacology; Mood Disorders; Anxiety Disorders; **Hospital:** NY-Presby/Weill Cornell Med Ctr, NY (page 102); **Address:** 525 E 68th St, Box 140, New York, NY 10021-4885; **Phone:** 212-746-5913; **Board Cert:** Psychiatry 1977; **Med School:** Cornell Univ-Weill Med Coll 1968; **Resid:** Psychiatry, NY Hosp 1975; **Fac Appt:** Prof Psyc, Cornell Univ-Weill Med Coll

Kowallis, George MD (Psyc) - **Spec Exp:** Depression; Anxiety Disorders; ADD/ADHD; **Address:** 162 W 56th St, Ste 407, New York, NY 10019-3831; **Phone:** 212-757-0324; **Board Cert:** Psychiatry 1977; Child & Adolescent Psychiatry 1978; **Med School:** Univ Pennsylvania 1969; **Resid:** Psychiatry, St Luke's-Roosevelt Hosp Ctr 1974; **Fac Appt:** Asst Clin Prof Psyc, NY Med Coll

Kranzler, Elliot MD (Psyc) - **Spec Exp:** Anxiety & Depression; Bereavement/Traumatic Grief; ADD/ADHD; **Hospital:** NY-Presby/Columbia Univ Med Ctr, NY (page 102); **Address:** 451 West End Ave, New York, NY 10024-5329; **Phone:** 212-580-9758; **Board Cert:** Psychiatry 1984; Child & Adolescent Psychiatry 1986; **Med School:** Albert Einstein Coll Med 1978; **Resid:** Psychiatry, Payne-Whitney Clin 1982; **Fellow:** Child & Adolescent Psychiatry, NY-Presby/Columbia Univ Med Ctr 1984; Research, NY-Presby/Columbia-NIMH; **Fac Appt:** Asst Prof Psyc, Columbia P&S

Kremberg, M Roy MD (Psyc) - **Spec Exp:** Mood Disorders; Anxiety Disorders; ADD/ADHD; **Hospital:** Mt Sinai St. Luke's; **Address:** 2109 Broadway, Ste 8144, New York, NY 10023-2106; **Phone:** 212-875-8568; **Board Cert:** Psychiatry 1980; Child & Adolescent Psychiatry 1982; **Med School:** Columbia P&S 1976; **Resid:** Psychiatry, St Luke's Hosp 1978; **Fellow:** Child & Adolescent Psychiatry, St Luke's Hosp 1980

Krueger, Richard B MD (Psyc) - **Spec Exp:** Sexual Behavior-Compulsive; **Hospital:** NY State Psychiatric Inst, NY-Presby/Columbia Univ Med Ctr, NY (page 102); **Address:** 210 E 68th St, Ste 1H, New York, NY 10065; **Phone:** 917-750-1596; **Board Cert:** Psychiatry 1984; Internal Medicine 1980; Addiction Psychiatry 2007; Forensic Psychiatry 2006; **Med School:** Harvard Med Sch 1977; **Resid:** Internal Medicine, Boston VA Hosp 1980; Psychiatry, Boston Med Ctr 1983; **Fac Appt:** Assoc Clin Prof Psyc, Columbia P&S

Levitan, Stephan MD (Psyc) - **Spec Exp:** Psychotherapy; Psychopharmacology; Couples Therapy; Psychoanalysis; **Hospital:** NY-Presby/Columbia Univ Med Ctr, NY (page 102); **Address:** 185 E 85th St, Ste 29J, New York, NY 10028-2143; **Phone:** 212-722-4311; **Board Cert:** Psychiatry 1974; **Med School:** SUNY Buffalo 1965; **Resid:** Psychiatry, Hillside Hosp 1969; **Fellow:** Psychoanalysis, Columbia Psychoanalysis Training Ctr 1973; **Fac Appt:** Clin Prof Psyc, Columbia P&S

Lindenmayer, Jean-Pierre MD (Psyc) - **Spec Exp:** Psychopharmacology; Schizophrenia; Bipolar/Mood Disorders; **Hospital:** Lenox Hill Hosp; **Address:** 18 E 77th St, Ste B, New York, NY 10021-1700; **Phone:** 212-249-2720; **Board Cert:** Psychiatry 1975; **Med School:** Switzerland 1967; **Resid:** Psychiatry, Univ Hosp-Geneva Med Sch 1969; Psychiatry, SUNY Downstate Med Ctr 1973; **Fellow:** Research, SUNY Downstate Med Ctr 1975; **Fac Appt:** Clin Prof Psyc, NYU Sch Med

Lipton, Brian P MD (Psyc) - **Spec Exp:** Psychotherapy; Psychopharmacology; Anxiety & Mood Disorders; Psychosomatic Disorders; **Hospital:** Lenox Hill Hosp; **Address:** 1111 Park Ave, Ste 1A, New York, NY 10128-1234; **Phone:** 212-427-4499; **Board Cert:** Psychiatry 1970; **Med School:** SUNY Downstate 1964; **Resid:** Psychiatry, Hillside Hosp 1968; **Fac Appt:** Asst Clin Prof Psyc, NYU Sch Med

Malaspina, Dolores MD (Psyc) - **Spec Exp:** Anxiety Disorders; Depression; Trauma Psychiatry; **Hospital:** NYU Langone Med Ctr (page 104); **Address:** 136 E 57th St, Ste 1201, New York, NY 10022; **Phone:** 718-877-5708; **Board Cert:** Psychiatry 1989; **Med School:** UMDNJ-NJ Med Sch, Newark 1983; **Resid:** Psychiatry, NY-Presby/Columbia Univ Med Ctr 1987; **Fellow:** Psychiatry, NY State Psych Inst 1989; **Fac Appt:** Prof Psyc, NYU Sch Med

Manevitz, Alan MD (Psyc) - **Spec Exp:** Marital/Family/Sex Therapy; Depression-TMS Therapy; ADD/PTSD; Fibromyalgia Syndrome (FMS); **Hospital:** NY-Presby/Weill Cornell Med Ctr, NY (page 102), Lenox Hill Hosp; **Address:** 60 Sutton Place South, Ste 1CN, New York, NY 10022; **Phone:** 212-751-5072; **Board Cert:** Psychiatry 1987; **Med School:** Columbia P&S 1980; **Resid:** Psychiatry, NY Hosp 1984; **Fellow:** Psychopharmacology, NY Hosp 1985; **Fac Appt:** Assoc Clin Prof Psyc, Cornell Univ-Weill Med Coll

Mann, J. John MD/PhD (Psyc) - **Spec Exp:** Mood Disorders; Clinical Trials; Suicide; **Hospital:** NY-Presby/Columbia Univ Med Ctr, NY (page 102); **Address:** Neurological Inst of NY, 710 W 168th St, rm 1209, New York, NY 10032; **Phone:** 646-774-7553; **Board Cert:** Psychiatry 1980; **Med School:** Australia 1971; **Resid:** Psychiatry, Royal Melbourne Hosp 1976; **Fac Appt:** Prof Psyc, Columbia P&S

Marin, Deborah B MD (Psyc) - **Spec Exp:** Memory Disorders; Depression; Depression in the Elderly; Geriatric Psychiatry; **Hospital:** Mt Sinai Hosp; **Address:** Mt Sinai, Psychiatry, 1425 Madison Ave Fl 5, New York, NY 10029; **Phone:** 212-659-8092; **Board Cert:** Psychiatry 1990; **Med School:** Mount Sinai Sch Med 1984; **Resid:** Psychiatry, Mt Sinai Hosp 1988; **Fellow:** Psychiatry, NY-Presby/Weill Cornell Med Ctr 1991; **Fac Appt:** Prof Psyc, Mount Sinai-Icahn Sch of Med

Markowitz, John C MD (Psyc) - **Spec Exp:** Depression; Post Traumatic Stress Disorder; Cognitive Psychotherapy; Psychopharmacology; **Hospital:** NY-Presby/Columbia Univ Med Ctr, NY (page 102), NY State Psychiatric Inst; **Address:** 40 E 83rd St, New York, NY 10028; **Phone:** 212-288-3070; **Board Cert:** Psychiatry 1987; **Med School:** Columbia P&S 1982; **Resid:** Psychiatry, Payne Whitney Clin/New York Hosp 1987; **Fac Appt:** Prof Psyc, Columbia P&S

Massie, Mary Jane MD (Psyc) - **Spec Exp:** Psychiatry in Cancer; Depression; **Hospital:** Meml Sloan Kettering Canc Ctr (page 110); **Address:** Meml Sloan-Kettering Cancer Ctr, Dept Psychiatry, 1275 York Ave, New York, NY 10065; **Phone:** 646-888-0181; **Board Cert:** Psychiatry 1978; Psychosomatic Medicine 2005; **Med School:** SUNY Buffalo 1973; **Resid:** Psychiatry, Montefiore Med Ctr 1977; **Fellow:** Psychiatry, Meml Sloan-Kettering Cancer Ctr 1978

McGrath, Patrick J MD (Psyc) - **Spec Exp:** Psychopharmacology-Consultation; Depression-Consultation; **Hospital:** NY-Presby/Columbia Univ Med Ctr, NY (page 102), NY State Psychiatric Inst; **Address:** 710 W 168th St, New York, NY 10032; **Phone:** 646-774-8076; **Board Cert:** Psychiatry 1979; **Med School:** Columbia P&S 1974; **Resid:** Psychiatry, NY State Psych Inst 1978; **Fac Appt:** Clin Prof Psyc, Columbia P&S

McMullen Jr, Robert MD (Psyc) - **Spec Exp:** Psychopharmacology; Anxiety Disorders; Bipolar/Mood Disorders; **Address:** 171 W 79th St, Ste 2, New York, NY 10024-6449; **Phone:** 212-362-9635; **Board Cert:** Psychiatry 1982; **Med School:** Georgetown Univ 1976; **Resid:** Psychiatry, NY State Psychiatric Inst 1980; **Fac Appt:** Asst Prof Psyc, Columbia P&S

Mellman, Lisa A MD (Psyc) - **Spec Exp:** Anxiety & Depression; Relationship Problems; **Hospital:** NY-Presby/Columbia Univ Med Ctr, NY (page 102), NY State Psychiatric Inst; **Address:** NY-Presby/Columbia Univ Med Ctr, Dept Psychiatry, 630 W 168th St, rm 3-401, New York, NY 10032; **Phone:** 917-620-6010; **Board Cert:** Psychiatry 1986; **Med School:** Case West Res Univ 1981; **Resid:** Psychiatry, NY-Presby/Columbia Univ Med Ctr 1985; **Fellow:** Psychoanalysis, NY-Presby/Columbia Univ Med Ctr 1991; **Fac Appt:** Clin Prof Psyc, Columbia P&S

Michels, Robert MD (Psyc) - **Spec Exp:** Psychoanalysis; **Hospital:** NY-Presby/Weill Cornell Med Ctr, NY (page 102); **Address:** 418 E 71st St, New York, NY 10021-4894; **Phone:** 212-746-6001; **Board Cert:** Psychiatry 1964; **Med School:** Northwestern Univ 1958; **Resid:** Psychiatry, Columbia-Presby/NY Psych Inst 1962; **Fac Appt:** Prof Psyc, Cornell Univ-Weill Med Coll

Moore, Joanne MD (Psyc) - **Spec Exp:** Eating Disorders; Anxiety & Depression; Addiction/Substance Abuse; Geriatric Psychiatry; **Hospital:** NY-Presby/Columbia Univ Med Ctr, NY (page 102); **Address:** NY-Presby, Psychiatry Dept, 635 W 165th St, Ste 303, New York, NY 10032; **Phone:** 212-305-9499; **Board Cert:** Psychiatry 1988; Addiction Psychiatry 2006; **Med School:** Harvard Med Sch 1982; **Resid:** Psychiatry, NY-Presby/Columbia Univ Med Ctr 1987; **Fellow:** Geriatric Psychiatry, NY-Presby/Columbia Univ Med Ctr 1984; **Fac Appt:** Assoc Prof Psyc, Columbia P&S

Muskin, Philip R MD (Psyc) - **Spec Exp:** Psychopharmacology; Anxiety & Depression; Psychiatry in Physical Illness; Psychoanalysis; **Hospital:** NY-Presby/Columbia Univ Med Ctr, NY (page 102); **Address:** 1700 York Ave, New York, NY 10128-7820; **Phone:** 212-722-8438; **Board Cert:** Psychiatry 1979; Geriatric Psychiatry 2011; Psychosomatic Medicine 2005; **Med School:** NY Med Coll 1974; **Resid:** Psychiatry, NYS Psych Inst 1978; **Fellow:** Psychosomatic Medicine, Columbia-Presby Hosp 1979; Psychopharmacology, NY State Psych Inst 1979; **Fac Appt:** Prof Psyc, Columbia P&S

Nininger, James MD (Psyc) - **Spec Exp:** Psychotherapy; Psychopharmacology; Adolescent Psychiatry; Geriatric Psychiatry; **Hospital:** NY-Presby/Weill Cornell Med Ctr, NY (page 102); **Address:** 10 E 78th St, Ste 5A, New York, NY 10075; **Phone:** 212-879-8338; **Board Cert:** Psychiatry 1978; **Med School:** Univ Cincinnati 1974; **Resid:** Psychiatry, Mount Sinai Hosp 1978; **Fac Appt:** Assoc Clin Prof Psyc, Cornell Univ-Weill Med Coll

Nunes, Edward MD (Psyc) - **Spec Exp:** Depression; Substance Abuse; **Hospital:** NY State Psychiatric Inst, NY-Presby/Columbia Univ Med Ctr, NY (page 102); **Address:** 617 West End Ave, Ste 1B, New York, NY 10032; **Phone:** 212-579-0339; **Board Cert:** Psychiatry 1986; Addiction Psychiatry 2013; **Med School:** Univ Conn 1981; **Resid:** Psychiatry, NYS Psychiatric Inst 1985; **Fellow:** Psychopharmacology, NYS Psychiatric Inst 1988; **Fac Appt:** Prof Psyc, Columbia P&S

Oberfield, Richard MD (Psyc) - **Spec Exp:** Child & Adolescent Psychiatry; Divorce/Family Issues; ADD/ADHD; **Hospital:** NYU Langone Med Ctr (page 104); **Address:** 200 E 33rd St, Ste 2J, New York, NY 10016-4874; **Phone:** 212-684-0148; **Board Cert:** Psychiatry 1979; Child & Adolescent Psychiatry 1980; **Med School:** Mount Sinai Sch Med 1974; **Resid:** Psychiatry, Bellevue Hosp 1976; **Fellow:** Child & Adolescent Psychiatry, Bellevue Hosp 1978; **Fac Appt:** Clin Prof Psyc, NYU Sch Med

Olds, David D MD (Psyc) - **Spec Exp:** Psychoanalysis; Psychotherapy; **Hospital:** NY-Presby/Columbia Univ Med Ctr, NY (page 102); **Address:** 108 E 96th St, Ste 6F, New York, NY 10128; **Phone:** 212-427-9688; **Board Cert:** Psychiatry 1975; **Med School:** Columbia P&S 1967; **Resid:** Psychiatry, NY State Psych Inst 1971; **Fellow:** Psychoanalysis, NY-Presby/Columbia Univ Med Ctr 1978; **Fac Appt:** Clin Prof Psyc, Columbia P&S

Papp, Laszlo A MD (Psyc) - **Spec Exp:** Anxiety & Depression; Mood Disorders; Psychotherapy & Psychopharmacology; Diagnostic Second Opinions; **Hospital:** NY-Presby/Columbia Univ Med Ctr, NY (page 102); **Address:** 124 E 84th St, Ste 1B, New York, NY 10028; **Phone:** 212-360-5750; **Board Cert:** Psychiatry 1993; **Med School:** Hungary 1978; **Resid:** Internal Medicine, Natl Inst Rheumatology 1981; Psychiatry, Beth Israel Med Ctr 1986; **Fellow:** Psychopharmacology, NY-Presby/Columbia Univ Med Ctr 1989; **Fac Appt:** Assoc Clin Prof Psyc, Columbia P&S

Pawel, Michael A MD (Psyc) - **Spec Exp:** Adolescent Psychiatry; **Hospital:** Mt Sinai St. Luke's; **Address:** 15 W 72nd St, Ste 1J, New York, NY 10023; **Phone:** 212-873-9170; **Board Cert:** Psychiatry 1977; **Med School:** Albert Einstein Coll Med 1971; **Resid:** Psychiatry, Montefiore Hosp Med Ctr 1974; **Fac Appt:** Asst Prof Psyc, Columbia P&S

Pfeffer, Cynthia R MD (Psyc) - **Spec Exp:** Child & Adolescent Psychiatry; Bereavement/Traumatic Grief; Anxiety & Depression; ADD/ADHD; **Hospital:** NY-Presby/Weill Cornell Med Ctr, NY (page 102), NYU Langone Med Ctr (page 104); **Address:** 1100 Park Ave, Ste 1B, New York, NY 10128; **Phone:** 212-717-2334; **Board Cert:** Psychiatry 1975; Child & Adolescent Psychiatry 1976; **Med School:** NYU Sch Med 1968; **Resid:** Psychiatry, Montefiore Med Ctr 1973; **Fellow:** Child & Adolescent Psychiatry, Montefiore Med Ctr 1973; **Fac Appt:** Prof Psyc, Cornell Univ-Weill Med Coll

Pines, Jeffrey M MD (Psyc) - **Spec Exp:** Substance Abuse; **Hospital:** NY-Presby/Columbia Univ Med Ctr, NY (page 102); **Address:** Columbia Univ Med Ctr, 161 Fort Washington Ave, New York, NY 10032; **Phone:** 212-579-1913; **Board Cert:** Psychiatry 1982; **Med School:** Columbia P&S 1973; **Resid:** Internal Medicine, NY-Presby/Columbia Univ Med Ctr 1976; Psychiatry, NYS Psych Inst 1980; **Fellow:** Rheumatology, Hosp Special Surgery 1977; Liaison Psychiatry, NY-Presby/Columbia Univ Med Ctr 1981; **Fac Appt:** Assoc Clin Prof Psyc, Columbia P&S

Preter, Maurice MD (Psyc) - **Spec Exp:** Neuro-Psychiatry; Bipolar/Mood Disorders; Panic Disorder; Personality Disorders; **Hospital:** NY-Presby/Columbia Univ Med Ctr, NY (page 102), Mt Sinai Hosp; **Address:** 1160 Fifth Ave, New York, NY 10029; **Phone:** 212-713-5336; **Board Cert:** Psychiatry 2004; Neurology 2004; **Med School:** Germany 1991; **Resid:** Psychiatry, Montefiore Med Ctr 1999; Neurology, Montefiore Med Ctr 1999; **Fac Appt:** Asst Clin Prof Psyc, Columbia P&S

Preven, David W MD (Psyc) - **Spec Exp:** Anxiety & Mood Disorders; Psychopharmacology; Psychotherapy; Forensic Psychiatry; **Hospital:** Montefiore Med Ctr-Moses Campus (page 100); **Address:** 451 West End Ave, Ste 2H, New York, NY 10024; **Phone:** 212-799-4907; **Board Cert:** Psychiatry 1969; Forensic Psychiatry 2005; **Med School:** Harvard Med Sch 1963; **Resid:** Psychiatry, Jacobi Med Ctr 1967; **Fellow:** Psychiatry, Albert Einstein Coll Med 1971; **Fac Appt:** Clin Prof Psyc, Albert Einstein Coll Med

Rees, Ellen MD (Psyc) - **Spec Exp:** Psychoanalysis; Psychotherapy; **Hospital:** NY-Presby/Weill Cornell Med Ctr, NY (page 102); **Address:** 108 E 96th St Fl 7 - Ste F, New York, NY 10128-6217; **Phone:** 212-722-5988; **Board Cert:** Psychiatry 1979; **Med School:** Albert Einstein Coll Med 1974; **Resid:** Psychiatry, Mt Sinai Hosp 1977; **Fellow:** Psychiatry, NY Hosp-Cornell 1978; Psychoanalysis, Columbia Univ Ctr Psych Trng 1991; **Fac Appt:** Assoc Clin Prof Psyc, Cornell Univ-Weill Med Coll

Roose, Steven MD (Psyc) - **Spec Exp:** Depression in the Elderly; Psychoanalysis; **Hospital:** NY State Psychiatric Inst, NY-Presby/Columbia Univ Med Ctr, NY (page 102); **Address:** NYS Psychiatric Inst, 1051 Riverside Drive, rm 2211, Box 98, New York, NY 10032; **Phone:** 212-831-8644; **Board Cert:** Psychiatry 1979; **Med School:** Mount Sinai Sch Med 1974; **Resid:** Psychiatry, NYS Psychiatric Inst 1978; **Fellow:** Research, NY-Presby/Columbia Univ Med Ctr 1981; **Fac Appt:** Prof Psyc, Columbia P&S

Rosen, Arnold M MD (Psyc) - **Spec Exp:** Depression; Psychopharmacology; **Address:** 200 E 78th St, New York, NY 10075; **Phone:** 212-288-6380; **Board Cert:** Psychiatry 1976; **Med School:** Univ Tex SW, Dallas 1968; **Resid:** Psychiatry, Metropolitan Hosp Ctr 1974; **Fellow:** Psychiatry, Metropolitan Hosp Ctr 1975

Rosenthal, Jesse S MD (Psyc) - **Spec Exp:** ADD/ADHD; Anxiety Disorders; Depression; **Hospital:** Mt Sinai Beth Israel; **Address:** 21 E 93rd St, New York, NY 10128; **Phone:** 212-876-3080; **Board Cert:** Psychiatry 1978; **Med School:** Geo Wash Univ 1973; **Resid:** Psychiatry, Mt Sinai Hosp 1976; **Fac Appt:** Asst Clin Prof Psyc, Mount Sinai-Icahn Sch of Med

Rosenthal, Richard N MD (Psyc) - **Spec Exp:** Anxiety & Mood Disorders; Addiction/Substance Abuse; **Hospital:** Mt Sinai Roosevelt, Mt Sinai Beth Israel; **Address:** 425 W 59th St, Ste 7C, New York, NY 10019; **Phone:** 212-523-5366; **Board Cert:** Psychiatry 1985; Addiction Psychiatry 2012; **Med School:** SUNY Downstate 1980; **Resid:** Psychiatry, Mount Sinai Med Ctr 1984; **Fac Appt:** Prof Psyc, Columbia P&S

Rosner, Richard MD (Psyc) - **Spec Exp:** Adolescent Psychiatry; Forensic Psychiatry; Addiction/Substance Abuse; **Hospital:** NYU Langone Med Ctr (page 104), Bellevue Hosp Ctr; **Address:** 140 E 83rd St, Ste 6A, New York, NY 10028-1928; **Phone:** 212-988-6014; **Board Cert:** Psychiatry 1974; Forensic Psychiatry 2004; Addiction Medicine 2004; **Med School:** NYU Sch Med 1966; **Resid:** Psychiatry, Mount Sinai Hosp 1970; **Fac Appt:** Clin Prof Psyc, NYU Sch Med

Ross, Stephen MD (Psyc) - **Spec Exp:** Addiction/Substance Abuse; Alcohol Abuse; Adolescent Psychiatry; Psychiatry in Cancer; **Hospital:** NYU Langone Med Ctr (page 104), Bellevue Hosp Ctr; **Address:** 462 1st Ave, rm NBV 20E-7, New York, NY 10016; **Phone:** 212-562-4097; **Board Cert:** Psychiatry 2012; Addiction Psychiatry 2014; **Med School:** UCLA-David Geffen Sch Med 1996; **Resid:** Psychiatry, NY-Presby/Columbia Univ Med Ctr 2000; **Fellow:** Addiction Psychiatry, Bellevue Hosp Ctr 2003; **Fac Appt:** Asst Prof Psyc, NYU Sch Med

Roth, Andrew J MD (Psyc) - **Spec Exp:** Psychiatry of Prostate Cancer; Geriatric Psychiatry; **Hospital:** Meml Sloan Kettering Canc Ctr (page 110); **Address:** MSKCC, Psychiatry, 641 Lexington Ave, Fl 7, New York, NY 10022; **Phone:** 646-888-0024; **Board Cert:** Psychiatry 1993; Geriatric Psychiatry 2007; Psychosomatic Medicine 2005; **Med School:** NY Med Coll 1988; **Resid:** Psychiatry, Mt Sinai Hosp 1992; **Fellow:** Liaison Psychiatry, Meml Sloan-Kettering Cancer Ctr 1994; **Fac Appt:** Clin Prof Psyc, Cornell Univ-Weill Med Coll

Rubinstein, Morton E MD (Psyc) - **Spec Exp:** Psychopharmacology; **Hospital:** VA NY Harbor Hlthcare Sys-Manhattan Campus; **Address:** 423 E 23rd St, New York, NY 10010-5013; **Phone:** 212-686-7500 x7991; **Board Cert:** Psychiatry 1988; **Med School:** NY Med Coll 1976; **Resid:** Psychiatry, Bellevue Hosp 1979; **Fellow:** Psychiatry, Mount Sinai Med Ctr 1980; **Fac Appt:** Assoc Clin Prof Psyc, NYU Sch Med

Sacks, Michael MD (Psyc) - **Spec Exp:** Personality Disorders; Relationship Problems; Anxiety & Depression; **Hospital:** NY-Presby/Weill Cornell Med Ctr, NY (page 102); **Address:** 525 E 68th St, Box 140, New York, NY 10021-4870; **Phone:** 212-746-3710; **Board Cert:** Psychiatry 1973; **Med School:** NYU Sch Med 1967; **Resid:** Psychiatry, NY State Psych Inst 1971; **Fellow:** Psychiatry, Natl Inst Mental Hlth 1973; **Fac Appt:** Prof Psyc, Cornell Univ-Weill Med Coll

Sadock, Virginia MD (Psyc) - **Spec Exp:** Psychotherapy; Sexual Dysfunction; Anxiety & Depression; Marital/Family/Sex Therapy; **Hospital:** NYU Langone Med Ctr (page 104); **Address:** 4 E 89th St, Ste 1E, New York, NY 10128; **Phone:** 212-427-0885; **Board Cert:** Psychiatry 1975; **Med School:** NY Med Coll 1970; **Resid:** Psychiatry, Metropolitan Hosp Ctr 1973; **Fac Appt:** Clin Prof Psyc, NYU Sch Med

Samberg, Eslee MD (Psyc) - **Spec Exp:** Psychoanalysis; Personality Disorders; Psychotherapy; **Hospital:** NY-Presby/Weill Cornell Med Ctr, NY (page 102); **Address:** 165 W End Ave, Ste 1M, New York, NY 10024; **Phone:** 212-874-7725; **Board Cert:** Psychiatry 1983; **Med School:** Cornell Univ-Weill Med Coll 1978; **Resid:** Psychiatry, NY-Presby/Weill Cornell Med Ctr 1982; **Fac Appt:** Assoc Clin Prof Psyc, Cornell Univ-Weill Med Coll

Sawyer, David MD (Psyc) - **Spec Exp:** Psychoanalysis; Child & Adolescent Psychiatry; Psychosomatic Disorders; Anxiety & Mood Disorders; **Address:** 1 W 64th St, Ste 1C, New York, NY 10023; **Phone:** 212-787-8260; **Board Cert:** Psychiatry 1982; Child & Adolescent Psychiatry 1984; **Med School:** NY Med Coll 1977; **Resid:** Psychiatry, NY Hosp-Cornell/Westchester 1980; **Fellow:** Child & Adolescent Psychiatry, NY Hosp-Cornell/Westchester 1982

Scharf, Robert D MD (Psyc) - **Spec Exp:** Psychotherapy; Psychopharmacology; Psychoanalysis; **Hospital:** Mt Sinai Roosevelt, Mt Sinai St. Luke's; **Address:** 207 E 74th St, Ste 1L, New York, NY 10021-3341; **Phone:** 212-988-4145; **Board Cert:** Psychiatry 1976; **Med School:** Albert Einstein Coll Med 1960; **Resid:** Internal Medicine, Barnes Hosp 1961; Psychiatry, Kings Co Hosp 1964; **Fellow:** Psychoanalysis, NY Psychoanalytic Inst 1973

Schein, Jonah MD (Psyc) - **Spec Exp:** Depression; Anxiety Disorders; Psychotherapy; **Hospital:** NY-Presby/Weill Cornell Med Ctr, NY (page 102); **Address:** 1349 Lexington Ave, Ste 1E, New York, NY 10128-1514; **Phone:** 212-876-2324; **Board Cert:** Psychiatry 1975; **Med School:** NYU Sch Med 1969; **Resid:** Psychiatry, NY State Psychiatric Inst 1973; **Fac Appt:** Assoc Clin Prof Psyc, Cornell Univ-Weill Med Coll

Seaman, Cheryl MD (Psyc) - **Spec Exp:** Psychotherapy; Anxiety Disorders; Depression; Psychopharmacology; **Address:** 286 Madison Ave, PH, New York, NY 10017; **Phone:** 917-687-8901; **Board Cert:** Psychiatry 1986; **Med School:** Columbia P&S 1979; **Resid:** Psychiatry, NY Hosp-Westchester Div 1983

Shapiro, Peter A MD (Psyc) - **Spec Exp:** Depression; Psychiatry in Physical Illness; Liaison Psychiatry; **Hospital:** NY-Presby/Columbia Univ Med Ctr, NY (page 102); **Address:** 239 Central Park West, Ste 1-BW, New York, NY 10024; **Phone:** 212-874-6030; **Board Cert:** Psychiatry 1985; Psychosomatic Medicine 2005; **Med School:** Columbia P&S 1980; **Resid:** Psychiatry, NY State Psych Inst 1984; **Fellow:** Liaison Psychiatry, NY-Presby/Columbia Univ Med Ctr 1986; **Fac Appt:** Clin Prof Psyc, Columbia P&S

Shaw, Ronda R MD (Psyc) - **Spec Exp:** Psychoanalysis; Psychotherapy; **Hospital:** Mt Sinai Hosp; **Address:** 35 E 85th St, Ste 2, New York, NY 10028; **Phone:** 212-772-0321; **Board Cert:** Psychiatry 1977; **Med School:** Wayne State Univ 1966; **Resid:** Psychiatry, Jacobi Med Ctr 1970; **Fac Appt:** Assoc Clin Prof Psyc, Mount Sinai Sch Med

Shinbach, Kent D MD (Psyc) - **Spec Exp:** Depression; Psychopharmacology; Geriatric Psychiatry; **Hospital:** Gracie Square Hosp, NY-Presby/Lower Manhattan Hosp (page 102); **Address:** 14 E 75th St, Ste 1A, New York, NY 10021; **Phone:** 212-744-7100; **Board Cert:** Psychiatry 1970; **Med School:** Jefferson Med Coll 1963; **Resid:** Psychiatry, NY Med Coll 1968; **Fac Appt:** Asst Clin Prof Psyc, Cornell Univ-Weill Med Coll

Siever, Larry J MD (Psyc) - **Spec Exp:** Psychopharmacology; Depression; Personality Disorders; **Hospital:** Mt Sinai Hosp, James J. Peters VA Med Ctr-Bronx; **Address:** 1 Gustave L Levy Pl, Box 1230, New York, NY 10029-6500; **Phone:** 212-774-1722; **Board Cert:** Psychiatry 1980; **Med School:** Stanford Univ 1975; **Resid:** Psychiatry, McLean Hosp 1978; **Fellow:** Biological Psychiatry, Natl Inst Mental Hlth 1982; **Fac Appt:** Prof Psyc, Mount Sinai Sch Med

Silver, Jonathan M MD (Psyc) - **Spec Exp:** Neuro-Psychiatry; Psychopharmacology; **Address:** 40 E 83rd St, Ste 1E, New York, NY 10028; **Phone:** 212-874-6453; **Board Cert:** Psychiatry 1984; Behavioral Neurology & Neuropsychiatry 2006; **Med School:** Albert Einstein Coll Med 1979; **Resid:** Psychiatry, NY State Psych Inst 1983; **Fellow:** Research, NY State Psych Inst 1985; **Fac Appt:** Clin Prof Psyc, NYU Sch Med

Snyder, Stephen L MD (Psyc) - **Spec Exp:** Sexual Dysfunction; Relationship Problems; Couples Therapy; **Hospital:** Mt Sinai Hosp; **Address:** 115 Central Park W, Ste 15, New York, NY 10023; **Phone:** 212-875-9800; **Board Cert:** Psychiatry 1989; **Med School:** UCSF 1983; **Resid:** Psychiatry, Payne Whitney Psych Clin 1987; **Fellow:** Behavioral Medicine, Mt Sinai Hosp 1989; **Fac Appt:** Assoc Clin Prof Psyc, Mount Sinai-Icahn Sch of Med

Spitz, Henry MD (Psyc) - **Spec Exp:** Family & Couples Therapy; Addiction/Substance Abuse; Anxiety & Depression; **Hospital:** NY-Presby/Columbia Univ Med Ctr, NY (page 102); **Address:** 101 Central Park W, Ste 1C, New York, NY 10023; **Phone:** 212-873-1415; **Board Cert:** Psychiatry 1973; **Med School:** NY Med Coll 1965; **Resid:** Psychiatry, NY Med Coll Hosp 1969; **Fellow:** Psychiatry, NY Med Coll Hosp 1971; **Fac Appt:** Clin Prof Psyc, Columbia P&S

Stein, Stefan MD (Psyc) - **Spec Exp:** Couples Therapy; Psychotherapy & Psychopharmacology; **Hospital:** NY-Presby/Weill Cornell Med Ctr, NY (page 102); **Address:** 850 Park Ave, Ste 1E, New York, NY 10075; **Phone:** 212-249-0200; **Board Cert:** Psychiatry 1970; **Med School:** NYU Sch Med 1963; **Resid:** Internal Medicine, Boston City Hosp 1964; Psychiatry, Albert Einstein Coll Med 1968; **Fellow:** Psychiatry, Mass Genl Hosp 1965; Psychoanalysis, NY Psychoan Inst 1974; **Fac Appt:** Prof Psyc, Cornell Univ-Weill Med Coll

Stone, Michael H MD (Psyc) - **Spec Exp:** Personality Disorders; Psychoanalysis; Forensic Psychiatry; Addiction/Substance Abuse; **Address:** 225 Central Park West, Ste 114, New York, NY 10024-6027; **Phone:** 212-758-2000; **Board Cert:** Psychiatry 1971; **Med School:** Cornell Univ-Weill Med Coll 1958; **Resid:** Internal Medicine, Bellevue Hosp 1961; Psychiatry, NY State Psychiatric Inst 1966; **Fellow:** Hematology, Meml Sloan-Kettering Cancer Ctr 1962; Medical Oncology, Meml Sloan-Kettering Cancer Ctr 1963; **Fac Appt:** Prof Emeritus Psyc, Columbia P&S

Strain, James J MD (Psyc) - **Spec Exp:** Psychiatry in Physical Illness; Psychoanalysis; **Hospital:** Mt Sinai Hosp; **Address:** 1425 Madison Ave, Ste 6-24, New York, NY 10029; **Phone:** 212-659-8728; **Board Cert:** Psychiatry 1969; **Med School:** Case West Res Univ 1962; **Resid:** Psychiatry, Univ Hosps 1966; **Fellow:** Psychiatric Research, Univ Hosps 1967; Psychoanalysis, NY Psychoanalytic Inst 1972; **Fac Appt:** Prof Psyc, Mount Sinai Sch Med

Sussman, Norman MD (Psyc) - **Spec Exp:** Psychopharmacology; Anxiety & Mood Disorders; Bipolar/Mood Disorders; **Hospital:** NYU Langone Med Ctr (page 104); **Address:** 150 E 58th St Fl 27, New York, NY 10155; **Phone:** 212-588-9722; **Board Cert:** Psychiatry 1980; **Med School:** NY Med Coll 1975; **Resid:** Psychiatry, Metropolitan Hosp Ctr 1977; Psychiatry, Westchester Med Ctr 1978; **Fac Appt:** Prof Psyc, NYU Sch Med

Swiller, Hillel MD (Psyc) - **Spec Exp:** Psychotherapy; Couples Therapy; **Hospital:** Mt Sinai Hosp; **Address:** 108 E 96th St, Ste 9F, New York, NY 10128; **Phone:** 212-534-5588; **Board Cert:** Psychiatry 1972; **Med School:** Cornell Univ-Weill Med Coll 1965; **Resid:** Psychiatry, Jacobi Med Ctr 1969; **Fac Appt:** Clin Prof Psyc, Mount Sinai Sch Med

Tancredi, Laurence R MD (Psyc) - **Spec Exp:** Forensic Psychiatry; Anxiety & Depression; **Hospital:** Lenox Hill Hosp; **Address:** 129-B E 71st St, New York, NY 10021-4201; **Phone:** 212-288-5197; **Board Cert:** Psychiatry 1979; **Med School:** Univ Pennsylvania 1966; **Resid:** Psychiatry, NY State Psychiatric Inst 1975; Psychiatry, Yale-New Haven Hosp 1977; **Fac Appt:** Clin Prof Psyc, NYU Sch Med

Taylor, Noel MD (Psyc) - **Spec Exp:** Anxiety Disorders; Mood Disorders; **Address:** 150 E 58 St, Fl 27, New York, NY 10155; **Phone:** 212-888-9038; **Board Cert:** Psychiatry 1985; **Med School:** Johns Hopkins Univ 1980; **Resid:** Psychiatry, Johns Hopkins Hosp 1984; **Fellow:** Psychiatry, Beth Israel Med Ctr 1986; **Fac Appt:** Asst Prof Psyc, Albert Einstein Coll Med

Teusink, J. Paul MD (Psyc) - **Spec Exp:** Geriatric Psychiatry; Depression; Dementia; **Hospital:** Mt Sinai Beth Israel; **Address:** 88 University Pl, Ste 705, New York, NY 10003; **Phone:** 347-466-2521; **Board Cert:** Psychiatry 1976; **Med School:** Univ Mich Med Sch 1969; **Resid:** Psychiatry, Topeka State Hosp 1971; Psychiatry, CF Menninger Meml Hosp 1973; **Fac Appt:** Asst Clin Prof Psyc, Albert Einstein Coll Med

Tolchin, Joan MD (Psyc) - **Spec Exp:** Child & Adolescent Psychiatry; Psychotherapy; Anxiety & Depression; **Hospital:** NY-Presby/Weill Cornell Med Ctr, NY (page 102); **Address:** 35 E 84th St, New York, NY 10028-0871; **Phone:** 212-744-1446; **Board Cert:** Psychiatry 1979; Child & Adolescent Psychiatry 1982; **Med School:** NYU Sch Med 1972; **Resid:** Psychiatry, Bronx Muni Hosp 1975; **Fellow:** Child & Adolescent Psychiatry, NY Hosp/Cornell 1977; **Fac Appt:** Assoc Clin Prof Psyc, Cornell Univ-Weill Med Coll

Wachtel, Alan B MD (Psyc) - **Spec Exp:** ADD/ADHD; Mood Disorders; Learning Disorders; **Hospital:** NYU Langone Med Ctr (page 104); **Address:** 201 E 87th St, Ste 16J, New York, NY 10128; **Phone:** 212-348-0175; **Board Cert:** Psychiatry 1977; **Med School:** Mount Sinai Sch Med 1972; **Resid:** Psychiatry, Mt Sinai Hosp 1976; **Fellow:** Liaison Psychiatry, NY-Presby/Weill Cornell Med Ctr 1977; **Fac Appt:** Assoc Clin Prof Psyc, NYU Sch Med

Wager, Steven G MD (Psyc) - **Spec Exp:** Psychopharmacology; Depression; Anxiety Disorders; **Address:** 145 W 86th St, Ste 1B, New York, NY 10024-3421; **Phone:** 212-769-9620; **Board Cert:** Psychiatry 1986; **Med School:** Case West Res Univ 1980; **Resid:** Psychiatry, NY-Presby/Columbia Univ Med Ctr 1984; **Fellow:** Psychopharmacology, NY-Presby/Columbia Univ Med Ctr 1986

Wallack, Joel J MD (Psyc) - **Spec Exp:** Psychopharmacology; Psychiatry in Physical Illness; Anxiety & Depression; **Hospital:** Mt Sinai Beth Israel, Mt Sinai Hosp; **Address:** Mount Sinai Beth Israel Med Ctr, 10 Union Square E, Ste 3B, New York, NY 10003; **Phone:** 212-420-2398; **Board Cert:** Psychiatry 1979; Psychosomatic Medicine 2005; **Med School:** UMDNJ-NJ Med Sch, Newark 1974; **Resid:** Psychiatry, St Lukes Hosp 1978; **Fellow:** Consultation Psychiatry, Montefiore Med Ctr 1979; Psychosomatic Medicine, Mt Sinai Hosp 1980; **Fac Appt:** Prof Psyc, Mount Sinai Sch Med

Walsh, B. Timothy MD (Psyc) - **Spec Exp:** Eating Disorders; Obesity; **Hospital:** NY State Psychiatric Inst, NY-Presby/Columbia Univ Med Ctr, NY (page 102); **Address:** NY State Psychiatric Inst, 1051 Riverside Drive, rm 2306, Box 98, New York, NY 10032; **Phone:** 646-774-8066; **Board Cert:** Psychiatry 1978; **Med School:** Harvard Med Sch 1972; **Resid:** Psychiatry, Bronx Muni Hosp Ctr 1977; **Fac Appt:** Prof Psyc, Columbia P&S

Weill, Terry L MD (Psyc) - **Spec Exp:** Bipolar/Mood Disorders; Psychiatry in Physical Illness; **Hospital:** Mt Sinai Hosp, Mt Sinai Beth Israel; **Address:** 350 Central Park West, New York, NY 10023-6547; **Phone:** 212-316-5818; **Board Cert:** Psychiatry 1985; **Med School:** Hahnemann Univ 1980; **Resid:** Psychiatry, Mount Sinai Med Ctr 1984; **Fellow:** Psychoanalysis, NYS Psyc Inst 1991; **Fac Appt:** Asst Prof Psyc, Mount Sinai Sch Med

Welsh, Howard K MD (Psyc) - **Spec Exp:** Psychotherapy; Psychoanalysis; **Hospital:** NYU Langone Med Ctr (page 104); **Address:** 27 W 86th St, Ste 1C, New York, NY 10024-3615; **Phone:** 212-362-5846; **Board Cert:** Psychiatry 1976; **Med School:** Albert Einstein Coll Med 1971; **Resid:** Psychiatry, Kings County Hosp 1974; **Fac Appt:** Clin Prof Psyc, NYU Sch Med

Winters, Richard A MD (Psyc) - **Spec Exp:** Psychopharmacology; Crisis Intervention; Psychodynamic Psychotherapy; **Address:** 201 E 87th St, Ste 12-B, New York, NY 10128; **Phone:** 212-744-1346; **Board Cert:** Psychiatry 1977; **Med School:** NY Med Coll 1972; **Resid:** Psychiatry, Metropolitan Hosp Ctr 1975; **Fac Appt:** Asst Prof Psyc, NY Med Coll

Zimberg, Sheldon MD (Psyc) - **Spec Exp:** Addiction Psychiatry; Hypnosis; Geriatric Psychiatry; **Address:** 245-A E 61st St, New York, NY 10065; **Phone:** 212-988-5139; **Board Cert:** Psychiatry 1969; Addiction Psychiatry 2004; **Med School:** SUNY Downstate 1961; **Resid:** Psychiatry, NYS Psych Inst 1965; **Fellow:** Community Psychiatry, Columbia Univ Sch Pub Hlth 1966; **Fac Appt:** Clin Prof Psyc, Columbia P&S

Pulmonary Disease

Acquista, Angelo J MD (Pul) - **Spec Exp:** Asthma; Disaster Preparedness; **Hospital:** Lenox Hill Hosp; **Address:** 110 E 59th St, Ste 9C, New York, NY 10022; **Phone:** 212-583-2850; **Board Cert:** Internal Medicine 1984; Pulmonary Disease 1986; **Med School:** NYU Sch Med 1981; **Resid:** Internal Medicine, Lenox Hill Hosp 1984; **Fellow:** Pulmonary Disease, Lenox Hill Hosp 1986

Adams, Francis V MD (Pul) - **Spec Exp:** Asthma; Chronic Obstructive Lung Disease (COPD); Pulmonary Fibrosis; Sarcoidosis; **Hospital:** NYU Langone Med Ctr (page 104); **Address:** 650 First Ave, New York, NY 10016-3240; **Phone:** 212-447-0088; **Board Cert:** Internal Medicine 1974; Pulmonary Disease 1976; **Med School:** Cornell Univ-Weill Med Coll 1971; **Resid:** Internal Medicine, Georgetown Univ Hosp 1973; **Fellow:** Pulmonary Disease, Bellevue Hosp 1975; **Fac Appt:** Asst Prof Med, NYU Sch Med

Addrizzo-Harris, Doreen MD (Pul) - **Spec Exp:** Bronchoscopy; Tuberculosis; Lung Cancer; Interstitial Lung Disease; **Hospital:** NYU Langone Med Ctr (page 104); **Address:** 530 First Ave, rm 5D, New York, NY 10016; **Phone:** 212-263-7951; **Board Cert:** Pulmonary Disease 2006; Critical Care Medicine 2007; **Med School:** Cornell Univ-Weill Med Coll 1989; **Resid:** Internal Medicine, Bellevue Hosp/NYU Med Ctr 1993; **Fellow:** Pulmonary Critical Care Medicine, Bellevue Hosp/NYU Med Ctr 1996; **Fac Appt:** Assoc Prof Med, NYU Sch Med

Arcasoy, Selim M MD (Pul) - **Spec Exp:** Transplant Medicine-Lung; Interstitial Lung Disease; Chronic Obstructive Lung Disease (COPD); Pulmonary Embolism; **Hospital:** NY-Presby/Columbia Univ Med Ctr, NY (page 102); **Address:** Ctr for Advanced Lung Dis/Transp, 622 W 168th St, PH Bldg - Fl 14E, rm 104, New York, NY 10032-3720; **Phone:** 212-305-6589; **Board Cert:** Internal Medicine 2013; Pulmonary Disease 2006; Critical Care Medicine 2007; **Med School:** Turkey 1990; **Resid:** Internal Medicine, SUNY Downstate Med Ctr 1994; **Fellow:** Pulmonary Critical Care Medicine, Univ Pittsburgh Med Ctr 1998; **Fac Appt:** Prof Med, Columbia P&S

Baskin, Martin MD (Pul) - **Spec Exp:** Asthma; Pneumonia; Emphysema; **Hospital:** Mt Sinai Roosevelt; **Address:** 185 W End Ave, Ste 1M, New York, NY 10023-5567; **Phone:** 212-595-7701; **Board Cert:** Internal Medicine 1985; Pulmonary Disease 1988; **Med School:** Mount Sinai Sch Med 1981; **Resid:** Internal Medicine, Beth Israel Med Ctr 1984; **Fellow:** Pulmonary Disease, St Luke's Roosevelt Hosp Ctr 1988; Critical Care Medicine, St Luke's Roosevelt Hosp Ctr 1989

Basner, Robert C MD (Pul) - **Spec Exp:** Sleep Disorders/Apnea; **Hospital:** NY-Presby/Columbia Univ Med Ctr, NY (page 102); **Address:** 622 W 168th, Ste 859, Columbia University Medical Center, New York, NY 10032; **Phone:** 212-305-7591; **Board Cert:** Internal Medicine 1986; Pulmonary Disease 1988; Sleep Medicine 2009; **Med School:** Columbia P&S 1983; **Resid:** Internal Medicine, Beth Israel Hosp 1986; **Fellow:** Pulmonary Disease, Brigham & Women's Hosp 1989; **Fac Appt:** Prof Med, Columbia P&S

Bevelaqua, Frederick MD (Pul) - **Spec Exp:** Asthma; Lung Cancer; Chronic Obstructive Lung Disease (COPD); Sarcoidosis; **Hospital:** NYU Langone Med Ctr (page 104); **Address:** 245A E 35th St, New York, NY 10016; **Phone:** 212-213-6796; **Board Cert:** Internal Medicine 1978; Pulmonary Disease 1980; **Med School:** NYU Sch Med 1974; **Resid:** Internal Medicine, NYU Med Ctr 1978; **Fellow:** Pulmonary Disease, NYU Med Ctr 1980; **Fac Appt:** Asst Clin Prof Med, NYU Sch Med

Blair, Lester W MD (Pul) - **Spec Exp:** Asthma; Sarcoidosis; Bronchitis; Chronic Obstructive Lung Disease (COPD); **Hospital:** NY-Presby/Lower Manhattan Hosp (page 102), NY-Presby/Weill Cornell Med Ctr, NY (page 102); **Address:** Weill Cornell Physicians, 156 William St Fl 7, New York, NY 10038; **Phone:** 212-312-5920; **Board Cert:** Internal Medicine 1987; Pulmonary Disease 1980; Critical Care Medicine 2009; **Med School:** Columbia P&S 1974; **Resid:** Internal Medicine, Columbia-Presby Med Ctr 1977; **Fellow:** Pulmonary Disease, Bellevue Hosp 1979; **Fac Appt:** Assoc Clin Prof Med, Cornell Univ-Weill Med Coll

Burschtin, Omar E MD (Pul) - **Spec Exp:** Sleep Medicine; Sleep Disorders/Apnea; **Hospital:** NYU Langone Med Ctr (page 104); **Address:** Sleep Med Assocs of NYC, 11 E 26th St Fl 13, New York, NY 10010; **Phone:** 212-481-1818; **Board Cert:** Pulmonary Disease 2008; Sleep Medicine 2009; **Med School:** Uruguay 1988; **Resid:** Internal Medicine, NYU Med Ctr 1994; **Fellow:** Pulmonary Critical Care Medicine, NYU Med Ctr 1997; Sleep Medicine, Bellevue Hosp 1998; **Fac Appt:** Asst Clin Prof Med, NYU Sch Med

DePalo, Louis R MD (Pul) - **Spec Exp:** Critical Care; Lung Cancer; **Hospital:** Mt Sinai Hosp; **Address:** 1130 Park Ave, Ste 3, New York, NY 10128; **Phone:** 212-289-3627; **Board Cert:** Internal Medicine 1985; Pulmonary Disease 1988; Critical Care Medicine 2009; **Med School:** NY Med Coll 1982; **Resid:** Internal Medicine, Mt Sinai Med Ctr 1985; **Fellow:** Pulmonary Disease, Univ Penn Hosps 1988; **Fac Appt:** Asst Clin Prof Med, Mount Sinai Sch Med

DiFabrizio, Larry MD (Pul) - **Hospital:** Mt Sinai Hosp; **Address:** Mt Sinai, Pulmonary Dept, 5 E 98 St Fl 8, New York, NY 10029; **Phone:** 212-241-5656; **Board Cert:** Internal Medicine 1987; Pulmonary Disease 2012; Critical Care Medicine 2012; Sleep Medicine 2009; **Med School:** Washington Univ, St Louis 1984; **Resid:** Internal Medicine, Brigham & Womens Hosp 1987; **Fellow:** Pulmonary Critical Care Medicine, Brigham & Womens Hosp 1988; Rheumatology, NY-Presby/Columbia Univ Med Ctr 1990

DiMango, Angela MD (Pul) - **Hospital:** NY-Presby/Columbia Univ Med Ctr, NY (page 102); **Address:** 161 Ft Washington Ave Fl 3, New York, NY 10032; **Phone:** 212-305-5730; **Board Cert:** Pulmonary Disease 2006; **Med School:** SUNY Downstate 1989; **Resid:** Internal Medicine, NY Presby-Columbia Med Ctr 1992; **Fellow:** Pulmonary Disease, NY Presby-Columbia Med Ctr 1995; Critical Care Medicine, NY Presby-Columbia Med Ctr 1996; **Fac Appt:** Assoc Prof Med, Columbia P&S

Dimango, Emily A MD (Pul) - **Spec Exp:** Cystic Fibrosis; Asthma; Chronic Obstructive Lung Disease (COPD); Bronchiectasis; **Hospital:** NY-Presby/Columbia Univ Med Ctr, NY (page 102); **Address:** NY-Presbyterian, Pulmonology, 622 W 168th St, rm 859, New York, NY 10032; **Phone:** 212-305-0631; **Board Cert:** Internal Medicine 2006; Pulmonary Disease 2005; **Med School:** NYU Sch Med 1989; **Resid:** Internal Medicine, NY-Presby/Columbia Univ Med Ctr 1992; **Fellow:** Pulmonary Disease, NY-Presby/Columbia Univ Med Ctr 1995; **Fac Appt:** Asst Prof Med, Columbia P&S

Eden, Edward MD (Pul) - **Spec Exp:** Emphysema; Asthma; Sarcoidosis; Emphysema/Alpha-1 Antitrypsin Deficiency; **Hospital:** Mt Sinai Roosevelt; **Address:** 425 W 59th St, Ste 8A, New York, NY 10019-1104; **Phone:** 212-492-5500; **Board Cert:** Internal Medicine 1980; Pulmonary Disease 1982; Critical Care Medicine 2007; **Med School:** England, UK 1975; **Resid:** Internal Medicine, Univ Hosp 1980; **Fellow:** Pulmonary Disease, Mount Sinai Hosp 1982; Pulmonary Disease, Columbia-Presby Med Ctr 1984; **Fac Appt:** Assoc Prof Med, Columbia P&S

Fishman, Donald R MD (Pul) - **Spec Exp:** Asthma; Chronic Obstructive Lung Disease (COPD); Bronchoscopy; Interstitial Lung Disease; **Hospital:** Mt Sinai Roosevelt, Lenox Hill Hosp; **Address:** 200 W 57th St, Ste 1201, New York, NY 10019; **Phone:** 212-765-5151; **Board Cert:** Internal Medicine 1976; Pulmonary Disease 1978; **Med School:** Univ Pennsylvania 1973; **Resid:** Internal Medicine, Univ Mich Med Ctr 1976; **Fellow:** Pulmonary Disease, NYU Med Ctr 1978; **Fac Appt:** Asst Clin Prof Med, Mount Sinai Sch Med

Garay, Stuart M MD (Pul) - **Spec Exp:** Asthma; Chronic Obstructive Lung Disease (COPD); Sleep Apnea; **Hospital:** NYU Langone Med Ctr (page 104); **Address:** New York Pulmonary Associates, 463 Third Ave Fl 2, New York, NY 10016-6025; **Phone:** 212-685-6001; **Board Cert:** Internal Medicine 1977; Pulmonary Disease 1980; **Med School:** Harvard Med Sch 1974; **Resid:** Internal Medicine, Mt Sinai Hosp 1977; **Fellow:** Pulmonary Disease, Bellevue Hosp 1979; **Fac Appt:** Clin Prof Med, NYU Sch Med

Gelbman, Brian D MD (Pul) - **Spec Exp:** Asthma; Chronic Obstructive Lung Disease (COPD); Lung Cancer; **Hospital:** NY-Presby/Weill Cornell Med Ctr, NY (page 102), Hosp For Special Surgery (page 109); **Address:** Pulmonary Consultants of NY, 635 Madison Ave, Ste 1101, New York, NY 10022; **Phone:** 212-628-6611; **Board Cert:** Internal Medicine 2013; Pulmonary Disease 2005; Critical Care Medicine 2006; Sleep Medicine 2013; **Med School:** Vanderbilt Univ 2000; **Resid:** Internal Medicine, NY-Presby/Weill Cornell Univ Med Ctr 2003; **Fellow:** Pulmonary Critical Care Medicine, NY-Presby/Weill Cornell Univ Med Ctr 2006; **Fac Appt:** Assoc Clin Prof Med, Cornell Univ-Weill Med Coll

Kaplan, Rana MD (Pul) - **Hospital:** Meml Sloan Kettering Canc Ctr (page 110), NY-Presby/Weill Cornell Med Ctr, NY (page 102); **Address:** 1275 York Ave, Ste A3, New York, NY 10065; **Phone:** 212-639-8025; **Board Cert:** Critical Care Medicine 2004; **Med School:** Cornell Univ-Weill Med Coll 1996; **Resid:** Internal Medicine, New Eng Med Ctr 1999; **Fellow:** Pulmonary Critical Care Medicine, NY Presby Hosp 2003

Klapholz, Ari MD (Pul) - **Spec Exp:** Sleep Disorders/Apnea; Emphysema; **Hospital:** Mt Sinai Beth Israel; **Address:** 275 7th Ave Fl 3, New York, NY 10001; **Phone:** 646-660-9999; **Board Cert:** Internal Medicine 1987; Pulmonary Disease 2010; Critical Care Medicine 2011; Sleep Medicine 2007; **Med School:** NY Med Coll 1984; **Resid:** Internal Medicine, Beth Israel Med Ctr 1987; **Fellow:** Pulmonary Disease, Beth Israel Med Ctr 1989; Critical Care Medicine, Mount Sinai Med Ctr 1990; **Fac Appt:** Assoc Clin Prof Med, NY Med Coll

Kolodny, Erwin MD (Pul) - **Spec Exp:** Asthma; Emphysema; Bronchitis; **Hospital:** NYU Langone Med Ctr (page 104); **Address:** 650 1st Ave, New York, NY 10016-3240; **Phone:** 212-213-0090; **Board Cert:** Internal Medicine 1977; Pulmonary Disease 1978; **Med School:** NYU Sch Med 1973; **Resid:** Internal Medicine, Bellevue Hosp 1976; **Fellow:** Pulmonary Disease, NYU Med Ctr 1978; **Fac Appt:** Asst Clin Prof Med, NYU Sch Med

Krieger, Ana C MD (Pul) - **Spec Exp:** Sleep Disorders/Apnea; Narcolepsy; Pulmonary Hypertension; **Hospital:** NY-Presby/Weill Cornell Med Ctr, NY (page 102); **Address:** Weill Cornell Center for Sleep Medicine, 425 E 61st St, Fl 5, New York, NY 10065; **Phone:** 646-962-7378; **Board Cert:** Internal Medicine 2011; Pulmonary Disease 2011; **Med School:** Brazil 1992; **Resid:** Internal Medicine, Univ Chicago Hosps 1996; **Fellow:** Critical Care Medicine, Franklin/Chicago Med Sch 1998; Pulmonary Disease, NYU Sch of Med 2000; **Fac Appt:** Assoc Prof Med, Cornell Univ-Weill Med Coll

Lederer, David J MD (Pul) - **Spec Exp:** Transplant-Lung; Pulmonary Fibrosis; Interstitial Lung Disease; **Hospital:** NY-Presby/Columbia Univ Med Ctr, NY (page 102); **Address:** 622 W 168th St, rm 104, PH-14, New York, NY 10032; **Phone:** 212-305-7771; **Board Cert:** Internal Medicine 2012; Pulmonary Disease 2005; Critical Care Medicine 2006; **Med School:** SUNY Downstate 1999; **Resid:** Internal Medicine, NY Presby/Columbia Med Ctr 2003; **Fellow:** Pulmonary Critical Care Medicine, NY Presby/Columbia Med Ctr 2006; **Fac Appt:** Asst Prof Med, Columbia P&S

Lee, Marjorie MD (Pul) - **Spec Exp:** Emphysema & Asthma; Sarcoidosis; **Hospital:** Mt Sinai Beth Israel; **Address:** 247 3rd Ave, Ste 403, New York, NY 10010-7455; **Phone:** 212-533-1185; **Board Cert:** Internal Medicine 1976; Pulmonary Disease 1978; **Med School:** SUNY Hlth Sci Ctr 1973; **Resid:** Internal Medicine, Kaiser Hosp 1976; Pulmonary Disease, Cabrini Hosp 1977; **Fellow:** Pulmonary Disease, Yale-New Haven Hosp 1979

Lessnau, Klaus-Dieter MD (Pul) - **Spec Exp:** Sleep Disorders/Apnea; **Hospital:** Lenox Hill Hosp; **Address:** 110 E 59th St, Ste 9C, New York, NY 10022; **Phone:** 212-583-2969; **Board Cert:** Internal Medicine 2012; Pulmonary Disease 2000; Critical Care Medicine 2000; Sleep Medicine 2009; **Med School:** Germany 1985; **Resid:** Internal Medicine, Cabrini Med Ctr 1991; **Fellow:** Pulmonary Disease, Cabrini Med Ctr 1993; Critical Care Medicine, Mount Sinai Hosp 1995; **Fac Appt:** Asst Clin Prof Med, NYU Sch Med

Libby, Daniel M MD (Pul) - **Spec Exp:** Asthma; Lung Cancer; Interstitial Lung Disease; Chronic Obstructive Lung Disease (COPD); **Hospital:** NY-Presby/Weill Cornell Med Ctr, NY (page 102); **Address:** Pulmonary Consultants of NY, 635 Madison Ave, Ste 1101, New York, NY 10022; **Phone:** 212-628-6611; **Board Cert:** Internal Medicine 1977; Pulmonary Disease 1980; **Med School:** Baylor Coll Med 1974; **Resid:** Internal Medicine, NY-Presby/Weill Cornell Med Ctr 1977; **Fellow:** Pulmonary Disease, NY-Presby/Weill Cornell Med Ctr 1979; **Fac Appt:** Prof Med, Cornell Univ-Weill Med Coll

Lowy, Joseph MD (Pul) - **Spec Exp:** Lung Cancer; Palliative Care; Chronic Obstructive Lung Disease (COPD); Pulmonary Fibrosis; **Hospital:** NYU Langone Med Ctr (page 104); **Address:** NYU Med Ctr, Pulmonology, 530 1st Ave, Ste HCC-5D, New York, NY 10016; **Phone:** 212-263-6202; **Board Cert:** Internal Medicine 1983; Pulmonary Disease 1986; Hospice & Palliative Medicine 2008; **Med School:** Univ Rochester 1980; **Resid:** Internal Medicine, NYU-Bellevue Hosp 1983; **Fellow:** Pulmonary Disease, UCSD Med Ctr 1986; **Fac Appt:** Asst Clin Prof Med, NYU Sch Med

Maxfield, Roger A MD (Pul) - **Spec Exp:** Emphysema & Asthma; Occupational Lung Disease; Lung Cancer; Bronchoscopy; **Hospital:** NY-Presby/Columbia Univ Med Ctr, NY (page 102); **Address:** 51 W 51st St, Ste 360, New York, NY 10019; **Phone:** 212-326-8415; **Board Cert:** Internal Medicine 1980; Pulmonary Disease 1986; **Med School:** Brown Univ 1977; **Resid:** Internal Medicine, Georgetown Univ Hosp 1980; **Fellow:** Pulmonary Disease, Bellevue Hosp 1985; **Fac Appt:** Prof Med, Columbia P&S

Miller, Rachel L MD (Pul) - **Spec Exp:** Asthma; **Hospital:** NY-Presby/Columbia Univ Med Ctr, NY (page 102); **Address:** 622 W 168th St - PH8, New York, NY 10032; **Phone:** 212-305-0631; **Board Cert:** Pulmonary Disease 2006; Critical Care Medicine 2007; Allergy & Immunology 2009; **Med School:** NYU Sch Med 1990; **Resid:** Internal Medicine, NY Presby/Columbia Med Ctr 1993; **Fellow:** Pulmonary Critical Care Medicine, NY Presby/Columbia Med Ctr 1995

Mina, Bushra A MD (Pul) - **Hospital:** Lenox Hill Hosp; **Address:** 155 E 76th St, Ste 1C, New York, NY 10021; **Phone:** 212-794-2800; **Board Cert:** Internal Medicine 2005; Pulmonary Disease 2005; Critical Care Medicine 2005; **Med School:** Egypt 1986; **Resid:** Internal Medicine, Muhlenberg Regl Med Ctr 1990; Internal Medicine, Lenox Hill Hosp 1991; **Fellow:** Critical Care Medicine, Meml Sloan Kettering Cancer Ctr 1992; Pulmonary Disease, St Vincent's Hosp 1993

Multz, Alan S MD (Pul) - **Spec Exp:** Respiratory Distress Syndrome; Chronic Obstructive Lung Disease (COPD); Critical Care Medicine; Sepsis; **Hospital:** Mt Sinai St. Luke's; **Address:** Mount Sinai St Luke's, Pulmonary Div, 1111 Amsterdam Ave, New York, NY 10025; **Phone:** 212-523-9422; **Board Cert:** Internal Medicine 1988; Pulmonary Disease 2010; Critical Care Medicine 2011; **Med School:** Boston Univ 1985; **Resid:** Internal Medicine, Montefiore Med Ctr 1988; **Fellow:** Pulmonary Disease, Montefiore Med Ctr 1990; Critical Care Medicine, Montefiore Med Ctr 1991; **Fac Appt:** Prof Med, Hofstra N Shore-LIJ Sch Med

Nash, Thomas MD (Pul) - **Spec Exp:** Asthma; Cough; Pneumonia; **Hospital:** NY-Presby/Weill Cornell Med Ctr, NY (page 102); Hosp For Special Surgery (page 109); **Address:** 310 E 72nd St, New York, NY 10021; **Phone:** 212-734-6612; **Board Cert:** Internal Medicine 1981; Infectious Disease 1984; Pulmonary Disease 1988; **Med School:** NYU Sch Med 1978; **Resid:** Internal Medicine, NY-Presby/Weill Cornell Med Ctr 1981; **Fellow:** Infectious Disease, NY-Presby/Weill Cornell Med Ctr 1983; Pulmonary Disease, Meml Sloan-Kettering Cancer Ctr 1985; **Fac Appt:** Assoc Clin Prof Med, NYU Sch Med

Nelson, Judith E MD (Pul) - **Spec Exp:** Palliative Care; **Hospital:** Mt Sinai Hosp; **Address:** Mt Sinai Medical Ctr, One Gustave Levy Pl, Box 1232, New York, NY 10029; **Phone:** 212-241-2587; **Board Cert:** Internal Medicine 1989; Pulmonary Disease 2012; Critical Care Medicine 2003; Hospice & Palliative Medicine 2012; **Med School:** NYU Sch Med 1986; **Resid:** Internal Medicine, Mt Sinai Med Ctr 1989; **Fellow:** Pulmonary Critical Care Medicine, Mt Sinai Med Ctr 1992; **Fac Appt:** Prof Med, Mount Sinai Sch Med

Padilla, Maria L MD (Pul) - **Spec Exp:** Sarcoidosis; Pulmonary Hypertension; Cystic Fibrosis; **Hospital:** Mt Sinai Hosp; **Address:** Mount Sinai Med Ctr, Pulmonary Assocs, 5 E 98th St Fl 8, New York, NY 10029; **Phone:** 212-241-5656; **Board Cert:** Internal Medicine 1978; Pulmonary Disease 1980; **Med School:** Mount Sinai Sch Med 1975; **Resid:** Internal Medicine, Mount Sinai Med Ctr 1978; **Fellow:** Pulmonary Disease, Mount Sinai Med Ctr 1980; **Fac Appt:** Prof Med, Mount Sinai Sch Med

Pastores, Stephen M MD (Pul) - **Spec Exp:** Respiratory Failure; Respiratory Distress Syndrome (ARDS); Sepsis; Critical Care Medicine; **Hospital:** Meml Sloan Kettering Canc Ctr (page 110); **Address:** 1275 York Ave, New York, NY 10021; **Phone:** 212-639-6673; **Board Cert:** Internal Medicine 1989; Pulmonary Disease 2006; Critical Care Medicine 2007; **Med School:** Philippines 1982; **Resid:** Internal Medicine, Metropolitan Hosp Ctr 1989; **Fellow:** Pulmonary Disease, Bellevue Hosp Ctr 1992; Critical Care Medicine, Mount Sinai Hosp 1993; **Fac Appt:** Prof Med, Cornell Univ-Weill Med Coll

Posner, David H MD (Pul) - **Spec Exp:** Interstitial Lung Disease; Lung Cancer; Sarcoidosis; Pulmonary Fibrosis; **Hospital:** Lenox Hill Hosp; **Address:** 178 E 85th St, Fl 3, New York, NY 10028; **Phone:** 212-737-0470; **Board Cert:** Internal Medicine 1984; Pulmonary Disease 1988; **Med School:** NY Med Coll 1981; **Resid:** Internal Medicine, Lenox Hill Hosp 1985; **Fellow:** Pulmonary Disease, LIJ Med Ctr 1987; **Fac Appt:** Assoc Clin Prof Med, NYU Sch Med

Powell, Charles A MD (Pul) - **Spec Exp:** Lung Cancer; Bronchoscopy; **Hospital:** Mt Sinai Hosp; **Address:** Mount Sinai, Pulmonary Dept, 5 E 98 St Fl 8, New York, NY 10029; **Phone:** 212-241-5656; **Board Cert:** Internal Medicine 2012; Pulmonary Disease 2006; Critical Care Medicine 2010; **Med School:** Univ Chicago-Pritzker Sch Med 1989; **Resid:** Internal Medicine, NY-Presby/Columbia Univ Med Ctr 1993; **Fellow:** Pulmonary Critical Care Medicine, Bostom Med Ctr 1996; **Fac Appt:** Prof Med, Mount Sinai Sch Med

Prager, Kenneth MD (Pul) - **Spec Exp:** Lung Disease; Asthma; Ethics; **Hospital:** NY-Presby/Columbia Univ Med Ctr, NY (page 102); **Address:** 161 Ft Washington Ave, Ste 312, New York, NY 10032; **Phone:** 212-305-5535; **Board Cert:** Internal Medicine 1973; **Med School:** Harvard Med Sch 1968; **Resid:** Internal Medicine, Columbia-Presby Med Ctr 1972; Internal Medicine, Billings Hosp 1973; **Fac Appt:** Clin Prof Med, Columbia P&S

Raskin, Jonathan MD (Pul) - **Spec Exp:** Asthma; Chronic Obstructive Lung Disease (COPD); Pulmonary Rehabilitation; **Hospital:** Mt Sinai Beth Israel, Lenox Hill Hosp; **Address:** 1000 Park Ave, New York, NY 10028-0934; **Phone:** 212-288-4600; **Board Cert:** Internal Medicine 1982; Pulmonary Disease 1984; **Med School:** Mexico 1978; **Resid:** Internal Medicine, Beth Israel Med Ctr 1982; **Fellow:** Pulmonary Disease, Mount Sinai Hosp 1985; **Fac Appt:** Asst Clin Prof Med, Albert Einstein Coll Med

Sanders, Abraham MD (Pul) - **Hospital:** NY-Presby/Weill Cornell Med Ctr, NY (page 102), Hosp For Special Surgery (page 109); **Address:** 425 E 61st St Fl 4, New York, NY 10021; **Phone:** 646-962-2333; **Board Cert:** Internal Medicine 1979; Pulmonary Disease 1982; Critical Care Medicine 2008; **Med School:** SUNY Downstate 1976; **Resid:** Internal Medicine, Univ Hosp/Kings County Hosp 1980; **Fellow:** Pulmonary Disease, Kings County Hosp 1981; **Fac Appt:** Assoc Prof Med, Cornell Univ-Weill Med Coll

Schluger, Neil MD (Pul) - **Spec Exp:** Tuberculosis; **Hospital:** NY-Presby/Columbia Univ Med Ctr, NY (page 102); **Address:** NY-Presby, Pulmonology Dept, 161 Fort Washington Ave Fl 3, New York, NY 10032; **Phone:** 212-305-1544; **Board Cert:** Internal Medicine 1988; Pulmonary Disease 2013; **Med School:** Univ Pennsylvania 1985; **Resid:** Internal Medicine, St Lukes Hosp 1989; **Fellow:** Pulmonary Critical Care Medicine, NY-Presby/Weill Cornell Med Ctr 1992; **Fac Appt:** Prof Med, Columbia P&S

Schultz, Barbara L MD (Pul) - **Hospital:** Mt Sinai Hosp; **Address:** 1120 Park Ave, New York, NY 10028; **Phone:** 212-517-8680; **Board Cert:** Internal Medicine 1986; Pulmonary Disease 1988; **Med School:** Mount Sinai Sch Med 1983; **Resid:** Internal Medicine, Mt Sinai Hosp 1986; **Fellow:** Pulmonary Disease, Mt Sinai Hosp 1988; **Fac Appt:** Asst Clin Prof Med, Mount Sinai-Icahn Sch of Med

Steiger, David MD (Pul) - **Spec Exp:** Rheumatologic Diseases of the Lung; Thromboembolic Disorders; Pulmonary Hypertension; Critical Care; **Hospital:** NYU Hosp For Joint Dis (page 104), NYU Langone Med Ctr (page 104); **Address:** 301 E 17th St Fl 5 - Ste 550, New York, NY 10003; **Phone:** 212-598-6422; **Board Cert:** Internal Medicine 1987; Critical Care Medicine 2005; Pulmonary Disease 2013; **Med School:** England, UK 1981; **Resid:** Internal Medicine, St Thomas Hosp 1984; Internal Medicine, St Lukes-Roosevelt Hosp 1989; **Fellow:** Pulmonary Disease, UCSF Med Ctr 1994; **Fac Appt:** Asst Prof Med, NYU Sch Med

Stein, Sidney K MD (Pul) - **Spec Exp:** Asthma; Bronchitis; Emphysema; Hiccups-Chronic; **Hospital:** Mt Sinai Beth Israel; **Address:** 55 E 34th St Fl 6, New York, NY 10016-4337; **Phone:** 212-879-7777; **Board Cert:** Internal Medicine 1982; Pulmonary Disease 1988; **Med School:** SUNY Hlth Sci Ctr 1979; **Resid:** Internal Medicine, Beth Israel Med Ctr 1982; **Fellow:** Pulmonary Disease, Beth Israel Med Ctr 1984; **Fac Appt:** Asst Clin Prof Med, Albert Einstein Coll Med

Stover-Pepe, Diane E MD (Pul) - **Spec Exp:** Interstitial Lung Disease; Pulmonary Infections; Pulmonary Disease/Immunocompromised; Bronchiolitis Obliterans; **Hospital:** Meml Sloan Kettering Canc Ctr (page 110); **Address:** 1275 York Ave, New York, NY 10065; **Phone:** 212-639-8380; **Board Cert:** Internal Medicine 1975; Pulmonary Disease 1978; **Med School:** Albert Einstein Coll Med 1970; **Resid:** Internal Medicine, Harlem Hosp Ctr 1972; Internal Medicine, NY Hosp-Cornell Med Ctr 1975; **Fellow:** Pulmonary Disease, Montefiore Med Ctr 1977; **Fac Appt:** Prof Med, Cornell Univ-Weill Med Coll

Sukumaran, Muthiah MD (Pul) - **Spec Exp:** Asthma; Chronic Obstructive Lung Disease (COPD); Lung Cancer; Tuberculosis; **Hospital:** NYU Langone Med Ctr (page 104); **Address:** Trinty Medical Centre, 111 Broadway Fl 2, New York, NY 10006; **Phone:** 212-263-9700; **Board Cert:** Internal Medicine 1976; Pulmonary Disease 1980; **Med School:** India 1973; **Resid:** Internal Medicine, Elmhurst City Hosp 1976; **Fellow:** Pulmonary Disease, Elmhurst City Hosp 1977; **Fac Appt:** Assoc Clin Prof Med, NY Med Coll

Thomashow, Byron MD (Pul) - **Spec Exp:** Emphysema & Asthma; Respiratory Failure; Chronic Obstructive Lung Disease (COPD); Interstitial Lung Disease; **Hospital:** NY-Presby/Columbia Univ Med Ctr, NY (page 102); **Address:** NY-Presby, Pulmonology, 161 Fort Washington Ave, Ste 311, New York, NY 10032; **Phone:** 212-305-5261; **Board Cert:** Internal Medicine 1977; Pulmonary Disease 1980; **Med School:** Columbia P&S 1974; **Resid:** Internal Medicine, St Lukes-Roosevelt Hosp 1977; Pulmonary Disease, St Lukes-Roosevelt Hosp 1978; **Fellow:** Pulmonary Disease, Harlem Hosp Ctr 1979; **Fac Appt:** Clin Prof Med, Columbia P&S

Yip, Chun K MD (Pul) - **Spec Exp:** Asthma; Emphysema; Chronic Obstructive Lung Disease (COPD); **Hospital:** NY-Presby/Columbia Univ Med Ctr, NY (page 102); **Address:** 67 Hudson St, Ste 1A, New York, NY 10013; **Phone:** 212-305-8548; **Board Cert:** Internal Medicine 1979; Pulmonary Disease 1984; **Med School:** Albert Einstein Coll Med 1976; **Resid:** Internal Medicine, Columbia-Presby Med Ctr 1979; **Fellow:** Pulmonary Disease, Bellevue Hosp Ctr 1981; **Fac Appt:** Clin Prof Med, Columbia P&S

Radiation Oncology

Chadha, Manjeet MD (RadRO) - **Spec Exp:** Breast Cancer; Gynecologic Cancer; Intensity Modulated Radiotherapy (IMRT); **Hospital:** Mt Sinai Beth Israel, Mt Sinai St. Luke's; **Address:** BIMC, Radiation Oncology, 10 Union Square E, Ste 4G, New York, NY 10003; **Phone:** 212-844-8022; **Board Cert:** Therapeutic Radiology 1985; **Med School:** India 1980; **Resid:** Radiation Oncology, NY-Presby/Columbia Univ Med Ctr 1983; Radiation Oncology, Meml Sloan-Kettering Cancer Ctr 1986; **Fac Appt:** Prof RadRO, Albert Einstein Coll Med

Chao, K.S. Clifford MD (RadRO) - **Spec Exp:** Intensity Modulated Radiotherapy (IMRT); Head & Neck Cancer; Prostate Cancer; **Hospital:** NY-Presby/Weill Cornell Med Ctr, NY (page 102); **Address:** NY-Presby, Radiation Oncology, 525 E 68th St, rm N046, New York, NY 10065; **Phone:** 212-746-3608; **Board Cert:** Radiation Oncology 2010; **Med School:** Taiwan 1982; **Resid:** Radiation Oncology, Mallinckrodt Radiation Inst 1993; **Fellow:** Radiation Oncology, Mallinckrodt Radiation Inst 1994; **Fac Appt:** Prof RadRO, Cornell Univ-Weill Med Coll

Cohen, Richard F MD (RadRO) - **Spec Exp:** Chemo-Radiation Combined Therapy; Cancer Survivors-Late Effects of Therapy; **Hospital:** NYU Langone Med Ctr (page 104); **Address:** NYU, Radiation Oncology, 160 E 34th St, rm LL1, New York, NY 10016; **Phone:** 212-731-5003; **Board Cert:** Radiation Oncology 2012; **Med School:** NY Med Coll 1990; **Resid:** Surgery, Univ Conn Hlth Ctr 1991; Otolaryngology, Univ Conn Hlth Ctr 1994; **Fellow:** Radiation Oncology, NYU Med Ctr 1998; **Fac Appt:** Asst Prof RadRO, NYU Sch Med

Ennis, Ronald D MD (RadRO) - **Spec Exp:** Prostate Cancer; Brachytherapy; Breast Cancer; Stereotactic Radiosurgery; **Hospital:** Mt Sinai Roosevelt, Mt Sinai Beth Israel; **Address:** Mt Sinai Roosevelt, Dept Radiation Oncology, 1000 10th Ave, Lower Level, New York, NY 10019; **Phone:** 212-636-3345; **Board Cert:** Radiation Oncology 2004; **Med School:** Yale Univ 1990; **Resid:** Therapeutic Radiology, Yale-New Haven Hosp 1994; **Fac Appt:** Assoc Prof RadRO, Mount Sinai-Icahn Sch of Med

Evans, Andrew MD (RadRO) - **Spec Exp:** Breast Cancer; Lung Cancer; Thoracic Cancers; **Hospital:** Mt Sinai Roosevelt; **Address:** Roosevelt Hosp, Radiation Oncology, 1000 10th Ave, New York, NY 10019; **Phone:** 212-523-7166; **Board Cert:** Radiation Oncology 2011; **Med School:** South Africa 1988; **Resid:** Radiation Oncology, Montefiore Med Ctr 1993; **Fellow:** Radiation Oncology, Cross Cancer Inst 1994; Radiation Oncology, Montefiore Med Ctr 1996; **Fac Appt:** Asst Prof RadRO, Albert Einstein Coll Med

Formenti, Silvia C MD (RadRO) - **Spec Exp:** Breast Cancer; Chemo-Radiation Combined Therapy; **Hospital:** NYU Langone Med Ctr (page 104); **Address:** NYU Med Ctr, Radiation Oncology, 160 E 34th St, New York, NY 10016; **Phone:** 212-263-2601; **Board Cert:** Radiation Oncology 1991; **Med School:** Italy 1980; **Resid:** Internal Medicine, San Carlo Borromeo Hosp 1983; Medical Oncology, Univ Pavia Med Ctr 1985; **Fellow:** Radiation Oncology, LAC & USC Med Ctr 1990; **Fac Appt:** Prof RadRO, NYU Sch Med

Goodman, Karyn MD (RadRO) - **Spec Exp:** Gastrointestinal Cancer; Stereotactic Radiosurgery; Chemo-Radiation Combined Therapy; Brachytherapy; **Hospital:** Meml Sloan Kettering Canc Ctr (page 110); **Address:** MSKCC, Radiation Oncology, 1275 York Ave, Box 22, New York, NY 10065; **Phone:** 212-639-3983; **Board Cert:** Radiation Oncology 2005; **Med School:** Stanford Univ 1999; **Resid:** Radiation Oncology, Meml Sloan-Kettering Cancer Ctr 2004

Harrison, Louis B MD (RadRO) - **Spec Exp:** Brachytherapy; Head & Neck Cancer; Radiation Therapy-Intraoperative; Melanoma; **Hospital:** Mt Sinai Beth Israel, Mt Sinai St. Luke's; **Address:** BIMC, Radiation Oncology, 10 Union Square E, Ste 4G, New York, NY 10003; **Phone:** 212-844-8087; **Board Cert:** Therapeutic Radiology 1986; **Med School:** SUNY Downstate 1982; **Resid:** Therapeutic Radiology, Yale-New Haven Hosp 1986; **Fac Appt:** Prof RadRO, Albert Einstein Coll Med

Hu, Kenneth S MD (RadRO) - **Spec Exp:** Head & Neck Cancer; Gastrointestinal Cancer; Brachytherapy; **Hospital:** Mt Sinai Beth Israel; **Address:** Mt Sinai Beth Israel, Radiation Onc Dept, 10 Union Square E, Ste 4F, New York, NY 10003; **Phone:** 212-844-2022; **Board Cert:** Radiation Oncology 2010; **Med School:** Harvard Med Sch 1994; **Resid:** Radiation Oncology, Meml Sloan-Kettering Cancer Ctr 1998; **Fellow:** Brachytherapy, Meml Sloan-Kettering Cancer Ctr 1999; **Fac Appt:** Assoc Prof RadRO, Albert Einstein Coll Med

Isaacson, Steven R MD (RadRO) - **Spec Exp:** Brain Tumors; Neuro-Oncology; Stereotactic Radiosurgery; Gliomas; **Hospital:** NY-Presby/Columbia Univ Med Ctr, NY (page 102); **Address:** NY Presby, Radiation Oncology, 622 W 168th St BHN Bldg - rm B-11, New York, NY 10032; **Phone:** 212-305-2611; **Board Cert:** Radiation Oncology 1988; Otolaryngology 1978; **Med School:** Jefferson Med Coll 1973; **Resid:** Otolaryngology, Hosp Univ Penn 1978; Radiation Oncology, SUNY Hlth Sci Ctr 1988; **Fac Appt:** Clin Prof RadRO, Columbia P&S

Lee, Nancy MD (RadRO) - **Spec Exp:** Intensity Modulated Radiotherapy (IMRT); Head & Neck Cancer; Thyroid Cancer; Nasopharyngeal Cancer; **Hospital:** Meml Sloan Kettering Canc Ctr (page 110); **Address:** MSKCC, Radiation Oncology, 1275 York Ave, New York, NY 10065; **Phone:** 212-639-3341; **Board Cert:** Radiation Oncology 2010; **Med School:** UMDNJ-NJ Med Sch, Newark 1995; **Resid:** Radiation Oncology, NY-Presby/Columbia Univ Med Ctr 2000

Lymberis, Stella C MD (RadRO) - **Spec Exp:** Gynecologic Cancer; Cancer Survivors-Late Effects of Therapy; Chemo-Radiation Combined Therapy; **Hospital:** NYU Langone Med Ctr (page 104); **Address:** NYU Clin Cancer Ctr, Radiation Oncology, 160 E 34th St, rm LL1, New York, NY 10016; **Phone:** 212-731-5003; **Board Cert:** Radiation Oncology 2006; **Med School:** Albert Einstein Coll Med 2000; **Resid:** Radiation Oncology, NYU Med Ctr 2005; **Fac Appt:** Asst Clin Prof RadRO, NYU Sch Med

McCormick, Beryl MD (RadRO) - **Spec Exp:** Breast Cancer; Eye Tumors/Cancer; **Hospital:** Meml Sloan Kettering Canc Ctr (page 110); **Address:** MSKCC, Radiation Oncology, 1275 York Ave, New York, NY 10065; **Phone:** 212-639-6828; **Board Cert:** Therapeutic Radiology 1977; **Med School:** UMDNJ-NJ Med Sch, Newark 1973; **Resid:** Therapeutic Radiology, Meml Sloan-Kettering Cancer Ctr 1977; **Fac Appt:** Prof RadRO, Cornell Univ-Weill Med Coll

Ng, John Paul Tracy MD (RadRO) - **Spec Exp:** Prostate Cancer; Head & Neck Cancer; **Hospital:** Lenox Hill Hosp, NY-Presby/Lower Manhattan Hosp (page 102); **Address:** Tribeca Radiation, 408 Broadway, New York, NY 10013; **Phone:** 212-925-8882; **Board Cert:** Radiation Oncology 1993; **Med School:** Albert Einstein Coll Med 1988; **Resid:** Radiation Oncology, Meml Sloan Kettering Cancer Ctr 1992

Nori, Dattatreyudu MD (RadRO) - **Spec Exp:** Prostate Cancer; Brachytherapy; Lung Cancer; Breast Cancer; **Hospital:** NY-Presby/Weill Cornell Med Ctr, NY (page 102), NY Hosp Queens (page 498); **Address:** 525 E 68th St, New York, NY 10065; **Phone:** 212-746-3679; **Board Cert:** Therapeutic Radiology 1979; **Med School:** India 1970; **Resid:** Radiation Oncology, Meml Sloan Kettering Cancer Ctr 1975; **Fellow:** Radiation Oncology, Meml Sloan Kettering Cancer Ctr 1978; **Fac Appt:** Prof RadRO, Cornell Univ-Weill Med Coll

Parashar, Bhupesh MD (RadRO) - **Spec Exp:** Head & Neck Cancer; Lung Cancer; **Hospital:** NY-Presby/Weill Cornell Med Ctr, NY (page 102); **Address:** NY Presby/Weill Cornell Med Ctr, 525 E 68th St, rm N-046, Stitch Radiation Ctr, New York, NY 10065; **Phone:** 212-746-3612; **Board Cert:** Radiation Oncology 2006; **Med School:** India 1995; **Resid:** Radiation Oncology, Montefiore Med Ctr 2005; **Fac Appt:** Assoc Clin Prof RadRO, Cornell Univ-Weill Med Coll

Pollack, Jed M MD (RadRO) - **Spec Exp:** Head & Neck Cancer; Prostate Cancer; Brain Tumors; **Hospital:** Lenox Hill Hosp; **Address:** Lenox Hill Hosp-Radiation Medicine, 100 E 77th St, New York, NY 10075; **Phone:** 516-321-3000; **Board Cert:** Therapeutic Radiology 1985; **Med School:** Univ New Mexico 1981; **Resid:** Therapeutic Radiology, Meml Sloan-Kettering Cancer Ctr 1985; **Fac Appt:** Asst Clin Prof

Rosenbaum, Alfred MD (RadRO) - **Spec Exp:** Breast Cancer; Prostate Cancer; Intensity Modulated Radiotherapy (IMRT); **Hospital:** Mt Sinai Hosp, Lenox Hill Hosp; **Address:** Rosetta Radiology, 1421 Third Ave, New York, NY 10028; **Phone:** 212-744-5538; **Board Cert:** Diagnostic Radiology 1973; **Med School:** Germany 1966; **Resid:** Diagnostic Radiology, Maimonides Med Ctr 1970; Radiation Oncology, Mount Sinai Hosp 1972; **Fellow:** Radiology, Montefiore Med Ctr 1973; **Fac Appt:** Asst Clin Prof Rad, Mount Sinai Sch Med

Schiff, Peter B MD/PhD (RadRO) - **Spec Exp:** Prostate Cancer; Gynecologic Cancer; Lung Cancer; **Hospital:** NYU Langone Med Ctr (page 104); **Address:** NYU Clinical Cancer Ctr, 160 E 34th St Fl 1, New York, NY 10016; **Phone:** 212-731-5003; **Board Cert:** Radiation Oncology 1990; **Med School:** Albert Einstein Coll Med 1984; **Resid:** Radiation Oncology, Meml Sloan Kettering Cancer Ctr 1988; **Fac Appt:** Prof RadRO, NYU Sch Med

Stock, Richard MD (RadRO) - **Spec Exp:** Prostate Cancer; Urologic Cancer; Intensity Modulated Radiotherapy (IMRT); **Hospital:** Mt Sinai Hosp; **Address:** Eastside Radiation Oncology, 61 E 77th St, New York, NY 10075; **Phone:** 212-772-2130; **Board Cert:** Radiation Oncology 1993; **Med School:** Mount Sinai Sch Med 1988; **Resid:** Radiation Oncology, Meml Sloan-Kettering Cancer Ctr 1992; **Fac Appt:** Prof RadRO, Mount Sinai-Icahn Sch of Med

Wolden, Suzanne L MD (RadRO) - **Spec Exp:** Pediatric Cancers; Sarcoma-Soft Tissue; Brain Tumors; Head & Neck Cancer; **Hospital:** Meml Sloan Kettering Canc Ctr (page 110); **Address:** MSK Cancer Ctr, Radiation Oncology, 1275 York Ave Fl 4, New York, NY 10065; **Phone:** 212-639-5148; **Board Cert:** Radiation Oncology 2010; **Med School:** UCSF 1994; **Resid:** Radiation Oncology, Stanford Univ Med Ctr 1998

Yahalom, Joachim MD (RadRO) - **Spec Exp:** Lymphoma; Hodgkin's Lymphoma; Multiple Myeloma; **Hospital:** Meml Sloan Kettering Canc Ctr (page 110); **Address:** MSKCC, Radiation Oncology, 1275 York Ave, New York, NY 10065; **Phone:** 212-639-5999; **Board Cert:** Radiation Oncology 1988; **Med School:** Israel 1976; **Resid:** Internal Medicine, Hadassah Hosp 1979; Radiation Oncology, Hadassah Hosp 1984; **Fellow:** Radiation Oncology, Meml Sloan-Kettering Canc Ctr 1986; **Fac Appt:** Prof RadRO, Cornell Univ-Weill Med Coll

Yamada, Yoshiya MD (RadRO) - **Spec Exp:** Brain Tumors; Stereotactic Radiosurgery; Brachytherapy; Genitourinary Cancer; **Hospital:** Meml Sloan Kettering Canc Ctr (page 110); **Address:** MSKCC, Radiation Oncology, 1275 York St, New York, NY 10021; **Phone:** 212-639-2950; **Board Cert:** Radiation Oncology 2010; **Med School:** Canada 1993; **Resid:** Radiation Oncology, Princess Margaret Hosp 1998; **Fellow:** Radiation Oncology, Meml Sloan-Kettering Cancer Ctr 1999

Zelefsky, Michael J MD (RadRO) - **Spec Exp:** Prostate Cancer; Brachytherapy; Head & Neck Cancer; **Hospital:** Meml Sloan Kettering Canc Ctr (page 110); **Address:** MSKCC, Radiation Oncology, 1275 York Ave, New York, NY 10065; **Phone:** 212-639-3716; **Board Cert:** Radiation Oncology 1991; **Med School:** Albert Einstein Coll Med 1986; **Resid:** Radiation Oncology, Meml Sloan-Kettering Cancer Ctr 1990; **Fac Appt:** Prof RadRO, Cornell Univ-Weill Med Coll

Reproductive Endocrinology

Brown, Jessica Rosenberg MD (RE) - **Spec Exp:** Infertility-IVF; Polycystic Ovarian Syndrome; Menopause Problems; **Hospital:** NYU Langone Med Ctr (page 104); **Address:** Madison Womens Hlth & Fertility, 50 E 77 St, New York, NY 10075; **Phone:** 212-639-9122; **Board Cert:** Obstetrics & Gynecology 2013; Reproductive Endocrinology 2013; **Med School:** NYU Sch Med 1987; **Resid:** Obstetrics & Gynecology, NY-Presby/Weill Cornell Med Ctr 1991; **Fellow:** Reproductive Endocrinology, Univ Hosp-UMDNJ 1993; **Fac Appt:** Asst Clin Prof ObG, NYU Sch Med

Chang, Peter L MD (RE) - **Spec Exp:** Infertility-IVF; Polycystic Ovarian Syndrome; Ovarian Failure; **Hospital:** Mt Sinai Beth Israel; **Address:** Center Infertility & Reproductive Health, 10 Union Square East, Ste 2E, New York, NY 10003; **Phone:** 212-844-8587; **Board Cert:** Obstetrics & Gynecology 2013; Reproductive Endocrinology/Infertility 2013; **Med School:** Univ Tex, San Antonio 1992; **Resid:** Obstetrics & Gynecology, Univ Hosp 1996; **Fellow:** Reproductive Endocrinology, Columbia P&S 1998; **Fac Appt:** Asst Prof ObG, Albert Einstein Coll Med

Choi, Janet M K MD (RE) - **Spec Exp:** Infertility-IVF; Fertility Preservation; Infertility-Advanced Maternal Age; Pregnancy Loss-Recurrent; **Hospital:** NY-Presby/Columbia Univ Med Ctr, NY (page 102); **Address:** Center for Women's Reproductive Care, 1790 Broadway Fl 2, New York, NY 10019; **Phone:** 646-756-8282; **Board Cert:** Obstetrics & Gynecology 2014; Reproductive Endocrinology/Infertility 2004; **Med School:** Columbia P&S 1996; **Resid:** Obstetrics & Gynecology, NY Presby Hosp/Columbia 2000; **Fellow:** Reproductive Endocrinology, NY Presby Hosp/Weill Cornel 2003; **Fac Appt:** Asst Prof ObG, Columbia P&S

Cholst, Ina N MD (RE) - **Spec Exp:** Laparoscopic Surgery; Infertility-IVF; **Hospital:** NY-Presby/Weill Cornell Med Ctr, NY (page 102); **Address:** Ctr for Reproductive Med & Infertility, 1305 York Ave Fl 6, New York, NY 10021; **Phone:** 646-962-3025; **Board Cert:** Obstetrics & Gynecology 1984; Reproductive Endocrinology 1985; **Med School:** NYU Sch Med 1977; **Resid:** Obstetrics & Gynecology, Yale-New Haven Hosp 1981; **Fellow:** Reproductive Endocrinology, Columbia-Presby Med Ctr 1983; **Fac Appt:** Assoc Prof ObG, Cornell Univ-Weill Med Coll

Copperman, Alan B MD (RE) - **Spec Exp:** Fertility Preservation in Cancer; Infertility; Infertility-Female; Infertility-IVF; **Hospital:** Mt Sinai Hosp; **Address:** Reproductive Medicine Associates of NY, 635 Madison Ave Fl 10, New York, NY 10022; **Phone:** 212-756-5777; **Board Cert:** Obstetrics & Gynecology 2014; Reproductive Endocrinology 2013; **Med School:** NY Med Coll 1989; **Resid:** Obstetrics & Gynecology, Yale-New Haven Hosp 1993; **Fellow:** Reproductive Endocrinology, Mt Sinai Hosp 1995; **Fac Appt:** Clin Prof ObG, Mount Sinai-Icahn Sch of Med

David, Sami MD (RE) - **Spec Exp:** Infertility; Miscarriage-Recurrent; Endometriosis; Uterine Fibroids; **Hospital:** Mt Sinai Hosp; **Address:** 1045 Fifth Ave, Ste 1A, New York, NY 10028; **Phone:** 212-831-0430; **Board Cert:** Obstetrics & Gynecology 1980; **Med School:** Columbia P&S 1971; **Resid:** Obstetrics & Gynecology, New York Hosp 1976; **Fellow:** Reproductive Endocrinology, Hosp Univ Penn 1978; **Fac Appt:** Prof ObG, Mount Sinai Sch Med

Davis, Owen K MD (RE) - **Spec Exp:** Infertility-IVF; Reproductive Surgery; Menstrual Disorders; **Hospital:** NY-Presby/Weill Cornell Med Ctr, NY (page 102); **Address:** Ctr for Reproductive Med, 1305 York Ave, Fl 6, New York, NY 10021; **Phone:** 646-962-3765; **Board Cert:** Obstetrics & Gynecology 2013; Reproductive Endocrinology/Infertility 2013; **Med School:** Wake Forest Univ 1982; **Resid:** Obstetrics & Gynecology, NY-Presby/Weill Cornell Med Ctr 1986; **Fellow:** Reproductive Endocrinology, Brigham & Womens Hosp 1988; **Fac Appt:** Prof ObG, Cornell Univ-Weill Med Coll

Fateh, Majid MD (RE) - **Spec Exp:** Infertility-IVF; Laparoscopic Surgery; Endometriosis; **Hospital:** Lenox Hill Hosp; **Address:** New York Fertility Institute, 1016 5th Ave, New York, NY 10028-0132; **Phone:** 212-734-5555; **Board Cert:** Obstetrics & Gynecology 2013; **Med School:** West Indies 1980; **Resid:** Obstetrics & Gynecology, Lenox Hill Hosp 1984; **Fellow:** Reproductive Endocrinology, Univ Penn 1986

Flisser, Eric D MD (RE) - **Spec Exp:** Infertility-IVF; Polycystic Ovarian Syndrome; Preimplantation Genetic Diagnosis; Gynecologic Surgery; **Hospital:** Lenox Hill Hosp, Winthrop Univ Hosp (page 536); **Address:** Reproductive Medical Assocs of New York, 635 Madison Ave Fl 10, New York, NY 10022; **Phone:** 212-756-5777; **Board Cert:** Obstetrics & Gynecology 2013; Reproductive Endocrinology 2013; **Med School:** NYU Sch Med 1999; **Resid:** Obstetrics & Gynecology, NY Presby-Columbia Med Ctr 2003; **Fellow:** Reproductive Endocrinology, NYU Med Ctr 2006

Gleicher, Norbert MD (RE) - **Spec Exp:** Infertility-IVF; **Address:** Ctr Human Reproduction, 21 E 69 St, New York, NY 10021; **Phone:** 212-994-4400; **Board Cert:** Obstetrics & Gynecology 1998; **Med School:** Israel 1973; **Resid:** Obstetrics & Gynecology, Mount Sinai Med Ctr 1978; **Fellow:** Reproductive Immunology, Mount Sinai Med Ctr 1975

Grifo, James A MD/PhD (RE) - **Spec Exp:** Preimplantation Genetic Diagnosis; Fertility Preservation in Cancer; Hysteroscopic Surgery; Laparoscopic Surgery; **Hospital:** NYU Langone Med Ctr (page 104); **Address:** NYU Fertility Ctr, 660 1st Ave Fl 5, New York, NY 10016; **Phone:** 212-263-7978; **Board Cert:** Obstetrics & Gynecology 2013; Reproductive Endocrinology 2013; **Med School:** Case West Res Univ 1984; **Resid:** Obstetrics & Gynecology, NY-Presby/Weill Cornell Med Ctr 1988; **Fellow:** Reproductive Endocrinology, Yale-New Haven Hosp 1990; **Fac Appt:** Prof ObG, NYU Sch Med

Grunfeld, Lawrence MD (RE) - **Spec Exp:** Infertility-IVF; Fertility Preservation; **Hospital:** Mt Sinai Hosp; **Address:** Reproductive Medicine Associates of NY, 635 Madison Ave, Fl 10, New York, NY 10022; **Phone:** 212-756-5777; **Board Cert:** Obstetrics & Gynecology 2013; Reproductive Endocrinology 2013; **Med School:** Mount Sinai Sch Med 1979; **Resid:** Obstetrics & Gynecology, Montefiore Med Ctr 1984; **Fellow:** Reproductive Endocrinology, Montefiore Med Ctr 1987; **Fac Appt:** Assoc Clin Prof ObG, Mount Sinai-Icahn Sch of Med

Keefe, David L MD (RE) - **Spec Exp:** Infertility-IVF; Infertility-Advanced Maternal Age; **Hospital:** NYU Langone Med Ctr (page 104); **Address:** NYU Fertility Ctr, 660 1st Ave Fl 5, New York, NY 10016; **Phone:** 212-263-3360; **Board Cert:** Obstetrics & Gynecology 2013; Reproductive Endocrinology 2013; **Med School:** Georgetown Univ 1980; **Resid:** Psychiatry, Cambridge Hosp 1983; Obstetrics & Gynecology, Yale-New Haven Hosp 1989; **Fellow:** Neuroendocrinology, Northwestern Meml Hosp 1985; Reproductive Endocrinology, Yale-New Haven Hosp 1992; **Fac Appt:** Prof ObG, NYU Sch Med

Keltz, Martin D MD (RE) - **Spec Exp:** Infertility-IVF; Pregnancy Loss-Recurrent; **Hospital:** Mt Sinai Roosevelt; **Address:** 425 W 59th St, Ste 5A, New York, NY 10019; **Phone:** 212-523-7751; **Board Cert:** Obstetrics & Gynecology 2013; Reproductive Endocrinology 2013; **Med School:** NYU Sch Med 1989; **Resid:** Obstetrics & Gynecology, NYU-Bellevue Hosp 1993; **Fellow:** Reproductive Endocrinology, Yale-New Haven Hosp 1995; **Fac Appt:** Assoc Clin Prof ObG, Columbia P&S

Licciardi, Frederick L MD (RE) - **Spec Exp:** Fertility Preservation in Cancer; Reproductive Surgery; Infertility; Infertility-IVF; **Hospital:** NYU Langone Med Ctr (page 104); **Address:** NYU Fertility Ctr, 660 First Ave, 5th Fl, New York, NY 10016; **Phone:** 212-263-7754; **Board Cert:** Obstetrics & Gynecology 2013; Reproductive Endocrinology 2013; **Med School:** UMDNJ-Rutgers Med Sch 1986; **Resid:** Obstetrics & Gynecology, St Barnabas Med Ctr 1990; **Fellow:** Reproductive Endocrinology, NY Hosp-Cornell Med Ctr 1992; **Fac Appt:** Assoc Prof ObG, NYU Sch Med

Matera, Cristina MD (RE) - **Spec Exp:** Infertility; Miscarriage-Recurrent; Laparoscopic Surgery; Endometriosis; **Hospital:** NY-Presby/Columbia Univ Med Ctr, NY (page 102); **Address:** Madison Womens Hlth & Fertility, 50 E 77th St, New York, NY 10075; **Phone:** 212-639-9122; **Board Cert:** Obstetrics & Gynecology 2013; Reproductive Endocrinology 2013; **Med School:** NYU Sch Med 1986; **Resid:** Obstetrics & Gynecology, NY-Presby/Columbia Univ Med Ctr 1990; **Fellow:** Reproductive Endocrinology, NY-Presby/Columbia Univ Med Ctr 1992; **Fac Appt:** Asst Clin Prof ObG, Columbia P&S

McConnell, Rachel A MD (RE) - **Spec Exp:** Infertility-IVF; Fertility Preservation; Uterine Fibroids; **Hospital:** NY-Presby/Columbia Univ Med Ctr, NY (page 102), NY-Presby/Westchester Div, NY (page 102); **Address:** NY Presby, Womens Reproductive Care, 1790 Broadway Fl 4, New York, NY 10019; **Phone:** 646-756-8282; **Board Cert:** Obstetrics & Gynecology 2013; Reproductive Endocrinology/Infertility 2013; **Med School:** Louisiana State U, Shrevport 1986; **Resid:** Obstetrics & Gynecology, Tulane Univ Med Ctr 1990; **Fellow:** Reproductive Endocrinology, LAC & USC Med Ctr 1992; **Fac Appt:** Assoc Prof ObG, Columbia P&S

Mukherjee, Tanmoy MD (RE) - **Spec Exp:** Infertility-IVF; Endometriosis; Uterine Fibroids; **Hospital:** Mt Sinai Hosp; **Address:** Reproductive Medicine Associates of NY, 635 Madison Ave, Fl 10, New York, NY 10022; **Phone:** 212-756-5777; **Board Cert:** Obstetrics & Gynecology 2013; Reproductive Endocrinology 2013; **Med School:** Albert Einstein Coll Med 1990; **Resid:** Obstetrics & Gynecology, Montefiore Med Ctr 1994; **Fellow:** Reproductive Endocrinology, Mt Sinai Hosp 1996; **Fac Appt:** Asst Clin Prof ObG, Mount Sinai-Icahn Sch of Med

Noyes, Nicole MD (RE) - **Spec Exp:** Fertility Preservation in Cancer; Infertility-IVF; Infertility; **Hospital:** NYU Langone Med Ctr (page 104), Bellevue Hosp Ctr; **Address:** NYU Fertility Ctr, 660 First Ave, 5th FL, New York, NY 10016; **Phone:** 212-263-7981; **Board Cert:** Obstetrics & Gynecology 2013; Reproductive Endocrinology 2013; **Med School:** Univ VT Coll Med 1986; **Resid:** Obstetrics & Gynecology, NY Hosp-Cornell Med Ctr 1990; **Fellow:** Reproductive Endocrinology, NY Hosp-Cornell Med Ctr 1992; **Fac Appt:** Assoc Prof ObG, NYU Sch Med

Pfeifer, Samantha M MD (RE) - **Spec Exp:** Infertility-Female; Fertility Preservation; Laparoscopic Surgery; Congenital Anomalies-Gynecologic; **Hospital:** NY-Presby/Weill Cornell Med Ctr, NY (page 102); **Address:** 40 Worth St Fl 4, New York, NY 10013; **Phone:** 646-962-7499; **Board Cert:** Obstetrics & Gynecology 2013; Reproductive Endocrinology 2013; **Med School:** Univ Pennsylvania 1986; **Resid:** Obstetrics & Gynecology, Hosp Univ Penn 1990; **Fellow:** Reproductive Endocrinology, Univ Penn 1993; **Fac Appt:** Assoc Clin Prof ObG, Cornell Univ-Weill Med Coll

Quagliarello, John R MD (RE) - **Spec Exp:** Infertility; Gynecologic Surgery; Uterine Fibroids; Menopause Problems; **Hospital:** NYU Langone Med Ctr (page 104), Bellevue Hosp Ctr; **Address:** 530 1st Ave, Ste 10-Q, New York, NY 10016-6402; **Phone:** 212-263-6358; **Board Cert:** Obstetrics & Gynecology 1979; Reproductive Endocrinology/Infertility 1981; **Med School:** McGill Univ 1970; **Resid:** Obstetrics & Gynecology, NYU Med Ctr 1977; **Fellow:** Reproductive Endocrinology, NYU Med Ctr 1979; **Fac Appt:** Assoc Prof ObG, NYU Sch Med

Rosenwaks, Zev MD (RE) - **Spec Exp:** Infertility-IVF; Genetic Disorders; Fertility Preservation in Cancer; **Hospital:** NY-Presby/Weill Cornell Med Ctr, NY (page 102); **Address:** Ctr for Reproductive Med & Infertility, 1305 York Ave Fl 6, New York, NY 10021; **Phone:** 646-962-3743; **Board Cert:** Obstetrics & Gynecology 1978; Reproductive Endocrinology 1981; **Med School:** SUNY Downstate 1972; **Resid:** Obstetrics & Gynecology, LIJ Med Ctr 1976; **Fellow:** Reproductive Endocrinology, Johns Hopkins Hosp 1978; **Fac Appt:** Prof ObG, Cornell Univ-Weill Med Coll

Sauer, Mark V MD (RE) - **Spec Exp:** Infertility-IVF; Fertility Preservation in Cancer; **Hospital:** NY-Presby/Columbia Univ Med Ctr, NY (page 102); **Address:** Ctr for Womens Reproductive Care, 1790 Broadway Fl 2, New York, NY 10019; **Phone:** 646-756-8282; **Board Cert:** Obstetrics & Gynecology 2013; Reproductive Endocrinology 2013; **Med School:** Univ IL Coll Med 1980; **Resid:** Obstetrics & Gynecology, Univ IL Med Ctr 1984; **Fellow:** Reproductive Endocrinology, Harbor-UCLA Med Ctr 1986; **Fac Appt:** Prof ObG, Columbia P&S

Schattman, Glenn L MD (RE) - **Spec Exp:** Infertility; Robotic Assisted Laparoscopic Surgery; Minimally Invasive Surgery; Congenital Anomalies-Gynecologic; **Hospital:** NY-Presby/Weill Cornell Med Ctr, NY (page 102); **Address:** Ctr for Reproductive Med & Infertility, 1305 York Ave Fl 6, New York, NY 10021; **Phone:** 646-962-3836; **Board Cert:** Obstetrics & Gynecology 2013; Reproductive Endocrinology/Infertility 2013; **Med School:** SUNY Downstate 1987; **Resid:** Obstetrics & Gynecology, Geo Wash Univ Med Ctr 1991; **Fellow:** Reproductive Endocrinology/Infertility, New York Hosp/Cornell 1993; **Fac Appt:** Assoc Prof ObG, Cornell Univ-Weill Med Coll

Schmidt-Sarosi, Cecilia MD (RE) - **Spec Exp:** Infertility-IVF; Menopause Problems; Polycystic Ovarian Syndrome; Uterine Fibroids; **Hospital:** NYU Langone Med Ctr (page 104); **Address:** 51 E 67th St, New York, NY 10065; **Phone:** 212-535-5350; **Board Cert:** Obstetrics & Gynecology 2009; Reproductive Endocrinology/Infertility 2009; **Med School:** NYU Sch Med 1976; **Resid:** Obstetrics & Gynecology, NYU Med Ctr 1980; **Fellow:** Reproductive Endocrinology, NYU Med Ctr 1982; **Fac Appt:** Prof ObG, NYU Sch Med

Spandorfer, Steven MD (RE) - **Spec Exp:** Infertility-IVF; Laparoscopic Surgery; **Hospital:** NY-Presby/Weill Cornell Med Ctr, NY (page 102); **Address:** Ctr for Reproductive Med & Infertility, 1305 York Ave Fl 6, New York, NY 10021; **Phone:** 646-962-3638; **Board Cert:** Obstetrics & Gynecology 2013; Reproductive Endocrinology 2013; **Med School:** Emory Univ 1988; **Resid:** Obstetrics & Gynecology, Univ Penn Affil Hosp 1996; **Fellow:** Reproductive Endocrinology, New York Hosp 1998; **Fac Appt:** Asst Prof ObG, Cornell Univ-Weill Med Coll

Stein, Daniel E MD (RE) - **Spec Exp:** Infertility-IVF; Polycystic Ovarian Syndrome; Laparoscopic Surgery; Hormonal Disorders; **Hospital:** Mt Sinai Roosevelt; **Address:** RMA Westside, 425 W 59th St, Ste 5A, New York, NY 10019; **Phone:** 212-523-7751; **Board Cert:** Obstetrics & Gynecology 2013; Reproductive Endocrinology/Infertility 2013; **Med School:** NY Med Coll 1989; **Resid:** Obstetrics & Gynecology, Thomas Jefferson Univ Hosp 1995; **Fellow:** Reproductive Endocrinology, UMDNJ-New Jersey Med Sch 1997

Sultan, Khalid M MD (RE) - **Spec Exp:** Infertility-IVF; Laparoscopic Surgery; **Hospital:** Lenox Hill Hosp; **Address:** New York Fertility Inst, 1016 5th Ave, New York, NY 10028; **Phone:** 212-734-5555; **Board Cert:** Obstetrics & Gynecology 2014; Reproductive Endocrinology 2014; **Med School:** NY Med Coll 1988; **Resid:** Obstetrics & Gynecology, Lenox Hill Hosp 1992; **Fellow:** Reproductive Endocrinology, New York Hosp 1994; **Fac Appt:** Asst Clin Prof ObG, NYU Sch Med

Tortoriello, Drew MD (RE) - **Spec Exp:** Infertility-IVF; Polycystic Ovarian Syndrome; **Hospital:** Mt Sinai Roosevelt; **Address:** 425 5th Ave, Fl 3, New York, NY 10016; **Phone:** 646-792-7476; **Board Cert:** Obstetrics & Gynecology 2014; Reproductive Endocrinology 2014; **Med School:** SUNY Downstate 1992; **Resid:** Obstetrics & Gynecology, NY Presby Hosp/Cornell 1996; **Fellow:** Reproductive Endocrinology, UMDNJ Affil Hosp 1998; Reproductive Endocrinology, Mass Genl Hosp

Warren, Michelle P MD (RE) - **Spec Exp:** Menopause Problems; Infertility; Menstrual Disorders; Women's Health; **Hospital:** NY-Presby/Columbia Univ Med Ctr, NY (page 102); **Address:** Center for Menopause,, Hormonal Disorders & Women's Health, 134 E 73rd St, New York, NY 10021; **Phone:** 212-737-4664; **Board Cert:** Internal Medicine 1972; Endocrinology 1973; **Med School:** Cornell Univ 1965; **Resid:** Internal Medicine, Bellevue Hosp Ctr 1968; Internal Medicine, Meml Hosp Cancer Ctr 1968; **Fellow:** Endocrinology, Columbia Presby Med Ctr 1971; **Fac Appt:** Prof ObG, Columbia P&S

Rheumatology

Adlersberg, Jay B MD (Rhu) - **Spec Exp:** Rheumatoid Arthritis; Psoriatic Arthritis; Osteoarthritis; Pain-Back; **Hospital:** Lenox Hill Hosp; **Address:** Medical Assocs East, 220 E 69th St, Ground FL, New York, NY 10021-5737; **Phone:** 212-570-1800; **Board Cert:** Internal Medicine 1972; Rheumatology 1980; **Med School:** Univ Pennsylvania 1969; **Resid:** Internal Medicine, Bellevue Hosp 1972; **Fellow:** Rheumatology/Immunology, Bellevue Hosp 1974; **Fac Appt:** Asst Clin Prof Med, NYU Sch Med

Agus, Bertrand MD (Rhu) - **Spec Exp:** Lupus/SLE; Rheumatoid Arthritis; Sarcoidosis; Gout; **Hospital:** NYU Langone Med Ctr (page 104); **Address:** 251 E 33rd St, Fl 4, New York, NY 10016-4804; **Phone:** 212-779-8421; **Board Cert:** Internal Medicine 1972; Rheumatology 1972; **Med School:** NYU Sch Med 1965; **Resid:** Internal Medicine, NYU Med Ctr 1970; **Fellow:** Rheumatology, NYU Med Ctr 1972; **Fac Appt:** Assoc Clin Prof Med, NYU Sch Med

Aizer, Juliet B MD (Rhu) - **Spec Exp:** Osteoporosis; Rheumatoid Arthritis; Osteoarthritis; Psoriatic Arthritis; **Hospital:** Hosp For Special Surgery (page 109); **Address:** Hospital Special Surgery, Rheumatology, 535 E 70th St, New York, NY 10021; **Phone:** 212-774-7056; **Board Cert:** Internal Medicine 2004; Rheumatology 2007; **Med School:** Cornell Univ 2001; **Resid:** Internal Medicine, Brigham & Women's Hosp 2004; **Fellow:** Rheumatology, Hosp for Special Surgery 2007; **Fac Appt:** Asst Prof Med, Cornell Univ-Weill Med Coll

Ali, Yousaf MD (Rhu) - **Spec Exp:** Gout; Osteoporosis; Behcet's Syndrome; **Hospital:** Mt Sinai Hosp; **Address:** Mt Sinai Faculty Practice Assocs, 5 E 98th St, Fl 11, New York, NY 10029; **Phone:** 212-241-1671; **Board Cert:** Internal Medicine 2008; Rheumatology 2009; **Med School:** England, UK 1992; **Resid:** Internal Medicine, OR Hlth & Sci Univ Hosp 1997; **Fellow:** Rheumatology, Yale-New Haven Hosp 1999; **Fac Appt:** Assoc Prof Med, Mount Sinai-Icahn Sch of Med

Ashany, Dalit MD (Rhu) - **Spec Exp:** Lupus/SLE; Rheumatoid Arthritis; Osteoarthritis; **Hospital:** Hosp For Special Surgery (page 109); **Address:** Hosp for Special Surg-Rheum Div, 525 E 71th St Fl 7, New York, NY 10021; **Phone:** 212-606-1671; **Board Cert:** Internal Medicine 1988; Rheumatology 2003; **Med School:** Albert Einstein Coll Med 1985; **Resid:** Internal Medicine, NY-Presby/Columbia Univ Med Ctr 1988; **Fellow:** Rheumatology, Hosp For Special Surgery 1991; **Fac Appt:** Asst Prof Med, Cornell Univ-Weill Med Coll

Bass, Anne R MD (Rhu) - **Spec Exp:** Lupus/SLE; Lyme Disease; Rheumatoid Arthritis; Vasculitis; **Hospital:** Hosp For Special Surgery (page 109), NY-Presby/Weill Cornell Med Ctr, NY (page 102); **Address:** Hosp for Special Surgery, Rheumatology, 535 E 70th St Fl 7, New York, NY 10021; **Phone:** 212-774-7043; **Board Cert:** Internal Medicine 1988; Rheumatology 2012; **Med School:** Columbia P&S 1985; **Resid:** Internal Medicine, NY Presby-Columbia Med Ctr 1988; **Fellow:** Rheumatology, NYU Med Ctr 1991; **Fac Appt:** Assoc Clin Prof Med, Cornell Univ-Weill Med Coll

Belmont, H. Michael MD (Rhu) - **Spec Exp:** Lupus/SLE; Antiphospholipid Syndrome (APS); Wegener's Granulomatosis; Rheumatoid Arthritis; **Hospital:** NYU Hosp For Joint Dis (page 104), NYU Langone Med Ctr (page 104); **Address:** NYU, Ctr Musculoskeletal Care, 333 E 38th St, Fl 4, New York, NY 10016; **Phone:** 646-501-7400; **Board Cert:** Internal Medicine 1983; Rheumatology 1986; **Med School:** Univ Pittsburgh 1980; **Resid:** Internal Medicine, Mount Sinai Med Ctr 1983; **Fellow:** Rheumatology, Bellevue Hosp Ctr 1985; **Fac Appt:** Assoc Prof Med, NYU Sch Med

Belostotsky, Olga MD/PhD (Rhu) - **Spec Exp:** Autoimmune Disorders; Asthma; Food & Drug Allergy; Immunodeficiency Disorders; **Hospital:** Lenox Hill Hosp, NS-LIJ Hlth Sys; **Address:** 47 E 77th St, Ste 201, New York, NY 10075; **Phone:** 646-688-3443; **Board Cert:** Internal Medicine 2005; Rheumatology 2010; **Med School:** Russia 1983; **Resid:** Allergy & Immunology, Brigham & Womens Hosp 1999; Internal Medicine, Lenox Hill Hosp 2002; **Fellow:** Rheumatology, N Shore Univ Hosp 2005; Allergy & Immunology, LIJ Med Ctr 2005; **Fac Appt:** Asst Clin Prof A&I, NYU Sch Med

Blume, Ralph S MD (Rhu) - **Spec Exp:** Vasculitis; Lupus/SLE; Rheumatoid Arthritis; **Hospital:** NY-Presby/Columbia Univ Med Ctr, NY (page 102); **Address:** NY-Presby, Rheumatology Dept, 161 Fort Washington Ave, Ste 638, New York, NY 10032; **Phone:** 212-305-5512; **Board Cert:** Internal Medicine 1972; Rheumatology 1974; **Med School:** Columbia P&S 1964; **Resid:** Internal Medicine, NY-Presby/Columbia Univ Med Ctr 1968; **Fellow:** Rheumatology, NY-Presby/Columbia Univ Med Ctr 1970; **Fac Appt:** Prof Med, Columbia P&S

Buyon, Jill P MD (Rhu) - **Spec Exp:** Lupus/SLE in Pregnancy; Lupus/SLE in Menopause; **Hospital:** NYU Hosp For Joint Dis (page 104), NYU Langone Med Ctr (page 104); **Address:** NYU Musculoskeletal Care, 333 E 38th St Fl 4, New York, NY 10016; **Phone:** 646-501-7400; **Board Cert:** Internal Medicine 1981; Rheumatology 1984; **Med School:** Albert Einstein Coll Med 1978; **Resid:** Internal Medicine, Montefiore Med Ctr 1981; **Fellow:** Rheumatology, NYU Med Ctr 1983; **Fac Appt:** Prof Med, NYU Sch Med

Crane, Richard P MD (Rhu) - **Spec Exp:** Rheumatoid Arthritis; Gout; Osteoarthritis; Arthritis; **Hospital:** Mt Sinai Hosp; **Address:** 1088 Park Ave, New York, NY 10128-1132; **Phone:** 212-860-8282; **Board Cert:** Internal Medicine 1984; Rheumatology 1986; **Med School:** Mount Sinai Sch Med 1981; **Resid:** Internal Medicine, Mt Sinai Hosp 1984; **Fellow:** Rheumatology, Mt Sinai Hosp 1986

Faller, Jason MD (Rhu) - **Spec Exp:** Gout; Rheumatoid Arthritis; Lyme Disease; Lupus/SLE; **Hospital:** Mt Sinai Roosevelt, Lenox Hill Hosp; **Address:** 333 W 57th St, Ste 104, New York, NY 10019; **Phone:** 212-307-6880; **Board Cert:** Internal Medicine 1980; Rheumatology 1982; **Med School:** Univ Pennsylvania 1977; **Resid:** Internal Medicine, Rush Presby St Lukes Med Ctr 1980; **Fellow:** Rheumatology, Univ Michigan Med Ctr 1982; **Fac Appt:** Asst Clin Prof Med, Mount Sinai-Icahn Sch of Med

Fields, Theodore R MD (Rhu) - **Spec Exp:** Gout; Rheumatoid Arthritis; Osteoarthritis; **Hospital:** Hosp For Special Surgery (page 109), NY-Presby/Weill Cornell Med Ctr, NY (page 102); **Address:** 535 E 70th St, Fl 8, Ste 848F, New York, NY 10021-4872; **Phone:** 212-606-1286; **Board Cert:** Internal Medicine 1979; Rheumatology 1982; **Med School:** SUNY Downstate 1976; **Resid:** Internal Medicine, Nassau Co Med Ctr 1979; **Fellow:** Rheumatology, Univ Hosp 1982; **Fac Appt:** Clin Prof Med, Cornell Univ-Weill Med Coll

Fischer, Harry D MD (Rhu) - **Spec Exp:** Lupus/SLE; Rheumatoid Arthritis; Vasculitis; **Hospital:** Mt Sinai Beth Israel; **Address:** 10 Union Square East, Ste 3D, New York, NY 10003-3314; **Phone:** 212-844-8101; **Board Cert:** Internal Medicine 1983; Rheumatology 2010; **Med School:** Mount Sinai Sch Med 1979; **Resid:** Internal Medicine, Beth Israel Med Ctr 1983; **Fellow:** Rheumatology, Hosp Joint Diseases 1985; **Fac Appt:** Assoc Prof Med, Mount Sinai-Icahn Sch of Med

Gibofsky, Allan MD (Rhu) - **Spec Exp:** Rheumatic Fever; Rheumatoid Arthritis; Inflammatory Arthritis; Behcet's Syndrome; **Hospital:** Hosp For Special Surgery (page 109), NY-Presby/Weill Cornell Med Ctr, NY (page 102); **Address:** 535 E 70th St, New York, NY 10021-4872; **Phone:** 212-606-1423; **Board Cert:** Internal Medicine 1977; Rheumatology 1980; **Med School:** Cornell Univ 1973; **Resid:** Internal Medicine, New York Hosp 1977; **Fellow:** Rheumatology/Immunology, Hosp for Special Surgery 1979; **Fac Appt:** Prof Med, Cornell Univ-Weill Med Coll

Golden, Brian D MD (Rhu) - **Spec Exp:** Rheumatoid Arthritis; **Hospital:** NYU Langone Med Ctr (page 104), NYU Hosp For Joint Dis (page 104); **Address:** NYU Rheumatology & Infusion Practice, 333 E 38th St Fl 4, New York, NY 10016; **Phone:** 646-501-7400; **Board Cert:** Internal Medicine 2004; Rheumatology 2006; **Med School:** Mount Sinai Sch Med 1991; **Resid:** Internal Medicine, Mount Sinai Hosp 1994; **Fellow:** Rheumatology, Hosp for Joint Diseases 1996

Goodman, Susan M MD (Rhu) - **Spec Exp:** Ankylosing Spondylitis; Rheumatoid Arthritis; Psoriatic Arthritis; **Hospital:** Hosp For Special Surgery (page 109), NY-Presby/Weill Cornell Med Ctr, NY (page 102); **Address:** Hosp for Special Surgery, 535 E 70th St, New York, NY 10021; **Phone:** 212-606-1163; **Board Cert:** Internal Medicine 1980; Rheumatology 1982; **Med School:** Univ Cincinnati 1977; **Resid:** Internal Medicine, Lenox Hill Hosp 1980; **Fellow:** Rheumatology, Columbia Presby Hosp 1983; **Fac Appt:** Asst Clin Prof Med, Cornell Univ-Weill Med Coll

Gorevic, Peter D MD (Rhu) - **Spec Exp:** Autoimmune Disease; Amyloidosis/Joint Disease; Cryoglobulinemia; **Hospital:** Mt Sinai Hosp; **Address:** Mount Sinai Med Ctr, Rheumatology Dept, 5 E 98th St Fl 11, New York, NY 10029; **Phone:** 212-241-1671; **Board Cert:** Internal Medicine 1973; Rheumatology 1976; Allergy & Immunology 1977; Diagnostic Lab Immunology 1986; **Med School:** NYU Sch Med 1970; **Resid:** Internal Medicine, NYU Med Ctr 1973; **Fellow:** Rheumatology, NYU Med Ctr 1975; Allergy & Immunology, NYU Med Ctr 1977; **Fac Appt:** Prof Med, Mount Sinai Sch Med

Greisman, Stewart G MD (Rhu) - **Spec Exp:** Lupus/SLE; Rheumatoid Arthritis; **Hospital:** Mt Sinai Roosevelt, Hosp For Special Surgery (page 109); **Address:** 457 W 57th St, Ste 106, New York, NY 10019; **Phone:** 212-265-1471; **Board Cert:** Internal Medicine 1984; Rheumatology 1986; **Med School:** Yale Univ 1981; **Resid:** Internal Medicine, Yale-New Haven Hosp 1984; **Fellow:** Rheumatology, Hosp Special Surgery 1986; **Fac Appt:** Assoc Clin Prof Med, Columbia P&S

Honig, Stephen MD (Rhu) - **Spec Exp:** Osteoporosis; Rheumatoid Arthritis; Osteoarthritis; **Hospital:** NYU Hosp For Joint Dis (page 104), NYU Langone Med Ctr (page 104); **Address:** 301 E 17th St, Ste 1100, New York, NY 10003-3804; **Phone:** 212-598-6367; **Board Cert:** Internal Medicine 1975; Rheumatology 1978; **Med School:** Univ Tenn Coll Med 1972; **Resid:** Internal Medicine, St Vincent's Hosp Med Ctr 1975; **Fellow:** Rheumatology, NYU Med Ctr 1977; **Fac Appt:** Assoc Clin Prof Med, NYU Sch Med

Horowitz, Mark D MD (Rhu) - **Spec Exp:** Lupus/SLE; Rheumatoid Arthritis; Fibromyalgia; **Hospital:** Mt Sinai Hosp; **Address:** 21 E 90th St, Ground Fl, New York, NY 10128-0654; **Phone:** 212-860-3077; **Board Cert:** Internal Medicine 1986; **Med School:** NE Ohio Univ 1983; **Resid:** Internal Medicine, Mt Sinai Med Ctr 1986; **Fellow:** Rheumatology, Mt Sinai Med Ctr 1989

Kerr, Leslie D MD (Rhu) - **Spec Exp:** Connective Tissue Disorders; Geriatric Rheumatology; Gout; Rheumatoid Arthritis; **Hospital:** Mt Sinai Hosp; **Address:** Mount Sinai Med Ctr, 5 E 98th St, 11th Fl, New York, NY 10029; **Phone:** 212-241-1671; **Board Cert:** Internal Medicine 1983; Rheumatology 1986; **Med School:** Columbia P&S 1980; **Resid:** Internal Medicine, Mt Sinai Hosp 1983; **Fellow:** Rheumatology, Mt Sinai Hosp 1985; **Fac Appt:** Assoc Prof Med, Mount Sinai Sch Med

Lee, Sicy H MD (Rhu) - **Spec Exp:** Rheumatoid Arthritis; Psoriatic Arthritis; Lupus/SLE; **Hospital:** NYU Hosp For Joint Dis (page 104), NYU Langone Med Ctr (page 104); **Address:** 333 E 38th St, Fl 4, New York, NY 10016; **Phone:** 646-501-7400; **Board Cert:** Internal Medicine 1982; Rheumatology 1984; **Med School:** Univ Cincinnati 1979; **Resid:** Internal Medicine, Good Samaritan 1982; **Fellow:** Rheumatology, Hosp for Joint Diseases 1985; **Fac Appt:** Asst Clin Prof Med, NYU Sch Med

Lipschitz, Robin L MD (Rhu) - **Spec Exp:** Osteoarthritis; Rheumatoid Arthritis; Osteoporosis; **Hospital:** Mt Sinai Roosevelt; **Address:** Upper Manhattan Medical Group, 1049 Fifth Ave, Ste 2A, New York, NY 10028; **Phone:** 212-772-7686; **Board Cert:** Internal Medicine 1989; Rheumatology 2013; **Med School:** South Africa 1980; **Resid:** Internal Medicine, Albert Einstein Med Ctr 1986; **Fellow:** Rheumatology, SUNY Stonybrook Med Ctr 1988

MacKenzie, C Ronald MD (Rhu) - **Hospital:** Hosp For Special Surgery (page 109), NY-Presby/Weill Cornell Med Ctr, NY (page 102); **Address:** 535 E 70th St, New York, NY 10021; **Phone:** 212-606-1669; **Board Cert:** Internal Medicine 1981; Rheumatology 2012; **Med School:** Univ Calgary 1977; **Resid:** Family Medicine, Calgary Gen Hosp 1978; Internal Medicine, Univ Manitoba Hosp 1981; **Fellow:** Internal Medicine, New York Hosp/Cornell 1983; Rheumatology, Hosp For Spec Surg 1993; **Fac Appt:** Assoc Clin Prof Med, Cornell Univ-Weill Med Coll

Magid, Steven K MD (Rhu) - **Spec Exp:** Rheumatoid Arthritis; Osteoarthritis; Lyme Disease; Polymyalgia Rheumatica; **Hospital:** Hosp For Special Surgery (page 109); **Address:** HSS, Rheumatology, 535 E 70th St, Fl 7, New York, NY 10021; **Phone:** 212-606-1060; **Board Cert:** Internal Medicine 1979; Rheumatology 1984; **Med School:** Cornell Univ 1976; **Resid:** Internal Medicine, NY-Presby/Weill Cornell Med Ctr 1979; **Fellow:** Rheumatology, Hosp Special Surgery 1981; **Fac Appt:** Clin Prof Med, Cornell Univ-Weill Med Coll

Marchetta, Paula A MD (Rhu) - **Spec Exp:** Rheumatoid Arthritis; Psoriatic Arthritis; Sjogren's Syndrome; Osteoarthritis; **Hospital:** NYU Langone Med Ctr (page 104); **Address:** Concorde Med Grp, 40 Park Ave, New York, NY 10016; **Phone:** 212-696-5415; **Board Cert:** Internal Medicine 1986; Rheumatology 2010; **Med School:** NYU Sch Med 1983; **Resid:** Internal Medicine, NYU-Bellevue Hosp 1986; **Fellow:** Rheumatology, NYU Med Ctr 1989; **Fac Appt:** Assoc Clin Prof Med, NYU Sch Med

Markenson, Joseph A MD (Rhu) - **Spec Exp:** Rheumatoid Arthritis; Lupus/SLE; Osteoarthritis; **Hospital:** Hosp For Special Surgery (page 109), NY-Presby/Weill Cornell Med Ctr, NY (page 102); **Address:** Hosp for Special Surgery, 535 E 70th St, Ste 659W, New York, NY 10021-4892; **Phone:** 212-606-1261; **Board Cert:** Internal Medicine 1976; Rheumatology 1978; **Med School:** SUNY Downstate 1970; **Resid:** Internal Medicine, New York Hosp 1975; **Fellow:** Rheumatology, Hosp For Special Surg 1976; **Fac Appt:** Clin Prof Med, Cornell Univ-Weill Med Coll

Mayer, Elizabeth W MD (Rhu) - **Spec Exp:** Autoimmune Rheumatic Disorders; **Hospital:** NY-Presby/Columbia Univ Med Ctr, NY (page 102); **Address:** 161 Fort Washington Ave, Herbert Irving Pavilion, Fl 2, New York, NY 10032; **Phone:** 212-305-5213; **Board Cert:** Internal Medicine 2005; Rheumatology 2007; **Med School:** Columbia P&S 1992; **Resid:** Internal Medicine, NY-Presby/Columbia Univ Med Ctr 1995; **Fellow:** Rheumatology, NY-Presby/Columbia Univ Med Ctr 1998; **Fac Appt:** Assoc Clin Prof Med, Columbia P&S

Meed, Steven D MD (Rhu) - **Spec Exp:** Lyme Disease; Chronic Fatigue Syndrome; Acupuncture; Fibromyalgia; **Hospital:** Lenox Hill Hosp, Mt Sinai Roosevelt; **Address:** Advantage Care Physicians, 215 E 95th St, New York, NY 10128; **Phone:** 212-996-8000; **Board Cert:** Internal Medicine 1978; Rheumatology 1986; **Med School:** NYU Sch Med 1975; **Resid:** Internal Medicine, Brookdale Hosp 1977; **Fellow:** Rheumatology, Barnes Hosp-Wash Univ 1979; **Fac Appt:** Asst Clin Prof Med, NYU Sch Med

Mitnick, Hal J MD (Rhu) - **Spec Exp:** Rheumatoid Arthritis; Psoriatic Arthritis; Osteoporosis; Dermatomyositis; **Hospital:** NYU Langone Med Ctr (page 104); **Address:** 333 E 34th St, Ste 1C, New York, NY 10016; **Phone:** 212-889-7217; **Board Cert:** Internal Medicine 1976; Rheumatology 1978; **Med School:** NYU Sch Med 1972; **Resid:** Internal Medicine, NYU-Bellevue Hosp 1976; **Fellow:** Rheumatology, NYU Med Ctr 1978; **Fac Appt:** Clin Prof Med, NYU Sch Med

Nickerson, Katherine G MD (Rhu) - **Spec Exp:** Lupus/SLE; Rheumatoid Arthritis; Vasculitis; **Hospital:** NY-Presby/Columbia Univ Med Ctr, NY (page 102); **Address:** NY-Presby, Rheumatology, 161 Fort Washington Ave Fl 2, New York, NY 10032; **Phone:** 212-305-4308; **Board Cert:** Internal Medicine 1984; Rheumatology 1986; **Med School:** UCSF 1981; **Resid:** Internal Medicine, Beth Israel Deaconess Med Ctr 1984; **Fellow:** Rheumatology, NY-Presby/Columbia Univ Med Ctr 1986; **Fac Appt:** Prof Med, Columbia P&S

Paget, Stephen MD (Rhu) - **Spec Exp:** Rheumatoid Arthritis; Lupus/SLE; Vasculitis; Connective Tissue Disorders; **Hospital:** Hosp For Special Surgery (page 109); **Address:** HSS, Rheumatology Dept, 535 E 70th St Fl 7, New York, NY 10021; **Phone:** 212-606-1845; **Board Cert:** Internal Medicine 1974; Rheumatology 2009; **Med School:** SUNY Downstate 1971; **Resid:** Internal Medicine, Johns Hopkins Hosp 1973; **Fellow:** Rheumatology, Hosp Special Surgery 1975; **Fac Appt:** Prof Med, Cornell Univ-Weill Med Coll

Parrish, Edward MD (Rhu) - **Spec Exp:** Musculoskeletal Disorders in HIV/AIDS; Autoimmune Disease; **Hospital:** Hosp For Special Surgery (page 109), NY-Presby/Weill Cornell Med Ctr, NY (page 102); **Address:** 525 E 71st St Fl 7, New York, NY 10021; **Phone:** 212-606-1743; **Board Cert:** Internal Medicine 1983; Rheumatology 1986; **Med School:** Wake Forest Univ 1980; **Resid:** Internal Medicine, Columbia-Presby Med Ctr 1983; **Fellow:** Rheumatology/Immunology, Columbia-Presby Med Ctr 1985; **Fac Appt:** Asst Prof Med, Cornell Univ-Weill Med Coll

Rackoff, Paula J MD (Rhu) - **Spec Exp:** Osteoporosis; Sjogren's Syndrome; Arthritis; Lupus/SLE; **Hospital:** NYU Langone Med Ctr (page 104); **Address:** NYU Langone Med Ctr, Ctr for Musculoskeletal Care, 333 E 38th St Fl 4, New York, NY 10016; **Phone:** 646-501-7400; **Board Cert:** Internal Medicine 1989; Rheumatology 2004; **Med School:** Yale Univ 1986; **Resid:** Internal Medicine, Yale-New Haven Hosp 1989; **Fellow:** Rheumatology, Yale-New Haven Hosp 1992; **Fac Appt:** Assoc Prof Med, Albert Einstein Coll Med

Russell, Linda MD (Rhu) - **Spec Exp:** Arthritis; Osteoporosis; Gout; **Hospital:** Hosp For Special Surgery (page 109); **Address:** HSS, Rheumatology, 535 E 70th St, New York, NY 10021; **Phone:** 212-606-1305; **Board Cert:** Internal Medicine 2012; Rheumatology 2004; **Med School:** Tufts Univ 1989; **Resid:** Internal Medicine, NY-Presby/Weill Cornell Med Ctr 1992; **Fellow:** Rheumatology, Hosp Special Surgery 1995; **Fac Appt:** Asst Prof Med, Cornell Univ-Weill Med Coll

Salmon, Jane E MD (Rhu) - **Spec Exp:** Lupus/SLE; Antiphospholipid Syndrome (APS); Rheumatoid Arthritis; **Hospital:** Hosp For Special Surgery (page 109); **Address:** HSS, Rheumatology, 535 E 70th St, New York, NY 10021; **Phone:** 212-606-1728; **Board Cert:** Internal Medicine 1981; Rheumatology 1984; **Med School:** Columbia P&S 1978; **Resid:** Internal Medicine, NY-Presby/Weill Cornell Med Ctr 1981; **Fellow:** Rheumatology, Hosp Special Surgery 1983; **Fac Appt:** Prof Med, Cornell Univ-Weill Med Coll

Samuels, Jonathan MD (Rhu) - **Spec Exp:** Rheumatoid Arthritis; Osteoarthritis; Musculoskeletal Disorders; Musculoskeletal Ultrasound; **Hospital:** NYU Langone Med Ctr (page 104); **Address:** Center for Musculoskeletal Care, 333 E 38th St, Fl 4, New York, NY 10016; **Phone:** 646-501-7400; **Board Cert:** Rheumatology 2014; **Med School:** Cornell Univ 1999; **Resid:** Internal Medicine, University Hosp 2002; **Fellow:** Rheumatology, Weill-Cornell Med Ctr 2005; **Fac Appt:** Asst Prof Med, NYU Sch Med

Schwartzfarb, Lanny S MD (Rhu) - **Spec Exp:** Rheumatoid Arthritis; Psoriatic Arthritis; Osteoarthritis; Lupus/SLE; **Hospital:** NYU Langone Med Ctr (page 104), Mt Sinai Beth Israel; **Address:** 315 E 69th St, Lobby, Ste J, New York, NY 10021; **Phone:** 212-734-5670; **Board Cert:** Internal Medicine 1975; Rheumatology 1978; **Med School:** NYU Sch Med 1972; **Resid:** Internal Medicine, Beth Israel Med Ctr 1975; **Fellow:** Rheumatology, NY-Presby/Columbia Univ Med Ctr 1977

Silverman, Jill Anne MD (Rhu) - **Hospital:** NY-Presby/Columbia Univ Med Ctr, NY (page 102); **Address:** 635 Madison Ave Fl 8, New York Physicians, New York, NY 10022; **Phone:** 212-857-4590; **Board Cert:** Internal Medicine 1984; Rheumatology 1986; **Med School:** Yale Univ 1979; **Resid:** Internal Medicine, Yale-New Haven Hosp 1982; **Fellow:** Rheumatology, G Washington Univ Hosp 1985; **Fac Appt:** Assoc Clin Prof Med, Columbia P&S

Smiles, Stephen A MD (Rhu) - **Spec Exp:** Arthritis; Osteoporosis; Lupus/SLE; Gout; **Hospital:** NYU Langone Med Ctr (page 104); **Address:** Ctr for Arthritis & Autoimmunity, 333 E 38th St Fl 4, New York, NY 10016; **Phone:** 646-501-7400; **Board Cert:** Internal Medicine 1977; Rheumatology 1980; **Med School:** SUNY Buffalo 1973; **Resid:** Internal Medicine, Bellevue Hosp Ctr 1977; **Fellow:** Rheumatology, Bellevue Hosp Ctr 1979; **Fac Appt:** Assoc Clin Prof Med, NYU Sch Med

Solitar, Bruce M MD (Rhu) - **Spec Exp:** Arthritis; Fibromyalgia; Reiter's Syndrome; Retroperitoneal Fibrosis; **Hospital:** NYU Langone Med Ctr (page 104), NYU Hosp For Joint Dis (page 104); **Address:** NYU Med Ctr, Rheumatology Dept, 333 E 34th St, Ste 1C, New York, NY 10016; **Phone:** 212-889-7217; **Board Cert:** Internal Medicine 2012; Rheumatology 2004; **Med School:** NYU Sch Med 1988; **Resid:** Internal Medicine, Bellevue Hosp 1992; **Fellow:** Rheumatology, Bellevue Hosp 1994; **Fac Appt:** Assoc Clin Prof Med, NYU Sch Med

Solomon, Gary MD (Rhu) - **Spec Exp:** Psoriatic Arthritis; Rheumatoid Arthritis; Autoimmune Disease; **Hospital:** NYU Langone Med Ctr (page 104), NYU Hosp For Joint Dis (page 104); **Address:** NYU Musculoskeletal Care, 333 E 38th St, New York, NY 10016; **Phone:** 646-501-7400; **Board Cert:** Internal Medicine 1980; Rheumatology 1982; **Med School:** Mount Sinai Sch Med 1977; **Resid:** Internal Medicine, Mt Sinai Hosp 1980; **Fellow:** Rheumatology, Montefiore Med Ctr 1982; **Fac Appt:** Assoc Clin Prof Med, NYU Sch Med

Spiera, Harry MD (Rhu) - **Spec Exp:** Lupus/SLE; Scleroderma; Vasculitis; Behcet's Syndrome; **Hospital:** Mt Sinai Hosp; **Address:** Rheumatology Assocs, 1088 Park Ave, New York, NY 10128-1132; **Phone:** 212-860-4000 x2; **Board Cert:** Internal Medicine 1965; Rheumatology 1972; **Med School:** NYU Sch Med 1958; **Resid:** Internal Medicine, VA Med Ctr 1960; Internal Medicine, Mt Sinai Hosp 1961; **Fellow:** Rheumatology, Columbia-Presby Med Ctr 1963; **Fac Appt:** Clin Prof Med, Mount Sinai Sch Med

Spiera, Robert MD (Rhu) - **Spec Exp:** Vasculitis; Lupus/SLE; Scleroderma; Sjogren's Syndrome; **Hospital:** Hosp For Special Surgery (page 109), NY-Presby/Weill Cornell Med Ctr, NY (page 102); **Address:** Rheumatology Assocs, 1088 Park Ave, New York, NY 10128; **Phone:** 212-860-4000; **Board Cert:** Rheumatology 2004; **Med School:** Yale Univ 1989; **Resid:** Internal Medicine, NY-Presby/Weill Cornell Med Ctr 1992; **Fellow:** Rheumatology, Hosp Special Surgery 1995; **Fac Appt:** Clin Prof Med, Cornell Univ-Weill Med Coll

Stern, Richard MD (Rhu) - **Spec Exp:** Rheumatoid Arthritis; Polymyalgia Rheumatica; Osteoarthritis; Osteoporosis; **Hospital:** Hosp For Special Surgery (page 109), NY-Presby/Weill Cornell Med Ctr, NY (page 102); **Address:** 420 E 72nd St, New York, NY 10021; **Phone:** 212-879-2282; **Board Cert:** Internal Medicine 1973; Rheumatology 1976; **Med School:** Tufts Univ 1970; **Resid:** Internal Medicine, New York Hosp 1973; **Fellow:** Immunology, Rockefeller Univ Hosp 1975; Rheumatology, Hosp Special Surgery 1975; **Fac Appt:** Assoc Clin Prof Med, Cornell Univ-Weill Med Coll

Whitman III, Hendricks H MD (Rhu) - **Spec Exp:** Rheumatoid Arthritis; Scleroderma; Osteoarthritis; **Hospital:** Hosp For Special Surgery (page 109), NY-Presby/Weill Cornell Med Ctr, NY (page 102); **Address:** Hospital for Special Surgery, 525 E 71st St Fl 7, New York, NY 10021; **Phone:** 212-774-2802; **Board Cert:** Internal Medicine 1978; Rheumatology 1980; **Med School:** Univ NC Sch Med 1975; **Resid:** Internal Medicine, New York Hosp 1978; **Fellow:** Rheumatology, Hosp for Special Surg 1980; **Fac Appt:** Asst Clin Prof Med, Cornell Univ-Weill Med Coll

Yee, Arthur M F MD/PhD (Rhu) - **Spec Exp:** Sarcoidosis; Gout; Spondyloarthropathies; Vasculitis; **Hospital:** Hosp For Special Surgery (page 109), NY-Presby/Weill Cornell Med Ctr, NY (page 102); **Address:** Hosp for Special Surgery, 535 E 70th St, New York, NY 10021; **Phone:** 212-606-1171; **Board Cert:** Internal Medicine 2004; Rheumatology 2006; **Med School:** NYU Sch Med 1991; **Resid:** Internal Medicine, New York Hosp 1994; **Fellow:** Rheumatology, Hosp Special Surg 1996; **Fac Appt:** Asst Prof Med, Cornell Univ-Weill Med Coll

Sports Medicine

Altchek, David MD (SM) - **Spec Exp:** Shoulder Surgery; Elbow Surgery; Knee Surgery; Arthroscopic Surgery; **Hospital:** Hosp For Special Surgery (page 109); **Address:** HSS, Sports Med, 525 E 71st St, New York, NY 10021; **Phone:** 212-606-1909; **Board Cert:** Orthopaedic Surgery 2011; **Med School:** Cornell Univ-Weill Med Coll 1982; **Resid:** Orthopaedic Surgery, Hosp Special Surgery 1987; **Fellow:** Sports Medicine, Hosp Special Surgery 1988; **Fac Appt:** Prof OrS, Cornell Univ-Weill Med Coll

Callahan, Lisa MD (SM) - **Spec Exp:** Primary Care Sports Medicine; Sports Medicine-Women; Fractures-Stress; **Hospital:** Hosp For Special Surgery (page 109), NY-Presby/Weill Cornell Med Ctr, NY (page 102); **Address:** Hospital for Special Surgery, 523 E 72nd St, New York, NY 10021; **Phone:** 212-606-1532; **Board Cert:** Family Medicine 2014; Sports Medicine 2013; **Med School:** E Carolina Univ 1987; **Resid:** Family Medicine, San Jose Med Ctr 1990; **Fellow:** Sports Medicine, San Jose Med Ctr 1991; **Fac Appt:** Assoc Prof FMed, Cornell Univ-Weill Med Coll

Cleeman, Edmond MD (SM) - **Spec Exp:** Shoulder Surgery; Rotator Cuff Surgery; Arthroscopic Surgery; **Hospital:** Mt Sinai Hosp; **Address:** Manhattan Orthopedic & Sports Medicine Grp, 1065 Park Ave Fl 2, New York, NY 10128; **Phone:** 212-289-0700; **Board Cert:** Orthopaedic Surgery 2015; Orthopaedic Sports Medicine 2015; **Med School:** Mount Sinai Sch Med 1996; **Resid:** Orthopaedic Surgery, Mt Sinai Med Ctr 2001; **Fellow:** Sports Medicine & Arthroscopic Surgery, Virginia/Arlington Hosp 2002; **Fac Appt:** Asst Clin Prof OrS, Mount Sinai Sch Med

Halpern, Brian MD (SM) - **Spec Exp:** Primary Care Sports Medicine; Knee Injuries; Shoulder Injuries; Overuse Injuries; **Hospital:** Hosp For Special Surgery (page 109); **Address:** 525 E 71st St, New York, NY 10021; **Phone:** 212-606-1329; **Board Cert:** Family Medicine 2008; Sports Medicine 2004; **Med School:** Cornell Univ 1981; **Resid:** Family Medicine, Univ Md Med Ctr 1984; **Fellow:** Sports Medicine, Hughston Ortho Clinic 1985; **Fac Appt:** Assoc Clin Prof Med, Cornell Univ-Weill Med Coll

Hershman, Elliott B MD (SM) - **Spec Exp:** Knee Injuries; Knee Surgery; Arthroscopic Surgery; Ligament Reconstruction; **Hospital:** Lenox Hill Hosp; **Address:** Manhattan Orthopaedics, 130 E 77th St, Fl 7, New York, NY 10075; **Phone:** 212-744-8114; **Board Cert:** Orthopaedic Surgery 2008; **Med School:** Univ Rochester 1979; **Resid:** Orthopaedic Surgery, Lenox Hill Hosp 1984; **Fellow:** Orthopaedic Sports Medicine, Cleveland Clin 1985; **Fac Appt:** Asst Clin Prof OrS, Mount Sinai-Icahn Sch of Med

Jazrawi, Laith M MD (SM) - **Spec Exp:** Sports Medicine; Arthroscopic Surgery; Cartilage Damage & Transplant; Knee Surgery; **Hospital:** NYU Langone Med Ctr (page 104); **Address:** NYU, Sports Med, 333 E 38th St Fl 4, New York, NY 10016; **Phone:** 646-501-7223; **Board Cert:** Orthopaedic Surgery 2015; Orthopaedic Sports Medicine 2015; **Med School:** Mount Sinai Sch Med 1995; **Resid:** Orthopaedic Surgery, NYU Hosp Joint Diseases 2001; **Fellow:** Sports Medicine, Ameri Sports Med Inst 2002; **Fac Appt:** Assoc Prof OrS, NYU Sch Med

Levine, William N MD (SM) - **Spec Exp:** Arthroscopic Surgery; Shoulder & Elbow Surgery; **Hospital:** NY-Presby/Columbia Univ Med Ctr, NY (page 102); **Address:** NY-Presby, Sports Med, 51 W 51st St, Ste 370, New York, NY 10019; **Phone:** 212-305-0762; **Board Cert:** Orthopaedic Surgery 2010; Orthopaedic Sports Medicine 2008; **Med School:** Case West Res Univ 1990; **Resid:** Surgery, Beth Israel Deaconess Med Ctr 1991; Orthopaedic Surgery, Tufts Med Ctr 1995; **Fellow:** Shoulder Surgery, NY-Presby/Columbia Univ Med Ctr 1996; Sports Medicine, Univ MD Med Ctr 1998; **Fac Appt:** Prof OrS, Columbia P&S

Maharam, Lewis G MD (SM) - **Spec Exp:** Primary Care Sports Medicine; Running Injuries; Pain-Back; Musculoskeletal Injuries; **Hospital:** Mt Sinai Hosp; **Address:** Head Shoulders Knees & Toes Medicine Doc, 24 W 57th St, Ste 605, New York, NY 10019-3918; **Phone:** 212-765-5763; **Board Cert:** Sports Medicine 1991; **Med School:** Emory Univ 1985; **Resid:** Internal Medicine, Danbury Hosp 1987; Internal Medicine, NY Infirm/Beekman Downtown 1989; **Fellow:** Sports Medicine, Pascack Valley Hosp 1990; **Fac Appt:** Asst Clin Prof Med, Mount Sinai Sch Med

Metzl, Jordan D MD (SM) - **Spec Exp:** Adolescent Sports Medicine; Running Injuries; Dance/Ballet Injuries; **Hospital:** Hosp For Special Surgery (page 109); **Address:** 519 E 72nd St, Ste 206, New York, NY 10021; **Phone:** 212-606-1678; **Board Cert:** Sports Medicine 2012; **Med School:** Univ MO-Columbia Sch Med 1993; **Resid:** Pediatrics, Tufts Med Ctr 1996; **Fellow:** Sports Medicine, Vanderbilt Univ Med Ctr 1997; Sports Medicine, Harvard Med Sch 1998; **Fac Appt:** Assoc Prof Ped, Cornell Univ-Weill Med Coll

Nisonson, Barton MD (SM) - **Spec Exp:** Shoulder & Knee Surgery; Arthroscopic Surgery; **Hospital:** Lenox Hill Hosp; **Address:** Lenox Hill Hosp, Orthopaedics, 130 E 77th St, Fl 8, New York, NY 10021; **Phone:** 212-570-9120; **Board Cert:** Orthopaedic Surgery 1974; **Med School:** Columbia P&S 1966; **Resid:** Surgery, NY-Presby/Columbia Univ Med Ctr 1968; Orthopaedic Surgery, NY-Presby/Columbia Univ Med Ctr 1973

Noy, Ron MD (SM) - **Spec Exp:** Knee Ligament Reconstruction; Knee Injuries/ACL/Meniscus Tears; Arthroscopic Surgery; Rotator Cuff Surgery; **Hospital:** Mt Sinai Beth Israel; **Address:** 424 Madison Ave Fl 9, New York, NY 10017; **Phone:** 646-862-0180; **Board Cert:** Orthopaedic Surgery 2014; Orthopaedic Sports Medicine 2014; **Med School:** UMDNJ-NJ Med Sch, Newark 1991; **Resid:** Orthopaedic Surgery, Kingsbrook Jewish Med Ctr 2000; **Fellow:** Orthopaedic Sports Medicine, IU Hlth Univ Hosp 2001

Rodeo, Scott A MD (SM) - **Spec Exp:** Knee Injuries; Cartilage Damage; Shoulder Surgery; **Hospital:** Hosp For Special Surgery (page 109); **Address:** HSS, Sports Med, 535 E 70th St, New York, NY 10021; **Phone:** 212-606-1513; **Board Cert:** Orthopaedic Surgery 2009; Orthopaedic Sports Medicine 2007; **Med School:** Cornell Univ-Weill Med Coll 1989; **Resid:** Orthopaedic Surgery, Hosp Special Surgery 1994; **Fellow:** Sports Medicine, Hosp Special Surgery 1996; **Fac Appt:** Prof OrS, Cornell Univ-Weill Med Coll

Rokito, Andrew MD (SM) - **Spec Exp:** Shoulder & Elbow Surgery; Rotator Cuff Surgery; Knee Injuries/ACL; **Hospital:** NYU Hosp For Joint Dis (page 104), NYU Langone Med Ctr (page 104); **Address:** NYU, Musculoskeletal Care, 333 E 38 St Fl 4, New York, NY 10016; **Phone:** 646-501-7223; **Board Cert:** Orthopaedic Surgery 2007; **Med School:** Boston Univ 1988; **Resid:** Orthopaedic Surgery, NYU Hosp Joint Diseases 1993; **Fellow:** Sports Medicine, Kerlan-Jobe Orthopaedic Clin 1994; **Fac Appt:** Assoc Prof OrS, NYU Sch Med

Roth, Neil S MD (SM) - **Spec Exp:** Shoulder Surgery; Rotator Cuff Surgery; Knee Surgery; Fractures; **Hospital:** Lenox Hill Hosp, White Plains Hosp (page 652); **Address:** 130 E 77th St Fl 8, New York, NY 10075; **Phone:** 212-861-2300; **Board Cert:** Orthopaedic Surgery 2012; Orthopaedic Sports Medicine 2008; **Med School:** Duke Univ 1991; **Resid:** Orthopaedic Surgery, NY-Presby/Columbia Univ Med Ctr 1997; **Fellow:** Orthopaedic Sports Medicine, Kerlan-Jobe Ortho Clin 1999; **Fac Appt:** Asst Prof OrS, Columbia P&S

Seneviratne, Aruna M MD (SM) - **Spec Exp:** Shoulder Surgery; Rotator Cuff Surgery; Elbow Surgery; Knee Surgery; **Hospital:** Lenox Hill Hosp; **Address:** 800A 5th Ave, Ste 300, New York, NY 10065; **Phone:** 212-960-8887; **Board Cert:** Orthopaedic Surgery 2007; Orthopaedic Sports Medicine 2008; **Med School:** NY Med Coll 1995; **Resid:** Surgery, Lenox Hill Hosp 1997; Orthopaedic Surgery, Hosp Special Surgery 2003; **Fellow:** Orthopaedic Sports Medicine, Lenox Hill Hosp 2004

Wickiewicz, Thomas L MD (SM) - **Spec Exp:** Knee Injuries/ACL; Shoulder Surgery; Rotator Cuff Surgery; Cartilage Damage & Transplant; **Hospital:** Hosp For Special Surgery (page 109), NY-Presby/Weill Cornell Med Ctr, NY (page 102); **Address:** HSS, Sports Med, 525 E 71st St, New York, NY 10021; **Phone:** 212-606-1450; **Board Cert:** Orthopaedic Surgery 1984; **Med School:** UMDNJ-NJ Med Sch, Newark 1976; **Resid:** Orthopaedic Surgery, Hosp Special Surgery 1981; **Fellow:** Sports Medicine, UCLA Med Ctr 1981; **Fac Appt:** Prof OrS, Cornell Univ-Weill Med Coll

Williams III, Riley J MD (SM) - **Spec Exp:** Cartilage Damage & Transplant; Shoulder Arthroscopic Surgery; Knee Injuries/ACL; Knee Surgery; **Hospital:** Hosp For Special Surgery (page 109), NY-Presby/Weill Cornell Med Ctr, NY (page 102); **Address:** HSS, Sports Med, 525 E 71st St, New York, NY 10021; **Phone:** 212-606-1855; **Board Cert:** Orthopaedic Sports Medicine 2012; Orthopaedic Surgery 2012; **Med School:** Stanford Univ 1992; **Resid:** Orthopaedic Surgery, Hosp Special Surgery 1997; **Fellow:** Sports Medicine & Shoulder Surgery, Hosp Special Surgery 1998; **Fac Appt:** Assoc Prof OrS, Cornell Univ-Weill Med Coll

Surgery

Alden, Dmitri MD (S) - **Spec Exp:** Robotic Surgery; Liver Surgery; Pancreatic & Biliary Surgery; Liver & Biliary Cancer; **Hospital:** Lenox Hill Hosp, Vassar Bros Med Ctr; **Address:** 186 E 76th St, New York, NY 10021; **Phone:** 212-434-6216; **Board Cert:** Surgery 2008; **Med School:** Russia 1991; **Resid:** Surgery, St Vincents Hosp 2003; **Fellow:** Hepatopancreatobiliary Surgery, Paul Brousse Hosp 1995; Research, Mount Sinai Med Ctr 1999

Allen, Peter J MD (S) - **Spec Exp:** Pancreatic Cancer; Pancreatic Surgery; Liver Cancer; Gastrointestinal Cancer; **Hospital:** Meml Sloan Kettering Canc Ctr (page 110); **Address:** Meml Sloan-Kettering Cancer Ctr, 1275 York Ave, New York, NY 10065; **Phone:** 212-639-5132; **Board Cert:** Surgery 2012; **Med School:** Dartmouth Med Sch 1993; **Resid:** Surgery, Walter Reed Army Med Ctr 1999; **Fellow:** Surgical Oncology, Meml Sloan Kettering Cancer Ctr 2004

Amory, Spencer E MD (S) - **Spec Exp:** Laparoscopic Surgery; Gastrointestinal Surgery; Hernia; **Hospital:** NY-Presby Hosp/The Allen Hosp (page 102); **Address:** 5141 Broadway, Ste 3-178, New York, NY 10034; **Phone:** 212-305-5221; **Board Cert:** Surgery 2010; **Med School:** Johns Hopkins Univ 1983; **Resid:** Surgery, NY-Presby/Columbia Univ Med Ctr 1989; **Fellow:** Emergency Medicine, Peninsula Hosp 1990; **Fac Appt:** Assoc Clin Prof S, Columbia P&S

Attiyeh, Fadi F MD (S) - **Spec Exp:** Colon & Rectal Cancer; Hepatobiliary Surgery; Pancreatic Surgery; **Hospital:** Mt Sinai Roosevelt; **Address:** 425 W 59th St, Ste 8B-1, New York, NY 10019; **Phone:** 212-307-1144; **Board Cert:** Surgery 1975; Colon & Rectal Surgery 1982; **Med School:** Amer Univ Beirut 1969; **Resid:** Surgery, Amer Univ Hosp 1973; **Fellow:** Surgical Oncology, Meml Sloan Kettering Canc Ctr 1976; **Fac Appt:** Prof S, Mount Sinai-Icahn Sch of Med

Axelrod, Deborah M MD (S) - **Spec Exp:** Breast Cancer & Surgery; **Hospital:** NYU Langone Med Ctr (page 104); **Address:** NYU, Cancer Ctr, 160 E 34th St Fl 3, New York, NY 10016; **Phone:** 212-731-5366; **Board Cert:** Surgery 2008; **Med School:** Israel 1982; **Resid:** Surgery, Beth Israel Med Ctr 1988; **Fellow:** Surgical Oncology, Meml Sloan-Kettering Cancer Ctr 1986; **Fac Appt:** Assoc Prof S, NYU Sch Med

Barie, Philip MD (S) - **Spec Exp:** Trauma; Critical Care; Hernia; Gastrointestinal Surgery; **Hospital:** NY-Presby/Weill Cornell Med Ctr, NY (page 102); **Address:** NY-Presby, Surgery Dept, 525 E 68th St, Box 116, New York, NY 10065; **Phone:** 212-746-5401; **Board Cert:** Surgery 2004; Surgical Critical Care 2005; **Med School:** Boston Univ 1977; **Resid:** Surgery, NY-Presby/Weill Cornell Med Ctr 1984; **Fellow:** Trauma, Albany Med Coll Affil Hosp 1981; **Fac Appt:** Prof S, Cornell Univ-Weill Med Coll

Berman, Russell S MD (S) - **Spec Exp:** Melanoma; Gastrointestinal Cancer; Sarcoma-Soft Tissue; Liver Cancer; **Hospital:** NYU Langone Med Ctr (page 104); **Address:** NYU Cancer Ctr, 160 E 34th St Fl 9, New York, NY 10016; **Phone:** 212-731-5415; **Board Cert:** Surgery 2007; **Med School:** NYU Sch Med 1990; **Resid:** Surgery, NYU-Bellevue Hosp 1997; **Fellow:** Surgical Oncology, Meml Sloan-Kettering Cancer Ctr 1994; Surgical Oncology, UT MD Anderson Cancer Ctr 2000; **Fac Appt:** Assoc Prof S, NYU Sch Med

Bernik, Stephanie F MD (S) - **Spec Exp:** Breast Cancer & Surgery; Breast Disease; Phyllodes Tumors; Angiosarcoma; **Hospital:** Lenox Hill Hosp; **Address:** Lenox Hill Hosp - Dept Surgery, 100 E 77th St Wollman Bldg Fl 3, New York, NY 10075; **Phone:** 212-434-6900; **Board Cert:** Surgery 2011; **Med School:** Yale Univ 1993; **Resid:** Surgery, St Vincents Hosp 1999; **Fellow:** Breast Surgery, Meml Sloan Kettering Canc Ctr 2000

Bessey, Palmer Q MD (S) - **Spec Exp:** Burn Care; Wound Healing/Care; Trauma; **Hospital:** NY-Presby/Weill Cornell Med Ctr, NY (page 102); **Address:** NY-Presby, Burn Ctr, 525 E 68th St Fl 7, New York, NY 10065; **Phone:** 212-746-0242; **Board Cert:** Surgery 2011; Surgical Critical Care 2005; **Med School:** Univ VT Coll Med 1975; **Resid:** Surgery, UAB Hosp 1979; **Fellow:** Nutrition & Metabolism, Brigham & Womens Hosp 1983; **Fac Appt:** Prof S, Cornell Univ-Weill Med Coll

Bessler, Marc MD (S) - **Spec Exp:** Obesity/Bariatric Surgery; Laparoscopic Surgery; Gastrointestinal Metabolic Surgery; Natural Orifice Surgery (NOTES); **Hospital:** NY-Presby/Columbia Univ Med Ctr, NY (page 102), Valley Hosp (page 739); **Address:** NY-Presby, Metabolic/Weight-Loss Surgery, 161 Fort Washington Ave, Ste 5-524, New York, NY 10032; **Phone:** 212-305-9506; **Board Cert:** Surgery 2007; **Med School:** NYU Sch Med 1989; **Resid:** Surgery, NY-Presby/Columbia Univ Med Ctr 1996; **Fac Appt:** Clin Prof S, Columbia P&S

Bloom, Norman D MD (S) - **Spec Exp:** Breast Cancer; Sarcoma; Cancer Surgery; **Hospital:** Mt Sinai Beth Israel; **Address:** The Gramercy, 61 Irving Place, Ste LL-B, New York, NY 10003; **Phone:** 212-505-6167; **Board Cert:** Surgery 2010; **Med School:** SUNY Downstate 1974; **Resid:** Surgery, Maimonides Med Ctr 1978; **Fellow:** Surgical Oncology, Meml Sloan Kettering Canc Ctr 1979; **Fac Appt:** Clin Prof S, NYU Sch Med

Boolbol, Susan K MD (S) - **Spec Exp:** Breast Cancer; Breast Surgery; Sentinel Node Surgery; **Hospital:** Mt Sinai Beth Israel; **Address:** BIMC, Breast Surgery, 10 Union Square E, Ste 4E, New York, NY 10003; **Phone:** 212-844-6231; **Board Cert:** Surgery 2011; **Med School:** Geo Wash Univ 1994; **Resid:** Surgery, NY-Presby/Weill Cornell Med Ctr 2000; **Fellow:** Breast Surgery, Meml Sloan-Kettering Cancer Ctr 2001

Brady, Mary Sue MD (S) - **Spec Exp:** Melanoma; Merkel Cell Carcinoma; Sarcoma-Soft Tissue; **Hospital:** Meml Sloan Kettering Canc Ctr (page 110); **Address:** MSKCC, Surgery, 160 E 53rd St Fl 3, New York, NY 10019; **Phone:** 646-497-9072; **Board Cert:** Surgery 2009; **Med School:** Univ Miami Sch Med 1983; **Resid:** Surgery, NY-Presby/Weill Cornell Med Ctr 1988; **Fellow:** Surgical Oncology, Meml Sloan-Kettering Cancer Ctr 1990; Immunology, Meml Sloan-Kettering Cancer Ctr 1992; **Fac Appt:** Assoc Prof S, Cornell Univ-Weill Med Coll

Brower, Steven T MD (S) - **Spec Exp:** Gastrointestinal Cancer; Liver Cancer; Minimally Invasive Surgery; Pancreatic Cancer; **Hospital:** Mt Sinai Beth Israel; **Address:** BIMC, Surgical Oncology, 10 Union Square E, Ste 4C, New York, NY 10003; **Phone:** 212-420-4335; **Board Cert:** Surgery 2007; **Med School:** SUNY Buffalo 1978; **Resid:** Surgery, Boston Univ Med Ctr 1981; **Fellow:** Surgical Oncology, National Cancer Inst 1983; Surgical Oncology, Boston Univ Med Ctr 1986; **Fac Appt:** Prof S, Albert Einstein Coll Med

Cassell, Lauren S MD (S) - **Spec Exp:** Breast Surgery; Breast Cancer; Nipple Sparing Mastectomy; **Hospital:** Lenox Hill Hosp; **Address:** 114A E 78th St, New York, NY 10075; **Phone:** 212-535-4040; **Board Cert:** Surgery 2003; **Med School:** NY Med Coll 1977; **Resid:** Surgery, Lenox Hill Hosp 1982

Chabot, John A MD (S) - **Spec Exp:** Liver & Biliary Surgery; Pancreatic Cancer; Pancreatic Surgery; Thyroid & Parathyroid Surgery; **Hospital:** NY-Presby/Columbia Univ Med Ctr, NY (page 102); **Address:** NY-Presby, Surgery, 161 Fort Washington Ave, Ste 8-819, New York, NY 10032; **Phone:** 212-305-9468; **Board Cert:** Surgery 2010; **Med School:** Dartmouth Med Sch 1983; **Resid:** Surgery, NY-Presby/Columbia Univ Med Ctr 1990; **Fac Appt:** Prof S, Columbia P&S

Cioroiu, Michael G MD (S) - **Spec Exp:** Breast Disease; Wound Healing/Care; Endoscopy; **Hospital:** Mt Sinai Hosp of Queens, Mt Sinai Beth Israel; **Address:** 247 3rd Ave, Ste LL3, New York, NY 10010-7453; **Phone:** 212-995-8099; **Board Cert:** Surgery 2004; **Med School:** Romania 1971; **Resid:** Surgery, Cabrini Med Ctr 1985; **Fac Appt:** Asst Clin Prof S, Mount Sinai Sch Med

Coit, Daniel G MD (S) - **Spec Exp:** Melanoma; Pancreatic Cancer; Stomach Cancer; **Hospital:** Meml Sloan Kettering Canc Ctr (page 110); **Address:** MSKCC, Surgery, 1275 York Ave, New York, NY 10065; **Phone:** 212-639-8411; **Board Cert:** Surgery 2004; **Med School:** Univ Cincinnati 1976; **Resid:** Internal Medicine, Beth Israel Deaconess Med Ctr 1978; Surgery, Beth Israel Deaconess Med Ctr 1983; **Fellow:** Surgical Oncology, Meml Sloan-Kettering Cancer Ctr 1985; **Fac Appt:** Prof S, Cornell Univ-Weill Med Coll

Dakin, Gregory F MD (S) - **Spec Exp:** Obesity/Bariatric Surgery; Laparoscopic Surgery; Gastrointestinal Surgery; **Hospital:** NY-Presby/Weill Cornell Med Ctr, NY (page 102); **Address:** GI, Metabolic & Bariatric Surgery, 525 E 68th St, Fl 8, New York, NY 10065; **Phone:** 212-746-5294; **Board Cert:** Surgery 2013; **Med School:** NYU Sch Med 1997; **Resid:** Surgery, Mount Sinai Med Ctr 2003; **Fac Appt:** Assoc Prof S, Cornell Univ-Weill Med Coll

DeMatteo, Ronald P MD (S) - **Spec Exp:** Liver Cancer; Gallbladder & Biliary Cancer; Pancreatic Cancer; Pancreatic Surgery; **Hospital:** Meml Sloan Kettering Canc Ctr (page 110); **Address:** MSKCC, Surgery Dept, 1275 York Ave, rm C896, New York, NY 10065; **Phone:** 212-639-5726; **Board Cert:** Surgery 2008; **Med School:** Cornell Univ-Weill Med Coll 1990; **Resid:** Surgery, Hosp U Penn 1997; **Fellow:** Surgical Oncology, Meml Sloan-Kettering Cancer Ctr 1999; **Fac Appt:** Prof S, Cornell Univ-Weill Med Coll

Divino, Celia M MD (S) - **Spec Exp:** Hernia; Gastrointestinal Surgery; Gallbladder Surgery; Laparoscopic Surgery; **Hospital:** Mt Sinai Hosp; **Address:** Surgical Assocs, 5 E 98th St, Fl 14, Ste A, New York, NY 10029; **Phone:** 212-241-3348; **Board Cert:** Surgery 2008; **Med School:** SUNY Downstate 1992; **Resid:** Surgery, Mt Sinai Med Ctr 1997; **Fac Appt:** Prof S, Mount Sinai Sch Med

El-Tamer, Mahmoud B MD (S) - **Spec Exp:** Breast Cancer; **Hospital:** Meml Sloan Kettering Canc Ctr (page 110); **Address:** Meml Sloan Kettering Canc Ctr, 300 E 66th St, New York, NY 10065; **Phone:** 646-888-4753; **Board Cert:** Surgery 2001; **Med School:** Amer Univ Beirut 1981; **Resid:** Surgery, American Univ Hosp 1985; Surgery, SUNY Downstate Med Ctr 1992; **Fellow:** Surgical Oncology, Meml Sloan Kettering Canc Ctr 1989; **Fac Appt:** Assoc Prof S, Columbia P&S

Emond, Jean C MD (S) - **Spec Exp:** Transplant-Liver; Liver Cancer; Liver & Biliary Cancer; Hepatobiliary Surgery; **Hospital:** NY-Presby/Columbia Univ Med Ctr, NY (page 102); **Address:** NY-Presby, Surgery, 622 W 168th St, rm PH-14C, New York, NY 10032; **Phone:** 212-305-9691; **Board Cert:** Surgery 2006; **Med School:** Univ Chicago-Pritzker Sch Med 1979; **Resid:** Surgery, Cook County Hosp 1984; **Fellow:** Surgery, Hosp de Paris 1985; Transplant Surgery, Univ Chicago Hosp 1987; **Fac Appt:** Prof S, Columbia P&S

Estabrook, Alison MD (S) - **Spec Exp:** Breast Cancer; Breast Surgery; Breast Cancer-High Risk Women; **Hospital:** Mt Sinai Roosevelt; **Address:** Mt Sinai-Roosevelt, Breast Ctr, 425 W 59th St, Ste 7A, New York, NY 10019; **Phone:** 212-523-7500; **Board Cert:** Surgery 2004; **Med School:** NYU Sch Med 1978; **Resid:** Surgery, NY-Presby/Columbia Univ Med Ctr 1984; **Fellow:** Surgical Oncology, NY-Presby/Columbia Univ Med Ctr 1982; **Fac Appt:** Prof S, Columbia P&S

Fahey III, Thomas J MD (S) - **Spec Exp:** Endocrine Surgery; Pheochromocytoma; Pancreatic Cancer; Minimally Invasive Surgery; **Hospital:** NY-Presby/Weill Cornell Med Ctr, NY (page 102); **Address:** NY-Presby, Surgery, 525 E 68th St, rm Starr 8, Box 249, New York, NY 10065; **Phone:** 212-746-5130; **Board Cert:** Surgery 2012; **Med School:** Cornell Univ-Weill Med Coll 1986; **Resid:** Surgery, NY-Presby/Weill Cornell Med Ctr 1992; **Fellow:** Endocrine Surgery, Royal N Shore Hosp 1993; **Fac Appt:** Prof S, Cornell Univ-Weill Med Coll

Feldman, Sheldon M MD (S) - **Spec Exp:** Breast Surgery; Breast Cancer; Complementary Medicine; Minimally Invasive Surgery; **Hospital:** NY-Presby/Columbia Univ Med Ctr, NY (page 102); **Address:** NY-Presby-Columbia Univ Med Ctr, Div Surgical Oncology, 161 Fort Washington Ave, Fl 10, Ste 1005, New York, NY 10032; **Phone:** 212-305-9676; **Board Cert:** Surgery 2011; **Med School:** NYU Sch Med 1975; **Resid:** Surgery, Bellevue Hosp Ctr 1980; **Fellow:** Peripheral Vascular Surgery, Beth Israel Med Ctr 1981; **Fac Appt:** Assoc Clin Prof S, Columbia P&S

Geller, Peter MD (S) - **Spec Exp:** Gastrointestinal Surgery; Hernia; **Hospital:** NY-Presby/Columbia Univ Med Ctr, NY (page 102); **Address:** Columbia Doctors Midtown, 51 W 51st St, Ste 380, New York, NY 10019; **Phone:** 212-326-5547; **Board Cert:** Surgery 2004; **Med School:** Columbia P&S 1980; **Resid:** Surgery, NY-Presby/Columbia Univ Med Ctr 1985; **Fellow:** Vascular Surgery, NY-Presby/Columbia Univ Med Ctr 1986; **Fac Appt:** Clin Prof S, Columbia P&S

Goldfarb, Alisan B MD (S) - **Spec Exp:** Breast Surgery; Breast Cancer; Sentinel Node Surgery; **Hospital:** Mt Sinai Hosp; **Address:** 1185 Park Ave, Ste 1A, New York, NY 10128; **Phone:** 212-987-5000; **Board Cert:** Surgery 2011; **Med School:** Mount Sinai Sch Med 1975; **Resid:** Surgery, Mt Sinai Med Ctr 1980; **Fac Appt:** Asst Clin Prof S, Mount Sinai Sch Med

Heerdt, Alexandra S MD (S) - **Spec Exp:** Breast Cancer; **Hospital:** Meml Sloan Kettering Canc Ctr (page 110); **Address:** MSKCC, Surgery, 300 E 66th St, New York, NY 10065; **Phone:** 646-888-5253; **Board Cert:** Surgery 2012; **Med School:** Jefferson Med Coll 1987; **Resid:** Surgery, NY-Presby/Weill Cornell Med Ctr 1992; **Fellow:** Surgical Oncology, Meml Sloan-Kettering Cancer Ctr 1993

Herron, Daniel M MD (S) - **Spec Exp:** Obesity/Bariatric Surgery; Laparoscopic Surgery; Endoscopic Surgery; **Hospital:** Mt Sinai Hosp; **Address:** Mt Sinai, Metabolic/Endocrine Surgery, 17 E 102nd St Fl 5, New York, NY 10029; **Phone:** 212-824-7891; **Board Cert:** Surgery 2008; **Med School:** Univ Pennsylvania 1992; **Resid:** Surgery, New England Med Ctr 1998; **Fellow:** Laparoscopic Surgery, Legacy Emanuel Hosp 1999; **Fac Appt:** Prof S, Mount Sinai-Icahn Sch of Med

Hiotis, Spiros P MD/PhD (S) - **Spec Exp:** Liver Cancer; Gallbladder & Biliary Cancer; Pancreatic Cancer; Stomach Cancer; **Hospital:** Mt Sinai Hosp; **Address:** Surgical Oncology Assocs, 1470 Madison Ave Fl 3rd, New York, NY 10029; **Phone:** 212-241-2891; **Board Cert:** Surgery 2010; **Med School:** Univ MD Sch Med 1992; **Resid:** Surgery, USF Med Ctr 1998; **Fellow:** Surgical Oncology, Meml Sloan Kettering Cancer Ctr 2000; **Fac Appt:** Assoc Prof S, Mount Sinai Sch Med

Hofstetter, Steven MD (S) - **Spec Exp:** Laparoscopic Abdominal Surgery; Gastrointestinal Surgery; Hernia; **Hospital:** NYU Langone Med Ctr (page 104); **Address:** NYU Med Ctr, Dept Surgery, 550 1st Ave Fl 6 - Ste 6C, New York, NY 10016-6402; **Phone:** 212-263-7302; **Board Cert:** Surgery 2011; **Med School:** SUNY Hlth Sci Ctr 1971; **Resid:** Surgery, Bellevue Hosp/NYU Med Ctr 1976; **Fac Appt:** Assoc Prof S, NYU Sch Med

Inabnet, William B MD (S) - **Spec Exp:** Thyroid Surgery; Adrenal Surgery; Pancreatic Surgery; Minimally Invasive Surgery; **Hospital:** Mt Sinai Hosp; **Address:** 5 E 98th St Fl 15, Box 1259, New York, NY 10029; **Phone:** 212-241-5339; **Board Cert:** Surgery 2007; **Med School:** Univ NC Sch Med 1991; **Resid:** Surgery, Rush Univ Med Ctr 1996; **Fellow:** Endocrine Surgery, Cochin Hosp 1997; **Fac Appt:** Prof S, Columbia P&S

Jacob, Brian P MD (S) - **Spec Exp:** Hernia; Obesity/Bariatric Surgery; Laparoscopic Surgery; **Hospital:** Mt Sinai Hosp; **Address:** Laparoscopic Surgical Ctr of NY, 1010 5th Ave, New York, NY 10028; **Phone:** 212-879-6677; **Board Cert:** Surgery 2005; **Med School:** Wayne State Univ 1998; **Resid:** Surgery, Mt Sinai Hosp 2004; **Fellow:** Minimally Invasive Surgery, NY-Presby/Columbia Univ Med Ctr 2005; **Fac Appt:** Assoc Clin Prof S, Mount Sinai-Icahn Sch of Med

Jarnagin, William MD (S) - **Spec Exp:** Hepatobiliary Surgery; Liver Cancer; Pancreatic Cancer; Gallbladder & Biliary Cancer; **Hospital:** Meml Sloan Kettering Canc Ctr (page 110); **Address:** Memorial Sloan Kettering Cancer Ctr, Dept Surgery, 1275 York Ave, New York, NY 10065; **Phone:** 212-639-7601; **Board Cert:** Surgery 2006; **Med School:** Rush Med Coll 1988; **Resid:** Surgery, UCSF Med Ctr 1996; **Fellow:** Hepatopancreatobiliary Surgery, Meml Sloan-Kettering Cancer Ctr 1997; **Fac Appt:** Prof S, Cornell Univ-Weill Med Coll

Kapur, Sandip MD (S) - **Spec Exp:** Transplant-Kidney; Transplant-Pancreas; **Hospital:** NY-Presby/Weill Cornell Med Ctr, NY (page 102); **Address:** NY-Presby, Transplant Surgery, 520 E 70th St Fl 8, New York, NY 10065; **Phone:** 212-746-5330; **Board Cert:** Surgery 2007; **Med School:** Cornell Univ-Weill Med Coll 1990; **Resid:** Surgery, NY-Presby/Weill Cornell Med Ctr 1996; **Fellow:** Research, Rogosin Inst 1994; Transplant Surgery, Thomas E Starzl Transplant Inst 1998; **Fac Appt:** Assoc Prof S, Cornell Univ-Weill Med Coll

Karpeh Jr, Martin S MD (S) - **Spec Exp:** Gastrointestinal Cancer; Esophageal Cancer; Pancreatic Cancer; Liver Cancer; **Hospital:** Mt Sinai Beth Israel; **Address:** BIMC, Surgery, 10 Union Square E, Ste 4D, New York, NY 10003; **Phone:** 212-420-4041; **Board Cert:** Surgery 2006; **Med School:** Penn State Coll Med 1983; **Resid:** Surgery, Hosp Univ Penn 1989; **Fellow:** Surgical Oncology, Meml Sloan-Kettering Cancer Ctr 1991; **Fac Appt:** Prof S, Mount Sinai-Icahn Sch of Med

Kato, Tomoaki MD (S) - **Spec Exp:** Transplant-Liver; Transplant Surgery-Pediatric; Transplant-Multi Organ; Transplant-Auto Transplantation; **Hospital:** NY-Presby/Columbia Univ Med Ctr, NY (page 102); **Address:** NY-Presby, Surgery, 622 W 168th St PH 14 Bldg, New York, NY 10032; **Phone:** 212-305-5101; **Med School:** Japan 1991; **Resid:** Surgery, Itami City Hosp 1995; **Fellow:** Transplant Surgery, Jackson Meml Hosp 1997; **Fac Appt:** Prof S, Columbia P&S

Katz, Lester B MD (S) - **Spec Exp:** Laparoscopic Abdominal Surgery; Esophageal Surgery; Hernia; **Hospital:** Mt Sinai Hosp; **Address:** 1010 Fifth Ave, New York, NY 10028; **Phone:** 212-879-6677; **Board Cert:** Surgery 2011; **Med School:** South Africa 1975; **Resid:** Surgery, Mount Sinai Hosp 1982; **Fac Appt:** Assoc Clin Prof S, Mount Sinai Sch Med

Kimmelstiel, Fred M MD (S) - **Spec Exp:** Laparoscopic Surgery; Breast Disease; Cancer Surgery; Hernia; **Hospital:** Mt Sinai Roosevelt, Mt Sinai St. Luke's; **Address:** 225 W 71st St, New York, NY 10023; **Phone:** 212-362-6060; **Board Cert:** Surgery 2006; **Med School:** NY Med Coll 1980; **Resid:** Surgery, St. Luke's - Roosevelt Hosp Ctr - St Luke's Hosp 1985; **Fellow:** Transplant Surgery, Stony Brook Univ Med Ctr 1986; **Fac Appt:** Asst Clin Prof S, Mount Sinai-Icahn Sch of Med

Kini, Subhash U MD (S) - **Spec Exp:** Obesity/Bariatric Surgery; Laparoscopic Surgery; **Hospital:** Mt Sinai Hosp; **Address:** Mount Sinai, Bariatric Surgery, 17 E 102 St Fl 5, New York, NY 10029; **Phone:** 212-824-2350; **Board Cert:** Surgery 2013; **Med School:** India 1986; **Resid:** Surgery, Our Lady Mercy Med Ctr 2003; **Fellow:** Laparoscopic Surgery, NY Med Coll 2004; **Fac Appt:** Asst Prof S, Mount Sinai Sch Med

Labow, Daniel M MD (S) - **Spec Exp:** Pancreatic Cancer; Gastrointestinal Cancer; Liver Cancer; **Hospital:** Mt Sinai Hosp; **Address:** Mt Sinai Hosp, Surgical Oncology, 1470 Madison Ave Fl 3, New York, NY 10029; **Phone:** 212-241-2891; **Board Cert:** Surgery 2003; **Med School:** Brown Univ 1995; **Resid:** Surgery, Univ Chicago Hosp 1997; Research, NY-Presby/Weill Cornell Med Ctr 1999; **Fellow:** Surgical Oncology, Meml Sloan-Kettering Cancer Ctr 2004; **Fac Appt:** Assoc Prof S, Mount Sinai-Icahn Sch of Med

Lee, James A MD (S) - **Spec Exp:** Adrenal Surgery; Endocrine Cancers; Thyroid & Parathyroid Cancer & Surgery; Pancreatic Surgery; **Hospital:** NY-Presby/Columbia Univ Med Ctr, NY (page 102); **Address:** NY-Presby, GI Endocrine Surgery, 161 Fort Washington Ave, Ste 819, New York, NY 10032; **Phone:** 212-305-0444; **Board Cert:** Surgery 2005; **Med School:** Columbia P&S 1999; **Resid:** Surgery, NY-Presby/Columbia Univ Med Ctr 2005; **Fellow:** Endocrine Surgery, UCSF Med Ctr 2006; **Fac Appt:** Assoc Prof S, Columbia P&S

Leitman, I. Michael MD (S) - **Spec Exp:** Hernia; Obesity/Bariatric Surgery; Laparoscopic Surgery; **Hospital:** Mt Sinai Beth Israel; **Address:** BIMC, Surgery, 10 Union Square E, Ste 2M, New York, NY 10003; **Phone:** 212-844-8570; **Board Cert:** Surgery 2009; Surgical Critical Care 2010; **Med School:** Boston Univ 1985; **Resid:** Surgery, NY-Presby/Weill Cornell Med Ctr 1990; **Fellow:** Surgical Critical Care, N Shore Univ Hosp 1991; **Fac Appt:** Prof S, Albert Einstein Coll Med

Lieberman, Michael D MD (S) - **Spec Exp:** Gastrointestinal Cancer; Colon & Rectal Cancer & Surgery; Hepatobiliary Surgery; Pancreatic Cancer; **Hospital:** NY-Presby/Weill Cornell Med Ctr, NY (page 102); **Address:** NY-Presby, Jay Monahan Ctr, 1315 York Ave, New York, NY 10021; **Phone:** 212-746-5434; **Board Cert:** Surgery 2013; **Med School:** UMDNJ-NJ Med Sch, Newark 1985; **Resid:** Surgery, Hosp Univ Penn 1992; **Fellow:** Surgical Oncology, Hosp Univ Penn 1990; Surgical Oncology, Meml Sloan-Kettering Cancer Ctr 1994; **Fac Appt:** Assoc Prof S, Cornell Univ-Weill Med Coll

McGinty Jr, James J MD (S) - **Spec Exp:** Laparoscopic Surgery; Minimally Invasive Surgery; Obesity/Bariatric Surgery; **Hospital:** Mt Sinai Roosevelt, Mt Sinai St. Luke's; **Address:** 1111 Amsterdam Ave Fl 4 - Ste 4W, New York, NY 10025; **Phone:** 212-636-1000; **Board Cert:** Surgery - 2013; **Med School:** Hahnemann Univ 1997; **Resid:** Surgery, Allegheny Genl Hosp 2002; **Fellow:** Minimally Invasive Surgery, NY-Presby/Columbia Univ Med Ctr 2003; **Fac Appt:** Asst Clin Prof S, Columbia P&S

Michelassi, Fabrizio MD (S) - **Spec Exp:** Gastrointestinal Cancer; Crohn's Disease; Ulcerative Colitis; Colon Cancer; **Hospital:** NY-Presby/Weill Cornell Med Ctr, NY (page 102); **Address:** NY-Presby, Surgery, 525 E 68th St, rm Starr 8, New York, NY 10065; **Phone:** 212-746-6006; **Board Cert:** Surgery 2002; **Med School:** Italy 1975; **Resid:** Surgery, NYU Med Ctr 1981; **Fellow:** Research, Mass Genl Hosp 1983; **Fac Appt:** Prof S, Cornell Univ-Weill Med Coll

Mills, Christopher B MD (S) - **Spec Exp:** Breast Cancer; Breast Surgery; **Hospital:** Mt Sinai Beth Israel; **Address:** 325 W 15th St, New York, NY 10011; **Phone:** 212-604-6006; **Board Cert:** Surgery 2009; **Med School:** UMDNJ-NJ Med Sch, Newark 1973; **Resid:** Surgery, St Vincent's Hosp 1978; **Fellow:** Nutrition & Metabolism, Ravenswood Hosp Med Ctr 1979; **Fac Appt:** Assoc Prof S, NY Med Coll

Morrow, Monica MD (S) - **Spec Exp:** Breast Cancer; **Hospital:** Meml Sloan Kettering Canc Ctr (page 110); **Address:** MSKCC, Breast Surgery, 300 E 66th St Fl 4, New York, NY 10065; **Phone:** 646-497-9064; **Board Cert:** Surgery 2011; **Med School:** Jefferson Med Coll 1976; **Resid:** Surgery, Med Ctr Hosp 1981; **Fellow:** Surgical Oncology, Meml Sloan Kettering Cancer Ctr 1983; **Fac Appt:** Prof S, Cornell Univ-Weill Med Coll

Newman, Elliot MD (S) - **Spec Exp:** Gastrointestinal Cancer; Robotic Surgery; Liver & Biliary Cancer; Colon & Rectal Cancer; **Hospital:** NYU Langone Med Ctr (page 104); **Address:** NYU Cancer Ctr, 160 E 34th St Fl 9, New York, NY 10016; **Phone:** 212-731-5466; **Board Cert:** Surgery 2004; **Med School:** NYU Sch Med 1986; **Resid:** Surgery, NYU Med Ctr 1993; **Fellow:** Research, Meml Sloan-Kettering Cancer Ctr 1991; Surgical Oncology, Meml Sloan-Kettering Cancer Ctr 1995; **Fac Appt:** Prof S, NYU Sch Med

Nowak, Eugene J MD (S) - **Spec Exp:** Breast Cancer; Hernia; Sentinel Node Surgery; Gastrointestinal Surgery; **Hospital:** NY-Presby/Weill Cornell Med Ctr, NY (page 102); **Address:** 325 E 79th St, Ground Fl, New York, NY 10075-0954; **Phone:** 212-517-6693; **Board Cert:** Surgery 2012; **Med School:** UMDNJ-NJ Med Sch, Newark 1975; **Resid:** Surgery, New York Hosp 1980; **Fac Appt:** Asst Clin Prof S, Cornell Univ-Weill Med Coll

Pachter, H. Leon MD (S) - **Spec Exp:** Gastrointestinal Surgery; Pancreatic Cancer; Colon Cancer; Minimally Invasive Surgery; **Hospital:** NYU Langone Med Ctr (page 104); **Address:** NYU Med Ctr, Surgery, 530 1st Ave, Ste 6C, New York, NY 10016; **Phone:** 212-263-7302; **Board Cert:** Surgery 2009; **Med School:** NYU Sch Med 1971; **Resid:** Surgery, NYU Med Ctr 1976; **Fac Appt:** Prof S, NYU Sch Med

Paty, Philip B MD (S) - **Spec Exp:** Colon & Rectal Cancer; Gastrointestinal Cancer; Pelvic Tumors; **Hospital:** Meml Sloan Kettering Canc Ctr (page 110); **Address:** MSKCC, Surgery, 1275 York Ave, New York, NY 10065; **Phone:** 212-639-6703; **Board Cert:** Surgery 2011; **Med School:** Stanford Univ 1983; **Resid:** Surgery, UCSF Med Ctr 1990; **Fellow:** Surgical Oncology, Meml Sloan-Kettering Cancer Ctr 1992; **Fac Appt:** Prof S, Cornell Univ-Weill Med Coll

Pomp, Alfons MD (S) - **Spec Exp:** Obesity/Bariatric Surgery; Laparoscopic Abdominal Surgery; Hernia; **Hospital:** NY-Presby/Weill Cornell Med Ctr, NY (page 102); **Address:** NY-Presby, Surgery, 525 E 68th St, Box 294, New York, NY 10065; **Phone:** 212-746-5294; **Board Cert:** Surgery 2010; **Med School:** Univ Sherbrooke 1980; **Resid:** Surgery, Univ Montreal Med Ctr 1985; **Fellow:** Nutrition, Rhode Island Hosp 1988; **Fac Appt:** Prof S, Cornell Univ-Weill Med Coll

Port, Elisa R MD (S) - **Spec Exp:** Breast Cancer & Surgery; Sentinel Node Surgery; Nipple Sparing Mastectomy; Breast Cancer-Male; **Hospital:** Mt Sinai Hosp; **Address:** Mt Sinai, Dubin Breast Ctr, 1176 5th Ave, New York, NY 10029; **Phone:** 212-241-3806; **Board Cert:** Surgery 2011; **Med School:** Mount Sinai Sch Med 1992; **Resid:** Surgery, Cedars-Sinai Med Ctr 1995; Surgery, LIJ Med Ctr 1997; **Fac Appt:** Assoc Prof S, Mount Sinai-Icahn Sch of Med

Ratner, Lloyd E MD (S) - **Spec Exp:** Transplant-Kidney; Transplant-Pancreas; Pancreatic Surgery; **Hospital:** NY-Presby/Columbia Univ Med Ctr, NY (page 102); **Address:** NY-Presby/Columbia Univ Med Ctr, 622 W 168th St PH Bldg - rm 14-408, New York, NY 10032; **Phone:** 212-305-6469; **Board Cert:** Surgery 2009; **Med School:** Hahnemann Univ 1983; **Resid:** Surgery, Long Is Jewish Med Ctr 1988; **Fellow:** Transplant Surgery, Barnes-Jewish Hosp 1990; **Fac Appt:** Assoc Prof S, Columbia P&S

Reiner, Mark A MD (S) - **Spec Exp:** Laparoscopic Surgery; Hernia; Esophageal Surgery; Pancreatic Surgery; **Hospital:** Mt Sinai Hosp; **Address:** Laparoscopic Surgical Ctr of NY, 1010 5th Ave, New York, NY 10028; **Phone:** 212-879-6677; **Board Cert:** Surgery 2011; **Med School:** SUNY Downstate 1974; **Resid:** Surgery, Mt Sinai Hosp 1979; **Fac Appt:** Clin Prof S, Mount Sinai-Icahn Sch of Med

Rosenberg, Vladimiro MD (S) - **Spec Exp:** Breast Cancer; Melanoma; Sarcoma-Soft Tissue; **Hospital:** Mt Sinai Hosp, Lenox Hill Hosp; **Address:** 1440 York Ave, Ste P-10, New York, NY 10075; **Phone:** 212-772-0010; **Med School:** Argentina 1965; **Resid:** Surgery, Mt Sinai Hosp 1977; **Fellow:** Surgical Oncology, MD Anderson Cancer Ctr 1978; **Fac Appt:** Asst Clin Prof S, Mount Sinai Sch Med

Roses, Daniel F MD (S) - **Spec Exp:** Breast Cancer; Melanoma; Thyroid & Parathyroid Surgery; **Hospital:** NYU Langone Med Ctr (page 104); **Address:** NYU Med Ctr, Surgery, 530 1st Ave, Ste 6B, New York, NY 10016; **Phone:** 212-263-7329; **Board Cert:** Surgery 1975; **Med School:** NYU Sch Med 1969; **Resid:** Surgery, NYU-Bellevue Hosp 1974; **Fellow:** Surgical Oncology, NYU-Bellevue Hosp 1978; **Fac Appt:** Prof Surg & Onc, NYU Sch Med

Salky, Barry A MD (S) - **Spec Exp:** Laparoscopic Abdominal Surgery; Gastroesophageal Reflux Disease (GERD); Colon Cancer; Ulcerative Colitis; **Hospital:** Mt Sinai Hosp; **Address:** Mount Sinai Med Ctr, Surgery Dept, 5 E 98th St Fl 14 - Ste C, Box 1259, New York, NY 10029; **Phone:** 212-241-6156; **Board Cert:** Surgery 2010; **Med School:** Univ Tenn Coll Med 1970; **Resid:** Surgery, Mount Sinai Med Ctr 1973; Surgery, Mount Sinai Med Ctr 1978; **Fac Appt:** Prof S, Mount Sinai Sch Med

Schnabel, Freya MD (S) - **Spec Exp:** Breast Cancer; Breast Cancer-High Risk Women; **Hospital:** NYU Langone Med Ctr (page 104); **Address:** NYU Cancer Ctr, 160 E 34th St Fl 3, New York, NY 10016; **Phone:** 212-731-5367; **Board Cert:** Surgery 2008; **Med School:** NYU Sch Med 1982; **Resid:** Surgery, NYU Med Ctr 1987; **Fellow:** Research, SUNY Hlth Sci Ctr 1988; **Fac Appt:** Prof S, NYU Sch Med

Schwartz, Myron E MD (S) - **Spec Exp:** Gastrointestinal Cancer; Liver Cancer; Hepatobiliary Surgery; Transplant-Liver; **Hospital:** Mt Sinai Hosp; **Address:** Mt Sinai Hosp, Liver Transplant, 5 E 98th St Fl 12, Box 1104, New York, NY 10029; **Phone:** 212-659-8084; **Board Cert:** Surgery 2009; **Med School:** Jefferson Med Coll 1976; **Resid:** Surgery, Mt Sinai Hosp 1986; Vascular Surgery, Mt Sinai Hosp 1987; **Fac Appt:** Prof S, Mount Sinai-Icahn Sch of Med

Shah, Jatin P MD/PhD (S) - **Spec Exp:** Head & Neck Cancer & Surgery; Thyroid Cancer; Skull Base Tumors; Salivary Gland Tumors & Surgery; **Hospital:** Meml Sloan Kettering Canc Ctr (page 110); **Address:** 1275 York Ave, New York, NY 10065; **Phone:** 646-497-9161; **Board Cert:** Surgery 1975; **Med School:** India 1964; **Resid:** Surgery, SSG Hosp 1967; Surgery, NY Eye & Ear Infirm 1974; **Fellow:** Head & Neck Surgical Oncology, Meml Sloan-Kettering Hosp 1972; **Fac Appt:** Prof S, Cornell Univ-Weill Med Coll

Shah, Paresh C MD (S) - **Spec Exp:** Laparoscopic Surgery; Obesity/Bariatric Surgery; Minimally Invasive Surgery; **Hospital:** NYU Langone Med Ctr (page 104); **Address:** NYU Med Ctr, Surgery, 530 1st Ave, Ste 6C, New York, NY 10016; **Phone:** 212-263-7302; **Board Cert:** Surgery 2010; **Med School:** SUNY Downstate 1991; **Resid:** Surgery, SUNY Downstate Med Ctr 1993; Surgery, Mass Genl Hosp 1995; **Fellow:** Laparoscopic Surgery, Lahey Clin 1999

Shapiro, Richard L MD (S) - **Spec Exp:** Breast Cancer; Melanoma; Thyroid & Parathyroid Surgery; Cancer Surgery; **Hospital:** NYU Langone Med Ctr (page 104); **Address:** NYU Cancer Ctr, 160 E 34th St Fl 4, New York, NY 10016; **Phone:** 212-731-5347; **Board Cert:** Surgery 2004; **Med School:** NYU Sch Med 1988; **Resid:** Surgery, NYU Med Ctr 1993; **Fellow:** Surgical Oncology, NYU Med Ctr 1995; **Fac Appt:** Assoc Prof S, NYU Sch Med

Simmons, Rache M MD (S) - **Spec Exp:** Breast Cancer; Breast Surgery; **Hospital:** NY-Presby/Weill Cornell Med Ctr, NY (page 102); **Address:** NY-Presby, Breast Surgery, 425 E 61st St Fl 10, New York, NY 10065; **Phone:** 212-821-0853; **Board Cert:** Surgery 2005; **Med School:** Duke Univ 1988; **Resid:** Surgery, NC Meml Hosp-UNC 1993; **Fellow:** Surgical Oncology, NY-Presby/Weill Cornell Med Ctr 1994; **Fac Appt:** Assoc Prof S, Cornell Univ-Weill Med Coll

Singer, Samuel MD (S) - **Spec Exp:** Sarcoma-Soft Tissue; Gastrointestinal Stromal Tumors; **Hospital:** Meml Sloan Kettering Canc Ctr (page 110); **Address:** MSCC, GMT Surgery Dept, 1275 York Ave, Ste H1210, New York, NY 10065; **Phone:** 212-639-2940; **Board Cert:** Surgery 2010; **Med School:** Harvard Med Sch 1982; **Resid:** Surgery, Brigham & Womens Hosp 1988; **Fellow:** Surgical Oncology, Dana Farber Cancer Inst 1990; **Fac Appt:** Assoc Prof S, Cornell Univ-Weill Med Coll

Slater, Gary I MD (S) - **Spec Exp:** Colon & Rectal Surgery; Inflammatory Bowel Disease; Hernia; Laparoscopic Surgery; **Hospital:** Mt Sinai Hosp; **Address:** 5 E 98th St Fl 3, New York, NY 10029-6501; **Phone:** 212-241-9281; **Board Cert:** Surgery 1975; **Med School:** NYU Sch Med 1968; **Resid:** Surgery, Mt Sinai Med Ctr 1974; **Fac Appt:** Prof S, Mount Sinai Sch Med

Swistel, Alexander J MD (S) - **Spec Exp:** Breast Cancer & Surgery; Cancer Reconstruction; Nipple Sparing Mastectomy; **Hospital:** NY-Presby/Weill Cornell Med Ctr, NY (page 102), Mt Sinai Roosevelt; **Address:** Weill Cornell Breast Surgery, 425 E 61st St, Fl 10, New York, NY 10065; **Phone:** 212-821-0602; **Board Cert:** Surgery 2005; **Med School:** Brown Univ 1975; **Resid:** Surgery, St Lukes-Roosevelt Hosp Ctr 1981; **Fellow:** Surgical Oncology, Meml Sloan-Kettering Cancer Ctr 1983; **Fac Appt:** Assoc Clin Prof S, Cornell Univ-Weill Med Coll

Tartter, Paul I MD (S) - **Spec Exp:** Breast Cancer; Breast Cancer in Elderly; Sentinel Node Surgery; **Hospital:** Mt Sinai Roosevelt; **Address:** Comprehensive Breast Center, 425 W 59th St, Ste 7A, New York, NY 10019-1104; **Phone:** 212-523-7500; **Board Cert:** Surgery 2011; **Med School:** Brown Univ 1977; **Resid:** Surgery, Mt Sinai Hosp 1982; **Fac Appt:** Assoc Prof S, Columbia P&S

Teperman, Lewis W MD (S) - **Spec Exp:** Transplant-Liver; Transplant-Kidney; Liver Cancer; Hepatobiliary Surgery; **Hospital:** NYU Langone Med Ctr (page 104); **Address:** NYU Transplant Assocs, 403 E 34th St, Fl 3, New York, NY 10016; **Phone:** 212-263-8134; **Board Cert:** Surgery 2007; **Med School:** Mount Sinai Sch Med 1981; **Resid:** Surgery, NY-Presby/Columbia Univ Med Ctr 1984; Surgery, LIJ Med Ctr 1986; **Fellow:** Transplant Surgery, UPMC 1988; **Fac Appt:** Assoc Prof S, NYU Sch Med

Van Zee, Kimberly J MD (S) - **Spec Exp:** Breast Cancer; **Hospital:** Meml Sloan Kettering Canc Ctr (page 110); **Address:** MSKCC, Breast Surgery, 300 E 66th St, New York, NY 10065; **Phone:** 646-888-5241; **Board Cert:** Surgery 2003; **Med School:** Harvard Med Sch 1987; **Resid:** Surgery, NY-Presby/Weill Cornell Med Ctr 1990; Surgery, NY-Presby/Weill Cornell Med Ctr 1994; **Fellow:** Research, NY-Presby/Weill Cornell Med Ctr 1993; **Fac Appt:** Prof S, Cornell Univ-Weill Med Coll

Vine, Anthony J MD (S) - **Spec Exp:** Laparoscopic Abdominal Surgery; Gastroesophageal Reflux Disease (GERD); Colon & Rectal Surgery; **Hospital:** Mt Sinai Hosp; **Address:** Laparoscopic Surgical Ctr of NY, 1010 5th Ave, New York, NY 10028; **Phone:** 212-879-6677; **Board Cert:** Surgery 2009; **Med School:** Vanderbilt Univ 1989; **Resid:** Surgery, Mt Sinai Hosp 1996; **Fellow:** Colon & Rectal Surgery, Mass Genl Hosp 1994; **Fac Appt:** Asst Clin Prof S, Mount Sinai-Icahn Sch of Med

Wallack, Marc MD (S) - **Spec Exp:** Melanoma; Breast Surgery; **Hospital:** Metropolitan Hosp Ctr - NY; **Address:** 1901 1st Ave Fl 3 - rm 3B, New York, NY 10029; **Phone:** 212-423-7118; **Board Cert:** Surgery 2011; **Med School:** Univ Pittsburgh 1970; **Resid:** Surgery, Hosp Univ Penn - UPHS 1976; **Fellow:** Medical Oncology, Wistar Inst Anatomy & Biology 1977; **Fac Appt:** Prof S, NY Med Coll

Wedderburn, Raymond V MD (S) - **Spec Exp:** Trauma; Critical Care; Laparoscopic Surgery; **Hospital:** Mt Sinai Roosevelt; **Address:** Mt Sinai, Surgery, 1111 Amsterdam Ave, Ste MU208, New York, NY 10025; **Phone:** 212-523-5295; **Board Cert:** Surgery 2012; Surgical Critical Care 2013; **Med School:** Cornell Univ-Weill Med Coll 1986; **Resid:** Surgery, St Lukes-Roosevelt Hosp Ctr 1991; **Fellow:** Surgical Critical Care, Jackson Meml Hosp 1993; **Fac Appt:** Asst Clin Prof S, Columbia P&S

Weltz, Christina R MD (S) - **Spec Exp:** Breast Cancer & Surgery; **Hospital:** Mt Sinai Hosp; **Address:** Mt Sinai, Dubin Breast Ctr, 1176 Fifth Ave, New York, NY 10029; **Phone:** 212-241-3806; **Board Cert:** Surgery 2008; **Med School:** Univ Pennsylvania 1989; **Resid:** Surgery, UCSF Med Ctr 1992; Surgery, Duke Univ Med Ctr 1996; **Fac Appt:** Asst Prof S, Mount Sinai Sch Med

Yurt, Roger W MD (S) - **Spec Exp:** Burn Care; Wound Healing/Care; Hyperbaric Medicine; Critical Care; **Hospital:** NY-Presby/Weill Cornell Med Ctr, NY (page 102); **Address:** NY-Presby, Burn Ctr, 525 E 68th St, rm L706, New York, NY 10021; **Phone:** 212-746-5410; **Board Cert:** Surgery 2008; **Med School:** Univ Miami Sch Med 1972; **Resid:** Surgery, Parkland Meml Hosp 1974; Surgery, NY-Presby/Weill Cornell Med Ctr 1980; **Fellow:** Internal Medicine, Brigham & Womens Hosp 1978; **Fac Appt:** Prof S, Cornell Univ-Weill Med Coll

Zarnegar, Rasa MD (S) - **Spec Exp:** Minimally Invasive Surgery; Endocrine Surgery; Gallbladder & Biliary Disease; Stomach Cancer; **Hospital:** NY-Presby/Weill Cornell Med Ctr, NY (page 102); **Address:** 525 E 68th St, Starr Bldg Fl 8, New York, NY 10065; **Phone:** 212-746-5130; **Board Cert:** Surgery 2006; **Med School:** Univ Chicago-Pritzker Sch Med 1999; **Resid:** Surgery, Univ Chicago Affil Hosps 2003; Surgery, Case West Res Univ Affil Hosps 2005; **Fellow:** Endocrine Surgery, UCSF Med Ctr 2006; Minimally Invasive Surgery, UCSF Med Ctr 2006; **Fac Appt:** Asst Prof S, Cornell Univ-Weill Med Coll

Zoland, Mark P MD (S) - **Spec Exp:** Minimally Invasive Surgery; Laparoscopic Surgery; Hernia; Hernia-Sports; **Hospital:** Lenox Hill Hosp; **Address:** GLSNY, 122 E 76th St, Ste 1B, New York, NY 10021; **Phone:** 212-628-8771; **Board Cert:** Surgery 2008; **Med School:** Cornell Univ-Weill Med Coll 1993; **Resid:** Surgery, Lenox Hill Hosp 1998

Thoracic & Cardiac Surgery

Adams, David H MD (T&CS) - **Spec Exp:** Mitral Valve Surgery; Heart Valve Surgery; Minimally Invasive Cardiac Surgery; Aortic Surgery; **Hospital:** Mt Sinai Hosp; **Address:** Mt Sinai, Cardiothoracic Surgery, 1190 5th Ave, Ste GP2-West, New York, NY 10029; **Phone:** 212-659-6820; **Board Cert:** Thoracic & Cardiac Surgery 2014; **Med School:** Duke Univ 1983; **Resid:** Surgery, Brigham & Womens Hosp 1990; Thoracic & Cardiac Surgery, Brigham & Womens Hosp 1992; **Fellow:** Research, Harvard Med Sch 1988; Surgery, Brigham & Womens Hosp 1992; **Fac Appt:** Prof T&CS, Mount Sinai-Icahn Sch of Med

Altorki, Nasser K MD (T&CS) - **Spec Exp:** Esophageal Cancer; Lung Cancer; Thoracic Cancers; **Hospital:** NY-Presby/Weill Cornell Med Ctr, NY (page 102); **Address:** NY-Presby, Cardiothoracic Surgery, 525 E 68th St, Ste M-404, New York, NY 10065; **Phone:** 212-746-5156; **Board Cert:** Surgery 2006; Thoracic & Cardiac Surgery 2007; **Med School:** Egypt 1978; **Resid:** Surgery, Univ Chicago Hosp 1985; **Fellow:** Cardiothoracic Surgery, Univ Chicago Hosp 1987; **Fac Appt:** Prof S, Cornell Univ-Weill Med Coll

Argenziano, Michael MD (T&CS) - **Spec Exp:** Robotic Cardiac Surgery; Coronary Artery Surgery; Maze Procedure for Atrial Fibrillation; **Hospital:** NY-Presby/Columbia Univ Med Ctr, NY (page 102); **Address:** NY Presby Med Ctr, Milstein Bldg, 177 Fort Washington Ave, rm 7-435, New York, NY 10032; **Phone:** 212-305-5888; **Board Cert:** Thoracic & Cardiac Surgery 2013; **Med School:** Columbia P&S 1992; **Resid:** Surgery, Columbia Presby Med Ctr 1998; **Fellow:** Cardiothoracic Surgery, Columbia Presby Med Ctr 2000; **Fac Appt:** Asst Prof S, Columbia P&S

Bacha, Emile A MD (T&CS) - **Spec Exp:** Pediatric Cardiac Surgery; Congenital Heart Disease; Neonatal & Infant Cardiac Surgery; Minimally Invasive Cardiac Surgery; **Hospital:** NY-Presby/Columbia Univ Med Ctr, NY (page 102), Morgan Stanley Chldns Hosp of NY-Presby, NY (page 102); **Address:** NY-Presby, Ped Cardiothoracic Surgery, 3959 Broadway, rm 276, New York, NY 10032; **Phone:** 212-305-2688; **Board Cert:** Thoracic & Cardiac Surgery 2009; Congenital Cardiac Surgery 2009; **Med School:** Germany 1989; **Resid:** Thoracic Surgery, Mass Genl Hosp 1993; Surgery, Emory Univ Med Ctr 1995; **Fellow:** Pediatric Cardiac Surgery, Hosp Marie Lanne Longe 1996; Pediatric Cardiac Surgery, Mass Genl Hosp 1998; **Fac Appt:** Prof S, Columbia P&S

Bains, Manjit MD (T&CS) - **Spec Exp:** Cardiothoracic Surgery; Esophageal Cancer; Lung Cancer; Mesothelioma; **Hospital:** Meml Sloan Kettering Canc Ctr (page 110); **Address:** MSKCC, Thoracic Surgery, 1275 York Ave, rm C861, New York, NY 10065; **Phone:** 646-497-9163; **Board Cert:** Surgery 1971; Thoracic Surgery 1972; **Med School:** India 1963; **Resid:** Surgery, Rochester Genl Hosp 1970; **Fellow:** Thoracic Surgery, Meml Sloan-Kettering Cancer Ctr 1972; **Fac Appt:** Clin Prof S, Cornell Univ-Weill Med Coll

Bhora, Faiz Y MD (T&CS) - **Spec Exp:** Lung Cancer; Esophageal Cancer; Thoracic Cancers; Robotic Surgery; **Hospital:** Mt Sinai Roosevelt; **Address:** Mt Sinai, Cancer Ctr, 325 W 15th St, New York, NY 10011; **Phone:** 212-523-7475; **Board Cert:** Thoracic & Cardiac Surgery 2014; **Med School:** Pakistan 1992; **Resid:** Surgery, G Washington Univ Med Ctr 2000; Cardiothoracic Surgery, UCLA Med Ctr 2002; **Fellow:** Transplant Surgery, UCLA Med Ctr 2004; Thoracic Oncology, Hosp Univ Penn 2005; **Fac Appt:** Assoc Clin Prof S, Columbia P&S

Chai, Paul J MD (T&CS) - **Spec Exp:** Cardiac Surgery-Adult & Pediatric; Congenital Heart Surgery; Transplant-Heart; **Hospital:** NY-Presby/Columbia Univ Med Ctr, NY (page 102), Muhlenberg Regional Med Ctr; **Address:** 3959 Broadway, Ste CHN-276, New York, NY 10032; **Phone:** 212-305-5975; **Board Cert:** Thoracic Surgery 2006; Congenital Cardiac Surgery 2009; **Med School:** Duke Univ 1994; **Resid:** Surgery, Duke Univ Med Ctr 2001; **Fellow:** Cardiothoracic Surgery, Duke Univ Med Ctr 2003; Pediatric Cardiac Surgery, Univ MI/Mott Chldn's Hosp 2004; **Fac Appt:** Asst Clin Prof S, Columbia P&S

Crawford Jr, Bernard K MD (T&CS) - **Spec Exp:** Lung Cancer; Minimally Invasive Surgery; Chest Wall Tumors; Mediastinal Tumors; **Hospital:** NYU Langone Med Ctr (page 104); **Address:** NYU Med Ctr, Cardiothoracic Surgery, 160 E 34th St Fl 8, New York, NY 10016; **Phone:** 212-731-5580; **Board Cert:** Thoracic & Cardiac Surgery 2009; **Med School:** Geo Wash Univ 1980; **Resid:** Surgery, NYU Med Ctr 1985; **Fellow:** Cardiothoracic Surgery, NYU Med Ctr 1987; **Fac Appt:** Asst Prof T&CS, NYU Sch Med

DeAnda Jr, Abelardo MD (T&CS) - **Spec Exp:** Aneurysm-Aortic; Heart Valve Surgery; Cardiothoracic Surgery; **Hospital:** NYU Langone Med Ctr (page 104), Bellevue Hosp Ctr; **Address:** NYU Medical Ctr, Cardiothoracic Surgery, 530 First Ave, Ste 9V, New York, NY 10016; **Phone:** 212-263-6516; **Board Cert:** Thoracic Surgery 2011; **Med School:** Stanford Univ 1990; **Resid:** Surgery, Stanford Med Ctr 1997; **Fellow:** Cardiothoracic Surgery, Stanford Med Ctr 2000; Cardiothoracic Research, Stanford Med Ctr 1994; **Fac Appt:** Assoc Prof TS, NYU Sch Med

Donington, Jessica Scott MD (T&CS) - **Spec Exp:** Cardiac Tumors/Cancer; Thoracic Cancers; Mesothelioma; Barrett's Esophagus; **Hospital:** Bellevue Hosp Ctr, NYU Langone Med Ctr (page 104); **Address:** Bellevue, Cardiothoracic Surgery, 462 1st Ave, Ste 10S1, New York, NY 10016; **Phone:** 212-562-2227; **Board Cert:** Thoracic & Cardiac Surgery 2011; **Med School:** Rush Med Coll 1992; **Resid:** Surgery, Georgetown Univ Hosp 1994; **Fellow:** Surgical Oncology, Natl Inst Hlth 1996; Thoracic & Cardiac Surgery, Mayo Clin 2002; **Fac Appt:** Assoc Prof T&CS, NYU Sch Med

Downey, Robert J MD (T&CS) - **Spec Exp:** Lung Cancer; Thoracic Cancers; Mesothelioma; **Hospital:** Meml Sloan Kettering Canc Ctr (page 110); **Address:** MSKCC, Thoracic Surgery, 1275 York Ave, New York, NY 10065; **Phone:** 212-639-8124; **Board Cert:** Thoracic & Cardiac Surgery 2005; Surgical Critical Care 2006; **Med School:** Columbia P&S 1985; **Resid:** Surgery, NY-Presby/Columbia Univ Med Ctr 1991; **Fellow:** Thoracic Surgery, Mayo Clin 1992; Thoracic Surgery, NY-Presby/Columbia Univ Med Ctr 1994

Flores, Raja M MD (T&CS) - **Spec Exp:** Mesothelioma; Lung Cancer; Video Assisted Thoracic Surgery (VATS); Esophageal Cancer; **Hospital:** Mt Sinai Hosp; **Address:** Mt Sinai, Cardiothoracic Surgery, 1470 Madison Ave Fl 3, New York, NY 10029; **Phone:** 212-241-9466; **Board Cert:** Surgery 2009; Thoracic & Cardiac Surgery 2010; **Med School:** Albert Einstein Coll Med 1992; **Resid:** Surgery, NY-Presby/Columbia Univ Med Ctr 1997; **Fellow:** Thoracic Surgery, Dana Faber Cancer Inst 2000; **Fac Appt:** Prof TS, Mount Sinai-Icahn Sch of Med

Fontana, Gregory MD (T&CS) - **Spec Exp:** Minimally Invasive Surgery; Pediatric Cardiac Surgery; Mitral Valve Surgery; Coronary Artery Surgery; **Hospital:** Lenox Hill Hosp; **Address:** Lenox Hill Hosp, Cardiothoracic Dept, 130 E 77th St Fl 4, New York, NY 10075; **Phone:** 212-434-3792; **Board Cert:** Thoracic & Cardiac Surgery 2004; **Med School:** UCLA-David Geffen Sch Med 1984; **Resid:** Surgery, Duke Univ Med Ctr 1989; Thoracic Surgery, Duke Univ Med Ctr 1993; **Fellow:** Pediatric Cardiac Surgery, UCLA Med Ctr 1994; Pediatric Cardiac Surgery, Chldns Hosp 1994

Galloway, Aubrey MD (T&CS) - **Spec Exp:** Minimally Invasive Heart Valve Surgery; Mitral Valve Surgery; Coronary Artery Surgery; Robotic Surgery; **Hospital:** NYU Langone Med Ctr (page 104); **Address:** NYU Med Ctr, Cardiothoracic Surgery, 560 1st Ave, Ste 9V, New York, NY 10016; **Phone:** 212-263-7185; **Board Cert:** Thoracic & Cardiac Surgery 2006; **Med School:** Tulane Univ 1978; **Resid:** Surgery, Univ CO Hosp 1983; **Fellow:** Cardiothoracic Surgery, NYU Med Ctr 1985; **Fac Appt:** Prof TS, NYU Sch Med

Ginsburg, Mark E MD (T&CS) - **Spec Exp:** Thoracic Surgery; Transplant-Lung; Emphysema-Lung Volume Reduction; **Hospital:** NY-Presby/Columbia Univ Med Ctr, NY (page 102), Good Samaritan Regional Med Ctr; **Address:** NY-Presby, Cardiothoracic Surgery, 161 Fort Washington Ave Fl 3, New York, NY 10032; **Phone:** 212-305-3408; **Board Cert:** Surgery 2005; Thoracic & Cardiac Surgery 2006; **Med School:** Tufts Univ 1980; **Resid:** Surgery, Univ Rochester-Strong Meml Hosp 1985; **Fellow:** Thoracic & Cardiac Surgery, Univ Rochester-Strong Meml Hosp 1987; **Fac Appt:** Assoc Clin Prof S, Columbia P&S

Girardi, Leonard N MD (T&CS) - **Spec Exp:** Aneurysm-Aortic; Cardiac Surgery; Marfan's Syndrome; **Hospital:** NY-Presby/Weill Cornell Med Ctr, NY (page 102); **Address:** NY-Presby, Cardiothoracic Surgery, 525 E 68th St, Ste M-404, New York, NY 10065; **Phone:** 212-746-5194; **Board Cert:** Surgery 2005; Thoracic & Cardiac Surgery 2007; **Med School:** Cornell Univ-Weill Med Coll 1989; **Resid:** Surgery, New York Hosp 1994; **Fellow:** Cardiothoracic Surgery, New York Hosp 1996; Cardiovascular Surgery, Baylor Coll Affil Hosp 1997; **Fac Appt:** Prof TS, Cornell Univ-Weill Med Coll

Gorenstein, Lyall A MD (T&CS) - **Spec Exp:** Minimally Invasive Thoracic Surgery; Thoracic Surgery; Hyperhidrosis-Palmar; Lung Cancer; **Hospital:** NY-Presby/Columbia Univ Med Ctr, NY (page 102), Nyack Hosp; **Address:** Rockland Thoracic & Vascular Assocs, 161 Fort Washington Ave, Irving Pavilion Fl 3, New York, NY 10032; **Phone:** 212-305-3408; **Board Cert:** Surgery 2009; Thoracic Surgery 2013; **Med School:** Univ Toronto 1983; **Resid:** Surgery, Univ Toronto Affil Hosps 1988; Surgery, Ontario Canc Inst 1989; **Fellow:** Thoracic Surgery, MD Anderson Canc Ctr 1990; Cardiothoracic Surgery, Univ Toronto Affil Hosps 1992; **Fac Appt:** Asst Clin Prof S, Columbia P&S

Grossi, Eugene A MD (T&CS) - **Spec Exp:** Minimally Invasive Cardiac Surgery; Mitral Valve Surgery; Cardiac Tumors, Myxomas; **Hospital:** NYU Langone Med Ctr (page 104); **Address:** NYU Med Ctr, Cardiothoracic Surgery, 530 1st Ave, Ste 9V, New York, NY 10016; **Phone:** 212-263-7452; **Board Cert:** Thoracic & Cardiac Surgery 2011; **Med School:** Columbia P&S 1981; **Resid:** Surgery, NYU Med Ctr 1987; **Fellow:** Cardiothoracic Surgery, NYU Med Ctr 1989; **Fac Appt:** Prof S, NYU Sch Med

Hoffman, Darryl M MD (T&CS) - **Spec Exp:** Coronary Artery Surgery; Heart Valve Surgery; Atrial Fibrillation; Pacemakers; **Hospital:** Mt Sinai Beth Israel, Mt Sinai Roosevelt; **Address:** Division of Cardiac Surgery, 317 E 17th St, Fierman Hall, 11th Fl, New York, NY 10003; **Phone:** 212-420-2584; **Med School:** South Africa 1983; **Resid:** Surgery 1989Edinburgh Royal Infirm 1989; **Fellow:** Cardiac Surgery, Allegheny Genl Hosp 1993; Cardiothoracic Transplant Surg, Mayo Clinic 1994; **Fac Appt:** Asst Prof S, Albert Einstein Coll Med

Isom, O. Wayne MD (T&CS) - **Spec Exp:** Cardiac Surgery; Coronary Artery Surgery; Heart Valve Surgery; **Hospital:** NY-Presby/Weill Cornell Med Ctr, NY (page 102), NY Hosp Queens (page 498); **Address:** NY-Presby, Cardiothoracic Surgery, 525 E 68th St, Ste M-404, New York, NY 10065; **Phone:** 212-746-5151; **Board Cert:** Surgery 1971; Thoracic Surgery 1972; **Med School:** Univ Tex, Houston 1965; **Resid:** Surgery, Parkland Meml Hosp 1970; **Fellow:** Thoracic & Cardiac Surgery, NYU Med Ctr 1972; **Fac Appt:** Prof TS, Cornell Univ-Weill Med Coll

Jones, David R MD (T&CS) - **Spec Exp:** Lung Cancer; Esophageal Cancer; Minimally Invasive Thoracic Surgery; **Hospital:** Meml Sloan Kettering Canc Ctr (page 110); **Address:** Meml Sloan-Kettering Canc Ctr, 1275 York Ave, Box 7, New York, NY 10065; **Phone:** 212-639-6428; **Board Cert:** Surgery 2005; Thoracic Surgery 2007; **Med School:** W VA Univ 1989; **Resid:** Surgery, W VA Univ Affil Hosp 1995; **Fellow:** Thoracic Surgery, Univ NC Affil Hosp 1998; **Fac Appt:** Prof S, Cornell Univ-Weill Med Coll

Krieger, Karl H MD (T&CS) - **Spec Exp:** Heart Valve Surgery; Coronary Artery Surgery; Cardiac Surgery-Adult; **Hospital:** NY-Presby/Weill Cornell Med Ctr, NY (page 102); **Address:** NY-Presby, Cardiothoracic Surgery, 525 E 68th St, Ste M-404, New York, NY 10065; **Phone:** 212-746-5152; **Board Cert:** Thoracic & Cardiac Surgery 2004; **Med School:** Johns Hopkins Univ 1975; **Resid:** Surgery, NYU-Bellevue Hosp 1979; **Fellow:** Thoracic & Cardiac Surgery, NYU-Bellevue Hosp 1981; **Fac Appt:** Prof S, Cornell Univ-Weill Med Coll

Lazzaro, Richard S MD (T&CS) - **Spec Exp:** Thoracic Surgery; Robotic Surgery; Minimally Invasive Surgery; Thoracic Surgery; **Hospital:** Lenox Hill Hosp, N Shore Univ Hosp; **Address:** Lenox Hill Hosp, Cardiothoracic Surgery, 130 E 77th St, Fl 4, New York, NY 10075; **Phone:** 212-434-3000; **Board Cert:** Surgery 2006; Thoracic & Cardiac Surgery 2007; **Med School:** Albany Med Coll 1988; **Resid:** Surgery, N Shore Univ Hosp 1994; **Fellow:** Cardiothoracic Surgery, Maimonides Med Ctr 1997; Thoracic Surgery, UPMC 1998; **Fac Appt:** Asst Prof T&CS, Hofstra N Shore-LIJ Sch Med

Loulmet, Didier F MD (T&CS) - **Spec Exp:** Heart Valve Surgery; Robotic Cardiac Surgery; Minimally Invasive Cardiac Surgery; Aneurysm-Aortic; **Hospital:** NYU Langone Med Ctr (page 104); **Address:** NYU Med Ctr, Cardiothoracic Surgery, 530 1st Ave, Ste 9V, New York, NY 10016; **Phone:** 212-263-2329; **Med School:** France 1984; **Resid:** Surgery, Paris Univ Hosp 1990; **Fellow:** Cardiothoracic Surgery, Brigham & Womens Hosp 1991; Pediatric Cardiac Surgery, Chdns Hosp 1992; **Fac Appt:** Assoc Prof TS, NYU Sch Med

Mosca, Ralph S MD (T&CS) - **Spec Exp:** Congenital Heart Disease-Adult & Child; Pediatric Cardiac Surgery; Heart Valve Surgery; **Hospital:** NYU Langone Med Ctr (page 104); **Address:** NYU Med Ctr, Cardiothoracic Surgery, 530 1st Ave, Ste 9V, New York, NY 10016; **Phone:** 212-263-5989; **Board Cert:** Thoracic & Cardiac Surgery 2011; **Med School:** SUNY Upstate Med Univ 1985; **Resid:** Surgery, SUNY Upstate Med Univ Hosp 1990; **Fellow:** Cardiothoracic Surgery, NY-Presby/Columbia Univ Med Ctr 1992; Pediatric Cardiac Surgery, Univ Mich Med Ctr 1993; **Fac Appt:** Prof TS, NYU Sch Med

Naka, Yoshifumi MD/PhD (T&CS) - **Spec Exp:** Transplant-Heart; Ventricular Assist Device (LVAD); Heart Failure & Ventricular Containment; Mitral Valve Surgery; **Hospital:** NY-Presby/Columbia Univ Med Ctr, NY (page 102); **Address:** NY-Presby, Cardiothoracic Surgery, 177 Fort Washington Ave, Ste 7-435, New York, NY 10032; **Phone:** 212-305-0828; **Med School:** Japan 1984; **Resid:** Surgery, Osaka Police Hosp 1991; **Fellow:** Cardiovascular Surgery, Osaka Police Hosp 1993; Cardiothoracic Surgery, NY-Presby/Columbia Univ Med Ctr 1998; **Fac Appt:** Prof S, Columbia P&S

Nguyen, Khanh H MD (T&CS) - **Spec Exp:** Pediatric Cardiac Surgery; Congenital Heart Disease-Adult & Child; **Hospital:** Mt Sinai Hosp; **Address:** Mt Sinai, Cardiothoracic Surgery, 1190 5th Ave Fl 2, Box 1028, New York, NY 10029; **Phone:** 212-659-9472; **Board Cert:** Thoracic & Cardiac Surgery 2006; Congenital Cardiac Surgery 2013; **Med School:** UC Irvine 1985; **Resid:** Surgery, Flushing Hosp 1992; Thoracic & Cardiac Surgery, Mt Sinai Hosp 1995; **Fellow:** Pediatric Cardiac Surgery, Great Ormond St Hosp 1996; **Fac Appt:** Assoc Prof T&CS, Mount Sinai-Icahn Sch of Med

Oz, Mehmet C MD (T&CS) - **Spec Exp:** Transplant-Heart; Heart Valve Surgery; Minimally Invasive Cardiac Surgery; **Hospital:** NY-Presby/Columbia Univ Med Ctr, NY (page 102); **Address:** NY-Presby, Cardiothoracic Surgery, 177 Fort Washington Ave, Ste 7-435, New York, NY 10032; **Phone:** 212-305-4434; **Board Cert:** Thoracic Surgery 2003; **Med School:** Univ Pennsylvania 1986; **Resid:** Surgery, NY-Presby/Columbia Univ Med Ctr 1991; **Fellow:** Cardiothoracic Surgery, NY-Presby/Columbia Univ Med Ctr 1993; **Fac Appt:** Prof S, Columbia P&S

Park, Bernard J MD (T&CS) - **Spec Exp:** Lung Cancer; Esophageal Cancer; Mediastinal Tumors; Robotic Surgery; **Hospital:** Meml Sloan Kettering Canc Ctr (page 110); **Address:** MSKCC, Cardiothoracic Surgery, 1275 York Ave, Box 533, New York, NY 10065; **Phone:** 646-888-3346; **Board Cert:** Surgery 2011; Thoracic Surgery 2013; **Med School:** Univ Pennsylvania 1993; **Resid:** Surgery, NY-Presby/Weill Cornell Med Ctr 2000; **Fellow:** Cardiothoracic Surgery, NY-Presby/Weill Cornell Med Ctr 2002; Thoracic Surgery, Meml Sloan-Kettering Cancer Ctr 2002; **Fac Appt:** Prof T&CS, Cornell Univ-Weill Med Coll

Pass, Harvey I MD (T&CS) - **Spec Exp:** Lung Cancer; Mesothelioma; Clinical Trials; Robotic Surgery; **Hospital:** NYU Langone Med Ctr (page 104); **Address:** NYU Cancer Ctr, 160 E 34th St, Fl 8, New York, NY 10016; **Phone:** 212-731-5414; **Board Cert:** Thoracic & Cardiac Surgery 2014; **Med School:** Duke Univ 1973; **Resid:** Surgery, Duke Univ Hosp 1975; Surgery, Univ Mississippi Med Ctr 1980; **Fellow:** Cardiothoracic Surgery, MUSC Med Ctr 1982; Thoracic Oncology, Natl Cancer Inst 1985; **Fac Appt:** Prof T&CS, NYU Sch Med

Patel, Nirav C MD (T&CS) - **Spec Exp:** Robotic Cardiac Surgery; Minimally Invasive Heart Valve Surgery; Coronary Artery Surgery; **Hospital:** Lenox Hill Hosp; **Address:** Lenox Hill Hosp, Cardiothoracic Surgery, 130 E 77th St Fl 4, New York, NY 10075; **Phone:** 212-434-6833; **Med School:** India 1992; **Resid:** Surgery, BYL Nair Charitable Hosp 1996; **Fellow:** Thoracic & Cardiac Surgery, Univ Liverpool Med Ctr 1998; Robotic Surgery, Lenox Hill Hosp 1999

Port, Jeffrey L MD (T&CS) - **Spec Exp:** Lung Cancer; Esophageal Cancer; Mesothelioma; **Hospital:** NY-Presby/Weill Cornell Med Ctr, NY (page 102); **Address:** NY-Presby, Cardiothoracic Surgery, 525 E 68th St, Ste M-404, New York, NY 10065; **Phone:** 212-746-5197; **Board Cert:** Surgery 2009; Thoracic & Cardiac Surgery 2009; **Med School:** NYU Sch Med 1991; **Resid:** Surgery, NYU Med Ctr 1998; **Fellow:** Thoracic Surgery, Meml Sloan-Kettering Cancer Ctr 2000; **Fac Appt:** Prof TS, Cornell Univ-Weill Med Coll

Puskas, John D MD (T&CS) - **Spec Exp:** Maze Procedure for Atrial Fibrillation; Aortic Surgery; Coronary Artery Surgery; Heart Valve Surgery; **Hospital:** Mt Sinai Beth Israel; **Address:** 1190 Fifth Ave, Box 1028, Guggenheim Pavilion 2 West, New York, NY 10029; **Phone:** 212-659-6800; **Board Cert:** Surgery 2004; Thoracic & Cardiac Surgery 2006; **Med School:** Harvard Med Sch 1986; **Resid:** Surgery, Mass Genl Hosp 1993; **Fellow:** Research, Toronto Genl Hosp 1991; Cardiothoracic Surgery, Emory Univ Hosp 1996; **Fac Appt:** Prof T&CS, Mount Sinai-Icahn Sch of Med

Rizk, Nabil P MD (T&CS) - **Spec Exp:** Esophageal Cancer; Lung Cancer; Thoracic Cancers; Minimally Invasive Surgery; **Hospital:** Meml Sloan Kettering Canc Ctr (page 110); **Address:** Meml Sloan-Kettering Cancer Ctr, 1275 York Ave, New York, NY 10021; **Phone:** 212-639-8357; **Board Cert:** Surgery 2009; Thoracic Surgery 2005; **Med School:** Yale Univ 1992; **Resid:** Surgery, Univ PA Hlth Systm 1999; **Fellow:** Thoracic Surgery, NY-Presby Hosp 2004; Thoracic Surgery, Meml Sloan-Kettering Canc Ctr 2005

Rusch, Valerie MD (T&CS) - **Spec Exp:** Mesothelioma; Lung Cancer; Esophageal Cancer; Thoracic Cancers; **Hospital:** Meml Sloan Kettering Canc Ctr (page 110); **Address:** MSKCC, Thoracic Surgery, 1275 York Ave, New York, NY 10021; **Phone:** 212-639-5873; **Board Cert:** Surgery 2011; Thoracic Surgery 2013; **Med School:** Columbia P&S 1975; **Resid:** Surgery, Univ Washington Med Ctr 1980; Cardiothoracic Surgery, Univ Washington Med Ctr 1982; **Fac Appt:** Prof TS, Cornell Univ-Weill Med Coll

Smith Jr, Craig R MD (T&CS) - **Spec Exp:** Mitral Valve Surgery; Minimally Invasive Cardiac Surgery; Robotic Cardiac Surgery; Coronary Artery Surgery; **Hospital:** NY-Presby/Columbia Univ Med Ctr, NY (page 102); **Address:** NY-Presby, Cardiothoracic Surgery, 177 Fort Washington Ave, Ste 7-435, New York, NY 10032; **Phone:** 212-305-8312; **Board Cert:** Thoracic & Cardiac Surgery 2004; **Med School:** Case West Res Univ 1977; **Resid:** Surgery, Univ Rochester-Strong Meml Hosp 1982; **Fellow:** Cardiothoracic Surgery, NY-Presby/Columbia Univ Med Ctr 1984; **Fac Appt:** Prof S, Columbia P&S

Sonett, Joshua R MD (T&CS) - **Spec Exp:** Minimally Invasive Thoracic Surgery; Transplant-Lung; Thoracic Cancers; Emphysema-Lung Volume Reduction; **Hospital:** NY-Presby/Columbia Univ Med Ctr, NY (page 102); **Address:** NY-Presby, Cardiothoracic Surgery, 161 Fort Washington Ave, Ste 301, New York, NY 10032; **Phone:** 212-305-8086; **Board Cert:** Surgery 2004; Thoracic & Cardiac Surgery 2007; **Med School:** E Carolina Univ 1988; **Resid:** Surgery, UMass Med Ctr 1993; **Fellow:** Cardiothoracic Surgery, UPMC 1994; Thoracic Surgery, Meml Sloan-Kettering Cancer Ctr; **Fac Appt:** Prof S, Columbia P&S

Stelzer, Paul MD (T&CS) - **Spec Exp:** Heart Valve Surgery; Aneurysm-Thoracic Aortic; Ross Procedure/Aortic Valve Disease; **Hospital:** Mt Sinai Hosp; **Address:** Mt Sinai, Cardiothoractic Surgery, 1190 Fifth Ave, Guggenheim Bldg - Fl GP2W, New York, NY 10029; **Phone:** 212-659-6871; **Board Cert:** Thoracic & Cardiac Surgery 2013; **Med School:** Columbia P&S 1972; **Resid:** Surgery, St Luke's Roosevelt Hosp 1977; Thoracic Surgery, NY Hosp 1981; **Fac Appt:** Prof T&CS, Mount Sinai-Icahn Sch of Med

Stewart, Allan S MD (T&CS) - **Spec Exp:** Cardiac Surgery; Aortic Surgery-Complex; Aortic Valve Replacement; Minimally Invasive Heart Valve Surgery; **Hospital:** Mt Sinai Hosp; **Address:** Mt Sinai, Cardiothoracic Surgery, 1190 5th Ave, Fl 2, New York, NY 10029; **Phone:** 212-659-6807; **Board Cert:** Thoracic & Cardiac Surgery 2006; **Med School:** UMDNJ-NJ Med Sch, Newark 1995; **Resid:** Surgery, Hosp Univ Penn 2002; **Fellow:** Thoracic Surgery, NY-Presby/Columbia Univ Med Ctr 2004; **Fac Appt:** Assoc Prof TS, Mount Sinai-Icahn Sch of Med

Swistel, Daniel MD (T&CS) - **Spec Exp:** Coronary Artery Surgery; Minimally Invasive Surgery; Heart Valve Surgery; Hypertrophic Cardiomyopathy; **Hospital:** Mt Sinai St. Luke's; **Address:** St Lukes Hosp, Cardiothoracic Surgery, 1090 Amsterdam Ave, Ste 8B, New York, NY 10025; **Phone:** 212-523-4088; **Board Cert:** Thoracic & Cardiac Surgery 2006; **Med School:** Rutgers R W Johnson Med Sch 1979; **Resid:** Surgery, St Lukes-Roosevelt Hosp 1984; Cardiothoracic Surgery, Montefiore Med Ctr 1986; **Fac Appt:** Assoc Clin Prof TS, Columbia P&S

Tranbaugh, Robert F MD (T&CS) - **Spec Exp:** Coronary Artery Surgery; Heart Valve Surgery; Aneurysm-Thoracic Aortic; **Hospital:** Mt Sinai Beth Israel, Mt Sinai Roosevelt; **Address:** Beth Israel Med Ctr, Division of Cardiac Surgery, 317 E 17th St, Fl 11, New York, NY 10003; **Phone:** 212-420-2584; **Board Cert:** Thoracic & Cardiac Surgery 2004; **Med School:** Univ Pennsylvania 1976; **Resid:** Surgery, UCSF Med Ctr 1983; Cardiothoracic Surgery, UCSF Med Ctr 1985; **Fac Appt:** Assoc Clin Prof T&CS, Albert Einstein Coll Med

Williams, Mathew R MD (T&CS) - **Spec Exp:** Interventional Cardiology; Heart Valve Surgery; **Hospital:** NYU Langone Med Ctr (page 104); **Address:** 530 First Ave, New York, NY 10016; **Phone:** 646-501-0197; **Board Cert:** Thoracic & Cardiac Surgery 2007; **Med School:** Columbia P&S 1996; **Resid:** Surgery, NY-Presby/Columbia Univ Med Ctr 2003; Cardiothoracic Surgery, NY-Presby/Columbia Univ Med Ctr 2005; **Fellow:** Research, NY-Presby/Columbia Univ Med Ctr 2001; Interventional Cardiology, NY-Presby/Columbia Univ Med Ctr 2006; **Fac Appt:** Asst Prof S, Columbia P&S

Urology

Armenakas, Noel A MD (U) - **Spec Exp:** Genitourinary Reconstruction; Trauma; **Hospital:** Lenox Hill Hosp, NY-Presby/Weill Cornell Med Ctr, NY (page 102); **Address:** New York Urological Assocs, 880 5th Ave, New York, NY 10021-4951; **Phone:** 212-535-1950; **Board Cert:** Urology 2012; **Med School:** Greece 1985; **Resid:** Urology, Monmouth Med Ctr 1987; Urology, Lenox Hill Hosp 1991; **Fellow:** Trauma, UCSF Med Ctr 1992; Reconstructive Surgery, UCSF Med Ctr 1992; **Fac Appt:** Clin Prof U, Cornell Univ-Weill Med Coll

Badani, Ketan K MD (U) - **Spec Exp:** Robotic Surgery; Prostate Cancer/Robotic Surgery; Minimally Invasive Urologic Surgery; Kidney Cancer; **Hospital:** Mt Sinai Hosp, Mt Sinai Roosevelt; **Address:** NYC Robotic Inst, 5 E 98th St Fl 6, New York, NY 10032; **Phone:** 212-241-3919; **Board Cert:** Urology 2009; **Med School:** Case West Res Univ 2001; **Resid:** Urology, Henry Ford Hosp 2005; **Fellow:** Robotic Surgery, Vattikuti Urology Inst 2007; **Fac Appt:** Prof U, Mount Sinai-Icahn Sch of Med

Bar-Chama, Natan MD (U) - **Spec Exp:** Infertility-Male; Erectile Dysfunction; Vasectomy Reversal; Varicocele Microsurgery; **Hospital:** Mt Sinai Hosp; **Address:** Reproductive Med Assocs of NY, 635 Madison Ave Fl 10, New York, NY 10022; **Phone:** 212-756-5777; **Board Cert:** Urology 2006; **Med School:** Albert Einstein Coll Med 1987; **Resid:** Urology, Montefiore Med Ctr 1993; **Fellow:** Male Infertility, Baylor Med Ctr 1994; **Fac Appt:** Assoc Prof U, Mount Sinai-Icahn Sch of Med

Benson, Mitchell C MD (U) - **Spec Exp:** Prostate Cancer/Robotic Surgery; Bladder Cancer; Kidney Cancer; Continent Urinary Diversions; **Hospital:** NY-Presby/Columbia Univ Med Ctr, NY (page 102); **Address:** NY-Presby, Urology, 161 Fort Washington Ave Fl 11, New York, NY 10032; **Phone:** 212-305-0114; **Board Cert:** Urology 1984; **Med School:** Columbia P&S 1977; **Resid:** Surgery, Mt Sinai Hosp 1979; Urology, NY-Presby/Columbia Univ Med Ctr 1982; **Fellow:** Oncology, Johns Hopkins Hosp 1984; **Fac Appt:** Prof U, Columbia P&S

Berman, Steven M MD (U) - **Spec Exp:** Prostate Cancer; Minimally Invasive Urologic Surgery; Kidney Cancer; Bladder Cancer; **Hospital:** Mt Sinai Beth Israel, NY-Presby/Weill Cornell Med Ctr, NY (page 102); **Address:** Advanced Urology Ctrs NY, 201 E 19th St, New York, NY 10003; **Phone:** 212-673-7300; **Board Cert:** Urology 2006; **Med School:** SUNY Downstate 1981; **Resid:** Surgery, Montefiore Med Ctr 1983; Urology, Montefiore Med Ctr 1986

Birns, Douglas R MD (U) - **Spec Exp:** Prostate Cancer; Urologic Cancer; Minimally Invasive Surgery; Kidney Stones; **Hospital:** Mt Sinai Hosp, Mt Sinai Beth Israel; **Address:** 157 E 72nd St, Ground Fl, New York, NY 10021-4331; **Phone:** 212-744-8700; **Board Cert:** Urology 2006; **Med School:** SUNY Downstate 1981; **Resid:** Urology, Mt Sinai Med Ctr 1986; **Fac Appt:** Asst Clin Prof U, Mount Sinai Sch Med

Blaivas, Jerry G MD (U) - **Spec Exp:** Genitourinary Reconstruction; Uro-Gynecology; Prostate Benign Disease; Urodynamics; **Hospital:** NY-Presby/Weill Cornell Med Ctr, NY (page 102), Lenox Hill Hosp; **Address:** UroCenter of NY, 445 E 77th St, New York, NY 10075; **Phone:** 212-772-3900; **Board Cert:** Urology 1978; **Med School:** Tufts Univ 1968; **Resid:** Surgery, Boston Med Ctr 1971; Urology, Tufts Med Ctr 1976; **Fac Appt:** Clin Prof U, Cornell Univ-Weill Med Coll

Bochner, Bernard H MD (U) - **Spec Exp:** Bladder Cancer; Urinary Reconstruction; **Hospital:** Meml Sloan Kettering Canc Ctr (page 110); **Address:** Kimmel Ctr for Urologic Cancers, 353 E 68th St, New York, NY 10065; **Phone:** 646-422-4387; **Board Cert:** Urology 2011; **Med School:** UCLA 1990; **Resid:** Surgery, LAC-USC Med Ctr 1992; Urology, LAC-USC Med Ctr 1996; **Fellow:** Urologic Oncology, USC/Norris Comp Canc Ctr 1998

Boczko, Stanley MD (U) - **Spec Exp:** Prostate Cancer; Impotence; Prostate Disease; **Hospital:** Montefiore Med Ctr-Moses Campus (page 100), Lenox Hill Hosp; **Address:** 23 E 79th St, New York, NY 10021; **Phone:** 212-628-1800; **Board Cert:** Urology 1981; **Med School:** Albert Einstein Coll Med 1973; **Resid:** Surgery, Montefiore Med Ctr 1975; Urology, Montefiore Med Ctr 1979; **Fellow:** Transplant Surgery, Montefiore Med Ctr 1975

Brodherson, Michael S MD (U) - **Spec Exp:** Urologic Cancer; Kidney Stones; **Hospital:** Lenox Hill Hosp; **Address:** 4 E 76th St, New York, NY 10021-2611; **Phone:** 212-794-2749; **Board Cert:** Urology 1981; **Med School:** SUNY Downstate 1973; **Resid:** Urology, Lenox Hill Hosp 1979

Coleman, Jonathan A MD (U) - **Spec Exp:** Prostate Cancer; Kidney Cancer; Adrenal Cancer; Minimally Invasive Surgery; **Hospital:** Meml Sloan Kettering Canc Ctr (page 110); **Address:** MSKCC, Urology, 1275 York Ave, New York, NY 10065; **Phone:** 646-422-4432; **Board Cert:** Urology 2006; **Med School:** Cornell Univ-Weill Med Coll 1996; **Resid:** Surgery, NY-Presby/Weill Cornell Med Ctr 1998; **Fellow:** Urology, NY-Presby/Weill Cornell Med Ctr 2002; Urology, Natl Cancer Inst 2003

Cooper, Kimberly L MD (U) - **Spec Exp:** Urology-Female; Incontinence; Neuro-Urology; Voiding Dysfunction; **Hospital:** NY-Presby/Columbia Univ Med Ctr, NY (page 102); **Address:** Columbia Dept Urology, 161 Fort Washington Ave Fl 11, New York, NY 10032; **Phone:** 212-305-0114; **Board Cert:** Urology 2014; **Med School:** Columbia P&S 1997; **Resid:** Urology, Columbia Univ Med Ctr 2002; **Fellow:** Female Urology, Columbia Univ Med Ctr 2003; Neurourology, Columbia Univ Med Ctr 2003; **Fac Appt:** Asst Prof U, Columbia P&S

Del Pizzo, Joseph J MD (U) - **Spec Exp:** Laparoscopic Kidney Surgery; Robotic Surgery; Kidney Cancer; Kidney Stones; **Hospital:** NY-Presby/Weill Cornell Med Ctr, NY (page 102); **Address:** Brady Urologic Health Ctr, 525 E 68th St Fl 9, New York, NY 10021; **Phone:** 212-746-5250; **Board Cert:** Urology 2013; **Med School:** Albert Einstein Coll Med 1994; **Resid:** Surgery, Mercy Med Ctr 1996; Urology, Univ Maryland Med Ctr 1999; **Fellow:** Laparoscopic Surgery, Univ Maryland 2000; **Fac Appt:** Assoc Prof U, Cornell Univ-Weill Med Coll

Dillon, Robert W MD (U) - **Spec Exp:** Kidney Stones; Urologic Cancer; Urology-Female; **Hospital:** Mt Sinai Hosp; **Address:** 1120 Park Ave, New York, NY 10128; **Phone:** 212-794-9000; **Board Cert:** Urology 1980; **Med School:** NY Med Coll 1973; **Resid:** Surgery, Mt Sinai Hosp 1975; Urology, Mt Sinai Hosp 1978; **Fac Appt:** Asst Clin Prof U, Mount Sinai Sch Med

Dinlenc, Caner Z MD (U) - **Spec Exp:** Kidney Stones; Kidney Cancer; Robotic Surgery; Prostate Cancer; **Hospital:** Mt Sinai Beth Israel; **Address:** Beth Israel Dept Urology, 10 Union Square E, Ste 3A, New York, NY 10003; **Phone:** 212-844-8900; **Board Cert:** Urology 2011; **Med School:** Boston Univ 1993; **Resid:** Urology, Boston Univ Med Ctr 1999; **Fellow:** Endourology, LIJ Med Ctr 2000; **Fac Appt:** Assoc Prof U, Mount Sinai-Icahn Sch of Med

Droller, Michael J MD (U) - **Spec Exp:** Urologic Cancer; Bladder Cancer; Prostate Cancer; Kidney Cancer; **Hospital:** Mt Sinai Hosp; **Address:** 5 E 98th St Fl 6, Box 1272, New York, NY 10029-6501; **Phone:** 212-241-3868; **Board Cert:** Urology 2001; **Med School:** Harvard Med Sch 1968; **Resid:** Surgery, Peter Bent Brigham Hosp 1970; Urology, Stanford Univ Med Ctr 1976; **Fellow:** Research, Univ Stockholm 1977; **Fac Appt:** Prof U, Mount Sinai Sch Med

Eastham, James A MD (U) - **Spec Exp:** Prostate Cancer; Prostate Cancer/Robotic Surgery; **Hospital:** Meml Sloan Kettering Canc Ctr (page 110); **Address:** Kimmel Ctr for Urologic Cancers, 353 E 68th St, New York, NY 10065; **Phone:** 646-422-4390; **Board Cert:** Urology 2005; **Med School:** USC Sch Med 1987; **Resid:** Urology, LAC-USC Med Ctr 1993; **Fellow:** Urologic Oncology, Baylor Coll Med 1995

Fine, Eugene M MD (U) - **Spec Exp:** Prostate Cancer; Prostate Disease; Erectile Dysfunction; Kidney Stones; **Hospital:** Mt Sinai Hosp, Lenox Hill Hosp; **Address:** Prostate HealthCare of NY, 12 E 86th St, New York, NY 10028; **Phone:** 212-517-9555; **Board Cert:** Urology 2005; **Med School:** Mexico 1978; **Resid:** Surgery, Downstate Med Ctr 1981; Urology, Mount Sinai Hosp 1985; **Fac Appt:** Asst Clin Prof U, Mount Sinai Sch Med

Fisch, Harry MD (U) - **Spec Exp:** Infertility-Male; Microsurgery; Vasectomy Reversal; **Hospital:** NY-Presby/Weill Cornell Med Ctr, NY (page 102), Lenox Hill Hosp; **Address:** 944 Park Ave, Ste 1C, New York, NY 10028; **Phone:** 212-879-0800; **Board Cert:** Urology 2010; **Med School:** Mount Sinai Sch Med 1983; **Resid:** Surgery, Montefiore Med Ctr 1985; Urology, Montefiore Med Ctr 1989; **Fac Appt:** Prof U, Columbia P&S

Fracchia, John A MD (U) - **Spec Exp:** Urologic Cancer; Prostate Benign Disease; Kidney Stones; **Hospital:** Lenox Hill Hosp, NY-Presby/Weill Cornell Med Ctr, NY (page 102); **Address:** NY Urological Assocs, 245 E 54th St, Ste 2N, New York, NY 10022; **Phone:** 212-570-6800 x185; **Board Cert:** Urology 1981; **Med School:** UMDNJ-NJ Med Sch, Newark 1973; **Resid:** Urology, New York Hosp 1979; Urology, Meml Sloan Kettering Cancer Ctr 1980; **Fac Appt:** Clin Prof U, Cornell Univ-Weill Med Coll

Goldstein, Marc MD (U) - **Spec Exp:** Infertility-Male; Varicocele Microsurgery; Vasectomy & Vasectomy Reversal; Microsurgery; **Hospital:** NY-Presby/Weill Cornell Med Ctr, NY (page 102); **Address:** NY-Presby, Urology, 525 E 68th St, Box 269, Ste STARR 900, New York, NY 10065; **Phone:** 212-746-5470; **Board Cert:** Urology 1982; **Med School:** SUNY Downstate 1972; **Resid:** Surgery, NY-Presby/Columbia Univ Med Ctr 1974; Urology, SUNY Downstate Med Ctr 1980; **Fellow:** Microsurgery, Rockefeller Univ 1982; Reproductive Medicine, Rockefeller Univ 1982; **Fac Appt:** Prof U, SUNY Downstate

Grasso III, Michael MD (U) - **Spec Exp:** Urologic Cancer; Kidney Cancer; Laparoscopic Kidney Surgery; Kidney Stones; **Hospital:** Lenox Hill Hosp, Westchester Med Ctr; **Address:** Lenox Hill Hosp, Endourology, 100 E 77th St, East Bldg - Fl 4, New York, NY 10075; **Phone:** 212-434-6300; **Board Cert:** Urology 2013; **Med School:** Jefferson Med Coll 1986; **Resid:** Surgery, Jefferson Univ Hosp 1988; Urology, Jefferson Univ Hosp 1992; **Fac Appt:** Prof U, NY Med Coll

Gribetz, Michael Elliot MD (U) - **Spec Exp:** Prostate Disease; Urology-Female; Sexual Dysfunction; Bladder Cancer; **Hospital:** Mt Sinai Hosp; **Address:** 1155 Park Ave, New York, NY 10128; **Phone:** 212-831-1300; **Board Cert:** Urology 1980; **Med School:** Albert Einstein Coll Med 1973; **Resid:** Surgery, Montefiore Med Ctr 1975; Urology, Mt Sinai Hosp 1978; **Fac Appt:** Asst Clin Prof U, Mount Sinai Sch Med

Gupta, Mantu MD (U) - **Spec Exp:** Kidney Stones; Endourology; Minimally Invasive Urologic Surgery; **Hospital:** Mt Sinai Roosevelt, Mt Sinai St. Luke's; **Address:** 625 Madison Ave Fl 2, New York, NY 10022; **Phone:** 212-241-1272; **Board Cert:** Urology 2007; **Med School:** Northwestern Univ 1989; **Resid:** Urology, UCSF Med Ctr 1995; **Fellow:** Endourology, LI Jewish Med Ctr 1996; **Fac Appt:** Prof U, Mount Sinai-Icahn Sch of Med

Hall, Simon J MD (U) - **Spec Exp:** Urologic Cancer; Minimally Invasive Urologic Surgery; Continent Urinary Diversions; Prostate Cancer; **Hospital:** Mt Sinai Hosp; **Address:** Mt Sinai, Urology, 5 E 98th St, Box 1272, New York, NY 10029; **Phone:** 212-241-4812; **Board Cert:** Urology 2009; **Med School:** Columbia P&S 1988; **Resid:** Surgery, Mt Sinai Hosp 1990; Urology, Boston Med Ctr 1994; **Fellow:** Urology, Baylor Med Ctr 1996; **Fac Appt:** Assoc Prof U, Mount Sinai-Icahn Sch of Med

Herr, Harry W MD (U) - **Spec Exp:** Bladder Cancer; Prostate Cancer; Testicular Cancer; **Hospital:** Meml Sloan Kettering Canc Ctr (page 110), NY-Presby/Weill Cornell Med Ctr, NY (page 102); **Address:** 1275 York Avenue, New York, NY 10021; **Phone:** 646-422-4411; **Board Cert:** Urology 1976; **Med School:** UCSF 1969; **Resid:** Urology, UC Irvine Med Ctr 1974; **Fellow:** Urology, Meml Sloan Kettering Cancer Ctr 1976; **Fac Appt:** Assoc Prof S, Cornell Univ-Weill Med Coll

Huang, William C MD (U) - **Spec Exp:** Urologic Cancer; Robotic Surgery; Bladder Cancer; Kidney Cancer; **Hospital:** NYU Langone Med Ctr (page 104), Bellevue Hosp Ctr; **Address:** 150 E 32nd St, Fl 2, NYU Urology Assocs, New York, NY 10016; **Phone:** 646-744-1503; **Board Cert:** Urology 2009; **Med School:** Jefferson Med Coll 1998; **Resid:** Surgery, Lahey Clin Med Ctr 2000; Urologic Surgery, Lahey Clin Med Ctr 2004; **Fellow:** Urologic Oncology, Meml Sloan-Kettering Cancer Ctr 2007; **Fac Appt:** Asst Prof U, NYU Sch Med

Kaminetsky, Jed C MD (U) - **Spec Exp:** Sexual Dysfunction; Prostate Cancer; Kidney Stones; Prostate Disease; **Hospital:** NYU Langone Med Ctr (page 104); **Address:** University Urology, 215 Lexington Ave Fl 20, New York, NY 10016; **Phone:** 212-686-9015; **Board Cert:** Urology 2010; **Med School:** NYU Sch Med 1984; **Resid:** Urology, NYU Med Ctr 1990; **Fac Appt:** Asst Clin Prof U, NYU Sch Med

Kaplan, Steven A MD (U) - **Spec Exp:** Prostate Disease; Voiding Dysfunction; Incontinence; **Hospital:** NY-Presby/Weill Cornell Med Ctr, NY (page 102); **Address:** 425 E 61 St, Fl 12, New York, NY 10065; **Phone:** 646-962-4811; **Board Cert:** Urology 2011; **Med School:** Mount Sinai Sch Med 1982; **Resid:** Surgery, Mount Sinai Hosp 1984; Urology, Columbia Presby Med Ctr 1988; **Fellow:** Urology, Columbia Presby Med Ctr 1990; **Fac Appt:** Prof U, Cornell Univ-Weill Med Coll

Kavaler, Elizabeth MD (U) - **Spec Exp:** Urology-Female; Incontinence; Uro-Gynecology; Pelvic Organ Prolapse Repair; **Hospital:** NY-Presby/Weill Cornell Med Ctr, NY (page 102), Lenox Hill Hosp; **Address:** NY Urological Assocs, 245 E 54th St, Ste 2N, New York, NY 10022; **Phone:** 212-570-6800; **Board Cert:** Urology 2013; Female Pelvic Medicine & Reconstuctive Surgery 2013; **Med School:** SUNY Downstate 1992; **Resid:** Urology, Mt Sinai Med Ctr 1998; **Fellow:** Female Urology, UCLA Med Ctr 2000; **Fac Appt:** Asst Clin Prof U, Cornell Univ-Weill Med Coll

Kirschenbaum, Alexander M MD (U) - **Spec Exp:** Prostate Cancer; Bladder Cancer; Kidney Cancer; Bladder Reconstruction; **Hospital:** Mt Sinai Hosp; **Address:** 229 E 79th St, Ste 1A, New York, NY 10075; **Phone:** 646-422-0926; **Board Cert:** Urology 2006; **Med School:** Mount Sinai Sch Med 1980; **Resid:** Surgery, Mt Sinai Hosp 1982; Urology, Mt Sinai Hosp 1985; **Fellow:** Urologic Oncology, Mt Sinai Hosp 1987; **Fac Appt:** Assoc Clin Prof U, Mount Sinai-Icahn Sch of Med

Klein, George MD (U) - **Spec Exp:** Kidney Stones; Sexual Dysfunction; Prostate Cancer; **Hospital:** Mt Sinai Hosp, Mt Sinai Beth Israel; **Address:** 157 E 72nd St, Ground Fl, New York, NY 10021; **Phone:** 212-744-8700; **Board Cert:** Urology 1983; **Med School:** Cornell Univ 1976; **Resid:** Surgery, N Shore Univ Hosp 1978; Urology, Mount Sinai Med Ctr 1981; **Fac Appt:** Asst Prof U, Mount Sinai Sch Med

Laudone, Vincent P MD (U) - **Spec Exp:** Robotic Surgery; Prostate Cancer; Bladder Cancer; Genitourinary Cancer; **Hospital:** Meml Sloan Kettering Canc Ctr (page 110); **Address:** Kimmel Ctr for Urologic Cancers, 353 E 68th St, New York, NY 10065; **Phone:** 646-422-4306; **Board Cert:** Urology 2009; **Med School:** Georgetown Univ 1981; **Resid:** Urology, Univ Virginia Med Ctr 1986; **Fellow:** Urologic Oncology, Meml Sloan-Kettering Cancer Ctr 1988

Lepor, Herbert MD (U) - **Spec Exp:** Prostate Cancer; **Hospital:** NYU Langone Med Ctr (page 104); **Address:** NYU Urology Assocs, 150 E 32nd St Fl 2, New York, NY 10016; **Phone:** 646-825-6327; **Board Cert:** Urology 2006; **Med School:** Johns Hopkins Univ 1975; **Resid:** Urology, Johns Hopkins Hosp 1986; **Fac Appt:** Prof U, NYU Sch Med

Lizza, Eli F MD (U) - **Spec Exp:** Impotence; Infertility-Male; **Hospital:** Lenox Hill Hosp, NY-Presby/Weill Cornell Med Ctr, NY (page 102); **Address:** New York Urological Assocs, 245 E 54th St, Fl 2, Ste 2N, New York, NY 10022; **Phone:** 212-570-6800 x180; **Board Cert:** Urology 2006; **Med School:** UMDNJ-NJ Med Sch, Newark 1979; **Resid:** Surgery, Lenox Hill Hosp 1981; Urology, W VA Med Ctr 1984; **Fellow:** Infertility, NY-Presby/Columbia Univ Med Ctr 1985

Loo, Marcus Hsieu-Hong MD (U) - **Spec Exp:** Prostate Disease; Kidney Stones; Voiding Dysfunction; Prostate Cancer; **Hospital:** NY-Presby/Weill Cornell Med Ctr, NY (page 102); **Address:** 254 Canal St, Ste 3001, New York, NY 10013-3501; **Phone:** 212-925-8388; **Board Cert:** Urology 2008; **Med School:** Cornell Univ-Weill Med Coll 1981; **Resid:** Surgery, NY Hosp-Cornell Med Ctr 1983; Urology, NY Hosp-Cornell Med Ctr 1988; **Fac Appt:** Clin Prof U, Cornell Univ-Weill Med Coll

Lowe, Franklin Charles MD (U) - **Spec Exp:** Prostate Disease; Complementary Medicine; Prostate Cancer; Kidney Stones; **Hospital:** Mt Sinai Roosevelt, Mt Sinai St. Luke's; **Address:** 425 W 59th St, Ste 3A, New York, NY 10019; **Phone:** 212-523-7790; **Board Cert:** Urology 2006; **Med School:** Columbia P&S 1979; **Resid:** Surgery, Johns Hopkins Hosp 1981; Urology, Johns Hopkins Hosp 1984; **Fac Appt:** Prof U, Mount Sinai-Icahn Sch of Med

Marks, Jon O MD (U) - **Spec Exp:** Kidney Stones; Interstitial Cystitis; **Hospital:** Mt Sinai Beth Israel; **Address:** Advanced Urology Ctrs NY, 201 E 19th St, New York, NY 10003; **Phone:** 212-673-7300; **Board Cert:** Urology 1983; **Med School:** NY Med Coll 1976; **Resid:** Surgery, Lenox Hill Hosp 1978; Urology, Lenox Hill Hosp 1981

McGovern, Thomas P MD (U) - **Spec Exp:** Prostate Cancer; Prostate Disease; Bladder Cancer; **Hospital:** NY-Presby/Weill Cornell Med Ctr, NY (page 102); **Address:** 525 E 68 St, Ste F9 West, New York, NY 10065-6310; **Phone:** 212-772-7411; **Board Cert:** Urology 1983; **Med School:** Cornell Univ 1974; **Resid:** Surgery, Mass Genl Hosp 1976; Urology, New York Hosp 1980

McKiernan, James M MD (U) - **Spec Exp:** Kidney Cancer; Bladder Cancer; Prostate Cancer; Testicular Cancer; **Hospital:** NY-Presby/Columbia Univ Med Ctr, NY (page 102); **Address:** Columbia Univ Med Ctr - Dept Urology, 161 Ft Washington Ave Fl 11, Herbert Irving Pavilion, New York, NY 10032; **Phone:** 212-305-5526; **Board Cert:** Urology 2012; **Med School:** Columbia P&S 1993; **Resid:** Surgery, NY-Presby/Columbia Univ Med Ctr 1995; Urology, NY-Presby/Columbia Univ Med Ctr 1999; **Fellow:** Urologic Oncology, Meml Sloan-Kettering Canc Ctr 2001; **Fac Appt:** Prof U, Columbia P&S

Mulhall, John P MD (U) - **Spec Exp:** Erectile Dysfunction; Sexual Dysfunction-Post Surgical; Penile Prostheses; Incontinence After Prostate Cancer; **Hospital:** Meml Sloan Kettering Canc Ctr (page 110); **Address:** MSKCC, Urology Dept, 16 E 60th St, New York, NY 10022; **Phone:** 646-888-6024; **Board Cert:** Urology 2008; **Med School:** Ireland 1985; **Resid:** Urology, Univ Conn Hlth Ctr 1995; **Fellow:** Urology, Boston Med Ctr 1996; **Fac Appt:** Assoc Prof U, Cornell Univ-Weill Med Coll

Nagler, Harris M MD (U) - **Spec Exp:** Vasectomy Reversal; Infertility-Male; Varicocele Microsurgery; Erectile Dysfunction; **Hospital:** Mt Sinai Beth Israel; **Address:** Beth Israel Med Ctr, Dept Urology, 10 Union Square E, Ste 3A, New York, NY 10003-3314; **Phone:** 212-844-8700; **Board Cert:** Urology 1982; **Med School:** Temple Univ 1975; **Resid:** Urology, Columbia Presby Med Ctr 1980; **Fellow:** Reproductive Medicine, Columbia Presby Med Ctr 1981; **Fac Appt:** Prof U, Albert Einstein Coll Med

Nitti, Victor MD (U) - **Spec Exp:** Urology-Female; Incontinence-Male & Female; Urodynamics; Voiding Dysfunction; **Hospital:** NYU Langone Med Ctr (page 104); **Address:** NYU Urology Assocs, 150 E 32nd St Fl 2, New York, NY 10016; **Phone:** 646-825-6324; **Board Cert:** Urology 2013; Female Pelvic Medicine & Reconstuctive Surgery 2013; **Med School:** UMDNJ-NJ Med Sch, Newark 1985; **Resid:** Surgery, SUNY Downstate Med Ctr 1987; Urology, SUNY Downstate Med Ctr 1991; **Fellow:** Female Urology, UCLA Med Ctr 1992; **Fac Appt:** Prof U, NYU Sch Med

Nobert, Craig F MD (U) - **Spec Exp:** Laparoscopic Surgery; Robotic Surgery; Urologic Cancer; **Hospital:** Mt Sinai Roosevelt; **Address:** Mount Sinai Roosevelt Hosp, Dept Urology, 425 W 59th St, Ste 3A, New York, NY 10019; **Phone:** 212-523-7586; **Board Cert:** Urology 2007; **Med School:** Tufts Univ 1998; **Resid:** Surgery, New York Hosp 2000; Urology, New York Hosp 2004; **Fellow:** Urologic Oncology, Meml Sloan Kettering Cancer Ctr 2004

Palese, Michael A MD (U) - **Spec Exp:** Kidney Cancer; Laparoscopic Surgery; Robotic Surgery; Kidney Stones; **Hospital:** Mt Sinai Hosp; **Address:** Mt Sinai, Urology, 5 E 98th St Fl 6, New York, NY 10029; **Phone:** 212-241-3868; **Board Cert:** Urology 2006; **Med School:** Mount Sinai Sch Med 1997; **Resid:** Surgery, Univ MD Med Ctr 1999; Urology, Univ MD Med Ctr 2003; **Fellow:** Urologic Oncology, NY-Presby/Weill Cornell Med Ctr 2004; Robotic Surgery, NY-Presby/Weill Cornell Med Ctr 2004; **Fac Appt:** Assoc Prof U, Mount Sinai-Icahn Sch of Med

Peng, Benjamin C.H. MD (U) - **Spec Exp:** Prostate Disease; Kidney Stones; Urologic Cancer; Erectile Dysfunction; **Hospital:** NY-Presby/Lower Manhattan Hosp (page 102), NYU Langone Med Ctr (page 104); **Address:** 168 Canal St, Ste 310, New York, NY 10013-4503; **Phone:** 212-226-2200; **Board Cert:** Urology 2011; **Med School:** Columbia P&S 1984; **Resid:** Surgery, Mount Sinai Med Ctr 1986; Urology, Columbia-Presby Hosp 1990; **Fac Appt:** Asst Clin Prof U, NYU Sch Med

Provet, John A MD (U) - **Spec Exp:** Urologic Cancer; Kidney Stones; Prostate Disease; Kidney Cancer; **Hospital:** NYU Langone Med Ctr (page 104); **Address:** University Urology, 215 Lexington Ave Fl 20, New York, NY 10016; **Phone:** 212-686-9015; **Board Cert:** Urology 2009; **Med School:** NYU Sch Med 1983; **Resid:** Surgery, NYU Med Ctr 1985; Urology, NYU Med Ctr 1989; **Fac Appt:** Assoc Clin Prof U, NYU Sch Med

Reckler, Jon M MD (U) - **Spec Exp:** Urologic Cancer; Adrenal Surgery; **Hospital:** NY-Presby/Weill Cornell Med Ctr, NY (page 102), Lenox Hill Hosp; **Address:** NY Urological Assocs, 880 5th Ave, New York, NY 10021; **Phone:** 212-535-1950; **Board Cert:** Urology 1976; **Med School:** Harvard Med Sch 1966; **Resid:** Surgery, Univ Hosps 1968; Urology, Peter Bent Brigham Hosp 1974

Russo, Paul MD (U) - **Spec Exp:** Kidney Cancer; Adrenal Cancer; Penile Cancer; Bladder Cancer; **Hospital:** Meml Sloan Kettering Canc Ctr (page 110); **Address:** Kimmel Ctr for Urologic Cancers, 353 E 68th St, New York, NY 10065; **Phone:** 646-422-4391; **Board Cert:** Urology 2014; **Med School:** Columbia P&S 1979; **Resid:** Surgery, Barnes-Jewish Hosp 1984; Urology, Barnes-Jewish Hosp 1984; **Fellow:** Urologic Oncology, Mem Sloan Kettering Canc Ctr 1986; **Fac Appt:** Assoc Prof U, Cornell Univ-Weill Med Coll

Samadi, David B MD (U) - **Spec Exp:** Prostate Cancer/Robotic Surgery; Prostate Cancer; Prostate Benign Disease; Prostate Disease; **Hospital:** Lenox Hill Hosp; **Address:** 485 Madison Ave, Fl 21, New York, NY 10022; **Phone:** 212-365-5000; **Board Cert:** Urology 2013; **Med School:** SUNY Stony Brook 1994; **Resid:** Surgery, Montefiore Med Ctr 1996; Urology, Montefiore Med Ctr 2000; **Fellow:** Urologic Oncology, Meml Sloan Kettering Cancer Ctr 2001; Laparoscopic Surgery, Henri Mondor Hosp 2003; **Fac Appt:** Prof U, Hofstra N Shore-LIJ Sch Med

Sandhu, Jaspreet S MD (U) - **Spec Exp:** Voiding Dysfunction; Incontinence After Prostate Cancer; Bladder Reconstruction; Urinary Reconstruction; **Hospital:** Meml Sloan Kettering Canc Ctr (page 110); **Address:** 1275 York Ave, Dept Urology, New York, NY 10065; **Phone:** 646-422-4399; **Board Cert:** Urology 2007; **Med School:** Wake Forest Univ 1998; **Resid:** Surgery, NY-Presby-Cornell Med Ctr 2000; **Fellow:** Urology, NY-Presby-Cornell Med Ctr 2004

Scardino, Peter T MD (U) - **Spec Exp:** Prostate Cancer; Bladder Cancer; Urologic Cancer; Urinary Reconstruction; **Hospital:** Meml Sloan Kettering Canc Ctr (page 110); **Address:** MSKCC, Urology, 353 E 68th St, Ste 501A, New York, NY 10065; **Phone:** 646-422-4329; **Board Cert:** Urology 1981; **Med School:** Duke Univ 1971; **Resid:** Surgery, Mass Genl Hosp 1973; Urology, UCLA Med Ctr 1979; **Fellow:** Urology, Natl Cancer Inst 1976; **Fac Appt:** Prof U, Cornell Univ-Weill Med Coll

Scherr, Douglas S MD (U) - **Spec Exp:** Prostate Cancer/Robotic Surgery; Bladder Cancer; Robotic Surgery; Testicular Cancer; **Hospital:** NY-Presby/Weill Cornell Med Ctr, NY (page 102); **Address:** NY-Presby, Urology, 525 E 68th St, Starr 900, New York, NY 10065; **Phone:** 212-746-5788; **Board Cert:** Urology 2013; **Med School:** Geo Wash Univ 1994; **Resid:** Urology, NY-Presby/Weill Cornell Med Ctr 2000; **Fellow:** Urologic Oncology, Meml Sloan-Kettering Canc Ctr 2002; **Fac Appt:** Assoc Prof U, Cornell Univ-Weill Med Coll

Schiff, Howard I MD (U) - **Spec Exp:** Infertility-Male; Erectile Dysfunction; Bladder Cancer; Prostate Cancer; **Hospital:** Mt Sinai Hosp, NY-Presby/Weill Cornell Med Ctr, NY (page 102); **Address:** 1120 Park Ave, Ste 1E, New York, NY 10128-1242; **Phone:** 212-996-6660; **Board Cert:** Urology 1982; **Med School:** W VA Univ 1975; **Resid:** Surgery, Montefiore Med Ctr 1977; Urology, Mt Sinai Med Ctr 1980; **Fac Appt:** Asst Clin Prof U, Mount Sinai Sch Med

Schiff, Jonathan D MD (U) - **Spec Exp:** Infertility-Male; Erectile Dysfunction; Pelvic Pain Syndrome; Kidney Stones; **Hospital:** Mt Sinai Hosp, NY-Presby/Weill Cornell Med Ctr, NY (page 102); **Address:** 1120 Park Ave, New York, NY 10128; **Phone:** 212-996-6660; **Board Cert:** Urology 2008; **Med School:** Mount Sinai Sch Med 1999; **Resid:** Surgery, NY Presby-Cornell Med Ctr 2001; Urology, NY Presby-Cornell Med Ctr 2005; **Fellow:** Male Reproductive Medicine/Surgery, Mount Sinai Hosp 2006; **Fac Appt:** Asst Clin Prof U, Mount Sinai Sch Med

Schlegel, Peter N MD (U) - **Spec Exp:** Prostate Cancer; Fertility Preservation in Cancer; Infertility-Male; Testicular Cancer; **Hospital:** NY-Presby/Weill Cornell Med Ctr, NY (page 102), Hosp For Special Surgery (page 109); **Address:** Brady Urology Associates, 525 E 68th St, Starr Bldg - Fl 9 - Ste 900, New York, NY 10065-4870; **Phone:** 212-746-5491; **Board Cert:** Urology 2011; **Med School:** Univ Mass Sch Med 1983; **Resid:** Surgery, Johns Hopkins Hosp 1985; Urology, Johns Hopkins Hosp 1989; **Fellow:** Medical Oncology, Johns Hopkins Hosp 1987; Male Reproduction, NY-Presby/Weill Cornell Med Ctr 1991; **Fac Appt:** Prof U, Cornell Univ-Weill Med Coll

Shabsigh, Ridwan MD (U) - **Spec Exp:** Erectile Dysfunction; Hypogonadism; Clinical Trials; Incontinence; **Hospital:** NY-Presby/Weill Cornell Med Ctr, NY (page 102), St. Barnabas Hosp - Bronx; **Address:** 944 Park Ave, New York, NY 10028; **Phone:** 212-249-6060; **Board Cert:** Urology 2011; **Med School:** Syria 1976; **Resid:** Urology, Seepark Hosp 1983; Urology, Baylor Med Ctr 1990; **Fellow:** Urology, Baylor Med Ctr 1987; **Fac Appt:** Prof U, Cornell Univ-Weill Med Coll

Sheinfeld, Joel MD (U) - **Spec Exp:** Testicular Cancer; Fertility Preservation in Cancer; **Hospital:** Meml Sloan Kettering Canc Ctr (page 110); **Address:** MSKCC, Urology, 353 E 68th St, New York, NY 10065; **Phone:** 646-422-4311; **Board Cert:** Urology 2009; **Med School:** Univ Fla Coll Med 1981; **Resid:** Urology, Univ Rochester Strong Meml Hosp 1986; **Fellow:** Urologic Oncology, Meml Sloan-Kettering Cancer Ctr 1989; **Fac Appt:** Assoc Prof U, Cornell Univ-Weill Med Coll

Shemtov, M Mendel MD (U) - **Spec Exp:** Prostate Cancer; Urologic Cancer; Laser Surgery; **Hospital:** NY-Presby/Weill Cornell Med Ctr, NY (page 102); **Address:** 115 E 61st St Fl 11, New York, NY 10065; **Phone:** 212-813-1112; **Board Cert:** Urology 2010; **Med School:** Univ Pennsylvania 1989; **Resid:** Surgery, Mount Sinai Med Ctr 1991; Urology, Mount Sinai Med Ctr 1995; **Fellow:** Urologic Oncology, Weill Cornell Med Ctr 1997; **Fac Appt:** Assoc Clin Prof U, Cornell Univ-Weill Med Coll

Sogani, Pramod C MD (U) - **Spec Exp:** Prostate Cancer; Penile Cancer; Bladder Cancer; Kidney Cancer; **Hospital:** Meml Sloan Kettering Canc Ctr (page 110); **Address:** Kimmel Ctr for Urologic Cancers, 353 E 68th St, New York, NY 10065; **Phone:** 646-422-4395; **Board Cert:** Urology 1976; **Med School:** India 1960; **Resid:** Urology, NYU Med Ctr 1969; Urology, Geo Wash Univ Med Ctr 1971; **Fellow:** Surgical Oncology, Meml Sloan Kettering Cancer Ctr 1973; **Fac Appt:** Prof U, Cornell Univ-Weill Med Coll

Stein, Mark MD (U) - **Spec Exp:** Incontinence; Erectile Dysfunction; Voiding Dysfunction; **Hospital:** Mt Sinai Beth Israel, NY-Presby/Weill Cornell Med Ctr, NY (page 102); **Address:** Advanced Urology Ctrs NY, 201 E 19th St, New York, NY 10003; **Phone:** 212-673-7300; **Board Cert:** Urology 2011; **Med School:** Yale Univ 1984; **Resid:** Surgery, Montefiore Med Ctr 1986; Urology, Montefiore Med Ctr 1990

Stifelman, Michael D MD (U) - **Spec Exp:** Robotic Surgery; Reconstructive Surgery; Minimally Invasive Urologic Surgery; Kidney Cancer; **Hospital:** NYU Langone Med Ctr (page 104), Englewood Hosp & Med Ctr; **Address:** 150 E 32nd St, Fl 2, NYU Urology Assocs, New York, NY 10016-6024; **Phone:** 646-825-6325; **Board Cert:** Urology 2011; **Med School:** Albert Einstein Coll Med 1993; **Resid:** Surgery, NY Presbyterian/Columbia Med Ctr 1995; Urology, NY Presbyterian/Columbia Med Ctr 1999; **Fellow:** Minimally Invasive Surgery, NY Presbyterian/Weill Cornell Med Ctr 2000; **Fac Appt:** Assoc Prof U, NYU Sch Med

Taneja, Samir S MD (U) - **Spec Exp:** Prostate Cancer; Kidney Cancer; Robotic Urologic Surgery; Bladder Cancer; **Hospital:** NYU Langone Med Ctr (page 104); **Address:** NYU Urology Assocs, 150 E 32nd St, Fl 2, New York, NY 10016; **Phone:** 646-825-6321; **Board Cert:** Urology 2009; **Med School:** Northwestern Univ 1990; **Resid:** Urology, UCLA Med Ctr 1996; **Fac Appt:** Prof U, NYU Sch Med

Te, Alexis E MD (U) - **Spec Exp:** Prostate Benign Disease; Prostate Cancer; Incontinence; Neuro-Urology; **Hospital:** NY-Presby/Weill Cornell Med Ctr, NY (page 102); **Address:** Cantor Mens Health Centr, 425 E 61st St Fl 12, New York, NY 10065; **Phone:** 646-962-4811; **Board Cert:** Urology 2006; **Med School:** Cornell Univ 1988; **Resid:** Urology, Columbia Presby Med Ctr 1994; **Fellow:** Neurourology, Columbia Univ 1995; Urodynamics, Columbia Univ 1995; **Fac Appt:** Prof U, Cornell Univ-Weill Med Coll

Tewari, Ashutosh K MD (U) - **Spec Exp:** Prostate Cancer/Robotic Surgery; **Hospital:** Mt Sinai Hosp; **Address:** 625 Madison Ave Fl 2, New York, NY 10019; **Phone:** 212-241-9955; **Board Cert:** Urology 2014; **Med School:** India 1984; **Resid:** Surgery, GSVM Med Coll 1990; Urology, Henry Ford Hosp 2003; **Fellow:** Transplant Surgery, Liverpool Univ Med Ctr 1993; Urologic Oncology, UF Hlth Shands Hosp 1995; **Fac Appt:** Assoc Prof U, Mount Sinai-Icahn Sch of Med

Vapnek, Jonathan M MD (U) - **Spec Exp:** Incontinence; Neurogenic Bladder; Urodynamics; Urinary Tract Infections; **Hospital:** Mt Sinai Hosp; **Address:** 229 E 79th St, Ste 1A, New York, NY 10075; **Phone:** 212-717-9500; **Board Cert:** Urology 2005; **Med School:** UCSD 1986; **Resid:** Surgery, UCSD Med Ctr 1988; Urology, UCSF Med Ctr 1992; **Fellow:** Neurourology, UC Davis Med Ctr 1993; **Fac Appt:** Assoc Clin Prof U, Mount Sinai-Icahn Sch of Med

Weiner, David M MD (U) - **Spec Exp:** Kidney Stones; Prostate Benign Disease; **Hospital:** Mt Sinai Roosevelt, Mt Sinai St. Luke's; **Address:** Mount Sinai Roosevelt Hosp, Dept Urology, 425 W 59th St, Ste 3A, New York, NY 10019; **Phone:** 212-523-7016; **Board Cert:** Urology 2011; **Med School:** UMDNJ-NJ Med Sch, Newark 1994; **Resid:** Surgery, St Lukes-Roosevelt Hosp 1996; Urology, Columbia-Presby Med Ctr 2000

Young, George P H MD (U) - **Spec Exp:** Incontinence; Voiding Dysfunction; Urology-Female; Pelvic Floor Disorders; **Hospital:** Lenox Hill Hosp, NY Hosp Queens (page 498); **Address:** 1060 5th Ave, Ste 1E-F, New York, NY 10128; **Phone:** 212-876-9811; **Board Cert:** Urology 2006; **Med School:** Brazil 1983; **Resid:** Surgery, Staten Island Univ Hosp 1989; Urology, New York Hosp 1993; **Fellow:** Female Urology, UCLA Med Ctr 1994

Vascular & Interventional Radiology

Brown, Karen T MD (VIR) - **Spec Exp:** Liver Cancer; Radiofrequency Tumor Ablation; **Hospital:** Meml Sloan Kettering Canc Ctr (page 110); **Address:** 1275 York Ave, New York, NY 10065; **Phone:** 212-639-5882; **Board Cert:** Diagnostic Radiology 1984; Vascular & Interventional Radiology 2004; **Med School:** Boston Univ 1979; **Resid:** Diagnostic Radiology, Mass Genl Hosp 1984; **Fellow:** Vascular & Interventional Radiology, Mass Genl Hosp 1985; **Fac Appt:** Clin Prof Rad, Cornell Univ-Weill Med Coll

Covey, Anne M MD (VIR) - **Spec Exp:** Liver Tumors; Chemoembolization & Tumor Ablation; Biliary Disorders; **Hospital:** Meml Sloan Kettering Canc Ctr (page 110); **Address:** Memorial Sloan Kettering Cancer Ctr, Interventional Radiology, 1275 York Ave, New York, NY 10065; **Phone:** 212-639-6746; **Board Cert:** Diagnostic Radiology 1999; Vascular & Interventional Radiology 2011; **Med School:** Columbia P&S 1994; **Resid:** Diagnostic Radiology, Yale-New Haven Hosp 1999; **Fellow:** Vascular & Interventional Radiology, Yale-New Haven Hosp 2001

Dreifuss, Ronald M MD (VIR) - **Hospital:** Mt Sinai St. Luke's, Mt Sinai Beth Israel; **Address:** St Lukes Hospital, Interventional Radiology, 440 W 114th St, New York, NY 10025; **Phone:** 212-523-4446; **Board Cert:** Diagnostic Radiology 1996; **Med School:** Mount Sinai Sch Med 1987; **Resid:** Diagnostic Radiology, Mount Sinai Med Ctr 1993; **Fellow:** Vascular & Interventional Radiology, New York Hosp-Cornell 1994; **Fac Appt:** Asst Clin Prof Rad, Mount Sinai-Icahn Sch of Med

Friedman, Adie MD (VIR) - **Spec Exp:** Interventional Radiology; **Hospital:** Mt Sinai Roosevelt; **Address:** Roosevelt Interventional Radiology, 1000 10th Ave Fl 4, New York, NY 10019; **Phone:** 212-523-7257; **Board Cert:** Diagnostic Radiology 1997; Vascular & Interventional Radiology 2000; **Med School:** UMDNJ-NJ Med Sch, Newark 1992; **Resid:** Diagnostic Radiology, Tufts-New Eng Med Ctr Hosps 1997; **Fellow:** Vascular & Interventional Radiology, NY Hosp-Cornell Med Ctr 1998; **Fac Appt:** Asst Clin Prof Rad, Mount Sinai Sch Med

Getrajdman, George I MD (VIR) - **Spec Exp:** Chemoembolization & Tumor Ablation; Biliary Disorders; **Hospital:** Meml Sloan Kettering Canc Ctr (page 110); **Address:** Meml Sloan Kettering Cancer Ctr, Interventional Radiology, 1275 York Ave, New York, NY 10065; **Phone:** 212-639-2598; **Board Cert:** Diagnostic Radiology 1988; **Med School:** Johns Hopkins Univ 1980; **Resid:** Diagnostic Radiology, Columbia-Presby Med Ctr 1985; **Fellow:** Vascular & Interventional Radiology, Columbia-Presby Med Ctr

Javit, Daniel J MD (VIR) - **Hospital:** Lenox Hill Hosp; **Address:** Lenox Hill Hospital, Interventional Radiology, 100 E 77th St, New York, NY 10075; **Phone:** 212-434-2908; **Board Cert:** Diagnostic Radiology 1993; Vascular & Interventional Radiology 2005; **Med School:** Cornell Univ 1988; **Resid:** Diagnostic Radiology, Mt Sinai Med Ctr 1993; **Fellow:** Interventional Radiology, New York Hosp 1994

Khilnani, Neil M MD (VIR) - **Spec Exp:** Varicose Veins; Vein Disorders; Iliac Vein Obstruction; **Hospital:** NY-Presby/Weill Cornell Med Ctr, NY (page 102); **Address:** Weill Cornell Vascular Comp Vein Care, 2315 Broadway at 84th ST, Fl 4, New York, NY 10024; **Phone:** 646-962-9179; **Board Cert:** Diagnostic Radiology 1991; Vascular & Interventional Radiology 2008; Venous & Lymphatic Medicine 2009; **Med School:** Mount Sinai Sch Med 1986; **Resid:** Diagnostic Radiology, NY-Presby/Columbia Univ Med Ctr 1991; **Fellow:** Vascular & Interventional Radiology, NY-Presby/Columbia Univ Med Ctr 1992; **Fac Appt:** Assoc Prof Rad, Cornell Univ-Weill Med Coll

Lookstein, Robert A MD (VIR) - **Spec Exp:** Arterial & Venous Stents; Renovascular Disease; Endovascular Surgery; Vein Disorders; **Hospital:** Mt Sinai Hosp; **Address:** Mt Sinai Radiology Assocs, 1176 5th Ave, New York, NY 10029; **Phone:** 212-241-7409; **Board Cert:** Diagnostic Radiology 2001; Vascular & Interventional Radiology 2003; **Med School:** SUNY Downstate 1995; **Resid:** Surgery, Mt Sinai Hosp 1997; Diagnostic Radiology, Mt Sinai Hosp 2001; **Fellow:** Vascular & Interventional Radiology, Mt Sinai Hosp 2002; **Fac Appt:** Prof Rad, Mount Sinai-Icahn Sch of Med

Nowakowski, Francis Scott MD (VIR) - **Spec Exp:** Uterine Fibroid Embolization; Interventional Oncology; Portal Hypertension; Dialysis Access; **Hospital:** Mt Sinai Hosp; **Address:** Radiology Assocs, Interventional Rad, 1468 Madison Ave, MC Level, 801, New York, NY 10029; **Phone:** 212-241-7409; **Board Cert:** Diagnostic Radiology 1999; Vascular & Interventional Radiology 2012; **Med School:** Univ Pennsylvania 1994; **Resid:** Diagnostic Radiology, Pennsylvania Hosp 1999; **Fellow:** Vascular & Interventional Radiology, Christiana Care Med Ctr 2000; **Fac Appt:** Asst Prof Rad, Mount Sinai Sch Med

Rosen, Robert J MD (VIR) - **Spec Exp:** Vascular Malformations; Chemoembolization & Tumor Ablation; **Hospital:** Lenox Hill Hosp; **Address:** Lenox Hill Heart & Vascular Inst, 130 E 77th St Fl 9, New York, NY 10075; **Phone:** 212-434-2606; **Board Cert:** Diagnostic Radiology 1980; **Med School:** Hahnemann Univ 1976; **Resid:** Diagnostic Radiology, Hahnemann Univ Hosp 1979; **Fellow:** Vascular & Interventional Radiology, Univ Penn 1980

Saboeiro, Gregory R MD (VIR) - **Spec Exp:** Musculoskeletal Imaging; Ultrasound; **Hospital:** Hosp For Special Surgery (page 109); **Address:** Hosp for Special Surgery, Dept Radiology, 535 E 70th St Fl 3, New York, NY 10021; **Phone:** 212-606-1566; **Board Cert:** Diagnostic Radiology 1993; **Med School:** St Louis Univ 1989; **Resid:** Radiology, St Louis Univ Hosp 1993; **Fellow:** Interventional Radiology, Mallinckrodt Inst 1994; Musculoskeletal Imaging, Hosp Special Surgery 2005; **Fac Appt:** Assoc Clin Prof Rad, Cornell Univ-Weill Med Coll

Shams, Joseph N MD (VIR) - **Spec Exp:** Spinal Imaging & Intervention; Uterine Fibroid Embolization; Liver Tumors; Chemoembolization & Tumor Ablation; **Hospital:** Mt Sinai Beth Israel, Mt Sinai Roosevelt; **Address:** Union Square Diagnostic Imaging, 144 Fourth Ave, New York, NY 10003; **Phone:** 212-420-2509; **Board Cert:** Diagnostic Radiology 1993; Vascular & Interventional Radiology 2006; **Med School:** SUNY Downstate 1988; **Resid:** Diagnostic Radiology, Beth Israel Med Ctr 1993; **Fellow:** Vascular & Interventional Radiology, Yale-New Haven Hosp 1994; **Fac Appt:** Asst Clin Prof Rad, Albert Einstein Coll Med

Silberzweig, James MD (VIR) - **Spec Exp:** Uterine Fibroid Embolization; Interventional Radiology; **Hospital:** Mt Sinai Beth Israel; **Address:** Mt Sinai Beth Israel, Dept Radiology, First Ave at 16th St, New York, NY 10003; **Phone:** 212-420-2409; **Board Cert:** Diagnostic Radiology 1994; Vascular & Interventional Radiology 2006; **Med School:** Northwestern Univ 1989; **Resid:** Diagnostic Radiology, SUNY Downstate Med Ctr 1994; **Fellow:** Vascular & Interventional Radiology, Montefiore Med Ctr 1995; **Fac Appt:** Clin Prof Rad, Albert Einstein Coll Med

Sofocleous, Constantinos T MD/PhD (VIR) - **Spec Exp:** Interventional Oncology; Chemoembolization & Tumor Ablation; Liver Tumors; Lung Cancer; **Hospital:** Meml Sloan Kettering Canc Ctr (page 110); **Address:** Meml Sloan-Kettering Cancer Ctr, Interventional Radiology, 1275 York Ave, New York, NY 10065; **Phone:** 212-639-3379; **Board Cert:** Diagnostic Radiology 1999; Vascular & Interventional Radiology 2012; **Med School:** Greece 1991; **Resid:** Diagnostic Radiology, St Lukes-Roosevelt Hosp 1998; **Fellow:** Vascular & Interventional Radiology, NYU Med Ctr 1999

Solomon, Stephen B MD (VIR) - **Spec Exp:** Radiofrequency Tumor Ablation; Kidney Cancer; Liver Cancer; Lung Cancer; **Hospital:** Meml Sloan Kettering Canc Ctr (page 110); **Address:** MSKCC, Interventional Radiology, 1275 York Ave, rm H118, New York, NY 10021; **Phone:** 212-639-5012; **Board Cert:** Diagnostic Radiology 1998; **Med School:** Yale Univ 1993; **Resid:** Diagnostic Radiology, Johns Hopkins Hosp 1998

Sperling, David C MD (VIR) - **Spec Exp:** Varicose Veins; Uterine Fibroid Embolization; Pelvic Congestion Syndrome; Angioplasty; **Hospital:** NY-Presby/Columbia Univ Med Ctr, NY (page 102); **Address:** Columbia Endovascular Assocs, Interventional Radiology, 51 W 51st St, Ste 301, New York, NY 10019; **Phone:** 212-326-8874; **Board Cert:** Diagnostic Radiology 1998; Vascular & Interventional Radiology 2010; **Med School:** SUNY Downstate 1993; **Resid:** Diagnostic Radiology, Thomas Jefferson Univ Hosp 1998; **Fellow:** Vascular & Interventional Radiology, Thomas Jefferson Univ Hosp 1999; **Fac Appt:** Assoc Clin Prof Rad, Columbia P&S

Susman, Jonathan MD (VIR) - **Spec Exp:** Chemoembolization & Tumor Ablation; Uterine Fibroid Embolization; **Hospital:** NY-Presby/Columbia Univ Med Ctr, NY (page 102); **Address:** NY Presby-Columbia Univ Med Ctr, Dept Radiology, 177 Fort Washington Ave, 4th Fl, Ste 100, New York, NY 10032; **Phone:** 212-305-7094; **Board Cert:** Diagnostic Radiology 1996; Vascular & Interventional Radiology 2011; **Med School:** Albert Einstein Coll Med 1991; **Resid:** Diagnostic Radiology, LI Jewish Med Ctr 1996; **Fellow:** Vascular & Interventional Radiology, NYU Med Ctr 1997; **Fac Appt:** Assoc Clin Prof Rad, Columbia P&S

Thornton, Raymond H MD (VIR) - **Spec Exp:** Chemoembolization & Tumor Ablation; Liver Cancer; Kidney Cancer; **Hospital:** Meml Sloan Kettering Canc Ctr (page 110); **Address:** Meml Sloan Kettering Cancer Ctr, Interventional Radiology, 1275 York Ave, New York, NY 10065; **Phone:** 212-639-2463; **Board Cert:** Diagnostic Radiology 2003; Vascular & Interventional Radiology 2005; **Med School:** Univ Pittsburgh 1998; **Resid:** Diagnostic Radiology, UCSF Med Ctr 2003; **Fellow:** Vascular & Interventional Radiology, UCSF Med Ctr 2004

Weintraub, Joshua L MD (VIR) - **Spec Exp:** Gastrointestinal Cancer; Chemoembolization & Tumor Ablation; Uterine Fibroid Embolization; Vascular Malformations; **Hospital:** NY-Presby/Columbia Univ Med Ctr, NY (page 102); **Address:** NY Presbyterian-Columbia Med Ctr, Dept Radiology, 622 W 168th St, New York, NY 10032; **Phone:** 212-305-7094; **Board Cert:** Diagnostic Radiology 1996; Vascular & Interventional Radiology 2009; **Med School:** Wayne State Univ 1991; **Resid:** Diagnostic Radiology, Beth Israel Hosp 1996; **Fellow:** Vascular & Interventional Radiology, Hosp Univ Penn 1997; **Fac Appt:** Assoc Prof Rad, Columbia P&S

Westcott, Mark A MD (VIR) - **Spec Exp:** Uterine Fibroid Embolization; **Hospital:** Lenox Hill Hosp; **Address:** Lenox Hill Hospital, Interventional Radiology, 100 E 77th St, New York, NY 10075; **Phone:** 212-434-2908; **Board Cert:** Diagnostic Radiology 1993; Vascular & Interventional Radiology 2006; **Med School:** Georgetown Univ 1988; **Resid:** Diagnostic Radiology, Northwestern Meml Hosp 1993; **Fellow:** Vascular & Interventional Radiology, Thomas Jefferson Univ Hosp 1994

Vascular Surgery

Adelman, Mark Alan MD (VascS) - **Spec Exp:** Carotid Artery Surgery; Aneurysm-Abdominal Aortic; Vein Disorders; Endovascular Surgery; **Hospital:** NYU Langone Med Ctr (page 104); **Address:** NYU Vascular Assocs, 530 1st Ave, Ste 6F, New York, NY 10016; **Phone:** 212-263-7311; **Board Cert:** Vascular Surgery 2012; **Med School:** NYU Sch Med 1985; **Resid:** Surgery, NYU Med Ctr 1990; **Fellow:** Vascular Surgery, NYU Med Ctr 1991; **Fac Appt:** Prof VascS, NYU Sch Med

Bajakian, Danielle MD (VascS) - **Spec Exp:** Endovascular Surgery; Peripheral Vascular Disease; Arterial Disease; Vein Disorders; **Hospital:** NY-Presby/Columbia Univ Med Ctr, NY (page 102); **Address:** NY-Presby, Vascular Surgery, 161 Fort Washington Ave Fl 5, New York, NY 10032; **Phone:** 212-932-5169; **Board Cert:** Vascular Surgery 2004; **Med School:** SUNY Downstate 1996; **Resid:** Surgery, Mt Sinai Hosp 2001; **Fellow:** Vascular Surgery, NYU Med Ctr 2003; Endovascular Surgery, Cleveland Clin 2003; **Fac Appt:** Asst Prof S, Columbia P&S

Benvenisty, Alan I MD (VascS) - **Spec Exp:** Renovascular Disease; Aneurysm-Aortic; Endovascular Surgery; Minimally Invasive Vascular Surgery; **Hospital:** Mt Sinai St. Luke's, Mt Sinai Roosevelt; **Address:** Mt Sinai, Vascular Surgery, 1090 Amsterdam Ave Fl 12, New York, NY 10025; **Phone:** 212-523-4706; **Board Cert:** Surgery 2013; Vascular Surgery 2009; **Med School:** Columbia P&S 1978; **Resid:** Surgery, NY-Presby/Columbia Univ Med Ctr 1983; **Fellow:** Vascular Surgery, NY-Presby/Columbia Univ Med Ctr 1984; Transplant Surgery, NY-Presby/Columbia Univ Med Ctr 1984; **Fac Appt:** Prof S, Columbia P&S

Bernik, Thomas R MD (VascS) - **Spec Exp:** Carotid Artery Surgery; Aneurysm-Aortic; Peripheral Vascular Disease; Endovascular Surgery; **Hospital:** Mt Sinai Beth Israel; **Address:** Beth Israel Vascular Surgery, 317 E 17th St Fl 12, New York, NY 10003; **Phone:** 212-844-5555; **Board Cert:** Surgery 2012; Vascular Surgery 2005; **Med School:** Geo Wash Univ 1994; **Resid:** Surgery, St Vincents Hosp 2000; **Fellow:** Vascular Surgery, N Shore Univ Hosp 2002; Endovascular Surgery, Univ Rochester 2002

Carroccio, Alfio MD (VascS) - **Spec Exp:** Aneurysm-Aortic; Minimally Invasive Surgery; Endovascular Surgery; **Hospital:** Lenox Hill Hosp; **Address:** Lenox Hill Hosp, Vascular Surgery, 130 E 77th St, Black Hall Fl 13, New York, NY 10075; **Phone:** 212-434-3420; **Board Cert:** Surgery 2010; Vascular Surgery 2005; **Med School:** Mount Sinai Sch Med 1996; **Resid:** Surgery, Mt Sinai Hosp 2001; **Fellow:** Vascular Surgery, Mt Sinai Hosp 2003

Cayne, Neal S MD (VascS) - **Spec Exp:** Endovascular Surgery; Aneurysm-Abdominal & Thoracic Aortic; Carotid Artery Surgery; Endovascular Stent Grafts; **Hospital:** NYU Langone Med Ctr (page 104); **Address:** NYU Vascular Assocs, 530 1st Ave, Ste 6F, MS 10016, New York, NY 10016; **Phone:** 212-263-7311; **Board Cert:** Surgery 2010; Vascular Surgery 2013; **Med School:** NY Med Coll 1995; **Resid:** Surgery, Montefiore Med Ctr 2000; **Fellow:** Vascular Surgery, Montefiore Med Ctr 2002; **Fac Appt:** Assoc Prof VascS, NYU Sch Med

Chideckel, Norman J MD (VascS) - **Spec Exp:** Vein Disorders; Varicose Veins; Sclerotherapy; **Hospital:** Mt Sinai Beth Israel; **Address:** Vascular Surgery & Vein Ctr, 380 2nd Ave, Ste 1004, New York, NY 10010; **Phone:** 212-473-1877; **Board Cert:** Surgery 2007; **Med School:** SUNY Downstate 1979; **Resid:** Surgery, Beth Israel Med Ctr 1984; **Fellow:** Vascular Surgery, Lutheran Med Ctr 1985

Ellozy, Sharif Hamed MD (VascS) - **Spec Exp:** Endovascular Surgery; Aneurysm-Aortic; **Hospital:** Mt Sinai Hosp; **Address:** Mt Sinai, Vascular Surgery, 5 E 98th St Fl 3, New York, NY 10029; **Phone:** 212-241-5315; **Board Cert:** Surgery 2004; Vascular Surgery 2005; **Med School:** NYU Sch Med 1996; **Resid:** Surgery, Mt Sinai Hosp 2002; **Fellow:** Vascular Surgery, Mt Sinai Hosp 2003; **Fac Appt:** Assoc Prof S, Mount Sinai-Icahn Sch of Med

Faries, Peter L MD (VascS) - **Spec Exp:** Aneurysm-Abdominal Aortic; Carotid Artery Surgery; Renovascular Disease; Peripheral Vascular Disease; **Hospital:** Mt Sinai Hosp; **Address:** 5 E 98th St Fl 3, New York, NY 10029; **Phone:** 212-241-5386; **Board Cert:** Surgery 2008; Vascular Surgery 2009; **Med School:** Univ Pennsylvania 1992; **Resid:** Surgery, Montefiore Med Ctr 1998; **Fellow:** Vascular Surgery, Beth Israel Deaconess Med Ctr 2000; **Fac Appt:** Prof S, Mount Sinai Sch Med

Giangola, Gary MD (VascS) - **Spec Exp:** Carotid Artery Surgery; Aneurysm-Aortic; Diabetic Leg/Foot; Vein Disorders; **Hospital:** Lenox Hill Hosp; **Address:** Lenox Hill Hosp-Vascular Surgery, 130 E 77th St, Black Hall Fl 13, New York, NY 10075; **Phone:** 212-434-3420; **Board Cert:** Vascular Surgery 2008; **Med School:** NYU Sch Med 1980; **Resid:** Surgery, NYU Med Ctr 1985; **Fellow:** Vascular Surgery, NYU 1986

Green, Richard M MD (VascS) - **Spec Exp:** Aneurysm-Abdominal Aortic; Carotid Artery Surgery; Percutaneous Vascular Interventions; **Hospital:** NY-Presby/Columbia Univ Med Ctr, NY (page 102); **Address:** NY-Presby, Vascular Surgery Dept, 161 Fort Washington Ave, rm 532, New York, NY 10032; **Phone:** 212-305-1165; **Board Cert:** Vascular Surgery 2013; **Med School:** Univ Rochester 1970; **Resid:** Surgery, Strong Meml Hosp 1976

Grossi, Robert J MD (VascS) - **Spec Exp:** Carotid Artery Surgery; Aneurysm-Abdominal Aortic; Wound Healing/Care; Endovascular Surgery; **Hospital:** Mt Sinai Beth Israel, NY-Presby/Lower Manhattan Hosp (page 102); **Address:** Beth Israel Med Ctr, Div Vasc Surg, 317 E 17th St, New York, NY 10003; **Phone:** 212-844-5559; **Board Cert:** Surgery 2006; Vascular Surgery 2008; **Med School:** UMDNJ-NJ Med Sch, Newark 1981; **Resid:** Surgery, St Vincent's Hosp 1986; **Fellow:** Vascular Surgery, Temple Univ Hosp 1987

Harrington, Elizabeth MD (VascS) - **Spec Exp:** Carotid Artery Surgery; Aneurysm-Aortic; Arterial Bypass Surgery-Leg; Varicose Veins; **Hospital:** Mt Sinai Hosp; **Address:** 2 E 93rd St, Ste 1C, New York, NY 10128; **Phone:** 212-876-7400; **Board Cert:** Surgery 2009; Vascular Surgery 2006; **Med School:** NY Med Coll 1975; **Resid:** Surgery, Mt Sinai Hosp 1980; **Fellow:** Vascular Surgery, Mt Sinai Hosp 1981; **Fac Appt:** Assoc Prof S, Mount Sinai-Icahn Sch of Med

Harrington, Martin E MD (VascS) - **Spec Exp:** Peripheral Vascular Disease; Limb Sparing Surgery; Aneurysm-Aortic; Carotid Artery Disease; **Hospital:** Mt Sinai Hosp; **Address:** 2 E 93rd St, New York, NY 10128; **Phone:** 212-876-7400; **Board Cert:** Internal Medicine 1978; Hematology 1980; Surgery 2013; Vascular Surgery 2007; **Med School:** Harvard Med Sch 1975; **Resid:** Internal Medicine, St Luke's Roosevelt Hosp Ctr 1979; Surgery, Mt Sinai Med Ctr 1984; **Fellow:** Surgical Oncology, Meml Sloan Kettering Canc Ctr 1986; Vascular Surgery, Mt Sinai Med Ctr 1989

Jacobowitz, Glenn R MD (VascS) - **Spec Exp:** Varicose Veins; Minimally Invasive Vascular Surgery; Carotid Artery Surgery; Aneurysm-Abdominal Aortic; **Hospital:** NYU Langone Med Ctr (page 104), Bellevue Hosp Ctr; **Address:** NYU Vascular Assocs, 530 First Ave, Ste 6F, New York, NY 10016; **Phone:** 212-263-7311; **Board Cert:** Surgery 2006; Vascular Surgery 2005; **Med School:** NYU Sch Med 1989; **Resid:** Surgery, NYU Langone Med Ctr 1995; **Fellow:** Vascular Surgery, NYU Langone Med Ctr 1996; **Fac Appt:** Prof S, NYU Sch Med

Kabnick, Lowell S MD (VascS) - **Spec Exp:** Varicose Veins; Vein Disorders; Minimally Invasive Vascular Surgery; Laser Surgery; **Hospital:** NYU Langone Med Ctr (page 104); **Address:** NYU Vein Center, 530 1st Ave, Fl 6, Ste D, New York, NY 10016; **Phone:** 212-263-8346; **Board Cert:** Surgery 2009; **Med School:** Geo Wash Univ 1976; **Resid:** Surgery, NYU Med Ctr 1978; Surgery, Long Island Jewish Med Ctr 1981; **Fellow:** Vascular Surgery, Mount Sinai Med Ctr 1982; **Fac Appt:** Assoc Prof S, NYU Sch Med

Lantis II, John C MD (VascS) - **Spec Exp:** Limb Sparing Surgery; Wound Healing/Care; Endovascular Surgery; Carotid Artery Surgery; **Hospital:** Mt Sinai St. Luke's, Mt Sinai Roosevelt; **Address:** Mt Sinai, Vascular Surgery, 1090 Amsterdam Ave, Ste 7A, New York, NY 10025; **Phone:** 212-523-4797; **Board Cert:** Surgery 2009; Vascular Surgery 2010; **Med School:** Albany Med Coll 1993; **Resid:** Surgery, Tufts Med Ctr 1999; **Fellow:** Vascular Surgery, Brigham & Womens Hosp 2000; **Fac Appt:** Prof S, Mount Sinai-Icahn Sch of Med

Maldonado, Thomas MD (VascS) - **Spec Exp:** Endovascular Surgery; Endovascular Stent Grafts; Aneurysm; Reconstructive Surgery; **Hospital:** NYU Langone Med Ctr (page 104); **Address:** NYU Vascular Assocs, 530 1st Ave, Ste 6F, New York, NY 10016; **Phone:** 212-263-7311; **Board Cert:** Surgery 2003; Vascular Surgery 2005; **Med School:** NYU Sch Med 1995; **Resid:** Surgery, NYU Med Ctr 2002; **Fellow:** Research, NYU Med Ctr 2000; Vascular Surgery, NYU Med Ctr 2003; **Fac Appt:** Assoc Prof S, NYU Sch Med

Marin, Michael L MD (VascS) - **Spec Exp:** Aneurysm-Aortic; Peripheral Vascular Disease; Limb Sparing Surgery; Endovascular Surgery; **Hospital:** Mt Sinai Hosp; **Address:** Mt Sinai, Vascular Surgery, 5 E 98th St Fl 3, Box 1259, New York, NY 10029; **Phone:** 212-241-0737; **Board Cert:** Surgery 2011; **Med School:** Mount Sinai Sch Med 1984; **Resid:** Surgery, NY-Presby/Columbia Univ Med Ctr 1990; **Fellow:** Transplant Surgery, NY-Presby/Columbia Univ Med Ctr 1988; Vascular Surgery, Montefiore Med Ctr 1992; **Fac Appt:** Prof S, Mount Sinai-Icahn Sch of Med

McKinsey, James F MD (VascS) - **Spec Exp:** Aneurysm-Abdominal Aortic; Endovascular Surgery; Carotid Artery Surgery; **Hospital:** Mt Sinai Roosevelt; **Address:** 1000 10th Ave, Ste 5G77, New York, NY 10019; **Phone:** 212-523-7460; **Board Cert:** Surgery 2013; Vascular Surgery 2003; **Med School:** Univ Fla Coll Med 1987; **Resid:** Surgery, GA Baptist Med Ctr 1992; **Fellow:** Vascular Surgery, Univ Chicago Hosp 1993; **Fac Appt:** Assoc Prof S, Columbia P&S

Mendes, Donna M MD (VascS) - **Spec Exp:** Limb Sparing Surgery; Endovascular Surgery; Varicose Veins; **Hospital:** Mt Sinai Roosevelt; **Address:** 10 W 66th St, Ste 1B, New York, NY 10023; **Phone:** 212-302-3051; **Board Cert:** Surgery 2004; Vascular Surgery 2011; **Med School:** Columbia P&S 1977; **Resid:** Surgery, St Lukes-Roosevelt Hosp Ctr 1982; **Fellow:** Vascular Surgery, Englewood Hosp 1984; **Fac Appt:** Assoc Prof S, Mount Sinai-Icahn Sch of Med

Morrissey, Nicholas J MD (VascS) - **Spec Exp:** Endovascular Surgery; Aneurysm-Abdominal & Thoracic Aortic; Carotid Artery Surgery; **Hospital:** NY-Presby/Columbia Univ Med Ctr, NY (page 102); **Address:** 161 Fort Washington Ave, Herbert Irving Pavilion Fl 5 - rm 538, New York, NY 10032; **Phone:** 212-342-2929; **Board Cert:** Surgery 2009; Vascular Surgery 2012; **Med School:** Univ Rochester 1992; **Resid:** Surgery, Strong Meml Hosp 1999; **Fellow:** Vascular Surgery, Mount Sinai Hosp 2001; **Fac Appt:** Assoc Prof S, Columbia P&S

Nalbandian, Matthew M MD (VascS) - **Spec Exp:** Spinal Access Surgery; Endovascular Surgery; Varicose Veins; Vein Disorders; **Hospital:** NYU Langone Med Ctr (page 104), Holy Name Med Ctr (page 738); **Address:** Northern Valley Vascular Assocs, 247 Third Ave, Ste 504, New York, NY 10010; **Phone:** 212-254-6882; **Board Cert:** Surgery 2009; Vascular Surgery 2008; **Med School:** Rutgers-NJ Med Sch 1993; **Resid:** Surgery, Boston Med Ctr 1998; **Fellow:** Vascular Surgery, NYU Med Ctr 2000; **Fac Appt:** Asst Prof S, NYU Sch Med

Rockman, Caron B MD (VascS) - **Spec Exp:** Carotid Artery Surgery; Aneurysm-Abdominal Aortic; Peripheral Vascular Disease; Vein Disorders; **Hospital:** NYU Langone Med Ctr (page 104); **Address:** NYU Vascular Assocs, 530 1st Ave Fl 6, New York, NY 10016; **Phone:** 212-263-7311; **Board Cert:** Surgery 2006; Vascular Surgery 2007; **Med School:** NYU Sch Med 1990; **Resid:** Surgery, NYU Med Ctr 1995; **Fellow:** Vascular Surgery, NYU Med Ctr 1997; **Fac Appt:** Prof S, NYU Sch Med

Schneider, Darren B MD (VascS) - **Spec Exp:** Endovascular Surgery; Minimally Invasive Vascular Surgery; Aneurysm-Aortic; Peripheral Vascular Disease; **Hospital:** NY-Presby/Weill Cornell Med Ctr, NY (page 102); **Address:** NY-Presby, Vascular Surgery, 525 E 68th St Starr Bldg Fl 8, New York, NY 10065; **Phone:** 212-746-5122; **Board Cert:** Vascular Surgery 2013; **Med School:** UCSD 1992; **Resid:** Surgery, UCSF Med Ctr 2000; **Fellow:** Interventional Radiology, UCSF Med Ctr 2001; Vascular Surgery, UCSF Med Ctr 2002; **Fac Appt:** Assoc Prof S, Cornell Univ-Weill Med Coll

Stein, Jeffrey S MD (VascS) - **Spec Exp:** Aneurysm-Aortic; Arterial Disease; Varicose Veins; **Hospital:** Mt Sinai Hosp; **Address:** 12 E 97th St, Ste 1C, New York, NY 10029; **Phone:** 212-396-0500; **Board Cert:** Surgery 2009; Vascular Surgery 2013; **Med School:** Washington Univ, St Louis 1982; **Resid:** Surgery, Mt Sinai Med Ctr 1988; **Fellow:** Surgical Critical Care, Mt Sinai Med Ctr 1989; Vascular Surgery, Mt Sinai Med Ctr 1990; **Fac Appt:** Asst Clin Prof S, Mount Sinai Sch Med

Teodorescu, Victoria J MD (VascS) - **Spec Exp:** Dialysis Access Surgery; Aneurysm; Diabetic Leg/Foot; Peripheral Vascular Disease; **Hospital:** Mt Sinai Hosp; **Address:** 5 E 98th St Fl 3, New York, NY 10029; **Phone:** 212-241-5315; **Board Cert:** Surgery 2011; Vascular Surgery 2003; **Med School:** NYU Sch Med 1985; **Resid:** Surgery, Mt Sinai Hosp 1991; **Fellow:** Vascular Surgery, Mt Sinai Hosp 1992; **Fac Appt:** Assoc Prof S, Mount Sinai Sch Med

Todd, George J MD (VascS) - **Spec Exp:** Minimally Invasive Vascular Surgery; Aneurysm-Abdominal Aortic; Carotid Artery Surgery; **Hospital:** Mt Sinai Roosevelt; **Address:** 1000 10th Ave, rm 5G77, New York, NY 10019; **Phone:** 212-523-7481; **Board Cert:** Surgery 2010; Vascular Surgery 2006; **Med School:** Penn State Coll Med 1974; **Resid:** Surgery, NY-Presby/Columbia Univ Med Ctr 1979; **Fellow:** Vascular Surgery, NY-Presby/Columbia Univ Med Ctr 1980; **Fac Appt:** Prof S, Columbia P&S

Yang, Paul MD (VascS) - **Spec Exp:** Endovascular Surgery; Arterial Disease; Peripheral Vascular Disease; **Hospital:** Mt Sinai Beth Israel; **Address:** Phillips Ambulatory Care Ctr, Vascular Surgery, 10 Union Square E, New York, NY 10003; **Phone:** 212-420-4343; **Board Cert:** Surgery 2004; Vascular Surgery 2005; **Med School:** NYU Sch Med 1988; **Resid:** Surgery, Montefiore Med Ctr 1993; **Fellow:** Vascular Surgery, Long Island Jewish Med Ctr 1994

Bronx

Adolescent Medicine

Alderman, Elizabeth MD (AM) - **Spec Exp:** Adolescent Gynecology; Eating Disorders; Parenting Issues; **Hospital:** Montefiore Med Ctr-Moses Campus (page 100), Chldns Hosp at Montefiore; **Address:** CHAM, Adolescent Med, 3415 Bainbridge Rd, Bronx, NY 10467; **Phone:** 718-920-6781; **Board Cert:** Pediatrics 2012; Adolescent Medicine 2008; **Med School:** SUNY Stony Brook 1987; **Resid:** Pediatrics, Montefiore Med Ctr 1990; **Fellow:** Adolescent Medicine, Montefiore Med Ctr 1992; **Fac Appt:** Prof Ped, Albert Einstein Coll Med

Coupey, Susan MD (AM) - **Spec Exp:** Adolescent Gynecology; Menstrual Disorders; **Hospital:** Montefiore Med Ctr-Moses Campus (page 100), Chldns Hosp at Montefiore; **Address:** CHAM, Adolescent Med, 3415 Bainbridge Rd Fl 4, Bronx, NY 10467; **Phone:** 718-920-6781; **Board Cert:** Pediatrics 1979; Adolescent Medicine 2008; **Med School:** Canada 1975; **Resid:** Pediatrics, Chldns Hosp 1978; **Fellow:** Adolescent Medicine, Montefiore Med Ctr 1979; **Fac Appt:** Prof Ped, Albert Einstein Coll Med

Rieder, Jessica MD (AM) - **Spec Exp:** Obesity; Vaccines; Eating Disorders; **Hospital:** Chldns Hosp at Montefiore; **Address:** Chldns Hosp Montefiore, Adolescent Med, 3415 Bainbridge Ave, Bronx, NY 10467; **Phone:** 718-741-2450; **Board Cert:** Pediatrics 2013; Adolescent Medicine 2008; **Med School:** Univ Alberta 1994; **Resid:** Pediatrics, Montefiore Med Ctr 1998; **Fellow:** Adolescent Medicine, Montefiore Med Ctr 2001; **Fac Appt:** Assoc Clin Prof Ped, Albert Einstein Coll Med

Allergy & Immunology

Bernstein, Larry J MD (A&I) - **Spec Exp:** Asthma; Immune Deficiency; Sinus Disorders; Food Allergy; **Hospital:** Montefiore Med Ctr-Moses Campus (page 100), NY Hosp Queens (page 498); **Address:** 72-35 112th St, Ste pr-5, Forest Hills, NY 10461; **Phone:** 718-544-6641; **Board Cert:** Pediatrics 1981; Allergy & Immunology 1985; **Med School:** Albert Einstein Coll Med 1977; **Resid:** Pediatrics, Jacobi Med Ctr 1981; **Fellow:** Allergy & Immunology, Albert Einstein Coll Med 1983; **Fac Appt:** Assoc Clin Prof Ped, Albert Einstein Coll Med

Kaufman, Alan MD (A&I) - **Spec Exp:** Asthma; Sinus Disorders; Urticaria; Immunodeficiency Disorders; **Hospital:** Montefiore Med Ctr-Moses Campus (page 100), Lawrence Hosp Ctr (page 102); **Address:** 3626 E Tremont Ave, Ste 202, Bronx, NY 10465-2030; **Phone:** 718-597-9000; **Board Cert:** Internal Medicine 1988; Allergy & Immunology 2009; **Med School:** West Indies 1984; **Resid:** Internal Medicine, Metropolitan Hosp Ctr 1987; **Fellow:** Allergy & Immunology, Albert Einstein Coll Med 1989

Lehach, Joan G MD (A&I) - **Spec Exp:** Asthma; **Hospital:** St. Barnabas Hosp - Bronx, Montefiore Med Ctr-Einstein Campus (page 100); **Address:** 1488 Metropolitan Ave, Ste 12, Bronx, NY 10462; **Phone:** 718-918-1991; **Board Cert:** Internal Medicine 2010; **Med School:** Dominican Republic 1985; **Resid:** Internal Medicine, St Barnabas Hosp 1988; **Fellow:** Allergy & Immunology, Jacobi Med Ctr 1990

Rosenstreich, David L MD (A&I) - **Spec Exp:** Urticaria; Sinusitis; Atopic Dermatitis; **Hospital:** Montefiore Med Ctr-Moses Campus (page 100), Jacobi Med Ctr; **Address:** 1515 Blondell Ave, Fl 2, Ste 220, Bronx, NY 10461; **Phone:** 866-633-8255; **Board Cert:** Internal Medicine 1972; Allergy & Immunology 1975; Clinical & Laboratory Immunology 1990; **Med School:** NYU Sch Med 1967; **Resid:** Internal Medicine, Albert Einstein Med Ctr 1969; **Fellow:** Allergy & Immunology, Natl Inst Hlth 1972; **Fac Appt:** Prof Med, Albert Einstein Coll Med

Rubinstein, Arye MD/PhD (A&I) - **Spec Exp:** Immune Deficiency; Asthma; Drug Sensitivity; **Hospital:** Montefiore Med Ctr-Moses Campus (page 100), Montefiore Med Ctr-Einstein Campus (page 100); **Address:** Montefiore, Allergy & Immunology, 1180 Morris Park Ave Fl 3, Bronx, NY 10461; **Phone:** 347-498-2410; **Board Cert:** Pediatrics 1976; Allergy & Immunology 1977; **Med School:** Switzerland 1962; **Resid:** Pediatrics, Tel Aviv Univ Hosp 1967; **Fellow:** Allergy & Immunology, Univ Bern 1969; Allergy & Immunology, Harvard Med Sch 1973; **Fac Appt:** Prof Ped, Albert Einstein Coll Med

Cardiac Electrophysiology

Ferrick, Kevin J MD (CE) - **Spec Exp:** Arrhythmias; Sudden Death Prevention; Pacemakers; **Hospital:** Montefiore Med Ctr-Moses Campus (page 100), Stamford Hosp (page 971); **Address:** Montefiore Medical Center, Arrhythmia Service, 111 E 210th St, Bronx, NY 10467; **Phone:** 718-920-4148; **Board Cert:** Internal Medicine 1981; Cardiovascular Disease 1983; Cardiac Electrophysiology 2013; **Med School:** Med Coll Wisc 1977; **Resid:** Internal Medicine, Montefiore Hosp 1980; **Fellow:** Cardiovascular Disease, Columbia-Presby Med Ctr 1981; Cardiac Electrophysiology, Columbia-Presby Med Ctr 1983; **Fac Appt:** Prof Med, Albert Einstein Coll Med

Gross, Jay MD (CE) - **Spec Exp:** Pacemakers; **Hospital:** Montefiore Med Ctr-Moses Campus (page 100); **Address:** Montefiore, Arrhythmia Svc, 111 E 210th St Fl 2, Bronx, NY 10467; **Phone:** 718-920-6190; **Board Cert:** Internal Medicine 1986; Cardiovascular Disease 1989; Cardiac Electrophysiology 2013; **Med School:** Albert Einstein Coll Med 1983; **Resid:** Internal Medicine, Montefiore Med Ctr 1986; **Fellow:** Cardiovascular Disease, Montrfiore Med Ctr 1988; **Fac Appt:** Prof Med, Albert Einstein Coll Med

Krumerman, Andrew K MD (CE) - **Spec Exp:** Atrial Fibrillation; Arrhythmias; Catheter Ablation; **Hospital:** Montefiore Med Ctr-Moses Campus (page 100); **Address:** Montefiore, Arrhythmia Svc, 111 E 210th St Fl 2, Bronx, NY 10467; **Phone:** 718-920-4776; **Board Cert:** Cardiovascular Disease 2013; Cardiac Electrophysiology 2004; **Med School:** Israel 1996; **Resid:** Internal Medicine, Montefiore Med Ctr 1999; **Fellow:** Cardiovascular Disease, N Shore Univ Hosp 2001; Cardiac Electrophysiology, Montefiore Med Ctr 2002; **Fac Appt:** Asst Prof Med, Albert Einstein Coll Med

Palma, Eugen C MD (CE) - **Spec Exp:** Arrhythmias; Atrial Fibrillation; Catheter Ablation; **Hospital:** Montefiore Med Ctr-Einstein Campus (page 100), Montefiore Med Ctr-Moses Campus (page 100); **Address:** 1825 Eastchester Rd, Weiler Bldg - Fl 2ND - Ste RAU, Bronx, NY 10461; **Phone:** 718-904-2588; **Board Cert:** Cardiovascular Disease 2007; Cardiac Electrophysiology 2010; **Med School:** Philippines 1989; **Resid:** Internal Medicine, SUNY Hlth Sci Ctr 1993; **Fellow:** Cardiovascular Disease, Montefiore Med Ctr-Moses Div 1997; Cardiac Electrophysiology, UCSF Med Ctr 1999; **Fac Appt:** Assoc Clin Prof Med, Albert Einstein Coll Med

Cardiovascular Disease

Cohen, Martin N MD (Cv) - **Spec Exp:** Preventive Cardiology; **Hospital:** Montefiore Med Ctr-Einstein Campus (page 100); **Address:** 1628 Eastchester Road, Bronx, NY 10461; **Phone:** 718-904-2927; **Board Cert:** Internal Medicine 1968; Cardiovascular Disease 1972; **Med School:** Columbia P&S 1961; **Resid:** Internal Medicine, Peter Bent Brigham Hosp 1965; **Fellow:** Cardiovascular Disease, Peter Bent Brigham Hosp 1968; **Fac Appt:** Prof Med, Albert Einstein Coll Med

Forman, Robert MD (Cv) - **Spec Exp:** Heart Valve Disease; Coronary Artery Disease; **Hospital:** Montefiore Med Ctr-Einstein Campus (page 100); **Address:** 1628 Eastchester Rd, Einstein Ctr for Heart/Vascular Care, Bronx, NY 10461-2301; **Phone:** 646-670-5120; **Med School:** Africa 1961; **Fellow:** Cardiovascular Disease, Peter Bent Brigham Hosp 1970; **Fac Appt:** Prof Med, Albert Einstein Coll Med

Garcia, Mario J MD (Cv) - **Spec Exp:** Echocardiography-Transesophageal; Echocardiography; **Hospital:** Montefiore Med Ctr-Moses Campus (page 100); **Address:** Montefiore Einstein Heart/Cardiovascular Care, 111 E 210th St, Bronx, NY 10467; **Phone:** 718-920-4172; **Board Cert:** Cardiovascular Disease 2013; **Med School:** Dominican Republic 1986; **Resid:** Internal Medicine, St Vincent's Med Ctr 1990; **Fellow:** Nuclear Cardiology, Mass Genl Hosp 1994; Cardiovascular Disease, Cleveland Clinic 1996; **Fac Appt:** Prof Med, Albert Einstein Coll Med

Greenberg, Mark A MD (Cv) - **Spec Exp:** Interventional Cardiology; Cardiac Catheterization; Heart Valve Disease; **Hospital:** Montefiore Med Ctr-Moses Campus (page 100), White Plains Hosp (page 652); **Address:** Cardiac Catherization Office, 111 E 210th St, Bronx, NY 10467; **Phone:** 718-920-4212; **Board Cert:** Internal Medicine 1976; Cardiovascular Disease 1979; Interventional Cardiology 2012; **Med School:** Univ IL Coll Med 1973; **Resid:** Internal Medicine, Montefiore Med Ctr 1976; **Fellow:** Cardiovascular Disease, Montefiore Med Ctr 1978; **Fac Appt:** Clin Prof Med, Albert Einstein Coll Med

Jorde, Ulrich Peter MD (Cv) - **Spec Exp:** Heart Failure; Cardiomyopathy; Transplant Medicine-Heart; **Hospital:** Montefiore Med Ctr-Moses Campus (page 100), Montefiore Med Ctr-Einstein Campus (page 100); **Address:** Montefiore Med Ctr, Cardiology, 210 E 210th St, MAP Bldg - Fl 7, Bronx, NY 10467; **Phone:** 212-920-2248; **Board Cert:** Cardiovascular Disease 2011; Advanced Heart Failure & Transplant Cardiology 2012; **Med School:** Germany 1991; **Resid:** Internal Medicine, Mt Sinai Hosp 1995; **Fellow:** Cardiovascular Disease, Albert Einstein Coll Med 1999; Advanced Heart Failure & Transplant Cardiology, NY-Presby/Columbia Univ Med Ctr 1999; **Fac Appt:** Prof Med, Albert Einstein Coll Med

Kaufman, David B MD (Cv) - **Spec Exp:** Nuclear Cardiology; **Hospital:** Montefiore Med Ctr-Einstein Campus (page 100); **Address:** Riverdale Heart Ctr, 2600 Netherland Ave, Ste 121, Riverdale, NY 10463; **Phone:** 718-548-1590; **Board Cert:** Internal Medicine 1980; Cardiovascular Disease 1983; **Med School:** Cornell Univ-Weill Med Coll 1977; **Resid:** Internal Medicine, Montefiore Med Ctr 1980; **Fellow:** Cardiovascular Disease, Montefiore Med Ctr 1983

Keller, Peter Karl MD (Cv) - **Spec Exp:** Congestive Heart Failure; Coronary Artery Disease; Arrhythmias; **Hospital:** Montefiore Med Ctr-Einstein Campus (page 100), Montefiore Westchester Sq (page 100); **Address:** Montefiore, Cardiology Dept, 1578 Williamsbridge Rd Fl 1, Bronx, NY 10461; **Phone:** 718-892-7817; **Board Cert:** Internal Medicine 1988; Cardiovascular Disease 2011; **Med School:** Mount Sinai Sch Med 1985; **Resid:** Internal Medicine, Jacobi Med Ctr 1988; **Fellow:** Cardiovascular Disease, Jacobi Med Ctr 1991; **Fac Appt:** Assoc Clin Prof Med, Albert Einstein Coll Med

Lucariello, Richard MD (Cv) - **Spec Exp:** Congestive Heart Failure; Angina; Hypertension; **Hospital:** Montefiore Med Ctr-Wakefield Campus (page 100); **Address:** Montefiore, Cardiovascular Disease, 4256 Bronx Blvd, Bronx, NY 10466; **Phone:** 646-329-8200; **Board Cert:** Internal Medicine 1987; Cardiovascular Disease 2011; **Med School:** NY Med Coll 1984; **Resid:** Internal Medicine, Westchester Med Ctr 1987; **Fellow:** Cardiovascular Disease, St Vincents Hosp 1989; Cardiovascular Disease, Westchester Med Ctr 1990

Menegus, Mark A MD (Cv) - **Spec Exp:** Acute Coronary Syndromes; Cardiac Catheterization; Interventional Cardiology; Heart Valve Disease; **Hospital:** Montefiore Med Ctr-Moses Campus (page 100), St. Barnabas Hosp - Bronx; **Address:** Montefiore Medical Center-Div Cardiology, 111 E 210th St, Bronx, NY 10467-2401; **Phone:** 718-920-5528; **Board Cert:** Internal Medicine 1984; Cardiovascular Disease 1987; **Med School:** Rutgers R W Johnson Med Sch 1981; **Resid:** Internal Medicine, Montefiore Med Ctr 1984; **Fellow:** Cardiovascular Disease, Montefiore Med Ctr 1987; **Fac Appt:** Clin Prof Med, Albert Einstein Coll Med

Monrad, E. Scott MD (Cv) - **Spec Exp:** Coronary Artery Disease; Heart Valve Disease; Cardiac Catheterization; **Hospital:** Montefiore Med Ctr-Einstein Campus (page 100), Jacobi Med Ctr; **Address:** Montefiore, Cardiovascular Disease, 1628 Eastchester Rd, Bronx, NY 10461; **Phone:** 646-670-5120; **Board Cert:** Internal Medicine 1982; Cardiovascular Disease 1985; **Med School:** McGill Univ 1979; **Resid:** Internal Medicine, New England Med Ctr 1982; **Fellow:** Cardiovascular Disease, Beth Israel Deaconess Med Ctr 1985; **Fac Appt:** Prof Med, Albert Einstein Coll Med

Neuberg, Gerald W MD (Cv) - **Spec Exp:** Congestive Heart Failure; Preventive Cardiology; **Hospital:** NY-Presby/Columbia Univ Med Ctr, NY (page 102), NY-Presby Hosp/The Allen Hosp (page 102); **Address:** 3050 Corlear Ave, Ste 204, Bronx, NY 10463; **Phone:** 646-317-0130; **Board Cert:** Internal Medicine 1986; Cardiovascular Disease 1989; **Med School:** Columbia P&S 1983; **Resid:** Internal Medicine, NY Presby Hosp 1986; **Fellow:** Cardiovascular Disease, Westchester Med Ctr 1988; Cardiovascular Disease, Mt Sinai Med Ctr 1989; **Fac Appt:** Clin Prof Med, Columbia P&S

Phillips, Malcolm C MD (Cv) - **Spec Exp:** Preventive Cardiology; Echocardiography; Cardiac Stress Testing; **Hospital:** St. Barnabas Hosp - Bronx; **Address:** 4422 3rd Ave, Bronx, NY 10457-2545; **Phone:** 718-960-6205; **Board Cert:** Internal Medicine 1979; Cardiovascular Disease 1981; **Med School:** Columbia P&S 1976; **Resid:** Internal Medicine, New York Hosp 1978; **Fellow:** Cardiovascular Disease, New York Hosp 1980; **Fac Appt:** Asst Clin Prof Med, Cornell Univ-Weill Med Coll

Sahar, David I MD (Cv) - **Spec Exp:** Arrhythmias; Atrial Fibrillation; Heart Valve Disease; Coronary Artery Disease; **Hospital:** NY-Presby/Columbia Univ Med Ctr, NY (page 102); **Address:** 3050 Corlear Ave, Ste 204, Bronx, NY 10463; **Phone:** 212-305-4567; **Board Cert:** Internal Medicine 1983; Cardiovascular Disease 1987; **Med School:** Columbia P&S 1980; **Resid:** Internal Medicine, Ohio State Univ Hosp 1983; **Fellow:** Cardiovascular Disease, St Lukes-Roosevelt Hosp 1985; Cardiac Electrophysiology, NY-Presby/Columbia Univ Med Ctr 1987; **Fac Appt:** Assoc Prof Med, Columbia P&S

Silverman, Rubin MD (Cv) - **Spec Exp:** Echocardiography; **Hospital:** St. Barnabas Hosp - Bronx, Montefiore Med Ctr-Einstein Campus (page 100); **Address:** 1250 Waters Pl, Ste 1207, Bronx, NY 10461; **Phone:** 718-409-3335; **Board Cert:** Internal Medicine 1981; Cardiovascular Disease 1983; **Med School:** Albert Einstein Coll Med 1978; **Resid:** Internal Medicine, Jacobi Med Ctr 1981; **Fellow:** Cardiovascular Disease, Montefiore Med Ctr 1983; **Fac Appt:** Asst Prof Med, Albert Einstein Coll Med

Taub, Cynthia C MD (Cv) - **Spec Exp:** Echocardiography; Heart Disease in Women; Heart Disease in Pregnancy; Heart Valve Disease; **Hospital:** Montefiore Med Ctr-Einstein Campus (page 100); **Address:** Montefiore Cardiology, 1628 Eastchester Rd, Bronx, NY 10461-2663; **Phone:** 646-670-5120; **Board Cert:** Internal Medicine ; Cardiovascular Disease 2004; Echocardiography 2006; **Med School:** China 1993; **Resid:** Internal Medicine, Jersey Shore Med Ctr 2001; **Fellow:** Cardiovascular Disease, Hartford Hosp/U Conn 2004; Echocardiography, Mass General Hosp 2005; **Fac Appt:** Assoc Clin Prof Med, Albert Einstein Coll Med

Child Neurology

Moshe, Solomon L MD (ChiN) - **Spec Exp:** Epilepsy/Seizure Disorders; **Hospital:** Montefiore Med Ctr-Moses Campus (page 100); **Address:** 3415 Bainbridge Ave Fl 4, Bronx, NY 10467; **Phone:** 718-920-4378; **Board Cert:** Pediatrics 1978; Child Neurology 1979; Clinical Neurophysiology 2013; **Med School:** Greece 1972; **Resid:** Pediatrics, Univ MD Hosp 1975; **Fellow:** Pediatric Neurology, Jacobi Med Ctr 1978; **Fac Appt:** Prof N, Albert Einstein Coll Med

Shinnar, Shlomo MD/PhD (ChiN) - **Spec Exp:** Epilepsy/Seizure Disorders; Infantile Spasms-West Syndrome; Electrical Status Epilepticus Of Sleep; Clinical Trials; **Hospital:** Montefiore Med Ctr-Moses Campus (page 100); **Address:** Montefiore Med Ctr, Pediatric Neurology and Epilepsy, 111 E 210th St, Fl 4, Bronx, NY 10467; **Phone:** 718-920-2906; **Board Cert:** Neurology 1984; Pediatrics 1984; Clinical Neurophysiology 2005; Epilepsy 2013; **Med School:** Albert Einstein Coll Med 1978; **Resid:** Pediatrics, Johns Hopkins Hosp 1980; Neurology, Johns Hopkins Hosp 1983; **Fac Appt:** Prof N, Albert Einstein Coll Med

Clinical Genetics

Marion, Robert W MD (CG) - **Spec Exp:** Spina Bifida; Williams Syndrome; Marfan's Syndrome; Down Syndrome; **Hospital:** Montefiore Med Ctr-Moses Campus (page 100), Blythedale Children's Hosp; **Address:** 3415 Bainbridge Ave, Bronx, NY 10467; **Phone:** 718-741-2323; **Board Cert:** Pediatrics 1985; Clinical Genetics 1987; **Med School:** Albert Einstein Coll Med 1979; **Resid:** Pediatrics, Jacobi Med Ctr 1982; **Fellow:** Clinical Genetics, Jacobi Med Ctr 1984; **Fac Appt:** Prof Ped, Albert Einstein Coll Med

Ostrer, Harry MD (CG) - **Spec Exp:** Genetic Disorders; Hereditary Cancer; **Hospital:** Montefiore Med Ctr-Wakefield Campus (page 100); **Address:** Albert Einstein College of Medicine, 1300 Morris Park Ave, Ullman Blg, rm 819, Bronx, NY 10461; **Phone:** 718-430-8605; **Board Cert:** Clinical Genetics 1984; Pediatrics 1985; Clinical Cytogenetics 1990; Clinical Molecular Genetics 2010; **Med School:** Columbia P&S 1976; **Resid:** Pediatrics, Johns Hopkins Hosp 1978; **Fellow:** Molecular Genetics, Natl Inst Health 1981; Clinical Genetics, Johns Hopkins Hosp 1984; **Fac Appt:** Prof Path, Albert Einstein Coll Med

Critical Care Medicine

Siegel, Robert MD (CCM) - **Spec Exp:** Pneumonia; Infectious Disease; **Hospital:** James J. Peters VA Med Ctr-Bronx, Mt Sinai Hosp; **Address:** 130 W Kingsbridge Rd, Ste 8C-100, Bronx, NY 10468-3992; **Phone:** 718-584-9000 x6723; **Board Cert:** Internal Medicine 1982; Pulmonary Disease 1986; Critical Care Medicine 2009; **Med School:** Columbia P&S 1979; **Resid:** Internal Medicine, St Luke's Hosp 1982; Internal Medicine, Booth Meml Hosp 1983; **Fellow:** Pulmonary Disease, Bronx Municipal Hosp 1985; **Fac Appt:** Assoc Prof Med, Mount Sinai Sch Med

Dermatology

Cohen, Steven R MD (D) - **Spec Exp:** Occupational Dermatology; Contact Dermatitis; Psoriasis; **Hospital:** Montefiore Med Ctr-Moses Campus (page 100); **Address:** 3514 Bainbridge Ave Fl 1, Bronx, NY 10467; **Phone:** 866-633-8255; **Board Cert:** Dermatology 2009; **Med School:** Univ Pennsylvania 1971; **Resid:** Dermatology, Yale-New Haven Hosp 1974; Preventive Medicine, Yale-New Haven Hosp 1977; **Fac Appt:** Prof D, Albert Einstein Coll Med

Lerman, Jay S MD (D) - **Spec Exp:** Acne; Eczema; **Hospital:** Montefiore Med Ctr-Einstein Campus (page 100), Montefiore Med Ctr-Moses Campus (page 100); **Address:** 2426 Eastchester Rd, Bronx, NY 10469; **Phone:** 718-865-8733; **Board Cert:** Dermatology 1974; **Med School:** SUNY Downstate 1969; **Resid:** Dermatology, Jacobi Med Ctr 1973; **Fac Appt:** Asst Clin Prof D, Albert Einstein Coll Med

Liteplo, Ronald R MD (D) - **Spec Exp:** Melanoma; Skin Diseases-Immunologic; **Hospital:** Montefiore Med Ctr-Moses Campus (page 100); **Address:** 4238 Bronx Blvd, Bronx, NY 10466; **Phone:** 718-325-9532; **Board Cert:** Internal Medicine 1975; Dermatology 1978; **Med School:** NYU Sch Med 1972; **Resid:** Internal Medicine, SUNY Buffalo Affil Hosp 1975; Dermatology, SUNY Buffalo Affil Hosp 1978; **Fellow:** Immunology, SUNY Buffalo Affil Hosp 1976; **Fac Appt:** Asst Clin Prof Med, Albert Einstein Coll Med

Rosen, Douglas MD (D) - **Spec Exp:** Skin Cancer; Hair Removal-Laser; Acne; **Hospital:** Montefiore Westchester Sq (page 100); **Address:** 3620 E Tremont Ave, FL 2, Bronx, NY 10465; **Phone:** 718-792-4700; **Board Cert:** Dermatology 1984; **Med School:** Albert Einstein Coll Med 1980; **Resid:** Dermatology, Montefiore Hosp Med Ctr 1984; **Fac Appt:** Assoc Prof D, Albert Einstein Coll Med

Rudikoff, Donald MD (D) - **Spec Exp:** AIDS Related Skin Disorders; Skin Infections; Smallpox; **Hospital:** Bronx Lebanon Hosp Ctr; **Address:** 1650 Selwyn Ave, Bronx, NY 10457; **Phone:** 718-960-1234; **Board Cert:** Internal Medicine 1980; Dermatology 2009; **Med School:** NY Med Coll 1973; **Resid:** Internal Medicine, Beth Israel Med Ctr 1980; Dermatology, Mount Sinai Med Ctr 1982; **Fac Appt:** Assoc Clin Prof D, Albert Einstein Coll Med

Diagnostic Radiology

Amis Jr, E Stephen MD (DR) - **Spec Exp:** Urologic Imaging; **Hospital:** Montefiore Med Ctr-Moses Campus (page 100); **Address:** Montefiore Med Ctr, Dept Radiology, 111 E 210th St, Bronx, NY 10467; **Phone:** 718-920-5113; **Board Cert:** Urology 1975; Diagnostic Radiology 1979; **Med School:** Northwestern Univ 1967; **Resid:** Urology, US Naval Hosp 1972; Diagnostic Radiology, US Naval Hosp 1978; **Fellow:** Urologic Radiology, Mass General Hosp 1981; **Fac Appt:** Prof Rad, Albert Einstein Coll Med

Haramati, Linda B MD (DR) - **Spec Exp:** Cardiac Imaging; Thoracic Imaging; Congenital Heart Disease; **Hospital:** Montefiore Med Ctr-Moses Campus (page 100), Jacobi Med Ctr; **Address:** Montefiore Med Ctr, Dept Radiology, 111 E 210th St, Bronx, NY 10467-2401; **Phone:** 718-920-5250; **Board Cert:** Diagnostic Radiology 1990; **Med School:** Albert Einstein Coll Med 1985; **Resid:** Diagnostic Radiology, Montefiore Med Ctr 1990; **Fellow:** Thoracic Radiology, Columbia-Presby Med Ctr 1991; **Fac Appt:** Clin Prof Rad, Albert Einstein Coll Med

Haramati, Nogah MD (DR) - **Spec Exp:** Orthopaedic Imaging; Rheumatology; Musculoskeletal Imaging; **Hospital:** Montefiore Med Ctr-Einstein Campus (page 100), Jacobi Med Ctr; **Address:** 1825 Eastchester Rd, rm 3-006, Bronx, NY 10461; **Phone:** 718-904-2965; **Board Cert:** Diagnostic Radiology 1990; **Med School:** SUNY Hlth Sci Ctr 1985; **Resid:** Diagnostic Radiology, Montefiore Hosp Med Ctr 1990; **Fellow:** Musculoskeletal Imaging, Columbia-Presby Med Ctr 1991; **Fac Appt:** Clin Prof Rad, Albert Einstein Coll Med

Laks, Mitchell P MD/PhD (DR) - **Spec Exp:** MRI; Ultrasound; CT Body Scan; **Hospital:** Montefiore Med Ctr-Moses Campus (page 100); **Address:** 111 E 210th St, Bronx, NY 10467; **Phone:** 718-920-4396; **Board Cert:** Diagnostic Radiology 1990; **Med School:** Harvard Med Sch 1985; **Resid:** Diagnostic Radiology, Einstein Affil Hosp 1990; **Fellow:** Magnetic Resonance Imaging, Brigham & Womens Hosp 1991; **Fac Appt:** Asst Prof Rad, Albert Einstein Coll Med

Rozenblit, Alla MD (DR) - **Spec Exp:** CT Scan; MRI; **Hospital:** Montefiore Med Ctr-Moses Campus (page 100); **Address:** 111 E 210th St, Bronx, NY 10467-2401; **Phone:** 718-920-4396; **Board Cert:** Diagnostic Radiology 1984; **Med School:** Russia 1971; **Resid:** Diagnostic Radiology, Queens Hosp Ctr 1984; **Fellow:** Ultrasound/CT, LI Jewish Med Ctr 1985; **Fac Appt:** Clin Prof Rad, Albert Einstein Coll Med

Spindola-Franco, Hugo MD (DR) - **Spec Exp:** Thoracic Radiology; Cardiac Imaging; Congenital Heart Disease; **Hospital:** Montefiore Med Ctr-Moses Campus (page 100); **Address:** 111 E 210th St, Bronx, NY 10467-2401; **Phone:** 718-920-4872; **Board Cert:** Diagnostic Radiology 1970; **Med School:** Mexico 1966; **Resid:** Diagnostic Radiology, Montefiore Hosp Med Ctr 1970; **Fellow:** Cardiovascular Radiology, Brigham Hosp/Harvard Med Sch 1971; **Fac Appt:** Prof Rad, Albert Einstein Coll Med

Stern, Harvey MD (DR) - **Spec Exp:** Nuclear Medicine; **Hospital:** Bronx Lebanon Hosp Ctr; **Address:** Bronx-Lebanon Hosp, Dept Radiology, 1650 Grand Concourse, Bronx, NY 10457-7606; **Phone:** 718-960-4522; **Board Cert:** Diagnostic Radiology 1975; Nuclear Radiology 1978; **Med School:** Albert Einstein Coll Med 1971; **Resid:** Diagnostic Radiology, Bronx Municipal Hosp 1975; **Fac Appt:** Asst Prof Rad, Albert Einstein Coll Med

Wolf, Ellen L MD (DR) - **Spec Exp:** Gastrointestinal Imaging; Abdominal Imaging; **Hospital:** Montefiore Med Ctr-Moses Campus (page 100); **Address:** 111 E 210th St, Bronx, NY 10467; **Phone:** 718-920-4851; **Board Cert:** Diagnostic Radiology 1976; **Med School:** Mount Sinai Sch Med 1972; **Resid:** Diagnostic Radiology, Columbia Presby Med Ctr 1974; Diagnostic Radiology, Johns Hopkins Univ 1976; **Fellow:** Pediatric Radiology, Columbia Presby Med Ctr 1977; **Fac Appt:** Clin Prof Rad, Albert Einstein Coll Med

Endocrinology, Diabetes & Metabolism

Cohen, Charmian D MD (EDM) - **Spec Exp:** Diabetes; Thyroid Disorders; Obesity; **Hospital:** Montefiore Med Ctr-Einstein Campus (page 100); **Address:** 1200 Waters Pl, Ste M105, Bronx, NY 10461; **Phone:** 718-892-7033; **Board Cert:** Internal Medicine 1987; Endocrinology, Diabetes & Metabolism 1989; **Med School:** South Africa 1977; **Resid:** Internal Medicine, G Schuer Hosp 1984; **Fellow:** Endocrinology, Diabetes & Metabolism, Albert Einstein Affil Hosp 1986

Grajower, Martin M MD (EDM) - **Spec Exp:** Diabetes; Osteoporosis; Thyroid Disorders; Metabolic Disorders; **Hospital:** Montefiore Med Ctr-Moses Campus (page 100); **Address:** 3736 Henry Hudson Pkwy E, Riverdale, NY 10463; **Phone:** 718-549-6268; **Board Cert:** Internal Medicine 1987; Endocrinology, Diabetes & Metabolism 1981; **Med School:** Albert Einstein Coll Med 1973; **Resid:** Internal Medicine, Montefiore Med Ctr 1975; Internal Medicine, Boston Med Ctr 1976; **Fellow:** Endocrinology, Diabetes & Metabolism, Montefiore Med Ctr 1978; **Fac Appt:** Assoc Clin Prof Med, Albert Einstein Coll Med

Guzman, Rodolfo MD (EDM) - **Spec Exp:** Endocrinology; Diabetes; Thyroid Disorders; **Hospital:** Bronx Lebanon Hosp Ctr; **Address:** 860 Grand Concourse, Ste 1K, Bronx, NY 10451; **Phone:** 718-585-5060; **Board Cert:** Internal Medicine 2013; Endocrinology, Diabetes & Metabolism 2000; **Med School:** Dominican Republic 1979; **Resid:** Internal Medicine, Bronx-Lebanon Hosp 1990; **Fellow:** Endocrinology, Diabetes & Metabolism, Lincoln Med Ctr 1992

Shamoon, Harry MD (EDM) - **Hospital:** Montefiore Med Ctr-Einstein Campus (page 100); **Address:** 1575 Blondell Ave, Ste 200, Bronx, NY 10461-2601; **Phone:** 718-405-8260; **Board Cert:** Internal Medicine 1977; Endocrinology, Diabetes & Metabolism 1979; **Med School:** Yale Univ 1974; **Resid:** Internal Medicine, Jacobi Med Ctr 1977; **Fellow:** Endocrinology, Diabetes & Metabolism, Yale-New Haven Hosp 1979; **Fac Appt:** Prof Med, Albert Einstein Coll Med

Surks, Martin I MD (EDM) - **Spec Exp:** Thyroid Disorders; **Hospital:** Montefiore Med Ctr-Moses Campus (page 100), N Central Bronx Hosp; **Address:** 3400 Bainbridge Ave Fl 2, Bronx, NY 10467; **Phone:** 866-633-8255; **Board Cert:** Internal Medicine 1967; Endocrinology, Diabetes & Metabolism 1977; **Med School:** NYU Sch Med 1960; **Resid:** Internal Medicine, Montefiore Med Ctr 1962; Internal Medicine, VA Hosp 1964; **Fac Appt:** Prof Med, Albert Einstein Coll Med

Zonszein, Joel MD (EDM) - **Spec Exp:** Diabetes; Thyroid Disorders; Heart Disease in Diabetes Patients; **Hospital:** Montefiore Med Ctr-Moses Campus (page 100); **Address:** 1575 Blondell Ave, Ste 200, Bronx, NY 10461; **Phone:** 866-633-8255; **Board Cert:** Nuclear Medicine 1976; Internal Medicine 1977; Endocrinology 1977; **Med School:** Mexico 1969; **Resid:** Internal Medicine, Maimonides Med Ctr 1972; Internal Medicine, Jacobi Med Ctr 1973; **Fellow:** Endocrinology, Northwestern Univ 1974; Endocrinology, Georgetown Univ 1975; **Fac Appt:** Prof Med, Albert Einstein Coll Med

Family Medicine

Biagiotti, Wendy L MD (FMed) *PCP* - **Hospital:** Montefiore Med Ctr-Moses Campus (page 100); **Address:** 3101 E Tremont Ave, Bronx, NY 10461; **Phone:** 718-863-7925; **Board Cert:** Family Medicine 2009; **Med School:** Mexico 1988; **Resid:** Family Medicine, St Joseph's Hosp&Med Ctr 1994; **Fac Appt:** Asst Clin Prof FMed, Albert Einstein Coll Med

Coloka-Kump, Rodika DO (FMed) *PCP* - **Spec Exp:** Preventive Medicine; **Hospital:** Saint Joseph's Med Ctr - Yonkers, St. John's Riverside Hosp-Andrus Pavil; **Address:** 530 W 236th St, rm #1D, Bronx, NY 10463; **Phone:** 718-548-4560; **Board Cert:** Family Medicine 2014; **Med School:** NY Coll Osteo Med 1988; **Resid:** Family Medicine, St Joseph's Med Ctr 1991

Cordero, Evelyn MD (FMed) *PCP* - **Hospital:** Montefiore Med Ctr-Wakefield Campus (page 100), Montefiore Med Ctr-Einstein Campus (page 100); **Address:** 941 Castle Hill Ave, Bronx, NY 10473; **Phone:** 718-792-3117; **Med School:** SUNY Hlth Sci Ctr 1979; **Resid:** Family Medicine, St Joseph's Med Ctr 1982

Delaney, Brian MD (FMed) *PCP* - **Spec Exp:** Geriatric Care; **Hospital:** Montefiore Med Ctr-Moses Campus (page 100), St. Barnabas Hosp - Bronx; **Address:** 2371 Arthur Ave, Bronx, NY 10458; **Phone:** 718-364-6199; **Board Cert:** Family Medicine 2007; Geriatric Medicine 2012; **Med School:** Albert Einstein Coll Med 1983; **Resid:** Family Medicine, Montefiore Med Ctr 1986; **Fac Appt:** Asst Prof FMed, Albert Einstein Coll Med

Duggan, Mary F MD (FMed) *PCP* - **Hospital:** Montefiore Med Ctr-Moses Campus (page 100), Montefiore Med Ctr-Einstein Campus (page 100); **Address:** Bronx Family Health Ctr, 360 E 193rd St, Bronx, NY 10458; **Phone:** 718-933-2400; **Board Cert:** Family Medicine 2008; **Med School:** Univ IL Coll Med 1997; **Resid:** Family Medicine, Montefiore Med Ctr 2000; **Fac Appt:** Asst Prof FMed, Albert Einstein Coll Med

Franzetti, Carl J DO (FMed) *PCP* - **Spec Exp:** Diabetes; **Hospital:** Saint Joseph's Med Ctr - Yonkers, NY-Presby Hosp/The Allen Hosp (page 102); **Address:** 3050 Corlear Ave, Ste 201, Bronx, NY 10463; **Phone:** 718-543-2700; **Board Cert:** Family Medicine 2005; **Med School:** NY Coll Osteo Med 1984; **Resid:** Family Medicine, Warren Hosp 1987

Gold, Marji MD (FMed) *PCP* - **Hospital:** Montefiore Med Ctr-Moses Campus (page 100); **Address:** Montefiore Med Ctr, 360 E 193rd St, Bronx, NY 10458; **Phone:** 718-933-2400; **Board Cert:** Family Medicine 2010; **Med School:** NYU Sch Med 1973; **Resid:** Family Medicine, Montefiore Med Ctr 1976

Morrow, Robert MD (FMed) *PCP* - **Spec Exp:** Preventive Medicine; Geriatric Medicine; Autism; **Hospital:** Montefiore Med Ctr-Moses Campus (page 100), Saint Joseph's Med Ctr - Yonkers; **Address:** 5997 Riverdale Ave, Bronx, NY 10471-1602; **Phone:** 718-884-9803; **Board Cert:** Family Medicine 2009; **Med School:** Mount Sinai Sch Med 1974; **Resid:** Family Medicine, Montefiore Med Ctr 1977; **Fac Appt:** Assoc Clin Prof FMed, Albert Einstein Coll Med

Soloway, Bruce H MD (FMed) *PCP* - **Spec Exp:** AIDS/HIV; **Hospital:** Montefiore Med Ctr-Moses Campus (page 100); **Address:** Montefiore Medical Center, 360 E 193 St, Bronx, NY 10458; **Phone:** 718-933-2400; **Board Cert:** Family Medicine 2007; **Med School:** Albert Einstein Coll Med 1985; **Resid:** Family Medicine, Montefiore Med Ctr 1988; **Fac Appt:** Assoc Prof FMed, Albert Einstein Coll Med

Gastroenterology

Abelow, Arthur MD (Ge) - **Spec Exp:** Endoscopy; Nutrition; **Hospital:** Montefiore Med Ctr-Einstein Campus (page 100), Montefiore Westchester Sq (page 100); **Address:** New York Associates in Gastroenterology, 1250 Waters Pl Fl 12 - Ste 1201, Bronx, NY 10461; **Phone:** 718-863-7397; **Board Cert:** Internal Medicine 1983; Gastroenterology 1985; **Med School:** Albert Einstein Coll Med 1980; **Resid:** Internal Medicine, Bronx Muni Hosp Ctr 1983; **Fellow:** Gastroenterology, Montefiore Med Ctr 1985; **Fac Appt:** Asst Clin Prof Med, Albert Einstein Coll Med

Brandt, Lawrence MD (Ge) - **Spec Exp:** Inflammatory Bowel Disease; Clostridium Difficile Disease; **Hospital:** Montefiore Med Ctr-Moses Campus (page 100); **Address:** 3400 Bainbridge Ave Fl 2, Bronx, NY 10467-2401; **Phone:** 866-633-8255; **Board Cert:** Internal Medicine 1972; Gastroenterology 2006; **Med School:** SUNY Downstate 1968; **Resid:** Internal Medicine, Mt Sinai Med Ctr 1972; **Fellow:** Gastroenterology, Mt Sinai Med Ctr 1972; **Fac Appt:** Prof Emeritus Med, Albert Einstein Coll Med

Frager, Joseph D MD (Ge) - **Spec Exp:** Colon Cancer; Endoscopy; Laser Surgery; **Hospital:** Montefiore Med Ctr-Moses Campus (page 100), NY Hosp Queens (page 498); **Address:** 277 Van Cortlandt Ave E, Bronx, NY 10467-3011; **Phone:** 718-798-8867; **Board Cert:** Internal Medicine 1983; Gastroenterology 1985; **Med School:** Univ Pennsylvania 1980; **Resid:** Internal Medicine, Montefiore Med Ctr 1983; **Fellow:** Gastroenterology, Montefiore Med Ctr 1985; **Fac Appt:** Asst Clin Prof Med, Albert Einstein Coll Med

Gaglio, Paul J MD (Ge) - **Spec Exp:** Transplant Medicine-Liver; Liver Disease; Hepatitis B & C; **Hospital:** Montefiore Med Ctr-Moses Campus (page 100); **Address:** Montefiore Einstein Liver Ctr, 111 E 210th St, Rosenthal Bldg, Fl 2, Bronx, NY 10467; **Phone:** 718-920-6240; **Board Cert:** Internal Medicine 2011; Gastroenterology 2003; Transplant Hepatology 2006; **Med School:** UMDNJ-NJ Med Sch, Newark 1988; **Resid:** Internal Medicine, Mt Sinai Med Ctr 1991; **Fellow:** Gastroenterology, UMDNJ-NJ Med Sch 1993; **Fac Appt:** Prof Med, Albert Einstein Coll Med

Greenwald, David A MD (Ge) - **Spec Exp:** Endoscopy; Gastroesophageal Reflux Disease (GERD); Peptic Ulcer Disease; **Hospital:** Montefiore Med Ctr-Moses Campus (page 100), Montefiore Med Ctr-Einstein Campus (page 100); **Address:** Montefiore Med Ctr, Div Gastroenterology, 111 E 210th St, Bronx, NY 10467; **Phone:** 718-920-4846; **Board Cert:** Internal Medicine 1989; Gastroenterology 2013; **Med School:** Albert Einstein Coll Med 1986; **Resid:** Internal Medicine, Columbia Presby Med Ctr 1989; **Fellow:** Gastroenterology, Columbia Presby Med Ctr 1993; **Fac Appt:** Clin Prof Med, Albert Einstein Coll Med

Gupta, Sanjeev MD (Ge) - **Spec Exp:** Hepatitis; Liver Failure; Liver Disease; **Hospital:** Montefiore Med Ctr-Einstein Campus (page 100); **Address:** Montefiore Hepatology Division, 1180 Morris Park Ave, Bronx, NY 10461; **Phone:** 888-795-4837; **Board Cert:** Internal Medicine 1989; **Med School:** India 1977; **Resid:** Internal Medicine, PGIMER 1980; Internal Medicine, Hammersmith Hosp 1982; **Fellow:** Gastroenterology, Hammersmith Hosp 1985; Hepatology, LAC-USC Med Ctr 1987; **Fac Appt:** Prof Med, Albert Einstein Coll Med

Gutwein, Isadore P MD (Ge) - **Spec Exp:** Pancreatic/Biliary Endoscopy (ERCP); Colonoscopy; Hepatitis; Inflammatory Bowel Disease/Crohn's; **Hospital:** Montefiore Med Ctr-Moses Campus (page 100); **Address:** Riverdale Gastro & Liver Diseases, 3765 Riverdale Ave, Ste 7, Bronx, NY 10463-1845; **Phone:** 718-543-3636; **Board Cert:** Internal Medicine 1976; Gastroenterology 1979; **Med School:** Albert Einstein Coll Med 1973; **Resid:** Internal Medicine, Montefiore Hosp Med Ctr 1976; **Fellow:** Gastroenterology, St Luke's Hosp 1978; **Fac Appt:** Asst Clin Prof Med, Albert Einstein Coll Med

Hertan, Hilary I MD (Ge) - **Spec Exp:** Endoscopic Ultrasound; **Hospital:** Montefiore Med Ctr-Wakefield Campus (page 100); **Address:** 4256 Bronx Blvd, Bronx, NY 10466; **Phone:** 646-329-8220; **Board Cert:** Internal Medicine 1986; Gastroenterology 1989; **Med School:** NY Med Coll 1982; **Resid:** Internal Medicine, North Shore Univ Hosp 1985; **Fellow:** Gastroenterology, Our Lady of Mercy Med Ctr 1990; **Fac Appt:** Asst Prof Med, NY Med Coll

Ho, Sammy MD (Ge) - **Spec Exp:** Pancreatic/Biliary Endoscopy (ERCP); Endoscopic Ultrasound; Endoscopy; **Hospital:** Montefiore Med Ctr-Moses Campus (page 100); **Address:** 111 E 210th St, Bronx, NY 10467; **Phone:** 718-920-4846; **Board Cert:** Gastroenterology 2005; **Med School:** SUNY Stony Brook 1998; **Resid:** Internal Medicine, Kaiser Fdn Hosp 2001; **Fellow:** Gastroenterology, Winthrop Univ Hosp 2004; **Fac Appt:** Asst Prof Med, Albert Einstein Coll Med

Korsten, Mark A MD (Ge) - **Spec Exp:** Constipation; Gastrointestinal Motility Disorders; Spinal Cord Injury & Colonic Motility; Liver Disease; **Hospital:** James J. Peters VA Med Ctr-Bronx; **Address:** 130 W Kingsbridge Rd, Ste 3H, Bronx, NY 10468; **Phone:** 718-584-9000 x6753; **Board Cert:** Internal Medicine 1973; Gastroenterology 1975; **Med School:** Yale Univ 1970; **Resid:** Internal Medicine, Mt Sinai Hosp 1973; **Fellow:** Gastroenterology, Mt Sinai Hosp 1975; **Fac Appt:** Prof Med, Mount Sinai Sch Med

Remy, Prospere MD (Ge) - **Spec Exp:** Liver Disease; **Hospital:** Bronx Lebanon Hosp Ctr; **Address:** 860 Grand Concourse, Ste 1K, Bronx, NY 10451-2815; **Phone:** 718-585-5060; **Board Cert:** Internal Medicine 2004; Gastroenterology 2004; **Med School:** Mexico 1984; **Resid:** Internal Medicine, Bronx-Lebanon Hosp 1990; **Fellow:** Gastroenterology, Bronx-Lebanon Hosp 1992; **Fac Appt:** Asst Prof Med, Albert Einstein Coll Med

Sable, Robert A MD (Ge) - **Spec Exp:** Hepatitis B & C; Gastroesophageal Reflux Disease (GERD); Inflammatory Bowel Disease; Irritable Bowel Syndrome; **Hospital:** Montefiore Med Ctr-Moses Campus (page 100), St. Barnabas Hosp - Bronx; **Address:** 3765 Riverdale Ave, Ste 7, Bronx, NY 10463-1845; **Phone:** 718-543-3636; **Board Cert:** Internal Medicine 1987; Gastroenterology 2000; **Med School:** Albert Einstein Coll Med 1973; **Resid:** Internal Medicine, Montefiore Hosp Med Ctr 1976; **Fellow:** Gastroenterology, NY Med Coll 1978; **Fac Appt:** Asst Clin Prof Med, Albert Einstein Coll Med

Sherman, Howard I MD (Ge) - **Spec Exp:** Colonoscopy; **Hospital:** Montefiore Med Ctr-Einstein Campus (page 100), Montefiore Westchester Sq (page 100); **Address:** NY Assocs in Gastroenterology, 1250 Waters Pl Fl 12, Bronx, NY 10461-3000; **Phone:** 718-863-7397; **Board Cert:** Internal Medicine 1976; Gastroenterology 1979; **Med School:** Albert Einstein Coll Med 1973; **Resid:** Internal Medicine, Emory Univ Hosp 1976; **Fellow:** Gastroenterology, Emory Univ Hosp 1978; **Fac Appt:** Assoc Clin Prof Med, Albert Einstein Coll Med

Stein, David F MD (Ge) - **Spec Exp:** Liver Disease; Hepatitis B & C; AIDS/HIV-Gastrointestinal Complications; Crohn's Disease; **Hospital:** Montefiore Med Ctr-Moses Campus (page 100), St. Barn-abas Hosp - Bronx; **Address:** Riverdale Gastro & Liver Diseases, 3765 Riverdale Ave, Ste 7, Bronx, NY 10463; **Phone:** 718-543-3636; **Board Cert:** Gastroenterology 2008; **Med School:** SUNY Downstate 1990; **Resid:** Internal Medicine, NYU Med Ctr 1994; **Fellow:** Gastroenterology, NYU Med Ctr 1996; **Fac Appt:** Asst Clin Prof Med, Albert Einstein Coll Med

Geriatric Medicine

Dharmarajan, Thiruvinvamvalai S MD (Ger) - **Spec Exp:** Kidney Disease; Kidney Failure; Preventive Medicine; **Hospital:** Montefiore Med Ctr-Wakefield Campus (page 100); **Address:** YDR Geriatrics & Nephrology, 3050 Westchester Ave, Ste 101, Bronx, NY 10461; **Phone:** 718-518-9304; **Board Cert:** Internal Medicine 1977; Geriatric Medicine 2010; Nephrology 1980; **Med School:** India 1967; **Resid:** Internal Medicine, Misericordia Hosp 1977; **Fellow:** Nephrology, Misericordia Hosp 1979; **Fac Appt:** Prof Med, NY Med Coll

Goldberg, Roy J MD (Ger) *PCP* - **Spec Exp:** Long Term Care; Medications in the Elderly; Palliative Care; **Hospital:** Montefiore Med Ctr-Einstein Campus (page 100), Montefiore New Rochelle Hosp (page 100); **Address:** Kings Harbor Multicare Ctr, 2000 E Gunhill Rd, Bronx, NY 10469; **Phone:** 718-405-3535; **Board Cert:** Internal Medicine 1985; Geriatric Medicine 2012; **Med School:** Albert Einstein Coll Med 1982; **Resid:** Internal Medicine, Montefiore Med Ctr 1985

Jacobs, Laurie G MD (Ger) *PCP* - **Spec Exp:** Abuse/Neglect; Frail Elderly; **Hospital:** Montefiore Med Ctr-Moses Campus (page 100); **Address:** Montefiore Med Ctr, Dept Geriatrics, 111 E 210th St, Bronx, NY 10467; **Phone:** 718-920-6471; **Board Cert:** Internal Medicine 1988; Geriatric Medicine 2012; **Med School:** Columbia P&S 1985; **Resid:** Internal Medicine, Montefiore Med Ctr 1988; **Fellow:** Geriatric Medicine, Montefiore Med Ctr 1990; **Fac Appt:** Prof Med, Albert Einstein Coll Med

Malik, Rubina A MD (Ger) *PCP* - **Spec Exp:** Osteoporosis; Falls in the Elderly; Frail Elderly; Palliative Care; **Hospital:** Montefiore Med Ctr-Moses Campus (page 100); **Address:** Montefiore Med Ctr-Div of Geriatric Med, 3400 Bainbridge Ave, Montefiore Greene Med Arts Pavilion, Bronx, NY 10467; **Phone:** 718-920-6723; **Board Cert:** Internal Medicine 2006; Geriatric Medicine 2009; Hospice & Palliative Medicine 2012; **Med School:** SUNY Stony Brook 1992; **Resid:** Internal Medicine, Univ Hosp 1995; **Fellow:** Geriatric Medicine, Univ Hosp 1996; **Fac Appt:** Asst Prof Med, Albert Einstein Coll Med

Russell, Robin O MD (Ger) - **Spec Exp:** Kidney Failure; Kidney Disease; Preventive Medicine; **Hospital:** Montefiore Med Ctr-Wakefield Campus (page 100); **Address:** YDR Geriatrics & Nephrology, 4256 Bronx Blvd, Bronx, NY 10466; **Phone:** 646-329-8220; **Board Cert:** Internal Medicine 1974; Nephrology 1980; **Med School:** Univ New Mexico 1971; **Resid:** Internal Medicine, Harlem Hosp 1974; **Fellow:** Nephrology, Harlem Hosp 1976; **Fac Appt:** Asst Prof Med, NY Med Coll

Geriatric Psychiatry

Kennedy, Gary J MD (GerPsy) - **Spec Exp:** Alzheimer's Disease; Dementia; Depression; **Hospital:** Montefiore Med Ctr-Moses Campus (page 100); **Address:** Montefiore Med Ctr, Psychiatry, 111 E 210th St, rm 3A, Bronx, NY 10467; **Phone:** 718-920-6270; **Board Cert:** Psychiatry 1980; Geriatric Psychiatry 2010; Psychosomatic Medicine 2005; **Med School:** Univ Tex, San Antonio 1975; **Resid:** Psychiatry, Univ Hosp 1979; **Fellow:** Geriatric Psychiatry, Montefiore Med Ctr 1981; Psychosomatic Medicine, Montefiore Med Ctr 1983; **Fac Appt:** Prof Psyc, Albert Einstein Coll Med

Gynecologic Oncology

Einstein, Mark H MD (GO) - **Spec Exp:** Cervical Cancer; HPV-Human Papilloma Virus; Vulvar & Vaginal Cancer; **Hospital:** Montefiore Med Ctr-Moses Campus (page 100); **Address:** 1695 Eastchester Rd, rm 601, Bronx, NY 10461; **Phone:** 718-405-8082; **Board Cert:** Obstetrics & Gynecology 2013; Gynecologic Oncology 2013; **Med School:** Univ Miami Sch Med 1995; **Resid:** Obstetrics & Gynecology, St Barnabas Med Ctr 1999; **Fellow:** Gynecologic Oncology, Albert Einstein Affil Hosp 2002; **Fac Appt:** Prof ObG, Albert Einstein Coll Med

Goldberg, Gary L MD (GO) - **Spec Exp:** Ovarian Cancer; Uterine Cancer; **Hospital:** Montefiore Med Ctr-Moses Campus (page 100); **Address:** 1695 Eastchester Rd, Ste L2, Bronx, NY 10461; **Phone:** 718-405-8082; **Board Cert:** Obstetrics & Gynecology 2013; Gynecologic Oncology 2013; **Med School:** South Africa 1975; **Resid:** Obstetrics & Gynecology, Groote Schuur Hosp 1982; **Fellow:** Gynecologic Oncology, Groote Schuur Hosp 1983; **Fac Appt:** Prof ObG, Albert Einstein Coll Med

Smith, Harriet O MD (GO) - **Spec Exp:** Uterine Cancer; Pelvic Reconstruction; Ovarian Cancer; Clinical Trials; **Hospital:** Montefiore Med Ctr-Moses Campus (page 100), Jacobi Med Ctr; **Address:** 1695 Eastchester Rd, Ste L2, Bronx, NY 10461; **Phone:** 718-405-8082; **Board Cert:** Obstetrics & Gynecology 2013; Gynecologic Oncology 2013; **Med School:** Med Coll GA 1980; **Resid:** Obstetrics & Gynecology, Emory Univ Hosp 1986; Gynecologic Oncology, MD Anderson Cancer Ctr 1988; **Fellow:** Reconstructive Pelvic Surgery, Emory Univ 1989; Gynecologic Oncology, Montefiore Med Ctr 1990; **Fac Appt:** Prof ObG, Albert Einstein Coll Med

Smotkin, David MD/PhD (GO) - **Spec Exp:** Gynecologic Cancer; Gynecologic Cancer-Rare; **Hospital:** Montefiore Med Ctr-Moses Campus (page 100); **Address:** Montefiore Women's Ctr, 3332 Rochambeau Ave, Bronx, NY 10467; **Phone:** 718-920-4794; **Board Cert:** Obstetrics & Gynecology 2013; Gynecologic Oncology 2013; **Med School:** Yale Univ 1980; **Resid:** Obstetrics & Gynecology, Univ Colorado Hosp 1984; **Fellow:** Gynecologic Oncology, UCLA Med Ctr 1987; **Fac Appt:** Asst Prof ObG, Albert Einstein Coll Med

Hand Surgery

Kulick, Roy G MD (HS) - **Spec Exp:** Carpal Tunnel Syndrome; Arthritis; Tendon Surgery; Hand & Upper Extremity Surgery; **Hospital:** Montefiore Med Ctr-Einstein Campus (page 100); **Address:** Montefiore Med Ctr, Orthopaedic Surgery, 1250 Waters Pl Fl 11, Bronx, NY 10461; **Phone:** 718-920-2060; **Board Cert:** Orthopaedic Surgery 1980; Hand Surgery 2011; **Med School:** Cornell Univ-Weill Med Coll 1973; **Resid:** Surgery, St Lukes-Roosevelt Hosp 1975; Orthopaedic Surgery, NY-Presby/Columbia Univ Med Ctr 1978; **Fellow:** Hand Surgery, Hosp Special Surgery 1979; **Fac Appt:** Assoc Prof OrS, Albert Einstein Coll Med

Hematology

Billett, Henny H MD (Hem) - **Spec Exp:** Bleeding/Coagulation Disorders; Thrombotic Disorders; Platelet Disorders; Sickle Cell Disease; **Hospital:** Montefiore Med Ctr-Einstein Campus (page 100), Montefiore Med Ctr-Moses Campus (page 100); **Address:** 1695 Eastchester Rd, Bronx, NY 10461-2601; **Phone:** 718-405-8323; **Board Cert:** Internal Medicine 1979; Hematology 1982; **Med School:** Mount Sinai Sch Med 1974; **Resid:** Internal Medicine, Montefiore Hosp Med Ctr 1979; **Fellow:** Tropical Medicine, London Sch Hygiene/Trop Med 1977; Hematology, Montefiore Hosp Med Ctr 1981; **Fac Appt:** Prof Med, Albert Einstein Coll Med

Landau, Leon C MD (Hem) - **Spec Exp:** Leukemia & Lymphoma; **Hospital:** Montefiore Med Ctr-Moses Campus (page 100), St. John's Riverside Hosp-Dobbs Ferry Pavil; **Address:** 75 E Gun Hill Rd, Bronx, NY 10467-2103; **Phone:** 718-655-3932; **Board Cert:** Internal Medicine 1977; Hematology 1978; Medical Oncology 1981; **Med School:** Albert Einstein Coll Med 1971; **Resid:** Internal Medicine, Montefiore Med Ctr 1973; Internal Medicine, Metropolitan Hosp Ctr 1974; **Fellow:** Hematology, Montefiore Med Ctr 1978; Medical Oncology, Montefiore Med Ctr 1978; **Fac Appt:** Asst Prof Med, Albert Einstein Coll Med

Infectious Disease

Berger, Judith J MD (Inf) - **Spec Exp:** AIDS/HIV; Travel Medicine; **Hospital:** St. Barnabas Hosp - Bronx; **Address:** St Barnabas Hosp, Dept Med, 4422 Third Ave, Bronx, NY 10457; **Phone:** 718-960-6205; **Board Cert:** Internal Medicine 1984; Infectious Disease 1986; **Med School:** Mount Sinai Sch Med 1980; **Resid:** Internal Medicine, Brookdale Univ Med Ctr 1984; **Fellow:** Infectious Disease, SUNY Downstate Med Ctr 1986; **Fac Appt:** Assoc Clin Prof Med, Albert Einstein Coll Med

Berman, Daniel S MD (Inf) - **Spec Exp:** Lyme Disease; Tuberculosis; Viral Infections; **Hospital:** Montefiore Med Ctr-Einstein Campus (page 100), Montefiore Med Ctr-Wakefield Campus (page 100); **Address:** 340 City Island Ave, Bronx, NY 10464; **Phone:** 914-524-8138; **Board Cert:** Internal Medicine 1985; Infectious Disease 1988; **Med School:** NYU Sch Med 1982; **Resid:** Internal Medicine, VA Hosp/NYU Med Ctr 1983; Internal Medicine, NYU Med Ctr 1985; **Fellow:** Infectious Disease, NYU Med Ctr 1987

Corpuz, Marilou O MD (Inf) - **Spec Exp:** Hospital Acquired Infections; **Hospital:** Montefiore Med Ctr-Wakefield Campus (page 100); **Address:** Montefiore Med Grp, 4256 Bronx Blvd, Bronx, NY 10466-2604; **Phone:** 646-329-8220; **Board Cert:** Internal Medicine 1988; Infectious Disease 2012; **Med School:** Philippines 1985; **Resid:** Internal Medicine, Griffin Hosp 1988; **Fellow:** Infectious Disease, LI Jewish Med Ctr 1991; **Fac Appt:** Assoc Prof Med, NY Med Coll

Keller, Marla MD (Inf) - **Spec Exp:** AIDS/HIV in Women; **Hospital:** Montefiore Med Ctr-Einstein Campus (page 100); **Address:** 1300 Morris Park Ave, rm 512, Bronx, NY 10461; **Phone:** 718-430-3240; **Board Cert:** Internal Medicine 2006; Infectious Disease 2008; **Med School:** NYU Sch Med 1993; **Resid:** Internal Medicine, Beth Israel Deaconess Med Ctr 1996; **Fellow:** Infectious Disease, Beth Israel/Brigham & Women's Hosp 1998; **Fac Appt:** Prof Med, Albert Einstein Coll Med

Robbins, Noah MD (Inf) - **Spec Exp:** AIDS/HIV; Sexually Transmitted Diseases; **Hospital:** Montefiore Med Ctr-Moses Campus (page 100); **Address:** Montefiore Med Grp, 3400 Bainbridge Ave Fl 8th, Bronx, NY 10467-2490; **Phone:** 718-920-8888; **Board Cert:** Internal Medicine 1974; Infectious Disease 1980; **Med School:** McGill Univ 1969; **Resid:** Internal Medicine, Albany Meml Hosp 1974; **Fellow:** Infectious Disease, Montefiore Hosp Med Ctr 1980; **Fac Appt:** Clin Prof Med, Albert Einstein Coll Med

Telzak, Edward E MD (Inf) - **Spec Exp:** AIDS/HIV; Tuberculosis; Infections-Opportunistic; Clinical Trials; **Hospital:** St. Barnabas Hosp - Bronx, Bronx Lebanon Hosp Ctr; **Address:** St Barnabas Hosp, Dept Internal Med, 4422 Third Ave, Mills Bldg, Fl 3, Bronx, NY 10457-7606; **Phone:** 718-960-6205; **Board Cert:** Internal Medicine 1983; Infectious Disease 1988; **Med School:** Albert Einstein Coll Med 1980; **Resid:** Internal Medicine, Tufts-New England Med Ctr 1983; **Fellow:** Infectious Disease, Brigham & Womens Hosp 1986; Tropical Medicine, Tufts-New England Med Ctr 1988; **Fac Appt:** Prof Med, Albert Einstein Coll Med

Weiss, Louis M MD (Inf) - **Spec Exp:** Parasitic Infections; AIDS/HIV; **Hospital:** Montefiore Med Ctr-Einstein Campus (page 100); **Address:** 1575 Blondell Ave, Ste 200, Bronx, NY 10461; **Phone:** 718-405-8311; **Board Cert:** Internal Medicine 1985; Infectious Disease 1988; **Med School:** Johns Hopkins Univ 1982; **Resid:** Internal Medicine, Univ Chicago Affil Hosp 1985; **Fellow:** Infectious Disease, Montefiore Med Ctr 1987; **Fac Appt:** Prof Med, Albert Einstein Coll Med

Internal Medicine

Ernst, Jerome A MD (IM) - **Spec Exp:** Asthma; Emphysema; Chronic Obstructive Lung Disease (COPD); AIDS/HIV; **Hospital:** Bronx Lebanon Hosp Ctr; **Address:** BronxCare-Avalon Med Ctr, 199 Mt Eden Pkwy Fl 6, Bronx, NY 10457; **Phone:** 718-518-5581; **Board Cert:** Internal Medicine 1978; Pulmonary Disease 1982; **Med School:** Israel 1969; **Resid:** Internal Medicine, Tel Hashomer Hosp 1970; Internal Medicine, Montefiore Med Ctr 1972; **Fellow:** Pulmonary Disease, Montefiore Med Ctr 1977; **Fac Appt:** Assoc Prof Med, Albert Einstein Coll Med

Fojas Jr, Antonio C MD (IM) *PCP* - **Spec Exp:** Preventive Medicine; **Hospital:** Montefiore Med Ctr-Wakefield Campus (page 100); **Address:** 4350 Van Cortlandt Park E, Bronx, NY 10470; **Phone:** 718-231-4444; **Board Cert:** Internal Medicine 2013; **Med School:** Philippines 1984; **Resid:** Internal Medicine, Our Lady of Mercy Med Ctr 1987; **Fellow:** Internal Medicine, Our Lady of Mercy Med Ctr 1988; **Fac Appt:** Asst Prof Med, NY Med Coll

Sander Jr, Norbert W MD (IM) *PCP* - **Spec Exp:** Preventive Medicine; Sports Medicine; **Hospital:** Montefiore New Rochelle Hosp (page 100); **Address:** 340 City Island Ave, Bronx, NY 10464; **Phone:** 718-885-0333; **Board Cert:** Internal Medicine 1981; **Med School:** Albert Einstein Coll Med 1971; **Resid:** Internal Medicine, Metropolitan Hosp Ctr 1973; Internal Medicine, Lincoln Med & Mental Hlth Ctr 1974

Selwyn, Peter MD (IM) - **Spec Exp:** AIDS/HIV; Palliative Care; Addiction/Substance Abuse; **Hospital:** Montefiore Med Ctr-Moses Campus (page 100); **Address:** Montfiore Family Hlth Ctr, 360 E 193rd St Fl 2, Bronx, NY 10458; **Phone:** 718-933-2400; **Board Cert:** Family Medicine 2005; Hospice & Palliative Medicine 2012; **Med School:** Harvard Med Sch 1981; **Resid:** Family Medicine, Montefiore Med Ctr 1984; **Fac Appt:** Prof Med, Albert Einstein Coll Med

Swiderski, Deborah M MD (IM) *PCP* - **Spec Exp:** Preventive Medicine; **Hospital:** Montefiore Med Ctr-Moses Campus (page 100); **Address:** Montefiore Med Grp, Primary Care, 305 E 161 St, Bronx, NY 10451; **Phone:** 718-579-2500; **Board Cert:** Internal Medicine 1986; **Med School:** Columbia P&S 1980; **Resid:** Internal Medicine, Montefiore Med Ctr 1983; **Fac Appt:** Assoc Clin Prof Med, Albert Einstein Coll Med

Teffera, Fassil MD (IM) *PCP* - **Spec Exp:** Diabetes; Hypertension; Preventive Medicine; **Hospital:** Montefiore Med Ctr-Wakefield Campus (page 100), Montefiore Med Ctr-Moses Campus (page 100); **Address:** 2426 Eastchester Rd, Ste 101, Bronx, NY 10469; **Phone:** 718-708-4726; **Board Cert:** Internal Medicine 2013; **Med School:** Ethiopia 1976; **Resid:** Internal Medicine, Our Lady of Mercy Med Ctr 1993; **Fac Appt:** Asst Clin Prof Med, NY Med Coll

Maternal & Fetal Medicine

Chazotte, Cynthia MD (MF) - **Spec Exp:** Pregnancy-High Risk; Asthma in Pregnancy; **Hospital:** Montefiore Med Ctr-Einstein Campus (page 100); **Address:** Montefiore, Inst Women's Hlth, 1695 Eastchester Rd, Ste L2, Bronx, NY 10461; **Phone:** 718-405-8200; **Board Cert:** Obstetrics & Gynecology 2013; Maternal & Fetal Medicine 2013; **Med School:** NY Med Coll 1981; **Resid:** Obstetrics & Gynecology, Montefiore Med Ctr 1985; **Fellow:** Maternal & Fetal Medicine, Montefiore Med Ctr 1987; **Fac Appt:** Prof ObG, Albert Einstein Coll Med

Dayal, Ashlesha MD (MF) - **Spec Exp:** Pregnancy-High Risk; **Hospital:** Montefiore Med Ctr-Einstein Campus (page 100); **Address:** Montefiore, Inst Women's Hlth, 1695 Eastchester Rd, Ste L2, Bronx, NY 10462; **Phone:** 718-405-8200; **Board Cert:** Obstetrics & Gynecology 2013; Maternal & Fetal Medicine 2013; **Med School:** Boston Univ 1993; **Resid:** Obstetrics & Gynecology, LIJ Med Ctr 1997; **Fellow:** Maternal & Fetal Medicine, NY-Presby/Columbia Univ Med Ctr 1999; **Fac Appt:** Assoc Clin Prof ObG, Albert Einstein Coll Med

Einstein, Francine H MD (MF) - **Spec Exp:** Obstetric Ultrasound; Diabetes in Pregnancy; **Hospital:** Montefiore Med Ctr-Einstein Campus (page 100); **Address:** 1695 Eastchester Rd, Ste L4, Women's Health Ctr, Bronx, NY 10461; **Phone:** 718-405-8200; **Board Cert:** Internal Medicine 2009; Maternal & Fetal Medicine 2009; **Med School:** Jefferson Med Coll 1997; **Resid:** Obstetrics & Gynecology, St Barnabas Med Ctr 2001; **Fellow:** Maternal & Fetal Medicine, Montefiore Med Ctr 2004; **Fac Appt:** Assoc Prof ObG, Albert Einstein Coll Med

Henderson, Cassandra E MD (MF) - **Spec Exp:** Pregnancy-High Risk; Diabetes in Pregnancy; **Hospital:** Lincoln Med & Mental Hlth Ctr, Harlem Hosp Ctr; **Address:** Lincoln Med Ctr, Ob/Gyn, 234 E 149th St, rm 518, Bronx, NY 10451; **Phone:** 718-579-5513; **Board Cert:** Obstetrics & Gynecology 2014; Maternal & Fetal Medicine 2014; **Med School:** Loyola Univ-Stritch Sch Med 1980; **Resid:** Obstetrics & Gynecology, Univ Chicago Hosp 1984; **Fellow:** Maternal & Fetal Medicine, Montefiore Med Ctr 1986

Medical Oncology

Bruckner, Howard W MD (Onc) - **Spec Exp:** Pancreatic Cancer; **Hospital:** Montefiore Med Ctr-Moses Campus (page 100), Mt Sinai Hosp; **Address:** 2330 Eastchester Rd, Bronx, NY 10469; **Phone:** 718-732-4050; **Board Cert:** Internal Medicine 1972; Medical Oncology 1973; **Med School:** Albert Einstein Coll Med 1966; **Resid:** Internal Medicine, Montefiore Med Ctr 1971; **Fellow:** Medical Oncology, Yale-New Haven Hosp 1971

Camacho, Fernando J MD (Onc) - **Spec Exp:** Breast Cancer; Lymphoma; Bladder Cancer; **Hospital:** Montefiore Med Ctr-Moses Campus (page 100), Saint Joseph's Med Ctr - Yonkers; **Address:** 60 E 208th St, Bronx, NY 10467; **Phone:** 718-405-1700; **Board Cert:** Internal Medicine 1976; Hematology 1978; Medical Oncology 1981; **Med School:** SUNY Buffalo 1973; **Resid:** Internal Medicine, Montefiore Med Ctr 1976; Hematology, Montefiore Med Ctr 1977; **Fellow:** Medical Oncology, Meml Sloan-Kettering Cancer Ctr 1979; **Fac Appt:** Asst Clin Prof Med, Albert Einstein Coll Med

Fuks, Joachim MD (Onc) - **Spec Exp:** Lung Cancer; Breast Cancer; Colon Cancer; **Hospital:** Montefiore Westchester Sq (page 100), Montefiore Med Ctr-Einstein Campus (page 100); **Address:** Montefiore Advanced Oncology, 1578 Williamsbridge Rd Fl 2, Bronx, NY 10461; **Phone:** 718-931-2290; **Board Cert:** Internal Medicine 1981; Medical Oncology 1983; **Med School:** Spain 1975; **Resid:** Internal Medicine, Mt Sinai Hosp 1978; **Fellow:** Medical Oncology, Natl Cancer Inst 1981

Perez-Soler, Roman MD (Onc) - **Spec Exp:** Lung Cancer; Mesothelioma; Drug Development; **Hospital:** Montefiore Med Ctr-Einstein Campus (page 100), Montefiore Med Ctr-Moses Campus (page 100); **Address:** Montefiore, Oncology, 1695 Eastchester Rd Fl 2, Bronx, NY 10461; **Phone:** 718-405-8404; **Board Cert:** Internal Medicine 1987; Medical Oncology 1989; **Med School:** Spain 1977; **Resid:** Internal Medicine, Univ Autonoma Med Ctr 1982; **Fellow:** Medical Oncology, UT MD Anderson Cancer Ctr 1985; **Fac Appt:** Prof Med, Albert Einstein Coll Med

Ramirez, Mark Anthony MD (Onc) - **Spec Exp:** Lymphoma, Non-Hodgkin's; Breast Cancer; Lung Cancer; **Hospital:** Montefiore Med Ctr-Moses Campus (page 100), Saint Joseph's Med Ctr - Yonkers; **Address:** 60 E 208th St, Bronx, NY 10467; **Phone:** 718-405-1700; **Board Cert:** Internal Medicine 1985; Medical Oncology 1989; Hematology 2005; **Med School:** Cornell Univ-Weill Med Coll 1982; **Resid:** Internal Medicine, Montefiore Med Ctr 1985; **Fellow:** Hematology & Oncology, Montefiore Med Ctr 1988; **Fac Appt:** Asst Clin Prof Med, Albert Einstein Coll Med

Sparano, Joseph A MD (Onc) - **Spec Exp:** Breast Cancer; Lymphoma; **Hospital:** Montefiore Med Ctr-Einstein Campus (page 100); **Address:** Montefiore, Oncology, 1695 Eastchester Rd Fl 2, Bronx, NY 10461; **Phone:** 718-405-8404; **Board Cert:** Internal Medicine 1986; Medical Oncology 1989; **Med School:** NY Med Coll 1982; **Resid:** Internal Medicine, St Vincents Hosp 1986; **Fellow:** Medical Oncology, Montefiore Med Ctr 1988; **Fac Appt:** Prof Med, Albert Einstein Coll Med

Vogl, Steven E MD (Onc) - **Spec Exp:** Breast Cancer; Lung Cancer; **Hospital:** Montefiore Med Ctr-Einstein Campus (page 100), White Plains Hosp (page 652); **Address:** 2220 Tiemann Ave, Bronx, NY 10469; **Phone:** 718-519-7774; **Board Cert:** Internal Medicine 1975; Medical Oncology 1975; **Med School:** Cornell Univ-Weill Med Coll 1970; **Resid:** Internal Medicine, Jacobi Med Ctr 1972; **Fellow:** Medical Oncology, Mt Sinai Med Ctr 1975

Neonatal-Perinatal Medicine

Campbell, Deborah E MD (NP) - **Spec Exp:** Prematurity/Low Birth Weight Infants; Neurodevelopmental Disabilities; Neonatal Nutrition; Ethics; **Hospital:** Montefiore Med Ctr-Einstein Campus (page 100), Montefiore Med Ctr-Wakefield Campus (page 100); **Address:** Montefiore-Weiler Hosp, Neonatology, 1601 Tenbroeck Ave, Bronx, NY 10461; **Phone:** 718-904-4105; **Board Cert:** Pediatrics 1983; Neonatal-Perinatal Medicine 1985; **Med School:** SUNY Buffalo 1978; **Resid:** Pediatrics, Montefiore Med Ctr 1981; **Fellow:** Neonatal-Perinatal Medicine, Montefiore Med Ctr 1983; **Fac Appt:** Prof Ped, Albert Einstein Coll Med

Nephrology

Coco, Maria MD (Nep) - **Spec Exp:** Hypertension; Kidney Disease; **Hospital:** Montefiore Med Ctr-Moses Campus (page 100); **Address:** 111 E 210th St, Bronx, NY 10467; **Phone:** 718-920-4136; **Board Cert:** Internal Medicine 1985; Nephrology 1988; **Med School:** Italy 1982; **Resid:** Internal Medicine, Bronx Lebanon Hosp 1985; **Fellow:** Nephrology, Montefiore Med Ctr 1988; **Fac Appt:** Prof Med, Albert Einstein Coll Med

Croll, James E MD (Nep) - **Spec Exp:** Dialysis Care; Hypertension; Kidney Failure-Chronic; **Hospital:** St. Barnabas Hosp - Bronx; **Address:** 2016 Bronxdale Ave, Ste 301, Bronx, NY 10462; **Phone:** 718-918-1356; **Board Cert:** Internal Medicine 1978; Nephrology 1982; **Med School:** Belgium 1975; **Resid:** Internal Medicine, Genesee Hosp 1978; **Fellow:** Nephrology, VA Med Ctr 1981

Gorkin, Janet U MD (Nep) - **Spec Exp:** Hypertension; Diabetic Kidney Disease; Kidney Failure; **Hospital:** Montefiore Med Ctr-Moses Campus (page 100); **Address:** 3327 Bainbridge Ave, Bronx, NY 10467; **Phone:** 718-881-7100; **Board Cert:** Internal Medicine 1976; Nephrology 1980; **Med School:** Mount Sinai Sch Med 1973; **Resid:** Internal Medicine, Mt Sinai Hosp 1976; **Fellow:** Nephrology, Mt Sinai Hosp 1978; **Fac Appt:** Prof Med, Albert Einstein Coll Med

Laitman, Robert MD (Nep) - **Spec Exp:** Diabetic Kidney Disease; Cholesterol/Lipid Disorders; **Hospital:** Montefiore Med Ctr-Einstein Campus (page 100); **Address:** Bronx Westchester Med Grp, 2510 Westchester Ave, Ste 106, Bronx, NY 10461; **Phone:** 718-518-1276; **Board Cert:** Internal Medicine 1986; Nephrology 1988; Geriatric Medicine 2010; **Med School:** Washington Univ, St Louis 1983; **Resid:** Internal Medicine, Jacobi Med Ctr 1986; **Fellow:** Nephrology, Montefiore Med Ctr 1988

Lynn, Robert I MD (Nep) - **Spec Exp:** Hypertension; Dialysis Care; **Hospital:** Montefiore Med Ctr-Einstein Campus (page 100); **Address:** 1200 Waters Pl, Ste M104, Bronx, NY 10461; **Phone:** 718-794-1200; **Board Cert:** Internal Medicine 1977; Nephrology 1980; **Med School:** Columbia P&S 1974; **Resid:** Internal Medicine, NY-Presby/Columbia Univ Med Ctr 1977; **Fellow:** Nephrology, Yale-New Haven Hosp 1979; **Fac Appt:** Assoc Prof Med, Albert Einstein Coll Med

Neugarten, Joel MD (Nep) - **Hospital:** Montefiore Med Ctr-Moses Campus (page 100), Montefiore Med Ctr-Einstein Campus (page 100); **Address:** Montefiore Med Ctr, Nephrology, 111 E 210th St, rm 605, Bronx, NY 10467; **Phone:** 718-920-5442; **Board Cert:** Internal Medicine 1978; Nephrology 1980; **Med School:** Albert Einstein Coll Med 1975; **Resid:** Internal Medicine, Mt Sinai Hosp 1978; **Fellow:** Nephrology, NYU Med Ctr 1980; **Fac Appt:** Prof Med, Albert Einstein Coll Med

Uday, Kalpana MD (Nep) - **Spec Exp:** Hypertension; Kidney Disease-Chronic; **Hospital:** Bronx Lebanon Hosp Ctr; **Address:** Health & Wellness Ctr, 199 W Mount Eden Pkwy Fl 8, Bronx, NY 10452; **Phone:** 718-992-7669; **Board Cert:** Internal Medicine 1989; Nephrology 2013; **Med School:** India 1980; **Resid:** Internal Medicine, Jamaica Med Ctr 1989; **Fellow:** Nephrology, Montefiore Med Ctr 1991; **Fac Appt:** Asst Prof Med, Albert Einstein Coll Med

Yoo, Jinil MD (Nep) - **Spec Exp:** Kidney Disease; Hypertension; Diabetes; **Hospital:** Montefiore Med Ctr-Wakefield Campus (page 100); **Address:** 4141 Carpenter Ave, Medical Village, Montefiore N, Bronx, NY 10466; **Phone:** 347-341-4340; **Board Cert:** Internal Medicine 1974; Nephrology 1976; **Med School:** South Korea 1967; **Resid:** Internal Medicine, Lahey Clinic 1973; Internal Medicine, Metropolitan Hosp Ctr 1974; **Fellow:** Nephrology, NY Med Coll 1976; **Fac Appt:** Prof Med, Albert Einstein Coll Med

Neurological Surgery

Flamm, Eugene S MD (NS) - **Spec Exp:** Aneurysm-Cerebral; Brain Tumors; Cerebrovascular Neurosurgery; **Hospital:** Montefiore Med Ctr-Moses Campus (page 100); **Address:** Montefiore, Neurosurgery, 3316 Rochambeau Ave, Bronx, NY 10467; **Phone:** 718-920-2339; **Board Cert:** Neurological Surgery 1973; **Med School:** SUNY Buffalo 1962; **Resid:** Surgery, NY-Presby/Weill Cornell Med Ctr 1964; Neurological Surgery, NYU Med Ctr 1970; **Fellow:** Neurological Surgery, Univ Zurich 1971; **Fac Appt:** Prof NS, Albert Einstein Coll Med

LaSala, Patrick A MD (NS) - **Spec Exp:** Brain Tumors; Epilepsy; Stereotactic Radiosurgery; **Hospital:** Montefiore Med Ctr-Moses Campus (page 100); **Address:** Montefiore, Neurosurgery, 3316 Rochambeau Ave, Bronx, NY 10467; **Phone:** 718-920-7466; **Board Cert:** Neurological Surgery 1991; **Med School:** Columbia P&S 1980; **Resid:** Neurological Surgery, NY-Presby/Columbia Univ Med Ctr 1987; **Fac Appt:** Assoc Prof NS, Albert Einstein Coll Med

Neurology

Boro, Alexis MD (N) - **Spec Exp:** Epilepsy/Seizure Disorders; **Hospital:** Montefiore Med Ctr-Moses Campus (page 100); **Address:** 111 E 210th St, Bronx, NY 10467; **Phone:** 718-920-4898; **Board Cert:** Neurology 2004; Epilepsy 2013; Clinical Neurophysiology 2013; **Med School:** SUNY Stony Brook 1998; **Resid:** Neurology, Mt Sinai Med Ctr 2002; **Fellow:** Epilepsy, Montefiore Med Ctr 2003; **Fac Appt:** Asst Prof N, Albert Einstein Coll Med

Cohen, Joel S MD (N) - **Spec Exp:** Epilepsy; Headache; Stroke; Parkinson's Disease; **Hospital:** Montefiore Med Ctr-Moses Campus (page 100), Montefiore Med Ctr-Einstein Campus (page 100); **Address:** ProHlth Care Assocs, 1610 Williamsbridge Rd Fl 3, Bronx, NY 10461; **Phone:** 718-597-8000; **Board Cert:** Neurology 1992; **Med School:** Albert Einstein Coll Med 1983; **Resid:** Neurology, Montefiore Med Ctr 1987; **Fellow:** Neurology, Montefiore Med Ctr 1988; **Fac Appt:** Assoc Prof N, Albert Einstein Coll Med

Freddo, Lorenza MD (N) - **Spec Exp:** Pain Management; Multiple Sclerosis; Peripheral Neuropathy; **Hospital:** St. Barnabas Hosp - Bronx; **Address:** Belmont Med Assocs, 2371 Arthur Ave, Bronx, NY 10458; **Phone:** 718-364-6199; **Board Cert:** Neurology 1992; **Med School:** Italy 1980; **Resid:** Neurology, NY-Presby/Columbia Univ Med Ctr 1990; Neurology; **Fac Appt:** Asst Prof NPath, Albert Einstein Coll Med

Grenell, Steven L MD (N) - **Spec Exp:** Pain Management; Headache; **Hospital:** Montefiore Med Ctr-Moses Campus (page 100), Lawrence Hosp Ctr (page 102); **Address:** 3975 Sedgewick Ave, Ste 1-F, Bronx, NY 10463; **Phone:** 718-796-6055; **Board Cert:** Neurology 1989; **Med School:** UMDNJ-Rutgers Med Sch 1977; **Resid:** Internal Medicine, Montefiore Med Ctr 1979; Neurology, Montefiore Med Ctr 1982; **Fellow:** Internal Medicine, Montefiore Med Ctr 1982; **Fac Appt:** Asst Prof N, Albert Einstein Coll Med

Herskovitz, Steven MD (N) - **Spec Exp:** Electromyography; Neuromuscular Disorders; Peripheral Neuropathy; **Hospital:** Montefiore Med Ctr-Moses Campus (page 100); **Address:** 111 E 210th St, Bronx, NY 10467; **Phone:** 718-920-4930; **Board Cert:** Internal Medicine 1983; Neurology 1987; Neuromuscular Medicine 2008; **Med School:** Cornell Univ-Weill Med Coll 1980; **Resid:** Internal Medicine, Montefiore Med Ctr 1983; Neurology, Montefiore Med Ctr 1986; **Fellow:** Electromyography, Montefiore Med Ctr 1987; **Fac Appt:** Prof N, Albert Einstein Coll Med

Kaufman, David Myland MD (N) - **Spec Exp:** Movement Disorders; **Hospital:** Montefiore Med Ctr-Moses Campus (page 100); **Address:** Montefiore, Neurology, 3400 Bainbridge Ave, Bronx, NY 10467; **Phone:** 718-920-4730; **Board Cert:** Internal Medicine 1972; Neurology 1976; **Med School:** Univ Chicago-Pritzker Sch Med 1968; **Resid:** Internal Medicine, Montefiore Med Ctr 1971; Neurology, Montefiore Med Ctr 1974; **Fac Appt:** Prof N, Albert Einstein Coll Med

Kirchoff, Kathryn MD (N) - **Spec Exp:** Stroke; **Hospital:** Montefiore Med Ctr-Moses Campus (page 100); **Address:** Montefiore, Stern Stroke Ctr, 111 E 210th St, Bronx, NY 10467; **Phone:** 718-920-6444; **Board Cert:** Neurology 2008; Vascular Neurology 2011; **Med School:** SUNY Stony Brook 2004; **Resid:** Neurology, Mt Sinai Hosp 2008; **Fac Appt:** Asst Prof N, Albert Einstein Coll Med

Lipton, Richard B MD (N) - **Spec Exp:** Headache; Clinical Trials; **Hospital:** Montefiore Med Ctr-Einstein Campus (page 100); **Address:** Montefiore Headache Ctr, 1575 Blondale Ave, rm 225, Bronx, NY 10461-1900; **Phone:** 718-405-8360; **Board Cert:** Neurology 1985; **Med School:** Univ Chicago-Pritzker Sch Med 1980; **Resid:** Neurology, Montefiore Med Ctr 1984; **Fellow:** Neurophysiology, Montefiore Med Ctr 1985; NeuroEpidemiology, Columbia Univ 1990; **Fac Appt:** Prof N, Albert Einstein Coll Med

Selman, Jay E MD (N) - **Spec Exp:** Pediatric Neurology; Epilepsy/Seizure Disorders; Headache; Tourette's Syndrome; **Hospital:** Blythedale Children's Hosp, Bronx Lebanon Hosp Ctr; **Address:** Bronxcare Poe Med & Dental Pediatrics, 2432 Grand Concourse, Bronx, NY 10458; **Phone:** 718-579-7337; **Board Cert:** Pediatrics 1978; Sleep Medicine 2007; Neurodevelopmental Disabilities 2012; **Med School:** Univ Tex SW, Dallas 1973; **Resid:** Pediatrics, Jacobi Med Ctr 1975; Neurology, Jacobi Med Ctr 1978; **Fellow:** Child Neurology, Jacobi Med Ctr 1977; **Fac Appt:** Assoc Clin Prof N, Columbia P&S

Sparr, Steven MD (N) - **Spec Exp:** Vascular Neurology; Pain Management; **Hospital:** Montefiore Med Ctr-Moses Campus (page 100); **Address:** Montefiore, Stern Stroke Ctr, 111 E 210th St, Bronx, NY 10467; **Phone:** 718-920-6402; **Board Cert:** Internal Medicine 1984; Neurology 1987; Vascular Neurology 2008; **Med School:** SUNY Buffalo 1980; **Resid:** Internal Medicine, Boston City Hosp 1983; Neurology, Albert Einstein 1986; **Fellow:** Neurological Rehabilitation, Burke Rehabilitation Hosp 1987; **Fac Appt:** Assoc Prof N, Albert Einstein Coll Med

Swerdlow, Michael L MD (N) - **Spec Exp:** Myasthenia Gravis; Spinal Disorders; Multiple Sclerosis; **Hospital:** Montefiore Med Ctr-Moses Campus (page 100); **Address:** Montefiore Med Ctr, Neurology, 3400 Bainbridge Ave, Bronx, NY 10467; **Phone:** 718-920-4178; **Board Cert:** Neurology 1975; **Med School:** Univ Pennsylvania 1967; **Resid:** Internal Medicine, Mt Sinai Hosp 1969; Neurology, Montefiore Med Ctr 1972; **Fellow:** Neurology, Natl Inst Hlth 1974; **Fac Appt:** Prof N, Albert Einstein Coll Med

Nuclear Medicine

Freeman, Leonard M MD (NuM) - **Spec Exp:** Nuclear Oncology; Gastrointestinal Disorders; PET Imaging; CT Scan; **Hospital:** Montefiore Med Ctr-Moses Campus (page 100); **Address:** 111 E 210th St Foreman Bldg Fl 4, Bronx, NY 10467-2401; **Phone:** 718-920-6060; **Board Cert:** Radiology 1966; Nuclear Medicine 2013; Nuclear Radiology 1974; **Med School:** Ros Franklin Univ/Chicago Med Sch 1961; **Resid:** Radiology, Bronx Municipal Hosp 1965; **Fac Appt:** Prof NuM, Albert Einstein Coll Med

Milstein, David M MD (NuM) - **Hospital:** Montefiore Med Ctr-Einstein Campus (page 100); Montefiore Med Ctr-Moses Campus (page 100); **Address:** Montefiore, Nuclear Medicine, 1695A Eastchester Rd, Bronx, NY 10461; **Phone:** 718-405-8455; **Board Cert:** Nuclear Medicine 1972; Diagnostic Radiology 1972; **Med School:** Albert Einstein Coll Med 1967; **Resid:** Diagnostic Radiology, Bronx Muni Hosp Ctr 1972; **Fellow:** Nuclear Medicine, Bronx Muni Hosp Ctr 1972; **Fac Appt:** Prof NuM, Albert Einstein Coll Med

Obstetrics & Gynecology

Dar, Pe'er MD (ObG) - **Spec Exp:** Fetal Diagnosis & Therapy; Fetal Ultrasound/Obstetrical Imaging; Prenatal Diagnosis; Pregnancy-High Risk; **Hospital:** Montefiore Med Ctr-Einstein Campus (page 100); **Address:** Montefiore Medical Park, 1695 Eastchester Rd, Ste L4, Bronx, NY 10461; **Phone:** 718-405-8218; **Board Cert:** Clinical Genetics 2013; Obstetrics & Gynecology 2013; **Med School:** Israel 1987; **Resid:** Obstetrics & Gynecology, Assaf Harofeh Hosp 1998; Obstetrics & Gynecology, Montefiore Med Ctr 2005; **Fellow:** Clinical Genetics, Albert Einstein/Montefiore Med Ctr 2000; **Fac Appt:** Assoc Clin Prof ObG, Albert Einstein Coll Med

Friedman, Ronit B MD (ObG) - **Spec Exp:** Pregnancy; **Hospital:** Montefiore Med Ctr-Moses Campus (page 100); **Address:** Montefiorev Women's Ctr, Obstetrics, 3332 Rochambeau Ave, Bronx, NY 10467; **Phone:** 718-920-5157; **Board Cert:** Obstetrics & Gynecology 2013; **Med School:** Columbia P&S 1999; **Resid:** Obstetrics & Gynecology, Beth Israel Deaconess Med Ctr 2003

Levy, Judith MD (ObG) *PCP* - **Hospital:** Montefiore Med Ctr-Einstein Campus (page 100); **Address:** 1695 Eastchester Rd, Ste L2, Bronx, NY 10461; **Phone:** 718-405-8200; **Board Cert:** Obstetrics & Gynecology 2013; **Med School:** Albert Einstein Coll Med 1981; **Resid:** Obstetrics & Gynecology, Bronx Muni Hosp 1985; **Fac Appt:** Asst Prof ObG, Albert Einstein Coll Med

Pali, Rozafa L MD (ObG) - **Spec Exp:** Women's Health; **Hospital:** Montefiore Med Ctr-Wakefield Campus (page 100), Montefiore New Rochelle Hosp (page 100); **Address:** 789 Waring Ave, Bronx, NY 10467; **Phone:** 718-231-5111; **Board Cert:** Obstetrics & Gynecology 2013; **Med School:** Albania 1981; **Resid:** Obstetrics & Gynecology, Univ Hosp 1985; Obstetrics & Gynecology, Our Lady of Mercy Med Ctr 2000

Ophthalmology

Chess, Jeremy MD (Oph) - **Spec Exp:** Retina/Vitreous Surgery; **Hospital:** Montefiore Med Ctr-Moses Campus (page 100); **Address:** Retina Grp, 2221 Boston Rd, Bronx, NY 10467; **Phone:** 718-798-3030; **Board Cert:** Ophthalmology 1977; **Med School:** Boston Univ 1970; **Resid:** Ophthalmology, Boston Univ Med Ctr 1974; **Fellow:** Vitreoretinal Surgery, Boston Univ Med Ctr 1983; **Fac Appt:** Assoc Clin Prof Oph, Albert Einstein Coll Med

Chuck Jr, Roy MD/PhD (Oph) - **Spec Exp:** Refractive Surgery; Corneal Disease & Surgery; **Hospital:** Montefiore Med Ctr-Moses Campus (page 100); **Address:** Montefiore, Dept of Ophthalmology, 3400 Bainbridge Ave, Bronx, NY 10467; **Phone:** 718-920-2020; **Board Cert:** Ophthalmology 2010; **Med School:** Columbia P&S 1993; **Resid:** Ophthalmology, Barnes-Jewish Hosp 1996; **Fellow:** Cornea & Refractive Surgery, Keck Med Ctr of USC 1999; **Fac Appt:** Prof Oph, Albert Einstein Coll Med

Katz, Barrett MD (Oph) - **Spec Exp:** Neuro-Ophthalmology; Optic Nerve Disorders; Eye Muscle Disorders; **Hospital:** Montefiore Med Ctr-Moses Campus (page 100); **Address:** 3400 Bainbridge Ave, Bronx, NY 10467; **Phone:** 718-920-2020; **Board Cert:** Ophthalmology 1984; **Med School:** Case West Res Univ 1973; **Resid:** Neurology, Brigham and Women's Hosp 1978; Ophthalmology, Tufts Med Ctr 1981; **Fellow:** Neuro-Ophthalmology, UCSF Med Ctr 1982; **Fac Appt:** Prof Oph, Albert Einstein Coll Med

Katz, Steven J MD (Oph) - **Spec Exp:** Cataract Surgery; Refractive Surgery; Diabetic Eye Disease/Retinopathy; **Hospital:** Montefiore Med Ctr-Einstein Campus (page 100); **Address:** 1931 Williamsbridge Rd, Bronx, NY 10461; **Phone:** 718-792-2700; **Board Cert:** Ophthalmology 1987; **Med School:** NYU Sch Med 1981; **Resid:** Ophthalmology, Long Island Jewish Med Ctr 1985

Mayers, Martin MD (Oph) - **Spec Exp:** Cataract Surgery; Cornea Transplant; Eye Infections; **Hospital:** Bronx Lebanon Hosp Ctr, Montefiore Med Ctr-Wakefield Campus (page 100); **Address:** Bronx-Lebanon Hosp Ctr, 1650 Grand Concourse, Milstein Bldg - rm 1C, Bronx, NY 10456; **Phone:** 718-518-8008; **Board Cert:** Ophthalmology 1985; **Med School:** Albert Einstein Coll Med 1979; **Resid:** Ophthalmology, SUNY Downstate Med Ctr 1983; **Fellow:** Cornea, Proctor Fdn-UCSF 1984; **Fac Appt:** Assoc Prof Oph, Albert Einstein Coll Med

Medow, Norman B MD (Oph) - **Spec Exp:** Cataract-Pediatric; Glaucoma-Pediatric; Corneal Disease-Pediatric; **Hospital:** Montefiore Med Ctr-Moses Campus (page 100); **Address:** Montefiore Hosp Ctr, Dept Ophthalmology, 3400 Bainbridge Ave, Bronx, NY 10467; **Phone:** 718-920-2020; **Board Cert:** Ophthalmology 1975; **Med School:** SUNY Downstate 1966; **Resid:** Ophthalmology, Manhattan EE&T Hosp 1972; **Fellow:** Cataract/Lens Implant Surgery, Charles Kelman, MD 1973; **Fac Appt:** Clin Prof Oph, Cornell Univ-Weill Med Coll

Odrich, Marc G MD (Oph) - **Spec Exp:** LASIK-Refractive Surgery; Cataract Surgery; Corneal Disease & Surgery; **Hospital:** Montefiore Med Ctr-Moses Campus (page 100), Lenox Hill Hosp (Manh Eye, Ear & Throat Hosp); **Address:** 3765 Riverdale Ave, Bronx, NY 10463; **Phone:** 718-432-2020; **Board Cert:** Ophthalmology 1989; **Med School:** Columbia P&S 1984; **Resid:** Ophthalmology, Columbia Harkness Eye Inst 1988; **Fellow:** Cornea & Ext Eye Disease, Mass Eye & Ear Infirm 1990

Rosenbaum, Pearl S MD (Oph) - **Spec Exp:** Cataract Surgery; Glaucoma; Eye Tumors/Cancer; Ophthalmic Pathology; **Hospital:** Montefiore Med Ctr-Moses Campus (page 100), Bronx Lebanon Hosp Ctr; **Address:** 1250 Waters Pl, Ste 502, Bronx, NY 10461; **Phone:** 718-518-0060; **Board Cert:** Ophthalmology 1988; **Med School:** Albert Einstein Coll Med 1982; **Resid:** Ophthalmology, Albert Einstein 1986; **Fellow:** Ophthalmic Pathology, Baylor Coll of Med Affil Hosp 1988; Ophthalmic Oncology, Baylor Coll of Med Affil Hosp 1988; **Fac Appt:** Prof Oph, Albert Einstein Coll Med

Slamovits, Thomas L MD (Oph) - **Spec Exp:** Neuro-Ophthalmology; Optic Nerve Disorders; Vision Loss-Unexplained Loss; Diabetic Eye Disease/Retinopathy; **Hospital:** Montefiore Med Ctr-Moses Campus (page 100), Hackensack Univ Med Ctr (page 96); **Address:** 1250 Pelham Pkwy S, Bronx, NY 10461; **Phone:** 718-794-1500; **Board Cert:** Ophthalmology 1980; **Med School:** Ohio State Univ 1975; **Resid:** Internal Medicine, Ohio State Univ Hosp 1976; Ophthalmology, Univ Pitts Eye & Ear Hosp 1979; **Fellow:** Neuro-Ophthalmology, Washington Univ-Barnes Hosp 1980; **Fac Appt:** Clin Prof Oph, Albert Einstein Coll Med

Terraciano, Anthony J MD (Oph) - **Spec Exp:** Cornea & External Eye Disease; **Hospital:** New York Eye & Ear Infirm of Mt Sinai; **Address:** 2241 Esplanade, Bronx, NY 10469; **Phone:** 718-654-7122; **Board Cert:** Ophthalmology 2014; **Med School:** Tufts Univ 1998; **Resid:** Ophthalmology, NY Eye & Ear Infirmary 2002; **Fellow:** Cornea & Ext Eye Disease, NY Eye & Ear Infirmary 2003

Tiwari, Ram P MD (Oph) - **Spec Exp:** Diabetic Eye Disease/Retinopathy; Glaucoma; Dry Eye Syndrome; **Hospital:** Montefiore Med Ctr-Wakefield Campus (page 100), NY-Presby/Columbia Univ Med Ctr, NY (page 102); **Address:** Bronx Ophthalmology, 1739 Williamsbridge Rd, Bronx, NY 10461-6203; **Phone:** 718-824-1560; **Board Cert:** Ophthalmology 1977; **Med School:** India 1966; **Resid:** Ophthalmology, Maulana Azad Med Coll Affil Hosp 1971; **Fellow:** Retina, Columbia-Presby Med Ctr 1978; **Fac Appt:** Asst Clin Prof Oph, Columbia P&S

Wolf, Kenneth J MD (Oph) - **Spec Exp:** Diabetic Eye Disease/Retinopathy; Cataract Surgery; **Hospital:** Montefiore Westchester Sq (page 100); **Address:** 1776 Eastchester Rd, Ste 235, Bronx, NY 10461; **Phone:** 718-892-6110; **Board Cert:** Ophthalmology 1980; **Med School:** Albert Einstein Coll Med 1974; **Resid:** Ophthalmology, Montefiore Hosp Med Ctr 1978; **Fac Appt:** Asst Clin Prof Oph, Albert Einstein Coll Med

Orthopaedic Surgery

Cobelli, Neil MD (OrS) - **Spec Exp:** Knee Replacement; Hip Replacement; Reconstructive Surgery; **Hospital:** Montefiore Med Ctr-Einstein Campus (page 100), Montefiore Med Ctr-Wakefield Campus (page 100); **Address:** 1250 Waters Pl Fl 11, Bronx, NY 10461; **Phone:** 718-920-2060; **Board Cert:** Orthopaedic Surgery 1985; **Med School:** Dartmouth Med Sch 1976; **Resid:** Orthopaedic Surgery, Montefiore Med Ctr 1983; **Fac Appt:** Prof OrS, Albert Einstein Coll Med

Geller, David S MD (OrS) - **Spec Exp:** Bone Cancer; Sarcoma; Sarcoma-Soft Tissue; Musculoskeletal Tumors; **Hospital:** Montefiore Med Ctr-Moses Campus (page 100); **Address:** MMC Medical Arts Pavilion, 3400 Bainbridge Ave Fl 6, Bronx, NY 10467; **Phone:** 718-920-5722; **Board Cert:** Orthopaedic Surgery 2008; **Med School:** Israel 2000; **Resid:** Orthopaedic Surgery, Montefiore Med Ctr 2005; **Fellow:** Orthopaedic Oncology, Mass Genl Hosp 2006; **Fac Appt:** Asst Prof OrS, Albert Einstein Coll Med

Hoang, Bang H MD (OrS) - **Spec Exp:** Musculoskeletal Tumors; Sarcoma; Reconstructive Surgery; Bone & Soft Tissue Tumors; **Hospital:** Montefiore Med Ctr-Einstein Campus (page 100); **Address:** Montefiore Greene Med Arts Pavilion, 3400 Bainbridge Ave, Bronx, NY 10467; **Phone:** 718-920-2060; **Board Cert:** Orthopaedic Surgery 2006; **Med School:** UCLA 1995; **Resid:** Orthopaedic Surgery, Univ Med Ctr 2001; **Fellow:** Orthopaedic Surgery, Univ Med Ctr 1997; Orthopaedic Oncology, Meml Sloan-Kettering Cancer Ctr 2003

Kleinman, Paul G MD (OrS) - **Spec Exp:** Pediatric Orthopaedic Surgery; Hand Surgery; Trauma; Sports Medicine; **Hospital:** St. Barnabas Hosp - Bronx; **Address:** 2016 Bronxdale Ave, Ste 202, Bronx, NY 10462-3365; **Phone:** 718-863-8695; **Board Cert:** Orthopaedic Surgery 2009; **Med School:** Stanford Univ 1979; **Resid:** Orthopaedic Surgery, Columbia-Presby Hosp 1985; **Fellow:** Hand Surgery, Allegheny Genl Hosp 1986; Pediatric Orthopaedic Surgery, Hosp Joint Diseases 1990

Kulsakdinun, Chaiyaporn MD (OrS) - **Spec Exp:** Foot & Ankle Surgery; Foot & Ankle Deformities; Sports Injuries; **Hospital:** Montefiore Med Ctr-Einstein Campus (page 100); **Address:** 1250 Waters Pl Fl 11 - Ste C, Bronx, NY 10461; **Phone:** 718-920-2060; **Board Cert:** Orthopaedic Surgery 2014; **Med School:** Yale Univ 1993; **Resid:** Orthopaedic Surgery, Yale-New Haven Hosp 1998; **Fellow:** Foot & Ankle Surgery, Hosp Special Surgery 1999; **Fac Appt:** Asst Prof OrS, Albert Einstein Coll Med

Levy, I Martin MD (OrS) - **Spec Exp:** Sports Medicine; Arthroscopic Surgery; Knee Meniscal Repair; Knee Injuries/ACL; **Hospital:** Montefiore Med Ctr-Einstein Campus (page 100); **Address:** 1250 Waters Pl Fl 11, Bronx, NY 10461; **Phone:** 347-577-4411; **Board Cert:** Orthopaedic Surgery 1982; **Med School:** NY Med Coll 1976; **Resid:** Orthopaedic Surgery, Bronx Municipal Hosps 1980; **Fellow:** Sports Medicine, Hosp for Special Surg 1981; **Fac Appt:** Clin Prof OrS, Albert Einstein Coll Med

Olsewski, John M MD (OrS) - **Spec Exp:** Spinal Reconstructive Surgery; Scoliosis; Spinal Surgery-Neck; Cervical Myelopathy; **Hospital:** Montefiore Med Ctr-Einstein Campus (page 100), Montefiore New Rochelle Hosp (page 100); **Address:** 2157 Tomlinson Ave, Bronx, NY 10461; **Phone:** 718-794-2501; **Board Cert:** Orthopaedic Surgery 2007; **Med School:** SUNY Buffalo 1986; **Resid:** Orthopaedic Surgery, SUNY Buffalo Affil Hosp 1992; **Fellow:** Spine Surgery, Twin Cities Scoliosis/Spine Ctr 1994; **Fac Appt:** Clin Prof OrS, Albert Einstein Coll Med

Sharan, Alok D MD (OrS) - **Spec Exp:** Spinal Tumors; Spinal Surgery; **Hospital:** Montefiore Med Ctr-Einstein Campus (page 100); **Address:** Montefiore, Orthopaedic Surgery, 1250 Waters Pl Fl 11, Bronx, NY 10461; **Phone:** 718-920-2060; **Board Cert:** Orthopaedic Surgery 2008; **Med School:** UMDNJ-NJ Med Sch, Newark 2000; **Resid:** Orthopaedic Surgery, Albany Med Ctr 2005; **Fellow:** Spine Surgery, NYU Hosp Joint Diseases 2006; **Fac Appt:** Asst Prof OrS, Albert Einstein Coll Med

Otolaryngology

Feghali, Joseph G MD (Oto) - **Spec Exp:** Ear Disorders/Surgery; Acoustic Neuroma; Hearing Disorders; Cholesteatoma; **Hospital:** Montefiore Med Ctr-Moses Campus (page 100); **Address:** ENT & Allergy Assocs, 1200 Waters Pl, Ste 110, Bronx, NY 10461; **Phone:** 718-863-4366; **Board Cert:** Otolaryngology 1990; **Med School:** Lebanon 1978; **Resid:** Surgery, Meml Sloan-Kettering Cancer Ctr 1986; Otolaryngology, Montefiore Med Ctr 1990; **Fellow:** Otology & Neurotology, House Ear Inst 1983; Neurological Surgery, Meml Sloan-Kettering Cancer Ctr 1985; **Fac Appt:** Clin Prof Oto, Albert Einstein Coll Med

Fried, Marvin P MD (Oto) - **Spec Exp:** Endoscopic Sinus Surgery; Head & Neck Tumors; Laryngeal & Voice Disorders; Sinus Disorders/Surgery; **Hospital:** Montefiore Med Ctr-Moses Campus (page 100), Montefiore Med Ctr-Einstein Campus (page 100); **Address:** Montefiore Greene Med Arts Pavilion, 3400 Bainbridge Ave Fl 3, Bronx, NY 10467; **Phone:** 718-920-4646; **Board Cert:** Otolaryngology 1975; **Med School:** Tufts Univ 1969; **Resid:** Surgery, Barnes-Jewish Hosp 1971; Otolaryngology, Barnes-Jewish Hosp 1975; **Fellow:** Washington Univ 1976; **Fac Appt:** Prof Oto, Albert Einstein Coll Med

Goldstein, Steven I MD (Oto) - **Spec Exp:** Sinus Surgery; Nasal Surgery; **Hospital:** Montefiore Westchester Sq (page 100), Montefiore Med Ctr-Einstein Campus (page 100); **Address:** 1200 Waters Pl, Bronx, NY 10461; **Phone:** 718-863-4366; **Board Cert:** Otolaryngology 1987; **Med School:** SUNY Buffalo 1982; **Resid:** Surgery, NYU Med Ctr 1984; Otolaryngology, NYU Med Ctr 1987; **Fellow:** Facial Plastic Surgery, Mt Sinai Hosp 1988

Park, Steven Y MD (Oto) - **Spec Exp:** Sleep Disorders/Apnea/Snoring; Nasal & Sinus Disorders; **Hospital:** Montefiore Med Ctr-Einstein Campus (page 100), Montefiore Med Ctr-Moses Campus (page 100); **Address:** 3400 Bainbridge Ave, Montefiore Greene Med Arts Pavilion, Bronx, NY 10467; **Phone:** 718-920-4646; **Board Cert:** Otolaryngology 1999; Sleep Medicine 2012; **Med School:** Columbia P&S 1993; **Resid:** Otolaryngology, Montefiore Med Ctr 1998; **Fac Appt:** Asst Prof Oto, Albert Einstein Coll Med

Smith, Jonathan C MD (Oto) - **Spec Exp:** Endoscopic Sinus Surgery; Thyroid & Parathyroid Cancer & Surgery; **Hospital:** Montefiore Med Ctr-Einstein Campus (page 100); **Address:** ENT & Allergy Assocs, 1200 Waters Pl Fl 1 - Ste 110, Bronx, NY 10461; **Phone:** 718-863-4366; **Board Cert:** Otolaryngology 2014; **Med School:** Vanderbilt Univ 1998; **Resid:** Otolaryngology, UPMC 2003

Smith, Richard V MD (Oto) - **Spec Exp:** Head & Neck Cancer; Thyroid & Parathyroid Surgery; Salivary Gland Tumors; Robotic Surgery; **Hospital:** Montefiore Med Ctr-Moses Campus (page 100), Montefiore Med Ctr-Einstein Campus (page 100); **Address:** Montefiore Med Ctr, Otolaryngology, 3400 Bainbridge Ave, Fl 3, Bronx, NY 10467; **Phone:** 718-920-4646; **Board Cert:** Otolaryngology 1996; **Med School:** Univ VT Coll Med 1990; **Resid:** Otolaryngology, Georgetown Univ Hosp 1995; **Fac Appt:** Prof Oto, Albert Einstein Coll Med

Yankelowitz, Stanley M MD (Oto) - **Spec Exp:** Nasal & Sinus Surgery; Pediatric Otolaryngology; **Hospital:** Montefiore Med Ctr-Moses Campus (page 100), Montefiore Westchester Sq (page 100); **Address:** 1200 Waters Pl, Ste 110, Bronx, NY 10461; **Phone:** 718-863-4366; **Med School:** South Africa 1974; **Resid:** Otolaryngology, Univ Stellenbosch 1985; Otolaryngology, Univ Cape Town 1987; **Fellow:** Pediatric Otolaryngology, Montefiore Med Ctr-Weiler Div 1988

Pediatric Allergy & Immunology

Wiznia, Andrew A MD (PA&I) - **Hospital:** Jacobi Med Ctr, N Central Bronx Hosp; **Address:** Jacobi Medical Ctr, Bldg 1, 1400 Pelham Pkwy S, Bronx, NY 10461; **Phone:** 718-918-5222; **Board Cert:** Pediatrics 1986; **Med School:** Columbia P&S 1980; **Resid:** Pediatrics, Bronx Muni Hosp Ctr 1983; Pediatrics, Bronx-Lebanon Hosp Ctr 1984; **Fellow:** Allergy & Immunology, Montefiore-Weiler Einstein Div 1986; **Fac Appt:** Prof Ped, Albert Einstein Coll Med

Pediatric Cardiology

Hsu, Daphne T MD (PCd) - **Spec Exp:** Interventional Cardiology; Heart Failure; Transplant Medicine-Heart; **Hospital:** Montefiore Med Ctr-Moses Campus (page 100), Chldns Hosp at Montefiore; **Address:** CHAM, Cardiology, 3415 Bainbridge Ave, Bronx, NY 10467; **Phone:** 718-741-2538; **Board Cert:** Pediatrics 1988; Pediatric Cardiology 2010; **Med School:** Yale Univ 1982; **Resid:** Pediatrics, Columbia Babies & Chldns Hosp 1985; **Fellow:** Pediatric Cardiology, Columbia Babies & Chldns Hosp 1988; **Fac Appt:** Prof Ped, Albert Einstein Coll Med

Pass, Robert H MD (PCd) - **Spec Exp:** Arrhythmias; Cardiac Electrophysiology; Cardiac Catheterization; **Hospital:** Montefiore Med Ctr-Moses Campus (page 100), Chldns Hosp at Montefiore; **Address:** Chldn's Hosp at Montefiore, Cardiology, 3415 Bainbridge Ave, Bronx, NY 10467; **Phone:** 718-741-2183; **Board Cert:** Pediatric Cardiology 2013; **Med School:** Boston Univ 1991; **Resid:** Pediatrics, NY Presby-Cornell Med Ctr 1994; **Fellow:** Cardiovascular Disease, Children's Hosp 1998; **Fac Appt:** Assoc Prof Ped, Albert Einstein Coll Med

Schiller, Myles S MD (PCd) - **Spec Exp:** Congenital Heart Disease & Acquired; Exercise Physiology; **Hospital:** Montefiore Med Ctr-Moses Campus (page 100), St. Barnabas Hosp - Bronx; **Address:** Children's Hosp Montefiore, 3415 Bainbridge Ave, Bronx, NY 10467; **Phone:** 718-741-2254; **Board Cert:** Pediatrics 1978; Pediatric Cardiology 1979; **Med School:** Ros Franklin Univ/Chicago Med Sch 1973; **Resid:** Pediatrics, New York Hosp-Cornell 1975; **Fellow:** Pediatric Cardiology, New York Hosp-Cornell 1977; **Fac Appt:** Assoc Clin Prof Ped, Albert Einstein Coll Med

Shenoy, Rajesh U MD (PCd) - **Spec Exp:** Echocardiography; Fetal Echocardiography; Congenital Heart Disease; **Hospital:** Mt Sinai Hosp, Queens Hosp Ctr - Jamaica; **Address:** 1 Gustave L. Levy Pl Fl 3, New York, NY 10029; **Phone:** 212-241-0424; **Board Cert:** Pediatric Cardiology 2007; **Med School:** India 1995; **Resid:** Pediatrics, Univ Illinois Med Ctr 1997; **Fellow:** Pediatric Cardiology, N Shore Hosp 2000; **Fac Appt:** Asst Prof Ped, Mount Sinai Sch Med

Walsh, Christine A MD (PCd) - **Spec Exp:** Arrhythmias; Congenital Heart Disease; Sudden Infant Death Syndrome (SIDS); Syncope; **Hospital:** Montefiore Med Ctr-Moses Campus (page 100); **Address:** 3415 Bainbridge Ave Fl 5, Bronx, NY 10467-2401; **Phone:** 718-741-2343; **Board Cert:** Pediatrics 1978; Pediatric Cardiology 2010; **Med School:** Yale Univ 1973; **Resid:** Pediatrics, Columbia-Presby Med Ctr 1976; **Fellow:** Pediatric Cardiology, Columbia-Presby Med Ctr 1980; **Fac Appt:** Clin Prof Ped, Albert Einstein Coll Med

Pediatric Critical Care Medicine

Singer, Lewis P MD (PCCM) - **Spec Exp:** Respiratory Failure; Airway Disorders; **Hospital:** Montefiore Med Ctr-Moses Campus (page 100); **Address:** 111 E 210th St, Rosenthal Pavilion Fl 4, Bronx, NY 10467; **Phone:** 718-741-2440; **Board Cert:** Pediatrics 1981; Neonatal-Perinatal Medicine 1983; Pediatric Critical Care Medicine 2012; **Med School:** UMDNJ-NJ Med Sch, Newark 1977; **Resid:** Pediatrics, Montefiore Hosp Med Ctr 1980; **Fellow:** Neonatology, Montefiore Hosp Med Ctr 1983; **Fac Appt:** Clin Prof Ped, Albert Einstein Coll Med

Ushay, H Michael MD/PhD (PCCM) - **Spec Exp:** Respiratory Failure; Sepsis & Septic Shock; Cardiac Critical Care; **Hospital:** Montefiore Med Ctr-Moses Campus (page 100); **Address:** 111 E 210th St, Rosenthal Pavilion Fl 4, Bronx, NY 10467; **Phone:** 718-741-2440; **Board Cert:** Pediatrics 2012; Pediatric Critical Care Medicine 2008; **Med School:** UMDNJ-NJ Med Sch, Newark 1986; **Resid:** Pediatrics, Montefiore/Bronx Muni Hosp 1990; **Fellow:** Pediatric Pulmonology, Montefiore Med Ctr 1991; Pediatric Critical Care Medicine, NY Hosp-Cornell Univ Med Ctr 1993; **Fac Appt:** Clin Prof Ped, Albert Einstein Coll Med

Weingarten-Arams, Jacqueline S MD (PCCM) - **Spec Exp:** Heart Disease; Lung Disease; Nutrition; **Hospital:** Montefiore Med Ctr-Moses Campus (page 100); **Address:** 111 E 210th St, Rosenthal Bldg - Fl 4, Bronx, NY 10467; **Phone:** 718-741-2440; **Board Cert:** Pediatrics 2011; Pediatric Critical Care Medicine 2011; **Med School:** Cornell Univ-Weill Med Coll 1986; **Resid:** Pediatrics, Columbia-Presby Med Ctr 1990; **Fellow:** Pediatric Critical Care Medicine, Cornell/NY Hosp 1996; **Fac Appt:** Assoc Clin Prof Ped, Albert Einstein Coll Med

Pediatric Endocrinology

Heptulla, Rubina A MD (PEn) - **Spec Exp:** Adrenal Disorders; Diabetes; Thyroid Disorders; **Hospital:** Montefiore Med Ctr-Moses Campus (page 100), Chldns Hosp at Montefiore; **Address:** Children's Hosp at Montefiore, Div Pediatric Endocrinology, 3415 Bainbridge Ave Fl 4, Bronx, NY 10467; **Phone:** 718-741-2450; **Board Cert:** Pediatrics 2010; Pediatric Endocrinology 2008; **Med School:** India 1989; **Resid:** Pediatrics, Rhode Island Hosp 1994; Pediatrics, Baystate Med Ctr 1995; **Fellow:** Pediatric Endocrinology, Yale-New Haven Hosp 1997; **Fac Appt:** Prof Ped, Albert Einstein Coll Med

Pediatric Gastroenterology

Thompson, John F MD (PGe) - **Spec Exp:** Inflammatory Bowel Disease/Crohn's; Short Bowel Syndrome; Transplant Medicine-Bowel; **Hospital:** Montefiore Med Ctr-Moses Campus (page 100); **Address:** Children's Hosp at Montefiore, 3415 Bainbridge Ave, Bronx, NY 10467; **Phone:** 718-741-2450; **Board Cert:** Pediatrics 1983; Pediatric Gastroenterology 2012; **Med School:** Loyola Univ-Stritch Sch Med 1977; **Resid:** Pediatrics, Wylers Chldns Hosp-Univ Chicago 1980; **Fellow:** Pediatric Gastroenterology, Babies Hosp-Columbia Univ 1985; Nutrition, Babies Hosp-Columbia Univ 1985; **Fac Appt:** Prof Ped, Albert Einstein Coll Med

Pediatric Hematology-Oncology

Dasgupta, Indira K MD (PHO) - **Spec Exp:** Leukemia & Lymphoma; **Hospital:** Montefiore Med Ctr-Wakefield Campus (page 100); **Address:** 600 E 233rd St, Fl 4, Bronx, NY 10466-2697; **Phone:** 718-920-9014; **Board Cert:** Pediatrics 1981; Pediatric Hematology-Oncology 1984; **Med School:** India 1967; **Resid:** Pediatrics, New York Methodist Hosp 1974; **Fellow:** Pediatric Hematology-Oncology, Meml Sloan Kettering Cancer Ctr 1979; Pediatric Hematology-Oncology, Mount Sinai Hosp 1981

Gorlick, Richard G MD (PHO) - **Spec Exp:** Bone Tumors; Sarcoma; Solid Tumors; **Hospital:** Montefiore Med Ctr-Moses Campus (page 100); **Address:** The Chdns Hosp at Montefiore, 3415 Bainbridge Ave, rm 300, Rosenthal Pavilion, Bronx, NY 10467; **Phone:** 718-741-2342; **Board Cert:** Pediatrics 2007; Pediatric Hematology-Oncology 2011; **Med School:** SUNY Downstate 1990; **Resid:** Pediatrics, Columbia-Presby Med Ctr 1993; **Fellow:** Pediatric Hematology-Oncology, Meml Sloan Kettering Cancer Ctr 1996; **Fac Appt:** Prof Ped, Albert Einstein Coll Med

Levy, Adam S MD (PHO) - **Spec Exp:** Brain Tumors; Spinal Cord Tumors; Neuro-Oncology; **Hospital:** Montefiore Med Ctr-Moses Campus (page 100); **Address:** The Chldns Hosp at Montefiore, 3415 Bainbridge Ave, Rosenthal Pavilion, Bronx, NY 10467; **Phone:** 718-741-2342; **Board Cert:** Pediatrics 2012; Pediatric Hematology-Oncology 2010; **Med School:** NYU Sch Med 1994; **Resid:** Pediatrics, Mt Sinai Hosp 1997; **Fellow:** Pediatric Hematology-Oncology, Meml Sloan Kettering Cancer Ctr 2000; **Fac Appt:** Assoc Clin Prof Ped, Albert Einstein Coll Med

Moulton, Thomas A MD (PHO) - **Spec Exp:** Sickle Cell Disease; **Hospital:** Bronx Lebanon Hosp Ctr; **Address:** 2432 Grand Concourse, Bronx, NY 10458; **Phone:** 718-579-7337; **Board Cert:** Pediatric Hematology-Oncology 2012; **Med School:** Loyola Univ-Stritch Sch Med 1984; **Resid:** Pediatrics, Rainbow Babies-Chldns Hosp 1987; **Fellow:** Pediatric Hematology-Oncology, Babies Hosp 1990

Pediatric Infectious Disease

Herold, Betsy C MD (PInf) - **Spec Exp:** AIDS/HIV; HPV-Human Papilloma Virus; **Hospital:** Montefiore Med Ctr-Einstein Campus (page 100); **Address:** 1300 Morris Park Ave, Forchheimer Bldg, Ste 702, Bronx, NY 10461; **Phone:** 718-741-2470; **Board Cert:** Pediatrics 1986; Pediatric Infectious Disease 2012; **Med School:** Univ Pennsylvania 1982; **Resid:** Pediatrics, Northwestern Meml Hosp 1986; **Fellow:** Infectious Disease, Northwestern Meml Hosp 1989; **Fac Appt:** Prof Ped, Albert Einstein Coll Med

Litman, Nathan MD (PInf) - **Spec Exp:** Infections in Immunocompromised Patients; Hospital Acquired Infections; **Hospital:** Montefiore Med Ctr-Moses Campus (page 100); **Address:** The Chldns Hosp at Montefiore, 3415 Bainbridge Ave, Bronx, NY 10467-2401; **Phone:** 718-741-2470; **Board Cert:** Pediatrics 1978; Pediatric Infectious Disease 2008; **Med School:** Albert Einstein Coll Med 1971; **Resid:** Pediatrics, Montefiore Med Ctr 1974; **Fellow:** Infectious Disease, Montefiore Med Ctr 1978; **Fac Appt:** Prof Ped, Albert Einstein Coll Med

Rosenberg, Michael G MD/PhD (PInf) - **Spec Exp:** AIDS/HIV; **Hospital:** Jacobi Med Ctr; **Address:** 1400 Pelham Pkwy S, Bronx, NY 10461; **Phone:** 718-918-4677; **Board Cert:** Pediatrics 2014; Pediatric Infectious Disease 2012; **Med School:** Univ Iowa Coll Med 1991; **Resid:** Pediatrics, Montefiore Med Ctr 1993; **Fellow:** Pediatric Infectious Disease, Montefiore Med Ctr 1996; **Fac Appt:** Assoc Prof Ped, Albert Einstein Coll Med

Pediatric Nephrology

Del Rio, Marcela MD (PNep) - **Spec Exp:** Dialysis Care; Transplant Medicine-Kidney; **Hospital:** Montefiore Med Ctr-Moses Campus (page 100); **Address:** Chldns Hosp, Ped Nephrology Div, 3415 Bainbridge Ave Fl 4, Bronx, NY 10467; **Phone:** 718-655-1120; **Board Cert:** Pediatrics 2009; Pediatric Nephrology 2011; **Med School:** Argentina 1987; **Resid:** Pediatrics, Richmond Meml Hosp 1997; **Fellow:** Pediatric Nephrology, Montefiore Med Ctr 2000; **Fac Appt:** Asst Prof Ped, Albert Ein-stein Coll Med

Goilav, Beatrice MD (PNep) - **Spec Exp:** Polycystic Kidney Disease; Lupus/SLE; Kidney Failure; **Hospital:** Chldns Hosp at Montefiore; **Address:** Chldns Hosp, Ped Nephrology Div, 3415 Bainbridge Ave Fl 4, Bronx, NY 10467; **Phone:** 718-741-2450; **Board Cert:** Pediatrics 2012; Pediatric Nephrology 2010; **Med School:** Switzerland 1998; **Resid:** Pediatrics, Jacobi Med Ctr 2004; **Fellow:** Pediatric Nephrology, Mt Sinai Hosp 2007; **Fac Appt:** Asst Prof Ped, Albert Einstein Coll Med

Kaskel, Frederick J MD/PhD (PNep) - **Spec Exp:** Kidney Disease-Chronic; Dialysis Care; Polycystic Kidney Disease; **Hospital:** Montefiore Med Ctr-Moses Campus (page 100), Chldns Hosp at Montefiore; **Address:** CHAM, Ped Nephrology, 3415 Bainbridge Ave, Fl 4, Bronx, NY 10467; **Phone:** 718-741-2450; **Board Cert:** Pediatrics 1980; Pediatric Nephrology 2010; **Med School:** Univ Cincinnati 1975; **Resid:** Pediatrics, Montefiore Med Ctr 1977; **Fellow:** Pediatric Nephrology, Montefiore Med Ctr 1981; **Fac Appt:** Prof Ped, Albert Einstein Coll Med

Reidy, Kimberly J MD (PNep) - **Spec Exp:** Kidney Disease-Chronic; Glomerulonephritis; **Hospital:** Chldns Hosp at Montefiore; **Address:** Chldns Hosp, Ped Nephrology Div, 3415 Bainbridge Ave Fl 4, Bronx, NY 10467; **Phone:** 718-655-1120; **Board Cert:** Pediatrics 2013; Pediatric Nephrology 2010; **Med School:** Albert Einstein Coll Med 2002; **Resid:** Pediatrics, NY-Presby/Chldns Hosp 2005; **Fellow:** Pediatric Nephrology, Montefiore Med Ctr 2008

Pediatric Otolaryngology

Bent III, John P MD (PO) - **Spec Exp:** Airway Reconstruction; Sinus Disorders/Surgery; Minimally Invasive Surgery; Cochlear Implants; **Hospital:** Montefiore Med Ctr-Moses Campus (page 100); **Address:** Children's Hospital at Montefiore, 3415 Bainbridge Ave Fl 5, Bronx, NY 10467-2490; **Phone:** 718-920-4646; **Board Cert:** Otolaryngology 1995; **Med School:** Wake Forest Univ 1989; **Resid:** Surgery, Wake Forest Univ Baptist Med Ctr 1990; Otolaryngology, Med Coll GA Affil Hosp 1994; **Fellow:** Pediatric Otolaryngology, Univ Iowa Affil Hosp 1995; **Fac Appt:** Prof Oto, Albert Einstein Coll Med

Pediatric Pulmonology

Arens, Raanan MD (PPul) - **Spec Exp:** Sleep Disorders/Apnea; **Hospital:** Montefiore Med Ctr-Einstein Campus (page 100); **Address:** Chldns Hosp at Montefiore, Respiratory & Sleep Medicine Div, 3415 Bainbridge Ave, Bronx, NY 10467; **Phone:** 718-741-2450; **Board Cert:** Pediatrics 2010; Pediatric Pulmonology 2011; Sleep Medicine 2009; **Med School:** Israel 1986; **Resid:** Pediatrics, Shera Med Ctr 1990; Pediatrics, Chldns Hosp 1995; **Fellow:** Pediatric Pulmonology, Chldns Hosp 1994; **Fac Appt:** Assoc Prof Ped, Albert Einstein Coll Med

Pediatric Rheumatology

Ilowite, Norman T MD (PRhu) - **Spec Exp:** Juvenile Arthritis; Lyme Disease; Lupus/SLE; Dermatomyositis; **Hospital:** Montefiore Med Ctr-Moses Campus (page 100), Chldns Hosp at Montefiore; **Address:** CHAM, Ped Rheumatology, 3415 Bainbridge Ave Fl 4, Bronx, NY 10467; **Phone:** 718-741-2450; **Board Cert:** Pediatrics 1985; Clinical & Laboratory Immunology 1990; Pediatric Rheumatology 2014; **Med School:** SUNY Downstate 1979; **Resid:** Pediatrics, Chldns Hosp Natl Med Ctr 1982; **Fellow:** Pediatric Rheumatology, Univ Washington Med Ctr 1984; **Fac Appt:** Prof Ped, Albert Einstein Coll Med

Pediatric Surgery

Jan, Dominique M MD/PhD (PS) - **Spec Exp:** Transplant-Bowel; Transplant-Liver; Transplant Surgery-Pediatric; **Hospital:** Montefiore Med Ctr-Moses Campus (page 100), Chldns Hosp at Montefiore; **Address:** Children's Hosp at Montefiore, Pediatric Surgery, 3415 Bainbridge Ave Fl 5, Bronx, NY 10467; **Phone:** 718-920-7200; **Med School:** France 1984; **Resid:** Surgery, Assistance Poblique Hosp 1989; **Fellow:** Pediatric Surgery, Necker Malades Hosp; **Fac Appt:** Prof S, Albert Einstein Coll Med

Muensterer, Oliver J MD/PhD (PS) - **Spec Exp:** Endoscopic Surgery; Minimally Invasive Surgery; Congenital Anomalies-Gastrointestinal; Trauma; **Hospital:** Montefiore Med Ctr-Moses Campus (page 100); **Address:** Montefiore Children's Hosp, 3415 Bainbridge Ave, Fl 3, Bronx, NY 10467; **Phone:** 718-920-7200; **Board Cert:** Pediatrics 2008; **Med School:** Germany 1995; **Resid:** Surgery, Univ Munich 1999; Pediatrics, Duke Univ Hosp 1999; **Fellow:** Pediatric Surgery, UAB Med Ctr 2002; **Fac Appt:** Prof S, Albert Einstein Coll Med

Statter, Mindy B MD (PS) - **Spec Exp:** Neonatal Surgery; Trauma; **Hospital:** Montefiore Med Ctr-Moses Campus (page 100); **Address:** Childrens Hosp at Montefiore, 3415 Bainbridge Ave Fl 5, Bronx, NY 10467; **Phone:** 718-920-7200; **Board Cert:** Surgery 2010; Pediatric Surgery 2005; Surgical Critical Care 2013; **Med School:** Emory Univ 1983; **Resid:** Surgery, Univ Illinois Med Ctr 1990; **Fellow:** Surgical Research, Mass Genl Hosp 1987; Pediatric Surgery, Univ Michigan 1992; **Fac Appt:** Assoc Clin Prof S, Albert Einstein Coll Med

Weinberg, Gerard MD (PS) - **Spec Exp:** Abdominal Wall Reconstruction; Trauma; Neonatal Surgery; **Hospital:** Montefiore Med Ctr-Moses Campus (page 100); **Address:** 3355 Bainbridge Ave, Bronx, NY 10467; **Phone:** 718-920-7200; **Board Cert:** Surgery 2009; Pediatric Surgery 2009; **Med School:** Albert Einstein Coll Med 1973; **Resid:** Surgery, Albert Einstein Affil Hosps 1976; Pediatric Surgery, Childrens Hosp 1977; **Fellow:** Pediatric Surgery, Univ of Miami Hosps 1979; **Fac Appt:** Clin Prof S, Albert Einstein Coll Med

Pediatrics

Andrade, Joseph R MD (Ped) *PCP* - **Spec Exp:** Preventive Medicine; **Hospital:** Montefiore Med Ctr-Wakefield Campus (page 100); **Address:** 1163 Manor Ave, Bronx, NY 10472; **Phone:** 718-589-3501; **Board Cert:** Pediatrics 2014; Internal Medicine 2011; **Med School:** Ecuador 1981; **Resid:** Pediatrics, Our Lady of Mercy Med Ctr 1986; Internal Medicine, Our Lady of Mercy Med Ctr 1988

Arnstein, Ellis J MD (Ped) *PCP* - **Spec Exp:** Developmental Disorders; **Hospital:** Bronx Lebanon Hosp Ctr; **Address:** Bronx Lebanon Hosp Ctr, 2432 Grand Concourse, Bronx, NY 10458; **Phone:** 718-579-7337; **Board Cert:** Pediatrics 1975; Neurodevelopmental Disabilities 2012; **Med School:** SUNY Downstate 1969; **Resid:** Pediatrics, Univ Wash Med Ctr 1973; **Fellow:** Child & Adolescent Psychiatry, Tufts-New England Med Ctr 1974; **Fac Appt:** Asst Prof Ped, NY Med Coll

Balk, Sophie J MD (Ped) *PCP* - **Spec Exp:** Preventive Medicine; **Hospital:** Montefiore Med Ctr-Moses Campus (page 100), Montefiore Med Ctr-Einstein Campus (page 100); **Address:** Comprehensive Family Care Ctr, 1621 Eastchester Rd, Bronx, NY 10461-2604; **Phone:** 718-405-8040; **Board Cert:** Pediatrics 2010; **Med School:** Albert Einstein Coll Med 1974; **Resid:** Pediatrics, Montefiore Med Ctr 1977; **Fac Appt:** Clin Prof Ped, Albert Einstein Coll Med

Belamarich, Peter F MD (Ped) - **Spec Exp:** Cholesterol/Lipid Disorders; Nutrition; Preventive Medicine; **Hospital:** Montefiore Med Ctr-Einstein Campus (page 100); **Address:** Chldn's Hosp at Montefiore, 3415 Bainbridge Ave, Fl 4, Bronx, NY 10467; **Phone:** 718-741-2450; **Board Cert:** Pediatrics 2010; **Med School:** Boston Univ 1983; **Resid:** Pediatrics, Brookdale Univ Hosp 1986; **Fellow:** Pediatric Gastroenterology, NY-Presby/Columbia Univ Med Ctr 1989; **Fac Appt:** Assoc Clin Prof Ped, Albert Einstein Coll Med

Bloomfield, Diane E MD (Ped) *PCP* - **Spec Exp:** Preventive Medicine; **Hospital:** Montefiore Med Ctr-Moses Campus (page 100); **Address:** Montefiore Family Care Ctr, 3444 Kossuth Ave, DTC Bldg Fl 1 - Ste 1B, Bronx, NY 10467-2461; **Phone:** 718-920-2273; **Board Cert:** Pediatrics 1987; **Med School:** Cornell Univ-Weill Med Coll 1982; **Resid:** Pediatrics, NY Hosp 1985; **Fellow:** Ambulatory Pediatrics, NY Hosp 1986; **Fac Appt:** Asst Prof Ped, Albert Einstein Coll Med

Cahill, Linda T MD (Ped) - **Spec Exp:** Child Abuse; Preventive Medicine; **Hospital:** Montefiore Med Ctr-Moses Campus (page 100); **Address:** Montefiore Child Advocacy Ctr, Chldns Hosp-Montefiore, 3314 Steuben Ave, Bronx, NY 10467; **Phone:** 718-920-5833; **Board Cert:** Pediatrics 2010; Child Abuse Pediatrics 2009; **Med School:** Med Coll PA 1969; **Resid:** Internal Medicine, LI Coll Hosp 1970; Pediatrics, Beth Israel Med Ctr 1972; **Fellow:** Pediatric Infectious Disease, Mt Sinai Hosp 1974; **Fac Appt:** Assoc Clin Prof Ped, Albert Einstein Coll Med

Chambers, Hazel J MD (Ped) *PCP* - **Spec Exp:** Preventive Medicine; **Hospital:** Montefiore Med Ctr-Moses Campus (page 100); **Address:** Montefiore Med Grp, Pediatrics, 1500 Astor Ave Fl 2, Bronx, NY 10469; **Phone:** 718-881-0100; **Board Cert:** Pediatrics 1976; **Med School:** Howard Univ 1969; **Resid:** Pediatrics, Jacobi Med Ctr 1972

Esteban-Cruciani, Nora V MD (Ped) - **Spec Exp:** Chronic Illness; **Hospital:** Chldns Hosp at Montefiore; **Address:** 3415 Bainbridge Ave, Department of Pediatrics, Rosenthal-3, Bronx, NY 10467; **Phone:** 718-741-2549; **Board Cert:** Pediatrics 2008; **Med School:** Argentina 1980; **Resid:** Pediatrics, Italian Hosp 1983; Pediatrics, Albert Einstein Coll Med 1993; **Fellow:** Research, Nat Inst Hlth 1991; Research, Albert Einstein Coll Med 2005; **Fac Appt:** Assoc Clin Prof Ped, Albert Einstein Coll Med

Haber, Patricia L MD (Ped) *PCP* - **Spec Exp:** Preventive Medicine; **Hospital:** Montefiore Med Ctr-Moses Campus (page 100); **Address:** 1500 Astor Ave Fl 2, Bronx, NY 10469-5900; **Phone:** 718-881-0100; **Board Cert:** Pediatrics 2009; **Med School:** Johns Hopkins Univ 1976; **Resid:** Pediatrics, Johns Hopkins Hosp 1979; **Fellow:** Immunology, Univ Alabama Hosp 1982; Pediatric Rheumatology, Univ Alabama Hosp 1984

Hirschman, Alan M MD (Ped) *PCP* - **Spec Exp:** Preventive Medicine; **Hospital:** Montefiore Med Ctr-Moses Campus (page 100); **Address:** 3765 Riverdale Ave, Ste 4, Bronx, NY 10463-1845; **Phone:** 718-548-7300; **Board Cert:** Pediatrics 1981; **Med School:** UMDNJ-NJ Med Sch, Newark 1976; **Resid:** Pediatrics, Montefiore Med Ctr 1980; **Fac Appt:** Asst Clin Prof Ped, Albert Einstein Coll Med

Igel, Gerard J MD (Ped) *PCP* - **Spec Exp:** Chronic Illness; Behavioral Disorders; Developmental Disorders; Preventive Medicine; **Hospital:** Montefiore Med Ctr-Moses Campus (page 100), Jacobi Med Ctr; **Address:** Montefiore Med Grp, 1500 Astor Ave, Bronx, NY 10469; **Phone:** 718-881-0100; **Board Cert:** Pediatrics 1986; **Med School:** Israel 1981; **Resid:** Pediatrics, Jacobi Med Ctr 1984; **Fac Appt:** Asst Clin Prof Ped, Albert Einstein Coll Med

Mayers, Marguerite M MD (Ped) *PCP* - **Spec Exp:** Tuberculosis; AIDS/HIV; Travel Medicine; Preventive Medicine; **Hospital:** Montefiore Med Ctr-Moses Campus (page 100); **Address:** Montefiore Family Care Ctr, 3444 Kossuth Ave, Bronx, NY 10467-2401; **Phone:** 718-920-2273; **Board Cert:** Pediatrics 1978; Pediatric Infectious Disease 2008; **Med School:** Albert Einstein Coll Med 1971; **Resid:** Pediatrics, Montefiore Med Ctr 1974; **Fellow:** Infectious Disease, Montefiore Med Ctr 1976; **Fac Appt:** Clin Prof Ped, Albert Einstein Coll Med

Oppedisano, Carlyn A MD (Ped) *PCP* - **Spec Exp:** Preventive Medicine; **Hospital:** Morgan Stanley Chldns Hosp of NY-Presby, NY (page 102); **Address:** Riverdale Pediatrics, 2600 Netherland Ave, Ste 120, Century Bldg, Riverdale, NY 10463-4813; **Phone:** 718-796-3580; **Board Cert:** Pediatrics 2009; **Med School:** Columbia P&S 1981; **Resid:** Pediatrics, Babies Hosp/NY-Presby Hosp 1985; **Fac Appt:** Assoc Clin Prof Ped, Columbia P&S

Schechter, Miriam B MD (Ped) *PCP* - **Spec Exp:** Asthma; Vaccines; Preventive Medicine; **Hospital:** Montefiore Med Ctr-Moses Campus (page 100), Chldns Hosp at Montefiore; **Address:** Comprehensive Family Care Ctr, 1621 Eastchester Rd, Bronx, NY 10461-2604; **Phone:** 718-405-8040; **Board Cert:** Pediatrics 2014; **Med School:** NYU Sch Med 1989; **Resid:** Pediatrics, Mt Sinai Med Ctr 1992; **Fac Appt:** Asst Prof Ped, Albert Einstein Coll Med

Stein, Ruth E K MD (Ped) - **Spec Exp:** Chronic Illness; Developmental & Behavioral Disorders; **Hospital:** Montefiore Med Ctr-Moses Campus (page 100); **Address:** 1225 Morris Park Ave, VE Bldg - rm 6B27, Bronx, NY 10461; **Phone:** 718-839-7057; **Board Cert:** Pediatrics 1971; Developmental-Behavioral Pediatrics 2012; **Med School:** Albert Einstein Coll Med 1966; **Resid:** Pediatrics, Bronx Muni Hosp 1968; Pediatrics, Chldns Hosp Natl Med Ctr 1969; **Fellow:** Community Medicine, Chldns Hosp Natl Med Ctr 1969; **Fac Appt:** Prof Ped, Albert Einstein Coll Med

Strassberg, Barbara E MD (Ped) *PCP* - **Spec Exp:** Developmental Disorders; Preventive Medicine; **Hospital:** Morgan Stanley Chldns Hosp of NY-Presby, NY (page 102); **Address:** Riverdale Pediatrics, 2600 Netherland Ave, Ste 120, Bronx, NY 10463-4813; **Phone:** 718-796-3580; **Board Cert:** Pediatrics 2009; **Med School:** SUNY Upstate Med Univ 1981; **Resid:** Pediatrics, NY-Presbyterian Hosp 1984; **Fac Appt:** Assoc Clin Prof Ped, Columbia P&S

Sullivan, Christina K MD (Ped) *PCP* - **Spec Exp:** Preventive Medicine; **Hospital:** Montefiore Med Ctr-Moses Campus (page 100); **Address:** Comprehensive Family Care Ctr, 1621 Eastchester Rd, Bronx, NY 10461-2604; **Phone:** 718-405-8040; **Board Cert:** Pediatrics 2007; **Med School:** Univ Conn 1990; **Resid:** Pediatrics, Mt Sinai Med Ctr 1993; **Fac Appt:** Asst Clin Prof Ped, Albert Einstein Coll Med

Weiner, Richard L MD (Ped) *PCP* - **Spec Exp:** Adolescent Medicine; Preventive Medicine; **Hospital:** Montefiore Med Ctr-Moses Campus (page 100), Montefiore Med Ctr-Einstein Campus (page 100); **Address:** Montefiore Medical Group, 2300 Westchester Ave, Bronx, NY 10462; **Phone:** 718-409-8000; **Board Cert:** Pediatrics 1991; **Med School:** Albert Einstein Coll Med 1975; **Resid:** Pediatrics, Jacobi Med Ctr 1978; **Fac Appt:** Assoc Prof Ped, Albert Einstein Coll Med

Zoltan, Irving MD (Ped) *PCP* - **Spec Exp:** Diagnostic Problems; Asthma; Infectious Disease; Preventive Medicine; **Hospital:** Jacobi Med Ctr, Montefiore Med Ctr-Moses Campus (page 100); **Address:** Jacobi Med Ctr, Dept Peds, 1400 Pelham Pkway S, Bronx, NY 10461; **Phone:** 718-918-6981; **Board Cert:** Pediatrics 1979; **Med School:** Albert Einstein Coll Med 1974; **Resid:** Pediatrics, Bronx Muni Hosp 1978; **Fac Appt:** Asst Clin Prof Ped, Albert Einstein Coll Med

Physical Medicine & Rehabilitation

Inwald, Gary DO (PMR) - **Spec Exp:** Musculoskeletal Disorders; Pain Management; **Hospital:** Montefiore Med Ctr-Einstein Campus (page 100); **Address:** Montefiore Med Ctr-Dept of Rehab, 1825 Eastchester Rd, Bronx, NY 10461; **Phone:** 718-904-2296; **Board Cert:** Physical Medicine & Rehabilitation 1983; **Med School:** Mich State Univ Coll Osteo Med 1976; **Resid:** Physical Medicine & Rehabilitation, St Vincents Hosp 1982

Levin, Sheryl MD (PMR) - **Spec Exp:** Neuro-Rehabilitation; Pain-Musculoskeletal; Arthritis; **Hospital:** Montefiore Med Ctr-Moses Campus (page 100); **Address:** 3435 Dekalb Ave, Bronx, NY 10467-2301; **Phone:** 718-547-8899; **Board Cert:** Physical Medicine & Rehabilitation 1989; **Med School:** Cornell Univ-Weill Med Coll 1984; **Resid:** Physical Medicine & Rehabilitation, New York Hosp 1988; **Fac Appt:** Asst Clin Prof PMR, Albert Einstein Coll Med

Thomas, Mark Alvin MD (PMR) - **Hospital:** Montefiore Med Ctr-Moses Campus (page 100); **Address:** 150 E 210th St Fl 1, Bronx, NY 10467; **Phone:** 718-920-2753; **Board Cert:** Physical Medicine & Rehabilitation 1988; **Med School:** Mexico 1982; **Resid:** Physical Medicine & Rehabilitation, Nassau Co Med Ctr 1986; **Fac Appt:** Assoc Prof PMR, Albert Einstein Coll Med

Plastic Surgery

Garfein, Evan S MD (PlS) - **Spec Exp:** Breast Cosmetic & Reconstructive Surgery; Micro-surgery; **Hospital:** Montefiore Med Ctr-Moses Campus (page 100); **Address:** Montefiore Med Ctr, Div Plastic Surgery, 1625 Poplar St, Bronx, NY 10461; **Phone:** 718-405-8444; **Board Cert:** Plastic Surgery 2009; **Med School:** Columbia P&S 1999; **Resid:** Surgery, Brigham and Women's Hosp 2004; **Fellow:** Plastic Surgery, Brigham and Women's Hosp 2007; **Fac Appt:** Asst Prof S, Albert Einstein Coll Med

Goldstein, Robert D MD (PlS) - **Spec Exp:** Breast Surgery; Cosmetic Surgery-Face; Nasal Surgery; Abdominoplasty; **Hospital:** Montefiore Med Ctr-Einstein Campus (page 100), Montefiore Med Ctr-Moses Campus (page 100); **Address:** Bronx Plastic Surgery, 2425 Eastchester Rd, Bronx, NY 10469; **Phone:** 718-405-7500; **Board Cert:** Plastic Surgery 1985; **Med School:** Penn State Coll Med 1977; **Resid:** Surgery, Montefiore Med Ctr 1981; Plastic Surgery, Jacobi Med Ctr 1984; **Fellow:** Hand Surgery, Montefiore Med Ctr-Einstein Div 1982; **Fac Appt:** Assoc Clin Prof PlS, Albert Einstein Coll Med

Greenstein, Bruce MD (PlS) - **Spec Exp:** Burn Care; Burns-Reconstructive Plastic Surgery; **Hospital:** Jacobi Med Ctr, N Central Bronx Hosp; **Address:** Jacobi Med Ctr, Dept Plastic Surgery, 1400 Pelham Pkwy S, Bldg 1 - rm 209, Bronx, NY 10461; **Phone:** 718-918-5970; **Board Cert:** Plastic Surgery 1984; **Med School:** SUNY Upstate Med Univ 1975; **Resid:** Surgery, Montefiore Med Ctr 1980; Plastic Surgery, Montefiore Med Ctr 1982; **Fellow:** Hand Surgery, Montefiore Med Ctr 1983; **Fac Appt:** Assoc Clin Prof PlS, Albert Einstein Coll Med

Liebling, Ralph W MD (PlS) - **Spec Exp:** Reconstructive Surgery; Microsurgery; Hand Surgery; Burn Care; **Hospital:** Jacobi Med Ctr, N Central Bronx Hosp; **Address:** Jacobi Med Ctr, Dept Plastic & Reconstructive Surg, 1400 Pelham Pkwy S, Bronx, NY 10461; **Phone:** 718-918-7000; **Board Cert:** Plastic Surgery 1988; **Med School:** Albert Einstein Coll Med 1977; **Resid:** Surgery, Montefiore Med Ctr 1981; Plastic Surgery, Montefiore Med Ctr 1983; **Fellow:** Reconstructive Microsurgery, NYU/Bellevue Hosp Ctr 1984; **Fac Appt:** Assoc Clin Prof PlS, Albert Einstein Coll Med

Psychiatry

Gelfand, Janice MD (Psyc) - **Spec Exp:** Depression; Anxiety Disorders; Psychosomatic Disorders; Personality Disorders; **Hospital:** NY-Presby/Columbia Univ Med Ctr, NY (page 102); **Address:** 3765 Riverdale Ave, Bronx, NY 10463; **Phone:** 718-361-3482; **Board Cert:** Psychiatry 1990; **Med School:** NYU Sch Med 1985; **Resid:** Psychiatry, NYU Med Ctr 1989; **Fellow:** Psychiatry, Beth Israel Med Ctr 1991; **Fac Appt:** Asst Prof Psyc, Columbia P&S

Heiman, Peter L MD (Psyc) - **Spec Exp:** Psychiatry in Physical Illness; **Hospital:** Montefiore Med Ctr-Moses Campus (page 100); **Address:** 4465 Douglas Ave, Ste 1K, Bronx, NY 10471; **Phone:** 212-472-8885; **Board Cert:** Psychiatry 1975; **Med School:** Albert Einstein Coll Med 1968; **Resid:** Psychiatry, Montefiore Med Ctr 1972; **Fac Appt:** Asst Clin Prof Psyc, Albert Einstein Coll Med

Lebinger, Martin B MD (Psyc) - **Spec Exp:** Depression; Anxiety Disorders; Panic Disorder; **Hospital:** Bronx Psych Ctr; **Address:** 1540 Pelham Pkwy S, Ste 1A, Bronx, NY 10461-1130; **Phone:** 718-518-0222; **Board Cert:** Psychiatry 1980; **Med School:** Albert Einstein Coll Med 1976; **Resid:** Psychiatry, Montefiore Med Ctr 1979; **Fellow:** Psychiatry, LI Jewish-Hillside Med Ctr 1981; **Fac Appt:** Asst Clin Prof Psyc, Albert Einstein Coll Med

Osei-Tutu, John MD (Psyc) - **Spec Exp:** Anxiety & Depression; Addiction/Substance Abuse; **Hospital:** Bronx Lebanon Hosp Ctr; **Address:** 1154 Wheeler Ave, Bronx, NY 10472; **Phone:** 718-991-9200; **Board Cert:** Psychiatry 1990; Addiction Psychiatry 2013; **Med School:** Ghana 1976; **Resid:** Psychiatry, Bronx-Lebanon Hosp 1983; **Fac Appt:** Asst Prof Psyc, Albert Einstein Coll Med

Schwartz, Bruce J MD (Psyc) - **Spec Exp:** Depression; Bipolar/Mood Disorders; Schizophrenia; Anxiety & Depression; **Hospital:** Montefiore Med Ctr-Moses Campus (page 100); **Address:** Montefiore Med Ctr, Psychiatry, 111 E 210th St, Bronx, NY 10467; **Phone:** 718-920-4040; **Board Cert:** Psychiatry 1980; **Med School:** SUNY Downstate 1975; **Resid:** Psychiatry, Bronx Muni Hosp 1979; **Fac Appt:** Clin Prof Psyc, Albert Einstein Coll Med

Wyszynski, Bernard MD (Psyc) - **Hospital:** Montefiore Med Ctr-Moses Campus (page 100); **Address:** Montefore Medical Ctr, KLAU 2, 111 E 210th St, Bronx, NY 10467; **Phone:** 718-920-4737; **Board Cert:** Psychiatry 1987; Neurology 1985; **Med School:** Univ Pennsylvania 1980; **Resid:** Neurology, Mt Sinai Med Ctr 1984; Psychiatry, Mt Sinai Med Ctr 1987; **Fac Appt:** Assoc Prof Psyc, Albert Einstein Coll Med

Pulmonary Disease

Aldrich, Thomas K MD (Pul) - **Spec Exp:** Asthma; Chronic Obstructive Lung Disease (COPD); Sickle Cell Disease-Lung; Sarcoidosis; **Hospital:** Montefiore Med Ctr-Moses Campus (page 100); **Address:** 3400 Bainbridge Ave, Fl 2nd, Bronx, NY 10467-2401; **Phone:** 866-633-8255; **Board Cert:** Internal Medicine 1978; Pulmonary Disease 1980; **Med School:** Univ Minn 1975; **Resid:** Internal Medicine, UC Irvine Med Ctr 1978; **Fellow:** Pulmonary Disease, Univ Virginia Med Ctr 1980; Physiology, Univ Penn 1982; **Fac Appt:** Prof Med, Albert Einstein Coll Med

Appel, David W MD (Pul) - **Spec Exp:** Sleep Disorders/Apnea; Asthma; Smoking Cessation; **Hospital:** Montefiore Med Ctr-Moses Campus (page 100); **Address:** 3400 Bainbridge Ave, Bronx, NY 10467; **Phone:** 866-633-8255; **Board Cert:** Internal Medicine 1976; **Med School:** Albert Einstein Coll Med 1973; **Resid:** Internal Medicine, Bronx Municipal Hosp 1976; **Fellow:** Pulmonary Disease, Bronx Municipal Hosp 1978; **Fac Appt:** Assoc Prof Med, Albert Einstein Coll Med

Casper, Theodore MD (Pul) - **Spec Exp:** Emphysema & Asthma; **Hospital:** Montefiore Med Ctr-Einstein Campus (page 100), Montefiore Med Ctr-Wakefield Campus (page 100); **Address:** Pulmonary Medicine, 1250 Waters Pl, Ste 506, Bronx, NY 10461; **Phone:** 718-892-1200; **Board Cert:** Internal Medicine 1983; Pulmonary Disease 1986; **Med School:** Columbia P&S 1980; **Resid:** Internal Medicine, St Lukes Hosp 1983; **Fellow:** Pulmonary Disease, St Lukes Hosp 1985; **Fac Appt:** Asst Clin Prof Med, Albert Einstein Coll Med

Karetzky, Monroe MD (Pul) - **Spec Exp:** Asthma; Sleep Disorders; **Hospital:** Hackensack Univ Med Ctr (page 96), Englewood Hosp & Med Ctr; **Address:** Bronx Pulmonary Center, 441 E Tremont Ave, Bronx, NY 10457; **Phone:** 718-583-9240; **Board Cert:** Internal Medicine 1971; Pulmonary Disease 1974; Critical Care Medicine 2011; Sleep Medicine 2013; **Med School:** Cornell Univ-Weill Med Coll 1963; **Resid:** Internal Medicine, Mary I Bassett Hosp 1965; **Fellow:** Cardiopulmonary Disease, Mary I Bassett Hosp 1967; **Fac Appt:** Assoc Clin Prof Med, UMDNJ-NJ Med Sch, Newark

Klapper, Philip MD (Pul) - **Spec Exp:** Asthma; Emphysema; Chronic Obstructive Lung Disease (COPD); **Hospital:** Montefiore Med Ctr-Moses Campus (page 100), Lawrence Hosp Ctr (page 102); **Address:** 3322 Bainbridge Ave, Bronx, NY 10467; **Phone:** 718-882-0090; **Board Cert:** Internal Medicine 1986; Pulmonary Disease 2010; Critical Care Medicine 2013; **Med School:** Albert Einstein Coll Med 1983; **Resid:** Internal Medicine, Montefiore Hosp Med Ctr 1986; **Fellow:** Pulmonary Disease, SUNY Downstate Med Ctr 1990; Critical Care Medicine, Montefiore Hosp Med Ctr 1991; **Fac Appt:** Asst Clin Prof Med, Albert Einstein Coll Med

Prezant, David MD (Pul) - **Spec Exp:** Asthma; **Hospital:** Montefiore Med Ctr-Moses Campus (page 100); **Address:** 111 E 210th St, Bronx, NY 10467-2401; **Phone:** 718-920-6095; **Board Cert:** Internal Medicine 1984; Pulmonary Disease 1986; **Med School:** Albert Einstein Coll Med 1981; **Resid:** Internal Medicine, Harlem Hosp 1984; **Fellow:** Pulmonary Disease, Montefiore Hosp Med Ctr 1986; **Fac Appt:** Prof Med, Albert Einstein Coll Med

Sender, Joel MD (Pul) - **Spec Exp:** Asthma; Sarcoidosis; **Hospital:** St. Barnabas Hosp - Bronx; **Address:** 2016 Bronxdale Ave, Ste 301, Bronx, NY 10462-3300; **Phone:** 718-409-2222; **Board Cert:** Internal Medicine 1978; Pulmonary Disease 1980; Geriatric Medicine 2005; **Med School:** Albany Med Coll 1975; **Resid:** Internal Medicine, Mount Sinai Hosp 1978; **Fellow:** Pulmonary Disease, Mount Sinai Hosp 1980; **Fac Appt:** Asst Clin Prof Med, NY Med Coll

Radiation Oncology

Bodner, William R MD (RadRO) - **Spec Exp:** Brachytherapy; Stereotactic Radiosurgery; **Hospital:** Montefiore Med Ctr-Einstein Campus (page 100); **Address:** Montefiore Med Park, Ctr for Radiology, 1625 Poplar St, Bronx, NY 10461; **Phone:** 718-405-8550; **Board Cert:** Radiation Oncology 2005; **Med School:** Wake Forest Univ 1987; **Resid:** Radiation Oncology, NY Med Coll Affil Hosp 1995; **Fac Appt:** Assoc Prof RadRO, Albert Einstein Coll Med

Garg, Madhur MD (RadRO) - **Spec Exp:** Head & Neck Cancer; Genitourinary Cancer; Central Nervous System Cancer; Brain & Spinal Cord Tumors; **Hospital:** Montefiore Med Ctr-Moses Campus (page 100); **Address:** Montefiore Med Ctr, Radiation Oncology, 111 E 210th St, Bronx, NY 10467; **Phone:** 718-920-4140; **Board Cert:** Radiation Oncology 2003; **Med School:** India 1996; **Resid:** Radiation Oncology, Rush Presby St Lukes Med Ctr 1999; Radiation Oncology, Montefiore Med Ctr 2003; **Fac Appt:** Assoc Prof RadRO, Albert Einstein Coll Med

Kalnicki, Shalom MD (RadRO) - **Spec Exp:** Lung Cancer; Head & Neck Cancer; Breast Cancer; Image Guided Radiotherapy (IGRT); **Hospital:** Montefiore Med Ctr-Moses Campus (page 100), Montefiore Med Ctr-Einstein Campus (page 100); **Address:** Montefiore Med Grp, 1625 Poplar St Fl 2, Bronx, NY 10461; **Phone:** 718-920-5280; **Board Cert:** Therapeutic Radiology 1979; **Med School:** Brazil 1974; **Resid:** Radiation Oncology, Montefiore Med Ctr 1979; **Fac Appt:** Prof Rad, Albert Einstein Coll Med

Reproductive Endocrinology

Zinaman, Michael J MD (RE) - **Spec Exp:** Endometriosis; Infertility; Uterine Fibroids; **Hospital:** Jacobi Med Ctr; **Address:** Jacobi Med Ctr, OB/GYN Dept, 1400 Pelham Pkwy S, Bronx, NY 10461; **Phone:** 718-918-5700; **Board Cert:** Obstetrics & Gynecology 2012; Reproductive Endocrinology 2012; **Med School:** SUNY Downstate 1981; **Resid:** Obstetrics & Gynecology, Univ Chicago Affil Hosps 1986; **Fellow:** Reproductive Endocrinology, Georgetown Univ Affil Hosps 1989; **Fac Appt:** Prof ObG, Tufts Univ

Rheumatology

Fomberstein, Barry MD (Rhu) - **Spec Exp:** Rheumatoid Arthritis; Gout; **Hospital:** Montefiore Med Ctr-Wakefield Campus (page 100); **Address:** Wakefield Medical Village, 4234 Bronx Blvd, Bronx, NY 10466; **Phone:** 347-341-4340; **Board Cert:** Internal Medicine 1979; Rheumatology 1982; **Med School:** Albert Einstein Coll Med 1976; **Resid:** Internal Medicine, LIJ Med Ctr 1979; **Fellow:** Rheumatology, LIJ Med Ctr 1981; **Fac Appt:** Assoc Clin Prof Med, NY Med Coll

Keiser, Harold D MD (Rhu) - **Spec Exp:** Connective Tissue Disorders; Gout; **Hospital:** Monte-fiore Med Ctr-Einstein Campus (page 100), Jacobi Med Ctr; **Address:** 1575 Blondell Ave, Ste 220, Bronx, NY 10461-2662; **Phone:** 866-633-8255 x4811; **Board Cert:** Internal Medicine 1972; Rheumatology 1972; **Med School:** NYU Sch Med 1964; **Resid:** Internal Medicine, Metro Genl Hosp 1968; **Fellow:** Rheumatology, Albert Einstein Coll Med 1972; **Fac Appt:** Prof Med, Albert Einstein Coll Med

Weinstein, Joshua W MD (Rhu) - **Spec Exp:** Lupus/SLE; Rheumatoid Arthritis; Gout; **Hospital:** Montefiore Med Ctr-Einstein Campus (page 100), NY Hosp Queens (page 498); **Address:** 7235 112 St, Forest Hills, NY 11375; **Phone:** 718-575-0649; **Board Cert:** Internal Medicine 1975; Rheumatology 1978; **Med School:** SUNY Downstate 1972; **Resid:** Internal Medicine, Maimonides Med Ctr 1975; **Fellow:** Rheumatology, Montefiore Med Ctr 1977; **Fac Appt:** Asst Prof Med, Albert Einstein Coll Med

Surgery

Agarwal, Nanakram MD (S) - **Spec Exp:** Breast Surgery; Colon & Rectal Surgery; **Hospital:** Montefiore Med Ctr-Wakefield Campus (page 100); **Address:** 600 E 233rd St, Fl 4, Bronx, NY 10466; **Phone:** 718-920-9143; **Board Cert:** Surgery 2011; Critical Care Medicine 2005; **Med School:** India 1973; **Resid:** Surgery, Our Lady of Mercy Med Ctr 1981; **Fellow:** Critical Care Medicine, Westchester Co Med Ctr 1982; **Fac Appt:** Prof S, NY Med Coll

Bellemare, Sarah MD (S) - **Spec Exp:** Hepatobiliary Surgery; Transplant-Liver; Hepatobiliary Surgery; Laparoscopic Surgery; **Hospital:** Montefiore Med Ctr-Einstein Campus (page 100), Monte-fiore Med Ctr-Moses Campus (page 100); **Address:** Montefiore Med Ctr, Surgery, 111 E 210th St Rosenthal Bldg Fl 2, Bronx, NY 10467; **Phone:** 718-904-2047; **Board Cert:** Surgery 2001; **Med School:** Canada 1996; **Resid:** Surgery, Montreal Univ Med Ctr 2001; **Fellow:** Hepatobiliary Surgery, NY-Presby/Columbia Univ Med Ctr 2003; Transplant Surgery, NY-Presby/Columbia Univ Med Ctr 2004; **Fac Appt:** Asst Clin Prof S, Albert Einstein Coll Med

Greenstein, Stuart M MD (S) - **Spec Exp:** Laparoscopic Surgery; Dialysis Access Surgery; Transplant-Kidney; **Hospital:** Montefiore Med Ctr-Moses Campus (page 100); **Address:** Montefiore Med Ctr - Dept Surgery, 111 E 210th St Fl 2, Bronx, NY 10467; **Phone:** 877-287-3536; **Board Cert:** Surgery 2003; **Med School:** Harvard Med Sch 1979; **Resid:** Surgery, UMDNJ, NJ Med Sch Affil Hosp 1984; **Fellow:** Vascular Surgery, Hosp Univ Penn - UPHS 1985; Transplant Surgery, SUNY Downstate Med Ctr 1986; **Fac Appt:** Prof S, Albert Einstein Coll Med

Kennedy, Timothy J MD (S) - **Spec Exp:** Laparoscopic Surgery; Pancreatic Cancer; Stomach Cancer; **Hospital:** Montefiore Med Ctr-Einstein Campus (page 100), Montefiore Med Ctr-Moses Cam-pus (page 100); **Address:** 1521 Jarett Place Fl 1, Bronx, NY 10461; **Phone:** 718-862-8840; **Board Cert:** Surgery 2007; **Med School:** Georgetown Univ 1999; **Resid:** Surgery, Northwestern Meml Hosp 2006; **Fellow:** Surgical Oncology, Meml Sloan Kettering Canc Ctr 2007; **Fac Appt:** Asst Prof S, Albert Einstein Coll Med

Kinkhabwala, Milan M MD (S) - **Spec Exp:** Transplant-Liver; Hepatobiliary Surgery; Liver & Biliary Surgery; **Hospital:** Montefiore Med Ctr-Moses Campus (page 100), Montefiore Med Ctr-Ein-stein Campus (page 100); **Address:** Montefiore Medical Ctr, 111 E 210th St, Rosenthal Section Fl 2, Bronx, NY 10467; **Phone:** 718-920-6659; **Board Cert:** Surgery 2004; **Med School:** Cornell Univ-Weill Med Coll 1989; **Resid:** Surgery, NY-Presby/Weil Cornell Med Ctr 1994; **Fellow:** Hepatobiliary Surgery, UCLA Med Ctr 1996; **Fac Appt:** Prof S, Albert Einstein Coll Med

Libutti, Steven K MD (S) - **Spec Exp:** Neuroendocrine Tumors; Gastrointestinal Cancer; **Hospital:** Montefiore Med Ctr-Einstein Campus (page 100), Montefiore Med Ctr-Moses Campus (page 100); **Address:** Montefiore Med Ctr, Cancer Care, 1521 Jarret Pl, Bronx, NY 10461; **Phone:** 718-862-8840; **Board Cert:** Surgery 2004; **Med School:** Columbia P&S 1990; **Resid:** Surgery, NY-Presby/Columbia Univ Med Ctr 1995; **Fellow:** Surgical Oncology, Natl Cancer Inst 1996; **Fac Appt:** Prof S, Albert Einstein Coll Med

Melvin, W. Scott MD (S) - **Spec Exp:** Liver & Biliary Surgery; Pancreatic Cancer; Hepatobiliary Cancer; Minimally Invasive Surgery; **Hospital:** Montefiore Med Ctr-Moses Campus (page 100); **Address:** Greene Medical Arts Bldg, 3400 Bainbridge Ave Fl 4, Bronx, NY 10467; **Phone:** 718-920- 4800; **Board Cert:** Surgery 2012; **Med School:** Med Coll OH 1987; **Resid:** Surgery, Univ Maryland 1992; **Fellow:** Gastrointestinal Surgery, Grant Med Ctr 1993; **Fac Appt:** Prof S, Albert Einstein Coll Med

Montgomery, Leslie L MD (S) - **Spec Exp:** Breast Cancer & Surgery; Sentinel Node Surgery; Clinical Trials; **Hospital:** Montefiore Med Ctr-Einstein Campus (page 100); **Address:** Montefiore-Einstein Ctr for Cancer, 1521 Jarret Pl, Bronx, NY 10461; **Phone:** 718-862-8846; **Board Cert:** Surgery 2006; **Med School:** UCSF 1991; **Resid:** Surgery, NY-Presby/Weill Cornell Med Ctr 1996; **Fellow:** Surgical Oncology, Brigham & Womens Hosp; Surgical Oncology, Meml Sloan-Kettering Cancer Ctr

Sas, Norman S MD (S) - **Spec Exp:** Breast Cancer; Laparoscopic Surgery; Hernia; **Hospital:** Montefiore Med Ctr-Moses Campus (page 100), Lawrence Hosp Ctr (page 102); **Address:** 3220 Fairfield Ave, Riverdale, NY 10463-3240; **Phone:** 718-549-0700; **Board Cert:** Surgery 2009; **Med School:** NY Med Coll 1974; **Resid:** Surgery, Montefiore Med Ctr 1978; **Fac Appt:** Asst Clin Prof S, Albert Einstein Coll Med

Shamamian, Peter MD (S) - **Spec Exp:** Pancreatic Cancer; **Hospital:** Montefiore Med Ctr-Moses Campus (page 100), Montefiore Med Ctr-Einstein Campus (page 100); **Address:** 3400 Bainbridge Ave Fl 4, Bronx, NY 10467; **Phone:** 718-920-4089; **Board Cert:** Surgery 2005; **Med School:** Rutgers R W Johnson Med Sch 1989; **Resid:** Surgery, NYU Langone Med Ctr 1995; **Fellow:** Surgical Oncology, Natl Inst Hlth 1996; **Fac Appt:** Prof S, Albert Einstein Coll Med

Thoracic & Cardiac Surgery

D'Alessandro, David A MD (T&CS) - **Spec Exp:** Cardiac Surgery; Transplant-Heart; Mechanical Assist Devices; Heart Valve Surgery; **Hospital:** Montefiore Med Ctr-Moses Campus (page 100), Montefiore Med Ctr-Einstein Campus (page 100); **Address:** Montefiore, Cardiothoracic Surgery, 3400 Bainbridge Ave MAP Bldg - Ste 5A, Bronx, NY 10467; **Phone:** 718-920-6515; **Board Cert:** Surgery 2004; Thoracic & Cardiac Surgery 2006; **Med School:** Columbia P&S 1997; **Resid:** Surgery, NY-Presby/Columbia Univ Med Ctr 2002; **Fellow:** Thoracic & Cardiac Surgery, NY-Presby/Columbia Univ Med Ctr 2004; Renal Transplant, NY-Presby/Columbia Univ Med Ctr 2006; **Fac Appt:** Asst Prof TS, Albert Einstein Coll Med

DeRose Jr, Joseph J MD (T&CS) - **Spec Exp:** Robotic Cardiac Surgery; Aortic Valve Replacement; Mitral Valve Surgery; Minimally Invasive Heart Valve Surgery; **Hospital:** Montefiore Med Ctr-Einstein Campus (page 100), Montefiore Med Ctr-Moses Campus (page 100); **Address:** Montefiore, Cardiothoracic Surgery, 1575 Blondell Ave, Ste 125, Bronx, NY 10461; **Phone:** 718-405-8371; **Board Cert:** Thoracic & Cardiac Surgery 2011; **Med School:** Columbia P&S 1993; **Resid:** Surgery, NY-Presby/Columbia Univ Med Ctr 1999; **Fellow:** Cardiothoracic Surgery, NY-Presby/Columbia Univ Med Ctr 2001; **Fac Appt:** Assoc Prof TS, Albert Einstein Coll Med

Goldstein, Daniel J MD (T&CS) - **Spec Exp:** Mechanical Assist Devices; Transplant-Heart; Coronary Artery Surgery; Aortic Surgery; **Hospital:** Montefiore Med Ctr-Moses Campus (page 100), Montefiore Med Ctr-Einstein Campus (page 100); **Address:** Montefiore, Cardiothoracic Surgery, 3400 Bainbridge Ave MAP Bldg - Ste 5A, Bronx, NY 10467; **Phone:** 718-920-2144; **Board Cert:** Thoracic Surgery 2010; **Med School:** Mount Sinai Sch Med 1991; **Resid:** Surgery, NY-Presby/Columbia Univ Med Ctr 1997; **Fellow:** Cardiothoracic Surgery, NY-Presby/Columbia Univ Med Ctr 1999; **Fac Appt:** Prof T&CS, Albert Einstein Coll Med

Keller, Steven M MD (T&CS) - **Spec Exp:** Lung Cancer; Esophageal Cancer; Mediastinal Tumors; Hyperhidrosis-Palmar; **Hospital:** Montefiore Med Ctr-Einstein Campus (page 100); **Address:** Montefiore, Cardiothoracic Surgery, 1575 Blondell Ave, Ste 125, Bronx, NY 10461; **Phone:** 718-405-8378; **Board Cert:** Thoracic Surgery 2007; **Med School:** Albany Med Coll 1977; **Resid:** Surgery, Mt Sinai Hosp 1985; Thoracic Surgery, Mem Sloan-Kettering Cancer Ctr 1987; **Fellow:** Surgical Oncology, Natl Cancer Inst 1983; **Fac Appt:** Prof TS, Albert Einstein Coll Med

Michler, Robert E MD (T&CS) - **Spec Exp:** Heart Valve Surgery; Coronary Artery Surgery; Atrial Fibrillation; Aneurysm-Aortic; **Hospital:** Montefiore Med Ctr-Moses Campus (page 100), Montefiore Med Ctr-Einstein Campus (page 100); **Address:** Montefiore, Dept Cardio/Thoracic Surgery, Green Medical Arts Pavilion, 3400 Bainbridge Ave, Ste 5, New York, NY 10467; **Phone:** 718-920-2100; **Board Cert:** Thoracic & Cardiac Surgery 2010; **Med School:** Dartmouth Med Sch 1981; **Resid:** Surgery, Columbia Presby Med Ctr 1987; **Fellow:** Cardiothoracic Surgery, Columbia Presby Med Ctr 1989; Congenital Heart Surgery, Boston Children's Hosp 1990; **Fac Appt:** Prof T&CS, Albert Einstein Coll Med

Weinstein, Samuel MD (T&CS) - **Spec Exp:** Pediatric Cardiac Surgery; Congenital Heart Disease-Adult; Transplant-Heart; **Hospital:** Montefiore Med Ctr-Moses Campus (page 100), Montefiore Med Ctr-Einstein Campus (page 100); **Address:** Montefiore Med Ctr, Moses Div, Dept Cardiothoracic Surgery, 3400 Bainbridge Ave Fl 5 - Ste 5A, Bronx, NY 10467; **Phone:** 718-920-7745; **Board Cert:** Surgery 2004; Thoracic Surgery 2007; Congenital Cardiac Surgery 2009; **Med School:** SUNY Stony Brook 1989; **Resid:** Surgery, NY-Presby/Columbia Univ Med Ctr 1996; Cardiothoracic Surgery, NY-Presby/Columbia Univ Med Ctr 1998; **Fellow:** Pediatric Cardiothoracic Surgery, Chldns Hosp 1999; **Fac Appt:** Assoc Prof TS, Albert Einstein Coll Med

Urology

Ghavamian, Reza MD (U) - **Spec Exp:** Urologic Cancer; Prostate Cancer/Robotic Surgery; Minimally Invasive Surgery; Clinical Trials; **Hospital:** Montefiore Med Ctr-Moses Campus (page 100); **Address:** MMC Medical Arts Pavilion, 3400 Bainbridge Ave Fl 5, Bronx, NY 10467; **Phone:** 718-920-8475; **Board Cert:** Urology 2008; **Med School:** Boston Univ 1991; **Resid:** Urology, Univ Mass Med Ctr 1996; **Fellow:** Urologic Oncology, Mayo Clinic 1998; **Fac Appt:** Clin Prof U, Albert Einstein Coll Med

Schoenberg, Mark P MD (U) - **Spec Exp:** Bladder Cancer; Urinary Reconstruction; **Hospital:** Montefiore Med Ctr-Moses Campus (page 100), Montefiore Med Ctr-Einstein Campus (page 100); **Address:** Montefiore Med Ctr, Dept Urology, Medical Arts Pavilion Fl 5, 111 E 210th St, Bronx, NY 10467; **Phone:** 718-920-5402; **Board Cert:** Urology 2005; **Med School:** Univ Tex, Houston 1986; **Resid:** Surgery, Hosp Univ Penn 1988; Urologic Surgery, Hosp Univ Penn 1992; **Fellow:** Urologic Oncology, Brady Inst/Johns Hopkins 1994; **Fac Appt:** Prof U, Albert Einstein Coll Med

Vascular & Interventional Radiology

Cynamon, Jacob MD (VIR) - Spec Exp: Peripheral Vascular Disease; Uterine Fibroid Embolization; Liver Cancer; Dialysis Access; **Hospital:** Montefiore Med Ctr-Moses Campus (page 100), Montefiore Med Ctr-Einstein Campus (page 100); **Address:** Montefiore Med Ctr, Interventional Radiology, 111 E 210th St, Bronx, NY 10467; **Phone:** 718-920-5729; **Board Cert:** Diagnostic Radiology 1987; Vascular & Interventional Radiology 2004; **Med School:** Albert Einstein Coll Med 1983; **Resid:** Surgery, Montefiore Med Ctr 1984; Diagnostic Radiology, Montefiore Med Ctr 1987; **Fellow:** Vascular & Interventional Radiology, New York Hosp-Cornell 1988; **Fac Appt:** Clin Prof Rad, Albert Einstein Coll Med

Vascular Surgery

Lipsitz, Evan C MD (VascS) - Spec Exp: Aneurysm-Abdominal & Thoracic Aortic; Endovascular Surgery; Limb Sparing Surgery; Peripheral Vascular Disease; **Hospital:** Montefiore Med Ctr-Moses Campus (page 100); **Address:** Montefiore Med Ctr-Vascular Surgery, 3400 Bainbridge Ave Fl 4, Bronx, NY 10467; **Phone:** 718-920-2016; **Board Cert:** Vascular Surgery 2008; **Med School:** Columbia P&S 1990; **Resid:** Surgery, Columbia-Presby Med Ctr 1996; **Fellow:** Vascular Surgery, Montefiore Med Ctr 1999; **Fac Appt:** Assoc Prof VascS, Albert Einstein Coll Med

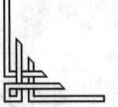

The Best in American Medicine
www.CastleConnolly.com

NEW YORK METHODIST HOSPITAL

506 Sixth Street, Brooklyn, N.Y. 11215
Phone (718) 780-3000, Fax (718) 780-3770
http://www.nym.org

Sponsorship	Voluntary, Not-for-Profit
Beds	591; 60 bassinets
Accreditation	The Joint Commission, Council on Graduate Medical Education

GENERAL DESCRIPTION

New York Methodist Hospital (NYM), a member of the NewYork-Presbyterian Healthcare System, has served the neighborhoods of Brooklyn for over 130 years. NYM's medical programs have recently expanded significantly and the Hospital's campus facilities in Park Slope have been extensively renovated. In addition, New York Methodist maintains satellite outpatient health centers throughout Brooklyn.

MEDICAL STAFF

NYM has over 1,200 physicians on staff; 90 percent are board certified or board eligible. Many physicians at NYM are known for the impressive and outstanding work they have done in their individual fields. New York Methodist Hospital offers medical residency programs in internal medicine, surgery, pediatrics, obstetrics/gynecology, radiation oncology, nuclear medicine, anesthesiology, emergency medicine, podiatry and dentistry. The Hospital also offers fellowships in several medical subspecialties.

SPECIAL PROGRAMS

Emergency Medicine: The Emergency Department houses a pediatric emergency room and private rooms for obstetrics/gynecology patients. The Hospital is a State-designated Stroke Center, an AHA Heart Center and EMS 911 Receiving Hospital. 718 780-3148.

Institute for Advanced and Minimally Invasive Surgery: 866 DOCS-14U.

Institute for Advanced Otolaryngology: 844 ENT-DOCS.

Institute for Asthma and Other Lung Diseases: See Centers of Excellence Section. 866 ASK-LUNG.

Institute for Cancer Care: 866 411-ONCO.

Institute for Cardiology and Cardiac Surgery: See Centers of Excellence Section. 866 84-HEART.

Institute for Diabetes and Other Endocrine Disorders: 866 4-GLAND-2.

Institute for Digestive and Liver Disorders: See Centers of Excellence Section. 866 DIGEST-1.

Institute for Healthy Aging: 844 780-9355.

Institute for Neurosciences: See Centers of Excellence Section. 866 DO-NEURO.

Institute for Orthopedic Medicine and Surgery: See Centers of Excellence Section. 866 ORTHO-11.

Institute for Vascular Medicine and Surgery: 866 438-VEIN.

Institute for Women's Health: 877 41-WOMAN.

Birthing Center: Spacious, private birthing rooms allow women to experience a "home-like" birth with the reassurance that high-tech medical equipment and specialists are instantly accessible if needed. Full-time lactation services are available for new mothers.

Physician Referral: The Hospital has a free seven-day, 24-hour telephone and computer on-line physician referral service. To find a doctor in any specialty with a convenient office location, area of specialization and insurance and billing policies, call 718 499-CARE or go to http://www.nym.org.

Adolescent Medicine

Birnbaum, Jeffrey MD (AM) - **Spec Exp:** AIDS/HIV in Adolescents; Adolescent Behavior-High Risk; Sexually Transmitted Diseases; **Hospital:** SUNY Downstate Med Ctr (Univ Hosp Brooklyn) (page 449); **Address:** SUNY Downstate, Adolescent Med, 450 Clarkson Blvd, Brooklyn, NY 11203; **Phone:** 718-282-1199; **Board Cert:** Pediatrics 2013; **Med School:** SUNY Downstate 1986; **Resid:** Pediatrics, SUNY Downstate Med Ctr 1989; **Fac Appt:** Assoc Prof Ped, SUNY Downstate

Hayes, Leslie A MD (AM) - **Spec Exp:** Nutrition; Adolescent Gynecology; **Hospital:** New York Methodist Hosp (page 448); **Address:** 1 Prospect Park W, Brooklyn, NY 11215; **Phone:** 718-636-3960; **Board Cert:** Adolescent Medicine 2012; **Med School:** Mount Sinai Sch Med 1986; **Resid:** Pediatrics, Chldns Hosp Natl Med Ctr 1989; **Fellow:** Adolescent Medicine, Univ Hosp-UMDNJ 1991

Seigel, Warren MD (AM) - **Hospital:** Maimonides Med Ctr (page 98); **Address:** 2601 Ocean Pkwy, Brooklyn, NY 11235; **Phone:** 718-616-3223; **Board Cert:** Adolescent Medicine 2014; **Med School:** Dominican Republic 1982; **Resid:** Pediatrics, Brookdale Univ Hosp 1987; **Fellow:** Adolescent Medicine, Brookdale Univ Hosp 1989

Allergy & Immunology

Greeley, Norman H MD (A&I) - **Spec Exp:** Asthma; **Hospital:** Maimonides Med Ctr (page 98), Lenox Hill Hosp (Manh Eye, Ear & Throat Hosp); **Address:** 140 Clinton St, Fl 1, Brooklyn, NY 11201-4701; **Phone:** 718-624-4465; **Board Cert:** Internal Medicine 1985; Allergy & Immunology 1987; Clinical & Laboratory Immunology 1988; **Med School:** Mexico 1980; **Resid:** Internal Medicine, Long Is Coll Hosp 1985; **Fellow:** Allergy & Immunology, SUNY Downstate Med Ctr 1987

Joks, Rauno MD (A&I) - **Spec Exp:** Asthma & Allergy; **Hospital:** SUNY Downstate Med Ctr (Univ Hosp Brooklyn) (page 449); **Address:** SUNY Downstate, Allergy & Immun, 450 Clarkson Ave, Brooklyn, NY 10093; **Phone:** 718-270-2156; **Board Cert:** Allergy & Immunology 2013; Rheumatology 2004; **Med School:** SUNY Stony Brook 1987; **Resid:** Internal Medicine, St Lukes-Roosevelt Hosp 1990; **Fellow:** Allergy Immunology & Rheumatology, SUNY Hlth Sci Hosp 1993

Klein, Norman MD (A&I) - **Spec Exp:** Asthma; Food Allergy; Hay Fever; Immune Deficiency; **Hospital:** Brookdale Univ Hosp Med Ctr, Brooklyn Hosp Ctr; **Address:** 1648 E 14th St, Ste 5, Brooklyn, NY 11229; **Phone:** 718-627-0183; **Board Cert:** Pediatrics 1981; Allergy & Immunology 1983; **Med School:** SUNY Downstate 1976; **Resid:** Pediatrics, Brookdale Univ Hosp 1979; **Fellow:** Allergy & Immunology, Montefiore Med Ctr 1980; **Fac Appt:** Asst Prof Ped, SUNY Downstate

Manvar, Dolly MD (A&I) - **Spec Exp:** Pediatric Allergy & Immunology; **Hospital:** Brooklyn Hosp Ctr; **Address:** 6414 Bay Pky, Brooklyn, NY 11204; **Phone:** 718-234-2300; **Board Cert:** Pediatrics 1982; Allergy & Immunology 1983; **Med School:** India 1977; **Resid:** Pediatrics, Interfaith Med Ctr 1981; **Fellow:** Allergy & Immunology, St Lukes-Roosevelt Hosp 1983

Silverman, Bernard A MD (A&I) - **Spec Exp:** Eczema; Food Allergy; Urticaria; Atopic Dermatitis; **Hospital:** Mt Sinai Hosp; **Address:** 2044 Ocean Ave, Ste A7, Brooklyn, NY 11230; **Phone:** 718-998-5556; **Board Cert:** Pediatrics 1984; Allergy & Immunology 1985; **Med School:** Wayne State Univ 1979; **Resid:** Pediatrics, Brookdale Univ Hosp Med Ctr 1982; **Fellow:** Allergy & Immunology, Montefiore Med Ctr 1984; **Fac Appt:** Asst Clin Prof Ped, Mount Sinai Sch Med

Vassallo, Milo F MD (A&I) - **Spec Exp:** Allergic Rhinitis; Asthma; Hives; Skin Allergies; **Hospital:** New York Methodist Hosp (page 448); **Address:** ENT and Allergy Assocs, 300 Cadman Plaza W (1 Pierrepont Pl), Ste 1301, Brooklyn, NY 11201; **Phone:** 718-208-4449; **Board Cert:** Pediatrics 2008; Allergy & Immunology 2010; **Med School:** NYU Sch Med 2003; **Resid:** Pediatrics, Mass Genl Hosp 2007; **Fellow:** Allergy & Immunology, Mass Genl Hosp 2009

Cardiac Electrophysiology

Greenberg, Yisachar MD (CE) - **Hospital:** Maimonides Med Ctr (page 98); **Address:** 421 Ocean Pkwy Fl 2, Brooklyn, NY 11218; **Phone:** 718-283-6842; **Board Cert:** Cardiovascular Disease 2008; Cardiac Electrophysiology 2008; **Med School:** SUNY Downstate 1989; **Resid:** Internal Medicine, LI Jewish Med Ctr 1993; **Fellow:** Cardiovascular Disease, Yale-New Haven Hosp 1995

Kassotis, John MD (CE) - **Spec Exp:** Arrhythmias; Atrial Fibrillation; Ventricular Tachycardia Ablation; Congenital Heart Disease; **Hospital:** SUNY Downstate Med Ctr (Univ Hosp Brooklyn) (page 449); **Address:** 450 Clarkson Ave, Box 1199, Brooklyn, NY 11203; **Phone:** 718-270-4147; **Board Cert:** Internal Medicine 2007; Cardiovascular Disease 2008; Cardiac Electrophysiology 2009; **Med School:** Columbia P&S 1990; **Resid:** Internal Medicine, NY-Presby/Columbia Univ Med Ctr 1993; **Fellow:** Cardiovascular Disease, NY-Presby/Columbia Univ Med Ctr 1996; Cardiac Electrophysiology, NY-Presby/Columbia Univ Med Ctr 1997; **Fac Appt:** Assoc Prof Med, SUNY Downstate

Turitto, Gioia MD (CE) - **Spec Exp:** Pacemakers; Defibrillators; Arrhythmias; **Hospital:** New York Methodist Hosp (page 448); **Address:** NY Methodist Hosp, Div Cardiology, 506 Sixth St, Fl 2, Brooklyn, NY 11215; **Phone:** 718-780-3626; **Board Cert:** Internal Medicine 2013; Cardiovascular Disease 2013; Cardiac Electrophysiology 2004; **Med School:** Italy 1981; **Resid:** Internal Medicine, SUNY Downstate Med Ctr 1992; **Fellow:** Cardiovascular Disease, SUNY Downstate Med Ctr 1987; **Fac Appt:** Assoc Clin Prof Med, Cornell Univ-Weill Med Coll

Wilbur, Sabrina L MD (CE) - **Spec Exp:** Arrhythmias; Pacemakers/Defibrillators; **Hospital:** New York Methodist Hosp (page 448), Mt Sinai Beth Israel; **Address:** 185 Montague St Fl 3, Brooklyn, NY 11201; **Phone:** 718-855-7223; **Board Cert:** Cardiovascular Disease 2005; Cardiac Electrophysiology 2009; **Med School:** Dominican Republic 1987; **Resid:** Internal Medicine, Temple Univ-Episcopal Hosp 1991; **Fellow:** Cardiovascular Disease, Temple Univ-Episcopal Hosp 1994; Cardiac Electrophysiology, Hosp Univ Penn 1995

Cardiovascular Disease

Borer, Jeffrey S MD (Cv) - **Spec Exp:** Heart Valve Disease; Heart Failure; Nuclear Cardiology; Coronary Artery Disease; **Hospital:** SUNY Downstate Med Ctr (Univ Hosp Brooklyn) (page 449), NY-Presby/Weill Cornell Med Ctr, NY (page 102); **Address:** SUNY Downstate Med Ctr, Div Cardiology, Howard Gilman Institute, 635 Madison Ave Fl 3, New York, NY 10022; **Phone:** 212-289-7777; **Board Cert:** Internal Medicine 1973; Cardiovascular Disease 1975; **Med School:** Cornell Univ-Weill Med Coll 1969; **Resid:** Internal Medicine, Mass Genl Hosp 1971; **Fellow:** Cardiovascular Disease, Natl Heart, Lung & Blood Inst 1974; Cardiovascular Disease, Guy's Hosp 1975; **Fac Appt:** Prof Med, SUNY Downstate

Charnoff, Judah A MD (Cv) - **Spec Exp:** Coronary Artery Disease; Congestive Heart Failure; Cholesterol/Lipid Disorders; **Hospital:** Lenox Hill Hosp, Maimonides Med Ctr (page 98); **Address:** Cross County Medical, 1262 Ocean Pkwy, Brooklyn, NY 11230; **Phone:** 718-859-5843; **Board Cert:** Internal Medicine 1987; Cardiovascular Disease 2005; **Med School:** NYU Sch Med 1984; **Resid:** Internal Medicine, Brookdale Hosp 1987; **Fellow:** Cardiovascular Disease, Maimonides Med Ctr 1989; **Fac Appt:** Asst Prof Med, SUNY Downstate

Dilmanian, Hajir E MD (Cv) - **Spec Exp:** Echocardiography; Heart Failure; Hypertension; Atrial Fibrillation; **Hospital:** New York Methodist Hosp (page 448); **Address:** NY Methodist Hosp, Cardiology Dept, 506 6th St, Fl 2, Brooklyn, NY 11215; **Phone:** 718-780-7830; **Board Cert:** Internal Medicine 2004; Cardiovascular Disease 2007; **Med School:** SUNY Downstate 2001; **Resid:** Internal Medicine, NYU Med Ctr 2004; **Fellow:** Cardiovascular Disease, Westchester Med Ctr 2007

Feit, Alan MD (Cv) - **Spec Exp:** Interventional Cardiology; **Hospital:** SUNY Downstate Med Ctr. (Univ Hosp Brooklyn) (page 449); **Address:** SUNY Downstate Med Ctr, Dept Cardiology, 450 Clarkson Ave, Box 1199, Brooklyn, NY 11203-2012; **Phone:** 718-270-2631; **Board Cert:** Internal Medicine 1978; Cardiovascular Disease 1981; Interventional Cardiology 2009; **Med School:** Columbia P&S 1975; **Resid:** Internal Medicine, Roosevelt Hosp Ctr 1978; **Fellow:** Cardiovascular Disease, Roosevelt Hosp Ctr 1980

Friedman, Howard S MD (Cv) - **Spec Exp:** Atrial Fibrillation; Coronary Artery Disease; Hypertension; **Hospital:** Brooklyn Hosp Ctr; **Address:** Dept Cardiology, 121 DeKalb Ave Fl 2 - Ste DPO, Brooklyn, NY 11201; **Phone:** 718-250-8317; **Board Cert:** Internal Medicine 1971; Cardiovascular Disease 1974; Geriatric Medicine 2004; **Med School:** SUNY Buffalo 1966; **Resid:** Internal Medicine, Barnes-Jewish Hosp 1968; **Fellow:** Cardiovascular Disease, Mt Sinai Med Ctr 1970; Cardiovascular Disease, Mt Sinai Med Ctr 1973; **Fac Appt:** Clin Prof Med, NYU Sch Med

Gelbfish, Joseph S MD (Cv) - **Spec Exp:** Preventive Cardiology; Heart Valve Disease; **Hospital:** New York Methodist Hosp (page 448), NY-Presby/Columbia Univ Med Ctr, NY (page 102); **Address:** 2500 Avenue I, Brooklyn, NY 11210; **Phone:** 718-951-0100; **Board Cert:** Internal Medicine 1986; Cardiovascular Disease 1989; **Med School:** NYU Sch Med 1980; **Resid:** Surgery, Maimonides Med Ctr 1984; Internal Medicine, Maimonides Med Ctr 1985; **Fellow:** Cardiovascular Disease, Maimonides Med Ctr 1988; Cardiovascular Disease, Beth Israel Deaconess Med Ctr 1989

Gelles, Jeremiah MD (Cv) - **Spec Exp:** Heart Failure; Hypertension; Arrhythmias; Preventive Cardiology; **Hospital:** New York Methodist Hosp (page 448), Maimonides Med Ctr (page 98); **Address:** 263 7th Ave, Ste 5H, Brooklyn, NY 11215-3690; **Phone:** 718-246-8800; **Board Cert:** Internal Medicine 1972; Cardiovascular Disease 1975; **Med School:** NYU Sch Med 1966; **Resid:** Internal Medicine, Mount Sinai Hosp 1970; Internal Medicine, Montefiore Med Ctr 1969; **Fellow:** Cardiovascular Disease, Mount Sinai Hosp 1971; Cardiac Electrophysiology, Columbia Presby Med Ctr 1973; **Fac Appt:** Asst Clin Prof Med, Cornell Univ-Weill Med Coll

Greengart, Alvin MD (Cv) - **Spec Exp:** Echocardiography; Non-Invasive Cardiology; **Hospital:** Maimonides Med Ctr (page 98); **Address:** Cardiology Assocs of Brooklyn, 4802 10th Ave Fl 4, Brooklyn, NY 11219; **Phone:** 718-283-6473; **Board Cert:** Internal Medicine 1977; Cardiovascular Disease 1979; **Med School:** Mount Sinai Sch Med 1974; **Resid:** Internal Medicine, Brookdale Med Ctr 1977; **Fellow:** Cardiovascular Disease, Brookdale Med Ctr 1979

Hanley, Gerard MD (Cv) - **Hospital:** Mt Sinai Beth Israel-BK; **Address:** 3131 Kings Hwy, Ste B1, Brooklyn, NY 11234; **Phone:** 718-421-1212; **Board Cert:** Internal Medicine 1989; **Med School:** SUNY Stony Brook 1984; **Resid:** Internal Medicine, SUNY Hlth Sci Ctr 1987; **Fellow:** Cardiovascular Disease, SUNY Hlth Sci Ctr 1990; Cardiovascular Disease, Westchester Med Ctr 1991

Heitner, John F MD (Cv) - **Spec Exp:** Nuclear Cardiology; Cardiac MRI; **Hospital:** New York Methodist Hosp (page 448); **Address:** Div Cardiology, 506 Sixth St, Brooklyn, NY 11215; **Phone:** 718-780-5037; **Board Cert:** Internal Medicine 2013; Cardiovascular Disease 2004; **Med School:** Albert Einstein Coll Med 1997; **Resid:** Internal Medicine, Duke Univ Hosps 2000; **Fellow:** Cardiovascular Disease, Emory Univ Hosp 2002; Cardiovascular Disease, Duke Univ Hosps 2004

Hollander, Gerald MD (Cv) - **Spec Exp:** Coronary Artery Disease; Heart Failure; Echocardiography; **Hospital:** Maimonides Med Ctr (page 98); **Address:** Cardiology Assocs-Brooklyn, 4802 10th Ave Fl 4, Brooklyn, NY 11219; **Phone:** 718-283-7643; **Board Cert:** Internal Medicine 1976; Cardiovascular Disease 1979; **Med School:** SUNY Downstate 1973; **Resid:** Internal Medicine, Brookdale Hosp 1976; **Fellow:** Cardiovascular Disease, Brookdale Hosp 1978; **Fac Appt:** Clin Prof Med, SUNY Hlth Sci Ctr

Kabalkin, Chaim MD (Cv) - **Spec Exp:** Non-Invasive Cardiology; Cardiac Imaging; Echocardiology; Atrial Fibrillation; **Hospital:** Maimonides Med Ctr (page 98); **Address:** Cardiology Assocs, 421 Ocean Pkwy, Brooklyn, NY 11218; **Phone:** 718-871-4742; **Board Cert:** Internal Medicine 2008; Cardiovascular Disease 2010; Echocardiography ; **Med School:** Israel 1994; **Resid:** Internal Medicine, Maimonides Med Ctr 1997; **Fellow:** Cardiovascular Disease, Maimonides Med Ctr 2000; **Fac Appt:** Asst Prof Med, Mount Sinai-Icahn Sch of Med

Kang, Pritpal S MD (Cv) - **Spec Exp:** Nuclear Cardiology; **Hospital:** Lutheran Med Ctr - Brooklyn; **Address:** 705 86th St, Ste M3, Brooklyn, NY 11228; **Phone:** 718-836-0600; **Board Cert:** Internal Medicine 1979; Cardiovascular Disease 1981; **Med School:** India 1972; **Resid:** Internal Medicine, Methodist Hosp 1978; **Fellow:** Cardiovascular Disease, VA Med Ctr 1980

Kerstein, Joshua MD (Cv) - **Spec Exp:** Atrial Fibrillation; Coronary Artery Disease; Brugada Syndrome; Long QT Syndrome; **Hospital:** Maimonides Med Ctr (page 98); **Address:** Maimonides Med Ctr, Cardiology Assocs, 4802 10th Ave Fl 4, Brooklyn, NY 11219; **Phone:** 718-283-8614; **Board Cert:** Cardiovascular Disease 2005; Nuclear Cardiology 2002; **Med School:** SUNY Downstate 1989; **Resid:** Internal Medicine, Maimonides Med Ctr 1992; **Fellow:** Cardiovascular Disease, Maimonides Med Ctr 1995; **Fac Appt:** Asst Prof Med, SUNY Downstate

Konka, Sudarsanam MD (Cv) - **Hospital:** New York Methodist Hosp (page 448); **Address:** 100 Clinton St, Ste 20, Brooklyn, NY 11201; **Phone:** 718-935-9837; **Board Cert:** Internal Medicine 1974; Cardiovascular Disease 1977; **Med School:** India 1970; **Resid:** Internal Medicine, Long Island Coll Hosp 1974; **Fellow:** Cardiovascular Disease, Nassau Univ Med Ctr 1975; Cardiovascular Disease, Long Island Coll Hosp 1976

Moskovits, Norbert MD (Cv) - **Spec Exp:** Heart Failure; Coronary Artery Disease; Preventive Cardiology; Cholesterol/Lipid Disorders; **Hospital:** Maimonides Med Ctr (page 98); **Address:** Maimonides Med Ctr, Div Cardiology, 4802 10 Ave, Fl 4, Brooklyn, NY 11219; **Phone:** 718-283-7948; **Board Cert:** Advanced Heart Failure & Transplant Cardiology 2012; Cardiovascular Disease 2005; **Med School:** Germany 1986; **Resid:** Internal Medicine, Maimonides Med Ctr 1992; **Fellow:** Cardiovascular Disease, Beth Israel Med Ctr 1995; **Fac Appt:** Asst Prof Med, Albert Einstein Coll Med

Paiusco, Augusto Dino MD (Cv) - **Spec Exp:** Preventive Cardiology; **Hospital:** Mt Sinai Beth Israel-BK; **Address:** University Heart Assocs, 3131 Kings Hwy, Ste B-8, Brooklyn, NY 11234; **Phone:** 718-998-2323; **Board Cert:** Internal Medicine 1989; **Med School:** Mexico 1984; **Resid:** Internal Medicine, SUNY Hlth Sci Ctr 1989; **Fellow:** Cardiovascular Disease, SUNY Hlth Sci Ctr 1992

Prabhu, H. Sudhakar MD (Cv) - **Spec Exp:** Echocardiography; Nuclear Cardiology; **Hospital:** Lutheran Med Ctr - Brooklyn; **Address:** 699 92nd St, Brooklyn, NY 11228; **Phone:** 718-833-2620; **Board Cert:** Internal Medicine 1978; Cardiovascular Disease 1981; Nuclear Cardiology 2006; Echocardiography 2008; **Med School:** India 1971; **Resid:** Internal Medicine, LI Coll Hosp 1976; **Fellow:** Cardiovascular Disease, LI Coll Hosp 1978; **Fac Appt:** Asst Prof Med, SUNY Downstate

Qadir, Shuja MD (Cv) - **Spec Exp:** Heart Failure; Arrhythmias; Coronary Artery Disease; **Hospital:** NY Hosp Queens (page 498), N Shore Univ Hosp; **Address:** 934 Manhattan Ave, Brooklyn, NY 11222; **Phone:** 718-275-6061; **Board Cert:** Internal Medicine 1984; Cardiovascular Disease 1987; **Med School:** Pakistan 1977; **Resid:** Internal Medicine, Catholic Med Ctr 1985; **Fellow:** Cardiovascular Disease, Catholic Med Ctr 1987; **Fac Appt:** Asst Prof Med, NY Med Coll

Traube, Charles MD (Cv) - **Spec Exp:** Cholesterol/Lipid Disorders; Hypertension; **Hospital:** Maimonides Med Ctr (page 98); **Address:** 2270 Kimball St, Ste 210, Brooklyn, NY 11234; **Phone:** 718-692-2700; **Board Cert:** Internal Medicine 1978; Cardiovascular Disease 1981; **Med School:** Albert Einstein Coll Med 1975; **Resid:** Internal Medicine, Brookdale Univ Hosp Med Ctr 1978; **Fellow:** Cardiovascular Disease, Brookdale Univ Hosp Med Ctr 1980; **Fac Appt:** Asst Clin Prof Med, Albert Einstein Coll Med

Wein, Paul K MD (Cv) - **Spec Exp:** Preventive Cardiology; Hypertension; Cholesterol/Lipid Disorders; Coronary Artery Disease; **Hospital:** Mt Sinai Beth Israel-BK, Long Is Jewish Med Ctr; **Address:** 3131 Kings Highway, Suite D6, Brooklyn, NY 11234; **Phone:** 718-338-2283; **Board Cert:** Internal Medicine 1979; Cardiovascular Disease 1983; **Med School:** SUNY Downstate 1976; **Resid:** Internal Medicine, Norwalk Hosp 1979; **Fellow:** Cardiovascular Disease, LI Jewish Med Ctr 1981

Zaloom, Robert MD (Cv) - **Spec Exp:** Cardiac Catheterization; Angiography-Coronary; Nutrition; Cardiac Stress Testing; **Hospital:** Lutheran Med Ctr - Brooklyn, Lenox Hill Hosp; **Address:** Bay Ridge Hearts, 217 Ovington Ave, Brooklyn, NY 11209; **Phone:** 718-238-0098; **Board Cert:** Internal Medicine 1986; Cardiovascular Disease 1989; **Med School:** France 1983; **Resid:** Internal Medicine, Lutheran Med Ctr 1986; **Fellow:** Cardiovascular Disease, SUNY Downstate Med Ctr 1988; **Fac Appt:** Asst Prof Med, Mount Sinai Sch Med

Child & Adolescent Psychiatry

Engel, Lenore MD (ChAP) - **Hospital:** Kings Co Hosp Ctr, SUNY Downstate Med Ctr (Univ Hosp Brooklyn) (page 449); **Address:** 115 Henry St, Ste 1G, Brooklyn, NY 11201-2562; **Phone:** 718-855-8911; **Board Cert:** Psychiatry 1983; Child & Adolescent Psychiatry 1985; Forensic Psychiatry 2008; **Med School:** SUNY Downstate 1978; **Resid:** Psychiatry, Kings Co Hosp 1982; **Fellow:** Child & Adolescent Psychiatry, SUNY Downstate Med Ctr 1984; **Fac Appt:** Asst Clin Prof Psyc, SUNY Downstate

Holzer, Barry D MD (ChAP) - **Spec Exp:** ADD/ADHD; Anxiety & Depression; Behavioral Disorders; Bipolar/Mood Disorders; **Address:** 2350 Ocean Ave, Ste 2J, Brooklyn, NY 11229; **Phone:** 718-743-7600; **Board Cert:** Psychiatry 1990; **Med School:** Albert Einstein Coll Med 1984; **Resid:** Psychiatry, Hillside Hosp-LIJ 1988; **Fellow:** Child & Adolescent Psychiatry, Schneider Chldns Hosp-LIJ 1990

Child Neurology

Hasson, Henry MD (ChiN) - **Spec Exp:** Epilepsy/Seizure Disorders; **Hospital:** Maimonides Med Ctr (page 98); **Address:** 2769 Coney Island Ave, Brooklyn, NY 11235; **Phone:** 718-785-9828; **Board Cert:** Child Neurology 2008; Clinical Neurophysiology 2009; **Med School:** Albert Einstein Coll Med 2001; **Resid:** Pediatrics, Maimonides Med Ctr 2004; **Fellow:** Child Neurology, Albert Einstein Coll Med Affil Hosp 2005; **Fac Appt:** Asst Prof Ped, SUNY Downstate

Pavlakis, Steven G MD (ChiN) - **Spec Exp:** Cerebrovascular Disease-Pediatric; Stroke; Stroke in Children; ADD/ADHD; **Hospital:** Brooklyn Hosp Ctr, Mt Sinai Hosp; **Address:** Brooklyn Hospital Ctr, Dept Ped Neurology, 240 Willoughby St, Ste 9K, Brooklyn, NY 11201; **Phone:** 718-250-6987; **Board Cert:** Pediatrics 1985; Child Neurology 1987; Neurodevelopmental Disabilities 2011; **Med School:** Brown Univ 1979; **Resid:** Pediatrics, NY-Presby/Columbia Univ Med Ctr 1981; **Fellow:** Pediatric Neurology, NY-Presby/Columbia Univ Med Ctr 1984; **Fac Appt:** Prof N, Mount Sinai Sch Med

Schubert, Romaine MD (ChiN) - **Spec Exp:** Epilepsy/Seizure Disorders; Developmental Disorders; Tourette's Syndrome; **Hospital:** New York Methodist Hosp (page 448); **Address:** 263 7th Ave, Ste 4A, Brooklyn, NY 11215; **Phone:** 718-246-8590; **Board Cert:** Child Neurology 1991; Clinical Neurophysiology 2010; Neurodevelopmental Disabilities 2012; **Med School:** Germany 1984; **Resid:** Pediatrics, SUNY Downstate/Kings Co Med Ctr 1987; **Fellow:** Child Neurology, SUNY Downstate/Kings Co Med Ctr 1990; **Fac Appt:** Asst Clin Prof Ped, Cornell Univ-Weill Med Coll

Clinical Genetics

Gilbert, Fred MD (CG) - **Spec Exp:** Cancer Genetics; Dysmorphology; **Hospital:** NY-Presby/Weill Cornell Med Ctr, NY (page 102), Brooklyn Hosp Ctr; **Address:** Pediatric Genetics, 240 Willoughby St, Ste 9K, Brooklyn, NY 11201; **Phone:** 718-250-6227; **Board Cert:** Clinical Genetics 1982; Clinical Cytogenetics 1982; **Med School:** Albert Einstein Coll Med 1966; **Resid:** Internal Medicine, Barnes-Jewish Hosp 1968; Internal Medicine, Natl Inst Hlth 1971; **Fellow:** Clinical Genetics, Yale-New Haven Hosp 1974; **Fac Appt:** Assoc Prof Ped, Cornell Univ-Weill Med Coll

Colon & Rectal Surgery

Asarian, Armand P MD (CRS) - **Spec Exp:** Colon Cancer; Breast Cancer; **Hospital:** Brooklyn Hosp Ctr; **Address:** Brooklyn Hosp Ctr, 121 DeKalb Ave, Dept Surg, Brooklyn, NY 11201; **Phone:** 718-250-6088; **Board Cert:** Surgery 2005; Colon & Rectal Surgery 2009; **Med School:** SUNY Downstate 1991; **Resid:** Surgery, Brooklyn Hosp Ctr 1996; **Fellow:** Colon & Rectal Surgery, Baylor Univ Med Ctr 1997; **Fac Appt:** Asst Clin Prof S, Cornell Univ-Weill Med Coll

Fleischer, Marian MD (CRS) - **Spec Exp:** Colonoscopy; Colon & Rectal Cancer; Pelvic & Perineal Surgery; Pelvic Organ Prolapse Repair; **Hospital:** Maimonides Med Ctr (page 98), New York Methodist Hosp (page 448); **Address:** 9707 4th Ave, Brooklyn, NY 11209-8129; **Phone:** 718-836-3603; **Board Cert:** Colon & Rectal Surgery 1984; **Med School:** Italy 1972; **Resid:** Surgery, Maimonides Med Ctr 1981; Colon & Rectal Surgery, Baltimore Med Ctr 1982

Dermatology

Baldwin, Hilary MD (D) - **Spec Exp:** Acne & Rosacea; Cosmetic Dermatology; **Address:** 142 Joralemon St, Ste 3A, Brooklyn, NY 11201; **Phone:** 718-797-3340; **Board Cert:** Dermatology 1988; **Med School:** Boston Univ 1984; **Resid:** Dermatology, NYU Med Ctr 1988; **Fac Appt:** Assoc Prof D, SUNY Downstate

Berry, Richard MD (D) - **Spec Exp:** Skin Cancer; Laser Hair Removal; Botox Therapy; **Address:** 2820 Ocean Pkwy, Brooklyn, NY 11235-7958; **Phone:** 718-996-3000; **Board Cert:** Dermatology 1978; **Med School:** SUNY Hlth Sci Ctr 1974; **Resid:** Dermatology, SUNY Downstate Med Ctr 1978; **Fac Appt:** Asst Clin Prof D, SUNY Hlth Sci Ctr

Biro, David MD/PhD (D) - **Spec Exp:** Mohs Surgery; Skin Laser Surgery; Cosmetic Dermatology; **Hospital:** SUNY Downstate Med Ctr (Univ Hosp Brooklyn) (page 449); **Address:** 9921 4th Ave, Fl 1, Brooklyn, NY 11209-8347; **Phone:** 718-833-7616; **Board Cert:** Dermatology 2013; **Med School:** Columbia P&S 1991; **Resid:** Dermatology, SUNY Hlth Sci Ctr 1995; **Fac Appt:** Asst Clin Prof D, SUNY Hlth Sci Ctr

Brancaccio, Ronald R MD (D) - **Spec Exp:** Contact Dermatitis; Skin Laser Surgery; Cosmetic Dermatology; **Hospital:** NYU Langone Med Ctr (page 104); **Address:** Skin Inst of NY, 7901 Fourth Ave, Brooklyn, NY 11209-3957; **Phone:** 718-491-5800; **Board Cert:** Dermatology 1977; **Med School:** Geo Wash Univ 1972; **Resid:** Dermatology, Univ Oregon Hlth Sci Ctr 1976; **Fellow:** Tropical Medicine, Univ Sao Paulo 1976; **Fac Appt:** Clin Prof D, NYU Sch Med

Danziger, Stephen MD (D) - **Spec Exp:** Skin Cancer & Moles; Acne & Rosacea; Psoriasis/Eczema; Warts; **Hospital:** New York Methodist Hosp (page 448); **Address:** 20 Plaza St E, Ste A17, Brooklyn, NY 11238; **Phone:** 718-638-3640; **Board Cert:** Dermatology 1975; **Med School:** SUNY Downstate 1968; **Resid:** Internal Medicine, St Luke's-Roosevelt Hosp Ctr 1969; Dermatology, SUNY Downstate Med Ctr/Kings County Med Ctr 1974; **Fac Appt:** Asst Clin Prof D, SUNY Downstate

Deitz, Marcia MD (D) - **Spec Exp:** Acne; Psoriasis; Warts; Eczema; **Hospital:** Coney Island Hosp; **Address:** 1486 Ocean Pkwy, Brooklyn, NY 11230-6453; **Phone:** 718-627-3024; **Board Cert:** Dermatology 1984; **Med School:** SUNY Downstate 1980; **Resid:** Internal Medicine, Brookdale Hosp 1981; Dermatology, NY Med Coll Affil Hosps 1984; **Fac Appt:** Asst Clin Prof Med, NY Coll Osteo Med

Feldman, Philip MD (D) - **Spec Exp:** Acne; Eczema; Psoriasis; **Hospital:** SUNY Downstate Med Ctr (Univ Hosp Brooklyn) (page 449); **Address:** 142 Joralemon St, Ste 4B, Brooklyn, NY 11201-4709; **Phone:** 718-237-0404; **Board Cert:** Dermatology 1970; **Med School:** Switzerland 1963; **Resid:** Dermatology, NY Presby Hosp 1967; **Fac Appt:** Asst Clin Prof D, SUNY Downstate

Frankel, David H MD (D) - **Spec Exp:** Skin Cancer; Eczema; Contact Dermatitis; **Hospital:** New York Methodist Hosp (page 448), Maimonides Med Ctr (page 98); **Address:** 263 7th Ave, Ste 5F, Brooklyn, NY 11215; **Phone:** 718-369-3559; **Board Cert:** Internal Medicine 1985; Dermatology 2004; **Med School:** Boston Univ 1982; **Resid:** Internal Medicine, Univ Chicago Hosps 1985; Dermatology, Univ Chicago Hosps 1988; **Fellow:** Mohs Surgery, Amer Coll Mohs Micro Surg 1989; **Fac Appt:** Asst Clin Prof D, Mount Sinai Sch Med

Glick, Sharon A MD (D) - **Spec Exp:** Pediatric Dermatology; **Hospital:** SUNY Downstate Med Ctr (Univ Hosp Brooklyn) (page 449), Kings Co Hosp Ctr; **Address:** SUNY Downstate Med Ctr, Dept Dermatology, 450 Clarkson Ave, Box 46, Brooklyn, NY 11203; **Phone:** 718-270-1230; **Board Cert:** Dermatology 2013; Pediatric Dermatology 2004; **Med School:** Albert Einstein Coll Med 1988; **Resid:** Pediatrics, Yale-New Haven Hosp 1991; Dermatology, Yale-New Haven Hosp 1994; **Fac Appt:** Assoc Prof D, SUNY Downstate

Levit, Eyal K MD (D) - **Spec Exp:** Laser Surgery; Botox Therapy; Cosmetic Surgery; Facial Rejuvenation; **Hospital:** Mt Sinai St. Luke's; **Address:** Advanced Derm Laser & Cosmetic Surg, 1220 Avenue P, Brooklyn, NY 11229; **Phone:** 718-375-7546; **Board Cert:** Dermatology 2007; **Med School:** Albert Einstein Coll Med 1995; **Resid:** Dermatology, NY-Presby/Columbia Univ Med Ctr 1999; **Fellow:** Mohs Surgery, Hosp Univ Penn 2000; Laser Surgery, NY-Presby/Columbia Univ Med Ctr 2002; **Fac Appt:** Assoc Clin Prof D, Columbia P&S

Shapiro, Michael D MD (D) - **Spec Exp:** Mohs Surgery; Cosmetic Dermatology; Skin Cancer; **Hospital:** Mt Sinai Hosp; **Address:** Vanguard Dermatology, 2408 Ocean Ave, Brooklyn, NY 11229; **Phone:** 718-332-2999; **Board Cert:** Dermatology 2012; **Med School:** Univ Pennsylvania 1999; **Resid:** Dermatology, Hosp Univ Penn-UPHS 2004; **Fellow:** Mohs Surgery, Univ CO Hlth Science Ctr 2005

Simon, Steven I MD (D) - **Spec Exp:** Skin Cancer; Botox Therapy; Laser Hair Removal; **Hospital:** SUNY Downstate Med Ctr (Univ Hosp Brooklyn) (page 449), Franklin Hosp; **Address:** 2270 Kimball St, rm 201, Brooklyn, NY 11234-5139; **Phone:** 718-253-4550; **Board Cert:** Dermatology 1981; **Med School:** Mexico 1975; **Resid:** Internal Medicine, Brookdale Hosp 1978; Dermatology, Downstate Med Ctr 1981; **Fac Appt:** Assoc Clin Prof D, SUNY Hlth Sci Ctr

Diagnostic Radiology

Amodio, John B MD (DR) - **Spec Exp:** Pediatric Radiology; **Hospital:** Kings Co Hosp Ctr, SUNY Downstate Med Ctr (Univ Hosp Brooklyn) (page 449); **Address:** SUNY Downstate Med Ctr, Dept Radiology, 450 Clarkson Ave, Box 1198, Brooklyn, NY 11203; **Phone:** 718-270-1603; **Board Cert:** Diagnostic Radiology 1984; Pediatric Radiology 2005; **Med School:** NY Med Coll 1980; **Resid:** Diagnostic Radiology, Montefiore Med Ctr 1984; **Fellow:** Pediatric Radiology, Columbia-Presby Med Ctr 1985

Garner, Steven Charles MD (DR) - **Spec Exp:** Trauma Radiology; **Hospital:** New York Methodist Hosp (page 448); **Address:** 506 6th St, Brooklyn, NY 11215; **Phone:** 718-780-5870; **Board Cert:** Diagnostic Radiology 1984; **Med School:** Ros Franklin Univ/Chicago Med Sch 1976; **Resid:** Diagnostic Radiology, Mt Sinai Hosp 1983

Lerman, Jay E MD (DR) - **Spec Exp:** Urologic Imaging; Musculoskeletal Imaging; **Address:** Lerman Diagnostic Imaging, 6511 Fort Hamilton Pkwy, Brooklyn, NY 11219; **Phone:** 718-491-4545; **Board Cert:** Diagnostic Radiology 1991; **Med School:** Albert Einstein Coll Med 1986; **Resid:** Diagnostic Radiology, Montefiore Med Ctr 1991; **Fellow:** Cross Sectional Imaging, Thomas Jefferson Univ Hosp 1992

Endocrinology, Diabetes & Metabolism

Brickman, Alan M MD (EDM) - **Spec Exp:** Diabetes; Thyroid Disorders; Cholesterol/Lipid Disorders; Calcium Disorders; **Hospital:** Maimonides Med Ctr (page 98); **Address:** 1318 52nd St, Brooklyn, NY 11219-3802; **Phone:** 718-436-9898; **Board Cert:** Internal Medicine 1979; Endocrinology, Diabetes & Metabolism 1981; **Med School:** Albert Einstein Coll Med 1976; **Resid:** Internal Medicine, Maimonides Med Ctr 1979; **Fellow:** Endocrinology, Diabetes & Metabolism, Yale-New Haven Hosp 1981

Giegerich, Edmund W MD (EDM) - **Spec Exp:** Thyroid Disorders; Diabetes; **Hospital:** New York Methodist Hosp (page 448); **Address:** 263 7th Ave, Ste 5A, Brooklyn, NY 11215; **Phone:** 718-246-8600; **Board Cert:** Internal Medicine 1980; Endocrinology, Diabetes & Metabolism 1983; **Med School:** SUNY Downstate 1977; **Resid:** Internal Medicine, Rhode Island Hosp 1980; **Fellow:** Endocrinology, Diabetes & Metabolism, Mount Sinai Hosp 1982; **Fac Appt:** Assoc Clin Prof Med, SUNY Hlth Sci Ctr

Goldman, Joel M MD (EDM) - **Spec Exp:** Thyroid Disorders; Diabetes; Calcium Disorders; **Hospital:** Brookdale Univ Hosp Med Ctr, Mt Sinai Beth Israel-BK; **Address:** 1 Brookdale Plaza, rm 101A-SBSI, Brooklyn, NY 11212-3132; **Phone:** 718-240-5378; **Board Cert:** Internal Medicine 1976; Endocrinology, Diabetes & Metabolism 1979; **Med School:** Univ Ariz Coll Med 1973; **Resid:** Internal Medicine, UMDNJ-Newark Affil Hosps 1975; Internal Medicine, Albert Einstein Coll Med 1976; **Fellow:** Endocrinology, Diabetes & Metabolism, NIAMDD-Natl Inst Hlth 1979; **Fac Appt:** Assoc Prof Med, SUNY Downstate

Park, Patricia MD (EDM) - **Spec Exp:** Diabetes; Thyroid Disorders; Osteoporosis; Pituitary Disorders; **Hospital:** Maimonides Med Ctr (page 98); **Address:** 984 50th St Fl 2, Brooklyn, NY 11219; **Phone:** 718-283-5923; **Board Cert:** Endocrinology, Diabetes & Metabolism 2008; Pediatrics 2012; Pediatric Endocrinology 2007; **Med School:** NY Med Coll 1999; **Resid:** Internal Medicine & Pediatrics, Penn State Med Ctr 2003; **Fellow:** Pediatric Endocrinology, UCLA Med Ctr 2006; Endocrinology, Diabetes & Metabolism, Cedars Sinai Med Ctr 2008

Resta, Christine MD (EDM) - **Spec Exp:** Diabetes; Thyroid Disorders; Osteoporosis; **Hospital:** Maimonides Med Ctr (page 98); **Address:** 984 50th St Fl 2, Brooklyn, NY 11219; **Phone:** 718-283-5923; **Board Cert:** Internal Medicine 2012; Endocrinology, Diabetes & Metabolism 2005; **Med School:** Albert Einstein Coll Med 1989; **Resid:** Internal Medicine, Montefiore Med Ctr 1992; **Fellow:** Endocrinology, Diabetes & Metabolism, Montefiore Med Ctr 1994

Silverberg, Arnold MD (EDM) - **Spec Exp:** Thyroid Disorders; Osteoporosis; Diabetes; **Hospital:** Maimonides Med Ctr (page 98); **Address:** 1301 57th St, Brooklyn, NY 11219; **Phone:** 718-283-6200; **Board Cert:** Internal Medicine 1968; Endocrinology 1977; **Med School:** Albert Einstein Coll Med 1961; **Resid:** Internal Medicine, Montefiore Med Ctr 1965; Internal Medicine, Mt Sinai Med Ctr 1964; **Fellow:** Endocrinology, Diabetes & Metabolism, Mt Sinai Med Ctr 1968

Warman, Jacob MD (EDM) - **Spec Exp:** Pituitary Disorders; Calcium Disorders; Thyroid Disorders; **Hospital:** Brooklyn Hosp Ctr; **Address:** 121 DeKalb Ave Fl 2, Brooklyn, NY 11201; **Phone:** 718-250-8000; **Board Cert:** Internal Medicine 1976; Endocrinology, Diabetes & Metabolism 1979; **Med School:** SUNY Downstate 1973; **Resid:** Internal Medicine, Maimonides Med Ctr 1976; **Fellow:** Endocrinology, Diabetes & Metabolism, Jewish Hosp 1978

Weinerman, Stuart A MD (EDM) - **Spec Exp:** Osteoporosis; Calcium Disorders; Paget's Disease of Bone; **Hospital:** N Shore Univ Hosp, Long Is Jewish Med Ctr; **Address:** 865 Northern Blvd, Ste 203, Great Neck, NY 11201; **Phone:** 516-708-2540; **Board Cert:** Internal Medicine 1987; Endocrinology, Diabetes & Metabolism 1989; **Med School:** Albert Einstein Coll Med 1984; **Resid:** Internal Medicine, N Shore Univ Hosp 1987; **Fellow:** Endocrinology, Diabetes & Metabolism, NY Hosp/Meml Sloan Kettering Cancer Ctr 1989

Family Medicine

Grady, Laura DO (FMed) *PCP* - **Hospital:** Lutheran Med Ctr - Brooklyn; **Address:** Family Physician Health Ctr, 5616 6th Ave, Brooklyn, NY 11220; **Phone:** 718-439-5440; **Board Cert:** Family Medicine 2008; **Med School:** NY Coll Osteo Med 1998; **Resid:** Family Medicine, Lutheran Med Ctr 2001

Krotowski, Mark MD (FMed) *PCP* - **Spec Exp:** Caribbean Health Care; Hypertension; Diabetes; **Hospital:** Brookdale Univ Hosp Med Ctr, SUNY Downstate Med Ctr (Univ Hosp Brooklyn) (page 449); **Address:** 8923 Avenue A, Brooklyn, NY 11236-1206; **Phone:** 718-385-8181; **Board Cert:** Family Medicine 2008; **Med School:** Israel 1976; **Resid:** Pediatrics, Brookdale Univ Hosp 1977; Family Medicine, Brookdale Univ Hosp 1979; **Fac Appt:** Assoc Clin Prof FMed, SUNY Downstate

Lopez, Clark R MD (FMed) *PCP* - **Hospital:** New York Methodist Hosp (page 448), Lutheran Med Ctr - Brooklyn; **Address:** 60 Plaza St E, Brooklyn, NY 11238; **Phone:** 718-783-3919; **Board Cert:** Family Medicine 2013; **Med School:** SUNY Downstate 1972; **Resid:** Family Medicine, Kings County Hosp 1976; **Fellow:** Family Medicine, Kings County Hosp 1977

Lyon, Claudia DO (FMed) *PCP* - **Hospital:** Lutheran Med Ctr - Brooklyn; **Address:** Family Physician Health Ctr, 5616 6th Ave, Brooklyn, NY 11220; **Phone:** 718-439-5440; **Board Cert:** Family Medicine 2013; **Med School:** NY Coll Osteo Med 1988; **Resid:** Family Medicine, Lutheran Med Ctr 1991

Sadovsky, Richard MD (FMed) *PCP* - **Spec Exp:** Preventive Medicine; Diabetes; Hepatitis; Thyroid Disorders; **Hospital:** SUNY Downstate Med Ctr (Univ Hosp Brooklyn) (page 449); **Address:** 450 Clarkson Ave, Ste B, Box 67, Brooklyn, NY 11203-2012; **Phone:** 718-270-2697; **Board Cert:** Family Medicine 2008; **Med School:** SUNY Hlth Sci Ctr 1974; **Resid:** Family Medicine, SUNY Hosp 1977; **Fac Appt:** Assoc Prof FMed, SUNY Hlth Sci Ctr

Schiowitz, Emanuel DO (FMed) *PCP* - **Hospital:** Maimonides Med Ctr (page 98); **Address:** 1701 59th St, Brooklyn, NY 11204-2254; **Phone:** 718-259-0222; **Board Cert:** Family Medicine 1968; **Med School:** Philadelphia Coll Osteo Med 1963; **Resid:** Family Medicine, Interboro Med Ctr 1964; **Fac Appt:** Asst Clin Prof FMed, NY Coll Osteo Med

Vincent, Miriam MD/PhD (FMed) *PCP* - **Spec Exp:** Diabetes; Arthritis; Preventive Medicine; **Hospital:** SUNY Downstate Med Ctr (Univ Hosp Brooklyn) (page 449), Kings Co Hosp Ctr; **Address:** 470 Clarkson Ave, Ste B, Brooklyn, NY 11203-2012; **Phone:** 718-270-1801; **Board Cert:** Family Medicine 2008; **Med School:** SUNY Hlth Sci Ctr 1985; **Resid:** Family Medicine, SUNY Downstate Med Ctr 1988; **Fac Appt:** Prof FMed, SUNY Hlth Sci Ctr

Gastroenterology

Erber, William MD (Ge) - **Spec Exp:** Endoscopy; Inflammatory Bowel Disease/Crohn's; Gastrointestinal Cancer; Capsule Endoscopy; **Hospital:** Maimonides Med Ctr (page 98), Mt Sinai Beth Israel; **Address:** 591 Ocean Pkwy, Brooklyn, NY 11218-5913; **Phone:** 718-972-8500; **Board Cert:** Internal Medicine 1975; Gastroenterology 1979; **Med School:** Ros Franklin Univ/Chicago Med Sch 1967; **Resid:** Internal Medicine, Maimonides Med Ctr 1969; Internal Medicine, Maimonides Med Ctr 1973; **Fellow:** Research, Hadassah Hosp 1972; Gastroenterology, Albert Einstein Coll Med 1975; **Fac Appt:** Asst Clin Prof Med, SUNY Downstate

Gamss, Jeffrey S MD (Ge) - **Spec Exp:** Colonoscopy; **Hospital:** NYU Langone Med Ctr (page 104); **Address:** 1630 E 14th St, Brooklyn, NY 11229; **Phone:** 718-692-1198; **Board Cert:** Internal Medicine 1986; Gastroenterology 1989; **Med School:** SUNY Downstate 1983; **Resid:** Internal Medicine, Brookdale Hosp 1986; **Fellow:** Gastroenterology, SUNY Downstate 1988

Gettenberg, Gary S MD (Ge) - **Spec Exp:** Gastrointestinal Cancer; Colon Cancer Screening; Gastroesophageal Reflux Disease (GERD); Celiac Disease; **Hospital:** Maimonides Med Ctr (page 98), New York Methodist Hosp (page 448); **Address:** 1630 E 14th St, Brooklyn, NY 11229-1104; **Phone:** 718-339-0391; **Board Cert:** Internal Medicine 1987; Gastroenterology 1989; **Med School:** NY Med Coll 1983; **Resid:** Internal Medicine, Maimonides Med Ctr 1986; **Fellow:** Gastroenterology, Maimonides Med Ctr 1989

Gupta, Jagdish K MD (Ge) - **Spec Exp:** Colon Cancer; Hepatitis; Peptic Ulcer Disease; **Hospital:** New York Methodist Hosp (page 448); **Address:** 207 Berkeley Pl, Brooklyn, NY 11217; **Phone:** 718-638-3150; **Board Cert:** Internal Medicine 1975; Gastroenterology 1977; **Med School:** India 1970; **Resid:** Internal Medicine, LI Coll Hosp 1975; **Fellow:** Gastroenterology, LI Coll Hosp 1977; **Fac Appt:** Asst Clin Prof Med, SUNY Downstate

Iswara, Kadirawelpillai MD (Ge) - **Spec Exp:** Pancreatic/Biliary Endoscopy (ERCP); Colonoscopy; Endoscopy; Hepatitis; **Hospital:** Maimonides Med Ctr (page 98); **Address:** 6010 Bay Pkwy, Ste 801, Brooklyn, NY 11204; **Phone:** 718-615-0400; **Board Cert:** Internal Medicine 1980; Gastroenterology 1975; **Med School:** Sri Lanka 1968; **Resid:** Internal Medicine, Coney Island Hosp 1972; Internal Medicine, Bronx VA Hosp 1973; **Fellow:** Gastroenterology, Maimonides Med Ctr 1976; **Fac Appt:** Asst Clin Prof Med, Mount Sinai Sch Med

Leb, Alvin D MD (Ge) - **Spec Exp:** Endoscopy; **Hospital:** Mt Sinai Beth Israel-BK; **Address:** 2985 Quentin Rd, Brooklyn, NY 11229; **Phone:** 718-336-2218; **Board Cert:** Internal Medicine 1985; Gastroenterology 1989; **Med School:** SUNY Downstate 1982; **Resid:** Internal Medicine, Brookdale Univ Hosp 1985; **Fellow:** Gastroenterology, Brookdale Univ Hosp 1988

Maizel, Barry MD (Ge) - **Spec Exp:** Endoscopy; Inflammatory Bowel Disease; Liver Disease; **Hospital:** New York Methodist Hosp (page 448), NY Hosp Queens (page 498); **Address:** 90 8th Ave, Brooklyn, NY 11215-1553; **Phone:** 718-622-8255; **Board Cert:** Internal Medicine 1979; Gastroenterology 1981; **Med School:** Italy 1975; **Resid:** Internal Medicine, Jewish Hosp 1978; **Fellow:** Gastroenterology, NY Med Coll-Metropolitan Hosp 1980

Mayer, Ira E MD (Ge) - **Spec Exp:** Inflammatory Bowel Disease/Crohn's; Gastroesophageal Reflux Disease (GERD); Gastrointestinal Motility Disorders; **Hospital:** Maimonides Med Ctr (page 98); **Address:** 575 Kings Hwy, Brooklyn, NY 11223; **Phone:** 718-891-0100; **Board Cert:** Internal Medicine 1978; Gastroenterology 1981; **Med School:** NY Med Coll 1975; **Resid:** Internal Medicine, Metropolitan Hosp Ctr 1978; **Fellow:** Gastroenterology, Emory Univ Hosp 1980; **Fac Appt:** Asst Clin Prof Med, SUNY Downstate

Notar-Francesco, Vincent J MD (Ge) - **Hospital:** New York Methodist Hosp (page 448); **Address:** 263 7th Ave, Ste 5A, Brooklyn, NY 11215; **Phone:** 718-246-8600; **Board Cert:** Internal Medicine 1989; Gastroenterology 2011; **Med School:** Mount Sinai Sch Med 1986; **Resid:** Internal Medicine, Stony Brook Univ Hosp 1989; **Fellow:** Gastroenterology, SUNY Downstate Med Ctr 1991

Piccione, Paul R MD (Ge) - **Hospital:** Lutheran Med Ctr - Brooklyn; **Address:** 560 Bay Ridge Pkwy, Brooklyn, NY 11209-2702; **Phone:** 718-748-5219; **Board Cert:** Internal Medicine 1985; Gastroenterology 1987; **Med School:** Italy 1981; **Resid:** Internal Medicine, Lutheran Med Ctr 1985; **Fellow:** Gastroenterology, St Luke's-Roosevelt Hosp 1987

Sohn, Won MD (Ge) - **Spec Exp:** Endoscopy; Pancreatic/Biliary Endoscopy (ERCP); **Hospital:** New York Methodist Hosp (page 448); **Address:** 213-33 39th Ave, Ste 428, Bayside, NY 11361; **Phone:** 718-428-5333; **Board Cert:** Internal Medicine 2010; Gastroenterology 2010; **Med School:** SUNY Downstate 1994; **Resid:** Internal Medicine, Yale-New Haven Hosp 1997; **Fellow:** Gastroenterology, NY-Presby Med Ctr 2000

Sorra, Toomas Mihkel MD (Ge) - **Spec Exp:** Colon & Rectal Cancer; Hepatitis; Gastroesophageal Reflux Disease (GERD); **Hospital:** SUNY Downstate Med Ctr (Univ Hosp Brooklyn) (page 449); **Address:** 166 Clinton St, Brooklyn, NY 11201-4618; **Phone:** 718-834-0100; **Board Cert:** Internal Medicine 1981; Gastroenterology 1983; **Med School:** Mexico 1975; **Resid:** Internal Medicine, LI Coll Hosp 1980; **Fellow:** Gastroenterology, LI Coll Hosp 1982; **Fac Appt:** Asst Prof Med, SUNY Downstate

Stollman, Yacov MD (Ge) - **Spec Exp:** Endoscopy & Colonoscopy; **Hospital:** New York Methodist Hosp (page 448); **Address:** 7124 18th Ave, Brooklyn, NY 11204; **Phone:** 718-234-3333; **Board Cert:** Internal Medicine 1980; Gastroenterology 1983; **Med School:** Albert Einstein Coll Med 1977; **Resid:** Internal Medicine, Brookdale Univ Hosp 1980; **Fellow:** Gastroenterology, Albert Einstein Coll Med Affil Hosp 1982

Vignesh, Shivakumar MD (Ge) - **Spec Exp:** Endoscopic Ultrasound; Interventional Endoscopy; **Hospital:** SUNY Downstate Med Ctr (Univ Hosp Brooklyn) (page 449); **Address:** SUNY Downstate Med Ctr, Gastroenterology, 470 Clarkson Ave, Ste A, Brooklyn, NY 11203; **Phone:** 718-270-4772; **Board Cert:** Gastroenterology 2013; **Med School:** India 1996; **Resid:** Internal Medicine, RWJ Univ Hosp 2000; **Fellow:** Gastroenterology, Thomas Jefferson Univ/Albert Einstein Med Ctr 2002; Endoscopy, Yale-New Haven Hosp 2003; **Fac Appt:** Assoc Prof Med, SUNY Downstate

Zimbalist, Eliot MD (Ge) - **Spec Exp:** Colon Cancer Screening; Hepatitis C; Irritable Bowel Syndrome; Inflammatory Bowel Disease; **Hospital:** Maimonides Med Ctr (page 98), Lutheran Med Ctr - Brooklyn; **Address:** 452 77 St, Brooklyn, NY 11209-3206; **Phone:** 718-921-5548; **Board Cert:** Internal Medicine 1983; Gastroenterology 1985; **Med School:** Mount Sinai Sch Med 1980; **Resid:** Internal Medicine, Maimonides Med Ctr 1983; **Fellow:** Gastroenterology, Meml Sloan-Kettering Cancer Ctr 1985

Geriatric Medicine

Baccash Jr, Emil G MD (Ger) *PCP* - **Spec Exp:** Geriatric Care; Preventive Medicine; **Hospital:** New York Methodist Hosp (page 448); **Address:** 20 8th Ave, Brooklyn, NY 11217; **Phone:** 718-622-7000; **Board Cert:** Internal Medicine 1981; Geriatric Medicine 2005; **Med School:** Italy 1978; **Resid:** Internal Medicine, NY Methodist Hosp 1981

Paris, Barbara E MD (Ger) *PCP* - **Spec Exp:** Preventive Medicine; Frail Elderly; Cognitive Loss in Aging; **Hospital:** Maimonides Med Ctr (page 98), Mt Sinai Hosp; **Address:** Maimonides Med Ctr, Geriatrics, 4802 10th Ave, Brooklyn, NY 11219; **Phone:** 718-283-7071; **Board Cert:** Internal Medicine 1982; Geriatric Medicine 2008; **Med School:** SUNY Downstate 1977; **Resid:** Internal Medicine, St Vincents Hosp 1980; **Fellow:** Geriatric Medicine, Mt Sinai Hosp 1986; **Fac Appt:** Clin Prof Med, Mount Sinai-Icahn Sch of Med

Geriatric Psychiatry

Amin, Ravindra N MD (GerPsy) - **Spec Exp:** Alzheimer's Disease; Anxiety Disorders; Depression; Memory Disorders; **Address:** 161 Atlantic Ave, Brooklyn, NY 11201; **Phone:** 718-237-2150; **Board Cert:** Psychiatry 1993; Geriatric Psychiatry 2004; Addiction Psychiatry 2006; **Med School:** India 1985; **Resid:** Psychiatry, Elmhurst Hosp 1992; **Fellow:** Geriatric Psychiatry, Mt Sinai Med Ctr 1994

Cohen, Carl MD (GerPsy) - **Spec Exp:** Alzheimer's Disease; Schizophrenia; Depression in the Elderly; **Hospital:** SUNY Downstate Med Ctr (Univ Hosp Brooklyn) (page 449); **Address:** SUNY Downstate Med Ctr, Psychiatry, 370 Lenox Rd, Brooklyn, NY 11226; **Phone:** 718-287-4806; **Board Cert:** Psychiatry 1977; Geriatric Psychiatry 2009; **Med School:** SUNY Buffalo 1971; **Resid:** Psychiatry, NYU Med Ctr 1974; **Fellow:** Geriatric Psychiatry, NYU Med Ctr 1975; **Fac Appt:** Prof Psyc, SUNY Hlth Sci Ctr

Greenberg, Robert M MD (GerPsy) - **Spec Exp:** Electroconvulsive Therapy (ECT); Neuro-Psychiatry; **Hospital:** Lutheran Med Ctr - Brooklyn; **Address:** Lutheran Med Ctr, Psychiatry Dept, 150 55th St, Brooklyn, NY 11220; **Phone:** 718-630-8600; **Board Cert:** Psychiatry 1986; Geriatric Psychiatry 2011; **Med School:** Mount Sinai Sch Med 1978; **Resid:** Psychiatry, NY-Presby/Westchester Div 1983

Rosen, Evelyn MD (GerPsy) - **Hospital:** New York Methodist Hosp (page 448); **Address:** 583 5th St, Brooklyn, NY 11215-3503; **Phone:** 212-813-9410; **Board Cert:** Psychiatry 1992; **Med School:** Mexico 1986; **Resid:** Psychiatry, SUNY Hlth Sci Ctr 1991; **Fellow:** Geriatric Psychiatry, SUNY Hlth Sci Ctr 1992

Gynecologic Oncology

Khulpateea, Neekianund MD (GO) - **Spec Exp:** Hysterectomy Alternatives; Gynecologic Cancer; **Hospital:** Maimonides Med Ctr (page 98); **Address:** Maimonides Med Ctr, Div Gyn Onc, 953 49th St Fl 2, Brooklyn, NY 11219-2923; **Phone:** 718-283-7370; **Board Cert:** Obstetrics & Gynecology 1981; **Med School:** Israel 1972; **Resid:** Obstetrics & Gynecology, NY Methodist Hosp 1976; **Fellow:** Gynecologic Oncology, SUNY Downstate Med Ctr 1978; **Fac Appt:** Assoc Prof ObG, SUNY Downstate

Serur, Eli MD (GO) - **Spec Exp:** Gynecologic Cancer; Laparoscopic Surgery; Nutrition & Cancer; **Hospital:** Brooklyn Hosp Ctr, Richmond Univ Med Ctr; **Address:** 240 Willoughby St, Ste 3A, Brooklyn, NY 11201; **Phone:** 718-250-8106; **Board Cert:** Obstetrics & Gynecology 2013; Gynecologic Oncology 2013; **Med School:** NYU Sch Med 1985; **Resid:** Obstetrics & Gynecology, Kings County Hosp 1989; **Fellow:** Gynecologic Oncology, Kings County Hosp 1991; **Fac Appt:** Asst Clin Prof ObG, Cornell Univ-Weill Med Coll

Hand Surgery

Choueka, Jack MD (HS) - **Spec Exp:** Hand & Upper Extremity Surgery; Rotator Cuff Surgery; Wrist Surgery; Shoulder Surgery; **Hospital:** Maimonides Med Ctr (page 98); **Address:** Maimonides Bone & Joint Ctr, 6010 Bay Pkwy Fl 7, Brooklyn, NY 11204; **Phone:** 718-283-7400; **Board Cert:** Orthopaedic Surgery 2011; Hand Surgery 2011; **Med School:** SUNY Hlth Sci Ctr 1991; **Resid:** Orthopaedic Surgery, NYU Hosp Joint Diseases 1996; **Fellow:** Hand Surgery, Univ Chicago Med Ctr 1998

Hematology

Cook, Perry C MD (Hem) - **Spec Exp:** Bone Marrow Transplant; Leukemia; Lymphoma; **Hospital:** New York Methodist Hosp (page 448); **Address:** 343 4th Ave, Brooklyn, NY 11215; **Phone:** 718-780-5246; **Board Cert:** Internal Medicine 1980; Hematology 1982; Medical Oncology 1983; **Med School:** Univ Iowa Coll Med 1977; **Resid:** Internal Medicine, St Luke's-Roosevelt Hosp Ctr 1979; Internal Medicine, NY-Presby/Columbia Univ Med Ctr 1980; **Fellow:** Hematology & Oncology, NY-Presby/Columbia Univ Med Ctr 1983; **Fac Appt:** Assoc Prof Med, NYU Sch Med

Dosik, Harvey MD (Hem) - **Spec Exp:** Leukemia & Lymphoma; Anemia; Multiple Myeloma; **Hospital:** New York Methodist Hosp (page 448); **Address:** 500 4th Ave, Ste 1, Brooklyn, NY 11215-3609; **Phone:** 718-208-1820; **Board Cert:** Internal Medicine 1970; Hematology 1976; **Med School:** NYU Sch Med 1963; **Resid:** Internal Medicine, Kings County Hosp 1967; **Fellow:** Hematology, Maimonides Med Ctr 1969

Solomon, William B MD (Hem) - **Spec Exp:** Sickle Cell Disease; Lymphoma; Clinical Trials; **Hospital:** Maimonides Med Ctr (page 98); **Address:** Maimonides Med Ctr, Hem/Onc Dept, 6300 8th Ave Fl 2, Brooklyn, NY 11220; **Phone:** 718-765-2613; **Board Cert:** Internal Medicine 1978; Hematology 1982; Medical Oncology 1985; **Med School:** Columbia P&S 1975; **Resid:** Internal Medicine, Montefiore Med Ctr 1978; **Fellow:** Hematology, Beth Israel Deaconess Med Ctr 1981; Molecular Biology, Mass Inst Tech; **Fac Appt:** Prof Med, SUNY Downstate

Hospice & Palliative Medicine

Popp, Beth MD (H & PM) - **Spec Exp:** Palliative Care; Pain-Cancer; Pain-Chronic; Pain Management; **Hospital:** Maimonides Med Ctr (page 98); **Address:** 6300 Eighth Ave, Brooklyn, NY 11220; **Phone:** 718-765-2600; **Board Cert:** Medical Oncology 2008; Hospice & Palliative Medicine 2010; **Med School:** Indiana Univ 1988; **Resid:** Internal Medicine, IU Hlth Affil Hosp 1991; **Fellow:** Medical Oncology, IU Hlth Affil Hosp 1993; Hospice & Palliative Medicine, Meml Sloan-Kettering Cancer Ctr 1995

Infectious Disease

Augenbraun, Michael H MD (Inf) - **Spec Exp:** AIDS/HIV; Sexually Transmitted Diseases; Infections-Opportunistic; **Hospital:** SUNY Downstate Med Ctr (Univ Hosp Brooklyn) (page 449), Kings Co Hosp Ctr; **Address:** 450 Clarkson Ave, rm B5-302, Box 56, Brooklyn, NY 11203; **Phone:** 718-270-1432; **Board Cert:** Internal Medicine 1988; Infectious Disease 2010; **Med School:** Univ Rochester 1985; **Resid:** Internal Medicine, North Shore Univ Hosp 1986; Internal Medicine, Meml Sloan-Kettering Cancer Ctr 1988; **Fellow:** Infectious Disease, SUNY Downstate Med Ctr 1990; **Fac Appt:** Prof Med, SUNY Hlth Sci Ctr

Berkowitz, Leonard B MD (Inf) - **Spec Exp:** AIDS/HIV; **Hospital:** Brooklyn Hosp Ctr; **Address:** 121 DeKalb Ave, Ste 5H, Brooklyn, NY 11201-5425; **Phone:** 718-250-6922; **Board Cert:** Internal Medicine 1980; Infectious Disease 1984; **Med School:** SUNY Downstate 1977; **Resid:** Internal Medicine, Kings Co Hosp Ctr 1981; **Fellow:** Infectious Disease, Kings Co Hosp Ctr 1983; **Fac Appt:** Asst Clin Prof Med, SUNY Hlth Sci Ctr

Chapnick, Edward K MD (Inf) - **Spec Exp:** AIDS/HIV; Travel Medicine; Antibiotic Resistance; **Hospital:** Maimonides Med Ctr (page 98); **Address:** Maimonides Med Ctr, Div Infectious Dis, 4802 10th Ave, Brooklyn, NY 11219-2844; **Phone:** 718-283-7492; **Board Cert:** Internal Medicine 1988; Infectious Disease 2012; **Med School:** SUNY Downstate 1985; **Resid:** Internal Medicine, Maimonides Med Ctr 1989; **Fellow:** Infectious Disease, Maimonides Med Ctr 1991; **Fac Appt:** Assoc Prof Med, SUNY Downstate

Cofsky, Richard D MD (Inf) - **Spec Exp:** Meningitis; Tuberculosis; AIDS/HIV; **Hospital:** Brookdale Univ Hosp Med Ctr; **Address:** Brookdale Univ Hosp, 1 Brookdale Plaza, rm 596, Brooklyn, NY 11212-3139; **Phone:** 718-240-5096; **Board Cert:** Internal Medicine 1981; Infectious Disease 1984; **Med School:** Univ MD Sch Med 1978; **Resid:** Internal Medicine, Maimonides Med Ctr 1981; **Fellow:** Infectious Disease, Downstate Med Ctr 1984

Landesman, Sheldon H MD (Inf) - **Spec Exp:** AIDS/HIV; Clinical Trials; **Hospital:** SUNY Downstate Med Ctr (Univ Hosp Brooklyn) (page 449); **Address:** SUNY Downstate Med Ctr, 450 Clarkson Ave, MS 97, Brooklyn, NY 11203; **Phone:** 718-270-3034; **Board Cert:** Internal Medicine 1976; **Med School:** SUNY Downstate 1972; **Resid:** Interventional Cardiology, Tufts-New England Med Ctr 1976; **Fellow:** Research, Baltimore Cancer Rsrch Inst/NCI 1977; Infectious Disease, Tufts-New England Med Ctr 1978; **Fac Appt:** Prof Med, SUNY Downstate

Pujol-Morato, Fernando A MD (Inf) - **Spec Exp:** AIDS/HIV; **Hospital:** New York Methodist Hosp (page 448); **Address:** 460 13th St, Brooklyn, NY 11215; **Phone:** 718-636-7400; **Board Cert:** Internal Medicine 1986; Infectious Disease 1988; **Med School:** Dominican Republic 1979; **Resid:** Internal Medicine, LI College Hosp 1985; **Fellow:** Infectious Disease, LI College Hosp 1987; **Fac Appt:** Asst Prof Med, Cornell Univ-Weill Med Coll

Stein, Alan J MD (Inf) - **Spec Exp:** AIDS/HIV; Travel Medicine; **Hospital:** New York Methodist Hosp (page 448), Brooklyn Hosp Ctr; **Address:** 348 13th St, Ste 201, Brooklyn, NY 11215; **Phone:** 718-369-4850; **Board Cert:** Internal Medicine 1976; Infectious Disease 1978; **Med School:** NY Med Coll 1972; **Resid:** Internal Medicine, Lenox Hill Hosp 1974; Internal Medicine, Metropolitan Hosp Ctr 1976; **Fellow:** Infectious Disease, NYU Med Ctr 1978; **Fac Appt:** Assoc Clin Prof Med, NYU Sch Med

Internal Medicine

Behm, Dutsi MD (IM) *PCP* - **Hospital:** New York Methodist Hosp (page 448), Maimonides Med Ctr (page 98); **Address:** 421 Ocean Pkwy, Ste 2A, Brooklyn, NY 11218-2408; **Phone:** 718-438-8585; **Med School:** Ukraine 1973; **Resid:** Internal Medicine, NY Methodist Hosp 1983

Bharathan, Thayyullathil MD (IM) *PCP* - **Spec Exp:** Alzheimer's Disease; Dementia; Palliative Care; Pain Management; **Hospital:** New York Methodist Hosp (page 448); **Address:** 263 7th Ave, Ste 5A, Brooklyn, NY 11215-3691; **Phone:** 718-246-8561; **Board Cert:** Internal Medicine 1976; **Med School:** India 1962; **Resid:** Internal Medicine, NY Methodist Hosp 1973; **Fac Appt:** Asst Clin Prof Med, Cornell Univ-Weill Med Coll

Butt, Ahmar A MD (IM) *PCP* - **Spec Exp:** Hypertension; Congestive Heart Failure; Cholesterol/Lipid Disorders; Diabetes; **Hospital:** Brooklyn Hosp Ctr; **Address:** Health Styles Medical, 55 Greene Ave, Ste 1-A, Brooklyn, NY 11238; **Phone:** 718-857-0404; **Board Cert:** Internal Medicine 2005; **Med School:** Pakistan 1983; **Resid:** Internal Medicine, Brooklyn Hosp 1994; **Fac Appt:** Asst Clin Prof Med, Cornell Univ-Weill Med Coll

Cohen, Barry A MD (IM) *PCP* - **Spec Exp:** Preventive Medicine; **Hospital:** Mt Sinai Beth Israel-BK; **Address:** 151A West End Ave, Brooklyn, NY 11235-4808; **Phone:** 718-934-1222; **Board Cert:** Internal Medicine 1986; **Med School:** Dominican Republic 1982; **Resid:** Internal Medicine, Mt Sinai Serv/City Hosp Ctr 1986

Ditchek, Alan MD (IM) *PCP* - **Spec Exp:** Chronic Fatigue Syndrome; Diabetes; Lyme Disease; Hypertension; **Hospital:** Mt Sinai Beth Israel-BK, New York Methodist Hosp (page 448); **Address:** 2516 Ocean Ave, Brooklyn, NY 11229-3916; **Phone:** 718-769-0444; **Board Cert:** Internal Medicine 1986; Infectious Disease 2007; **Med School:** Mexico 1981; **Resid:** Internal Medicine, Lutheran Med Ctr 1985; **Fellow:** Infectious Disease, Nassau Co Med Ctr 1986; Infectious Disease, SUNY Downstate 1995; **Fac Appt:** Asst Prof Med, SUNY Downstate

Ellis, Earl A MD (IM) *PCP* - **Spec Exp:** Geriatric Care; Geriatric Medicine; Preventive Medicine; **Hospital:** Brooklyn Hosp Ctr, SUNY Downstate Med Ctr (Univ Hosp Brooklyn) (page 449); **Address:** 66 Rutland Rd, Brooklyn, NY 11225-5313; **Phone:** 718-282-4412; **Board Cert:** Internal Medicine 1984; **Med School:** Howard Univ 1980; **Resid:** Internal Medicine, Elmhurst City Hosp 1983

Gambarin, Boris L MD/PhD (IM) *PCP* - **Spec Exp:** Cardiovascular Disease; Diabetes; **Hospital:** New York Methodist Hosp (page 448); **Address:** 5923 16th Ave, Brooklyn, NY 11204; **Phone:** 718-259-6122; **Board Cert:** Internal Medicine 2005; **Med School:** Russia 1969; **Resid:** Internal Medicine, Interfaith Med Ctr 1995; **Fac Appt:** Asst Prof Med, Cornell Univ-Weill Med Coll

Grunzweig, Milton J MD (IM) *PCP* - **Spec Exp:** Preventive Medicine; **Hospital:** Brookdale Univ Hosp Med Ctr; **Address:** 2000 Ocean Ave, Ste 1, Brooklyn, NY 11230; **Phone:** 718-769-7900; **Board Cert:** Internal Medicine 1989; **Med School:** SUNY Downstate 1986; **Resid:** Internal Medicine, Brookdale Hosp 1989

Hsuih, Terence C H MD (IM) *PCP* - **Spec Exp:** Preventive Medicine; **Hospital:** Maimonides Med Ctr (page 98); **Address:** 775 57th St, Brooklyn, NY 11220; **Phone:** 718-439-6163; **Board Cert:** Internal Medicine 2008; **Med School:** Mount Sinai Sch Med 1995; **Resid:** Internal Medicine, New York Hosp 1998

Hyman, Jeffrey S MD (IM) *PCP* - **Hospital:** Staten Island Univ Hosp - North; **Address:** 8012 3rd Ave, Brooklyn, NY 11209; **Phone:** 718-745-5600; **Board Cert:** Internal Medicine 2007; **Med School:** Mexico 1980; **Resid:** Internal Medicine, Maimonides Med Ctr 1984

Joy, Mark MD (IM) *PCP* - **Spec Exp:** Diabetes; Thyroid Disorders; **Hospital:** VA NY Harbor Hlthcr Sys-Brooklyn Campus; **Address:** VA NY Harbor Healthcare Sys, Dept Medicine, 800 Poly Pl, Brooklyn, NY 11209; **Phone:** 718-630-3766; **Board Cert:** Internal Medicine 1983; **Med School:** W VA Univ 1979; **Resid:** Internal Medicine, Mercy Hosp 1982; **Fac Appt:** Asst Clin Prof Med, NY Med Coll

Kaiser, Stephen J MD (IM) *PCP* - **Spec Exp:** Diabetes; Hypertension; Preventive Medicine; **Hospital:** Maimonides Med Ctr (page 98); **Address:** 1335 Ocean Pkwy, Brooklyn, NY 11230; **Phone:** 718-382-8900; **Board Cert:** Internal Medicine 1972; **Med School:** SUNY Buffalo 1964; **Resid:** Internal Medicine, Kings County Hosp 1967; **Fellow:** Hematology, Maimonides Med Ctr 1969

Katzenelenbogen, Moshe MD (IM) *PCP* - **Hospital:** Mt Sinai Beth Israel-BK; **Address:** 3901 Nostrand Ave, Brooklyn, NY 11235; **Phone:** 718-646-1422; **Board Cert:** Internal Medicine 1984; **Med School:** Romania 1980; **Resid:** Internal Medicine, Coney Island Hosp 1984

Levey, Robert L MD (IM) *PCP* - **Spec Exp:** Chronic Obstructive Lung Disease (COPD); Alzheimer's Disease; **Hospital:** SUNY Downstate Med Ctr (Univ Hosp Brooklyn) (page 449); **Address:** SUNY Downstate Med Ctr, Dept Internal Med, 450 Clarkson Ave, Brooklyn, NY 11203; **Phone:** 718-780-2838; **Board Cert:** Internal Medicine 1977; **Med School:** Univ Mich Med Sch 1970; **Resid:** Internal Medicine, Long Island Coll Hosp 1977

Lu, Bing MD/PhD (IM) *PCP* - **Spec Exp:** Chinese Community Health; Acupuncture; Sinusitis; Irritable Bowel Syndrome; **Hospital:** Maimonides Med Ctr (page 98), SUNY Downstate Med Ctr (Univ Hosp Brooklyn) (page 449); **Address:** Universal Medical Services, 4506 8th Ave, Brooklyn, NY 11220; **Phone:** 718-972-1233; **Board Cert:** Internal Medicine 2007; **Med School:** China 1982; **Resid:** Internal Medicine, Miriam Hosp 1997; **Fac Appt:** Asst Prof Med, Mount Sinai Sch Med

Malik, Asim R MD (IM) *PCP* - **Spec Exp:** Peptic Acid Disorders; **Hospital:** New York Methodist Hosp (page 448); **Address:** 1224 8th Ave, Brooklyn, NY 11215; **Phone:** 718-788-5588; **Board Cert:** Internal Medicine 2004; Gastroenterology 2007; **Med School:** Pakistan 1976; **Resid:** Surgery, NY Methodist Hosp 1978; Internal Medicine, NY Methodist Hosp 1981; **Fellow:** Gastroenterology, Wayne County Genl Hosp 1983

Mehta, Viplov K MD (IM) *PCP* - **Spec Exp:** Hypertension/Kidney Disease; Dialysis Care; Diabetes; Geriatric Care; **Hospital:** Kingsbrook Jewish Med Ctr, Brooklyn Hosp Ctr; **Address:** 894 Eastern Pkwy, Brooklyn, NY 11213-3618; **Phone:** 718-774-6060; **Board Cert:** Internal Medicine 1985; Nephrology 2005; **Med School:** India 1980; **Resid:** Internal Medicine, Kingsbrook Jewish Med Ctr 1985; **Fellow:** Nephrology, SUNY Downstate Med Ctr 1987; **Fac Appt:** Assoc Clin Prof Med, SUNY Downstate

Peterson, Stephen J MD (IM) *PCP* - **Hospital:** New York Methodist Hosp (page 448); **Address:** NY Methodist Hosp, Dept Medicine, 506 Sixth St, East Pavil Bldg - Fl 3rd, Brooklyn, NY 11215; **Phone:** 718-780-5246; **Board Cert:** Internal Medicine 1985; **Med School:** Philippines 1982; **Resid:** Internal Medicine, Metropolitan Hosp Ctr 1986; **Fac Appt:** Prof Med, NY Med Coll

Ratner, Ina MD (IM) *PCP* - **Hospital:** Maimonides Med Ctr (page 98); **Address:** 745 64th St, Brooklyn, NY 11220; **Phone:** 718-765-2583; **Board Cert:** Internal Medicine 1989; **Med School:** Univ Mass Sch Med 1986; **Resid:** Internal Medicine, Mount Auburn Hosp 1989

Sherman, Frederic M MD (IM) - **Spec Exp:** Cardiovascular Disease; Alzheimer's Disease; Preventive Medicine; **Hospital:** Lutheran Med Ctr - Brooklyn, Brooklyn Hosp Ctr; **Address:** 8672 Bay Pkwy, Brooklyn, NY 11214-4102; **Phone:** 718-372-2234; **Board Cert:** Internal Medicine 1976; Hospice & Palliative Medicine 2012; **Med School:** NY Med Coll 1972; **Resid:** Internal Medicine, Mount Sinai Hosp 1975Long Island Coll Hosp 1976; **Fellow:** Cardiovascular Disease, Long Island Coll Hosp 1977

Simon, Todd L MD (IM) *PCP* - **Spec Exp:** Preventive Medicine; Asthma; **Hospital:** New York Methodist Hosp (page 448); **Address:** 263 7th Ave, Ste 5A, Brooklyn, NY 11215; **Phone:** 718-246-8561; **Board Cert:** Internal Medicine 2006; **Med School:** NYU Sch Med 1991; **Resid:** Internal Medicine, Mt Sinai Hosp 1994; **Fac Appt:** Assoc Prof Med, Cornell Univ-Weill Med Coll

Tal, Avraham MD (IM) *PCP* - **Spec Exp:** Hypertension; Cholesterol/Lipid Disorders; Diabetes; **Hospital:** Coney Island Hosp; **Address:** 2601 Ocean Pkwy, Ste 4N39, Brooklyn, NY 11235-7745; **Phone:** 718-616-3880; **Board Cert:** Internal Medicine 1983; **Med School:** Italy 1975; **Resid:** Internal Medicine, LI College Hosp 1977; Internal Medicine, Kingsbrook Jewish Med Ctr 1979

Walfish, Jacob S MD (IM) *PCP* - **Spec Exp:** Gastrointestinal Disorders; Irritable Bowel Syndrome; Diagnostic Problems; **Hospital:** NYU Langone Med Ctr (page 104); **Address:** NYU Langone of Williamsburg, 101 Broadway, Ste 301, Brooklyn, NY 11249; **Phone:** 718-384-5179; **Board Cert:** Internal Medicine 1977; Gastroenterology 1979; **Med School:** Harvard Med Sch 1974; **Resid:** Internal Medicine, Mt Sinai Hosp 1977; **Fellow:** Gastroenterology, Mt Sinai Hosp 1979; **Fac Appt:** Asst Clin Prof Med, NYU Sch Med

Interventional Cardiology

Borgen, Elliot J MD (IC) - **Spec Exp:** Angioplasty & Stent Placement; **Hospital:** Maimonides Med Ctr (page 98); **Address:** Maimonides Med Ctr, Div Cardiology, 4802 10th Ave, Brooklyn, NY 11219; **Phone:** 718-283-6257; **Board Cert:** Cardiovascular Disease 2009; Interventional Cardiology 2010; **Med School:** Albert Einstein Coll Med 1992; **Resid:** Internal Medicine, Montefiore Med Ctr 1995; **Fellow:** Cardiovascular Disease, Montefiore Med Ctr 1999; Interventional Cardiology, Maimonides Med Ctr 2000; **Fac Appt:** Asst Prof Med, Mount Sinai Sch Med

Brener, Sorin MD (IC) - **Spec Exp:** Angioplasty & Stent Placement; **Hospital:** New York Methodist Hosp (page 448); **Address:** New York Methodist Hosp, 506 6th St, Brooklyn, NY 11215; **Phone:** 718-780-7830; **Board Cert:** Internal Medicine 2012; Cardiovascular Disease 2005; Interventional Cardiology 2009; **Med School:** Israel 1984; **Resid:** Internal Medicine, Cleveland Clin 1992; **Fellow:** Cardiovascular Disease, Cleveland Clin 1996

Frankel, Robert A MD (IC) - **Spec Exp:** Angioplasty & Stent Placement; **Hospital:** Maimonides Med Ctr (page 98); **Address:** Maimonides Med Ctr, Div Cardiology, 4802 10th Ave, Brooklyn, NY 11219; **Phone:** 718-283-7480; **Board Cert:** Internal Medicine 1987; Cardiovascular Disease 1989; Interventional Cardiology 2010; **Med School:** Mexico 1982; **Resid:** Internal Medicine, Maimonides Med Ctr 1987; **Fellow:** Cardiovascular Disease, Maimonides Med Ctr 1989; Interventional Cardiology, Maimonides Med Ctr 1990; **Fac Appt:** Assoc Clin Prof Med, SUNY Downstate

Friedman, Michael S MD (IC) - **Hospital:** Maimonides Med Ctr (page 98); **Address:** Maimonides Med Ctr, Cardiology, 4802 10th Ave Fl 4, Brooklyn, NY 11219; **Phone:** 718-283-6843; **Board Cert:** Internal Medicine 1989; Cardiovascular Disease 2012; Interventional Cardiology 2013; **Med School:** Israel 1986; **Resid:** Internal Medicine, LIJ Med Ctr 1989; **Fellow:** Cardiovascular Disease, Lenox Hill Hosp 1992; Interventional Cardiology, Lenox Hill Hosp 1993; **Fac Appt:** Asst Prof Med, SUNY Hlth Sci Ctr

Marmur, Jonathan MD (IC) - **Spec Exp:** Coronary Artery Disease; Cardiac Catheterization; **Hospital:** SUNY Downstate Med Ctr (Univ Hosp Brooklyn) (page 449); **Address:** SUNY Hlth Science Ctr, 450 Clarkson Ave, Box 1199, Brooklyn, NY 11203; **Phone:** 718-270-7383; **Board Cert:** Internal Medicine 1986; Cardiovascular Disease 1989; Interventional Cardiology 2010; **Med School:** Laval Univ, Quebec 1982; **Resid:** Internal Medicine, McGill Univ/Montreal Genl Hosp 1986; **Fellow:** Cardiovascular Disease, Univ Toronto/St Michael's Hosp 1988; Interventional Cardiology, Mt Sinai Med Ctr 1992; **Fac Appt:** Prof Med, SUNY Downstate

Shani, Jacob MD (IC) - **Spec Exp:** Cardiac Catheterization; Angioplasty & Stent Placement; Percutaneous Valve Repair; Aortic Valve Replacement; **Hospital:** Maimonides Med Ctr (page 98); **Address:** Maimonides Med Ctr, Cardiology, 4802 10th Ave, Brooklyn, NY 11219; **Phone:** 718-283-7480; **Board Cert:** Internal Medicine 1981; Cardiovascular Disease 1983; Interventional Cardiology 2009; **Med School:** Israel 1977; **Resid:** Internal Medicine, Maimonides Med Ctr 1981; **Fellow:** Cardiovascular Disease, Beth Israel Deaconess Med Ctr 1983; **Fac Appt:** Prof Med, SUNY Downstate

Maternal & Fetal Medicine

Bush, Jacqueline MD (MF) - **Spec Exp:** Pregnancy-High Risk; Diabetes in Pregnancy; **Hospital:** New York Methodist Hosp (page 448); **Address:** 263 7th Ave, Ste 3A, Brooklyn, NY 11215; **Phone:** 718-246-8500; **Board Cert:** Obstetrics & Gynecology 2007; **Med School:** SUNY Stony Brook 1989; **Resid:** Obstetrics & Gynecology, SUNY Hlth Sci Ctr 1993; Obstetrics & Gynecology, Kings Co Hosp Ctr 1996

Chandra, Prasanta C MD (MF) - **Spec Exp:** Pregnancy-High Risk; Premature Labor; Pregnancy-Teenage; **Hospital:** Wyckoff Heights Med Ctr; **Address:** 220A Saint Nicholas Ave, Brooklyn, NY 11237; **Phone:** 718-418-8745; **Board Cert:** Obstetrics & Gynecology 1979; Maternal & Fetal Medicine 1980; **Med School:** India 1969; **Resid:** Surgery, Bronx Muni Hosp-Albert Einstein Med Ctr 1972; Obstetrics & Gynecology, Bronx Muni Hosp-Albert Einstein Med Ctr 1976; **Fellow:** Maternal & Fetal Medicine, Bronx Muni Hosp-Albert Einstein Med Ctr 1978

Medical Oncology

Astrow, Alan B MD (Onc) - **Spec Exp:** Ovarian Cancer; Breast Cancer; **Hospital:** Maimonides Med Ctr (page 98); **Address:** Maimonides Cancer Ctr, Hem/Onc, 6300 8th Ave Fl 2, Brooklyn, NY 11220; **Phone:** 718-765-2653; **Board Cert:** Internal Medicine 1983; Hematology 1986; Medical Oncology 1987; **Med School:** Yale Univ 1980; **Resid:** Internal Medicine, Boston Med Ctr 1983; **Fellow:** Hematology & Oncology, NYU Med Ctr 1986; **Fac Appt:** Assoc Clin Prof Med, NY Med Coll

Bashevkin, Michael L MD (Onc) - **Spec Exp:** Solid Tumors; Hematologic Malignancies; **Hospital:** Maimonides Med Ctr (page 98); **Address:** Hematology Oncology Assocs, 1660 E 14th St, Ste 501, Brooklyn, NY 11229; **Phone:** 718-382-8500; **Board Cert:** Internal Medicine 1976; Hematology 1978; Medical Oncology 1979; **Med School:** SUNY Downstate 1973; **Resid:** Internal Medicine, VA Med Ctr 1976; **Fellow:** Hematology & Oncology, Maimonides Med Ctr 1979

Dosik, David MD (Onc) - **Spec Exp:** Breast Cancer; Lung Cancer; Colon Cancer; **Hospital:** New York Methodist Hosp (page 448), New York Comm Hosp; **Address:** 500 4th Ave, Ste 1, Brooklyn, NY 11215; **Phone:** 718-780-5240; **Board Cert:** Hematology 2006; Medical Oncology 2007; **Med School:** SUNY Downstate 1990; **Resid:** Internal Medicine, Staten Island Univ Hosp 1993; **Fellow:** Hematology & Oncology, NYU Med Ctr 1996

Flaherty, Brian MD (Onc) - **Hospital:** Lutheran Med Ctr - Brooklyn, New York Methodist Hosp (page 448); **Address:** 9920 4th Ave, Ste 311, Brooklyn, NY 11209; **Phone:** 718-921-1672; **Board Cert:** Internal Medicine 2013; Medical Oncology 2013; Hematology 2004; **Med School:** Mexico 1985; **Resid:** Internal Medicine, Lutheran Med Ctr 1989; **Fellow:** Hematology & Oncology, Stony Brook Univ Med Ctr 1992

Lebowicz, Joseph MD (Onc) - **Spec Exp:** Lung Cancer; Breast Cancer; Gastrointestinal Cancer; Hematologic Malignancies; **Hospital:** Maimonides Med Ctr (page 98); **Address:** Hem/Onc Assocs, 1660 E 14th St, Ste 501, Brooklyn, NY 11229; **Phone:** 718-382-8500; **Board Cert:** Internal Medicine 1978; Hematology 1980; Medical Oncology 1981; **Med School:** Albert Einstein Coll Med 1975; **Resid:** Internal Medicine, Maimonides Med Ctr 1978; **Fellow:** Hematology & Oncology, Maimonides Med Ctr 1981

Lichter, Stephen M MD (Onc) - **Spec Exp:** Breast Cancer; Lung Cancer; Gastrointestinal Cancer; Prostate Cancer; **Hospital:** Mt Sinai Beth Israel-BK, New York Comm Hosp; **Address:** HemOnCare, 2935 Ave S, Brooklyn, NY 11229; **Phone:** 718-616-0801; **Board Cert:** Internal Medicine 1978; Medical Oncology 1981; **Med School:** Ros Franklin Univ/Chicago Med Sch 1975; **Resid:** Internal Medicine, Brookdale Hosp 1978; **Fellow:** Hematology & Oncology, Brookdale Hosp 1980; **Fac Appt:** Asst Clin Prof Med, SUNY Hlth Sci Ctr

Neonatal-Perinatal Medicine

Gudavalli, Madhu R MD (NP) - **Spec Exp:** Prematurity/Low Birth Weight Infants; **Hospital:** New York Methodist Hosp (page 448); **Address:** NY Methodist Hosp, NICU, 506 6th St, Brooklyn, NY 11215; **Phone:** 718-780-3727; **Board Cert:** Pediatrics 1980; Neonatal-Perinatal Medicine 2009; **Med School:** India 1972; **Resid:** Pediatrics, NY Infirm 1976; Pediatrics, Booth Meml Hosp 1977; **Fellow:** Neonatal-Perinatal Medicine, NYU-Bellevue Hosp 1979

Sokal, Myron MD (NP) - **Spec Exp:** Neonatal Care; **Hospital:** Brookdale Univ Hosp Med Ctr; **Address:** Brookdale Univ Hosp, Neonatalogy, 1 Brookdale Plaza, rm 244, Brooklyn, NY 11212; **Phone:** 718-240-5629; **Board Cert:** Pediatrics 1972; Neonatal-Perinatal Medicine 1975; **Med School:** Albert Einstein Coll Med 1967; **Resid:** Pediatrics, Yale-New Haven Hosp 1969; **Fellow:** Neonatal-Perinatal Medicine, Columbia-Presby Med Ctr 1971; **Fac Appt:** Prof Ped, SUNY Hlth Sci Ctr

Nephrology

Chou, Shyan-Yih MD (Nep) - **Spec Exp:** Kidney Disease; Hypertension; Dialysis Care; **Hospital:** Brookdale Univ Hosp Med Ctr; **Address:** Brookdale Univ Hosp, Nephrology, 1 Brookdale Plaza, rm 169-CHC, Brooklyn, NY 11212; **Phone:** 718-240-5615; **Board Cert:** Internal Medicine 1972; Nephrology 1974; **Med School:** Taiwan 1966; **Resid:** Internal Medicine, Brookdale Hosp 1970; Internal Medicine, Brookdale Hosp 1970; **Fellow:** Nephrology, Brookdale Hosp 1973; **Fac Appt:** Prof Med, SUNY Downstate

Delano, Barbara G MD (Nep) - **Spec Exp:** Dialysis Care; Kidney Failure-Chronic; Kidney Disease-Acute; **Hospital:** SUNY Downstate Med Ctr (Univ Hosp Brooklyn) (page 449), Kings Co Hosp Ctr; **Address:** SUNY Downstate, Nephrology, 450 Clarkson Ave, Box 52, Brooklyn, NY 11203; **Phone:** 718-270-3174; **Board Cert:** Internal Medicine 2010; **Med School:** SUNY Hlth Sci Ctr 1965; **Resid:** Internal Medicine, SUNY Downstate Med Ctr 1967; **Fellow:** Nephrology, SUNY Downstate Med Ctr 1969; **Fac Appt:** Prof Med, SUNY Downstate

Lipner, Henry I MD (Nep) - **Spec Exp:** Kidney Disease; Hypertension; Dialysis Care; **Hospital:** Maimonides Med Ctr (page 98); **Address:** 1435 86th St, Brooklyn, NY 11228; **Phone:** 718-648-0101; **Board Cert:** Internal Medicine 1974; Nephrology 1976; **Med School:** NYU Sch Med 1968; **Resid:** Internal Medicine, Brooklyn Jewish Hosp 1971; **Fellow:** Nephrology, Montefiore Med Ctr 1972

Markell, Mariana S MD (Nep) - **Spec Exp:** Transplant Medicine-Kidney; Complementary Medicine; **Hospital:** SUNY Downstate Med Ctr (Univ Hosp Brooklyn) (page 449), Kings Co Hosp Ctr; **Address:** SUNY Downstate, Nephrology, 450 Clarkson Ave, Box 52, Brooklyn, NY 11203; **Phone:** 718-270-3174; **Board Cert:** Internal Medicine 1984; Nephrology 1986; **Med School:** NY Med Coll 1981; **Resid:** Internal Medicine, NY-Presby/Columbia Univ Med Ctr 1984; **Fellow:** Nephrology, NY-Presby/Columbia Univ Med Ctr 1985UCLA Med Ctr 1986; **Fac Appt:** Assoc Prof Med, SUNY Downstate

Neelakantappa, Kotresha H MD (Nep) - **Spec Exp:** Kidney Disease; Hypertension; **Hospital:** New York Methodist Hosp (page 448); **Address:** 9920 4th Ave, Ste 309, Brooklyn, NY 11209; **Phone:** 718-745-3079; **Board Cert:** Internal Medicine 1977; Nephrology 1978; **Med School:** India 1969; **Resid:** Internal Medicine, NY Methodist Hosp 1974; **Fellow:** Nephrology, NYU Med Ctr 1976; **Fac Appt:** Asst Prof Med, NYU Sch Med

Pannone, John MD (Nep) - **Spec Exp:** Dialysis Care; Kidney Disease-Chronic; Hypertension; **Hospital:** Lutheran Med Ctr - Brooklyn; **Address:** 61 Oliver St, Ste PR-1, Brooklyn, NY 11209; **Phone:** 718-238-4980; **Board Cert:** Internal Medicine 1978; Nephrology 1980; **Med School:** Italy 1974; **Resid:** Internal Medicine, Lutheran Med Ctr 1977; **Fellow:** Nephrology, Brookdale Hosp 1979; Nephrology, NY-Presby/Weill Cornell Med Ctr 1980

Parnes, Eliezer MD (Nep) - **Spec Exp:** Hypertension; Dialysis Care; Diabetic Kidney Disease; **Hospital:** Mt Sinai Beth Israel-BK; **Address:** 3131 Kings Hwy, rm D-5, Brooklyn, NY 11234; **Phone:** 718-338-2283; **Board Cert:** Internal Medicine 1989; Nephrology 2013; **Med School:** SUNY Downstate 1986; **Resid:** Internal Medicine, Brookdale Hosp 1989; **Fellow:** Nephrology, Brookdale Hosp 1992

Salifu, Moro O MD (Nep) - **Spec Exp:** Kidney Disease; **Hospital:** SUNY Downstate Med Ctr (Univ Hosp Brooklyn) (page 449); **Address:** SUNY Downstate, Nephrology, 450 Clarkson Ave, Box 52, Brooklyn, NY 11203; **Phone:** 718-270-3174; **Board Cert:** Internal Medicine 2009; Nephrology 2010; **Med School:** Turkey 1994; **Resid:** Internal Medicine, SUNY Hlth Sci Ctr 1998; **Fellow:** Nephrology, SUNY Hlth Sci Ctr 2001

Shapiro, Warren B MD (Nep) - **Spec Exp:** Kidney Failure-Chronic; Kidney Failure; Hypertension; Dialysis Care; **Hospital:** Brookdale Univ Hosp Med Ctr; **Address:** Brookdale Univ Hosp, Nephrology, 1 Brookdale Plaza, Ste 169-CHC, Brooklyn, NY 11212; **Phone:** 718-240-5615; **Board Cert:** Internal Medicine 1972; Nephrology 1974; **Med School:** Ros Franklin Univ/Chicago Med Sch 1966; **Resid:** Internal Medicine, UCSF Med Ctr 1968; Internal Medicine, NY Med Coll 1970; **Fellow:** Nephrology, NY Med Coll 1971; **Fac Appt:** Assoc Clin Prof Med, SUNY Downstate

Shein, Leon MD (Nep) - **Spec Exp:** Hypertension; Diabetic Kidney Disease; Electrolyte Disorders; Nutrition; **Hospital:** New York Methodist Hosp (page 448); **Address:** Prospect Med Grp, 1545 Atlantic Ave, Brooklyn, NY 11213; **Phone:** 718-552-2069; **Board Cert:** Internal Medicine 1989; Nephrology 2014; **Med School:** Philippines 1983; **Resid:** Internal Medicine, Woodhull Med Ctr 1986; **Fellow:** Nephrology, Brookdale Hosp 1988

Spitalewitz, Samuel MD (Nep) - **Spec Exp:** Diabetic Kidney Disease; Hypertension; **Hospital:** Brookdale Univ Hosp Med Ctr; **Address:** Brookdale Univ Hosp, Nephrology, 1 Brookdale Plaza, Ste 169-CHC, Brooklyn, NY 11212; **Phone:** 718-240-5615; **Board Cert:** Internal Medicine 1978; Nephrology 1980; **Med School:** NYU Sch Med 1975; **Resid:** Internal Medicine, Brookdale Hosp 1978; **Fellow:** Nephrology, Brookdale Hosp 1981; **Fac Appt:** Assoc Clin Prof Med, SUNY Downstate

Stam, Lawrence MD (Nep) - **Spec Exp:** Dialysis Care; Glomerulonephritis; **Hospital:** New York Methodist Hosp (page 448); **Address:** NY Methodist Hosp, Nephrology, 506 6th St, Ste 5A, Brooklyn, NY 11215; **Phone:** 718-830-7109; **Board Cert:** Internal Medicine 1981; Nephrology 1984; **Med School:** SUNY Stony Brook 1978; **Resid:** Internal Medicine, St Elizabeths Med Ctr 1981; **Fellow:** Nephrology, Kingsbrook Jewish Med Ctr 1982; **Fac Appt:** Asst Clin Prof Med, Cornell Univ-Weill Med Coll

Tan, Reynaldo G MD (Nep) - **Hospital:** Lutheran Med Ctr - Brooklyn; **Address:** Cambridge Nephrology, 8122 7th Ave, Brooklyn, NY 11209; **Phone:** 718-836-0225; **Board Cert:** Internal Medicine 2004; Nephrology 2006; **Med School:** Philippines 1988; **Resid:** Internal Medicine, Lutheran Med Ctr 1993; **Fellow:** Nephrology, Temple Univ Hosp 1994

Neurological Surgery

Cardoso, Erico R MD (NS) - **Spec Exp:** Pituitary Tumors; Spinal Cord Disorders; Hydrocephalus; **Hospital:** Wyckoff Heights Med Ctr; **Address:** Wyckoff Heights Med Ctr, Neurosurgery, 374 Stockholm St, rm 409, Brooklyn, NY 11237; **Phone:** 718-508-4640; **Board Cert:** Neurological Surgery 1994; **Med School:** Brazil 1973; **Resid:** Surgery, Ottawa Civic Hosp 1976; Neurological Surgery, Ottawa Civic Hosp 1980; **Fellow:** Neurological Surgery, Clin Rsch Fellowship Univ Hosp 1981; Neurological Surgery, Inst Neurol Scis 1982; **Fac Appt:** Assoc Prof NS, SUNY Downstate

Cohen, Anders DO (NS) - **Spec Exp:** Minimally Invasive Spinal Surgery; Pediatric Neurosurgery; **Hospital:** Brooklyn Hosp Ctr; **Address:** Brooklyn Hosp, Neurosurgery, 240 Willoughby St, Ste 4E, Brooklyn, NY 11201; **Phone:** 718-250-8103; **Board Cert:** Neurological Surgery 2009; **Med School:** NY Coll Osteo Med 1997; **Resid:** Neurological Surgery, LIJ Med Ctr 2002; **Fellow:** Spine Surgery, NY-Presby/Weill Cornell Med Ctr 2003; Pediatric Neurological Surgery, NY-Presby/Weill Cornell Med Ctr 2005; **Fac Appt:** Asst Prof NS, Cornell Univ-Weill Med Coll

Schwartz, Amit Y MD (NS) - **Spec Exp:** Skull Base Surgery; Brain Tumors; Pituitary Tumors; Spinal Disorders; **Hospital:** Maimonides Med Ctr (page 98); **Address:** Maimonides Med Ctr, Neurosurgery, 948 48th St Fl 2, Brooklyn, NY 11219; **Phone:** 718-283-7219; **Board Cert:** Neurological Surgery 2005; **Med School:** Mount Sinai Sch Med 1995; **Resid:** Neurological Surgery, Mt Sinai Hosp 2001; **Fellow:** Skull Base Surgery, Jackson Meml Hosp 2002; **Fac Appt:** Asst Clin Prof NS, Mount Sinai Sch Med

Zonenshayn, Martin MD (NS) - **Spec Exp:** Parkinson's Disease; Stereotactic Radiosurgery; Carpal Tunnel Syndrome; Trigeminal Neuralgia; **Hospital:** New York Methodist Hosp (page 448); **Address:** NY Methodist Hosp, Neurosurgery, 263 7th Ave, Ste 4D, Brooklyn, NY 11215; **Phone:** 718-246-8660; **Board Cert:** Neurological Surgery 2008; **Med School:** NYU Sch Med 1996; **Resid:** Neurological Surgery, NY-Presby/Weill Cornell Med Ctr 2002; **Fellow:** Stereotactic Neurological Surgery, NYU Hosp Joint Diseases 2003; **Fac Appt:** Assoc Clin Prof NS, Cornell Univ-Weill Med Coll

Neurology

Abou-Fayssal, Nada MD (N) - **Spec Exp:** Multiple Sclerosis; Vascular Neurology; Clinical Neurophysiology; **Hospital:** Lutheran Med Ctr - Brooklyn; **Address:** Lutheran HlthCare, Neurology, 8714 5th Ave, Brooklyn, NY 11209; **Phone:** 718-630-8600; **Board Cert:** Neurotology 2011; Vascular Neurology 2005; **Med School:** Lebanon 1991; **Resid:** Neurology, Mt Sinai Med Ctr 1998

Azhar, Salman MD (N) - **Spec Exp:** Stroke; Neuro-Rehabilitation; Dementia; Spasticity Management; **Hospital:** Lutheran Med Ctr - Brooklyn; **Address:** Lutheran HlthCare, Neurology, 8714 5th Ave, Brooklyn, NY 11209; **Phone:** 718-630-8600; **Board Cert:** Neurology 2008; Vascular Neurology 2008; **Med School:** Med Coll VA 1993; **Resid:** Neurology, Med Coll Va Hosp 1995; Neurology, Mt Sinai Hosp 1997; **Fellow:** Stroke, Natl Inst Hlth 1999; **Fac Appt:** Asst Prof N, SUNY Downstate

Benjamin, Jeffrey L MD (N) - **Hospital:** New York Methodist Hosp (page 448); **Address:** NY Methodist Hosp, Neurology, 263 7th Ave, Ste 4A, Brooklyn, NY 11215; **Phone:** 718-246-8614; **Board Cert:** Neurology 1990; **Med School:** Dominica 1983; **Resid:** Neurology, SUNY Downstate Med Ctr 1984

Bodis-Wollner, Ivan G MD (N) - **Spec Exp:** Parkinson's Disease; Neuro-Ophthalmology; Behavioral Neurology; **Hospital:** SUNY Downstate Med Ctr (Univ Hosp Brooklyn) (page 449), Kings Co Hosp Ctr; **Address:** SUNY Downstate, Neurology, 450 Clarkson Ave, Ste A, Box 35, Brooklyn, NY 11203; **Phone:** 718-270-2734; **Board Cert:** Neurology 1977; **Med School:** Austria 1965; **Resid:** Neurology, Mt Sinai Hosp 1974; **Fellow:** Clinical Neurophysiology, Mass Genl Hosp 1974; **Fac Appt:** Prof N, SUNY Downstate

Buckner, Cary D MD (N) - **Spec Exp:** Neuromuscular Disorders; Peripheral Neuropathy; Clinical Neurophysiology; **Hospital:** New York Methodist Hosp (page 448); **Address:** NY Methodist Hosp, Neurology, 263 7th Ave, Ste 4A, Brooklyn, NY 11215; **Phone:** 718-246-8614; **Board Cert:** Neurology 2009; Clinical Neurophysiology 2011; **Med School:** Georgetown Univ 1994; **Resid:** Neurology, NY-Presby/Columbia Univ Med Ctr 1998; **Fellow:** Neuromuscular Disease, NY-Presby/Columbia Univ Med Ctr 1999

Crystal, Howard A MD (N) - **Spec Exp:** Alzheimer's Disease; Dementia; **Hospital:** SUNY Downstate Med Ctr (Univ Hosp Brooklyn) (page 449), Kings Co Hosp Ctr; **Address:** SUNY Downstate, Neurology, 450 Clarkson Ave, Box 1213, Brooklyn, NY 11203; **Phone:** 718-221-5188; **Board Cert:** Neurology 1981; **Med School:** Univ Pennsylvania 1976; **Resid:** Neurology, Montefiore Med Ctr 1980; **Fellow:** Neurological Pathology, Montefiore Med Ctr 1982; **Fac Appt:** Prof N, SUNY Downstate

Drexler, Ellen MD (N) - **Spec Exp:** Headache; **Hospital:** Maimonides Med Ctr (page 98); **Address:** Maimonides Med Ctr, Neurology, 883 65th St, Brooklyn, NY 11210; **Phone:** 718-283-7470; **Board Cert:** Neurology 1983; **Med School:** SUNY Downstate 1978; **Resid:** Neurology, Montefiore Med Ctr 1982; **Fac Appt:** Assoc Prof N, Mount Sinai Sch Med

Grant, Arthur C MD/PhD (N) - **Spec Exp:** Epilepsy; **Hospital:** SUNY Downstate Med Ctr (Univ Hosp Brooklyn) (page 449); **Address:** SUNY Downstate, Neurology, 470 Clarkson Ave, Brooklyn, NY 11203; **Phone:** 718-270-2959; **Board Cert:** Neurology 2010; Clinical Neurophysiology 2011; **Med School:** Case West Res Univ 1993; **Resid:** Neurology, Emory Univ Hosp 1997; **Fellow:** Clinical Neurophysiology, Emory Univ Hosp 1999; **Fac Appt:** Assoc Prof N, SUNY Downstate

Kay, Arthur D MD (N) - **Spec Exp:** Alzheimer's Disease; Parkinson's Disease; Dementia; Stroke; **Hospital:** Brookdale Univ Hosp Med Ctr; **Address:** Brookdale Univ Hosp, Neurology, 1 Brookdale Plaza, Ste 475, Brooklyn, NY 11212; **Phone:** 718-240-5622; **Board Cert:** Neurology 1983; **Med School:** SUNY Downstate 1978; **Resid:** Neurology, Brookdale Hosp 1982; **Fellow:** Research, Natl Inst Hlth 1984; **Fac Appt:** Assoc Prof N, SUNY Downstate

Keilson, Marshall MD (N) - **Spec Exp:** Alzheimer's Disease; Epilepsy; **Hospital:** NYU Langone Med Ctr (page 104); **Address:** 2044 Ocean Ave, Ste A8, Brooklyn, NY 11230; **Phone:** 718-759-6065; **Board Cert:** Neurology 1982; **Med School:** Albert Einstein Coll Med 1977; **Resid:** Internal Medicine, Montefiore Med Ctr 1978; Neurology, Jacobi Med Ctr 1981; **Fellow:** Clinical Neurophysiology, Brookdale Hosp 1983

Koziorynska, Ewa MD (N) - **Spec Exp:** Epilepsy; Sleep Disorders; Clinical Neurophysiology; **Hospital:** SUNY Downstate Med Ctr (Univ Hosp Brooklyn) (page 449); **Address:** SUNY Downstate, Epilepsy Ctr, 450 Clarkson Ave, Box 1213, Brooklyn, NY 11203; **Phone:** 718-270-2959; **Board Cert:** Neurology 2006; Sleep Medicine 2009; **Med School:** Poland 1994; **Resid:** Neurology, RWJ Univ Hosp 2003; **Fellow:** Clinical Neurophysiology, Yale-New Haven Hosp 2005

Levine, Steven R MD (N) - **Spec Exp:** Stroke; Cerebrovascular Disease; **Hospital:** SUNY Downstate Med Ctr (Univ Hosp Brooklyn) (page 449); **Address:** SUNY Downstate, Neurology, 450 Clarkson Ave, Ste B6-307, Box 1213, Brooklyn, NY 11203; **Phone:** 718-250-6940; **Board Cert:** Neurology 1986; Vascular Neurology 2005; **Med School:** Med Coll Wisc 1981; **Resid:** Neurology, Univ Michigan Med Ctr 1985; **Fellow:** Cerebrovascular Disease, Henry Ford Hosp 1987; **Fac Appt:** Prof N, SUNY Downstate

Maccabee, Paul J MD (N) - **Spec Exp:** Neuromuscular Disorders; Electromyography; Peripheral Neuropathy; **Hospital:** SUNY Downstate Med Ctr (Univ Hosp Brooklyn) (page 449); **Address:** SUNY Downstate, Neurology, 450 Clarkson Ave, Box 35, Brooklyn, NY 11203; **Phone:** 718-270-2502; **Board Cert:** Neurology 1977; Clinical Neurophysiology 2013; **Med School:** Boston Univ 1970; **Resid:** Neurology, Boston Med Ctr 1976; **Fellow:** Clinical Neurophysiology, Mass Genl Hosp 1978; Clinical Neurophysiology, Mt Sinai Hosp 1979; **Fac Appt:** Prof N, SUNY Downstate

Maniscalco, Anthony MD (N) - **Spec Exp:** Movement Disorders; Cerebrovascular Disease; Neuromuscular Disorders; **Hospital:** Mt Sinai Beth Israel-BK, Lutheran Med Ctr - Brooklyn; **Address:** Neurology Assocs, 117 70th St, Brooklyn, NY 11209; **Phone:** 718-836-8800; **Board Cert:** Internal Medicine 1982; Neurology 1988; **Med School:** Italy 1978; **Resid:** Internal Medicine, Maimonides Med Ctr 1981; Neurology, St Vincents Hosp 1984

Nouri, Shahin MD (N) - **Spec Exp:** Epilepsy/Seizure Disorders; **Hospital:** New York Methodist Hosp (page 448); **Address:** NY Methodist Hosp, Neurology, 263 7th Ave, Ste 4A, Brooklyn, NY 11215; **Phone:** 718-246-8614; **Board Cert:** Neurology 2004; Clinical Neurophysiology 2005; **Med School:** Germany 1994; **Resid:** Internal Medicine, Staten Island Univ Hosp 1998; Neurology, Georgetown Univ Hosp 2001; **Fellow:** Clinical Neurophysiology, NYU Med Ctr 2002

Rudolph, Steven H MD (N) - **Spec Exp:** Stroke; Neuro-Ophthalmology; Cerebrovascular Disease; **Hospital:** Maimonides Med Ctr (page 98); **Address:** Maimonides Med Ctr, Neurology, 948 48th St Fl 2, Brooklyn, NY 11219; **Phone:** 718-283-7670; **Board Cert:** Neurology 1981; Vascular Neurology 2005; **Med School:** SUNY Hlth Sci Ctr 1976; **Resid:** Neurology, Mt Sinai Hosp 1980; **Fellow:** Neuro-Ophthalmology, Mt Sinai Hosp 1982; **Fac Appt:** Asst Clin Prof N, Mount Sinai-Icahn Sch of Med

Salgado, Miran W MD (N) - **Spec Exp:** Movement Disorders; Parkinson's Disease; Balance Disorders; Headache; **Hospital:** New York Methodist Hosp (page 448); **Address:** NY Methodist Hosp, Neurology, 263 7th Ave, Ste 4A, Brooklyn, NY 11215; **Phone:** 718-246-8614; **Board Cert:** Neurology 2004; Vascular Neurology 2006; **Med School:** Sri Lanka 1990; **Resid:** Neurology, SUNY Downstate Med Ctr 1994; **Fellow:** Movement Disorders, NY-Presby/Columbia Univ Med Ctr 1995

Sobol, Norman J MD (N) - **Spec Exp:** Headache; Stroke; Parkinson's Disease; **Hospital:** Mt Sinai Beth Israel-BK, Maimonides Med Ctr (page 98); **Address:** 3131 Kings Hwy, Ste C7, Brooklyn, NY 11234; **Phone:** 718-677-0009; **Board Cert:** Neurology 1980; Internal Medicine 1977; **Med School:** Univ Chicago-Pritzker Sch Med 1974; **Resid:** Internal Medicine, Kings Co Hosp 1976; Neurology, Kings Co Hosp 1978; **Fellow:** Clinical Neurophysiology, Kings Co Hosp 1980; **Fac Appt:** Asst Prof N, SUNY Downstate

Vas, George A MD (N) - **Spec Exp:** Stroke; Multiple Sclerosis; **Hospital:** SUNY Downstate Med Ctr (Univ Hosp Brooklyn) (page 449), Kings Co Hosp Ctr; **Address:** SUNY Downstate, Neurology, 450 Clarkson Ave N, Ste A, Brooklyn, NY 11203; **Phone:** 718-270-2502; **Board Cert:** Internal Medicine 1973; Neurology 1977; **Med School:** Univ Pittsburgh 1970; **Resid:** Internal Medicine, NY-Presby/Weill Cornell Med Ctr 1972; Neurology, NY-Presby/Weill Cornell Med Ctr 1975; **Fac Appt:** Prof N, SUNY Downstate

Yellin, Joseph C DO (N) - **Spec Exp:** Headache; Memory Disorders; Dementia; **Hospital:** Lenox Hill Hosp, New York Comm Hosp; **Address:** 1599 E 15th St Fl 3, Brooklyn, NY 11230; **Phone:** 718-377-2223; **Med School:** Univ Osteo Med & Hlth Sci, Des Moines 1978; **Resid:** Neurology, Kings Co Hosp/Downstate Med Ctr 1982

Nuclear Medicine

Strashun, Arnold M MD (NuM) - **Spec Exp:** Neurological Imaging; Nuclear Cardiology; Thyroid Disorders; PET Imaging-Brain; **Hospital:** SUNY Downstate Med Ctr (Univ Hosp Brooklyn) (page 449), Kings Co Hosp Ctr; **Address:** SUNY Downstate, Nuclear Med, 450 Clarkson Ave, Box 1210, Brooklyn, NY 11203; **Phone:** 718-270-1603; **Board Cert:** Internal Medicine 1977; Nuclear Medicine 1979; **Med School:** Baylor Coll Med 1974; **Resid:** Internal Medicine, Baylor Med Ctr 1977; **Fellow:** Nuclear Medicine, VA Med Ctr 1978; Nuclear Medicine, Mt Sinai Hosp 1979; **Fac Appt:** Prof Rad, SUNY Downstate

Obstetrics & Gynecology

Arnouk, Issam MD (ObG) - **Hospital:** Lutheran Med Ctr - Brooklyn; **Address:** 355 Ovington Ave, Brooklyn, NY 11209; **Phone:** 718-745-5777; **Board Cert:** Obstetrics & Gynecology 1983; **Med School:** Syria 1974; **Resid:** Surgery, NY Methodist Hosp 1978; Obstetrics & Gynecology, Lutheran Med Ctr 1981

Comrie, Millicent A MD (ObG) *PCP* - **Spec Exp:** Menopause Problems; Uterine Fibroids; Prenatal Diagnosis; **Hospital:** Maimonides Med Ctr (page 98); **Address:** 148 Pierrepont St, Brooklyn, NY 11201; **Phone:** 718-852-9180; **Board Cert:** Obstetrics & Gynecology 1983; **Med School:** SUNY Hlth Sci Ctr 1976; **Resid:** Obstetrics & Gynecology, Long Island Coll Hosp 1980; **Fellow:** Public Health, NY-Presby/Columbia Univ Med Ctr 1981; **Fac Appt:** Asst Clin Prof ObG, SUNY Downstate

Dor, Nathan MD (ObG) - **Spec Exp:** Pregnancy-High Risk; **Hospital:** Maimonides Med Ctr (page 98); **Address:** Maimonides Med Ctr, Ob/Gyn, 943 48th St, Brooklyn, NY 11219; **Phone:** 718-853-1535; **Board Cert:** Obstetrics & Gynecology 2013; Maternal & Fetal Medicine 2013; **Med School:** Israel 1973; **Resid:** Obstetrics & Gynecology, Montefiore Med Ctr 1977; **Fellow:** Perinatal Medicine, Westchester Co Med Ctr 1979; **Fac Appt:** Asst Prof ObG, SUNY Downstate

Haratz-Rubinstein, Natan MD (ObG) - **Spec Exp:** Obstetric Ultrasound; Pregnancy-High Risk; **Hospital:** New York Methodist Hosp (page 448); **Address:** NY Methodist Hosp, Ob/Gyn, 506 6th St Fl 4, Brooklyn, NY 11215; **Phone:** 718-780-5799; **Board Cert:** Obstetrics & Gynecology 2013; **Med School:** Venezuela 1989; **Resid:** Obstetrics & Gynecology, Conception Palacio Maternity Hosp 1994; Obstetrics & Gynecology, NY-Presby/Columbia Univ Med Ctr 1997; **Fac Appt:** Asst Prof ObG, SUNY Downstate

Maher, John T MD (ObG) - **Hospital:** New York Methodist Hosp (page 448); **Address:** Brooklyn Women's Healthcare, 110 4th Ave, Brooklyn, NY 11217; **Phone:** 718-852-5810; **Board Cert:** Obstetrics & Gynecology 2013; **Med School:** UMDNJ-NJ Med Sch, Newark 1989; **Resid:** Obstetrics & Gynecology, NY-Presby/Weill Cornell Med Ctr 1993

Minkoff, Howard L MD (ObG) - **Spec Exp:** AIDS/HIV in Pregnancy; Pregnancy-High Risk; **Hospital:** Maimonides Med Ctr (page 98); **Address:** Maimonides, Womens Primary Care, 4422 9th Ave, Brooklyn, NY 11219; **Phone:** 718-283-8930; **Board Cert:** Obstetrics & Gynecology 1995; Maternal & Fetal Medicine 1995; **Med School:** Penn State Coll Med 1975; **Resid:** Obstetrics & Gynecology, Kings Co Hosp Ctr 1979; **Fellow:** Maternal & Fetal Medicine, Kings Co Hosp Ctr 1981; **Fac Appt:** Prof ObG, SUNY Downstate

Postell, Scott MD (ObG) - **Hospital:** Mt Sinai Beth Israel; **Address:** ODA Professionals, 420 Broadway, Brooklyn, NY 11201; **Phone:** 718-384-3475; **Board Cert:** Obstetrics & Gynecology 2013; **Med School:** NYU Sch Med 1986; **Resid:** Obstetrics & Gynecology, Brooke Army Med Ctr 1990

Reizis, Igal MD (ObG) - **Spec Exp:** Gynecology Only; **Hospital:** Maimonides Med Ctr (page 98); **Address:** 5925 15th Ave, Brooklyn, NY 11219; **Phone:** 718-972-2700; **Board Cert:** Obstetrics & Gynecology 1984; **Med School:** Israel 1977; **Resid:** Obstetrics & Gynecology, Maimonides Med Ctr 1984

Ophthalmology

Ackerman, Jacob L MD (Oph) - **Spec Exp:** Glaucoma; Cataract Surgery-Lens Implant; Eyelid Cosmetic Surgery; Macular Degeneration; **Address:** Brook Plaza Ophthalmology Assocs, 1987 Utica Ave, Brooklyn, NY 11234; **Phone:** 718-968-8700; **Board Cert:** Ophthalmology 1976; **Med School:** Albert Einstein Coll Med 1971; **Resid:** Ophthalmology, LI Jewish Hillside Med Ctr 1975; **Fac Appt:** Asst Clin Prof Oph, SUNY Downstate

Berman, David H MD (Oph) - **Spec Exp:** Retinal Detachment; Diabetic Eye Disease/Retinopathy; Macular Degeneration; **Hospital:** New York Eye & Ear Infirm of Mt Sinai, Brooklyn Hosp Ctr; **Address:** Brooklyn Retinal Vascular Ctr, 185 Montague St, Ste PH, Brooklyn, NY 11201; **Phone:** 718-222-3050; **Board Cert:** Ophthalmology 1989; **Med School:** SUNY Downstate 1982; **Resid:** Internal Medicine, Kings Co Hosp 1984; Ophthalmology, Kings Co Hosp 1987; **Fellow:** Ophthalmology, Kings Co Hosp 1988; Retina/Vitreous Surgery, Hermann Eye Ctr 1989; **Fac Appt:** Assoc Clin Prof Oph, SUNY Downstate

Brecher, Rubin MD (Oph) - **Spec Exp:** Diabetic Eye Disease/Retinopathy; Macular Degeneration; **Hospital:** Maimonides Med Ctr (page 98); **Address:** 736 Ocean Pkwy, Brooklyn, NY 11230; **Phone:** 718-851-1186; **Board Cert:** Ophthalmology 1991; **Med School:** Albert Einstein Coll Med 1984; **Resid:** Ophthalmology, Montefiore Med Ctr 1988; **Fellow:** Medical Retina, Moorefields Eye Hosp 1989

Deutsch, James A MD (Oph) - **Spec Exp:** Strabismus; Cataract Surgery; Glaucoma; Pediatric Ophthalmology; **Hospital:** SUNY Downstate Med Ctr (Univ Hosp Brooklyn) (page 449); **Address:** 110 Remsen St, Ste 1B, Brooklyn, NY 11201; **Phone:** 718-855-8700; **Board Cert:** Ophthalmology 1989; **Med School:** NYU Sch Med 1984; **Resid:** Ophthalmology, Mt Sinai Hosp 1988; **Fellow:** Pediatric Ophthalmology, Wills Eye Hosp 1989; **Fac Appt:** Asst Clin Prof Oph, Mount Sinai-Icahn Sch of Med

Douros, Stella MD (Oph) - **Spec Exp:** Diabetic Eye Disease/Retinopathy; Macular Degeneration; Retina/Vitreous Surgery; **Hospital:** New York Eye & Ear Infirm of Mt Sinai, Mt Sinai Hosp; **Address:** 7501 6th Ave, Brooklyn, NY 11209; **Phone:** 718-238-2336; **Board Cert:** Ophthalmology 2009; **Med School:** Albert Einstein Coll Med 1991; **Resid:** Ophthalmology, Lenox Hill Hosp 1995; **Fellow:** Vitreoretinal Surgery, Joslin Diabetes Ctr 1996

Dweck, Monica M MD (Oph) - **Spec Exp:** Eyelid Surgery; Tear Duct Problems; Orbital Diseases; **Hospital:** Mt Sinai Hosp, New York Eye & Ear Infirm of Mt Sinai; **Address:** Mt Sinai Brooklyn Heights Med Grp, 300 Cadman Plaza W, Fl 17, Brooklyn, NY 11201; **Phone:** 929-210-6200; **Board Cert:** Ophthalmology 2008; **Med School:** SUNY Downstate 1986; **Resid:** Ophthalmology, NY Eye & Ear Infirm 1990; **Fellow:** Oculoplastic Surgery, The Cleveland Clinic 1991

Feinstein, Neil C MD (Oph) - **Spec Exp:** Cataract Surgery; Glaucoma; Diabetic Eye Disease/Retinopathy; Macular Degeneration; **Hospital:** Maimonides Med Ctr (page 98); **Address:** 919 48th St, Brooklyn, NY 11219; **Phone:** 718-435-1800; **Board Cert:** Ophthalmology 1979; **Med School:** Albert Einstein Coll Med 1974; **Resid:** Internal Medicine, Maimonides Med Ctr 1975; Ophthalmology, SUNY Downstate Med Ctr 1978

Freedman, Jeffrey MD/PhD (Oph) - **Spec Exp:** Glaucoma; Uveitis; Retinal Disorders; **Hospital:** Kingsbrook Jewish Med Ctr; **Address:** 161 Atlantic Ave, Ste 203, Brooklyn, NY 11201; **Phone:** 718-596-9086; **Board Cert:** Ophthalmology 1975; **Med School:** South Africa 1964; **Resid:** Internal Medicine, Baragwanat Genl Hosp 1966; Ophthalmology, Transvaal Genl Hosp 1967; **Fellow:** Ophthalmology, SUNY Downstate Med Ctr 1970; **Fac Appt:** Prof Oph, SUNY Downstate

Hyman, George F MD (Oph) - **Spec Exp:** Corneal Disease; Glaucoma; **Address:** Brooklyn Eye Inst, 2460 Flatbush Ave, Ste 4, Brooklyn, NY 11234; **Phone:** 718-252-1200; **Board Cert:** Ophthalmology 1976; **Med School:** Univ MD Sch Med 1968; **Resid:** Ophthalmology, SUNY Downstate Med Ctr 1974; **Fellow:** Anterior Segment - External Disease, Univ Witwatersrand 1975; **Fac Appt:** Asst Clin Prof Oph, SUNY Downstate

Lazzaro, Douglas R MD (Oph) - **Spec Exp:** Corneal Disease & Surgery; Cornea Transplant; Refractive Surgery; **Hospital:** SUNY Downstate Med Ctr (Univ Hosp Brooklyn) (page 449), Lutheran Med Ctr - Brooklyn; **Address:** 7901 4th Ave, Brooklyn, NY 11209; **Phone:** 718-748-1334; **Board Cert:** Ophthalmology 2007; **Med School:** SUNY Downstate 1990; **Resid:** Ophthalmology, SUNY Downstate Med Ctr 1994; **Fellow:** Cornea & Refractive Surgery, Manhattan Eye & Ear Infirmary 1995; **Fac Appt:** Prof Oph, SUNY Downstate

Lebowitz, Mark A MD (Oph) - **Spec Exp:** LASIK-Refractive Surgery; Cataract Surgery; Corneal Disease & Surgery; **Hospital:** Lenox Hill Hosp (Manh Eye, Ear & Throat Hosp); **Address:** KLM Ophthalmology, 1301 Avenue J, Brooklyn, NY 11230; **Phone:** 718-284-1921; **Board Cert:** Ophthalmology 2006; **Med School:** NYU Sch Med 1982; **Resid:** Internal Medicine, Beth Israel Med Ctr 1983; Ophthalmology, SUNY Downstate Med Ctr 1986; **Fellow:** Cornea & Ext Eye Disease, Manhattan Eye & Ear Hosp 1987

Lish, Adam MD (Oph) - **Spec Exp:** Glaucoma; **Hospital:** Mt Sinai Beth Israel-BK; **Address:** Brook Plaza Ophthalmology, 1987 Utica Ave, Brooklyn, NY 11234; **Phone:** 718-968-8700; **Board Cert:** Ophthalmology 2006; **Med School:** Boston Univ 1989; **Resid:** Ophthalmology, SUNY Hlth Sci Ctr 1993; **Fellow:** Glaucoma, Mt Sinai Med Ctr 1994

Lombardo, James J MD (Oph) - **Spec Exp:** Diabetic Eye Disease/Retinopathy; Glaucoma; **Hospital:** SUNY Downstate Med Ctr (Univ Hosp Brooklyn) (page 449); **Address:** 7801 4th Ave, Brooklyn, NY 11209; **Phone:** 718-836-6661; **Board Cert:** Ophthalmology 1982; **Med School:** NYU Sch Med 1976; **Resid:** Internal Medicine, St Vincents Hosp 1977; Ophthalmology, NY Eye & Ear Infirmary 1980

Metz, Dennis MD (Oph) - **Hospital:** New York Comm Hosp; **Address:** Brook Plaza Ophthalmology, 1987 Utica Ave, Brooklyn, NY 11234; **Phone:** 718-968-8700; **Board Cert:** Ophthalmology 1983; **Med School:** Albert Einstein Coll Med 1978; **Resid:** Ophthalmology, Brookdale Univ Hosp Med Ctr 1982

Mogil, Laurey G MD (Oph) - **Spec Exp:** Glaucoma; **Hospital:** Mt Sinai Hosp; **Address:** KLM Ophthalmology, 1301 Avenue J, Brooklyn, NY 11230; **Phone:** 718-284-1921; **Board Cert:** Ophthalmology 2006; **Med School:** Albert Einstein Coll Med 1980; **Resid:** Ophthalmology, Mt Sinai Hosp 1984; **Fellow:** Glaucoma, Mt Sinai Hosp 1985; **Fac Appt:** Asst Clin Prof Oph, Mount Sinai-Icahn Sch of Med

Reich, Raymond MD (Oph) - **Spec Exp:** Cataract Surgery; Ophthalmic Plastic Surgery; Laser Refractive Surgery; **Hospital:** Maimonides Med Ctr (page 98); **Address:** 1575 E 19th St, Brooklyn, NY 11230; **Phone:** 718-332-6200; **Board Cert:** Ophthalmology 1978; **Med School:** Albert Einstein Coll Med 1973; **Resid:** Ophthalmology, Univ Hosp 1977; **Fellow:** Ophthalmic Plastic Surgery, Mass Eye & Ear Infirm 1978; **Fac Appt:** Asst Prof Oph, SUNY Downstate

Saffra, Norman MD (Oph) - **Spec Exp:** Microsurgery; Retinal Disorders; Diabetic Eye Disease/Retinopathy; **Hospital:** Maimonides Med Ctr (page 98); **Address:** 902 49th St, Brooklyn, NY 11219; **Phone:** 718-283-8000; **Board Cert:** Ophthalmology 2005; **Med School:** Albert Einstein Coll Med 1988; **Resid:** Ophthalmology, Montefiore Med Ctr 1992; **Fellow:** Retina/Vitreous Surgery, SUNY Downstate Med Ctr 1993; **Fac Appt:** Clin Prof Oph, Mount Sinai-Icahn Sch of Med

Sciortino, Patrick J MD (Oph) - **Spec Exp:** LASIK-Refractive Surgery; Cataract Surgery; Laser Vision Surgery; **Hospital:** New York Comm Hosp; **Address:** Eye Care Ctr, 914 Bay Ridge Pkwy, Brooklyn, NY 11228; **Phone:** 718-748-5700; **Board Cert:** Ophthalmology 2009; **Med School:** NY Med Coll 1978; **Resid:** Ophthalmology, St Vincents Hosp 1980; Ophthalmology, Catholic Med Ctr 1983; **Fellow:** Neuro-Ophthalmology, SUNY Downstate Med Ctr 1984

Seidman, Mitchell S DO (Oph) - **Spec Exp:** Cataract Surgery; **Hospital:** New York Methodist Hosp (page 448); **Address:** 2989 Ocean Pkwy, Brooklyn, NY 11235; **Phone:** 718-332-2020; **Board Cert:** Ophthalmology 1979; **Med School:** Philadelphia Coll Osteo Med 1974; **Resid:** Ophthalmology, Temple Univ Hosp 1978; **Fellow:** Anterior Segment - External Disease, Med Ctr Hosp 1979

Sherman, Steven I DO (Oph) - **Spec Exp:** Glaucoma; Anterior Segment Surgery; **Hospital:** New York Methodist Hosp (page 448), Interfaith Med Ctr; **Address:** 2303 Avenue Z, Brooklyn, NY 11235; **Phone:** 718-934-6600; **Board Cert:** Ophthalmology 1990; **Med School:** Univ Osteo Med & Hlth Sci, Des Moines 1977; **Resid:** Internal Medicine, Coney Island Hosp 1979; Ophthalmology, UHPHS Hosp 1982; **Fellow:** Glaucoma, Kings Co Hosp Ctr 1983; **Fac Appt:** Asst Clin Prof Oph, Touro Coll Osteopathic Med-NY

Smith, Edward F MD (Oph) - **Spec Exp:** Cataract Surgery; Neuro-Ophthalmology; **Hospital:** SUNY Downstate Med Ctr (Univ Hosp Brooklyn) (page 449), Kingsbrook Jewish Med Ctr; **Address:** Downstate Ophthalmology Assocs, 34 Plaza St E, Brooklyn, NY 11238; **Phone:** 718-638-2020; **Board Cert:** Ophthalmology 1989; **Med School:** SUNY Downstate 1984; **Resid:** Ophthalmology, SUNY Downstate Med Ctr 1988; **Fellow:** Neuro-Ophthalmology, SUNY Downstate Med Ctr 1989; **Fac Appt:** Assoc Clin Prof Oph, SUNY Downstate

Stein, Arnold Jay MD (Oph) - **Spec Exp:** Retinal Disorders; Glaucoma; Cataract Surgery; Laser Surgery; **Hospital:** Mt Sinai Beth Israel-BK, Long Is Jewish Med Ctr; **Address:** 1226 Ocean Pkwy, Brooklyn, NY 11230; **Phone:** 718-692-0400; **Board Cert:** Ophthalmology 1987; **Med School:** SUNY Downstate 1982; **Resid:** Ophthalmology, LIJ Med Ctr 1986; **Fac Appt:** Asst Clin Prof Oph, Albert Einstein Coll Med

Unterricht, Sam L MD (Oph) - **Spec Exp:** Macular Disease/Degeneration; Retinal Disorders; Optic Nerve Disorders; Neuro-Ophthalmology; **Hospital:** New York Methodist Hosp (page 448), Kingsbrook Jewish Med Ctr; **Address:** 20 Plaza St E, Brooklyn, NY 11238; **Phone:** 718-622-5800; **Board Cert:** Ophthalmology 1982; **Med School:** SUNY Downstate 1976; **Resid:** Ophthalmology, SUNY Downstate Med Ctr 1980; **Fellow:** Neuro-Ophthalmology, Kingsbrook Jewish Med Ctr 1981; Retina/Vitreous Surgery, SUNY Downstate Med Ctr 1982; **Fac Appt:** Asst Clin Prof Oph, SUNY Downstate

Zellner, James H MD (Oph) - **Spec Exp:** Laser Refractive Surgery; Cataract Surgery; **Hospital:** New York Eye & Ear Infirm of Mt Sinai; **Address:** 7817 5th Ave, Brooklyn, NY 11209; **Phone:** 718-748-2020; **Board Cert:** Ophthalmology 1982; **Med School:** Albert Einstein Coll Med 1977; **Resid:** Ophthalmology, SUNY Downstate Med Ctr 1981

Orthopaedic Surgery

Kolker, Dov M MD (OrS) - **Spec Exp:** Foot & Ankle Surgery; Knee Injuries; Trauma; Sports Medicine; **Hospital:** Maimonides Med Ctr (page 98), Mt Sinai Hosp; **Address:** 6010 Bay Pkwy Fl 7, Brooklyn, NY 11204; **Phone:** 212-744-2200; **Board Cert:** Orthopaedic Surgery 2008; **Med School:** Tufts Univ 1994; **Resid:** Surgery, Beth Israel Deaconess Med Ctr 1995; Orthopaedic Surgery, UMass Med Ctr 1999; **Fellow:** Trauma, AO Trauma Prog 2000; Foot & Ankle Surgery, Mt Sinai Hosp 2001

Mani, John Vijay MD (OrS) - **Spec Exp:** Hip Replacement; Knee Replacement; **Hospital:** Lutheran Med Ctr - Brooklyn; **Address:** 161 Atlantic Ave, Brooklyn, NY 11201; **Phone:** 718-855-0088; **Board Cert:** Orthopaedic Surgery 1977; **Med School:** India 1970; **Resid:** Orthopaedic Surgery, Brookdale Hosp 1976; **Fellow:** Arthritis Surgery, Hosp Special Surgery 1978; **Fac Appt:** Assoc Clin Prof OrS, SUNY Downstate

Menezes, Placido A MD (OrS) - **Spec Exp:** Knee Replacement; Fractures; Joint Replacement; **Hospital:** New York Methodist Hosp (page 448); **Address:** 543 2nd St, Brooklyn, NY 11215; **Phone:** 718-788-7600; **Board Cert:** Orthopaedic Surgery 1980; **Med School:** India 1970; **Resid:** Surgery, NY Methodist Hosp 1976; Orthopaedic Surgery, Brooklyn Jewish Hosp & Med Ctr 1978

Merola, Andrew A MD (OrS) - **Spec Exp:** Spinal Surgery; Scoliosis; **Hospital:** New York Methodist Hosp (page 448), Mt Sinai Hosp; **Address:** 567 1st St, Brooklyn, NY 11215; **Phone:** 718-783-5542; **Board Cert:** Orthopaedic Surgery 2009; **Med School:** Howard Univ 1990; **Resid:** Orthopaedic Surgery, SUNY Downstate Med Ctr 1995; **Fellow:** Spine Surgery, Univ CO Hosp 1996; **Fac Appt:** Assoc Prof OrS, SUNY Downstate

Morgan, Daniel J MD (OrS) - **Spec Exp:** Arthroscopic Surgery; Hip & Knee Replacement; Shoulder Surgery; PRP (Platelet Rich Plasma); **Hospital:** Mt Sinai Beth Israel-BK; **Address:** Kings Hwy Orthopedic Assocs, 3131 Kings Hwy, Ste C11, Brooklyn, NY 11234; **Phone:** 718-258-2588; **Board Cert:** Orthopaedic Surgery 2011; **Med School:** Univ MD Sch Med 1985; **Resid:** Surgery, Washington Hosp Ctr 1986; Orthopaedic Surgery, Kingsbrook Jewish Med Ctr 1997

Soifer, Todd B MD (OrS) - **Spec Exp:** Arthritis; Knee Injuries; Arthroscopic Surgery; Rotator Cuff Surgery; **Hospital:** Mt Sinai Beth Israel-BK; **Address:** Kings Hwy Orthopedic Assocs, 3131 Kings Hwy, Ste C11, Brooklyn, NY 11234; **Phone:** 718-258-2588; **Board Cert:** Orthopaedic Surgery 2007; **Med School:** Mount Sinai Sch Med 1989; **Resid:** Orthopaedic Surgery, Beth Israel Med Ctr 1994

Splain, Shepard H DO (OrS) - **Spec Exp:** Arthroscopic Surgery; Shoulder & Knee Reconstruction; Sports Medicine; Joint Replacement; **Hospital:** Brookdale Univ Hosp Med Ctr; **Address:** Brookdale Univ Hosp, Orthopaedic Surgery, 1 Brookdale Plaza, Ste 152, Brooklyn, NY 11212; **Phone:** 718-240-5888; **Board Cert:** Orthopaedic Surgery 1980; **Med School:** Mich State Univ Coll Osteo Med 1973; **Resid:** Orthopaedic Surgery, Brookdale Hosp 1978; **Fellow:** Sports Medicine, Oklahoma Hlth Scis Ctr 1979; **Fac Appt:** Assoc Clin Prof OrS, SUNY Downstate

Tepler, Melvin MD (OrS) - **Spec Exp:** Fractures; **Hospital:** Maimonides Med Ctr (page 98); **Address:** 1252 E 9th St, Brooklyn, NY 11230; **Phone:** 718-677-6000; **Board Cert:** Orthopaedic Surgery 2009; **Med School:** NY Med Coll 1980; **Resid:** Surgery, Maimonides Med Ctr 1981; Orthopaedic Surgery, Maimonides Med Ctr 1985

Urban Jr, William P MD (OrS) - **Spec Exp:** Sports Medicine; Arthroscopic Surgery; Shoulder & Knee Surgery; Knee Injuries/ACL/Meniscus Tears; **Hospital:** SUNY Downstate Med Ctr (Univ Hosp Brooklyn) (page 449); **Address:** SUNY Downstate Med Ctr, Orthopaedics, 450 Clarkson Ave, Box 30, Brooklyn, NY 11203; **Phone:** 718-270-4540; **Board Cert:** Orthopaedic Surgery 2009; Orthopaedic Sports Medicine 2013; **Med School:** SUNY Downstate 1990; **Resid:** Orthopaedic Surgery, SUNY Downstate Medical Ctr 1994; **Fellow:** Orthopaedic Sports Medicine, Univ Kentucky Med Ctr 1995; **Fac Appt:** Assoc Prof OrS, SUNY Downstate

Walsh, Raymond B MD (OrS) - **Spec Exp:** Hip Replacement; Knee Replacement; **Hospital:** Lutheran Med Ctr - Brooklyn; **Address:** Ovington Orthopedic Assocs, 6900 4th Ave Fl 2, Brooklyn, NY 11209; **Phone:** 718-238-6400; **Board Cert:** Orthopaedic Surgery 1981; **Med School:** England, UK 1974; **Resid:** Surgery, Maimonides Med Ctr 1976; Orthopaedic Surgery, Maimonides Med Ctr 1980

Otolaryngology

Branovan, Daniel Igor MD (Oto) - **Spec Exp:** Sinus Disorders/Surgery; Endoscopic Sinus Surgery; Minimally Invasive Surgery; **Address:** NY Ear, Nose & Throat Inst, 1810 Voorhies Ave, Brooklyn, NY 11235; **Phone:** 718-616-1000; **Board Cert:** Otolaryngology 1999; **Med School:** Stanford Univ 1992; **Resid:** Surgery, St Vincents Hosp 1993; Otolaryngology, NY Eye & Ear Infirm 1997

Chaudhry, M. Rashid MD (Oto) - **Spec Exp:** Cosmetic Surgery-Face; Sinus Surgery; Head & Neck Cancer Reconstruction; **Hospital:** Brookdale Univ Hosp Med Ctr; **Address:** Brookdale Univ Hosp, Otolaryngology, 1 Brookdale Plaza, Ste 157-CHC, Brooklyn, NY 11212; **Phone:** 718-240-6366; **Board Cert:** Otolaryngology 1978; **Med School:** Pakistan 1969; **Resid:** Surgery, Downstate Med Ctr-Kings Co 1974; Otolaryngology, Downstate Med Ctr-Kings Co 1978; **Fac Appt:** Asst Prof Oto, SUNY Downstate

Habib, Ramez MD (Oto) - **Hospital:** New York Methodist Hosp (page 448); **Address:** ENT and Allergy Assocs, 7333 6th Ave, Brooklyn, NY 11209-2607; **Phone:** 718-833-0515; **Board Cert:** Otolaryngology 2005; **Med School:** Mount Sinai-Icahn Sch of Med 1999; **Resid:** Otolaryngology, SUNY Downstate Med Ctr 2004

Hanson, Matthew B MD (Oto) - **Spec Exp:** Otology; **Hospital:** SUNY Downstate Med Ctr (Univ Hosp Brooklyn) (page 449); **Address:** SUNY Downstate Med Ctr, Otolaryngology, 470 Clarkson Ave, Ste H, Box 126, Brooklyn, NY 11203; **Phone:** 718-270-4701; **Board Cert:** Otolaryngology 1997; Neurotology 2008; **Med School:** Univ Iowa Coll Med 1989; **Resid:** Otolaryngology, NY-Presby/Columbia Univ Med Ctr 1995; **Fellow:** Neurotology, Baptist Hosp 1997; **Fac Appt:** Asst Prof Oto, SUNY Downstate

Lagmay, Victor M MD (Oto) - **Spec Exp:** Thyroid & Parathyroid Surgery; Head & Neck Cancer & Surgery; Endoscopic Sinus Surgery; **Hospital:** Maimonides Med Ctr (page 98); **Address:** Maimonides Med Ctr, Otolaryngology, 919 49th St, Brooklyn, NY 11219; **Phone:** 718-283-6260; **Board Cert:** Otolaryngology 1999; **Med School:** NYU Sch Med 1992; **Resid:** Otolaryngology, NYU Med Ctr 1998; **Fellow:** Head and Neck Surgery, Beth Israel Med Ctr 1999; **Fac Appt:** Asst Clin Prof S, SUNY Downstate

Song, Christopher S MD (Oto) - **Hospital:** New York Methodist Hosp (page 448), SUNY Downstate Med Ctr (Univ Hosp Brooklyn) (page 449); **Address:** ENT and Allergy Assocs, 7333 6th Ave, Brooklyn, NY 11209-2607; **Phone:** 718-833-0515; **Board Cert:** Otolaryngology 2005; **Med School:** Tufts Univ 1999; **Resid:** Otolaryngology, SUNY Hlth Sci Ctr 2004

Vastola, A Paul MD (Oto) - **Spec Exp:** Throat Disorders; Pediatric Otolaryngology; Cleft Palate/Lip; **Hospital:** Maimonides Med Ctr (page 98); **Address:** ENT & Allergy Assocs, 300 Cadman Plaza W, Ste 1301, Brooklyn, NY 11201; **Phone:** 718-208-4449; **Board Cert:** Otolaryngology 1995; **Med School:** Boston Univ 1988; **Resid:** Surgery, NY Hosp-Cornell Med Ctr 1990; Otolaryngology, Manhattan Eye, Ear & Throat Hosp 1993; **Fellow:** Pediatric Otolaryngology, Texas Chldn's Hosp 1994; **Fac Appt:** Asst Clin Prof Oto, SUNY Downstate

Pain Medicine

Agarwal, Sanjeev MD (PM) - **Spec Exp:** Pain-Interventional Techniques; Pain-After Spinal Intervention; Pain-Back & Neck; Pain-Low Back; **Hospital:** SUNY Downstate Med Ctr (Univ Hosp Brooklyn)(page 449), Brooklyn Hosp Ctr; **Address:** Orthopedics Assocs at SUNY Downstate, 710 Parkside Ave, Brooklyn, NY 11203; **Phone:** 718-270-4540; **Board Cert:** Physical Medicine & Rehabilitation 2007; Pain Medicine 2007; Sports Medicine 2011; Hospice & Palliative Medicine 2012; **Med School:** India 1989; **Resid:** Internal Medicine, Flushing Hosp Med Crt 2003; Physical Medicine & Rehabilitation, Nassau Community Med ctr 2006; **Fellow:** Pain Medicine, Univ Cincinnati Hosp 2007; **Fac Appt:** Asst Prof PMR, SUNY Downstate

Lefkowitz, Mathew MD (PM) - **Spec Exp:** Pain-Low Back; Pain-After Spinal Intervention; Sciatica; Pain-Back & Neck; **Hospital:** New York Methodist Hosp (page 448); **Address:** 185 Montague St Fl 6, Brooklyn, NY 11201; **Phone:** 718-625-4244; **Board Cert:** Anesthesiology 1993; Pain Medicine 2005; **Med School:** Belgium 1983; **Resid:** Anesthesiology, Mt Sinai Hosp 1986; **Fellow:** Pain Medicine, Mt Sinai Hosp 1987

Reyfman, Leonid MD (PM) - **Spec Exp:** Pain Rehabilitation & Psychiatry; Pain Management; Pain-Interventional Techniques; **Hospital:** SUNY Downstate Med Ctr (Univ Hosp Brooklyn) (page 449); **Address:** Pain Phys of NY, 2279 Coney Island Ave, Ste 2A, Brooklyn, NY 11223; **Phone:** 718-998-9890; **Board Cert:** Anesthesiology 2007; Pain Medicine 2007; **Med School:** Dominica 2002; **Resid:** Anesthesiology, Maimonides Med Ctr 2006; **Fellow:** Pain Medicine, St Lukes-Roosevelt Hosp 2007; **Fac Appt:** Asst Clin Prof Anes, SUNY Downstate

Pathology

Vigorita, Vincent J MD (Path) - **Spec Exp:** Bone Pathology; Surgical Pathology; **Hospital:** Maimonides Med Ctr (page 98), SUNY Downstate Med Ctr (Univ Hosp Brooklyn) (page 449); **Address:** SUNY Downstate Med Ctr, Pathology, 4802 10th Ave, Brooklyn, NY 11219; **Phone:** 917-648-5945; **Board Cert:** Anatomic Pathology 1980; **Med School:** NY Med Coll 1976; **Resid:** Pathology, Johns Hopkins Hosp 1978; **Fellow:** Pathology, Meml Sloan Kettering Cancer Ctr 1979; **Fac Appt:** Prof Path, SUNY Downstate

Pediatric Cardiology

Kaplovitz, Harry S MD (PCd) - **Spec Exp:** Syncope; Echocardiography; Heart Failure; **Hospital:** Maimonides Med Ctr (page 98); **Address:** Maimonides-Chldns Hosp, Ped Cardiology, 4802 10th Ave, rm G1, Brooklyn, NY 11219; **Phone:** 718-283-7500; **Board Cert:** Pediatrics 1988; Pediatric Cardiology 2014; **Med School:** Albert Einstein Coll Med 1981; **Resid:** Pediatrics, N Shore Univ Hosp 1984; **Fellow:** Pediatric Cardiology, NYU Med Ctr 1986

Ramaswamy, Prema MD (PCd) - **Spec Exp:** Fetal Echocardiography; Congenital Heart Disease; **Hospital:** Maimonides Med Ctr (page 98); **Address:** Maimonides-Chldns Hosp, Ped Cardiology, 4802 10th Ave, rm G1, Brooklyn, NY 11219; **Phone:** 718-283-7500; **Board Cert:** Pediatrics 2008; Pediatric Cardiology 2011; **Med School:** India 1986; **Resid:** Pediatrics, M Y Hosp 1990; Pediatrics, Montefiore Med Ctr 1993; **Fellow:** Pediatric Cardiology, NY-Presby/Weill Cornell Med Ctr 1996

Pediatric Endocrinology

Agdere, Levon MD (PEn) - **Spec Exp:** Diabetes; Short Stature in Children; Thyroid Disorders; **Hospital:** New York Methodist Hosp (page 448); **Address:** 263 7th Ave, Ste 3B, Brooklyn, NY 11215; **Phone:** 718-246-8540; **Board Cert:** Pediatric Endocrinology 2013; **Med School:** Turkey 1981; **Resid:** Pediatrics, Lutheran Med Ctr 1986; **Fellow:** Pediatric Endocrinology, NY-Presby/Weill Cornell Med Ctr 1989

Avruskin, Theodore W MD (PEn) - **Spec Exp:** Growth Disorders; Diabetes; Thyroid Disorders; **Hospital:** Brookdale Univ Hosp Med Ctr, SUNY Downstate Med Ctr (Univ Hosp Brooklyn) (page 449); **Address:** 1 Brookdale Plaza, Ste 222, Brooklyn, NY 11212; **Phone:** 718-240-5960; **Board Cert:** Pediatrics 1965; **Med School:** Univ Toronto 1960; **Resid:** Pediatrics, Montreal Chldns Hosp 1962; Pediatrics, Chldns Hosp Med Ctr 1964; **Fellow:** Pediatric Endocrinology, Chldns Hosp Med Ctr 1968

Pediatric Gastroenterology

Breglio, Keith J MD (PGe) - **Spec Exp:** Crohn's Disease; Ulcerative Colitis; Gastroesophageal Reflux Disease (GERD); **Hospital:** Maimonides Med Ctr (page 98); **Address:** Maimonides-Chldns Hosp, Ped Gastro, 4802 10th Ave Fl 3, Brooklyn, NY 11219; **Phone:** 718-283-8260; **Board Cert:** Pediatrics 2006; Pediatric Gastroenterology 2009; **Med School:** SUNY Upstate Med Univ 2002; **Resid:** Pediatrics, Schneider Chldns Hosp 2006; **Fellow:** Pediatric Gastroenterology, Mt Sinai Hosp 2009; **Fac Appt:** Asst Prof Ped, Mount Sinai Sch Med

Jelin, Abraham MD (PGe) - **Spec Exp:** Nutrition; Breast Feeding Problems; Gastroesophageal Reflux Disease (GERD); Constipation; **Hospital:** Brooklyn Hosp Ctr; **Address:** 121 DeKalb Ave, Brooklyn, NY 11201; **Phone:** 718-250-6277; **Board Cert:** Pediatrics 1978; Pediatric Gastroenterology 2012; **Med School:** NYU Sch Med 1972; **Resid:** Pediatrics, Montefiore Med Ctr 1974; Pediatrics, Brookdale Univ Hosp 1975; **Fellow:** Pediatric Gastroenterology, Emory Univ Hosp 1977; **Fac Appt:** Asst Clin Prof Ped, NYU Sch Med

McFarlane-Ferreira, Yvonne B MD (PGe) - **Spec Exp:** Pain-Abdominal Recurrent; Failure to Thrive; Constipation; Inflammatory Bowel Disease; **Hospital:** New York Methodist Hosp (page 448); **Address:** 263 7th Ave, Ste 3B, Brooklyn, NY 11215; **Phone:** 718-246-8515; **Board Cert:** Pediatrics 2012; Pediatric Gastroenterology 2010; **Med School:** West Indies 1983; **Resid:** Anesthesiology, Princess Margaret Hosp 1986; Pediatrics, Brooklyn Hosp 1989; **Fellow:** Pediatric Gastroenterology, Mt Sinai Hosp 1992; **Fac Appt:** Asst Clin Prof Ped, Cornell Univ-Weill Med Coll

Rabinowitz, Simon S MD/PhD (PGe) - **Spec Exp:** Inflammatory Bowel Disease; Hepatitis; Gastroesophageal Reflux Disease (GERD); Gastrointestinal Disorders; **Hospital:** SUNY Downstate Med Ctr (Univ Hosp Brooklyn) (page 449); **Address:** SUNY Downstate Med Ctr, 445 Lenox Rd, Box 49, Brooklyn, NY 11203; **Phone:** 718-270-8884; **Board Cert:** Pediatrics 2009; Pediatric Gastroenterology 2013; **Med School:** Univ Miami Sch Med 1983; **Resid:** Pediatrics, Mt Sinai Hosp 1985; **Fellow:** Pediatric Gastroenterology, Mt Sinai Hosp 1987

Schwarz, Steven M MD (PGe) - **Spec Exp:** Gastroesophageal Reflux Disease (GERD); Nutrition; Endoscopy; Inflammatory Bowel Disease; **Hospital:** SUNY Downstate Med Ctr (Univ Hosp Brooklyn) (page 449), Mt Sinai Beth Israel; **Address:** SUNY Chldns Hosp, Ped Gastroenterology, 445 Lenox Rd Fl 4, Box 49, Brooklyn, NY 11203; **Phone:** 718-270-4714; **Board Cert:** Pediatrics 1979; Pediatric Gastroenterology 2012; **Med School:** Columbia P&S 1974; **Resid:** Pediatrics, NY-Presby/Columbia Univ Med Ctr 1977; **Fellow:** Pediatric Gastroenterology, Stanford Univ Hosp & Clins 1978; Pediatric Gastroenterology, NY-Presby/Columbia Univ Med Ctr 1980; **Fac Appt:** Prof Ped, SUNY Downstate

Wetzler, Graciela MD (PGe) - **Spec Exp:** Gastroesophageal Reflux Disease (GERD); Inflammatory Bowel Disease/Crohn's; Peptic Ulcer Disease; **Hospital:** Maimonides Med Ctr (page 98); **Address:** Maimonides-Chlds Hosp, Ped Gastro, 948 48th St Fl 3, Brooklyn, NY 11219; **Phone:** 718-283-7500; **Board Cert:** Pediatric Gastroenterology 2010; **Med School:** Argentina 1984; **Resid:** Pediatrics, Montefiore Med Ctr 1992; **Fellow:** Pediatric Gastroenterology, NY-Presby/Weill Cornell Med Ctr 1995; **Fac Appt:** Assoc Clin Prof Ped, SUNY Downstate

Pediatric Hematology-Oncology

Guarini, Ludovico MD (PHO) - **Spec Exp:** Leukemia; Solid Tumors; **Hospital:** Maimonides Med Ctr (page 98); **Address:** Maimonides Med Ctr, Pediatrics, 6300 8th Ave Fl 2, Brooklyn, NY 11220; **Phone:** 718-765-2671; **Board Cert:** Pediatrics 1984; Pediatric Hematology-Oncology 2014; **Med School:** Italy 1974; **Resid:** Pediatrics, Beth Israel Med Ctr 1981; **Fellow:** Pediatric Hematology-Oncology, NY-Presby/Columbia Univ Med Ctr 1984; **Fac Appt:** Assoc Prof Ped, SUNY Hlth Sci Ctr

Kulpa, Jolanta MD (PHO) - **Spec Exp:** Sickle Cell Disease; Leukemia; Thalassemia; Bleeding/Coagulation Disorders; **Hospital:** New York Methodist Hosp (page 448); **Address:** Park Slope Pediatrics, 263 7th Ave, Ste 3B, Brooklyn, NY 11215; **Phone:** 718-780-3066; **Board Cert:** Pediatrics 1983; Pediatric Hematology-Oncology 1984; **Med School:** Med Coll PA 1972; **Resid:** Pediatrics, Lenox Hill Hosp 1975; **Fellow:** Blood Banking Transfusion Medicine, NY Blood Center 1977; Pediatric Hematology-Oncology, NY Hosp/Cornell/Sloan Kettering 1979

Sadanandan, Swayam MD (PHO) - **Spec Exp:** Sickle Cell Disease; Bleeding/Coagulation Disorders; Anemia; Pediatric Cancers; **Hospital:** Brooklyn Hosp Ctr; **Address:** 121 DeKalb Ave Fl 10, Brooklyn, NY 11201; **Phone:** 718-250-6074; **Board Cert:** Pediatrics 1980; Pediatric Hematology-Oncology 1984; **Med School:** India 1972; **Resid:** Pediatrics, St Vincents Hosp 1979; **Fellow:** Pediatric Hematology-Oncology, NYU Med Ctr 1981

Sundaram, Revathy MD (PHO) - **Spec Exp:** Thalassemia; Sickle Cell Disease; Leukemia; **Hospital:** New York Methodist Hosp (page 448); **Address:** Park Slope Pediatrics, 263 7th Ave, Ste 3B, Brooklyn, NY 11215; **Phone:** 718-780-3066; **Board Cert:** Pediatrics 1980; Pediatric Hematology-Oncology 1984; **Med School:** India 1973; **Resid:** Pediatrics, Rutgers Univ Hosp 1978; Pediatrics, Long Island Hosp 1980; **Fellow:** Pediatric Hematology-Oncology, Long Island Hosp 1983; **Fac Appt:** Asst Prof Ped, SUNY Hlth Sci Ctr

Viswanathan, Kusum MD (PHO) - **Spec Exp:** Sickle Cell Disease; Pediatric Cancers; Anemia; **Hospital:** Brookdale Univ Hosp Med Ctr; **Address:** Brookdale Univ Hosp, Ped Hem/Onc, 1 Brookdale Plaza, rm 346-CHC, Brooklyn, NY 11212; **Phone:** 718-240-5904; **Board Cert:** Pediatrics 1986; Pediatric Hematology-Oncology 1987; **Med School:** India 1980; **Resid:** Pediatrics, Long Island Coll Hosp 1984; **Fellow:** Pediatric Hematology-Oncology, Long Island Coll Hosp 1986

Pediatric Nephrology

Kaplan, Matthew R MD (PNep) - **Spec Exp:** Hypertension; Glomerulonephritis; **Hospital:** Brooklyn Hosp Ctr; **Address:** Brooklyn Hosp Ctr, Ped Nephrology, 240 Willoughby St Fl 9, Brooklyn, NY 11201; **Phone:** 718-250-6911; **Board Cert:** Pediatrics 1974; Pediatric Nephrology 1976; **Med School:** SUNY Downstate 1969; **Resid:** Pediatrics, NY-Presby/Weill Cornell Med Ctr 1973; **Fellow:** Pediatric Nephrology, NY-Presby/Weill Cornell Med Ctr 1976; **Fac Appt:** Assoc Clin Prof Ped, SUNY Downstate

Pediatric Otolaryngology

Goldsmith, Ari J MD (PO) - **Spec Exp:** Voice Disorders; Airway Disorders; Hearing Loss; Sleep Apnea; **Hospital:** Maimonides Med Ctr (page 98); **Address:** 921 49th St, Brooklyn, NY 11219; **Phone:** 718-283-6260; **Board Cert:** Otolaryngology 1994; **Med School:** Albert Einstein Coll Med 1988; **Resid:** Otolaryngology, LIJ Hosp 1993; **Fellow:** Pediatric Otolaryngology, Chldns Hosp 1994; **Fac Appt:** Assoc Prof Oto, SUNY Downstate

Rosenfeld, Richard M MD (PO) - **Spec Exp:** Sinus Disorders/Surgery; Head & Neck Surgery; Ear Disorders/Surgery; **Hospital:** SUNY Downstate Med Ctr (Univ Hosp Brooklyn) (page 449); **Address:** SUNY Downstate, Otolaryngology, 134 Atlantic Ave, Brooklyn, NY 11201; **Phone:** 718-780-1498; **Board Cert:** Otolaryngology 1989; **Med School:** SUNY Buffalo 1984; **Resid:** Surgery, Mt Sinai Hosp 1986; Otolaryngology, Mt Sinai Hosp 1989; **Fellow:** Pediatric Otolaryngology, Chldns Hosp 1991; **Fac Appt:** Prof Oto, SUNY Downstate

Pediatric Pulmonology

Giusti, Robert J MD (PPul) - **Spec Exp:** Cystic Fibrosis; Asthma; Cough-Chronic; **Hospital:** NYU Langone Med Ctr (page 104); **Address:** NYU Med Ctr, Ped Pulmonology, 160 E 32nd St, L-3, New York, NY 10016; **Phone:** 212-263-5940; **Board Cert:** Pediatrics 1987; Pediatric Pulmonology 2011; **Med School:** SUNY Downstate 1981; **Resid:** Pediatrics, NYU-Bellevue Hosp 1985; **Fac Appt:** Assoc Clin Prof Ped, NYU Sch Med

Lee, Haesoon MD (PPul) - **Spec Exp:** Asthma; Sleep Apnea; Tuberculosis; Airway Disorders; **Hospital:** SUNY Downstate Med Ctr (Univ Hosp Brooklyn) (page 449), Kings Co Hosp Ctr; **Address:** SUNY Downstate, Pediatrics, 450 Clarkson Ave, Box 49, Brooklyn, NY 11203; **Phone:** 718-221-5316; **Board Cert:** Pediatrics 1979; Pediatric Pulmonology 2011; **Med School:** South Korea 1972; **Resid:** Pediatrics, St Francis Hosp 1975; **Fellow:** Pediatric Pulmonology, Albert Einstein Affil Hosp 1977; **Fac Appt:** Assoc Prof Ped, SUNY Downstate

Marcus, Michael MD (PPul) - **Spec Exp:** Asthma; Sleep Apnea; Chronic Lung Disease; Gastroesophageal Reflux Disease (GERD); **Hospital:** Maimonides Med Ctr (page 98), Richmond Univ Med Ctr; **Address:** 948 48th St, Brooklyn, NY 11219; **Phone:** 718-980-5864; **Board Cert:** Pediatrics 1984; Allergy & Immunology 1987; Pediatric Pulmonology 2008; **Med School:** SUNY Stony Brook 1980; **Resid:** Pediatrics, Nassau Co Med Ctr 1983; **Fellow:** Pediatric Pulmonology, Chldns Hosp 1985; Allergy & Immunology, Chldns Hosp 1985; **Fac Appt:** Assoc Clin Prof Ped, NYU Sch Med

Narula, Pramod MD (PPul) - **Spec Exp:** Asthma; Chronic Lung Disease; **Hospital:** New York Methodist Hosp (page 448); **Address:** 501 6th St, Brooklyn, NY 11215; **Phone:** 718-780-5941; **Board Cert:** Pediatrics 2012; Pediatric Pulmonology 2008; **Med School:** India 1977; **Resid:** Pediatrics, Winthrop Univ Hosp 1990; **Fellow:** Pediatric Pulmonology, NY-Presby/Columbia Univ Med Ctr 1994; **Fac Appt:** Clin Prof Ped, Cornell Univ-Weill Med Coll

Needleman, Joshua MD (PPul) - **Spec Exp:** Asthma & Chronic Lung Disease; Cystic Fibrosis; Bronchoscopy; Exercise Physiology; **Hospital:** Maimonides Med Ctr (page 98); **Address:** Maimonides-Chldns Hosp, Ped Pulmonology, 948 48th St Fl 3, Brooklyn, NY 11219; **Phone:** 718-283-7500; **Board Cert:** Pediatric Pulmonology 2013; **Med School:** Temple Univ 1991; **Resid:** Pediatrics, Univ MD Med Ctr 1995; **Fellow:** Pediatric Pulmonology, St Christophers Hosp Chldn 1998

Pediatric Urology

Friedman, Steven C MD (Ped Uro) - **Spec Exp:** Urinary Tract Infections; Robotic Urologic Surgery; Urinary Reconstruction; Genital Reconstruction-Pediatric; **Hospital:** Maimonides Med Ctr (page 98), NS-LIJ Hlth Sys; **Address:** Pediatric Urology Assocs, 745 64th St Fl 4, Brooklyn, NY 11220; **Phone:** 718-833-2600; **Board Cert:** Urology 2010; Pediatric Urology 2010; **Med School:** SUNY Downstate 1983; **Resid:** Surgery, Beth Israel Med Ctr 1985; Urology, Maimonides Med Ctr 1988; **Fellow:** Pediatric Urology, Chldns Hosp 1991

Pediatrics

Ajl, Stephen MD (Ped) *PCP* - **Spec Exp:** Child Abuse; **Hospital:** Brooklyn Hosp Ctr; **Address:** 121 DeKalb Ave, Brooklyn, NY 11201; **Phone:** 718-250-8764; **Board Cert:** Pediatrics 1980; Child Abuse Pediatrics 2009; **Med School:** Temple Univ 1975; **Resid:** Pediatrics, NY-Presby Hosp/Weill Cornell Med Ctr 1978; **Fellow:** Ambulatory Pediatrics, Mt Sinai Hosp 1979

Bulmash, Max A MD (Ped) *PCP* - **Hospital:** Maimonides Med Ctr (page 98), NYU Langone Med Ctr (page 104); **Address:** Kensington Pediatrics, 3904 16th Ave, Brooklyn, NY 11218; **Phone:** 718-851-8080; **Board Cert:** Pediatrics 1987; **Med School:** Univ MD Sch Med 1978; **Resid:** Pediatrics, Maimonides Med Ctr 1984; **Fac Appt:** Asst Clin Prof Ped, SUNY Downstate

Feldman, Saul MD (Ped) *PCP* - **Spec Exp:** ADD/ADHD; Weight Management; **Hospital:** Maimonides Med Ctr (page 98), NYU Langone Med Ctr (page 104); **Address:** Kensington Pediatrics, 3904 16th Ave, Brooklyn, NY 11218; **Phone:** 718-851-8080; **Board Cert:** Pediatrics 2012; **Med School:** Albert Einstein Coll Med 2001; **Resid:** Pediatrics, Maimonides Med Ctr 2004

Glaser, Amy L MD (Ped) *PCP* - **Hospital:** NYU Langone Med Ctr (page 104); **Address:** Slope Pediatrics, 60 8th Ave, Brooklyn, NY 11217; **Phone:** 718-636-0019; **Board Cert:** Pediatrics 1985; **Med School:** Mount Sinai Sch Med 1979; **Resid:** Pediatrics, Montefiore Med Ctr 1983; **Fellow:** Adolescent Medicine, Mt Sinai Hosp 1985

Jackson, Rosemary M MD (Ped) *PCP* - **Spec Exp:** Diabetes; Obesity; **Hospital:** SUNY Downstate Med Ctr (Univ Hosp Brooklyn) (page 449); **Address:** 900 Lenox Rd, Brooklyn, NY 11203; **Phone:** 718-363-6646; **Board Cert:** Pediatrics 2006; **Med School:** SUNY Upstate Med Univ 1985; **Resid:** Pediatrics, SUNY Downstate Med Ctr 1988; **Fac Appt:** Asst Clin Prof Ped, SUNY Downstate

Laraque, Danielle MD (Ped) *PCP* - **Spec Exp:** Child Abuse; **Hospital:** Maimonides Med Ctr (page 98); **Address:** Maimonides Med Ctr, Pediatrics, 977 48th St, Brooklyn, NY 11219; **Phone:** 718-283-6150; **Board Cert:** Pediatrics 1986; Child Abuse Pediatrics 2009; **Med School:** UCLA 1981; **Resid:** Pediatrics, Chldns Hosp 1984; **Fellow:** Academic Pediatrics, Chldns Hosp 1986

Oghia, Hady MD (Ped) *PCP* - **Hospital:** Richmond Univ Med Ctr; **Address:** 7506 16th Ave, Brooklyn, NY 11214; **Phone:** 718-331-3166; **Med School:** Mexico 1979; **Resid:** Pediatrics, Sisters of Charity Hlth Sys 1983

Oppenheim, Jennifer A MD (Ped) *PCP* - **Spec Exp:** Special Health Care Needs; **Hospital:** NYU Langone Med Ctr (page 104); **Address:** Pediatric Assocs NYC, 20 Plaza St E, Ste A7, Brooklyn, NY 11238; **Phone:** 718-857-5500; **Board Cert:** Pediatrics 2007; **Med School:** Cornell Univ 1996; **Resid:** Pediatrics, Bellevue Hosp/NYU Med Ctr 1999

Preis, Oded MD (Ped) *PCP* - **Spec Exp:** Prematurity/Low Birth Weight Infants; **Hospital:** Maimonides Med Ctr (page 98); **Address:** 1729 E 12th St, Brooklyn, NY 11229; **Phone:** 718-339-4919; **Board Cert:** Pediatrics 1978; Neonatal-Perinatal Medicine 1981; **Med School:** Israel 1971; **Resid:** Pediatrics, Maimonides Med Ctr 1975; **Fellow:** Neonatal-Perinatal Medicine, SUNY Downstate Med Ctr 1977; **Fac Appt:** Assoc Clin Prof Ped, SUNY Downstate

Sergiou, Harry G MD (Ped) *PCP* - **Hospital:** New York Methodist Hosp (page 448); **Address:** 554 Henry St, Brooklyn, NY 11231; **Phone:** 718-625-5591; **Board Cert:** Pediatrics 2011; **Med School:** Greece 1979; **Resid:** Pediatrics, LI Coll Hosp 1985

Wu, Jason J MD/PhD (Ped) *PCP* - **Spec Exp:** Chinese Community Health; **Hospital:** Maimonides Med Ctr (page 98); **Address:** 781 47th St, Brooklyn, NY 11220; **Phone:** 718-435-5980; **Board Cert:** Pediatrics 2010; **Med School:** China 1982; **Resid:** Pediatrics, Maimonides Med Ctr 2001; **Fac Appt:** Asst Clin Prof Ped, Mount Sinai Sch Med

Physical Medicine & Rehabilitation

Gifford, Irina MD (PMR) - **Spec Exp:** Musculoskeletal Disorders; Neurologic Rehabilitation; Pediatric Rehabilitation; **Hospital:** Kingsbrook Jewish Med Ctr; **Address:** Kingsbrook Rehab Inst, 585 Schenectady Ave, rm 221, Brooklyn, NY 11203; **Phone:** 718-604-5341; **Board Cert:** Physical Medicine & Rehabilitation 1990; **Med School:** Romania 1960; **Resid:** Physical Medicine & Rehabilitation, Mt Sinai Hosp 1989; **Fellow:** Pediatric Rehabilitation Medicine, Albert Einstein Med Sch 1990

Harris, Philip MD (PMR) - **Hospital:** Brookdale Univ Hosp Med Ctr; **Address:** Brookdale Hosp, Physical Med & Rehab, 1 Brookdale Plaza, Brooklyn, NY 11212; **Phone:** 718-240-6126; **Board Cert:** Physical Medicine & Rehabilitation 1991; **Med School:** NYU Sch Med 1986; **Resid:** Physical Medicine & Rehabilitation, NYU Rusk Inst 1990

Pipia, Paul A MD (PMR) - **Spec Exp:** Neuromuscular Disorders; Pain-Back; Stroke Rehabilitation; Sports Medicine; **Hospital:** SUNY Downstate Med Ctr (Univ Hosp Brooklyn) (page 449); **Address:** Univ Orthopaedic Assocs, 710 Parkside Ave, Brooklyn, NY 11226; **Phone:** 718-282-7800; **Board Cert:** Physical Medicine & Rehabilitation 2006; Sports Medicine 2011; **Med School:** SUNY Downstate 1989; **Resid:** Physical Medicine & Rehabilitation, NYU Rusk Inst 1993; **Fac Appt:** Asst Prof PMR, SUNY Downstate

Ross, Marc MD (PMR) - **Spec Exp:** Sports Medicine; Pain-Back; Gait Disorders; **Hospital:** Kingsbrook Jewish Med Ctr, Mt Sinai Hosp; **Address:** Kingsbrook Rehab Inst, 585 Schenectady Ave, rm 221, Brooklyn, NY 11203; **Phone:** 718-604-5341; **Board Cert:** Physical Medicine & Rehabilitation 2014; **Med School:** NY Med Coll 1989; **Resid:** Physical Medicine & Rehabilitation, Mt Sinai Hosp 1993; **Fac Appt:** Asst Clin Prof PMR, Mount Sinai-Icahn Sch of Med

Stein, Perry MD (PMR) - **Spec Exp:** Pain Management; Palliative Care; **Hospital:** Mercy Med Ctr-Rockville Centre, Maimonides Med Ctr (page 98); **Address:** 383 Ocean Pkwy, Brooklyn, NY 11218; **Phone:** 718-941-6000; **Board Cert:** Physical Medicine & Rehabilitation 1991; Hospice & Palliative Medicine 2012; **Med School:** Mexico 1985; **Resid:** Physical Medicine & Rehabilitation, SUNY Downstate Med Ctr 1990

Psychiatry

Berkowitz, Howard L MD (Psyc) - **Spec Exp:** Anxiety & Depression; Geriatric Psychiatry; **Hospital:** Maimonides Med Ctr (page 98); **Address:** 4715 Fort Hamilton Pkwy, Brooklyn, NY 11219; **Phone:** 718-633-2025; **Board Cert:** Psychiatry 1977; Geriatric Psychiatry 2004; **Med School:** Albert Einstein Coll Med 1972; **Resid:** Internal Medicine, Beth Israel Med Ctr 1973; Psychiatry, Kings Co Hosp 1976; **Fellow:** Liaison Psychiatry, Kings Co Hosp 1977; **Fac Appt:** Assoc Prof Psyc, SUNY Downstate

Colah, Jessy J MD (Psyc) - **Spec Exp:** Geriatric Psychiatry; Depression; **Hospital:** New York Methodist Hosp (page 448); **Address:** NY Methodist Hosp, Psychiatry, 517 6th St, Brooklyn, NY 11215; **Phone:** 718-780-3771; **Board Cert:** Psychiatry 1992; **Med School:** India 1979; **Resid:** Psychiatry, Brookdale Univ Med Ctr 1987

Coplan, Jeremy MD (Psyc) - **Spec Exp:** Anxiety Disorders; Psychosomatic Disorders; Bipolar/Mood Disorders; **Hospital:** SUNY Downstate Med Ctr (Univ Hosp Brooklyn) (page 449); **Address:** SUNY Downstate, Psychiatry, 450 Clarkson Ave, Box 1203, Brooklyn, NY 11203; **Phone:** 718-270-1476; **Board Cert:** Psychiatry 1990; **Med School:** South Africa 1983; **Resid:** Psychiatry, SUNY-Downstate Med Ctr 1989; **Fellow:** Biological Psychiatry, NY-Presby/Columbia Univ Med Ctr 1990; **Fac Appt:** Prof Psyc, SUNY Downstate

Eitan, Noam MD (Psyc) - **Hospital:** Woodhull Med & Mental Hlth Ctr; **Address:** 760 Broadway, Brooklyn, NY 11206; **Phone:** 718-963-8000; **Board Cert:** Psychiatry 2008; **Med School:** Israel 1986; **Resid:** Psychiatry, Shalvata Hosp 1991; **Fellow:** Psychoanalysis, Sackler Sch Med 1995

Goldberg, Jeffrey DO (Psyc) - **Spec Exp:** Geriatric Psychiatry; Anxiety & Depression; Mood Disorders; **Hospital:** Coney Island Hosp; **Address:** 5025 Ft Hamilton Pkwy, Brooklyn, NY 11219; **Phone:** 718-633-8183; **Board Cert:** Psychiatry 2013; Geriatric Psychiatry 2013; **Med School:** NY Coll Osteo Med 1981; **Resid:** Psychiatry, Maimonides Med Ctr 1985; **Fac Appt:** Asst Clin Prof Psyc, SUNY Downstate

Heisman, Alexander MD (Psyc) - **Spec Exp:** Addiction/Substance Abuse; Liaison Psychiatry; Pain-Chronic; Anxiety & Depression; **Hospital:** Mt Sinai Beth Israel-BK, New York Methodist Hosp (page 448); **Address:** 3045 Ocean Pkwy, Ste 1A, Brooklyn, NY 11235; **Phone:** 718-449-1705; **Board Cert:** Psychiatry 2007; Psychosomatic Medicine 2008; **Med School:** Russia 1976; **Resid:** Psychiatry, Montefiore Med Ctr 1996

Viswanathan, Ramaswamy MD (Psyc) - **Spec Exp:** Depression; Anxiety Disorders; **Hospital:** SUNY Downstate Med Ctr (Univ Hosp Brooklyn) (page 449), Kings Co Hosp Ctr; **Address:** SUNY Downstate, Psychiatry, 450 Clarkson Ave, Ste 5-350, MS 127, Brooklyn, NY 11203; **Phone:** 718-270-2352; **Board Cert:** Psychiatry 1978; Geriatric Psychiatry 2012; Psychosomatic Medicine 2005; Forensic Psychiatry 2009; **Med School:** India 1972; **Resid:** Internal Medicine, Queens Hosp Ctr 1974; Psychiatry, SUNY Hlth Sci Ctr 1977; **Fellow:** Psychiatry, SUNY Hlth Sci Ctr 1978; **Fac Appt:** Assoc Prof Psyc, SUNY Downstate

Pulmonary Disease

Abott, Michael L MD (Pul) - **Spec Exp:** Asthma; Emphysema; **Hospital:** Lutheran Med Ctr - Brooklyn, New York Methodist Hosp (page 448); **Address:** Lutheran HlthCare, Pulmonology, 8714 5th Ave, Brooklyn, NY 11209; **Phone:** 718-630-8600; **Board Cert:** Internal Medicine 1983; Pulmonary Disease 1986; **Med School:** Mexico 1978; **Resid:** Internal Medicine, Coney Island Hosp 1982; **Fellow:** Pulmonary Disease, Montefiore Med Ctr 1984

Amin, Hossam H MD (Pul) - **Spec Exp:** Asthma & Allergy; Critical Care; Sleep Medicine; **Hospital:** Metropolitan Hosp Ctr - NY, New York Methodist Hosp (page 448); **Address:** 6903 4th Ave, Brooklyn, NY 11209; **Phone:** 718-238-6161; **Board Cert:** Internal Medicine 2006; Pulmonary Disease 2008; Critical Care Medicine 2009; Sleep Medicine 2013; **Med School:** Egypt 1988; **Resid:** Internal Medicine, Interfaith Med Ctr 1996; **Fellow:** Pulmonary Disease, Interfaith Med Ctr 1998; Critical Care Medicine, Mt Sinai Hosp 1999; **Fac Appt:** Assoc Prof Med, NY Med Coll

Bergman, Michael Ira MD (Pul) - **Spec Exp:** Asthma; Bronchitis; Respiratory Failure; Pneumonia; **Hospital:** Maimonides Med Ctr (page 98); **Address:** Maimonides Med Ctr, Pulmonology, 953 49th St, Ste 511, Brooklyn, NY 11219; **Phone:** 718-283-8380; **Board Cert:** Internal Medicine 1981; Pulmonary Disease 1984; Critical Care Medicine 2007; **Med School:** Albert Einstein Coll Med 1978; **Resid:** Internal Medicine, Brookdale Hosp 1981; **Fellow:** Pulmonary Critical Care Medicine, Mt Sinai Hosp 1984; **Fac Appt:** Asst Prof Med, Albert Einstein Coll Med

Bernstein, Chaim MD (Pul) - **Spec Exp:** Asthma; Chronic Obstructive Lung Disease (COPD); Emphysema; **Hospital:** Mt Sinai Beth Israel-BK; **Address:** Kings Pulmonary Assocs, 3131 Kings Hwy, Ste D10, Brooklyn, NY 11234; **Phone:** 718-252-3590; **Board Cert:** Internal Medicine 1977; Pulmonary Disease 1982; Critical Care Medicine 2007; **Med School:** NYU Sch Med 1974; **Resid:** Internal Medicine, Brookdale Med Ctr 1977; Pulmonary Disease, Manhattan VA Hosp 1979; **Fellow:** Pulmonary Disease, NYU-Bellevue Hosp 1979

Bondi, Elliott MD (Pul) - **Spec Exp:** Asthma; Tuberculosis; Pneumonia; **Hospital:** Brookdale Univ Hosp Med Ctr; **Address:** Brookdale Hosp, Pulmonology, 1 Brookdale Plaza, rm A107, Brooklyn, NY 11212; **Phone:** 718-240-5236; **Board Cert:** Internal Medicine 1987; Pulmonary Disease 1982; **Med School:** Univ MD Sch Med 1971; **Resid:** Internal Medicine, Maimonides Med Ctr 1973; **Fellow:** Pulmonary Disease, Jacobi Med Ctr 1976; **Fac Appt:** Assoc Clin Prof Med, SUNY Downstate

Demetis, Spiro MD (Pul) - **Spec Exp:** Sarcoidosis; Lung Cancer; Asthma & Emphysema; Pulmonary Hypertension; **Hospital:** SUNY Downstate Med Ctr (Univ Hosp Brooklyn) (page 449), Lutheran Med Ctr - Brooklyn; **Address:** 9001 Fort Hamilton Pkwy, Brooklyn, NY 11209; **Phone:** 718-748-4446; **Board Cert:** Internal Medicine 1989; Pulmonary Disease 2005; Critical Care Medicine 2005; **Med School:** Mexico 1983; **Resid:** Internal Medicine, SUNY Hlth Sci Ctr 1988; **Fellow:** Pulmonary Disease, SUNY Hlth Sci Ctr 1990; Critical Care Medicine, SUNY Hlth Sci Ctr 1991; **Fac Appt:** Assoc Prof Med, SUNY Hlth Sci Ctr

George, Liziamma MD (Pul) - **Spec Exp:** Smoking Cessation; Critical Care Medicine; Pulmonary Hypertension; Sleep Disorders; **Hospital:** New York Methodist Hosp (page 448); **Address:** NY Methodist Hosp, Pulmonology, 506 6th St, Brooklyn, NY 11215; **Phone:** 718-780-5941; **Board Cert:** Internal Medicine 1987; Critical Care Medicine 2011; Pulmonary Disease 2010; Sleep Medicine 2009; **Med School:** India 1980; **Resid:** Internal Medicine, St Joseph's Med Ctr 1987; **Fellow:** Pulmonary Disease, St Joseph's Med Ctr 1989

Gulrajani, Ramesh MD (Pul) - **Spec Exp:** Asthma; Sarcoidosis; Lung Cancer; **Hospital:** Brooklyn Hosp Ctr; **Address:** Brooklyn Hosp, Pulmonology, 240 Willoughby St, Ste 7F, Brooklyn, NY 11201; **Phone:** 718-250-6100; **Board Cert:** Internal Medicine 1979; Pulmonary Disease 1984; **Med School:** India 1974; **Resid:** Internal Medicine, Brooklyn Cumberland Med Ctr 1979; **Fellow:** Pulmonary Disease, Brooklyn Cumberland Med Ctr 1981; **Fac Appt:** Assoc Clin Prof Med, Cornell Univ-Weill Med Coll

Hammer, Arthur MD (Pul) - **Spec Exp:** Asthma; Sleep Disorders; Pulmonary Fibrosis; **Hospital:** Mt Sinai Beth Israel-BK; **Address:** Kings Pulmonary Assocs, 3131 Kings Hwy, Ste D10, Brooklyn, NY 11234; **Phone:** 718-252-3590; **Board Cert:** Internal Medicine 2006; Pulmonary Disease 2009; **Med School:** Mexico 1970; **Resid:** Internal Medicine, Brookdale Hosp 1974; **Fellow:** Pulmonary Disease, NYU Med Ctr 1976

Kupfer, Yizhak MD (Pul) - **Spec Exp:** Sleep & Snoring Disorders; **Hospital:** Maimonides Med Ctr (page 98); **Address:** Maimonides Med Ctr, Pulmonology, 953 49th St, Ste 511, Brooklyn, NY 11219; **Phone:** 718-283-8380; **Board Cert:** Internal Medicine 1989; Pulmonary Disease 2012; Critical Care Medicine 2013; Sleep Medicine 2007; **Med School:** SUNY Downstate 1986; **Resid:** Internal Medicine, Maimonides Med Ctr 1989; **Fellow:** Pulmonary Disease, Maimonides Med Ctr 1991; Critical Care Medicine, Maimonides Med Ctr 1992; **Fac Appt:** Assoc Clin Prof Med, SUNY Downstate

Lombardo, Gerard T MD (Pul) - **Spec Exp:** Sleep Apnea; Sleep & Snoring Disorders; **Hospital:** New York Methodist Hosp (page 448); **Address:** 808 8th Ave, Brooklyn, NY 11215; **Phone:** 718-369-1818; **Board Cert:** Internal Medicine 1984; Pulmonary Disease 1986; Sleep Medicine 2009; **Med School:** Grenada 1981; **Resid:** Internal Medicine, NY Methodist Hosp 1984; **Fellow:** Pulmonary Disease, NY Methodist Hosp 1986; **Fac Appt:** Asst Clin Prof Med, Cornell Univ-Weill Med Coll

Miarrostami, Rameen M MD (Pul) - **Spec Exp:** Asthma; Chronic Obstructive Lung Disease (COPD); Emphysema; Cough; **Hospital:** Maimonides Med Ctr (page 98); **Address:** 7124 18th Ave, Brooklyn, NY 11204; **Phone:** 718-234-3333; **Board Cert:** Internal Medicine 2011; Pulmonary Disease 2004; **Med School:** Dominican Republic 1985; **Resid:** Internal Medicine, Lincoln Med Ctr 1991; **Fellow:** Pulmonary Disease, LI Coll Hosp 1993

Saleh, Anthony MD (Pul) - **Spec Exp:** Asthma; Interstitial Lung Disease; Chronic Obstructive Lung Disease (COPD); Lung Cancer; **Hospital:** New York Methodist Hosp (page 448); **Address:** 7206 7th Ave, Brooklyn, NY 11209; **Phone:** 718-745-1200; **Board Cert:** Internal Medicine 1988; Pulmonary Disease 2010; **Med School:** Grenada 1985; **Resid:** Internal Medicine, NY Methodist Hosp 1988; **Fellow:** Pulmonary Disease, NY Methodist Hosp 1990; **Fac Appt:** Assoc Clin Prof Med, Cornell Univ-Weill Med Coll

Smith, Peter R MD (Pul) - **Spec Exp:** Chronic Obstructive Lung Disease (COPD); Smoking Cessation; Sarcoidosis; Wegener's Granulomatosis; **Hospital:** Brooklyn Hosp Ctr; **Address:** Brooklyn Hosp, Pulmonology, 121 DeKalb Ave, Ste 14J, Brooklyn, NY 11201; **Phone:** 718-250-6950; **Board Cert:** Internal Medicine 1973; Pulmonary Disease 1974; Critical Care Medicine 2009; **Med School:** Columbia P&S 1968; **Resid:** Internal Medicine, Downstate Med Ctr 1970; Internal Medicine, Jacobi Med Ctr 1971; **Fellow:** Pulmonary Disease, Downstate Med Ctr 1974; **Fac Appt:** Clin Prof Med, SUNY Hlth Sci Ctr

Radiation Oncology

Ashamalla, Hani MD (RadRO) - **Spec Exp:** Stereotactic Body Radiotherapy; Prostate Cancer; Breast Cancer; **Hospital:** New York Methodist Hosp (page 448); **Address:** NY Methodist Hosp, Radiation Oncology, 506 6th St, Brooklyn, NY 11215; **Phone:** 718-780-3677; **Board Cert:** Radiation Oncology 2004; **Med School:** Egypt 1983; **Resid:** Radiation Oncology, NY Methodist Hosp 1994; **Fellow:** Radiation Oncology, NY Methodist Hosp 1995; Pediatric Oncology, Chldns Hosp 1995; **Fac Appt:** Clin Prof RadRO, Cornell Univ-Weill Med Coll

Cooper, Jay S MD (RadRO) - **Spec Exp:** Head & Neck Cancer; Skin Cancer; Chemo-Radiation Combined Therapy; Intensity Modulated Radiotherapy (IMRT); **Hospital:** Maimonides Med Ctr (page 98); **Address:** Maimonides Cancer Ctr, Radiation Onc, 6300 8th Ave, Brooklyn, NY 11220; **Phone:** 718-765-2741; **Board Cert:** Therapeutic Radiology 1977; **Med School:** NYU Sch Med 1973; **Resid:** Radiation Oncology, NYU Med Ctr 1977; **Fac Appt:** Prof RadRO, Albert Einstein Coll Med

Donahue, Bernadine R MD (RadRO) - **Spec Exp:** Brain Tumors; Pediatric Cancers; **Hospital:** Maimonides Med Ctr (page 98); **Address:** Maimonides Cancer Ctr, Radiation Onc, 6300 8th Ave, LL, Brooklyn, NY 11220; **Phone:** 718-765-2700; **Board Cert:** Internal Medicine 1987; Radiation Oncology 1991; Hospice & Palliative Medicine 2012; **Med School:** Boston Univ 1984; **Resid:** Internal Medicine, Boston Med Ctr 1987; **Fellow:** Radiation Oncology, NYU Med Ctr 1990

Gliedman, Paul R MD (RadRO) - **Spec Exp:** Breast Cancer; Prostate Cancer; Brain Tumors; Stereotactic Radiosurgery; **Hospital:** Mt Sinai Roosevelt, Mt Sinai Beth Israel-BK; **Address:** Brooklyn Radiation Oncology, 2101 Avenue X, Brooklyn, NY 11235; **Phone:** 718-512-2160; **Board Cert:** Radiation Oncology 1987; **Med School:** Columbia P&S 1983; **Resid:** Radiation Oncology, NYU Med Ctr 1987

Rotman, Marvin Z MD (RadRO) - **Spec Exp:** Bladder Cancer; Gynecologic Cancer; Eye Tumors/Cancer; Prostate Cancer; **Hospital:** SUNY Downstate Med Ctr (Univ Hosp Brooklyn) (page 449), VA NY Harbor Hlthcr Sys-Brooklyn Campus; **Address:** SUNY Downstate, Radiation Oncology, 450 Clarkson Ave, Box 1211, Brooklyn, NY 11203; **Phone:** 718-270-2181; **Board Cert:** Diagnostic Radiology 1966; **Med School:** Jefferson Med Coll 1958; **Resid:** Internal Medicine, Albert Einstein Med Ctr 1962; Radiation Oncology, Montefiore Hosp Med Ctr 1966; **Fac Appt:** Prof RadRO, SUNY Downstate

Schwartz, David Lawrence MD (RadRO) - **Spec Exp:** Prostate Cancer; Brachytherapy; Breast Cancer; **Hospital:** SUNY Downstate Med Ctr (Univ Hosp Brooklyn) (page 449), VA NY Harbor Hlthcr Sys-Brooklyn Campus; **Address:** Metropolitan Radiation Oncology, 800 Poly Pl, Brooklyn, NY 11209; **Phone:** 718-630-3605; **Board Cert:** Radiation Oncology 1993; **Med School:** SUNY Downstate 1988; **Resid:** Radiation Oncology, SUNY Downstate Med Ctr 1992

Sherr, David L MD (RadRO) - **Spec Exp:** Intensity Modulated Radiotherapy (IMRT); Stereotactic Radiosurgery; Image Guided Radiotherapy (IGRT); Stereotactic Body Radiotherapy; **Hospital:** Brooklyn Hosp Ctr; **Address:** Brooklyn Hosp, Radiation Oncology, 121 Dekalb Ave, Brooklyn, NY 11201; **Phone:** 718-250-8248; **Board Cert:** Radiation Oncology 1987; **Med School:** Albert Einstein Coll Med 1981; **Resid:** Internal Medicine, Brookdale Hosp Med Ctr 1983; Radiation Oncology, NY-Presby/Columbia Univ Med Ctr 1986; **Fellow:** Epidemiology, NY-Presby/Weill Cornell Med Ctr 2014; **Fac Appt:** Assoc Clin Prof RadRO, Mount Sinai-Icahn Sch of Med

Reproductive Endocrinology

Grazi, Richard MD (RE) - **Spec Exp:** Infertility-IVF; Preimplantation Genetic Diagnosis; Fertility Preservation in Cancer; Infertility-Advanced Maternal Age; **Hospital:** Maimonides Med Ctr (page 98); **Address:** Genesis Fertility & Reproductive Med, 6010 Bay Pkwy, Brooklyn, NY 11228; **Phone:** 718-283-8600; **Board Cert:** Obstetrics & Gynecology 2006; Reproductive Endocrinology/Infertility 2006; **Med School:** SUNY Buffalo 1981; **Resid:** Obstetrics & Gynecology, NYU Med Ctr 1985; **Fellow:** Reproductive Endocrinology, Univ Med Ctr-UMDNJ 1987; **Fac Appt:** Assoc Clin Prof ObG, Mount Sinai-Icahn Sch of Med

Kofinas, George D MD (RE) - **Spec Exp:** Infertility-IVF; Fertility Preservation; Robotic Assisted Laparoscopic Surgery; Hysteroscopic Surgery; **Hospital:** New York Methodist Hosp (page 448); **Address:** Kofinas Fertility Inst, 506 6th St, WKP Bldg - Fl 4, Brooklyn, NY 11215; **Phone:** 718-780-5065; **Board Cert:** Obstetrics & Gynecology 2013; Reproductive Endocrinology 2013; **Med School:** Greece 1975; **Resid:** Obstetrics & Gynecology, NY Methodist Hosp 1982; Obstetrics & Gynecology, Brooklyn Caledonian Hosp 1984; **Fellow:** Reproductive Endocrinology, SUNY Hlth Sci Ctr 1986

Rheumatology

Efthimiou, Petros MD (Rhu) - **Spec Exp:** Rheumatoid Arthritis; Autoimmune Disease; Psoriatic Arthritis; Spondyloarthropathies; **Hospital:** New York Methodist Hosp (page 448); **Address:** 1 Prospect Park St W, Ste 1D, Brooklyn, NY 11215; **Phone:** 718-622-3563; **Board Cert:** Internal Medicine 2011; Rheumatology 2013; **Med School:** Greece 1996; **Resid:** Internal Medicine, Brown Univ/Rhode Island Hosp 2001; **Fellow:** Rheumatology, Hosp for Special Surg 2004; Rheumatology, NY-Presby/Weill Cornell Med Ctr 2004; **Fac Appt:** Assoc Prof Med, Cornell Univ-Weill Med Coll

Garner, Bruce F MD (Rhu) - **Spec Exp:** Rheumatoid Arthritis; Osteoporosis; Osteoarthritis; Lupus/SLE; **Hospital:** Lutheran Med Ctr - Brooklyn; **Address:** 7901 4th Ave, Ste A5, Brooklyn, NY 11209; **Phone:** 718-921-5239; **Board Cert:** Internal Medicine 1987; Rheumatology 1988; **Med School:** Mexico 1981; **Resid:** Internal Medicine, Lutheran Med Ctr 1985; **Fellow:** Rheumatology, Washington Hosp Ctr 1987; **Fac Appt:** Asst Clin Prof Med, SUNY Downstate

Green, Stuart A MD (Rhu) - **Spec Exp:** Rheumatoid Arthritis; Osteoporosis; Lupus/SLE; **Hospital:** Brooklyn Hosp Ctr; **Address:** Brooklyn Hosp, Rheumatology, 121 DeKalb Ave Fl 7, Brooklyn, NY 11201; **Phone:** 718-250-6921; **Board Cert:** Internal Medicine 1982; Rheumatology 1986; **Med School:** Georgetown Univ 1979; **Resid:** Internal Medicine, St Lukes-Roosevelt Hosp 1982; **Fellow:** Rheumatology, SUNY Downstate Med Ctr 1985; **Fac Appt:** Asst Clin Prof Med, NYU Sch Med

Lesser, Robert S MD (Rhu) - **Spec Exp:** Polymyalgia Rheumatica; Rheumatoid Arthritis; Lupus/SLE; **Hospital:** Mt Sinai Beth Israel-BK; **Address:** 4015 Avenue U, Brooklyn, NY 11234; **Phone:** 718-252-5151; **Board Cert:** Internal Medicine 1985; Rheumatology 1988; **Med School:** Univ Hlth Scis, Chicago Med Sch 1982; **Resid:** Internal Medicine, Hahnemann Univ Hosp 1985; **Fellow:** Rheumatology, Hahnemann Univ Hosp 1987; **Fac Appt:** Assoc Clin Prof Med, SUNY Downstate

Patel, Jitendra K MD (Rhu) - **Spec Exp:** Arthritis; Fibromyalgia; Pain-Back; **Hospital:** Kingsbrook Jewish Med Ctr, Mt Sinai Beth Israel-BK; **Address:** 3420 Ave N, Brooklyn, NY 11234; **Phone:** 718-258-7019; **Board Cert:** Internal Medicine 1979; Rheumatology 1982; **Med School:** India 1975; **Resid:** Internal Medicine, Mem Univ Newfoundland Affil Hosp 1979; **Fellow:** Rheumatology, Georgetown Univ Hosp 1982

Schiff, Carl F MD (Rhu) - **Spec Exp:** Rheumatoid Arthritis; Osteoporosis; **Hospital:** Maimonides Med Ctr (page 98); **Address:** 4915 10th Ave, Brooklyn, NY 11219; **Phone:** 718-283-8519; **Board Cert:** Internal Medicine 1983; Rheumatology 1986; **Med School:** Yale Univ 1980; **Resid:** Internal Medicine, Mt Sinai Hosp 1983; **Fellow:** Rheumatology, NY-Presby/Columbia Univ Med Ctr 1986; **Fac Appt:** Asst Clin Prof Med, SUNY Hlth Sci Ctr

Surgery

Adler, Harry L MD (S) - **Spec Exp:** Biliary Surgery; Laparoscopic Surgery; Hernia; Colon Surgery; **Hospital:** Maimonides Med Ctr (page 98); **Address:** Maimonides Med Ctr, Surgery, 948 48th St Fl 3, Brooklyn, NY 11219; **Phone:** 718-283-7952; **Board Cert:** Surgery 2005; Surgical Critical Care 2008; **Med School:** NYU Sch Med 1980; **Resid:** Surgery, NYU-Bellevue Med Ctr 1985; **Fellow:** Surgical Critical Care, Maimonides Med Ctr 1986; **Fac Appt:** Asst Clin Prof S, SUNY Downstate

Alfonso II, Antonio E MD (S) - **Spec Exp:** Thyroid Cancer; Head & Neck Surgery; Breast Cancer; **Hospital:** SUNY Downstate Med Ctr (Univ Hosp Brooklyn) (page 449); **Address:** SUNY Downstate, Surgery, 450 Clarkson Ave, Brooklyn, NY 11203; **Phone:** 718-875-3244; **Board Cert:** Surgery 1973; **Med School:** Philippines 1968; **Resid:** Surgery, Temple Univ Hosp 1972; **Fellow:** Surgical Oncology, Meml Sloan-Kettering Cancer Ctr 1974; **Fac Appt:** Prof Emeritus S, SUNY Downstate

Bernstein, Michael O MD (S) - **Spec Exp:** Breast Cancer; Hernia; Gastrointestinal Surgery; **Hospital:** Richmond Univ Med Ctr; **Address:** 11 Ralph Pl, Ste 204, Staten Island, NY 10301; **Phone:** 718-273-5954; **Board Cert:** Surgery 2007; **Med School:** Penn State Coll Med 1983; **Resid:** Surgery, SUNY-Kings Co Hosp 1988; **Fac Appt:** Assoc Clin Prof S, SUNY Downstate

Borriello, Raffaele MD (S) - **Spec Exp:** Laparoscopic Surgery; Hernia; Gastrointestinal Surgery; **Hospital:** New York Methodist Hosp (page 448); **Address:** 100 Clinton St, Ste 2, Brooklyn, NY 11201; **Phone:** 718-625-0767; **Board Cert:** Surgery 2005; **Med School:** SUNY Downstate 1981; **Resid:** Surgery, Kings Co Hosp Ctr 1986; **Fac Appt:** Asst Clin Prof S, SUNY Downstate

Dresner, Lisa S MD (S) - **Spec Exp:** Breast Surgery; Critical Care; **Hospital:** SUNY Downstate Med Ctr (Univ Hosp Brooklyn) (page 449); **Address:** SUNY Downstate, Surgery, 445 Lenox Rd, Brooklyn, NY 11203; **Phone:** 718-270-1973; **Board Cert:** Surgery 2011; Surgical Critical Care 2013; **Med School:** SUNY Downstate 1985; **Resid:** Surgery, SUNY Downstate Med Ctr 1992; **Fellow:** Surgical Critical Care, Jackson Meml Hosp 1993; **Fac Appt:** Assoc Prof S, SUNY Downstate

Fahoum, Bashar H MD (S) - **Spec Exp:** Laparoscopic Surgery; Critical Care; Trauma; **Hospital:** New York Methodist Hosp (page 448); **Address:** NY Methodist Hosp, Surgery, 506 6th St, Brooklyn, NY 11215; **Phone:** 718-780-3288; **Board Cert:** Surgery 2013; Surgical Critical Care 2012; **Med School:** Syria 1987; **Resid:** Surgery, NY Methodist Hosp 1993; **Fac Appt:** Asst Prof S, Cornell Univ-Weill Med Coll

Genato, Romulo L MD (S) - **Spec Exp:** Breast Surgery; Laparoscopic Surgery; Hernia; **Hospital:** Brooklyn Hosp Ctr; **Address:** 240 Willoughby St, Ste 8E, Brooklyn, NY 11201; **Phone:** 718-250-8970; **Board Cert:** Surgery 2010; **Med School:** Philippines 1972; **Resid:** Surgery, Brooklyn Hosp 1979

Gorecki, Piotr J MD (S) - **Hospital:** New York Methodist Hosp (page 448); **Address:** 263 7th Ave, Ste 5A, Brooklyn, NY 11215; **Phone:** 718-246-8600; **Board Cert:** Surgery 2009; **Med School:** Poland 1991; **Resid:** Surgery, NY Methodist Hosp 1998; **Fellow:** Laparoscopic Surgery, Mayo Clin 1999; **Fac Appt:** Asst Prof S, Cornell Univ-Weill Med Coll

Kaleya, Ronald N MD (S) - **Spec Exp:** Pancreatic Cancer; Breast Cancer; Colon & Rectal Cancer; **Hospital:** Maimonides Med Ctr (page 98); **Address:** Maimonides Med Ctr, Surgery, 948 48th St Fl 3, Brooklyn, NY 11219; **Phone:** 718-283-7952; **Board Cert:** Surgery 2008; **Med School:** Cornell Univ-Weill Med Coll 1980; **Resid:** Surgery, Montefiore Med Ctr 1985; **Fellow:** Surgical Oncology, Meml Sloan-Kettering Cancer Ctr 1987

Lewis, Theophilus MD (S) - **Spec Exp:** Breast Cancer & Surgery; **Hospital:** SUNY Downstate Med Ctr (Univ Hosp Brooklyn) (page 449); **Address:** SUNY Downstate, Surgery, 451 Clarkson Ave, rm B4121, Brooklyn, NY 11203; **Phone:** 718-270-2155; **Board Cert:** Surgery 2013; **Med School:** SUNY Downstate 1978; **Resid:** Surgery, Kings Co Hosp Ctr 1983

Lois, William A MD (S) - **Spec Exp:** Dialysis Access Surgery; Vascular Surgery; Wound Healing/Care; **Hospital:** Kingsbrook Jewish Med Ctr; **Address:** 5723 Avenue N, Brooklyn, NY 11234; **Phone:** 718-251-1111; **Board Cert:** Surgery 2010; **Med School:** Spain 1982; **Resid:** Surgery, Interfaith Med Ctr 1987

Manasseh, Donna-Marie MD (S) - **Spec Exp:** Breast Surgery; **Hospital:** Maimonides Med Ctr (page 98); **Address:** Maimonides Breast Ctr, 745 64th St, Brooklyn, NY 11220; **Phone:** 718-765-2570; **Board Cert:** Surgery 2005; **Med School:** Harvard Med Sch 1996; **Resid:** Surgery, NY Presby Hosp 2002; **Fellow:** Surgical Breast Oncology, Meml Sloan Kettering Canc Ctr 2005; **Fac Appt:** Asst Clin Prof S, Columbia P&S

Rajpal, Sanjeev MD (S) - **Spec Exp:** Laparoscopic Surgery; Obesity/Bariatric Surgery; Cancer Surgery; Robotic Surgery; **Hospital:** Mt Sinai Beth Israel-BK, Flushing Hosp Med Ctr; **Address:** 2060 Utica Ave, Brooklyn, NY 11234; **Phone:** 718-676-5309; **Board Cert:** Surgery 2013; **Med School:** India 1975; **Resid:** Surgery, Brookdale Hosp Med Ctr 1980; **Fellow:** Surgical Oncology, Roswell Park Meml Inst 1982; Laparoscopic Surgery, Yale-New Haven Hosp 2001; **Fac Appt:** Asst Prof S, SUNY Downstate

Schwartzman, Alexander MD (S) - **Spec Exp:** Breast Cancer; Colon Surgery; Laparoscopic Surgery; Gallbladder Surgery; **Hospital:** SUNY Downstate Med Ctr (Univ Hosp Brooklyn) (page 449); **Address:** SUNY Downstate, Surgery, 445 Lenox Rd, Brooklyn, NY 11203; **Phone:** 718-270-1973; **Board Cert:** Surgery 2010; **Med School:** Dominican Republic 1983; **Resid:** Surgery, Brooklyn Hosp Ctr 1988

Thoracic & Cardiac Surgery

Abrol, Sunil MD (T&CS) - **Spec Exp:** Cardiac Surgery; Aneurysm-Thoracic Aortic; Heart Valve Surgery; Aortic Surgery; **Hospital:** Maimonides Med Ctr (page 98), Brookdale Univ Hosp Med Ctr; **Address:** Maimonides Med Ctr, Cardiothoracic Surg, 4802 10th Ave Fl 4, Brooklyn, NY 11219; **Phone:** 718-283-7686; **Board Cert:** Surgery 2009; Thoracic Surgery 2011; **Med School:** India 1986; **Resid:** Surgery, Maimonides Med Ctr 1998; **Fellow:** Thoracic Surgery, SUNY Hlth Sci Ctr 2001; **Fac Appt:** Asst Prof S, Mount Sinai-Icahn Sch of Med

Crooke, Gregory A MD (T&CS) - **Spec Exp:** Cardiac Surgery-Adult & Pediatric; Minimally Invasive Heart Valve Surgery; Transplant-Heart; Thoracic Aortic Surgery; **Hospital:** Maimonides Med Ctr (page 98); **Address:** Maimonides Med Ctr, Cardiothoracic dept, 4802 10th Ave, Administration Bldg Fl 4, Brooklyn, NY 11219; **Phone:** 718-283-7686; **Board Cert:** Thoracic & Cardiac Surgery 2014; **Med School:** Cornell Univ-Weill Med Coll 1984; **Resid:** Surgery, Northwestern Meml Hosp 1989; **Fellow:** Cardiothoracic Surgery, NYU Med Ctr 1992; **Fac Appt:** Asst Prof TS, NYU Sch Med

Harris, Loren MD (T&CS) - **Spec Exp:** Minimally Invasive Thoracic Surgery; Robotic Surgery; Lung Cancer; Esophageal Tumors; **Hospital:** Maimonides Med Ctr (page 98); **Address:** Maimonides Med Ctr, Cardiothoracic Surg, 4802 10th Ave Fl 4, Brooklyn, NY 11219; **Phone:** 718-283-7686; **Board Cert:** Surgery 2013; Thoracic & Cardiac Surgery 2006; **Med School:** NYU Sch Med 1987; **Resid:** Surgery, NYU Med Ctr 1994; **Fellow:** Cardiovascular Surgery, NYU Med Ctr 1996; **Fac Appt:** Assoc Prof S, SUNY Downstate

Ribakove, Greg MD (T&CS) - **Spec Exp:** Minimally Invasive Cardiac Surgery; Heart Valve Surgery; Coronary Artery Surgery; **Hospital:** Maimonides Med Ctr (page 98); **Address:** Maimonides, Cardiothoracic Surgery, 4802 10th Ave Fl 4, Brooklyn, NY 11219; **Phone:** 718-283-7686; **Board Cert:** Thoracic Surgery 2010; **Med School:** Univ Chicago-Pritzker Sch Med 1980; **Resid:** Surgery, NYU Med Ctr 1982; **Fellow:** Cardiovascular Surgery, Natl Inst Hlth 1984; Thoracic Surgery, Stanford Univ Hosp & Clins 1994; **Fac Appt:** Assoc Prof T&CS, NYU Sch Med

Shaw, Jason P MD (T&CS) - **Spec Exp:** Minimally Invasive Thoracic Surgery; Lung Cancer; Esophageal Cancer; Mediastinal Tumors; **Hospital:** Maimonides Med Ctr (page 98); **Address:** Maimonides Med Ctr, Cardiothoracic Surg, 4802 10th Ave Fl 4, Brooklyn, NY 11219; **Phone:** 718-283-7686; **Board Cert:** Surgery 2006; Thoracic & Cardiac Surgery 2010; **Med School:** McGill Univ 1998; **Resid:** Surgery, North Shore Univ/LIJ Hlth Sys 2005; **Fellow:** Thoracic Surgery, Jackson Meml Hosp 2007; Minimally Invasive Surgery, Mt Sinai Hosp 2008

Tortolani, Anthony J MD (T&CS) - **Spec Exp:** Transfusion Free Surgery; Heart Valve Surgery; Coronary Artery Surgery; **Hospital:** New York Methodist Hosp (page 448), NY-Presby/Weill Cornell Med Ctr, NY (page 102); **Address:** NY Methodist Hosp, Cardiothoracic Surg, 506 6th St Fl 6, Brooklyn, NY 11215; **Phone:** 718-780-5990; **Board Cert:** Surgery 1975; Thoracic Surgery 2009; **Med School:** Geo Wash Univ 1969; **Resid:** Surgery, N Shore Univ Hosp 1974; **Fellow:** Cardiothoracic Surgery, NYU Med Ctr 1978; **Fac Appt:** Assoc Prof S, Cornell Univ-Weill Med Coll

Urology

Colon, Ivan MD (U) - **Spec Exp:** Kidney Cancer; Prostate Cancer; Laparoscopic Surgery; Robotic Surgery; **Hospital:** New York Methodist Hosp (page 448); **Address:** Brooklyn Urology, 1 Prospect Park W, Ste C, Brooklyn, NY 11215; **Phone:** 718-230-7788; **Board Cert:** Urology 2013; **Med School:** Univ Wisc 1994; **Resid:** Urology, Brookdale Univ Hosp 2001; **Fellow:** Urologic Laparoscopic Surg-Endourology, Cedars-Sinai Med Ctr 2002

Grunberger, Ivan MD (U) - **Spec Exp:** Prostate Cancer; Impotence; Minimally Invasive Surgery; Kidney Stones; **Hospital:** New York Methodist Hosp (page 448); **Address:** Brooklyn Urology, 1 Prospect Park W, Ste C, Brooklyn, NY 11215; **Phone:** 718-230-7788; **Board Cert:** Urology 2007; **Med School:** NYU Sch Med 1980; **Resid:** Surgery, N Shore Univ Hosp 1982; Urology, NYU Med Ctr 1988; **Fac Appt:** Clin Prof U, Cornell Univ-Weill Med Coll

Meisenberg, Gene MD (U) - **Spec Exp:** Prostate Disease; Kidney Stones; Impotence; **Hospital:** NY-Presby/Weill Cornell Med Ctr, NY (page 102), New York Methodist Hosp (page 448); **Address:** 1523 Voorhies Ave Fl 5, Brooklyn, NY 11235; **Phone:** 718-743-2200; **Board Cert:** Urology 2011; **Med School:** Russia 1981; **Resid:** Surgery, Beth Israel Med Ctr 1993; Urology, RWJ Univ Hosp 1998

Rosenthal, Sheldon MD (U) - **Spec Exp:** Kidney Stones; Prostate Disease; **Hospital:** Wyckoff Heights Med Ctr; **Address:** 359 Stockholm St Fl 1, Brooklyn, NY 11237; **Phone:** 718-821-3200; **Board Cert:** Urology 1977; **Med School:** Ros Franklin Univ/Chicago Med Sch 1967; **Resid:** Surgery, Albert Einstein Coll Med Affil Hosps 1970; Urology, NY Med Coll Affil Hosps 1975

Saada, Simon MD (U) - **Spec Exp:** Kidney Stones; Prostate Cancer; Kidney Cancer; **Hospital:** Maimonides Med Ctr (page 98), Richmond Univ Med Ctr; **Address:** 705 86th St, Ste M2, Brooklyn, NY 11228; **Phone:** 718-238-1075; **Board Cert:** Urology 1981; **Med School:** Egypt 1970; **Resid:** Surgery, LI Coll Med Ctr 1974; Urology, Charleston Area Med Ctr 1981

Sharaby, Jacob S MD (U) - **Hospital:** Maimonides Med Ctr (page 98), Mt Sinai Beth Israel-BK; **Address:** 770 Ocean Pkwy, Brooklyn, NY 11217; **Phone:** 718-941-2002; **Board Cert:** Urology 2011; **Med School:** Israel 1992; **Resid:** Surgery, Beth Israel Med Ctr 1994; Urology, Maimonides Med Ctr 1999

Silver, David A MD (U) - **Spec Exp:** Laparoscopic Surgery; Urologic Cancer; Robotic Surgery; Continent Urinary Diversions; **Hospital:** Maimonides Med Ctr (page 98), Lutheran Med Ctr - Brooklyn; **Address:** 6323 7th Ave, Brooklyn, NY 11220; **Phone:** 718-283-7153; **Board Cert:** Urology 2007; **Med School:** Albert Einstein Coll Med 1989; **Resid:** Urology, Maimonides Med Ctr 1995; **Fellow:** Urologic Oncology, Meml Sloan-Kettering Canc Ctr 1997

Wainstein, Sasha MD (U) - **Spec Exp:** Impotence; Voiding Dysfunction; Endourology; **Hospital:** Maimonides Med Ctr (page 98), Forest Hills Hosp; **Address:** 4720 Fort Hamilton Pkwy, Brooklyn, NY 11219; **Phone:** 718-436-3900; **Board Cert:** Urology 1977; **Med School:** Colombia 1969; **Resid:** Urology, Maimonides Med Ctr 1975

Vascular Surgery

Ascher, Enrico MD (VascS) - **Spec Exp:** Endovascular Surgery; Carotid Artery Surgery; Limb Sparing Surgery; Aneurysm; **Hospital:** Lutheran Med Ctr - Brooklyn; **Address:** Vascular Inst, 960 50th St, Brooklyn, NY 11219; **Phone:** 718-438-3800; **Board Cert:** Vascular Surgery 2004; **Med School:** Brazil 1974; **Resid:** Surgery, NY Med Coll 1981; **Fellow:** Vascular Surgery, Montefiore Med Ctr 1982; **Fac Appt:** Prof S, SUNY Downstate

D'Ayala, Marcus D MD (VascS) - **Spec Exp:** Endovascular Surgery; Aneurysm-Abdominal Aortic; Carotid Artery Surgery; Peripheral Vascular Disease; **Hospital:** New York Methodist Hosp (page 448); **Address:** NY Methodist Hosp, Vascular Surgery, 506 6th St, Brooklyn, NY 11215; **Phone:** 718-780-3288; **Board Cert:** Surgery 2008; Vascular Surgery 2009; **Med School:** Univ Wisc 1992; **Resid:** Surgery, Montefiore Med Ctr 1997; **Fellow:** Vascular Surgery, Mt Sinai Hosp 1998; **Fac Appt:** Assoc Clin Prof S, Cornell Univ-Weill Med Coll

Gelbfish, Gary A MD (VascS) - **Spec Exp:** Dialysis Access; **Hospital:** Mt Sinai Beth Israel-BK; **Address:** 2502 Avenue I, Brooklyn, NY 11210; **Phone:** 718-258-3004; **Board Cert:** Surgery 2013; **Med School:** Columbia P&S 1982; **Resid:** Surgery, Maimonides Med Ctr 1989; **Fellow:** Vascular Surgery, Maimonides Med Ctr 1990; **Fac Appt:** Asst Clin Prof S, Mount Sinai-Icahn Sch of Med

Menezes, Nelson MD (VascS) - **Spec Exp:** Varicose Veins; Peripheral Vascular Disease; Carotid Artery Surgery; **Hospital:** Brooklyn Hosp Ctr, New York Methodist Hosp (page 448); **Address:** 186 Joralemon St, Ste 1002, Brooklyn, NY 11201; **Phone:** 718-625-4100; **Board Cert:** Surgery 2006; Vascular Surgery 2007; **Med School:** India 1984; **Resid:** Surgery, Brooklyn Hosp Ctr 1995; **Fellow:** Vascular Surgery, Baptist Meml Hosp 1996; Vascular Surgery, SUNY Stony Brook Univ Med Ctr 1997; **Fac Appt:** Asst Clin Prof VascS, Cornell Univ-Weill Med Coll

Rhee, Robert MD (VascS) - **Spec Exp:** Aneurysm-Aortic; Carotid Artery Disease; Peripheral Vascular Disease; Minimally Invasive Vascular Surgery; **Hospital:** Maimonides Med Ctr (page 98); **Address:** 947 49th St, Brooklyn, NY 11219; **Phone:** 718-283-7957; **Board Cert:** Vascular Surgery 2005; **Med School:** Univ Rochester 1988; **Resid:** Surgery, Strong Meml Hosp 1993; **Fellow:** Vascular Surgery, Mayo Clinic 1995

Weiser, Robert MD (VascS) - **Spec Exp:** Lower Limb Arterial Disease; Carotid Artery Surgery; Lower Limb Ulcers; **Hospital:** New York Methodist Hosp (page 448); **Address:** 186 Joralemon St Fl 7, Brooklyn, NY 11201; **Phone:** 718-797-1101; **Board Cert:** Surgery 2005; **Med School:** Albert Einstein Coll Med 1977; **Resid:** Surgery, Montefiore Med Ctr 1982; **Fellow:** Vascular Surgery, Montefiore Med Ctr 1983

The Best in American Medicine
www.CastleConnolly.com

Queens

Sponsored Page

Allergy & Immunology

Menchell, David L MD (A&I) - **Spec Exp:** Asthma; Nasal Allergy; Sinus Disorders; **Hospital:** NY Hosp Queens (page 498); **Address:** 73-03 198th St, Fresh Meadows, NY 11366; **Phone:** 718-465-4100; **Board Cert:** Internal Medicine 1980; Allergy & Immunology 1983; **Med School:** NYU Sch Med 1977; **Resid:** Internal Medicine, NY Hosp Queens 1980; **Fellow:** Allergy & Immunology, NY Hosp Queens 1983

Cardiovascular Disease

Akinboboye, Olakunle MD (Cv) - **Spec Exp:** Diabetes & Heart Disease; Nuclear Stress Testing; Hypertension; Coronary Artery Disease; **Hospital:** NY Hosp Queens (page 498), St. Francis Hosp - The Heart Ctr (page 111); **Address:** Laurelton Heart Specialists, 234-36 Merrick Blvd Fl 2, Rosedale, NY 11422; **Phone:** 718-949-9400; **Board Cert:** Internal Medicine 2005; Cardiovascular Disease 2005; Nuclear Cardiology 1996; **Med School:** Nigeria 1984; **Resid:** Internal Medicine, Nassau County Med Ctr 1991; **Fellow:** Cardiovascular Disease, NY-Presby/Columbia Univ Med Ctr 1995; Nuclear Cardiology, NY-Presby/Columbia Univ Med Ctr 1994; **Fac Appt:** Asst Clin Prof Med, NYU Sch Med

Golduber, Gary MD (Cv) - **Spec Exp:** Coronary Artery Disease; Congestive Heart Failure; **Hospital:** NYU Langone Med Ctr (page 104); **Address:** NYU Columbia Med, 9785 Queens Blvd, Rego Park, NY 11374; **Phone:** 718-261-9100; **Board Cert:** Internal Medicine 2005; Cardiovascular Disease 2008; Nuclear Cardiology 2007; Echocardiography 2008; **Med School:** SUNY Downstate 2002; **Resid:** Internal Medicine, Montefiore Med Ctr 2005; **Fellow:** Cardiovascular Disease, Maimonides Med Ctr 2008

Hsueh, John Tzu-Lang MD (Cv) - **Spec Exp:** Coronary Artery Disease; Heart Valve Disease; **Hospital:** NY Hosp Queens (page 498), Flushing Hosp Med Ctr; **Address:** 136-17 39th Ave, Fl 4 - Ste CF-E, Flushing, NY 11354; **Phone:** 718-559-3600; **Board Cert:** Internal Medicine 1987; Cardiovascular Disease 1979; **Med School:** Taiwan 1970; **Resid:** Internal Medicine, Flushing Hosp Med Ctr 1976; **Fellow:** Cardiovascular Disease, Wayne State Univ 1978

Kerwin, Todd Christopher MD (Cv) - **Spec Exp:** Nuclear Cardiology; Non-Invasive Cardiology; Hypertension; **Hospital:** NY Hosp Queens (page 498); **Address:** NYHQ, Cardiology, 56-45 Main St, Flushing, NY 11355; **Phone:** 718-670-1130; **Board Cert:** Nuclear Cardiology 2004; Cardiovascular Disease 2013; **Med School:** Georgetown Univ 1997; **Resid:** Internal Medicine, Univ Hosps Case Med Ctr 2000; **Fellow:** Cardiovascular Disease, Rush Univ Med Ctr 2003; **Fac Appt:** Asst Prof Med, Cornell Univ-Weill Med Coll

Kirtane, Sanjay S MD (Cv) - **Spec Exp:** Coronary Artery Disease; Nuclear Cardiology; Heart Failure; **Hospital:** St. John's Episcopal Hosp - Queens, South Nassau Comm Hosp; **Address:** 114-12 Beach Channel Drive, Ste 7, Rockaway Park, NY 11694; **Phone:** 718-318-1029; **Board Cert:** Internal Medicine 1980; Cardiovascular Disease 1983; Nuclear Cardiology 2009; **Med School:** India 1974; **Resid:** Internal Medicine, St John's Episcopal Hosp 1980; **Fellow:** Cardiovascular Disease, LI Jewish Med Ctr 1981; Cardiovascular Disease, St John's Episcopal Hosp 1982

Robbins, Michael J MD (Cv) - **Spec Exp:** Echocardiography; Non-Invasive Cardiology; **Hospital:** Mt Sinai Hosp; **Address:** 94-36 58th Ave, Ste G4, Elmhurst, NY 11373; **Phone:** 718-760-0011; **Board Cert:** Internal Medicine 1984; Cardiovascular Disease 1987; **Med School:** Cornell Univ 1981; **Resid:** Internal Medicine, Albert Einstein Coll Med Affil Hosp 1985; **Fellow:** Cardiovascular Disease, Mount Sinai Med Ctr 1987; **Fac Appt:** Assoc Prof Med, Mount Sinai Sch Med

Rydzinski, Mayer MD (Cv) - **Spec Exp:** Echocardiography; **Hospital:** NY Hosp Queens (page 498), Forest Hills Hosp; **Address:** 80-02 Kew Gardens Road, Ste 323, Kew Gardens, NY 11415; **Phone:** 718-268-7633; **Board Cert:** Internal Medicine 1979; Cardiovascular Disease 1981; Echocardiography 2008; **Med School:** Albert Einstein Coll Med 1976; **Resid:** Internal Medicine, Metropolitan Hosp Ctr 1977; Internal Medicine, Montefiore Hosp Med Ctr 1979; **Fellow:** Cardiovascular Disease, LI Jewish Hosp 1981

Siskind, Steven J MD (Cv) - **Spec Exp:** Angina; Heart Failure; Arrhythmias; Non-Invasive Cardiology; **Hospital:** NYU Langone Med Ctr (page 104), NY Hosp Queens (page 498); **Address:** NYU Cardiovascular Assocs, 142-42 Booth Memorial Ave, Flushing, NY 11355; **Phone:** 718-353-4004; **Board Cert:** Internal Medicine 1979; Cardiovascular Disease 1981; **Med School:** Albert Einstein Coll Med 1976; **Resid:** Internal Medicine, Jacobi Med Ctr 1979; **Fellow:** Cardiovascular Disease, Albert Einstein Med Coll Affil Hosp 1981; **Fac Appt:** Asst Prof, Cornell Univ-Weill Med Coll

Child & Adolescent Psychiatry

Fornari, Victor M MD (ChAP) - **Spec Exp:** Eating Disorders; Trauma Psychiatry; Post Traumatic Stress Disorder; **Hospital:** Zucker Hillside Hosp, Steven & Alexandra Cohen Chldn's Med Ctr of NY; **Address:** Zucker Hillside Hosp, Ambulatory Care Pav Lower Level, 75-59 263rd St, Glen Oaks, NY 11004; **Phone:** 718-470-3510; **Board Cert:** Psychiatry 1984; Child & Adolescent Psychiatry 1985; **Med School:** SUNY Downstate 1979; **Resid:** Psychiatry, Hosp Univ Penn - UPHS 1982; **Fellow:** Child & Adolescent Psychiatry, NS-LIJ Hlth Sys 1984; **Fac Appt:** Prof Psyc, Hofstra N Shore-LIJ Sch Med

Kafantaris, Vivian P MD (ChAP) - **Spec Exp:** Bipolar/Mood Disorders; ADD/ADHD; Aggression Disorders; Clinical Trials; **Hospital:** Zucker Hillside Hosp; **Address:** The Zucker Hillside Hospital, 75-59 263rd St, Glen Oaks, NY 11004; **Phone:** 718-470-3503; **Board Cert:** Psychiatry 1989; Child & Adolescent Psychiatry 1990; Addiction Psychiatry 2007; **Med School:** Albert Einstein Coll Med 1983; **Resid:** Psychiatry, Albert Einstein Coll Med 1987; **Fellow:** Child & Adolescent Psychiatry, NYU/Bellevue Hosp Ctr 1989; Research, NYU/Bellevue Hosp Ctr 1991

Colon & Rectal Surgery

Tiszenkel, Howard I MD (CRS) - **Spec Exp:** Colon & Rectal Cancer; Laparoscopic Surgery; **Hospital:** NY Hosp Queens (page 498); **Address:** 56-45 Main St, rm WLL300, Flushing, NY 11355-5000; **Phone:** 718-445-0220; **Board Cert:** Surgery 2006; Colon & Rectal Surgery 1988; **Med School:** NY Med Coll 1981; **Resid:** Surgery, St Luke's Hosp 1986; Colon & Rectal Surgery, Carle Clinic 1987

Dermatology

Beyda, Bernadette A MD (D) - **Hospital:** NY Hosp Queens (page 498); **Address:** 141-23 59th Ave, Flushing, NY 11355-5304; **Phone:** 718-445-0566; **Board Cert:** Dermatology 1982; **Med School:** France 1976; **Resid:** Pathology, Booth Meml Med Ctr 1979; Dermatology, NY Hosp 1982

Fox, Joshua MD (D) - **Spec Exp:** Skin Cancer; Cosmetic Dermatology; **Hospital:** Long Is Jewish Med Ctr; **Address:** Advanced Dermatology, 58-47 188th St, Fresh Meadows, NY 11365; **Phone:** 718-357-8200; **Board Cert:** Dermatology 1986; **Med School:** Mount Sinai Sch Med 1982; **Resid:** Dermatology, NYU Med Ctr 1986

Gladstein, Michael J MD (D) - **Hospital:** Maimonides Med Ctr (page 98); **Address:** 3062 36th Street, Astoria, NY 11103-4798; **Phone:** 718-728-8979; **Board Cert:** Dermatology 1987; **Med School:** NYU Sch Med 1979; **Resid:** Dermatology, NYU Med Ctr 1983

Pereira, Frederick A MD (D) - **Spec Exp:** Skin Cancer; Geriatric Dermatology; **Hospital:** NY Hosp Queens (page 498), Mt Sinai Hosp; **Address:** 51-14 Kissena Blvd, Flushing, NY 11355-4163; **Phone:** 718-359-4425; **Board Cert:** Dermatology 2009; **Med School:** UMDNJ-NJ Med Sch, Newark 1968; **Resid:** Dermatology, Mt Sinai Hosp 1974; Dermatology, Metro Hosp 1975

Diagnostic Radiology

Choi, Mark Hyeok-Je MD (DR) - **Spec Exp:** Musculoskeletal Imaging; **Hospital:** Mt Sinai Hosp of Queens; **Address:** 2916 Astoria Blvd, Astoria, NY 11102; **Phone:** 718-204-5800; **Board Cert:** Diagnostic Radiology 2005; **Med School:** Tufts Univ 2000; **Resid:** Diagnostic Radiology, Nassau Univ Med Ctr 2005; **Fellow:** Musculoskeletal Imaging, Hosp Univ Penn 2006

Mollin, Joel MD (DR) - **Spec Exp:** Ultrasound; CT Scan; **Hospital:** Elmhurst Hosp Ctr; **Address:** 79-01 Broadway, E1-18, Radiology, Elmhurst, NY 11373; **Phone:** 718-334-2061; **Board Cert:** Psychiatry 1976; Diagnostic Radiology 1985; **Med School:** SUNY Downstate 1969; **Resid:** Diagnostic Radiology, USPHS Hosp 1981; Diagnostic Radiology, Mt Sinai Hosp 1983; **Fac Appt:** Asst Prof, Mount Sinai Sch Med

Tartell, Jay D MD (DR) - **Hospital:** Mt Sinai Hosp of Queens; **Address:** Advanced Radiological Imaging, 89-40 56th Ave, Elmhurst, NY 11373-4943; **Phone:** 718-335-5532; **Board Cert:** Diagnostic Radiology 1987; **Med School:** NY Med Coll 1982; **Resid:** Diagnostic Radiology, Bronx Muni Hosp 1986; **Fellow:** Ultrasound/CT/MRI, North Shore Univ Hosp 1987

Youner, Craig J MD (DR) - **Hospital:** Mt Sinai Hosp of Queens; **Address:** Advanced Radiological Imaging, 29-16 Astoria Blvd, Astoria, NY 11102; **Phone:** 718-204-5800; **Board Cert:** Diagnostic Radiology 1978; **Med School:** Albany Med Coll 1973; **Resid:** Internal Medicine, N Shore Univ Hosp 1975; Diagnostic Radiology, N Shore Univ Hosp 1978; **Fac Appt:** Asst Clin Prof Rad, Mount Sinai Sch Med

Endocrinology, Diabetes & Metabolism

Lorber, Daniel L MD (EDM) - **Spec Exp:** Diabetes; **Hospital:** NY Hosp Queens (page 498); **Address:** Queens Diabetes and Endocrinology, 59-45 161st St, Fresh Meadows, NY 11365-1414; **Phone:** 718-762-3111; **Board Cert:** Internal Medicine 1987; Endocrinology, Diabetes & Metabolism 1977; **Med School:** Albert Einstein Coll Med 1972; **Resid:** Internal Medicine, Jacobi Med Ctr 1975; **Fellow:** Endocrinology, Diabetes & Metabolism, Vanderbilt Univ Hosp 1977; **Fac Appt:** Assoc Clin Prof Med, Cornell Univ-Weill Med Coll

Rosman, Lawrence D MD (EDM) - **Spec Exp:** Thyroid Disorders; Osteoporosis; Diabetes; Pituitary Disorders; **Hospital:** NY Hosp Queens (page 498), NYU Langone Med Ctr (page 104); **Address:** 112-03 Queens Blvd, Ste 207, Forest Hills, NY 11375-5550; **Phone:** 718-263-3718; **Board Cert:** Internal Medicine 1978; Endocrinology 1983; **Med School:** NYU Sch Med 1975; **Resid:** Internal Medicine, NYU Langone Med Ctr 1978; **Fellow:** Endocrinology, Diabetes & Metabolism, NYU Langone Med Ctr 1980; **Fac Appt:** Asst Clin Prof Med, NYU Sch Med

Tibaldi, Joseph M MD (EDM) - **Spec Exp:** Diabetes; Thyroid Disorders; Geriatric Endocrinology; **Hospital:** NY Hosp Queens (page 498); **Address:** Queens Diabetes and Endocrinology, 59-45 161st St, Fresh Meadows, NY 11365-1414; **Phone:** 718-762-3111; **Board Cert:** Internal Medicine 1982; Endocrinology, Diabetes & Metabolism 1985; **Med School:** Mount Sinai Sch Med 1979; **Resid:** Internal Medicine, Mount Sinai Med Ctr 1982; **Fellow:** Endocrinology, Montefiore Med Ctr 1984; **Fac Appt:** Asst Clin Prof Med, Cornell Univ-Weill Med Coll

Family Medicine

Di Scala, Reno G MD (FMed) *PCP* - **Hospital:** Mt Sinai Hosp of Queens; **Address:** Steinway Medical Group, 22-02 Steinway St, Astoria, NY 11105; **Phone:** 347-242-2684; **Board Cert:** Family Medicine 2008; **Med School:** Italy 1982; **Resid:** Surgery, Catholic Med Ctr 1985; Family Medicine, Community Hosp 1987

Fisher, George C MD (FMed) *PCP* - **Spec Exp:** Preventive Medicine; Hypertension; Cholesterol/Lipid Disorders; Diabetes; **Hospital:** Mt Sinai Hosp of Queens, Mt Sinai Hosp; **Address:** 22-33 33rd St, Astoria, NY 11105; **Phone:** 718-726-1000; **Board Cert:** Family Medicine 2008; **Med School:** England, UK 1979; **Resid:** Family Medicine, St Joseph Med Ctr 1993

Istrico, Richard A DO (FMed) *PCP* - **Spec Exp:** Primary Care Sports Medicine; **Hospital:** Long Is Jewish Med Ctr; **Address:** 158-01 Crossbay Blvd, Howard Beach, NY 11414-3137; **Phone:** 718-738-9115; **Board Cert:** Family Medicine 1981; **Med School:** Philadelphia Coll Osteo Med 1978; **Resid:** Family Medicine, Interboro Hosp 1979; Sports Medicine, Baptist Med Ctr 1980

Molnar, Thomas G MD (FMed) *PCP* - **Spec Exp:** Hypertension; Diabetes; **Hospital:** NY Hosp Queens (page 498), Flushing Hosp Med Ctr; **Address:** 83-39 Daniels St, Jamaica, NY 11435-1208; **Phone:** 718-291-5151; **Board Cert:** Family Medicine 2007; **Med School:** Hungary 1982; **Resid:** Surgery, Flushing Hosp 1985; Family Medicine, Downstate Med Ctr 1988

Muraca, Glenn J DO (FMed) *PCP* - **Spec Exp:** Sports Medicine; Nutrition; **Hospital:** Flushing Hosp Med Ctr, Wyckoff Heights Med Ctr; **Address:** 104-01 Corona Ave, Corona, NY 11368; **Phone:** 718-271-2020; **Board Cert:** Family Medicine 1994; **Med School:** NY Coll Osteo Med 1990; **Resid:** Family Medicine, Peninsula Hosp 1994

Reddy, Mallikarjuna D MD (FMed) *PCP* - **Spec Exp:** Geriatric Care; **Hospital:** NY Hosp Queens (page 498); **Address:** 72-18 164th St, Flushing, NY 11365-4222; **Phone:** 718-969-6640; **Board Cert:** Family Medicine 2009; **Med School:** India 1981; **Resid:** Family Medicine, Catholic Med Ctr 1990

Roth, Alan R DO (FMed) *PCP* - **Spec Exp:** Palliative Care; Diabetes; Hypertension; **Hospital:** Jamaica Hosp Med Ctr, Flushing Hosp Med Ctr; **Address:** 11940 Metropolitan Ave, Kew Gardens, NY 11415; **Phone:** 718-849-0624; **Board Cert:** Family Medicine 2009; Hospice & Palliative Medicine 2008; **Med School:** NY Coll Osteo Med 1986; **Resid:** Family Medicine, Jamaica Hosp Med Ctr 1989; **Fac Appt:** Asst Clin Prof FMed, Albert Einstein Coll Med

Gastroenterology

Augello, Sabino MD (Ge) - **Spec Exp:** Colon Cancer Screening; Endoscopy & Colonoscopy; Liver Disease; Biliary Disease; **Hospital:** Mt Sinai Hosp of Queens; **Address:** Metropolitan Gastroenterology, 23-18 31st St, Ste 300, Astoria, NY 11105; **Phone:** 718-932-6000; **Board Cert:** Gastroenterology 2005; **Med School:** SUNY Downstate 1998; **Resid:** Internal Medicine, Beth Israel Med Ctr 2002; **Fellow:** Gastroenterology, Beth Israel Med Ctr 2005

Esposito, Stephen P MD (Ge) - **Hospital:** NY Hosp Queens (page 498), NY-Presby/Columbia Univ Med Ctr, NY (page 102); **Address:** 26-19 Francis Lewis Blvd, Bayside, NY 11358; **Phone:** 718-224-7186; **Board Cert:** Internal Medicine 1989; Gastroenterology 2002; **Med School:** SUNY Upstate Med Univ 1986; **Resid:** Internal Medicine, LI Jewish Hosp 1989; **Fellow:** Gastroenterology, Booth Meml Hosp 1991

Harooni, Robert B MD (Ge) - **Spec Exp:** Colonoscopy; Peptic Ulcer Disease; Capsule Endoscopy; **Hospital:** NY Hosp Queens (page 498); **Address:** 55-16 Main St, Lower Level, Flushing, NY 11355; **Phone:** 718-461-6161; **Board Cert:** Internal Medicine 1981; Gastroenterology 1985; **Med School:** Iran 1973; **Resid:** Internal Medicine, Booth Meml Hosp 1982; **Fellow:** Gastroenterology, Booth Meml Hosp 1984; **Fac Appt:** Asst Prof Med, Cornell Univ-Weill Med Coll

Nussbaum, Michel E MD (Ge) - **Spec Exp:** Endoscopy & Colonoscopy; Colon Cancer Screening; Inflammatory Bowel Disease; Peptic Ulcer Disease; **Hospital:** NY Hosp Queens (page 498); **Address:** 142-43 Booth Memorial Ave, Flushing, NY 11355; **Phone:** 718-886-1919; **Board Cert:** Internal Medicine 1981; Gastroenterology 1983; **Med School:** Belgium 1977; **Resid:** Internal Medicine, NY Hosp Queens 1980; **Fellow:** Gastroenterology, NY Hosp Queens 1982

Ramgopal, Mekala MD (Ge) - **Spec Exp:** Peptic Acid Disorders; Inflammatory Bowel Disease; Colon & Rectal Cancer Detection; **Hospital:** St. John's Episcopal Hosp - Queens, Mercy Med Ctr-Rockville Centre; **Address:** 21-24 Camp Rd, Far Rockaway, NY 11691; **Phone:** 718-327-0207; **Board Cert:** Internal Medicine 1978; Gastroenterology 1979; **Med School:** India 1974; **Resid:** Internal Medicine, Jersey City Med Ctr 1976; Internal Medicine, VA Med Ctr 1977; **Fellow:** Gastroenterology, Univ Hosp 1979

Rand, James A MD (Ge) - **Spec Exp:** Colonoscopy; Endoscopy; **Hospital:** NY Hosp Queens (page 498); **Address:** 200-12 44th Ave, Bayside, NY 11361; **Phone:** 718-224-7454; **Board Cert:** Internal Medicine 1978; Gastroenterology 1981; **Med School:** Albert Einstein Coll Med 1975; **Resid:** Internal Medicine, Strong Meml Hosp 1977; Internal Medicine, NY-Presby/Columbia Univ Med Ctr 1978; **Fellow:** Gastroenterology, Montefiore Med Ctr 1980

Vogelman, Arthur MD (Ge) - **Spec Exp:** Colon Cancer; Peptic Ulcer Disease; Gastroesophageal Reflux Disease (GERD); **Hospital:** Forest Hills Hosp, NY Hosp Queens (page 498); **Address:** 7146 110th St, Forest Hills, NY 11375-4842; **Phone:** 718-261-2500; **Board Cert:** Internal Medicine 1979; Gastroenterology 1981; **Med School:** Univ Pittsburgh 1975; **Resid:** Internal Medicine, Mt Sinai Hosp 1978; **Fellow:** Gastroenterology, Mt Sinai Hosp 1980

Weg, Arnold L MD (Ge) - **Spec Exp:** Endoscopy; Inflammatory Bowel Disease/Crohn's; **Hospital:** NY-Presby/Weill Cornell Med Ctr, NY (page 102); **Address:** 71-36 110th St, Ste 1G, Forest Hills, NY 11375-4836; **Phone:** 718-520-2210; **Board Cert:** Internal Medicine 1985; Gastroenterology 1987; **Med School:** NYU Sch Med 1982; **Resid:** Internal Medicine, NY-Presby/Columbia Univ Med Ctr 1985; **Fellow:** Gastroenterology, NY-Presby/Weill Cornell Med Ctr 1987

Geriatric Medicine

Brody, Samuel A MD (Ger) - **Spec Exp:** Frail Elderly; Geriatric Care; Preventive Medicine; **Hospital:** Forest Hills Hosp, NY Hosp Queens (page 498); **Address:** 69-15 Yellowstone Blvd, Forest Hills, NY 11375; **Phone:** 718-268-4500; **Board Cert:** Internal Medicine 1980; Gastroenterology 1983; Geriatric Medicine 2008; **Med School:** Vanderbilt Univ 1977; **Resid:** Internal Medicine, Vanderbilt Med Ctr 1980; **Fellow:** Gastroenterology, Temple Univ Hosp 1983

Geriatric Psychiatry

Greenwald, Blaine MD (GerPsy) - **Spec Exp:** Depression; Dementia; **Hospital:** Zucker Hillside Hosp, N Shore Univ Hosp; **Address:** Zucker Hillside Hosp, Psychiatry, 75-59 263rd St, Ambulatory Care Pavilion, rm 2102, Glen Oaks, NY 11004; **Phone:** 718-470-8159; **Board Cert:** Psychiatry 1983; Geriatric Psychiatry 2011; **Med School:** NY Med Coll 1978; **Resid:** Psychiatry, Mt Sinai Hosp 1982; **Fellow:** Geriatric Psychiatry, Mt Sinai Hosp 1983; **Fac Appt:** Assoc Prof Psyc, Hofstra N Shore-LIJ Sch Med

Koppel, Jeremy L MD (GerPsy) - **Hospital:** Zucker Hillside Hosp, NS-LIJ Hlth Sys; **Address:** Zucker Hillside Hosp, Psychiatry, 75-59 263rd St, Glen Oaks, NY 11004; **Phone:** 718-470-8140; **Board Cert:** Psychiatry 2005; Geriatric Psychiatry 2006; **Med School:** Indiana Univ 1999; **Resid:** Psychiatry, LIJ Med Ctr 2003; **Fellow:** Geriatric Psychiatry, LIJ Med Ctr 2004; **Fac Appt:** Asst Prof Psyc, Hofstra N Shore-LIJ Sch Med

Kremen, Neil J MD (GerPsy) - **Spec Exp:** Depression; Dementia; **Hospital:** Zucker Hillside Hosp, NS-LIJ Hlth Sys; **Address:** Zucker Hillside Hosp, Psychiatry, 75-59 263rd St, Behavioral Health Pavilion, 2 South, Glen Oaks, NY 11004; **Phone:** 718-470-8559; **Board Cert:** Psychiatry 1990; Geriatric Psychiatry 2013; **Med School:** Univ Rochester 1985; **Resid:** Psychiatry, Long Island Jewish Med Ctr 1990

Gynecologic Oncology

Hagopian, George MD (GO) - **Spec Exp:** Gynecologic Cancer; Minimally Invasive Surgery; **Hospital:** Elmhurst Hosp Ctr, Queens Hosp Ctr - Jamaica; **Address:** Elmhurst Hosp, Dept Ob/Gyn, 79-01 Broadway, Elmhurst, NY 11373; **Phone:** 718-334-5366; **Board Cert:** Obstetrics & Gynecology 2013; Gynecologic Oncology 2013; **Med School:** Wayne State Univ 1998; **Resid:** Obstetrics & Gynecology, Northwestern Univ Med Ctr 2002; **Fellow:** Gynecologic Oncology, Mount Sinai Hosp 2004; Gynecologic Oncology, UT MD Anderson Cancer Ctr 2005

Hand Surgery

Caligiuri, Daniel A MD (HS) - **Spec Exp:** Hand & Wrist Surgery; Nerve & Tendon Reconstruction; **Hospital:** Kings Co Hosp Ctr; **Address:** 23-18 31st St, Ste 210, Astoria, NY 11105; **Phone:** 718-777-1885; **Board Cert:** Orthopaedic Surgery 2005; Hand Surgery 2005; **Med School:** SUNY Downstate 1986; **Resid:** Orthopaedic Surgery, SUNY Downstate Med Ctr 1991; **Fellow:** Hand Surgery, Thomas Jefferson Univ Hosp 1992; **Fac Appt:** Asst Prof OrS, SUNY Downstate

Kamler, Kenneth M MD (HS) - **Spec Exp:** Carpal Tunnel Syndrome; Arthritis; Fractures; **Hospital:** Long Is Jewish Med Ctr; **Address:** 66-55 Fresh Pond Rd, Ridgewood, NY 11385; **Phone:** 516-326-2266; **Med School:** France 1975; **Resid:** Orthopaedic Surgery, LIJ Med Ctr 1979; **Fellow:** Hand Surgery, NY-Presby/Columbia Univ Med Ctr 1981

Paksima, Nader DO (HS) - **Spec Exp:** Hand & Wrist Surgery; Microsurgery; **Hospital:** Jamaica Hosp Med Ctr, NYU Hosp For Joint Dis (page 104); **Address:** 133-03 Jamaica Ave, Richmond Hill, NY 11418; **Phone:** 718-206-6923; **Board Cert:** Orthopaedic Surgery 1999; Hand Surgery 2000; **Med School:** NY Coll Osteo Med 1992; **Resid:** Orthopaedic Surgery, Ohio Univ Med Ctr 1998; **Fellow:** Hand Surgery, NYU Hosp for Joint Diseases 1999; **Fac Appt:** Assoc Prof OrS, NYU Sch Med

Hospice & Palliative Medicine

Pan, Cynthia X MD (H & PM) - **Spec Exp:** Palliative Care; Pain Management; Geriatric Care; **Hospital:** NY Hosp Queens (page 498); **Address:** NY Hosp Queens-Dept of Medicine, 56-45 Main St, Flushing, NY 11355; **Phone:** 718-670-2413; **Board Cert:** Internal Medicine 2005; Geriatric Medicine 2008; Hospice & Palliative Medicine 2008; **Med School:** SUNY Stony Brook 1988; **Resid:** Internal Medicine, Univ Rochester Med Ctr 1995; **Fellow:** Geriatric Medicine, Harvard Univ Affil Hosp 1996; **Fac Appt:** Assoc Clin Prof Med, Cornell Univ-Weill Med Coll

Infectious Disease

Asnis, Deborah S MD (Inf) - **Spec Exp:** West Nile Virus; AIDS/HIV; Meningitis; **Hospital:** Flushing Hosp Med Ctr; **Address:** Flushing Hosp Med Ctr, 4500 Parsons Blvd, Dept of Medicine, Fl 3, Flushing, NY 11355; **Phone:** 718-670-3012; **Board Cert:** Internal Medicine 1985; Infectious Disease 1988; **Med School:** Northwestern Univ 1981; **Resid:** Ophthalmology, LI Jewish Hosp 1983; Internal Medicine, LI Jewish Hosp 1985; **Fellow:** Infectious Disease, LI Jewish Hosp 1987; **Fac Appt:** Asst Clin Prof Med, Cornell Univ-Weill Med Coll

Rubin, David S MD (Inf) - **Spec Exp:** AIDS/HIV; **Hospital:** NY Hosp Queens (page 498); **Address:** 138-47 Horace Harding Expy, Flushing, NY 11367; **Phone:** 718-461-5813; **Board Cert:** Internal Medicine 1986; Infectious Disease 1988; **Med School:** Cornell Univ-Weill Med Coll 1983; **Resid:** Internal Medicine, Beth Israel Med Ctr 1986; **Fellow:** Infectious Disease, VA Med Ctr 1988

Segal-Maurer, Sorana MD (Inf) - **Spec Exp:** AIDS/HIV; Viral Infections; Tuberculosis; **Hospital:** NY Hosp Queens (page 498); **Address:** NY Hosp Queens, Div Infectious Dis, 56-45 Main St, Flushing, NY 11355-5000; **Phone:** 718-670-1525; **Board Cert:** Infectious Disease 2000; **Med School:** Mount Sinai Sch Med 1988; **Resid:** Internal Medicine, Jacobi Med Ctr 1991; **Fellow:** Infectious Disease, Montefiore Med Ctr 1993

Internal Medicine

Amin, Mahendra MD (IM) *PCP* - **Hospital:** Long Is Jewish Med Ctr; **Address:** 89-02 Springfield Blvd, Queens Village, NY 11427-2514; **Phone:** 718-776-4444; **Board Cert:** Internal Medicine 1984; **Med School:** India 1978; **Resid:** Internal Medicine, Metropolitan Hosp Ctr 1984

Beyda, Allan E MD (IM) *PCP* - **Spec Exp:** Preventive Medicine; Cholesterol/Lipid Disorders; **Hospital:** NY Hosp Queens (page 498), N Shore Univ Hosp; **Address:** 141-23 59th Ave, Flushing, NY 11355-5304; **Phone:** 718-359-7406; **Board Cert:** Internal Medicine 1979; **Med School:** France 1976; **Resid:** Internal Medicine, New York Hosp Med Ctr 1979

Blum, Daniel N MD (IM) *PCP* - **Spec Exp:** Geriatric Care; Hypertension; Diabetes; Complex Diagnosis; **Hospital:** NY Hosp Queens (page 498); **Address:** 13806 Jewel Ave, Flushing, NY 11367-1933; **Phone:** 718-520-0248; **Board Cert:** Internal Medicine 1984; **Med School:** Albert Einstein Coll Med 1980; **Resid:** Internal Medicine, NY Hosp 1984

Brewer, Marlon E MD (IM) *PCP* - **Spec Exp:** Diabetes; Hypertension; Preventive Medicine; **Hospital:** Elmhurst Hosp Ctr; **Address:** 79-01 Broadway, rm A1-16, Elmhurst, NY 11373; **Phone:** 718-334-2490; **Board Cert:** Internal Medicine 2004; **Med School:** Spain 1986; **Resid:** Internal Medicine, Elmhurst Hosp 1992; **Fac Appt:** Asst Prof Med, Mount Sinai Sch Med

Fukilman, Oscar J MD (IM) *PCP* - **Spec Exp:** Preventive Medicine; **Hospital:** Mt Sinai Hosp of Queens; **Address:** 25-31 30th Road, Ste 1A, Astoria, NY 11102; **Phone:** 718-267-1102; **Board Cert:** Internal Medicine 1979; **Med School:** Argentina 1968; **Resid:** Internal Medicine, Elmhurst Hosp/Mt Sinai Hosp Svc 1972

Hundert, Michael MD (IM) *PCP* - **Spec Exp:** Geriatric Medicine; **Hospital:** N Shore Univ Hosp, St. Francis Hosp - The Heart Ctr (page 111); **Address:** 46-19 Little Neck, Flushing, NY 11362; **Phone:** 718-428-7400; **Board Cert:** Internal Medicine 1978; Geriatric Medicine 2004; **Med School:** Rush Med Coll 1975; **Resid:** Internal Medicine, NY-Presby/Weill Cornell Med Ctr 1978

Joseph, John L MD (IM) - **Spec Exp:** Rheumatology; Osteoporosis; Arthritis; **Hospital:** NY Hosp Queens (page 498); **Address:** 66-20 108th St, Ste 1A, Forest Hills, NY 11375; **Phone:** 718-896-8920; **Board Cert:** Internal Medicine 1983; **Med School:** Mexico 1977; **Resid:** Internal Medicine, Coney Island Hosp 1982; **Fellow:** Rheumatology, Long Island Coll Hosp 1984

Mastrangelo, Ralph MD (IM) *PCP* - **Hospital:** N Shore Univ Hosp; **Address:** 4619 Little Neck Pky, Flushing, NY 11362; **Phone:** 718-428-7400; **Board Cert:** Internal Medicine 1989; **Med School:** SUNY Buffalo 1982; **Resid:** Internal Medicine, N Shore Univ Hosp 1985

Messana, Ida MD (IM) *PCP* - **Spec Exp:** Geriatric Medicine; Preventive Medicine; **Hospital:** Long Is Jewish Med Ctr; **Address:** 109-33 71st Rd, Ste 2E, Forest Hills, NY 11375; **Phone:** 718-263-4345; **Board Cert:** Internal Medicine 1988; **Med School:** SUNY Stony Brook 1984; **Resid:** Internal Medicine, Montefiore Med Ctr 1987; **Fellow:** Geriatric Medicine, Montefiore Med Ctr 1989

Pasquale, Jack MD (IM) - **Spec Exp:** Nutrition; Nutrition & Cancer Prevention/Control; Nutrition in Cancer Therapy; **Hospital:** NY Hosp Queens (page 498); **Address:** Clinical Nutrition Service, 73-03 198th St, Fresh Meadows, NY 11366-1818; **Phone:** 718-465-0041; **Board Cert:** Internal Medicine 1987; **Med School:** Grenada 1981; **Resid:** Internal Medicine, Millard Fillmore Hosp 1984; **Fellow:** Nutrition, Hosp Univ Penn 1985

Somogyi, Anthony MD (IM) *PCP* - **Hospital:** NY Hosp Queens (page 498); **Address:** 42-23 Francis Lewis Blvd, Ste 201, Bayside, NY 11361; **Phone:** 718-224-5687; **Board Cert:** Internal Medicine 1979; **Med School:** Belgium 1976; **Resid:** Internal Medicine, NY Hosp Queens 1980

Interventional Cardiology

Papadakos, Stylianos P MD (IC) - **Spec Exp:** Cardiac Catheterization; Percutaneous Myocardial Revasc (PMR); Angioplasty & Stent Placement; **Hospital:** NYU Langone Med Ctr (page 104), NS-LIJ Hlth Sys; **Address:** Cardiovascular Assocs of New York, 44-01 Francis Lewis Blvd, Level 3, Bayside, NY 11361; **Phone:** 718-423-3355; **Board Cert:** Cardiovascular Disease 2004; Interventional Cardiology 2010; **Med School:** Greece 1985; **Resid:** Internal Medicine, Booth Meml Med Ctr 1989; Internal Medicine, Mt Sinai Hosp 1990; **Fellow:** Cardiovascular Disease, Univ Conn Hosp 1994; **Fac Appt:** Asst Clin Prof Med, Cornell Univ-Weill Med Coll

Maternal & Fetal Medicine

Eglinton, Gary Scott MD (MF) - **Spec Exp:** Obstetric Ultrasound; Fetal Diagnosis & Therapy; Pregnancy-High Risk; **Hospital:** NY Hosp Queens (page 498); **Address:** NY Hosp Queens, Ob/Gyn Dept, 56-45 Main St, rm M365, Flushing, NY 11355; **Phone:** 718-670-1534; **Board Cert:** Obstetrics & Gynecology 2013; Maternal & Fetal Medicine 2013; **Med School:** Univ Ariz Coll Med 1976; **Resid:** Obstetrics & Gynecology, David Grant USAF Med Ctr 1980; **Fellow:** Maternal & Fetal Medicine, LAC-USC Med Ctr 1982; **Fac Appt:** Assoc Prof ObG, Cornell Univ-Weill Med Coll

Inglis, Steven R MD (MF) - **Spec Exp:** Pregnancy-High Risk; Obstetric Ultrasound; Prenatal Diagnosis; **Hospital:** Jamaica Hosp Med Ctr; **Address:** Jamaica Hosp, Dept Ob/Gyn, 89-06 135th St, Ste 6A, Jamaica, NY 11418; **Phone:** 718-206-7642; **Board Cert:** Obstetrics & Gynecology 2013; Maternal & Fetal Medicine 2013; **Med School:** NY Med Coll 1986; **Resid:** Obstetrics & Gynecology, Albany Med Ctr 1990; **Fellow:** Maternal & Fetal Medicine, NY-Presby/Weill Cornell Med Ctr 1992; **Fac Appt:** Assoc Prof ObG, Cornell Univ-Weill Med Coll

Skupski, Daniel MD (MF) - **Spec Exp:** Fetal Diagnosis & Therapy; Multiple Gestation; **Hospital:** NY Hosp Queens (page 498), NY-Presby/Weill Cornell Med Ctr, NY (page 102); **Address:** 56-45 Main St, Flushing, NY 11355-5060; **Phone:** 718-670-1534; **Board Cert:** Obstetrics & Gynecology 2013; Maternal & Fetal Medicine 2013; **Med School:** Univ Mich Med Sch 1985; **Resid:** Obstetrics & Gynecology, Hurley Med Ctr 1989; **Fellow:** Maternal & Fetal Medicine, NY-Presby/Weill Cornell Med Ctr 1994; **Fac Appt:** Prof ObG, Cornell Univ-Weill Med Coll

Medical Oncology

Abramowitz, Avram L MD (Onc) - **Spec Exp:** Breast Cancer; Colon & Rectal Cancer; Lung Cancer; Leukemia & Lymphoma; **Hospital:** Mt Sinai Hosp, Forest Hills Hosp; **Address:** Queens Med Assocs, 176-60 Union Tpke, Ste 360, Fresh Meadows, NY 11366; **Phone:** 718-460-2300; **Board Cert:** Internal Medicine 1987; Hematology 2004; Medical Oncology 2004; **Med School:** NY Med Coll 1984; **Resid:** Internal Medicine, Roosevelt Hosp 1987; **Fellow:** Hematology & Oncology, Roosevelt Hosp 1989; Bone Marrow Transplant, Mt Sinai Hosp 1993

Benisovich, Vladimir I MD (Onc) - **Spec Exp:** Breast Cancer; Lung Cancer; Colon Cancer; **Hospital:** Elmhurst Hosp Ctr, Mt Sinai Hosp; **Address:** Elmhurst Hosp, Med Oncology, 79-01 Broadway, Ste H2-04, Elmhurst, NY 11373; **Phone:** 718-334-6731; **Board Cert:** Internal Medicine 1982; Hematology 1984; Medical Oncology 1985; **Med School:** Russia 1966; **Resid:** Internal Medicine, Bronx Lebanon Hosp 1980; **Fellow:** Hematology, NYU Med Ctr 1982; Medical Oncology, Mt Sinai Hosp 1983

Cortes, Engracio P MD (Onc) - **Spec Exp:** Breast Cancer; Gastrointestinal Cancer; Lung Cancer; Lymphoma; **Hospital:** NY Hosp Queens (page 498), Long Is Jewish Med Ctr; **Address:** 200-20 44th Ave, Bayside, NY 11361; **Phone:** 718-279-9101; **Board Cert:** Internal Medicine 1976; Medical Oncology 1977; **Med School:** Philippines 1964; **Resid:** Internal Medicine, Lemuel Shattuck Hosp 1968; **Fellow:** Medical Oncology, Roswell Park Cancer Inst 1971; **Fac Appt:** Assoc Clin Prof Med, Cornell Univ-Weill Med Coll

Daly, Jane E MD (Onc) - **Hospital:** NY Hosp Queens (page 498); **Address:** 87-23 Myrtle Ave, Glendale, NY 11385; **Phone:** 718-441-5581; **Board Cert:** Internal Medicine 1978; Hematology 1980; Medical Oncology 1981; **Med School:** NY Med Coll 1975; **Resid:** Internal Medicine, Kings County Hosp 1978; **Fellow:** Hematology, LI Jewish Med Ctr 1980; Medical Oncology, Albert Einstein Coll Med Affil Hosp 1981

Greenberg, Howard J MD (Onc) - **Spec Exp:** Breast Cancer; Colon Cancer; Lymphoma Consultation; Coagulation/Bleeding Disorders; **Hospital:** Mt Sinai Hosp of Queens, Mt Sinai Hosp; **Address:** Mt Sinai, Hem/Onc, 27-15 30th Ave, Astoria, NY 11102; **Phone:** 718-278-3569; **Board Cert:** Internal Medicine 1976; Hematology 1978; Medical Oncology 1979; **Med School:** SUNY Downstate 1973; **Resid:** Internal Medicine, Mt Sinai Hosp 1976; **Fellow:** Hematology, Mt Sinai Hosp 1978; Medical Oncology, Meml Sloan-Kettering Cancer Ctr 1979; **Fac Appt:** Assoc Prof Onc, Mount Sinai-Icahn Sch of Med

Shum, Kee Y MD (Onc) - **Spec Exp:** Breast Cancer; Lung Cancer; Colon Cancer; **Hospital:** NY Hosp Queens (page 498), Flushing Hosp Med Ctr; **Address:** 136-25 Maple Ave, Ste 205, Flushing, NY 11355; **Phone:** 718-463-2245; **Board Cert:** Internal Medicine 1984; Medical Oncology 1987; **Med School:** Cornell Univ-Weill Med Coll 1981; **Resid:** Internal Medicine, Kings County Hosp 1985; **Fellow:** Medical Oncology, Meml Sloan-Kettering Cancer Ctr 1987

Neonatal-Perinatal Medicine

Hand, Ivan L MD (NP) - **Spec Exp:** Respiratory Distress Syndrome; Prematurity/Low Birth Weight Infants; Nutrition; Breast Feeding Problems; **Hospital:** Kings Co Hosp Ctr, Queens Hosp Ctr - Jamaica; **Address:** Kings Co Hosp, Neonatology, 451 Clarkson Ave, D5 North, Brooklyn, NY 11203; **Phone:** 718-245-4753; **Board Cert:** Pediatrics 1986; Neonatal-Perinatal Medicine 2011; **Med School:** Albert Einstein Coll Med 1982; **Resid:** Pediatrics, Montefiore Med Ctr 1985; Pediatrics, Bronx Lebanon Hosp 1986; **Fellow:** Neonatal-Perinatal Medicine, NY-Presby/Weill Cornell Med Ctr 1988; **Fac Appt:** Assoc Prof Ped, SUNY Downstate

Nephrology

Charytan, Chaim MD (Nep) - **Spec Exp:** Hypertension; Diabetic Kidney Disease; Kidney Stones; Nephrotic Syndrome; **Hospital:** NY Hosp Queens (page 498); **Address:** 56-45 Main St, Flushing, NY 11355; **Phone:** 718-670-1151; **Board Cert:** Internal Medicine 1969; Nephrology 1974; **Med School:** Albert Einstein Coll Med 1964; **Resid:** Internal Medicine, Jacobi Med Ctr 1967; **Fellow:** Nephrology, Boston Med Ctr 1968; **Fac Appt:** Clin Prof Med, Cornell Univ-Weill Med Coll

Galler, Marilyn MD (Nep) - **Spec Exp:** Hypertension; Kidney Disease; **Hospital:** NY Hosp Queens (page 498); **Address:** 56-45 Main St, rm M201, Flushing, NY 11355; **Phone:** 718-670-1151; **Board Cert:** Internal Medicine 1979; Nephrology 1984; **Med School:** NYU Sch Med 1975; **Resid:** Internal Medicine, Bronx Muni Hosp 1979; **Fellow:** Nephrology, Montefiore Med Ctr 1981; **Fac Appt:** Asst Clin Prof Med, Cornell Univ-Weill Med Coll

Spinowitz, Bruce S MD (Nep) - **Spec Exp:** Diabetic Kidney Disease; Hypertension; Kidney Stones; **Hospital:** NY Hosp Queens (page 498), Montefiore Med Ctr-Einstein Campus (page 100); **Address:** 56-45 Main St, rm M201, Flushing, NY 11355; **Phone:** 718-670-1151; **Board Cert:** Internal Medicine 1976; Nephrology 1978; **Med School:** NYU Sch Med 1973; **Resid:** Internal Medicine, Bellevue Hosp 1976; **Fellow:** Nephrology, Bellevue Hosp 1978; **Fac Appt:** Assoc Clin Prof Med, Cornell Univ-Weill Med Coll

Neurology

Appelbaum, Jeffrey C DO (N) - **Spec Exp:** Multiple Sclerosis; Peripheral Neuropathy; **Hospital:** NY Hosp Queens (page 498), Long Is Jewish Med Ctr; **Address:** ProHlth Care Assocs, 59-07 175 Pl, Flushing, NY 11365; **Phone:** 718-939-0800; **Board Cert:** Neurology 1982; **Med School:** Philadelphia Coll Osteo Med 1977; **Resid:** Neurology, SUNY Downstate Med Ctr 1981; **Fac Appt:** Assoc Prof N, NY Coll Osteo Med

Casson, Ira R MD (N) - **Spec Exp:** Sports Neurology; Headache; Head Injury; Concussion; **Hospital:** Long Is Jewish Med Ctr; **Address:** 112-03 Queens Blvd, Ste 201, Forest Hills, NY 11375; **Phone:** 718-544-6633; **Board Cert:** Neurology 1980; **Med School:** NYU Sch Med 1975; **Resid:** Neurology, NYU Med Ctr 1979; **Fac Appt:** Asst Prof N, Albert Einstein Coll Med

Edgar, Ellen I MD (N) - **Spec Exp:** Neuromuscular Disorders; Headache; Spasticity Management; Botox Therapy; **Hospital:** Montefiore Med Ctr-Moses Campus (page 100); **Address:** Complete Neurological Care, 112-47 Queens Blvd, Ste 206, Forest Hills, NY 11375; **Phone:** 718-521-4251; **Board Cert:** Neurology 2010; Clinical Neurophysiology 2011; **Med School:** Uzbekistan 1996; **Resid:** Neurology, SUNY Hlth Sci Ctr 2009; **Fellow:** Clinical Neurophysiology, G Washington Univ Hosp 2010

Oribe, Emilio M MD (N) - **Spec Exp:** Movement Disorders; Stroke; **Hospital:** NY Hosp Queens (page 498), NY-Presby/Weill Cornell Med Ctr, NY (page 102); **Address:** NY Neurological Assocs, 27-47 Crescent St, Astoria, NY 11102; **Phone:** 718-606-9193; **Board Cert:** Therapeutic Radiology 1986; Neurology 1991; **Med School:** Uruguay 1981; **Resid:** Internal Medicine, NYU Downtown Hosp 1986; Neurology, Mt Sinai Hosp 1989; **Fellow:** Movement Disorders, Mt Sinai Hosp 1991

Obstetrics & Gynecology

Benedicto, Milagros A MD (ObG) - **Hospital:** Wyckoff Heights Med Ctr; **Address:** 68-52 Fresh Pond Rd, Ridgewood, NY 11385; **Phone:** 718-381-7016; **Board Cert:** Obstetrics & Gynecology 2013; **Med School:** Philippines 1964; **Resid:** Obstetrics & Gynecology, Wyckoff Heights Med Ctr 1969; **Fellow:** Wyckoff Heights Med Ctr 1971

Sarabanchong, Voravut O MD (ObG) - **Spec Exp:** Hysteroscopic Surgery; Endometriosis; HPV-Human Papillomavirus; Gynecologic Surgery; **Hospital:** Mt Sinai Hosp of Queens; **Address:** Mt Sinai, Ob/Gyn, 30-16 30th Drive Fl 5, Astoria, NY 11105; **Phone:** 718-545-0948; **Board Cert:** Obstetrics & Gynecology 2013; Public Health & Genl Preventive Med 2008; **Med School:** Cornell Univ-Weill Med Coll 1993; **Resid:** Obstetrics & Gynecology, Univ Hosp Penn 1997; Preventive Medicine, Mt Sinai Sch Med 2007; **Fac Appt:** Asst Prof ObG, Mount Sinai-Icahn Sch of Med

Ophthalmology

Aharon, Raphael MD (Oph) - **Spec Exp:** Diagnostic Problems; Eye Infections; Cataract Surgery; Glaucoma; **Address:** 108-37 71st Ave, Forest Hills, NY 11375; **Phone:** 718-268-6120; **Board Cert:** Ophthalmology 1987; **Med School:** Albert Einstein Coll Med 1980; **Resid:** Internal Medicine, Brookdale Hosp 1981; Ophthalmology, Albert Einstein Coll Med Affil Hosp 1984; **Fac Appt:** Asst Clin Prof Oph, Albert Einstein Coll Med

Fishman, Allen J MD (Oph) - **Spec Exp:** Cataract Surgery-Lens Implant; LASIK-Refractive Surgery; **Hospital:** Flushing Hosp Med Ctr; **Address:** 92-29 Queens Blvd, Ste 2I, Rego Park, NY 11374; **Phone:** 718-261-7007; **Board Cert:** Ophthalmology 1981; **Med School:** Ros Franklin Univ/Chicago Med Sch 1976; **Resid:** Surgery, Beth Israel Med Ctr 1977; Ophthalmology, Brookdale Hosp 1980

Grasso, Cono M MD (Oph) - **Spec Exp:** Cataract Surgery; Glaucoma; Oculoplastic Surgery; **Hospital:** Jamaica Hosp Med Ctr, Flushing Hosp Med Ctr; **Address:** Comprehensive Ophthalmology, 83-05 Grand Ave, Elmhurst, NY 11373; **Phone:** 718-429-0300; **Board Cert:** Ophthalmology 1979; **Med School:** NY Med Coll 1974; **Resid:** Internal Medicine, Metropolitan Hosp Ctr 1975; Ophthalmology, Wills Eye 1978; **Fac Appt:** Assoc Prof Oph, NY Med Coll

Haller, Melvin MD (Oph) - **Spec Exp:** Cataract Surgery; Diabetic Eye Disease/Retinopathy; Refractive Surgery; Oculoplastic & Reconstructive Surgery; **Hospital:** Mt Sinai Hosp of Queens; **Address:** 30-74 36th St, Astoria, NY 11103; **Phone:** 718-728-0224; **Board Cert:** Ophthalmology 1976; **Med School:** SUNY Downstate 1971; **Resid:** Ophthalmology, Montefiore Med Ctr 1975

Hirshfield, Gary MD (Oph) - **Spec Exp:** Cataract Surgery; Laser Surgery; Anterior Segment Surgery; Refractive Surgery; **Hospital:** Lenox Hill Hosp (Manh Eye, Ear & Throat Hosp); **Address:** 176-60 Union Tpke, Ste 110, Fresh Meadows, NY 11366; **Phone:** 718-460-1200; **Board Cert:** Ophthalmology 1991; **Med School:** Yale Univ 1986; **Resid:** Ophthalmology, Manhattan EET Hosp 1990

Kaufmann, Cheryl MD (Oph) - **Spec Exp:** Cataract Surgery; Laser Refractive Surgery; Glaucoma; **Hospital:** NY Hosp Queens (page 498), Lenox Hill Hosp (Manh Eye, Ear & Throat Hosp); **Address:** 43-70 Kissena Blvd, Flushing, NY 11355; **Phone:** 718-353-5970; **Board Cert:** Ophthalmology 1977; **Med School:** NYU Sch Med 1972; **Resid:** Ophthalmology, Manhattan EET Hosp 1976

Mackool Sr, Richard J MD (Oph) - **Spec Exp:** Cataract Surgery; LASIK-Refractive Surgery; Lens Implants-Multifocal; Corneal Disease & Surgery; **Hospital:** New York Eye & Ear Infirm of Mt Sinai, NYU Langone Med Ctr (page 104); **Address:** 31-27 41st St, Astoria, NY 11103; **Phone:** 718-728-3400; **Board Cert:** Ophthalmology 1975; **Med School:** Boston Univ 1968; **Resid:** Ophthalmology, NY Eye & Ear Infirm 1973; **Fac Appt:** Asst Clin Prof Oph, NY Med Coll

Winterkorn, Jacqueline S MD/PhD (Oph) - **Spec Exp:** Neuro-Ophthalmology; Brain Tumors; Eye Muscle Disorders; **Address:** 161-10 Union Tpke, Flushing, NY 11366; **Phone:** 718-380-5346; **Board Cert:** Ophthalmology 1989; **Med School:** Cornell Univ-Weill Med Coll 1983; **Resid:** Ophthalmology, Mt Sinai Hosp 1987; **Fellow:** Neuro-Ophthalmology, NY-Presby/Columbia Univ Med Ctr 1988; **Fac Appt:** Clin Prof Oph, Cornell Univ-Weill Med Coll

Orthopaedic Surgery

Besser Sr, Walter A MD (OrS) - **Spec Exp:** Joint Replacement; Fractures; Trauma; **Hospital:** Mt Sinai Hosp of Queens, NY Hosp Queens (page 498); **Address:** 30-71 29th St, Astoria, NY 11102; **Phone:** 718-204-7752; **Board Cert:** Orthopaedic Surgery 1977; **Med School:** Spain 1968; **Resid:** Orthopaedic Surgery, LIJ Hosp 1971; Orthopaedic Surgery, Brooklyn Jewish Hosp 1974; **Fellow:** Orthopaedic Surgery, Hosp Special Surgery 1977

Schwartz, Evan G MD (OrS) - **Spec Exp:** Sports Medicine; Shoulder Surgery; Knee Surgery; Joint Replacement; **Hospital:** Lenox Hill Hosp; **Address:** Park Lenox Orthopaedics, 30-16 30th Drive, Ste 1B, Astoria, NY 11102; **Phone:** 718-558-1975; **Board Cert:** Orthopaedic Surgery 2010; **Med School:** SUNY Buffalo 1981; **Resid:** Orthopaedic Surgery, Montefiore Med Ctr 1986; **Fellow:** Sports Medicine, Hosp Special Surgery 1987; Shoulder Surgery, Hosp Special Surgery 1987; **Fac Appt:** Asst Prof OrS, NY Med Coll

Touliopoulos, Steven J MD (OrS) - **Spec Exp:** Sports Medicine; Fractures; Hip Replacement; Knee Replacement; **Hospital:** Mt Sinai Hosp of Queens, NY-Presby/Lower Manhattan Hosp (page 102); **Address:** Univ Orthopedics of NY, 23-18 31st St, Ste 210, Astoria, NY 11105; **Phone:** 718-777-1885; **Board Cert:** Orthopaedic Surgery 2010; Orthopaedic Sports Medicine 2007; **Med School:** SUNY Downstate 1991; **Resid:** Orthopaedic Surgery, SUNY Hlth Sci Ctr 1996; **Fellow:** Orthopaedic Sports Medicine, Lenox Hill Hosp 1997

Yang, Edward C MD (OrS) - **Spec Exp:** Musculoskeletal Injuries; Arthritis; Joint Replacement; Geriatric Orthopaedic Surgery; **Hospital:** Mt Sinai Hosp of Queens; **Address:** Mt Sinai Advanced Surgery Grp, 30-74 31st St Fl 5, Long Island City, NY 11102; **Phone:** 718-808-7700; **Board Cert:** Orthopaedic Surgery 2010; **Med School:** NYU Sch Med 1982; **Resid:** Orthopaedic Surgery, NYU Hosp Joint Diseases 1987; **Fac Appt:** Prof OrS, Mount Sinai-Icahn Sch of Med

Otolaryngology

Huo, Jerry MD (Oto) - **Spec Exp:** Endoscopic Sinus Surgery; Thyroid Surgery; Parotid Gland Surgery; Vocal Cord Disorders; **Hospital:** NY Hosp Queens (page 498); **Address:** 136-20 38th Ave, Ste 7J, Flushing, NY 11354; **Phone:** 718-670-0006; **Board Cert:** Otolaryngology 1998; **Med School:** Mount Sinai Sch Med 1991; **Resid:** Surgery, Lenox Hill Hosp 1993; Otolaryngology, Manhattan EET Hosp 1997; **Fac Appt:** Asst Clin Prof Oto, Cornell Univ-Weill Med Coll

La Marca, Charles A MD (Oto) - **Hospital:** Glen Cove Hosp; **Address:** 75-06 Eliot Ave, Middle Village, NY 11379; **Phone:** 718-335-2224; **Board Cert:** Otolaryngology 1984; **Med School:** Mexico 1977; **Resid:** Otolaryngology, SUNY Downstate Med Ctr 1982

Mittleman, Myles MD (Oto) - **Spec Exp:** Sinus Surgery; Vertigo; Hearing Loss; Head & Neck Surgery; **Hospital:** NY Hosp Queens (page 498), Flushing Hosp Med Ctr; **Address:** 5847 Francis Lewis Blvd, Oakland Gardens, NY 11364; **Phone:** 718-225-5400; **Med School:** Med Coll Wisc 1975; **Resid:** Otolaryngology, NYU Med Ctr 1979

Pediatric Cardiology

Rutkovsky, Lisa E MD (PCd) - **Spec Exp:** Congenital Heart Disease; Arrhythmias; **Hospital:** NY Hosp Queens (page 498); **Address:** 142-23 Booth Memorial Ave, Flushing, NY 11355; **Phone:** 718-460-9776; **Board Cert:** Pediatrics 2007; Pediatric Cardiology 2007; **Med School:** NYU Sch Med 1986; **Resid:** Pediatrics, N Shore Univ Hosp 1989; **Fellow:** Pediatric Cardiology, NYU-Bellevue Hosp 1992; **Fac Appt:** Asst Prof Ped, NYU Sch Med

Pediatrics

Abularrage, Joseph J MD (Ped) *PCP* - **Hospital:** NY Hosp Queens (page 498); **Address:** NYHQ, Pediatrics, 56-34 Main St, Flushing, NY 11355; **Phone:** 718-670-1813; **Board Cert:** Pediatrics 1981; **Med School:** NYU Sch Med 1975; **Resid:** Pediatrics, NYU-Bellevue Hosp 1979; **Fellow:** Public Health & Genl Preventive Med, NY-Presby/Columbia Univ Med Ctr 1981

Goldstein, Steven J MD (Ped) *PCP* - **Spec Exp:** Nutrition; Asthma; Vaccines; **Hospital:** Long Is Jewish Med Ctr, NY Hosp Queens (page 498); **Address:** Kew Garden Hills Pediatrics, 141-49 70th Rd, Flushing, NY 11367; **Phone:** 718-268-5282; **Board Cert:** Pediatrics 1983; **Med School:** SUNY Downstate 1978; **Resid:** Pediatrics, LIJ Med Ctr 1981

Physical Medicine & Rehabilitation

Dauhajre, Richard MD (PMR) - **Hospital:** Mt Sinai Hosp of Queens; **Address:** Family Hlth Assocs, 31-60 21st St, Astoria, NY 11106; **Phone:** 718-932-2110; **Board Cert:** Pediatric Rehabilitation Medicine 2013; **Med School:** Mount Sinai Sch Med 1997; **Resid:** Surgery, Lenox Hill Hosp 1999; Physical Medicine & Rehabilitation, NYU Med Ctr 2002

Vallarino, Ramon MD (PMR) - **Spec Exp:** Functional Ability Loss; Electromyography; Musculoskeletal Disorders; **Hospital:** New York Methodist Hosp (page 448); **Address:** 37-04 91st St, Jackson Heights, NY 11372; **Phone:** 516-418-0675; **Board Cert:** Physical Medicine & Rehabilitation 1977; **Med School:** Peru 1966; **Resid:** Physical Medicine & Rehabilitation, Mt Sinai Hosp 1968; **Fellow:** Rheumatology, Mt Sinai Hosp 1968; **Fac Appt:** Asst Clin Prof PMR, SUNY Hlth Sci Ctr

Psychiatry

Kalash, Glenn DO (Psyc) - **Spec Exp:** Forensic Psychiatry; Psychosomatic Disorders; Addiction Psychiatry; Liaison Psychiatry; **Hospital:** Jamaica Hosp Med Ctr, St. Francis Hosp - The Heart Ctr (page 111); **Address:** Jamaica Hosp, Psychiatry, 8900 Van Wyck Expressway, Jamaica, NY 11418; **Phone:** 718-206-7167; **Board Cert:** Psychiatry 2008; Forensic Psychiatry 2009; Psychosomatic Medicine 2005; **Med School:** NY Coll Osteo Med 1992; **Resid:** Psychiatry, NS-LIJ Hlth Sys 1996; **Fellow:** Liaison Psychiatry, Meml Sloan-Kettering Cancer Ctr 1997; **Fac Appt:** Assoc Clin Prof Psyc, NY Coll Osteo Med

Mendelowitz, Alan MD (Psyc) - **Spec Exp:** Schizophrenia; Psychopharmacology; **Hospital:** Zucker Hillside Hosp; **Address:** Zucker Hillside Hosp, Psychiatry, 75-59 263rd St, rm 208, Glen Oaks, NY 11004; **Phone:** 718-470-8397; **Board Cert:** Psychiatry 1992; **Med School:** UMDNJ-Rutgers Med Sch 1987; **Resid:** Psychiatry, Hillside Hosp 1991

Rajput, Ashok MD (Psyc) - **Spec Exp:** Geriatric Psychiatry; Depression; **Hospital:** Mt Sinai Hosp of Queens; **Address:** 84-04 Penelope Ave, Flushing, NY 11379; **Phone:** 718-894-6963; **Board Cert:** Psychiatry 1990; **Med School:** India 1978; **Resid:** Psychiatry, Elmhurst Hosp Ctr 1988; **Fac Appt:** Asst Clin Prof Psyc, Mount Sinai-Icahn Sch of Med

Vivek, Seeth MD (Psyc) - **Spec Exp:** Depression; Panic Disorder; Obsessive-Compulsive Disorder; Liaison Psychiatry; **Hospital:** Jamaica Hosp Med Ctr, Flushing Hosp Med Ctr; **Address:** 75-58 113th St, Ste 1A, Forest Hills, NY 11375; **Phone:** 718-268-9595; **Board Cert:** Psychiatry 1980; Addiction Psychiatry 2011; Geriatric Psychiatry 2011; Psychosomatic Medicine 2005; **Med School:** India 1972; **Resid:** Psychiatry, Natl Inst Mental Hlth 1976; Psychiatry, Mt Sinai Hosp 1979; **Fellow:** Liaison Psychiatry, Montefiore Med Ctr 1981; **Fac Appt:** Prof Psyc, NY Coll Osteo Med

Pulmonary Disease

Chadha, Jang MD (Pul) - **Spec Exp:** Sleep Disorders; Asthma; Emphysema; Critical Care Medicine; **Hospital:** Flushing Hosp Med Ctr, Forest Hills Hosp; **Address:** 11203 Queens Blvd, Ste 201, Forest Hills, NY 11375; **Phone:** 718-544-6660; **Board Cert:** Internal Medicine 1982; Pulmonary Disease 1984; Critical Care Medicine 2008; Sleep Medicine 2007; **Med School:** India 1976; **Resid:** Internal Medicine, Lincoln Hosp 1982; **Fellow:** Pulmonary Disease, NY Med Coll 1984

Kassapidis, Sotirios MD (Pul) - **Hospital:** Mt Sinai Hosp of Queens, N Shore Univ Hosp; **Address:** 22-31 33rd St, Astoria, NY 11105; **Phone:** 718-278-6595; **Board Cert:** Critical Care Medicine 2010; **Med School:** Grenada 1987; **Resid:** Internal Medicine, SUNY Hlth Sci Ctr 1993; **Fellow:** Pulmonary Disease, SUNY Hlth Sci Ctr 1995; Critical Care Medicine, SUNY Hlth Sci Ctr 1996; **Fac Appt:** Asst Clin Prof Med, NYU Sch Med

Mehrishi, Sandeep MD (Pul) - **Spec Exp:** Critical Care Medicine; Sleep Medicine; **Hospital:** N Shore Univ Hosp; **Address:** 250-12 Hillside Ave, Ste 12B, Bellrose, NY 11426; **Phone:** 718-347-0411; **Board Cert:** Internal Medicine 2007; Pulmonary Disease 2009; Critical Care Medicine 2010; Sleep Medicine 2007; **Med School:** India 1993; **Resid:** Internal Medicine, Nassau Univ Med Ctr 1997; **Fellow:** Pulmonary Critical Care Medicine, N Shore Univ Hosp 2000

Nath, Sunil MD (Pul) - **Spec Exp:** Asthma; Emphysema; Lung Cancer; **Hospital:** NY Hosp Queens (page 498); **Address:** 55-14 Main St, Flushing, NY 11355; **Phone:** 718-359-3131; **Board Cert:** Internal Medicine 1980; Pulmonary Disease 1982; **Med School:** India 1976; **Resid:** Internal Medicine, Booth Meml Med Ctr 1980; **Fellow:** Pulmonary Disease, Booth Meml Med Ctr 1982

Silverman, Joel R MD (Pul) - **Spec Exp:** Emphysema; Asthma; Pulmonary Rehabilitation; Sarcoidosis; **Hospital:** Flushing Hosp Med Ctr, N Shore Univ Hosp; **Address:** 111-20 Queens Blvd, Forest Hills, NY 11375; **Phone:** 718-544-4224; **Board Cert:** Internal Medicine 1977; Pulmonary Disease 1980; Critical Care Medicine 2005; **Med School:** Univ Okla Coll Med 1974; **Resid:** Internal Medicine, N Shore Univ Hosp 1977; **Fellow:** Pulmonary Disease, Bellevue Hosp 1979

Thurm, Craig A MD (Pul) - **Spec Exp:** Asthma; Chronic Obstructive Lung Disease (COPD); Interstitial Lung Disease; Pulmonary Fibrosis; **Hospital:** Jamaica Hosp Med Ctr; **Address:** Jamaica Hosp, Pulmonology, 134-20 Jamaica Ave, Jamaica, NY 11418; **Phone:** 718-206-8776; **Board Cert:** Pulmonary Disease 2012; Critical Care Medicine 2013; **Med School:** Albert Einstein Coll Med 1987; **Resid:** Internal Medicine, Francis Scott Key Med Ctr 1990; **Fellow:** Pulmonary Critical Care Medicine, Univ MD Med Ctr 1993

Radiation Oncology

Katz, Alan J MD (RadRO) - **Spec Exp:** Stereotactic Body Radiotherapy; Prostate Cancer; Intensity Modulated Radiotherapy (IMRT); **Hospital:** NS-LIJ Hlth Sys; **Address:** 40-20 Main St Fl 4, Queens, NY 11354; **Phone:** 888-880-6646; **Board Cert:** Therapeutic Radiology 1981; **Med School:** NYU Sch Med 1977; **Resid:** Therapeutic Radiology, NYU Med Ctr 1981

Lipsztein, Roberto MD (RadRO) - **Hospital:** Lenox Hill Hosp, Mt Sinai Hosp; **Address:** NY Radiation Assocs, 106-14 70th Ave, Forest Hills, NY 11375; **Phone:** 718-520-6620; **Board Cert:** Therapeutic Radiology 1982; **Med School:** Brazil 1974; **Resid:** Radiation Oncology, Mt Sinai Hosp 1981; **Fellow:** Radiation Oncology, Mt Sinai Hosp 1981; **Fac Appt:** Asst Clin Prof RadRO, Mount Sinai-Icahn Sch of Med

Rheumatology

Sonpal, Girish M MD (Rhu) - **Spec Exp:** Osteoporosis; Rheumatoid Arthritis; Lupus/SLE; Autoimmune Disease; **Hospital:** NY Hosp Queens (page 498), Flushing Hosp Med Ctr; **Address:** 149-65 24th Ave, Flushing, NY 11357; **Phone:** 718-445-0500; **Board Cert:** Internal Medicine 1974; Rheumatology 1976; **Med School:** India 1969; **Resid:** Internal Medicine, Catholic Med Ctr 1974; **Fellow:** Rheumatology, Worcester City Hosp 1975; Rheumatology, Queens Hosp Ctr 1976; **Fac Appt:** Asst Prof Med, Cornell Univ-Weill Med Coll

Sullivan, Catherine L MD (Rhu) - **Spec Exp:** Rheumatoid Arthritis; **Address:** 2619 Francis Lewis Blvd, Bayside, NY 11358; **Phone:** 718-224-7186; **Board Cert:** Rheumatology 2004; **Med School:** SUNY Stony Brook 1989; **Resid:** Internal Medicine, Winthrop Univ Hosp 1992; **Fellow:** Rheumatology, Winthrop Univ Hosp 1993

Viennas, Stelios MD (Rhu) - **Spec Exp:** Autoimmune Rheumatic Disorders; **Hospital:** NYU Langone Med Ctr (page 104); **Address:** 38-02 31st, Astoria, NY 11103; **Phone:** 718-728-5951; **Med School:** NY Med Coll 1992; **Resid:** Internal Medicine, NY Med Coll Affil Hosp 1997; **Fellow:** Rheumatology, St Vincents Hosp 2001

Sports Medicine

Rosen, Jeffrey E MD (SM) - **Spec Exp:** Pediatric Sports Medicine; **Hospital:** NY Hosp Queens (page 498), NYU Hosp For Joint Dis (page 104); **Address:** NYHQ, Orthopaedic & Rehab Med, 163-03 Horace Harding Expy Fl 2, Fresh Meadows, NY 11365; **Phone:** 866-670-6824; **Board Cert:** Orthopaedic Surgery 2012; **Med School:** Columbia P&S 1993; **Resid:** Orthopaedic Surgery, NYU-Hosp Joint Diseases 1998; **Fellow:** Sports Medicine & Arthroscopic Surgery, Kerlan-Jobe Ortho Clin 1999; **Fac Appt:** Asst Prof OrS, NYU Sch Med

Surgery

Kemeny, M. Margaret MD (S) - **Spec Exp:** Liver Cancer; Pancreatic Cancer; Colon & Rectal Cancer; Cancer Surgery; **Hospital:** Queens Hosp Ctr - Jamaica; **Address:** Queens Hosp-Cancer Ctr, Surgery, 82-68 164th St, rm A531, Jamaica, NY 11432; **Phone:** 718-883-4031; **Board Cert:** Surgery 2013; **Med School:** Columbia P&S 1972; **Resid:** Surgery, NY-Presby/Columbia Univ Med Ctr 1974; Surgery, Univ CO Hosp 1976; **Fellow:** Surgery, Meml Sloan-Kettering Cancer Ctr 1977; Surgical Oncology, Natl Cancer Inst 1981; **Fac Appt:** Prof S, Mount Sinai-Icahn Sch of Med

Manolas, Panagiotis A MD (S) - **Spec Exp:** Breast Cancer; Laparoscopic Surgery; **Hospital:** Mt Sinai Hosp of Queens, Mt Sinai Hosp; **Address:** 30-16 30th Drive, Astoria, NY 11102; **Phone:** 718-626-0707; **Board Cert:** Surgery 2009; **Med School:** Greece 1982; **Resid:** Surgery, NY Methodist Hosp 1989; **Fac Appt:** Asst Clin Prof S, Mount Sinai-Icahn Sch of Med

Mendoza, Ernesto A MD (S) - **Spec Exp:** Parathyroid Surgery; Throat Disorders; Head & Neck Surgery; **Hospital:** New York Methodist Hosp (page 448); **Address:** 40-45 78th St, Elmhurst, NY 11373; **Phone:** 718-397-9058; **Board Cert:** Surgery 2009; **Med School:** Peru 1974; **Resid:** Surgery, Kingsbrook Jewish Med Ctr 1983; **Fellow:** Head and Neck Surgery, Tulane Med Ctr 1985; Surgical Oncology, Roswell Park Cancer Inst 1986

Pace, Benjamin W MD (S) - **Spec Exp:** Breast Surgery; Breast Cancer; **Hospital:** Queens Hosp Ctr - Jamaica; **Address:** Queens Hosp, Surgery, 82-68 164th St, rm A365, Jamaica, NY 11432; **Phone:** 718-883-4640; **Board Cert:** Surgery 2004; **Med School:** Mexico 1977; **Resid:** Surgery, LIJ Med Ctr 1983; **Fac Appt:** Assoc Prof S, Mount Sinai-Icahn Sch of Med

Siegel, Beth M MD (S) - **Spec Exp:** Breast Cancer; Breast Disease; **Hospital:** NY Hosp Queens (page 498); **Address:** NYHQ, Breast Ctr, 56-26 Main St, Flushing, NY 11355; **Phone:** 718-670-1185; **Board Cert:** Surgery 2011; **Med School:** Dominica 1982; **Resid:** Surgery, NY Hosp Queens 1988

Sung, Kap-Jae MD (S) - **Spec Exp:** Breast Cancer; Ultrasound; **Hospital:** NY Hosp Queens (page 498), Forest Hills Hosp; **Address:** 66-83 70 St, Middle Village, NY 11379; **Phone:** 718-651-2929; **Board Cert:** Surgery 2005; **Med School:** South Korea 1973; **Resid:** Surgery, Wyckoff Heights Hosp 1986; **Fac Appt:** Asst Prof S, NY Med Coll

Zeitlin, Alan P MD (S) - **Spec Exp:** Vascular Surgery; Breast Cancer; Laparoscopic Abdominal Surgery; Gastrointestinal Surgery; **Hospital:** Flushing Hosp Med Ctr; **Address:** 69-60 108th St, Ste 107, Forest Hills, NY 11375; **Phone:** 718-544-0442; **Board Cert:** Surgery 2012; **Med School:** Univ Miami Sch Med 1974; **Resid:** Surgery, Montefiore Med Ctr 1979

Thoracic & Cardiac Surgery

Graver, L. Michael MD (T&CS) - **Spec Exp:** Minimally Invasive Cardiac Surgery; Coronary Artery Surgery; Aortic Surgery; Heart Valve Surgery; **Hospital:** Long Is Jewish Med Ctr; **Address:** LIJ Med Ctr, Cardiothoracic Surgery, 270-05 76th Ave, Ste O-4000, New Hyde Park, NY 11040; **Phone:** 718-470-7460; **Board Cert:** Surgery 2003; Thoracic & Cardiac Surgery 2004; **Med School:** Albany Med Coll 1977; **Resid:** Surgery, St Lukes-Roosevelt Hosp Ctr 1982; **Fellow:** Cardiovascular Surgery, Beth Israel Deaconess Med Ctr 1985; **Fac Appt:** Prof TS, Hofstra N Shore-LIJ Sch Med

Lang, Samuel J MD (T&CS) - **Spec Exp:** Minimally Invasive Cardiac Surgery; Heart Valve Surgery; Cardiothoracic Surgery; **Hospital:** NY Hosp Queens (page 498), NY-Presby/Weill Cornell Med Ctr, NY (page 102); **Address:** NYHQ, Cardiothoracic Surgery, 56-45 Main St, rm 387, Flushing, NY 11355; **Phone:** 718-670-1137; **Board Cert:** Thoracic & Cardiac Surgery 2006; **Med School:** UAB Sch Med 1978; **Resid:** Surgery, UCLA Med Ctr 1982; Thoracic Surgery, NYU Med Ctr 1983; **Fellow:** Cardiothoracic Surgery, UCLA Med Ctr 1985; Pediatric Cardiac Surgery, Hosp Sick Chldn 1986; **Fac Appt:** Prof S, Cornell Univ-Weill Med Coll

Lee, Paul C MD (T&CS) - **Spec Exp:** Lung Cancer; Esophageal Cancer; Gastroesophageal Reflux Disease (GERD); Minimally Invasive Thoracic Surgery; **Hospital:** NY Hosp Queens (page 498), NY-Presby/Weill Cornell Med Ctr, NY (page 102); **Address:** NYHQ, Cardiothoracic Surgery, 56-45 Main St, Ste A100, Flushing, NY 11355; **Phone:** 718-670-2707; **Board Cert:** Surgery 2010; Thoracic Surgery 2013; **Med School:** Johns Hopkins Univ 1995; **Resid:** Surgery, UPMC 2001; **Fellow:** Thoracic & Cardiac Surgery, NY-Presby/Weill Cornell Med Ctr 2003; Minimally Invasive Surgery, Meml Sloan-Kettering Cancer Ctr 2004; **Fac Appt:** Prof T&CS, Cornell Univ-Weill Med Coll

Urology

Farrell, Robert M MD (U) - **Spec Exp:** Endourology; Urologic Cancer; **Hospital:** NY Hosp Queens (page 498), Flushing Hosp Med Ctr; **Address:** NYHQ, Urology, 58-42 Main St, Flushing, NY 11355; **Phone:** 718-353-3710; **Board Cert:** Urology 1976; **Med School:** Cornell Univ-Weill Med Coll 1966; **Resid:** Surgery, NY-Presby/Weill Cornell Med Ctr 1968; Urology, NY-Presby/Weill Cornell Med Ctr 1975

Sandhaus, Jeffrey J MD (U) - **Spec Exp:** Prostate Cancer; Minimally Invasive Surgery; Vasectomy-Scalpelless; **Hospital:** Mt Sinai Hosp of Queens, NY-Presby/Weill Cornell Med Ctr, NY (page 102); **Address:** 36-01 31st Ave, Astoria, NY 11106; **Phone:** 718-932-3535; **Board Cert:** Urology 1976; **Med School:** NY Med Coll 1966; **Resid:** Urology, Kings Co Hosp Ctr 1973; **Fac Appt:** Asst Clin Prof U, Mount Sinai-Icahn Sch of Med

Shafizadeh, Farshad A MD (U) - **Spec Exp:** Urology-Female; Pelvic Organ Prolapse Repair; **Hospital:** NY Hosp Queens (page 498); **Address:** NY Hospital of Queens, Urology, 5645 Main St, Basement, WLL 300, Queens, NY 11355; **Phone:** 718-303-3720; **Board Cert:** Urology 2013; **Med School:** SUNY Downstate 1995; **Resid:** Surgery, Montefiore Med Ctr 1997; Urology, Montefiore Med Ctr 2001

Tarasuk, Albert P MD (U) - **Spec Exp:** Prostate Disease; Bladder Surgery; Kidney Stones; **Hospital:** NY Hosp Queens (page 498), Flushing Hosp Med Ctr; **Address:** NYHQ, Urology, 58-42 Main St, Flushing, NY 11355; **Phone:** 718-353-3710; **Board Cert:** Urology 1972; **Med School:** Geo Wash Univ 1964; **Resid:** Urology, Beth Israel Med Ctr 1971

Tillem, Steven M MD (U) - **Hospital:** Mt Sinai Hosp of Queens, NY Hosp Queens (page 498); **Address:** 31-19 Newton Ave, Ste 801, Astoria, NY 11102; **Phone:** 718-777-2111; **Board Cert:** Urology 2009; **Med School:** UMDNJ-NJ Med Sch, Newark 1992; **Resid:** Surgery, LIJ Med Ctr 1994; Urology, LIJ Med Ctr 1998

Vascular & Interventional Radiology

Rogers, David M MD (VIR) - **Spec Exp:** Interventional Radiology; **Hospital:** NY Hosp Queens (page 498), Wyckoff Heights Med Ctr; **Address:** NYHQ, Radiology, 56-45 Main St, Flushing, NY 11355; **Phone:** 718-670-1496; **Board Cert:** Diagnostic Radiology 1987; **Med School:** Columbia P&S 1981; **Resid:** Diagnostic Radiology, Mt Sinai Hosp 1987; **Fellow:** Vascular & Interventional Radiology, NYU Med Ctr 1988

Vascular Surgery

Lee, Andy Ming Hai MD (VascS) - **Spec Exp:** Aneurysm-Abdominal & Thoracic Aortic; Peripheral Vascular Disease; Endovascular Surgery; **Hospital:** NY Hosp Queens (page 498); **Address:** NYHQ, Vascular Surgery, 56-45 Main St, Ste LL300, Flushing, NY 11355; **Phone:** 718-445-0220; **Board Cert:** Surgery 2007; Vascular Surgery 2008; **Med School:** UMDNJ-Rutgers Med Sch 1992; **Resid:** Surgery, NYU Med Ctr 1997; **Fellow:** Vascular Surgery, NYU Med Ctr 1999; **Fac Appt:** Asst Clin Prof VascS, Cornell Univ-Weill Med Coll

The Best in American Medicine
www.CastleConnolly.com

Richmond (Staten Island)

Richmond (Staten Island)

Adolescent Medicine

Lee, April C MD (AM) - **Hospital:** Staten Island Univ Hosp - North, NS-LIJ Hlth Sys; **Address:** Staten Island Univ Hosp, Adolescent Med, 242 Mason Ave, Staten Island, NY 10305; **Phone:** 718-226-6294; **Board Cert:** Pediatrics 1986; Adolescent Medicine 2008; **Med School:** NYU Sch Med 1980; **Resid:** Pediatrics, NYU Med Ctr 1983; **Fellow:** Adolescent Medicine, Brookdale Hosp 1986; **Fac Appt:** Asst Clin Prof Ped, SUNY Hlth Sci Ctr

Allergy & Immunology

Rao, Yalamanchili A.K. MD (A&I) - **Spec Exp:** Asthma & Allergy; **Hospital:** Staten Island Univ Hosp - North, Richmond Univ Med Ctr; **Address:** 896 Targee St, Staten Island, NY 10304; **Phone:** 718-816-8200; **Board Cert:** Internal Medicine 1977; Allergy & Immunology 1977; Pediatrics 1976; **Med School:** India 1968; **Resid:** Pediatrics, LI Coll Hosp 1973; Internal Medicine, LI Coll Hosp 1977; **Fellow:** Allergy & Immunology, LI Coll Hosp 1977; **Fac Appt:** Asst Clin Prof A&I, SUNY Downstate

Cardiovascular Disease

Besser, Louis M MD (Cv) - **Spec Exp:** Coronary Artery Disease; Arrhythmias; Acute Coronary Syndromes; Atrial Fibrillation; **Hospital:** Richmond Univ Med Ctr, Staten Island Univ Hosp - North; **Address:** Primary Cardiology, 11 Ralph Pl, Ste 310, Staten Island, NY 10304-4419; **Phone:** 718-442-1777; **Board Cert:** Internal Medicine 1988; Cardiovascular Disease 1989; Nuclear Cardiology 2007; **Med School:** Mexico 1981; **Resid:** Internal Medicine, St Vincents Med Ctr 1986; **Fellow:** Cardiovascular Disease, St Vincents Med Ctr 1988; **Fac Appt:** Asst Clin Prof Med, NY Med Coll

Bogin, Marc MD (Cv) - **Spec Exp:** Echocardiography; Cardiac Catheterization; **Hospital:** Staten Island Univ Hosp - North, Richmond Univ Med Ctr; **Address:** Heart, Lung & Surgery Ctr, 501 Seaview Ave, Ste 200, Staten Island, NY 10305; **Phone:** 718-663-6400; **Board Cert:** Internal Medicine 1989; Cardiovascular Disease 2013; **Med School:** Mexico 1985; **Resid:** Internal Medicine, Booth Meml Hosp 1990; **Fellow:** Cardiovascular Disease, St Vincent's Hosp & Med Ctr 1993; **Fac Appt:** Asst Clin Prof Med, NY Med Coll

Grodman, Richard S MD (Cv) - **Spec Exp:** Echocardiography; Cardiac Catheterization; **Hospital:** Richmond Univ Med Ctr; **Address:** Richmond University Medical Center, 355 Bard Ave, Staten Island, NY 10310-1664; **Phone:** 718-818-4642; **Board Cert:** Internal Medicine 1976; Cardiovascular Disease 1979; **Med School:** SUNY Downstate 1973; **Resid:** Internal Medicine, SUNY Downstate 1976; Critical Care Medicine, SUNY Downstate 1977; **Fellow:** Cardiovascular Disease, Rhode Island Hosp-Brown 1979; **Fac Appt:** Assoc Clin Prof Med, NY Med Coll

Lafferty, James C MD (Cv) - **Spec Exp:** Electrophysiologic Testing; **Hospital:** Staten Island Univ Hosp - North; **Address:** Staten Island Heart, 501 Seaview Ave, Ste 300, Staten Island, NY 10305; **Phone:** 718-663-7000 x6; **Board Cert:** Internal Medicine 1985; Cardiovascular Disease 1987; Cardiac Electrophysiology 2006; **Med School:** SUNY Hlth Sci Ctr 1982; **Resid:** Internal Medicine, Staten Island Hosp 1985; **Fellow:** Cardiovascular Disease, Downstate Med Ctr 1987; **Fac Appt:** Assoc Prof Med, SUNY Downstate

Schwartz, Charles A MD (Cv) - **Spec Exp:** Echocardiography; Stress Echocardiography; Transesophageal Echocardiogram (TEE); **Hospital:** Staten Island Univ Hosp - North; **Address:** Staten Island Heart, 501 Seaview Ave, Ste 300, Staten Island, NY 10305; **Phone:** 718-663-7000; **Board Cert:** Internal Medicine 1983; Cardiovascular Disease 1985; Echocardiography 2011; **Med School:** SUNY Downstate 1980; **Resid:** Internal Medicine, Staten Island Hosp 1983; **Fellow:** Cardiovascular Disease, St Vincents Hosp & Med Ctr 1985

Vazzana, Thomas MD (Cv) - **Spec Exp:** Interventional Cardiology; Non-Invasive Cardiology; **Hospital:** Staten Island Univ Hosp - North; **Address:** Heart, Lung & Surgery Ctr, 501 Seaview Ave, Ste 200, Staten Island, NY 10305; **Phone:** 718-663-6400; **Board Cert:** Internal Medicine 1989; Cardiovascular Disease 2011; **Med School:** Grenada 1985; **Resid:** Internal Medicine, St Joseph's Hosp & Med Ctr 1989; **Fellow:** Cardiovascular Disease, St Vincent's Hosp & Med Ctr 1991

Winter, Steven MD (Cv) - **Spec Exp:** Cholesterol/Lipid Disorders; Preventive Cardiology; Non-Invasive Cardiology; **Hospital:** Staten Island Univ Hosp - North, Richmond Univ Med Ctr; **Address:** 2627 Hylan Blvd, B Bldg, Staten Island, NY 10306-4339; **Phone:** 718-351-5600; **Board Cert:** Internal Medicine 1979; Cardiovascular Disease 1981; **Med School:** UMDNJ-NJ Med Sch, Newark 1976; **Resid:** Internal Medicine, N Shore Univ Hosp 1979; **Fellow:** Cardiovascular Disease, Rhode Island Hosp 1981; **Fac Appt:** Asst Clin Prof Med, SUNY Hlth Sci Ctr

Child Neurology

De Carlo, Regina MD (ChiN) - **Spec Exp:** Autism & Developmental Disorders; Headache; Learning Disorders; ADD/ADHD; **Hospital:** Richmond Univ Med Ctr, NYU Langone Med Ctr (page 104); **Address:** 2550 Victory Blvd, Staten Island, NY 10314-6635; **Phone:** 718-983-0923; **Board Cert:** Pediatrics 1984; Child Neurology 1984; **Med School:** UMDNJ-NJ Med Sch, Newark 1977; **Resid:** Pediatrics, NYU Med Ctr 1979; Neurology, NYU Med Ctr 1981; **Fellow:** Child Neurology, NYU Med Ctr 1982; **Fac Appt:** Asst Clin Prof N, NYU Sch Med

Colon & Rectal Surgery

Lacqua, Frank MD (CRS) - **Spec Exp:** Colonoscopy; Colon Cancer; Anal Disorders & Reconstruction; **Hospital:** Richmond Univ Med Ctr, Lutheran Med Ctr - Brooklyn; **Address:** 2372 Victory Blvd, Staten Island, NY 10314; **Phone:** 718-761-3700; **Board Cert:** Colon & Rectal Surgery 2011; Surgery 2009; **Med School:** SUNY Buffalo 1985; **Resid:** Surgery, St Luke's-Roosevelt Hosp 1990; **Fellow:** Colon & Rectal Surgery, Univ Tex Hlth Sci Ctr 1991

Dermatology

Bernstein, Charles MD (D) - **Hospital:** Staten Island Univ Hosp - North; **Address:** 244 Buel Ave, Fl 2, Staten Island, NY 10305; **Phone:** 718-980-5767; **Board Cert:** Internal Medicine 1983; Dermatology 1987; **Med School:** SUNY Downstate 1980; **Resid:** Internal Medicine, Staten Island Hosp 1984; Dermatology, Downstate Med Ctr 1987; **Fac Appt:** Assoc Clin Prof D, SUNY Hlth Sci Ctr

Lederman, Josiane MD (D) - **Spec Exp:** Cosmetic Dermatology; Skin Cancer; Laser Surgery; **Address:** 116 Lamberts Ln, Staten Island, NY 10314-7210; **Phone:** 718-370-0422; **Board Cert:** Dermatology 1986; **Med School:** France 1981; **Resid:** Dermatology, Saint Louis Hosp 1983; **Fellow:** Dermatology, Mass Genl Hosp/Harvard 1986

Diagnostic Radiology

Raia, Carolyn MD (DR) - **Spec Exp:** Breast Imaging; Breast Cancer; Mammography; **Hospital:** Staten Island Univ Hosp - North; **Address:** SIUH Breast Imaging Ctr, 256 B Mason Ave, Staten Island, NY 10305; **Phone:** 718-226-1333; **Board Cert:** Diagnostic Radiology 1994; **Med School:** SUNY Downstate 1989; **Resid:** Diagnostic Radiology, St Lukes-Roosevelt Hosp 1994; **Fellow:** Breast Surgery, Columbia-Presby Med Ctr 1995

Endocrinology, Diabetes & Metabolism

Cohen, Neil D MD (EDM) - **Spec Exp:** Diabetes; Thyroid Disorders; Osteoporosis; Thyroid Cancer; **Hospital:** Staten Island Univ Hosp - North, Staten Island Univ Hosp - South; **Address:** 1460 Victory Blvd, Staten Island, NY 10301-3914; **Phone:** 718-442-0300; **Board Cert:** Internal Medicine 2013; Endocrinology, Diabetes & Metabolism 2005; **Med School:** Med Coll PA Hahnemann 1990; **Resid:** Internal Medicine, N Shore Univ Hosp 1993; **Fellow:** Endocrinology, Diabetes & Metabolism, Montefiore Med Ctr 1995

Das, Seshadri MD (EDM) - **Spec Exp:** Diabetes; Thyroid Disorders; Polycystic Ovarian Syndrome; Calcium Disorders; **Hospital:** Richmond Univ Med Ctr, Staten Island Univ Hosp - South; **Address:** 774 Manor Rd Fl 2 - Ste 208, Staten Island, NY 10314; **Phone:** 718-273-5522; **Board Cert:** Internal Medicine 1983; Endocrinology, Diabetes & Metabolism 2008; **Med School:** India 1968; **Resid:** Internal Medicine, North Middlesex Hosp 1975; Internal Medicine, Whittington Hosp/Royal Free Hosp 1977; **Fellow:** Endocrinology, Diabetes & Metabolism, SUNY Downstate 1980; **Fac Appt:** Assoc Clin Prof Med, Mount Sinai-Icahn Sch of Med

Hoffman, Richard S MD (EDM) - **Spec Exp:** Diabetes; Thyroid Disorders; Parathyroid Disorders; Adrenal Disorders; **Hospital:** Staten Island Univ Hosp - North; **Address:** 1460 Victory Blvd, Staten Island, NY 10301; **Phone:** 718-442-0300; **Board Cert:** Internal Medicine 1971; Endocrinology, Diabetes & Metabolism 1975; **Med School:** SUNY Hlth Sci Ctr 1965; **Resid:** Internal Medicine, Long Island Coll Hosp 1967; Internal Medicine, Boston City Hosp 1968; **Fellow:** Endocrinology, Boston City Hosp 1970

Rothman, Jeffrey G MD (EDM) - **Spec Exp:** Diabetes; Osteoporosis; Thyroid Disorders; **Hospital:** Staten Island Univ Hosp - North, Staten Island Univ Hosp - South; **Address:** 1460 Victory Blvd, Staten Island, NY 10301-3914; **Phone:** 718-442-0300; **Board Cert:** Internal Medicine 1973; Endocrinology, Diabetes & Metabolism 1977; **Med School:** SUNY Buffalo 1970; **Resid:** Internal Medicine, Hosp Univ Penn 1973; **Fellow:** Endocrinology, Diabetes & Metabolism, Hosp Univ Penn 1977

Family Medicine

Nepola, Neil MD (FMed) *PCP* - **Hospital:** Staten Island Univ Hosp - South; **Address:** 217 Rose Ave, Staten Island, NY 10306-2918; **Phone:** 718-667-6767; **Board Cert:** Family Medicine 2004; **Med School:** Philippines 1979; **Resid:** Family Medicine, UMDNJ-St Peter's Hosp 1983

Gastroenterology

Bruckstein, Alex H MD (Ge) - **Spec Exp:** Colonoscopy; Gastroscopy; Gastroesophageal Reflux Disease (GERD); Hepatitis; **Hospital:** Staten Island Univ Hosp - North, Staten Island Univ Hosp - South; **Address:** 2627 Hylan Blvd, Staten Island, NY 10306; **Phone:** 718-667-3200; **Board Cert:** Internal Medicine 1979; Gastroenterology 1983; **Med School:** Albert Einstein Coll Med 1975; **Resid:** Internal Medicine, Roosevelt Hosp 1977; Internal Medicine, St Luke's Hosp 1978; **Fellow:** Gastroenterology, NY VA Med Ctr 1980; **Fac Appt:** Asst Clin Prof Med, SUNY Downstate

Fazio, Richard A MD (Ge) - **Spec Exp:** Colonoscopy; Gastroesophageal Reflux Disease (GERD); **Hospital:** Richmond Univ Med Ctr; **Address:** 78 Todt Hill Rd, Ste 203, Staten Island, NY 10314-4528; **Phone:** 718-448-1122; **Board Cert:** Internal Medicine 1982; Gastroenterology 1983; **Med School:** Italy 1978; **Resid:** Internal Medicine, Maimonides Med Ctr 1981; **Fellow:** Gastroenterology, St Vincent's Med Ctr 1983

Wickremesinghe, Prasanna C MD (Ge) - **Spec Exp:** Inflammatory Bowel Disease/Crohn's; Hepatitis; Endoscopy; **Hospital:** Richmond Univ Med Ctr; **Address:** 481 Bard Ave, Staten Island, NY 10310; **Phone:** 718-448-0865; **Board Cert:** Internal Medicine 1980; Gastroenterology 1975; **Med School:** Sri Lanka 1968; **Resid:** Internal Medicine, Coney Island Hosp 1972; **Fellow:** Gastroenterology, Maimonides Medical Ctr 1975

Geriatric Medicine

Seminara, Donna P MD (Ger) - **Spec Exp:** Geriatric Care; Frail Elderly; Preventive Medicine; **Hospital:** Staten Island Univ Hosp - North; **Address:** Island Internists, 420 Lyndale Ave, Staten Island, NY 10312-6131; **Phone:** 718-967-5630; **Board Cert:** Internal Medicine 2010; Geriatric Medicine 2000; **Med School:** Mexico 1986; **Resid:** Internal Medicine, Staten Island Univ Hosp 1990

Gynecologic Oncology

Maiman, Mitchell MD (GO) - **Spec Exp:** Cervical Cancer; Ovarian Cancer; Uterine Cancer; **Hospital:** Staten Island Univ Hosp - North; **Address:** 256 Mason Ave, Ste C, Staten Island, NY 10305-3408; **Phone:** 718-226-9269; **Board Cert:** Obstetrics & Gynecology 2013; Gynecologic Oncology 2013; **Med School:** SUNY Downstate 1981; **Resid:** Obstetrics & Gynecology, Montefiore Med Ctr 1985; **Fellow:** Gynecologic Oncology, SUNY Downstate Med Ctr 1987; **Fac Appt:** Prof ObG, SUNY Downstate

Infectious Disease

Glaser, Jordan B MD (Inf) - **Spec Exp:** AIDS/HIV; **Hospital:** Staten Island Univ Hosp - North, Staten Island Univ Hosp - South; **Address:** 1408 Richmond Rd, Staten Island, NY 10304; **Phone:** 718-979-5646; **Board Cert:** Internal Medicine 1982; Infectious Disease 1984; **Med School:** SUNY Downstate 1979; **Resid:** Internal Medicine, Staten Island Hosp 1982; **Fellow:** Infectious Disease, SUNY Downstate Med Ctr 1984; **Fac Appt:** Assoc Clin Prof Med, SUNY Hlth Sci Ctr

Internal Medicine

Gazzara, Paul MD (IM) *PCP* - **Spec Exp:** Complementary Medicine; Acupuncture; Addiction/Substance Abuse; **Hospital:** Staten Island Univ Hosp - North; **Address:** South Shore Physicians, 3589 Hylan Blvd, Staten Island, NY 10308; **Phone:** 718-966-3700; **Board Cert:** Internal Medicine 1986; **Med School:** SUNY Downstate 1983; **Resid:** Internal Medicine, Staten Island Hosp 1986; **Fac Appt:** Asst Clin Prof Med, SUNY Hlth Sci Ctr

Strange, Theodore MD (IM) *PCP* - **Spec Exp:** Geriatric Medicine; **Hospital:** Staten Island Univ Hosp - South, Staten Island Univ Hosp - North; **Address:** 68 Seguine Ave, Staten Island, NY 10309; **Phone:** 718-356-6500; **Board Cert:** Internal Medicine 2001; Geriatric Medicine 2012; **Med School:** SUNY Hlth Sci Ctr 1985; **Resid:** Internal Medicine, Staten Island Univ Hosp 1988; **Fac Appt:** Assoc Clin Prof Med, SUNY Downstate

Interventional Cardiology

Malpeso, James V MD (IC) - **Spec Exp:** Cardiac Catheterization; Angioplasty & Stent Placement; Cardiac CT Angiography; **Hospital:** Staten Island Univ Hosp - North; **Address:** Univ Cardiology, 501 Seaview Ave HLS Bldg - Ste 200, Staten Island, NY 10305; **Phone:** 718-226-9600; **Board Cert:** Internal Medicine 1979; Cardiovascular Disease 1981; Cardiovascular Computed Tomography 2008; **Med School:** Albert Einstein Coll Med 1975; **Resid:** Internal Medicine, Kings County Hosp 1978; **Fellow:** Cardiovascular Disease, St Vincent Hosp Med Ctr 1980; **Fac Appt:** Asst Prof Med, SUNY Downstate

Medical Oncology

Forlenza, Thomas J MD (Onc) - **Spec Exp:** Palliative Care; Bleeding/Coagulation Disorders; Breast Cancer; Lung Cancer; **Hospital:** Richmond Univ Med Ctr; **Address:** 1366 Victory Blvd, Ste A, Staten Island, NY 10301; **Phone:** 718-816-4949; **Board Cert:** Internal Medicine 1981; Hematology 1984; Blood Banking 1984; Medical Oncology 1985; **Med School:** Boston Univ 1977; **Resid:** Internal Medicine, Univ Kentucky Med Ctr 1980; **Fellow:** Hematology, NYU Med Ctr 1982; Medical Oncology, Kings Co Hosp 1983; **Fac Appt:** Asst Prof Med, NYU Sch Med

Friscia, Philip MD (Onc) - **Spec Exp:** Lung Cancer; Colon Cancer; Hematology; **Hospital:** Staten Island Univ Hosp - North, Staten Island Univ Hosp - South; **Address:** Nalitt Cancer Inst, 256 Mason Ave C Bldg Fl 1, Staten Island, NY 10305; **Phone:** 718-226-6400; **Board Cert:** Internal Medicine 1978; Medical Oncology 1981; **Med School:** Italy 1972; **Resid:** Internal Medicine, LI Coll Hosp 1976; **Fellow:** Hematology & Oncology, LI Coll Hosp 1979; **Fac Appt:** Asst Clin Prof Med, SUNY Downstate

Odaimi, Marcel MD (Onc) - **Spec Exp:** Brain Tumors; **Hospital:** Staten Island Univ Hosp - North; **Address:** Nalitt Cancer Inst, 256 Mason Ave C Bldg Fl 1, Staten Island, NY 10305; **Phone:** 718-226-6400; **Board Cert:** Internal Medicine 1987; Medical Oncology 1989; **Med School:** Amer Univ Beirut 1981; **Resid:** Internal Medicine, American Univ 1983; Internal Medicine, Staten Island Hosp 1987; **Fellow:** Medical Oncology, UT MD Anderson Cancer Ctr 1985

Terjanian, Terenig O MD (Onc) - **Hospital:** Staten Island Univ Hosp - North; **Address:** Nalitt Cancer Inst, 256 Mason Ave C Bldg Fl 1, Staten Island, NY 10305; **Phone:** 718-226-6400; **Board Cert:** Internal Medicine 1984; Medical Oncology 1987; Hematology 1988; **Med School:** France 1978; **Resid:** Anatomic Pathology, Amer Univ Beirut 1981; Internal Medicine, Staten Island Univ Hosp 1984; **Fellow:** Medical Oncology, Univ Tex-MD Anderson Cancer Ctr 1986; Hematology, NYU Med Ctr 1988

Neonatal-Perinatal Medicine

Roth, Philip MD/PhD (NP) - **Spec Exp:** Neonatal Care; Neonatal Infections/Immunity; **Hospital:** Staten Island Univ Hosp - North; **Address:** SIUH, NICU, 475 Seaview Ave Fl 4 East, Staten Island, NY 10305; **Phone:** 718-226-9796; **Board Cert:** Pediatrics 1987; Neonatal-Perinatal Medicine 2011; **Med School:** Columbia P&S 1982; **Resid:** Pediatrics, Chldns Hosp 1986; **Fellow:** Neonatal-Perinatal Medicine, Hosp Univ Penn 1988; **Fac Appt:** Assoc Prof Ped, SUNY Downstate

Nephrology

Grossman, Susan D MD (Nep) - **Hospital:** Richmond Univ Med Ctr; **Address:** 1366 Victory Blvd, Staten Island, NY 10310; **Phone:** 718-273-3400; **Board Cert:** Internal Medicine 1980; Nephrology 1982; **Med School:** UMDNJ-NJ Med Sch, Newark 1977; **Resid:** Internal Medicine, Univ Hosp 1980; **Fellow:** Nephrology, New England Med Ctr 1982

Kleiner, Morton MD (Nep) - **Spec Exp:** Hypertension; Kidney Disease; **Hospital:** Staten Island Univ Hosp - North; **Address:** Staten Island Dialysis Ctr, 470 Seaview Ave, Staten Island, NY 10305; **Phone:** 718-987-5942; **Board Cert:** Internal Medicine 1977; Nephrology 1982; **Med School:** NY Med Coll 1974; **Resid:** Internal Medicine, N Shore Univ Hosp 1977; **Fellow:** Nephrology, NY-Presby/Weill Cornell Med Ctr 1979; **Fac Appt:** Asst Clin Prof Med, SUNY Downstate

Pepe, John M MD (Nep) - **Spec Exp:** Transplant Medicine-Kidney; **Hospital:** Richmond Univ Med Ctr, Staten Island Univ Hosp - South; **Address:** 1550 Richmond Ave, Ste 205, Staten Island, NY 10314; **Phone:** 718-982-7800; **Board Cert:** Internal Medicine 1978; Nephrology 1980; **Med School:** Med Coll PA Hahnemann 1975; **Resid:** Internal Medicine, Univ Hosp 1978; **Fellow:** Nephrology, Bronx Muni Hosp 1980; **Fac Appt:** Asst Prof Med, NY Med Coll

Neurology

Jutkowitz, Robert S MD (N) - **Spec Exp:** Headache; Seizure Disorders; **Hospital:** Richmond Univ Med Ctr; **Address:** 78 Todt Hill Rd, Ste 205, Staten Island, NY 10314; **Phone:** 718-442-7133; **Board Cert:** Neurology 1976; **Med School:** Univ Louisville Sch Med 1968; **Resid:** Internal Medicine, St Viincents Hosp 1970; Neurology, Mt Sinai Hosp 1974

Mesad, Salah MD (N) - **Spec Exp:** Epilepsy/Seizure Disorders; **Hospital:** Richmond Univ Med Ctr; **Address:** Northeast Regional Epilepsy Group, 737 Castleton Ave, Staten Island, NY 10310; **Phone:** 718-655-6595; **Board Cert:** Neurology 2006; **Med School:** Germany 1987; **Resid:** Neurology, Univ Minn Hosp & Clin 1995

Najjar, Souhel MD (N) - **Spec Exp:** Epilepsy/Seizure Disorders; Pediatric Neurology; Migraine; **Hospital:** Staten Island Univ Hosp - North, NYU Langone Med Ctr (page 104); **Address:** 501 Seaview Ave, Ste 104, Staten Island, NY 10305; **Phone:** 718-683-3766; **Board Cert:** Neurology 1993; **Med School:** Syria 1983; **Resid:** Pathology, Albany Med Ctr 1988; Neurology, Albany Med Ctr 1992; **Fellow:** Neurological Pathology, NYU Med Ctr 1994; **Fac Appt:** Assoc Clin Prof N, NYU Sch Med

Neuroradiology

Raden, Mark J MD (NRad) - **Spec Exp:** Invertentional Radiology; Vascular Malformations; **Hospital:** Staten Island Univ Hosp - North; **Address:** Staten Island Univ Hosp, Neuroradiology, 475 Seaview Ave, Staten Island, NY 10305; **Phone:** 718-226-1784; **Board Cert:** Diagnostic Radiology 1995; Neuroradiology 2010; **Med School:** Albert Einstein Coll Med 1989; **Resid:** Diagnostic Radiology, UMDNJ Affil Hosp 1994; **Fellow:** Neurological Radiology, Montefiore Med Ctr 1995

Obstetrics & Gynecology

Ponterio, Jane M MD (ObG) *PCP* - **Spec Exp:** Menopause Problems; Hysterectomy Alternatives; Adolescent Gynecology; HPV-Human Papilloma Virus; **Hospital:** Richmond Univ Med Ctr, Staten Island Univ Hosp - North; **Address:** 1583 Richmond Ave, Staten Island, NY 10314; **Phone:** 718-983-0204; **Board Cert:** Obstetrics & Gynecology 2013; **Med School:** NY Med Coll 1981; **Resid:** Obstetrics & Gynecology, St Luke's Hosp Ctr 1985; **Fac Appt:** Asst Prof ObG, NY Med Coll

Reilly, James G DO (ObG) - **Spec Exp:** Colposcopy; Laparoscopic Surgery; Hysterectomy Alternatives; **Hospital:** Richmond Univ Med Ctr, Staten Island Univ Hosp - North; **Address:** 668 Castleton Ave, Staten Island, NY 10301-2044; **Phone:** 718-448-4300; **Board Cert:** Obstetrics & Gynecology 2013; **Med School:** NY Coll Osteo Med 1991; **Resid:** Obstetrics & Gynecology, St Vincent Cath Med Ctr 1996; **Fac Appt:** Asst Clin Prof ObG, NY Coll Osteo Med

Ophthalmology

Derespinis Sr, Patrick A MD (Oph) - **Spec Exp:** Eye Muscle Disorders; Pediatric Ophthalmology; Eye Disorders-Congenital; **Hospital:** Staten Island Univ Hosp - South, Univ Hosp-Newark; **Address:** Pediatric Eye Care of Staten Island, 2504 Richmond Rd, Staten Island, NY 10306; **Phone:** 718-667-1010; **Board Cert:** Ophthalmology 1989; **Med School:** Mexico 1981; **Resid:** Internal Medicine, NY Hosp Med Ctr 1983; Ophthalmology, UMDNJ 1987; **Fellow:** Pediatric Ophthalmology, Manhattan EE&T Hosp 1988; **Fac Appt:** Assoc Clin Prof Oph, UMDNJ-NJ Med Sch, Newark

Kramer, Philip W MD (Oph) - **Spec Exp:** Diabetic Eye Disease/Retinopathy; Cataract Surgery; Glaucoma; **Hospital:** Staten Island Univ Hosp - South, New York Eye & Ear Infirm of Mt Sinai; **Address:** Ophthalmology Assocs of Staten Island, 1460 Victory Blvd, Staten Island, NY 10301-3914; **Phone:** 718-447-0022; **Board Cert:** Ophthalmology 1985; **Med School:** Temple Univ 1980; **Resid:** Ophthalmology, NY Eye & Ear Infirmary 1984

Zerykier, Abraham L MD (Oph) - **Spec Exp:** Cataract Surgery; Diabetic Eye Disease/Retinopathy; Glaucoma; **Hospital:** Staten Island Univ Hosp - South, Mt Sinai Beth Israel-BK; **Address:** 16 Ross Ave, Staten Island, NY 10306-2216; **Phone:** 718-667-4444; **Board Cert:** Ophthalmology 1980; **Med School:** Hahnemann Univ 1975; **Resid:** Internal Medicine, Brookdale Hosp 1976; Ophthalmology, Jewish Hosp 1979; **Fac Appt:** Asst Clin Prof Oph, SUNY Downstate

Orthopaedic Surgery

Drucker, David A MD (OrS) - **Spec Exp:** Hip & Knee Replacement; Joint Replacement; Arthritis; **Hospital:** Mt Sinai Beth Israel, Staten Island Univ Hosp - North; **Address:** New York Hip & Knee, 11 Ralph Pl, Ste 103A, Staten Island, NY 10304; **Phone:** 718-727-6945; **Board Cert:** Orthopaedic Surgery 2014; **Med School:** Univ Chicago-Pritzker Sch Med 1983; **Resid:** Orthopaedic Surgery, UNDMJ Univ Hosp 1989; **Fellow:** Reconstructive Surgery, Indiana Univ Affil Hosp 1990; Joint Replacement Surgery, Mass Genl Hosp 1991; **Fac Appt:** Asst Clin Prof OrS, UMDNJ-NJ Med Sch, Newark

Flynn, Maryirene MD (OrS) - **Spec Exp:** Arthroscopic Surgery; Sports Medicine; **Hospital:** Richmond Univ Med Ctr, Staten Island Univ Hosp - North; **Address:** Staten Island Orthopedics, 2052 Richmond Rd, Staten Island, NY 10306; **Phone:** 718-351-6500 x101; **Board Cert:** Orthopaedic Surgery 2005; **Med School:** Albert Einstein Coll Med 1986; **Resid:** Orthopaedic Surgery, Montefiore Hosp Med Ctr 1991; **Fellow:** Sports Medicine, Staten Island Hosp 1992

Jayaram, Nadubeethi MD (OrS) - **Spec Exp:** Hand Surgery; **Hospital:** Richmond Univ Med Ctr; **Address:** Richmond Orthopaedic Assocs, 11 Ralph Pl, Ste 102, Staten Island, NY 10304; **Phone:** 718-447-6545; **Board Cert:** Orthopaedic Surgery 2014; **Med School:** India 1973; **Resid:** Surgery, Univ Hosp 1981; Orthopaedic Surgery, Univ Hosp 1985; **Fellow:** Vascular Surgery, Lutheran Med Ctr 1982; Hand Surgery, Univ Alabama Hosp 1988

Reilly, John P MD (OrS) - **Spec Exp:** Sports Medicine; Trauma; **Hospital:** Staten Island Univ Hosp - North; **Address:** Ortho Assocs of NY, 3333 Hylan Blvd, Staten Island, NY 10306; **Phone:** 718-667-7500; **Board Cert:** Orthopaedic Surgery 2010; **Med School:** SUNY Downstate 1981; **Resid:** Orthopaedic Surgery, Lenox Hill Hosp 1986; **Fellow:** Trauma, Univ MD Hosp 1987

Otolaryngology

Castellano, Bartolomeo V MD (Oto) - **Hospital:** Mt Sinai Hosp; **Address:** 2052 Richmond Rd, Ste 1C, Box 4, Staten Island, NY 10306; **Phone:** 718-420-1279; **Board Cert:** Otolaryngology 1985; **Med School:** Mexico 1979; **Resid:** Otolaryngology, NYU Med Ctr 1984; **Fellow:** Facial Plastic Surgery, Mt Sinai Med Ctr 1985; **Fac Appt:** Asst Clin Prof Oto, NYU Sch Med

Sinnreich, Abraham MD (Oto) - **Spec Exp:** Sinus Disorders; Sleep Disorders/Apnea; **Hospital:** Richmond Univ Med Ctr, Mt Sinai Hosp; **Address:** 1 Teleport Drive, Ste 200, Staten Island, NY 10314; **Phone:** 718-370-0072; **Board Cert:** Otolaryngology 1984; **Med School:** Albert Einstein Coll Med 1979; **Resid:** Otolaryngology, Mount Sinai Hosp 1983; **Fac Appt:** Asst Clin Prof Oto, SUNY Downstate

Sperling, Neil M MD (Oto) - **Spec Exp:** Otosclerosis; Hearing Loss; Meniere's Disease; **Hospital:** New York Eye & Ear Infirm of Mt Sinai, SUNY Downstate Med Ctr (Univ Hosp Brooklyn) (page 449); **Address:** New York Otolaryngology Group, 2205 Hylan Blvd, Staten Island, NY 10306; **Phone:** 718-967-6696; **Board Cert:** Otolaryngology 1990; **Med School:** NY Med Coll 1985; **Resid:** Otolaryngology, NY Eye & Ear Infirm 1990; **Fellow:** Otology, Minnesota Ear Clinic 1991; **Fac Appt:** Assoc Prof Oto, SUNY Downstate

Pain Medicine

Stilwell, Anne Marie MD (PM) - **Spec Exp:** Pain-Spine; Pain-After Spinal Intervention; **Hospital:** Richmond Univ Med Ctr; **Address:** 45 McLean Ave, Staten Island, NY 10305; **Phone:** 718-448-6373; **Board Cert:** Anesthesiology 2009; Pain Medicine 2007; **Med School:** Univ Rochester 1990; **Resid:** Anesthesiology, NY Hosp-Cornell Med Ctr 1994; **Fellow:** Pain Management, NY Hosp-Cornell Med Ctr 1996

Pediatric Endocrinology

Torrado-Jule, Carmen MD (PEn) - **Spec Exp:** Diabetes; Thyroid Disorders; Growth Disorders; Obesity; **Hospital:** Staten Island Univ Hosp - North, N Shore Univ Hosp; **Address:** 2460 Highland Blvd, Staten Island, NY 10306; **Phone:** 718-226-5613; **Board Cert:** Pediatrics 2007; Pediatric Endocrinology 2012; **Med School:** Dominican Republic 1983; **Resid:** Pediatrics, Kings County Hosp 1987; **Fellow:** Pediatric Endocrinology, Kings County Hosp 1990; **Fac Appt:** Asst Prof Ped, SUNY Hlth Sci Ctr

Pediatric Pulmonology

Chan, Siu-Pun MD (PPul) - **Spec Exp:** Asthma; Critical Care; Sleep Medicine; **Hospital:** Staten Island Univ Hosp - North; **Address:** Chldns Subspecialty Ctr, 2460 Hylan Blvd, Staten Island, NY 10306; **Phone:** 718-226-5619; **Board Cert:** Pediatrics 2012; Pediatric Pulmonology 2008; Sleep Medicine 2007; **Med School:** Hong Kong 1980; **Resid:** Pediatrics, Univ Hosp 1990; **Fellow:** Pediatric Pulmonology, Univ Hosp 1993

Pediatric Urology

Horowitz, Mark MD (Ped Uro) - **Spec Exp:** Urodynamics; Urinary Reflux/Obstruction; Laparoscopic Surgery; **Hospital:** Staten Island Univ Hosp - North, NY Hosp Queens (page 498); **Address:** Pediatric Urology Assocs, 500 Seaview Ave, Ste 130, Staten Island, NY 10305; **Phone:** 718-226-1271; **Board Cert:** Urology 2006; **Med School:** NY Med Coll 1986; **Resid:** Urology, SUNY Downstate Med Ctr 1992; **Fellow:** Pediatric Urology, Chldns Hosp 1994; **Fac Appt:** Assoc Prof U, SUNY Downstate

Pediatrics

Bastawros, Mary N MD (Ped) *PCP* - **Spec Exp:** Preventive Medicine; **Hospital:** Richmond Univ Med Ctr, Staten Island Univ Hosp - North; **Address:** 314 Seaview Ave, Staten Island, NY 10305; **Phone:** 718-668-3417; **Board Cert:** Pediatrics 1985; **Med School:** Egypt 1966; **Resid:** Pediatrics, NY Methodist Hosp 1975; Pediatrics, Kingsbrook Jewish Med Ctr 1976

Duchnowska, Alicja B MD (Ped) *PCP* - **Spec Exp:** Preventive Medicine; **Hospital:** Staten Island Univ Hosp - North; **Address:** 934 Ionia Ave, Staten Island, NY 10309-2308; **Phone:** 718-984-5255; **Board Cert:** Pediatrics 1985; **Med School:** Poland 1965; **Resid:** Pediatrics, Natl Inst of Mother & Child 1970; Pediatrics, Staten Island Hosp 1982; **Fellow:** Pediatrics, Staten Island Hosp 1984

Visconti, Ernest B MD (Ped) *PCP* - **Spec Exp:** Infectious Disease; Preventive Medicine; **Hospital:** Lutheran Med Ctr - Brooklyn, Richmond Univ Med Ctr; **Address:** 314 Seaview Ave, Staten Island, NY 10305-2246; **Phone:** 718-668-3417; **Board Cert:** Pediatrics 1992; Pediatric Infectious Disease 2008; **Med School:** SUNY Upstate Med Univ 1971; **Resid:** Pediatrics, NY Hosp 1974; **Fellow:** Infectious Disease, Rhode Island Hosp 1978

Physical Medicine & Rehabilitation

Weinberg, Jeffrey B MD (PMR) - **Spec Exp:** Geriatric Rehabilitation; Musculoskeletal Injuries; **Hospital:** Staten Island Univ Hosp - North; **Address:** Staten Island Univ Hosp, Medical Arts Pavilion, 242 Mason Ave, Staten Island, NY 10305; **Phone:** 718-226-6362; **Board Cert:** Physical Medicine & Rehabilitation 1985; **Med School:** NY Med Coll 1980; **Resid:** Physical Medicine & Rehabilitation, NYU Med Ctr 1983; **Fellow:** Geriatric Medicine, NYU Med Ctr 1986; **Fac Appt:** Asst Clin Prof PMR, SUNY Downstate

Weiner, Kevin H MD (PMR) - **Hospital:** Morristown Med Ctr (page 92), NS-LIJ Hlth Sys; **Address:** 262 Nelson Ave, Staten Island, NY 10308; **Phone:** 718-442-4422; **Board Cert:** Physical Medicine & Rehabilitation 2009; **Med School:** Univ Hlth Scis, Chicago Med Sch 1994; **Resid:** Physical Medicine & Rehabilitation, NYU Med Ctr 1998

Plastic Surgery

Cherofsky, Alan MD (PlS) - **Spec Exp:** Breast Cosmetic & Reconstructive Surgery; Liposuction & Body Contouring; Pediatric Plastic Surgery; **Hospital:** Staten Island Univ Hosp - South, Richmond Univ Med Ctr; **Address:** 4546 Hylan Blvd, Staten Island, NY 10312-6400; **Phone:** 718-967-3300; **Board Cert:** Plastic Surgery 1993; **Med School:** SUNY Downstate 1982; **Resid:** Surgery, Staten Island Univ Hosp 1987; Plastic Surgery, Univ Missouri Hosp 1989

Cutolo Jr, Louis C MD (PlS) - **Spec Exp:** Breast Augmentation; Liposuction; Eyelid Surgery; Cosmetic Surgery-Face & Neck; **Hospital:** Staten Island Univ Hosp - North, Richmond Univ Med Ctr; **Address:** 1557 Victory Blvd, Staten Island, NY 10314; **Phone:** 718-720-9400; **Board Cert:** Plastic Surgery 2003; **Med School:** SUNY Downstate 1985; **Resid:** Surgery, Staten Island Hosp 1990; **Fellow:** Plastic Surgery, Univ Florida/Shands Hosp 1992

Psychiatry

Di Buono, Mark MD (Psyc) - **Spec Exp:** Geriatric Psychiatry; Depression; Autism; **Hospital:** Staten Island Univ Hosp - South; **Address:** Richmond Behavioral Assocs, 4349 Hylan Blvd, Staten Island, NY 10312; **Phone:** 718-227-1897; **Board Cert:** Psychiatry 1990; Geriatric Psychiatry 2008; **Med School:** Mexico 1981; **Resid:** Psychiatry, Stony Brook Univ Med Ctr 1987; **Fac Appt:** Asst Clin Prof Psyc, SUNY Downstate

Sullivan, Timothy B MD (Psyc) - **Spec Exp:** Bipolar/Mood Disorders; Schizophrenia; Psychiatry in Physical Illness; Psychotherapy & Psychopharmacology; **Hospital:** Staten Island Univ Hosp - North; **Address:** Staten Island Univ Hosp North, Dept Psychiatry, 450 Seaview Ave Fl 2, Staten Island, NY 10305; **Phone:** 718-226-8910; **Board Cert:** Internal Medicine 1981; Psychiatry 1986; **Med School:** Dartmouth Med Sch 1977; **Resid:** Internal Medicine, St Vincent's Hosp 1980; Psychiatry, New York Hosp-Westchester 1984; **Fellow:** Hematology & Oncology, St Vincent's Hosp 1981; **Fac Appt:** Assoc Prof Psyc, NY Med Coll

Pulmonary Disease

Castellano, Michael A MD (Pul) - **Spec Exp:** Asthma; Emphysema; **Hospital:** Staten Island Univ Hosp - North; **Address:** 501 Seaview Ave, Ste 102, Staten Island, NY 10305; **Phone:** 718-980-5700; **Board Cert:** Internal Medicine 1974; Pulmonary Disease 1978; Critical Care Medicine 2007; Geriatric Medicine 2004; **Med School:** Italy 1968; **Resid:** Internal Medicine, Staten Island Hosp 1972; **Fellow:** Pulmonary Disease, NYU-Bellvue Hosp 1974; **Fac Appt:** Asst Prof Med, SUNY Downstate

Maniatis, Theodore MD (Pul) - **Spec Exp:** Asthma; Lung Cancer; Chronic Obstructive Lung Disease (COPD); Interstitial Lung Disease; **Hospital:** Staten Island Univ Hosp - North, Staten Island Univ Hosp - South; **Address:** Staten Island Pulmonary Assocs, 501 Seaview Ave, Ste 102, Staten Island, NY 10305; **Phone:** 718-980-5700; **Board Cert:** Internal Medicine 1983; Pulmonary Disease 1986; Critical Care Medicine 2007; **Med School:** SUNY Hlth Sci Ctr 1980; **Resid:** Internal Medicine, Staten Island Univ Hosp 1983; **Fellow:** Pulmonary Disease, Univ Med Ctr-UMDNJ 1985; **Fac Appt:** Asst Clin Prof Med, SUNY Downstate

Martins, Publius MD (Pul) - **Spec Exp:** Asthma; Emphysema; **Hospital:** Richmond Univ Med Ctr; **Address:** 283 Bard Ave, Staten Island, NY 10310-1664; **Phone:** 718-816-8068; **Board Cert:** Internal Medicine 1984; **Med School:** Portugal 1975; **Resid:** Internal Medicine, St Vincent's Hosp 1981; **Fellow:** Pulmonary Disease, Meml Hosp 1983; **Fac Appt:** Assoc Clin Prof Med, NY Med Coll

Sasso, Louis MD (Pul) - **Spec Exp:** Asthma; Chronic Obstructive Lung Disease (COPD); Interstitial Lung Disease; **Hospital:** Staten Island Univ Hosp - North; **Address:** 501 Seaview Ave, Ste 102, Staten Island, NY 10305-3400; **Phone:** 718-980-5700; **Board Cert:** Internal Medicine 1976; Pulmonary Disease 1978; Critical Care Medicine 2005; Geriatric Medicine 2009; **Med School:** UMDNJ-NJ Med Sch, Newark 1972; **Resid:** Internal Medicine, St Vincent's Hosp & Med Ctr 1974; Internal Medicine, CMDNJ-Martland Hosp 1975; **Fellow:** Pulmonary Disease, Bellevue Hosp/NYU Med Ctr 1977; **Fac Appt:** Asst Clin Prof Med, SUNY Downstate

Radiation Oncology

Adams, Marc T MD (RadRO) - **Spec Exp:** Prostate Cancer; Breast Cancer; Lung Cancer; Brain Tumors; **Hospital:** Richmond Univ Med Ctr; **Address:** Regional Radiology, 360 Bard Ave, Staten Island, NY 10310; **Phone:** 718-876-2023; **Board Cert:** Radiation Oncology 1990; **Med School:** UAB Sch Med 1985; **Resid:** Radiation Oncology, St Barnabas Hosp 1989; **Fac Appt:** Asst Prof Rad, NY Med Coll

Rheumatology

Goldstein, Mark A MD (Rhu) - **Spec Exp:** Rheumatoid Arthritis; Osteoporosis; Lupus/SLE; **Hospital:** Staten Island Univ Hosp - South, Staten Island Univ Hosp - North; **Address:** 1534 Victory Blvd, Staten Island, NY 10314; **Phone:** 718-447-0055; **Board Cert:** Internal Medicine 1982; Rheumatology 1988; **Med School:** NY Med Coll 1979; **Resid:** Internal Medicine, Montefiore Med Ctr 1982; **Fellow:** Rheumatology, Montefiore Med Ctr 1987

Surgery

D'Anna Jr, John A MD (S) - **Spec Exp:** Vascular Surgery; **Hospital:** Staten Island Univ Hosp - North, Staten Island Univ Hosp - South; **Address:** 375 Seguine Ave, Staten Island, NY 10309; **Phone:** 718-226-2950; **Board Cert:** Surgery 2011; **Med School:** Georgetown Univ 1977; **Resid:** Surgery, St Vincent's Hosp Med Ctr 1982; **Fellow:** Vascular Surgery, St Vincent's Hosp Med Ctr 1983; **Fac Appt:** Assoc Clin Prof S, SUNY Downstate

Hornyak, Stephen W MD (S) - **Spec Exp:** Breast Surgery; Laparoscopic Surgery; Gastrointestinal Surgery; **Hospital:** Staten Island Univ Hosp - North, Richmond Univ Med Ctr; **Address:** 1130 Victory Blvd, Staten Island, NY 10301; **Phone:** 718-442-3400; **Board Cert:** Surgery 2010; **Med School:** SUNY Hlth Sci Ctr 1974; **Resid:** Surgery, Kings County Hosp 1979; **Fellow:** Thoracic Surgery, Meml Sloan Kettering Cancer Ctr 1980; **Fac Appt:** Asst Clin Prof S, SUNY Downstate

Lutchman, Gordon MD (S) - **Spec Exp:** Wound Healing/Care; Vein Disorders; Laser Surgery; **Hospital:** Maimonides Med Ctr (page 98); **Address:** Laser & Varicose Vein Treatment Ctr, 500 Seaview Ave, Ste 240, Staten Island, NY 10305; **Phone:** 718-667-1777; **Board Cert:** Surgery 2007; **Med School:** Jamaica 1976; **Resid:** Surgery, Royal United Hosp 1982; Surgery, Maimonides Med Ctr 1987; **Fellow:** Vascular Surgery, Maimonides Med Ctr 1988

Pahuja, Murlidhar MD (S) - **Spec Exp:** Breast Cancer; Laparoscopic Surgery; Wound Healing/Care; **Hospital:** Staten Island Univ Hosp - North, Staten Island Univ Hosp - South; **Address:** 4287 Richmond Ave, Staten Island, NY 10312; **Phone:** 718-967-6230; **Board Cert:** Surgery 2013; **Med School:** Pakistan 1971; **Resid:** Surgery, Stamford Hosp 1978; Surgery, Staten Island Hosp 1982; **Fellow:** Burn Surgery, NY Hosp 1980

Thoracic & Cardiac Surgery

McGinn Jr, Joseph T MD (T&CS) - **Spec Exp:** Minimally Invasive Cardiac Surgery; Heart Valve Surgery; **Hospital:** Staten Island Univ Hosp - North; **Address:** Staten Is Univ Hosp, Heart Inst, 501 Seaview Ave, Ste 202, Staten Island, NY 10305; **Phone:** 718-226-1612; **Board Cert:** Surgery 2009; Thoracic & Cardiac Surgery 2009; Surgical Critical Care 2003; **Med School:** SUNY Downstate 1981; **Resid:** Surgery, SUNY Downstate Med Ctr 1986; Cardiothoracic Surgery, LIJ Med Ctr 1988

Rosell, Frank M MD (T&CS) - **Spec Exp:** Coronary Artery Surgery; Heart Valve Surgery; **Hospital:** Staten Island Univ Hosp - North; **Address:** 501 Seaview Ave, Ste 202, Staten Island, NY 10305; **Phone:** 718-226-1612; **Board Cert:** Surgery 2006; Thoracic Surgery 2010; **Med School:** NYU Sch Med 1992; **Resid:** Surgery, NY Med Coll Affil Hosp 1997; **Fellow:** Thoracic Surgery, Long Is Jewish Med Ctr 2000

Urology

Karanikolas, Nicholas T MD (U) - **Spec Exp:** Prostate Cancer/Robotic Surgery; Bladder Cancer; Kidney Cancer; Testicular Cancer; **Hospital:** Staten Island Univ Hosp - North; **Address:** Nalitt Cancer Ctr, 256 Mason Ave, Staten Island, NY 10305; **Phone:** 718-226-6031; **Board Cert:** Urology 2008; **Med School:** SUNY Downstate 1998; **Resid:** Urology, SUNY Hlth Sci Ctr 2004; **Fellow:** Urologic Oncology, Meml Sloan Kettering Cancer Ctr 2008

Lessing, Jeffrey A MD (U) - **Spec Exp:** Prostate Disease; Impotence; Kidney Stones; Infertility-Male; **Hospital:** Staten Island Univ Hosp - North, Staten Island Univ Hosp - South; **Address:** Todt Hill Urlogic Group, 78 Todt Hill Rd, Ste 112, Staten Island, NY 10314; **Phone:** 718-448-3880; **Board Cert:** Urology 1982; **Med School:** NYU Sch Med 1975; **Resid:** Surgery, NYU Med Ctr 1977; Urology, Mt Sinai Med Ctr 1980

Raboy, Adley MD (U) - **Spec Exp:** Prostate Disease; Prostate Cancer; Minimally Invasive Surgery; Kidney Stones; **Hospital:** Staten Island Univ Hosp - North, Staten Island Univ Hosp - South; **Address:** Staten Island Urological Assocs, 1460 Victory Blvd, Staten Island, NY 10301-3914; **Phone:** 718-273-8100; **Board Cert:** Urology 2012; **Med School:** SUNY Downstate 1984; **Resid:** Surgery, Staten Island Hosp 1986; Urology, SUNY Downstate Med Ctr 1990; **Fac Appt:** Assoc Clin Prof U, SUNY Downstate

Savino, Michael A MD (U) - **Spec Exp:** Robotic Surgery; Prostate Cancer; Kidney Stones; Laparoscopic Surgery; **Hospital:** Staten Island Univ Hosp - North, Maimonides Med Ctr (page 98); **Address:** 375 Seguine Ave, Fl 1, Staten Island, NY 10309; **Phone:** 718-226-2950; **Board Cert:** Urology 2007; **Med School:** Mexico 1979; **Resid:** Surgery, Maimonides Med Ctr 1982; Urology, Maimonides Med Ctr 1985; **Fac Appt:** Assoc Clin Prof

Vascular & Interventional Radiology

Scheiner, Jonathan E MD (VIR) - **Spec Exp:** Carotid Artery Stent Placement; Endovascular Surgery; Tumor Embolization; Urinary Tract Interventions; **Hospital:** Staten Island Univ Hosp - North; **Address:** Staten Island Univ Hosp-North, Interventional Radiology, 475 Seaview Ave, Staten Island, NY 10305; **Phone:** 718-226-9181; **Board Cert:** Diagnostic Radiology 1999; **Med School:** Albert Einstein Coll Med 1994; **Resid:** Diagnostic Radiology, Montefiore Med Ctr 1999; **Fellow:** Vascular & Interventional Radiology, New York Hosp/Sloan-Kettering Cancer Ctr 2000; **Fac Appt:** Asst Clin Prof Rad, Hofstra N Shore-LIJ Sch Med

Vascular Surgery

Deitch, Jonathan MD (VascS) - **Spec Exp:** Aortic Surgery; Carotid Artery Disease; Endovascular Surgery; Aneurysm; **Hospital:** Staten Island Univ Hosp - North; **Address:** 501 Seaview Ave, Ste 302, Staten Island, NY 10305; **Phone:** 718-226-6800; **Board Cert:** Vascular Surgery 2009; **Med School:** NY Med Coll 1991; **Resid:** Surgery, Montefiore Med Ctr 1996; **Fellow:** Vascular Surgery, Wake Forest Univ Med Ctr 1998

Rodino, William MD (VascS) - **Spec Exp:** Endovascular Surgery; Aneurysm-Aortic; Carotid Artery Disease; Peripheral Vascular Disease; **Hospital:** Richmond Univ Med Ctr, New York Methodist Hosp (page 448); **Address:** Verrazano Vascular Assocs, 2025 Richmond Ave, Ste 1LL, Staten Island, NY 10314; **Phone:** 718-370-0307; **Board Cert:** Surgery 2006; Vascular Surgery 2007; **Med School:** SUNY Downstate 1990; **Resid:** Surgery, SUNY Downstate Med Ctr 1995; **Fellow:** Vascular Surgery, SUNY Downstate Med Ctr 1997

The Best in American Medicine
www.CastleConnolly.com

Sponsorship: Voluntary, Not-for-Profit
Beds: 591
Accreditation: The Joint Commission

General Overview

Founded in 1896 by a group of local physicians and concerned citizens, Winthrop-University Hospital is Long Island's first voluntary and second largest hospital. The university-affiliated medical center and New York State-designated Regional Trauma Center offers sophisticated diagnostic and therapeutic care in virtually every specialty and subspecialty of medicine and surgery. Winthrop has earned many prestigious accreditations, including designations as a New York State (NYS) Stroke Center and NYS Regional Perinatal Center, and is known across the State for its excellent outcomes in interventional cardiology and cardiac surgery. In addition to its leading cardiology and specialty care services such as Orthopaedic Surgery, Winthrop boasts several specialized Centers that are dedicated to Cancer Care, Digestive Disorders, Family Care including Women's and Children's Health Services, Lung Care and Neurosciences.

Patient care, academics and research are the three components of Winthrop's mission. Because research is so essential, Winthrop will soon open a new four-floor, 95,000-square-foot Research and Academic Center which will house basic science research, clinical/translational research, outcomes research, medical education classrooms and support services.

Staff

The Hospital employs over 7,200 dedicated and caring individuals, including nearly 1,900 nurses. Winthrop's medical staff – which includes 1,900 full-time and voluntary attending physicians – cared for close to 32,000 inpatients, handled nearly 70,000 emergency visits, and conducted more than 960,000 outpatient appointments in 2013.

Academic and Clinical Affiliations

Winthrop is an affiliated member of the New York-Presbyterian Healthcare System and is the Clinical Campus of Stony Brook University School of Medicine.

Research and Clinical Trials

Winthrop has been spearheading pioneering research that holds the promise of major ramifications in the understanding and treatment of many serious medical conditions. From diabetes, multiple sclerosis, rheumatoid arthritis and lupus, to cardiovascular diseases, obstetrics and premature births, Winthrop's researchers and clinicians have been at the forefront of important discoveries.

No Place Like Home

Winthrop's award-winning certified home health care agency offers nursing, as well as physical, speech and occupational therapies in conjunction with medical social work and home health aide services to Nassau and Suffolk Counties as well as for Queens residents.

Special Programs and Services

Advances in Neuroscience

Within Winthrop's Department of Neuroscience, an interdisciplinary team of healthcare professionals are pioneering the use of advanced approaches for diagnosis and treatment, including computerized imaging systems, state-of-the-art surgical interventions such as deep brain stimulation and the latest generation of medication therapies. In addition to a 14-bed Neurosciences Special Care Unit, the Department boasts comprehensive resources for the diagnosis and treatment of a wide range of conditions, including aneurysms, blood clots and tumors and special programs for conditions including multiple sclerosis, movement disorders, and epilepsy.

A Leader in Men's Health

At Winthrop, prostate cancer patients are offered a full array of treatment options. Minimally invasive surgery using the daVinci Surgical Robot System is available, as well as intensity-modulated radiation therapy (IMRT), cryotherapy and more. In addition, Winthrop pioneered the use of CyberKnife® for prostate cancer – a technology that takes radiotherapy to new levels of accuracy. Last year, Winthrop treated over 2,100 cancer patients with CyberKnife, making it one of the busiest CyberKnife centers in the world. Additionally, in the latest step to provide the residents of Manhattan and the entire tri-state region with greater access to the Hospital's leading edge CyberKnife services, Winthrop recently opened New York City's first CyberKnife facility at 150 Amsterdam Avenue at 66th Street.

In addition, Winthrop's Men's Health Center provides comprehensive, coordinated men's services – from urological to cardiac services – making it easy for the men of Long Island to receive multispecialty preventive care and medical management.

Excellence in Women's Healthcare

Winthrop is a nationally recognized, regional leader in women's health services. The experts at the Winthrop Breast Health Center – the first center in Nassau County to earn accreditation by the National Accreditation Program for Breast Centers (NAPBC) – provide comprehensive risk assessment, diagnosis, treatment and follow-up care to patients. Winthrop is also the only site in the tri-state area to earn accreditation by the American Institute of Ultrasound in Medicine (AIUM) for fetal echocardiograms.

In its continuing mission to expand and improve treatment options for patients with breast cancer, Winthrop recently completed an Institutional Review Board-approved clinical trial with very positive outcomes. The trial utilized the CyberKnife Radiosurgery system as a follow-up to lumpectomy in select women with breast cancer who desire breast conservation after resection of their breast tumor.

Select National Performance Recognitions	
• **2014-15 Best Regional Hospitals in the New York Metro Area -** *U.S. News & World Report* with 10 high-performing specialties	• **NAEC Level 4 Epilepsy Center**
• **2014-15 Best Children's Hospitals -** *U.S. News & World Report* for excellence in pediatric diabetes & endocrinology and pediatric pulmonology.	• **NAPBC National Breast Center**
	• **National Association of Children's Hospitals and Related Institutions** (NACHRI) Designated Children's Hospital
• Recipient of Healthgrades® Cardiac Care Excellence Award, 6 Years in a Row (2010-2015)	• **New York State Designated Regional Trauma Center**
• Five-Star Recipient of Healthgrades® Award for Coronary Interventional Procedure, 13 Years in a Row (2003-2015)	• **New York State Regional Perinatal Center**
• **HCM Center of Excellence** by The National Hypertrophic Cardiomyopathy Association	• **New York State Stroke Center**
• **Long Island Health Network**, Member	• **The Joint Commission:** *Accreditation – Hospital, Certified Home Health Agency*
"Most Wired" Hospital by *Hospitals & Health Networks* Magazine, 3 years in a row	• **The Joint Commission:** *Gold Seal of Approval™ for Advanced Certification* - Inpatient Diabetes Care

Adolescent Medicine

Arden, Martha MD (AM) - **Spec Exp:** Adolescent Gynecology; Nutrition; Eating Disorders; **Hospital:** Steven & Alexandra Cohen Chldn's Med Ctr of NY, N Shore Univ Hosp; **Address:** 2001 Marcus Ave, Ste N204, New Hyde Park, NY 11040; **Phone:** 347-882-1321; **Board Cert:** Adolescent Medicine 2008; **Med School:** Yale Univ 1984; **Resid:** Pediatrics, NY-Presby/Columbia Univ Med Ctr 1987; **Fellow:** Adolescent Medicine, Schneider Chldns Hosp 1990; **Fac Appt:** Assoc Clin Prof Ped, Albert Einstein Coll Med

Carmine, Linda MD (AM) - **Spec Exp:** Eating Disorders; Menstrual Disorders; Sexually Transmitted Diseases; **Hospital:** Steven & Alexandra Cohen Chldn's Med Ctr of NY; **Address:** 410 Lakeville Rd, Ste 108, New Hyde Park, NY 11042; **Phone:** 516-465-3270; **Board Cert:** Pediatrics 1987; Adolescent Medicine 2008; **Med School:** NYU Sch Med 1982; **Resid:** Pediatrics, Montefiore Med Ctr 1985; **Fellow:** Adolescent Medicine, Montefiore Med Ctr 1986; **Fac Appt:** Assoc Prof Ped, Hofstra N Shore-LIJ Sch Med

Feinstein, Ronald A MD (AM) - **Spec Exp:** Weight Management; Obesity; Eating Disorders; **Hospital:** Steven & Alexandra Cohen Chldn's Med Ctr of NY; **Address:** 410 Lakeville Rd, Ste 108, New Hyde Park, NY 11042; **Phone:** 516-465-3270; **Board Cert:** Pediatrics 1981; Adolescent Medicine 2008; **Med School:** NY Med Coll 1976; **Resid:** Pediatrics, LI Jewish Med Ctr 1979; **Fellow:** Adolescent Medicine, UAB Hosp 1981; **Fac Appt:** Prof Ped, Hofstra N Shore-LIJ Sch Med

Fisher, Martin M MD (AM) - **Spec Exp:** Eating Disorders; Chronic Fatigue Syndrome; **Hospital:** Steven & Alexandra Cohen Chldn's Med Ctr of NY, N Shore Univ Hosp; **Address:** 410 Lakeville Rd, Ste 108, New Hyde Park, NY 11042; **Phone:** 516-465-3270; **Board Cert:** Pediatrics 1979; Adolescent Medicine 2008; **Med School:** Albert Einstein Coll Med 1975; **Resid:** Pediatrics, LI Jewish Med Ctr 1978; **Fellow:** Adolescent Medicine, LI Jewish Med Ctr 1980

Jacobson, Marc S MD (AM) - **Spec Exp:** Nutrition; Obesity; Preventive Cardiology; Metabolic Syndrome; **Hospital:** Long Is Jewish Med Ctr, N Shore Univ Hosp; **Address:** ProHealth Care Assocs, 2 Prohealth Plaza, Ste 201, Lake Success, NY 11042; **Phone:** 516-304-3950; **Board Cert:** Pediatrics 1983; Adolescent Medicine 2008; **Med School:** Univ Kansas 1973; **Resid:** Pediatrics, Univ Kansas Hosp 1976; **Fellow:** Adolescent Medicine, Univ MD Med Ctr 1979; **Fac Appt:** Prof Ped, Albert Einstein Coll Med

Swedler, Jane MD (AM) - **Spec Exp:** Adolescent Gynecology; **Hospital:** Winthrop Univ Hosp (page 536); **Address:** Winthrop Pediatric Associates, 222 Station Plaza N, Ste 611, Mineola, NY 11501; **Phone:** 516-663-2532; **Board Cert:** Family Medicine 2009; Adolescent Medicine 2011; **Med School:** McGill Univ 1987; **Resid:** Family Medicine, Queen Elizabeth Hosp 1989; Family Medicine, Stony Brook Univ Med Ctr 1990; **Fellow:** Adolescent Medicine, Montefiore Med Ctr 1992; **Fac Appt:** Asst Prof Med, Mount Sinai Sch Med

Allergy & Immunology

Boxer, Mitchell MD (A&I) - **Spec Exp:** Asthma; Drug Sensitivity; Churg-Strauss Vasculitis; Sinusitis; **Hospital:** Long Is Jewish Med Ctr; **Address:** 2001 Marcus Ave, Ste N220, Lake Success, NY 11042; **Phone:** 516-482-0910; **Board Cert:** Internal Medicine 1984; Allergy & Immunology 1987; **Med School:** NY Med Coll 1981; **Resid:** Internal Medicine, LI Jewish Med Ctr 1984; **Fellow:** Allergy & Immunology, Northwestern Meml Hosp 1987; **Fac Appt:** Asst Clin Prof Med, Albert Einstein Coll Med

Corriel, Robert N MD (A&I) - **Spec Exp:** Asthma & Allergy; Sinus Disorders; Rhinitis; Food Allergy; **Hospital:** N Shore Univ Hosp, Long Is Jewish Med Ctr; **Address:** Manhasset Allergy & Asthma Associates, 1129 Northern Blvd, Ste 300, Manhasset, NY 11030; **Phone:** 516-365-6077; **Board Cert:** Pediatrics 1983; Allergy & Immunology 1985; **Med School:** Wake Forest Univ 1976; **Resid:** Pediatrics, N Shore Univ Hosp 1979; **Fellow:** Allergy & Immunology, Univ Hosp 1981; **Fac Appt:** Asst Clin Prof Ped, Hofstra N Shore-LIJ Sch Med

Edwards, Bruce L MD (A&I) - **Spec Exp:** Asthma; Sinus Disorders; Food Allergy; **Hospital:** Long Is Jewish Med Ctr, Plainview Hosp; **Address:** 700 Old Country Rd, Ste 105, Plainview, NY 11803-4932; **Phone:** 516-933-1125; **Board Cert:** Allergy & Immunology 2009; **Med School:** Case West Res Univ 1984; **Resid:** Pediatrics, Babies Hosp/Columbia Presby 1987; **Fellow:** Allergy & Immunology, Schneider Chldns Hosp-LIJ 1989

Fonacier, Luz MD (A&I) - **Spec Exp:** Skin Allergies; Drug Sensitivity; Asthma & Allergy; **Hospital:** Winthrop Univ Hosp (page 536); **Address:** 210 Mineola Blvd, Ste 410, Mineola, NY 11501; **Phone:** 516-663-2097; **Board Cert:** Internal Medicine 1989; Allergy & Immunology 2011; **Med School:** Philippines 1978; **Resid:** Dermatology, Univ Philippines 1983; Internal Medicine, Lutheran Med Ctr 1989; **Fellow:** Dermatology, NYU Med Ctr 1986; Allergy & Immunology, NY Hosp-Cornell Med Ctr 1991; **Fac Appt:** Clin Prof A&I, SUNY Stony Brook

Frieri, Marianne MD/PhD (A&I) - **Spec Exp:** Asthma; Food Allergy; Immune Deficiency; Rhinitis; **Hospital:** N Shore Univ Hosp, Nassau Univ Med Ctr; **Address:** 566 Broadway, Massapequa, NY 11758; **Phone:** 516-541-6262; **Board Cert:** Internal Medicine 1984; Allergy & Immunology 1985; Diagnostic Lab Immunology 1990; **Med School:** Loyola Univ-Stritch Sch Med 1978; **Resid:** Internal Medicine, St Josephs Hosp 1980; **Fellow:** Allergy & Immunology, NIH/NIAID 1983; **Fac Appt:** Prof A&I, SUNY Stony Brook

Goldstein, Stanley MD (A&I) - **Spec Exp:** Asthma; Pulmonary Disease; **Hospital:** Long Is Jewish Med Ctr, Mercy Med Ctr-Rockville Centre; **Address:** Allergy & Asthma Care-Long Island, 242 Merrick Rd, Ste 401, Rockville Centre, NY 11570; **Phone:** 516-536-7336; **Board Cert:** Pediatrics 1979; Allergy & Immunology 1981; **Med School:** NY Med Coll 1975; **Resid:** Pediatrics, LI Jewish Med Ctr 1978; **Fellow:** Allergy & Immunology, Chldns Hosp 1982

Lang, Paul MD (A&I) - **Spec Exp:** Asthma; Food Allergy; Insect Allergies; **Hospital:** N Shore Univ Hosp, Winthrop Univ Hosp (page 536); **Address:** N Shore Allergy Asthma Inst, 1 Hollow Ln, Ste 110, New Hyde Park, NY 11042; **Phone:** 516-365-6666; **Board Cert:** Pediatrics 1978; Allergy & Immunology 1979; **Med School:** Cornell Univ-Weill Med Coll 1973; **Resid:** Pediatrics, LAC & USC Med Ctr 1975; Allergy & Immunology, St Lukes-Roosevelt Hosp 1977; **Fac Appt:** Assoc Clin Prof Ped, NYU Sch Med

Markovics, Sharon B MD (A&I) - **Spec Exp:** Allergy; Asthma; Rhinitis; Sinus Disorders; **Hospital:** N Shore Univ Hosp, Long Is Jewish Med Ctr; **Address:** Manhasset Allergy & Asthma Associates, 1129 Northern Blvd, Ste 300, Manhasset, NY 11030-3527; **Phone:** 516-365-6077; **Board Cert:** Pediatrics 1979; Allergy & Immunology 1981; **Med School:** Albert Einstein Coll Med 1975; **Resid:** Pediatrics, Bellevue Hosp 1977; **Fellow:** Allergy & Immunology, Montreal Chldns Hosp 1979; **Fac Appt:** Asst Clin Prof Ped, NYU Sch Med

Novick, Brian MD (A&I) - **Spec Exp:** Asthma; Sinus Disorders; Food Allergy; Hives; **Hospital:** Nassau Univ Med Ctr, Lenox Hill Hosp; **Address:** ProHealth Care Assocs, Allergy Testing, 30 Newbridge Rd, Ste 100, East Meadow, NY 11554; **Phone:** 516-731-5740; **Board Cert:** Pediatrics 1984; Allergy & Immunology 2012; **Med School:** Mexico 1978; **Resid:** Pediatrics, Albert Einstein Coll Med Affil Hosp 1982; **Fellow:** Allergy & Immunology, Albert Einstein Coll Med Affil Hosp 1984; **Fac Appt:** Asst Clin Prof A&I, Albert Einstein Coll Med

Sicklick, Marc MD (A&I) - **Spec Exp:** Asthma; Immune Deficiency; Insect Allergies; **Hospital:** N Shore Univ Hosp, Long Is Jewish Med Ctr; **Address:** 123 Grove Ave, Ste 110, Cedarhurst, NY 11516; **Phone:** 516-569-5550; **Board Cert:** Pediatrics 1979; Allergy & Immunology 1987; **Med School:** Albert Einstein Coll Med 1974; **Resid:** Pediatrics, Bronx Muni Hosp Ctr 1977; **Fellow:** Allergy & Immunology, Montefiore Med Ctr 1979; **Fac Appt:** Assoc Clin Prof Ped, Albert Einstein Coll Med

Weinstock, Gary A MD (A&I) - **Spec Exp:** Asthma; Allergy; Hives; **Hospital:** N Shore Univ Hosp, Glen Cove Hosp; **Address:** 310 E Shore Rd, Ste 207, Great Neck, NY 11023; **Phone:** 516-487-1073; **Board Cert:** Internal Medicine 1982; Pulmonary Disease 1984; Allergy & Immunology 1985; **Med School:** Albany Med Coll 1979; **Resid:** Internal Medicine, N Shore Univ Hosp 1982; **Fellow:** Pulmonary Disease, Stony Brook Univ Med Ctr 1983; Allergy & Immunology, Stony Brook Univ Med Ctr 1986; **Fac Appt:** Asst Clin Prof Med, NYU Sch Med

Wertheim, David MD (A&I) - **Spec Exp:** Pediatric Allergy & Immunology; **Hospital:** Long Is Jewish Med Ctr, St. Francis Hosp - The Heart Ctr (page 111); **Address:** ProHealth Care Assocs, Allergy & Imm, 2800 Marcus Ave, Ste 202, Lake Success, NY 11042; **Phone:** 516-608-2898; **Board Cert:** Allergy & Immunology 2006; **Med School:** Med Coll PA 1988; **Resid:** Pediatrics, Schneider Chldns Hosp 1992; **Fellow:** Allergy & Immunology, LI Jewish Med Ctr 1994; **Fac Appt:** Asst Clin Prof Ped, Albert Einstein Coll Med

Cardiac Electrophysiology

Beldner, Stuart Jay MD (CE) - **Spec Exp:** Arrhythmias; Pacemakers; Defibrillators; **Hospital:** N Shore Univ Hosp; **Address:** N Shore Univ Hosp, Dept Cardiology, 300 Community Drive, Manhassett, NY 11030; **Phone:** 516-562-4100; **Board Cert:** Cardiovascular Disease 2013; Cardiac Electrophysiology 2005; **Med School:** Israel 1997; **Resid:** Internal Medicine, N Shore Univ Hosp 2000; **Fellow:** Cardiovascular Disease, N Shore Univ Hosp 2003; Cardiac Electrophysiology, Univ Penn 2005

Jadonath, Ram L MD (CE) - **Spec Exp:** Arrhythmias; Atrial Fibrillation; Pacemakers/Defibrillators; Syncope; **Hospital:** N Shore Univ Hosp; **Address:** N Shore Univ Hosp, Cardiology Dept, 300 Community Drive, Manhasset, NY 11030; **Phone:** 516-562-4100; **Board Cert:** Internal Medicine 1989; Cardiovascular Disease 2006; Cardiac Electrophysiology 2006; **Med School:** Columbia P&S 1986; **Resid:** Internal Medicine, St Lukes-Roosevelt Hosp 1989; **Fellow:** Cardiovascular Disease, St Lukes-Roosevelt Hosp 1992; Cardiac Electrophysiology, Philadelphia Heart Inst 1993; **Fac Appt:** Assoc Prof Med, Albert Einstein Coll Med

Levine, Joseph H MD (CE) - **Spec Exp:** Arrhythmias; Sudden Death Prevention; Atrial Fibrillation; Pacemakers; **Hospital:** St. Francis Hosp - The Heart Ctr (page 111); **Address:** 100 Port Washington Blvd, Roslyn, NY 11576; **Phone:** 516-622-1011; **Board Cert:** Internal Medicine 1983; Cardiovascular Disease 1987; **Med School:** Univ Rochester 1980; **Resid:** Internal Medicine, Yale-New Haven Hosp 1983; **Fellow:** Cardiovascular Disease, Johns Hopkins Hosp 1986; Cardiac Electrophysiology, Hosp Univ Penn 1987

Slotwiner, David J MD (CE) - **Spec Exp:** Arrhythmias; Pacemakers; Defibrillators; Atrial Fibrillation; **Hospital:** Long Is Jewish Med Ctr; **Address:** 270-05 76th Ave, New Hyde Park, NY 11040; **Phone:** 718-470-7246; **Board Cert:** Cardiovascular Disease 2008; Cardiac Electrophysiology 2009; **Med School:** Univ Chicago-Pritzker Sch Med 1992; **Resid:** Internal Medicine, NY-Presby-Cornell Med Ctr 1995; **Fellow:** Cardiovascular Disease, NY-Presby-Cornell Med Ctr 1997; Cardiac Electrophysiology, NY-Presby-Cornell Med Ctr 1999

Cardiovascular Disease

Anto, Maliakal Joseph MD (Cv) - **Spec Exp:** Hypertension; Coronary Artery Disease; Non-Invasive Cardiology; Congestive Heart Failure; **Hospital:** Syosset Hosp, Plainview Hosp; **Address:** 8 Greenfield Rd, Syosset, NY 11791; **Phone:** 516-496-7900; **Board Cert:** Internal Medicine 1980; Cardiovascular Disease 1989; **Med School:** India 1974; **Resid:** Internal Medicine, Our Lady of Mercy Med Ctr 1979; **Fellow:** Cardiovascular Disease, Nassau County Med Ctr 1981

Bhansali, Rohan D MD (Cv) - **Spec Exp:** Echocardiography; Nuclear Cardiology; Nuclear Stress Testing; **Hospital:** Long Is Jewish Med Ctr, N Shore Univ Hosp; **Address:** LIJ Med Ctr, Cardiology Dept, 270-05 76th Ave Fl 4, New Hyde Park, NY 11040; **Phone:** 718-470-7330; **Board Cert:** Cardiovascular Disease 2004; **Med School:** SUNY Upstate Med Univ 1998; **Resid:** Internal Medicine, LIJ Med Ctr 2001; **Fellow:** Cardiovascular Disease, LIJ Med Ctr 2004

Breen, William John MD (Cv) - **Spec Exp:** Echocardiography; **Hospital:** Plainview Hosp; **Address:** 43 Crossways Park Drive, Woodbury, NY 11797; **Phone:** 516-938-3000; **Board Cert:** Internal Medicine 1980; Cardiovascular Disease 1983; **Med School:** NY Med Coll 1977; **Resid:** Internal Medicine, North Shore Univ Hosp 1980; **Fellow:** Cardiovascular Disease, North Shore Univ Hosp 1982; **Fac Appt:** Assoc Prof Med, NYU Sch Med

Chen, Timothy T MD (Cv) - **Spec Exp:** Congestive Heart Failure; Pacemakers; **Hospital:** Winthrop Univ Hosp (page 536), South Nassau Comm Hosp; **Address:** South Shore Heart Assocs, 242 Merrick Rd, Ste 402, Rockville Center, NY 11570; **Phone:** 516-763-2800; **Board Cert:** Cardiovascular Disease 2004; **Med School:** Columbia P&S 1998; **Resid:** Internal Medicine, Montefiore Med Ctr 2001; **Fellow:** Cardiovascular Disease, Montefiore Med Ctr 2004

Chesner, Michael D MD (Cv) - **Spec Exp:** Preventive Cardiology; Cholesterol/Lipid Disorders; Cardiac Stress Testing; **Address:** 325 W Park Ave, Long Beach, NY 11561; **Phone:** 516-432-2004; **Board Cert:** Internal Medicine 2004; Cardiovascular Disease 2007; **Med School:** Albert Einstein Coll Med 1987; **Resid:** Internal Medicine, Bronx Municipal Hosp 1990; **Fellow:** Cardiovascular Disease, LI Jewish Hosp 1993; **Fac Appt:** Assoc Prof Med, NY Coll Osteo Med

Cramer, Marvin MD (Cv) - **Spec Exp:** Coronary Artery Disease; Echocardiography; Stress Echocardiography; **Hospital:** N Shore Univ Hosp, St. Francis Hosp - The Heart Ctr (page 111); **Address:** 225 Community Drive, Ste 130, Great Neck, NY 11021; **Phone:** 516-504-0474; **Board Cert:** Internal Medicine 1974; Cardiovascular Disease 1977; Nuclear Cardiology 2005; Echocardiography 2007; **Med School:** Jefferson Med Coll 1969; **Resid:** Internal Medicine, St Lukes Med Ctr 1973; **Fellow:** Cardiovascular Disease, Columbia-Presby Med Ctr 1976; **Fac Appt:** Assoc Clin Prof Med, NYU Sch Med

D'Agostino, Ronald DO (Cv) - **Spec Exp:** Hypertension; Cholesterol/Lipid Disorders; Mitral Valve Disease; **Hospital:** Long Is Jewish Med Ctr, N Shore Univ Hosp; **Address:** Long Island Cardiovascular Consultants, 1983 Marcus Ave, Ste E124, Lake Success, NY 11042; **Phone:** 516-627-2121; **Board Cert:** Internal Medicine 2000; Cardiovascular Disease 2011; **Med School:** NY Coll Osteo Med 1985; **Resid:** Internal Medicine, LI Jewish Med Ctr 1989; Internal Medicine, LI Jewish Med Ctr 1993; **Fellow:** Cardiovascular Disease, LI Jewish Med Ctr 1992; **Fac Appt:** Asst Prof Med, NY Coll Osteo Med

Dresdale, Robert J MD (Cv) - **Spec Exp:** Heart Disease in Women; Pulmonary Hypertension; **Hospital:** N Shore Univ Hosp, St. Francis Hosp - The Heart Ctr (page 111); **Address:** 225 Community Drive, Ste 130, Great Neck, NY 11021-5506; **Phone:** 516-504-0474; **Board Cert:** Internal Medicine 1975; Cardiovascular Disease 1977; **Med School:** Columbia P&S 1972; **Resid:** Internal Medicine, Columbia-Presby Med Ctr 1974; **Fellow:** Cardiovascular Disease, Columbia-Presby Med Ctr 1976; **Fac Appt:** Assoc Clin Prof Med, NYU Sch Med

Ezratty, Ari M MD (Cv) - **Spec Exp:** Interventional Cardiology; **Hospital:** St. Francis Hosp - The Heart Ctr (page 111); **Address:** 100 Port Washington Blvd, Roslyn, NY 11576; **Phone:** 516-570-6907; **Board Cert:** Internal Medicine 1988; Cardiovascular Disease 2014; **Med School:** Mount Sinai Sch Med 1985; **Resid:** Internal Medicine, Mt Sinai Hosp 1989; **Fellow:** Cardiovascular Disease, Brigham & Womens Hosp 1992; Interventional Cardiology, Mt Sinai Hosp 1994

Fein, Frederick S MD (Cv) - **Spec Exp:** Heart Disease; **Hospital:** Winthrop Univ Hosp (page 536); **Address:** 120 Mineola Blvd, Ste 500, Mineola, NY 11501; **Phone:** 516-663-4480; **Board Cert:** Internal Medicine 1975; Cardiovascular Disease 1977; **Med School:** NYU Sch Med 1972; **Resid:** Internal Medicine, Montefiore Hosp Med Ctr 1975; **Fellow:** Cardiovascular Disease, Montefiore Hosp Med Ctr 1977; **Fac Appt:** Assoc Prof Med, Albert Einstein Coll Med

Gindea, Aaron J MD (Cv) - **Spec Exp:** Heart Valve Disease; Congestive Heart Failure; Congenital Heart Disease; **Hospital:** N Shore Univ Hosp, St. Francis Hosp - The Heart Ctr (page 111); **Address:** 800 Community Drive, Manhasset, NY 11030-3803; **Phone:** 516-627-6622; **Board Cert:** Internal Medicine 1985; Cardiovascular Disease 1989; **Med School:** NYU Sch Med 1982; **Resid:** Internal Medicine, Bellevue Hosp 1985; **Fellow:** Cardiovascular Disease, Bellevue Hosp 1987; **Fac Appt:** Assoc Prof Med, Hofstra N Shore-LIJ Sch Med

Gleckel, Louis W MD (Cv) - **Spec Exp:** Preventive Cardiology; Cardiac Stress Testing; Cholesterol/Lipid Disorders; Hypertension; **Hospital:** Long Is Jewish Med Ctr; **Address:** 2 Ohio Drive, Fl 2, Lake Success, NY 11042-1052; **Phone:** 516-622-6060; **Board Cert:** Internal Medicine 1986; **Med School:** SUNY Downstate 1983; **Resid:** Internal Medicine, LIJ Med Ctr 1986; **Fellow:** Cardiovascular Disease, LIJ Med Ctr 1989

Goldberg, Steven Mark MD (Cv) - **Spec Exp:** Cholesterol/Lipid Disorders; Preventive Cardiology; **Hospital:** N Shore Univ Hosp; **Address:** 1010 Northern Blvd, Ste 110, Great Neck, NY 11021-5306; **Phone:** 516-390-2430; **Board Cert:** Internal Medicine 1982; Cardiovascular Disease 1985; **Med School:** Univ Pennsylvania 1979; **Resid:** Internal Medicine, N Shore Univ Hosp 1982; **Fellow:** Cardiovascular Disease, N Shore Univ Hosp 1984

Gomez, Henry Esteban MD (Cv) - **Spec Exp:** Echocardiography; Non-Invasive Cardiology; **Hospital:** N Shore Univ Hosp; **Address:** Long Island Cardiovascular Consultants, 1983 Markus Ave, Ste E124, Lake Success, NY 11042; **Phone:** 516-627-2121; **Board Cert:** Internal Medicine 2004; Cardiovascular Disease 2008; **Med School:** Mount Sinai Sch Med 1990; **Resid:** Internal Medicine, Montefiore Med Ctr 1993; **Fellow:** Cardiovascular Disease, Long Island Jewish Med Ctr 1996

Goodman, Mark A MD (Cv) - **Spec Exp:** Cholesterol/Lipid Disorders; Pacemakers/Defibrillators; Coronary Artery Disease; Congestive Heart Failure; **Hospital:** Winthrop Univ Hosp (page 536), N Shore Univ Hosp; **Address:** 975 Stewart Ave, Garden City, NY 11530-4816; **Phone:** 516-222-8610; **Board Cert:** Internal Medicine 1972; Cardiovascular Disease 1973; **Med School:** SUNY Upstate Med Univ 1967; **Resid:** Internal Medicine, Montefiore Med Ctr 1969; Internal Medicine, Mt Sinai Hosp 1970; **Fellow:** Cardiovascular Disease, Montefiore Med Ctr 1972; **Fac Appt:** Assoc Clin Prof Med, SUNY Stony Brook

Green, Stephen J MD (Cv) - **Spec Exp:** Heart Attack; Angioplasty; Cholesterol/Lipid Disorders; Interventional Cardiology; **Hospital:** Winthrop Univ Hosp (page 536); **Address:** Winthrop Cardiology Associates, 120 Mineola Blvd, Ste 500, Mineola, NY 11501; **Phone:** 516-663-4480; **Board Cert:** Internal Medicine 1983; Cardiovascular Disease 1985; Interventional Cardiology 2009; **Med School:** Tufts Univ 1980; **Resid:** Internal Medicine, N Shore Univ Hosp 1983; **Fellow:** Cardiovascular Disease, N Shore Univ Hosp 1985

Hershman, Ronnie MD (Cv) - **Spec Exp:** Invasive Cardiology; **Hospital:** St. Francis Hosp - The Heart Ctr (page 111); **Address:** 1 Hollow Ln, Ste 103, Lake Success, NY 11042; **Phone:** 516-869-5400; **Board Cert:** Internal Medicine 1985; Cardiovascular Disease 1987; **Med School:** Mount Sinai Sch Med 1982; **Resid:** Internal Medicine, Mt Sinai Med Ctr 1985; **Fellow:** Cardiovascular Disease, Mt Sinai Med Ctr 1989

Jauhar, Rajiv MD (Cv) - **Spec Exp:** Angioplasty & Stent Placement; Cardiac Catheterization; Cardiac Imaging; Interventional Cardiology; **Hospital:** Long Is Jewish Med Ctr; **Address:** LIJ Med Ctr, Cardiology Dept, 270-05 76 Ave Fl 4, New Hyde Park, NY 11040; **Phone:** 718-470-7330; **Board Cert:** Cardiovascular Disease 2009; Interventional Cardiology 2010; **Med School:** Univ Chicago-Pritzker Sch Med 1991; **Resid:** Internal Medicine, UCSD Med Ctr 1994; **Fellow:** Cardiovascular Disease, NY-Presby/Weill Cornell Med Ctr 1999

Kalman, Jill MD (Cv) - **Spec Exp:** Heart Failure; Cardiomyopathy; Heart Disease in Women; **Hospital:** Lenox Hill Hosp; **Address:** 270-05 76th Ave, New Hyde Park, NY 11040; **Phone:** 718-470-7469; **Board Cert:** Cardiovascular Disease 2005; **Med School:** Mount Sinai Sch Med 1987; **Resid:** Internal Medicine, Mount Sinai Med Ctr 1991; **Fellow:** Cardiovascular Disease, Mount Sinai Med Ctr 1995; **Fac Appt:** Assoc Prof Med, Mount Sinai Sch Med

Kobren, Steven M MD (Cv) - **Spec Exp:** Heart Failure; Mitral Valve Prolapse; Nuclear Stress Testing; **Hospital:** NYU Langone Med Ctr (page 104), Long Is Jewish Med Ctr; **Address:** 488 Great Neck Rd, Great Neck, NY 11021; **Phone:** 516-482-6747; **Board Cert:** Internal Medicine 1986; Cardiovascular Disease 1989; Critical Care Medicine 2011; **Med School:** SUNY Downstate 1983; **Resid:** Internal Medicine, LIJ Med Ctr 1986; **Fellow:** Cardiovascular Disease, LIJ Med Ctr 1988

Koss, Jerome MD (Cv) - **Spec Exp:** Interventional Cardiology; Heart Valve Disease; Nuclear Cardiology; Atrial Fibrillation; **Hospital:** Long Is Jewish Med Ctr, St. Francis Hosp - The Heart Ctr (page 111); **Address:** 3003 New Hyde Park Rd, Ste 406, New Hyde Park, NY 11042; **Phone:** 516-358-5401; **Board Cert:** Internal Medicine 1977; Cardiovascular Disease 1981; Interventional Cardiology 2010; **Med School:** Albert Einstein Coll Med 1974; **Resid:** Internal Medicine, Jacobi Med Ctr 1978; **Fellow:** Cardiovascular Disease, Montefiore Med Ctr 1980; **Fac Appt:** Asst Prof Med, Albert Einstein Coll Med

Lituchy, Andrew MD (Cv) - **Spec Exp:** Coronary Artery Disease; Peripheral Vascular Disease; Interventional Cardiology; **Hospital:** St. Francis Hosp - The Heart Ctr (page 111), South Nassau Comm Hosp; **Address:** 100 Port Washington Blvd, Ste G-05, Roslyn, NY 11576-1353; **Phone:** 516-365-4888; **Board Cert:** Cardiovascular Disease 2005; **Med School:** Hahnemann Univ 1988; **Resid:** Internal Medicine, Bronx Muni/Albert Einstein Med Ctr 1991; **Fellow:** Cardiovascular Disease, NY-Cornell Med Ctr 1994; Interventional Cardiology, NY-Cornell Med Ctr 1995

Marzo, Kevin P MD (Cv) - **Spec Exp:** Cardiac Catheterization; **Hospital:** Winthrop Univ Hosp (page 536); **Address:** Winthrop Cardiology Associates, 120 Mineola Blvd, Ste 500, Mineola, NY 11501; **Phone:** 516-663-4480; **Board Cert:** Internal Medicine 1988; Cardiovascular Disease 2013; Interventional Cardiology 2009; **Med School:** Northwestern Univ 1985; **Resid:** Internal Medicine, Columbia Presby Med Ctr 1988; **Fellow:** Cardiovascular Disease, Hosp U Penn 1991; Interventional Cardiology, Hosp U Penn 1992

Mintz, Guy L MD (Cv) - **Spec Exp:** Preventive Cardiology; Cholesterol/Lipid Disorders; Coronary Artery Disease; Hypertension; **Hospital:** N Shore Univ Hosp, St. Francis Hosp - The Heart Ctr (page 111); **Address:** 287 Northern Blvd, Ste 211, Great Neck, NY 11021; **Phone:** 516-482-3401; **Board Cert:** Internal Medicine 1987; **Med School:** Boston Univ 1984; **Resid:** Internal Medicine, N Shore Univ Hosp 1987; **Fellow:** Cardiovascular Disease, N Shore Univ Hosp 1989; **Fac Appt:** Assoc Clin Prof Med, NYU Sch Med

Nicosia, Thomas A MD (Cv) - **Spec Exp:** Coronary Artery Disease; Congestive Heart Failure; **Hospital:** St. Francis Hosp - The Heart Ctr (page 111), N Shore Univ Hosp; **Address:** Manhasset Medical Associates, 1615 Northern Blvd, Ste 301, Manhasset, NY 11030; **Phone:** 516-627-9355; **Board Cert:** Internal Medicine 1979; Cardiovascular Disease 1981; **Med School:** Univ Cincinnati 1974; **Resid:** Internal Medicine, University Hosp 1978; **Fellow:** Cardiovascular Disease, Bellevue Hosp 1980

Pappas, Thomas W MD (Cv) - **Spec Exp:** Interventional Cardiology; Coronary Angioplasty/Stents; Angiography-Coronary; Cardiac Imaging; **Hospital:** St. Francis Hosp - The Heart Ctr (page 111); **Address:** 1155 Northern Blvd, Ste 330, Manhasset, NY 11030; **Phone:** 516-726-7575; **Board Cert:** Internal Medicine 1986; Cardiovascular Disease 1989; Interventional Cardiology 2010; **Med School:** Cornell Univ-Weill Med Coll 1983; **Resid:** Internal Medicine, New York Hosp 1986; **Fellow:** Cardiovascular Disease, New York Hosp-Cornell 1988; Interventional Cardiology, NYU Med Ctr 1990

Ragno, Philip D MD (Cv) - **Spec Exp:** Cholesterol/Lipid Disorders; Congestive Heart Failure; **Hospital:** Winthrop Univ Hosp (page 536); **Address:** 1401 Franklin Ave, Garden City, NY 11501; **Phone:** 516-877-2626; **Board Cert:** Internal Medicine 1987; Cardiovascular Disease 1989; **Med School:** SUNY Stony Brook 1984; **Resid:** Internal Medicine, Winthrop Univ Hosp 1987; **Fellow:** Cardiovascular Disease, Winthrop Univ Hosp 1989

Rutkovsky, Edward V MD (Cv) - **Spec Exp:** Nuclear Stress Testing; Echocardiography; **Hospital:** N Shore Univ Hosp, St. Francis Hosp - The Heart Ctr (page 111); **Address:** N Shore Cardiac Imaging, PC, 2035 Lakeville Rd, Ste 101, New Hyde Park, NY 11040-1661; **Phone:** 516-328-9797; **Board Cert:** Internal Medicine 1987; Cardiovascular Disease 1989; **Med School:** NYU Sch Med 1984; **Resid:** Internal Medicine, NYU Med Ctr 1987; **Fellow:** Cardiovascular Disease, N Shore Univ Hosp 1989; **Fac Appt:** Asst Clin Prof Med, NYU Sch Med

Schreiber, Carl MD (Cv) - **Spec Exp:** Coronary Artery Disease; Nuclear Cardiology; Non-Invasive Cardiology; **Hospital:** Glen Cove Hosp, N Shore Univ Hosp; **Address:** North Nassau Cardiology Associates, 70 Glen St, Ste 200, Glen Cove, NY 11542-2853; **Phone:** 516-484-7893; **Board Cert:** Internal Medicine 1982; Cardiovascular Disease 1985; **Med School:** Med Coll GA 1979; **Resid:** Internal Medicine, Columbia-Presby Med Ctr 1982; **Fellow:** Cardiovascular Disease, Westchester Med Ctr 1984

Shayani, Steven S MD (Cv) - **Spec Exp:** Coronary Artery Disease; Congestive Heart Failure; Nuclear Cardiology; Cholesterol/Lipid Disorders; **Hospital:** Mt Sinai Hosp, St. Francis Hosp - The Heart Ctr (page 111); **Address:** Long Island Heart Associates, 200 Old Country Rd, Ste 278, Mineola, NY 11501; **Phone:** 516-877-0977; **Board Cert:** Cardiovascular Disease 2005; **Med School:** SUNY Upstate Med Univ 1988; **Resid:** Internal Medicine, Winthrop Univ Hosp 1991; **Fellow:** Cardiovascular Disease, Winthrop Univ Hosp 1994; **Fac Appt:** Asst Clin Prof Med, Mount Sinai Sch Med

Shlofmitz, Richard A MD (Cv) - **Spec Exp:** Interventional Cardiology; Cardiac Catheterization; **Hospital:** St. Francis Hosp - The Heart Ctr (page 111); **Address:** 100 Port Washington Blvd, Roslyn, NY 11576; **Phone:** 516-390-9640; **Board Cert:** Internal Medicine 1984; Cardiovascular Disease 1987; **Med School:** NYU Sch Med 1980; **Resid:** Internal Medicine, N Shore Univ Hosp 1984; **Fellow:** Cardiovascular Disease, Presby/Columbia Univ Med Ctr 1987

Sokol, Sergio MD (Cv) - **Spec Exp:** Echocardiography; **Hospital:** St. John's Episcopal Hosp - Queens; **Address:** Five Towns Heart Imaging, 650 Central Ave, Ste K, Cedarhurst, NY 11516; **Phone:** 516-804-8590; **Board Cert:** Cardiovascular Disease 2004; Internal Medicine 2013; **Med School:** Israel 1994; **Resid:** Internal Medicine, Montefiore Med Ctr 1998; **Fellow:** Cardiovascular Disease, N Shore Univ Hosp 2001

Spadaro, Louise A MD (Cv) - **Spec Exp:** Preventive Cardiology; Heart Disease in Women; **Hospital:** St. Francis Hosp - The Heart Ctr (page 111); **Address:** 100 Port Washington Blvd, Roslyn, NY 11576; **Phone:** 516-562-6653; **Board Cert:** Internal Medicine 1987; Cardiovascular Disease 1989; **Med School:** NYU Sch Med 1984; **Resid:** Internal Medicine, Bellevue Hosp 1987; **Fellow:** Cardiovascular Disease, Bellevue Hosp/NYU Med Ctr 1989

Tenet, William MD (Cv) - **Spec Exp:** Congestive Heart Failure; Coronary Artery Disease; **Hospital:** N Shore Univ Hosp, Lenox Hill Hosp; **Address:** NYU Langone Cardiovascular Associates, 1155 Northern Blvd, Ste 330, Manhasset, NY 11030; **Phone:** 516-627-4330; **Board Cert:** Internal Medicine 1983; Cardiovascular Disease 1987; **Med School:** Italy 1980; **Resid:** Internal Medicine, Booth Meml Med Ctr 1984; **Fellow:** Cardiovascular Disease, Univ Conn Hlth Ctr 1986; **Fac Appt:** Asst Clin Prof Med, Cornell Univ-Weill Med Coll

Weg, Ira L MD (Cv) - **Spec Exp:** Congestive Heart Failure; Coronary Artery Disease; **Hospital:** South Nassau Comm Hosp; **Address:** N Shore LIJ Internal Medicine, 158 Hempstead Ave, Lynbrook, NY 11563; **Phone:** 516-593-3541; **Board Cert:** Internal Medicine 1979; Cardiovascular Disease 1981; **Med School:** SUNY Hlth Sci Ctr 1976; **Resid:** Internal Medicine, Kings County Hosp 1979; **Fellow:** Cardiovascular Disease, Montefiore Med Ctr 1981; **Fac Appt:** Asst Clin Prof Med, Albert Einstein Coll Med

Child & Adolescent Psychiatry

Foley, Carmel A MD (ChAP) - **Spec Exp:** Mood Disorders; **Hospital:** Steven & Alexandra Cohen Chldn's Med Ctr of NY; **Address:** 420 Lakeville Rd, Ste 110, New Hyde Park, NY 11040; **Phone:** 718-470-3550; **Board Cert:** Psychiatry 1979; Child & Adolescent Psychiatry 1981; Psychosomatic Medicine 2009; **Med School:** Ireland 1972; **Resid:** Psychiatry, Lafayette Clin 1977; **Fellow:** Child & Adolescent Psychiatry, Lafayette Clin 1979; Child & Adolescent Psychiatry, LIJ Med Ctr 1980

Williams, Daniel T MD (ChAP) - **Spec Exp:** Neuro-Psychiatry; Psychopharmacology; Psychosomatic Disorders; **Hospital:** NY-Presby/Columbia Univ Med Ctr, NY (page 102), NS-LIJ Hlth Sys; **Address:** 2001 Marcus Ave, Ste N-218, New Hyde Park, NY 11042; **Phone:** 516-488-3636; **Board Cert:** Psychiatry 1975; Child & Adolescent Psychiatry 1976; **Med School:** Cornell Univ-Weill Med Coll 1969; **Resid:** Psychiatry, Mount Sinai Hosp 1972; **Fellow:** Child & Adolescent Psychiatry, Columbia-Presby Hosp 1974

Child Neurology

Atluru, Vijaya MD (ChiN) - **Spec Exp:** Epilepsy; Migraine; Developmental Disorders; Autism; **Hospital:** Winthrop Univ Hosp (page 536); **Address:** Winthrop Child Neurology Associates, 173 Mineola Blvd, Ste 101, Mineola, NY 11501; **Phone:** 516-663-9494; **Board Cert:** Pediatrics 1979; Child Neurology 1983; **Med School:** India 1973; **Resid:** Pediatrics, Nassau Co Med Ctr 1977; **Fellow:** Child Neurology, Stony Brook Univ Med Ctr 1980; **Fac Appt:** Assoc Prof N, SUNY Stony Brook

Bergtraum, Marcia MD (ChiN) - **Hospital:** Long Is Jewish Med Ctr; **Address:** 2001 Marcus Ave, Ste N-218, New Hyde Park, NY 11042-1214; **Phone:** 516-488-2323; **Board Cert:** Pediatrics 1981; Child Neurology 1988; **Med School:** Georgetown Univ 1974; **Resid:** Pediatrics, LI Jewish Hosp 1977; **Fellow:** Pediatric Hematology-Oncology, LI Jewish Hosp 1978; Pediatric Neurology, LI Jewish Hosp 1982

Gould, Robert MD (ChiN) - **Hospital:** N Shore Univ Hosp, Steven & Alexandra Cohen Chldn's Med Ctr of NY; **Address:** Metropolitan Pediatric Neurology, 1000 Northern Blvd, Ste 240, Great Neck, NY 11021; **Phone:** 516-829-3100; **Board Cert:** Pediatrics 1984; Child Neurology 1984; **Med School:** Columbia P&S 1977; **Resid:** Pediatrics, Babies Hosp-Columbia P&S 1979; Neurology, Neuro Inst-Columbia P&S 1980; **Fellow:** Pediatric Neurology, Neuro Inst-Columbia P&S 1982; **Fac Appt:** Assoc Clin Prof N, Cornell Univ-Weill Med Coll

LaJoie, Josiane M MD (ChiN) - **Spec Exp:** Epilepsy/Seizure Disorders; Neurophysiology; **Hospital:** Steven & Alexandra Cohen Chldn's Med Ctr of NY; **Address:** CCMC, Pediatric Neurology, 410 Lakeville Rd, Ste 105, New Hyde Park, NY 11042; **Phone:** 516-465-5255; **Board Cert:** Pediatrics 2013; Child Neurology 2012; Clinical Neurophysiology 2005; **Med School:** Univ Pennsylvania 1996; **Resid:** Pediatrics, Montefiore Med Ctr 1998; **Fellow:** Child Neurology, Montefiore Med Ctr 2001; Clinical Neurophysiology, Montefiore Med Ctr 2002; **Fac Appt:** Asst Prof N, NYU Sch Med

Maytal, Joseph MD (ChiN) - **Spec Exp:** Epilepsy/Seizure Disorders; Migraine; **Hospital:** Steven & Alexandra Cohen Chldn's Med Ctr of NY; **Address:** Div Pediatric Neurology, 410 Lakeville Rd, Ste 105, Lake Success, NY 11042; **Phone:** 516-465-5255; **Board Cert:** Pediatrics 1986; Child Neurology 1988; **Med School:** Israel 1979; **Resid:** Pediatrics, Brookdale Univ Hosp Med Ctr 1983; Child Neurology, Montefiore Med Ctr 1986; **Fellow:** Neurophysiology, Montefiore Med Ctr 1987; **Fac Appt:** Clin Prof N, Albert Einstein Coll Med

Smith, Robin E MD (ChiN) - **Spec Exp:** Cerebral Palsy; Neuromuscular Disorders; Headache; Epilepsy/Seizure Disorders; **Hospital:** Steven & Alexandra Cohen Chldn's Med Ctr of NY; **Address:** NRAD Medical Assocs, 105 Froehlich Farm Blvd, Woodbury, NY 11797; **Phone:** 516-222-2022 x7776; **Board Cert:** Pediatrics 2013; Child Neurology 2008; **Med School:** South Africa 1985; **Resid:** Pediatrics, Johannesburg Hosp 1993; Pediatrics, Schneider Childrens Hosp 1998; **Fellow:** Child Neurology, Schneider Childrens Hosp 1997; **Fac Appt:** Asst Prof N, Hofstra N Shore-LIJ Sch Med

Sy-Kho, Rosemarie MD (ChiN) - **Spec Exp:** Epilepsy; **Hospital:** Steven & Alexandra Cohen Chldn's Med Ctr of NY, NS-LIJ Hlth Sys; **Address:** Cohens Chldns Med Ctr, Child Neurology, 410 Lakeville Rd, Ste 105, New Hyde Park, NY 11040; **Phone:** 516-465-5255; **Board Cert:** Child Neurology 1993; **Med School:** Philippines 1978; **Resid:** Pediatrics, SUNY Stony Brook Univ Med Ctr 1988; **Fellow:** Child Neurology, LIJ Med Ctr 1991; **Fac Appt:** Asst Prof Ped, Hofstra N Shore-LIJ Sch Med

Clinical Genetics

Bialer, Martin G MD/PhD (CG) - **Spec Exp:** Marfan's Syndrome; Neurofibromatosis; Metabolic Genetic Disorders; Cancer Genetics; **Hospital:** Steven & Alexandra Cohen Chldn's Med Ctr of NY, NS-LIJ Hlth Sys; **Address:** 1554 Northern Blvd, Ste 204, Manhasset, NY 11030; **Phone:** 516-365-3996; **Board Cert:** Pediatrics 1987; Clinical Biochemical Genetics 1990; Clinical Genetics 1990; **Med School:** Med Univ SC 1983; **Resid:** Pediatrics, N Shore Univ Hosp 1986; **Fellow:** Clinical Genetics, Univ of VA Med Ctr 1989; **Fac Appt:** Clin Prof Ped, NYU Sch Med

Fox, Joyce MD (CG) - **Hospital:** Steven & Alexandra Cohen Chldn's Med Ctr of NY, Long Is Jewish Med Ctr; **Address:** 1554 Northern Blvd, Ste 204, Manhasset, NY 11030; **Phone:** 516-365-3996; **Board Cert:** Pediatrics 1986; Clinical Genetics 1987; **Med School:** Columbia P&S 1980; **Resid:** Pediatrics, Case Western Univ Hosp 1983; **Fellow:** Clinical Genetics, Yale-New Haven Hosp 1986; **Fac Appt:** , Albert Einstein Coll Med

Colon & Rectal Surgery

Greenwald, Marc MD (CRS) - **Spec Exp:** Laparoscopic Surgery; Colonoscopy; Anorectal Disorders; Colon & Rectal Cancer; **Hospital:** N Shore Univ Hosp, St. Francis Hosp - The Heart Ctr (page 111); **Address:** North Shore Surgical Specialists, 310 E Shore Rd, Ste 203, Great Neck, NY 11023-2432; **Phone:** 516-482-8657; **Board Cert:** Surgery 2009; Colon & Rectal Surgery 2011; **Med School:** Albert Einstein Coll Med 1985; **Resid:** Surgery, Montefiore Hosp Med Ctr 1990; **Fellow:** Colon & Rectal Surgery, St Francis Hosp 1991

Moseson, Michael D MD (CRS) - **Spec Exp:** Anorectal Disorders; Colonoscopy/Polypectomy; **Hospital:** St. Francis Hosp - The Heart Ctr (page 111), N Shore Univ Hosp; **Address:** 3 Vermont Drive, Lake Success, NY 11042; **Phone:** 516-608-6848; **Board Cert:** Colon & Rectal Surgery 1982; **Med School:** Spain 1975; **Resid:** Surgery, North Shore Univ Hosp 1980; Colon & Rectal Surgery, UMDNJ-RWJohnson Med Ctr 1981

Pappas, Dean P MD (CRS) - **Spec Exp:** Minimally Invasive Surgery; Colon & Rectal Cancer; Colonoscopy; Gastrointestinal Cancer; **Hospital:** Winthrop Univ Hosp (page 536), South Nassau Comm Hosp; **Address:** Colorectal Surgical Specialists of NY, 1100 Franklin Ave, Ste 203, Garden City, NY 11530; **Phone:** 516-248-2422; **Board Cert:** Surgery 2009; Colon & Rectal Surgery 2010; **Med School:** SUNY Stony Brook 1994; **Resid:** Surgery, Stony Brook Univ Med Ctr 1999; **Fellow:** Colon & Rectal Surgery, Orlando Regl Med Ctr 2000

Procaccino Jr, John A MD (CRS) - **Spec Exp:** Inflammatory Bowel Disease/Crohn's; Colon & Rectal Cancer; Anorectal Disorders; Colon & Rectal Cancer-Familial Polyposis; **Hospital:** N Shore Univ Hosp, Long Is Jewish Med Ctr; **Address:** 900 Northern Blvd, Ste 100, Great Neck, NY 11021; **Phone:** 516-730-2100; **Board Cert:** Surgery 2009; Colon & Rectal Surgery 2011; **Med School:** NY Med Coll 1984; **Resid:** Surgery, N Shore Univ Hosp 1989; **Fellow:** Colon & Rectal Surgery, Cleveland Clin 1990; **Fac Appt:** Asst Clin Prof S, Cornell Univ-Weill Med Coll

Rivadeneira, David E MD (CRS) - **Spec Exp:** Colon & Rectal Cancer & Surgery; Inflammatory Bowel Disease; Gastrointestinal Surgery; Laparoscopic Surgery; **Hospital:** Huntington Hosp, Southside Hosp; **Address:** North Shore - LIJ Colorectal Surgery, 321 Crossways Park Drive, Woodbury, NY 11797; **Phone:** 631-470-1450; **Board Cert:** Surgery 2013; Colon & Rectal Surgery 2004; **Med School:** Howard Univ 1995; **Resid:** Surgery, NY-Presby/Weill Cornell Med Ctr 2002; **Fellow:** Colon & Rectal Surgery, Lahey Clin 2003; **Fac Appt:** Prof S, Hofstra N Shore-LIJ Sch Med

Sullivan III, James D MD (CRS) - **Spec Exp:** Cancer Surgery; Colon & Rectal Cancer & Surgery; Gastrointestinal Cancer; Robotic Surgery; **Hospital:** N Shore Univ Hosp, St. Francis Hosp - The Heart Ctr (page 111); **Address:** North Shore Surgical Oncology, 450 lakeville Rd, New Hyde Park, NY 11042; **Phone:** 516-487-9488; **Board Cert:** Surgery 2004; Colon & Rectal Surgery 2005; **Med School:** NY Med Coll 1987; **Resid:** Surgery, N Shore Univ Hosp 1992; **Fellow:** Colon & Rectal Surgery, Cleveland Clinic 1993

Dermatology

Aprile, Georgette MD (D) - **Spec Exp:** Acne; Atopic Dermatitis; Laser Surgery; Laser Hair Removal; **Hospital:** Glen Cove Hosp; **Address:** 8 Medical Plaza, Lower Level, Ste 103, Glen Cove, NY 11542; **Phone:** 516-759-9200; **Board Cert:** Dermatology 1978; **Med School:** NY Med Coll 1974; **Resid:** Dermatology, New York Hosp 1978

Barazani, Lance A MD (D) - **Spec Exp:** Cosmetic Dermatology; **Hospital:** Long Is Jewish Med Ctr; **Address:** Advanced Dermatology, 175 IU Willets Rd, Albertson, NY 11507; **Phone:** 516-625-6222; **Board Cert:** Internal Medicine 1989; Dermatology 2013; **Med School:** NY Med Coll 1986; **Resid:** Internal Medicine, N Shore Univ Hosp 1989; Dermatology, NY Presby-Cornell Med Ctr 1994; **Fellow:** Dermatologic Research, Rockefeller Univ 1991

Bruckstein, Robert MD (D) - **Spec Exp:** Acne; Skin Cancer; Cosmetic Dermatology; Skin Laser Surgery; **Hospital:** St. John's Episcopal Hosp - Queens; **Address:** 290 Central Ave, Ste 206, Lawrence, NY 11559-8507; **Phone:** 516-239-2332; **Board Cert:** Dermatology 1977; **Med School:** NYU Sch Med 1972; **Resid:** Dermatology, Bellevue Hosp Ctr 1975; **Fac Appt:** Asst Clin Prof D, NYU Sch Med

De Pietro, William MD (D) - **Spec Exp:** Skin Laser Surgery; Dermatologic Surgery; **Hospital:** Glen Cove Hosp; **Address:** 10 Medical Plaza, Ste 102, Glen Cove, NY 11542; **Phone:** 516-671-1780; **Board Cert:** Dermatology 1980; **Med School:** Georgetown Univ 1976; **Resid:** Dermatology, St Luke's Hosp 1980

Demento, Frank MD (D) - **Spec Exp:** Dermatologic Surgery; Skin Cancer; **Hospital:** Winthrop Univ Hosp (page 536), NY-Presby/Columbia Univ Med Ctr, NY (page 102); **Address:** 520 Franklin Ave, Ste 229, Garden City, NY 11530; **Phone:** 516-746-1227; **Board Cert:** Dermatology 1969; **Med School:** UMDNJ-NJ Med Sch, Newark 1964; **Resid:** Dermatology, USPHS Hosp 1966; **Fellow:** Dermatology, Columbia-Presby Hosp 1968

Dolitsky, Charisse MD (D) - **Spec Exp:** Acne; Skin Cancer; Botox Therapy; Facial Rejuvenation; **Address:** 604 E Park Ave, Long Beach, NY 11561; **Phone:** 516-432-0011; **Board Cert:** Dermatology 1989; **Med School:** SUNY Downstate 1985; **Resid:** Dermatology, SUNY Downstate Med Ctr 1989

Falcon, Ronald MD (D) - **Spec Exp:** Skin Cancer; Acne; Psoriasis; **Address:** 604 E Park Ave, Long Beach, NY 11561; **Phone:** 516-432-0011; **Board Cert:** Dermatology 1989; **Med School:** SUNY Downstate 1985; **Resid:** Dermatology, SUNY Downstate Med Ctr 1989

Franck, Jeanne M MD (D) - **Spec Exp:** Mohs Surgery; **Hospital:** NY-Presby/Columbia Univ Med Ctr, NY (page 102); **Address:** 520 Franklin Ave, Ste 207, Garden City, NY 11530; **Phone:** 516-741-1055; **Board Cert:** Dermatology 2013; **Med School:** Columbia P&S 1991; **Resid:** Dermatology, Columbia Presby Med Ctr 1995; **Fellow:** Mohs Surgery, Univ Minn Med Ctr 1996

Hefter, Harold MD (D) - **Spec Exp:** Cosmetic Dermatology; Dermatologic Surgery; Acne; **Hospital:** Franklin Hosp, Jacobi Med Ctr; **Address:** 135 Rockaway Tpke, Ste 100, Lawrence, NY 11559-1033; **Phone:** 516-371-1600; **Board Cert:** Dermatology 1985; **Med School:** Albert Einstein Coll Med 1981; **Resid:** Dermatology, Albert Einstein Affil Hosp 1985; **Fac Appt:** Asst Prof D, Albert Einstein Coll Med

Hisler, Barbara M MD (D) - **Spec Exp:** Skin Cancer; Acne; Psoriasis; **Hospital:** Long Is Jewish Med Ctr; **Address:** 1300 Union Tpke, Ste 303, New Hyde Park, NY 11040-1759; **Phone:** 516-326-0333; **Board Cert:** Internal Medicine 1986; Dermatology 1989; **Med School:** NY Med Coll 1983; **Resid:** Internal Medicine, LI Jewish Med Ctr 1985; Dermatology, Detroit Med Ctr 1988

Levine, Laurie J MD (D) - **Spec Exp:** Skin Laser Surgery; Botox Therapy; Cosmetic Dermatology; **Hospital:** Winthrop Univ Hosp (page 536); **Address:** 200 Old Country Rd, Ste 140, Mineola, NY 11501-4237; **Phone:** 516-742-6136; **Board Cert:** Dermatology 1988; **Med School:** SUNY Stony Brook 1984; **Resid:** Dermatology, Thomas Jefferson Univ Hosp 1988; **Fellow:** Dermatologic Surgery, Thomas Jefferson Univ Hosp 1989; **Fac Appt:** Asst Clin Prof D, SUNY Stony Brook

Paltzik, Robert L MD (D) - **Spec Exp:** Pediatric Dermatology; Dermatologic Surgery; Facial Rejuvenation; **Hospital:** N Shore Univ Hosp, Winthrop Univ Hosp (page 536); **Address:** 2 Hillside Ave, Ste G, Williston Park, NY 11596; **Phone:** 516-747-2230; **Board Cert:** Dermatology 1977; Pediatrics 1976; **Med School:** NYU Sch Med 1971; **Resid:** Pediatrics, Yale-New Haven Hosp 1973; Dermatology, SUNY Downstate Med Ctr 1977; **Fac Appt:** Asst Prof D, NYU Sch Med

Sarnoff, Deborah S MD (D) - **Spec Exp:** Mohs Surgery; Skin Cancer; Dermatologic Surgery; Skin Laser Surgery; **Hospital:** NYU Langone Med Ctr (page 104); **Address:** 31 Northern Blvd, Greenvale, NY 11548; **Phone:** 516-484-9000; **Board Cert:** Dermatology 2009; **Med School:** Geo Wash Univ 1980; **Resid:** Dermatology, NYU Med Ctr 1984; **Fellow:** Dermatologic Surgery, NYU Med Ctr 1986; **Fac Appt:** Clin Prof D, NYU Sch Med

Silverman, Mark K MD (D) - **Spec Exp:** Melanoma; Skin Cancer; Skin Laser Surgery; **Hospital:** South Nassau Comm Hosp; **Address:** South Nassau Dermatology, 258 Merrick Rd, Oceanside, NY 11572; **Phone:** 516-766-0345; **Board Cert:** Internal Medicine 1989; Dermatology 2012; **Med School:** Tufts Univ 1986; **Resid:** Internal Medicine, Montefiore Med Ctr 1989; Dermatology, Albert Einstein Coll of Med Affil Hosp 1994; **Fellow:** Research, NYU 1991

Sklar, Jeffrey Alan MD (D) - **Spec Exp:** Facial Rejuvenation; Cosmetic Dermatology; Botox Therapy; **Hospital:** NY-Presby/Columbia Univ Med Ctr, NY (page 102), Syosset Hosp; **Address:** Center for Aesthetic Dermatology, 800 Woodbury Rd, Ste A, Woodbury, NY 11797-2503; **Phone:** 516-496-9400; **Board Cert:** Dermatology 1986; **Med School:** Columbia P&S 1982; **Resid:** Dermatology, Columbia Presby Hosp 1986; **Fac Appt:** Asst Clin Prof D, Columbia P&S

Walczyk, John MD (D) - **Spec Exp:** Cosmetic Dermatology; **Hospital:** NY-Presby/Columbia Univ Med Ctr, NY (page 102), Plainview Hosp; **Address:** 1165 Northern Blvd, Ste 405, Manhasset, NY 11030; **Phone:** 516-365-8030; **Board Cert:** Dermatology 2013; **Med School:** Columbia P&S 1990; **Resid:** Dermatology, Columbia Presby Hosp 1994

Diagnostic Radiology

Goodman, Kenneth J MD (DR) - **Spec Exp:** Urologic Imaging; Ultrasound; CT Scan; **Hospital:** St. Francis Hosp - The Heart Ctr (page 111); **Address:** St Francis Hosp-The Heart Ctr, Dept Radiology, 100 Port Washington Blvd, Roslyn, NY 11576-1353; **Phone:** 516-562-6500; **Board Cert:** Diagnostic Radiology 1977; **Med School:** Univ Tex, San Antonio 1972; **Resid:** Diagnostic Radiology, Cornell Med Ctr 1977; **Fellow:** Brain Imaging, Cornell Med Ctr 1978

Hammel, Jay D MD (DR) - **Spec Exp:** MRI; **Hospital:** N Shore Univ Hosp, Syosset Hosp; **Address:** 4277 Hempstead Tpke, Ste 200, Bethpage, NY 11714; **Phone:** 516-796-4340; **Board Cert:** Diagnostic Radiology 1989; **Med School:** SUNY Upstate Med Univ 1984; **Resid:** Diagnostic Radiology, St Vincent's Med Ctr 1989

Hoffman, Janet C MD (DR) - **Hospital:** Long Is Jewish Med Ctr; **Address:** 270-05 76th Ave, rm C-204, New Hyde Park, NY 11040; **Phone:** 718-470-3456; **Board Cert:** Diagnostic Radiology 1978; **Med School:** SUNY Downstate 1974; **Resid:** Diagnostic Radiology, Columbia Presby Hosp 1978; **Fellow:** Ultrasound, NY Hosp-Cornell Med Ctr 1979

Khan, Arfa MD (DR) - **Spec Exp:** Thoracic Radiology; **Hospital:** Long Is Jewish Med Ctr, Syosset Hosp; **Address:** 270-05 76th Ave, rm C204, New Hyde Park, NY 11040; **Phone:** 718-470-3456; **Board Cert:** Diagnostic Radiology 1971; **Med School:** India 1964; **Resid:** Diagnostic Radiology, Queens Hosp 1970; **Fellow:** Diagnostic Radiology, LI Jewish Med Ctr 1971; **Fac Appt:** Prof Rad, Albert Einstein Coll Med

Luchs, Jonathan S MD (DR) - **Spec Exp:** Musculoskeletal Imaging; Interventional Radiology; **Address:** ProHealth Care Assocs-Radiology, 2800 Marcus Ave, Lake Success, NY 11042; **Phone:** 516-622-6000; **Board Cert:** Diagnostic Radiology 2013; **Med School:** Israel 1996; **Resid:** Surgery, Maimonides Med Ctr 1999; **Fellow:** Diagnostic Radiology, Winthrop Univ Hosp 2003; Musculoskeletal Imaging, Hosp for Special Surgery 2004

Port, Abraham MD (DR) - **Spec Exp:** Breast Cancer; Mammography; **Hospital:** South Nassau Comm Hosp; **Address:** Complete Women's Imaging, 990 Stewart Ave, Ste 100, Garden City, NY 11530; **Phone:** 516-222-4294; **Board Cert:** Diagnostic Radiology 1985; **Med School:** Albert Einstein Coll Med 1981; **Resid:** Diagnostic Radiology, Montefiore Med Ctr 1985; **Fellow:** Body Imaging, NY Hosp-Cornell Med Ctr 1986

Rifkin, Matthew D MD (DR) - **Spec Exp:** CT Scan; MRI; Ultrasound; **Hospital:** South Nassau Comm Hosp; **Address:** S Nassau Comm Hosp, Radiology, 1 Healthy Way, Oceanside, NY 11572; **Phone:** 516-632-3921; **Board Cert:** Diagnostic Radiology 1978; **Med School:** Albert Einstein Coll Med 1974; **Resid:** Diagnostic Radiology, Montefiore Hosp 1978; **Fellow:** Ultrasound/CT, Johns Hopkins Hosp 1979

Rossi, Dennis R MD (DR) - **Spec Exp:** MRI; **Address:** Elmont Open MRI, 545 Elmont Rd, Elmont, NY 11003; **Phone:** 516-328-7200; **Board Cert:** Diagnostic Radiology 1973; **Med School:** SUNY Downstate 1968; **Resid:** Diagnostic Radiology, Montefiore Hosp Med Ctr 1972; **Fac Appt:** Asst Prof Rad, SUNY Stony Brook

Sherman, Scott J MD (DR) - **Spec Exp:** CT Scan; PET Imaging; **Hospital:** St. Francis Hosp - The Heart Ctr (page 111), St. Joseph's Hosp-Nassau; **Address:** St Francis Hosp-The Heart Ctr, 100 Port Washington Blvd, Roslyn, NY 11576; **Phone:** 516-562-6500; **Board Cert:** Diagnostic Radiology 1983; Nuclear Medicine 1984; **Med School:** Northwestern Univ 1979; **Resid:** Diagnostic Radiology, NY Hosp 1983; Nuclear Medicine, NY Hosp 1984; **Fellow:** Ultrasound, NY Hosp 1985

Yoon, Sydney S MD (DR) - **Spec Exp:** MRI; CT Scan; Neuroradiology; Interventional Radiology; **Hospital:** South Nassau Comm Hosp; **Address:** South Nassau Comm Hosp, Dept Radiology, 1 Healthy Way, Oceanside, NY 11572; **Phone:** 516-632-4660; **Board Cert:** Internal Medicine 1989; Diagnostic Radiology 1993; Vascular & Interventional Radiology 2011; Neuroradiology 2006; **Med School:** Univ Chicago-Pritzker Sch Med 1986; **Resid:** Internal Medicine, Johns Hopkins Hosp 1989; Diagnostic Radiology, UCLA Ronald Reagan Med Ctr 1993; **Fellow:** Neuroradiology, NY-Presby/Columbia Univ Med Ctr 1995; Vascular & Interventional Radiology, UCLA Ronald Reagan Med Ctr 1997

Endocrinology, Diabetes & Metabolism

Bhatt, Anjani A MD (EDM) - **Spec Exp:** Thyroid Disorders; Diabetes; **Address:** 871 E Park Ave, Long Beach, NY 11561; **Phone:** 516-889-8853; **Board Cert:** Internal Medicine 1983; Endocrinology, Diabetes & Metabolism 1985; **Med School:** India 1976; **Resid:** Internal Medicine, Brooklyn Hosp 1981; **Fellow:** Endocrinology, Brooklyn Hosp 1984

Bitton, Rachelle N MD (EDM) - **Spec Exp:** Osteoporosis; Thyroid Disorders; Diabetes; Pituitary Disorders; **Hospital:** Long Is Jewish Med Ctr, N Shore Univ Hosp; **Address:** ProHealth Care Assocs, 2 Ohio Drive, Lake Success, NY 11042; **Phone:** 516-390-5760; **Board Cert:** Internal Medicine 1981; Endocrinology, Diabetes & Metabolism 1985; **Med School:** SUNY Downstate 1978; **Resid:** Internal Medicine, Brookdale Hosp 1981; **Fellow:** Endocrinology, Diabetes & Metabolism, Univ Hosp 1984

Friedman, Seth G MD (EDM) - **Spec Exp:** Thyroid Disorders; Pituitary Disorders; Diabetes; Osteoporosis; **Hospital:** NS-LIJ Hlth Sys; **Address:** 560 Northern Blvd, Ste 207, Great Neck, NY 11021; **Phone:** 516-466-6165; **Board Cert:** Endocrinology, Diabetes & Metabolism 2013; **Med School:** Mount Sinai Sch Med 1988; **Resid:** Internal Medicine, LI Jewish Med Ctr 1991; **Fellow:** Endocrinology, Diabetes & Metabolism, Albert Einstein Affil Hosp 1993

Gordon, Jeffrey H MD (EDM) - **Spec Exp:** Diabetes; Thyroid Disorders; Pituitary Disorders; **Hospital:** St. Francis Hosp - The Heart Ctr (page 111), N Shore Univ Hosp; **Address:** 3 School St, Ste 306, Glen Cove, NY 11542-2548; **Phone:** 516-759-2420; **Board Cert:** Internal Medicine 1972; Endocrinology, Diabetes & Metabolism 1973; **Med School:** Cornell Univ-Weill Med Coll 1965; **Resid:** Internal Medicine, Bellevue Hosp 1967; **Fellow:** Endocrinology, Duke Univ Med Ctr 1970; Endocrinology, VA Hosp 1972; **Fac Appt:** Asst Clin Prof Med, NYU Sch Med

Greenfield, Martin MD (EDM) - **Spec Exp:** Diabetes; Thyroid Disorders; Osteoporosis; Adrenal Disorders; **Hospital:** Long Is Jewish Med Ctr, N Shore Univ Hosp; **Address:** ProHealth Care Assocs, 2 Ohio Drive, Lake Success, NY 11042; **Phone:** 516-608-6823; **Board Cert:** Internal Medicine 1987; Endocrinology, Diabetes & Metabolism 1979; **Med School:** SUNY Downstate 1968; **Resid:** Internal Medicine, LI Jewish Med Ctr 1971; **Fellow:** Endocrinology, Diabetes & Metabolism, Brigham & Womens Hosp 1975

Hupart, Kenneth H MD (EDM) - **Spec Exp:** Thyroid Disorders; Osteoporosis; Diabetes; Cholesterol/Lipid Disorders; **Hospital:** Nassau Univ Med Ctr; **Address:** Nassau Univ Med Ctr, Div Endocrinology, 2201 Heampstead Tpke, East Meadow, NY 11554; **Phone:** 516-572-4848; **Board Cert:** Internal Medicine 1985; Endocrinology 1989; **Med School:** SUNY Stony Brook 1982; **Resid:** Internal Medicine, Montefiore Hosp Med Ctr 1986; **Fellow:** Endocrinology, Diabetes & Metabolism, Montefiore Hosp Med Ctr 1988; **Fac Appt:** Assoc Clin Prof Med, Albert Einstein Coll Med

Kaplan, Jonathan MD (EDM) - **Spec Exp:** Diabetes; **Hospital:** N Shore Univ Hosp; **Address:** 1000 Northern Blvd, Ste 240, Great Neck, NY 11021; **Phone:** 516-829-0802; **Board Cert:** Internal Medicine 2006; Endocrinology, Diabetes & Metabolism 2008; **Med School:** Israel 1990; **Resid:** Internal Medicine, Rambam Med Ctr 1994; Internal Medicine, N Shore Univ Hosp 1996; **Fellow:** Endocrinology, Diabetes & Metabolism, Albert Einstein Affil Hosp 1998

Lomasky, Steven MD (EDM) - **Spec Exp:** Diabetes; Cholesterol/Lipid Disorders; Thyroid Disorders; **Hospital:** South Nassau Comm Hosp; **Address:** 242 Merrick Rd, rm 403, Rockville Ctr, NY 11570; **Phone:** 516-536-3700; **Board Cert:** Endocrinology, Diabetes & Metabolism 1989; Internal Medicine 1985; **Med School:** Israel 1982; **Resid:** Internal Medicine, Montefiore Med Ctr 1986; **Fellow:** Endocrinology, Diabetes & Metabolism, Montefiore Med Ctr 1987; **Fac Appt:** Asst Clin Prof Med, Albert Einstein Coll Med

Margulies, Paul MD (EDM) - **Spec Exp:** Thyroid Disorders; Adrenal Disorders; Pituitary Disorders; Addison's Disease; **Hospital:** N Shore Univ Hosp; **Address:** 444 Community Drive, Ste 312, Manhasset, NY 11030-3820; **Phone:** 516-627-1366; **Board Cert:** Internal Medicine 1975; Endocrinology, Diabetes & Metabolism 1977; **Med School:** Univ Chicago-Pritzker Sch Med 1970; **Resid:** Internal Medicine, New YorkHosp/Cornell 1974; Endocrinology, Diabetes & Metabolism, New York Hosp/Cornell 1975; **Fellow:** Endocrinology, Diabetes & Metabolism, New York Hosp/Cornell 1976; **Fac Appt:** Assoc Prof Med, NYU Sch Med

Rosenthal, David S MD (EDM) - **Spec Exp:** Thyroid Disorders; Pituitary Disorders; Adrenal Disorders; Osteoporosis; **Hospital:** Nassau Univ Med Ctr; **Address:** Nassau Univ Med Ctr, Div Endocrinology, 2201 Hempstead Tpke, Box 49, East Meadow, NY 11554; **Phone:** 516-572-4848; **Board Cert:** Internal Medicine 1969; Endocrinology, Diabetes & Metabolism 1972; **Med School:** NYU Sch Med 1963; **Resid:** Internal Medicine, Wilford Hall USAF Med Ctr 1967; **Fellow:** Endocrinology, Diabetes & Metabolism, Boston Univ Med Ctr 1972; Nuclear Medicine, Boston Univ Med Ctr 1972; **Fac Appt:** Asst Prof Med, SUNY Stony Brook

Shapiro, Lawrence E MD (EDM) - **Spec Exp:** Thyroid Disorders; Diabetes; **Hospital:** Winthrop Univ Hosp (page 536); **Address:** 1300 Franklin Ave, Ste ML6, Garden City, NY 11530; **Phone:** 516-663-3511; **Board Cert:** Internal Medicine 1975; Endocrinology 1977; **Med School:** SUNY Downstate 1971; **Resid:** Internal Medicine, Bellevue Hosp 1974; **Fellow:** Endocrinology, Diabetes & Metabolism, NYU Med Ctr 1975; **Fac Appt:** Prof Med, SUNY Stony Brook

Family Medicine

Arcati, Anthony T MD (FMed) *PCP* - **Hospital:** Winthrop Univ Hosp (page 536); **Address:** 530 Hicksville Rd, Bethpage, NY 11714; **Phone:** 516-937-5000; **Med School:** Mexico 1975; **Resid:** Family Medicine, Nassau Co Med Ctr 1979

Arcati, Robert J MD (FMed) *PCP* - **Hospital:** Winthrop Univ Hosp (page 536); **Address:** 530 Hicksville Rd, Bethpage, NY 11714; **Phone:** 516-937-5000; **Board Cert:** Family Medicine 2008; **Med School:** Mount Sinai Sch Med 1986; **Resid:** Family Medicine, Somerset Med Ctr 1989

Capobianco, Luigi MD (FMed) *PCP* - **Spec Exp:** Geriatric Care; **Hospital:** Glen Cove Hosp; **Address:** One School St, Ste 203, Glen Cove, NY 11542; **Phone:** 516-671-9800; **Board Cert:** Family Medicine 2007; Geriatric Medicine 2008; **Med School:** Italy 1984; **Resid:** Family Medicine, N Shore Univ Hosp 1988

Edelstein, Martin P MD (FMed) *PCP* - **Spec Exp:** Preventive Medicine; **Hospital:** N Shore Univ Hosp; **Address:** 11 Beverly Rd, Great Neck, NY 11021; **Phone:** 516-487-1614; **Board Cert:** Family Medicine 2008; **Med School:** McGill Univ 1971; **Resid:** Family Medicine, Jewish Genl Hosp 1973; **Fac Appt:** Asst Clin Prof FMed, Albert Einstein Coll Med

Moynihan, Brian T DO (FMed) *PCP* - **Spec Exp:** Hypertension; Diabetes; Skin Diseases; **Hospital:** St. Joseph's Hosp-Nassau, N Shore Univ Hosp; **Address:** East Meadow Family Practice, 2840 Jerusalem Ave, Wantagh, NY 11793-2017; **Phone:** 516-781-1141; **Board Cert:** Family Medicine ; **Med School:** NY Coll Osteo Med 1983; **Resid:** Family Medicine, Kennedy Meml Hosp 1986; **Fac Appt:** Asst Prof FMed, NY Coll Osteo Med

Rechter, Lesley MD (FMed) *PCP* - **Hospital:** Stony Brook Univ Hosp; **Address:** 54 Birchwood Park Drive, Jericho, NY 11753; **Phone:** 516-933-6850; **Med School:** NY Med Coll 1976; **Resid:** Family Medicine, Nassau County Med Ctr 1979; **Fac Appt:** Assoc Clin Prof FMed, SUNY Stony Brook

Soskel, Neil DO (FMed) *PCP* - **Spec Exp:** Primary Care Sports Medicine; **Hospital:** South Nassau Comm Hosp; **Address:** 185 Merrick Rd, Ste 1B, Lynbrook, NY 11563; **Phone:** 516-887-0077; **Board Cert:** Family Medicine 2008; **Med School:** NY Coll Osteo Med 1986; **Resid:** Family Medicine, S Nassau Comm Hosp 1989; **Fac Appt:** Assoc Clin Prof FMed, Hofstra N Shore-LIJ Sch Med

Gastroenterology

Bartolomeo, Robert S MD (Ge) - **Spec Exp:** Colonoscopy; Inflammatory Bowel Disease; Gastroesophageal Reflux Disease (GERD); Colon Cancer Screening; **Hospital:** Winthrop Univ Hosp (page 536); **Address:** Gastroenterology Assocs, 1103 Stewart Ave, Ste 300, Garden City, NY 11530; **Phone:** 516-248-3737; **Board Cert:** Internal Medicine 1974; Gastroenterology 1977; **Med School:** NY Med Coll 1971; **Resid:** Internal Medicine, Metropolitan Hosp Ctr 1973; Internal Medicine, Beth Israel Hosp 1974; **Fellow:** Gastroenterology, Bridgeport Hosp 1977

Bernstein, David E MD (Ge) - **Spec Exp:** Liver Disease; Hepatitis; **Hospital:** N Shore Univ Hosp; **Address:** North Shore Univ Hosp, Div Gastroenterology, 300 Community Drive, Manhasset, NY 11030-3816; **Phone:** 516-562-4281; **Board Cert:** Internal Medicine 2011; Gastroenterology 2013; **Med School:** SUNY Stony Brook 1988; **Resid:** Internal Medicine, Montefiore Med Ctr 1991; **Fellow:** Gastroenterology, Jackson Meml Hosp 1993

Blumstein, Meyer MD (Ge) - **Spec Exp:** Endoscopy; Gastroesophageal Reflux Disease (GERD); Inflammatory Bowel Disease; Colon & Rectal Cancer Detection; **Hospital:** Long Is Jewish Med Ctr, South Nassau Comm Hosp; **Address:** 158 Hempstead Ave, Lynbrook, NY 11563-1605; **Phone:** 516-593-3541; **Board Cert:** Internal Medicine 1989; **Med School:** SUNY Hlth Sci Ctr 1986; **Resid:** Internal Medicine, LI Jewish Med Ctr 1989; **Fellow:** Gastroenterology, LI Jewish Med Ctr 1991; **Fac Appt:** Asst Prof Med, Hofstra N Shore-LIJ Sch Med

Caccese, William J MD (Ge) - **Spec Exp:** Endoscopy; Colon Cancer; **Hospital:** Plainview Hosp; **Address:** 700 Old Country Rd, Ste 104, Plainview, NY 11803-4932; **Phone:** 516-681-1200; **Board Cert:** Internal Medicine 1981; Gastroenterology 1983; **Med School:** SUNY Hlth Sci Ctr 1978; **Resid:** Internal Medicine, N Shore Univ Hosp 1981; **Fellow:** Gastroenterology, N Shore Univ Hosp 1983

Cerulli, Maurice A MD (Ge) - **Spec Exp:** Inflammatory Bowel Disease; Gastroesophageal Reflux Disease (GERD); Colon Cancer Screening; Hepatitis B & C; **Hospital:** Long Is Jewish Med Ctr, N Shore Univ Hosp; **Address:** 410 Lakeville Rd, Ste 107, New Hyde Park, NY 11040; **Phone:** 718-470-7281; **Board Cert:** Internal Medicine 1975; Gastroenterology 1977; **Med School:** SUNY Hlth Sci Ctr 1972; **Resid:** Internal Medicine, Kings County Hosp 1975; **Fellow:** Gastroenterology, Johns Hopkins Hosp 1977; **Fac Appt:** Assoc Prof Med, Hofstra N Shore-LIJ Sch Med

DeVito, Bethany S MD (Ge) - **Spec Exp:** Women's Health; Capsule Endoscopy; **Hospital:** N Shore Univ Hosp, Long Is Jewish Med Ctr; **Address:** North Shore Univ Hosp, Div Gastroenterology, 300 Community Drive, Manhasset, NY 11030; **Phone:** 516-562-4281; **Board Cert:** Gastroenterology 2007; **Med School:** SUNY Upstate Med Univ 1992; **Resid:** Internal Medicine, St Vincents Hosp 1995; **Fellow:** Gastroenterology, NY Hosp 1997

Eskreis, David S MD (Ge) - **Spec Exp:** Ulcerative Colitis/Crohn's; Endoscopy & Colonoscopy; **Hospital:** N Shore Univ Hosp, Long Is Jewish Med Ctr; **Address:** 2001 Marcus Ave, Ste W85, Lake Success, NY 11042; **Phone:** 516-326-2700; **Board Cert:** Internal Medicine 1986; Gastroenterology 1987; **Med School:** Geo Wash Univ 1982; **Resid:** Internal Medicine, Bronx Muni Hosp Ctr 1985; **Fellow:** Gastroenterology, Montefiore Med Ctr 1987

Farber, Charles S MD (Ge) - **Spec Exp:** Colon Cancer; Gastroesophageal Reflux Disease (GERD); **Hospital:** Plainview Hosp; **Address:** Plainview Manetto Gastro, 146 A Manetto Hill Rd, Ste 205, Plainview, NY 11803; **Phone:** 516-822-4404; **Board Cert:** Internal Medicine 1981; Gastroenterology 1983; **Med School:** SUNY Hlth Sci Ctr 1978; **Resid:** Internal Medicine, N Shore Univ Hosp 1981; **Fellow:** Gastroenterology, Jacobi Med Ctr 1983

Goldblum, Lester F DO (Ge) - **Spec Exp:** Endoscopy; Colon Cancer; Capsule Endoscopy; **Hospital:** Plainview Hosp; **Address:** Massapequa Gastroenterology Assocs, 850 Hicksville Rd, Ste 100, Seaford, NY 11783; **Phone:** 516-796-9000; **Board Cert:** Internal Medicine 1983; **Med School:** Univ Osteo Med & Hlth Sci, Des Moines 1979; **Resid:** Internal Medicine, Nassau Univ Med Ctr 1983; **Fellow:** Gastroenterology, Nassau Univ Med Ctr 1985

Gould, Perry C MD (Ge) - **Spec Exp:** Ulcerative Colitis; Colon & Rectal Cancer; Gastroesophageal Reflux Disease (GERD); Capsule Endoscopy; **Hospital:** Winthrop Univ Hosp (page 536); **Address:** Gastroenterology Assocs, 1103 Stewart Ave, Ste 300, Garden City, NY 11530; **Phone:** 516-248-3737; **Board Cert:** Internal Medicine 1980; Gastroenterology 1983; **Med School:** NY Med Coll 1977; **Resid:** Internal Medicine, LI Jewish Hosp 1980; **Fellow:** Gastroenterology, NY Med Coll Affil Hosp 1983; **Fac Appt:** Asst Clin Prof Med, SUNY Stony Brook

Greenberg, Ronald MD (Ge) - **Spec Exp:** Inflammatory Bowel Disease; Peptic Acid Disorders; **Hospital:** Long Is Jewish Med Ctr, N Shore Univ Hosp; **Address:** 410 Lakeville Rd, Ste 107, New Hyde Park, NY 11040; **Phone:** 718-470-7281; **Board Cert:** Internal Medicine 1982; Gastroenterology 1985; **Med School:** Hahnemann Univ 1979; **Resid:** Internal Medicine, Albany Med Ctr 1982; **Fellow:** Gastroenterology, St Lukes-Roosevelt Hosp Ctr 1985

Grendell, James H MD (Ge) - **Spec Exp:** Pancreatic Disease; Nutrition; Liver Disease; **Hospital:** Winthrop Univ Hosp (page 536); **Address:** Winthrop Gastroenterology, 222 Station Plaza N, Ste 428, Mineola, NY 11501-3819; **Phone:** 516-663-2066; **Board Cert:** Internal Medicine 1978; Gastroenterology 1981; **Med School:** Ohio State Univ 1975; **Resid:** Internal Medicine, Beth Israel Hosp 1978; **Fellow:** Gastroenterology, UCSF Med Ctr 1981; **Fac Appt:** Prof Med, SUNY Stony Brook

Katz, Seymour MD (Ge) - **Spec Exp:** Inflammatory Bowel Disease; Colonoscopy; Endoscopy; **Hospital:** N Shore Univ Hosp, Long Is Jewish Med Ctr; **Address:** Nassau Gastroenterology Assocs, 1000 Northern Blvd, Ste 140, Great Neck, NY 11021; **Phone:** 516-466-2340; **Board Cert:** Internal Medicine 1971; Gastroenterology 1972; **Med School:** NYU Sch Med 1964; **Resid:** Internal Medicine, Albert Einstein Sch Med Affil Hosp 1966; Internal Medicine, Bronx Muni Hosp 1969; **Fellow:** Gastroenterology, Cornell Med Ctr 1971; **Fac Appt:** Clin Prof Med, NYU Sch Med

McKinley, Matthew John MD (Ge) - **Spec Exp:** Gastroesophageal Reflux Disease (GERD); Barrett's Esophagus; Biliary Disease; **Hospital:** N Shore Univ Hosp, Glen Cove Hosp; **Address:** ProHealth Care Assocs, 2800 Marcus Ave, Ste 201, Lake Success, NY 11042; **Phone:** 516-622-6076; **Board Cert:** Internal Medicine 1978; Gastroenterology 1981; **Med School:** Creighton Univ 1975; **Resid:** Internal Medicine, N Shore Univ Hosp 1978; Internal Medicine, Meml Sloan-Kettering Cancer Ctr 1978; **Fellow:** Gastroenterology, Hosp St Raphael 1980; **Fac Appt:** Assoc Prof Med, NYU Sch Med

Miller, Larry S MD (Ge) - **Spec Exp:** Endoscopy; Endoscopic Therapies; **Hospital:** Long Is Jewish Med Ctr; **Address:** LIJ Med Ctr, Gastroenterology, 270-05 76th Ave, New Hyde Park, NY 11040; **Phone:** 516-562-4281; **Board Cert:** Internal Medicine 1984; Gastroenterology 1989; **Med School:** Ros Franklin Univ/Chicago Med Sch 1981; **Resid:** Internal Medicine, Univ Chicago Hosps 1984; **Fellow:** Gastroenterology, Georgetown Univ Hosp 1986; Endoscopy, Wellesley Hosp 1987; **Fac Appt:** Prof Med, Hofstra N Shore-LIJ Sch Med

Miller, Seth L MD (Ge) - **Spec Exp:** Endoscopy & Colonoscopy; Gastrointestinal Disorders; **Hospital:** South Nassau Comm Hosp; **Address:** 206 West Park Ave, Long Beach, NY 11561; **Phone:** 516-432-8021; **Board Cert:** Internal Medicine 1983; Gastroenterology 1987; **Med School:** Mount Sinai Sch Med 1980; **Resid:** Internal Medicine, Beth Israel Med Ctr 1983; **Fellow:** Gastroenterology, Beth Israel Med Ctr 1985

Milman, Perry J MD (Ge) - **Spec Exp:** Gastroesophageal Reflux Disease (GERD); Colon Cancer; Inflammatory Bowel Disease; Endoscopy; **Hospital:** Long Is Jewish Med Ctr, N Shore Univ Hosp; **Address:** 2001 Marcus Ave, Ste N18, Lake Success, NY 11042-1011; **Phone:** 516-775-7770; **Board Cert:** Internal Medicine 1976; Gastroenterology 1979; **Med School:** SUNY Downstate 1973; **Resid:** Internal Medicine, LI Jewish Med Ctr 1976; **Fellow:** Gastroenterology, VA Hosp/NYU 1978; **Fac Appt:** Asst Clin Prof Med, Albert Einstein Coll Med

Schwartz, Gary J MD (Ge) - **Spec Exp:** Colon Cancer Screening; Gastroesophageal Reflux Disease (GERD); **Hospital:** Winthrop Univ Hosp (page 536); **Address:** Gastroenterology Assocs, 1103 Stewart Ave, Ste 300, Garden City, NY 11530; **Phone:** 516-248-3737; **Board Cert:** Internal Medicine 1985; Gastroenterology 1987; **Med School:** Mexico 1979; **Resid:** Internal Medicine, Winthrop Univ Hosp 1983; **Fellow:** Gastroenterology, Univ Hosp/SUNY Hlth Sci Ctr 1986

Talansky, Arthur L MD (Ge) - **Spec Exp:** Crohn's Disease; Ulcerative Colitis; Colonoscopy; **Hospital:** N Shore Univ Hosp, St. Francis Hosp - The Heart Ctr (page 111); **Address:** North Shore Gastroenterology Assocs, 233 E Shore Rd, Ste 101, Great Neck, NY 11023-2433; **Phone:** 516-487-2444; **Board Cert:** Internal Medicine 1980; Gastroenterology 1983; **Med School:** Mount Sinai Sch Med 1977; **Resid:** Internal Medicine, Meml Sloan-Kettering Cancer Ctr 1980; **Fellow:** Gastroenterology, Mount Sinai Hosp 1982; **Fac Appt:** Assoc Clin Prof Med, Hofstra N Shore-LIJ Sch Med

Weissman, Gary S MD (Ge) - **Spec Exp:** Gastrointestinal Cancer; Inflammatory Bowel Disease; Esophageal Disorders; Irritable Bowel Syndrome; **Hospital:** N Shore Univ Hosp, Long Is Jewish Med Ctr; **Address:** ProHealth Care Assocs, 2800 Marcus Ave, Ste 201, Lake Success, NY 11042; **Phone:** 516-622-6076; **Board Cert:** Internal Medicine 1980; Gastroenterology 1983; **Med School:** NY Med Coll 1976; **Resid:** Internal Medicine, N Shore Univ Hosp 1980; **Fellow:** Gastroenterology, Meml Sloan-Kettering Cancer Ctr 1982

Geriatric Medicine

Gomolin, Irving H MD (Ger) - **Spec Exp:** Medications in the Elderly; Dementia; Polypharmacology (Excess Medications); **Hospital:** Winthrop Univ Hosp (page 536); **Address:** Winthrop Geriatric Med Assocs, 222 Station Plaza N, Fl 5th, Ste 518, Mineola, NY 11501-3893; **Phone:** 516-663-2588; **Board Cert:** Internal Medicine 1979; Geriatric Medicine 2008; **Med School:** McGill Univ 1976; **Resid:** Internal Medicine, Jewish Genl Hosp 1978; Internal Medicine, Beth Israel Hosp 1981; **Fellow:** Clinical Pharmacology, Harvard Med Sch Affil Hosp 1980; **Fac Appt:** Clin Prof Med, SUNY Stony Brook

Guzik, Howard J MD (Ger) *PCP* - **Spec Exp:** Palliative Care; Geriatric Care; Preventive Medicine; **Hospital:** N Shore Univ Hosp, Long Is Jewish Med Ctr; **Address:** 865 Northern Blvd, Ste 201, Great Neck, NY 11021; **Phone:** 516-708-2520; **Board Cert:** Internal Medicine 1984; Geriatric Medicine 2008; Hospice & Palliative Medicine 2010; **Med School:** Albert Einstein Coll Med 1981; **Resid:** Internal Medicine, Montefiore Med Ctr 1984; **Fellow:** Geriatric Medicine, Montefiore Med Ctr 1986

Lanman, Geraldine M MD (Ger) *PCP* - **Spec Exp:** Geriatric Care; Preventive Medicine; **Hospital:** Long Is Jewish Med Ctr; **Address:** 1 Delaware Drive, Ste 48, New Hyde Park, NY 11042; **Phone:** 516-326-5320; **Board Cert:** Internal Medicine 1983; **Med School:** Univ Calgary 1980; **Resid:** Internal Medicine, LIJ Med Ctr 1983; **Fellow:** Geriatric Medicine, Parker Jewish Inst for Hlthcare & Rehab 1985; **Fac Appt:** Asst Clin Prof Med, Albert Einstein Coll Med

Macina, Lucy O MD (Ger) *PCP* - **Spec Exp:** Frail Elderly; Dementia; Geriatric Care; **Hospital:** Winthrop Univ Hosp (page 536); **Address:** Winthrop Geriatric Med Assocs, 222 Station Plaza N Fl 5 - Ste 518, Mineola, NY 11501-3893; **Phone:** 516-663-2588; **Board Cert:** Internal Medicine 1982; Geriatric Medicine 2012; **Med School:** Loyola Univ-Stritch Sch Med 1978; **Resid:** Internal Medicine, VA Hosp 1980; Internal Medicine, Loyola Univ Med Ctr 1982; **Fellow:** Geriatric Medicine, Roger Williams Hosp 1985; **Fac Appt:** Asst Clin Prof Med, SUNY Stony Brook

Wolf-Klein, Gisele P MD (Ger) *PCP* - **Spec Exp:** Dementia; Falls in the Elderly; Alzheimer's Disease; **Hospital:** Long Is Jewish Med Ctr; **Address:** 865 Northern Blvd, Ste 201, Great Neck, NY 11021; **Phone:** 516-708-2520; **Board Cert:** Internal Medicine 1984; Geriatric Medicine 2012; **Med School:** Switzerland 1975; **Resid:** Internal Medicine, LIJ Med Ctr 1978; **Fellow:** Geriatric Medicine, Parker Jewish Inst 1979; **Fac Appt:** Clin Prof Med, Albert Einstein Coll Med

Gynecologic Oncology

Chalas, Eva MD (GO) - **Spec Exp:** Gynecologic Cancer; Minimally Invasive Surgery; **Hospital:** Winthrop Univ Hosp (page 536); **Address:** Winthrop LI Gyn Onc Assocs, 200 Old Country Rd, Ste 365, Mineola, NY 11501; **Phone:** 516-294-5440; **Board Cert:** Obstetrics & Gynecology 2013; Gynecologic Oncology 2013; **Med School:** SUNY Stony Brook 1981; **Resid:** Obstetrics & Gynecology, Univ Hosp 1985; **Fellow:** Gynecologic Oncology, Meml Sloan Kettering Canc Ctr 1987; **Fac Appt:** Prof ObG, SUNY Stony Brook

Lovecchio, John L MD (GO) - **Spec Exp:** Ovarian Cancer; Uterine Cancer; Cervical Cancer; Vulvar Disease/Cancer; **Hospital:** N Shore Univ Hosp, Long Is Jewish Med Ctr; **Address:** North Shore Univ Hosp-Div Gyn Onc, 300 Community Drive, Monti Pavilion, Fl 10, Manhasset, NY 11030-3816; **Phone:** 516-562-4438; **Board Cert:** Obstetrics & Gynecology 2005; Gynecologic Oncology 2005; **Med School:** SUNY Buffalo 1975; **Resid:** Obstetrics & Gynecology, Case Western Reserve Univ Hosp 1979; **Fellow:** Gynecologic Oncology, Jackson Meml Hosp 1982; **Fac Appt:** Prof ObG, Hofstra N Shore-LIJ Sch Med

Menzin, Andrew W MD (GO) - **Spec Exp:** Uterine Cancer; Ovarian Cancer; Robotic Surgery; **Hospital:** N Shore Univ Hosp, Long Is Jewish Med Ctr; **Address:** N Shore Univ Hosp-Div Gyn Onc, 300 Community Drive,, Monti Pavilion, Fl 10, Manhasset, NY 11030-3816; **Phone:** 516-562-4438; **Board Cert:** Obstetrics & Gynecology 2013; Gynecologic Oncology 2013; **Med School:** NYU Sch Med 1989; **Resid:** Obstetrics & Gynecology, Hosp Univ Penn 1993; **Fellow:** Gynecologic Oncology, Hosp Univ Penn 1995; **Fac Appt:** Prof ObG, Hofstra N Shore-LIJ Sch Med

Hand Surgery

Gluck, Robert I MD (HS) - **Spec Exp:** Hand & Upper Extremity Surgery; Dupuytren's Contracture; Carpal Tunnel Syndrome; Arthritis Hand Surgery; **Hospital:** Long Is Jewish Med Ctr; **Address:** Healthy Hands Ctr, 410 Lakeville Rd, Ste 303, New Hyde Park, NY 11042; **Phone:** 516-280-5844; **Board Cert:** Hand Surgery 2012; **Med School:** Albert Einstein Coll Med 1982; **Resid:** Surgery, Long Is Jewish Hosp 1987; **Fellow:** Hand & Microvascular Surgery, Stony Brook Univ Med Ctr 1989; **Fac Appt:** Asst Clin Prof S, Albert Einstein Coll Med

Lane, Lewis B MD (HS) - **Spec Exp:** Carpal Tunnel Syndrome; Arthritis; Sports Injuries; Hand Reconstruction; **Hospital:** N Shore Univ Hosp; **Address:** Univ Orthopaedics, 611 Northern Blvd, Ste 200, Great Neck, NY 11021; **Phone:** 516-723-2663; **Board Cert:** Orthopaedic Surgery 1981; Hand Surgery 2010; **Med School:** Columbia P&S 1974; **Resid:** Orthopaedic Surgery, Hosp Special Surgery 1979; **Fellow:** Research, Hosp Special Surgery 1976; Hand Surgery, St Lukes-Roosevelt Hosp Ctr 1980; **Fac Appt:** Prof OrS, Hofstra N Shore-LIJ Sch Med

Stein, Peter D MD (HS) - **Spec Exp:** Hand & Wrist Surgery; Carpal Tunnel Syndrome; Fractures-Complex; Dupuytren's Contracture; **Hospital:** N Shore Univ Hosp, St. Francis Hosp - The Heart Ctr (page 111); **Address:** Orthopaedic Assocs of Manhasset, 600 Northern Blvd, Ste 300, Great Neck, NY 11021; **Phone:** 516-627-8717; **Board Cert:** Orthopaedic Surgery 2007; Hand Surgery 2007; **Med School:** Cornell Univ-Weill Med Coll 1987; **Resid:** Orthopaedic Surgery, St Lukes-Roosevelt Med Ctr 1992; **Fellow:** Hand Surgery, NYU Langone Med Ctr 1993; **Fac Appt:** Asst Clin Prof OrS, Hofstra N Shore-LIJ Sch Med

Teplitz, Glenn A MD (HS) - **Spec Exp:** Carpal Tunnel Syndrome; Fractures; Sports Injuries; Wrist/Hand Injuries; **Hospital:** Winthrop Univ Hosp (page 536); **Address:** Winthrop Orthopaedic Assocs, 1300 Franklin Ave, Ste UL-3A, Garden City, NY 11530; **Phone:** 516-747-8900; **Board Cert:** Orthopaedic Surgery 2007; **Med School:** Tulane Univ 1987; **Resid:** Orthopaedic Surgery, UMDNJ Med Ctr 1993; **Fellow:** Hand Surgery, Hosp for Special Surg 1994; **Fac Appt:** Asst Clin Prof OrS, SUNY Stony Brook

Tuckman, David V MD (HS) - **Spec Exp:** Carpal Tunnel Syndrome; **Hospital:** Long Is Jewish Med Ctr, St. Francis Hosp - The Heart Ctr (page 111); **Address:** Orthopedic Assocs-Manhasset, 600 Northern Blvd, Ste 300, Great Neck, NY 11021; **Phone:** 516-627-8717; **Board Cert:** Orthopaedic Surgery 2007; Hand Surgery 2009; **Med School:** Albert Einstein Coll Med 1998; **Resid:** Orthopaedic Surgery, Long Is Jewish Med Ctr 2003; **Fellow:** Sports Medicine & Hand Surgery, NYU Hosp For Joint Dis 2004; Hand Surgery, NYU Hosp For Joint Dis 2005; **Fac Appt:** Asst Clin Prof OrS, Hofstra N Shore-LIJ Sch Med

Hematology

Allen, Steven L MD (Hem) - **Spec Exp:** Bleeding/Coagulation Disorders; Leukemia & Lymphoma; Multiple Myeloma; Gaucher Disease; **Hospital:** N Shore Univ Hosp, Long Is Jewish Med Ctr; **Address:** Monter Canc Ctr, 450 Lakeville Rd, Lake Success, NY 11042; **Phone:** 516-734-8970; **Board Cert:** Internal Medicine 1980; Hematology 1982; Medical Oncology 1983; **Med School:** Johns Hopkins Univ 1977; **Resid:** Internal Medicine, NY-Presby/Weill Cornell Med Ctr 1980; **Fellow:** Hematology & Oncology, NY-Presby/Weill Cornell Med Ctr 1983; **Fac Appt:** Prof Hem & Onc, Hofstra N Shore-LIJ Sch Med

Kolitz, Jonathan E MD (Hem) - **Spec Exp:** Leukemia & Lymphoma; Hodgkin's Lymphoma; Multiple Myeloma; Myelodysplastic Syndromes; **Hospital:** N Shore Univ Hosp, Long Is Jewish Med Ctr; **Address:** Monter Cancer Ctr, 450 Lakeville Rd, Lake Success, NY 11042; **Phone:** 516-734-8970; **Board Cert:** Internal Medicine 1982; Medical Oncology 1985; Hematology 1988; **Med School:** Yale Univ 1979; **Resid:** Internal Medicine, N Shore Univ Hosp 1982; **Fellow:** Hematology & Oncology, Meml Sloan-Kettering Canc Ctr 1985; **Fac Appt:** Prof Hem, Hofstra N Shore-LIJ Sch Med

Rai, Kanti R MD (Hem) - **Spec Exp:** Leukemia; Lymphoma; **Hospital:** Long Is Jewish Med Ctr; **Address:** LIJ Med Ctr, Hem/Onc, 410 Lakeville Rd, Ste 212, New Hyde Park, NY 10042; **Phone:** 718-470-4050; **Board Cert:** Pediatrics 1959; **Med School:** India 1955; **Resid:** Pediatrics, Lincoln Hosp 1958; Pediatrics, North Shore Univ Hosp 1959; **Fellow:** Hematology, LI Jewish Med Ctr 1960; **Fac Appt:** Prof Onc, Hofstra N Shore-LIJ Sch Med

Staszewski, Harry MD (Hem) - **Spec Exp:** Hematologic Malignancies; Clinical Trials; **Hospital:** Winthrop Univ Hosp (page 536); **Address:** Winthrop Hematology Oncology Assocs, 200 Old Country Rd, Ste 450, Mineola, NY 11501; **Phone:** 516-663-9500; **Board Cert:** Internal Medicine 1981; Medical Oncology 1983; Hematology 1984; **Med School:** Yale Univ 1978; **Resid:** Internal Medicine, N Shore Univ Hosp 1981; **Fellow:** Medical Oncology, Meml Sloan Kettering Canc Ctr 1983; Hematology, LI Jewish Hosp 1984; **Fac Appt:** Assoc Clin Prof Med, SUNY Stony Brook

Infectious Disease

Cervia, Joseph S MD (Inf) - **Spec Exp:** AIDS/HIV; Travel Medicine; Pediatric Infections; Immune Deficiency; **Hospital:** N Shore Univ Hosp, Steven & Alexandra Cohen Chldn's Med Ctr of NY; **Address:** N Shore Univ Hosp-Div Infect Dis, 400 Community Drive, Manhasset, NY 11030; **Phone:** 516-562-4280; **Board Cert:** Internal Medicine 1989; Pediatrics 2010; Infectious Disease 2010; Pediatric Infectious Disease 2008; **Med School:** NY Med Coll 1984; **Resid:** Internal Medicine & Pediatrics, Brookdale Univ Hosp Med Ctr 1988; **Fellow:** Infectious Disease, NY-Presby/Weill Cornell Med Ctr 1990; **Fac Appt:** Clin Prof Med, Hofstra N Shore-LIJ Sch Med

Cunha, Burke A MD (Inf) - **Spec Exp:** Infections in Immunocompromised Patients; Pneumonia; Fevers of Unknown Origin; Chronic Fatigue Syndrome; **Hospital:** Winthrop Univ Hosp (page 536); **Address:** Winthrop Univ Hosp-Div Infect Dis, 222 Station Plaza N, Ste 432, Mineola, NY 11501; **Phone:** 516-663-2507; **Board Cert:** Internal Medicine 1977; Infectious Disease 1978; **Med School:** Penn State Coll Med 1972; **Resid:** Internal Medicine, Hartford Hosp 1975; **Fellow:** Infectious Disease, Hartford Hosp 1977; **Fac Appt:** Prof Med, SUNY Stony Brook

Epstein, Marcia E MD (Inf) - **Spec Exp:** Infections in Immunocompromised Patients; Antibiotic Resistance; **Hospital:** N Shore Univ Hosp; **Address:** N Shore Univ Hosp-Div Infect Dis, 400 Community Drive, Manhasset, NY 11030; **Phone:** 516-562-4280; **Board Cert:** Internal Medicine 1987; Infectious Disease 2012; **Med School:** Harvard Med Sch 1983; **Resid:** Internal Medicine, Montefiore Med Ctr-Moses Campus 1986; **Fellow:** Infectious Disease, Montefiore Med Ctr-Moses Campus 1990

Farber, Bruce F MD (Inf) - **Spec Exp:** Lyme Disease; Malaria; **Hospital:** N Shore Univ Hosp, Long Is Jewish Med Ctr; **Address:** N Shore Univ Hosp-Div Infect Dis, 400 Community Drive, Manhasset, NY 11030; **Phone:** 516-562-4280; **Board Cert:** Internal Medicine 1979; Infectious Disease 1984; **Med School:** Northwestern Univ 1976; **Resid:** Internal Medicine, Univ Virginia Hlth Sys 1979; **Fellow:** Infectious Disease, Mass Genl Hosp 1982; **Fac Appt:** Assoc Prof Med, NYU Sch Med

Hirsch, Bruce E MD (Inf) - **Spec Exp:** Infectious Disease in Elderly; **Hospital:** N Shore Univ Hosp, Long Is Jewish Med Ctr; **Address:** N Shore Univ Hosp-Div Infect Dis, 400 Community Drive, Manhasset, NY 11030; **Phone:** 516-562-4280; **Board Cert:** Internal Medicine 1986; Geriatric Medicine 2007; Infectious Disease 2004; **Med School:** Cornell Univ-Weill Med Coll 1982; **Resid:** Internal Medicine, N Shore Univ Hosp 1986; Geriatric Medicine, NY-Presby/Weill Cornell Med Ctr 1988; **Fellow:** Infectious Disease, Jacobi Med Ctr 1989; Infectious Disease, N Shore Univ Hosp 1994

Johnson, Diane H MD (Inf) - **Spec Exp:** AIDS/HIV; Sexually Transmitted Diseases; Travel Medicine; **Hospital:** Winthrop Univ Hosp (page 536); **Address:** Winthrop Infect Dis Assocs, 222 Station Plaza N, Ste 432, Mineola, NY 11501; **Phone:** 516-663-2507; **Board Cert:** Internal Medicine 2004; Infectious Disease 2004; **Med School:** Univ VT Coll Med 1989; **Resid:** Internal Medicine, Winthrop Univ Hosp 1992; **Fellow:** Infectious Disease, Winthrop Univ Hosp 1994; **Fac Appt:** Asst Prof Med, SUNY Stony Brook

Klein, Natalie C MD (Inf) - **Spec Exp:** HIV; Lyme Disease; Tuberculosis; **Hospital:** Winthrop Univ Hosp (page 536); **Address:** Winthrop Infect Dis Assocs, 222 Station Plaza N, Ste 432, Mineola, NY 11501-3957; **Phone:** 516-663-2507; **Board Cert:** Internal Medicine 1982; Infectious Disease 1984; **Med School:** Jefferson Med Coll 1979; **Resid:** Internal Medicine, Mt Sinai Hosp 1982; **Fellow:** Infectious Disease, Mt Sinai Hosp 1984; **Fac Appt:** Assoc Clin Prof Med, SUNY Stony Brook

McGowan, Joseph MD (Inf) - **Spec Exp:** AIDS/HIV; HIV in Pregnancy; HIV & Hepatitis co-infection; AIDS/HIV in Elderly; **Hospital:** N Shore Univ Hosp; **Address:** N Shore Univ Hosp-Div Infect Dis, 400 Community Drive, Manhasset, NY 11030; **Phone:** 516-562-4280; **Board Cert:** Infectious Disease 2012; **Med School:** Mount Sinai Sch Med 1987; **Resid:** Internal Medicine, Montefiore Med Ctr-Moses Campus 1990; **Fellow:** Infectious Disease, Montefiore Med Ctr-Moses Campus 1993

Scheer, Max S MD (Inf) - **Spec Exp:** Skin/Soft Tissue Infections; Infections-Respiratory; Sexually Transmitted Diseases; **Hospital:** N Shore Univ Hosp; **Address:** Woodmere Med Assocs, 15 Irving Pl, Woodmere, NY 11598-1229; **Phone:** 516-374-6750; **Board Cert:** Internal Medicine 1979; Infectious Disease 1982; **Med School:** SUNY Downstate 1975; **Resid:** Family Medicine, Kings Co Hosp-SUNY 1978; Internal Medicine, Morristown Meml Hosp 1979; **Fellow:** Infectious Disease, Mt Sinai Hosp 1981; **Fac Appt:** Asst Clin Prof Med, NYU Sch Med

Internal Medicine

Berbari, Nicholas E MD (IM) *PCP* - **Hospital:** Winthrop Univ Hosp (page 536); **Address:** Winthrop Internal Med, 222 Station Plaza N, Ste 310, Mineola, NY 11501; **Phone:** 516-663-2051; **Board Cert:** Internal Medicine 2006; **Med School:** SUNY Stony Brook 1993; **Resid:** Internal Medicine, Winthrop Univ Hosp 1997; **Fac Appt:** Asst Prof Med, SUNY Stony Brook

Berger, Jeffrey T MD (IM) *PCP* - **Spec Exp:** Ethics; Palliative Care; Geriatric Care; **Hospital:** Winthrop Univ Hosp (page 536); **Address:** Winthrop Geriatrics, 222 Station Plaza N, Ste 518, Mineola, NY 11501; **Phone:** 516-663-2588; **Board Cert:** Internal Medicine 2011; Hospice & Palliative Medicine 2008; **Med School:** SUNY Stony Brook 1988; **Resid:** Internal Medicine, Winthrop Univ Hosp 1991; **Fac Appt:** Prof Med, SUNY Stony Brook

Corapi, Mark J MD (IM) *PCP* - **Hospital:** Winthrop Univ Hosp (page 536); **Address:** Winthrop Internal Med, 222 Station Plaza N, Ste 310, Mineola, NY 11501; **Phone:** 516-663-2051; **Board Cert:** Internal Medicine 1985; **Med School:** SUNY Downstate 1982; **Resid:** Internal Medicine, LIJ Med Ctr 1985; **Fac Appt:** Assoc Prof Med, SUNY Stony Brook

Cusumano, Stephen P MD (IM) *PCP* - **Spec Exp:** Hypertension; Asthma; **Hospital:** St. Joseph's Hosp-Nassau, NS-LIJ Hlth Sys; **Address:** 850 Hicksville Rd, Ste 104, Seaford, NY 11783; **Phone:** 516-735-5454; **Board Cert:** Internal Medicine 1988; **Med School:** Univ Hlth Scis, Chicago Med Sch 1985; **Resid:** Internal Medicine, Winthrop Univ Hosp 1988

Edelson, David G MD (IM) *PCP* - **Spec Exp:** Concierge Medicine; Obesity; **Hospital:** N Shore Univ Hosp; **Address:** Healthbridge, 1000 Northern Blvd, Ste 230, Great Neck, NY 11021; **Phone:** 516-627-4433; **Board Cert:** Internal Medicine 1985; Obesity Medicine 2005; **Med School:** Northwestern Univ 1982; **Resid:** Internal Medicine, LIJ Med Ctr 1987; **Fac Appt:** Asst Clin Prof Med, Hofstra N Shore-LIJ Sch Med

Federbush, Richard MD (IM) *PCP* - **Spec Exp:** Hypertension; Cholesterol/Lipid Disorders; Diabetes; **Hospital:** Plainview Hosp, Syosset Hosp; **Address:** 175 Jericho Tpke, Ste 216, Syosset, NY 11791; **Phone:** 516-364-9800; **Board Cert:** Internal Medicine 2012; **Med School:** Mexico 1985; **Resid:** Internal Medicine, SUNY Stony Brook Univ Med Ctr 1990; **Fac Appt:** Asst Clin Prof Med, Hofstra N Shore-LIJ Sch Med

Gelberg, Burt W MD (IM) *PCP* - **Spec Exp:** Preventive Medicine; Colonoscopy; Gastroscopy; **Hospital:** Franklin Hosp; **Address:** 401 Franklin Ave, Franklin Square, NY 11010; **Phone:** 516-326-2255; **Board Cert:** Internal Medicine 1975; **Med School:** SUNY Downstate 1972; **Resid:** Internal Medicine, Montefiore Med Ctr 1973; Internal Medicine, Lenox Hill Hosp 1975; **Fellow:** Gastroenterology, Lenox Hill Hosp 1977

Goodman, Michael MD (IM) *PCP* - **Spec Exp:** Concierge Medicine; **Hospital:** South Nassau Comm Hosp; **Address:** 2495 Newbridge Rd, Bellmore, NY 11710; **Phone:** 516-826-1200; **Board Cert:** Internal Medicine 1980; **Med School:** Italy 1975; **Resid:** Internal Medicine, Nassau Univ Med Ctr 1978

Internal Medicine

Gorski, Lydia E MD (IM) *PCP* - **Spec Exp:** Women's Health; Geriatric Medicine; Preventive Medicine; **Hospital:** Winthrop Univ Hosp (page 536), N Shore Univ Hosp; **Address:** Physicians Medical Care, 820 Jericho Tpke, New Hyde Park, NY 11040; **Phone:** 516-352-0430; **Board Cert:** Internal Medicine 1988; **Med School:** Poland 1982; **Resid:** Internal Medicine, St Vincent Hosp Med Ctr 1987

Gottridge, Joanne MD (IM) *PCP* - **Hospital:** NS-LIJ Hlth Sys, Long Is Jewish Med Ctr; **Address:** NS-LIJ Hlth, Primary Care, 865 Northern Blvd, Ste 102, Great Neck, NY 11021; **Phone:** 516-622-5000; **Board Cert:** Internal Medicine 1983; **Med School:** Case West Res Univ 1980; **Resid:** Internal Medicine, N Shore Univ Hosp 1983; **Fac Appt:** Assoc Prof Med, Hofstra N Shore-LIJ Sch Med

Hotchkiss, Edward MD (IM) *PCP* - **Hospital:** South Nassau Comm Hosp, NS-LIJ Hlth Sys; **Address:** 158 Hempstead Ave, Lynbrook, NY 11563; **Phone:** 516-593-3541; **Board Cert:** Internal Medicine 1972; **Med School:** SUNY Downstate 1965; **Resid:** Internal Medicine, LI Jewish Med Ctr 1970; **Fellow:** Psychiatry, SUNY Downstate Med Ctr 1971; **Fac Appt:** Assoc Prof Med, Albert Einstein Coll Med

Klein, William M MD (IM) *PCP* - **Spec Exp:** Concierge Medicine; **Hospital:** N Shore Univ Hosp, Long Is Jewish Med Ctr; **Address:** Healthbridge, 1000 Northern Blvd, Ste 230, Great Neck, NY 11021; **Phone:** 516-627-4433; **Board Cert:** Internal Medicine 2013; **Med School:** Mount Sinai Sch Med 1994; **Resid:** Internal Medicine, Mt Sinai Hosp 1997

Leong, Pauline MD (IM) *PCP* - **Hospital:** NS-LIJ Hlth Sys; **Address:** NS-LIJ Hlth, Primary Care, 865 Northern Blvd, Ste 102, Great Neck, NY 11021; **Phone:** 516-622-5000; **Board Cert:** Internal Medicine 1988; **Med School:** NYU Sch Med 1983; **Resid:** Internal Medicine, NY Hosp Queens 1988

Newitz, Deborah K MD (IM) - **Hospital:** Winthrop Univ Hosp (page 536); **Address:** Winthrop Internal Med, 222 Station Plaza N, Ste 310, Mineola, NY 11051; **Phone:** 516-663-2051; **Board Cert:** Internal Medicine 2005; **Med School:** Albert Einstein Coll Med 1991; **Resid:** Internal Medicine, Mt Sinai Hosp 1994

Rubenstein, Jack MD (IM) *PCP* - **Spec Exp:** Complex Diagnosis; Kidney Failure-Chronic; Geriatric Care; Hypertension; **Hospital:** Franklin Hosp, N Shore Univ Hosp; **Address:** 70 Glen Cove Rd, Ste 301, Roslyn Heights, NY 11577; **Phone:** 516-621-1502; **Board Cert:** Internal Medicine 2008; Nephrology 2009; Geriatric Medicine 2008; **Med School:** NY Med Coll 1976; **Resid:** Internal Medicine, N Shore Univ Hosp 1979; Nephrology, N Shore Univ Hosp 1980; **Fellow:** Nephrology, NYU Med Ctr 1982; **Fac Appt:** Assoc Clin Prof Med, Hofstra N Shore-LIJ Sch Med

Rucker, Steve MD (IM) *PCP* - **Spec Exp:** Hypertension; Kidney Disease; Kidney Stones; **Hospital:** St. Francis Hosp - The Heart Ctr (page 111), NS-LIJ Hlth Sys; **Address:** 1999 Marcus Ave, Ste 216, Lake Success, NY 11042; **Phone:** 516-775-4545; **Board Cert:** Internal Medicine 1986; Nephrology 1988; **Med School:** Univ Pittsburgh 1983; **Resid:** Internal Medicine, Long Is Jewish Med Ctr 1986; **Fellow:** Nephrology, Mt Sinai Hosp 1988

Taubman, Lowell B MD (IM) *PCP* - **Spec Exp:** Dementia; Alzheimer's Disease; Preventive Medicine; Geriatric Care; **Address:** 206 Riverside Blvd, Long Beach, NY 11561; **Phone:** 516-432-5670; **Board Cert:** Internal Medicine 1988; **Med School:** Mexico 1980; **Resid:** Internal Medicine, Univ Pittsburg Med Ctr 1983; Internal Medicine, St Clares Hosp 1984; **Fellow:** Geriatric Medicine, Jewish Inst Geriatric Care 1986

Timpone, Leonard MD (IM) *PCP* - **Spec Exp:** Geriatric Medicine; Headache; Preventive Medicine; **Hospital:** Franklin Hosp, Mercy Med Ctr-Rockville Centre; **Address:** 1051 Adams Ave, Franklin Square, NY 11010; **Phone:** 516-354-4858; **Board Cert:** Internal Medicine 2004; **Med School:** France 1984; **Resid:** Internal Medicine, NY-Presby/Lower Manhattan Hosp 1988

Weinstein, Mark J MD (IM) *PCP* - **Spec Exp:** Hypertension; Diabetes; Cholesterol/Lipid Disorders; **Hospital:** Plainview Hosp; **Address:** 4045 Hempstead Tpke, Fl 3, Bethpage, NY 11714; **Phone:** 516-731-7770; **Board Cert:** Internal Medicine 1978; Infectious Disease 1980; **Med School:** Harvard Med Sch 1975; **Resid:** Internal Medicine, Univ Hosp 1978; **Fellow:** Infectious Disease, Univ Hosp 1980

Wolff, Edward MD (IM) *PCP* - **Spec Exp:** Asthma; Heart Disease; **Hospital:** St. Francis Hosp - The Heart Ctr (page 111), N Shore Univ Hosp; **Address:** 107 Northern Blvd, Ste 404, Great Neck, NY 11021; **Phone:** 516-498-1818; **Board Cert:** Internal Medicine 1987; **Med School:** Georgetown Univ 1966; **Resid:** Internal Medicine, Metropolitan Hosp Ctr 1970; **Fellow:** Pulmonary Disease, Metropolitan Hosp Ctr 1971

Zupnick, Henry Michael MD (IM) *PCP* - **Spec Exp:** Asthma; Airway Disorders; Critical Care Medicine; **Hospital:** Long Is Jewish Med Ctr, Franklin Hosp; **Address:** South Shore Int Med Assocs, 158 Hempstead Ave, Lynbrook, NY 11563; **Phone:** 516-593-3541; **Board Cert:** Internal Medicine 1983; Pulmonary Disease 1988; **Med School:** Albert Einstein Coll Med 1980; **Resid:** Internal Medicine, Brookdale Hosp Med Ctr 1983; **Fellow:** Pulmonary Disease, Columbia-Presby Med Ctr 1985; Critical Care Medicine, Mount Sinai Hosp 1987; **Fac Appt:** Asst Prof Med, Hofstra N Shore-LIJ Sch Med

Interventional Cardiology

Abittan, Meyer H MD (IC) - **Spec Exp:** Angiography-Coronary; Preventive Cardiology; **Hospital:** St. Francis Hosp - The Heart Ctr (page 111); **Address:** St Francis Hosp, Cardiology, 100 Port Washington Blvd, Ste G-03, Roslyn, NY 11576; **Phone:** 516-627-1155; **Board Cert:** Internal Medicine 1989; **Med School:** Mount Sinai Sch Med 1986; **Resid:** Internal Medicine, Brookdale Univ Hosp Med Ctr 1989; **Fellow:** Cardiovascular Disease, Mt Sinai Med Ctr 1990; Interventional Cardiology, Maimonides Med Ctr

Berke, Andrew D MD (IC) - **Hospital:** St. Francis Hosp - The Heart Ctr (page 111); **Address:** St Francis Hosp-Vizza Pavilion, 100 Port Washington Blvd, Ste G-04, Roslyn, NY 11576; **Phone:** 516-365-2211; **Board Cert:** Internal Medicine 1982; Cardiovascular Disease 1985; Interventional Cardiology 2009; **Med School:** Brown Univ 1979; **Resid:** Internal Medicine, NY-Presby/Columbia Univ Med Ctr 1982; **Fellow:** Cardiovascular Disease, NY-Presby/Columbia Univ Med Ctr 1985; **Fac Appt:** Asst Clin Prof Med, Columbia P&S

Kaplan, Barry M MD (IC) - **Spec Exp:** Angioplasty & Stent Placement; **Hospital:** N Shore Univ Hosp; **Address:** NShore Univ Med Ctr, Cardiology, 300 Community Drive, Manhasset, NY 11030; **Phone:** 516-562-4100; **Board Cert:** Cardiovascular Disease 2005; Interventional Cardiology 2009; **Med School:** Israel 1987; **Resid:** Internal Medicine, NYU Langone Med Ctr 1991; **Fellow:** Cardiovascular Disease, Montefiore Med Ctr 1994; Interventional Cardiology, William Beaumont Hosp 1995; **Fac Appt:** Asst Prof Med, Hofstra N Shore-LIJ Sch Med

Petrossian, George A MD (IC) - **Spec Exp:** Carotid Artery Stent Placement; Peripheral Vascular Disease; Coronary Angioplasty/Stents; Renovascular Disease; **Hospital:** St. Francis Hosp - The Heart Ctr (page 111), South Nassau Comm Hosp; **Address:** 1405 Old Northern Blvd, Roslyn, NY 11576; **Phone:** 516-484-6777; **Board Cert:** Internal Medicine 1986; Cardiovascular Disease 1989; Interventional Cardiology 2010; **Med School:** Mount Sinai Sch Med 1983; **Resid:** Internal Medicine, NY-Presby/Columbia Univ Med Ctr 1987; **Fellow:** Cardiovascular Disease, NY-Presby/Columbia Univ Med Ctr 1989; Interventional Cardiology, Mass Genl Hosp 1990

Zisfein, Jerome B MD (IC) - **Spec Exp:** Coronary Angioplasty/Stents; Pacemakers; Cardiac Catheterization; **Hospital:** Winthrop Univ Hosp (page 536), South Nassau Comm Hosp; **Address:** S Shore Heart Assocs, 242 Merrick Rd, Ste 402, Rockville Centre, NY 11570; **Phone:** 516-763-2800; **Board Cert:** Internal Medicine 1984; Cardiovascular Disease 1987; Interventional Cardiology 2010; **Med School:** NY Med Coll 1981; **Resid:** Internal Medicine, Rhode Is Hosp 1984; **Fellow:** Cardiovascular Disease, Mass Genl Hosp 1989

Maternal & Fetal Medicine

Chavez, Martin R MD (MF) - **Spec Exp:** Pregnancy-High Risk; Obstetric Ultrasound; Fetal Surgery; **Hospital:** Winthrop Univ Hosp (page 536); **Address:** Perinatal Assocs, 120 Mineola Blvd, Ste 110, Mineola, NY 11501; **Phone:** 516-663-3020; **Board Cert:** Obstetrics & Gynecology 2013; Maternal & Fetal Medicine 2013; **Med School:** Rutgers R W Johnson Med Sch 1996; **Resid:** Obstetrics & Gynecology, UMDNJ-R Wood Johnson Med Ctr 2002; **Fellow:** Maternal & Fetal Medicine, UMDNJ-R Wood Johnson Med Ctr 2003

Meirowitz, Natalie MD (MF) - **Spec Exp:** Prenatal Diagnosis; Pregnancy Loss; Pregnancy-High Risk; **Hospital:** Long Is Jewish Med Ctr; **Address:** NS-LIJ Med Ctr-Dept Ob/Gyn, 270-05 76th Ave, Ste T-457A, New Hyde Park, NY 11040; **Phone:** 718-470-5466; **Board Cert:** Obstetrics & Gynecology 2013; Maternal & Fetal Medicine 2013; **Med School:** Harvard Med Sch 1993; **Resid:** Obstetrics & Gynecology, N Shore Univ Med Ctr 1997; **Fellow:** Maternal & Fetal Medicine, Univ Hosp-UMDNJ 2000; **Fac Appt:** Asst Prof ObG, Albert Einstein Coll Med

Rochelson, Burton L MD (MF) - **Spec Exp:** Pregnancy-High Risk; Ultrasound; Prenatal Diagnosis; **Hospital:** N Shore Univ Hosp; **Address:** N Shore Univ Hosp, Maternal-Fetal Med, 300 Community Drive, Levitt Bldg - Fl 3, Manhasset, NY 11030; **Phone:** 516-562-2892; **Board Cert:** Obstetrics & Gynecology 2013; Maternal & Fetal Medicine 2013; **Med School:** Univ Mich Med Sch 1978; **Resid:** Obstetrics & Gynecology, LI Jewish Med Ctr 1982; **Fellow:** Maternal & Fetal Medicine, Univ Hosp 1986; **Fac Appt:** Prof ObG, Hofstra N Shore-LIJ Sch Med

Sicuranza, Genevieve B MD (MF) - **Spec Exp:** Prenatal Diagnosis; **Hospital:** Winthrop Univ Hosp (page 536), St. Joseph's Hosp-Nassau; **Address:** Perinatal Assocs, 120 Mineola Blvd, Ste 110, Mineola, NY 11501; **Phone:** 516-663-3020; **Board Cert:** Obstetrics & Gynecology 2013; Maternal & Fetal Medicine 2013; **Med School:** Puerto Rico 1985; **Resid:** Obstetrics & Gynecology, Catholic Med Ctr 1991; **Fellow:** Maternal & Fetal Medicine, SUNY Hlth Sci Ctr 1993; **Fac Appt:** Asst Prof ObG, SUNY Stony Brook

Vintzileos, Anthony M MD (MF) - **Spec Exp:** Ultrasound; Fetal Therapy; **Hospital:** Winthrop Univ Hosp (page 536); **Address:** Women's Contemporary Care Assocs, 120 Mineola Blvd Ste 100, Mineola, NY 11501; **Phone:** 516-663-3010; **Board Cert:** Obstetrics & Gynecology 1999; Maternal & Fetal Medicine 1999; **Med School:** Greece 1975; **Resid:** Obstetrics & Gynecology, St Joseph's Hosp Med Ctr 1981; **Fellow:** Maternal & Fetal Medicine, Univ Conn Hlth Ctr 1983; **Fac Appt:** Prof ObG, SUNY Stony Brook

Vohra, Nidhi MD (MF) - **Spec Exp:** Prenatal Diagnosis; **Hospital:** N Shore Univ Hosp; **Address:** North Shore Univ Hosp, Maternal Fetal Med, 300 Community Drive, Manhasset, NY 11030; **Phone:** 516-562-4458; **Board Cert:** Obstetrics & Gynecology 2013; Maternal & Fetal Medicine 2013; **Med School:** India 1985; **Resid:** Obstetrics & Gynecology, LIJ Med Ctr 1993; **Fellow:** Maternal & Fetal Medicine, LIJ Med Ctr 1996

Medical Oncology

Arena, Francis P MD (Onc) - **Spec Exp:** Breast Cancer; **Hospital:** N Shore Univ Hosp, NYU Langone Med Ctr (page 104); **Address:** NYU Langone Arena Onc/Rheum, 1999 Marcus Ave, Ste 120, Lake Success, NY 11042; **Phone:** 516-466-6611; **Board Cert:** Internal Medicine 1978; Medical Oncology 2006; **Med School:** Cornell Univ-Weill Med Coll 1975; **Resid:** Internal Medicine, NY-Presby/Weill Cornell Med Ctr 1978; Internal Medicine, Meml Sloan-Kettering Canc Ctr 1979; **Fellow:** Hematology & Oncology, Meml Sloan-Kettering Canc Ctr 1980; **Fac Appt:** Assoc Clin Prof Med, NYU Sch Med

Bradley, Thomas P MD (Onc) - **Spec Exp:** Bladder Cancer; Prostate Cancer; Kidney Cancer; **Hospital:** N Shore Univ Hosp; **Address:** NS-LIJ Hlth, Monter Cancer Ctr, 450 Lakeville Rd, Lake Success, NY 11042; **Phone:** 516-734-8900; **Board Cert:** Internal Medicine 1987; Medical Oncology 2011; Hematology 2012; **Med School:** Mexico 1982; **Resid:** Internal Medicine, SUNY Downstate Med Ctr 1988; **Fellow:** Hematology & Oncology, SUNY Downstate Med Ctr 1991; **Fac Appt:** Assoc Prof Med, Albert Einstein Coll Med

Budman, Daniel R MD (Onc) - **Spec Exp:** Breast Cancer; Lymphoma; Drug Discovery & Development; Psychopharmacology; **Hospital:** N Shore Univ Hosp, Long Is Jewish Med Ctr; **Address:** NS-LIJ Hlth, Monter Cancer Ctr, 450 Lakeville Rd, Lake Success, NY 11042; **Phone:** 516-734-8900; **Board Cert:** Internal Medicine 1975; Hematology 1978; Medical Oncology 1979; **Med School:** Albert Einstein Coll Med 1972; **Resid:** Internal Medicine, Hosp Univ Penn 1974; Hematology, Natl Inst Hlth 1976; **Fellow:** Medical Oncology, Meml Sloan-Kettering Cancer Ctr 1977; Hematology, NYU Med Ctr 1978; **Fac Appt:** Prof Med, Hofstra N Shore-LIJ Sch Med

Citron, Marc L MD (Onc) - **Spec Exp:** Breast Cancer; Lung Cancer; **Hospital:** Long Is Jewish Med Ctr; **Address:** ProHealth Care Assocs, Div Oncology, 2800 Marcus Ave, Ste 200, Lake Success, NY 11042-1008; **Phone:** 516-622-6150; **Board Cert:** Internal Medicine 1977; Medical Oncology 1979; **Med School:** Wayne State Univ 1974; **Resid:** Internal Medicine, Georgetown Univ Hosp 1977; **Fellow:** Medical Oncology, Georgetown Univ Hosp 1979; **Fac Appt:** Clin Prof Med, Albert Einstein Coll Med

D'Olimpio, James MD (Onc) - **Spec Exp:** Palliative Care; Pancreatic Cancer; Pain-Cancer; **Hospital:** N Shore Univ Hosp; **Address:** Monter Cancer Ctr, N Shore Univ Hosp, 450 Lakeville Rd, Lake Success, NY 11042; **Phone:** 516-734-8906; **Board Cert:** Internal Medicine 1983; Medical Oncology 2006; Hospice & Palliative Medicine 2008; **Med School:** Mexico 1978; **Resid:** Internal Medicine, Mt Sinai/Elmhurst Hosp 1982; Medical Oncology, Montefiore Med Ctr 1984

Hindenburg, Alexander A MD (Onc) - **Spec Exp:** Pancreatic Cancer; Breast Cancer; Gynecologic Cancer; Myelodysplastic Syndromes; **Hospital:** Winthrop Univ Hosp (page 536); **Address:** Winthrop Hem/Onc Assocs, 200 Old Country Rd, Ste 450, Mineola, NY 11501; **Phone:** 516-663-9500; **Board Cert:** Internal Medicine 1981; Medical Oncology 1983; Hematology 1988; **Med School:** Rutgers R W Johnson Med Sch 1978; **Resid:** Internal Medicine, Mt Sinai Hosp 1981; **Fellow:** Hematology & Oncology, NY-Presby/Columbia Univ Med Ctr 1984; **Fac Appt:** Asst Prof Med, SUNY Stony Brook

Kappel, Bruce I MD (Onc) - **Spec Exp:** Breast Cancer; Colon Cancer; **Hospital:** Plainview Hosp, St. Joseph's Hosp-Nassau; **Address:** Med Oncology Assocs, 40 Crossways Park Drive, Ste 103, Woodbury, NY 11797; **Phone:** 516-921-5533; **Board Cert:** Internal Medicine 1985; Medical Oncology 1987; Hematology 1988; **Med School:** Emory Univ 1982; **Resid:** Internal Medicine, Emory Univ Hosp 1985; **Fellow:** Medical Oncology, NY-Presby/Columbia Univ Med Ctr 1988

Kessler, Leonard MD (Onc) - **Hospital:** South Nassau Comm Hosp, Mercy Med Ctr-Rockville Centre; **Address:** 242 Merrick Rd, Ste 301, Rockville Centre, NY 11570; **Phone:** 516-536-1455; **Board Cert:** Internal Medicine 1979; Medical Oncology 1981; Hematology 1982; **Med School:** Albert Einstein Coll Med 1975; **Resid:** Internal Medicine, Montefiore Med Ctr 1977; **Fellow:** Hematology, Montefiore Med Ctr 1981; Medical Oncology, Meml Sloan-Kettering Cancer Ctr 1980

Marino, John S MD (Onc) - **Spec Exp:** Breast Cancer; Colon Cancer; Lung Cancer; **Hospital:** N Shore Univ Hosp, St. Francis Hosp - The Heart Ctr (page 111); **Address:** 2001 Marcus Ave, Ste S265, Lake Success, NY 11042; **Phone:** 516-883-0122; **Board Cert:** Internal Medicine 1982; Medical Oncology 1985; **Med School:** NY Med Coll 1979; **Resid:** Internal Medicine, N Shore Univ Hosp 1982; **Fellow:** Medical Oncology, Jacobi Med Ctr 1983; Medical Oncology, N Shore Univ Hosp 1984; **Fac Appt:** Asst Clin Prof Med, Hofstra N Shore-LIJ Sch Med

Mehrotra, Bhoomi MD (Onc) - **Spec Exp:** Lung Cancer; Head & Neck Cancer; Gastrointestinal Cancer; **Hospital:** St. Francis Hosp - The Heart Ctr (page 111); **Address:** St Francis Hosp, Cancer Inst, 100 Port Washington Blvd, Roslyn, NY 11576; **Phone:** 516-325-7500; **Board Cert:** Hematology 2004; Medical Oncology 2013; **Med School:** India 1986; **Resid:** Internal Medicine, LIJ Med Ctr 1990; **Fellow:** Hematology & Oncology, UCSF Med Ctr 1993; **Fac Appt:** Assoc Prof Med, Hofstra N Shore-LIJ Sch Med

Raptis, George MD (Onc) - **Spec Exp:** Breast Cancer; **Hospital:** N Shore Univ Hosp, Long Is Jewish Med Ctr; **Address:** N Shore LIJ-Monter Cancer Ctr, 450 Lakeville Rd, Lake Success, NY 11042; **Phone:** 516-734-8900; **Board Cert:** Medical Oncology 2014; **Med School:** Mount Sinai Sch Med 1987; **Resid:** Internal Medicine, Mt Sinai Hosp 1990; **Fellow:** Hematology & Oncology, Meml Sloan-Kettering Cancer Ctr 1993; **Fac Appt:** Assoc Prof Med, Hofstra N Shore-LIJ Sch Med

Schneider, Jeffrey G MD (Onc) - **Spec Exp:** Lung Cancer; Solid Tumors; **Hospital:** Winthrop Univ Hosp (page 536); **Address:** 200 Old Country Rd, Ste 450, Mineola, NY 11501; **Phone:** 516-663-9500; **Board Cert:** Internal Medicine 1989; Medical Oncology 2012; Hematology 2004; **Med School:** Yale Univ 1986; **Resid:** Internal Medicine, Bellevue Hosp/NYU Langone Med Ctr 1989; **Fellow:** Hematology & Oncology, Meml Sloan Kettering Canc Ctr 1994; **Fac Appt:** Asst Prof Med, SUNY Stony Brook

Schwartz, Paula R MD (Onc) - **Spec Exp:** Breast Cancer; Colon Cancer; **Hospital:** N Shore Univ Hosp, Long Is Jewish Med Ctr; **Address:** 3003 New Hyde Park Rd, Ste 401, New Hyde Park, NY 11042; **Phone:** 516-354-5700; **Board Cert:** Internal Medicine 1986; Hematology 1988; **Med School:** SUNY Downstate 1980; **Resid:** Internal Medicine, LIJ Med Ctr 1983; **Fellow:** Hematology, Mt Sinai Hosp 1985; Hematology, N Shore Univ Hosp 1989

Tomao, Frank A MD (Onc) - **Spec Exp:** Lung Cancer; Breast Cancer; **Hospital:** N Shore Univ Hosp, St. Francis Hosp - The Heart Ctr (page 111); **Address:** NYU Langone Oncology, 2001 Marcus Ave, Ste S265, Lake Success, NY 11042; **Phone:** 516-883-0122; **Board Cert:** Internal Medicine 1974; Medical Oncology 1975; **Med School:** Cornell Univ-Weill Med Coll 1965; **Resid:** Internal Medicine, Meml Sloan-Kettering Canc Ctr 1967; Internal Medicine, Bellevue Hosp 1968; **Fellow:** Medical Oncology, Meml Sloan-Kettering Canc Ctr 1969

Vinciguerra, Vincent P MD (Onc) - **Spec Exp:** Breast Cancer; Gastrointestinal Cancer; Lung Cancer; Cancer Prevention; **Hospital:** N Shore Univ Hosp, Glen Cove Hosp; **Address:** N Shore LIJ-Monter Cancer Ctr, 450 Lakeville Rd, Lake Success, NY 11042; **Phone:** 516-734-8900; **Board Cert:** Internal Medicine 1971; Hematology 1974; Medical Oncology 1975; **Med School:** Georgetown Univ 1966; **Resid:** Internal Medicine, NY-Presby/Weill Cornell Med Ctr 1969; Internal Medicine, N Shore Univ Hosp 1971; **Fellow:** Hematology & Oncology, NY-Presby/Weill Cornell Med Ctr 1973; Hematology & Oncology, N Shore Univ Hosp 1974; **Fac Appt:** Prof Med, NYU Sch Med

Weiselberg, Lora R MD (Onc) - **Spec Exp:** Breast Cancer; Cancer Prevention; **Hospital:** N Shore Univ Hosp, Long Is Jewish Med Ctr; **Address:** NS-LIJ Hlth, Monter Cancer Ctr, 450 Lakeville Rd, Lake Success, NY 11042; **Phone:** 516-734-8900; **Board Cert:** Internal Medicine 1978; Medical Oncology 1981; Hematology 1982; **Med School:** NY Med Coll 1975; **Resid:** Internal Medicine, Stamford Hosp 1978; **Fellow:** Medical Oncology, N Shore Univ Hosp 1980; Hematology, N Shore Univ Hosp 1981; **Fac Appt:** Assoc Prof Med, Hofstra N Shore-LIJ Sch Med

Weiss, Rita MD/PhD (Onc) - **Hospital:** St. Francis Hosp - The Heart Ctr (page 111), N Shore Univ Hosp; **Address:** 107 Northern Blvd, Ste 306, Great Neck, NY 11021; **Phone:** 516-482-0080; **Board Cert:** Internal Medicine 1984; Medical Oncology 1989; **Med School:** Mexico 1977; **Resid:** Internal Medicine, Winthrop Univ Hosp 1980; **Fellow:** Medical Oncology, Mt Sinai Hosp 1982

Neonatal-Perinatal Medicine

Boxer, Harriet S MD (NP) - **Spec Exp:** Prematurity/Low Birth Weight Infants; Chronic Obstructive Lung Disease (COPD); **Hospital:** Nassau Univ Med Ctr; **Address:** Nassau Univ Med Ctr, Neonatology, 2201 Hempstead Tpke, Box 30, East Meadow, NY 11554; **Phone:** 516-572-3318; **Board Cert:** Pediatrics 1978; Neonatal-Perinatal Medicine 1977; **Med School:** SUNY Downstate 1972; **Resid:** Pediatrics, Babies Hosp 1974; Pediatrics, Chldns Hosp 1975; **Fellow:** Neonatal-Perinatal Medicine, LIJ-Hillside Med Ctr 1977; **Fac Appt:** Asst Prof Ped, SUNY Stony Brook

Schanler, Richard J MD (NP) - **Spec Exp:** Neonatal Care; **Hospital:** Steven & Alexandra Cohen Chldn's Med Ctr of NY, N Shore Univ Hosp; **Address:** Cohen Chldns Med Ctr, NICU, 269-01 76th Ave, rm CH344, New Hyde Park, NY 11040; **Phone:** 718-470-3440; **Board Cert:** Pediatrics 1979; Neonatal-Perinatal Medicine 2009; **Med School:** UMDNJ-NJ Med Sch, Newark 1974; **Resid:** Pediatrics, Univ Colorado Hosp 1977; **Fellow:** Neonatology, Women & Infants Hosp 1980; **Fac Appt:** Prof Ped, Albert Einstein Coll Med

Steele, Andrew M MD (NP) - **Spec Exp:** Lung Disease in Newborns; Sudden Infant Death Syndrome (SIDS); Breathing Disorders; **Hospital:** Steven & Alexandra Cohen Chldn's Med Ctr of NY, N Shore Univ Hosp; **Address:** Steven & Alexandra Cohen Chldn's Med Ctr, 269-01 76th Ave, New Hyde Park, NY 11040-1433; **Phone:** 718-470-3013; **Board Cert:** Pediatrics 1981; Neonatal-Perinatal Medicine 2009; **Med School:** SUNY Downstate 1976; **Resid:** Pediatrics, LI Jewish Med Ctr 1978; **Fellow:** Neonatal-Perinatal Medicine, LI Jewish Med Ctr 1980; **Fac Appt:** Assoc Prof Ped, Hofstra N Shore-LIJ Sch Med

Nephrology

Balsam, Leah MD (Nep) - **Spec Exp:** Hypertension; **Hospital:** Nassau Univ Med Ctr; **Address:** Nassau Univ Med Ctr, Nephrology, 2201 Hempstead Blvd, East Meadow, NY 11554; **Phone:** 516-572-4848; **Board Cert:** Internal Medicine 1987; Nephrology 2010; **Med School:** SUNY Downstate 1984; **Resid:** Internal Medicine, Montefiore Med Ctr 1987; **Fellow:** Nephrology, NYU Med Ctr 1989; **Fac Appt:** Assoc Clin Prof Med, SUNY Stony Brook

Bourla, Steven L MD (Nep) - **Spec Exp:** Kidney Disease; **Hospital:** Plainview Hosp, St. Joseph's Hosp-Nassau; **Address:** Island Med Grp, 789 Old Country Rd, Plainview, NY 11803; **Phone:** 516-433-3600; **Board Cert:** Internal Medicine 1979; Nephrology 1982; **Med School:** NY Med Coll 1975; **Resid:** Internal Medicine, LIJ Med Ctr 1979; **Fellow:** Nephrology, NYU Med Ctr 1981

Mailloux, Lionel U MD (Nep) - **Spec Exp:** Hypertension; Dialysis Care; Fluid/Electrolyte Balance; Hypertension/Kidney Disease; **Hospital:** N Shore Univ Hosp, Glen Cove Hosp; **Address:** 50 Seaview Blvd, Port Washington, NY 11050; **Phone:** 516-484-6093; **Board Cert:** Internal Medicine 1977; Nephrology 1972; **Med School:** Hahnemann Univ 1962; **Resid:** Internal Medicine, Hartford Hosp 1965; **Fellow:** Nephrology, Hahnemann Hosp 1966; **Fac Appt:** Clin Prof Med, Hofstra N Shore-LIJ Sch Med

Masani, Naveed N MD (Nep) - **Spec Exp:** Dialysis Care; **Hospital:** Winthrop Univ Hosp (page 536); **Address:** Winthrop Nephrology Assocs, 200 Old Country Rd, Ste 135, Mineola, NY 11501; **Phone:** 516-663-2169; **Board Cert:** Nephrology 2004; **Med School:** SUNY Stony Brook 1999; **Resid:** Internal Medicine, Winthrop Univ Hosp 2002; **Fellow:** Nephrology, Winthrop Univ Hosp 2004

Mattana, Joseph MD (Nep) - **Spec Exp:** Diabetic Kidney Disease; Hypertension; Glomerulonephritis; **Hospital:** Winthrop Univ Hosp (page 536); **Address:** Winthrop Nephrology Assocs, 200 Old Country Rd, Ste 135, Mineola, NY 11501; **Phone:** 516-663-2169; **Board Cert:** Nephrology 2004; **Med School:** SUNY Hlth Sci Ctr 1987; **Resid:** Internal Medicine, LIJ Hosp 1990; **Fellow:** Nephrology, LIJ Hosp 1993

Singhal, Pravin C MD (Nep) - **Spec Exp:** Hypertension; Diabetic Kidney Disease; HIV Related Kidney Disease; **Hospital:** Long Is Jewish Med Ctr, N Shore Univ Hosp; **Address:** NS-LIJ Hlth, Nephrology, 100 Community Drive Fl 2, Great Neck, NY 11021; **Phone:** 516-465-3010; **Board Cert:** Internal Medicine 1983; Nephrology 1986; **Med School:** India 1970; **Resid:** Internal Medicine, Postgrad Inst Med Ed 1972; Internal Medicine, Brigham & Womens Hosp 1983; **Fellow:** Nephrology, Montefiore Med Ctr 1985; **Fac Appt:** Prof Med, Albert Einstein Coll Med

Neurological Surgery

Brisman, Jonathan L MD (NS) - **Spec Exp:** Aneurysm-Cerebral; Arteriovenous Malformations; Carotid Stenosis; Endovascular Neurosurgery; **Hospital:** Winthrop Univ Hosp (page 536), St. Francis Hosp - The Heart Ctr (page 111); **Address:** NSPC, 1991 Marcus Ave, Ste 108, Lake Success, NY 11042; **Phone:** 516-442-2250; **Board Cert:** Neurological Surgery 2008; **Med School:** Columbia P&S 1995; **Resid:** Surgery, Mass Genl Hosp 1996; Neurological Surgery, Mass Genl Hosp 2002; **Fellow:** Interventional Neuroradiology, St Lukes-Roosevelt Hosp Ctr 2003; Cerebrovascular Neurosurgery, Swedish Med Ctr 2005

Brown, Jeffrey A MD (NS) - **Spec Exp:** Trigeminal Neuralgia; Pain-Chronic; **Hospital:** Winthrop Univ Hosp (page 536), N Shore Univ Hosp; **Address:** NSPC, 600 Northern Blvd, Ste 118, Great Neck, NY 11021; **Phone:** 516-478-0008; **Board Cert:** Neurological Surgery 1986; **Med School:** Univ Chicago-Pritzker Sch Med 1976; **Resid:** Neurological Surgery, Univ Chicago Hosp 1982

Eisenberg, Mark B MD (NS) - **Spec Exp:** Skull Base Surgery; Spinal Surgery-Minimally Invasive; Pituitary Tumors; Brain Tumors; **Hospital:** N Shore Univ Hosp; **Address:** NS-LIJ Hlth, Neurosurgery, 900 Northern Blvd, Ste 260, Great Neck, NY 11021; **Phone:** 516-773-7737; **Board Cert:** Neurological Surgery 2010; **Med School:** Univ Miami Sch Med 1988; **Resid:** Neurological Surgery, Mt Sinai Hosp 1994; **Fellow:** Skull Base Surgery, Univ Arkansas Med Ctr 1995; **Fac Appt:** Asst Clin Prof NS, NYU Sch Med

Grant, John A MD (NS) - **Spec Exp:** Pediatric Neurosurgery; Epilepsy; **Hospital:** Winthrop Univ Hosp (page 536), Good Samaritan Hosp Med Ctr - West Islip; **Address:** NSPC, 100 Merrick Rd, Ste 200, Rockville Centre, NY 11570; **Phone:** 516-632-7050; **Board Cert:** Neurological Surgery 1998; **Med School:** Ireland 1985; **Resid:** Surgery, Johns Hopkins Hosp 1987; Neurological Surgery, NY-Presby/Columbia Univ Med Ctr 1992; **Fellow:** Pediatric Neurological Surgery, Chldns Meml Hosp 1993

Holtzman, Robert N MD (NS) - **Spec Exp:** Brain & Spinal Cord Tumors; Spinal Surgery; Aneurysm-Cerebral; Chiari's Deformity; **Hospital:** Winthrop Univ Hosp (page 536); **Address:** NSPC, 1991 Marcus Ave, Ste 108, Lake Success, NY 11042; **Phone:** 516-442-2250; **Board Cert:** Neurology 1978; Neurological Surgery 1980; **Med School:** Columbia P&S 1969; **Resid:** Surgery, Harbor Genl Hosp 1973; Neurological Surgery, Neurological Inst 1976; **Fac Appt:** Assoc Clin Prof NS, Columbia P&S

Levine, Mitchell E MD (NS) - **Spec Exp:** Brain Tumors; Minimally Invasive Spinal Surgery; Cerebrovascular Surgery; **Hospital:** Lenox Hill Hosp, N Shore Univ Hosp; **Address:** Lenox Hill Hosp, Neurosurgery, 130 E 77th St, Great Neck, NY 11021; **Phone:** 212-434-3900; **Board Cert:** Neurological Surgery 1987; **Med School:** Mount Sinai Sch Med 1977; **Resid:** Neurological Surgery, Mt Sinai Hosp 1983; **Fac Appt:** Asst Prof NS, Mount Sinai Sch Med

Mittler, Mark A MD (NS) - **Spec Exp:** Pediatric Neurosurgery; Brain & Spinal Cord Tumors; Vascular Malformations; Hydrocephalus; **Hospital:** Steven & Alexandra Cohen Chldn's Med Ctr of NY, N Shore Univ Hosp; **Address:** LI Neurosurgical Assocs, 410 Lakeville Rd, Ste 204, New Hyde Park, NY 11042; **Phone:** 516-354-3401; **Board Cert:** Neurological Surgery 2012; Pediatric Neurological Surgery 2013; **Med School:** Univ Rochester 1991; **Resid:** Neurological Surgery, Rhode Island Hosp 1998; **Fellow:** Pediatric Neurological Surgery, Chldns Hosp 1999; **Fac Appt:** Asst Prof NS, Hofstra N Shore-LIJ Sch Med

Onesti, Stephen T MD (NS) - **Spec Exp:** Spinal Surgery; Minimally Invasive Spinal Surgery; Spinal Disorders-Degenerative; Pain-Chronic; **Hospital:** Winthrop Univ Hosp (page 536), South Nassau Comm Hosp; **Address:** NSPC, 100 Merrick Rd, Ste 200, Rockville Centre, NY 11570; **Phone:** 516-632-7050; **Board Cert:** Neurological Surgery 1995; **Med School:** Harvard Med Sch 1986; **Resid:** Neurological Surgery, NY-Presby/Columbia Univ Med Ctr 1993; **Fac Appt:** Prof NS, SUNY Downstate

Rekate, Harold L MD (NS) - **Spec Exp:** Chiari's Deformity; Hydrocephalus; Pediatric Neurosurgery; Brain Tumors; **Hospital:** N Shore Univ Hosp; **Address:** Chiari Inst, 611 Northern Blvd, Ste 150, Great Neck, NY 11021; **Phone:** 516-570-4400; **Board Cert:** Neurological Surgery 1980; **Med School:** Med Coll VA 1970; **Resid:** Neurological Surgery, Univ Hosps 1978; **Fac Appt:** Prof NS, Hofstra N Shore-LIJ Sch Med

Schulder, Michael MD (NS) - **Spec Exp:** Brain Tumors; Movement Disorders; Skull Base Surgery; **Hospital:** N Shore Univ Hosp; **Address:** N Shore, Brain Tumor Ctr, 450 Lakeville Rd, New Hyde Park, NY 11042; **Phone:** 516-941-1260; **Board Cert:** Neurological Surgery 1991; **Med School:** Columbia P&S 1982; **Resid:** Neurological Surgery, Montefiore Hosp Med Ctr 1988; **Fac Appt:** Assoc Prof NS, UMDNJ-NJ Med Sch, Newark

Neurology

Blanck, Richard H MD (N) - **Spec Exp:** Multiple Sclerosis; Pain-Back; **Hospital:** N Shore Univ Hosp, St. Francis Hosp - The Heart Ctr (page 111); **Address:** Neurological Associates of Long Island, 1991 Marcus Ave, Ste 110, Lake Success, NY 11042; **Phone:** 516-466-4700; **Board Cert:** Internal Medicine 1976; Neurology 1980; **Med School:** UMDNJ-NJ Med Sch, Newark 1973; **Resid:** Internal Medicine, N Shore Univ Hosp 1975; Neurology, N Shore Univ Hosp 1978; **Fac Appt:** Assoc Clin Prof N, NYU Sch Med

Ettinger, Alan MD (N) - **Spec Exp:** Epilepsy; Seizure Disorders; **Hospital:** Winthrop Univ Hosp (page 536), Huntington Hosp; **Address:** NSPC, 1991 Marcus Ave, Ste 108, Lake Success, NY 11042; **Phone:** 516-442-2250; **Board Cert:** Neurology 1989; **Med School:** Boston Univ 1983; **Resid:** Internal Medicine, Hartford Hosp 1985; Neurology, Montefiore Med Ctr 1988; **Fellow:** Epilepsy, Montefiore Med Ctr 1989; **Fac Appt:** Prof N, Albert Einstein Coll Med

Gordon, Marc L MD (N) - **Spec Exp:** Dementia; Headache; Multiple Sclerosis; Alzheimer's Disease; **Hospital:** Zucker Hillside Hosp; **Address:** LIJ Cushing Neuroscience Inst, 611 Northern Blvd, Ste 150, Great Neck, NY 11021-5207; **Phone:** 516-325-7000; **Board Cert:** Neurology 1990; **Med School:** Columbia P&S 1985; **Resid:** Neurology, Monetefiore Med Ctr 1989; **Fellow:** Neuropsychopharmacology, Monetefiore Med Ctr 1990; **Fac Appt:** Assoc Prof N, Hofstra N Shore-LIJ Sch Med

Gottesman, Malcolm MD (N) - **Spec Exp:** Multiple Sclerosis; Stroke; **Hospital:** Winthrop Univ Hosp (page 536); **Address:** Winthrop Neuroscience, 200 Old Country Rd, Ste 370, Mineola, NY 11501; **Phone:** 516-663-4525; **Board Cert:** Neurology 1989; Psychiatry 1983; **Med School:** Albany Med Coll 1978; **Resid:** Psychiatry, Boston Med Ctr 1982; Neurology, LIJ Med Ctr 1988; **Fellow:** Behavioral Medicine, Boston Med Ctr 1983; **Fac Appt:** Assoc Prof N, SUNY Stony Brook

Haimovic, Itzhak C MD (N) - **Spec Exp:** Spinal Disorders; Epilepsy; Headache; **Hospital:** N Shore Univ Hosp, Long Is Jewish Med Ctr; **Address:** Neurological Specialities, 170 Great Neck Rd, Great Neck, NY 11021; **Phone:** 516-487-4464; **Board Cert:** Neurology 1981; Clinical Neurophysiology 2010; **Med School:** NY Med Coll 1975; **Resid:** Internal Medicine, N Shore Univ Hosp 1977; Neurology, N Shore Univ Hosp 1980; **Fac Appt:** Assoc Clin Prof N, NYU Sch Med

Harden, Cynthia L MD (N) - **Spec Exp:** Epilepsy/Seizure Disorders; **Hospital:** Long Is Jewish Med Ctr, N Shore Univ Hosp; **Address:** LIJ Cushing Neuroscience Inst, 611 Northern Blvd, Ste 150, Great Neck, NY 11021; **Phone:** 516-325-7000; **Board Cert:** Neurology 1989; Epilepsy 2013; **Med School:** Univ Wisc 1983; **Resid:** Internal Medicine, St Lukes Hosp 1985; Neurology, Mt Sinai Hosp 1988; **Fellow:** Clinical Neurophysiology, Montefiore Med Ctr 1989

Kadakia, Satish K MD (N) - **Spec Exp:** Child Neurology; Ataxia; Bell's Palsy; **Hospital:** Nassau Univ Med Ctr; **Address:** 2201 Hempstead Tpke Fl 7 - Ste 772, East Meadow, NY 11554-1859; **Phone:** 516-572-3107; **Board Cert:** Pediatrics 1987; Child Neurology 1992; Neurodevelopmental Disabilities 2005; **Med School:** India 1980; **Resid:** Pediatrics, Jersey Shore Univ Med Ctr 1986; Neurology, Nassau Univ Med Ctr 1989; **Fellow:** Child Neurology, Nassau Univ Med Ctr 1990; **Fac Appt:** Prof N, SUNY Stony Brook

Kanner, Ronald M MD (N) - **Spec Exp:** Headache; Pain-Chronic; Migraine; **Hospital:** Long Is Jewish Med Ctr; **Address:** LIJ Cushing Neuroscience Inst, 611 Northern Blvd, Ste 150, Great Neck, NY 11021; **Phone:** 516-325-7000; **Board Cert:** Neurology 1980; **Med School:** Spain 1975; **Resid:** Internal Medicine, Univ Hosp Penn 1976; Neurology, Jacobi Med Ctr 1979; **Fellow:** Neuro-Oncology, Meml Sloan-Kettering Cancer Ctr 1981; **Fac Appt:** Prof N, Hofstra N Shore-LIJ Sch Med

Kelemen, John MD (N) - **Spec Exp:** Electromyography; Neuromuscular Disorders; Botox for Muscle Overactivity; Dystonia; **Hospital:** Plainview Hosp; **Address:** Island Neurological Assocs, 824 Old Country Rd, Plainview, NY 11803; **Phone:** 516-822-2230; **Board Cert:** Neurology 1979; **Med School:** Georgetown Univ 1974; **Resid:** Neurology, Nassau Univ Med Ctr 1978; Neurology, New England Med Ctr 1980

Kessler, Jeffrey T MD (N) - **Spec Exp:** Parkinson's Disease; Dementia; Pain-Facial; **Hospital:** N Shore Univ Hosp, St. Francis Hosp - The Heart Ctr (page 111); **Address:** Neurological Assocs, 1991 Marcus Ave, Ste 110, Lake Success, NY 11042; **Phone:** 516-466-4700; **Board Cert:** Internal Medicine 1974; Neurology 1976; **Med School:** Cornell Univ-Weill Med Coll 1969; **Resid:** Internal Medicine, NY-Presby/Weill Cornell Med Ctr 1971; Neurology, NY-Presby/Weill Cornell Med Ctr 1974; **Fac Appt:** Assoc Clin Prof N, NYU Sch Med

Kula, Roger W MD (N) - **Spec Exp:** Neuromuscular Disorders; Chiari's Deformity; Syringomyelia & Spinal Cord Diseases; Myasthenia Gravis; **Hospital:** N Shore Univ Hosp; **Address:** Chiari Inst, 611 Northern Blvd, Ste 150, Great Neck, NY 11021; **Phone:** 516-570-4400; **Board Cert:** Internal Medicine 1975; Neurology 1977; Neuromuscular Medicine 2008; **Med School:** Johns Hopkins Univ 1970; **Resid:** Neurology, UCSF Med Ctr 1974; Neurology, Natl Inst Hlth 1975; **Fellow:** Neuromuscular Medicine, Natl Inst Hlth 1977; **Fac Appt:** Assoc Prof N, Hofstra N Shore-LIJ Sch Med

Levy, Lewis A MD (N) - **Spec Exp:** Tourette's Syndrome; Parkinson's Disease; **Hospital:** South Nassau Comm Hosp; **Address:** LI Neurology Consultants, 777 Sunrise Hwy, Ste 200, Lynbrook, NY 11563; **Phone:** 516-887-3516; **Board Cert:** Neurology 1979; **Med School:** SUNY Downstate 1973; **Resid:** Neurology, Jacobi Med Ctr 1977; **Fac Appt:** Asst Clin Prof N, Albert Einstein Coll Med

Newman, Stephen M MD (N) - **Spec Exp:** Multiple Sclerosis; Migraine; **Hospital:** Plainview Hosp; **Address:** Island Neurological Assocs, 824 Old Country Rd, Plainview, NY 11803; **Phone:** 516-822-2230; **Board Cert:** Neurology 1978; **Med School:** SUNY Buffalo 1972; **Resid:** Neurology, Nassau Co Med Ctr 1976

Ragone, Philip S MD (N) - **Spec Exp:** Electromyography; **Hospital:** St. Francis Hosp - The Heart Ctr (page 111), N Shore Univ Hosp; **Address:** 1010 Northern Blvd, Ste 136, Great Neck, NY 11021; **Phone:** 516-482-4100; **Board Cert:** Internal Medicine 1985; Neurology 1989; Electrodiagnostic Medicine 1990; **Med School:** NY Med Coll 1982; **Resid:** Internal Medicine, Lenox Hill Hosp 1985; Neurology, Montefiore Med Ctr 1988; **Fellow:** Electromyography, Montefiore Med Ctr 1989

Schaul, Neil S MD (N) - **Spec Exp:** Epilepsy/Seizure Disorders; Electrodiagnosis; **Hospital:** NY Hosp Queens (page 498); **Address:** 1575 Hillside Ave, Ste 100, New Hyde Park, NY 11040; **Phone:** 516-616-6286; **Board Cert:** Neurology 1976; **Med School:** SUNY Hlth Sci Ctr 1966; **Resid:** Internal Medicine, DC Genl Hosp 1968; Neurology, Montreal Neur Hosp 1974; **Fellow:** Neurophysiology, Montreal Neur Hosp 1977; **Fac Appt:** Assoc Prof Med, Cornell Univ-Weill Med Coll

Turner, Ira MD (N) - **Spec Exp:** Headache; **Hospital:** Plainview Hosp; **Address:** Island Neurological Assocs, 824 Old Country Rd, Plainview, NY 11803; **Phone:** 516-822-2230; **Board Cert:** Neurology 1978; Headache Medicine 2007; **Med School:** SUNY Downstate 1972; **Resid:** Neurology, Nassau Co Med Ctr 1976

Neuroradiology

Johnson, Alan A MD (NRad) - **Hospital:** Long Is Jewish Med Ctr; **Address:** LIJ Med Ctr, Radiology, 270-05 76th Ave, New Hyde Park, NY 11040; **Phone:** 718-470-7175; **Board Cert:** Neuroradiology 2007; Diagnostic Radiology 2001; **Med School:** SUNY Upstate Med Univ 1996; **Resid:** Diagnostic Radiology, Columbia Presby Med Ctr 2001; **Fellow:** Neuroradiology, Columbia Presby Med Ctr 2003; **Fac Appt:** Asst Prof Rad, Hofstra N Shore-LIJ Sch Med

Ortiz, Orlando MD (NRad) - **Spec Exp:** Interventional Neuroradiology; Spine Imaging & Intervention; **Hospital:** Winthrop Univ Hosp (page 536); **Address:** Winthrop Univ Hosp, Neuroradiology, 259 1st St, Mineola, NY 11501; **Phone:** 516-663-2123; **Board Cert:** Diagnostic Radiology 1990; Neuroradiology 2006; **Med School:** Harvard Med Sch 1985; **Resid:** Diagnostic Radiology, LIJ Med Ctr 1990; **Fellow:** Neurological Radiology, NY-Presby/Columbia Univ Med Ctr 1992; **Fac Appt:** Clin Prof Rad, SUNY Stony Brook

Pile-Spellman, John M MD (NRad) - **Spec Exp:** Interventional Neuroradiology; Cerebrovascular Disease; Arteriovenous Malformations; Endovascular Neurosurgery; **Hospital:** Winthrop Univ Hosp (page 536); **Address:** NSPC, Radiology, 1991 Marcus Ave, Ste 108, Lake Success, NY 11042; **Phone:** 516-442-2250; **Board Cert:** Diagnostic Radiology 1984; **Med School:** Tufts Univ 1978; **Resid:** Neurological Surgery, Tufts Med Ctr 1981; **Fellow:** Neurological Radiology, Mass Genl Hosp 1984; Interventional Neuroradiology, NYU Med Ctr 1986; **Fac Appt:** Prof Rad, Columbia P&S

Sanelli, Pina MD (NRad) - **Spec Exp:** Spine Imaging & Intervention; MRI & CT of Brain & Spine; MRI; **Hospital:** NS-LIJ Hlth Sys; **Address:** NS-LIJ Hlth, Radiology, 300 Community Drive, Manhasset, NY 11030; **Phone:** 516-562-2815; **Board Cert:** Diagnostic Radiology 1999; Neuroradiology 2011; **Med School:** SUNY Buffalo 1994; **Resid:** Diagnostic Radiology, Albany Med Ctr 1997; Diagnostic Radiology, N Shore Univ Hosp 1999; **Fellow:** Neurological Radiology, Mass Genl Hosp 2001

Setton, Avi MD (NRad) - **Spec Exp:** Cerebrovascular Disease; Stroke; **Hospital:** N Shore Univ Hosp; **Address:** N Shore Univ Hosp, Neuroradiology, 300 Community Drive, 9 Tower, Manhasset, NY 11030; **Phone:** 516-562-3021; **Med School:** Israel 1978; **Resid:** Diagnostic Radiology, Bellevue Med Ctr 1991; **Fellow:** Neurological Radiology, NYU Med Ctr 1992

Nuclear Medicine

Palestro, Christopher J MD (NuM) - **Spec Exp:** Nuclear Imaging; Thyroid & Parathyroid Imaging; Thyroid Cancer; PET Imaging; **Hospital:** Long Is Jewish Med Ctr, N Shore Univ Hosp; **Address:** LIJ Med Ctr, Nuclear Med, 270-05 76th Ave Research Bldg Fl 4, New Hyde Park, NY 11040; **Phone:** 718-470-7080; **Board Cert:** Nuclear Medicine 1982; **Med School:** Mexico 1975; **Resid:** Diagnostic Radiology, Roosevelt Hosp 1980; **Fellow:** Nuclear Medicine, Meml Sloan-Kettering Cancer Ctr 1982; **Fac Appt:** Prof Rad, Hofstra N Shore-LIJ Sch Med

Obstetrics & Gynecology

Benedict, Leonard A MD (ObG) - **Spec Exp:** Gynecology Only; Gynecologic Surgery; **Hospital:** N Shore Univ Hosp; **Address:** 433 Uniondale Ave, Uniondale, NY 11553; **Phone:** 516-483-8798; **Board Cert:** Obstetrics & Gynecology 1981; **Med School:** Scotland, UK 1972; **Resid:** Obstetrics & Gynecology, Brooklyn Jewish Hosp 1978; **Fac Appt:** Asst Clin Prof ObG, NYU Sch Med

Haselkorn, Joan MD (ObG) *PCP* **- Spec Exp:** Laparoscopic Surgery; Hysteroscopic Surgery; Uterine Fibroids; Gynecology Only; **Hospital:** South Nassau Comm Hosp; **Address:** 556 Merrick Rd, Ste 200, Rockville Centre, NY 11570; **Phone:** 516-255-2044; **Board Cert:** Obstetrics & Gynecology 2013; **Med School:** Israel 1982; **Resid:** Obstetrics & Gynecology, NYU Med Ctr 1986

Jacob, Jessica MD (ObG) *PCP* **- Hospital:** N Shore Univ Hosp; **Address:** 3003 New Hyde Park Rd, Ste 407, New Hyde Park, NY 11042-1214; **Phone:** 516-488-8145; **Board Cert:** Obstetrics & Gynecology 2013; **Med School:** NYU Sch Med 1983; **Resid:** Obstetrics & Gynecology, N Shore Univ Hosp 1987; **Fac Appt:** Asst Clin Prof ObG, NYU Sch Med

Klein, Victor R MD (ObG) **- Spec Exp:** Multiple Gestation; Genetic Disorders; Pregnancy-High Risk; **Hospital:** N Shore Univ Hosp, Long Is Jewish Med Ctr; **Address:** NS-LIJ Med Grp, 600 Northern Blvd, Ste 212, Great Neck, NY 11021; **Phone:** 516-472-5700; **Board Cert:** Obstetrics & Gynecology 2013; Maternal & Fetal Medicine 2013; Clinical Genetics 1987; **Med School:** SUNY Downstate 1980; **Resid:** Internal Medicine, Kings Co Hosp Ctr 1981; Obstetrics & Gynecology, Johns Hopkins Hosp 1985; **Fellow:** Clinical Genetics, Univ Texas SW Med Ctr 1987; Maternal & Fetal Medicine, Univ Texas SW Med Ctr 1987; **Fac Appt:** Assoc Clin Prof ObG, Hofstra N Shore-LIJ Sch Med

Krim, Eileen Y MD (ObG) **- Spec Exp:** Menopause Problems; Adolescent Gynecology; Osteoporosis; Laparoscopic Surgery; **Hospital:** N Shore Univ Hosp; **Address:** 3111 New Hyde Park Rd, North Hills, NY 11040-3500; **Phone:** 516-365-6100; **Board Cert:** Obstetrics & Gynecology 1982; **Med School:** NY Med Coll 1975; **Resid:** Obstetrics & Gynecology, Beth Israel Med Ctr 1979; **Fellow:** Maternal & Fetal Medicine, N Shore Univ Hosp 1981; **Fac Appt:** Assoc Clin Prof ObG, NYU Sch Med

Leong, Mary MD (ObG) **- Spec Exp:** Uterine Fibroids; Gynecologic Surgery; Women's Health; Robotic Surgery; **Hospital:** Long Is Jewish Med Ctr; **Address:** A & J Gottlieb Women's Comprehensive Hlth Ctr, 1554 Northern Blvd, Fl 5th, Manhasset, NY 11030; **Phone:** 516-390-9242; **Board Cert:** Obstetrics & Gynecology 2013; **Med School:** NYU Sch Med 1978; **Resid:** Obstetrics & Gynecology, Bellevue Hosp Ctr 1982; **Fac Appt:** Asst Prof ObG, Albert Einstein Coll Med

Lind, Lawrence R MD (ObG) **- Spec Exp:** Uro-Gynecology; Pelvic Reconstruction; **Hospital:** N Shore Univ Hosp, Long Is Jewish Med Ctr; **Address:** 865 Northern Blvd, Ste 202, Great Neck, NY 11021; **Phone:** 516-622-5114; **Board Cert:** Obstetrics & Gynecology 2013; **Med School:** Cornell Univ-Weill Med Coll 1990; **Resid:** Obstetrics & Gynecology, N Shore Univ Hosp 1994; **Fellow:** Gynecologic Urology, UCLA Med Ctr 1996

Mack, Laurence F MD (ObG) *PCP* **- Spec Exp:** Infertility; Pregnancy-High Risk; Autoimmune Disease in Pregnancy; Pap Smear Abnormalities; **Hospital:** Plainview Hosp, Mercy Med Ctr-Rockville Centre; **Address:** 1130 N Broadway, North Massapequa, NY 11758-0910; **Phone:** 516-799-3462; **Board Cert:** Obstetrics & Gynecology 2013; **Med School:** Univ Hlth Scis, Chicago Med Sch 1985; **Resid:** Obstetrics & Gynecology, Brookdale Hosp 1989

Nimaroff, Michael L MD (ObG) *PCP* **- Spec Exp:** Laparoscopic Surgery; Hysterectomy Alternatives; Hysteroscopic Surgery; **Hospital:** N Shore Univ Hosp; **Address:** 600 Northern Blvd, Ste 212, Great Neck, NY 11021; **Phone:** 516-472-5700; **Board Cert:** Obstetrics & Gynecology 2013; **Med School:** UMDNJ-NJ Med Sch, Newark 1987; **Resid:** Obstetrics & Gynecology, N Shore Univ Hosp 1991; **Fac Appt:** Asst Clin Prof ObG, NYU Sch Med

Salzman, Ronnie M MD (ObG) **- Spec Exp:** Gynecology Only; **Hospital:** Long Is Jewish Med Ctr; **Address:** Long Island Women's Healthcare Assocs, 2428 Merrick Rd Unit A, Bellmore, NY 11710; **Phone:** 516-379-2689; **Board Cert:** Obstetrics & Gynecology 2013; **Med School:** SUNY Stony Brook 1980; **Resid:** Obstetrics & Gynecology, Mass Genl Hosp 1984

Toles, Allen W MD (ObG) - **Spec Exp:** Pregnancy-High Risk; **Hospital:** Long Is Jewish Med Ctr; **Address:** A & J Gottlieb Women's Comprehensive Hlth Ctr, 1554 Northern Blvd Fl 5th, Manhasset, NY 11030; **Phone:** 516-390-9242; **Board Cert:** Obstetrics & Gynecology 2013; **Med School:** Meharry Med Coll 1986; **Resid:** Obstetrics & Gynecology, Howard Univ Hosp 1990; **Fac Appt:** Asst Prof ObG, Albert Einstein Coll Med

Vasudeva, Kusum MD (ObG) - **Spec Exp:** Gynecology Only; **Hospital:** N Shore Univ Hosp; **Address:** 2 Ohio Drive, Ste 200, Pro Health Plaza, Lake Success, NY 11042; **Phone:** 516-608-6800; **Board Cert:** Obstetrics & Gynecology 1975; **Med School:** India 1967; **Resid:** Obstetrics & Gynecology, N Shore Univ Hosp 1974; **Fellow:** Maternal & Fetal Medicine, N Shore Univ Hosp 1976

Occupational Medicine

Mendelsohn, Sara L MD (OM) - **Spec Exp:** Travel Medicine; Occupational Disease & Injury; Preventive Medicine; Asbestos-Related Lung Disease; **Hospital:** Stony Brook Univ Hosp; **Address:** 800 Woodbury Rd, Ste K, Woodbury, NY 11797; **Phone:** 516-682-9142; **Board Cert:** Occupational Medicine 1993; **Med School:** Boston Univ 1988; **Resid:** Occupational Medicine, Univ IL Med Ctr 1991; **Fac Appt:** Asst Clin Prof OM, SUNY Stony Brook

Wilkenfeld, Marc MD (OM) - **Spec Exp:** Environmental Medicine; **Hospital:** Winthrop Univ Hosp (page 536); **Address:** 1300 Franklin Ave, Ste UL4A, Garden City, NY 11530; **Phone:** 516-663-8890; **Board Cert:** Occupational Medicine 1991; **Med School:** Univ VT Coll Med 1985; **Resid:** Occupational Medicine, Mt Sinai Med Ctr 1989; **Fac Appt:** Asst Clin Prof OM, Columbia P&S

Ophthalmology

Berke, Stanley J MD (Oph) - **Spec Exp:** Glaucoma; Cataract Surgery-Lens Implant; Laser Surgery; **Hospital:** Long Is Jewish Med Ctr, Nassau Univ Med Ctr; **Address:** Berke Eye Care, 1600 Stewart Ave, Ste 306, Westbury, NY 11590; **Phone:** 516-794-2020; **Board Cert:** Ophthalmology 1987; **Med School:** SUNY Buffalo 1981; **Resid:** Ophthalmology, Nassau Univ Med Ctr 1985; **Fellow:** Cataract/Lens Implant Surgery, Mass Eye & Ear Infirm 1986; **Fac Appt:** Assoc Clin Prof Oph, Albert Einstein Coll Med

Boniuk, Vivien MD (Oph) - **Spec Exp:** Diagnostic Problems; **Hospital:** Long Is Jewish Med Ctr, Queens Hosp Ctr - Jamaica; **Address:** 600 Northern Blvd, Ste 214, Great Neck, NY 11021; **Phone:** 516-470-2020; **Board Cert:** Ophthalmology 1969; **Med School:** Dalhousie Univ 1964; **Resid:** Ophthalmology, Barnes Jewish Hosp 1967; **Fellow:** Ophthalmological Pathology, Baylor Coll Affil Hosp 1968; **Fac Appt:** Assoc Prof Oph, Hofstra N Shore-LIJ Sch Med

D'Aversa, Gerard MD (Oph) - **Spec Exp:** Cataract Surgery; Refractive Surgery; Corneal Disease; **Address:** Ophthalmic Consultants of LI, 65 Roosevelt Ave, rm 204, Valley Stream, NY 11580-1106; **Phone:** 516-374-4199; **Board Cert:** Ophthalmology 2006; **Med School:** Albert Einstein Coll Med 1989; **Resid:** Ophthalmology, LI Jewish Med Ctr 1993; **Fellow:** Cornea & Ext Eye Disease, Shands Hosp 1994; **Fac Appt:** Asst Prof Oph, Albert Einstein Coll Med

Fastenberg, David M MD (Oph) - **Spec Exp:** Retina/Vitreous Surgery; Macular Degeneration; Diabetic Eye Disease/Retinopathy; **Hospital:** Syosset Hosp, Long Is Jewish Med Ctr; **Address:** Long Island Vitreoretinal Consultants, 600 Northern Blvd, Ste 216, Great Neck, NY 11021; **Phone:** 516-466-0390; **Board Cert:** Ophthalmology 1981; **Med School:** NY Med Coll 1976; **Resid:** Ophthalmology, Northwestern Meml Hosp 1980; **Fellow:** Retina, USC-Doheny Eye Inst 1982; **Fac Appt:** Assoc Clin Prof Oph, Albert Einstein Coll Med

Ferrone, Philip J MD (Oph) - **Spec Exp:** Retinal Disorders; Retina/Vitreous Surgery; Retinal Disorders-Pediatric; **Hospital:** Syosset Hosp, Long Is Jewish Med Ctr; **Address:** Long Island Vitreoretinal Consultants, 600 Northern Blvd, Ste 216, Great Neck, NY 11021; **Phone:** 516-466-0390; **Board Cert:** Ophthalmology 2006; **Med School:** Harvard Med Sch 1989; **Resid:** Ophthalmology, Duke Univ Eye Ctr 1993; **Fellow:** Vitreoretinal Surgery, Associated Retinal Consultants 1995

Girardi, Anthony MD (Oph) - **Spec Exp:** Cataract Surgery; Glaucoma; **Hospital:** Glen Cove Hosp; **Address:** 8 Medical Plaza, Ste 201, Glen Cove, NY 11542; **Phone:** 516-676-4596; **Board Cert:** Ophthalmology 1985; **Med School:** SUNY Stony Brook 1980; **Resid:** Ophthalmology, Kings Co Hosp 1984; **Fac Appt:** Asst Clin Prof Oph, SUNY Downstate

Goldberg, Leslie P MD (Oph) - **Spec Exp:** Cataract Surgery; LASIK-Refractive Surgery; Eyelid Cosmetic Surgery; **Hospital:** St. Francis Hosp - The Heart Ctr (page 111), N Shore Univ Hosp; **Address:** Long Island Eye Surgeons, 1981 Marcus Ave, Ste E115, Lake Success, NY 11042; **Phone:** 516-627-5113; **Board Cert:** Ophthalmology 1977; **Med School:** Ros Franklin Univ/Chicago Med Sch 1970; **Resid:** Ophthalmology, NYU Med Ctr 1976; **Fac Appt:** Asst Clin Prof Oph, NYU Sch Med

Hatsis, Alexander MD (Oph) - **Spec Exp:** LASIK-Refractive Surgery; Cataract Surgery; Corneal Disease; Keratoconus; **Hospital:** South Nassau Comm Hosp, Nassau Univ Med Ctr; **Address:** 2 Lincoln Ave, Ste 401, Rockville Centre, NY 11570; **Phone:** 516-763-4106; **Board Cert:** Ophthalmology 2013; **Med School:** Italy 1978; **Resid:** Surgery, Nassau Co Med Ctr 1980; Ophthalmology, Nassau Co Med Ctr 1981; **Fellow:** Ophthalmology, Nassau Co Med Ctr 1983; **Fac Appt:** Asst Clin Prof Oph, SUNY Stony Brook

Hufnagel, Thierry J MD (Oph) - **Spec Exp:** Corneal Disease & Surgery; Cornea & External Eye Disease; LASIK-Refractive Surgery; **Hospital:** N Shore Univ Hosp; **Address:** Stahl Eyecare Experts, 450 Endo Blvd, Garden City, NY 11530; **Phone:** 516-832-8000; **Board Cert:** Ophthalmology 2005; Anatomic Pathology 1986; **Med School:** France 1981; **Resid:** Anatomic & Clinical Pathology, Hosp U Penn 1984; Ophthalmology, Yale-New Haven Hosp 1988; **Fellow:** Ophthalmic Pathology, New Haven Children's Hosp 1991

Kasper, William S MD (Oph) - **Spec Exp:** Cataract Surgery; Glaucoma; Cornea & External Eye Disease; **Hospital:** Winthrop Univ Hosp (page 536); **Address:** 520 Franklin Ave, Ste L9, Garden City, NY 11530; **Phone:** 516-742-3937; **Board Cert:** Ophthalmology 1974; **Med School:** Belgium 1967; **Resid:** Ophthalmology, Nassau Univ Med Ctr 1971; **Fac Appt:** Assoc Clin Prof Oph, Belgium

Kodsi, Sylvia R MD (Oph) - **Spec Exp:** Pediatric Ophthalmology; **Hospital:** Long Is Jewish Med Ctr; **Address:** 600 Northern Blvd, Ste 220, Great Neck, NY 11021; **Phone:** 516-470-2020; **Board Cert:** Ophthalmology 2013; **Med School:** NYU Sch Med 1987; **Resid:** Ophthalmology, St Vincent's Hosp & Med Ctr 1991; **Fellow:** Neuro-Ophthalmology, Mayo Clinic 1992; Pediatric Ophthalmology, U Minn Med Ctr 1993

Malik, Sajid MD (Oph) - **Spec Exp:** Cataract Surgery; Lens Implants-Multifocal; **Hospital:** Winthrop Univ Hosp (page 536); **Address:** Woodbury Optical, 185 Woodbury Rd, Hicksville, NY 11801; **Phone:** 516-681-3937; **Board Cert:** Ophthalmology 2010; **Med School:** SUNY Stony Brook 1989; **Resid:** Ophthalmology, Columbia Presby/Harlem Hosp 1994

Marks, Alan B MD (Oph) - **Spec Exp:** Cataract Surgery; Laser-Refractive Surgery; Eyelid Cosmetic Surgery; **Hospital:** St. Francis Hosp - The Heart Ctr (page 111), Syosset Hosp; **Address:** Long Island Eye Surgeons, 1981 Marcus Ave, Ste E115, Lake Success, NY 11042; **Phone:** 516-627-5113; **Board Cert:** Ophthalmology 1983; **Med School:** NY Med Coll 1978; **Resid:** Ophthalmology, N Shore Univ Hosp 1982

Nauheim, Richard MD (Oph) - **Spec Exp:** Corneal Disease; Cataract Surgery; **Hospital:** South Nassau Comm Hosp, NS-LIJ Hlth Sys; **Address:** 2025 Merrick Ave, Merrick, NY 11566; **Phone:** 516-868-7110; **Board Cert:** Ophthalmology 1989; **Med School:** SUNY Buffalo 1984; **Resid:** Ophthalmology, Nassau Univ Med Ctr 1988; **Fellow:** Cornea & Ext Eye Disease, Eye & Ear Inst - UPMC 1989; **Fac Appt:** Asst Prof Oph, SUNY Stony Brook

Nelson, David B MD (Oph) - **Spec Exp:** Cataract Surgery; **Hospital:** Mercy Med Ctr-Rockville Centre; **Address:** Ophthalmic Consultants of LI, 2000 N Village Ave, Ste 402, Ryan Medical Arts Bldg, Rockville Center, NY 11570-1001; **Phone:** 516-766-2519; **Board Cert:** Ophthalmology 1977; **Med School:** SUNY Hlth Sci Ctr 1972; **Resid:** Ophthalmology, NY Ear & Eye Infirm 1976; **Fac Appt:** Asst Prof Oph, SUNY Stony Brook

Packer, Samuel MD (Oph) - **Hospital:** Long Is Jewish Med Ctr; **Address:** 600 Northern Blvd, Ste 214, Great Neck, NY 11021; **Phone:** 516-465-8406; **Board Cert:** Ophthalmology 1973; **Med School:** SUNY Downstate 1966; **Resid:** Ophthalmology, Yale-New Haven Hosp 1971; **Fac Appt:** Clin Prof Oph, NYU Sch Med

Perry, Henry D MD (Oph) - **Spec Exp:** Laser-Refractive Surgery; Cornea Transplant; Cataract Surgery; Eyelid/Tear Duct Disorders; **Hospital:** Mercy Med Ctr-Rockville Centre, N Shore Univ Hosp; **Address:** Ophthalmic Consultants of LI, 2000 N Village Ave, Ste 402, Ryan Medical Arts Bldg, Rockville Centre, NY 11570-1001; **Phone:** 516-766-2519; **Board Cert:** Ophthalmology 1976; **Med School:** Univ Cincinnati 1971; **Resid:** Ophthalmology, Nassau Univ Med Ctr 1975; Ophthalmology, Hosp Univ Penn 1974; **Fellow:** Cornea, Mass Eye & Ear Infirmary 1977; **Fac Appt:** Assoc Clin Prof Oph, Cornell Univ-Weill Med Coll

Prywes, Arnold S MD (Oph) - **Spec Exp:** Glaucoma; Cataract Surgery; **Hospital:** N Shore Univ Hosp; **Address:** Eye Care Assocs & Glaucoma Consultants LI, 4212 Hempstead Tpke, Bethpage, NY 11714-5709; **Phone:** 516-731-4800; **Board Cert:** Ophthalmology 1978; **Med School:** Mount Sinai Sch Med 1972; **Resid:** Ophthalmology, Mount Sinai Hosp 1977; **Fellow:** Ophthalmology, Mount Sinai Hosp 1974; **Fac Appt:** Assoc Clin Prof Oph, Albert Einstein Coll Med

Rosenthal, Kenneth J MD (Oph) - **Spec Exp:** Intraocular Lenses; Cataract Surgery; Laser Surgery; Cosmetic Surgery-Face; **Hospital:** New York Eye & Ear Infirm of Mt Sinai, St. Francis Hosp - The Heart Ctr (page 111); **Address:** 310 E Shore Rd, Ste 102, Great Neck, NY 11023; **Phone:** 516-466-8989; **Board Cert:** Ophthalmology 1986; **Med School:** Albany Med Coll 1978; **Resid:** Ophthalmology, N Shore Univ Hosp 1983

Rubin, Laurence MD (Oph) - **Spec Exp:** Cataract Surgery; Intraocular Lens; Glaucoma; **Hospital:** N Shore Univ Hosp; **Address:** Mid-Island Eye Phys & Surgeons, 4277 Hempstead Tpke, Ste 109, Bethpage, NY 11714-5706; **Phone:** 516-796-4030; **Board Cert:** Ophthalmology 1987; **Med School:** NY Med Coll 1980; **Resid:** Ophthalmology, New York Eye & Ear Infirm 1984

Rubin, Steven E MD (Oph) - **Spec Exp:** Strabismus; Pediatric Ophthalmology; Amblyopia; **Hospital:** Long Is Jewish Med Ctr; **Address:** NSLIJ Div Pediatric Ophthalmology, 600 Northern Blvd, Ste 220, Great Neck, NY 11021-5200; **Phone:** 516-465-8444; **Board Cert:** Ophthalmology 1983; **Med School:** SUNY Downstate 1978; **Resid:** Ophthalmology, Univ Penn-Scheie Eye Inst 1982; **Fellow:** Pediatric Ophthalmology, Wills Eye Hosp 1983; **Fac Appt:** Prof Oph, NYU Sch Med

Schlessinger, David A MD (Oph) - **Spec Exp:** Eyelid Cosmetic & Reconstructive Surgery; Oculoplastic Surgery; Neuro-Ophthalmology; Eyelid Surgery/Blepharoplasty; **Hospital:** Syosset Hosp; **Address:** Schlessinger Eye & Face, 75 Froehlich Farm Blvd, Woodbury, NY 11797; **Phone:** 516-496-2122; **Board Cert:** Ophthalmology 2005; **Med School:** Univ Pittsburgh 1988; **Resid:** Ophthalmology, Interfaith Med Ctr 1992; **Fellow:** Ophthalmic Plastic & Reconstructive Surgery, Univ Minn Med Ctr 1993; Neuro-Ophthalmology, Univ Minn Med Ctr 1993

Sturm, Richard T MD (Oph) - **Spec Exp:** Glaucoma; Cataract Surgery; **Hospital:** Mercy Med Ctr-Rockville Centre; **Address:** 360 Merrick Rd Fl 3, Lynbrook, NY 11563; **Phone:** 516-593-7709; **Board Cert:** Ophthalmology 1989; **Med School:** NY Med Coll 1983; **Resid:** Ophthalmology, St Luke's-Roosevelt Hosp Ctr 1987; **Fellow:** Glaucoma, Mass Eye & Ear Infirm 1988; **Fac Appt:** Asst Clin Prof Oph, Albert Einstein Coll Med

Svitra, Paul P MD (Oph) - **Spec Exp:** Diabetic Eye Disease/Retinopathy; Macular Degeneration; Retinal Detachment; Retinal Disorders; **Hospital:** N Shore Univ Hosp, Long Is Jewish Med Ctr; **Address:** 3003 New Hyde Park Rd, Ste 203, New Hyde Park, NY 11042; **Phone:** 516-327-0505; **Board Cert:** Ophthalmology 1990; **Med School:** Cornell Univ-Weill Med Coll 1984; **Resid:** Ophthalmology, Mass Eye & Ear Infirmary 1989; **Fellow:** Retina/Vitreous Surgery, Duke Eye Ctr 1990; **Fac Appt:** Asst Prof Oph, Cornell Univ-Weill Med Coll

Udell, Ira J MD (Oph) - **Spec Exp:** Cornea Transplant; Corneal Disease; Keratoconus; PROSE Contact Lens; **Hospital:** Long Is Jewish Med Ctr, N Shore Univ Hosp; **Address:** 600 Northern Blvd, Ste 214, Great Neck, NY 11021; **Phone:** 516-470-2020; **Board Cert:** Ophthalmology 1980; **Med School:** Tulane Univ 1974; **Resid:** Ophthalmology, LIJ Med Ctr 1979; **Fellow:** Cornea, Mass Eye & Ear Infirm 1981; **Fac Appt:** Prof Oph, Hofstra N Shore-LIJ Sch Med

Weinstein, Joseph MD (Oph) - **Spec Exp:** Cataract Surgery; Refractive Surgery; Botox Therapy; **Hospital:** N Shore Univ Hosp, Syosset Hosp; **Address:** Eye Care Assocs & Glaucoma Consultants LI, 4212 Hempstead Tpke, Bethpage, NY 11714-5712; **Phone:** 516-731-4800; **Board Cert:** Ophthalmology 1982; **Med School:** Albert Einstein Coll Med 1977; **Resid:** Ophthalmology, Long Island Jewish Med Ctr 1981

Orthopaedic Surgery

Amaral, Terry MD (OrS) - **Spec Exp:** Pediatric Orthopaedic Surgery; **Hospital:** Steven & Alexandra Cohen Chldn's Med Ctr of NY; **Address:** Steven & Alexandra Cohen Children's Hosp, 269-01 76th Ave Fl 1 - rm 161, New Hyde Park, NY 11040; **Phone:** 718-470-3570; **Board Cert:** Orthopaedic Surgery 2006; **Med School:** Albert Einstein Coll Med 1998; **Resid:** Orthopaedic Surgery, Montefiore Med Ctr 2003; **Fellow:** Pediatric Orthopaedic Surgery, Hosp for Special Surgery 2004

Angel, Michael J MD (OrS) - **Spec Exp:** Sports Medicine; Shoulder & Knee Surgery; Ankle Reconstruction; Arthroscopic Surgery; **Hospital:** St. Francis Hosp - The Heart Ctr (page 111); **Address:** Orthopaedic Assocs of Manhasset, 600 Northern Blvd, Ste 300, Great Neck, NY 11021; **Phone:** 516-627-8717; **Board Cert:** Orthopaedic Surgery 2012; **Med School:** Albert Einstein Coll Med 2003; **Resid:** Orthopaedic Surgery, N Shore/LI Jewish Med Ctr 2008; **Fellow:** Orthopaedic Sports Medicine, Kerlan-Jobe Orthopaedic Clinic 2009

Asnis, Stanley E MD (OrS) - **Spec Exp:** Hip Replacement; Knee Replacement; Joint Replacement; **Hospital:** N Shore Univ Hosp; **Address:** Univ Orthopaedic Assocs, 611 Northern Blvd, Ste 200, Great Neck, NY 11021; **Phone:** 516-723-2663; **Board Cert:** Orthopaedic Surgery 1976; **Med School:** Washington Univ, St Louis 1968; **Resid:** Surgery, NY Hosp 1971; Orthopaedic Surgery, Hosp for Special Surg 1975; **Fac Appt:** Assoc Prof OrS, Albert Einstein Coll Med

Capozzi, James D MD (OrS) - **Spec Exp:** Joint Replacement; Fractures in the Elderly; Arthroscopic Surgery; **Hospital:** Winthrop Univ Hosp (page 536); **Address:** Winthrop Ortho Assocs of Long Island, 1300 Franklin Ave, Ste UL3A/B, Garden City, NY 11530; **Phone:** 516-747-8900; **Board Cert:** Orthopaedic Surgery 2010; **Med School:** Mount Sinai Sch Med 1981; **Resid:** Orthopaedic Surgery, Mount Sinai Hosp 1986; **Fellow:** Joint Replacement Surgery, New England Baptist Hosp 1987; **Fac Appt:** Asst Clin Prof OrS, Mount Sinai Sch Med

D'Agostino, Richard J MD (OrS) - **Spec Exp:** Sports Medicine; Knee Surgery; Shoulder Surgery; Arthroscopic Surgery; **Hospital:** St. Francis Hosp - The Heart Ctr (page 111), N Shore Univ Hosp; **Address:** Orthopaedic Assocs of Manhasset, 600 Northern Blvd, Ste 300, Great Neck, NY 11021; **Phone:** 516-627-8717; **Board Cert:** Orthopaedic Surgery 2011; **Med School:** Mount Sinai Sch Med 1982; **Resid:** Orthopaedic Surgery, Mt Sinai Med Ctr 1987; **Fellow:** Sports Medicine, New Eng Baptist Hosp 1988; **Fac Appt:** Asst Clin Prof OrS, Albert Einstein Coll Med

Dines, David M MD (OrS) - **Spec Exp:** Shoulder Arthroscopic Surgery; Shoulder Surgery; Shoulder Replacement; Sports Medicine; **Hospital:** Long Is Jewish Med Ctr, Hosp For Special Surgery (page 109); **Address:** 333 Earl Ovington Blvd, Ste 106, Uniondale, NY 11553; **Phone:** 516-482-1037; **Board Cert:** Orthopaedic Surgery 1980; **Med School:** UMDNJ-NJ Med Sch, Newark 1974; **Resid:** Surgery, NY-Presby/Weill Cornell Med Ctr 1976; Orthopaedic Surgery, Hosp Special Surgery 1979; **Fac Appt:** Clin Prof OrS, Cornell Univ-Weill Med Coll

Dines, Joshua S MD (OrS) - **Spec Exp:** Sports Medicine; Shoulder & Knee Reconstruction; Arthroscopic Surgery; Shoulder Replacement; **Hospital:** Hosp For Special Surgery (page 109), Long Is Jewish Med Ctr; **Address:** 333 Earle Ovington Blvd, Ste 106, Uniondale, NY 11553; **Phone:** 516-482-1037; **Board Cert:** Orthopaedic Surgery 2009; **Med School:** Cornell Univ-Weill Med Coll 2001; **Resid:** Orthopaedic Surgery, Hosp for Special Surgery 2006; **Fellow:** Orthopaedic Sports Medicine, Kerlan-Jobe Orthopaedic Clinic 2007; **Fac Appt:** Assoc Prof OrS, Cornell Univ-Weill Med Coll

Godfried, David H MD (OrS) - **Spec Exp:** Pediatric Orthopaedic Surgery; Reconstructive Surgery; Scoliosis; Cerebral Palsy; **Hospital:** NYU Hosp For Joint Dis (page 104), NS-LIJ Hlth Sys; **Address:** NY Pediatric Ortho Surg & Scoliosis, 333 E Shore Rd, Ste 101, Manhasset, NY 11030; **Phone:** 516-439-4766; **Board Cert:** Orthopaedic Surgery 2012; **Med School:** Columbia P&S 1991; **Resid:** Internal Medicine, Univ Minnesota Hosp 1992; Orthopaedic Surgery, Univ Minnesota Hosp 1996; **Fellow:** Pediatric Orthopaedic Surgery, Shriners Hosp Chldn 1997; Pediatric Orthopaedic Surgery, Northwestern Univ Chldns Meml Hosp 1998; **Fac Appt:** Assoc Clin Prof OrS, NYU Sch Med

Kenan, Samuel MD (OrS) - **Spec Exp:** Bone Tumors; Limb Sparing Surgery; Pediatric Orthopaedic Surgery; Reconstructive Surgery-Complex; **Hospital:** Lenox Hill Hosp, N Shore Univ Hosp; **Address:** 1001 Franklin Ave, Ste 110, Garden City, NY 11530; **Phone:** 212-684-5511; **Med School:** Israel 1976; **Resid:** Orthopaedic Surgery, Hadassah Univ Hosp 1984; **Fellow:** Orthopaedic Pathology, Hosp for Joint Diseases 1987; **Fac Appt:** Prof OrS, NYU Sch Med

Kipnis, James MD (OrS) - **Spec Exp:** Knee Surgery; Hip Surgery; Shoulder Surgery; Sports Surgery; **Hospital:** N Shore Univ Hosp, Long Is Jewish Med Ctr; **Address:** Orthopaedic Care of Long Island, 1000 Northern Blvd, Ste 110, Great Neck, NY 11021; **Phone:** 516-482-0302; **Board Cert:** Orthopaedic Surgery 2006; **Med School:** UCSF 1986; **Resid:** Orthopaedic Surgery, Montefiore Med Ctr 1991; **Fellow:** Orthopaedic Sports Medicine, Tufts Univ Med Ctr 1992

Levitz, Craig L MD (OrS) - **Spec Exp:** Sports Medicine; Shoulder Surgery; Knee Injuries/ACL; Cartilage Damage & Transplant; **Hospital:** South Nassau Comm Hosp; **Address:** Orlin & Cohen Orthopaedic Grp, 36 Lincoln Ave Fl 3rd, Rockville Centre, NY 11570; **Phone:** 516-536-2800; **Board Cert:** Orthopaedic Surgery 2011; Orthopaedic Sports Medicine 2007; **Med School:** Univ Pennsylvania 1992; **Resid:** Orthopaedic Surgery, Hosp Univ Penn 1997; **Fellow:** Sports Medicine, Amer Sports Med Inst 1998

Mauri, Thomas M MD (OrS) - **Spec Exp:** Spinal Surgery; Scoliosis; Spinal Disc Replacement; **Hospital:** N Shore Univ Hosp, Long Is Jewish Med Ctr; **Address:** Univ Orthopaedic Assocs, 611 Northern Blvd, Ste 200, Great Neck, NY 11021; **Phone:** 516-723-2663; **Board Cert:** Orthopaedic Surgery 2009; **Med School:** Albany Med Coll 1980; **Resid:** Neurological Surgery, North Shore Univ Hosp 1982; Orthopaedic Surgery, Hosp for Special Surgery 1985; **Fellow:** Spine Surgery, Rancho Los Amigos Natl Rehab Ctr 1986

Montero, Carlos F MD (OrS) - **Spec Exp:** Hand Surgery; **Hospital:** St. Joseph's Hosp-Nassau, Plainview Hosp; **Address:** ProHEALTH Care Assocs, 2920 Hempstead Tpke, Ste 7, Levittown, NY 11756; **Phone:** 516-735-4048; **Board Cert:** Orthopaedic Surgery 1974; **Med School:** Argentina 1968; **Resid:** Surgery, Bronx VA Hosp 1970; Orthopaedic Surgery, Nassau County Med Ctr 1973; **Fellow:** Hand Surgery, Nassau County Med Ctr 1974; **Fac Appt:** Asst Clin Prof OrS, SUNY Stony Brook

Rich, Daniel Stephen MD (OrS) - **Spec Exp:** Knee Replacement; Hip Replacement; **Hospital:** Hosp For Special Surgery (page 109), St. Francis Hosp - The Heart Ctr (page 111); **Address:** 585 Plandome Rd, Ste 103, Manhasset, NY 11030-1971; **Phone:** 516-627-1525; **Board Cert:** Orthopaedic Surgery 1984; **Med School:** Harvard Med Sch 1977; **Resid:** Surgery, St Luke's-Roosevelt Hosp Ctr 1979; Orthopaedic Surgery, Hosp for Special Surgery 1982; **Fac Appt:** Asst Clin Prof OrS, Cornell Univ-Weill Med Coll

Ruotolo, Charles J MD (OrS) - **Spec Exp:** Rotator Cuff Surgery; Shoulder Injuries; Arthroscopic Surgery; **Hospital:** Nassau Univ Med Ctr, Massapequa Gen Hosp; **Address:** Total Orthopaedics & Sports Medicine, 5500 Merrick Rd, Massapequa, NY 11758; **Phone:** 516-795-3033; **Board Cert:** Orthopaedic Surgery 2005; **Med School:** NY Med Coll 1995; **Resid:** Surgery, Univ Hosp 1996; Orthopaedic Surgery, Univ Hosp 2000

Seideman, Bruce MD (OrS) - **Spec Exp:** Hip Replacement; Knee Replacement; Arthritis; **Hospital:** St. Francis Hosp - The Heart Ctr (page 111), N Shore Univ Hosp; **Address:** Orthopaedic Assocs of Manhasset, 600 Northern Blvd, Ste 300, Great Neck, NY 11021; **Phone:** 516-627-8717; **Board Cert:** Orthopaedic Surgery 2010; **Med School:** Albany Med Coll 1981; **Resid:** Orthopaedic Surgery, NY Presby/Columbia Med Ctr 1986; **Fellow:** Joint Replacement Surgery, Mayo Clinic 1987

Sgaglione, Nicholas A MD (OrS) - **Spec Exp:** Sports Medicine; Shoulder Surgery; Elbow Surgery; Arthroscopic Surgery; **Hospital:** N Shore Univ Hosp, Long Is Jewish Med Ctr; **Address:** Univ Orthopaedic Assocs, 611 Northern Blvd, Ste 200, Great Neck, NY 11021; **Phone:** 516-723-2663; **Board Cert:** Orthopaedic Surgery 2012; **Med School:** Mount Sinai Sch Med 1983; **Resid:** Orthopaedic Surgery, Hosp Special Surg 1988; **Fellow:** Sports Medicine, Southern CA Ortho Inst 1989; **Fac Appt:** Prof OrS, Hofstra N Shore-LIJ Sch Med

Shapiro, Jeffrey F MD (OrS) - **Spec Exp:** Knee Surgery; Knee Replacement; **Hospital:** N Shore Univ Hosp, Long Is Jewish Med Ctr; **Address:** Orthopaedic Care of Long Island, 1000 Northern Blvd, Ste 110, Great Neck, NY 11021; **Phone:** 516-482-0302; **Board Cert:** Orthopaedic Surgery 2009; **Med School:** NY Med Coll 1977; **Resid:** Orthopaedic Surgery, LIJ Med Ctr 1983; **Fellow:** Joint Replacement Surgery, Johns Hopkins Hosp 1984

Shebairo, Raymond A MD (OrS) - **Spec Exp:** Arthroscopic Surgery; Shoulder & Knee Surgery; Joint Replacement; Sports Medicine; **Hospital:** Long Is Jewish Med Ctr; **Address:** 1575 Hillside Ave, Ste 303, New Hyde Park, NY 11040; **Phone:** 516-437-5500; **Board Cert:** Orthopaedic Surgery 1982; **Med School:** Med Coll Wisc 1973; **Resid:** Orthopaedic Surgery, LIJ Med Ctr 1977

Simonson, Barry G MD (OrS) - **Spec Exp:** Sports Medicine; Arthroscopic Surgery; Hip & Knee Reconstruction; Hip & Knee Replacement; **Hospital:** Glen Cove Hosp, NS-LIJ Hlth Sys; **Address:** Orthopaedic Assocs of Great Neck, 825 Northern Blvd, Ste 201, Great Neck, NY 11021-5323; **Phone:** 516-773-7535; **Board Cert:** Orthopaedic Surgery 2014; **Med School:** Mount Sinai-Icahn Sch of Med 1984; **Resid:** Surgery, LI Jewish Med Ctr 1986; Orthopaedic Surgery, LI Jewish Med Ctr 1990; **Fellow:** Sports Medicine, NYU Med Ctr 1991

Ticker, Jonathan B MD (OrS) - **Spec Exp:** Shoulder Surgery; Shoulder Arthroscopic Surgery; Rotator Cuff Surgery; Sports Medicine; **Hospital:** South Nassau Comm Hosp, Long Is Jewish Med Ctr; **Address:** Orlin & Cohen Orthopaedic Group, 1728 Sunrise Hwy, Merrick, NY 11566; **Phone:** 516-992-4700; **Board Cert:** Orthopaedic Surgery 2008; **Med School:** UMDNJ-NJ Med Sch, Newark 1988; **Resid:** Orthopaedic Surgery, NY-Presby/Columbia Univ Med Ctr 1994; **Fellow:** Shoulder Surgery, NY-Presby/Columbia Univ Med Ctr 1991; Sports Medicine & Shoulder Surgery, UPMC 1995; **Fac Appt:** Asst Prof OrS, Columbia P&S

Otolaryngology

Draizin, Dennis L MD (Oto) - **Spec Exp:** Hearing Disorders; Nasal & Sinus Disorders; Voice Disorders; **Hospital:** South Nassau Comm Hosp, Winthrop Univ Hosp (page 536); **Address:** 195 N Village Ave, Ste 1, Rockville Centre, NY 11570-3814; **Phone:** 516-536-7777; **Board Cert:** Otolaryngology 1980; **Med School:** Univ VA Sch Med 1975; **Resid:** Surgery, Northshore Univ Hosp 1977; Otolaryngology, Mt Sinai Sch Med 1980

Durante, Anthony J MD (Oto) - **Hospital:** Winthrop Univ Hosp (page 536); **Address:** Mineola ENT, 134 Mineola Blvd, Ste 201, Mineola, NY 11501; **Phone:** 516-294-9363; **Board Cert:** Otolaryngology 1975; **Med School:** Italy 1967; **Resid:** Surgery, Nassau Hosp 1970; Otolaryngology, Montefiore Med Ctr 1975; **Fac Appt:** Asst Clin Prof S, SUNY Stony Brook

Frank, Douglas K MD (Oto) - **Spec Exp:** Head & Neck Cancer & Surgery; Thyroid & Parathyroid Surgery; Salivary Gland Tumors & Surgery; Skull Base Surgery; **Hospital:** Long Is Jewish Med Ctr, N Shore Univ Hosp; **Address:** 430 Lakeville Rd, New Hyde Park, NY 11042; **Phone:** 718-470-7552; **Board Cert:** Otolaryngology 1997; **Med School:** Univ Pennsylvania 1990; **Resid:** Surgery, St Vincent Hosp 1992; Otolaryngology, NY Ear & Ear Infirm 1996; **Fellow:** Head & Neck Surgical Oncology, UT MD Anderson Cancer Ctr 1999; **Fac Appt:** Assoc Prof Oto, Albert Einstein Coll Med

Gordon, Michael A MD (Oto) - **Spec Exp:** Balance Disorders; Hearing Disorders; Otosclerosis; Ear Surgery; **Hospital:** Long Is Jewish Med Ctr; **Address:** ENT & Allergy Assocs, 990 Stewart Ave, Ste 610, Garden City, NY 11530; **Phone:** 516-222-1881; **Board Cert:** Otolaryngology 1993; **Med School:** Albert Einstein Coll Med 1986; **Resid:** Otolaryngology, Montefiore Hosp Med Ctr 1992; **Fellow:** Otology & Neurotology, Ear Research Foundation 1993; **Fac Appt:** Asst Prof Oto, Albert Einstein Coll Med

Grosso, John J MD (Oto) - **Spec Exp:** Pediatric Otolaryngology; Otology; **Hospital:** Plainview Hosp, Syosset Hosp; **Address:** Long Island ENT Assocs, 875 Old Country Rd, Ste 200, Plainview, NY 11803-4934; **Phone:** 516-931-5552; **Board Cert:** Otolaryngology 1993; **Med School:** SUNY Upstate Med Univ 1986; **Resid:** Otolaryngology, Univ Hosp 1992

Jacono, Andrew A MD (Oto) - **Spec Exp:** Cosmetic & Reconstructive Surgery-Face; Rhinoplasty; Eyelid Surgery/Blepharoplasty; **Hospital:** N Shore Univ Hosp, Lenox Hill Hosp; **Address:** NY Ctr-Facial Plastic & Laser Surgery, 440 Northern Blvd, Great Neck, NY 11021; **Phone:** 212-570-2500; **Board Cert:** Otolaryngology 2012; Facial Plastic & Reconstr Surgery 2013; **Med School:** Albert Einstein Coll Med 1996; **Resid:** Otolaryngology, New York Eye & Ear Infirmary 2001; **Fellow:** Facial Plastic Surgery, Univ Rochester 2002; **Fac Appt:** Asst Prof Oto, Albert Einstein Coll Med

Moisa, Idel MD (Oto) - **Spec Exp:** Thyroid Surgery; Sinus Disorders; Snoring/Sleep Apnea; Endoscopic Sinus Surgery; **Hospital:** Glen Cove Hosp, Winthrop Univ Hosp (page 536); **Address:** ProHlth Care Assocs, ENT, 3 School St, Ste 304, Glen Cove, NY 11542; **Phone:** 516-671-0085; **Board Cert:** Otolaryngology 1988; **Med School:** Albert Einstein Coll Med 1983; **Resid:** Otolaryngology, Montefiore Med Ctr 1988; **Fellow:** Head and Neck Surgery, Montefiore Med Ctr 1990; **Fac Appt:** Asst Clin Prof Oto, NYU Sch Med

Perlman, Philip W MD (Oto) - **Spec Exp:** Pediatric & Adult Otolaryngology; Endoscopic Sinus Surgery; Head & Neck Surgery; Snoring/Sleep Apnea; **Hospital:** St. Francis Hosp - The Heart Ctr (page 111), N Shore Univ Hosp; **Address:** Progressive Ear, Nose & Throat Assocs, 333 E Shore Rd, Ste 102, Manhasset, NY 11030-2911; **Phone:** 516-466-5100; **Board Cert:** Otolaryngology 1988; Facial Plastic & Reconstr Surgery 1994; **Med School:** SUNY Downstate 1983; **Resid:** Surgery, Staten Island Hosp 1985; Otolaryngology, Albany Meml Hosp 1988; **Fellow:** Facial Plastic & Reconstr Surgery, AAFPRS 1989

Rosner, Louis M MD (Oto) - **Spec Exp:** Rhinoplasty; Endoscopic Sinus Surgery; Head & Neck Cancer; **Hospital:** South Nassau Comm Hosp, Mercy Med Ctr-Rockville Centre; **Address:** 176 N Village Ave, Ste 1A, Rockville Centre, NY 11570-3800; **Phone:** 516-678-0303; **Board Cert:** Otolaryngology 1982; **Med School:** Ros Franklin Univ/Chicago Med Sch 1978; **Resid:** Otolaryngology, NY Eye & Ear Infirm 1982

Scioscia, Kenneth A MD (Oto) - **Spec Exp:** Sinus Disorders/Surgery; Nasal & Sinus Disorders; **Hospital:** Long Is Jewish Med Ctr, Winthrop Univ Hosp (page 536); **Address:** ProHealth Care Assocs, 2800 Marcus Ave, Lake Success, NY 11042; **Phone:** 516-622-3377; **Board Cert:** Otolaryngology 1999; **Med School:** SUNY Stony Brook 1993; **Resid:** Surgery, UPMC McKeesport Hosp 1994; Otolaryngology, Univ Hlth Ctr/Eye & Ear Hosp 1998

Setzen, Michael MD (Oto) - **Spec Exp:** Nasal & Sinus Surgery; Rhinoplasty; Sleep Disorders/Apnea; Snoring/Sleep Apnea; **Hospital:** N Shore Univ Hosp, St. Francis Hosp - The Heart Ctr (page 111); **Address:** 600 Northern Blvd, Ste 312, Great Neck, NY 11021; **Phone:** 516-829-0045; **Board Cert:** Otolaryngology 1982; **Med School:** South Africa 1974; **Resid:** Surgery, Cleveland Clin 1978; Otolaryngology, Barnes-Jewish Hosp 1982; **Fac Appt:** Assoc Clin Prof Oto, NYU Sch Med

Shikowitz, Mark J MD (Oto) - **Spec Exp:** Pituitary Tumors; Rhinoplasty; Head & Neck Surgery; Facial Plastic Surgery; **Hospital:** Long Is Jewish Med Ctr, N Shore Univ Hosp; **Address:** 430 Lakeville Rd, Hearing & Speech Bldg, New Hyde Park, NY 11042; **Phone:** 718-470-7552; **Board Cert:** Otolaryngology 1987; **Med School:** Dominica 1981; **Resid:** Otolaryngology, LI Jewish Med Ctr 1986; **Fac Appt:** Prof Oto, Albert Einstein Coll Med

Snyder, Gary M MD (Oto) - **Spec Exp:** Endoscopic Sinus Surgery; Facial Plastic & Reconstructive Surgery; Voice Disorders; Balance Disorders; **Hospital:** Plainview Hosp, N Shore Univ Hosp; **Address:** Ear, Nose & Throat Assocs of NY, 146 A Manetto Hill Rd, Plainview, NY 11803; **Phone:** 516-931-5353; **Board Cert:** Otolaryngology 1983; **Med School:** NY Med Coll 1979; **Resid:** Surgery, North Shore Univ Hosp 1980; Otolaryngology, Manhattan Eye & Ear Hosp 1983

Soletic, Raymond MD (Oto) - **Spec Exp:** Endoscopic Sinus Surgery; Cosmetic Surgery-Face; **Hospital:** St. Francis Hosp - The Heart Ctr (page 111); **Address:** 1615 Northern Blvd, Ste 201, Manhasset, NY 11030; **Phone:** 516-365-7952; **Board Cert:** Otolaryngology 1990; **Med School:** Mexico 1982; **Resid:** Surgery, Baystate/Tufts 1985; Otolaryngology, Manhattan EE&T Hosp 1989

Turk, Jon B MD (Oto) - **Spec Exp:** Facial Plastic & Reconstructive Surgery; Cosmetic Surgery-Face; **Hospital:** N Shore Univ Hosp; **Address:** 173 Froehlich Farm Blvd, Woodbury, NY 11797; **Phone:** 516-921-8989; **Board Cert:** Otolaryngology 1995; Facial Plastic & Reconstr Surgery 1997; **Med School:** SUNY Downstate 1988; **Resid:** Otolaryngology, Mt Sinai Hosp 1993; **Fellow:** Facial Plastic Surgery, University Hosp of Bern 1994

Vambutas, Andrea MD (Oto) - **Spec Exp:** Hearing & Balance Disorders; Pediatric Otolaryngology; Cochlear Implants; **Hospital:** Long Is Jewish Med Ctr, N Shore Univ Hosp; **Address:** 430 Lakeville Rd, Hearing & Speech Bldg, New Hyde Park, NY 11042; **Phone:** 718-470-7552; **Board Cert:** Otolaryngology 1998; **Med School:** Albert Einstein Coll Med 1992; **Resid:** Otolaryngology, LIJ Med Ctr 1997; **Fellow:** Otology, Minnesota Ear Head & Neck Clin 1998; **Fac Appt:** Assoc Clin Prof Oto, Albert Einstein Coll Med

Youngerman, Jay S MD (Oto) - **Spec Exp:** Pediatric Otolaryngology; Head & Neck Surgery; Sleep & Snoring Disorders; Ear Disorders/Surgery; **Hospital:** Plainview Hosp, Syosset Hosp; **Address:** Long Island ENT Assocs, 875 Old Country Rd, Ste 200, Plainview, NY 11803-4934; **Phone:** 516-931-5552; **Board Cert:** Otolaryngology 1984; **Med School:** Med Coll VA 1979; **Resid:** Otolaryngology, LI Jewish Med Ctr 1983

Zahtz, Gerald D MD (Oto) - **Spec Exp:** Sinus Disorders/Surgery; Pediatric Otolaryngology; **Hospital:** Long Is Jewish Med Ctr, N Shore Univ Hosp; **Address:** 430 Lakeville Rd, New Hyde Park, NY 11040; **Phone:** 718-470-7552; **Board Cert:** Otolaryngology 1981; **Med School:** St Louis Univ 1977; **Resid:** Otolaryngology, LIJ-Hillside Med Ctr 1981; **Fac Appt:** Assoc Clin Prof Oto, Albert Einstein Coll Med

Zelman, Warren H MD (Oto) - **Spec Exp:** Head & Neck Surgery; Sinus Disorders/Surgery; Pediatric & Adult Otolaryngology; **Hospital:** Winthrop Univ Hosp (page 536); **Address:** 990 Stewart Ave, Ste 610, Garden City, NY 11530; **Phone:** 516-739-3999; **Board Cert:** Otolaryngology 1987; **Med School:** Ros Franklin Univ/Chicago Med Sch 1982; **Resid:** Surgery, Univ Hosp-SUNY 1984; Otolaryngology, Manhattan EE&T Hosp 1987

Pain Medicine

Agin, Carole A MD (PM) - **Spec Exp:** Acupuncture; Complex Regional Pain Syndromes; Pain-Neuropathic; Pain-Back; **Address:** ProHealth Care Assocs, Pain Med, 3 Delaware Drive, Lake Success, NY 11042; **Phone:** 516-622-6105; **Board Cert:** Anesthesiology 1991; Pain Medicine 2014; **Med School:** Ros Franklin Univ/Chicago Med Sch 1986; **Resid:** Anesthesiology, Beth Israel Med Ctr 1990; **Fellow:** Pain Medicine, Meml Sloan-Kettering Cancer Ctr 1991

Pinsky, Steven H MD (PM) - **Hospital:** Mercy Med Ctr-Rockville Centre; **Address:** 55 Maple Ave, Ste 106, Rockville Centre, NY 11570; **Phone:** 516-764-4875; **Board Cert:** Anesthesiology 1994; Pain Medicine 2007; **Med School:** Albert Einstein Coll Med 1989; **Resid:** Anesthesiology, SUNY Downstate 1993; **Fellow:** Pain Medicine, St Lukes Roosevelt Med Ctr 1994

Pathology

Crawford, James M MD/PhD (Path) - **Spec Exp:** Liver Pathology; Gastrointestinal Pathology; Gastrointestinal Cancer; **Hospital:** N Shore Univ Hosp, Long Is Jewish Med Ctr; **Address:** N Shore-LIJHS Laboratories, 10 Nevada Drive, Lake Success, NY 11042-1114; **Phone:** 516-719-1061; **Board Cert:** Anatomic Pathology 1987; **Med School:** Duke Univ 1982; **Resid:** Pathology, Duke Univ Med Ctr 1983; Pathology, Brigham & Women's Hosp 1987; **Fellow:** Gastrointestinal Pathology, Brigham & Women's Hosp 1987; Research, Royal Free hosp 1989; **Fac Appt:** Prof Path, Hofstra N Shore-LIJ Sch Med

Esposito, Michael John MD (Path) - **Hospital:** N Shore Univ Hosp; **Address:** 6 Ohio Drive, Ste 202, Lake Success, NY 11042; **Phone:** 516-304-7271; **Board Cert:** Anatomic & Clinical Pathology 1995; **Med School:** NE Ohio Univ 1989; **Resid:** Anatomic & Clinical Pathology, LI Jewish Med Ctr 1994

Kahn, Leonard B MD (Path) - **Spec Exp:** Bone Pathology; Head & Neck Pathology; Soft Tissue Tumors; Jaw Tumors; **Hospital:** Long Is Jewish Med Ctr, N Shore Univ Hosp; **Address:** 6 Ohio Drive, Ste 202 - rm 21, Lake Success, NY 10042; **Phone:** 516-304-7264; **Board Cert:** Anatomic Pathology 1980; **Med School:** South Africa 1960; **Resid:** Pathology, Univ Cape Town Affil Hosp 1966; **Fellow:** Surgical Pathology, Washington Univ Affil Hosp 1969; **Fac Appt:** Prof Path, Albert Einstein Coll Med

Pediatric Allergy & Immunology

Bonagura, Vincent R MD (PA&I) - **Hospital:** Long Is Jewish Med Ctr, NS-LIJ Hlth Sys; **Address:** LIJMC, Ped Allergy & Immunology, 865 Northern Blvd, Ste 101, Great Neck, NY 11021; **Phone:** 516-622-5070; **Board Cert:** Pediatrics 1979; Allergy & Immunology 1981; Diagnostic Lab Immunology 1986; **Med School:** Columbia P&S 1975; **Resid:** Pediatrics, NY-Presby/Columbia Univ Med Ctr 1978; **Fellow:** Allergy & Immunology, NY-Presby/Columbia Univ Med Ctr 1981; **Fac Appt:** Prof Ped, Hofstra N Shore-LIJ Sch Med

Fagin, James C MD (PA&I) - **Spec Exp:** Asthma; Allergy; Immunodeficiency Disorders; Rhinitis; **Hospital:** N Shore Univ Hosp; **Address:** Manhasset Allergy & Asthma, 1129 Northern Blvd, Ste 300, Manhasset, NY 11030; **Phone:** 516-365-6077; **Board Cert:** Pediatrics 1980; Allergy & Immunology 1983; **Med School:** Belgium 1976; **Resid:** Pediatrics, N Shore Univ Hosp 1979; **Fellow:** Allergy & Immunology, Chldns Hosp Pittsburgh 1981

Pediatric Cardiology

Better, Donna J MD (PCd) - **Spec Exp:** Echocardiography; Fetal Echocardiography; Congenital Heart Disease; **Hospital:** Winthrop Univ Hosp (page 536); **Address:** 120 Mineola Blvd, Ste 210, Mineola, NY 11501; **Phone:** 516-663-4600; **Board Cert:** Pediatric Cardiology 2011; **Med School:** Albert Einstein Coll Med 1989; **Resid:** Pediatrics, Mt Sinai Hosp 1992; **Fellow:** Pediatric Cardiology, Columbia-Presby Med Ctr 1995

Blaufox, Andrew D MD (PCd) - **Hospital:** Steven & Alexandra Cohen Chldn's Med Ctr of NY, NS-LIJ Hlth Sys; **Address:** Steven & Alexandra Cohen Children's Med Ctr, 269-01 76th Ave, New Hyde Park, NY 11040; **Phone:** 718-470-7350; **Board Cert:** Pediatric Cardiology 2007; **Med School:** Albert Einstein Coll Med 1993; **Resid:** Pediatrics, Mt Sinai Med Ctr 1996; **Fellow:** Pediatric Cardiology, Mt Sinai Med Ctr 1999; **Fac Appt:** Clin Prof Ped, Albert Einstein Coll Med

Cooper, Rubin S MD (PCd) - **Spec Exp:** Congenital Heart Disease; Rheumatic Heart Disease; Kawasaki Disease; **Hospital:** Steven & Alexandra Cohen Chldn's Med Ctr of NY, Long Is Jewish Med Ctr; **Address:** CCMC, Pediatric Cardiology, 269-01 76th Ave, Ste 139, New Hyde Park, NY 11040; **Phone:** 718-470-7350; **Board Cert:** Pediatrics 1976; Pediatric Cardiology 1979; **Med School:** NY Med Coll 1971; **Resid:** Pediatrics, Univ Rochester Strong Meml Hosp 1973; **Fellow:** Pediatric Cardiology, Univ Rochester Strong Meml Hosp 1975; **Fac Appt:** Prof Ped, Hofstra N Shore-LIJ Sch Med

Kholwadwala, Dipak MD (PCd) - **Spec Exp:** Congenital Heart Disease; **Hospital:** Steven & Alexandra Cohen Chldn's Med Ctr of NY; **Address:** The Children's Heart Ctr, 269-01 76 Ave, rm 139, New Hyde Park, NY 11040; **Phone:** 718-470-7350; **Board Cert:** Pediatric Cardiology 2014; **Med School:** India 1984; **Resid:** Pediatrics, Univ of New Mexico Med Ctr 1989; **Fellow:** Pediatric Cardiology, Yale-New Haven Hosp 1992

Levchuck, Sean G MD (PCd) - **Spec Exp:** Interventional Cardiology; Congenital Heart Disease; Atrial Septal Defect; Percutaneous ASD/PFO Closure; **Hospital:** St. Francis Hosp - The Heart Ctr (page 111), Steven & Alexandra Cohen Chldn's Med Ctr of NY; **Address:** 100 Port Washington Blvd, Ste 108, Roslyn, NY 11576-1353; **Phone:** 516-365-3340; **Board Cert:** Pediatrics 2007; Pediatric Cardiology 2011; **Med School:** Grenada 1989; **Resid:** Pediatrics, Winthrop Univ Hosp 1992; **Fellow:** Pediatric Cardiology, St Christophers Hosp 1995

Luxenberg, Douglas M DO (PCd) - **Spec Exp:** Echocardiography; Congenital Heart Disease; **Hospital:** St. Francis Hosp - The Heart Ctr (page 111); **Address:** St Francis Hosp, Ped Cardiology, 100 Port Washington Blvd, Ste 108, Roslyn, NY 11576; **Phone:** 516-365-3340; **Board Cert:** Pediatrics 2012; Pediatric Cardiology 2014; **Med School:** Philadelphia Coll Osteo Med 1999; **Resid:** Pediatrics, Winthrop Univ Hosp 2003; **Fellow:** Pediatric Cardiology, St Christophers Hosp Chldn 2004; Pediatric Cardiology, Univ Chicago Med Ctr 2006

Montoya-Iraheta, Carlos MD (PCd) - **Spec Exp:** Congenital Heart Disease; Echocardiography; **Hospital:** Winthrop Univ Hosp (page 536); **Address:** Winthrop Pediatric Assocs, 120 Mineola Blvd, Ste 210, Mineola, NY 11501; **Phone:** 516-663-4600; **Board Cert:** Pediatric Cardiology 2007; **Med School:** Guatemala 1982; **Resid:** Pediatrics, SUNY Downstate Med Ctr 1987; **Fellow:** Pediatric Cardiology, NY-Presby/Weill Cornell Med Ctr 1992; **Fac Appt:** Asst Prof Ped, Columbia P&S

Romano, Angela MD (PCd) - **Spec Exp:** Echocardiography; Marfan's Syndrome; Kawasaki Disease; **Hospital:** Steven & Alexandra Cohen Chldn's Med Ctr of NY, NS-LIJ Hlth Sys; **Address:** CCMC, Pediatric Cardiology, 269-01 76th Ave, Ste 139, New Hyde Park, NY 11040; **Phone:** 718-470-7350; **Board Cert:** Pediatrics 1984; Pediatric Cardiology 2010; **Med School:** Columbia P&S 1980; **Resid:** Pediatrics, Chldns & Babies Hosp 1984; **Fellow:** Pediatric Cardiology, Chldns Hosp 1987

Schiff, Russell J MD (PCd) - **Spec Exp:** Echocardiography; Fetal Echocardiography; Cardiomyopathy; Congenital Heart Disease; **Hospital:** Huntington Hosp, Steven & Alexandra Cohen Chldn's Med Ctr of NY; **Address:** 43 Crossways Park Drive W, Woodbury, NY 11797; **Phone:** 516-992-5205; **Board Cert:** Pediatrics 1986; Pediatric Cardiology 2010; **Med School:** SUNY Stony Brook 1981; **Resid:** Pediatrics, Long Island Jewish Med Ctr 1984; **Fellow:** Pediatric Cardiology, Long Island Jewish Med Ctr 1986

Shapir, Yehuda MD (PCd) - **Spec Exp:** Congenital Heart Disease & Acquired; Echocardiography; Fetal Echocardiography; **Hospital:** Steven & Alexandra Cohen Chldn's Med Ctr of NY; **Address:** Steven & Alexandra Cohen Chldn's Med Ctr, 269-01 76th Ave, New Hyde Park, NY 11040-1433; **Phone:** 718-470-7350; **Board Cert:** Pediatric Cardiology 2013; **Med School:** Israel 1977; **Resid:** Pediatrics, Rambam Med Ctr 1981; **Fellow:** Pediatric Cardiology, UCLA Med Ctr 1985

Vallone, Ambrose M MD (PCd) - **Spec Exp:** Cardiac Catheterization; Syncope; Fetal Echocardiography; **Hospital:** St. Francis Hosp - The Heart Ctr (page 111), NS-LIJ Hlth Sys; **Address:** 100 Port Washington Blvd, Ste 108, Roslyn, NY 11576-1353; **Phone:** 516-365-3340; **Board Cert:** Pediatrics 1983; Pediatric Cardiology 2010; **Med School:** Johns Hopkins Univ 1977; **Resid:** Pediatrics, Johns Hopkins Hosp 1980; **Fellow:** Pediatric Cardiology, Yale-New Haven Hosp 1983

Pediatric Endocrinology

Accacha, Siham D MD (PEn) - **Spec Exp:** Diabetes; Growth Disorders; Metabolic Syndrome; **Hospital:** Winthrop Univ Hosp (page 536); **Address:** Winthrop Pediatric Assocs, 120 Mineola Blvd, Ste 210, Mineola, NY 11501; **Phone:** 516-663-4600; **Board Cert:** Pediatric Endocrinology 2013; **Med School:** France 1993; **Resid:** Pediatrics, Westchester Med Ctr 2001; **Fellow:** Pediatric Endocrinology, Winthrop Univ Hosp 2005

Carey, Dennis E MD (PEn) - **Spec Exp:** Diabetes; Calcium Disorders; Growth Disorders; Thyroid Disorders; **Hospital:** Steven & Alexandra Cohen Chldn's Med Ctr of NY, NS-LIJ Hlth Sys; **Address:** 1991 Marcus Ave, Ste M100, Lake Success, NY 11042-2057; **Phone:** 516-472-3750; **Board Cert:** Pediatrics 1979; Pediatric Endocrinology 1983; **Med School:** SUNY Downstate 1973; **Resid:** Pediatric Surgery, LI Jewish Med Ctr 1976; **Fellow:** Pediatric Endocrinology, UCSD Med Ctr 1979

Castro-Magana, Mariano S MD (PEn) - **Spec Exp:** Growth/Development Disorders; Adrenal Disorders; Sexual Development Problems; **Hospital:** Winthrop Univ Hosp (page 536); **Address:** Winthrop Univ Hosp, Ped Endocrinology, 120 Mineola Blvd, Ste 210, Mineola, NY 11501; **Phone:** 516-663-4600; **Board Cert:** Pediatrics 1983; Pediatric Endocrinology 1983; **Med School:** El Salvador 1976; **Resid:** Pediatrics, Nassau Univ Med Ctr 1980; **Fellow:** Pediatric Endocrinology, Nassau Univ Med Ctr 1982; **Fac Appt:** Prof Ped, SUNY Stony Brook

Frank, Graeme R MD (PEn) - **Spec Exp:** Pubertal Disorders; Growth/Development Disorders; Diabetes; Thyroid Disorders; **Hospital:** Steven & Alexandra Cohen Chldn's Med Ctr of NY; **Address:** 1991 Marcus Ave, Ste M100, Lake Success, NY 11042-2057; **Phone:** 516-472-3750; **Board Cert:** Pediatrics 2012; Pediatric Endocrinology 2010; **Med School:** South Africa 1982; **Resid:** Pediatrics, LIJ-Schneider Chldns Hosp 1991; **Fellow:** Pediatric Endocrinology, Chldns Hosp 1994

Kreitzer, Paula M MD (PEn) - **Spec Exp:** Diabetes; Growth/Development Disorders; **Hospital:** Steven & Alexandra Cohen Chldn's Med Ctr of NY, Long Is Jewish Med Ctr; **Address:** 1991 Marcus Ave, Ste M100, Lake Success, NY 11042-2057; **Phone:** 516-472-3750; **Board Cert:** Pediatrics 1987; Pediatric Endocrinology 2011; **Med School:** Univ NC Sch Med 1982; **Resid:** Pediatrics, LIJ-Schneider Chldns Hosp 1985; **Fellow:** Pediatric Endocrinology, LIJ-Schneider Chldns Hosp 1987

Speiser, Phyllis W MD (PEn) - **Spec Exp:** Pubertal Disorders; Growth/Development Disorders; Adrenal Disorders; Thyroid Disorders; **Hospital:** Steven & Alexandra Cohen Chldn's Med Ctr of NY, N Shore Univ Hosp; **Address:** Cohen Children's Med Ctr of NY, Pediatric Endocrinology, 1991 Marcus Ave, Ste M100, Lake Success, NY 11042; **Phone:** 516-472-3750; **Board Cert:** Pediatrics 1984; Pediatric Endocrinology 2009; **Med School:** Columbia P&S 1979; **Resid:** Pediatrics, Jacobi Med Ctr 1982; **Fellow:** Pediatric Endocrinology, NY-Presby/Weill Cornell Med Ctr 1984; **Fac Appt:** Prof Ped, Hofstra N Shore-LIJ Sch Med

Pediatric Gastroenterology

Daum, Fredric MD (PGe) - **Spec Exp:** Colitis; Nutrition in Bowel Disorders; Nutrition in Autism; Encopresis (fecal soiling); **Hospital:** Winthrop Univ Hosp (page 536); **Address:** Winthrop Pediatric Assocs, 120 Mineola Blvd, Ste 210, Mineola, NY 11501; **Phone:** 516-663-4600; **Board Cert:** Pediatrics 1972; Pediatric Gastroenterology 2012; **Med School:** Tufts Univ 1967; **Resid:** Pediatrics, Jacobi Med Ctr 1970; **Fellow:** Adolescent Medicine, Montefiore Med Ctr 1973; **Fac Appt:** Prof Ped, SUNY Stony Brook

Marciano, Tuvia A DO (PGe) - **Spec Exp:** Endoscopy; Nutrition; Nutrition in Autism; Liver Disease; **Hospital:** Winthrop Univ Hosp (page 536); **Address:** Winthrop Pediatric Assocs, 120 Mineola Blvd, Ste 210, Mineola, NY 11501; **Phone:** 516-663-4600; **Board Cert:** Pediatrics 2004; Pediatric Gastroenterology 2007; **Med School:** NY Coll Osteo Med 2000; **Resid:** Pediatrics, SUNY Downstate Med Ctr 2004; **Fellow:** Pediatric Gastroenterology, Montefiore Med Ctr 2007; **Fac Appt:** Asst Prof Ped, SUNY Stony Brook

Markowitz, James F MD (PGe) - **Spec Exp:** Inflammatory Bowel Disease/Crohn's; Gastroesophageal Reflux Disease (GERD); **Hospital:** Steven & Alexandra Cohen Chldn's Med Ctr of NY, Long Is Jewish Med Ctr; **Address:** 1991 Marcus Ave, Ste M100, Lake Success, NY 11042; **Phone:** 516-472-3650; **Board Cert:** Pediatrics 1981; Pediatric Gastroenterology 2012; **Med School:** Cornell Univ-Weill Med Coll 1977; **Resid:** Pediatrics, NY Hosp 1980; **Fellow:** Pediatric Gastroenterology, N Shore Univ Hosp 1983; **Fac Appt:** Prof Ped, Hofstra N Shore-LIJ Sch Med

Pettei, Michael J MD/PhD (PGe) - **Spec Exp:** Nutrition; Celiac Disease; **Hospital:** Steven & Alexandra Cohen Chldn's Med Ctr of NY, N Shore Univ Hosp; **Address:** 1991 Marcus Ave, Ste M100, Lake Success, NY 11042; **Phone:** 516-472-3650; **Board Cert:** Pediatrics 1986; Pediatric Gastroenterology 2012; **Med School:** Univ Miami Sch Med 1980; **Resid:** Pediatrics, Mt Sinai Hosp 1983; **Fellow:** Pediatric Gastroenterology, NY-Presby/Columbia Univ Med Ctr 1986; **Fac Appt:** Assoc Prof Ped, Hofstra N Shore-LIJ Sch Med

Weinstein, Toba A MD (PGe) - **Spec Exp:** Inflammatory Bowel Disease/Crohn's; Gastroesophageal Reflux Disease (GERD); Irritable Bowel Syndrome; Constipation; **Hospital:** Steven & Alexandra Cohen Chldn's Med Ctr of NY, Long Is Jewish Med Ctr; **Address:** 1991 Marcus Ave, Ste M100, Lake Success, NY 11042; **Phone:** 516-472-3650; **Board Cert:** Pediatrics 2014; Pediatric Gastroenterology 2014; **Med School:** Columbia P&S 1986; **Resid:** Pediatrics, Chldn's Hosp Natl Med Ctr 1989; **Fellow:** Pediatric Gastroenterology, Schneider Children's Hosp-LIJ 1991; **Fac Appt:** Assoc Prof Ped, Hofstra N Shore-LIJ Sch Med

Pediatric Hematology-Oncology

Atlas, Mark P MD (PHO) - **Spec Exp:** Brain Tumors-Pediatric; Thalassemia; Neuro-Oncology; **Hospital:** Steven & Alexandra Cohen Chldn's Med Ctr of NY, NS-LIJ Hlth Sys; **Address:** CCMC, Ped Hem/Onc Dept, 269-01 76th Ave, rm 253, New Hyde Park, NY 11040; **Phone:** 718-470-3460; **Board Cert:** Pediatric Hematology-Oncology 2013; Pediatrics 2014; **Med School:** Albert Einstein Coll Med 1985; **Resid:** Pediatrics, Children's Hosp 1992; **Fellow:** Pediatric Hematology-Oncology, Northwestern Meml Hosp 1996; **Fac Appt:** Asst Prof Ped, Hofstra N Shore-LIJ Sch Med

Lipton, Jeffrey M MD/PhD (PHO) - **Spec Exp:** Bone Marrow Failure Disorders; Stem Cell Transplant; Bone Marrow Transplant; **Hospital:** Steven & Alexandra Cohen Chldn's Med Ctr of NY, N Shore Univ Hosp; **Address:** Cohen Chldn's Med Ctr of New York, Pediatric Hem/Onc & Stem Cell, 269-01 76th Ave, Ste 255, New Hyde Park, NY 11040; **Phone:** 718-470-3470; **Board Cert:** Pediatrics 1981; **Med School:** St Louis Univ 1975; **Resid:** Pediatrics, Chldns Hosp 1978; **Fellow:** Pediatric Hematology-Oncology, Dana Farber Cancer Inst 1981; **Fac Appt:** Prof Ped, Hofstra N Shore-LIJ Sch Med

Redner, Arlene S MD (PHO) - **Spec Exp:** Leukemia; Brain Tumors; Solid Tumors; Neuro-Oncology; **Hospital:** Steven & Alexandra Cohen Chldn's Med Ctr of NY; **Address:** CCMC, Dept Pediatric Hem/Onc, 269-01 76th Ave, rm 253, New Hyde Park, NY 11040-1434; **Phone:** 718-470-3460; **Board Cert:** Pediatrics 1982; Pediatric Hematology-Oncology 1984; **Med School:** Univ Pennsylvania 1977; **Resid:** Pediatrics, Boston Floating Hosp 1980; **Fellow:** Pediatric Hematology-Oncology, Meml Sloan Kettering Hosp 1985; **Fac Appt:** Prof Ped, Hofstra N Shore-LIJ Sch Med

Sabatino, Dominick P MD (PHO) - **Spec Exp:** Cooley's Anemia; Thalassemia; Sickle Cell Disease; **Hospital:** Nassau Univ Med Ctr; **Address:** Nassau Univ Med Ctr, Dept Peds, 2201 Hempstead Tpke, East Meadow, NY 11554; **Phone:** 516-572-3305; **Board Cert:** Pediatrics 1975; Pediatric Hematology-Oncology 1982; **Med School:** Italy 1968; **Resid:** Pediatrics, LI College Hosp 1973; **Fellow:** Pediatric Hematology-Oncology, LI College Hosp 1976

Weinblatt, Mark E MD (PHO) - **Spec Exp:** Leukemia & Lymphoma; Sickle Cell Disease; Bleeding/Coagulation Disorders; Thalassemia; **Hospital:** Winthrop Univ Hosp (page 536); **Address:** Winthrop Univ Hosp, Pediatric Hem/Onc, 120 Mineola Blvd, Ste 460, Mineola, NY 11501; **Phone:** 516-663-9400; **Board Cert:** Pediatrics 1980; Pediatric Hematology-Oncology 1982; **Med School:** Albert Einstein Coll Med 1976; **Resid:** Pediatrics, Jacobi Med Ctr 1979; **Fellow:** Pediatric Hematology-Oncology, Chldns Hosp 1981; **Fac Appt:** Prof Ped, SUNY Stony Brook

Wolfe, Lawrence C MD (PHO) - **Spec Exp:** Palliative Care; Neuroblastoma; Adrenal Cancer; Congenital Hemolytic Anemia; **Hospital:** Steven & Alexandra Cohen Chldn's Med Ctr of NY; **Address:** Steven & Alexandra Cohen Chldn's Med Ctr, Div Pediatric Hematology/Oncology, 269-01 76th Ave, New Hyde Park, NY 11040; **Phone:** 718-470-3460; **Board Cert:** Pediatrics 1981; Pediatric Hematology-Oncology 1987; Hospice & Palliative Medicine 2010; **Med School:** Harvard Med Sch 1976; **Resid:** Pediatrics, Chldns Hosp 1978; **Fellow:** Pediatric Hematology-Oncology, Chldns Hosp 1981; **Fac Appt:** Prof Ped

Pediatric Infectious Disease

Krilov, Leonard R MD (PInf) - **Spec Exp:** Infections-Respiratory; Infections in Int'l Adopted Children; Chronic Fatigue Syndrome; Lyme Disease; **Hospital:** Winthrop Univ Hosp (page 536), Good Samaritan Hosp Med Ctr - West Islip; **Address:** Winthrop Univ Hosp, Out-Patient Clinic, 120 Mineola Blvd, Ste 210, Mineola, NY 11501; **Phone:** 516-663-3090; **Board Cert:** Pediatrics 1983; Pediatric Infectious Disease 2008; **Med School:** Columbia P&S 1978; **Resid:** Pediatrics, Johns Hopkins Hosp 1981; **Fellow:** Pediatric Infectious Disease, Chldns Hosp 1984; **Fac Appt:** Prof Ped, SUNY Stony Brook

Rubin, Lorry G MD (PInf) - **Spec Exp:** Kawasaki Disease; Tuberculosis; Fevers of Unknown Origin; **Hospital:** Steven & Alexandra Cohen Chldn's Med Ctr of NY, N Shore Univ Hosp; **Address:** CCMC, Ped Infectious Disease, 269-01 76th Ave, rm 160, New Hyde Park, NY 11040; **Phone:** 718-470-3480; **Board Cert:** Pediatrics 1983; Pediatric Infectious Disease 2008; **Med School:** Rush Med Coll 1978; **Resid:** Pediatrics, Chldns Hosp 1981; **Fellow:** Pediatric Infectious Disease, Johns Hopkins Hosp 1984; **Fac Appt:** Prof Ped, Hofstra N Shore-LIJ Sch Med

Sood, Sunil K MD (PInf) - **Spec Exp:** Fevers of Unknown Origin; Tuberculosis; Lyme Disease; **Hospital:** Steven & Alexandra Cohen Chldn's Med Ctr of NY, Southside Hosp; **Address:** CCMC, Div Pediatric Infectious Dis, 269-01 76th Ave, New Hyde Park, NY 11040-1433; **Phone:** 718-470-3480; **Board Cert:** Pediatrics 1987; Pediatric Infectious Disease 2008; **Med School:** India 1976; **Resid:** Pediatrics, Mercy Med Ctr 1983; Pediatrics, Georgetown Univ Hosp 1985; **Fellow:** Infectious Disease, Tulane Univ Hosp 1988; **Fac Appt:** , Albert Einstein Coll Med

Pediatric Otolaryngology

Mendelsohn, Michael G MD (PO) - **Spec Exp:** Head & Neck Tumors; Sinus Disorders; **Hospital:** Long Is Jewish Med Ctr, Steven & Alexandra Cohen Chldn's Med Ctr of NY; **Address:** ENT & Allergy Assocs, 990 Stewart Ave, Ste 610, Garden City, NY 11530; **Phone:** 516-222-1881; **Board Cert:** Otolaryngology 1999; **Med School:** Boston Univ 1990; **Resid:** Otolaryngology, LI Jewish Med Ctr 1995; **Fellow:** Pediatric Otolaryngology, Univ Virginia Med Ctr 1996; **Fac Appt:** Asst Prof Oto, SUNY Downstate

Smith, Lee P MD (PO) - **Spec Exp:** Airway Disorders; Head & Neck Tumors; Tonsil/Adenoid Disorders; Ear Infections; **Hospital:** Steven & Alexandra Cohen Chldn's Med Ctr of NY, Long Is Jewish Med Ctr; **Address:** Steven & Alexandra Cohen Chldn's Med Ctr, Pediatric Otolaryngology Div, 430 Lakeville Rd, New Hyde Park, NY 11042; **Phone:** 718-470-7550; **Board Cert:** Otolaryngology 2008; **Med School:** NYU Sch Med 2002; **Resid:** Surgery, Jackson Meml Hosp 2003; Otolaryngology, Jackson Meml Hosp 2007; **Fellow:** Pediatric Otolaryngology, Chldns Hosp 2009; **Fac Appt:** Asst Prof Oto, Hofstra N Shore-LIJ Sch Med

Pediatric Pulmonology

Pirzada, Melodi B MD (PPul) - **Spec Exp:** Asthma; Cystic Fibrosis; Breathing Disorders; **Hospital:** Winthrop Univ Hosp (page 536), South Nassau Comm Hosp; **Address:** Winthrop Pediatric Assocs, 120 Mineola Blvd, Ste 210, Mineola, NY 11501; **Phone:** 516-663-4600; **Board Cert:** Pediatric Pulmonology 2008; **Med School:** Turkey 1986; **Resid:** Pediatrics, Winthrop Univ Hosp 1991; **Fellow:** Pediatric Pulmonology, NY-Presby/Columbia Univ Med Ctr 1994; **Fac Appt:** Assoc Clin Prof Ped, SUNY Stony Brook

Schaeffer, Janis I MD (PPul) - **Spec Exp:** Asthma; Cough-Chronic; Lung Disorders-Congenital; **Hospital:** Steven & Alexandra Cohen Chldn's Med Ctr of NY, N Shore Univ Hosp; **Address:** Pediatric Asthma & Pulmo Assocs of NY, 3003 New Hyde Park Rd, Ste 204, New Hyde Park, NY 11042-1214; **Phone:** 516-488-7575; **Board Cert:** Pediatrics 1984; **Med School:** SUNY Downstate 1979; **Resid:** Pediatrics, LI Jewish Med Ctr 1982; **Fellow:** Pediatric Pulmonology, Columbia-Presby Med Ctr 1985; **Fac Appt:** Asst Prof Ped, Albert Einstein Coll Med

Pediatric Rheumatology

Gottlieb, Beth S MD (PRhu) - **Spec Exp:** Juvenile Arthritis; Lupus/SLE; Dermatomyositis; Vasculitis; **Hospital:** Steven & Alexandra Cohen Chldn's Med Ctr of NY, NS-LIJ Hlth Sys; **Address:** 1991 Marcus Ave, Ste M100, Lake Success, NY 11042; **Phone:** 516-472-3700; **Board Cert:** Pediatric Rheumatology 2013; **Med School:** Israel 1992; **Resid:** Pediatrics, LIJ Med Ctr 1995; **Fellow:** Pediatric Rheumatology, LIJ Med Ctr 1998; **Fac Appt:** Assoc Prof Ped, Hofstra N Shore-LIJ Sch Med

Pediatric Surgery

Coren, Charles V MD (PS) - **Spec Exp:** Necrotizing Enterocolitis; Neonatal Surgery; **Hospital:** Winthrop Univ Hosp (page 536), NY Hosp Queens (page 498); **Address:** Chldns Surgical Grp, 320 Post Ave, Ste 101, Westbury, NY 11590; **Phone:** 516-997-1199; **Board Cert:** Pediatric Surgery 2013; **Med School:** Univ Cincinnati 1978; **Resid:** Surgery, NYU Med Ctr 1983; **Fellow:** Pediatric Surgery, Univ Hosp 1985; **Fac Appt:** Assoc Prof S, Columbia P&S

Dolgin, Stephen E MD (PS) - **Spec Exp:** Neonatal Surgery; Ulcerative Colitis; Inflammatory Bowel Disease/Crohn's; Ovarian Masses in Children/Adolescents; **Hospital:** Steven & Alexandra Cohen Chldn's Med Ctr of NY, N Shore Univ Hosp; **Address:** 269-01 76th Ave, Ste 158, New Hyde Park, NY 11040; **Phone:** 718-470-3636; **Board Cert:** Surgery 2011; Pediatric Surgery 2013; **Med School:** NYU Sch Med 1977; **Resid:** Surgery, Brigham & Womens Hosp 1982; **Fellow:** Pediatric Surgery, Chldns Meml Hosp 1984; **Fac Appt:** Prof S, Hofstra N Shore-LIJ Sch Med

Hong, Andrew R MD (PS) - **Spec Exp:** Neonatal Surgery; Minimally Invasive Surgery; Chest Wall Deformities; **Hospital:** Steven & Alexandra Cohen Chldn's Med Ctr of NY, N Shore Univ Hosp; **Address:** NS LIJ, Div Ped Surgery, 269-01 76th Ave, New Hyde Park, NY 11040; **Phone:** 718-470-3636; **Board Cert:** Surgery 2012; Pediatric Surgery 2011; **Med School:** Univ Wisc 1985; **Resid:** Surgery, Med Ctr Hosp 1991; **Fellow:** Pediatric Surgery, Montreal Chldns Hosp 1993; **Fac Appt:** Asst Prof S, Hofstra N Shore-LIJ Sch Med

Pediatric Urology

Gitlin, Jordan S MD (Ped Uro) - **Spec Exp:** Reconstructive Surgery; Minimally Invasive Surgery; Varicocele; **Hospital:** Steven & Alexandra Cohen Chldn's Med Ctr of NY, Winthrop Univ Hosp (page 536); **Address:** Pediatric Urology Assocs, 1999 Marcus Ave, Ste M18, Lake Success, NY 11042; **Phone:** 516-466-6953; **Board Cert:** Urology 2008; Pediatric Urology 2008; **Med School:** SUNY Upstate Med Univ 1994; **Resid:** Urology, NYU Med Ctr 2001; **Fellow:** Pediatric Urology, Riley Chldn's Hosp 2002; **Fac Appt:** Assoc Clin Prof U, Hofstra N Shore-LIJ Sch Med

Pediatrics

Adesman, Andrew R MD (Ped) - **Spec Exp:** Autism; Asperger's Syndrome; Developmental & Behavioral Disorders; Tourette's Syndrome; **Hospital:** Steven & Alexandra Cohen Chldn's Med Ctr of NY; **Address:** 1983 Marcus Ave Fl 1 - Ste 130, Lake Success, NY 11042; **Phone:** 516-802-6100; **Board Cert:** Pediatrics 1987; Neurodevelopmental Disabilities 2012; Developmental-Behavioral Pediatrics 2010; **Med School:** Univ Pennsylvania 1981; **Resid:** Pediatrics, Chldn's Hosp Natl Med Ctr 1984; **Fellow:** Developmental-Behavioral Pediatrics, Chldn's Hosp 1986; **Fac Appt:** Assoc Prof Ped, Albert Einstein Coll Med

Amer, Jeffrey A MD (Ped) *PCP* - **Hospital:** Winthrop Univ Hosp (page 536), Long Is Jewish Med Ctr; **Address:** 38 S Oyster Bay Rd, Syosset, NY 11791; **Phone:** 516-682-0555; **Board Cert:** Pediatrics 2009; **Med School:** Jefferson Med Coll 1981; **Resid:** Pediatrics, Bronx Municipal Hosp 1984

Chianese, Maurice J MD (Ped) *PCP* - **Spec Exp:** Pediatric Sports Medicine; Asthma; Developmental & Behavioral Disorders; Preventive Medicine; **Hospital:** Steven & Alexandra Cohen Chldn's Med Ctr of NY, N Shore Univ Hosp; **Address:** ProHealthCare Assocs, 7 Vermont Drive, Lake Success, NY 11042; **Phone:** 516-622-7337; **Board Cert:** Pediatrics 2011; **Med School:** NY Med Coll 1986; **Resid:** Pediatrics, N Shore Univ Hosp 1989; **Fac Appt:** Assoc Clin Prof Ped, Hofstra N Shore-LIJ Sch Med

Cooper, Seymour M MD (Ped) *PCP* - **Hospital:** Winthrop Univ Hosp (page 536), Steven & Alexandra Cohen Chldn's Med Ctr of NY; **Address:** 1101 Stewart Ave, Ste 306, Garden City, NY 11530; **Phone:** 516-746-2299; **Board Cert:** Pediatrics 2010; **Med School:** NY Med Coll 1972; **Resid:** Pediatrics, Montefiore Hosp Med Ctr 1975

Friedman, Eugene B MD (Ped) *PCP* - **Spec Exp:** Preventive Medicine; **Hospital:** Steven & Alexandra Cohen Chldn's Med Ctr of NY, Winthrop Univ Hosp (page 536); **Address:** Park Pediatrics, 271 Jericho Tpke, Floral Park, NY 11002; **Phone:** 516-354-7575; **Board Cert:** Pediatrics 1973; **Med School:** NY Med Coll 1968; **Resid:** Pediatrics, Metropolitan Hosp Ctr 1971; **Fac Appt:** Asst Clin Prof Ped, Albert Einstein Coll Med

Gerberg, Lynda F MD (Ped) *PCP* - **Spec Exp:** Sports Medicine; Preventive Medicine; **Hospital:** N Shore Univ Hosp, NS-LIJ Hlth Sys; **Address:** Kings Point Pediatrics, 200 Middle Neck Rd, Great Neck, NY 11021; **Phone:** 516-466-3311; **Board Cert:** Pediatrics 2009; **Med School:** Mexico 1987; **Resid:** Pediatrics, Schneider Chldns Hosp 1992; **Fellow:** Sports Medicine, Chldns Hosp 1993; **Fac Appt:** Asst Prof Ped, Albert Einstein Coll Med

Gould, Eric F MD (Ped) *PCP* - **Spec Exp:** Developmental Disorders; Preventive Medicine; **Hospital:** Long Is Jewish Med Ctr, N Shore Univ Hosp; **Address:** 225 Community Drive, Ste 105, Great Neck, NY 11021-2229; **Phone:** 516-829-9409; **Board Cert:** Pediatrics 1976; **Med School:** NY Med Coll 1970; **Resid:** Pediatrics, LIJ Med Ctr 1972; Pediatrics, Bellevue Hosp Ctr 1974; **Fellow:** Child Development, Montefiore Med Ctr 1976

Green, Abraham I MD (Ped) *PCP* - **Spec Exp:** Asthma; Nutrition; ADD/ADHD; **Hospital:** Long Is Jewish Med Ctr, Winthrop Univ Hosp (page 536); **Address:** Ped Hlthcare of LI, 145 Franklin Pl, Woodmere, NY 11598; **Phone:** 516-295-1200; **Board Cert:** Pediatrics 2009; **Med School:** Albert Einstein Coll Med 1979; **Resid:** Pediatrics, Jacobi Med Ctr 1983

Grijnsztein, Jacob MD (Ped) *PCP* - **Hospital:** Long Is Jewish Med Ctr, N Shore Univ Hosp; **Address:** Kidz Kare of Great Neck LLP, 107 Northern Blvd, Ste 201, Great Neck, NY 11021; **Phone:** 516-487-6565; **Board Cert:** Pediatrics 1979; **Med School:** NYU Sch Med 1973; **Resid:** Pediatrics, Bellevue Hosp 1976

Hankin, Dorie E MD (Ped) - **Spec Exp:** Developmental Disorders; Behavioral Disorders; **Hospital:** Winthrop Univ Hosp (page 536), Steven & Alexandra Cohen Chldn's Med Ctr of NY; **Address:** 173 Mineola Blvd, Ste 301B, Mineola, NY 11501; **Phone:** 516-739-1936; **Board Cert:** Pediatrics 1980; Neurodevelopmental Disabilities 2012; Developmental-Behavioral Pediatrics 2010; **Med School:** Albert Einstein Coll Med 1974; **Resid:** Pediatrics, Montefiore Med Ctr 1978; **Fellow:** Child Development, Montefiore Med Ctr 1980; **Fac Appt:** Asst Clin Prof Ped, SUNY Stony Brook

Leavens-Maurer, Jill MD (Ped) *PCP* - **Hospital:** Winthrop Univ Hosp (page 536); **Address:** Winthrop Pediatric Assocs, 222 Station Plaza N, Ste 611, Mineola, NY 11501-3893; **Phone:** 516-663-2532; **Board Cert:** Pediatrics 2011; **Med School:** SUNY Upstate Med Univ 1984; **Resid:** Pediatrics, NY-Presby/Weill Cornell Med Ctr 1987

Marino, Ronald V DO (Ped) *PCP* - **Spec Exp:** Developmental & Behavioral Disorders; **Hospital:** Winthrop Univ Hosp (page 536), Good Samaritan Hosp Med Ctr - West Islip; **Address:** Winthrop Pediatric Assocs, 222 Station Plaza N, Ste 611, Mineola, NY 11501-3808; **Phone:** 516-663-2532; **Board Cert:** Pediatrics 1985; **Med School:** Mich State Univ 1978; **Resid:** Pediatrics, Doctors Hosp 1981; **Fellow:** Behavioral Pediatrics, Univ Maryland Med Ctr 1985; **Fac Appt:** Clin Prof Ped, SUNY Stony Brook

Milanaik, Ruth L DO (Ped) - **Spec Exp:** Developmental & Behavioral Disorders; ADD/ADHD; **Hospital:** Steven & Alexandra Cohen Chldn's Med Ctr of NY, NS-LIJ Hlth Sys; **Address:** 1983 Marcus Ave Fl 1 - Ste 130, Lake Success, NY 11042; **Phone:** 516-802-6100; **Board Cert:** Pediatrics 2008; Developmental-Behavioral Pediatrics 2012; **Med School:** NY Coll Osteo Med 1997; **Resid:** Pediatrics, Winthrop Univ Hosp 2001; **Fellow:** Developmental-Behavioral Pediatrics, NS-LIJ Hlth Sys 2004

Nerwen, Clifford B MD (Ped) *PCP* - **Spec Exp:** Preventive Medicine; **Hospital:** Steven & Alexandra Cohen Chldn's Med Ctr of NY, N Shore Univ Hosp; **Address:** 410 Lakeville Rd, Ste 108, New Hyde Park, NY 11040; **Phone:** 516-465-4377 x2; **Board Cert:** Pediatrics 2010; **Med School:** Univ Conn 1991; **Resid:** Pediatrics, Schneider Chldns Hosp 1994

Rabinowicz, Morris MD (Ped) *PCP* - **Spec Exp:** Preventive Medicine; **Hospital:** Plainview Hosp, Steven & Alexandra Cohen Chldn's Med Ctr of NY; **Address:** 995 Old Country Rd, Plainview, NY 11803; **Phone:** 516-935-7333; **Board Cert:** Pediatrics 1985; **Med School:** SUNY Downstate 1978; **Resid:** Surgery, LIJ Med Ctr 1982; Pediatrics, Brookdale Hosp 1983; **Fac Appt:** Asst Prof Ped, Hofstra N Shore-LIJ Sch Med

Resmovits, Marvin MD (Ped) *PCP* - **Hospital:** Steven & Alexandra Cohen Chldn's Med Ctr of NY, N Shore Univ Hosp; **Address:** Kidz Kare of Great Neck, 107 NE Northern Blvd, Fl S, Ste 201, Great Neck, NY 11021-4309; **Phone:** 516-487-6565; **Board Cert:** Pediatrics 2010; **Med School:** SUNY Buffalo 1979; **Resid:** Pediatrics, LI Jewish Hosp 1982

Turow, Victor D MD (Ped) *PCP* - **Hospital:** N Shore Univ Hosp, Long Is Jewish Med Ctr; **Address:** 833 Northern Blvd, Ste 110, Great Neck, NY 11021; **Phone:** 516-504-0606; **Board Cert:** Pediatrics 1983; **Med School:** SUNY Downstate 1978; **Resid:** Pediatrics, LIJ Med Ctr 1981

Physical Medicine & Rehabilitation

Beer, Jeffry R MD (PMR) - **Spec Exp:** Spinal Rehabilitation; Pain Medicine; Pain-Interventional Techniques; Pain-Musculoskeletal; **Hospital:** N Shore Univ Hosp, NS-LIJ Hlth Sys; **Address:** Long Island Spine Rehabilitation Med, 801 Merrick Ave, East Meadow, NY 11554; **Phone:** 516-393-8941; **Board Cert:** Physical Medicine & Rehabilitation 2005; Pain Medicine 2005; **Med School:** SUNY Downstate 2000; **Resid:** Physical Medicine & Rehabilitation, Long Island Jewish Med Ctr 2004; **Fellow:** Interventional Spine Medicine, Beth Israel Med Ctr - Petrie Division 2005

Lipetz, Jason S MD (PMR) - **Spec Exp:** Spinal Rehabilitation; Pain-Spine; **Hospital:** Long Is Jewish Med Ctr, N Shore Univ Hosp; **Address:** Long Island Spine Rehabilitation Med, 801 Merrick Ave, East Meadow, NY 11554; **Phone:** 516-393-8941; **Board Cert:** Physical Medicine & Rehabilitation 2009; Pain Medicine 2012; **Med School:** Columbia P&S 1994; **Resid:** Physical Medicine & Rehabilitation, Kessler Inst-UMDNJ 1998; **Fellow:** Interventional Spine Medicine, Univ Penn Affil Hosp 1999; **Fac Appt:** Asst Prof PMR, Albert Einstein Coll Med

Root, Barry C MD (PMR) - **Spec Exp:** Pain Management; Electromyography; Spinal Cord Injury; Spinal Rehabilitation; **Hospital:** N Shore Univ Hosp, St. Francis Hosp - The Heart Ctr (page 111); **Address:** 101 St Andrew's Ln Fl 1-North, Glen Cove, NY 11542-2254; **Phone:** 516-674-7501; **Board Cert:** Physical Medicine & Rehabilitation 1988; **Med School:** Ohio State Univ 1984; **Resid:** Physical Medicine & Rehabilitation, Nassau County Med Ctr 1987

Stein, Adam B MD (PMR) - **Spec Exp:** Spinal Cord Injury; Multiple Sclerosis; Stroke Rehabilitation; **Hospital:** Glen Cove Hosp, Long Is Jewish Med Ctr; **Address:** North Shore-LIJ Med Grp, Dept Physical Med & Rehab, 1554 Northern Blvd Fl 4, Manhasset, NY 11030; **Phone:** 516-321-6400; **Board Cert:** Physical Medicine & Rehabilitation 1992; Spinal Cord Injury Medicine 2013; **Med School:** NYU Sch Med 1987; **Resid:** Physical Medicine & Rehabilitation, Rusk Inst-NYU Med Ctr 1991

Weiss, Lyn D MD (PMR) - **Spec Exp:** Electrodiagnosis; Electromyography; **Hospital:** Nassau Univ Med Ctr; **Address:** Nassau Univ Med Ctr, Phys Med & Rehab, 2201 Hempstead Tpke, East Meadow, NY 11554; **Phone:** 516-572-6525; **Board Cert:** Physical Medicine & Rehabilitation 1990; **Med School:** SUNY Downstate 1985; **Resid:** Physical Medicine & Rehabilitation, Nassau Univ Med Ctr 1989; **Fac Appt:** Clin Prof PMR, Hofstra N Shore-LIJ Sch Med

Plastic Surgery

Addona, Tommaso MD (PlS) - **Spec Exp:** Microvascular Surgery; Breast Reconstruction; **Hospital:** Winthrop Univ Hosp (page 536), South Nassau Comm Hosp; **Address:** Long Island Plastic Surg Grp, 999 Franklin Ave, Garden City, NY 11530; **Phone:** 516-504-3014; **Board Cert:** Plastic Surgery 2010; **Med School:** Albert Einstein Coll Med 2002; **Resid:** Surgery, Mt. Sinai Hosp 2005; Plastic Surgery, Mt. Sinai Hosp 2008; **Fellow:** Microvascular Surgery, Meml Sloan Kettering Cancer Ctr 2009

Alizadeh, Kaveh MD (PlS) - **Spec Exp:** Breast Cosmetic & Reconstructive Surgery; Facial Plastic & Reconstructive Surgery; Liposuction & Body Contouring; Migraine; **Hospital:** Westchester Med Ctr, N Shore Univ Hosp; **Address:** 833 Northern Blvd, Ste 240, Great Neck, NY 11021; **Phone:** 929-800-1887; **Board Cert:** Plastic Surgery 2011; **Med School:** Cornell Univ 1993; **Resid:** Plastic Surgery, Univ Chicago Hosps 1999; **Fellow:** Microsurgery, Meml Sloan-Kettering Cancer Ctr 2000; Cosmetic Plastic Surgery, Manhattan Eye, Ear & Throat Hosp 2000

Breitbart, Arnold MD (PlS) - **Spec Exp:** Cosmetic Surgery-Face & Body; Liposuction; Breast Reconstruction; Cosmetic Surgery-Breast; **Hospital:** N Shore Univ Hosp, NY-Presby/Weill Cornell Med Ctr, NY (page 102); **Address:** 1155 Northern Blvd, Ste 110, Manhasset, NY, 11030; **Phone:** 516-365-3511; **Board Cert:** Surgery 2003; Plastic Surgery 2004; **Med School:** NYU Sch Med 1985; **Resid:** Surgery, NYU Med Ctr 1991; Plastic Surgery, NYU Med Ctr 1993; **Fellow:** Craniofacial Surgery, NYU Med Ctr 1994; Microsurgery, Meml Sloan-Kettering Cancer Ctr 1995; **Fac Appt:** Asst Prof S, Cornell Univ-Weill Med Coll

Davenport, Thomas Andrew MD (PlS) - **Spec Exp:** Cosmetic & Reconstructive Surgery; Burns-Reconstructive Plastic Surgery; Wound Healing/Care; **Hospital:** Winthrop Univ Hosp (page 536), South Nassau Comm Hosp; **Address:** Long Island Plastic Surgical Group, 999 Franklin Ave, Ste 226, Garden City, NY 11530; **Phone:** 516-742-3404; **Board Cert:** Plastic Surgery 2006; **Med School:** Yale Univ 1993; **Resid:** Surgery, Mass General Hosp 1996; Plastic Surgery, Mass General Hosp 1998; **Fellow:** Reconstructive Surgery, Meml Sloan-Kettering Cancer Ctr 2000; Burn Surgery, Shriners Hosp Chdn 2002

DeVita, Gregory A MD (PlS) - **Spec Exp:** Rhinoplasty; Rhinoplasty Revision; Cosmetic Surgery-Face; Cosmetic Surgery-Breast; **Hospital:** St. Francis Hosp - The Heart Ctr (page 111), N Shore Univ Hosp; **Address:** The Plastic Surgery Group, 650 Northern Blvd, Great Neck, NY 11021-5204; **Phone:** 516-466-7000; **Board Cert:** Plastic Surgery 1989; **Med School:** SUNY Downstate 1980; **Resid:** Surgery, St Luke's Hosp 1982; Surgery, Jersey City Med Ctr 1983; **Fellow:** Plastic Surgery, New York Methodist Hosp 1984; Plastic Surgery, SUNY Downstate Med Ctr 1986

DiGregorio, Vincent R MD (PlS) - **Spec Exp:** Rhinoplasty Revision; Cosmetic Surgery-Face; Breast Reconstruction & Augmentation; Eyelid Surgery; **Hospital:** Winthrop Univ Hosp (page 536), Mercy Med Ctr-Rockville Centre; **Address:** Long Island Plastic Surgical Grp, 999 Franklin Ave, Garden City, NY 11530; **Phone:** 516-742-3404; **Board Cert:** Plastic Surgery 1978; **Med School:** Albany Med Coll 1968; **Resid:** Surgery, Thomas Jefferson Univ Hosp 1974; Plastic Surgery, Nassau Co Med Ctr 1976; **Fac Appt:** Assoc Prof PlS, SUNY Stony Brook

Dubner, Sanford MD (PlS) - **Spec Exp:** Head & Neck Tumors; Melanoma; Reconstructive Plastic Surgery; **Hospital:** Long Is Jewish Med Ctr, N Shore Univ Hosp; **Address:** Long Island Surgical Specialists, 410 Lakeville Rd, Ste 310, Lake Success, NY 11042; **Phone:** 516-437-1111; **Board Cert:** Surgery 2006; Plastic Surgery 1992; **Med School:** SUNY Stony Brook 1982; **Resid:** Surgery, Booth Meml Med Ctr 1987; Plastic Surgery, Montefiore Med Ctr 1989; **Fellow:** Head and Neck Surgery, Meml Sloan-Kettering Cancer Ctr 1990; **Fac Appt:** Clin Prof S, Hofstra N Shore-LIJ Sch Med

Elkowitz, Marc J MD (PlS) - **Spec Exp:** Cosmetic Surgery; Reconstructive Surgery; **Hospital:** Long Is Jewish Med Ctr, N Shore Univ Hosp; **Address:** Plastic Surgery of New York, 107 Northern Blvd, Ste 203, Great Neck, NY 11021; **Phone:** 516-773-9200; **Board Cert:** Surgery 2007; Plastic Surgery 2012; **Med School:** Albany Med Coll 1993; **Resid:** Surgery, NY Med Coll 1998; **Fellow:** Plastic Surgery, Montefiore Med Ctr 2000; **Fac Appt:** Asst Clin Prof PlS, Albert Einstein Coll Med

Feinberg, Joseph MD (PlS) - **Spec Exp:** Cosmetic Surgery-Face & Eyes; Breast Augmentation; Abdominoplasty; **Hospital:** St. Francis Hosp - The Heart Ctr (page 111), N Shore Univ Hosp; **Address:** 1201 Northern Blvd, Ste 202, Manhasset, NY 11030; **Phone:** 516-869-6200; **Board Cert:** Plastic Surgery 1980; **Med School:** Cornell Univ-Weill Med Coll 1973; **Resid:** Surgery, NY Hosp 1976; Plastic Surgery, NY Hosp 1978; **Fellow:** Plastic/Reconstructive Surgery, Meml Sloan-Kettering Cancer Ctr 1978; **Fac Appt:** Asst Clin Prof S, Cornell Univ-Weill Med Coll

Funt, David K MD (PlS) - **Spec Exp:** Cosmetic Surgery-Face & Body; Botox Therapy; Facial Rejuvenation; **Hospital:** South Nassau Comm Hosp, N Shore Univ Hosp; **Address:** 19 Irving Pl, Woodmere, NY 11598; **Phone:** 516-295-0404; **Board Cert:** Plastic Surgery 1987; **Med School:** Geo Wash Univ 1979; **Resid:** Surgery, Montefiore Med Ctr 1983; Plastic Surgery, Montefiore Med Ctr 1985; **Fac Appt:** Asst Clin Prof PlS, Albert Einstein Coll Med

Gallagher, Pamela M MD (PlS) - **Spec Exp:** Breast Augmentation; Abdominoplasty; Facial Rejuvenation; Body Contouring; **Hospital:** Good Samaritan Hosp Med Ctr - West Islip, Long Is Jewish Med Ctr; **Address:** Island Plastic Surgery & Aesthetics, 190 E Jericho Tpke, Mineola, NY 11501; **Phone:** 516-977-9922; **Board Cert:** Plastic Surgery 1980; **Med School:** Univ Chicago-Pritzker Sch Med 1974; **Resid:** Surgery, NY-Presby/Weill Cornell Med Ctr 1977; Plastic Surgery, NY-Presby/Weill Cornell Med Ctr 1979

Gold, Alan H MD (PlS) - **Spec Exp:** Cosmetic Surgery-Face & Eyes; Cosmetic Surgery-Breast; Cosmetic Surgery-Body; Nasal Surgery; **Hospital:** N Shore Univ Hosp, Long Is Jewish Med Ctr; **Address:** 833 Northern Blvd, Ste 240, Great Neck, NY 11021-5322; **Phone:** 516-498-2800; **Board Cert:** Plastic Surgery 1979; **Med School:** SUNY Downstate 1971; **Resid:** Surgery, N Shore Univ Hosp 1975; Plastic Surgery, Kings County-SUNY Med Ctr 1978; **Fellow:** Hand Surgery, Nassau County Med Ctr 1976

Groeger, William E MD (PlS) - **Spec Exp:** Skin Cancer; **Hospital:** South Nassau Comm Hosp, Mercy Med Ctr-Rockville Centre; **Address:** 1490 Broadway Fl 2, Hewlett, NY 11557-1645; **Phone:** 516-887-5502; **Board Cert:** Plastic Surgery 1982; **Med School:** SUNY Downstate 1972; **Resid:** Surgery, Beth Israel Med Ctr 1977; Plastic Surgery, SUNY Downstate Med Ctr 1979

Israeli, Ron MD (PlS) - **Spec Exp:** Plastic & Reconstructive Surgery; Breast Reconstruction; Microsurgery; **Hospital:** N Shore Univ Hosp, St. Francis Hosp - The Heart Ctr (page 111); **Address:** Aesthetic Plastic Surgery, 833 Northern Blvd, Ste 160, Great Neck, NY 11021; **Phone:** 516-498-8400; **Board Cert:** Plastic Surgery 2009; **Med School:** Boston Univ 1990; **Resid:** Surgery, Mt Sinai Hosp 1995; Plastic Surgery, Mass Genl Hosp 1997; **Fellow:** Microsurgery, Mt Sinai Hosp 1992

Kasabian, Armen K MD (PlS) - **Spec Exp:** Hand Reconstruction; Plastic & Reconstructive Surgery; Microsurgery; **Hospital:** Long Is Jewish Med Ctr, NS-LIJ Hlth Sys; **Address:** 1991 Marcus Ave, Ste 102, Lake Success, NY 11042; **Phone:** 516-497-7900; **Board Cert:** Plastic Surgery 1992; Hand Surgery 2004; **Med School:** Cornell Univ-Weill Med Coll 1982; **Resid:** Surgery, NYU Med Ctr 1987; Plastic Surgery, NYU Med Ctr 1989; **Fellow:** Microsurgery, NYU Med Ctr 1990; **Fac Appt:** Asst Prof PlS, NYU Sch Med

Kessler, Martin E MD (PlS) - **Spec Exp:** Cosmetic Surgery-Face & Body; Reconstructive Surgery-Face; Breast Reconstruction; Hand Surgery; **Hospital:** South Nassau Comm Hosp, N Shore Univ Hosp; **Address:** The Plastic Surgery Group, 242 Merrick Rd, Ste 302, Rockville Centre, NY 11570-5254; **Phone:** 516-536-5858; **Board Cert:** Plastic Surgery 1987; **Med School:** Cornell Univ-Weill Med Coll 1980; **Resid:** Surgery, NY Hosp 1983; Plastic Surgery, NY Hosp 1985; **Fellow:** Hand Surgery, Cleveland Clin 1986; Microsurgery, Univ Louisville Hosp 1986; **Fac Appt:** Assoc Clin Prof PlS, Cornell Univ-Weill Med Coll

Kilgo, Matthew S MD (PlS) - **Spec Exp:** Breast Cosmetic & Reconstructive Surgery; Body Contouring; Cancer Reconstruction; **Hospital:** Winthrop Univ Hosp (page 536); **Address:** Long Island Plastic Surgical Group, 999 Franklin Ave, Garden City, NY 11530; **Phone:** 516-742-3404; **Board Cert:** Plastic Surgery 2013; **Med School:** Univ Chicago-Pritzker Sch Med 1993; **Resid:** Surgery, Univ WI Hosp & Clins 1998; Plastic Surgery, UI Hlth Univ Hosp 2001; **Fellow:** Breast Surgery, Gloucestershire Royal Hosp 1999; Plastic/Reconstructive Surgery, Meml Sloan-Kettering Cancer Ctr 2003

Leipziger, Lyle S MD (PlS) - **Spec Exp:** Cosmetic Surgery-Face & Eyes; Cosmetic Surgery-Breast; Breast Reconstruction; Liposuction & Body Contouring; **Hospital:** N Shore Univ Hosp, Long Is Jewish Med Ctr; **Address:** 900 Northern Blvd, Ste 130, Great Neck, NY 11021; **Phone:** 516-465-8787; **Board Cert:** Plastic Surgery 1994; **Med School:** Cornell Univ-Weill Med Coll 1985; **Resid:** Plastic Surgery, NY Hosp 1990; **Fellow:** Craniofacial Surgery, Johns Hopkins Hosp 1991

Lukash, Frederick N MD (PlS) - **Spec Exp:** Pediatric Plastic Surgery; Cosmetic Surgery-Face; Breast Cosmetic & Reconstructive Surgery; Rhinoplasty; **Hospital:** Long Is Jewish Med Ctr, Steven & Alexandra Cohen Chldn's Med Ctr of NY; **Address:** Long Island Plastic Surgical Grp, 2110 Northern Blvd, Ste 210, Manhasset, NY 11030-3022; **Phone:** 516-439-5500; **Board Cert:** Plastic Surgery 1982; **Med School:** Tulane Univ 1973; **Resid:** Surgery, Emory Univ Hosp 1975; Surgery, Univ Hosp 1980; **Fellow:** Plastic Surgery, Mass Genl Hosp 1981; **Fac Appt:** Asst Prof S, Albert Einstein Coll Med

Ruotolo, Rachel A MD (PlS) - **Spec Exp:** Pediatric Plastic Surgery; Craniofacial Surgery-Pediatric; Cleft Palate/Lip; Vascular Malformations; **Hospital:** Winthrop Univ Hosp (page 536), N Shore Univ Hosp; **Address:** Long Island Plastic Surg Grp, 999 Franklin Ave, Garden City, NY 11530; **Phone:** 516-504-3014; **Board Cert:** Plastic Surgery 2008; **Med School:** Geo Wash Univ 1999; **Resid:** Plastic Surgery, Univ PA Med Sch 2006; **Fellow:** Craniofacial Surgery, Med City Dallas Hosp 2007

Sasson, Homayoun N MD (PlS) - **Spec Exp:** Cosmetic & Reconstructive Surgery; Body Contouring; Facial Rejuvenation; **Hospital:** Franklin Hosp, Plainview Hosp; **Address:** 1000 Northern Blvd Ste 370, Great Neck, NY 11021; **Phone:** 516-487-5017; **Board Cert:** Plastic Surgery 2009; **Med School:** Univ Mass Sch Med 1988; **Resid:** Surgery, Cedars-Sinai Med Ctr 1993; Plastic Surgery, Yale-New Haven Hosp 1996; **Fac Appt:** Clin Prof PlS, Hofstra N Shore-LIJ Sch Med

Silberman, Mark Illan MD (PlS) - **Spec Exp:** Cosmetic Surgery-Face; Breast Cosmetic & Reconstructive Surgery; Facial Rejuvenation; Body Contouring; **Hospital:** N Shore Univ Hosp, St. Francis Hosp - The Heart Ctr (page 111); **Address:** The Plastic Surgery Group, 650 Northern Blvd, Great Neck, NY 11021-5204; **Phone:** 516-466-7000; **Board Cert:** Plastic Surgery 1988; **Med School:** SUNY Downstate 1980; **Resid:** Surgery, Beth Israel Med Ctr 1983; Plastic Surgery, SUNY Downstate Med Ctr 1985

Simpson, Roger MD (PlS) - **Spec Exp:** Eyelid Surgery; Liposuction & Body Contouring; Cosmetic Surgery-Face & Breast; Burn Care; **Hospital:** Winthrop Univ Hosp (page 536), NS-LIJ Hlth Sys; **Address:** Long Island Plastic Surgical Grp, 999 Franklin Ave, Garden City, NY 11530; **Phone:** 516-742-3404; **Board Cert:** Plastic Surgery 1981; **Med School:** Belgium 1974; **Resid:** Surgery, Nassau Co Med Ctr 1978; Plastic Surgery, Nassau Co Med Ctr 1980; **Fellow:** Hand Surgery, St Luke's-Roosevelt Hosp Ctr 1981; **Fac Appt:** Asst Clin Prof S, SUNY Stony Brook

Psychiatry

Bailine, Samuel MD (Psyc) - **Spec Exp:** Depression; Psychopharmacology; Electroconvulsive Therapy (ECT); **Hospital:** Zucker Hillside Hosp; **Address:** 5 Ridgeway Rd, Port Washington, NY 11050; **Phone:** 516-883-3304; **Board Cert:** Psychiatry 1970; **Med School:** NYU Sch Med 1964; **Resid:** Psychiatry, Tulane Med Ctr 1968; **Fac Appt:** Assoc Prof Psyc, Hofstra N Shore-LIJ Sch Med

Behr, Raymond MD (Psyc) - **Spec Exp:** Depression; Bipolar/Mood Disorders; Addiction/Substance Abuse; **Hospital:** Long Is Jewish Med Ctr; **Address:** 81-A Arleigh Rd, Great Neck, NY 11021-1442; **Phone:** 516-482-1980; **Board Cert:** Psychiatry 1981; Child & Adolescent Psychiatry 1982; **Med School:** South Africa 1973; **Resid:** Psychiatry, LI Jewish Med Ctr 1978; **Fellow:** Child & Adolescent Psychiatry, LI Jewish Med Ctr 1980; **Fac Appt:** Asst Clin Prof Psyc, Albert Einstein Coll Med

Benjamin, John MD (Psyc) - **Spec Exp:** Depression; Anxiety Disorders; Schizophrenia; **Hospital:** N Shore Univ Hosp; **Address:** 1983 Marcus Ave, Ste E132, Lake Success, NY 11042; **Phone:** 516-216-1780; **Board Cert:** Psychiatry 1983; **Med School:** India 1969; **Resid:** Psychiatry, N Shore Univ Hosp 1981; **Fac Appt:** Asst Clin Prof Psyc, NYU Sch Med

Berman, Sheldon S MD (Psyc) - **Spec Exp:** Psychodynamic Psychotherapy; Psychopharmacology; Palliative Care; **Address:** 8 Payne Circle, Hewlett Harbor, NY 11557-2735; **Phone:** 516-374-4417; **Board Cert:** Psychiatry 1979; **Med School:** Ros Franklin Univ/Chicago Med Sch 1969; **Resid:** Psychiatry, Brookdale Hosp 1973; **Fac Appt:** Asst Clin Prof Psyc, SUNY Downstate

Bhatt, Ashok MD (Psyc) - **Spec Exp:** Depression; Psychopharmacology; **Address:** 871 E Park Ave, Long Beach, NY 11561; **Phone:** 516-889-8844; **Board Cert:** Psychiatry 1985; **Med School:** India 1976; **Resid:** Psychiatry, LI Jewish Med Ctr 1981; **Fellow:** Psychiatry, LI Jewish Med Ctr 1983

Brenner, Ronald L MD (Psyc) - **Spec Exp:** Depression; Dementia; Panic Disorder; Geriatric Psychiatry; **Hospital:** St. John's Episcopal Hosp - Queens, Mercy Med Ctr-Rockville Centre; **Address:** Neurobehavioral Research, 74 Carman Ave, Cedarhurst, NY 11516; **Phone:** 516-295-7230; **Board Cert:** Psychiatry 1979; Geriatric Psychiatry 2006; **Med School:** Spain 1974; **Resid:** Psychiatry, St Luke's Hosp 1978; **Fellow:** Pharmacology, New York Univ Med Ctr 1979; **Fac Appt:** Clin Prof Psyc, SUNY Hlth Sci Ctr

Budman, Cathy L MD (Psyc) - **Spec Exp:** Tourette's Syndrome; ADD/ADHD; Obsessive-Compulsive Disorder; Neuro-Psychiatry; **Hospital:** N Shore Univ Hosp, Long Is Jewish Med Ctr; **Address:** 400 Community Drive, Manhasset, NY 11030; **Phone:** 516-562-3223; **Board Cert:** Psychiatry 1991; **Med School:** SUNY Buffalo 1984; **Resid:** Psychiatry, Langley Porter Psych Inst/UCSF 1986; Psychiatry, N Shore Univ Hosp 1990; **Fellow:** Family Medicine, Sydney Univ-Royal Price Albert Hosp 1988; Neuropsychiatry, N Shore Univ Hosp 1991; **Fac Appt:** Prof Psyc, Hofstra N Shore-LIJ Sch Med

Crasta, Jovita M MD (Psyc) - **Spec Exp:** Anxiety Disorders; Depression; Bipolar/Mood Disorders; Women's Health-Mental Health; **Hospital:** South Nassau Comm Hosp; **Address:** 2277 Grand Ave, Baldwin, NY 11510-3148; **Phone:** 516-377-5400; **Board Cert:** Psychiatry 1991; **Med School:** India 1981; **Resid:** Psychiatry, Nassau County Med Ctr 1987

Gupta, Adarsh K MD (Psyc) - **Spec Exp:** Psychosomatic Disorders; Sleep Medicine; Neuro-Psychiatry; Psychopharmacology; **Hospital:** Long Is Jewish Med Ctr; **Address:** Great Neck Psychiatry, 1010 Northern Blvd, Ste 208, Great Neck, NY 11021; **Phone:** 516-336-2544; **Board Cert:** Psychiatry 2007; Psychosomatic Medicine 2005; Sleep Medicine 2011; Behavioral Neurology & Neuropsychiatry 2006; **Med School:** India 1978; **Resid:** Psychiatry, NYU Med Ctr 1995

Gurevich, Michael I MD (Psyc) - **Spec Exp:** Psychotherapy & Psychopharmacology; Complementary Medicine; Addiction/Substance Abuse; Psychiatry in Physical Illness; **Address:** 997 Glen Cove Avenue, Glen Head, NY 11545-1584; **Phone:** 516-674-9489; **Board Cert:** Psychiatry 1989; **Med School:** Lithuania 1974; **Resid:** Psychiatry, Elmhurst Hosp Ctr 1987; **Fellow:** Child Psychiatry, Elmhurst Hosp Ctr 1989

Katus, Eli Margrethe MD (Psyc) - **Spec Exp:** Psychopharmacology; Psychotherapy; Child & Adolescent Psychiatry; **Hospital:** N Shore Univ Hosp, Winthrop Univ Hosp (page 536); **Address:** 1035 Route 106, East Norwich, NY 11732-1005; **Phone:** 516-922-5607; **Board Cert:** Psychiatry 1990; Child & Adolescent Psychiatry 1991; **Med School:** Germany 1982; **Resid:** Psychiatry, N Shore Univ Hosp 1986; **Fellow:** Child & Adolescent Psychiatry, N Shore Univ Hosp 1988

Katz, Jack L MD (Psyc) - **Spec Exp:** Eating Disorders; Depression; Anxiety Disorders; Bipolar/Mood Disorders; **Hospital:** N Shore Univ Hosp, Long Is Jewish Med Ctr; **Address:** 1010 Northern Blvd, Ste 208, Great Neck, NY 11021; **Phone:** 516-336-2565; **Board Cert:** Psychiatry 1968; **Med School:** Albert Einstein Coll Med 1960; **Resid:** Psychiatry, Montefiore Med Ctr 1966; Internal Medicine, Jackson Meml Hosp 1961; **Fellow:** Psychiatric Research, Montefiore Med Ctr-Einstein 1968; **Fac Appt:** Prof Psyc, Hofstra N Shore-LIJ Sch Med

Liang, Vera T MD (Psyc) - **Spec Exp:** Women's Health-Mental Health; Depression; Anxiety Disorders; **Hospital:** Long Is Jewish Med Ctr; **Address:** 1 Expressway Plaza, Ste 201, Roslyn Heights, NY 11577; **Phone:** 516-484-5869; **Board Cert:** Psychiatry 1977; Child & Adolescent Psychiatry 1981; **Med School:** Hong Kong 1969; **Resid:** Psychiatry, LI Jewish Med Ctr 1973; **Fellow:** Child & Adolescent Psychiatry, Jacobi Med Ctr 1975

Sami, Sherif F MD (Psyc) - **Spec Exp:** Depression; Anxiety & Mood Disorders; Geriatric Psychiatry; **Hospital:** Winthrop Univ Hosp (page 536), N Shore Univ Hosp; **Address:** 7 Bond St, Ste 1A, Great Neck, NY 11021; **Phone:** 516-487-9191; **Board Cert:** Psychiatry 1973; **Med School:** Egypt 1961; **Resid:** Psychiatry, Cairo Univ Hosp 1966; Psychiatry, Elmhurst Hosp 1969; **Fellow:** Community Psychiatry, Albert Einstein 1970

Selzer, Jeffrey A MD (Psyc) - **Spec Exp:** Mood Disorders; Depression; Addiction/Substance Abuse; Addiction Psychiatry; **Hospital:** Zucker Hillside Hosp, N Shore Univ Hosp; **Address:** Phys Resource Network, 333 E Shore Rd, Ste 204, Manhasset, NY 11030; **Phone:** 516-876-7175; **Board Cert:** Psychiatry 1985; **Med School:** Univ Mich Med Sch 1979; **Resid:** Psychiatry, UCLA Med Ctr 1983; **Fac Appt:** Assoc Prof Psyc, Hofstra N Shore-LIJ Sch Med

Pulmonary Disease

Altus, Jonathan D MD (Pul) - **Spec Exp:** Breathing Disorders; Asthma; Chronic Obstructive Lung Disease (COPD); Cough-Chronic; **Hospital:** South Nassau Comm Hosp, Franklin Hosp; **Address:** South Shore Pulmonary Medicine, 920 Atlantic Ave, Baldwin Harbor, NY 11510; **Phone:** 516-623-8700; **Board Cert:** Internal Medicine 1988; Pulmonary Disease 2012; **Med School:** SUNY Downstate 1984; **Resid:** Internal Medicine, Beth Israel Med Ctr 1987; **Fellow:** Pulmonary Disease, New York Univ Med Ctr 1989

Blum, Alan I MD (Pul) - **Spec Exp:** Critical Care Medicine; Asthma; **Hospital:** South Nassau Comm Hosp, Franklin Hosp; **Address:** Pulmonary & Critical Care Cons, 444 Merrick Rd, Lower Level 1, Lynbrook, NY 11563-2400; **Phone:** 516-593-9500; **Board Cert:** Internal Medicine 1981; Pulmonary Disease 1984; **Med School:** Mexico 1977; **Resid:** Internal Medicine, Mt Sinai Hosp Ctr 1981; **Fellow:** Pulmonary Disease, Mt Sinai Hosp Ctr 1983

Breidbart, David M MD (Pul) - **Spec Exp:** Asthma; Chronic Obstructive Lung Disease (COPD); Sarcoidosis; **Hospital:** N Shore Univ Hosp, St. Francis Hosp - The Heart Ctr (page 111); **Address:** North Shore Pulmonary Assocs, 6 Ohio Drive, Ste 201, LSQ Med Bldg, Lake Success, NY 11042-1129; **Phone:** 516-328-8700; **Board Cert:** Internal Medicine 1982; Pulmonary Disease 1984; **Med School:** SUNY Downstate 1979; **Resid:** Internal Medicine, North Shore Univ Hosp 1982; **Fellow:** Pulmonary Disease, Meml Sloan-Kettering Hosp 1983; Pulmonary Disease, Montefiore Hosp 1985

Cohen, Michael L MD (Pul) - **Spec Exp:** Asthma; Bronchitis; Emphysema; **Hospital:** N Shore Univ Hosp; **Address:** N Shore Internal Med Assocs, 560 Northern Blvd, Ste 203, Great Neck, NY 11021-5100; **Phone:** 516-482-0600; **Board Cert:** Internal Medicine 1972; Pulmonary Disease 1974; **Med School:** SUNY Upstate Med Univ 1967; **Resid:** Internal Medicine, Montefiore Hosp Med Ctr 1970; Internal Medicine, Queens Hosp Cntr 1974; **Fellow:** Pulmonary Disease, Montefiore Hosp Med Ctr 1971; Pulmonary Disease, LI Jewish Med Ctr 1974; **Fac Appt:** Asst Clin Prof Med, NYU Sch Med

Donath, Joseph MD (Pul) - **Spec Exp:** Asthma; Lung Cancer; Critical Care; Mycobacterial Infections; **Hospital:** NY Hosp Queens (page 498), South Nassau Comm Hosp; **Address:** South Shore Pulmonary Med, 360 Central Ave, Ste 113, Lawrence, NY 11559; **Phone:** 516-569-6966; **Board Cert:** Internal Medicine 1980; Pulmonary Disease 1982; Critical Care Medicine 2009; **Med School:** Hungary 1972; **Resid:** Internal Medicine, VA Med Ctr 1980; **Fellow:** Pulmonary Disease, Mt Sinai Hosp 1982

Fein, Alan M MD (Pul) - **Spec Exp:** Chronic Obstructive Lung Disease (COPD); Asthma; Pneumonia; Critical Care Medicine; **Hospital:** N Shore Univ Hosp, Long Is Jewish Med Ctr; **Address:** ProHealth Care Assocs, 2800 Marcus Ave, Ste 202, Lake Success, NY 11042; **Phone:** 516-608-2890; **Board Cert:** Internal Medicine 1997; Pulmonary Disease 1999; Critical Care Medicine 2008; **Med School:** SUNY Downstate 1973; **Resid:** Internal Medicine, Jacobi Med Ctr 1976; **Fellow:** Pulmonary Disease, UCSF Med Ctr 1978; **Fac Appt:** Clin Prof Med, NYU Sch Med

Feinsilver, Steven H MD (Pul) - **Spec Exp:** Sleep Medicine; Sleep Disorders/Apnea; **Hospital:** Mt Sinai Hosp; **Address:** Mt Sinai, Pulmonology-Sleep Medicine, 98th St, between 5th and Madison Ave Fl 8, New York, NY 10029; **Phone:** 212-241-5656; **Board Cert:** Internal Medicine 1980; Pulmonary Disease 1982; Sleep Medicine 2009; **Med School:** Brown Univ 1977; **Resid:** Internal Medicine, Boston Univ Hosp 1980; **Fellow:** Pulmonary Disease, Stanford Univ Med Ctr 1982

Gordon, Richard E MD (Pul) - **Spec Exp:** Emphysema; Asthma; Airway Disorders; **Hospital:** St. Joseph's Hosp-Nassau, Plainview Hosp; **Address:** Island Pulmonary Associates, 4271 Hempstead Tpke, Ste 1, Bethpage, NY 11714-5718; **Phone:** 516-796-3700; **Board Cert:** Internal Medicine 1984; Pulmonary Disease 1986; **Med School:** Mount Sinai Sch Med 1980; **Resid:** Internal Medicine, Beth Israel Med Ctr 1983; **Fellow:** Pulmonary Disease, Queens Hosp Ctr 1985

Greenberg, Harly MD (Pul) - **Spec Exp:** Sleep Disorders/Apnea; **Hospital:** Long Is Jewish Med Ctr, N Shore Univ Hosp; **Address:** NS-LIJ Sleep Disorders Ctr, 410 Lakeville Rd, Ste 107, New Hyde Park, NY 11042; **Phone:** 516-465-3899; **Board Cert:** Internal Medicine 1985; Pulmonary Disease 1988; Sleep Medicine 2011; **Med School:** NYU Sch Med 1982; **Resid:** Internal Medicine, N Shore Univ Hosp 1985; **Fellow:** Pulmonary Disease, NYU-Bellevue Hosp 1987; **Fac Appt:** Prof Med, Hofstra N Shore-LIJ Sch Med

Leeman, Benjamin J MD (Pul) - **Spec Exp:** Asthma; Pneumonia; Chronic Obstructive Lung Disease (COPD); **Hospital:** Franklin Hosp, South Nassau Comm Hosp; **Address:** 20 W Lincoln Ave, Ste 306, Valley Stream, NY 11580; **Phone:** 516-599-8787; **Board Cert:** Internal Medicine 2006; Pulmonary Disease 2007; **Med School:** SUNY Stony Brook 1988; **Resid:** Internal Medicine, Montefiore Med Ctr-Weiler Div 1991; **Fellow:** Pulmonary Disease, NY Presby-Columbia Med Ctr 1993

Mermelstein, Steve A MD (Pul) - **Spec Exp:** Asthma; Chronic Obstructive Lung Disease (COPD); Cough-Chronic; **Hospital:** South Nassau Comm Hosp, Franklin Hosp; **Address:** Pulmonary & Critical Care Cons, 444 Merrick Rd, Lower Level 1, Lynbrook, NY 11563-2456; **Phone:** 516-593-9500; **Board Cert:** Internal Medicine 1980; Pulmonary Disease 1982; **Med School:** Albert Einstein Coll Med 1977; **Resid:** Internal Medicine, Metropolitan Hosp Ctr 1980; **Fellow:** Pulmonary Disease, St Luke's-Roosevelt Hosp Ctr 1982

Newmark, Ian H MD (Pul) - **Spec Exp:** Critical Care Medicine; Asthma; Lung Cancer; **Hospital:** N Shore Univ Hosp, Plainview Hosp; **Address:** 8 Greenfield Rd, Syosset, NY 11791-4831; **Phone:** 516-496-3001; **Board Cert:** Internal Medicine 1982; Pulmonary Disease 1986; Critical Care Medicine 2010; **Med School:** SUNY Downstate 1979; **Resid:** Internal Medicine, Nassau Univ Med Ctr 1982; **Fellow:** Pulmonary Intensive Care, Nassau Univ Med Ctr 1984; **Fac Appt:** Asst Clin Prof Med, Hofstra N Shore-LIJ Sch Med

Niederman, Michael S MD (Pul) - **Spec Exp:** Infections-Respiratory; Emphysema; Respiratory Failure; Pneumonia; **Hospital:** Winthrop Univ Hosp (page 536); **Address:** Winthrop Univ Hosp, Pulmonology Div, 222 Station Plaza N, Ste 400, Mineola, NY 11501; **Phone:** 516-663-2834; **Board Cert:** Internal Medicine 1980; Pulmonary Disease 1982; Critical Care Medicine 2007; **Med School:** Boston Univ 1977; **Resid:** Internal Medicine, Northwestern Univ Med Ctr 1980; **Fellow:** Pulmonary Disease, Yale-New Haven Hosp 1983; **Fac Appt:** Prof Med, SUNY Stony Brook

Schulster, Rita B MD (Pul) - **Hospital:** South Nassau Comm Hosp; **Address:** 442 E Waukena Ave, Oceanside, NY 11572; **Phone:** 516-599-8234; **Board Cert:** Internal Medicine 1977; Pulmonary Disease 1978; **Med School:** Albert Einstein Coll Med 1970; **Resid:** Internal Medicine, Beth Israel Med Ctr 1973; Internal Medicine, Beth Israel Med Ctr 1974; **Fellow:** Pulmonary Disease, LI Jewish Med Ctr 1975; Pulmonary Disease, Beth Israel Med Ctr 1976

Steinberg, Harry N MD (Pul) - **Spec Exp:** Asthma; Emphysema; Lung Cancer; Pulmonary Hypertension; **Hospital:** Long Is Jewish Med Ctr, N Shore Univ Hosp; **Address:** NS-LIJ Sleep Disorders Ctr, 410 Lakeville Rd, Ste 107, New Hyde Park, NY 11042; **Phone:** 516-465-5400; **Med School:** Temple Univ 1966; **Resid:** Internal Medicine, Temple Univ Hosp 1967; Internal Medicine, LI Jewish Med Ctr 1969; **Fellow:** Pulmonary Critical Care Medicine, Hosp Univ Penn 1974; **Fac Appt:** Prof Med, Hofstra N Shore-LIJ Sch Med

Wyner, Perry A MD (Pul) - **Spec Exp:** Asthma; Cough-Chronic; Emphysema; Critical Care Medicine; **Hospital:** Mercy Med Ctr-Rockville Centre, N Shore Univ Hosp; **Address:** Long Island Int Med, 2 Lincoln Ave, Ste 201, Rockville Centre, NY 11570; **Phone:** 516-536-4960; **Board Cert:** Internal Medicine 1980; Pulmonary Disease 1982; **Med School:** Cornell Univ-Weill Med Coll 1977; **Resid:** Internal Medicine, Med Coll Virginia Hosps 1980; **Fellow:** Pulmonary Disease, Bellevue Hosp 1982

Radiation Oncology

Bosworth, Jay L MD (RadRO) - **Spec Exp:** Breast Cancer; Prostate Cancer; **Hospital:** St. Francis Hosp - The Heart Ctr (page 111), N Shore Univ Hosp; **Address:** NRAD Med Assocs, 6 Ohio Drive, Ste 103, Lake Success, NY 11042; **Phone:** 516-222-2022; **Board Cert:** Therapeutic Radiology 1974; **Med School:** Albert Einstein Coll Med 1970; **Resid:** Radiation Oncology, Bronx Muni Hosp Ctr 1974

Diamond, Ezriel MD (RadRO) - **Spec Exp:** Breast Cancer; Lung Cancer; Prostate Cancer; **Hospital:** Plainview Hosp, N Shore Univ Hosp; **Address:** Advanced Radiation Centers of New York, 688 Old Country Rd, Plainview, NY 11803; **Phone:** 516-932-6007; **Board Cert:** Therapeutic Radiology 1982; **Med School:** NYU Sch Med 1978; **Resid:** Radiation Oncology, NYU Med Ctr 1981; Therapeutic Radiology, NY Methodist Hosp 1982

Gewanter, Richard M MD (RadRO) - **Spec Exp:** Prostate Cancer; Lung Cancer; **Hospital:** Meml Sloan Kettering Canc Ctr (page 110); **Address:** MSKCC-Dept Rad Oncology, 1000 N Village Ave, Rockville Centre, NY 11570; **Phone:** 516-256-3600; **Board Cert:** Radiation Oncology 2012; **Med School:** Albert Einstein Coll Med 1995; **Resid:** Radiation Oncology, Columbia Presby Med Ctr 2002

Ghaly, Maged M MD (RadRO) - **Spec Exp:** Brachytherapy; Stereotactic Body Radiotherapy; Radiation Therapy-Intraoperative; **Hospital:** Long Is Jewish Med Ctr, N Shore Univ Hosp; **Address:** Ctr for Advanced Medicine, 450 Lakeville Rd, Lake Success, NY 11042; **Phone:** 516-321-3000; **Board Cert:** Radiation Oncology 2013; **Med School:** Egypt 1992; **Resid:** Radiation Oncology, New York Methodist Hosp 2002; **Fellow:** Radiation Oncology, New York Methodist Hsop 2003

Haas, Jonathan A MD (RadRO) - **Spec Exp:** Brachytherapy; Prostate Cancer; Gynecologic Cancer; Intensity Modulated Radiotherapy (IMRT); **Hospital:** Winthrop Univ Hosp (page 536); **Address:** Winthrop Univ Hosp, Dept Radiation Oncology, 264 Old Country Rd, Mineola, NY 11501; **Phone:** 516-663-2501; **Board Cert:** Radiation Oncology 2009; **Med School:** Washington Univ, St Louis 1993; **Resid:** Radiation Oncology, Hosp Univ Penn 1998; **Fac Appt:** Asst Clin Prof RadRO, SUNY Stony Brook

Knisely, Jonathan P S MD (RadRO) - **Spec Exp:** Brain Tumors; Stereotactic Radiosurgery; Skull Base Tumors; **Hospital:** N Shore Univ Hosp, Glen Cove Hosp; **Address:** Radiation Medicine, 450 Lakeville Rd, New Hyde Park, NY 11042; **Phone:** 516-321-3000; **Board Cert:** Internal Medicine 1989; Radiation Oncology 1993; **Med School:** Univ Pennsylvania 1986; **Resid:** Internal Medicine, Michael Reese Hosp 1989; Radiation Oncology, Univ Toronto Med Ctr 1992; **Fac Appt:** Assoc Prof RadRO, Hofstra N Shore-LIJ Sch Med

Lee, Lucille N MD (RadRO) - **Spec Exp:** Breast Cancer; Prostate Cancer; **Hospital:** Long Is Jewish Med Ctr, NS-LIJ Hlth Sys; **Address:** Ctr for Advanced Med, Dept of Rad Med, 450 Lakeville Rd, Lake Success, NY 11042; **Phone:** 855-927-6622; **Board Cert:** Radiation Oncology 2011; **Med School:** Rutgers R W Johnson Med Sch 1996; **Resid:** Radiation Oncology, Mount Sinai Med Ctr 2001

Marienberg, Evelyn S MD (RadRO) - **Spec Exp:** Breast Cancer; Head & Neck Cancer; Vulvar & Vaginal Cancer; **Hospital:** Glen Cove Hosp; **Address:** Glen Cove Hosp, Dept Radiation Medicine, 101 St Andrews Ln, Glen Cove, NY 11542; **Phone:** 516-470-7190; **Board Cert:** Radiation Oncology 1996; **Med School:** SUNY Stony Brook 1988; **Resid:** Radiation Oncology, Univ of Miami Hosp & Clins/Sylvester Comp Canc Ctr 1994; **Fac Appt:** Asst Prof RadRO, SUNY Downstate

Mullen Jr, Edward E MD (RadRO) - **Spec Exp:** Brain Tumors; Breast Cancer; Stereotactic Radiosurgery; **Hospital:** South Nassau Comm Hosp; **Address:** South Nassau Comm Hosp, Dept Radiation Oncology, One Healthy Way, Oceanside, NY 11572; **Phone:** 516-632-3370; **Board Cert:** Radiation Oncology 1991; **Med School:** Univ VA Sch Med 1986; **Resid:** Radiation Oncology, Columbia-Presby Med Ctr 1991

Potters, Louis MD (RadRO) - **Spec Exp:** Prostate Cancer; Intensity Modulated Radiotherapy (IMRT); Brachytherapy; **Hospital:** Long Is Jewish Med Ctr, NS-LIJ Hlth Sys; **Address:** Ctr for Advanced Medicine- Dept Rad Med, 450 Lakeville Rd, Lake Success, NY 11042; **Phone:** 855-927-6622; **Board Cert:** Internal Medicine 1988; Radiation Oncology 1999; **Med School:** UMDNJ-NJ Med Sch, Newark 1985; **Resid:** Internal Medicine, Beth Israel Med Ctr 1988; Radiation Oncology, SUNY Downstate Med Ctr 1991; **Fac Appt:** Prof RadRO, Hofstra N Shore-LIJ Sch Med

Reproductive Endocrinology

Brenner, Steven H MD (RE) - **Spec Exp:** Infertility-IVF; Fertility Preservation; Preimplantation Genetic Diagnosis; **Hospital:** Long Is Jewish Med Ctr, John T Mather Meml Hosp; **Address:** Long Island IVF, 2001 Marcus Ave, Ste N213, Lake Success, NY 11042; **Phone:** 718-358-6363; **Board Cert:** Obstetrics & Gynecology 1985; Reproductive Endocrinology/Infertility 1987; **Med School:** SUNY Downstate 1978; **Resid:** Obstetrics & Gynecology, Beth Israel Med Ctr 1982; **Fellow:** Reproductive Endocrinology/Infertility, NYU Med Ctr 1984; **Fac Appt:** Assoc Clin Prof ObG, Albert Einstein Coll Med

Rheumatology

Belilos, Elise MD (Rhu) - **Spec Exp:** Polymyalgia Rheumatica; Giant Cell Arteritis; Rheumatoid Arthritis; **Hospital:** Winthrop Univ Hosp (page 536); **Address:** Winthrop Univ Hosp, Div Rheum, 120 Mineola Blvd, Ste 410, Mineola, NY 11501; **Phone:** 516-663-2097; **Board Cert:** Internal Medicine 1989; Rheumatology 2004; **Med School:** SUNY Stony Brook 1986; **Resid:** Internal Medicine, Winthrop Univ Hosp 1990; **Fellow:** Rheumatology, Winthrop UnivHosp 1993; **Fac Appt:** Asst Clin Prof Med, SUNY Stony Brook

Carsons, Steven E MD (Rhu) - **Spec Exp:** Rheumatoid Arthritis; Sjogren's Syndrome; Vasculitis; **Hospital:** Winthrop Univ Hosp (page 536); **Address:** Winthrop Univ Hosp, Div Rhematology, 120 Mineola Blvd, Ste 410, Mineola, NY 11501; **Phone:** 516-663-2097; **Board Cert:** Internal Medicine 1978; Rheumatology 1980; Clinical & Laboratory Immunology 1988; **Med School:** NY Med Coll 1975; **Resid:** Internal Medicine, Maimonides Med Ctr 1978; **Fellow:** Rheumatology, SUNY Brooklyn Med Ctr 1980; **Fac Appt:** Prof Med, SUNY Hlth Sci Ctr

Cohen, Daniel Henry MD (Rhu) - **Spec Exp:** Osteoporosis; Amyloidosis; **Hospital:** South Nassau Comm Hosp, Franklin Hosp; **Address:** 1157 Broadway, Hewlett, NY 11557; **Phone:** 516-295-4481; **Board Cert:** Internal Medicine 1981; Rheumatology 1984; **Med School:** NYU Sch Med 1978; **Resid:** Internal Medicine, Columbia-Presby Med Ctr 1981; **Fellow:** Rheumatology, NYU Med Ctr 1983

Furie, Richard A MD (Rhu) - **Spec Exp:** Lupus/SLE; Antiphospholipid Syndrome (APS); Rheumatoid Arthritis; **Hospital:** N Shore Univ Hosp, Long Is Jewish Med Ctr; **Address:** 865 Northern Blvd, Ste 302, Great Neck, NY 11021; **Phone:** 516-708-2550; **Board Cert:** Internal Medicine 1982; Rheumatology 1984; **Med School:** Cornell Univ-Weill Med Coll 1979; **Resid:** Internal Medicine, NY Hosp 1982; **Fellow:** Rheumatology, Hosp Spec Surg 1984; **Fac Appt:** Assoc Prof Med, Albert Einstein Coll Med

Lipstein-Kresch, Esther MD (Rhu) - **Spec Exp:** Rheumatoid Arthritis; Osteoarthritis; Osteoporosis; Fibromyalgia; **Hospital:** Long Is Jewish Med Ctr, N Shore Univ Hosp; **Address:** ProHealth Care Assocs, 2 ProHealth Plaza, Ste 103, Lake Success, NY 11042-1111; **Phone:** 516-622-6090; **Board Cert:** Internal Medicine 1982; Rheumatology 1984; **Med School:** SUNY Hlth Sci Ctr 1979; **Resid:** Internal Medicine, LI Jewish Med Ctr 1982; **Fellow:** Rheumatology, LI Jewish Med Ctr 1984; **Fac Appt:** Asst Prof Med, Mount Sinai Sch Med

Meredith, Gary S MD (Rhu) - **Spec Exp:** Gout; Lupus/SLE; Rheumatoid Arthritis; **Hospital:** St. Francis Hosp - The Heart Ctr (page 111); **Address:** 2 ProHEALTH Plaza, Ste 200, Lake Success, NY 11042; **Phone:** 516-622-6125; **Board Cert:** Internal Medicine 1984; Rheumatology 1986; **Med School:** NYU Sch Med 1981; **Resid:** Internal Medicine, Bellevue Hosp 1984; **Fellow:** Rheumatology, NYU Med Ctr 1986; **Fac Appt:** Asst Clin Prof Med, NYU Sch Med

Porges, Andrew J MD (Rhu) - **Spec Exp:** Osteoporosis; Rheumatoid Arthritis; Vasculitis; Lupus/SLE; **Hospital:** N Shore Univ Hosp, Glen Cove Hosp; **Address:** 1044 Northern Blvd, Ste 104, Roslyn, NY 11576; **Phone:** 516-484-6880; **Board Cert:** Internal Medicine 1989; Rheumatology 2012; **Med School:** Cornell Univ 1986; **Resid:** Internal Medicine, New York Hosp 1989; **Fellow:** Rheumatology, Hosp Special Surg 1992

Sullivan, James M MD (Rhu) - **Spec Exp:** Rheumatoid Arthritis; Lupus/SLE; Osteoarthritis; **Hospital:** Winthrop Univ Hosp (page 536); **Address:** 711 Stewart Ave, Ste 100, Garden City, NY 11530; **Phone:** 516-222-8654; **Board Cert:** Internal Medicine 1977; Rheumatology 1980; **Med School:** SUNY Upstate Med Univ 1974; **Resid:** Internal Medicine, Univ Michigan Med Ctr 1977; **Fellow:** Rheumatology, Univ Michigan Med Ctr 1979

Tiger, Louis MD (Rhu) - **Spec Exp:** Rheumatoid Arthritis; Lupus/SLE; Osteoarthritis; **Hospital:** Winthrop Univ Hosp (page 536); **Address:** 566 Broadway, Massapequa, NY 11758; **Phone:** 516-541-6262; **Board Cert:** Internal Medicine 1975; Rheumatology 1976; **Med School:** Univ Louisville Sch Med 1967; **Resid:** Internal Medicine, Maimonides Medical Ctr 1970; **Fellow:** Rheumatology, Albert Einstein Med Ctr 1974

Sports Medicine

Briner Jr, William W MD (SM) - **Spec Exp:** Primary Care Sports Medicine; **Hospital:** Hosp For Special Surgery (page 109); **Address:** 333 Earle Ovington Blvd, Omni Bldg - Ste 106, Uniondale, NY 11553; **Phone:** 516-222-6803; **Board Cert:** Family Medicine 2007; Sports Medicine 2013; **Med School:** Ohio State Univ 1985; **Resid:** Family Medicine, Macneal Meml Hosp 1988; **Fellow:** Sports Medicine, Marshall Univ 1990; **Fac Appt:** Asst Clin Prof FMed, Univ IL Coll Med

Surgery

Adamo, Alfred MD (S) - **Spec Exp:** Gastrointestinal Cancer & Surgery; Breast Cancer & Surgery; Head & Neck Cancer & Surgery; Laparoscopic Surgery; **Hospital:** Winthrop Univ Hosp (page 536); **Address:** Winthrop Univ Hosp, Surgery, 120 Mineola Blvd, Ste 320, Mineola, NY 11501; **Phone:** 516-663-3300; **Board Cert:** Surgery 2007; **Med School:** SUNY Downstate 1974; **Resid:** Surgery, Nassau Univ Med Ctr 1978; **Fac Appt:** Asst Clin Prof S, SUNY Stony Brook

Allendorf, John D MD (S) - **Spec Exp:** Cancer Surgery; Pancreatic Cancer; Hepatobiliary Surgery; Endocrine Surgery; **Hospital:** Winthrop Univ Hosp (page 536); **Address:** Winthrop Surgical Assocs, 120 Mineola Blvd, Ste 320, Mineola, NY 11501; **Phone:** 516- 66-32436; **Board Cert:** Surgery 2012; **Med School:** Columbia P&S 1997; **Resid:** Surgery, NY Presby Hosp/Columbia 2002; **Fellow:** Hepatobiliary Surgery, NY Presby Hosp/Columbia 2003

Auguste, Louis J MD (S) - **Spec Exp:** Breast Disease; Melanoma; Thyroid & Parathyroid Surgery; Hernia; **Hospital:** Long Is Jewish Med Ctr, N Shore Univ Hosp; **Address:** 2035 Lakeville Rd, Ste 206, New Hyde Park, NY 11042-1102; **Phone:** 516-775-2070; **Board Cert:** Surgery 2011; **Med School:** Haiti 1973; **Resid:** Surgery, Long Is Jewish Med Ctr 1980; **Fellow:** Surgical Oncology, Roswell Park Canc Inst 1982; **Fac Appt:** Assoc Clin Prof S, Albert Einstein Coll Med

Bank, Matthew A MD (S) - **Spec Exp:** Trauma; **Hospital:** N Shore Univ Hosp, NS-LIJ Hlth Sys; **Address:** 1999 Marcus Ave, Ste 106C, Lake Success, NY 11030; **Phone:** 516-233-3610; **Board Cert:** Surgery 2011; Surgical Critical Care 2013; **Med School:** NY Med Coll 1995; **Resid:** Surgery, Long Is Jewish Med Ctr 2000; **Fellow:** Surgical Critical Care, Yale-New Haven Hosp 2001; **Fac Appt:** Asst Prof S, Hofstra N Shore-LIJ Sch Med

Benowitz, Joel MD (S) - **Spec Exp:** Breast Cancer; Breast Disease; Minimally Invasive Surgery; Breast Reconstruction; **Hospital:** Mercy Med Ctr-Rockville Centre; **Address:** 1000 North Village Ave, Rockville Centre, NY 11570; **Phone:** 516-889-9100; **Board Cert:** Surgery 2012; **Med School:** Mexico 1975; **Resid:** Surgery, Brookdale Hosp Med Ctr 1981

Brathwaite, Collin MD (S) - **Spec Exp:** Obesity/Bariatric Surgery; Trauma; Minimally Invasive Surgery; Gastrointestinal Surgery; **Hospital:** Winthrop Univ Hosp (page 536); **Address:** Winthrop Surgical Weight Loss, 120 Mineola Blvd, Ste 320, Mineola, NY 11501; **Phone:** 516-663-3300; **Board Cert:** Surgery 2011; **Med School:** Howard Univ 1983; **Resid:** Surgery, St Vincents Hosp & Med Ctr 1988; **Fellow:** Trauma/Critical Care, Shock Trauma Ctr 1989; **Fac Appt:** Assoc Prof S, SUNY Stony Brook

Chorost, Mitchell I MD (S) - **Spec Exp:** Cancer Surgery; Gastrointestinal Cancer; **Hospital:** St. Francis Hosp - The Heart Ctr (page 111); **Address:** NY Surgical Partners, 139 Plandome Rd, Manhasset, NY 11030; **Phone:** 516-627-5262; **Board Cert:** Surgery 2009; **Med School:** UMDNJ-Rutgers Med Sch 1993; **Resid:** Surgery, SUNY Stony Brook Univ Med Ctr 1998; **Fellow:** Surgical Oncology, Roswell Park Cancer Inst 2000

Conte, Charles C MD (S) - **Spec Exp:** Cancer Surgery; Breast Cancer; Pancreatic Cancer; **Hospital:** N Shore Univ Hosp, Forest Hills Hosp; **Address:** North Shore-LIJ Cancer Inst, Dept Surgical Oncology, 450 Lakeville Rd, Lake Success, NY 11042; **Phone:** 516-487-9454; **Board Cert:** Surgery 2005; **Med School:** Dartmouth Med Sch 1981; **Resid:** Surgery, Hartford Hosp 1986; **Fellow:** Surgical Oncology, Roswell Park Cancer Inst 1988; **Fac Appt:** Asst Prof S, Hofstra N Shore-LIJ Sch Med

Coppa, Gene F MD (S) - **Spec Exp:** Minimally Invasive Surgery; Hepatobiliary Surgery; Gastrointestinal Surgery; Pancreatic Surgery; **Hospital:** N Shore Univ Hosp; **Address:** N Shore Univ Hosp, 300 Community Drive, Manhasset, NY 11030; **Phone:** 516-562-2870; **Board Cert:** Surgery 2010; **Med School:** NYU Sch Med 1974; **Resid:** Surgery, NYU/Bellevue Med Ctr 1979; **Fac Appt:** Prof S, Hofstra N Shore-LIJ Sch Med

Datta, Rajiv V MD (S) - **Spec Exp:** Breast Cancer; Colon & Rectal Cancer; Gastrointestinal Cancer; Head & Neck Cancer; **Hospital:** South Nassau Comm Hosp; **Address:** South Nassau Comm Hosp Canc Ctr, 1 S Central Ave, Valley Stream, NY 11580; **Phone:** 516-632-3350; **Board Cert:** Surgery 2009; **Med School:** India 1984; **Resid:** Surgery, Maimonides Med Ctr 1998; **Fellow:** Surgical Oncology, Roswell Park Canc Inst 1999; Head and Neck Surgery, Roswell Park Canc Inst 2000; **Fac Appt:** Asst Clin Prof S, Hofstra N Shore-LIJ Sch Med

Gecelter, Gary R MD (S) - **Spec Exp:** Pancreatic Cancer; Esophageal Surgery; Laparoscopic Surgery; Biliary Surgery; **Hospital:** St. Francis Hosp - The Heart Ctr (page 111); **Address:** 139 Plandome Rd, Manhasset, NY 11030; **Phone:** 516-627-5262; **Med School:** South Africa 1981; **Resid:** Surgery, Johannesburg Hosp 1990; **Fellow:** Gastroenterology, Johannesburg Hosp 1992

Grieco, Michael B MD (S) - **Spec Exp:** Breast Surgery; Laparoscopic Abdominal Surgery; Hernia; Laparoscopic Cholecystectomy; **Hospital:** Glen Cove Hosp, St. Francis Hosp - The Heart Ctr (page 111); **Address:** 10 Medical Plaza, Ste 105, Glen Cove, NY 11542; **Phone:** 516-676-1060; **Board Cert:** Surgery 2010; Colon & Rectal Surgery 1982; **Med School:** Albany Med Coll 1974; **Resid:** Surgery, N Shore Univ Hosp 1979; **Fellow:** Surgery, Lahey Clinic 1980; Colon & Rectal Surgery, Greater Baltimore Med Ctr 1981

Halpern, David K MD (S) - **Spec Exp:** Laparoscopic Surgery-Advanced; Hernia; Breast Cancer & Surgery; Cancer Surgery; **Hospital:** Winthrop Univ Hosp (page 536); **Address:** Nassau Surgical Assocs, 300 Old Country Rd, Ste 101, Mineola, NY 11501; **Phone:** 516-741-4138; **Board Cert:** Surgery 2006; **Med School:** Northwestern Univ 1990; **Resid:** Surgery, SUNY Stony Brook Univ Med Ctr 1995; **Fac Appt:** Asst Clin Prof S, SUNY Stony Brook

Khalife, Michael E MD (S) - **Spec Exp:** Laparoscopic Surgery; Breast Surgery; Minimally Invasive Surgery; **Hospital:** Winthrop Univ Hosp (page 536), N Shore Univ Hosp; **Address:** Nassau Surgical Assocs, 300 Old Country Rd, Ste 101, Mineola, NY 11501; **Phone:** 516-741-4138; **Board Cert:** Surgery 2013; **Med School:** Lebanon 1978; **Resid:** Surgery, Stony Brook Univ Med Ctr 1984; **Fac Appt:** Asst Clin Prof S, SUNY Stony Brook

Kurtz, Lewis M MD (S) - **Spec Exp:** Breast Surgery; Gallbladder Surgery; Hernia; **Hospital:** St. Francis Hosp - The Heart Ctr (page 111), Long Is Jewish Med Ctr; **Address:** 310 E Shore Rd, Ste 203, Great Neck, NY 11023; **Phone:** 516-482-8657; **Board Cert:** Surgery 2010; **Med School:** Italy 1971; **Resid:** Surgery, Long Is Jewish Med Ctr 1978

Mansouri, Hormoz MD (S) - **Spec Exp:** Varicose Veins; **Hospital:** N Shore Univ Hosp; **Address:** 175 Jericho Tpke, Ste 201, Syosset, NY 11791; **Phone:** 516-682-4800; **Board Cert:** Surgery 1980; **Med School:** Iran 1964; **Resid:** Surgery, Henry Ford Hosp 1969; Surgery, Nassau Univ Med Ctr 1971; **Fac Appt:** Asst Prof S, SUNY Stony Brook

Molmenti, Ernesto P MD/PhD (S) - **Spec Exp:** Transplant-Kidney; **Hospital:** Long Is Jewish Med Ctr, NS-LIJ Hlth Sys; **Address:** 1554 Northern Blvd, Manhasset, NY 11030; **Phone:** 516-472-5800; **Board Cert:** Surgery 2006; **Med School:** Boston Univ 1989; **Resid:** Surgery, Barnes Jewish Med Ctr 1996; **Fellow:** Research, Wash Univ Affil Hosp 1994; Research, Thomas E. Starzl Transplantation Inst 1998; **Fac Appt:** Prof S, Boston Univ

Reiner, Dan S MD (S) - **Spec Exp:** Laparoscopic Surgery; Hernia; Gastrointestinal Surgery; **Hospital:** N Shore Univ Hosp, Syosset Hosp; **Address:** 2800 Marcus Ave, Ste 204, Lake Success, NY 11042-1008; **Phone:** 516-622-6120; **Board Cert:** Surgery 2005; Surgical Critical Care 2007; **Med School:** St Louis Univ 1980; **Resid:** Surgery, St Louis Univ Hosp 1985; **Fellow:** Surgical Critical Care, UMDNJ-NJ Med Sch Affil Hosp 1986; **Fac Appt:** Assoc Clin Prof S, NYU Sch Med

Vitale, Gerard F MD (S) - **Spec Exp:** Aneurysm; Carotid Artery Surgery; Varicose Veins; Arterial Bypass Surgery; **Hospital:** Glen Cove Hosp; **Address:** 10 Medical Plaza, Ste 305, Glen Cove, NY 11542; **Phone:** 516-759-5559; **Board Cert:** Surgery 2010; **Med School:** SUNY Buffalo 1982; **Resid:** Surgery, N Shore Univ Hosp 1987; **Fellow:** Vascular Surgery, St Vincents Hosp 1988

Thoracic & Cardiac Surgery

Andaz, Shahriyour MD (T&CS) - **Spec Exp:** Thoracic Cancers; Lung Cancer; **Hospital:** South Nassau Comm Hosp, Franklin Hosp; **Address:** 444 Merrick Rd, Ste 380, Lynbrook, NY 11563; **Phone:** 516-255-5010; **Board Cert:** Surgery 2009; Thoracic & Cardiac Surgery 2010; **Med School:** India 1983; **Resid:** Surgery, Bronx Lebanon Hosp Ctr 1998; **Fellow:** Thoracic Surgery, SUNY Hlth Sci Ctr 2001

Barrett, Leonard Octavius MD (T&CS) - **Spec Exp:** Chest Trauma; Esophageal Tumors; Critical Care; **Hospital:** Nassau Univ Med Ctr; **Address:** Nassau Univ Med Ctr, 2201 Hempstead Tpke, Fl 8, East Meadow, NY 11554; **Phone:** 516-572-6703; **Board Cert:** Surgery 2009; Surgical Critical Care 2010; Thoracic & Cardiac Surgery 2005; **Med School:** SUNY Downstate 1983; **Resid:** Surgery, SUNY Stony Brook Med Ctr 1989; **Fellow:** Surgical Critical Care, Winthrop Univ Med Ctr 1990; Cardiothoracic Surgery, Beth Israel Med Ctr 1993

Esposito, Rick A MD (T&CS) - **Spec Exp:** Cardiac Surgery; Coronary Artery Surgery; Mitral Valve Minimally Invasive Surgery; **Hospital:** N Shore Univ Hosp; **Address:** N Shore Univ Hosp, Dept Cardiothoracic Surgery, 300 Community Drive, Ste 1DSU, Manhasset, NY 11030; **Phone:** 516-562-4970; **Board Cert:** Thoracic Surgery 2006; **Med School:** Univ Chicago-Pritzker Sch Med 1979; **Resid:** Surgery, NYU Langone Med Ctr 1984; **Fellow:** Cardiothoracic Surgery, NYU Langone Med Ctr 1986; **Fac Appt:** Prof T&CS, Hofstra N Shore-LIJ Sch Med

Glassman, Lawrence R MD (T&CS) - **Spec Exp:** Lung Cancer; Esophageal Cancer; Emphysema; Tracheal Surgery; **Hospital:** N Shore Univ Hosp; **Address:** NS-LIJ, Cardiothoracic Surgery, 225 Community Drive, Ste 110, Great Neck, NY 11021; **Phone:** 516-918-4388; **Board Cert:** Thoracic & Cardiac Surgery 2013; **Med School:** NYU Sch Med 1981; **Resid:** Surgery, Univ Minn Med Ctr 1983; Surgery, NYU Med Ctr 1985; **Fellow:** Thoracic Oncology, Meml Sloan-Kettering Cancer Ctr 1988; Cardiothoracic Surgery, NYU Med Ctr 1990

Hyman, Kevin M MD (T&CS) - **Spec Exp:** Lung Cancer; Esophageal Cancer; Emphysema; Minimally Invasive Thoracic Surgery; **Hospital:** N Shore Univ Hosp; **Address:** NS-LIJ Med Grp, Div Thoracic Surg, 225 Community Drive, Ste 110, Great Neck, NY 11021; **Phone:** 516-918-4388; **Board Cert:** Surgery 2006; Thoracic & Cardiac Surgery 2007; **Med School:** Cornell Univ-Weill Med Coll 1997; **Resid:** Surgery, NYU Med Ctr 2004; **Fellow:** Cardiothoracic Surgery, NYU Med Ctr 2006; Thoracic Surgery, Mount Sinai Med Ctr 2007; **Fac Appt:** Asst Prof S, Hofstra N Shore-LIJ Sch Med

Meyer, David B MD (T&CS) - **Spec Exp:** Pediatric Cardiac Surgery; Congenital Heart Disease-Adult & Child; Minimally Invasive Cardiac Surgery; **Hospital:** Steven & Alexandra Cohen Chldn's Med Ctr of NY; **Address:** CCMC, Ped Cardiothoracic Surgery, 269-01 76th Ave, Ste 139, New Hyde Park, NY 11040; **Phone:** 718-470-3580; **Board Cert:** Surgery 2003; Thoracic & Cardiac Surgery 2014; Congenital Cardiac Surgery 2010; **Med School:** Yale Univ 1997; **Resid:** Surgery, NYU Med Ctr 2002; **Fellow:** Cardiothoracic Surgery, NYU Med Ctr 2004; **Fac Appt:** Asst Prof T&CS, NYU Sch Med

Parnell Jr, Vincent A MD (T&CS) - **Spec Exp:** Pediatric Cardiothoracic Surgery; Congenital Heart Disease; **Hospital:** Steven & Alexandra Cohen Chldn's Med Ctr of NY, N Shore Univ Hosp; **Address:** 269-01 76th Ave, Ste 139, New Hyde Park, NY 11040; **Phone:** 718-470-3580; **Board Cert:** Thoracic & Cardiac Surgery 2014; Congenital Cardiac Surgery 2011; **Med School:** SUNY Downstate 1976; **Resid:** Surgery, N Shore Univ Hosp 1981; Thoracic Surgery, Harper Hosp 1983; **Fellow:** Pediatric Cardiac Surgery, Chldns Hosp 1984; **Fac Appt:** Assoc Prof T&CS, Hofstra N Shore-LIJ Sch Med

Pogo, Gustave J MD (T&CS) - **Spec Exp:** Aneurysm-Aortic; **Hospital:** N Shore Univ Hosp; **Address:** N Shore, Thoracic & Cardiac Surgery, 300 Community Drive, Ste 1DSU, Manhasset, NY 11030; **Phone:** 516-562-4970; **Board Cert:** Thoracic & Cardiac Surgery 2011; **Med School:** NYU Sch Med 1983; **Resid:** Surgery, N Shore Univ Hosp 1988; Cardiothoracic Surgery, Mount Sinai Med Ctr 1991; **Fac Appt:** Asst Prof S, Hofstra N Shore-LIJ Sch Med

Robinson, Newell B MD (T&CS) - **Spec Exp:** Minimally Invasive Cardiac Surgery; Maze Procedure for Atrial Fibrillation; Heart Valve Surgery; **Hospital:** St. Francis Hosp - The Heart Ctr (page 111); **Address:** St Francis Hosp-The Heart Ctr, 100 Port Washington Blvd, Ste G01, Roslyn, NY 11576; **Phone:** 516-627-2173; **Board Cert:** Surgery 2005; Thoracic & Cardiac Surgery 2006; **Med School:** Univ Miss 1973; **Resid:** Surgery, NY-Presby/Weill Cornell Med Ctr 1984; Surgery, Meml Sloan-Kettering Cancer Ctr 1984; **Fellow:** Trauma, Univ Washington Med Ctr 1981; Cardiothoracic Surgery, NY-Presby/Weill Cornell Med Ctr 1986

Scheinerman, Samuel Jacob MD (T&CS) - **Spec Exp:** Minimally Invasive Surgery; Aortic Valve Replacement; Heart Valve Surgery; Coronary Artery Surgery; **Hospital:** Long Is Jewish Med Ctr; **Address:** LI Jewish Med Ctr, Dept Thoracic Surg, 270-05 76th Ave, Oncology Bldg Fl 4, New Hyde Park, NY 11040; **Phone:** 718-470-7460; **Board Cert:** Thoracic & Cardiac Surgery 2009; **Med School:** NYU Sch Med 1981; **Resid:** Surgery, NYU Med Ctr 1986; **Fellow:** Cardiothoracic Surgery, NYU Med Ctr 1988; **Fac Appt:** Asst Clin Prof S, Cornell Univ-Weill Med Coll

Schubach, Scott L MD (T&CS) - **Spec Exp:** Cardiac Surgery; Coronary Artery Surgery; Heart Valve Surgery; Minimally Invasive Surgery; **Hospital:** Winthrop Univ Hosp (page 536); **Address:** Winthrop Univ Hosp, Cardiothoracic, 120 Mineola Blvd, Ste 300, Mineola, NY 11501; **Phone:** 516-663-4400; **Board Cert:** Surgery 2007; Thoracic Surgery 2010; Surgical Critical Care 2010; **Med School:** Baylor Coll Med 1983; **Resid:** Surgery, Dartmouth-Hitchcock Med Ctr 1988; Cardiothoracic Surgery, UPMC 1991; **Fac Appt:** Asst Prof T&CS, SUNY Stony Brook

Zeltsman, Vadim MD (T&CS) - **Spec Exp:** Thoracic Cancers; Video Assisted Thoracic Surgery (VATS); **Hospital:** Long Is Jewish Med Ctr, N Shore Univ Hosp; **Address:** 225 Community Drive, Ste 110, Great Neck, NY 11021; **Phone:** 516-918-4388; **Board Cert:** Surgery 2011; Thoracic Surgery 2013; **Med School:** Russia 1986; **Resid:** Surgery, Mercy Catholic Med Ctr 1998; **Fellow:** Cardiothoracic Surgery, UMDNJ Affil Hosp 2001; **Fac Appt:** Asst Prof T&CS, Hofstra N Shore-LIJ Sch Med

Urology

Ashley, Richard N MD (U) - **Spec Exp:** Urologic Cancer; Kidney Stones; Incontinence; **Hospital:** N Shore Univ Hosp; **Address:** Smith Institute for Urology, 233 7th St, Ste 203, Garden City, NY 11530; **Phone:** 516-294-7666; **Board Cert:** Urology 1980; **Med School:** NY Med Coll 1972; **Resid:** Surgery, St Vincents Hosp 1975; Urology, SUNY Downstate Med Ctr 1978

Bruno, Anthony M MD (U) - **Spec Exp:** Prostate Cancer; Kidney Stones; Voiding Dysfunction; **Hospital:** Winthrop Univ Hosp (page 536); **Address:** Advanced Urology Ctrs of NY, 1305 Franklin Ave, Ste 100, Garden City, NY 11530; **Phone:** 516-746-5550; **Board Cert:** Urology 1977; **Med School:** Italy 1968; **Resid:** Surgery, Winthrop Univ Hosp 1972; Urology, Bellevue Hosp Ctr 1975; **Fac Appt:** Asst Clin Prof U, SUNY Stony Brook

D'Esposito, Robert F MD (U) - **Hospital:** Winthrop Univ Hosp (page 536); **Address:** Urological Surgeons of Long Island, 601 Franklin Ave, Ste 300, Garden City, NY 11530-5759; **Phone:** 516-742-3200; **Board Cert:** Urology 1981; **Med School:** Italy 1971; **Resid:** Surgery, Nassau Hosp 1972; Urology, Nassau Hosp 1976; **Fac Appt:** Assoc Clin Prof U, SUNY Stony Brook

Edelman, Robert A MD (U) - **Hospital:** Winthrop Univ Hosp (page 536); **Address:** Urological Surgeons of Long Island, 601 Franklin Ave, Ste 300, Garden City, NY 11530-5729; **Phone:** 516-742-3200; **Board Cert:** Urology 1981; **Med School:** SUNY Upstate Med Univ 1974; **Resid:** Surgery, Montefiore Med Ctr 1976; Urology, Montefiore Med Ctr 1979; **Fac Appt:** Assoc Clin Prof U, SUNY Stony Brook

Gershbaum, Meyer D MD (U) - **Spec Exp:** Robotic Surgery; Minimally Invasive Surgery; Prostate Cancer/Robotic Surgery; **Hospital:** Winthrop Univ Hosp (page 536), N Shore Univ Hosp; **Address:** Urological Surgeons of Long Island, 601 Franklin Ave, Ste 300, Garden City, NY 11530; **Phone:** 516-742-3200; **Board Cert:** Urology 2013; **Med School:** Albert Einstein Coll Med 1996; **Resid:** Surgery, LI Jewish Med Ctr 1998; Urology, LI Jewish Med Ctr 2002; **Fellow:** Laparoscopic Surgery, VA Med Ctr 2003

Girardi, Sarah K MD (U) - **Spec Exp:** Infertility-Male; Microsurgery; Female Urology; **Hospital:** N Shore Univ Hosp, St. Francis Hosp - The Heart Ctr (page 111); **Address:** Urology Associates, 535 Plandome Rd, Ste 3, Manhasset, NY 11030; **Phone:** 516-627-6188; **Board Cert:** Urology 2006; **Med School:** Univ NC Sch Med 1987; **Resid:** Urology, New York Hosp 1995; **Fellow:** Male Infertility, Cornell Univ 1996; **Fac Appt:** Assoc Prof U, Cornell Univ-Weill Med Coll

Hanna, Moneer K MD (U) - **Spec Exp:** Pediatric Urology; Reconstructive Surgery; Hypospadias; Bladder Surgery; **Hospital:** Steven & Alexandra Cohen Chldn's Med Ctr of NY, NY-Presby/Weill Cornell Med Ctr, NY (page 102); **Address:** 935 Northern Blvd, Ste 303, Great Neck, NY 11021; **Phone:** 516-466-6950; **Board Cert:** Urology 1978; **Med School:** Egypt 1963; **Resid:** Urology, London Univ Affil Hosp 1972; Urology, Univ West Ont Affil Hosps 1976; **Fellow:** Pediatric Urology, Hosp For Sick Chldn 1975; **Fac Appt:** Clin Prof U, Cornell Univ-Weill Med Coll

Harris, Steven M MD (U) - **Spec Exp:** Prostate Disease; Kidney Stones; **Hospital:** South Nassau Comm Hosp, Mercy Med Ctr-Rockville Centre; **Address:** Advanced Urology, 143 N Long Beach Rd, Ste 1, Rockville Centre, NY 11570; **Phone:** 516-766-2929; **Board Cert:** Urology 1984; **Med School:** Albert Einstein Coll Med 1976; **Resid:** Urology, Mt Sinai Med Ctr 1981

Katz, Aaron E MD (U) - **Spec Exp:** Prostate Cancer-Cryosurgery; Kidney Cancer-Cryosurgery; Complementary Medicine; Nutrition & Cancer Prevention; **Hospital:** Winthrop Univ Hosp (page 536); **Address:** Winthrop Urology, 1300 Franklin Ave, Ste ML6, Garden City, NY 11530; **Phone:** 516-535-1900; **Board Cert:** Urology 2006; **Med School:** NY Med Coll 1986; **Resid:** Urology, Maimonides Med Ctr 1992; **Fellow:** Urologic Oncology, NY-Presby/Columbia Univ Med Ctr 1993; **Fac Appt:** Assoc Clin Prof U, SUNY Stony Brook

Kavoussi, Louis R MD (U) - **Spec Exp:** Robotic Surgery; Urologic Cancer; Prostate Cancer; Kidney Cancer; **Hospital:** Long Is Jewish Med Ctr, N Shore Univ Hosp; **Address:** Smith Inst for Urology, 450 Lakeville Rd, B Bldg, Ste M-41, New Hyde Park, NY 11042; **Phone:** 516-734-8558; **Board Cert:** Urology 2009; **Med School:** SUNY Buffalo 1983; **Resid:** Surgery, Barnes-Jewish Hosp 1985; Urology, Barnes-Jewish Hosp 1989; **Fac Appt:** Prof U, Hofstra N Shore-LIJ Sch Med

Layne, Jeffrey T MD (U) - **Spec Exp:** Kidney Stones; Incontinence; Impotence; **Hospital:** Plainview Hosp, St. Joseph's Hosp-Nassau; **Address:** Advn Urology Ctrs NY, 1181 Old Country Rd, Ste 1, Plainview, NY 11803-5018; **Phone:** 516-933-6060; **Board Cert:** Urology 2007; **Med School:** SUNY Stony Brook 1989; **Resid:** Surgery, Tufts-New England Med Ctr 1991; Urology, Tufts-New England Med CtrTufts-New England Med Ctr 1995

Levine, Michael A MD (U) - **Spec Exp:** Urologic Cancer; Kidney Stones; Erectile Dysfunction; Incontinence; **Hospital:** Long Is Jewish Med Ctr, N Shore Univ Hosp; **Address:** Lake Success Urological Assocs, 2001 Marcus Ave, Ste N214, Lake Success, NY 11042; **Phone:** 516-437-4228; **Board Cert:** Urology 2008; **Med School:** SUNY Downstate 1992; **Resid:** Urology, NYU Med Ctr 1998; **Fac Appt:** Asst Clin Prof U, SUNY Upstate Med Univ

Lieberman, Elliott MD (U) - **Hospital:** Plainview Hosp; **Address:** Advanced Urology Ctrs NY, 875 Old Country Rd, Ste 301, Plainview, NY 11803-4934; **Phone:** 516-931-1710; **Board Cert:** Urology 1983; **Med School:** SUNY Downstate 1976; **Resid:** Surgery, Mt Sinai Med Ctr 1978; Urology, SUNY Downstate Med Ctr 1981

Lumerman, Jeffrey H MD (U) - **Spec Exp:** Prostate Cancer; Prostate Disease; Kidney Stones; Men's Health; **Hospital:** Winthrop Univ Hosp (page 536), N Shore Univ Hosp; **Address:** ProHealthcare Associates Urology, 2 ProHealth Plaza, lake Success, NY 11042; **Phone:** 516-622-6110; **Board Cert:** Urology 2009; **Med School:** Albert Einstein Coll Med 1993; **Resid:** Surgery, LIJ Med Ctr 1995; Urology, LIJ Med Ctr 1999; **Fac Appt:** Asst Clin Prof U, SUNY Stony Brook

Mellinger, Brett C MD (U) - **Spec Exp:** Infertility-Male; Erectile Dysfunction; Peyronie's Disease; Incontinence; **Hospital:** Winthrop Univ Hosp (page 536), N Shore Univ Hosp; **Address:** Advanced Urology Ctrs of NY, 100 Garden City Plaza, Ste 101, Garden City, NY 11530; **Phone:** 516-873-5353; **Board Cert:** Urology 2010; **Med School:** Indiana Univ 1981; **Resid:** Urology, Univ Hosp 1985; **Fellow:** Male Infertility, New York Hosp-Cornell 1988; **Fac Appt:** Assoc Clin Prof U, SUNY Stony Brook

Moldwin, Robert M MD (U) - **Spec Exp:** Interstitial Cystitis; Pain-Pelvic; Urologic Infectious Disease; **Hospital:** Long Is Jewish Med Ctr, NS-LIJ Hlth Sys; **Address:** Smith Institute for Urology, 450 Lakeville Rd, Bldg B, Ste M41, New Hyde Park, NY 11040-1433; **Phone:** 516-734-8500; **Board Cert:** Urology 2012; **Med School:** Univ Chicago-Pritzker Sch Med 1984; **Resid:** Urology, LI Jewish Med Ctr 1989; **Fellow:** Urologic Infectious Disease, Jefferson Med Coll 1991; **Fac Appt:** Assoc Prof U, Hofstra N Shore-LIJ Sch Med

Paul, Elliot M MD (U) - **Spec Exp:** Prostate Cancer; Kidney Stones; Laparoscopic Surgery; Incontinence-Female; **Hospital:** Long Is Jewish Med Ctr, St. Francis Hosp - The Heart Ctr (page 111); **Address:** Lake Success Urological Assocs, 2001 Marcus Ave, Ste N214, Lake Success, NY 11042; **Phone:** 516-437-4228; **Board Cert:** Urology 2007; **Med School:** Albert Einstein Coll Med 2000; **Resid:** Urology, LI Jewish Med Ctr 2005

Richstone, Lee MD (U) - **Spec Exp:** Robotic Surgery; Laparoscopic Surgery; Prostate Cancer; Urologic Cancer; **Hospital:** N Shore Univ Hosp, Long Is Jewish Med Ctr; **Address:** Smith Institute for Urology, 450 Lakeville Rd, B Bldg, Ste M41, New Hyde Park, NY 11042; **Phone:** 516-734-8500; **Board Cert:** Urology 2009; **Med School:** Cornell Univ 2000; **Resid:** Urology, Weill Cornell Med Ctr 2006

Shepard, Barry R MD (U) - **Spec Exp:** Kidney Stones; Urologic Cancer; **Hospital:** Winthrop Univ Hosp (page 536), N Shore Univ Hosp; **Address:** Urological Surgeons of Long Island, 601 Franklin Ave, Ste 300, Garden City, NY 11530; **Phone:** 516-742-3200; **Board Cert:** Urology 2006; **Med School:** SUNY Downstate 1979; **Resid:** Surgery, LI Jewish Med Ctr 1981; Urology, Columbia-Presby Med Ctr 1984

Sunshine, Robert D MD (U) - **Spec Exp:** Vasectomy-Scalpelless; Prostate Disease; **Hospital:** St. Joseph's Hosp-Nassau, Plainview Hosp; **Address:** Advn Urology Ctrs NY, 480 Hicksville Rd, Bethpage, NY 11714-5700; **Phone:** 516-796-2222; **Board Cert:** Urology 2005; **Med School:** Mexico 1977; **Resid:** Surgery, Long Island Jewish Hosp 1981; Urology, Mount Sinai Med Ctr 1985

Ziegelbaum, Michael M MD (U) - **Spec Exp:** Incontinence-Male & Female; Prostate Disease; Laparoscopic Surgery; Kidney Stones; **Hospital:** Long Is Jewish Med Ctr, St. Francis Hosp - The Heart Ctr (page 111); **Address:** Lake Success Urological Assocs, 2001 Marcus Ave, Ste N214, Lake Success, NY 11042; **Phone:** 516-437-4228; **Board Cert:** Urology 2010; **Med School:** Cornell Univ 1982; **Resid:** Urology, Cleveland Clinic 1988; **Fellow:** Stone Disease, Stony Brook Univ Med Ctr 1989; **Fac Appt:** Asst Clin Prof U, Albert Einstein Coll Med

Vascular & Interventional Radiology

Cooper, Stanley G MD (VIR) - **Spec Exp:** Interventional Radiology; Dialysis Access; **Address:** ProHEALTH Care Associates, 2800 Marcus Ave, Lake Success, NY 11042; **Phone:** 516-622-7485; **Board Cert:** Diagnostic Radiology 1989; Vascular & Interventional Radiology 2006; **Med School:** Albert Einstein Coll Med 1984; **Resid:** Diagnostic Radiology, Norwalk Hosp 1989; **Fellow:** Vascular & Interventional Radiology, Yale-New Haven Hosp 1990

Crystal, Kenneth S MD (VIR) - **Spec Exp:** Interventional Radiology; Uterine Fibroid Embolization; Angioplasty; **Hospital:** St. Francis Hosp - The Heart Ctr (page 111); **Address:** St Francis Hosp, 100 Port Washington Blvd, Roslyn, NY 11576; **Phone:** 516-562-6500; **Board Cert:** Diagnostic Radiology 1986; **Med School:** Univ Rochester 1981; **Resid:** Diagnostic Radiology, NYU Med Ctr 1985; **Fellow:** Vascular & Interventional Radiology, NYU Med Ctr; **Fac Appt:** Asst Prof Rad, NYU Sch Med

Hon, Man MD (VIR) - **Spec Exp:** Uterine Fibroid Embolization; Chemoembolization & Tumor Ablation; **Hospital:** Winthrop Univ Hosp (page 536); **Address:** Winthrop Univ Hosp, Interventional Radiology, 259 1st St, Mineola, NY 11501; **Phone:** 516-663-2452; **Board Cert:** Diagnostic Radiology 1990; Vascular & Interventional Radiology 2009; **Med School:** Albert Einstein Coll Med 1985; **Resid:** Diagnostic Radiology, Jacobi Med Ctr 1990; **Fellow:** Vascular & Interventional Radiology, New York Hosp-Cornell 1991; **Fac Appt:** Asst Prof Rad, SUNY Stony Brook

Siegel, David N MD (VIR) - **Spec Exp:** Uterine Fibroid Embolization; **Hospital:** Long Is Jewish Med Ctr; **Address:** LIJMC, Radiology, 270-05 76th Ave, New Hyde Park, NY 11040; **Phone:** 718-470-7134; **Board Cert:** Diagnostic Radiology 1991; Vascular & Interventional Radiology 2006; **Med School:** UMDNJ-NJ Med Sch, Newark 1986; **Resid:** Diagnostic Radiology, Hackensack Univ Med Ctr 1991; **Fellow:** Vascular & Interventional Radiology, LIJ Med Ctr 1996; **Fac Appt:** Asst Prof Rad, Albert Einstein Coll Med

Vascular Surgery

Chaudhry, Saqib S MD (VascS) - **Spec Exp:** Dialysis Access Surgery; Vein Disorders; Sclerotherapy; Vein Disorders; **Hospital:** Forest Hills Hosp, Flushing Hosp Med Ctr; **Address:** 1044 Northern Blvd, Ste 302, Roslyn, NY 11576; **Phone:** 516-621-1313; **Board Cert:** Vascular Surgery 2009; Thoracic & Cardiac Surgery 2011; **Med School:** Iraq 1972; **Resid:** Surgery, Flushing Hosp Med Ctr 1978; Thoracic Surgery, Wayne State Univ Affil Hosps 1980

Faust, Glenn R MD (VascS) - **Spec Exp:** Aneurysm-Abdominal Aortic; Carotid Artery Disease; Peripheral Vascular Disease; Vein Disorders; **Hospital:** Nassau Univ Med Ctr; **Address:** Nassau Univ Med Ctr-Vascular Surgery, 2201 Hempstead Tpke, East Meadow, NY 11554; **Phone:** 516-572-4848; **Board Cert:** Vascular Surgery 2004; **Med School:** Yale Univ 1986; **Resid:** Surgery, LI Jewish Med Ctr 1991; **Fellow:** Vascular Surgery, LI Jewish Med Ctr 1992; **Fac Appt:** Asst Prof S, Albert Einstein Coll Med

Landis, Gregg S MD (VascS) - **Spec Exp:** Endovascular Surgery; Peripheral Vascular Disease; Aneurysm-Aortic; Carotid Artery Surgery; **Hospital:** Long Is Jewish Med Ctr; **Address:** 1999 Marcus Ave, Ste 106B, New Hyde Park, NY 11042; **Phone:** 516-470-4505; **Board Cert:** Surgery 2009; Vascular Surgery 2011; **Med School:** UMDNJ-Rutgers Med Sch 1995; **Resid:** Surgery, Montefiore Med Ctr 2000; **Fellow:** Vascular Surgery, SUNY Downstate Med Ctr 2002; **Fac Appt:** Assoc Prof S, Hofstra N Shore-LIJ Sch Med

Purtill, William A MD (VascS) - **Spec Exp:** Arterial Disease; Endovascular Surgery; Aneurysm-Abdominal Aortic; Carotid Artery Disease; **Hospital:** N Shore Univ Hosp, St. Francis Hosp - The Heart Ctr (page 111); **Address:** 990 Stewart Ave, Ste L32, Garden City, NY 11530; **Phone:** 516-466-0485; **Board Cert:** Surgery 2007; Vascular Surgery 2007; **Med School:** Ireland 1989; **Resid:** Surgery, Johns Hopkins Hosp 1993; Surgery, Stony Brook Univ Med Ctr 1996; **Fellow:** Vascular Surgery, Univ MD Med Ctr 1997; **Fac Appt:** Asst Clin Prof S, SUNY Stony Brook

Rockland

Rockland

Allergy & Immunology

Bosso, John MD (A&I) - **Spec Exp:** Asthma; Food Allergy; Drug Sensitivity; **Hospital:** Nyack Hosp; **Address:** Allergy & Asthma Consut. - Rockland/Bergen, 2 Crosfield Ave, Ste 406, West Nyack, NY 10994; **Phone:** 845-353-9600; **Board Cert:** Internal Medicine 1988; Allergy & Immunology 2011; **Med School:** SUNY Buffalo 1985; **Resid:** Internal Medicine, Staten Island Univ Hosp 1988; **Fellow:** Allergy & Immunology, Scripps Green Hosp 1990

LoGalbo, Peter MD (A&I) - **Spec Exp:** Asthma; Food Allergy; **Hospital:** Good Samaritan Regional Med Ctr, Nyack Hosp; **Address:** ENT & Allergy Assocs, 1 Crosfield Ave, Ste 201, West Nyack, NY 10994; **Phone:** 845-727-1370; **Board Cert:** Pediatrics 1983; Allergy & Immunology 1983; **Med School:** SUNY Stony Brook 1978; **Resid:** Pediatrics, Mt Sinai Hosp 1980; **Fellow:** Pediatric Allergy & Immunology, Duke Univ Hosp 1982; **Fac Appt:** Asst Clin Prof Ped, Albert Einstein Coll Med

Cardiovascular Disease

Beniaminovitz, Ainat MD (Cv) - **Spec Exp:** Heart Failure; Transplant Medicine-Heart; Women's Health; **Hospital:** Good Samaritan Regional Med Ctr; **Address:** Columbia Doctors Hudson Vly, 222 Route 59, Ste 302, Suffern, NY 10901; **Phone:** 845-368-0100; **Board Cert:** Internal Medicine 2003; Cardiovascular Disease 2007; **Med School:** Columbia P&S 1990; **Resid:** Internal Medicine, NY-Presby/Columbia Univ Med Ctr 1994; **Fellow:** Cardiovascular Disease, NY-Presby/Columbia Univ Med Ctr 1997; **Fac Appt:** Asst Prof Med, Columbia P&S

Roth, Richard L MD (Cv) - **Spec Exp:** Cholesterol/Lipid Disorders; Non-Invasive Cardiology; **Hospital:** Good Samaritan Regional Med Ctr, Nyack Hosp; **Address:** Columbia Doctors of Hudson Valley, 222 Route 59, Ste 302, Suffern, NY 10901; **Phone:** 845-368-0100; **Board Cert:** Internal Medicine 1978; Cardiovascular Disease 1981; **Med School:** Yale Univ 1975; **Resid:** Internal Medicine, Boston Med Ctr 1978; **Fellow:** Cardiovascular Disease, Boston Med Ctr 1980; **Fac Appt:** Asst Clin Prof Med, Columbia P&S

Southren, David MD (Cv) - **Spec Exp:** Cholesterol/Lipid Disorders; Non-Invasive Cardiology; Preventive Cardiology; **Hospital:** Nyack Hosp, Good Samaritan Regional Med Ctr; **Address:** Advanced Cardiovascular Care, 206 Route 303, Valley Cottage, NY 10989; **Phone:** 845-268-0880; **Board Cert:** Internal Medicine 1984; Cardiovascular Disease 1987; Critical Care Medicine 2011; **Med School:** NY Med Coll 1981; **Resid:** Internal Medicine, Barnes-Jewish Hosp 1984; **Fellow:** Cardiovascular Disease, Emory Univ Hosp 1985; Cardiovascular Disease, Westchester Med Ctr 1986

Child Neurology

Sherbany, Ariel A MD (ChiN) - **Spec Exp:** Epilepsy/Seizure Disorders; Neurometabolic Disorders; Neurodevelopmental Disabilities; **Hospital:** Nyack Hosp; **Address:** Pediatric Neurology of Hudson Valley, 55 Old Nyach Tpke, Ste 101, Nanuet, NY 10954; **Phone:** 845-627-0723; **Board Cert:** Pediatrics 1985; Child Neurology 1988; **Med School:** NYU Sch Med 1979; **Resid:** Pediatrics, St Louis Chldns Hosp 1981; Neurology, NY-Presby/Columbia Univ Med Ctr 1982; **Fellow:** Pediatric Neurology, NY-Presby/Columbia Univ Med Ctr 1984

Dermatology

Waldorf, Donald MD (D) - **Spec Exp:** Skin Cancer; Acne; Psoriasis; Cosmetic Dermatology; **Hospital:** Rockland Psych Ctr; **Address:** 57 N Middletown Rd, Nanuet, NY 10954-2312; **Phone:** 845-623-7077; **Board Cert:** Dermatology 1967; **Med School:** Univ Pennsylvania 1962; **Resid:** Dermatology, Hosp Univ Penn 1964; Dermatology, NYU Medical Center 1967; **Fellow:** Dermatology, Natl Cancer Inst 1966

Waldorf, Heidi A MD (D) - **Spec Exp:** Cosmetic Dermatology; Skin Laser Surgery; Mohs Surgery; **Hospital:** Mt Sinai Hosp; **Address:** Waldorf Dermatology, 57 N Middletown Rd, Nanuet, NY 10954; **Phone:** 845-623-7077; **Board Cert:** Dermatology 2013; **Med School:** Univ Pennsylvania 1990; **Resid:** Dermatology, Mass Genl Hosp 1994; **Fellow:** Mohs Surgery, Laser & Skin Surg Ctr 1995; **Fac Appt:** Assoc Clin Prof D, Mount Sinai-Icahn Sch of Med

Diagnostic Radiology

Bobroff, Lewis M MD (DR) - **Spec Exp:** Breast Imaging; Thyroid Ultrasound; PET Imaging; Interventional Radiology; **Hospital:** Good Samaritan Regional Med Ctr; **Address:** Ramapo Radiology Assocs, 255 Lafayette Ave, Suffern, NY 10901; **Phone:** 845-368-5196; **Board Cert:** Diagnostic Radiology 1974; **Med School:** Harvard Med Sch 1969; **Resid:** Diagnostic Radiology, Montefiore Med Ctr 1973; **Fellow:** Interventional Radiology, Montefiore Med Ctr 1973

Geller, Mark E MD (DR) - **Spec Exp:** MRI; CT Scan; Nuclear Radiology; **Hospital:** Nyack Hosp; **Address:** Hudson Vly Radiology Assocs, 18 Squadron Blvd, New City, NY 10956; **Phone:** 845-634-9729; **Board Cert:** Diagnostic Radiology 1989; **Med School:** SUNY Downstate 1985; **Resid:** Diagnostic Radiology, Westchester Med Ctr 1989

Endocrinology, Diabetes & Metabolism

Cosman, Felicia MD (EDM) - **Spec Exp:** Osteoporosis; **Hospital:** Helen Hayes Hosp; **Address:** Helen Hayes Hosp, Bone Ctr, 51-55 N Route 9W, West Haverstraw, NY 10993; **Phone:** 845-786-4489; **Board Cert:** Internal Medicine 1986; Endocrinology, Diabetes & Metabolism 1989; **Med School:** SUNY Stony Brook 1983; **Resid:** Internal Medicine, NY-Presby/Columbia Univ Med Ctr 1986; **Fellow:** Endocrinology, NY-Presby/Columbia Univ Med Ctr 1988; **Fac Appt:** Prof Med, Columbia P&S

Family Medicine

Ibelli, Vincent MD (FMed) *PCP* - **Spec Exp:** Asthma; Hypertension; Osteoporosis; Gastroesophageal Reflux Disease (GERD); **Hospital:** Nyack Hosp; **Address:** Orangetown Family Practice, 97 Route 303, Tappan, NY 10983; **Phone:** 845-359-5005; **Board Cert:** Family Medicine 2007; **Med School:** Italy 1983; **Resid:** Family Medicine, JFK Med Ctr 1986

Ingrassia, Joseph T MD (FMed) *PCP* - **Hospital:** Good Samaritan Regional Med Ctr; **Address:** 36 College Ave, Nanuet, NY 10954; **Phone:** 845-623-2456; **Board Cert:** Family Medicine 2013; **Med School:** Mexico 1974; **Resid:** Family Medicine, Nassau Univ Med Ctr 1978

Gastroenterology

May, Louis D MD (Ge) - **Spec Exp:** Hepatitis; Endoscopy; Pancreatic/Biliary Endoscopy (ERCP); **Hospital:** Good Samaritan Regional Med Ctr, Nyack Hosp; **Address:** Gastrointestinal Assocs of Rockland, 500 New Henpstead Rd, New City, NY 10956; **Phone:** 845-362-3200; **Board Cert:** Internal Medicine 1981; Gastroenterology 1983; **Med School:** Univ Miami Sch Med 1978; **Resid:** Internal Medicine, Univ Utah Med Ctr 1981; **Fellow:** Gastroenterology, Univ Utah Med Ctr 1983

Hand Surgery

Shuren, Neal H MD (HS) - **Spec Exp:** Hand & Upper Extremity Surgery; Carpal Tunnel Syndrome; Arthroscopic Wrist Surgery; Upper Extremity Trauma; **Hospital:** Good Samaritan Regional Med Ctr; **Address:** Rockland Orthopedics & Sports Medicine, 327 Route 59, Colonial Square, Airmont, NY 10952; **Phone:** 845-356-2900; **Board Cert:** Orthopaedic Surgery 2009; Hand Surgery 2009; **Med School:** Boston Univ 1990; **Resid:** Orthopaedic Surgery, NYU Med Ctr 1995; **Fellow:** Hand Surgery, Loma Linda Med Ctr 1996

Internal Medicine

Ferrara, Lisa MD (IM) - **Hospital:** Nyack Hosp; **Address:** Rockland Pulmonary & Med Assocs, 2 Crosfield Ave, Ste 318, West Nyack, NY 10994; **Phone:** 845-353-5600; **Board Cert:** Internal Medicine 2013; **Med School:** UMDNJ-Rutgers Med Sch 1990; **Resid:** Internal Medicine, UMDNJ-RWJ Med Ctr 1993

Glassman, Charles F MD (IM) *PCP* - **Spec Exp:** Concierge Medicine; Preventive Medicine; Complementary Medicine; **Hospital:** Good Samaritan Regional Med Ctr, Nyack Hosp; **Address:** 7C Medical Park Drive, Pomona, NY 10970; **Phone:** 845-362-1110; **Board Cert:** Internal Medicine 1989; **Med School:** NY Med Coll 1985; **Resid:** Internal Medicine, Westchester Co Med Ctr 1988; **Fac Appt:** Asst Clin Prof Med, NY Med Coll

Handelsman, Richard E DO (IM) *PCP* - **Spec Exp:** Concierge Medicine; Preventive Medicine; **Hospital:** Nyack Hosp, Good Samaritan Regional Med Ctr; **Address:** 7 Medical Park Drive, Ste C, Pomona, NY 10970; **Phone:** 845-362-1169; **Board Cert:** Internal Medicine 1981; **Med School:** Univ Osteo Med & Hlth Sci, Des Moines 1976; **Resid:** Internal Medicine, UMDNJ Med Ctr 1978; Internal Medicine, Norwalk Hosp 1980; **Fac Appt:** Asst Clin Prof Med, NY Med Coll

Interventional Cardiology

Brogno, David MD (IC) - **Spec Exp:** Cardiac Catheterization; Angioplasty; Coronary Angioplasty/Stents; Coronary Artery Disease-Complex; **Hospital:** NY-Presby/Columbia Univ Med Ctr, NY (page 102), Good Samaritan Regional Med Ctr; **Address:** Columbia Doctors Hudson Vly, 222 Route 59, Ste 302, Suffern, NY 10901; **Phone:** 845-368-0100; **Board Cert:** Internal Medicine 1986; Cardiovascular Disease 1989; Interventional Cardiology 2009; **Med School:** Univ Mich Med Sch 1983; **Resid:** Internal Medicine, St Lukes-Roosevelt Hosp Ctr 1987; **Fellow:** Cardiovascular Disease, St Lukes-Roosevelt Hosp Ctr 1989; Interventional Cardiology, St Lukes-Roosevelt Hosp Ctr 1991; **Fac Appt:** Asst Prof Med, Columbia P&S

Innerfield, Michael MD (IC) - **Spec Exp:** Coronary Artery Disease; Preventive Cardiology; Peripheral Vascular Disease; **Hospital:** Good Samaritan Regional Med Ctr, Nyack Hosp; **Address:** 257 Lafayette Ave, Ste 330, Suffern, NY 10901; **Phone:** 845-368-0048; **Board Cert:** Internal Medicine 1984; Cardiovascular Disease 1987; Interventional Cardiology 2009; **Med School:** NY Med Coll 1981; **Resid:** Internal Medicine, Jacobi Med Ctr 1984; **Fellow:** Cardiovascular Disease, Montefiore Med Ctr 1986; Interventional Cardiology, Cooper Univ Hosp 1987; **Fac Appt:** Asst Prof S, Mount Sinai-Icahn Sch of Med

Medical Oncology

Goldberg, Robert MD (Onc) - **Spec Exp:** Brain Tumors; Bone Tumors; **Hospital:** Good Samaritan Regional Med Ctr, Nyack Hosp; **Address:** 10 Esquire Rd, Ste 6, New City, NY 10956; **Phone:** 845-634-2727; **Board Cert:** Internal Medicine 1982; Medical Oncology 1985; Hematology 1984; **Med School:** Mount Sinai Sch Med 1979; **Resid:** Internal Medicine, Beth Israel Med Ctr 1982; **Fellow:** Hematology & Oncology, Univ Minn Med Ctr 1985

Lonberg, Mathew MD (Onc) - **Spec Exp:** Lung Cancer; Breast Cancer; Lymphoma; Melanoma; **Hospital:** Nyack Hosp; **Address:** Hematology Oncology Assocs, 255 5th Ave, Nyack, NY 10960; **Phone:** 845-362-1750; **Board Cert:** Internal Medicine 1984; Medical Oncology 1987; Hematology 1988; **Med School:** Univ VA Sch Med 1981; **Resid:** Internal Medicine, NYU-Bellevue Hosp 1984; **Fellow:** Hematology & Oncology, Meml Sloan-Kettering Cancer Ctr 1985; **Fac Appt:** Asst Clin Prof Med, Columbia P&S

Zimmerman, Marc MD (Onc) - **Hospital:** Nyack Hosp, Good Samaritan Regional Med Ctr; **Address:** 974 Rte 45, Ste 1200, Pomona, NY 10970; **Phone:** 845-362-3970; **Board Cert:** Internal Medicine 1980; Medical Oncology 1981; Hematology 1984; **Med School:** Albany Med Coll 1977; **Resid:** Internal Medicine, Albany Med Ctr 1979; **Fellow:** Medical Oncology, Albany Med Ctr 1982

Neonatal-Perinatal Medicine

Katzenstein, Martin S MD (NP) - **Spec Exp:** Neonatal Nutrition; Gastroesophageal Reflux Disease (GERD); **Hospital:** Good Samaritan Regional Med Ctr, Westchester Med Ctr; **Address:** Good Samaritan Hosp, Neonatology, 255 Lafayette Ave, Ste 370 & 390, Suffern, NY 10901; **Phone:** 845-368-5705; **Board Cert:** Pediatrics 2011; **Med School:** NY Med Coll 1978; **Resid:** Pediatrics, NY-Presby/Weill Cornell Med Ctr 1981; **Fellow:** Neonatal-Perinatal Medicine, NY-Presby/Weill Cornell Med Ctr 1982; Neonatal-Perinatal Medicine, Westchester Co Med Ctr 1984; **Fac Appt:** Assoc Clin Prof Ped, NY Med Coll

Mendoza, Glenn MD (NP) - **Hospital:** Good Samaritan Regional Med Ctr, Children's & Women's Phys.of Westchester; **Address:** Good Samaritan Hosp, Neonatology, 255 Lafayette Ave, Suffern, NY 10901; **Phone:** 914-493-8431; **Board Cert:** Pediatrics 1985; **Med School:** Philippines 1976; **Resid:** Family Medicine, Elyria Meml Hosp 1980; Pediatrics, Brooklyn Jewish Med Ctr 1983; **Fellow:** Neonatal-Perinatal Medicine, Mt Sinai Hosp 1985; **Fac Appt:** Asst Prof Ped, Columbia P&S

Nephrology

Kozin, Arthur M MD (Nep) - **Spec Exp:** Hypertension; Kidney Failure-Chronic; Diabetic Kidney Disease; **Hospital:** Nyack Hosp, Good Samaritan Regional Med Ctr; **Address:** Rockland Renal Assocs, 2 Crosfield Ave, Ste 212, West Nyack, NY 10994; **Phone:** 845-358-2400; **Board Cert:** Internal Medicine 1985; Nephrology 1988; **Med School:** Albert Einstein Coll Med 1982; **Resid:** Internal Medicine, Montefiore Hosp Med Ctr 1985; **Fellow:** Nephrology, Bellevue Hosp 1987

Shapiro, Kenneth S MD (Nep) - **Spec Exp:** Hypertension; Diabetic Kidney Disease; Transplant Medicine-Kidney; **Hospital:** Nyack Hosp, Good Samaritan Regional Med Ctr; **Address:** Rockland Renal Assocs, 2 Crosfield Ave, Ste 312, West Nyack, NY 10994; **Phone:** 845-358-2400; **Board Cert:** Internal Medicine 1978; Nephrology 1980; **Med School:** Rush Med Coll 1975; **Resid:** Internal Medicine, Albany Meml Hosp 1978; **Fellow:** Nephrology, Tufts Med Ctr 1980; **Fac Appt:** Asst Clin Prof Med, NY Med Coll

Tracz, Michal MD (Nep) - **Hospital:** Good Samaritan Regional Med Ctr; **Address:** Rockland Renal Assocs, 2 Crosfield Ave, West Nyack, NY 10994; **Phone:** 845-358-2400; **Board Cert:** Internal Medicine 2007; Nephrology 2009; **Med School:** SUNY Stony Brook 2002; **Resid:** Internal Medicine, Mayo Clinic 2005; **Fellow:** Nephrology, Mayo Clinic 2008

Yablon, Steven MD (Nep) - **Spec Exp:** Hypertension; Kidney Failure; Dialysis Care; **Hospital:** Nyack Hosp, Good Samaritan Regional Med Ctr; **Address:** Rockland Renal Assocs, 2 Crosfield Ave, Ste 312, West Nyack, NY 10994; **Phone:** 845-358-2400; **Board Cert:** Internal Medicine 1976; Nephrology 1978; **Med School:** UMDNJ-NJ Med Sch, Newark 1973; **Resid:** Internal Medicine, Tufts Med Ctr 1975; **Fellow:** Renal Disease, Hosp Univ Penn 1977

Neurological Surgery

Degen, Jeffrey W MD (NS) - **Spec Exp:** Neuro-Endoscopy; Minimally Invasive Spinal Surgery; Brain & Spinal Tumors; **Hospital:** St. Luke's Cornwall Hosp-Cornwall Campus, Nyack Hosp; **Address:** Hudson Vly Brain & Spine Surgery, 222 Route 59, Ste 205, Suffern, NY 10901; **Phone:** 845-368-0286; **Board Cert:** Neurological Surgery 2007; **Med School:** Cornell Univ-Weill Med Coll 1998; **Resid:** Neurological Surgery, Georgetown Univ Hosp 2005; **Fac Appt:** Asst Clin Prof NS, NY Med Coll

Oppenheim, Jeffrey S MD (NS) - **Spec Exp:** Spinal Disorders-Degenerative; Brain Tumors; Spinal Surgery; Microsurgery; **Hospital:** Nyack Hosp, Good Samaritan Regional Med Ctr; **Address:** Hudson Vly Brain & Spine Surgery, 222 Route 59, Ste 205, Suffern, NY 10901; **Phone:** 845-368-0286; **Board Cert:** Neurological Surgery 1996; **Med School:** Cornell Univ-Weill Med Coll 1988; **Resid:** Neurological Surgery, Mt Sinai Hosp 1994

Neurology

Etienne, Mill MD (N) - **Spec Exp:** Clinical Neurophysiology; Epilepsy; Behavioral Neurology; Stroke Prevention; **Hospital:** Good Samaritan Regional Med Ctr; **Address:** Bon Secours Neuorology, 257 Lafeyette Ave, Ste 360, Suffern, NY 10901; **Phone:** 845-368-8808; **Board Cert:** Neurology 2007; Clinical Neurophysiology 2011; Epilepsy 2013; **Med School:** NY Med Coll 2002; **Resid:** Neurology, NY-Presby/Columbia Univ Med Ctr 2006; **Fellow:** Clinical Neurophysiology, NY-Presby/Columbia Univ Med Ctr 2009

Ferro, John A MD (N) - **Spec Exp:** Neuromuscular Disorders; Stroke Prevention; Women's Health; Neurophysiology; **Hospital:** Nyack Hosp; **Address:** Rockland Neurological Assocs, 2 Crosfield Ave, Ste 202, West Nyack, NY 10994; **Phone:** 845-353-4344; **Board Cert:** Neurology 1993; **Med School:** Albert Einstein Coll Med 1988; **Resid:** Neurology, NY-Presby/Weill Cornell Med Ctr 1992; **Fellow:** Neurophysiology, Hosp Special Surgery 1994

Ober, David T MD (N) - **Spec Exp:** Neuromuscular Disorders; Botox Therapy; Electrodiagnosis; **Hospital:** Nyack Hosp; **Address:** Rockland Neurological Assocs, 2 Crosfield Ave, Ste 202, West Nyack, NY 10994; **Phone:** 845-353-4344; **Board Cert:** Neurology 2009; **Med School:** Albany Med Coll 1994; **Resid:** Neurology, Mt Sinai Hosp 1998; **Fellow:** Neuroelectrophysiology, St Elizabeths Med Ctr 1999

Seliger, Glenn M MD (N) - **Spec Exp:** Head Injury; **Hospital:** Helen Hayes Hosp; **Address:** Helen Hayes Hosp, Neurology, 51-55 Route 9W, West Haverstraw, NY 10993; **Phone:** 845-786-4459; **Board Cert:** Neurology 1988; **Med School:** SUNY Downstate 1983; **Resid:** Neurology, NY-Presby/Columbia Univ Med Ctr 1987; **Fellow:** Neurological Rehabilitation, Braintree Rehab Hosp 1988; **Fac Appt:** Asst Prof N, Columbia P&S

Neuroradiology

Schwartz, Joel M MD (NRad) - **Spec Exp:** Head & Neck Imaging; **Hospital:** Nyack Hosp; **Address:** Hudson Vly Radiology Assocs, 18 Squadron Blvd, New City, NY 10956; **Phone:** 845-634-9729; **Board Cert:** Diagnostic Radiology 1990; Neuroradiology 2006; **Med School:** SUNY Upstate Med Univ 1985; **Resid:** Diagnostic Radiology, NYU Med Ctr 1990; **Fellow:** Neuroradiology, NYU Med Ctr 1993

Obstetrics & Gynecology

Hostin, Helen MD (ObG) - **Hospital:** Nyack Hosp; **Address:** Comprehensive Ob/Gyn, 26 Firemans Memorial Drive, Ste 120, Pomona, NY 10970; **Phone:** 845-362-5900; **Board Cert:** Obstetrics & Gynecology 2013; **Med School:** NYU Sch Med 1997; **Resid:** Obstetrics & Gynecology, Westchester Med Ctr 2001

Ophthalmology

Weingarten, Phyllis E MD (Oph) - **Spec Exp:** Pediatric Ophthalmology; Strabismus; **Hospital:** Good Samaritan Regional Med Ctr, Mt Sinai Beth Israel; **Address:** Pomona Eye Assocs, 4A Medical Park Drive, Pomona, NY 10970; **Phone:** 845-354-6225; **Board Cert:** Ophthalmology 1991; **Med School:** NY Med Coll 1986; **Resid:** Internal Medicine, Lenox Hill Hosp 1987; Ophthalmology, Brookdale Univ Hosp Med Ctr 1990; **Fellow:** Strabismus, SUNY Downstate Med Ctr 1991; Pediatric Ophthalmology, Johns Hopkins Hosp 1992

Orthopaedic Surgery

Austin, Kenneth S MD (OrS) - **Spec Exp:** Hip Replacement & Revision; Knee Replacement; Sports Medicine; Trauma; **Hospital:** Good Samaritan Regional Med Ctr; **Address:** Rockland Orthopedics & Sports Medicine, 327 Route 59, Colonial Square, Airmont, NY 10952; **Phone:** 845-356-2900; **Board Cert:** Orthopaedic Surgery 2007; **Med School:** NYU Sch Med 1988; **Resid:** Surgery, Bellevue/NYU Med Ctr 1989; Orthopaedic Surgery, Bellevue/NYU Med Ctr 1993; **Fellow:** Sports Medicine/Knee Surgery, Mass Genl Hosp 1994

Fond, Jason E MD (OrS) - **Spec Exp:** Joint Reconstruction; Fractures-Complex; Pediatric Sports Medicine; Sports Medicine; **Hospital:** Good Samaritan Regional Med Ctr, Nyack Hosp; **Address:** Advanced Orthopaedics & Sports Med, 408 Airport Executive Park, Nanuet, NY 10954; **Phone:** 845-425-0555; **Board Cert:** Orthopaedic Surgery 2014; **Med School:** Albert Einstein Coll Med 1995; **Resid:** Orthopaedic Surgery, Montefiore Med Ctr 2000; **Fellow:** Sports Medicine, Nirschl Ortho & Sports Med Clin 2001

Medici, Mark D MD (OrS) - **Spec Exp:** Sports Medicine; Joint Replacement; Trauma; **Hospital:** Nyack Hosp, Good Samaritan Regional Med Ctr; **Address:** Clarkstown Orthopedics, 2 Crosfield Ave, Ste 422, West Nyack, NY 10994; **Phone:** 845-358-1000; **Board Cert:** Orthopaedic Surgery 2012; **Med School:** NY Med Coll 1993; **Resid:** Orthopaedic Surgery, Montefiore Med Ctr 1998; **Fellow:** Sports Medicine, Staten Island Orthopedics & Sports Med 1999

Rubin, Cheryl J MD (OrS) - **Spec Exp:** Shoulder Arthroscopic Surgery; Knee Surgery; **Hospital:** Good Samaritan Regional Med Ctr; **Address:** Rockland Ortho & Sports Med, 327 Route 59, Colonial Square, Airmont, NY 10952; **Phone:** 845-356-2900; **Board Cert:** Orthopaedic Surgery 2013; **Med School:** Mount Sinai Sch Med 1983; **Resid:** Orthopaedic Surgery, Montefiore Hosp Med Ctr 1988; **Fellow:** Arthroscopic Surgery, Ortho Research Of Virginia 1989

Pain Medicine

Burns, Paul MD (PM) - **Spec Exp:** Pain-Cancer; Pain-Chronic; **Hospital:** Good Samaritan Regional Med Ctr; **Address:** Ramapo Med Assocs, 100 Route 59, Ste 105, Suffern, NY 10901; **Phone:** 845-357-5745; **Board Cert:** Anesthesiology 1984; Pain Medicine 2007; **Med School:** SUNY Buffalo 1978; **Resid:** Anesthesiology, NY-Presby/Weill Cornell Med Ctr 1981

Mims, Timothy T MD (PM) - **Spec Exp:** Pain-Spine; Pain-Back, Head & Neck; Pain-After Spinal Intervention; **Hospital:** Good Samaritan Regional Med Ctr, Hackensack UMC-Mountainside (page 802); **Address:** Ramapo Pain Mgmt, 100 Route 59, Ste 105, Suffern, NY 10901; **Phone:** 845-357-5745; **Board Cert:** Anesthesiology 2005; Pain Medicine 2006; **Med School:** Dominica 1999; **Resid:** Internal Medicine, Brookdale Hosp Med Ctr 2001; Anesthesiology, Mt Sinai Med Ctr 2004; **Fellow:** Pain Medicine, Meml Sloan-Kettering Cancer Ctr 2006

Patel, Neil P MD (PM) - **Spec Exp:** Pain Management; Critical Care; **Hospital:** Nyack Hosp; **Address:** Northeastern Pain Mgmt, 160 N Midland Ave Fl 5, Nyack, NY 10960; **Phone:** 845-348-2243; **Board Cert:** Physical Medicine & Rehabilitation 2004; Pain Medicine 2005; **Med School:** Dominica 1999; **Resid:** Physical Medicine & Rehabilitation, Mt Sinai Med Ctr 2003; **Fellow:** Pain Medicine, Meml Sloan-Kettering Cancer Ctr 2004

Pediatric Infectious Disease

Arlievsky, Nina Z MD (PInf) - **Spec Exp:** Lyme Disease; HIV; Fevers of Unknown Origin; Hospital Acquired Infections; **Hospital:** Westchester Med Ctr; **Address:** CWPW, Ped Infectious Disease, 19 Bradhurst Ave, Ste 1400, Hawthorne, NY 10532; **Phone:** 914-493-8333; **Board Cert:** Pediatric Infectious Disease 2012; **Med School:** Mount Sinai Sch Med 1989; **Resid:** Pediatrics, N Shore Univ Hosp 1992; **Fellow:** Pediatric Infectious Disease, NYU Bellevue Hosp 1994; **Fac Appt:** Asst Prof Ped, NY Med Coll

Pediatrics

Bernstein, William H MD (Ped) *PCP* - **Spec Exp:** Preventive Medicine; **Hospital:** Nyack Hosp, Good Samaritan Regional Med Ctr; **Address:** Gomathi Pediatrics, 67 N Main St Fl 2, New City, NY 10956; **Phone:** 845-634-8911; **Board Cert:** Pediatrics 1966; **Med School:** Vanderbilt Univ 1960; **Resid:** Pediatrics, Bellevue Hosp 1962; Pediatrics, Mt Sinai Hosp 1965; **Fellow:** Neonatology, Mt Sinai Hosp 1966

Cohen, Daniel H MD (Ped) *PCP* - **Spec Exp:** Preventive Medicine; **Hospital:** Nyack Hosp, Good Samaritan Regional Med Ctr; **Address:** N Rockland Pediatrics, 171 Ramapo Rd, Ste 4, Garnerville, NY 10923; **Phone:** 845-947-1772; **Board Cert:** Pediatrics 2010; **Med School:** SUNY Downstate 1974; **Resid:** Pediatrics, Emory Univ Hosp 1977

Diamant, Esther P MD (Ped) *PCP* - **Spec Exp:** Infectious Disease; Preventive Medicine; **Address:** Refuah Hlth Ctr, Pediatrics Dept, 728 N Main St Fl 4, Spring Valley, NY 10977; **Phone:** 845-354-9300; **Board Cert:** Pediatrics 2010; **Med School:** Mount Sinai Sch Med 1987; **Resid:** Pediatrics, Mount Sinai Med Ctr 1990; **Fellow:** Pediatric Infectious Disease, Mount Sinai Med Ctr 1993

Puder, Douglas R MD (Ped) *PCP* - **Spec Exp:** Asthma; Developmental Disorders; **Hospital:** Nyack Hosp; **Address:** Clarkstown Pediatrics, 35 Smith St, Nanuet, NY 10954; **Phone:** 845-623-7100; **Board Cert:** Pediatrics 2010; **Med School:** NYU Sch Med 1982; **Resid:** Pediatrics, NYU/Bellevue Hosp 1985; **Fellow:** Ambulatory Pediatrics, NYU Med Ctr 1987; **Fac Appt:** Assoc Clin Prof Ped, Columbia P&S

Siegal, Elliot J MD (Ped) *PCP* - **Spec Exp:** Thyroid Disorders; Growth Disorders; Diabetes; Preventive Medicine; **Hospital:** Nyack Hosp; **Address:** Clarkstown Pediatrics, 200 E Eckerson Rd, New City, NY 10956-7169; **Phone:** 845-352-5511; **Board Cert:** Pediatrics 1973; Pediatric Endocrinology 1978; **Med School:** Univ Pennsylvania 1968; **Resid:** Pediatrics, NY Hosp 1971; **Fellow:** Pediatric Endocrinology, NY Hosp 1972

Physical Medicine & Rehabilitation

Brief, Rochelle MD (PMR) - **Spec Exp:** Electrodiagnosis; **Hospital:** Nyack Hosp; **Address:** 365 Route 304, Bardonia, NY 10954-2042; **Phone:** 845-623-7949; **Board Cert:** Physical Medicine & Rehabilitation 2013; **Med School:** Albert Einstein Coll Med 1987; **Resid:** Physical Medicine & Rehabilitation, Montefiore Med Ctr 1992

Guarracini, Mary MD (PMR) - **Spec Exp:** Amputee Rehabilitation; **Hospital:** Helen Hayes Hosp; **Address:** Helen Hayes Hosp, Rehab, 51-55 Route 9W, West Haverstraw, NY 10993; **Phone:** 845-786-4967; **Board Cert:** Physical Medicine & Rehabilitation 1986; **Med School:** St Louis Univ 1982; **Resid:** Physical Medicine & Rehabilitation, Northwestern Meml Hosp 1985

Robinson, Michael D MD (PMR) - **Spec Exp:** Pain-Neuropathic; Pain-Back & Neck; Electrodiagnosis; Pain-Interventional Techniques; **Hospital:** Good Samaritan Regional Med Ctr; **Address:** Rockland Orthopedics & Sports Med, 327 Rte 59, Colonial Square, Airmont, NY 10952; **Phone:** 845-356-2900; **Board Cert:** Physical Medicine & Rehabilitation 2013; Pain Medicine 2011; Electrodiagnostic Medicine 2010; **Med School:** Tufts Univ 1988; **Resid:** Rehabilitation, Walter Reed Army Med Ctr 1992

Slaten, Warren K MD (PMR) - **Spec Exp:** Pain-Neck; Pain-Back; Electrodiagnosis; **Hospital:** Good Samaritan Regional Med Ctr; **Address:** Rockland Orthopedics & Sports Medicine, 327 Route 59, Colonial Square, Airmont, NY 10952; **Phone:** 845-356-2900; **Board Cert:** Physical Medicine & Rehabilitation 2005; Pain Medicine 2011; Electrodiagnostic Medicine 2009; **Med School:** Washington Univ, St Louis 1990; **Resid:** Physical Medicine & Rehabilitation, UMDNJ Med Ctr & Kessler Inst 1994; **Fellow:** Pain Medicine, Florida Spine Inst 1999

Plastic Surgery

Fiorillo Jr, Michael A MD (PlS) - **Spec Exp:** Breast Augmentation; Breast Cosmetic & Reconstructive Surgery; **Hospital:** Hackensack Univ Med Ctr (page 96); **Address:** 150 S Pearl St, Pearl River, NY 10965; **Phone:** 845-623-6141; **Board Cert:** Plastic Surgery 2009; **Med School:** Ros Franklin Univ/Chicago Med Sch 1991; **Resid:** Surgery, Staten Island Hosp 1996; **Fellow:** Plastic Surgery, Univ Hosp-UMDNJ 1998

Psychiatry

Levy, Michael I MD (Psyc) - **Spec Exp:** Psychopharmacology; Geriatric Psychiatry; Anxiety & Depression; **Hospital:** Nyack Hosp; **Address:** 160 N Midland Ave, Nyack, NY 10960; **Phone:** 845-348-2116; **Board Cert:** Psychiatry 1982; **Med School:** Albert Einstein Coll Med 1977; **Resid:** Psychiatry, Mt Sinai Hosp 1981

Schroeder, Karl J MD (Psyc) - **Spec Exp:** Addiction/Substance Abuse; Psychiatry in Physical Illness; Post Traumatic Stress Disorder; **Address:** 104 Montebello Rd, Suffern, NY 10901; **Phone:** 845-357-9367; **Board Cert:** Psychiatry 1980; **Med School:** Columbia P&S 1974; **Resid:** Psychiatry, NYS Psych Inst 1977; **Fac Appt:** Asst Clin Prof Med, Columbia P&S

Pulmonary Disease

Chang, Benjamin G MD (Pul) - **Spec Exp:** Sleep Disorders/Apnea; Critical Care; **Hospital:** Nyack Hosp, Good Samaritan Regional Med Ctr; **Address:** Rockland Pulmonary & Med Assocs, 2 Crosfield Ave, Ste 318, West Nyack, NY 10994; **Phone:** 845-353-5600; **Board Cert:** Internal Medicine 2011; Pulmonary Disease 2013; Critical Care Medicine 2004; Sleep Medicine 2007; **Med School:** Columbia P&S 1998; **Resid:** Internal Medicine, Georgetown Univ Hosp 2001; **Fellow:** Pulmonary Disease, NYU Med Ctr 2004

Harris, Leon MD (Pul) - **Hospital:** Good Samaritan Regional Med Ctr; **Address:** 2 Crossfield Ave, Ste 318, West Nyack, NY 10994-2212; **Phone:** 845-353-5600; **Board Cert:** Internal Medicine 1979; Pulmonary Disease 1982; Critical Care Medicine 2004; **Med School:** Mount Sinai Sch Med 1976; **Resid:** Internal Medicine, Mt Sinai Hosp 1979; **Fellow:** Pulmonary Disease, Mass Genl Hosp 1981

Hodes, David L MD (Pul) - **Hospital:** Nyack Hosp, Good Samaritan Regional Med Ctr; **Address:** 2 Medical Park Drive, Ste 3, West Nyack, NY 10994; **Phone:** 845-727-7733; **Board Cert:** Internal Medicine 1976; Pulmonary Disease 1978; **Med School:** NYU Sch Med 1973; **Resid:** Internal Medicine, St Luke's Hosp 1976; **Fellow:** Pulmonary Disease, Bellevue Hosp/NYU 1978

Menitove, Stephen MD (Pul) - **Hospital:** Nyack Hosp, Good Samaritan Regional Med Ctr; **Address:** Rockland Pulmonary & Med Assocs, 2 Crosfield Ave, Ste 318, West Nyack, NY 10994; **Phone:** 845-353-5600; **Board Cert:** Internal Medicine 1980; Pulmonary Disease 1982; **Med School:** Mount Sinai Sch Med 1977; **Resid:** Internal Medicine, Mt Sinai Hosp 1983; **Fellow:** Pulmonary Disease, NYU Bellevue Med Ctr 1982

Pellicone, John MD (Pul) - **Hospital:** Helen Hayes Hosp, Nyack Hosp; **Address:** Helen Hayes Hosp, Pulmonary Dept, 51-55 Route 9W, West Haverstraw, NY 10993; **Phone:** 845-786-4060; **Board Cert:** Internal Medicine 1984; Pulmonary Disease 2010; Critical Care Medicine 2012; **Med School:** Columbia P&S 1981; **Resid:** Internal Medicine, Montefiore Med Ctr 1984; **Fellow:** Pulmonary Disease, Bellevue Hosp 1986; **Fac Appt:** Asst Clin Prof Med, Columbia P&S

Rheumatology

Kurucz, Oliver MD (Rhu) - **Spec Exp:** Rheumatoid Arthritis; Immunodeficiency Disorders; **Hospital:** Nyack Hosp; **Address:** 300 N Middletown Rd, Ste 11, Pearl River, NY 10965; **Phone:** 845-735-4114; **Board Cert:** Rheumatology 2004; **Med School:** SUNY Downstate 1999; **Resid:** Internal Medicine, St Vincents Hosp 2002; **Fellow:** Rheumatology, NYU Med Ctr 2004

Sports Medicine

Berezin, Marc A MD (SM) - **Spec Exp:** Arthroscopic Surgery; Knee Surgery; **Hospital:** Nyack Hosp, Good Samaritan Regional Med Ctr; **Address:** Orangetown Orthopaedic Assocs, 99 Dutch Hill Rd, Orangeburg, NY 10962-2106; **Phone:** 845-359-1877; **Board Cert:** Orthopaedic Surgery 2013; **Med School:** NY Med Coll 1985; **Resid:** Orthopaedic Surgery, NY Med Coll Affil Hosps 1990; **Fellow:** Sports Medicine, Orthopaedic Assocs 1991

Davis Jr, William L MD (SM) - **Spec Exp:** Sports Injuries; Arthroscopic Surgery; Shoulder & Knee Injuries; **Hospital:** Good Samaritan Regional Med Ctr; **Address:** Rockland Orthopedics & Sports Med, 327 Route 59, Airmont, NY 10952; **Phone:** 845-356-2900; **Board Cert:** Orthopaedic Surgery 2012; **Med School:** SUNY Stony Brook 1993; **Resid:** Orthopaedic Surgery, Univ Hosp 1998; **Fellow:** Orthopaedic Sports Medicine, Univ Conn Hlth Ctr 1999

Kraushaar, Barry S MD (SM) - **Spec Exp:** Shoulder Arthroscopic Surgery; Rotator Cuff Surgery; Knee Injuries; Sports Injuries; **Hospital:** Nyack Hosp, Good Samaritan Regional Med Ctr; **Address:** Advanced Orthopedics & Sports Med, 408 Airport Executive Park, Nanuet, NY 10954; **Phone:** 845-425-0555; **Board Cert:** Orthopaedic Surgery 2009; Orthopaedic Sports Medicine 2007; **Med School:** Albert Einstein Coll Med 1990; **Resid:** Orthopaedic Surgery, Bronx Lebanon Hosp Ctr 1995; **Fellow:** Sports Medicine, Virginia Sports Med Inst 1996

Surgery

Fleischer, Lee S MD (S) - **Spec Exp:** Breast Disease; Laparoscopic Surgery-Advanced; Gastrointestinal Surgery; Hernia; **Hospital:** Nyack Hosp; **Address:** Highland Surgical Assocs, 1 Crosfield Ave, Ste 105, West Nyack, NY 10994; **Phone:** 845-535-3362; **Board Cert:** Surgery 2012; **Med School:** McGill Univ 1987; **Resid:** Surgery, Beth Israel Med Ctr 1992

Joseph, Patricia K MD (S) - **Spec Exp:** Breast Cancer; **Hospital:** Nyack Hosp; **Address:** Nyack Breast & Women's Hlth Ctr, 160 N Midland Ave, Nyack, NY 10960; **Phone:** 845-348-8507; **Board Cert:** Surgery 2005; **Med School:** Univ Fla Coll Med 1979; **Resid:** Surgery, Montefiore Med Ctr-Einstein Campus 1985

Urology

Giella, John G MD (U) - **Spec Exp:** Kidney Stones; Prostate Cancer; Prostate Disease; **Hospital:** Nyack Hosp, Good Samaritan Regional Med Ctr; **Address:** Advanced Urology Ctrs NY, 2 Medical Park Drive, Ste 10, West Nyack, NY 10994; **Phone:** 845-354-5000; **Board Cert:** Urology 2012; **Med School:** Harvard Med Sch 1986; **Resid:** Surgery, St Vincents Hosp 1988; Urology, NY-Presby/Columbia Univ Med Ctr 1992

Vascular Surgery

Choi, H Michael MD (VascS) - **Spec Exp:** Endovascular Surgery; Limb Salvage; Dialysis Access; Carotid Artery Disease; **Hospital:** Good Samaritan Regional Med Ctr, Englewood Hosp & Med Ctr; **Address:** Rockland Thoracic & Vascular Assocs, 5A Medical Park Drive, Pomona, NY 10970; **Phone:** 845-362-0075; **Board Cert:** Surgery 2004; Vascular Surgery 2006; **Med School:** Mount Sinai Sch Med 1996; **Resid:** Surgery, Univ Hosp-UMDNJ 2002; **Fellow:** Vascular Surgery, Univ Hosp-UMDNJ 2004

Suffolk

Suffolk

Allergy & Immunology

Guida Jr, Louis E MD (A&I) - **Spec Exp:** Allergy; Urticaria; Asthma; Cystic Fibrosis; **Hospital:** Good Samaritan Hosp Med Ctr - West Islip, St. Charles Hosp; **Address:** Bay Shore Allergy & Asthma Spec Practice, 649 Montauk Hwy, West Bay Shore, NY 11706; **Phone:** 631-665-2700; **Board Cert:** Pediatrics 2011; **Med School:** Grenada 1984; **Resid:** Pediatrics, Monmouth Med Ctr 1987; Allergy & Immunology, Nassau Co Med Ctr 1993; **Fellow:** Pediatric Pulmonology, Hahnemann Univ Hosp 1990

Lusman, Paul A MD (A&I) - **Spec Exp:** Asthma; Sinus Disorders; Hives; Nasal Allergy; **Hospital:** John T Mather Meml Hosp, St. Charles Hosp; **Address:** 120 N Country Rd, Port Jefferson, NY 11777; **Phone:** 631-928-4990; **Board Cert:** Pediatrics 1971; Allergy & Immunology 1974; **Med School:** Albert Einstein Coll Med 1965; **Resid:** Pediatrics, Bellevue Hosp 1968; **Fellow:** Allergy & Immunology, Duke Univ Hosp 1972

Mayer, Daniel L MD (A&I) - **Spec Exp:** Asthma; Allergic Rhinitis; Food Allergy; Sinusitis; **Hospital:** Stony Brook Univ Hosp, St. Catherine's of Siena Med Ctr; **Address:** 263 E Main St, Smithtown, NY 11787; **Phone:** 631-366-5252; **Board Cert:** Pediatrics 1983; Allergy & Immunology 2013; **Med School:** Italy 1978; **Resid:** Pediatrics, Albany Med Ctr 1985; **Fellow:** Allergy & Immunology, LI Coll Hosp 1987; **Fac Appt:** Asst Prof A&I, SUNY Stony Brook

Richheimer, Michael Steven MD (A&I) - **Spec Exp:** Asthma; Skin Allergies; Sinus Disorders; Immunodeficiency Disorders; **Hospital:** Stony Brook Univ Hosp, Maimonides Med Ctr (page 98); **Address:** 1855 Union Blvd, Bayshore, NY 11706; **Phone:** 631-665-6363; **Board Cert:** Allergy & Immunology 2006; **Med School:** Grenada 1985; **Resid:** Internal Medicine, St Joseph's Hosp-Seton Hall Univ 1988; **Fellow:** Allergy & Immunology, SUNY Stony Brook Med Ctr 1990; **Fac Appt:** Assoc Clin Prof A&I, SUNY Stony Brook

Satnick, Steven MD (A&I) - **Spec Exp:** Asthma; Urticaria; **Hospital:** Stony Brook Univ Hosp; **Address:** 900 Main St, Ste 102, Holbrook, NY 11741-1813; **Phone:** 631-588-4486; **Board Cert:** Internal Medicine 1983; Allergy & Immunology 1987; **Med School:** SUNY Downstate 1980; **Resid:** Internal Medicine, SUNY Downstate Med Ctr 1984; **Fellow:** Allergy & Immunology, SUNY Downstate Med Ctr 1987

Cardiac Electrophysiology

Fan, Roger MD (CE) - **Spec Exp:** Arrhythmias; Atrial Fibrillation; Radiofrequency Ablation; Pacemakers; **Hospital:** Stony Brook Univ Hosp; **Address:** Cardiology, 200 Motor Parkway, Suite C16, Hauppauge, NY 11788-5100; **Phone:** 631-444-9600; **Board Cert:** Internal Medicine 2004; Cardiovascular Disease 2007; Cardiac Electrophysiology 2008; **Med School:** Yale Univ 2001; **Resid:** Internal Medicine, Brigham and Women's Hosp 2004; **Fellow:** Cardiovascular Disease, Pennsylvania Hosp-UPHS 2007; Cardiac Electrophysiology, Pennsylvania Hosp-UPHS 2008; **Fac Appt:** Asst Prof Med, SUNY Stony Brook

Rashba, Eric J MD (CE) - **Spec Exp:** Arrhythmias; Pacemakers; Syncope; Atrial Fibrillation; **Hospital:** Stony Brook Univ Hosp; **Address:** 200 Motor Pkwy, Ste C16, Hauppauge, NY 11788; **Phone:** 631-444-9600; **Board Cert:** Internal Medicine 2006; Cardiovascular Disease 2008; Cardiac Electrophysiology 2009; **Med School:** Yale Univ 1992; **Resid:** Internal Medicine, Strong Meml Hosp 1995; **Fellow:** Cardiovascular Disease, New England Med Ctr 1999; Cardiac Electrophysiology, New England Med Ctr 1999; **Fac Appt:** Prof Med, SUNY Stony Brook

Cardiovascular Disease

Altschul, Larry MD (Cv) - **Spec Exp:** Non-Invasive Cardiology; Echocardiography; Nuclear Cardiology; **Hospital:** St. Francis Hosp - The Heart Ctr (page 111), Good Samaritan Hosp Med Ctr - West Islip; **Address:** St Francis, South Bay Cardiovascular, 540 Union Blvd, West Islip, NY 11795; **Phone:** 631-669-2555; **Board Cert:** Internal Medicine 1980; Cardiovascular Disease 1983; **Med School:** SUNY Buffalo 1977; **Resid:** Internal Medicine, Nassau Univ Med Ctr 1980; **Fellow:** Cardiovascular Disease, Nassau Univ Med Ctr 1982

Borek, Mark G MD (Cv) - **Spec Exp:** Nuclear Cardiology; Echocardiography; Cardiac Catheterization; **Hospital:** Stony Brook Univ Hosp; **Address:** Island Cardiovascular Assocs, 496 Smithtown ByPass, Ste 101, Smithtown, NY 11787; **Phone:** 631-979-8880; **Board Cert:** Internal Medicine 1985; Cardiovascular Disease 1987; **Med School:** SUNY Downstate 1981; **Resid:** Internal Medicine, Nassau Univ Med Ctr 1984; **Fellow:** Cardiovascular Disease, Long Island Coll Hosp 1987; **Fac Appt:** Asst Prof Med, SUNY Stony Brook

Chengot, Mathew T MD (Cv) - **Spec Exp:** Nuclear Cardiology; Interventional Cardiology; Heart Failure; Echocardiography; **Hospital:** Good Samaritan Hosp Med Ctr - West Islip, St. Joseph's Hosp-Nassau; **Address:** Amityville Heart Ctr, 129 Broadway, Amityville, NY 11701; **Phone:** 631-598-3434; **Board Cert:** Internal Medicine 1983; Cardiovascular Disease 1985; **Med School:** India 1976; **Resid:** Internal Medicine, Lincoln Med Ctr 1982; **Fellow:** Cardiovascular Disease, Mount Sinai Med Ctr 1984

Dervan, John MD (Cv) - **Spec Exp:** Interventional Cardiology; Cholesterol/Lipid Disorders; Heart Failure; **Hospital:** Stony Brook Univ Hosp, St. Charles Hosp; **Address:** Heart Associates of Long Island, 220 Belle Mead Rd, Ste A, East Setauket, NY 11733; **Phone:** 631-941-2273; **Board Cert:** Internal Medicine 1979; Cardiovascular Disease 1985; Interventional Cardiology 2009; **Med School:** St Louis Univ 1976; **Resid:** Internal Medicine, Faulkner Hosp 1980; **Fellow:** Cardiovascular Disease, Beth Israel Deaconess Med Ctr 1983; **Fac Appt:** Assoc Clin Prof Med, SUNY Stony Brook

Falco, Thomas MD (Cv) - **Hospital:** Peconic Bay Med Ctr, Eastern Long Island Hosp; **Address:** East End Cardiology, 1279 E Main St, Riverhead, NY 11901; **Phone:** 631-727-2100; **Board Cert:** Internal Medicine 1985; Cardiovascular Disease 1987; **Med School:** Mexico 1980; **Resid:** Internal Medicine, Winthrop Univ Hosp 1985; **Fellow:** Cardiovascular Disease, Albany Med Ctr 1987

Jeremias, Allen MD (Cv) - **Spec Exp:** Interventional Cardiology; Peripheral Vascular Disease; Percutaneous Vascular Interventions; Vascular Disease; **Hospital:** Stony Brook Univ Hosp; **Address:** Stony Brook Univ Med Ctr, Div Cardiology, 26 Research Way, Stony Brook, NY 11733; **Phone:** 631-444-9970; **Board Cert:** Cardiovascular Disease 2005; Interventional Cardiology 2006; **Med School:** Germany 1995; **Resid:** Internal Medicine, Cleveland Clinic Hosp 2002; **Fellow:** Cardiovascular Disease, Beth Israel-Deaconess Med Ctr 2004; Interventional Cardiology, Beth Israel-Deaconess Med Ctr 2005; **Fac Appt:** Assoc Prof Med, SUNY Stony Brook

Lense, Lloyd D MD (Cv) - **Spec Exp:** Cholesterol/Lipid Disorders; Hypertension; Coronary Artery Disease; Congestive Heart Failure; **Hospital:** Stony Brook Univ Hosp; **Address:** Stony Brook Univ Med Ctr, Div Cardiology, 26 Research Way, East Setauket, NY 11733; **Phone:** 631-444-9970; **Board Cert:** Internal Medicine 1980; Cardiovascular Disease 1983; **Med School:** NYU Sch Med 1977; **Resid:** Internal Medicine, Mt Sinai Hosp 1980; **Fellow:** Cardiovascular Disease, Montefiore Med Ctr 1983; **Fac Appt:** Assoc Clin Prof Med, SUNY Stony Brook

Masciello, Michael A MD (Cv) - **Spec Exp:** Coronary Artery Disease; Congestive Heart Failure; **Hospital:** Southside Hosp, Good Samaritan Hosp Med Ctr - West Islip; **Address:** 540 Union Blvd, West Islip, NY 11795; **Phone:** 631-669-2555; **Board Cert:** Internal Medicine 1983; Cardiovascular Disease 1985; **Med School:** Univ Miami Sch Med 1980; **Resid:** Internal Medicine, Nassau County Med Ctr 1983; **Fellow:** Cardiovascular Disease, Nassau County Med Ctr 1985

Matilsky, Michael A MD (Cv) - **Spec Exp:** Cholesterol/Lipid Disorders; Hypertension; Coronary Artery Disease; Atrial Fibrillation; **Hospital:** St. Charles Hosp, John T Mather Meml Hosp; **Address:** Three Village Cardiology, 210 Belle Mead Rd, East Setauket, NY 11733-3327; **Phone:** 631-689-1400; **Board Cert:** Internal Medicine 1985; Cardiovascular Disease 1987; **Med School:** SUNY Stony Brook 1982; **Resid:** Internal Medicine, Mt Sinai Hosp 1985; **Fellow:** Cardiovascular Disease, New York Hosp-Cornell 1988

Skopicki, Hal A MD/PhD (Cv) - **Spec Exp:** Heart Failure; Cardiomyopathy; **Hospital:** Stony Brook Univ Hosp; **Address:** Stony Brook Cardiology, 200 Motor Pkwy, Ste C-16, Hauppauge, NY 11788; **Phone:** 631-444-9600; **Board Cert:** Cardiovascular Disease 2007; Advanced Heart Failure & Transplant Cardiology 2012; **Med School:** Ros Franklin Univ/Chicago Med Sch 1990; **Resid:** Internal Medicine, Yale-New Haven Hosp 1993; **Fellow:** Cardiovascular Disease, Mass Genl Hosp 1994; **Fac Appt:** Asst Prof Med, SUNY Stony Brook

Weinberg, Marc MD (Cv) - **Hospital:** Huntington Hosp; **Address:** West Carver Med Assocs, 200 W Carver St, Ste 8, Huntington, NY 11743-3303; **Phone:** 631-421-0020; **Board Cert:** Internal Medicine 1976; Cardiovascular Disease 1979; Critical Care Medicine 2007; **Med School:** Yale Univ 1973; **Resid:** Internal Medicine, New Haven Hosp 1977; **Fellow:** Cardiovascular Disease, New Haven Hosp 1979

Child & Adolescent Psychiatry

Carlson, Gabrielle A MD (ChAP) - **Spec Exp:** Child Psychiatry; Bipolar/Mood Disorders; ADD/ADHD; **Hospital:** Stony Brook Univ Hosp; **Address:** Stony Brook Psychiatric Assocs, Div Child & Adolescent Psych, Putnam Hall, rm 103, Stony Brook, NY 11794-8790; **Phone:** 631-632-8850; **Board Cert:** Psychiatry 1975; Child & Adolescent Psychiatry 1978; **Med School:** Cornell Univ-Weill Med Coll 1968; **Resid:** Psychiatry, Barnes Hosp-Washington Univ 1970; Psychiatry, Nat Inst Mental Hlth 1972; **Fellow:** Child & Adolescent Psychiatry, UCLA Med Ctr 1978; **Fac Appt:** Prof Psyc, SUNY Stony Brook

Gandhi, Lajpat R MD (ChAP) - **Spec Exp:** Anxiety & Mood Disorders; ADD/ADHD; **Hospital:** Huntington Hosp; **Address:** 110 E Main St, Ste 5, Huntington, NY 11743; **Phone:** 631-427-6411; **Board Cert:** Psychiatry 1981; Child & Adolescent Psychiatry 1985; **Med School:** India 1975; **Resid:** Psychiatry, Metropolitan Hosp 1979; **Fellow:** Psychiatry, Elmhurst Hosp-Mt Sinai 1980; Child & Adolescent Psychiatry, LI Jewish-Hillside Med Ctr 1981

Weisbrot, Deborah M MD (ChAP) - **Spec Exp:** Anxiety & Mood Disorders; Neuro-Psychiatry; **Hospital:** Stony Brook Univ Hosp; **Address:** Stony Brook Psychiatric Assocs, Div Child & Adolescent Psych, Putnam Hall, rm 103, Stony Brook, NY 11794-8790; **Phone:** 631-632-8850; **Board Cert:** Psychiatry 1985; Child & Adolescent Psychiatry 1991; **Med School:** SUNY Buffalo 1979; **Resid:** Psychiatry, Yale-New Haven Hosp 1983; **Fellow:** Child Psychiatry, NY Hosp-Payne Whitney Clin 1986; **Fac Appt:** Assoc Prof Psyc, SUNY Stony Brook

Child Neurology

Andriola, Mary R MD (ChiN) - **Spec Exp:** Epilepsy; ADD/ADHD; Headache; Developmental Disorders; **Hospital:** Stony Brook Univ Hosp; **Address:** Neurology Associates of Stony Brook, 179 N Belle Mead Rd, East Setauket, NY 11733; **Phone:** 631-444-2599; **Board Cert:** Pediatrics 1970; Child Neurology 1972; Clinical Neurophysiology 2012; Neurodevelopmental Disabilities 2005; **Med School:** Duke Univ 1965; **Resid:** Pediatrics, Univ Fla Shands Hosp 1967; **Fellow:** Neurology, Univ Fla Shands Hosp 1970; **Fac Appt:** Prof N, SUNY Stony Brook

Clinical Genetics

McGovern, Margaret Mary MD/PhD (CG) - **Hospital:** Stony Brook Univ Hosp; **Address:** Stony Brook Childrens Services, 37 Research Way, East Setauket, NY 11733; **Phone:** 631-444-2710; **Board Cert:** Pediatrics 2012; Clinical Genetics 1990; **Med School:** Mount Sinai Sch Med 1986; **Resid:** Pediatrics, Mt Sinai Hosp 1988; **Fellow:** Genetics, Mt Sinai Hosp 1990; **Fac Appt:** Prof Ped, SUNY Stony Brook

Colon & Rectal Surgery

Leiboff, Arnold R MD (CRS) - **Hospital:** John T Mather Meml Hosp, St. Charles Hosp; **Address:** 3400 Nesconset Hwy, Ste 100, East Setauket, NY 11733; **Phone:** 631-689-2600; **Board Cert:** Surgery 2007; Colon & Rectal Surgery 2010; **Med School:** NY Med Coll 1978; **Resid:** Surgery, SUNY at Stony Brook 1987; **Fellow:** Colon & Rectal Surgery, Carle Foundation Hosp-Univ Ill 1989

Smithy, William B MD (CRS) - **Spec Exp:** Colon & Rectal Cancer; Anorectal Disorders; Colonoscopy; **Hospital:** Stony Brook Univ Hosp, St. Catherine's of Siena Med Ctr; **Address:** 222 Middle Country Rd, Ste 209, Smithtown, NY 11787; **Phone:** 631-638-2800; **Board Cert:** Surgery 2009; Colon & Rectal Surgery 1989; **Med School:** Columbia P&S 1981; **Resid:** Surgery, Roosevelt Hosp 1987; **Fellow:** Colon & Rectal Surgery, RWJ Univ Hosp 1988; **Fac Appt:** Asst Clin Prof S, SUNY Stony Brook

Dermatology

Basuk, Pamela MD (D) - **Spec Exp:** Cosmetic Dermatology; Melanoma; Skin Laser Surgery; Skin Cancer; **Hospital:** Southside Hosp; **Address:** 2011 Union Blvd, Ste 1, Bayshore, NY 11706; **Phone:** 631-666-2900; **Board Cert:** Dermatology 1988; **Med School:** NYU Sch Med 1984; **Resid:** Dermatology, Brown Univ Hosp 1988

Berger, Bernard W MD (D) - ; **Address:** 319 Hampton Rd, Southampton, NY 11968-5029; **Phone:** 631-283-7722; **Board Cert:** Dermatology 1975; **Med School:** UC Irvine 1963; **Resid:** Dermatology, Mount Sinai Hosp 1971

Clark, Richard A MD (D) - **Spec Exp:** Eczema; Contact Dermatitis; Skin Cancer; **Hospital:** Stony Brook Univ Hosp; **Address:** 181 N Belle Mead Rd, Ste 5, East Setauket, NY 11733; **Phone:** 631-444-4200; **Board Cert:** Internal Medicine 1974; Allergy & Immunology 1977; Dermatology 1980; **Med School:** Univ Rochester 1971; **Resid:** Internal Medicine, Strong Meml Hosp 1973; **Fellow:** Allergy & Immunology, Nat Inst Health 1976; Dermatology, Mass Genl Hosp 1980; **Fac Appt:** Prof D, SUNY Stony Brook

Huh, Julie MD (D) - **Spec Exp:** Acne; Skin Cancer; Eczema; **Hospital:** Good Samaritan Hosp Med Ctr - West Islip, Southside Hosp; **Address:** 332 E Main St, Bayshore, NY 11706-8404; **Phone:** 631-666-0500; **Board Cert:** Dermatology 2013; **Med School:** Columbia P&S 1991; **Resid:** Dermatology, Columbia-Presby Med Ctr 1995

Kristal, Leonard MD (D) - **Spec Exp:** Pediatric Dermatology; **Hospital:** Stony Brook Univ Hosp, Steven & Alexandra Cohen Chldn's Med Ctr of NY; **Address:** Stony Brook Dermatology Associates, 181 N Belle Mead Rd, Ste 5, East Setauket, NY 11733; **Phone:** 631-444-4200; **Board Cert:** Pediatrics 2011; Dermatology 2015; Pediatric Dermatology 2015; **Med School:** Univ Hlth Scis, Chicago Med Sch 1986; **Resid:** Pediatrics, Chldn's Hosp 1989; Dermatology, SUNY Stony Brook Univ Hosp 1993; **Fellow:** Pediatric Dermatology, CHOP 1994; **Fac Appt:** Asst Prof Ped, SUNY Stony Brook

Marghoob, Ashfaq A MD (D) - **Spec Exp:** Skin Cancer; Melanoma; **Hospital:** Meml Sloan Kettering Canc Ctr (page 110); **Address:** Meml Sloan Kettering Cancer Ctr, 800 Veterans Memorial Hwy, Fl 2, Hauppage, NY 11788; **Phone:** 631-863-5150; **Board Cert:** Dermatology 2005; **Med School:** SUNY Stony Brook 1987; **Resid:** Family Medicine, SUNY Stony Brook Med Ctr 1990; **Fellow:** Dermatology, SUNY Stony Brook Med Ctr 1995

Moynihan, Gavan D MD (D) - **Spec Exp:** Melanoma; Skin Cancer; **Hospital:** Good Samaritan Hosp Med Ctr - West Islip, Southside Hosp; **Address:** 332 E Main St, Bay Shore, NY 11706-8404; **Phone:** 631-666-0500; **Board Cert:** Dermatology 2009; **Med School:** Howard Univ 1973; **Resid:** Dermatology, USPHS Hosp 1976; **Fellow:** Dermatology, Columbia-Presby Med Ctr 1977; **Fac Appt:** Asst Prof D, SUNY Stony Brook

Notaro, Antoinette MD (D) - **Spec Exp:** Skin Cancer; Botox Therapy; Psoriasis; Acne; **Hospital:** Eastern Long Island Hosp, Peconic Bay Med Ctr; **Address:** 13405 Main Rd, Mattituck, NY 11952-0093; **Phone:** 631-298-1122; **Board Cert:** Dermatology 1982; **Med School:** SUNY Downstate 1978; **Resid:** Dermatology, Montefiore Med Ctr 1982; **Fac Appt:** Asst Clin Prof D, SUNY Stony Brook

Siegel, Daniel M MD (D) - **Spec Exp:** Mohs Surgery; Dermatologic Surgery; Skin Cancer; **Hospital:** SUNY Downstate Med Ctr (Univ Hosp Brooklyn) (page 449), VA NY Harbor Hlthcr Sys-Brooklyn Campus; **Address:** 994 W Jericho Tpke, Ste 103, Smithtown, NY 11787; **Phone:** 631-864-6647; **Board Cert:** Dermatology 2009; **Med School:** Albany Med Coll 1981; **Resid:** Dermatology, Parkland Univ Texas SW Med Ctr 1985; **Fellow:** Mohs Surgery, Baylor Coll Med 1986; **Fac Appt:** Clin Prof D, SUNY Downstate

Skrokov, Robert MD (D) - **Spec Exp:** Vascular Malformations/Birthmarks; Psoriasis; Skin Cancer; **Hospital:** Good Samaritan Hosp Med Ctr - West Islip, Southside Hosp; **Address:** 332 E Main St, Bay Shore, NY 11706-8404; **Phone:** 631-666-0500; **Board Cert:** Dermatology 2009; **Med School:** SUNY Downstate 1982; **Resid:** Dermatology, SUNY-Downstate Med Ctr 1986; **Fac Appt:** Asst Clin Prof D, SUNY Stony Brook

Tom, Jack MD (D) - **Spec Exp:** Acne; Geriatric Dermatology; **Hospital:** Mt Sinai Hosp; **Address:** 207 Hallock Rd, Ste 210, Stony Brook, NY 11790-3076; **Phone:** 631-444-0004; **Board Cert:** Dermatology 1986; **Med School:** NYU Sch Med 1982; **Resid:** Internal Medicine, NYU Med Ctr 1983; Dermatology, Mount Sinai Med Ctr 1986; **Fac Appt:** Asst Clin Prof D, Mount Sinai Sch Med

Wong, Anthony L MD (D) - **Spec Exp:** Mohs Surgery; Skin Cancer; **Address:** Skin Cancer & Dermatologic Surgery, 994 W Jericho Tpke, Ste 103, Smithtown, NY 11787; **Phone:** 631-864-6647; **Board Cert:** Dermatology 2004; **Med School:** SUNY Downstate 2000; **Resid:** Dermatology, SUNY Hlth Sci Ctr 2004; **Fellow:** Mohs Surgery, SUNY Hlth Sci Ctr 2005

Diagnostic Radiology

Gould, Elaine S MD (DR) - **Spec Exp:** Musculoskeletal Imaging; **Hospital:** Stony Brook Univ Hosp; **Address:** Stony Brook University Hospital, Level 4, Room 120, Nicolls Rd, Stony Brook, NY 11794-8460; **Phone:** 631-638-2121; **Board Cert:** Diagnostic Radiology 1985; **Med School:** SUNY Downstate 1980; **Resid:** Diagnostic Radiology, Winthrop Univ Hosp 1982; Diagnostic Radiology, SUNY Stony Brook Univ Hosp 1985; **Fellow:** Skeletal Radiology, Hosp for Joint Diseases 1986; **Fac Appt:** Clin Prof Rad, SUNY Stony Brook

Kirshy, David MD (DR) - **Spec Exp:** CT Scan; MRI; PET Imaging; **Hospital:** Southampton Hosp; **Address:** 1333 Roanoke Ave, Riverhead, NY 11901; **Phone:** 631-727-2755; **Board Cert:** Diagnostic Radiology 1993; **Med School:** SUNY Downstate 1988; **Resid:** Diagnostic Radiology, SUNY Hlth Sci Ctr 1993

Mankes, Seth O MD (DR) - **Hospital:** Stony Brook Univ Hosp; **Address:** Stony Brook Univ Med Ctr, Radiology Dept, HSC Level 4, rm 120, Stony Brook, NY 11794-8460; **Phone:** 631-638-2121; **Board Cert:** Diagnostic Radiology 1981; **Med School:** NYU Sch Med 1976; **Resid:** Diagnostic Radiology, NYU Med Ctr 1981; **Fellow:** Abdominal Imaging, NYU Med Ctr 1982; **Fac Appt:** Assoc Clin Prof Rad, SUNY Stony Brook

Schweitzer, Mark MD (DR) - **Spec Exp:** Musculoskeletal Imaging; Bone Imaging; **Hospital:** Stony Brook Univ Hosp; **Address:** Stony Brook Dept Radiology, HSC Level 4, Room 120, Stony Brook, NY 11794-8460; **Phone:** 631-444-7901; **Board Cert:** Diagnostic Radiology 1990; **Med School:** SUNY Buffalo 1986; **Resid:** Diagnostic Radiology, Stony Brook Univ Hosp/Nassau Co Med Ctr 1990; **Fellow:** Musculoskeletal Imaging, UCSF Med Ctr 1991; **Fac Appt:** Prof Rad, SUNY Stony Brook

Endocrinology, Diabetes & Metabolism

Balkin, Michael S MD (EDM) - **Spec Exp:** Diabetes; Thyroid Disorders; Hirsutism (Excessive Body Hair); Osteoporosis; **Hospital:** Huntington Hosp, Nassau Univ Med Ctr; **Address:** 191 E Main St, Huntington, NY 11743-2921; **Phone:** 631-549-2525; **Board Cert:** Internal Medicine 1976; Endocrinology 1977; **Med School:** Mount Sinai Sch Med 1972; **Resid:** Internal Medicine, Kings County Med Ctr 1975; **Fellow:** Endocrinology, Diabetes & Metabolism, Mt Sinai Med Ctr 1977; Endocrinology, Diabetes & Metabolism, Meml Sloan Kettering Cancer Ctr 1980

Brand, Howard A MD (EDM) - **Spec Exp:** Thyroid Disorders; Pituitary Disorders; Diabetes; Cholesterol/Lipid Disorders; **Hospital:** St. Catherine's of Siena Med Ctr; **Address:** 2500 Nesconset Hwy, Bldg 3C, Stony Brook, NY 11790; **Phone:** 631-751-2400; **Board Cert:** Internal Medicine 1987; Endocrinology, Diabetes & Metabolism 2011; **Med School:** UMDNJ-Rutgers Med Sch 1984; **Resid:** Internal Medicine, Mt Sinai Hosp 1987; Internal Medicine, Bronx VA Med Ctr 1988; **Fellow:** Endocrinology, Diabetes & Metabolism, NYU Med Ctr 1990

Carlson, Harold E MD (EDM) - **Spec Exp:** Thyroid Disorders; Pituitary Disorders; Gynecomastia; **Hospital:** Stony Brook Univ Hosp; **Address:** Stony Brook Univ Med Ctr, Div Endocrinology & Metabolism, 26 Research Way, East Setauket, NY 11733-3453; **Phone:** 631-444-0580; **Board Cert:** Internal Medicine 1974; Endocrinology, Diabetes & Metabolism 1975; **Med School:** Cornell Univ-Weill Med Coll 1968; **Resid:** Internal Medicine, Barnes-Jewish Hosp 1970; Internal Medicine, Natl Inst Hlth 1972; **Fellow:** Endocrinology, Washington Univ 1974; **Fac Appt:** Prof Med, SUNY Stony Brook

Gelato, Marie MD (EDM) - **Spec Exp:** Thyroid Disorders; Pituitary Disorders; Adrenal Disorders; Polycystic Ovarian Syndrome; **Hospital:** Stony Brook Univ Hosp; **Address:** Stony Brook Internist, Specialty Care, 26 Research Way, East Setauket, NY 11733; **Phone:** 631-444-0580; **Board Cert:** Internal Medicine 1982; Endocrinology 1985; **Med School:** Mich State Univ 1979; **Resid:** Internal Medicine, Dartmouth Med Ctr 1982; **Fellow:** Endocrinology, Natl Inst Hlth 1985; **Fac Appt:** Prof Med, SUNY Stony Brook

Gioia, Leonard V MD (EDM) - **Spec Exp:** Diabetes; Thyroid Disorders; **Hospital:** Southside Hosp, Good Samaritan Hosp Med Ctr - West Islip; **Address:** 53 Brentwood Rd, Ste E, Bay Shore, NY 11706; **Phone:** 631-666-6275; **Board Cert:** Internal Medicine 1979; Endocrinology, Diabetes & Metabolism 1981; **Med School:** SUNY Downstate 1976; **Resid:** Internal Medicine, St Vincent's Hosp & Med Ctr 1979; **Fellow:** Endocrinology, Diabetes & Metabolism, Boston Univ Med Ctr 1981

Goldenberg, Alan MD (EDM) - **Spec Exp:** Diabetes; Thyroid Disorders; Hormonal Disorders; Addison's Disease; **Hospital:** Southampton Hosp, Peconic Bay Med Ctr; **Address:** East End Endocrine Assocs, 189 Main Rd, Riverhead, NY 11901; **Phone:** 631-288-7120; **Board Cert:** Internal Medicine 2008; Endocrinology, Diabetes & Metabolism 2008; **Med School:** SUNY Stony Brook 1993; **Resid:** Internal Medicine, Winthrop Univ Hosp 1996; **Fellow:** Endocrinology, Diabetes & Metabolism, Winthrop Univ Hosp 1998

Wexler, Craig B MD (EDM) - **Spec Exp:** Diabetes; Thyroid Disorders; Hormonal Disorders; Cholesterol/Lipid Disorders; **Hospital:** Southside Hosp, NS-LIJ Hlth Sys; **Address:** 1723A North Ocean Ave, Medford, NY 11763; **Phone:** 631-758-5858; **Board Cert:** Internal Medicine 1981; Endocrinology, Diabetes & Metabolism 1989; **Med School:** Ros Franklin Univ/Chicago Med Sch 1978; **Resid:** Internal Medicine, LIJ-Hillside Med Ctr 1981; **Fellow:** Endocrinology, Diabetes & Metabolism, LIJ-Hillside Med Ctr 1989

Family Medicine

Aponte, Alex M MD (FMed) *PCP* - **Spec Exp:** Preventive Medicine; **Hospital:** Southampton Hosp; **Address:** Westhampton Primary Care, 80 Old Riverhead Rd, Westhampton Beach, NY 11978; **Phone:** 631-288-7746; **Board Cert:** Family Medicine 2009; **Med School:** SUNY Buffalo 1992; **Resid:** Family Medicine, Overlook Hosp 1995

Baltus, Michele N MD (FMed) *PCP* - **Hospital:** Huntington Hosp; **Address:** Huntington Medical Group, 180 E Pulaski Rd, Huntington Station, NY 11746-1998; **Phone:** 631-425-2236; **Board Cert:** Family Medicine 2012; **Med School:** UMDNJ-Univ Med Dent NJ 1988; **Resid:** Family Medicine, Somerset Med Ctr 1991

Ebarb, Raymond MD (FMed) *PCP* - **Spec Exp:** Cholesterol/Lipid Disorders; **Hospital:** Southside Hosp, Good Samaritan Hosp Med Ctr - West Islip; **Address:** 213 Montauk Hwy, West Sayville, NY 11796; **Phone:** 631-563-6205; **Board Cert:** Family Medicine 2005; **Med School:** Mexico 1982; **Resid:** Family Medicine, Southside Hosp 1987; **Fac Appt:** Asst Clin Prof FMed, SUNY Stony Brook

Fishkin, Michael DO (FMed) *PCP* - **Hospital:** John T Mather Meml Hosp, St. Charles Hosp; **Address:** 2500 Nesconset Hwy, Building 7D, Stony Brook, NY 11790-2566; **Phone:** 631-751-3322; **Board Cert:** Family Medicine 2006; **Med School:** Univ Osteo Med & Hlth Sci, Des Moines 1973; **Resid:** Family Medicine, Nassau County Med Ctr 1976

Giugliano Sr, James E DO (FMed) *PCP* - **Spec Exp:** Lyme Disease; **Hospital:** Southampton Hosp; **Address:** 290 N Sea Rd, Southampton, NY 11968; **Phone:** 631-283-5900; **Board Cert:** Family Medicine 2012; **Med School:** NY Coll Osteo Med 1988; **Resid:** Family Medicine, Southside Hosp 1991; **Fac Appt:** Clin Prof FMed, NY Coll Osteo Med

Greenblatt, Louis L DO (FMed) *PCP* - **Spec Exp:** Preventive Medicine; Geriatric Medicine; **Hospital:** St. Catherine's of Siena Med Ctr, Stony Brook Univ Hosp; **Address:** 533 Rte 111, Hauppauge, NY 11788; **Phone:** 631-366-1788; **Board Cert:** Family Medicine 2007; Geriatric Medicine 2006; **Med School:** NY Coll Osteo Med 1983; **Resid:** Family Medicine, Stony Brook Med Ctr 1986; **Fac Appt:** Asst Clin Prof FMed, SUNY Stony Brook

Johnson, Sabrina MD (FMed) *PCP* - **Hospital:** Brookhaven Meml Hosp & Med Ctr; **Address:** South Brookhaven Family Health Ctr, 365 E Main St, Patchogue, NY 11772; **Phone:** 631-854-1300; **Board Cert:** Family Medicine 2013; **Med School:** SUNY Downstate 1987; **Resid:** Family Medicine, Stony Brook Univ Hosp 1991

Schwinn, Hans D MD (FMed) *PCP* - **Hospital:** Southampton Hosp; **Address:** Westhampton Primary Care Center, 80 Old Riverhead Rd, Westhampton Beach, NY 11978-1401; **Phone:** 631-288-7746; **Board Cert:** Family Medicine 2007; **Med School:** Germany 1978; **Resid:** Family Medicine, Community Hosp 1981

Trilling, Jeffrey S MD (FMed) *PCP* - **Hospital:** Stony Brook Univ Hosp; **Address:** Stony Brook Family Medical Group, 181 N Belle Mead Rd, Ste 2, East Setauket, NY 11733; **Phone:** 631-444-5858; **Board Cert:** Family Medicine 2007; **Med School:** NY Med Coll 1973; **Resid:** Family Medicine, Deaconess Hosp 1976; **Fac Appt:** Assoc Prof FMed, SUNY Stony Brook

Gastroenterology

Buscaglia, Jonathan M MD (Ge) - **Spec Exp:** Endoscopy; Pancreatic/Biliary Endoscopy (ERCP); **Hospital:** Stony Brook Univ Hosp; **Address:** Stony Brook Univ Gastro & Hepatology, 3 Technology Drive, Ste 300, East Setauket, NY 11733-4073; **Phone:** 631-444-5220; **Board Cert:** Internal Medicine 2004; Gastroenterology 2007; **Med School:** SUNY Buffalo 2001; **Resid:** Internal Medicine, Montefiore Med Ctr 2004; **Fellow:** Gastroenterology, Johns Hopkins Hosp 2007; Advanced Endoscopy, Johns Hopkins Hosp 2008; **Fac Appt:** Asst Prof Med, SUNY Stony Brook

Cohn, William J MD (Ge) - **Spec Exp:** Liver Disease; **Hospital:** John T Mather Meml Hosp, St. Charles Hosp; **Address:** LI Digestive Disease Consultants, 3400 Nesconset Hwy, Ste 101, East Setauket, NY 11733; **Phone:** 631-751-8700; **Board Cert:** Internal Medicine 1975; Gastroenterology 1979; **Med School:** Med Coll VA 1972; **Resid:** Internal Medicine, Med Coll VA Affil Hosp 1975; **Fellow:** Gastroenterology, A Einstein Coll Med Affil Hosp 1978; **Fac Appt:** Asst Clin Prof Med, SUNY Stony Brook

Duva, Joseph M MD (Ge) - **Spec Exp:** Endoscopy & Colonoscopy; Gastroesophageal Reflux Disease (GERD); Irritable Bowel Syndrome; Colonoscopy/Polypectomy; **Hospital:** Eastern Long Island Hosp, Peconic Bay Med Ctr; **Address:** 887 Old Country Rd, Ste A, Riverhead, NY 11901-2115; **Phone:** 631-727-6122; **Board Cert:** Internal Medicine 1981; Gastroenterology 2007; **Med School:** Mount Sinai Sch Med 1978; **Resid:** Internal Medicine, Nassau County Med Ctr 1981; **Fellow:** Gastroenterology, Nassau County Med Ctr 1983

Glanzman, Barry MD (Ge) - **Spec Exp:** Colonoscopy; Gastroesophageal Reflux Disease (GERD); Endoscopy; **Hospital:** Huntington Hosp; **Address:** 152 E Main St, Ste C, Huntington, NY 11743; **Phone:** 631-421-2185; **Board Cert:** Gastroenterology 1989; Internal Medicine 1984; **Med School:** SUNY Downstate 1980; **Resid:** Internal Medicine, LI Jewish hosp 1983; **Fellow:** Gastroenterology, Med Coll of VA 1986

Harrison, Aaron R MD (Ge) - **Spec Exp:** Gastroesophageal Reflux Disease (GERD); Colon Cancer; Crohn's Disease; **Hospital:** Southside Hosp; **Address:** NS-LIJ Western Suffolk Gastro Assocs, 375 E Main St, Ste 21, Bay Shore, NY 11706; **Phone:** 631-968-8288; **Board Cert:** Internal Medicine 1977; Gastroenterology 1979; **Med School:** Albert Einstein Coll Med 1974; **Resid:** Internal Medicine, Jacobi Med Ctr 1977; **Fellow:** Gastroenterology, UCLA Med Ctr 1979; **Fac Appt:** Asst Clin Prof Med, SUNY Stony Brook

Khokhar, Asim S MD (Ge) - **Spec Exp:** Liver Disease; Hepatitis B & C; Colon Cancer Screening; **Hospital:** Stony Brook Univ Hosp; **Address:** Univ Gastroenterology & Hepatology, 3 Technology Drive, Ste 300, East Setauket, NY 11733; **Phone:** 631-444-5220; **Board Cert:** Gastroenterology 2008; **Med School:** Pakistan 1999; **Resid:** Internal Medicine, Parkridge Hosp 2003; **Fellow:** Hepatology, Beth Israel Deaconess Med Ctr 2005; Gastroenterology, Beth Isreal Deaconess Med Ctr 2008; **Fac Appt:** Asst Prof Med, SUNY Stony Brook

Lazar, Robert M MD (Ge) - **Spec Exp:** Endoscopy; Colonoscopy; **Hospital:** St. Catherine's of Siena Med Ctr; **Address:** 48 Route 25A, Ste 107, Smithtown, NY 11787-1431; **Phone:** 631-862-3680; **Board Cert:** Internal Medicine 1986; Gastroenterology 2011; **Med School:** Mexico 1981; **Resid:** Internal Medicine, Univ Hosp/SUNY Hlth Sci Ctr 1986

Spielberg, Alan L MD (Ge) - **Spec Exp:** Inflammatory Bowel Disease; Colitis; **Hospital:** St. Catherine's of Siena Med Ctr; **Address:** 48 Route 25A, Ste 203, Smithtown, NY 11787-1448; **Phone:** 631-724-1178; **Board Cert:** Internal Medicine 1977; Gastroenterology 1979; **Med School:** Belgium 1974; **Resid:** Internal Medicine, Albany Med Ctr 1977; **Fellow:** Gastroenterology, Albany Med Ctr 1979; **Fac Appt:** Asst Clin Prof Med, SUNY Stony Brook

Zaffer, Imran MD (Ge) - **Hospital:** Huntington Hosp; **Address:** Park Avenue Gastroenterology, 755 Park Ave, Ste 200, Huntington, NY 11743; **Phone:** 631-683-4235; **Board Cert:** Gastroenterology 2014; **Med School:** India 1992; **Resid:** Internal Medicine, Nassau Univ Med Ctr 1999; **Fellow:** Gastroenterology, Nassau Univ Med Ctr 2002

Zinkin, Noah T MD (Ge) - **Spec Exp:** Celiac Disease; Crohn's Disease; Hepatitis; **Hospital:** Huntington Hosp; **Address:** 775 Park Ave, Ste 225, Huntington, NY 11743; **Phone:** 631-923-1420; **Board Cert:** Internal Medicine 2013; Gastroenterology 2006; **Med School:** Univ Rochester 2000; **Resid:** Internal Medicine, Brigham & Women's Hosp 2003; **Fellow:** Gastroenterology, Beth Israel Deaconess Med Ctr 2006

Geriatric Medicine

Fields, Suzanne D MD (Ger) *PCP* - **Spec Exp:** Geriatric Care; Preventive Medicine; Palliative Care; **Hospital:** Stony Brook Univ Hosp; **Address:** 205 N Belle Mead Rd, East Setauket, NY 11733; **Phone:** 631-444-4630; **Board Cert:** Internal Medicine 1982; Geriatric Medicine 2008; Hospice & Palliative Medicine 2012; **Med School:** Univ Conn 1979; **Resid:** Internal Medicine, Waterbury Hosp 1983; **Fellow:** Internal Medicine, NY-Presby/Weill Cornell Med Ctr 1985; **Fac Appt:** Prof Med, SUNY Stony Brook

Gynecologic Oncology

Pearl, Michael L MD (GO) - **Spec Exp:** Gynecologic Cancers; Gynecologic Surgery-Complex; **Hospital:** Stony Brook Univ Hosp, Winthrop Univ Hosp (page 536); **Address:** Stony Brook, Div Gynecologic Oncology, 3 Edmund D Pellegrino Rd, Stony Brook, NY 11794-9456; **Phone:** 631-444-2989; **Board Cert:** Obstetrics & Gynecology 2013; Gynecologic Oncology 2013; Hospice & Palliative Medicine 2010; **Med School:** UCSF 1986; **Resid:** Obstetrics & Gynecology, UCSF Med Ctr 1990; **Fellow:** Gynecologic Oncology, Univ Michigan Affil Hosps 1994; **Fac Appt:** Prof ObG, SUNY Stony Brook

Hand Surgery

Hurst, Lawrence C MD (HS) - **Spec Exp:** Microvascular Surgery; Nerve Disorders/Surgery; Dupuytren's Contracture; **Hospital:** Stony Brook Univ Hosp; **Address:** Stony Brook Orthopaedic Assocs, 14 Technology Drive, Ste 11, East Setauket, NY 11733-3464; **Phone:** 631-444-3145; **Board Cert:** Orthopaedic Surgery 1980; Hand Surgery 2010; **Med School:** Univ VT Coll Med 1973; **Resid:** Orthopaedic Surgery, NC Meml Hosp-UNC 1978; **Fellow:** Hand Surgery, NY-Presby/Columbia Univ Med Ctr 1979; **Fac Appt:** Prof OrS, SUNY Stony Brook

Wang, Edward D MD (HS) - **Spec Exp:** Hand & Upper Extremity Surgery; Arthritis; Wrist Surgery; Shoulder Surgery; **Hospital:** Stony Brook Univ Hosp; **Address:** Stony Brook Orthopaedic Assocs, 14 Technology Drive, Ste 11, East Setauket, NY 11733-3464; **Phone:** 631-444-4233; **Board Cert:** Orthopaedic Surgery 2009; Headache Medicine 2009; **Med School:** Yale Univ 1990; **Resid:** Orthopaedic Surgery, Hosp Univ Penn 1995; **Fellow:** Hand Surgery, Mass Genl Hosp 1996; **Fac Appt:** Assoc Prof OrS, SUNY Stony Brook

Hematology

Avvento, Louis J MD (Hem) - **Spec Exp:** Breast Cancer; Lymphoma; **Hospital:** Peconic Bay Med Ctr, Southampton Hosp; **Address:** Eastern Long Is Hematology/Oncology, 1333 E Main St, Riverhead, NY 11901; **Phone:** 631-727-8500; **Board Cert:** Internal Medicine 1985; Medical Oncology 1987; Hematology 2004; Hospice & Palliative Medicine 2012; **Med School:** Italy 1981; **Resid:** Internal Medicine, Jamaica Med Ctr 1985; **Fellow:** Hematology, Univ Hosp-SUNY 1988

Schuster, Michael W MD (Hem) - **Spec Exp:** Bone Marrow Transplant; Hematologic Malignancies; Myelodysplastic Syndromes; Anemia-Aplastic; **Hospital:** Stony Brook Univ Hosp; **Address:** Stony Brook Univ Canc Ctr, 3 Edmund D Pellegrino Rd, Stony Brook, NY 11794; **Phone:** 631-444-3577; **Board Cert:** Internal Medicine 1984; Hematology 1986; **Med School:** Dartmouth Med Sch 1980; **Resid:** Internal Medicine, Beth Israel Deaconess Med Ctr 1983; **Fellow:** Hematology & Oncology, Beth Israel Deaconess Med Ctr 1987; **Fac Appt:** Prof Hem & Onc, SUNY Stony Brook

Hospice & Palliative Medicine

Hallarman, Lynn E MD (H & PM) - **Spec Exp:** Palliative Care; Pain-Cancer; Ethics; **Hospital:** Stony Brook Univ Hosp; **Address:** Stony Brook Univ Med Ctr-Palliative Care, 101 Nicolls Rd, Stony Brook, NY 11794; **Phone:** 631-638-2801; **Board Cert:** Internal Medicine 2006; Hospice & Palliative Medicine 2008; **Med School:** Yale Univ 1993; **Resid:** Internal Medicine, Strong Meml Hosp 1996; **Fellow:** Hospice & Palliative Medicine, Harvard Med Sch Affil Hosps 1998; **Fac Appt:** Asst Prof Med, SUNY Stony Brook

Infectious Disease

Collins, Adriane J DO (Inf) - **Hospital:** Good Samaritan Hosp Med Ctr - West Islip, Southside Hosp; **Address:** South Shore Infectious Disease, 125 Sunrise Hwy, West Islip, NY 11795; **Phone:** 631-376-6075; **Board Cert:** Infectious Disease 2009; **Med School:** NY Coll Osteo Med 1990; **Resid:** Internal Medicine, Long Is Jewish Med Ctr 1993; **Fellow:** Infectious Disease, Long Is Jewish Med Ctr 1995

Fernando, Rajeev MD (Inf) - **Spec Exp:** HIV; Wound Healing/Care; **Hospital:** Southampton Hosp; **Address:** 325 Meeting House Ln, Southampton, NY 11968; **Phone:** 631-283-4048; **Board Cert:** Internal Medicine 2008; Infectious Disease 2011; **Med School:** India 2001; **Resid:** Internal Medicine, Brooklyn Hosp 2008; **Fellow:** Infectious Disease, Mary Hitchcock Meml Hosp 2010

Nash, Bernard J MD (Inf) - **Spec Exp:** Hospital Acquired Infections; Viral Infections; **Hospital:** Good Samaritan Hosp Med Ctr - West Islip, Southside Hosp; **Address:** Suffolk Int Med Assocs, 500 Montauk Hwy, Ste S, West Islip, NY 11795; **Phone:** 631-587-7733; **Board Cert:** Internal Medicine 1978; Infectious Disease 1982; **Med School:** Georgetown Univ 1975; **Resid:** Internal Medicine, St Elizabeth Hosp 1978; **Fellow:** Infectious Disease, Boston Univ Med Ctr 1981

Internal Medicine

Balot, Barry H DO (IM) *PCP* - **Spec Exp:** Geriatric Medicine; Preventive Medicine; **Hospital:** Good Samaritan Hosp Med Ctr - West Islip, Southside Hosp; **Address:** 150 E Sunrise Hwy, Ste 101, Lindenhurst, NY 11757; **Phone:** 631-225-6200; **Board Cert:** Internal Medicine 1989; **Med School:** NY Coll Osteo Med 1985; **Resid:** Internal Medicine, Univ Hosp 1987; Internal Medicine, Overlook Med Ctr 1989

Covey, Alexander J MD (IM) - **Spec Exp:** Aging Skin; **Address:** East End Laser Care, 445 Main St, Center Moriches, NY 11934; **Phone:** 631-878-9200; **Board Cert:** Internal Medicine 1988; **Med School:** Ros Franklin Univ/Chicago Med Sch 1985; **Resid:** Internal Medicine, Winthrop Univ Hosp 1988

Friedling, Steven P MD (IM) *PCP* - **Spec Exp:** Preventive Medicine; Chronic Illness; Concierge Medicine; **Hospital:** St. Catherine's of Siena Med Ctr, Stony Brook Univ Hosp; **Address:** 267 E Main St A Bldg, Smithtown, NY 11787; **Phone:** 631-724-8348; **Board Cert:** Internal Medicine 1973; Infectious Disease 1980; **Med School:** SUNY Downstate 1968; **Resid:** Medical Oncology, Natl Canc Inst 1971; Internal Medicine, Barnes-Jewish Hosp 1973; **Fellow:** Infectious Disease, Barnes-Jewish Hosp 1974; **Fac Appt:** Asst Prof Med, SUNY Stony Brook

German, Harold J MD (IM) *PCP* - **Spec Exp:** Hematology; Preventive Medicine; **Hospital:** Huntington Hosp; **Address:** 150 Main St, Huntington, NY 11743; **Phone:** 631-271-8700; **Board Cert:** Internal Medicine 1973; Hematology 1978; **Med School:** Columbia P&S 1967; **Resid:** Internal Medicine, Harlem Hosp Med Ctr 1971; Internal Medicine, NY-Presby/Columbia Univ Med Ctr 1972; **Fellow:** Hematology, NY-Presby/Columbia Univ Med Ctr 1973

Hallal Jr, Edward J MD (IM) *PCP* - **Hospital:** Southside Hosp; **Address:** 180 E Main St, Bay Shore, NY 11706; **Phone:** 631-665-0027; **Board Cert:** Internal Medicine 1987; **Med School:** Grenada 1984; **Resid:** Internal Medicine, NY Methodist Hosp 1987

Lalli, Corradino Michael MD (IM) *PCP* - **Spec Exp:** Geriatric Medicine; **Hospital:** St. Catherine's of Siena Med Ctr; **Address:** N Shore Med Grp, 59 Southern Blvd, Nesconset, NY 11767; **Phone:** 631-659-1700; **Board Cert:** Internal Medicine 1979; Geriatric Medicine 2008; **Med School:** Albert Einstein Coll Med 1976; **Resid:** Internal Medicine, Nassau Co Med Ctr 1979; **Fellow:** Pulmonary Disease, Nassau Co Med Ctr 1980; **Fac Appt:** Asst Clin Prof Med, SUNY Stony Brook

Oppenheimer, John MD (IM) *PCP* - **Spec Exp:** Geriatric Medicine; AIDS/HIV; Concierge Medicine; **Hospital:** Southampton Hosp; **Address:** 60 Bay St, Sag Harbor, NY 11963; **Phone:** 631-725-4600; **Board Cert:** Internal Medicine 1984; Geriatric Medicine 2009; **Med School:** Tulane Univ 1981; **Resid:** Internal Medicine, Tulane Univ Hosp 1982; Internal Medicine, Harlem Hosp 1983

Romano, Rosario MD (IM) *PCP* - **Spec Exp:** Geriatric Care; Cholesterol/Lipid Disorders; **Hospital:** John T Mather Meml Hosp, St. Charles Hosp; **Address:** 5225-15 Rte 347, Port Jefferson Station, NY 11776; **Phone:** 631-331-1000; **Board Cert:** Internal Medicine 1977; **Med School:** NY Med Coll 1973; **Resid:** Internal Medicine, Lenox Hill Hosp 1977; **Fac Appt:** Asst Clin Prof Med, SUNY Stony Brook

Simon, Lloyd D MD (IM) *PCP* - **Spec Exp:** Addiction/Substance Abuse; Preventive Medicine; **Hospital:** Eastern Long Island Hosp; **Address:** East End Phys Svcs, 44210 County Road 48, Ste C, Southold, NY 11971; **Phone:** 631-765-4150; **Board Cert:** Internal Medicine 1983; **Med School:** SUNY Buffalo 1980; **Resid:** Internal Medicine, UMass Memorial Med Ctr 1983

Singer, Mark DO (IM) *PCP* - **Hospital:** Huntington Hosp; **Address:** Mt Sinai/N Shore Med Grp, 325 Park Ave, Huntington, NY 11743; **Phone:** 631-351-8487; **Board Cert:** Internal Medicine 2009; **Med School:** NY Coll Osteo Med 1995; **Resid:** Internal Medicine, N Shore Univ Hosp 1999

Stallone, James A DO (IM) *PCP* - **Spec Exp:** Preventive Medicine; **Hospital:** Good Samaritan Hosp Med Ctr - West Islip; **Address:** 400 W Main St, Ste 234, Babylon, NY 11702; **Phone:** 631-321-4200; **Board Cert:** Internal Medicine 1989; **Med School:** NY Coll Osteo Med 1986; **Resid:** Internal Medicine, Booth Meml Med Ctr/Einstein 1989; **Fac Appt:** Asst Clin Prof Med, NY Coll Osteo Med

Weiss, Deborah MD (IM) *PCP* - **Hospital:** Huntington Hosp, NS-LIJ Hlth Sys; **Address:** Mt Sinai/N Shore Med Grp, 325 Park Ave, Huntington, NY 11743; **Phone:** 631-367-5024; **Board Cert:** Internal Medicine 2010; **Med School:** Cornell Univ-Weill Med Coll 1997; **Resid:** Internal Medicine, N Shore Univ Hosp 2000

Wertheim, William A MD (IM) *PCP* - **Spec Exp:** Geriatric Care; **Hospital:** Stony Brook Univ Hosp; **Address:** Stony Brook Internists, 205 N Belle Mead Rd, East Setauket, NY 11733; **Phone:** 631-444-4630; **Board Cert:** Internal Medicine 2013; **Med School:** NYU Sch Med 1989; **Resid:** Internal Medicine, Univ Michigan Med Ctr 1992; **Fac Appt:** Clin Prof Med, SUNY Stony Brook

Interventional Cardiology

Lawson, William E MD (IC) - **Spec Exp:** Angioplasty & Stent Placement; Preventive Cardiology; Non-Invasive Cardiology; Heart Failure; **Hospital:** Stony Brook Univ Hosp; **Address:** Stony Brook Heart Ctr, 101 Nicholls Rd, Stony Brook, NY 11794; **Phone:** 631-444-1066; **Board Cert:** Internal Medicine 1980; Cardiovascular Disease 1983; Interventional Cardiology 2009; Advanced Heart Failure & Transplant Cardiology 2010; **Med School:** UMDNJ-Rutgers Med Sch 1977; **Resid:** Internal Medicine, Nassau Univ Med Ctr 1980; **Fellow:** Cardiovascular Disease, SUNY Stony Brook Univ Med Ctr 1982; **Fac Appt:** Prof Med, SUNY Stony Brook

Ong, Lawrence MD (IC) - **Spec Exp:** Angioplasty & Stent Placement; **Hospital:** Huntington Hosp, N Shore Univ Hosp; **Address:** Huntington Hosp, Cardiology, 270 Park Ave, Huntington, NY 11743; **Phone:** 631-351-7948; **Board Cert:** Internal Medicine 1979; Cardiovascular Disease 1981; Interventional Cardiology 2009; **Med School:** UCSF 1976; **Resid:** Internal Medicine, N Shore Univ Hosp 1979; **Fellow:** Cardiovascular Disease, N Shore Univ Hosp 1981; **Fac Appt:** Assoc Prof Med, Hofstra N Shore-LIJ Sch Med

Maternal & Fetal Medicine

Bernasko, James MD (MF) - **Spec Exp:** Pregnancy-High Risk; Diabetes in Pregnancy; Prenatal Diagnosis; **Hospital:** Stony Brook Univ Hosp; **Address:** Stony Brook Ob/Gyn, 4875 Sunrise Hwy, Bohemia, NY 11716; **Phone:** 631-444-4686; **Board Cert:** Obstetrics & Gynecology 2013; Maternal & Fetal Medicine 2013; **Med School:** Ghana 1987; **Resid:** Obstetrics & Gynecology, Columbia/Harlem Hosp Ctr 1994; **Fellow:** Maternal & Fetal Medicine, Mt Sinai Hosp 1996; **Fac Appt:** Assoc Prof ObG, SUNY Stony Brook

Medical Oncology

Akhund, Birjis G MD (Onc) - **Spec Exp:** Breast Cancer; Lymphoma; Lung Cancer; **Hospital:** Huntington Hosp; **Address:** Huntington Med Grp, Hem/Onc, 180 E Pulaski Rd, Huntington Station, NY 11746; **Phone:** 631-425-2280; **Board Cert:** Internal Medicine 1989; Medical Oncology 2013; Hematology 2004; **Med School:** Lebanon 1986; **Resid:** Internal Medicine, Beth Israel Med Ctr 1990; **Fellow:** Hematology & Oncology, NYU Med Ctr 1992; Hematology Research, NYU Med Ctr 1993

Buchholtz, Michael MD (Onc) - **Spec Exp:** Hematologic Malignancies; Breast Cancer; **Hospital:** Huntington Hosp; **Address:** North Shore-LIJ Canc Inst, 270 Pulaski Rd, Ste D, Greenlawn, NY 11740; **Phone:** 631-427-6060; **Board Cert:** Medical Oncology 2013; **Med School:** Italy 1983; **Resid:** Internal Medicine, VA Med Ctr 1986; **Fellow:** Medical Oncology, N Shore Univ Hosp 1989; **Fac Appt:** Asst Prof Med, Hofstra N Shore-LIJ Sch Med

Caruso, Rocco MD (Onc) - **Spec Exp:** Lymphoma; **Hospital:** St. Catherine's of Siena Med Ctr, St. Charles Hosp; **Address:** North Island Hem/Onc, 2500 Nesconset Hwy 26-B Bldg, Stony Brook, NY 11790; **Phone:** 631-751-8305; **Board Cert:** Internal Medicine 1982; Hematology 1984; Medical Oncology 2005; **Med School:** Univ Pennsylvania 1979; **Resid:** Internal Medicine, St Lukes-Roosevelt Hosp Ctr 1982; **Fellow:** Hematology, NYU Med Ctr 1985; Medical Oncology, LIJ Med Ctr 1994; **Fac Appt:** Asst Prof Med, SUNY Stony Brook

DaCosta, Noshir Anthony MD (Onc) - **Spec Exp:** Breast Cancer; Hematologic Malignancies; **Hospital:** Stony Brook Univ Hosp, John T Mather Meml Hosp; **Address:** N Shore Hem/Onc Assocs, 235 N Belle Mead Rd, East Setauket, NY 11733; **Phone:** 631-751-3000; **Board Cert:** Internal Medicine 1989; Hematology 2012; Medical Oncology 2012; **Med School:** India 1985; **Resid:** Internal Medicine, LaGuardia Hosp 1989; **Fellow:** Hematology & Oncology, SUNY Stony Brook Univ Med Ctr 1992; **Fac Appt:** Asst Clin Prof Onc, SUNY Stony Brook

Fiore, John J MD (Onc) - **Spec Exp:** Lung Cancer; **Hospital:** St. Catherine's of Siena Med Ctr; **Address:** Meml Sloan-Kettering Ctr, 650 Commack Rd, Commack, NY 11725; **Phone:** 631-623-4100; **Board Cert:** Internal Medicine 1978; Hematology 1982; Medical Oncology 1983; **Med School:** Tufts Univ 1975; **Resid:** Internal Medicine, VA Med Ctr 1979; **Fellow:** Hematology, VA Med Ctr 1981; Medical Oncology, Meml Sloan-Kettering Canc Ctr 1984

Kudelka, Andrzej P MD (Onc) - **Spec Exp:** Head & Neck Cancer; Breast Cancer; Pancreatic Cancer; Palliative Care; **Hospital:** Stony Brook Univ Hosp; **Address:** Stony Brook, Cancer Ctr, 3 Edmund D Pellegrino Rd, Stony Brook, NY 11794; **Phone:** 631-638-1000; **Board Cert:** Internal Medicine 1987; Medical Oncology 1989; Hospice & Palliative Medicine 2010; **Med School:** Poland 1982; **Resid:** Internal Medicine, Coney Is Hosp 1987; **Fellow:** Hematology & Oncology, Stony Brook Univ Hosp 1990

Ostrow, Stanley MD (Onc) - **Spec Exp:** Breast Cancer; Leukemia; Carcinoid Tumors; Lung Cancer; **Hospital:** John T Mather Meml Hosp, Brookhaven Meml Hosp & Med Ctr; **Address:** NShore Hem/Onc Assocs, 235 N Belle Mead Rd, East Setauket, NY 11733; **Phone:** 631-751-3000; **Board Cert:** Internal Medicine 1978; Medical Oncology 1979; Hematology 1982; **Med School:** SUNY Downstate 1974; **Resid:** Internal Medicine, Jewish Meml Hosp 1976; **Fellow:** Hematology & Oncology, Natl Canc Inst 1980; **Fac Appt:** Asst Prof Med, SUNY Stony Brook

Strauss, Barry MD (Onc) - **Spec Exp:** Lung Cancer; Breast Cancer; Colon Cancer; Ovarian Cancer; **Hospital:** Southampton Hosp; **Address:** 353 Meeting House Ln, Southampton, NY 11968; **Phone:** 631-283-6611; **Board Cert:** Internal Medicine 1975; Medical Oncology 1975; **Med School:** Geo Wash Univ 1971; **Resid:** Internal Medicine, Beth Israel Med Ctr 1973; **Fellow:** Medical Oncology, Natl Cancer Inst 1975

Neonatal-Perinatal Medicine

Davidson, Dennis MD (NP) - **Spec Exp:** Lung Disease in Newborns; **Hospital:** Stony Brook Univ Hosp; **Address:** Stony Brook Phys, Neonatal-Perinatal, 101 Nicholls Rd, HSC T11-060, Stony Brook, NY 11794; **Phone:** 631-444-7653; **Board Cert:** Pediatrics 1980; Neonatal-Perinatal Medicine 2009; **Med School:** Loyola Univ-Stritch Sch Med 1974; **Resid:** Pediatrics, NY-Presby/Morgan Stanley Chldns Hosp 1978; **Fellow:** Neonatal-Perinatal Medicine, NY-Presby/Morgan Stanley Chldns Hosp 1981; **Fac Appt:** Clin Prof Ped, SUNY Stony Brook

Parekh, Aruna J MD (NP) - **Hospital:** Stony Brook Univ Hosp; **Address:** Stony Brook NICU, 37 Research Way, East Setauket, NY 11733; **Phone:** 631-444-7653; **Board Cert:** Pediatrics 1976; Neonatal-Perinatal Medicine 1985; **Med School:** India 1970; **Resid:** Pediatrics, LI Coll Hosp 1975; **Fellow:** Neonatal-Perinatal Medicine, N Shore Univ Hosp 1977

Neurological Surgery

Davis, Raphael P MD (NS) - **Spec Exp:** Acoustic Neuroma; Skull Base Surgery; Spinal Disc Replacement; Brain & Spinal Surgery; **Hospital:** Stony Brook Univ Hosp, St. Charles Hosp; **Address:** NY Spine & Brain Surgery, 24 Research Way, Ste 200, East Setauket, NY 11733; **Phone:** 631-444-1213; **Board Cert:** Neurological Surgery 1990; **Med School:** Mount Sinai Sch Med 1981; **Resid:** Neurological Surgery, Mt Sinai Hosp 1987; **Fac Appt:** Prof NS, SUNY Stony Brook

Leon, Steven P MD (NS) - **Spec Exp:** Minimally Invasive Spinal Surgery; Spinal Disorders-Degenerative; Spinal Disc Replacement; Spinal Tumors; **Hospital:** St. Charles Hosp, Brookhaven Meml Hosp & Med Ctr; **Address:** Long Island Neuroscience Specialists, 100 Hospital Rd, Ste 216, East Patchogue, NY 11772; **Phone:** 631-475-5511; **Board Cert:** Neurological Surgery 2004; **Med School:** Harvard Med Sch 1994; **Resid:** Neurological Surgery, Brigham & Womens Hosp 2000; **Fellow:** Spine Surgery, Cleveland Clin 2001; **Fac Appt:** Asst Clin Prof NS, Cornell Univ-Weill Med Coll

Woo, Henry H MD (NS) - **Spec Exp:** Brain Tumors; Aneurysm-Cerebral; Cerebrovascular Surgery; Stroke; **Hospital:** Stony Brook Univ Hosp; **Address:** Stony Brook, Neurosurgery, 101 Nicolls Rd, Ste 430, Stony Brook, NY 11794; **Phone:** 631-444-1213; **Board Cert:** Neurological Surgery 2008; **Med School:** NYU Sch Med 1995; **Resid:** Neurological Surgery, NYU Med Ctr 2002; **Fellow:** Interventional Neuroradiology, NYU Med Ctr 2003; **Fac Appt:** Prof NS, SUNY Stony Brook

Neurology

Cohen, Daniel H MD/PhD (N) - **Spec Exp:** Stroke; Neuromuscular Disorders; Multiple Sclerosis; Dementia; **Hospital:** Good Samaritan Hosp Med Ctr - West Islip, Southside Hosp; **Address:** LI Neurosurgery, 370 E Main St, Bay Shore, NY 11706; **Phone:** 631-666-4767; **Board Cert:** Neurology 1986; **Med School:** Univ Miami Sch Med 1980; **Resid:** Neurology, Jackson Meml Hosp 1984

Coyle, Patricia K MD (N) - **Spec Exp:** Multiple Sclerosis; Neuro-Immunology; Lyme Disease; Infections-Neurologic; **Hospital:** Stony Brook Univ Hosp; **Address:** Neurology Assocs of Stony Brook, 179 N Belle Mead Rd, East Setauket, NY 11733; **Phone:** 631-444-2599; **Board Cert:** Neurology 2004; **Med School:** Johns Hopkins Univ 1974; **Resid:** Neurology, Johns Hopkins Hosp 1978; **Fellow:** Neurological Immunology, Johns Hopkins Hosp 1980; **Fac Appt:** Prof N, SUNY Stony Brook

Moreta, Henry G MD (N) - **Hospital:** Peconic Bay Med Ctr; **Address:** South Shore Neurologic Assocs, 877 E Main St, Ste 106, Riverhead, NY 11901; **Phone:** 631-727-0660; **Board Cert:** Neurology 1987; **Med School:** Harvard Med Sch 1977; **Resid:** Internal Medicine, N Shore Univ Hosp 1979; Neurology, N Shore Univ Hosp 1980

Neuroradiology

Fiorella, David J MD (NRad) - **Spec Exp:** Stroke; Endovascular Surgery; Arteriovenous Malformations; Interventional Neuroradiology; **Hospital:** Stony Brook Univ Hosp; **Address:** NY Spine & Brain Surgery, 101 Nicolls Rd, L4 Rm 430, Stony Brook, NY 11794; **Phone:** 631-444-1213; **Board Cert:** Diagnostic Radiology 2001; Neuroradiology 2014; **Med School:** SUNY Buffalo 1996; **Resid:** Diagnostic Radiology, Duke Univ Hosp 2001; **Fellow:** Neurological Radiology, St Joseph Hosp & Med Ctr 2004; **Fac Appt:** Prof NS, SUNY Stony Brook

Peyster, Robert MD (NRad) - **Hospital:** Stony Brook Univ Hosp; **Address:** Stony Brook, Radiology, 101 Nicolls Rd, L4 Rm 120, Stony Brook, NY 11794; **Phone:** 631-638-2121; **Board Cert:** Diagnostic Radiology 1977; Neuroradiology 2007; **Med School:** SUNY Downstate 1973; **Resid:** Diagnostic Radiology, Mass Genl Hosp 1977; **Fellow:** Neurological Radiology, Mass Genl Hosp 1979; **Fac Appt:** Prof Rad, SUNY Stony Brook

Obstetrics & Gynecology

Baker, David A MD (ObG) - **Spec Exp:** Infectious Disease; Premature Labor; Vulvar & Vaginal Disorders; Sexually Transmitted Diseases; **Hospital:** Stony Brook Univ Hosp; **Address:** University Assocs in Ob/Gyn, 6 Technology Drive, Ste 200, East Setauket, NY 11733-9254; **Phone:** 631-444-4686; **Board Cert:** Obstetrics & Gynecology 1979; Maternal & Fetal Medicine 1981; **Med School:** SUNY Downstate 1973; **Resid:** Obstetrics & Gynecology, Hosp Univ Penn 1977; **Fellow:** Maternal & Fetal Medicine, Med Ctr Hosp 1979; **Fac Appt:** Prof ObG, SUNY Stony Brook

Berlin, Scott F MD (ObG) - **Hospital:** Southside Hosp; **Address:** 2330 Union Blvd, Islip, NY 11751; **Phone:** 631-224-4200; **Board Cert:** Obstetrics & Gynecology 2013; **Med School:** Univ Chicago-Pritzker Sch Med 1990; **Resid:** Obstetrics & Gynecology, Univ Illinois Hosps 1994

Davenport, Deborah M MD (ObG) - **Spec Exp:** Menopause Problems; **Hospital:** Stony Brook Univ Hosp; **Address:** Three Village Women's Health Care, 100-16 S Jersey Ave, East Setauket, NY 11733-2036; **Phone:** 631-689-6400; **Board Cert:** Obstetrics & Gynecology 2009; **Med School:** Univ Pennsylvania 1975; **Resid:** Obstetrics & Gynecology, Univ Hosp 1983; **Fac Appt:** Asst Clin Prof ObG, SUNY Stony Brook

Gentilesco, Michael MD (ObG) *PCP* - **Spec Exp:** Gynecology Only; **Hospital:** St. Catherine's of Siena Med Ctr, Stony Brook Univ Hosp; **Address:** 48 Route 25A, Ste 207, Smithtown, NY 11787; **Phone:** 631-862-3800; **Board Cert:** Obstetrics & Gynecology 2013; **Med School:** Albert Einstein Coll Med 1980; **Resid:** Obstetrics & Gynecology, NY-Presby/Columbia Univ Med Ctr 1984

Hirt, Paula Sue MD (ObG) - **Spec Exp:** Gynecology Only; **Hospital:** Good Samaritan Hosp Med Ctr - West Islip; **Address:** 83 W Main St, East Islip, NY 11730; **Phone:** 631-277-5800; **Board Cert:** Obstetrics & Gynecology 1985; **Med School:** NYU Sch Med 1979; **Resid:** Obstetrics & Gynecology, NYU Med Ctr 1983

Kramer, Mitchell MD (ObG) - **Spec Exp:** Gynecologic Surgery-Complex; Menopause Problems; Minimally Invasive Surgery; Pregnancy-High Risk; **Hospital:** Huntington Hosp; **Address:** Huntington Medical Grp, 180 E Pulaski Rd, Huntington Station, NY 11746; **Phone:** 631-425-2218; **Board Cert:** Obstetrics & Gynecology 2013; **Med School:** NY Med Coll 1985; **Resid:** Obstetrics & Gynecology, LI Jewish Med Ctr 1989; **Fac Appt:** Asst Clin Prof ObG, Hofstra N Shore-LIJ Sch Med

Lee, Douglas S MD (ObG) *PCP* - **Spec Exp:** Gynecology Only; Menopause Problems; Cervical Disease; **Hospital:** John T Mather Meml Hosp, St. Charles Hosp; **Address:** 118 N Country Road, Port Jefferson, NY 11777; **Phone:** 631-473-7171; **Board Cert:** Obstetrics & Gynecology 1979; **Med School:** NYU Sch Med 1973; **Resid:** Obstetrics & Gynecology, Bronx Municipal Hosp 1977; **Fac Appt:** Asst Clin Prof ObG, SUNY Stony Brook

Ott, Allen Edwin MD (ObG) - **Spec Exp:** Infertility; Colposcopy; Gynecology Only; **Hospital:** Southampton Hosp; **Address:** 595 Hampton Rd, Southampton, NY 11968-3021; **Phone:** 631-283-0918; **Board Cert:** Obstetrics & Gynecology 1979; **Med School:** Boston Univ 1972; **Resid:** Obstetrics & Gynecology, Hosp Univ Penn 1976

San Roman, Gerardo A MD (ObG) - **Spec Exp:** Minimally Invasive Surgery; Robotic Surgery; **Hospital:** St. Charles Hosp, John T Mather Meml Hosp; **Address:** Suffolk Ob/Gyn, 118 N Country Rd, Port Jefferson, NY 11777; **Phone:** 631-473-7171; **Board Cert:** Obstetrics & Gynecology 2013; **Med School:** Johns Hopkins Univ 1981; **Resid:** Obstetrics & Gynecology, NY Hosp 1985

Segarra, Pedro R MD (ObG) - **Spec Exp:** Pelvic Organ Prolapse Repair; Breast Disease; Gynecologic Surgery; Vaginal Reconstruction; **Hospital:** Southampton Hosp; **Address:** 595 Hampton Rd, Southampton, NY 11968; **Phone:** 631-283-0918; **Board Cert:** Obstetrics & Gynecology 2013; **Med School:** NY Med Coll 1983; **Resid:** Obstetrics & Gynecology, Lenox Hill Hosp 1987

Ophthalmology

Aries, Philip M MD (Oph) - **Spec Exp:** Diabetic Eye Disease; Glaucoma; **Hospital:** Southside Hosp, Good Samaritan Hosp Med Ctr - West Islip; **Address:** Suffolk Ophthalmology Assocs, 375 E Main St, Ste 24, Bay Shore, NY 11706; **Phone:** 631-665-1330; **Board Cert:** Ophthalmology 1975; **Med School:** NY Med Coll 1967; **Resid:** Ophthalmology, Nassau Univ Med Ctr 1973

Cossari Jr, Alfred J MD (Oph) - **Spec Exp:** Pediatric Ophthalmology; Strabismus; **Hospital:** John T Mather Meml Hosp, St. Charles Hosp; **Address:** Village Eye Care, 311 Barnum Ave, Port Jefferson, NY 11777-1682; **Phone:** 631-928-6400; **Board Cert:** Ophthalmology 1976; **Med School:** Italy 1969; **Resid:** Ophthalmology, Nassau Co Med Ctr 1974; **Fellow:** Retina, Johns Hopkins Hosp 1974; Pediatric Ophthalmology, Chldns Natl Med Ctr 1975

Di Leo, Frank MD (Oph) - **Spec Exp:** Oculoplastic Surgery; **Hospital:** Southampton Hosp, Mt Sinai Roosevelt; **Address:** 1601 County Rd 39, Ste 10, Southampton, NY 11968-5243; **Phone:** 631-283-3677; **Board Cert:** Ophthalmology 1987; **Med School:** Albert Einstein Coll Med 1981; **Resid:** Ophthalmology, St Luke's-Roosevelt Hosp Ctr 1985

El Baba, Fadi Z MD (Oph) - **Spec Exp:** Retina/Vitreous Surgery; Diabetic Eye Disease/Retinopathy; Macular Degeneration; HIV Retinitis; **Hospital:** Stony Brook Univ Hosp; **Address:** Stony Brook Ophthalmology, 33 Research Way, Ste 13, East Setauket, NY 11733; **Phone:** 631-444-4090; **Board Cert:** Ophthalmology 2013; **Med School:** Amer Univ Beirut 1982; **Resid:** Ophthalmology, Doheny Eye Inst/USC Med Ctr 1991; **Fellow:** Eye Pathology, Wilmer Eye Inst/Johns Hopkins 1986; Retina, Oregon Lions Sight & Hearing Inst 1987; **Fac Appt:** Assoc Clin Prof Oph, SUNY Stony Brook

Martin, Jeffrey Lawrence MD (Oph) - **Spec Exp:** Cataract Surgery; Laser Vision Surgery; **Hospital:** Syosset Hosp, Stony Brook Univ Hosp; **Address:** North Shore Eye Care, 260 Middle Country Rd, Ste 201, Smithtown, NY 11787; **Phone:** 631-265-8780; **Board Cert:** Ophthalmology 2010; **Med School:** SUNY Stony Brook 1994; **Resid:** Ophthalmology, Nassau Co Med Ctr 1998; **Fac Appt:** Asst Clin Prof Oph, SUNY Stony Brook

Nattis, Richard J MD (Oph) - **Spec Exp:** Cataract Surgery; Laser Vision Surgery; **Hospital:** Southside Hosp, Syosset Hosp; **Address:** Lindenhurst Eye Physicians & Surgeons, 500 W Main St, Ste 210, Babylon, NY 11702; **Phone:** 631-957-3355; **Board Cert:** Ophthalmology 1985; **Med School:** NY Med Coll 1980; **Resid:** Ophthalmology, St Vincent's Hosp 1984; **Fac Appt:** Asst Clin Prof Oph, NY Coll Osteo Med

O'Malley, Grace M MD (Oph) - **Spec Exp:** Cataract Surgery; **Hospital:** Southampton Hosp; **Address:** North Shore Eye Care & Hampton Eye, 186 Old Towne Rd, Southampton, NY 11968; **Phone:** 631-283-3533; **Board Cert:** Ophthalmology 1987; **Med School:** NY Med Coll 1981; **Resid:** Ophthalmology, NY Med Coll 1985

Pizzarello, Louis MD (Oph) - **Spec Exp:** Diabetic Eye Disease/Retinopathy; Oculoplastic Surgery; **Hospital:** Southampton Hosp, Eastern Long Island Hosp; **Address:** 137 Hampton Rd, Southampton, NY 11968; **Phone:** 631-283-5152; **Board Cert:** Ophthalmology 1980; **Med School:** Univ VA Sch Med 1975; **Resid:** Ophthalmology, Columbia-Presby Med Ctr 1979

Romanelli, John F MD (Oph) - **Spec Exp:** Cataract Surgery; Glaucoma; **Hospital:** St. Catherine's of Siena Med Ctr, Stony Brook Univ Hosp; **Address:** 222 E Main St, Ste 330, Smithtown, NY 11787-2814; **Phone:** 631-724-4488; **Board Cert:** Ophthalmology 2013; **Med School:** Harvard Med Sch 1987; **Resid:** Ophthalmology, Manhattan Eye, Ear, Throat Hosp 1991

Rothberg, Charles MD (Oph) - **Spec Exp:** Cataract Surgery; Glaucoma; **Hospital:** Brookhaven Meml Hosp & Med Ctr; **Address:** 331 E Main St, Patchogue, NY 11772-3114; **Phone:** 631-758-5300; **Board Cert:** Ophthalmology 1989; **Med School:** SUNY Downstate 1983; **Resid:** Ophthalmology, SUNY Downstate Med Ctr 1987

Schneck, Gideon L MD (Oph) - **Spec Exp:** Eyelid Cosmetic Surgery; Thyroid Eye Disease; Orbital Surgery; **Hospital:** Stony Brook Univ Hosp, St. Charles Hosp; **Address:** 2500 Nesconset Hwy, Bldg 17 B, Stony Brook, NY 11790; **Phone:** 631-246-9140; **Board Cert:** Ophthalmology 1991; **Med School:** Boston Univ 1986; **Resid:** Ophthalmology, Northwestern Meml Hosp 1990; **Fellow:** Oculoplastic Surgery, IL Eye & Ear Infirmary 1991; **Fac Appt:** Asst Clin Prof Oph, SUNY Stony Brook

Sibony, Patrick A MD (Oph) - **Spec Exp:** Neuro-Ophthalmology; Orbital Diseases; **Hospital:** Stony Brook Univ Hosp; **Address:** Stony Brook Ophthalmology, 33 Research Way, Ste 13, East Setauket, NY 11733; **Phone:** 631-444-4090; **Board Cert:** Ophthalmology 1982; **Med School:** Boston Univ 1977; **Resid:** Ophthalmology, Boston Univ Med Ctr 1981; **Fellow:** Ophthalmology, Eye & Ear Hosp 1982; **Fac Appt:** Prof Oph, SUNY Stony Brook

Weber, Pamela A MD (Oph) - **Spec Exp:** Retinal Disorders; Macular Degeneration; Diabetic Eye Disease/Retinopathy; **Hospital:** Stony Brook Univ Hosp; **Address:** Island Retina, 1500 William Floyd Pkwy, Ste 304, Shirley, NY 11967; **Phone:** 631-924-4300; **Board Cert:** Ophthalmology 1989; **Med School:** Columbia P&S 1984; **Resid:** Ophthalmology, New York Eye & Ear Infirm 1988; **Fellow:** Vitreoretinal Surgery, Retina Assoc 1990; **Fac Appt:** Asst Prof Oph, SUNY Stony Brook

Zweibel, Lawrence C MD (Oph) - **Spec Exp:** LASIK-Refractive Surgery; Cataract Surgery; Glaucoma; **Hospital:** St. Catherine's of Siena Med Ctr; **Address:** North Shore Eye Care, 260 Middle Country Rd, Ste 201, Smithtown, NY 11787-2982; **Phone:** 631-265-8780; **Board Cert:** Ophthalmology 1977; **Med School:** Albany Med Coll 1972; **Resid:** Ophthalmology, French-Polyclinic Hosp 1976

Orthopaedic Surgery

Arvan, Glenn D MD (OrS) - **Spec Exp:** Trauma; Pediatric Orthopaedic Surgery; Joint Replacement; Geriatric Orthopaedic Surgery; **Hospital:** Good Samaritan Hosp Med Ctr - West Islip; **Address:** 400 W Main St, Ste 120, Babylon, NY 11702; **Phone:** 631-661-0202; **Board Cert:** Orthopaedic Surgery 1979; **Med School:** Duke Univ 1972; **Resid:** Orthopaedic Surgery, NY Hosp 1974; Orthopaedic Surgery, Case Western Res Med Ctr 1977

Divaris, Nicholas MD (OrS) - **Spec Exp:** Fractures-Complex; Trauma; Shoulder Arthroscopic Surgery; Knee Surgery; **Hospital:** Stony Brook Univ Hosp; **Address:** Stony Brook Orthopaedic Assocs, 14 Technology Drive, Ste 11, East Setauket, NY 11733-3464; **Phone:** 631-444-4233; **Board Cert:** Orthopaedic Surgery 2014; **Med School:** SUNY Stony Brook 1995; **Resid:** Orthopaedic Surgery, Albany Med Ctr 2000; **Fellow:** Trauma, R. Adams Cowley Shock Trauma Ctr 2002; **Fac Appt:** Asst Prof OrS, SUNY Stony Brook

Dowling Jr, Thomas J MD (OrS) - **Spec Exp:** Spinal Surgery; Spinal Deformity; **Hospital:** St. Catherine's of Siena Med Ctr, Huntington Hosp; **Address:** Long Island Spine Specialists PC, 763 Larkfield Rd Fl 2, Commack, NY 11725-2900; **Phone:** 631-462-2225; **Board Cert:** Orthopaedic Surgery 2011; **Med School:** Boston Univ 1981; **Resid:** Surgery, North Shore Univ Hosp 1983; Orthopaedic Surgery, SUNY Univ Hosp 1987; **Fellow:** Spine Surgery, Toronto Genl Hosp 1988; **Fac Appt:** Asst Clin Prof OrS, Hofstra N Shore-LIJ Sch Med

Gurtowski, James P MD (OrS) - **Spec Exp:** Cartilage Damage & Transplant; Joint Preservation; Hip & Knee Surgery; Joint Replacement; **Hospital:** Huntington Hosp; **Address:** Huntington Med Grp, 180 E Pulaski Rd, Huntington Station, NY 11746; **Phone:** 631-425-2140; **Board Cert:** Orthopaedic Surgery 2012; **Med School:** SUNY Stony Brook 1984; **Resid:** Surgery, Univ Hosp 1985; Orthopaedic Surgery, Univ Hosp 1989; **Fac Appt:** Asst Prof OrS, Hofstra N Shore-LIJ Sch Med

Kottmeier, Stephen A MD (OrS) - **Spec Exp:** Trauma; Sports Injuries; **Hospital:** Stony Brook Univ Hosp; **Address:** Stony Brook Orthopaedic Associates, 14 Technology Drive, Ste 11, East Setauket, NY 11733; **Phone:** 631-444-4233; **Board Cert:** Orthopaedic Surgery 2014; **Med School:** SUNY Downstate 1984; **Resid:** Orthopaedic Surgery, SUNY Downstate Med Ctr 1989; **Fellow:** Sports Medicine, Penn State Hershey Med Ctr 1990; Orthopaedic Trauma, Southern NJ Regl Trauma Ctr 1991; **Fac Appt:** Prof OrS, SUNY Stony Brook

Lewis, Ronald MD (OrS) - **Spec Exp:** Pediatric Orthopaedic Surgery; Arthroscopic Surgery; Sports Medicine; Scoliosis; **Hospital:** Winthrop Univ Hosp (page 536), Huntington Hosp; **Address:** Pediatric Orthopaedics of LI, 205 E Main St, Ste 2-6, Huntington, NY 11743; **Phone:** 631-923-2370; **Board Cert:** Orthopaedic Surgery 2012; **Med School:** SUNY Stony Brook 1993; **Resid:** Orthopaedic Surgery, Univ Hosp-SUNY Stony Brook 1998; **Fellow:** Pediatric Orthopaedic Surgery, Chldns Hosp Med Ctr 1999

Sampson, Steven P MD (OrS) - **Spec Exp:** Hand & Wrist Surgery; Foot & Ankle Surgery; **Hospital:** Stony Brook Univ Hosp; **Address:** Stony Brook Orthopaedic Assocs, 14 Technology Drive, Ste 11, East Setauket, NY 11733-3464; **Phone:** 631-444-4233; **Board Cert:** Orthopaedic Surgery 2008; Hand Surgery 2008; **Med School:** UMDNJ-Rutgers Med Sch 1978; **Resid:** Orthopaedic Surgery, Hosp Univ Penn 1983; **Fellow:** Hand Surgery, St Luke's-Roosevelt Hosp 1984; **Fac Appt:** Assoc Prof OrS, SUNY Stony Brook

Tabershaw, Richard J MD (OrS) - **Spec Exp:** Shoulder Surgery; Sports Medicine; Arthroscopic Surgery; **Address:** Suffolk Orthopaedic Assocs, 375 E Main St, Ste 1, Bay Shore, NY 11706-8418; **Phone:** 631-665-8790; **Board Cert:** Orthopaedic Surgery 2009; **Med School:** Georgetown Univ 1980; **Resid:** Surgery, St Vincent Med Ctr 1983; Orthopaedic Surgery, NY-Presby/Columbia Univ Med Ctr 1986

Otolaryngology

Gargano, Robert M MD (Oto) - **Spec Exp:** Ear Disorders/Surgery; Nasal Surgery; **Hospital:** Southside Hosp, Good Samaritan Hosp Med Ctr - West Islip; **Address:** 375 E Main St, Ste 17, Bay Shore, NY 11706; **Phone:** 631-665-2430; **Board Cert:** Otolaryngology 1989; **Med School:** Tufts Univ 1984; **Resid:** Otolaryngology, New England Med Ctr 1989

Lipinsky, Edward J MD (Oto) - **Hospital:** St. Catherine's of Siena Med Ctr; **Address:** 300 E Main St Fl 2 - Ste 1, Smithtown, NY 11787-2900; **Phone:** 631-265-3727; **Board Cert:** Otolaryngology 1976; **Med School:** NYU Sch Med 1972; **Resid:** Otolaryngology, Washington Hosp 1976

Litman, Richard S MD (Oto) - **Spec Exp:** Pediatric Otolaryngology; Head & Neck Surgery; Otology; Sinus Surgery; **Hospital:** John T Mather Meml Hosp, St. Charles Hosp; **Address:** ENT & Allergy Assocs, 251 E Oakland Ave, Port Jefferson, NY 11777; **Phone:** 631-928-0188; **Board Cert:** Otolaryngology 1976; **Med School:** Wake Forest Univ 1971; **Resid:** Surgery, LIJ Med Ctr 1973; Otolaryngology, Bronx Muni Hosp 1976; **Fac Appt:** Asst Clin Prof Oto, SUNY Stony Brook

Pain Medicine

Gargiulo, Juan J MD (PM) - **Spec Exp:** Pain-Chronic; Pain-Back; Pain-Cancer; **Hospital:** Southampton Hosp; **Address:** 365 County Rd 39A, Ste 15-16, Southampton, NY 11968; **Phone:** 631-702-2300; **Board Cert:** Anesthesiology 1993; Pain Medicine 2009; **Med School:** Uruguay 1984; **Resid:** Anesthesiology, Westchester Med Ctr 1991

Litman, Steven J MD (PM) - **Spec Exp:** Pain-Back & Neck; **Hospital:** Good Samaritan Hosp Med Ctr - West Islip, St. Charles Hosp; **Address:** All Island Pain Consultants, 387 E Main St, Ste 102, Bay Shore, NY 11706; **Phone:** 631-665-0075; **Board Cert:** Anesthesiology 1993; Pain Medicine 2007; **Med School:** NY Med Coll 1987; **Resid:** Anesthesiology, Westchester Co Med Ctr 1991

Vaillancourt, Philippe D MD (PM) - **Spec Exp:** Headache; Pain-Chronic; **Hospital:** Southampton Hosp, Peconic Bay Med Ctr; **Address:** 877 E Main St, Ste 106, Riverhead, NY 11901; **Phone:** 631-727-0660; **Board Cert:** Neurology 1986; Pain Medicine 2010; **Med School:** McGill Univ 1978; **Resid:** Neurology, Mount Sinai Med Ctr 1983

Pathology

Tornos, Carmen MD (Path) - **Spec Exp:** Gynecologic Cancer; Breast Cancer; Ovarian Cancer; **Hospital:** Stony Brook Univ Hosp; **Address:** Stony Brook Univ Hosp, Pathology, 101 Nicolls Rd, rm 749, Stony Brook, NY 11794; **Phone:** 631-444-2222; **Board Cert:** Anatomic & Clinical Pathology 1989; **Med School:** Spain 1977; **Resid:** Hematology, Ciudad Sanitaria Valle de Hebron 1982; Anatomic & Clinical Pathology, Univ Texas Affil Hosp 1989; **Fellow:** Surgical Pathology, UT MD Anderson Cancer Ctr 1990; **Fac Appt:** Prof Path, SUNY Stony Brook

Pediatric Cardiology

Biancaniello, Thomas MD (PCd) - **Spec Exp:** Congenital Heart Disease; Fetal Echocardiography; Interventional Cardiology; Cardiac Catheterization; **Hospital:** Morgan Stanley Chldns Hosp of NY-Presby, NY (page 102), Good Samaritan Hosp Med Ctr - West Islip; **Address:** 57 Southern Blvd, Ste 3, Nesconset, NY 11767; **Phone:** 631-265-3300; **Board Cert:** Pediatrics 1979; Pediatric Cardiology 1981; **Med School:** NY Med Coll 1975; **Resid:** Pediatrics, North Shore Univ Hosp 1977; **Fellow:** Pediatric Cardiology, Cincinnati Chldns Hosp 1980; **Fac Appt:** Prof Ped, Columbia P&S

Pediatric Endocrinology

Wilson, Thomas A MD (PEn) - **Spec Exp:** Growth Disorders; Adrenal Disorders; Sexual Differentiation Disorders; Thyroid Disorders; **Hospital:** Stony Brook Univ Hosp; **Address:** SBUMC, Pediatric Endocrinology, 37 Research Way, East Setauket, NY 11733; **Phone:** 631-444-5437; **Board Cert:** Pediatrics 1978; Pediatric Endocrinology 2009; **Med School:** Univ Pennsylvania 1973; **Resid:** Pediatrics, Drew Med Ctr 1975; Pediatrics, Chldns Hosp 1976; **Fellow:** Pediatric Endocrinology, Univ Virginia Med Ctr 1982; **Fac Appt:** Prof Ped, SUNY Stony Brook

Pediatric Gastroenterology

Chawla, Anupama MD (PGe) - **Spec Exp:** Gastroesophageal Reflux Disease (GERD); Crohn's Disease; Inflammatory Bowel Disease; **Hospital:** Stony Brook Univ Hosp; **Address:** Stony Brook Children's Services, 4 Technology Drive, Ste 250, East Setauket, NY 11733; **Phone:** 631-444-5437; **Board Cert:** Pediatrics 2007; Pediatric Gastroenterology 2014; **Med School:** India 1980; **Resid:** Pediatrics, Stony Brook Med Ctr 1987; **Fellow:** Pediatric Gastroenterology, N Shore Univ Hosp 1990; **Fac Appt:** Assoc Prof Ped, SUNY Stony Brook

Gold, David M MD (PGe) - **Spec Exp:** Gastroesophageal Reflux Disease (GERD); Irritable Bowel Syndrome; Ulcerative Colitis/Crohn's; **Hospital:** Good Samaritan Hosp Med Ctr - West Islip; **Address:** 655 Deer Park Ave, Babylon, NY 11702; **Phone:** 631-321-2190; **Board Cert:** Pediatric Gastroenterology 2010; **Med School:** Albert Einstein Coll Med 1987; **Resid:** Pediatrics, LI Jewish Med Ctr 1990; **Fellow:** Pediatric Gastroenterology, LI Jewish Med Ctr 1993

Kessler, Bradley H MD (PGe) - **Spec Exp:** Inflammatory Bowel Disease/Crohn's; Liver Disease; Malabsorption; **Hospital:** Good Samaritan Hosp Med Ctr - West Islip, Mercy Med Ctr-Rockville Centre; **Address:** 655 Deer Park Ave, Babylon, NY 11702; **Phone:** 631-321-2190; **Board Cert:** Pediatrics 1988; Pediatric Gastroenterology 2012; **Med School:** SUNY Downstate 1982; **Resid:** Pediatrics, N Shore Univ Hosp 1985; **Fellow:** Pediatric Gastroenterology, Baylor-TX Chldns Hosp 1987; **Fac Appt:** Assoc Prof Ped, NY Coll Osteo Med

Pediatric Hematology-Oncology

Laver, Joseph H MD (PHO) - **Spec Exp:** Stem Cell Transplant; Lymphoma, Non-Hodgkin's; **Hospital:** Stony Brook Univ Hosp; **Address:** Stony Brook Univ Hosp, 3 Edmund D Pellegrino Rd, Stony Brook, NY 11794; **Phone:** 631-638-1000; **Board Cert:** Pediatrics 1985; Pediatric Hematology-Oncology 1987; **Med School:** Israel 1979; **Resid:** Pediatrics, Assaf Harofeh Med Ctr 1982; **Fellow:** Pediatric Hematology-Oncology, Meml Sloan Kettering Cancer Ctr 1985; **Fac Appt:** Prof Ped, SUNY Stony Brook

Parker, Robert I MD (PHO) - **Spec Exp:** Pediatric Cancers; Bleeding/Coagulation Disorders; Platelet Disorders; Lymphoma; **Hospital:** Stony Brook Univ Hosp; **Address:** SBUMC, Pediatric Hem/Onc, 3 Edmund D Pellegrino Rd Fl 4, Stony Brook, NY 11794; **Phone:** 631-638-1000; **Board Cert:** Pediatrics 1983; Pediatric Hematology-Oncology 1984; **Med School:** Brown Univ 1976; **Resid:** Pediatrics, Rhode Island Hosp 1979; Clinical Pathology, Natl Inst Hlth Clin Ctr 1984; **Fellow:** Pediatric Hematology-Oncology, Rhode Island Hosp 1980; Pediatric Hematology-Oncology, Natl Inst Hlth Clin Ctr 1981; **Fac Appt:** Prof Ped, SUNY Stony Brook

Pediatric Infectious Disease

Nachman, Sharon A MD (PInf) - **Spec Exp:** Lyme Disease; AIDS/HIV; **Hospital:** Stony Brook Univ Hosp; **Address:** Stony Brook Children's Services, 37 Research Way, Stony Brook, NY 11794-3465; **Phone:** 631-444-7692; **Board Cert:** Pediatrics 1987; Pediatric Infectious Disease 2008; **Med School:** SUNY Stony Brook 1983; **Resid:** Pediatrics, Schneiders Chldns Hosp 1986; **Fellow:** Pediatric Infectious Disease, NY Med Coll Affil Hosp 1987; Pediatric Infectious Disease, Rockefeller Univ Affil Hosp 1989; **Fac Appt:** Prof Ped, SUNY Stony Brook

Pediatric Nephrology

Whyte, Dilys A MD (PNep) - **Spec Exp:** Glomerulonephritis; Urinary Tract Infections; **Hospital:** Good Samaritan Hosp Med Ctr - West Islip; **Address:** 655 Deer Park Ave, Babylon, NY 11702; **Phone:** 631-321-2100; **Board Cert:** Pediatrics 2012; **Med School:** SUNY Buffalo 1991; **Resid:** Pediatrics, Kaleida Hlth/Chldns Hosp 1994; **Fellow:** Pediatric Nephrology, Yale-New Haven Hosp 1998

Pediatric Pulmonology

Kier, Catherine E MD (PPul) - **Spec Exp:** Cystic Fibrosis; Asthma & Chronic Lung Disease; **Hospital:** Stony Brook Univ Hosp; **Address:** 4 Technology Drive Fl 2 - Ste 250, East Setauket, NY 11733; **Phone:** 631-444-5437; **Board Cert:** Pediatric Pulmonology 2007; **Med School:** Philippines 1990; **Resid:** Pediatrics, N Shore Univ Hosp 1995; **Fellow:** Pediatric Pulmonology, Chldns Hosp 2000; **Fac Appt:** Assoc Prof Ped, SUNY Stony Brook

Pediatric Surgery

Lee, Thomas Kang-Ming MD (PS) - **Spec Exp:** Hernia; Pediatric Cancers; Minimally Invasive Surgery; **Hospital:** Stony Brook Univ Hosp; **Address:** Stony Brook Surgical Assocs, Stony Brook Univ Med Ctr, Surg Care Ctr, 37 Research Way, East Setauket, NY 11733; **Phone:** 631-444-4545; **Board Cert:** Surgery 2005; Pediatric Surgery 2007; **Med School:** Univ Chicago-Pritzker Sch Med 1988; **Resid:** Surgery, NY Hosp-Cornell Med Ctr 1995; **Fellow:** Surgery, Hosps Univ Pittsburgh 1992; Pediatric Surgery, Cardinal Glennon Chldns Hosp/St Louis Univ 1997; **Fac Appt:** Prof S, SUNY Stony Brook

Scriven, Richard J MD (PS) - **Spec Exp:** Hernia; Minimally Invasive Surgery; Necrotizing Enterocolitis; Tumor Surgery; **Hospital:** Stony Brook Univ Hosp; **Address:** Stony Brook Surgical Assocs, Stony Brook Univ Med Ctr, Surg Care Ctr, 37 Research Way, East Setauket, NY 11733; **Phone:** 631-444-4545; **Board Cert:** Surgery 2007; Pediatric Surgery 2009; **Med School:** Albert Einstein Coll Med 1990; **Resid:** Surgery, SUNY Hlth Sci Ctr 1997; **Fellow:** Pediatric Surgery, SUNY Hlth Sci Ctr 1999; **Fac Appt:** Assoc Prof S, SUNY Stony Brook

Pediatric Urology

Wasnick, Robert MD (Ped Uro) - **Spec Exp:** Undescended Testis; Hydronephrosis; Hypospadias; **Hospital:** Stony Brook Univ Hosp, St. Charles Hosp; **Address:** Stony Brook Urology, 24 Research Way, Ste 500, East Setauket, NY 11733; **Phone:** 631-444-1910; **Board Cert:** Urology 1982; Pediatric Urology 2008; **Med School:** Jefferson Med Coll 1974; **Resid:** Surgery, St Vincents Hosp Med Ctr 1977; Urology, Downstate Med Ctr 1980; **Fellow:** Pediatric Urology, Alder Hey Chldns Hosp 1981; **Fac Appt:** Clin Prof U, SUNY Stony Brook

Pediatrics

Chernobilsky, Lev MD (Ped) *PCP* - **Spec Exp:** Asthma; Preventive Medicine; **Hospital:** Stony Brook Univ Hosp, St. Catherine's of Siena Med Ctr; **Address:** Smith Haven Peds, 269 E Main St D Bldg, Smithtown, NY 11787; **Phone:** 631-361-2121; **Board Cert:** Pediatrics 1987; **Med School:** Ukraine 1974; **Resid:** Pediatrics, Stony Brook Univ Med Ctr 1985; **Fac Appt:** Assoc Clin Prof Ped, SUNY Stony Brook

Cusumano, Barbara Jane MD (Ped) *PCP* - **Hospital:** Southampton Hosp; **Address:** Southampton Pediatric Associates, 5 Squiretown Rd, Hampton Bays, NY 11946; **Phone:** 631-728-5300; **Board Cert:** Pediatrics 2008; **Med School:** Ros Franklin Univ/Chicago Med Sch 1984; **Resid:** Pediatrics, New York Hosp 1987

Festa, Robert S MD (Ped) *PCP* - **Spec Exp:** Anemia; Bleeding/Coagulation Disorders; Preventive Medicine; **Hospital:** Stony Brook Univ Hosp, St. Charles Hosp; **Address:** Pediatrics & Adolescent Med-Holbrook, 270 Union Ave, Holbrook, NY 11741; **Phone:** 631-588-4442 x5; **Board Cert:** Pediatrics 1978; Pediatric Hematology-Oncology 1980; **Med School:** SUNY Downstate 1972; **Resid:** Pediatrics, Montefiore Med Ctr 1975; **Fellow:** Pediatric Hematology-Oncology, Chldns Hosp 1978

Kaplan, Martin P MD (Ped) *PCP* - **Spec Exp:** Asthma; Developmental Disorders; ADD/ADHD; **Hospital:** Stony Brook Univ Hosp, St. Charles Hosp; **Address:** Pediatrics & Adolescent Medicine, 125 Oakland Ave, Ste 103, Port Jefferson, NY 11777; **Phone:** 631-331-6200; **Board Cert:** Pediatrics 1977; **Med School:** NYU Sch Med 1972; **Resid:** Pediatrics, Bellevue Hosp 1974; Pediatrics, Duke Univ Med Ctr 1975; **Fac Appt:** Asst Clin Prof Ped, SUNY Stony Brook

Kurfist, Lee A MD (Ped) *PCP* - **Spec Exp:** Adolescent Medicine; Metabolic Disorders; Preventive Medicine; **Hospital:** Huntington Hosp, Long Is Jewish Med Ctr; **Address:** ProHEALTH Care Assocs, 205 E Main St, Ste 2-8, Huntington, NY 11743; **Phone:** 631-424-1741; **Board Cert:** Pediatrics 2014; **Med School:** Italy 1985; **Resid:** Pediatrics, Nassau Univ Med Ctr 1988; **Fellow:** Pediatric Gastroenterology, Mt Sinai Hosp 1991

Manners, Richard E MD (Ped) *PCP* - **Spec Exp:** Preventive Medicine; **Hospital:** St. Charles Hosp, Stony Brook Univ Hosp; **Address:** Mid-Suffolk Pediatric Assocs, 1770 Motor Pkwy, Islandia, NY 11749; **Phone:** 631-434-1770; **Board Cert:** Pediatrics 1980; **Med School:** Albert Einstein Coll Med 1975; **Resid:** Pediatrics, Univ Minn Med Ctr 1978; **Fellow:** Ambulatory Pediatrics, Univ Minn Med Ctr 1979

McMahon, Donna-Marie DO (Ped) *PCP* - **Spec Exp:** Preventive Medicine; **Hospital:** Good Samaritan Hosp Med Ctr - West Islip, Southside Hosp; **Address:** Family Health Care Center, 267 Carleton Ave Fl 1, Central Islip, NY 11722; **Phone:** 631-348-3254; **Board Cert:** Pediatrics 2013; **Med School:** NY Coll Osteo Med 1987; **Resid:** Pediatrics, Winthrop Hosp 1990; Pediatrics, Chldn's Hosp 1991; **Fac Appt:** Asst Prof Ped, NY Coll Osteo Med

Parles, James G MD (Ped) *PCP* - **Spec Exp:** Preventive Medicine; **Hospital:** Stony Brook Univ Hosp, St. Catherine's of Siena Med Ctr; **Address:** Smithtown Pediatric Grp, 260 Middle Country Rd, Ste 107, Smithtown, NY 11787; **Phone:** 631-979-7222; **Board Cert:** Pediatrics 2008; **Med School:** NYU Sch Med 1985; **Resid:** Pediatrics, Mt Sinai Hosp 1988; **Fac Appt:** Asst Clin Prof Ped, SUNY Stony Brook

Quinn, Joseph B MD (Ped) *PCP* - **Spec Exp:** ADD/ADHD; Preventive Medicine; **Hospital:** Southampton Hosp; **Address:** Southampton Pediatric Assocs, 325 Meetinghouse Ln Bldg 2 - Ste J, Southampton, NY 11968; **Phone:** 631-283-7733; **Board Cert:** Pediatrics 1987; **Med School:** Univ VT Coll Med 1981; **Resid:** Pediatrics, Univ MD Med Ctr 1982; Pediatrics, NY Hosp 1984

Quinn, Leslie M MD (Ped) *PCP* - **Spec Exp:** Child Abuse; Pneumonia; **Hospital:** Stony Brook Univ Hosp; **Address:** 4 Technology Drive, Ste 250, East Setauket, NY 11733; **Phone:** 631-444-5437; **Board Cert:** Pediatrics 2011; Child Abuse Pediatrics 2011; **Med School:** SUNY Downstate 1984; **Resid:** Pediatrics, NY-Presby/Weill Cornell Med Ctr 1987; **Fellow:** Child Abuse & Neglect, Bellevue Hosp 2011; **Fac Appt:** Assoc Prof Ped, SUNY Stony Brook

Sosulski, Richard MD (Ped) *PCP* - **Spec Exp:** Lung Disease in Newborns; Neonatal Critical Care; Neonatology; Preventive Medicine; **Hospital:** Stony Brook Univ Hosp, St. Catherine's of Siena Med Ctr; **Address:** Smith Haven Pediatrics, 269 E Main St D Bldg, Smithtown, NY 11787-2807; **Phone:** 631-361-2121; **Board Cert:** Pediatrics 2010; Neonatal-Perinatal Medicine 1983; **Med School:** SUNY Downstate 1977; **Resid:** Pediatrics, LI Jewish Med Ctr 1980; **Fellow:** Neonatal-Perinatal Medicine, Chldns Hosp 1982; **Fac Appt:** Assoc Clin Prof Ped, SUNY Stony Brook

Physical Medicine & Rehabilitation

John, Sylvia T MD (PMR) - **Spec Exp:** Trauma Rehabilitation; Brain Injury Rehabilitation; **Hospital:** Southside Hosp; **Address:** 301 E Main St, Bay Shore, NY 11706; **Phone:** 631-968-3100; **Board Cert:** Pediatric Rehabilitation Medicine 2004; **Med School:** India 1990; **Resid:** Physical Medicine & Rehabilitation, LIJ Med Ctr 2003

Rosenberg, Craig H MD (PMR) - **Spec Exp:** Pain-Back & Neck; Spasticity Management; Electromyography; Acupuncture; **Hospital:** Southside Hosp, Stony Brook Univ Hosp; **Address:** 301 E Main St, Bay Shore, NY 11706; **Phone:** 631-968-3100; **Board Cert:** Physical Medicine & Rehabilitation 1987; **Med School:** Mexico 1981; **Resid:** Physical Medicine & Rehabilitation, NYU Med Ctr/Rusk Inst 1985; **Fac Appt:** Asst Prof PMR, Hofstra N Shore-LIJ Sch Med

Plastic Surgery

Anton, John R MD (PlS) - **Spec Exp:** Cosmetic Surgery-Face; Eyelid Surgery; Liposuction; **Hospital:** Southampton Hosp, Peconic Bay Med Ctr; **Address:** 138 Old Town Rd, Southampton, NY 11968-5011; **Phone:** 631-283-9100; **Board Cert:** Plastic Surgery 1992; **Med School:** Univ VT Coll Med 1981; **Resid:** Surgery, Mass Genl Hosp 1986; Plastic Surgery, Wayne State Univ Affil Hosp 1987; **Fellow:** Surgery, Mass Genl Hosp 1986; Plastic Surgery, Nassau Co Med Ctr 1988

Dagum, Alexander B MD (PlS) - **Spec Exp:** Reconstructive Plastic Surgery; Cleft Palate/Lip; Hand Surgery; Microsurgery; **Hospital:** Stony Brook Univ Hosp; **Address:** SBUMC, Plastic Surgery, 24 Research Way, Ste 100, East Setauket, NY 11733; **Phone:** 631-444-4666; **Board Cert:** Plastic Surgery 2013; Hand Surgery 2012; **Med School:** Canada 1987; **Resid:** Surgery, Univ Ottawa Civic Hosp 1988; Plastic Surgery, Univ Toronto Med Ctr 1993; **Fellow:** Microsurgery, Univ Toronto Med Ctr 1984; Hand Surgery, Stony Brook Univ Med Ctr 1995; **Fac Appt:** Prof S, SUNY Stony Brook

Duboys, Elliot B MD (PlS) - **Spec Exp:** Cosmetic & Reconstructive Surgery; Pediatric Plastic Surgery; Cosmetic Surgery-Breast; Birth Defects; **Hospital:** Plainview Hosp, Stony Brook Univ Hosp; **Address:** Associated Plastic Surgeons/Consultants, 864 W Jericho Tpke, Huntington, NY 11743; **Phone:** 631-423-1000; **Board Cert:** Plastic Surgery 1985; **Med School:** Belgium 1977; **Resid:** Surgery, Stony Brook Univ Med Ctr 1982; Plastic Surgery, Nassau County Med Ctr 1984; **Fac Appt:** Assoc Prof PlS, SUNY Stony Brook

Marotta, James C MD (PlS) - **Spec Exp:** Facial Plastic & Reconstructive Surgery; Cosmetic Surgery-Face; **Hospital:** Stony Brook Univ Hosp, St. Catherine's of Siena Med Ctr; **Address:** 895 W Jericho Tpke, Smithtown, NY 11787; **Phone:** 631-982-2022; **Board Cert:** Otolaryngology 2005; Facial Plastic & Reconstr Surgery 2008; **Med School:** SUNY Stony Brook 1999; **Resid:** Otolaryngology, Yale-New Haven Hosp 2004; **Fellow:** Facial Plastic & Reconstr Surgery, Quatela Ctr for Plastic Surg 2005; **Fac Appt:** Asst Clin Prof Oto, SUNY Stony Brook

Psychiatry

Aronson, Thomas A MD (Psyc) - **Spec Exp:** Depression; Bipolar/Mood Disorders; Personality Disorders-Borderline; **Hospital:** St. Catherine's of Siena Med Ctr; **Address:** Smithtown Psychiatric Services, 2 Brooksite Drive, Ste 220, Smithtown, NY 11787-3400; **Phone:** 631-265-0909; **Board Cert:** Psychiatry 1985; **Med School:** Washington Univ, St Louis 1980; **Resid:** Psychiatry, Hosp Univ Penn 1984; **Fac Appt:** Assoc Clin Prof Psyc, SUNY Stony Brook

Koreen, Amy R MD (Psyc) - ; **Address:** 28 Elm St, Huntington, NY 11743; **Phone:** 631-423-8368; **Board Cert:** Psychiatry 1993; **Med School:** Mount Sinai Sch Med 1988; **Resid:** Psychiatry, Univ Maryland Med Ctr 1991; Psychiatry, LI Jewish Med Ctr 1992; **Fellow:** Neuropsychopharmacology, LI Jewish Med Ctr 1993

Lee, Kwang Soo MD (Psyc) - ; **Address:** 221 Broadway, Ste 303, Amityville, NY 11701-2726; **Phone:** 631-789-7448; **Board Cert:** Psychiatry 1979; **Med School:** South Korea 1965; **Resid:** Internal Medicine, Booth Meml Hosp 1967; Psychiatry, Bellevue Hosp 1969; **Fellow:** Psychiatry, Amer Inst Psychoanalysis 1969

Nass, Jack MD (Psyc) - **Spec Exp:** Geriatric Rehabilitation; Bipolar/Mood Disorders; Depression; Neuro-Psychiatry; **Hospital:** Good Samaritan Hosp Med Ctr - West Islip; **Address:** 2100 Deer Park Ave, Ste 8, Deer Park, NY 11729; **Phone:** 631-321-7697; **Board Cert:** Psychiatry 1980; **Med School:** Belgium 1975; **Resid:** Psychiatry, LI Jewish Med Ctr 1979

Rosen, Bruce I MD (Psyc) - **Spec Exp:** Depression; Anxiety Disorders; Bipolar/Mood Disorders; Psychopharmacology; **Address:** North Shore Psychiatric Consultants, 222 Middle Country Rd, Ste 210, Smithtown, NY 11787-2814; **Phone:** 631-265-6868; **Board Cert:** Psychiatry 1976; **Med School:** Loyola Univ-Stritch Sch Med 1971; **Resid:** Psychiatry, LI Jewish-Hillside Med Ctr 1974; **Fellow:** Psychiatry, LI Jewish-Hillside Med Ctr 1975; **Fac Appt:** Assoc Clin Prof Psyc, SUNY Stony Brook

Schwartz, Michael MD (Psyc) - **Spec Exp:** Forensic Psychiatry; Psychotherapy & Psychopharmacology; Mood Disorders; Anxiety Disorders; **Hospital:** Stony Brook Univ Hosp; **Address:** 150 Broadhollow Rd, Ste 204, Melville, NY 11747; **Phone:** 631-385-3313; **Board Cert:** Psychiatry 1984; **Med School:** Univ Miami Sch Med 1977; **Resid:** Internal Medicine, Mount Sinai Hosp 1978; Psychiatry, Mount Sinai Hosp 1981; **Fellow:** Research, Natl Inst Aging 1983; **Fac Appt:** Assoc Prof Psyc, SUNY Stony Brook

Pulmonary Disease

Baram, Daniel MD (Pul) - **Spec Exp:** Critical Care Medicine; Lung Cancer; **Hospital:** John T Mather Meml Hosp; **Address:** 70 North Country Rd, Ste 101, Port Jefferson, NY 11777; **Phone:** 631-473-0037; **Board Cert:** Internal Medicine 2004; Critical Care Medicine 2007; Pulmonary Disease 2008; **Med School:** Jefferson Med Coll 1990; **Resid:** Internal Medicine, New York Hosp 1993; **Fellow:** Critical Care Medicine, Natl Inst of Health 1996; Pulmonary Disease, NYU/Bellevue Hosps 1998

Bernardini, Dennis L MD (Pul) - **Spec Exp:** Chronic Obstructive Lung Disease (COPD); Asthma; Sarcoidosis; Pulmonary Fibrosis; **Hospital:** Huntington Hosp; **Address:** 175 E Main St, Huntington, NY 11743-2939; **Phone:** 631-424-3787; **Board Cert:** Internal Medicine 1983; Pulmonary Disease 1986; **Med School:** Johns Hopkins Univ 1980; **Resid:** Internal Medicine, St Luke's Hosp 1983; **Fellow:** Pulmonary Disease, Univ Hospital 1985; Critical Care Medicine, Univ Hospital 1985

Glaser, Morton L MD (Pul) - **Spec Exp:** Emphysema & Asthma; Interstitial Lung Disease; Lung Cancer; Pulmonary Hypertension; **Hospital:** St. Charles Hosp, John T Mather Meml Hosp; **Address:** Suffolk Pulmonary Assocs, 60 N Country Rd, Ste 203, Port Jefferson, NY 11777; **Phone:** 631-509-1888; **Board Cert:** Internal Medicine 1980; Pulmonary Disease 1984; Critical Care Medicine 2010; Undersea & Hyperbaric Medicine 2005; **Med School:** Med Coll Wisc 1976; **Resid:** Internal Medicine, Roger Williams Med Ctr 1979; **Fellow:** Pulmonary Disease, Univ Hosp 1981

Sklarek, Howard M MD (Pul) - **Spec Exp:** Asthma; Cough; Chronic Obstructive Lung Disease (COPD); Interstitial Lung Disease; **Hospital:** Southampton Hosp, Eastern Long Island Hosp; **Address:** Southampton Pulmonary Med, 325 Meeting House Ln Bldg 1 - Ste K, Southampton, NY 11968; **Phone:** 631-283-8008; **Board Cert:** Internal Medicine 1984; Pulmonary Disease 1986; Critical Care Medicine 2010; Hospice & Palliative Medicine 2012; **Med School:** SUNY Buffalo 1981; **Resid:** Internal Medicine, Winthrop Univ Hosp 1984; **Fellow:** Pulmonary Critical Care Medicine, Winthrop Univ Hosp 1986

Walser, Lawrence A MD (Pul) - **Spec Exp:** Critical Care Medicine; Respiratory Failure; Respiratory Distress Syndrome; **Hospital:** Peconic Bay Med Ctr; **Address:** Peconic Bay Primary Med, 185 Old Country Rd, Ste 3, Riverhead, NY 11901; **Phone:** 631-727-2523; **Board Cert:** Internal Medicine 1982; Pulmonary Disease 2007; Critical Care Medicine 2007; **Med School:** SUNY Downstate 1979; **Resid:** Internal Medicine, Berkshire Med Ctr 1982; **Fellow:** Pulmonary Disease, Stony Brook Univ Hosp 1984

Wohlberg, Gary MD (Pul) - **Spec Exp:** Critical Care Medicine; Sleep Medicine; Cystic Fibrosis; Respiratory Distress Syndrome; **Hospital:** Southside Hosp, Good Samaritan Hosp Med Ctr - West Islip; **Address:** Long Island Lung Ctr, 370 E Main St, Ste 5, Bay Shore, NY 11706-8405; **Phone:** 631-666-5864; **Board Cert:** Internal Medicine 1985; Pulmonary Disease 1986; Critical Care Medicine 2010; Sleep Medicine 2007; **Med School:** SUNY Hlth Sci Ctr 1981; **Resid:** Internal Medicine, Long Island Jewish Hosp 1984; **Fellow:** Pulmonary Disease, Montefiore Hosp Med Ctr 1986

Radiation Oncology

Park, Tae L MD (RadRO) - **Spec Exp:** Prostate Cancer; Breast Cancer; Gynecologic Cancer; **Hospital:** Stony Brook Univ Hosp; **Address:** Stony Brook Univ Med Ctr-Rad Oncology, 100 Nicolls Rd, Level 2, rm 643, Stony Brook, NY 11794; **Phone:** 631-444-2210; **Board Cert:** Therapeutic Radiology 1984; **Med School:** South Korea 1976; **Resid:** Radiation Oncology, Kings Co Med Ctr 1984; Radiation Oncology, MD Anderson Cancer Ctr 1985; **Fac Appt:** Assoc Clin Prof RadRO, SUNY Stony Brook

Ryu, Samuel MD (RadRO) - **Spec Exp:** Central Nervous System Cancer; Brain & Spinal Cord Tumors; Stereotactic Radiosurgery; Stereotactic Body Radiotherapy; **Hospital:** Stony Brook Univ Hosp; **Address:** Stony Brook Univ Hosp, 101 Nicolls Rd, Hosp Level 2, rm 664, Stony Brook, NY 11794-7028; **Phone:** 631-444-7770; **Board Cert:** Radiation Oncology 2008; **Med School:** South Korea 1982; **Resid:** Radiation Oncology, Henry Ford Hosp 1996; **Fac Appt:** Prof RadRO, SUNY Stony Brook

Reproductive Endocrinology

Bronson, Richard A MD (RE) - **Spec Exp:** Infertility-IVF; Pregnancy Loss-Recurrent; Reproductive Immunology; **Hospital:** Stony Brook Univ Hosp; **Address:** Reproductive Specialists of New York, 2500 Nesconset Highway, Bldg 23, Stony Brook, NY 11790; **Phone:** 631-246-9100; **Board Cert:** Obstetrics & Gynecology 1976; Reproductive Endocrinology 1980; **Med School:** NYU Sch Med 1966; **Resid:** Surgery, NYU Med Ctr 1971; Obstetrics & Gynecology, Hosp Univ Penn 1974; **Fellow:** Reproductive Endocrinology, Pennsylvania Hosp 1976; **Fac Appt:** Prof ObG, SUNY Stony Brook

Kenigsberg, Daniel J MD (RE) - **Spec Exp:** Infertility-IVF; Preimplantation Genetic Diagnosis; Fertility Preservation; **Hospital:** Long Is Jewish Med Ctr, Stony Brook Univ Hosp; **Address:** Long Island IVF, 8 Corporate Center Drive, Ste 101, Melville, NY 11747; **Phone:** 631-331-7575; **Board Cert:** Obstetrics & Gynecology 1995; Reproductive Endocrinology/Infertility 1995; **Med School:** NY Med Coll 1978; **Resid:** Obstetrics & Gynecology, Johns Hopkins Hosp 1982; **Fellow:** Reproductive Endocrinology/Infertility, Natl Inst Hlth 1984; **Fac Appt:** Assoc Clin Prof ObG, SUNY Stony Brook

Lydic, Michael L MD (RE) - **Spec Exp:** Polycystic Ovarian Syndrome; Pregnancy Loss-Recurrent; Infertility; Infertility-IVF; **Hospital:** Stony Brook Univ Hosp; **Address:** Reproductive Specialists of NY, 2500 Nesconset Hwy Bldg 23, Stony Brook, NY 11790; **Phone:** 631-246-9100; **Board Cert:** Obstetrics & Gynecology 2013; Reproductive Endocrinology/Infertility 2013; **Med School:** Hahnemann Univ 1989; **Resid:** Obstetrics & Gynecology, Hahnemann Univ Hosp 1993; **Fellow:** Reproductive Endocrinology/Infertility, Univ of Cincinnati 1995; **Fac Appt:** Assoc Clin Prof ObG, SUNY Stony Brook

Pena, Joseph E MD (RE) - **Spec Exp:** Infertility-IVF; Preimplantation Genetic Diagnosis; Fertility Preservation; Polycystic Ovarian Syndrome; **Hospital:** Good Samaritan Hosp Med Ctr - West Islip, Syosset Hosp; **Address:** Long Island IVF, 500 Montauk Hwy, Ste A, West Islip, NY 11795; **Phone:** 631-661-5437; **Board Cert:** Obstetrics & Gynecology 2013; Reproductive Endocrinology/Infertility 2013; **Med School:** NYU Sch Med 1996; **Resid:** Obstetrics & Gynecology, Pennsylvania Hosp 2000; **Fellow:** Reproductive Endocrinology/Infertility, NY Presby-Columbia Med Ctr 2003

Rheumatology

Hamburger, Max Ira MD (Rhu) - **Spec Exp:** Rheumatoid Arthritis; Gout; Vasculitis; **Hospital:** St. Charles Hosp, John T Mather Meml Hosp; **Address:** 1895 Walt Whitman Rd, Rheumatology Associates of Long Island, Melville, NY 11747; **Phone:** 631-249-9525; **Board Cert:** Internal Medicine 1977; Rheumatology 1980; **Med School:** Albert Einstein Coll Med 1973; **Resid:** Internal Medicine, Bellevue Hosp 1976; **Fellow:** Allergy & Immunology, Nat Inst Health 1979; **Fac Appt:** Asst Clin Prof Med, SUNY Stony Brook

Repice, Michael MD (Rhu) - **Spec Exp:** Arthritis; Connective Tissue Disorders; **Hospital:** Huntington Hosp; **Address:** 195 E Main St, Ste B, Huntington, NY 11743-2812; **Phone:** 631-271-1640; **Board Cert:** Internal Medicine 1976; Rheumatology 1980; **Med School:** Georgetown Univ 1973; **Resid:** Internal Medicine, Worcester City Hosp 1977; **Fellow:** Rheumatology, Northwestern Univ 1979

Sports Medicine

Putterman, Eric A MD (SM) - **Spec Exp:** Arthroscopic Surgery; **Hospital:** Glen Cove Hosp; **Address:** Premier Ortho Surgery & Sports Medicine, 1800 Walt Whitman Rd, Ste 120, Melville, NY 11747; **Phone:** 631-293-9540; **Board Cert:** Orthopaedic Surgery 2009; **Med School:** Mount Sinai Sch Med 1980; **Resid:** Orthopaedic Surgery, NYU-Bellevue Med Ctr 1985; **Fellow:** Sports Medicine, NYU-Bellevue Med Ctr 1985

Surgery

Busch-Devereaux, Erna MD (S) - **Spec Exp:** Breast Cancer; Breast Surgery; **Hospital:** Huntington Hosp, N Shore Univ Hosp; **Address:** 270 Pulaski Rd, Ste A, Greenlawn, NY 11740; **Phone:** 631-423-1414; **Board Cert:** Surgery 2010; **Med School:** UMDNJ-NJ Med Sch, Newark 1985; **Resid:** Surgery, St Vincent Cath Med Ctr 1990; **Fellow:** Surgical Oncology, Roswell Park Canc Inst 1993; **Fac Appt:** Asst Prof S, NYU Sch Med

Cohen, Bradley D MD (S) - **Spec Exp:** Breast Cancer; Laparoscopic Surgery; Sentinel Node Surgery; Melanoma; **Hospital:** Good Samaritan Hosp Med Ctr - West Islip, Southside Hosp; **Address:** 15 Park Ave, Bay Shore, NY 11706; **Phone:** 631-581-4400; **Board Cert:** Surgery 2009; **Med School:** Mount Sinai Sch Med 1983; **Resid:** Surgery, Lenox Hill Hosp 1988; **Fellow:** Surgical Oncology, Meml Sloan Kettering Cancer Ctr 1989

Cosgrove, John M MD (S) - **Spec Exp:** Laparoscopic Surgery; Endoscopy; Biliary Surgery; Gastrointestinal Surgery; **Hospital:** Eastern Long Island Hosp; **Address:** 201 Manor Place, Greenport, NY 11944; **Phone:** 631-477-5386; **Board Cert:** Surgery 2008; **Med School:** NY Med Coll 1983; **Resid:** Surgery, Beth Israel Med Ctr 1988; **Fac Appt:** Clin Prof S, Albert Einstein Coll Med

O'Hea, Brian J MD (S) - **Spec Exp:** Breast Cancer; Sentinel Node Surgery; **Hospital:** Stony Brook Univ Hosp; **Address:** Stony Brook Univ Med Ctr, Breast Cancer Ctr, 3 Edmund D Pellegrino Rd, Stony Brook, NY 11794; **Phone:** 631-444-1795; **Board Cert:** Surgery 2012; **Med School:** Georgetown Univ 1986; **Resid:** Surgery, St Vincent's Hosp 1991; **Fellow:** Breast Disease, Meml Sloan-Kettering Cancer Ctr 1996; **Fac Appt:** Asst Prof S, SUNY Stony Brook

Pryor, Aurora D MD (S) - **Spec Exp:** Laparoscopic Surgery-Advanced; Obesity/Bariatric Surgery; Gastroesophageal Reflux Disease (GERD); Achalasia; **Hospital:** Stony Brook Univ Hosp; **Address:** Stony Brook Surgical Associates, Stony Brook Univ Med Ctr, Surg Care Ctr, 37 Research Way, East Setauket, NY 11733-3465; **Phone:** 631-444-4545; **Board Cert:** Surgery 2012; **Med School:** Duke Univ 1995; **Resid:** Surgery, Duke Univ Med Ctr 2002; **Fellow:** Laparoscopic Surgery, Duke Univ Med Ctr 2003; **Fac Appt:** Prof S, SUNY Stony Brook

Sclafani, Lisa M MD (S) - **Spec Exp:** Breast Surgery; Breast Cancer; **Hospital:** Meml Sloan Kettering Canc Ctr (page 110); **Address:** Meml Sloan-Kettering Canc Ctr - Commack, 650 Commack Rd, Commack, NY 11725; **Phone:** 631-623-4050; **Board Cert:** Surgery 2007; **Med School:** NYU Sch Med 1982; **Resid:** Surgery, Montefiore Med Ctr-Moses Campus 1987; **Fellow:** Surgical Oncology, Meml Sloan Kettering Canc Ctr 1988; **Fac Appt:** Assoc Clin Prof S, Cornell Univ-Weill Med Coll

Shapiro, Marc J MD (S) - **Spec Exp:** Laparoscopic Surgery; Gastrointestinal Surgery; Burn Care; Trauma; **Hospital:** Stony Brook Univ Hosp; **Address:** 37 Research Way, East Setauket, NY 11733; **Phone:** 631-444-4545; **Board Cert:** Surgery 2004; Surgical Critical Care 2005; **Med School:** Univ Mich Med Sch 1979; **Resid:** Surgery, Henry Ford Hosp 1984; **Fellow:** Critical Care Medicine, Univ Pittsburgh Hosp 1985; **Fac Appt:** Prof S, SUNY Stony Brook

Talamini, Mark A MD (S) - **Spec Exp:** Robotic Surgery; Minimally Invasive Surgery; Gastrointestinal Cancer; Cancer Surgery; **Hospital:** Stony Brook Univ Hosp; **Address:** Stony Brook Cancer & Breast Ctr, 37 Research Way, East Setauket, NY 11733; **Phone:** 631-444-8113; **Board Cert:** Surgery 2008; **Med School:** Johns Hopkins Univ 1981; **Resid:** Surgery, Johns Hopkins Hosp 1987; **Fellow:** Surgery, Univ Cincinnati Affil Hosp 1985; **Fac Appt:** Prof S, UCSD

Zingale, Robert MD (S) - **Hospital:** Huntington Hosp; **Address:** 158 E Main St, Ste 7, Huntington, NY 11743-2988; **Phone:** 631-271-1822; **Board Cert:** Surgery 2007; Surgical Critical Care 2010; **Med School:** SUNY Downstate 1983; **Resid:** Surgery, Maimonides Med Ctr 1988; **Fellow:** Trauma, Coney Is Hosp 1989; **Fac Appt:** Assoc Clin Prof S, NY Med Coll

Thoracic & Cardiac Surgery

Bilfinger, Thomas V MD (T&CS) - **Spec Exp:** Cardiac Surgery-Adult; Lung Cancer; **Hospital:** Stony Brook Univ Hosp; **Address:** Health Science Center, 3 Edmund D Pellegrino Rd, rm 80, Stony Brook, NY 11794; **Phone:** 631-444-1820; **Board Cert:** Surgery 2006; Thoracic & Cardiac Surgery 2008; Surgical Critical Care 2010; **Med School:** Switzerland 1978; **Resid:** Surgery, Univ TX Med Branch Hosp 1986; **Fellow:** Thoracic Surgery, Univ TX Med Branch Hosp 1988; **Fac Appt:** Prof T&CS, SUNY Stony Brook

Fernandez, Harold A MD (T&CS) - **Spec Exp:** Cardiac Surgery-High Risk; Minimally Invasive Heart Valve Surgery; Ventricular Assist Device (LVAD); Atrial Fibrillation; **Hospital:** Stony Brook Univ Hosp; **Address:** Stony Brook Surgical Assocs, 101 Nicolls Rd, Level 19 HSC, rm 080, Stony Brook, NY 11794; **Phone:** 631-444-6590; **Board Cert:** Surgery 2012; Thoracic Surgery 2005; **Med School:** Harvard Med Sch 1993; **Resid:** Surgery, NYU Med Ctr 1999; **Fellow:** Cardiothoracic Surgery, NYU Med Ctr 2001; **Fac Appt:** Prof S, SUNY Stony Brook

Hartman, Alan R MD (T&CS) - **Spec Exp:** Minimally Invasive Heart Valve Surgery; Aneurysm-Thoracic Aortic; **Hospital:** N Shore Univ Hosp, Southside Hosp; **Address:** Southside Hosp, Cardiothoracic Surgery, 301 E Main St, Ste 2North, Bay Shore, NY 11706; **Phone:** 631-968-3525; **Board Cert:** Surgery 2004; Thoracic & Cardiac Surgery 2005; Surgical Critical Care 2010; **Med School:** Mount Sinai Sch Med 1979; **Resid:** Surgery, NYU-Bellevue Hosp 1984; **Fellow:** Cardiothoracic Surgery, NYU-Bellevue Hosp 1986; **Fac Appt:** Assoc Prof S, NYU Sch Med

Palatt, Terry MD (T&CS) - **Spec Exp:** Lung Cancer; Video Assisted Thoracic Surgery (VATS); **Hospital:** Good Samaritan Hosp Med Ctr - West Islip, Southside Hosp; **Address:** Island Surgical & Vascular Group, 15 Park Ave, Bay Shore, NY 11706; **Phone:** 631-581-4400; **Board Cert:** Thoracic Surgery 2008; **Med School:** Grenada 1981; **Resid:** Surgery, Maimonides Med Ctr 1986; **Fellow:** Cardiothoracic Surgery, SUNY Hlth Sci Ctr 1988

Taylor Jr, James R MD (T&CS) - **Spec Exp:** Thoracic Aortic Surgery; Aneurysm-Aortic; Minimally Invasive Heart Valve Surgery; **Hospital:** Stony Brook Univ Hosp; **Address:** Stony Brook Cardiothoracic Surgery, 101 Nicolls Rd, Level 19 HSC, rm 080, Stony Brook, NY 11794; **Phone:** 631-444-6590; **Board Cert:** Surgery 2008; Thoracic & Cardiac Surgery 2013; **Med School:** Med Univ SC 1984; **Resid:** Surgery, New York Hosp 1989; **Fellow:** Cardiothoracic Surgery, New York Hosp 1991; **Fac Appt:** Prof T&CS, SUNY Stony Brook

Urology

Mills II, Carl MD (U) - **Spec Exp:** Urologic Cancer; **Hospital:** St. Charles Hosp, Brookhaven Meml Hosp & Med Ctr; **Address:** 635 Belle Terre Rd, Ste 201, Port Jefferson, NY 11777; **Phone:** 631-509-4805; **Board Cert:** Urology 1984; **Med School:** Geo Wash Univ 1975; **Resid:** Surgery, New York Hosp/Cornell 1978; Urology, New York Hosp/Cornell 1982

Spears, Thomas E MD (U) - **Hospital:** Huntington Hosp; **Address:** Huntington Medical Group, 180 E Pulaski Rd, Huntington Station, NY 11746; **Phone:** 631-425-2125; **Board Cert:** Urology 2013; **Med School:** NY Med Coll 1986; **Resid:** Surgery, Metropolitan Hosp/NY Med Coll 1988; Urology, Metropolitan Hosp/NY Med Coll 1993

Waltzer, Wayne MD (U) - **Spec Exp:** Urologic Cancer; Reconstructive Urology Surgery; Transplant-Kidney; **Hospital:** Stony Brook Univ Hosp, St. Catherine's of Siena Med Ctr; **Address:** Stony Brook Urology, 24 Research Way, Suite 500, East Setauket, NY 11733-3453; **Phone:** 631-444-1910; **Board Cert:** Urology 1980; **Med School:** Univ Pittsburgh 1973; **Resid:** Urology, UPMC=Presbyterian Med Ctr 1978; **Fellow:** Renal Transplant, Mayo Clinic 1979; **Fac Appt:** Prof U, SUNY Stony Brook

Vascular Surgery

Arnold, Thomas E MD (VascS) - **Spec Exp:** Peripheral Vascular Disease; Endovascular Surgery; Endovascular Stent Grafts; **Hospital:** John T Mather Meml Hosp, St. Charles Hosp; **Address:** Ssuffolk Vascular Assocs, 1110 Hallock Ave, Port Jefferson Station, NY 11776; **Phone:** 631-476-9100; **Board Cert:** Surgery 2003; Vascular Surgery 2003; **Med School:** SUNY Downstate 1985; **Resid:** Surgery, Presbyterian Med Ctr 1987; Surgery, MCP Affil Hosp 1991; **Fellow:** Vascular Surgery, Hahnemann Univ Hosp 1993

Pollina, Robert M MD (VascS) - **Spec Exp:** Peripheral Vascular Disease; Endovascular Surgery; Endovascular Stent Grafts; **Hospital:** John T Mather Meml Hosp, St. Charles Hosp; **Address:** Suffolk Vascular Assocs, 1110 Hallock Ave, Port Jefferson Station, NY 11776; **Phone:** 631-476-9100; **Board Cert:** Vascular Surgery 2007; **Med School:** SUNY Downstate 1988; **Resid:** Surgery, Kings Co Hosp Ctr 1993; **Fellow:** Vascular Surgery, Maimonides Med Ctr 1995

Tassiopoulos, Apostolos K MD (VascS) - **Spec Exp:** Endovascular Surgery; Aneurysm-Aortic; Peripheral Vascular Disease; Carotid Artery Disease; **Hospital:** Stony Brook Univ Hosp; **Address:** Stony Brook Surgical Assocs, 37 Research Way, East Setauket, NY 11733; **Phone:** 631-444-4545; **Board Cert:** Surgery 2010; Vascular Surgery 2012; **Med School:** Greece 1989; **Resid:** Surgery, SUNY Upstate Med Ctr 1999; **Fellow:** Vascular Surgery, Loyola Univ Med Ctr 2001; **Fac Appt:** Prof S, SUNY Stony Brook

White Plains Hospital

41 East Post Road
White Plains, NY 10601
Tel: (914) 681-0600
www.wphospital.org

Sponsorship: Private, Not-for-Profit
Beds: 292
Accreditation: Joint Commission on Accreditation of Healthcare Organizations, Commission on Cancer of the American College of Surgeons, National Accreditation Program for Breast Centers, College of American Pathologists, American Registry of Radiological Technology, American Society of Radiological Technology, Intersocietal Commission for the Accreditation of Echocardiography Laboratories, American Institute of Ultrasound Medicine, American Academy of Sleep Medicine.

A LEADING COMMUNITY HOSPITAL White Plains Hospital (WPH) is a 292-bed facility that has served Westchester County and the surrounding area since 1893. The Hospital offers much of the technology of large urban specialty teaching hospitals, and combines it with compassionate and personalized care close to home. In addition to a wide range of general acute care services, WPH offers highly sophisticated specialty programs in Oncology, Orthopedics & Joint Replacement, Obstetrics, Neonatal Intensive Care, Radiology, Minimally Invasive & Robotic Surgery, Cardiology, and Stroke Care. An enhanced Emergency Department opened in 2010 and a state-of-the-art Cardiac Catheterization Lab opened in 2008.

The Hospital is an twelve-time winner of the Consumer Choice Award for Westchester County, and the Hospital received Magnet® recognition from the American Nurses Credentialing Center (ANCC) in 2012.

CENTERS OF EXCELLENCE

• WILLIAM & SYLVIA SILBERSTEIN NEONATAL & MATERNITY CENTER A Labor & Delivery unit, backed up by a state-of-the-art Level III Mastronardi Neonatal Intensive Care Unit – the highest designation available to a community hospital – is part of the reason why WPH leads Westchester County in number of deliveries, year after year.

• DICKSTEIN CANCER TREATMENT CENTER Part of the Hospital's comprehensive Cancer Program, the Dickstein Center anchors a wide range of services including two linear accelerators for radiation therapy, a new state of the art infusion center for chemotherapy and other intravenous treatments, and complementary care programs. Clinical navigation services provide a personal guide for patients at each stage of diagnosis, treatment and follow up care. The Cancer Program has repeatedly received an Outstanding Achievement Award from the American College of Surgeons Commission on Cancer and was recognized by the National Accreditation Program for Breast Centers (NAPBC) in 2012.

• MINIMALLY INVASIVE & ROBOTIC SURGERY White Plains Hospital's surgeons perform more minimally invasive surgeries than any other hospital in Westchester. The Hospital was also the first community hospital in the Westchester-Fairfield region to use the da Vinci® Robotic Surgical System for prostate cancer surgery.

• ORTHOPEDICS More hip and knee replacement surgeries – many of them using minimally invasive techniques – have been performed at WPH than at any other hospital in Westchester.

• CARDIOLOGY The Hospital's cardiology program includes a new and expansive non-invasive testing center, Joan and Alan Herfort, M.D. Cardiac Catheterization Laboratory, and an eight-bed inpatient coronary care unit.

• THE RUTH AND JEROME A. SIEGEL STROKE CENTER The Hospital was the first in Westchester County to receive Stroke Center designation from the New York State Department of Health and the first in the County to receive Gold (Sustained) Award Recognition from the American Stroke Association's Get with the Guidelines℠ – Stroke program.

PHYSICIAN REFERRAL:
For a physician referral or more information about our services,
please call (914) 681-1010 or visit www.wphospital.org

Addiction Psychiatry

Bisaga, Adam MD (AdP) - **Spec Exp:** Opiate Addiction; Alcohol Abuse; Drug Abuse; Dual Diagnosis; **Hospital:** NY-Presby/Columbia Univ Med Ctr, NY (page 102), NY State Psychiatric Inst; **Address:** 547 Saw Mill River Rd, Fl 3, Ste PH, Ardsley, NY 10502; **Phone:** 914-419-8921; **Board Cert:** Psychiatry 2008; Addiction Psychiatry 2011; **Med School:** Poland 1989; **Resid:** Psychiatry, N Shore Univ Hosp 1997; **Fellow:** Addiction Psychiatry, NYSPI-Columbia Univ 1999; **Fac Appt:** Prof Psyc, Columbia P&S

Adolescent Medicine

Nackenson, Marcia J MD (AM) - **Spec Exp:** Adolescent Gynecology; Eating Disorders; **Hospital:** Westchester Med Ctr; **Address:** Chldns & Women's Physicians Westchester, 503 Grasslands Rd, Ste 200, Valhalla, NY 10595; **Phone:** 914-304-5288; **Board Cert:** Pediatrics 1987; Adolescent Medicine 2012; **Med School:** Israel 1983; **Resid:** Pediatrics, Brookdale Hosp Med Ctr 1986; **Fellow:** Adolescent Medicine, Brookdale Hosp Med Ctr 1987; **Fac Appt:** Assoc Clin Prof Ped, NY Med Coll

Allergy & Immunology

Deener, Avi M MD (A&I) - **Spec Exp:** Asthma & Allergy; **Hospital:** White Plains Hosp (page 652); **Address:** Westchester Med Group, 210 Westchester Ave, White Plains, NY 10604; **Phone:** 914-831-6850; **Board Cert:** Internal Medicine 2005; Allergy & Immunology 2008; **Med School:** UMDNJ-NJ Med Sch, Newark 2002; **Resid:** Internal Medicine, UMDNJ Med Ctr 2005; **Fellow:** Allergy & Immunology, Montefiore Med Ctr 2008

Geraci-Ciardullo, Kira MD (A&I) - **Spec Exp:** Asthma; Sinus Disorders; Food Allergy; Insect Allergies; **Hospital:** White Plains Hosp (page 652); **Address:** 1600 Harrison Ave, Ste 304, Rockledge Plaza, Mamaroneck, NY 10543-3145; **Phone:** 914-777-1179; **Board Cert:** Pediatrics 1984; Allergy & Immunology 2008; **Med School:** Columbia P&S 1980; **Resid:** Pediatrics, NY-Cornell Hosp 1983; **Fellow:** Allergy & Immunology, NY-Cornell Hosp 1985

Goldman, Neil C MD (A&I) - **Spec Exp:** Asthma; Drug Sensitivity; Sinusitis; Insect Allergies; **Hospital:** Hudson Valley Hosp Ctr; **Address:** Hudson Valley Asthma & Allergy Assocs, 35 S Riverside Ave, Ste 106, Croton On Hudson, NY 10520; **Phone:** 914-271-0001; **Board Cert:** Allergy & Immunology 1977; **Med School:** NY Med Coll 1966; **Resid:** Internal Medicine, Beth Israel Hosp 1968; Internal Medicine, Metropolitan Hosp Ctr 1969; **Fellow:** Allergy & Immunology, Jewish Med Ctr 1970

Maloney, Patrick F MD (A&I) - **Spec Exp:** Food Allergy; **Hospital:** White Plains Hosp (page 652), Westchester Med Ctr; **Address:** Westchester Hlth Assocs, 1600 Harrison Ave, Ste 304, Mamaroneck, NY 10543; **Phone:** 914-777-1179; **Board Cert:** Allergy & Immunology 2005; **Med School:** SUNY Stony Brook 1999; **Resid:** Internal Medicine, Stony Brook Univ Med Ctr 2002; **Fellow:** Allergy & Immunology, Stony Brook Univ Med Ctr 2004

Mechanic, Laura MD (A&I) - **Spec Exp:** Allergic Rhinitis; Eczema; Hives; Immunodeficiency Disorders; **Hospital:** White Plains Hosp (page 652); **Address:** Westchester Medical Group, 210 Westchester Ave, White Plains, NY 10604; **Phone:** 914-831-6850; **Board Cert:** Allergy & Immunology 2005; **Med School:** NYU Sch Med 1989; **Resid:** Internal Medicine, Mt Sinai Med Ctr 1992; **Fellow:** Allergy & Immunology, Mt Sinai Med Ctr 1995

Osleeb, Craig MD (A&I) - **Hospital:** Northern Westchester Hosp; **Address:** Mount Kisco Medical Group, 110 S Bedford Rd, Mt. Kisco, NY 10549; **Phone:** 914-242-1580; **Board Cert:** Allergy & Immunology 2013; Pediatrics 2013; **Med School:** Univ Wisc 1988; **Resid:** Pediatrics, UConn Med Ctr 1991; **Fellow:** Allergy & Immunology, Chldns Natl Med Ctr 1993

Pollowitz, James Allen MD (A&I) - **Spec Exp:** Asthma; Food Allergy; Hives; Drug Sensitivity; **Hospital:** White Plains Hosp (page 652), Lawrence Hosp Ctr (page 102); **Address:** 281 Garth Rd, Ste A, Scarsdale, NY 10583-4034; **Phone:** 914-472-3833; **Board Cert:** Pediatrics 1978; Allergy & Immunology 1979; **Med School:** NYU Sch Med 1973; **Resid:** Pediatrics, Bronx Muni Hosp Ctr 1976; **Fellow:** Allergy & Immunology, St Vincent Med Ctr 1978; **Fac Appt:** Asst Clin Prof Ped, NY Med Coll

Tuerk-Mendelsohn, Lois MD (A&I) - **Spec Exp:** Asthma; Hay Fever; Food Allergy; Eczema; **Hospital:** Northern Westchester Hosp; **Address:** MKMG, Allergy & Immunology, 103 S Bedford Rd, Ste 208, Mt Kisco, NY 10549; **Phone:** 914-666-7171; **Board Cert:** Internal Medicine 1989; **Med School:** NY Med Coll 1986; **Resid:** Internal Medicine, Lenox Hill Hosp 1989; **Fellow:** Allergy & Immunology, Mount Sinai Med Ctr 1991

Cardiac Electrophysiology

Cohen, Martin B MD (CE) - **Spec Exp:** Arrhythmias; Pacemakers; Defibrillators; Coronary Angioplasty/Stents; **Hospital:** Westchester Med Ctr, White Plains Hosp (page 652); **Address:** Westchester Heart & Vascular, 19 Bradhurst Ave Fl 3 - Ste 3850 South, Hawthorne, NY 10532-2140; **Phone:** 914-909-6900; **Board Cert:** Internal Medicine 1983; Cardiovascular Disease 1985; Cardiac Electrophysiology 2006; Interventional Cardiology 2004; **Med School:** SUNY Downstate 1980; **Resid:** Internal Medicine, Univ Hosp 1983; **Fellow:** Cardiovascular Disease, Univ Hosp 1985; Interventional Cardiology, Westchester Co Med Ctr 1986; **Fac Appt:** Assoc Prof Med, NY Med Coll

Iwai, Sei MD (CE) - **Spec Exp:** Catheter Ablation; Pacemakers/Defibrillators; Atrial Fibrillation; Defibrillator Cable Extraction; **Hospital:** Westchester Med Ctr; **Address:** Westchester Heart & Vascular, 19 Bradhurst Ave, Fl 3, Ste 3850 South, Hawthorne, NY 10532; **Phone:** 914-909-6900; **Board Cert:** Cardiovascular Disease 2011; Cardiac Electrophysiology 2011; **Med School:** Columbia P&S 1994; **Resid:** Internal Medicine, NY-Presby/Columbia Univ Med Ctr 1997; **Fellow:** Cardiovascular Disease, NY-Presby/Weill Cornell Med Ctr 2000; Cardiac Electrophysiology, NY-Presby/Weill Cornell Med Ctr 2001; **Fac Appt:** Prof Med, NY Med Coll

Rubin, David A MD (CE) - **Spec Exp:** Arrhythmias; Radiofrequency Ablation; Pacemakers/Defibrillators; **Hospital:** NY-Presby/Columbia Univ Med Ctr, NY (page 102), White Plains Hosp (page 652); **Address:** 222 Westchester Ave, White Plains, NY 10604; **Phone:** 914-428-3888; **Board Cert:** Internal Medicine 1978; Cardiovascular Disease 1981; Cardiac Electrophysiology 2012; **Med School:** Columbia P&S 1975; **Resid:** Internal Medicine, NY-Presby/Columbia Univ Med Ctr 1978; **Fellow:** Cardiovascular Disease, Mount Sinai Med Ctr 1980; **Fac Appt:** Clin Prof Med, Columbia P&S

Sorbera, Carmine A MD (CE) - **Spec Exp:** Arrhythmias; Cardiac Catheterization; **Hospital:** Northern Westchester Hosp; **Address:** Columbia Med Grp, 19 Bradhurst Ave, Ste 700, Hawthorne, NY 10532; **Phone:** 914-593-7800; **Board Cert:** Internal Medicine 1987; Cardiovascular Disease 1989; Cardiac Electrophysiology 2004; **Med School:** NY Med Coll 1983; **Resid:** Internal Medicine, Westchester Med Ctr 1987; **Fellow:** Cardiovascular Disease, Westchester Med Ctr 1989; Cardiac Electrophysiology, Westchester Med Ctr 1990

Cardiovascular Disease

Cappucci, Roger Vincent MD (Cv) - **Spec Exp:** Echocardiography; Cardiac Stress Testing; **Hospital:** White Plains Hosp (page 652); **Address:** Scarsdale Medical Group, 600 Mamaroneck Ave, Ste 200, Harrison, NY 10528; **Phone:** 914-723-8100; **Board Cert:** Internal Medicine 2013; Cardiovascular Disease 2005; **Med School:** Cornell Univ-Weill Med Coll 1989; **Resid:** Internal Medicine, NY-Presby/Weill Cornell Med Ctr 1992; **Fellow:** Cardiovascular Disease, Montefiore Med Ctr 1995

Catanese, James W MD (Cv) - **Spec Exp:** Coronary Artery Disease; Congestive Heart Failure; Heart Valve Disease; **Hospital:** Northern Westchester Hosp, Westchester Med Ctr; **Address:** Westchester Health- Cardiology, 105 S Bedford Rd, Ste 320, Mt Kisco, NY 10549; **Phone:** 914-242-9400; **Board Cert:** Cardiovascular Disease 2005; **Med School:** Albany Med Coll 1988; **Resid:** Internal Medicine, Montefiore Med Ctr 1991; **Fellow:** Cardiovascular Disease, Montefiore Med Ctr 1994

Charney, Richard MD (Cv) - **Spec Exp:** Interventional Cardiology; Heart Valve Disease; Coronary Artery Disease; Peripheral Vascular Disease; **Hospital:** Montefiore New Rochelle Hosp (page 100), NY-Presby/Weill Cornell Med Ctr, NY (page 102); **Address:** Sound Shore Cardiology Assocs, 175 Memorial Hwy, Ste 1-1, New Rochelle, NY 10801; **Phone:** 914-235-3535; **Board Cert:** Internal Medicine 1989; Cardiovascular Disease 2011; Interventional Cardiology 2010; **Med School:** Mount Sinai Sch Med 1986; **Resid:** Internal Medicine, Mt Sinai Hosp 1989; **Fellow:** Cardiovascular Disease, Montefiore Med Ctr 1992; Interventional Cardiology, Montefiore Med Ctr 1993; **Fac Appt:** Asst Prof Med, Cornell Univ-Weill Med Coll

Cooper, Jerome MD (Cv) - **Spec Exp:** Coronary Artery Disease; Hypertension; Heart Valve Disease; **Hospital:** Montefiore New Rochelle Hosp (page 100), NY-Presby/Columbia Univ Med Ctr, NY (page 102); **Address:** Westchester Heart Specialists, 150 Lockwood Ave, Ste 28, New Rochelle, NY 10801; **Phone:** 914-633-7870; **Board Cert:** Internal Medicine 1968; Cardiovascular Disease 1973; **Med School:** SUNY Hlth Sci Ctr 1961; **Resid:** Internal Medicine, Baltimore City Hosps 1963; Internal Medicine, Montefiore Hosp Med Ctr 1965; **Fellow:** Cardiovascular Disease, Johns Hopkins Univ Hosp 1967; **Fac Appt:** Assoc Clin Prof Med, Columbia P&S

Cziner, David MD (Cv) - **Spec Exp:** Coronary Artery Disease; Cholesterol/Lipid Disorders; **Hospital:** White Plains Hosp (page 652), Greenwich Hosp (page 970); **Address:** WestMed Medical Group, 210 Westchester Ave, White Plains, NY 10604; **Phone:** 914-305-2700; **Board Cert:** Internal Medicine 1989; Cardiovascular Disease 2011; Nuclear Cardiology 2003; **Med School:** NYU Sch Med 1986; **Resid:** Internal Medicine, Bellevue/NYU Med Ctr 1989; **Fellow:** Cardiovascular Disease, Bellevue/NYU Med Ctr 1992

DeLuca, Albert J MD (Cv) - **Spec Exp:** Coronary Artery Disease; Cholesterol/Lipid Disorders; **Hospital:** NY-Presby/Columbia Univ Med Ctr, NY (page 102), White Plains Hosp (page 652); **Address:** Columbia Doctors Medical Grp, 15 N Broadway Fl 2, White Plains, NY 10601-2225; **Phone:** 914-428-2600; **Board Cert:** Cardiovascular Disease 2013; Internal Medicine 1989; **Med School:** SUNY Downstate 1986; **Resid:** Internal Medicine, Mount Sinai Med Ctr 1989; **Fellow:** Cardiovascular Disease, Westchester Med Ctr 1991; **Fac Appt:** Asst Prof Med, NY Med Coll

Fass, Arthur MD (Cv) - **Spec Exp:** Preventive Cardiology; Coronary Artery Disease; Hypertension; Cholesterol/Lipid Disorders; **Hospital:** Phelps Meml Hosp Ctr, Westchester Med Ctr; **Address:** 465 N State Rd, Briarcliff Manor, NY 10510; **Phone:** 914-762-5810; **Board Cert:** Internal Medicine 1979; Cardiovascular Disease 1981; **Med School:** NY Med Coll 1976; **Resid:** Internal Medicine, Metropolitan Hosp 1979; **Fellow:** Cardiovascular Disease, Westchester Med Ctr 1981

Feld, Michael MD (Cv) - **Spec Exp:** Pacemakers; Coronary Artery Disease; Congestive Heart Failure; **Hospital:** Phelps Meml Hosp Ctr, St. John's Riverside Hosp-Dobbs Ferry Pavil; **Address:** 150 White Plains Rd, Tarrytown, NY 10591-4500; **Phone:** 914-631-2895; **Board Cert:** Internal Medicine 1980; Cardiovascular Disease 1983; **Med School:** Penn State Coll Med 1977; **Resid:** Internal Medicine, Montefiore Med Ctr 1981; **Fellow:** Cardiovascular Disease, Montefiore Med Ctr 1983; **Fac Appt:** Asst Clin Prof Med, Albert Einstein Coll Med

Fishbach, Mitchell MD (Cv) - **Spec Exp:** Non-Invasive Cardiology; Sports Medicine; Nuclear Cardiology; **Hospital:** Lawrence Hosp Ctr (page 102), NY-Presby/Columbia Univ Med Ctr, NY (page 102); **Address:** Westmed Med Grp, Cardiology, 73 Market St, Yonkers, NY 10710; **Phone:** 914-831-6880; **Board Cert:** Internal Medicine 1980; Cardiovascular Disease 1983; **Med School:** Albert Einstein Coll Med 1977; **Resid:** Internal Medicine, Montefiore Med Ctr 1980; **Fellow:** Cardiovascular Disease, Montefiore Med Ctr 1982

Frishman, William MD (Cv) - **Spec Exp:** Coronary Artery Disease; Preventive Cardiology; Hypertension; Heart Failure; **Hospital:** Westchester Med Ctr; **Address:** 19 Bradhurst Ave, Ste 3070 North, Hawthorne, NY 10532; **Phone:** 914-372-7887; **Board Cert:** Internal Medicine 1997; Cardiovascular Disease 1997; **Med School:** Boston Univ 1969; **Resid:** Internal Medicine, Montefiore Med Ctr 1971; Internal Medicine, Bronx Muni Hosp 1972; **Fellow:** Cardiovascular Disease, NY Hosp 1974; **Fac Appt:** Prof Med, NY Med Coll

Gabelman, Gary S MD (Cv) - **Spec Exp:** Non-Invasive Cardiology; Echocardiography; Nuclear Cardiology; Preventive Cardiology; **Hospital:** Lawrence Hosp Ctr (page 102), NY-Presby/Columbia Univ Med Ctr, NY (page 102); **Address:** Westmed Med Grp, Cardiology, 73 Market St, Yonkers, NY 10710; **Phone:** 914-831-6880; **Board Cert:** Internal Medicine 1988; Cardiovascular Disease 2011; **Med School:** Mount Sinai Sch Med 1985; **Resid:** Internal Medicine, Montefiore Med Ctr 1989; **Fellow:** Cardiovascular Disease, Montefiore Med Ctr 1991; **Fac Appt:** Assoc Clin Prof Med, Columbia P&S

Ganem, Amanda R MD (Cv) - **Spec Exp:** Coronary Artery Disease; Cardiac CT Angiography; Transesophageal Echocardiogram (TEE); Nuclear Cardiology; **Hospital:** Greenwich Hosp (page 970), White Plains Hosp (page 652); **Address:** WestMed Medical Group, Cardiology, 1 Theal Rd, Rye, NY 10580; **Phone:** 914-848-8760; **Board Cert:** Cardiovascular Disease 2007; Echocardiography 2007; **Med School:** NY Med Coll 2000; **Resid:** Internal Medicine, Long Island Jewish Med Ctr 2004; **Fellow:** Cardiovascular Disease, N Shore Univ Hosp 2007

Gass, Alan MD (Cv) - **Spec Exp:** Heart Failure; Transplant Medicine-Heart; **Hospital:** Westchester Med Ctr; **Address:** 19 Bradhurst Ave, Ste 3850 South, Hawthorne, NY 10532; **Phone:** 914-909-6900; **Board Cert:** Cardiovascular Disease 2012; Advanced Heart Failure & Transplant Cardiology 2012; **Med School:** Italy 1984; **Resid:** Internal Medicine, LIJ Med Ctr 1987; **Fellow:** Cardiovascular Disease, Beth Israel Med Ctr 1988; Transplant Medicine, Stanford Univ Med Ctr 1989; **Fac Appt:** Assoc Prof Med, NY Med Coll

Gitler, Bernard MD (Cv) - **Spec Exp:** Coronary Artery Disease; Heart Valve Disease; Congestive Heart Failure; Atrial Fibrillation; **Hospital:** Montefiore New Rochelle Hosp (page 100), Montefiore Med Ctr-Moses Campus (page 100); **Address:** Westchester Heart Specialists, 150 Lockwood Ave, Ste 28, New Rochelle, NY 10801-4913; **Phone:** 914-633-7870; **Board Cert:** Internal Medicine 2009; Cardiovascular Disease 2009; Critical Care Medicine 2010; Advanced Heart Failure & Transplant Cardiology 2012; **Med School:** Cornell Univ-Weill Med Coll 1976; **Resid:** Internal Medicine, Jacobi Med Ctr 1979; **Fellow:** Cardiovascular Disease, Montefiore Med Ctr 1981; **Fac Appt:** Assoc Prof Med, Albert Einstein Coll Med

Greif, Richard H MD (Cv) - **Hospital:** Saint Joseph's Med Ctr - Yonkers; **Address:** 127 S Broadway Fl 4th - Ste 409, Yonkers, NY 10701; **Phone:** 914-378-7583; **Board Cert:** Internal Medicine 1978; Cardiovascular Disease 1981; **Med School:** NY Med Coll 1975; **Resid:** Internal Medicine, Metropolitan Hosp 1978; **Fellow:** Cardiovascular Disease, St Vincents Hosp 1981; **Fac Appt:** Assoc Clin Prof Med, NY Med Coll

Hamroff, Glenn S MD (Cv) - **Spec Exp:** Heart Failure; **Hospital:** Hudson Valley Hosp Ctr, NYU Langone Med Ctr (page 104); **Address:** NYU Langone at Hudson Valley Cardiology, 1985 Crompound Rd, Cortland Manor, NY 10567; **Phone:** 914-736-0703; **Board Cert:** Cardiovascular Disease 2007; **Med School:** SUNY Downstate 1990; **Resid:** Internal Medicine, Montefiore Med Ctr 1993; **Fellow:** Cardiovascular Disease, Montefiore Med Ctr 1996; Heart Failure, Montefiore Med Ctr 1997

Hart, Douglas J MD (Cv) - **Spec Exp:** Non-Invasive Cardiology; Nuclear Cardiology; Echocardiography; Congestive Heart Failure; **Hospital:** Lawrence Hosp Ctr (page 102), NY-Presby/Columbia Univ Med Ctr, NY (page 102); **Address:** WestMed Med Grp, Ridge Hill, 73 Market St, Ste 215, Yonkers, NY 10710; **Phone:** 914-831-6880; **Board Cert:** Cardiovascular Disease 2007; **Med School:** Univ Mich Med Sch 1990; **Resid:** Internal Medicine, NY-Presby/Columbia Univ Med Ctr 1993; **Fellow:** Cardiovascular Disease, NY-Presby/Columbia Univ Med Ctr 1994; Nuclear Cardiology, Georgetown Med Ctr; **Fac Appt:** Asst Clin Prof Med, Columbia P&S

Kaplan, Kenneth C MD (Cv) - **Hospital:** Phelps Meml Hosp Ctr; **Address:** 160 N State Rd, Briarcliff Manor, NY 10510; **Phone:** 914-762-3821; **Board Cert:** Internal Medicine 1970; Cardiovascular Disease 1975; Echocardiography 1996; **Med School:** NYU Sch Med 1962; **Resid:** Internal Medicine, Bellevue Hosp 1966; **Fellow:** Cardiovascular Disease, Bellevue Hosp/NYU 1969; **Fac Appt:** Asst Clin Prof Med, NY Med Coll

Kay, Richard H MD (Cv) - **Spec Exp:** Preventive Cardiology; Congestive Heart Failure; Non-Invasive Cardiology; **Hospital:** White Plains Hosp (page 652), NY-Presby/Columbia Univ Med Ctr, NY (page 102); **Address:** Columbia Doctors Medical Group, 19 Bradhurst Ave, Ste 700, Hawthorne, NY 10532-2140; **Phone:** 914-593-7800; **Board Cert:** Internal Medicine 1979; Cardiovascular Disease 1981; **Med School:** Johns Hopkins Univ 1976; **Resid:** Internal Medicine, Columbia-Presby Med Ctr 1979; **Fellow:** Cardiovascular Disease, Mount Sinai Hosp 1981; **Fac Appt:** Assoc Prof Med, NY Med Coll

Keating, Richard J MD (Cv) - **Hospital:** Northern Westchester Hosp; **Address:** 110 S Bedford Rd, Mount Kisco, NY 10549; **Phone:** 914-241-1050; **Board Cert:** Internal Medicine 2004; Cardiovascular Disease 2008; Echocardiography 2009; Nuclear Cardiology 2009; **Med School:** Georgetown Univ 2001; **Resid:** Internal Medicine, Mayo Clinic 2004; **Fellow:** Cardiovascular Disease, NY-Presby/Weill Cornell Med Ctr 2008

Keltz, Theodore N MD (Cv) - **Spec Exp:** Coronary Artery Disease; Heart Valve Disease; Arrhythmias; Preventive Cardiology; **Hospital:** Montefiore New Rochelle Hosp (page 100), Montefiore Med Ctr-Moses Campus (page 100); **Address:** Westchester Heart Specialists, 150 Lockwood Ave, Ste 28, New Rochelle, NY 10801; **Phone:** 914-633-7870; **Board Cert:** Internal Medicine 1983; Cardiovascular Disease 1985; Echocardiography 2006; Nuclear Cardiology 1996; **Med School:** Albany Med Coll 1980; **Resid:** Internal Medicine, Mt Sinai Med Ctr 1983; **Fellow:** Cardiovascular Disease, Montefiore Med Ctr 1985; **Fac Appt:** Assoc Clin Prof Med, Albert Einstein Coll Med

Kupersmith, Andrew C MD (Cv) - **Hospital:** Westchester Med Ctr, White Plains Hosp (page 652); **Address:** Columbia Doctors Medical Group, 19 Bradhurst Ave, Ste 700, Hawthorne, NY 10532; **Phone:** 914-593-7800; **Board Cert:** Cardiovascular Disease 2014; **Med School:** Univ MD Sch Med 1995; **Resid:** Internal Medicine, LIJ Med Ctr 1998; **Fellow:** Cardiovascular Disease, Wesctchester Med Ctr 2001; **Fac Appt:** Asst Prof Med, NY Med Coll

Leonard, Daniel MD (Cv) - **Hospital:** Northern Westchester Hosp, Westchester Med Ctr; **Address:** Mt Kisco Med Grp, 110 S Bedford Rd Bldg 110, Mt Kisco, NY 10549-3433; **Phone:** 914-241-1050; **Board Cert:** Internal Medicine 1984; Cardiovascular Disease 1987; **Med School:** Univ Cincinnati 1981; **Resid:** Internal Medicine, NY-Presby/Weil Cornell Med Ctr 1984; **Fellow:** Cardiovascular Disease, Montefiore Med Ctr 1986; **Fac Appt:** Assoc Clin Prof Med, NY Med Coll

Levine, Evan MD (Cv) - **Spec Exp:** Cardiac Stress Testing; **Hospital:** Montefiore Med Ctr-Moses Campus (page 100), St. John's Riverside Hosp-Andrus Pavil; **Address:** 530 Yonkers Ave, Yonkers, NY 10704; **Phone:** 914-308-7350; **Board Cert:** Internal Medicine 1988; Cardiovascular Disease 2011; **Med School:** Mount Sinai Sch Med 1985; **Resid:** Internal Medicine, Montefiore Med Ctr 1988; **Fellow:** Cardiovascular Disease, Montefiore Med Ctr 1990; **Fac Appt:** Asst Clin Prof Med, Albert Einstein Coll Med

Lieb, Mark MD (Cv) - **Hospital:** Northern Westchester Hosp; **Address:** Mount Kisco Medical Group, 110 S Bedford Rd Fl 2, Mt Kisco, NY 10549-3412; **Phone:** 914-241-1050; **Board Cert:** Cardiovascular Disease 2006; **Med School:** Boston Univ 1988; **Resid:** Internal Medicine, Mt Sinai Med Ctr 1991; **Fellow:** Cardiovascular Disease, Mt Sinai Med Ctr 1995

Matos, Marshall MD (Cv) - **Spec Exp:** Coronary Artery Disease; Preventive Cardiology; Arrhythmias; Cholesterol/Lipid Disorders; **Hospital:** Montefiore New Rochelle Hosp (page 100), Lenox Hill Hosp; **Address:** 140 Lockwood Ave, Ste 310, New Rochelle, NY 10801-4909; **Phone:** 914-576-7171; **Board Cert:** Internal Medicine 1980; Cardiovascular Disease 1985; **Med School:** Albert Einstein Coll Med 1977; **Resid:** Internal Medicine, Bronx Muni Hosp 1981; **Fellow:** Cardiovascular Disease, Albert Einstein Coll Med 1983; **Fac Appt:** Asst Prof Med, NYU Sch Med

McClung, John Arthur MD (Cv) - **Spec Exp:** Echocardiography; **Hospital:** Westchester Med Ctr; **Address:** 19 Bradhurst Ave, Ste 3850 South, Hawthorne, NY 10532; **Phone:** 914-909-6900; **Board Cert:** Internal Medicine 1980; Cardiovascular Disease 1983; **Med School:** NY Med Coll 1975; **Resid:** Internal Medicine, Misericordia Hosp Med Ctr 1976; Internal Medicine, Lincoln Med & Mental Hlth Ctr 1979; **Fellow:** Cardiovascular Disease, Westchester Med Ctr 1982; **Fac Appt:** Prof Med, NY Med Coll

Medina, Emma MD (Cv) - **Spec Exp:** Non-Invasive Cardiology; **Hospital:** Montefiore New Rochelle Hosp (page 100), Montefiore Med Ctr-Einstein Campus (page 100); **Address:** 140 Lockwood Ave, Ste 310, New Rochelle, NY 10801-4909; **Phone:** 914-632-1600; **Board Cert:** Internal Medicine 1982; Cardiovascular Disease 1985; **Med School:** NYU Sch Med 1979; **Resid:** Internal Medicine, Jacobi Med Ctr 1982; **Fellow:** Cardiovascular Disease, Jacobi Med Ctr 1984; **Fac Appt:** Asst Clin Prof Med, Albert Einstein Coll Med

Mercando, Anthony MD (Cv) - **Spec Exp:** Cholesterol/Lipid Disorders; Preventive Cardiology; **Hospital:** Lawrence Hosp Ctr (page 102), NY-Presby/Columbia Univ Med Ctr, NY (page 102); **Address:** Westmed Med Grp, Cardiology, 73 Market St, Yonkers, NY 10710; **Phone:** 914-831-6880; **Board Cert:** Internal Medicine 1983; Cardiovascular Disease 1987; **Med School:** Harvard Med Sch 1980; **Resid:** Internal Medicine, Montefiore Med Ctr 1984; **Fellow:** Cardiovascular Disease, Montefiore Med Ctr 1986; **Fac Appt:** Clin Prof Med, Albert Einstein Coll Med

Paley, Ari J MD (Cv) - **Spec Exp:** Coronary Artery Disease; **Hospital:** White Plains Hosp (page 652); **Address:** 30 Davis Ave, White Plains, NY 10605; **Phone:** 914-328-2355; **Board Cert:** Integrative Medicine 2006; Cardiovascular Disease 2009; **Med School:** Albert Einstein Coll Med 2002; **Resid:** Internal Medicine, NY Presby-Columbia Med Ctr 2006; **Fellow:** Cardiovascular Disease, NYU Med Ctr 2009

Perry-Bottinger, Lynne V MD (Cv) - **Spec Exp:** Cardiac Catheterization; Coronary Angioplasty/Stents; Heart Disease in Women; Heart Disease in African Americans; **Hospital:** NY-Presby/Columbia Univ Med Ctr, NY (page 102), Montefiore New Rochelle Hosp (page 100); **Address:** Clinical & Interventional Cardiology, 140A Lockwood Ave, New Rochelle, NY 10801; **Phone:** 914-576-7577; **Med School:** Yale Univ 1986; **Resid:** Internal Medicine, Yale-New Haven Hosp 1990; **Fellow:** Cardiovascular Disease, Johns Hopkins Hosp 1993; Interventional Cardiology, Johns Hopkins Hosp 1994; **Fac Appt:** Asst Clin Prof Med, Columbia P&S

Pilchik, Robert M MD (Cv) - **Spec Exp:** Cardiac Catheterization; Echocardiography; Nuclear Cardiology; **Hospital:** Northern Westchester Hosp, White Plains Hosp (page 652); **Address:** Westchester Health Associates, 1888 Commerce St, Yorktown Heights, NY 10598; **Phone:** 914-962-4000; **Board Cert:** Cardiovascular Disease 2013; Nuclear Cardiology 2006; **Med School:** Mount Sinai Sch Med 1995; **Resid:** Internal Medicine, St Lukes-Roosevelt Hosp 1998; **Fellow:** Cardiovascular Disease, St Lukes-Roosevelt Hosp 2001

Price Jr, Thomas J MD (Cv) - **Hospital:** Montefiore Mt Vernon Hosp (page 100), Montefiore New Rochelle Hosp (page 100); **Address:** 105 Stevens Ave, Ste 603, Mt Vernon, NY 10550; **Phone:** 914-664-4052; **Board Cert:** Internal Medicine 1984; Cardiovascular Disease 1987; **Med School:** Univ Cincinnati 1975; **Resid:** Internal Medicine, Harlem Hosp 1979; **Fellow:** Cardiovascular Disease, Harlem Hosp 1983; **Fac Appt:** Asst Clin Prof Med, Columbia P&S

Pucillo, Anthony MD (Cv) - **Spec Exp:** Coronary Angioplasty/Stents; Peripheral Vascular Disease; Cardiac Catheterization; **Hospital:** NY-Presby/Columbia Univ Med Ctr, NY (page 102), Westchester Med Ctr; **Address:** 19 Bradhurst Ave, Ste 700, Hawthorne, NY 10532; **Phone:** 914-593-7800; **Board Cert:** Internal Medicine 1981; Cardiovascular Disease 1983; **Med School:** Mount Sinai Sch Med 1978; **Resid:** Internal Medicine, Columbia-Presby Med Ctr 1981; **Fellow:** Cardiovascular Disease, Columbia-Presby Med Ctr 1984; **Fac Appt:** Assoc Prof Med, NY Med Coll

Sheikh, Shahid H MD (Cv) - **Hospital:** St. John's Riverside Hosp-Andrus Pavil, Montefiore Med Ctr-Wakefield Campus (page 100); **Address:** 970 N Broadway, Ste 210, Yonkers, NY 10701-1311; **Phone:** 914-963-0111; **Board Cert:** Internal Medicine 1977; Cardiovascular Disease 1979; **Med School:** Pakistan 1971; **Resid:** Internal Medicine, Our Lady of Mercy Med Ctr 1977

Silver, Michael M MD (Cv) - **Spec Exp:** Hypertension; Cholesterol/Lipid Disorders; Coronary Artery Disease; **Hospital:** White Plains Hosp (page 652), Greenwich Hosp (page 970); **Address:** WestMed Medical Group, 210 Westchester Ave, White Plains, NY 10604; **Phone:** 914-305-2700 x2; **Board Cert:** Internal Medicine 1980; Cardiovascular Disease 1983; **Med School:** SUNY Downstate 1977; **Resid:** Internal Medicine, Thomas Jefferson Univ Hosp 1980; **Fellow:** Cardiovascular Disease, Presby-Hosp Univ Penn 1982

Tarkin, Howard N MD (Cv) - **Spec Exp:** Pacemakers/Defibrillators; **Hospital:** Hudson Valley Hosp Ctr, NYU Langone Med Ctr (page 104); **Address:** NYU Langone at Hudson Valley Cardiology, 1985 Crompound Rd, Cortlandt Manor, NY 10567; **Phone:** 914-736-0703; **Board Cert:** Cardiovascular Disease 2005; **Med School:** SUNY Downstate 1987; **Resid:** Internal Medicine, Montefiore Med Ctr 1990; **Fellow:** Cardiovascular Disease, Univ Conn Med Ctr 1994; **Fac Appt:** Asst Clin Prof Med, NYU Sch Med

Tartaglia, Joseph J MD (Cv) - **Spec Exp:** Angina; Congestive Heart Failure; Arrhythmias; **Hospital:** White Plains Hosp (page 652), Greenwich Hosp (page 970); **Address:** 311 North St, Ste 402, White Plains, NY 10605-2232; **Phone:** 914-946-3388; **Board Cert:** Internal Medicine 1988; Cardiovascular Disease 2011; Geriatric Medicine 2004; **Med School:** Italy 1984; **Resid:** Internal Medicine, Our Lady of Mercy Med Ctr 1988; **Fellow:** Cardiovascular Disease, N Shore Univ Hosp 1990; **Fac Appt:** Asst Clin Prof Med, NY Med Coll

Wallach, Ronald MD (Cv) - **Hospital:** Northern Westchester Hosp; **Address:** Mount Kisco Medical Group, 110 S Bedford Rd Fl 2, Mount Kisco, NY 10549; **Phone:** 914-241-1050; **Board Cert:** Internal Medicine 1975; Cardiovascular Disease 1977; **Med School:** Columbia P&S 1970; **Resid:** Internal Medicine, NY-Preby/Columbia Univ Med Ctr 1975; **Fellow:** Cardiovascular Disease, Univ of Alabama Hosp 1977

Weissman, Ronald MD (Cv) - **Spec Exp:** Coronary Artery Disease; Congestive Heart Failure; Arrhythmias; Hypertrophic Cardiomyopathy; **Hospital:** White Plains Hosp (page 652), Westchester Med Ctr; **Address:** 15 N Broadway Fl 2, White Plains, NY 10601; **Phone:** 914-428-6000; **Board Cert:** Internal Medicine 1980; Cardiovascular Disease 1983; **Med School:** NY Med Coll 1977; **Resid:** Internal Medicine, LI Jewish Hosp 1980; **Fellow:** Cardiovascular Disease, LI Jewish Hosp 1982; **Fac Appt:** Assoc Clin Prof Med, NY Med Coll

Yuen, Jeannette MD (Cv) - **Spec Exp:** Coronary Artery Disease; **Hospital:** White Plains Hosp (page 652); **Address:** Scarsdale Medical Group, 600 Mamaroneck Ave Fl 2, Harrison, NY 10583; **Phone:** 914-723-8100; **Board Cert:** Internal Medicine 2009; Cardiovascular Disease 2006; **Med School:** Northwestern Univ 1988; **Resid:** Internal Medicine, Michael Reese Hosp 1991; **Fellow:** Cardiovascular Disease, Montefiore Med Ctr 1994

Zimmerman, Franklin Harrison MD (Cv) - **Spec Exp:** Preventive Cardiology; Sports Medicine-Cardiology; Cholesterol/Lipid Disorders; Hypertension; **Hospital:** Phelps Meml Hosp Ctr, Westchester Med Ctr; **Address:** Phelps Cardiology at Briarcliff, 465 N State Rd, Briarcliff Manor, NY 10510-1468; **Phone:** 914-762-5810; **Board Cert:** Internal Medicine 1983; Cardiovascular Disease 1987; Critical Care Medicine 2006; **Med School:** Brown Univ 1980; **Resid:** Internal Medicine, St Lukes-Roosevelt Hosp 1983; **Fellow:** Cardiovascular Disease, St Lukes-Roosevelt Hosp Ctr 1988; **Fac Appt:** Asst Prof Med, Columbia P&S

Child & Adolescent Psychiatry

Cohen, Lee Steven MD (ChAP) - **Spec Exp:** Anxiety & Mood Disorders; Psychopharmacology; ADD/ADHD; Autism; **Hospital:** Morgan Stanley Chldns Hosp of NY-Presby, NY (page 102), NY-Presby/Columbia Univ Med Ctr, NY (page 102); **Address:** 623 Warburton Ave, Hastings On Hudson, NY 10706-1523; **Phone:** 914-478-1330; **Board Cert:** Psychiatry 1987; Child & Adolescent Psychiatry 1988; **Med School:** SUNY Stony Brook 1982; **Resid:** Psychiatry, Mt Sinai Med Ctr 1985; **Fellow:** Child & Adolescent Psychiatry, Columbia-Presby Med Ctr 1987; **Fac Appt:** Asst Clin Prof Psyc, Columbia P&S

Fink, Candida A MD (ChAP) - **Spec Exp:** Anxiety & Mood Disorders; ADD/ADHD; Developmental Disorders; **Address:** 4 Stanton Cir, New Rochelle, NY 10804; **Phone:** 877-534-1090; **Board Cert:** Psychiatry 1994; Child & Adolescent Psychiatry 2006; **Med School:** Boston Univ 1987; **Resid:** Psychiatry, Beth Israel Deaconess Hosp 1990; **Fellow:** Child & Adolescent Psychiatry, Children's Hosp 1992

Greenhill, Laurence L MD (ChAP) - **Spec Exp:** ADD/ADHD; Depression; **Hospital:** NY State Psychiatric Inst, NY-Presby/Columbia Univ Med Ctr, NY (page 102); **Address:** 9 Country Rd, Mamaroneck, NY 10543; **Phone:** 914-381-2436; **Board Cert:** Psychiatry 1975; Child & Adolescent Psychiatry 1976; **Med School:** Albert Einstein Coll Med 1967; **Resid:** Psychiatry, Bronx Muni Hosp Ctr 1972; Psychiatry, Bronx Muni Hosp Ctr 1974; **Fellow:** Child & Adolescent Psychiatry, Natl Inst Mental Hlth 1971; **Fac Appt:** Prof Psyc, Columbia P&S

Hyler, Irene MD (ChAP) - **Spec Exp:** Psychotherapy; Psychoanalysis; **Hospital:** NY-Presby/Weill Cornell Med Ctr, NY (page 102); **Address:** 2A Berkeley Rd, Scarsdale, NY 10583-1102; **Phone:** 914-472-8447; **Board Cert:** Psychiatry 1984; Child & Adolescent Psychiatry 1986; **Med School:** Albert Einstein Coll Med 1979; **Resid:** Psychiatry, Bronx Muni Hosp 1982; **Fellow:** Child & Adolescent Psychiatry, Albert Einstein Coll Med 1984; **Fac Appt:** Asst Clin Prof Psyc, Cornell Univ-Weill Med Coll

Kalikow, Kevin T MD (ChAP) - ; **Address:** 83 S Bedford Rd, Mt Kisco, NY 10549; **Phone:** 914-666-3000; **Board Cert:** Psychiatry 1984; Child & Adolescent Psychiatry 1986; **Med School:** Tulane Univ 1979; **Resid:** Psychiatry, NY Hosp-Westchester Div 1983; **Fellow:** Child & Adolescent Psychiatry, NY State Psych Inst 1985; **Fac Appt:** Asst Clin Prof Psyc, NY Med Coll

Lomonaco, Salvatore MD (ChAP) - **Hospital:** Montefiore Med Ctr-Moses Campus (page 100); **Address:** 1815 Palmer Ave, Larchmont, NY 10538; **Phone:** 914-834-0085; **Board Cert:** Psychiatry 1976; **Med School:** SUNY Downstate 1966; **Resid:** Psychiatry, Montefiore Med Ctr 1971; Child Psychiatry, Montefiore Med Ctr 1972

Rabinowitz, Ilene MD (ChAP) - **Spec Exp:** Psychopharmacology; Mood Disorders; Anxiety; **Address:** 50 Main St, Ste 1000, White Plains, NY 10606; **Phone:** 914-682-2047; **Board Cert:** Psychiatry 1993; Child & Adolescent Psychiatry 2008; **Med School:** Mount Sinai Sch Med 1988; **Resid:** Psychiatry, NY-Presby/Westchester Div 1992; **Fellow:** Child & Adolescent Psychiatry, NY-Presby/Columbia Univ Med Ctr 1994

Rubinstein, Boris MD (ChAP) - **Spec Exp:** Psychopharmacology; Neuro-Psychiatry; Anxiety & Mood Disorders; Developmental Disorders; **Hospital:** NY-Presby/Weill Cornell Med Ctr, NY (page 102), Mt Sinai St. Luke's; **Address:** 623 Warburton Ave, Hastings On Hudson, NY 10706; **Phone:** 914-478-1330; **Board Cert:** Pediatrics 1976; Psychiatry 1979; Child & Adolescent Psychiatry 1981; **Med School:** Mexico 1970; **Resid:** Pediatrics, Chldns Hosp 1974; Psychiatry, Jacobi Med Ctr 1976; **Fellow:** Child & Adolescent Psychiatry, Jacobi Med Ctr 1978

Schreiber, Klaus MD (ChAP) - **Spec Exp:** Developmental Disorders; **Address:** 1 Neperan Rd, Tarrytown, NY 10591; **Phone:** 914-332-0270; **Board Cert:** Psychiatry 1976; Child & Adolescent Psychiatry 1986; **Med School:** Germany 1966; **Resid:** Psychiatry, Elmhurst City Hosp Ctr 1971; Psychiatry, Westchester Med Ctr 1972; **Fellow:** Child & Adolescent Psychiatry, Westchester Med Ctr 1973; Child & Adolescent Psychiatry, Albert Einstein Coll Med 1982; **Fac Appt:** Asst Prof Psyc, NY Med Coll

Seaver, Robert MD (ChAP) - **Spec Exp:** Forensic Psychiatry; Art & Creativity; Psychopharmacology; **Address:** 83 S Bedford Rd Fl 2nd, Mt Kisco, NY 10549; **Phone:** 914-241-8979; **Board Cert:** Pediatrics 1978; Psychiatry 1984; Child & Adolescent Psychiatry 1986; **Med School:** Mount Sinai Sch Med 1973; **Resid:** Pediatrics, Mount Sinai Med Ctr 1975; Pediatrics, St Lukes-Roosevelt Hosp 1976; **Fellow:** Psychiatry, NY-Presby/Westchester Div 1984; Child & Adolescent Psychiatry, Jacobi Med Ctr 1985

Silva, Raul R MD (ChAP) - **Spec Exp:** Autism; ADD/ADHD; Depression; Psychopharmacology; **Address:** 2975 Westchester Ave, Ste 308, Purchase, NY 10577; **Phone:** 201-218-1380; **Board Cert:** Psychiatry 1991; Child & Adolescent Psychiatry 1992; **Med School:** Mexico 1983; **Resid:** Psychiatry, St Vincent's Medical Ctr 1988; **Fellow:** Child & Adolescent Psychiatry, St Luke's Hosp 1990; Research, Bellevue Hosp Ctr 1992

Silverman, Amy MD (ChAP) - **Spec Exp:** Anxiety & Depression; ADD/ADHD; **Hospital:** NY-Presby/Westchester Div, NY (page 102); **Address:** 600 Mamaroneck Ave, Ste 400, Harrison, NY 10528; **Phone:** 914-301-9465; **Board Cert:** Psychiatry 2013; Child & Adolescent Psychiatry 2013; **Med School:** Mount Sinai Sch Med 1998; **Resid:** Psychiatry, Brigham and Women's Hosp 2001; **Fellow:** Child Psychiatry, NY Presby/Cornell Med Ctr 2003; **Fac Appt:** Asst Clin Prof ChAP, Cornell Univ

Slater, Jonathan Allen MD (ChAP) - **Spec Exp:** Psychopharmacology; Psychiatry in Physical Illness; **Hospital:** Morgan Stanley Chldns Hosp of NY-Presby, NY (page 102); **Address:** 1 Bridge St, Ste 24, Irvington, NY 10533; **Phone:** 914-591-4040; **Board Cert:** Psychiatry 1991; Child & Adolescent Psychiatry 1993; Psychosomatic Medicine 2006; **Med School:** Columbia P&S 1985; **Resid:** Psychiatry, NY State Psych Inst 1990; **Fellow:** Research, Columbia Univ 1986; Child & Adolescent Psychiatry, NY Presby-Columbia Med Ctr 1992; **Fac Appt:** Clin Prof Psyc, Columbia P&S

Walker, Audrey MD (ChAP) - **Spec Exp:** Psychosomatic Disorders; **Hospital:** Montefiore Med Ctr-Moses Campus (page 100); **Address:** 2005 Palmer Ave, Larchmont, NY 10538; **Phone:** 914-834-2214; **Board Cert:** Psychiatry 1992; Child & Adolescent Psychiatry 1994; Psychosomatic Medicine 2005; **Med School:** Albert Einstein Coll Med 1985; **Resid:** Psychiatry, NY Presby-Columbia Med Ctr 1990

Child Neurology

Alshansky, Anna MD (ChiN) - **Hospital:** Northern Westchester Hosp; **Address:** Mount Kisco Medical Group, 225 Veterans Rd, Yorktown Heights, NY 10598; **Phone:** 914-302-8059; **Board Cert:** Child Neurology 2009; **Med School:** Russia 1983; **Resid:** Pediatrics, City Chldns Hosp 1986; Pediatrics, Long Island Jewish Med Ctr 1995; **Fellow:** Child Neurology, Long Island Jewish Med Ctr 1998

Cantor, Liliah MD (ChiN) - **Spec Exp:** Headache; **Hospital:** Westchester Med Ctr; **Address:** Pediatric Neurological Assocs, 755 N Broadway, Medical Services Bldg, Ste 540, Sleepy Hollow, NY 10591; **Phone:** 914-358-0188; **Board Cert:** Pediatrics 2007; Child Neurology 2007; **Med School:** Russia 1986; **Resid:** Pediatrics, Bronx Lebanon Hosp 1997; **Fellow:** Child Neurology, NYU Med Ctr 2004

Jacobson, Ronald I MD (ChiN) - **Spec Exp:** Epilepsy; Headache; ADD/ADHD; Autism; **Hospital:** Westchester Med Ctr, Children's & Women's Phys.of Westchester; **Address:** Pediatric Neurology Associates, 755 N Broadway, Medical Services Bldg, Ste 540, Sleepy Hollow, NY 10591; **Phone:** 914-358-0190; **Board Cert:** Pediatrics 1981; Child Neurology 1984; **Med School:** Albert Einstein Coll Med 1975; **Resid:** Pediatrics, Yale-New Haven Hosp 1978; **Fellow:** Neurological Immunology, Yale Univ School of Med 1979; Pediatric Neurology, Univ Minn Med Ctr 1982; **Fac Appt:** Assoc Clin Prof N, NY Med Coll

Kang, Harriet MD (ChiN) - **Spec Exp:** Epilepsy/Seizure Disorders; **Hospital:** Mt Sinai Beth Israel; **Address:** 141 S Central Park Ave, Hartsdale, NY 10530; **Phone:** 914-428-0529; **Board Cert:** Pediatrics 1979; Child Neurology 1981; Clinical Neurophysiology 2006; **Med School:** Johns Hopkins Univ 1974; **Resid:** Pediatrics, Johns Hopkins Hosp 1976; Child Neurology, Univ Minn Med Ctr 1979; **Fellow:** Clinical Neurophysiology, Univ Minn Med Ctr 1980; **Fac Appt:** Assoc Prof N, Albert Einstein Coll Med

Kutscher, Martin MD (ChiN) - **Spec Exp:** ADD/ADHD; Asperger's Syndrome; Autism; **Hospital:** Westchester Med Ctr; **Address:** 800 Westchester Ave, Ste N641, Rye Brook, NY 10573; **Phone:** 914-232-1810; **Board Cert:** Pediatrics 1986; Child Neurology 1989; **Med School:** Columbia P&S 1981; **Resid:** Pediatrics, St Christopher's Hosp 1984; **Fellow:** Child Neurology, Montefiore Med Ctr 1987; **Fac Appt:** Asst Clin Prof Ped, NY Med Coll

Roseman, Bruce MD (ChiN) - **Spec Exp:** Asperger's Syndrome; **Hospital:** Westchester Med Ctr; **Address:** 125 S Broadway, White Plains, NY 10605-1405; **Phone:** 914-997-2032; **Board Cert:** Pediatrics 1978; Child Neurology 1982; **Med School:** Georgetown Univ 1973; **Resid:** Pediatrics, Johns Hopkins Hosp 1976; **Fellow:** Child Neurology, NY-Presby/Columbia Univ Med Ctr 1979

Sweeney, Tanya-Marie MD (ChiN) - **Spec Exp:** Neurodevelopmental Disabilities; **Hospital:** Northern Westchester Hosp; **Address:** Mount Kisco Medical Group, 110 S Bedford Rd, Mount Kisco, NY 10549-3412; **Phone:** 914-241-1050; **Board Cert:** Child Neurology 2008; **Med School:** SUNY Stony Brook 2002; **Resid:** Pediatrics, Winthrop Univ Hosp 2005; **Fellow:** Child Neurology, N Shore-LIJ Hlth System 2008

Clinical Genetics

Kronn, David F MD (CG) - **Spec Exp:** Bone Disorders-Metabolic; Bone Disorders-Inherited; **Hospital:** Westchester Med Ctr, Children's & Women's Phys.of Westchester; **Address:** Regional Medical Genetics, 503 Grasslands Rd, Ste 200, Valhalla, NY 10595; **Phone:** 914-304-5280; **Board Cert:** Clinical Genetics 2010; Clinical Biochemical Genetics 2010; **Med School:** Ireland 1989; **Resid:** Pediatrics, NYU Med Ctr 1996; **Fellow:** Clinical Genetics, NYU Med Ctr 1996; **Fac Appt:** Assoc Prof CG, NY Med Coll

Colon & Rectal Surgery

Krakovitz, Evan K MD (CRS) - **Spec Exp:** Colon & Rectal Cancer & Surgery; Hemorrhoids; Laparoscopic Surgery; Hernia; **Hospital:** Greenwich Hosp (page 970), White Plains Hosp (page 652); **Address:** Westmed Medical Group, 210 Westchester Ave, Ste 106, White Plains, NY 10604; **Phone:** 914-682-6557; **Board Cert:** Surgery 2005; Colon & Rectal Surgery 2007; **Med School:** Hahnemann Univ 1989; **Resid:** Surgery, Graduate Hospital 1994; **Fellow:** Colon & Rectal Surgery, RWJ Univ Hosp 1995; **Fac Appt:** Clin Prof CRS, Cornell Univ-Weill Med Coll

Wishner, Jerald D MD (CRS) - **Spec Exp:** Colon & Rectal Cancer; Laparoscopic Surgery; **Hospital:** Northern Westchester Hosp; **Address:** Mount Kisco Med Grp, 110 S Bedford Rd, Mount Kisco, NY 10549; **Phone:** 914-241-1050; **Board Cert:** Surgery 2004; Colon & Rectal Surgery 2006; **Med School:** Northwestern Univ 1988; **Resid:** Surgery, St Luke's-Roosevelt Hosp Ctr 1993; Colon & Rectal Surgery, Grtr Baltimore Med Ctr 1994; **Fellow:** Minimally Invasive Surgery, Eastern Va Med Sch 1995; **Fac Appt:** Asst Prof S, Columbia P&S

Dermatology

Bank, David MD (D) - **Spec Exp:** Liposuction; Skin Laser Surgery; Botox Therapy; **Hospital:** Northern Westchester Hosp, NY-Presby/Columbia Univ Med Ctr, NY (page 102); **Address:** 359 E Main St, Ste 4G, Mt Kisco, NY 10549; **Phone:** 914-241-3003; **Board Cert:** Dermatology 1989; **Med School:** Columbia P&S 1985; **Resid:** Dermatology, Columbia-Presby Med Ctr 1989; **Fac Appt:** Assoc Clin Prof D, Columbia P&S

Berkowitz, Rhonda K MD (D) - **Spec Exp:** Melanoma; Skin Cancer; **Hospital:** NY-Presby/Columbia Univ Med Ctr, NY (page 102); **Address:** 325 S Highland Ave, Briarcliff Manor, NY 10510-2031; **Phone:** 914-941-5769; **Board Cert:** Dermatology 1986; **Med School:** NYU Sch Med 1982; **Resid:** Internal Medicine, N Shore Univ Hosp 1983; Dermatology, Columbia-Presby Med Ctr 1986

Bronin, Andrew MD (D) - **Spec Exp:** Melanoma; Skin Cancer; Complex Diagnosis; **Hospital:** Greenwich Hosp (page 970), Yale-New Haven Hosp; **Address:** 4 Rye Ridge Plaza, Rye Brook, NY 10573; **Phone:** 914-253-8080; **Board Cert:** Dermatology 1981; **Med School:** NY Med Coll 1975; **Resid:** Dermatology, NY-Presby/Weill Cornell Med Ctr 1979; **Fac Appt:** Assoc Clin Prof D, Yale Univ

Burack, Lauren H MD (D) - **Hospital:** Northern Westchester Hosp, Putnam Hosp Ctr; **Address:** Mount Kisco Medical Group, 90 S Bedford Rd, Mount Kisco, NY 10549; **Phone:** 914-242-1355; **Board Cert:** Dermatology 2009; **Med School:** Georgetown Univ 1995; **Resid:** Dermatology, NY-Presby Cornell Med Ctr 2000; **Fellow:** Research, Investigative Dermatology Lab, Cornell 1999

Davis, Ira C MD (D) - **Spec Exp:** Mohs Surgery; Skin Cancer; Laser Surgery; Cosmetic Dermatology; **Hospital:** Westchester Med Ctr; **Address:** 280 N Central Park Ave, Ste 114, Hartsdale, NY 10530; **Phone:** 914-288-0500; **Board Cert:** Dermatology 1990; **Med School:** NYU Sch Med 1986; **Resid:** Dermatology, Duke Univ Med Ctr 1990; **Fellow:** Dermatologic Pharmacology, NYU Med Ctr 1991; Mohs Surgery, Wake Forest Baptist Med Ctr 1994; **Fac Appt:** Asst Clin Prof D, NY Med Coll

Evans, Lydia Marion MD (D) - **Spec Exp:** Cosmetic Dermatology; Mohs Surgery; Facial Rejuvenation; Skin Laser Surgery; **Hospital:** NY-Presby/Columbia Univ Med Ctr, NY (page 102); **Address:** 229 King Street, Chappaqua, NY 10514; **Phone:** 914-238-1500; **Board Cert:** Dermatology 2013; Internal Medicine 1982; **Med School:** Penn State Coll Med 1979; **Resid:** Internal Medicine, Fletcher Allen Hlth Care 1983; Dermatology, NY-Presby/Columbia Univ Med Ctr 1993; **Fellow:** Medical Oncology, Meml Sloan-Kettering Cancer Ctr 1986

Felsenstein, Jerome M MD (D) - **Hospital:** Phelps Meml Hosp Ctr, NYU Langone Med Ctr (page 104); **Address:** 449 N State Rd, Ste 203, Briar Cliff Manor, NY 10510; **Phone:** 914-941-5770; **Board Cert:** Dermatology 1976; **Med School:** NYU Sch Med 1971; **Resid:** Dermatology, Kings County Hosp 1975

Goldberg, Neil S MD (D) - **Spec Exp:** Pediatric Dermatology; Acne; **Hospital:** Lawrence Hosp Ctr (page 102); **Address:** 222 Westchester Ave, Ste 203, White Plains, NY 10604-2926; **Phone:** 914-761-8140; **Board Cert:** Dermatology 1986; **Med School:** Northwestern Univ 1982; **Resid:** Dermatology, Northwestern Meml Hosp 1986

Goldwasser, Jennifer H MD (D) - **Spec Exp:** Hair & Nail Disorders; Acne & Rosacea; **Hospital:** White Plains Hosp (page 652); **Address:** Scarsdale Medical Group, 259 Heathcote Rd, Scarsdale, NY 10583; **Phone:** 914-723-8100; **Board Cert:** Dermatology 2011; **Med School:** SUNY Downstate 1989; **Resid:** Dermatology, SUNY Downstate Med Ctr 1993

Grossman, Marc E MD (D) - **Spec Exp:** Skin Diseases in Transplants/Cancer; Psoriasis; Rare Skin Disorders; Cutaneous Lymphoma; **Hospital:** NY-Presby/Columbia Univ Med Ctr, NY (page 102), White Plains Hosp (page 652); **Address:** 12 Greenridge Ave, White Plains, NY 10605-1238; **Phone:** 914-946-1101; **Board Cert:** Internal Medicine 1977; Dermatology 2009; **Med School:** Univ Pennsylvania 1974; **Resid:** Internal Medicine, Hosp Univ Penn 1976; **Fellow:** Dermatology, Columbia-Presby Med Ctr 1979; **Fac Appt:** Prof D, Columbia P&S

Howanitz, Nancy C MD (D) - **Spec Exp:** Melanoma; Skin Cancer; Rosacea; Cosmetic Dermatology; **Hospital:** Lawrence Hosp Ctr (page 102); **Address:** 700 White Plains Rd, Scarsdale, NY 10583-5013; **Phone:** 914-725-5150; **Board Cert:** Dermatology 1980; **Med School:** Baylor Coll Med 1975; **Resid:** Anatomic Pathology, Texas Houston Med Ctr 1977; Dermatology, NYU Med Ctr 1980; **Fac Appt:** Asst Clin Prof D, NYU Sch Med

Hurwitz, Diana S MD (D) - ; **Address:** Westchester Medical Group, 1 Theall Rd, Ste 211, Rye, NY 10580; **Phone:** 914-848-8840; **Board Cert:** Dermatology 2013; **Med School:** Mount Sinai Sch Med 1992; **Resid:** Dermatology, Mt Sinai Med Ctr 1996

Kaplan, Sherri KO MD (D) - **Hospital:** St. John's Riverside Hosp-Dobbs Ferry Pavil; **Address:** 1055 Saw Mill River Rd, Ste 208, Ardsley, NY 10502-1046; **Phone:** 914-693-7191; **Board Cert:** Dermatology 1987; **Med School:** NY Med Coll 1983; **Resid:** Dermatology, Westchester Med Ctr 1987

Kaporis, Athena G MD (D) - **Spec Exp:** Cosmetic Dermatology; Skin Cancer; Laser Surgery; **Hospital:** Northern Westchester Hosp; **Address:** 185 Kisco Ave, Ste 300, Mt Kisco, NY 10549; **Phone:** 914-242-2020; **Board Cert:** Dermatology 2006; **Med School:** NYU Sch Med 1994; **Resid:** Dermatology, SUNY Downstate Med Ctr 1998

Klar, Tobi MD (D) - **Spec Exp:** Skin Cancer; **Hospital:** Montefiore New Rochelle Hosp (page 100); **Address:** 150 Lockwood Ave, Ste 20, New Rochelle, NY 10801; **Phone:** 914-636-2039; **Board Cert:** Dermatology 1989; **Med School:** SUNY Downstate 1981; **Resid:** Dermatology, Downstate Med Ctr 1986

Levy, Ross S MD (D) - **Spec Exp:** Skin Laser Surgery; Dermatologic Surgery; Skin Cancer; **Hospital:** Northern Westchester Hosp, Montefiore Med Ctr-Moses Campus (page 100); **Address:** Mt Kisco Med Group, 110 S Bedford Rd, Mt Kisco, NY 10549; **Phone:** 914-242-1355; **Board Cert:** Dermatology 1981; **Med School:** Albert Einstein Coll Med 1976; **Resid:** Internal Medicine, Montefiore Med Ctr 1978; **Fellow:** Dermatology, Montefiore Med Ctr 1981; **Fac Appt:** Assoc Clin Prof Med, Albert Einstein Coll Med

Lukash, Barbara MD (D) - **Spec Exp:** Skin Cancer; Acne; Psoriasis; Melanoma; **Hospital:** NY-Presby/Columbia Univ Med Ctr, NY (page 102); **Address:** 14 Lawton St, New Rochelle, NY 10801; **Phone:** 914-712-2800; **Board Cert:** Dermatology 1980; **Med School:** Tulane Univ 1976; **Resid:** Dermatology, Univ Chicago Hosps 1980; **Fac Appt:** Assoc Clin Prof D, Columbia P&S

Mackler, Karen MD (D) - **Spec Exp:** Pediatric Dermatology; Skin Cancer; **Hospital:** Montefiore New Rochelle Hosp (page 100), Montefiore Med Ctr-Moses Campus (page 100); **Address:** 150 Lockwood Ave, Ste 34, New Rochelle, NY 10801-4914; **Phone:** 914-576-7070; **Board Cert:** Pediatrics 1978; Dermatology 1983; **Med School:** NYU Sch Med 1973; **Resid:** Pediatrics, NY Hosp 1976; Dermatology, Montefiore Hosp Med Ctr 1983; **Fac Appt:** Asst Prof D, Albert Einstein Coll Med

Marsh, Elizabeth MD (D) - **Spec Exp:** Botox Therapy; **Hospital:** White Plains Hosp (page 652); **Address:** Scarsdale Medical Group, 550 Mamaroneck Ave, Ste 101, Harrison, NY 10528; **Phone:** 914-698-2190; **Board Cert:** Dermatology 2006; **Med School:** NYU Sch Med 1993; **Resid:** Dermatology, NY Hosp Med Ctr-Cornell Univ 1997

Mermelstein, Harold MD (D) - **Spec Exp:** Cosmetic Dermatology; Aging Skin; Sclerotherapy; Laser Surgery; **Hospital:** NYU Langone Med Ctr (page 104), Lawrence Hosp Ctr (page 102); **Address:** 1075 Central Park Ave Fl 3 - Ste 304, Scarsdale, NY 10583; **Phone:** 914-667-2242; **Board Cert:** Dermatology 1979; **Med School:** NY Med Coll 1975; **Resid:** Dermatology, NYU Med Ctr 1979; **Fellow:** Dermatologic Surgery, NYU Med Ctr 1980; **Fac Appt:** Assoc Clin Prof D, NYU Sch Med

Mizrachi-Jonisch, Ayelet MD (D) - **Spec Exp:** Cosmetic Dermatology; Laser Surgery; Laser Hair Removal; **Hospital:** Northern Westchester Hosp; **Address:** Mount Kisco Medical Group, 111 Bedford Rd, Katonah, NY 10536-2115; **Phone:** 914-232-3135; **Board Cert:** Dermatology 2007; **Med School:** NYU Sch Med 2003; **Resid:** Dermatology, Montefiore Med Ctr 2007

Narins, Rhoda S MD (D) - **Spec Exp:** Liposuction; Cosmetic Dermatology; Botox Therapy; Facial Rejuvenation; **Hospital:** White Plains Hosp (page 652), NYU Langone Med Ctr (page 104); **Address:** 222 Westchester Ave, Ste 300, White Plains, NY 10604-2925; **Phone:** 914-684-1000; **Board Cert:** Dermatology 1970; **Med School:** NYU Sch Med 1965; **Resid:** Dermatology, NYU Med Ctr 1969; **Fac Appt:** Clin Prof D, NYU Sch Med

Newburger, Amy E MD (D) - **Spec Exp:** Contact Dermatitis; Cosmetic Dermatology; **Address:** 2 Overhill Rd, Ste 330, Scarsdale, NY 10583; **Phone:** 914-725-1800; **Board Cert:** Dermatology 1979; **Med School:** NYU Sch Med 1974; **Resid:** Dermatology, Univ Miami Hosps 1978

Rosenberg, Benjamin N MD (D) - **Spec Exp:** Cosmetic Dermatology; Skin Laser Surgery; Pigmented Lesions; Skin Cancer & Moles; **Hospital:** Northern Westchester Hosp; **Address:** Mount Kisco Medical Group, 110 S Bedford Rd, Mount Kisco, NY 10549; **Phone:** 914-241-1050; **Board Cert:** Dermatology 2013; **Med School:** NYU Sch Med 2001; **Resid:** Dermatology, NYU Med Ctr 2005

Schachne, Jeffrey P MD (D) - **Spec Exp:** Skin Laser Surgery; **Hospital:** Hudson Valley Hosp Ctr; **Address:** Mount Kisco Medical Group, 3680 Hill Blvd, Jefferson Valley, NY 10535; **Phone:** 914-962-6222; **Board Cert:** Dermatology 1988; **Med School:** SUNY Downstate 1984; **Resid:** Dermatology, Einstein Affil Hosp 1988

Schliftman, Alan B MD (D) - **Spec Exp:** Skin Laser Surgery; Skin Cancer; Cosmetic Dermatology; **Hospital:** Westchester Med Ctr; **Address:** 244 Westchester Ave, Ste 211, White Plains, NY 10604-2926; **Phone:** 914-761-1400; **Board Cert:** Dermatology 1981; **Med School:** Geo Wash Univ 1977; **Resid:** Dermatology, Montefiore Med Ctr 1981; **Fac Appt:** Asst Clin Prof D, NY Med Coll

Sturza, Jeffrey MD (D) - **Spec Exp:** Psoriasis; Skin Laser Surgery; Cosmetic Dermatology; **Hospital:** Phelps Meml Hosp Ctr; **Address:** Advanced Dermatology, 150 White Plains Rd, Ste 210, Tarrytown, NY 10591; **Phone:** 914-631-4666; **Board Cert:** Dermatology 1988; **Med School:** SUNY Hlth Sci Ctr 1984; **Resid:** Dermatology, Cook Co Hosp 1988

Treiber, Ruth K MD (D) - **Spec Exp:** Botox Therapy; Acne & Rosacea; Facial Rejuvenation; Skin Cancer & Moles; **Hospital:** NY-Presby/Columbia Univ Med Ctr, NY (page 102); **Address:** 175 Purchase St, Rye, NY 10580; **Phone:** 914-967-2153; **Board Cert:** Dermatology 1983; **Med School:** Cornell Univ-Weill Med Coll 1978; **Resid:** Internal Medicine, NY-Presby/Columbia Univ Med Ctr 1980; Dermatology, NY-Presby/Columbia Univ Med Ctr 1983; **Fac Appt:** Assoc Clin Prof D, Columbia P&S

Young, Saryna P MD (D) - **Spec Exp:** Cosmetic Dermatology; **Hospital:** White Plains Hosp (page 652); **Address:** Westchester Medical Group, 210 Westchester Ave, White Plains, NY 10601; **Phone:** 914-682-6426; **Board Cert:** Dermatology 2007; **Med School:** Albert Einstein Coll Med 2003; **Resid:** Dermatology, Montefiore Med Ctr 2007

Zeltser, Ross MD (D) - **Spec Exp:** Mohs Surgery; Skin Cancer; **Hospital:** Northern Westchester Hosp; **Address:** 185 Kisco Ave, Ste 300, Mt Kisco, NY 10549; **Phone:** 914-242-2020; **Board Cert:** Dermatology 2006; **Med School:** Univ Rochester 2002; **Resid:** Internal Medicine, Lenox Hill Hosp 2003; Dermatology, Boston Med Ctr/Tufts Med Ctr 2006; **Fellow:** Mohs Surgery, Tufts Med Ctr 2007

Zweibel, Stuart M MD/PhD (D) - **Spec Exp:** Mohs Surgery; Skin Cancer; Skin Laser Surgery; Cosmetic Dermatology; **Hospital:** Northern Westchester Hosp; **Address:** 185 Kisco Ave, Ste 300, Mt Kisco, NY 10549; **Phone:** 914-242-2020; **Board Cert:** Dermatology 2009; **Med School:** Mount Sinai Sch Med 1985; **Resid:** Dermatology, Rhode Island Hosp 1989; **Fellow:** Mohs Surgery, Univ WI Hosps & Clinics 1991

Diagnostic Radiology

Hertz, Marc MD (DR) - **Spec Exp:** CT Scan; MRI; **Address:** Mount Kisco Medical Group, Radiology, 90 S Bedford Rd, Mount Kisco, NY 10549; **Phone:** 914-242-1395; **Board Cert:** Diagnostic Radiology 1985; **Med School:** Howard Univ 1979; **Resid:** Pathology, Lenox Hill Hosp 1981; Diagnostic Radiology, Montefiore Med Ctr 1984; **Fellow:** Ultrasound/CT, North Shore Univ Hosp 1985

Hibbard, Claire A MD (DR) - **Spec Exp:** Women's Imaging; Mammography; **Address:** Mount Kisco Medical Group, Radiology, 90 S Bedford Rd, Mount Kisco, NY 10549-3412; **Phone:** 914-241-1050; **Board Cert:** Diagnostic Radiology 1989; **Med School:** Columbia P&S 1984; **Resid:** Diagnostic Radiology, Hosp Univ Penn 1988; **Fellow:** Musculoskeletal Imaging, Hosp Univ Penn 1989; **Fac Appt:** Asst Clin Prof Rad, Albert Einstein Coll Med

Khoury, Paul MD (DR) - **Hospital:** White Plains Hosp (page 652); **Address:** White Plains Hosp Ctr, Dept Radiology, 41 E Post Rd, White Plains, NY 10601; **Phone:** 914-681-1219; **Board Cert:** Diagnostic Radiology 1979; Nuclear Radiology 1980; **Med School:** Lebanon 1973; **Resid:** Diagnostic Radiology, Hotel Dieu de France Hosp 1975; Diagnostic Radiology, St Luke's-Roosevelt Hosp Ctr 1979

Kutcher, Rosalyn MD (DR) - **Spec Exp:** Mammography; Ultrasound; Women's Imaging; **Hospital:** White Plains Hosp (page 652); **Address:** Women's Imaging Ctr, 90 S Ridge Ave, Rye Brook, NY 10573; **Phone:** 914-935-0011; **Board Cert:** Diagnostic Radiology 1975; **Med School:** SUNY Hlth Sci Ctr 1970; **Resid:** Diagnostic Radiology, Montefiore Med Ctr 1974; **Fac Appt:** Prof Rad, Albert Einstein Coll Med

Lefkovitz, Zvi MD (DR) - **Spec Exp:** Thoracic Radiology; **Hospital:** Westchester Med Ctr; **Address:** WMC Advanced Physician Services, 100 Woods Rd, Valhalla, NY 10595; **Phone:** 914-493-6692; **Board Cert:** Diagnostic Radiology 1986; **Med School:** Ros Franklin Univ/Chicago Med Sch 1982; **Resid:** Diagnostic Radiology, Maimonides Med Ctr 1986; **Fellow:** Interventional Radiology, Univ Hosp 1987; **Fac Appt:** Clin Prof Rad, NY Med Coll

Leslie, Denise MD (DR) - **Spec Exp:** Neuroradiology; **Hospital:** Good Samaritan Regional Med Ctr; **Address:** Hartsdale Imaging, 141 S Central Ave, Hartsdale, NY 10530; **Phone:** 914-345-0376; **Board Cert:** Diagnostic Radiology 1985; **Med School:** SUNY Buffalo 1981; **Resid:** Diagnostic Radiology, Metropolitan Med Ctr 1985; **Fellow:** Neuroradiology, Westchester Co Med Ctr 1987

Lisi-DeMartino, Virna MD (DR) - **Spec Exp:** Women's Imaging; Breast Imaging; MRI; **Hospital:** Northern Westchester Hosp; **Address:** Mount Kisco Medical Group, 90 S Bedford Rd, Mount Kisco, NY 10549; **Phone:** 914-241-1050; **Board Cert:** Diagnostic Radiology 2006; **Med School:** NYU Sch Med 2001; **Resid:** Diagnostic Radiology, NY Presby-Cornell Med Ctr 2006; **Fellow:** Breast Imaging, Meml Sloan-Kettering Ctr 2007

LoRusso, Diane MD (DR) - **Spec Exp:** Breast Imaging; Women's Health; Ultrasound; Mammography-Digital; **Address:** Rye Radiology Assoc, 30 Rye Ridge Plaza, Rye Brook, NY 10573-2830; **Phone:** 914-253-9200; **Board Cert:** Diagnostic Radiology 1974; **Med School:** SUNY Upstate Med Univ 1969; **Resid:** Diagnostic Radiology, Montefiore Med Ctr 1974

Poplausky, Maurice R MD (DR) - **Spec Exp:** Interventional Radiology; **Hospital:** Hudson Valley Hosp Ctr; **Address:** Hudsonj Valley Imaging, P.C., 1980 Crompound Rd, Cortland Manor, NY 10567; **Phone:** 914-734-3680; **Board Cert:** Diagnostic Radiology 1995; Vascular & Interventional Radiology 2008; **Med School:** SUNY Buffalo 1990; **Resid:** Diagnostic Radiology, SUNY Downstate Med Ctr 1995; **Fellow:** Vascular & Interventional Radiology, Mass Genl Hosp 1996; **Fac Appt:** Assoc Prof Rad, NY Med Coll

Staeger-Hirsch, Christine N MD (DR) - **Spec Exp:** Breast Imaging; **Address:** Rye Radiology, 30 Rye Ridge Plaza, Rye Brook, NY 10573-2830; **Phone:** 914-253-9200; **Board Cert:** Diagnostic Radiology 2006; **Med School:** NYU Sch Med 2001; **Resid:** Diagnostic Radiology, St Luke's Roosevelt Med Ctr 2006; **Fellow:** Breast Imaging, NYU Med Ctr 2007

Swirsky, Michael H MD (DR) - **Spec Exp:** Mammography; Gastrointestinal Imaging; CT Scan; Abdominal Imaging; **Hospital:** White Plains Hosp (page 652), Phelps Meml Hosp Ctr; **Address:** White Plains Hosp-Dept Radiology, 41 E Post Rd, White Plains, NY 10601; **Phone:** 914-681-1069; **Board Cert:** Diagnostic Radiology 1979; **Med School:** Case West Res Univ 1975; **Resid:** Diagnostic Radiology, Strong Meml Hosp 1979

Wald, Leonard A MD (DR) - **Spec Exp:** Body Imaging; Women's Imaging; **Hospital:** Northern Westchester Hosp; **Address:** Mount Kisco Medical Group, 90 S Bedford Rd, Mt Kisco, NY 10549; **Phone:** 914-241-1050; **Board Cert:** Diagnostic Radiology 1985; **Med School:** Albert Einstein Coll Med 1981; **Resid:** Diagnostic Radiology, Montefiore/Einstein Med Ctr 1985; **Fellow:** Ultrasound/CT/MRI, Thomas Jefferson Univ Hosp 1986

Weiss, Jonathan D MD (DR) - ; **Address:** WestMed Medical Group, Radiology, 210 Westchester Ave, White Plains, NY 10601; **Phone:** 914-682-6430; **Board Cert:** Diagnostic Radiology 1987; **Med School:** Tufts Univ 1983; **Resid:** Diagnostic Radiology, SUNY Downstate Med Ctr 1987; **Fellow:** Interventional Radiology, SUNY Downstate Med Ctr 1988

Endocrinology, Diabetes & Metabolism

Bloomgarden, David K MD (EDM) - **Spec Exp:** Diabetes; Osteoporosis; Thyroid Disorders; Hypogonadism-Male; **Hospital:** White Plains Hosp (page 652); **Address:** Scarsdale Medical Group, 550 Mamaroneck Ave, Ste 101, Harrison, NY 10528; **Phone:** 914-723-8100 x302; **Board Cert:** Internal Medicine 1980; Endocrinology, Diabetes & Metabolism 1983; **Med School:** NYU Sch Med 1977; **Resid:** Internal Medicine, Albert Einstein/Jacobi Med Ctr 1980; **Fellow:** Endocrinology, Diabetes & Metabolism, Montefiore Med Ctr 1982

Blum, David MD (EDM) - **Spec Exp:** Diabetes; Osteoporosis; Thyroid Disorders; **Hospital:** Montefiore New Rochelle Hosp (page 100); **Address:** Diabetes Center - 5th Floor, 16 Guion Pl, New Rochelle, NY 10801; **Phone:** 914-633-8680; **Board Cert:** Internal Medicine 1977; Endocrinology, Diabetes & Metabolism 1979; **Med School:** Northwestern Univ 1974; **Resid:** Internal Medicine, Mt Sinai Hosp 1977; **Fellow:** Endocrinology, Mt Sinai Hosp 1979; **Fac Appt:** Asst Clin Prof Med, NY Med Coll

Gitler, Ellen S MD (EDM) - **Hospital:** Burke Rehab Hosp; **Address:** 785 Mamaroneck Ave, White Plains, NY 10605-2523; **Phone:** 914-597-2409; **Board Cert:** Internal Medicine 1980; Endocrinology, Diabetes & Metabolism 1983; **Med School:** Cornell Univ-Weill Med Coll 1977; **Resid:** Internal Medicine, Bronx Municipal Hosp 1980; **Fellow:** Endocrinology, Diabetes & Metabolism, Mount Sinai Med Ctr 1982

Greenwald, Bonnie Wolf MD (EDM) - **Spec Exp:** Thyroid Disorders; Diabetes; Osteoporosis; Weight Management; **Hospital:** White Plains Hosp (page 652); **Address:** Maple Medical Group, 30 Davis Ave, White Plains, NY 10605; **Phone:** 914-328-2355; **Board Cert:** Internal Medicine 2010; Endocrinology, Diabetes & Metabolism 2004; **Med School:** NYU Sch Med 1997; **Resid:** Internal Medicine, NY Presby-Columbia Med Ctr 2000; **Fellow:** Endocrinology, Diabetes & Metabolism, Emory Univ Med Ctr 2004

Hellerman, James MD (EDM) - **Spec Exp:** Thyroid Disorders; Diabetes; Calcium Disorders; **Hospital:** Phelps Meml Hosp Ctr; **Address:** 200 S Broadway, Ste 100, Tarrytown, NY 10591-4504; **Phone:** 914-631-9300; **Board Cert:** Internal Medicine 1979; Endocrinology 1983; **Med School:** Univ Rochester 1976; **Resid:** Internal Medicine, Montefiore Med Ctr 1980; **Fellow:** Endocrinology, Diabetes & Metabolism, Mass Genl Hosp 1984

Kantor, Alan MD (EDM) - **Spec Exp:** Thyroid Disorders; Osteoporosis; Diabetes; Endocrine Tumors; **Hospital:** Northern Westchester Hosp; **Address:** 1940 Commerce St, Ste 310, Yorktown Heights, NY 10598; **Phone:** 914-245-1111; **Board Cert:** Internal Medicine 1981; Endocrinology, Diabetes & Metabolism 1983; **Med School:** South Africa 1975; **Resid:** Internal Medicine, La Guardia Hosp 1980; Internal Medicine, LI Jewish-Hillside Med Ctr 1981; **Fellow:** Endocrinology, Diabetes & Metabolism, Meml Sloan Kettering Cancer Ctr 1983; **Fac Appt:** Asst Clin Prof Med, NY Med Coll

Kleinbaum, Jerry I MD (EDM) - **Spec Exp:** Diabetes; **Hospital:** Hudson Valley Hosp Ctr; **Address:** Mount Kisco Medical Group-Endocrinology, 46 Route 6 at Mahopac Ave, Ste 103, Yorktown Heights, NY 10598; **Phone:** 914-248-5556; **Board Cert:** Internal Medicine 1979; Endocrinology 1985; **Med School:** Tufts Univ 1976; **Resid:** Internal Medicine, Montefiore Med Ctr 1980; **Fellow:** Endocrinology, Diabetes & Metabolism, Montefiore Med Ctr 1981

Leibowitz, Jonas MD (EDM) - **Spec Exp:** Diabetes; Osteoporosis; Thyroid Disorders; Nutrition; **Hospital:** Lawrence Hosp Ctr (page 102), White Plains Hosp (page 652); **Address:** 770 B McLean Ave, Yonkers, NY 10704; **Phone:** 914-237-3636; **Board Cert:** Internal Medicine 2005; Endocrinology, Diabetes & Metabolism 2007; **Med School:** SUNY Downstate 1992; **Resid:** Internal Medicine, Mt Sinai Med Ctr 1995; **Fellow:** Endocrinology, Mt Sinai Med Ctr 1997; **Fac Appt:** Asst Clin Prof Med, NY Med Coll

Powell, Jeffrey S MD (EDM) - **Hospital:** Northern Westchester Hosp; **Address:** MKMG, Endocrinology, 90 S Bedford Rd, Mount Kisco, NY 10549; **Phone:** 914-241-1050; **Board Cert:** Internal Medicine 2008; Endocrinology, Diabetes & Metabolism 2010; **Med School:** Albert Einstein Coll Med 1995; **Resid:** Internal Medicine, NY-Presby/Columbia Univ Med Ctr 1998; **Fellow:** Endocrinology, Diabetes & Metabolism, NY-Presby/Columbia Univ Med Ctr 2001

Pretto, Zorayda MD (EDM) - **Hospital:** White Plains Hosp (page 652); **Address:** Mid-Westchester Medical Assocs, 210 Westchester Ave, White Plains, NY 10605; **Phone:** 914-831-4150; **Board Cert:** Internal Medicine 2005; Endocrinology, Diabetes & Metabolism 2006; **Med School:** Panama 1986; **Resid:** Internal Medicine, St John's Episcopal Hosp 1991; **Fellow:** Endocrinology, Diabetes & Metabolism, Beth Israel Hosp 1993

Rudin, Eric A MD (EDM) - **Spec Exp:** Diabetes; **Hospital:** Northern Westchester Hosp; **Address:** MKMG, Endocrinology, 111 Bedford Rd, Katonah, NY 10549; **Phone:** 914-232-3135; **Board Cert:** Internal Medicine 2013; Endocrinology, Diabetes & Metabolism 2005; **Med School:** Mount Sinai Sch Med 2000; **Resid:** Internal Medicine, Thomas Jefferson Univ Hosp` 2003; **Fellow:** Endocrinology, Diabetes & Metabolism, Montefiore Med Ctr 2005

Stein, Randy MD (EDM) - **Spec Exp:** Diabetes; Osteoporosis; **Hospital:** White Plains Hosp (page 652); **Address:** Westchester Medical Group-Endocrinology, 210 Westchester Ave, White Plains, NY 10604; **Phone:** 914-831-4150; **Board Cert:** Internal Medicine 1981; Endocrinology, Diabetes & Metabolism 1983; **Med School:** Albert Einstein Coll Med 1978; **Resid:** Internal Medicine, Montefiore Med Ctr 1981; **Fellow:** Endocrinology, Diabetes & Metabolism, Montefiore Med Ctr 1983

Weiser, Kenneth R MD (EDM) - **Spec Exp:** Diabetes; Osteoporosis; **Hospital:** White Plains Hosp (page 652); **Address:** Westchester Med Group-Endocrinolgy, 210 Westchester Ave, White Plains, NY 10604; **Phone:** 914-831-4150; **Board Cert:** Internal Medicine 2013; Endocrinology, Diabetes & Metabolism 2005; **Med School:** Albert Einstein Coll Med 1990; **Resid:** Internal Medicine, Jacobi Med Ctr 1993; **Fellow:** Endocrinology, Diabetes & Metabolism, Mt Sinai Med Ctr 1995

Family Medicine

Annabi, Iyad N MD (FMed) *PCP* - **Spec Exp:** Diabetes; Geriatric Care; Preventive Cardiology; Preventive Medicine; **Hospital:** St. John's Riverside Hosp-Andrus Pavil; **Address:** Westchester Family Medicine Practice, 472 Palmer Rd, Yonkers, NY 10701-5207; **Phone:** 914-375-2300; **Board Cert:** Family Medicine 2008; **Med School:** Mexico 1988; **Resid:** Family Medicine, St Joseph Med Ctr 1995; **Fac Appt:** Assoc Clin Prof FMed, NY Med Coll

Apuzzo, Thomas R MD (FMed) *PCP* - **Hospital:** St. John's Riverside Hosp-Andrus Pavil, Saint Joseph's Med Ctr - Yonkers; **Address:** 955 Yonkers Ave, Yonkers, NY 10704; **Phone:** 914-237-0994; **Board Cert:** Family Medicine 2009; **Med School:** Italy 1985; **Resid:** Family Medicine, St Joseph's Med Ctr 1989

Carniciu, Stere MD (FMed) *PCP* - **Hospital:** Phelps Meml Hosp Ctr; **Address:** 20 Beacon Hill Drive, Ste 2B, Dobbs Ferry, NY 10522; **Phone:** 914-591-6888; **Board Cert:** Family Medicine 2013; **Med School:** Romania 1982; **Resid:** Family Medicine, Bronx Lebanon Hosp Ctr 1996

Gottesfeld, Peter Michael MD (FMed) *PCP* - **Spec Exp:** Aging; Preventive Medicine; ADD/ADHD; **Hospital:** Northern Westchester Hosp, Hudson Valley Hosp Ctr; **Address:** 101 S Bedford Rd, Ste 412, Mt Kisco, NY 10549-3455; **Phone:** 914-241-7800; **Board Cert:** Family Medicine 2010; **Med School:** Rutgers R W Johnson Med Sch 1985; **Resid:** Family Medicine, Thomas Jefferson Univ Hosp 1988; **Fac Appt:** Assoc Clin Prof FMed, NY Med Coll

Merker, Edward L MD (FMed) *PCP* - **Spec Exp:** Geriatric Care; **Hospital:** Phelps Meml Hosp Ctr, NY-Presby/Columbia Univ Med Ctr, NY (page 102); **Address:** Columbia Doctors, 180 Marble Ave, Pleasantville, NY 10570; **Phone:** 914-769-7300 x202; **Board Cert:** Family Medicine 2012; **Med School:** Albert Einstein Coll Med 1981; **Resid:** Family Medicine, Overlook Hosp 1984; **Fac Appt:** Asst Prof Med, Columbia P&S

Miller, Daniel MD (FMed) *PCP* - **Hospital:** St. John's Riverside Hosp-Andrus Pavil, Saint Joseph's Med Ctr - Yonkers; **Address:** Hudson River HealthCare, 503 S Broadway, Yonkers, NY 10705; **Phone:** 914-965-9771; **Board Cert:** Family Medicine 2007; **Med School:** Univ Cincinnati 1984; **Resid:** Family Medicine, Montefiore Med Ctr 1987; **Fac Appt:** Asst Prof FMed, NY Med Coll

Palekar, Shashishekhar S MD (FMed) *PCP* - **Hospital:** White Plains Hosp (page 652); **Address:** 106 Calvert St, Harrison, NY 10528; **Phone:** 914-835-0073; **Board Cert:** Family Medicine 2013; **Med School:** India 1980; **Resid:** Family Medicine, St Joseph's Med Ctr 1996

Piccirilli, Dora C MD (FMed) *PCP* - **Hospital:** Phelps Meml Hosp Ctr, NY-Presby/Columbia Univ Med Ctr, NY (page 102); **Address:** Columbia Doctors, 180 Marble Ave, Pleasantville, NY 10570; **Phone:** 914-769-7300; **Board Cert:** Family Medicine 2005; **Med School:** SUNY Hlth Sci Ctr 1988; **Resid:** Family Medicine, Overlook Hosp 1991; **Fac Appt:** Asst Prof Med, Columbia P&S

Sharpe, Arleen S MD (FMed) *PCP* - **Hospital:** White Plains Hosp (page 652); **Address:** WestMed Group, 73 Market St, Yonkers, NY 10710; **Phone:** 914-693-1660; **Board Cert:** Family Medicine 2005; **Med School:** SUNY Stony Brook 1988; **Resid:** Family Medicine, Montefiore Med Ctr 1991

Strongwater, Richard F MD (FMed) *PCP* - **Spec Exp:** Travel Medicine; **Hospital:** Phelps Meml Hosp Ctr, NY-Presby/Columbia Univ Med Ctr, NY (page 102); **Address:** Columbia Doctors, 180 Marble Ave, Pleasantville, NY 10570; **Phone:** 914-769-7300; **Board Cert:** Family Medicine 2012; **Med School:** SUNY Upstate Med Univ 1981; **Resid:** Family Medicine, Overlook Hosp 1984; **Fac Appt:** Asst Prof Med, Columbia P&S

Sutton, Ira MD (FMed) *PCP* - **Spec Exp:** Preventive Medicine; Skin Diseases; **Hospital:** White Plains Hosp (page 652), Montefiore New Rochelle Hosp (page 100); **Address:** 2 Overhill Rd, Ste 225, Scarsdale, NY 10583; **Phone:** 914-636-0077; **Board Cert:** Family Medicine 2008; **Med School:** Albert Einstein Coll Med 1980; **Resid:** Family Medicine, Brown Univ/Memorial Hosp 1983

Yudin, Howard MD (FMed) *PCP* - **Hospital:** Greenwich Hosp (page 970); **Address:** 3010 Westchester Ave, Ste 401, Purchase, NY 10577; **Phone:** 914-251-1261; **Board Cert:** Family Medicine 2008; **Med School:** Univ Montreal 1974; **Resid:** Family Medicine, Jewish Genl Hosp 1976

Gastroenterology

Abemayor, Elie M MD (Ge) - **Spec Exp:** Inflammatory Bowel Disease; Endoscopy; Irritable Bowel Syndrome; Gastroesophageal Reflux Disease (GERD); **Hospital:** Northern Westchester Hosp; **Address:** Westchester Health, 91 Smith Ave, Mt Kisco, NY 10549; **Phone:** 914-241-9026; **Board Cert:** Internal Medicine 1988; Gastroenterology 2005; **Med School:** SUNY Stony Brook 1985; **Resid:** Internal Medicine, Bellevue Hosp/NYU 1988; **Fellow:** Gastroenterology, VA NY Habor Hlthcare Sys 1990

Antonelle, Robert W MD (Ge) - **Spec Exp:** Gastroesophageal Reflux Disease (GERD); Liver & Biliary Disease; Colonoscopy; **Hospital:** White Plains Hosp (page 652), Montefiore Mt Vernon Hosp (page 100); **Address:** White Plains Gastroenterologists, 311 North St, rm 403, White Plains, NY 10605-2232; **Phone:** 914-949-7171; **Board Cert:** Gastroenterology 2006; **Med School:** NY Med Coll 1989; **Resid:** Internal Medicine, Westchester Med Ctr 1992; **Fellow:** Gastroenterology, Westchester Med Ctr 1995

Auerbach, Mitchell E MD (Ge) - **Spec Exp:** Colonoscopy; Crohn's Disease; Ulcerative Colitis; **Hospital:** Saint Joseph's Med Ctr - Yonkers, St. John's Riverside Hosp-Andrus Pavil; **Address:** Westchester Digestive Dis Grp, 469 N Broadway, Yonkers, NY 10701-1923; **Phone:** 914-969-1115; **Board Cert:** Gastroenterology 2008; **Med School:** Tufts Univ 1991; **Resid:** Internal Medicine, Mt Sinai Hosp 1994; **Fellow:** Gastroenterology, Mt Sinai Hosp 1997

Byfield, Floyd C MD (Ge) - **Spec Exp:** Endoscopy & Colonoscopy; **Hospital:** Phelps Meml Hosp Ctr; **Address:** Phelps Med Assocs, 777 N Broadway, Ste 305, Sleepy Hollow, NY 10591; **Phone:** 914-366-6120; **Board Cert:** Internal Medicine 2006; Gastroenterology 2009; **Med School:** Mount Sinai Sch Med 1993; **Resid:** Internal Medicine, Ny-Presby/Cornell Med Ctr 1996; **Fellow:** Gastroenterology, NY-Presby/Cornell Med Ctr 1998

Chinitz, Marvin A MD (Ge) - **Spec Exp:** Colonoscopy; Inflammatory Bowel Disease; Liver Disease; Gastroesophageal Reflux Disease (GERD); **Hospital:** Northern Westchester Hosp; **Address:** Mount Kisco Med Grp, 90 S Bedford Rd, Mt Kisco, NY 10549-3422; **Phone:** 914-241-1050; **Board Cert:** Internal Medicine 1981; Gastroenterology 1985; **Med School:** Boston Univ 1978; **Resid:** Internal Medicine, Boston Med Ctr 1981; **Fellow:** Gastroenterology, Montefiore Med Ctr 1984; **Fac Appt:** Asst Prof Med, Albert Einstein Coll Med

Close, Georgia M MD (Ge) - **Hospital:** Putnam Hosp Ctr; **Address:** Mount Kisco Medical Group, 225 Veterans Rd, Yorktown Heights, NY 10598; **Phone:** 914-302-8059; **Board Cert:** Internal Medicine 2007; Gastroenterology 2011; **Med School:** Cornell Univ-Weill Med Coll 2004; **Resid:** Internal Medicine, NY Presby-Cornell Med Ctr 2007; **Fellow:** Gastroenterology & Nutrition, Meml Sloan Kettering Cancer Ctr 2009

Dworkin, Brad M MD (Ge) - **Spec Exp:** Gastrointestinal Motility Disorders; Nutrition; Inflammatory Bowel Disease; **Hospital:** Westchester Med Ctr; **Address:** Gastro & Hepatobiliary Cons, 19 Bradhurst Ave, Ste 2550 S, Hawthorne, NY 10595; **Phone:** 914-493-7337; **Board Cert:** Internal Medicine 1979; Gastroenterology 1981; **Med School:** Jefferson Med Coll 1976; **Resid:** Internal Medicine, New York Hosp 1979; **Fellow:** Gastroenterology, Meml Sloan Kettering Cancer Ctr 1981; Nutrition, Meml Sloan Kettering Cancer Ctr 1982; **Fac Appt:** Prof Med, NY Med Coll

Ehrlich, James B MD (Ge) - **Spec Exp:** Esophageal Disorders; Gastroesophageal Reflux Disease (GERD); Gastrointestinal Motility Disorders; **Hospital:** Lawrence Hosp Ctr (page 102); **Address:** WestMed Medical Group, Ridge Hill, 73 Market St, Ste 219, Yonkers, NY 10710; **Phone:** 914-831-6820; **Board Cert:** Internal Medicine 1983; Gastroenterology 1985; **Med School:** Univ Hlth Scis, Chicago Med Sch 1980; **Resid:** Internal Medicine, Univ Illinois Med Ctr 1983; **Fellow:** Gastroenterology, Michael Reese Hosp 1985

Fath Jr, Robert B MD (Ge) - **Spec Exp:** Endoscopy; Colonoscopy; **Hospital:** White Plains Hosp (page 652); **Address:** Scarsdale Med Grp, 600 Mamaroneck Ave, Ste 301, Harrison, NY 10528; **Phone:** 914-723-8100 x309; **Board Cert:** Internal Medicine 1981; Gastroenterology 1983; **Med School:** Univ Miss 1978; **Resid:** Internal Medicine, N Shore Hosp 1981; **Fellow:** Gastroenterology, Meml Sloan-Kettering Cancer Ctr 1983; **Fac Appt:** Med, Cornell Univ-Weill Med Coll

Field, Barry E MD (Ge) - **Spec Exp:** Ulcerative Colitis; Crohn's Disease; **Hospital:** Phelps Meml Hosp Ctr; **Address:** Phelps Med Assocs, 777 N Broadway Fl 3 - Ste 305, Sleepy Hollow, NY 10591-1040; **Phone:** 914-366-6120; **Board Cert:** Internal Medicine 1976; Gastroenterology 1979; **Med School:** Albert Einstein Coll Med 1972; **Resid:** Internal Medicine, Metropolitan Hosp Ctr 1976; **Fellow:** Gastroenterology, Harbor Genl Hosp 1978

Finegold, Jonathan MD (Ge) - **Spec Exp:** Barrett's Esophagus; Colon Cancer; Inflammatory Bowel Disease/Crohn's; **Hospital:** Lawrence Hosp Ctr (page 102); **Address:** WestMed Medical Group, Ridge Hill, 73 Market St, Ste 219, Yonkers, NY 10710; **Phone:** 914-831-6820; **Board Cert:** Internal Medicine 2005; Gastroenterology 2007; **Med School:** Univ Miami Sch Med 1991; **Resid:** Internal Medicine, NY-Presby/Columbia Med Ctr 1994; **Fellow:** Gastroenterology, NY-Presby/Columbia Med Ctr 1997

Geders, Jane M MD/PhD (Ge) - **Spec Exp:** Hepatitis C; Nutrition; Colon Cancer Screening; **Hospital:** Northern Westchester Hosp; **Address:** Mount Kisco Medical Group, 90 S Bedford Rd, Mt Kisco, NY 10549; **Phone:** 914-242-1307; **Med School:** Univ S Fla Coll Med 1987; **Resid:** Internal Medicine, Meml Sloan Kettering Cancer Ctr 1990; **Fellow:** Gastroenterology, Mt Sinai Med Ctr 1992; Hepatology, Mt Sinai Med Ctr 1993

Gendler, Seth L MD (Ge) - **Spec Exp:** Pancreatic/Biliary Endoscopy (ERCP); Biliary Disease; Pancreatic Disease; **Hospital:** White Plains Hosp (page 652); **Address:** 1296 North Ave Fl 2, New Rochelle, NY 10804; **Phone:** 914-235-0918; **Board Cert:** Internal Medicine 1986; Gastroenterology 2011; **Med School:** Rush Med Coll 1983; **Resid:** Internal Medicine, St Lukes Hosp 1986; **Fellow:** Gastroenterology, St Lukes Hosp 1988; Endoscopy, Univ Hosp 1989

Genn, David A MD (Ge) - **Spec Exp:** Colon Cancer Screening; Biliary Disease; Gastroesophageal Reflux Disease (GERD); Barrett's Esophagus; **Hospital:** Hudson Valley Hosp Ctr, NY-Presby/Columbia Univ Med Ctr, NY (page 102); **Address:** Hudson Vlly Ctr Digestive Hlth, 1985 Crompond Rd, D Bldg, Cortlandt Manor, NY 10567; **Phone:** 914-739-2400; **Board Cert:** Gastroenterology 2014; **Med School:** Boston Univ 1988; **Resid:** Internal Medicine, Montefiore Med Ctr 1991; **Fellow:** Gastroenterology, Westchester Med Ctr 1993

Goldblatt, Robert S MD (Ge) - **Spec Exp:** Liver Disease; Biliary Disease; Endoscopy; Inflammatory Bowel Disease; **Hospital:** White Plains Hosp (page 652), Greenwich Hosp (page 970); **Address:** Northeast Med Grp, 3010 Westchester Ave, Ste 400, Purchase, NY 10577; **Phone:** 914-253-9252; **Board Cert:** Internal Medicine 1978; Gastroenterology 1979; **Med School:** Geo Wash Univ 1974; **Resid:** Internal Medicine, Univ FL-Shands Hosp 1977; **Fellow:** Gastroenterology, Yale-New Haven Hosp 1979; **Fac Appt:** Assoc Prof Med, Cornell Univ-Weill Med Coll

Heier, Stephen K MD (Ge) - **Spec Exp:** Colonoscopy/Polypectomy; Gastric & Esophageal Disorders; Pancreatic/Biliary Endoscopy (ERCP); **Hospital:** Phelps Meml Hosp Ctr; **Address:** Phelps Memorial Hosp, Advanced Endoscopy & Gastroenterology, 755 N Broadway, Ste 530, Sleepy Hollow, NY 10591; **Phone:** 914-366-1190; **Board Cert:** Internal Medicine 1979; Gastroenterology 1981; **Med School:** Albany Med Coll 1976; **Resid:** Internal Medicine, Metro Hosp Ctr 1979; **Fellow:** Gastroenterology, Tufts New England Med Ctr 1981; **Fac Appt:** Clin Prof Med, NY Med Coll

Hillman, Deborah L MD (Ge) - **Spec Exp:** Women's Health; Irritable Bowel Syndrome; **Hospital:** Northern Westchester Hosp; **Address:** Mount Kisco Medical Group, 90 S Bedford Rd, Mount Kisco, NY 10549-3412; **Phone:** 914-241-1050; **Board Cert:** Gastroenterology 2006; **Med School:** NYU Sch Med 1999; **Resid:** Internal Medicine, Columbia Presby Med Ctr 2002; **Fellow:** Gastroenterology, Montefiore Med Ctr 2005

Jaffe, Alan H MD (Ge) - **Spec Exp:** Endoscopy & Colonoscopy; Gastroesophageal Reflux Disease (GERD); **Hospital:** White Plains Hosp (page 652), Greenwich Hosp (page 970); **Address:** WestMed Med Grp, 210 Westchester Ave Fl 2 - Ste 205, White Plains, NY 10604; **Phone:** 914-682-6466; **Board Cert:** Internal Medicine 1977; Gastroenterology 1979; **Med School:** Cornell Univ-Weill Med Coll 1974; **Resid:** Internal Medicine, N Shore U Med Ctr 1977; **Fellow:** Gastroenterology, St Raphael Hosp 1979

Kahn, Oren MD (Ge) - **Spec Exp:** Inflammatory Bowel Disease; Peptic Ulcer Disease; Gastroesophageal Reflux Disease (GERD); Colonoscopy; **Hospital:** Northern Westchester Hosp; **Address:** Mount Kisco Med Grp, 90 S Bedford Rd, Mount Kisco, NY 10549; **Phone:** 914-241-1050; **Board Cert:** Internal Medicine 2004; Gastroenterology 2007; **Med School:** Albert Einstein Coll Med 1990; **Resid:** Internal Medicine, Mt Sinai Med Ctr 1994; **Fellow:** Gastroenterology, Mt Sinai Med Ctr 1996; **Fac Appt:** Assoc Clin Prof Med, Mount Sinai Sch Med

Katz, Henry J MD (Ge) - **Hospital:** Montefiore Med Ctr-Moses Campus (page 100), St. John's Riverside Hosp-Dobbs Ferry Pavil; **Address:** 1234 Central Park Ave, Ste 3A, Yonkers, NY 10704; **Phone:** 914-793-1600; **Board Cert:** Internal Medicine 1983; Gastroenterology 1985; **Med School:** Albany Med Coll 1980; **Resid:** Internal Medicine, Bellevue Hosp 1983; **Fellow:** Gastroenterology, Montefiore Med Ctr 1985

Kozicky, Orest J MD (Ge) - **Spec Exp:** Colitis; Peptic Ulcer Disease; Gastroesophageal Reflux Disease (GERD); **Hospital:** St. John's Riverside Hosp-Andrus Pavil; **Address:** Westchester Digestive Dis Grp, 469 N Broadway Fl 1, Yonkers, NY 10701-1923; **Phone:** 914-969-1115; **Board Cert:** Internal Medicine 1985; Gastroenterology 1987; **Med School:** NY Med Coll 1981; **Resid:** Internal Medicine, Jacobi Med Ctr 1985; **Fellow:** Gastroenterology, Montefiore Med Ctr 1987; **Fac Appt:** Assoc Clin Prof Med, Albert Einstein Coll Med

Kressner, Michael MD (Ge) - **Spec Exp:** Colon Cancer; Inflammatory Bowel Disease; Biliary Disease; **Hospital:** Montefiore New Rochelle Hosp (page 100), Montefiore Mt Vernon Hosp (page 100); **Address:** 140 Lockwood Ave, Ste 110, New Rochelle, NY 10801-4907; **Phone:** 914-636-5222; **Board Cert:** Internal Medicine 1980; Gastroenterology 1983; **Med School:** SUNY Buffalo 1977; **Resid:** Internal Medicine, Jacobi Med Ctr 1980; **Fellow:** Gastroenterology, Jacobi Med Ctr 1982

Landau, Steven R MD (Ge) - **Spec Exp:** Inflammatory Bowel Disease; Colon Cancer; **Hospital:** White Plains Hosp (page 652); **Address:** 30 Greenridge Ave, White Plains, NY 10605; **Phone:** 914-328-8555; **Board Cert:** Internal Medicine 1984; Gastroenterology 1987; **Med School:** NYU Sch Med 1981; **Resid:** Internal Medicine, Jacobi Med Ctr 1984; **Fellow:** Gastroenterology, Mount Sinai Hosp 1986; **Fac Appt:** Asst Prof Med, Columbia P&S

Lebovics, Edward MD (Ge) - **Spec Exp:** Hepatitis B & C; Pancreatic/Biliary Endoscopy (ERCP); Crohn's Disease; Liver Disease; **Hospital:** Westchester Med Ctr; **Address:** Gastroenterology & Hepatobiliary Cons, 19 Bradhurst Ave, Ste 2550 S, Hawthorne, NY 10595; **Phone:** 914-493-7337; **Board Cert:** Internal Medicine 1983; Gastroenterology 1985; **Med School:** NYU Sch Med 1980; **Resid:** Internal Medicine, Barnes-Jewish Hosp 1983; **Fellow:** Hepatology, Mt Sinai Hosp 1984; Gastroenterology, NY Med Coll Affil Hosp 1986; **Fac Appt:** Prof Med, NY Med Coll

Lee, Sang Y MD (Ge) - **Spec Exp:** Liver Disease; **Hospital:** Northern Westchester Hosp; **Address:** Mount Kisco Med Grp, 111 Bedford Rd, Katonah, NY 10536; **Phone:** 914-232-3135; **Board Cert:** Gastroenterology 2007; **Med School:** Tufts Univ 2000; **Resid:** Internal Medicine, Montefiore Med Ctr 2003; **Fellow:** Gastroenterology, Montefiore Med Ctr 2007

Liss, Mark MD (Ge) - **Spec Exp:** Endoscopy; Peptic Acid Disorders; Inflammatory Bowel Disease; **Hospital:** Montefiore New Rochelle Hosp (page 100); **Address:** 140 Lockwood Ave, Ste 318, New Rochelle, NY 10801; **Phone:** 914-633-0888; **Board Cert:** Internal Medicine 1980; Gastroenterology 1983; **Med School:** Mount Sinai Sch Med 1977; **Resid:** Internal Medicine, Mt Sinai Hosp 1980; **Fellow:** Gastroenterology, Montefiore Med Ctr 1982; **Fac Appt:** Asst Clin Prof Med, Albert Einstein Coll Med

Martin, Christopher A MD (Ge) - **Spec Exp:** Endoscopy; Pancreatic/Biliary Endoscopy (ERCP); **Hospital:** Phelps Meml Hosp Ctr; **Address:** Phelps Med Assocs, 777 N Broadway, Ste 305, Physicians Professional Bldg, Sleepy Hollow, NY 10591; **Phone:** 914-366-6120; **Board Cert:** Internal Medicine 2012; Gastroenterology 2005; **Med School:** Cornell Univ-Weill Med Coll 1999; **Resid:** Internal Medicine, NY-Presby/Weill Cornell Med Ctr 2002; **Fellow:** Gastroenterology, St Luke's-Roosevelt Hosp Ctr 2005

Pais, Shireen Andrade MD (Ge) - **Spec Exp:** Pancreatic/Biliary Endoscopy (ERCP); Pancreatic Disease; Biliary Disease; Barrett's Esophagus; **Hospital:** Westchester Med Ctr; **Address:** 19 Bradhurst Ave, Ste 2550 South, Hawthorne, NY 10532; **Phone:** 914-493-7337; **Board Cert:** Gastroenterology 2006; **Med School:** India 1996; **Resid:** Internal Medicine, St Lukes-Roosevelt Hosp Ctr 2002; **Fellow:** Gastroenterology, LAC & USC Med Ctr 2005; Advanced Endoscopy, UI Hlth Univ Hosp 2006; **Fac Appt:** Assoc Prof Med, NY Med Coll

Rosemarin, Jack I MD (Ge) - **Spec Exp:** Colonoscopy; Peptic Acid Disorders; Nutrition; **Hospital:** White Plains Hosp (page 652); **Address:** Digestive Disease & Nutrition Ctr-Westchester, 2 Gannett Drive, Ste L1, White Plains, NY 10604; **Phone:** 914-683-1555; **Board Cert:** Internal Medicine 1982; Gastroenterology 1983; **Med School:** NY Med Coll 1978; **Resid:** Internal Medicine, NY Med Coll Affil Hosp 1981; **Fellow:** Gastroenterology, Yale Affil Hosp 1983

Roston, Alfred D MD (Ge) - **Spec Exp:** Barrett's Esophagus; Gastroesophageal Reflux Disease (GERD); Inflammatory Bowel Disease; Irritable Bowel Syndrome; **Hospital:** White Plains Hosp (page 652); **Address:** Digestive Disease & Nutrition Ctr-Westchester, 2 Gannett Drive, Ste L1, White Plains, NY 10604; **Phone:** 914-683-1555; **Board Cert:** Gastroenterology 2005; **Med School:** NYU Sch Med 1989; **Resid:** Internal Medicine, Mt Sinai Hosp 1992; **Fellow:** Gastroenterology, NY Hosp-Cornell Univ Med 1994; Endoscopy, Brigham & Women's Hospital 1995

Sgouros, Anthony Peter MD (Ge) - **Spec Exp:** Inflammatory Bowel Disease; Gastrointestinal Cancer; **Hospital:** Northern Westchester Hosp; **Address:** Westchester Health Assocs, 322 Underhill Ave, Yorktown Heights, NY 10598; **Phone:** 914-269-9632; **Board Cert:** Gastroenterology 2005; **Med School:** Mount Sinai Sch Med 1990; **Resid:** Internal Medicine, NY-Presby/Columbia Univ Med Ctr 1993; **Fellow:** Gastroenterology, Montefiore Med Ctr 1995

Shapiro, Neil H MD (Ge) - **Spec Exp:** Endoscopy; Liver Disease; Inflammatory Bowel Disease; **Hospital:** White Plains Hosp (page 652), Greenwich Hosp (page 970); **Address:** Sound Shore Gastroenterology, 3010 Westchester Ave, Ste 400, Purchase, NY 10577; **Phone:** 914-253-9252; **Board Cert:** Internal Medicine 1978; Gastroenterology 1981; **Med School:** Wayne State Univ 1975; **Resid:** Internal Medicine, Beth Israel Med Ctr 1978; **Fellow:** Gastroenterology, Montefiore Med Ctr 1980; **Fac Appt:** Asst Clin Prof Med, Cornell Univ-Weill Med Coll

Taffet, Sanford L MD (Ge) - **Spec Exp:** Inflammatory Bowel Disease; Colon Cancer; Liver Disease; **Hospital:** Montefiore New Rochelle Hosp (page 100), Montefiore Mt Vernon Hosp (page 100); **Address:** 140 Lockwood Ave, Ste 110, New Rochelle, NY 10801-4907; **Phone:** 914-636-5222; **Board Cert:** Internal Medicine 1980; Gastroenterology 1981; **Med School:** NY Med Coll 1976; **Resid:** Internal Medicine, Maimonides Med Ctr 1979; **Fellow:** Gastroenterology, Albert Einstein Med Ctr 1981

Torman, Julie A MD (Ge) - **Spec Exp:** Colon Cancer Screening; Swallowing Disorders; **Hospital:** Phelps Meml Hosp Ctr; **Address:** 2005 Albany Post Rd, Ste 15, Croton-on-Hudson, NY 10520; **Phone:** 914-271-4212; **Board Cert:** Internal Medicine 1983; Gastroenterology 1989; **Med School:** Univ Nevada 1980; **Resid:** Internal Medicine, Brigham & Womens Hosp 1983; **Fellow:** Gastroenterology, Stanford Univ Med Ctr 1985

Wayne, Peter K MD (Ge) - **Spec Exp:** Hepatitis; Pancreatic/Biliary Endoscopy (ERCP); Liver Disease; Colonoscopy; **Hospital:** Saint Joseph's Med Ctr - Yonkers, St. John's Riverside Hosp-Andrus Pavil; **Address:** Westchester Digestive Dis Grp, 469 N Broadway, Yonkers, NY 10701-1923; **Phone:** 914-969-1115; **Board Cert:** Internal Medicine 1979; Gastroenterology 1981; **Med School:** Albert Einstein Coll Med 1976; **Resid:** Internal Medicine, Montefiore Hosp Med Ctr 1979; **Fellow:** Gastroenterology, Mount Sinai Hosp 1981

Wolf, David C MD (Ge) - **Spec Exp:** Liver Failure; Transplant Medicine-Liver; Liver Disease; Hepatitis B & C; **Hospital:** Westchester Med Ctr; **Address:** Westchester Medical Ctr, Liver Transplant Ctr, 100 Woods Rd, BHC Lower Level, Valhalla, NY 10595; **Phone:** 914-493-8916; **Board Cert:** Internal Medicine 1988; Gastroenterology 2011; Transplant Hepatology 2006; **Med School:** Columbia P&S 1985; **Resid:** Internal Medicine, NY Presby Hosp 1988; **Fellow:** Gastroenterology, Montefiore Med Ctr 1991; **Fac Appt:** Clin Prof Med, NY Med Coll

Geriatric Medicine

Banc, Tobe E MD (Ger) - **Spec Exp:** Geriatric Care; Preventive Medicine; **Hospital:** Phelps Meml Hosp Ctr; **Address:** 755 N Broadway, Ste 100, Sleepy Hollow, NY 10510; **Phone:** 914-366-3677; **Board Cert:** Internal Medicine 2010; Geriatric Medicine 2012; **Med School:** NYU Sch Med 1993; **Resid:** Internal Medicine, Hartford Hosp 1996; **Fellow:** Geriatric Medicine, Mt Sinai Med Ctr 1998

Devons, Cathryn A MD (Ger) - **Spec Exp:** Alzheimer's Disease; Memory Disorders; Dementia; Osteoporosis; **Hospital:** Phelps Meml Hosp Ctr, Mt Sinai Hosp; **Address:** Phelps Memorial Hosp, Div Geriatrics, 755 N Broadway, Sleepy Hollow, NY 10591; **Phone:** 914-366-3669; **Board Cert:** Geriatric Medicine 2004; **Med School:** Israel 1988; **Resid:** Internal Medicine, Montefiore Med Ctr 1991; **Fellow:** Geriatric Medicine, Mt Sinai Med Ctr 1993; **Fac Appt:** Asst Prof Med, Mount Sinai Sch Med

Escher, Jeffrey E MD (Ger) - **Spec Exp:** Geriatric Care; **Hospital:** Saint Joseph's Med Ctr - Yonkers, Westchester Med Ctr; **Address:** IPC The Hospitalist Company, 3 Barker Ave, White Plains, NY 10601; **Phone:** 914-949-1199; **Med School:** Belgium 1980; **Resid:** Internal Medicine, New Britain Genl Hosp 1983; **Fellow:** Geriatric Medicine, NYU Med Ctr 1985

Fader, Andrew MD (Ger) - **Hospital:** St. John's Riverside Hosp-Dobbs Ferry Pavil; **Address:** 128 Ashford Ave, Dobbs Ferry, NY 10522; **Phone:** 914-693-6500; **Board Cert:** Internal Medicine 1987; Geriatric Medicine 2010; **Med School:** Mexico 1982; **Resid:** Internal Medicine, Metropolitan Hosp 1987; **Fellow:** Geriatric Medicine, Westchester Co Med Ctr 1988

Grimshaw Jr, Robert S MD (Ger) *PCP* - **Spec Exp:** Geriatric Functional Assessment; Frail Elderly; **Hospital:** Hudson Valley Hosp Ctr, Westchester Med Ctr; **Address:** Mount Kisco Medical Group, 3680 Hill Blvd Fl 1, Jefferson Valley, NY 10535; **Phone:** 914-242-1370; **Board Cert:** Internal Medicine 1982; Geriatric Medicine 2004; **Med School:** Albert Einstein Coll Med 1979; **Resid:** Internal Medicine, Jacobi Med Ctr 1982; **Fac Appt:** Assoc Prof Med, NY Med Coll

Martimucci, William A MD (Ger) *PCP* - **Spec Exp:** Geriatric Care; Preventive Medicine; **Hospital:** White Plains Hosp (page 652); **Address:** WESTMED Med Grp, 1 Theall Rd, Ste 206, Rye, NY 10580; **Phone:** 914-848-8700; **Board Cert:** Internal Medicine 1989; **Med School:** Grenada 1985; **Resid:** Internal Medicine, Caledonian Hosp 1988; **Fellow:** Geriatric Medicine, Mt Sinai Med Ctr 1990

Vaughan, Margaret E MD (Ger) *PCP* - **Spec Exp:** Geriatric Functional Assessment; Frail Elderly; Falls in the Elderly; **Hospital:** Northern Westchester Hosp; **Address:** Mt Kisco Med Grp, Geriatric Med, 111 Bedford Rd, Katonah, NY 10536; **Phone:** 914-232-3135; **Board Cert:** Internal Medicine 2012; Geriatric Medicine 2013; **Med School:** SUNY Upstate Med Univ 1994; **Resid:** Anesthesiology, NY-Presby/Weill Cornell Med Ctr 1998; Internal Medicine, St Vincents Hosp 2001; **Fellow:** Geriatric Medicine, St Vincents Hosp 2002

Gynecologic Oncology

Chuang, Linus T MD (GO) - **Spec Exp:** Gynecologic Cancers; Ovarian Cancer; Uterine Cancer; Cervical Cancer; **Hospital:** St. John's Riverside Hosp-Andrus Pavil, White Plains Hosp (page 652); **Address:** 15 N Broadway N, Ste G, White Plains, NY 10601; **Phone:** 914-761-8901; **Board Cert:** Obstetrics & Gynecology 2013; Gynecologic Oncology 2013; **Med School:** Taiwan 1981; **Resid:** Obstetrics & Gynecology, Flushing Hosp 1990; **Fellow:** Gynecologic Oncology, MD Anderson Cancer Ctr 1994; **Fac Appt:** Prof ObG, Mount Sinai Sch Med

Gretz III, Herbert F MD (GO) - **Spec Exp:** Gynecologic Cancer; Minimally Invasive Surgery; Robotic Surgery; **Hospital:** White Plains Hosp (page 652), Greenwich Hosp (page 970); **Address:** WestMed Medical Grp, 2 Longview Ave, Ste 302, White Plains, NY 10601; **Phone:** 914-305-2730; **Board Cert:** Obstetrics & Gynecology 2013; Gynecologic Oncology 2013; **Med School:** NY Med Coll 1986; **Resid:** Obstetrics & Gynecology, NYU Med Ctr 1990; **Fellow:** Gynecologic Oncology, Univ Michigan Med Ctr 1993; **Fac Appt:** Assoc Clin Prof ObG, Mount Sinai Sch Med

Tedjarati, Sean S MD (GO) - **Spec Exp:** Uterine Cancer; Ovarian Cancer; Cervical Cancer; **Hospital:** Westchester Med Ctr; **Address:** 19 Bradhurst Ave, rm 2575 South, Hawthorne, NY 10532; **Phone:** 914-493-2181; **Board Cert:** Obstetrics & Gynecology 2013; Gynecologic Oncology 2013; **Med School:** West Indies 1994; **Resid:** Family Medicine, Ohio State Univ Med Ctr 1997; Obstetrics & Gynecology, Ohio State Univ Med Ctr 2000; **Fellow:** Gynecologic Oncology, MD Anderson Cancer Ctr 2003; **Fac Appt:** Assoc Prof ObG, NY Med Coll

Wertheim, Iris MD (GO) - **Spec Exp:** Gynecologic Cancers; **Hospital:** Northern Westchester Hosp; **Address:** Mt Kisco Med Grp, 400 E Main St, Mount Kisco, NY 10549; **Phone:** 914-242-2991; **Board Cert:** Obstetrics & Gynecology 2013; Gynecologic Oncology 2013; **Med School:** Columbia P&S 1989; **Resid:** Obstetrics & Gynecology, Brigham & Women's Hosp 1993; **Fellow:** Gynecologic Oncology, Brigham & Women's Hosp 1996; **Fac Appt:** Asst Prof S, Columbia P&S

Hand Surgery

Fragner, Paul D MD (HS) - **Spec Exp:** Hand & Wrist Surgery; Elbow Surgery; **Hospital:** White Plains Hosp (page 652); **Address:** White Plains Physician Assocs Orthopedic Specialists, 222 Westchester Ave, Ste 101, White Plains, NY 10604; **Phone:** 914-946-1010; **Board Cert:** Orthopaedic Surgery 2006; Hand Surgery 2006; **Med School:** SUNY Upstate Med Univ 1986; **Resid:** Orthopaedic Surgery, SUNY Downstate Med Ctr 1991; **Fellow:** Hand Surgery, Hosp U Penn 1992

Ilan, Doron MD (HS) - **Spec Exp:** Hand & Upper Extremity Surgery; Shoulder Surgery; Arthroscopic Surgery; Rotator Cuff Surgery; **Hospital:** St. John's Riverside Hosp-Dobbs Ferry Pavil, Nyack Hosp; **Address:** Premier Othropedics of Westchester & Rockland, 128 Ashford Ave, Lower Level Dobbs Ferry Hosp, Dobbs Ferry, NY 10522; **Phone:** 914-693-2057; **Board Cert:** Orthopaedic Surgery 2005; Hand Surgery 2007; **Med School:** Tulane Univ 1997; **Resid:** Surgery, NYU-Hosp Joint Diseases 1998; Orthopaedic Surgery, NYU-Hosp Joint Diseases 2002; **Fellow:** Hand Surgery, Stanford Univ Med Ctr 2004

Magill Jr, Richard M MD (HS) - **Spec Exp:** Hand & Upper Extremity Surgery; Microvascular Surgery; Shoulder Surgery; **Hospital:** Westchester Med Ctr, Phelps Meml Hosp Ctr; **Address:** University Orthopaedics, 19 Bradhurst Ave, Ste 1300-N, Hawthorne, NY 10532; **Phone:** 914-789-2733; **Board Cert:** Orthopaedic Surgery 2006; Hand Surgery 2006; **Med School:** Temple Univ 1983; **Resid:** Surgery, Temple Univ Hosp 1985; Orthopaedic Surgery, Maimonides Med Ctr 1992; **Fellow:** Hand Surgery, Duke Univ Med Ctr 1993

Pianka, George MD (HS) - **Spec Exp:** Hand & Wrist Surgery; Hand & Upper Extremity Surgery; Arthroscopic Surgery; Dupuytren's Contracture; **Hospital:** Phelps Meml Hosp Ctr; **Address:** Hudson Valley Bone & Joint Surgeons, 24 Saw Mill River Rd, Ste 206, Hawthorne, NY 10532; **Phone:** 914-631-7777; **Board Cert:** Orthopaedic Surgery 2013; Hand Surgery 2013; **Med School:** Univ Conn 1984; **Resid:** Orthopaedic Surgery, Lenox Hill Hosp 1989; **Fellow:** Hand Surgery, NYU Hosp For Joint Diseases 1990

Schefer, Alan J MD (HS) - **Spec Exp:** Hand & Upper Extremity Surgery; **Hospital:** Northern Westchester Hosp; **Address:** MKMG, Div Hand Surgery, 90 S Bedford Rd, Mount Kisco, NY 10549; **Phone:** 914-241-1050; **Board Cert:** Orthopaedic Surgery 2009; Hand Surgery 2009; **Med School:** Hahnemann Univ 1990; **Resid:** Orthopaedic Surgery, Mt Sinai Med Ctr 1995; **Fellow:** Hand Surgery, Stony Brook Univ Med Ctr 1996

Hematology

Ambinder, Jeffrey M MD (Hem) - **Hospital:** Putnam Hosp Ctr, Hudson Valley Hosp Ctr; **Address:** Hudson Vly Hematology & Onc Assocs, 2649 Strang Blvd, Ste 208, Yorktown Heights, NY 10598; **Phone:** 914-245-6000; **Board Cert:** Internal Medicine 1978; Hematology 1980; Medical Oncology 1983; **Med School:** NYU Sch Med 1975; **Resid:** Internal Medicine, Duke Univ Med Ctr 1978; **Fellow:** Hematology & Oncology, Duke Univ Med Ctr 1981

Lederman, Carol A MD (Hem) - **Spec Exp:** Hematology-Benign; Coagulation/Bleeding Disorders; Hematologic Malignancies; Transfusion Medicine; **Hospital:** White Plains Hosp (page 652); **Address:** Cancer & Blood Specialists of New York, 2 Longview Ave, Ste 201, White Plains, NY 10601; **Phone:** 914-684-2779; **Board Cert:** Hematology 2006; Medical Oncology 2007; **Med School:** Cornell Univ-Weill Med Coll 1989; **Resid:** Internal Medicine, Mt Sinai Med Ctr 1991; Internal Medicine, City Hosp Ctr at Elmhurst 1992; **Fellow:** Hematology & Oncology, Westchester Medical Ctr 1996

Liu, DeLong MD/PhD (Hem) - **Spec Exp:** Leukemia & Lymphoma; Multiple Myeloma; Lung Cancer; Anemia-Aplastic; **Hospital:** Westchester Med Ctr, Phelps Meml Hosp Ctr; **Address:** Hudson Valley Hem/Onc Assocs, 19 Bradhurst Ave, Ste 2100, Hawthorne, NY 10532; **Phone:** 914-493-8375; **Board Cert:** Internal Medicine 2006; Medical Oncology 2011; Hematology 2013; **Med School:** China 1984; **Resid:** Internal Medicine, Montefiore Med Ctr 1996; **Fellow:** Hematology & Oncology, Meml Sloan Kettering Cancer Ctr 1999; **Fac Appt:** Prof Med, NY Med Coll

Nelson, John C MD (Hem) - **Spec Exp:** Hematologic Malignancies; **Hospital:** Westchester Med Ctr, Phelps Meml Hosp Ctr; **Address:** Hudson Vly Hematology & Onc Assocs, 19 Bradhurst Ave, Ste 2100, Hawthorne, NY 10532; **Phone:** 914-493-8375; **Board Cert:** Internal Medicine 1974; Hematology 1976; **Med School:** Harvard Med Sch 1971; **Resid:** Internal Medicine, Mt Sinai Med Ctr 1974; **Fellow:** Hematology, Westchester Med Ctr 1976; **Fac Appt:** Asst Prof Med, NY Med Coll

Infectious Disease

Berkey, Peter B MD (Inf) - **Spec Exp:** Immune Deficiency; Tick-borne Diseases; Travel Medicine; HIV; **Hospital:** St. John's Riverside Hosp-Andrus Pavil, Saint Joseph's Med Ctr - Yonkers; **Address:** 970 N Broadway, Ste 212, Yonkers, NY 10701-1311; **Phone:** 914-376-1543; **Board Cert:** Internal Medicine 1985; Infectious Disease 1988; **Med School:** Univ Puerto Rico 1980; **Resid:** Internal Medicine, NY Med Coll/Univ Hosp 1984; **Fellow:** Infectious Disease, MD Anderson Cancer Ctr 1988

Kesh, Sandra MD (Inf) - **Spec Exp:** Hospital Acquired Infections; Antibiotic Resistance; Staphylococcal Infections; **Hospital:** White Plains Hosp (page 652), Greenwich Hosp (page 970); **Address:** WestMed Medical Grp, 210 Westchester Ave, White Plains, NY 10604; **Phone:** 914-682-6511; **Board Cert:** Internal Medicine 2013; Infectious Disease 2007; **Med School:** Cornell Univ-Weill Med Coll 2000; **Resid:** Internal Medicine, NY Presby-Cornell Med Ctr 2003; **Fellow:** Infectious Disease, NY Presby-Cornell Med Ctr 2007

Lederman, Jeffrey A MD (Inf) - **Spec Exp:** Travel Medicine; HIV; Lyme Disease; Tuberculosis; **Hospital:** Montefiore New Rochelle Hosp (page 100); **Address:** Montefiore New Rochelle Hosp, Div Infectious Dis, 16 Guion Pl Fl 2, New Rochelle, NY 10802; **Phone:** 914-365-4657; **Board Cert:** Internal Medicine 2011; Infectious Disease 2000; **Med School:** Jefferson Med Coll 1988; **Resid:** Internal Medicine, Mt Sinai Hosp 1991; **Fellow:** Infectious Disease, Montefiore Med Ctr 1995

Moorjani, Harish MD (Inf) - **Spec Exp:** Lyme Disease; AIDS/HIV; **Hospital:** Montefiore Mt Vernon Hosp (page 100), Phelps Meml Hosp Ctr; **Address:** Hudson Infectious Dis Assocs, 127 Woodside Ave, Ste 204, Briarcliff Manor, NY 10510; **Phone:** 914-762-2276; **Board Cert:** Internal Medicine 2014; Infectious Disease 2004; **Med School:** India 1986; **Resid:** Internal Medicine, UMDNJ Med Ctr 1992; **Fellow:** Infectious Disease, Stony Brook Univ Med Ctr 1994

Nadelman, Robert B MD (Inf) - **Spec Exp:** Tick-borne Diseases; Lyme Disease; **Hospital:** Westchester Med Ctr; **Address:** 19 Bradhurst Ave, Ste 200N, Hawthorne, NY 10532; **Phone:** 914-493-8865; **Board Cert:** Internal Medicine 1983; Infectious Disease 1988; **Med School:** Albert Einstein Coll Med 1980; **Resid:** Internal Medicine, Beth Israel Hosp 1983; **Fellow:** Infectious Disease, Beth Israel Hosp 1985; **Fac Appt:** Prof Med, NY Med Coll

Raffalli, John T MD (Inf) - **Spec Exp:** Lyme Disease; Tick-borne Diseases; **Hospital:** Northern Westchester Hosp; **Address:** MKMG, Infectious Disease, 90 S Bedford Rd, Mount Kisco, NY 10549; **Phone:** 914-241-1050; **Board Cert:** Internal Medicine 2005; Infectious Disease 2005; **Med School:** SUNY Downstate 1989; **Resid:** Internal Medicine, VA NY Harbor Hlthcare Sys 1992; **Fellow:** Infectious Disease, Meml Sloan-Kettering Cancer Ctr 1992; **Fac Appt:** Assoc Clin Prof Med, NY Med Coll

Rush, Thomas J MD (Inf) - **Spec Exp:** AIDS/HIV; Lyme Disease; Travel Medicine; **Hospital:** Phelps Meml Hosp Ctr, Putnam Hosp Ctr; **Address:** Hudson Infectious Dis Assocs, 127 Woodside Ave, Ste 204, Briarcliff Manor, NY 10510; **Phone:** 914-762-2276; **Board Cert:** Internal Medicine 1981; Infectious Disease 1984; **Med School:** Rush Med Coll 1978; **Resid:** Internal Medicine, Genesee Hosp 1981; **Fellow:** Infectious Disease, Strong Meml Hosp 1983; **Fac Appt:** Asst Clin Prof Med, NY Med Coll

Spicehandler, Debra A MD (Inf) - **Spec Exp:** Viral Infections; Antibiotic Resistance; Lyme Disease; **Hospital:** Northern Westchester Hosp; **Address:** 16 Bessel Ln, Chappaqua, NY 10514; **Phone:** 914-238-6330; **Board Cert:** Internal Medicine 1983; Infectious Disease 2007; **Med School:** Univ Cincinnati 1980; **Resid:** Internal Medicine, NYU Med Ctr 1983; **Fellow:** Infectious Disease, NYU Med Ctr 1985

Wormser, Gary P MD (Inf) - **Spec Exp:** Lyme Disease; AIDS/HIV; Diagnostic Problems; **Hospital:** Westchester Med Ctr; **Address:** 19 Bradhurst Ave, Ste 200N, Hawthorne, NY 10532; **Phone:** 914-493-8865; **Board Cert:** Internal Medicine 1978; Infectious Disease 1982; **Med School:** Johns Hopkins Univ 1972; **Resid:** Internal Medicine, Mt Sinai Hosp 1975; **Fellow:** Infectious Disease, Mt Sinai Hosp 1977; **Fac Appt:** Prof Med, NY Med Coll

Internal Medicine

Abdoo, Robert A MD (IM) *PCP* - **Hospital:** Hudson Valley Hosp Ctr; **Address:** 3630 Hill Blvd, Ste 402, Jefferson Valley, NY 10535-1506; **Phone:** 914-245-8808; **Board Cert:** Internal Medicine 1982; **Med School:** Univ Rochester 1979; **Resid:** Internal Medicine, Westchester Co Med Ctr 1982; **Fac Appt:** Asst Prof Med, NY Med Coll

Abenavoli, Tancredi J MD (IM) *PCP* - **Hospital:** White Plains Hosp (page 652); **Address:** 446 Westchester Ave, Port Chester, NY 10573; **Phone:** 914-939-1573; **Board Cert:** Internal Medicine 1979; Cardiovascular Disease 1981; **Med School:** NYU Sch Med 1976; **Resid:** Internal Medicine, VA Hosp/NYU Med Ctr 1979; **Fellow:** Cardiovascular Disease, VA Hosp/NYU Med Ctr 1981

Ades, Joseph R MD (IM) *PCP* - **Spec Exp:** Acupuncture; Complementary Medicine; **Hospital:** Phelps Meml Hosp Ctr; **Address:** 150 White Plains Rd, Ste 207, Tarrytown, NY 10591; **Phone:** 914-631-2480; **Board Cert:** Internal Medicine 1985; **Med School:** Albert Einstein Coll Med 1982; **Resid:** Internal Medicine, LAC & USC Med Ctr 1986

Alpert, Barbara MD (IM) *PCP* - **Spec Exp:** Osteoporosis; Lyme Disease; **Hospital:** Northern Westchester Hosp; **Address:** MKMG, Primary Care, 90 S Bedford Rd, Mount Kisco, NY 10549; **Phone:** 914-241-1050; **Board Cert:** Internal Medicine 1987; **Med School:** Univ Pennsylvania 1984; **Resid:** Internal Medicine, NY-Cornell Hosp 1987; **Fac Appt:** Asst Clin Prof Med, Mount Sinai Sch Med

Altholz, Jeffrey D MD (IM) - **Spec Exp:** Occupational Medicine; Addiction/Substance Abuse; **Hospital:** Phelps Meml Hosp Ctr; **Address:** Westchester Med Care, 150 White Plains Rd, Tarrytown, NY 10591; **Phone:** 914-345-3135; **Med School:** Albert Einstein Coll Med 1986; **Resid:** Internal Medicine, St Vincents Hosp 1989; **Fellow:** Internal Medicine, St Vincents Hosp 1990

Andersen, Margaret MD (IM) *PCP* - **Hospital:** Northern Westchester Hosp; **Address:** Westchester Health Int Med for Women, 645 Marble Ave, Thornwood, NY 10594; **Phone:** 914-769-1600; **Board Cert:** Internal Medicine 1997; **Med School:** SUNY Stony Brook 1994; **Resid:** Internal Medicine, Mount Sinai Med Ctr 1997; **Fac Appt:** Asst Clin Prof Med, NY Med Coll

Aversa, Alphonse R MD (IM) *PCP* - **Hospital:** Northern Westchester Hosp; **Address:** MKMG, Primary Care, 90 S Bedford Rd, Mount Kisco, NY 10549; **Phone:** 914-241-1050; **Board Cert:** Internal Medicine 1999; **Med School:** SUNY Downstate 1977; **Resid:** Internal Medicine, Kings Co Hosp Ctr 1981

Bennett, Stanford W MD (IM) *PCP* - **Hospital:** Northern Westchester Hosp; **Address:** Westchester Health Assocs, 1838 Commerce St, Yorktown Heights, NY 10598; **Phone:** 914-962-3500; **Board Cert:** Internal Medicine 2005; **Med School:** Dominica 2001; **Resid:** Internal Medicine, Stamford Hosp 2005

Beran, Nancy R MD (IM) *PCP* - **Spec Exp:** Women's Health; **Hospital:** Northern Westchester Hosp; **Address:** Westchester Hlth Internal Med for Women, 645 Marble Ave, Thornwood, NY 10594; **Phone:** 914-769-1600; **Board Cert:** Internal Medicine 2009; **Med School:** Thomas Jefferson Univ 1995; **Resid:** Internal Medicine, Parkland Meml Hosp 1998

Carosella, Christine MD (IM) *PCP* - **Spec Exp:** Hypertension; Asthma; Cholesterol/Lipid Disorders; **Hospital:** Westchester Med Ctr; **Address:** 19 Bradhurst Ave, Ste 3090 North, Hawthorne, NY 10532; **Phone:** 914-592-2400; **Board Cert:** Internal Medicine 2005; **Med School:** NY Med Coll 1992; **Resid:** Internal Medicine, Westchester Med Ctr 1995; **Fac Appt:** Asst Prof Med, NY Med Coll

Colangelo, Daniel A MD (IM) *PCP* - **Hospital:** White Plains Hosp (page 652); **Address:** Scarsdale Med Grp, 600 Mamaroneck Ave, Ste 200, Mamaroneck, NY 10528; **Phone:** 914-698-4466; **Board Cert:** Internal Medicine 2004; **Med School:** NYU Sch Med 1980; **Resid:** Internal Medicine, Lenox Hill Hosp 1983

Croen, Kenneth MD (IM) *PCP* - **Spec Exp:** Infectious Disease; **Hospital:** White Plains Hosp (page 652); **Address:** Scarsdale Med Grp, 600 Mamaroneck Ave, Ste 200, Harrison, NY 10583; **Phone:** 914-723-8100; **Board Cert:** Internal Medicine 1984; Infectious Disease 1988; **Med School:** Albert Einstein Coll Med 1980; **Resid:** Internal Medicine, NY-Presby/Columbia Univ Med Ctr 1983; Infectious Disease, Presby Hosp 1984; **Fellow:** Infectious Disease, Natl Inst Hlth 1989

D'Ascanio, Alfredo MD (IM) *PCP* - **Spec Exp:** Endocrinology; **Hospital:** Northern Westchester Hosp; **Address:** Westchester Health, One S Greeley Ave, Ste 303, Chappaqua, NY 10514; **Phone:** 914-238-0801; **Board Cert:** Internal Medicine 2006; **Med School:** Italy 1983; **Resid:** Internal Medicine, Bridgeport Hosp 1987; **Fellow:** Endocrinology, Westchester Co Med Ctr 1989

Dennett, Ronald MD (IM) *PCP* - **Hospital:** Lawrence Hosp Ctr (page 102); **Address:** WestMed Med Group, Ridge Hill, 73 Market St, Fl 2, Yonkers, NY 10710; **Phone:** 914-831-6840; **Board Cert:** Internal Medicine 1980; **Med School:** Univ VT Coll Med 1977; **Resid:** Internal Medicine, Univ Colorado Hosp 1980; **Fac Appt:** Asst Clin Prof Med, Albert Einstein Coll Med

Engelhardt III, Martin B DO (IM) *PCP* - **Hospital:** White Plains Hosp (page 652); **Address:** North Ridge Medical Group, 1296 North Ave, New Rochelle, NY 10804; **Phone:** 914-235-8224; **Board Cert:** Internal Medicine 2009; **Med School:** Philadelphia Coll Osteo Med 1993; **Resid:** Internal Medicine, Albert Einstein Affil Hosp 1998

Ennis, David T MD (IM) *PCP* - **Hospital:** Northern Westchester Hosp; **Address:** Westchester Health Assocs, 1838 Commerce St, Yorktown Heights, NY 10598; **Phone:** 914-962-3500; **Board Cert:** Internal Medicine 1986; **Med School:** NY Med Coll 1983; **Resid:** Internal Medicine, Westchester Co Med Ctr 1986

Fazio, Nelson M MD (IM) *PCP* - **Spec Exp:** Skin Diseases; Hypertension; Obesity; Infectious Disease; **Hospital:** Lawrence Hosp Ctr (page 102); **Address:** 133 Montgomery Ave, Scarsdale, NY 10583; **Phone:** 914-713-8517; **Board Cert:** Internal Medicine 1986; **Med School:** NY Med Coll 1981; **Resid:** Internal Medicine, Westchester Co Med Ctr 1984; **Fellow:** Infectious Disease, Montefiore Med Ctr 1994

Fenster, Mitchell MD (IM) *PCP* - **Hospital:** White Plains Hosp (page 652); **Address:** Westchester Hlth Assocs, 401 Columbus Ave, Valhalla, NY 10595; **Phone:** 914-769-0268; **Board Cert:** Internal Medicine 1987; **Med School:** Mount Sinai Sch Med 1981; **Resid:** Internal Medicine, NYU-Bellevue Med Ctr 1984

Fiorentino, Thomas MD (IM) *PCP* - **Spec Exp:** Palliative Care; **Hospital:** St. John's Riverside Hosp-Andrus Pavil, Mt Sinai Hosp; **Address:** Mt Sinai Riverside Med Grp, 1010 N Broadway, Yonkers, NY 10701; **Phone:** 914-969-0770; **Board Cert:** Internal Medicine 1975; Hospice & Palliative Medicine 2008; **Med School:** NY Med Coll 1972; **Resid:** Internal Medicine, Metropolitan Hosp 1976

Glickstein, Shari MD (IM) *PCP* - **Hospital:** White Plains Hosp (page 652); **Address:** Maple Medical, 30 Davis Ave, White Plains, NY 10601; **Phone:** 914-328-2355; **Board Cert:** Internal Medicine 1986; **Med School:** Mount Sinai Sch Med 1983; **Resid:** Internal Medicine, Mt Sinai Med Ctr 1986

Goldman, Jack S MD (IM) *PCP* - **Spec Exp:** Colonoscopy/Polypectomy; Liver Disease; Endoscopy; **Address:** 750 McLean Ave, Yonkers, NY 10704; **Phone:** 914-237-8686; **Board Cert:** Internal Medicine 1975; Gastroenterology 1979; **Med School:** Albert Einstein Coll Med 1961; **Resid:** Internal Medicine, Bronx Lebanon Hosp 1963; Internal Medicine, VA Med Ctr 1966; **Fellow:** Gastroenterology, VA Med Ctr 1965

Gross, Jeffrey D MD (IM) *PCP* - **Hospital:** Northern Westchester Hosp; **Address:** MKMG, Primary Care, 90 S Bedford Rd, Mt Kisco, NY 10549; **Phone:** 914-241-1050; **Board Cert:** Internal Medicine 2005; **Med School:** SUNY Hlth Sci Ctr 1992; **Resid:** Internal Medicine, Montefiore Med Ctr 1996

Herzog, David A MD (IM) *PCP* - **Spec Exp:** Cholesterol/Lipid Disorders; Preventive Medicine; **Hospital:** White Plains Hosp (page 652); **Address:** WestMed Med Grp, 1 Theall Rd, Ste 204, Rye, NY 10580; **Phone:** 914-848-8700; **Board Cert:** Internal Medicine 1984; **Med School:** Mount Sinai Sch Med 1981; **Resid:** Internal Medicine, St Luke's Hosp 1984

Hopkins, Arthur J MD (IM) *PCP* - **Spec Exp:** Preventive Medicine; **Hospital:** Montefiore Med Ctr-Moses Campus (page 100); **Address:** Montefiore Med Grp, Primary Care, 1010 Central Park Ave, Yonkers, NY 10704; **Phone:** 914-964-4133; **Board Cert:** Internal Medicine 1986; **Med School:** Univ Pennsylvania 1983; **Resid:** Internal Medicine, Hosp Univ Penn 1986; **Fac Appt:** Asst Prof Med, Albert Einstein Coll Med

Jacobowitz, Marilyn MD (IM) *PCP* - **Hospital:** Northern Westchester Hosp; **Address:** Mt Kisco Med Grp, 90 S Bedford Rd, Mt Kisco, NY 10549-3412; **Phone:** 914-241-1050; **Board Cert:** Internal Medicine 2012; Pulmonary Disease 2004; Critical Care Medicine 2005; **Med School:** NYU Sch Med 1989; **Resid:** Internal Medicine, Mt Sinai Hosp 1992; **Fellow:** Pulmonary Disease, Mt Sinai Hosp 1995

Kapoor, Satish MD (IM) *PCP* - **Spec Exp:** Asthma; Emphysema; Preventive Medicine; **Hospital:** Phelps Meml Hosp Ctr; **Address:** 362 N Broadway Fl 2, Sleepy Hollow, NY 10591; **Phone:** 914-631-2070; **Board Cert:** Internal Medicine 1979; **Med School:** India 1972; **Resid:** Internal Medicine, Kingsbrook Jewish Med Ctr 1979; **Fellow:** Pulmonary Disease, Queens Hosp 1981

Karmen, Carol L MD (IM) *PCP* - **Spec Exp:** Preventive Medicine; **Hospital:** Westchester Med Ctr; **Address:** 19 Bradhurst Ave, Ste 3090 North, Hawthorne, NY 10532; **Phone:** 914-592-2400; **Board Cert:** Internal Medicine 2007; **Med School:** Albert Einstein Coll Med 1986; **Resid:** Internal Medicine, Westchester Med Ctr 1990; **Fac Appt:** Assoc Prof Med, NY Med Coll

Krieger, Sharon MD (IM) *PCP* - **Hospital:** Northern Westchester Hosp; **Address:** MKMG, Primary Care, 90 S Bedford Rd, Mt Kisco, NY 10549; **Phone:** 914-241-1050; **Board Cert:** Internal Medicine 2004; **Med School:** Louisiana State U, New Orleans 1991; **Resid:** Internal Medicine, NY-Presby/Weill Cornell Med Ctr 1994

Kubersky, Steven MD (IM) *PCP* - **Hospital:** White Plains Hosp (page 652), Lawrence Hosp Ctr (page 102); **Address:** WestMed Med Grp, 73 Market St Fl 2, Yonkers, NY 10710; **Phone:** 914-831-6860; **Board Cert:** Internal Medicine 2013; **Med School:** NYU Sch Med 1988; **Resid:** Internal Medicine, Mt Sinai Hosp 1992

Lechner, Michael MD (IM) *PCP* - **Spec Exp:** Geriatric Medicine; Geriatric Rehabilitation; **Hospital:** Phelps Meml Hosp Ctr; **Address:** 14 Church St, Ste 208, Ossining, NY 10562; **Phone:** 914-631-0866; **Board Cert:** Internal Medicine 1980; **Med School:** Albert Einstein Coll Med 1961; **Resid:** Internal Medicine, Westchester Med Ctr 1964; **Fellow:** Hematology, LIJ Med Ctr 1965

Lodish, Galya S MD (IM) *PCP* - **Hospital:** Northern Westchester Hosp; **Address:** Westchester Health Int Medicine, 105 S Bedford Rd, Ste 302, Mount Kisco, NY 10549; **Phone:** 914-769-1600; **Board Cert:** Internal Medicine 2004; **Med School:** Univ Tex, Houston 2000; **Resid:** Internal Medicine, Mount Auburn Hosp 2004

Margulis, Steven M MD (IM) *PCP* - **Hospital:** Northern Westchester Hosp; **Address:** MKMG, Primary Care, 90 S Bedford Rd, Mt Kisco, NY 10549; **Phone:** 914-241-1050; **Board Cert:** Internal Medicine 2010; **Med School:** Albert Einstein Coll Med 1997; **Resid:** Internal Medicine, Mt Sinai Hosp 2000

Melman, Martin MD (IM) *PCP* - **Spec Exp:** Hypertension; Asthma; Geriatric Medicine; **Hospital:** Phelps Meml Hosp Ctr; **Address:** 87 Grand St, Croton-on-Hudson, NY 10520; **Phone:** 914-271-4845; **Board Cert:** Internal Medicine 1977; **Med School:** NY Med Coll 1974; **Resid:** Internal Medicine, Metropolitan Hosp Ctr 1977; Internal Medicine, Westchester Med Ctr 1978; **Fac Appt:** Asst Clin Prof Med, NY Med Coll

Morrison, Donna E MD (IM) *PCP* - **Hospital:** Northern Westchester Hosp; **Address:** Mount Kisco Medical Group, PC, 537 N State Rd, Briarcliff Manor, NY 10510-1573; **Phone:** 914-940-2500; **Board Cert:** Internal Medicine 2012; **Med School:** Cornell Univ-Weill Med Coll 1999; **Resid:** Internal Medicine, Mount Sinai Hosp 2002

Pappas, Steven MD (IM) *PCP* - **Spec Exp:** Occupational Medicine; Preventive Medicine; **Hospital:** Montefiore New Rochelle Hosp (page 100); **Address:** 266 White Plains Rd, Ste 1A, Eastchester, NY 10709; **Phone:** 914-793-1115; **Board Cert:** Internal Medicine 1982; **Med School:** Albert Einstein Coll Med 1978; **Resid:** Internal Medicine, St Lukes-Roosevelt Hosp Ctr 1981

Pomerantz, Daniel MD (IM) *PCP* - **Spec Exp:** Palliative Care; Ethics; **Hospital:** Montefiore New Rochelle Hosp (page 100); **Address:** Montefiore, Primary Care, 29 Glover Johnson Pkwy, New Rochelle, NY 10801; **Phone:** 914-365-3160; **Board Cert:** Internal Medicine 2013; Hospice & Palliative Medicine 2010; **Med School:** Harvard Med Sch 1990; **Resid:** Internal Medicine, NYU Med Ctr 1994

Ridge, Gerald A MD (IM) *PCP* - **Spec Exp:** Geriatric Medicine; Preventive Medicine; **Hospital:** Lawrence Hosp Ctr (page 102), NY-Presby/Columbia Univ Med Ctr, NY (page 102); **Address:** Lawrence Med Assocs, 685 White Plains Rd, Eastchester, NY 10709; **Phone:** 914-787-4100; **Board Cert:** Internal Medicine 2008; Geriatric Medicine 2008; **Med School:** UCSF 1979; **Resid:** Internal Medicine, Bronx Muni Hosp 1981; Internal Medicine, NY-Presby/Columbia Univ Med Ctr 1982; **Fellow:** Neurology, NY-Presby/Columbia Univ Med Ctr 1983; **Fac Appt:** Clin Prof Med, Columbia P&S

Rie, Jonathan MD (IM) *PCP* - **Spec Exp:** Hypertension; Kidney Stones; **Hospital:** White Plains Hosp (page 652); **Address:** 33 Davis Ave, White Plains, NY 10605; **Phone:** 914-831-2900; **Board Cert:** Internal Medicine 1988; Nephrology 2010; **Med School:** NY Med Coll 1985; **Resid:** Internal Medicine, Montefiore Med Ctr 1988; **Fellow:** Nephrology, Montefiore Med Ctr 1990

Rosch, Elliott MD (IM) *PCP* - **Spec Exp:** Preventive Medicine; Cholesterol/Lipid Disorders; Hypertension; Weight Management; **Hospital:** St. John's Riverside Hosp-Andrus Pavil, Mt Sinai Hosp; **Address:** Mt Sinai Riverside Med Grp, 1010 N Broadway, Yonkers, NY 10701; **Phone:** 914-965-4424; **Board Cert:** Internal Medicine 1981; **Med School:** Univ Pennsylvania 1978; **Resid:** Internal Medicine, Hosp Univ Penn 1981; **Fac Appt:** Asst Prof Med, Mount Sinai-Icahn Sch of Med

Saltzman-Gabelman, Lori MD (IM) *PCP* - **Hospital:** White Plains Hosp (page 652); **Address:** WestMed Med Grp, 210 Westchester Ave Fl 2, White Plains, NY 10604; **Phone:** 914-682-0700; **Board Cert:** Internal Medicine 1989; **Med School:** NY Med Coll 1986; **Resid:** Internal Medicine, Westchester Med Ctr 1989

Soltren, Rafael MD (IM) *PCP* - **Spec Exp:** Diabetes; Hypertension; **Hospital:** Phelps Meml Hosp Ctr; **Address:** Phelps Med Assocs, 100 S Highland Ave, Ossining, NY 10562; **Phone:** 914-941-1277; **Board Cert:** Internal Medicine 1985; **Med School:** Cornell Univ-Weill Med Coll 1981; **Resid:** Internal Medicine, Montefiore Med Ctr 1984

Starke, Charles L MD (IM) *PCP* - **Hospital:** Phelps Meml Hosp Ctr, Westchester Med Ctr; **Address:** 302 Chappaqua Rd, Briarcliff Manor, NY 10510; **Phone:** 914-762-4460; **Board Cert:** Internal Medicine 1978; **Med School:** Albert Einstein Coll Med 1975; **Resid:** Internal Medicine, Georgetown Univ Hosp 1978; **Fac Appt:** Prof Med, Columbia P&S

Tang, David J MD (IM) *PCP* - **Hospital:** St. John's Riverside Hosp-Andrus Pavil, Mt Sinai Hosp; **Address:** Mt Sinai Riverside Med Grp, 1010 N Broadway, Yonkers, NY 10701; **Phone:** 914-965-4424; **Board Cert:** Internal Medicine 2005; **Med School:** Meharry Med Coll 2002; **Resid:** Internal Medicine, LIJ Med Ctr 2005

Turro, James J MD (IM) *PCP* - **Hospital:** Northern Westchester Hosp; **Address:** MKMG, Primary Care, 90 S Bedford Rd, Mt Kisco, NY 10549; **Phone:** 914-241-1050; **Board Cert:** Internal Medicine 1985; **Med School:** Cornell Univ-Weill Med Coll 1982; **Resid:** Internal Medicine, Bronx Muni Hosp 1986

Warshafsky, Stephen MD (IM) *PCP* - **Spec Exp:** Lyme Disease; Cholesterol/Lipid Disorders; Preventive Cardiology; Preventive Medicine; **Hospital:** Westchester Med Ctr; **Address:** 1055 Saw Mill River Rd, Ste 206, Ardsley, NY 10502; **Phone:** 914-591-0733; **Board Cert:** Internal Medicine 2004; **Med School:** NY Med Coll 1989; **Resid:** Internal Medicine, Westchester Med Ctr 1992; **Fac Appt:** Assoc Clin Prof Med, NY Med Coll

Wein, Michael S MD (IM) - **Hospital:** Northern Westchester Hosp; **Address:** 111 Bedford Rd, Katonah, NY 10536; **Phone:** 914-232-3135; **Board Cert:** Internal Medicine 2013; **Med School:** NYU Sch Med 2000; **Resid:** Internal Medicine, Beth Israel Deconess Med Ctr 2003

Wolfe, Mary J MD (IM) *PCP* - **Hospital:** Phelps Meml Hosp Ctr; **Address:** Columbia Doctors, 14 Church St, Ste 208, Ossining, NY 10562; **Phone:** 914-941-1334; **Board Cert:** Internal Medicine 1980; **Med School:** Penn State Coll Med 1976; **Resid:** Internal Medicine, Westchester Med Ctr 1979

Wolfson, Robert A MD (IM) *PCP* - **Hospital:** Northern Westchester Hosp; **Address:** MKMG, Primary Care, 90 S Bedford Rd, Mount Kisco, NY 10549; **Phone:** 914-241-1050; **Board Cert:** Internal Medicine 1980; **Med School:** SUNY Downstate 1977; **Resid:** Internal Medicine, Kings Co Hosp 1981

Zarowitz, William MD (IM) *PCP* - **Spec Exp:** Occupational Medicine; Preventive Medicine; **Hospital:** White Plains Hosp (page 652); **Address:** 143 Maple Ave, White Plains, NY 10601; **Phone:** 914-683-8610; **Board Cert:** Internal Medicine 1981; **Med School:** NY Med Coll 1978; **Resid:** Internal Medicine, Montefiore Med Ctr 1981; **Fac Appt:** Assoc Clin Prof Med, NY Med Coll

Interventional Cardiology

Hjemdahl-Monsen, Craig MD (IC) - **Spec Exp:** Cardiac Catheterization; Percutaneous Coronary Intervention; Coronary Angioplasty/Stents; **Hospital:** NY-Presby/Columbia Univ Med Ctr, NY (page 102), White Plains Hosp (page 652); **Address:** Columbia Doctors Med Grp, Cardiology, 19 Bradhurst Ave, Ste 700, Hawthorne, NY 10532; **Phone:** 914-593-7800; **Board Cert:** Internal Medicine 1983; Cardiovascular Disease 1985; Interventional Cardiology 2009; **Med School:** Johns Hopkins Univ 1980; **Resid:** Internal Medicine, Univ Hosp 1983; **Fellow:** Cardiovascular Disease, Mt Sinai Hosp 1985; Interventional Cardiology, Mt Sinai Hosp 1987; **Fac Appt:** Asst Clin Prof Med, Columbia P&S

Kalapatapu, Kumar S MD (IC) - **Hospital:** NY-Presby/Columbia Univ Med Ctr, NY (page 102), White Plains Hosp (page 652); **Address:** Columbia Doctors, 19 Bradhurst Ave, Ste 700, Hawthorne, NY 10532; **Phone:** 914-593-7800; **Board Cert:** Cardiovascular Disease 2008; Interventional Cardiology 2013; **Med School:** India 1985; **Resid:** Internal Medicine, Advocate Christ Med Ctr 1993; **Fellow:** Cardiovascular Disease, St Vincents Hosp 1994; Interventional Cardiology, Westchester Med Ctr 1996

Messinger, David MD (IC) - **Spec Exp:** Coronary Angioplasty/Stents; **Hospital:** NY-Presby/Weill Cornell Med Ctr, NY (page 102), Westchester Med Ctr; **Address:** Sound Shore, Cardiology, 175 Memorial Hwy, New Rochelle, NY 10801; **Phone:** 914-235-3535; **Board Cert:** Cardiovascular Disease 2005; Interventional Cardiology 2009; **Med School:** Cornell Univ-Weill Med Coll 1987; **Resid:** Internal Medicine, NY-Presby/Weill Cornell Med Ctr 1990; **Fellow:** Cardiovascular Disease, NY-Presby/Weill Cornell Med Ctr 1993; Interventional Cardiology, NY-Presby/Weill Cornell Med Ctr 1994

Weiss, Melvin MD (IC) - **Spec Exp:** Cardiac Imaging; Congestive Heart Failure; Diabetes & Heart Disease; Coronary Artery Disease; **Hospital:** NY-Presby/Columbia Univ Med Ctr, NY (page 102), White Plains Hosp (page 652); **Address:** Columbia Doctors, 19 Bradhurst Ave, Ste 700, Hawthorne, NY 10532; **Phone:** 914-593-7800; **Board Cert:** Internal Medicine 1972; Cardiovascular Disease 1975; **Med School:** SUNY Hlth Sci Ctr 1967; **Resid:** Internal Medicine, New York Hosp 1971; **Fellow:** Cardiovascular Disease, NY-Presby/Columbia Univ Med Ctr 1972; **Fac Appt:** Prof Med, NY Med Coll

Maternal & Fetal Medicine

Berck, David J MD (MF) - **Spec Exp:** Ultrasound; Pregnancy-High Risk; **Hospital:** Northern Westchester Hosp; **Address:** MKMG, Maternal & Fetal Med, 90 S Bedford Rd, Mount Kisco, NY 10549; **Phone:** 914-241-1050; **Board Cert:** Obstetrics & Gynecology 2013; Maternal & Fetal Medicine 2013; **Med School:** Harvard Med Sch 1991; **Resid:** Obstetrics & Gynecology, Mass Genl Hosp 1995; **Fellow:** Maternal & Fetal Medicine, NY-Presby/Columbia Univ Med Ctr 1998

Cape, Alison MD (MF) - **Hospital:** Northern Westchester Hosp; **Address:** MKMG, Maternal-Fetal Med, 90 S Bedford Rd, Mount Kisco, NY 10549; **Phone:** 914-241-1050; **Board Cert:** Obstetrics & Gynecology 2014; Maternal & Fetal Medicine 2014; **Med School:** Harvard Med Sch 2003; **Resid:** Obstetrics & Gynecology, Brigham & Womens Hosp 2007; **Fellow:** Maternal & Fetal Medicine, Brigham & Womens Hosp 2010

Devine, Patricia Ann MD (MF) - **Spec Exp:** Pregnancy-High Risk; Prenatal Diagnosis; Diabetes in Pregnancy; Premature Labor; **Hospital:** Montefiore New Rochelle Hosp (page 100); **Address:** Montefiore, Maternal Fetal Med, 16 Guion Pl Fl 4, New Rochelle, NY 10802; **Phone:** 914-365-4263; **Board Cert:** Obstetrics & Gynecology 2013; Maternal & Fetal Medicine 2013; **Med School:** Mount Sinai Sch Med 1987; **Resid:** Obstetrics & Gynecology, Beth Israel Med Ctr 1991; **Fellow:** Maternal & Fetal Medicine, Westchester Co Med Ctr 1993; **Fac Appt:** Assoc Clin Prof ObG, NY Med Coll

Gallousis, Francene MD (MF) - **Hospital:** Northern Westchester Hosp; **Address:** NWH, Maternal Fetal Med, 400 E Main St, rm 310, Mount Kisco, NY 10549; **Phone:** 914-666-1010; **Board Cert:** Obstetrics & Gynecology 2014; Maternal & Fetal Medicine 2014; **Med School:** SUNY Downstate 1990; **Resid:** Obstetrics & Gynecology, Westchester Med Ctr 1994

Lescale, Keith B MD (MF) - **Spec Exp:** Pregnancy-High Risk; Prenatal Diagnosis; Fetal Ultrasound/Obstetrical Imaging; Genetic Disorders; **Hospital:** White Plains Hosp (page 652), Phelps Meml Hosp Ctr; **Address:** Hudson Valley Perinatal Consulting, 600 Mamaroneck Ave, Ste 110, Harrison, NY 10528; **Phone:** 914-670-0500; **Board Cert:** Obstetrics & Gynecology 2013; Maternal & Fetal Medicine 2013; **Med School:** Louisiana State U, New Orleans 1987; **Resid:** Obstetrics & Gynecology, LSU Interim Public Hosp 1991; **Fellow:** Maternal & Fetal Medicine, NY-Presby/Weill Cornell Med Ctr 1994

Medical Oncology

Ahmed, Tauseef MD (Onc) - **Spec Exp:** Bone Marrow Transplant; Lymphoma; Brain Tumors; Genitourinary Cancer; **Hospital:** Westchester Med Ctr; **Address:** Hudson Vly Hem/Onc Assocs, 19 Bradhurst Ave, Ste 2100, Hawthorne, NY 10532; **Phone:** 914-493-8375; **Board Cert:** Internal Medicine 1980; Hematology 1982; Medical Oncology 1983; **Med School:** Pakistan 1976; **Resid:** Internal Medicine, Sinai-Grace Hosp 1980; **Fellow:** Medical Oncology, Meml Sloan-Kettering Cancer Ctr 1983; **Fac Appt:** Prof Med, NY Med Coll

Bernhardt, Bernard MD (Onc) - **Spec Exp:** Lung Cancer; Lymphoma; Leukemia-Chronic Lymphocytic; Anemias & Red Blood Cell Disorders; **Hospital:** Montefiore New Rochelle Hosp (page 100), Montefiore Med Ctr-Einstein Campus (page 100); **Address:** Advanced Oncology Assocs, 50 Guion Pl, Ste 32, New Rochelle, NY 10801; **Phone:** 914-632-5397; **Board Cert:** Internal Medicine 1968; Hematology 1972; Medical Oncology 1973; **Med School:** Northwestern Univ 1961; **Resid:** Internal Medicine, DC Genl Hosp 1963; Internal Medicine, NY Med Coll 1966; **Fellow:** Hematology, Montefiore Hosp Med Ctr 1968; **Fac Appt:** Clin Prof Med, NY Med Coll

Caron, Philip C MD/PhD (Onc) - **Spec Exp:** Lymphoma; Gastrointestinal Cancer; **Hospital:** Phelps Meml Hosp Ctr, Meml Sloan Kettering Canc Ctr (page 110); **Address:** MSKCC, Sleepy Hollow Oncology Svc, 777 N Broadway, Ste 102, Sleepy Hollow, NY 10591; **Phone:** 914-366-0664; **Board Cert:** Internal Medicine 1989; Medical Oncology 2013; Hematology 2007; **Med School:** NY Med Coll 1986; **Resid:** Internal Medicine, Mt Sinai Hosp 1989; **Fellow:** Hematology & Oncology, Meml Sloan-Kettering Cancer Ctr 1992

Casper, Ephraim S MD (Onc) - **Spec Exp:** Gastrointestinal Cancer; Pancreatic Cancer; Sarcoma-Soft Tissue; Solid Tumors; **Hospital:** Meml Sloan Kettering Canc Ctr (page 110); **Address:** MSKCC West Harrison, 500 Westchester Ave, West Harrison, NY 10604; **Phone:** 914-367-7220; **Board Cert:** Internal Medicine 1977; Medical Oncology 1979; **Med School:** Rush Med Coll 1974; **Resid:** Internal Medicine, Rush Univ Med Ctr 1977; **Fellow:** Medical Oncology, Meml Sloan-Kettering Cancer Ctr 1979

Feldman, Stuart P MD (Onc) - **Spec Exp:** Breast Cancer; Lymphoma; **Hospital:** White Plains Hosp (page 652), Greenwich Hosp (page 970); **Address:** WestMed Med Grp, Hem/Onc, 210 Westchester Ave, White Plains, NY 10604; **Phone:** 914-681-5200; **Board Cert:** Internal Medicine 1980; Hematology 1982; Medical Oncology 1985; **Med School:** Geo Wash Univ 1977; **Resid:** Internal Medicine, NY-Presby/Weill Cornell Med Ctr 1980; **Fellow:** Hematology & Oncology, Meml Sloan-Kettering Cancer Ctr 1983; **Fac Appt:** Asst Clin Prof Med, Cornell Univ-Weill Med Coll

Fialk, Mark A MD (Onc) - **Spec Exp:** Hematologic Malignancies; **Hospital:** White Plains Hosp (page 652); **Address:** Scarsdale Med Grp, 600 Mamaroneck Ave Fl 2, Harrison, NY 10528; **Phone:** 914-723-8100; **Board Cert:** Internal Medicine 1976; Medical Oncology 1977; Hematology 1978; **Med School:** Tufts Univ 1973; **Resid:** Internal Medicine, NY-Presby/Weill Cornell Med Ctr 1975; Internal Medicine, Meml Sloan-Kettering Cancer Ctr 1976; **Fellow:** Hematology & Oncology, NY-Presby/Weill Cornell Med Ctr 1978; Infectious Disease, Meml Sloan-Kettering Cancer Ctr 1979; **Fac Appt:** Asst Clin Prof Med, NY Med Coll

Gold, Julie M MD (Onc) - **Hospital:** Northern Westchester Hosp; **Address:** MKMG, Hem/Onc, 400 E Main St, Mount Kisco, NY 10549; **Phone:** 914-242-2991; **Board Cert:** Internal Medicine 2005; Hematology 2009; Medical Oncology 2009; **Med School:** Cornell Univ-Weill Med Coll 2002; **Resid:** Internal Medicine, NY-Presby/Weill Cornell Med Ctr 2005; **Fellow:** Hematology & Oncology, Brigham & Womens Hosp 2009

Goldberg, Jonathan S MD (Onc) - **Spec Exp:** Breast Cancer; Lymphoma; Gastrointestinal Cancer; Lung Cancer; **Hospital:** Northern Westchester Hosp, Putnam Hosp Ctr; **Address:** MKMG, Hem/Onc, 90 S Bedford Rd, Mount Kisco, NY 10549; **Phone:** 914-241-1050; **Board Cert:** Internal Medicine 2007; Hematology 2011; Medical Oncology 2011; **Med School:** Mount Sinai Sch Med 1994; **Resid:** Internal Medicine, NY-Presby/Columbia Univ Med Ctr 1997; **Fellow:** Hematology & Oncology, NY-Presby/Columbia Univ Med Ctr 1999

Halaas, Jeffrey L MD (Onc) - **Spec Exp:** Breast Cancer; Leukemia & Lymphoma; Ovarian Cancer; Lung Cancer; **Hospital:** Northern Westchester Hosp, Putnam Hosp Ctr; **Address:** MKMG, Hem/Onc, 90 S Bedford Rd, Mt Kisco, NY 10549; **Phone:** 914-241-1050; **Board Cert:** Hematology 2005; Medical Oncology 2005; **Med School:** Cornell Univ-Weill Med Coll 1999; **Resid:** Internal Medicine, NY-Presby/Weill Cornell Med Ctr 2001; **Fellow:** Hematology & Oncology, Meml Sloan-Kettering Cancer Ctr 2005

Mellacheruvu, Smitha MD (Onc) - **Hospital:** St. John's Riverside Hosp-Andrus Pavil; **Address:** 984 N Broadway, Ste 311, Yonkers, NY 10701-1308; **Phone:** 914-965-2060; **Board Cert:** Hematology 2006; Medical Oncology 2009; **Med School:** India 1999; **Resid:** Internal Medicine, Univ CT Med Ctr 2003; **Fellow:** Hematology & Oncology, Montefiore Med Ctr 2006

Mills, Nancy Ellyn MD (Onc) - **Spec Exp:** Breast Cancer; Gynecologic Cancer; **Hospital:** Phelps Meml Hosp Ctr, Meml Sloan Kettering Canc Ctr (page 110); **Address:** MSKCC, Sleepy Hollow Med Oncology Svc, 777 N Broadway, Ste 102, Sleepy Hollow, NY 10591; **Phone:** 914-366-0664; **Board Cert:** Internal Medicine 2010; Medical Oncology 2013; Hematology 2004; **Med School:** Mount Sinai Sch Med 1987; **Resid:** Internal Medicine, Mt Sinai Hosp 1990; **Fellow:** Hematology & Oncology, NYU Med Ctr 1993; **Fac Appt:** Asst Clin Prof Med, Cornell Univ-Weill Med Coll

Phillips, Elizabeth MD (Onc) - **Spec Exp:** Breast Cancer; Hematology; Lymphoma; Leukemia; **Hospital:** Montefiore New Rochelle Hosp (page 100), Montefiore Med Ctr-Moses Campus (page 100); **Address:** Advanced Oncology Assocs, 50 Guion Pl, Ste 32, New Rochelle, NY 10801; **Phone:** 914-632-5397; **Board Cert:** Internal Medicine 1974; Hematology 1976; Medical Oncology 1977; **Med School:** Univ Wash 1969; **Resid:** Internal Medicine, Harlem Hosp 1972; Hematology, Montefiore Med Ctr 1973; **Fellow:** Hematology & Oncology, Mem Sloan-Kettering Cancer Ctr 1976; **Fac Appt:** Assoc Clin Prof Med, NY Med Coll

Provenzano, Anthony F MD (Onc) - **Spec Exp:** Lung Cancer; Breast Cancer; Cancer Genetics; Gastrointestinal Cancer; **Hospital:** Lawrence Hosp Ctr (page 102), Montefiore Mt Vernon Hosp (page 100); **Address:** Lawrence Med Assocs, 1 Pondfield Rd W, Ste 1, Bronxville, NY 10708; **Phone:** 914-961-3421; **Board Cert:** Internal Medicine 1979; Medical Oncology 1981; **Med School:** Cornell Univ-Weill Med Coll 1976; **Resid:** Internal Medicine, Lenox Hill Hosp 1978; **Fellow:** Medical Oncology, St Vincents Hosp 1979; Medical Oncology, Lenox Hill Hosp 1981; **Fac Appt:** Asst Clin Prof Med, NY Med Coll

Puccio, Carmelo A MD (Onc) - **Spec Exp:** Breast Cancer; Lung Cancer; Solid Tumors; Gynecologic Cancer; **Hospital:** Westchester Med Ctr; **Address:** Hudson Vly Hem/Onc Assocs, 19 Bradhurst Ave, Ste 2100, Hawthorne, NY 10532; **Phone:** 914-493-8375; **Board Cert:** Internal Medicine 1984; Medical Oncology 1989; **Med School:** Mexico 1979; **Resid:** Internal Medicine, Maimonides Med Ctr 1984; **Fellow:** Medical Oncology, Westchester Co Med Ctr 1985; **Fac Appt:** Asst Prof Med, NY Med Coll

Raff, Joshua P MD (Onc) - **Hospital:** White Plains Hosp (page 652); **Address:** Oncology & Hematology of White Plains, 244 Westchester Ave, Ste 411, White Plains, NY 10604; **Phone:** 914-684-8100; **Board Cert:** Internal Medicine 2010; Hematology 2013; Medical Oncology 2013; **Med School:** Israel 1997; **Resid:** Internal Medicine, Montefiore Med Ctr 2000; **Fellow:** Hematology & Oncology, Montefiore Med Ctr 2003

Rosen, Norman MD (Onc) - **Spec Exp:** Lung Cancer; Breast Cancer; **Hospital:** St. John's Riverside Hosp-Andrus Pavil; **Address:** 984 N Broadway, Ste 311, Yonkers, NY 10701; **Phone:** 914-965-2060; **Board Cert:** Internal Medicine 1975; Medical Oncology 1977; **Med School:** Tufts Univ 1972; **Resid:** Internal Medicine, Montefiore Med Ctr 1975; **Fellow:** Hematology & Oncology, Montefiore Med Ctr 1977; **Fac Appt:** Asst Clin Prof Med, Albert Einstein Coll Med

Sadan, Sara MD (Onc) - **Spec Exp:** Breast Cancer; Gynecologic Cancer; Gastrointestinal Cancer; Lymphoma; **Hospital:** White Plains Hosp (page 652); **Address:** Oncology & Hematology of White Plains, 244 Westchester Ave, Ste 411, White Plains, NY 10604; **Phone:** 914-684-8100; **Board Cert:** Medical Oncology 2005; **Med School:** Israel 1984; **Resid:** Internal Medicine, St Lukes-Roosevelt Hosp 1991; **Fellow:** Hematology & Oncology, Meml Sloan-Kettering Cancer Ctr 1994

Saponara, Eduardo M MD (Onc) - **Spec Exp:** Breast Cancer; Hematology; Gastrointestinal Cancer; Hematologic Malignancies; **Hospital:** Lawrence Hosp Ctr (page 102), Mt Sinai Hosp; **Address:** Lawrence Medical Associates, 77 Pondfield Rd, Bronxville, NY 10708-3809; **Phone:** 914-793-1500; **Board Cert:** Internal Medicine 1977; Hematology 1978; Medical Oncology 1979; **Med School:** Peru 1973; **Resid:** Internal Medicine, Westchester Med Ctr 1976; **Fellow:** Hematology & Oncology, Flower Fifth Ave Hospital/NY Med Coll 1978; Oncology, Mount Sinai Hosp 1979; **Fac Appt:** Asst Clin Prof Onc, Mount Sinai-Icahn Sch of Med

Schneider, Robert Jay MD (Onc) - **Spec Exp:** Breast Cancer; Genitourinary Cancer; **Hospital:** Northern Westchester Hosp; **Address:** 101 S Bedford, Ste 202A, Mt Kisco, NY 10549-3456; **Phone:** 914-666-8976; **Board Cert:** Internal Medicine 1979; Medical Oncology 1985; **Med School:** Albert Einstein Coll Med 1975; **Resid:** Internal Medicine, Jacobi Med Ctr 1978; **Fellow:** Medical Oncology, Meml Sloan Kettering Cancer Ctr 1980

Seiter, Karen MD (Onc) - **Spec Exp:** Hematologic Malignancies; Leukemia; Myelodysplastic Syndromes; **Hospital:** Westchester Med Ctr; **Address:** Hudson Vly Hem/Onc Assocs, 19 Bradhurst Ave, Ste 2100, Hawthorne, NY 10532; **Phone:** 914-493-8375; **Board Cert:** Internal Medicine 1988; Medical Oncology 2011; Hematology 2012; **Med School:** NY Med Coll 1985; **Resid:** Internal Medicine, Jacobi Med Ctr 1988; **Fellow:** Hematology & Oncology, Meml Sloan-Kettering Cancer Ctr 1991; **Fac Appt:** Prof Med, NY Med Coll

Wasserheit, Carolyn MD (Onc) - **Spec Exp:** Solid Tumors; Breast Cancer; Gynecologic Cancer; **Hospital:** Phelps Meml Hosp Ctr, Meml Sloan Kettering Canc Ctr (page 110); **Address:** MSKCC, Sleep Hollow Med Oncology Svc, 777 N Broadway, Ste 102, Sleepy Hollow, NY 10591; **Phone:** 914-366-0664; **Board Cert:** Internal Medicine 1988; Medical Oncology 2011; **Med School:** Mount Sinai Sch Med 1985; **Resid:** Internal Medicine, Mt Sinai Hosp 1988; **Fellow:** Hematology, Mt Sinai Hosp 1990; Medical Oncology, Meml Sloan-Kettering Cancer Ctr 1992

Neonatal-Perinatal Medicine

Brumberg, Heather L MD (NP) - **Spec Exp:** Neonatology; Nutrition; **Hospital:** Westchester Med Ctr; **Address:** WMC, Maria Fareri Chldns Hosp, 100 Woods Rd, rm 2215, Valhalla, NY 10595; **Phone:** 914-493-8558; **Board Cert:** Pediatrics 2014; Neonatal-Perinatal Medicine 2011; **Med School:** Tufts Univ 1996; **Resid:** Pediatrics, Floating Hosp Chldn 1999; **Fellow:** Neonatal-Perinatal Medicine, Yale-New Haven Hosp 2002; **Fac Appt:** Assoc Prof Ped, NY Med Coll

Golombek, Sergio G MD (NP) - **Spec Exp:** Prematurity/Low Birth Weight Infants; Lung Disease in Newborns; **Hospital:** Westchester Med Ctr, Children's & Women's Phys.of Westchester; **Address:** Maria Fareri Children's Hosp, 100 Woods Rd, rm 2215, Valhalla, NY 10595; **Phone:** 914-493-8558; **Board Cert:** Neonatal-Perinatal Medicine 2012; Pediatrics 2008; **Med School:** Argentina 1983; **Resid:** Pediatrics, Dr Ignacio Pirovano Hosp 1987; Pediatrics, Raymond Blank Meml Hosp Chldn 1991; **Fellow:** Neonatal-Perinatal Medicine, Chldns Mercy Hosp 1996; **Fac Appt:** Prof Ped, NY Med Coll

Jaile-Marti, Jesus MD (NP) - **Spec Exp:** Lung Disease in Newborns; Neonatal Nutrition; **Hospital:** White Plains Hosp (page 652), Nyack Hosp; **Address:** White Plains Hosp, Neonatology, Davis Ave at East Post Rd, White Plains, NY 10601; **Phone:** 914-681-1253; **Board Cert:** Pediatrics 2012; Neonatal-Perinatal Medicine 2012; **Med School:** Columbia P&S 1987; **Resid:** Pediatrics, NY-Presby/Columbia Univ Med Ctr 1990; **Fellow:** Neonatology, NY-Presby/Columbia Univ Med Ctr 1993

Kase, Jordan MD (NP) - **Spec Exp:** Neonatal Critical Care; **Hospital:** Westchester Med Ctr, Children's & Women's Phys.of Westchester; **Address:** CWPW, Neonatalology, 19 Bradhurst Ave, Ste 1400, Hawthorne, NY 10532; **Phone:** 914-493-8431; **Board Cert:** Neonatal-Perinatal Medicine 2013; Pediatrics 2009; **Med School:** Geo Wash Univ 1998; **Resid:** Pediatrics, NYU Med Ctr 2001; **Fellow:** Neonatology, Morgan Stanley Children's Hosp 2004; **Fac Appt:** Asst Prof Ped, NY Med Coll

La Gamma, Edmund F MD (NP) - **Spec Exp:** Neonatal Infections; Prematurity/Low Birth Weight Infants; Necrotizing Enterocolitis; **Hospital:** Westchester Med Ctr, Children's & Women's Phys.of Westchester; **Address:** Westchester Med Ctr, Newborn Med, 100 Woods Rd, rm 2215, Valhalla, NY 10595; **Phone:** 914-493-8558; **Board Cert:** Pediatrics 1981; Neonatal-Perinatal Medicine 1981; **Med School:** NY Med Coll 1976; **Resid:** Pediatrics, NY-Presby/Weill Cornell Med Ctr 1978; **Fellow:** Neonatal-Perinatal Medicine, NY-Presby/Weill Cornell Med Ctr 1980; Cardiovascular Research, UCSF Med Ctr 1981; **Fac Appt:** Prof Ped, NY Med Coll

Stafford Jr, John R MD (NP) - **Spec Exp:** Neonatal Care; **Hospital:** Northern Westchester Hosp; **Address:** 400 E Main St Fl 3, Mt Kisco, NY 10549; **Phone:** 914-666-1272; **Board Cert:** Pediatrics 2007; Neonatal-Perinatal Medicine 2007; **Med School:** SUNY Downstate 1986; **Resid:** Pediatrics, NY-Presby/Columbia Univ Med Ctr 1989; **Fellow:** Neonatology, NY-Presby/Columbia Univ Med Ctr 1992; **Fac Appt:** Clin Prof Ped, Columbia P&S

Nephrology

Adler, Stephen MD (Nep) - **Spec Exp:** Kidney Failure; Glomerulonephritis; Hypertension; Dialysis Care; **Hospital:** Westchester Med Ctr, White Plains Hosp (page 652); **Address:** Nephrology Assocs of Westchester, 19 Bradhurst Ave, Ste 200N, Hawthorne, NY 10532; **Phone:** 914-493-7701; **Board Cert:** Internal Medicine 1979; Nephrology 1982; **Med School:** NYU Sch Med 1976; **Resid:** Internal Medicine, Mt Sinai Hosp 1979; **Fellow:** Nephrology, Boston Med Ctr 1982; **Fac Appt:** Prof Med, NY Med Coll

Buzzeo, Louis MD (Nep) - **Spec Exp:** Hypertension; Kidney Disease; **Hospital:** Phelps Meml Hosp Ctr; **Address:** 777 N Broadway, Ste 203, Sleepy Hollow, NY 10591; **Phone:** 914-332-9100; **Board Cert:** Internal Medicine 1975; Nephrology 1978; **Med School:** Tufts Univ 1972; **Resid:** Internal Medicine, St Vincents Hosp 1975; **Fellow:** Nephrology, NYU Med Ctr 1977

Delaney, Veronica MD/PhD (Nep) - **Spec Exp:** Transplant Medicine-Kidney; Kidney Failure; **Hospital:** Westchester Med Ctr; **Address:** Nephrology Assocs of Westchester, 19 Bradhurst Ave, Ste 200N, Hawthorne, NY 10532; **Phone:** 914-493-7701; **Board Cert:** Internal Medicine 1981; Nephrology 1982; **Med School:** England, UK 1973; **Resid:** Internal Medicine, Dublin Univ Hosps; **Fellow:** Nephrology, UPMC 1983; **Fac Appt:** Assoc Prof Med, NY Med Coll

Garrick, Renee MD (Nep) - **Spec Exp:** Hypertension; Kidney Disease-Chronic; Dialysis Care; Fluid/Electrolyte Balance; **Hospital:** Westchester Med Ctr, White Plains Hosp (page 652); **Address:** Nephrology Assocs of Westchester, 19 Bradhurst Ave, Ste 200N, Hawthorne, NY 10532; **Phone:** 914-493-7701; **Board Cert:** Internal Medicine 1981; Nephrology 1984; **Med School:** Rush Med Coll 1978; **Resid:** Internal Medicine, Jacobi Med Ctr 1981; **Fellow:** Nephrology, Hosp Univ Penn 1984; **Fac Appt:** Prof Med, NY Med Coll

Klein, Michael D MD (Nep) - **Spec Exp:** Kidney Disease; **Hospital:** Westchester Med Ctr; **Address:** Nephrology Assocs of Westchester, 19 Bradhurst Ave, Ste 200N, Hawthorne, NY 10532; **Phone:** 914-493-7701; **Board Cert:** Internal Medicine 2006; Nephrology 2008; **Med School:** Univ IL Coll Med 1993; **Resid:** Internal Medicine, Jacobi Med Ctr 1996; **Fellow:** Nephrology, NY Presby Hosp 1998

Kolbovsky, Iosif MD (Nep) - **Hospital:** White Plains Hosp (page 652); **Address:** WestMed Med Grp, 3020 Westchester Ave Fl 3, Purchase, NY 10577; **Phone:** 914-682-6454; **Board Cert:** Internal Medicine 2005; Nephrology 2007; **Med School:** Russia 1984; **Resid:** Internal Medicine, Brookdale Univ Hosp Med Ctr 1995; **Fellow:** Nephrology, Brookdale Univ Hosp Med Ctr 1997

Korosi, Anthony MD (Nep) - **Hospital:** White Plains Hosp (page 652); **Address:** 3020 Westchester Ave Fl 3, WestMed Medical Group, Nephrology, Purchase, NY 10577; **Phone:** 914-683-6474; **Board Cert:** Internal Medicine 2007; Nephrology 2009; **Med School:** Univ Pittsburgh 1994; **Resid:** Internal Medicine, Mount Sinai Hosp 1997; **Fellow:** Nephrology, Mount Sinai Hosp 2000

Monahan, Marianne MD (Nep) - **Hospital:** Greenwich Hosp (page 970); **Address:** WestMed Med Grp, Nephrology, 3020 Westchester Ave Fl 3, Purchase, NY 10577; **Phone:** 914-831-4100; **Board Cert:** Internal Medicine 2011; Nephrology 2003; **Med School:** Tufts Univ 1998; **Resid:** Internal Medicine, Mount Sinai Med Ctr 2001; **Fellow:** Nephrology, Mount Sinai Med Ctr 2004

Reda, Dominick F MD (Nep) - **Spec Exp:** Hypertension; Kidney Disease; **Hospital:** Saint Joseph's Med Ctr - Yonkers; **Address:** 136 S Broadway, Yonkers, NY 10701; **Phone:** 914-965-0621; **Board Cert:** Internal Medicine 1987; Nephrology 2010; **Med School:** Italy 1983; **Resid:** Internal Medicine, Our Lady of Mercy 1987; **Fellow:** Nephrology, Lincoln Med Ctr 1989; **Fac Appt:** Asst Clin Prof Med, NY Med Coll

Rosen, Michael A MD (Nep) - **Spec Exp:** Kidney Disease-Pediatric & Adult; **Hospital:** Northern Westchester Hosp; **Address:** MKMG, Nephrology, 90 S Bedford Rd, Mount Kisco, NY 10549; **Phone:** 914-241-1050; **Board Cert:** Internal Medicine 2004; Nephrology 2007; **Med School:** Indiana Univ 2000; **Resid:** Internal Medicine & Pediatrics, Mt Sinai Hosp 2004; **Fellow:** Nephrology, Mt Sinai Hosp 2008

Saltzman, Martin MD (Nep) - **Spec Exp:** Kidney Disease; Hypertension; Dialysis Care; **Hospital:** Northern Westchester Hosp; **Address:** MKMG, Nephrology, 90 S Bedford Rd, Mount Kisco, NY 10549; **Phone:** 914-241-1050; **Board Cert:** Internal Medicine 1977; Nephrology 1978; **Med School:** SUNY Downstate 1972; **Resid:** Internal Medicine, Kings Co Hosp 1973; Internal Medicine, Harlem Hosp 1974; **Fellow:** Nephrology, SUNY Downstate Med Ctr 1976

Neurological Surgery

Benzil, Deborah L MD (NS) - **Spec Exp:** Brain Tumors; Peripheral Nerve Surgery; **Hospital:** Putnam Hosp Ctr, Northern Westchester Hosp; **Address:** MKMG, Neurosurgery, 90 S Bedford Rd, Mount Kisco, NY 10530; **Phone:** 914-241-1050; **Board Cert:** Neurological Surgery 1997; **Med School:** Univ MD Sch Med 1985; **Resid:** Neurological Surgery, Rhode Island Hosp 1993; **Fac Appt:** Assoc Prof NS, NY Med Coll

De Lotbiniere, Alain MD (NS) - **Spec Exp:** Movement Disorders; Brain Tumors; Pituitary Tumors; Deep Brain Stimulation; **Hospital:** Northern Westchester Hosp, White Plains Hosp (page 652); **Address:** Brain & Spine Surgeons of NY, 244 Westchester Ave, Ste 310, White Plains, NY 10604; **Phone:** 914-948-6688; **Board Cert:** Neurological Surgery 1994; **Med School:** McGill Univ 1981; **Resid:** Surgery, Royal Victoria Hosp 1983; Neurological Surgery, Royal Victoria Hosp 1988; **Fellow:** Neurological Surgery, Univ Cambridge 1989

Kornel, Ezriel MD (NS) - **Spec Exp:** Spinal Surgery-Minimally Invasive; Brain Tumors; Spinal Cord Tumors; **Hospital:** Northern Westchester Hosp, White Plains Hosp (page 652); **Address:** Brain & Spine Surgeons of NY, 244 Westchester Ave, Ste 310, White Plains, NY 10604; **Phone:** 914-948-6688; **Board Cert:** Neurological Surgery 1987; **Med School:** Rush Med Coll 1978; **Resid:** Surgery, Washington Hosp Ctr 1979; Neurological Surgery, G Washington Univ Hosp 1984; **Fac Appt:** Asst Clin Prof NS, Columbia P&S

Lee, Thomas T MD (NS) - **Spec Exp:** Spinal Surgery; Minimally Invasive Spinal Surgery; Stereotactic Radiosurgery; **Hospital:** St. John's Riverside Hosp-Andrus Pavil, Phelps Meml Hosp Ctr; **Address:** 150 White Plains Rd, Ste 110, Tarrytown, NY 10591; **Phone:** 914-631-9207; **Board Cert:** Neurological Surgery 2012; **Med School:** UCLA 1993; **Resid:** Neurological Surgery, Jackson Meml Med Ctr 1999; **Fac Appt:** Asst Clin Prof NS, Mount Sinai Sch Med

Murali, Raj MD (NS) - **Spec Exp:** Trigeminal Neuralgia; Skull Base Surgery; Aneurysm-Cerebral; Pituitary Tumors; **Hospital:** Westchester Med Ctr; **Address:** Westchester Med Ctr, Neurosurgery, 19 Bradhurst Ave, Ste 2800, Valhalla, NY 10532; **Phone:** 914-345-8111; **Board Cert:** Neurological Surgery 1982; **Med School:** India 1968; **Resid:** Neurological Surgery, Royal Infirm-Univ Edinburgh 1974; Neurological Surgery, NYU Med Ctr 1979; **Fac Appt:** Prof NS, NY Med Coll

Robbins, John B MD (NS) - **Spec Exp:** Spinal Surgery; Brain Tumors; **Hospital:** Phelps Meml Hosp Ctr, St. John's Riverside Hosp-Andrus Pavil; **Address:** 755 N Broadway, Ste 520, Sleepy Hollow, NY 10591; **Phone:** 914-366-1144; **Board Cert:** Neurological Surgery 1991; **Med School:** Brown Univ 1978; **Resid:** Surgery, Montefiore Med Ctr 1986; Neurological Surgery, NY Hosp 1989

Rosner, Saran S MD (NS) - **Spec Exp:** Spinal Surgery; Brain & Spinal Cord Tumors; **Hospital:** Hudson Valley Hosp Ctr, Phelps Meml Hosp Ctr; **Address:** 245 Saw Mill River Rd, Hawthorne, NY 10532; **Phone:** 914-741-2666; **Board Cert:** Neurological Surgery 1986; **Med School:** Columbia P&S 1976; **Resid:** Surgery, Johns Hopkins Hosp 1978; Neurological Surgery, Columbia-Presby Med Ctr 1983

Neurology

Ahluwalia, Brij M.S. MD (N) - **Spec Exp:** Dementia; Cerebrovascular Disease; Multiple Sclerosis; **Hospital:** Westchester Med Ctr; **Address:** Neurology Assocs of Westchester, 19 Bradhurst Ave, Ste 2850, Hawthorne, NY 10532; **Phone:** 914-345-1313; **Board Cert:** Neurology 1974; **Med School:** India 1961; **Resid:** Internal Medicine, Beekman Downtown Hosp 1969; Neurology, Metropolitan Hosp 1972; **Fac Appt:** Prof N, NY Med Coll

Caporaso, Gregg L MD/PhD (N) - **Spec Exp:** Alzheimer's Disease; Multiple Sclerosis; **Hospital:** Northern Westchester Hosp; **Address:** 91 Smith Ave, Neurology Assocs, Mount Kisco, NY 10549-2815; **Phone:** 914-241-1717; **Board Cert:** Neurology 2009; **Med School:** Cornell Univ-Weill Med Coll 1994; **Resid:** Neurology, NY Presby/Weill Cornell Med Ctr 1999; **Fellow:** Memory Disorders, NY Presby/Weill Cornell Med Ctr

Carniciu, Sanda I MD (N) - **Spec Exp:** Electrodiagnosis; Clinical Neurophysiology; **Hospital:** Phelps Meml Hosp Ctr; **Address:** 245 N Broadway, Ste 102, Sleepy Hollow, NY 10591; **Phone:** 914-631-6888; **Board Cert:** Neurology 2008; Clinical Neurophysiology 2010; Electrodiagnostic Medicine 2000; **Med School:** Romania 1987; **Resid:** Internal Medicine, VA Med Ctr 1994; Neurology, NYU Med Ctr 1997; **Fellow:** Clinical Neurophysiology, NY Presby-Cornell Med Ctr 1998

Dickoff, David J MD (N) - **Spec Exp:** Epilepsy/Seizure Disorders; Neuromuscular Disorders; Parkinson's Disease; Trigeminal Neuralgia; **Hospital:** St. John's Riverside Hosp-Andrus Pavil, Mt Sinai Hosp; **Address:** Metro Neurology Consultants, 984 N Broadway, Ste 509, Yonkers, NY 10701; **Phone:** 914-968-0620; **Board Cert:** Neurology 1987; Electrodiagnostic Medicine 1989; **Med School:** Albany Med Coll 1982; **Resid:** Neurology, Mt Sinai Hosp 1986; **Fellow:** Neuromuscular Disease, NY-Presby/Columbia Univ Med Ctr 1987; **Fac Appt:** Asst Clin Prof N, Mount Sinai-Icahn Sch of Med

Dousmanis, Athanasios G MD (N) - **Spec Exp:** Movement Disorders; Clinical Neurophysiology; Nerve Injuries; Seizure Disorders; **Hospital:** Lawrence Hosp Ctr (page 102); **Address:** WestMed Med Grp, Neurology, 73 Market St, Ste 217, Yonkers, NY 10710; **Phone:** 914-831-2970; **Board Cert:** Neurology 2012; **Med School:** Cornell Univ 1997; **Resid:** Internal Medicine, Mt Sinai Hosp 1998; Neurology, NY-Presby/Columbia Univ Med Ctr 2001; **Fellow:** Clinical Neurophysiology, NY-Presby/Columbia Univ Med Ctr 2002

Gross, Elliott George MD (N) - **Spec Exp:** Alzheimer's Disease; Parkinson's Disease; Headache; Pain-Back & Neck; **Hospital:** Montefiore Med Ctr-Moses Campus (page 100); **Address:** 3020 Westchester Ave, Ste 104, Purchase, NY 10577; **Phone:** 914-251-1010; **Board Cert:** Neurology 1969; **Med School:** Albert Einstein Coll Med 1962; **Resid:** Neurology, Jacobi Med Ctr 1966; **Fellow:** Neurology, Albert Einstein Med Coll 1970; **Fac Appt:** Asst Clin Prof N, Columbia P&S

Jordan, Barry D MD (N) - **Spec Exp:** Brain Injury; Sports Neurology; Concussion; Memory Disorders; **Hospital:** Burke Rehab Hosp; **Address:** Burke Rehabilitation Hosp, 785 Mamaroneck Ave, White Plains, NY 10605; **Phone:** 914-597-2332; **Board Cert:** Neurology 1989; **Med School:** Harvard Med Sch 1981; **Resid:** Neurology, NY-Presby/Weill Cornell Med Ctr 1986; **Fellow:** Sports Medicine, Hosp Special Surgery 1987; Behavioral Neurology, UCLA Med Ctr 1998; **Fac Appt:** Assoc Prof N, Cornell Univ-Weill Med Coll

Kranzler, L. Stephan MD (N) - **Hospital:** White Plains Hosp (page 652); **Address:** WestMed Med Grp, 244 Westchester Ave, Ste 315, White Plains, NY 10604; **Phone:** 914-946-9444; **Board Cert:** Neurology 1990; **Med School:** Univ Pennsylvania 1985; **Resid:** Neurology, NY-Presby/Columbia Univ Med Ctr 1989

Laban-Grant, Olgica MD (N) - **Spec Exp:** Epilepsy; Epilepsy in Women; Clinical Neurophysiology; **Hospital:** White Plains Hosp (page 652); **Address:** NE Regional Epilepsy Grp, 333 Westchester Ave, Ste E104, White Plains, NY 10604; **Phone:** 914-428-9213; **Board Cert:** Neurology 2013; Clinical Neurophysiology 2005; **Med School:** Yugoslavia 1991; **Resid:** Neurology, NYU Med Ctr 2002; **Fellow:** Clinical Neurophysiology, NYU Med Ctr 2003

Lambrakis, Christos C MD (N) - **Spec Exp:** Epilepsy/Seizure Disorders; Deep Brain Stimulation; **Hospital:** Orange Regl Med Ctr, White Plains Hosp (page 652); **Address:** NE Regional Epilepsy Group, 333 Westchester Ave, Ste E104, White Plains, NY 10604; **Phone:** 914-428-9213; **Board Cert:** Neurology 2008; **Med School:** NY Med Coll 1993; **Resid:** Neurology, Westchester Med Ctr 1997; **Fellow:** Epilepsy, Westchester Med Ctr 1998

Marks, Stephen J MD (N) - **Spec Exp:** Stroke; Alzheimer's Disease; Dementia; Vascular Neurology; **Hospital:** Westchester Med Ctr; **Address:** Neurology Assocs of Westchester, 19 Bradhurst Ave, Ste 2850, Hawthorne, NY 10532; **Phone:** 914-345-1313; **Board Cert:** Neurology 1985; Vascular Neurology 2006; **Med School:** NY Med Coll 1980; **Resid:** Neurology, Mt Sinai Hosp 1984; **Fellow:** Stroke, Duke Univ Hosp 1985; **Fac Appt:** Prof N, NY Med Coll

Morris, James R MD/PhD (N) - **Spec Exp:** Stroke; Headache; Epilepsy; Parkinson's Disease; **Hospital:** Greenwich Hosp (page 970); **Address:** 3020 Westchester Ave, Ste 305, Purchase, NY 10577; **Phone:** 203-629-8029; **Board Cert:** Neurology 2006; **Med School:** Indiana Univ 1990; **Resid:** Neurology, NY-Presby/Columbia Univ Med Ctr 1994; **Fellow:** Clinical Neurophysiology, NY-Presby/Columbia Univ Med Ctr 1995

Rosenkilde, Carl E MD/PhD (N) - **Spec Exp:** Electrodiagnosis; **Hospital:** Northern Westchester Hosp; **Address:** Neurology Assocs, 91 Smith Ave, Mt Kisco, NY 10549; **Phone:** 914-241-1717; **Board Cert:** Neurology 1992; **Med School:** Albert Einstein Coll Med 1985; **Resid:** Neurology, Yale-New Haven Hosp 1989; **Fellow:** Neurology, UCLA Med Ctr 1979

Sangiorgio, Maria R MD (N) - **Spec Exp:** Movement Disorders; **Hospital:** Putnam Hosp Ctr; **Address:** Mount Kisco Medical Group, 111 Bedford Rd, Katonah, NY 10536; **Phone:** 914-232-3156; **Board Cert:** Neurology 2010; **Med School:** Albany Med Coll 1992; **Resid:** Internal Medicine, NYU Med Ctr 1995; **Fellow:** Neurology, Strong Memorial Hosp 1998

Silverman, Ronald M MD (N) - **Spec Exp:** Stroke; **Hospital:** Lawrence Hosp Ctr (page 102); **Address:** WestMed Med Grp, Neurology, 73 Market St, Ste 217, Yonkers, NY 10710; **Phone:** 914-831-2970; **Board Cert:** Neurology 1978; **Med School:** Albert Einstein Coll Med 1972; **Resid:** Internal Medicine, Metropolitan Hosp 1973; Neurology, Mt Sinai Hosp 1976

Singh, Avtar MD (N) - **Spec Exp:** Stroke; Epilepsy; Headache; **Hospital:** White Plains Hosp (page 652); **Address:** Scarsdale Med Grp, 600 Mamaroneck Ave, Ste 200, Harrison, NY 10605; **Phone:** 914-723-8100; **Board Cert:** Neurology 1978; **Med School:** India 1967; **Resid:** Neurology, Metropolitan Hosp Ctr 1976; **Fac Appt:** Assoc Clin Prof N, NY Med Coll

Szabo, Albert MD (N) - **Spec Exp:** Clinical Neurophysiology; Neuromuscular Disorders; **Hospital:** Northern Westchester Hosp; **Address:** MKMG, Neurology, 90 S Bedford Rd, Mount Kisco, NY 10549; **Phone:** 914-241-1050; **Board Cert:** Neurology 2007; **Med School:** Hungary 1989; **Resid:** Neurology, Mt Sinai Hosp 1994; **Fellow:** Neuromuscular Disease, Thomas Jefferson Univ Hosp 1996; Clinical Neurophysiology, SUNY Downstate Med Ctr 1997

Tolunsky, Eugene MD (N) - **Spec Exp:** Clinical Neurophysiology; **Hospital:** Northern Westchester Hosp; **Address:** MKMG, Neurology, 90 S Bedford Rd, Mount Kisco, NY 10549; **Phone:** 914-241-1050; **Board Cert:** Neurology 2012; **Med School:** Univ Pennsylvania 1997; **Resid:** Neurology, Mtr Sinai Hosp 2001; **Fellow:** Neurophysiology, Mt Sinai Hosp 2002

Weintraub, Michael Ira MD (N) - **Spec Exp:** Carpal Tunnel Syndrome; Peripheral Neuropathy; Pain-Back & Neck; Diabetic Neuropathy; **Address:** 325 S Highland Ave, Briarcliff Manor, NY 10510; **Phone:** 914-941-0788; **Board Cert:** Neurology 1972; **Med School:** SUNY Buffalo 1966; **Resid:** Neurology, Yale-New Haven Hosp 1970; **Fac Appt:** Clin Prof N, NY Med Coll

Neuroradiology

Berger, Scott B MD/PhD (NRad) - **Spec Exp:** Cerebrovascular Disease; Stroke; **Hospital:** Northern Westchester Hosp; **Address:** MKMG, Radiology, 90 S Bedford Rd, Mount Kisco, NY 10549; **Phone:** 914-241-1050; **Board Cert:** Diagnostic Radiology 2010; Neuroradiology 2010; **Med School:** Cornell Univ-Weill Med Coll 1992; **Resid:** Diagnostic Radiology, Yale-New Haven Hosp 1997; **Fellow:** Neurological Radiology, Yale-New Haven Hosp 1998

Mehta, Hasit MD (NRad) - **Spec Exp:** Brain Imaging; Cardiac CT Angiography; MRI & CT of Brain & Spine; **Hospital:** Westchester Med Ctr; **Address:** WMC Advanced Physicians Services, 100 Woods Way, Valhalla, NY 10595; **Phone:** 914-493-8158; **Board Cert:** Diagnostic Radiology 2005; Neuroradiology 2007; **Med School:** SUNY Buffalo 2000; **Resid:** Diagnostic Radiology, Parkland Hosp,UT SW Med Ctr 2004; **Fellow:** Neuroradiology, NY Presy-Columbia Med Ctr 2006; **Fac Appt:** Asst Prof Rad, NY Med Coll

Tenner, Michael MD (NRad) - **Spec Exp:** Stroke; Aneurysm-Cerebral; Carotid Artery Stent Placement; Arteriovenous Malformations; **Hospital:** Westchester Med Ctr; **Address:** WMC Advanced Physicians Svcs, 100 Woods Rd, Valhalla, NY 10595; **Phone:** 914-493-8158; **Board Cert:** Diagnostic Radiology 1967; Neuroradiology 2007; **Med School:** Univ MD Sch Med 1960; **Resid:** Diagnostic Radiology, Univ MD Med Ctr 1962; Diagnostic Radiology, Univ MD Med Ctr 1966; **Fellow:** Neuroradiology, Neurological Inst-Columbia Presby 1968; **Fac Appt:** Prof Rad, NY Med Coll

Nuclear Medicine

Gerard, Perry S MD (NuM) - **Spec Exp:** PET Imaging; CT Scan; Nuclear Imaging; Nuclear Oncology; **Hospital:** Westchester Med Ctr; **Address:** 100 Woods Rd, Valhalla, NY 10595; **Phone:** 914-493-8260; **Board Cert:** Diagnostic Radiology 1987; Nuclear Radiology 1989; Nuclear Cardiology 2008; **Med School:** Dominica 1980; **Resid:** Diagnostic Radiology, Maimonides Med Ctr 1984; **Fellow:** Diagnostic Imaging, Maimonides Med Ctr 1985; **Fac Appt:** Assoc Prof Rad, NY Med Coll

Obstetrics & Gynecology

Armbruster, Robert G MD (ObG) - **Hospital:** Greenwich Hosp (page 970); **Address:** 73 Market St, Ste 212, Yonkers, NY 10710; **Phone:** 914-337-3229; **Board Cert:** Obstetrics & Gynecology 1984; **Med School:** Washington Univ, St Louis 1977; **Resid:** Obstetrics & Gynecology, UCLA Med Ctr 1979; Obstetrics & Gynecology, NY-Cornell Hosp 1981

Burns, Elisa MD (ObG) - **Spec Exp:** Minimally Invasive Surgery; Robotic Surgery; Colposcopy; Menopause Problems; **Hospital:** Northern Westchester Hosp; **Address:** Mount Kisco Med Grp, Ob/Gyn, 90 S Bedford Rd, Mt Kisco, NY 10549; **Phone:** 914-241-1050; **Board Cert:** Obstetrics & Gynecology 2013; **Med School:** Columbia P&S 1982; **Resid:** Obstetrics & Gynecology, NY-Presby/Columbia Univ Med Ctr 1986

Dweck, Alyssa MD (ObG) - **Spec Exp:** Gynecology Only; **Hospital:** Northern Westchester Hosp; **Address:** Mount Kisco Medical Group, 90 S Bedford Rd, Mount Kisco, NY 10549; **Phone:** 914-241-1050; **Board Cert:** Obstetrics & Gynecology 2013; **Med School:** Hahnemann Univ 1990; **Resid:** Obstetrics & Gynecology, Lankenau Hosp 1994

Eilen, Bonnie D MD (ObG) *PCP* - **Hospital:** White Plains Hosp (page 652); **Address:** 210 Westchester Ave Fl 3 - rm 306, White Plains, NY 10605; **Phone:** 914-831-6800; **Board Cert:** Obstetrics & Gynecology 2013; **Med School:** Albert Einstein Coll Med 1977; **Resid:** Obstetrics & Gynecology, Bronx Municipal Hosp 1981; **Fac Appt:** Asst Clin Prof ObG, Albert Einstein Coll Med

Florio, Philip L MD (ObG) *PCP* - **Spec Exp:** Laparoscopic Surgery; Colposcopy; **Hospital:** St. John's Riverside Hosp-Andrus Pavil; **Address:** 1022 N Broadway, Yonkers, NY 10701-1303; **Phone:** 914-963-0284; **Board Cert:** Obstetrics & Gynecology 1981; **Med School:** SUNY Upstate Med Univ 1974; **Resid:** Obstetrics & Gynecology, St Barnabas Med Ctr 1978

Gannon, Jennifer B MD (ObG) - **Spec Exp:** Adolescent Gynecology; **Hospital:** Northern Westchester Hosp; **Address:** Mount Kisco Medical Group, 90 S Bedford Rd, Mount Kisco, NY 10549; **Phone:** 914-242-1380; **Board Cert:** Obstetrics & Gynecology 2013; **Med School:** Univ Conn 2001; **Resid:** Obstetrics & Gynecology, Women & Infants Hosp 2005

Giuffrida, Regina MD (ObG) *PCP* - **Spec Exp:** Menopause Problems; Gynecologic Surgery; Gynecology Only; **Hospital:** Northern Westchester Hosp; **Address:** Mount Kisco Med Grp, Ob/Gyn, 90 S Bedford Rd, Mt Kisco, NY 10549; **Phone:** 914-241-1050; **Board Cert:** Obstetrics & Gynecology 2013; **Med School:** NY Med Coll 1980; **Resid:** Obstetrics & Gynecology, UCSD Med Ctr 1984

Grano, Vanessa A MD (ObG) - **Spec Exp:** Laparoscopic Surgery; Pap Smear Abnormalities; Colposcopy; **Hospital:** Greenwich Hosp (page 970); **Address:** Westchester Medical Grp, 1 Theall Rd, Rye, NY 10580; **Phone:** 914-253-4912; **Board Cert:** Obstetrics & Gynecology 2013; **Med School:** SUNY Downstate 1988; **Resid:** Obstetrics & Gynecology, NY-Presby/Columbia Univ Med Ctr 1992

Grecco, Dominic M MD (ObG) - **Spec Exp:** Pregnancy-High Risk; Hysterectomy Alternatives; Robotic Surgery; **Hospital:** Northern Westchester Hosp; **Address:** 59 Kensico Drive, Mount Kisco, NY 10549; **Phone:** 914-241-4900; **Board Cert:** Obstetrics & Gynecology 2013; **Med School:** Grenada 1985; **Resid:** Obstetrics & Gynecology, LI Coll Hosp 1990

Hayworth, Scott D MD (ObG) - **Spec Exp:** Minimally Invasive Surgery; Endometriosis; Menopause Problems; **Hospital:** Northern Westchester Hosp; **Address:** Mount Kisco Medical Group, 90 S Bedford Rd, Mt Kisco, NY 10549-3412; **Phone:** 914-241-1050; **Board Cert:** Obstetrics & Gynecology 2014; **Med School:** Cornell Univ-Weill Med Coll 1984; **Resid:** Obstetrics & Gynecology, Mount Sinai Med Ctr 1988; **Fac Appt:** Asst Clin Prof ObG, Mount Sinai Sch Med

Keller, Adina Holand MD (ObG) - **Spec Exp:** Robotic Surgery; Minimally Invasive Surgery; Menopause Problems; **Hospital:** Northern Westchester Hosp; **Address:** 90 S Bedford Rd, Mount Kisco, NY 10549; **Phone:** 914-241-1050; **Board Cert:** Obstetrics & Gynecology 2013; **Med School:** Mount Sinai Sch Med 1993; **Resid:** Obstetrics & Gynecology, Mount Sinai Med Ctr 1997

Malley, Susan S MD (ObG) - **Spec Exp:** Gynecology Only; Adolescent Gynecology; Menstrual Disorders; Menopause Problems; **Hospital:** Putnam Hosp Ctr; **Address:** Northern Medical Specialists, 340 Rte 202, Somers, NY 10589; **Phone:** 914-277-4544; **Board Cert:** Obstetrics & Gynecology 2013; **Med School:** Wayne State Univ 1991; **Resid:** Obstetrics & Gynecology, Cedars-Siani Med Ctr 1995

McGovern, Catherine A MD (ObG) - **Hospital:** White Plains Hosp (page 652); **Address:** 210 Westchester Ave Fl 3 - Ste 306, White Plains, NY 10605; **Phone:** 914-831-6800; **Board Cert:** Obstetrics & Gynecology 2013; **Med School:** Albany Med Coll 1985; **Resid:** Obstetrics & Gynecology, Albany Med Ctr 1989

Meacham, Kevin L MD (ObG) - **Spec Exp:** Pregnancy-High Risk; Laparoscopic Surgery; Gynecologic Surgery; **Hospital:** White Plains Hosp (page 652); **Address:** 2071 Boston Post Rd, Larchmont, NY 10538; **Phone:** 914-834-4123; **Board Cert:** Obstetrics & Gynecology 2013; **Med School:** NY Med Coll 1986; **Resid:** Obstetrics & Gynecology, LIJ Med Ctr 1990

Mendelowitz, Lawrence G MD (ObG) - **Spec Exp:** Osteoporosis; Gynecologic Surgery; Pelvic Organ Prolapse Repair; Pregnancy-High Risk; **Hospital:** Phelps Meml Hosp Ctr, Westchester Med Ctr; **Address:** Sleepy Hollow Medical Group at Phelps, 755 N Broadway, Ste 560, Sleepy Hollow, NY 10591; **Phone:** 914-631-0337; **Board Cert:** Obstetrics & Gynecology 2013; **Med School:** NYU Sch Med 1976; **Resid:** Obstetrics & Gynecology, Bellevue Hosp-NYU 1980; **Fac Appt:** Asst Prof ObG, NY Med Coll

Mieszerski, Laura E MD (ObG) - **Spec Exp:** Adolescent Gynecology; Pregnancy-High Risk; **Hospital:** Hudson Valley Hosp Ctr; **Address:** Hudson Valley Health Ctr, Women's Health, 1037 Main St, Peekskill, NY 10566; **Phone:** 914-734-8790; **Board Cert:** Obstetrics & Gynecology 2013; **Med School:** Albany Med Coll 1992; **Resid:** Obstetrics & Gynecology, UTSA Affil Hosp 1996

Nelson, William S MD (ObG) - **Spec Exp:** Menopause Problems; **Hospital:** Greenwich Hosp (page 970); **Address:** Westchester Medical Grp, 1 Theall Rd, Rye, NY 10580; **Phone:** 914-253-4912; **Board Cert:** Obstetrics & Gynecology 1981; **Med School:** Albert Einstein Coll Med 1960; **Resid:** Obstetrics & Gynecology, Maimonides Med Ctr 1965; **Fac Appt:** Asst Clin Prof ObG, Albert Einstein Coll Med

Regard, Monique M MD (ObG) - **Spec Exp:** Pediatric & Adolescent Gynecology Only; Birth Defects-Vaginal; Ovarian Masses in Children/Adolescents; **Hospital:** Westchester Med Ctr, Children's & Women's Phys.of Westchester; **Address:** Chldn's/Women's Physicians Westchester, 503 Grasslands Rd, Ste 200, Valhalla, NY 10595; **Phone:** 914-304-5254; **Board Cert:** Obstetrics & Gynecology 2013; **Med School:** Baylor Coll Med 1989; **Resid:** Obstetrics & Gynecology, Univ Minn Med Ctr 1993; **Fac Appt:** Asst Clin Prof Ped, NY Med Coll

Simon, Beth J MD (ObG) - **Spec Exp:** Gynecologic Surgery; Laparoscopic Surgery; **Hospital:** Greenwich Hosp (page 970); **Address:** Scarsdale Medical Grp, 600 Mamaroneck Ave, Harrison, NY 10528; **Phone:** 914-723-8100; **Board Cert:** Obstetrics & Gynecology 2013; **Med School:** Albert Einstein Coll Med 1998; **Resid:** Obstetrics & Gynecology, Montefiore Med Ctr 2002; **Fac Appt:** Asst Clin Prof ObG, Mount Sinai-Icahn Sch of Med

Ullman, Joel MD (ObG) - **Spec Exp:** Laparoscopic Surgery-Complex; Uro-Gynecology; Vulvar Disease; Vaginal Surgery; **Hospital:** Montefiore New Rochelle Hosp (page 100); **Address:** 1 Madison Ave, Larchmont, NY 10538; **Phone:** 914-833-1000; **Board Cert:** Obstetrics & Gynecology 1978; **Med School:** NY Med Coll 1963; **Resid:** Obstetrics & Gynecology, Beth Israel Med Ctr 1969; **Fac Appt:** Asst Clin Prof ObG, Albert Einstein Coll Med

Wysoki, Randee S MD (ObG) - **Hospital:** White Plains Hosp (page 652); **Address:** 210 Westchester Ave, Westmed Medical Group, White Plains, NY 10604; **Phone:** 914-831-6800; **Board Cert:** Obstetrics & Gynecology 2013; **Med School:** Georgetown Univ 1982; **Resid:** Obstetrics & Gynecology, Emory Univ Med Ctr 1986

Ophthalmology

Biser, Seth A MD (Oph) - **Spec Exp:** Corneal Disease & Surgery; Cataract Surgery; Refractive Surgery; **Hospital:** Lawrence Hosp Ctr (page 102); **Address:** 654 Gramatan Ave, Fleetwood, NY 10552; **Phone:** 914-664-2300; **Board Cert:** Ophthalmology 2014; **Med School:** Univ Pennsylvania 1997; **Resid:** Ophthalmology, Wilmer Eye Inst 2001; **Fellow:** Refractive Surgery, North Shore Hosp 2002; **Fac Appt:** Asst Clin Prof Oph, NYU Sch Med

Bortz, John G MD (Oph) - **Spec Exp:** Oculoplastic & Orbital Surgery; Neuro-Ophthalmology; Orbital & Eyelid Tumors/Cancer; Eyelid Cosmetic & Reconstructive Surgery; **Hospital:** Westchester Med Ctr; **Address:** 811 N Broadway, White Plains, NY 10603-2403; **Phone:** 914-686-0006; **Board Cert:** Ophthalmology 1989; Internal Medicine 1982; **Med School:** Johns Hopkins Univ 1979; **Resid:** Internal Medicine, St Lukes-Roosevelt Hosp 1982; Ophthalmology, Westchester Co Med Ctr 1987; **Fellow:** Oculoplastic & Reconstructive Surgery, Albany Med Ctr 1988

Bromberg, Beth S MD (Oph) - **Hospital:** Northern Westchester Hosp, White Plains Hosp (page 652); **Address:** WestMed Medical Group, 1 Theall Rd, Rye, NY 10580; **Phone:** 914-848-8999; **Board Cert:** Ophthalmology 2006; **Med School:** Johns Hopkins Univ 1985; **Resid:** Internal Medicine, Rush Univ Med Ctr 1986; Ophthalmology, Univ Illinois Eye & Ear Infirm 1989

Brustein, Harris C MD (Oph) - **Spec Exp:** Pediatric Ophthalmology; **Hospital:** Montefiore New Rochelle Hosp (page 100); **Address:** 77 Quaker Ridge Rd, Ste 203, New Rochelle, NY 10804-2821; **Phone:** 914-235-0022; **Board Cert:** Ophthalmology 1976; **Med School:** Albert Einstein Coll Med 1970; **Resid:** Ophthalmology, Montefiore Med Ctr 1974; **Fellow:** Pediatric Ophthalmology, Chldns Hosp 1975

Charles, Howard C MD (Oph) - **Spec Exp:** Retinal Disorders; Retina/Vitreous Surgery; **Hospital:** Northern Westchester Hosp; **Address:** Mount Kisco Medical Group, 101 S Bedford Rd, Ste 404, Mt Kisco, NY 10549; **Phone:** 914-666-2001; **Board Cert:** Ophthalmology 1987; **Med School:** Albany Med Coll 1981; **Resid:** Ophthalmology, Montefiore Med Ctr 1983; Ophthalmology, Jacobi Med Ctr 1984; **Fellow:** Retinal Surgery, Univ Illinois Hosp & Clinic 1987; **Fac Appt:** Asst Clin Prof Oph, Albert Einstein Coll Med

Dieck, William MD (Oph) - **Spec Exp:** Cataract Surgery; Glaucoma; Lens Implants-Multifocal; Dry Eye Syndrome; **Hospital:** Northern Westchester Hosp; **Address:** 185 Kisco Ave, Ste 500, Mt Kisco, NY 10549; **Phone:** 914-666-4939; **Board Cert:** Ophthalmology 1990; **Med School:** NY Med Coll 1983; **Resid:** Internal Medicine, Westchester Co Med Ctr 1985; Ophthalmology, Westchester Co Med Ctr 1988

Fern, Craig MD (Oph) - **Spec Exp:** Retinal Disorders; Retina/Vitreous Surgery; **Hospital:** Northern Westchester Hosp; **Address:** 105 S Bedford Rd, Ste 311, Mt Kisco, NY 10549; **Phone:** 914-244-3800; **Board Cert:** Ophthalmology 2005; **Med School:** NYU Sch Med 1987; **Resid:** Internal Medicine, Bellevue Med Ctr 1989; Ophthalmology, Bellevue Med Ctr 1993; **Fellow:** Vitreoretinal Disease, UC Davis Med Ctr 1995; **Fac Appt:** Asst Prof Oph, NYU Sch Med

Fleischman, Jay MD (Oph) - **Spec Exp:** Diabetic Eye Disease/Retinopathy; Macular Degeneration; Uveitis; **Hospital:** Montefiore Med Ctr-Moses Campus (page 100), Stamford Hosp (page 971); **Address:** 600 Mamaroneck Ave, Ste 103, Harrison, NY 10528-1613; **Phone:** 914-315-5111; **Board Cert:** Ophthalmology 1980; **Med School:** Columbia P&S 1975; **Resid:** Ophthalmology, Johns Hopkins Hosp 1979; **Fellow:** Retina/Vitreous Surgery, Med Coll Wisc Affil Hosps 1980; **Fac Appt:** Assoc Prof Oph, Albert Einstein Coll Med

Forman, Scott MD (Oph) - **Spec Exp:** Botox Therapy; Neuro-Ophthalmology; **Hospital:** Westchester Med Ctr; **Address:** Westchester Med Ctr, Ophthalmology, 100 Woods Rd, Macy Pav, Ste 1100, Valhalla, NY 10595; **Phone:** 914-493-7666; **Board Cert:** Ophthalmology 1989; **Med School:** Rutgers R W Johnson Med Sch 1981; **Resid:** Ophthalmology, Westchester Med Ctr 1987; **Fellow:** Neuro-Ophthalmology, NY-Presby/Columbia Univ Med Ctr 1988; **Fac Appt:** Assoc Prof Oph, NY Med Coll

Glassman, Morris I MD (Oph) - **Spec Exp:** Laser Surgery; Glaucoma; **Hospital:** Northern Westchester Hosp, Montefiore Med Ctr-Moses Campus (page 100); **Address:** 1940 Commerce St, Yorktown Heights, NY 10598; **Phone:** 914-962-5506; **Board Cert:** Ophthalmology 1975; **Med School:** NYU Sch Med 1968; **Resid:** Ophthalmology, Jacobi Med Ctr 1974; **Fac Appt:** Asst Clin Prof Oph, Albert Einstein Coll Med

Gordon, James R MD (Oph) - **Spec Exp:** Oculoplastic Surgery; Eyelid Cosmetic & Reconstructive Surgery; **Hospital:** White Plains Hosp (page 652); **Address:** Westchester Eye Assocs, 450 Mamaroneck Ave, Harrison, NY 10528; **Phone:** 914-949-9200; **Board Cert:** Ophthalmology 2004; **Med School:** Israel 1996; **Resid:** Ophthalmology, St Vincent's Hosp & Med Ctr 2000

Greenbaum, Allen S MD (Oph) - **Spec Exp:** Laser Refractive Surgery; Cataract Surgery; **Hospital:** White Plains Hosp (page 652); **Address:** Westchester Eye Assocs, 450 Mamaroneck Rd, Harrison, NY 10528; **Phone:** 914-949-9200; **Board Cert:** Ophthalmology 1985; **Med School:** Mount Sinai Sch Med 1979; **Resid:** Ophthalmology, Mount Sinai Hosp 1984

Greenberg, Steven C MD (Oph) - **Spec Exp:** Pediatric Ophthalmology; **Hospital:** Putnam Hosp Ctr, White Plains Hosp (page 652); **Address:** WestMed Medical Grp, 1 Theall Rd, Rye, NY 10580; **Phone:** 914-848-8999; **Board Cert:** Ophthalmology 1987; **Med School:** Univ Conn 1982; **Resid:** Ophthalmology, NYU Med Ctr 1986; **Fellow:** Pediatric Ophthalmology, Manhattan EE&T Hosp 1987

Horowitz, Marc A MD (Oph) - **Spec Exp:** Pediatric Ophthalmology; Strabismus; Retinopathy of Prematurity; Eye Muscle Disorders; **Hospital:** Westchester Med Ctr, White Plains Hosp (page 652); **Address:** 14 Harwood Ct, Ste 209, Scarsdale, NY 10583; **Phone:** 914-723-5511; **Board Cert:** Ophthalmology 1983; **Med School:** Mount Sinai Sch Med 1978; **Resid:** Ophthalmology, St Luke's Roosevelt Hosp Ctr 1982; **Fellow:** Pediatric Ophthalmology, Chldns Hosp 1983; **Fac Appt:** Asst Clin Prof Oph, NY Med Coll

Lederman, Martin E MD (Oph) - **Spec Exp:** Pediatric Ophthalmology; Eye Muscle Disorders; Diagnostic Problems; Tear Duct Problems; **Hospital:** White Plains Hosp (page 652), NY-Presby/Columbia Univ Med Ctr, NY (page 102); **Address:** 3020 Westchester Ave, Ste 402, Purchase, NY 10577; **Phone:** 914-417-6441; **Board Cert:** Ophthalmology 2005; **Med School:** Albert Einstein Coll Med 1964; **Resid:** Ophthalmology, Albert Einstein Affil Hosp 1968; **Fellow:** Pediatric Ophthalmology, Chldns Hosp Natl Med Ctr 1969; **Fac Appt:** Assoc Prof Oph, Columbia P&S

Lippman, Jay I MD (Oph) - **Spec Exp:** Cataract Surgery; LASIK-Refractive Surgery; **Hospital:** New York Eye & Ear Infirm of Mt Sinai; **Address:** 828 Pelhamdale Ave, New Rochelle, NY 10801; **Phone:** 914-636-3600; **Board Cert:** Ophthalmology 1972; **Med School:** Ros Franklin Univ/Chicago Med Sch 1964; **Resid:** Ophthalmology, Montefiore Med Ctr 1970; **Fac Appt:** Clin Prof Oph, NY Med Coll

McKee, Heather C MD (Oph) - **Spec Exp:** Cataract Surgery; Glaucoma; **Hospital:** St. John's Riverside Hosp-Dobbs Ferry Pavil; **Address:** 200 S Broadway, Ste 202, Tarrytown, NY 10591-4504; **Phone:** 914-631-7300; **Board Cert:** Ophthalmology 1981; **Med School:** Duke Univ 1976; **Resid:** Ophthalmology, Strong Meml Hosp 1980; **Fac Appt:** Asst Clin Prof Oph, NY Med Coll

Mignone, Biagio V MD (Oph) - **Spec Exp:** Retinal Disorders; Glaucoma; Cataract Surgery; **Hospital:** Montefiore Mt Vernon Hosp (page 100), Lawrence Hosp Ctr (page 102); **Address:** 955 Yonkers Ave, Ste 105, Yonkers, NY 10704; **Phone:** 914-237-2002; **Board Cert:** Ophthalmology 1980; **Med School:** NY Med Coll 1975; **Resid:** Ophthalmology, UMDNJ Med Ctr 1979; **Fac Appt:** Asst Clin Prof Oph, NY Med Coll

Morello, Robert F MD (Oph) - **Spec Exp:** Geriatric Ophthalmology; **Hospital:** Montefiore New Rochelle Hosp (page 100); **Address:** Southern Westchester Ophthalmology, Westchester Eye MDs, 120 Warren St, New Rochelle, NY 10801; **Phone:** 914-633-7214; **Board Cert:** Ophthalmology 1985; **Med School:** Mexico 1976; **Resid:** Internal Medicine, Bronx Lebanon Hosp 1978; Ophthalmology, Bronx Lebanon Hosp 1981

Most, Richard W MD (Oph) - **Spec Exp:** Pediatric Ophthalmology; Strabismus-Adult & Pediatric; Tear Duct Problems; **Hospital:** Mt Sinai Hosp; **Address:** 101 S Bedford Rd, Bldg 400 - Ste 401, Mt Kisco, NY 10549; **Phone:** 914-241-2206; **Board Cert:** Ophthalmology 1977; Pediatric Ophthalmology 1978; **Med School:** Italy 1971; **Resid:** Pathology, Maimonides Med Ctr 1973; Ophthalmology, Lenox Hill Hosp 1976; **Fellow:** Pediatric Ophthalmology, NYU Med Ctr/Bellevue Hosp 1977; Pediatric Ophthalmology, Chldns Hosp Natl Med Ctr 1978; **Fac·Appt:** Assoc Clin Prof Oph, Mount Sinai Sch Med

Phillips, Howard P MD (Oph) - **Spec Exp:** Corneal Disease; **Hospital:** Phelps Meml Hosp Ctr; **Address:** Hudson Valley Eye Assocs, 24 Saw Mill River Rd, Ste 202, Hawthorne, NY 10532; **Phone:** 914-345-3937; **Board Cert:** Ophthalmology 1982; **Med School:** NYU Sch Med 1977; **Resid:** Ophthalmology, NYU Med Ctr 1981; **Fellow:** Retina, Bellevue Hosp 1982

Ray, Audell W MD (Oph) - **Spec Exp:** Glaucoma; **Hospital:** Lawrence Hosp Ctr (page 102); **Address:** Bronxville Eye Assocs, 77 Pondfield Rd, Bronxville, NY 10708-3809; **Phone:** 914-337-8844; **Board Cert:** Ophthalmology 1979; **Med School:** Columbia P&S 1974; **Resid:** Internal Medicine, St Lukes-Roosevelt Hosp 1975; Ophthalmology, Manhattan EE & T Hosp 1978

Salzman, Jacqueline G MD (Oph) - **Spec Exp:** Diabetic Eye Disease; Glaucoma; Macular Degeneration; **Hospital:** Phelps Meml Hosp Ctr; **Address:** 200 S Broadway, Ste 211, Tarrytown, NY 10591-4504; **Phone:** 914-332-5394; **Board Cert:** Ophthalmology 1985; **Med School:** NYU Sch Med 1979; **Resid:** Ophthalmology, Bellevue Hosp 1983; **Fellow:** Retina, Bellevue Hosp 1984

Solomon, Ira S MD (Oph) - **Spec Exp:** Glaucoma; Laser Surgery; Microsurgery; **Hospital:** New York Eye & Ear Infirm of Mt Sinai, Montefiore Med Ctr-Moses Campus (page 100); **Address:** Scarsdale Ophthalmology Associates PLLC, 700 White Plains Rd, Ste 343, Scarsdale, NY 10583; **Phone:** 914-725-5400; **Board Cert:** Ophthalmology 1989; **Med School:** Jefferson Med Coll 1982; **Resid:** Internal Medicine, Lenox Hill Hosp 1983; Ophthalmology, Montefiore Med Ctr 1986; **Fellow:** Glaucoma, New York E&E Infirm 1987

Solomon, Sherry K MD (Oph) - **Spec Exp:** Diabetic Eye Disease/Retinopathy; Macular Degeneration; Retinitis Pigmentosa; **Hospital:** Lawrence Hosp Ctr (page 102); **Address:** Scarsdale Ophthalmology Assocs, 700 White Plains Rd, Ste 343, Scarsdale, NY 10583; **Phone:** 914-725-5400; **Board Cert:** Ophthalmology 1991; **Med School:** Albert Einstein Coll Med 1986; **Resid:** Internal Medicine, Lenox Hill Hosp 1987; Ophthalmology, Montefiore Hosp Med Ctr 1990; **Fellow:** Retina, NYU Med Ctr 1991

Stein, Mitchell B MD (Oph) - **Spec Exp:** Cataract Surgery; Cornea & External Eye Disease; **Hospital:** Northern Westchester Hosp; **Address:** 69 S Moger Ave, Mount Kisco, NY 10549-2217; **Phone:** 914-666-2961; **Board Cert:** Internal Medicine 1982; Ophthalmology 2005; **Med School:** Albert Einstein Coll Med 1979; **Resid:** Internal Medicine, Bronx Muni Hosp 1982; Ophthalmology, SUNY-Downstate Med Ctr 1986; **Fellow:** Cornea, Mt Sinai Hosp/Beth Israel Hosp 1987; **Fac Appt:** Asst Clin Prof Med, Albert Einstein Coll Med

Tindel-Kahn, Lori J MD (Oph) - **Spec Exp:** Retinal Disorders; Diabetic Eye Disease/Retinopathy; **Hospital:** White Plains Hosp (page 652); **Address:** WestMed Medical Group, 210 Westchester Ave, Fl 3, Ste 301, White Plains, NY 10604; **Phone:** 914-682-6560; **Board Cert:** Ophthalmology 1991; **Med School:** NY Med Coll 1986; **Resid:** Ophthalmology, Brookdale Hosp Med Ctr 1990; **Fellow:** Retina, NYU Med Ctr 1991

Tostanoski, Jean R MD (Oph) - **Spec Exp:** Corneal Disease & Transplant; Refractive Surgery; Cataract Surgery; Glaucoma; **Hospital:** Phelps Meml Hosp Ctr; **Address:** Hudson Valley Eye Assocs, 24 Saw Mill River Rd, Ste 202, Hawthorne, NY 10532; **Phone:** 914-345-3937; **Board Cert:** Ophthalmology 2006; **Med School:** Albert Einstein Coll Med 1989; **Resid:** Ophthalmology, Bronx Lebanon Hosp Ctr 1993; Ophthalmology, Manhattan EE&T Hosp 1994

Trivedi, Gaurang MD (Oph) - **Spec Exp:** Glaucoma; Cataract Surgery; **Hospital:** Northern Westchester Hosp; **Address:** Mt Kisco Medical Group, Ophthalmology, 90 S Bedford Rd, Mount Kisco, NY 10549; **Phone:** 914-242-1355; **Board Cert:** Ophthalmology 2007; **Med School:** Loyola Univ-Stritch Sch Med 2002; **Resid:** Ophthalmology, NY Eye & Ear Infirm 2006; **Fellow:** Glaucoma, NY Eye & Ear Infirm 2007

Zabin, Steven MD (Oph) - **Spec Exp:** Cataract Surgery-Lens Implant; Trauma; **Hospital:** White Plains Hosp (page 652), Westchester Med Ctr; **Address:** WestMed Medical Group, 210 Westchester Ave Fl 3 - Ste 301, White Plains, NY 10604; **Phone:** 914-682-6560; **Board Cert:** Ophthalmology 1987; **Med School:** SUNY Upstate Med Univ 1980; **Resid:** Ophthalmology, Westchester Med Ctr 1984; **Fac Appt:** Asst Prof Oph, NY Med Coll

Zaidman, Gerald W MD (Oph) - **Spec Exp:** Laser Vision Surgery; Cornea Transplant; Cataract Surgery; Corneal Disease-Pediatric; **Hospital:** Westchester Med Ctr; **Address:** Westchester Med Ctr, Dept Ophthalmology, Macy Pavilion, rm 1100, Valhalla, NY 10595; **Phone:** 914-493-1599; **Board Cert:** Ophthalmology 1981; **Med School:** Albert Einstein Coll Med 1975; **Resid:** Ophthalmology, Beth Abraham Hosp 1977; Ophthalmology, Lenox Hill Hosp 1980; **Fellow:** Cornea & Ext Eye Disease, Univ Pittsburgh Affil Hosp 1982; **Fac Appt:** Assoc Prof Oph, NY Med Coll

Orthopaedic Surgery

Asprinio, David E MD (OrS) - **Spec Exp:** Trauma; **Hospital:** Westchester Med Ctr; **Address:** University Orthopaedics, 19 Bradhurst Ave, Ste 1300-N, Hawthorne, NY 10595; **Phone:** 914-789-2734; **Board Cert:** Orthopaedic Surgery 2008; **Med School:** Univ VT Coll Med 1986; **Resid:** Orthopaedic Surgery, Rhode Island Hosp 1992; **Fellow:** Trauma, Hosp for Special Surg 1993

Bavaro, Nicholas A MD (OrS) - **Spec Exp:** Sports Medicine; Knee Surgery; Hip Surgery; Hip & Knee Replacement; **Hospital:** St. John's Riverside Hosp-Dobbs Ferry Pavil, Nyack Hosp; **Address:** Premier Othopaedics of Westchester & Rockland, Community Hosp-Dobbs Ferry, Lower Level, 128 Ashford Ave, Dobbs Ferry, NY 10522; **Phone:** 914-693-2057; **Board Cert:** Orthopaedic Surgery 2014; **Med School:** NY Med Coll 1993; **Resid:** Orthopaedic Surgery, St Lukes Roosevelt Hosp 1998; **Fellow:** Sports Medicine, NYU Hosp for Joint Diseases 1999

Burak, Corey F MD (OrS) - **Spec Exp:** Hip Replacement; Knee Surgery; Minimally Invasive Surgery; Joint Replacement; **Hospital:** Phelps Meml Hosp Ctr; **Address:** Hudson Valley Bone & Joint Surgeons, 24 Saw Mill River Rd, Rte 9A, Ste 206, Hawthorne, NY 10532; **Phone:** 914-631-7777; **Board Cert:** Orthopaedic Surgery 2008; **Med School:** SUNY Upstate Med Univ 1999; **Resid:** Surgery, St Vincent's Hosp & Med Ctr 2001; Orthopaedic Surgery, Tulane Med Ctr 2005; **Fellow:** Research, Tulane Med Ctr 2006; Hip & Knee Surgery, Dorr Arthritis Inst 2008

Burak, George MD (OrS) - **Spec Exp:** Sports Injuries; Arthritis; **Hospital:** Phelps Meml Hosp Ctr; **Address:** Hudson Valley Bone & Joint Surgeons, 24 Saw Mill River Rd, Ste 206, Hawthorne, NY 10532-1541; **Phone:** 914-631-7777; **Board Cert:** Orthopaedic Surgery 1971; **Med School:** SUNY Upstate Med Univ 1964; **Resid:** Orthopaedic Surgery, Kings County Hosp 1969; **Fac Appt:** Asst Prof OrS, SUNY Downstate

Buschmann, William R MD (OrS) - **Spec Exp:** Foot & Ankle Surgery; **Hospital:** White Plains Hosp (page 652); **Address:** White Plains Physician Assocs Orthopedic Specialists, 222 Westchester Ave, Ste 101, White Plains, NY 10604; **Phone:** 914-946-1010; **Board Cert:** Orthopaedic Surgery 2007; **Med School:** NY Med Coll 1978; **Resid:** Orthopaedic Surgery, Hershey Med Ctr 1983; **Fellow:** Foot & Ankle Surgery, Hosp for Joint Diseases 1991

Cristofaro, Robert L MD (OrS) - **Spec Exp:** Pediatric Orthopaedic Surgery; Pediatric Sports Medicine; Foot & Hip Disorders-Complex Pediatric; Neuromuscular Disorders; **Hospital:** Westchester Med Ctr, Montefiore New Rochelle Hosp (page 100); **Address:** 3010 Westchester Ave, Ste 104, Purchase, NY 10577; **Phone:** 914-967-8708; **Board Cert:** Orthopaedic Surgery 1978; **Med School:** SUNY Downstate 1971; **Resid:** Surgery, Montefiore Hosp 1973; Orthopaedic Surgery, Montefiore Hosp 1976; **Fellow:** Pediatric Orthopaedic Surgery, Rancho Los Amigos Med Ctr 1977; **Fac Appt:** Assoc Clin Prof OrS, NY Med Coll

Cushner, Michael A MD (OrS) - **Hospital:** Mt Sinai Beth Israel, St. John's Riverside Hosp-Dobbs Ferry Pavil; **Address:** WestMed Medical Group, 73 Market St, Ridge Hill, Yonkers, NY 10801; **Phone:** 914-682-6540; **Board Cert:** Orthopaedic Surgery 2012; **Med School:** Univ MD Sch Med 1993; **Resid:** Orthopaedic Surgery, Med Univ SC 1998; **Fellow:** Trauma, S Tahoe Sports Med Group 1999

Edelson, Charles MD (OrS) - **Spec Exp:** Reconstructive Surgery; Sports Medicine; Joint Replacement; Knee Replacement; **Hospital:** St. John's Riverside Hosp-Andrus Pavil, Saint Joseph's Med Ctr - Yonkers; **Address:** S Westchester Ortho & Sports Med Assocs, 970 N Broadway, Ste 204, Yonkers, NY 10701-1310; **Phone:** 914-476-4343; **Board Cert:** Orthopaedic Surgery 1979; **Med School:** NY Med Coll 1973; **Resid:** Surgery, Montefiore Med Ctr 1975; Orthopaedic Surgery, Montefiore Med Ctr 1978

Gundy, Edward V MD (OrS) - **Spec Exp:** Geriatric Orthopaedic Surgery; Sports Medicine; **Hospital:** White Plains Hosp (page 652), Greenwich Hosp (page 970); **Address:** WESTMED Medical Group, 1 Theall Rd, Rye, NY 10580; **Phone:** 914-682-6540; **Board Cert:** Orthopaedic Surgery 1983; **Med School:** Cornell Univ-Weill Med Coll 1976; **Resid:** Surgery, St Lukes-Roosevelt Hosp 1978; Orthopaedic Surgery, Hosp Special Surg 1981

Hoisington, Samuel A MD (OrS) - **Spec Exp:** Foot & Ankle Surgery; Fractures; Foot & Ankle Deformities; **Hospital:** Phelps Meml Hosp Ctr; **Address:** Hudson Valley Bone & Joint Surgeons, 24 Saw Mill River Rd, Ste 206, Hawthorne, NY 10532; **Phone:** 914-631-7777; **Board Cert:** Orthopaedic Surgery 2011; **Med School:** Albany Med Coll 1991; **Resid:** Orthopaedic Surgery, Montefiore Med Ctr 1996; **Fellow:** Foot & Ankle Surgery, Allegheny Univ Med Ctr 1997

Holder, Jonathan L MD (OrS) - **Spec Exp:** Sports Medicine; Foot & Ankle Surgery; Joint Replacement; **Hospital:** White Plains Hosp (page 652), Westchester Med Ctr; **Address:** 170 Maple Ave, Ste 109, White Plains, NY 10601; **Phone:** 914-421-0600; **Board Cert:** Orthopaedic Surgery 2013; **Med School:** NY Med Coll 1985; **Resid:** Orthopaedic Surgery, Metropolitan Hosp Ctr 1990

Karas, Evan H MD (OrS) - **Spec Exp:** Shoulder Surgery; Sports Medicine; **Hospital:** Northern Westchester Hosp; **Address:** Mt Kisco Med Grp, 90 S Bedford Rd, Mt Kisco, NY 10549; **Phone:** 914-241-1050; **Board Cert:** Orthopaedic Surgery 2010; Orthopaedic Sports Medicine 2011; **Med School:** NYU Sch Med 1991; **Resid:** Orthopaedic Surgery, Mt Sinai Hosp 1996; **Fellow:** Sports Medicine, Hosp Univ Penn 1997

Khabie, Victor MD (OrS) - **Spec Exp:** Sports Medicine; Shoulder Surgery; Elbow Surgery; Knee Surgery; **Hospital:** Northern Westchester Hosp, Putnam Hosp Ctr; **Address:** Somers Ortho Surgery & Sports Med Group, 657 E Main St, Ste 3, Mt Kisco, NY 10549; **Phone:** 914-666-5550; **Board Cert:** Orthopaedic Surgery 2010; Orthopaedic Sports Medicine 2008; **Med School:** Harvard Med Sch 1991; **Resid:** Orthopaedic Surgery, Hosp for Joint Dis 1996; **Fellow:** Orthopaedic Sports Medicine, Kerlan-Jobe Ortho Clinic 1997; **Fac Appt:** Asst Clin Prof OrS, NYU Sch Med

Lent, David E MD (OrS) - **Spec Exp:** Knee Replacement; Knee Surgery; Arthroscopic Surgery; **Hospital:** St. John's Riverside Hosp-Andrus Pavil; **Address:** S Westchester Ortho & Sports Med Assocs, 970 N Broadway, Ste 204, Yonkers, NY 10701-1310; **Phone:** 914-476-4343; **Board Cert:** Orthopaedic Surgery 2010; **Med School:** NYU Sch Med 1991; **Resid:** Orthopaedic Surgery, Jacobi Med Ctr 1996

Maddalo, Anthony V MD (OrS) - **Spec Exp:** Sports Medicine; Shoulder & Knee Injuries; Rotator Cuff Surgery; **Hospital:** Phelps Meml Hosp Ctr, NYU Langone Med Ctr (page 104); **Address:** 24 Saw Mill River Rd, Ste 206, Hawthorne, NY 10532; **Phone:** 914-631-7777; **Board Cert:** Orthopaedic Surgery 2009; **Med School:** NY Med Coll 1981; **Resid:** Orthopaedic Surgery, Lenox Hill Hosp 1986

Mann, Ronald L MD (OrS) - **Spec Exp:** Pediatric Orthopaedic Surgery; Fractures; Sports Medicine; **Hospital:** Northern Westchester Hosp; **Address:** 1888 Commerce St, Yorktown Heights, NY 10598-4431; **Phone:** 914-962-7712; **Board Cert:** Orthopaedic Surgery 2009; **Med School:** Univ Pennsylvania 1980; **Resid:** Orthopaedic Surgery, Mount Sinai Hosp 1985; **Fellow:** Pediatric Orthopaedic Surgery, Hosp for Special Surgery 1986

Nelson Jr, John M MD (OrS) - **Spec Exp:** Pediatric Orthopaedic Surgery; Clubfoot/Foot Deformities in Children; Pediatric Sports Medicine; **Hospital:** Montefiore New Rochelle Hosp (page 100), Westchester Med Ctr; **Address:** Superior Orthopaedic Care, 3010 Westchester Ave, Ste 104, Purchase, NY 10577; **Phone:** 914-632-4420; **Board Cert:** Orthopaedic Surgery 2008; **Med School:** Mount Sinai Sch Med 1979; **Resid:** Orthopaedic Surgery, Hosp for Joint Diseases 1984; **Fellow:** Pediatric Orthopaedic Surgery, Scottish Rite Chldn's Hosp 1985

Oh, Young Don MD (OrS) - **Spec Exp:** Sports Medicine; Arthroscopic Surgery; Joint Replacement; **Hospital:** White Plains Hosp (page 652), Greenwich Hosp (page 970); **Address:** WestMed Med Grp, Orthopaedic Surgery, 210 Westchester Ave, White Plains, NY 10604; **Phone:** 914-682-6540; **Board Cert:** Orthopaedic Surgery 2012; **Med School:** NYU Sch Med 1993; **Resid:** Orthopaedic Surgery, LIJ Med Ctr 1998; **Fellow:** Orthopaedic Sports Medicine, UCLA Med Ctr 1999

Pidoriano, Arthur J MD (OrS) - **Spec Exp:** Sports Medicine; Arthroscopic Surgery; Rotator Cuff Surgery; Knee Ligament Reconstruction; **Hospital:** Hudson Valley Hosp Ctr; **Address:** Mt Kisco Med Grp, 1978 Crompond Rd, Ste 201, Cortlandt Manor, NY 10567; **Phone:** 914-739-2121; **Board Cert:** Orthopaedic Surgery 2008; **Med School:** NY Med Coll 1989; **Resid:** Orthopaedic Surgery, Westchester Med Ctr 1994; **Fellow:** Sports Medicine, Univ Conn Sch Med Affil Hosp 1995

Seebacher, J Robert MD (OrS) - **Spec Exp:** Hip Replacement; Knee Replacement; Arthritis; **Hospital:** Phelps Meml Hosp Ctr; **Address:** Hudson Valley Bone & Joint Surgeons, 24 Saw Mill River Rd, Ste 206, Hawthorne, NY 10532; **Phone:** 914-631-7777; **Board Cert:** Orthopaedic Surgery 1984; **Med School:** Georgetown Univ 1976; **Resid:** Surgery, Mount Sinai Hosp 1978; Orthopaedic Surgery, Hosp for Special Surgery 1981; **Fellow:** Pediatric Orthopaedic Surgery, Hosp for Sick Children 1982

Small, Robert D MD (OrS) - Spec Exp: Knee Replacement; Hip Replacement; **Hospital:** White Plains Hosp (page 652); **Address:** White Plains Physician Assocs Orthopedic Specialists, 222 Westchester Ave, Ste 101, White Plains, NY 10604; **Phone:** 914-946-1010; **Board Cert:** Orthopaedic Surgery 1985; **Med School:** NY Med Coll 1977; **Resid:** Orthopaedic Surgery, Hosp for Joint Diseases 1982; **Fellow:** Hip Surgery, Hosp for Special Surgery 1983

Small, Steven R MD (OrS) - Spec Exp: Sports Medicine; **Hospital:** Hudson Valley Hosp Ctr; **Address:** Mt Kisco Med Grp, 1978 Crompond Rd, Ste 201, Cortland Manor, NY 10567; **Phone:** 914-739-2121; **Board Cert:** Orthopaedic Surgery 2011; **Med School:** NY Med Coll 1979; **Resid:** Orthopaedic Surgery, Westchester Med Ctr 1984

Spencer, Eric M MD (OrS) - Spec Exp: Hand Surgery; **Hospital:** St. John's Riverside Hosp-Andrus Pavil; **Address:** S Westchester Ortho & Sports Med Assocs, 970 N Broadway, Ste 204, Yonkers, NY 10701; **Phone:** 914-476-4343; **Board Cert:** Orthopaedic Surgery 2006; **Med School:** Columbia P&S 1998; **Resid:** Orthopaedic Surgery, Lenox Hill Hosp 2002; **Fellow:** Hand Surgery, Hosp for Joint Disease 2003

Voellmicke, Kurt V MD (OrS) - Spec Exp: Foot & Ankle Surgery; **Hospital:** Northern Westchester Hosp; **Address:** Mt Kisco Med Grp, 90 S Bedford Rd, Mount Kisco, NY 10549; **Phone:** 914-241-1050; **Board Cert:** Orthopaedic Surgery 2014; **Med School:** Cornell Univ-Weill Med Coll 1996; **Resid:** Orthopaedic Surgery, Hosp for Special Surgery 2001; **Fellow:** Foot & Ankle Surgery, Hosp for Special Surgery 2002

Weinstein, Richard N MD (OrS) - Spec Exp: Shoulder Surgery; Rotator Cuff Surgery; Sports Medicine; Knee Surgery; **Hospital:** White Plains Hosp (page 652); **Address:** 1133 Westchester Ave, Ste N008, White Plains, NY 10604; **Phone:** 914-358-9700; **Board Cert:** Orthopaedic Surgery 2010; Orthopaedic Sports Medicine 2007; **Med School:** NYU Sch Med 1991; **Resid:** Orthopaedic Surgery, Bronx Lebanon Hosp 1996; **Fellow:** Sports Medicine, Univ Conn Hlth Syst 1997; **Fac Appt:** , Albert Einstein Coll Med

Yasgur, David J MD (OrS) - Spec Exp: Knee Replacement; Joint Replacement; Sports Medicine; **Hospital:** Northern Westchester Hosp; **Address:** Mount Kisco Med Grp, 111 Bedford Rd, Katonah, NY 10536; **Phone:** 914-232-3135; **Board Cert:** Orthopaedic Surgery 2010; **Med School:** Cornell Univ 1991; **Resid:** Orthopaedic Surgery, Hosp Joint Diseases 1996; **Fellow:** Knee Reconstruction, ISK Ortho Inst/Beth Israel North Med Ctr 1997

Zelicof, Steven B MD/PhD (OrS) - Spec Exp: Joint Reconstruction; Arthritis; Sports Medicine; Hip & Knee Replacement; **Hospital:** Montefiore New Rochelle Hosp (page 100), Westchester Med Ctr; **Address:** Specialty Orthopedics, 600 Mamaroneck Ave, Ste 101, Harrison, NY 10528; **Phone:** 914-686-0111; **Board Cert:** Orthopaedic Surgery 2013; **Med School:** Univ Pennsylvania 1983; **Resid:** Orthopaedic Surgery, Hosp Special Surg 1989; **Fellow:** Orthopaedic Surgery, Brigham & Women's Hosp 1990; **Fac Appt:** Clin Prof OrS, NY Med Coll

Otolaryngology

Fox, Mark L MD (Oto) - Spec Exp: Thyroid Surgery; Salivary Gland Surgery; Head & Neck Cancer; Sinus Surgery; **Hospital:** Lawrence Hosp Ctr (page 102), Montefiore New Rochelle Hosp (page 100); **Address:** ENT & Allergy Assocs, 1 Elm St, Ste 2A, Tuckahoe, NY 10707; **Phone:** 914-961-2515; **Board Cert:** Otolaryngology 1979; **Med School:** NY Med Coll 1973; **Resid:** Otolaryngology, Manhattan EET Hosp 1979; **Fac Appt:** Asst Clin Prof Oto, Columbia P&S

Kase, Steven B MD (Oto) - **Spec Exp:** Sinus Disorders; Pediatric Otolaryngology; **Hospital:** White Plains Hosp (page 652), Mt Sinai Hosp; **Address:** 75 S Broadway Fl 3, White Plains, NY 10601; **Phone:** 914-949-3888; **Board Cert:** Otolaryngology 1981; **Med School:** Loyola Univ-Stritch Sch Med 1976; **Resid:** Otolaryngology, NY E&E Infirmary 1980

Kates, Matthew J MD (Oto) - **Spec Exp:** Sinus Disorders/Surgery; Sleep Disorders/Apnea; Balance Disorders; **Hospital:** Montefiore New Rochelle Hosp (page 100), Lawrence Hosp Ctr (page 102); **Address:** 145 Huguenot St, rm 610, New Rochelle, NY 10801-4914; **Phone:** 914-235-1888; **Board Cert:** Otolaryngology 1992; **Med School:** Cornell Univ-Weill Med Coll 1986; **Resid:** Surgery, St Vincent's Hosp 1988; Otolaryngology, Manhattan EET Hosp 1991

Meiteles, Lawrence Z MD (Oto) - **Spec Exp:** Cochlear Implants; Skull Base Surgery; Otology & Neuro-Otology; Balance Disorders; **Hospital:** Westchester Med Ctr; **Address:** The Balance Ctr, 480 Bedford Rd, Chappaqua, NY 10514; **Phone:** 914-242-8111; **Board Cert:** Otolaryngology 1992; **Med School:** Albert Einstein Coll Med 1986; **Resid:** Otolaryngology, New York Eye & Ear 1991; **Fellow:** Otology & Neurotology, Univ Michigan Med Ctr 1993; **Fac Appt:** Assoc Clin Prof Oto, NY Med Coll

Ryback, Hyman MD (Oto) - **Spec Exp:** Endoscopic Sinus Surgery; Laryngeal Disorders; Snoring/Sleep Apnea; Reconstructive Surgery; **Hospital:** White Plains Hosp (page 652); **Address:** 75 S Broadway Fl 3, White Plains, NY 10601; **Phone:** 914-949-3888; **Board Cert:** Otolaryngology 1977; **Med School:** McGill Univ 1970; **Resid:** Surgery, Jewish Genl Hosp 1973; Otolaryngology, Mount Sinai Hosp 1977

Scott, John C MD (Oto) - **Spec Exp:** Head & Neck Surgery; Facial Plastic Surgery; Thyroid Surgery; Cosmetic Surgery-Face; **Hospital:** Northern Westchester Hosp; **Address:** MKMG, Otolaryngology, 110 S Bedford Rd Fl 2, Mt Kisco, NY 10549; **Phone:** 914-242-1355; **Board Cert:** Otolaryngology 1994; Facial Plastic & Reconstr Surgery 1997; **Med School:** Univ Mich Med Sch 1988; **Resid:** Otolaryngology, Johns Hopkins Hosp 1993; **Fellow:** Facial Plastic & Reconstr Surgery, Mt Sinai Hosp 1994

Shapiro, Barry M MD (Oto) - **Spec Exp:** Endoscopic Sinus Surgery; Sleep Disorders/Apnea; **Hospital:** Phelps Meml Hosp Ctr, St. John's Riverside Hosp-Andrus Pavil; **Address:** West Med Medical Group, Ridge Hill, 73 Market St, Yonkers, NY 10510-1469; **Phone:** 914-945-0505; **Board Cert:** Otolaryngology 1983; **Med School:** Mount Sinai Sch Med 1978; **Resid:** Otolaryngology, Mount Sinai Med Ctr 1982; **Fac Appt:** , Mount Sinai Sch Med

Siglock, Timothy J MD (Oto) - **Spec Exp:** Ear Disorders/Surgery; Sinus Surgery; Voice Disorders; **Hospital:** Hudson Valley Hosp Ctr; **Address:** Mount Kisco Medical Group, 3680 Hill Blvd, Ste 202, Jefferson Valley, NY 10535-1502; **Phone:** 914-245-7700; **Board Cert:** Otolaryngology 1986; **Med School:** Belgium 1981; **Resid:** Otolaryngology, New York Eye & Ear Infirm 1986; **Fellow:** Research, House Ear Inst 1987

Stidham, Katrina Ruth MD (Oto) - **Spec Exp:** Cochlear Implants; Ear Disorders/Surgery; Otology & Neuro-Otology; Dizziness/Vertigo; **Hospital:** Westchester Med Ctr, New York Eye & Ear Infirm of Mt Sinai; **Address:** 19 Bradhurst Ave, Ste 3600S, Hawthorne, NY 10532; **Phone:** 914-909-4578; **Board Cert:** Otolaryngology 1999; **Med School:** Duke Univ 1993; **Resid:** Otolaryngology, Stanford Univ Hosp 1998; **Fellow:** Neurotology, CA Inst 2000; **Fac Appt:** Assoc Prof Oto, NY Med Coll

Zalvan, Craig H MD (Oto) - **Spec Exp:** Voice Disorders; Swallowing Disorders; Airway Disorders; Vocal Cord Disorders; **Hospital:** Phelps Meml Hosp Ctr, Westchester Med Ctr; **Address:** Inst Voice & Swallowing Disorders, 777 N Broadway, Ste 303, North Tarrytown, NY 10591; **Phone:** 914-366-3636; **Board Cert:** Otolaryngology 2012; **Med School:** Albert Einstein Coll Med 1995; **Resid:** Otolaryngology, Manhattan EE&T 1999; Otolaryngology, NY-Presby/Columbia Univ Med Ctr 2001; **Fellow:** Laryngology, St Lukes-Roosevelt Hosp 2002; **Fac Appt:** Assoc Prof Oto, NY Med Coll

Pain Medicine

Kizelshteyn, Grigory MD (PM) - **Spec Exp:** Pain-Back & Neck; Pain-Spine; **Hospital:** White Plains Hosp (page 652); **Address:** Pain Medicine Wellness Ctr of New York, 220 Westchester Ave, Ground Floor, White Plains, NY 10604; **Phone:** 914-289-1507; **Board Cert:** Anesthesiology 1991; **Med School:** Russia 1977; **Resid:** Anesthesiology, Westchester Med Ctr 1985; **Fellow:** Pain Medicine, Westchester Med Ctr 1987

Lu, Gabriel P MD/PhD (PM) - **Spec Exp:** Acupuncture; Pain-Back & Neck; **Address:** 112 Penn Rd, Scarsdale, NY 10583; **Phone:** 914-725-4240; **Board Cert:** Anesthesiology 1984; **Med School:** China 1968; **Resid:** Surgery, St Lukes Hospital 1976; Anesthesiology, Montefiore Med Ctr 1978; **Fellow:** Anesthesiology, Montefiore Med Ctr 1979; **Fac Appt:** Prof Anes, Albert Einstein Coll Med

Malits, Bella M MD (PM) - **Spec Exp:** Pain-Chronic; Reflex Sympathetic Dystrophy (RSD); **Hospital:** Northern Westchester Hosp; **Address:** MKMG, Pain Med, 34 S Bedford Rd, Ste 201, Mt Kisco, NY 10549; **Phone:** 914-242-4400; **Board Cert:** Anesthesiology 1995; Pain Medicine 2007; **Med School:** NY Med Coll 1990; **Resid:** Anesthesiology, Mt Sinai Hosp 1994; **Fellow:** Pain Management, Mt Sinai Hosp 1995

Pediatric Cardiology

Bierman, Fredrick Zachary MD (PCd) - **Spec Exp:** Fetal Echocardiography; Kawasaki Disease; Congenital Heart Disease; Echocardiography; **Hospital:** Westchester Med Ctr; **Address:** NY Medical College, Pediatric Cardiology, 40 Sunshine Cottage Rd, Ste 1NJ26, Valhalla, NY 10595; **Phone:** 914-594-2222; **Board Cert:** Pediatrics 1978; Pediatric Cardiology 1981; **Med School:** SUNY Downstate 1973; **Resid:** Pediatrics, Mount Sinai Med Ctr 1976; **Fellow:** Pediatric Cardiology, Harvard Chldns Hosp 1979; **Fac Appt:** Prof Ped, NY Med Coll

Crowe, David MD (PCd) - **Spec Exp:** Congenital Heart Disease; **Hospital:** Northern Westchester Hosp; **Address:** Northern Westchester Hosp, 480 N Bedford Rd, Chappaqua, NY 10514; **Phone:** 914-458-8800; **Board Cert:** Pediatric Cardiology 2010; **Med School:** NY Med Coll 1994; **Resid:** Pediatrics, NY-Presby/Weill Cornell Med Ctr 1997; **Fellow:** Pediatric Cardiology, NY-Presby/Columbia Univ Med Ctr 2000

Fish, Bernard G MD (PCd) - **Spec Exp:** Cardiac Imaging; Fetal Echocardiography; **Hospital:** Westchester Med Ctr, Children's & Women's Phys.of Westchester; **Address:** NY Medical College, Pediatric Cardiology, 19 Bradhurst Ave, Ste 1400, Hawthorne, NY 10532; **Phone:** 914-594-2222; **Board Cert:** Pediatrics 1974; Pediatric Cardiology 1975; **Med School:** Univ Chicago-Pritzker Sch Med 1969; **Resid:** Pediatrics, Montefiore Hosp Med Ctr 1971; Pediatric Cardiology, Montefiore Hosp Med Ctr 1973; **Fellow:** Pediatric Cardiology, Yale-New Haven Hosp 1975; **Fac Appt:** Assoc Prof Ped, NY Med Coll

Friedman, Deborah M MD (PCd) - **Spec Exp:** Fetal Cardiology; Echocardiography; Fetal Echocardiography; Congenital Heart Disease; **Hospital:** Westchester Med Ctr, Children's & Women's Phys.of Westchester; **Address:** NY Medical College, Pediatric Cardiology, 19 Bradhurst Ave, rm 1400, Hawthorne, NY 10532; **Phone:** 914-594-2222; **Board Cert:** Pediatrics 1982; Pediatric Cardiology 1983; Pediatric Critical Care Medicine 2014; **Med School:** Univ Chicago-Pritzker Sch Med 1977; **Resid:** Pediatrics, Bronx Muni Hosp Ctr 1980; **Fellow:** Pediatric Cardiology, NYU Med Ctr 1983; **Fac Appt:** Prof Ped, NY Med Coll

Gewitz, Michael H MD (PCd) - **Spec Exp:** Neonatal Cardiology; Kawasaki Disease; Echocardiography; Heart Failure; **Hospital:** Westchester Med Ctr, Children's & Women's Phys.of Westchester; **Address:** NY Medical College, Pediatric Cardiology, 19 Bradhurst Ave, Ste 1400, Valhalla, NY 10532; **Phone:** 914-594-2222; **Board Cert:** Pediatrics 1979; Pediatric Cardiology 1981; **Med School:** Hahnemann Univ 1974; **Resid:** Pediatrics, Chldns Hosp 1976; Pediatrics, Hosp Sick Chldn 1977; **Fellow:** Pediatric Cardiology, Yale-New Haven Hosp 1980; **Fac Appt:** Prof Ped, NY Med Coll

Issenberg, Henry J MD (PCd) - **Spec Exp:** Fetal Echocardiography; Congenital Heart Disease-Adult & Child; Kawasaki Disease; Arrhythmias-Fetal; **Hospital:** Westchester Med Ctr, Children's & Women's Phys.of Westchester; **Address:** NY Medical College, Pediatric Cardiology, 19 Bradhurst Ave, rm 1400, Hawthorne, NY 10532; **Phone:** 914-594-2222; **Board Cert:** Pediatrics 1979; Pediatric Cardiology 1979; **Med School:** Emory Univ 1974; **Resid:** Pediatrics, Jacobi Med Ctr 1977; **Fellow:** Pediatric Cardiology, Childrens Med Ctr 1980; **Fac Appt:** Assoc Prof Ped, NY Med Coll

Pediatric Critical Care Medicine

Goltzman, Carey S MD (PCCM) - **Spec Exp:** Respiratory Failure; Sepsis & Septic Shock; **Hospital:** Westchester Med Ctr, Children's & Women's Phys.of Westchester; **Address:** Marla Fareri Children's Hosp, 100 Woods Rd, Valhalla, NY 10595; **Phone:** 914-493-7513; **Board Cert:** Pediatrics 2014; **Med School:** Mexico 1981; **Resid:** Pediatrics, Westchester Med Ctr 1987; **Fellow:** Pediatric Critical Care Medicine, Henry Ford Hosp 1989; **Fac Appt:** Asst Prof Ped, NY Med Coll

Pediatric Endocrinology

Agarwal, Chhavi MD (PEn) - **Spec Exp:** Thyroid Disorders; Rett Syndrome; Calcium Disorders; Obesity; **Hospital:** Montefiore Med Ctr-Moses Campus (page 100), White Plains Hosp (page 652); **Address:** Pediatric Endocrinology of NY, 495 Central Park Ave, Ste 208, Scarsdale, NY 10583; **Phone:** 914-713-8774; **Board Cert:** Pediatric Endocrinology 2007; Pediatrics 2011; **Med School:** India 1990; **Resid:** Pediatrics, Royal College of Physicians A 1999; Pediatrics, Flushing Hosp Med Ctr 2004; **Fellow:** Pediatric Endocrinology, NY-Presby/Columbia Univ Med Ctr 2007; Research, Albert Einstein Coll of Med: Yeshiva Univ 2013

DiMartino-Nardi, Joan MD (PEn) - **Spec Exp:** Thyroid Disorders; Diabetes; **Hospital:** Northern Westchester Hosp; **Address:** Pediatrics at Chappaqua Crossings, 480 Bedford Rd, Chappaqua, NY 10514; **Phone:** 914-458-8800; **Board Cert:** Pediatrics 1985; Pediatric Endocrinology 1986; **Med School:** SUNY Downstate 1980; **Resid:** Pediatrics, Montefiore Med Ctr 1983; **Fellow:** Pediatric Endocrinology, New York Hosp 1986; **Fac Appt:** Clin Prof Ped, Albert Einstein Coll Med

Noto, Richard MD (PEn) - **Spec Exp:** Growth/Development Disorders; Diabetes; Lead Poisoning; Thyroid Disorders; **Hospital:** Westchester Med Ctr, Children's & Women's Phys.of Westchester; **Address:** Children's Physicians of Westchester, 755 N Broadway, Ste 400, Sleepy Hollow, NY 10591; **Phone:** 914-366-3400; **Board Cert:** Pediatrics 1981; Pediatric Endocrinology 1983; **Med School:** Mount Sinai Sch Med 1976; **Resid:** Pediatrics, Beth Israel Med Ctr 1978; **Fellow:** Pediatric Endocrinology, NY-Presby/Weill Cornell Med Ctr 1979; Pediatric Endocrinology, N Shore Univ Hosp 1981; **Fac Appt:** Asst Prof Ped, NY Med Coll

Romano, Alicia A MD (PEn) - **Spec Exp:** Growth/Development Disorders; Diabetes; **Hospital:** Westchester Med Ctr; **Address:** Chldn's Physicians of Westchester, 755 N Broadway, Ste 400, Sleepy Hollow, NY 10591; **Phone:** 914-366-3400; **Board Cert:** Pediatric Endocrinology 2013; **Med School:** SUNY Stony Brook 1985; **Resid:** Pediatrics, Schneider Chldns Hosp 1988; **Fellow:** Pediatric Endocrinology, Schneider Chldns Hosp 1991; **Fac Appt:** Asst Prof Ped, NY Med Coll

Saenger, Paul H MD (PEn) - **Spec Exp:** Short Stature in Children; Turner Syndrome; Sexual Differentiation Disorders; **Hospital:** Winthrop Univ Hosp (page 536); **Address:** 150 Lockwood Ave, Ste 34, New Rochelle, NY 10801; **Phone:** 914-636-5924; **Board Cert:** Pediatrics 1973; Pediatric Endocrinology 1978; **Med School:** Germany 1967; **Resid:** Pediatrics, Montefiore Hosp Med Ctr 1970; Pediatrics, Albert Einstein Coll Med 1971; **Fellow:** Pediatric Endocrinology, Cornell Univ Med Ctr 1975

Pediatric Gastroenterology

Berezin, Stuart H MD (PGe) - **Spec Exp:** Gastroesophageal Reflux Disease (GERD); Celiac Disease; Inflammatory Bowel Disease; **Hospital:** Westchester Med Ctr, Children's & Women's Phys.of Westchester; **Address:** CWPW, Pediatric Gastroenterology Dept, 503 Grasslands Rd, Ste 201, Valhalla, NY 10595; **Phone:** 914-367-0000; **Board Cert:** Pediatrics 1980; Pediatric Gastroenterology 2012; **Med School:** Hahnemann Univ 1976; **Resid:** Pediatrics, MetroHealth Med Ctr 1980; **Fellow:** Gastroenterology, Chldns Hosp 1983; **Fac Appt:** Asst Prof Ped, NY Med Coll

Birnbaum, Audrey H MD (PGe) - **Spec Exp:** Food Allergy; Inflammatory Bowel Disease/Crohn's; **Hospital:** Northern Westchester Hosp; **Address:** Mt Kisco Med Grp, 110 S Bedford Rd, Mount Kisco, NY 10549; **Phone:** 914-241-1050; **Board Cert:** Pediatric Gastroenterology 2014; **Med School:** NYU Sch Med 1986; **Resid:** Pediatrics, Mount Sinai Med Ctr 1989; **Fellow:** Pediatric Gastroenterology, Mount Sinai Med Ctr 1991

Halata, Michael S MD (PGe) - **Spec Exp:** Inflammatory Bowel Disease; Functional Bowel Disorders; Gastroesophageal Reflux Disease (GERD); **Hospital:** Westchester Med Ctr, Children's & Women's Phys.of Westchester; **Address:** 503 Grasslands Rd, Ste 201, Valhalla, NY 10595; **Phone:** 914-367-0000; **Board Cert:** Pediatrics 1980; Pediatric Gastroenterology 2012; **Med School:** UMDNJ-NJ Med Sch, Newark 1974; **Resid:** Pediatrics, Westchester Med Ctr 1977; **Fellow:** Pediatric Gastroenterology, Westchester Med Ctr 1980; **Fac Appt:** Assoc Prof Ped, NY Med Coll

Sunku, Bhanu K MD (PGe) - **Hospital:** Northern Westchester Hosp; **Address:** MKMG, Ped Gastroenterology, 90 S Bedford Rd, Mount Kisco, NY 10549; **Phone:** 914-241-1050; **Board Cert:** Pediatric Gastroenterology 2007; **Med School:** Boston Univ 1998; **Resid:** Pediatrics, Winthrop Univ Hosp 2001; **Fellow:** Pediatric Gastroenterology, Chldns Meml Hosp 2004

Pediatric Hematology-Oncology

Cairo, Mitchell S MD (PHO) - **Spec Exp:** Bone Marrow Transplant; Stem Cell Transplant; Leukemia & Lymphoma; **Hospital:** Westchester Med Ctr, Children's & Women's Phys.of Westchester; **Address:** CWPW, Pediatric Hem/Onc, 19 Bradhurst Ave, Ste 800S, Hawthorne, NY 10532; **Phone:** 914-493-7997; **Board Cert:** Pediatrics 1980; Pediatric Hematology-Oncology 1982; **Med School:** UCSF 1976; **Resid:** Pediatrics, UCLA Med Ctr 1979; **Fellow:** Pediatric Hematology-Oncology, IU Hlth Hosp 1981; **Fac Appt:** Prof Ped, NY Med Coll

Ozkaynak, Mehmet F MD (PHO) - **Spec Exp:** Bone Marrow Transplant; **Hospital:** Westchester Med Ctr, Children's & Women's Phys.of Westchester; **Address:** 19 Bradhurst Ave, Ste 1400, Hawthorne, NY 10532; **Phone:** 914-493-7997; **Board Cert:** Pediatric Hematology-Oncology 2014; **Med School:** Turkey 1978; **Resid:** Pediatrics, Hacettepe Chldn's Hosp 1982; Pediatrics, Chldn's Hosp 1991; **Fellow:** Hematology & Oncology, Chldn's Hosp 1989; **Fac Appt:** Prof Ped, NY Med Coll

Sandoval, Claudio MD (PHO) - **Spec Exp:** Leukemia & Lymphoma; Ataxia Telangiectasia; **Hospital:** Westchester Med Ctr, Children's & Women's Phys.of Westchester; **Address:** 19 Bradhurst Ave, Ste 1400, Hawthorne, NY 10532; **Phone:** 914-493-7997; **Board Cert:** Pediatric Hematology-Oncology 2008; **Med School:** NY Med Coll 1987; **Resid:** Pediatrics, Schneider Chldns Hosp 1990; **Fellow:** Pediatric Hematology-Oncology, St Jude Chldns Rsch Hosp 1994; **Fac Appt:** Prof Ped, NY Med Coll

Tugal, Oya L MD (PHO) - **Spec Exp:** Leukemia & Lymphoma; Langerhans Cell Histiocytoma; **Hospital:** Westchester Med Ctr, Children's & Women's Phys.of Westchester; **Address:** 19 Bradhurst Ave, Ste 1400, Hawthorne, NY 10532; **Phone:** 914-493-7997; **Board Cert:** Pediatrics 1986; Pediatric Hematology-Oncology 1987; **Med School:** Turkey 1974; **Resid:** Pediatrics, Hacettepe Med Ctr 1977; Pediatrics, Westchester Med Ctr 1985; **Fellow:** Allergy & Immunology, Hacettepe Med Ctr 1978; Pediatric Hematology-Oncology, Mount Sinai Hosp 1987; **Fac Appt:** Prof Ped, NY Med Coll

Pediatric Infectious Disease

Li, Karl I-Ming MD (PInf) - **Spec Exp:** Lyme Disease; Tick-borne Diseases; **Hospital:** Westchester Med Ctr, Children's & Women's Phys.of Westchester; **Address:** 19 Bradhurst Ave Fl 1 - Ste 1400, Hawthorne, NY 10532; **Phone:** 914-493-8333; **Board Cert:** Pediatric Infectious Disease 2012; **Med School:** Univ Mass Sch Med 1979; **Resid:** Pediatrics, Penn State Hershey Med Ctr 1982; Pediatrics, Miami Children's Hosp 1983; **Fellow:** Pediatric Infectious Disease, Univ Pittsburgh Med Ctr 1986; **Fac Appt:** Asst Prof Ped, NY Med Coll

Nolan, Sheila MD (PInf) - **Hospital:** Westchester Med Ctr; **Address:** 19 Bradhurst Ave, Ground FL, rm 1400, Hawthorne, NY 10532; **Phone:** 914-493-8333; **Board Cert:** Pediatrics 2009; Pediatric Infectious Disease 2009; **Med School:** Temple Univ 1998; **Resid:** Pediatrics, Univ S FL Coll of Med 2001; **Fellow:** Reproductive Toxicology, Natl Inst of Health 2006; Pediatric Infectious Disease, CHOP 2009; **Fac Appt:** Asst Prof Ped, NY Med Coll

Pediatric Nephrology

Samsonov, Dmitry V MD (PNep) - **Spec Exp:** Transplant Medicine-Kidney; Kidney Disease-Chronic; **Hospital:** Westchester Med Ctr, Metropolitan Hosp Ctr - NY; **Address:** Chldn & Women's Physicians, 19 Bradhurst Ave, Hawthorne, NY 10532; **Phone:** 914-493-7583; **Board Cert:** Pediatrics 2010; Pediatric Nephrology 2012; **Med School:** Russia 1989; **Resid:** Pediatrics, Hadassah Univ Hosp 1999; Pediatrics, Univ KY Affil Hosp 2010; **Fellow:** Pediatric Nephrology, Chldn's Hosp 2002; Transplant Medicine, Chldn's Hosp 2003; **Fac Appt:** Asst Prof Med, NY Med Coll

Pediatric Otolaryngology

Bernstein, Joseph M MD (PO) - **Spec Exp:** Airway Disorders; Sleep Apnea; Craniofacial Surgery; Cleft Palate/Lip; **Hospital:** New York Eye & Ear Infirm of Mt Sinai, Mt Sinai Beth Israel; **Address:** 244 Westchester Ave, Ste 215, White Plains, NY 10604; **Phone:** 914-997-9100; **Board Cert:** Otolaryngology 1998; **Med School:** NYU Sch Med 1991; **Resid:** Surgery, NYU Med Ctr 1993; Otolaryngology, NYU Med Ctr 1997; **Fellow:** Pediatric Otolaryngology, Texas Chldns Hosp 1998

De Serres, Lianne M MD (PO) - **Spec Exp:** Airway Disorders; Sinus Disorders; Ear Infections; Craniofacial Surgery; **Hospital:** Westchester Med Ctr, Phelps Meml Hosp Ctr; **Address:** ENT Faculty Practice, 1055 Saw Mill River Rd, Ste 101, Ardsley, NY 10502; **Phone:** 914-693-7636; **Board Cert:** Otolaryngology 1997; **Med School:** Univ NC Sch Med 1990; **Resid:** Otolaryngology, Univ Wash Med Ctr 1996; **Fellow:** Pediatric Otolaryngology, Univ Wash Med Ctr 1998; **Fac Appt:** Assoc Clin Prof Oto, NY Med Coll

Keller, Jeffrey L MD (PO) - **Spec Exp:** Otitis Media; Sinusitis; Sleep Disorders/Apnea; **Hospital:** Northern Westchester Hosp; **Address:** MKMG, Pediatric Otolaryngology, 110 S Bedford Rd Fl 2, Mount Kisco, NY 10549; **Phone:** 914-241-1050 x3006; **Board Cert:** Otolaryngology 1996; **Med School:** Stanford Univ 1990; **Resid:** Otolaryngology, Mount Sinai Med Ctr 1995; **Fellow:** Pediatric Otolaryngology, Chldns Hosp 1996; **Fac Appt:** Asst Prof Oto, Mount Sinai Sch Med

Merer, David M MD (PO) - **Spec Exp:** Airway Disorders; Hearing Disorders; Sinus Disorders; Head & Neck Tumors; **Hospital:** Westchester Med Ctr; **Address:** ENT Faculty Practice, 1055 Saw Mill River Rd, Ste 101, Ardsley, NY 10502; **Phone:** 914-693-7636; **Board Cert:** Otolaryngology 1996; **Med School:** Albert Einstein Coll Med 1990; **Resid:** Surgery, Montefiore Med Ctr 1991; Otolaryngology, Montefiore Med Ctr 1995; **Fellow:** Pediatric Otolaryngology, Montefiore Med Ctr 1996; **Fac Appt:** Assoc Prof Oto, NY Med Coll

Pediatric Pulmonology

Amin, Nikhil S MD (PPul) - **Spec Exp:** Cystic Fibrosis; Asthma; Lung Disorders-Congenital; Primary Ciliary Dyskinesia; **Hospital:** Westchester Med Ctr; **Address:** Pediatric Specialty Ctr, 19 Bradhurst Ave, Ste 1400, Hawthorne, NY 10532; **Phone:** 914-493-7585; **Board Cert:** Pediatric Pulmonology 2008; **Med School:** India 1980; **Resid:** Pediatrics, Baroda Med Coll-SSG Hosp 1984; Pediatrics, NY Med Coll 1988; **Fellow:** Pediatric Pulmonology, NY Med Coll 1994; **Fac Appt:** Assoc Prof Ped, NY Med Coll

Boyer, Joseph T MD (PPul) - **Spec Exp:** Asthma; Cystic Fibrosis; **Hospital:** Westchester Med Ctr; **Address:** 19 Bradhurst Ave, Ste 1400, Hawthorne, NY 10532; **Phone:** 914-493-7585; **Board Cert:** Pediatric Pulmonology 2013; **Med School:** SUNY Downstate 1988; **Resid:** Pediatrics, Westchester Med Ctr 1991; **Fellow:** Pediatric Pulmonology, Westchester Med Ctr 1995

Dozor, Allen J MD (PPul) - **Spec Exp:** Asthma; Cystic Fibrosis; **Hospital:** Westchester Med Ctr, Children's & Women's Phys.of Westchester; **Address:** CWPW, Ped Pulmonology, 19 Bradhurst Ave Fl 1 - Ste 1400, Hawthorne, NY 10532; **Phone:** 914-493-7585; **Board Cert:** Pediatrics 1981; Pediatric Pulmonology 2010; **Med School:** Penn State Coll Med 1977; **Resid:** Pediatrics, St Vincents Hosp & Med Ctr 1980; **Fellow:** Pediatric Pulmonology, Chldns Hosp 1982; **Fac Appt:** Prof Ped, NY Med Coll

Kass, Lewis J MD (PPul) - **Spec Exp:** Sleep Disorders/Apnea; Asthma & Chronic Lung Disease; Cystic Fibrosis; **Hospital:** Northern Westchester Hosp, Norwalk Hosp; **Address:** Westchester Ped Pulmo & Sleep Med, 103 S Bedford Rd, Ste 111, Mount Kisco, NY 10549; **Phone:** 914-242-0445; **Board Cert:** Pediatric Pulmonology 2012; Sleep Medicine 2007; **Med School:** SUNY Downstate 1991; **Resid:** Pediatrics, Chldns Med Ctr 1995; **Fellow:** Pediatric Pulmonology, Yale-New Haven Hosp 1998

Krishnan, Sankaran S MD (PPul) - **Spec Exp:** Cystic Fibrosis; Bronchoscopy; Asthma; **Hospital:** Westchester Med Ctr; **Address:** CWPW, Pediatric Pulmonology Dept, 19 Bradhurst Ave Fl 1 - Ste 1400, Hawthorne, NY 10532; **Phone:** 914-493-7585; **Board Cert:** Pediatrics 2008; Pediatric Pulmonology 2013; **Med School:** India 1990; **Resid:** Pediatrics, Lincoln Med & Mental Hlth Ctr 1994; **Fellow:** Pediatric Pulmonology, Westchester Med Ctr 1997; **Fac Appt:** Asst Prof Ped, NY Med Coll

Lowenthal, Diana B MD (PPul) - **Spec Exp:** Asthma; Cystic Fibrosis; Cough-Chronic; **Hospital:** Westchester Med Ctr; **Address:** 19 Bradhurst Ave Fl 1 - Ste 1400, Hawthorne, NY 10532; **Phone:** 914-493-7585; **Board Cert:** Pediatric Pulmonology 2014; **Med School:** Albert Einstein Coll Med 1986; **Resid:** Pediatrics, Montefiore Med Ctr 1989; **Fellow:** Pediatric Pulmonology, Mount Sinai Hosp 1992; **Fac Appt:** Asst Prof Ped, NY Med Coll

Quittell, Lynne M MD (PPul) - **Spec Exp:** Cystic Fibrosis; Asthma; **Hospital:** Morgan Stanley Chldns Hosp of NY-Presby, NY (page 102), NY-Presby/Columbia Univ Med Ctr, NY (page 102); **Address:** Northern Westchester Hospital, 480 Bedford Rd, Chappaqua, NY 10514; **Phone:** 212-305-5122; **Board Cert:** Pediatrics 1986; Pediatric Pulmonology 2011; **Med School:** Israel 1981; **Resid:** Pediatrics, Schneider Chldns Hosp 1984; **Fellow:** Pediatric Pulmonology, St Christopher's Hosp 1988

Pediatric Rheumatology

Chao, Chun T MD (PRhu) - **Spec Exp:** Juvenile Arthritis; Lupus/SLE; Dermatomyositis; Arthritis in Lyme Disease; **Hospital:** Westchester Med Ctr; **Address:** 19 Bradhurst Ave, First Fl, Ste 1400, Hawthorne, NY 10532; **Phone:** 914-594-2270; **Board Cert:** Pediatric Rheumatology 2008; **Med School:** Philippines 1982; **Resid:** Pediatrics, St Lukes-Roosevelt Hosp 1988; Pediatrics, Duke Univ Med Ctr 1990; **Fellow:** Pediatric Rheumatology, Univ Tennessee Med Ctr 1993; **Fac Appt:** Asst Prof Ped, NY Med Coll

Pediatric Surgery

McBride, Whitney J MD (PS) - **Spec Exp:** Neonatal Surgery; Laparoscopic Surgery; **Hospital:** Westchester Med Ctr, Phelps Meml Hosp Ctr; **Address:** 19 Bradhurst Ave, Ste 1400, Hawthorne, NY 10532; **Phone:** 914-493-7620; **Board Cert:** Surgery 2011; **Med School:** Univ VT Coll Med 1992; **Resid:** Surgery, Fletcher Allen Hlthcare/Univ VT 1998

Stringel, Gustavo L MD (PS) - **Spec Exp:** Minimally Invasive Surgery; Cancer Surgery; Neonatal Surgery; **Hospital:** Westchester Med Ctr, Phelps Meml Hosp Ctr; **Address:** CWPW, Pediatric Surgery Dept, 19 Bradhurst Ave, Ste 1400, Hawthorne, NY 10532; **Phone:** 914-493-7620; **Board Cert:** Surgery 2007; Pediatric Surgery 2005; Surgical Critical Care 2007; **Med School:** Mexico 1971; **Resid:** Surgery, Univ Toronto Affil Hosp 1977; **Fellow:** Pediatric Surgery, Hosp Sick Chldn 1979; **Fac Appt:** Prof S, NY Med Coll

Zitsman, Jeffrey MD (PS) - **Spec Exp:** Minimally Invasive Surgery; Chest Wall Deformities; Obesity/Bariatric Surgery; **Hospital:** Morgan Stanley Chldns Hosp of NY-Presby, NY (page 102), Greenwich Hosp (page 970); **Address:** 688 White Plains Rd, Ste 223, Scarsdale, NY 10583; **Phone:** 914-722-6737; **Board Cert:** Surgery 2013; Pediatric Surgery 2005; **Med School:** Tufts Univ 1976; **Resid:** Surgery, Tufts Med Ctr 1981; **Fellow:** Pediatric Surgery, NY-Presby/Columbia Univ Med Ctr 1985; **Fac Appt:** Assoc Clin Prof S, Columbia P&S

Pediatric Urology

Franco, Israel MD (Ped Uro) - **Spec Exp:** Voiding Dysfunction-Pediatric; Laparoscopic Surgery; Prune Belly Syndrome; Neurogenic Bladder; **Hospital:** Westchester Med Ctr, Northern Westchester Hosp; **Address:** Pediatric Urology Assocs, 150 White Plains Rd, Ste 306, Tarrytown, NY 10591; **Phone:** 914-493-8628; **Board Cert:** Urology 2008; Pediatric Urology 2008; **Med School:** Albert Einstein Coll Med 1983; **Resid:** Pediatrics, St Vincent's Hosp 1985; Urology, New York Med Coll Affil Hosp 1989; **Fellow:** Pediatric Urology, Chldns Meml hosp 1991; **Fac Appt:** Assoc Prof U, NY Med Coll

Reda, Edward F MD (Ped Uro) - **Spec Exp:** Reconstructive Urologic Surgery; Hypospadias; Incontinence; **Hospital:** Westchester Med Ctr; **Address:** Pediatric Urology Assocs, 150 White Plains Rd, Ste 306, Tarrytown, NY 10591; **Phone:** 914-493-8628; **Board Cert:** Urology 1984; **Med School:** Mexico 1976; **Resid:** Surgery, Bronx Lebanon Hosp 1979; Urology, Montefiore Med Ctr 1982; **Fellow:** Pediatric Urology, Chldns Hosp 1984; **Fac Appt:** Assoc Prof U, NY Med Coll

Pediatrics

Acker, Peter J MD (Ped) *PCP* - **Spec Exp:** Pediatric Dermatology; Adolescent Medicine; Learning Disorders; **Hospital:** Greenwich Hosp (page 970), Westchester Med Ctr; **Address:** Pediatric Assocs, 26 Rye Ridge Plaza, Rye Brook, NY 10573; **Phone:** 914-251-1100; **Board Cert:** Pediatrics 2009; **Med School:** Israel 1982; **Resid:** Pediatrics, NYU/Bellevue Hosp Ctr 1985; **Fellow:** Ambulatory Pediatrics, NYU/Bellevue Hosp Ctr 1987

Altman, Robin L MD (Ped) *PCP* - **Hospital:** Westchester Med Ctr, Children's & Women's Phys.of Westchester; **Address:** CWPW Pediatrics, 19 Bradhurst Ave, Ste 2400, Hawthorne, NY 10532; **Phone:** 914-593-8850; **Board Cert:** Pediatrics 1987; **Med School:** Rutgers R W Johnson Med Sch 1983; **Resid:** Pediatrics, NY-Presby/Columbia Univ Med Ctr 1986; **Fac Appt:** Assoc Prof Ped, NY Med Coll

Angello, Thomas A MD (Ped) *PCP* - **Hospital:** Lawrence Hosp Ctr (page 102); **Address:** WestMed Medical Group, Pediatrics, 73 Market St, Ridge Hill, NY 10710; **Phone:** 914-607-4730; **Board Cert:** Pediatrics 2014; **Med School:** Grenada 1996; **Resid:** Pediatrics, St Luke's-Roosevelt Hosp 1999

Avvocato, Gloria P MD (Ped) *PCP* - **Spec Exp:** Adolescent Medicine; **Hospital:** White Plains Hosp (page 652); **Address:** Westchester Park Pediatrics, 222 N Westchester Ave, Ste 202, White Plains, NY 10604; **Phone:** 914-761-1717; **Board Cert:** Pediatrics 2008; **Med School:** Mexico 1987; **Resid:** Pediatrics, LIJ Med Ctr 1994

Bailey, Michele L MD (Ped) *PCP* - **Spec Exp:** Adolescent Medicine; Preventive Medicine; **Hospital:** Montefiore Med Ctr-Wakefield Campus (page 100), Lawrence Hosp Ctr (page 102); **Address:** Mayfield Pediatrics, 16 N Broadway, Ste LMG, White Plains, NY 10601; **Phone:** 914-686-1848; **Board Cert:** Pediatrics 2008; **Med School:** West Indies 1989; **Resid:** Pediatrics, Lincoln Med Ctr 1994; **Fac Appt:** Asst Clin Prof Ped, NY Med Coll

Barsh, Elliot B MD (Ped) *PCP* - **Spec Exp:** Preventive Medicine; **Hospital:** Northern Westchester Hosp; **Address:** Mount Kisco Medical Group, 110 S Bedford Rd, Mt Kisco, NY 10549; **Phone:** 914-242-1580; **Board Cert:** Pediatrics 2011; **Med School:** NYU Sch Med 1984; **Resid:** Pediatrics, Montefiore Med Ctr 1987; Pediatrics, Bronx-Lebanon Hosp 1988

Baskind, Lawrence J MD (Ped) *PCP* - **Spec Exp:** Preventive Medicine; **Hospital:** Hudson Valley Hosp Ctr; **Address:** The Westchester Med Practice, 35 S Riverside Ave, Ste 101, Croton-On-Hudson, NY 10520; **Phone:** 914-271-2424; **Board Cert:** Pediatrics 2010; **Med School:** Rutgers-NJ Med Sch 1983; **Resid:** Pediatrics, Univ Hosp-UMDNJ 1987; **Fac Appt:** Assoc Clin Prof Ped, NY Med Coll

Berkowitz, Norman MD (Ped) *PCP* - **Spec Exp:** Developmental & Mood Disorders; Preventive Medicine; **Hospital:** Greenwich Hosp (page 970), Westchester Med Ctr; **Address:** Ped Assocs, 26 Rye Ridge Plaza, Rye Brook, NY 10573-2820; **Phone:** 914-251-1100; **Board Cert:** Pediatrics 1972; **Med School:** SUNY Buffalo 1967; **Resid:** Pediatrics, Mount Sinai Med Ctr 1970; **Fellow:** Psychoanalysis, St Christopher Hosp Chldn 1973

Berman, Morton H MD (Ped) *PCP* - **Spec Exp:** Developmental Disorders; **Hospital:** White Plains Hosp (page 652); **Address:** 244 Westchester Ave, Ste 210, White Plains, NY 10604; **Phone:** 914-948-7016; **Board Cert:** Pediatrics 1972; **Med School:** NYU Sch Med 1966; **Resid:** Pediatrics, Bellevue Hosp 1968; Pediatric Neurology, Bellevue Hosp 1971; **Fac Appt:** Asst Clin Prof Ped, NYU Sch Med

Bomback, Fredric MD (Ped) *PCP* - **Spec Exp:** Infectious Disease; Complex Diagnosis; Adolescent Medicine; **Hospital:** White Plains Hosp (page 652), NY-Presby/Columbia Univ Med Ctr, NY (page 102); **Address:** WestMed Med Grp Pediatrics, 99 Fieldstone Drive, Hartsdale, NY 10530; **Phone:** 914-428-2120; **Board Cert:** Pediatrics 2010; **Med School:** NYU Sch Med 1969; **Resid:** Pediatrics, Jacobi Med Ctr 1972; **Fellow:** Genetics and Metabolism, Albert Einstein Coll Med 1976; **Fac Appt:** Clin Prof Ped, Columbia P&S

Bookner, Scott D MD (Ped) *PCP* - **Hospital:** White Plains Hosp (page 652); **Address:** Scarsdale Pediatric Assocs, 7 Popham Rd, Ste 301, Scarsdale, NY 10583; **Phone:** 914-725-0800; **Board Cert:** Pediatrics 2014; **Med School:** SUNY Buffalo 1989; **Resid:** Pediatrics, Chldns Hosp 1992; **Fac Appt:** Asst Clin Prof Ped, NY Med Coll

Collins, Margaret A MD (Ped) *PCP* - **Spec Exp:** Preventive Medicine; **Hospital:** Northern Westchester Hosp; **Address:** Mount Kisco Medical Group, 110 S Bedford Rd, Mt Kisco, NY 10549; **Phone:** 914-242-1580; **Board Cert:** Pediatrics 2013; **Med School:** Geo Wash Univ 1988; **Resid:** Pediatrics, N Shore Univ Hosp 1992; **Fac Appt:** Asst Clin Prof Ped, NY Med Coll

Coven, Barbara J MD (Ped) *PCP* - **Spec Exp:** Preventive Medicine; **Hospital:** Greenwich Hosp (page 970), White Plains Hosp (page 652); **Address:** Westchester Med Grp, Dept Pediatrics, 210 Westchester Ave Fl 2, White Plains, NY 10604; **Phone:** 914-682-0731; **Board Cert:** Pediatrics 2010; **Med School:** Boston Univ 1980; **Resid:** Pediatrics, Boston City Hosp 1983; **Fellow:** Psychosomatic Medicine, Chldns Hosp Med Ctr 1983

Cowan, Stephen MD (Ped) - **Spec Exp:** Developmental Disorders; ADD/ADHD; Autism; Complementary Medicine; **Hospital:** Hudson Valley Hosp Ctr; **Address:** The Westchester Ctr for Holistic Families, 491 Lexington Ave, Mt Kisco, NY 10049; **Phone:** 914-864-1976; **Board Cert:** Pediatrics 2010; **Med School:** Italy 1984; **Resid:** Pediatrics, St Lukes-Roosevelt Hosp Ctr 1987; **Fellow:** Developmental-Behavioral Pediatrics, Developmental Disabilities Ctr-Roosevelt Hosp 1989

Eisenberg, Amy B MD (Ped) *PCP* - **Spec Exp:** Developmental Disorders; **Hospital:** White Plains Hosp (page 652); **Address:** Westchester Park Pediatrics, 222 N Westchester Ave, Ste 202, White Plains, NY 10604; **Phone:** 914-761-1717; **Board Cert:** Pediatrics 2011; **Med School:** Mount Sinai Sch Med 1993; **Resid:** Pediatrics, Mt Sinai Med Ctr 1996

Hartz, Cindi L MD (Ped) *PCP* - **Spec Exp:** Preventive Medicine; **Hospital:** Montefiore New Rochelle Hosp (page 100); **Address:** Larchmont Pediatrics, 1415 Boston Post Rd, Larchmont, NY 10538; **Phone:** 914-833-1502; **Med School:** Mount Sinai Sch Med 1983; **Resid:** Pediatrics, Mt Sinai Hosp 1986; **Fellow:** Pediatric Hematology-Oncology, Mt Sinai Hosp 1987

Levinson, William MD (Ped) - **Spec Exp:** Developmental & Behavioral Disorders; ADD/ADHD; Autism; **Hospital:** Westchester Med Ctr; **Address:** 503 Grasslands Rd, Ste 200, Valhalla, NY 10595; **Phone:** 914-304-5250; **Board Cert:** Developmental-Behavioral Pediatrics 2012; **Med School:** Albert Einstein Coll Med 1976; **Resid:** Pediatrics, Bronx Municipal Hosp 1979; **Fellow:** Developmental-Behavioral Pediatrics, Albert Einstein Coll of Med 1980; Developmental-Behavioral Pediatrics, Chldn's Hosp 1982; **Fac Appt:** Assoc Clin Prof Ped, NY Med Coll

Levitt, Miriam MD (Ped) *PCP* - **Spec Exp:** Travel Medicine; Preventive Medicine; **Hospital:** Lawrence Hosp Ctr (page 102), Montefiore Med Ctr-Moses Campus (page 100); **Address:** 1 Pondfield Rd, Ste 303, Bronxville, NY 10708-3706; **Phone:** 914-961-3604; **Board Cert:** Pediatrics 1975; **Med School:** Albert Einstein Coll Med 1971; **Resid:** Pediatrics, Montefiore Med Ctr 1974; **Fac Appt:** Asst Clin Prof Ped, Albert Einstein Coll Med

London, Ronald MD (Ped) *PCP* - **Spec Exp:** Developmental Disorders; Preventive Medicine; **Hospital:** Montefiore Med Ctr-Moses Campus (page 100), Montefiore Med Ctr-Einstein Campus (page 100); **Address:** WestMed Medical Grp, 171 Huguenot St, New Rochelle, NY 10801; **Phone:** 914-607-4720; **Board Cert:** Pediatrics 2010; **Med School:** Israel 1984; **Resid:** Pediatrics, Montefiore Med Ctr 1987; **Fellow:** Child Development, Albert Einstein Coll Med Affil Hosp Affil Hosp 1988

Lubell, Harry R MD (Ped) *PCP* - **Spec Exp:** Preventive Medicine; **Hospital:** Phelps Meml Hosp Ctr, Westchester Med Ctr; **Address:** Pediatrics of Sleepy Hollow, 150 White Plains Rd, Ste 101, Tarrytown, NY 10591-2657; **Phone:** 914-332-4141; **Board Cert:** Pediatrics 1969; **Med School:** Ros Franklin Univ/Chicago Med Sch 1964; **Resid:** Pediatrics, Montefiore Med Ctr 1967; **Fellow:** Pediatric Hematology-Oncology, Babies Hosp-Columbia Presby Hosp 1970; **Fac Appt:** Assoc Clin Prof Ped, NY Med Coll

Meisler, Susan H MD (Ped) *PCP* - **Spec Exp:** Adolescent Medicine; Preventive Medicine; **Hospital:** Montefiore Med Ctr-Einstein Campus (page 100), Montefiore New Rochelle Hosp (page 100); **Address:** Ped Assocs of Southern Westchester, 145 Hugenot St, Ste 200, New Rochelle, NY 10801-5011; **Phone:** 914-235-1400; **Board Cert:** Pediatrics 2011; **Med School:** SUNY Stony Brook 1984; **Resid:** Pediatrics, Schneider Chldn's Hosp 1987

Proskin, Wendy MD (Ped) *PCP* - **Hospital:** White Plains Hosp (page 652), Greenwich Hosp (page 970); **Address:** WestMed, Pediatrics & Adolescent Med, 210 Westchester Ave, White Plains, NY 10604; **Phone:** 914-682-0731; **Board Cert:** Pediatrics 2010; **Med School:** SUNY Downstate 1999; **Resid:** Pediatrics, Montefiore Med Ctr 2002

Richel, Peter L MD (Ped) *PCP* - **Spec Exp:** Preventive Medicine; **Hospital:** Northern Westchester Hosp; **Address:** 36 Smith Ave, Mt Kisco, NY 10549; **Phone:** 914-666-6655; **Board Cert:** Pediatrics 2007; **Med School:** Dominican Republic 1983; **Resid:** Pediatrics, Chldns Hosp-Albany Med Ctr 1987; **Fellow:** Ambulatory Pediatrics, St Luke's-Roosevelt Hosp Ctr 1988; **Fac Appt:** Asst Clin Prof Ped, Albert Einstein Coll Med

Ross, Jody A MD (Ped) *PCP* - **Hospital:** White Plains Hosp (page 652); **Address:** Westchester Park Pediatrics, 222 N Westchester Ave, Ste 202, White Plains, NY 10604; **Phone:** 914-761-1717; **Board Cert:** Pediatrics 1986; **Med School:** St Louis Univ 1981; **Resid:** Pediatrics, Mt Sinai Med Ctr 1984; **Fellow:** Pediatric Endocrinology, Mt Sinai Med Ctr 1986

Versfelt, Mary MD (Ped) *PCP* - **Spec Exp:** Chronic Illness; Neonatal Care; Adolescent Medicine; **Hospital:** Greenwich Hosp (page 970), Westchester Med Ctr; **Address:** Pediatric Assocs, 26 Rye Ridge Plaza, Rye Brook, NY 10573; **Phone:** 914-251-1100; **Board Cert:** Pediatrics 2010; **Med School:** Columbia P&S 1978; **Resid:** Pediatrics, NY-Presby/Columbia Univ Med Ctr 1981; **Fac Appt:** Assoc Clin Prof Ped, Columbia P&S

Wager, Marc D MD (Ped) *PCP* - **Spec Exp:** Adolescent Medicine; **Hospital:** Montefiore New Rochelle Hosp (page 100); **Address:** Pediatric Grp-New Rochelle, 140 Lockwood Ave, Ste 115, New Rochelle, NY 10801; **Phone:** 914-235-3800; **Board Cert:** Pediatrics 1986; **Med School:** Albert Einstein Coll Med 1981; **Resid:** Pediatrics, Jacobi Med Ctr 1984; **Fellow:** Adolescent Medicine, Montefiore Med Ctr 1986; **Fac Appt:** Asst Clin Prof Ped, Albert Einstein Coll Med

Weissbrot, Jay M MD (Ped) *PCP* - **Spec Exp:** Adolescent Medicine; **Hospital:** White Plains Hosp (page 652); **Address:** Westchester Hlth, Pediatrics, 410 N Broadway, White Plains, NY 10603; **Phone:** 914-948-0353; **Board Cert:** Pediatrics 1986; **Med School:** SUNY Downstate 1980; **Resid:** Pediatrics, Brookdale Univ Hosp 1983; **Fellow:** Adolescent Medicine, Brookdale Univ Hosp 1984

Wurzel, Carol L MD (Ped) *PCP* - **Spec Exp:** Special Health Care Needs; **Hospital:** White Plains Hosp (page 652); **Address:** Westchester Park Pediatrics, 222 N Westchester Ave, Ste 202, White Plains, NY 10604; **Phone:** 914-761-1717; **Board Cert:** Pediatrics 1987; **Med School:** Mount Sinai Sch Med 1982; **Resid:** Pediatrics, Schneider Children's Hosp 1986; **Fellow:** Pediatric Infectious Disease, SChneider Children's Hosp 1987

Physical Medicine & Rehabilitation

Gross, Stacy B S MD (PMR) - **Spec Exp:** Sports Injuries; **Hospital:** Northern Westchester Hosp; **Address:** Mount Kisco Medical Group, 90 S Bedford Rd, Mount Kisco, NY 10549; **Phone:** 914-241-1050; **Board Cert:** Physical Medicine & Rehabilitation 2006; Sports Medicine 2013; **Med School:** Israel 2001; **Resid:** Physical Medicine & Rehabilitation, NYU Med Ctr 2005

Pechman, Karen M MD (PMR) - **Spec Exp:** Electrodiagnosis; Musculoskeletal Disorders; Amputee Rehabilitation; Pain Management; **Hospital:** Burke Rehab Hosp; **Address:** 170 Maple Ave, Ste 510, White Plains, NY 10601; **Phone:** 914-683-0020; **Board Cert:** Physical Medicine & Rehabilitation 1987; Electrodiagnostic Medicine 1989; **Med School:** Boston Univ 1980; **Resid:** Physical Medicine & Rehabilitation, Jacobi Med Ctr 1986; **Fellow:** Research, NYU Med Ctr 1982; **Fac Appt:** Asst Clin Prof PMR, Cornell Univ-Weill Med Coll

Pici, Ralph A MD (PMR) - **Spec Exp:** Musculoskeletal Disorders; **Hospital:** Lawrence Hosp Ctr (page 102); **Address:** Lawrence Hosp Ctr, Physical Med & Rehab, 55 Palmer Ave Fl 2, Bronxville, NY 10708; **Phone:** 914-787-3374; **Board Cert:** Physical Medicine & Rehabilitation 1974; **Med School:** Italy 1965; **Resid:** Pediatrics, Westchester Med Ctr 1967; Physical Medicine & Rehabilitation, Jacobi Med Ctr 1972

Randolph, Audrey L MD (PMR) - **Spec Exp:** Musculoskeletal Disorders; Pain-Back & Neck; **Hospital:** Westchester Med Ctr; **Address:** 19 Bradhurst Ave, Ste 1700 South, Hawthorne, NY 10532; **Phone:** 914-909-4168; **Board Cert:** Physical Medicine & Rehabilitation 1970; **Med School:** Med Coll PA Hahnemann 1964; **Resid:** Physical Medicine & Rehabilitation, NYU Med Ctr 1968; **Fac Appt:** Prof PMR, NY Med Coll

Plastic Surgery

Beran, Samuel J MD (PlS) - **Spec Exp:** Reconstructive Surgery; Liposuction; Breast Augmentation; **Hospital:** White Plains Hosp (page 652); **Address:** Cosmetic Surgery Assocs of NY, 440 Mamaroneck Ave, Ste 412, Harrison, NY 10528; **Phone:** 914-761-8667; **Board Cert:** Plastic Surgery 2009; **Med School:** Albany Med Coll 1990; **Resid:** Surgery, Thomas Jefferson Univ Hosp 1995; Plastic Surgery, UT Southwestern Med Ctr 1997

Chin, Simon H MD (PlS) - **Spec Exp:** Hand Surgery; Cosmetic Surgery-Face & Body; Plastic & Reconstructive Surgery; **Hospital:** Putnam Hosp Ctr, Northern Westchester Hosp; **Address:** Mount Kisco Med Grp, Plastic Surg, 111 Bedford Rd, Katonah, NY 10536; **Phone:** 914-232-3135 x2317; **Board Cert:** Plastic Surgery 2009; Hand Surgery 2010; **Med School:** Vanderbilt Univ 2000; **Resid:** Surgery, Yale-New Haven Hosp 2003; Plastic Surgery, Yale-New Haven Hosp 2006; **Fellow:** Hand Surgery, Univ Washington Med Ctr 2007; Cosmetic Plastic Surgery, NYU Med Ctr 2008

Greenwald, Joshua Adam MD (PlS) - **Spec Exp:** Breast Augmentation; Rhinoplasty; Liposuction & Body Contouring; **Hospital:** White Plains Hosp (page 652); **Address:** Cosmetic Surgery Assocs of NY, 440 Mamaroneck Ave, Ste 412, Harrison, NY 10528; **Phone:** 914-761-8667; **Board Cert:** Plastic Surgery 2005; **Med School:** NYU Sch Med 1995; **Resid:** Surgery, NYU Med Ctr 2001; **Fellow:** Plastic Surgery, Emory Univ Hosp 2004

Khoury, F. Frederic MD (PlS) - **Spec Exp:** Pediatric Plastic Surgery; Cosmetic Surgery-Breast; Cosmetic Surgery-Face; **Hospital:** White Plains Hosp (page 652), Greenwich Hosp (page 970); **Address:** 22 Rye Ridge Plaza, Rye Brook, NY 10573-2820; **Phone:** 914-253-9300; **Board Cert:** Plastic Surgery 2014; **Med School:** Lebanon 1971; **Resid:** Surgery, St Luke's-Roosevelt Hosp Ctr 1976; Plastic Surgery, St Luke's-Roosevelt Hosp Ctr 1979; **Fellow:** Plastic Surgery, St Louis Hosp 1977

Kleinman, Andrew MD (PlS) - **Spec Exp:** Cosmetic Surgery; Breast Augmentation; Eyelid Surgery; **Hospital:** Montefiore New Rochelle Hosp (page 100); **Address:** Kleinman Plastic Surgery, 800 Westchester Ave, Ste S-512, Rye Brook, NY 10573; **Phone:** 914-253-0700; **Board Cert:** Plastic Surgery 1989; **Med School:** Univ Rochester 1979; **Resid:** Surgery, Harvard Surg Svcs 1982; **Fellow:** Plastic Surgery, Baylor Coll Med 1985

Koch, Robert Michael MD (PlS) - **Spec Exp:** Cosmetic Surgery; Breast Cosmetic & Reconstructive Surgery; Microsurgery; Reconstructive Plastic Surgery; **Hospital:** Westchester Med Ctr; **Address:** NY Group for Plastic Surgery, 155 White Plains Rd, Tarrytown, NY 10591; **Phone:** 914-366-6139; **Board Cert:** Plastic Surgery 2013; **Med School:** Hahnemann Univ 1993; **Resid:** Surgery, George Washington Univ Med Ctr 1997; Plastic Surgery, UCLA Med Ctr 1999; **Fellow:** Cosmetic Plastic Surgery, Lenox Hill Hosp 2000; Research, Natl Inst Health 2001; **Fac Appt:** Asst Prof S, NY Med Coll

Newman, Scott E MD (PlS) - **Spec Exp:** Breast Reconstruction & Augmentation; Cosmetic Surgery-Breast; Cosmetic Surgery-Body; Abdominoplasty; **Hospital:** St. John's Riverside Hosp-Andrus Pavil, Montefiore Med Ctr-Einstein Campus (page 100); **Address:** 1 Odell Plaza, Yonkers, NY 10701; **Phone:** 914-423-9000; **Board Cert:** Plastic Surgery 2004; **Med School:** NY Med Coll 1985; **Resid:** Surgery, Westchester Med Ctr 1990; Plastic Surgery, Mt Sinai Med Ctr 1993; **Fac Appt:** Asst Clin Prof PlS, Albert Einstein Coll Med

Palaia, David A MD (PlS) - **Spec Exp:** Cosmetic Surgery-Face; Breast Reconstruction; Rhinoplasty; Reconstructive Surgery; **Hospital:** Northern Westchester Hosp; **Address:** 400 E Main St, North Bldg, Fl 2, Mt Kisco, NY 10549; **Phone:** 914-242-7610; **Board Cert:** Plastic Surgery 1993; **Med School:** UMDNJ-NJ Med Sch, Newark 1985; **Resid:** Surgery, Montefiore-Weiler Einstein Div 1989; Plastic Surgery, Montefiore-Weiler Einstein Div 1991

Pisarenko, Vadim MD (PlS) - **Spec Exp:** Cosmetic Surgery; **Hospital:** Lawrence Hosp Ctr (page 102), Montefiore New Rochelle Hosp (page 100); **Address:** Plastic Surgery of Westchester, 500 Mamaroneck Ave, Ste 211, Harrison, NY 10528; **Phone:** 914-771-7373; **Board Cert:** Surgery 2010; Plastic Surgery 2013; **Med School:** Univ Minn 2003; **Resid:** Surgery, UMDNJ Med Ctr 2009; Plastic Surgery, Montefiore Med Ctr 2011

Reiffel, Robert S MD (PlS) - **Spec Exp:** Cosmetic & Reconstructive Surgery; Hand Surgery; Cosmetic Surgery-Face & Nose; Breast Reconstruction & Augmentation; **Hospital:** White Plains Hosp (page 652); **Address:** 12 Greenridge Ave, Ste 203, White Plains, NY 10605; **Phone:** 914-683-1400; **Board Cert:** Plastic Surgery 1981; **Med School:** Columbia P&S 1972; **Resid:** Surgery, St Lukes-Roosevelt Hosp Ctr 1977; Plastic Surgery, NYU Med Ctr 1979; **Fellow:** Hand Surgery, NYU Med Ctr 1980

Rosenberg, Michael H MD (PlS) - **Spec Exp:** Cosmetic Surgery-Face; Liposuction & Body Contouring; Breast Surgery; **Hospital:** Northern Westchester Hosp, Westchester Med Ctr; **Address:** Northern Westchester Surgical Services, 400 E Main St, Fl 2 North, Mount Kisco, NY 10549; **Phone:** 914-242-7610; **Board Cert:** Surgery 2006; Plastic Surgery 2008; **Med School:** Columbia P&S 1987; **Resid:** Surgery, Columbia Presby Med Ctr 1992; Plastic/Reconstructive Surgery, Columbia Presby Med Ctr 1994; **Fac Appt:** Asst Clin Prof PlS, NY Med Coll

Roth, Douglas A MD (PlS) - **Spec Exp:** Cosmetic Surgery-Face; Cosmetic Surgery-Breast; Facial Plastic & Reconstructive Surgery; Skin Cancer; **Hospital:** Northern Westchester Hosp; **Address:** Mount Kisco Med Grp, Plastic Surgery, 110 S Bedford Rd, Mt Kisco, NY 10549; **Phone:** 914-242-5647; **Board Cert:** Surgery 2008; Plastic Surgery 2010; **Med School:** NYU Sch Med 1990; **Resid:** Surgery, NYU Med Ctr 1996; Plastic Surgery, NYU Med Ctr 1998; **Fellow:** Microvascular Surgery, NYU Med Ctr 1999; **Fac Appt:** Asst Clin Prof S, Mount Sinai Sch Med

Suzman, Michael S MD (PlS) - **Spec Exp:** Rhinoplasty; Facial Plastic & Reconstructive Surgery; Breast Surgery; **Hospital:** Greenwich Hosp (page 970), White Plains Hosp (page 652); **Address:** WestMed, Plastic Surgery, 1 Theall Rd, Ste 211, Rye, NY 10580; **Phone:** 914-848-8880; **Board Cert:** Plastic Surgery 2013; **Med School:** Cornell Univ-Weill Med Coll 1996; **Resid:** Surgery, NY Presby Hosp 2000; Surgical Oncology, Meml Sloan-Kettering Cancer Ctr 2000; **Fellow:** Plastic Surgery, NY Presby Hosp 2002

Psychiatry

Addonizio, Gerard C MD (Psyc) - **Spec Exp:** Psychotherapy; Psychopharmacology; Depression; Anxiety & Mood Disorders; **Hospital:** NY-Presby/Westchester Div, NY (page 102); **Address:** 21 Bloomingdale Rd, White Plains, NY 10605; **Phone:** 914-997-5864; **Board Cert:** Psychiatry 1983; **Med School:** Columbia P&S 1978; **Resid:** Psychiatry, Yale-New Haven Hosp 1982; **Fac Appt:** Prof Psyc, Cornell Univ-Weill Med Coll

Badikian, Arthur V MD (Psyc) - **Spec Exp:** Mood Disorders; Aging; Women's Health-Mental Health; Psychiatry in Cancer; **Hospital:** St. Vincent Cath Med Ctrs - Westchester; **Address:** 600 Mamaroneck Ave, Ste 106, Harrison, NY 10528; **Phone:** 914-948-4277; **Board Cert:** Psychiatry 1981; **Med School:** Univ Fla Coll Med 1976; **Resid:** Psychiatry, Westchester Med Ctr 1980; **Fac Appt:** Assoc Prof Psyc, NY Med Coll

Bauman, Jonathan H MD (Psyc) - **Spec Exp:** Mood Disorders; Anxiety Disorders; Personality Disorders; **Hospital:** Four Winds Hosp; **Address:** 892 Rt 35, Box 121, Cross River, NY 10518; **Phone:** 914-719-3210; **Board Cert:** Psychiatry 1978; **Med School:** Georgetown Univ 1974; **Resid:** Psychiatry, Univ VA Med Ctr 1975; Psychiatry, Georgetown Univ Hosp 1977; **Fac Appt:** Asst Prof Psyc, Albert Einstein Coll Med

Bogen, Steven MD (Psyc) - **Spec Exp:** Anxiety & Depression; Addiction Psychiatry; **Hospital:** Phelps Meml Hosp Ctr; **Address:** Phelps Meml Hosp, Dept Psychiatry, 701 N Broadway, Sleepy Hollow, NY 10591-1096; **Phone:** 914-366-3024; **Board Cert:** Psychiatry 2005; Addiction Psychiatry 2006; **Med School:** SUNY Downstate 1988; **Resid:** Psychiatry, Montefiore Med Ctr 1992

Breindel, David S MD (Psyc) - **Hospital:** NY-Presby/Westchester Div, NY (page 102); **Address:** 234 Elk Ave, New Rochelle, NY 10804-4217; **Phone:** 914-235-5520; **Board Cert:** Psychiatry 1981; **Med School:** Albert Einstein Coll Med 1976; **Resid:** Psychiatry, Bronx Muni Hosps 1980

Dulit, Rebecca A MD (Psyc) - **Spec Exp:** Personality Disorders-Borderline; Special Needs-Parental Therapy; Anxiety Disorders; Depression; **Hospital:** NY-Presby/Westchester Div, NY (page 102); **Address:** 45 Popham Rd, Ste D, Scarsdale, NY 10583; **Phone:** 914-722-0608; **Board Cert:** Psychiatry 1991; **Med School:** Mount Sinai Sch Med 1985; **Resid:** Psychiatry, Payne Whitney Clin 1989; **Fellow:** Research, Payne Whitney Clin 1992; **Fac Appt:** Assoc Clin Prof Psyc, Cornell Univ-Weill Med Coll

Gabel, Richard H MD (Psyc) - **Spec Exp:** Psychopharmacology; Psychotherapy; **Hospital:** White Plains Hosp (page 652); **Address:** 12 Greenridge Ave, White Plains, NY 10605; **Phone:** 914-681-0202; **Board Cert:** Psychiatry 1982; **Med School:** NYU Sch Med 1976; **Resid:** Psychiatry, Mass Genl Hosp 1980

Harlam, Dean MD (Psyc) - **Spec Exp:** Depression; Bipolar/Mood Disorders; Psychopharmacology; Schizophrenia; **Hospital:** Saint Joseph's Med Ctr - Yonkers; **Address:** St Vincent's Hosp, 275 North St, Harrison, NY 10528; **Phone:** 914-925-5490; **Board Cert:** Psychiatry 1979; **Med School:** Albert Einstein Coll Med 1972; **Resid:** Psychiatry, Bronx Muni Hosp 1976; **Fellow:** Psychiatry, NY Hosp-Cornell Med Ctr 1977; **Fac Appt:** Assoc Clin Prof Psyc, NY Med Coll

Kahn, Jeffrey P MD (Psyc) - **Spec Exp:** Anxiety & Depression; Psychotherapy; Work/Career Problems; Couples Therapy; **Hospital:** NY-Presby/Weill Cornell Med Ctr, NY (page 102), NY-Presby/Westchester Div, NY (page 102); **Address:** 45 Popham Rd, Ste 1F, Scarsdale, NY 10583; **Phone:** 914-725-6303; **Board Cert:** Psychiatry 1986; **Med School:** Columbia P&S 1979; **Resid:** Psychiatry, NY-Presby/Columbia Univ Med Ctr 1983; **Fellow:** Psychiatric Research, NY-Presby/Columbia Univ Med Ctr 1985; **Fac Appt:** Assoc Clin Prof Psyc, Cornell Univ-Weill Med Coll

Kaufmann, Charles A MD (Psyc) - **Spec Exp:** Schizophrenia; Bipolar/Mood Disorders; Alcohol Abuse; **Hospital:** NY-Presby/Columbia Univ Med Ctr, NY (page 102), NY State Psychiatric Inst; **Address:** 16 Dakin Ave, Mt Kisco, NY 10543; **Phone:** 914-238-7909; **Board Cert:** Psychiatry 1982; **Med School:** Columbia P&S 1977; **Resid:** Psychiatry, NY-Presby/Weill Cornell Med Ctr 1981; **Fellow:** Research, Natl Inst Hlth 1985; Research, Ctr for Neurobio & Behavior 1988; **Fac Appt:** Assoc Prof Psyc, Columbia P&S

Klagsbrun, Samuel C MD (Psyc) - **Spec Exp:** Psychiatry in Cancer; Psychiatry in Terminal Illness; **Hospital:** Four Winds Hosp; **Address:** 800 Cross River Rd, Katonah, NY 10536; **Phone:** 914-763-8151 x2222; **Board Cert:** Psychiatry 1977; **Med School:** Ros Franklin Univ/Chicago Med Sch 1962; **Resid:** Psychiatry, Yale-New Haven Hosp 1966; **Fac Appt:** Clin Prof Psyc, Albert Einstein Coll Med

Levin, Andrew P MD (Psyc) - **Spec Exp:** Post Traumatic Stress Disorder; Forensic Psychiatry; Psychopharmacology; Cognitive Psychotherapy; **Hospital:** NY-Presby/Columbia Univ Med Ctr, NY (page 102); **Address:** 141 N Central Ave, Hartsdale, NY 10530-1912; **Phone:** 914-949-7699 x376; **Board Cert:** Psychiatry 1985; Forensic Psychiatry 2006; **Med School:** Univ Pennsylvania 1980; **Resid:** Psychiatry, NY State Psych Inst 1984; **Fellow:** Anxiety Disorder, NY State Psych Inst 1986; **Fac Appt:** Asst Clin Prof Psyc, Columbia P&S

Lew, Arthur MD (Psyc) - **Spec Exp:** Child & Adolescent Psychiatry; Psychoanalysis; **Address:** 225 Lyncroft Rd, New Rochelle, NY 10804-4120; **Phone:** 914-632-9679; **Board Cert:** Psychiatry 1974; Child & Adolescent Psychiatry 1979; **Med School:** SUNY Downstate 1968; **Resid:** Psychiatry, SUNY Downstate Med Ctr 1972; **Fellow:** Child & Adolescent Psychiatry, SUNY Downstate Med Ctr 1975; **Fac Appt:** Clin Prof Psyc, NYU Sch Med

Meyers, Barnett S MD (Psyc) - **Spec Exp:** Depression; Psychopharmacology; Psychotherapy; Geriatric Psychiatry; **Hospital:** NY-Presby/Westchester Div, NY (page 102); **Address:** NY-Presby, Psychiatry Dept, 21 Bloomingdale Rd, White Plains, NY 10605; **Phone:** 914-997-5721; **Board Cert:** Psychiatry 1975; Geriatric Psychiatry 2010; **Med School:** NYU Sch Med 1966; **Resid:** Psychiatry, Bronx Muni Hosp 1972; **Fac Appt:** Prof Psyc, Cornell Univ-Weill Med Coll

Milone, Richard D MD (Psyc) - **Spec Exp:** Depression; Psychopharmacology; **Hospital:** Saint Joseph's Med Ctr - Yonkers; **Address:** 275 North St, Harrison, NY 10528; **Phone:** 914-925-5311; **Board Cert:** Psychiatry 1970; **Med School:** Creighton Univ 1963; **Resid:** Psychiatry, St Vincent's Hosp & Med Ctr 1967; **Fac Appt:** Assoc Clin Prof Psyc, NY Med Coll

Neschis, Ronald MD (Psyc) - **Spec Exp:** Geriatric Psychiatry; **Hospital:** Saint Joseph's Med Ctr - Yonkers; **Address:** 18 Linden Ave, Larchmont, NY 10538-4139; **Phone:** 914-834-3470; **Board Cert:** Psychiatry 1972; **Med School:** SUNY Downstate 1963; **Resid:** Psychiatry, Montefiore Hosp Med Ctr 1969

Opler, Lewis A MD/PhD (Psyc) - **Spec Exp:** Psychopharmacology; Psychotherapy; **Hospital:** NY-Presby/Columbia Univ Med Ctr, NY (page 102); **Address:** 765 Gramatan Ave, Mount Vernon, NY 10552-1043; **Phone:** 914-668-4799; **Board Cert:** Psychiatry 1983; **Med School:** Albert Einstein Coll Med 1976; **Resid:** Psychiatry, Bronx Muni Hosp 1979; **Fac Appt:** Prof Psyc, Columbia P&S

Perlman, Barry B MD (Psyc) - **Hospital:** Saint Joseph's Med Ctr - Yonkers; **Address:** St Joseph's Med Ctr, Dept Psychiatry, 127 S Broadway, Yonkers, NY 10701-4006; **Phone:** 914-378-7342; **Board Cert:** Psychiatry 1977; **Med School:** Yale Univ 1971; **Resid:** Psychiatry, Mount Sinai Hosp 1975; **Fac Appt:** Assoc Clin Prof Psyc, NY Med Coll

Perry, Bradford MD (Psyc) - **Spec Exp:** Anxiety & Mood Disorders; Psychopharmacology; **Hospital:** NY-Presby/Westchester Div, NY (page 102), White Plains Hosp (page 652); **Address:** 455 Central Park Ave, Ste 214, Scarsdale, NY 10583; **Phone:** 914-472-2167; **Board Cert:** Psychiatry 1989; **Med School:** Univ Miami Sch Med 1984; **Resid:** Psychiatry, NY-Presby/Westchester Div 1988; **Fellow:** Psychiatry, NY-Presby/Columbia Univ Med Ctr 1989; **Fac Appt:** Assoc Clin Prof Psyc, Cornell Univ-Weill Med Coll

Raff, Adam N MD (Psyc) - **Spec Exp:** Depression; Child & Adolescent Psychiatry; Geriatric Psychiatry; Psychoanalysis; **Hospital:** White Plains Hosp (page 652), Northern Westchester Hosp; **Address:** Psychiatric Solutions of Westchester, 45 Popham Rd, Ste 1D, Scarsdale, NY 10583; **Phone:** 917-369-1841; **Board Cert:** Psychiatry 2012; Forensic Psychiatry 2012; **Med School:** Israel 1997; **Resid:** Psychiatry, NYU Med Ctr 2001

Russakoff, L. Mark MD (Psyc) - **Spec Exp:** Anxiety & Mood Disorders; **Hospital:** Phelps Meml Hosp Ctr; **Address:** Phelps Meml Hosp, Psychiatry Dept, 755 N Broadway, Ste 250, Sleepy Hollow, NY 10591; **Phone:** 914-366-3604; **Board Cert:** Psychiatry 1976; **Med School:** SUNY Downstate 1971; **Resid:** Psychiatry, Yale-New Haven Hosp 1975

Zolkind, Neil A MD (Psyc) - **Spec Exp:** Depression; Anxiety Disorders; **Hospital:** Westchester Med Ctr; **Address:** 150 White Plains Rd, Ste 102, Tarrytown, NY 10591; **Phone:** 914-909-5838; **Board Cert:** Psychiatry 1981; **Med School:** Geo Wash Univ 1976; **Resid:** Psychiatry, UCLA Neuropsych Hosp 1980; **Fac Appt:** Assoc Prof Psyc, NY Med Coll

Pulmonary Disease

Binder, Ralph E MD (Pul) - **Spec Exp:** Asthma; Chronic Obstructive Lung Disease (COPD); Interstitial Lung Disease; **Hospital:** Lawrence Hosp Ctr (page 102); **Address:** 329 Whiteplains Rd, Ste 100, Eastchester, NY 10709; **Phone:** 914-337-1610; **Board Cert:** Internal Medicine 1978; Pulmonary Disease 1980; **Med School:** Yale Univ 1975; **Resid:** Internal Medicine, Bronx Muni Hosp 1978; **Fellow:** Pulmonary Disease, Boston Med Ctr 1980; **Fac Appt:** Asst Prof Med, Columbia P&S

Brill, Joseph J MD (Pul) - **Spec Exp:** Sarcoidosis; Chronic Obstructive Lung Disease (COPD); Asthma; **Hospital:** St. John's Riverside Hosp-Andrus Pavil, Saint Joseph's Med Ctr - Yonkers; **Address:** Pulmonary Disease Group of Westchester, 1034 N Broadway Ave, Yonkers, NY 10708; **Phone:** 914-968-1611; **Board Cert:** Internal Medicine 1988; Pulmonary Disease 2012; **Med School:** Mexico 1981; **Resid:** Internal Medicine, Elmhurst City Hosp 1986; **Fellow:** Pulmonary Disease, Mt Sinai 1988

Bures, Sergio MD (Pul) - **Spec Exp:** Lung Cancer; Bronchoscopy; Asthma & Emphysema; **Hospital:** Northern Westchester Hosp; **Address:** Mount Kisco Medical Group, 111 Bedford Rd, Katonah, NY 10536; **Phone:** 914-232-3135; **Board Cert:** Internal Medicine 2010; Pulmonary Disease 2005; Critical Care Medicine 2006; **Med School:** Albany Med Coll 1994; **Resid:** Internal Medicine, Tripler Army Med Ctr 1999; **Fellow:** Critical Care Medicine, Meml Sloan Kettering Cancer Ctr 2003; Pulmonary Critical Care Medicine, Meml Sloan Kettering Cancer Ctr 2005

Casino, Joseph E MD (Pul) - **Spec Exp:** Asthma; Sleep Disorders; **Hospital:** Montefiore New Rochelle Hosp (page 100); **Address:** 2365 Boston Post Rd, Ste 103, Larchmont, NY 10538; **Phone:** 914-833-2020; **Board Cert:** Internal Medicine 1989; Pulmonary Disease 2010; Critical Care Medicine 2011; **Med School:** Italy 1984; **Resid:** Internal Medicine, New Rochelle Med Ctr 1988; **Fellow:** Pulmonary Critical Care Medicine, RW Johnson Univ Hosp 1991

De Matteo, Robert E MD (Pul) - **Spec Exp:** Asthma; Emphysema; Lung Cancer-Early Detection; **Hospital:** St. John's Riverside Hosp-Andrus Pavil, Saint Joseph's Med Ctr - Yonkers; **Address:** 970 N Broadway, Ste 209, Yonkers, NY 10701; **Phone:** 914-965-3366; **Board Cert:** Internal Medicine 1988; Pulmonary Disease 2010; **Med School:** Dominican Republic 1982; **Resid:** Internal Medicine, Mount Sinai/Bronx VA Hosp 1985; **Fellow:** Pulmonary Disease, Westchester Med Ctr 1988

Delorenzo, Lawrence J MD (Pul) - **Spec Exp:** Asthma; Emphysema; **Hospital:** Westchester Med Ctr; **Address:** Westchester Med Ctr, Pulmonology Dept, 100 Woods Rd, Macy Pav - rm 1042, Valhalla, NY 10595; **Phone:** 914-493-7518; **Board Cert:** Internal Medicine 1979; Pulmonary Disease 1982; Critical Care Medicine 2009; **Med School:** NY Med Coll 1976; **Resid:** Internal Medicine, Metropolitan Hosp Ctr 1979; **Fellow:** Pulmonary Disease, Metropolitan Hosp Ctr 1981; **Fac Appt:** Prof Med, NY Med Coll

DiCosmo, Bruno F MD (Pul) - **Spec Exp:** Pulmonary Fibrosis; Bronchoscopy; Lung Cancer; Sleep Disorders; **Hospital:** White Plains Hosp (page 652), Greenwich Hosp (page 970); **Address:** WestMed, Pulmonology, 1 Theall Rd, Rye, NY 10580; **Phone:** 914-848-8777; **Board Cert:** Internal Medicine 2011; Pulmonary Disease 2004; Critical Care Medicine 2005; Sleep Medicine 2011; **Med School:** Univ Conn 1988; **Resid:** Internal Medicine, Univ Conn Hlth Ctr 1991; **Fellow:** Pulmonary Critical Care Medicine, Yale-New Haven Hosp 1994; **Fac Appt:** Asst Clin Prof Med, Cornell Univ-Weill Med Coll

Frimer, Richard B MD (Pul) - **Hospital:** White Plains Hosp (page 652); **Address:** 170 Maple Ave, Ste G1, White Plains, NY 10601-4710; **Phone:** 914-328-0932; **Board Cert:** Internal Medicine 1983; Pulmonary Disease 1986; Critical Care Medicine 2010; **Med School:** SUNY Buffalo 1980; **Resid:** Internal Medicine, Montefiore Med Ctr 1983; **Fellow:** Pulmonary Disease, NYU Med Ctr 1985

Klares, Scott M MD (Pul) - **Spec Exp:** Asthma; Cough; **Hospital:** Northern Westchester Hosp; **Address:** MKMG, Pulmonary & Critical Care Med, 90 S Bedford Rd, Mount Kisco, NY 10549; **Phone:** 914-241-1050; **Board Cert:** Internal Medicine 2006; Pulmonary Disease 2007; Critical Care Medicine 2008; **Med School:** NY Med Coll 1992; **Resid:** Internal Medicine, Beth Israel Deaconess Med Ctr 1995; **Fellow:** Pulmonary Critical Care Medicine, Boston Med Ctr 1998; **Fac Appt:** Asst Clin Prof Med, Mount Sinai Sch Med

Lehrman, Gary R MD (Pul) - **Spec Exp:** Sleep Disorders; **Hospital:** Phelps Meml Hosp Ctr; **Address:** 160 N State Rd, Briarcliff Manor, NY 10510-1443; **Phone:** 914-762-8383; **Board Cert:** Internal Medicine 1982; Pulmonary Disease 1986; Critical Care Medicine 2004; Sleep Medicine 2007; **Med School:** NYU Sch Med 1979; **Resid:** Internal Medicine, LI Jewish Med Ctr 1982; **Fellow:** Pulmonary Disease, LIJ Med Ctr/Queens Hosp Affil 1985; **Fac Appt:** Asst Prof Med, Columbia P&S

Lehrman, Stuart MD (Pul) - **Spec Exp:** Lung Cancer; Asthma; **Hospital:** Westchester Med Ctr; **Address:** Westchester Med Ctr, Macys Pavilon-Pulmonary Lab, 100 Woods Rd, Valhalla, NY 10595; **Phone:** 914-493-7518; **Board Cert:** Internal Medicine 1981; Pulmonary Disease 1984; Critical Care Medicine 2007; Sleep Medicine 2007; **Med School:** SUNY Downstate 1978; **Resid:** Internal Medicine, Cedars-Sinai Med Ctr 1981; **Fellow:** Pulmonary Disease, Cedars-Sinai Med Ctr 1983; **Fac Appt:** Assoc Clin Prof Med, NY Med Coll

Mandel, Michael MD (Pul) - **Spec Exp:** Sleep Disorders/Apnea; Chronic Obstructive Lung Disease (COPD); Asthma; **Hospital:** Montefiore New Rochelle Hosp (page 100); **Address:** 2365 Boston Post Rd, Ste 103, Larchmont, NY 10538; **Phone:** 914-833-2020; **Board Cert:** Internal Medicine 1986; Pulmonary Disease 2010; Critical Care Medicine 2011; Sleep Medicine 2009; **Med School:** Columbia P&S 1983; **Resid:** Internal Medicine, St Lukes Roosevelt Hosp 1987; **Fellow:** Pulmonary Critical Care Medicine, UMDNJ Med Ctr 1989; **Fac Appt:** Asst Clin Prof Med, NY Med Coll

Meixler, Steven M MD (Pul) - **Spec Exp:** Asthma; Emphysema; Cough-Chronic; **Hospital:** White Plains Hosp (page 652), Greenwich Hosp (page 970); **Address:** WestMed, Pulmonology, 210 Westchester Ave, White Plains, NY 10604; **Phone:** 914-682-6511; **Board Cert:** Internal Medicine 1987; Pulmonary Disease 2010; Critical Care Medicine 2011; **Med School:** Boston Univ 1984; **Resid:** Internal Medicine, VA Med Ctr 1988; **Fellow:** Pulmonary Disease, Bellevue Hosp/NYU 1990

Novitch, Richard MD (Pul) - **Spec Exp:** Pulmonary Rehabilitation; **Hospital:** Burke Rehab Hosp; **Address:** 785 Mamaroneck Ave, White Plains, NY 10605; **Phone:** 914-597-2226; **Board Cert:** Internal Medicine 1987; **Med School:** Mexico 1983; **Resid:** Internal Medicine, UMDNJ Med Ctr 1987; **Fellow:** Pulmonary Disease, UMDNJ Med Ctr 1989; **Fac Appt:** Asst Clin Prof Med, Cornell Univ-Weill Med Coll

Pechman, Paul MD (Pul) - **Hospital:** White Plains Hosp (page 652); **Address:** Scarsdale Medical Group, 259 Heathcote Rd, Scarsdale, NY 10583; **Phone:** 914-723-8100; **Board Cert:** Internal Medicine 1980; Pulmonary Disease 1982; Critical Care Medicine 2008; Geriatric Medicine 2012; **Med School:** Boston Univ 1977; **Resid:** Internal Medicine, Boston Med Ctr 1980; **Fellow:** Pulmonary Disease, Bronx Muni Hosp 1982

Schreiber, Michael E MD (Pul) - **Spec Exp:** Asthma; Emphysema; **Hospital:** St. John's Riverside Hosp-Andrus Pavil, Saint Joseph's Med Ctr - Yonkers; **Address:** 970 N Broadway, Ste 209, Yonkers, NY 10701; **Phone:** 914-423-8517; **Board Cert:** Internal Medicine 1976; Pulmonary Disease 1978; Sleep Medicine 2011; **Med School:** Univ Ariz Coll Med 1973; **Resid:** Internal Medicine, Montefiore Med Ctr 1976; **Fellow:** Pulmonary Disease, NYU Med Ctr 1978; **Fac Appt:** Asst Clin Prof Med, NY Med Coll

Sherling, Bruce E MD (Pul) - **Hospital:** White Plains Hosp (page 652), Greenwich Hosp (page 970); **Address:** Westchester Medical Group, 1 Theall Rd, Rye, NY 10580; **Phone:** 914-848-8777; **Board Cert:** Internal Medicine 1976; Pulmonary Disease 1978; **Med School:** NY Med Coll 1973; **Resid:** Internal Medicine, Metropolitan Hosp Ctr 1976; **Fellow:** Pulmonary Disease, Lenox Hill Hosp 1978; Pulmonary Disease

Volcovici, Guido MD (Pul) - **Spec Exp:** Asthma; Emphysema; **Hospital:** Saint Joseph's Med Ctr - Yonkers; **Address:** 127 S Broadway, Ste 406, Yonkers, NY 10710; **Phone:** 914-968-5446; **Board Cert:** Internal Medicine 1985; Pulmonary Disease 1988; **Med School:** Romania 1962; **Resid:** Internal Medicine, Jewish Hosp 1974; **Fellow:** Pulmonary Disease, VA Med Ctr 1976

Wurm, Emanuel DO (Pul) - **Spec Exp:** Chronic Obstructive Lung Disease (COPD); Asthma; Interstitial Lung Disease; Sarcoidosis; **Hospital:** White Plains Hosp (page 652), Greenwich Hosp (page 970); **Address:** WestMed Med Group, Pulmonology, 210 Westchester Ave, White Plains, NY 10604; **Phone:** 914-682-6511; **Board Cert:** Internal Medicine 2006; Pulmonary Disease 2009; Critical Care Medicine 2010; **Med School:** NY Coll Osteo Med 1991; **Resid:** Internal Medicine, Beth Israel Med Ctr 1996; **Fellow:** Pulmonary Critical Care Medicine, Beth Israel Med Ctr 1999

Radiation Oncology

Choi, Julie MD (RadRO) - **Hospital:** Northern Westchester Hosp; **Address:** Cancer Treatment & Wellness Ctr, 400 E Main St, Mount Kisco, NY 10549; **Phone:** 914-242-8115; **Board Cert:** Radiation Oncology 2010; **Med School:** Univ MO-Kansas City 1992; **Resid:** Internal Medicine, Beth Israel Med Ctr 1995; Radiation Oncology, NY Presby-Columbia Med Ctr 1997

Fass, Daniel E MD (RadRO) - **Spec Exp:** Prostate Cancer; Breast Cancer; Head & Neck Cancer; **Address:** WestMed, Radiation Oncology, 1 Theall Rd, Ste 107, Rye, NY 10580; **Phone:** 914-848-8950; **Board Cert:** Radiation Oncology 1987; **Med School:** Howard Univ 1983; **Resid:** Radiation Oncology, NYU Med Ctr 1986; **Fellow:** Brachytherapy, Meml Sloan-Kettering Cancer Ctr 1987; **Fac Appt:** Asst Prof RadRO, Cornell Univ-Weill Med Coll

Lee, Henry J MD/PhD (RadRO) - **Spec Exp:** Prostate Cancer; Brachytherapy; **Hospital:** White Plains Hosp (page 652); **Address:** Dickstein Cancer Ctr, 2 Longview Ave, Lower Level, White Plains, NY 10601; **Phone:** 914-681-2727; **Board Cert:** Radiation Oncology 2012; **Med School:** Univ Chicago-Pritzker Sch Med 1993; **Resid:** Radiation Oncology, Meml Sloan Kettering Cancer Ctr 1997; **Fellow:** Radiation Oncology, Meml Sloan Kettering Cancer Ctr 2001

Moorthy, Chitti MD (RadRO) - **Spec Exp:** Prostate Cancer; Breast Cancer; Brain Tumors; Pediatric Radiology; **Hospital:** Westchester Med Ctr; **Address:** Westchester Med Ctr, Radiation Med, 100 Woods Rd, Macy Pav - rm 1297, Valhalla, NY 10595; **Phone:** 914-493-8561; **Board Cert:** Therapeutic Radiology 1979; **Med School:** India 1974; **Resid:** Surgery, Michael Reese Hosp & Med Ctr 1976; Radiation Oncology, Michael Reese Hosp & Med Ctr 1979; **Fellow:** Brachytherapy, Meml Sloan-Kettering Cancer Ctr 1980; **Fac Appt:** Prof RadRO, NY Med Coll

Stevens, Randy E MD (RadRO) - **Spec Exp:** Breast Cancer; **Hospital:** White Plains Hosp (page 652); **Address:** Dickstein Cancer Ctr, 2 Longview Ave, Lower Level, White Plains, NY 10601; **Phone:** 914-681-2727; **Board Cert:** Internal Medicine 1989; Radiation Oncology 1993; **Med School:** NYU Sch Med 1986; **Resid:** Radiation Oncology, NYU Med Ctr 1992

Tinger, Alfred MD (RadRO) - **Spec Exp:** Prostate Cancer; Breast Cancer; Skin Cancer; Gynecologic Cancer; **Hospital:** Northern Westchester Hosp; **Address:** Cancer Treatment & Wellness Ctr, 400 E Main St, Mount Kisco, NY 10549; **Phone:** 914-242-8115; **Board Cert:** Radiation Oncology 2008; **Med School:** SUNY Downstate 1992; **Resid:** Radiation Oncology, Washington Univ Med Ctr 1997

Reproductive Endocrinology

Bennett, Rachel MD (RE) - Spec Exp: Infertility-IVF; Hysteroscopic Surgery; Polycystic Ovarian Syndrome; **Hospital:** Northern Westchester Hosp, Hudson Valley Hosp Ctr; **Address:** Westchester Reproductive Med, 344 E Main St, Ste 403, Mt Kisco, NY 10549; **Phone:** 914-218-8955; **Board Cert:** Obstetrics & Gynecology 2013; Reproductive Endocrinology 2013; **Med School:** Mount Sinai Sch Med 1989; **Resid:** Obstetrics & Gynecology, NY-Presby/Weill Cornell Med Ctr 1993; **Fellow:** Reproductive Endocrinology, Brigham & Womens Hosp 1995; **Fac Appt:** Asst Clin Prof Med, Mount Sinai Sch Med

Klein, Jeffrey MD (RE) - Spec Exp: Infertility-IVF; Infertility; Polycystic Ovarian Syndrome; Endometriosis; **Hospital:** White Plains Hosp (page 652); **Address:** Reproductive Medicine Associates of NY, 15 N Broadway, Garden Level, Ste G, White Plains, NY 10601; **Phone:** 914-997-6200; **Board Cert:** Obstetrics & Gynecology 2014; Reproductive Endocrinology 2014; **Med School:** Albert Einstein Coll Med 1995; **Resid:** Obstetrics & Gynecology, G Washington Univ Med Ctr 1999; **Fellow:** Reproductive Endocrinology, NY-Presby/Columbia Univ Med Ctr 2002

Lieman, Harry J MD (RE) - Spec Exp: Infertility-IVF; Polycystic Ovarian Syndrome; Preimplantation Genetic Diagnosis; **Hospital:** Montefiore Med Ctr-Einstein Campus (page 100), Montefiore Med Ctr-Moses Campus (page 100); **Address:** Montefiore Inst for Reproductive Med, 141 S Central Ave, Ste 201, Hartsdale, NY 10530; **Phone:** 914-997-1060; **Board Cert:** Obstetrics & Gynecology 2013; Reproductive Endocrinology/Infertility 2013; **Med School:** SUNY Downstate 1990; **Resid:** Obstetrics & Gynecology, Jacobi Med Ctr 1994; **Fellow:** Reproductive Endocrinology/Infertility, UMDNJ Affil Hosp 1996; **Fac Appt:** Assoc Prof ObG, Albert Einstein Coll Med

Stangel, John MD (RE) - Spec Exp: Infertility-IVF; Endometriosis; Miscarriage-Recurrent; **Address:** Reproductive Medicine Associates of NY, 15 N Broadway, Ste G, White Plains, NY 10601; **Phone:** 914-997-6200; **Board Cert:** Obstetrics & Gynecology 1976; Reproductive Endocrinology 1981; **Med School:** NY Med Coll 1969; **Resid:** Obstetrics & Gynecology, Mount Sinai Med Ctr 1974; **Fellow:** Reproductive Endocrinology, Metropolitan Hosp Ctr 1976

Rheumatology

Barone, Richard P MD (Rhu) - Spec Exp: Rheumatoid Arthritis; Lupus/SLE; Psoriatic Arthritis; **Hospital:** Montefiore New Rochelle Hosp (page 100); **Address:** 421 Huguenot St Fl 4 - Ste 44, New Rochelle, NY 10801-7004; **Phone:** 914-235-3065; **Med School:** Italy 1971; **Resid:** Internal Medicine, Brooklyn Jewish Hosp & Med Ctr 1974; **Fellow:** Rheumatology, Brooklyn Jewish Hosp & Med Ctr 1976; **Fac Appt:** Assoc Clin Prof Med, NY Med Coll

Berger, Jack J MD (Rhu) - Spec Exp: Rheumatoid Arthritis; Psoriatic Arthritis; Spondylitis; Gout; **Hospital:** White Plains Hosp (page 652); **Address:** 210 Westchester Ave, White Plains, NY 10604; **Phone:** 914-682-6532; **Board Cert:** Internal Medicine 1979; Rheumatology 1982; **Med School:** Albert Einstein Coll Med 1976; **Resid:** Internal Medicine, Bellevue Hosp 1979; **Fellow:** Rheumatology, Bellevue Hosp 1981

Burns, Mark R MD (Rhu) - Spec Exp: Lupus Nephritis; Rheumatoid Arthritis; **Hospital:** Montefiore New Rochelle Hosp (page 100); **Address:** 421 Huguenot St, rm 44, New Rochelle, NY 10801; **Phone:** 914-235-3065; **Board Cert:** Internal Medicine 1980; Rheumatology 1984; **Med School:** UCSF 1977; **Resid:** Internal Medicine, Montefiore Med Ctr 1980; **Fellow:** Rheumatology, Montefiore Med Ctr 1983; **Fac Appt:** Asst Clin Prof Med, Albert Einstein Coll Med

Foto, Frank MD (Rhu) - **Spec Exp:** Rheumatoid Arthritis; Lupus/SLE; Gout; Fibromyalgia; **Hospital:** Phelps Meml Hosp Ctr; **Address:** 310 N Highland Ave, Ste 7, Ossining, NY 10562; **Phone:** 914-762-5555; **Board Cert:** Internal Medicine 1989; Rheumatology 2007; **Med School:** Mexico 1983; **Resid:** Internal Medicine, Nassau Univ Med Ctr 1988; **Fellow:** Rheumatology, Univ Iowa Hosp & Clinics 1991

Lans, David M DO (Rhu) - **Spec Exp:** Rheumatoid Arthritis; Lupus/SLE; Asthma; Osteoporosis; **Hospital:** Lawrence Hosp Ctr (page 102), Montefiore New Rochelle Hosp (page 100); **Address:** 838 Pelhamdale Ave, New Rochelle, NY 10801-1032; **Phone:** 914-235-5577; **Board Cert:** Internal Medicine 1984; Allergy & Immunology 1987; Rheumatology 1988; **Med School:** Univ Osteo Med & Hlth Sci, Des Moines 1981; **Resid:** Internal Medicine, Downstate Univ Hosp 1985; **Fellow:** Allergy & Immunology, New Eng Med Ctr 1987; Rheumatology, Hosp For Special Surgery 1989; **Fac Appt:** Asst Clin Prof Med, NY Med Coll

Lenci, Margaret M MD (Rhu) - **Hospital:** Northern Westchester Hosp; **Address:** MKMG, Rheumatology, 90 S Bedford Rd, Mount Kisco, NY 10549; **Phone:** 914-242-1370; **Board Cert:** Internal Medicine 1983; Rheumatology 1988; **Med School:** SUNY Downstate 1980; **Resid:** Internal Medicine, Montefiore Med Ctr 1983; **Fellow:** Rheumatology, Montefiore Med Ctr 1988

Marmur, Ronen MD/PhD (Rhu) - **Spec Exp:** Autoimmune Disorders; Psoriatic Arthritis; Connective Tissue Disorders; Gout; **Hospital:** Northern Westchester Hosp, Putnam Hosp Ctr; **Address:** 90 S Bedford Rd, Mount Kisco, NY 10549; **Phone:** 914-241-1050; **Board Cert:** Internal Medicine 2012; Rheumatology 2013; **Med School:** Albert Einstein Coll Med 1998; **Resid:** Internal Medicine, NY-Presby/Weill Cornell Univ Med Ctr 2000; **Fellow:** Rheumatology, Hosp for Special Surgery/ Weill Cornell 2004; Neurological Immunology, Rockefeller Univ Hosp 2002

Reinitz, Elizabeth MD (Rhu) - **Spec Exp:** Rheumatoid Arthritis; Lupus/SLE; Osteoarthritis; Gout; **Hospital:** White Plains Hosp (page 652); **Address:** Scarsdale Medical Group, 600 Mamaroneck Ave, Ste 200, Harrison, NY 10528; **Phone:** 914-723-8100; **Board Cert:** Internal Medicine 1979; Rheumatology 1982; **Med School:** Albert Einstein Coll Med 1976; **Resid:** Internal Medicine, Boston City Hosp 1979; **Fellow:** Rheumatology, Montefiore Med Ctr 1981

Sloane, Lori E MD (Rhu) - **Spec Exp:** Lupus/SLE; Rheumatoid Arthritis; **Hospital:** Northern Westchester Hosp; **Address:** Westchester Hlth Assocs, 322 Underhill Ave, Yorktown Heights, NY 10598; **Phone:** 914-962-5501; **Board Cert:** Internal Medicine 1989; **Med School:** SUNY Downstate 1986; **Resid:** Internal Medicine, Jacobi Med Ctr 1989; **Fellow:** Rheumatology, Montefiore Hosp Med Ctr 1991

Wallis, Susan M MD (Rhu) - **Hospital:** Montefiore New Rochelle Hosp (page 100); **Address:** 421 Huguenot St, rm 44, New Rochelle, NY 10801; **Phone:** 914-235-3065; **Board Cert:** Internal Medicine 2006; Rheumatology 2008; **Med School:** Israel 2003; **Resid:** Internal Medicine, Montefiore Med Ctr 2006; **Fellow:** Rheumatology, Univ Michigan Hosps 2008

Yegudin-Ash, Julia MD (Rhu) - **Spec Exp:** Lupus/SLE; Rheumatoid Arthritis; Psoriatic Arthritis; Scleroderma; **Hospital:** Westchester Med Ctr; **Address:** MRA Physicians, Endocrinology Rheumatology, 19 Bradhurst Ave, Ste 3070N, Hawthorne, NY 10532; **Phone:** 914-594-4444; **Board Cert:** Rheumatology 2006; **Med School:** SUNY Stony Brook 1987; **Resid:** Internal Medicine, Winthrop Univ Hosp 1990; **Fellow:** Rheumatology, Mass Genl Hosp 1992; Rheumatology, NYU Hosp Joint Diseases 1993; **Fac Appt:** Assoc Prof Med, NY Med Coll

Sports Medicine

Cavaliere, Gregg MD (SM) - **Spec Exp:** Rotator Cuff Surgery; Knee Injuries/Ligament Surgery; Shoulder Instability; Arthroscopic Surgery; **Hospital:** Phelps Meml Hosp Ctr, St. John's Riverside Hosp-Dobbs Ferry Pavil; **Address:** Hudson Valley Bone & Joint Surgeons, 24 Saw Mill River Rd, Ste 206, Hawthorne, NY 10532; **Phone:** 914-631-7777; **Board Cert:** Orthopaedic Surgery 2006; **Med School:** NY Med Coll 1987; **Resid:** Orthopaedic Surgery, Lenox Hill Hosp 1992; **Fellow:** Sports Medicine, NYU Med Ctr 1993

Luks, Howard J MD (SM) - **Spec Exp:** Knee Injuries/ACL; Cartilage Damage; Knee Replacement; **Hospital:** Westchester Med Ctr; **Address:** Univ Orthopaedics, 19 Bradhurst Ave, Ste 1300N, Hawthorne, NY 10532; **Phone:** 914-789-2735; **Board Cert:** Orthopaedic Surgery 2010; **Med School:** NY Med Coll 1991; **Resid:** Orthopaedic Surgery, LIJ Med Ctr 1996; **Fellow:** Orthopaedic Sports Medicine, NYU Hosp Joint Diseases 1997; **Fac Appt:** Asst Prof OrS, NY Med Coll

Shifrin, Seth P MD (SM) - **Spec Exp:** Primary Care Sports Medicine; Pediatric Sports Medicine; **Hospital:** Northern Westchester Hosp; **Address:** MKMG, Sports Med, 110 S Bedford Rd Fl 3, Mount Kisco, NY 10549; **Phone:** 914-241-1050; **Board Cert:** Internal Medicine 2004; Sports Medicine 2005; Pediatrics 2013; **Med School:** Univ Chicago-Pritzker Sch Med 2000; **Resid:** Internal Medicine & Pediatrics, Chldns Hosp 2004; **Fellow:** Primary Care Sports Medicine, MacNeal Hosp 2005

Small, Eric W MD (SM) - **Spec Exp:** Primary Care Sports Medicine; Concussion; **Hospital:** Northern Westchester Hosp, Mt Sinai Beth Israel; **Address:** Westchester Hlth, 666 Lexington Ave, Mt Kisco, NY 10549; **Phone:** 914-666-7900; **Board Cert:** Sports Medicine 2007; **Med School:** UMDNJ-NJ Med Sch, Newark 1989; **Resid:** Pediatrics, Montefiore Med Ctr 1992; **Fellow:** Pediatric Sports Medicine, McMaster Univ/Hamilton 1994; Sports Medicine, Chldns Hosp 1995; **Fac Appt:** Asst Clin Prof Ped, Mount Sinai-Icahn Sch of Med

Vaidya, Sudhir P MD (SM) - **Spec Exp:** Primary Care Sports Medicine; Pain Management; Geriatric Rehabilitation; **Hospital:** Burke Rehab Hosp, Saint Joseph's Med Ctr - Yonkers; **Address:** Burke Rehab Hosp, 785 Mamaroneck Ave, White Plains, NY 10605; **Phone:** 914-597-2332; **Board Cert:** Family Medicine 2005; Sports Medicine 2011; **Med School:** India 1979; **Resid:** Physical Medicine & Rehabilitation, NHS Hosps-Leicester, Milton Keynes-Bedford 1995; Family Medicine, St Joseph's Hosp 1998; **Fac Appt:** Asst Clin Prof Med, Cornell Univ-Weill Med Coll

Zelazny, Daniel MD (SM) - **Spec Exp:** Sports Medicine; **Hospital:** Westchester Med Ctr, Mid-Hudson Regl Hosp; **Address:** 19 Bradhurst Ave, Ste 1300N, Hawthorne, NY 10532; **Phone:** 914-789-2732; **Board Cert:** Orthopaedic Surgery 2004; Orthopaedic Sports Medicine 2007; **Med School:** Hahnemann Univ 1994; **Resid:** Surgery, St Vincent Cath Med Ctr 1995; Orthopaedic Surgery, Westchester Med Ctr 1999; **Fellow:** Sports Medicine, Graduate Hosp 2000

Surgery

Arthur, Karen S MD (S) - **Spec Exp:** Breast Cancer & Surgery; **Hospital:** Northern Westchester Hosp; **Address:** Northern Westchester Hosp Breast Inst, 400 E Main St, Mount Kisco, NY 10549; **Phone:** 914-242-7640; **Board Cert:** Surgery 2011; **Med School:** Mount Sinai Sch Med 1974; **Resid:** Surgery, Mount Sinai Hosp 1979

Ashikari, Andrew Y MD (S) - **Spec Exp:** Breast Cancer; Breast Disease; Nipple Sparing Mastectomy; **Hospital:** St. John's Riverside Hosp-Dobbs Ferry Pavil; **Address:** St John's Riverside, Dobbs Ferry Pav, 128 Ashford Ave, Ashikari Breast Ctr, Dobbs Ferry, NY 10522; **Phone:** 914-693-5025; **Board Cert:** Surgery 2006; **Med School:** Univ Pittsburgh 1991; **Resid:** Surgery, Montefiore Med Ctr 1996; **Fellow:** Surgical Oncology, Univ Chicago Med Ctr 1999; **Fac Appt:** Asst Prof S, NY Med Coll

Cahan, Anthony C MD (S) - **Spec Exp:** Breast Surgery; Breast Cancer; **Hospital:** Northern Westchester Hosp; **Address:** Northern Westchester Surgical Svcs, 3010 Westchester Ave, Ste 201, Purchase, NY 10577; **Phone:** 914-517-8220; **Board Cert:** Surgery 2008; **Med School:** Cornell Univ-Weill Med Coll 1982; **Resid:** Surgery, NY-Presby/Weill Cornell Med Ctr 1987; **Fac Appt:** Asst Clin Prof Med, NY Med Coll

Charny, Caleb K MD/PhD (S) - **Spec Exp:** Laparoscopic Surgery-Advanced; Hernia; Breast Surgery; Gastrointestinal Surgery; **Hospital:** White Plains Hosp (page 652), Greenwich Hosp (page 970); **Address:** WestMed Medical Grp, 210 Westchester Ave Fl 3, White Plains, NY 10604; **Phone:** 914-682-6557; **Board Cert:** Surgery 2011; **Med School:** NYU Sch Med 1995; **Resid:** Surgery, New York Hosp 2000

Chefitz, Allen B MD (S) - **Spec Exp:** Gastrointestinal Cancer & Surgery; Hernia; Laparoscopic Surgery; **Hospital:** Lawrence Hosp Ctr (page 102), NY-Presby Hosp/The Allen Hosp (page 102); **Address:** Lawrence Hosp, Ctr for Advanced Surgery, 55 Palmer Ave Fl 5, Bronxville, NY 10708; **Phone:** 914-787-4000; **Board Cert:** Surgery 2013; **Med School:** Univ Mass Sch Med 1987; **Resid:** Surgery, Montefiore Med Ctr 1992

Diflo, Thomas MD (S) - **Spec Exp:** Transplant-Kidney; Transplant-Liver; **Hospital:** Westchester Med Ctr; **Address:** Westchester Medical Ctr, 100 Woods Rd, Taylor Pavilion, Room O-127, Valhalla, NY 10595; **Phone:** 914-493-1169; **Board Cert:** Surgery 2012; Surgical Critical Care 2005; **Med School:** Boston Univ 1984; **Resid:** Surgery, Boston Univ Med Ctr 1991; **Fellow:** Transplant Surgery, New England Deaconess Hosp 1992; **Fac Appt:** Prof S, NY Med Coll

Fou, Adora C MD (S) - **Spec Exp:** Breast Disease; Minimally Invasive Surgery; Breast Cancer-High Risk Women; **Hospital:** White Plains Hosp (page 652), Greenwich Hosp (page 970); **Address:** Westchester Med Grp, 1 Theall Rd, Ste 103, Rye, NY 10580; **Phone:** 914-848-8960; **Board Cert:** Surgery 2007; **Med School:** Univ Tex, Houston 2000; **Resid:** Surgery, NY Med Coll Affil Hosps 2005; **Fellow:** Breast Surgery, Columbia/Presby Hosp 2006

Gordon, Mark S MD (S) - **Spec Exp:** Breast Cancer; Melanoma; Colon Cancer; Soft Tissue Tumors; **Hospital:** White Plains Hosp (page 652); **Address:** White Plains Physicians Assocs, 33 Davis Ave, Upper Level, White Plains, NY 10605; **Phone:** 914-684-5884; **Board Cert:** Surgery 2006; **Med School:** Northwestern Univ 1982; **Resid:** Surgery, NY Hosp 1987; **Fellow:** Surgical Oncology, Meml Sloan-Kettering Cancer Ctr 1989; **Fac Appt:** Asst Clin Prof S, NY Med Coll

Kaul, Ashutosh MD (S) - **Spec Exp:** Obesity/Bariatric Surgery; Minimally Invasive Surgery; **Hospital:** Westchester Med Ctr; **Address:** Advanced Surgeons, 19 Bradhurst Ave, Ste 1700, Hawthorne, NY 10532; **Phone:** 914-347-0162; **Board Cert:** Surgery 2010; **Med School:** India 1988; **Resid:** Surgery, Bronx Lebanon Hosp 1998; Surgery, St Barnabas Med Ctr 2000; **Fac Appt:** Asst Prof S, NY Med Coll

Lau, Har Chi MD (S) - **Spec Exp:** Laparoscopic Surgery; Hernia; **Hospital:** Phelps Meml Hosp Ctr; **Address:** Hudson Valley Surgical Grp, 777 N Broadway, Ste 204, Sleepy Hollow, NY 10591; **Phone:** 914-631-3660; **Board Cert:** Surgery 2007; **Med School:** Univ Pennsylvania 1992; **Resid:** Surgery, Allegheny Genl Hosp 1998

Lemercier, Maud L MD (S) - **Spec Exp:** Breast Cancer; **Hospital:** Northern Westchester Hosp; **Address:** Mount Kisco Medical Group, Surgery, 111 Bedford Rd, Katonah, NY 10536; **Phone:** 914-232-3135; **Board Cert:** Surgery 2006; **Med School:** Temple Univ 1999; **Resid:** Surgery, Univ Conn Hlth Ctr 2005

Maffucci, Leonard MD (S) - **Spec Exp:** Obesity/Bariatric Surgery; **Hospital:** Montefiore New Rochelle Hosp (page 100); **Address:** Montefiore-New Rochelle Hosp, 16 Guion Pl, Fl 8, New Rochelle, NY 10801; **Phone:** 914-365-3284; **Board Cert:** Surgery 2011; **Med School:** NY Med Coll 1985; **Resid:** Surgery, Westchester Med Ctr 1990

Messina, Amanda L MD (S) - **Spec Exp:** Laparoscopic Surgery-Advanced; Colon & Rectal Surgery; Obesity/Bariatric Surgery; **Hospital:** Northern Westchester Hosp; **Address:** Mount Kisco Medical Group, Surgery, 110 S Bedford Rd, Fl 3rd, Mount Kisco, NY 10549; **Phone:** 914-864-4551; **Board Cert:** Surgery 2008; **Med School:** Temple Univ 2003; **Resid:** Surgery, NYU Med Ctr 2008

Rajdeo, Heena P MD (S) - **Spec Exp:** Dialysis Access Surgery; Thyroid & Parathyroid Surgery; Trauma; Laparoscopic Surgery; **Hospital:** Westchester Med Ctr; **Address:** 100 Wood Rd, Taylor Pavilion, Ste E130, Valhalla, NY 10595; **Phone:** 914-372-7196; **Board Cert:** Surgery 2012; **Med School:** India 1969; **Resid:** Surgery, KEM Hosp 1972; Surgery, Westchester Med Ctr 1982; **Fac Appt:** Asst Prof S, NY Med Coll

Raniolo, Robert J MD (S) - **Spec Exp:** Breast Surgery; Gastrointestinal Surgery; Hernia; **Hospital:** Phelps Meml Hosp Ctr; **Address:** Hudson Vly Surgical Grp, 777 N Broadway, Ste 204, Sleepy Hollow, NY 10591; **Phone:** 914-631-3660; **Board Cert:** Surgery 2007; **Med School:** Mexico 1981; **Resid:** Surgery, Lincoln Hosp 1988

Weber, Kaare J MD (S) - **Spec Exp:** Endocrine Surgery; Thyroid & Parathyroid Cancer & Surgery; Minimally Invasive Surgery; **Hospital:** White Plains Hosp (page 652); **Address:** White Plains Hospital Physician Associates, 170 Maple Ave, Ste 502, White Plains, NY 10601; **Phone:** 914-948-1000; **Board Cert:** Surgery 2004; **Med School:** Albert Einstein Coll Med 1997; **Resid:** Surgery, Mount Sinai Med Ctr 2003; **Fellow:** Endocrine Surgery, Rush Univ Med Ctr 2004; **Fac Appt:** Asst Prof S, Mount Sinai Sch Med

Thoracic & Cardiac Surgery

Berman, Scott K MD (T&CS) - **Spec Exp:** Thoracic Surgery; Thoracic Cancers; Esophageal Surgery; Minimally Invasive Thoracic Surgery; **Hospital:** White Plains Hosp (page 652), Hudson Valley Hosp Ctr; **Address:** 4 Lyons Pl, White Plains, NY 10601; **Phone:** 914-948-6633; **Board Cert:** Thoracic Surgery 2001; **Med School:** UMDNJ-Rutgers Med Sch 1983; **Resid:** Surgery, St Francis Med Ctr 1988; Thoracic & Cardiac Surgery, SUNY Upstate Med Ctr 1990

Lafaro, Rocco J MD (T&CS) - **Spec Exp:** Minimally Invasive Cardiac Surgery; **Hospital:** Westchester Med Ctr, Phelps Meml Hosp Ctr; **Address:** Westchester Med Ctr Heart Institute, 100 Woods Way, Valhalla, NY 10595; **Phone:** 914-493-8793; **Board Cert:** Thoracic Surgery 2011; **Med School:** NY Med Coll 1982; **Resid:** Surgery, Metropolitan Hosp Ctr 1984; Surgery, Westchester Med Ctr 1986; **Fellow:** Thoracic Surgery, Bronx Muni Hosp Ctr 1991; Thoracic Surgery, Montefiore Med Ctr 1993

Lansman, Steven L MD/PhD (T&CS) - **Spec Exp:** Coronary Artery Surgery; Heart Valve Surgery; Ventricular Assist Device (LVAD); Transplant-Heart; **Hospital:** Westchester Med Ctr; **Address:** Westchester Med Ctr, Heart Inst, 100 Woods Rd, Macy Pav, rm 114, Valhalla, NY 10595; **Phone:** 914-493-8793; **Board Cert:** Thoracic & Cardiac Surgery 2004; **Med School:** SUNY Hlth Sci Ctr 1977; **Resid:** Surgery, Montefiore Med Ctr 1982; **Fellow:** Thoracic Surgery, Univ Hosp 1984; **Fac Appt:** Prof S, NY Med Coll

Merav, Avraham D MD (T&CS) - **Spec Exp:** Minimally Invasive Thoracic Surgery; Lung Surgery; Esophageal Surgery; Cardiothoracic Surgery; **Hospital:** Phelps Meml Hosp Ctr, Westchester Med Ctr; **Address:** 755 N Broadway, Sleepy Hollow, NY 10591; **Phone:** 914-366-2333; **Board Cert:** Surgery 1974; Thoracic Surgery 2004; **Med School:** Switzerland 1964; **Resid:** Surgery, Montefiore Med Ctr 1973; **Fellow:** Cardiothoracic Surgery, Montefiore Med Ctr 1975; **Fac Appt:** Assoc Clin Prof TS, Albert Einstein Coll Med

Sett, Suvro S MD (T&CS) - **Spec Exp:** Pediatric Cardiac Surgery; Congenital Heart Disease; Congenital Heart Disease-Adult; **Hospital:** Westchester Med Ctr; **Address:** Maria Fareri Chldn's Hosp, 100 Woods Rd, Valhalla, NY 10595; **Phone:** 914-594-2222; **Med School:** Canada 1983; **Resid:** Surgery, Univ Saskatchewan Affil Hosps 1988; Cardiovascular Surgery, Univ British Columbia Affil Hosps 1991; **Fellow:** Pediatric Cardiac Surgery, Hosp for Sick Chld 1993

Spielvogel, David MD (T&CS) - **Spec Exp:** Aneurysm-Aortic; Transplant-Heart; Coronary Artery Surgery; Heart Valve Surgery; **Hospital:** Westchester Med Ctr; **Address:** Westchester Med Ctr, Heart Inst, 100 Woods Rd, Macy Pav, rm 114, Valhalla, NY 10595; **Phone:** 914-493-8793; **Board Cert:** Thoracic & Cardiac Surgery 2009; **Med School:** SUNY Downstate 1990; **Resid:** Surgery, SUNY Downtown Med Ctr 1995; Thoracic Surgery, Mt Sinai Hosp 1998; **Fellow:** Cardiac Surgery, Harefield Hosp 1999; **Fac Appt:** Prof T&CS, NY Med Coll

Weiser, Todd S MD (T&CS) - **Spec Exp:** Lung Cancer; Esophageal Cancer; Minimally Invasive Surgery; Mediastinal Tumors; **Hospital:** White Plains Hosp (page 652); **Address:** White Plains Phys, 33 Davis Ave, Fl 1, White Plains, NY 10605; **Phone:** 914-681-2750; **Board Cert:** Thoracic & Cardiac Surgery 2007; Surgery 2013; **Med School:** Jefferson Med Coll 1996; **Resid:** Surgery, St Vincent's Hosp & Med Ctr 2003; **Fellow:** Surgical Oncology, Natl Cancer Inst 2000; Thoracic & Cardiac Surgery, Mass Genl Hosp 2005

Urology

Axelrod, Sheldon L MD (U) - **Spec Exp:** Prostate Cancer; Prostate Disease; Robotic Surgery; Bladder Cancer; **Hospital:** Northern Westchester Hosp, Putnam Hosp Ctr; **Address:** MKMG, Urology, 111 Bedford Rd, Katonah, NY 10536; **Phone:** 914-232-3135; **Board Cert:** Urology 2012; **Med School:** Albert Einstein Coll Med 1982; **Resid:** Surgery, Montefiore Med Ctr 1984; Urology, NY-Presby/Columbia Med Ctr 1988

Biggs, Grace MD (U) - **Spec Exp:** Urology-Female; Voiding Dysfunction; Pelvic Organ Prolapse Repair; Incontinence; **Hospital:** Greenwich Hosp (page 970); **Address:** WestMed Med Group, Urology, 210 Westchester Ave, White Plains, NY 10580; **Phone:** 914-682-6470; **Board Cert:** Urology 2011; **Med School:** SUNY Upstate Med Univ 2001; **Resid:** Surgery, Montefiore Med Ctr 2006; Urology, Meml Sloan Kettering Cancer Ctr 2007; **Fellow:** Reconstructive Pelvic Surgery, NYU Med Ctr 2009

Blair, Bryan P MD (U) - **Hospital:** White Plains Hosp (page 652); **Address:** WestMed Medical Group, 210 Westchester Ave, White Plains, NY 10604; **Phone:** 914-682-6470; **Board Cert:** Urology 2013; **Med School:** Tulane Univ 1994; **Resid:** Urology, Natl Naval Med Ctr 2001

Boczko, Judd MD (U) - **Spec Exp:** Prostate Cancer/Robotic Surgery; Robotic Urologic Surgery; Minimally Invasive Urologic Surgery; Prostate Benign Disease; **Hospital:** Greenwich Hosp (page 970), White Plains Hosp (page 652); **Address:** WestMed Medical Group, 210 Westchester Ave, White Plains, NY 10604; **Phone:** 914-682-6470; **Board Cert:** Urology 2008; **Med School:** Albert Einstein Coll Med 1999; **Resid:** Surgery, Montefiore Med Ctr 2001; Urology, Montefiore Med Ctr 2005; **Fellow:** Robotic Surgery, Univ Rochester 2006; **Fac Appt:** Asst Prof U, NY Med Coll

Breslin, David S MD (U) - **Spec Exp:** Urology-Female; Incontinence; Urodynamics; **Hospital:** Hudson Valley Hosp Ctr; **Address:** Mount Kisco Medical Group, 1978 Crompond Rd, Cortlandt Manor, NY 10567; **Phone:** 914-737-8675; **Board Cert:** Urology 2007; **Med School:** Mount Sinai Sch Med 1987; **Resid:** Surgery, Mount Sinai Med Ctr 1989; Urology, Lenox Hill Hosp 1994; **Fellow:** Female Urology, Beth Israel Deaconess Med Ctr 1995; **Fac Appt:** Asst Clin Prof U, NY Med Coll

Choudhury, Muhammad S MD (U) - **Spec Exp:** Urologic Cancer; Bladder Reconstruction; Prostate Cancer; Testicular Cancer; **Hospital:** Westchester Med Ctr, Montefiore New Rochelle Hosp (page 100); **Address:** Urology Ctr of Westchester, 19 Bradhurst Ave, Ste 1900, Hawthorne, NY 10532-2144; **Phone:** 914-347-1900; **Board Cert:** Urology 1982; **Med School:** Bangladesh 1972; **Resid:** Urology, Columbia-Presby Med Ctr 1978; **Fellow:** Urologic Oncology, Roswell Park Cancer Inst 1981; **Fac Appt:** Prof U, NY Med Coll

Eshghi, A Majid MD (U) - **Spec Exp:** Kidney Stones; Endourology; Minimally Invasive Surgery; **Hospital:** Westchester Med Ctr, Montefiore New Rochelle Hosp (page 100); **Address:** Urology Center of Westchester, 19 Bradhurst Ave, Ste 1900, Hawthorne, NY 10532; **Phone:** 914-347-1900; **Board Cert:** Urology 2005; **Med School:** Iran 1976; **Resid:** Urology, LI Jewish Med Ctr 1985; **Fac Appt:** Prof U, NY Med Coll

Fleischmann, Nicole B MD (U) - **Spec Exp:** Voiding Dysfunction; Pelvic Organ Prolapse Repair; Neurogenic Bladder; Urology-Female; **Hospital:** White Plains Hosp (page 652); **Address:** 170 Maple Ave, White Plains, NY 10605; **Phone:** 914-949-7556; **Board Cert:** Urology 2013; Female Pelvic Medicine & Reconstuctive Surgery 2013; **Med School:** SUNY Hlth Sci Ctr 1997; **Resid:** Surgery, Montefiore Med Ctr 1999; Urology, Montefiore Med Ctr 2003; **Fellow:** Female Urology, NYU Med Ctr 2004

Glassman, Charles N MD (U) - **Spec Exp:** Pediatric Urology; Minimally Invasive Surgery; Prostate Disease; Erectile Dysfunction; **Hospital:** White Plains Hosp (page 652); **Address:** 170 Maple Ave, Ste 104, White Plains, NY 10601-4707; **Phone:** 914-949-7556; **Board Cert:** Urology 1980; **Med School:** Tufts Univ 1973; **Resid:** Surgery, UCSF Med Ctr 1975; Urology, UCSF Med Ctr 1978; **Fellow:** Pediatric Urology, Mayo Clinic 1979

Housman, Arno D MD (U) - **Spec Exp:** Urologic Cancer; Kidney Stones; Prostate Cancer; **Hospital:** Phelps Meml Hosp Ctr; **Address:** 325 S Highland Ave, Briarcliff Manor, NY 10510; **Phone:** 914-941-0617; **Board Cert:** Urology 2009; **Med School:** SUNY Downstate 1980; **Resid:** Surgery, SUNY Downstate Med Ctr 1983; Urology, Yale-New Haven Hosp 1986

Lerner, Seth E MD (U) - **Spec Exp:** Prostate Cancer/Robotic Surgery; Urologic Cancer; Minimally Invasive Surgery; **Hospital:** White Plains Hosp (page 652); **Address:** 170 Maple Ave, Ste 104, White Plains, NY 10601; **Phone:** 914-949-7556; **Board Cert:** Urology 2005; **Med School:** SUNY Downstate 1988; **Resid:** Surgery, Montefiore Med Ctr 1990; Urology, Montefiore Med Ctr 1994; **Fellow:** Urologic Oncology, Mayo Clinic 1995

Matthews, Gerald J MD (U) - **Spec Exp:** Infertility-Male; Impotence; Sexual Dysfunction; Vasectomy & Vasectomy Reversal; **Hospital:** Westchester Med Ctr, Montefiore Med Ctr-Wakefield Campus (page 100); **Address:** Urology Center of Westchester, 19 Bradhurst Ave, Ste 1900, Hawthorne, NY 10532-2144; **Phone:** 914-347-1900; **Board Cert:** Urology 2006; **Med School:** NY Med Coll 1986; **Resid:** Surgery, St Francis Hosp 1988; Urology, Lenox Hill Hosp 1993; **Fellow:** Urology, Cornell Univ 1995; **Fac Appt:** Assoc Prof U, NY Med Coll

Nogueira, Mark A MD (U) - **Spec Exp:** Robotic Surgery; Prostate Cancer; Urologic Cancer; **Hospital:** Putnam Hosp Ctr, Northern Westchester Hosp; **Address:** Mount Kisco Medical Group-Urology, 110 S Bedford Rd, Mount Kisco, NY 10549; **Phone:** 914-241-1050; **Board Cert:** Urology 2009; **Med School:** Mount Sinai Sch Med 2001; **Resid:** Urology, SUNY-Buffalo Affil Hosps 2006; **Fellow:** Urologic Oncology, Roswell Park Cancer Inst 2007

Owens, George F MD (U) - **Spec Exp:** Prostate Disease; Erectile Dysfunction; Incontinence; Minimally Invasive Surgery; **Hospital:** White Plains Hosp (page 652), Westchester Med Ctr; **Address:** Advn Urology Ctrs NY, 311 North St, Ste 406, White Plains, NY 10605-2232; **Phone:** 914-946-1406; **Board Cert:** Urology 2005; **Med School:** NY Med Coll 1979; **Resid:** Surgery, Montefiore Med Ctr 1981; Urology, Montefiore Med Ctr 1984; **Fellow:** Urology, NY Med College 1985; **Fac Appt:** Assoc Clin Prof U, NY Med Coll

Phillips, John L MD (U) - **Spec Exp:** Robotic Surgery; Prostate Cancer; Urologic Cancer; **Hospital:** Westchester Med Ctr; **Address:** 19 Bradhurst Ave, Ste 1900, Hawthorne, NY 10532-2144; **Phone:** 914-347-1900; **Board Cert:** Urology 2012; **Med School:** Yale Univ 1992; **Resid:** Surgery, Yale-New Haven Hosp 1994; Urology, Yale-New Haven Hosp 1997; **Fellow:** Urologic Oncology, NIH 2000; **Fac Appt:** Assoc Prof U, NY Med Coll

Riechers, Roger N MD (U) - **Spec Exp:** Robotic Urologic Surgery; Minimally Invasive Surgery; Prostate Cancer; **Hospital:** Northern Westchester Hosp; **Address:** Columbia Doctors Medical Group, 19 Bradhurst Ave, Ste 700, Hawthorne, NY 10532; **Phone:** 914-593-7800; **Board Cert:** Urology 1976; **Med School:** NYU Sch Med 1968; **Resid:** Urology, Mt Sinai Med Ctr 1973

Roberts, Larry P MD (U) - **Spec Exp:** Erectile Dysfunction; Incontinence; Prostate Disease; Urology-Female; **Hospital:** Montefiore New Rochelle Hosp (page 100); **Address:** 175 Memorial Hwy, Ste 3-2, New Rochelle, NY 10801-5641; **Phone:** 914-235-2929; **Board Cert:** Urology 1981; **Med School:** Univ Miami Sch Med 1974; **Resid:** Surgery, Univ Miami Hosps 1976; Urology, Einstein Affil Hosps 1979; **Fac Appt:** Asst Clin Prof U, Albert Einstein Coll Med

Schrager, Alan MD (U) - **Spec Exp:** Prostate Disease; Urology-Female; Urologic Cancer; Voiding Dysfunction; **Hospital:** Greenwich Hosp (page 970), Montefiore New Rochelle Hosp (page 100); **Address:** 1600 Harrison Ave, Ste 102-G, Mamaroneck, NY 10543-3124; **Phone:** 914-698-8106; **Board Cert:** Urology 1975; **Med School:** Univ Hlth Scis, Chicago Med Sch 1966; **Resid:** Surgery, Maimonides Med Ctr 1970; Urology, SUNY Downstate Med Ctr 1973

Siegel, Judy F MD (U) - **Spec Exp:** Voiding Dysfunction-Female; Voiding Dysfunction-Pediatric; **Hospital:** St. John's Riverside Hosp-Andrus Pavil, Phelps Meml Hosp Ctr; **Address:** Family Urology, 623 Warburton Ave, Ste 102, Hastings-on-Hudson, NY 10706; **Phone:** 914-478-3001; **Board Cert:** Urology 2009; **Med School:** Univ VT Coll Med 1988; **Resid:** Surgery, LI Jewish Med Ctr 1990; Urology, LI Jewish Med Ctr 1994; **Fellow:** Pediatric Urology, Schneider Chldns Hosp 1996

Trauzzi, Stephen J MD (U) - **Spec Exp:** Prostate Disease; Prostate Cancer/Robotic Surgery; **Hospital:** Montefiore New Rochelle Hosp (page 100), White Plains Hosp (page 652); **Address:** Advanced Urology Centers of NY, 120 Warren St, New Rochelle, NY 10801; **Phone:** 914-636-2121; **Board Cert:** Urology 2006; **Med School:** Georgetown Univ 1988; **Resid:** Urology, St. Lukes Roosevelt Hosp Ctr - Roosevelt Div 1994

Weinberg, Jerry MD (U) - **Spec Exp:** Prostate Cancer; Urologic Cancer; Robotic Surgery; Minimally Invasive Surgery; **Hospital:** Northern Westchester Hosp; **Address:** 666 Lexington Ave, Ste 100, Mount Kisco, NY 10549; **Phone:** 914-666-4346; **Board Cert:** Urology 2010; **Med School:** SUNY Downstate 1983; **Resid:** Surgery, LIJ Med Ctr 1985; Urology, LIJ Med Ctr 1989

Werner, Michael A MD (U) - **Spec Exp:** Infertility-Male; Sexual Dysfunction; **Hospital:** White Plains Hosp (page 652); **Address:** 2975 Westchester Ave, Purchase, NY 10577; **Phone:** 914-997-4100; **Board Cert:** Urology 2005; **Med School:** UCSF 1986; **Resid:** Surgery, Beth Israel Med Ctr 1989; Urology, Mount Sinai Med Ctr 1993; **Fellow:** Male Infertility, Boston Univ Med Ctr 1994

Vascular & Interventional Radiology

Hamet, Marc R MD (VIR) - **Spec Exp:** Osteoporosis Spine-Vertebroplasty; Uterine Fibroid Embolization; Endovascular Surgery; Carotid Artery Stent Placement; **Hospital:** White Plains Hosp (page 652), Lawrence Hosp Ctr (page 102); **Address:** White Plains Radiology Assocs, White Plains Hospital, 41 E Post Rd, White Plains, NY 10601; **Phone:** 914-681-1273; **Board Cert:** Diagnostic Radiology 1995; Vascular & Interventional Radiology 2009; Neuroradiology 2010; **Med School:** Univ MD Sch Med 1991; **Resid:** Diagnostic Radiology, Univ Maryland Affil Hosp 1995; **Fellow:** Neuroradiology, Univ Maryland 1996; Interventional Radiology, Johns Hopkins Hosp 1998

Maddineni, Shekher MD (VIR) - **Spec Exp:** Uterine Fibroid Embolization; Chemoembolization & Tumor Ablation; Varicose Veins; **Hospital:** Westchester Med Ctr; **Address:** Advanced Imaging, Vascular & Interventional Radiology, 100 Woods Way, Valhalla, NY 10595; **Phone:** 914-493-7563; **Board Cert:** Diagnostic Radiology 1997; Vascular & Interventional Radiology 2010; **Med School:** NYU Sch Med 1988; **Resid:** Surgery, Beth Israel Med Ctr 1992; Diagnostic Radiology, Harlem Hosp 1996; **Fellow:** Vascular & Interventional Radiology, Montefiore Med Ctr 1998

Tulla, Carlos A MD (VIR) - **Hospital:** White Plains Hosp (page 652); **Address:** White Plains Hospital, Interventional Radiology, 41 E Post Rd, White Plains, NY 10601; **Phone:** 914-681-1273; **Board Cert:** Diagnostic Radiology 1986; Vascular & Interventional Radiology 2006; **Med School:** Univ Puerto Rico 1980; **Resid:** Diagnostic Radiology, Univ Hosp 1985; **Fellow:** Interventional Radiology, NYU Med Ctr 1986

Vascular Surgery

Babu, Sateesh C MD (VascS) - **Spec Exp:** Carotid Artery Surgery; Aneurysm-Abdominal Aortic; Lower Limb Arterial Disease; Vein Disorders; **Hospital:** Westchester Med Ctr, Northern Westchester Hosp; **Address:** Westchester Heart & Vascular, 19 Bradhurst Ave, Ste 3850S, Hawthorne, NY 10532; **Phone:** 914-909-6900; **Board Cert:** Vascular Surgery 2013; **Med School:** India 1969; **Resid:** Surgery, Jewish Meml Hosp 1972; Surgery, Metropolitan Hosp 1975; **Fellow:** Vascular Surgery, Metropolitan Hosp 1977; **Fac Appt:** Clin Prof S, NY Med Coll

Fishman, Eric MD (VascS) - **Spec Exp:** Aneurysm-Aortic; Endovascular Surgery; **Hospital:** White Plains Hosp (page 652), Greenwich Hosp (page 970); **Address:** WestMed Med Group-Vascular Surgery, 1 Theall Road, Rye, NY 10580; **Phone:** 914-723-7737; **Board Cert:** Surgery 2005; Vascular Surgery 2012; **Med School:** Mount Sinai Sch Med 1997; **Resid:** Surgery, Mount Sinai Med Ctr 2003; **Fellow:** Vascular Surgery, Mount Sinai Med Ctr 2011

Goyal, Arun MD (VascS) - **Spec Exp:** Minimally Invasive Vascular Surgery; Varicose Veins; Laser Surgery; **Hospital:** Westchester Med Ctr; **Address:** Westchester Heart & Vascular, 19 Bradhurst Ave, Ste 3850 S, Hawthorne, NY 10532; **Phone:** 914-909-6900; **Board Cert:** Surgery 2006; Vascular Surgery 2008; **Med School:** NY Med Coll 1990; **Resid:** Surgery, Mount Sinai Hosp 1995; **Fellow:** Vascular Surgery, Mount Sinai Hosp 1996; **Fac Appt:** Asst Prof S, NY Med Coll

Laskowski, Igor A MD (VascS) - **Spec Exp:** Endovascular Surgery; Carotid Artery Surgery; Aneurysm-Aortic; Peripheral Vascular Disease; **Hospital:** Westchester Med Ctr; **Address:** Westchester Heart & Vascular, 19 Bradhurst Ave, Ste 3750, Hawthorne, NY 10532; **Phone:** 914-909-6900; **Board Cert:** Surgery 2007; Vascular Surgery 2009; **Med School:** Poland 1996; **Resid:** Surgery, Columbia-Presby Hosp 2006; **Fellow:** Vascular Surgery, NYU Med Ctr 2007; Transplant Immunology, Harvard Univ; **Fac Appt:** Asst Prof S, NY Med Coll

Mateo, Romeo B MD (VascS) - **Spec Exp:** Endovascular Surgery; Minimally Invasive Surgery; Carotid Artery Surgery; Aneurysm; **Hospital:** Westchester Med Ctr; **Address:** Westchester Heart & Vascular Ctr, 19 Bradhurst Ave, Ste 3850 S, Hawthorne, NY 10532; **Phone:** 914-909-6900; **Board Cert:** Surgery 2010; Vascular Surgery 2010; **Med School:** Brown Univ 1988; **Resid:** Surgery, Rhode Island Hosp 1996; **Fellow:** Vascular Surgery, Cleveland Clinic 1998; **Fac Appt:** Asst Prof S, NY Med Coll

Suggs, William D MD (VascS) - **Spec Exp:** Minimally Invasive Surgery; Aneurysm-Abdominal & Thoracic Aortic; Carotid Artery Surgery; **Hospital:** White Plains Hosp (page 652); **Address:** Vascular Assocs, 4 Lyon Pl, Lobby Level, Ste 2, White Plains, NY 10601; **Phone:** 914-948-6633; **Board Cert:** Vascular Surgery 2012; **Med School:** Wake Forest Univ 1983; **Resid:** Surgery, G Washington Univ Hosp 1989; **Fellow:** Vascular Surgery, Emory Univ Hosp 1991; **Fac Appt:** Assoc Prof VascS, Albert Einstein Coll Med

The State of New Jersey

The Best in American Medicine
www.CastleConnolly.com

Bergen

Hackensack
University Health Network

30 Prospect Avenue, Hackensack, NJ 07601 • 551-996-2000
www.HackensackUHN.org

HackensackUMC *(Hackensack University Medical Center)*
HackensackUMC at Pascack Valley
HackensackUMC Mountainside
Palisades Medical Center

Year Founded: 2010
Number of hospital and nursing home beds: 1,697
Number of employees: 11,355
2013 Admissions: 67,352
Number of Hospitals in System: 4

Nursing: Magnet® Recognized for Nursing Excellence

Academic Affiliations: Georgetown University School of Medicine, St. George's University, Stevens Institute of Technology, Rutgers Medical School

Clinical Affiliations: Georgetown Lombardi Comprehensive Cancer Center, MedStar Georgetown University Hospital, Good Samaritan Regional Medical Center, CentraState Healthcare System, NYU Langone Medical Center's Division of Pediatric Surgery, MinuteClinic, CityMD, United Surgical Partners International

Strategic Alliance: North Shore-LIJ Health System

• **Network Alliance:** AllSpire Health Partners - seven health systems with a total of 28 hospitals: Atlantic Health System (Morristown, NJ), Hackensack University Health Network (Hackensack, NJ), Lancaster General Health (Lancaster, PA), Lehigh Valley Health Network (Allentown, PA), Meridian Health (Neptune, NJ), Reading Health System (Reading, PA), and WellSpan Health (York, PA).

Hackensack University Health Network (HackensackUHN) is the non-profit, New Jersey-based parent company of HackensackUMC, the HackensackUMC Foundation, Hackensack University HealthPartners Medical Group, and corporate joint venture partners with LHP Hospital Group (Plano, TX) in ownership of two hospitals: HackensackUMC at Pascack Valley (Westwood, NJ) and HackensackUMC Mountainside (Montclair, NJ).

• **Hackensack University Medical Groups:** HackensackUHN enjoys various models of employment partnerships with 500 physicians in practices throughout the region. Ranging from sub-specialists to pediatric specialists, these medical groups help to improve efficiency and streamline care. The Hackensack University Medical Group is the largest member of the HackensackAlliance ACO.

• **Accountable Care Organization (ACO):** In April 2012, HackensackAlliance ACO announced it was one of 27 ACOs selected to participate in the Medicare Shared Savings Program (Shared Savings Program) ACO. The ACO started with covering 13,000 lives and has now grown to nearly 40,000. In September 2014, CMS reported that HackensackAlliance ACO has generated $10.75 million in savings and is receiving a $5.27 million payment for Earned Shared Savings

• **United Surgical Partners International (USPI):** HackensackUHN entered into a joint venture partnership with community physicians and USPI in the acquisition and operation of two ambulatory surgery centers in Bergen County.

• **HackensackUMC Fitness & Wellness Powered by the Giants:** HackensackUMC teamed up with the New York Football Giants and Fitness & Wellness Professional Services to open a state-of-the-art wellness center on Route 17 in Maywood, NJ. This dynamic center offers everything to get and keep the community well, and is one of the largest of its kind in New Jersey; with 75,000-square-feet of fitness space and 35,000-square feet of space dedicated to wellness and medical needs.

For more information, please visit www.HackensackUHN.org.

HackensackUMC
at Pascack Valley

250 Old Hook Road, Westwood, NJ 07675 • 201-383-1035
www.HackensackUMCPV.com

Number of beds: 128
Number of employees: 603 (including per diem)

HackensackUMC at Pascack Valley is a full service 128-bed hospital that serves the Pascack Valley and Northern Valley communities with a caliber of care that is consistent with Hackensack University Health Network's world-class standard. The hospital is a joint venture of the Hackensack University Health Network and the LHP Hospital Group Inc., one of the country's leading private hospital management companies. This state-of-the-art healthcare facility features fully renovated and brand new private rooms at no additional costs to the patient. Services include:

- Bariatric Surgery
- Breast Health Services
- Cancer Services
- Cardiac Services
- Cardiac & Pulmonary Rehabilitation
- Emergency Department
- Imaging and Diagnostics
- Maternity Unit
- Orthopedics and the Center for Joint Replacement
- Surgical Services
- Sleep Center
- Inpatient Therapy Services
- Wound Care

Each all-private, fully-renovated room features a variety of amenities and specialty features for advanced patient care. Special service offerings to help alleviate stress during a patient stay include:

- **Parking** – Valet parking is offered at our front main entrance and at our side entrance near labor and delivery. This service is provided free of charge to all patients at HackensackUMC at Pascack Valley.

- **Concierge** – Patient concierge is available to all patients from 10 a.m. – 2 p.m., Monday through Friday. Patients can choose from a variety of services including dry-cleaning, prescription and pajama orders, car washes, and more.

- **Room Service** – Room service is offered to our patients as an added convenience. After a long surgery, procedure or delivery our courteous staff will deliver a (medically approved) hot meal to patient rooms at their request from our in-room dining menu.

- **Wi-Fi** – This service is provided to all patients at no additional cost.

HackensackUMC at Pascack Valley proudly offers a number of outreach programs to the local community including Mommy University and the Be Well Community Lecture Series. Mommy University features a series of lectures designed to educate and provide support for new parents or caregivers. These pre and post natal programs are designed to take the mystery out of the birthing process and help expectant parents for one of life's most precious moments, the birth of a child. All lectures are free and conveniently located in the HackensackUMC at Pascack Valley Community Classroom.

The Be Well Community Lecture Series is designed to educate members of the local community about ways to stay well and lead healthier, more fulfilling lives. These seminars are taught by physicians and offered free of charge to the community.

For more information, please call 201-383-1035 or visit www.HackensackUMCPV.com.

For more information about Holy Name Medical Center or for a physician referral, call 877-HOLY-NAME. Please mention "Castle Connolly Guide."

Holy Name Medical Center

718 Teaneck Road
Teaneck, NJ 07666
877-HOLY-NAME
(465-9626)
holyname.org

THE HOLY NAME HEALING TRADITION

Holy Name Medical Center (HNMC) is a fully accredited, not-for-profit healthcare facility based in Teaneck, New Jersey, with off-site locations throughout Bergen County, and in Hudson and Passaic counties. Founded and sponsored by the Sisters of St. Joseph of Peace in 1925, the comprehensive 361-bed medical center offers leading-edge medical practice and technology administered in an environment rooted in a tradition of compassion and respect for every patient.

COMPREHENSIVE PROGRAMS AND SERVICES

HNMC provides high-quality health care across a continuum that encompasses education, prevention, early intervention, comprehensive treatment options, rehabilitation and wellness maintenance—from conception through end-of-life.

In addition to patient care, HNMC's School of Nursing is renowned for the education of registered nurses and licensed practical nurses.

PERFORMANCE RECOGNITION

- **Top Performer on Key Quality Measures**
  THE JOINT COMMISSION
- **Best Regional Hospitals**
  US NEWS & WORLD REPORT
- **Magnet Recognition**
  AMERICAN NURSES CREDENTIALING ASSOCIATION
- **Beacon Award**
  AMERICAN ASSOCIATION OF CRITICAL-CARE NURSES
- **Primary Stroke Care Center**
  THE JOINT COMMISSION
- **Gold Plus Achievement Award**
  AMERICAN HEART ASSOCIATION/AMERICAN STROKE ASSOCIATION
- **Hospital Safety Score "A"**
  THE LEAPFROG GROUP
- **Community Value Five Star**
  CLEVERLEY + ASSOCIATES
- **"Best Places to Work in New Jersey"**
  NJ BIZ MAGAZINE

Centers of Excellence

- Bone and Joint Center
- Cardiovascular Services
- Emergency Care Center
- Interventional Institute
- Maternal/Child Health
- Regional Cancer Center

Robotic and Minimally Invasive Surgery

Breast Services

Center for Healthy Living

Center for Sleep Medicine

Post-Acute Services:
– Home Health Care
– Palliative Care
– Community Hospice
– Villa Marie Claire residential hospice
– Adult Medical Day Care

Institute for Clinical Research

Culturally Sensitive Health Care:
– Korean Medical Program
– Hispanic Outreach Program
– Jewish Patient Services

Center for Physical Rehabilitation

HNH Fitness® Medically Based Fitness Center

MS Center

THE VALLEY HOSPITAL

223 North Van Dien Avenue, Ridgewood, NJ 07450
Phone: 201-447-8000 • www.ValleyHealth.com
www.Facebook.com/ValleyHospital • www.Twitter.com/ValleyHospital

Sponsorship: Voluntary Not-for-Profit   **Beds:** 451 Acute Care Beds
Accredited by The Joint Commission

■ PROFILE

The Valley Hospital is affiliated with the NewYork-Presbyterian Healthcare System. Valley has been recognized 10 consecutive times under the J.D. Power and Associates Distinguished Hospital Program and is a three-time recipient of the Magnet Award for Nursing Excellence.

Healthgrades has named Valley one of America's 100 Best Hospitals for Orthopedic Surgery, Joint Replacement, and Cardiac Surgery, and recognized the hospital for clinical excellence in gynecologic surgery, maternity care, joint replacement, orthopedic surgery, and overall patient experience.

Valley has earned an impressive 12 Disease-Specific Care Certifications for healthcare quality from the Joint Commission: acute myocardial infarction, heart failure, total hip replacement, total knee replacement, stroke, breast cancer, lung cancer, colorectal cancer, prostate cancer, pancreatic cancer, and uterine-ovarian cancer, and chronic obstructive pulmonary disease. No hospital in the nation has more Gold Seals of Approval in cancer care than Valley.

■ MEDICAL STAFF

The Valley Hospital has more than 1,000 physicians on its Active Medical Staff, 92 percent of whom are board certified.

■ CARDIOLOGY

The Valley Heart and Vascular Institute is a leader in the field of cardiology services, including cardiac surgery; coronary angioplasty and other interventional procedures; electrophysiology studies; and cardiac research. Valley is among only 1.7 percent of hospitals nationwide to receive The Society of Thoracic Surgeons' highest ratings in three procedures: coronary artery bypass, aortic valve surgery, and a combination of the two procedures.

■ SURGERY

The Valley Hospital is also known for its comprehensive surgical program, including pioneering dvances in surgical oncology, gastrointestinal surgery, gyncologic oncology, thoracic surgery, and its Center for Minimally Invasive and Robotic Surgery. The hospital has also been designated as a Bariatric Surgery Center of Excellence.

■ ONCOLOGY

Valley is known for its centers specializing in the diagnosis, care and treatment of breast, lung, and prostate cancers; its surgical oncology, neuro-oncology, and gynecologic oncology programs; its comprehensive oncology clinical trials program and its Department of Radiation Oncology, including Tomotherapy. Valley was the first hospital in northern New Jersey to offer Gamma Knife radiosurgery, a noninvasive tool designed to treat cancer and neurological conditions in the brain

■ WOMEN'S & CHILDREN'S SERVICES

The hospital is well known for its women's and children's services, including the Fertility Center, Maternal-Fetal Medicine program, the Center for Holistic Birth, an enhanced Neonatal Intensive Care Unit, a maternal & child health home care program, and The Kireker Center for Child Development that offers a full spectrum of services.

Physician Referral: Information on physicians affiliated with The Valley Hospital is available by phone at 1-800-VALLEY 1 (1-800-825-5391) or by visiting **www.ValleyMedicalStaff.com.**

Adolescent Medicine

Imbornone, Peter J MD (AM) - **Spec Exp:** Preventive Medicine; Chronic Illness; **Hospital:** Hackensack Univ Med Ctr (page 96); **Address:** Rochelle Park Med Ctr, 96 Parkway, Bldg B, Rochelle Park, NJ 07662; **Phone:** 201-291-1010; **Board Cert:** Internal Medicine 1986; **Med School:** Italy 1980; **Resid:** Internal Medicine, St. Joseph's Hosp Med Ctr 1986; **Fellow:** Adolescent Medicine, St. Joseph's Hosp Med Ctr 1989

Allergy & Immunology

Blume, Jessica W MD (A&I) - **Spec Exp:** Food Allergy; **Hospital:** Valley Hosp (page 739), Hackensack UMC-Pascack Valley (page 737); **Address:** Bergen Medical Associates, 466 Old Hook Rd, Ste 1, Emerson, NJ 07630; **Phone:** 201-967-8221; **Board Cert:** Internal Medicine 2005; Allergy & Immunology 2007; **Med School:** Rutgers R W Johnson Med Sch 2002; **Resid:** Internal Medicine, SUNY Buffalo Med Ctr 2005; **Fellow:** Allergy & Immunology, SUNY Buffalo Med Ctr 2007

Chang, Cindy Ching MD (A&I) - **Spec Exp:** Asthma & Allergy; Allergic Rhinitis; Sinus Disorders; **Hospital:** Hackensack Univ Med Ctr (page 96), Valley Hosp (page 739); **Address:** Forest Hlthcare Assocs, 277 Forest Ave, Ste 120, Paramus, NJ 07652; **Phone:** 201-986-1881; **Board Cert:** Allergy & Immunology 2014; **Med School:** SUNY Stony Brook 1997; **Resid:** Internal Medicine, Stony Brook Univ Hosp 2000; **Fellow:** Allergy & Immunology, Stony Brook Univ Hosp 2002

Falk, Theodore MD (A&I) - **Spec Exp:** Asthma; Pediatric Allergy & Immunology; Immunodeficiency Disorders; Chronic Fatigue Syndrome; **Hospital:** Holy Name Med Ctr (page 738), Englewood Hosp & Med Ctr; **Address:** 63 Grand Ave, Ste 100, River Edge, NJ 07661-1930; **Phone:** 201-487-2900; **Board Cert:** Pediatrics 1982; **Med School:** Belgium 1977; **Resid:** Pediatrics, Long Island Jewish Med Ctr 1980; **Fellow:** Allergy & Immunology, Nassau Co Med Ctr 1982

From, Stuart B MD (A&I) - **Spec Exp:** Asthma & Allergy; Urticaria; Skin Allergies; Food & Drug Allergy; **Hospital:** Englewood Hosp & Med Ctr; **Address:** Englewood Allergy Associates, 309 Engle St, Ste 2, Englewood, NJ 07631; **Phone:** 201-568-1480; **Board Cert:** Allergy & Immunology 2003; **Med School:** NY Med Coll 1987; **Resid:** Internal Medicine, Montefiore Med Ctr 1990; **Fellow:** Allergy & Immunology, NY-Presby/Weill Cornell Med Ctr 1992

Geller, Debora K MD (A&I) - **Spec Exp:** Pediatric Allergy & Immunology; Sinus Disorders; Food Allergy; Allergic Rhinitis; **Hospital:** Chilton Med Ctr (page 92); **Address:** 466 Old Hook Rd, Ste 24-E, Emerson, NJ 07630; **Phone:** 201-265-7515; **Board Cert:** Allergy & Immunology 2005; **Med School:** Univ Rochester 1999; **Resid:** Pediatrics, Univ Hosp 2002; **Fellow:** Allergy & Immunology, Chldns Hosp 2005

Goodstein, Carolyn E MD (A&I) - **Spec Exp:** Pediatric Allergy & Immunology; Rhinitis; Urticaria; Sinusitis; **Hospital:** Englewood Hosp & Med Ctr, Hackensack Univ Med Ctr (page 96); **Address:** 180 N Dean St, Englewood, NJ 07631; **Phone:** 201-871-4755; **Board Cert:** Internal Medicine 1974; Allergy & Immunology 1980; **Med School:** SUNY Downstate 1964; **Resid:** Internal Medicine, Montefiore Med Ctr 1967; Allergy & Immunology, St Lukes-Roosevelt Hosp 1971

Harish, Ziv MD (A&I) - **Spec Exp:** Asthma & Sinusitis; Hay Fever; Urticaria; Hives; **Hospital:** Englewood Hosp & Med Ctr, Hackensack Univ Med Ctr (page 96); **Address:** 200 Engle St, Ste 18, Englewood, NJ 07631; **Phone:** 201-871-7475; **Board Cert:** Allergy & Immunology 2012; **Med School:** Israel 1983; **Resid:** Pediatrics, Montefiore Med Ctr 1989; **Fellow:** Allergy & Immunology, Montefiore Med Ctr 1991; **Fac Appt:** Clin Prof Med, Albert Einstein Coll Med

Michelis, Mary Ann MD (A&I) - **Spec Exp:** Asthma; Immune Deficiency; **Hospital:** Hackensack Univ Med Ctr (page 96); **Address:** 360 Essex St, Ste 302, Hackensack, NJ 07601; **Phone:** 551-996-2065; **Board Cert:** Internal Medicine 1978; Allergy & Immunology 1981; Diagnostic Lab Immunology 1988; **Med School:** Univ Pittsburgh 1975; **Resid:** Internal Medicine, Lenox Hill Hosp 1978; **Fellow:** Allergy & Immunology, NY-Presby/Weill Cornell Med Ctr 1980; **Fac Appt:** Assoc Clin Prof Med, UMDNJ-NJ Med Sch, Newark

Minikes, Neil I MD (A&I) - **Spec Exp:** Eczema; Food Allergy; Hay Fever; Asthma; **Hospital:** Englewood Hosp & Med Ctr, Hackensack Univ Med Ctr (page 96); **Address:** Allergy & Asthma Ctr North NJ, 500 Piermont Rd, Ste 304, Closter, NJ 7624; **Phone:** 201-564-7777; **Board Cert:** Pediatrics 1986; Allergy & Immunology 2011; **Med School:** Columbia P&S 1980; **Resid:** Pediatrics, NY-Presby/Columbia Univ Med Ctr 1983; **Fellow:** Allergy & Immunology, LI Jewish Med Ctr 1990; **Fac Appt:** Asst Clin Prof Ped, Columbia P&S

Perin, Patrick MD (A&I) - **Spec Exp:** Allergy; Asthma; Pediatric Allergy & Immunology; **Hospital:** Holy Name Med Ctr (page 738), St. Joseph's Regl Med Ctr - Paterson; **Address:** Advanced Asthma Allergy Care, 185 Cedar Ln, Ste L2, Teaneck, NJ 07666; **Phone:** 201-836-6400; **Board Cert:** Allergy & Immunology 2013; **Med School:** Grenada 1987; **Resid:** Pediatrics, Univ Hosp-UMDNJ 1990; **Fellow:** Allergy & Immunology, Thomas Jefferson Univ Hosp 1992

Selvaggi, Thomas A MD (A&I) - **Spec Exp:** Autoimmune Disease; Asthma & Allergy; **Hospital:** Hackensack Univ Med Ctr (page 96); **Address:** Hackensack Allergy & Asthma, 211 Essex St, Ste 401, Hackensack, NJ 07601-3245; **Phone:** 201-343-6673; **Board Cert:** Internal Medicine 2012; Allergy & Immunology 2005; **Med School:** Med Coll PA 1989; **Resid:** Internal Medicine, Univ Pittsburgh Med Ctr 1992; **Fellow:** Allergy & Immunology, Clinical Ctr at the NIH 1995; Clinical & Laboratory Immunology, Clinical Ctr at the NIH 1997

Skripak, Justin M MD (A&I) - **Spec Exp:** Asthma & Allergy; Food Allergy; Immune Deficiency; Pediatric Allergy & Immunology; **Hospital:** Valley Hosp (page 739), Hoboken Univ Med Ctr - Hoboken; **Address:** ENT & Allergy Assocs, 690 Kinderkamack Rd, Ste 101, Oradell, NJ 07649; **Phone:** 201-722-9850; **Board Cert:** Allergy & Immunology 2008; **Med School:** UMDNJ-NJ Med Sch, Newark 2001; **Resid:** Pediatrics, St Christopher's Hosp for Chldn 2004; **Fellow:** Allergy & Immunology, Johns Hopkins Hosp 2006

Cardiac Electrophysiology

Feigenblum, David Yehuda MD/PhD (CE) - **Spec Exp:** Atrial Fibrillation; **Hospital:** Englewood Hosp & Med Ctr; **Address:** North Jersey Electrophysiology Assocs, 350 Engle St, Englewood, NJ 07631; **Phone:** 201-894-3533; **Board Cert:** Cardiovascular Disease 2013; Cardiac Electrophysiology 2004; **Med School:** NYU Sch Med 1997; **Resid:** Internal Medicine, NYU Med Ctr/ Tisch Hosp 2000; **Fellow:** Cardiovascular Disease, NYU Med Ctr/ Tisch Hosp 2003; Cardiac Electrophysiology, NYU Med Ctr/ Tisch Hosp 2004; **Fac Appt:** Asst Clin Prof Med, Mount Sinai Sch Med

Mittal, Suneet MD (CE) - **Spec Exp:** Syncope; Atrial Fibrillation; Catheter Ablation; Defibrillator Cable Extraction; **Hospital:** Valley Hosp (page 739); **Address:** 223 N Van Dien Ave, Ridgewood, NJ 07450; **Phone:** 201-432-7837; **Board Cert:** Internal Medicine 2004; Cardiovascular Disease 2007; Cardiac Electrophysiology 2008; **Med School:** Boston Univ 1991; **Resid:** Internal Medicine, Hosp U Penn 1994; **Fellow:** Cardiovascular Disease, Hosp U Penn 1996; Cardiac Electrophysiology, NY Presbyterian/Weill Cornell Med Ctr 1998

Preminger, Mark W MD (CE) - **Spec Exp:** Arrhythmias; Pacemakers/Defibrillators; **Hospital:** Valley Hosp (page 739), Mt Sinai St. Luke's; **Address:** Valley Hosp, Arrhythmia Dept, 223 N Van Dien Ave, Ridgewood, NJ 07450; **Phone:** 201-432-7837; **Board Cert:** Internal Medicine 1989; Cardiovascular Disease 2011; Cardiac Electrophysiology 2012; **Med School:** Hahnemann Univ 1985; **Resid:** Internal Medicine, N Shore Univ Hosp 1989; **Fellow:** Cardiovascular Disease, NY-Presby/Weill Cornell Med Ctr 1991; Cardiac Electrophysiology, Philedelphia Heart Inst 1992; **Fac Appt:** Assoc Prof Med, Columbia P&S

Ruffo, Scott D MD (CE) - **Spec Exp:** Pacemakers; **Hospital:** Hackensack Univ Med Ctr (page 96), Holy Name Med Ctr (page 738); **Address:** Mulkay Cardiology Consultants, 493 Essex St, Hackensack, NJ 07601; **Phone:** 201-996-9244; **Board Cert:** Cardiovascular Disease 2003; Cardiac Electrophysiology 2010; **Med School:** NYU Sch Med 1994; **Resid:** Internal Medicine, NYU Med Ctr/Bellevue Hosp 1997; **Fellow:** Cardiovascular Disease, NYU Med Ctr/Bellevue Hosp 2000; Cardiac Electrophysiology, NYU Med Ctr/Bellevue Hosp 2001

Shukla, Gunjan J MD (CE) - **Spec Exp:** Atrial Fibrillation; Pacemakers; Arrhythmias; **Hospital:** Hackensack Univ Med Ctr (page 96); **Address:** Electrophysiology Assocs of Northern NJ, 20 Prospect Ave, Ste 701, Hackensack, NJ 07601; **Phone:** 201-996-2997; **Board Cert:** Cardiovascular Disease 2005; Cardiac Electrophysiology 2006; **Med School:** India 1996; **Resid:** Internal Medicine, St Elizabeth's Med Ctr 2001; **Fellow:** Cardiovascular Disease, St Elizabeth's Med Ctr 2005; Cardiac Electrophysiology, St Elizabeth's Med Ctr 2006

Simons, Grant R MD (CE) - **Spec Exp:** Arrhythmias; **Hospital:** Englewood Hosp & Med Ctr, Hackensack Univ Med Ctr (page 96); **Address:** Englewood Hosp Arrhythmia Ctr, 350 Engle St, Englewood, NJ 07631; **Phone:** 201-894-3533; **Board Cert:** Cardiovascular Disease 2007; Cardiac Electrophysiology 2008; **Med School:** Duke Univ 1990; **Resid:** Internal Medicine, Brigham & Women's Hosp 1993; **Fellow:** Cardiovascular Disease, Duke Univ Med Ctr 1996; Cardiac Electrophysiology, Duke Univ Med Ctr 1997; **Fac Appt:** Assoc Clin Prof Med, Mount Sinai Sch Med

Steinberg, Jonathan S MD (CE) - **Spec Exp:** Atrial Fibrillation; Catheter Ablation; Defibrillators; Arrhythmias; **Hospital:** Valley Hosp (page 739); **Address:** Valley Hospital, Bergen Bldg, Lower Level, 223 N Van Dien Ave, Ridgewood, NJ 07450; **Phone:** 201-432-7837; **Board Cert:** Internal Medicine 1983; Cardiovascular Disease 1987; Cardiac Electrophysiology 2012; **Med School:** Mount Sinai Sch Med 1980; **Resid:** Internal Medicine, NYU Med Ctr/Manhattan VA Hosp 1984; **Fellow:** Cardiovascular Disease, Geo Wash Univ Med Ctr 1986; Cardiac Electrophysiology, Columbia Presby Med Ctr 1988; **Fac Appt:** Prof Med, Columbia P&S

Zaim, Sina MD (CE) - **Spec Exp:** Atrial Fibrillation; Arrhythmias; **Hospital:** Hackensack Univ Med Ctr (page 96), Newark Beth Israel Med Ctr (page 94); **Address:** 255 W Spring Valley Ave, Ste 205, Maywood, NJ 07607; **Phone:** 201-546-8746; **Board Cert:** Internal Medicine 1985; Cardiovascular Disease 1989; Cardiac Electrophysiology 2004; Critical Care Medicine 2013; **Med School:** Cornell Univ-Weill Med Coll 1981; **Resid:** Internal Medicine, Roosevelt Hosp 1984; **Fellow:** Cardiovascular Disease, Roosevelt Hosp 1987; Cardiac Electrophysiology, MA Genl Hosp 1994; **Fac Appt:** Asst Prof Med, Hahnemann Univ

Cardiovascular Disease

Adibi, Baback MD (Cv) - **Spec Exp:** Cardiac CT Angiography; Coronary Angioplasty/Stents; Cardiac Catheterization; **Hospital:** Hackensack Univ Med Ctr (page 96); **Address:** Bergen Cardiology Assocs, 400 Frank W Burr Blvd, Ste 22, Teaneck, NJ 07666; **Phone:** 201-907-0442; **Board Cert:** Cardiovascular Disease 2005; **Med School:** Univ Pittsburgh 1999; **Resid:** Internal Medicine, Thomas Jefferson Univ Hosp 2002; **Fellow:** Cardiovascular Disease, Thomas Jefferson Univ Hosp 2005

Andrews, Paul M MD (Cv) - **Spec Exp:** Interventional Cardiology; **Hospital:** Hackensack Univ Med Ctr (page 96), Holy Name Med Ctr (page 738); **Address:** Bergen Cardiology Assocs, 400 Frank Burr Blvd, Teaneck, NJ 07666; **Phone:** 201-907-0442; **Board Cert:** Cardiovascular Disease 2010; Interventional Cardiology 2011; **Med School:** SUNY Hlth Sci Ctr 1994; **Resid:** Internal Medicine, Mt Sinai Hosp 1997; **Fellow:** Cardiovascular Disease, Mt Sinai Hosp 2000

Bareket, Yaron MD (Cv) - **Spec Exp:** Nuclear Cardiology; **Hospital:** Hackensack Univ Med Ctr (page 96), Englewood Hosp & Med Ctr; **Address:** Cross County Cardiology, 103 River Rd, Ste 201, Edgewater, NJ 07020; **Phone:** 201-941-8100; **Board Cert:** Cardiovascular Disease 2005; **Med School:** Australia 1987; **Resid:** Internal Medicine, Beth Israel Med Ctr 1992; **Fellow:** Cardiovascular Disease, Montefiore Med Ctr 1995

Berkowitz, Walter D MD (Cv) - **Spec Exp:** Arrhythmias; Coronary Artery Disease; Hypertension; **Hospital:** Englewood Hosp & Med Ctr, Hackensack Univ Med Ctr (page 96); **Address:** 2200 Fletcher Ave, Fort Lee, NJ 07024-5005; **Phone:** 201-461-6200; **Board Cert:** Internal Medicine 1969; Cardiovascular Disease 1972; **Med School:** SUNY Downstate 1962; **Resid:** Internal Medicine, Maimonides Hosp 1964; Internal Medicine, Mt Sinai Hosp 1965; **Fellow:** Cardiovascular Disease, Montefiore Med Ctr 1967

Cocke, Thomas P MD (Cv) - **Spec Exp:** Interventional Cardiology; **Hospital:** Hackensack Univ Med Ctr (page 96), Valley Hosp (page 739); **Address:** Westwood Cardiology Assocs, 333 Old Hook Rd, Ste 200, Westwood, NJ 07675; **Phone:** 201-664-0201; **Board Cert:** Internal Medicine 1988; **Med School:** SUNY Stony Brook 1985; **Resid:** Internal Medicine, Jacobi Hosp 1988; **Fellow:** Cardiovascular Disease, NY-Presby/Columbia Univ Med Ctr 1991; Interventional Cardiology, Mt Sinai Hosp 1992

Conroy Jr, Daniel P MD (Cv) - **Spec Exp:** Non-Invasive Cardiology; Hypertension; Cholesterol/Lipid Disorders; Diabetes & Heart Disease; **Hospital:** St. Mary's Hosp - Passaic, Hackensack Univ Med Ctr (page 96); **Address:** 358 Valley Brook Ave, Lyndhurst, NJ 07071; **Phone:** 201-460-0142; **Board Cert:** Internal Medicine 1979; Cardiovascular Disease 1981; **Med School:** Mexico 1975; **Resid:** Internal Medicine, St Michaels Med Ctr 1978; **Fellow:** Cardiovascular Disease, St Michaels Med Ctr 1980

Dardashti, Omid A MD (Cv) - **Spec Exp:** Echocardiography; Coronary Artery Disease; **Hospital:** Valley Hosp (page 739); **Address:** Valley Med Grp Cardiology, 1124 E Ridgewood Ave, Ste 202, Ridgewood, NJ 07450; **Phone:** 201-689-8070; **Board Cert:** Internal Medicine 2004; Cardiovascular Disease 2007; **Med School:** UMDNJ-Rutgers Med Sch 2001; **Resid:** Internal Medicine, UMDNJ R W Johnson Hosp 2004; **Fellow:** Cardiovascular Disease, St Vincent"s Hosp 2007

DiVagno, Leonardo J MD (Cv) - **Spec Exp:** Cholesterol/Lipid Disorders; Hypertension; **Hospital:** Englewood Hosp & Med Ctr, Hackensack Univ Med Ctr (page 96); **Address:** 218 Route 17 N, Ste 310, Rochelle, NJ 07662; **Phone:** 201-845-3535; **Board Cert:** Cardiovascular Disease 2003; **Med School:** Italy 1991; **Resid:** Internal Medicine, St Vincent's Hosp 1995; **Fellow:** Cardiovascular Disease, NY Med Coll Affil Hosp 1998

Eichman, Gerard MD (Cv) - **Spec Exp:** Coronary Angioplasty/Stents; Cardiac Catheterization; Heart Valve Disease; **Hospital:** Holy Name Med Ctr (page 738), Hackensack Univ Med Ctr (page 96); **Address:** Cardiovascular Assocs of Teaneck, 954 Teaneck Rd, Teaneck, NJ 7666; **Phone:** 201-833-2300; **Board Cert:** Cardiovascular Disease 2005; **Med School:** Dominica 1988; **Resid:** Internal Medicine, Monmouth Med Ctr 1991; **Fellow:** Cardiovascular Disease, Seton Hall Affil Hosp 1992

Eisenberg, Sheldon B MD (Cv) - **Spec Exp:** Nuclear Cardiology; Preventive Cardiology; Coronary Artery Disease; Non-Invasive Cardiology; **Hospital:** Hackensack UMC-Pascack Valley (page 737), Hackensack Univ Med Ctr (page 96); **Address:** Westwood Cardiology Associates, 333 Old Hook Rd, Ste 200, Westwood, NJ 07675-3200; **Phone:** 201-664-0201; **Board Cert:** Internal Medicine 1979; Cardiovascular Disease 1981; **Med School:** Cornell Univ-Weill Med Coll 1976; **Resid:** Internal Medicine, N Shore Univ Hosp 1979; **Fellow:** Cardiovascular Disease, N Shore Univ Hosp 1981

Erlebacher, Jay A MD (Cv) - **Spec Exp:** Pacemakers; Congestive Heart Failure; Cardiac Stress Testing; Echocardiography; **Hospital:** Englewood Hosp & Med Ctr; **Address:** Englewood Cardiology Consultants, 177 N Dean St, Englewood, NJ 07631; **Phone:** 201-569-4901; **Board Cert:** Internal Medicine 1978; Cardiovascular Disease 1981; **Med School:** SUNY Upstate Med Univ 1975; **Resid:** Internal Medicine, Jacobi Med Ctr 1978; **Fellow:** Cardiovascular Disease, Johns Hopkins Hosp 1980; **Fac Appt:** Asst Clin Prof Med, Cornell Univ-Weill Med Coll

Gardin, Julius M MD (Cv) - **Spec Exp:** Echocardiography; Geriatric Cardiology; Preventive Cardiology; Non-Invasive Cardiology; **Hospital:** Hackensack Univ Med Ctr (page 96); **Address:** Hackensack Univ Med Ctr, Dept Medicine, 30 Prospect Ave, 1 Main, Ste 1647, Hackensack, NJ 07601; **Phone:** 551-996-4747; **Board Cert:** Internal Medicine 1975; Cardiovascular Disease 1977; **Med School:** Univ Mich Med Sch 1972; **Resid:** Internal Medicine, Univ Mich Hosp 1975; **Fellow:** Cardiovascular Disease, Georgetown Univ Hosp 1977; **Fac Appt:** Prof Med, UMDNJ-Rutgers Med Sch

Goldschmidt, Howard Z MD (Cv) - **Spec Exp:** Heart Valve Disease; Pacemakers; Cardiomyopathy; Atrial Fibrillation; **Hospital:** Valley Hosp (page 739); **Address:** Valley Heart Grp, 1200 E Ridgewood Ave Fl 2, Ridgewood, NJ 07450; **Phone:** 201-670-8660; **Board Cert:** Internal Medicine 1986; Cardiovascular Disease 1989; **Med School:** Columbia P&S 1983; **Resid:** Internal Medicine, Mt Sinai Hosp 1986; **Fellow:** Cardiovascular Disease, Mt Sinai Hosp 1988

Goldweit, Richard S MD (Cv) - **Spec Exp:** Interventional Cardiology; Sleep Disorders/Cardiac Risk; Peripheral Vascular Disease; Cardiac Catheterization; **Hospital:** Englewood Hosp & Med Ctr; **Address:** Englewood Cardiology Consultants, 177 N Dean St, Englewood, NJ 07631; **Phone:** 201-569-4901; **Board Cert:** Internal Medicine 1985; Cardiovascular Disease 1987; Interventional Cardiology 2009; **Med School:** Cornell Univ-Weill Med Coll 1982; **Resid:** Internal Medicine, NY-Presby/Weill Cornell Med Ctr 1985; **Fellow:** Cardiovascular Disease, NY-Presby/Weill Cornell Med Ctr 1987

Hodges, David MD (Cv) - **Spec Exp:** Stress Management; **Hospital:** Englewood Hosp & Med Ctr; **Address:** 200 Grand Ave, Ste 202, Engelwood, NJ 07631; **Phone:** 201-816-9266; **Board Cert:** Internal Medicine 1987; Cardiovascular Disease 2014; **Med School:** NYU Sch Med 1984; **Resid:** Internal Medicine, Boston Med Ctr 1987; Internal Medicine, Beth Israel Deaconess Med Ctr 1989; **Fellow:** Cardiovascular Disease, Brigham & Womens Hosp 1991; **Fac Appt:** Asst Prof Med, Columbia P&S

Hollywood, Jacqueline MD (Cv) - **Spec Exp:** Coronary Artery Disease; Vascular Disease; Ischemic Heart Disease; **Hospital:** Hackensack Univ Med Ctr (page 96), Englewood Hosp & Med Ctr; **Address:** Advanced Cardiology Inst, 2200 Fletcher Ave, Fort Lee, NJ 07024; **Phone:** 201-461-6200; **Board Cert:** Cardiovascular Disease 2012; **Med School:** Mount Sinai Sch Med 1996; **Resid:** Internal Medicine, NY-Presby/Weill Cornell Med Ctr 1999; **Fellow:** Cardiovascular Disease, NY-Presby/Weill Cornell Med Ctr 2002

Issa, Ebrahim S MD (Cv) - **Spec Exp:** Coronary Artery Disease; Vascular Disease; Cholesterol/Lipid Disorders; **Hospital:** Holy Name Med Ctr (page 738), Hackensack Univ Med Ctr (page 96); **Address:** North Jersey Heart, 800 Grange Rd, Teaneck, NJ 07666; **Phone:** 201-907-0995; **Board Cert:** Internal Medicine 2005; Cardiovascular Disease 2005; **Med School:** India 1982; **Resid:** Internal Medicine, Erie County Med Ctr 1990; **Fellow:** Cardiovascular Disease, Univ Of Buffalo Affil Hosp 1993

Jacowitz, Joel MD (Cv) - **Spec Exp:** Echocardiography; Interventional Cardiology; **Hospital:** Valley Hosp (page 739); **Address:** Old Hook Med Assocs, 452 Old Hook Rd, Emerson, NJ 07630; **Phone:** 201-666-3900 x201; **Board Cert:** Internal Medicine 1981; Cardiovascular Disease 1985; Echocardiography 2013; **Med School:** SUNY Downstate 1977; **Resid:** Internal Medicine, Metropolitan Hosp 1980; Internal Medicine, Harlem Hosp 1981; **Fellow:** Cardiovascular Disease, Harlem Hosp 1985; Interventional Cardiology, Dartmouth-Hitchcock Med Ctr 1993; **Fac Appt:** Assoc Clin Prof Med, Seton Hall Univ Sch Hlth & Med Scis

Kanarek, Steven E MD (Cv) - **Spec Exp:** Coronary Artery Disease; Vascular Disease; **Hospital:** Hackensack Univ Med Ctr (page 96); **Address:** HUMC Cardiovascular Partners, 920 Main St, Ste 2, Hackensack, NJ 07601; **Phone:** 201-342-7733; **Board Cert:** Internal Medicine 2009; Cardiovascular Disease 2012; Echocardiography 2013; Nuclear Cardiology 2014; **Med School:** Albert Einstein Coll Med 1996; **Resid:** Internal Medicine, LI Jewish Med Ctr 1999; **Fellow:** Cardiovascular Disease, LI Jewish Med Ctr 2001

Katechis, Dennis DO (Cv) - **Spec Exp:** Coronary Artery Disease; Cholesterol/Lipid Disorders; Heart Valve Disease; **Hospital:** Englewood Hosp & Med Ctr; **Address:** Englewood Cardiology Consultants, 177 N Dean St, Englewood, NJ 07631; **Phone:** 201-816-2508; **Board Cert:** Cardiovascular Disease 2004; **Med School:** NY Coll Osteo Med 1997; **Resid:** Internal Medicine, North Shore Univ Hosp 2000; **Fellow:** Cardiovascular Disease, North Shore Univ Hosp 2003

Kim, Steve S MD (Cv) - **Spec Exp:** Interventional Cardiology; Angioplasty & Stent Placement; Acute Coronary Syndromes; **Hospital:** Hackensack Univ Med Ctr (page 96), Englewood Hosp & Med Ctr; **Address:** Advanced Cardiology Inst, 2200 Fletcher Ave, Fort Lee, NJ 07024; **Phone:** 201-461-6200; **Board Cert:** Cardiovascular Disease 2004; Interventional Cardiology 2005; **Med School:** Case West Res Univ 1998; **Resid:** Internal Medicine, NY-Presby Hosp/Weill Cornell Med Ctr 2001; **Fellow:** Cardiovascular Disease, NY-Presby Hosp/Weill Cornell Med Ctr 2004; Interventional Cardiology, NY-Presby Hosp/Weill Cornell Med Ctr 2005

Krasikov, Tatiana MD (Cv) - **Spec Exp:** Echocardiography; Nuclear Cardiology; **Hospital:** Hackensack Univ Med Ctr (page 96), Englewood Hosp & Med Ctr; **Address:** Advanced Cardiology Inst, 2200 Fletcher Ave, Fort Lee, NJ 07024; **Phone:** 201-461-6200; **Board Cert:** Internal Medicine 2012; Cardiovascular Disease 2005; **Med School:** Harvard Med Sch 1998; **Resid:** Internal Medicine, NY-Presby/Weill Cornell Med Ctr 2002; **Fellow:** Cardiovascular Disease, NY-Presby/Weill Cornell Med Ctr 2005; Nuclear Cardiology, NY-Presby/Weill Cornell Med Ctr 2006

Landers, David B MD (Cv) - **Spec Exp:** Cardiac Catheterization; Coronary Angioplasty/Stents; Angioplasty; Interventional Cardiology; **Hospital:** Hackensack Univ Med Ctr (page 96), Holy Name Med Ctr (page 738); **Address:** 400 Frank Burr Blvd, Teaneck, NJ 07666; **Phone:** 201-928-2300; **Board Cert:** Internal Medicine 1983; Cardiovascular Disease 1987; Interventional Cardiology 2010; **Med School:** Georgetown Univ 1979; **Resid:** Internal Medicine, St Vincents Hosp 1982; **Fellow:** Cardiovascular Disease, Westchester Co Med Ctr 1985; **Fac Appt:** Asst Clin Prof Med, UMDNJ-NJ Med Sch, Newark

Landzberg, Joel S MD (Cv) - **Spec Exp:** Preventive Cardiology; Coronary Artery Disease; Heart Failure; Heart Valve Disease; **Hospital:** Hackensack Univ Med Ctr (page 96), Valley Hosp (page 739); **Address:** Westwood Cardiology Associates, 333 Old Hook Rd, Ste 200, Westwood, NJ 07675-3200; **Phone:** 201-664-0201; **Board Cert:** Internal Medicine 1986; Cardiovascular Disease 1989; Interventional Cardiology 2012; **Med School:** Columbia P&S 1983; **Resid:** Internal Medicine, Vanderbilt Univ Hosp 1986; **Fellow:** Cardiology Research, Moffit Hosp 1987; Cardiovascular Disease, Brigham & Womens Hosp 1991; **Fac Appt:** Assoc Clin Prof Med, UMDNJ-NJ Med Sch, Newark

Lee, Nellie U MD (Cv) - **Spec Exp:** Preventive Cardiology; Cholesterol/Lipid Disorders; **Hospital:** Holy Name Med Ctr (page 738); **Address:** 190 Euclid Ave, Ridgefield Park, NJ 07660-1742; **Phone:** 201-440-3366; **Board Cert:** Internal Medicine 1973; Cardiovascular Disease 1977; **Med School:** Philippines 1966; **Resid:** Internal Medicine, Mt Sinai Hosp 1970Washington DC VA Med Ctr 1971; **Fellow:** Cardiovascular Disease, St Luke's Hosp 1974

Lichtstein, Elliott S MD (Cv) - **Spec Exp:** Heart Attack; Congestive Heart Failure; Heart Valve Disease; Heart Failure; **Hospital:** Hackensack Univ Med Ctr (page 96), Valley Hosp (page 739); **Address:** Westwood Cardiology, 333 Old Hook Rd, Ste 200, Westwood, NJ 07675; **Phone:** 201-664-0201; **Board Cert:** Internal Medicine 1984; Cardiovascular Disease 1987; **Med School:** Temple Univ 1981; **Resid:** Internal Medicine, Albany Med Ctr Hosp 1984; **Fellow:** Cardiovascular Disease, LI Jewish Med Ctr 1986

Matican, Jeffrey S MD (Cv) - **Spec Exp:** Interventional Cardiology; Nuclear Cardiology; **Hospital:** Englewood Hosp & Med Ctr, Hackensack Univ Med Ctr (page 96); **Address:** 309 Engle St, Ste 5, Englewood, NJ 07631-1822; **Phone:** 201-503-1920; **Board Cert:** Internal Medicine 1987; Cardiovascular Disease 1989; Interventional Cardiology 2009; **Med School:** NYU Sch Med 1982; **Resid:** Internal Medicine, St Lukes-Roosevelt Hosp 1986; **Fellow:** Cardiovascular Disease, St Lukes-Roosevelt Hosp 1989; Interventional Cardiology, NYU Med Ctr/Tisch Hosp 1990

Patel, Sanjeev N MD (Cv) - **Spec Exp:** Congestive Heart Failure; Coronary Artery Disease; **Hospital:** Hackensack Univ Med Ctr (page 96); **Address:** Heart Care Ctr, 38 Mayhill St, Saddle Brook, NJ 07663; **Phone:** 201-843-1019; **Board Cert:** Internal Medicine 2009; Cardiovascular Disease 2009; **Med School:** UMDNJ-NJ Med Sch, Newark 1993; **Resid:** Internal Medicine, Univ Hosp 1996; **Fellow:** Cardiovascular Disease, Univ Hosp 1999; **Fac Appt:** Asst Prof Med, UMDNJ-Rutgers Med Sch

Pumill, Rick MD (Cv) - **Spec Exp:** Coronary Artery Disease; Hypertension; Congestive Heart Failure; **Hospital:** Hackensack Univ Med Ctr (page 96); **Address:** Cross County Cardiology, 103 River Rd Fl 2, Edgewater, NJ 07020; **Phone:** 201-941-8100; **Board Cert:** Internal Medicine 1988; Cardiovascular Disease 2013; **Med School:** Dominica 1984; **Resid:** Internal Medicine, Jersey City Med Ctr 1988; **Fellow:** Cardiovascular Disease, Jersey City Med Ctr 1990

Reison, Dennis S MD (Cv) - **Spec Exp:** Interventional Cardiology; **Hospital:** Valley Hosp (page 739); **Address:** Valley Heart Grp, 1200 E Ridgewood Ave Fl 2, Ridgewood, NJ 07450; **Phone:** 201-670-8660; **Board Cert:** Internal Medicine 1978; Cardiovascular Disease 1981; **Med School:** Stanford Univ 1975; **Resid:** Internal Medicine, NY-Presby/Columbia Univ Med Ctr 1978; **Fellow:** Cardiovascular Disease, Mount Sinai Med Ctr 1979; Cardiovascular Disease, NY-Presby/Columbia Univ Med Ctr 1981; **Fac Appt:** Asst Clin Prof Med, Columbia P&S

Rossakis, Constantine MD (Cv) - **Spec Exp:** Interventional Cardiology; Nuclear Cardiology; **Hospital:** Hackensack Univ Med Ctr (page 96); **Address:** 357 Prospect Ave, Hackensack, NJ 07601; **Phone:** 201-489-3440; **Board Cert:** Internal Medicine 1986; Cardiovascular Disease 1989; Nuclear Cardiology 2009; **Med School:** NYU Sch Med 1983; **Resid:** Internal Medicine, NY-Presby/Weill Cornell Med Ctr 1986; **Fellow:** Cardiovascular Disease, NY-Presby/Weill Cornell Med Ctr 1989; **Fac Appt:** Asst Clin Prof Med, Cornell Univ-Weill Med Coll

Rothman, Howard C MD (Cv) - **Spec Exp:** Cholesterol/Lipid Disorders; Angina; Preventive Medicine; **Hospital:** Hackensack Univ Med Ctr (page 96), Englewood Hosp & Med Ctr; **Address:** Advanced Cardiology Inst, 2200 Fletcher Ave, Fort Lee, NJ 07024-5005; **Phone:** 201-461-6200; **Board Cert:** Internal Medicine 1975; Cardiovascular Disease 1979; **Med School:** Univ Cincinnati 1970; **Resid:** Internal Medicine, NY Hosp-Cornell Med Ctr 1975; **Fellow:** Cardiovascular Disease, NY Hosp-Cornell Med Ctr 1976; **Fac Appt:** Asst Clin Prof Med, Mount Sinai Sch Med

Sagar, Yogesh MD (Cv) - **Spec Exp:** Invasive Cardiology; Echocardiography; Pacemakers; Cholesterol/Lipid Disorders; **Hospital:** Hackensack Univ Med Ctr (page 96), Holy Name Med Ctr (page 738); **Address:** Bergen Cardiology Associates, 400 Frank W Burr Blvd, Ste 22, Teaneck, NJ 07666; **Phone:** 201-907-0442; **Board Cert:** Internal Medicine 2006; **Med School:** Hahnemann Univ 1991; **Resid:** Internal Medicine, Hahnemann Univ Hosp 1994; **Fellow:** Cardiovascular Disease, Hahnemann Univ Hosp 1997

Salerno, William D MD (Cv) - **Spec Exp:** Vein Disorders; Echocardiography; Critical Care Medicine; **Hospital:** Hackensack Univ Med Ctr (page 96); **Address:** Heartcare Ctr, 38 Mayhill St, Saddle Brook, NJ 07663; **Phone:** 201-843-1019; **Board Cert:** Internal Medicine 1987; Cardiovascular Disease 1989; Critical Care Medicine 2011; **Med School:** Mexico 1982; **Resid:** Internal Medicine, Hackensack Univ Med Ctr 1986; Critical Care Medicine, Norwalk Hosp 1987; **Fellow:** Cardiovascular Disease, Hackensack Univ Med Ctr 1989; Interventional Cardiology, Hackensack Univ Med Ctr 1990; **Fac Appt:** Assoc Clin Prof Med, UMDNJ-Rutgers Med Sch

Sotsky, Gerald MD (Cv) - **Hospital:** Valley Hosp (page 739); **Address:** Valley Heart Grp, 1200 E Ridgewood Ave Fl 2, Ridgewood, NJ 07450; **Phone:** 201-670-8660; **Board Cert:** Internal Medicine 1984; Cardiovascular Disease 1987; **Med School:** Mount Sinai Sch Med 1981; **Resid:** Internal Medicine, Mount Sinai Med Ctr 1984; **Fellow:** Cardiovascular Disease, Mount Sinai Med Ctr 1986

Stoupakis, George MD (Cv) - **Spec Exp:** Interventional Cardiology; Angioplasty & Stent Placement; **Hospital:** Hackensack Univ Med Ctr (page 96), Englewood Hosp & Med Ctr; **Address:** Metropolitan Cardiovascular Cons, 5 Summit Ave, Ste 200, Hackensack, NJ 07601; **Phone:** 201-343-7001; **Board Cert:** Cardiovascular Disease 2004; Interventional Cardiology 2005; **Med School:** Grenada 1998; **Resid:** Internal Medicine, UMDNJ/ Univ Hosp 2001; **Fellow:** Cardiovascular Disease, UMDNJ/ Univ Hosp 2004; Interventional Cardiology, North Shore Univ Hosp 2005

Teichholz, Louis E MD (Cv) - **Spec Exp:** Mitral Valve Disease; Complementary Medicine; Echocardiography; Cholesterol/Lipid Disorders; **Hospital:** Hackensack Univ Med Ctr (page 96); **Address:** Hackensack Univ Med Ctr, Cardiology, 30 Prospect Ave, 4-Main, rm 4655, Hackensack, NJ 07601; **Phone:** 551-996-2314; **Board Cert:** Internal Medicine 1972; Cardiovascular Disease 1975; **Med School:** Harvard Med Sch 1966; **Resid:** Internal Medicine, Brigham & Womens Hosp 1968; **Fellow:** Cardiovascular Disease, Brigham & Womens Hosp 1972; **Fac Appt:** Prof Med, UMDNJ-NJ Med Sch, Newark

Wild, David MD (Cv) - **Hospital:** Holy Name Med Ctr (page 738), Hackensack Univ Med Ctr (page 96); **Address:** Cardiovascular Assocs of Teaneck, 954 Teaneck Rd, Teaneck, NJ 7666; **Phone:** 201-833-2300; **Board Cert:** Cardiovascular Disease 2008; Internal Medicine 2005; **Med School:** Rutgers R W Johnson Med Sch 2002; **Resid:** Internal Medicine, Montefiore Med Ctr 2005; **Fellow:** Cardiovascular Disease, St Lukes-Roosevelt Hosp Ctr 2008

Williams, Marcus L MD (Cv) - **Spec Exp:** Cholesterol/Lipid Disorders; Hypertension; Atrial Fibrillation; Coronary Artery Disease; **Hospital:** Chilton Med Ctr (page 92), Valley Hosp (page 739); **Address:** Cardiac Assocs N Jersey, 43 Yawpo Ave, Ste 2, Oakland, NJ 07436; **Phone:** 201-337-0066; **Board Cert:** Internal Medicine 1985; Cardiovascular Disease 1989; **Med School:** Geo Wash Univ 1982; **Resid:** Internal Medicine, NC Meml Hosp 1985; **Fellow:** Cardiovascular Disease, NC Meml Hosp 1988

Child & Adolescent Psychiatry

Kotler, Lisa A MD (ChAP) - **Spec Exp:** Eating Disorders; ADD/ADHD; Depression; Anxiety Disorders; **Hospital:** NYU Langone Med Ctr (page 104); **Address:** NYU Child Study Ctr-Hackensack, 411 Hackensack Ave Fl 7, Hackensack, NJ 07601; **Phone:** 201-465-8111; **Board Cert:** Psychiatry 2008; Child & Adolescent Psychiatry 2009; **Med School:** Yale Univ 1993; **Resid:** Psychiatry, Mt Sinai Med Ctr 1996; **Fellow:** Child & Adolescent Psychiatry, Columbia-Presby Med Ctr 1998; Eating Disorders Research, NY State Psyc Inst-Columbia Presby MC 1999; **Fac Appt:** Asst Clin Prof Psyc, NYU Sch Med

Pincus, Emile I MD (ChAP) - **Spec Exp:** Substance Abuse; Suicide; ADD/ADHD; Anxiety & Depression; **Address:** 912 Kinderkamack Rd Fl 2, River Edge, NJ 07661; **Phone:** 201-615-1352; **Board Cert:** Psychiatry 1986; Child & Adolescent Psychiatry 2004; **Med School:** Mount Sinai Sch Med 1978; **Resid:** Psychiatry, St Lukes Hosp Ctr 1979; Psychiatry, Mt Sinai Med Ctr 1982; **Fellow:** Child & Adolescent Psychiatry, New York Hosp-Cornell Med Ctr 1984

Child Neurology

Cope, Jennifer A MD (ChiN) - **Spec Exp:** Epilepsy/Seizure Disorders; **Hospital:** Valley Hosp (page 739); **Address:** Neurology Grp of Bergen County, 1200 E Ridgewood Ave, Ste 208, Fl 2, East Wing, Ridgewood, NJ 07450; **Phone:** 201-444-0868; **Board Cert:** Child Neurology 2005; **Med School:** SUNY Hlth Sci Ctr 1995; **Resid:** Pediatrics, Schneider Chldns Hosp/LIJ Med Ctr 1997; **Fellow:** Pediatric Neurology, Mount Sinai Hosp 2000; Neurophysiology, NYU Affil Hosp 2001

Heilbroner, Peter L MD/PhD (ChiN) - **Spec Exp:** Pediatric Neurology; ADD/ADHD; **Hospital:** Valley Hosp (page 739); **Address:** Neurology Group Of Bergen County, 1200 E Ridgewood Ave, W Wing Fl 2, Ridgewood, NJ 07450; **Phone:** 201-444-0868; **Board Cert:** Child Neurology 2011; **Med School:** Rutgers R W Johnson Med Sch 1993; **Resid:** Pediatric Neurology, NYU Med Ctr 1997

Sousa, Rolando MD (ChiN) - **Spec Exp:** Epilepsy; Autism; Neurofibromatosis; **Hospital:** NYU Langone Med Ctr (page 104); **Address:** 20 Prospect Ave, Hackensack, NJ 07601; **Phone:** 201-518-7290; **Board Cert:** Pediatrics 2009; **Med School:** Panama 1990; **Resid:** Pediatrics, Newark Beth Israel Med Ctr 1998; **Fellow:** Child Neurology, NYU Med Ctr 2002; Clinical Neurophysiology, NYU Med Ctr 2003; **Fac Appt:** Asst Clin Prof N, NYU Sch Med

Clinical Genetics

Pedro, Helio F MD (CG) - **Spec Exp:** Pediatric Clinical Genetics; Chromosome Disorders; Inherited Disorders; **Hospital:** Hackensack Univ Med Ctr (page 96); **Address:** 30 Prospect Ave, Don Imus Bldg, Ste 210, Hackensack, NJ 07601; **Phone:** 551-996-5264; **Board Cert:** Clinical Genetics 2005; Clinical Biochemical Genetics 2007; **Med School:** Grenada 1995; **Resid:** Pediatrics, UMDNJ Univ Hosp 1999; **Fellow:** Clinical Genetics, UMDNJ Univ Hosp 2003; **Fac Appt:** Asst Prof Ped, UMDNJ-Rutgers Med Sch

Colon & Rectal Surgery

Gallina, Gregory J MD (CRS) - **Spec Exp:** Minimally Invasive Surgery; Incontinence-Fecal; Colon Cancer Screening; Robotic Surgery; **Hospital:** Hackensack Univ Med Ctr (page 96), St. Joseph's Regl Med Ctr - Paterson; **Address:** 255 W Spring Valley Ave, Ste 103, Maywood, NJ 07607; **Phone:** 201-525-1031; **Board Cert:** Colon & Rectal Surgery 2011; **Med School:** Geo Wash Univ 1992; **Resid:** Surgery, Univ Hosp-UMDNJ 1997; **Fellow:** Colon & Rectal Surgery, SUNY Buffalo Affil Hosp 1998

Helbraun, Mark E MD (CRS) - **Hospital:** Hackensack Univ Med Ctr (page 96); **Address:** 20 Prospect Ave, Ste 811, Hackensack, NJ 07601; **Phone:** 201-525-1660; **Board Cert:** Colon & Rectal Surgery 1978; **Med School:** Wayne State Univ 1972; **Resid:** Surgery, New York Hosp-Cornell 1977; **Fellow:** Colon & Rectal Surgery, Lahey Clin 1978

Nizin, Joel S MD (CRS) - **Spec Exp:** Colon Cancer; Inflammatory Bowel Disease; **Hospital:** Valley Hosp (page 739), Chilton Med Ctr (page 92); **Address:** 85 Harristown Rd, Ste 105, Glenrock, NJ 07452; **Phone:** 201-689-9100; **Board Cert:** Colon & Rectal Surgery 1987; Surgery 2008; **Med School:** Howard Univ 1978; **Resid:** Surgery, St Luke's Hosp 1983; **Fellow:** Colon & Rectal Surgery, Univ Minn Med Ctr 1984

Waxenbaum, Steven I MD (CRS) - **Spec Exp:** Laparoscopic Surgery; Hemorrhoids; Colon Cancer; Rectal Cancer; **Hospital:** Valley Hosp (page 739), Englewood Hosp & Med Ctr; **Address:** 216 Engle St, Englewood, NJ 07631; **Phone:** 201-567-7615; **Board Cert:** Surgery 2003; Colon & Rectal Surgery 2006; **Med School:** Rutgers R W Johnson Med Sch 1988; **Resid:** Surgery, Westchester Med Ctr 1993; **Fellow:** Colon & Rectal Surgery, Lehigh Valley Hosp 1994

White, Ronald A MD (CRS) - **Spec Exp:** Hemorrhoids; Colon & Rectal Cancer; Colonoscopy; **Hospital:** Englewood Hosp & Med Ctr, Valley Hosp (page 739); **Address:** 216 Engle St, Ste 203, Englewood, NJ 07631-2428; **Phone:** 201-567-7615; **Board Cert:** Colon & Rectal Surgery 1988; **Med School:** Boston Univ 1981; **Resid:** Surgery, Montefiore Hosp 1986; **Fellow:** Colon & Rectal Surgery, RW Johnson Med Sch 1987

Dermatology

Andrews, Alan D MD (D) - **Spec Exp:** Skin Cancer; Phototherapy; **Hospital:** NY-Presby/Columbia Univ Med Ctr, NY (page 102), Holy Name Med Ctr (page 738); **Address:** 500 Piermont Rd, Ste 101, Closter, NJ 07624; **Phone:** 201-767-0501; **Board Cert:** Dermatology 1979; **Med School:** Univ VA Sch Med 1972; **Resid:** Dermatology, Natl Canc Inst 1975; **Fellow:** Dermatology, Columbia-Presby Med Ctr 1979

Ashinoff, Robin MD (D) - **Spec Exp:** Mohs Surgery; Laser Surgery; Cosmetic Dermatology; Melanoma; **Hospital:** Hackensack Univ Med Ctr (page 96), NYU Langone Med Ctr (page 104); **Address:** 360 Essex St, Ste 201, Hackensack, NJ 07601; **Phone:** 551-996-8660; **Board Cert:** Dermatology 2009; **Med School:** NYU Sch Med 1985; **Resid:** Dermatology, NYU Med Ctr 1989; **Fellow:** Mohs Surgery, NYU Med Ctr 1991; **Fac Appt:** Assoc Clin Prof D, NYU Sch Med

Brauner, Gary J MD (D) - **Spec Exp:** Skin Laser Surgery; Black/Asian Skin Care; Cosmetic Dermatology; Hair Removal-Laser; **Hospital:** Englewood Hosp & Med Ctr, Mt Sinai Hosp; **Address:** 1625 Anderson Ave, Ste 201, Fort Lee, NJ 07024; **Phone:** 201-461-5522; **Board Cert:** Dermatology 1972; Dermatopathology 1978; **Med School:** Harvard Med Sch 1967; **Resid:** Dermatology, Mass Genl Hosp 1971; **Fac Appt:** Assoc Clin Prof D, Mount Sinai Sch Med

Fishman, Miriam MD (D) - **Spec Exp:** Pediatric Dermatology; Skin Cancer; **Hospital:** Englewood Hosp & Med Ctr; **Address:** 216 Engle St, Ste 104, Englewood, NJ 07631-2428; **Phone:** 201-569-5678; **Board Cert:** Dermatology 2009; **Med School:** NYU Sch Med 1978; **Resid:** Pediatrics, Montefiore Med Ctr 1981; Dermatology, Montefiore Med Ctr 1984

Fried, Sharon Z MD (D) - **Spec Exp:** Skin Cancer; Acne; Psoriasis; **Hospital:** Englewood Hosp & Med Ctr; **Address:** 180 N Dean St, Ste 2 South, Englewood, NJ 07631-2534; **Phone:** 201-569-9800; **Board Cert:** Internal Medicine 1983; Dermatology 2009; **Med School:** NYU Sch Med 1980; **Resid:** Internal Medicine, NYU Med Ctr 1983; Dermatology, SUNY Downstate HSC 1985

Giardina-Beckett, MarieAnn MD (D) - **Spec Exp:** Acne; Botox Therapy; **Hospital:** Meadowlands Hosp Med Ctr, St. Mary's Hosp - Passaic; **Address:** 71 Union Ave, Ste 108, Rutherford, NJ 07070; **Phone:** 201-804-8900; **Board Cert:** Dermatology 2009; **Med School:** NY Med Coll 1986; **Resid:** Dermatology, New York Med Coll 1990

Grodberg, Michele MD (D) - **Spec Exp:** Cosmetic Dermatology; Hair Removal-Laser; Botox Therapy; Facial Rejuvenation; **Hospital:** Englewood Hosp & Med Ctr; **Address:** 106 Grand Ave Fl 3, Englewood, NJ 07631-3574; **Phone:** 201-567-8884; **Board Cert:** Dermatology 2009; **Med School:** NYU Sch Med 1987; **Resid:** Dermatology, NYU Med Ctr 1991

Heldman, Jay MD (D) - **Spec Exp:** Dermatologic Surgery; **Hospital:** Valley Hosp (page 739); **Address:** 23-00 Route 208 S, Fair Lawn, NJ 07410-1559; **Phone:** 201-797-7770; **Board Cert:** Dermatology 1981; **Med School:** Columbia P&S 1977; **Resid:** Dermatology, Mount Sinai Hosp 1981

Morman, Manuel R MD/PhD (D) - **Spec Exp:** Mohs Surgery; Skin Cancer; Reconstructive Surgery; **Hospital:** St. Mary's Hosp - Passaic; **Address:** 47 Orient Way, Rutherford, NJ 07070-2040; **Phone:** 201-460-0280; **Board Cert:** Dermatology 2009; **Med School:** Jefferson Med Coll 1976; **Resid:** Dermatology, Hosp Univ Penn 1979; **Fellow:** Chemosurgery, Cleveland Clinic 1980

Possick, Paul MD (D) - **Spec Exp:** Skin Cancer; Contact Dermatitis; Eczema; Psoriasis; **Hospital:** NYU Langone Med Ctr (page 104); **Address:** 390 Old Hook Rd Fl 2, Westwood, NJ 07675-2616; **Phone:** 201-666-9550; **Board Cert:** Dermatology 2009; **Med School:** Tufts Univ 1964; **Resid:** Internal Medicine, Montefiore Hosp 1966; Dermatology, Univ Hosp 1968; **Fac Appt:** Asst Prof D, NYU Sch Med

Rapaport, Jeffrey A MD (D) - **Spec Exp:** Cosmetic Dermatology; Scar Revision; Laser Surgery; Skin Laser Surgery; **Hospital:** Holy Name Med Ctr (page 738), Englewood Hosp & Med Ctr; **Address:** 333 Sylvan Ave Fl 2 - Ste 207, Englewood Cliffs, NJ 07632; **Phone:** 201-227-1555; **Board Cert:** Dermatology 1983; **Med School:** Emory Univ 1978; **Resid:** Dermatology, Jefferson Univ Hosp 1982

Scherl, Sharon MD (D) - **Spec Exp:** Acne; Cosmetic Dermatology; Photodynamic Therapy; Tattoo Removal; **Hospital:** Englewood Hosp & Med Ctr; **Address:** 45 Central Ave, Tenafly, NJ 07670; **Phone:** 201-568-8400; **Board Cert:** Dermatology 2010; **Med School:** NY Med Coll 1988; **Resid:** Dermatology, Metropolitian Hosp Ctr 1992

Shin, Helen T MD (D) - **Spec Exp:** Pediatric Dermatology; **Hospital:** Hackensack Univ Med Ctr (page 96); **Address:** 155 Polifly Rd, Ste 101, Hackensack, NJ 07601; **Phone:** 551-996-8697; **Board Cert:** Dermatology 2014; Pediatric Dermatology 2014; **Med School:** Cornell Univ-Weill Med Coll 1995; **Resid:** Pediatric Surgery, Mt Sinai Med Ctr 1997; Dermatology, NY Presby Hosp/Cornell 2000; **Fellow:** Pediatric Dermatology, NYU Med Ctr 2001

Sweeney, Eugene W MD (D) - **Spec Exp:** Skin Cancer; Pediatric Dermatology; Acne; **Hospital:** Holy Name Med Ctr (page 738), Englewood Hosp & Med Ctr; **Address:** 757 N Teaneck Rd, Teaneck, NJ 07666-4241; **Phone:** 201-837-3939; **Board Cert:** Dermatology 1967; **Med School:** NY Med Coll 1960; **Resid:** Dermatology, Columbia-Presby Med Ctr 1966; **Fac Appt:** Assoc Clin Prof D, Columbia P&S

Weiss, Darryl S MD (D) - **Spec Exp:** Hair Restoration/Transplant; Cosmetic Dermatology; Skin Laser Surgery; **Hospital:** Valley Hosp (page 739); **Address:** 23-00 Route 208 S, Fairlawn, NJ 07410; **Phone:** 201-797-7770; **Board Cert:** Dermatology 1990; **Med School:** Med Coll VA 1986; **Resid:** Dermatology, Jackson Meml Hosp 1990

Diagnostic Radiology

Arams, Ronald S MD (DR) - **Spec Exp:** Body Imaging; Interventional Radiology; **Hospital:** Valley Hosp (page 739); **Address:** Radiology Assocs of Ridgewood, 20 Franklin Tpke, Waldwick, NJ 07463; **Phone:** 201-445-8822; **Board Cert:** Diagnostic Radiology 1990; Vascular & Interventional Radiology 2008; **Med School:** Cornell Univ-Weill Med Coll 1985; **Resid:** Diagnostic Radiology, NYU Med Ctr/Bellevue Hosp 1990; **Fellow:** Vascular & Interventional Radiology, NYU Med Ctr/Bellevue Hosp 1993; Brain Imaging, NYU Med Ctr/Bellevue Hosp 1994

Budin, Joel A MD (DR) - **Spec Exp:** Neuroradiology; **Hospital:** Hackensack Univ Med Ctr (page 96); **Address:** 30 Prospect Ave, Hackensack, NJ 07601; **Phone:** 201-488-2660; **Board Cert:** Diagnostic Radiology 1975; **Med School:** Columbia P&S 1969; **Resid:** Diagnostic Radiology, Columbia-Presby Med Ctr 1975

Calem-Grunat, Jaclyn A MD (DR) - **Spec Exp:** Breast Imaging; Ultrasound; **Hospital:** Valley Hosp (page 739); **Address:** Radiology Assocs of Ridgewood, 20 Franklin Tpke, Waldwick, NJ 07463; **Phone:** 201-445-8822; **Board Cert:** Diagnostic Radiology 1994; **Med School:** Mount Sinai Sch Med 1988; **Resid:** Internal Medicine, Beth Israel Med Ctr 1990; Diagnostic Radiology, Harbor-UCLA Med Ctr 1994; **Fellow:** Breast Imaging, UCLA Med Ctr 1995

Chu, Regina W MD (DR) - **Spec Exp:** Mammography; MRI; Thoracic Imaging; Breast Imaging; **Hospital:** Hackensack Univ Med Ctr (page 96); **Address:** 20 Prospect Ave, Ste 513, Hackensack, NJ 07601-1914; **Phone:** 551-996-2200; **Board Cert:** Diagnostic Radiology 1998; **Med School:** Albany Med Coll 1993; **Resid:** Internal Medicine, Lenox Hill Hosp 1994; Diagnostic Radiology, St Luke's-Roosevelt Hosp Ctr 1998

Goldfischer, Mindy A MD (DR) - **Spec Exp:** Breast Imaging; Ultrasound; **Hospital:** Englewood Hosp & Med Ctr; **Address:** 350 Engle St, Englewood, NJ 07631; **Phone:** 201-894-3480; **Board Cert:** Diagnostic Radiology 1986; **Med School:** NYU Sch Med 1982; **Resid:** Diagnostic Radiology, Montefiore Med Ctr 1986; **Fellow:** Diagnostic Radiology, Thomas Jefferson Univ Hosp 1987

Gross, Joshua David MD (DR) - **Spec Exp:** Breast Imaging; Breast Cancer; **Hospital:** Holy Name Med Ctr (page 738); **Address:** Holy Name Hosp, Breast Imaging, 718 Teaneck Rd, Teaneck, NJ 07666; **Phone:** 201-833-7100; **Board Cert:** Diagnostic Radiology 1984; **Med School:** Albert Einstein Coll Med 1980; **Resid:** Diagnostic Radiology, Einstein/Jacobi Hosp 1984

Krinsky, Glenn MD (DR) - **Spec Exp:** MRI; Musculoskeletal Imaging; Gastrointestinal Imaging; **Hospital:** Valley Hosp (page 739); **Address:** Radiology Assocs of Ridgewood, 20 Franklin Tpke, Waldwick, NJ 07463; **Phone:** 201-445-8822; **Board Cert:** Diagnostic Radiology 1994; **Med School:** NYU Sch Med 1988; **Resid:** Surgical Pathology, Bellevue Hosp 1990; Diagnostic Radiology, Bellevue Hosp 1993; **Fellow:** Magnetic Resonance Imaging, NYU/Bellevue Hosp 1994

Levy, Lauren S MD (DR) - **Spec Exp:** Mammography; Breast MRI; Breast Imaging; **Hospital:** Valley Hosp (page 739); **Address:** Radiology Assocs of Ridgewood, 20 Franklin Tpke, Waldwick, NJ 07463; **Phone:** 201-445-8822; **Board Cert:** Diagnostic Radiology 1996; **Med School:** SUNY Downstate 1991; **Resid:** Diagnostic Radiology, NYU-Bellevue Hosp 1996; **Fellow:** Mammography, NYU-Bellevue Hosp 1997

Liebling, Melissa Schubach MD (DR) - **Spec Exp:** Pediatric Radiology; **Hospital:** Hackensack Univ Med Ctr (page 96); **Address:** Hackensack Univ Med Ctr, Dept Radiology, 30 Prospect Ave, Hackensack, NJ 07601; **Phone:** 201-996-2200; **Board Cert:** Diagnostic Radiology 1992; Pediatric Radiology 2006; **Med School:** Albany Med Coll 1987; **Resid:** Diagnostic Radiology, Columbia-Presby Med Ctr 1992; **Fellow:** Pediatric Radiology, Columbia-Presby/Babies Hosp 1994

Lubat, Edward MD (DR) - **Spec Exp:** Abdominal Imaging; Thoracic Radiology; Musculoskeletal Imaging; Nuclear Medicine; **Hospital:** Valley Hosp (page 739); **Address:** Radiology Assocs of Ridgewood, 20 Franklin Tpke, Waldwick, NJ 07463-1749; **Phone:** 201-445-8822; **Board Cert:** Diagnostic Radiology 1989; Nuclear Medicine 1989; **Med School:** Jefferson Med Coll 1982; **Resid:** Diagnostic Radiology, Beth Israel Med Ctr 1984; Diagnostic Radiology, NYU Med Ctr 1988; **Fellow:** Nuclear Medicine, NYU Med Ctr 1985

Panush, David MD (DR) - **Spec Exp:** Neuroradiology; **Hospital:** Hackensack Univ Med Ctr (page 96); **Address:** Hackensack Radiology Group, 30 Prospect Ave, Hackensack, NJ 07601; **Phone:** 551-996-2254; **Board Cert:** Diagnostic Radiology 1990; **Med School:** Albert Einstein Coll Med 1985; **Resid:** Radiology, Montefiore Med Ctr 1990; **Fellow:** Neuroradiology, Yale-New Haven Hosp 1992

Rakow, Joel Ivan MD (DR) - **Spec Exp:** Ultrasound; **Hospital:** Hackensack Univ Med Ctr (page 96); **Address:** Hackensack Univ Med Ctr, Dept Radiology, 30 Prospect Ave, Hackensack, NJ 07601; **Phone:** 201-996-2200; **Board Cert:** Diagnostic Radiology 1986; **Med School:** Albert Einstein Coll Med 1982; **Resid:** Diagnostic Radiology, Montefiore Med Ctr 1986; **Fellow:** Ultrasound, Thomas Jefferson Med Ctr 1987

Rambler, Louis MD (DR) - **Spec Exp:** Ultrasound; **Hospital:** Valley Hosp (page 739); **Address:** Radiology Assocs of Ridgewood, 20 Franklin Tpke, Waldwick, NJ 07463-1749; **Phone:** 201-445-8822; **Board Cert:** Diagnostic Radiology 1977; **Med School:** Cornell Univ-Weill Med Coll 1971; **Resid:** Diagnostic Radiology, Columbia-Presby Med Ctr 1977

Shapiro, Mark Linden MD (DR) - **Hospital:** Englewood Hosp & Med Ctr; **Address:** Englewood Hosp, Dept Radiology, 350 Engle St, Englewood, NJ 07631; **Phone:** 201-894-3480; **Board Cert:** Diagnostic Radiology 1993; **Med School:** SUNY Hlth Sci Ctr 1988; **Resid:** Diagnostic Radiology, North Shore Univ Hosp 1993; **Fellow:** Magnetic Resonance Imaging, Hosp U Penn 1994

Toth, Patrick J MD (DR) - **Spec Exp:** Abdominal Imaging; Thoracic Radiology; Interventional Radiology; Nuclear Radiology; **Hospital:** Hackensack Univ Med Ctr (page 96); **Address:** Hackensack Univ Med Ctr, Dept Radiology, 30 Prospect Ave, Hackensack, NJ 07601; **Phone:** 201-996-2200; **Board Cert:** Diagnostic Radiology 1988; **Med School:** Yale Univ 1982; **Resid:** Surgery, Yale-New Haven Hosp 1984; Diagnostic Radiology, NYU Med Ctr 1987; **Fellow:** Body Imaging, NYU Med Ctr 1988; Interventional Radiology, NYU Med Ctr 1989; **Fac Appt:** Asst Clin Prof Rad, NYU Sch Med

Endocrinology, Diabetes & Metabolism

Cobin, Rhoda H MD (EDM) - **Spec Exp:** Thyroid Disorders; Diabetes; Pituitary Disorders; **Hospital:** Valley Hosp (page 739), Mt Sinai Hosp; **Address:** 75 N Maple Ave, Ste 202, Ridgewood, NJ 07450; **Phone:** 201-444-5552; **Board Cert:** Internal Medicine 1972; Endocrinology, Diabetes & Metabolism 1975; **Med School:** Univ Puerto Rico 1969; **Resid:** Internal Medicine, Beth Israel Med Ctr 1972; **Fellow:** Endocrinology, Diabetes & Metabolism, Mt Sinai Hosp 1974; **Fac Appt:** Clin Prof Med, Mount Sinai Sch Med

Daud-Ahmad, Sameera MD (EDM) - **Spec Exp:** Thyroid Disorders; Diabetes; Polycystic Ovarian Syndrome; **Hospital:** Hackensack Univ Med Ctr (page 96), Valley Hosp (page 739); **Address:** Old Hook Medical Assocs, 452 Old Hook Rd, Emerson, NJ 07630; **Phone:** 201-666-3900 x307; **Board Cert:** Internal Medicine 2007; Endocrinology, Diabetes & Metabolism 2009; **Med School:** Pakistan 2002; **Resid:** Internal Medicine, Loma Linda Univ Med Ctr 2006; Internal Medicine, Overlook Hosp 2007; **Fellow:** Endocrinology, Cleveland Clin 2009

Goldman, Michael MD (EDM) - **Spec Exp:** Thyroid Disorders; Diabetes; Pituitary Disorders; Cholesterol/Lipid Disorders; **Hospital:** Englewood Hosp & Med Ctr; **Address:** 600 E Palisade Ave, Ste 1, Englewood Cliffs, NJ 07632-1826; **Phone:** 201-568-1108; **Board Cert:** Internal Medicine 1980; Endocrinology, Diabetes & Metabolism 1981; **Med School:** NY Med Coll 1973; **Resid:** Internal Medicine, Englewood Hosp 1978; **Fellow:** Endocrinology, Diabetes & Metabolism, Columbia-Presby Med Ctr 1980; **Fac Appt:** Asst Prof Med, Mount Sinai Sch Med

Schwartz, Joseph J MD (EDM) - **Hospital:** Holy Name Med Ctr (page 738), Englewood Hosp & Med Ctr; **Address:** 229 Engle St, Englewood, NJ 07631; **Phone:** 201-567-8999; **Board Cert:** Internal Medicine 2011; Endocrinology, Diabetes & Metabolism 2013; **Med School:** Albert Einstein Coll Med 1998; **Resid:** Internal Medicine, LIJ Med Ctr 2001; **Fellow:** Endocrinology, Diabetes & Metabolism, Mt Sinai Med Ctr 2003

Tohme, Jack F MD (EDM) - **Spec Exp:** Osteoporosis; Thyroid Disorders; Diabetes; **Hospital:** Valley Hosp (page 739); **Address:** 265 Ackerman Ave, Ste 101, Ridgewood, NJ 07450-4203; **Phone:** 201-444-4363; **Board Cert:** Internal Medicine 1978; Endocrinology, Diabetes & Metabolism 1979; **Med School:** Amer Univ Beirut 1974; **Resid:** Internal Medicine, American Univ Hosp 1976; **Fellow:** Endocrinology, Diabetes & Metabolism, Columbia-Presby Med Ctr 1977; Endocrinology, Diabetes & Metabolism, Barnes Jewish Hosp 1978; **Fac Appt:** Assoc Clin Prof Med, Columbia P&S

Wehmann, Robert MD/PhD (EDM) - **Spec Exp:** Diabetes; Thyroid Disorders; Pituitary Disorders; **Hospital:** Valley Hosp (page 739), Hackensack Univ Med Ctr (page 96); **Address:** 54 Orchard St, Hillsdale, NJ 07642; **Phone:** 201-666-1400; **Board Cert:** Internal Medicine 1977; Endocrinology 1979; **Med School:** Albany Med Coll 1974; **Resid:** Internal Medicine, VA Med Ctr 1976; **Fellow:** Endocrinology, Natl Inst Hlth 1979

Wiesen, Mark MD (EDM) - **Spec Exp:** Diabetes; Thyroid Disorders; Osteoporosis; **Hospital:** Hackensack Univ Med Ctr (page 96), Holy Name Med Ctr (page 738); **Address:** 870 Palisade Ave, Ste 203, Teaneck, NJ 07666; **Phone:** 201-836-5655; **Board Cert:** Internal Medicine 1978; Endocrinology, Diabetes & Metabolism 1981; **Med School:** Columbia P&S 1975; **Resid:** Internal Medicine, Brookdale Hosp 1978; **Fellow:** Endocrinology, Diabetes & Metabolism, Mt Sinai Hosp 1981; **Fac Appt:** Asst Clin Prof Med, UMDNJ-NJ Med Sch, Newark

Family Medicine

Beauchamp, Donald P MD (FMed) *PCP* - **Hospital:** Valley Hosp (page 739); **Address:** Prospect Medical Office, 301 Godwin Ave, Midland Park, NJ 07432; **Phone:** 201-444-4526; **Board Cert:** Family Medicine 2010; **Med School:** Temple Univ 2000; **Resid:** Family Medicine, Chestnut Hill Hosp 2003

Bello, Mary R MD (FMed) *PCP* - **Spec Exp:** Adolescent Medicine; Geriatric Medicine; **Hospital:** Valley Hosp (page 739); **Address:** 400 Franklin Tpke, Ste 106, Mahwah, NJ 07430-3517; **Phone:** 201-327-3333; **Board Cert:** Family Medicine 2010; **Med School:** Dominica 1984; **Resid:** Family Medicine, St Joseph's Hosp 1987; **Fac Appt:** Asst Clin Prof FMed, UMDNJ-NJ Med Sch, Newark

Cassotta, Joseph MD (FMed) *PCP* - **Spec Exp:** Preventive Medicine; **Hospital:** Holy Name Med Ctr (page 738); **Address:** 1600 Center Ave, Fort Lee, NJ 07024-4731; **Phone:** 201-585-7511; **Board Cert:** Family Medicine 2006; **Med School:** Mexico 1979; **Resid:** Family Medicine, John F Kennedy Med Ctr 1985

Gross, Harvey MD (FMed) *PCP* - **Spec Exp:** Geriatric Medicine; Dementia; Myasthenia Gravis; **Hospital:** Englewood Hosp & Med Ctr, Holy Name Med Ctr (page 738); **Address:** 370 Grand Ave, Ste 102, Englewood, NJ 07631; **Phone:** 201-567-3370; **Board Cert:** Family Medicine 2005; Geriatric Medicine 2010; **Med School:** Boston Univ 1970; **Resid:** Family Medicine, Southside Hosp 1974; **Fac Appt:** Asst Clin Prof Med, Mount Sinai Sch Med

Karatoprak, Ohan MD (FMed) *PCP* - **Spec Exp:** Nutrition; Asthma; Obesity; Geriatric Medicine; **Hospital:** Holy Name Med Ctr (page 738); **Address:** 420 Deerwood Rd, Fort Lee, NJ 07024-1643; **Phone:** 201-886-8877; **Board Cert:** Family Medicine 2005; **Med School:** Turkey 1977; **Resid:** Surgery, Brookdale Univ Hosp 1983; Family Medicine, Southside Hosp 1986; **Fac Appt:** Asst Clin Prof FMed, UMDNJ-NJ Med Sch, Newark

Leipsner, George MD (FMed) *PCP* - **Hospital:** Hackensack Univ Med Ctr (page 96); **Address:** 57 W Pleasant Ave, Maywood, NJ 07607-1334; **Phone:** 201-488-2111; **Board Cert:** Family Medicine 2001; **Med School:** Italy 1966; **Resid:** Family Medicine, Hackensack Hosp 1968; **Fac Appt:** Asst Clin Prof FMed, UMDNJ-Rutgers Med Sch

McConnell, Julie W MD (FMed) - **Spec Exp:** Preventive Medicine; **Hospital:** Hackensack UMC-Pascack Valley (page 737); **Address:** Bergen Medical Assocs, 466 Old Hook Rd, Ste 1, Emerson, NJ 07630; **Phone:** 201-967-8221; **Board Cert:** Family Medicine 2013; **Med School:** Univ Miami Sch Med 2000; **Resid:** Family Medicine, Jackson Meml Hosp 2003

Wilkin, Daniel J DO (FMed) *PCP* - **Spec Exp:** Geriatric Care; Palliative Care; **Hospital:** Valley Hosp (page 739), Englewood Hosp & Med Ctr; **Address:** Bergen Primary Care Assocs, 680 Kinderkamack Rd, Ste 205, Oradell, NJ 07649; **Phone:** 201-262-0608; **Board Cert:** Family Medicine 2005; Hospice & Palliative Medicine 2012; **Med School:** Philadelphia Coll Osteo Med 2002; **Resid:** Family Medicine, JFK Med Ctr 2005

Gastroenterology

Avezzano, Eric S MD (Ge) - **Spec Exp:** Endoscopy; Peptic Acid Disorders; Celiac Disease; Gastroesophageal Reflux Disease (GERD); **Hospital:** Valley Hosp (page 739), Hackensack UMC-Pascack Valley (page 737); **Address:** Bergen Gastroenterology, 466 Old Hook Rd, Ste 1, Emerson, NJ 07630; **Phone:** 201-967-8221; **Board Cert:** Internal Medicine 1988; Gastroenterology 2011; **Med School:** SUNY Stony Brook 1985; **Resid:** Internal Medicine, G Washington Univ Hosp 1988; **Fellow:** Gastroenterology, Georgetown Univ 1990

Broussard, Crystal N MD (Ge) - **Spec Exp:** Women's Health; **Hospital:** Valley Hosp (page 739), Hackensack UMC-Pascack Valley (page 737); **Address:** Bergen Gastroenterology, 466 Old Hook Rd, Ste 1, Emerson, NJ 07630; **Phone:** 201-967-8221; **Board Cert:** Internal Medicine 2008; Gastroenterology 2009; **Med School:** Case West Res Univ 1992; **Resid:** Internal Medicine, Johns Hopkins Bayview Med Ctr 1995; **Fellow:** Gastroenterology, Cleveland Clinic 1998

DeLillo, Anthony R MD (Ge) - **Spec Exp:** Inflammatory Bowel Disease; Esophageal Disorders; **Hospital:** Valley Hosp (page 739), Hackensack UMC-Pascack Valley (page 737); **Address:** Bergen Gastroenterology, 466 Old Hook Rd, Ste 1, Emerson, NJ 07630; **Phone:** 201-967-8221; **Board Cert:** Gastroenterology 2011; **Med School:** Cornell Univ-Weill Med Coll 1994; **Resid:** Internal Medicine, Mt Sinai Med Ctr 1997; **Fellow:** Gastroenterology, Mt Sinai Med Ctr 2001

Fried, Harry A MD (Ge) - **Hospital:** Englewood Hosp & Med Ctr; **Address:** 333 Old Hook Rd, Ste 101, Westwood, NJ 07675; **Phone:** 201-594-0535; **Board Cert:** Internal Medicine 1989; Gastroenterology 2005; **Med School:** SUNY Downstate 1986; **Resid:** Internal Medicine, St Lukes Hosp 1989; **Fellow:** Gastroenterology, Cooper Hosp 1995

Friedrich, Ivan MD (Ge) - **Spec Exp:** Colonoscopy; Inflammatory Bowel Disease; Constipation; Gastroesophageal Reflux Disease (GERD); **Hospital:** Englewood Hosp & Med Ctr, Holy Name Med Ctr (page 738); **Address:** 420 Grand Ave, Englewood, NJ 07631-4152; **Phone:** 201-569-7044; **Board Cert:** Internal Medicine 1979; Gastroenterology 1981; **Med School:** Albany Med Coll 1976; **Resid:** Internal Medicine, Montefiore Med Ctr 1979; **Fellow:** Gastroenterology, Mt Sinai Med Ctr 1982; **Fac Appt:** Asst Clin Prof Med, Mount Sinai Sch Med

Goldfarb, Joel A MD (Ge) - **Spec Exp:** Colonoscopy/Polypectomy; Colon Cancer; Hepatitis; Liver Disease; **Hospital:** Holy Name Med Ctr (page 738), Englewood Hosp & Med Ctr; **Address:** 1086 Teaneck Rd, Ste 4C, Teaneck, NJ 07666; **Phone:** 201-837-9449; **Board Cert:** Internal Medicine 1978; Gastroenterology 1981; **Med School:** NYU Sch Med 1975; **Resid:** Internal Medicine, NYU Med Ctr 1978; Hepatology, Yale-New Haven Hosp 1979; **Fellow:** Gastroenterology, NY-Presby/Columbia Univ Med Ctr 1981; **Fac Appt:** Asst Clin Prof Med, Mount Sinai-Icahn Sch of Med

Klein, Walter A MD (Ge) - **Spec Exp:** Esophageal Disorders; Gastroesophageal Reflux Disease (GERD); Colon Polyps & Cancer; **Hospital:** Englewood Hosp & Med Ctr; **Address:** The Park Medical Group, 274 County Rd, Ste A, Tenafly, NJ 07670; **Phone:** 201-568-0493; **Board Cert:** Internal Medicine 2010; Gastroenterology 2013; **Med School:** Cornell Univ-Weill Med Coll 1987; **Resid:** Internal Medicine, NY Hosp-Cornell Med Ctr 1990; **Fellow:** Gastroenterology, Temple Univ Hosp 1992; **Fac Appt:** Asst Clin Prof Med, Mount Sinai Sch Med

Levine, Robert S MD (Ge) - **Spec Exp:** Pancreatic/Biliary Endoscopy (ERCP); Pancreatic & Biliary Disease; **Hospital:** Valley Hosp (page 739), Hackensack UMC-Pascack Valley (page 737); **Address:** Bergen Gastroenterology, 466 Old Hook Rd, Ste 1, Emerson, NJ 07630; **Phone:** 201-967-8221; **Board Cert:** Gastroenterology 2014; **Med School:** Georgetown Univ 1987; **Resid:** Internal Medicine, George Washington Univ 1990; **Fellow:** Gastroenterology, George Washington Univ 1993

Margulis, Stephen J MD (Ge) - **Spec Exp:** Hepatitis; Colonoscopy/Polypectomy; Peptic Ulcer Disease; Inflammatory Bowel Disease; **Hospital:** Valley Hosp (page 739), Hackensack UMC-Pascack Valley (page 737); **Address:** Bergen Gastroenterology, 467 Old Hook Rd, Ste 1, Emerson, NJ 07630; **Phone:** 201-967-8221; **Board Cert:** Internal Medicine 1984; Gastroenterology 1987; **Med School:** Brown Univ 1981; **Resid:** Internal Medicine, New York Hosp-Cornell 1984; **Fellow:** Digestive Diseases, New York Hosp-Cornell 1986

Nikias, George A MD (Ge) - **Spec Exp:** Liver Disease; Hepatitis; Endoscopy; **Hospital:** Hackensack Univ Med Ctr (page 96); **Address:** 130 Kinderkamack Rd, Ste 301, River Edge, NJ 07661; **Phone:** 201-489-7772; **Board Cert:** Gastroenterology 2005; **Med School:** NY Med Coll 1989; **Resid:** Internal Medicine, North Shore Univ Hosp 1992; **Fellow:** Hepatology, Mayo Clinic 1993; Gastroenterology, Meml Sloan-Kettering Cancer Ctr 1995; **Fac Appt:** Asst Clin Prof Med, UMDNJ-NJ Med Sch, Newark

Panella, Vincent S MD (Ge) - **Spec Exp:** Colon & Rectal Cancer; Hepatitis C; Inflammatory Bowel Disease; Endoscopy; **Hospital:** Englewood Hosp & Med Ctr, Holy Name Med Ctr (page 738); **Address:** Englewood Endoscopic Associates, 420 Grand Ave, Englewood, NJ 07631-4141; **Phone:** 201-569-7044; **Board Cert:** Internal Medicine 1985; Gastroenterology 1987; **Med School:** NY Med Coll 1982; **Resid:** Internal Medicine, North Shore Univ Hosp 1985; **Fellow:** Gastroenterology, Mem Sloan-Kettering Cancer Cntr 1987; **Fac Appt:** Asst Clin Prof Med, Mount Sinai Sch Med

Pittman, Robert H MD (Ge) - **Spec Exp:** Capsule Endoscopy; Endoscopic Therapies; **Hospital:** Valley Hosp (page 739), Hackensack UMC-Pascack Valley (page 737); **Address:** Bergen Gastroenterology, 466 Old Hook Rd, Ste 1, Emerson, NJ 07630; **Phone:** 201-967-8221; **Board Cert:** Gastroenterology 2006; **Med School:** NYU Sch Med 1999; **Resid:** Internal Medicine, Mount Sinai Med Ctr 2002; **Fellow:** Gastroenterology, Mount Sinai Med Ctr 2006

Rahmin, Michael G MD (Ge) - **Spec Exp:** Endoscopy; Hepatitis; **Hospital:** Valley Hosp (page 739); **Address:** 140 Chestnut St, Ste 300, Ridgewood, NJ 07452; **Phone:** 201-444-2600; **Board Cert:** Gastroenterology 2005; **Med School:** NYU Sch Med 1989; **Resid:** Internal Medicine, Mt Sinai Hosp 1992; **Fellow:** Gastroenterology, New York Hosp 1995; Hepatology, Mt Sinai Hosp 1995

Roth, Joseph M MD (Ge) - **Spec Exp:** Endoscopy; Inflammatory Bowel Disease; **Hospital:** St. Mary's Hosp - Passaic, St. Joseph's Regl Med Ctr - Paterson; **Address:** 71 Union Ave, Rutherford, NJ 07070-1272; **Phone:** 201-842-0020; **Board Cert:** Internal Medicine 1984; Gastroenterology 1987; **Med School:** Univ Pittsburgh 1981; **Resid:** Internal Medicine, Lenox Hill Hosp 1984; **Fellow:** Gastroenterology, Univ Conn Hlth Ctr 1986

Rubin, Kenneth Phillip MD (Ge) - **Spec Exp:** Gastroesophageal Reflux Disease (GERD); Endoscopy; Inflammatory Bowel Disease; Colon Cancer; **Hospital:** Englewood Hosp & Med Ctr, Mt Sinai Hosp; **Address:** 420 Grand Ave, Englewood, NJ 07631-4152; **Phone:** 201-569-7044; **Board Cert:** Internal Medicine 1978; Gastroenterology 1981; **Med School:** UMDNJ-NJ Med Sch, Newark 1975; **Resid:** Internal Medicine, Bronx Muni Hosp 1979; **Fellow:** Gastroenterology, Mount Sinai Hosp 1981; **Fac Appt:** Asst Clin Prof Med, Mount Sinai Sch Med

Rubinoff, Mitchell J MD (Ge) - **Spec Exp:** Hepatitis; Gastroesophageal Reflux Disease (GERD); **Hospital:** Valley Hosp (page 739); **Address:** 140 Chestnut St, Ste 300, Ridgewood, NJ 07450-2536; **Phone:** 201-444-2600; **Board Cert:** Internal Medicine 1982; Gastroenterology 1985; **Med School:** Mount Sinai Sch Med 1979; **Resid:** Internal Medicine, Columbia-Presby Med Ctr 1982; **Fellow:** Gastroenterology, Columbia-Presby Med Ctr 1985

Spinnell, Mitchell K MD (Ge) - **Spec Exp:** Inflammatory Bowel Disease; Colonoscopy; **Hospital:** Englewood Hosp & Med Ctr; **Address:** Advanced Gastro of Bergen County, 140 Sylvan Ave, Ste 101A, Englewood Cliffs, NJ 07632; **Phone:** 201-945-6564; **Board Cert:** Internal Medicine 2009; Gastroenterology 2009; **Med School:** SUNY Buffalo 1991; **Resid:** Internal Medicine, Montefiore Med Ctr 1995; **Fellow:** Gastroenterology, Montefiore Med Ctr 1999

Zingler, Barry M MD (Ge) - **Spec Exp:** Colon Cancer; Hepatitis; Gastroesophageal Reflux Disease (GERD); **Hospital:** Englewood Hosp & Med Ctr, Holy Name Med Ctr (page 738); **Address:** Advanced Gastroenterology of Bergen Cty, 140 Sylvan Ave, Ste 101A, Englewood Cliffs, NJ 7632; **Phone:** 201-945-6564; **Board Cert:** Internal Medicine 1988; Gastroenterology 2011; **Med School:** UMDNJ-Rutgers Med Sch 1985; **Resid:** Internal Medicine, NYU Med Ctr 1988; **Fellow:** Gastroenterology, NYU Med Ctr 1990

Zucker, Ira I MD (Ge) - **Spec Exp:** Colon Cancer; Gastroesophageal Reflux Disease (GERD); Ulcerative Colitis/Crohn's; Hepatitis; **Hospital:** Valley Hosp (page 739), Hackensack Univ Med Ctr (page 96); **Address:** 452 Old Hook Rd, Emerson, NJ 07630; **Phone:** 201-666-3900; **Board Cert:** Internal Medicine 1984; Gastroenterology 1987; **Med School:** Ros Franklin Univ/Chicago Med Sch 1981; **Resid:** Internal Medicine, St Vincents Hosp 1984; **Fellow:** Gastroenterology, St Vincents Hosp 1986

Geriatric Medicine

Chavez, Laura M DO (Ger) *PCP* - **Spec Exp:** Alzheimer's Disease; **Hospital:** Holy Name Med Ctr (page 738), Hackensack Univ Med Ctr (page 96); **Address:** IMA of Bergen County, 15 Anderson St, Hackensack, NJ 07601; **Phone:** 201-487-3355; **Board Cert:** Internal Medicine 2011; Geriatric Medicine 2004; **Med School:** NY Coll Osteo Med 1998; **Resid:** Internal Medicine, UMDNJ Univ Hosp 2001; **Fellow:** Geriatric Medicine, UMDNJ Univ Hosp 2002

Katz, Terri F MD (Ger) - **Spec Exp:** Frail Elderly; Dementia; Alzheimer's Disease; **Hospital:** Englewood Hosp & Med Ctr, Holy Name Med Ctr (page 738); **Address:** Ctr for Dynamic Aging, 1530 Palisades Ave, Fort Lee, NJ 07024; **Phone:** 201-363-8871; **Board Cert:** Internal Medicine 1989; Geriatric Medicine 2004; **Med School:** Geo Wash Univ 1986; **Resid:** Internal Medicine, G Washington Univ Hosp 1987; Internal Medicine, St Francis Hosp 1989; **Fac Appt:** Asst Clin Prof Med, Albert Einstein Coll Med

Leifer, Bennett MD (Ger) *PCP* - **Spec Exp:** Geriatric Medicine; Medications in the Elderly; **Hospital:** Valley Hosp (page 739); **Address:** Prospect Medical Offices LLC., 301 Godwin Ave, Midland Park, NJ 07432; **Phone:** 201-444-4526; **Board Cert:** Internal Medicine 2011; **Med School:** SUNY Upstate Med Univ 1986; **Resid:** Internal Medicine, Hartford Hosp 1989; **Fellow:** Geriatric Medicine, Mt Sinai Hosp 1991

Pantagis, Stefanos G MD (Ger) *PCP* - **Spec Exp:** Palliative Care; Frail Elderly; Falls in the Elderly; Alzheimer's Disease; **Hospital:** Hackensack Univ Med Ctr (page 96), Englewood Hosp & Med Ctr; **Address:** 810 Main St, Hackensack, NJ 07601; **Phone:** 201-633-7375; **Board Cert:** Family Medicine 2012; Geriatric Medicine 2009; Hospice & Palliative Medicine 2012; **Med School:** UMDNJ-Rutgers Med Sch 1993; **Resid:** Family Medicine, RWJ Univ Hosp 1998; **Fellow:** Geriatric Medicine, Georgetown Univ Hosp 1999

Parulekar, Manisha S MD (Ger) *PCP* - **Spec Exp:** Palliative Care; Frail Elderly; Alzheimer's Disease; Dementia; **Hospital:** Hackensack Univ Med Ctr (page 96); **Address:** Ctr for Healthy Senior Living, 360 Essex St, Ste 401, Hackensack, NJ 07601; **Phone:** 551-996-1140; **Board Cert:** Internal Medicine 2012; Geriatric Medicine 2013; Hospice & Palliative Medicine 2012; **Med School:** India 1994; **Resid:** Internal Medicine, NY Methodist Hosp 2002; **Fellow:** Geriatric Medicine, UMDNJ Univ Hosp 2003

Tank, Lisa K MD (Ger) *PCP* - **Spec Exp:** Cancer in the Elderly; **Hospital:** Hackensack Univ Med Ctr (page 96); **Address:** HUMC, Geriatric Med, 360 Essex St, Ste 401, Hackensack, NJ 07601; **Phone:** 551-996-1140; **Board Cert:** Internal Medicine 2011; Geriatric Medicine 2013; **Med School:** India 1996; **Resid:** Internal Medicine, NY Methodist Hosp 2001; **Fellow:** Geriatric Medicine, Hackensack Univ Med Ctr 2003

Villongco, Raymond M MD (Ger) - **Spec Exp:** Diabetes; Hypertension; **Hospital:** Mt Sinai Hosp, Holy Name Med Ctr (page 738); **Address:** Salus Medical, 121 Cedar Ln, Ste 2B, Teaneck, NJ 07666; **Phone:** 201-836-4228; **Board Cert:** Internal Medicine 2004; **Med School:** Philippines 1989; **Resid:** Internal Medicine, Jersey City Med Ctr 1994; **Fellow:** Geriatric Medicine, Mt Sinai Med Ctr 1996; **Fac Appt:** Asst Clin Prof H & PM, Mount Sinai Sch Med

Gynecologic Oncology

Goldman, Noah A MD (GO) - **Spec Exp:** Gynecologic Cancer; Minimally Invasive Surgery; Robotic Surgery; **Hospital:** Valley Hosp (page 739); **Address:** Valley Hospital Luckow Pavilion, 1 Valley Health Plaza, Paramus, NJ 07652; **Phone:** 201-634-5401; **Board Cert:** Obstetrics & Gynecology 2012; Gynecologic Oncology 2012; **Med School:** UMDNJ-NJ Med Sch, Newark 1996; **Resid:** Obstetrics & Gynecology, Mount Sinai Med Ctr 2000; **Fellow:** Gynecologic Oncology, Montefiore Med Ctr 2003

Vaidya, Ami MD (GO) - **Spec Exp:** Minimally Invasive Gynecologic Surgery; Robotic Surgery; Gynecologic Cancer; Gynecologic Surgery; **Hospital:** Hackensack Univ Med Ctr (page 96); **Address:** John Theurer Cancer Ctr-Gyn Oncology, 92 2nd St, Hackensack, NJ 07601; **Phone:** 551-996-5811; **Board Cert:** Obstetrics & Gynecology 2013; Gynecologic Oncology 2013; Hospice & Palliative Medicine 2012; **Med School:** Columbia P&S 1999; **Resid:** Obstetrics & Gynecology, NYU Med Ctr 2003; **Fellow:** Gynecologic Oncology, Mass General Hosp 2006

Hand Surgery

Fakharzadeh, Frederick F MD (HS) - **Hospital:** Hackensack Univ Med Ctr (page 96), Valley Hosp (page 739); **Address:** 22 Madison Ave, Ste 301, Paramus, NJ 07652; **Phone:** 201-587-7767; **Board Cert:** Orthopaedic Surgery 2009; Hand Surgery 2009; **Med School:** Columbia P&S 1980; **Resid:** Surgery, St Lukes-Roosevelt Hosp 1982; Orthopaedic Surgery, NY-Presby/Columbia Univ Med Ctr 1985; **Fellow:** Hand Surgery, Thomas Jefferson Univ Hosp 1986

Gurland, Mark MD (HS) - **Spec Exp:** Carpal Tunnel Syndrome; Wrist/Hand Injuries; Arthritis Hand Surgery; **Hospital:** Hackensack Univ Med Ctr (page 96), Englewood Hosp & Med Ctr; **Address:** 216 Engle St, Englewood, NJ 07631-2448; **Phone:** 201-568-4066; **Board Cert:** Orthopaedic Surgery 2009; Hand Surgery 2009; **Med School:** NYU Sch Med 1979; **Resid:** Orthopaedic Surgery, Hosp for Joint Diseases 1984; **Fellow:** Hand Surgery, Thomas Jefferson Univ Hosp 1985

Kim, Richard Young-Jin MD (HS) - **Spec Exp:** Wrist Surgery; Carpal Tunnel Syndrome; Microvascular Surgery; **Hospital:** Hackensack Univ Med Ctr (page 96); **Address:** HUMC, Plastic & Orthopedic Surgery, 360 Essex St, Ste 303, Hackensack, NJ 07601; **Phone:** 551-996-5439; **Board Cert:** Plastic Surgery 2008; Hand Surgery 2010; **Med School:** Mount Sinai Sch Med 1999; **Resid:** Plastic/Reconstructive Surgery, Rhode Island Hosp 2005; **Fellow:** Hand & Microvascular Surgery, NY-Presby/Columbia Univ Med Ctr 2007; **Fac Appt:** Asst Clin Prof PlS, Columbia P&S

Miller-Breslow, Anne J MD (HS) - **Spec Exp:** Rheumatoid Arthritis; Wrist/Hand Injuries; Arthroscopic Surgery; Carpal Tunnel Syndrome; **Hospital:** Englewood Hosp & Med Ctr; **Address:** Englewood Orthopedic Assocs, 401 S Van Brunt St Fl 3, Englewood, NJ 07631; **Phone:** 201-569-2770; **Board Cert:** Orthopaedic Surgery 2012; Hand Surgery 2012; **Med School:** Harvard Med Sch 1983; **Resid:** Orthopaedic Surgery, Montefiore Med Ctr 1988; **Fellow:** Hand Surgery, Tufts Med Ctr 1989

Rosenstein, Roger G MD (HS) - **Hospital:** Valley Hosp (page 739), Hackensack Univ Med Ctr (page 96); **Address:** 22 Madison Ave, Ste 301, Paramus, NJ 07652; **Phone:** 201-587-7767; **Board Cert:** Orthopaedic Surgery 1984; Hand Surgery 2010; **Med School:** Columbia P&S 1975; **Resid:** Surgery, St Lukes-Roosevelt Hosp 1977; Orthopaedic Surgery, NY-Presby/Columbia Univ Med Ctr 1980; **Fellow:** Hand Surgery, Thomas Jefferson Univ Hosp 1981; **Fac Appt:** Assoc Clin Prof OrS, UMDNJ-NJ Med Sch, Newark

Hematology

Feldman, Tatyana A MD (Hem) - **Spec Exp:** Lymphoma; **Hospital:** Hackensack Univ Med Ctr (page 96); **Address:** John Pheurer Cancer Ctr, 92 2nd St, Ste 210, Hackensack, NJ 07601; **Phone:** 201-996-5900; **Board Cert:** Internal Medicine 2008; Hematology 2012; Medical Oncology 2012; **Med School:** Ukraine 1992; **Resid:** Internal Medicine, Beth Israel Med Ctr 1998; Internal Medicine, Montefiore Med Ctr 1999; **Fellow:** Hematology & Oncology, NYU Med Ctr 2001

Fernbach, Barry R MD (Hem) - **Hospital:** Valley Hosp (page 739); **Address:** 1 Valley Health Plaza, Paramus, NJ 07652; **Phone:** 201-634-5353; **Board Cert:** Internal Medicine 1974; Medical Oncology 1977; Hematology 1982; **Med School:** Harvard Med Sch 1971; **Resid:** Internal Medicine, Mt Sinai Hosp 1974; Hematology, Mt Sinai Hosp 1976; **Fellow:** Neoplastic Diseases, Mt Sinai Hosp 1977

Israel, Alan M MD (Hem) - **Hospital:** Valley Hosp (page 739); **Address:** 270 Old Hook Rd, Westwood, NJ 07675-3102; **Phone:** 201-666-4949; **Board Cert:** Internal Medicine 1982; Medical Oncology 1985; Hematology 1986; **Med School:** NYU Sch Med 1979; **Resid:** Internal Medicine, Mt Sinai Hosp 1982; **Fellow:** Hematology & Oncology, Meml Sloan Kettering Cancer Ctr 1984; Hematology, LI Jewish Hosp 1985

Rowley, Scott D MD (Hem) - **Spec Exp:** Stem Cell Transplant; Bone Marrow Transplant; Graft vs Host Disease; **Hospital:** Hackensack Univ Med Ctr (page 96); **Address:** John Theuer Cancer Ctr, 92 2nd St, Ste 230, Hackensack, NJ 07601; **Phone:** 551-996-8297; **Board Cert:** Internal Medicine 1981; Medical Oncology 1983; Hematology 1984; **Med School:** Univ Mass Sch Med 1978; **Resid:** Internal Medicine, Rhode Island Hosp 1981; **Fellow:** Hematology & Oncology, Rhode Island Hosp 1984; **Fac Appt:** Assoc Prof Med, UMDNJ-NJ Med Sch, Newark

Vesole, David H MD/PhD (Hem) - **Spec Exp:** Multiple Myeloma; Stem Cell Transplant; Amyloidosis; Waldenstrom's Macroglobulinemia; **Hospital:** Hackensack Univ Med Ctr (page 96), MedStar Georgetown Univ Hosp; **Address:** 92 Second St, Hackensack, NJ 07601; **Phone:** 551-996-8704; **Board Cert:** Internal Medicine 1987; **Med School:** Northwestern Univ 1984; **Resid:** Internal Medicine, Univ Iowa Hosp 1987; **Fellow:** Hematology & Oncology, Univ Iowa Hosp 1990; **Fac Appt:** Prof Med, UMDNJ-NJ Med Sch, Newark

Infectious Disease

Birch, Thomas MD (Inf) - **Spec Exp:** AIDS/HIV; Lyme Disease; West Nile Virus; Antibiotic Resistance; **Hospital:** Holy Name Med Ctr (page 738), Englewood Hosp & Med Ctr; **Address:** Birch Tree Med Assocs, 718 Teaneck Rd, Teaneck, NJ 07666; **Phone:** 201-541-6315; **Board Cert:** Internal Medicine 1986; Infectious Disease 2004; **Med School:** Univ Wisc 1983; **Resid:** Internal Medicine, Montefiore Med Ctr 1986; **Fellow:** Infectious Disease, Montefiore Med Ctr 1993

Cicogna, Cristina E MD (Inf) - **Spec Exp:** Infections in Immunocompromised Patients; Hospital Acquired Infections; **Hospital:** Hackensack Univ Med Ctr (page 96); **Address:** 20 Prospect Ave Fl 5 - Ste 507, Hackensack, NJ 07601; **Phone:** 201-487-4088; **Board Cert:** Infectious Disease 2004; **Med School:** Switzerland 1986; **Resid:** Internal Medicine, St Luke's-Roosevelt Hosp 1992; **Fellow:** Infectious Disease, Meml Sloan-Kettering Cancer Ctr 1995; **Fac Appt:** Asst Prof Med, Rutgers R W Johnson Med Sch

Desai, Amita J MD (Inf) - **Spec Exp:** Infections in Transplant Patients; Tropical Diseases; Tuberculosis; **Hospital:** Holy Name Med Ctr (page 738); **Address:** Birch Tree Medical Associates, 718 Teaneck Rd, Teaneck, NJ 07666; **Phone:** 201-541-6315; **Board Cert:** Internal Medicine 1987; Infectious Disease 2004; **Med School:** NY Med Coll 1983; **Resid:** Internal Medicine, Montefiore Med Ctr 1986; **Fellow:** Infectious Disease, Mount Sinai Med Ctr 1994

Knackmuhs, Gary G MD (Inf) - **Spec Exp:** Travel Medicine; **Hospital:** Valley Hosp (page 739); **Address:** Ridgewood Infectious Disease Assocs, 947 Lynwood Ave, Ste 2E, Ridgewood, NJ 07450-4407; **Phone:** 201-447-6468; **Board Cert:** Internal Medicine 1979; Infectious Disease 1982; **Med School:** NY Med Coll 1976; **Resid:** Internal Medicine, Mt Sinai Hosp 1979; **Fellow:** Infectious Disease, Montefiore Med Ctr 1981

Kocher, Jeffrey MD (Inf) - **Spec Exp:** Hepatitis B & C; AIDS/HIV; Fungal Infections; Lyme Disease; **Hospital:** Englewood Hosp & Med Ctr; **Address:** 25 Rockwood Pl, Ste 120, Englewood, NJ 07631; **Phone:** 201-568-3335; **Board Cert:** Internal Medicine 1983; Infectious Disease 1986; **Med School:** Cornell Univ-Weill Med Coll 1980; **Resid:** Internal Medicine, NY-Presby/Weill Cornell Med Ctr 1983; Internal Medicine, St Barnabas Hosp 1984; **Fellow:** Infectious Disease, NY-Presby/Weill Cornell Med Ctr 1986; **Fac Appt:** Assoc Clin Prof Med, Mount Sinai-Icahn Sch of Med

O'Hagan Sotsky, Carol A MD (Inf) - **Hospital:** Valley Hosp (page 739); **Address:** Ridgewood Infectious Disease Assocs, 947 Linwood Ave, Ste 2E, Ridgewood, NJ 07450; **Phone:** 201-447-6468; **Board Cert:** Internal Medicine 1986; Infectious Disease 2010; **Med School:** NY Med Coll 1982; **Resid:** Pediatrics, NY Presby-Columbia Med Ctr 1984; Internal Medicine, St Lukes Roosevelt Hosp 1986; **Fellow:** Infectious Disease, Montefiore Med Ctr 1989

Sperber, Steven J MD (Inf) - **Hospital:** Hackensack Univ Med Ctr (page 96); **Address:** 20 Prospect Ave, Ste 507, Hackensack, NJ 07601; **Phone:** 201-487-4088; **Board Cert:** Internal Medicine 1985; Infectious Disease 1988; **Med School:** NYU Sch Med 1982; **Resid:** Internal Medicine, SUNY Stony Brook Med Ctr 1985; **Fellow:** Infectious Disease, Univ Va Med Ctr 1988; **Fac Appt:** Assoc Clin Prof Med, UMDNJ-NJ Med Sch, Newark

Tsiouris, Simon J MD (Inf) - **Spec Exp:** Tuberculosis; Travel Medicine; Tropical Diseases; AIDS/HIV; **Hospital:** Valley Hosp (page 739); **Address:** Ridgewood Infectious Disease Assocs, 947 Linwood Ave, Ste 2E, Ridgewood, NJ 07450; **Phone:** 201-447-6468; **Board Cert:** Infectious Disease 2004; **Med School:** Johns Hopkins Univ 1998; **Resid:** Internal Medicine, NY-Presby/Weill Cornell Med Ctr 2001; **Fellow:** Infectious Disease, Columbia Univ Med Ctr 2003

Weisholtz, Steven J MD (Inf) - **Spec Exp:** AIDS/HIV; Antibiotic Resistance; Travel Medicine; **Hospital:** Englewood Hosp & Med Ctr; **Address:** 25 Rockwood Pl, Ste 120, Englewood, NJ 07631-4957; **Phone:** 201-568-3335; **Board Cert:** Internal Medicine 1981; Infectious Disease 1984; **Med School:** Univ Pennsylvania 1978; **Resid:** Internal Medicine, New York Hosp 1981; **Fellow:** Infectious Disease, New York Hosp 1983; **Fac Appt:** Asst Clin Prof Med, Mount Sinai Sch Med

Internal Medicine

Brunnquell, Stephen MD (IM) *PCP* - **Hospital:** Englewood Hosp & Med Ctr; **Address:** Park Med Grp, 24 Elm St, Harrington Park, NJ 07640; **Phone:** 201-784-0123; **Board Cert:** Internal Medicine 2012; **Med School:** UMDNJ-NJ Med Sch, Newark 1989; **Resid:** Internal Medicine, Montefiore Med Ctr 1992; **Fac Appt:** Asst Clin Prof Med, Mount Sinai-Icahn Sch of Med

Cacciola, Thomas A MD (IM) *PCP* - **Spec Exp:** Preventive Medicine; Complementary Medicine; **Hospital:** Hackensack Univ Med Ctr (page 96); **Address:** 403 N Farview Ave, Paramus, NJ 07652; **Phone:** 201-261-8386; **Board Cert:** Internal Medicine 1988; **Med School:** Jefferson Med Coll 1983; **Resid:** Internal Medicine, Hackensack Med Ctr 1986

Flanzman, Susan A MD (IM) *PCP* - **Spec Exp:** Women's Health; Anxiety & Depression; Menopause Problems; Nutrition & Obesity; **Hospital:** Valley Hosp (page 739), Hackensack UMC-Pascack Valley (page 737); **Address:** Bergen Medical Assocs, 1 W Ridgewood Ave, Ste 301, Paramus, NJ 07652; **Phone:** 201-445-1660; **Board Cert:** Internal Medicine 2012; **Med School:** Mount Sinai Sch Med 1987; **Resid:** Internal Medicine, Montefiore Med Ctr 1991

Giangola, Joseph MD (IM) *PCP* - **Spec Exp:** Diabetes; **Hospital:** Hackensack Univ Med Ctr (page 96); **Address:** Forest Hlthcare Assocs, 277 Forest Ave, Ste 200, Paramus, NJ 07652; **Phone:** 201-986-1881; **Board Cert:** Internal Medicine 1981; **Med School:** Italy 1978; **Resid:** Internal Medicine, Long Island Coll Hosp 1981; **Fellow:** Diabetes, Joslin Clin 1982

Glaubiger, Carol MD (IM) *PCP* - **Hospital:** Valley Hosp (page 739); **Address:** Old Hook Med Assocs, 452 Old Hook Rd, Emerson, NJ 7630; **Phone:** 201-666-3900; **Board Cert:** Internal Medicine 2010; **Med School:** Mich State Univ 1986; **Resid:** Internal Medicine, Scranton-Temple Residency Program 1989

Kushner, Evan G MD (IM) *PCP* - **Spec Exp:** Geriatric Medicine; **Hospital:** Hackensack Univ Med Ctr (page 96), Valley Hosp (page 739); **Address:** Forest Hlthcare Assocs, 277 Forest Ave, Ste 200, Paramus, NJ 7652; **Phone:** 201-986-1881; **Board Cert:** Internal Medicine 1989; Geriatric Medicine 2005; **Med School:** SUNY Upstate Med Univ 1986; **Resid:** Internal Medicine, Univ Hosp 1989

Lan, Vivian E MD (IM) *PCP* - **Spec Exp:** Women's Health; Eating Disorders; **Hospital:** Valley Hosp (page 739), Hackensack UMC-Pascack Valley (page 737); **Address:** Bergen Medical Associates, 466 Old Hook Rd, Ste 1, Emerson, NJ 07630; **Phone:** 201-967-8221; **Board Cert:** Internal Medicine 2007; **Med School:** Mount Sinai Sch Med 1994; **Resid:** Internal Medicine, Mt Sinai Med Ctr 1997

Lauricella, Joseph MD (IM) *PCP* - **Spec Exp:** Coronary Artery Disease; **Hospital:** Holy Name Med Ctr (page 738); **Address:** 292 Columbia Ave, Fort Lee, NJ 07024-4124; **Phone:** 201-224-0050; **Board Cert:** Internal Medicine 1985; **Med School:** Mexico 1978; **Resid:** Internal Medicine, Rutgers Univ Med Ctr 1985

Miguel, Eduardo E MD (IM) *PCP* - **Spec Exp:** Rheumatoid Arthritis; **Hospital:** Englewood Hosp & Med Ctr; **Address:** 200 Grand Ave, Ste 202, Englewood, NJ 07631; **Phone:** 201-871-3280; **Board Cert:** Internal Medicine 1982; **Med School:** Paraguay 1966; **Resid:** Internal Medicine, VA Med Ctr 1969; Internal Medicine, NY Polyclinic Hosp 1972; **Fellow:** Rheumatology, Abraham Jacobi Hosp 1973

Pelavin, Martin MD (IM) *PCP* - **Hospital:** Valley Hosp (page 739), Englewood Hosp & Med Ctr; **Address:** 215 Old Tappan Rd, Old Tappan, NJ 07675-7428; **Phone:** 201-666-1000; **Board Cert:** Internal Medicine 1976; **Med School:** NYU Sch Med 1973; **Resid:** Internal Medicine, Montefiore Hosp Med Ctr 1976

Schuster, Joseph C MD (IM) *PCP* - **Hospital:** Holy Name Med Ctr (page 738), Hackensack Univ Med Ctr (page 96); **Address:** 175 Cedar Ln, Teaneck, NJ 07666-4315; **Phone:** 201-692-7766; **Board Cert:** Internal Medicine 1984; **Med School:** Albany Med Coll 1981; **Resid:** Internal Medicine, Kings County Hosp 1984

Scibetta, Maria MD (IM) *PCP* - **Hospital:** Valley Hosp (page 739); **Address:** 470 N Franklin Tpke, Ramsey, NJ 07446-2034; **Phone:** 201-327-8765; **Board Cert:** Internal Medicine 2014; **Med School:** Rutgers R W Johnson Med Sch 1990; **Resid:** Internal Medicine, Mount Sinai Hosp 1993

Valinoti, Anne Marie MD (IM) *PCP* - **Spec Exp:** Women's Health; **Hospital:** Valley Hosp (page 739); **Address:** Prospect Medical Office, 301 Godwin Ave, Midland Park, NJ 07432; **Phone:** 201-444-4526; **Board Cert:** Internal Medicine 2004; **Med School:** Columbia P&S 1991; **Resid:** Internal Medicine, New York Hosp 1994

Volpe, Anthony P MD (IM) *PCP* - **Spec Exp:** Hypertension; **Hospital:** Valley Hosp (page 739); **Address:** 466 Old Hook Rd, Ste 14, Emerson, NJ 07630-1368; **Phone:** 201-262-6485; **Board Cert:** Internal Medicine 2005; **Med School:** Mexico 1981; **Resid:** Internal Medicine, Texas Tech Hlth Scis Ctr 1986

Wasserman, Kenneth H MD (IM) *PCP* - **Hospital:** Englewood Hosp & Med Ctr, Holy Name Med Ctr (page 738); **Address:** 177 N Dean St Fl 1, Englewood, NJ 07631; **Phone:** 201-567-1140 x10; **Board Cert:** Internal Medicine 1982; **Med School:** Albert Einstein Coll Med 1979; **Resid:** Internal Medicine, Lenox Hill Hosp 1982

Interventional Cardiology

Angeli, Stephen J MD (IC) - **Spec Exp:** Angioplasty & Stent Placement; Cardiac Catheterization; Coronary Artery Disease; **Hospital:** Holy Name Med Ctr (page 738); **Address:** Cardiovascular Assocs of Teaneck, 954 Teaneck Rd, Teaneck, NJ 07666; **Phone:** 201-833-2300; **Board Cert:** Internal Medicine 1984; Cardiovascular Disease 1987; Interventional Cardiology 2009; **Med School:** SUNY Downstate 1981; **Resid:** Internal Medicine, Kings Co Hosp 1984; **Fellow:** Cardiovascular Disease, St Michael Med Ctr 1986

Syed, Tariqshah M MD (IC) - **Spec Exp:** Cardiac Catheterization; Angiography-Coronary; Angioplasty & Stent Placement; Coronary Artery Disease; **Hospital:** Holy Name Med Ctr (page 738), Hackensack Univ Med Ctr (page 96); **Address:** Holy Name Cardiology Assocs, 954 Teaneck Rd, Teaneck, NJ 07666; **Phone:** 201-833-2300; **Board Cert:** Internal Medicine 2004; Cardiovascular Disease 2007; Interventional Cardiology 2008; Echocardiography 2007; **Med School:** Pakistan 1999; **Resid:** Internal Medicine, St Luke-Roosevelt Hosp Ctr 2004; **Fellow:** Cardiovascular Disease, Mt Sinai Hosp 2007; Interventional Cardiology, St Luke-Roosevelt Hosp Ctr 2008

Maternal & Fetal Medicine

Al-Khan, Abdulla M MD (MF) - **Spec Exp:** Pregnancy-High Risk; Fetal Surgery; Critical Care; Fetal Ultrasound/Obstetrical Imaging; **Hospital:** Hackensack Univ Med Ctr (page 96); **Address:** Hackensack Univ Med Ctr, 30 Prospect Ave, Fl 2, rm 73, Hackensack, NJ 07601; **Phone:** 551-996-2453; **Board Cert:** Obstetrics & Gynecology 2013; Maternal & Fetal Medicine 2013; **Med School:** Grenada 1995; **Resid:** Obstetrics & Gynecology, Seton Hall Univ Med Ctr 1999; **Fellow:** Maternal & Fetal Medicine, UMDNJ Med Ctr 2003; **Fac Appt:** Asst Prof ObG, UMDNJ-Rutgers Med Sch

Alvarez, Manuel MD (MF) - **Spec Exp:** Multiple Gestation; Pregnancy-High Risk; **Hospital:** Hackensack Univ Med Ctr (page 96), NYU Langone Med Ctr (page 104); **Address:** 20 Prospect Ave, Ste 601, Hackensack, NJ 07601; **Phone:** 551-996-2765; **Board Cert:** Obstetrics & Gynecology 2013; Maternal & Fetal Medicine 2013; **Med School:** Dominican Republic 1981; **Resid:** Obstetrics & Gynecology, St Joseph Hosp 1987; **Fellow:** Maternal & Fetal Medicine, Mount Sinai Med Ctr 1989; Critical Care Obstetrics, Mount Sinai Med Ctr 1990

Frieden, Faith J MD (MF) - **Spec Exp:** Prenatal Ultrasound; Prenatal Diagnosis; **Hospital:** Englewood Hosp & Med Ctr; **Address:** EHMC, Ob/Gyn, 350 Engle St, Ste 4215, Englewood, NJ 07631; **Phone:** 201-894-3669; **Board Cert:** Obstetrics & Gynecology 2013; Maternal & Fetal Medicine 2013; **Med School:** Mount Sinai Sch Med 1984; **Resid:** Obstetrics & Gynecology, Beth Israel Med Ctr 1988; **Fellow:** Maternal & Fetal Medicine, Bellevue Hosp-NYU 1990; **Fac Appt:** Asst Prof ObG, Mount Sinai-Icahn Sch of Med

Principe, David L MD (MF) - **Spec Exp:** Pregnancy-High Risk; **Hospital:** St. Joseph's Regl Med Ctr - Paterson, Palisades Med Ctr; **Address:** St Joseph's Perinatal Ctr, 1 Broadway, Ste 203, Elmwood Park, NJ 07407; **Phone:** 973-569-6264; **Board Cert:** Obstetrics & Gynecology 2013; Maternal & Fetal Medicine 2013; **Med School:** Grenada 1991; **Resid:** Obstetrics & Gynecology, St Joseph Hosp 1995; **Fellow:** Maternal & Fetal Medicine, Univ Chicago/Chicago Lying in Hosp 1997; Maternal & Fetal Medicine, Yale New Haven Hosp 1998

Saphier, Carl J MD (MF) - **Spec Exp:** Pregnancy-High Risk; Prenatal Diagnosis; Prematurity/Low Birth Weight Infants; **Hospital:** Englewood Hosp & Med Ctr, Holy Name Med Ctr (page 738); **Address:** 498 Engle St, Englewood, NJ 07631; **Phone:** 201-569-0121; **Board Cert:** Obstetrics & Gynecology 2013; Maternal & Fetal Medicine 2013; **Med School:** Brown Univ 1992; **Resid:** Obstetrics & Gynecology, Brigham & Womens Hosp 1996; **Fellow:** Maternal & Fetal Medi-cine, Brigham & Womens Hosp 1999

Zelop, Carolyn M MD (MF) - **Spec Exp:** Prenatal Diagnosis; Fetal Echocardiography; Pregnancy-High Risk; **Hospital:** Valley Hosp (page 739); **Address:** Valley Hospital, 15 Essex Rd, Ste 204, Paramus, NJ 07652; **Phone:** 201-291-6321; **Board Cert:** Obstetrics & Gynecology 2013; Maternal & Fetal Medicine 2013; **Med School:** Tufts Univ 1987; **Resid:** Obstetrics & Gynecology, Brigham and Women's Hosp 1991; **Fellow:** Maternal & Fetal Medicine, Brigham and Women's Hosp 1993

Medical Oncology

Attas, Lewis MD (Onc) - **Spec Exp:** Breast Cancer; Lymphoma; Bleeding/Coagulation Disorders; Gaucher Disease; **Hospital:** Englewood Hosp & Med Ctr, Holy Name Med Ctr (page 738); **Address:** EHMC, Med Oncology, 350 Engle St Berrie Bldg, Englewood, NJ 07631; **Phone:** 201-568-5250; **Board Cert:** Internal Medicine 1985; Medical Oncology 1987; Hematology 1988; Hospice & Palliative Medicine 2012; **Med School:** Mount Sinai Sch Med 1982; **Resid:** Internal Medicine, Montefiore Med Ctr 1985; **Fellow:** Hematology & Oncology, N Shore Univ Hosp 1988; **Fac Appt:** Assoc Clin Prof Med, Mount Sinai-Icahn Sch of Med

Condemi, Giuseppe MD (Onc) - **Spec Exp:** Breast Cancer; Prostate Cancer; Colon Cancer; **Hospital:** Holy Name Med Ctr (page 738), Englewood Hosp & Med Ctr; **Address:** Medical Oncology Dept, 718 Teaneck Rd, Teaneck, NJ 07666; **Phone:** 201-227-6008; **Board Cert:** Internal Medicine 2003; Medical Oncology 2005; **Med School:** Dominica 1998; **Resid:** Internal Medicine, Mt. Sinai Sch Med 2001; **Fellow:** Hematology & Oncology, A Einstein Coll Med 2004

Forte, Francis A MD (Onc) - **Spec Exp:** Breast Cancer; Hematologic Malignancies; Coagulation/Bleeding Disorders; Solid Tumors; **Hospital:** Englewood Hosp & Med Ctr, Holy Name Med Ctr (page 738); **Address:** 350 Engle St Berrie Bldg Fl 1, Englewood, NJ 07631; **Phone:** 201-568-5250; **Board Cert:** Internal Medicine 1971; Hematology 1972; Medical Oncology 1973; **Med School:** Albert Einstein Coll Med 1964; **Resid:** Internal Medicine, Mount Sinai Hosp 1968; **Fellow:** Hematology, Mount Sinai Hosp 1969; **Fac Appt:** Assoc Clin Prof Med, Mount Sinai Sch Med

Goldberg, Stuart L MD (Onc) - **Spec Exp:** Leukemia; Stem Cell Transplant; Myelodysplastic Syndromes; Bone Marrow Failure Disorders; **Hospital:** Hackensack Univ Med Ctr (page 96); **Address:** John Theurer Cancer Ctr, HUMC, 92 Second St Fl 2, Hackensack, NJ 07601; **Phone:** 551-996-3925; **Board Cert:** Internal Medicine 1989; **Med School:** Penn State Coll Med 1986; **Resid:** Internal Medicine, G Washington Univ Hosp 1989; **Fellow:** Hematology & Oncology, G Washington Univ Hosp 1991; Bone Marrow Transplant, Mayo Clin 1992; **Fac Appt:** Assoc Clin Prof Med, UMDNJ-NJ Med Sch, Newark

Goy, Andre MD (Onc) - **Spec Exp:** Lymphoma; Hodgkin's Lymphoma; **Hospital:** Hackensack Univ Med Ctr (page 96); **Address:** Hackensack Canc Ctr, 92 2nd St, Hackensack, NJ 07601; **Phone:** 201-996-5900; **Med School:** France 1988; **Resid:** Internal Medicine, Grenoble Univ Med Ctr 1992; **Fellow:** Hematology & Oncology, Grenoble Univ Med Ctr 1993

Harper, Harry D MD (Onc) - **Spec Exp:** Lung Cancer; **Hospital:** Hackensack Univ Med Ctr (page 96); **Address:** John Theurer Cancer Ctr, 92 2nd St, Ste 310, Hackensack, NJ 07601; **Phone:** 551-996-5087; **Board Cert:** Internal Medicine 1980; Hematology 1982; Medical Oncology 1983; **Med School:** Baylor Coll Med 1977; **Resid:** Internal Medicine, NY-Presby/Weill Cornell Med Ctr 1980; **Fellow:** Hematology & Oncology, Meml Sloan-Kettering Cancer Ctr 1983

Jennis, Andrew A MD (Onc) - **Spec Exp:** Gastrointestinal Cancer; **Hospital:** Hackensack Univ Med Ctr (page 96); **Address:** John Theurer Cancer Ctr, HUMC, 92 Second St, Hackensack, NJ 07601; **Phone:** 551-996-5900; **Board Cert:** Internal Medicine 1988; Medical Oncology 2011; **Med School:** Columbia P&S 1985; **Resid:** Internal Medicine, Mount Sinai Hosp 1988; **Fellow:** Hematology & Oncology, Beth Israel Hosp 1992

Krutchik, Allan N MD (Onc) - **Spec Exp:** Breast Cancer; **Hospital:** St. Joseph's Wayne Hosp, Chilton Med Ctr (page 92); **Address:** John Theurer Cancer Ctr, Bldg C, 795 Franklin Ave Fl 1, Franklin Lakes, NJ 07417; **Phone:** 201-848-8791; **Board Cert:** Internal Medicine 1976; Medical Oncology 2001; **Med School:** Ros Franklin Univ/Chicago Med Sch 1973; **Resid:** Internal Medicine, Beth Israel Hosp 1976; **Fellow:** Medical Oncology, MD Anderson Cancer Ctr 1978; **Fac Appt:** Asst Clin Prof Med, UMDNJ-NJ Med Sch, Newark

Ligresti, Louise G MD (Onc) - **Spec Exp:** Breast Cancer; **Hospital:** Valley Hosp (page 739), Chilton Med Ctr (page 92); **Address:** One Valley Hlth Plaza, Luckow Pavillion, Paramus, NJ 07652; **Phone:** 201-634-5353; **Board Cert:** Medical Oncology 2008; Hematology 2008; **Med School:** SUNY Upstate Med Univ 1991; **Resid:** Internal Medicine, NY Hosp-Cornell Med Ctr 1994; **Fellow:** Hematology & Oncology, Meml Sloan Kettering Cancer Ctr 1995

Pascal, Mark S MD (Onc) - **Spec Exp:** Lung Cancer; Breast Cancer; Neuro-Oncology; **Hospital:** Hackensack Univ Med Ctr (page 96), Holy Name Med Ctr (page 738); **Address:** John Theurer Cancer Ctr, HUMC, 92 Second St, Hackensack, NJ 07601; **Phone:** 551-996-5266; **Board Cert:** Internal Medicine 1977; Medical Oncology 1979; **Med School:** Jefferson Med Coll 1973; **Resid:** Pathology, NY Hosp-Cornell Univ Med Ctr 1976; Internal Medicine, NY Hosp-Cornell Univ Med Ctr 1977; **Fellow:** Hematology & Oncology, Meml Sloan-Kettering Cancer Ctr 1979

Pecora, Andrew L MD (Onc) - **Spec Exp:** Stem Cell Transplant; Myelodysplastic Syndromes; Melanoma; Immunotherapy; **Hospital:** Hackensack Univ Med Ctr (page 96); **Address:** 92 2nd St, Hackensack, NJ 07601; **Phone:** 201-996-5900; **Board Cert:** Internal Medicine 1986; Hematology 1988; Medical Oncology 1989; **Med School:** UMDNJ-NJ Med Sch, Newark 1983; **Resid:** Internal Medicine, New York Presby Hosp 1986; **Fellow:** Hematology & Oncology, Meml Sloan Kettering Cancer Ctr 1988; **Fac Appt:** Prof Med, UMDNJ-NJ Med Sch, Newark

Pieczara, Beata K MD (Onc) - **Hospital:** Holy Name Med Ctr (page 738); **Address:** Regional Cancer Ctr at Holy Name, 718 Teaneck Rd, Teaneck, NJ 07666; **Phone:** 201-227-6008; **Board Cert:** Hematology 2003; **Med School:** Poland 1993; **Resid:** Internal Medicine, Bronx Lebanon Hosp 1999; **Fellow:** Hematology & Oncology, Westchester Med Ctr 2002

Rakowski, Thomas J MD (Onc) - **Spec Exp:** Breast Cancer; Lung Cancer; Colon Cancer; **Hospital:** Valley Hosp (page 739); **Address:** One Valley Health Plaza, Luckow Pavilion, Paramus, NJ 07652; **Phone:** 201-634-5578; **Board Cert:** Internal Medicine 1979; Medical Oncology 1981; **Med School:** SUNY Upstate Med Univ 1976; **Resid:** Internal Medicine, SUNY Hlth Sci Ctr 1979; **Fellow:** Hematology & Oncology, NY Presby Hosp-Columbia Campus 1981

Rivera, Yadyra MD (Onc) - **Spec Exp:** Breast Cancer; Colon Cancer; Lung Cancer; **Hospital:** Holy Name Med Ctr (page 738); **Address:** Regional Cancer Ctr at Holy Name, 718 Teaneck Rd, Teaneck, NJ 07666; **Phone:** 201-227-6008; **Board Cert:** Internal Medicine 2005; Medical Oncology 2008; Hematology 2009; **Med School:** Univ del Caribe Escuela Med 1992; **Resid:** Internal Medicine, Cabrini Med Ctr 1995; **Fellow:** Hematology, Cabrini Med Ctr 1997

Rosenbluth, Richard J MD (Onc) - **Spec Exp:** Breast Cancer in Elderly; Leukemia & Lymphoma; Palliative Care; Cancer Risk Assessment; **Hospital:** Hackensack Univ Med Ctr (page 96); **Address:** 92 2nd St, Hackensack, NJ 07601; **Phone:** 551-996-5857; **Board Cert:** Medical Oncology 1973; Hematology 1976; Medical Oncology 1977; Hospice & Palliative Medicine 2012; **Med School:** NYU Sch Med 1970; **Resid:** Internal Medicine, Bellevue Hosp Ctr 1973; **Fellow:** Hematology, Hosp Univ Penn 1976; Medical Oncology, Hosp Univ Penn 1977; **Fac Appt:** Asst Clin Prof Onc, NYU Sch Med

Schleider, Michael A MD (Onc) - **Spec Exp:** Breast Cancer; Colon Cancer; Bleeding/Coagulation Disorders; **Hospital:** Englewood Hosp & Med Ctr, Holy Name Med Ctr (page 738); **Address:** 350 Engle St Berrie Bldg Fl 1, Englewood, NJ 07631; **Phone:** 201-568-5250; **Board Cert:** Internal Medicine 1974; Hematology 1976; Medical Oncology 1977; **Med School:** Univ Pennsylvania 1969; **Resid:** Internal Medicine, New York Hosp 1974; **Fellow:** Hematology & Oncology, New York Hosp 1977

Waintraub, Stanley E MD (Onc) - **Spec Exp:** Breast Cancer; Bleeding/Coagulation Disorders; **Hospital:** Hackensack Univ Med Ctr (page 96); **Address:** 92 2nd St, Hackensack, NJ 07601; **Phone:** 551-996-5864; **Board Cert:** Internal Medicine 1980; Hematology 1982; Medical Oncology 1983; **Med School:** NY Med Coll 1977; **Resid:** Internal Medicine, Metropolitan Hosp Ctr 1980; **Fellow:** Hematology, Montefiore Hosp Med Ctr 1982; Medical Oncology, Meml Sloan Kettering Cancer Ctr 1983

Neonatal-Perinatal Medicine

Carlin, Elizabeth B MD (NP) - **Spec Exp:** Nutrition; **Hospital:** Englewood Hosp & Med Ctr, Mt Sinai Hosp; **Address:** Englewood Hosp & Med Ctr, 350 Engle St, Englewood, NJ 07631-1808; **Phone:** 201-894-3472; **Board Cert:** Neonatal-Perinatal Medicine 2013; **Med School:** Boston Univ 1990; **Resid:** Pediatrics, Boston City Hosp 1993; **Fellow:** Neonatal-Perinatal Medicine, Mt Sinai Med Ctr 1996; **Fac Appt:** Asst Prof Ped, Mount Sinai Sch Med

Chhabra, Rakesh S MD (NP) - **Spec Exp:** Multiple Gestation; Prematurity/Low Birth Weight Infants; **Hospital:** Hackensack Univ Med Ctr (page 96); **Address:** HUMC, Neonatology, 30 Prospect Ave, Hackensack, NJ 07601; **Phone:** 551-996-5362; **Board Cert:** Pediatrics 2008; **Med School:** India 1985; **Resid:** Pediatrics, Montefiore Med Ctr 1990; **Fellow:** Neonatal-Perinatal Medicine, Montefiore Med Ctr 1993

Giuliano, Michael A MD (NP) - **Hospital:** Hackensack Univ Med Ctr (page 96); **Address:** Hackensack Univ Med Ctr, 30 Prospect Ave Imus Bldg - rm 220, Hackensack, NJ 07601; **Phone:** 551-996-5362; **Board Cert:** Pediatrics 2010; Neonatal-Perinatal Medicine 2010; **Med School:** SUNY Downstate 1981; **Resid:** Pediatrics, New York Hosp 1984; **Fellow:** Neonatal-Perinatal Medicine, New York Hosp/Cornell 1986; **Fac Appt:** Assoc Prof Ped, UMDNJ-NJ Med Sch, Newark

Manginello, Frank P MD (NP) - **Spec Exp:** Prematurity/Low Birth Weight Infants; Lung Disease in Newborns; Developmental Disorders; **Hospital:** Valley Hosp (page 739); **Address:** Ctr for Child Development, 505 Goffle Rd Fl 2, Ridgewood, NJ 07450; **Phone:** 201-447-8388; **Board Cert:** Pediatrics 1978; Neonatal-Perinatal Medicine 1979; **Med School:** Georgetown Univ 1973; **Resid:** Pediatrics, Georgetown Univ Hosp 1975; **Fellow:** Perinatal Medicine, NY-Presby/Weill Cornell Med Ctr 1977

Perl, Harold MD (NP) - **Spec Exp:** Pulmonary Disease; Jaundice & Bilirubin Metabolism; Sudden Infant Death Syndrome (SIDS); **Hospital:** Hackensack Univ Med Ctr (page 96); **Address:** Hackensack Univ Med Ctr, Dept Pediatrics, 30 Prospect Ave Imus Bldg - rm 220, Hackensack, NJ 07601-1914; **Phone:** 551-996-5362; **Board Cert:** Pediatrics 1980; Neonatal-Perinatal Medicine 2010; **Med School:** Albert Einstein Coll Med 1975; **Resid:** Pediatrics, Montefiore Med Ctr 1978; **Fellow:** Neonatal-Perinatal Medicine, Montefiore Med Ctr 1980; **Fac Appt:** Assoc Prof Ped, UMDNJ-NJ Med Sch, Newark

Planer II, Benjamin C MD (NP) - **Spec Exp:** Lung Disease in Newborns; Neonatal Infections; Neonatal Nutrition; **Hospital:** Hackensack Univ Med Ctr (page 96); **Address:** HUMC, Neonatology, 30 Prospect Ave, Hackensack, NJ 07601; **Phone:** 551-996-5362; **Board Cert:** Pediatrics 2007; Neonatal-Perinatal Medicine 2010; **Med School:** South Africa 1986; **Resid:** Pediatrics, LIJ Med Ctr 1992; **Fellow:** Neonatal-Perinatal Medicine, Chldns Hosp 1995; **Fac Appt:** Assoc Prof Ped, UMDNJ-NJ Med Sch, Newark

Raziuddin, Khaja MD (NP) - **Spec Exp:** Prematurity/Low Birth Weight Infants; Breathing Disorders; **Hospital:** Holy Name Med Ctr (page 738), Hackensack Univ Med Ctr (page 96); **Address:** 70 Pearl St, Dumont, NJ 07628; **Phone:** 201-387-2627; **Board Cert:** Pediatrics 1976; Neonatal-Perinatal Medicine 2007; **Med School:** India 1966; **Resid:** Pediatrics, Kings Co Hosp 1974; **Fellow:** Neonatal-Perinatal Medicine, Kings Co Hosp 1976; **Fac Appt:** Asst Prof Ped, SUNY Downstate

Nephrology

Fein, Deborah A MD (Nep) - **Spec Exp:** Hypertension; Kidney Disease; Transplant Medicine-Kidney; Lupus Nephritis; **Hospital:** Englewood Hosp & Med Ctr, Holy Name Med Ctr (page 738); **Address:** 177 N Dean St, Ste 207, Englewood, NJ 07631; **Phone:** 201-567-0446; **Board Cert:** Internal Medicine 1983; Nephrology 2004; **Med School:** Tufts Univ 1980; **Resid:** Internal Medicine, St Lukes-Roosevelt Hosp Ctr 1983; **Fellow:** Nephrology, NY-Presby/Weill Cornell Med Ctr 1986

Joseph, Rosy E MD (Nep) - **Hospital:** Hackensack Univ Med Ctr (page 96); **Address:** 360 Essex St Fl 3 - Ste 304, Hackensack, NJ 07601; **Phone:** 201-646-0110; **Board Cert:** Internal Medicine 2008; Nephrology 2009; **Med School:** Columbia P&S 1990; **Resid:** Internal Medicine, Univ of Toronto 1997; **Fellow:** Nephrology, NY Presby-Columbia Med Ctr 1999

Kozlowski, Jeffrey P MD (Nep) - **Spec Exp:** Hypertension; Dialysis Care; Diabetic Kidney Disease; **Hospital:** Valley Hosp (page 739), Hackensack Univ Med Ctr (page 96); **Address:** 44 Godwin Ave, Ste 301, Midland Park, NJ 07432; **Phone:** 201-447-0013; **Board Cert:** Internal Medicine 1981; Nephrology 1984; **Med School:** NYU Sch Med 1978; **Resid:** Internal Medicine, VA Med Ctr 1981; **Fellow:** Nephrology, NYU Med Ctr 1984

Levin, David N MD (Nep) - **Spec Exp:** Hypertension; Dialysis Care; **Hospital:** Holy Name Med Ctr (page 738), Hackensack Univ Med Ctr (page 96); **Address:** 870 Palisade Ave, Ste 202, Teaneck, NJ 07666-3419; **Phone:** 201-836-0897; **Board Cert:** Internal Medicine 1979; Nephrology 1982; **Med School:** UMDNJ-NJ Med Sch, Newark 1976; **Resid:** Internal Medicine, Jacobi Med Ctr 1979; **Fellow:** Nephrology, Albert Einstein Coll Med 1981

Pattner, Austin M MD (Nep) - **Spec Exp:** Hypertension; Dialysis Care; Kidney Disease; **Hospital:** Englewood Hosp & Med Ctr, Hackensack Univ Med Ctr (page 96); **Address:** 177 N Dean St, Ste 207, Englewood, NJ 07631; **Phone:** 201-567-0446; **Board Cert:** Internal Medicine 1974; Nephrology 1976; **Med School:** SUNY Upstate Med Univ 1966; **Resid:** Internal Medicine, Roosevelt Hosp 1969; Internal Medicine, Columbia-Presby Med Ctr 1970; **Fellow:** Nephrology, Columbia-Presby Med Ctr 1972; **Fac Appt:** Asst Clin Prof Med, Mount Sinai Sch Med

Rigolosi, Robert S MD (Nep) - **Spec Exp:** Kidney Disease; Hypertension; Dialysis Care; **Hospital:** Holy Name Med Ctr (page 738), Valley Hosp (page 739); **Address:** Renal Medicine Associates, 718 Teaneck Rd, Teaneck, NJ 07666-4281; **Phone:** 201-833-3223; **Med School:** Italy 1963; **Resid:** Internal Medicine, Bronx VA Hosp 1967; **Fellow:** Renal Disease, Georgetown Univ Hosp 1969

Salazer, Thomas L MD (Nep) - **Hospital:** Hackensack Univ Med Ctr (page 96), Holy Name Med Ctr (page 738); **Address:** Nephrology Assocs, 870 Palisade Ave, Ste 202, Teaneck, NJ 07666; **Phone:** 201-836-0897; **Board Cert:** Internal Medicine 2012; Nephrology 2004; **Med School:** SUNY Stony Brook 1989; **Resid:** Internal Medicine, Mayo Clin 1992; **Fellow:** Nephrology, Mayo Clin 1994

Tartini, Albert MD (Nep) - **Spec Exp:** Kidney Disease; Hypertension; Dialysis Care; Anemia; **Hospital:** Valley Hosp (page 739), Holy Name Med Ctr (page 738); **Address:** 400 Franklin Tpke, Ste 208, Mahwah, NJ 07430; **Phone:** 201-825-3322; **Board Cert:** Internal Medicine 1988; Nephrology 2010; **Med School:** Grenada 1984; **Resid:** Internal Medicine, St Joseph Hosp Med Ctr 1988; **Fellow:** Nephrology, Univ Vermont Med Ctr 1990

Weizman, Howard B MD (Nep) - **Spec Exp:** Dialysis Care; Hypertension; **Hospital:** Hackensack Univ Med Ctr (page 96), Valley Hosp (page 739); **Address:** Bergen Hypertension & Renal Assocs, 44 Godwin Ave, Ste 301, Midland Park, NJ 07432-1976; **Phone:** 201-447-0013; **Board Cert:** Internal Medicine 1985; Nephrology 2012; **Med School:** Albert Einstein Coll Med 1982; **Resid:** Internal Medicine, Bronx Muni Hosp 1985; **Fellow:** Nephrology, Mount Sinai Med Ctr 1987; **Fac Appt:** Asst Clin Prof Med, UMDNJ-Rutgers Med Sch

Neurological Surgery

Arginteanu, Marc MD (NS) - **Spec Exp:** Spinal Surgery; Spinal Deformity; Spinal Reconstructive Surgery; Skull Base Surgery; **Hospital:** Englewood Hosp & Med Ctr, Mt Sinai Hosp; **Address:** 309 Engle St Fl 2 - Ste 6, Englewood, NJ 07631; **Phone:** 201-569-7737; **Board Cert:** Neurological Surgery 2013; **Med School:** Univ Pennsylvania 1993; **Resid:** Neurological Surgery, Mt Sinai Med Ctr 1999; **Fellow:** Spine Surgery, Beth Israel Med Ctr 2001; **Fac Appt:** Assoc Clin Prof NS, Mount Sinai Sch Med

Carpenter, Duncan B MD (NS) - **Spec Exp:** Spinal Surgery; Spinal Reconstructive Surgery; **Hospital:** Valley Hosp (page 739); **Address:** 225 Dayton St, Ridgewood, NJ 07450-4407; **Phone:** 201-612-0020; **Board Cert:** Neurological Surgery 1987; **Med School:** Columbia P&S 1978; **Resid:** Surgery, St Lukes Hosp 1980; Neurological Surgery, NY Neuro Inst-Columbia 1985

Fried, Arno H MD (NS) - **Spec Exp:** Epilepsy; Brain Tumors; Head Injury; Pediatric Neurosurgery; **Hospital:** Hackensack Univ Med Ctr (page 96), St. Peter's Univ Hosp; **Address:** Advanced Neurosurgery Assocs, 201 Route 17 N, Ste 501, Rutherford, NJ 07070; **Phone:** 201-457-0044; **Board Cert:** Neurological Surgery 1990; **Med School:** Meharry Med Coll 1980; **Resid:** Neurological Surgery, Montefiore Med Ctr 1986; Neurological Surgery, Univ Utah Hlth Care 1987; **Fellow:** Pediatric Neurological Surgery, Chldns Hosp 1987

Moore, Frank M MD (NS) - **Spec Exp:** Aneurysm-Cerebral; Brain Tumors; Spinal Cord Tumors; Spinal Surgery; **Hospital:** Englewood Hosp & Med Ctr, Mt Sinai Hosp; **Address:** Metropolitan Neurosurgery Assocs, 309 Engle St, Ste 6, Englewood, NJ 07631; **Phone:** 201-569-7737; **Board Cert:** Neurological Surgery 1992; **Med School:** France 1983; **Resid:** Neurological Surgery, Mt Sinai Hosp 1988; **Fac Appt:** Assoc Prof NS, Mount Sinai Sch Med

Peterson, Thomas R MD (NS) - **Spec Exp:** Spinal Surgery-Low Back; Cerebrovascular Malformations; Spinal Surgery-Cervical; **Hospital:** Hackensack Univ Med Ctr (page 96); **Address:** 140 Prospect Ave, Ste 18, Hackensack, NJ 07601-1262; **Phone:** 201-525-0500; **Board Cert:** Neurological Surgery 1987; **Med School:** Tufts Univ 1976; **Resid:** Surgery, Hosp Univ Penn 1977; Neurological Surgery, New England Med Ctr 1982

Roth, Patrick A MD (NS) - **Spec Exp:** Spinal Surgery; Brain Tumors; Pain-Back; **Hospital:** Hackensack Univ Med Ctr (page 96), Valley Hosp (page 739); **Address:** 680 Kinderkamack Rd, Ste 300, Oradell, NJ 07649; **Phone:** 201-342-2550; **Board Cert:** Neurological Surgery 1997; **Med School:** Albert Einstein Coll Med 1987; **Resid:** Neurological Surgery, New England Med Ctr 1994; **Fac Appt:** Asst Clin Prof NS, UMDNJ-NJ Med Sch, Newark

Steinberger, Alfred A MD (NS) - **Spec Exp:** Spinal Cord Tumors; Aneurysm; Brain Tumors; Spinal Surgery; **Hospital:** Mt Sinai Hosp, Englewood Hosp & Med Ctr; **Address:** 309 Engle St, Ste 6, Englewood, NJ 07631; **Phone:** 201-569-7737; **Board Cert:** Neurological Surgery 1985; **Med School:** Columbia P&S 1976; **Resid:** Neurological Surgery, Neuro Inst-Columbia-Presby 1982; **Fac Appt:** Asst Clin Prof NS, Mount Sinai Sch Med

Vingan, Roy D MD (NS) - **Spec Exp:** Spinal Surgery; Minimally Invasive Spinal Surgery; **Hospital:** Hackensack Univ Med Ctr (page 96), Valley Hosp (page 739); **Address:** North Jersey Brain and Spine Center, 680 Kinderkamack Rd, Ste 300, Oradell, NJ 07649; **Phone:** 201-342-2550; **Board Cert:** Neurological Surgery 1995; **Med School:** SUNY Downstate 1985; **Resid:** Neurological Surgery, SUNY Hlth Sci Ctr 1992

Neurology

Alweiss, Gary S MD (N) - **Spec Exp:** Electromyography; Carpal Tunnel Syndrome; Headache; Nerve Injuries; **Hospital:** Englewood Hosp & Med Ctr; **Address:** Bergen Neurology Consultants, 25 Rockwood Pl, Ste 110, Englewood, NJ 07631; **Phone:** 201-894-5805; **Board Cert:** Neurology 1993; Electrodiagnostic Medicine 2005; **Med School:** Mount Sinai Sch Med 1988; **Resid:** Neurology, Mount Sinai Hosp 1992; **Fellow:** Neuromuscular Disease, NY-Presby/Columbia Univ Med Ctr 1993; **Fac Appt:** Asst Clin Prof N, Columbia P&S

Citak, Kenneth A MD (N) - **Spec Exp:** Neuromuscular Disorders; Electromyography; Cerebrovascular Disease; Pain Management; **Hospital:** Valley Hosp (page 739); **Address:** Neurology Group of Bergen County, 1200 E Ridgewood Ave, W Wing Fl 2, Ridgewood, NJ 07450; **Phone:** 201-444-0868; **Board Cert:** Psychiatry 1992; **Med School:** NYU Sch Med 1986; **Resid:** Neurology, Mount Sinai Med Ctr 1990; **Fellow:** Neuromuscular Medicine, Mount Sinai Med Ctr 1991

Duncan, David B MD (N) - **Spec Exp:** Multiple Sclerosis; Neurodegenerative Disorders; **Hospital:** Holy Name Med Ctr (page 738); **Address:** Holy Name Med Ctr, Multiple Sclerosis, 718 Teaneck Rd, Teaneck, NJ 07666; **Phone:** 201-837-0727; **Board Cert:** Neurology 2008; **Med School:** Indiana Univ 1988; **Resid:** Neurology, Univ KY Med Ctr 1992

Effron, Charles R MD (N) - **Spec Exp:** Peripheral Neuropathy; **Hospital:** Mt Sinai Hosp; **Address:** 365 W Passaic St, Ste 105, Rochelle Park, NJ 07662; **Phone:** 201-845-6500; **Board Cert:** Neurology 1989; **Med School:** Brown Univ 1983; **Resid:** Internal Medicine, Beth Israel Med Ctr 1984; Neurology, Mt Sinai Hosp 1987

Fellman, Damon MD (N) - **Spec Exp:** Vascular Neurology; Headache; Pediatric Neurology; Epilepsy; **Hospital:** Hackensack Univ Med Ctr (page 96); **Address:** Hackensack Neurology Group, 211 Essex St, Ste 202, Hackensack, NJ 07601-3245; **Phone:** 201-488-1515; **Board Cert:** Neurology 1977; Vascular Neurology 2005; Headache Medicine 2009; **Med School:** Univ Cincinnati 1970; **Resid:** Neurology, Mount Sinai Hosp 1974; Pediatrics, Mount Sinai Hosp 1975; **Fellow:** Neurology, Johns Hopkins Hosp 1976

Klein, Patricia G MD (N) - **Spec Exp:** Headache; Dizziness; Stroke; **Address:** 680 Kinderkamack Rd, Ste 302, Oradell, NJ 07649; **Phone:** 201-261-6222; **Board Cert:** Neurology 1980; **Med School:** UMDNJ-NJ Med Sch, Newark 1976; **Resid:** Neurology, UMDNJ 1979

Levin, Kenneth A MD (N) - **Spec Exp:** Stroke; Alzheimer's Disease; Parkinson's Disease; Epilepsy; **Hospital:** Valley Hosp (page 739); **Address:** Neurology Group of Bergen County, 1200 E Ridgewood Ave, E Wing Fl 2, Ridgewood, NJ 07450; **Phone:** 201-444-0868; **Board Cert:** Neurology 1987; **Med School:** Indiana Univ 1982; **Resid:** Neurology, IU Hlth Univ Hosp 1986

Levy, Kirk MD (N) - **Spec Exp:** Epilepsy; **Hospital:** Englewood Hosp & Med Ctr; **Address:** Bergen Neurology Consultants, 25 Rockwood Pl, Ste 110, Englewood, NJ 07631; **Phone:** 201-894-5805; **Board Cert:** Neurology 1998; Clinical Neurophysiology 2008; **Med School:** SUNY Stony Brook 1993; **Resid:** Neurology, Barnes Jewish Hosp 1997; **Fellow:** Clinical Neurophysiology, Univ Mich Hosps 1999

Lijtmaer, Hugo N MD (N) - **Hospital:** Valley Hosp (page 739); **Address:** Neurology Group of Bergen County, 1200 E Ridgewood Ave, E Wing Fl 2, Ridgewood, NJ 07450; **Phone:** 201-444-0868; **Board Cert:** Neurology 1976; **Med School:** Argentina 1968; **Resid:** Neurology, Montefiore Med Ctr 1974

Noskin, Olga MD (N) - **Spec Exp:** Stroke; Vascular Neurology; **Hospital:** Valley Hosp (page 739); **Address:** Neurology Group of Bergen County, 1200 E Ridgewood Ave Fl 2, E Wing Fl 2, Ridgewood, NJ 07450; **Phone:** 201-444-0868; **Board Cert:** Neurology 2007; Vascular Neurology 2008; **Med School:** Albert Einstein Coll Med 2002; **Resid:** Neurology, NS-LIJ Hlth System 2006; **Fellow:** Vascular Neurology, NY-Presby/Columbia Univ Med Ctr 2007

Perron, Reed C MD (N) - **Hospital:** Valley Hosp (page 739); **Address:** Neurology Group of Bergen Co, 1200 E Ridgewood Ave Fl 2, E Wing, Ste 208, Ridgewood, NJ 07450; **Phone:** 201-444-0868; **Board Cert:** Neurology 1974; **Med School:** Univ Rochester 1966; **Resid:** Internal Medicine, Cleveland Clinic 1970; Neurology, Albert Einstein Coll Med 1973

Rabin, Aaron MD/PhD (N) - **Spec Exp:** Parkinson's Disease; Dementia; Peripheral Neuropathy; **Hospital:** Englewood Hosp & Med Ctr; **Address:** 700 E Palisade Ave, Englewood Cliffs, NJ 07632; **Phone:** 201-568-3412; **Board Cert:** Neurology 1981; **Med School:** Albert Einstein Coll Med 1976; **Resid:** Internal Medicine, Brookdale Hosp Med Ctr 1980; Neurology, Albert Einstein Coll Med Affil Hosps 1980; **Fellow:** Neuroelectrophysiology, Neur Inst-Columbia Presby 1981; **Fac Appt:** Asst Clin Prof Med, Mount Sinai Sch Med

Van Engel, Daniel R MD (N) - **Spec Exp:** Electromyography; Neuromuscular Disorders; Spinal Disorders; **Hospital:** Valley Hosp (page 739); **Address:** Neurology Group of Bergen County, 1200 E Ridgewood Ave, E Wing Fl 2 - Ste 208, Ridgewood, NJ 07450; **Phone:** 201-444-0868; **Board Cert:** Neurology 1980; **Med School:** SUNY Upstate Med Univ 1973; **Resid:** Internal Medicine, N Shore-LIJ Med Ctr 1975; Neurology, Montefiore Med Ctr 1978

Van Slooten, David D MD (N) - **Spec Exp:** Electromyography; Headache; Dementia; Brain & Spinal Imaging; **Hospital:** Holy Name Med Ctr (page 738), Valley Hosp (page 739); **Address:** 680 Kinderkamack Rd, Ste 302, Oradell, NJ 07649-1500; **Phone:** 201-261-6222; **Board Cert:** Neurology 1989; Clinical Neurophysiology 2004; Electrodiagnostic Medicine 2004; **Med School:** UMDNJ-NJ Med Sch, Newark 1984; **Resid:** Neurology, UMDNJ Univ Hosp 1988; **Fellow:** Clinical Neurophysiology, VA Med Ctr 1989

Willner, Joseph H MD (N) - **Spec Exp:** Multiple Sclerosis; Myasthenia Gravis; Peripheral Neuropathy; **Hospital:** Englewood Hosp & Med Ctr; **Address:** 25 Rockwood Pl, Ste 110, Englewood, NJ 07631-4363; **Phone:** 201-894-5805; **Board Cert:** Neurology 1978; **Med School:** NYU Sch Med 1970; **Resid:** Neurology, Columbia-Presby Hosp 1977; **Fac Appt:** Clin Prof N, Columbia P&S

Neuroradiology

Lerner, Elliot J MD (NRad) - **Spec Exp:** Brain & Spinal Imaging; Head & Neck Imaging; **Hospital:** Valley Hosp (page 739); **Address:** Radiology Assocs of Ridgewood, 20 Franklin Tpke, Waldwick, NJ 7463; **Phone:** 201-445-8822; **Board Cert:** Diagnostic Radiology 1990; Neuroradiology 2004; **Med School:** Brown Univ 1985; **Resid:** Diagnostic Radiology, Hosp Univ Penn 1989; **Fellow:** Neuroradiology, Hosp Univ Penn 1991

Pierce, Sean D MD (NRad) - **Spec Exp:** Neuro-Oncology; **Hospital:** Hackensack Univ Med Ctr (page 96); **Address:** HackensackUMC-Radiology, 30 Prospect Ave, Hackensack, NJ 07601; **Phone:** 551-996-2194; **Board Cert:** Diagnostic Radiology 1999; Neuroradiology 2012; **Med School:** Harvard Med Sch 1994; **Resid:** Internal Medicine, Mt Auburn Hosp 1995; Diagnostic Radiology, Barnes Hosp 1999; **Fellow:** Neurological Radiology, NYU Med Ctr 2001

Nuclear Medicine

Agress Jr, Harry MD (NuM) - **Spec Exp:** PET Imaging; Cancer Detection & Staging; Nuclear Oncology; CT Scan; **Hospital:** Hackensack Univ Med Ctr (page 96); **Address:** Hackensack University Medical Center, 30 Prospect Ave, Hackensack, NJ 07601; **Phone:** 201-996-2200; **Board Cert:** Nuclear Medicine 1976; Diagnostic Radiology 1978; **Med School:** Tufts Univ 1972; **Resid:** Radiology, Columbia-Presby Med Ctr 1978; **Fellow:** Nuclear Medicine, Natl Inst Hlth 1975; **Fac Appt:** Clin Prof Rad, Columbia P&S

Obstetrics & Gynecology

Butler, David G MD (ObG) *PCP* - **Spec Exp:** Gynecologic Surgery; Menopause Problems; **Hospital:** Holy Name Med Ctr (page 738), Englewood Hosp & Med Ctr; **Address:** 420 Grand Ave, Ste 201, Englewood, NJ 07631-4152; **Phone:** 201-871-4040; **Board Cert:** Obstetrics & Gynecology 1972; **Med School:** SUNY Downstate 1965; **Resid:** Obstetrics & Gynecology, St Vincents Hosp 1970

Cavallaro, Barbara A MD (ObG) - **Hospital:** Hackensack Univ Med Ctr (page 96); **Address:** 170 Prospect Ave, Bldg 2, Ste 4, Hackensack, NJ 07601-2255; **Phone:** 201-488-2288; **Board Cert:** Obstetrics & Gynecology 2014; **Med School:** NYU Sch Med 1986; **Resid:** Obstetrics & Gynecology, Mt Sinai Med Ctr 1991

Coven, Roger MD (ObG) - **Hospital:** Valley Hosp (page 739); **Address:** 581 N Franklin Tpke, Ramsey, NJ 07446; **Phone:** 201-236-2100; **Board Cert:** Obstetrics & Gynecology 2013; **Med School:** UMDNJ-NJ Med Sch, Newark 1980; **Resid:** Obstetrics & Gynecology, Thomas Jefferson Univ Hosp 1984

Englert, Christopher A MD (ObG) - **Spec Exp:** Gynecologic Surgery; Laparoscopic Surgery; Robotic Surgery; Vulvar & Vaginal Disorders; **Hospital:** Holy Name Med Ctr (page 738); **Address:** 420 Grand Ave, Ste 201, Englewood, NJ 07631; **Phone:** 201-871-4040; **Board Cert:** Obstetrics & Gynecology 2013; **Med School:** Univ Cincinnati 1985; **Resid:** Obstetrics & Gynecology, Thomas Jefferson Univ Hosp 1990

Faust, Michael G MD (ObG) - **Spec Exp:** Gynecologic Surgery; Menopause Problems; Minimally Invasive Surgery; Gynecology Only; **Hospital:** Valley Hosp (page 739); **Address:** Valley Ctr for Womens Hlth, 581 N Franklin Tpke Fl 2, Ramsey, NJ 07446; **Phone:** 201-236-2100; **Board Cert:** Obstetrics & Gynecology 2013; **Med School:** Univ Pittsburgh 1983; **Resid:** Obstetrics & Gynecology, Thomas Jefferson Univ Hosp 1988

Fernandez, Jacinto J MD (ObG) - **Spec Exp:** Women's Health; Uro-Gynecology; **Hospital:** Holy Name Med Ctr (page 738); **Address:** 222 Cedar Ln, Ste 207, Teaneck, NJ 07666; **Phone:** 201-833-7087; **Board Cert:** Obstetrics & Gynecology 1976; **Med School:** Spain 1967; **Resid:** Obstetrics & Gynecology, St. Joseph's Hosp 1975

Hurst, Wendy R MD (ObG) - **Spec Exp:** Gynecology Only; Laparoscopic Surgery; Menopause Problems; Adolescent Gynecology; **Hospital:** Englewood Hosp & Med Ctr; **Address:** 370 Grand Ave, Ste 202, Englewood, NJ 07631-4109; **Phone:** 201-894-9599; **Board Cert:** Obstetrics & Gynecology 2013; **Med School:** Tufts Univ 1986; **Resid:** Obstetrics & Gynecology, Hosp Univ Penn - UPHS 1991

Meyer, Monica L MD (ObG) - **Spec Exp:** Gynecology Only; Adolescent Gynecology; Menopause Problems; Gynecologic Surgery; **Hospital:** Valley Hosp (page 739); **Address:** Bergen Medical Associates, 1 W Ridgewood Ave, Ste 211, Paramus, NJ 07652; **Phone:** 201-251-2323; **Board Cert:** Obstetrics & Gynecology 2013; **Med School:** SUNY Hlth Sci Ctr 1991; **Resid:** Obstetrics & Gynecology, Lenox Hill Hosp 1995

Miller, Lisa Ann B MD (ObG) - **Spec Exp:** Gynecology Only; **Hospital:** Hackensack Univ Med Ctr (page 96); **Address:** Excelsior Women's Care, 170 Prospect Ave, Ste 4, Hackensack, NJ 07601-1931; **Phone:** 201-488-2288; **Board Cert:** Obstetrics & Gynecology 2013; **Med School:** Med Coll PA Hahnemann 1988; **Resid:** Obstetrics & Gynecology, Lenox Hill Hosp 1992

Rezvani, Fred F MD (ObG) - **Spec Exp:** Pregnancy-High Risk; Minimally Invasive Surgery; Congenital Anomalies-Gynecologic; **Hospital:** Valley Hosp (page 739); **Address:** 119 Prospect St, Ridgewood, NJ 07450; **Phone:** 201-444-1600; **Board Cert:** Obstetrics & Gynecology 2013; **Med School:** Grenada 1983; **Resid:** Obstetrics & Gynecology, Lincoln Med & Mental Hlth Ctr 1988

Rubenstein, Andrew F MD (ObG) - **Hospital:** Hackensack Univ Med Ctr (page 96); **Address:** 82 E Allendale Rd, Ste 1A, Saddle River, NJ 07458; **Phone:** 201-934-5050; **Board Cert:** Obstetrics & Gynecology 2013; **Med School:** Hahnemann Univ 1990; **Resid:** Obstetrics & Gynecology, Mt Sinai Hosp 1995

Schulze, Ruth J MD (ObG) - **Spec Exp:** Vulvar Disease; Osteoporosis; Adolescent Gynecology; Women's Health over age 40; **Hospital:** Valley Hosp (page 739); **Address:** Women's Total Hlth, 577 Chestnut Ridge Rd Fl 2, Woodcliff Lake, NJ 7677; **Phone:** 201-391-5770; **Board Cert:** Obstetrics & Gynecology 2013; **Med School:** SUNY Stony Brook 1983; **Resid:** Obstetrics & Gynecology, Baystate Med Ctr 1987

Ophthalmology

Angioletti, Louis Scott MD (Oph) - **Spec Exp:** Retina/Vitreous Surgery; Retinal Disorders; Retinal Disorders-Pediatric; **Hospital:** Hackensack Univ Med Ctr (page 96); **Address:** Angioletti Retina Assocs, 1617 Palisade Ave, Fort Lee, NJ 07024; **Phone:** 201-947-1900; **Board Cert:** Ophthalmology 2014; **Med School:** Georgetown Univ 1986; **Resid:** Internal Medicine, N Shore Univ Hosp 1987; Ophthalmology, NY Eye & Ear Infirm 1990; **Fellow:** Vitreoretinal Surgery, Baylor Med Ctr 1992; **Fac Appt:** Assoc Clin Prof Oph, NY Med Coll

Brown, Andrew C MD (Oph) - **Spec Exp:** LASIK-Refractive Surgery; Cataract Surgery; Macular Degeneration; **Hospital:** Hackensack Univ Med Ctr (page 96); **Address:** Brown Eye Care Assocs, 751 Teaneck Rd, Teaneck, NJ 07666; **Phone:** 201-833-0006; **Board Cert:** Ophthalmology 2009; **Med School:** Boston Univ 2002; **Resid:** Ophthalmology, New York Eye & Ear Infirm 2007

Brown, Christopher D MD (Oph) - **Spec Exp:** Corneal Disease; Diabetic Eye Disease/Retinopathy; LASIK-Refractive Surgery; **Hospital:** Englewood Hosp & Med Ctr, Holy Name Med Ctr (page 738); **Address:** Brown Eye Care Assocs, 751 Teaneck Rd, Teaneck, NJ 07666; **Phone:** 201-833-0006; **Med School:** Boston Univ 1996; **Resid:** Ophthalmology, Wills Eye Hosp 2001; **Fellow:** Cornea, Vision Correction Ctr 2002

Burke, Patricia A MD (Oph) - **Spec Exp:** Corneal Disease; Cataract Surgery; **Hospital:** Holy Name Med Ctr (page 738); **Address:** One Sears Drive, Paramus, NJ 07652; **Phone:** 201-599-0123; **Board Cert:** Ophthalmology 1991; **Med School:** UMDNJ-NJ Med Sch, Newark 1986; **Resid:** Ophthalmology, NY-Presby/Columbia Univ Med Ctr 1990; **Fellow:** Cornea, Lenox Hill Hosp (Manh Eye, Ear & Throat Hosp) 1991

Chin, Patrick K MD (Oph) - **Spec Exp:** Laser Vision Surgery; Cataract Surgery; Refractive Surgery; **Hospital:** Valley Hosp (page 739); **Address:** Westwood Ophthalmology Assocs, 300 Fairview Ave, Westwood, NJ 07675; **Phone:** 201-666-4014; **Board Cert:** Ophthalmology 2007; **Med School:** UMDNJ-NJ Med Sch, Newark 1989; **Resid:** Ophthalmology, NYU Langone Med Ctr 1994; **Fellow:** Refractive Surgery, Gimbel Eye Ctr 1995

DeLuca, Joseph A MD (Oph) - **Spec Exp:** Cataract Surgery; Laser Refractive Surgery; Anterior Segment Surgery; Trauma; **Hospital:** Clara Maass Med Ctr (page 94); **Address:** 20 Park Ave Fl 1, Lyndhurst, NJ 07071-1012; **Phone:** 201-896-0096; **Board Cert:** Ophthalmology 1991; **Med School:** UMDNJ-Rutgers Med Sch 1985; **Resid:** Ophthalmology, United Hosp Med Ctr 1990; **Fac Appt:** Asst Clin Prof Oph, UMDNJ-NJ Med Sch, Newark

Geller, Bradley D MD (Oph) - **Spec Exp:** Corneal Disease & Surgery; LASIK-Refractive Surgery; Cataract Surgery; Glaucoma; **Hospital:** Hackensack Univ Med Ctr (page 96); **Address:** 466 Old Hook Rd, Ste 24E, Emerson, NJ 07630; **Phone:** 201-265-7515; **Board Cert:** Ophthalmology 2014; **Med School:** Univ Rochester 1998; **Resid:** Ophthalmology, SUNY Health Sci Ctr 2002; **Fellow:** Cornea & Refractive Surgery, Piedmont Hosp 2003

Hersh, Peter S MD (Oph) - **Spec Exp:** LASIK-Refractive Surgery; Cornea Transplant; Keratoconus; **Hospital:** Univ Hosp-Newark; **Address:** Cornea & Laser Eye Inst-Hersh Vision Grp, Glenpointe Center East, 300 Frank W Burr Blvd, Ste 71, Teaneck, NJ 07666-6704; **Phone:** 201-883-0505; **Board Cert:** Ophthalmology 1987; **Med School:** Johns Hopkins Univ 1982; **Resid:** Internal Medicine, Lenox Hill Hosp 1983; Ophthalmology, Mass Eye & Ear Infirm 1986; **Fellow:** Cornea & Ext Eye Disease, Mass Eye & Ear Infirm 1987; **Fac Appt:** Clin Prof Oph, UMDNJ-NJ Med Sch, Newark

Liva, Douglas MD (Oph) - **Spec Exp:** LASIK-Refractive Surgery; Cataract Surgery; Glaucoma; **Hospital:** Valley Hosp (page 739); **Address:** Liva Eye Center, 625 Franklin Tpke, Ridgewood, NJ 07450-2350; **Phone:** 201-444-7770; **Board Cert:** Ophthalmology 1987; **Med School:** Univ Miami Sch Med 1981; **Resid:** Ophthalmology, UMDNJ Affil Hosps 1986

Norden, Richard A MD (Oph) - **Spec Exp:** LASIK-Refractive Surgery; Laser Vision Surgery; Botox Therapy; **Address:** Norden Laser Eye Associates, 1144 E Ridgewood Ave, Ridgewood, NJ 07450-3915; **Phone:** 201-444-2442; **Board Cert:** Ophthalmology 1985; **Med School:** Southern IL Univ 1980; **Resid:** Ophthalmology, UMDNJ Med Ctr 1984; **Fellow:** Cornea & Refractive Surgery, NY Eye & Ear Infirm 1986; **Fac Appt:** Asst Clin Prof Oph, NY Med Coll

Rosenberg, Michael E MD (Oph) - **Spec Exp:** Corneal Disease & Surgery; Cataract Surgery; Cataract Surgery-Lens Implant; Cornea Transplant; **Hospital:** Hackensack Univ Med Ctr (page 96); **Address:** 301 Bridge Plaza N, Fort Lee, NJ 07024; **Phone:** 201-947-5929; **Board Cert:** Ophthalmology 2008; **Med School:** NYU Sch Med 1992; **Resid:** Internal Medicine, Dartmouth Hitchcock Med Ctr 1993; Ophthalmology, NY E & E Infirm 1996; **Fellow:** Cornea & Ext Eye Disease, St Barnabas Med Ctr 1997

Silbert, Glenn R MD (Oph) - **Hospital:** Hackensack Univ Med Ctr (page 96), New York Eye & Ear Infirm of Mt Sinai; **Address:** 316 State St, Hackensack, NJ 07601-5529; **Phone:** 201-342-8115; **Board Cert:** Ophthalmology 1985; **Med School:** Columbia P&S 1979; **Resid:** Surgery, Beth Israel Med Ctr 1980; Ophthalmology, NYU Langone Med Ctr 1983; **Fac Appt:** Assoc Clin Prof Oph, Mount Sinai-Icahn Sch of Med

Stabile, John R MD (Oph) - **Spec Exp:** Cataract Surgery; Oculoplastic Surgery; LASIK-Refractive Surgery; **Hospital:** Englewood Hosp & Med Ctr; **Address:** Tenafly Eye Assocs, 111 Dean Drive, Tenafly, NJ 07670; **Phone:** 201-567-5995; **Board Cert:** Ophthalmology 1981; **Med School:** NY Med Coll 1976; **Resid:** Ophthalmology, St Lukes-Roosevelt Hosp Ctr 1980; **Fellow:** Oculoplastic & Reconstructive Surgery, NY-Presby/Columbia Univ Med Ctr 1981

Topilow, Harvey W MD (Oph) - **Spec Exp:** Retinal Disorders; Macular Degeneration; Retinopathy of Prematurity; **Hospital:** New York Eye & Ear Infirm of Mt Sinai; **Address:** 301 Bridge Plaza N, Fort Lee, NJ 07024; **Phone:** 212-288-3860; **Board Cert:** Ophthalmology 1980; **Med School:** Columbia P&S 1975; **Resid:** Internal Medicine, Montefiore Med Ctr 1976; Ophthalmology, Albert Einstein Coll Med Affil Hosps 1979; **Fellow:** Vitreoretinal Surgery, Mass Eye & Ear Infirm 1980; **Fac Appt:** Assoc Clin Prof Oph, Albert Einstein Coll Med

Weinberg, Martin R MD (Oph) - **Spec Exp:** Neuro-Ophthalmology; Glaucoma; **Hospital:** Englewood Hosp & Med Ctr, Hackensack Univ Med Ctr (page 96); **Address:** 405 Cedar Ln, Ste 5, Teaneck, NJ 07666-1715; **Phone:** 201-836-8333; **Board Cert:** Ophthalmology 1989; **Med School:** Eastern VA Med Sch 1979; **Resid:** Surgery, Albany Meml Hosp 1981; Ophthalmology, Kings Co Hosp Ctr 1986; **Fellow:** Ophthalmic Pathology, Scheie Eye Inst-Univ Penn 1983; Oncology, Lenox Hill Hosp (Manh Eye, Ear & Throat Hosp) 1988

Orthopaedic Surgery

Altman, Wayne J MD (OrS) - **Spec Exp:** Carpal Tunnel Syndrome; Knee Injuries; Hand & Wrist Injuries; Shoulder Injuries; **Hospital:** St. Mary's Hosp - Passaic, Meadowlands Hosp Med Ctr; **Address:** 85 Orient Way, FL 1, Rutherford, NJ 07070; **Phone:** 201-438-5888; **Board Cert:** Orthopaedic Surgery 2009; **Med School:** UMDNJ-NJ Med Sch, Newark 1978; **Resid:** Orthopaedic Surgery, UMDNJ-NJ Med Sch Affil Hosp 1983; **Fellow:** Hand Surgery, Thomas Jefferson Univ Hosp 1984

Berberian, Wayne S MD (OrS) - **Spec Exp:** Bone Infections; Foot & Ankle Deformities; Foot & Ankle Surgery-Complex; Tendon Surgery; **Hospital:** Hackensack Univ Med Ctr (page 96), Univ Hosp-Newark; **Address:** Hackensack University Medical Center, Medical Plaza Building, 20 Prospect Ave, Ste 901, Hackensack, NJ 07601; **Phone:** 973-972-8464; **Board Cert:** Orthopaedic Surgery 2013; **Med School:** Med Coll PA 1991; **Resid:** Surgery, St Lukes Roosevelt Hosp 1992; Orthopaedic Surgery, UMDNJ Univ Hosp 1998; **Fellow:** Orthopaedic Research, Hosp for Special Surgery 1994; Foot & Ankle Reconstruction, Hahnemann Univ Hosp 1999; **Fac Appt:** Assoc Prof OrS, UMDNJ-Rutgers Med Sch

Berman, Mark S MD (OrS) - **Spec Exp:** Knee Surgery; Shoulder Surgery; Rotator Cuff Surgery; Sports Medicine; **Hospital:** Hackensack Univ Med Ctr (page 96), Holy Name Med Ctr (page 738); **Address:** 920 Main St Fl 2, Hackensack, NJ 07601-3246; **Phone:** 201-489-8250; **Board Cert:** Orthopaedic Surgery 2010; **Med School:** Mount Sinai Sch Med 1981; **Resid:** Surgery, Mt Sinai Med Ctr 1983; Orthopaedic Surgery, SUNY Downstate Med Ctr (Univ Hosp Brooklyn) 1986; **Fellow:** Sports Medicine, Lenox Hill Hosp 1987

Cahill, James W MD (OrS) - **Spec Exp:** Arthroscopic Surgery-Knee; Joint Replacement; Shoulder Arthroscopic Surgery; Cartilage Damage; **Hospital:** Hackensack Univ Med Ctr (page 96), Holy Name Med Ctr (page 738); **Address:** 87 Summit Ave, Hackensack, NJ 07601; **Phone:** 201-489-0022; **Board Cert:** Orthopaedic Surgery 2010; **Med School:** Columbia P&S 1990; **Resid:** Orthopaedic Surgery, Montefiore Med Ctr 1995; **Fellow:** Sports Medicine, NYU Hosp For Joint Dis 1996

Distefano, Michael C MD (OrS) - **Spec Exp:** Fractures-Stress; Shoulder & Knee Surgery; Trauma; Sports Medicine; **Hospital:** Hackensack Univ Med Ctr (page 96), Valley Hosp (page 739); **Address:** 140 Route 17 N, Ste 255, Paramus, NJ 07652; **Phone:** 201-261-5501; **Board Cert:** Orthopaedic Surgery 1983; Orthopaedic Sports Medicine 2007; **Med School:** Albert Einstein Coll Med 1977; **Resid:** Orthopaedic Surgery, Montefiore Med Ctr 1981; **Fellow:** Orthopaedic Sports Medicine, Montefiore Med Ctr 2007

Doidge, Robert W DO (OrS) - **Spec Exp:** Knee Surgery; Shoulder Surgery; Sports Medicine; **Hospital:** Englewood Hosp & Med Ctr; **Address:** 370 Grand Ave, Ste 100, Englewood, NJ 07631-4109; **Phone:** 201-567-5700; **Board Cert:** Orthopaedic Surgery 2006; **Med School:** Philadelphia Coll Osteo Med 1986; **Resid:** Orthopaedic Surgery, St. John Macomb-Oakland Hosp-Oakland Campus 1992; **Fellow:** Sports Medicine, Michigan State Univ Affil Hosp 1993

Esformes, Ira MD (OrS) - **Spec Exp:** Sports Medicine; Arthroscopic Surgery; Joint Replacement; **Hospital:** Valley Hosp (page 739), Hackensack Univ Med Ctr (page 96); **Address:** 440 Old Hook Rd Fl 2, Emerson, NJ 07630-1325; **Phone:** 201-261-3333; **Board Cert:** Orthopaedic Surgery 1985; Orthopaedic Sports Medicine 2009; **Med School:** Albany Med Coll 1977; **Resid:** Surgery, N Shore Univ Hosp 1979; Orthopaedic Surgery, Hosp for Joint Diseases 1983

Gennace, Ronald E MD (OrS) - **Hospital:** Clara Maass Med Ctr (page 94), Saint Michael's Med Ctr; **Address:** 312 Belleville Tpke, Ste 2A, North Arlington, NJ 07031; **Phone:** 201-997-8777; **Board Cert:** Orthopaedic Surgery 1982; **Med School:** UMDNJ-NJ Med Sch, Newark 1976; **Resid:** Orthopaedic Surgery, St. Joseph's Regl Med Ctr 1982

Hale, James J MD (OrS) - **Spec Exp:** Spinal Surgery; Pain-Back; Minimally Invasive Spinal Surgery; **Hospital:** Holy Name Med Ctr (page 738), NYU Hosp For Joint Dis (page 104); **Address:** 222 Cedar Ln, Ste 120, Teaneck, NJ 07666; **Phone:** 201-836-5332; **Board Cert:** Orthopaedic Surgery 2007; **Med School:** NYU Sch Med 1998; **Resid:** Orthopaedic Surgery, NYU Med Ctr 2003; **Fellow:** Spine Surgery, NYU Med Ctr 2004; **Fac Appt:** Asst Clin Prof OrS, NYU Sch Med

Hartzband, Mark A MD (OrS) - **Spec Exp:** Knee Replacement; Hip Replacement; **Hospital:** Hackensack Univ Med Ctr (page 96), Holy Name Med Ctr (page 738); **Address:** 10 Forest Ave, Paramus, NJ 07652; **Phone:** 201-291-4040; **Board Cert:** Orthopaedic Surgery 2007; **Med School:** McGill Univ 1978; **Resid:** Surgery, Montefiore Med Ctr 1981; Orthopaedic Surgery, Montefiore Med Ctr 1984

Implicito, Dante A MD (OrS) - **Spec Exp:** Spinal Surgery; Spinal Disorders-Degenerative; **Hospital:** Hackensack Univ Med Ctr (page 96); **Address:** 266 Harristown Rd, Glen Rock, NJ 07452; **Phone:** 201-251-7725; **Board Cert:** Orthopaedic Surgery 2009; **Med School:** UMDNJ-NJ Med Sch, Newark 1990; **Resid:** Orthopaedic Surgery, UMDNJ Med Ctr 1995; **Fellow:** Spine Surgery, St Marys Hosp 1996

Kayal, Robert A MD (OrS) - **Spec Exp:** Elbow Surgery; Hip & Knee Surgery; Joint Reconstruction; Minimally Invasive Surgery; **Hospital:** Valley Hosp (page 739), Chilton Med Ctr (page 92); **Address:** Kayal Orthopaedic Ctr, 385 S Maple Ave, Ste 206, Ridgewood, NJ 07450; **Phone:** 201-447-3880; **Board Cert:** Orthopaedic Surgery 2012; **Med School:** UMDNJ-Rutgers Med Sch 1994; **Resid:** Surgery, LI Jewish Med Ctr 1995; Orthopaedic Surgery, LI Jewish Med Ctr 1999

Kelly, Michael A MD (OrS) - **Spec Exp:** Knee Surgery; Knee Replacement; Arthroscopic Surgery; **Hospital:** Hackensack Univ Med Ctr (page 96), Lenox Hill Hosp; **Address:** 360 Essex St, Ste 303, Hackensack, NJ 07601; **Phone:** 551-996-8867; **Board Cert:** Orthopaedic Surgery 2009; **Med School:** Georgetown Univ 1979; **Resid:** Surgery, St Vincents Hosp 1981; Orthopaedic Surgery, NY-Presby/Columbia Univ Med Ctr 1984; **Fellow:** Knee Surgery, Hosp for Special Surgery 1985

Longobardi, Raphael MD (OrS) - **Spec Exp:** Shoulder Surgery; Rotator Cuff Surgery; Knee Surgery; Sports Medicine; **Hospital:** Holy Name Med Ctr (page 738), Hackensack Univ Med Ctr (page 96); **Address:** 433 Hackensack Ave Fl 2, Hackensack, NJ 07601; **Phone:** 201-343-1717; **Board Cert:** Orthopaedic Surgery 2009; Orthopaedic Sports Medicine 2011; **Med School:** NYU Sch Med 1990; **Resid:** Orthopaedic Surgery, NYU Med Ct 1995; **Fellow:** Sports Medicine, Univ of Tennessee Med Ctr 1996

McIlveen, Stephen J MD (OrS) - **Spec Exp:** Joint Replacement; Sports Medicine; Shoulder Surgery; Knee Surgery; **Hospital:** Valley Hosp (page 739), Hackensack Univ Med Ctr (page 96); **Address:** 1 W Ridgewood Ave, Ste 307, Paramus, NJ 07652; **Phone:** 201-670-6702; **Board Cert:** Orthopaedic Surgery 1983; **Med School:** NYU Sch Med 1973; **Resid:** Surgery, NY-Presby/Columbia Univ Med Ctr 1975; Orthopaedic Surgery, NY-Presby/Columbia Univ Med Ctr 1978; **Fellow:** Joint Replacement Surgery, NY-Presby/Columbia Univ Med Ctr 1979; Elbow & Shoulder Surgery, NY-Presby/Columbia Univ Med Ctr 1979; **Fac Appt:** Asst Prof OrS, Columbia P&S

Pollock, Roger G MD (OrS) - **Spec Exp:** Rotator Cuff Surgery; Shoulder Injuries; Shoulder Arthroscopic Surgery; **Hospital:** NY-Presby/Columbia Univ Med Ctr, NY (page 102), Valley Hosp (page 739); **Address:** 1 W Ridgewood Ave, Ste 202, Paramus, NJ 07652; **Phone:** 201-612-9774; **Board Cert:** Orthopaedic Surgery 2005; **Med School:** Columbia P&S 1985; **Resid:** Surgery, St Lukes-Roosevelt Hosp 1987; Orthopaedic Surgery, NY-Presby/Columbia Univ Med Ctr 1991; **Fellow:** Shoulder Surgery, NY-Presby/Columbia Univ Med Ctr 1992; **Fac Appt:** Asst Prof OrS, Columbia P&S

Salzer Jr, Richard L MD (OrS) - **Spec Exp:** Hip & Knee Replacement; Knee Surgery; Joint Replacement; Minimally Invasive Surgery; **Hospital:** Englewood Hosp & Med Ctr, Palisades Med Ctr; **Address:** Englewood Orthopedic Assocs, 401 S Van Brunt St Fl 3, Englewood, NJ 07631-4800; **Phone:** 201-569-2770; **Board Cert:** Orthopaedic Surgery 1979; **Med School:** Tufts Univ 1973; **Resid:** Surgery, UT Southwestern Med Ctr-St. Paul Campus 1975; Orthopaedic Surgery, Hosp Special Surg 1978

Wittig, James C MD (OrS) - **Spec Exp:** Bone Tumors; Sarcoma-Soft Tissue; Reconstructive Surgery; Pediatric Orthopaedic Cancers; **Hospital:** Hackensack Univ Med Ctr (page 96); **Address:** HUMC, Orthopaedic Surgery, 20 Prospect Ave, Ste 501, Hackensack, NJ 07601; **Phone:** 551-996-2533; **Board Cert:** Orthopaedic Surgery 2014; **Med School:** NYU Sch Med 1994; **Resid:** Orthopaedic Surgery, NY-Presby/Columbia Univ Med Ctr 1999; **Fellow:** Orthopaedic Oncology, Washington Cancer Inst 2001; Orthopaedic Oncology, Natl Inst Hlth 2001

Otolaryngology

Benson, Brian E MD (Oto) - **Spec Exp:** Vocal Cord Disorders; Voice Disorders; Throat Disorders; **Hospital:** Hackensack Univ Med Ctr (page 96); **Address:** 20 Prospect Ave, Ste 909, Hackensack, NJ 07601; **Phone:** 551-996-2750; **Board Cert:** Otolaryngology 2009; **Med School:** Columbia P&S 2003; **Resid:** Otolaryngology, UMDNJ Med Ctr 2008

Henick, David H MD (Oto) - **Spec Exp:** Nasal & Sinus Surgery; Endoscopic Sinus Surgery; Head & Neck Surgery; **Hospital:** Englewood Hosp & Med Ctr, Hackensack Univ Med Ctr (page 96); **Address:** 301 Bridge Plaza N Fl 3, Fort Lee, NJ 07024-5059; **Phone:** 201-592-8200; **Board Cert:** Otolaryngology 1993; **Med School:** SUNY Buffalo 1987; **Resid:** Otolaryngology, Montefiore Med Ctr 1992; **Fellow:** Head and Neck Surgery, Montefiore Med Ctr 1993; Endocrine Surgery, Hosp Univ Penn - UPHS 1994; **Fac Appt:** Asst Clin Prof Oto, Mount Sinai Sch Med

Ho, Bryan MD (Oto) - **Spec Exp:** Sinus Surgery; Thyroid & Parathyroid Surgery; **Hospital:** Englewood Hosp & Med Ctr, Holy Name Med Ctr (page 738); **Address:** Englewood ENT, 216 Engle St, Ste 101, Englewood, NJ 07631; **Phone:** 201-816-9800; **Board Cert:** Otolaryngology 1995; **Med School:** Mount Sinai Sch Med 1989; **Resid:** Surgery, Mt Sinai Hosp 1990; Otolaryngology, Mt Sinai Hosp 1994

Inouye, Masayuki MD (Oto) - **Spec Exp:** Thyroid Disorders; Thyroid Cancer & Surgery; **Hospital:** Hackensack Univ Med Ctr (page 96); **Address:** 20 Prospect Ave, Ste 909, Hackensack, NJ 07601; **Phone:** 201-489-6520; **Board Cert:** Otolaryngology 2012; **Med School:** SUNY Stony Brook 1996; **Resid:** Otolaryngology, Stanford Univ Med Ctr 2001

Katz, Harry MD (Oto) - **Spec Exp:** Nasal & Sinus Disorders; **Hospital:** Valley Hosp (page 739); **Address:** 44 Godwin Ave, Ste 300, Midland Park, NJ 07432-1959; **Phone:** 201-445-2900; **Board Cert:** Otolaryngology 1982; **Med School:** NYU Sch Med 1977; **Resid:** Surgery, LIJ Med Ctr 1978; Otolaryngology, NYU Langone Med Ctr 1981

Low, Ronald B MD (Oto) - **Spec Exp:** Sinus Disorders/Surgery; **Hospital:** Hackensack Univ Med Ctr (page 96); **Address:** 20 Prospect Ave, Ste 909, Hackensack, NJ 07601-5013; **Phone:** 201-489-6520; **Board Cert:** Otolaryngology 1974; **Med School:** UMDNJ-NJ Med Sch, Newark 1969; **Resid:** Surgery, Montefiore Med Ctr 1971; Otolaryngology, Bellevue Hosp Ctr 1974; **Fac Appt:** Asst Clin Prof Oto, UMDNJ-NJ Med Sch, Newark

Milgrim, Laurence M MD (Oto) - **Spec Exp:** Facial Plastic Surgery; **Hospital:** Holy Name Med Ctr (page 738), Valley Hosp (page 739); **Address:** 1 Degraw Ave, Teaneck, NJ 07666; **Phone:** 201-837-2174; **Board Cert:** Otolaryngology 1995; Facial Plastic & Reconstr Surgery 2000; **Med School:** UMDNJ-Rutgers Med Sch 1989; **Resid:** Otolaryngology, Montefiore Med Ctr 1995; **Fellow:** Facial Plastic & Reconstr Surgery, Mt Sinai Med Ctr 1995

Rosen, Arie MD (Oto) - **Spec Exp:** Head & Neck Tumors; Sinus Disorders; Facial Plastic Surgery; Ear Surgery; **Hospital:** Hackensack Univ Med Ctr (page 96), Englewood Hosp & Med Ctr; **Address:** 2 S Summit Ave, Hackensack, NJ 07601-1117; **Phone:** 201-996-9200; **Board Cert:** Otolaryngology 1995; **Med School:** Israel 1979; **Resid:** Otolaryngology, Univ Chicago-Pritzker Sch Affil Hosp 1994; **Fac Appt:** Assoc Clin Prof S, UMDNJ-NJ Med Sch, Newark

Scherl, Michael P MD (Oto) - **Spec Exp:** Hearing Loss/Tinnitus; Nasal & Sinus Disorders; **Hospital:** Englewood Hosp & Med Ctr; **Address:** 354 Old Hook Rd, Ste 204, Westwood, NJ 07675; **Phone:** 201-666-8787; **Board Cert:** Otolaryngology 1987; **Med School:** Albany Med Coll 1982; **Resid:** Surgery, Mount Sinai Med Ctr 1984; Otolaryngology, Mount Sinai Med Ctr 1987; **Fac Appt:** , Mount Sinai Sch Med

Shaari, Christopher M MD (Oto) - **Spec Exp:** Sinus Disorders/Surgery; Thyroid & Parathyroid Cancer & Surgery; **Hospital:** Hackensack Univ Med Ctr (page 96); **Address:** 20 Prospect Ave, Ste 712, Hackensack, NJ 07601; **Phone:** 201-342-8060; **Board Cert:** Otolaryngology 1997; **Med School:** Albany Med Coll 1991; **Resid:** Otolaryngology, Mt Sinai Hosp 1996; **Fellow:** Head and Neck Surgery, Mt Sinai Hosp 1997

Surow, Jason B MD (Oto) - **Spec Exp:** Pediatric Otolaryngology; Sinus Disorders; Voice Disorders; **Hospital:** Valley Hosp (page 739), Good Samaritan Regional Med Ctr; **Address:** 690 Kinderkamack Rd, Ste 101, Oradell, NJ 07649; **Phone:** 201-722-9850; **Board Cert:** Otolaryngology 1987; **Med School:** Univ Pennsylvania 1982; **Resid:** Surgery, Hosp Univ Penn - UPHS 1984; Otolaryngology, Hosp Univ Penn - UPHS 1987

Tobias, Geoffrey W MD (Oto) - **Spec Exp:** Rhinoplasty; Rhinoplasty Revision; Nasal Reconstruction; **Hospital:** Englewood Hosp & Med Ctr, Mt Sinai Hosp; **Address:** 214 Engle St, Ste 22, Englewood, NJ 07631; **Phone:** 201-567-6770; **Board Cert:** Otolaryngology 1978; **Med School:** Tufts Univ 1973; **Resid:** Otolaryngology, Mt Sinai Med Ctr 1978; **Fac Appt:** Asst Clin Prof Oto, Mount Sinai Sch Med

Pain Medicine

Datta, Samyadev MD (PM) - **Spec Exp:** Complex Regional Pain Syndromes; Pain-Cancer; Pain-Back; **Hospital:** Holy Name Med Ctr (page 738); **Address:** Ctr for Pain Management, 294 State St, Ste 1, Hackensack, NJ 07601; **Phone:** 201-488-7246; **Board Cert:** Anesthesiology 1996; Pain Medicine 2009; **Med School:** India 1979; **Resid:** Anesthesiology, NY-Presby/Columbia Univ Med Ctr 1994

Park, Kenneth H DO (PM) - **Spec Exp:** Pain-Chronic; Pain-Back; Pain-Neuropathic; Pain-Cancer; **Hospital:** Holy Name Med Ctr (page 738); **Address:** 680 Kinderkamack Rd, Ste 207, Oradell, NJ 07649; **Phone:** 201-487-7246; **Board Cert:** Anesthesiology 2007; Pain Medicine 2007; **Med School:** NY Coll Osteo Med 2002; **Resid:** Anesthesiology, Brigham & Women's Hosp 2006; **Fellow:** Pain Medicine, Brigham & Women's Hosp 2007

Ragukonis, Thomas P MD (PM) - ; **Address:** Bergen Pain Mngmt, 37 W Century Rd, Ste 101, Paramus, NJ 07652; **Phone:** 201-634-9000; **Board Cert:** Anesthesiology 1999; Pain Medicine 2000; **Med School:** UMDNJ-NJ Med Sch, Newark 1991; **Resid:** Anesthesiology, NY-Presby/Columbia Univ Med Ctr 1996

Silverman, Robert S MD (PM) - **Spec Exp:** Pain Management; Trauma Rehabilitation; **Hospital:** Valley Hosp (page 739); **Address:** Vally Inst for Pain, 1 Valley Health Plaza, Paramus, NJ 07652; **Phone:** 201-634-5555; **Board Cert:** Anesthesiology 1999; Pain Medicine 2011; **Med School:** NE Ohio Univ 1993; **Resid:** Anesthesiology, Cleveland Clin 1997; **Fellow:** Pain Medicine, Cleveland Clin 2000

Pathology

Bhattacharyya, Pritish K MD (Path) - **Spec Exp:** Leukemia & Lymphoma; Fine Needle Aspiration Biopsy; Lymph Node Pathology; **Hospital:** Hackensack Univ Med Ctr (page 96); **Address:** Hackensack Pathology Assocs, 30 Prospect Ave, rm 1000D, Hackensack, NJ 07601; **Phone:** 551-996-4811; **Board Cert:** Anatomic & Clinical Pathology 2001; Hematology 2002; Molecular Genetic Pathology 2007; **Med School:** India 1979; **Resid:** Pathology, Univ Hosp 1999; **Fellow:** Surgical Pathology, SUNY Univ Hosp 2000; Hematology, Albert Einstein Coll Med Affil Hosp 2001; **Fac Appt:** Clin Prof Path, Rutgers-NJ Med Sch

Olsen, Drew A MD (Path) - **Spec Exp:** Gynecologic Pathology; **Hospital:** Holy Name Med Ctr (page 738); **Address:** 718 Teaneck Rd, Teaneck, NJ 07666; **Phone:** 201-833-3246; **Board Cert:** Anatomic & Clinical Pathology 2000; **Med School:** NY Med Coll 1995; **Resid:** Anatomic & Clinical Pathology, Yale-New Haven Hosp 1999; **Fellow:** Surgical Pathology, Yale-New Haven Hosp 2000

Sanchez, Miguel A MD (Path) - **Spec Exp:** Breast Cancer; Thyroid Cancer; **Hospital:** Englewood Hosp & Med Ctr; **Address:** Englewood Hosp, Pathology, 350 Engle St Dean Bldg Fl LL1, Englewood, NJ 07631; **Phone:** 201-894-3423; **Board Cert:** Anatomic Pathology 1975; Clinical Pathology 1979; Cytopathology 1991; **Med School:** Spain 1969; **Resid:** Pathology, Englewood Hosp 1972; Pathology, Temple Univ Hosp 1973; **Fellow:** Pathology, Meml Sloan-Kettering Cancer Ctr 1974; Clinical Pathology, St Vincents Hosp 1975; **Fac Appt:** Assoc Prof Path, Mount Sinai Sch Med

Pediatric Allergy & Immunology

Colenda, Maryann J MD (PA&I) - **Spec Exp:** Asthma-Adult & Pediatric; Allergy; **Hospital:** Englewood Hosp & Med Ctr, Meadowlands Hosp Med Ctr; **Address:** 811 Abbott Blvd, Fort Lee, NJ 07024-4116; **Phone:** 201-224-2256; **Board Cert:** Pediatrics 2012; Allergy & Immunology 1979; **Med School:** NY Med Coll 1971; **Resid:** Pediatrics, NY-Presby/Columbia Univ Med Ctr 1974; **Fellow:** Allergy & Immunology, NY-Presby/Columbia Univ Med Ctr 1978; **Fac Appt:** Assoc Clin Prof Ped, Columbia P&S

Hicks, Patricia M MD (PA&I) - **Spec Exp:** Asthma & Sinusitis; Asthma in Pregnancy; **Hospital:** Valley Hosp (page 739); **Address:** 119 1st St, Ste 5, Ho Ho Kus, NJ 07423; **Phone:** 201-444-5277; **Board Cert:** Pediatrics 1978; Allergy & Immunology 2001; **Med School:** Penn State Coll Med 1973; **Resid:** Pediatrics, NY-Presby/Columbia Univ Med Ctr 1976; **Fellow:** Allergy & Immunology, NY-Presby/Columbia Univ Med Ctr 1981

Pediatric Cardiology

Apfel, Howard D MD (PCd) - **Spec Exp:** Congenital Heart Disease; Echocardiography; Fetal Echocardiography; **Hospital:** Valley Hosp (page 739), NY-Presby/Columbia Univ Med Ctr, NY (page 102); **Address:** 205 Robin Rd, Ste 100, Paramus, NJ 07652; **Phone:** 201-599-0026; **Board Cert:** Pediatric Cardiology 2011; **Med School:** SUNY Hlth Sci Ctr 1989; **Resid:** Pediatrics, LI Jewish Med Ctr 1992; **Fellow:** Pediatric Cardiology, NY-Presby/Columbia Univ Med Ctr 1995

Dyme, Joshua L MD (PCd) - **Spec Exp:** Congenital Heart Disease; Fetal Echocardiography; **Hospital:** Hackensack Univ Med Ctr (page 96); **Address:** HUMC Pediatric Heart Ctr, 155 Poilfly Rd, Ste 106, Hackensack, NJ 07601; **Phone:** 201-487-7617; **Board Cert:** Pediatrics 2011; Pediatric Cardiology 2006; **Med School:** Univ Rochester 2000; **Resid:** Pediatrics, St Christopher's Hosp for Children 2004; **Fellow:** Pediatric Cardiology, NY Presby-Columbia Med Ctr 2006

Messina, John J MD (PCd) - **Spec Exp:** Critical Care; Interventional Cardiology; Congenital Heart Disease; **Hospital:** St. Joseph's Regl Med Ctr - Paterson; **Address:** 1 Broadway, Ste 203, Elmwood Park, NJ 07407-1844; **Phone:** 973-569-6250; **Board Cert:** Pediatrics 2009; Pediatric Cardiology 2008; **Med School:** Grenada 1986; **Resid:** Pediatrics, St. Joseph's Regl Med Ctr 1989; **Fellow:** Pediatric Cardiology, NY-Presby/Weill Cornell Med Ctr 1992

Solowiejczyk, David E MD (PCd) - **Spec Exp:** Echocardiography; Congenital Heart Disease; **Hospital:** Morgan Stanley Chldns Hosp of NY-Presby, NY (page 102); **Address:** Pediatric Cardiology, 205 Robin Rd, Ste 100, Paramus, NJ 07652; **Phone:** 201-599-0026; **Board Cert:** Pediatric Cardiology 2011; **Med School:** NYU Sch Med 1986; **Resid:** Pediatrics, Mt Sinai Med Ctr 1989; **Fellow:** Cardiovascular Disease, NY Presby Hosp-Columbia Med Ctr 1993; **Fac Appt:** Assoc Prof Ped, Columbia P&S

Tozzi, Robert J MD (PCd) - **Spec Exp:** Hypertrophic Cardiomyopathy; Fetal Echocardiography; Cholesterol/Lipid Disorders; Heart Failure; **Hospital:** Hackensack Univ Med Ctr (page 96); **Address:** HUMC, Pediatric Heart Ctr, 155 Polifly Rd, Ste 106, Hackensack, NJ 07601; **Phone:** 201-487-7617; **Board Cert:** Pediatrics 1987; Pediatric Cardiology 2013; **Med School:** UMDNJ-NJ Med Sch, Newark 1983; **Resid:** Pediatrics, Univ Hosp-UMDNJ 1986; **Fellow:** Pediatric Cardiology, NYU Med Ctr 1988

Wong, Austin H MD (PCd) - **Spec Exp:** Congenital Heart Disease; Arrhythmias; **Hospital:** Hackensack Univ Med Ctr (page 96); **Address:** Pediatric Ctr for Heart Disease, 155 Polifly Rd, Ste 106, Hackensack, NJ 07601; **Phone:** 201-487-7617; **Board Cert:** Pediatrics 2007; Pediatric Cardiology 2012; **Med School:** Albert Einstein Coll Med 1997; **Resid:** Pediatrics, Montefiore Med Ctr 2000; **Fellow:** Pediatric Cardiology, Mt Sinai Med Ctr 2003

Pediatric Endocrinology

Aisenberg, Javier E MD (PEn) - **Spec Exp:** Diabetes; Growth Disorders; **Hospital:** Hackensack Univ Med Ctr (page 96); **Address:** HUMC, Pediatric Endocrinology, 30 Prospect Ave WFAN Bldg - rm 251, Hackensack, NJ 07601; **Phone:** 551-996-5329; **Board Cert:** Pediatrics 2008; Pediatric Endocrinology 2010; **Med School:** Argentina 1987; **Resid:** Pediatrics, NYU-Bellevue Hosp Ctr 1991; **Fellow:** Pediatric Endocrinology, NY-Presby/Weill Cornell Med Ctr 1994

Novogroder, Michael MD (PEn) - **Spec Exp:** Growth/Development Disorders; Pubertal Disorders; Thyroid Disorders; **Hospital:** Englewood Hosp & Med Ctr; **Address:** Metropolitan Pediatric Grp, 704 Palisade Ave, Teaneck, NJ 07666; **Phone:** 201-836-4301; **Board Cert:** Pediatrics 1974; Pediatric Endocrinology 1980; **Med School:** SUNY Hlth Sci Ctr 1969; **Resid:** Pediatrics, Jacobi Med Ctr 1973; **Fellow:** Pediatric Endocrinology, NY-Presby/Weill Cornell Med Ctr 1976; **Fac Appt:** Prof Ped, Columbia P&S

Pediatric Gastroenterology

Jeshion, Wendy C MD (PGe) - **Spec Exp:** Inflammatory Bowel Disease/Crohn's; Celiac Disease; Peptic Ulcer Disease; Nutrition; **Hospital:** Hackensack Univ Med Ctr (page 96); **Address:** HUMC, Pediatric Gastroenterology, 155 Polifly Rd, Ste 102, Hackensack, NJ 07601; **Phone:** 551-996-8840; **Board Cert:** Pediatric Gastroenterology 2014; **Med School:** Mount Sinai Sch Med 1992; **Resid:** Pediatrics, Chldns Hosp 1995; **Fellow:** Pediatric Gastroenterology, Chldns Hosp 1998; **Fac Appt:** Asst Prof Ped, UMDNJ-NJ Med Sch, Newark

Moustafellos, Elaine MD (PGe) - **Spec Exp:** Esophageal Disorders; Malabsorption Syndrome; Inflammatory Bowel Disease; **Hospital:** Hackensack Univ Med Ctr (page 96); **Address:** HUMC, Ctr Gastroenterology & Nutrition, 155 Polifly Rd, Ste 102, Hackensack, NJ 07601; **Phone:** 551-996-8840; **Board Cert:** Pediatric Gastroenterology 2014; Pediatrics 2013; **Med School:** SUNY Hlth Sci Ctr 1992; **Resid:** Pediatrics, NY-Presby/Weill Cornell Med Ctr 1995; **Fellow:** Pediatric Gastroenterology, NY-Presby/Weill Cornell Med Ctr 1998

Pediatric Hematology-Oncology

Diamond, Steven H MD (PHO) - **Spec Exp:** Pediatric Cancers; Sickle Cell Disease; Hemophilia; **Hospital:** Hackensack Univ Med Ctr (page 96); **Address:** Hackensack Univ Med Ctr, Div Ped Hem/Onc, 30 Prospect Ave, Hackensack, NJ 07601-1914; **Phone:** 551-996-5437; **Board Cert:** Pediatrics 1979; Pediatric Hematology-Oncology 1980; **Med School:** Univ Pennsylvania 1974; **Resid:** Pediatrics, Mount Sinai Med Ctr 1977; **Fellow:** Pediatric Hematology-Oncology, Beth Israel Med Ctr - Petrie Div 1979; **Fac Appt:** Asst Prof Ped, UMDNJ-NJ Med Sch, Newark

Flug, Frances MD (PHO) - **Spec Exp:** Bleeding/Coagulation Disorders; Sickle Cell Disease; Pediatric Cancers; **Hospital:** Hackensack Univ Med Ctr (page 96), Saint Michael's Med Ctr; **Address:** Hackensack Univ Med Ctr, Div Ped Hem/Onc, 30 Prospect Ave, Hackensack, NJ 07601-2129; **Phone:** 551-996-5437; **Board Cert:** Pediatrics 1984; Pediatric Hematology-Oncology 1984; **Med School:** SUNY Downstate 1979; **Resid:** Pediatrics, NYU Langone Med Ctr 1982; **Fellow:** Pediatric Hematology-Oncology, NYU Langone Med Ctr 1984; **Fac Appt:** Assoc Prof Ped, UMDNJ-NJ Med Sch, Newark

Gillio III, Alfred P MD (PHO) - **Spec Exp:** Leukemia & Lymphoma; Bleeding/Coagulation Disorders; **Hospital:** Hackensack Univ Med Ctr (page 96); **Address:** Inst for Pediatric Cancer & Blood Disorders, 30 Prospect Ave Fl 1, Don Imus Ctr, Hackensack, NJ 07601; **Phone:** 551-996-5600; **Board Cert:** Pediatric Hematology-Oncology 2012; **Med School:** Med Coll VA 1981; **Resid:** Pediatrics, Med Coll VA Hosp 1984; **Fellow:** Pediatric Hematology-Oncology, Meml Sloan-Kettering Cancer Ctr 1987

Halpern, Steven L MD (PHO) - **Spec Exp:** Leukemia & Lymphoma; Brain Tumors; Hodgkin's Lymphoma; Hemophilia; **Hospital:** Goryeb Children's Hosp (page 92), Overlook Med Ctr (page 92); **Address:** Goryeb Chldns Hosp, 100 Madison Ave, Morristown, NJ 07960; **Phone:** 973-971-6720; **Board Cert:** Pediatrics 1981; Pediatric Hematology-Oncology 1982; **Med School:** Ros Franklin Univ/Chicago Med Sch 1976; **Resid:** Pediatrics, St Christophers Hosp for Children 1979; **Fellow:** Pediatric Hematology-Oncology, Chldns Hosp 1982; **Fac Appt:** Asst Prof Ped, UMDNJ-NJ Med Sch, Newark

Harris, Michael B MD (PHO) - **Spec Exp:** Leukemia & Lymphoma; Bone Tumors; Cancer Survivors-Late Effects of Therapy; **Hospital:** Hackensack Univ Med Ctr (page 96); **Address:** HUMC, Inst Ped Cancer & Blood Disorders, 30 Prospect Ave, rm WFAN-PC116, Hackensack, NJ 07601; **Phone:** 551-996-5437; **Board Cert:** Pediatrics 1974; Pediatric Hematology-Oncology 1974; **Med School:** Albert Einstein Coll Med 1969; **Resid:** Pediatrics, Chldns Hosp 1971; **Fellow:** Pediatric Hematology-Oncology, Chldns Hosp 1974; **Fac Appt:** Prof Ped, UMDNJ-NJ Med Sch, Newark

Pediatric Infectious Disease

Boscamp, Jeffrey R MD (PInf) - **Spec Exp:** Fevers of Unknown Origin; Lyme Disease; **Hospital:** Hackensack Univ Med Ctr (page 96); **Address:** Hackensack Univ Med Ctr, 30 Prospect Ave, WFAN Bldg, PC 360, Hackensack, NJ 07601; **Phone:** 551-996-5308; **Board Cert:** Pediatrics 1986; Pediatric Infectious Disease 2009; **Med School:** NY Med Coll 1981; **Resid:** Pediatrics, NY-Presby/Columbia Univ Med Ctr 1984; Internal Medicine, Greenwich Hosp 1985; **Fellow:** Infectious Disease, Montefiore Med Ctr 1987; **Fac Appt:** Assoc Prof Ped, UMDNJ-Univ Med Dent NJ

Piwoz, Julia A MD (PInf) - **Spec Exp:** AIDS/HIV; Congenital Infections; Infections in Transplant Patients; **Hospital:** Hackensack Univ Med Ctr (page 96); **Address:** HUMC, Ped Infectious Disease, 30 Prospect Ave WFAN Bldg - rm PC360, Hackensack, NJ 07601; **Phone:** 551-996-5308; **Board Cert:** Pediatrics 2008; Pediatric Infectious Disease 2014; **Med School:** Hahnemann Univ 1991; **Resid:** Pediatrics, Mt Sinai Hosp 1994; **Fellow:** Pediatric Infectious Disease, Mt Sinai Hosp 1995; **Fac Appt:** Asst Prof Ped, UMDNJ-NJ Med Sch, Newark

Slavin, Kevin A MD (PInf) - **Spec Exp:** Antibiotic Resistance; Travel Medicine; Infection Control; **Hospital:** Hackensack Univ Med Ctr (page 96); **Address:** HUMC, Ped Infectious Disease, 30 Prospect Ave WFAN Bldg - rm PC360, Hackensack, NJ 07601; **Phone:** 551-996-5308; **Board Cert:** Pediatrics 2012; Pediatric Infectious Disease 2014; **Med School:** UCLA 1993; **Resid:** Pediatrics, UCSF Med Ctr 1996; **Fellow:** Clinical Pharmacology, UCSF Med Ctr 1997; Pediatric Infectious Disease, UCSF Med Ctr 1999; **Fac Appt:** Asst Prof Ped, UMDNJ-NJ Med Sch, Newark

Pediatric Nephrology

Ettinger, Leigh MD (PNep) - **Spec Exp:** Kidney Disease; Hypertension in Children; **Hospital:** Hackensack Univ Med Ctr (page 96); **Address:** HUMC Ped Nephrology, 30 Prospect Ave, WFAN Bldg, rm PC239, Hackensack, NJ 07601; **Phone:** 551-996-8228; **Board Cert:** Pediatrics 2009; Pediatric Nephrology 2013; **Med School:** Tufts Univ 1998; **Resid:** Pediatrics, Dartmouth Univ Chldn's Hosp 2001; **Fellow:** Pediatric Nephrology, Mt Sinai Med Ctr 2002; Pediatric Nephrology, Albert Einstein Affil Hosp 2004

Lieberman, Kenneth V MD (PNep) - **Spec Exp:** Nephrotic Syndrome; Glomerulonephritis; Kidney Failure-Chronic; Hypertension; **Hospital:** Hackensack Univ Med Ctr (page 96); **Address:** HUMC, Ped Nephrology, 30 Prospect Ave WFAN Bldg - rm PC239, Hackensack, NJ 07601; **Phone:** 551-996-8228; **Board Cert:** Pediatrics 1981; Pediatric Nephrology 2009; **Med School:** Albert Einstein Coll Med 1977; **Resid:** Pediatrics, Mt Sinai Hosp 1979; **Fellow:** Pediatric Nephrology, NY-Presby/Weill Cornell Med Ctr 1981; **Fac Appt:** Prof Ped, UMDNJ-NJ Med Sch, Newark

Pediatric Otolaryngology

Quraishi, Huma A MD (PO) - **Spec Exp:** Throat Disorders; Rhinitis; Otitis Media; **Hospital:** Hackensack Univ Med Ctr (page 96), Univ Hosp-Newark; **Address:** 30 Prospect Ave, WFAN Bldg, Rm 312, Hackensack, NJ 07601; **Phone:** 551-996-5515; **Board Cert:** Otolaryngology 1999; **Med School:** Mount Sinai Sch Med 1993; **Resid:** Otolaryngology, WV Univ Med Ctr 1998; **Fellow:** Pediatric Otolaryngology, Chldns Nat'l Med Ctr 1999

Respler, Don S MD (PO) - **Spec Exp:** Airway Disorders; Sinus Disorders; Head & Neck Tumors; Sleep Disorders/Apnea; **Hospital:** Hackensack Univ Med Ctr (page 96), Valley Hosp (page 739); **Address:** 2 S Summit Ave, Hackensack, NJ 07601-1117; **Phone:** 201-996-9200; **Board Cert:** Otolaryngology 1986; **Med School:** Mount Sinai Sch Med 1981; **Resid:** Surgery, Beth Israel Med Ctr - Petrie Div 1983; Otolaryngology, UMDNJ-Univ Hosp 1986; **Fellow:** Pediatric Otolaryngology, Chldns Hosp 1988; **Fac Appt:** Asst Clin Prof Oto, UMDNJ-NJ Med Sch, Newark

Samadi, Sharyar D MD (PO) - **Spec Exp:** Ear Infections; Sinusitis; Tonsil/Adenoid Disorders; Sleep Apnea; **Hospital:** Hackensack Univ Med Ctr (page 96); **Address:** 10 Forest Ave, Ste 100, Paramus, NJ 07652; **Phone:** 201-996-1505; **Board Cert:** Otolaryngology 2012; **Med School:** Johns Hopkins Univ 1996; **Resid:** Otolaryngology, Univ Penn Med Ctr 2001; **Fellow:** Pediatric Otolaryngology, Chldns Hosp of Philadelphia 2003

Pediatric Pulmonology

Kanengiser, Steven MD (PPul) - **Spec Exp:** Asthma; Cough-Chronic; Pneumonia; **Hospital:** Valley Hosp (page 739); **Address:** 505 Goffle Rd, Ridgewood, NJ 07450-4027; **Phone:** 201-447-8026; **Board Cert:** Pediatric Pulmonology 2008; **Med School:** UCSF 1984; **Resid:** Pediatrics, Children's Hosp 1987; **Fellow:** Pediatric Pulmonology, Westchester Med Ctr 1994; **Fac Appt:** Asst Clin Prof Ped, Columbia P&S

Kaplan, Ellen B MD (PPul) - **Spec Exp:** Asthma & Chronic Lung Disease; Allergy; Cystic Fibrosis; **Hospital:** Hackensack Univ Med Ctr (page 96); **Address:** HUMC, Dept Peds, 30 Prospect Ave, WFAN PC375, Hackensack, NJ 07601; **Phone:** 551-996-5207; **Board Cert:** Pediatrics 1987; Allergy & Immunology 2012; Pediatric Pulmonology 2011; **Med School:** SUNY Hlth Sci Ctr 1983; **Resid:** Pediatrics, Montefiore Med Ctr 1986; **Fellow:** Allergy & Immunology, Chldns Hosp 1988; Pediatric Pulmonology, Chldns Hosp 1995

Lee, Donna J MD (PPul) - **Spec Exp:** Pulmonary Infections; Asthma; **Hospital:** Hackensack Univ Med Ctr (page 96); **Address:** HUMC, Ped Pulmonology, 30 Prospect Ave WFAN Bldg - rm TC375, Hackensack, NJ 07601; **Phone:** 551-996-5207; **Board Cert:** Pediatrics 2011; Pediatric Pulmonology 2007; **Med School:** UMDNJ-NJ Med Sch, Newark 1993; **Resid:** Pediatrics, Univ Hosp-UMDNJ 1996; **Fellow:** Pediatric Pulmonology, Babies & Chldns Hosp 1999; **Fac Appt:** Asst Prof Ped, UMDNJ-NJ Med Sch, Newark

Ngai, Pakkay MD (PPul) - **Spec Exp:** Asthma; Sleep Disorders; Sleep Medicine; **Hospital:** Hackensack Univ Med Ctr (page 96); **Address:** 30 Prospect Ave WFAN Bldg - rm TC375, Hackensack, NJ 07601; **Phone:** 551-996-5207; **Board Cert:** Pediatrics 2014; Pediatric Pulmonology 2010; Sleep Medicine 2007; **Med School:** NYU Sch Med 1995; **Resid:** Pediatrics, NY Presby/Columbia Med Ctr 1998; **Fellow:** Pediatric Pulmonology, NY Presby/Columbia Med Ctr 2002

Pediatric Rheumatology

Haines, Kathleen A MD (PRhu) - **Spec Exp:** Juvenile Arthritis; Lupus/SLE; Immune Deficiency; Scleroderma; **Hospital:** Hackensack Univ Med Ctr (page 96), NYU Langone Med Ctr (page 104); **Address:** Pediatric Ctr, Ped Rheumatology, 30 Prospect Ave, rm PC360, Hackensack, NJ 07601; **Phone:** 551-996-5306; **Board Cert:** Pediatrics 1980; Allergy & Immunology 1981; Pediatric Rheumatology 2014; **Med School:** Albert Einstein Coll Med 1975; **Resid:** Pediatrics, NY-Presby/Weill Cornell Med Ctr 1977; **Fellow:** Allergy & Immunology, NY-Presby/Weill Cornell Med Ctr 1980; Rheumatology, NYU Med Ctr 1982

Kimura, Yukiko MD (PRhu) - **Spec Exp:** Juvenile Arthritis; Lupus/SLE; Dermatomyositis; Vasculitis; **Hospital:** Hackensack Univ Med Ctr (page 96); **Address:** Dan Imus Pediatric Ctr, Ped Rheumatology, 30 Prospect Ave, Ste PC360, Hackensack, NJ 07601; **Phone:** 551-996-5306; **Board Cert:** Pediatrics 1987; Pediatric Rheumatology 2014; **Med School:** Albert Einstein Coll Med 1982; **Resid:** Pediatrics, Babies Hosp/Columbia Presby 1985; **Fellow:** Pediatric Rheumatology, Babies Hosp/Columbia Presby 1991; **Fac Appt:** Prof Ped, UMDNJ-NJ Med Sch, Newark

Li, Suzanne C MD/PhD (PRhu) - **Spec Exp:** Scleroderma; Juvenile Arthritis; Lupus/SLE; Dermatomyositis; **Hospital:** Hackensack Univ Med Ctr (page 96); **Address:** Hackensack Univ Med Ctr, 30 Prospect Ave, Imus Bldg - rm PC360, Hackensack, NJ 07601; **Phone:** 551-996-5306; **Board Cert:** Pediatric Rheumatology 2011; **Med School:** Columbia P&S 1985; **Resid:** Pediatrics, Babies Hosp/Columbia Presby Med Ctr 1988; **Fellow:** Pediatric Rheumatology, Babies Hosp/Columbia 1992; **Fac Appt:** Assoc Prof Ped, UMDNJ-Rutgers Med Sch

Weiss, Jennifer E MD (PRhu) - **Spec Exp:** Juvenile Arthritis; Lupus/SLE; **Hospital:** Hackensack Univ Med Ctr (page 96); **Address:** Don Imas Pediatric Ctr, Ped Rheumatology, 30 Prospect Ave, Ste PC360, Hackensack, NJ 07601; **Phone:** 551-996-5306; **Board Cert:** Pediatric Rheumatology 2012; **Med School:** Grenada 1998; **Resid:** Pediatrics, LIJ Med Ctr 2001; **Fellow:** Pediatric Rheumatology, LIJ Med Ctr 2003

Pediatric Surgery

Alexander, Frederick MD (PS) - **Spec Exp:** Gastrointestinal Surgery; Thoracic Surgery; Solid Tumors; Congenital Anomalies-Gastrointestinal; **Hospital:** Hackensack Univ Med Ctr (page 96), Valley Hosp (page 739); **Address:** 140 Route 17, Ste 321, Paramus, NJ 07652; **Phone:** 201-225-9700; **Board Cert:** Pediatric Surgery 2010; **Med School:** Columbia P&S 1977; **Resid:** Surgery, Brigham & Womens Hosp 1984; **Fellow:** Pediatric Surgery, Chldns Hosp 1986

Friedman, David L MD (PS) - **Spec Exp:** Neonatal Surgery; Gastroesophageal Reflux Disease (GERD); Laparoscopic Surgery; **Hospital:** Valley Hosp (page 739), Hackensack Univ Med Ctr (page 96); **Address:** 30 W Century Rd, Ste 235, Paramus, NJ 07652-1433; **Phone:** 201-225-9440; **Board Cert:** Pediatric Surgery 2009; **Med School:** SUNY Downstate 1971; **Resid:** Surgery, SUNY Downstate Med Ctr 1976; **Fellow:** Pediatric Surgery, SUNY Downstate Med Ctr 1977; **Fac Appt:** Asst Clin Prof S, Columbia P&S

Gandhi, Rajinder P MD (PS) - **Spec Exp:** Gastrointestinal Surgery; Laparoscopic Surgery; Chest Wall Deformities; **Hospital:** Valley Hosp (page 739); **Address:** 30 W Century Rd, Ste 235, Paramus, NJ 07652; **Phone:** 201-225-9440; **Board Cert:** Surgery 1975; Pediatric Surgery 2007; **Med School:** Burma 1966; **Resid:** Surgery, Montefiore Med Ctr-Einstein Div 1974; **Fellow:** Pediatric Surgery, Columbia-Presby Med Ctr 1976

Kuenzler, Keith A MD (PS) - **Spec Exp:** Minimally Invasive Surgery; Neonatal Surgery; Congenital Anomalies; **Hospital:** Hackensack Univ Med Ctr (page 96); **Address:** Hackensack Univ Med Ctr, 30 Prospect Ave WSAN Bldg Fl 3, Hackensack, NJ 07601; **Phone:** 551-996-2921; **Board Cert:** Surgery 2005; Pediatric Surgery 2008; **Med School:** Jefferson Med Coll 1997; **Resid:** Surgery, Thomas Jefferson Univ Hosp 2004; **Fellow:** Pediatric Surgery, NY Presby-Columbia Med Ctr 2006; **Fac Appt:** Asst Prof S, NYU Sch Med

Pediatric Urology

Hensle, Terry W MD (Ped Uro) - **Spec Exp:** Pediatric Urology; Hypospadias; Urinary Reconstruction; Wilms' Tumor; **Hospital:** Hackensack Univ Med Ctr (page 96); **Address:** 699 Teaneck Rd, Ste 103, Teaneck, NJ 07666; **Phone:** 201-645-3362; **Board Cert:** Urology 1978; **Med School:** Cornell Univ-Weill Med Coll 1968; **Resid:** Surgery, Boston Med Ctr 1973; Urology, Mass Genl Hosp 1976; **Fellow:** Pediatric Urology, Mass Genl Hosp 1977; Pediatric Urology, Great Ormond St Hosp 1978; **Fac Appt:** Prof U, Columbia P&S

Koo, Harry P MD (Ped Uro) - **Spec Exp:** Congenital Anomalies-Genitourinary; Reconstructive Surgery; Hydronephrosis; **Hospital:** Hackensack Univ Med Ctr (page 96); **Address:** Urology Health-Partners, Hackensack Univ Med Ctr, 360 Essex St, Ste 403, Hackensack, NJ 07601; **Phone:** 551-996-8090; **Board Cert:** Urology 2007; **Med School:** Univ Rochester 1987; **Resid:** Surgery, Ny-Presby Hosp/Columbia 1989; Urology, Ny-Presby Hosp/Columbia 1993; **Fellow:** Pediatric Urology, Chldns Hosp 1995; **Fac Appt:** Prof U, Va Commonwealth Univ Sch Med

Pediatrics

Berkowitz, Irwin H MD (Ped) *PCP* - **Spec Exp:** Asthma; ADD/ADHD; Parenting Issues; **Hospital:** Valley Hosp (page 739), Hackensack UMC-Pascack Valley (page 737); **Address:** Chestnut Ridge Pediatric Assocs, 595 Chestnut Ridge Rd, Ste 4, Woodcliff Lake, NJ 07677; **Phone:** 201-391-2020; **Board Cert:** Pediatrics 2010; **Med School:** SUNY Downstate 1972; **Resid:** Pediatrics, Lenox Hill Hosp 1976; **Fac Appt:** Asst Clin Prof Ped, NY Med Coll

Bienstock, Jeffrey M MD (Ped) *PCP* - **Spec Exp:** Child Abuse; Preventive Medicine; **Hospital:** Valley Hosp (page 739); **Address:** PediatriCare Assocs, 20-20 Fair Lawn Ave, Fair Lawn, NJ 07410; **Phone:** 201-791-4545; **Board Cert:** Pediatrics 2011; **Med School:** Mexico 1983; **Resid:** Pediatrics, LIJ Med Ctr 1988

Buchalter, Maury MD (Ped) *PCP* - **Spec Exp:** Asthma; Infectious Disease; ADD/ADHD; **Hospital:** Hackensack Univ Med Ctr (page 96), Englewood Hosp & Med Ctr; **Address:** Tenafly Pediatrics, 301 Bridge Plaza N, Fort Lee, NJ 07670; **Phone:** 201-592-8787; **Board Cert:** Pediatrics 2010; **Med School:** Mount Sinai Sch Med 1984; **Resid:** Pediatrics, Mt Sinai Hosp 1987; **Fellow:** Infectious Disease, Chldns Hosp 1988

Harlow, Paul J MD (Ped) *PCP* - **Spec Exp:** Anemia; Bleeding/Coagulation Disorders; **Hospital:** Hackensack Univ Med Ctr (page 96), Valley Hosp (page 739); **Address:** Pediatric Specialties, 90 Prospect Ave, Ste 1A, Hackensack, NJ 07601; **Phone:** 201-342-4001 x107; **Board Cert:** Pediatrics 1979; Pediatric Hematology-Oncology 1980; **Med School:** SUNY Downstate 1974; **Resid:** Pediatrics, Bronx Municipal Hosp 1977; **Fellow:** Pediatric Hematology-Oncology, Chldn's Hosp 1979

Kanter, Alan I MD (Ped) *PCP* - **Spec Exp:** ADD/ADHD; Autism; **Hospital:** Englewood Hosp & Med Ctr, Morgan Stanley Chldns Hosp of NY-Presby, NY (page 102); **Address:** 704 Palisade Ave, Teaneck, NJ 07666-3198; **Phone:** 201-836-4301; **Board Cert:** Pediatrics 1978; **Med School:** Albert Einstein Coll Med 1970; **Resid:** Pediatrics, Montefiore Med Ctr 1975

Kolsky, Neil Harris MD (Ped) *PCP* - **Spec Exp:** Neonatology; Infectious Disease; **Hospital:** Holy Name Med Ctr (page 738), Hackensack Univ Med Ctr (page 96); **Address:** Pedimedica, 870 Palisade Ave, Ste 201, Teaneck, NJ 07666-3419; **Phone:** 201-692-1661; **Board Cert:** Pediatrics 1972; **Med School:** UMDNJ-NJ Med Sch, Newark 1966; **Resid:** Pediatrics, Johns Hopkins Hosp 1969

Kushner, Susan C MD (Ped) *PCP* - **Spec Exp:** Atopic Dermatitis; Allergic Rhinitis; Asthma; Otitis Media; **Hospital:** Hackensack Univ Med Ctr (page 96), Valley Hosp (page 739); **Address:** Forrest Pediatrics, 299 Forrest Ave Fl 3, Paramus, NJ 07652; **Phone:** 201-267-0888; **Board Cert:** Pediatrics 2011; **Med School:** SUNY Upstate Med Univ 1986; **Resid:** Pediatrics, Schneider Chldns Hosp 1989

Namerow, David M MD (Ped) *PCP* - **Spec Exp:** Behavioral Disorders; Adolescent Medicine; **Hospital:** Valley Hosp (page 739), St. Joseph's Regl Med Ctr - Paterson; **Address:** PediatriCare Associates, 2020 Fair Lawn Ave, Fair Lawn, NJ 07410-2319; **Phone:** 201-791-4545; **Board Cert:** Pediatrics 1978; **Med School:** Univ Louisville Sch Med 1972; **Resid:** Pediatrics, Chldn's Hosp 1975; **Fellow:** Adolescent Medicine, Univ MD Hosp 1977; **Fac Appt:** Asst Clin Prof Ped, NY Med Coll

O'Brien, Daryl H MD (Ped) *PCP* - **Spec Exp:** Developmental & Behavioral Disorders; **Hospital:** Valley Hosp (page 739); **Address:** Broadway Pediatric Assocs, 336 Center Ave, Westwood, NJ 07675; **Phone:** 201-664-7444; **Board Cert:** Pediatrics 1986; **Med School:** Dartmouth Med Sch 1979; **Resid:** Pediatrics, Duke Univ Med Ctr 1982

Rabinowitz, Arnold H MD (Ped) *PCP* - **Spec Exp:** Allergy; **Hospital:** Hackensack Univ Med Ctr (page 96); **Address:** 22 Madison Ave, Ste 303, Paramus, NJ 07652; **Phone:** 201-291-9797; **Board Cert:** Pediatrics 2011; **Med School:** Mexico 1979; **Resid:** Pediatrics, Brookdale Univ Hosp Med Ctr 1983; **Fellow:** Pediatric Allergy, NY-Presby/Columbia Univ Med Ctr 1985

Schuss, Steven A MD (Ped) *PCP* - **Hospital:** Englewood Hosp & Med Ctr, Hackensack Univ Med Ctr (page 96); **Address:** Teaneck Pediatric Assocs, 197 Cedar Ln, Teaneck, NJ 07666; **Phone:** 201-836-7171; **Board Cert:** Pediatrics 1986; **Med School:** Albert Einstein Coll Med 1979; **Resid:** Pediatrics, Montefiore Med Ctr 1983

Sugarman, Lynn B MD (Ped) *PCP* - **Hospital:** Englewood Hosp & Med Ctr, Hackensack Univ Med Ctr (page 96); **Address:** Tenafly Pediatrics, 32 Franklin St, Tenafly, NJ 07670-2005; **Phone:** 201-569-2400; **Board Cert:** Pediatrics 2010; **Med School:** Harvard Med Sch 1977; **Resid:** Pediatrics, Bronx Muni Hos 1981; **Fellow:** Pediatric Critical Care Medicine, Bronx Muni Hosp 1983

Tantawi, Mohamed A MD (Ped) *PCP* - **Hospital:** Hackensack Univ Med Ctr (page 96); **Address:** Hackensack Pediatrics, 177 Summit Ave, Hackensack, NJ 07601; **Phone:** 201-487-8222; **Board Cert:** Pediatrics 2014; **Med School:** UMDNJ-Rutgers Med Sch 2000; **Resid:** Pediatrics, NY-Presby/Weill Cornell Med Ctr 2003

Weiss, Christopher A DO (Ped) *PCP* - **Hospital:** Hackensack Univ Med Ctr (page 96), Englewood Hosp & Med Ctr; **Address:** Washington Ave Pediatrics, 95 N Washington Ave, Bergenfield, NJ 07621; **Phone:** 201-384-0300; **Board Cert:** Pediatrics 2008; **Med School:** Nova SE Univ, Coll Osteo Med 1996; **Resid:** Pediatrics, Long Island Jewish Med Ctr 2001

Wisotsky, David H MD (Ped) *PCP* - **Hospital:** Englewood Hosp & Med Ctr, Hackensack Univ Med Ctr (page 96); **Address:** Tenafly Pediatrics, 32 Franklin St, Tenafly, NJ 07670; **Phone:** 201-569-2400; **Board Cert:** Pediatrics 2010; **Med School:** Albert Einstein Coll Med 1974; **Resid:** Pediatrics, Bronx Muni Hosp 1978; **Fac Appt:** Asst Clin Prof Ped, Columbia P&S

Physical Medicine & Rehabilitation

Averill, Allison M MD (PMR) - **Spec Exp:** Neuro-Rehabilitation; Brain Injury Rehabilitation; Stroke Rehabilitation; Acupuncture; **Hospital:** Kessler Inst for Rehab - Saddle Brook; **Address:** Kessler Institute for Rehab, Saddle Brook Campus, 300 Market St, Saddle Brook, NJ 07663; **Phone:** 201-368-6043; **Board Cert:** Physical Medicine & Rehabilitation 2013; **Med School:** Rutgers R W Johnson Med Sch 1988; **Resid:** Physical Medicine & Rehabilitation, Univ Penn Hosp 1992; **Fac Appt:** Asst Clin Prof PMR, UMDNJ-NJ Med Sch, Newark

Liss, Donald MD (PMR) - **Spec Exp:** Pain-Back; Sports Medicine; Osteoarthritis; **Hospital:** NY-Presby/Columbia Univ Med Ctr, NY (page 102), Englewood Hosp & Med Ctr; **Address:** 500 Grand Ave, Fl 1st, Englewood, NJ 07631-2920; **Phone:** 201-567-2277; **Board Cert:** Physical Medicine & Rehabilitation 1984; **Med School:** Wayne State Univ 1979; **Resid:** Physical Medicine & Rehabilitation, Columbia-Presby Med Ctr 1982; **Fac Appt:** Assoc Clin Prof PMR, Columbia P&S

Liss, Howard MD (PMR) - **Spec Exp:** Pain Management; **Hospital:** NY-Presby/Columbia Univ Med Ctr, NY (page 102), Englewood Hosp & Med Ctr; **Address:** Physical Medicine & Rehabilitation Ctr, 500 Grand Ave Fl 1, Englewood, NJ 07631-2920; **Phone:** 201-567-2277; **Board Cert:** Physical Medicine & Rehabilitation 1982; **Med School:** Wayne State Univ 1977; **Resid:** Physical Medicine & Rehabilitation, NY-Presby/Columbia Univ Med Ctr 1981; **Fac Appt:** Asst Clin Prof PMR, Columbia P&S

Zimmerman, Jerald R MD (PMR) - **Spec Exp:** Post Polio Syndrome/Rehabilitation; Musculoskeletal Disorders; Pain Management; **Hospital:** Englewood Hosp & Med Ctr, Holy Name Med Ctr (page 738); **Address:** 370 Grand Ave, Ste 102, Englewood, NJ 07631; **Phone:** 201-567-3370; **Board Cert:** Physical Medicine & Rehabilitation 1989; **Med School:** Univ IL Coll Med 1982; **Resid:** Orthopaedic Surgery, Univ Minn Med Ctr 1985; Physical Medicine & Rehabilitation, Columbia-Presby Med Ctr 1988; **Fac Appt:** Asst Clin Prof PMR, Mount Sinai Sch Med

Plastic Surgery

Boss Jr, William K MD (PlS) - **Spec Exp:** Cosmetic & Reconstructive Surgery; Liposuction; Breast Augmentation; Blepharoplasty; **Hospital:** Hackensack Univ Med Ctr (page 96); **Address:** Cosmetic Surgery & Rejuvenation Ctr, 305 Route 17, Paramus, NJ 07652; **Phone:** 201-967-1100; **Board Cert:** Plastic Surgery 1984; **Med School:** UMDNJ-NJ Med Sch, Newark 1975; **Resid:** Surgery, UMDNJ Med Ctr 1980; Plastic Surgery, Yale-New Haven Hosp 1982; **Fellow:** Hand & Microvascular Surgery, RK Davies Med Ctr 1983; **Fac Appt:** Asst Clin Prof S, UMDNJ-NJ Med Sch, Newark

Breslow, Gary D MD (PlS) - **Spec Exp:** Breast Reconstruction; Cosmetic Surgery-Breast; Cosmetic Surgery-Face; **Hospital:** Valley Hosp (page 739); **Address:** Bergen Med Ctr Bldg, 1 W Ridgewood Ave, Ste 110, Paramus, NJ 07652; **Phone:** 201-444-9522; **Board Cert:** Plastic Surgery 2006; **Med School:** NYU Sch Med 1998; **Resid:** Plastic Surgery, Hosp U Penn 2004; **Fellow:** Plastic/Reconstructive Surgery, NYU Med Ctr 2005

Cozzone, John T MD (PlS) - **Spec Exp:** Cosmetic Surgery-Face & Body; Breast Cosmetic & Reconstructive Surgery; Liposuction & Body Contouring; **Hospital:** Hackensack Univ Med Ctr (page 96), Valley Hosp (page 739); **Address:** Art Plastic Surgery, 1 W Ridgewood Ave, Ste 302, Paramus, NJ 07652; **Phone:** 201-251-6622; **Board Cert:** Plastic Surgery 1990; **Med School:** Italy 1978; **Resid:** Surgery, Jersey City Medical Center 1983; **Fellow:** Plastic/Reconstructive Surgery, Ohio State Med Ctr 1985

D'Amico, Richard A MD (PlS) - **Spec Exp:** Cosmetic Surgery-Face; Liposuction & Body Contouring; Breast Augmentation; Facial Rejuvenation; **Hospital:** Englewood Hosp & Med Ctr, Holy Name Med Ctr (page 738); **Address:** 180 N Dean St, Ste 3N, Englewood, NJ 07631-2534; **Phone:** 201-567-9595; **Board Cert:** Plastic Surgery 1986; **Med School:** NYU Sch Med 1976; **Resid:** Surgery, Tulsa Med Ctr 1979; Surgery, Strong Meml Hosp 1981; **Fellow:** Plastic/Reconstructive Surgery, Columbia-Presby Med Ctr 1983; **Fac Appt:** Asst Clin Prof PlS, Mount Sinai Sch Med

Lipson, David E MD (PlS) - **Spec Exp:** Breast Augmentation; Body Contouring; Facial Rejuvenation; **Hospital:** Valley Hosp (page 739); **Address:** 2300 Route 208 South, Fair Lawn, NJ 07410; **Phone:** 201-797-7770; **Board Cert:** Plastic Surgery 1981; **Med School:** Albert Einstein Coll Med 1971; **Resid:** Surgery, Bellevue/NYU Med Ctr 1976; Plastic Surgery, Bellevue/NYU Med Ctr 1978

Ponamgi, Suri B MD (PlS) - **Spec Exp:** Cosmetic & Reconstructive Surgery; Breast Reconstruction; **Hospital:** Palisades Med Ctr, Holy Name Med Ctr (page 738); **Address:** 1101 Palisades Ave, Fort Lee, NJ 07024-6329; **Phone:** 201-224-8831; **Board Cert:** Plastic Surgery 1984; **Med School:** India 1970; **Resid:** Surgery, Bronx Lebonon Hosp 1979; Plastic Surgery, NY Methodist Hosp 1982; **Fellow:** Surgery, Bronx Lebonon Hosp 1980

Sternschein, Michael J MD (PlS) - **Spec Exp:** Cosmetic Surgery-Face & Breast; Liposuction & Body Contouring; Laser Surgery; **Hospital:** Hackensack Univ Med Ctr (page 96), Valley Hosp (page 739); **Address:** 1200 E Ridgewood Ave, Fl 2 W Wing, Ridgewood, NJ 07450; **Phone:** 201-444-1188; **Board Cert:** Plastic Surgery 1985; **Med School:** Columbia P&S 1976; **Resid:** Surgery, Columbia-Presby Med Ctr 1980; Plastic Surgery, Columbia-Presby Med Ctr 1982; **Fellow:** Microsurgery, Columbia-Presby Med Ctr 1983

Winters, Richard M MD (PlS) - **Spec Exp:** Cosmetic & Reconstructive Surgery; Rhinoplasty; Cosmetic Surgery-Face & Breast; Breast Reconstruction; **Hospital:** Hackensack Univ Med Ctr (page 96); **Address:** Aesthetic & Reconstructive Surgeons, 113 W Essex St, Ste 202, Maywood, NJ 07607; **Phone:** 201-487-3400; **Board Cert:** Plastic Surgery 2009; **Med School:** Univ Conn 1990; **Resid:** Surgery, Univ Conn Affil Hosp 1995; **Fellow:** Plastic/Reconstructive Surgery, NY-Presby/Weill Cornell Med Ctr 1997; Microsurgery, CA Pacific Med Ctr - Davies Campus 1998

Zapiach, Luis MD (PlS) - **Spec Exp:** Cosmetic & Reconstructive Surgery; Breast Cosmetic & Reconstructive Surgery; Cosmetic Surgery-Face & Body; **Hospital:** Hackensack Univ Med Ctr (page 96), Valley Hosp (page 739); **Address:** Art Plastic Surgery, 1 W Ridgewood Ave, Ste 302, Paramus, NJ 07652; **Phone:** 201-251-6622; **Board Cert:** Surgery 2005; Plastic Surgery 2008; **Med School:** NYU Sch Med 1998; **Resid:** Surgery, UMDNJ Med Ctr 2004; **Fellow:** Plastic Surgery, Emory Univ Hosp 2007

Zubowski, Robert I MD (PlS) - **Spec Exp:** Breast Augmentation; Liposuction & Body Contouring; Cosmetic Surgery-Face; **Hospital:** Valley Hosp (page 739); **Address:** 1 Sears Drive Fl 1, Paramus, NJ 07652; **Phone:** 201-261-7550; **Board Cert:** Plastic Surgery 2015; **Med School:** Mexico 1983; **Resid:** Surgery, Westchester Co Med Ctr 1990; **Fellow:** Plastic Surgery, Cleveland Clinic 1992; **Fac Appt:** Asst Clin Prof S, NY Med Coll

Psychiatry

Chertoff, Harvey R MD (Psyc) - **Spec Exp:** Anxiety & Mood Disorders; Psychoanalysis; **Hospital:** Englewood Hosp & Med Ctr, NY-Presby/Columbia Univ Med Ctr, NY (page 102); **Address:** 205 Engle St, Englewood, NJ 07631-2409; **Phone:** 201-567-4970; **Board Cert:** Psychiatry 1978; **Med School:** Albert Einstein Coll Med 1966; **Resid:** Psychiatry, NY Psychoanalytic Inst 1970; **Fac Appt:** Asst Clin Prof Psyc, Columbia P&S

Coira, Diego L MD (Psyc) - **Spec Exp:** Psychosomatic Disorders; **Hospital:** Hackensack Univ Med Ctr (page 96); **Address:** Hackensack Univ, dept Psychiatry, 30 Prospect Ave, 6 St John, rm 6706, Hackensack, NJ 07601; **Phone:** 551-996-3428; **Board Cert:** Psychiatry 2009; Psychosomatic Medicine 2009; **Med School:** Dominica 1983; **Resid:** Psychiatry, Harlem Hosp 1996; **Fac Appt:** Assoc Prof Psyc, UMDNJ-NJ Med Sch, Newark

Farkas, Edward L MD (Psyc) - **Spec Exp:** Depression in the Elderly; Psychotherapy-Men's Issues; Panic Disorder; **Hospital:** Holy Name Med Ctr (page 738); **Address:** 175 Cedar Ln, Ste A, Teaneck, NJ 07666-4315; **Phone:** 201-692-8354; **Board Cert:** Psychiatry 1988; **Med School:** Italy 1979; **Resid:** Psychiatry, Bronx Lebanon Hosp 1981; Psychiatry, St Luke's-Roosevelt Hosp Ctr 1983; **Fellow:** Psychiatry, William Allison White Inst 1983

Gurland, Frances Effron MD (Psyc) - **Spec Exp:** Eating Disorders; ADD/ADHD; **Address:** 216 Engle St, Englewood, NJ 07631; **Phone:** 201-568-4066; **Board Cert:** Psychiatry 2005; **Med School:** SUNY Downstate 1989; **Resid:** Psychiatry, St Lukes-Roosevelt Hosp Ctr 1991; **Fellow:** Child & Adolescent Psychiatry, Mount Sinai Hosp 1994

Narula, Amarjot S MD (Psyc) - **Spec Exp:** Geriatric Psychiatry; Mood Disorders; **Hospital:** Valley Hosp (page 739), Bergen Regl Med Ctr; **Address:** 65 N Maple Ave, Ridgewood, NJ 07450-1600; **Phone:** 201-670-4423; **Board Cert:** Psychiatry 1992; Geriatric Psychiatry 2007; **Med School:** India 1980; **Resid:** Psychiatry, Middletown Psychiatric Ctr 1988; **Fellow:** Psychiatry, Metropolitan Hosp 1989

Rosenfeld, David N MD (Psyc) - **Spec Exp:** Mood Disorders; Anxiety Disorders; Personality Disorders; Geriatric Psychiatry; **Hospital:** Valley Hosp (page 739); **Address:** 265 Ackerman Ave, Ste 202, Ridgewood, NJ 07450-4200; **Phone:** 201-447-5630; **Board Cert:** Psychiatry 2005; **Med School:** Rutgers R W Johnson Med Sch 1988; **Resid:** Psychiatry, Mount Sinai Sch Med 1990; Psychiatry, Bergen Pines Co 1994

Samuels, Steven MD (Psyc) - **Spec Exp:** Dementia; Anxiety & Depression; Geriatric Psychiatry; Electroconvulsive Therapy (ECT); **Hospital:** Englewood Hosp & Med Ctr; **Address:** Medical Director Behavioral Health Unit, Fl 4 East, 350 Engle St, Fl 4 East, Psychiatric Medicine Consultants-NJ, Englewood, NJ 07631; **Phone:** 201-681-2915; **Board Cert:** Psychiatry 2014; Geriatric Psychiatry 2006; **Med School:** SUNY Buffalo 1989; **Resid:** Psychiatry, St Vincents Hosp & Med Ctr 1993; **Fellow:** Geriatric Psychiatry, Hosp Univ Penn 1995; **Fac Appt:** Asst Prof Psyc, Mount Sinai Sch Med

Shah, Pritesh J MD (Psyc) - **Spec Exp:** Geriatric Psychiatry; **Hospital:** Holy Name Med Ctr (page 738); **Address:** 354 Old Hook Rd, Ste 102, Westwood, NJ 07675; **Phone:** 201-358-0400; **Board Cert:** Psychiatry 2014; **Med School:** India 1985; **Resid:** Psychiatry, Bergen Regl Med Ctr 1991

Wagle, Sharad D MD (Psyc) - **Spec Exp:** Anxiety Disorders; Forensic Psychiatry; Geriatric Psychiatry; **Hospital:** Holy Name Med Ctr (page 738); **Address:** 718 Teaneck Rd, Teaneck, NJ 07666; **Phone:** 201-833-3291; **Board Cert:** Psychiatry 2006; **Med School:** India 1972; **Resid:** Psychiatry, Hackensack Univ Med Ctr 1976; Psychiatry, Albert Einstein Coll Med 1978; **Fellow:** Child & Adolescent Psychiatry, Psychoanalytic Inst 1978

Zaidi, Syed A R MD (Psyc) - **Spec Exp:** Addiction Psychiatry; **Hospital:** Holy Name Med Ctr (page 738); **Address:** 294 State St, Ste 2, Hackensack, NJ 07601; **Phone:** 201-342-4004; **Board Cert:** Psychiatry 2009; **Med School:** Pakistan 1984; **Resid:** Psychiatry, Temple Univ Hosp 1996; **Fellow:** Geriatric Psychiatry, Mount Sinai Med Ctr 1997

Pulmonary Disease

Barasch, Jeffrey P MD (Pul) - **Spec Exp:** Sleep Disorders; Lung Cancer; Asthma; Chronic Obstructive Lung Disease (COPD); **Hospital:** Valley Hosp (page 739); **Address:** 140 Chestnut St, Ste 200, Ridgewood, NJ 07450; **Phone:** 201-447-3866; **Board Cert:** Sleep Medicine 2007; Pulmonary Disease 1984; Internal Medicine 1982; **Med School:** NYU Sch Med 1979; **Resid:** Internal Medicine, NYU-Bellevue Hosp 1980; Internal Medicine, St Lukes-Roosevelt Hosp Ctr 1982; **Fellow:** Pulmonary Disease, NYU Med Ctr 1984

Benoff, Brian A MD (Pul) - **Spec Exp:** Sleep Medicine; Critical Care Medicine; **Hospital:** Holy Name Med Ctr (page 738), Englewood Hosp & Med Ctr; **Address:** Holy Name Pulmonary Assocs, 180 N Dean St, Ste 2N, Englewood, NJ 07631; **Phone:** 201-871-8366; **Board Cert:** Internal Medicine 2007; Pulmonary Disease 2009; Critical Care Medicine 2010; Sleep Medicine 2011; **Med School:** Albert Einstein Coll Med 1994; **Resid:** Internal Medicine, LIJ Med Ctr 1997; **Fellow:** Pulmonary Critical Care Medicine, LIJ Med Ctr 2000

Brauntuch, Glenn R MD (Pul) - **Spec Exp:** Chronic Obstructive Lung Disease (COPD); Asthma; Lung Cancer; **Hospital:** Englewood Hosp & Med Ctr, Holy Name Med Ctr (page 738); **Address:** Bergen Medical Alliance, 180 Engle St, Englewood, NJ 07631-2507; **Phone:** 201-568-8010; **Board Cert:** Internal Medicine 1981; Pulmonary Disease 1984; **Med School:** Columbia P&S 1978; **Resid:** Internal Medicine, St Lukes-Roosevelt Hosp 1982; **Fellow:** Pulmonary Disease, NYU Med Ctr 1984

Bromberg, Assia MD (Pul) - **Spec Exp:** Asthma; Emphysema; Women's Health; **Hospital:** Valley Hosp (page 739); **Address:** 19-20 Fair Lawn Ave, Fairlawn, NJ 07410; **Phone:** 201-794-1963; **Board Cert:** Internal Medicine 1989; Pulmonary Disease 2004; **Med School:** Moldova 1974; **Resid:** Anesthesiology, Chaim Sheba Med Ctr 1981; Internal Medicine, Englewood Hosp 1989; **Fellow:** Pulmonary Disease, Bellevue-NYU Med Ctr 1992

Engler, Mitchell S MD (Pul) - **Spec Exp:** Sleep Disorders; **Hospital:** Holy Name Med Ctr (page 738), Englewood Hosp & Med Ctr; **Address:** Bergen Medical Alliance, 180 Engle St, Englewood, NJ 07631-2507; **Phone:** 201-568-8010; **Board Cert:** Internal Medicine 1981; Pulmonary Disease 1988; Sleep Medicine 2003; **Med School:** Boston Univ 1978; **Resid:** Internal Medicine, St Lukes Hosp 1981; **Fellow:** Pulmonary Disease, St Lukes Hosp 1983

Glassman, Adam MD (Pul) - **Spec Exp:** Sleep Disorders/Apnea; Chronic Obstructive Lung Disease (COPD); **Hospital:** Holy Name Med Ctr (page 738), Englewood Hosp & Med Ctr; **Address:** 180 N Dean St Fl 2, Englewood, NJ 07631; **Phone:** 201-871-8366; **Board Cert:** Pulmonary Disease 2007; Sleep Medicine 2011; **Med School:** Grenada 1987; **Resid:** Internal Medicine, UMDNJ-Univ Hosp 1991; **Fellow:** Pulmonary Disease, UMDNJ Univ Hosp 1993; Pulmonary Critical Care Medicine, UMDNJ Univ Hosp 1994

Goss, Deborah A MD (Pul) - **Spec Exp:** Lung Cancer; Sleep Disorders; **Hospital:** Hackensack Univ Med Ctr (page 96); **Address:** Hackensack Sleep & Pulmonary Ctr, 170 Prospect Ave, Ste 20, Hackensack, NJ 07601; **Phone:** 201-996-0232; **Board Cert:** Internal Medicine 2010; Pulmonary Disease 2012; Critical Care Medicine 2013; Sleep Medicine 2007; **Med School:** Creighton Univ 1997; **Resid:** Internal Medicine, UMDNJ-Univ Hosp 2000; **Fellow:** Pulmonary Critical Care Medicine, UMDNJ 2003

Levine, Selwyn E MD (Pul) - **Spec Exp:** Chronic Obstructive Lung Disease (COPD); Lung Cancer; Asthma; Pneumonia; **Hospital:** Holy Name Med Ctr (page 738), Englewood Hosp & Med Ctr; **Address:** Pulmonary Assocs of Northern NJ, 200 Grand Ave, Ste 102, Englewood, NJ 07631; **Phone:** 201-871-3636; **Board Cert:** Internal Medicine 1985; Pulmonary Disease 1988; **Med School:** NYU Sch Med 1982; **Resid:** Internal Medicine, Bellevue Hosp/NYU Med Ctr 1985; **Fellow:** Pulmonary Disease, Montefiore Med Ctr 1987

Malovany, Robert J MD (Pul) - **Spec Exp:** Exercise Physiology; Interventional Pulmonology; **Hospital:** Englewood Hosp & Med Ctr; **Address:** Bergen Medical Alliance, 180 Engle St, Englewood, NJ 07631-2507; **Phone:** 201-568-8010; **Board Cert:** Internal Medicine 1973; Pulmonary Disease 1976; **Med School:** Jefferson Med Coll 1970; **Resid:** Internal Medicine, Montefiore Med Ctr 1973; **Fellow:** Pulmonary Disease, Montefiore Med Ctr 1975; **Fac Appt:** Asst Clin Prof Med, Mount Sinai Sch Med

Polkow, Melvin S MD (Pul) - **Spec Exp:** Asthma; Sarcoidosis; Pulmonary Fibrosis; **Hospital:** Hackensack Univ Med Ctr (page 96); **Address:** 211 Essex St, Ste 302, Hackensack, NJ 07601; **Phone:** 201-498-1311; **Board Cert:** Internal Medicine 1980; Pulmonary Disease 1982; Critical Care Medicine 2007; **Med School:** SUNY Downstate 1977; **Resid:** Internal Medicine, Lenox Hill Hosp 1980; **Fellow:** Pulmonary Critical Care Medicine, Univ Hosp 1982; **Fac Appt:** Asst Clin Prof Med, UMDNJ-NJ Med Sch, Newark

Simon, Clifford J MD (Pul) - **Spec Exp:** Asthma; Lung Cancer; Bronchoscopy; **Hospital:** Englewood Hosp & Med Ctr, Holy Name Med Ctr (page 738); **Address:** 180 Engle St, Englewood, NJ 07631-2507; **Phone:** 201-567-2050; **Board Cert:** Internal Medicine 1976; Pulmonary Disease 1980; **Med School:** Cornell Univ-Weill Med Coll 1973; **Resid:** Internal Medicine, Dartmouth Affil Hosps 1975; **Fellow:** Pulmonary Disease, Bellevue Hosp 1977

Radiation Oncology

Dubin, David M MD (RadRO) - **Spec Exp:** Breast Cancer; **Hospital:** Englewood Hosp & Med Ctr; **Address:** Englewood Hosp, Dept Radiation Oncology, 350 Engle St, Englewood, NJ 07631-1808; **Phone:** 201-894-3125; **Board Cert:** Radiation Oncology 1991; **Med School:** Albert Einstein Coll Med 1986; **Resid:** Radiation Oncology, St Barnabas Hosp 1990

Gejerman, Glen MD (RadRO) - **Spec Exp:** Prostate Cancer; Breast Cancer; Image Guided Radiotherapy (IGRT); Brachytherapy; **Hospital:** Hackensack Univ Med Ctr (page 96); **Address:** Regl Cancer Care Assocs, Hackensack Univ Med Ctr, 92 Second St, Hackensack, NJ 07601; **Phone:** 551-996-2464; **Board Cert:** Radiation Oncology 2006; **Med School:** UMDNJ-NJ Med Sch, Newark 1990; **Resid:** Radiation Oncology, Montefiore Med Ctr 1995; **Fac Appt:** Asst Clin Prof RadRO, Albert Einstein Coll Med

Ingenito, Anthony C MD (RadRO) - **Spec Exp:** Brain Tumors; Stereotactic Radiosurgery; Lung Cancer; Central Nervous System Cancer; **Hospital:** Hackensack Univ Med Ctr (page 96); **Address:** John Theurer Cancer Ctr, 92 Second St, Hackensack, NJ 07601; **Phone:** 201-996-2210; **Board Cert:** Radiation Oncology 2008; **Med School:** UMDNJ-NJ Med Sch, Newark 1991; **Resid:** Anesthesiology, NY-Presby Hosp 1993; Radiation Oncology, NY-Presby Hosp 1996

Rosenbluth, Benjamin D MD (RadRO) - **Spec Exp:** Prostate Cancer; Breast Cancer; **Hospital:** Holy Name Med Ctr (page 738); **Address:** Holy Name Med Ctr, Radiation Oncology, 718 Teaneck Rd, Teaneck, NJ 07666; **Phone:** 201-541-5900; **Board Cert:** Radiation Oncology 2008; **Med School:** Harvard Med Sch 2001; **Resid:** Radiation Oncology, Meml Sloan Kettering Cancer Ctr 2006

Vialotti, Charles P MD (RadRO) - **Spec Exp:** Lung Cancer; Palliative Care; **Hospital:** Holy Name Med Ctr (page 738); **Address:** Holy Name Med Ctr, Radiation Oncology, 718 Teaneck Rd, Teaneck, NJ 07666; **Phone:** 201-541-5900; **Board Cert:** Therapeutic Radiology 1975; **Med School:** NY Med Coll 1971; **Resid:** Radiology, NYU Med Ctr 1974; **Fellow:** Therapeutic Radiology, NYU Med Ctr 1975

Reproductive Endocrinology

Lesorgen, Philip R MD (RE) - **Spec Exp:** Infertility-IVF; Endometriosis; **Hospital:** Englewood Hosp & Med Ctr, Holy Name Med Ctr (page 738); **Address:** 106 Grand Ave, Ste 400, Englewood, NJ 07631-3570; **Phone:** 201-569-6979; **Board Cert:** Obstetrics & Gynecology 1984; **Med School:** Boston Univ 1977; **Resid:** Obstetrics & Gynecology, LI Jewish Med Ctr 1981; **Fellow:** Reproductive Endocrinology, Thomas Jefferson Univ Hosp 1983; **Fac Appt:** Asst Clin Prof ObG, Seton Hall Univ Sch Hlth & Med Scis

McGovern, Peter G MD (RE) - **Spec Exp:** Infertility-IVF; Fertility Preservation in Cancer; **Hospital:** Univ Hosp-Newark, Hackensack Univ Med Ctr (page 96); **Address:** University Reproductive Assocs, 214 Terrace Ave, Hasbrouck Heights, NJ 07604; **Phone:** 201-288-6330; **Board Cert:** Obstetrics & Gynecology 2014; Reproductive Endocrinology/Infertility 201; **Med School:** NYU Sch Med 1986; **Resid:** Obstetrics & Gynecology, NYU-Bellevue Hosp Ctr 1990; **Fellow:** Reproductive Endocrinology, UMDNJ-Newark Affil Hosp 1992; **Fac Appt:** Prof ObG, UMDNJ-NJ Med Sch, Newark

Miller, Jane E MD (RE) - **Spec Exp:** Infertility-IVF; Laparoscopic Surgery; Hysteroscopic Surgery; **Hospital:** Holy Name Med Ctr (page 738); **Address:** North Hudson IVF Ctr, 385 Sylvan Ave, Ste 12, Englewood Cliffs, NJ 07632; **Phone:** 201-871-1999; **Board Cert:** Obstetrics & Gynecology 2013; Reproductive Endocrinology/Infertility 2013; **Med School:** SUNY Downstate 1978; **Resid:** Obstetrics & Gynecology, Beth Israel Deaconess Med Ctr 1983; Obstetrics & Gynecology, Erlanger Med Ctr 1984; **Fellow:** Reproductive Endocrinology, SUNY Downstate Med Ctr 1989

Rheumatology

Chung, Jeff MD (Rhu) - **Spec Exp:** Arthritis; Autoimmune Disease; Inflammatory Arthritis; Musculoskeletal Disorders; **Hospital:** Valley Hosp (page 739), Hackensack UMC-Pascack Valley (page 737); **Address:** Bergen Medical Associates, 466 Old Hook Rd, Ste 1, Emerson, NJ 07630; **Phone:** 201-967-8221; **Board Cert:** Rheumatology 2005; **Med School:** SUNY Hlth Sci Ctr 1998; **Resid:** Internal Medicine, Yale-New Haven Hosp 2001; **Fellow:** Rheumatology, Yale-New Haven Hosp 2004

Gonter, Neil J MD (Rhu) - **Spec Exp:** Rheumatoid Arthritis; Gout; Osteoporosis; Osteoarthritis; **Hospital:** Hackensack Univ Med Ctr (page 96), Holy Name Med Ctr (page 738); **Address:** Rheumatology Associates of North Jersey, 1415 Queen Anne Rd, Teaneck, NJ 07666; **Phone:** 201-837-7788; **Board Cert:** Rheumatology 2013; Internal Medicine 2013; **Med School:** SUNY Upstate Med Univ 1998; **Resid:** Internal Medicine, UMDNJ Univ Hosp 2001; **Fellow:** Rheumatology, SUNY Downstate Med Ctr 2003; **Fac Appt:** Asst Clin Prof Med, Columbia P&S

Guma, Michael DO (Rhu) - **Spec Exp:** Arthritis; Autoimmune Disease; Inflammatory Muscle Disease; Osteoporosis; **Hospital:** Saint Michael's Med Ctr; **Address:** North Jersey Rheumatology Assocs, 312 Belleville Tpke, Ste 3A, North Arlington, NJ 07031; **Phone:** 201-998-2800; **Board Cert:** Internal Medicine 2013; Rheumatology 2004; **Med School:** Kirksville Coll Osteo Med 1989; **Resid:** Internal Medicine, St Michaels Med Ctr 1992; **Fellow:** Rheumatology, St Michaels Med Ctr 1994

Kepecs, Gilbert MD (Rhu) - **Hospital:** Hackensack Univ Med Ctr (page 96), Holy Name Med Ctr (page 738); **Address:** Hackensack Rheumatology, 385 Prospect Ave Fl 2, Hackensack, NJ 07601; **Phone:** 201-498-9060; **Board Cert:** Internal Medicine 1989; Rheumatology 2012; **Med School:** Albert Einstein Coll Med 1986; **Resid:** Internal Medicine, St Lukes Hosp 1989; **Fellow:** Rheumatology, Montefiore Med Ctr 1993; Research, Albert Einstein Coll Med 1995; **Fac Appt:** Asst Clin Prof Med, UMDNJ-NJ Med Sch, Newark

Kopelman, Rima G MD (Rhu) - **Spec Exp:** Rheumatoid Arthritis; Lupus/SLE; Vasculitis; **Hospital:** Valley Hosp (page 739), NY-Presby/Columbia Univ Med Ctr, NY (page 102); **Address:** 301 Godwin Ave, Midland Park, NJ 07432-1544; **Phone:** 201-444-4526; **Board Cert:** Internal Medicine 1980; Rheumatology 1984; **Med School:** Columbia P&S 1977; **Resid:** Internal Medicine, Columbia-Presby Med Ctr 1981; **Fellow:** Rheumatology, Columbia-Presby Med Ctr 1983; **Fac Appt:** Asst Clin Prof Med, Columbia P&S

Leibowitz, Evan H MD (Rhu) - **Spec Exp:** Rheumatoid Arthritis; Gout; Lupus/SLE; **Hospital:** Valley Hosp (page 739); **Address:** Prospect Medical Office, 301 Godwin Ave, Midland Park, NJ 07432; **Phone:** 201-444-4526; **Board Cert:** Rheumatology 2011; **Med School:** UMDNJ-NJ Med Sch, Newark 1996; **Resid:** Internal Medicine, New York Hosp 1999; **Fellow:** Rheumatology, Hosp for Special Surg 2002

Marcus, Ralph E MD (Rhu) - **Spec Exp:** Rheumatoid Arthritis; Osteoporosis; Lupus/SLE; Sclero-derma; **Hospital:** Hackensack Univ Med Ctr (page 96), Holy Name Med Ctr (page 738); **Address:** Rheumatology Assocs of North Jersey, 1450 Queen Anne Rd, Teaneck, NJ 07666-3521; **Phone:** 201-837-7788; **Board Cert:** Internal Medicine 1975; Rheumatology 1976; **Med School:** Albert Einstein Coll Med 1969; **Resid:** Internal Medicine, Mount Sinai Hosp 1974; **Fellow:** Rheumatology, Natl Inst Hlth 1972; Rheumatology, Hosp Special Surg 1976; **Fac Appt:** Assoc Clin Prof Med, Rutgers R W Johnson Med Sch

Salem, Noel B MD (Rhu) - **Spec Exp:** Fibromyalgia; **Hospital:** Englewood Hosp & Med Ctr; **Address:** 285 Engle St, Englewood, NJ 07631-2406; **Phone:** 201-871-0223; **Board Cert:** Internal Medicine 1976; Rheumatology 1998; Geriatric Medicine 2004; **Med School:** SUNY Buffalo 1972; **Resid:** Internal Medicine, US Public Hlth Svc Hosp 1973; Internal Medicine, Columbia-Presby Med Ctr 1974; **Fellow:** Rheumatology, Columbia-Presby Med Ctr 1976; **Fac Appt:** Asst Clin Prof Med, Mount Sinai Sch Med

Zalkowitz, Alan MD (Rhu) - **Spec Exp:** Rheumatoid Arthritis; Gout; Collagen Vascular Disor-ders; **Hospital:** Valley Hosp (page 739); **Address:** 31-00 Broadway, Fl 2nd, Fair Lawn, NJ 07410-2331; **Phone:** 201-796-2255; **Board Cert:** Internal Medicine 1977; Rheumatology 1982; **Med School:** Belgium 1970; **Resid:** Internal Medicine, Yale New Haven Hosp 1971; Internal Medicine, Stamford Hosp 1972; **Fellow:** Rheumatology, Mount Sinai Hosp 1974

Sports Medicine

Alberta, Francis G MD (SM) - **Spec Exp:** Elbow Reconstruction; Shoulder & Knee Injuries; Knee Injuries; **Hospital:** Hackensack Univ Med Ctr (page 96); **Address:** 266 Harristown Rd, Ste 100, Glen Rock, NJ 07452; **Phone:** 201-493-8990; **Board Cert:** Orthopaedic Surgery 2006; Or-thopaedic Sports Medicine 2009; **Med School:** UMDNJ-NJ Med Sch, Newark 1997; **Resid:** Or-thopaedic Surgery, Univ Conn Med Ctr 2002; **Fellow:** Orthopaedic Sports Medicine, Kerlan-Jobe Ortho Clin 2005

Delfico, Anthony J MD (SM) - **Spec Exp:** Arthroscopic Surgery; Shoulder & Knee Surgery; Knee Replacement; Knee Injuries/ACL; **Hospital:** Valley Hosp (page 739); **Address:** Ridgewood Or-thopedic Grp, 85 S Maple Ave, Ridgewood, NJ 07450; **Phone:** 201-445-2830; **Board Cert:** Or-thopaedic Surgery 2011; **Med School:** Rutgers R W Johnson Med Sch 1992; **Resid:** Orthopaedic Surgery, Robert Wood Johnson Univ Hosp 1997; **Fellow:** Sports Medicine, Duke Univ Hosp 1998

Savatsky, Gary J MD (SM) - **Spec Exp:** Shoulder & Knee Injuries; **Hospital:** Hackensack Univ Med Ctr (page 96); **Address:** Orthopedic Spine & Sports Med Ctr, 2 Forest Ave, Paramus, NJ 07652; **Phone:** 201-587-1111; **Board Cert:** Orthopaedic Surgery 2007; **Med School:** Columbia P&S 1975; **Resid:** Surgery, St Luke's-Roosevelt Hosp Ctr 1978; Orthopaedic Surgery, Hosp for Special Surg 1980; **Fellow:** Orthopaedic Surgery, Hosp for Special Surg 1983

Surgery

Ahlborn, Thomas N MD (S) - **Spec Exp:** Gastrointestinal Surgery; Laparoscopic Surgery; Gall-bladder Surgery; **Hospital:** Valley Hosp (page 739); **Address:** Valley Med Grp, Surgery, 385 S Maple Ave, Ste 202, Glen Rock, NJ 07452; **Phone:** 201-444-5757; **Board Cert:** Surgery 2005; **Med School:** Columbia P&S 1980; **Resid:** Surgery, NY-Presby/Columbia Univ Med Ctr 1985; **Fel-low:** Vascular Surgery, NY-Presby/Columbia Univ Med Ctr 1986

Fried, Kenneth S MD (S) - **Spec Exp:** Carotid Artery Surgery; Laparoscopic Surgery; **Hospital:** Englewood Hosp & Med Ctr, Holy Name Med Ctr (page 738); **Address:** 180 N Dean St, Ste 2 South, Englewood, NJ 07631-2541; **Phone:** 201-568-8666; **Board Cert:** Surgery 2004; **Med School:** NYU Sch Med 1978; **Resid:** Surgery, NYU Med Ctr 1983; **Fellow:** Peripheral Vascular Surgery, NYU Med Ctr 1984

Harris, Michael T MD (S) - **Spec Exp:** Colon & Rectal Cancer & Surgery; Gastrointestinal Surgery; **Hospital:** Englewood Hosp & Med Ctr; **Address:** Englewood Hospital and Medical Center, 350 Engle St, Englewood, NJ 07639; **Phone:** 201-608-2800; **Board Cert:** Surgery 2003; **Med School:** Columbia P&S 1988; **Resid:** Surgery, Mt Sinai Med Ctr 1993; **Fac Appt:** Assoc Clin Prof S, Mount Sinai Sch Med

Licata Jr, Joseph J MD (S) - **Spec Exp:** Laparoscopic Surgery; Breast Surgery; **Hospital:** Valley Hosp (page 739); **Address:** 245 E Main St, Ramsey, NJ 07446; **Phone:** 201-327-0220; **Board Cert:** Surgery 2011; **Med School:** Mexico 1984; **Resid:** Surgery, Westchester Med Ctr 1991

McCain, Donald A MD/PhD (S) - **Spec Exp:** Gastrointestinal Cancer; Melanoma; Sarcomas; Colon & Rectal Cancer; **Hospital:** Hackensack Univ Med Ctr (page 96); **Address:** 20 Prospect Ave, Ste 603, Hackensack, NJ 07601; **Phone:** 201-342-1010; **Board Cert:** Surgery 2010; **Med School:** Albert Einstein Coll Med 1991; **Resid:** Surgery, Mt Sinai Med Ctr 1996; **Fellow:** Surgical Oncology, Meml Sloan-Kettering Cancer Ctr 1998; **Fac Appt:** Asst Clin Prof S, UMDNJ-NJ Med Sch, Newark

Pereira, Stephen G MD (S) - **Spec Exp:** Minimally Invasive Surgery; Robotic Surgery; **Hospital:** Hackensack Univ Med Ctr (page 96); **Address:** 90 Prospect Ave, Ste 1D, Hackensack, NJ 07601; **Phone:** 201-343-3433; **Board Cert:** Surgery 2007; **Med School:** Rutgers R W Johnson Med Sch 1991; **Resid:** Surgery, Northwestern Meml Hosp 1996; **Fellow:** Laparoscopic Surgery, Hackensack Univ Med Ctr 1999

Poole, John W MD (S) - **Hospital:** Holy Name Med Ctr (page 738); **Address:** 83 Summit Ave, Hackensack, NJ 07601; **Phone:** 201-646-0010; **Board Cert:** Surgery 2008; **Med School:** Univ VA Sch Med 1982; **Resid:** Surgery, Montefiore Med Ctr 1987

Schmidt, Hans J MD (S) - **Spec Exp:** Obesity/Bariatric Surgery; Laparoscopic Abdominal Surgery; **Hospital:** Hackensack Univ Med Ctr (page 96); **Address:** 81 Route 4 W, Ste 401, Paramus, NJ 07652; **Phone:** 201-646-1121; **Board Cert:** Surgery 2008; **Med School:** UMDNJ-NJ Med Sch, Newark 1991; **Resid:** Surgery, Univ Hosp-UMDNJ 1997

Sussman, Barry C MD (S) - **Spec Exp:** Laparoscopic Surgery; Breast Surgery; **Hospital:** Englewood Hosp & Med Ctr; **Address:** 375 Engle St, Englewood, NJ 07631-1823; **Phone:** 201-894-0400; **Board Cert:** Surgery 2008; **Med School:** NYU Sch Med 1973; **Resid:** Surgery, NYU Med Ctr 1978; **Fellow:** Vascular Surgery, Englewood Hosp 1979; **Fac Appt:** Asst Clin Prof S, Mount Sinai Sch Med

Yang, Hee K MD (S) - **Spec Exp:** Laparoscopic Surgery; Vascular Surgery; **Hospital:** Holy Name Med Ctr (page 738); **Address:** 464 Hudson Terr, Ste 101, Englewood Cliff, NJ 07632; **Phone:** 201-567-7747; **Board Cert:** Surgery 2006; **Med School:** Rush Med Coll 1989; **Resid:** Surgery, Lenox Hill Hosp 1994

Yiengpruksawan, Anusak MD (S) - **Spec Exp:** Liver & Biliary Surgery; Endoscopic Ultrasound; Robotic Surgery; Minimally Invasive Surgery; **Hospital:** Valley Hosp (page 739), Chilton Med Ctr (page 92); **Address:** Valley Hosp, Surgery Dept, 1 Valley Health Plaza, Paramus, NJ 07652; **Phone:** 201-634-5438; **Board Cert:** Surgery 2011; **Med School:** Japan 1978; **Resid:** Surgery, Harlem Hosp 1989; **Fellow:** Surgical Oncology, Meml Sloan-Kettering Cancer Ctr 1991

Thoracic & Cardiac Surgery

Elmann, Elie M MD (T&CS) - **Spec Exp:** Robotic Cardiac Surgery; Minimally Invasive Cardiac Surgery; Heart Valve Surgery; Atrial Fibrillation; **Hospital:** Hackensack Univ Med Ctr (page 96), Englewood Hosp & Med Ctr; **Address:** Hackensack Univ Med Ctr, Cardiothoracic, 20 Prospect Ave, Ste 900, Hackensack, NJ 07601; **Phone:** 201-996-2261; **Board Cert:** Surgery 2004; Thoracic & Cardiac Surgery 2005; **Med School:** NY Med Coll 1987; **Resid:** Surgery, Cabrini Med Ctr 1992; **Fellow:** Cardiothoracic Surgery, SUNY Downstate Med Ctr 1995; **Fac Appt:** Asst Prof S, UMDNJ-NJ Med Sch, Newark

Klein, James J MD (T&CS) - **Spec Exp:** Aneurysm-Thoracic Aortic; **Hospital:** Englewood Hosp & Med Ctr; **Address:** Englewood Cardiac Surgery Assocs, 350 Engle St, Ste 5200, Englewood, NJ 07631; **Phone:** 201-894-3636; **Board Cert:** Thoracic Surgery 2007; Surgery 2004; **Med School:** SUNY Stony Brook 1990; **Resid:** Surgery, SUNY Downstate Med Ctr 1995; **Fellow:** Thoracic & Cardiac Surgery, Mount Sinai Med Ctr 1998

Kline, Gary M MD (T&CS) - **Spec Exp:** Lung Cancer; Emphysema; Mediastinal Tumors; **Hospital:** Holy Name Med Ctr (page 738); **Address:** Summit Surgical Inst, 332 Summit Ave, Hackensack, NJ 07601; **Phone:** 201-488-6445; **Board Cert:** Surgery 2004; Thoracic & Cardiac Surgery 2005; **Med School:** Wayne State Univ 1986; **Resid:** Surgery, Detroit Med Ctr 1991; **Fellow:** Thoracic Surgery, Hosp Univ Penn 1994

McCullough, Jock N MD (T&CS) - **Spec Exp:** Heart Valve Surgery; Minimally Invasive Heart Valve Surgery; Coronary Artery Surgery; Cardiac Surgery; **Hospital:** Hackensack Univ Med Ctr (page 96); **Address:** The Heart & Vascular Hosp at Hackensack, 20 Prospect Ave, Ste 406, Hackensack, NJ 07601; **Phone:** 551-996-5388; **Board Cert:** Surgery 2004; Thoracic Surgery 2005; **Med School:** UMDNJ-NJ Med Sch, Newark 1987; **Resid:** Surgery, UMDNJ Affil Hosp 1993; **Fellow:** Cardiothoracic Surgery, Mt Sinai Med Ctr 1996

Zairis, Ignatios S MD (T&CS) - **Spec Exp:** Endovascular Surgery; Minimally Invasive Thoracic Surgery; Vascular Surgery; **Hospital:** Englewood Hosp & Med Ctr, Holy Name Med Ctr (page 738); **Address:** 741 Teaneck Rd, Teaneck, NJ 07666; **Phone:** 201-837-8282; **Board Cert:** Surgery 2011; **Med School:** Greece 1973; **Resid:** Surgery, Kings Co Hosp 1984; Thoracic Surgery, SUNY Hlth Sci Ctr 1983; **Fellow:** Cardiothoracic Surgery, SUNY Hlth Sci Ctr 1984

Zapolanski, Alex MD (T&CS) - **Spec Exp:** Minimally Invasive Heart Valve Surgery; Aortic Surgery; Coronary Artery Surgery; **Hospital:** Valley Hosp (page 739); **Address:** Valley Hosp, Heart Ctr, 223 N Van Dien Ave, Ridgewood, NJ 07450; **Phone:** 201-447-8377; **Board Cert:** Thoracic Surgery 2004; **Med School:** Argentina 1973; **Resid:** Surgery, Cleveland Clin 1979; Cardiothoracic Surgery, Toronto Genl Hosp 1981

Urology

Agarwal, Saurabh MD (U) - **Spec Exp:** Robotic Urologic Surgery; Prostate Cancer/Robotic Surgery; **Hospital:** Valley Hosp (page 739); **Address:** Urology Group, 4 Godwin Ave, Midland Park, NJ 07432; **Phone:** 201-444-7070; **Board Cert:** Urology 2007; **Med School:** Boston Univ 1999; **Resid:** Surgery, Rhode Island Hosp 2000; Urology, Rhode Island Hosp 2004

Ahmed, Mutahar MD (U) - **Spec Exp:** Robotic Surgery; Prostate Cancer; Minimally Invasive Surgery; Kidney Cancer; **Hospital:** Hackensack Univ Med Ctr (page 96), Holy Name Med Ctr (page 738); **Address:** NJ Ctr Prostate Cancer & Urology, 255 W Spring Valley Ave, Ste 101, Maywood, NJ 07607; **Phone:** 201-487-8866; **Board Cert:** Urology 2013; **Med School:** SUNY Hlth Sci Ctr 1997; **Resid:** Surgery, Univ Hosp-UMDNJ 1999; **Fellow:** Urology, Univ Hosp-UMDNJ 2003; **Fac Appt:** Asst Clin Prof U, UMDNJ-NJ Med Sch, Newark

Andronaco, Raymond B MD (U) - **Spec Exp:** Voiding Dysfunction; Incontinence; **Hospital:** Englewood Hosp & Med Ctr; **Address:** Urologic Specialties, 177 N Dean St, South Tower, Ste 305, Englewood, NJ 07631; **Phone:** 201-569-7777; **Board Cert:** Urology 2003; **Med School:** Mexico 1976; **Resid:** Surgery, Beth Israel Med Ctr 1979; Urology, NYU Med Ctr 1983

Basralian, Kevin R MD (U) - **Spec Exp:** Infertility-Male; Prostate Benign Disease; Minimally Invasive Surgery; Reconstructive Urologic Surgery; **Hospital:** Hackensack Univ Med Ctr (page 96); **Address:** HUMC, Urology Dept, 360 Essex St, Ste 403, Hackensack, NJ 07601; **Phone:** 551-996-8090; **Board Cert:** Urology 2010; **Med School:** Mexico 1979; **Resid:** Surgery, Lenox Hill Hosp 1982; Urology, Lenox Hill Hosp 1985; **Fellow:** Reconstructive Pelvic Surgery, Univ Edinburgh 1986

Baum, Richard D MD (U) - **Spec Exp:** Kidney Stones; **Hospital:** Valley Hosp (page 739); **Address:** Urology Group, 4 Godwin Ave, Midland Park, NJ 07432-1921; **Phone:** 201-444-7070; **Board Cert:** Urology 2010; **Med School:** Tulane Univ 1981; **Resid:** Surgery, NYU Med Ctr 1983; Urology, NYU Med Ctr 1987

Chun, Thomas Y MD (U) - **Spec Exp:** Prostate Cancer; Kidney Stones; Erectile Dysfunction; **Hospital:** Englewood Hosp & Med Ctr, Holy Name Med Ctr (page 738); **Address:** Urology Ctr, 300 Grand Ave, Ste 202, Englewood, NJ 07631; **Phone:** 201-816-1900; **Board Cert:** Urology 2008; **Med School:** Geo Wash Univ 1991; **Resid:** Surgery, NYU Med Ctr 1993; Urology, NYU Med Ctr 1997

DeTorres, Wayne R MD (U) - **Spec Exp:** Minimally Invasive Urologic Surgery; Prostate Cancer; Prostate Disease; Voiding Dysfunction; **Hospital:** Valley Hosp (page 739); **Address:** Urology Group, 4 Godwin Ave, Midland Park, NJ 07432; **Phone:** 201-444-7070; **Board Cert:** Urology 2007; **Med School:** Tufts Univ 1988; **Resid:** Urology, Univ NC Hosp 1996

Esposito, Michael P MD (U) - **Spec Exp:** Laparoscopic Kidney Surgery; Prostate Cancer/Robotic Surgery; Minimally Invasive Urologic Surgery; Adrenal Surgery; **Hospital:** Hackensack Univ Med Ctr (page 96), Monmouth Med Ctr (page 94); **Address:** NJ Ctr Prostate Cancer & Urology, 255 W Spring Valley Ave, Ste 101, Maywood, NJ 07607; **Phone:** 201-487-8866; **Board Cert:** Urology 2012; **Med School:** UMDNJ-NJ Med Sch, Newark 1994; **Resid:** Urology, Univ Hosp-UMDNJ 2000; **Fellow:** Minimally Invasive Surgery, Univ Hosp-UMDNJ 2002; Urologic Laparoscopic Surg-Endourology, Royal Infirm/Western Genl Hosp 2003; **Fac Appt:** Asst Clin Prof S, UMDNJ-NJ Med Sch, Newark

Frey, Howard L MD (U) - **Spec Exp:** Prostate Cancer; Bladder Cancer; Kidney Cancer; Microsurgery; **Hospital:** Valley Hosp (page 739); **Address:** Urology Grp, 4 Godwin Ave, Midland Park, NJ 07432; **Phone:** 201-444-7070; **Board Cert:** Urology 2013; **Med School:** Johns Hopkins Univ 1977; **Resid:** Surgery, Johns Hopkins Hosp 1979; Urology, UCLA Med Ctr 1983

Katz, Steven A MD (U) - **Spec Exp:** Transfusion Free Surgery; Prostate Cancer; Laparoscopic Surgery; **Hospital:** Englewood Hosp & Med Ctr, Holy Name Med Ctr (page 738); **Address:** Urology Ctr-Englewood, 300 Grand Ave, Ste 202, Englewood, NJ 7631; **Phone:** 201-816-1900; **Board Cert:** Urology 1978; **Med School:** SUNY Buffalo 1969; **Resid:** Urology, Metropolitan Hosp Ctr 1976

Kerns, John MD (U) - **Spec Exp:** Urologic Cancer; Incontinence; Infertility-Male; **Hospital:** Holy Name Med Ctr (page 738); **Address:** Urologic Specialists, 177 N Dean St, South Tower, Ste 305, Englewood, NJ 07631; **Phone:** 201-569-7777; **Board Cert:** Urology 1983; **Med School:** Georgetown Univ 1975; **Resid:** Surgery, Georgetown Univ Hosp 1977; Urology, Georgetown Univ Hosp 1981

Lanteri, Vincent J MD (U) - **Spec Exp:** Prostate Cancer/Robotic Surgery; Urologic Cancer; **Hospital:** Hackensack Univ Med Ctr (page 96), Holy Name Med Ctr (page 738); **Address:** NJ Ctr for Prostate Cancer & Urology, 255 W Spring Valley Ave, Ste 101, Maywood, NJ 07607; **Phone:** 201-487-8866; **Board Cert:** Urology 1982; **Med School:** Mexico 1974; **Resid:** Surgery, UMDNJ Med Ctr 1976; Urology, UMDNJ Med Ctr 1980; **Fellow:** Urologic Oncology, Roswell Park Cancer Inst 1981

Mackey, Timothy J MD (U) - **Hospital:** Valley Hosp (page 739); **Address:** Urology Group, 4 Godwin Ave, Midland Park, NJ 07432; **Phone:** 201-444-7070; **Board Cert:** Urology 2011; **Med School:** Univ VA Sch Med 1993; **Resid:** Surgery, Univ MD Med Ctr 1996; Urology, Univ MD Med Ctr 1999

Margolis, Eric J MD (U) - **Spec Exp:** Urologic Cancer; Prostate Disease; Robotic Surgery; Pelvic Organ Prolapse Repair; **Hospital:** Englewood Hosp & Med Ctr; **Address:** Urology Ctr-Englewood, 300 Grand Ave, Ste 202, Englewood, NJ 7631; **Phone:** 201-816-1900; **Board Cert:** Urology 2008; **Med School:** SUNY Upstate Med Univ 1990; **Resid:** Urologic Surgery, Mt Sinai Hosp 1996

Munver, Ravi MD (U) - **Spec Exp:** Robotic Surgery; Prostate Cancer; Kidney Cancer; Kidney Stones; **Hospital:** Hackensack Univ Med Ctr (page 96); **Address:** Hackensack University Medical Center, Department of Urology, 360 Essex St, Ste 403, Hackensack, NJ 07601; **Phone:** 551-996-8090; **Board Cert:** Urology 2013; **Med School:** Cornell Univ-Weill Med Coll 1996; **Resid:** Urology, Duke Univ Med Ctr 2002; **Fellow:** Robotic Surgery, NY-Presby/Cornell Univ Med Ctr 2003; **Fac Appt:** Assoc Prof U, UMDNJ-NJ Med Sch, Newark

Rosenberg, Gene S MD (U) - **Spec Exp:** Minimally Invasive Surgery; Prostate Cancer-Cryosurgery; Kidney Cancer-Cryosurgery; **Hospital:** Hackensack Univ Med Ctr (page 96), Holy Name Med Ctr (page 738); **Address:** University Urology Assocs, 20 Prospect Ave, Ste 719, Hackensack, NJ 07601; **Phone:** 201-343-0082; **Board Cert:** Urology 1982; **Med School:** NYU Sch Med 1974; **Resid:** Pathology, Kings Co Hosp 1976; Urology, Bellevue Hosp 1980

Sadeghi-Nejad, Hossein MD (U) - **Spec Exp:** Erectile Dysfunction; Peyronie's Disease; Prostate Disease; Infertility-Male; **Hospital:** Hackensack Univ Med Ctr (page 96), Univ Hosp-Newark; **Address:** 20 Prospect Ave, rm 711, Hackensack, NJ 07601; **Phone:** 201-342-7977 x214; **Board Cert:** Urology 2009; **Med School:** McGill Univ 1989; **Resid:** Surgery, UCSF Med Ctr 1991; Urology, Boston Univ Med Ctr 1996; **Fellow:** Microsurgery, Boston Univ Med Ctr 1997; Reproductive Medicine, Boston Univ Med Ctr 1997; **Fac Appt:** Prof U, UMDNJ-Rutgers Med Sch

Sawczuk, Ihor S MD (U) - **Spec Exp:** Bladder Cancer; Kidney Cancer; Prostate Cancer/Robotic Surgery; **Hospital:** Hackensack Univ Med Ctr (page 96), NY-Presby/Columbia Univ Med Ctr, NY (page 102); **Address:** HUMC, Urology, 360 Essex St, Ste 403, Hackensack, NJ 07601; **Phone:** 551-996-8090; **Board Cert:** Urology 2005; **Med School:** Med Coll PA Hahnemann 1979; **Resid:** Surgery, St Vincents Hosp 1981; Urology, NY-Presby/Columbia Univ Med Ctr 1984; **Fellow:** Urologic Oncology, NY-Presby/Columbia Univ Med Ctr 1986; **Fac Appt:** Prof U, UMDNJ-NJ Med Sch, Newark

Siegel, Andrew L MD (U) - **Spec Exp:** Urology-Female; Incontinence; Urodynamics; Voiding Dysfunction; **Hospital:** Hackensack Univ Med Ctr (page 96); **Address:** Bergen Urological Assocs, 20 Prospect Ave, Ste 715, Hackensack, NJ 07601; **Phone:** 201-342-6600; **Board Cert:** Urology 2013; Female Pelvic Medicine & Reconstuctive Surgery 2013; **Med School:** Ros Franklin Univ/Chicago Med Sch 1981; **Resid:** Urology, Hosp Univ Penn-UPHS 1987; **Fellow:** Female Urology, UCLA Med Ctr 1988; **Fac Appt:** Asst Clin Prof U, UMDNJ-Rutgers Med Sch

Wasserman, Gary D MD (U) - **Spec Exp:** Kidney Stones; Incontinence; Voiding Dysfunction; **Hospital:** Englewood Hosp & Med Ctr, Holy Name Med Ctr (page 738); **Address:** Urology Ctr-Englewood, 300 Grand Ave, Ste 202, Englewood, NJ 7631; **Phone:** 201-816-1900; **Board Cert:** Urology 2012; **Med School:** Tulane Univ 1985; **Resid:** Surgery, G Washington Univ Hosp 1987; Urology, Tulane Med Ctr 1991

Vascular & Interventional Radiology

Albert, Arthur MD (VIR) - **Spec Exp:** Interventional Radiology; **Hospital:** Hackensack Univ Med Ctr (page 96); **Address:** HackensackUMC-Dept of Radiology, 30 Prospect Ave, Hackensack, NJ 07601; **Phone:** 551-996-2194; **Board Cert:** Diagnostic Radiology 1982; **Med School:** Penn State Coll Med 1978; **Resid:** Diagnostic Radiology, Hosp Univ Penn 1982; **Fellow:** Vascular & Interventional Radiology, Alexandria Hosp 1983

Rundback, John H MD (VIR) - **Spec Exp:** Angioplasty; Chemoembolization & Tumor Ablation; Peripheral Vascular Disease; **Hospital:** Holy Name Med Ctr (page 738); **Address:** Holy Name Med Ctr, Radiology, 718 Teaneck Rd, Ste 1E, Teaneck, NJ 07666; **Phone:** 201-833-7268; **Board Cert:** Diagnostic Radiology 1992; Vascular & Interventional Radiology 2006; **Med School:** SUNY Downstate 1987; **Resid:** Diagnostic Radiology, Beth Israel Med Ctr 1992; **Fellow:** Interventional Radiology, Washington Hosp Ctr 1993; **Fac Appt:** Assoc Prof Rad, Columbia P&S

Vascular Surgery

Char, Daniel J MD (VascS) - **Spec Exp:** Endovascular Surgery; Aneurysm-Abdominal & Thoracic Aortic; **Hospital:** Valley Hosp (page 739); **Address:** 1124 E Ave, Ste 104, Ridgewood, NJ 07450; **Phone:** 201-444-5353; **Board Cert:** Surgery 2011; Vascular Surgery 2013; **Med School:** SUNY Stony Brook 1995; **Resid:** Surgery, Stony Brook Univ Med Ctr 2000; **Fellow:** Vascular Surgery, Stony Brook Univ Med Ctr 2002

Elias, Steven M MD (VascS) - **Spec Exp:** Vein Disorders; Wound Healing/Care; Minimally Invasive Surgery; Varicose Veins; **Hospital:** Englewood Hosp & Med Ctr, NY-Presby/Columbia Univ Med Ctr, NY (page 102); **Address:** Englewood Hosp & Med Ctr, Ctr Vein Disease, 350 Engle St, Englewood, NJ 07631-2541; **Phone:** 201-894-3252; **Board Cert:** Surgery 2007; **Med School:** SUNY Buffalo 1979; **Resid:** Surgery, Millard Filmore Hosp 1981; **Fellow:** Peripheral Vascular Surgery, Englewood Hosp 1985; **Fac Appt:** Asst Prof S, Columbia P&S

Geuder, James W MD (VascS) - **Spec Exp:** Vein Disorders; Carotid Artery Surgery; Aneurysm-Aortic; Endovascular Surgery; **Hospital:** Hackensack Univ Med Ctr (page 96); **Address:** Vein Center of Oradell, 680 Kinderkamack Rd, Ste 306, Oradell, NJ 07649; **Phone:** 201-262-8346; **Board Cert:** Surgery 2007; Vascular Surgery 2009; **Med School:** Med Coll Wisc 1981; **Resid:** Surgery, Univ Hosp-UMDNJ 1986; **Fellow:** Vascular Surgery, NYU Med Ctr 1988

Kagan, Peter E MD (VascS) - **Spec Exp:** Aneurysm-Abdominal Aortic; Carotid Artery Surgery; Endovascular Surgery; **Hospital:** Hackensack Univ Med Ctr (page 96), Holy Name Med Ctr (page 738); **Address:** North Jersey Surgical Specialists, 83 Summit Ave, Hackensack, NJ 07601; **Phone:** 201-646-0010; **Board Cert:** Surgery 2011; Vascular Surgery 2006; **Med School:** Grenada 1997; **Resid:** Surgery, Univ Hosp-UMDNJ 2002; **Fellow:** Vascular Surgery, Newark Beth Israel Med Ctr 2004

Manno, Joseph MD (VascS) - **Spec Exp:** Arterial Disease; Angioplasty; Limb Sparing Surgery; **Hospital:** Hackensack Univ Med Ctr (page 96), Holy Name Med Ctr (page 738); **Address:** North Jersey Surgical Specialists, 83 Summit Ave, Hackensack, NJ 07601; **Phone:** 201-646-0010; **Board Cert:** Surgery 2009; Vascular Surgery 2012; **Med School:** Oral Roberts Sch Med 1982; **Resid:** Surgery, Univ Hosp-UMDNJ 1987; **Fellow:** Vascular Surgery, Univ Hosp-UMDNJ 1989

Napolitano, Massimo MD (VascS) - **Spec Exp:** Aneurysm-Abdominal & Thoracic Aortic; Endovascular Surgery; Carotid Artery Surgery; **Hospital:** Hackensack Univ Med Ctr (page 96); **Address:** Bergen Surgical Specialists, 20 Prospect Ave, Ste 707, Hackensack, NJ 07601; **Phone:** 201-343-0040; **Board Cert:** Vascular Surgery 2004; Surgery 2012; **Med School:** Italy 1984; **Resid:** Surgery, UMDNJ Affil Hosp 1987; Surgery, Monmouth Med Ctr 1989; **Fellow:** Surgery, Henry Ford Hosp 1992; Vascular Surgery, Henry Ford Hosp 1994

Simonian, Gregory T MD (VascS) - **Spec Exp:** Endovascular Surgery; Aneurysm; **Hospital:** Hackensack Univ Med Ctr (page 96); **Address:** Bergen Surgical Specialists, 211 Essex St, Ste 102, Hackensack, NJ 07601; **Phone:** 201-487-8882; **Board Cert:** Vascular Surgery 2011; **Med School:** UMDNJ-NJ Med Sch, Newark 1992; **Resid:** Surgery, Univ Hosp-UMDNJ 1997; **Fellow:** Vascular Surgery, Univ Hosp-UMDNJ 2000

Wolodiger, Fred A MD (VascS) - **Spec Exp:** Arterial Bypass Surgery-Leg; Carotid Artery Surgery; Aneurysm-Aortic; Endovascular Surgery; **Hospital:** Englewood Hosp & Med Ctr; **Address:** Englewood Surgical Assocs, 375 Engle St, Englewood, NJ 07631; **Phone:** 201-894-0400; **Board Cert:** Surgery 2004; Vascular Surgery 2008; **Med School:** SUNY Downstate 1980; **Resid:** Surgery, N Shore Univ Hosp 1985; **Fellow:** Peripheral Vascular Surgery, Englewood Hosp & Med Ctr 1987

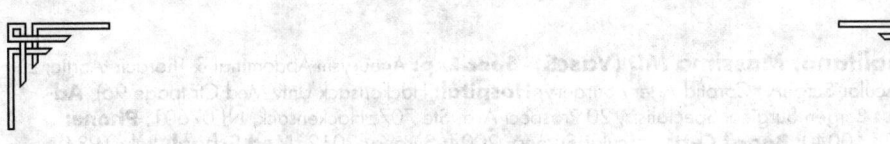

The Best in American Medicine
www.CastleConnolly.com

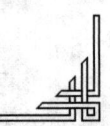

HackensackUMC
Mountainside

1 Bay Avenue, Montclair, NJ 07042 • 973-429-6000
www.mountainsidehosp.com

Number of beds: 365
Number of employees: 1,644
2013 Admissions: 11,208

HackensackUMC Mountainside continues to build on its distinguished 123-year-old tradition of service and deliver on its commitment to provide convenient, local access to world-class healthcare. In fact, this 365-bed facility is successfully adapting to the changing healthcare landscape and committed to offering comprehensive, coordinated outpatient and inpatient care.

Clinical integration with the Hackensack University Health Network's renowned flagship hospital is ongoing and HackensackUMC Mountainside is involved in numerous activities that will contribute to its vitality. Most notable are the establishment of the Mountainside Medical Group, an employed physician practice intended to make primary care readily available at offices throughout the hospital's service area; construction of a new medical office building; participation in the Bundled Payments for Care Initiative Model 2, a pilot project of the Centers for Medicare and Medicaid; and completion of several important energy efficiency projects in collaboration with PSE&G's Hospital Efficiency Program.

On the hospital's main campus, patients have immediate access to state-of-the-art diagnostic technologies, including high-speed, 3-D CT imaging. The most current treatment alternatives for diverse conditions are available at specialized centers dedicated to women's health, cancer care, cardiology, surgery, stroke, chronic kidney disease, wound care and sleep disorders.

HackensackUMC Mountainside's Center for Advanced Bariatric Surgery is a Metabolic and Bariatric Surgery Accreditation and Quality Improvement Program Center of Excellence, and the Breast Health Program is an American College of Radiology Center of Excellence. Other distinguished programs include the Cancer Center, accredited with special commendation by the American College of Surgeons.

- Metabolic and Bariatric Surgery Accreditation and Quality Improvement Program Center of Excellence
- Joint Commission National Quality Approval
- American College of Radiology for Radiation Oncology and Mammography
- American Heart Association/American Stroke Association Get with the Guidelines Gold Plus Achievement Award
- New Jersey Department of Health and Senior Services-designated Primary Stroke Center
- Federal Drug Administration's Mammography Quality Standards Act for Mammography Services
- American College of Surgeons for the Cancer Center
- College of American Pathologists for Laboratory Services
- National League for Nursing Accrediting Commission for the Mountainside Nursing School
- Intersocietal Commission for the Accreditation of Echocardiography Laboratories

For more information, please call 973-429-6000 or visit www.Mountainsidehosp.com.

Addiction Psychiatry

Westreich, Laurence M MD (AdP) - **Spec Exp:** Addiction/Substance Abuse; Cocaine Addiction; Alcohol Abuse; Psychopharmacology; **Address:** Park West Assocs, 33 Plymouth St, Ste 104, Montclair, NJ 07042; **Phone:** 973-509-1444; **Board Cert:** Psychiatry 1993; Addiction Psychiatry 2013; Forensic Psychiatry 2014; **Med School:** Univ Minn 1988; **Resid:** Internal Medicine, Hennepin County Med Ctr 1989; Psychiatry, Beth Israel Med Ctr 1992; **Fellow:** Addiction Psychiatry, NYU Med Ctr/Bellevue Hosp 1994; **Fac Appt:** Assoc Clin Prof Psyc, NYU Sch Med

Adolescent Medicine

Johnson, Robert L MD (AM) - **Spec Exp:** AIDS/HIV; Abuse/Neglect; Behavioral Disorders; **Hospital:** Univ Hosp-Newark; **Address:** Univ Hosp, Adolescent Med, 90 Bergen St, Ste 4300, Newark, NJ 07103; **Phone:** 973-972-2100; **Board Cert:** Pediatrics 1978; **Med School:** UMDNJ-NJ Med Sch, Newark 1972; **Resid:** Pediatrics, Martland Hosp 1974; **Fellow:** Adolescent Medicine, NYU Med Ctr 1976; **Fac Appt:** Prof Ped, UMDNJ-NJ Med Sch, Newark

Neal, Wendy P MD (AM) - **Spec Exp:** Adolescent Gynecology; **Hospital:** Chldns Hosp NJ at Newark (page 94); **Address:** Pediatric Hlth Ctr, 166 Lyons Ave Fl 1, Newark, NJ 07112; **Phone:** 973-926-7282; **Board Cert:** Pediatrics 2010; Adolescent Medicine 2011; **Med School:** Tulane Univ 1991; **Resid:** Pediatrics, Montefiore Med Ctr 1994; **Fellow:** Adolescent Medicine, Montefiore Med Ctr 1995

Stanford, Paulette D MD (AM) - **Spec Exp:** AIDS/HIV in Adolescents; Adolescent Gynecology; Adolescent Behavior-High Risk; **Hospital:** Univ Hosp-Newark; **Address:** Univ Hosp, Adolescent Med, 90 Bergen St, Ste 4300, Newark, NJ 07103; **Phone:** 973-972-2100; **Board Cert:** Pediatrics 1984; Adolescent Medicine 2008; **Med School:** UMDNJ-NJ Med Sch, Newark 1975; **Resid:** Pediatrics, UMDNJ-Univ Hosp 1977; **Fellow:** Adolescent Medicine, UMDNJ-Univ Hosp 1979; **Fac Appt:** Prof Ped, UMDNJ-NJ Med Sch, Newark

Allergy & Immunology

Perlman, Donald B MD (A&I) - **Spec Exp:** Asthma; Urticaria; Drug Sensitivity; **Hospital:** St. Barnabas Med Ctr (page 94), Newark Beth Israel Med Ctr (page 94); **Address:** Assocs Otolaryngology NJ, 741 Northfield Ave, Ste 104, West Orange, NJ 7052; **Phone:** 973-736-7722; **Board Cert:** Pediatrics 1978; Allergy & Immunology 1979; **Med School:** Mount Sinai Sch Med 1973; **Resid:** Pediatrics, Mount Sinai Med Ctr 1976; **Fellow:** Allergy & Immunology, Duke Univ Hosp 1978; **Fac Appt:** Asst Clin Prof Ped, UMDNJ-NJ Med Sch, Newark

Weiss, Steven J MD (A&I) - **Spec Exp:** Asthma; Sinus Disorders; Drug Sensitivity; **Hospital:** St. Barnabas Med Ctr (page 94); **Address:** 209 S Livingston Ave, Ste 6, Livingston, NJ 07039-4042; **Phone:** 973-992-4171; **Board Cert:** Internal Medicine 1985; Allergy & Immunology 1987; **Med School:** Ros Franklin Univ/Chicago Med Sch 1982; **Resid:** Internal Medicine, St Lukes Roosevelt Hosp 1985; **Fellow:** Allergy & Immunology, St Lukes Roosevelt Hosp 1987; **Fac Appt:** Asst Clin Prof A&I, UMDNJ-Rutgers Med Sch

Cardiac Electrophysiology

Correia, Joaquim J MD (CE) - **Spec Exp:** Arrhythmias; Pacemakers/Defibrillators; Syncope; **Hospital:** Saint Michael's Med Ctr; **Address:** 243 Chestnut St, Ste 2L, Newark, NJ 07105; **Phone:** 973-589-8668; **Board Cert:** Internal Medicine 1989; Cardiac Electrophysiology 2004; Cardiovascular Disease 2013; **Med School:** NYU Sch Med 1986; **Resid:** Internal Medicine, NY-Presby/Columbia Univ Med Ctr 1989; **Fellow:** Cardiovascular Disease, NY-Presby/Columbia Univ Med Ctr 1992; Cardiac Electrophysiology, NY-Presby/Columbia Univ Med Ctr 1993; **Fac Appt:** Asst Prof Med, UMDNJ-NJ Med Sch, Newark

Costeas, Constantinos A MD (CE) - **Spec Exp:** Arrhythmias; Radiofrequency Ablation; Pacemakers; **Hospital:** Saint Michael's Med Ctr, St. Barnabas Med Ctr (page 94); **Address:** NJ Cardiology Assocs, 375 Mount Pleasant Ave Fl 2, West Orange, NJ 07052; **Phone:** 973-731-9598; **Board Cert:** Cardiac Electrophysiology 2008; Cardiovascular Disease 2008; **Med School:** SUNY Stony Brook 1989; **Resid:** Internal Medicine, Stony Brook Univ Med Ctr 1992; **Fellow:** Cardiovascular Disease, St Vincents Hosp 1996; Cardiac Electrophysiology, NY-Presby/Columbia Univ Med Ctr 1998

Roelke, Marc MD (CE) - **Spec Exp:** Pacemakers/Defibrillators; Cardiac Catheterization; **Hospital:** Newark Beth Israel Med Ctr (page 94), St. Barnabas Med Ctr (page 94); **Address:** NJ Cardiology Assocs, 375 Mount Pleasant Ave Fl 2, West Orange, NJ 07052; **Phone:** 973-731-9598; **Board Cert:** Cardiovascular Disease 2013; Cardiac Electrophysiology 2006; **Med School:** Columbia P&S 1987; **Resid:** Internal Medicine, Univ Chicago Med Ctr 1990; **Fellow:** Cardiovascular Disease, Mass Genl Hosp 1992; Cardiac Electrophysiology, Mass Genl Hosp 1994

Sauberman, Roy B MD (CE) - **Spec Exp:** Radiofrequency Ablation; Pacemakers/Defibrillators; Syncope; **Hospital:** St. Barnabas Med Ctr (page 94), Morristown Med Ctr (page 92); **Address:** Summit Medical Group, 161 Millburn Ave, Millburn, NJ 07041; **Phone:** 973-467-4220; **Board Cert:** Cardiovascular Disease 2008; Cardiac Electrophysiology 2008; **Med School:** Yale Univ 1990; **Resid:** Internal Medicine, NY-Presby/Weill Cornell Med Ctr 1993; **Fellow:** Cardiovascular Disease, NY-Presby/Columbia Univ Med Ctr 1996; Cardiac Electrophysiology, Beth Israel Med Ctr 1998

Cardiovascular Disease

Criscito, Mario A MD (Cv) - **Spec Exp:** Cholesterol/Lipid Disorders; Congestive Heart Failure; Hypertension; **Hospital:** St. Barnabas Hosp - Bronx, Clara Maass Med Ctr (page 94); **Address:** Cardiology Ctr of NJ, 50 Newark Ave, Ste 204, Belleville, NJ 07109-3565; **Phone:** 973-450-2158; **Board Cert:** Internal Medicine 1973; Cardiovascular Disease 1979; **Med School:** Italy 1969; **Resid:** Internal Medicine, St barnabas Med Ctr 1973; **Fellow:** Cardiovascular Disease, St Barnabas Med Ctr 1976

Fisk, Marc S DO (Cv) - **Spec Exp:** Preventive Cardiology; Nuclear Cardiology; **Hospital:** Clara Maass Med Ctr (page 94), Newark Beth Israel Med Ctr (page 94); **Address:** NJ Cardiology Assocs, 5 Franklin Ave, Ste 502, Belleville, NJ 07109; **Phone:** 973-429-8333; **Board Cert:** Cardiovascular Disease 2012; **Med School:** NY Coll Osteo Med 1992; **Resid:** Internal Medicine, Coney Island Hosp 1993; Internal Medicine, Univ MA Meml Hosp 1995; **Fellow:** Cardiovascular Disease, Lahey Clin 1998

Klapholz, Marc MD (Cv) - **Spec Exp:** Congestive Heart Failure; Angioplasty; Interventional Cardiology; Pulmonary Hypertension; **Hospital:** Univ Hosp-Newark; **Address:** Univ Hosp, Cardiology Dept, 90 Bergen St, Ste 3500, Newark, NJ 07103; **Phone:** 973-972-2573; **Board Cert:** Internal Medicine 1989; Cardiovascular Disease 2012; Interventional Cardiology 2009; Advanced Heart Failure & Transplant Cardiology 2010; **Med School:** Albert Einstein Coll Med 1986; **Resid:** Internal Medicine, Bronx Muni Hosp 1989; **Fellow:** Cardiovascular Disease, Bronx Muni Hosp 1992; Interventional Cardiology, Montefiore Med Ctr 1995; **Fac Appt:** Prof Med, UMDNJ-NJ Med Sch, Newark

Rogal, Gary J MD (Cv) - **Spec Exp:** Echocardiography; Coronary Artery Disease; Heart Valve Disease; **Hospital:** St. Barnabas Med Ctr (page 94), Newark Beth Israel Med Ctr (page 94); **Address:** NJ Cardiology Assocs, 375 Mount Pleasant Ave, West Orange, NJ 07052; **Phone:** 973-731-9442; **Board Cert:** Internal Medicine 1981; Cardiovascular Disease 1983; **Med School:** Geo Wash Univ 1978; **Resid:** Internal Medicine, Zucker Hillside Hosp 1981; **Fellow:** Cardiovascular Disease, Univ Rochester Strong Meml Hosp 1984

Saroff, Alan L MD (Cv) - **Spec Exp:** Heart Valve Disease; Cholesterol/Lipid Disorders; Arrhythmias; Preventive Cardiology; **Hospital:** Hackensack UMC-Mountainside (page 802), NY-Presby/Columbia Univ Med Ctr, NY (page 102); **Address:** Montclair Cardiology Group, 123 Highland Ave, Ste 302, Glen Ridge, NJ 07028-1522; **Phone:** 973-748-9555; **Board Cert:** Internal Medicine 1972; Cardiovascular Disease 1975; **Med School:** SUNY Upstate Med Univ 1965; **Resid:** Internal Medicine, SUNY-Syracuse Med Ctr 1967; Internal Medicine, NY Hosp 1970; **Fellow:** Cardiovascular Disease, Columbia Presby Med Ctr 1972; Cardiac Electrophysiology, Columbia Presby Med Ctr 1973; **Fac Appt:** Assoc Clin Prof Med, Columbia P&S

Shamoon, Fayez E MD (Cv) - **Spec Exp:** Interventional Cardiology; Coronary Artery Disease; Nuclear Cardiology; Angioplasty & Stent Placement; **Hospital:** Saint Michael's Med Ctr, Trinitas Reg Med Ctr (page 946); **Address:** Saint Michaels Med Ctr - Cardiology, 111 Central Ave, Newark, NJ 07102; **Phone:** 973-877-5160; **Board Cert:** Internal Medicine 2006; Cardiovascular Disease 2006; Interventional Cardiology 2009; **Med School:** Jordan 1981; **Resid:** Internal Medicine, Jordan Univ Hosp 1985; Internal Medicine, St Michael's Med Ctr 1992; **Fellow:** Cardiovascular Disease, St Michael's Med Ctr 1995; Interventional Cardiology, St Michael's Med Ctr 1996; **Fac Appt:** Prof Med, Seton Hall Univ Sch Hlth & Med Scis

Wangenheim, Paul M MD (Cv) - **Spec Exp:** Echocardiography; Coronary Angioplasty/Stents; Interventional Cardiology; **Hospital:** St. Barnabas Med Ctr (page 94); **Address:** Consultants in Cardiology, 741 Northfield Ave, Ste 205, West Orange, NJ 7052; **Phone:** 973-467-1544; **Board Cert:** Internal Medicine 1985; Cardiovascular Disease 1987; Echocardiography 1997; **Med School:** UMDNJ-NJ Med Sch, Newark 1982; **Resid:** Internal Medicine, Univ Hosp-UMDNJ 1985; **Fellow:** Cardiovascular Disease, Newark Beth Israel Med Ctr 1987

Zucker, Mark J MD (Cv) - **Spec Exp:** Transplant Medicine-Heart; Heart Failure; Pulmonary Hypertension; Amyloid Heart Disease; **Hospital:** Newark Beth Israel Med Ctr (page 94), St. Barnabas Med Ctr (page 94); **Address:** NBIMC, Cardiac Transplant Ctr, 201 Lyons Ave, Ste L4, Newark, NJ 07112; **Phone:** 973-926-7205; **Board Cert:** Internal Medicine 1984; Cardiovascular Disease 1987; Advanced Heart Failure & Transplant Cardiology 2010; **Med School:** Northwestern Univ 1981; **Resid:** Internal Medicine, Northwestern Meml Hosp 1984; **Fellow:** Cardiovascular Disease, Northwestern Meml Hosp 1987

Child & Adolescent Psychiatry

Cammarata, Sandra MD (ChAP) - **Spec Exp:** ADD/ADHD; Bipolar/Mood Disorders; **Hospital:** Hackensack UMC-Mountainside (page 802); **Address:** N Jersey Ctr for Comprehensive Mental Hlth, 14 Smull Ave Fl 2, Caldwell, NJ 07110; **Phone:** 973-618-0100; **Board Cert:** Psychiatry 2007; Child & Adolescent Psychiatry 2007; **Med School:** Italy 1983; **Resid:** Psychiatry, New England Med Ctr 1987; **Fellow:** Child & Adolescent Psychiatry, New England Med Ctr 1989

Child Neurology

Goldberg, Rina F MD (ChiN) - **Spec Exp:** Epilepsy; **Hospital:** St. Barnabas Med Ctr (page 94); **Address:** Inst of Neurology & Outpatient EEG dept, St Barnabas Ambulatory Care Ctr, 200 S Orange Ave, Ste 101, Livingston, NJ 07039; **Phone:** 973-322-7580; **Board Cert:** Pediatrics 2013; Child Neurology 2008; Clinical Neurophysiology 2009; Epilepsy 2013; **Med School:** Albert Einstein Coll Med 1992; **Resid:** Pediatrics, NY Presby-Columbia Med Ctr 1995; **Fellow:** Child Neurology, Montefiore Med Ctr 1997; Clinical Neurophysiology, Montefiore Med Ctr 1998

Pak, Jayoung MD (ChiN) - **Spec Exp:** Epilepsy/Seizure Disorders; **Hospital:** Univ Hosp-Newark; **Address:** 90 Bergen St, Ste 8100, Newark, NJ 07103-2406; **Phone:** 973-972-2922; **Board Cert:** Child Neurology 1993; **Med School:** South Korea 1978; **Resid:** Pediatrics, UMDNJ-Univ Hosp 1988; **Fellow:** Child Neurology, UMDNJ-Univ Hosp 1991; **Fac Appt:** Asst Prof N, UMDNJ-NJ Med Sch, Newark

Clinical Genetics

Desposito, Franklin MD (CG) - **Spec Exp:** Birth Defects; Genetic Disorders; **Hospital:** Univ Hosp-Newark, St. Barnabas Med Ctr (page 94); **Address:** 90 Bergen St, Ste 5400, Newark, NJ 07103; **Phone:** 973-972-3300; **Board Cert:** Pediatrics 1986; Clinical Genetics 1982; Clinical Cytogenetics 1990; Clinical Molecular Genetics 2010; **Med School:** Ros Franklin Univ/Chicago Med Sch 1957; **Resid:** Pediatrics, Long Island Jewish Hosp 1961; **Fellow:** Hematology, Univ Wisc Sch Med 1963; **Fac Appt:** Prof Ped, UMDNJ-NJ Med Sch, Newark

Colon & Rectal Surgery

Gilder, Mark E MD (CRS) - **Spec Exp:** Laparoscopic Surgery; Inflammatory Bowel Disease; **Hospital:** St. Barnabas Med Ctr (page 94), Morristown Med Ctr (page 92); **Address:** Assocs in Colon & Rectal Diseases, Barnabas Health Ambulatory Care Ctr, 200 S Orange Ave, Ste 232, Livingston, NJ 07039; **Phone:** 973-322-0250; **Board Cert:** Colon & Rectal Surgery 2013; **Med School:** NY Med Coll 1987; **Resid:** Surgery, North Shore Univ Hosp 1992; **Fellow:** Colon & Rectal Surgery, St Francis Hosp 1993

Orringer, Robert D MD (CRS) - **Hospital:** St. Barnabas Med Ctr (page 94), Overlook Med Ctr (page 92); **Address:** Assocs in Colon & Rectal Disease, Barnabas Health Ambulatory Care Ctr, 200 S Orange Ave, Ste 232, Livingston, NJ 07039; **Phone:** 973-322-0250; **Board Cert:** Colon & Rectal Surgery 1983; **Med School:** Univ Pittsburgh 1975; **Resid:** Surgery, New England Deaconess Hosp 1981; **Fellow:** Colon & Rectal Surgery, Lahey Clinic 1982

Rothberg, Robert M MD (CRS) - **Spec Exp:** Colon & Rectal Cancer; Colonoscopy; Diverticulitis; **Hospital:** Hackensack UMC-Mountainside (page 802), St. Barnabas Med Ctr (page 94); **Address:** 39 S Fullerton Ave, Montclair, NJ 07042-6303; **Phone:** 973-744-0550; **Board Cert:** Colon & Rectal Surgery 1978; **Med School:** NYU Sch Med 1972; **Resid:** Surgery, Bellevue Hospital Center 1974; Surgery, Hackensack Hosp 1977; **Fellow:** Colon & Rectal Surgery, Muhlenberg Hosp 1978

Tarantino, Debra R MD (CRS) - **Spec Exp:** Laparoscopic Surgery; Anorectal Disorders; Inflammatory Bowel Disease; Pelvic Floor Disorders; **Hospital:** St. Barnabas Med Ctr (page 94), Overlook Med Ctr (page 92); **Address:** Assocs in Colon & Rectal Disease, Barnabas Health Ambulatory Care Ctr, 200 S Orange Ave, Ste 232, Livingston, NJ 07039; **Phone:** 973-322-0250; **Board Cert:** Surgery 2008; Colon & Rectal Surgery 2001; **Med School:** SUNY Buffalo 1994; **Resid:** Surgery, Univ Hosp Cleveland 1999; **Fellow:** Colon & Rectal Surgery, St Luke's Roosevelt Hosp Ctr 2000

Dermatology

Connolly, Adrian L MD (D) - **Spec Exp:** Mohs Surgery; Skin Cancer; **Hospital:** St. Barnabas Med Ctr (page 94); **Address:** 101 Old Short Hills Rd, Ste 503, West Orange, NJ 07052-1023; **Phone:** 973-731-9131; **Board Cert:** Dermatology 2009; **Med School:** UMDNJ-NJ Med Sch, Newark 1975; **Resid:** Dermatology, NYU Med Ctr 1979; **Fac Appt:** Asst Clin Prof D, UMDNJ-NJ Med Sch, Newark

Downie, Jeanine B MD (D) - **Spec Exp:** Cosmetic Dermatology; Botox Therapy; Black/Asian Skin Care; Skin Laser Surgery; **Hospital:** Overlook Med Ctr (page 92), Hackensack UMC-Mountain-side (page 802); **Address:** 51 Park St, Montclair, NJ 07042; **Phone:** 973-509-6900; **Board Cert:** Dermatology 2006; **Med School:** SUNY Downstate 1992; **Resid:** Pediatrics, New York Hosp 1994; Dermatology, Mt Sinai Med Ctr 1997

Liftin, Alan J MD (D) - **Spec Exp:** Cosmetic Dermatology; Botox Therapy; Facial Rejuvenation; Acne & Rosacea; **Hospital:** St. Barnabas Med Ctr (page 94); **Address:** 22 Old Short Hills Rd, Ste 103, Livingston, NJ 07039-5605; **Phone:** 973-535-5800; **Board Cert:** Dermatology 2009; Anatomic Pathology 1987; Dermatopathology 1989; **Med School:** Mount Sinai Sch Med 1982; **Resid:** Pathology, Mt Sinai Hosp 1985; Dermatology, Mt Sinai Hosp 1990; **Fellow:** Dermatopathology, Hosp Univ Penn 1986

Rozanski, Reuben MD (D) - **Spec Exp:** Cosmetic Dermatology; Acne; Rosacea; **Hospital:** Hackensack UMC-Mountainside (page 802); **Address:** 200 Highland Ave, Glen Ridge, NJ 07028-1528; **Phone:** 973-748-9474; **Board Cert:** Dermatology 1979; Internal Medicine 1974; **Med School:** Boston Univ 1970; **Resid:** Internal Medicine, Montefiore Med Ctr 1973; Dermatology, Albert Einstein Coll Med 1976

Schwartz, Robert A MD (D) - **Spec Exp:** Skin Cancer; Atopic Dermatitis; Tuberous Sclerosis; Rare Skin Disorders; **Hospital:** Univ Hosp-Newark; **Address:** 185 S Orange Ave, Newark, NJ 07103; **Phone:** 973-972-6255; **Board Cert:** Dermatology 1978; Clinical & Laboratory Dematologic Immunology 1985; **Med School:** NY Med Coll 1974; **Resid:** Dermatology, Univ Hosp 1977; Dermatology, Roswell Park Meml Inst 1978; **Fellow:** Dermatopathology, NJ Med Sch Affil Hosps 1990; **Fac Appt:** Prof D, UMDNJ-Rutgers Med Sch

Siegel, Eric S MD (D) - **Spec Exp:** Cosmetic Dermatology; Skin Laser Surgery; **Hospital:** St. Barnabas Med Ctr (page 94), Overlook Med Ctr (page 92); **Address:** Millburn Laser Center, 12 E Willow St, Millburn, NJ 07041; **Phone:** 973-376-8500; **Board Cert:** Dermatology 2007; **Med School:** SUNY Downstate 1993; **Resid:** Internal Medicine, Staten Island Univ Hosp 1996; Dermatology, Downstate Med Ctr 1999; **Fac Appt:** Assoc Clin Prof D, SUNY Downstate

Diagnostic Radiology

Lee, Huey-Jen MD (DR) - **Spec Exp:** Brain Imaging; Head & Neck Imaging; Spine Neuroradiologic Diagnosis; Brain Tumors; **Hospital:** Univ Hosp-Newark; **Address:** 150 Bergen St, Ste C320, Dept of Radiology, Newark, NJ 07103; **Phone:** 973-972-6900; **Board Cert:** Diagnostic Radiology 1990; Neuroradiology 2004; **Med School:** Taiwan 1976; **Resid:** Pediatrics, Taipei Jen-Ai Hosp 1979; Diagnostic Radiology, Beth Israel Med Ctr 1988; **Fellow:** Neuroradiology, NY Med Coll Affil Hosp 1989; **Fac Appt:** Prof Rad, UMDNJ-NJ Med Sch, Newark

Levy, Daniel MD (DR) - **Spec Exp:** Neuroradiology; **Hospital:** Chilton Med Ctr (page 92); **Address:** Montclair Radiology, 116 Park St, Montclair, NJ 07042; **Phone:** 973-746-2525; **Board Cert:** Diagnostic Radiology 1982; **Med School:** NY Med Coll 1978; **Resid:** Diagnostic Radiology, Mt Sinai Med Ctr 1982; **Fellow:** Neurological Radiology, NY Presby Hosp/Columbia 1983

Moses, Stuart MD (DR) - **Spec Exp:** Nuclear Radiology; MRI; CT Body Scan; Musculoskeletal Imaging; **Hospital:** Chilton Med Ctr (page 92); **Address:** Montclair Radiology, 116 Park St, Montclair, NJ 07042; **Phone:** 973-746-2525; **Board Cert:** Diagnostic Radiology 1982; Nuclear Radiology 1983; **Med School:** Mount Sinai Sch Med 1978; **Resid:** Diagnostic Radiology, Mt Sinai Med Ctr 1982; **Fellow:** Nuclear Medicine, Montefiore Med Ctr 1983

Sanders, Linda M MD (DR) - **Spec Exp:** Breast Imaging; **Hospital:** St. Barnabas Med Ctr (page 94); **Address:** St Barnabas Breast Center, 200 S Orange Ave, Livingston, NJ 07039; **Phone:** 973-322-7800; **Board Cert:** Diagnostic Radiology 1986; **Med School:** Univ Pennsylvania 1982; **Resid:** Diagnostic Radiology, Columbia-Presby Med Ctr 1986; **Fellow:** Mammography, Meml Sloan-Kettering Cancer Ctr 1987

Spektor, Vadim Y MD (DR) - **Spec Exp:** Head & Neck Imaging; Neuroradiology; **Hospital:** Newark Beth Israel Med Ctr (page 94); **Address:** Newark Beth Israel, Radiology, 201 Lyons Ave, Newark, NJ 07112; **Phone:** 973-926-8510; **Board Cert:** Diagnostic Radiology 2005; Neuroradiology 2008; **Med School:** Boston Univ 2000; **Resid:** Diagnostic Radiology, NY Univ Med Ctr 2005; **Fellow:** Neurological Radiology, NY Univ Med Ctr 2007

Endocrinology, Diabetes & Metabolism

Baranetsky, Nicholas G MD (EDM) - **Spec Exp:** Thyroid Disorders; Pituitary Disorders; Adrenal Disorders; **Hospital:** Saint Michael's Med Ctr, Clara Maass Med Ctr (page 94); **Address:** St Michaels Med Ctr - Endocrinology, 306 Dr Martin Luther King Blvd, Newark, NJ 07102; **Phone:** 973-877-5185; **Board Cert:** Internal Medicine 1977; Endocrinology, Diabetes & Metabolism 1981; **Med School:** NY Med Coll 1974; **Resid:** Internal Medicine, Stamford Hosp 1977; **Fellow:** Endocrinology, Diabetes & Metabolism, VA Med Ctr-Wadsworth 1979; **Fac Appt:** Prof Med, Seton Hall Univ Sch Hlth & Med Scis

Bleich, David MD (EDM) - **Spec Exp:** Diabetes; Metabolic Disorders; Thyroid Disorders; **Hospital:** Univ Hosp-Newark; **Address:** Univ Hosp, Endocrinology Dept, 90 Bergen St, Ste 4500, Newark, NJ 07103; **Phone:** 973-972-2500; **Board Cert:** Internal Medicine 1986; Endocrinology, Diabetes & Metabolism 1989; **Med School:** NY Med Coll 1983; **Resid:** Internal Medicine, Maimonides Med Ctr 1986; **Fellow:** Endocrinology, Diabetes & Metabolism, Brigham & Womens Hosp 1990; Research, Joslin Diabetes Ctr 1992; **Fac Appt:** Assoc Prof Med, UMDNJ-Rutgers Med Sch

Dower, Samuel M MD (EDM) - **Hospital:** St. Barnabas Med Ctr (page 94); **Address:** 200 S Orange Ave, Ste 219, Livingston, NJ 07039; **Phone:** 973-322-7200; **Board Cert:** Internal Medicine 1984; Endocrinology 1987; **Med School:** NYU Sch Med 1981; **Resid:** Internal Medicine, Bronx Muni Hosp 1984; **Fellow:** Endocrinology, Mount Sinai Hosp 1985

Gewirtz, George P MD (EDM) - **Spec Exp:** Diabetes; Thyroid Disorders; Osteoporosis; **Hospital:** St. Barnabas Med Ctr (page 94); **Address:** 200 S Orange Ave, Ste 219, Livingston, NJ 07039; **Phone:** 973-322-7200; **Board Cert:** Internal Medicine 1972; Endocrinology 1975; **Med School:** Harvard Med Sch 1965; **Resid:** Internal Medicine, Bellevue Hosp Ctr 1967; Internal Medicine, Columbia-Presby Med Ctr 1971; **Fellow:** Endocrinology, Diabetes & Metabolism, Mt Sinai Hosp 1973

Family Medicine

Cirello, Richard MD (FMed) *PCP* - **Hospital:** Hackensack UMC-Mountainside (page 802); **Address:** Town Medical Associates, 271 Grove Ave, Verona, NJ 07044-1730; **Phone:** 973-239-2600; **Board Cert:** Family Medicine 2014; **Med School:** Mexico 1975; **Resid:** Family Medicine, Mountainside Hosp 1979; **Fac Appt:** Asst Clin Prof FMed, UMDNJ-Rutgers Med Sch

Gorman, Robert T MD (FMed) *PCP* - **Hospital:** Hackensack UMC-Mountainside (page 802), St. Barnabas Med Ctr (page 94); **Address:** Town Medical Assocs, 271 Grove Ave, Verona, NJ 07044; **Phone:** 973-239-2600; **Board Cert:** Family Medicine 2005; **Med School:** UMDNJ-NJ Med Sch, Newark 1982; **Resid:** Family Medicine, Mountainside Hosp 1985; **Fac Appt:** Asst Clin Prof FMed, UMDNJ-NJ Med Sch, Newark

Schlam, Everett W MD (FMed) *PCP* - **Spec Exp:** Travel Medicine; **Hospital:** Hackensack UMC-Mountainside (page 802); **Address:** Mountainside Family Practice Assocs, 799 Bloomfield Ave, Verona, NJ 07044; **Phone:** 973-746-7050; **Board Cert:** Family Medicine 2007; Sports Medicine 2011; **Med School:** Rutgers R W Johnson Med Sch 1986; **Resid:** Family Medicine, Mountainside Hosp 1989

Gastroenterology

Bains, Yatinder MD (Ge) - **Spec Exp:** Liver Disease; Inflammatory Bowel Disease; Gastroesophageal Reflux Disease (GERD); **Hospital:** Clara Maass Med Ctr (page 94), Jersey City Med Ctr (page 94); **Address:** 116 Millburn Ave, Ste 102, Millburn, NJ 07041; **Phone:** 973-376-2121; **Board Cert:** Internal Medicine 2013; Gastroenterology 2013; **Med School:** UMDNJ-NJ Med Sch, Newark 1987; **Resid:** Internal Medicine, Univ Hosp-UMDNJ 1990; **Fellow:** Gastroenterology, Univ Hosp-UMDNJ 1992

Finkelstein, Warren MD (Ge) - **Spec Exp:** Crohn's Disease; Ulcerative Colitis; Inflammatory Bowel Disease; **Hospital:** Hackensack UMC-Mountainside (page 802); **Address:** Gastroenterology Grp of NJ, 123 Highland Ave, Ste 103, Glen Ridge, NJ 7028; **Phone:** 973-429-8800; **Board Cert:** Internal Medicine 1975; Gastroenterology 1983; **Med School:** Med Coll VA 1972; **Resid:** Internal Medicine, Boston Med Ctr 1974; Internal Medicine, VA Hlthcare Sys 1975; **Fellow:** Gastroenterology, Mass Genl Hosp 1977; **Fac Appt:** Assoc Clin Prof Med, UMDNJ-NJ Med Sch, Newark

Fiske, Steven C MD (Ge) - **Spec Exp:** Colon Cancer Screening; Colonoscopy; Peptic Acid Disorders; Gastroesophageal Reflux Disease (GERD); **Hospital:** St. Barnabas Med Ctr (page 94), Clara Maass Med Ctr (page 94); **Address:** 1500 Pleasant Valley Way, Ste 306, West Orange, NJ 07052-1104; **Phone:** 973-325-5775; **Board Cert:** Internal Medicine 1977; Gastroenterology 1979; **Med School:** NYU Sch Med 1974; **Resid:** Internal Medicine, NYU-Bellevue Hosp Ctr 1976; **Fellow:** Gastroenterology, Harvard /Brigham & Womens Hosp 1978; **Fac Appt:** Assoc Prof Med, Seton Hall Univ Sch Hlth & Med Scis

Kenny, Raymond MD (Ge) - **Spec Exp:** Liver Disease; Hepatitis B & C; Inflammatory Bowel Disease/Crohn's; Ulcerative Colitis; **Hospital:** Hackensack UMC-Mountainside (page 802); **Address:** The Gastroenterology Group of New Jersey, 123 Highland Ave, Ste 103, Glen Ridge, NJ 07028; **Phone:** 973-429-8800; **Board Cert:** Internal Medicine 1984; Gastroenterology 1987; **Med School:** SUNY Stony Brook 1981; **Resid:** Internal Medicine, Mayo Clinic 1984; **Fellow:** Gastroenterology, Univ Penn Med Ctr 1986; **Fac Appt:** Asst Clin Prof Med, UMDNJ-NJ Med Sch, Newark

Mogan, Glen R MD (Ge) - **Spec Exp:** Inflammatory Bowel Disease; Peptic Ulcer Disease; Gastroesophageal Reflux Disease (GERD); **Hospital:** St. Barnabas Med Ctr (page 94); **Address:** 741 N Field Ave, Ste 204, West Orange, NJ 07052-1104; **Phone:** 973-731-8686; **Board Cert:** Internal Medicine 1978; Gastroenterology 1981; **Med School:** SUNY Upstate Med Univ 1975; **Resid:** Internal Medicine, Mount Sinai Hosp 1977; **Fellow:** Gastroenterology, Mount Sinai Hosp 1980; **Fac Appt:** Assoc Clin Prof Med, UMDNJ-Rutgers Med Sch

Spira, Robert S MD (Ge) - **Spec Exp:** Liver Disease; Inflammatory Bowel Disease; Endoscopy; **Hospital:** Saint Michael's Med Ctr, Clara Maass Med Ctr (page 94); **Address:** 5 Franklin Ave, Ste 109, Claremont Professional Bldg, Belleville, NJ 07109; **Phone:** 973-759-7240; **Board Cert:** Internal Medicine 1978; Gastroenterology 1981; **Med School:** NYU Sch Med 1975; **Resid:** Internal Medicine, Bellevue Hosp/NYU Med Ctr 1979; **Fellow:** Gastroenterology, VA Med Ctr 1981; **Fac Appt:** Asst Prof Med, UMDNJ-NJ Med Sch, Newark

Geriatric Medicine

Arunachalam, Muthu R MD (Ger) - **Spec Exp:** Preventive Medicine; Palliative Care; **Hospital:** Hackensack UMC-Mountainside (page 802); **Address:** 22 Old Short Hills Rd, Ste 110, Livingston, NJ 07039; **Phone:** 973-994-0899; **Board Cert:** Geriatric Medicine 2004; **Med School:** India 1993; **Resid:** Internal Medicine, Flushing Hosp Med Ctr 1999; **Fellow:** Geriatric Medicine, Flushing Hosp Med Ctr 2000

Redling, Theresa M DO (Ger) *PCP* - **Spec Exp:** Palliative Care; Frail Elderly; Alzheimer's Disease; Dementia; **Hospital:** St. Barnabas Med Ctr (page 94); **Address:** Geriatric Hlth Ctr, 101 Old Short Hills Rd, Ste 302, West Orange, NJ 07052; **Phone:** 973-322-6457; **Board Cert:** Internal Medicine 2010; Geriatric Medicine 2012; Hospice & Palliative Medicine 2010; **Med School:** UMDNJ Sch Osteo Med 1987; **Resid:** Internal Medicine, Morristown Meml Hosp 1990; **Fellow:** Geriatric Medicine, Mt Sinai Hosp 1992; **Fac Appt:** Asst Prof Med, Albert Einstein Coll Med

Schor, Joshua D MD (Ger) - **Spec Exp:** Alzheimer's Disease; **Hospital:** St. Barnabas Med Ctr (page 94); **Address:** Daughters of Israel, 1155 Pleasant Valley Way, West Orange, NJ 07052; **Phone:** 877-209-2041; **Board Cert:** Internal Medicine 1988; Geriatric Medicine 2011; **Med School:** Yale Univ 1985; **Resid:** Internal Medicine, Mass General Hosp 1988; **Fellow:** Geriatric Medicine, Beth Israel Med Ctr 1990

Umakanthan, Suganthini MD (Ger) *PCP* - **Spec Exp:** Dementia; Delirium; Palliative Care; **Hospital:** Newark Beth Israel Med Ctr (page 94); **Address:** Newark Beth Israel Geriatrics, 156 Lyons Ave, Newark, NJ 07112; **Phone:** 973-926-6775; **Board Cert:** Internal Medicine 2006; Geriatric Medicine 2008; **Med School:** Sri Lanka 1989; **Resid:** Internal Medicine, Coney Island Hosp 1996; **Fellow:** Geriatric Medicine, UMDNJ Univ Hosp 1997

Gynecologic Oncology

Anderson, Patrick S MD (GO) - **Spec Exp:** Gynecologic Cancer; Robotic Surgery; **Hospital:** Holy Name Med Ctr (page 738); **Address:** Ctr for Gyn Oncology & Women's Hlth, 120 Irvington Ave, South Orange, NJ 07079; **Phone:** 973-762-7270; **Board Cert:** Obstetrics & Gynecology 2013; Gynecologic Oncology 2013; **Med School:** UMDNJ-NJ Med Sch, Newark 1988; **Resid:** Obstetrics & Gynecology, Montefiore Med Ctr 1992; **Fellow:** Gynecologic Oncology, Montefiore Med Ctr 1998; **Fac Appt:** Asst Clin Prof ObG, Albert Einstein Coll Med

Cracchiolo, Bernadette M MD (GO) - **Hospital:** Univ Hosp-Newark; **Address:** UMDNJ-New Jersey Med Sch, Dept OB/Gyn, 185 S Orange Ave, rm E 506, ACC Level C, Newark, NJ 07101; **Phone:** 973-972-5055; **Board Cert:** Obstetrics & Gynecology 2013; Gynecologic Oncology 2013; Hospice & Palliative Medicine 2008; **Med School:** Univ Hlth Scis, Chicago Med Sch 1991; **Resid:** Obstetrics & Gynecology, Columbia Presby Hosp 1995; **Fellow:** Gynecologic Oncology, Yale-New Haven Hosp 1997; **Fac Appt:** Asst Prof ObG, UMDNJ-NJ Med Sch, Newark

Denehy, Thad R MD (GO) - **Spec Exp:** Robotic Surgery; Ovarian Cancer; Gynecologic Surgery-Complex; Pelvic Organ Prolapse Repair; **Hospital:** St. Barnabas Med Ctr (page 94), St. Clare's Hosp-Denville; **Address:** Gyn Cancer & Pelvic Surgery, LLC, 101 Old Short Hills Rd, Ste 400, West Orange, NJ 07052; **Phone:** 973-243-9300; **Board Cert:** Obstetrics & Gynecology 2013; Gynecologic Oncology 2013; **Med School:** Wake Forest Univ 1984; **Resid:** Obstetrics & Gynecology, St Barnabas Med Ctr 1988; **Fellow:** Gynecologic Oncology, Strong Meml Hosp 1990

Taylor, Robert R MD (GO) - **Spec Exp:** Pelvic Reconstruction; Gynecologic Cancer; Laparoscopic Surgery; Robotic Surgery; **Hospital:** St. Barnabas Med Ctr (page 94); **Address:** Gynecologic Cancer & Pelvic Surgery, 101 Old Short Hills Rd, Ste 400, West Orange, NJ 07052; **Phone:** 973-243-9300; **Board Cert:** Obstetrics & Gynecology 2013; Gynecologic Oncology 2013; **Med School:** Uniformed Srvs Univ, Bethesda 1985; **Resid:** Obstetrics & Gynecology, United Naval Med Ctr 1989; **Fellow:** Gynecologic Oncology, Walter Reed Army Med Ctr 1994

Hand Surgery

Tan, Virak MD (HS) - **Spec Exp:** Hand & Upper Extremity Surgery; Microvascular Surgery; Nerve Disorders/Surgery; **Hospital:** Univ Hosp-Newark, Overlook Med Ctr (page 92); **Address:** 90 Bergen St, Ste 1200, Newark, NJ 07103; **Phone:** 973-972-0763; **Board Cert:** Orthopaedic Surgery 2014; Hand Surgery 2014; **Med School:** Univ Pennsylvania 1994; **Resid:** Orthopaedic Surgery, Hosp U Penn 2000; **Fellow:** Hand Surgery, Hosp for Special Surgery 2001; Microvascular Surgery, Chang Gung Meml Hosp 2001; **Fac Appt:** Prof OrS, UMDNJ-NJ Med Sch, Newark

Hematology

Cohen, Alice J MD (Hem) - **Spec Exp:** Bleeding/Coagulation Disorders; **Hospital:** Newark Beth Israel Med Ctr (page 94), St. Barnabas Med Ctr (page 94); **Address:** Newark Beth Israel Med Ctr, Hematology, 201 Lyons Ave, Ste D2, Newark, NJ 07112; **Phone:** 973-926-7230; **Board Cert:** Internal Medicine 1984; Hematology 1986; Medical Oncology 2011; **Med School:** Ros Franklin Univ/Chicago Med Sch 1981; **Resid:** Internal Medicine, VA Harbor Hlthcare Sys 1984; **Fellow:** Hematology & Oncology, G Washington Univ Hosp 1986; Hematology & Oncology, NY-Presby/Columbia Univ Med Ctr 1987; **Fac Appt:** Assoc Clin Prof Med, Columbia P&S

Sabnani, Indu MD (Hem) - **Spec Exp:** Lymphoma; **Hospital:** Newark Beth Israel Med Ctr (page 94); **Address:** Newark Beth Israel Med Ctr, 2130 Milburn Ave, Ste C11, Maplewood, NJ 07040; **Phone:** 973-762-7676; **Board Cert:** Internal Medicine 1987; Medical Oncology 1989; **Med School:** India 1980; **Resid:** Internal Medicine, United Hosp 1987; **Fellow:** Hematology & Oncology, UMDNJ-Newark 1990

Zauber, N Peter MD (Hem) - **Hospital:** St. Barnabas Med Ctr (page 94); **Address:** 22 Old Short Hills Rd, Ste 108, Livingston, NJ 07039; **Phone:** 973-533-9299; **Board Cert:** Internal Medicine 1976; Hematology 1978; **Med School:** Johns Hopkins Univ 1971; **Resid:** Internal Medicine, New York Meml Hosp 1973; Internal Medicine, Mercy Med Ctr 1976; **Fellow:** Hematology & Oncology, Presby Hosp-Univ Pittsburgh 1978

Infectious Disease

Slim, Jihad G MD (Inf) - **Spec Exp:** AIDS/HIV; Hepatitis C; Hospital Acquired Infections; Osteomyelitis; **Hospital:** Saint Michael's Med Ctr, Newark Beth Israel Med Ctr (page 94); **Address:** Saint Michaels Med Ctr, 111 Central Ave, Newark, NJ 07102; **Phone:** 973-877-5644; **Board Cert:** Internal Medicine 1986; Infectious Disease 1988; **Med School:** Lebanon 1980; **Resid:** Internal Medicine, Broussais Hosp 1983; Internal Medicine, Saint Michael's Med Ctr 1986; **Fellow:** Infectious Disease, Saint Michaels Med Ctr 1988; **Fac Appt:** Asst Prof Med, Seton Hall Univ Sch Hlth & Med Scis

Smith, Leon G MD (Inf) - **Spec Exp:** Fevers of Unknown Origin; Bone/Joint Infections; Hepatitis; Chronic Fatigue Syndrome; **Hospital:** St. Barnabas Med Ctr (page 94); **Address:** 189 Eagle Rock Ave, Roseland, NJ 07068; **Phone:** 973-226-3359; **Board Cert:** Internal Medicine 1963; Infectious Disease 1974; **Med School:** Georgetown Univ 1956; **Resid:** Infectious Disease, Nat Inst Hlth 1959; Internal Medicine, Yale-New Haven Hosp 1962; **Fellow:** Infectious Disease, Yale-New Haven Hosp 1960; **Fac Appt:** Prof Med, UMDNJ-NJ Med Sch, Newark

Smith, Stephen M MD (Inf) - **Spec Exp:** AIDS/HIV; Diagnostic Problems; Hepatitis; Sexually Transmitted Diseases; **Hospital:** St. Barnabas Med Ctr (page 94), Saint Michael's Med Ctr; **Address:** 189 Eagle Rock Ave, Roseland, NJ 07068; **Phone:** 973-226-3359; **Board Cert:** Infectious Disease 2004; **Med School:** Yale Univ 1989; **Resid:** Internal Medicine, Univ Virginia Med Ctr 1992; **Fellow:** Infectious Disease, NIH 1995; **Fac Appt:** Asst Prof Med, Seton Hall Univ Sch Hlth & Med Scis

Soroko, Theresa A MD (Inf) - **Spec Exp:** AIDS/HIV; Lyme Disease; Skin/Soft Tissue Infections; **Hospital:** Hackensack UMC-Mountainside (page 802), Clara Maass Med Ctr (page 94); **Address:** 199 Broad St, Ste 2A, Bloomfield, NJ 07003-2635; **Phone:** 973-748-4583; **Board Cert:** Internal Medicine 1988; Infectious Disease 2012; **Med School:** Grenada 1985; **Resid:** Internal Medicine, St Michael's Med Ctr 1988; **Fellow:** Infectious Disease, St Michael's Med Ctr 1990; **Fac Appt:** Asst Clin Prof Med, UMDNJ-NJ Med Sch, Newark

Youssef-Bessler, Manal F MD (Inf) - **Spec Exp:** AIDS/HIV; Fevers of Unknown Origin; Staphylococcal Infections; **Hospital:** Morristown Med Ctr (page 92), St. Barnabas Med Ctr (page 94); **Address:** 22 Old Short Hills Rd, Ste 106, Livingston, NJ 07039; **Phone:** 973-535-8355; **Board Cert:** Internal Medicine 2013; Infectious Disease 2005; **Med School:** Egypt 1992; **Resid:** Internal Medicine, UMDNJ-Univ Hosp 2003; **Fellow:** Infectious Disease, UMDNJ-Univ Hosp 2005

Internal Medicine

Chrisanderson, Donna A MD (IM) - **Spec Exp:** Nutrition; **Hospital:** St. Barnabas Med Ctr (page 94); **Address:** 2040 Millburn Ave, Ste 402, Maplewood, NJ 07040; **Phone:** 973-378-9070; **Board Cert:** Internal Medicine 2004; **Med School:** Med Coll GA 1988; **Resid:** Internal Medicine, Greenwich Hosp 1991; **Fellow:** Internal Medicine, Univ Alabama Affil Hosp 1993

Fortunato, Franklin D MD (IM) *PCP* - **Spec Exp:** Asthma; **Hospital:** Hackensack UMC-Mountainside (page 802), Clara Maass Med Ctr (page 94); **Address:** 127 Pine St, Montclair, NJ 07042-4835; **Phone:** 973-744-4075; **Board Cert:** Internal Medicine 1978; Pulmonary Disease 1980; **Med School:** UMDNJ-NJ Med Sch, Newark 1975; **Resid:** Internal Medicine, St Michael's Med Ctr 1977; **Fellow:** Pulmonary Disease, St Michael's Med Ctr 1979

Gribbon, John MD (IM) *PCP* - **Spec Exp:** Hypertension; Diabetes; Cholesterol/Lipid Disorders; Diagnostic Problems; **Hospital:** Hackensack UMC-Mountainside (page 802); **Address:** 62 S Fullerton Ave, Montclair, NJ 07042-2686; **Phone:** 973-744-3382; **Board Cert:** Internal Medicine 1980; **Med School:** UMDNJ-NJ Med Sch, Newark 1977; **Resid:** Internal Medicine, UMDNJ-Univ Hosp 1980; **Fac Appt:** Asst Clin Prof Med, UMDNJ-NJ Med Sch, Newark

Rommer, James A MD (IM) *PCP* - **Spec Exp:** Preventive Medicine; **Hospital:** St. Barnabas Med Ctr (page 94); **Address:** 349 E Northfield Rd, Ste 110, Livingston, NJ 07039-4807; **Phone:** 973-992-2227; **Board Cert:** Internal Medicine 1981; **Med School:** Cornell Univ-Weill Med Coll 1978; **Resid:** Internal Medicine, NY Hosp-Cornell Med Ctr 1981; **Fellow:** Internal Medicine, Johns Hopkins Med Sch 1982; **Fac Appt:** Asst Clin Prof Med, Mount Sinai Sch Med

Russo, John A MD (IM) *PCP* - **Hospital:** St. Barnabas Med Ctr (page 94); **Address:** 1500 Pleasant Valley Way, Ste 302, West Orange, NJ 07052; **Phone:** 973-736-8119; **Board Cert:** Internal Medicine 1988; **Med School:** Mexico 1981; **Resid:** Internal Medicine & Pediatrics, UMDNJ Affil Hosp 1987

Interventional Cardiology

Cohen, Marc MD (IC) - **Hospital:** Newark Beth Israel Med Ctr (page 94); **Address:** Newark Beth Israel Med Ctr, 201 Lyons Ave, Ste C2, Newark, NJ 07112; **Phone:** 973-926-7852; **Board Cert:** Internal Medicine 1980; Cardiovascular Disease 1983; Interventional Cardiology 2009; **Med School:** NYU Sch Med 1977; **Resid:** Internal Medicine, Mt Sinai Hosp 1980; **Fellow:** Cardiovascular Disease, Mt Sinai Hosp 1982; **Fac Appt:** Prof Med, Mount Sinai-Icahn Sch of Med

Goldstein, Jonathan E MD (IC) - **Spec Exp:** Cardiac Catheterization; **Hospital:** Saint Michael's Med Ctr, Christ Hosp - Jersey City; **Address:** St Michaels Med Ctr, Cardiology Dept, 111 Central Ave Fl 5, Newark, NJ 07102; **Phone:** 973-877-5430; **Board Cert:** Internal Medicine 1978; Cardiovascular Disease 1981; **Med School:** UMDNJ-NJ Med Sch, Newark 1973; **Resid:** Internal Medicine, Jackson Meml Hosp 1976; **Fellow:** Cardiovascular Disease, Boston Med Ctr 1978; **Fac Appt:** Assoc Prof Med, Seton Hall Univ Sch Hlth & Med Scis

Kaid, Khalil A MD (IC) - **Spec Exp:** Heart Valve Disease; Coronary Angioplasty/Stents; Pacemakers; **Hospital:** Newark Beth Israel Med Ctr (page 94), St. Barnabas Med Ctr (page 94); **Address:** Cardiology & Vascular Consultants of NJ, 2168 Millburn Ave, Ste 204, Maplewood, NJ 07040; **Phone:** 973-762-3353; **Board Cert:** Internal Medicine 2006; Cardiovascular Disease 2009; Interventional Cardiology 2010; **Med School:** Dominica 2003; **Resid:** Internal Medicine, Newark Beth Israel Med Ctr 2006; Cardiovascular Disease, Newark Beth Israel Med Ctr 2009; **Fellow:** Interventional Cardiology, Newark Beth Israel Med Ctr 2010

Miller, Kenneth P MD (IC) - **Spec Exp:** Angioplasty & Stent Placement; **Hospital:** Hackensack UMC-Mountainside (page 802), St. Barnabas Med Ctr (page 94); **Address:** 62 S Fullerton Ave, Montclair, NJ 07042-2629; **Phone:** 973-746-8585; **Board Cert:** Internal Medicine 1985; Cardiovascular Disease 1989; Interventional Cardiology 2012; **Med School:** NYU Sch Med 1982; **Resid:** Internal Medicine, Bronx Muni Hosp 1986; **Fellow:** Cardiovascular Disease, Columbia Presby Med Ctr 1988

Torre, Sabino R MD (IC) - **Spec Exp:** Angioplasty & Stent Placement; Cardiac Catheterization; **Hospital:** St. Barnabas Med Ctr (page 94); **Address:** NJ Cardiology Associates, 375 Mount Pleasant Ave, West Orange, NJ 07052; **Phone:** 973-731-9442; **Board Cert:** Internal Medicine 1988; Cardiovascular Disease 2011; Interventional Cardiology 2009; **Med School:** SUNY Buffalo 1985; **Resid:** Internal Medicine, NY Presby-Weill Cornell Med Ctr 1988; **Fellow:** Cardiovascular Disease, Mt Sinai Med Ctr 1991; Interventional Cardiology, Mt Sinai Med Ctr 1992; **Fac Appt:** Asst Prof Med, Mount Sinai Sch Med

Maternal & Fetal Medicine

Apuzzio, Joseph J MD (MF) - **Spec Exp:** Prenatal Diagnosis; Pregnancy-High Risk; Infectious Disease; **Hospital:** Univ Hosp-Newark; **Address:** Univ Hosp, Ob/Gyn, 140 Bergen St, Level C, Newark, NJ 07101; **Phone:** 973-972-2700; **Board Cert:** Obstetrics & Gynecology 2013; Maternal & Fetal Medicine 2013; **Med School:** UMDNJ-NJ Med Sch, Newark 1973; **Resid:** Obstetrics & Gynecology, UMDNJ-Univ Hosp 1976; **Fellow:** Maternal & Fetal Medicine, UMDNJ-Univ Hosp 1982; **Fac Appt:** Prof ObG, UMDNJ-NJ Med Sch, Newark

Gimovsky, Martin L MD (MF) - **Spec Exp:** Pregnancy-High Risk; **Hospital:** Newark Beth Israel Med Ctr (page 94); **Address:** OB/GYN Ultrasound, 201 Lyons Ave, Newark, NJ 07112; **Phone:** 973-926-4882; **Board Cert:** Obstetrics & Gynecology 2013; Maternal & Fetal Medicine 2013; **Med School:** NYU Sch Med 1976; **Resid:** Obstetrics & Gynecology, Sloane Hosp/Columbia Presby hop 1980; **Fellow:** Maternal & Fetal Medicine, USC Med Ctr 1982; **Fac Appt:** Clin Prof ObG, Mount Sinai Sch Med

Smith Jr, Leon G MD (MF) - **Spec Exp:** Ultrasound; Prenatal Diagnosis; Perinatal Infections; Amniocentesis; **Hospital:** St. Barnabas Med Ctr (page 94), Clara Maass Med Ctr (page 94); **Address:** NJ Perinatal Associates, 94 Old Short Hills Rd, East Wing, Ste 402, Livingston, NJ 07039-5672; **Phone:** 973-322-5287; **Board Cert:** Obstetrics & Gynecology 2013; Maternal & Fetal Medicine 2013; **Med School:** Georgetown Univ 1985; **Resid:** Obstetrics & Gynecology, Tulane Univ Hosp 1989; **Fellow:** Maternal & Fetal Medicine, Baylor Univ Hosp 1991

Terrone, Dom A MD (MF) - **Spec Exp:** Fetal Therapy; Prematurity Prevention; Prematurity/Low Birth Weight Infants; Perinatal Medicine; **Hospital:** St. Barnabas Med Ctr (page 94), Clara Maass Med Ctr (page 94); **Address:** NJ Perinatal Assocs, 94 Old Short Hills Rd, Ste 402, Livingston, NJ 07039; **Phone:** 973-322-5287; **Board Cert:** Obstetrics & Gynecology 2013; Maternal & Fetal Medicine 2013; **Med School:** UMDNJ-NJ Med Sch, Newark 1993; **Resid:** Obstetrics & Gynecology, St Barnabas Med Ctr 1997; **Fellow:** Maternal & Fetal Medicine, Univ Mississippi Med Ctr 2000; **Fac Appt:** Asst Prof ObG, Mount Sinai Sch Med

Warren, Wendy B MD (MF) - **Spec Exp:** Pregnancy-High Risk; **Hospital:** St. Barnabas Med Ctr (page 94); **Address:** NJ Perinatal Associates, 94 Old Short Hills Rd, East Wing, Ste 402, Livingston, NJ 07039; **Phone:** 973-322-5287; **Board Cert:** Obstetrics & Gynecology 2013; Maternal & Fetal Medicine 2013; **Med School:** Cornell Univ 1982; **Resid:** Obstetrics & Gynecology, T Jefferson Univ Hosp 1986; **Fellow:** Maternal & Fetal Medicine, Columbia Presby Hosp 1991

Wolf, Edward J MD (MF) - **Spec Exp:** Multiple Gestation; Premature Labor; Prematurity/Low Birth Weight Infants; Perinatal Medicine; **Hospital:** St. Barnabas Med Ctr (page 94), Clara Maass Med Ctr (page 94); **Address:** NJ Perinatal Associates, 94 Old Short Hills Rd, Ste 402, Livingston, NJ 07039; **Phone:** 973-322-5287; **Board Cert:** Obstetrics & Gynecology 2012; Maternal & Fetal Medicine 2012; **Med School:** Georgetown Univ 1984; **Resid:** Obstetrics & Gynecology, US Naval Hosp 1989; **Fellow:** Maternal & Fetal Medicine, Univ Conn Hlth Ctr 1992

Medical Oncology

Conti, John A MD (Onc) - **Spec Exp:** Bone Marrow Failure Disorders; Leukemia & Lymphoma; **Hospital:** Clara Maass Med Ctr (page 94), Hackensack UMC-Mountainside (page 802); **Address:** Essex Oncology of North Jersey, 36 Newark Ave, Ste 304, Belleville, NJ 07109; **Phone:** 973-751-8880; **Board Cert:** Internal Medicine 1989; Medical Oncology 2013; Hospice & Palliative Medicine 2008; **Med School:** Rutgers-NJ Med Sch 1986; **Resid:** Internal Medicine, UMDNJ-Univ Hosp 1989; **Fellow:** Medical Oncology, Meml Sloan-Kettering Cancer Ctr 1992

Leitner, Stuart P MD (Onc) - **Spec Exp:** Urologic Cancer; Breast Cancer; **Hospital:** St. Barnabas Med Ctr (page 94); **Address:** SMBC Med Oncology Assocs, 94 Old Short Hills Rd Fl 2, Livingston, NJ 07039; **Phone:** 973-322-5200; **Board Cert:** Internal Medicine 1982; Medical Oncology 1985; **Med School:** Mount Sinai Sch Med 1979; **Resid:** Internal Medicine, Univ Tex SW Med Ctr 1982; **Fellow:** Medical Oncology, Meml Sloan Kettering Cancer Ctr 1985

Lippman, Alan J MD (Onc) - **Hospital:** Clara Maass Med Ctr (page 94), St. Barnabas Med Ctr (page 94); **Address:** 36 Newark Ave, Ste 304, Belleville, NJ 07109; **Phone:** 973-751-8880; **Board Cert:** Internal Medicine 1973; Medical Oncology 1975; **Med School:** Hahnemann Univ 1965; **Resid:** Internal Medicine, Newark Beth Israel Med Ctr 1971; **Fellow:** Medical Oncology, Meml Sloan-Kettering Cancer Ctr 1972; **Fac Appt:** Assoc Clin Prof Med, UMDNJ-NJ Med Sch, Newark

Michaelson, Richard A MD (Onc) - **Spec Exp:** Breast Cancer; **Hospital:** St. Barnabas Med Ctr (page 94); **Address:** SBMC, Med Oncology Assocs, 94 Old Short Hills Rd Fl 2, Livingston, NJ 07039; **Phone:** 973-322-5200; **Board Cert:** Internal Medicine 1979; Medical Oncology 1981; **Med School:** Univ Pennsylvania 1976; **Resid:** Internal Medicine, Hosp Univ Penn 1979; **Fellow:** Medical Oncology, Meml Sloan-Kettering Cancer Ctr 1981

Radovich, Delia MD (Onc) - **Spec Exp:** Gastrointestinal Cancer; Breast Cancer; Clinical Trials; **Hospital:** St. Barnabas Med Ctr (page 94); **Address:** Med Oncology Assocs of SBMC, 94 Old Short Hills Rd Fl 2, Livingston, NJ 07039; **Phone:** 973-322-5658; **Board Cert:** Medical Oncology 2004; **Med School:** Brown Univ 1998; **Resid:** Internal Medicine, Yale-New Haven Hosp 2001; **Fellow:** Medical Oncology, Meml Sloan-Kettering Cancer Ctr 2004

Sagorin, Charles E MD (Onc) - **Hospital:** Hackensack UMC-Mountainside (page 802), Clara Maass Med Ctr (page 94); **Address:** 70 Park St, Ste 310, Montclair, NJ 07042-2960; **Phone:** 973-783-3300; **Board Cert:** Internal Medicine 1981; Medical Oncology 1983; Hematology 1986; **Med School:** SUNY Downstate 1971; **Resid:** Internal Medicine, Bronx Municipal Hosp 1973; **Fellow:** Hematology, Montefiore Med Ctr 1974; Medical Oncology, Montefiore Med Ctr 1978

Scoppetuolo, Michael MD (Onc) - **Spec Exp:** Sarcoma; Palliative Care; Hematologic Malignancies; Lung Cancer; **Hospital:** St. Barnabas Med Ctr (page 94); **Address:** SBMC Med Oncology Assocs, 94 Old Short Hills Rd Fl 2, Livingston, NJ 07039; **Phone:** 973-322-5200; **Board Cert:** Internal Medicine 1982; Medical Oncology 1985; **Med School:** Univ Hlth Scis, Chicago Med Sch 1979; **Resid:** Internal Medicine, Univ Hosp 1982; **Fellow:** Hematology & Oncology, Meml Sloan Kettering Cancer Ctr 1984

Neonatal-Perinatal Medicine

Rai, Bellipady C MD (NP) - **Spec Exp:** Breathing Disorders; Neonatology; Neonatal Nutrition; Prematurity/Low Birth Weight Infants; **Hospital:** Newark Beth Israel Med Ctr (page 94), Clara Maass Med Ctr (page 94); **Address:** Newark Beth Israel, Neonatology, 201 Lyons Ave, Ste C9, Newark, NJ 07112; **Phone:** 973-926-7203; **Board Cert:** Neonatal-Perinatal Medicine 2010; **Med School:** India 1979; **Resid:** Pediatrics, Interfaith Med Ctr 1988; **Fellow:** Neonatal-Perinatal Medicine, Jacobi Med Ctr 1990

Sun, Shyan C MD (NP) - **Spec Exp:** Prematurity/Low Birth Weight Infants; Breathing Disorders; Respiratory Distress Syndrome; **Hospital:** St. Barnabas Med Ctr (page 94); **Address:** Dept Neonatology, 94 Old Short Hills Rd, Ste 121, Livingston, NJ 07039; **Phone:** 973-322-5437; **Board Cert:** Pediatrics 1969; Neonatal-Perinatal Medicine 1975; **Med School:** Taiwan 1960; **Resid:** Pediatrics, Univ London 1967; Pediatrics, Harlem Hosp 1970; **Fellow:** Neonatology, LI Jewish Med Ctr 1972; **Fac Appt:** Clin Prof Ped, UMDNJ-NJ Med Sch, Newark

Vangvanichyakorn, Kamtorn MD (NP) - **Spec Exp:** Neonatal Nutrition; Neonatology; Neonatal Infections; **Hospital:** St. Barnabas Med Ctr (page 94); **Address:** St Barnabas, Neonatology, 94 Old Short Hills Rd, rm 121, Livingston, NJ 07039; **Phone:** 973-322-5213; **Board Cert:** Pediatrics 1980; Neonatal-Perinatal Medicine 1981; **Med School:** Thailand 1974; **Resid:** Pediatrics, Univ Hosp 1978; Pediatrics, Chldns Hosp 1979; **Fellow:** Neonatal-Perinatal Medicine, Chldns Hosp 1981; **Fac Appt:** Asst Prof Ped, UMDNJ-NJ Med Sch, Newark

Nephrology

Grasso, Michael A MD (Nep) - **Spec Exp:** Kidney Disease; Hypertension; Dialysis Care; Transplant Medicine-Kidney; **Hospital:** Newark Beth Israel Med Ctr (page 94), St. Barnabas Med Ctr (page 94); **Address:** 111 Northfield Ave, Ste 311, West Orange, NJ 07052-4703; **Phone:** 973-325-2103; **Board Cert:** Internal Medicine 1974; Nephrology 1976; **Med School:** Univ MD Sch Med 1970; **Resid:** Internal Medicine, Univ MD Hosp 1974; **Fellow:** Nephrology, Newark Beth Israel Hosp 1976

Mulgaonkar, Shamkant P MD (Nep) - **Spec Exp:** Transplant Medicine-Kidney; **Hospital:** St. Barnabas Med Ctr (page 94), Newark Beth Israel Med Ctr (page 94); **Address:** St Barnabas Med Ctr, 94 Old Short Hills Rd, Ste 303, Livingston, NJ 07039; **Phone:** 973-322-8216; **Board Cert:** Internal Medicine 1981; Nephrology 1982; **Med School:** India 1975; **Resid:** Internal Medicine, Morristown Meml Hosp 1980; **Fellow:** Nephrology, St Barnabas Med Ctr 1982; **Fac Appt:** Assoc Clin Prof Med, UMDNJ-NJ Med Sch, Newark

Sipzner, Robert J MD (Nep) - **Spec Exp:** Hypertension; Kidney Failure; **Hospital:** Bayonne Med Ctr, St. Barnabas Med Ctr (page 94); **Address:** 22 Old Short Hills Rd, Ste 212, Livingston, NJ 07039; **Phone:** 973-994-4550; **Board Cert:** Internal Medicine 1985; Nephrology 1988; **Med School:** NYU Sch Med 1982; **Resid:** Internal Medicine, SUNY Downstate Med Ctr 1985; **Fellow:** Nephrology, Univ Tenn Hlth Sci Ctr 1987

Neurological Surgery

Clemente, Roderick J MD (NS) - **Spec Exp:** Cerebrovascular Neurosurgery; Meningioma; **Hospital:** Hackensack Univ Med Ctr (page 96), Clara Maass Med Ctr (page 94); **Address:** Neurosurgical Care New Jersey, 96 Gates Ave, Montclair, NJ 07042-2511; **Phone:** 973-744-3166; **Board Cert:** Neurological Surgery 1989; **Med School:** Italy 1978; **Resid:** Surgery, Washington Hosp Ctr 1980; Neurological Surgery, George Washington Univ Hosp 1985

Heary, Robert F MD (NS) - **Spec Exp:** Spinal Surgery; Spinal Cord Injury; Spinal Deformity; **Hospital:** Univ Hosp-Newark, Overlook Med Ctr (page 92); **Address:** Mountainside Hosp, 1 Bay Ave, Montclair, NJ 07042; **Phone:** 973-259-3548; **Board Cert:** Neurological Surgery 2010; **Med School:** Univ Pittsburgh 1986; **Resid:** Surgery, UMDNJ Univ Hosp 1989; Neurological Surgery, UMDNJ Univ Hosp 1994; **Fellow:** Orthopaedic Surgery, Thomas Jefferson Univ Hosp 1995; **Fac Appt:** Prof NS, UMDNJ-NJ Med Sch, Newark

Neurology

Blady, David MD (N) - **Spec Exp:** Parkinson's Disease; Dementia; Multiple Sclerosis; Stroke; **Hospital:** Hackensack UMC-Mountainside (page 802), Clara Maass Med Ctr (page 94); **Address:** 230 Sherman Ave, Ste L, Glen Ridge, NJ 07028-1520; **Phone:** 973-743-9555; **Board Cert:** Neurology 1990; **Med School:** SUNY Downstate 1983; **Resid:** Neurology, Bellevue Hosp/NYU Med Ctr 1987

Cook, Stuart D MD (N) - **Spec Exp:** Multiple Sclerosis; Infectious & Demyelinating Diseases; **Hospital:** Univ Hosp-Newark; **Address:** 65 Bergen St, rm 1435, Newark, NJ 07103; **Phone:** 973-972-9181; **Board Cert:** Neurology 1970; **Med School:** Univ VT Coll Med 1962; **Resid:** Neurology, Montefiore Med Ctr 1968; **Fac Appt:** Prof N, UMDNJ-NJ Med Sch, Newark

Geller, Eric B MD (N) - **Spec Exp:** Epilepsy; **Hospital:** St. Barnabas Med Ctr (page 94); **Address:** St Barnabas Inst Neurolgy/Neurosurgery, 200 S Orange Ave, Ste 101, Livingston, NJ 07039; **Phone:** 973-322-7580; **Board Cert:** Neurology 2005; Clinical Neurophysiology 2006; **Med School:** Brown Univ 1989; **Resid:** Neurology, Harvard Med Sch Prog 1993; **Fellow:** Clinical Neurophysiology, Cleveland Clinic 1995

Marks, David A MD (N) - **Spec Exp:** Epilepsy/Seizure Disorders; Headache; Migraine; **Hospital:** Univ Hosp-Newark; **Address:** 90 Bergen St Fl 8th - Ste 8100, Newark, NJ 07103; **Phone:** 973-972-2550; **Board Cert:** Neurology 1989; **Med School:** South Africa 1983; **Resid:** Neurology, Boston Med Ctr 1988; **Fellow:** Neurophysiology, New England Med Ctr 1989; Epilepsy, Yale-New Haven Hosp 1991; **Fac Appt:** Assoc Prof Med, UMDNJ-NJ Med Sch, Newark

Ruderman, Marvin I MD (N) - **Spec Exp:** Neuromuscular Disorders; Peripheral Neuropathy; Myasthenia Gravis; Demyelinating Neuropathy; **Hospital:** St. Barnabas Med Ctr (page 94); **Address:** 1099 Bloomfield Ave, West Caldwell, NJ 07006-7129; **Phone:** 973-439-7000; **Board Cert:** Neurology 1981; **Med School:** Columbia P&S 1976; **Resid:** Neurology, Barnes Hosp 1980; **Fellow:** Neuromuscular Disease, Neuro Inst 1981

Nuclear Medicine

Lutzker, Letty G MD (NuM) - **Spec Exp:** Nuclear Radiology; **Hospital:** St. Barnabas Med Ctr (page 94); **Address:** St Barnabas Med Ctr, Dept Radiology, 94 Old Short Hills Rd, Livingston, NJ 07039-5672; **Phone:** 973-322-5957; **Board Cert:** Diagnostic Radiology 1973; Nuclear Medicine 2013; Nuclear Radiology 1977; **Med School:** Albert Einstein Coll Med 1968; **Resid:** Diagnostic Radiology, Montefiore Med Ctr 1973

Obstetrics & Gynecology

Cooperman, Alan S MD (ObG) - **Spec Exp:** Infertility; Menopause Problems; Osteoporosis; Incontinence; **Hospital:** Overlook Med Ctr (page 92), St. Barnabas Med Ctr (page 94); **Address:** 235 Millburn Ave, Ste 101, Millburn, NJ 07041-1738; **Phone:** 973-467-9440; **Board Cert:** Obstetrics & Gynecology 1979; **Med School:** Italy 1968; **Resid:** Obstetrics & Gynecology, Newark Beth Israel Med Ctr 1972

Crane, Stephen E MD (ObG) - **Spec Exp:** Minimally Invasive Gynecologic Surgery; Robotic Surgery; Gynecologic Cancer; **Hospital:** St. Barnabas Med Ctr (page 94); **Address:** Summit Med Grp, Ob/Gyn, 375 Mount Pleasant Ave, Ste 202, West Orange, NJ 07052; **Phone:** 973-731-7707; **Board Cert:** Obstetrics & Gynecology 2014; **Med School:** UMDNJ-NJ Med Sch, Newark 1986; **Resid:** Obstetrics & Gynecology, St Barnabas Med Ctr 1990

Luciani, Richard L MD (ObG) - **Spec Exp:** Laparoscopic Surgery; Pregnancy-High Risk; Endometriosis; **Hospital:** Overlook Med Ctr (page 92), St. Barnabas Med Ctr (page 94); **Address:** 235 Millburn Ave, Ste 101, Millburn, NJ 07041; **Phone:** 973-467-9440; **Board Cert:** Obstetrics & Gynecology 2013; **Med School:** UMDNJ-NJ Med Sch, Newark 1976; **Resid:** Obstetrics & Gynecology, St Barnabas Hosp 1980

Quartell, Anthony C MD (ObG) - **Spec Exp:** Minimally Invasive Surgery; Pelvic Reconstruction; Robotic Surgery; Laparoscopic Surgery-Complex; **Hospital:** St. Barnabas Med Ctr (page 94); **Address:** 316 Eisenhower Pkwy, Ste 202, Livingston, NJ 07039-1718; **Phone:** 973-716-9600; **Board Cert:** Obstetrics & Gynecology 1978; **Med School:** UMDNJ-NJ Med Sch, Newark 1969; **Resid:** Surgery, Univ Hosp 1971; Obstetrics & Gynecology, St Barnabas Med Ctr 1976

Ophthalmology

Bhagat, Neelakshi MD (Oph) - **Spec Exp:** Retinal Detachment; Trauma; Diabetic Eye Disease/Retinopathy; Macular Degeneration; **Hospital:** Univ Hosp-Newark; **Address:** NJ, Univ Hosp - Dept Ophthalmology, 90 Bergen St, DOC Bldg - Fl 6th, Newark, NJ 07103; **Phone:** 973-972-2032; **Board Cert:** Ophthalmology 2010; **Med School:** SUNY Stony Brook 1994; **Resid:** Ophthalmology, UMDNJ-NJ Med Sch Affil Hosp 1998; **Fellow:** Retina, Doheny Eye Inst - USC 1999; **Fac Appt:** Asst Prof Oph, UMDNJ-NJ Med Sch, Newark

Cangemi, Francis E MD (Oph) - **Spec Exp:** Diabetic Eye Disease/Retinopathy; Macular Degeneration; Retinal Detachment; Retinopathy of Prematurity; **Hospital:** Clara Maass Med Ctr (page 94), Valley Hosp (page 739); **Address:** 36 Newark Ave, Ste 212, Belleville, NJ 07109-4121; **Phone:** 973-751-8808; **Board Cert:** Ophthalmology 1976; **Med School:** NY Med Coll 1969; **Resid:** Internal Medicine, Mayo Clin 1971; Ophthalmology, New York Eye & Ear Infirm 1975; **Fellow:** Retina/Vitreous Surgery, Mass Eye & Ear Infirmary 1972; Vitreoretinal Surgery, Mass Eye & Ear Infirmary 1976; **Fac Appt:** Assoc Clin Prof Oph, UMDNJ-NJ Med Sch, Newark

Caputo, Anthony R MD (Oph) - **Spec Exp:** Pediatric Ophthalmology; Strabismus; **Hospital:** Clara Maass Med Ctr (page 94); **Address:** 556 Eagle Rock Ave, Ste 203, Roseland, NJ 07068-1500; **Phone:** 973-228-3111; **Board Cert:** Ophthalmology 1976; **Med School:** Italy 1969; **Resid:** Ophthalmology, UMDNJ-Univ Hosp 1974; **Fellow:** Pediatric Ophthalmology, Wills Eye Hosp 1975; **Fac Appt:** Prof Oph, UMDNJ-NJ Med Sch, Newark

Cohen, Steven B MD (Oph) - **Spec Exp:** Retina/Vitreous Surgery; Diabetic Eye Disease; Macular Degeneration; **Hospital:** St. Barnabas Med Ctr (page 94); **Address:** Retina-Vitreous Consultants, 349 E Northfield Rd, Ste 100, Livingston, NJ 07039; **Phone:** 973-716-0123; **Board Cert:** Ophthalmology 1984; **Med School:** NYU Sch Med 1978; **Resid:** Internal Medicine, LA Co-USC Med Ctr 1979; Ophthalmology, LIJ Med Ctr 1982; **Fellow:** Vitreoretinal Surgery, Univ Chicago Med Ctr 1985

Davidson, Lawrence M MD (Oph) - **Spec Exp:** Cataract Surgery; Glaucoma; **Hospital:** Hackensack UMC-Mountainside (page 802), St. Barnabas Med Ctr (page 94); **Address:** 825 Bloomfield Ave Fl 1, Fells Plaza, Verona, NJ 07044-1300; **Phone:** 973-239-4000; **Board Cert:** Ophthalmology 1975; **Med School:** SUNY Downstate 1969; **Resid:** Ophthalmology, Lenox Hill Hosp (Manh Eye, Ear & Throat Hosp) 1974

Eichler, Joel D MD (Oph) - **Spec Exp:** Diabetic Eye Disease/Retinopathy; Macular Degeneration; Retinal Disorders; **Hospital:** Clara Maass Med Ctr (page 94); **Address:** Eye Inst of Essex, 5 Franklin Ave, Ste 209, Belleville, NJ 07109; **Phone:** 973-751-6060; **Board Cert:** Ophthalmology 2014; **Med School:** Geo Wash Univ 1988; **Resid:** Internal Medicine, Santa Barbara Cottage Hosp 1989; Ophthalmology, UMDNJ-NJ Med Sch Affil Hosp 1992; **Fellow:** Vitreoretinal Surgery, Touro Infirm 1993

Frohman, Larry P MD (Oph) - **Spec Exp:** Neuro-Ophthalmology; Sarcoidosis; Vision Loss-Unexplained Loss; **Hospital:** Univ Hosp-Newark; **Address:** NJ, Univ Hosp - Dept Ophthalmology, 90 Bergen St, DOC Bldg, Ste 6174, Newark, NJ 07103; **Phone:** 973-972-2065; **Board Cert:** Ophthalmology 1985; **Med School:** Univ Pennsylvania 1980; **Resid:** Ophthalmology, Bellevue Hosp Ctr 1984; **Fellow:** Neuro-Ophthalmology, Bellevue Hosp Ctr 1985; **Fac Appt:** Prof Oph, UMDNJ-NJ Med Sch, Newark

Glatt, Herbert L MD (Oph) - **Spec Exp:** Cataract Surgery-Lens Implant; Glaucoma; **Hospital:** Hackensack UMC-Mountainside (page 802), Clara Maass Med Ctr (page 94); **Address:** 1025 Broad St, Bloomfield, NJ 07003-2844; **Phone:** 973-338-1001; **Board Cert:** Ophthalmology 1991; **Med School:** Mexico 1979; **Resid:** Ophthalmology, UMDNJ-NJ Med Sch Affil Hosps 1983; **Fac Appt:** Asst Clin Prof Oph, UMDNJ-NJ Med Sch, Newark

Langer, Paul D MD (Oph) - **Spec Exp:** Diplopia; Orbital Tumors/Cancer; Thyroid Eye Disease; Ophthalmic Plastic Surgery; **Hospital:** Univ Hosp-Newark; **Address:** NJ, Univ Hosp - Dept Ophthalmology, 90 Bergen St DOC Bldg - Ste 6174, Newark, NJ 07103; **Phone:** 973-972-2065; **Board Cert:** Ophthalmology 2005; **Med School:** Johns Hopkins Univ 1989; **Resid:** Ophthalmology, UCSF Med Ctr 1993; **Fellow:** Ophthalmic Plastic Surgery, Univ Utah Affil Hosp 1995; Orbital Surgery, Moorfields Eye Hosp 1995; **Fac Appt:** Asst Prof Oph, UMDNJ-NJ Med Sch, Newark

Turbin, Roger E MD (Oph) - **Spec Exp:** Neuro-Ophthalmology; Orbital Tumors/Cancer; Oculoplastic & Orbital Surgery; **Hospital:** Univ Hosp-Newark, St. Barnabas Med Ctr (page 94); **Address:** NJ, Univ Hosp - Dept Ophthalmology, 90 Bergen St DOC Bldg - Ste 6174, Newark, NJ 07103; **Phone:** 973-972-2065; **Board Cert:** Ophthalmology 2010; **Med School:** Washington Univ, St Louis 1993; **Resid:** Ophthalmology, NYU Langone Med Ctr 1997; **Fellow:** Neuro-Ophthalmology, NY Eye & Ear/Beth Israel 1998; Oculoplastic Surgery, Allegheny Genl Hosp 1999; **Fac Appt:** Asst Prof Oph, UMDNJ-NJ Med Sch, Newark

Wagner, Rudolph S MD (Oph) - **Spec Exp:** Strabismus; Eye Disorders-Congenital; Strabismus; Pediatric Ophthalmology; **Hospital:** Clara Maass Med Ctr (page 94), Univ Hosp-Newark; **Address:** Chldns Eye Care Ctr New Jersey, 1 Clara Maass Drive, Belleville, NJ 07109; **Phone:** 973-751-1702; **Board Cert:** Ophthalmology 1983; **Med School:** UMDNJ-NJ Med Sch, Newark 1978; **Resid:** Ophthalmology, UMDNJ-NJ Med Sch Affil Hosp 1982; **Fellow:** Pediatric Ophthalmology, Wills Eye Hosp 1983; **Fac Appt:** Clin Prof Oph, UMDNJ-NJ Med Sch, Newark

Zarbin, Marco A MD/PhD (Oph) - **Spec Exp:** Macular Degeneration; Diabetic Eye Disease/Retinopathy; Eye Trauma; Retinal Detachment; **Hospital:** Univ Hosp-Newark, St. Barnabas Med Ctr (page 94); **Address:** NJ, Univ Hosp - Dept Ophthalmology, 90 Bergen St, DOC Bldg, Ste 6174, Newark, NJ 07103-2499; **Phone:** 973-972-2065; **Board Cert:** Ophthalmology 1989; **Med School:** Johns Hopkins Univ 1984; **Resid:** Ophthalmology, Johns Hopkins Hosp 1988; **Fellow:** Vitreoretinal Surgery, Johns Hopkins Hosp 1989; **Fac Appt:** Prof Oph, UMDNJ-NJ Med Sch, Newark

Orthopaedic Surgery

Benevenia, Joseph MD (OrS) - **Spec Exp:** Limb Sparing Surgery; Bone Cancer; Sarcoma-Soft Tissue; Musculoskeletal Cancer; **Hospital:** Univ Hosp-Newark; **Address:** Univ Hosp, Orthopaedics, 90 Bergen St, Ste 1200, Newark, NJ 07103; **Phone:** 973-972-2153; **Board Cert:** Orthopaedic Surgery 2013; **Med School:** UMDNJ-NJ Med Sch, Newark 1984; **Resid:** Orthopaedic Surgery, Univ Hosp-UMDNJ 1989; **Fellow:** Musculoskeletal Oncology, Case Western Reserve Univ 1991; **Fac Appt:** Prof OrS, UMDNJ-NJ Med Sch, Newark

Chase, Mark D MD (OrS) - **Spec Exp:** Sports Medicine; **Hospital:** Hackensack UMC-Mountainside (page 802); **Address:** Montclair Orthopaedic Grp, 200 Highland Ave, Glen Ridge, NJ 07028-1521; **Phone:** 973-746-2200; **Board Cert:** Orthopaedic Surgery 2012; **Med School:** Boston Univ 1983; **Resid:** Orthopaedic Surgery, Boston Med Ctr 1988; **Fellow:** Orthopaedic Surgery, Harlem Hosp 1989

Decter, Edward M MD (OrS) - **Spec Exp:** Knee Reconstruction; Shoulder Reconstruction; Sports Medicine; **Hospital:** St. Barnabas Med Ctr (page 94); **Address:** Ctr for Orthopaedics, 1500 Pleasant Vly Way, Ste 101, West Orange, NJ 07052; **Phone:** 973-669-5600; **Board Cert:** Orthopaedic Surgery 1982; **Med School:** Creighton Univ 1975; **Resid:** Surgery, Temple Univ Hosp 1976; Orthopaedic Surgery, NYU Hosp For Joint Dis 1980

Mendes, John F MD (OrS) - **Spec Exp:** Hip & Knee Replacement; Foot & Ankle Surgery; Spinal Disorders; **Hospital:** Hackensack UMC-Mountainside (page 802), Clara Maass Med Ctr (page 94); **Address:** Montclair Orthopaedic Group, 200 Highland Ave, Glen Ridge, NJ 07028-1521; **Phone:** 973-746-2200; **Board Cert:** Orthopaedic Surgery 1984; **Med School:** Cornell Univ-Weill Med Coll 1976; **Resid:** Surgery, Bryn Mawr Hosp 1978; Orthopaedic Surgery, Hosp Special Surg 1981; **Fellow:** Adult Reconstructive Surgery, Pennsylvania Hosp-UPHS 1982

Patterson, Francis R MD (OrS) - **Spec Exp:** Musculoskeletal Tumors; Bone Cancer; Limb Sparing Surgery; Soft Tissue Tumors; **Hospital:** Univ Hosp-Newark; **Address:** 90 Bergen St DOC Bldg - Ste 1200, Newark, NJ 07103; **Phone:** 973-972-1993; **Board Cert:** Orthopaedic Surgery 2012; **Med School:** SUNY Buffalo 1993; **Resid:** Orthopaedic Surgery, SUNY Hlth Sci Ctr 1998; **Fellow:** Musculoskeletal Oncology, Univ Chicago Affil Hosps 1999; **Fac Appt:** Prof OrS, UMDNJ-NJ Med Sch, Newark

Queler, Seth R MD (OrS) - **Spec Exp:** Adolescent Sports Medicine; **Hospital:** Clara Maass Med Ctr (page 94); **Address:** 45 Franklin Ave, Nutley, NJ 07110; **Phone:** 973-751-0111; **Board Cert:** Orthopaedic Surgery 2008; **Med School:** Northwestern Univ 2000; **Resid:** Orthopaedic Surgery, UMDNJ Med Ctr 2005; **Fellow:** Foot & Ankle Surgery, Univ PA Hlth Sys 2006

Rieber, Michael MD (OrS) - **Spec Exp:** Hip & Knee Replacement; Hip & Knee Reconstruction; Shoulder Surgery; Shoulder Replacement; **Hospital:** St. Barnabas Med Ctr (page 94); **Address:** 200 S Orange Ave, Ste 230, Ambulatory Care Ctr, Livingston, NJ 07039; **Phone:** 973-322-7400; **Board Cert:** Orthopaedic Surgery 2011; **Med School:** NY Med Coll 1992; **Resid:** Orthopaedic Surgery, Albany Med Ctr 1999; **Fellow:** Sports Medicine, Penn State Univ Med Ctr 2000

Rosa, Richard A MD (OrS) - **Spec Exp:** Joint Replacement; Knee Replacement; Arthroscopic Surgery; Knee Surgery; **Hospital:** St. Barnabas Med Ctr (page 94); **Address:** 741 Northfield Ave, Ste 200, MC 07052, West Orange, NJ 07052; **Phone:** 973-736-9980; **Board Cert:** Orthopaedic Surgery 2007; **Med School:** UMDNJ-NJ Med Sch, Newark 1978; **Resid:** Orthopaedic Surgery, UMDNJ-Univ Hosp 1983; **Fellow:** Joint Replacement Surgery, Hosp for Special Surgery 1984

Sabharwal, Sanjeev MD (OrS) - **Spec Exp:** Pediatric Orthopaedic Surgery; Limb Lengthening (Ilizarov Procedure); Limb Deformities; **Hospital:** Univ Hosp-Newark, Overlook Med Ctr (page 92); **Address:** 90 Bergen St DOC Bldg - Ste 1200, Newark, NJ 07103; **Phone:** 973-972-0246; **Board Cert:** Orthopaedic Surgery 2010; **Med School:** India 1985; **Resid:** Surgery, St Elizabeth Hosp 1988; Orthopaedic Surgery, Univ British Columbia Affil Hosp 1994; **Fellow:** Pediatric Orthopaedic Surgery, Chldns Hosp/Shriners Hosp 1996; Reconstructive Surgery, Md Ctr for Limb Lengthening & Reconstruction 1996; **Fac Appt:** Prof OrS, UMDNJ-NJ Med Sch, Newark

Schob, Clifford J MD (OrS) - **Spec Exp:** Sports Medicine; Shoulder & Knee Surgery; **Hospital:** Overlook Med Ctr (page 92), St. Barnabas Med Ctr (page 94); **Address:** 235 Millburn Ave, Ste 102, Millburn, NJ 07041; **Phone:** 973-258-1177; **Board Cert:** Orthopaedic Surgery 2013; **Med School:** Rutgers R W Johnson Med Sch 1982; **Resid:** Surgery, NS-LIJ Hlth Sys 1984; Orthopaedic Surgery, NS-LIJ Hlth Sys 1988; **Fellow:** Sports Medicine, Amer Sports Med Inst 1990

Otolaryngology

Holzberg, Norman MD (Oto) - **Hospital:** St. Barnabas Med Ctr (page 94); **Address:** 741 Northfield Ave, Ste 104, West Orange, NJ 07052; **Phone:** 973-243-0600; **Board Cert:** Otolaryngology 1990; **Med School:** Ros Franklin Univ/Chicago Med Sch 1985; **Resid:** Surgery, Saint Barnabas Md Ctr 1987; Otolaryngology, Manhattan EE&T Hosp 1990

Morrow, Todd A MD (Oto) - **Spec Exp:** Cosmetic Surgery-Face; Rhinoplasty; Laser Surgery; Botox Therapy; **Hospital:** St. Barnabas Med Ctr (page 94), Newark Beth Israel Med Ctr (page 94); **Address:** Tomorrow's Face, 741 Northfield Ave, Ste 104, West Orange, NJ 07052; **Phone:** 973-243-0600; **Board Cert:** Otolaryngology 1992; Facial Plastic & Reconstr Surgery 1995; **Med School:** Jefferson Med Coll 1986; **Resid:** Otolaryngology, UMDNJ-Univ Hosp 1991; **Fellow:** Facial Plastic & Reconstr Surgery, Univ Toronto Affil Hosps 1992

Zbar, Lloyd I.S. MD (Oto) - **Spec Exp:** Hearing & Balance Disorders; Nasal & Sinus Disorders; Voice Disorders; **Hospital:** Hackensack UMC-Mountainside (page 802), Overlook Med Ctr (page 92); **Address:** 200 Highland Ave, Ste 250, Glen Ridge, NJ 07028-1528; **Phone:** 973-744-2424; **Board Cert:** Otolaryngology 1970; **Med School:** Queens Univ 1964; **Resid:** Surgery, Beth Israel Deaconess Med Ctr 1966; Otolaryngology, Bellevue Hosp Ctr 1969; **Fellow:** Otolaryngology, Bellevue Hosp Ctr 1970; **Fac Appt:** Assoc Clin Prof Oto, NYU Sch Med

Pain Medicine

Kaufman, Andrew G MD (PM) - **Spec Exp:** Complex Regional Pain Syndromes; Pain-Back & Neck; Pain-Cancer; Pain-Neuropathic; **Hospital:** Univ Hosp-Newark, Overlook Med Ctr (page 92); **Address:** 90 Bergen St, Ste 3400, Newark, NJ 07103; **Phone:** 973-972-2085; **Board Cert:** Anesthesiology 1993; Pain Medicine 2015; **Med School:** Univ VA Sch Med 1988; **Resid:** Anesthesiology, NY-Presby/Columbia Univ Med Ctr 1992; **Fellow:** Pain Medicine, Beth Israel Deaconess Hosp 1993; **Fac Appt:** Assoc Prof Anes, UMDNJ-NJ Med Sch, Newark

Pathology

Heller, Debra S MD (Path) - **Spec Exp:** Gynecologic Pathology; Pediatric Pathology; Perinatal Pathology; **Hospital:** Univ Hosp-Newark; **Address:** UMDNJ-NJ Med Sch Dept Pathology, 185 S Orange Ave, Newark, NJ 07101; **Phone:** 973-972-0751; **Board Cert:** Anatomic Pathology 1988; Obstetrics & Gynecology 2013; Pediatric Pathology 1999; Pathology 2014; **Med School:** NY Med Coll 1977; **Resid:** Obstetrics & Gynecology, Beth Israel Med Ctr 1981; Anatomic Pathology, Mt Sinai Med Ctr 1988; **Fellow:** Pediatric Pathology, Mt Sinai Med Ctr 1987; Gynecologic Pathology, Mt Sinai Med Ctr 1989; **Fac Appt:** Prof Path, UMDNJ-NJ Med Sch, Newark

Lara, Jonathan F MD (Path) - **Hospital:** St. Barnabas Med Ctr (page 94); **Address:** St Barnabas Med Ctr, Dept Pathology, 94 Old Short Hills Rd, Livingston, NJ 07039-5672; **Phone:** 973-322-5762; **Board Cert:** Anatomic & Clinical Pathology 1988; Cytopathology 1997; **Med School:** Philippines 1984; **Resid:** Pathology, St Barnabas Med Ctr 1988; **Fellow:** Surgical Pathology, Meml Sloan Kettering Canc Ctr 1989; **Fac Appt:** Asst Clin Prof Path, UMDNJ-NJ Med Sch, Newark

Pediatric Allergy & Immunology

Fost, Arthur F MD (PA&I) - **Spec Exp:** Asthma; Sinusitis; Urticaria; **Hospital:** Clara Maass Med Ctr (page 94); **Address:** 197 Bloomfield Ave, Verona, NJ 07044-2702; **Phone:** 973-857-0330; **Board Cert:** Pediatrics 1968; Allergy & Immunology 1972; **Med School:** Jefferson Med Coll 1963; **Resid:** Pediatrics, Chldns Hosp 1965; Pediatrics, Hosp Univ Penn 1966; **Fellow:** Allergy & Immunology, St Vincent's Hosp 1968; **Fac Appt:** Assoc Clin Prof Ped, UMDNJ-NJ Med Sch, Newark

Morrison, Susan H MD (PA&I) - **Hospital:** Clara Maass Med Ctr (page 94); **Address:** 36 Newark Ave, Ste 322, Belleville, NJ 07109; **Phone:** 973-450-0100; **Board Cert:** Pediatrics 1986; Allergy & Immunology 2008; Pediatric Infectious Disease 2009; **Med School:** UMDNJ-NJ Med Sch, Newark 1981; **Resid:** Pediatrics, Univ Hosp-UMDNJ 1985; **Fellow:** Pediatric Allergy & Immunology, Univ Hosp-UMDNJ 1988; **Fac Appt:** Asst Clin Prof Ped, UMDNJ-NJ Med Sch, Newark

Torre, Arthur J MD (PA&I) - **Spec Exp:** Asthma & Allergy; Diving Medicine; Rhinitis; Sinusitis; **Hospital:** St. Joseph's Regl Med Ctr - Paterson; **Address:** 25 Hollywood Ave, Fairfield, NJ 07004-1113; **Phone:** 973-882-0880; **Board Cert:** Pediatrics 1975; **Med School:** UMDNJ-NJ Med Sch, Newark 1970; **Resid:** Pediatrics, Martland Hosp 1974; **Fellow:** Pediatric Allergy & Immunology, Martland Hosp 1975; **Fac Appt:** Assoc Clin Prof Ped, UMDNJ-NJ Med Sch, Newark

Pediatric Cardiology

Fernandes, John MD (PCd) - **Spec Exp:** Congenital Heart Disease; Fetal Cardiology; Echocardiography; **Hospital:** St. Barnabas Med Ctr (page 94), Morgan Stanley Chldns Hosp of NY-Presby, NY (page 102); **Address:** 349 E Northfield Rd, Ste 201, Livingston, NJ 07039-4086; **Phone:** 973-533-1031; **Board Cert:** Pediatric Cardiology 2013; **Med School:** India 1983; **Resid:** Pediatrics, Hahnemann Univ Hosp 1988; **Fellow:** Pediatric Cardiology, NYU Med Ctr 1991; **Fac Appt:** Assoc Clin Prof Ped, Columbia P&S

O'Connor, Brian K MD (PCd) - **Hospital:** Newark Beth Israel Med Ctr (page 94), Chldns Hosp NJ at Newark (page 94); **Address:** Newark Beth Israel - Chldns Hrt Ctr, 201 Lyons Ave, Ste L-5, Newark, NJ 07112; **Phone:** 973-926-3500; **Board Cert:** Pediatric Cardiology 2015; **Med School:** Georgetown Univ 1985; **Resid:** Pediatrics, New England Med Ctr 1988; **Fellow:** Pediatric Cardiology, Mott Chldns Hosp 1991; Pediatric Cardiology, Chldns Hosp 1994

Verma, Rajiv MD (PCd) - **Spec Exp:** Congenital Heart Disease-Adult & Child; Kawasaki Disease; **Hospital:** Newark Beth Israel Med Ctr (page 94); **Address:** Newark Beth Israel - Chldns Hrt Ctr, 201 Lyons Ave, Ste L-5, Newark, NJ 07112; **Phone:** 973-926-3500; **Board Cert:** Pediatric Cardiology 2009; **Med School:** Zambia 1984; **Resid:** Surgery, Chldn's Hosp of Philadelphia 1997; Pediatrics, NYU Langone Med Ctr 1991; **Fellow:** Pediatric Cardiology, NYU Langone Med Ctr 1994; Interventional Cardiology, Chldns Hosp 1996; **Fac Appt:** Assoc Clin Prof Ped, NYU Sch Med

Pediatric Critical Care Medicine

Yeh, Timothy S MD (PCCM) - **Hospital:** St. Barnabas Med Ctr (page 94), Monmouth Med Ctr (page 94); **Address:** St Barnabas Med Ctr, 94 Old Short Hills Rd, Fl 4th, rm 4134A, Livingston, NJ 07039; **Phone:** 973-322-5691; **Board Cert:** Pediatrics 1982; Pediatric Critical Care Medicine 2010; **Med School:** UC Davis 1976; **Resid:** Pediatrics, UC Davis Med Ctr 1979; **Fellow:** Pediatric Critical Care Medicine, Chldns Natl Med Ctr 1981

Pediatric Endocrinology

Brenner, Dennis J MD (PEn) - **Spec Exp:** Growth Disorders; Pubertal Disorders; Diabetes; Turner Syndrome; **Hospital:** St. Barnabas Med Ctr (page 94), Newark Beth Israel Med Ctr (page 94); **Address:** 375 Mt Pleasant Ave, Ste 105, West Orange, NJ 07052; **Phone:** 973-322-7600; **Board Cert:** Pediatric Endocrinology 2011; **Med School:** SUNY Downstate 1997; **Resid:** Pediatrics, Steven & Alexandra Cohen Chldn's Med Ctr of NY 2000; **Fellow:** Pediatric Endocrinology, Steven & Alexandra Cohen Chldn's Med Ctr of NY 2003; **Fac Appt:** Asst Clin Prof Ped, SUNY Downstate

Oppenheimer, Ellen MD (PEn) - **Spec Exp:** Pubertal Disorders; Growth Disorders; Adrenal Disorders; **Hospital:** St. Barnabas Med Ctr (page 94); **Address:** Pediatric Spec Ctr at St Barnabas, 375 Mount Pleasant Ave, Ste 105, West Orange, NJ 07052; **Phone:** 973-322-7600 x4; **Board Cert:** Pediatric Endocrinology 2010; **Med School:** Albert Einstein Coll Med 1985; **Resid:** Pediatrics, Montefiore Med Ctr 1989; **Fellow:** Pediatric Endocrinology, Montefiore Med Ctr 1992

Sivitz, Jennifer N MD (PEn) - **Spec Exp:** Diabetes; Obesity; **Hospital:** Hackensack Univ Med Ctr (page 96), Newark Beth Israel Med Ctr (page 94); **Address:** 30 Prospect Ave WFAN Bldg - rm 251, Hackensack, NJ 07601; **Phone:** 551-996-5329; **Board Cert:** Pediatrics 2013; Pediatric Endocrinology 2009; **Med School:** NY Med Coll 2002; **Resid:** Pediatrics, LIJ Med Ctr 2005; **Fellow:** Pediatric Endocrinology, Mass Genl Hosp 2007

Pediatric Gastroenterology

Sunaryo, Francis P MD (PGe) - **Spec Exp:** Inflammatory Bowel Disease; Gastroesophageal Reflux Disease (GERD); Celiac Disease; **Hospital:** Newark Beth Israel Med Ctr (page 94), St. Barnabas Med Ctr (page 94); **Address:** Newark Beth Israel Med Ctr, Div Pediatric Gastroenterology, 201 Lyons Ave, Newark, NJ 07112; **Phone:** 973-926-7280; **Board Cert:** Pediatrics 1982; Pediatric Gastroenterology 2012; **Med School:** Indonesia 1973; **Resid:** Pediatrics, N Shore Univ Hosp 1979; **Fellow:** Pediatric Gastroenterology, Chldns Hosp 1982; **Fac Appt:** Asst Clin Prof Ped, UMDNJ-Univ Med Dent NJ

Pediatric Hematology-Oncology

Bekele, Wondwessen MD (PHO) - **Spec Exp:** Leukemia & Lymphoma; Bleeding/Coagulation Disorders; Bone Marrow Failure Disorders; **Hospital:** Newark Beth Israel Med Ctr (page 94), Monmouth Med Ctr (page 94); **Address:** Chldns Hosp NJ, Dept Hem/Onc, 201 Lyons Ave, Ste L5, Newark, NJ 07112; **Phone:** 973-926-7161; **Board Cert:** Pediatrics 1979; Pediatric Hematology-Oncology 1980; **Med School:** Ethiopia 1972; **Resid:** Internal Medicine, Brooklyn-Cumberland Hosp 1975; Pediatrics, Brooklyn-Cumberland Hosp 1977; **Fellow:** Pediatric Hematology-Oncology, Mt Sinai Hosp 1980; **Fac Appt:** Asst Clin Prof Ped, UMDNJ-NJ Med Sch, Newark

Kamalakar, Peri MD (PHO) - **Hospital:** Newark Beth Israel Med Ctr (page 94), Monmouth Med Ctr (page 94); **Address:** Valerie Fund Chldns Ctr, 201 Lyons Ave, Ste L5, Newark, NJ 07112-2027; **Phone:** 973-926-7161; **Board Cert:** Pediatrics 1975; Pediatric Hematology-Oncology 1997; **Med School:** India 1967; **Resid:** Pediatrics, Beth Israel Med Ctr 1973; **Fellow:** Pediatric Hematology-Oncology, Chldns Hosp 1976; **Fac Appt:** Asst Clin Prof Ped, UMDNJ-NJ Med Sch, Newark

Pediatric Nephrology

Roberti, M. Isabel D A MD/PhD (PNep) - **Spec Exp:** Transplant Medicine-Kidney; Kidney Failure; Hypertension; Kidney Stones; **Hospital:** St. Barnabas Med Ctr (page 94); **Address:** SBMC - Pediatric Nephrology, 94 Old Short Hills Rd, Ste 304, Livingston, NJ 07039; **Phone:** 973-322-5264; **Board Cert:** Pediatrics 2010; Pediatric Nephrology 2012; **Med School:** Brazil 1983; **Resid:** Pediatrics, Hosp Sao Paulo 1986; **Fellow:** Pediatric Nephrology, Hosp Sao Paulo 1989; Pediatric Nephrology, Mount Sinai Med Ctr 1995; **Fac Appt:** Assoc Clin Prof Ped, Mount Sinai Sch Med

Vyas, Shefali MD (PNep) - **Spec Exp:** Transplant Medicine-Kidney; Hypertension in Children; Dialysis Care; Kidney Disease; **Hospital:** St. Barnabas Med Ctr (page 94), Chldns Hosp NJ at Newark (page 94); **Address:** Barnabas Hlth, Chldns Kidney Ctr, 94 Old Short Hills Rd, Ste 304, Livingston, NJ 07039; **Phone:** 973-322-5264; **Board Cert:** Pediatrics 2012; Pediatric Nephrology 2008; **Med School:** India 1990; **Resid:** Pediatrics, Govt Med Hosp 1994; Pediatrics, SUNY Downstate Med Ctr 1997; **Fellow:** Pediatric Nephrology, SUNY Downstate Med Ctr 2000; Research, NY-Presby/Weill Cornell Med Ctr 2000; **Fac Appt:** Asst Prof Ped, UMDNJ-Univ Med Dent NJ

Pediatric Pulmonology

Aguila, Helen A MD (PPul) - **Spec Exp:** Asthma; Tuberculosis; **Hospital:** Univ Hosp-Newark, Columbus Hosp; **Address:** UMDNJ-Univ Hosp-Newark, 90 Bergen St Fl 5th - rm 5100, Dept Ped Pulmonology, Newark, NJ 07103; **Phone:** 973-972-5779; **Board Cert:** Pediatrics 1983; Pediatric Pulmonology 2014; **Med School:** Philippines 1974; **Resid:** Pediatrics, Staten Island Hosp 1979; Pediatrics, Kings Co Hosp/Downstate Med Ctr 1980; **Fellow:** Pediatric Pulmonology, Chldns Hosp Michigan 1983; **Fac Appt:** Asst Prof Ped, UMDNJ-NJ Med Sch, Newark

Bisberg, Dorothy S MD (PPul) - **Spec Exp:** Asthma; Cystic Fibrosis; **Hospital:** St. Barnabas Med Ctr (page 94), Newark Beth Israel Med Ctr (page 94); **Address:** Pediatric Specialty Center, 375 Mount Pleasant Ave, Ste 105, West Orange, NJ 07052; **Phone:** 973-322-7600 x6; **Board Cert:** Pediatrics 1978; Pediatric Pulmonology 2014; **Med School:** Cornell Univ-Weill Med Coll 1972; **Resid:** Pediatrics, Montefiore Med Ctr 1974; Pediatrics, Bronx Lebanon Hosp 1975; **Fac Appt:** Asst Clin Prof Ped, UMDNJ-NJ Med Sch, Newark

Kottler, William F MD (PPul) - **Spec Exp:** Asthma; Cystic Fibrosis; **Hospital:** St. Barnabas Med Ctr (page 94), Overlook Med Ctr (page 92); **Address:** 48 Essex St, Millburn, NJ 07041; **Phone:** 973-218-0900; **Board Cert:** Pediatric Pulmonology 2009; **Med School:** Dominica 1987; **Resid:** Pediatrics, Overlook Hosp 1990; **Fellow:** Pediatric Pulmonology, Newark Beth Israel Hosp 1991; Pediatric Pulmonology, Univ Florida Shands Hosp 1993; **Fac Appt:** Asst Clin Prof Ped, UMDNJ-NJ Med Sch, Newark

Mikkilineni, Sushmita MD (PPul) - **Spec Exp:** Critical Care; Sleep Medicine; **Hospital:** Chldns Hosp NJ at Newark (page 94); **Address:** 201 Lyons Ave, Ste L-5, Newark, NJ 07112; **Phone:** 973-926-4273; **Board Cert:** Pediatrics 2008; Pediatric Pulmonology 2014; Pediatric Critical Care Medicine 2010; Sleep Medicine 2007; **Med School:** India 1979; **Resid:** Pediatrics, RW Johnson Univ Hosp 1987; **Fellow:** Pediatric Pulmonary & Critical Care, RW Johnson Univ Hosp 1988; Pediatric Pulmonology, NY-Presby/Columbia Univ Med Ctr 1991; **Fac Appt:** Assoc Clin Prof Ped, Rutgers R W Johnson Med Sch

Montalvo Stanton, Evelyn MD (PPul) - **Spec Exp:** Cystic Fibrosis; Asthma; **Hospital:** Univ Hosp-Newark; **Address:** Univ Hosp, Ped Pulmonary Dept, 90 Bergen St Fl 5 - Ste 5100, Newark, NJ 07103; **Phone:** 973-972-5779; **Board Cert:** Pediatrics 2008; Pediatric Pulmonology 2011; **Med School:** UMDNJ-NJ Med Sch, Newark 1981; **Resid:** Pediatrics, Univ Hosp-UMDNJ 1989; **Fellow:** Pediatric Pulmonology, NY-Presby/Columbia Univ Med Ctr 1993; **Fac Appt:** Asst Prof Ped, UMDNJ-NJ Med Sch, Newark

Pediatric Rheumatology

Chalom, Elizabeth C MD (PRhu) - **Spec Exp:** Juvenile Arthritis; **Hospital:** St. Barnabas Med Ctr (page 94); **Address:** 375 Mount Pleasant Ave, Ste 105, West Orange, NJ 07052; **Phone:** 973-322-7600; **Board Cert:** Pediatrics 2008; Pediatric Rheumatology 2013; **Med School:** Columbia P&S 1991; **Resid:** Pediatrics, Chldns Hosp 1994; **Fellow:** Pediatric Rheumatology, Chldns Hosp 1995; **Fac Appt:** Asst Clin Prof S, UMDNJ-NJ Med Sch, Newark

Pediatric Surgery

Bethel, Colin A MD (PS) - **Spec Exp:** Minimally Invasive Surgery; Neonatal Surgery; **Hospital:** Newark Beth Israel Med Ctr (page 94), St. Joseph's Regl Med Ctr - Paterson; **Address:** Pediatric Surgery Group, 2130 Millburn Ave, Ste C-1, Maplewood, NJ 07040; **Phone:** 973-313-3115; **Board Cert:** Surgery 2005; Pediatric Surgery 2007; **Med School:** Columbia P&S 1987; **Resid:** Surgery, Yale-New Haven Hosp 1990; Surgery, Yale-New Haven Hosp 1995; **Fellow:** Pediatric Surgery, Chldns Hosp 1997; **Fac Appt:** Asst Prof S, UMDNJ-NJ Med Sch, Newark

Pediatric Urology

Stock, Jeffrey A MD (Ped Uro) - **Spec Exp:** Robotic Surgery-Pediatric; Minimally Invasive Surgery-Pediatric; Hypospadias; **Hospital:** Newark Beth Israel Med Ctr (page 94), Mt Sinai Hosp; **Address:** 101 Old Short Hills Rd, Ste 203, West Orange, NJ 07052; **Phone:** 973-325-7188; **Board Cert:** Urology 2010; Pediatric Urology 2010; **Med School:** Mount Sinai Sch Med 1988; **Resid:** Surgery, Univ Hosp-UMDNJ 1990; Urology, Univ Hosp-UMDNJ 1993; **Fellow:** Pediatric Urology, UCSD Med Ctr 1994; **Fac Appt:** Assoc Clin Prof S, UMDNJ-NJ Med Sch, Newark

Pediatrics

Colyer-Aversa, Lori A MD (Ped) *PCP* - **Spec Exp:** Developmental Disorders; Autism; Neonatal Care; **Hospital:** Hackensack UMC-Mountainside (page 802); **Address:** 399 Hoover Ave, Ste 5, Bloomfield, NJ 07003; **Phone:** 973-748-9500; **Board Cert:** Pediatrics 2014; **Med School:** UMDNJ-NJ Med Sch, Newark 1989; **Resid:** Pediatrics, Columbia-Presby Med Ctr 1992

Gruenwald, Laurence D MD (Ped) *PCP* - **Spec Exp:** Asthma; Behavioral Disorders; **Hospital:** St. Barnabas Med Ctr (page 94); **Address:** 90 Millburn Ave, Ste 101, Millburn, NJ 07041-1933; **Phone:** 973-378-7990; **Board Cert:** Pediatrics 1981; **Med School:** UMDNJ-NJ Med Sch, Newark 1975; **Resid:** Pediatrics, Chldns Hosp Natl Med Ctr 1978; **Fac Appt:** Asst Clin Prof Ped, UMDNJ-NJ Med Sch, Newark

Marcus, Richard W MD (Ped) *PCP* - **Spec Exp:** ADD/ADHD; **Hospital:** Clara Maass Med Ctr (page 94); **Address:** Nutley Pediatrics Associates, 242 Washington Ave, Ste A, Nutley, NJ 07110-1994; **Phone:** 973-667-6676; **Board Cert:** Pediatrics 1988; **Med School:** UMDNJ-NJ Med Sch, Newark 1982; **Resid:** Pediatrics, Univ Hosp-UMDNJ 1985; **Fac Appt:** Asst Clin Prof Ped, UMDNJ-NJ Med Sch, Newark

Rosenblatt, Joshua S MD (Ped) *PCP* - **Spec Exp:** Pain Management; **Hospital:** Newark Beth Israel Med Ctr (page 94); **Address:** NBIMC, Pediatrics Dept, 201 Lyons Ave, Newark, NJ 07112; **Phone:** 973-926-7273; **Board Cert:** Pediatrics 2010; **Med School:** UMDNJ-NJ Med Sch, Newark 1984; **Resid:** Pediatrics, Newark Beth Israel Med Ctr 1987; **Fac Appt:** Asst Clin Prof Ped, UMDNJ-NJ Med Sch, Newark

Physical Medicine & Rehabilitation

Bach, John R MD (PMR) - **Spec Exp:** Neuromuscular Disorders; Amyotrophic Lateral Sclerosis (ALS); Post Polio Syndrome/Rehabilitation; **Hospital:** Univ Hosp-Newark; **Address:** UHNJ, Physical Med & Rehab, 90 Bergen St, Ste 3100, Newark, NJ 07103; **Phone:** 973-972-2809; **Board Cert:** Physical Medicine & Rehabilitation 1986; **Med School:** UMDNJ-Rutgers Med Sch 1976; **Resid:** Physical Medicine & Rehabilitation, NYU Med Ctr 1980; **Fellow:** Neuromuscular Disease, Univ Hosp 1983; **Fac Appt:** Prof PMR, UMDNJ-NJ Med Sch, Newark

Cole, Jeffrey L MD (PMR) - **Spec Exp:** Pain Management; Neuromuscular Disorders; Electromyography; Electrodiagnosis; **Hospital:** Kessler Inst for Rehab - W Orange; **Address:** Kessler Inst for Rehabilitation, 1199 Pleasant Valley Way, West Orange, NJ 07052; **Phone:** 973-243-6943; **Board Cert:** Physical Medicine & Rehabilitation 1983; Pain Medicine 2014; **Med School:** Mexico 1977; **Resid:** Internal Medicine, NY Hosp-Queens Med Ctr 1979; Physical Medicine & Rehabilitation, Montefiore Med Ctr 1982; **Fellow:** Electrodiagnosis, Booth Meml Med Ctr 1983; **Fac Appt:** Assoc Clin Prof PMR, UMDNJ-NJ Med Sch, Newark

Francis, Kathleen D MD (PMR) - **Spec Exp:** Lymphedema; **Address:** Lymphedema Physician Services, 200 S Orange Ave, Ste 111, Livingston, NJ 07039; **Phone:** 973-322-7366; **Board Cert:** Physical Medicine & Rehabilitation 2004; **Med School:** UMDNJ-NJ Med Sch, Newark 1989; **Resid:** Physical Medicine & Rehabilitation, UMDNJ-Kessler Inst Rehab 1993; **Fac Appt:** Asst Clin Prof PMR, UMDNJ-NJ Med Sch, Newark

Kirshblum, Steven C MD (PMR) - **Spec Exp:** Spinal Cord Injury; Spasticity Management; **Hospital:** Kessler Inst for Rehab - W Orange, St. Barnabas Med Ctr (page 94); **Address:** Kessler Inst Rehab, 1199 Pleasant Valley Way, West Orange, NJ 07052; **Phone:** 973-731-3600; **Board Cert:** Physical Medicine & Rehabilitation 1991; Spinal Cord Injury Medicine 2008; **Med School:** Univ Hlth Scis, Chicago Med Sch 1986; **Resid:** Physical Medicine & Rehabilitation, Mt Sinai Hosp 1990; **Fac Appt:** Prof PMR, UMDNJ-Rutgers Med Sch

Shumko, John Z MD/PhD (PMR) - **Spec Exp:** Sports Medicine; **Hospital:** St. Barnabas Med Ctr (page 94); **Address:** Sports & Physical Med Inst, 200 S Orange Ave, Ste 230, Livingston, NJ 07039; **Phone:** 973-322-7909; **Board Cert:** Physical Medicine & Rehabilitation 2007; **Med School:** UMDNJ-NJ Med Sch, Newark 1992; **Resid:** Physical Medicine & Rehabilitation, Kessler Inst Rehab 1996

Plastic Surgery

Ablaza, Valerie J MD (PlS) - **Spec Exp:** Cosmetic Surgery-Breast; Breast Reconstruction; Liposuction & Body Contouring; **Hospital:** St. Barnabas Med Ctr (page 94), Hackensack UMC-Mountainside (page 802); **Address:** The Plastic Surgery Group, 37 N Fullerton Ave, Montclair, NJ 07042; **Phone:** 973-233-1933; **Board Cert:** Plastic Surgery 2010; **Med School:** Med Coll PA 1989; **Resid:** Surgery, Albert Einstein Med Ctr 1994; Plastic Surgery, New York Hosp 1996; **Fellow:** Breast Surgery, Nashville Plastic Surgery 1997

DiBernardo, Barry E MD (PlS) - **Spec Exp:** Laser Surgery; Hair Restoration/Transplant; Cosmetic Surgery-Face & Body; Body Contouring After Weight Loss; **Hospital:** Hackensack UMC-Mountainside (page 802), Clara Maass Med Ctr (page 94); **Address:** 29 Park St, Montclair, NJ 07042; **Phone:** 973-509-2000; **Board Cert:** Plastic Surgery 1994; **Med School:** Cornell Univ-Weill Med Coll 1984; **Resid:** Surgery, Mt Sinai Med Ctr 1989; Plastic Surgery, Montefiore Med Ctr 1991; **Fac Appt:** Assoc Clin Prof PlS, UMDNJ-NJ Med Sch, Newark

Granick, Mark S MD (PlS) - **Spec Exp:** Reconstructive Surgery; Cosmetic Surgery; Skin Cancer; Wound Healing/Care; **Hospital:** Univ Hosp-Newark, Newark Beth Israel Med Ctr (page 94); **Address:** 140 Bergen St, rm E-1620, Newark, NJ 07103; **Phone:** 973-972-5377; **Board Cert:** Otolaryngology 1982; Plastic Surgery 1985; **Med School:** Harvard Med Sch 1977; **Resid:** Otolaryngology, Mass E&E Hosp 1982; Plastic Surgery, Univ Pittsburgh Med Ctr 1984; **Fac Appt:** Prof PlS, UMDNJ-NJ Med Sch, Newark

LoVerme, Paul J MD (PlS) - **Spec Exp:** Cosmetic Surgery-Face; Liposuction & Body Contouring; Breast Reconstruction & Augmentation; **Hospital:** Hackensack UMC-Mountainside (page 802), St. Barnabas Med Ctr (page 94); **Address:** 825 Bloomfield Ave, Ste 205, Verona, NJ 07044; **Phone:** 973-857-9499; **Board Cert:** Plastic Surgery 1987; **Med School:** UMDNJ-NJ Med Sch, Newark 1978; **Resid:** Surgery, UMDNJ Univ Hosp 1983; Plastic Surgery, Med Coll Hosp 1985; **Fac Appt:** Asst Clin Prof PlS, UMDNJ-NJ Med Sch, Newark

Rosen, Allen D MD (PlS) - **Spec Exp:** Cosmetic Surgery-Face & Breast; Breast Reconstruction; Liposuction & Body Contouring; Eyelid Surgery; **Hospital:** St. Barnabas Med Ctr (page 94), Hackensack UMC-Mountainside (page 802); **Address:** The Plastic Surgery Group, 37 N Fullerton Ave, Montclair, NJ 07042; **Phone:** 973-233-1933; **Board Cert:** Plastic Surgery 1991; **Med School:** SUNY Buffalo 1983; **Resid:** Surgery, Columbia Presby Med Ctr 1986; Plastic Surgery, Columbia Presby Med Ctr 1988; **Fellow:** Hand Surgery, Columbia Presby Med Ctr 1987; **Fac Appt:** Asst Clin Prof PlS, UMDNJ-NJ Med Sch, Newark

Psychiatry

Caracci, Giovanni MD (Psyc) - **Spec Exp:** Geriatric Psychiatry; Psychopharmacology; Psychotherapy; Post Traumatic Stress Disorder; **Hospital:** Univ Hosp-Newark; **Address:** 183 S Orange Ave, rm F-1555, Newark, NJ 07101; **Phone:** 973-972-0829; **Board Cert:** Psychiatry 1990; **Med School:** Italy 1977; **Resid:** Psychiatry, Metropolitan Hosp 1984; **Fac Appt:** Assoc Prof Psyc, UMDNJ-NJ Med Sch, Newark

Faber, Mark P MD (Psyc) - **Spec Exp:** Child Psychiatry; Anxiety Disorders; Depression; ADD/ADHD; **Hospital:** St. Barnabas Med Ctr (page 94), Hackensack UMC-Mountainside (page 802); **Address:** 594 Valley Rd, Upper Montclair, NJ 07043-1882; **Phone:** 973-746-6711; **Board Cert:** Psychiatry 1993; Child & Adolescent Psychiatry 2005; **Med School:** Dominica 1988; **Resid:** Psychiatry, CT Valley Hosp 1991; **Fellow:** Child & Adolescent Psychiatry, UMDNJ-RW Johnson Sch Med 1994; Sleep Medicine, UMDNJ-RW Johnson Sch Med 1996

Hindin, Lee E MD (Psyc) - **Spec Exp:** Addiction Psychiatry; **Hospital:** St. Barnabas Med Ctr (page 94); **Address:** Creative Intervention, 22 Old Short Hills Rd, Ste 217, Livingston, NJ 07039; **Phone:** 973-365-2300; **Board Cert:** Psychiatry 1984; **Med School:** UMDNJ-NJ Med Sch, Newark 1977; **Resid:** Psychiatry, UCLA-Neuropsych Inst 1982

Nucci, Annamaria MD/PhD (Psyc) - **Spec Exp:** Psychopharmacology; Relationship Problems; Depression; **Address:** 5 Westview Terr, Cedar Grove, NJ 07009; **Phone:** 973-857-2609; **Board Cert:** Psychiatry 1978; **Med School:** Italy 1971; **Resid:** Psychiatry, VA Hosp-NYU 1973; Psychiatry, Payne Whitney Clin 1976; **Fellow:** Child & Adolescent Psychiatry, NY-Presby/Weill Cornell Med Ctr 1976

Schleifer, Steven J MD (Psyc) - **Spec Exp:** Depression; Psychoneuroimmunology; Anxiety Disorders; **Hospital:** Univ Hosp-Newark; **Address:** 183 S Orange Ave Bldg BHSB F1430, Newark, NJ 07103; **Phone:** 973-972-5023; **Board Cert:** Psychiatry 1980; **Med School:** Mount Sinai Sch Med 1975; **Resid:** Psychiatry, Mount Sinai Med Ctr 1979; **Fac Appt:** Prof Psyc, UMDNJ-NJ Med Sch, Newark

Zornitzer, Michael R MD (Psyc) - **Spec Exp:** Psychopharmacology; Anxiety & Depression; Psychotherapy; ADD/ADHD; **Hospital:** St. Barnabas Med Ctr (page 94); **Address:** 2 W Northfield Rd, Ste 305, Livingston, NJ 07039-3789; **Phone:** 973-992-6090; **Board Cert:** Psychiatry 1976; **Med School:** SUNY Downstate 1971; **Resid:** Psychiatry, NYU Med Ctr 1972; Psychiatry, Albert Einstein Coll of Med 1975; **Fac Appt:** Asst Clin Prof Psyc, NY Coll Osteo Med

Pulmonary Disease

Greenberg, Martin J MD (Pul) - **Spec Exp:** Asthma; Emphysema; **Hospital:** St. Barnabas Med Ctr (page 94); **Address:** 124 East Mt Pleasant Ave, Livingston, NJ 07039; **Phone:** 973-994-4130; **Board Cert:** Internal Medicine 1987; **Med School:** Dominica 1983; **Resid:** Internal Medicine, Univ Hosp UMDNJ 1986; **Fellow:** Pulmonary Disease, Newark Beth Israel 1988

Miller, Richard A MD (Pul) - **Spec Exp:** Sarcoidosis; Asthma; Sleep Medicine; **Hospital:** Saint Michael's Med Ctr; **Address:** St Michaels Medical Center, 111 Central Ave, Newark, NJ 07102; **Phone:** 973-877-5493; **Board Cert:** Internal Medicine 1989; Pulmonary Disease 2013; Critical Care Medicine 2005; **Med School:** NY Med Coll 1983; **Resid:** Internal Medicine, St Michaels Med Ctr 1988; **Fellow:** Pulmonary Critical Care Medicine, St Michaels Med Ctr 1991

Safirstein, Benjamin MD (Pul) - **Spec Exp:** Asthma; Sarcoidosis; **Hospital:** Hackensack UMC-Mountainside (page 802), Saint Michael's Med Ctr; **Address:** 123 Highland Ave, Ste 101, Glen Ridge, NJ 07028; **Phone:** 973-744-9125; **Board Cert:** Internal Medicine 1970; Pulmonary Disease 1974; **Med School:** Ros Franklin Univ/Chicago Med Sch 1965; **Resid:** Internal Medicine, Mount Sinai Hosp 1969; **Fellow:** Pulmonary Disease, Brompton Hosp 1972; **Fac Appt:** Assoc Clin Prof Med, Mount Sinai Sch Med

Shah, Smita S MD (Pul) - **Spec Exp:** Chronic Obstructive Lung Disease (COPD); Lung Cancer; Pulmonary Hypertension; Sleep Apnea; **Hospital:** St. Barnabas Med Ctr (page 94); **Address:** 96 Millburn Ave, Ste 200-A, Millburn, NJ 07040; **Phone:** 973-763-6800; **Board Cert:** Internal Medicine 1986; Pulmonary Disease 2010; Sleep Medicine 2009; **Med School:** India 1980; **Resid:** Internal Medicine, St Marys Hosp 1986; **Fellow:** Pulmonary Critical Care Medicine, Temple Univ Hosp 1988

Radiation Oncology

Grann, Alison MD (RadRO) - **Spec Exp:** Breast Cancer; Brain Tumors; **Hospital:** St. Barnabas Med Ctr (page 94); **Address:** St Barnabas, Radiation Onc Dept, 94 Old Short Hills Rd, Livingston, NJ 07039; **Phone:** 973-322-5638; **Board Cert:** Radiation Oncology 2010; **Med School:** Geo Wash Univ 1991; **Resid:** Internal Medicine, Beth Israel Deaconess Med Ctr 1994; Radiation Oncology, Meml Sloan-Kettering Cancer Ctr 1998

Wagman, Raquel T MD (RadRO) - **Spec Exp:** Breast Cancer; Gynecologic Cancer; Gastrointestinal Cancer; **Hospital:** St. Barnabas Med Ctr (page 94); **Address:** St Barnabas Med Ctr, 94 Old Short Hills Rd, Livingston, NJ 07039; **Phone:** 973-322-5630; **Board Cert:** Radiation Oncology 2010; **Med School:** Univ Mich Med Sch 1995; **Resid:** Radiation Oncology, Meml Sloan Kettering Cancer Ctr 2000

Reproductive Endocrinology

Chen, Serena H MD (RE) - **Spec Exp:** Infertility-IVF; Laparoscopic Surgery; Hysteroscopic Surgery; Fertility Preservation in Cancer; **Hospital:** St. Barnabas Med Ctr (page 94); **Address:** IRMS at Saint Barnabas, 94 Old Short Hills Rd, East Wing, Ste 403, Livingston, NJ 07039; **Phone:** 973-322-8286; **Board Cert:** Obstetrics & Gynecology 2013; Reproductive Endocrinology 2013; **Med School:** Duke Univ 1988; **Resid:** Obstetrics & Gynecology, Johns Hopkins Hosp 1992; **Fellow:** Reproductive Endocrinology, Johns Hopkins Hosp 1994

Rheumatology

Cannarozzi, Nicholas A MD (Rhu) - **Spec Exp:** Rheumatoid Arthritis; Lupus Nephritis; Osteoporosis; Vasculitis; **Hospital:** Hackensack UMC-Mountainside (page 802); **Address:** 127 Pine St, Montclair, NJ 07042-4835; **Phone:** 973-783-6000; **Board Cert:** Internal Medicine 1980; Rheumatology 1972; **Med School:** Hahnemann Univ 1965; **Resid:** Internal Medicine, Philadelphia Genl Hosp 1967; Internal Medicine, St Michaels Med Ctr 1968; **Fellow:** Rheumatology, Yale-New Haven Hosp 1969; Rheumatology, Yale-New Haven Hosp 1972

Lahita, Robert G MD/PhD (Rhu) - **Spec Exp:** Lupus/SLE; Inflammatory Arthritis-Consult; Arthritis; Autoimmune Disorders; **Hospital:** Newark Beth Israel Med Ctr (page 94); **Address:** Newark Beth Israel Med Ctr, Rheumatology, 201 Lyons Ave, Fl 4, Newark, NJ 07112; **Phone:** 973-926-7472; **Board Cert:** Internal Medicine 2004; Rheumatology 2007; **Med School:** Jefferson Med Coll 1973; **Resid:** Internal Medicine, New York Hosp-Cornell 1976; **Fellow:** Rheumatology, Rockefeller Hosp 1978; **Fac Appt:** Prof Med, UMDNJ-Rutgers Med Sch

Ritter, Jill M MD (Rhu) - **Hospital:** St. Barnabas Med Ctr (page 94); **Address:** 200 S Orange Ave, Livingston, NJ 07039; **Phone:** 973-322-0234; **Board Cert:** Rheumatology 2004; **Med School:** NYU Sch Med 1989; **Resid:** Internal Medicine, Mt Sinai Med Ctr 1992; **Fellow:** Rheumatology, Mt Sinai Med Ctr 1994

Simon, Jonathan M MD (Rhu) - **Hospital:** Hackensack UMC-Mountainside (page 802); **Address:** 1018 Broad St, Bloomfield, NJ 07003-2807; **Phone:** 973-338-3383; **Board Cert:** Internal Medicine 1981; Rheumatology 1984; **Med School:** NYU Sch Med 1978; **Resid:** Internal Medicine, UMDNJ Univ Hosp 1981; **Fellow:** Rheumatology, UMDNJ Univ Hosp 1983

Sports Medicine

Gehrmann, Robin M MD (SM) - **Spec Exp:** Cartilage Damage & Transplant; Knee Ligament Reconstruction; Shoulder Injuries; Arthroscopic Surgery; **Hospital:** Univ Hosp-Newark; **Address:** 33 Bleeker St, Millburn, NJ 07041; **Phone:** 973-689-6266; **Board Cert:** Orthopaedic Surgery 2015; Orthopaedic Sports Medicine 2015; **Med School:** Hahnemann Univ 1995; **Resid:** Surgery, Univ Med Ctr-UMDNJ 1996; Orthopaedic Surgery, Univ Med Ctr-UMDNJ 2000; **Fellow:** Orthopaedic Sports Medicine, Univ Hosp Penn 2001; **Fac Appt:** Asst Prof OrS, UMDNJ-NJ Med Sch, Newark

Levy, Andrew S MD (SM) - **Spec Exp:** Cartilage Damage & Transplant; Ligament Reconstruction; Shoulder Surgery; **Hospital:** St. Barnabas Med Ctr (page 94), Morristown Med Ctr (page 92); **Address:** 90 Milburn Ave, Ste 204A, Milburn, NJ 07041; **Phone:** 908-598-9199; **Board Cert:** Orthopaedic Surgery 2008; **Med School:** Temple Univ 1987; **Resid:** Orthopaedic Surgery, Albert Einstein Med Ctr 1994; **Fellow:** Sports Medicine & Shoulder Surgery, Duke Univ Med Ctr 1995

Surgery

Andrei, Valeriu E MD (S) - **Spec Exp:** Obesity/Bariatric Surgery; Laparoscopic Surgery; **Hospital:** Robert Wood Johnson Univ Hosp - New Brunswick, St. Barnabas Med Ctr (page 94); **Address:** Bariatric Assocs, 200 S Orange Ave, Ste 123, Livingston, NJ 07039; **Phone:** 973-322-7265; **Board Cert:** Surgery 2009; **Med School:** Romania 1987; **Resid:** Surgery, Methodist Hosp 1988; **Fellow:** Minimally Invasive Surgery, Mount Sinai Med Ctr 1999

Blackwood, M. Michele MD (S) - **Spec Exp:** Breast Cancer; Breast Surgery; Sentinel Node Surgery; Breast Cancer-High Risk Women; **Hospital:** St. Barnabas Med Ctr (page 94); **Address:** St Barnabas, Breast Ctr, 200 S Orange Ave, Ste 102, Livingston, NJ 07039; **Phone:** 973-322-7020; **Board Cert:** Surgery 2003; **Med School:** Med Univ SC 1988; **Resid:** Surgery, Stamford Hosp 1993; **Fellow:** Surgical Oncology, Meml Sloan-Kettering Cancer Ctr 1994; **Fac Appt:** Asst Clin Prof S, Columbia P&S

Chamberlain, Ronald S MD (S) - **Spec Exp:** Liver & Biliary Surgery; Cancer Surgery; Laparoscopic Surgery; Pancreatic Cancer; **Hospital:** St. Barnabas Med Ctr (page 94); **Address:** St Barnabas Med Ctr, Surgery, 94 Old Short Hills Rd, Ste 1172, Livingston, NJ 07039; **Phone:** 973-322-5195; **Board Cert:** Surgery 2009; **Med School:** Geo Wash Univ 1991; **Resid:** Surgery, G Washington Univ Hosp 1997; **Fellow:** Surgical Oncology, Natl Cancer Inst 1996; Hepatobiliary Surgery, Meml Sloan-Kettering Canc Ctr 1999; **Fac Appt:** Prof S, UMDNJ-NJ Med Sch, Newark

Elliott, Nancy MD (S) - **Spec Exp:** Breast Cancer & Surgery; **Hospital:** St. Barnabas Med Ctr (page 94); **Address:** Montclair Breast Ctr, 37 N Fullerton Ave, Montclair, NJ 07042; **Phone:** 973-509-1818; **Board Cert:** Surgery 2010; **Med School:** Mount Sinai Sch Med 1981; **Resid:** Surgery, St Vincents Hosp 1988; **Fellow:** Breast Surgery, RWJ-UMDNJ Hosp 1989

Fletcher, H. Stephen MD (S) - **Spec Exp:** Vascular Surgery; Breast Surgery; **Hospital:** St. Barnabas Med Ctr (page 94); **Address:** 94 Old Short Hills Rd, Ste 1172, Livingston, NJ 07039; **Phone:** 973-322-5195; **Board Cert:** Surgery 1973; **Med School:** Geo Wash Univ 1967; **Resid:** Surgery, G Washington Univ Med Ctr 1972; **Fac Appt:** Assoc Clin Prof S, UMDNJ-NJ Med Sch, Newark

Hertz, Marcie MD (S) - **Spec Exp:** Breast Cancer & Surgery; **Hospital:** St. Barnabas Med Ctr (page 94); **Address:** Montclair Breast Ctr, 37 N Fullerton Ave, Montclair, NJ 07042; **Phone:** 973-509-1818; **Board Cert:** Surgery 2010; **Med School:** Albert Einstein Coll Med 1984; **Resid:** Surgery, Montefiore Med Ctr 1989

Huston, Jan A MD (S) - **Spec Exp:** Breast Surgery; Breast Disease; **Hospital:** Hackensack UMC-Mountainside (page 802); **Address:** Summit Breast Care, UMCHackensack Mountainside Breast Ctr, 1 Bay Ave, Harries Pavilion Fl 2 - Ste 4, Montclair, NJ 07042; **Phone:** 973-259-3505; **Board Cert:** Surgery 2007; **Med School:** Mich State Univ 1982; **Resid:** Surgery, St Barnabas Hosp 1987; **Fellow:** Vascular Surgery, Lehigh Valley Hosp 1988

Maheshwari, Vivek MD (S) - **Spec Exp:** Gastrointestinal Cancer; Endocrine Tumors; Cancer Surgery; Breast Cancer; **Hospital:** St. Barnabas Med Ctr (page 94), Newark Beth Israel Med Ctr (page 94); **Address:** Prof Assocs in Surgery, 101 Old Short Hills Rd, Ste 206, West Orange, NJ 7052; **Phone:** 973-731-5005; **Board Cert:** Surgery 2003; **Med School:** India 1992; **Resid:** Surgery, Beth Israel Med Ctr 2002; **Fellow:** Surgical Oncology, UPMC 2004

Petrone, Sylvia J MD (S) - **Spec Exp:** Burn Care; Critical Care; **Hospital:** St. Barnabas Med Ctr (page 94); **Address:** St Barnabas Med Ctr, Burn Ctr, 94 Old Short Hills Rd, Livingston, NJ 07039; **Phone:** 973-322-5924; **Board Cert:** Surgery 2011; Surgical Critical Care 2008; **Med School:** Loyola Univ-Stritch Sch Med 1977; **Resid:** Surgery, Boston Med Ctr 1982; **Fellow:** Burn Surgery, NY-Presby/Weill Cornell Med Ctr 1983

Shack, Robert P MD (S) - **Spec Exp:** Vascular Surgery; **Hospital:** St. Barnabas Med Ctr (page 94); **Address:** 745 Northfield Ave, West Orange, NJ 07052; **Phone:** 973-325-7705; **Board Cert:** Surgery 2005; **Med School:** Jefferson Med Coll 1969; **Resid:** Surgery, Mount Sinai Med Ctr 1975

Shapiro, Michael E MD (S) - **Spec Exp:** Transplant-Kidney; Transplant-Pancreas; Parathyroid Surgery; Dialysis Access Surgery; **Hospital:** Hackensack Univ Med Ctr (page 96); **Address:** 90 Bergen St, Ste 7100, Newark, NJ 07103; **Phone:** 973-972-2400; **Board Cert:** Surgery 2005; **Med School:** Univ Rochester 1977; **Resid:** Surgery, Beth Israel Med Ctr 1983; **Fac Appt:** Assoc Prof S, UMDNJ-NJ Med Sch, Newark

Thoracic & Cardiac Surgery

Camacho, Margarita T MD (T&CS) - **Spec Exp:** Mechanical Assist Devices; Transplant-Heart; Heart Failure; **Hospital:** Newark Beth Israel Med Ctr (page 94); **Address:** NBIMC, Cardiothoracic Surgery Dept, 201 Lyons Ave, Ste G5, Newark, NJ 07112; **Phone:** 973-926-6938; **Board Cert:** Thoracic & Cardiac Surgery 2008; **Med School:** NY Med Coll 1984; **Resid:** Surgery, Lenox Hill Hosp 1989; Cardiothoracic Surgery, Albert Einstein Affil Hosp 1991; **Fellow:** Pediatric Cardiothoracic Surgery, LI Jewish Med Ctr 1992; Transplantation/Mechanical Assist Devices, Cleveland Clin 1994

Forman, Mark MD (T&CS) - **Spec Exp:** Lung Cancer; Lung Surgery; Vascular Surgery; Video Assisted Thoracic Surgery (VATS); **Hospital:** St. Barnabas Med Ctr (page 94), Overlook Med Ctr (page 92); **Address:** 1500 Pleasant Valley Way, Ste 302, West Orange, NJ 07052; **Phone:** 973-324-0988; **Board Cert:** Thoracic & Cardiac Surgery 2007; **Med School:** Tulane Univ 1976; **Resid:** Surgery, LI Jewish Med Ctr 1981; **Fellow:** Cardiothoracic Surgery, Montefiore Med Ctr 1984

Goldenberg, Bruce MD (T&CS) - **Spec Exp:** Minimally Invasive Thoracic Surgery; Cardiac Surgery-Adult; Pacemakers; Arrhythmias; **Hospital:** St. Clare's Hosp-Denville, Hackensack UMC-Mountainside (page 802); **Address:** 30 Chatham Rd, Ste 377, Short Hills, NJ 07078; **Phone:** 973-467-5550; **Board Cert:** Thoracic & Cardiac Surgery 2003; **Med School:** Northwestern Univ 1976; **Resid:** Surgery, NYU Med Ctr 1981; **Fellow:** Thoracic & Cardiac Surgery, NYU Med Ctr 1983; **Fac Appt:** Asst Clin Prof S, UMDNJ-NJ Med Sch, Newark

Saunders, Craig R MD (T&CS) - **Spec Exp:** Cardiac Surgery; Minimally Invasive Surgery; **Hospital:** Newark Beth Israel Med Ctr (page 94), St. Barnabas Med Ctr (page 94); **Address:** NBIMC, Cardiothoracic Surgery Dept, 201 Lyons Ave, Ste G5, Newark, NJ 07112; **Phone:** 973-926-6938; **Board Cert:** Thoracic & Cardiac Surgery 2011; **Med School:** Univ Iowa Coll Med 1970; **Resid:** Surgery, Univ Iowa Hosps & Clins 1978; Cardiothoracic Surgery, Cleveland Clin 1980

Urology

Boorjian, Peter C MD (U) - **Spec Exp:** Kidney Stones; Prostate Benign Disease; Urinary Tract Infections; Urologic Cancer; **Hospital:** Hackensack UMC-Mountainside (page 802); **Address:** Montclair Urological Group, 777 Bloomfield Ave, Glen Ridge, NJ 07028; **Phone:** 973-429-0462; **Board Cert:** Urology 1978; **Med School:** SUNY Downstate 1971; **Resid:** Surgery, Med Coll VA 1973; Urology, SUNY Downstate 1976

Ciccone, Patrick N MD (U) - **Spec Exp:** Prostate Cancer; Genitourinary Cancer; **Hospital:** Clara Maass Med Ctr (page 94), St. Barnabas Med Ctr (page 94); **Address:** NJ Urology, 36 Newark Ave, Ste 200, Belleville, NJ 07109; **Phone:** 973-759-6180; **Board Cert:** Urology 1975; **Med School:** Georgetown Univ 1967; **Resid:** Surgery, VA Med Ctr 1969; Urology, VA Med Ctr 1972

Katz, Jeffrey I MD (U) - **Spec Exp:** Prostate Disease; Kidney Stones; Urologic Cancer; **Hospital:** St. Barnabas Med Ctr (page 94); **Address:** Summit Medical Group, 741 Northfield Ave, Ste 206, Livingston, NJ 07039; **Phone:** 973-436-1070; **Board Cert:** Urology 1978; **Med School:** Italy 1970; **Resid:** Surgery, Mount Sinai Hosp 1973; Urology, Montefiore Med Ctr 1976

Linsenmeyer, Todd A MD (U) - **Spec Exp:** Infertility-Male in Spinal Cord Injury; Voiding Dysfunction/Spinal Cord Injury; Urodynamics in Spinal Cord Injury; **Hospital:** Kessler Inst for Rehab - W Orange; **Address:** Kessler Inst Rehab, 1199 Pleasant Valley Way, West Orange, NJ 07052; **Phone:** 973-731-3600 x2274; **Board Cert:** Urology 2005; Physical Medicine & Rehabilitation 1990; Spinal Cord Injury Medicine 2013; **Med School:** Univ Hawaii JA Burns Sch Med 1979; **Resid:** Urology, Tripler AMC 1984; **Fellow:** Physical Medicine & Rehabilitation, Stanford Univ Hosp & Clins 1989; **Fac Appt:** Prof S, UMDNJ-NJ Med Sch, Newark

Saidi, James MD (U) - **Spec Exp:** Minimally Invasive Surgery; Prostate Cancer; Robotic Urologic Surgery; **Hospital:** Hackensack UMC-Mountainside (page 802); **Address:** Montclair Urological Group, 777 Bloomfield Ave, Glen Ridge, NJ 07028; **Phone:** 973-429-0462; **Board Cert:** Urology 2012; **Med School:** Univ Tex SW, Dallas 1994; **Resid:** Surgery, NY Presby Hosp/Columbia 1996; Urology, NY Presby Hosp/Columbia 2000

Savatta, Domenico J MD (U) - **Spec Exp:** Robotic Urologic Surgery; Prostate Cancer; Kidney Cancer; Bladder Cancer; **Hospital:** Newark Beth Israel Med Ctr (page 94), St. Barnabas Med Ctr (page 94); **Address:** Urology Grp of NJ, 375 Mt Pleasant Ave, Ste 250, West Orange, NJ 7052; **Phone:** 732-499-0111; **Board Cert:** Urology 2014; **Med School:** SUNY Stony Brook 1997; **Resid:** Surgery, IU Hlth Hosp 1999; Urologic Surgery, IU Hlth Hosp 2003

Vascular Surgery

Brener, Bruce J MD (VascS) - **Spec Exp:** Endovascular Surgery; Minimally Invasive Vascular Surgery; Carotid Artery Surgery; Aneurysm-Aortic; **Hospital:** Newark Beth Israel Med Ctr (page 94), St. Barnabas Med Ctr (page 94); **Address:** Vascular Assocs of NJ, 200 S Orange Ave, Ste 109, Livingston, NJ 07039; **Phone:** 973-322-7233; **Board Cert:** Surgery 1972; Vascular Surgery 2005; **Med School:** Harvard Med Sch 1966; **Resid:** Surgery, Chldns Hosp 1968; Surgery, Brigham & Women's Hosp 1972; **Fellow:** Vascular Surgery, Mass Genl Hosp 1973; **Fac Appt:** Assoc Clin Prof S, Columbia P&S

Hertz, Steven MD (VascS) - **Hospital:** St. Barnabas Med Ctr (page 94); **Address:** 1500 Pleasant Valley Way, Ste 302, West Orange, NJ 07052; **Phone:** 973-324-0988; **Board Cert:** Vascular Surgery 2012; **Med School:** Albert Einstein Coll Med 1987; **Resid:** Surgery, Mount Sinai Med Ctr 1992; **Fellow:** Vascular Surgery, Hosp U Penn 1993

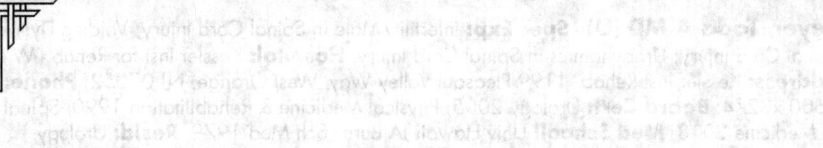 

Hudson

Hudson

Cardiovascular Disease

Cruz, Merle C MD (Cv) - **Spec Exp:** Heart Disease; **Hospital:** Hoboken Univ Med Ctr - Hoboken; **Address:** 268 St Pauls Ave, Jersey City, NJ 07306; **Phone:** 201-653-7533; **Board Cert:** Internal Medicine 1983; Cardiovascular Disease 1985; **Med School:** Philippines 1976; **Resid:** Internal Medicine, Jersey City Med Ctr 1982; **Fellow:** Cardiovascular Disease, Brookdale Univ Hosp Med Ctr 1984

Elkind, Barry M MD (Cv) - **Spec Exp:** Non-Invasive Cardiology; Preventive Cardiology; Nutrition; **Hospital:** Bayonne Med Ctr, Newark Beth Israel Med Ctr (page 94); **Address:** Assocs Cardiovascular Care, 1061 Avenue C, Bayonne, NJ 07002; **Phone:** 201-858-0800; **Board Cert:** Internal Medicine 1979; Cardiovascular Disease 1981; **Med School:** UMDNJ-NJ Med Sch, Newark 1976; **Resid:** Internal Medicine, Boston Med Ctr 1979; **Fellow:** Cardiovascular Disease, Tufts Med Ctr 1982

Moussa, Ghias M MD (Cv) - **Spec Exp:** Heart Valve Disease; Congestive Heart Failure; **Hospital:** Christ Hosp - Jersey City; **Address:** 1815 Kennedy Blvd, Jersey City, NJ 07305; **Phone:** 201-333-3311; **Board Cert:** Internal Medicine 1989; **Med School:** Syria 1979; **Resid:** Internal Medicine, Jersey City Med Ctr 1989; **Fellow:** Cardiovascular Disease, Jersey City Med Ctr 1991; **Fac Appt:** Assoc Prof Med, UMDNJ-NJ Med Sch, Newark

Child Neurology

McAbee, Gary N DO (ChiN) - **Spec Exp:** Autism; Epilepsy; Headache; **Hospital:** Hoboken Univ Med Ctr - Hoboken; **Address:** 6017 Bergenline Ave, West New York, NJ 07093; **Phone:** 201-766-9666; **Board Cert:** Pediatrics 1988; Child Neurology 1988; **Med School:** Univ Osteo Med & Hlth Sci, Des Moines 1980; **Resid:** Pediatrics, NY Med Coll 1982; **Fellow:** Child Neurology, St Louis Chldns Hosp 1985; **Fac Appt:** Prof N, Seton Hall Univ Sch Hlth & Med Scis

Dermatology

Blank, Ellen MD (D) - **Spec Exp:** Acne; **Hospital:** Mt Sinai Hosp; **Address:** 333 Avenue C, Bayonne, NJ 07002; **Phone:** 201-858-4800; **Board Cert:** Dermatology 1979; **Med School:** Mount Sinai Sch Med 1975; **Resid:** Dermatology, Mount Sinai Hosp 1979

Kopec, Anna V MD (D) - **Spec Exp:** Cosmetic Dermatology; Hair & Nail Disorders; **Hospital:** Bayonne Med Ctr; **Address:** 730 Kennedy Blvd, Bayonne, NJ 07002-1838; **Phone:** 201-858-4300; **Board Cert:** Dermatology 2009; **Med School:** UMDNJ-NJ Med Sch, Newark 1975; **Resid:** Dermatology, Albert Einstein 1979; **Fac Appt:** Assoc Clin Prof D, Albert Einstein Coll Med

Endocrinology, Diabetes & Metabolism

Cam, Jenny Rose G MD (EDM) - **Spec Exp:** Diabetes; Thyroid Disorders; Osteoporosis; Adrenal Disorders; **Hospital:** Hoboken Univ Med Ctr - Hoboken, Christ Hosp - Jersey City; **Address:** 10 Huron Ave, Ste 1P, Jersey City, NJ 07306; **Phone:** 201-656-6003; **Board Cert:** Internal Medicine 1988; Endocrinology, Diabetes & Metabolism 1989; **Med School:** Philippines 1979; **Resid:** Internal Medicine, Interfaith Med Ctr 1987; **Fellow:** Endocrinology, Diabetes & Metabolism, UMDNJ-Univ Hosp 1989

Family Medicine

Levine, Martin S DO (FMed) *PCP* - **Spec Exp:** Primary Care Sports Medicine; Osteopathic Manipulation; **Hospital:** Christ Hosp - Jersey City, Bayonne Med Ctr; **Address:** 789 Avenue C, Bayonne, NJ 07002; **Phone:** 201-339-2620; **Board Cert:** Family Medicine 2007; Geriatric Medicine 2011; **Med School:** Kirksville Coll Osteo Med 1980; **Resid:** Family Medicine, Kennedy Meml Hosp 1983; **Fac Appt:** Prof FMed, Touro Coll Osteopathic Med-NY

Pollak, Joseph A MD (FMed) - **Spec Exp:** Preventive Medicine; Sports Medicine; Geriatric Medicine; **Hospital:** Hackensack Univ Med Ctr (page 96); **Address:** 232 Washington St, Hoboken, NJ 07030; **Phone:** 201-795-9909; **Board Cert:** Family Medicine 2005; Geriatric Medicine 2012; **Med School:** Rutgers-NJ Med Sch 1981; **Resid:** Family Medicine, St. Mary's Hosp 1984

Sklower, Jay A DO (FMed) *PCP* - **Spec Exp:** Geriatric Medicine; Diabetes; Cholesterol/Lipid Disorders; **Hospital:** Christ Hosp - Jersey City; **Address:** 100 Journal Square, Jersey City, NJ 07306-2929; **Phone:** 201-216-3040; **Board Cert:** Family Medicine 2005; **Med School:** SUNY Stony Brook 1971; **Resid:** Family Medicine, Union Meml Hosp 1973; **Fac Appt:** Assoc Prof Ped

Gastroenterology

Hahn, John C MD (Ge) - **Spec Exp:** Colonoscopy; Peptic Acid Disorders; **Hospital:** Bayonne Med Ctr; **Address:** 534 Avenue E, Ste 1C, Bayonne, NJ 07002; **Phone:** 201-823-0450; **Board Cert:** Internal Medicine 1988; Gastroenterology 2011; **Med School:** UMDNJ-NJ Med Sch, Newark 1985; **Resid:** Internal Medicine, Univ Hosp 1988; **Fellow:** Gastroenterology, Univ Hosp 1990

Prakash, Anaka MD (Ge) - **Spec Exp:** Pancreatic/Biliary Endoscopy (ERCP); Capsule Endoscopy; **Hospital:** Bayonne Med Ctr, Jersey City Med Ctr (page 94); **Address:** 534 Ave E, Ste 1A, Bayonne, NJ 07002; **Phone:** 201-858-8444; **Board Cert:** Internal Medicine 1976; Gastroenterology 1977; **Med School:** India 1970; **Resid:** Internal Medicine, St Joseph's Hosp 1975; **Fellow:** Gastroenterology, CMDNJ-Newark 1977

Geriatric Medicine

Brown, Mitchell Lee MD (Ger) *PCP* - **Spec Exp:** Alzheimer's Disease; **Hospital:** Bayonne Med Ctr, Jersey City Med Ctr (page 94); **Address:** 758 Broadway, Bayonne, NJ 07002; **Phone:** 201-339-2220; **Board Cert:** Internal Medicine 2013; Geriatric Medicine 2013; **Med School:** Dominica 1987; **Resid:** Internal Medicine, St Elizabeth Hosp 1990; **Fellow:** Geriatric Medicine, St Vincent's Hosp & Med Ctr 1992

Reisner, Michelle R MD (Ger) *PCP* - **Spec Exp:** Frail Elderly; **Hospital:** Jersey City Med Ctr (page 94); **Address:** 196 Jewitt Ave, Jersey City, NJ 07304; **Phone:** 201-433-3335; **Board Cert:** Internal Medicine 1989; Geriatric Medicine 2005; Hospice & Palliative Medicine 2008; **Med School:** South Africa 1983; **Resid:** Internal Medicine, Jersey City Med Ctr 1989; **Fac Appt:** Asst Prof Med, Mount Sinai Sch Med

Internal Medicine

Cardiello, Gary P MD (IM) *PCP* - **Spec Exp:** Diabetes; Hypertension; Hemochromatosis; **Hospital:** Clara Maass Med Ctr (page 94), Saint Michael's Med Ctr; **Address:** 744 Broadway, Bayonne, NJ 07002; **Phone:** 201-436-8888; **Board Cert:** Internal Medicine 1986; **Med School:** Italy 1983; **Resid:** Internal Medicine, St Michael's Med Ctr 1986

Condo, Dominick MD (IM) *PCP* - **Spec Exp:** Geriatric Care; **Hospital:** Bayonne Med Ctr, Overlook Med Ctr (page 92); **Address:** 622 Broadway, Bayonne, NJ 07002; **Phone:** 201-436-2800; **Board Cert:** Internal Medicine 1984; **Med School:** Mexico 1980; **Resid:** Internal Medicine, St Michaels Med Ctr 1984

Dedousis, John T MD (IM) *PCP* - **Hospital:** Bayonne Med Ctr; **Address:** 1166 Kennedy Blvd, Bayonne, NJ 07002-3112; **Phone:** 201-339-1133; **Board Cert:** Internal Medicine 2013; **Med School:** Dominica 1984; **Resid:** Internal Medicine, Univ Hosp 1988

Kozel, Joseph M MD (IM) *PCP* - **Spec Exp:** Asthma; Chronic Obstructive Lung Disease (COPD); Lung Cancer; Lung Disease in Pregnancy; **Hospital:** Hoboken Univ Med Ctr - Hoboken, Jersey City Med Ctr (page 94); **Address:** 331 Grand St, Fl Ground, Hoboken, NJ 07030; **Phone:** 201-656-3519; **Board Cert:** Internal Medicine 1984; **Med School:** Mexico 1973; **Resid:** Family Medicine, St Mary Hosp 1979; Internal Medicine, St Michaels Med Ctr 1980; **Fellow:** Pulmonary Disease, St Michaels Med Ctr 1982

Mutterperl, Mitchell MD (IM) *PCP* - **Spec Exp:** Hypertension; Cholesterol/Lipid Disorders; Cardiovascular Disease; **Hospital:** Bayonne Med Ctr, Jersey City Med Ctr (page 94); **Address:** 19 W 33rd St, Bayonne, NJ 07002-3916; **Phone:** 201-858-0090; **Board Cert:** Internal Medicine 1985; **Med School:** Italy 1981; **Resid:** Internal Medicine, UMDNJ-NJ Med Ctr 1985

Nephrology

Thomsen, Stephen MD (Nep) - **Spec Exp:** Diabetes; Hypertension; Kidney Disease; **Hospital:** Christ Hosp - Jersey City, Hackensack UMC-Mountainside (page 802); **Address:** 510 31st St, Union City, NJ 07087; **Phone:** 201-866-3322; **Board Cert:** Internal Medicine 1981; Nephrology 2006; **Med School:** Italy 1977; **Resid:** Internal Medicine, Mountainside Hosp 1980; **Fellow:** Nephrology, Univ Hosp-UMDNJ 1982

Neurology

Anselmi, Gregory D MD (N) - **Spec Exp:** Migraine; Multiple Sclerosis; Stroke; **Hospital:** Bayonne Med Ctr, Hoboken Univ Med Ctr - Hoboken; **Address:** 1222 Kennedy Blvd, Bayonne, NJ 07002-3822; **Phone:** 201-339-6531; **Board Cert:** Neurology 2009; Vascular Neurology 2009; **Med School:** Italy 1988; **Resid:** Internal Medicine, SUNY/Univ Hosp 1989; **Fellow:** Neurology, St Vincent's Hosp & Med Ctr 1992

Charles, James A MD (N) - **Spec Exp:** Headache; Clinical Neurophysiology; **Hospital:** Bayonne Med Ctr, Holy Name Med Ctr (page 738); **Address:** 956 Kennedy Blvd Fl 1st, Bayonne, NJ 07002; **Phone:** 201-858-2457; **Board Cert:** Neurology 1984; Clinical Neurophysiology 2005; **Med School:** UMDNJ-NJ Med Sch, Newark 1978; **Resid:** Neurology, UMDNJ Med Ctr 1982; **Fac Appt:** Asst Clin Prof N, UMDNJ-NJ Med Sch, Newark

Sadeghi, Hooshang W MD (N) - **Spec Exp:** Parkinson's Disease; Stroke; Multiple Sclerosis; Dystonia-Cervical; **Hospital:** Bayonne Med Ctr, Jersey City Med Ctr (page 94); **Address:** 631 Broadway, FL 3, Bayonne, NJ 07002-3846; **Phone:** 201-823-2888; **Board Cert:** Neurology 1977; **Med School:** Iran 1967; **Resid:** Neurology, UMDNJ Med Ctr 1975; **Fac Appt:** Asst Clin Prof N, UMDNJ-NJ Med Sch, Newark

Obstetrics & Gynecology

Banzon, Manuel B MD (ObG) - **Spec Exp:** Laparoscopic Surgery; Vaginal Surgery; Incontinence; **Hospital:** Meadowlands Hosp Med Ctr, Jersey City Med Ctr (page 94); **Address:** 1265 Paterson Plank Rd, Ste 3D, Secaucus, NJ 07094; **Phone:** 201-864-4442; **Board Cert:** Obstetrics & Gynecology 1979; **Med School:** Philippines 1962; **Resid:** Obstetrics & Gynecology, Jersey City Med Ctr 1969

Masson, Lalitha MD (ObG) - **Spec Exp:** Infertility; **Hospital:** Christ Hosp - Jersey City; **Address:** 634 Newark Ave, Main Fl, Jersey City, NJ 07306; **Phone:** 201-963-8554; **Board Cert:** Obstetrics & Gynecology 1973; **Med School:** India 1964; **Resid:** Obstetrics & Gynecology, Jersey City Med Ctr 1968; Obstetrics & Gynecology, St Clares Hosp 1970; **Fellow:** Infertility, UMDNJ-NJ Sch Med Affil Hosps 1971

Uy, Vena MD (ObG) *PCP* - **Hospital:** Christ Hosp - Jersey City, Meadowlands Hosp Med Ctr; **Address:** 142 Palisade Ave, Ste 102, Jersey City, NJ 07306; **Phone:** 201-653-0506; **Board Cert:** Obstetrics & Gynecology 1977; **Med School:** Philippines 1968; **Resid:** Obstetrics & Gynecology, Jersey Shore Univ Med Ctr 1973; **Fellow:** Gynecologic Pathology, Magee-Womens Hosp - UPMC 1974

Ophthalmology

Benedetto, Dominick A MD (Oph) - **Spec Exp:** LASIK-Refractive Surgery; Cataract Surgery; **Hospital:** Bayonne Med Ctr, Morristown Med Ctr (page 92); **Address:** EyeMD Assocs, 124 Avenue B, Ste 1, Bayonne, NJ 07002-2033; **Phone:** 201-436-1150; **Board Cert:** Ophthalmology 1982; **Med School:** Univ Fla Coll Med 1975; **Resid:** Ophthalmology, Wills Eye Hosp 1981

Constad, William H MD (Oph) - **Spec Exp:** Cornea Transplant; Cataract Surgery; Refractive Surgery; LASIK-Refractive Surgery; **Hospital:** Jersey City Med Ctr (page 94); **Address:** 600 Pavonia Ave Fl 6, Jersey City, NJ 07306; **Phone:** 201-963-3937; **Board Cert:** Ophthalmology 1985; **Med School:** Med Coll PA Hahnemann 1980; **Resid:** Ophthalmology, Univ Hosp-UMDNJ 1984; **Fellow:** Cornea, New York Eye & Ear Infirm 1985; **Fac Appt:** Clin Prof Oph, UMDNJ-NJ Med Sch, Newark

Orthopaedic Surgery

Granatir, Charles E MD (OrS) - **Spec Exp:** Joint Replacement; Arthroscopic Surgery-Knee; Shoulder Injuries; Sports Medicine; **Hospital:** Clara Maass Med Ctr (page 94); **Address:** 586 Kearny Ave, Kearny, NJ 07032; **Phone:** 201-997-7667; **Board Cert:** Orthopaedic Surgery 2010; **Med School:** Hahnemann Univ 1979; **Resid:** Orthopaedic Surgery, Montefiore Med Ctr 1984

Otolaryngology

Garay, Kenneth F MD (Oto) - **Spec Exp:** Nasal & Sinus Disorders; Sleep Disorders; Hearing Loss; Balance Disorders; **Hospital:** Jersey City Med Ctr (page 94); **Address:** 377 Jersey Ave, Ste 220, Jersey City, NJ 07302; **Phone:** 201-224-4155; **Board Cert:** Otolaryngology 1982; **Med School:** Temple Univ 1978; **Resid:** Surgery, Abington Meml Hosp 1979; Otolaryngology, NY-Presby/Columbia Univ Med Ctr 1982

Pediatrics

Baker, Azzam A MD (Ped) *PCP* - **Hospital:** Hackensack Univ Med Ctr (page 96), Palisades Med Ctr; **Address:** Riverside Pediatric Group, 714 10th St, Secaucus, NJ 07094-2921; **Phone:** 201-863-3346; **Board Cert:** Pediatrics 2011; **Med School:** Egypt 1972; **Resid:** Pediatrics, Jersey City Med Ctr 1978; **Fellow:** Neonatal-Perinatal Medicine, UMDNJ Univ Hosp 1980

Klos, Andrzej E MD (Ped) *PCP* - **Spec Exp:** Neonatal Care; Nutrition; Preventive Medicine; **Hospital:** Hoboken Univ Med Ctr - Hoboken, Hackensack Univ Med Ctr (page 96); **Address:** Hoboken Pediatrics, 1327 Willow Ave, Hoboken, NJ 07030; **Phone:** 201-963-5633; **Board Cert:** Pediatrics 2013; **Med School:** Poland 1977; **Resid:** Pediatrics, Jersey City Med Ctr 1994; **Fac Appt:** Asst Clin Prof Ped, UMDNJ-NJ Med Sch, Newark

Oko, Piotr W MD (Ped) *PCP* - **Hospital:** Christ Hosp - Jersey City, Hoboken Univ Med Ctr - Hoboken; **Address:** Hoboken Pediatrics, 1327 Willow Ave, Hoboken, NJ 07030; **Phone:** 201-963-5633; **Board Cert:** Pediatrics 2010; **Med School:** Poland 1987; **Resid:** Pediatrics, Jersey City Med Ctr 1995

Skripkus, Aldona J MD (Ped) *PCP* - **Hospital:** Clara Maass Med Ctr (page 94); **Address:** 381 Kearny Ave, Kearny, NJ 07032-2603; **Phone:** 201-991-4824; **Board Cert:** Pediatrics 1973; **Med School:** Med Coll PA Hahnemann 1966; **Resid:** Pediatrics, Chldns Hosp 1969

Physical Medicine & Rehabilitation

Filippone, Mark A MD (PMR) - **Spec Exp:** Electrodiagnosis; Electromyography; Pain Management; **Hospital:** Christ Hosp - Jersey City, Hoboken Univ Med Ctr - Hoboken; **Address:** 2012 John F Kennedy Blvd W, Jersey City, NJ 07305-1526; **Phone:** 201-332-6855; **Board Cert:** Physical Medicine & Rehabilitation 1980; **Med School:** Georgetown Univ 1974; **Resid:** Pediatrics, St Vincent's Hosp & Med Ctr 1976; Physical Medicine & Rehabilitation, Bronx Muni Hosp-Einstein 1979; **Fac Appt:** Asst Clin Prof PMR, Albert Einstein Coll Med

Psychiatry

Gewolb, Eric B MD (Psyc) - **Spec Exp:** Anxiety Disorders; Dementia; Bipolar/Mood Disorders; **Hospital:** Bayonne Med Ctr; **Address:** 830 Kennedy Blvd, Bayonne, NJ 07002-2872; **Phone:** 201-339-0200; **Board Cert:** Psychiatry 1979; **Med School:** Tulane Univ 1974; **Resid:** Psychiatry, Mount Sinai Hosp 1978

Jacoby, Jacob H MD/PhD (Psyc) - **Spec Exp:** Psychopharmacology; Mood Disorders; **Hospital:** Bayonne Med Ctr, St. Barnabas Med Ctr (page 94); **Address:** 654 Avenue C, Ste 201, Bayonne, NJ 07002-3899; **Phone:** 201-339-0323; **Board Cert:** Psychiatry 1993; **Med School:** SUNY Buffalo 1980; **Resid:** Psychiatry, Western Psychiatric Inst 1983; **Fellow:** Psychiatry, Montefiore Med Ctr 1984; **Fac Appt:** Assoc Clin Prof Psyc, UMDNJ-NJ Med Sch, Newark

Kurani, Devendra MD (Psyc) - **Spec Exp:** Depression; Anxiety Disorders; Panic Disorder; **Hospital:** St. Barnabas Med Ctr (page 94), Christ Hosp - Jersey City; **Address:** 221 Palisade Ave, Jersey City, NJ 07306; **Phone:** 201-656-3116; **Board Cert:** Psychiatry 1986; **Med School:** India 1975; **Resid:** Psychiatry, Warley Hosp 1981; Psychiatry, Harlem Hosp 1983

Moraille, Pascale MD (Psyc) - **Spec Exp:** Autism; Developmental Disorders; ADD/ADHD; **Hospital:** Hoboken Univ Med Ctr - Hoboken; **Address:** CMHC of Hoboken Univ Med Ctr, 506 Third St, Hoboken, NJ 07030; **Phone:** 201-792-8200; **Board Cert:** Psychiatry 1993; **Med School:** Ponce Med Sch 1988; **Resid:** Psychiatry, UMDNJ-Univ Hosp 1991; **Fellow:** Child & Adolescent Psychiatry, UMDNJ-Univ Hosp 1993

Pulmonary Disease

Elamir, Mazhar E MD (Pul) - **Spec Exp:** Sleep Disorders; Allergy; Asthma; **Hospital:** Christ Hosp - Jersey City, Hackensack Univ Med Ctr (page 96); **Address:** 192 Harrison Ave, Jersey City, NJ 07304; **Phone:** 201-333-5363; **Board Cert:** Internal Medicine 1987; Pulmonary Disease 2004; Sleep Medicine 2011; **Med School:** Egypt 1981; **Resid:** Internal Medicine, Jersey City Med Ctr 1987; **Fellow:** Pulmonary Disease, Interfaith Med Ctr 1990

Rheumatology

Scarpa, Nicholas P MD (Rhu) - **Spec Exp:** Lupus/SLE in Pregnancy; Rheumatoid Arthritis; Osteoporosis; **Hospital:** Christ Hosp - Jersey City; **Address:** Arthritis center of New Jersey, 600 Pavonia Ave Fl 5 - Ste 1, Jersey City, NJ 07306-2932; **Phone:** 201-216-3050; **Board Cert:** Internal Medicine 1983; Rheumatology 1986; **Med School:** UMDNJ-NJ Med Sch, Newark 1980; **Resid:** Internal Medicine, Hackensack Univ Med Ctr 1983; **Fellow:** Rheumatology, Hosp for Special Surgery 1985; **Fac Appt:** Asst Clin Prof Med, UMDNJ-NJ Med Sch, Newark

Surgery

Sultan, Ronald H MD (S) - **Spec Exp:** Thyroid Surgery; Breast Cancer & Surgery; Gallbladder Surgery; **Hospital:** Jersey City Med Ctr (page 94), Palisades Med Ctr; **Address:** 2255 John F Kennedy Blvd, Jersey City, NJ 07304-1428; **Phone:** 201-434-3305; **Board Cert:** Surgery 2009; **Med School:** NYU Sch Med 1973; **Resid:** Surgery, Bronx Muni Hosp 1977; Surgery, Albert Einstein Med Ctr 1980

Urology

Katz, Herbert I MD (U) - **Spec Exp:** Urologic Cancer; Erectile Dysfunction; Kidney Stones; Prostate Disease; **Hospital:** Bayonne Med Ctr; **Address:** Urology Grp of NJ, 534 Ave E, Ste 2A, Bayonne, NJ 7002; **Phone:** 201-823-1303; **Board Cert:** Urology 1981; **Med School:** Temple Univ 1974; **Resid:** Surgery, Abington Meml Hosp 1976; Urology, Montefiore Med Ctr 1979

Shulman, Yale MD (U) - **Spec Exp:** Urologic Cancer; Kidney Stones; Sexual Dysfunction; Incontinence; **Hospital:** Christ Hosp - Jersey City, Englewood Hosp & Med Ctr; **Address:** Shulman Urology, 2255 Kennedy Blvd, Jersey City, NJ 07304-1428; **Phone:** 201-433-1057; **Board Cert:** Urology 1984; **Med School:** Albert Einstein Coll Med 1976; **Resid:** Surgery, Montefiore Hosp Med Ctr 1978; Urology, NYU Med Ctr 1982; **Fac Appt:** Assoc Clin Prof U, NYU Sch Med

Steigman, Elliot G MD (U) - **Spec Exp:** Kidney Stones; Prostate Benign Disease; **Hospital:** Christ Hosp - Jersey City; **Address:** Sovereign Med Grp, Urology, 142 Palisade Ave, Ste 211, Jersey City, NJ 07306; **Phone:** 201-435-2244; **Board Cert:** Urology 1982; **Med School:** SUNY Downstate 1975; **Resid:** Surgery, Brookdale Hosp Med Ctr 1977; Urology, SUNY Downstate Med Ctr 1980

Vascular & Interventional Radiology

Smith, Peter L MD (VIR) - **Spec Exp:** Varicose Veins; Vein Disorders; **Hospital:** Bayonne Med Ctr; **Address:** Bayonne Med Ctr, Vein Treatment Ctr, 29 E 29th St, Bayonne, NJ 07002; **Phone:** 201-858-4590; **Board Cert:** Diagnostic Radiology 1992; Vascular & Interventional Radiology 2006; **Med School:** Washington Univ, St Louis 1987; **Resid:** Diagnostic Radiology, Mass Genl Hosp 1992; **Fellow:** Vascular & Interventional Radiology, Mass Geml Hosp 1995

Vascular Surgery

McGovern Jr, Patrick J MD (VascS) - **Spec Exp:** Dialysis Access Surgery; Aneurysm-Aortic; Carotid Artery Surgery; Endovascular Surgery; **Hospital:** Christ Hosp - Jersey City, Bayonne Med Ctr; **Address:** 17 Nardone Pl, Jersey City, NJ 07306; **Phone:** 201-656-0646; **Board Cert:** Surgery 2013; Vascular Surgery 2008; **Med School:** UMDNJ-NJ Med Sch, Newark 1978; **Resid:** Surgery, UMDNJ-Univ Hosp 1983; **Fellow:** Vascular Surgery, UMDNJ-RWJ Univ Hosp 1984

The Best in American Medicine
www.CastleConnolly.com

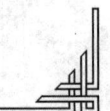

Mercer

Mercer

Allergy & Immunology

Ricketti, Anthony J MD (A&I) - **Spec Exp:** Asthma in Pregnancy; Allergic Aspergillosis; Eosinophilic Lung Disorders; **Hospital:** St. Francis Med Ctr - Trenton, Robert Wood Johnson Univ Hosp Hamilton; **Address:** Allergy & Pulmonary Assocs, 1542 Kuser Rd, Ste B7, Trenton, NJ 08619; **Phone:** 609-581-1400; **Board Cert:** Internal Medicine 1981; Allergy & Immunology 1983; Pulmonary Disease 1986; Critical Care Medicine 2009; **Med School:** Hahnemann Univ 1978; **Resid:** Internal Medicine, Cleveland Clin Fdn 1981; **Fellow:** Allergy & Immunology, Northwestern Meml Hosp 1982; Pulmonary Disease, Northwestern Meml Hosp 1984; **Fac Appt:** Asst Clin Prof Med, Rutgers R W Johnson Med Sch

Cardiovascular Disease

Costin, Andrew MD (Cv) - **Spec Exp:** Nuclear Cardiology; Echocardiography; **Hospital:** Univ Med Ctr Princeton at Plainsboro; **Address:** Princeton Med Grp, 419 N Harrison St, Princeton, NJ 08540; **Phone:** 609-924-9300; **Board Cert:** Internal Medicine 1989; Cardiovascular Disease 2013; Nuclear Cardiology 2007; Echocardiography 2011; **Med School:** Yale Univ 1986; **Resid:** Internal Medicine, NY-Presby/Weill Cornell Med Ctr 1989; **Fellow:** Cardiovascular Disease, Hosp Univ Penn 1993

Mahalingam, Banu MD (Cv) - **Spec Exp:** Heart Disease in Women; Echocardiography; Preventive Cardiology; Nuclear Cardiology; **Hospital:** Univ Med Ctr Princeton at Plainsboro, Robert Wood Johnson Univ Hosp - New Brunswick; **Address:** Cardiac Assocs Princeton, 731 Alexander Rd, Ste 202, Princeton, NJ 08542; **Phone:** 609-921-7456; **Board Cert:** Internal Medicine 2008; Cardiovascular Disease 2012; Echocardiography 2013; **Med School:** India 1995; **Resid:** Internal Medicine, RW Johnson Univ Hosp 1998; **Fellow:** Cardiovascular Disease, RW Johnson Univ Hosp 2001

Dermatology

Bagel, Jerry MD (D) - **Spec Exp:** Psoriasis; Atopic Dermatitis; Exfoliate Erythroderma; Skin Cancer & Moles; **Hospital:** Univ Med Ctr Princeton at Plainsboro; **Address:** 59 One Mile Rd, Ste G, East Windsor, NJ 08520-2505; **Phone:** 609-443-4500; **Board Cert:** Dermatology 1985; **Med School:** Mount Sinai Sch Med 1981; **Resid:** Dermatology, Columbia-Presby Med Ctr 1985

Notterman, Robyn MD (D) - **Spec Exp:** Melanoma; Skin Cancer; **Hospital:** Univ Med Ctr Princeton at Plainsboro; **Address:** Princeton Dermatology, 800 Bunn Drive, Ste 201, Princeton, NJ 08540; **Phone:** 609-924-1033; **Board Cert:** Dermatology 2013; **Med School:** Cornell Univ-Weill Med Coll 1983; **Resid:** Dermatology, NYU Med Ctr 1992

Diagnostic Radiology

Compito, Gerard A MD (DR) - **Hospital:** Univ Med Ctr Princeton at Plainsboro; **Address:** Princeton Radiology Assocs, 419 N Harrison St, Princeton, NJ 08540; **Phone:** 732-821-5563; **Board Cert:** Diagnostic Radiology 1990; Neuroradiology 2005; **Med School:** SUNY Upstate Med Univ 1985; **Resid:** Diagnostic Radiology, NY Hosp-Cornell 1990; **Fellow:** Neuroradiology, NY Hosp-Cornell 1992

Ford, Robert R MD (DR) - **Spec Exp:** CT Scan; MRI; Nuclear Medicine; Ultrasound; **Hospital:** Univ Med Ctr Princeton at Plainsboro; **Address:** Princeton Radiology Assocs, 419 N Harrison St, Princeton, NJ 08540; **Phone:** 732-821-5563; **Board Cert:** Diagnostic Radiology 1988; Neuroradiology 2009; **Med School:** UMDNJ-Rutgers Med Sch 1983; **Resid:** Diagnostic Radiology, NY Presby Hosp 1988

Endocrinology, Diabetes & Metabolism

Shelmet, John J MD (EDM) - **Spec Exp:** Diabetes; Metabolic Disorders; **Hospital:** Univ Med Ctr Princeton at Plainsboro; **Address:** 3131 Princeton Pike, Bldg 2B, Ste 104, Lawrenceville, NJ 08648-2526; **Phone:** 609-896-8050; **Board Cert:** Internal Medicine 1984; **Med School:** Rutgers R W Johnson Med Sch 1981; **Resid:** Internal Medicine, Middlesex Genl Hosp/Univ Hosp 1984; **Fellow:** Metabolism, Temple Univ 1986; Diabetes, Temple Univ 1988; **Fac Appt:** Clin Prof Med, Rutgers R W Johnson Med Sch

Family Medicine

Lansing, Martha MD (FMed) *PCP* - **Spec Exp:** Chronic Illness; Women's Health; Psychosomatic Disorders; **Hospital:** Capital Health Regl Med Ctr, Robert Wood Johnson Univ Hosp - New Brunswick; **Address:** 433 Bellevue Ave, Fl 4th, Trenton, NJ 08618; **Phone:** 609-278-5900; **Board Cert:** Family Medicine 2005; **Med School:** Univ Okla Coll Med 1982; **Resid:** Family Medicine, Univ Tenn Afill Hosp 1984; Family Medicine, Williamsport Hosp/Univ Penn 1985; **Fac Appt:** Assoc Prof FMed, UMDNJ-Rutgers Med Sch

Rednor, Jeffrey D DO (FMed) *PCP* - **Spec Exp:** Diabetes; Pain-Back; Preventive Cardiology; **Hospital:** Robert Wood Johnson Univ Hosp Hamilton; **Address:** 1 Washington Blvd, Ste A, Robbinsville, NJ 08691; **Phone:** 609-448-4353; **Board Cert:** Family Medicine 1992; **Med School:** UMDNJ Sch Osteo Med 1989; **Resid:** Family Medicine, Kennedy Meml Hosp 1992

Gastroenterology

Afridi, Shariq A MD (Ge) - **Spec Exp:** Liver Disease; Endoscopy; **Hospital:** Robert Wood Johnson Univ Hosp Hamilton, St. Francis Med Ctr - Trenton; **Address:** 1374 White Horse Square Rd, Yorkshire Bldg - Fl 2, Hamilton, NJ 08690; **Phone:** 609-586-1319; **Board Cert:** Gastroenterology 2013; **Med School:** Pakistan 1986; **Resid:** Internal Medicine, Bridgeport Hosp 1991; **Fellow:** Gastroenterology, Bridgeport Hosp 1993

De Antonio, Joseph R MD (Ge) - **Spec Exp:** Liver Disease; **Hospital:** Capital Health Regl Med Ctr; **Address:** 3100 Princeton Pike, Bldg 4 - Ste C, Lawrenceville, NJ 08648; **Phone:** 609-882-2185; **Board Cert:** Internal Medicine 1989; Gastroenterology 2004; **Med School:** St Louis Univ 1982; **Resid:** Internal Medicine, VA Med Ctr 1989; **Fellow:** Gastroenterology, Bellevue Hosp Ctr 1991

Meirowitz, Robert F MD (Ge) - **Spec Exp:** Inflammatory Bowel Disease; Colon Polyps & Cancer; Colonoscopy; Gastroesophageal Reflux Disease (GERD); **Hospital:** Univ Med Ctr Princeton at Plainsboro; **Address:** Princeton Gastroenterology Assocs, 731 Alexander Rd, Ste 100, Princeton, NJ 08540; **Phone:** 609-924-1422; **Board Cert:** Internal Medicine 1987; Gastroenterology 2012; **Med School:** NY Med Coll 1984; **Resid:** Internal Medicine, RW Johnson Univ Hosp 1988; **Fellow:** Gastroenterology, Univ MD Med Ctr 1990; **Fac Appt:** Asst Clin Prof Med, Rutgers R W Johnson Med Sch

Rosner, Bruce P MD (Ge) - **Spec Exp:** Liver Disease; Gastroesophageal Reflux Disease (GERD); Colon Cancer; **Hospital:** St. Francis Med Ctr - Trenton; **Address:** Gastroenterology Assocs, 2275 Whitehorse Mercerville Rd, Ste 6, Trenton, NJ 08619-2643; **Phone:** 609-890-0200; **Board Cert:** Internal Medicine 1979; Gastroenterology 1983; **Med School:** Univ Pennsylvania 1976; **Resid:** Internal Medicine, Penn Hosp 1979; **Fellow:** Gastroenterology, Hahnemann Univ 1981

Rubin, Marc R MD (Ge) - **Hospital:** St. Francis Med Ctr - Trenton; **Address:** Gastroenterology Assocs, 2275 Whitehorse Mercerville Rd, Ste 2, Trenton, NJ 08619-2643; **Phone:** 609-890-0200; **Board Cert:** Internal Medicine 1977; Gastroenterology 1979; **Med School:** Albert Einstein Coll Med 1974; **Resid:** Internal Medicine, Penn Hosp 1977; **Fellow:** Gastroenterology, Univ Hosp 1979

Hand Surgery

Ark, Jon Wong Tze-Jen MD (HS) - **Spec Exp:** Hand Surgery; Carpal Tunnel Syndrome; Foot & Ankle Surgery; Arthritis Hand Surgery; **Hospital:** Univ Med Ctr Princeton at Plainsboro; **Address:** 325 Princeton Ave, Princeton, NJ 08540; **Phone:** 609-924-8131; **Board Cert:** Orthopaedic Surgery 2007; Hand Surgery 2007; **Med School:** Rutgers R W Johnson Med Sch 1987; **Resid:** Orthopaedic Surgery, Columbia-Presby Med Ctr 1992; **Fellow:** Hand Surgery, Mass Genl Hosp 1993; Foot & Ankle Surgery, Jefferson Hosp 1995

Infectious Disease

Aufiero, Patrick MD (Inf) - **Spec Exp:** AIDS/HIV; Lyme Disease; Osteomyelitis; Skin/Soft Tissue Infections; **Hospital:** Robert Wood Johnson Univ Hosp Hamilton, Capital Health Med Ctr - Hopewell; **Address:** 2085 Klockner Rd, Hamilton, NJ 08690; **Phone:** 609-587-4122; **Board Cert:** Internal Medicine 2005; Infectious Disease 2006; **Med School:** Grenada 1984; **Resid:** Internal Medicine, St Michaels Med Ctr 1989; **Fellow:** Infectious Disease, St Michaels Med Ctr 1991

Gekowski, Kathleen MD (Inf) - **Spec Exp:** Travel Medicine; AIDS/HIV; Lyme Disease; **Hospital:** Capital Health Med Ctr - Hopewell, Robert Wood Johnson Univ Hosp Hamilton; **Address:** 1450 Parkside Ave, Ste 4, Ewing, NJ 08638; **Phone:** 609-882-3500; **Board Cert:** Internal Medicine 1979; Infectious Disease 1984; **Med School:** Hahnemann Univ 1976; **Resid:** Internal Medicine, Univ Illinois Hosp 1979; **Fellow:** Infectious Disease, Yale Univ 1982; **Fac Appt:** Assoc Clin Prof Med, Rutgers R W Johnson Med Sch

Porwancher, Richard B MD (Inf) - **Spec Exp:** Lyme Disease; AIDS/HIV; Disaster Preparedness; **Hospital:** St. Francis Med Ctr - Trenton, Robert Wood Johnson Univ Hosp Hamilton; **Address:** 1245 Whitehorse-Mercerville Rd, Ste 410-411, Hamilton, NJ 08619-3831; **Phone:** 609-581-2000; **Board Cert:** Internal Medicine 1980; Infectious Disease 1982; **Med School:** Northwestern Univ 1977; **Resid:** Internal Medicine, Med Coll Wisc Affil Hosps 1980; **Fellow:** Infectious Disease, VA Med Ctr 1982; **Fac Appt:** Assoc Clin Prof Med

Internal Medicine

Corazza, Douglas P MD (IM) *PCP* - **Hospital:** Univ Med Ctr Princeton at Plainsboro; **Address:** Montgomery Internal Med Grp, 727 State Rd, Princeton, NJ 08540; **Phone:** 609-921-6410; **Board Cert:** Internal Medicine 1988; **Med School:** UMDNJ-Rutgers Med Sch 1985; **Resid:** Internal Medicine, RW Johnson Univ Hosp 1988

Harman, John MD (IM) *PCP* - **Hospital:** Capital Health Med Ctr - Hopewell; **Address:** 850 Bear Tavern Rd, Ste 309, Ewing, NJ 08560; **Phone:** 609-656-8845; **Board Cert:** Internal Medicine 1972; **Med School:** Univ Pennsylvania 1969; **Resid:** Internal Medicine, Presby Hosp 1972; **Fellow:** Pulmonary Disease, U Penn Hosp 1975

Murray, Simon D MD (IM) *PCP* - **Spec Exp:** Concierge Medicine; Cholesterol/Lipid Disorders; Nutrition; Preventive Medicine; **Hospital:** Univ Med Ctr Princeton at Plainsboro; **Address:** 727 State Rd Fl 2, Princeton, NJ 08540; **Phone:** 609-921-7444; **Board Cert:** Internal Medicine 1985; **Med School:** Philippines 1980; **Resid:** Internal Medicine, UMDNJ/RWJ Univ Hosp 1984; **Fac Appt:** Asst Clin Prof Med, Rutgers R W Johnson Med Sch

Schaeffer, Mark A MD (IM) *PCP* - **Hospital:** Univ Med Ctr Princeton at Plainsboro; **Address:** 800 Bunn Drive, Ste 302, Princeton, NJ 08540; **Phone:** 609-921-1680; **Board Cert:** Internal Medicine 1989; **Med School:** NY Med Coll 1984; **Resid:** Internal Medicine, RW Johnson Univ Hosp 1989

Yamane, Michael H MD (IM) *PCP* - **Hospital:** Capital Health Med Ctr - Hopewell; **Address:** 2480 Pennington Rd, Ste 104, Pennington, NJ 08534-5227; **Phone:** 609-818-1000; **Board Cert:** Internal Medicine 1984; **Med School:** UCSF 1981; **Resid:** Internal Medicine, Univ Hawaii Med Ctr 1984

Interventional Cardiology

Shanahan, Andrew J MD (IC) - **Spec Exp:** Angioplasty; **Hospital:** Univ Med Ctr Princeton at Plainsboro, Robert Wood Johnson Univ Hosp - New Brunswick; **Address:** Cardiology Assocs of Princeton, 731 Alexander St, Ste 202, Princeton, NJ 08540; **Phone:** 609-921-7456; **Board Cert:** Internal Medicine 2005; Cardiovascular Disease 2005; Interventional Cardiology 2011; **Med School:** Med Coll Wisc 1989; **Resid:** Internal Medicine, St Lukes-Roosevelt Hosp 1992; **Fellow:** Cardiovascular Disease, St Lukes-Roosevelt Hosp 1995

Medical Oncology

Grossman, Bernard MD (Onc) - **Hospital:** Capital Health Med Ctr - Hopewell, Robert Wood Johnson Univ Hosp Hamilton; **Address:** Two Capital Way, Ste 220, Pennington, NJ 08534; **Phone:** 609-303-0747; **Board Cert:** Internal Medicine 1977; Medical Oncology 1979; Hematology 1980; Hospice & Palliative Medicine 2010; **Med School:** Temple Univ 1974; **Resid:** Internal Medicine, Albany Meml Hosp 1977; **Fellow:** Hematology & Oncology, George Wash Univ Hosp 1979; Oncology, Fox Chase Cancer Ctr 1980

Lerma, Pauline M MD (Onc) - **Spec Exp:** Breast Cancer; Hematologic Malignancies; **Hospital:** Robert Wood Johnson Univ Hosp Hamilton; **Address:** Cancer Inst NJ-Hamilton, 2575 Klockner Rd, Hamilton, NJ 08690; **Phone:** 609-631-6960; **Board Cert:** Internal Medicine 2006; Medical Oncology 2009; Hematology 2010; **Med School:** Philippines 1992; **Resid:** Internal Medicine, Abington Meml Hosp 1996; **Fellow:** Hematology & Oncology, Hahnemann Univ Hosp 1999; Bone Marrow Transplant, Hahnemann Univ Hosp 2000; **Fac Appt:** Asst Prof Med, Rutgers R W Johnson Med Sch

Schaebler, David L MD (Onc) - **Hospital:** Capital Health Med Ctr - Hopewell, Robert Wood Johnson Univ Hosp Hamilton; **Address:** Mercer Bucks Hem/Onc, Two Capital Way, Ste 220, Pennington, NJ 08534; **Phone:** 609-303-0747; **Board Cert:** Hospice & Palliative Medicine 2008; Medical Oncology 2013; **Med School:** Jefferson Med Coll 1988; **Resid:** Internal Medicine, Cooper Univ Med Ctr 1991; **Fellow:** Medical Oncology, Fox Chase 1994

Sierocki, John S MD (Onc) - **Spec Exp:** Breast Cancer; Lung Cancer; Lymphoma; Brain Tumors; **Hospital:** Univ Med Ctr Princeton at Plainsboro; **Address:** Princeton Med Grp, 419 N Harrison St, Ste 101, Princeton, NJ 08540-3521; **Phone:** 609-924-9300; **Board Cert:** Internal Medicine 1976; Medical Oncology 1979; **Med School:** Hahnemann Univ 1973; **Resid:** Internal Medicine, Hahnemann Univ Hosp 1976; **Fellow:** Medical Oncology, Meml Sloan-Kettering Cancer Ctr 1978

Yi, Peter I MD (Onc) - **Spec Exp:** Breast Cancer; Lymphoma; Prostate Cancer; Colon Cancer; **Hospital:** Univ Med Ctr Princeton at Plainsboro; **Address:** Princeton Medical Group, Princeton HealthCare Center, 419 N Harrison St, Ste 101, Princeton, NJ 8540; **Phone:** 609-924-9300; **Board Cert:** Internal Medicine 1987; Medical Oncology 1989; Hematology 2010; **Med School:** Cornell Univ-Weill Med Coll 1984; **Resid:** Internal Medicine, Brigham & Women's Hosp 1987; **Fellow:** Hematology & Oncology, NY Hosp-Cornell Med Ctr 1990; **Fac Appt:** Asst Clin Prof Med, Rutgers R W Johnson Med Sch

Nephrology

Cohen, Barry H MD (Nep) - **Hospital:** Capital Health Med Ctr - Hopewell; **Address:** 40 Fuld St, Ste 401, Trenton, NJ 08638-5247; **Phone:** 609-599-1004; **Board Cert:** Internal Medicine 1971; Nephrology 1974; **Med School:** Hahnemann Univ 1965; **Resid:** Internal Medicine, Hahnemann Univ Hosp 1968; **Fellow:** Nephrology, Hahnemann Univ 1969

Ruddy, Michael C MD (Nep) - **Spec Exp:** Hypertension; Renovascular Disease; Diabetic Kidney Disease; Pheochromocytoma; **Hospital:** Univ Med Ctr Princeton at Plainsboro, Robert Wood Johnson Univ Hosp - New Brunswick; **Address:** Princeton Hypertension-Nephrology Assocs, 88 Princeton Highstown Rd, Ste 203, Princeton Junction, NJ 08550; **Phone:** 609-750-7330; **Board Cert:** Internal Medicine 1977; Nephrology 1980; **Med School:** UMDNJ-NJ Med Sch, Newark 1974; **Resid:** Internal Medicine, UMDNJ-RW Johnson Med Affil Hosp 1977; **Fellow:** Nephrology, NY-Presby/Weill Cornell Med Ctr 1980

Sudhakar, Telechery A MD (Nep) - **Spec Exp:** Kidney Disease; **Hospital:** Capital Health Med Ctr - Hopewell, Capital Health Regl Med Ctr; **Address:** 40 Fuld St, Ste 401, Trenton, NJ 08638; **Phone:** 609-599-1004; **Board Cert:** Internal Medicine 1977; Nephrology 1978; **Med School:** India 1973; **Resid:** Internal Medicine, Helene Fuld Med Ctr 1976; **Fellow:** Nephrology, Washington VA Hosp 1978

Wei, Fong MD (Nep) - **Spec Exp:** Hypertension; Kidney Stones; **Hospital:** Univ Med Ctr Princeton at Plainsboro; **Address:** 419 N Harrison St, Princeton, NJ 08540; **Phone:** 609-924-9300; **Board Cert:** Internal Medicine 1976; Nephrology 1976; **Med School:** Tufts Univ 1967; **Resid:** Internal Medicine, Boston City Hosp 1969; Internal Medicine, Bronx Municipal Hosp 1970; **Fellow:** Nephrology, Univ NC Hosp 1972

Neurological Surgery

McLaughlin, Mark R MD (NS) - **Spec Exp:** Spinal Surgery-Complex; Spinal Surgery-Minimally Invasive; Trigeminal Neuralgia; **Hospital:** Univ Med Ctr Princeton at Plainsboro, St. Mary Med Ctr - Langhorne, PA; **Address:** Princeton Brain & Spine Care, 731 Alexander Rd, Ste 200, Princeton, NJ 08540; **Phone:** 609-921-9001; **Board Cert:** Neurological Surgery 2004; **Med School:** Med Coll VA 1992; **Resid:** Neurological Surgery, Univ Pittsburgh Med Ctr 1999; **Fellow:** Complex Spinal Surgery, Emory Univ Affil Hosp 2000

Neurology

Kaiser, Paul K MD (N) - **Hospital:** Univ Med Ctr Princeton at Plainsboro, Capital Health Med Ctr - Hopewell; **Address:** 3131 Princeton Pike, Building 3, Ste 202, Lawrenceville, NJ 08648-2526; **Phone:** 609-896-1701; **Board Cert:** Neurology 1993; Vascular Neurology 2009; **Med School:** Jefferson Med Coll 1988; **Resid:** Neurology, Temple Univ Hosp 1992; **Fellow:** Clinical Neurophysiology, Temple Univ Hosp 1993

Kososky, Charles S MD (N) - **Spec Exp:** Stroke; Alzheimer's Disease; **Hospital:** St. Francis Med Ctr - Trenton; **Address:** St Francis Med Ctr, Neurosci Inst, 601 Hamilton Ave, Ste 275, Trenton, NJ 08629; **Phone:** 609-599-5792; **Board Cert:** Neurology 1981; **Med School:** UMDNJ-NJ Med Sch, Newark 1975; **Resid:** Internal Medicine, Kings Co Hosp 1976; Neurology, UMDNJ-Univ Hosp 1979

Patchell, Roy A MD (N) - **Spec Exp:** Neuro-Oncology; Brain Tumors; Spinal Tumors; **Hospital:** Capital Health Med Ctr - Hopewell; **Address:** Capital Inst Neurosciences, 2 Capital Way, Ste 456, Pennington, NJ 08534; **Phone:** 609-537-7300; **Board Cert:** Neurology 1984; **Med School:** Univ KY Coll Med 1979; **Resid:** Neurology, Johns Hopkins Hosp 1983; **Fellow:** Neuro-Oncology, Meml Sloan-Kettering Cancer Ctr 1985

Vester, John W MD (N) - **Spec Exp:** Parkinson's Disease; Stroke; Peripheral Neuropathy; Epilepsy/Seizure Disorders; **Hospital:** Univ Med Ctr Princeton at Plainsboro; **Address:** 1000 Herrontown Rd, Princeton, NJ 08540; **Phone:** 609-497-0100; **Board Cert:** Neurology 1979; **Med School:** Georgetown Univ 1973; **Resid:** Internal Medicine, Hartford Hosp 1975; Neurology, Georgetown Univ Hosp 1978

Witte, Arnold S MD (N) - **Spec Exp:** Neuromuscular Disorders; Parkinson's Disease; Electromyography; **Hospital:** Capital Health Med Ctr - Hopewell, Capital Health Regl Med Ctr; **Address:** 2 Princess Rd, Ste 2F, Lawrenceville, NJ 08648; **Phone:** 609-895-9000; **Board Cert:** Internal Medicine 1981; Neurology 1983; **Med School:** Tufts Univ 1977; **Resid:** Internal Medicine, Univ Hosp of Cleveland 1979; Neurology, Hosp Univ Penn 1981; **Fellow:** Neurourology, Hosp Univ Penn 1982

Neuroradiology

Applbaum, Yaakov N MD (NRad) - **Spec Exp:** Vascular Interventional Radiology; Uterine Fibroid Embolization; **Hospital:** Capital Health Regl Med Ctr; **Address:** Capital Hlth, Radiology, 750 Brunswick Ave, Trenton, NJ 08638; **Phone:** 609-815-7532; **Board Cert:** Diagnostic Radiology 1985; Vascular & Interventional Radiology 2005; Neuroradiology 2008; **Med School:** Albert Einstein Coll Med 1980; **Resid:** Diagnostic Radiology, Maimonides Med Ctr 1985; **Fellow:** Interventional Radiology, UC Irvine Med Ctr 1987; Neurological Radiology, UC Irvine Med Ctr 1989

Obstetrics & Gynecology

Brickner, Gary R MD (ObG) *PCP* - **Spec Exp:** Gynecology Only; Menopause Problems; Minimally Invasive Surgery; Weight Management; **Hospital:** Capital Health Med Ctr - Hopewell; **Address:** Brickner-Martell Ctr Women's Hlth, Quakerbridge Plaza 1A Bldg, Hamilton, NJ 08619-1241; **Phone:** 609-689-9991; **Board Cert:** Obstetrics & Gynecology 1981; **Med School:** Univ Pittsburgh 1975; **Resid:** Obstetrics & Gynecology, Pennsylvania Hosp-UPHS 1980

Ophthalmology

Matossian, Cynthia MD (Oph) - **Spec Exp:** Cataract Surgery; Dry Eye Syndrome; **Hospital:** Capital Health Regl Med Ctr, Doylestown Hosp; **Address:** Two Capital Way, Ste 326, Pennington, NJ 08534; **Phone:** 609-882-8833; **Board Cert:** Ophthalmology 1987; **Med School:** Penn State Coll Med 1981; **Resid:** Ophthalmology, G Washington Univ Hosp 1986

Mulvey, Lauri D MD (Oph) - **Spec Exp:** Pediatric Ophthalmology; Amblyopia; Strabismus; Glaucoma-Pediatric; **Hospital:** Chldns Hosp of Philadelphia; **Address:** CHOP Princeton Specialty Care Ctr, 707 Alexander Rd, Ste 205, Princeton, NJ 08540; **Phone:** 609-520-1717; **Board Cert:** Ophthalmology 1983; **Med School:** Harvard Med Sch 1977; **Resid:** Ophthalmology, Barnes-Jewish Hosp 1981; **Fellow:** Pediatric Ophthalmology, Wills Eye Hosp 1983

Safran, Steven G MD (Oph) - **Spec Exp:** Cataract Surgery; Laser Vision Surgery; Glaucoma; LASIK-Refractive Surgery; **Hospital:** Capital Health Med Ctr - Hopewell, Robert Wood Johnson Univ Hosp Hamilton; **Address:** 132 Franklin Corner Rd, Ste A-1, Lawrenceville, NJ 08648-2523; **Phone:** 609-896-3931; **Board Cert:** Ophthalmology 2013; **Med School:** SUNY Downstate 1987; **Resid:** Ophthalmology, NYU Langone Med Ctr 1991; **Fellow:** Cornea & Ext Eye Disease, Duke Univ Hosp 1992

Wasserman, Barry N MD (Oph) - **Spec Exp:** Pediatric Ophthalmology; LASIK-Refractive Surgery; Eyelid Surgery; Botox Therapy; **Hospital:** St. Peter's Univ Hosp, Univ Med Ctr Princeton at Plainsboro; **Address:** 100 Canal Pointe Blvd, Ste 112, Princeton, NJ 08540; **Phone:** 609-243-8711; **Board Cert:** Ophthalmology 2009; **Med School:** UMDNJ-NJ Med Sch, Newark 1992; **Resid:** Ophthalmology, UMDNJ-NJ Med Sch Affil Hosps 1996; **Fellow:** Pediatric Ophthalmology, IU Hlth Univ Hosp 1997; **Fac Appt:** Asst Clin Prof Oph, Rutgers R W Johnson Med Sch

Wong, Richard H MD (Oph) - **Spec Exp:** Cataract Surgery-Lens Implant; LASIK-Refractive Surgery; **Hospital:** Univ Med Ctr Princeton at Plainsboro; **Address:** Princeton Eye Grp, 419 N Harrison St, Ste 104, Princeton, NJ 08540-3521; **Phone:** 609-921-9437; **Board Cert:** Internal Medicine 1982; Ophthalmology 1987; **Med School:** UMDNJ-NJ Med Sch, Newark 1979; **Resid:** Internal Medicine, Thomas Jefferson Univ Hosp 1982; Ophthalmology, Wills Eye Hosp 1986

Orthopaedic Surgery

Abrams, Jeffrey S MD (OrS) - **Spec Exp:** Shoulder Surgery; Sports Medicine; Arthroscopic Surgery; Rotator Cuff Surgery; **Hospital:** Univ Med Ctr Princeton at Plainsboro; **Address:** Princeton Orthopaedic Assocs, 325 Princeton Ave, Princeton, NJ 08540-1617; **Phone:** 609-924-8131; **Board Cert:** Orthopaedic Surgery 2009; **Med School:** SUNY Upstate Med Univ 1980; **Resid:** Orthopaedic Surgery, Thomas Jefferson Univ Hosp 1985; **Fellow:** Shoulder Surgery, Univ Western Ontario 1986; Sports Medicine, Hughston Sports Med Hosp 1986; **Fac Appt:** Assoc Clin Prof OrS, Seton Hall Univ Sch Hlth & Med Scis

Gomez, William MD (OrS) - **Spec Exp:** Sports Medicine; Arthroscopic Surgery; Arthritis; **Hospital:** Robert Wood Johnson Univ Hosp Hamilton, St. Francis Med Ctr - Trenton; **Address:** Trenton Orthopaedic Grp, 1225 Whitehorse Mercerville Rd, D Bldg - Ste 220, Mercerville, NJ 08619-3876; **Phone:** 609-581-2200; **Board Cert:** Orthopaedic Surgery 2011; **Med School:** Columbia P&S 1982; **Resid:** Surgery, St Vincent's Hosp 1984; Orthopaedic Surgery, NY-Presby/Columbia Univ Med Ctr 1987; **Fellow:** Sports Medicine, UPMC 1988

Grenis, Michael S MD (OrS) - **Spec Exp:** Carpal Tunnel Syndrome; Hand & Wrist Injuries; **Hospital:** Univ Med Ctr Princeton at Plainsboro, Capital Health Med Ctr - Hopewell; **Address:** Princeton Orthopaedic Assocs, 325 Princeton Ave, Princeton, NJ 08540; **Phone:** 609-924-8131; **Board Cert:** Orthopaedic Surgery 2013; **Med School:** NY Med Coll 1984; **Resid:** Surgery, Bellevue Hosp Ctr 1985; Orthopaedic Surgery, Bellevue Hosp Ctr 1989; **Fellow:** Hand Surgery, Bellevue Hosp Ctr 1990

Gutowski III, W. Thomas MD (OrS) - **Spec Exp:** Hip Replacement; Knee Replacement; Arthroscopic Surgery; Joint Replacement; **Hospital:** Univ Med Ctr Princeton at Plainsboro; **Address:** Princeton Orthopaedic Assocs, 325 Princeton Ave, Princeton, NJ 08540; **Phone:** 609-924-8131; **Board Cert:** Orthopaedic Surgery 2008; **Med School:** Cornell Univ-Weill Med Coll 1980; **Resid:** Orthopaedic Surgery, Yale-New Haven Hosp 1984

Taitsman, James P MD (OrS) - **Spec Exp:** Sports Medicine; Arthroscopic Surgery-Knee; Shoulder & Knee Surgery; Hand & Upper Extremity Surgery; **Hospital:** Capital Health Med Ctr - Hopewell, Robert Wood Johnson Univ Hosp Hamilton; **Address:** 123 Franklin Corner Rd, Ste 114, Lawrenceville, NJ 08648-2526; **Phone:** 609-896-0707; **Board Cert:** Orthopaedic Surgery 1977; **Med School:** Univ Rochester 1971; **Resid:** Surgery, Yale-New Haven Hosp 1973; Orthopaedic Surgery, Yale-New Haven Hosp 1976

Otolaryngology

Brunner, Eugenie MD (Oto) - **Spec Exp:** Cosmetic Surgery-Face; Rhinoplasty; Skin Laser Surgery; Blepharoplasty; **Hospital:** Univ Med Ctr Princeton at Plainsboro; **Address:** 256 Bunn Drive, Ste 4, Princeton, NJ 08540; **Phone:** 609-921-9497; **Board Cert:** Otolaryngology 1997; Facial Plastic & Reconstr Surgery 2012; **Med School:** Rutgers R W Johnson Med Sch 1990; **Resid:** Surgery, NYU Med Ctr 1992; Otolaryngology, NYU Med Ctr 1996; **Fellow:** Facial Plastic & Reconstr Surgery, Univ Toronto Affil Hosp 1997

Li, Ronald W MD (Oto) - **Spec Exp:** Pediatric & Adult Otolaryngology; Head & Neck Surgery; **Hospital:** Univ Med Ctr Princeton at Plainsboro; **Address:** 800 Bunn Drive, Ste 305, Princeton, NJ 08540; **Phone:** 609-921-1000; **Board Cert:** Otolaryngology 1990; **Med School:** Mount Sinai Sch Med 1984; **Resid:** Otolaryngology, Montefiore Med Ctr 1989

Pain Medicine

Loren, Gary M MD (PM) - **Spec Exp:** Pain-Back; Reflex Sympathetic Dystrophy (RSD); **Hospital:** St. Francis Med Ctr - Trenton; **Address:** 1666 Hamilton Ave, Ste 2, Hamilton Township, NJ 08629; **Phone:** 609-584-9080; **Board Cert:** Anesthesiology 1988; Pain Medicine 2013; **Med School:** Univ Pittsburgh 1984; **Resid:** Anesthesiology, Long Is Jewish Med Ctr 1988; **Fellow:** Pediatrics, Long Is Jewish Med Ctr 1990

Pediatric Gastroenterology

Farhath, Sabeena MD (PGe) - **Spec Exp:** Crohn's Disease; Diarrheal Diseases; Irritable Bowel Syndrome; **Hospital:** Capital Health Med Ctr - Hopewell; **Address:** PedsGastro Ctr, 2123 Klockner Rd, Hamilton, NJ 08690; **Phone:** 609-586-7337; **Board Cert:** Pediatrics 2007; Pediatric Gastroenterology 2013; **Med School:** India 1991; **Resid:** Pediatrics, Cooper Univ Hosp 1994; **Fellow:** Pediatric Gastroenterology, Alfred I duPont Hosp Chldn 1997

Pediatrics

Baiser, Dennis M MD (Ped) *PCP* - **Spec Exp:** Developmental Disorders; Asthma; **Hospital:** Capital Health Med Ctr - Hopewell, Robert Wood Johnson Univ Hosp Hamilton; **Address:** Hamilton Pediatrics, 3 Hamilton Health Pl, Ste A, Hamilton, NJ 08690; **Phone:** 609-581-4480; **Board Cert:** Pediatrics 1983; **Med School:** NY Med Coll 1978; **Resid:** Pediatrics, Chldns Hosp 1981

Boim, Marilynn D MD (Ped) *PCP* - **Hospital:** Capital Health Med Ctr - Hopewell, Robert Wood Johnson Univ Hosp Hamilton; **Address:** Hamilton Pediatrics, 3 Hamilton Health Pl, Ste A, Hamilton, NJ 08690; **Phone:** 609-581-4480; **Board Cert:** Pediatrics 2009; Pediatric Endocrinology 2011; **Med School:** Emory Univ 1982; **Resid:** Pediatrics, Mt Sinai Hosp 1985; **Fellow:** Pediatric Endocrinology, Mt Sinai Hosp 1987

Palsky, Glenn S MD (Ped) *PCP* - **Hospital:** Capital Health Med Ctr - Hopewell, Univ Med Ctr Princeton at Plainsboro; **Address:** Delaware Valley Pediatric Associates, 132 Franklin Corner Rd, Lawrenceville, NJ 08648-2526; **Phone:** 609-896-4141; **Board Cert:** Pediatrics 1978; **Med School:** Penn State Coll Med 1973; **Resid:** Pediatrics, Albany Med Ctr 1977

Raymond, Gerald M MD (Ped) *PCP* - **Hospital:** Univ Med Ctr Princeton at Plainsboro; **Address:** 196 Princeton Heights Town Rd, West Windsor, NJ 08550; **Phone:** 609-799-5335; **Board Cert:** Pediatrics 2010; **Med School:** Penn State Coll Med 1983; **Resid:** Pediatrics, Columbus Chldns Hosp 1986

Physical Medicine & Rehabilitation

Agri, Robyn F MD (PMR) - **Spec Exp:** Acupuncture; Pain Management; Botox Therapy; **Hospital:** St. Lawrence Rehab Ctr, Capital Health Med Ctr - Hopewell; **Address:** St Lawrence Rehabilitation Ctr, 2381 Lawrenceville Rd, Lawrenceville, NJ 08648-2024; **Phone:** 609-896-9500; **Board Cert:** Physical Medicine & Rehabilitation 1990; **Med School:** SUNY Hlth Sci Ctr 1985; **Resid:** Physical Medicine & Rehabilitation, Hosp Univ Penn 1989

Gribbin, Dorota M MD (PMR) - **Spec Exp:** Musculoskeletal Disorders; Pain Management; **Hospital:** Robert Wood Johnson Univ Hosp Hamilton, Univ Med Ctr Princeton at Plainsboro; **Address:** 2333 Whitehorse-Mercerville Rd, Ste 8, Mercerville, NJ 08619; **Phone:** 609-588-0540; **Board Cert:** Physical Medicine & Rehabilitation 2013; **Med School:** Poland 1984; **Resid:** Internal Medicine, Beth Israel Med Ctr 1989; Physical Medicine & Rehabilitation, New York Hosp 1992; **Fac Appt:** Asst Clin Prof PMR, Columbia P&S

Plastic Surgery

Drimmer, Marc A MD (PlS) - **Spec Exp:** Cosmetic Surgery; Skin Cancer Reconstruction; Burns-Reconstructive Plastic Surgery; Breast Reconstruction; **Hospital:** Univ Med Ctr Princeton at Plainsboro; **Address:** 842 State Rd, Princeton, NJ 08540; **Phone:** 609-924-1026; **Board Cert:** Plastic Surgery 1981; **Med School:** Belgium 1974; **Resid:** Surgery, Beth Israel Med Ctr 1977; Plastic Surgery, Univ Hosp 1979; **Fac Appt:** Asst Clin Prof S, UMDNJ-Rutgers Med Sch

Leach, Thomas A MD (PlS) - **Spec Exp:** Cosmetic Surgery-Face; Cosmetic Surgery-Breast; Liposuction; Facial Rejuvenation; **Hospital:** Univ Med Ctr Princeton at Plainsboro, Robert Wood Johnson Univ Hosp - New Brunswick; **Address:** 932 State Rd, Princeton, NJ 08540; **Phone:** 609-921-7161; **Board Cert:** Plastic Surgery 1994; **Med School:** UMDNJ-NJ Med Sch, Newark 1985; **Resid:** Surgery, UMDNJ Med Ctr 1990; **Fellow:** Plastic Surgery, UMDNJ Med Ctr 1992

Smotrich, Gary A MD (PlS) - **Hospital:** Capital Health Med Ctr - Hopewell, Robert Wood Johnson Univ Hosp Hamilton; **Address:** Lawrenceville Plastic Surgery, 3131 Princeton Pike, Bldg 5 - Ste 205, Lawrenceville, NJ 08648-2300; **Phone:** 609-896-2525; **Board Cert:** Plastic Surgery 1991; **Med School:** Univ Conn 1982; **Resid:** Surgery, Boston Univ Med Ctr 1987; Plastic Surgery, Univ Louisville Hosp 1989

Psychiatry

Leifer, Marvin W MD (Psyc) - **Spec Exp:** Psychopharmacology; Anxiety & Mood Disorders; Depression; Bipolar/Mood Disorders; **Hospital:** Univ Med Ctr Princeton at Plainsboro; **Address:** 42 N Tulane St, Princeton, NJ 08542; **Phone:** 609-683-7929; **Board Cert:** Psychiatry 1977; **Med School:** SUNY Downstate 1970; **Resid:** Psychiatry, Albert Einstein Coll Med Affil Hosp 1974; **Fellow:** Psychopharmacology, Albert Einstein Coll Med Affil Hosp 1976

Schneider, Samuel MD (Psyc) - **Spec Exp:** Mood Disorders; Personality Disorders; Addiction/Substance Abuse; **Hospital:** Univ Med Ctr Princeton at Plainsboro; **Address:** 33 State Rd, Ste J, Princeton, NJ 08540-1304; **Phone:** 609-924-3980; **Board Cert:** Psychiatry 1984; Internal Medicine 1978; **Med School:** Penn State Coll Med 1975; **Resid:** Internal Medicine, MS Hershey Med Ctr 1977; Psychiatry, UMDNJ-RW Johnson Univ Hosp 1982

Pulmonary Disease

Seelagy, Marc M MD (Pul) - **Spec Exp:** Sleep Disorders; Lung Disease; Critical Care Medicine; **Hospital:** St. Francis Med Ctr - Trenton, Robert Wood Johnson Univ Hosp Hamilton; **Address:** Allergy & Pulmonary Associates, 1542 Kuser Rd, Ste B7, Trenton, NJ 08619-3829; **Phone:** 609-581-1400; **Board Cert:** Internal Medicine 1989; Pulmonary Disease 2012; Critical Care Medicine 2013; Sleep Medicine 1995; **Med School:** Univ Chicago-Pritzker Sch Med 1986; **Resid:** Internal Medicine, Univ Colorado Hosp 1989; **Fellow:** Pulmonary Critical Care Medicine, Johns Hopkins Hosp 1993

Radiation Oncology

McKenna, Michael G MD (RadRO) - **Spec Exp:** Prostate Cancer; Breast Cancer; Head & Neck Cancer; **Hospital:** Robert Wood Johnson Univ Hosp Hamilton; **Address:** Cancer Inst NJ-Radiation Oncology, 2575 Klockner Rd, Hamilton, NJ 08690; **Phone:** 609-584-2800; **Board Cert:** Radiation Oncology 1993; **Med School:** Univ Mass Sch Med 1988; **Resid:** Radiation Oncology, Hosp Univ Penn 1992; **Fac Appt:** Asst Prof RadRO, UMDNJ-Robert Wood Johnson

Reproductive Endocrinology

O'Shaughnessy, Althea M MD (RE) - **Spec Exp:** Infertility; Laparoscopic Surgery; Minimally Invasive Surgery; **Hospital:** Univ Med Ctr Princeton at Plainsboro, Capital Health Med Ctr - Hopewell; **Address:** Princeton Center for Reproductive Med, 65 S Main St C Bldg - Ste 100, Pennington, NJ 08534; **Phone:** 609-818-1114; **Board Cert:** Obstetrics & Gynecology 2013; Reproductive Endocrinology/Infertility 2013; **Med School:** Univ Rochester 1982; **Resid:** Obstetrics & Gynecology, Univ Conn Hlth Ctr 1986; **Fellow:** Reproductive Endocrinology, Downstate Med Ctr 1988

Rheumatology

Carney, Alexander S MD (Rhu) - **Hospital:** Univ Med Ctr Princeton at Plainsboro; **Address:** 8 Quakerbridge Plaza, Ste H, Mercerville, NJ 08619; **Phone:** 609-588-9044; **Board Cert:** Internal Medicine 1972; Rheumatology 1978; **Med School:** Cornell Univ-Weill Med Coll 1966; **Resid:** Internal Medicine, Univ Iowa Hosp 1972; **Fellow:** Rheumatology, Univ Iowa Hosp 1974

Surgery

Dultz, Rachel P MD (S) - **Spec Exp:** Breast Surgery; Breast Cancer; **Hospital:** Univ Med Ctr Princeton at Plainsboro; **Address:** Breast Surgical Specialist, 300B Princeton Hightstown Rd, Ste 102, East Windsor, NJ 08520; **Phone:** 609-688-2700; **Board Cert:** Surgery 2006; **Med School:** SUNY Downstate 1991; **Resid:** Surgery, RW Johnson Univ Hosp 1997; **Fellow:** Breast Surgery, Baylor Med Ctr 1998; **Fac Appt:** Asst Clin Prof S, Rutgers R W Johnson Med Sch

Gannon, Christopher J MD (S) - **Spec Exp:** Liver & Biliary Surgery; Liver Cancer; Pancreatic Cancer; Thyroid Cancer; **Hospital:** Capital Health Med Ctr - Hopewell, Capital Health Regl Med Ctr; **Address:** Two Capital Way, Ste 356, Pennington, NJ 08534; **Phone:** 609-537-6000; **Board Cert:** Surgery 2005; **Med School:** Columbia P&S 1998; **Resid:** Surgery, Univ Maryland Med Ctr 2004; **Fellow:** Surgical Oncology, MD Anderson Cancer Ctr 2007; **Fac Appt:** Asst Prof S, UMDNJ-Robert Wood Johnson

Thoracic & Cardiac Surgery

Seinfeld, Fredric I MD (T&CS) - **Spec Exp:** Carotid Artery Surgery; Aneurysm; Esophageal Surgery; Cardiovascular Surgery; **Hospital:** St. Francis Med Ctr - Trenton, Univ Med Ctr Princeton at Plainsboro; **Address:** St Francis, Cardiothoracic Surgery, 601 Hamilton Ave, rm 109, Trenton, NJ 08629; **Phone:** 609-599-5308; **Board Cert:** Thoracic & Cardiac Surgery 2005; **Med School:** SUNY Buffalo 1976; **Resid:** Surgery, NYU Med Ctr 1981; Cardiothoracic Surgery, Yale-New Haven Hosp 1984

Urology

Rossman, Barry R MD (U) - **Spec Exp:** Kidney Stones; Incontinence-Female; Prostate Cancer; Erectile Dysfunction; **Hospital:** Univ Med Ctr Princeton at Plainsboro, Robert Wood Johnson Univ Hosp - New Brunswick; **Address:** Urology Grp of Princeton, 134 Stanhope St, Princeton, NJ 8540; **Phone:** 609-924-6487; **Board Cert:** Urology 2010; **Med School:** Boston Univ 1983; **Resid:** Surgery, Montefiore Med Ctr 1985; Urology, Montefiore Med Ctr 1989; **Fac Appt:** Assoc Clin Prof U, Rutgers R W Johnson Med Sch

Vasselli, Anthony J MD (U) - **Hospital:** Univ Med Ctr Princeton at Plainsboro; **Address:** 299 Witherspoon St, Princeton, NJ 08540; **Phone:** 609-252-0575; **Board Cert:** Urology 2006; **Med School:** NY Med Coll 1979; **Resid:** Urology, Albany Meml Hosp 1984

Vukasin, Alexander P MD (U) - **Spec Exp:** Laparoscopic Surgery; Urologic Cancer; Urology-Female; **Hospital:** Univ Med Ctr Princeton at Plainsboro, Robert Wood Johnson Univ Hosp - New Brunswick; **Address:** Urology Grp of Princeton, 134 Stanhope St, Princeton, NJ 8540; **Phone:** 609-924-6487; **Board Cert:** Urology 2006; **Med School:** Yale Univ 1989; **Resid:** Urology, NY-Presby/Weill Cornell Med Ctr 1995; **Fac Appt:** Asst Clin Prof U, Rutgers R W Johnson Med Sch

Vascular & Interventional Radiology

Choudhri, Ajay MD (VIR) - **Spec Exp:** Interventional Oncology; Aneurysm-Aortic; Vascular Disease; Endovascular Surgery; **Hospital:** Capital Health Med Ctr - Hopewell, Capital Health Regl Med Ctr; **Address:** 750 Brunswick Ave, Trenton, NJ 08638; **Phone:** 609-815-7532; **Board Cert:** Diagnostic Radiology 2000; Endovascular Medicine 2008; **Med School:** UMDNJ-NJ Med Sch, Newark 1995; **Resid:** Diagnostic Radiology, Montefiore Med Ctr 2000; **Fellow:** Vascular & Interventional Radiology, Miami Cardiac & Vascular Inst 2001

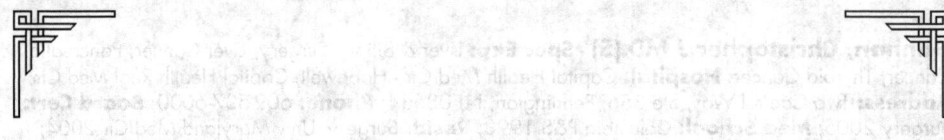

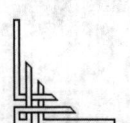

Middlesex

Addiction Psychiatry

Williams, Jill M MD (AdP) - **Spec Exp:** Addiction/Substance Abuse; Alcohol Abuse; Dual Diagnosis; Smoking Cessation; **Hospital:** Robert Wood Johnson Univ Hosp - New Brunswick; **Address:** 671 Hoes Ln, Piscataway, NJ 08855; **Phone:** 732-235-4402; **Board Cert:** Psychiatry 2008; Addiction Psychiatry 2012; **Med School:** Rutgers R W Johnson Med Sch 1993; **Resid:** Psychiatry, Duke Univ Hosp 1997; **Fellow:** Addiction Psychiatry, RW Johnson Univ Hosp 1999; **Fac Appt:** Assoc Prof Psyc, Rutgers R W Johnson Med Sch

Adolescent Medicine

Brill, Susan R MD (AM) - **Spec Exp:** Adolescent Gynecology; Eating Disorders; Preventive Medicine; **Hospital:** St. Peter's Univ Hosp; **Address:** 254 Easton Ave, Ste 3, New Brunswick, NJ 08901; **Phone:** 732-565-5487; **Board Cert:** Pediatrics 1990; Adolescent Medicine 2012; **Med School:** Albert Einstein Coll Med 1987; **Resid:** Pediatrics, North Shore Univ Hosp 1990; **Fac Appt:** Asst Clin Prof Ped, Rutgers-NJ Med Sch

Snyder, Barbara K MD (AM) - **Spec Exp:** Eating Disorders; Pediatric Gynecology; **Hospital:** Robert Wood Johnson Univ Hosp - New Brunswick; **Address:** Childrens Health Inst New Jersey, 89 French St, Ste 2230, New Brunswick, NJ 08901; **Phone:** 732-235-7896; **Board Cert:** Pediatrics 1985; Adolescent Medicine 2008; **Med School:** Geo Wash Univ 1979; **Resid:** Pediatrics, Chldns National Med Ctr 1981; Pediatrics, Upstate Med Ctr 1982; **Fellow:** Adolescent Medicine, Strong Meml Hosp 1988; **Fac Appt:** Assoc Prof Ped

Allergy & Immunology

Blum, Jay R MD (A&I) - **Spec Exp:** Rhinitis; Asthma; Hives; Urticaria; **Hospital:** St. Peter's Univ Hosp, Robert Wood Johnson Univ Hosp - New Brunswick; **Address:** 85 Raritan Ave, Highland Park, NJ 08904; **Phone:** 732-846-7861; **Board Cert:** Internal Medicine 1978; Allergy & Immunology 1979; **Med School:** Univ Pennsylvania 1974; **Resid:** Internal Medicine, Beth Israel Med Ctr 1977; **Fellow:** Allergy & Immunology, NY-Presby/Weill Cornell Med Ctr 1979

Jyonouchi, Harumi MD (A&I) - **Spec Exp:** Immunodeficiency Disorders; Food Allergy; Immunotherapy; **Hospital:** St. Peter's Univ Hosp; **Address:** 254 Easton Ave, Medical Office Bldg, 3rd Fl, New Brunswick, NJ 08901; **Phone:** 732-339-7780; **Board Cert:** Pediatrics 2010; Allergy & Immunology 2013; **Med School:** Japan 1976; **Resid:** Pediatrics, Oklahoma Meml Chldns Hosp 1985; Pediatrics, All Chldns Hosp 1987; **Fellow:** Allergy & Immunology, All Chldns Hosp 1989; **Fac Appt:** Assoc Prof Ped, UMDNJ-NJ Med Sch, Newark

Kesarwala, Hemant MD (A&I) - **Spec Exp:** Food Allergy; Asthma; Infectious Disease; **Hospital:** St. Peter's Univ Hosp, Robert Wood Johnson Univ Hosp - New Brunswick; **Address:** 3084 Rte 27, Unit 6, Kendall Park, NJ 08824; **Phone:** 732-821-0595; **Board Cert:** Pediatrics 1979; Allergy & Immunology 1979; **Med School:** India 1971; **Resid:** Pediatrics, Lincoln Hosp 1976; **Fellow:** Infectious Disease, RW Johnson Univ Hosp 1978; Allergy & Immunology, Chldns Hosp 1979; **Fac Appt:** Clin Prof Ped, Drexel Univ Coll Med

Leibner, Donald N MD (A&I) - **Spec Exp:** Asthma & Allergy; Cough-Chronic; Insect Allergies; Nasal & Sinus Disorders; **Hospital:** Robert Wood Johnson Univ Hosp - New Brunswick, St. Peter's Univ Hosp; **Address:** 579-A Cranbury Rd, Ste 103, East Brunswick, NJ 08816; **Phone:** 732-390-4900; **Board Cert:** Allergy & Immunology 2005; **Med School:** SUNY Downstate 1981; **Resid:** Pediatrics, UMDNJ-Rutgers 1984; **Fellow:** Allergy & Immunology, Long Island Coll Hosp 1986; **Fac Appt:** Asst Clin Prof Ped, Drexel Univ Coll Med

Mumneh, Nayla Z MD (A&I) - **Spec Exp:** Asthma & Allergy; Pediatric Allergy & Immunology; Hereditary Angioedema; Food Allergy & Eczema; **Hospital:** JFK Med Ctr - Edison, St. Peter's Univ Hosp; **Address:** Allergy Treatment Ctr of NJ, 530 Green St, Ste 2-East, Iselin, NJ 08830; **Phone:** 732-283-3040; **Board Cert:** Allergy & Immunology 2011; **Med School:** Lebanon 1992; **Resid:** Internal Medicine, Carney Hosp 1997; **Fellow:** Allergy & Immunology, Cornell Univ Med Ctr 1999; **Fac Appt:** Assoc Clin Prof Med, UMDNJ-Rutgers Med Sch

Cardiovascular Disease

Altmann, Dory B MD (Cv) - **Spec Exp:** Coronary Artery Disease; Heart Valve Disease; Interventional Cardiology; **Hospital:** Robert Wood Johnson Univ Hosp - New Brunswick, St. Peter's Univ Hosp; **Address:** Cardiology Assocs of New Brunswick, 593 Cranbury Rd, East Brunswick, NJ 8816; **Phone:** 732-390-3333; **Board Cert:** Internal Medicine 1989; Cardiovascular Disease 2011; Interventional Cardiology 2009; **Med School:** Yale Univ 1986; **Resid:** Internal Medicine, New England Med Ctr 1989; **Fellow:** Cardiovascular Disease, Mt Sinai Hosp 1992; Interventional Cardiology, Washington Hosp Ctr 1993; **Fac Appt:** Asst Clin Prof Med, Rutgers R W Johnson Med Sch

Kostis, John B MD (Cv) - **Spec Exp:** Coronary Artery Disease; Hypertension; Cholesterol/Lipid Disorders; **Hospital:** Robert Wood Johnson Univ Hosp - New Brunswick; **Address:** 125 Paterson St, CAB Bldg - Fl 5 - Ste 5200, New Brunswick, NJ 08901; **Phone:** 732-235-7685; **Board Cert:** Internal Medicine 1973; Cardiovascular Disease 1973; **Med School:** Greece 1960; **Resid:** Internal Medicine, Evanglismos Hosp 1964; Internal Medicine, Cumberland Med Ctr 1967; **Fellow:** Cardiovascular Disease, Philadelphia Genl Hosp 1969; **Fac Appt:** Prof Med, Rutgers R W Johnson Med Sch

Mermelstein, Erwin MD (Cv) - **Spec Exp:** Cholesterol/Lipid Disorders; Cardiac Catheterization; Congestive Heart Failure; Hypertension; **Hospital:** Robert Wood Johnson Univ Hosp - New Brunswick, St. Peter's Univ Hosp; **Address:** Cardiology Assocs of New Brunswick, 593 Cranbury Rd, East Brunswick, NJ 8816; **Phone:** 732-390-3333; **Board Cert:** Internal Medicine 1981; Cardiovascular Disease 1983; **Med School:** Cornell Univ 1978; **Resid:** Internal Medicine, NY-Presby/Weill Cornell Med Ctr 1981; **Fellow:** Cardiovascular Disease, Hosp Univ Penn 1983

Mondrow, Daniel N MD (Cv) - **Spec Exp:** Cardiac Catheterization; Nuclear Stress Testing; Critical Care Medicine; Hypertension; **Hospital:** JFK Med Ctr - Edison, Robert Wood Johnson Univ Hosp - New Brunswick; **Address:** 280 Main St, Metuchen, NJ 08840; **Phone:** 732-494-3177; **Board Cert:** Internal Medicine 1979; Cardiovascular Disease 1985; **Med School:** SUNY Downstate 1976; **Resid:** Internal Medicine, Brookdale Univ Med Ctr 1979; **Fellow:** Cardiovascular Disease, St Vincent Med Ctr 1981

Schanzer, Robert J MD (Cv) - **Spec Exp:** Hypertension; **Hospital:** Robert Wood Johnson Univ Hosp at Rahway, JFK Med Ctr - Edison; **Address:** Advanced Cardiovascular Medicine, 1 Ethel Rd, Ste 106D, Edison, NJ 08820; **Phone:** 732-650-0040; **Board Cert:** Internal Medicine 2009; Cardiovascular Disease 2013; Interventional Cardiology 2004; **Med School:** Albert Einstein Coll Med 1995; **Resid:** Internal Medicine, Mount Sinai Med Ctr 1998; **Fellow:** Cardiovascular Disease, NYU Med Ctr 2001; Interventional Cardiology, NYU Med Ctr 2002

Shell, Roger A MD (Cv) - **Spec Exp:** Coronary Artery Disease; Heart Valve Disease; Cholesterol/Lipid Disorders; Non-Invasive Cardiology; **Hospital:** Robert Wood Johnson Univ Hosp - New Brunswick, St. Peter's Univ Hosp; **Address:** Cardiology Assocs of New Brunswick, 593 Cranbury Rd, East Brunswick, NJ 8816; **Phone:** 732-390-3333; **Board Cert:** Internal Medicine 1980; Cardiovascular Disease 1983; **Med School:** UMDNJ-Rutgers Med Sch 1977; **Resid:** Internal Medicine, RW Johnson Univ Hosp 1980; **Fellow:** Cardiovascular Disease, Penn Presby Med Ctr 1982; **Fac Appt:** Asst Clin Prof Med, Rutgers R W Johnson Med Sch

Shindler, Daniel M MD (Cv) - **Spec Exp:** Echocardiography; Echocardiography-Trans-esophageal; Cardiac Tumors/Cancer; **Hospital:** Robert Wood Johnson Univ Hosp - New Brunswick; **Address:** Univ Med Group, 125 Paterson St, Fl 6th, Ste 6100, New Brunswick, NJ 08901; **Phone:** 732-235-7855; **Board Cert:** Internal Medicine 1987; **Med School:** Spain 1979; **Resid:** Internal Medicine, USPHS Hosp 1981; Internal Medicine, RW Johnson Hosp 1982; **Fellow:** Cardiovascular Disease, RW Johnson Hosp 1984; **Fac Appt:** Prof Med, Rutgers R W Johnson Med Sch

Child & Adolescent Psychiatry

Shampain, Lawrence R MD (ChAP) - **Spec Exp:** Pervasive Development Disorders; Anxiety Disorders; ADD/ADHD; Child Psychiatry; **Hospital:** Robert Wood Johnson Univ Hosp - Somerset, Univ Beh HC-Univ of Med/Dent of NJ; **Address:** 32 Wernik Place, Ste B, Metuchen, NJ 08840; **Phone:** 732-548-1600; **Board Cert:** Psychiatry 1988; Child & Adolescent Psychiatry 1990; **Med School:** Hahnemann Univ 1982; **Resid:** Psychiatry, Mt Sinai Med Ctr 1985; **Fellow:** Child Psychiatry, UCLA Neuropsych Inst 1987; **Fac Appt:** Assoc Clin Prof Psyc, Rutgers R W Johnson Med Sch

Child Neurology

Wollack, Jan B MD (ChiN) - **Spec Exp:** Epilepsy/Seizure Disorders; **Hospital:** Robert Wood Johnson Univ Hosp - New Brunswick; **Address:** 89 French St Fl 2, New Brunswick, NJ 08901; **Phone:** 732-235-7875; **Board Cert:** Pediatrics 1988; Child Neurology 1987; Epilepsy 2013; **Med School:** Columbia P&S 1981; **Resid:** Pediatrics, Columbia-Presby Med Ctr 1983; Neurology, Columbia-Presby Med Ctr 1986; **Fac Appt:** Assoc Prof Ped, Rutgers R W Johnson Med Sch

Clinical Genetics

Sklower Brooks, Susan MD (CG) - **Spec Exp:** Birth Defects; Inborn Errors of Metabolism; Developmental Disorders; Prenatal Diagnosis; **Hospital:** Robert Wood Johnson Univ Hosp - New Brunswick; **Address:** Robert Wood Johnson Med Grp, Child Hlth Inst of NJ, 89 French St Fl 2, New Brunswick, NJ 08903-2160; **Phone:** 732-235-6230; **Board Cert:** Pediatrics 1979; Clinical Genetics 1982; Clinical Biochemical Genetics 1984; **Med School:** Mount Sinai Sch Med 1975; **Resid:** Pediatrics, Mount Sinai Hosp 1977; **Fellow:** Clinical Genetics, Mount Sinai Hosp 1979; **Fac Appt:** Prof Ped, Rutgers R W Johnson Med Sch

Colon & Rectal Surgery

Eisenstat, Theodore E MD (CRS) - **Spec Exp:** Colon Cancer; Inflammatory Bowel Disease; Anorectal Disorders; Hemorrhoids; **Hospital:** Robert Wood Johnson Univ Hosp - New Brunswick, JFK Med Ctr - Edison; **Address:** Robert Wood Johnson Med Group, Clinical Academic Bldg, 125 Paterson St, Ste 4100, New Brunswick, NJ 08901; **Phone:** 732-235-7920; **Board Cert:** Surgery 1974; Colon & Rectal Surgery 2013; **Med School:** NY Med Coll 1968; **Resid:** Surgery, Thomas Jefferson Univ Hosp 1971; Surgery, Pennsylvania Hosp 1973; **Fellow:** Colon & Rectal Surgery, Muhlenberg Med Ctr 1978; **Fac Appt:** Clin Prof S, Rutgers R W Johnson Med Sch

Rezac, Craig MD (CRS) - **Spec Exp:** Colon & Rectal Cancer; Inflammatory Bowel Disease; Diverticulitis; Pelvic & Perineal Surgery; **Hospital:** Robert Wood Johnson Univ Hosp - New Brunswick; **Address:** 125 Patterson St, Ste 4100, New Brunswick, NJ 08903; **Phone:** 732-235-7920; **Board Cert:** Surgery 2011; Colon & Rectal Surgery 2012; **Med School:** Italy 1995; **Resid:** Surgery, RW Johnson Medical Ctr 2001; **Fellow:** Colon & Rectal Surgery, RW Johnson Med Ctr 2002; Laparoscopic Surgery, Hackensack Med Ctr 2003; **Fac Appt:** Asst Prof S, Rutgers R W Johnson Med Sch

Zinkin, Lewis D MD (CRS) - **Spec Exp:** Colon Cancer; Inflammatory Bowel Disease; **Hospital:** Robert Wood Johnson Univ Hosp - New Brunswick, St. Peter's Univ Hosp; **Address:** Princeton Surgical Assocs, 5 Plainsboro Rd, Ste 400, Plainsboro, NJ 08816; **Phone:** 609-936-9100; **Board Cert:** Colon & Rectal Surgery 1978; **Med School:** UMDNJ-NJ Med Sch, Newark 1970; **Resid:** Surgery, St Vincents Hosp 1977; Colon & Rectal Surgery, Greater Baltimore Med Ctr 1978; **Fac Appt:** Assoc Clin Prof S

Dermatology

Milgraum, Sandy S MD (D) - **Spec Exp:** Skin Laser Surgery; Tattoo Removal; Cosmetic Dermatology; Pediatric Dermatology; **Hospital:** Robert Wood Johnson Univ Hosp - New Brunswick; **Address:** Academic Dermatology Ctr, 81 Brunswick Woods Drive, East Brunswick, NJ 08816-5601; **Phone:** 732-613-0300; **Board Cert:** Dermatology 1986; Pediatric Dermatology 2006; **Med School:** Australia 1979; **Resid:** Dermatology, Univ Mich Hosp 1986; **Fac Appt:** Assoc Prof D, Rutgers R W Johnson Med Sch

Vine, John E MD (D) - **Spec Exp:** Mohs Surgery; Cosmetic Dermatology; Hyperhidrosis/Axillary Curettage; **Hospital:** Univ Med Ctr Princeton at Plainsboro, Robert Wood Johnson Univ Hosp - New Brunswick; **Address:** Medical Arts Pavilion, 4th floor, 5 Plainsboro Rd, Ste 460, Princeton, NJ 08536; **Phone:** 609-799-6222; **Board Cert:** Dermatology 2005; **Med School:** Brown Univ 1992; **Resid:** Dermatology, Meml Hermann Hosp 1996; **Fellow:** Mohs Surgery, Scripps Clinic 1997

Wrone, David A MD (D) - **Spec Exp:** Skin Laser Surgery; Cosmetic Surgery; Mohs Surgery; Skin Cancer; **Hospital:** Univ Med Ctr Princeton at Plainsboro, Robert Wood Johnson Univ Hosp - New Brunswick; **Address:** 1950 Highway 27, Ste A, North Brunswick, NJ 08902; **Phone:** 609-683-4999; **Board Cert:** Dermatology 2009; **Med School:** Stanford Univ 1996; **Resid:** Dermatology, Univ Wisconsin Med Ctr 1998; Dermatology, Mass Genl Hosp 2001; **Fellow:** Mohs Surgery, UCLA Med Ctr 2002

Diagnostic Radiology

Epstein, Robert E MD (DR) - **Spec Exp:** MRI; Musculoskeletal Imaging; **Hospital:** Robert Wood Johnson Univ Hosp - New Brunswick; **Address:** University Radiology Group, 579A Cranbury Rd Fl 3, East Brunswick, NJ 08816; **Phone:** 732-390-0040; **Board Cert:** Diagnostic Radiology 1995; **Med School:** Duke Univ 1990; **Resid:** Diagnostic Radiology, Thomas Jefferson Univ Hosp 1995; **Fellow:** Musculoskeletal Imaging, Hosp Univ Penn 1996; **Fac Appt:** Asst Clin Prof Rad, Rutgers R W Johnson Med Sch

Rosenfeld, David L MD (DR) - **Spec Exp:** Pediatric Radiology; **Hospital:** Robert Wood Johnson Univ Hosp - New Brunswick; **Address:** University Radiology Group, 579A Cranbury Rd Fl 3, East Brunswick, NJ 08816; **Phone:** 732-390-0040; **Board Cert:** Diagnostic Radiology 1972; **Med School:** Univ Pittsburgh 1967; **Resid:** Diagnostic Radiology, Montefiore Med Ctr 1971; **Fac Appt:** Clin Prof Rad, Rutgers R W Johnson Med Sch

Schlesinger, Scott D MD (DR) - **Spec Exp:** Interventional Neuroradiology; **Hospital:** Robert Wood Johnson Univ Hosp - New Brunswick; **Address:** Univ Radiology Grp, 483 Cranbury Rd, East Brunswick, NJ 08816; **Phone:** 732-390-0040; **Board Cert:** Diagnostic Radiology 1988; **Med School:** NE Ohio Univ 1983; **Resid:** Diagnostic Radiology, Univ Hosp 1988; **Fellow:** Neurological Radiology, NYU Med Ctr 1990

Underberg-Davis, Sharon J MD (DR) - **Spec Exp:** Pediatric Radiology; **Hospital:** Robert Wood Johnson Univ Hosp - New Brunswick; **Address:** Univ Radiology Grp, 579A Cranbury Rd Fl 3, East Brunswick, NJ 08816; **Phone:** 732-390-0040; **Board Cert:** Diagnostic Radiology 1993; Pediatric Radiology 2004; **Med School:** Harvard Med Sch 1988; **Resid:** Diagnostic Radiology, Hosp Univ Penn 1993; **Fellow:** Pediatric Radiology, Chldns Hosp 1995

Endocrinology, Diabetes & Metabolism

Agrin, Richard MD (EDM) - **Spec Exp:** Thyroid Disorders; Parathyroid Disorders; Diabetes; **Hospital:** Robert Wood Johnson Univ Hosp - New Brunswick, Robert Wood Johnson Univ Hosp - Somerset; **Address:** 78 Easton Ave, New Brunswick, NJ 08901; **Phone:** 732-545-1065; **Board Cert:** Internal Medicine 1974; Endocrinology 1977; **Med School:** Univ Pennsylvania 1971; **Resid:** Internal Medicine, USPHS Hosp 1975; **Fellow:** Endocrinology, Boston Univ Hosp 1977; **Fac Appt:** Assoc Clin Prof Med, Rutgers R W Johnson Med Sch

Bucholtz, Harvey K MD (EDM) - **Spec Exp:** Diabetes; Thyroid Disorders; Osteoporosis; **Hospital:** JFK Med Ctr - Edison, Newark Beth Israel Med Ctr (page 94); **Address:** 2 Lincoln Hwy, Ste 501, Edison, NJ 08820; **Phone:** 732-549-7470; **Board Cert:** Internal Medicine 1973; Endocrinology 1975; **Med School:** SUNY Upstate Med Univ 1968; **Resid:** Internal Medicine, Univ Michigan Med Ctr 1971; **Fellow:** Endocrinology, Duke Univ Med Ctr 1975; **Fac Appt:** Asst Clin Prof Med, UMDNJ-NJ Med Sch, Newark

Maman, Arie MD (EDM) - **Spec Exp:** Thyroid Disorders; Diabetes; Pituitary Disorders; **Hospital:** Robert Wood Johnson Univ Hosp - New Brunswick, St. Peter's Univ Hosp; **Address:** D3 Brier Hill Ct, East Brunswick, NJ 08816-3335; **Phone:** 732-613-0707; **Board Cert:** Internal Medicine 1977; Endocrinology, Diabetes & Metabolism 1979; **Med School:** France 1974; **Resid:** Internal Medicine, Jewish Hosp 1977; **Fellow:** Endocrinology, Univ Colorado Hosp 1979; **Fac Appt:** Assoc Clin Prof Med, Rutgers R W Johnson Med Sch

Schneider, Stephen H MD (EDM) - **Spec Exp:** Diabetes; Nutrition; Cholesterol/Lipid Disorders; **Hospital:** Robert Wood Johnson Univ Hosp - New Brunswick; **Address:** 125 Patterson St, Clinical Academic Bldg Fl 5 - Ste 5100B, New Brunswick, NJ 08901; **Phone:** 732-235-7219; **Board Cert:** Internal Medicine 1975; Endocrinology, Diabetes & Metabolism 1979; **Med School:** Boston Univ 1972; **Resid:** Internal Medicine, Boston Univ Hosp 1975; **Fellow:** Endocrinology, Diabetes & Metabolism, Boston Med Ctr 1976; **Fac Appt:** Prof Med, Rutgers R W Johnson Med Sch

Spiler, Ira MD (EDM) - **Spec Exp:** Pituitary Disorders; Thyroid Disorders; Calcium Disorders; **Hospital:** Raritan Bay Med Ctr - Perth Amboy, Robert Wood Johnson Univ Hosp - New Brunswick; **Address:** Endocrine Associates of Raritan Bay, 3 Hospital Plaza, Ste 307, Old Bridge, NJ 08857-3095; **Phone:** 732-360-1122; **Board Cert:** Internal Medicine 1976; Endocrinology, Diabetes & Metabolism 1979; **Med School:** Albert Einstein Coll Med 1971; **Resid:** Internal Medicine, Bronx Municipal Hosp 1973; Internal Medicine, Boston City Hosp 1976; **Fellow:** Endocrinology, Tufts-New England Med Ctr 1978; **Fac Appt:** Assoc Clin Prof Med, Rutgers R W Johnson Med Sch

Family Medicine

Metz, John P MD (FMed) *PCP* - **Spec Exp:** Primary Care Sports Medicine; **Hospital:** JFK Med Ctr - Edison; **Address:** JFK Fam Med Ctr, 65 James St, Edison, NJ 08818; **Phone:** 732-321-7487; **Board Cert:** Family Medicine 2013; Sports Medicine 2011; **Med School:** Jefferson Med Coll 1994; **Resid:** Family Medicine, Malcolm Grow Med Ctr 1997; **Fellow:** Primary Care Sports Medicine, Uniformed Srvs U Hlth Scis 2000

Picciano, Anne MD (FMed) *PCP* - **Spec Exp:** Adolescent Medicine; **Hospital:** JFK Med Ctr - Edison; **Address:** JFK Fam Med Ctr, 65 James St, Edison, NJ 08818; **Phone:** 732-321-7487; **Board Cert:** Family Medicine 2009; Adolescent Medicine 2013; **Med School:** Univ Pennsylvania 1987; **Resid:** Family Medicine, W Jersey Hlth 1990; **Fac Appt:** Asst Clin Prof FMed, Rutgers R W Johnson Med Sch

Swee, David E MD (FMed) *PCP* - **Hospital:** Robert Wood Johnson Univ Hosp - New Brunswick; **Address:** Family Medicine at Monument Square, 317 George St, Fl 1, Ste 100, New Brunswick, NJ 08901; **Phone:** 732-235-8993; **Board Cert:** Family Medicine 2007; **Med School:** Canada 1975; **Resid:** Family Medicine, Somerset Med Ctr 1977; **Fac Appt:** Prof FMed, Rutgers R W Johnson Med Sch

Tallia, Alfred F MD (FMed) *PCP* - **Hospital:** Robert Wood Johnson Univ Hosp - New Brunswick; **Address:** Family Med at Monument Square, 317 George St, Fl 1, Ste 100, New Brunswick, NJ 08901-2162; **Phone:** 732-235-8993; **Board Cert:** Family Medicine 2007; **Med School:** Rutgers R W Johnson Med Sch 1978; **Resid:** Family Medicine, Thomas Jefferson Univ Hosp 1981; **Fac Appt:** Prof FMed, Rutgers R W Johnson Med Sch

Tierney, Peter C MD (FMed) *PCP* - **Hospital:** Univ Med Ctr Princeton at Plainsboro; **Address:** 666 Plainsboro Rd, Ste 1316, Plainsboro, NJ 08536; **Phone:** 609-275-8100; **Board Cert:** Family Medicine 2005; **Med School:** Univ VA Sch Med 1983; **Resid:** Family Medicine, Hunterdon Med Ctr 1986

Winter, Robin O MD (FMed) *PCP* - **Spec Exp:** Geriatric Medicine; **Hospital:** JFK Med Ctr - Edison; **Address:** JFK Fam Med Ctr, 65 James St, Edison, NJ 08818; **Phone:** 732-321-7487; **Board Cert:** Family Medicine 2005; Geriatric Medicine 2006; **Med School:** Albert Einstein Coll Med 1978; **Resid:** Family Medicine, Hunterdon Med Ctr 1981; **Fac Appt:** Clin Prof FMed, Rutgers R W Johnson Med Sch

Gastroenterology

Hodes, Steven E MD (Ge) - **Hospital:** Raritan Bay Med Ctr - Perth Amboy, JFK Med Ctr - Edison; **Address:** 205 May St, Ste 201, Edison, NJ 08837; **Phone:** 732-661-9225; **Board Cert:** Internal Medicine 1977; Gastroenterology 1979; **Med School:** Albert Einstein Coll Med 1974; **Resid:** Internal Medicine, Montefiore Med Ctr 1977; **Fellow:** Gastroenterology, Mt Sinai-Bronx VA Hosps 1979

Pitchumoni, Capecomorin S MD (Ge) - **Spec Exp:** Pancreatic Disease; Gastroesophageal Reflux Disease (GERD); Pancreatic Cancer; Hepatitis C; **Hospital:** St. Peter's Univ Hosp; **Address:** St Peters Univ Hosp, 254 Easton Ave, CARES Bldg - Fl 4 - Ste 4013, New Brunswick, NJ 08901; **Phone:** 732-745-8600; **Board Cert:** Gastroenterology 1971; Internal Medicine 1977; **Med School:** India 1960; **Resid:** Internal Medicine, Norwalk Hosp 1968; **Fellow:** Gastroenterology, Yale New Haven Hosp 1969; **Fac Appt:** Clin Prof Med, India

Plumser, Allan B MD (Ge) - **Spec Exp:** Endoscopy; Pancreatic/Biliary Endoscopy (ERCP); Liver Disease; **Hospital:** Robert Wood Johnson Univ Hosp - New Brunswick, St. Peter's Univ Hosp; **Address:** 465 Cranbury Rd, Ste 102, East Brunswick, NJ 08816; **Phone:** 732-390-1995; **Board Cert:** Internal Medicine 1981; Gastroenterology 1983; **Med School:** NY Med Coll 1978; **Resid:** Internal Medicine, SUNY Stonybrook Med Ctr 1981; **Fellow:** Gastroenterology, SUNY Stonybrook Med Ctr 1983

Geriatric Medicine

Bullock, Richard B MD (Ger) *PCP* - **Spec Exp:** Hypertension; Cholesterol/Lipid Disorders; Dementia; **Hospital:** JFK Med Ctr - Edison; **Address:** 225 May St, Ste E, Edison, NJ 08837-3266; **Phone:** 732-661-2020; **Board Cert:** Internal Medicine 1984; Geriatric Medicine 2010; **Med School:** Mount Sinai Sch Med 1981; **Resid:** Internal Medicine, Mt Sinai Hosp 1984; **Fac Appt:** Asst Clin Prof Med, Rutgers R W Johnson Med Sch

Vigario, Jose C DO (Ger) *PCP* - **Spec Exp:** Frail Elderly; Dementia; Alzheimer's Disease; **Hospital:** Univ Med Ctr Princeton at Plainsboro; **Address:** Princeton Medicine, 2 Center Drive, Ste 200, Monroe Township, NJ 08831; **Phone:** 609-395-2470; **Board Cert:** Internal Medicine 2004; Geriatric Medicine 2009; **Med School:** NY Coll Osteo Med 1992; **Resid:** Internal Medicine, Union Hosp 1994; Internal Medicine, Overlook Med Ctr 1995; **Fellow:** Geriatric Medicine, RWJ Univ Hosp 1998; **Fac Appt:** Asst Clin Prof Med, Drexel Univ Coll Med

Gynecologic Oncology

Rodriguez, Lorna MD/PhD (GO) - **Spec Exp:** Robotic Surgery; Ovarian Cancer; Cervical Cancer; **Hospital:** Robert Wood Johnson Univ Hosp - New Brunswick; **Address:** Cancer Institute of New Jersey, 195 Little Albany St Fl 1 - rm 1100, New Brunswick, NJ 08903; **Phone:** 732-235-7615; **Board Cert:** Obstetrics & Gynecology 2013; Gynecologic Oncology 2013; **Med School:** Puerto Rico 1979; **Resid:** Obstetrics & Gynecology, Cooper Med Ctr 1983; **Fellow:** Gynecologic Oncology, Univ Michigan Hosps 1985; **Fac Appt:** Prof ObG, Rutgers R W Johnson Med Sch

Welshinger, Marie MD (GO) - **Spec Exp:** Gynecologic Cancer; **Hospital:** St. Peter's Univ Hosp; **Address:** St Peter's Physician Assocs, 78 Easton Ave, New Brunswick, NJ 08901-1865; **Phone:** 732-828-3504; **Board Cert:** Obstetrics & Gynecology 2013; Gynecologic Oncology 2013; **Med School:** Univ Minn 1988; **Resid:** Obstetrics & Gynecology, SUNY Stony Brook Hosp 1992; **Fellow:** Gynecologic Oncology, Meml Sloan-Kettering Cancer Ctr 1996

Hematology

Karp, George I MD (Hem) - **Spec Exp:** Coagulation/Bleeding Disorders; Anemia; Breast Cancer; **Hospital:** Robert Wood Johnson Univ Hosp - New Brunswick, St. Peter's Univ Hosp; **Address:** Natl Cancer Care Assocs, J-2 Brier Hill Ct, East Brunswick, NJ 08816; **Phone:** 732-390-7750; **Board Cert:** Internal Medicine 1979; Medical Oncology 1981; Hematology 1982; **Med School:** Columbia P&S 1976; **Resid:** Internal Medicine, Univ Chicago Med Ctr 1978; **Fellow:** Medical Oncology, Dana Farber Cancer Inst 1981; Hematology, Beth Israel Deaconess Hosp 1982; **Fac Appt:** Clin Prof Hem & Onc, Rutgers R W Johnson Med Sch

Philipp, Claire S MD (Hem) - **Spec Exp:** Bleeding/Coagulation Disorders; **Hospital:** Robert Wood Johnson Univ Hosp - New Brunswick; **Address:** Robert Wood Johnson Med School, 125 Paterson St, CAB5231, New Brunswick, NJ 08901; **Phone:** 732-235-6531; **Board Cert:** Internal Medicine 1981; Hematology 1984; Medical Oncology 1985; **Med School:** Brown Univ 1978; **Resid:** Internal Medicine, Beth Israel Med Ctr 1981; **Fellow:** Hematology & Oncology, NYU Med Ctr 1984; **Fac Appt:** Prof Med, Rutgers R W Johnson Med Sch

Strair, Roger MD/PhD (Hem) - **Spec Exp:** Leukemia; Lymphoma; Bone Marrow Transplant; Multiple Myeloma; **Hospital:** Robert Wood Johnson Univ Hosp - New Brunswick; **Address:** Cancer Inst of NJ, 195 Little Albany St, New Brunswick, NJ 08903; **Phone:** 732-235-7464; **Board Cert:** Internal Medicine 1984; Hematology 1986; Medical Oncology 1987; **Med School:** Albert Einstein Coll Med 1981; **Resid:** Internal Medicine, Brigham & Women's Hosp 1984; **Fellow:** Hematology & Oncology, Brigham & Women's Hosp 1988; **Fac Appt:** Assoc Prof Med, Rutgers R W Johnson Med Sch

Infectious Disease

Boruchoff, Susan E MD (Inf) - **Spec Exp:** Travel Medicine; AIDS/HIV; Viral Infections; **Hospital:** Robert Wood Johnson Univ Hosp - New Brunswick; **Address:** RWJ Div Infectious Disease/Travel Med, 125 Patterson St Fl 5 - Ste 5100B, New Brunswick, NJ 08901-1928; **Phone:** 732-235-7060; **Board Cert:** Internal Medicine 1985; Infectious Disease 1988; **Med School:** Columbia P&S 1982; **Resid:** Internal Medicine, Geo Wash Univ Hosp 1985; **Fellow:** Infectious Disease, Univ Mass Med Ctr 1988; **Fac Appt:** Prof Med, Rutgers R W Johnson Med Sch

Middleton, John R MD (Inf) - **Spec Exp:** AIDS/HIV; Osteomyelitis; **Hospital:** Raritan Bay Med Ctr - Perth Amboy; **Address:** ID Care, 3 Hospital Plaza, Ste 208, Old Bridge, NJ 08857-3093; **Phone:** 732-360-2700; **Board Cert:** Internal Medicine 1973; Infectious Disease 1980; **Med School:** UMDNJ-NJ Med Sch, Newark 1970; **Resid:** Internal Medicine, NY Hosp-Cornell Med Ctr 1973; **Fellow:** Infectious Disease, RWJ Univ Hosp 1977; **Fac Appt:** Assoc Clin Prof Med, UMDNJ-Rutgers Med Sch

Sensakovic, John W MD/PhD (Inf) - **Spec Exp:** Lyme Disease; Fevers of Unknown Origin; Bone Infections; **Hospital:** Saint Michael's Med Ctr, JFK Med Ctr - Edison; **Address:** 113 James St, Edison, NJ 08820; **Phone:** 732-549-3449; **Board Cert:** Internal Medicine 1982; Infectious Disease 1984; **Med School:** UMDNJ-NJ Med Sch, Newark 1977; **Resid:** Internal Medicine, St Michaels Med Ctr 1980; **Fellow:** Infectious Disease, St Michaels Med Ctr 1982; **Fac Appt:** Prof Med, Seton Hall Univ Sch Hlth & Med Scis

Snepar, Richard A MD (Inf) - **Hospital:** Robert Wood Johnson Univ Hosp - New Brunswick, St. Peter's Univ Hosp; **Address:** Highland Park Medical, 579A Cranbury Rd, Ste 102, East Brunswick, NJ 08816; **Phone:** 732-613-0711; **Board Cert:** Internal Medicine 1979; Infectious Disease 1982; **Med School:** Cornell Univ-Weill Med Coll 1976; **Resid:** Internal Medicine, Med Coll PA Affil Hosp 1979; **Fellow:** Infectious Disease, Med Coll PA Affil Hosp 1981; **Fac Appt:** Asst Clin Prof Med, Rutgers R W Johnson Med Sch

Weinstein, Melvin P MD (Inf) - **Spec Exp:** Bone/Joint Infections; Infective Endocarditis; Mycobacterial Infections; **Hospital:** Robert Wood Johnson Univ Hosp - New Brunswick; **Address:** 125 Patterson St, Fl 5, New Brunswick, NJ 08901-1928; **Phone:** 732-235-7713; **Board Cert:** Internal Medicine 1975; Infectious Disease 1978; Medical Microbiology 1983; **Med School:** Geo Wash Univ 1970; **Resid:** Internal Medicine, Hartford Hosp 1975; **Fellow:** Infectious Disease, Univ Colo Hosp 1977; **Fac Appt:** Prof Med, Rutgers R W Johnson Med Sch

Internal Medicine

Carson, Jeffrey L MD (IM) *PCP* - **Hospital:** Robert Wood Johnson Univ Hosp - New Brunswick; **Address:** 125 Paterson St, Ste 5100, New Brunswick, NJ 08901; **Phone:** 732-235-6968; **Board Cert:** Internal Medicine 1980; **Med School:** Hahnemann Univ 1977; **Resid:** Internal Medicine, Hahnemann Univ Hosp 1980; **Fellow:** Internal Medicine, Univ Penn 1982; **Fac Appt:** Prof Med, Rutgers R W Johnson Med Sch

Cassidy, Brian MD (IM) *PCP* - **Hospital:** JFK Med Ctr - Edison; **Address:** 3910 Park Ave, Ste 8, Edison, NJ 08820; **Phone:** 732-767-3130; **Board Cert:** Internal Medicine 1988; **Med School:** Grenada 1985; **Resid:** Internal Medicine, Muhlenberg Med Ctr 1988

DeSilva Jr, Derrick M MD (IM) *PCP* - **Spec Exp:** Complementary Medicine; **Hospital:** Raritan Bay Med Ctr - Perth Amboy; **Address:** 629 Amboy Ave, Fl 2, Edison, NJ 08837; **Phone:** 732-738-8801; **Med School:** Dominican Republic 1982; **Resid:** Internal Medicine, Raritan Bay Med Ctr-Perth Amboy Div 1988

Schaer, Teresa M MD (IM) *PCP* - **Spec Exp:** Concierge Medicine; Geriatric Medicine; **Hospital:** St. Peter's Univ Hosp, Robert Wood Johnson Univ Hosp - New Brunswick; **Address:** 12 Stults Rd, Ste 123, Dayton, NJ 08810; **Phone:** 732-230-3272; **Board Cert:** Internal Medicine 1984; Geriatric Medicine 2010; **Med School:** UCSD 1981; **Resid:** Internal Medicine, Bellevue Hosp Ctr 1984; **Fellow:** Geriatric Medicine, Geo Wash Univ Med Ctr 1986; **Fac Appt:** Assoc Clin Prof Med

Medical Oncology

Aisner, Joseph MD (Onc) - **Spec Exp:** Lung Cancer; Solid Tumors; Thymoma; Mesothelioma; **Hospital:** Robert Wood Johnson Univ Hosp - New Brunswick; **Address:** Cancer Inst of New Jersey, 195 Little Albany St, New Brunswick, NJ 08903-2681; **Phone:** 732-235-7464; **Board Cert:** Internal Medicine 1973; Medical Oncology 1975; **Med School:** Wayne State Univ 1970; **Resid:** Internal Medicine, Georgetown Univ Hosp 1972; **Fellow:** Hematology & Oncology, Natl Cancer Inst 1975; **Fac Appt:** Prof Med, Rutgers R W Johnson Med Sch

DiPaola, Robert S MD (Onc) - **Spec Exp:** Genitourinary Cancer; Prostate Cancer; Urologic Cancer; **Hospital:** Robert Wood Johnson Univ Hosp - New Brunswick; **Address:** Cancer Inst of New Jersey, 195 Little Albany St, New Brunswick, NJ 08903-2681; **Phone:** 732-235-3336; **Board Cert:** Internal Medicine 2011; Medical Oncology 2005; **Med School:** Univ Utah 1988; **Resid:** Internal Medicine, Duke Univ Med Ctr 1991; **Fellow:** Hematology & Oncology, Univ Penn Hosp 1994; **Fac Appt:** Assoc Prof Med, Rutgers R W Johnson Med Sch

Nissenblatt, Michael J MD (Onc) - **Spec Exp:** Breast Cancer; Colon Cancer; Lung Cancer; Hereditary Cancer; **Hospital:** Robert Wood Johnson Univ Hosp - New Brunswick, St. Peter's Univ Hosp; **Address:** Central Jersey Oncology Ctr, 1 Brier Hill Ct J2 Bldg, East Brunswick, NJ 08816; **Phone:** 732-390-7750; **Board Cert:** Internal Medicine 1976; Medical Oncology 1979; **Med School:** Columbia P&S 1973; **Resid:** Internal Medicine, Johns Hopkins Hosp 1976; **Fellow:** Medical Oncology, Johns Hopkins Hosp 1978; **Fac Appt:** Clin Prof Onc, Rutgers R W Johnson Med Sch

Shypula, Gregory J MD (Onc) - **Spec Exp:** Hematology; **Hospital:** Raritan Bay Med Ctr - Perth Amboy, JFK Med Ctr - Edison; **Address:** 1030 St Georges Ave, Ste 307, Avenel, NJ 07001-1330; **Phone:** 732-750-1200; **Board Cert:** Internal Medicine 1989; Medical Oncology 2011; Hematology 2007; **Med School:** Poland 1981; **Resid:** Internal Medicine, T Marciniak Univ 1984; Internal Medicine, Raritan Bay Med Ctr-Perth Amboy Div 1988; **Fellow:** Hematology & Oncology, St Luke's-Roosevelt Hosp Ctr 1992; **Fac Appt:** Asst Clin Prof Med, UMDNJ-Robert Wood Johnson

Toppmeyer, Deborah L MD (Onc) - **Spec Exp:** Breast Cancer; Hereditary Cancer; **Hospital:** Robert Wood Johnson Univ Hosp - New Brunswick; **Address:** Cancer Inst of New Jersey, 195 Little Albany St, New Brunswick, NJ 08903; **Phone:** 732-235-9692; **Board Cert:** Internal Medicine 1988; Medical Oncology 2006; **Med School:** Albany Med Coll 1985; **Resid:** Internal Medicine, Univ Pittsburgh Hlth Ctr Hosp 1988; **Fellow:** Medical Oncology, Dana Farber Cancer Inst 1993; **Fac Appt:** Assoc Prof Med

Neonatal-Perinatal Medicine

Hegyi, Thomas MD (NP) - **Spec Exp:** Sudden Infant Death Syndrome (SIDS); **Hospital:** Robert Wood Johnson Univ Hosp - New Brunswick; **Address:** R W Johnson Univ Hosp, NICU Div, 1 Robert Wood Johnson Pl, New Brunswick, NJ 08903-1766; **Phone:** 732-235-7354; **Board Cert:** Pediatrics 1977; Neonatal-Perinatal Medicine 2010; **Med School:** Albert Einstein Coll Med 1972; **Resid:** Pediatrics, NY-Presby/Columbia Univ Med Ctr 1975; **Fellow:** Neonatal-Perinatal Medicine, Jacobi Med Ctr 1977; **Fac Appt:** Prof Ped, Rutgers R W Johnson Med Sch

Hiatt, I Mark MD (NP) - **Spec Exp:** Respiratory Failure; Prematurity/Low Birth Weight Infants; Ethics; **Hospital:** St. Peter's Univ Hosp; **Address:** St Peter's Univ Hosp, Div Neonatal Med, 254 Easton Ave, New Brunswick, NJ 08902; **Phone:** 732-745-8523; **Board Cert:** Pediatrics 1978; Neonatal-Perinatal Medicine 1979; **Med School:** Cornell Univ-Weill Med Coll 1972; **Resid:** Pediatrics, NY Hosp-Cornell Med Ctr 1975; **Fellow:** Neonatal-Perinatal Medicine, Babies Hosp-Columbia Univ 1977

Kaur, Harpreet MD (NP) - **Spec Exp:** Neonatology; Breathing Disorders; Infections-Neonatal; **Hospital:** St. Peter's Univ Hosp; **Address:** St Peters Univ Hosp, Neonatology, 254 Easton Ave, New Brunswick, NJ 08901; **Phone:** 732-745-8600 x8448; **Board Cert:** Pediatrics 2007; Neonatal-Perinatal Medicine 2010; **Med School:** India 1997; **Resid:** Pediatrics, Flushing Hosp Med Ctr 2005; **Fellow:** Neonatal-Perinatal Medicine, Jacobi Med Ctr 2009

Mehta, Rajeev MD (NP) - **Spec Exp:** Neonatal Critical Care; **Hospital:** Robert Wood Johnson Univ Hosp - New Brunswick; **Address:** RW Johnson Med School, 125 Paterson St, New Brunswick, NJ 08903-1766; **Phone:** 732-235-7036; **Board Cert:** Neonatal-Perinatal Medicine 2007; **Med School:** India 1978; **Resid:** Pediatrics, Queens Park/St Mary's/Dudley Rd Hosps 1985; Pediatrics, Univ Hosp 1990; **Fellow:** Neonatology, Bradford Royal Infirmary 1989; Neonatology, North Shore Univ Hosp 1993; **Fac Appt:** Prof Ped, Rutgers R W Johnson Med Sch

Nephrology

Covit, Andrew B MD (Nep) - **Spec Exp:** Hypertension; Kidney Failure; Renovascular Disease; **Hospital:** Robert Wood Johnson Univ Hosp - New Brunswick, St. Peter's Univ Hosp; **Address:** Nephrology-Hypertension Assocs, 8 Old Bridge Tpke, South River, NJ 08882; **Phone:** 732-390-4888; **Board Cert:** Internal Medicine 1982; Nephrology 1986; **Med School:** SUNY Downstate 1979; **Resid:** Internal Medicine, NY-Presby/Weill Cornell Med Ctr 1982; **Fellow:** Nephrology, NY-Presby/Weill Cornell Med Ctr 1984

Sherman, Richard A MD (Nep) - **Spec Exp:** Dialysis Care; Electrolyte Disorders; **Hospital:** Robert Wood Johnson Univ Hosp - New Brunswick; **Address:** RWJ Div Nephrology, 125 Patterson St, Ste 5100, New Brunswick, NJ 08901; **Phone:** 732-235-6512; **Board Cert:** Internal Medicine 1978; Nephrology 1980; **Med School:** Albert Einstein Coll Med 1975; **Resid:** Internal Medicine, Metropolitan Hosp 1977; **Fellow:** Nephrology, Montefiore Med Ctr 1979; **Fac Appt:** Prof Med, Rutgers R W Johnson Med Sch

Neurological Surgery

Nosko, Michael G MD/PhD (NS) - **Spec Exp:** Aneurysm-Cerebral; Brain Tumors; Pituitary Tumors; Cerebrovascular Neurosurgery; **Hospital:** Robert Wood Johnson Univ Hosp - New Brunswick, Univ Med Ctr Princeton at Plainsboro; **Address:** University Neuro Assocs, 125 Paterson St Fl 2 - Ste 2100, New Brunswick, NJ 08901-1962; **Phone:** 732-235-7756; **Board Cert:** Neurological Surgery 1993; **Med School:** Univ Toronto 1982; **Resid:** Neurological Surgery, Univ Alberta Affil Hosp 1991; **Fellow:** Research, Alberta Heritage Fdn Med Rsch 1986; **Fac Appt:** Assoc Prof NS, Rutgers R W Johnson Med Sch

Przybylski, Gregory J MD (NS) - **Spec Exp:** Spinal Surgery; Multiple Sclerosis; Vascular Neurosurgery; Spinal Cord Tumors; **Hospital:** JFK Med Ctr - Edison, Jersey Shore Univ Med Ctr; **Address:** NJ Neuroscience Inst, 65 James St Fl 2nd, Edison, NJ 08820; **Phone:** 732-321-7010; **Board Cert:** Neurological Surgery 2011; **Med School:** Jefferson Med Coll 1987; **Resid:** Neurological Surgery, UPMC 1994; **Fellow:** Spine Surgery, UPMC 1995; Spine Surgery, Med Coll Wisc 1996; **Fac Appt:** Prof NS, Seton Hall Univ Sch Hlth & Med Scis

Neurology

Belsh, Jerry M MD (N) - **Spec Exp:** Neuromuscular Disorders; Amyotrophic Lateral Sclerosis (ALS); Myasthenia Gravis; Neuro-Pathology; **Hospital:** Robert Wood Johnson Univ Hosp - New Brunswick; **Address:** 125 Paterson St Fl 6, New Brunswick, NJ 08901; **Phone:** 732-235-7340; **Board Cert:** Neurology 1981; **Med School:** Jefferson Med Coll 1975; **Resid:** Neurology, Hahnemann Univ Hosp 1977; Neurology, SUNY-Dwnst Med Ctr 1979; **Fellow:** Neuromuscular Medicine, Mt Sinai Hosp 1980; **Fac Appt:** Prof N, Rutgers R W Johnson Med Sch

Gizzi, Martin S MD/PhD (N) - **Spec Exp:** Neuro-Ophthalmology; Stroke; Progressive Supranuclear Palsy (PSP); Stroke; **Hospital:** JFK Med Ctr - Edison; **Address:** NJ Neuroscience Institute, 65 James St, Edison, NJ 08820-3947; **Phone:** 732-321-7010; **Board Cert:** Neurology 1990; Vascular Neurology 2008; **Med School:** Univ Miami Sch Med 1985; **Resid:** Neurology, Mount Sinai Hosp 1989; **Fellow:** Neuro-Ophthalmology, Mount Sinai Hosp 1991; **Fac Appt:** Prof N, Seton Hall Univ Sch Hlth & Med Scis

Golbe, Lawrence I MD (N) - **Spec Exp:** Parkinson's Disease; Progressive Supranuclear Palsy (PSP); Movement Disorders; **Hospital:** Robert Wood Johnson Univ Hosp - New Brunswick; **Address:** 125 Paterson St, Fl 6, rm 6100, New Brunswick, NJ 08901-2160; **Phone:** 732-235-7733; **Board Cert:** Neurology 1984; **Med School:** NYU Sch Med 1978; **Resid:** Internal Medicine, Hahnemann Univ Hosp 1980; Neurology, Bellevue Hosp 1983; **Fac Appt:** Prof N, Rutgers R W Johnson Med Sch

Herman, Martin N MD (N) - **Spec Exp:** Epilepsy; Stroke; Behavioral Disorders; **Hospital:** JFK Med Ctr - Edison; **Address:** New Jersey Neuroscience Institute, 65 James St Fl 2, Edison, NJ 08818; **Phone:** 732-321-7010 x69130; **Board Cert:** Neurology 1973; Epilepsy 2013; **Med School:** Northwestern Univ 1964; **Resid:** Psychiatry, Strong Meml Hosp 1965; Neurology, Univ VA Hlth Sci Ctr 1970; **Fellow:** Clinical Neurophysiology, Columbia-Presby Hosp 1971

Lazar, Mark H MD (N) - **Spec Exp:** Headache; Pain Management; Acupuncture; Sarcoidosis; **Hospital:** Robert Wood Johnson Univ Hosp - New Brunswick; **Address:** 573 Cranbury Rd, Ste A5, East Brunswick, NJ 08816-4026; **Phone:** 732-254-5101; **Board Cert:** Neurology 1982; **Med School:** NYU Sch Med 1977; **Resid:** Neurology, NYU Med Ctr 1981; **Fellow:** Neurology, NY-Cornell Med Ctr 1982; Clinical Neurophysiology, Columbia-Presby Med Ctr 1983

Lepore, Frederick E MD (N) - **Spec Exp:** Neuro-Ophthalmology; Botox for Blepharospasm; Migraine; Pseudomotor Cerebri; **Hospital:** Robert Wood Johnson Univ Hosp - New Brunswick; **Address:** Dept Neurology, 125 Paterson St, rm 6210, New Brunswick, NJ 08901-2160; **Phone:** 732-235-7730; **Board Cert:** Neurology 1981; **Med School:** Univ Rochester 1975; **Resid:** Internal Medicine, Univ Michigan Med Ctr 1976; Neurology, Univ Virginia Hlth Sci Ctr 1979; **Fellow:** Neuro-Ophthalmology, Bascom Palmer Eye Inst 1980; **Fac Appt:** Prof N, Rutgers R W Johnson Med Sch

McKinney III, James S MD (N) - **Spec Exp:** Stroke; **Hospital:** Robert Wood Johnson Univ Hosp - New Brunswick; **Address:** Robert Wood Johnson Med Grp, Clinical Academic Bldg, 125 Paterson St, Ste 6100, New Brunswick, NJ 08901; **Phone:** 732-235-7733; **Board Cert:** Neurology 2008; **Med School:** Grenada 2004; **Resid:** Neurology, Seton Hall Univ-JFK Med Ctr 2008; **Fellow:** Stroke, Hosp U Penn 2009; **Fac Appt:** Asst Prof N, Rutgers R W Johnson Med Sch

Oh, Youn K MD (N) - **Spec Exp:** Headache; Stroke; Seizure Disorders; Parkinson's Disease; **Hospital:** JFK Med Ctr - Edison, Robert Wood Johnson Univ Hosp at Rahway; **Address:** 34-36 Progress St, Ste B3, Edison, NJ 08820-1197; **Phone:** 908-757-6633; **Board Cert:** Neurology 1979; Psychiatry 1981; **Med School:** South Korea 1964; **Resid:** Psychiatry, Harvard Psy Svc/Boston City Hosp 1973; Neurology, UMDNJ-NJ Med Sch 1975; **Fac Appt:** Assoc Clin Prof N, Rutgers R W Johnson Med Sch

Rosenberg, Michael L MD (N) - **Spec Exp:** Neuro-Ophthalmology; Neuro-Otology; Balance Disorders; **Hospital:** JFK Med Ctr - Edison; **Address:** New Jersey Neuroscience Institute, 65 James St Fl 2, Edison, NJ 08818; **Phone:** 732-321-7010 x69130; **Board Cert:** Neurology 1983; **Med School:** Baylor Coll Med 1976; **Resid:** Neurology, Letterman AMC 1980; **Fellow:** Neuro-Ophthal-mology, Bascom-Palmer Eye Inst 1981; **Fac Appt:** Prof N, Seton Hall Univ Sch Hlth & Med Scis

Sage, Jacob I MD (N) - **Spec Exp:** Parkinson's Disease; Dystonia; **Hospital:** Robert Wood Johnson Univ Hosp - New Brunswick; **Address:** 125 Paterson St Fl 6 - Ste 6100, New Brunswick, NJ 08901-2160; **Phone:** 732-235-7733; **Board Cert:** Neurology 1979; **Med School:** Univ Pittsburgh 1972; **Resid:** Neurology, Univ Pittsburgh Hosps 1978; **Fellow:** Neurological Chemistry, NY Hosp-Cornell 1980; **Fac Appt:** Prof N, Rutgers R W Johnson Med Sch

Neuroradiology

Fitzpatrick, Maurice MD (NRad) - **Spec Exp:** MRI & CT of Brain & Spine; **Hospital:** Robert Wood Johnson Univ Hosp at Rahway, St. Peter's Univ Hosp; **Address:** Univ Radiology Grp, 579A Cranbury Rd, East Brunswick, NJ 08816; **Phone:** 732-390-0040; **Board Cert:** Diagnostic Radiology 1996; Neuroradiology 2009; **Med School:** Georgetown Univ 1991; **Resid:** Internal Medicine, N Shore Univ Hosp 1992; Diagnostic Radiology, Beth Israel Med Ctr 1996; **Fellow:** Neuroradiology, Thomas Jefferson Univ Hosp 1997

Keller, Irwin A MD (NRad) - **Spec Exp:** Brain & Spinal Imaging; Interventional Neuroradiol-ogy; Aneurysm-Cerebral; **Hospital:** Robert Wood Johnson Univ Hosp - New Brunswick; **Address:** Univ Radiology Grp, 579A Cranbury Rd Fl 3, East Brunswick, NJ 08816; **Phone:** 732-390-0040; **Board Cert:** Diagnostic Radiology 1984; Neuroradiology 2005; **Med School:** NY Med Coll 1980; **Resid:** Diagnostic Radiology, Montefiore Med Ctr 1984; **Fellow:** Neuroradiology, NYU Med Ctr 1986; **Fac Appt:** Clin Prof Rad, Rutgers R W Johnson Med Sch

Roychowdhury, Sudipta MD (NRad) - **Spec Exp:** Interventional Neuroradiology; Pediatric Radiology; **Hospital:** Robert Wood Johnson Univ Hosp - New Brunswick; **Address:** University Radiol-ogy Group, 483 Cranbury Rd, East Brunswick, NJ 08816; **Phone:** 732-390-0040; **Board Cert:** Di-agnostic Radiology 1997; Neuroradiology 2010; **Med School:** Northwestern Univ 1992; **Resid:** Diagnostic Radiology, Northwestern Meml Hosp 1997; **Fellow:** Neuroradiology, Hosp Univ Penn 1999; **Fac Appt:** Asst Clin Prof Rad, Rutgers R W Johnson Med Sch

Schonfeld, Steven M MD (NRad) - **Spec Exp:** Spine Imaging & Intervention; Pediatric Neu-roradiology; Interventional Neuroradiology; **Hospital:** Robert Wood Johnson Univ Hosp - New Brunswick, St. Peter's Univ Hosp; **Address:** University Radiology Group, 579A Cranbury Rd, Fl 3, East Brunswick, NJ 08816; **Phone:** 732-390-0040; **Board Cert:** Diagnostic Radiology 1982; Neu-roradiology 2005; **Med School:** Mount Sinai Sch Med 1978; **Resid:** Internal Medicine, Jacobi Med Ctr 1979; Diagnostic Radiology, Montefiore Hosp Med Ctr 1982; **Fellow:** Neuroradiology, NYU Med Ctr 1984; **Fac Appt:** Clin Prof Rad, Rutgers R W Johnson Med Sch

Obstetrics & Gynecology

Bachmann, Gloria A MD (ObG) - **Spec Exp:** Menopause Problems; Sexual Dysfunction; Pelvic Surgery; Uterine Fibroids; **Hospital:** Robert Wood Johnson Univ Hosp - New Brunswick; **Address:** Women's Hlth Inst, 125 Paterson St CAB Bldg - Ste 4200, New Brunswick, NJ 89011962; **Phone:** 732-235-7633; **Board Cert:** Obstetrics & Gynecology 1981; **Med School:** Univ Pennsylvania 1974; **Resid:** Obstetrics & Gynecology, Hosp Univ Penn - UPHS 1978; **Fac Appt:** Prof ObG, Rutgers R W Johnson Med Sch

Bochner, Ronnie Z MD (ObG) - **Spec Exp:** Gynecologic Surgery; Laparoscopic Surgery; Uterine Fibroids; Menopause Problems; **Hospital:** Robert Wood Johnson Univ Hosp - New Brunswick; **Address:** RWJ OB/GYN Assocs, 3270 Rt 27, Ste 2200, Kendall Park, NJ 08824-1458; **Phone:** 732-422-8989; **Board Cert:** Obstetrics & Gynecology 2013; **Med School:** Mount Sinai Sch Med 1981; **Resid:** Obstetrics & Gynecology, LI Jewish Med Ctr 1985; **Fac Appt:** Assoc Clin Prof ObG, Rutgers R W Johnson Med Sch

Davis, Nicole D MD (ObG) - **Spec Exp:** Gynecology Only; **Hospital:** St. Peter's Univ Hosp; **Address:** 620 Cranbury Rd, Ste LL90, East Brunswick, NJ 08816; **Phone:** 732-257-0081; **Board Cert:** Obstetrics & Gynecology 2013; **Med School:** Yale Univ 1988; **Resid:** Obstetrics & Gynecology, NY-Presby/Weill Cornell Med Ctr 1992

Friedman, Alan L MD (ObG) - **Spec Exp:** Pregnancy-High Risk; Infertility; **Hospital:** Univ Med Ctr Princeton at Plainsboro; **Address:** Princeton OB/GYN, 5 Plainsboro Rd, Med Arts Pav, Ste 500, Plainsboro, NJ 08536; **Phone:** 609-936-0700; **Board Cert:** Obstetrics & Gynecology 2013; **Med School:** Univ Chicago-Pritzker Sch Med 1982; **Resid:** Obstetrics & Gynecology, NYU Bellevue Hospital 1986

Rathauser, Robert H MD (ObG) - **Hospital:** Robert Wood Johnson Univ Hosp - New Brunswick; **Address:** RWJ OB/GYN Assocs, 3270 Route 27, Ste 2200, MS 08824, Kendall Park, NJ 08824; **Phone:** 732-422-8989; **Board Cert:** Obstetrics & Gynecology 2013; **Med School:** NYU Sch Med 1979; **Resid:** Obstetrics & Gynecology, LI Jewish Med Ctr 1983

Occupational Medicine

Gochfeld, Michael MD/PhD (OM) - **Spec Exp:** Environmental Medicine; Mercury Toxic Exposure; Chemical Exposure; **Hospital:** Robert Wood Johnson Univ Hosp - New Brunswick; **Address:** EOHSI Clin Ctr, 170 Frelinghuysen Rd, Ste 200, Piscataway, NJ 08854; **Phone:** 848-445-0123; **Board Cert:** Occupational Medicine 1983; **Med School:** Albert Einstein Coll Med 1965; **Resid:** Pediatrics, Univ CO Med Ctr 1966; **Fellow:** Behavioral Medicine, Rockefeller Univ Affil Hosp 1977; **Fac Appt:** Prof OM, Rutgers R W Johnson Med Sch

Kipen, Howard M MD (OM) - **Spec Exp:** Environmental Medicine; Occupational Lung Disease; **Hospital:** Robert Wood Johnson Univ Hosp - New Brunswick; **Address:** EOHSI Clin Ctr, 170 Frelinghuysen Rd, Ste 200, Piscataway, NJ 08854; **Phone:** 848-445-0123; **Board Cert:** Internal Medicine 1982; Occupational Medicine 1986; **Med School:** UCSF 1979; **Resid:** Internal Medicine, Columbia Presby Med Ctr 1982; Occupational Medicine, Mt Sinai Hosp 1984; **Fac Appt:** Prof Med, Rutgers R W Johnson Med Sch

Ophthalmology

Blondo, Dennis L MD (Oph) - **Hospital:** Raritan Bay Med Ctr - Old Bridge Div; **Address:** 28 Throckmorton Ln, Old Bridge, NJ 08857-2558; **Phone:** 732-679-6100; **Board Cert:** Ophthalmology 1979; **Med School:** Med Coll VA 1973; **Resid:** Ophthalmology, NYU Langone Med Ctr 1978

Engel, J. Mark MD (Oph) - **Spec Exp:** Pediatric Ophthalmology; Strabismus; **Hospital:** Robert Wood Johnson Univ Hosp - New Brunswick, St. Peter's Univ Hosp; **Address:** Univ Chldns Eye Ctr, 4 Cornwall Ct, East Brunswick, NJ 08816; **Phone:** 732-613-9191; **Board Cert:** Ophthalmology 2013; **Med School:** Loyola Univ-Stritch Sch Med 1986; **Resid:** Internal Medicine, Evanston Hosp 1988; Ophthalmology, Interfaith Med Ctr 1991; **Fellow:** Pediatric Ophthalmology, Lurie Chldn's Hosp-Chicago 1992; **Fac Appt:** Assoc Clin Prof Oph, UMDNJ-NJ Med Sch, Newark

Grabowski, Wayne M MD (Oph) - **Spec Exp:** Diabetic Eye Disease; Laser Vision Surgery; Glaucoma; **Hospital:** Univ Med Ctr Princeton at Plainsboro; **Address:** 5 Centre Drive, Ste 1B, Monroe Township, NJ 08831; **Phone:** 609-409-2777; **Board Cert:** Ophthalmology 1982; **Med School:** Albany Med Coll 1977; **Resid:** Ophthalmology, Albany Med Ctr 1981; **Fellow:** Vitreoretinal Surgery, Wills Eye Hosp 1983

Milite, James P MD (Oph) - **Spec Exp:** Oculoplastic Surgery; Eyelid Tumors/Cancer; Thyroid Eye Disease; **Hospital:** New York Eye & Ear Infirm of Mt Sinai; **Address:** Omni Eye Svcs, 485 Route 1 S A Bldg, Iselin, NJ 08830; **Phone:** 732-750-0400; **Board Cert:** Ophthalmology 2006; **Med School:** NYU Sch Med 1990; **Resid:** Ophthalmology, New York Eye & Ear Infirm 1994; **Fellow:** Ocular Pathology, New York Eye & Ear Infirm 1995; Ophthalmic Plastic Surgery, New York Eye & Ear Infirm 1996

Napolitano, Joseph D MD (Oph) - **Spec Exp:** Pediatric Ophthalmology; Strabismus; **Hospital:** Robert Wood Johnson Univ Hosp - New Brunswick; **Address:** Omni Eye Svcs, 485 Route 1 South, A Bldg - Ste 140, Iselin, NJ 8830; **Phone:** 732-750-0400; **Board Cert:** Ophthalmology 2008; **Med School:** Rutgers R W Johnson Med Sch 1987; **Resid:** Ophthalmology, UMDNJ-NJ Med Sch Affil Hosp 1992; **Fellow:** Pediatric Ophthalmology, Chldns Hosp 1994

Prenner, Jonathan L MD (Oph) - **Spec Exp:** Retina/Vitreous Surgery; Macular Degeneration; Retinal Detachment; Diabetic Eye Disease/Retinopathy; **Hospital:** Robert Wood Johnson Univ Hosp - New Brunswick; **Address:** NJ Retina, 10 Plum St, Fl 6, New Brunswick, NJ 08901; **Phone:** 732-220-1600; **Board Cert:** Ophthalmology 2003; **Med School:** SUNY Stony Brook 1998; **Resid:** Ophthalmology, Scheie Eye Inst 2002; **Fellow:** Vitreoretinal Surgery & Disease, William Beaumont Hosp 2004; **Fac Appt:** Assoc Clin Prof Oph, Rutgers R W Johnson Med Sch

Santamaria II, Jaime MD (Oph) - **Spec Exp:** Cataract Surgery; LASIK-Refractive Surgery; Cornea Transplant; **Hospital:** Raritan Bay Med Ctr - Perth Amboy, NY-Presby/Columbia Univ Med Ctr, NY (page 102); **Address:** Santamaria Eye Center, 104 Market St, Perth Amboy, NJ 08861-4412; **Phone:** 732-826-5159; **Board Cert:** Ophthalmology 1979; **Med School:** Columbia P&S 1973; **Resid:** Ophthalmology, Columbia-Presby Med Ctr 1978; **Fellow:** Research, Columbia Physicians & Surgeons 1975; **Fac Appt:** Asst Clin Prof Oph, Columbia P&S

Orthopaedic Surgery

Garfinkel, Matthew J MD (OrS) - **Spec Exp:** Shoulder & Knee Surgery; Arthroscopic Surgery; Sports Medicine; **Hospital:** JFK Med Ctr - Edison; **Address:** Edison-Metuchen Orthopaedic Grp, 10 Parsonage Rd Fl 5 - Ste 500, Edison, NJ 08837-2429; **Phone:** 732-494-6226; **Board Cert:** Orthopaedic Surgery 2015; **Med School:** Cornell Univ-Weill Med Coll 1986; **Resid:** Surgery, Jacobi Med Ctr 1987; Orthopaedic Surgery, Montefiore/Weiler Einsten Med Ctr 1991; **Fellow:** Sports Medicine, Lankenau Hosp 1992

Lombardi, Joseph S MD (OrS) - **Spec Exp:** Spinal Surgery; Spinal Disc Replacement; **Hospital:** JFK Med Ctr - Edison; **Address:** Edison-Metuchen Orthopaedic Grp, 10 Parsonage Rd Fl 5 - Ste 500, Edison, NJ 08837-2475; **Phone:** 732-494-6226; **Board Cert:** Orthopaedic Surgery 2008; **Med School:** UMDNJ-NJ Med Sch, Newark 1978; **Resid:** Orthopaedic Surgery, UMDNJ-Univ Hosp 1983; **Fellow:** Spine Surgery, Long Beach Meml Med Ctr 1984

Piskun, Andrew MD (OrS) - **Spec Exp:** Trauma; Sports Injuries; Arthroscopic Surgery; **Hospital:** Robert Wood Johnson Univ Hosp - New Brunswick, St. Peter's Univ Hosp; **Address:** Zemsky and Piskun MD, PA, 1132 S Washington Ave, Piscataway, NJ 08854-3335; **Phone:** 732-752-8484; **Board Cert:** Orthopaedic Surgery 1984; **Med School:** Rutgers R W Johnson Med Sch 1977; **Resid:** Orthopaedic Surgery, UMDNJ-RW Johnson Univ Hosp 1982; **Fac Appt:** Asst Clin Prof OrS, Rutgers R W Johnson Med Sch

Reich, Steven Mark MD (OrS) - **Spec Exp:** Spinal Surgery; Spinal Disorders; **Hospital:** Robert Wood Johnson Univ Hosp - New Brunswick, St. Peter's Hosp - Albany; **Address:** Affil Orthopaedic Specialists, 2186 Route 27, Ste 1A, North Brunswick, NJ 08902; **Phone:** 732-422-1222; **Board Cert:** Orthopaedic Surgery 2005; **Med School:** Albert Einstein Coll Med 1986; **Resid:** Orthopaedic Surgery, NYU Hosp Joint Diseases 1991; **Fellow:** Spine Surgery, Thomas Jefferson Univ Hosp 1992; **Fac Appt:** Asst Clin Prof OrS, UMDNJ-Rutgers Med Sch

Otolaryngology

Edelman, Bruce A MD (Oto) - **Spec Exp:** Ear Disorders; Sinusitis; **Hospital:** St. Peter's Univ Hosp; **Address:** B3 Cornwall Drive, East Brunswick, NJ 08816; **Phone:** 732-238-0300; **Board Cert:** Otolaryngology 1990; **Med School:** NYU Sch Med 1984; **Resid:** Surgery, Albert Einstein Med Ctr 1986; Otolaryngology, NYU Langone Med Ctr 1990; **Fellow:** Pediatric Otolaryngology, Chldns Hosp 1991

Kay, Scott L MD (Oto) - **Spec Exp:** Facial Nerve Disorders; Otology; Hearing Loss; Sinus Surgery; **Hospital:** Univ Med Ctr Princeton at Plainsboro; **Address:** 7 Schalks Crossing Rd, Ste 324, Plainsboro, NJ 08536; **Phone:** 609-897-0203; **Board Cert:** Otolaryngology 1993; **Med School:** Univ Pennsylvania 1986; **Resid:** Surgery, Mt Sinai Med Ctr 1988; Otolaryngology, NY-Presby/Columbia Univ Med Ctr 1992; **Fellow:** Facial Plastic Surgery, UPMC Shadyside 1993

Mazzara, Carl A MD (Oto) - **Spec Exp:** Rhinoplasty; Eyelid Surgery; Cancer Reconstruction; Facial Plastic & Reconstructive Surgery; **Hospital:** JFK Med Ctr - Edison, Overlook Med Ctr (page 92); **Address:** Mazzara Aesthetics, 5 Lincoln Hwy, Ste 4, Edison, NJ 08820; **Phone:** 732-635-1800; **Board Cert:** Otolaryngology 1994; Facial Plastic & Reconstr Surgery 1997; **Med School:** Mount Sinai Sch Med 1988; **Resid:** Otolaryngology, UMDNJ-Univ Hosp 1992; **Fellow:** Facial Plastic & Reconstr Surgery, Inst Facial Plastic Surg 1993

Miller, Andrew J MD (Oto) - **Spec Exp:** Cosmetic Surgery-Face; **Hospital:** JFK Med Ctr - Edison; **Address:** Assocs in Plastic Surgery, 1150 Amboy Ave, Edison, NJ 08837; **Phone:** 732-548-3200; **Board Cert:** Otolaryngology 2000; Facial Plastic & Reconstr Surgery 2012; **Med School:** Baylor Coll Med 1994; **Resid:** Surgery, Tulane Med Ctr 2005; Otolaryngology, Tulane Med Ctr 1999

Rosenbaum, Jeffrey M MD (Oto) - **Spec Exp:** Head & Neck Surgery; Cosmetic Surgery-Face; Salivary Gland Surgery; Thyroid & Parathyroid Surgery; **Hospital:** St. Peter's Univ Hosp; **Address:** B3 Cornwall Drive, East Brunswick, NJ 08816; **Phone:** 732-238-0300; **Board Cert:** Otolaryngology 1978; **Med School:** Albany Med Coll 1973; **Resid:** Surgery, Hartford Hosp 1975; Otolaryngology, NYU Langone Med Ctr 1978; **Fellow:** Plastic Surgery, Wayne State Univ Hosp 1979

Pain Medicine

Grubb, William R MD/DDS (PM) - **Spec Exp:** Complex Regional Pain Syndromes; Pain-Cancer; **Hospital:** Robert Wood Johnson Univ Hosp - New Brunswick; **Address:** NJ Pain Inst, 125 Patterson St Fl 5 - Ste 5100, New Brunswick, NJ 08901; **Phone:** 732-235-7246; **Board Cert:** Anesthesiology 1990; Pain Medicine 2007; **Med School:** Geo Wash Univ 1985; **Resid:** Anesthesiology, G Washington Univ Med Ctr 1989; **Fellow:** Pain Management, G Washington Univ Med Ctr 1990; Cardiac Anesthesiology, Univ S Fla Coll Med 1994; **Fac Appt:** Assoc Prof Anes, Rutgers R W Johnson Med Sch

Levin, Alexander MD (PM) - **Spec Exp:** Pain-Chronic; **Hospital:** Robert Wood Johnson Univ Hosp - New Brunswick; **Address:** 561 Cranbury Road Fl Ground, East Brunswick, NJ 08816-5400; **Phone:** 732-651-1300; **Board Cert:** Anesthesiology 1990; Pain Medicine 2007; **Med School:** Russia 1977; **Resid:** Anesthesiology, Westchester Med Ctr 1986; **Fellow:** Pain Medicine, Univ Cincinnati Med Ctr 1988

Pathology

Barnard, Nicola J MD (Path) - **Spec Exp:** Breast Pathology; Surgical Pathology; **Hospital:** Robert Wood Johnson Univ Hosp - New Brunswick; **Address:** RJW Dept Surgical Pathology, 1 Robert Wood Johnson Pl, New Brunswick, NJ 08901; **Phone:** 732-937-8592; **Board Cert:** Anatomic Pathology 1981; **Med School:** England, UK 1975; **Resid:** Pathology, Yale-New Haven Hosp 1980; Anatomic Pathology, New England Deaconess Hosp 1982; **Fellow:** Clinical Pathology, Harvard Univ Affil Hosp 1982; **Fac Appt:** Prof Path, Rutgers R W Johnson Med Sch

Pediatric Cardiology

Agarwal, Kishan C MD (PCd) - **Spec Exp:** Echocardiography; Heart Disease in Adolescents; Arrhythmias; **Hospital:** JFK Med Ctr - Edison, Children's Specialized Hosp; **Address:** 450 Plainfield Rd, Edison, NJ 08820-2628; **Phone:** 732-494-9500; **Board Cert:** Pediatrics 1990; Pediatric Cardiology 1990; **Med School:** India 1969; **Resid:** Pediatrics, St John's Episcopal Hosp 1977; Pediatrics, SUNY Downstate Med Ctr 1979; **Fellow:** Pediatric Cardiology, Mayo Clinic 1981; **Fac Appt:** Clin Prof Ped, Rutgers R W Johnson Med Sch

Gaffney, Joseph W MD (PCd) - **Spec Exp:** Echocardiography; Fetal Echocardiography; Critical Care; **Hospital:** Robert Wood Johnson Univ Hosp - New Brunswick, Morgan Stanley Chldns Hosp of NY-Presby, NY (page 102); **Address:** RWJ Univ Hosp - Dept Ped Cardiology, 125 Paterson St Fl 6 - Ste 6100, Clin Academic Bldg, New Brunswick, NJ 08901; **Phone:** 732-235-7905; **Board Cert:** Pediatric Cardiology 2013; **Med School:** NY Med Coll 1981; **Resid:** Pediatrics, Brookdale Univ Hosp Med Ctr 1984; **Fellow:** Pediatric Cardiology, NY-Presby/Columbia Univ Med Ctr 1987; **Fac Appt:** Assoc Prof Ped, Rutgers R W Johnson Med Sch

Kurer, Cheryl C MD (PCd) - **Spec Exp:** Congenital Heart Disease; Arrhythmias; Syncope; **Hospital:** Chldns Hosp of Philadelphia, St. Peter's Univ Hosp; **Address:** St Peters Univ Hosp - CHOP Cardiac Ctr, 254 Easton Ave, Med Offc Bldg Fl 2, New Brunswick, NJ 08901-1766; **Phone:** 732-846-2855; **Board Cert:** Pediatrics 1987; Pediatric Cardiology 2013; **Med School:** Mount Sinai Sch Med 1983; **Resid:** Pediatrics, Mt Sinai Med Ctr 1986; **Fellow:** Pediatric Cardiology, Chldns Hosp 1989; **Fac Appt:** Clin Prof Ped, Univ Pennsylvania

Pediatric Critical Care Medicine

Anene, Okechukwu P MD (PCCM) - **Spec Exp:** Nutrition; **Hospital:** JFK Med Ctr - Edison; **Address:** Chldns Svc Dept, JFK Med Ctr, 65 James St, Edison, NJ 08820; **Phone:** 732-321-7000 x68080; **Board Cert:** Pediatric Critical Care Medicine 2011; Pediatrics 2009; **Med School:** Nigeria 1983; **Resid:** Pediatrics, UMDNJ-New Jersey Med Sch Affil Hosp 1991; **Fellow:** Pediatric Critical Care Medicine, Wayne St Univ Affil Hosp 1995; **Fac Appt:** Assoc Prof Ped, Seton Hall Univ Sch Hlth & Med Scis

Jonna, Siva P MD (PCCM) - **Hospital:** St. Peter's Univ Hosp; **Address:** 254 Easton Ave, rm 5094, New Brunswick, NJ 08901; **Phone:** 732-745-8600 x8152; **Board Cert:** Pediatrics 2013; Pediatric Critical Care Medicine 2013; **Med School:** India 1981; **Resid:** Pediatrics, Howard Univ Hosp 1995; **Fellow:** Pediatric Critical Care Medicine, MedStar Georgetown Univ Hosp 1996; **Fac Appt:** Assoc Prof Ped, Grenada

Pediatric Endocrinology

Marshall, Ian MD (PEn) - **Spec Exp:** Adrenal Disorders; Growth Disorders; Pubertal Disorders; Diabetes; **Hospital:** Robert Wood Johnson Univ Hosp - New Brunswick; **Address:** RWJ Univ Hosp, Div Pediatric Endocrinology, 89 French St Fl 2, New Brunswick, NJ 08901; **Phone:** 732-235-6230; **Board Cert:** Pediatric Endocrinology 2011; **Med School:** South Africa 1991; **Resid:** Pediatrics, Schneider Chldns's Hosp 1999; **Fellow:** Pediatric Endocrinology, NY Presby Hosp 2002; **Fac Appt:** Asst Prof Ped, UMDNJ-Robert Wood Johnson

Xu, Weizhen MD (PEn) - **Spec Exp:** Diabetes; Growth Disorders; Metabolic Syndrome; **Hospital:** St. Peter's Univ Hosp; **Address:** St Peter's Univ Hosp, Pediatrics Dept, 254 Easton Ave, Medical Office Bldg, 3rd FL, New Brunswick, NJ 08901; **Phone:** 732-745-8574; **Board Cert:** Pediatrics 2008; Pediatric Endocrinology 2011; **Med School:** China 1987; **Resid:** Pediatrics, Chldn's Hosp 2000; **Fellow:** Pediatric Endocrinology, Chldn's Hosp 2003; **Fac Appt:** Asst Prof Ped, Rutgers R W Johnson Med Sch

Pediatric Gastroenterology

Koniaris, Soula G MD (PGe) - **Spec Exp:** Nutrition; Inflammatory Bowel Disease; Celiac Disease; **Hospital:** Robert Wood Johnson Univ Hosp - New Brunswick; **Address:** Child Hlth Inst NJ, 89 French St Fl 2, New Brunswick, NJ 08901; **Phone:** 732-235-7885; **Board Cert:** Pediatric Gastroenterology 2005; **Med School:** Univ Tenn Coll Med 1988; **Resid:** Pediatrics, Montefiore Med Ctr 1991; **Fellow:** Pediatric Gastroenterology, N Shore Univ Hosp 1994; **Fac Appt:** Asst Prof Ped, Rutgers R W Johnson Med Sch

Pediatric Hematology-Oncology

Drachtman, Richard A MD (PHO) - **Spec Exp:** Pediatric Cancers; Sickle Cell Disease; **Hospital:** Robert Wood Johnson Univ Hosp - New Brunswick, Jersey Shore Univ Med Ctr; **Address:** Rutgers Cancer Instiute of New Jersey, 195 Little Albany St, Ste 2900, New Brunswick, NJ 08903; **Phone:** 732-235-5437; **Board Cert:** Pediatric Hematology-Oncology 2014; **Med School:** Ros Franklin Univ/Chicago Med Sch 1984; **Resid:** Pediatrics, N Shore Univ Hosp 1988; **Fellow:** Pediatric Hematology-Oncology, Mt Sinai Hosp 1991; **Fac Appt:** Prof Ped, UMDNJ-Rutgers Med Sch

Masterson, Margaret MD (PHO) - **Hospital:** Robert Wood Johnson Univ Hosp - New Brunswick; **Address:** Rutgers Cancer Inst of NJ, 195 Little Albany St, Pediatric Hem/Oncology, New Brunswick, NJ 08901; **Phone:** 732-235-8131; **Board Cert:** Pediatrics 1986; Pediatric Hematology-Oncology 2012; **Med School:** Eastern VA Med Sch 1982; **Resid:** Pediatrics, Children's Hosp of Pittsburgh 1986; **Fellow:** Pediatric Hematology-Oncology, Children's Hosp 1989; **Fac Appt:** Assoc Prof Ped, Rutgers R W Johnson Med Sch

Pediatric Infectious Disease

Whitley-Williams, Patricia N MD (PInf) - **Spec Exp:** AIDS/HIV; Lyme Disease; Neonatal Infections; Travel Medicine; **Hospital:** Robert Wood Johnson Univ Hosp - New Brunswick; **Address:** RWJ - Div Pediatric Infect Dis, 89 French St Fl 2, New Brunswick, NJ 08903; **Phone:** 732-235-7894; **Board Cert:** Pediatrics 1980; Pediatric Infectious Disease 2012; **Med School:** Johns Hopkins Univ 1975; **Resid:** Pediatrics, Chldns Hosp 1978; **Fellow:** Pediatric Infectious Disease, Boston Med Ctr 1981; **Fac Appt:** Prof Ped, Rutgers R W Johnson Med Sch

Pediatric Nephrology

Singh, Anup MD (PNep) - **Spec Exp:** Nephrotic Syndrome; Lupus/SLE; Hypertension in Children; Kidney Stones; **Hospital:** St. Peter's Univ Hosp, Staten Island Univ Hosp - South; **Address:** St Peter's Univ Hosp, 254 Easton Ave MOB-3, New Brunswick, NJ 08901; **Phone:** 732-565-5489; **Board Cert:** Pediatrics 2014; Pediatric Nephrology 2010; **Med School:** Philippines 1985; **Resid:** Pediatrics, SUNY-Downstate Med Ctr 1991; **Fellow:** Pediatric Nephrology, SUNY-Downstate Med Ctr 1994; **Fac Appt:** Assoc Prof Ped, Drexel Univ Coll Med

Weiss, Lynne S MD (PNep) - **Spec Exp:** Hypertension; Kidney Disease; Kidney Failure-Chronic; Kidney Stones; **Hospital:** Robert Wood Johnson Univ Hosp - New Brunswick; **Address:** RWJ Univ Hosp - Dept Ped Nephrology, 89 French St Fl 2, New Brunswick, NJ 08901; **Phone:** 732-235-7880; **Board Cert:** Pediatrics 1979; Pediatric Nephrology 1982; **Med School:** Hahnemann Univ 1974; **Resid:** Pediatrics, Michael Reese Hosp & Med Ctr 1977; **Fellow:** Pediatric Nephrology, Michael Reese Hosp & Med Ctr 1979; **Fac Appt:** Prof Ped, Rutgers R W Johnson Med Sch

Pediatric Otolaryngology

Traquina, Diana N MD (PO) - **Spec Exp:** Airway Disorders; Ear Disorders; Sinus Disorders; **Hospital:** Robert Wood Johnson Univ Hosp - New Brunswick; **Address:** Univ Otolaryngology Assocs, 181 Somerset St Fl 2, New Brunswick, NJ 08901; **Phone:** 732-247-2401; **Board Cert:** Otolaryngology 1989; **Med School:** Yale Univ 1984; **Resid:** Surgery, Yale-New Haven Hosp 1986; Otolaryngology, Yale-New Haven Hosp 1989; **Fellow:** Pediatric Otolaryngology, Montefiore Med Ctr 1990

Pediatric Rheumatology

Moorthy, Lakshmi N MD (PRhu) - **Spec Exp:** Lupus/SLE; Arthritis; **Hospital:** Robert Wood Johnson Univ Hosp - New Brunswick; **Address:** RWJ Univ Hosp, Chld Hlth Inst, 89 French St, Ste 2300, New Brunswick, NJ 08901; **Phone:** 732-235-6230 x6; **Board Cert:** Pediatrics 2007; Pediatric Rheumatology 2012; **Med School:** India 1995; **Resid:** Pediatrics, NY-Presby/Weill Cornell Med Ctr 2000; **Fellow:** Pediatric Rheumatology, Hosp Special Surgery 2003; **Fac Appt:** Asst Prof Ped, Rutgers R W Johnson Med Sch

Pediatric Surgery

Gallucci, John G MD (PS) - **Spec Exp:** Neonatal Surgery; Thoracic Surgery; Minimally Invasive Surgery; **Hospital:** St. Peter's Univ Hosp; **Address:** St Peters Univ Hosp, Surgery, 254 Easton Ave, MOB4, New Brunswick, NJ 08901; **Phone:** 732-565-5482; **Board Cert:** Pediatric Surgery 2009; **Med School:** Rutgers R W Johnson Med Sch 1990; **Resid:** Surgery, Cooper Univ Hosp 1996; **Fellow:** Pediatric Surgery, McGill Univ Chldns Hosp 2000

Pediatric Urology

Fleisher, Michael H MD (Ped Uro) - **Hospital:** St. Peter's Univ Hosp, Jersey Shore Univ Med Ctr; **Address:** Pediatric Urology Assocs, 557 Cranbury Rd, Ste 4, East Brunswick, NJ 08816-5400; **Phone:** 732-613-9144; **Board Cert:** Urology 1984; Pediatric Urology 2009; **Med School:** SUNY Downstate 1977; **Resid:** Surgery, Yale New Haven Hosp 1979; Urology, SUNY Downstate Med Ctr 1982; **Fellow:** Renal Transplant, Montefiore Hosp Med Ctr 1979; Pediatric Urology, Hosp Sick Chldn 1983; **Fac Appt:** Assoc Clin Prof U, UMDNJ-Robert Wood Johnson

Vates III, Thomas S MD (Ped Uro) - **Spec Exp:** Robotic Surgery; **Hospital:** Robert Wood Johnson Univ Hosp - New Brunswick, Monmouth Med Ctr (page 94); **Address:** Pediatric Urology Assocs, 557 Cranbury Rd, Ste 4, East Brunswick, NJ 08816; **Phone:** 732-613-9144; **Board Cert:** Urology 2009; Pediatric Urology 2009; **Med School:** Georgetown Univ 1989; **Resid:** Surgery, RW Johnson Univ Hosp 1991; Urology, RW Johnson Univ Hosp 1995; **Fellow:** Pediatric Urology, Chldns Hosp Michigan 1997; **Fac Appt:** Asst Clin Prof U, UMDNJ-Robert Wood Johnson

Pediatrics

Yalamanchi, Krishan MD (Ped) - **Spec Exp:** Neurodevelopmental Disabilities; Brain Injury; Pediatric Rehabilitation; **Hospital:** Children's Specialized Hosp, Robert Wood Johnson Univ Hosp - New Brunswick; **Address:** 200 Somerset St, New Brunswick, NJ 08901; **Phone:** 732-258-7065; **Board Cert:** Pediatrics 2011; Neurodevelopmental Disabilities 2004; **Med School:** India 1981; **Resid:** Pediatrics, Newark Beth Israel Med Ctr 1987; **Fac Appt:** Asst Clin Prof Ped, Rutgers R W Johnson Med Sch

Physical Medicine & Rehabilitation

Brown, David P DO (PMR) - **Spec Exp:** Sports Medicine; Electrodiagnosis; Electromyography; **Hospital:** JFK Med Ctr - Edison; **Address:** JFK Johnson Rehabilitation Inst, 65 James St, Edison, NJ 08820; **Phone:** 732-321-7070; **Board Cert:** Physical Medicine & Rehabilitation 1990; Sports Medicine 2007; **Med School:** Philadelphia Coll Osteo Med 1985; **Resid:** Physical Medicine & Rehabilitation, Walter Reed AMC 1989

Fantasia, Michele E MD (PMR) - **Spec Exp:** Pediatric Rehabilitation; Spinal Cord Injury-Pediatric; Cerebral Palsy; Neuromuscular Disorders; **Hospital:** Children's Specialized Hosp, Robert Wood Johnson Univ Hosp - New Brunswick; **Address:** Pediatric Phys Med & Rehab, 200 Somerset St, New Brunswick, NJ 08901; **Phone:** 732-258-7065; **Board Cert:** Pediatrics 2006; Physical Medicine & Rehabilitation 2010; Spinal Cord Injury Medicine 2012; Pediatric Rehabilitation Medicine 2010; **Med School:** UMDNJ-NJ Med Sch, Newark 1994; **Resid:** Pediatrics, Univ Hosp-UMDNJ 1996; Physical Medicine & Rehabilitation, Univ Hosp-UMDNJ 1999; **Fac Appt:** Asst Prof PMR, UMDNJ-NJ Med Sch, Newark

Greenwald, Brian D MD (PMR) - **Spec Exp:** Stroke Rehabilitation; Brain Injury Rehabilitation; **Hospital:** JFK Med Ctr - Edison; **Address:** JFK Johnson Rehab Inst, 65 James St, Edison, NJ 08818; **Phone:** 732-321-7000 x68121; **Board Cert:** Physical Medicine & Rehabilitation 2010; **Med School:** SUNY Stony Brook 1995; **Resid:** Physical Medicine & Rehabilitation, Univ Hosp 1999; **Fellow:** Physical Medicine & Rehabilitation, Med Coll Va 2000; **Fac Appt:** Assoc Clin Prof PMR, Rutgers R W Johnson Med Sch

Plastic Surgery

Borah, Gregory L MD (PlS) - **Spec Exp:** Cosmetic Surgery-Face; Cosmetic Surgery-Breast; Hand Surgery; Pediatric Plastic Surgery; **Hospital:** Robert Wood Johnson Univ Hosp - New Brunswick, St. Peter's Univ Hosp; **Address:** RWJ Med Grp, Clinical Academic Bldg, 125 Patterson St, Ste 4100, New Brunswick, NJ 08901-1928; **Phone:** 732-235-7865; **Board Cert:** Plastic Surgery 2008; **Med School:** Harvard Med Sch 1978; **Resid:** Surgery, Mass Genl Hosp 1983; Plastic Surgery, Yale-New Haven Hosp 1985; **Fac Appt:** Prof PlS, Rutgers R W Johnson Med Sch

Herbstman, Robert A MD (PlS) - **Spec Exp:** Breast Cosmetic & Reconstructive Surgery; Liposuction & Body Contouring; Facial Rejuvenation; Minimally Invasive Surgery; **Hospital:** Robert Wood Johnson Univ Hosp - New Brunswick, Riverview Med Ctr; **Address:** 579A Cranbury Rd, Ste 202, East Brunswick, NJ 08816; **Phone:** 732-254-1919; **Board Cert:** Plastic Surgery 1992; **Med School:** Univ Rochester 1982; **Resid:** Surgery, RW Johnson Univ Hosp 1987; Plastic Surgery, Univ Hosp 1989; **Fac Appt:** Asst Clin Prof S, Rutgers R W Johnson Med Sch

Kaufman, Matthew R MD (PlS) - **Spec Exp:** Rhinoplasty; Rhinoplasty Revision; Cosmetic Surgery-Breast; Peripheral Nerve Surgery; **Hospital:** Robert Wood Johnson Univ Hosp - Somerset, Jersey Shore Univ Med Ctr; **Address:** 30 Rehill Ave, Ste 3400, Somerville, NJ 08876; **Phone:** 908-927-8993; **Board Cert:** Plastic Surgery 2007; Otolaryngology 2014; **Med School:** SUNY Upstate Med Univ 1998; **Resid:** Surgery, Mount Sinai Med Ctr 1999; Otolaryngology, Mount Sinai Med Ctr 2003; **Fellow:** Plastic Surgery, UCLA Med Ctr 2005; **Fac Appt:** Asst Clin Prof S, Drexel Univ Coll Med

Nini, Kevin T MD (PlS) - **Spec Exp:** Cosmetic Surgery-Face; Cosmetic Surgery-Breast; Liposuction & Body Contouring; **Hospital:** St. Peter's Univ Hosp; **Address:** PSANJ, 78 Easton Ave Fl 2, New Brunswick, NJ 08901; **Phone:** 732-418-0709; **Board Cert:** Plastic Surgery 1994; **Med School:** Rutgers R W Johnson Med Sch 1984; **Resid:** Surgery, Hosp Univ Penn 1989; Plastic Surgery, Shands at Univ FL 1991; **Fellow:** Plastic Surgery, Univ Miami Hosp 1992

Wey, Philip D MD (PlS) - **Spec Exp:** Cosmetic Surgery-Face; Breast Cosmetic & Reconstructive Surgery; Liposuction & Body Contouring; **Hospital:** Robert Wood Johnson Univ Hosp - New Brunswick, St. Peter's Univ Hosp; **Address:** Plastic Surgery Arts of NJ, 78 Easton Ave, New Brunswick, NJ 08901; **Phone:** 732-418-0709; **Board Cert:** Plastic Surgery 2007; **Med School:** Brown Univ 1986; **Resid:** Surgery, Northwestern Meml Hosp 1990; Plastic Surgery, NY-Presby/Weill Cornell Med Ctr 1992; **Fellow:** Breast Surgery, Meml Sloan-Kettering Cancer Ctr 1993; **Fac Appt:** Assoc Clin Prof S, Rutgers R W Johnson Med Sch

Psychiatry

Jones Jr, Frank A MD (Psyc) - **Spec Exp:** Depression; Anxiety & Mood Disorders; Psychotherapy; **Address:** 2186 Route 27, Ste 2A, North Brunswick, NJ 08902; **Phone:** 732-422-0800; **Board Cert:** Psychiatry 1977; **Med School:** Case West Res Univ 1972; **Resid:** Psychiatry, Boston State Hosp 1973; Psychiatry, Worcester State Hosp 1975

Menza, Matthew A MD (Psyc) - **Spec Exp:** Psychopharmacology; Depression; Anxiety Disorders; **Hospital:** Robert Wood Johnson Univ Hosp - New Brunswick; **Address:** 671 Hoes Ln, Fl 3, Piscataway, NJ 08854; **Phone:** 732-235-7647; **Board Cert:** Psychiatry 1985; **Med School:** Temple Univ 1980; **Resid:** Psychiatry, NYU-Bellevue Hosp 1984; **Fellow:** Psychosomatic Medicine, Mass Genl Hosp 1985; **Fac Appt:** Prof Psyc, Rutgers R W Johnson Med Sch

Pulmonary Disease

Goldberg, Jory J MD (Pul) - **Spec Exp:** Lung Disease; Asthma; **Hospital:** Univ Med Ctr Princeton at Plainsboro; **Address:** 18 Centre Drive, Ste 103, Monroe Township, NJ 08831-1564; **Phone:** 609-655-1700; **Board Cert:** Internal Medicine 1981; Pulmonary Disease 1984; Critical Care Medicine 2007; **Med School:** Mexico 1976; **Resid:** Internal Medicine, City Hosp Ctr Elmhurst 1979; Internal Medicine, Monmouth Hosp 1980; **Fellow:** Pulmonary Disease, St Barnabas Med Ctr 1981; Pulmonary Disease, Bergen Reg Med Ctr 1982

Goldblatt, Kenneth H MD (Pul) - **Spec Exp:** Asthma; Emphysema; Sarcoidosis; **Hospital:** Univ Med Ctr Princeton at Plainsboro; **Address:** Princeton Healthcare Med Assoc, 5 Plainsboro Rd Fl 3 - Ste 300, Plainsboro, NJ 08536; **Phone:** 609-853-7272; **Board Cert:** Internal Medicine 1975; Pulmonary Disease 1978; **Med School:** NY Med Coll 1972; **Resid:** Internal Medicine, UMDNJ-Rutgers Affil Hosp 1975; **Fellow:** Pulmonary Disease, UMDNJ-Rutgers Affil Hosp 1977; **Fac Appt:** Assoc Prof Med, Rutgers R W Johnson Med Sch

Harangozo, Andrea M MD (Pul) - **Hospital:** Robert Wood Johnson Univ Hosp - New Brunswick, St. Peter's Univ Hosp; **Address:** Pulmonary/Intensive Care Specialists NJ, 593 Cranbury Rd, Ste 1-A, East Brunswick, NJ 08816-4029; **Phone:** 732-613-8880; **Board Cert:** Internal Medicine 1989; Pulmonary Disease 2005; Critical Care Medicine 2005; **Med School:** NYU Sch Med 1984; **Resid:** Internal Medicine, RW Johnson Univ Hosp 1987; **Fellow:** Pulmonary Critical Care Medicine, RW Johnson Univ Hosp 1990

Melillo, Nicholas G MD (Pul) - **Spec Exp:** Chronic Obstructive Lung Disease (COPD); Lung Cancer; Asthma; **Hospital:** JFK Med Ctr - Edison; **Address:** 106 James St, Edison, NJ 08820-3945; **Phone:** 732-906-0091; **Board Cert:** Internal Medicine 1983; Pulmonary Disease 1986; Critical Care Medicine 2007; **Med School:** UMDNJ-NJ Med Sch, Newark 1979; **Resid:** Internal Medicine, St Michael's Med Ctr 1983; **Fellow:** Pulmonary Disease, St Michael's Med Ctr 1985; Critical Care Medicine, St Michael's Med Ctr 1986; **Fac Appt:** Assoc Clin Prof Med, Seton Hall Univ Sch Hlth & Med Scis

Sotolongo, Anays M MD (Pul) - **Spec Exp:** Sleep Medicine; Sleep & Snoring Disorders; Interventional Pulmonology; Critical Care; **Hospital:** Robert Wood Johnson Univ Hosp - New Brunswick; **Address:** RWJ Medical Group-Pulmonary Disease, Clin Acad Bldg, 125 Patterson St, Ste 5200B, New Brunswick, NJ 08901; **Phone:** 732-235-7840; **Board Cert:** Internal Medicine 2008; Pulmonary Disease 2008; Critical Care Medicine 2009; Sleep Medicine 2009; **Med School:** SUNY Buffalo 1992; **Resid:** Internal Medicine, Robert Wood Johnson Univ Hosp 1995; **Fellow:** Pulmonary Critical Care Medicine, Robert Wood Johnson Univ Hosp 1999; **Fac Appt:** Asst Prof Med, UMDNJ-Rutgers Med Sch

Radiation Oncology

Baumann, John C MD (RadRO) - **Spec Exp:** Breast Cancer; Cervical Cancer; **Hospital:** Univ Med Ctr Princeton at Plainsboro, Hunterdon Med Ctr; **Address:** Univ Med Ctr Princeton-Dept Rad Onc, One Plainsboro Rd, Plainsboro, NJ 08536; **Phone:** 609-853-6770; **Board Cert:** Radiation Oncology 1981; **Med School:** Harvard Med Sch 1977; **Resid:** Internal Medicine, Walter Reed AMC 1978; Radiation Oncology, Harvard Joint Program 1981

Radiation Oncology

Haffty, Bruce G MD (RadRO) - **Spec Exp:** Breast Cancer; Head & Neck Cancer; **Hospital:** Robert Wood Johnson Univ Hosp - New Brunswick; **Address:** Cancer Inst of NJ, 195 Little Albany St, rm 2038, New Brunswick, NJ 08903; **Phone:** 732-253-3939; **Board Cert:** Radiation Oncology 1988; **Med School:** Yale Univ 1984; **Resid:** Therapeutic Radiology, Yale-New Haven Hosp 1985; Radiation Oncology, Yale-New Haven Hosp 1988; **Fac Appt:** Prof RadRO, Rutgers R W Johnson Med Sch

Macher, Mark S MD (RadRO) - **Hospital:** JFK Med Ctr - Edison; **Address:** JFK Med Ctr, Mid-State Rad Oncology, 65 James St, Edison, NJ 08818; **Phone:** 732-321-7167; **Board Cert:** Therapeutic Radiology 1986; **Med School:** Howard Univ 1982; **Resid:** Diagnostic Radiology, New York Univ Med Ctr 1985; **Fellow:** Radiation Oncology, Univ Hosp 1986

Soffen, Edward M MD (RadRO) - **Spec Exp:** Prostate Cancer; Breast Cancer; Brachytherapy; **Hospital:** Univ Med Ctr Princeton at Plainsboro, CentraState Med Ctr; **Address:** Med Ctr Princeton-Dept Rad Onc, One Plainsboro Rd, Plainsboro, NJ 08536; **Phone:** 609-853-6770; **Board Cert:** Radiation Oncology 1991; **Med School:** Temple Univ 1986; **Resid:** Radiation Oncology, Hosp Univ Penn 1990; **Fac Appt:** Asst Clin Prof RadRO, Rutgers R W Johnson Med Sch

Rheumatology

Lichtbroun, Alan S MD (Rhu) - **Spec Exp:** Rheumatoid Arthritis; Sjogren's Syndrome; Fibromyalgia; Acupuncture; **Hospital:** Robert Wood Johnson Univ Hosp - New Brunswick, St. Peter's Univ Hosp; **Address:** 63 Brunswick Woods Dr, East Brunswick, NJ 08816-5601; **Phone:** 732-613-1900; **Board Cert:** Internal Medicine 1980; Rheumatology 1984; **Med School:** SUNY Downstate 1977; **Resid:** Internal Medicine, LI Jewish-Hillside Med Ctr 1980; **Fellow:** Rheumatology, Mt Sinai Hosp 1982

Surgery

August, David A MD (S) - **Spec Exp:** Pancreatic Cancer; Esophageal Cancer; Stomach Cancer; Sarcoma-Soft Tissue; **Hospital:** Robert Wood Johnson Univ Hosp - New Brunswick; **Address:** Cancer Inst of New Jersey, 195 Little Albany St, New Brunswick, NJ 08903; **Phone:** 732-235-7701; **Board Cert:** Surgery 2005; **Med School:** Yale Univ 1980; **Resid:** Surgery, Yale-New Haven Hosp 1986; **Fellow:** Surgical Oncology, Natl Canc Inst 1984; **Fac Appt:** Prof S, Rutgers R W Johnson Med Sch

Chung-Loy, Harold E MD (S) - **Spec Exp:** Laparoscopic Surgery; Breast Surgery; Vascular Surgery; **Hospital:** JFK Med Ctr - Edison, Robert Wood Johnson Univ Hosp at Rahway; **Address:** 98 James St, Ste 202, Edison, NJ 08820-3902; **Phone:** 732-548-1000; **Board Cert:** Surgery 2007; **Med School:** Howard Univ 1980; **Resid:** Surgery, Mount Sinai Hosp 1985

Dasmahapatra, Kumar MD (S) - **Spec Exp:** Cancer Surgery; Breast Surgery; Laparoscopic Surgery; Pancreatic Surgery; **Hospital:** Raritan Bay Med Ctr - Perth Amboy, JFK Med Ctr - Edison; **Address:** Comprehensive Surgical Assocs, 225 May St, Ste A, Edison, NJ 08837; **Phone:** 732-346-5400; **Board Cert:** Surgery 2009; **Med School:** India 1973; **Resid:** Surgery, Grace Hosp 1979; **Fellow:** Surgical Oncology, Roswell Park Meml Inst 1982; **Fac Appt:** Assoc Clin Prof S, UMDNJ-NJ Med Sch, Newark

Goydos, James S MD (S) - **Spec Exp:** Cancer Surgery; Melanoma; Skin Cancer; Sarcoma-Soft Tissue; **Hospital:** Robert Wood Johnson Univ Hosp - New Brunswick, St. Peter's Univ Hosp; **Address:** Cancer Inst of New Jersey, 195 Little Albany St, Ste 3000, New Brunswick, NJ 8901; **Phone:** 732-235-7563; **Board Cert:** Surgery 2004; **Med School:** Rutgers R W Johnson Med Sch 1988; **Resid:** Surgery, New Britain Genl Hosp 1993; **Fellow:** Surgical Oncology, UPMC 1995; **Fac Appt:** Prof S, Rutgers R W Johnson Med Sch

Jordan III, Lawrence J MD (S) - **Spec Exp:** Laparoscopic Surgery; Endoscopic Surgery; Cancer Surgery; Hernia; **Hospital:** Univ Med Ctr Princeton at Plainsboro; **Address:** Princeton Surgical Assocs, 5 Plainsboro Rd, Ste 400, Princeton, NJ 08536; **Phone:** 609-936-9100; **Board Cert:** Surgery 2009; **Med School:** Cornell Univ-Weill Med Coll 1983; **Resid:** Surgery, NY-Presby/Columbia Univ Med Ctr 1988

Kaufman, Howard L MD (S) - **Spec Exp:** Cancer Surgery; Melanoma; Immunotherapy; Vaccine Therapy; **Hospital:** Robert Wood Johnson Univ Hosp - New Brunswick; **Address:** The Cancer Inst of NJ, 195 Little Albany St, New Brunswick, NJ 08901; **Phone:** 732-235-7563; **Board Cert:** Surgery 2007; **Med School:** Loyola Univ-Stritch Sch Med 1986; **Resid:** Internal Medicine, St Francis Hosp 1988; Surgery, Boston Med Ctr 1995; **Fellow:** Tumor Immunology, Natl Cancer Inst/Naval Med Ctr 1990; Surgical Oncology, Natl Cancer Inst/Naval Med Ctr 1997; **Fac Appt:** Prof S, Rutgers R W Johnson Med Sch

Kearney, Thomas J MD (S) - **Spec Exp:** Breast Cancer; **Hospital:** Robert Wood Johnson Univ Hosp - New Brunswick, St. Peter's Univ Hosp; **Address:** Cancer Inst of New Jersey, 195 Little Albany St, Ste 3000, New Brunswick, NJ 8901; **Phone:** 732-235-7563; **Board Cert:** Surgery 2012; **Med School:** Georgetown Univ 1984; **Resid:** Surgery, Cedars-Sinai Med Ctr 1992; **Fellow:** Surgical Oncology, Univ Chicago Med Ctr 1995; **Fac Appt:** Assoc Prof S, Rutgers R W Johnson Med Sch

McManus, Susan A MD (S) - **Spec Exp:** Breast Surgery; Cancer Surgery; **Hospital:** St. Peter's Univ Hosp; **Address:** Breast Ctr, 240 Easton Ave Fl 3, New Brunswick, NJ 08901; **Phone:** 732-846-3300; **Board Cert:** Surgery 2006; **Med School:** Mexico 1979; **Resid:** Surgery, Beth Israel Med Ctr 1985; **Fac Appt:** Asst Clin Prof S, Rutgers R W Johnson Med Sch

Trooskin, Stanley Z MD (S) - **Spec Exp:** Minimally Invasive Surgery; Thyroid Cancer; Gastrointestinal Cancer & Rare Tumors; **Hospital:** Robert Wood Johnson Univ Hosp - New Brunswick; **Address:** UMDNJ-RWJ, Surgery, 125 Paterson St, Ste 4100, New Brunswick, NJ 08901; **Phone:** 732-235-7920; **Board Cert:** Surgery 2010; **Med School:** Univ Pittsburgh 1975; **Resid:** Surgery, NYU Med Ctr 1980; **Fac Appt:** Prof S, Rutgers R W Johnson Med Sch

Thoracic & Cardiac Surgery

Heim, John A MD (T&CS) - **Spec Exp:** Cardiothoracic Surgery; Pacemakers; **Hospital:** Univ Med Ctr Princeton at Plainsboro; **Address:** Univ Med Ctr at Princeton, 5 Plainsboro Rd, Ste 260, Plainsboro, NJ 08536; **Phone:** 609-853-7200; **Board Cert:** Thoracic & Cardiac Surgery 2014; Surgery 2013; **Med School:** Rutgers R W Johnson Med Sch 1985; **Resid:** Surgery, Hartford Hosp 1991; **Fellow:** Thoracic Oncology, Meml Sloan-Kettering Cancer Ctr 1992; Cardiothoracic Surgery, Rush Presby-St Lukes Med Ctr 1994; **Fac Appt:** Prof S

Lee, Leonard Y MD (T&CS) - **Spec Exp:** Coronary Artery Surgery; Minimally Invasive Cardiac Surgery; Heart Failure; Gene Therapy-Cardiac Angiogenesis; **Hospital:** Robert Wood Johnson Univ Hosp - New Brunswick; **Address:** RWJ Univ Hosp, Cardiothoracic Surgery, 1 RW Johnson Pl, MEB 508, Box 19, New Brunswick, NJ 08903; **Phone:** 732-235-8725; **Board Cert:** Surgery 2011; Thoracic & Cardiac Surgery 2013; **Med School:** Rutgers R W Johnson Med Sch 1992; **Resid:** Surgery, St Vincents Hosp 1997; **Fellow:** Thoracic & Cardiac Surgery, NY-Presby/Weill Cornell Med Ctr 2001; **Fac Appt:** Assoc Prof T&CS, Rutgers R W Johnson Med Sch

Urology

Richards, Steven L MD (U) - **Spec Exp:** Kidney Stones; Erectile Dysfunction; Prostate Benign Disease; **Hospital:** St. Peter's Univ Hosp, Robert Wood Johnson Univ Hosp - New Brunswick; **Address:** Mid-Jersey Urology, 333 Forsgate Drive, Ste 202, Jamesburg, NJ 08831-1567; **Phone:** 732-561-2058; **Board Cert:** Urology 2009; **Med School:** Albert Einstein Coll Med 1993; **Resid:** Surgery, Montefiore Med Ctr 1995; Urology, Montefiore Med Ctr 1999

Weiss, Robert E MD (U) - **Spec Exp:** Bladder Cancer; Kidney Cancer; Testicular Cancer; Robotic Surgery; **Hospital:** Robert Wood Johnson Univ Hosp - New Brunswick; **Address:** Cancer Ctr Inst of NJ, Urology, 195 Little Albany St, New Brunswick, NJ 08901; **Phone:** 732-235-8515; **Board Cert:** Urology 2014; **Med School:** NYU Sch Med 1985; **Resid:** Urology, Mt Sinai Hosp 1991; **Fellow:** Urologic Oncology, Meml Sloan-Kettering Cancer Ctr 1994; **Fac Appt:** Assoc Prof U, Rutgers R W Johnson Med Sch

Vascular & Interventional Radiology

Censullo, Michael L MD (VIR) - **Spec Exp:** Interventional Radiology; Chemoembolization & Tumor Ablation; **Hospital:** Robert Wood Johnson Univ Hosp - New Brunswick; **Address:** 579A Cranbury Rd, East Brunswick, NJ 08816; **Phone:** 732-390-0040; **Board Cert:** Diagnostic Radiology 2002; Vascular & Interventional Radiology 2005; Nuclear Cardiology 2004; **Med School:** Georgetown Univ 1997; **Resid:** Diagnostic Radiology, Univ TX Hlth Sci Ctr 2002; **Fellow:** Vascular & Interventional Radiology, MD Anderson Cancer Ctr, TX Heart Inst 2003

Denny, Donald F MD (VIR) - **Spec Exp:** Uterine Fibroid Embolization; **Hospital:** Univ Med Ctr Princeton at Plainsboro; **Address:** Princeton Radiology Assocs, 1 Plainsboro Rd, Plainsboro, NJ 08536; **Phone:** 609-853-6500; **Board Cert:** Diagnostic Radiology 1982; Vascular & Interventional Radiology 2005; **Med School:** Hahnemann Univ 1978; **Resid:** Diagnostic Radiology, Yale-New Haven Hosp 1982; **Fellow:** Cardiovascular Radiology, Brigham & Womens Hosp 1983; **Fac Appt:** Assoc Clin Prof Rad, Yale Univ

Nosher, John L MD (VIR) - **Spec Exp:** Endovascular Surgery; Uterine Fibroid Embolization; Interventional Oncology; Liver Cancer; **Hospital:** Robert Wood Johnson Univ Hosp - New Brunswick; **Address:** RWJ Univ Hosp, Radiology, 125 Paterson St, MEB 404, New Brunswick, NJ 08901; **Phone:** 732-390-0040; **Board Cert:** Diagnostic Radiology 1975; Vascular & Interventional Radiology 2005; **Med School:** Jefferson Med Coll 1970; **Resid:** Diagnostic Radiology, NY-Presby/Columbia Univ Med Ctr 1975; **Fac Appt:** Clin Prof Rad, Rutgers R W Johnson Med Sch

Vascular Surgery

Goldman, Kenneth A MD (VascS) - **Spec Exp:** Carotid Artery Surgery; Aneurysm-Aortic; Varicose Veins; Endovascular Surgery; **Hospital:** Univ Med Ctr Princeton at Plainsboro; **Address:** Princeton Surgical Assocs, 5 Plainsboro Rd, Ste 400, Plainsboro, NJ 08536; **Phone:** 609-936-9100; **Board Cert:** Surgery 2013; Vascular Surgery 2004; **Med School:** NYU Sch Med 1988; **Resid:** Surgery, Bellevue Hosp 1993; **Fellow:** Vascular Surgery, NYU Med Ctr 1994

Monmouth

Monmouth

Allergy & Immunology

Gross, Gary L MD (A&I) - **Spec Exp:** Asthma; Cough-Chronic; Sinus Disorders; Atopic Dermatitis; **Hospital:** Jersey Shore Univ Med Ctr, Monmouth Med Ctr (page 94); **Address:** Atlantic Allergy, Asthma, & Immunology, 802 W Park Ave, Ste 213, Ocean Township, NJ 07712; **Phone:** 732-695-2555; **Board Cert:** Allergy & Immunology 1987; Pediatrics 1986; **Med School:** NYU Sch Med 1981; **Resid:** Pediatrics, Chldns Natl Med Ctr 1984; **Fellow:** Allergy & Immunology, Chldns Hosp 1986; **Fac Appt:** Asst Clin Prof Ped, Rutgers R W Johnson Med Sch

Picone, Frank J MD (A&I) - **Spec Exp:** Asthma; Sinus Disorders; Allergy; **Hospital:** Riverview Med Ctr, Monmouth Med Ctr (page 94); **Address:** Two River Allergy & Asthma Grp, 709 Sycamore Ave, Tinton Falls, NJ 07701; **Phone:** 732-747-8188; **Board Cert:** Pediatrics 1973; Allergy & Immunology 1975; **Med School:** UMDNJ-NJ Med Sch, Newark 1967; **Resid:** Pediatrics, Jackson Meml Hosp 1970; **Fellow:** Allergy & Immunology, Chldns Hosp 1974; **Fac Appt:** Asst Clin Prof Ped, Drexel Univ Coll Med

Sher, Ellen R MD (A&I) - **Spec Exp:** Asthma & Sinusitis; Nasal Allergy; Insect Allergies; Immune Deficiency; **Hospital:** Monmouth Med Ctr (page 94), Jersey Shore Univ Med Ctr; **Address:** Atlantic Allergy, Asthma & Immunology, 802 W Park Ave, Ste 213, Ocean Township, NJ 07712; **Phone:** 732-695-2555; **Board Cert:** Internal Medicine 1989; Allergy & Immunology 2014; **Med School:** Georgetown Univ 1986; **Resid:** Internal Medicine, Thomas Jefferson Univ Hosp 1989; **Fellow:** Pulmonary Disease, Thomas Jefferson Univ Hosp 1990; Allergy & Immunology, Natl Jewish Hlth 1992; **Fac Appt:** Asst Clin Prof Med, Drexel Univ Coll Med

Cardiovascular Disease

Daniels, Jeffrey S MD (Cv) - **Hospital:** Monmouth Med Ctr (page 94), Jersey Shore Univ Med Ctr; **Address:** Monmouth Cardiology Assocs, 215 Brighton Ave, Long Branch, NJ 07740; **Phone:** 732-222-5143; **Board Cert:** Internal Medicine 1983; Cardiovascular Disease 1985; **Med School:** Albany Med Coll 1980; **Resid:** Internal Medicine, Mt Sinai Hosp 1983; **Fellow:** Cardiovascular Disease, Mt Sinai Hosp 1985; **Fac Appt:** Asst Clin Prof Med, Drexel Univ Coll Med

Child Neurology

Barabas, Ronald E MD (ChiN) - **Spec Exp:** Pediatric Neurology; Developmental Disorders; Neurogenetics; Metabolic Disorders; **Hospital:** Monmouth Med Ctr (page 94); **Address:** CNNH, 3350 Highway 138W, Ste 117, Wall, NJ 07719; **Phone:** 855-852-8150; **Board Cert:** Child Neurology 2007; Clinical Genetics 2010; Neurodevelopmental Disabilities 2007; **Med School:** UMDNJ-Rutgers Med Sch 1986; **Resid:** Pediatrics, Buffalo Chldns Hosp 1988; **Fellow:** Pediatric Neurology, Chldns Hosp of Pittsburgh 1991; Pediatric Metabolism, Chldns Hosp of Philadelphia 1993; **Fac Appt:** Asst Clin Prof Ped, Drexel Univ Coll Med

Clinical Genetics

Santolaya, Joaquin MD/PhD (CG) - **Spec Exp:** Genetic Disorders; Prenatal Genetic Diagnosis; Fetal Therapy; **Hospital:** Robert Wood Johnson Univ Hosp - New Brunswick, Jersey Shore Univ Med Ctr; **Address:** Perinatal Inst, 1994 State Route 33, Neptune, NJ 07753; **Phone:** 732-776-4755; **Board Cert:** Clinical Genetics 2010; **Med School:** Spain 1980; **Resid:** Obstetrics & Gynecology, Fundacion Jimenez Diaz 1985; **Fellow:** Clinical Genetics, Univ IL Hosp 1994; Clinical Molecular Genetics, Yale-New Haven Hosp 1999; **Fac Appt:** Prof ObG, UMDNJ-Rutgers Med Sch

Colon & Rectal Surgery

Arvanitis, Michael L MD (CRS) - **Spec Exp:** Laparoscopic Surgery; Colon & Rectal Cancer; Ulcerative Colitis; **Hospital:** Monmouth Med Ctr (page 94), Riverview Med Ctr; **Address:** Specialty Surgical Assoc, 10 Industrial Way E, Ste 104, Eatontown, NJ 07724; **Phone:** 732-389-1331; **Board Cert:** Surgery 2008; Colon & Rectal Surgery 2008; **Med School:** Hahnemann Univ 1982; **Resid:** Surgery, St Vincent's Hosp 1987; **Fellow:** Colon & Rectal Surgery, Cleveland Clinic 1988; **Fac Appt:** Asst Clin Prof S, Hahnemann Univ

Dermatology

Grossman, Kenneth A MD (D) - **Spec Exp:** Psoriasis; Skin Cancer; Cutaneous Lymphoma; Cosmetic Dermatology; **Hospital:** Riverview Med Ctr; **Address:** 180 White Rd, Ste 103, Little Silver, NJ 07739-1166; **Phone:** 732-842-5222; **Board Cert:** Internal Medicine 1980; Dermatology 1983; **Med School:** SUNY Hlth Sci Ctr 1977; **Resid:** Internal Medicine, Nassau County Med Ctr 1980; Dermatology, Montefiore Med Ctr 1983

Hametz, Irwin MD (D) - **Hospital:** CentraState Med Ctr; **Address:** 77-55 Schanck Rd, Ste B-3, Freehold, NJ 07728; **Phone:** 732-462-9800; **Board Cert:** Dermatology 1978; **Med School:** NY Med Coll 1973; **Resid:** Pediatrics, Long Island Jewish-Hillside Med Ctr 1975; Dermatology, Brown Univ Affil Hosps 1978; **Fac Appt:** Asst Clin Prof Med, Rutgers R W Johnson Med Sch

Orsini, William J MD (D) - **Hospital:** Monmouth Med Ctr (page 94); **Address:** 223 Monmouth Rd, W Long Branch, NJ 07764; **Phone:** 732-870-2992; **Board Cert:** Internal Medicine 1975; Dermatology 1977; **Med School:** UMDNJ-NJ Med Sch, Newark 1972; **Resid:** Internal Medicine, Monmouth Med Ctr 1975; Dermatology, Albany Med Ctr 1977

Diagnostic Radiology

Chalal, Jeffrey M MD (DR) - **Hospital:** CentraState Med Ctr; **Address:** Freehold Radiology Grp, 901 W Main St, Ground Fl, Freehold, NJ 07728; **Phone:** 732-462-4844; **Board Cert:** Diagnostic Radiology 1982; **Med School:** Univ Pennsylvania 1977; **Resid:** Diagnostic Radiology, Columbia-Presby Med Ctr 1981

Endocrinology, Diabetes & Metabolism

Nassberg, Barton MD (EDM) - **Spec Exp:** Thyroid Disorders; Diabetes; **Hospital:** Bayshore Community Hosp; **Address:** 723 N Beers St, Ste 2G, Holmdel, NJ 07733-1512; **Phone:** 732-739-0200; **Board Cert:** Internal Medicine 1982; Endocrinology, Diabetes & Metabolism 1985; **Med School:** Belgium 1979; **Resid:** Internal Medicine, Mountainside Hosp 1982; **Fellow:** Endocrinology, Diabetes & Metabolism, Hershey Med Ctr 1984

Family Medicine

Bernardo Jr, Salvatore MD (FMed) *PCP* - **Hospital:** CentraState Med Ctr; **Address:** 4255 Rte 9 N, Ste B, Freehold, NJ 07728; **Phone:** 732-683-9897; **Board Cert:** Family Medicine 2009; **Med School:** UMDNJ-NJ Med Sch, Newark 1993; **Resid:** Family Medicine, Somerset Med Ctr 1996; **Fac Appt:** Asst Clin Prof FMed, UMDNJ-NJ Med Sch, Newark

Catanese, Vincent J MD (FMed) *PCP* - **Spec Exp:** Hypertension; Diabetes; Functional Bowel Disorders; **Address:** 733 N Beers St, Ste U3, Holmdel, NJ 07733; **Phone:** 732-264-8484; **Board Cert:** Family Medicine 2005; **Med School:** Penn State Coll Med 1978; **Resid:** Family Medicine, Conemaugh Valley Meml Hosp 1981

Gastroenterology

Binns, Joseph MD (Ge) - **Spec Exp:** Colonoscopy; **Hospital:** Riverview Med Ctr; **Address:** Red Bank Gastroenterology Assocs, 365 Broad St, Ste 1-E, Red Bank, NJ 07701; **Phone:** 732-842-4294; **Board Cert:** Gastroenterology 2013; **Med School:** Rutgers R W Johnson Med Sch 1987; **Resid:** Internal Medicine, Pennsylvania Hosp 1990; **Fellow:** Gastroenterology, Graduate Hosp 1992

Fiest, Thomas DO (Ge) - **Spec Exp:** Colitis; Liver Disease; **Hospital:** Monmouth Med Ctr (page 94), Jersey Shore Univ Med Ctr; **Address:** Monmouth Gastroenterology, 142 Highway 35, Ste 103, Eatontown, NJ 07724; **Phone:** 732-389-5004; **Board Cert:** Internal Medicine 1989; Gastroenterology 2005; **Med School:** Philadelphia Coll Osteo Med 1985; **Resid:** Internal Medicine, Monmouth Med Ctr 1990; **Fellow:** Gastroenterology, Jersey City Med Ctr 1993

Ludwig, Shelly L MD (Ge) - **Spec Exp:** Inflammatory Bowel Disease; Hepatitis C; Gastroesophageal Reflux Disease (GERD); Endoscopy; **Hospital:** CentraState Med Ctr; **Address:** 901 W Main St, Ste 106, Medical Arts Bldg, Freehold, NJ 07728; **Phone:** 732-303-3888; **Board Cert:** Internal Medicine 1977; Gastroenterology 1979; **Med School:** Albert Einstein Coll Med 1974; **Resid:** Internal Medicine, LAC-Harbor UCLA Med Ctr 1977; **Fellow:** Gastroenterology, Wadsworth VA Hosp/UCLA 1979; **Fac Appt:** Assoc Clin Prof Med, Rutgers R W Johnson Med Sch

Turtel, Penny S MD (Ge) - **Spec Exp:** Inflammatory Bowel Disease; Celiac Disease; Colon Polyps & Cancer; **Hospital:** Monmouth Med Ctr (page 94), Jersey Shore Univ Med Ctr; **Address:** Shore Gastroenterology, 1907 Route 35, Ste 1, Oakhurst, NJ 07755-2760; **Phone:** 732-517-0060; **Board Cert:** Internal Medicine 1989; Gastroenterology 2011; **Med School:** Cornell Univ-Weill Med Coll 1986; **Resid:** Internal Medicine, Mount Sinai Hosp 1989; **Fellow:** Gastroenterology, Mount Sinai Hosp 1991

Geriatric Medicine

Gohel, Rekha M MD (Ger) - **Spec Exp:** Preventive Medicine; Alzheimer's Disease; Dementia; **Hospital:** CentraState Med Ctr, Comm Med Ctr - Toms River (page 94); **Address:** Elite Medical Care, 318 Professional View Drive, Ste 300, Freehold, NJ 07728; **Phone:** 732-409-6440; **Board Cert:** Internal Medicine 2012; Geriatric Medicine 2013; **Med School:** India 1995; **Resid:** Internal Medicine, Flushing Hosp Med Ctr 2001; **Fellow:** Geriatric Medicine, Flushing Hosp Med Ctr 2003

Israel, Jessica L MD (Ger) - **Spec Exp:** Palliative Care; **Hospital:** Monmouth Med Ctr (page 94); **Address:** Monmouth Med Ctr, Dept Geriatrics, 300 Second Ave, Long Branch, NJ 07740; **Phone:** 732-923-7550; **Board Cert:** Geriatric Medicine 2006; **Med School:** Mount Sinai Sch Med 1995; **Resid:** Internal Medicine, Mt Sinai Med Ctr 1998; **Fellow:** Geriatric Medicine, Mt Sinai Med Ctr 2000

Hand Surgery

Lisser, Steven P MD (HS) - **Spec Exp:** Shoulder Surgery; Wrist/Hand Injuries; Ligament Reconstruction; Sports Medicine; **Hospital:** Riverview Med Ctr, Monmouth Med Ctr (page 94); **Address:** Orthopaedic, Sports Med & Rehab Ctr, 80 Oak Hill Rd, Red Bank, NJ 07701; **Phone:** 732-741-2313; **Board Cert:** Orthopaedic Surgery 2007; Hand Surgery 2007; Orthopaedic Sports Medicine 2007; **Med School:** Mount Sinai Sch Med 1987; **Resid:** Orthopaedic Surgery, Mt Sinai Med Ctr 1992; **Fellow:** Hand & Microvascular Surgery, Thom Jefferson Univ 1993; Sports Medicine & Shoulder Surgery, Univ Pennsylvania 1994; **Fac Appt:** Asst Clin Prof OrS, Mount Sinai Sch Med

Hematology

Lerner, William A MD (Hem) - **Spec Exp:** Palliative Care; **Hospital:** Jersey Shore Univ Med Ctr, Ocean Med Ctr; **Address:** 1707 Atlantic Ave, Manasquan, NJ 08736-1147; **Phone:** 732-528-0760; **Board Cert:** Internal Medicine 1980; Hematology 1982; Medical Oncology 1983; Hospice & Palliative Medicine 2008; **Med School:** Belgium 1977; **Resid:** Internal Medicine, Albert Einstein Med Ctr 1980; **Fellow:** Hematology & Oncology, NYU Med Ctr 1983

Topilow, Arthur A MD (Hem) - **Spec Exp:** Lymphoma; Multiple Myeloma; **Hospital:** Jersey Shore Univ Med Ctr, Ocean Med Ctr; **Address:** 1707 Atlantic Ave, Manasquan, NJ 08736-1147; **Phone:** 732-528-0760; **Board Cert:** Internal Medicine 1971; Hematology 1972; Medical Oncology 1981; **Med School:** NY Med Coll 1967; **Resid:** Internal Medicine, Flower/NY Metro Hosp 1970; **Fellow:** Hematology, Flower/NY Metro Hosp 1972; **Fac Appt:** Assoc Clin Prof Med, UMDNJ-NJ Med Sch, Newark

Infectious Disease

Eng, Margaret H MD (Inf) - **Spec Exp:** AIDS/HIV; **Hospital:** Monmouth Med Ctr (page 94); **Address:** Monmouth Family Hlth Ctr, 300 Second Ave, Long Branch, NJ 07740; **Phone:** 732-923-7139; **Board Cert:** Internal Medicine 1983; Infectious Disease 2010; **Med School:** Albert Einstein Coll Med 1980; **Resid:** Internal Medicine, Kings Co Hosp 1984; **Fellow:** Infectious Disease, Univ Maryland Med Ctr 1986

Internal Medicine

DeMartin, Robert MD (IM) *PCP* - **Hospital:** Jersey Shore Univ Med Ctr; **Address:** 1330 Laurel Ave, Ste 201, Sea Girt, NJ 08750; **Phone:** 732-449-6681; **Board Cert:** Internal Medicine 1986; **Med School:** Mexico 1982; **Resid:** Internal Medicine, Univ Hosp-UMDNJ 1986

Glowacki, Jan S MD (IM) *PCP* - **Spec Exp:** Preventive Medicine; Diagnostic Problems; **Hospital:** Riverview Med Ctr, Monmouth Med Ctr (page 94); **Address:** Fair Haven Internal Medicine, 569 River Rd, Fair Haven, NJ 07704-3262; **Phone:** 732-530-0100; **Board Cert:** Internal Medicine 1980; **Med School:** Jefferson Med Coll 1977; **Resid:** Internal Medicine, Monmouth Med Ctr 1980

Granet, Kenneth M MD (IM) *PCP* - **Hospital:** Monmouth Med Ctr (page 94); **Address:** 166 Morris Ave, Long Branch, NJ 07740; **Phone:** 732-229-2020; **Board Cert:** Internal Medicine 1987; **Med School:** SUNY Downstate 1984; **Resid:** Internal Medicine, N Shore Univ Hosp 1987; **Fac Appt:** Asst Clin Prof Med, Drexel Univ Coll Med

Masterson, Raymond M MD (IM) *PCP* - **Spec Exp:** Hypertension; Diabetes; Cholesterol/Lipid Disorders; Peripheral Vascular Disease; **Hospital:** Jersey Shore Univ Med Ctr; **Address:** 700 Highway 71, Ste 9, Sea Girt, NJ 08750-2804; **Phone:** 732-974-0340; **Board Cert:** Internal Medicine 1986; **Med School:** Philippines 1978; **Resid:** Internal Medicine, St Michaels Med Ctr 1982

Maternal & Fetal Medicine

Genc, Mehmet R MD/PhD (MF) - **Spec Exp:** Amniocentesis; Hypertension in Pregnancy; Pregnancy-High Risk; Fetal Abnormalities; **Hospital:** Jersey Shore Univ Med Ctr, Riverview Med Ctr; **Address:** 1944 Route 33, Ste 204, Neptune, NJ 07753; **Phone:** 732-776-4755; **Board Cert:** Obstetrics & Gynecology 2013; Maternal & Fetal Medicine 2013; **Med School:** Turkey 1994; **Resid:** Obstetrics & Gynecology, NY-Presby/Weill Cornell Med Ctr 2000; **Fellow:** Maternal & Fetal Medicine, NY-Presby/Weill Cornell Med Ctr 2001; Maternal & Fetal Medicine, Brigham & Women's Hosp 2003; **Fac Appt:** Asst Prof ObG, UMDNJ-Rutgers Med Sch

Gonzalez, David MD (MF) - **Spec Exp:** Pregnancy-High Risk; **Hospital:** Monmouth Med Ctr (page 94); **Address:** Monmouth Med Group, 73 S Bath Ave, Long Branch, NJ 07740; **Phone:** 732-870-3600; **Board Cert:** Obstetrics & Gynecology 2013; Maternal & Fetal Medicine 2013; **Med School:** Temple Univ 1990; **Resid:** Obstetrics & Gynecology, Univ Hosp-UMDNJ 1994; **Fellow:** Maternal & Fetal Medicine, Univ Hosp-UMDNJ 1996

Medical Oncology

Fitzgerald, Denis B MD (Onc) - **Spec Exp:** Breast Cancer; Lung Cancer; Colon Cancer; Lymphoma, Non-Hodgkin's; **Hospital:** Riverview Med Ctr; **Address:** 180 White Rd, Ste 101, Little Silver, NJ 07739; **Phone:** 732-530-8666; **Board Cert:** Internal Medicine 1981; Medical Oncology 1985; Hematology 1986; **Med School:** SUNY Downstate 1978; **Resid:** Internal Medicine, St Vincents Hosp Med Ctr 1982; **Fellow:** Hematology & Oncology, Univ Rochester 1985

Greenberg, Susan N MD (Onc) - **Spec Exp:** Breast Cancer; Lung Cancer; Palliative Care; **Hospital:** Jersey Shore Univ Med Ctr, Monmouth Med Ctr (page 94); **Address:** 39 Sycamore Ave, Little Silver, NJ 07739-1208; **Phone:** 732-576-8610; **Board Cert:** Internal Medicine 1981; Medical Oncology 1983; **Med School:** Med Coll PA Hahnemann 1978; **Resid:** Internal Medicine, Hosp Med Coll Penn 1981; **Fellow:** Hematology & Oncology, Columbia-Presby Med Ctr 1983

Sharon, David J MD (Onc) - **Spec Exp:** Breast Cancer; Lung Cancer; Gastrointestinal Cancer; Hematologic Malignancies; **Hospital:** Monmouth Med Ctr (page 94), CentraState Med Ctr; **Address:** The Cancer Ctr - Monmouth Med Ctr, 100 State Highway 36, Ste 1B, West Long Branch, NJ 07764-6205; **Phone:** 732-222-1711; **Board Cert:** Internal Medicine 1980; Medical Oncology 1983; **Med School:** NY Med Coll 1977; **Resid:** Internal Medicine, Beth Israel Med Ctr 1980; **Fellow:** Neoplastic Diseases, Mount Sinai Med Ctr 1982

Walsh, Christina M MD (Onc) - **Spec Exp:** Cancer Genetics; Breast Cancer; **Hospital:** Riverview Med Ctr; **Address:** Hematology Oncology of Cen NJ, 180 White Rd, Little Silver, NJ 07739; **Phone:** 732-530-8666; **Board Cert:** Internal Medicine 1980; Hematology 1982; Medical Oncology 1985; **Med School:** Georgetown Univ 1977; **Resid:** Internal Medicine, Georgetown Univ Hosp 1980; **Fellow:** Hematology, Georgetown Univ Hosp 1981; Hematology & Oncology, NYU Med Ctr 1984

Neonatal-Perinatal Medicine

Graff, Michael A MD (NP) - **Spec Exp:** Neonatology; **Hospital:** Jersey Shore Univ Med Ctr, Ocean Med Ctr; **Address:** Jersey Shore Univ Med Ctr, Dept Peds, 1945 State Rte 33, Neptune, NJ 07754; **Phone:** 732-776-4283; **Board Cert:** Pediatrics 1981; Neonatal-Perinatal Medicine 1983; **Med School:** Italy 1977; **Resid:** Pediatrics, NYU Med Ctr 1980; **Fellow:** Neonatology, Columbia-Presby Med Ctr 1982

Nephrology

Haratz, Alan MD (Nep) - **Spec Exp:** Kidney Disease; Hypertension; **Hospital:** Monmouth Med Ctr (page 94); **Address:** Hypertension & Nephrology Assocs, 6 Industrial Way W, Ste B, Eatontown, NJ 07724; **Phone:** 732-460-1200; **Board Cert:** Internal Medicine 1982; Nephrology 1984; **Med School:** Hahnemann Univ 1979; **Resid:** Internal Medicine, Monmouth Med Ctr 1982; **Fellow:** Nephrology, Hahneman Univ Med Ctr 1984

Manning, Eric C MD/PhD (Nep) - **Spec Exp:** Hypertension; Kidney Disease; Dialysis Care; **Hospital:** Robert Wood Johnson Univ Hosp - New Brunswick, Robert Wood Johnson Univ Hosp - Somerset; **Address:** 719 Route 206, Ste 100, Hillsborough, NJ 08844; **Phone:** 908-904-9055; **Board Cert:** Internal Medicine 1989; Nephrology 2012; **Med School:** UC Davis 1985; **Resid:** Internal Medicine, Boston Univ Hosp 1988; **Fellow:** Nephrology, Boston Univ Hosp 1992

Neurological Surgery

Maggio, William W MD (NS) - **Spec Exp:** Epilepsy; Spinal Surgery; Stroke; Brain Tumors-Metastatic; **Hospital:** Jersey Shore Univ Med Ctr, Ocean Med Ctr; **Address:** Meridian Surgical Assocs, 2101 Rte 34, Ste D, Wall Township, NJ 07719; **Phone:** 732-974-0003; **Board Cert:** Neurological Surgery 1993; **Med School:** Penn State Coll Med 1981; **Resid:** Neurological Surgery, Univ Virginia Hlth Sys 1988; **Fellow:** Neurological Surgery, Meml Sloan-Kettering Canc Ctr 1990

Rosenblum, Bruce R MD (NS) - **Spec Exp:** Spinal Surgery; Brain Tumors; Pain-Back & Neck; Chiari's Deformity; **Hospital:** Riverview Med Ctr, Bayshore Community Hosp; **Address:** 160 Ave at the Commons, Ste 2, Shrewsbury, NJ 07702; **Phone:** 732-460-1522; **Board Cert:** Neurological Surgery 1991; **Med School:** Mount Sinai Sch Med 1982; **Resid:** Neurological Surgery, Mount Sinai Med Ctr 1988; **Fellow:** Stroke, Natl Inst Health 1986

Neurology

Gainey, Patrick J MD (N) - **Hospital:** Robert Wood Johnson Univ Hosp - New Brunswick; **Address:** 23 Kilmer Drive Bldg 1 - Ste E, Morganville, NJ 07751; **Phone:** 732-617-0808; **Board Cert:** Neurology 1993; **Med School:** Rutgers R W Johnson Med Sch 1988; **Resid:** Neurology, UMDNJ Med Ctr 1990; **Fellow:** Neurology, UMDNJ Med Ctr 1993

Gilson, Noah R MD (N) - **Spec Exp:** Multiple Sclerosis; Headache; Parkinson's Disease; **Hospital:** Monmouth Med Ctr (page 94), Riverview Med Ctr; **Address:** Neurology Specialists of Monmouth County, 107 Monmouth Rd, Ste 110, West Long Branch, NJ 07764; **Phone:** 732-935-1850; **Board Cert:** Neurology 1987; Vascular Neurology 2009; **Med School:** Loyola Univ-Stritch Sch Med 1982; **Resid:** Neurology, Mount Sinai Hosp 1986

Silbert, Paul J MD (N) - **Spec Exp:** Parkinson's Disease; Headache; Carpal Tunnel Syndrome; Alzheimer's Disease; **Hospital:** Jersey Shore Univ Med Ctr; **Address:** 2100 Corlies Ave, Ste 5, Neptune, NJ 07753-6116; **Phone:** 732-776-8866; **Board Cert:** Neurology 1980; **Med School:** Jefferson Med Coll 1971; **Resid:** Neurology, Columbia-Presby Med Ctr 1975; **Fellow:** Neurology, Columbia Univ 1976

Neuroradiology

Lu, Stanley MD (NRad) - **Spec Exp:** Stroke; MRI-Brain & Spine; Spinal Cord Injury; Head & Neck Imaging; **Hospital:** Monmouth Med Ctr (page 94); **Address:** Monmouth Med Ctr-Neuroradiology, 300 Second Ave Stanley Bldg - Ste 113, Long Branch, NJ 07740; **Phone:** 732-923-6806; **Board Cert:** Diagnostic Radiology 2014; Neuroradiology 2006; **Med School:** NYU Sch Med 1999; **Resid:** Internal Medicine, Lenox Hill Hosp 2000; Diagnostic Radiology, NYU Langone Med Ctr 2004; **Fellow:** Neurological Radiology, Stanford Univ Hosp & Clins 2005

Obstetrics & Gynecology

Goldstein, Steven A MD (ObG) - **Spec Exp:** Ultrasound; Menopause Problems; Minimally Invasive Surgery; **Hospital:** CentraState Med Ctr, Monmouth Med Ctr (page 94); **Address:** 501 Iron Bridge Rd, Ste 4, Freehold, NJ 07728; **Phone:** 732-431-1807; **Board Cert:** Obstetrics & Gynecology 2013; **Med School:** SUNY Downstate 1985; **Resid:** Obstetrics & Gynecology, Robert Wood Johnson Univ Hosp 1990

Martens, Mark G MD (ObG) - **Spec Exp:** Infections in Pregnancy; Vulvar & Vaginal Disorders; Menopause Problems; Viral Infections; **Hospital:** Jersey Shore Univ Med Ctr; **Address:** Jersey Shore Univ Med Ctr, Dept Ob/Gyn, 1944 Rte 33, Ste 101B, Neptune, NJ 07754; **Phone:** 732-776-3797; **Board Cert:** Obstetrics & Gynecology 2013; **Med School:** Geo Wash Univ 1982; **Resid:** Obstetrics & Gynecology, Hartford Hosp 1986; **Fellow:** Ob/Gyn Infectious Diseases, Baylor Coll Med 1987

Seigel, Mark J MD (ObG) - **Spec Exp:** Adolescent Gynecology; Minimally Invasive Surgery; Menopause Problems; **Hospital:** CentraState Med Ctr, Monmouth Med Ctr (page 94); **Address:** 501 Iron Bridge Rd, Ste 4, Freehold, NJ 07728-5305; **Phone:** 732-431-1807; **Board Cert:** Obstetrics & Gynecology 2013; **Med School:** Geo Wash Univ 1980; **Resid:** Obstetrics & Gynecology, NY-Presby/Columbia Univ Med Ctr 1985

Ophthalmology

Goldberg, Daniel B MD (Oph) - **Spec Exp:** LASIK-Refractive Surgery; Cornea Transplant; Cataract Surgery; Lens Implant; **Hospital:** Monmouth Med Ctr (page 94); **Address:** Atlantic Eye Physicians, 180 White Rd, Ste 202, Little Silver, NJ 07739-1166; **Phone:** 732-219-9220; **Board Cert:** Ophthalmology 1979; **Med School:** SUNY Downstate 1974; **Resid:** Ophthalmology, SUNY Downstate Med Ctr 1978; **Fellow:** Cornea, Eye & Ear Hosp 1979; **Fac Appt:** Asst Clin Prof Oph, Drexel Univ Coll Med

Kristan, Ronald W MD (Oph) - **Spec Exp:** Cataract Surgery; Oculoplastic Surgery; Botox Therapy; Eyelid Cosmetic & Reconstructive Surgery; **Hospital:** Monmouth Med Ctr (page 94); **Address:** Atlantic Eye Physicians, 279 Third Ave, Ste 204, Long Branch, NJ 07740; **Phone:** 732-222-7373; **Board Cert:** Ophthalmology 1985; **Med School:** NYU Sch Med 1980; **Resid:** Ophthalmology, Albany Memorial Hosp 1984; **Fellow:** Oculoplastic Surgery, Albany Memorial Hosp 1985

Talansky, Marvin L MD (Oph) - **Spec Exp:** Cataract Surgery; Diabetic Eye Disease; LASIK-Refractive Surgery; **Hospital:** Jersey Shore Univ Med Ctr, Monmouth Med Ctr (page 94); **Address:** Eye Diag & Surgery Ctr, 3333 Fairmont Ave, Asbury Park, NJ 07712; **Phone:** 732-988-4000; **Board Cert:** Ophthalmology 1978; **Med School:** Med Univ SC 1973; **Resid:** Ophthalmology, Storm Eye Inst 1977; **Fellow:** Retina, Storm Eye Inst 1986

Turtel, Lawrence S MD (Oph) - **Spec Exp:** Pediatric Ophthalmology; Strabismus; **Hospital:** Jersey Shore Univ Med Ctr, Monmouth Med Ctr (page 94); **Address:** Eye Diag & Surgery Ctr, 3333 Fairmont Ave, Asbury Park, NJ 07712; **Phone:** 732-988-4000; **Board Cert:** Ophthalmology 2013; **Med School:** Columbia P&S 1986; **Resid:** Internal Medicine, Beth Israel Med Ctr 1987; Ophthalmology, St Vincents Hosp 1990; **Fellow:** Pediatric Ophthalmology, Lenox Hill Hosp (Manh Eye, Ear & Throat Hosp) 1992

Orthopaedic Surgery

Bade III, Harry A MD (OrS) - **Spec Exp:** Joint Replacement; Shoulder Arthroscopic Surgery; Hand Surgery; Arthroscopic Surgery-Knee; **Hospital:** Monmouth Med Ctr (page 94), Riverview Med Ctr; **Address:** Professional Orthopedics Assocs, 776 Shrewsbury Ave, Ste 201, Tinton Falls, NJ 77243006; **Phone:** 732-530-4949; **Board Cert:** Orthopaedic Surgery 1984; Orthopaedic Sports Medicine 2007; **Med School:** Jefferson Med Coll 1976; **Resid:** Surgery, St. Luke's - Roosevelt Hosp Ctr - Roosevelt Div 1978; Orthopaedic Surgery, Hosp for Special Surg 1981; **Fellow:** Shoulder Surgery, Hosp for Special Surg 1982; Hand Surgery, St. Luke's - Roosevelt Hosp Ctr - Roosevelt Div 1983

Grossman, Robert B MD (OrS) - **Spec Exp:** Knee Surgery; **Hospital:** Monmouth Med Ctr (page 94), Riverview Med Ctr; **Address:** Shore Orth Group, 35 Gilbert St S, Tinton Falls, NJ 07701-4917; **Phone:** 732-530-1515; **Board Cert:** Orthopaedic Surgery 1978; **Med School:** Univ MD Sch Med 1972; **Resid:** Orthopaedic Surgery, Univ Vermont Med Ctr 1976; **Fellow:** Sports Medicine, Lenox Hill Hosp 1977

Otolaryngology

Rossos, Apostolos A.P. MD (Oto) - **Spec Exp:** Pediatric Otolaryngology; Sinus Disorders; Hearing Disorders; Sleep Apnea; **Hospital:** CentraState Med Ctr, Robert Wood Johnson Univ Hosp Hamilton; **Address:** 501 Iron Bridge Rd, Ste 11, Freehold, NJ 07728-5305; **Phone:** 732-409-2500; **Board Cert:** Otolaryngology 1988; **Med School:** Grenada 1981; **Resid:** Surgery, UMDNJ-Univ Hosp 1983; Otolaryngology, UMDNJ-Univ Hosp 1986

Scaccia, Frank J MD (Oto) - **Spec Exp:** Cosmetic Surgery-Face; Rhinoplasty; Nasal & Sinus Surgery; Reconstructive Surgery; **Hospital:** Riverview Med Ctr, Bayshore Community Hosp; **Address:** Riverside Plastic Surgery & Sinus Ctr, 70 E Front St, Fl 3, Red Bank, NJ 07701; **Phone:** 732-747-5300; **Board Cert:** Otolaryngology 1993; Facial Plastic & Reconstr Surgery 1995; **Med School:** Wake Forest Univ 1985; **Resid:** Surgery, Monmouth Med Ctr 1988; Otolaryngology, Univ Hosp 1992

Shah, Darsit K MD (Oto) - **Spec Exp:** Head & Neck Cancer & Surgery; Thyroid & Parathyroid Surgery; Parotid Gland Tumors; Neuro-Otology; **Hospital:** Monmouth Med Ctr (page 94); **Address:** Cen Jersey Otolaryngology, 1131 Broad St, Ste 103, Shrewsbury, NJ 07702; **Phone:** 732-389-3388; **Board Cert:** Otolaryngology 1997; **Med School:** Med Coll PA 1991; **Resid:** Surgery, Mt Sinai Med Ctr 1992; Otolaryngology, Mt Sinai Med Ctr 1996; **Fellow:** Neurotology, Michigan Ear Inst 1997; **Fac Appt:** Asst Clin Prof Oto, Drexel Univ Coll Med

Pain Medicine

Bram, Harris N MD (PM) - **Spec Exp:** Pain-Back & Neck; Complex Regional Pain Syndromes; **Hospital:** Riverview Med Ctr, Monmouth Med Ctr - South (page 94); **Address:** NJ Pain Care Specialists, 1806 Highway 35, Ste 305, Oakhurst, NJ 07755; **Phone:** 732-720-0247; **Board Cert:** Anesthesiology 1993; Pain Medicine 2004; **Med School:** Univ Ark 1988; **Resid:** Anesthesiology, Hahnemann Univ Hosp 1992; **Fellow:** Pain Medicine, Thomas Jefferson Univ Hosp 1993

Daknis, Charles Brian MD (PM) - **Spec Exp:** Pain-Spine; Pain-Interventional Techniques; **Hospital:** Monmouth Med Ctr (page 94); **Address:** Spine & Pain Ctrs of NY & NJ, 655 Shrewsbury Ave, Ste 202, Shrewsbury, NJ 07702; **Phone:** 732-345-1180; **Board Cert:** Anesthesiology 1996; Pain Medicine 2007; **Med School:** Hahnemann Univ 1990; **Resid:** Neurological Surgery, Albany Med Ctr 1992; Anesthesiology, Albany Med Ctr 1994; **Fellow:** Pain Medicine, Harvard/Brigham & Women's Hosp 1995

Metzger, Scott E MD (PM) - **Spec Exp:** Pain-Back & Neck; **Hospital:** Riverview Med Ctr; **Address:** Premier Pain Ctrs, 160 Avenue at the Common, Ste 1, Shrewsbury, NJ 07702; **Phone:** 732-380-0200; **Board Cert:** Anesthesiology 1997; Pain Medicine 2009; **Med School:** Boston Univ 1992; **Resid:** Anesthesiology, Johns Hopkins Hosp 1996; **Fellow:** Pain Medicine, Johns Hopkins Hosp 1997

Staats, Peter MD (PM) - **Spec Exp:** Pain-Cancer; Pain-Back; **Hospital:** Riverview Med Ctr, CentraState Med Ctr; **Address:** Premier Pain Centers, 160 Avenue at the Commons, Ste 1, Shrewsbury, NJ 07702; **Phone:** 732-380-0200; **Board Cert:** Anesthesiology 1994; Pain Medicine 2005; **Med School:** Univ Mich Med Sch 1989; **Resid:** Anesthesiology, Johns Hopkins Hosp 1993; **Fellow:** Pain Medicine, Johns Hopkins Hosp 1994

Pediatric Infectious Disease

Fisher, Margaret C MD (PInf) - **Spec Exp:** Diarrheal Diseases; **Hospital:** Monmouth Med Ctr (page 94); **Address:** Chldns Hosp at Monmouth Med Ctr, 300 Second Ave Stanley Bldg - rm 209, Long Branch, NJ 07740; **Phone:** 732-923-7250; **Board Cert:** Pediatrics 1980; Pediatric Infectious Disease 2008; **Med School:** UCLA 1975; **Resid:** Pediatrics, St. Christopher's Hosp for Chldn 1978; **Fellow:** Pediatric Infectious Disease, St. Christopher's Hosp for Chldn 1980; **Fac Appt:** Prof Ped, Drexel Univ Coll Med

Pediatric Otolaryngology

Tavill, Michael A MD (PO) - **Hospital:** Monmouth Med Ctr (page 94); **Address:** Central Jersey Otolaryngology, 1131 Broad St, Ste 103, Shrewsbury, NJ 07702; **Phone:** 732-389-3388; **Board Cert:** Otolaryngology 1997; **Med School:** Case West Res Univ 1991; **Resid:** Otolaryngology, Hosp Univ Penn 1996; **Fellow:** Pediatric Otolaryngology, Childrens Hosp 1997; **Fac Appt:** Asst Clin Prof Oto, Drexel Univ Coll Med

Pediatrics

Murphy, Robert D MD (Ped) *PCP* - **Spec Exp:** ADD/ADHD; Asthma; Vaccines; Infectious Disease; **Hospital:** Monmouth Med Ctr (page 94); **Address:** Pediatric & Adolescent Med, 223 Monmouth Rd, Ste 2, West Long Branch, NJ 07764; **Phone:** 732-229-4540; **Board Cert:** Pediatrics 1982; **Med School:** Vanderbilt Univ 1977; **Resid:** Pediatrics, Yale-New Haven Hosp 1980

Smoller, Alison DO (Ped) - **Spec Exp:** Autism; Developmental & Behavioral Disorders; ADD/ADHD; Learning Disorders; **Hospital:** Children's Specialized Hosp-Toms River; **Address:** Developmental Pediatrics, 1806 Highway 35 S, Ste 107, Oakhurst, NJ 07755; **Phone:** 732-660-0220; **Board Cert:** Pediatrics 2013; Developmental-Behavioral Pediatrics 2011; **Med School:** Univ Hlth Sci, Coll Osteo Med 2002; **Resid:** Pediatrics, Newark Beth Israel Med Ctr 2005; **Fellow:** Developmental-Behavioral Pediatrics, NYU Med Ctr 2009

Plastic Surgery

Ashinoff, Russell L MD (PlS) - **Spec Exp:** Breast Reconstruction; Cosmetic Surgery; Lymphedema; Trauma-Reconstructive Plastic Surgery; **Hospital:** Jersey Shore Univ Med Ctr, Ocean Med Ctr; **Address:** Institute for Advanced Reconstruction, 535 Sycamore Ave, Shrewsbury, NJ 07702; **Phone:** 732-741-0970; **Board Cert:** Surgery 2006; Plastic Surgery 2009; **Med School:** SUNY Upstate Med Univ 1999; **Resid:** Surgery, NYU Med Ctr 2005; **Fellow:** Plastic/Reconstructive Surgery, Emory Univ Hosp 2008

Chidyllo, Stephen A MD/DDS (PlS) - **Spec Exp:** Cosmetic Surgery-Face; Cosmetic Surgery-Breast; Body Contouring; Breast Reconstruction; **Hospital:** Jersey Shore Univ Med Ctr, Southern Ocean Med Ctr; **Address:** Central Jersey Plastic Surgery, 107 Monmouth Rd, Ste 106, West Long Branch, NJ 07764; **Phone:** 732-460-9566; **Board Cert:** Plastic Surgery 2015; **Med School:** Hahnemann Univ 1987; **Resid:** Surgery, NY Infirm-Beekman Downtown Hosp 1990; Plastic Surgery, Univ Illinois Med Ctr 1992; **Fellow:** Craniofacial Surgery, Eastern Va Med Sch 1993; **Fac Appt:** Assoc Clin Prof S, Drexel Univ Coll Med

Dudick, Stephen T MD (PlS) - **Spec Exp:** Breast Reconstruction & Augmentation; Cosmetic Surgery; Cleft Palate/Lip; Body Contouring After Weight Loss; **Hospital:** Jersey Shore Univ Med Ctr, Mon-mouth Med Ctr (page 94); **Address:** 252 Broad St, Red Bank, NJ 07701; **Phone:** 732-741-1303; **Board Cert:** Plastic Surgery 1993; **Med School:** Mexico 1975; **Resid:** Surgery, St Vincents Hosp 1981; Plastic Surgery, Indiana Univ Med Ctr 1983

Elkwood, Andrew I MD (PlS) - **Spec Exp:** Cosmetic Surgery-Face; Peripheral Nerve Surgery; Reconstructive Surgery; Limb Surgery/Reconstruction; **Hospital:** Jersey Shore Univ Med Ctr, Monmouth Med Ctr (page 94); **Address:** The Plastic Surgery Center, 535 Sycamore Ave, Shrewsbury, NJ 07702; **Phone:** 732-741-0970; **Board Cert:** Surgery 2004; Plastic Surgery 2008; **Med School:** Albany Med Coll 1988; **Resid:** Surgery, NYU Med Ctr 1994; **Fellow:** Plastic/Reconstructive Surgery, NYU Med Ctr 1996; **Fac Appt:** Assoc Clin Prof S, Drexel Univ Coll Med

Glicksman, Caroline A MD (PlS) - **Spec Exp:** Breast Reconstruction & Augmentation; **Hospital:** Jersey Shore Univ Med Ctr; **Address:** 2164 Hwy 35, Bldg A, Sea Girt, NJ 08750; **Phone:** 732-974-2424; **Board Cert:** Plastic Surgery 1994; **Med School:** SUNY Downstate 1985; **Resid:** Surgery, Mt Sinai Hosp 1988; Plastic Surgery, NY Hosp-Cornell Med Ctr 1991; **Fellow:** Cosmetic Plastic Surgery, Mass Genl Hosp-Newton Wellesley Hosp 1992

Hetzler, Peter T MD (PlS) - **Spec Exp:** Breast Cosmetic & Reconstructive Surgery; Liposuction & Body Contouring; Skin Cancer; **Hospital:** Riverview Med Ctr, Monmouth Med Ctr (page 94); **Address:** 200 White Rd, Ste 211, Little Silver, NJ 07739-1162; **Phone:** 732-219-0447; **Board Cert:** Plastic Surgery 1991; **Med School:** Univ Mich Med Sch 1981; **Resid:** Surgery, MS Hershey Med Ctr 1986; Plastic/Reconstructive Surgery, MS Hershey Med Ctr 1988; **Fellow:** Microsurgery, York Hosp Trauma Ctr 1988; Cosmetic Plastic Surgery, Manhattan Eye & Ear Hosp 1989

Rose, Michael I MD (PlS) - **Spec Exp:** Body Contouring After Weight Loss; Breast Cosmetic & Reconstructive Surgery; Reconstructive Surgery; **Hospital:** Jersey Shore Univ Med Ctr, CentraState Med Ctr; **Address:** The Plastic Surgery Center, 535 Sycamore Ave, Shrewsbury, NJ 07702; **Phone:** 732-741-0970; **Board Cert:** Surgery 2009; Plastic Surgery 2013; **Med School:** NYU Sch Med 1994; **Resid:** Surgery, NYU/Bellevue Med Ctr 2000; **Fellow:** Plastic Surgery, Emory Univ Med Ctr 2002

Samra, Said A MD (PlS) - **Spec Exp:** Reconstructive Surgery; Hand Surgery; Cosmetic Surgery; **Hospital:** Bayshore Community Hosp, Raritan Bay Med Ctr - Perth Amboy; **Address:** 733 N Beers St, Ste U-1, Holmdel, NJ 07733-1528; **Phone:** 732-739-2100; **Board Cert:** Plastic Surgery 1988; **Med School:** Syria 1973; **Resid:** Surgery, UMDNJ-NJ Med Sch 1980; Plastic Surgery, St Barnabas Hosp 1982

Zaccaria, Alan MD (PlS) - **Spec Exp:** Breast Cosmetic & Reconstructive Surgery; Cosmetic Surgery-Face & Body; Botox Therapy; Wound Healing/Care; **Hospital:** Jersey Shore Univ Med Ctr, Monmouth Med Ctr (page 94); **Address:** 180 White Rd, Ste 102, Little Silver, NJ 07739; **Phone:** 732-530-8565; **Board Cert:** Plastic Surgery 2005; **Med School:** Rutgers R W Johnson Med Sch 1986; **Resid:** Surgery, Monmouth Med Ctr 1991; **Fellow:** Plastic/Reconstructive Surgery, Univ IL Med Ctr 1993

Psychiatry

Rubin, Kenneth J MD (Psyc) - **Spec Exp:** Mood Disorders; Anxiety Disorders; Dementia; **Hospital:** Monmouth Med Ctr (page 94); **Address:** 170 Morris Ave, Long Branch, NJ 07740-6660; **Phone:** 732-870-3535; **Board Cert:** Psychiatry 1979; **Med School:** SUNY Downstate 1974; **Resid:** Psychiatry, Kings County Hosp 1977

Pulmonary Disease

Davis, George C MD (Pul) - **Spec Exp:** Critical Care; Chronic Obstructive Lung Disease (COPD); Sepsis; **Hospital:** Monmouth Med Ctr (page 94); **Address:** 279 3rd Ave, Ste 510, Long Branch, NJ 07740; **Phone:** 732-870-0650; **Board Cert:** Internal Medicine 1976; Pulmonary Disease 1980; Critical Care Medicine 2013; **Med School:** Hahnemann Univ 1973; **Resid:** Internal Medicine, Monmouth Med Ctr 1977; **Fellow:** Pulmonary Disease, Monmouth Med Ctr 1979

Reproductive Endocrinology

Damien, Miguel MD (RE) - **Spec Exp:** Infertility-IVF; **Hospital:** Riverview Med Ctr, Monmouth Med Ctr (page 94); **Address:** 655 Shrewsbury Ave, Ste 300, Shrewsbury, NJ 07702; **Phone:** 732-758-6511; **Board Cert:** Obstetrics & Gynecology 2013; Reproductive Endocrinology 2013; **Med School:** Dartmouth Med Sch 1982; **Resid:** Obstetrics & Gynecology, Beth Israel Deaconess Hosp 1986; **Fellow:** Reproductive Endocrinology, Beth Israel Deaconess Hosp 1988; Reproductive Endocrinology, Univ Conn Hlth Ctr 1989

Rheumatology

Wasser, Kenneth B MD (Rhu) - **Spec Exp:** Rheumatoid Arthritis; Lupus Nephritis; Psoriatic Arthritis; **Hospital:** Riverview Med Ctr, Monmouth Med Ctr (page 94); **Address:** 43 Gilbert St N, Ste 7, Tinton Falls, NJ 07701; **Phone:** 732-530-7999; **Board Cert:** Internal Medicine 1981; Rheumatology 1982; **Med School:** Case West Res Univ 1977; **Resid:** Internal Medicine, Univ Hosps 1980; **Fellow:** Rheumatology, Univ Hosps 1982

Sports Medicine

Rice, Stephen G MD/PhD (SM) - **Spec Exp:** Primary Care Sports Medicine; Musculoskeletal Injuries; **Hospital:** Jersey Shore Univ Med Ctr; **Address:** Jersey Shore Sports Med Ctr, 51-02 Davis Ave, Ste 02, Neptune, NJ 07753; **Phone:** 732-776-2433; **Board Cert:** Pediatrics 1981; Sports Medicine 2014; **Med School:** NYU Sch Med 1974; **Resid:** Pediatrics, Chldn's Hosp Med Ctr 1977; **Fac Appt:** Clin Prof Ped, Rutgers R W Johnson Med Sch

Sclafani, Michael A MD (SM) - **Spec Exp:** Knee Injuries/Ligament Surgery; Shoulder Instability; Arthroscopic Surgery; **Hospital:** Jersey Shore Univ Med Ctr; **Address:** Orthopedic Institute of Central Jersey, 2315 Route 34 S, Manasquan, NJ 08736; **Phone:** 732-974-0404; **Board Cert:** Orthopaedic Surgery 2007; **Med School:** NYU Sch Med 1988; **Resid:** Orthopaedic Surgery, NYU Med Ctr 1993; **Fellow:** Sports Medicine & Shoulder Surgery, American Sports Med Inst 1994

Surgery

Borao, Frank J MD (S) - **Spec Exp:** Laparoscopic Abdominal Surgery; Obesity/Bariatric Surgery; Gastroesophageal Reflux Disease (GERD); Critical Care; **Hospital:** Monmouth Med Ctr (page 94); **Address:** Specialty Surgical Assocs, 10 Industrial Way E, Ste 104, Eatontown, NJ 07724; **Phone:** 732-389-1331; **Board Cert:** Surgery 2010; **Med School:** UMDNJ-NJ Med Sch, Newark 1994; **Resid:** Surgery, Monmouth Med Ctr 1999; **Fellow:** Laparoscopic Surgery, Inst for Minimally Invasive Surg 2000; **Fac Appt:** Asst Clin Prof S, Hahnemann Univ

Goldfarb, Michael A MD (S) - **Spec Exp:** Breast Cancer & Surgery; Telemedicine; **Hospital:** Monmouth Med Ctr (page 94); **Address:** 48 Pavilion Ave, Long Branch, NJ 07740; **Phone:** 732-870-6060; **Board Cert:** Surgery 1973; **Med School:** NYU Sch Med 1967; **Resid:** Surgery, Beth Israel Med Ctr 1972; **Fac Appt:** Prof S, Drexel Univ Coll Med

Johnson Miller, Denise L MD (S) - **Spec Exp:** Breast Cancer; Breast Cancer-High Risk Women; Melanoma; Neuroendocrine Tumors; **Hospital:** Jersey Shore Univ Med Ctr, Ocean Med Ctr; **Address:** Meridian Hlth Breast Surgery Assocs, 1945 Hwy 33, Ackerman 5, Neptune, NJ 07753; **Phone:** 732-776-4594; **Board Cert:** Surgery 2012; **Med School:** Washington Univ, St Louis 1978; **Resid:** Immunology, Univ Texas SW Med Ctr 1982; Surgery, Univ IL Med Ctr 1986; **Fellow:** Surgical Oncology, City of Hope Med Ctr 1988

Thoracic & Cardiac Surgery

Neibart, Richard M MD (T&CS) - **Spec Exp:** Coronary Artery Surgery; Cardiac Surgery; Aortic Surgery; **Hospital:** Jersey Shore Univ Med Ctr; **Address:** Mid-Atlantic Surgical Assocs, 1944 Rte 33, Ste 201, Neptune, NJ 07753; **Phone:** 732-776-4618; **Board Cert:** Thoracic & Cardiac Surgery 2011; **Med School:** Mount Sinai Sch Med 1982; **Resid:** Surgery, St Vincents Hosp 1987; **Fellow:** Thoracic Surgery, Jackson Meml Hosp 1989

Urology

Ebani, Jack MD (U) - **Spec Exp:** Prostate Cancer; Incontinence; **Hospital:** Jersey Shore Univ Med Ctr, Ocean Med Ctr; **Address:** 1820 Corlies Ave, Neptune, NJ 07753; **Phone:** 732-774-4551; **Board Cert:** Urology 2006; **Med School:** SUNY Hlth Sci Ctr 1979; **Resid:** Surgery, N Shore Univ Hosp 1981; Urology, NYU Med Ctr 1985

Geltzeiler, Jules MD (U) - **Spec Exp:** Prostate Cancer; Incontinence; **Hospital:** Monmouth Med Ctr (page 94), Jersey Shore Univ Med Ctr; **Address:** NJ Urologic Inst, 10 Industrial Way E, Ste 101, Eatontown, NJ 07724; **Phone:** 732-963-9091; **Board Cert:** Urology 2004; **Med School:** Hahnemann Univ 1979; **Resid:** Surgery, Monmouth Med Ctr 1981; Urology, G Washington Univ Hosp 1984; **Fac Appt:** Asst Clin Prof S, Drexel Univ Coll Med

Litvin, Y. Samuel MD (U) - **Spec Exp:** Infertility; Prostate Disease; **Hospital:** Monmouth Med Ctr (page 94), Riverview Med Ctr; **Address:** NJ Urologic Inst, 10 Industrial Way E, Ste 101, Eatontown, NJ 07724; **Phone:** 732-963-9091; **Board Cert:** Urology 2013; **Med School:** UCLA 1986; **Resid:** Surgery, Beth Israel Med Ctr 1988; Urology, Beth Israel Med Ctr 1991; **Fac Appt:** Asst Clin Prof U, Drexel Univ Coll Med

Rose, John G MD (U) - **Hospital:** Riverview Med Ctr, Bayshore Community Hosp; **Address:** Urology Assocs, 595 Shrewsbury Ave, Shrewsbury, NJ 07702; **Phone:** 732-741-5923; **Board Cert:** Urology 1977; **Med School:** Cornell Univ-Weill Med Coll 1968; **Resid:** Surgery, NY-Presby/Weill Cornell Med Ctr 1970; Urology, Univ Virginia Med Ctr 1974; **Fellow:** Urology, Univ Virginia Med Ctr

Rotolo, James MD (U) - **Spec Exp:** Prostate Disease; Urologic Cancer; Kidney Stones; **Hospital:** Ocean Med Ctr, Jersey Shore Univ Med Ctr; **Address:** Rotolo, Howard & Leitner Urologic Assocs, 2401 Highway 35, Manasquan, NJ 08736; **Phone:** 732-223-7877; **Board Cert:** Urology 2010; **Med School:** Georgetown Univ 1984; **Resid:** Surgery, Georgetown Univ Hosp 1986; Urology, Georgetown Univ Hosp 1990

Vascular Surgery

Weiswasser, Jonathan M MD (VascS) - **Spec Exp:** Varicose Veins; Vein Disorders; **Address:** The Plastic Surgery Ctr, 535 Sycamore Ave, Shrewsbury, NJ 07702; **Phone:** 732-741-0970; **Board Cert:** Surgery 2011; Vascular Surgery 2012; **Med School:** NYU Sch Med 1993; **Resid:** Surgery, NYU Med Ctr 2000; **Fellow:** Vascular Surgery, NYU Med Ctr 2001

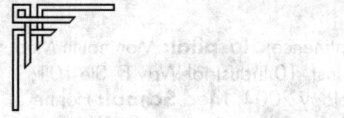

The Best in American Medicine
www.CastleConnolly.com

Morris

Addiction Psychiatry

Finkelstein, Mario MD (AdP) - **Spec Exp:** Addiction/Substance Abuse; Alcohol Abuse; Cocaine Addiction; Psychopharmacology; **Address:** 95 Madison Ave, Ste 103, Morristown, NJ 07960; **Phone:** 973-538-0111; **Board Cert:** Psychiatry 2014; Psychosomatic Medicine 2005; Addiction Psychiatry 2006; **Med School:** Argentina 1979; **Resid:** Psychiatry, St Luke's-Roosevelt Hosp 1994

Adolescent Medicine

Clark-Hamilton, Jill MD (AM) - **Spec Exp:** Eating Disorders; Adolescent Gynecology; Behavioral Disorders; **Hospital:** Goryeb Children's Hosp (page 92), Overlook Med Ctr (page 92); **Address:** Goryeb Chldn's Hosp at Morristown, 100 Madison Ave, Morristown, NJ 07962; **Phone:** 973-971-5199; **Board Cert:** Adolescent Medicine 2014; **Med School:** SUNY Upstate Med Univ 1983; **Resid:** Pediatrics, Montefiore Med Ctr 1987; **Fellow:** Adolescent Medicine, Montefiore Med Ctr 1989

Rosenfeld, Walter D MD (AM) - **Spec Exp:** Eating Disorders; **Hospital:** Goryeb Children's Hosp (page 92); **Address:** Goryeb Chldns Hosp, Adolescent Med, 100 Madison Ave, Morristown, NJ 07960; **Phone:** 973-971-5199; **Board Cert:** Pediatrics 1980; Adolescent Medicine 2008; **Med School:** Temple Univ 1975; **Resid:** Pediatrics, NY-Presby/Columbia Univ Med Ctr 1978; **Fellow:** Adolescent Medicine, Chldns Hosp 1979; **Fac Appt:** Prof Ped, UMDNJ-NJ Med Sch, Newark

Allergy & Immunology

Applebaum, Eric MD (A&I) - **Spec Exp:** Asthma; Food Allergy; Sinus Disorders; Rhinitis; **Hospital:** Morristown Med Ctr (page 92), St. Clare's Hosp-Denville; **Address:** 3799 Route 46 E, Parsippany, NJ 07054-1101; **Phone:** 973-335-1700; **Board Cert:** Allergy & Immunology 2014; **Med School:** Albert Einstein Coll Med 1987; **Resid:** Internal Medicine, LI Jewish Med Ctr 1990; **Fellow:** Allergy & Immunology, LI Jewish Med Ctr 1992

Chernack, William J MD (A&I) - **Spec Exp:** Asthma; Sinus Disorders; Insect Allergies; **Hospital:** Morristown Med Ctr (page 92), Morgan Stanley Chldns Hosp of NY-Presby, NY (page 102); **Address:** 28 Franklin Pl, Morristown, NJ 07960-5305; **Phone:** 973-538-7271; **Board Cert:** Pediatrics 1975; Allergy & Immunology 1977; **Med School:** NY Med Coll 1970; **Resid:** Pediatrics, Columbia-Presby Med Ctr 1972; **Fellow:** Allergy & Immunology, Columbia-Presby Med Ctr 1974; **Fac Appt:** Asst Clin Prof Ped, Columbia P&S

Hirsch, Andrew C MD (A&I) - **Spec Exp:** Asthma; Sinusitis; Allergic Rhinitis; Eczema; **Hospital:** Riverview Med Ctr, Monmouth Med Ctr (page 94); **Address:** 258 Broad St, Red Bank, NJ 07701-5623; **Phone:** 732-741-8900; **Board Cert:** Allergy & Immunology 2005; **Med School:** Temple Univ 1988; **Resid:** Pediatrics, New York Hosp 1991; **Fellow:** Allergy & Immunology, Thomas Jefferson Univ Hosp 1993

Kanumury, Sunita MD (A&I) - **Spec Exp:** Asthma; Eczema; Food & Drug Allergy; Sinusitis; **Hospital:** St. Clare's Hosp-Denville, Hackettstown Reg Med Ctr; **Address:** Asthma & Allergy Care, 496 E Main St, Ste 1, Denville, NJ 07834; **Phone:** 973-627-1000; **Board Cert:** Allergy & Immunology 2005; **Med School:** India 1986; **Resid:** Pediatrics, Univ Toledo Med Ctr 1991; **Fellow:** Allergy & Immunology, Univ Hosp-UMDNJ 1993

Cardiac Electrophysiology

Winters, Stephen L MD (CE) - **Spec Exp:** Pacemakers/Defibrillators; Catheter Ablation; Atrial Fibrillation; Syncope; **Hospital:** Morristown Med Ctr (page 92), Overlook Med Ctr (page 92); **Address:** Morristown Meml Hosp, 100 Madison Ave, Morristown, NJ 07962-1956; **Phone:** 973-971-4261; **Board Cert:** Internal Medicine 1982; Cardiovascular Disease 1985; Cardiac Electrophysiology 2012; **Med School:** Mount Sinai Sch Med 1979; **Resid:** Internal Medicine, Mt Sinai Med Ctr 1982; **Fellow:** Cardiovascular Disease, Mt Sinai Med Ctr 1985; Cardiac Electrophysiology, Mt Sinai Med Ctr 1986; **Fac Appt:** Assoc Prof Med, UMDNJ-NJ Med Sch, Newark

Cardiovascular Disease

Blick, Michael D MD (Cv) - **Spec Exp:** Cardiac Catheterization; **Hospital:** St. Clare's Hosp-Dover, Morristown Med Ctr (page 92); **Address:** Lakeland Cardiology, 765 Rte 10 E, Ste 104, Randolph, NJ 07869; **Phone:** 973-989-2566; **Board Cert:** Internal Medicine 1985; Cardiovascular Disease 1987; **Med School:** Geo Wash Univ 1982; **Resid:** Internal Medicine, LI Jewish Med Ctr 1985; **Fellow:** Cardiovascular Disease, Philadelphia Heart Inst 1987

Blum, Mark A MD (Cv) - **Spec Exp:** Interventional Cardiology; Cholesterol/Lipid Disorders; Hypertrophic Cardiomyopathy; Preventive Cardiology; **Hospital:** Morristown Med Ctr (page 92); **Address:** Cardiology Assocs-Morristown, 95 Madison Ave, Ste A10, Morristown, NJ 7960; **Phone:** 973-889-9001; **Board Cert:** Internal Medicine 1986; Cardiovascular Disease 1989; **Med School:** Mount Sinai Sch Med 1983; **Resid:** Internal Medicine, Montefiore Med Ctr 1985; Internal Medicine, Mount Sinai Med Ctr 1986; **Fellow:** Cardiovascular Disease, Mount Sinai Med Ctr 1988; Interventional Cardiology, Newark Beth Israel Hosp 1989; **Fac Appt:** Asst Clin Prof Med, Mount Sinai Sch Med

Fisch, Arthur P MD (Cv) - **Spec Exp:** Echocardiography; Coronary Artery Disease; Heart Valve Disease; **Hospital:** Morristown Med Ctr (page 92); **Address:** Morristown Cardiology Assocs, 435 South St, Ste 100, Morristown, NJ 07960; **Phone:** 973-267-3944; **Board Cert:** Internal Medicine 1972; Cardiovascular Disease 1975; **Med School:** Boston Univ 1969; **Resid:** Internal Medicine, UCLA Med Ctr 1972; **Fellow:** Cardiovascular Disease, Hosp Univ Penn 1974

Lowell, Barry H MD (Cv) - **Spec Exp:** Interventional Cardiology; Angioplasty; **Hospital:** St. Clare's Hosp-Dover, Morristown Med Ctr (page 92); **Address:** Morris Heart Assocs, 400 Valley Rd, Ste 102, Mount Arlington, NJ 07856; **Phone:** 973-770-7899; **Board Cert:** Internal Medicine 1986; Cardiovascular Disease 1989; Interventional Cardiology 2010; **Med School:** SUNY Stony Brook 1982; **Resid:** Internal Medicine, St Lukes-Roosevelt Hosp Ctr 1985; **Fellow:** Cardiovascular Disease, St Lukes-Roosevelt Hosp Ctr 1989

Raska, Karel MD (Cv) - **Spec Exp:** Preventive Cardiology; Hypertension; Echocardiography; **Hospital:** Morristown Med Ctr (page 92); **Address:** Morristown Cardiology Assocs, 435 South St, Ste 100, Morristown, NJ 07960; **Phone:** 973-267-3944; **Board Cert:** Cardiovascular Disease 2005; **Med School:** Harvard Med Sch 1989; **Resid:** Internal Medicine, Mass Genl Hosp 1992; **Fellow:** Cardiovascular Disease, Johns Hopkins Hosp 1995

Child Neurology

Bennett, Harvey S MD (ChiN) - **Spec Exp:** Concussion; Tourette's Syndrome; Cerebral Palsy; **Hospital:** Goryeb Children's Hosp (page 92), Overlook Med Ctr (page 92); **Address:** Goryeb Chldn's Hosp at Morristown, 100 Madison Ave, Box 24, Morristown, NJ 07960; **Phone:** 973-971-5700; **Board Cert:** Pediatrics 1979; Child Neurology 1991; Neurodevelopmental Disabilities 2009; **Med School:** Albert Einstein Coll Med 1975; **Resid:** Pediatrics, St Christopher's Hosp Chldn 1977; Child Neurology, Montefiore Med Ctr 1980; **Fac Appt:** Clin Prof N, Mount Sinai Sch Med

Desouza, Trevor MD (ChiN) - **Spec Exp:** Epilepsy; Neuromuscular Disorders; Cerebral Palsy; Tourette's Syndrome; **Hospital:** Goryeb Children's Hosp (page 92); **Address:** Advocare Pediatric Neurology Assocs, 25 Lindsley Drive, Ste 205, Morristown, NJ 07960; **Phone:** 973-993-8777; **Board Cert:** Pediatrics 1985; Child Neurology 1989; **Med School:** Kenya 1977; **Resid:** Pediatrics, Bronx-Lebanon Hosp Ctr 1983; **Fellow:** Pediatric Neurology, Montefiore Med Ctr 1986; Neuromuscular Medicine, Montefiore Med Ctr 1987; **Fac Appt:** Asst Prof Ped, UMDNJ-Univ Med Dent NJ

Grossman, Elliot A MD (ChiN) - **Spec Exp:** Migraine; ADD/ADHD; Tourette's Syndrome; Epilepsy; **Hospital:** St. Barnabas Med Ctr (page 94), Morristown Med Ctr (page 92); **Address:** 220 Ridgedale Ave, Ste A3, Florham Park, NJ 07932-1349; **Phone:** 973-966-6333; **Board Cert:** Pediatrics 1987; Child Neurology 1990; **Med School:** Meharry Med Coll 1980; **Resid:** Pediatrics, Bellevue Hosp 1982; Pediatrics, Boston City Hosp 1983; **Fellow:** Pediatric Neurology, Boston City Hosp 1986

Lazar, Lorraine M MD (ChiN) - **Spec Exp:** Epilepsy/Seizure Disorders; **Hospital:** Goryeb Children's Hosp (page 92), Overlook Med Ctr (page 92); **Address:** Goryeb Chldn's Hosp at Morristown, 100 Madison Ave, Morristown, NJ 07962; **Phone:** 973-971-5700; **Board Cert:** Child Neurology 2010; Clinical Neurophysiology 2011; **Med School:** Mount Sinai Sch Med 1993; **Resid:** Neurology, NY Presby Hosp/Cornell 1995; Child Neurology, NY Presby Hosp/Cornell 1997; **Fellow:** Clinical Neurophysiology, NY Presby Hosp/Cornell 1998

Clinical Genetics

Adams, Darius MD (CG) - **Spec Exp:** Fetal Abnormalities; Inherited Disorders; Metabolic Genetic Disorders; Dysmorphology; **Hospital:** Overlook Med Ctr (page 92); **Address:** 435 South St, Ste 220, Morristown, NJ 07960; **Phone:** 908-522-6289; **Board Cert:** Clinical Biochemical Genetics 2005; Clinical Genetics 2013; **Med School:** UMDNJ-NJ Med Sch, Newark 1997; **Resid:** Clinical Genetics, Mt Sinai Hosp 2002; **Fellow:** Clinical Biochemical Genetics, Mt Sinai Hosp 2003; **Fac Appt:** Asst Prof Ped, Albany Med Coll

Colon & Rectal Surgery

Moskowitz, Richard L MD (CRS) - **Spec Exp:** Colon & Rectal Cancer; Anorectal Disorders; Inflammatory Bowel Disease; **Hospital:** Morristown Med Ctr (page 92), St. Clare's Hosp-Dover; **Address:** 111 Madison Ave, Ste 312, Morristown, NJ 07960-6083; **Phone:** 973-267-1225; **Board Cert:** Surgery 2005; Colon & Rectal Surgery 1985; **Med School:** Penn State Coll Med 1978; **Resid:** Surgery, LI Jewish-Hillside Med Ctr 1983; Colon & Rectal Surgery, Greater Baltimore Med Ctr 1984; **Fellow:** Colon & Rectal Surgery, St Marks Hosp 1985

Dermatology

Almeida, Laila N MD (D) - Spec Exp: Psoriasis; Acne; Skin Cancer; **Hospital:** St. Clare's Hosp-Denville, NY-Presby/Columbia Univ Med Ctr, NY (page 102); **Address:** Dermatology Associates in Morris, 199 Baldwin Rd, Ste 230, Parsippany, NJ 07054-2043; **Phone:** 973-335-2560; **Board Cert:** Internal Medicine 1986; Dermatology 2009; **Med School:** Univ Mich Med Sch 1983; **Resid:** Internal Medicine, Columbia-Presby Hosp 1986; Dermatology, Columbia-Presby Hosp 1989

Cooper, Lauren M MD (D) - Spec Exp: Botox Therapy; Facial Rejuvenation; Skin Cancer; **Hospital:** Morristown Med Ctr (page 92); **Address:** Affil Dermatologists & Surgeons, 182 South St, Ste 3, Morristown, NJ 07960; **Phone:** 973-267-0300; **Board Cert:** Dermatology 1988; **Med School:** NYU Sch Med 1984; **Resid:** Dermatology, Bellevue/NYU Med Ctr 1988

Machler, Brian C MD (D) - Spec Exp: Contact Dermatitis; Laser Surgery; Skin Cancer; **Hospital:** St. Barnabas Med Ctr (page 94); **Address:** Center for Dermatology, 128 Columbia Tpke, Ste 200, Florham Park, NJ 07932; **Phone:** 973-736-9535; **Board Cert:** Dermatology 2004; **Med School:** UMDNJ-NJ Med Sch, Newark 1991; **Resid:** Dermatology, Jackson Meml Hosp 1995; **Fac Appt:** Asst Prof D, NYU Sch Med

Diagnostic Radiology

Murphy, Robyn C MD (DR) - Spec Exp: Pediatric Radiology; **Hospital:** Morristown Med Ctr (page 92); **Address:** Morristown Meml Hosp, Dept Radiology, 100 Madison Ave, Ste 408, Morristown, NJ 07960; **Phone:** 973-971-5370; **Board Cert:** Diagnostic Radiology 1997; Pediatric Radiology 2010; **Med School:** Med Coll VA 1992; **Resid:** Diagnostic Radiology, Columbia-Presby Med Ctr 1997; **Fellow:** Pediatric Radiology, NY-Presby Hosp 1998

Endocrinology, Diabetes & Metabolism

Nevin, Marie E MD (EDM) - Hospital: Morristown Med Ctr (page 92); **Address:** Summit Med Grp, 95 Madison Ave Fl 2 - Ste B, Morristown, NJ 07960; **Phone:** 973-775-5151; **Board Cert:** Internal Medicine 1989; Endocrinology, Diabetes & Metabolism 2013; **Med School:** UMDNJ-NJ Med Sch, Newark 1986; **Resid:** Internal Medicine, Morristown Meml Hosp 1989; **Fellow:** Endocrinology, Mount Sinai Med Ctr 1991

Family Medicine

Capio, Mario MD (FMed) *PCP* **- Hospital:** Chilton Med Ctr (page 92); **Address:** 230 W Parkway Unit 10, Pompton Plains, NJ 07444; **Phone:** 973-835-0800; **Board Cert:** Family Medicine 2012; **Med School:** UMDNJ-NJ Med Sch, Newark 1995; **Resid:** Family Medicine, Mountainside Hosp 1998; **Fac Appt:** Assoc Prof FMed, UMDNJ-NJ Med Sch, Newark

Holland Jr, Elbridge T MD (FMed) *PCP* **- Hospital:** Overlook Med Ctr (page 92); **Address:** 492 Main St, Chatham, NJ 07928; **Phone:** 973-635-2432; **Board Cert:** Family Medicine 2009; Geriatric Medicine 2007; **Med School:** Univ Chicago-Pritzker Sch Med 1975; **Resid:** Family Medicine, Overlook Hosp 1978; **Fac Appt:** Asst Clin Prof FMed, UMDNJ-NJ Med Sch, Newark

Gastroenterology

Dalena, John M MD (Ge) - **Spec Exp:** Colon Cancer Screening; Endoscopy; Gastroesophageal Reflux Disease (GERD); Inflammatory Bowel Disease; **Hospital:** Morristown Med Ctr (page 92); **Address:** Summit Medical Group, 65 Ridgedale Ave, Cedar Knolls, NJ 07927; **Phone:** 973-401-0500; **Board Cert:** Internal Medicine 1988; Gastroenterology 2011; **Med School:** UMDNJ-NJ Med Sch, Newark 1985; **Resid:** Internal Medicine, Mount Sinai Hosp 1988; **Fellow:** Gastroenterology, UMDNJ-Univ Hosp 1990

Samach, Michael MD (Ge) - **Spec Exp:** Colonoscopy; Gastroesophageal Reflux Disease (GERD); Hepatitis C; **Hospital:** Morristown Med Ctr (page 92); **Address:** Affiliates in Gastroenterology, 101 Madison Ave, Ste 100, Morristown, NJ 07960; **Phone:** 973-455-0404; **Board Cert:** Internal Medicine 1974; Gastroenterology 1979; **Med School:** NYU Sch Med 1971; **Resid:** Internal Medicine, Montefiore Med Ctr 1974; **Fellow:** Gastroenterology, Montefiore Med Ctr 1978; **Fac Appt:** Asst Clin Prof Med, Mount Sinai Sch Med

Soriano, John G MD (Ge) - **Hospital:** St. Clare's Hosp-Denville, Morristown Med Ctr (page 92); **Address:** 16 Pocono Rd, Ste 201, Denville, NJ 07834; **Phone:** 973-627-4430; **Board Cert:** Internal Medicine 1986; **Med School:** Mexico 1981; **Resid:** Internal Medicine, Morristown Meml Hosp 1987; **Fellow:** Gastroenterology, Long Island Coll Hosp 1989

Stein, Lawrence B MD (Ge) - **Spec Exp:** Hepatitis; Gastroesophageal Reflux Disease (GERD); Endoscopy; **Hospital:** Morristown Med Ctr (page 92), St. Barnabas Med Ctr (page 94); **Address:** 101 Madison Ave, Ste 102, Morristown, NJ 07960; **Phone:** 973-410-0960; **Board Cert:** Internal Medicine 1972; Gastroenterology 1973; **Med School:** Univ Minn 1965; **Resid:** Internal Medicine, Bronx Muni Hosp 1967; Internal Medicine, Bronx Muni Hosp 1970; **Fellow:** Gastroenterology, Einstein Med Ctr 1972

Gynecologic Oncology

Heller, Paul B MD (GO) - **Spec Exp:** Gynecologic Cancer; **Hospital:** Morristown Med Ctr (page 92), Overlook Med Ctr (page 92); **Address:** Morristown Meml Hosp, Women's Cancer Ctr, 100 Madison Ave, Morristown, NJ 07962; **Phone:** 973-971-5900; **Board Cert:** Obstetrics & Gynecology 1975; Gynecologic Oncology 1982; **Med School:** NY Med Coll 1968; **Resid:** Obstetrics & Gynecology, Metroplitan Hosp 1971; Obstetrics & Gynecology, Beth Israel Med Ctr 1973; **Fellow:** Gynecologic Oncology, Metropolitan Hosp 1977; **Fac Appt:** Clin Prof ObG, Temple Univ

Tobias, Daniel H MD (GO) - **Spec Exp:** Gynecologic Cancer; Uterine Cancer; Laparoscopic Surgery; **Hospital:** Morristown Med Ctr (page 92), Overlook Med Ctr (page 92); **Address:** Morristown Meml Hosp, Women's Cancer Ctr, 100 Madison Ave, Morristown, NJ 07962; **Phone:** 973-971-5900; **Board Cert:** Obstetrics & Gynecology 2013; Gynecologic Oncology 2013; **Med School:** Univ MO-Kansas City 1992; **Resid:** Obstetrics & Gynecology, Bronx Muni Hosp Ctr 1996; **Fellow:** Gynecologic Oncology, Mt Sinai Med Ctr 1999

Hand Surgery

Ende, Leigh S MD (HS) - **Spec Exp:** Arthritis; Carpal Tunnel Syndrome; Hand & Upper Extremity Surgery; **Hospital:** St. Clare's Hosp-Dover, Newton Med Ctr (page 92); **Address:** 121 Center Grove Rd, Ste 6, Randolph, NJ 07869; **Phone:** 973-366-5565; **Board Cert:** Orthopaedic Surgery 2010; Hand Surgery 2010; **Med School:** Tulane Univ 1978; **Resid:** Orthopaedic Surgery, UMDNJ-Univ Hosp 1983; **Fellow:** Hand Surgery, Columbia Presby Med Ctr 1984

Miller, Jeffrey K MD (HS) - **Spec Exp:** Carpal Tunnel Syndrome; Dupuytren's Contracture; Wrist/Hand Injuries; Elbow Surgery; **Hospital:** Morristown Med Ctr (page 92), St. Barnabas Med Ctr (page 94); **Address:** 111 Madison Ave, Ste 302, Morristown, NJ 07960; **Phone:** 973-538-5200; **Board Cert:** Orthopaedic Surgery 2010; Hand Surgery 2010; **Med School:** Univ Pittsburgh 1981; **Resid:** Orthopaedic Surgery, Boston Med Ctr 1986; **Fellow:** Hand Surgery, Thomas Jefferson Univ Hosp 1987

Infectious Disease

Allegra, Donald T MD (Inf) - **Spec Exp:** Tropical Diseases; AIDS/HIV; International Health; Travel Medicine; **Hospital:** St. Clare's Hosp-Denville, Morristown Med Ctr (page 92); **Address:** 765 Rte 10 E, Ste 201, Randolph, NJ 07869; **Phone:** 973-989-0068; **Board Cert:** Infectious Disease 1982; Internal Medicine 1978; **Med School:** Harvard Med Sch 1974; **Resid:** Internal Medicine, Univ CO Hosp 1978; **Fellow:** Infectious Disease, Emory Univ Hosp 1981

Krieger, Richard E MD (Inf) - **Spec Exp:** Lyme Disease; Endocarditis; **Hospital:** Chilton Med Ctr (page 92), St. Joseph's Wayne Hosp; **Address:** 765 Route 10 E, Randolph, NJ 07869; **Phone:** 973-989-0068; **Board Cert:** Internal Medicine 1981; Infectious Disease 1984; **Med School:** UMDNJ-NJ Med Sch, Newark 1978; **Resid:** Internal Medicine, Med Coll Penn Hosp 1981; **Fellow:** Infectious Disease, Med Coll Penn Hosp 1983

McManus, Edward J MD (Inf) - **Spec Exp:** Antibiotic Resistance; Wound Healing/Care; **Hospital:** St. Clare's Hosp-Denville, Morristown Med Ctr (page 92); **Address:** 765 Route 10 E, Ste 201, Randolph, NJ 07869; **Phone:** 973-989-0068; **Board Cert:** Internal Medicine 1985; Infectious Disease 1988; Undersea & Hyperbaric Medicine 2011; **Med School:** UMDNJ-NJ Med Sch, Newark 1982; **Resid:** Internal Medicine, Univ Wisconsin Hosp 1986; **Fellow:** Infectious Disease, Nat Inst Health 1989

Internal Medicine

Collum, Robert G MD (IM) *PCP* - **Hospital:** St. Clare's Hosp-Denville; **Address:** Denville Assocs of Internal Med, 16 Pocono Rd, Ste 317, Denville, NJ 07834; **Phone:** 973-627-2650; **Board Cert:** Internal Medicine 2005; **Med School:** Columbia P&S 1992; **Resid:** Internal Medicine, NY-Presby/Cornell Med Ctr 1995

Randazzo, Jean P MD (IM) *PCP* - **Spec Exp:** Women's Health; Arthritis; Hypertension; **Hospital:** Morristown Med Ctr (page 92); **Address:** Internal Med Morristown, 95 Madison Ave, Ste A-00, Morristown, NJ 07960; **Phone:** 973-538-1388; **Board Cert:** Internal Medicine 2013; **Med School:** Tufts Univ 1990; **Resid:** Internal Medicine, Morristown Meml Hosp 1994; **Fac Appt:** Asst Clin Prof Med, UMDNJ-NJ Med Sch, Newark

Raska, Anna Maria MD (IM) *PCP* - **Spec Exp:** Preventive Medicine; **Hospital:** Morristown Med Ctr (page 92); **Address:** Internal Med Fac Assocs, 435 South St, Ste 350, Morristown, NJ 07960; **Phone:** 973-971-7165; **Board Cert:** Internal Medicine 2005; **Med School:** Johns Hopkins Univ 1992; **Resid:** Internal Medicine, Johns Hopkins Hosp 1995

Scaduto, Philip MD (IM) *PCP* - **Spec Exp:** Hypertension; Diabetes; Geriatric Medicine; Preventive Medicine; **Hospital:** St. Clare's Hosp-Denville; **Address:** 223 W Main St, Boonton, NJ 07005-1166; **Phone:** 973-335-8656; **Board Cert:** Internal Medicine 1986; **Med School:** UMDNJ-NJ Med Sch, Newark 1983; **Resid:** Internal Medicine, UMDNJ-Univ Hosp 1986

Silva, Waldemar MD (IM) - **Hospital:** Chilton Med Ctr (page 92), St. Joseph's Regl Med Ctr - Paterson; **Address:** 488 Newark Pompton Tpke, Pompton Plains, NJ 07444; **Phone:** 973-835-9100; **Board Cert:** Internal Medicine 1987; **Med School:** Harvard Med Sch 1982; **Resid:** Internal Medicine, Bronx Muni Hosp 1985

Storch, Kenneth J MD/PhD (IM) - **Spec Exp:** Nutrition; Diabetes; Cholesterol/Lipid Disorders; **Hospital:** Morristown Med Ctr (page 92), Overlook Med Ctr (page 92); **Address:** Storch Med Nutrition Ctr, 147 Columbia Tpke, Ste 308, Florham Park, NJ 07932; **Phone:** 973-765-9355; **Board Cert:** Internal Medicine 1982; **Med School:** SUNY Downstate 1979; **Resid:** Internal Medicine, Staten Island Hosp 1982; **Fellow:** Nutrition & Metabolism, MIT Affil Hosp 1986; Nutrition & Metabolism, Beth Israel Deaconess Med Ctr 1988; **Fac Appt:** Asst Clin Prof Med, Mount Sinai Sch Med

Maternal & Fetal Medicine

Benito, Carlos W MD (MF) - **Spec Exp:** Pregnancy Loss; Prenatal Diagnosis; Premature Labor; **Hospital:** Morristown Med Ctr (page 92), Overlook Med Ctr (page 92); **Address:** 435 South St, Ste 308, Morristown, NJ 07960; **Phone:** 973-971-7080; **Board Cert:** Obstetrics & Gynecology 2013; Maternal & Fetal Medicine 2013; **Med School:** Rutgers R W Johnson Med Sch 1990; **Resid:** Obstetrics & Gynecology, UMDNJ-RWJ Med Ctr 1997; **Fellow:** Maternal & Fetal Medicine, UMDNJ-RWJ Med Ctr 1999

Lashley, Susan MD (MF) - **Hospital:** Morristown Med Ctr (page 92); **Address:** 435 South St, Ste 380, Morristown, NJ 07960; **Phone:** 973-971-7080; **Board Cert:** Obstetrics & Gynecology 2013; Maternal & Fetal Medicine 2016; **Med School:** SUNY Hlth Sci Ctr 1997; **Resid:** Obstetrics & Gynecology, UMDNJ-RWJ Univ Hosp 2004

Medical Oncology

Adler, Kenneth R MD (Onc) - **Spec Exp:** Breast Cancer; Myeloproliferative Disorders; Lymphoma; **Hospital:** Morristown Med Ctr (page 92); **Address:** Carol G Simon Cancer Ctr, 100 Madison Ave, Box 1089, Morristown, NJ 07962-1089; **Phone:** 973-538-5210; **Board Cert:** Internal Medicine 1976; Hematology 1978; **Med School:** Albany Med Coll 1973; **Resid:** Internal Medicine, Albany Med Ctr 1976; **Fellow:** Hematology & Oncology, Albany Med Ctr 1978; **Fac Appt:** Asst Clin Prof Med, UMDNJ-Rutgers Med Sch

Farber, Charles M MD/PhD (Onc) - **Spec Exp:** Leukemia & Lymphoma; Breast Cancer; Ovarian Cancer; Multiple Myeloma; **Hospital:** Morristown Med Ctr (page 92); **Address:** Carol G Simon Cancer Center, 100 Madison Ave Fl 2, Morristown, NJ 07962-1089; **Phone:** 973-538-5210; **Board Cert:** Medical Oncology 2000; **Med School:** NYU Sch Med 1986; **Resid:** Internal Medicine, NY Hosp 1988; **Fellow:** Hematology & Oncology, NY Hosp 1992; **Fac Appt:** Asst Clin Prof Med, UMDNJ-NJ Med Sch, Newark

Frank, Martin J MD (Onc) - **Hospital:** Chilton Med Ctr (page 92); **Address:** 97 West Pkwy, Pompton Plains, NJ 07444; **Phone:** 973-831-5451; **Board Cert:** Internal Medicine 1985; Medical Oncology 1989; **Med School:** Geo Wash Univ 1982; **Resid:** Internal Medicine, Montefiore Hosp 1986; **Fellow:** Medical Oncology, Montefiore Hosp 1987

Gurubhagavatula, Sarada MD (Onc) - **Spec Exp:** Lung Cancer; **Hospital:** Morristown Med Ctr (page 92), St. Clare's Hosp-Denville; **Address:** Hematology-Oncology Associates, 100 Madison Ave, Fl 2, Box 1089, Morristown, NJ 07962; **Phone:** 973-538-5210; **Board Cert:** Medical Oncology 2004; **Med School:** Johns Hopkins Univ 1998; **Resid:** Internal Medicine, Brigham & Women's Hosp 2001; **Fellow:** Hematology & Oncology, Dana Farber Cancer Inst 2004

Kane, Michael J MD (Onc) - **Spec Exp:** Breast Cancer; Colon Cancer; Lung Cancer; **Hospital:** Chilton Med Ctr (page 92), Newton Med Ctr (page 92); **Address:** Atlantic Med Oncology, 97 West Pkwy Fl 1, Pompton Plains, NJ 07444; **Phone:** 973-831-5055; **Board Cert:** Internal Medicine 1986; Medical Oncology 1989; **Med School:** UMDNJ-NJ Med Sch, Newark 1983; **Resid:** Internal Medicine, Thomas Jefferson Univ Hosp 1986; **Fellow:** Medical Oncology, Mount Sinai Hosp 1988; **Fac Appt:** Assoc Clin Prof Onc, Rutgers R W Johnson Med Sch

Papish, Steven W MD (Onc) - **Spec Exp:** Breast Cancer; Lymphoma; Gynecologic Cancer; **Hospital:** Morristown Med Ctr (page 92), **Address:** Carol G Simon Cancer Ctr, 100 Madison Ave Fl 2, Morristown, NJ 07962-1089; **Phone:** 973-538-5210; **Board Cert:** Internal Medicine 1977; Hematology 1980; Medical Oncology 1981; **Med School:** Univ Pennsylvania 1974; **Resid:** Internal Medicine, Geo Wash Univ Med Ctr 1978; **Fellow:** Hematology, New England Med Ctr 1979; Medical Oncology, Dana Farber Canc Inst 1981

Neonatal-Perinatal Medicine

Skolnick, Lawrence M MD (NP) - **Spec Exp:** Neonatal Care; Prematurity/Low Birth Weight Infants; **Hospital:** Morristown Med Ctr (page 92), Overlook Med Ctr (page 92); **Address:** 100 Madison Ave, Morristown, NJ 07960-6136; **Phone:** 973-971-5488; **Board Cert:** Pediatrics 1977; Neonatal-Perinatal Medicine 1977; **Med School:** NYU Sch Med 1972; **Resid:** Pediatrics, Albert Einstein 1975; **Fellow:** Neonatal-Perinatal Medicine, Duke Univ Med Ctr 1977

Nephrology

Byrd, Lawrence H MD (Nep) - **Spec Exp:** Hypertension; Pheochromocytoma; Kidney Tumors; Dialysis Care; **Hospital:** St. Barnabas Med Ctr (page 94), Bayonne Med Ctr; **Address:** 83 Hanover Rd, Ste 290, MS 07932, Florham Park, NJ 07932-5605; **Phone:** 973-736-2212; **Board Cert:** Internal Medicine 1977; Nephrology 1978; **Med School:** Med Coll PA 1973; **Resid:** Internal Medicine, Univ Hosp 1976; **Fellow:** Nephrology, New York Hosp-Cornell 1978; **Fac Appt:** Asst Clin Prof Med, UMDNJ-NJ Med Sch, Newark

Fine, Paul L MD (Nep) - **Spec Exp:** Hypertension; Kidney Failure; Dialysis Care; **Hospital:** Morristown Med Ctr (page 92), St. Clare's Hosp-Denville; **Address:** 2 Franklin Pl, Morristown, NJ 07960-5305; **Phone:** 973-267-7673; **Board Cert:** Internal Medicine 1982; Nephrology 1984; **Med School:** Yale Univ 1979; **Resid:** Internal Medicine, New York Hosp 1982; **Fellow:** Nephrology, Kidney Ctr-Cornell Univ Med Ctr 1984; **Fac Appt:** Asst Clin Prof Med, Mount Sinai Sch Med

Lyman, Neil W MD (Nep) - **Spec Exp:** Dialysis Care; Kidney Failure; **Hospital:** St. Barnabas Med Ctr (page 94), Clara Maass Med Ctr (page 94); **Address:** 83 Hanover Rd, Ste 290, MS 07932, Florham Park, NJ 07932; **Phone:** 973-736-2212; **Board Cert:** Internal Medicine 1976; Nephrology 1980; **Med School:** Albert Einstein Coll Med 1973; **Resid:** Internal Medicine, Mt Sinai Hosp 1976; Nephrology, Mt Sinai Hosp 1979; **Fellow:** Nephrology, Boston Med Ctr 1977; **Fac Appt:** Asst Prof Med, UMDNJ-NJ Med Sch, Newark

Najarian, James S MD (Nep) - **Spec Exp:** Hypertension; Kidney Failure; Transplant Medicine-Kidney; Dialysis Care; **Hospital:** Morristown Med Ctr (page 92), St. Clare's Hosp-Denville; **Address:** 121 Center Grove Rd, Ste 1314, Randolph, NJ 07869; **Phone:** 973-361-3737; **Board Cert:** Internal Medicine 1975; Nephrology 2006; **Med School:** Univ Wisc 1972; **Resid:** Internal Medicine, Beth Israel Hosp 1975; **Fellow:** Nephrology, Montefiore Med Ctr 1978

Zenenberg, Robert D DO (Nep) - **Spec Exp:** Kidney Disease; **Hospital:** St. Barnabas Med Ctr (page 94), Morristown Med Ctr (page 92); **Address:** Nephrology Assocs, 83 Hanover Rd, Ste 290, Florham Park, NJ 07932; **Phone:** 973-736-2212; **Board Cert:** Internal Medicine 2009; Nephrology 2011; **Med School:** Philadelphia Coll Osteo Med 1995; **Resid:** Internal Medicine, U Conn Hlth System 1999; **Fellow:** Nephrology, NYU Med Ctr 2000

Neurological Surgery

Benitez, Ronald P MD (NS) - **Spec Exp:** Endovascular Surgery; Cerebrovascular Neuro-surgery; Stroke; Aneurysm-Cerebral; **Hospital:** Overlook Med Ctr (page 92); **Address:** Atlantic Neu-rosurgery Specialists, 310 Madison Ave Fl 3 - Ste 300, Morristown, NJ 07960; **Phone:** 973-285-7800; **Board Cert:** Neurological Surgery 2006; **Med School:** Georgetown Univ 1994; **Resid:** Neurological Surgery, Thos Jefferson Univ Hosp 2000; **Fellow:** Cerebrovascular Neuro-surgery, Thos Jefferson Univ Hosp 2001

Beyerl, Brian D MD (NS) - **Spec Exp:** Brain Tumors; Stereotactic Radiosurgery; Arteriovenous Malformations; **Hospital:** Morristown Med Ctr (page 92), Overlook Med Ctr (page 92); **Address:** Atlantic Neurosurgical Specialists, 310 Madison Ave, Ste 300, Morristown, NJ 07960; **Phone:** 973-285-7800; **Board Cert:** Neurological Surgery 1990; **Med School:** Johns Hopkins Univ 1980; **Resid:** Surgery, Johns Hopkins Univ Hosp 1981; Neurological Surgery, Mass Genl Hosp 1986

Knightly, John J MD (NS) - **Spec Exp:** Spinal Surgery-Complex; Stereotactic Radiosurgery; Minimally Invasive Spinal Surgery; Trauma; **Hospital:** Overlook Med Ctr (page 92), Morristown Med Ctr (page 92); **Address:** Atlantic Neurosurgical Specialists, 310 Madison Ave, Ste 300, Morristown, NJ 07960; **Phone:** 973-285-7800; **Board Cert:** Neurological Surgery 1998; **Med School:** UMDNJ-NJ Med Sch, Newark 1985; **Resid:** Neurological Surgery, Bethesda Naval Hosp 1992; **Fellow:** Complex Spinal Surgery, Barrow Neurol Inst 1993

Mazzola, Catherine A MD (NS) - **Spec Exp:** Brain Injury-Traumatic; Congenital Nervous System Malformations; Pediatric Neurosurgery; Brain Tumors; **Hospital:** Morristown Med Ctr (page 92), Hackensack Univ Med Ctr (page 96); **Address:** NJ Pediatric Neuroscience Inst, 131 Madison Ave Fl 3, Morristown, NJ 07960; **Phone:** 973-326-9000; **Board Cert:** Neurological Surgery 2006; **Med School:** Rutgers-NJ Med Sch 1995; **Resid:** Surgery, Univ Hosp 1996; Neurological Surgery, Univ Hosp 2001; **Fellow:** Pediatric Neurological Surgery, Chldns Hosp 2002

Neurology

Fellus, Jonathan L MD (N) - **Spec Exp:** Brain Injury; Neuro-Rehabilitation; **Address:** Advanced Neurocare, 227 Route 206 N, Bldg 2, Ste 101, Flanders, NJ 07836; **Phone:** 732-494-7600; **Board Cert:** Neurology 2009; **Med School:** Rutgers R W Johnson Med Sch 1992; **Resid:** Neurology, Penn Hosp 1996; **Fellow:** Neurological Rehabilitation, Kernan Hosp/Univ MD Med Ctr 1997; **Fac Appt:** Asst Clin Prof N, UMDNJ-NJ Med Sch, Newark

Fox, Stuart W MD (N) - **Spec Exp:** Neuromuscular Disorders; Headache; **Hospital:** Morristown Med Ctr (page 92); **Address:** The Neuroscience Center of Northern NJ, 310 Madison Ave, Ste 120, Morristown, NJ 07960-6092; **Phone:** 973-285-1446; **Board Cert:** Internal Medicine 1978; Neurology 1982; **Med School:** Cornell Univ-Weill Med Coll 1975; **Resid:** Internal Medicine, Univ Mich Med Ctr 1978; Neurology, Albert Einstein 1981; **Fellow:** Clinical Neurophysiology, LI Jewish-Hillside Hosp 1982

Obstetrics & Gynecology

Banks, Judy L MD (ObG) - **Spec Exp:** Colposcopy; Cervical Cancer; Endometriosis; Ovarian Cancer; **Hospital:** Morristown Med Ctr (page 92); **Address:** 256 Columbia Tpke, Ste 212 North, Florham Park, NJ 07932; **Phone:** 973-377-3374; **Board Cert:** Obstetrics & Gynecology 2003; **Med School:** Meharry Med Coll 1975; **Resid:** Obstetrics & Gynecology, Univ Hosp-UMDNJ 1980

Culligan, Patrick J MD (ObG) - **Spec Exp:** Uro-Gynecology; **Hospital:** Overlook Med Ctr (page 92), Morristown Med Ctr (page 92); **Address:** 435 South St, Ste 370, Morristown, NJ 07960; **Phone:** 973-971-7267; **Board Cert:** Obstetrics & Gynecology 2013; **Med School:** Mercer Univ Sch Med 1993; **Resid:** Obstetrics & Gynecology, Greenville Hlth Sys 1997; **Fellow:** Uro-Gynecology, Evanston Hosp 1999

Dreyfuss, Patricia O MD (ObG) - **Hospital:** St. Clare's Hosp-Denville; **Address:** 115 Route 46 West, D Bldg - Ste 27, Mountain Lakes, NJ 07046; **Phone:** 973-334-3345; **Board Cert:** Obstetrics & Gynecology 1985; **Med School:** UMDNJ-Rutgers Med Sch 1979; **Resid:** Obstetrics & Gynecology, Saint Barnabas Med Ctr 1983

Gluck, Ian J MD (ObG) *PCP* - **Spec Exp:** Laparoscopic Surgery; Laparoscopic Hysterectomy; **Hospital:** Morristown Med Ctr (page 92); **Address:** Lifeline Med Assocs, 59 Franklin St, Morristown, NJ 07960; **Phone:** 973-538-1515; **Board Cert:** Obstetrics & Gynecology 1985; **Med School:** NY Med Coll 1979; **Resid:** Obstetrics & Gynecology, Emory Univ Hosp 1984

Mohr, Robert F MD (ObG) *PCP* - **Spec Exp:** Gynecologic Surgery; Laparoscopic Surgery; Menopause Problems; **Hospital:** Morristown Med Ctr (page 92), St. Clare's Hosp-Denville; **Address:** Lifeline Med Assocs, 390 Route 10, Ste 1, Randolph, NJ 07869; **Phone:** 973-328-1262; **Board Cert:** Obstetrics & Gynecology 2003; **Med School:** Hahnemann Univ 1977; **Resid:** Obstetrics & Gynecology, Northwestern Meml Hosp 1982

Steer, Robert L MD (ObG) - **Spec Exp:** Pregnancy-High Risk; Multiple Gestation; Laparoscopic Surgery; HPV-Human Papilloma Virus; **Hospital:** Morristown Med Ctr (page 92), Overlook Med Ctr (page 92); **Address:** 60 Franklin St, Morristown, NJ 07960-5217; **Phone:** 973-993-1919; **Board Cert:** Obstetrics & Gynecology 2014; **Med School:** Cornell Univ-Weill Med Coll 1986; **Resid:** Obstetrics & Gynecology, NY-Presby/Weill Cornell Med Ctr 1991; **Fac Appt:** Asst Clin Prof ObG, Mount Sinai Sch Med

Wallis, Joseph J DO (ObG) - **Spec Exp:** Laparoscopic Surgery; Endoscopy; Infertility; **Hospital:** St. Clare's Hosp-Denville, St. Clare's Hosp-Dover; **Address:** 16 Pocono Rd, Ste 309, Denville, NJ 07834; **Phone:** 973-989-9000; **Board Cert:** Obstetrics & Gynecology 1977; **Med School:** Philadelphia Coll Osteo Med 1970; **Resid:** Internal Medicine, St Michaels Med Ctr 1972; Obstetrics & Gynecology, St Michaels Med Ctr 1975

Ophthalmology

Chen, Lucy L MD (Oph) - **Spec Exp:** Pediatric Ophthalmology; Strabismus; **Hospital:** St. Clare's Hosp-Sussex, Morristown Med Ctr (page 92); **Address:** Advocare Ped Eye Phys, 95 Madison Ave, Ste 301, Morristown, NJ 07960-6092; **Phone:** 973-540-8814; **Board Cert:** Internal Medicine 1988; Ophthalmology 2004; **Med School:** Boston Univ 1985; **Resid:** Internal Medicine, NY-Presby/Columbia Univ Med Ctr 1988; Ophthalmology, Edward Harkness Eye Inst 1992; **Fellow:** Pediatric Ophthalmology, Wills Eye Hosp 1993

Kazam, Ezra S MD (Oph) - **Spec Exp:** Glaucoma; Cataract Surgery; Refractive Surgery; LASIK-Refractive Surgery; **Hospital:** Morristown Med Ctr (page 92); **Address:** 2 Washington Pl, Morristown, NJ 07960-4220; **Phone:** 973-267-8755; **Board Cert:** Ophthalmology 1978; **Med School:** SUNY Downstate 1973; **Resid:** Internal Medicine, Jacobi Med Ctr 1974; Ophthalmology, Montefiore Med Ctr 1977

Morgan, Charles F MD (Oph) - **Spec Exp:** Pediatric Ophthalmology; Strabismus; **Hospital:** Goryeb Children's Hosp (page 92); **Address:** Advocare Pediatric Eye Physicians, 95 Madison Ave, Ste 301, Morristown, NJ 07960-6389; **Phone:** 973-540-8814; **Board Cert:** Ophthalmology 2010; **Med School:** Vanderbilt Univ 1992; **Resid:** Internal Medicine, Evanston Hosp 1993; Ophthalmology, Anheuser-Busch Eye Inst 1996; **Fellow:** Pediatric Ophthalmology, Manhattan Eye & Ear Hosp 1999

Pinke, Robert S MD (Oph) - **Spec Exp:** Cataract Surgery; Glaucoma; **Hospital:** St. Clare's Hosp-Dover, St. Clare's Hosp-Denville; **Address:** 66 Sunset Strip, Ste 107, Succasunna, NJ 07876; **Phone:** 973-584-4451; **Board Cert:** Ophthalmology 1989; **Med School:** Mount Sinai Sch Med 1984; **Resid:** Internal Medicine, St Luke-Roosevelt Hsop 1985; Ophthalmology, Cullen Eye Inst 1988

Sachs, Ronald MD (Oph) - **Spec Exp:** Macular Degeneration; Diabetic Eye Disease/Retinopathy; Retinal Disorders; Retina/Vitreous Surgery; **Hospital:** Morristown Med Ctr (page 92), St. Clare's Hosp-Denville; **Address:** 8 Saddle Rd, Ste 201, Cedar Knolls, NJ 07927; **Phone:** 973-539-3600; **Board Cert:** Ophthalmology 2014; **Med School:** NYU Sch Med 1988; **Resid:** Ophthalmology, Montefiore Med Ctr 1992; **Fellow:** Retina, Albert Einstein Med Ctr 1993

Orthopaedic Surgery

Dowling, William J MD (OrS) - **Spec Exp:** Joint Replacement; Arthritis-Hip & Knee; Hip & Knee Replacement; Hip Resurfacing; **Hospital:** Morristown Med Ctr (page 92), Overlook Med Ctr (page 92); **Address:** 111 Madison Ave, Ste 400, Morristown, NJ 07960; **Phone:** 973-971-6895; **Board Cert:** Orthopaedic Surgery 1978; **Med School:** UMDNJ-NJ Med Sch, Newark 1971; **Resid:** Orthopaedic Surgery, UMDNJ-NJ Med Sch Affil Hosp 1976

Montgomery, Kenneth D MD (OrS) - **Spec Exp:** Hand Surgery; Shoulder Surgery; Knee Surgery; Rotator Cuff Surgery; **Hospital:** Morristown Med Ctr (page 92); **Address:** TriCounty Orthopaedics, Advanced Med Ctr, 197 Ridgedale Ave, Ste 300, Cedar Knolls, NJ 07927; **Phone:** 973-538-2334; **Board Cert:** Orthopaedic Surgery 2010; Orthopaedic Sports Medicine 2007; **Med School:** UCSF 1990; **Resid:** Orthopaedic Surgery, Hosp Special Surgery 1995; **Fellow:** Sports Medicine, Lenox Hill Hosp 1996; Obstetrics & Anesthesiology, Brigham & Women's Hosp 1997

Rieger, Kenneth J MD (OrS) - **Spec Exp:** Fractures-Pediatric; Scoliosis; Spinal Surgery; **Hospital:** Overlook Med Ctr (page 92), Morristown Med Ctr (page 92); **Address:** New Jersey Spine Center, 40 Main St, Chatham, NJ 07928; **Phone:** 973-635-0800; **Board Cert:** Orthopaedic Surgery 2009; **Med School:** Columbia P&S 2001; **Resid:** Orthopaedic Surgery, NY Presby Hosp 2006; **Fellow:** Spine Surgery, Leatherman Spine Inst 2007

Rieger, Mark A MD (OrS) - **Spec Exp:** Pediatric Orthopaedic Surgery; Scoliosis; Hip Disorders-Pediatric; Adolescent Sports Medicine; **Hospital:** Morristown Med Ctr (page 92), St. Barnabas Med Ctr (page 94); **Address:** Advocare Orthopedic Ctr, 218 Ridgedale Ave, Ste 104, Cedar Knolls, NJ 07927-2109; **Phone:** 973-538-7700; **Board Cert:** Orthopaedic Surgery 2012; **Med School:** Univ Conn 1983; **Resid:** Orthopaedic Surgery, NS-LIJ Hlth Sys 1988; **Fellow:** Pediatric Orthopaedic Surgery, Nemours/Alfred I. duPont Hosp for Chldn 1989; **Fac Appt:** Asst Clin Prof OrS, NYU Sch Med

Spielman, Joel H MD (OrS) - **Spec Exp:** Spinal Surgery; **Hospital:** St. Clare's Hosp-Dover, St. Clare's Hosp-Denville; **Address:** Ortho Assocs of West Jersey, 600 Mt Pleasant Ave, Dover, NJ 07801-1630; **Phone:** 973-989-0888; **Board Cert:** Orthopaedic Surgery 2005; **Med School:** Albert Einstein Coll Med 1986; **Resid:** Orthopaedic Surgery, Montefiore Med Ctr 1991; **Fellow:** Spine Surgery, Hosp for Special Surg 1993

Taffet, Berton MD (OrS) - **Spec Exp:** Arthritis; Hip & Knee Replacement; Hip Resurfacing; Joint Replacement; **Hospital:** Morristown Med Ctr (page 92); **Address:** 111 Madison Ave Fl 4 - Ste 400, Morristown, NJ 07960; **Phone:** 973-984-0404; **Board Cert:** Orthopaedic Surgery 2011; **Med School:** Albert Einstein Coll Med 1978; **Resid:** Orthopaedic Surgery, Mt Sinai Med Ctr 1983; **Fellow:** Joint Replacement Surgery, Univ Colorado Hosp 1984

Willis, Andrew A MD (OrS) - **Spec Exp:** Hand & Upper Extremity Surgery; Shoulder & Knee Surgery; Sports Injuries; Fractures; **Hospital:** Morristown Med Ctr (page 92); **Address:** Tri County Orthopaedics, 197 Rodgedale Ave, Cedar Knolls, NJ 07927; **Phone:** 973-538-2334; **Board Cert:** Orthopaedic Surgery 2007; Orthopaedic Sports Medicine 2008; Hand Surgery 2008; **Med School:** Columbia P&S 1997; **Resid:** Orthopaedic Surgery, Hosp for Special Surg 2002; **Fellow:** Hand Surgery, Mayo Grad School Med 2003; Sports Medicine, Hosp for Special Surg 2004

Otolaryngology

Fleming, Gregory J MD (Oto) - **Spec Exp:** Endoscopic Sinus Surgery; Sleep Disorders/Apnea; **Hospital:** Morristown Med Ctr (page 92), Overlook Med Ctr (page 92); **Address:** Morristown Otolaryngology Grp, 26 Madison Ave, Morristown, NJ 07960; **Phone:** 973-267-1850; **Board Cert:** Otolaryngology 1988; **Med School:** Univ Mass Sch Med 1982; **Resid:** Surgery, UMass Memorial Med Ctr 1984; Otolaryngology, Mass Eye & Ear Infirm 1988

Kanowitz, Seth J MD (Oto) - **Spec Exp:** Otology; Rhinitis; Meniere's Disease; **Hospital:** Morristown Med Ctr (page 92); **Address:** Advocare ENT of Morristown, 95 Madison Ave, Ste 105, Morristown, NJ 07960; **Phone:** 973-644-0808; **Board Cert:** Otolaryngology 2007; **Med School:** Univ S Fla Coll Med 2001; **Resid:** Otolaryngology, NYU Med Ctr 2006; **Fellow:** Otology, Cleveland Clinic 2007

Lachman, Reid A MD (Oto) - **Hospital:** Morristown Med Ctr (page 92); **Address:** Advocare ENT Specialists Morristown, 95 Madison Ave, Ste 105, Morristown, NJ 07960-7331; **Phone:** 973-644-0808; **Board Cert:** Otolaryngology 1986; **Med School:** NY Med Coll 1981; **Resid:** Surgery, Beth Israel Med Ctr 1982; Otolaryngology, Jacobi Med Ctr 1986

Taylor, Howard MD (Oto) - **Spec Exp:** Hearing Loss; Sinus Surgery; Throat Disorders; Voice Disorders; **Hospital:** Chilton Med Ctr (page 92); **Address:** 51 State Rte 23 S, Riverdale, NJ 07457-1625; **Phone:** 973-831-1220; **Board Cert:** Otolaryngology 1980; **Med School:** Columbia P&S 1976; **Resid:** Otolaryngology, Univ Chicago Affil Hosps 1980; **Fellow:** Facial Plastic Surgery, Med Coll PA Affil Hosps 1981

Pain Medicine

Rudman, Michael E MD (PM) - **Spec Exp:** Pain-Back; Pain-Chronic; Complex Regional Pain Syndromes; **Hospital:** Morristown Med Ctr (page 92); **Address:** NJ Pain Cons, 310 Madison Ave Fl 3 - Ste 301, Morristown, NJ 07960; **Phone:** 908-630-0175; **Board Cert:** Pain Medicine 2007; Anesthesiology 1993; **Med School:** Penn State Coll Med 1988; **Resid:** Anesthesiology, Hosp Univ Penn - UPHS 1992

Pediatric Allergy & Immunology

Barisciano, Lisa MD (PA&I) - **Spec Exp:** Asthma; Food Allergy; Allergy; Eczema; **Hospital:** Morristown Med Ctr (page 92); **Address:** 15 James St, Ste 4, Florham Park, NJ 07932; **Phone:** 973-503-0600; **Board Cert:** Pediatrics 2008; Allergy & Immunology 2013; **Med School:** UMDNJ-Rutgers Med Sch 1998; **Resid:** Pediatrics, NY-Presby/Weill Cornell Med Ctr 2001; **Fellow:** Allergy & Immunology, NY-Presby/Weill Cornell Med Ctr 2003

Pediatric Cardiology

Donnelly, Christine M MD (PCd) - **Spec Exp:** Fetal Echocardiography; Congenital Heart Disease; Cardiac Catheterization; Interventional Cardiology; **Hospital:** Morristown Med Ctr (page 92), Morgan Stanley Chldns Hosp of NY-Presby, NY (page 102); **Address:** Goryeb Chldns Hosp-Ped Cardiology, 100 Madison Ave, Morristown, NJ 07962; **Phone:** 973-971-5996; **Board Cert:** Pediatrics 1985; Pediatric Cardiology 1985; **Med School:** Columbia P&S 1978; **Resid:** Pediatrics, NY-Presby/Columbia Univ Med Ctr 1981; **Fellow:** Pediatric Cardiology, NY-Presby/Columbia Univ Med Ctr 1984; **Fac Appt:** Assoc Clin Prof Ped, Columbia P&S

Mone, Suzanne M MD (PCd) - **Spec Exp:** Arrhythmias; Heart Failure; Rheumatic Heart Disease; **Hospital:** Overlook Med Ctr (page 92), Morristown Med Ctr (page 92); **Address:** Overlook Med Ctr, Div Ped Cardiology, 100 Madison Ave, Morristown, NJ 07962; **Phone:** 973-971-5996; **Board Cert:** Pediatrics 2013; Pediatric Cardiology 2014; **Med School:** Grenada 1999; **Resid:** Pediatrics, Strong Meml Hosp 2003; **Fellow:** Pediatric Cardiology, Chldns Hosp Med Ctr 2005; Pediatric Cardiology, Stanford Hosp & Clin 2006; **Fac Appt:** Asst Clin Prof Ped, Mount Sinai Sch Med

Pediatric Endocrinology

Cerame, Barbara I MD (PEn) - **Spec Exp:** Diabetes; Thyroid Disorders; **Hospital:** Goryeb Children's Hosp (page 92), Overlook Med Ctr (page 92); **Address:** Goryeb Chldn's Hosp at Morristown, 100 Madison Ave, Box 53, Morristown, NJ 07960; **Phone:** 973-971-4340; **Board Cert:** Pediatrics 2011; Pediatric Endocrinology 2011; **Med School:** Philippines 1985; **Resid:** Pediatrics, Robert Wood Johnson Univ Hosp 1995; **Fellow:** Pediatric Endocrinology, NY Presby Hosp/Cornell 1998; **Fac Appt:** Asst Prof Ped, UMDNJ-Rutgers Med Sch

Chin, Daisy Y MD (PEn) - **Spec Exp:** Thyroid Disorders; Growth Disorders; Pubertal Disorders; Diabetes; **Hospital:** Goryeb Children's Hosp (page 92), Overlook Med Ctr (page 92); **Address:** Gorebny Chldn's Hosp at Morristown, 100 Madison Ave, Box 53, Morristown, NJ 07960; **Phone:** 973-971-4340; **Board Cert:** Pediatric Endocrinology 2014; **Med School:** SUNY Downstate 1992; **Resid:** Pediatrics, Columbia Presby Med Ctr 1995; **Fellow:** Pediatric Endocrinology, NYU Med Ctr 1998

Silverman, Lawrence A MD (PEn) - **Spec Exp:** Metabolic Syndrome; Adrenal Disorders; **Hospital:** Morristown Med Ctr (page 92), Overlook Med Ctr (page 92); **Address:** Morristown Meml Hosp, Dept of Ped Endocrinology, 100 Madison Ave, Morristown, NJ 07962; **Phone:** 973-971-4340; **Board Cert:** Pediatric Endocrinology 2010; **Med School:** UMDNJ-Rutgers Med Sch 1987; **Resid:** Pediatrics, LI Jewish Med Ctr 1990; **Fellow:** Pediatric Endocrinology, UCSF Med Ctr 1993; **Fac Appt:** Asst Prof Ped, UMDNJ-NJ Med Sch, Newark

Starkman, Harold S MD (PEn) - **Spec Exp:** Diabetes; Growth Disorders; **Hospital:** Goryeb Children's Hosp (page 92), Morristown Med Ctr (page 92); **Address:** Morristown Meml Hosp-Atlantic Hlth, 100 Madison Ave, Morristown, NJ 07962-6136; **Phone:** 973-971-4340; **Board Cert:** Pediatrics 1980; Pediatric Endocrinology 1983; **Med School:** Albert Einstein Coll Med 1976; **Resid:** Pediatrics, Mt Sinai Med Ctr 1978; Pediatrics, NY-Presby/Weill Cornell Med Ctr 1979; **Fellow:** Pediatric Endocrinology, NY-Presby/Weill Cornell Med Ctr 1980; Pediatric Endocrinology, Joslin Diabetes Ctr 1983; **Fac Appt:** Assoc Prof Ped, Mount Sinai Sch Med

Pediatric Gastroenterology

Rosh, Joel MD (PGe) - **Spec Exp:** Inflammatory Bowel Disease/Crohn's; Celiac Disease; Liver Disease; Constipation; **Hospital:** Morristown Med Ctr (page 92), Overlook Med Ctr (page 92); **Address:** Dept Peds Gastroenterology & Nutrition, 100 Madison Ave, Morristown, NJ 07960-6136; **Phone:** 973-971-5676; **Board Cert:** Pediatric Gastroenterology 2014; **Med School:** Albert Einstein Coll Med 1986; **Resid:** Pediatrics, Babies Hosp/Columbia-Presby Med Ctr 1989; **Fellow:** Pediatric Gastroenterology, Mount Sinai Med Ctr 1991; **Fac Appt:** Assoc Prof Ped, UMDNJ-NJ Med Sch, Newark

Pediatric Infectious Disease

Baorto, Elizabeth P MD (PInf) - **Spec Exp:** Lyme Disease; **Hospital:** Morristown Med Ctr (page 92); **Address:** Morristown Medical Ctr, Div Pediatric Infectious Disease, 100 Madison Ave, Morristown, NJ 07960; **Phone:** 973-971-6329; **Board Cert:** Pediatrics 2011; Pediatric Infectious Disease 2014; **Med School:** SUNY Downstate 1993; **Resid:** Pediatrics, St Louis Children's Hosp 1996

Pediatric Nephrology

Corey, Howard E MD (PNep) - **Spec Exp:** Kidney Disease; Hypertension; Glomerulonephritis; **Hospital:** Goryeb Children's Hosp (page 92), Overlook Med Ctr (page 92); **Address:** Chldns Kidney Ctr, 100 Madison Ave, Morristown, NJ 07962; **Phone:** 973-971-5649; **Board Cert:** Pediatric Nephrology 2013; **Med School:** SUNY Downstate 1983; **Resid:** Pediatrics, Jacobi Med Ctr 1986; **Fellow:** Pediatric Nephrology, Jacobi Med Ctr 1989

Pediatric Pulmonology

Atlas, Arthur B MD (PPul) - **Spec Exp:** Asthma; Cystic Fibrosis; Lung Disease; Allergy; **Hospital:** Morristown Med Ctr (page 92), Overlook Med Ctr (page 92); **Address:** Morristown Meml Hosp, Resp Ctr for Chldn, 100 Madison Ave, Box 107, Morristown, NJ 07962; **Phone:** 973-971-4142; **Board Cert:** Pediatric Pulmonology 2014; **Med School:** Mexico 1982; **Resid:** Pediatrics, St Louis Chldns Hosp 1986; **Fellow:** Allergy & Immunology, St Louis Chldns Hosp 1989; Pediatric Pulmonology, Chldns Hosp/Univ Pittsburgh 1991; **Fac Appt:** Asst Prof Ped, UMDNJ-NJ Med Sch, Newark

Bieler, Harvey P MD (PPul) - **Spec Exp:** Asthma; Chronic Lung Disease; Cystic Fibrosis; **Hospital:** Goryeb Children's Hosp (page 92), Overlook Med Ctr (page 92); **Address:** Goryeb Chldns Hosp, 100 Madison Ave, Ste 107, Morristown, NJ 07962; **Phone:** 973-971-4142; **Board Cert:** Pediatric Pulmonology 2007; **Med School:** McGill Univ 1990; **Resid:** Pediatrics, St Christopher Hosp for Chldn 1993; **Fellow:** Pediatric Pulmonology, Clarian Indiana Univ Hosp 1996

Pediatric Urology

Connor, John P MD (Ped Uro) - **Spec Exp:** Fetal Urology; Genitourinary Reconstruction; **Hospital:** Goryeb Children's Hosp (page 92), Overlook Med Ctr (page 92); **Address:** Adult & Pediatric Urology Group, 261 James St, Ste 3A, Morristown, NJ 07960; **Phone:** 973-539-0333; **Board Cert:** Urology 2008; Pediatric Urology 2008; **Med School:** Ireland 1983; **Resid:** Surgery, UCLA Med Ctr 1986; Urology, Columbia-Presby Hosp 1990; **Fellow:** Urologic Oncology, Meml Sloan Kettering 1992; Pediatric Urology, Chldns Hosp Mich 1993

Pediatrics

Ashton, Julie A MD (Ped) *PCP* - **Hospital:** Goryeb Children's Hosp (page 92), Morristown Med Ctr (page 92); **Address:** Franklin Pediatrics, 91 S Jefferson Rd, Whippany, NJ 07981; **Phone:** 973-538-6116; **Board Cert:** Pediatrics 2012; **Med School:** UMDNJ-NJ Med Sch, Newark 1987; **Resid:** Pediatrics, UMDNJ Chldn's Hosp 1990

Gotfried, Fern MD (Ped) *PCP* - **Hospital:** Goryeb Children's Hosp (page 92), Morristown Med Ctr (page 92); **Address:** Franklin Pediatrics, 91 S Jefferson Rd, Ste 200, Whippany, NJ 07981; **Phone:** 973-538-6116; **Board Cert:** Pediatrics 1986; Adolescent Medicine 2008; **Med School:** UMDNJ-Rutgers Med Sch 1980; **Resid:** Pediatrics, Strong Meml Hosp 1983; **Fellow:** Adolescent Medicine, Strong Meml Hosp 1985

Handler, Robert W MD (Ped) *PCP* - **Spec Exp:** Asthma; Allergy; Behavioral Disorders; **Hospital:** Morristown Med Ctr (page 92), St. Clare's Hosp-Denville; **Address:** Advocare Parsippany Pediatrics, 1140 Parsippany Blvd, Ste 102, Parsippany, NJ 07054; **Phone:** 973-263-0066; **Board Cert:** Pediatrics 1980; **Med School:** UMDNJ-NJ Med Sch, Newark 1975; **Resid:** Pediatrics, Chldns Hosp 1978

Lavaia-Marzano, Maria MD (Ped) *PCP* - **Hospital:** Goryeb Children's Hosp (page 92), Overlook Med Ctr (page 92); **Address:** Madison Pediatrics, 435 South St, Ste 200, Morristown, NJ 07960; **Phone:** 973-822-0003; **Board Cert:** Pediatrics 2011; **Med School:** SUNY Downstate 1993; **Resid:** Pediatrics, NY Presby Hosp/Cornell 1996

Lodish, Stephanie R MD (Ped) *PCP* - **Hospital:** Goryeb Children's Hosp (page 92), Overlook Med Ctr (page 92); **Address:** Madison Pediatrics, 435 South St, Ste 200, Morristown, NJ 07960; **Phone:** 973-822-0003; **Board Cert:** Pediatrics 2014; **Med School:** Case West Res Univ 1996; **Resid:** Pediatrics, Chldn's Hosp 1999

Meltzer, Alan J MD (Ped) *PCP* - **Hospital:** Goryeb Children's Hosp (page 92), Overlook Med Ctr (page 92); **Address:** Madison Pediatrics, 435 South St, Ste 200, Morristown, NJ 07960; **Phone:** 973-822-0003; **Board Cert:** Pediatrics 2009; **Med School:** SUNY Downstate 1981; **Resid:** Pediatrics, N Shore Univ Hosp 1984

Scherer, Susan D MD (Ped) *PCP* - **Hospital:** Goryeb Children's Hosp (page 92), Overlook Med Ctr (page 92); **Address:** Madison Pediatrics, 435 South St, Ste 200, Morristown, NJ 07940; **Phone:** 973-822-0003; **Board Cert:** Pediatrics 2007; **Med School:** Univ Tex, San Antonio 1997; **Resid:** Pediatrics, Johns Hopkins Hosp 2000

Shaw-Brachfeld, Jennifer MD (Ped) *PCP* - **Spec Exp:** Developmental & Behavioral Disorders; **Hospital:** Goryeb Children's Hosp (page 92), St. Barnabas Med Ctr (page 94); **Address:** Touchpoint Pediatrics, 17 Watchung Ave, Chatham, NJ 07928; **Phone:** 973-665-0900; **Board Cert:** Pediatrics 2007; Developmental-Behavioral Pediatrics 2010; **Med School:** Univ Conn 1989; **Resid:** Pediatrics, Schneider Chldn's Hosp 1992; **Fellow:** Developmental-Behavioral Pediatrics, Schneider Chldn's Hosp 1994

Suda, Anjuli K MD (Ped) *PCP* - **Spec Exp:** Pulmonary Disease; **Hospital:** Chilton Med Ctr (page 92); **Address:** 170 Kinnelon Rd, Ste 28, Kinnelon, NJ 07405; **Phone:** 973-838-0001; **Board Cert:** Pediatrics 1988; **Med School:** India 1976; **Resid:** Pediatrics, St Joseph's Hosp & Med Ctr 1985

Physical Medicine & Rehabilitation

Klecz, Robert J MD (PMR) - **Spec Exp:** Musculoskeletal Disorders; Stroke Rehabilitation; Spasticity Management; Electromyography; **Hospital:** Morristown Med Ctr (page 92); **Address:** Rehab Inst at Morristown Hosp, 95 Mount Kemble Ave, Thebaud Bldg Fl 4, Morristown, NJ 07960; **Phone:** 973-796-3600; **Board Cert:** Physical Medicine & Rehabilitation 2006; **Med School:** Poland 1990; **Resid:** Internal Medicine, UMDNJ Univ Hosp 1992; Physical Medicine & Rehabilitation, UMDNJ-Kessler Inst 1995; **Fac Appt:** Assoc Clin Prof PMR, UMDNJ-Univ Med Dent NJ

Mulford, Gregory J MD (PMR) - **Spec Exp:** Sports Medicine; Electrodiagnosis; **Hospital:** Morristown Med Ctr (page 92), Overlook Med Ctr (page 92); **Address:** Assocs in Rehab Medicine, 95 Mt Kemble Ave, Thebaud Bldg - Fl 4, Morristown, NJ 7960; **Phone:** 973-796-3600; **Board Cert:** Physical Medicine & Rehabilitation 1990; Sports Medicine 2011; **Med School:** Rutgers R W Johnson Med Sch 1985; **Resid:** Physical Medicine & Rehabilitation, Columbia-Presby Hosp 1989; **Fac Appt:** Assoc Clin Prof PMR, UMDNJ-Univ Med Dent NJ

Valenza, Joseph P MD (PMR) - **Spec Exp:** Pain Management; Complex Regional Pain Syndromes; Repetitive Strain Injuries; Spinal Cord Injury; **Hospital:** Kessler Inst for Rehab - Chester; **Address:** Kessler Inst for Rehab, Dept Pain Management, 201 Pleasant Hill Rd, Chester, NJ 07930; **Phone:** 973-252-6402; **Board Cert:** Physical Medicine & Rehabilitation 2007; Pain Medicine 2012; **Med School:** SUNY Downstate 1992; **Resid:** Physical Medicine & Rehabilitation, Vet Affairs Med Ctr 1996; **Fac Appt:** Asst Clin Prof PMR, UMDNJ-NJ Med Sch, Newark

Plastic Surgery

Colon, Francisco G MD (PlS) - **Spec Exp:** Cosmetic Surgery-Face & Body; Reconstructive Plastic Surgery; Breast Reconstruction; **Hospital:** St. Barnabas Med Ctr (page 94), Morristown Med Ctr (page 92); **Address:** PeerGroup Plastic Surgery Ctr, 124 Columbia Tpke, Florham Park, NJ 07932; **Phone:** 973-822-3000; **Board Cert:** Plastic Surgery 2007; **Med School:** Columbia P&S 1987; **Resid:** Surgery, St Lukes Roosevelt Hosp 1992; Plastic Surgery, Beth Israel Deaconess Med Ctr 1994; **Fellow:** Microvascular Surgery, Bet Israel Deaconess Med Ctr 1995

Lange, David J MD (PlS) - **Spec Exp:** Cosmetic Surgery-Breast; Liposuction & Body Contouring; Craniofacial Surgery/Reconstruction; **Hospital:** St. Barnabas Med Ctr (page 94), Morristown Med Ctr (page 92); **Address:** Peer Group, 124 Columbia Tpke, Florham Park, NJ 07932; **Phone:** 973-822-3000; **Board Cert:** Plastic Surgery 1990; **Med School:** Mexico 1979; **Resid:** Surgery, St Banabas Med Ctr 1985; **Fellow:** Plastic Surgery, St Louis Univ Hosp 1987

Pyo, Daniel J MD (PlS) - **Spec Exp:** Facial Rejuvenation; Craniofacial Surgery; Craniofacial Surgery-Pediatric; Microsurgery; **Hospital:** Morristown Med Ctr (page 92), St. Barnabas Med Ctr (page 94); **Address:** Plastic Surgery Ctr of NJ, 131 Madison Ave, Ste 120, Morristown, NJ 07960; **Phone:** 973-540-9055; **Board Cert:** Surgery 2009; Plastic Surgery 2009; **Med School:** Mount Sinai Sch Med 1990; **Resid:** Surgery, Strong Meml Hosp 1995; **Fellow:** Plastic Surgery, Yale-New Haven Hosp 1997

Rafizadeh, Farhad MD (PlS) - **Spec Exp:** Breast Reconstruction; Facial Rejuvenation; Cosmetic Surgery-Face & Breast; **Hospital:** Morristown Med Ctr (page 92), St. Barnabas Med Ctr (page 94); **Address:** 101 Madison Ave, Ste 105, Morristown, NJ 07960; **Phone:** 973-267-0928; **Board Cert:** Plastic Surgery 1986; **Med School:** Switzerland 1975; **Resid:** Surgery, St Barnabas Med Ctr 1981; Surgery, Morristown Meml Hosp 1982; **Fellow:** Plastic Surgery, New York Hosp-Cornell Med Ctr 1984

Starker, Isaac MD (PlS) - **Spec Exp:** Cosmetic Surgery-Face & Body; Cosmetic Surgery-Breast; Breast Reconstruction; **Hospital:** Morristown Med Ctr (page 92), St. Barnabas Med Ctr (page 94); **Address:** The Peer Group, 124 Columbia Tpke, Florham Park, NJ 07932; **Phone:** 973-822-3000; **Board Cert:** Plastic Surgery 1992; **Med School:** NYU Sch Med 1981; **Resid:** Surgery, St Lukes-Roosevelt Hosp Ctr 1986; Plastic Surgery, Montefiore Med Ctr 1988; **Fellow:** Hand Surgery, St Lukes-Roosevelt Hosp Ctr 1989

Weinstein, Larry P MD (PlS) - **Spec Exp:** Breast Cosmetic & Reconstructive Surgery; Cosmetic Surgery-Face; Liposuction & Body Contouring; Facial Rejuvenation; **Hospital:** Morristown Med Ctr (page 92), Overlook Med Ctr (page 92); **Address:** 385 State Rte 24, Ste 3K, Chester, NJ 07930-2910; **Phone:** 908-879-2222; **Board Cert:** Plastic Surgery 1993; **Med School:** Mexico 1979; **Resid:** Surgery, Univ Hosp/Morristown Meml Hosp 1984; Surgical Oncology, Meml Sloan-Kettering Cancer Ctr 1985; **Fellow:** Research, Univ Pittsburgh 1986; Plastic Surgery, SUNY-Brooklyn Med Ctr 1988

Psychiatry

Fennelly, Bryan W MD (Psyc) - **Spec Exp:** Child Psychiatry; ADD/ADHD; Depression; Bipolar/Mood Disorders; **Hospital:** Morristown Med Ctr (page 92); **Address:** 8 Shunpike Rd, Ste 9, Madison, NJ 07940-2740; **Phone:** 973-660-0084; **Board Cert:** Psychiatry 2004; Child & Adolescent Psychiatry 2005; **Med School:** UMDNJ-Univ Med Dent NJ 1989; **Resid:** Psychiatry, NYU Med Ctr 1992; **Fellow:** Child & Adolescent Psychiatry, NYU 1994

Pulmonary Disease

Benton, Marc L MD (Pul) - **Spec Exp:** Asthma & Emphysema; Sleep Disorders/Apnea; Cough; **Hospital:** Morristown Med Ctr (page 92), St. Barnabas Hosp - Bronx; **Address:** Atlantic Sleep & Pulmonary Associates, 300 Madison Ave Fl 3, Madison, NJ 07940; **Phone:** 973-822-2772; **Board Cert:** Internal Medicine 1985; Pulmonary Disease 1988; Critical Care Medicine 2005; Sleep Medicine 2011; **Med School:** Mount Sinai Sch Med 1982; **Resid:** Internal Medicine, Mt Sinai Hosp 1985; **Fellow:** Pulmonary Disease, NYU Med Ctr 1988; **Fac Appt:** Asst Clin Prof Med, Mount Sinai Sch Med

Fiel, Stanley B MD (Pul) - **Spec Exp:** Cystic Fibrosis; Chronic Obstructive Lung Disease (COPD); Asthma; Bronchiectasis; **Hospital:** Morristown Med Ctr (page 92), Overlook Med Ctr (page 92); **Address:** 435 South St, Ste 350, Morristown, NJ 07962; **Phone:** 973-971-7165; **Board Cert:** Internal Medicine 1976; Pulmonary Disease 1978; **Med School:** Med Coll PA 1973; **Resid:** Internal Medicine, Temple Univ Hosp 1976; **Fellow:** Pulmonary Disease, Hosp Univ Penn 1978; **Fac Appt:** Prof Med, Mount Sinai Sch Med

O'Donnell, Timothy DO (Pul) - **Spec Exp:** Asthma & Allergy; Lung Cancer; Interstitial Lung Disease; Chronic Obstructive Lung Disease (COPD); **Hospital:** Chilton Med Ctr (page 92), Morristown Med Ctr (page 92); **Address:** 63 Beaver Brook Rd, Ste 301, Lincoln Park, NJ 07035; **Phone:** 973-694-1300; **Board Cert:** Internal Medicine 1989; Pulmonary Disease 2012; Critical Care Medicine 2013; **Med School:** UMDNJ Sch Osteo Med 1985; **Resid:** Internal Medicine, Univ Hosp-UMDNJ 1989; **Fellow:** Pulmonary Critical Care Medicine, UMDNJ-Newark Beth Israel Med Ctr 1992

Radiation Oncology

Wong, James R MD (RadRO) - **Spec Exp:** Prostate Cancer; Head & Neck Cancer; Breast Cancer; Pancreatic Cancer; **Hospital:** Morristown Med Ctr (page 92); **Address:** Morristown Medical Center, Radiation Oncology Dept, 100 Madison Ave, Box 9, Morristown, NJ 07960; **Phone:** 973-971-5329; **Board Cert:** Radiation Oncology 1993; **Med School:** Harvard Med Sch 1986; **Resid:** Radiation Oncology, Harvard Jt Ctr for Rad Therapy 1992; **Fellow:** Radiation Oncology, NY-Presby/Weill Cornell Med Ctr 1997; **Fac Appt:** Assoc Clin Prof RadRO, Columbia P&S

Reproductive Endocrinology

Bergh, Paul A MD (RE) - **Spec Exp:** Fertility Preservation; **Hospital:** Morristown Med Ctr (page 92); **Address:** Reproductive Med Assocs of NJ, 140 Allen Rd, Basking Ridge, NJ 7920; **Phone:** 908-604-7800; **Board Cert:** Obstetrics & Gynecology 2013; Reproductive Endocrinology 2013; **Med School:** Rutgers R W Johnson Med Sch 1983; **Resid:** Diagnostic Radiology, Med Ctr Hosp Vermont 1985; Obstetrics & Gynecology, St Barnabas Hosp 1989; **Fellow:** Reproductive Endocrinology, Mount Sinai Med Ctr 1991

Rheumatology

Pasik, Deborah MD (Rhu) - **Spec Exp:** Rheumatoid Arthritis; Osteoporosis; Lupus/SLE; Fibromyalgia; **Hospital:** Morristown Med Ctr (page 92); **Address:** 8 Saddle Road, Ste 202, Cedar Knolls, NJ 07927; **Phone:** 973-984-9796; **Board Cert:** Internal Medicine 1985; Rheumatology 1988; **Med School:** Mount Sinai Sch Med 1982; **Resid:** Internal Medicine, Beth Israel Hosp 1985; **Fellow:** Rheumatology, NYU Med Ctr 1988; **Fac Appt:** Asst Clin Prof Med, Mount Sinai-Icahn Sch of Med

Sports Medicine

Feldman, David J MD (SM) - **Hospital:** St. Clare's Hosp-Denville; **Address:** 16 Pocono Rd, Ste 100, Denville, NJ 07834; **Phone:** 973-625-5700; **Board Cert:** Orthopaedic Surgery 1979; Orthopaedic Sports Medicine 2007; **Med School:** Boston Univ 1972; **Resid:** Surgery, Mt Sinai Med Ctr 1974; Orthopaedic Surgery, Mt Sinai Med Ctr 1977; **Fellow:** Pediatric Orthopaedic Surgery, Stanford Univ Med Ctr 1978

Ginsberg, Claudia L MD (SM) - **Spec Exp:** Primary Care Sports Medicine; Running Injuries; Knee Injuries; **Hospital:** Morristown Med Ctr (page 92); **Address:** 197 Ridgedale Ave, Atlantic Sports Health, Cedar Knolls, NJ 07927; **Phone:** 973-538-2334; **Board Cert:** Internal Medicine 2012; Sports Medicine 2013; **Med School:** Cornell Univ-Weill Med Coll 1999; **Resid:** Internal Medicine, NY Presby-Cornell Med Ctr 2002; **Fellow:** Sports Medicine, Univ Pittsburgh Med Ctr 2003

Martins, Damion MD (SM) - **Spec Exp:** Primary Care Sports Medicine; **Hospital:** Morristown Med Ctr (page 92); **Address:** Atlantic Sports Health, 111 Madison Ave, Ste 400, Morristown, NJ 07960; **Phone:** 973-971-6898; **Board Cert:** Internal Medicine 2011; Sports Medicine 2004; **Med School:** Georgetown Univ 1998; **Resid:** Internal Medicine, George Univ Med Ctr 2001; **Fellow:** Sports Medicine, Univ of Maryland Affil Hosp 2002

Surgery

Carter, Mitchel S MD (S) - **Spec Exp:** Laparoscopic Surgery; Laparoscopic Cholecystectomy; Gastroesophageal Reflux Disease (GERD); Hernia; **Hospital:** Morristown Med Ctr (page 92); **Address:** Allied Surgical Grp, 261 James St, Ste 2G, Morristown, NJ 07960; **Phone:** 973-267-6400; **Board Cert:** Surgery 2003; **Med School:** Ros Franklin Univ/Chicago Med Sch 1979; **Resid:** Surgery, Montefiore Med Ctr 1984

Diehl, William L MD (S) - **Spec Exp:** Breast Cancer; Pancreatic Cancer; Gastrointestinal Cancer; Colon Cancer; **Hospital:** Morristown Med Ctr (page 92); **Address:** Allied Surgical Grp, 261 James St, Ste 2G, Morristown, NJ 07960; **Phone:** 973-267-6400; **Board Cert:** Surgery 2009; **Med School:** Mexico 1981; **Resid:** Surgery, Morristown Med Ctr 1986; **Fellow:** Surgical Oncology, Meml Sloan-Kettering Cancer Ctr 1988

Rolandelli, Rolando H MD (S) - **Spec Exp:** Crohn's Disease; Inflammatory Bowel Disease; Gastrointestinal Surgery; Colon & Rectal Surgery; **Hospital:** Morristown Med Ctr (page 92), Overlook Med Ctr (page 92); **Address:** 435 South St, Ste 360, Morristown, NJ 07960; **Phone:** 973-971-7200; **Board Cert:** Surgery 2009; **Med School:** Argentina 1977; **Resid:** Surgery, Central Airforce Hosp 1982; Surgery, Univ Hosp Penn 1990; **Fellow:** Metabolism, Univ Hosp Penn 1984

Strutin, Millard D MD (S) - **Hospital:** St. Clare's Hosp-Denville; **Address:** NW Surgical Assocs, 121 Center Grove Rd, Randolph, NJ 07869; **Phone:** 973-328-1414; **Board Cert:** Surgery 2008; Surgical Critical Care 2012; **Med School:** Italy 1981; **Resid:** Surgery, Univ Hosp-UMDNJ 1986

Ward, David S MD (S) - **Spec Exp:** Obesity/Bariatric Surgery; **Hospital:** Morristown Med Ctr (page 92); **Address:** 435 South St, Ste 360, Morristown, NJ 07960-6392; **Phone:** 973-971-7609; **Board Cert:** Surgery 2011; **Med School:** Rutgers R W Johnson Med Sch 1994; **Resid:** Surgery, Morristown Meml Hosp 1999

Whitman, Eric D MD (S) - **Spec Exp:** Melanoma; Endocrine Tumors; Cancer Surgery; Sarcoma; **Hospital:** Morristown Med Ctr (page 92), Overlook Med Ctr (page 92); **Address:** Atlantic Hlth, Melanoma Ctr, 100 Madison Ave, Ste 3502, Morristown, NJ 07960; **Phone:** 973-971-7111; **Board Cert:** Surgery 2013; **Med School:** Penn State Coll Med 1985; **Resid:** Surgery, Hershey Med Ctr 1991; **Fellow:** Surgical Oncology, Natl Inst Hlth 1992

Thoracic & Cardiac Surgery

Brown III, John M MD (T&CS) - **Spec Exp:** Cardiac Surgery-Adult; Heart Valve Surgery; **Hospital:** Morristown Med Ctr (page 92); **Address:** Mid-Atlantic Surgical Assocs, 100 Madison Ave, Morristown, NJ 07960; **Phone:** 973-971-7300; **Board Cert:** Thoracic & Cardiac Surgery 2013; **Med School:** Cornell Univ-Weill Med Coll 1986; **Resid:** Surgery, NY-Presby/Weill Cornell Med Ctr 1991; **Fellow:** Cardiothoracic Surgery, Meml Sloan-Kettering Cancer Ctr 1993

Widmann, Mark D MD (T&CS) - **Spec Exp:** Minimally Invasive Thoracic Surgery; Video Assisted Thoracic Surgery (VATS); **Hospital:** Morristown Med Ctr (page 92), Overlook Med Ctr (page 92); **Address:** North Jersey Thoracic Surgical Assocs, 100 Madison Ave, Ste 4101, Morristown, NJ 07960; **Phone:** 973-644-4844; **Board Cert:** Thoracic & Cardiac Surgery 2007; **Med School:** Yale Univ 1987; **Resid:** Surgery, Yale-New Haven Hosp 1995; **Fellow:** Cardiothoracic Surgery, Univ Iowa Hosps & Clins 1998; **Fac Appt:** Asst Clin Prof S, Columbia P&S

Urology

Chaikin, David C MD (U) - **Spec Exp:** Voiding Dysfunction; Urology-Female; Neuro-Urology; **Hospital:** Morristown Med Ctr (page 92); **Address:** Morristown Urology, 261 James St, Ste 1A, Morristown, NJ 07960; **Phone:** 973-539-1050; **Board Cert:** Urology 2013; Female Pelvic Medicine & Reconstuctive Surgery 2013; **Med School:** Albert Einstein Coll Med 1992; **Resid:** Urology, Hosp Univ Penn 1997; **Fellow:** Female Urology, NY-Presby/Weill Cornell Med Ctr 1999; **Fac Appt:** Asst Clin Prof U, Cornell Univ-Weill Med Coll

Colton, Marc D MD (U) - **Spec Exp:** Prostate Cancer; Urologic Cancer; Kidney Stones; Robotic Urologic Surgery; **Hospital:** St. Clare's Hosp-Denville, Morristown Med Ctr (page 92); **Address:** Morris Urology, 16 Pocono Rd, Ste 205, Denville, NJ 07834; **Phone:** 973-627-0060; **Board Cert:** Urology 2006; **Med School:** Med Coll PA 1989; **Resid:** Surgery, Temple Univ Hosp 1991; Urology, Temple Univ Hosp 1995

Kaynan, Ayal MD (U) - **Spec Exp:** Robotic Surgery; Bladder Cancer; Urologic Cancer; **Hospital:** Morristown Med Ctr (page 92); **Address:** Adult & Pediatric Urology Grp, 261 James St, Ste 3A, Morristown, NJ 07960; **Phone:** 973-539-0333; **Board Cert:** Urology 2011; **Med School:** Duke Univ 1994; **Resid:** Urologic Surgery, Montefiore Med Ctr 2000; **Fellow:** Endourology, Stanford Univ Hosp & Clins 2001

Vascular & Interventional Radiology

Calhoun, Sean K DO (VIR) - **Hospital:** Morristown Med Ctr (page 92); **Address:** Memorial Radiology Associates, 100 Madison Ave, Morristown, NJ 07962; **Phone:** 973-971-5377; **Board Cert:** Diagnostic Radiology 2001; Vascular & Interventional Radiology 2007; **Med School:** UMDNJ Sch Osteo Med 1996; **Resid:** Diagnostic Radiology, Morristown Meml hosp 2001; **Fellow:** Vascular & Interventional Radiology, Montefiore Med Ctr 2002; **Fac Appt:** Assoc Clin Prof Rad, Mount Sinai Sch Med

Yablonsky, Thaddeus M MD (VIR) - **Spec Exp:** Interventional Radiology; **Hospital:** Morristown Med Ctr (page 92); **Address:** Memorial Radiology Associates, 100 Madison Ave, Morristown, NJ 07960; **Phone:** 973-971-5377; **Board Cert:** Diagnostic Radiology 1995; Vascular & Interventional Radiology 2009; **Med School:** Rutgers R W Johnson Med Sch 1990; **Resid:** Diagnostic Radiology, St Vincent's Hosp & Med Ctr 1992; Diagnostic Radiology, Morristown Meml Hosp 1995; **Fellow:** Interventional Radiology, New York Hosp 1996

Vascular Surgery

Patel, Amit V MD (VascS) - **Spec Exp:** Aneurysm-Aortic; Endovascular Surgery; Carotid Artery Surgery; **Hospital:** Morristown Med Ctr (page 92); **Address:** Advanced Vascular, 131 Madison Ave, Fl 2, Morristown, NJ 07960; **Phone:** 973-540-9700; **Board Cert:** Surgery 2004; Vascular Surgery 2006; **Med School:** Albert Einstein Coll Med 1988; **Resid:** Surgery, Montefiore Med Ctr 1993; **Fellow:** Vascular Surgery, Hosp Univ Penn 1994

Passaic

Passaic

Adolescent Medicine

Blaustein, Silvia A MD (AM) - **Spec Exp:** Preventive Medicine; Adolescent Gynecology; Adolescent Behavior-High Risk; Vaccines; **Hospital:** St. Joseph's Regl Med Ctr - Paterson; **Address:** 703 Main St, Paterson, NJ 07503; **Phone:** 973-754-2523; **Board Cert:** Pediatrics 2009; Adolescent Medicine 2012; **Med School:** Argentina 1990; **Resid:** Pediatrics, LIJ Med Ctr 1994

Allergy & Immunology

Klein, Robert Michael MD (A&I) - **Spec Exp:** Asthma & Sinusitis; Food Allergy; Urticaria; Cough-Chronic; **Hospital:** NY-Presby/Weill Cornell Med Ctr, NY (page 102), NYU Langone Med Ctr (page 104); **Address:** Allergy & Asthma Medical Associates, 1005 Clifton Ave, Ste 102, Clifton, NJ 07013-3520; **Phone:** 973-773-7400; **Board Cert:** Pediatrics 1981; **Med School:** NY Med Coll 1976; **Resid:** Pediatrics, Beth Israel Hosp 1979; **Fellow:** Allergy & Immunology, Columbia-Presby Med Ctr 1984; **Fac Appt:** Asst Clin Prof Ped, Columbia P&S

Cardiovascular Disease

Goyal, Neil K MD (Cv) - **Spec Exp:** Interventional Cardiology; Vascular Disease; Heart Valve Disease; **Hospital:** St. Mary's Hosp - Passaic, NY-Presby/Columbia Univ Med Ctr, NY (page 102); **Address:** New Jersey Physicians, 6 Brighton Rd Fl 2, Clifton, NJ 07012; **Phone:** 973-777-7911; **Board Cert:** Cardiovascular Disease 2005; Interventional Cardiology 2006; **Med School:** Columbia P&S 1999; **Resid:** Internal Medicine, NY-Presby/Columbia Univ Med Ctr 2002; **Fellow:** Cardiovascular Disease, NY-Presby/Columbia Univ Med Ctr 2005; Interventional Cardiology, NY-Presby/Columbia Univ Med Ctr 2006

Julie, Edward MD (Cv) - **Spec Exp:** Interventional Cardiology; **Hospital:** St. Mary's Hosp - Passaic, St. Joseph's Regl Med Ctr - Paterson; **Address:** 1030 Clifton Ave, Clifton, NJ 07013; **Phone:** 973-778-3777; **Board Cert:** Internal Medicine 1983; Cardiovascular Disease 1987; **Med School:** Albert Einstein Coll Med 1980; **Resid:** Internal Medicine, Mount Sinai Med Ctr 1983; **Fellow:** Cardiovascular Disease, NY-Presby/Weill Cornell Med Ctr 1986

Salimi, Mostafa MD (Cv) - **Hospital:** St. Joseph's Wayne Hosp, St. Joseph's Regl Med Ctr - Paterson; **Address:** Advanced Cardiology Prac, 246 Hamburg Tpke, Ste 201, Wayne, NJ 7470; **Phone:** 973-942-1141; **Board Cert:** Internal Medicine 1973; Cardiovascular Disease 1977; **Med School:** Iran 1964; **Resid:** Internal Medicine, VA Hosp 1970; **Fellow:** Cardiovascular Disease, G Washington Univ Hosp 1972

Siepser, Stuart L MD (Cv) - **Spec Exp:** Coronary Artery Disease; Hypertension; Nuclear Stress Testing; Cholesterol/Lipid Disorders; **Hospital:** Chilton Med Ctr (page 92), Morristown Med Ctr (page 92); **Address:** Cardilogy Assocs-North Jersey, 1777 Hamburg Tpke, Ste 102, Wayne, NJ 7470; **Phone:** 973-831-7455; **Board Cert:** Internal Medicine 1972; Cardiovascular Disease 1975; Nuclear Cardiology 2011; **Med School:** NYU Sch Med 1968; **Resid:** Internal Medicine, NYU Med Ctr 1970; Cardiovascular Disease, NYU Med Ctr 1972; **Fac Appt:** Asst Clin Prof Med, UMDNJ-NJ Med Sch, Newark

Weiss, E Michael MD (Cv) - **Spec Exp:** Preventive Cardiology; Hypertension; Coronary Artery Disease; Heart Failure; **Hospital:** St. Joseph's Regl Med Ctr - Paterson, St. Mary's Hosp - Passaic; **Address:** 842 Clifton Ave, Ste 5, Clifton, NJ 07013-1881; **Phone:** 973-777-2440; **Board Cert:** Internal Medicine 1984; Cardiovascular Disease 2007; **Med School:** Romania 1980; **Resid:** Internal Medicine, Hackensack Med Ctr 1983; **Fellow:** Cardiovascular Disease, Hackensack Med Ctr 1985; **Fac Appt:** Asst Clin Prof Med, UMDNJ-NJ Med Sch, Newark

Dermatology

Gold, Jonathan A MD (D) - **Spec Exp:** Acne & Rosacea; Eczema; Skin Cancer; **Hospital:** St. Mary's Hosp - Passaic; **Address:** 1033 Clifton Ave, Clifton, NJ 07013; **Phone:** 973-777-6444; **Board Cert:** Dermatology 1987; **Med School:** Canada 1982; **Resid:** Dermatology, McGill Univ Med Ctr 1986; Dermatology, Montefiore Med Ctr 1987; **Fellow:** Dermatologic Pharmacology, NYU Med Ctr 1988

Maier, Herbert MD (D) - **Spec Exp:** Acne; Connective Tissue Disorders; Rosacea; **Hospital:** St. Joseph's Wayne Hosp; **Address:** 220 Hamburg Tpke Fl 2 - Ste 22, Wayne, NJ 07470; **Phone:** 973-595-6338; **Board Cert:** Dermatology 1975; **Med School:** Geo Wash Univ 1967; **Resid:** Dermatology, Mount Sinai Med Ctr 1973

Pollack, Shoshannah S MD (D) - **Hospital:** Chilton Med Ctr (page 92); **Address:** 1777 Hamburg Tpke, Ste 102, Wayne, NJ 07470; **Phone:** 973-835-1823; **Board Cert:** Dermatology 1990; **Med School:** Albert Einstein Coll Med 1986; **Resid:** Dermatology, Montefiore Med Ctr 1990

Tanzer, Floyd R MD (D) - **Spec Exp:** Acne; Eczema; **Address:** 992 Clifton Ave, Clifton, NJ 07013-3502; **Phone:** 973-365-1800; **Board Cert:** Dermatology 1977; **Med School:** SUNY Downstate 1973; **Resid:** Dermatology, Kings Co Hosp 1977

Endocrinology, Diabetes & Metabolism

Berkowitz, Richard H MD (EDM) - **Spec Exp:** Diabetes; Cholesterol/Lipid Disorders; Thyroid Disorders; **Hospital:** Chilton Med Ctr (page 92); **Address:** 2025 Hamburg Tpke, Ste D, Wayne, NJ 07470-6250; **Phone:** 973-839-5070; **Board Cert:** Internal Medicine 1975; Endocrinology 1977; **Med School:** SUNY Hlth Sci Ctr 1970; **Resid:** Internal Medicine, Montefiore Med Ctr 1974; Internal Medicine, UMDNJ-Univ Hosp 1975; **Fellow:** Endocrinology, Beth Israel Med Ctr 1977

Sherry, Stephen H MD (EDM) - **Spec Exp:** Thyroid Disorders; Diabetes; Osteoporosis; **Hospital:** Hackensack UMC-Mountainside (page 802); **Address:** 123 Highland Ave, Ste G-1, Glen Ridge, NJ 07424; **Phone:** 973-744-3733; **Board Cert:** Internal Medicine 1979; Endocrinology, Diabetes & Metabolism 1981; **Med School:** Univ Conn 1976; **Resid:** Internal Medicine, New Eng Deaconess Med Ctr 1979; **Fellow:** Endocrinology, Diabetes & Metabolism, New Eng Deaconess Med Ctr 1981; **Fac Appt:** Asst Clin Prof Med, UMDNJ-NJ Med Sch, Newark

Gastroenterology

Bleicher, Robert MD (Ge) - **Spec Exp:** Inflammatory Bowel Disease; Irritable Bowel Syndrome; Liver Disease; **Hospital:** Chilton Med Ctr (page 92); **Address:** 1825 Route 23 South, Wayne, NJ 07470; **Phone:** 973-633-1484; **Board Cert:** Internal Medicine 1981; Gastroenterology 1983; **Med School:** Columbia P&S 1978; **Resid:** Internal Medicine, Northwestern Meml Hosp 1981; **Fellow:** Gastroenterology, Northwestern Meml Hosp 1983

Farkas, John J MD (Ge) - **Hospital:** St. Joseph's Regl Med Ctr - Paterson, St. Joseph's Wayne Hosp; **Address:** 716 Broad St Fl 1, Clifton, NJ 07013; **Phone:** 973-777-5717; **Board Cert:** Internal Medicine 1989; **Med School:** Dominica 1983; **Resid:** Internal Medicine, St Joseph's Hosp & Med Ctr 1986; **Fellow:** Gastroenterology, St Joseph's Hosp & Med Ctr 1988

Infectious Disease

Najjar, Sessine MD (Inf) - **Spec Exp:** Travel Medicine; **Hospital:** St. Mary's Hosp - Passaic, Valley Hosp (page 739); **Address:** 975 Clifton Ave Fl 2, Clifton, NJ 07013-2722; **Phone:** 973-778-8666; **Board Cert:** Internal Medicine 1979; Infectious Disease 1984; **Med School:** Lebanon 1974; **Resid:** Internal Medicine, Beekman Downtown Hosp 1977; **Fellow:** Infectious Disease, St Michaels Med Ctr 1979

Weiss, Gabriella A MD (Inf) - **Spec Exp:** Chronic Fatigue Syndrome; Lyme Disease; Bone Infections; **Hospital:** St. Mary's Hosp - Passaic; **Address:** Medical Specialties of NJ, 842 Clifton Ave, Clifton, NJ 07013-1800; **Phone:** 973-777-2440; **Board Cert:** Internal Medicine 1985; **Med School:** Romania 1979; **Resid:** Internal Medicine, Hackensack Med Ctr 1984; **Fellow:** Infectious Disease, Hackensack Med Ctr 1985

Internal Medicine

De Giacomo, Frank C MD (IM) *PCP* - **Spec Exp:** Cholesterol/Lipid Disorders; **Hospital:** St. Mary's Hosp - Passaic; **Address:** New Jersey Physicians, 6 Brighton Rd Fl 2, Clifton, NJ 07012; **Phone:** 973-472-2100; **Board Cert:** Internal Medicine 1972; **Med School:** Harvard Med Sch 1965; **Resid:** Internal Medicine, Bellevue Hosp 1968; **Fellow:** Cardiovascular Disease, VA Hosp 1969

Gajdos, Robert MD (IM) *PCP* - **Hospital:** Hackensack UMC-Mountainside (page 802), St. Mary's Hosp - Passaic; **Address:** 1005 Clifton Ave, Clifton, NJ 07013-3520; **Phone:** 973-777-2005; **Board Cert:** Internal Medicine 1989; **Med School:** Grenada 1985; **Resid:** Internal Medicine, Mountainside Hosp 1989

Gold, Jeffrey L MD (IM) *PCP* - **Hospital:** St. Joseph's Regl Med Ctr - Paterson; **Address:** 468 Parish Drive, Wayne, NJ 07470-5053; **Phone:** 973-305-8300; **Board Cert:** Internal Medicine 1983; **Med School:** Mexico 1977; **Resid:** Internal Medicine, St Josephs Hosp 1981; **Fac Appt:** Asst Clin Prof Med, UMDNJ-NJ Med Sch, Newark

Jawetz, Harold I MD (IM) - **Spec Exp:** Chronic Obstructive Lung Disease (COPD); Pulmonary Disease; Asthma; **Hospital:** St. Mary's Hosp - Passaic, St. Joseph's Regl Med Ctr - Paterson; **Address:** New Jersey Physicians, 6 Brighton Rd, Clifton, NJ 07012; **Phone:** 973-472-2100; **Board Cert:** Internal Medicine 1974; **Med School:** Albert Einstein Coll Med 1971; **Resid:** Internal Medicine, Montefiore Med Ctr 1974; **Fellow:** Pulmonary Disease, Montefiore Med Ctr 1978

Medical Oncology

Uhm, Kyudong MD (Onc) - **Hospital:** St. Mary's Hosp - Passaic, St. Joseph's Regl Med Ctr - Paterson; **Address:** Clifton R.46 E Hematology & Oncology Ctr, 1117 Route 46 E, Ste 205, Clifton, NJ 07013; **Phone:** 973-471-0981; **Board Cert:** Internal Medicine 1978; Medical Oncology 1979; Hematology 1980; **Med School:** South Korea 1969; **Resid:** Internal Medicine, Englewood 1977; Hematology, Montefiore Hosp Med Ctr 1978; **Fellow:** Medical Oncology, Montefiore Hosp Med Ctr 1980

Nephrology

Vitting, Kevin E MD (Nep) - **Spec Exp:** Hypertension; Kidney Failure; **Hospital:** St. Joseph's Regl Med Ctr - Paterson, St. Joseph's Wayne Hosp; **Address:** 342 Hamburg Tpke, Ste 201, Wayne, NJ 07470; **Phone:** 973-389-1119; **Board Cert:** Internal Medicine 1985; Nephrology 1988; **Med School:** Rutgers R W Johnson Med Sch 1982; **Resid:** Internal Medicine, Lenox Hill Hosp 1985; **Fellow:** Nephrology, Lenox Hill Hosp 1987; **Fac Appt:** Asst Clin Prof Med, Mount Sinai Sch Med

Neurology

Chodosh, Eliot H MD (N) - **Spec Exp:** Stroke; Multiple Sclerosis; **Hospital:** St. Joseph's Wayne Hosp, Chilton Med Ctr (page 92); **Address:** 220 Hamburg Tpke, Ste 16, Wayne, NJ 07470-2193; **Phone:** 973-942-4778; **Board Cert:** Neurology 1987; **Med School:** Mexico 1981; **Resid:** Neurology, Boston Univ Med Ctr 1986; **Fellow:** Cerebrovascular Disease, Boston Univ Med Ctr 1987

Knep, Stanley J MD (N) - **Spec Exp:** Electromyography; Parkinson's Disease; Headache; Stroke; **Address:** 905 Allwood Rd, Ste 105, Clifton, NJ 07013; **Phone:** 973-471-3680; **Board Cert:** Neurology 1977; **Med School:** South Africa 1965; **Resid:** Internal Medicine, Johannesburg Hosp 1970; Neurology, Albert Einstein Coll Med 1975; **Fac Appt:** Assoc Clin Prof N, Seton Hall Univ Sch Hlth & Med Scis

Padela, Mohammad F MD (N) - **Spec Exp:** Acupuncture; Balance Disorders; Multiple Sclerosis; Parkinson's Disease; **Hospital:** Holy Name Med Ctr (page 738); **Address:** North Jersey Neurology Care, 721 Clifton Ave, Ste 1B, Clifton, NJ 07013; **Phone:** 973-471-3730; **Board Cert:** Neurology 2005; **Med School:** Pakistan 1983; **Resid:** Internal Medicine, Univ Hosp-UMDNJ 1991; Neurology, Univ Hosp-UMDNJ 1994; **Fellow:** Neurology, NY Medical Coll-St Vincent Cath Med Ctrs 1995

Neuroradiology

Aluri-Vallabhaneni, Bhanu Sri MD (NRad) - **Spec Exp:** Pediatric Neuroradiology; Brain Imaging; Spinal Imaging; Head & Neck Imaging; **Hospital:** St. Joseph's Regl Med Ctr - Paterson, Hackensack UMC-Mountainside (page 802); **Address:** Imaging Subspecialists of North Jersey, 703 Main St Fl Ground, Paterson, NJ 7503; **Phone:** 973-754-2645; **Board Cert:** Diagnostic Radiology 1998; **Med School:** India 1988; **Resid:** Diagnostic Radiology, Harlem Hosp 1998; **Fellow:** Neurological Radiology, NY-Presby/Columbia Univ Med Ctr 2000

Obstetrics & Gynecology

Burns, Les A MD (ObG) *PCP* - **Spec Exp:** Menopause Problems; Pap Smear Abnormalities; Hysterectomy Alternatives; Pregnancy After Age 35; **Hospital:** Chilton Med Ctr (page 92), St. Joseph's Regl Med Ctr - Paterson; **Address:** 1784 Hamburg Tpke, Wayne, NJ 07470-4023; **Phone:** 973-831-9925; **Board Cert:** Obstetrics & Gynecology 2013; **Med School:** Hahnemann Univ 1981; **Resid:** Obstetrics & Gynecology, Danbury Hosp 1986

Ophthalmology

Giliberti, Orazio L MD (Oph) - **Spec Exp:** LASIK-Refractive Surgery; Cataract Surgery-Lens Implant; Corneal Disease & Surgery; Glaucoma; **Hospital:** Univ Hosp-Newark, Clara Maass Med Ctr (page 94); **Address:** Giliberti Eye and Laser Center, 415 Totowa Rd, Totowa, NJ 07512-2081; **Phone:** 973-595-0011; **Board Cert:** Ophthalmology 1989; **Med School:** Grenada 1982; **Resid:** Ophthalmology, UMDNJ Affil Hosps 1987; **Fellow:** Ophthalmology, Pennsylvania Hosp 1984; Refractive Surgery, Vision Sculpting; **Fac Appt:** Asst Clin Prof Oph, UMDNJ-NJ Med Sch, Newark

Vogel, Mitchell MD (Oph) - **Spec Exp:** Corneal Disease; Refractive Surgery; Uveitis; Cataract Surgery; **Hospital:** St. Mary's Hosp - Passaic, Overlook Med Ctr (page 92); **Address:** New Jersey Vision Assocs, 124 Gregory Ave, Ste 104, Passaic, NJ 07055-4856; **Phone:** 973-779-0808; **Board Cert:** Ophthalmology 2010; **Med School:** Temple Univ 1991; **Resid:** Internal Medicine, Mountainside Hosp 1992; Ophthalmology, Nassau Univ Med Ctr 1995; **Fellow:** Cornea, Univ Tex SW Affil Hosp 1996

Orthopaedic Surgery

Drillings, Gary J MD (OrS) - **Spec Exp:** Knee Injuries; Shoulder Injuries; Sports Medicine; **Hospital:** Chilton Med Ctr (page 92); **Address:** 1777 Hamburg Tpke, Ste 305, Wayne, NJ 07470; **Phone:** 973-831-6666; **Board Cert:** Orthopaedic Surgery 2014; **Med School:** SUNY Upstate Med Univ 1985; **Resid:** Orthopaedic Surgery, Northwestern Meml Hosp 1990; **Fellow:** Sports Medicine, Lenox Hill Hosp 1991

Emami, Arash MD (OrS) - **Spec Exp:** Spinal Surgery; Scoliosis; Minimally Invasive Spinal Surgery; Spinal Disc Replacement; **Hospital:** St. Joseph's Regl Med Ctr - Paterson, NYU Hosp For Joint Dis (page 104); **Address:** Univ Spine Ctr, 504 Valley Rd Fl 2 - Ste 203, Wayne, NJ 07470; **Phone:** 973-686-0700; **Board Cert:** Orthopaedic Surgery 2013; **Med School:** Univ Chicago-Pritzker Sch Med 1994; **Resid:** Orthopaedic Surgery, Univ Chicago Affil Hosps 1999; **Fellow:** Spine Surgery, UCSF Med Ctr 2000; **Fac Appt:** Asst Prof OrS, Seton Hall Univ Sch Hlth & Med Scis

Mc Inerney, Vincent K MD (OrS) - **Spec Exp:** Hip Replacement; Minimally Invasive Surgery; Knee Replacement; Shoulder Replacement; **Hospital:** St. Joseph's Regl Med Ctr - Paterson; **Address:** Northland Orthopedics, 504 Valley Rd, Ste 200, Wayne, NJ 07470; **Phone:** 973-694-2690; **Board Cert:** Orthopaedic Surgery 1984; **Med School:** UMDNJ-NJ Med Sch, Newark 1977; **Resid:** Orthopaedic Surgery, St. Joseph's Regl Med Ctr 1981; **Fellow:** Sports Medicine, Mass Genl Hosp 1982

Reicher, Oscar A MD (OrS) - **Spec Exp:** Reconstructive Surgery; Sports Medicine; Arthritis; **Hospital:** Chilton Med Ctr (page 92), St. Joseph's Wayne Hosp; **Address:** 2035 Hamburg Tpke, Ste D, Wayne, NJ 07470; **Phone:** 973-616-0200; **Board Cert:** Orthopaedic Surgery 2007; **Med School:** Univ Pittsburgh 1979; **Resid:** Orthopaedic Surgery, Vanderbilt Univ Med Ctr 1984

Strongwater, Allan M MD (OrS) - **Spec Exp:** Pediatric Orthopaedic Surgery; Cerebral Palsy; Deformity Reconstruction; **Hospital:** St. Joseph's Regl Med Ctr - Paterson; **Address:** St Josephs Chldns Hosp-Dept Ped Ortho Surg, 703 Main St Xavier Bldg - Ste 702, Paterson, NJ 07503; **Phone:** 973-754-2414; **Board Cert:** Orthopaedic Surgery 2007; **Med School:** Rush Med Coll 1978; **Resid:** Orthopaedic Surgery, Yale-New Haven Hosp 1983; **Fellow:** Pediatric Orthopaedic Surgery, Hosp Joint Diseases 1984; **Fac Appt:** Clin Prof OrS, NYU Sch Med

Otolaryngology

Cece, John A MD (Oto) - **Spec Exp:** Sinus Surgery; Cosmetic Surgery-Face; Rhinoplasty; **Hospital:** Chilton Med Ctr (page 92), St. Mary's Hosp - Passaic; **Address:** ENT & Allergy Assocs, 1211 Hamburg Tpke, Ste 205, Wayne, NJ 07470; **Phone:** 973-633-0808; **Board Cert:** Otolaryngology 1986; Facial Plastic & Reconstr Surgery 1992; **Med School:** Rutgers R W Johnson Med Sch 1981; **Resid:** Otolaryngology, Mt Sinai Med Ctr 1986

La Bagnara Jr, James MD (Oto) - **Spec Exp:** Thyroid & Parathyroid Surgery; Pediatric Otolaryngology; **Hospital:** St. Joseph's Regl Med Ctr - Paterson, St. Joseph's Wayne Hosp; **Address:** 311 Lexington Ave, Paterson, NJ 07502-1010; **Phone:** 973-942-1300; **Board Cert:** Otolaryngology 1978; **Med School:** UMDNJ-NJ Med Sch, Newark 1974; **Resid:** Otolaryngology, UMDNJ-NJ Med Sch Affil Hosp 1978

Pediatric Hematology-Oncology

Bonilla, Mary Ann MD (PHO) - **Hospital:** St. Joseph's Regl Med Ctr - Paterson; **Address:** SJCH, Hematology-Oncology Dept, 703 Main St Fl 7, Paterson, NJ 07503; **Phone:** 973-754-3230; **Board Cert:** Pediatrics 1986; Pediatric Hematology-Oncology 2012; **Med School:** Loyola Univ-Stritch Sch Med 1981; **Resid:** Pediatrics, Brookdale Univ Hosp Med Ctr 1984; **Fellow:** Pediatric Hematology-Oncology, Meml Sloan-Kettering Canc Ctr 1988

Pediatric Pulmonology

Nachajon, Roberto V MD (PPul) - **Spec Exp:** Asthma; Cystic Fibrosis; Sleep Disorders; Bronchoscopy; **Hospital:** St. Joseph's Regl Med Ctr - Paterson, Mt Sinai Hosp; **Address:** 11 Getty Ave, Paterson, NJ 07503; **Phone:** 973-754-2550; **Board Cert:** Pediatric Pulmonology 2011; Sleep Medicine 2007; **Med School:** Uruguay 1985; **Resid:** Pediatrics, Chldns Hosp Uruguay 1990; Pediatrics, Beth Israel Med Ctr 1993; **Fellow:** Pediatric Pulmonology, Chldns Hosp 1996; **Fac Appt:** Asst Clin Prof Ped, Mount Sinai Sch Med

Pediatric Surgery

Bhattacharyya, Nishith MD (PS) - **Spec Exp:** Cancer Surgery; Minimally Invasive Surgery; Chest Wall Deformities; Pediatric Plastic Surgery; **Hospital:** St. Joseph's Regl Med Ctr - Paterson, Newark Beth Israel Med Ctr (page 94); **Address:** 2130 Milburn Ave, Ste C-1, Maplewood, NJ 07470; **Phone:** 973-313-3115; **Board Cert:** Surgery 2013; Pediatric Surgery 2007; **Med School:** India 1984; **Resid:** Surgery, Univ Hawaii Med Ctr 1994; Surgery, Chldns Hosp 1991; **Fellow:** Pediatric Surgery, Chldns Hosp-Ohio 1996; **Fac Appt:** Asst Clin Prof PS, NY Med Coll

Pediatrics

Scofield, Lisa E MD (Ped) *PCP* - **Hospital:** St. Joseph's Regl Med Ctr - Paterson, Chilton Med Ctr (page 92); **Address:** 57 Willowbrook Blvd, Ste 421, Wayne, NJ 07470; **Phone:** 973-754-4025; **Board Cert:** Pediatrics 2008; **Med School:** UMDNJ-NJ Med Sch, Newark 1990; **Resid:** Pediatrics, New York Hosp-Cornell 1994

Plastic Surgery

Figlia, Paul M MD (PlS) - **Spec Exp:** Reconstructive Plastic Surgery; Facial Rejuvenation; Breast Augmentation; Body Contouring; **Hospital:** JFK Med Ctr - Edison, St. Barnabas Med Ctr (page 94); **Address:** 1500 Pleasant Vly Way, Ste 307, West Orange, NJ 07502; **Phone:** 973-324-5333; **Board Cert:** Plastic Surgery 2005; **Med School:** Rutgers R W Johnson Med Sch 1984; **Resid:** Surgery, St Barnabas Med Ctr 1986; Surgery, Washington Hosp Ctr 1989; **Fellow:** Plastic Surgery, OU Med Ctr 1992

Ganchi, Parham A MD/PhD (PlS) - **Spec Exp:** Cosmetic Surgery-Face & Body; Cosmetic Surgery-Breast; Facial Rejuvenation; Body Contouring; **Hospital:** Chilton Med Ctr (page 92), St. Joseph's Wayne Hosp; **Address:** 246 Hamburg Tpke, Ste 307, Wayne, NJ 07470; **Phone:** 973-942-6600; **Board Cert:** Plastic Surgery 2013; **Med School:** Duke Univ 1994; **Resid:** Surgery, Brigham & Womens Hosp 1999; **Fellow:** Plastic Surgery, Brigham & Womens Hosp 2002

Pulmonary Disease

Amoruso, Robert C MD (Pul) - **Spec Exp:** Asthma; Critical Care; **Hospital:** St. Joseph's Regl Med Ctr - Paterson, St. Joseph's Wayne Hosp; **Address:** 999 McBride Ave, Ste 201B, Woodland Park, NJ 07424; **Phone:** 973-256-0287; **Board Cert:** Internal Medicine 1979; Pulmonary Disease 1982; **Med School:** Italy 1975; **Resid:** Internal Medicine, St Joseph's Hosp Med Ctr 1979; **Fellow:** Pulmonary Disease, College Hosp-UMDNJ 1981; **Fac Appt:** Asst Clin Prof Med, Mount Sinai Sch Med

Grizzanti, Joseph N DO (Pul) - **Spec Exp:** Lung Cancer; Asthma & Allergy; Sarcoidosis; Immunologic Lung Disease; **Hospital:** Valley Hosp (page 739); **Address:** 297 Lafayette Ave, Hawthorne, NJ 07506; **Phone:** 973-790-4111; **Board Cert:** Internal Medicine 1979; Pulmonary Disease 1982; Allergy & Immunology 1985; **Med School:** Philadelphia Coll Osteo Med 1976; **Resid:** Internal Medicine, UMDNJ-Univ Hosp 1979; **Fellow:** Pulmonary Disease, Montefiore Med Ctr 1981; Allergy & Immunology, Montefiore Med Ctr 1984; **Fac Appt:** Assoc Clin Prof Med, Albert Einstein Coll Med

Radiation Oncology

Cole, Robert J MD (RadRO) - **Spec Exp:** Brachytherapy; Breast Cancer; Prostate Cancer; **Hospital:** St. Mary's Hosp - Passaic, Robert Wood Johnson Univ Hosp - New Brunswick; **Address:** St Mary's Hosp, Dept Oncology, 350 Boulevard, Passaic, NJ 07055; **Phone:** 973-365-5088; **Board Cert:** Therapeutic Radiology 1983; **Med School:** Wake Forest Univ 1979; **Resid:** Radiation Oncology, Univ VA Hlth Sci Ctr 1983

Rheumatology

Goldberg, Marc A MD (Rhu) - **Spec Exp:** Rheumatoid Arthritis; Osteoporosis; Osteoarthritis; **Hospital:** St. Mary's Hosp - Passaic; **Address:** 6 Brighton Rd, Clifton, NJ 07012; **Phone:** 973-473-2597; **Board Cert:** Internal Medicine 1972; Rheumatology 1976; **Med School:** Med Coll VA 1969; **Resid:** Internal Medicine, Univ Maryland Hosp 1972; Rheumatology, Johns Hopkins Hosp 1973; **Fellow:** Rheumatology, Hosp Univ Penn 1976

Lewko, Michael P MD (Rhu) - **Spec Exp:** Geriatric Rheumatology; Arthritis; Osteoporosis; Rheumatoid Arthritis; **Hospital:** St. Joseph's Regl Med Ctr - Paterson; **Address:** NJ Arthritis & Osteoporosis Ctr, 871 Allwood Rd, Clifton, NJ 07012; **Phone:** 973-405-5163; **Board Cert:** Internal Medicine 1988; Rheumatology 2012; Geriatric Medicine 2004; **Med School:** UMDNJ-Rutgers Med Sch 1985; **Resid:** Internal Medicine, RW Johnson Univ Hosp 1988; **Fellow:** Geriatric Medicine, Roger Williams Med Ctr 1989; Rheumatology, Hosp Univ Penn 1991; **Fac Appt:** Asst Clin Prof Med, Mount Sinai Sch Med

Surgery

Budd, Daniel C MD (S) - **Spec Exp:** Breast Disease; Endocrine Surgery; Hernia; **Hospital:** St. Joseph's Regl Med Ctr - Paterson, Valley Hosp (page 739); **Address:** General Surgeons of North Jersey, 707 Broadway, Paterson, NJ 07514; **Phone:** 973-742-3371; **Board Cert:** Surgery 1975; **Med School:** Duke Univ 1969; **Resid:** Surgery, Columbia-Presbyterian Hosp 1974; **Fac Appt:** Assoc Clin Prof S, UMDNJ-NJ Med Sch, Newark

Feigenbaum, Howard MD (S) - **Spec Exp:** Gastrointestinal Surgery; Colon Surgery; Laparoscopic Surgery; Breast Surgery; **Hospital:** Chilton Med Ctr (page 92), St. Joseph's Wayne Hosp; **Address:** 227 Hamburg Tpke, Pompton Lakes, NJ 07442-1838; **Phone:** 973-839-7999; **Board Cert:** Surgery 2009; **Med School:** NYU Sch Med 1971; **Resid:** Surgery, Bellevue Hosp 1977

Thoracic & Cardiac Surgery

Connolly, Mark W MD (T&CS) - **Spec Exp:** Minimally Invasive Cardiac Surgery; Coronary Artery Surgery; **Hospital:** St. Joseph's Regl Med Ctr - Paterson; **Address:** St Josephs, Cardiothoracic Surgery Dept, 703 Main St, Paterson, NJ 07503; **Phone:** 973-754-2486; **Board Cert:** Thoracic & Cardiac Surgery 2011; **Med School:** Northwestern Univ 1982; **Resid:** Surgery, NYU Med Ctr 1988; Cardiothoracic Surgery, Emory Univ Hosp 1991; **Fellow:** Surgical Research, Maimonides Med Ctr 1986

Pontoriero, Michael MD (T&CS) - **Hospital:** Clara Maass Med Ctr (page 94); **Address:** Cardiovascular Grp, 1401 Broad St, Clifton, NJ 07013; **Phone:** 973-759-9000; **Board Cert:** Thoracic & Cardiac Surgery 2013; Surgery 2010; **Med School:** UMDNJ-NJ Med Sch, Newark 1985; **Resid:** Surgery, Univ Hosp-UMDNJ 1990; **Fellow:** Cardiothoracic Surgery, Tufts Med Ctr 1993

Urology

Levine, Seth P MD (U) - **Spec Exp:** Prostate Cancer; Incontinence; **Hospital:** Chilton Med Ctr (page 92), Valley Hosp (page 739); **Address:** Assocs in Urology-North Jersey, 1777 Hamburg Tpke, Ste 304, Wayne, NJ 7470; **Phone:** 973-616-8400; **Board Cert:** Urology 1980; **Med School:** Tufts Univ 1971; **Resid:** Surgery, Mount Sinai Med Ctr 1973; Urology, Mount Sinai Med Ctr 1978

Somerset

Somerset

Allergy & Immunology

Caucino, Julie A DO (A&I) - **Spec Exp:** Asthma & Allergy; Drug Sensitivity; Sinusitis; **Hospital:** Univ Med Ctr Princeton at Plainsboro; **Address:** Princeton Allergy & Asthma Assocs, 24 Vreeland Drive, Skillman, NJ 08558; **Phone:** 609-921-2202; **Board Cert:** Allergy & Immunology 2013; **Med School:** Kirksville Coll Osteo Med 1987; **Resid:** Internal Medicine, RW Johnson Univ Hosp 1991; **Fellow:** Allergy & Immunology, Montefiore Med Ctr 1995

Fox, James A MD (A&I) - **Spec Exp:** Asthma; Urticaria; Food Allergy; Hereditary Angioedema; **Hospital:** Robert Wood Johnson Univ Hosp - Somerset, Hunterdon Med Ctr; **Address:** 3461 US Highway 22 E, D Bldg, Branchburg, NJ 08876-6021; **Phone:** 908-725-4777; **Board Cert:** Pediatrics 1981; Allergy & Immunology 1983; **Med School:** Yale Univ 1977; **Resid:** Pediatrics, Bronx Municipal Hosp Ctr 1980; **Fellow:** Allergy & Immunology, Columbia-Presby Med Ctr 1982

Krol, Kristine MD (A&I) - **Spec Exp:** Insect Allergies; Drug Sensitivity; Food Allergy; Asthma; **Hospital:** Staten Island Univ Hosp - South, Robert Wood Johnson Univ Hosp - Somerset; **Address:** AllerCare, 177 W High St, Somerville, NJ 08876; **Phone:** 908-725-8666; **Board Cert:** Internal Medicine 1987; Allergy & Immunology 2011; **Med School:** SUNY Downstate 1981; **Resid:** Internal Medicine, Staten Island Univ Hosp 1985; **Fellow:** Allergy & Immunology, Mass Genl Hosp 1987; **Fac Appt:** Asst Clin Prof Med, SUNY Downstate

Pedinoff, Andrew J MD (A&I) - **Spec Exp:** Rhinitis; Asthma; Hay Fever; **Hospital:** Univ Med Ctr Princeton at Plainsboro, Robert Wood Johnson Univ Hosp - New Brunswick; **Address:** Princeton Allergy & Asthma Assocs, 24 Vreeland Drive, Skilman, NJ 08558; **Phone:** 609-921-2202; **Board Cert:** Allergy & Immunology 2013; **Med School:** Dominican Republic 1984; **Resid:** Pediatrics, Georgetown Univ Hosp 1987; **Fellow:** Allergy & Immunology, Georgetown Univ Hosp 1988; **Fac Appt:** Asst Clin Prof Ped, Rutgers R W Johnson Med Sch

Schulhafer, Edwin MD (A&I) - **Spec Exp:** Asthma; Sinus Disorders; Allergy; Migraine; **Hospital:** Hunterdon Med Ctr, Robert Wood Johnson Univ Hosp - Somerset; **Address:** Allergy, Asthma & Sinus Ctr, 712 Courtyard Drive, Hillsborough, NJ 08844; **Phone:** 908-526-0200; **Board Cert:** Internal Medicine 1988; Allergy & Immunology 2006; **Med School:** UMDNJ-NJ Med Sch, Newark 1983; **Resid:** Internal Medicine, Overlook Hosp 1986; **Fellow:** Allergy & Immunology, Long Island Coll Hosp 1988

Southern, D Loren MD (A&I) - **Spec Exp:** Asthma & Allergy; Urticaria; Hereditary Angioedema; Food Allergy; **Hospital:** Univ Med Ctr Princeton at Plainsboro; **Address:** Princeton Allergy & Asthma Assocs, 24 Vreeland Drive, Skillman, NJ 08558; **Phone:** 609-921-2202; **Board Cert:** Pediatrics 1976; **Med School:** Columbia P&S 1971; **Resid:** Pediatrics, Columbia-Presby Med Ctr 1974; **Fellow:** Allergy & Immunology, Columbia-Presby Med Ctr 1976

Cardiac Electrophysiology

Ivanov, Alexander MD (CE) - **Spec Exp:** Arrhythmias; Atrial Fibrillation; Pacemakers; Defibrillators; **Hospital:** Robert Wood Johnson Univ Hosp - Somerset; **Address:** Cardiology Associates of Somerset County, 745 Route 202-206, Bridgewater, NJ 08807; **Phone:** 908-722-6410; **Board Cert:** Internal Medicine 2008; Cardiovascular Disease 2011; Cardiac Electrophysiology 2003; **Med School:** Russia 1983; **Resid:** Internal Medicine, Allegheny General Hosp 1997; **Fellow:** Cardiovascular Disease, Lankenau Hosp 1999; Cardiac Electrophysiology, Hahnemann Univ Med Ctr 2002

Cardiovascular Disease

Hall, Jason O MD (Cv) - **Spec Exp:** Interventional cardiology; **Hospital:** Robert Wood Johnson Univ Hosp - Somerset; **Address:** 225 Jackson St, Medicor, Bridgewater, NJ 08807; **Phone:** 908-526-8668; **Board Cert:** Internal Medicine 1989; Cardiovascular Disease 2013; Interventional Cardiology 2011; **Med School:** UMDNJ-Rutgers Med Sch 1985; **Resid:** Anatomic & Clinical Pathology, RWJ Univ Hosp 1986; Internal Medicine, RWJ Univ Hosp 1990; **Fellow:** Cardiovascular Disease, Cleveland Clinic 1993; Interventional Cardiology, Cleveland Clinic 1994

Kulkarni, Rachana A MD (Cv) - **Spec Exp:** Nuclear Cardiology; Echocardiography-Transesophageal; Hypertension; **Hospital:** Robert Wood Johnson Univ Hosp - Somerset, Robert Wood Johnson Univ Hosp - New Brunswick; **Address:** Medicor Cardiology, 225 Jackson St, Bridgewater, NJ 08807; **Phone:** 908-526-8668; **Board Cert:** Cardiovascular Disease 2010; Nuclear Cardiology 2012; **Med School:** India 1988; **Resid:** Internal Medicine, RW Johnson Univ Hosp 1995; **Fellow:** Cardiovascular Disease, RW Johnson Univ Hosp 1998

Lebenthal, Mark J MD (Cv) - **Spec Exp:** Heart Disease in Women; **Hospital:** Robert Wood Johnson Univ Hosp - Somerset; **Address:** Cardiology Assocs of Somerset County, 745 Rt 202-206, Bridgewater, NJ 08807; **Phone:** 908-722-6410; **Board Cert:** Internal Medicine 1980; Cardiovascular Disease 1983; **Med School:** Mexico 1976; **Resid:** Internal Medicine, CMDNJ-U Program 1980; **Fellow:** Cardiovascular Disease, Thos Jefferson U Hosp 1982

Saulino, Patrick F MD (Cv) - **Spec Exp:** Cardiac Catheterization; Invasive Cardiology; Non-Invasive Cardiology; **Hospital:** Robert Wood Johnson Univ Hosp - Somerset, Robert Wood Johnson Univ Hosp - New Brunswick; **Address:** Medicor, Cardiology, 3322 Rte 22 W, Ste 505, Branchburg, NJ 08876; **Phone:** 908-231-0041; **Board Cert:** Internal Medicine 1984; Cardiovascular Disease 1987; **Med School:** Georgetown Univ 1981; **Resid:** Internal Medicine, Georgetown Univ Hosp 1984; Cardiovascular Disease, Georgetown Univ Hosp 1985; **Fellow:** Cardiovascular Disease, RW Johnson Univ Hosp 1987; Cardiovascular Disease, Georgetown Univ Hosp 1988

Stroh, Jack A MD (Cv) - **Spec Exp:** Angioplasty & Stent Placement; Hypertension; Cholesterol/Lipid Disorders; **Hospital:** Robert Wood Johnson Univ Hosp - New Brunswick, St. Peter's Univ Hosp; **Address:** New Brunswick Cardiology Grp, 75 Veronica Ave, Ste 101, Somerset, NJ 08873-5002; **Phone:** 732-247-7444; **Board Cert:** Internal Medicine 1987; Cardiovascular Disease 1989; Interventional Cardiology 2009; **Med School:** Albert Einstein Coll Med 1984; **Resid:** Internal Medicine, Boston Univ Med Ctr 1987; **Fellow:** Cardiovascular Disease, NYU Med Ctr 1990; **Fac Appt:** Asst Clin Prof Med, Rutgers R W Johnson Med Sch

Dermatology

Fox, Alissa B MD (D) - **Spec Exp:** Acne; Psoriasis; **Hospital:** Robert Wood Johnson Univ Hosp - Somerset, Hunterdon Med Ctr; **Address:** 3461 US Highway 22, Branchburg, NJ 08876; **Phone:** 908-725-4777; **Board Cert:** Dermatology 1984; **Med School:** NYU Sch Med 1980; **Resid:** Dermatology, New York Hosp 1984

Pappert, Amy S MD (D) - **Spec Exp:** Contact Dermatitis; **Hospital:** Robert Wood Johnson Univ Hosp - New Brunswick; **Address:** RW Johnson Medical Group, Dept Dermatology, 1 World's Fair Drive, Ste 2400, Somerset, NJ 08873; **Phone:** 732-463-7546; **Board Cert:** Dermatology 2013; **Med School:** Rutgers R W Johnson Med Sch 1989; **Resid:** Dermatology, Columbia Presby Med Ctr 1994; **Fac Appt:** Asst Prof D, Rutgers R W Johnson Med Sch

Diagnostic Radiology

Greer, Jeannete G MD (DR) - **Spec Exp:** Breast Imaging; **Hospital:** Robert Wood Johnson Univ Hosp - Somerset; **Address:** Somerset Med Ctr, Dept Radiology, 110 Rehill Ave, Somerville, NJ 08876; **Phone:** 732-968-4899; **Board Cert:** Diagnostic Radiology 1994; **Med School:** Harvard Med Sch 1989; **Resid:** Diagnostic Radiology, T Jefferson Univ Hosp 1994, **Fellow:** Breast Imaging, T Jefferson Univ Hosp 1995

Melville, Gordon E MD (DR) - **Spec Exp:** Neuroradiology; MRI; **Hospital:** Robert Wood Johnson Univ Hosp - Somerset; **Address:** Somerset Medical Ctr, Dept Radiology, 100 Rehill Ave, Somerville, NJ 08876; **Phone:** 732-968-4899; **Board Cert:** Diagnostic Radiology 1984; Neuroradiology 2006; **Med School:** Univ NC Sch Med 1979; **Resid:** Diagnostic Radiology, G Washington Univ Hosp 1984; **Fellow:** Neuroradiology, Mass Genl Hosp 1985

Yang, Roger S MD (DR) - **Spec Exp:** Breast Imaging; Women's Imaging; **Hospital:** Robert Wood Johnson Univ Hosp - Somerset; **Address:** Somerset Med Ctr, Dept Radiology, 110 Rehill Ave, Somerville, NJ 08876; **Phone:** 732-968-4899; **Board Cert:** Diagnostic Radiology 1997; **Med School:** Northwestern Univ 1992; **Resid:** Diagnostic Radiology, Univ Hosp 1997; **Fellow:** Women's Imaging, Univ Hosp/Kings Co Hosp 1998; **Fac Appt:** Asst Clin Prof Rad, SUNY Downstate

Family Medicine

Corson, Richard L MD (FMed) *PCP* - **Hospital:** Robert Wood Johnson Univ Hosp - Somerset; **Address:** 313 Courtyard Drive, Hillsborough, NJ 08844; **Phone:** 908-722-9962; **Board Cert:** Family Medicine 2014; **Med School:** Rutgers R W Johnson Med Sch 1983; **Resid:** Family Medicine, Somerset Med Ctr 1986

Frisoli, Anthony MD (FMed) *PCP* - **Spec Exp:** Sports Medicine; Geriatric Care; **Hospital:** Robert Wood Johnson Univ Hosp - Somerset; **Address:** Martinsville Family Practice, 1973 Washington Valley Rd, Martinsville, NJ 08836; **Phone:** 732-560-9225; **Board Cert:** Family Medicine 2005; **Med School:** UMDNJ-Rutgers Med Sch 1983; **Resid:** Family Medicine, Somerset Med Ctr 1986

Steckel, Rebecca MD (FMed) *PCP* - **Spec Exp:** Women's Health; Preventive Medicine; **Hospital:** Robert Wood Johnson Univ Hosp - Somerset; **Address:** Franklin Family Practice, 29 Clyde Rd, Ste 101, Somerset, NJ 08873; **Phone:** 732-873-0330; **Board Cert:** Family Medicine 2014; **Med School:** NY Med Coll 1983; **Resid:** Family Medicine, Mountainside Hosp 1986; **Fellow:** Obstetrics, OSU Med Ctr 1987; **Fac Appt:** FMed

Ziering, Thomas S MD (FMed) *PCP* - **Spec Exp:** Concierge Medicine; Anxiety & Depression; Gay/Lesbian/Transgender Health; Complementary Medicine; **Hospital:** Morristown Med Ctr (page 92); **Address:** 39 Olcott Sq, Bernardsville, NJ 07924-2317; **Phone:** 908-221-1919; **Board Cert:** Family Medicine 2012; **Med School:** UMDNJ-NJ Med Sch, Newark 1987; **Resid:** Family Medicine, Somerset Med Ctr 1990; **Fac Appt:** Assoc Clin Prof FMed, Rutgers R W Johnson Med Sch

Gastroenterology

Accurso, Charles A MD (Ge) - **Spec Exp:** Colon Cancer Screening; Irritable Bowel Syndrome; Gastroesophageal Reflux Disease (GERD); Endoscopy; **Hospital:** Robert Wood Johnson Univ Hosp - Somerset; **Address:** 511 Courtyard Drive, Bldg 500, Hillsborough, NJ 08844-2017; **Phone:** 908-218-9222; **Board Cert:** Internal Medicine 1987; Gastroenterology 1989; **Med School:** UMDNJ-NJ Med Sch, Newark 1984; **Resid:** Internal Medicine, Univ Hosp 1987; **Fellow:** Gastroenterology, Univ Hosp/NJ Med Sch 1989; **Fac Appt:** Asst Clin Prof Med, UMDNJ-NJ Med Sch, Newark

Ferges, Mitchell L MD (Ge) - **Spec Exp:** Liver Disease; **Hospital:** St. Peter's Univ Hosp, Robert Wood Johnson Univ Hosp - New Brunswick; **Address:** 33 Clyde Rd, Ste 102, Somerset, NJ 08873; **Phone:** 732-873-9200; **Board Cert:** Internal Medicine 1978; Gastroenterology 1981; **Med School:** Rutgers R W Johnson Med Sch 1975; **Resid:** Internal Medicine, UMDNJ Rutgers Affil Hosps 1978; **Fellow:** Gastroenterology, UMDNJ Univ Hosp 1980

Hand Surgery

Boretz, Robert S MD (HS) - **Spec Exp:** Carpal Tunnel Syndrome; Arthritis; Wrist Surgery; Arthroscopic Surgery; **Hospital:** Robert Wood Johnson Univ Hosp - Somerset; **Address:** Summit Med Grp, 215 Union Ave, Ste B, Bridgewater, NJ 08807; **Phone:** 908-685-8500; **Board Cert:** Orthopaedic Surgery 2004; Hand Surgery 2007; **Med School:** SUNY Hlth Sci Ctr 1993; **Resid:** Surgery, LIJ Med Ctr 1996; Orthopaedic Surgery, LIJ Med Ctr 2000; **Fellow:** Hand Surgery, New England Med Ctr 2001

Coyle Jr, Michael P MD (HS) - **Spec Exp:** Arthritis Hand Surgery; Nerve Compression; Dupuytren's Contracture; Sports Injuries; **Hospital:** Robert Wood Johnson Univ Hosp - New Brunswick, St. Peter's Univ Hosp; **Address:** Univ Orthopaedic Assocs, 2 Worlds Fair Drive, Somerset, NJ 8873; **Phone:** 732-537-0909; **Board Cert:** Orthopaedic Surgery 2005; Hand Surgery 2010; Orthopaedic Sports Medicine 2007; **Med School:** Columbia P&S 1968; **Resid:** Surgery, UCSF-Moffitt Hosp 1970; Orthopaedic Surgery, NY Orth Hosp 1976; **Fellow:** Hand Surgery, NY Orth Hosp 1977; **Fac Appt:** Clin Prof OrS, Rutgers R W Johnson Med Sch

Infectious Disease

Herman, David J MD (Inf) - **Spec Exp:** Lyme Disease; AIDS/HIV; Travel Medicine; **Hospital:** Univ Med Ctr Princeton at Plainsboro, Robert Wood Johnson Univ Hosp - Somerset; **Address:** 105 Raider Blvd, Ste 101, Hillsborough, NJ 08844; **Phone:** 908-281-0221; **Board Cert:** Internal Medicine 1988; Infectious Disease 2010; **Med School:** Univ MO-Columbia Sch Med 1985; **Resid:** Internal Medicine, Northwestern Meml Hosp 1988; **Fellow:** Infectious Disease, Univ Minn Med Ctr 1991; **Fac Appt:** Assoc Clin Prof Med, Rutgers R W Johnson Med Sch

Nahass, Ronald G MD (Inf) - **Spec Exp:** HIV; Hepatitis B & C; Diagnostic Problems; **Hospital:** Robert Wood Johnson Univ Hosp - New Brunswick, Univ Med Ctr Princeton at Plainsboro; **Address:** ID Care Assocs, 105 Raider Blvd, Ste 101, Hillsborough, NJ 08844; **Phone:** 908-281-0221; **Board Cert:** Internal Medicine 1985; Infectious Disease 1988; **Med School:** Rutgers R W Johnson Med Sch 1982; **Resid:** Internal Medicine, RW Johnson Univ Hosp 1985; **Fellow:** Infectious Disease, RW Johnson Univ Hosp 1988; **Fac Appt:** Clin Prof Med, Rutgers R W Johnson Med Sch

Internal Medicine

Bell, Kevin E MD (IM) *PCP* - **Spec Exp:** Lyme Disease; Hypertension; **Hospital:** Overlook Med Ctr (page 92); **Address:** 10 Mountain Blvd, Warren, NJ 07059-2639; **Phone:** 908-226-9000; **Board Cert:** Internal Medicine 1978; **Med School:** Columbia P&S 1975; **Resid:** Internal Medicine, Univ Wisconsin Med Ctr 1979; **Fac Appt:** Asst Clin Prof Med, Columbia P&S

Bonaventura, Lisa M MD (IM) *PCP* - **Spec Exp:** Concierge Medicine; **Hospital:** Morristown Med Ctr (page 92); **Address:** 2345 Lamington Rd, Ste 104, Bedminster, NJ 07921-2612; **Phone:** 908-781-6333; **Board Cert:** Internal Medicine 1989; **Med School:** Univ Cincinnati 1986; **Resid:** Internal Medicine, Morristown Meml Hosp 1989

Catanzaro, Donna MD (IM) *PCP* - **Hospital:** Robert Wood Johnson Univ Hosp - Somerset; **Address:** Primary Care, 34 E Somerset St, Raritan, NJ 08869; **Phone:** 908-685-2532; **Med School:** UMDNJ-NJ Med Sch, Newark 1990; **Resid:** Internal Medicine, Baystate Med Ctr 1993

Ferrante, Maurice A MD (IM) *PCP* - **Hospital:** Overlook Med Ctr (page 92); **Address:** 8 Mountain Blvd, Warren, NJ 07059; **Phone:** 908-561-8600; **Board Cert:** Internal Medicine 2010; **Med School:** Jefferson Med Coll 1987; **Resid:** Internal Medicine, Univ Maryland Med Ctr 1990

Neiman, Deborah L MD (IM) *PCP* - **Spec Exp:** Weight Management; **Hospital:** Morristown Med Ctr (page 92), Hunterdon Med Ctr; **Address:** 311 Omni Drive, Hillsborough, NJ 08844; **Phone:** 908-281-0632; **Board Cert:** Internal Medicine 1987; **Med School:** NY Med Coll 1984; **Resid:** Internal Medicine, Morristown Meml Hosp 1987

Sanchez-Catanese, Betty MD (IM) *PCP* - **Hospital:** Robert Wood Johnson Univ Hosp - Somerset; **Address:** 315 E Main St, Somerville, NJ 08876-3109; **Phone:** 908-722-3442; **Board Cert:** Internal Medicine 1987; **Med School:** NY Med Coll 1983; **Resid:** Internal Medicine, Northshore Univ Hosp 1986

Interventional Cardiology

Rachofsky, Edward L MD (IC) - **Spec Exp:** Echocardiography; Angioplasty & Stent Placement; Cardiac Catheterization; Coronary Artery Disease; **Hospital:** Robert Wood Johnson Univ Hosp - Somerset, Morristown Med Ctr (page 92); **Address:** Medicor Cardiology, 225 Jackson St, Bridgewater, NJ 08807; **Phone:** 908-526-8668; **Board Cert:** Internal Medicine 2005; Cardiovascular Disease 2008; Interventional Cardiology 2009; **Med School:** Mount Sinai Sch Med 2002; **Resid:** Internal Medicine, NY Presby-Cornell Med Ctr Hosp 2005; **Fellow:** Cardiovascular Disease, NYU Med Ctr 2007; Interventional Cardiology, NYU Med Ctr 2008

Medical Oncology

Fang, Bruno S MD (Onc) - **Spec Exp:** Lung Cancer; Head & Neck Cancer; Breast Cancer; Colon Cancer; **Hospital:** Robert Wood Johnson Univ Hosp - New Brunswick, St. Peter's Univ Hosp; **Address:** Central Jersey Oncology Ctr, 454 Elizabeth Ave, Ste 240, Somerset, NJ 08873; **Phone:** 732-390-7750; **Board Cert:** Internal Medicine 2006; Hematology 2010; Medical Oncology 2010; **Med School:** Brazil 1991; **Resid:** Internal Medicine, Jackson Meml Hosp 1996; Internal Medicine, VA Med Ctr 1997; **Fellow:** Hematology & Oncology, Natl Cancer Inst/NIH 2000

Hamilton, Audrey M MD (Onc) - **Spec Exp:** Hematologic Malignancies; Multiple Myeloma; Lymphoma; Myeloproliferative Diseases; **Hospital:** Meml Sloan Kettering Canc Ctr (page 110); **Address:** Meml Sloan Kettering Cancer Ctr, 136 Mountain View Blvd, Basking Ridge, NJ 07920; **Phone:** 908-542-3000; **Board Cert:** Internal Medicine 1986; Hematology 2004; Medical Oncology 2005; **Med School:** Harvard Med Sch 1983; **Resid:** Internal Medicine, Brigham & Womens Hosp 1986; **Fellow:** Hematology & Oncology, NY Hosp-Cornell Med Ctr 1989

Salwitz, James C MD (Onc) - **Spec Exp:** Colon Cancer; Breast Cancer; Lung Cancer; Leukemia & Lymphoma; **Hospital:** Robert Wood Johnson Univ Hosp - New Brunswick, St. Peter's Univ Hosp; **Address:** Central Jersey Oncology Ctr, 454 Elizabeth Ave, Ste 240, Somerset, NJ 08873; **Phone:** 732-390-7750; **Board Cert:** Internal Medicine 1984; Medical Oncology 1987; Hospice & Palliative Medicine 2012; **Med School:** UMDNJ-Rutgers Med Sch 1981; **Resid:** Internal Medicine, Northwestern Univ/McGaw Med Ctr 1984; **Fellow:** Medical Oncology, NIH-Natl Canc Inst 1987

Toomey, Kathleen C MD (Onc) - **Spec Exp:** Breast Cancer; **Hospital:** Robert Wood Johnson Univ Hosp - Somerset; **Address:** Steepchase Cancer Ctr, 30 Rehill Ave, Ste 2500, Somerville, NJ 08876; **Phone:** 908-927-8700; **Board Cert:** Internal Medicine 1982; Medical Oncology 1987; **Med School:** Italy 1978; **Resid:** Internal Medicine, St Peters Med Ctr 1982; **Fellow:** Hematology & Oncology, UMDNJ-Rutgers Med Sch 1985

Nephrology

Kabis, Suzanne M MD (Nep) - **Spec Exp:** Lupus Nephritis; Hypertension; Glomerulonephritis; Kidney Disease in Pregnancy; **Hospital:** Robert Wood Johnson Univ Hosp - New Brunswick, St. Peter's Univ Hosp; **Address:** 1350 Hamilton St, Somerset, NJ 08873; **Phone:** 732-246-2626; **Board Cert:** Internal Medicine 1982; Nephrology 1988; **Med School:** UMDNJ-Rutgers Med Sch 1979; **Resid:** Internal Medicine, NC Meml Hosp 1982; **Fellow:** Nephrology, NC Meml Hosp 1985

Neurology

Friedlander, Devin S MD (N) - **Spec Exp:** Headache; Botox Therapy; Dizziness; **Hospital:** St. Peter's Univ Hosp; **Address:** Princeton & Rutgers Neurology, 77 Veronica Ave, Ste 102, Somerset, NJ 08873-3448; **Phone:** 732-246-1311; **Board Cert:** Neurology 2013; **Med School:** Rutgers R W Johnson Med Sch 1989; **Resid:** Internal Medicine, R W Johnson Univ Hosp 1991; Neurology, Albert Einstein Coll Med 1993; **Fellow:** Neurophysiology, Lyons VA Med Ctr 1994

Obstetrics & Gynecology

Levey, James A MD (ObG) - **Spec Exp:** HPV-Human Papilloma Virus; Robotic Surgery; Endometriosis; Menstrual Disorders; **Hospital:** Overlook Med Ctr (page 92); **Address:** Summit Med Grp, 34 Mountain Blvd, Warren, NJ 07059; **Phone:** 908-769-0100; **Board Cert:** Obstetrics & Gynecology 2013; **Med School:** Albany Med Coll 1991; **Resid:** Surgery, Montefiore Med Ctr 1992; Obstetrics & Gynecology, Med Ctr of DE 1996

Sanderson, Rhonda A MD (ObG) - **Spec Exp:** Gynecology Only; Menopause Problems; **Hospital:** Overlook Med Ctr (page 92); **Address:** 8 Mountain Blvd, Warren, NJ 07059; **Phone:** 908-754-5775; **Board Cert:** Obstetrics & Gynecology 2013; **Med School:** Hahnemann Univ 1980; **Resid:** Obstetrics & Gynecology, Women & Infants Hosp 1985

Ophthalmology

Angrist, Richard C MD (Oph) - **Spec Exp:** Cataract Surgery; Glaucoma; Eyelid/Tear Duct Disorders; Ophthalmic Plastic Surgery; **Hospital:** Robert Wood Johnson Univ Hosp - New Brunswick, Monmouth Med Ctr - South (page 94); **Address:** 1527 State Route 27, Ste 2600, Somerset, NJ 08873; **Phone:** 732-246-1050; **Board Cert:** Ophthalmology 1985; **Med School:** Albany Med Coll 1979; **Resid:** Ophthalmology, NY Eye& Ear Infirm 1983; **Fellow:** Ophthalmic Plastic & Reconstructive Surgery, Univ Wisconsin 1984

Salz, Alan G MD (Oph) - **Spec Exp:** LASIK-Refractive Surgery; Cataract Surgery-Lens Implant; Refractive Surgery; **Hospital:** Robert Wood Johnson Univ Hosp - Somerset; **Address:** The Eye Specialists, 31 Monroe St, Bridgewater, NJ 08807; **Phone:** 908-231-1110; **Board Cert:** Ophthalmology 1987; **Med School:** Boston Univ 1981; **Resid:** Ophthalmology, Wills Eye Hosp 1985

Orthopaedic Surgery

Butler, Mark S MD (OrS) - **Spec Exp:** Trauma; Foot & Ankle Surgery; **Hospital:** Robert Wood Johnson Univ Hosp - New Brunswick, St. Peter's Univ Hosp; **Address:** Univ Orthopaedic Assocs, 2 Worlds Fair Drive, Somerset, NJ 8873; **Phone:** 732-537-0909; **Board Cert:** Orthopaedic Surgery 2014; **Med School:** Rutgers R W Johnson Med Sch 1984; **Resid:** Orthopaedic Surgery, UMDNJ-RW Johnson Univ Hosp 1989; **Fellow:** Orthopaedic Trauma, Maryland Inst EMS 1990; Foot & Ankle Surgery, Maryland Inst EMS 1992; **Fac Appt:** Assoc Clin Prof OrS, Rutgers R W Johnson Med Sch

D'Agostini Jr, Robert J MD (OrS) - **Spec Exp:** Joint Replacement; Sports Medicine; **Hospital:** Morristown Med Ctr (page 92); **Address:** Tri-Co Orthopedics, 1590 Route 206 N, Bedminster, NJ 07921; **Phone:** 908-234-2002; **Board Cert:** Orthopaedic Surgery 2008; Sports Medicine 2009; **Med School:** Rutgers R W Johnson Med Sch 1980; **Resid:** Orthopaedic Surgery, MedStar Georgetown Univ Hosp 1986

Dwyer, James W MD (OrS) - **Spec Exp:** Spinal Surgery; Minimally Invasive Spinal Surgery; Spinal Disc Replacement; Spinal Reconstructive Surgery; **Hospital:** Robert Wood Johnson Univ Hosp - Somerset, Univ Hosp-Newark; **Address:** Somerset Orthopedic Assocs, 1081 Route 22 W, Bridgewater, NJ 08807; **Phone:** 908-722-0822; **Board Cert:** Orthopaedic Surgery 2013; Spine Surgery ; **Med School:** UMDNJ-NJ Med Sch, Newark 1982; **Resid:** Orthopaedic Surgery, UMDNJ Affil Hosps 1989; **Fellow:** Spine Surgery, Seton Med Ctr/St Marys Spine Ctr 1990; **Fac Appt:** Asst Clin Prof OrS, UMDNJ-NJ Med Sch, Newark

Otolaryngology

Lazar, Amy D MD (Oto) - **Spec Exp:** Sinus Disorders; **Hospital:** Robert Wood Johnson Univ Hosp - Somerset; **Address:** ENT and Allergy Associates, 245 US Hwy 22, Fl 3, Bridgewater, NJ 08807; **Phone:** 908-722-1022; **Board Cert:** Otolaryngology 1999; **Med School:** Ros Franklin Univ/Chicago Med Sch 1992; **Resid:** Otolaryngology, Manhattan EE & T Hosp 1995; Otolaryngology, Boston Med Ctr 1998

Pediatric Pulmonology

Turcios, Nelson L MD (PPul) - **Spec Exp:** Breathing Disorders; Cough-Chronic; Cystic Fibrosis; Ciliary Dyskinesia; **Hospital:** Robert Wood Johnson Univ Hosp - Somerset, St. Peter's Univ Hosp; **Address:** 282 E Main St, Somerville, NJ 08876; **Phone:** 908-526-5212; **Board Cert:** Pediatrics 1982; Pediatric Pulmonology 2014; **Med School:** El Salvador 1973; **Resid:** Pediatrics, Univ Mississippi Med Ctr 1978; Pediatrics, Univ Maryland Hosp 1980; **Fellow:** Pediatric Pulmonology, Childrens Hosp Natl Med Ctr 1982; **Fac Appt:** Assoc Prof Ped, UMDNJ-NJ Med Sch, Newark

Pediatric Urology

Barone, Joseph G MD (Ped Uro) - **Spec Exp:** Robotic Surgery-Pediatric; Urinary Reconstruction; Incontinence; Hypospadias; **Hospital:** Robert Wood Johnson Univ Hosp - New Brunswick, Univ Med Ctr Princeton at Plainsboro; **Address:** RWJUH Med Grp, Urology, 1 Worlds Fair Drive Fl 1, Somerset, NJ 08873; **Phone:** 732-235-7960; **Board Cert:** Urology 2009; Pediatric Urology 2009; **Med School:** UMDNJ-Rutgers Med Sch 1987; **Resid:** Urology, RWJ Univ Hosp 1993; **Fellow:** Pediatric Urology, Emory Univ Hosp 1994; **Fac Appt:** Assoc Prof S, Rutgers R W Johnson Med Sch

Pediatrics

Katz, Andrea G MD (Ped) *PCP* - **Spec Exp:** Developmental & Behavioral Disorders; Chronic Illness; Obesity; **Hospital:** Overlook Med Ctr (page 92); **Address:** 76 Stirling Rd, Ste 201, Warren, NJ 07059; **Phone:** 908-755-5437; **Board Cert:** Pediatrics 2013; **Med School:** NY Med Coll 1988; **Resid:** Pediatrics, NY Hosp-Cornell Med Ctr 1991

Yorke, Eric R MD (Ped) *PCP* - **Hospital:** Robert Wood Johnson Univ Hosp - Somerset, Morristown Med Ctr (page 92); **Address:** Somerset Pediatric Group, 2345 Lamington Rd, Ste 101, Bedminster, NJ 07921; **Phone:** 908-470-1124; **Board Cert:** Pediatrics 2009; **Med School:** Columbia P&S 1982; **Resid:** Pediatrics, Babies Hosp-Columbia 1986

Plastic Surgery

Olson, Robert M MD (PlS) - **Spec Exp:** Cleft Palate/Lip; Head & Neck Surgery; Wound Healing/Care; **Hospital:** St. Peter's Univ Hosp, Robert Wood Johnson Univ Hosp - New Brunswick; **Address:** 888 Easton Ave, Ste 6, Somerset, NJ 08873-1898; **Phone:** 732-418-1888; **Board Cert:** Plastic Surgery 1982; **Med School:** Univ Pennsylvania 1974; **Resid:** Surgery, Peter Bent Brigham Hosp 1979; Plastic Surgery, Mayo Clinic 1981; **Fac Appt:** Assoc Prof S, Rutgers R W Johnson Med Sch

Perry, Arthur W MD (PlS) - **Spec Exp:** Rhinoplasty; Eyelid Surgery; Liposuction; Abdominoplasty; **Hospital:** Robert Wood Johnson Univ Hosp - New Brunswick, Robert Wood Johnson Univ Hosp - Somerset; **Address:** 3055 Route 27, Franklin Park, NJ 08823-1315; **Phone:** 732-422-9600; **Board Cert:** Plastic Surgery 1989; **Med School:** Albany Med Coll 1981; **Resid:** Surgery, Beth Israel Hosp 1984; Plastic Surgery, Univ Chicago Hosps 1987; **Fellow:** Burn Surgery, New York Hosp-Cornell 1985; Cosmetic Plastic Surgery, Univ Miami/Baker-Gordon Assocs 1987; **Fac Appt:** Assoc Prof PlS, Columbia P&S

Psychiatry

Donnellan, Joseph A MD (Psyc) - **Spec Exp:** Eating Disorders; Obsessive-Compulsive Disorder; **Hospital:** Robert Wood Johnson Univ Hosp - Somerset; **Address:** 422 Courtyard Drive, Hillsborough, NJ 08844; **Phone:** 908-725-5595; **Board Cert:** Psychiatry 1991; **Med School:** UMDNJ-NJ Med Sch, Newark 1986; **Resid:** Psychiatry, UMDNJ Univ Hosp 1990

Rochford, Joseph MD (Psyc) - **Spec Exp:** Depression; Anxiety Disorders; Eating Disorders; **Hospital:** Robert Wood Johnson Univ Hosp - Somerset; **Address:** 407 Omni Drive, Hillsborough, NJ 08844; **Phone:** 908-359-2312; **Board Cert:** Psychiatry 1975; **Med School:** Yale Univ 1969; **Resid:** Psychiatry, Hosp Univ Penn 1973

Pulmonary Disease

Arno, Louis J MD (Pul) - **Spec Exp:** Critical Care; **Hospital:** Robert Wood Johnson Univ Hosp - Somerset; **Address:** RespaCare, 489 Union Ave, Bridgewater, NJ 08807; **Phone:** 732-356-9950; **Board Cert:** Pulmonary Disease 2006; Critical Care Medicine 2009; **Med School:** Grenada 1986; **Resid:** Internal Medicine, St Michaels Med Ctr 1990; **Fellow:** Pulmonary Disease, St Michaels Med Ctr 1992; Critical Care Medicine, St Michaels Med Ctr 1993

Gerhard, Harvey MD (Pul) - **Hospital:** Morristown Med Ctr (page 92); **Address:** The Pulmonary Group, 416 Mount Airy Rd, Basking Ridge, NJ 07920-2438; **Phone:** 908-766-6605; **Board Cert:** Internal Medicine 1977; **Med School:** Yale Univ 1974; **Resid:** Internal Medicine, Bellevue Hosp Ctr 1977; **Fellow:** Pulmonary Disease, Yale-New Haven Hosp 1979

Radiation Oncology

Braver, Joel K MD (RadRO) - **Spec Exp:** Prostate Cancer; Stereotactic Radiosurgery; Merkel Cell Carcinoma; Lung Cancer; **Hospital:** Robert Wood Johnson Univ Hosp - Somerset; **Address:** Steeplchase Cancer Center, 30 Rehill Ave, Ste 1100, Somerville, NJ 08876; **Phone:** 908-927-8777; **Board Cert:** Radiation Oncology 2006; **Med School:** Rutgers R W Johnson Med Sch 1991; **Resid:** Radiation Oncology, Montefiore Med Ctr 1996

Hug, Eugen B MD (RadRO) - **Spec Exp:** Pediatric Cancers; Proton Beam Therapy; Skull Base Tumors; Sarcoma; **Address:** ProCure Proton Therapy Ctr, 103 Cedar Grove Ln, Somerset, NJ 08873; **Phone:** 732-357-2600; **Board Cert:** Radiation Oncology 1994; **Med School:** Germany 1986; **Resid:** Radiation Oncology, Mass Genl Hosp 1992; **Fellow:** Radiation Oncology, Mass Genl Hosp 1993

Reproductive Endocrinology

Drews, Michael R MD (RE) - **Spec Exp:** Infertility-IVF; Miscarriage-Recurrent; **Hospital:** Morristown Med Ctr (page 92); **Address:** Reproductive Medical Assocs of NJ, 140 Allen Rd, Basking Ridge, NJ 07920; **Phone:** 908-604-7800; **Board Cert:** Obstetrics & Gynecology 2013; Reproductive Endocrinology 2013; **Med School:** Cornell Univ-Weill Med Coll 1986; **Resid:** Obstetrics & Gynecology, N Shore Univ Hosp 1990; **Fellow:** Reproductive Endocrinology, Mount Sinai Med Ctr 1992

Scott, Richard T MD (RE) - **Spec Exp:** Infertility; Infertility-IVF; Fertility Preservation in Cancer; **Hospital:** Morristown Med Ctr (page 92); **Address:** Reproductive Med Assocs of NJ, 140 Allen Rd, Basking Ridge, NJ 07920; **Phone:** 908-604-7800; **Board Cert:** Obstetrics & Gynecology 2013; Reproductive Endocrinology 2013; **Med School:** Univ VA Sch Med 1983; **Resid:** Obstetrics & Gynecology, Wilford Hall USAF Med Ctr 1987; **Fellow:** Reproductive Endocrinology, Jones Inst Reproductive Med 1989; **Fac Appt:** Prof ObG, Rutgers R W Johnson Med Sch

Treiser, Susan L MD/PhD (RE) - **Spec Exp:** Infertility; Infertility-IVF; **Hospital:** St. Peter's Univ Hosp; **Address:** IVF NJ Fertility & Gynecology Ctr, 81 Veronica Ave, Somerset, NJ 08873; **Phone:** 732-220-9060; **Board Cert:** Obstetrics & Gynecology 2013; Reproductive Endocrinology 2013; **Med School:** Georgetown Univ 1983; **Resid:** Obstetrics & Gynecology, UMDNJ Med Ctr 1988; **Fellow:** Reproductive Endocrinology, Columbia Presby Med Ctr 1990

Surgery

Drascher, Gary MD (S) - **Spec Exp:** Laparoscopic Surgery-Complex; Aneurysm; Carotid Artery Surgery; Vascular Surgery; **Hospital:** Robert Wood Johnson Univ Hosp - Somerset; **Address:** Surgical Assocs Central NJ, 30 Rehill Ave, Ste 3300, Somerville, NJ 08776; **Phone:** 908-927-8994; **Board Cert:** Surgery 2007; **Med School:** Mount Sinai Sch Med 1981; **Resid:** Internal Medicine, St Lukes-Roosevelt Hosp Ctr 1982; Surgery, St Lukes-Roosevelt Hosp Ctr 1987; **Fellow:** Vascular Surgery, Englewood Hosp 1989

Lanfranchi, Angela E MD (S) - **Spec Exp:** Breast Cancer; Breast Surgery; **Hospital:** Robert Wood Johnson Univ Hosp - Somerset; **Address:** Surgical Assocs Central NJ, 30 Rehill Ave, Ste 3300, Somerville, NJ 08776; **Phone:** 908-927-8994; **Board Cert:** Surgery 2012; **Med School:** Georgetown Univ 1975; **Resid:** Family Medicine, Somerset Hosp 1978; Surgery, Stony Brook Univ Med Ctr 1982; **Fellow:** Vascular Surgery, Nassau Hosp 1983

Thoracic & Cardiac Surgery

Batsides, George P MD (T&CS) - **Spec Exp:** Cardiac Surgery; Aortic Surgery; **Hospital:** Robert Wood Johnson Univ Hosp - New Brunswick, Robert Wood Johnson Univ Hosp - Somerset; **Address:** 125 Paterson St, Ste 4100, New Brunswick, NJ 08901; **Phone:** 732-235-7800; **Board Cert:** Surgery 2003; Thoracic & Cardiac Surgery 2006; **Med School:** UMDNJ-Robert Wood Johnson 1997; **Resid:** Surgery, RWJ Univ Med Ctr 2002; Thoracic & Cardiac Surgery, RWJ Univ Med Ctr 2005; **Fac Appt:** Asst Prof T&CS, Rutgers R W Johnson Med Sch

Caccavale, Robert J MD (T&CS) - **Spec Exp:** Video Assisted Thoracic Surgery (VATS); **Hospital:** Robert Wood Johnson Univ Hosp - Somerset, CentraState Med Ctr; **Address:** Thoracic Grp, 35 Clyde Rd, Ste 104, Somerset, NJ 08873; **Phone:** 732-247-3002; **Board Cert:** Thoracic & Cardiac Surgery 2008; **Med School:** SUNY Buffalo 1981; **Resid:** Surgery, NYU Med Ctr 1984; Surgery, Booth Meml Med Ctr 1986; **Fellow:** Thoracic Surgery, SUNY Downstate Med Ctr 1988; **Fac Appt:** Assoc Clin Prof T&CS, Rutgers R W Johnson Med Sch

Urology

Catanese, Anthony J MD (U) - **Spec Exp:** Urologic Cancer; Kidney Cancer; **Hospital:** Robert Wood Johnson Univ Hosp - Somerset, St. Peter's Univ Hosp; **Address:** Partners in Urology, 315 E Main St, Somerville, NJ 08876; **Phone:** 908-722-6900; **Board Cert:** Urology 2009; **Med School:** NY Med Coll 1983; **Resid:** Surgery, NYU Med Ctr 1985; Urology, NYU Med Ctr 1989

Vascular Surgery

Imegwu, Obi J MD (VascS) - **Spec Exp:** Endovascular Surgery; Peripheral Vascular Disease; **Hospital:** Robert Wood Johnson Univ Hosp - Somerset; **Address:** Somerset Surgical Assocs, 30 Rehill Ave, Ste 3400, Somerville, NJ 08876; **Phone:** 908-735-2400; **Board Cert:** Surgery 2009; Vascular Surgery 2010; **Med School:** Jefferson Med Coll 1992; **Resid:** Surgery, Montefiore Med Ctr 1999; Vascular Surgery, UMDNJ Univ Hosp-Newark 2001

Union

Trinitas Regional Medical Center

225 WILLIAMSON STREET | ELIZABETH, NEW JERSEY 07207
PH 908.994.5000 | WWW.TRINITASRMC.ORG

Caring For You In Every Way

SPONSORSHIP: Trinitas Regional Medical Center is a voluntary not-for-profit Catholic teaching hospital sponsored by the Sisters of Charity of Saint Elizabeth in partnership with Elizabethtown Healthcare Foundation.

BEDS: 556 *Accredited by The Joint Commission*

MEDICAL STAFF

Trinitas Regional Medical Center has nearly 500 physicians and over 40 residents on its medical staff. Trinitas is a major clinical site for the Seton Hall School of Health and Medical Sciences' Internal Medicine Residency Program.

CENTERS OF EXCELLENCE:

Behavioral Health & Psychiatry: Behavioral Health services at Trinitas are among the most comprehensive in New Jersey and include a full range of inpatient and outpatient psychiatric care for seniors, adults, adolescents and children.

Cancer Care: The Trinitas Comprehensive Cancer Center offers the most advanced medical and radiation technology available, including Rapid Arc radiotherapy, to cancer patients. An interdisciplinary team works with each patient to develop a care plan encompassing the latest diagnostic treatment options, medical technology, clinical trials and integrative therapy.

Cardiology: Trinitas maintains a full-service cardiac facility for the intensive care of patients with heart disease, including elective angioplasty, a cardiac care unit, intermediate coronary care unit, cardiac catheterization lab, non-invasive cardiology services, full-service emergency department, and cardiac rehabilitation services.

Maternal & Child Health: Trinitas offers a Level II Intermediate Care Nursery, a 24-hour in-house pediatrician and obstetrician, and midwifery services. Inpatient care for child/adolescent psychiatric patients is also offered.

Renal Care: Trinitas is committed to patients experiencing kidney failure, and initiated the THRIVE early intervention program to reach high-risk patients.

Seniors Services: The Trinitas commitment to seniors takes many forms, most recently the establishment of the Acute Care for the Elderly (ACE) nursing unit. The Seniors First Membership Program offers special gifts and invitations to special events.

School of Nursing: The third largest school of nursing in the United States, the Trinitas School of Nursing, affiliated with Union County College, is known for an outstanding nursing education program that was recently designated a Center of Excellence in Nursing Education by the National League for Nursing.

Sleep Disorders: The Comprehensive Sleep Disorders Center provides monitored, fully-attended diagnostic sleep studies designed to rule out physical, non-stress related symptoms that may prevent restful sleep in adults and children. Two locations are offered, including the first hotel-based sleep center in New Jersey.

Women's Services: In addition to the latest modalities in digital mammography, breast biopsy, breast MRI, bone density screening and ultrasound, women can visit Trinitas for cosmetic and reconstructive surgery and innovative surgical care using the da Vinci® Robotic Surgical System for female incontinence and prolapse.

Wound Healing/Diabetes Management: The Trinitas Center for Wound Healing and Hyperbaric Medicine has one of the highest heal rates in the nation. Specially-trained certified nurses and physicians treat those with chronic, hard-to-heal wounds. Recognized by the American Diabetes Association, the Diabetes Management Center offers a high quality education program for diabetics.

Adolescent Medicine

Sanders, Leslie MD (AM) - **Spec Exp:** Eating Disorders; **Hospital:** Overlook Med Ctr (page 92), Morristown Med Ctr (page 92); **Address:** Overlook Med Ctr, Eating Disoders Program, 99 Beauvoir Ave, Summit, NJ 07902; **Phone:** 908-522-5757; **Board Cert:** Adolescent Medicine 2012; **Med School:** Albert Einstein Coll Med 1984; **Resid:** Pediatrics, Univ Pittsburgh Med Ctr 1987

Allergy & Immunology

Bielory, Leonard MD (A&I) - **Spec Exp:** Dry Eye Syndrome; Asthma; Eye Allergy; Autoimmune Ocular Disorders; **Hospital:** St. Barnabas Med Ctr (page 94); **Address:** 400 Mountain Ave, Springfield, NJ 07081; **Phone:** 973-912-9817; **Board Cert:** Internal Medicine 1984; Allergy & Immunology 1985; Diagnostic Lab Immunology 1986; **Med School:** UMDNJ-NJ Med Sch, Newark 1980; **Resid:** Internal Medicine, Univ Md Hosp 1982; Internal Medicine, Natl Inst Hlth 1983; **Fellow:** Allergy & Immunology, Natl Inst Hlth 1985; **Fac Appt:** Prof A&I, UMDNJ-NJ Med Sch, Newark

Brown, David K MD (A&I) - **Spec Exp:** Asthma; Sinus Disorders; Headache; **Hospital:** Overlook Med Ctr (page 92); **Address:** Allergy Diagnostic & Treatment Ctr, 33 Overlook Rd, Ste 307, Summit, NJ 07901; **Phone:** 908-522-9696; **Board Cert:** Internal Medicine 1984; Allergy & Immunology 1987; **Med School:** Med Coll OH 1981; **Resid:** Internal Medicine, Overlook Hosp 1984; **Fellow:** Allergy & Immunology, St Lukes-Roosevelt Hosp 1986

Goodman, Alan J MD (A&I) - **Spec Exp:** Rhinitis; Sinus Disorders; Asthma; **Hospital:** St. Barnabas Med Ctr (page 94); **Address:** Summit Medical Group, 574 Springfield Ave, Westfield, NJ 07090; **Phone:** 908-688-6200; **Board Cert:** Internal Medicine 1985; Allergy & Immunology 2009; **Med School:** SUNY Upstate Med Univ 1982; **Resid:** Internal Medicine, Washington Hosp Ctr 1985; **Fellow:** Allergy & Immunology, St Luke's-Roosevelt Hosp Ctr 1988

LeBenger, Kerry S MD (A&I) - **Spec Exp:** Asthma; Allergy; **Hospital:** Overlook Med Ctr (page 92); **Address:** Summit Med Grp, ENT Allergy, 1 Diamond Hill Rd Fl 2, Lawrence Pav, Berkely Heights, NJ 07922; **Phone:** 908-277-8681; **Board Cert:** Internal Medicine 1983; Allergy & Immunology 1985; **Med School:** NY Med Coll 1980; **Resid:** Internal Medicine, Lenox Hill Hosp 1983; **Fellow:** Allergy & Immunology, NY-Presby/Weill Cornell Med Ctr 1985; **Fac Appt:** Asst Clin Prof Med, UMDNJ-Rutgers Med Sch

Maccia, Clement MD (A&I) - **Spec Exp:** Rhinitis; Asthma; Urticaria; Eczema; **Hospital:** JFK Med Ctr - Edison, Robert Wood Johnson Univ Hosp - New Brunswick; **Address:** Asthma, Sinus & Allergy Ctrs, 19 Holly St, Cranford, NJ 07016; **Phone:** 908-276-0666; **Board Cert:** Pediatrics 1980; Allergy & Immunology 1985; **Med School:** Italy 1971; **Resid:** Pediatrics, Muhlenberg Med Ctr 1974; **Fellow:** Allergy & Immunology, Univ Hosp 1976; **Fac Appt:** Clin Prof A&I, Rutgers R W Johnson Med Sch

Mendelson, Joel S MD (A&I) - **Spec Exp:** Infectious Disease; Food Allergy; Urticaria; Eczema; **Hospital:** St. Barnabas Med Ctr (page 94), Chldns Hosp NJ at Newark (page 94); **Address:** 1124 Springfield Ave, Mountainside, NJ 07092; **Phone:** 908-233-4477; **Board Cert:** Pediatrics 1987; Allergy & Immunology 2009; Pediatric Infectious Disease 2012; **Med School:** Dominican Republic 1982; **Resid:** Pediatrics, St Lukes-Roosevelt Hosp 1985; **Fellow:** Allergy & Immunology, Univ Hosp-UMDNJ 1987; Pediatric Infectious Disease, Univ Hosp-UMDNJ 1987; **Fac Appt:** Asst Prof Ped, Grenada

Cardiovascular Disease

Kalischer, Alan L MD (Cv) - **Spec Exp:** Echocardiography; Nuclear Cardiology; Coronary Artery Disease; Arrhythmias; **Hospital:** Overlook Med Ctr (page 92), JFK Med Ctr - Edison; **Address:** Fanwood-Westfield Cardiology, 313 South Ave, Ste 202, Fanwood, NJ 07023; **Phone:** 908-889-1900; **Board Cert:** Internal Medicine 1982; Cardiovascular Disease 1985; Echocardiography 2011; Nuclear Cardiology 2012; **Med School:** NY Med Coll 1977; **Resid:** Internal Medicine, SUNY Downstate Med Ctr 1980; **Fellow:** Cardiovascular Disease, NY-Presby/Columbia Univ Med Ctr 1984; **Fac Appt:** Asst Prof Med, Rutgers R W Johnson Med Sch

Sachs, R. Gregory MD (Cv) - **Spec Exp:** Heart Disease; Heart Valve Disease; Congenital Heart Disease-Adult; **Hospital:** Overlook Med Ctr (page 92), Morristown Med Ctr (page 92); **Address:** Summit Med Grp, Cardiology, 1 Diamond Hill Rd Fl 2, Berkeley Heights, NJ 07922; **Phone:** 908-277-8713; **Board Cert:** Internal Medicine 1972; Cardiovascular Disease 1976; **Med School:** Georgetown Univ 1966; **Resid:** Internal Medicine, Georgetown Univ Hosp 1968; **Fellow:** Cardiovascular Disease, Emory Univ Hosp 1970; **Fac Appt:** Asst Clin Prof Med, Columbia P&S

Sheris, Steven J MD (Cv) - **Spec Exp:** Stress Echocardiography; Nuclear Cardiology; **Hospital:** Overlook Med Ctr (page 92), Morristown Med Ctr (page 92); **Address:** Assocs in Cardiovascular Disease, 571 Central Ave, Ste 115, New Providence, NJ 7974; **Phone:** 908-464-4200; **Board Cert:** Internal Medicine 2014; Cardiovascular Disease 2007; Nuclear Cardiology 2013; **Med School:** UMDNJ-Rutgers Med Sch 1988; **Resid:** Internal Medicine, Natl Naval Med Ctr 1994; **Fellow:** Cardiovascular Disease, Natl Naval Med Ctr 1997

Slama, Robert D MD (Cv) - **Spec Exp:** Echocardiography; Preventive Cardiology; Nuclear Cardiology; **Hospital:** Overlook Med Ctr (page 92), Morristown Med Ctr (page 92); **Address:** Summit Med Grp, Cardiology, 1 Diamond Hill Rd, Berkeley Heights, NJ 07922; **Phone:** 908-277-8714; **Board Cert:** Internal Medicine 1974; Cardiovascular Disease 1977; **Med School:** Temple Univ 1971; **Resid:** Internal Medicine, Boston Med Ctr 1973; Internal Medicine, Georgetown Univ Hosp 1974; **Fellow:** Cardiovascular Disease, Boston Med Ctr 1976

Child & Adolescent Psychiatry

Greenberg, Rosalie MD (ChAP) - **Spec Exp:** Bipolar/Mood Disorders; ADD/ADHD; **Hospital:** Overlook Med Ctr (page 92); **Address:** 33 Overlook Rd, Ste 406, Summit, NJ 07901; **Phone:** 908-598-0200; **Board Cert:** Psychiatry 1982; Child & Adolescent Psychiatry 1983; **Med School:** Columbia P&S 1976; **Resid:** Psychiatry, Columbia-Presby Hosp 1979; **Fellow:** Child & Adolescent Psychiatry, Columbia-Presby Hosp 1981; **Fac Appt:** Asst Clin Prof Psyc, Columbia P&S

Child Neurology

Traeger, Eveline C MD (ChiN) - **Spec Exp:** Autism; ADD/ADHD; Learning Disorders; **Hospital:** Children's Specialized Hosp; **Address:** Chldns Specialized Hosp, 150 New Providence Rd, Mountainside, NJ 07092; **Phone:** 908-233-3720; **Board Cert:** Child Neurology 2014; Clinical Genetics 1990; **Med School:** SUNY Buffalo 1984; **Resid:** Child Neurology, Yeshiva Univ 1988; Pediatrics, Jacobi Med Ctr 1994

Colon & Rectal Surgery

Abir, Farshad MD (CRS) - **Spec Exp:** Colon & Rectal Cancer; Laparoscopic Surgery; **Hospital:** Overlook Med Ctr (page 92); **Address:** Summit Med Grp, 1 Diamond Hill Rd Fl 4, Berkeley Heights, NJ 07922; **Phone:** 908-277-8950; **Board Cert:** Surgery 2005; Colon & Rectal Surgery 2007; **Med School:** SUNY Downstate 2000; **Resid:** Surgery, Yale-New Haven Hosp 2005; **Fellow:** Colon & Rectal Surgery, Cleveland Clin 2008

Chinn, Bertram T MD (CRS) - **Spec Exp:** Laparoscopic Surgery; Colon & Rectal Cancer; Inflammatory Bowel Disease; Diverticulitis; **Hospital:** Overlook Med Ctr (page 92), Robert Wood Johnson Univ Hosp - New Brunswick; **Address:** Associated Colon & Rectal Surgeons, Overlook Medical Center, 99 Beauvoir Ave, Cancer Ctr Fl 6, Summit, NJ 07902; **Phone:** 732-494-6640; **Board Cert:** Surgery 2002; Colon & Rectal Surgery 2012; **Med School:** Jefferson Med Coll 1987; **Resid:** Surgery, Thomas Jefferson Univ Hosp 1992; **Fellow:** Colon & Rectal Surgery, UMDNJ-RW Johnson Med Ctr 1993; **Fac Appt:** Assoc Clin Prof S, Rutgers R W Johnson Med Sch

Groff, Walter L MD (CRS) - **Spec Exp:** Colonoscopy; Rectal Cancer/Sphincter Preservation; **Hospital:** Overlook Med Ctr (page 92), St. Barnabas Med Ctr (page 94); **Address:** 33 Overlook Rd, Ste 412, Summit, NJ 07901-3564; **Phone:** 908-598-0220; **Board Cert:** Colon & Rectal Surgery 1980; **Med School:** Albany Med Coll 1970; **Resid:** Surgery, St Vincent's Hosp 1979; Colon & Rectal Surgery, Muhlenberg Med Ctr 1980; **Fac Appt:** Assoc Prof S, Columbia P&S

Dermatology

Eisenberg, Richard R MD (D) - **Spec Exp:** Skin Cancer; Melanoma; Acne; **Hospital:** Overlook Med Ctr (page 92); **Address:** 40 Stirling Rd, Ste 203, Watchung, NJ 07069; **Phone:** 908-753-4144; **Board Cert:** Internal Medicine 1985; Dermatology 1989; **Med School:** Cornell Univ-Weill Med Coll 1982; **Resid:** Internal Medicine, NY Hosp-Cornell Med Ctr 1985; Dermatology, NY Hosp-Cornell/Meml Sloan Kettering Cancer Ctr 1989

Weinberger, George I MD (D) - **Spec Exp:** Skin Cancer; **Hospital:** St. Barnabas Med Ctr (page 94); **Address:** 190 Greenbrook Rd, North Plainfield, NJ 07060-3903; **Phone:** 908-561-8070; **Board Cert:** Dermatology 1977; **Med School:** UMDNJ-NJ Med Sch, Newark 1973; **Resid:** Dermatology, Henry Ford Hosp 1977

Zirvi, Monib A MD (D) - **Spec Exp:** Cosmetic Dermatology; Skin Cancer; **Hospital:** Morristown Med Ctr (page 92), Overlook Med Ctr (page 92); **Address:** 1 Diamond Hill Rd, Laurence Bldg-2nd Fl, Berkeley Heights, NJ 07922; **Phone:** 908-769-0100; **Board Cert:** Dermatology 2012; **Med School:** Cornell Univ 2000; **Resid:** Dermatology, Hosp Univ Penn 2004

Diagnostic Radiology

Grosso-Rivas, Sue Jane MD (DR) - **Spec Exp:** Breast Imaging; Nuclear Radiology; CT Body Scan; **Hospital:** Overlook Med Ctr (page 92); **Address:** Summit Med Grp, 1 Diamond Hill Rd, Berkeley Heights, NJ 07922; **Phone:** 908-273-4300; **Board Cert:** Diagnostic Radiology 1991; **Med School:** Harvard Med Sch 1985; **Resid:** Diagnostic Radiology, NYU Med Ctr 1990; **Fellow:** Nuclear Radiology, NYU Med Ctr 1991

Rokhsar, Michael H DO (DR) - **Spec Exp:** Brain Imaging; Spinal Imaging; MRI; Head & Neck Imaging; **Hospital:** Overlook Med Ctr (page 92); **Address:** Westfield Imaging Ctr, 118-122 Elm St, Westfield, NJ 07090; **Phone:** 908-232-0290; **Board Cert:** Diagnostic Radiology 2001; Neuroradiology 2013; **Med School:** NY Coll Osteo Med 1996; **Resid:** Diagnostic Radiology, Overlook Hosp 2001; **Fellow:** Neurological Radiology, Beth Israel Med Ctr 2003

Endocrinology, Diabetes & Metabolism

Fuhrman, Robert A MD (EDM) - **Spec Exp:** Diabetes; Thyroid Disorders; Osteoporosis; **Hospital:** Overlook Med Ctr (page 92); **Address:** 552 Westfield Ave, Westfield, NJ 07090-3312; **Phone:** 908-654-3377; **Board Cert:** Internal Medicine 1971; Endocrinology, Diabetes & Metabolism 1972; **Med School:** Ros Franklin Univ/Chicago Med Sch 1966; **Resid:** Internal Medicine, Mount Sinai Hosp 1970; Nuclear Medicine, VA Hospital 1970; **Fellow:** Endocrinology, Diabetes & Metabolism, Mount Sinai Hosp 1970

Rosenbaum, Robert L MD (EDM) - **Spec Exp:** Thyroid Disorders; Diabetes; Osteoporosis; **Hospital:** Overlook Med Ctr (page 92); **Address:** Summit Med Grp, One Diamond Hill Rd, Berkeley Heights, NJ 07922-2104; **Phone:** 908-277-8667; **Board Cert:** Internal Medicine 1978; Endocrinology, Diabetes & Metabolism 1981; **Med School:** Columbia P&S 1975; **Resid:** Internal Medicine, Montefiore Hosp Med Ctr 1978; **Fellow:** Endocrinology, Diabetes & Metabolism, Montefiore Hosp Med Ctr 1980; **Fac Appt:** Asst Clin Prof Med, Mount Sinai Sch Med

Selinger, Sharon E MD (EDM) - **Spec Exp:** Diabetes; Thyroid Disorders; Pituitary Disorders; Osteoporosis; **Hospital:** Overlook Med Ctr (page 92); **Address:** Summit Endocrinology & Diabetes, 1 Springfield Ave, Ste 1A, Summit, NJ 07901; **Phone:** 908-273-8300; **Board Cert:** Internal Medicine 1984; Endocrinology, Diabetes & Metabolism 1987; **Med School:** Cornell Univ-Weill Med Coll 1981; **Resid:** Internal Medicine, Montefiore Hosp Med Ctr 1984; **Fellow:** Endocrinology, Diabetes & Metabolism, Bellevue Hosp-NYU Med Ctr 1986

Silverman, Mitchell S MD (EDM) - **Spec Exp:** Diabetes; Thyroid Disorders; Adrenal Disorders; **Hospital:** Newark Beth Israel Med Ctr (page 94), St. Barnabas Med Ctr (page 94); **Address:** 2333 Morris Ave, Fl 1, Ste B-109, Union, NJ 07083; **Phone:** 908-964-5511; **Board Cert:** Internal Medicine 1983; Endocrinology 1987; **Med School:** Duke Univ 1980; **Resid:** Internal Medicine, Emory Univ Hosp 1983; **Fellow:** Endocrinology, Diabetes & Metabolism, NY Hosp-Meml Sloan-Kettering 1988

Family Medicine

Eisenstat, Steven DO (FMed) *PCP* - **Spec Exp:** Osteoporosis; Hypertension; Alzheimer's Disease; **Hospital:** Overlook Med Ctr (page 92); **Address:** 1050 Galloping Hill Rd, Ste 202, Union, NJ 07083-7980; **Phone:** 908-688-4845; **Board Cert:** Family Medicine 1993; Geriatric Medicine 1991; **Med School:** Ohio State Univ 1984; **Resid:** Family Medicine, Union Hosp 1986; **Fac Appt:** Asst Clin Prof FMed, NY Coll Osteo Med

Podell, Richard N MD (FMed) *PCP* - **Spec Exp:** Complementary Medicine; Nutrition & Disease Prevention/Control; Fibromyalgia; Chronic Fatigue Syndrome; **Hospital:** Overlook Med Ctr (page 92); **Address:** Medical Arts Center, 11 Overlook Rd, Ste 140, Summit, NJ 07901; **Phone:** 908-273-7770; **Board Cert:** Internal Medicine 1980; Family Medicine 2005; **Med School:** Harvard Med Sch 1969; **Resid:** Internal Medicine, Mt Sinai Hosp 1972; **Fellow:** Nutrition, Harvard Sch Pub Hlth 1973; **Fac Appt:** Clin Prof FMed, Rutgers R W Johnson Med Sch

Tabachnick, John F MD (FMed) *PCP* - **Hospital:** Overlook Med Ctr (page 92); **Address:** 563 Westfield Ave, Westfield, NJ 07090; **Phone:** 908-232-5858; **Board Cert:** Family Medicine 2007; **Med School:** Mount Sinai Sch Med 1979; **Resid:** Family Medicine, Overlook Hosp 1982; **Fac Appt:** Asst Clin Prof FMed, UMDNJ Sch Osteo Med

Wagner, Claudia A MD (FMed) *PCP* - **Hospital:** Overlook Med Ctr (page 92); **Address:** 563 Westfield Ave, Westfield Family Practice, Westfield, NJ 07090-3300; **Phone:** 908-232-5858; **Board Cert:** Family Medicine 2013; **Med School:** Mount Sinai Sch Med 1988; **Resid:** Family Medicine, Overlook Med Ctr 1991

Gastroenterology

Barrison, Adam F MD (Ge) - **Spec Exp:** Endoscopy; **Hospital:** Overlook Med Ctr (page 92); **Address:** Summit Medical Group, 1 Diamond Hill Rd, Berkeley Heights, NJ 07922; **Phone:** 908-277-8940; **Board Cert:** Gastroenterology 2011; **Med School:** NYU Sch Med 1995; **Resid:** Internal Medicine, Beth Israel Hosp 1998; **Fellow:** Gastroenterology, Boston Univ Med Ctr 2001

Ben-Menachem, Tamir MD (Ge) - **Spec Exp:** Endoscopy; Pancreatic/Biliary Endoscopy (ERCP); Endoscopic Ultrasound; **Hospital:** Overlook Med Ctr (page 92); **Address:** Summit Med Grp, Gastroenterology, 1 Diamond Hill Rd, Berkeley Heights, NJ 07922; **Phone:** 908-277-8940; **Board Cert:** Internal Medicine 2004; Gastroenterology 2007; **Med School:** Israel 1989; **Resid:** Internal Medicine, Henry Ford Hosp 1994; **Fellow:** Gastroenterology, Henry Ford Hosp 1997; **Fac Appt:** Assoc Prof Med, Rutgers R W Johnson Med Sch

Feit, David MD (Ge) - **Spec Exp:** Hepatitis; **Hospital:** Hackensack Univ Med Ctr (page 96); **Address:** Hackensack Digestive Diseases Assocs, 385 Prospect Ave, Hackensack, NJ 07061; **Phone:** 201-488-3003; **Board Cert:** Internal Medicine 1984; Gastroenterology 1989; **Med School:** Columbia P&S 1981; **Resid:** Internal Medicine, Columbia-Presby Med Ctr 1984; **Fellow:** Gastroenterology, Columbia-Presby Med Ctr 1987

Goldenberg, David MD (Ge) - **Spec Exp:** Inflammatory Bowel Disease/Crohn's; Biliary Disease; Gastroesophageal Reflux Disease (GERD); **Hospital:** JFK Med Ctr - Edison, Robert Wood Johnson Univ Hosp - Somerset; **Address:** Gastroenterology Assocs, 1165 Park Ave, Plainfield, NJ 70603010; **Phone:** 908-754-2992; **Board Cert:** Internal Medicine 1977; Gastroenterology 1981; **Med School:** NY Med Coll 1974; **Resid:** Internal Medicine, Metropolitan Hosp 1977; **Fellow:** Gastroenterology, Emory Univ Hosp 1980; **Fac Appt:** Asst Clin Prof Med, UMDNJ-NJ Med Sch, Newark

Kerner, Michael B MD (Ge) - **Spec Exp:** Colonoscopy; Biliary Disease; Gastroesophageal Reflux Disease (GERD); Inflammatory Bowel Disease; **Hospital:** Overlook Med Ctr (page 92), Morristown Med Ctr (page 92); **Address:** Assocs in Digestive Diseases, 25 Morris Ave, Springfield, NJ 07081-1406; **Phone:** 973-467-1313; **Board Cert:** Internal Medicine 1975; Gastroenterology 1977; **Med School:** Wake Forest Univ 1971; **Resid:** Internal Medicine, NYU Med Ctr 1974; **Fellow:** Gastroenterology, Manhattan VA-Bellevue Hosp 1976; **Fac Appt:** Asst Clin Prof Med, Mount Sinai Sch Med

Khan, Amber M MD (Ge) - **Spec Exp:** Colon & Rectal Cancer; Esophageal Disorders; Crohn's Disease; Liver Disease; **Hospital:** Overlook Med Ctr (page 92), Robert Wood Johnson Univ Hosp - Somerset; **Address:** 571 Central Ave Bldg 4 - Ste 112, New Providence, NJ 07974; **Phone:** 908-522-1313; **Board Cert:** Gastroenterology 2007; **Med School:** Philippines 1990; **Resid:** Internal Medicine, Mt Auburn Hosp 1995; **Fellow:** Gastroenterology, Univ Hosp-SUNY Stony Brook 1997

Mahal, Pradeep MD (Ge) - **Spec Exp:** Gastrointestinal Cancer; **Hospital:** Overlook Med Ctr (page 92), Trinitas Reg Med Ctr (page 946); **Address:** 1308 Morris Ave, Ste 202, Union, NJ 07083; **Phone:** 908-851-6767; **Board Cert:** Gastroenterology 1981; Internal Medicine 1978; Medical Oncology 1983; **Med School:** India 1975; **Resid:** Internal Medicine, UMDNJ Univ Hosp 1978; **Fellow:** Medical Oncology, MD Anderson Tumor Inst 1979

Tempera, Patrick G MD (Ge) - **Spec Exp:** Biliary Disease; Pancreatic Disease; Gastroesophageal Reflux Disease (GERD); **Hospital:** Overlook Med Ctr (page 92), Robert Wood Johnson Univ Hosp - Somerset; **Address:** 1308 Morris Ave, Ste 102, Union, NJ 07083; **Phone:** 908-851-2770; **Board Cert:** Gastroenterology 2004; **Med School:** Grenada 1986; **Resid:** Internal Medicine, Seton Hall Univ Hosp 1990; **Fellow:** Gastroenterology, Seton Hall Univ Hosp 1992; **Fac Appt:** Assoc Prof Med, Seton Hall Univ Sch Hlth & Med Scis

Geriatric Medicine

Khimani, Karim J MD (Ger) *PCP* - **Spec Exp:** Geriatric Medicine; Alzheimer's Disease; Dementia; Long Term Care; **Hospital:** Trinitas Reg Med Ctr (page 946); **Address:** 240 Williamson St, Ste 306, Elizabeth, NJ 07202; **Phone:** 908-352-5071; **Board Cert:** Internal Medicine 1986; Hospice & Palliative Medicine 2008; **Med School:** Dominica 1982; **Resid:** Internal Medicine, St Elizabeth Hosp 1985; **Fac Appt:** Asst Clin Prof Med, Seton Hall Univ Sch Hlth & Med Scis

Solomon, Robert B MD (Ger) *PCP* - **Spec Exp:** Alzheimer's Disease; Osteoporosis; **Hospital:** Trinitas Reg Med Ctr (page 946), Overlook Med Ctr (page 92); **Address:** 744 Galloping Hill Rd, Roselle Park, NJ 07204-1758; **Phone:** 908-241-0044; **Board Cert:** Internal Medicine 1980; Geriatric Medicine 2008; **Med School:** SUNY Hlth Sci Ctr 1977; **Resid:** Internal Medicine, Westchester Med Ctr 1980; **Fellow:** Geriatric Medicine, NY Hosp 1981

Hematology

Kessler, William W MD (Hem) - **Hospital:** Trinitas Reg Med Ctr (page 946); **Address:** 225 Williamson St, Elizabeth, NJ 07083; **Phone:** 908-994-8773; **Board Cert:** Internal Medicine 1978; Hematology 1980; **Med School:** Albert Einstein Coll Med 1975; **Resid:** Internal Medicine, UMDNJ-Newark 1978; **Fellow:** Hematology, VA Hosp 1979

Infectious Disease

Farrer, William Eric MD (Inf) - **Spec Exp:** AIDS/HIV; Diabetic Leg/Foot Infections; Travel Medicine; **Hospital:** Trinitas Reg Med Ctr (page 946); **Address:** Union County Infectious Disease Group, 240 Williamson St, Ste 502, Elizabeth, NJ 07202; **Phone:** 908-994-5300; **Board Cert:** Internal Medicine 1978; Infectious Disease 1980; **Med School:** Harvard Med Sch 1975; **Resid:** Internal Medicine, Montefiore Med Ctr 1978; **Fellow:** Infectious Disease, Montefiore Med Ctr 1980; **Fac Appt:** Assoc Prof Med, Seton Hall Univ Sch Hlth & Med Scis

Greenman, James L MD (Inf) - **Spec Exp:** AIDS/HIV; Lyme Disease; **Hospital:** Overlook Med Ctr (page 92); **Address:** Medical Diagnostic Associates, 525 Central Ave, Ste C, Westfield, NJ 07090; **Phone:** 908-233-0895; **Board Cert:** Internal Medicine 1985; Infectious Disease 1988; **Med School:** Albert Einstein Coll Med 1982; **Resid:** Internal Medicine, Columbia-Presby Med Ctr 1985; **Fellow:** Infectious Disease, Montefiore Med Ctr 1987

Roland, Robert DO (Inf) - **Spec Exp:** AIDS/HIV; Travel Medicine; Hepatitis C; **Hospital:** Overlook Med Ctr (page 92), Robert Wood Johnson Univ Hosp at Rahway; **Address:** Overlook Hosp Wound Healing Program, 11 Overlook Rd, Bldg II, Ste LL101, Summit, NJ 07901; **Phone:** 908-522-5900; **Board Cert:** Internal Medicine 1990; Infectious Disease 1992; **Med School:** Kirksville Coll Osteo Med 1985; **Resid:** Internal Medicine, Union Hosp 1989; **Fellow:** Infectious Disease, Kennedy Meml Hosp 1991; **Fac Appt:** Asst Clin Prof Med, NY Coll Osteo Med

Internal Medicine

Alterman, Lloyd H MD (IM) - **Spec Exp:** Hypertension; Kidney Disease-Chronic; **Hospital:** Overlook Med Ctr (page 92); **Address:** 1 Diamond Hill Rd, Berkeley Heights, NJ 07922; **Phone:** 908-277-8683; **Board Cert:** Internal Medicine 1980; Nephrology 1982; **Med School:** Wayne State Univ 1977; **Resid:** Internal Medicine, Overlook Hosp 1980; **Fellow:** Nephrology, Montefiore Med Ctr 1982

DiGiacomo, William A MD (IM) *PCP* - **Hospital:** Saint Michael's Med Ctr, Overlook Med Ctr (page 92); **Address:** 2801 Morris Ave, Union, NJ 07083; **Phone:** 908-851-2500; **Board Cert:** Internal Medicine 1978; **Med School:** Mexico 1974; **Resid:** Internal Medicine, St Michaels Med Ctr 1978; **Fac Appt:** Assoc Prof Med, Seton Hall Univ Sch Hlth & Med Scis

Feldman, Jeffrey N MD (IM) - **Spec Exp:** Kidney Disease-Chronic; Cholesterol/Lipid Disorders; Diabetes; Hypertension; **Hospital:** Overlook Med Ctr (page 92); **Address:** 440 Chestnut St, Fl 1, Union, NJ 07083-9306; **Phone:** 908-686-9330; **Board Cert:** Internal Medicine 1979; Nephrology 1982; **Med School:** Hahnemann Univ 1976; **Resid:** Internal Medicine, Bronx Municipal Hosp 1979; **Fellow:** Nephrology, SUNY Hlth Sci Ctr 1981

Goodgold, Abraham MD (IM) *PCP* - **Hospital:** Trinitas Reg Med Ctr (page 946), Robert Wood Johnson Univ Hosp at Rahway; **Address:** Union County Hlthcare Assocs, 310 W Jersey St, Elizabeth, NJ 07202-1832; **Phone:** 908-351-2222; **Board Cert:** Internal Medicine 1977; **Med School:** NYU Sch Med 1973; **Resid:** Internal Medicine, Montefiore Med Ctr 1976; **Fellow:** Endocrinology, Mt Sinai Med Ctr 1978

Maglaras, Nicholas C MD (IM) *PCP* - **Hospital:** Trinitas Reg Med Ctr (page 946); **Address:** 236 E Westfield Ave, Ste 5, Roselle Park, NJ 07204; **Phone:** 908-245-8222; **Board Cert:** Internal Medicine 2013; Pulmonary Disease 2006; **Med School:** Grenada 1987; **Resid:** Internal Medicine, Elmhurst Hosp 1990; **Fellow:** Pulmonary Disease, Elmhurst Hosp 1992

Interventional Cardiology

Lux, Michael S MD (IC) - **Hospital:** Overlook Med Ctr (page 92), Morristown Med Ctr (page 92); **Address:** Assocs in Cardiovascular Disease, 211 Mountain Ave, Springfield, NJ 07081-1581; **Phone:** 973-467-0005; **Board Cert:** Internal Medicine 1980; Cardiovascular Disease 1985; **Med School:** NYU Sch Med 1977; **Resid:** Internal Medicine, Johns Hopkins Hosp 1980; **Fellow:** Cardiovascular Disease, Johns Hopkins Hosp 1983; **Fac Appt:** Asst Prof Med, Columbia P&S

Mich, Robert J MD (IC) - **Spec Exp:** Arrhythmias; **Hospital:** Morristown Med Ctr (page 92), Overlook Med Ctr (page 92); **Address:** Assocs in Cardiovascular Disease, 571 Central Ave, Ste 115, New Providence, NJ 07974; **Phone:** 908-464-4200; **Board Cert:** Internal Medicine 1984; Cardiovascular Disease 1985; **Med School:** Johns Hopkins Univ 1979; **Resid:** Internal Medicine, John Hopkins Hosp 1982; **Fellow:** Cardiovascular Disease, Vanderbilt Univ Hosp 1984; Cardiovascular Disease, Mass Genl Hosp 1986

Medical Oncology

Guerin, Bonni L MD (Onc) - **Spec Exp:** Breast Cancer; **Hospital:** Overlook Med Ctr (page 92); **Address:** Medical Diagnostic Assocs, Overlook Oncology Ctr, 99 Beauvoir Ave Fl 5, Summit, NJ 07902; **Phone:** 908-608-0078; **Board Cert:** Internal Medicine 2005; Medical Oncology 2005; **Med School:** SUNY Stony Brook 1988; **Resid:** Internal Medicine, Vanderbilt Univ Med Ctr 1991; **Fellow:** Medical Oncology, UCSD Cancer Ctr 1993

Lowenthal, Dennis A MD (Onc) - **Spec Exp:** Lung Cancer; Hematology; Prostate Cancer; Leukemia & Lymphoma; **Hospital:** Overlook Med Ctr (page 92); **Address:** The Carol G. Simon Cancer Center, Overlook Medical Center, 99 Beauvoir Ave, Summit, NJ 07902; **Phone:** 908-608-0078; **Board Cert:** Internal Medicine 1982; Medical Oncology 1985; Hematology 1986; **Med School:** Boston Univ 1979; **Resid:** Internal Medicine, Montefiore Med Ctr 1982; **Fellow:** Hematology, Montefiore Med Ctr 1983; Medical Oncology, Mem Sloan Kettering Cancer Ctr 1986; **Fac Appt:** Asst Clin Prof Med, Mount Sinai Sch Med

Moriarty, Daniel J MD (Onc) - **Spec Exp:** Gastrointestinal Cancer; **Hospital:** Overlook Med Ctr (page 92); **Address:** Med Diagnostic Assocs, 99 Beauvoir Ave Fl 5, Summit, NJ 07902; **Phone:** 908-608-0078; **Board Cert:** Internal Medicine 1982; Medical Oncology 1987; **Med School:** Univ VT Coll Med 1976; **Resid:** Internal Medicine, Cambridge Hosp 1984; **Fellow:** Hematology & Oncology, St Elizabeth Hosp 1987

Wax, Michael B MD (Onc) - **Spec Exp:** Breast Cancer; Hematologic Malignancies; **Hospital:** Overlook Med Ctr (page 92); **Address:** Summit Med Grp, Med Oncology, 1 Diamond Hill Rd, Berkeley Heights, NJ 07922; **Phone:** 908-277-8890; **Board Cert:** Internal Medicine 1980; Medical Oncology 1983; **Med School:** Med Coll PA Hahnemann 1977; **Resid:** Internal Medicine, Hosp Univ Penn 1980; **Fellow:** Hematology & Oncology, Fred Hutchinson Cancer Rsch Ctr 1982; **Fac Appt:** Asst Prof Med, Mount Sinai-Icahn Sch of Med

Nephrology

Goldstein, Carl S MD (Nep) - **Spec Exp:** Hypertension; Hypertension in Pregnancy; Kidney Failure; Hypertension/Kidney Disease; **Hospital:** Overlook Med Ctr (page 92); **Address:** 215 North Ave W, Westfield, NJ 07090-1428; **Phone:** 908-232-4321; **Board Cert:** Internal Medicine 1981; Nephrology 1984; **Med School:** Washington Univ, St Louis 1978; **Resid:** Internal Medicine, Univ Minn Med Ctr 1981; **Fellow:** Nephrology, Hosp Univ Penn 1984; **Fac Appt:** Clin Prof Med, Mount Sinai Sch Med

McAnally, James F MD (Nep) - **Spec Exp:** Kidney Disease; Hypertension; Diabetes; **Hospital:** Trinitas Reg Med Ctr (page 946); **Address:** 240 Williamson St, Ste 307, Elizabeth, NJ 07202-3672; **Phone:** 908-994-9200; **Board Cert:** Internal Medicine 1978; Nephrology 1980; **Med School:** UMDNJ-NJ Med Sch, Newark 1975; **Resid:** Internal Medicine, UMDNJ-Newark Affil Hosp 1978; Internal Medicine, Georgetown Univ Hosp 1980; **Fellow:** Nephrology, Georgetown Univ Hosp 1980; **Fac Appt:** Assoc Clin Prof Med, Seton Hall Univ Sch Hlth & Med Scis

Neurological Surgery

Friedlander, Marvin E MD (NS) - **Spec Exp:** Spinal Surgery; **Hospital:** Trinitas Reg Med Ctr (page 946), Overlook Med Ctr (page 92); **Address:** 700 Rahway Ave, Union, NJ 07083; **Phone:** 908-688-1999; **Board Cert:** Neurological Surgery 1994; **Med School:** SUNY Downstate 1982; **Resid:** Neurological Surgery, Kings Co Hosp 1989

Hodosh, Richard M MD (NS) - **Spec Exp:** Spinal Surgery; Pain-Back; Carpal Tunnel Syndrome; Stroke; **Hospital:** Overlook Med Ctr (page 92), Morristown Med Ctr (page 92); **Address:** Atlantic Brain & Spine Institute, 99 Beauvoir Ave, MS 07902, Clinical Office MAC 1, ste 405, Summit, NJ 07901; **Phone:** 908-522-4979; **Board Cert:** Neurological Surgery 1980; **Med School:** Univ Cincinnati 1972; **Resid:** Neurological Surgery, Univ Tex Hlth Scis Ctr 1978; **Fellow:** Neuroradiology, Natl Hosp Neur Dis 1975; Neurological Surgery, Kantonsspital 1976

Neurology

Bansil, Shalini M MD (N) - **Spec Exp:** Stroke; **Hospital:** Overlook Med Ctr (page 92); **Address:** Overlook Med Ctr, Stroke Ctr, 99 Beauvoir Ave, Summit, NJ 07902; **Phone:** 908-522-5545; **Board Cert:** Neurology 1989; Vascular Neurology 2006; **Med School:** India 1983; **Resid:** Neurology, UMDNJ Med Ctr 1988; **Fellow:** Stroke, Beth Israel Med Ctr 1989

Coohill, Lisa M MD (N) - **Spec Exp:** Headache; Migraine; Memory Disorders; Alzheimer's Disease; **Hospital:** Overlook Med Ctr (page 92); **Address:** Summit Medical Grp, 1 Diamond Hill Rd, Whitman Pavilion Fl 2, Berkshire Heights, NJ 07922; **Phone:** 908-277-8639; **Board Cert:** Neurology 2010; **Med School:** UMDNJ-NJ Med Sch, Newark 1991; **Resid:** Internal Medicine, Monmouth Med Ctr 1992; Neurology, NYU Med Ctr 1995; **Fellow:** Neurological Rehabilitation, NYU Hosp for Joint Diseases 2002

Halperin, John MD (N) - **Spec Exp:** Neuromuscular Disorders; Lyme Disease; Neuro-Immunology; Neuromyelitis Optica; **Hospital:** Overlook Med Ctr (page 92), Morristown Med Ctr (page 92); **Address:** Overlook Med Ctr, Neurology, 99 Beauvoir Ave, Summit, NJ 07902; **Phone:** 908-522-2829; **Board Cert:** Internal Medicine 1978; Neurology 1982; Clinical Neurophysiology 2005; **Med School:** Harvard Med Sch 1975; **Resid:** Internal Medicine, Univ Chicago Med Ctr 1977; Neurology, Mass Genl Hosp 1980; **Fellow:** Neuromuscular Disease, Mass Genl Hosp 1983; **Fac Appt:** Prof N, Mount Sinai-Icahn Sch of Med

Kurlan, Roger M MD (N) - **Spec Exp:** ADD/ADHD; Tourette's Syndrome; **Hospital:** Overlook Med Ctr (page 92); **Address:** 99 Beauvoir Ave, Summit, NJ 07902; **Phone:** 908-522-6144; **Board Cert:** Neurology 1984; **Med School:** Washington Univ, St Louis 1978; **Resid:** Neurology, Univ Rochester Med Ctr 1983; **Fellow:** Movement Disorders, Univ Rochester 1984

Politsky, Jeffrey M MD (N) - **Spec Exp:** Epilepsy/Seizure Disorders; Critical Care; **Hospital:** Overlook Med Ctr (page 92), Morristown Med Ctr (page 92); **Address:** Atlantic Neuroscience Institute, Overlook Medical Center, 99 Beauvoir Ave, Summit, NJ 07901; **Phone:** 908-522-4990; **Board Cert:** Neurology 2005; **Med School:** Canada 1994; **Resid:** Neurology, Univ British Columbia 1999; **Fellow:** Epilepsy, Harvard Med Sch-Mass Genl Hosp 2001; **Fac Appt:** Assoc Clin Prof N, Mount Sinai Sch Med

Pollock, Jeffrey C MD (N) - **Hospital:** Overlook Med Ctr (page 92); **Address:** 47 Maple St, Ste 104, Summit, NJ 07901; **Phone:** 908-277-2722; **Board Cert:** Neurology 1987; **Med School:** Med Coll GA 1982; **Resid:** Psychiatry, UMDNJ Mental Hlth Ctr 1983; Neurology, UMDNJ Med Ctr 1986

Sachs, Stephen M MD (N) - **Spec Exp:** Headache; Stroke; Dementia; Parkinson's Disease; **Hospital:** Robert Wood Johnson Univ Hosp at Rahway, Trinitas Reg Med Ctr (page 946); **Address:** 700 N Broad St, Ste 201, Elizabeth, NJ 07208; **Phone:** 908-354-3994; **Board Cert:** Neurology 1977; **Med School:** Univ Pennsylvania 1971; **Resid:** Internal Medicine, Bellevue Hosp 1973; Neurology, Columbia-Presby Med Ctr 1976

Schanzer, Bernard MD (N) - **Spec Exp:** Stroke; Headache; Multiple Sclerosis; Amyotrophic Lateral Sclerosis (ALS); **Hospital:** Trinitas Reg Med Ctr (page 946), Robert Wood Johnson Univ Hosp at Rahway; **Address:** 700 N Broad St, Ste 201, Elizabeth, NJ 07208; **Phone:** 908-354-3994; **Board Cert:** Neurology 1972; **Med School:** Belgium 1962; **Resid:** Internal Medicine, Maimonides Med Ctr 1965; Neurology, Bronx Muni Med Ctr 1969; **Fac Appt:** Assoc Clin Prof N, UMDNJ-NJ Med Sch, Newark

Neuroradiology

Horner, Neil B MD (NRad) - **Spec Exp:** MRI & CT of Brain & Spine; Spine Imaging & Intervention; Brain Imaging; Head & Neck Imaging; **Hospital:** Overlook Med Ctr (page 92); **Address:** Overlook Med Ctr, Radiology, 99 Beauvoir Ave, Summit, NJ 07902; **Phone:** 908-522-2253; **Board Cert:** Diagnostic Radiology 1988; Nuclear Radiology 1989; Neuroradiology 2005; **Med School:** UMDNJ-Rutgers Med Sch 1983; **Resid:** Diagnostic Radiology, NYU Med Ctr 1988; **Fellow:** Neuroradiology, NYU Med Ctr 1989; Nuclear Radiology, NYU Med Ctr 1989; **Fac Appt:** Assoc Clin Prof Rad, Mount Sinai-Icahn Sch of Med

Obstetrics & Gynecology

Beim, Robert B MD (ObG) - **Spec Exp:** Laparoscopic Surgery; Minimally Invasive Surgery; Colposcopy; **Hospital:** St. Peter's Univ Hosp, JFK Med Ctr - Edison; **Address:** 190 Greenbrook Rd, N Plainfield, NJ 07060; **Phone:** 908-756-6812; **Board Cert:** Obstetrics & Gynecology 2013; **Med School:** SUNY Upstate Med Univ 1989; **Resid:** Obstetrics & Gynecology, Robert Wood Johnson Univ Hosp 1993; **Fac Appt:** Asst Clin Prof ObG, Drexel Univ Coll Med

Frattarola, Michael A MD (ObG) - **Hospital:** Overlook Med Ctr (page 92); **Address:** 950 W Chestnut St, Ste 102, Union, NJ 07083; **Phone:** 908-688-8545; **Board Cert:** Obstetrics & Gynecology 1984; **Med School:** UMDNJ-NJ Med Sch, Newark 1973; **Resid:** Obstetrics & Gynecology, Univ Hosp-UMDNJ 1976

Hyman, Martin C MD (ObG) - **Spec Exp:** Gynecology Only; **Hospital:** Overlook Med Ctr (page 92); **Address:** 950 W Chestnut St, Ste 102, Union, NJ 07083; **Phone:** 908-688-8545; **Board Cert:** Obstetrics & Gynecology 1983; **Med School:** Mexico 1976; **Resid:** Obstetrics & Gynecology, Newark Beth Israel 1981

Margulis, Elynne B MD (ObG) - **Spec Exp:** Infertility; **Hospital:** Overlook Med Ctr (page 92); **Address:** 522 E Broad St, Westfield, NJ 07090; **Phone:** 908-232-4449; **Board Cert:** Obstetrics & Gynecology 1985; **Med School:** Columbia P&S 1978; **Resid:** Obstetrics & Gynecology, Hosp Univ Penn 1982

Soffer, Jeffrey L MD (ObG) - **Hospital:** Overlook Med Ctr (page 92); **Address:** 522 E Broad St, Westfield, NJ 07090; **Phone:** 908-232-4449; **Board Cert:** Obstetrics & Gynecology 1983; **Med School:** Howard Univ 1975; **Resid:** Obstetrics & Gynecology, Pennsylvania Hosp-UPHS 1979

Ophthalmology

Confino, Joel MD (Oph) - **Spec Exp:** Laser Vision Surgery; Cataract Surgery; Corneal Disease & Transplant; LASIK-Refractive Surgery; **Hospital:** Overlook Med Ctr (page 92); **Address:** 592 Springfield Ave, Westfield, NJ 07090-1002; **Phone:** 908-789-8999; **Board Cert:** Ophthalmology 1985; **Med School:** Albert Einstein Coll Med 1980; **Resid:** Ophthalmology, Mt Sinai Med Ctr 1984; **Fellow:** Cornea & Ext Eye Disease, UCSD Med Ctr 1985

Natale, Benjamin P DO (Oph) - **Spec Exp:** Glaucoma; Cataract Surgery; Diabetic Eye Disease/Retinopathy; Macular Degeneration; **Hospital:** St. Barnabas Med Ctr (page 94); **Address:** Assoc Eye Phys & Surgeons of NJ, 1050 Galloping Hill Rd, Ste 104, Union, NJ 70837983; **Phone:** 908-964-7878; **Board Cert:** Ophthalmology 1991; **Med School:** Des Moines Univ 1980; **Resid:** Family Medicine, Union Hosp 1982; Ophthalmology, UMDNJ Affil Hosps 1985; **Fellow:** Refractive Surgery, Newark Eye & Ear Infirm 1986

Orthopaedic Surgery

Barmakian, Joseph T MD (OrS) - **Spec Exp:** Carpal Tunnel Syndrome; Nerve & Tendon Reconstruction; Shoulder Reconstruction; **Hospital:** Overlook Med Ctr (page 92); **Address:** 574 Springfield Ave, Westfield, NJ 07090-3300; **Phone:** 908-232-7797; **Board Cert:** Orthopaedic Surgery 2013; Hand Surgery 2013; **Med School:** Rutgers R W Johnson Med Sch 1984; **Resid:** Surgery, G Washington Univ Hosp 1986; Orthopaedic Surgery, NY-Presby/Columbia Univ Med Ctr 1989; **Fellow:** Hand Surgery, NYU Hosp For Joint Dis 1990

Botwin, Clifford A DO (OrS) - **Spec Exp:** Arthroscopic Surgery; **Hospital:** Overlook Med Ctr (page 92), Bayonne Med Ctr; **Address:** Assoc Orthopaedics, 1000 Galloping Hill Rd, Ste 202, Union, NJ 07083-6936; **Phone:** 908-964-6600; **Board Cert:** Orthopaedic Surgery 1985; **Med School:** Kansas City Univ of Med & Biosciences(Ostepathic) 1971; **Resid:** Orthopaedic Surgery, Delaware Valley Hosp 1976

Drzala, Mark R MD (OrS) - **Spec Exp:** Spinal Surgery; **Hospital:** Hackensack UMC-Mountainside (page 802), Overlook Med Ctr (page 92); **Address:** NJ Spine Specialists, 33 Overlook Rd, Ste 305, Summit, NJ 07901; **Phone:** 908-608-9610; **Board Cert:** Orthopaedic Surgery 2012; **Med School:** UMDNJ-NJ Med Sch, Newark 1991; **Resid:** Orthopaedic Surgery, UMDNJ-NJ Med Sch Affil Hosp 1997; **Fellow:** Spine Surgery, UCSF Med Ctr 1998; **Fac Appt:** Asst Clin Prof OrS, UMDNJ-NJ Med Sch, Newark

Gallick, Gregory S MD (OrS) - **Spec Exp:** Sports Medicine; Knee Reconstruction; Shoulder Reconstruction; Arthroscopic Surgery; **Hospital:** Overlook Med Ctr (page 92); **Address:** 2780 Morris Ave, Ste 2C, Union, NJ 07083; **Phone:** 908-686-6665; **Board Cert:** Orthopaedic Surgery 2009; **Med School:** UMDNJ-Rutgers Med Sch 1980; **Resid:** Surgery, UMDNJ Affil Hosps 1981; Orthopaedic Surgery, UMDNJ Affil Hosps 1985; **Fellow:** Interventional Cardiology, So CA Sports Med 1986

Innella, Robin R DO (OrS) - **Spec Exp:** Sports Medicine; Hip & Knee Replacement; Fractures; **Hospital:** Overlook Med Ctr (page 92); **Address:** Associated Orthopaedics, 1000 Galloping Hill Rd, Ste 202, Union, NJ 07083; **Phone:** 908-964-6600; **Board Cert:** Orthopaedic Surgery 1991; Sports Medicine 1998; **Med School:** Philadelphia Coll Osteo Med 1982; **Resid:** Orthopaedic Surgery, Kennedy Mem Hosp-Univ Med Ctr 1987; **Fac Appt:** Asst Clin Prof S, NY Coll Osteo Med

Mackessy, Richard P MD (OrS) - **Spec Exp:** Hand Surgery; **Hospital:** Trinitas Reg Med Ctr (page 946), Robert Wood Johnson Univ Hosp at Rahway; **Address:** Union City Orthopaedic Grp, 210 W St Georges Ave, Linden, NJ 07036; **Phone:** 908-486-1111; **Board Cert:** Orthopaedic Surgery 2007; Hand Surgery 2007; **Med School:** UMDNJ-NJ Med Sch, Newark 1978; **Resid:** Surgery, St Vincents Hosp 1980; Orthopaedic Surgery, St. Luke's - Roosevelt Hosp Ctr - St Luke's Hosp 1983; **Fellow:** Hand Surgery, Thomas Jefferson Univ Hosp 1984

Sarokhan, Alan J MD (OrS) - **Spec Exp:** Hip & Knee Replacement; Hand Surgery; **Hospital:** Overlook Med Ctr (page 92), St. Barnabas Med Ctr (page 94); **Address:** 33 Overlook Rd, Med Arts Bldg - Ste 201, Summit, NJ 07901-3562; **Phone:** 908-522-4555; **Board Cert:** Orthopaedic Surgery 2007; **Med School:** Harvard Med Sch 1977; **Resid:** Surgery, Brigham & Women's Hosp 1979; Orthopaedic Surgery, Harvard Affil Hosps 1982; **Fellow:** Hand Surgery, St. Luke's - Roosevelt Hosp Ctr - Roosevelt Div 1983

Otolaryngology

Carniol, Paul J MD (Oto) - **Spec Exp:** Facial Plastic & Reconstructive Surgery; Cosmetic Surgery; Skin Cancer; Melanoma; **Hospital:** Overlook Med Ctr (page 92), Univ Hosp-Newark; **Address:** Medical Arts Bldg, 33 Overlook Rd, Ste 401, Summit, NJ 07901; **Phone:** 908-598-1400; **Board Cert:** Otolaryngology 1981; Facial Plastic & Reconstr Surgery 1991; **Med School:** Univ Pennsylvania 1976; **Resid:** Surgery, Hosp of Univ of Pennsylvania 1977; Surgery, North SHore Univ Hosp 1978; **Fellow:** Otolaryngology, Mass Eye & Ear Infirm 1981; Plastic/Reconstructive Surgery, Hosp Univ Penn 1983; **Fac Appt:** Clin Prof Oto, UMDNJ-NJ Med Sch, Newark

Drake III, William MD (Oto) - **Spec Exp:** Endoscopic Sinus Surgery; Head & Neck Surgery; Thyroid & Parathyroid Cancer & Surgery; **Hospital:** Overlook Med Ctr (page 92); **Address:** 213 Summit Rd, Mountainside, NJ 07092; **Phone:** 908-233-2111; **Board Cert:** Otolaryngology 1995; **Med School:** UMDNJ-NJ Med Sch, Newark 1989; **Resid:** Otolaryngology, Mt Sinai Med Ctr 1994

Kwartler, Jed A MD (Oto) - **Spec Exp:** Acoustic Neuroma; Balance Disorders; Cochlear Implants; Cholesteatoma; **Hospital:** Overlook Med Ctr (page 92); **Address:** Summit Med Grp, 1 Diamond Hill Rd, Lawrence Pavillion Fl 2, Berkeley Heights, NJ 07922; **Phone:** 908-277-8681; **Board Cert:** Otolaryngology 1988; Neurotology 2010; **Med School:** UMDNJ-NJ Med Sch, Newark 1983; **Resid:** Surgery, UMDNJ/Univ Hosp 1985; Otolaryngology, UMDNJ/Univ Hosp 1988; **Fellow:** Otology & Neurotology, House Ear Clin and Inst 1990; **Fac Appt:** Assoc Clin Prof Oto, UMDNJ-NJ Med Sch, Newark

Presti, Paul MD (Oto) - **Spec Exp:** Head & Neck Surgery; Facial Plastic & Reconstructive Surgery; Cosmetic Surgery; **Hospital:** Overlook Med Ctr (page 92); **Address:** 213 Summit Rd, Mountainside, NJ 07092; **Phone:** 908-233-2111; **Board Cert:** Otolaryngology 2008; Facial Plastic & Reconstr Surgery 2011; **Med School:** Georgetown Univ 2002; **Resid:** Otolaryngology, NY Eye & Ear Infirm 2007; **Fellow:** Facial Plastic Surgery, Rousso Facial Plastic Surgery Clin 2008

Scharf, Richard C DO (Oto) - **Spec Exp:** Sinus Disorders/Surgery; Cosmetic Surgery-Face; Head & Neck Cancer; Sleep Apnea; **Hospital:** St. Barnabas Med Ctr (page 94), Bayonne Med Ctr; **Address:** 505 Chestnut St, Roselle Park, NJ 07204; **Phone:** 908-241-0200; **Board Cert:** Otolaryngology 1998; **Med School:** Univ Hlth Sci, Coll Osteo Med 1986; **Resid:** Otolaryngology, Genesys Regl Med Ctr 1992

Pediatric Allergy & Immunology

Pien, Gary C MD/PhD (PA&I) - **Spec Exp:** Asthma & Allergy; Food & Drug Allergy; Eczema; Immune Deficiency; **Hospital:** Overlook Med Ctr (page 92); **Address:** Summit Medical Group, 1 Diamond Hill Rd, Berkeley Heights, NJ 07922; **Phone:** 908-277-8681; **Board Cert:** Pediatrics 2007; Allergy & Immunology 2008; **Med School:** Brown Univ 2003; **Resid:** Pediatrics, Hasbro Chldns Hosp 2006; **Fellow:** Allergy & Immunology, Chldns Hosp-Philadelphia 2009

Pediatric Cardiology

Leichter, Donald A MD (PCd) - **Spec Exp:** Congenital Heart Disease; Fetal Echocardiography; Cardiac Electrophysiology; **Hospital:** Overlook Med Ctr (page 92), Morgan Stanley Chldns Hosp of NY-Presby, NY (page 102); **Address:** 47 Maple St, Ste 406, Summit, NJ 07901; **Phone:** 908-522-5566; **Board Cert:** Pediatrics 1988; Pediatric Cardiology 2010; **Med School:** Cornell Univ-Weill Med Coll 1980; **Resid:** Pediatrics, Chldns Natl Med Ctr 1983; **Fellow:** Pediatric Cardiology, NY-Presby/Columbia Univ Med Ctr 1986; **Fac Appt:** Assoc Clin Prof Ped, Columbia P&S

Pediatric Endocrinology

Anhalt, Henry DO (PEn) - **Spec Exp:** Diabetes; Obesity; Growth Disorders; **Address:** 140 Prospect Ave, Ste 2, Hackensack, NJ 07061; **Phone:** 201-996-0777; **Board Cert:** Pediatric Endocrinology 2012; **Med School:** NY Coll Osteo Med 1988; **Resid:** Pediatrics, Winthrop Univ Hosp 1992; **Fellow:** Pediatric Endocrinology, Stanford Univ Hosp & Clins 1995; **Fac Appt:** Assoc Prof Ped, SUNY Hlth Sci Ctr

Pediatric Gastroenterology

Tyshkov, Michael MD (PGe) - **Spec Exp:** Nutrition; Crohn's Disease; Colitis; Irritable Bowel Syndrome; **Hospital:** Overlook Med Ctr (page 92), Staten Island Univ Hosp - North; **Address:** Overlook Med Ctr - Kids Tummy, 33 Overlook Rd, Ste 208, Summit, NJ 07901; **Phone:** 908-273-7745; **Board Cert:** Pediatric Gastroenterology 2010; **Med School:** Russia 1977; **Resid:** Pediatrics, Flushing Hosp Med Ctr 1989; **Fellow:** Pediatric Gastroenterology, Westchester Med Ctr 1991; **Fac Appt:** Asst Clin Prof Ped, SUNY Downstate

Pediatric Pulmonology

Kohn, Gary L MD (PPul) - **Spec Exp:** Lung Disease; Cough; Asthma & Chronic Lung Disease; Pneumonia; **Hospital:** Overlook Med Ctr (page 92), Morristown Med Ctr (page 92); **Address:** Pulmonary & Allergy Assocs, 1 Diamond Hill Rd, Berkeley Heights, NJ 07922; **Phone:** 908-673-7220; **Board Cert:** Pediatrics 2015; Pediatric Pulmonology 2007; Pediatric Critical Care Medicine 2015; **Med School:** Ros Franklin Univ/Chicago Med Sch 1994; **Resid:** Pediatrics, U Chicago Hosps 1997; **Fellow:** Pediatric Pulmonology, Chldns Hosp Med Ctr 2000; Pediatric Critical Care Medicine, Schneider Chldns Hosp 2002; **Fac Appt:** Asst Clin Prof Ped, UMDNJ-NJ Med Sch, Newark

Pediatric Surgery

Bergman, Kerry S MD (PS) - **Hospital:** Overlook Med Ctr (page 92), Morristown Med Ctr (page 92); **Address:** Overlook Hospital, 99 Beauvoir Ave, Box 220, Summit, NJ 07902; **Phone:** 908-522-3523; **Board Cert:** Surgery 2007; Pediatric Surgery 2009; **Med School:** Albany Med Coll 1982; **Resid:** Surgery, New England Med Ctr 1988; **Fellow:** Pediatric Surgery, New England Med Ctr 1991; **Fac Appt:** Asst Clin Prof PS, Columbia P&S

Pediatrics

Ayyanathan, Karpukarasi MD (Ped) *PCP* - **Hospital:** Trinitas Reg Med Ctr (page 946), JFK Med Ctr - Edison; **Address:** Linden Pediatric Grp, 517 Rahway Ave, Elizabeth, NJ 07202-2308; **Phone:** 908-527-1247; **Board Cert:** Pediatrics 2010; **Med School:** India 1975; **Resid:** Pediatrics, St Elizabeth Hosp 1977; Pediatrics, Rahway Hosp 1979

Corbo, Emanuel MD (Ped) - **Spec Exp:** Vaccines; Asthma; Otitis Media; Pneumonia; **Hospital:** Overlook Med Ctr (page 92), Trinitas Reg Med Ctr (page 946); **Address:** 443 E Westfield Ave, Roselle Park, NJ 07204-2428; **Phone:** 908-245-2442; **Board Cert:** Pediatrics 2008; **Med School:** Grenada 1985; **Resid:** Pediatrics, Newark Beth Israel Med Ctr 1990; **Fellow:** Pediatric Trauma, Newark Beth Israel Med Ctr 1991

Davis, Kenneth J MD (Ped) *PCP* - **Hospital:** Overlook Med Ctr (page 92), Trinitas Reg Med Ctr (page 946); **Address:** 701 Newark Ave, Ste 212, Elizabeth, NJ 07208-3550; **Phone:** 908-354-9500; **Board Cert:** Pediatrics 1985; **Med School:** Albert Einstein Coll Med 1980; **Resid:** Pediatrics, Bellevue Hosp 1983

Panza, Robert A MD (Ped) - **Hospital:** Overlook Med Ctr (page 92); **Address:** Pediatric Associates of Westfield, 566 Westfield Ave, Westfield, NJ 07090; **Phone:** 908-233-7171; **Board Cert:** Pediatrics 2011; **Med School:** Italy 1985; **Resid:** Pediatrics, Overlook Hosp 1988

Panzner, Elizabeth A MD (Ped) *PCP* - **Spec Exp:** Acne; Allergy; Asthma; **Hospital:** St. Barnabas Med Ctr (page 94), Overlook Med Ctr (page 92); **Address:** Union Pediatric Medical Group, 1050 Galloping Hill Rd, Ste 200, Union, NJ 07083-9417; **Phone:** 908-688-9900; **Board Cert:** Pediatrics 2011; **Med School:** Mexico 1984; **Resid:** Pediatrics, UMDNJ-Univ Hosp 1988

Saraiya, Narendra N MD (Ped) *PCP* - **Spec Exp:** Asthma; Anemia; Sickle Cell Disease; **Hospital:** Trinitas Reg Med Ctr (page 946), JFK Med Ctr - Edison; **Address:** 817 Rahway Ave, Elizabeth, NJ 07202; **Phone:** 908-353-5750; **Board Cert:** Pediatrics 1988; **Med School:** India 1971; **Resid:** Pediatrics, NY Methodist Hosp 1980; **Fellow:** Pediatric Hematology-Oncology, Maimonides Med Ctr 1982; Pediatric Hematology-Oncology, Chldns Hosp Buffalo 1984

Physical Medicine & Rehabilitation

Armento, Michael J MD (PMR) - **Spec Exp:** Pediatric Rehabilitation; Cerebral Palsy; Spina Bifida; Spinal Cord Injury-Pediatric; **Hospital:** Children's Specialized Hosp, Newark Beth Israel Med Ctr (page 94); **Address:** Chldns Specialized Hosp, 150 New Providence Rd, Mountainside, NJ 07092; **Phone:** 908-301-5502; **Board Cert:** Physical Medicine & Rehabilitation 2013; Pediatric Rehabilitation Medicine 2013; Spinal Cord Injury Medicine 2013; **Med School:** UMDNJ-NJ Med Sch, Newark 1988; **Resid:** Physical Medicine & Rehabilitation, Univ Hosp-UMDNJ 1992; **Fellow:** Pediatric Rehabilitation Medicine, Chldns Specialized Hosp 2004; **Fac Appt:** Assoc Clin Prof Ped, UMDNJ-NJ Med Sch, Newark

Diamond, Martin MD (PMR) - **Spec Exp:** Cerebral Palsy; Neuromuscular Disorders; Electrodiagnosis; Spasticity Management; **Hospital:** Children's Specialized Hosp, Newark Beth Israel Med Ctr (page 94); **Address:** Chldns Specialized Hosp, 150 New Providence Rd, Mountainside, NJ 07092; **Phone:** 908-301-5502; **Board Cert:** Pediatrics 1983; Physical Medicine & Rehabilitation 1982; **Med School:** Univ Pittsburgh 1975; **Resid:** Pediatrics, Chldns Hosp Natl Med Ctr 1978; Physical Medicine & Rehabilitation, Sinai Hosp 1980; **Fac Appt:** Assoc Clin Prof PMR, UMDNJ-Rutgers Med Sch

Malanga, Gerard A MD (PMR) - **Spec Exp:** Pain-Back & Neck; Sports Injuries; Regenokine Therapy (PRP); Musculoskeletal Imaging; **Hospital:** Overlook Med Ctr (page 92); **Address:** NJ Sports Med, 197 Ridgedale Ave, Ste 210, Cedar Knolls, NJ 07927; **Phone:** 973-998-8301; **Board Cert:** Physical Medicine & Rehabilitation 2013; Pain Medicine 2013; Sports Medicine 2009; **Med School:** UMDNJ-NJ Med Sch, Newark 1983; **Resid:** Physical Medicine & Rehabilitation, Univ Hosp-UMDNJ 1992; **Fellow:** Sports Medicine, Mayo Clin 1993; **Fac Appt:** Prof PMR, UMDNJ-Univ Med Dent NJ

Plastic Surgery

Gardner, James N MD (PlS) - **Spec Exp:** Breast Cosmetic & Reconstructive Surgery; Abdominoplasty; Laser Surgery; **Hospital:** Overlook Med Ctr (page 92); **Address:** 33 Overlook Rd, Ste 310, Summit, NJ 07901; **Phone:** 908-918-1969; **Board Cert:** Plastic Surgery 2005; **Med School:** Rutgers R W Johnson Med Sch 1987; **Resid:** Surgery, UMDNJ Univ Hosp 1992; Plastic Surgery, UMDNJ Univ Hosp 1994

Hyans, Peter MD (PlS) - **Spec Exp:** Cosmetic Surgery-Breast; Breast Reconstruction; Cosmetic Surgery-Face; Liposuction & Body Contouring; **Hospital:** Overlook Med Ctr (page 92), St. Barnabas Med Ctr (page 94); **Address:** Summit Medical Grp, Plastic Surgery Ctr, Lawrence Pavilion, 1 Diamond Hill Rd Fl 1, Berkeley Heights, NJ 07922; **Phone:** 908-277-8759; **Board Cert:** Plastic Surgery 2015; **Med School:** Rutgers R W Johnson Med Sch 1986; **Resid:** Surgery, Thomas Jefferson Univ Hosp 1991; Plastic/Reconstructive Surgery, Univ Cincinnati Hosp 1993; **Fellow:** Cosmetic Surgery, Univ Miami Affil Hosp 1994

Tepper, Howard N MD (PlS) - **Spec Exp:** Cosmetic Surgery; Breast Surgery; Hand Surgery; **Hospital:** Overlook Med Ctr (page 92); **Address:** 955 S Springfield Ave, Ste 105, Westfield, NJ 07081; **Phone:** 908-654-6540; **Board Cert:** Plastic Surgery 1983; **Med School:** Albert Einstein Coll Med 1975; **Resid:** Surgery, Montefiore Hosp Med Ctr 1979; Plastic Surgery, Montefiore Hosp Med Ctr 1981; **Fellow:** Hand Surgery, St Luke's-Roosevelt Hosp Ctr 1979

Zeitels, Jerrold R MD (PlS) - **Spec Exp:** Liposuction & Body Contouring; Reconstructive Surgery; Hand Surgery; **Hospital:** Overlook Med Ctr (page 92), Robert Wood Johnson Univ Hosp at Rahway; **Address:** 522 E Broad St, Westfield, NJ 07090-2116; **Phone:** 908-654-6540; **Board Cert:** Plastic Surgery 1989; Hand Surgery 2009; **Med School:** Univ Chicago-Pritzker Sch Med 1980; **Resid:** Surgery, Univ Michigan Med Ctr 1985; Plastic Surgery, Hosp Univ Penn 1987

Psychiatry

Kaplan, Gabriel MD (Psyc) - **Spec Exp:** Psychopharmacology; ADD/ADHD; Depression; **Hospital:** Bergen Regl Med Ctr; **Address:** 535 Morris Ave, Springfield, NJ 07081-1426; **Phone:** 973-376-1020; **Board Cert:** Psychiatry 1987; Child & Adolescent Psychiatry 1989; **Med School:** Argentina 1980; **Resid:** Psychiatry, NY Hosp-Cornell 1986; Child Psychiatry, NY Hosp-Cornell 1988; **Fac Appt:** Assoc Clin Prof Psyc, UMDNJ-NJ Med Sch, Newark

Miller, David G MD (Psyc) - **Spec Exp:** Psychopharmacology; Depression; ADD/ADHD; Bipolar/Mood Disorders; **Address:** 28 Milburn Ave, Ste 5, Springfield, NJ 07081; **Phone:** 973-218-1770; **Board Cert:** Psychiatry 1985; **Med School:** Rutgers R W Johnson Med Sch 1980; **Resid:** Psychiatry, Strong Meml Hosp 1984

Richardson, William T MD (Psyc) - **Spec Exp:** Adolescent Psychiatry; Family Therapy; Psychopharmacology; **Hospital:** Overlook Med Ctr (page 92), Morristown Med Ctr (page 92); **Address:** 33 Overlook Rd, Ste 210, Summit, NJ 07901-3570; **Phone:** 908-598-0008; **Board Cert:** Psychiatry 1980; **Med School:** McGill Univ 1967; **Resid:** Psychiatry, Jewish Genl Hosp 1971; Psychiatry, Payne Whitney Clinic 1974

Silver, Bennett MD (Psyc) - **Spec Exp:** Child & Adolescent Psychiatry; ADD/ADHD; Anxiety Disorders; **Hospital:** Bergen Regl Med Ctr; **Address:** 535 Morris Ave, Springfield, NJ 07081; **Phone:** 973-376-1020; **Board Cert:** Psychiatry 1979; **Med School:** SUNY Downstate 1974; **Resid:** Psychiatry, Mount Sinai Hosp 1978; **Fellow:** Child & Adolescent Psychiatry, Mount Sinai Hosp 1980

Sofair, Jane MD (Psyc) - **Spec Exp:** Anxiety & Depression; Women's Health; **Hospital:** Morristown Med Ctr (page 92); **Address:** 597 Springfield Ave, Summit, NJ 07901; **Phone:** 973-292-0960; **Board Cert:** Psychiatry 1985; **Med School:** NYU Sch Med 1980; **Resid:** Psychiatry, NYU Med Ctr 1984

Villafranca, Manuel V MD (Psyc) - **Spec Exp:** Psychopharmacology; Depression; Anxiety Disorders; **Hospital:** Summit Oaks Hosp, Christ Hosp - Jersey City; **Address:** 220 Lenox Ave, Westfield, NJ 07090; **Phone:** 908-232-9369; **Board Cert:** Psychiatry 1982; **Med School:** Philippines 1971; **Resid:** Psychiatry, St Vincents Hosp 1978; **Fellow:** Child & Adolescent Psychiatry, St Vincents Hosp 1980

Pulmonary Disease

Cerrone, Federico MD (Pul) - **Spec Exp:** Sleep Disorders; Asthma; Chronic Obstructive Lung Disease (COPD); **Hospital:** Overlook Med Ctr (page 92), Morristown Med Ctr (page 92); **Address:** 1 Springfield Ave, Summit, NJ 07901; **Phone:** 908-934-0555; **Board Cert:** Internal Medicine 1989; Pulmonary Disease 2012; Critical Care Medicine 2013; Sleep Medicine 2007; **Med School:** Georgetown Univ 1986; **Resid:** Internal Medicine, Bronx Muni Hosp 1989; **Fellow:** Pulmonary Critical Care Medicine, Georgetown Univ Hosp 1992

Hwang, Cheng-hong DO/PhD (Pul) - **Hospital:** Robert Wood Johnson Univ Hosp at Rahway; **Address:** 1457 Raritan Rd, Ste 101, Clark, NJ 07066; **Phone:** 908-272-2270; **Board Cert:** Internal Medicine 1983; Pulmonary Disease 1984; Critical Care Medicine 2005; **Med School:** Des Moines Univ 1978; **Resid:** Internal Medicine, USPHS Hosp 1981; **Fellow:** Pulmonary Disease, UMDNJ-Univ Hosp 1983

Sussman, Robert MD (Pul) - **Spec Exp:** Asthma; Chronic Obstructive Lung Disease (COPD); Pulmonary Fibrosis; Lung Cancer; **Hospital:** Overlook Med Ctr (page 92), Morristown Med Ctr (page 92); **Address:** Pulmonary & Allergy Assocs, 1 Springfield Ave, Summit, NJ 07901; **Phone:** 908-934-0555; **Board Cert:** Internal Medicine 1984; Pulmonary Disease 1988; **Med School:** Albert Einstein Coll Med 1981; **Resid:** Internal Medicine, Montefiore Med Ctr 1984; **Fellow:** Pulmonary Disease, NYU-Bellevue Hosp 1987

Zimmerman, Mark I MD (Pul) - **Spec Exp:** Critical Care Medicine; Asthma & Allergy; Chronic Obstructive Lung Disease (COPD); **Hospital:** Overlook Med Ctr (page 92), Morristown Med Ctr (page 92); **Address:** Pulmonary & Allergy Assocs, 1 Springfield Ave, Summit, NJ 07901; **Phone:** 908-934-0555; **Board Cert:** Internal Medicine 1988; Critical Care Medicine 2013; Pulmonary Disease 2012; **Med School:** NYU Sch Med 1985; **Resid:** Internal Medicine, NYU Med Ctr 1988; **Fellow:** Pulmonary Critical Care Medicine, Mount Sinai Med Ctr 1992

Radiation Oncology

Schwartz, Louis E MD (RadRO) - **Spec Exp:** Stereotactic Radiosurgery; Prostate Cancer; Brain Tumors; **Hospital:** Overlook Med Ctr (page 92); **Address:** Overlook Hosp, Dept Rad Oncology, 33 Overlook Rd, Ste L05, Medical Arts Ctr 1, Summit, NJ 07901-3561; **Phone:** 908-522-2871; **Board Cert:** Therapeutic Radiology 1979; Pediatrics 1981; **Med School:** SUNY Hlth Sci Ctr 1974; **Resid:** Pediatrics, NY Methodist Hosp 1976; Pediatrics, Chldns Hosp Med Ctr 1977; **Fellow:** Therapeutic Radiology, Columbia-Presby Hosp 1979

Rheumatology

Brodman, Richard R MD (Rhu) - **Spec Exp:** Lupus/SLE; Rheumatoid Arthritis; Osteoporosis; Osteoarthritis; **Hospital:** JFK Med Ctr - Edison; **Address:** 345 Somerset St, Ste 107, North Plainfield, NJ 07060-4774; **Phone:** 908-561-7440; **Board Cert:** Internal Medicine 1976; Rheumatology 1982; **Med School:** SUNY Downstate 1973; **Resid:** Internal Medicine, Rhode Island Hosp 1976; **Fellow:** Rheumatology, Brigham & Womens Hosp 1978

Kramer, Neil MD (Rhu) - **Spec Exp:** Rheumatoid Arthritis; Lupus/SLE; Sjogren's Syndrome; Vasculitis; **Hospital:** Overlook Med Ctr (page 92); **Address:** Overlook Med Ctr, Rheumatology, 33 Overlook Rd, Ste L01, Summit, NJ 07901; **Phone:** 908-598-7940; **Board Cert:** Internal Medicine 1977; Rheumatology 1980; **Med School:** Univ Pennsylvania 1974; **Resid:** Internal Medicine, Manhattan VA Hosp 1978; **Fellow:** Rheumatology, NYU Med Ctr 1980; **Fac Appt:** Assoc Clin Prof Med, Mount Sinai-Icahn Sch of Med

Rosenstein, Elliot D MD (Rhu) - **Spec Exp:** Rheumatoid Arthritis; Lupus/SLE; Sjogren's Syndrome; Behcet's Syndrome; **Hospital:** Overlook Med Ctr (page 92), Atlantic Hlth (page 92); **Address:** Inst for Reheumatic & Autoimmune Disease, 33 Overlook Rd, Ste L01, Summit, NJ 07901; **Phone:** 908-598-7940; **Board Cert:** Internal Medicine 1981; Rheumatology 1984; **Med School:** Mount Sinai Sch Med 1978; **Resid:** Internal Medicine, NYU/Bellevue Hosp 1982; **Fellow:** Rheumatology, NYU/Bellevue Hosp 1984; **Fac Appt:** Assoc Clin Prof Med, Mount Sinai Sch Med

Worth, David A MD (Rhu) - **Spec Exp:** Rheumatoid Arthritis; Osteoporosis; **Hospital:** Overlook Med Ctr (page 92); **Address:** 2376 Morris Ave, Union, NJ 07083-5707; **Phone:** 908-686-6616; **Board Cert:** Internal Medicine 1974; Rheumatology 1978; **Med School:** Univ Rochester 1971; **Resid:** Internal Medicine, Montefiore Med Ctr 1975; **Fellow:** Rheumatology, Montefiore Med Ctr 1978

Surgery

Colaco, Rodolfo MD (S) - **Spec Exp:** Hernia; Gallbladder Surgery; Laparoscopic Surgery; Breast Surgery; **Hospital:** Trinitas Reg Med Ctr (page 946); **Address:** 431 Elmora Ave, Elizabeth, NJ 07208; **Phone:** 908-353-4177; **Board Cert:** Surgery 2011; **Med School:** India 1974; **Resid:** Surgery, St Vincent Hosp 1980; Surgery, St Elizabeth Hosp 1983

DiGioia, Julia M MD (S) - **Spec Exp:** Breast Disease; Breast Cancer; **Hospital:** Overlook Med Ctr (page 92), Jersey City Med Ctr (page 94); **Address:** Medical Arts Ctr, 33 Overlook Rd, Ste 205, Summit, NJ 07901; **Phone:** 908-522-3200; **Board Cert:** Surgery 2005; **Med School:** Italy 1979; **Resid:** Surgery, Jersey City Med Ctr 1984

Feteiha, Muhammad S MD (S) - **Spec Exp:** Minimally Invasive Surgery; Obesity/Bariatric Surgery; Colon & Rectal Surgery; **Hospital:** Overlook Med Ctr (page 92), Trinitas Reg Med Ctr (page 946); **Address:** Advanced Surgical Assocs, 155 Morris Ave Fl 2, Springfield, NJ 07081; **Phone:** 973-232-2300; **Board Cert:** Surgery 2009; **Med School:** Tufts Univ 1995; **Resid:** Surgery, Univ Hosp 2000; **Fellow:** Surgery, NY-Presby/Columbia Univ Med Ctr 2001

Frost, James H MD (S) - **Spec Exp:** Breast Cancer; Colon Surgery; Laparoscopic Surgery; Vein Disorders; **Hospital:** Overlook Med Ctr (page 92), Trinitas Reg Med Ctr (page 946); **Address:** Advanced Surgical Assocs, 155 Morris Ave Fl 2, Springfield, NJ 07081; **Phone:** 973-232-2300; **Board Cert:** Surgery 2007; **Med School:** Mexico 1982; **Resid:** Surgery, Univ IL Med Ctr 1988

Gumbs, Andrew MD (S) - **Spec Exp:** Gastrointestinal Surgery; Minimally Invasive Surgery; Hepatobiliary Surgery; Pancreatic & Biliary Surgery; **Hospital:** Overlook Med Ctr (page 92); **Address:** Summit Med Grp, Surgery, 1 Diamond Hill Rd Fl 4, Berkeley Heights, NJ 07922; **Phone:** 908-277-8950; **Board Cert:** Surgery 2006; **Med School:** Yale Univ 1998; **Resid:** Surgery, Yale-New Haven Hosp 2005; **Fellow:** Minimally Invasive Surgery, NY-Presby/Columbia Univ Med Ctr 2006; Hepatopancreatobiliary Surgery, Univ Rene Descartes Affil Hosp 2007

Lozner, Jerrold S MD (S) - **Spec Exp:** Breast Cancer & Surgery; Breast Surgery; **Hospital:** Overlook Med Ctr (page 92); **Address:** 1 Diamond Hill Rd, Berkeley Heights, NJ 07922; **Phone:** 908-277-8770; **Board Cert:** Surgery 2009; **Med School:** Univ Louisville Sch Med 1971; **Resid:** Surgery, Univ Cincinnati Med Ctr 1976; **Fellow:** Cardiothoracic Surgery, Univ Cincinnati Med Ctr 1978; **Fac Appt:** Assoc Clin Prof S, Columbia P&S

Mandel, Marc S MD (S) - **Spec Exp:** Gallbladder Surgery; Breast Cancer & Surgery; Cancer Surgery; Abdominal Wall Reconstruction; **Hospital:** Overlook Med Ctr (page 92); **Address:** 11 Overlook Rd, Ste 160, Summit, NJ 07901; **Phone:** 908-598-0966; **Board Cert:** Surgery 2009; **Med School:** Albert Einstein Coll Med 1985; **Resid:** Surgery, Montefiore Med Ctr 1988; Surgery, Yale-New Haven Hosp 1990

Nitzberg, Richard S MD (S) - **Spec Exp:** Laparoscopic Surgery; Vein Disorders; Hernia; Vascular Surgery; **Hospital:** Overlook Med Ctr (page 92); **Address:** Summit Med Grp, Surgery, 1 Diamond Hill Rd Fl 4, Berkeley Heights, NJ 07922; **Phone:** 908-277-8950; **Board Cert:** Surgery 2009; Vascular Surgery 2010; **Med School:** Harvard Med Sch 1983; **Resid:** Surgery, NY-Presby/Columbia Univ Med Ctr 1988; **Fellow:** Vascular Surgery, Tufts Med Ctr 1990

Sacco, Margaret M MD (S) - **Spec Exp:** Breast Cancer & Surgery; Breast Disease; **Hospital:** Overlook Med Ctr (page 92), Morristown Med Ctr (page 92); **Address:** Carol G Simon Cancer Ctr, 33 Overlook Rd, MAC-1 Building Ste 207, Summit, NJ 07901; **Phone:** 908-598-6610; **Board Cert:** Surgery 2011; **Med School:** Hahnemann Univ 1986; **Resid:** Surgery, Univ Hosp-UMDNJ 1991; **Fellow:** Surgical Oncology, Univ Hosp-UMDNJ 1993

Starker, Paul MD (S) - **Spec Exp:** Laparoscopic Surgery; **Hospital:** Overlook Med Ctr (page 92); **Address:** Overlook Surgical Associates, 11 Overlook Rd, Ste 160, Summit, NJ 07901; **Phone:** 908-608-9001; **Board Cert:** Surgery 2006; **Med School:** Columbia P&S 1980; **Resid:** Surgery, NY-Presby/Columbia Univ Med Ctr 1986; **Fellow:** Metabolism, NY-Presby/Columbia Univ Med Ctr 1982; **Fac Appt:** Clin Prof S, Columbia P&S

Urology

Lehrhoff, Bernard J MD (U) - **Spec Exp:** Prostate Cancer; Kidney Stones; Sexual Dysfunction; Bladder Cancer; **Hospital:** Overlook Med Ctr (page 92), Saint Michael's Med Ctr; **Address:** Premier Urology Grp, 275 Orchard St, Westfield, NJ 07090; **Phone:** 908-654-5100; **Board Cert:** Urology 1984; **Med School:** UMDNJ-NJ Med Sch, Newark 1976; **Resid:** Urology, Bellevue Hosp 1982; **Fac Appt:** Asst Clin Prof U, Columbia P&S

Miller, Mark I MD (U) - **Spec Exp:** Kidney Stones; Urology-Female; Urologic Cancer; **Hospital:** Trinitas Reg Med Ctr (page 946); **Address:** Premier Urology Grp, 275 Orchard St, Westfield, NJ 07090; **Phone:** 908-654-5100; **Board Cert:** Urology 2007; **Med School:** Cornell Univ 1991; **Resid:** Urology, NY-Presby/Columbia Univ Med Ctr 1997

Ring, Kenneth S MD (U) - **Spec Exp:** Pediatric Urology; Urologic Cancer; Kidney Stones; **Hospital:** Overlook Med Ctr (page 92); **Address:** Premier Urology Grp, 275 Orchard St, Westfield, NJ 07090; **Phone:** 908-654-5100; **Board Cert:** Urology 2012; **Med School:** Mount Sinai Sch Med 1985; **Resid:** Surgery, Mt Sinai Hosp 1987; Urology, NY-Presby/Columbia Univ Med Ctr 1991

Seidman, Barry MD (U) - **Spec Exp:** Sexual Dysfunction; Incontinence; Genitourinary Cancer; **Hospital:** Overlook Med Ctr (page 92); **Address:** 33 Overlook Rd, Ste 408, Summit, NJ 07901; **Phone:** 908-219-4479; **Board Cert:** Urology 2004; **Med School:** Mount Sinai Sch Med 1978; **Resid:** Urology, Mount Sinai Med Ctr 1983

Vascular Surgery

Addis, Michael D MD (VascS) - **Spec Exp:** Endovascular Surgery; Carotid Artery Surgery; **Hospital:** St. Barnabas Med Ctr (page 94), Overlook Med Ctr (page 92); **Address:** The Cardiovascular Care Group, 433 Central Ave, Westfield, NJ 07090; **Phone:** 973-759-9000; **Board Cert:** Surgery 2005; Vascular Surgery 2007; **Med School:** UMDNJ-NJ Med Sch, Newark 1999; **Resid:** Surgery, Mount Sinai Med Ctr 2004; **Fellow:** Vascular Surgery, Mount Sinai Med Ctr 2005

Kumar, Mark MD (VascS) - **Spec Exp:** Endovascular Surgery; **Hospital:** Overlook Med Ctr (page 92), St. Barnabas Med Ctr (page 94); **Address:** The Cardiovascular Care Group, 433 Central Ave, Westfield, NJ 07090; **Phone:** 973-759-9000; **Board Cert:** Vascular Surgery 2013; **Med School:** Univ VA Sch Med 1996; **Resid:** Surgery, Saint Barnabas Med Ctr 2001; Vascular Surgery, VA Commonwealth Univ Med Ctr 2002

Sales, Clifford M MD (VascS) - **Spec Exp:** Varicose Veins; Aneurysm-Abdominal Aortic; Peripheral Vascular Disease; Carotid Artery Surgery; **Hospital:** Overlook Med Ctr (page 92), Morristown Med Ctr (page 92); **Address:** Cardiovascular Care Grp, 433 Central Ave, Westfield, NJ 07090; **Phone:** 973-759-9000; **Board Cert:** Vascular Surgery 2013; **Med School:** Mount Sinai Sch Med 1986; **Resid:** Surgery, Montefiore Med Ctr 1991; **Fellow:** Vascular Surgery, Montefiore Med Ctr 1993; **Fac Appt:** Asst Clin Prof S, Mount Sinai-Icahn Sch of Med

The State of Connecticut

The Best in American Medicine
www.CastleConnolly.com

Fairfield

Greenwich Hospital

GENERAL OVERVIEW

Greenwich Hospital is a progressive regional medical center and teaching institution with an internal medicine residency, serving lower Fairfield and Westchester counties. Care is provided on a beautiful, modern campus designed to create a healing environment for patients and visitors.

ACADEMIC AND CLINICAL AFFILIATIONS

As a member of Yale New Haven Health System, Greenwich Hospital is a major affiliate of Yale School of Medicine and maintains affiliations with other leading medical providers. Patients have access to a comprehensive range of medical, surgical, diagnostic, integrative medicine and wellness programs. Greenwich Hospital also offers robotic surgery, hyperbaric medicine and wound healing. It has a state-certified and Joint Commission-accredited Stroke Center, and participates in international clinical trials. Greenwich Hospital is also certified in hip and knee replacement and spinal fusion.

OUTSTANDING CLINICAL SERVICES

Specialties include oncology care at the hospital's Bendheim Cancer Center; advanced breast care at the Breast Center; a comprehensive maternity program, including Level III NICU and fertility services; a Pediatric Specialty Center; a Weight Loss and Diabetes Center; expert neuroscience and spine services; and a wide range of surgical specialties including knee, hip and shoulder joint replacement, plus bariatric surgery.

SERVICE EXCELLENCE

Greenwich Hospital is renowned for service excellence and has been a recipient of Press Ganey's Summit Award for highest ratings in Patient Satisfaction.

greenwichhospital.org

5 Perryridge Road
Greenwich, CT
06830-4697

Tel: 203.863.3000

greenwichhospital.org

PHYSICIAN REFERRAL:

For a prompt, personal physician referral, please call Greenwich Hospital at 203-863-3627 or visit us online.

SPONSORSHIP:

Voluntary, not-for-profit

BEDS:

206

ACCREDITATION:

The Joint Commission

General Overview

Stamford Hospital provides area residents (Fairfield and Westchester Counties) access to the latest technology with a compassionate, patient-centered care approach in keeping with the Planetree philosophy. Stamford is a Level II trauma center with a nationally recognized adult intensive care unit. Our areas of expertise include:

Cancer Care   StamfordHospital.org/cancer
Heart Services   StamfordHospital.org/heart
Orthopedics   StamfordHospital.org/ortho
Women's Health   StamfordHospital.org/womenshealth

Comprehensive Specialty Centers

Bennett Cancer Center provides compassionate, patient-centered care from diagnosis through post-treatment.

Center for Integrative Medicine and Wellness blends conventional and complementary care for patients.

Center for Robotic Surgery using the *da Vinci* Surgical System, enables surgeons to perform even the most complex and delicate procedures through very small incisions with unmatched precision.

Center for Sleep Medicine offers experts in diagnosing and treating pediatric and adult sleep disorders, including snoring, sleep apnea, insomnia, narcolepsy and restless leg syndrome.

Center for Surgical Weight Loss offers the region's only comprehensive weight management program.

CyberKnife Center, located at the first and only hospital in Fairfield and Westchester Counties, provides the technology to destroy tumors with pinpoint accuracy.

Diabetes & Endocrine Center brings together consultative services and complete clinical care, including comprehensive patient education, medical management and treatment.

Women's Breast Center, first in the nation to receive accreditation from the American College of Surgeons for excellence in breast care, and proud to be the first comprehensive breast center in the region to offer 3-D tomosynthesis to all screening mammography patients.

Academic and Clinical Affiliations

Stamford Hospital is an affiliate of the New York–Presbyterian Healthcare System and a major teaching affiliate of the Columbia University College of Physicians & Surgeons.

Accreditation

The Joint Commission

Beds

305

Sponsorship

Voluntary, Not-for-Profit

For a Physician Referral or more information,

please call **1.877.233.9355** or visit StamfordHospital.org /doctor.

Stamford Hospital
30 Shelburne Road
Stamford, CT 06902
203.276.1000

StamfordHospital.org

Addiction Psychiatry

Collins, Eric D MD (AdP) - **Spec Exp:** Addiction/Substance Abuse; Opiate Addiction; Dual Diagnosis; Alcohol Abuse; **Hospital:** Silver Hill Hosp, NY-Presby/Columbia Univ Med Ctr, NY (page 102); **Address:** 208 Valley Rd, New Canaan, CT 06840; **Phone:** 203-801-2241; **Board Cert:** Psychiatry 2005; Addiction Psychiatry 2007; Psychosomatic Medicine 2008; **Med School:** Columbia P&S 1990; **Resid:** Psychiatry, NY State Psyc Inst 1994; **Fellow:** Psychosomatic Medicine, NY-Presby/Columbia Univ Med Ctr 1995; Addiction Psychiatry, NY State Psyc Inst 1996

Cooperman, Sheila A MD (AdP) - **Spec Exp:** Addiction/Substance Abuse; Opiate Addiction; **Hospital:** St. Vincent's Med Ctr - Bridgeport; **Address:** 47 Long Lots Rd, Westport, CT 06880; **Phone:** 203-227-1251; **Board Cert:** Psychiatry 1987; Addiction Psychiatry 2006; **Med School:** Grenada 1982; **Resid:** Psychiatry, Tufts Med Ctr 1985; Psychiatry, Norwich Hosp 1986

Adolescent Medicine

Schneider, Marcie B MD (AM) - **Spec Exp:** Eating Disorders; Obesity; Menstrual Disorders; **Hospital:** Greenwich Hosp (page 970); **Address:** Greenwich Adolescent Medicine, 239 Glenville Rd, Greenwich, CT 06831; **Phone:** 203-532-1919; **Board Cert:** Pediatrics 1987; Adolescent Medicine 2008; **Med School:** Albert Einstein Coll Med 1983; **Resid:** Pediatrics, Montefiore Med Ctr 1986; **Fellow:** Adolescent Medicine, N Shore Univ Hosp 1989

Zolkowski-Wynne, Joanna MD (AM) - **Spec Exp:** Nutrition; Eating Disorders; Parenting Issues; **Hospital:** Bridgeport Hosp, Yale-New Haven Hosp; **Address:** Bridgeport Hosp, 267 Grant St, Bridgeport, CT 06610; **Phone:** 203-384-3064; **Board Cert:** Pediatrics 1985; Adolescent Medicine 2008; **Med School:** SUNY Upstate Med Univ 1980; **Resid:** Pediatrics, Rhode Island Hosp 1983; **Fellow:** Ambulatory Pediatrics, Rhode Island Hosp 1985; Adolescent Medicine, Beth Israel Deaconess Med Ctr 1986; **Fac Appt:** Asst Clin Prof Ped, Yale Univ

Allergy & Immunology

Backman, Kenneth S MD (A&I) - **Spec Exp:** Nasal Allergy; Food Allergy; Asthma; Sinus Disorders; **Hospital:** Bridgeport Hosp, St. Vincent's Med Ctr - Bridgeport; **Address:** Allergy & Asthma Care Fairfield Co, 55 Walls Drive, Ste 405, Fairfield, CT 06824; **Phone:** 203-259-7070; **Board Cert:** Allergy & Immunology 2007; **Med School:** Cornell Univ-Weill Med Coll 1991; **Resid:** Internal Medicine, Univ Chicago Med Ctr 1994; **Fellow:** Allergy & Immunology, Northwestern Meml Hosp 1996

Bell, Jonathan B MD (A&I) - **Spec Exp:** Asthma; Insect Allergies; Sinusitis; Hives; **Hospital:** Danbury Hosp; **Address:** Advanced Specialty Care, 107 Newtown Rd, Ste 1B, Danbury, CT 06810; **Phone:** 203-748-7433; **Board Cert:** Pediatrics 1986; Allergy & Immunology 1987; **Med School:** Georgetown Univ 1980; **Resid:** Pediatrics, St Christophers Hosp Chldn 1983; **Fellow:** Pediatric Allergy & Immunology, Chldns Hosp 1987; **Fac Appt:** Asst Clin Prof A&I, NY Med Coll

Bloom, Katherine A MD (A&I) - **Spec Exp:** Food Allergy; Immune Deficiency; Asthma; **Hospital:** St. Vincent's Med Ctr - Bridgeport, Bridgeport Hosp; **Address:** Allergy & Asthma Care of Fairfield Co, 55 Walls Drive, Ste 405, Fairfield, CT 06824; **Phone:** 203-259-7070; **Board Cert:** Allergy & Immunology 2008; Internal Medicine 2006; **Med School:** Albert Einstein Coll Med 2003; **Resid:** Internal Medicine, NY-Presby/Columbia Univ Med Ctr 2006; **Fellow:** Allergy & Immunology, Mount Sinai Med Ctr 2008

Hemmers, Philip H DO (A&I) - **Spec Exp:** Pediatric Allergy & Immunology; Food Allergy; **Hospital:** St. Vincent's Med Ctr - Bridgeport, Norwalk Hosp; **Address:** Allergy Ctr of CT, 4 Corporate Drive, Shelton, CT 06484; **Phone:** 203-374-6103; **Board Cert:** Pediatrics 2012; Allergy & Immunology 2007; **Med School:** NY Coll Osteo Med 2001; **Resid:** Pediatrics, Mount Sinai Hosp 2004; **Fellow:** Allergy & Immunology, LI College Hosp 2007

Lee, Richard J MD (A&I) - **Spec Exp:** Pediatric Allergy & Immunology; Urticaria; **Hospital:** Danbury Hosp; **Address:** Advanced Allergy & Asthma Care, 107 Newtown Rd, Ste 1B, Danbury, CT 6810; **Phone:** 203-748-7433; **Board Cert:** Allergy & Immunology 1987; Internal Medicine 1985; **Med School:** Dominican Republic 1980; **Resid:** Internal Medicine, UMDNJ-Rutgers 1983; **Fellow:** Allergy & Immunology, Rhode Island Hosp 1986

Lindner, Paul S MD (A&I) - **Spec Exp:** Asthma & Sinusitis; Food & Drug Allergy; Immunodeficiency Disorders; Allergic Rhinitis; **Hospital:** Stamford Hosp (page 971); **Address:** Allergy & Asthma Ctr of Stamford, 22 5th St, Stamford, CT 06905-5030; **Phone:** 203-978-0072; **Board Cert:** Internal Medicine 1989; Allergy & Immunology 2011; **Med School:** SUNY Buffalo 1985; **Resid:** Internal Medicine, Stamford Hosp 1989; **Fellow:** Allergy & Immunology, Nassau Co Med Ctr 1991; **Fac Appt:** Assoc Clin Prof A&I, Columbia P&S

Litchman, Mark D MD (A&I) - **Spec Exp:** Asthma; Immune Deficiency; Lupus/SLE; Vasculitis; **Hospital:** Greenwich Hosp (page 970), Stamford Hosp (page 971); **Address:** Fairfield Co Allergy, Asthma & Immunology, 2 1/2 Dearfield Drive, Greenwich, CT 06831-5335; **Phone:** 203-869-2080; **Board Cert:** Internal Medicine 1987; Allergy & Immunology 2011; Rheumatology 1988; **Med School:** Rush Med Coll 1984; **Resid:** Internal Medicine, Greenwich Hosp 1987; **Fellow:** Allergy & Immunology, Yale-New Haven Hosp 1989; Rheumatology, Yale-New Haven Hosp 1989

Matczuk, Agnieszka MD (A&I) - **Spec Exp:** Pediatric Allergy & Immunology; **Hospital:** Greenwich Hosp (page 970); **Address:** Fairfield Co Allergy, Asthma, & Immunology, 2 1/2 Dearfield Drive, Greenwich, CT 06831; **Phone:** 203-869-2080; **Board Cert:** Pediatrics 2007; Allergy & Immunology 2013; **Med School:** Poland 1993; **Resid:** Pediatrics, Beth Israel Med Ctr 2000; **Fellow:** Allergy & Immunology, Yale-New Haven Hosp 2003

Santilli Jr, John MD (A&I) - **Spec Exp:** Allergy; Sinusitis; Pediatric Allergy & Immunology; **Hospital:** St. Vincent's Med Ctr - Bridgeport; **Address:** Allergy Ctr of CT, 4 Corporate Drive, Shelton, CT 06484; **Phone:** 203-374-6103; **Board Cert:** Pediatrics 1973; Allergy & Immunology 1983; **Med School:** Georgetown Univ 1968; **Resid:** Pediatrics, Medstar Georgetown Univ Hosp 1971; **Fellow:** Allergy & Immunology, Medstar Georgetown Univ Hosp 1973

Sproviero, Joseph MD/PhD (A&I) - **Spec Exp:** Asthma & Allergy; Autoimmune Disease; **Hospital:** Norwalk Hosp, Greenwich Hosp (page 970); **Address:** Fairfield Co Allergy, Asthma, & Immunology, 148 East Ave, Ste 3G, Norwalk, CT 06851; **Phone:** 203-838-4034; **Board Cert:** Allergy & Immunology 2012; Internal Medicine 1989; **Med School:** Columbia P&S 1985; **Resid:** Internal Medicine, Yale-New Haven Hosp 1988; **Fellow:** Allergy & Immunology, Yale-New Haven Hosp 1990; Rheumatology, Yale-New Haven Hosp 1991; **Fac Appt:** Asst Clin Prof Med, Yale Univ

Veksler-Offengenden, Irena MD (A&I) - **Spec Exp:** Asthma & Allergy; Rhinitis; Food & Drug Allergy; **Hospital:** Bridgeport Hosp, St. Vincent's Med Ctr - Bridgeport; **Address:** Allergy & Asthma Care Fairfield Co, 55 Walls Drive, Ste 405, Fairfield, CT 06824; **Phone:** 203-259-7070; **Board Cert:** Allergy & Immunology 2005; **Med School:** Cornell Univ-Weill Med Coll 2000; **Resid:** Internal Medicine, RWJ-UMDNJ Med Ctr 2003; **Fellow:** Allergy & Immunology, Stony Brook Univ Med Ctr 2005

Cardiac Electrophysiology

Chiravuri, Murali MD/PhD (CE) - **Spec Exp:** Arrhythmias; Atrial Fibrillation; Pacemakers; **Hospital:** Danbury Hosp, Bridgeport Hosp; **Address:** Cardiac Specialists, 25 Germantown Rd, Ste 2B, Danbury, CT 06810; **Phone:** 203-794-0090; **Board Cert:** Internal Medicine 2004; Cardiovascular Disease 2007; Cardiac Electrophysiology 2009; **Med School:** Tufts Univ 2001; **Resid:** Internal Medicine, Brigham & Womens Hosp 2003; **Fellow:** Cardiovascular Disease, Mass Genl Hosp 2007; Cardiac Electrophysiology, Brigham & Womens Hosp 2009

Dhruvakumar, Sandhya MD (CE) - **Spec Exp:** Arrhythmias; Atrial Fibrillation; **Hospital:** Stamford Hosp (page 971); **Address:** Tully Health Ctr, Div Cardiology, 32 Strawberry Hill Court Fl 4, Stamford, CT 06902; **Phone:** 203-276-2321; **Board Cert:** Cardiovascular Disease 2006; Cardiac Electrophysiology 2010; **Med School:** Univ Mass Sch Med 2000; **Resid:** Internal Medicine, Beth Israel Med Ctr 2003; **Fellow:** Cardiovascular Disease, NY-Presby/Weill Cornell Med Ctr 2006; Cardiac Electrophysiology, Pennsylvania Hosp-UPHS 2008

Lottick, Adam T MD (CE) - **Spec Exp:** Arrhythmias; Atrial Fibrillation; **Hospital:** St. Vincent's Med Ctr - Bridgeport, Bridgeport Hosp; **Address:** CT Heart & Vascular Ctr, 112 Quary Rd Fl 4 - Ste 400, Trumbull, CT 06611; **Phone:** 203-333-8800; **Board Cert:** Internal Medicine 2005; Cardiovascular Disease 2009; Cardiac Electrophysiology 2012; **Med School:** Washington Univ, St Louis 1991; **Resid:** Internal Medicine, Johns Hopkins Hosp 1994; **Fellow:** Cardiovascular Disease, Univ CO Hosp 1997; Cardiac Electrophysiology, Univ CO Hosp 1999

McPherson, Craig A MD (CE) - **Spec Exp:** Arrhythmias; Pacemakers/Defibrillators; Atrial Fibrillation; Syncope; **Hospital:** Bridgeport Hosp, Yale-New Haven Hosp; **Address:** Bridgeport Hosp, Div Electrophysiology, 267 Grant St, Fl 10, Bridgeport, CT 06610; **Phone:** 203-384-3442; **Board Cert:** Internal Medicine 1979; Cardiovascular Disease 1983; Cardiac Electrophysiology 2004; **Med School:** Tufts Univ 1976; **Resid:** Internal Medicine, Tufts-New England Med Ctr 1979; **Fellow:** Cardiovascular Disease, Yale-New Haven Hosp 1983; Cardiac Electrophysiology, Yale-New Haven Hosp 1984; **Fac Appt:** Clin Prof Med, Yale Univ

Pittaro, Michael R MD (CE) - **Spec Exp:** Arrhythmias; **Hospital:** St. Vincent's Med Ctr - Bridgeport, Norwalk Hosp; **Address:** Cardio Physicians Fairfield Co, 40 Cross St, Ste 200, Norwalk, CT 06851; **Phone:** 203-845-2160; **Board Cert:** Cardiac Electrophysiology 2012; Cardiovascular Disease 2011; **Med School:** Univ Pennsylvania 1995; **Resid:** Internal Medicine, Barnes-Jewish Hosp 1998; **Fellow:** Cardiovascular Disease, Beth Israel Deaconess Hosp 2000; Cardiac Electrophysiology, Beth Israel Deaconess Hosp 2002

Winslow, Robert D MD (CE) - **Spec Exp:** Arrhythmias; Atrial Fibrillation; Pacemakers; Defibrillators; **Hospital:** Bridgeport Hosp; **Address:** Cardiac Specialists, 1305 Post Rd, Fairfield, CT 06824; **Phone:** 203-292-2000; **Board Cert:** Cardiovascular Disease 2005; Cardiac Electrophysiology 2007; **Med School:** Northwestern Univ-Feinberg Sch Med 1999; **Resid:** Internal Medicine, Brigham & Women's Hosp 2002; **Fellow:** Cardiovascular Disease, Mount Sinai Hosp 2005; Cardiac Electrophysiology, Brigham & Women's Hosp 2007

Cardiovascular Disease

Augenbraun, Charles B MD (Cv) - **Spec Exp:** Hypertension; Cholesterol/Lipid Disorders; Preventive Cardiology; **Hospital:** Norwalk Hosp; **Address:** Cardio Assocs Fairfield Co, 40 Cross St, Ste 200, Norwalk, CT 06851; **Phone:** 203-845-2160; **Board Cert:** Internal Medicine 1981; Cardiovascular Disease 1985; **Med School:** Univ Pennsylvania 1978; **Resid:** Internal Medicine, Temple Univ Hosp 1981; **Fellow:** Cardiovascular Disease, Hosp Univ Penn 1985

Bloom, Gregory S MD (Cv) - **Spec Exp:** Nuclear Cardiology; Echocardiography; Non-Invasive Cardiology; **Hospital:** St. Vincent's Med Ctr - Bridgeport, Bridgeport Hosp; **Address:** CT Heart & Vascular Ctr, 112 Quary Rd, Ste 400, Trumbull, CT 06611; **Phone:** 203-333-8800; **Board Cert:** Internal Medicine 2004; Cardiovascular Disease 2007; Nuclear Cardiology 2007; **Med School:** Geo Wash Univ 2001; **Resid:** Internal Medicine, Beth Israel Med Ctr 2004; **Fellow:** Cardiovascular Disease, LIJ Med Ctr 2007

Casale, Linda R MD (Cv) - **Spec Exp:** Non-Invasive Cardiology; Women's Health; Echocardiography; **Hospital:** Bridgeport Hosp, Milford Hosp; **Address:** Cardiac Specs of Fairfield, 1305 Post Rd, Fairfield, CT 06824; **Phone:** 203-292-2000; **Board Cert:** Cardiovascular Disease 2013; **Med School:** NY Med Coll 1986; **Resid:** Internal Medicine, Montefiore Med Ctr 1989; **Fellow:** Cardiovascular Disease, UCSD Med Ctr 1991

Channamsetty, Venu MD (Cv) - **Spec Exp:** Echocardiography; Nuclear Cardiology; Diagnostic Problems; **Hospital:** St. Vincent's Med Ctr - Bridgeport; **Address:** Cardiology Physicians, 2979 Main St Fl 1, Bridgeport, CT 06606; **Phone:** 203-683-5100; **Board Cert:** Internal Medicine 2004; Cardiovascular Disease 2007; **Med School:** Albany Med Coll 2001; **Resid:** Internal Medicine, Rhode Island Hosp 2004; **Fellow:** Cardiovascular Disease, Westchester Med Ctr 2007

Choi, Joonun MD (Cv) - **Spec Exp:** Coronary Artery Disease; Heart Failure; **Hospital:** Stamford Hosp (page 971); **Address:** The Heart Physicians, 80 Mill River St, Ste 1300, Stamford, CT 06902; **Phone:** 203-348-7410; **Board Cert:** Cardiovascular Disease 2007; **Med School:** NY Med Coll 2001; **Resid:** Internal Medicine, St Vincent Med Ctr 2003; **Fellow:** Cardiovascular Disease, St Vincent Med Ctr 2007

Copen, David L MD (Cv) - **Spec Exp:** Cardiac Catheterization; Coronary Artery Disease; Congestive Heart Failure; Angioplasty & Stent Replacement; **Hospital:** Danbury Hosp; **Address:** Danbury WCMG, Cardiology, 111 Osborne St Fl 3 - Ste 131, Danbury, CT 06810; **Phone:** 203-739-7155; **Board Cert:** Internal Medicine 1972; Cardiovascular Disease 1975; **Med School:** SUNY Downstate 1969; **Resid:** Internal Medicine, Yale-New Haven Hosp 1972; **Fellow:** Cardiovascular Disease, Mass Genl Hosp 1974; **Fac Appt:** Assoc Clin Prof Med, Yale Univ

Cusack, Evelyn J MD (Cv) - **Spec Exp:** Echocardiography; Non-Invasive Cardiology; **Hospital:** Stamford Hosp (page 971); **Address:** The Heart Physicians, 80 Mill River St, Ste 1300, Stamford, CT 06902; **Phone:** 203-348-7410; **Board Cert:** Cardiovascular Disease 2004; **Med School:** Univ Mass Sch Med 1998; **Resid:** Internal Medicine, Rhode Island Hosp 2001; **Fellow:** Cardiovascular Disease, Westchester Med Ctr 2004; Echocardiography, NY-Presby/Columbia Univ Med Ctr 2005

Fisher, Lawrence I MD (Cv) - **Spec Exp:** Cardiac Catheterization; Pacemakers; Heart Valve Disease; **Hospital:** Danbury Hosp; **Address:** Cardiac Specialists, 25 Germantown Rd, Danbury, CT 06810; **Phone:** 203-794-0090; **Board Cert:** Internal Medicine 1988; Cardiovascular Disease 2011; **Med School:** SUNY Buffalo 1985; **Resid:** Internal Medicine, Bronx Muni Hosp 1988; **Fellow:** Cardiovascular Disease, Montefiore Med Ctr 1990

Green, Jeffrey A MD (Cv) - **Spec Exp:** Hypertension; Cholesterol/Lipid Disorders; Preventive Cardiology; **Hospital:** Stamford Hosp (page 971); **Address:** The Heart Physicians, 80 Mill River St, Ste 1300, Stamford, CT 06902; **Phone:** 203-348-7410; **Board Cert:** Cardiovascular Disease 2004; **Med School:** NY Med Coll 1998; **Resid:** Internal Medicine, Montefiore Med Ctr 2001; **Fellow:** Cardiovascular Disease, Montefiore Med Ctr 2004

Heiman, Mark D MD (Cv) - Spec Exp: Nuclear Cardiology; Cardiac CT Angiography; Clinical Trials; **Hospital:** Stamford Hosp (page 971), St. Vincent's Med Ctr - Bridgeport; **Address:** Cardio Assocs Fairfield Co, 1177 Summer St, Ste 5, Stamford, CT 06901; **Phone:** 203-353-1133; **Board Cert:** Internal Medicine 1989; Cardiovascular Disease 2011; **Med School:** Albert Einstein Coll Med 1986; **Resid:** Internal Medicine, Montefiore Med Ctr 1989; **Fellow:** Cardiovascular Disease, Montefiore Med Ctr 1991

Horowitz, Steven F MD (Cv) - Spec Exp: Nuclear Cardiology; Preventive Cardiology; Complementary Medicine; **Hospital:** Stamford Hosp (page 971); **Address:** Stamford Hospital, Dept Cardiology, 30 Shelburne Rd Fl 2, Stamford, CT 06904-9317; **Phone:** 203-276-7480; **Board Cert:** Internal Medicine 1975; Cardiovascular Disease 1979; **Med School:** NY Med Coll 1972; **Resid:** Internal Medicine, Beth Israel Hosp 1975; **Fellow:** Cardiovascular Disease, Mt Sinai Hosp 1978; Cardiology Research, Mt Sinai Hosp 1979

Keller, Andrew M MD (Cv) - Spec Exp: Echocardiography; Cardiac Imaging; **Hospital:** Danbury Hosp; **Address:** Danbury WCMG, Cardiology, 111 Osborne St Fl 3 - Ste 131, Danbury, CT 06810; **Phone:** 203-739-7155; **Board Cert:** Internal Medicine 1982; Cardiovascular Disease 1985; **Med School:** Ohio State Univ 1979; **Resid:** Internal Medicine, Duke Univ Hosp 1982; **Fellow:** Cardiovascular Disease, UT Southwestern Med Ctr 1985; **Fac Appt:** Assoc Clin Prof Med, Columbia P&S

Kosinski, Edward J MD (Cv) - Spec Exp: Angioplasty & Stent Placement; Coronary Artery Disease; Peripheral Vascular Disease; **Hospital:** St. Vincent's Med Ctr - Bridgeport; **Address:** Cardio Physicians, 2979 Main St Fl 1, Bridgeport, CT 06606-4201; **Phone:** 203-683-5100; **Board Cert:** Internal Medicine 1976; Cardiovascular Disease 1979; **Med School:** Wake Forest Univ 1973; **Resid:** Internal Medicine, Columbia-Presby Med Ctr 1976; **Fellow:** Cardiovascular Disease, Peter Bent Brigham Hosp 1979; **Fac Appt:** Assoc Clin Prof Med, Yale Univ

Kunkes, Steven H MD (Cv) - Spec Exp: Cardiovascular Imaging; Diagnostic Problems; **Hospital:** Bridgeport Hosp, Milford Hosp; **Address:** Cardiac Specialists, 1305 Post Rd, Fairfield, CT 06824; **Phone:** 203-292-2000; **Board Cert:** Internal Medicine 1976; Cardiovascular Disease 1979; Geriatric Medicine 2004; **Med School:** Mount Sinai Sch Med 1973; **Resid:** Internal Medicine, Bellevue Hosp Ctr 1976; **Fellow:** Cardiovascular Disease, Mt Sinai Med Ctr 1978; **Fac Appt:** Assoc Clin Prof Med, Yale Univ

Lomnitz, David J MD (Cv) - Spec Exp: Echocardiography; Nuclear Cardiology; **Hospital:** Norwalk Hosp, St. Vincent's Med Ctr - Bridgeport; **Address:** Cardio Assocs Fairfield Co, 40 Cross St, Ste 200, Norwalk, CT 06851; **Phone:** 203-845-2160; **Board Cert:** Cardiovascular Disease 2011; **Med School:** Univ Pennsylvania 1995; **Resid:** Internal Medicine, UCSF Med Ctr 1998; **Fellow:** Cardiovascular Disease, NY-Presby/Weill Cornell Med Ctr 2001

Mani, Susan MD (Cv) - Spec Exp: Heart Disease in Women; Cholesterol/Lipid Disorders; **Hospital:** Danbury Hosp; **Address:** Danbury WCMG, Cardiology, 111 Osborne St Fl 3 - Ste 131, Danbury, CT 06810; **Phone:** 203-739-7155; **Board Cert:** Cardiovascular Disease 2005; **Med School:** Johns Hopkins Univ 1998; **Resid:** Internal Medicine, Johns Hopkins Hosp 2001; **Fellow:** Cardiovascular Disease, NY-Presby/Columbia Univ Med Ctr 2005

Marshalko, Stephen J MD/PhD (Cv) - Spec Exp: Congenital Heart Disease; Coronary Artery Disease; Echocardiography; Mitral Valve Prolapse; **Hospital:** Bridgeport Hosp, St. Vincent's Med Ctr - Bridgeport; **Address:** Advanced Cardiovascular Specs, 439 Mill Hill Ave, Bridgeport, CT 06610; **Phone:** 203-334-2100; **Board Cert:** Internal Medicine 2010; Cardiovascular Disease 2013; Interventional Cardiology 2004; **Med School:** Yale Univ 1996; **Resid:** Internal Medicine, Yale-New Haven Hosp 1999; **Fellow:** Cardiovascular Disease, Yale-New Haven Hosp 2002

Meizlish, Jay Lewis MD (Cv) - **Spec Exp:** Interventional Cardiology; Preventive Cardiology; Cholesterol/Lipid Disorders; Nuclear Cardiology; **Hospital:** Bridgeport Hosp, Milford Hosp; **Address:** Cardiac Specs, 1305 Post Rd, Fairfield, CT 06824; **Phone:** 203-292-2000; **Board Cert:** Internal Medicine 1980; Cardiovascular Disease 1983; Nuclear Medicine 1984; Interventional Cardiology 2010; **Med School:** NYU Sch Med 1977; **Resid:** Internal Medicine, Harbor-UCLA Med Ctr 1980; **Fellow:** Cardiovascular Disease, Yale-New Haven Hosp 1983; Nuclear Medicine, Yale-New Haven Hosp 1984

Michaelson, Stephen MD (Cv) - **Spec Exp:** Congestive Heart Failure; Coronary Artery Disease; **Hospital:** Norwalk Hosp; **Address:** Cardio Assocs Fairfield Co, 40 Cross St, Ste 200, Norwalk, CT 06851; **Phone:** 203-845-2160; **Board Cert:** Internal Medicine 1975; Cardiovascular Disease 1977; **Med School:** SUNY Upstate Med Univ 1972; **Resid:** Internal Medicine, Univ VA Hosp 1975; **Fellow:** Cardiovascular Disease, Yale-New Haven Hosp 1977

Neeson, Francis J MD (Cv) - **Spec Exp:** Preventive Cardiology; Echocardiography; **Hospital:** Stamford Hosp (page 971), Greenwich Hosp (page 970); **Address:** Greenwich Med Grp, 75 Holly Hill Ln, Greenwich, CT 06830; **Phone:** 203-869-6960; **Board Cert:** Internal Medicine 1988; Cardiovascular Disease 2011; **Med School:** NYU Sch Med 1985; **Resid:** Internal Medicine, Montefiore Med Ctr 1988; **Fellow:** Cardiovascular Disease, Montefiore Med Ctr 1991

Pollack, Brian D MD (Cv) - **Spec Exp:** Nuclear Cardiology; Echocardiography; **Hospital:** Danbury Hosp; **Address:** 25 Germantown Rd, Ste 2B, Danbury, CT 06810; **Phone:** 203-794-0090; **Board Cert:** Cardiovascular Disease 2013; Echocardiography 2006; Nuclear Cardiology 2003; **Med School:** Mount Sinai Sch Med 1987; **Resid:** Internal Medicine, Mt Sinai Med Ctr 1990; **Fellow:** Cardiovascular Disease, Westchester Med Ctr 1993

Ronen, Alon MD (Cv) - **Spec Exp:** Echocardiography; Nuclear Cardiology; Preventive Cardiology; Invasive Cardiology; **Hospital:** St. Vincent's Med Ctr - Bridgeport, Bridgeport Hosp; **Address:** CT Heart Vascular Ctr, 112 Quary Rd, Ste 400, Trumbull, CT 06611; **Phone:** 203-333-8800; **Board Cert:** Cardiovascular Disease 2010; Nuclear Cardiology 2011; Echocardiography 2007; **Med School:** Med Coll PA 1994; **Resid:** Internal Medicine, UMass Genl Hosp 1997; **Fellow:** Cardiovascular Disease, UMass Genl Hosp 2000

Schmierer, Jeffrey A MD (Cv) - **Spec Exp:** Nutrition; **Hospital:** Danbury Hosp; **Address:** Danbury WCMG, Cardiology, 111 Osborne St Fl 3 - Ste 131, Danbury, CT 06810; **Phone:** 203-739-7155; **Board Cert:** Internal Medicine 1982; Cardiovascular Disease 1985; **Med School:** SUNY Downstate 1979; **Resid:** Internal Medicine, NY-Presby/Weill Cornell Med Ctr 1982; **Fellow:** Cardiovascular Disease, Tufts Med Ctr 1984

Schuster, Edward H MD (Cv) - **Spec Exp:** Hypertension; Heart Failure; Cholesterol/Lipid Disorders; **Hospital:** Stamford Hosp (page 971), Norwalk Hosp; **Address:** Tully Hlth Ctr, 32 Strawberry Hill Ct, Stamford, CT 06902; **Phone:** 203-276-2323; **Board Cert:** Internal Medicine 1980; Cardiovascular Disease 1981; **Med School:** Ros Franklin Univ/Chicago Med Sch 1976; **Resid:** Internal Medicine, Duke Univ Med Ctr 1979; **Fellow:** Cardiovascular Disease, Johns Hopkins Hosp 1981

Taikowski, Richard L MD (Cv) - **Spec Exp:** Echocardiography; Congenital Heart Disease-Adult; Nuclear Cardiology; **Hospital:** Bridgeport Hosp, Milford Hosp; **Address:** Cardiac Specs, 1305 Post Rd, Fairfield, CT 06824; **Phone:** 203-292-2000; **Board Cert:** Internal Medicine 1988; Cardiovascular Disease 2012; **Med School:** Boston Univ 1985; **Resid:** Internal Medicine, Boston Univ Med Ctr 1988; **Fellow:** Cardiovascular Disease, Mt Sinai Med Ctr 1991

Zarich, Stuart W MD (Cv) - **Spec Exp:** Echocardiography; Heart Disease in Women; Cardiac Catheterization; Mitral Valve Prolapse; **Hospital:** Bridgeport Hosp; **Address:** Northeast Med Grp, 267 Grant St, Fl 10, Bridgeport, CT 06610; **Phone:** 203-384-3844; **Board Cert:** Internal Medicine 1984; Cardiovascular Disease 1989; **Med School:** SUNY Upstate Med Univ 1981; **Resid:** Internal Medicine, Beth Israel Deaconess Hosp 1984; **Fellow:** Cardiovascular Disease, Beth Israel Deaconess Hosp/Harvard 1988; **Fac Appt:** Clin Prof Med, Yale Univ

Child & Adolescent Psychiatry

Lipschitz, Deborah S MD (ChAP) - **Spec Exp:** Developmental Disorders; Mood Disorders; Anxiety & Depression; Trauma Psychiatry; **Address:** 21 Sherman Ct, Fairfield, CT 06824-5825; **Phone:** 203-256-9926; **Board Cert:** Psychiatry 2008; Child & Adolescent Psychiatry 2010; **Med School:** Africa 1986; **Resid:** Psychiatry, Montefiore Med Ctr 1994; **Fellow:** Child & Adolescent Psychiatry, Montefiore Med Ctr 1995

Lustbader, Andrew MD (ChAP) - **Spec Exp:** ADD/ADHD; Anxiety & Depression; Parenting Issues; **Hospital:** Yale-New Haven Hosp; **Address:** Therapeutic Ctr for Chldn & Families, 215 Main St, Westport, CT 06880; **Phone:** 203-454-2428 x704; **Board Cert:** Child & Adolescent Psychiatry 2012; **Med School:** Albert Einstein Coll Med 1991; **Resid:** Pediatrics, Yale-New Haven Hosp 1994; Psychiatry, Yale-New Haven Hosp 1996; **Fellow:** Child & Adolescent Psychiatry, Yale-New Haven Hosp 1998; **Fac Appt:** Asst Clin Prof ChAP, Yale Univ

Poll, Joan MD (ChAP) - **Spec Exp:** Developmental Disorders; Anxiety Disorders; Psychotherapy; Psychoanalysis; **Address:** 16 Bushy Ridge Rd, Westport, CT 06880-2105; **Phone:** 203-222-1186; **Board Cert:** Psychiatry 1983; Child & Adolescent Psychiatry 1993; **Med School:** NY Med Coll 1976; **Resid:** Psychiatry, Jacobi Med Ctr 1980; **Fellow:** Child & Adolescent Psychiatry, Yale-New Haven Hosp 1982; **Fac Appt:** Asst Clin Prof Psyc, Yale Univ

Rosenfeld, Alvin A MD (ChAP) - **Spec Exp:** Psychotherapy; Sexual Development Problems; Overscheduled Children; Family Therapy; **Hospital:** NY-Presby/Weill Cornell Med Ctr, NY (page 102); **Address:** 17 Sherwood Pl, Greenwich, CT 06830; **Phone:** 203-861-0700; **Board Cert:** Psychiatry 1976; Child & Adolescent Psychiatry 1978; **Med School:** Harvard Med Sch 1970; **Resid:** Psychiatry, Mass Mental Hlth Ctr 1973; **Fellow:** Child & Adolescent Psychiatry, Beth Israel Hosp 1975; **Fac Appt:** Clin Prof Psyc, Cornell Univ-Weill Med Coll

Samanich, John G MD (ChAP) - **Spec Exp:** ADD/ADHD; Autism & Developmental Disorders; Eating Disorders; Substance Abuse; **Address:** Greenwich Child & Adolescent Psych, 239 Glenville Rd, Greenwich, CT 06831; **Phone:** 203-531-1031; **Board Cert:** Psychiatry 2006; Child & Adolescent Psychiatry 2007; **Med School:** SUNY Buffalo 2001; **Resid:** Psychiatry, Beth Israel Med Ctr 2004; **Fellow:** Child & Adolescent Psychiatry, St Vincent Med Ctr 2006

Colon & Rectal Surgery

Bussell, Stuart MD (CRS) - **Spec Exp:** Minimally Invasive Surgery; **Hospital:** Danbury Hosp; **Address:** Danbury, Colon-Rectal Surgery-WCMG, 111 Osborne St Fl 1, Danbury, CT 06810; **Phone:** 203-739-7131; **Board Cert:** Surgery 2012; Colon & Rectal Surgery 2013; **Med School:** Mich State Univ 1996; **Resid:** Surgery, Mich State Univ Hosp 2001; **Fellow:** Colon & Rectal Surgery, Greater Baltimore Med Ctr 2002

Littlejohn, Charles E MD (CRS) - **Spec Exp:** Colon & Rectal Cancer; **Hospital:** Stamford Hosp (page 971), Norwalk Hosp; **Address:** Colon & Rectal Surg of Southern CT, 70 Mill River St, Stamford, CT 06902; **Phone:** 203-323-8989; **Board Cert:** Colon & Rectal Surgery 1985; **Med School:** Dartmouth Med Sch 1978; **Resid:** Surgery, Rochester Genl Hosp 1980; Colon & Rectal Surgery, UMDNJ Med Ctr 1984

McClane, James M MD (CRS) - **Spec Exp:** Colon & Rectal Cancer; Laparoscopic Surgery; Inflammatory Bowel Disease; Diverticulitis; **Hospital:** Norwalk Hosp; **Address:** Colon & Rectal Surgical Care CT, 30 Stevens St, Ste D, Norwalk, CT 06856; **Phone:** 203-852-2262; **Board Cert:** Colon & Rectal Surgery 2011; **Med School:** Cornell Univ-Weill Med Coll 1995; **Resid:** Surgery, Thos Jefferson Univ Hosp 2000; **Fellow:** Colon & Rectal Surgery, Cleveland Clin Fdn 2001

Thornton, Scott C MD (CRS) - **Spec Exp:** Laparoscopic Surgery; Colon & Rectal Cancer; Minimally Invasive Surgery; Colostomy Avoidance; **Hospital:** Bridgeport Hosp; **Address:** Northeast Med Grp, 1305 Post Rd, Ste 215, Fairfield, CT 06824; **Phone:** 203-255-7088; **Board Cert:** Colon & Rectal Surgery 2012; Surgery 2011; **Med School:** Univ Pittsburgh 1986; **Resid:** Surgery, Univ Conn Sch Med Affil Hosp 1991; **Fellow:** Colon & Rectal Surgery, UMDNJ Med Ctr 1992; **Fac Appt:** Clin Prof S, Yale Univ

Dermatology

Connors, Richard C MD (D) - **Spec Exp:** Skin Cancer; Dermatopathology; **Hospital:** Greenwich Hosp (page 970); **Address:** 1 Perryridge Rd, Ste 2, Greenwich, CT 06830-4607; **Phone:** 203-622-0808; **Board Cert:** Dermatology 1974; Dermatopathology 1976; **Med School:** Cornell Univ-Weill Med Coll 1967; **Resid:** Dermatology, New York Hosp 1974; **Fellow:** Dermatopathology, NYU Med Ctr 1975; **Fac Appt:** Assoc Clin Prof D, NYU Sch Med

Dietz, Stephanie B MD (D) - **Spec Exp:** Pediatric Dermatology; Acne; Eczema; **Hospital:** Stamford Hosp (page 971), Yale-New Haven Hosp; **Address:** Dermatology Ctr Stamford, 1290 Summer St, Ste 3600, Stamford, CT 06905; **Phone:** 203-325-3576; **Board Cert:** Dermatology 2008; **Med School:** Univ Pennsylvania 1995; **Resid:** Internal Medicine, Hosp Univ Penn 1996; Dermatology, NYU Med Ctr 1999

Drugge, Rhett J MD (D) - **Spec Exp:** Melanoma; Psoriasis; Skin Cancer; **Hospital:** Stamford Hosp (page 971); **Address:** 50 Glenbrook Rd, Ste 1C, Stamford, CT 06902-2949; **Phone:** 203-324-5719; **Board Cert:** Dermatology 2013; **Med School:** NY Med Coll 1989; **Resid:** Dermatology, Univ Michigan Med Ctr 1992

Haven, Lynne Marie MD (D) - **Spec Exp:** Facial Rejuvenation; Cosmetic Dermatology; Botox Therapy; Laser Surgery; **Hospital:** Greenwich Hosp (page 970); **Address:** 49 Lake Ave, Greenwich, CT 06830; **Phone:** 203-869-4242; **Board Cert:** Dermatology 2008; **Med School:** Columbia P&S 1995; **Resid:** Internal Medicine, Mass Genl Hosp 1996; Dermatology, NYU Med Ctr 1999

Kolenik III, Steven A MD (D) - **Spec Exp:** Skin Cancer; Mohs Surgery; **Hospital:** Norwalk Hosp, Yale-New Haven Hosp; **Address:** CT Dermatology Grp, 761 Main Ave, Ste 102, Norwalk, CT 06851; **Phone:** 203-810-4151; **Board Cert:** Dermatology 2014; **Med School:** Yale Univ 1990; **Resid:** Dermatology, Yale-New Haven Hosp 1994; **Fellow:** Mohs Surgery, Yale-New Haven Hosp 1995; **Fac Appt:** Asst Clin Prof D, Yale Univ

Lipper, Graeme M MD (D) - **Spec Exp:** Pediatric Dermatology; Cosmetic Surgery; Skin Laser Surgery; Botox Therapy; **Hospital:** Danbury Hosp; **Address:** Advanced DermCare, 25 Tamarack Ave, Danbury, CT 06810; **Phone:** 203-797-8990; **Board Cert:** Dermatology 2010; **Med School:** Harvard Med Sch 1997; **Resid:** Dermatology, Mass Genl Hosp 2001; **Fellow:** Cosmetic Surgery, Mass Genl Hosp 2002

Maiocco, Kenneth J MD (D) - **Spec Exp:** Skin Cancer; Dermatologic Surgery; Botox Therapy; **Hospital:** St. Vincent's Med Ctr - Bridgeport, Bridgeport Hosp; **Address:** Moss & Maiocco, 4639 Main St, Ste 1, Bridgeport, CT 06606-1873; **Phone:** 203-374-5546; **Board Cert:** Dermatology 1976; **Med School:** Univ Rochester 1967; **Resid:** Internal Medicine, St Vincents Med Ctr 1971; Dermatology, Geisinger Med Ctr 1975

Mayer, Fern E MD (D) - **Spec Exp:** Skin Cancer; Pediatric Dermatology; Immune Deficiency-Skin Disorders; **Hospital:** Stamford Hosp (page 971), Yale-New Haven Hosp; **Address:** 132 Morgan St, Stamford, CT 06905; **Phone:** 203-969-0123; **Board Cert:** Dermatology 1990; **Med School:** NYU Sch Med 1986; **Resid:** Internal Medicine, Mt Sinai Hosp 1987; Dermatology, SUNY Downstate Med Ctr 1990

McAleer, Patricia A MD (D) - **Spec Exp:** Acne; Psoriasis; Skin Laser Surgery; Botox Therapy; **Hospital:** Norwalk Hosp, Stamford Hosp (page 971); **Address:** Skin Care Physicians of Fairfield County, 13 Park St, Norwalk, CT 06851; **Phone:** 203-847-2400; **Board Cert:** Dermatology 2008; **Med School:** Ros Franklin Univ/Chicago Med Sch 1995; **Resid:** Dermatology, Westchester Med Ctr 1999

Naidorf, Ellen S MD (D) - **Spec Exp:** Skin Cancer; Pediatric Dermatology; **Hospital:** Stamford Hosp (page 971), Yale-New Haven Hosp; **Address:** 22 Long Ridge Rd, Stamford, CT 06905-3812; **Phone:** 203-964-1103; **Board Cert:** Dermatology 2009; Pediatrics 1980; **Med School:** Columbia P&S 1975; **Resid:** Pediatrics, Yale-New Haven Hosp 1978; **Fellow:** Dermatology, Columbia Presby Hosp 1980

Oestreicher, Mark I MD (D) - **Spec Exp:** Skin Cancer; Hair Loss; Cosmetic Dermatology; **Hospital:** Bridgeport Hosp, St. Vincent's Med Ctr - Bridgeport; **Address:** Adult & Ped Derm Specs, 160 Hawley Ln, Ste 104, Trumbull, CT 06611; **Phone:** 203-377-0639; **Board Cert:** Internal Medicine 1977; Dermatology 1979; **Med School:** Albany Med Coll 1974; **Resid:** Internal Medicine, Albany Meml Hosp 1977; Dermatology, UCLA Med Ctr 1979; **Fac Appt:** Asst Prof D, Yale Univ

Oshman, Robin G MD/PhD (D) - **Spec Exp:** Skin Cancer; Cosmetic Dermatology; Pediatric Dermatology; **Hospital:** Yale-New Haven Hosp, Norwalk Hosp; **Address:** 101 Long Lots Rd, Westport, CT 06880-5426; **Phone:** 203-454-0743; **Board Cert:** Dermatology 1990; **Med School:** Brown Univ 1985; **Resid:** Dermatology, Mt Sinai Med Ctr 1989; **Fac Appt:** Asst Clin Prof D, Yale Univ

Pesce, Joseph R MD (D) - **Spec Exp:** Psoriasis; Rosacea; Skin Cancer; **Hospital:** St. Vincent's Med Ctr - Bridgeport, Bridgeport Hosp; **Address:** Assocs in Dermatology, 4699 Main St, Ste 212, Bridgeport, CT 06606-1830; **Phone:** 203-372-8949; **Board Cert:** Dermatology 1972; **Med School:** Belgium 1967; **Resid:** Internal Medicine, Hosp St Raphael 1968; Dermatology, Dartmouth-Hitchcock Med Ctr 1971

Pruzan-Clain, Debra L MD (D) - **Spec Exp:** Cosmetic Dermatology; Pediatric Dermatology; Skin Cancer; **Hospital:** Stamford Hosp (page 971); **Address:** Dermatology Ctr Stamford, 1290 Summer St, Ste 3600, Stamford, CT 06905; **Phone:** 203-325-3576; **Board Cert:** Dermatology 1990; **Med School:** Univ Pennsylvania 1986; **Resid:** Internal Medicine, Mt Sinai Hosp 1987; Dermatology, SUNY Downstate Med Ctr 1990; **Fac Appt:** Asst Prof D, Albert Einstein Coll Med

Sibrack, Laurence A MD/PhD (D) - **Spec Exp:** Skin Cancer; Cosmetic Dermatology; **Hospital:** Danbury Hosp; **Address:** Dermatology Assocs-W CT, 73 Sand Pit Rd, Ste 207, Danbury, CT 6810; **Phone:** 203-792-4151; **Board Cert:** Dermatology 1978; **Med School:** Univ Mich Med Sch 1974; **Resid:** Dermatology, Yale-New Haven Hosp 1978; **Fac Appt:** Assoc Clin Prof D, Yale Univ

Whitman, Gail B MD (D) - **Spec Exp:** Pediatric Dermatology; Acne; Skin Laser Surgery; **Hospital:** Norwalk Hosp; **Address:** Skin Care Physicians of Fairfield Co, 13 Park St, Norwalk, CT 06851; **Phone:** 203-847-2400; **Board Cert:** Dermatology 1986; **Med School:** UMDNJ-NJ Med Sch, Newark 1980; **Resid:** Pediatrics, Overlook Hosp 1983; Dermatology, NY Presby-Columbia Med Ctr 1986

Diagnostic Radiology

Cohen, Steven M MD (DR) - **Spec Exp:** Ultrasound; Women's Imaging; CT Body Scan; MRI; **Hospital:** Bridgeport Hosp, St. Vincent's Med Ctr - Bridgeport; **Address:** Advanced Radiology Cons, 3 Enterprise Drive, Shelton, CT 06484; **Phone:** 203-696-3672; **Board Cert:** Diagnostic Radiology 1987; **Med School:** NY Med Coll 1983; **Resid:** Internal Medicine, Stamford Hosp 1984; Diagnostic Radiology, Montefiore Med Ctr 1987; **Fellow:** Ultrasound/CT/MRI, Thos Jefferson Univ Hosp 1989; **Fac Appt:** Asst Prof Rad, Columbia P&S

Desai, Kapil R MD (DR) - **Spec Exp:** Musculoskeletal Imaging; Musculoskeletal Tumors; Ultrasound; Sports Medicine Radiology; **Hospital:** Greenwich Hosp (page 970); **Address:** Greenwich Radiological Grp, 49 Lake Ave, Ste 101, Greenwich, CT 06830; **Phone:** 203-869-6220; **Board Cert:** Diagnostic Radiology 2008; **Med School:** UMDNJ-NJ Med Sch, Newark 2003; **Resid:** Diagnostic Radiology, NYU Med Ctr 2008; **Fellow:** Musculoskeletal Imaging, NYU Med Ctr 2009

Donahue, John P MD (DR) - **Spec Exp:** MRI; Women's Imaging; CT Scan; **Hospital:** Bridgeport Hosp; **Address:** Robert Russo MD & Assocs Radiology, 2909 Main St Fl 1, Stratford, CT 06615; **Phone:** 203-683-4570; **Board Cert:** Diagnostic Radiology 1996; **Med School:** Georgetown Univ 1991; **Resid:** Diagnostic Radiology, St Vincents Med Ctr 1996; **Fellow:** Abdominal Imaging, NY-Presby/Columbia Univ Med Ctr 1997

Ehrlich, Conrad MD (DR) - **Spec Exp:** CT Scan; Mammography; Ultrasound; **Hospital:** Danbury Hosp; **Address:** Housatonic Valley Radiological Assocs, 67 Sand Pit Rd, Ste 105, Danbury, CT 06810-4032; **Phone:** 203-797-1770; **Board Cert:** Internal Medicine 1979; Nuclear Medicine 1981; Diagnostic Radiology 1983; **Med School:** Boston Univ 1976; **Resid:** Nuclear Medicine, Harvard Joint Program 1981; Diagnostic Radiology, Beth Israel Deaconess Med Ctr 1983; **Fellow:** Ultrasound/CT, Beth Israel Deaconess Med Ctr 1984

Ernberg, Lauren A MD (DR) - **Spec Exp:** Musculoskeletal Imaging; MRI; **Hospital:** Norwalk Hosp; **Address:** Norwalk Radiology & Mammography Ctr, 148 East Ave, Ste 1R, Norwalk, CT 06851; **Phone:** 203-838-4886; **Board Cert:** Diagnostic Radiology 2012; **Med School:** Cornell Univ-Weill Med Coll 1997; **Resid:** Diagnostic Radiology, NY-Presby/Weill Cornell Med Ctr 2002; **Fellow:** Musculoskeletal Imaging, Hosp Special Surg 2003

Fey, Christopher P MD (DR) - **Spec Exp:** Nuclear Radiology; Nuclear Medicine; MRI; CT Scan; **Hospital:** Greenwich Hosp (page 970); **Address:** Greenwich Radiological Grp, 49 Lake Ave, Ste 205, Greenwich, CT 06830; **Phone:** 203-869-6220; **Board Cert:** Diagnostic Radiology 1998; Nuclear Medicine 2009; **Med School:** Yale Univ 1993; **Resid:** Radiology, Beth Israel Deaconess Med Ctr 1998; **Fellow:** Nuclear Medicine, Harvard Univ Affil Hosp 1999

King, Michael H MD (DR) - **Spec Exp:** MRI; Ultrasound; Thoracic Imaging; **Hospital:** Stamford Hosp (page 971); **Address:** Stamford Radiological Assocs, 34 Shelburne Rd, Stamford, CT 06902; **Phone:** 203-276-7860; **Board Cert:** Diagnostic Radiology 1999; **Med School:** Ros Franklin Univ/Chicago Med Sch 1995; **Resid:** Diagnostic Radiology, Norwalk Hosp 1999; **Fellow:** Radiology, NY Presby Hosp 2000

Lee, Ronald P MD (DR) - **Spec Exp:** MRI; CT Scan; **Hospital:** Norwalk Hosp; **Address:** Norwalk Radiology & Mammography Ctr, 148 East Ave, Ste 1R, Norwalk, CT 06851; **Phone:** 203-851-5645; **Board Cert:** Diagnostic Radiology 1991; **Med School:** NYU Sch Med 1986; **Resid:** Diagnostic Radiology, Bellevue Hosp/NYU Med Ctr 1991; **Fellow:** Magnetic Resonance Imaging, Johns Hopkins Hosp 1992

Mullen, David J MD (DR) - **Spec Exp:** MRI; CT Body Scan; **Hospital:** Greenwich Hosp (page 970); **Address:** Greenwich Radiological Grp, 49 Lake Ave, Ste 205, Greenwich, CT 06830; **Phone:** 203-869-6220; **Board Cert:** Diagnostic Radiology 1987; **Med School:** Albert Einstein Coll Med 1983; **Resid:** Diagnostic Radiology, Columbia-Presby Med Ctr 1987

Pittaro, Denise I MD (DR) - **Spec Exp:** Neuroradiology; **Hospital:** St. Vincent's Med Ctr - Bridgeport, Bridgeport Hosp; **Address:** Advanced Radiology Cons, 3 Enterprise Drive, Ste 220, Shelton, CT 06484; **Phone:** 203-696-6125; **Board Cert:** Diagnostic Radiology 1999; **Med School:** Univ Pennsylvania 1995; **Resid:** Diagnostic Radiology, Mallinckrodt Inst of Radiology 1999; **Fellow:** Neuroradiology, Brigham & Womens Hosp 2001

Riccio, Gioia J MD (DR) - **Spec Exp:** Women's Imaging; Ultrasound; Mammography; **Hospital:** Bridgeport Hosp; **Address:** Robert Russo MD & Assocs Radiology, 4699 Main St, Ste 108, Bridgeport, CT 06606; **Phone:** 203-683-4550; **Board Cert:** Diagnostic Radiology 2000; **Med School:** Puerto Rico 1993; **Resid:** Diagnostic Radiology, St Vincents Med Ctr 1998; **Fellow:** Women's Imaging, Wake Forest Baptist Med Ctr 1999; Mammography, Wake Forest Baptist Med Ctr 1999

Salik, Erez MD (DR) - **Spec Exp:** Interventional Radiology; **Hospital:** Greenwich Hosp (page 970), Norwalk Hosp; **Address:** Greenwich Radiological Grp, 49 Lake Ave, Greenwich, CT 06830; **Phone:** 203-863-3960; **Board Cert:** Diagnostic Radiology 2004; **Med School:** Mount Sinai Sch Med 1999; **Resid:** Radiology, NYU Med Ctr 2004; **Fellow:** Vascular & Interventional Radiology, Yale-New Haven Hosp 2005

Endocrinology, Diabetes & Metabolism

Arden-Cordone, Mary MD (EDM) - **Spec Exp:** Osteoporosis; Thyroid Disorders; **Hospital:** Stamford Hosp (page 971), Greenwich Hosp (page 970); **Address:** Endocrinology Ctr Stamford, 1275 Summer St, Ste A1, Stamford, CT 06905; **Phone:** 203-359-2444; **Board Cert:** Internal Medicine 2005; Endocrinology, Diabetes & Metabolism 2006; **Med School:** NYU Sch Med 1989; **Resid:** Internal Medicine, NY-Presby/Columbia Univ Med Ctr 1992; **Fellow:** Endocrinology, Diabetes & Metabolism, NY-Presby/Columbia Univ Med Ctr 1995

Benaviv-Meskin, Danielle P MD (EDM) - **Spec Exp:** Thyroid Disorders; Pituitary Disorders; Diabetes; **Hospital:** St. Vincent's Med Ctr - Bridgeport, Bridgeport Hosp; **Address:** Endocrine & Diabetes Specs of CT, 112 Quarry Rd, Ste 250, Trumbull, CT 06611; **Phone:** 203-371-7048; **Board Cert:** Endocrinology, Diabetes & Metabolism 2006; **Med School:** Jefferson Med Coll 2000; **Resid:** Internal Medicine, Montefiore Med Ctr 2004; **Fellow:** Endocrinology, Diabetes & Metabolism, NYU Med Ctr 2006

Goldberg-Berman, Judith C MD/PhD (EDM) - **Spec Exp:** Thyroid Disorders; Osteoporosis; Diabetes; **Hospital:** Greenwich Hosp (page 970); **Address:** 56 Lafayette Pl, Ste A, Greenwich, CT 06830; **Phone:** 203-622-9160; **Board Cert:** Endocrinology, Diabetes & Metabolism 2013; **Med School:** Cornell Univ-Weill Med Coll 1987; **Resid:** Internal Medicine, NYU/Bellevue Hosp 1990; **Fellow:** Endocrinology, New York Hosp/Meml Sloan Kettering 1993

Rennert, Nancy J MD (EDM) - **Spec Exp:** Diabetes in Minority Populations; Thyroid Disorders; Endocrine Disorders in Pregnancy; **Hospital:** Norwalk Hosp; **Address:** Norwalk Community Hlth Ctr, 120 Connecticut Ave, Norwalk, CT 06854; **Phone:** 203-899-1770; **Board Cert:** Endocrinology, Diabetes & Metabolism 2014; **Med School:** Univ Pittsburgh 1987; **Resid:** Internal Medicine, Univ Pitt Hlth Ctr 1990; **Fellow:** Endocrinology, Diabetes & Metabolism, Yale-New Haven Hosp 1993

Rich, Glenn MD (EDM) - **Spec Exp:** Calcium Disorders; Diabetes; **Hospital:** Bridgeport Hosp, St. Vincent's Med Ctr - Bridgeport; **Address:** Fairfield Co Med Grp, 15 Corporate Drive, Ste 2-1, Trumbull, CT 06611; **Phone:** 203-459-5100; **Board Cert:** Internal Medicine 1989; Endocrinology, Diabetes & Metabolism 2011; **Med School:** Cornell Univ-Weill Med Coll 1986; **Resid:** Internal Medicine, St Lukes Hospital 1989; **Fellow:** Endocrinology, Diabetes & Metabolism, Brigham & Women's Hosp 1991

Rosa, Joseph A MD (EDM) - **Spec Exp:** Diabetes; Thyroid Disorders; **Hospital:** St. Vincent's Med Ctr - Bridgeport, Bridgeport Hosp; **Address:** Endocrine & Diabetes Specs of CT, 112 Quarry Rd, Ste 250, Trumbull, CT 06611; **Phone:** 203-371-7048; **Board Cert:** Internal Medicine 1987; Endocrinology, Diabetes & Metabolism 1989; **Med School:** Mexico 1982; **Resid:** Internal Medicine, St Vincents Med Ctr 1986; **Fellow:** Endocrinology, Diabetes & Metabolism, Univ Conn Med Ctr 1988

Savino, Robert R DO (EDM) - **Spec Exp:** Diabetes; Hypogonadism-Male; **Hospital:** Danbury Hosp; **Address:** Danbury WCMG, Endocrinology, 25 Germantown Rd, Ste 1A, Danbury, CT 06810; **Phone:** 203-794-5620; **Board Cert:** Endocrinology, Diabetes & Metabolism 2005; **Med School:** NY Coll Osteo Med 1988; **Resid:** Internal Medicine, LIJ Med Ctr 1992; **Fellow:** Endocrinology, Diabetes & Metabolism, Lahey-Hitchcock Med Ctr 1993; Endocrinology, Diabetes & Metabolism, Joslin Diabetes Ctr 1994; **Fac Appt:** Asst Clin Prof Med, Yale Univ

Yu, Yi-Hao MD/PhD (EDM) - **Spec Exp:** Osteoporosis in Men; Nutrition; **Hospital:** Greenwich Hosp (page 970), Yale-New Haven Hosp; **Address:** Northeast Med Grp, Endocrinology, 2015 W Main St, Ste 101, Stamford, CT 06902; **Phone:** 203-863-3750; **Board Cert:** Endocrinology, Diabetes & Metabolism 2012; **Med School:** NYU Sch Med 1996; **Resid:** Internal Medicine, NY-Presby/Columbia Univ Med Ctr 1998; **Fellow:** Endocrinology, Diabetes & Metabolism, NY-Presby/Columbia Univ Med Ctr 2001; **Fac Appt:** Assoc Prof Med, Columbia P&S

Family Medicine

Acosta, Rodrigo MD (FMed) *PCP* - **Spec Exp:** Geriatric Care; Preventive Medicine; **Hospital:** Stamford Hosp (page 971); **Address:** Stamford Family Prac, 32 Strawberry Hill Ct Fl 4 - Ste 6, Stamford, CT 06902; **Phone:** 203-977-2566; **Board Cert:** Family Medicine 2008; Geriatric Medicine 2012; **Med School:** Univ Tex SW, Dallas 1984; **Resid:** Family Medicine, St. Joseph Med Ctr 1987

Cigno, Thomas MD (FMed) *PCP* - **Hospital:** Danbury Hosp; **Address:** 10 South St, Ste 201, Ridgefield, CT 06877; **Phone:** 203-244-7848; **Board Cert:** Family Medicine 2009; **Med School:** Tufts Univ 1986; **Resid:** Family Medicine, St Francis Hosp & Med Ctr 1989

Duchen, Douglas MD (FMed) *PCP* - **Spec Exp:** Preventive Medicine; **Hospital:** St. Vincent's Med Ctr - Bridgeport, Bridgeport Hosp; **Address:** Primed Physicians, 112 Quarry Rd, Ste 120, Trumbull, CT 06611; **Phone:** 203-372-4065; **Board Cert:** Family Medicine 2011; **Med School:** South Africa 1983; **Resid:** Orthopaedic Surgery, Whittington Hosp 1987; Family Medicine, Brookhaven Meml Hosp 1991

Falkoff, Alan T MD (FMed) *PCP* - **Spec Exp:** Preventive Medicine; **Hospital:** Stamford Hosp (page 971); **Address:** High Ridge Family Practice, 30 Buxton Farms Rd, Ste 210, Stamford, CT 06905; **Phone:** 203-322-7070; **Board Cert:** Family Medicine 2007; **Med School:** Grenada 1985; **Resid:** Family Medicine, St Joseph's Med Ctr 1988

Farrell, Matthew M MD (FMed) *PCP* - **Spec Exp:** Primary Care Sports Medicine; **Hospital:** Danbury Hosp; **Address:** 60 Old New Milford Rd, Ste 2A, Brookfield, CT 06804; **Phone:** 203-775-6365; **Board Cert:** Geriatric Medicine 2006; Family Medicine 2007; **Med School:** Columbia P&S 1980; **Resid:** Family Medicine, Somerset Med Ctr 1983; **Fac Appt:** Asst Clin Prof FMed, Univ Conn

Filiberto, Cosmo MD (FMed) *PCP* - **Spec Exp:** Geriatric Care; Cholesterol/Lipid Disorders; Preventive Medicine; **Hospital:** St. Vincent's Med Ctr - Bridgeport, Bridgeport Hosp; **Address:** Primed Physicians, 112 Quarry Rd, Ste 120, Trumbull, CT 06611; **Phone:** 203-372-4065; **Board Cert:** Family Medicine 2006; **Med School:** Italy 1976; **Resid:** Family Medicine, Lutheran Med Ctr 1980; **Fac Appt:** Assoc Prof FMed, Quinnipiac Univ-Netter Sch Med

Herbert, Joshua B MD (FMed) *PCP* - **Spec Exp:** Preventive Medicine; **Hospital:** Stamford Hosp (page 971); **Address:** Fairfield Co Personal Med, 5 High Ridge Park, Ste 103, Stamford, CT 06905; **Phone:** 203-276-4644; **Board Cert:** Family Medicine 2006; **Med School:** Grenada 1996; **Resid:** Family Medicine, N Shore Univ Hosp 1999

Mallozzi, Angelo MD (FMed) *PCP* - **Spec Exp:** Preventive Medicine; **Hospital:** Stamford Hosp (page 971); **Address:** Stamford Family Practice, 32 Strawberry Hill Ct Fl 4 - Ste 6, Stamford, CT 06902; **Phone:** 203-977-2566; **Board Cert:** Family Medicine 2008; **Med School:** Italy 1978; **Resid:** Family Medicine, St Joseph's Hosp 1982

Miller, Leslie R DO (FMed) *PCP* - **Spec Exp:** Preventive Medicine; **Hospital:** Bridgeport Hosp, St. Vincent's Med Ctr - Bridgeport; **Address:** 52 Beach Rd, Ste 102, Fairfield, CT 06824; **Phone:** 203-256-9905; **Board Cert:** Family Medicine 2004; **Med School:** NY Coll Osteo Med 1985; **Resid:** Family Medicine, St Francis Hosp 1988; **Fellow:** Preventive Medicine, Yale Univ School of Med Affil Hosp 1989

O'Regan, Simon MD (FMed) *PCP* - **Hospital:** Danbury Hosp; **Address:** 21 South St, Ridgefield, CT 06877; **Phone:** 203-438-6541; **Board Cert:** Family Medicine 2005; **Med School:** South Africa 1988; **Resid:** Family Medicine, Grott Schuur Hosp 1991

Williams, Ann H MD (FMed) *PCP* - **Hospital:** Stamford Hosp (page 971); **Address:** Morgan St Family Med, 90 Morgan St, Ste 108, Stamford, CT 06905; **Phone:** 203-359-9997; **Board Cert:** Family Medicine 2008; **Med School:** England, UK 1988; **Resid:** Family Medicine, Stamford Hosp 2008

Gastroenterology

Barenberg, David MD (Ge) - **Hospital:** Danbury Hosp; **Address:** Danbury WCMG, Gastroenterology, 111 Osborne St, Ste 121, Danbury, CT 06810; **Phone:** 203-739-7038; **Board Cert:** Internal Medicine 1983; Gastroenterology 1985; **Med School:** SUNY Downstate 1980; **Resid:** Internal Medicine, NY-Presby/Columbia Univ Med Ctr 1983; **Fellow:** Gastroenterology, Brigham & Womens Hosp 1985

Barro, Jennifer L MD (Ge) - **Spec Exp:** Endoscopy; **Hospital:** Greenwich Hosp (page 970); **Address:** Ctr GI Med Fairfield & Westchester, 500 W Putnam Ave, Ste 100, Greenwich, CT 06830; **Phone:** 203-863-2900; **Board Cert:** Internal Medicine 2011; Gastroenterology 2004; **Med School:** Stanford Univ 1998; **Resid:** Internal Medicine, Beth Israel Deaconess Med Ctr 2001; **Fellow:** Gastroenterology, Stanford Univ Hosp & Clins 2004

Bonheim, Nelson A MD (Ge) - **Spec Exp:** Inflammatory Bowel Disease; Hepatitis C; Colon Cancer; **Hospital:** Greenwich Hosp (page 970); **Address:** Ctr for GI Med Fairfield & Westchester, 500 W Putnam Ave, Ste 100, Greenwich, CT 06830; **Phone:** 203-863-2900; **Board Cert:** Internal Medicine 1973; Gastroenterology 1975; **Med School:** Ros Franklin Univ/Chicago Med Sch 1970; **Resid:** Internal Medicine, Bronx Muni Hosp 1973; **Fellow:** Gastroenterology, NY Hosp-Cornell Med Ctr 1975; **Fac Appt:** Assoc Prof Med, Yale Univ

Burns, Bryan J MD (Ge) - **Spec Exp:** Inflammatory Bowel Disease; Endoscopic Therapies; Gastroesophageal Reflux Disease (GERD); **Hospital:** St. Vincent's Med Ctr - Bridgeport, Bridgeport Hosp; **Address:** Fairfield Co Endoscopy Ctr, 888 White Plains Rd, Ste 110, Trumbull, CT 06611; **Phone:** 203-459-4451; **Board Cert:** Internal Medicine 2010; Gastroenterology 2013; **Med School:** Albert Einstein Coll Med 1997; **Resid:** Internal Medicine, NY-Presby/Weill Cornell Med Ctr 2000; **Fellow:** Gastroenterology, Montefiore Med Ctr 2003

Dettmer, Robert M MD (Ge) - **Spec Exp:** Endoscopy; Colonoscopy/Polypectomy; **Hospital:** Stamford Hosp (page 971); **Address:** Tully Ctr, Div Gastroenterology, 32 Strawberry Hill Ct, Ste 41042, Stamford, CT 06902; **Phone:** 203-348-5355; **Board Cert:** Gastroenterology 2010; **Med School:** Albert Einstein Coll Med 1994; **Resid:** Internal Medicine, NY-Presby/Columbia Univ Med Ctr 1997; **Fellow:** Gastroenterology, NY-Presby/Columbia Univ Med Ctr 2000

Grossman, Edward T MD (Ge) - **Spec Exp:** Inflammatory Bowel Disease; Malabsorption; **Hospital:** St. Vincent's Med Ctr - Bridgeport, Bridgeport Hosp; **Address:** Gastro Assocs, 425 Post Rd Fl 1, Fairfield, CT 06824; **Phone:** 203-292-9000; **Board Cert:** Internal Medicine 1970; Gastroenterology 1973; **Med School:** Albert Einstein Coll Med 1963; **Resid:** Internal Medicine, Bronx Muni Hosp Ctr 1969; **Fellow:** Gastroenterology, NY-Presby/Weill Cornell Med Ctr 1972; **Fac Appt:** Assoc Clin Prof Med, Univ Conn

Gruss, Claudia B MD (Ge) - **Spec Exp:** Colonoscopy; Gastroesophageal Reflux Disease (GERD); Inflammatory Bowel Disease; Nutrition; **Hospital:** Norwalk Hosp; **Address:** Arbor Med Grp, 73 Redding Rd, Georgetown, CT 06896; **Phone:** 203-544-9517; **Board Cert:** Internal Medicine 1980; Gastroenterology 1983; **Med School:** Brown Univ 1977; **Resid:** Internal Medicine, Rhode Island Hosp 1980; **Fellow:** Gastroenterology, Rhode Island Hosp 1983

Hale, William B MD (Ge) - **Spec Exp:** Liver Disease; Gastrointestinal Disorders; **Hospital:** Norwalk Hosp; **Address:** Norwalk Hosp, Div Gastroenterology, 30 Steven St, Ste D, Norwalk, CT 06850; **Phone:** 203-852-2278; **Board Cert:** Internal Medicine 1983; Gastroenterology 1987; **Med School:** Univ Wisc 1980; **Resid:** Internal Medicine, Boston Med Ctr 1983; **Fellow:** Gastroenterology, Boston Med Ctr 1986

Kapel, Robert C MD (Ge) - **Hospital:** Danbury Hosp; **Address:** 2 Glen Hill Rd, Danbury, CT 06810; **Phone:** 203-748-7460; **Board Cert:** Gastroenterology 2005; **Med School:** Cornell Univ 1989; **Resid:** Internal Medicine, Mount Sinai Med Ctr 1993; **Fellow:** Gastroenterology, Univ Miami Hosp 1995

Khaghan, Neda MD (Ge) - **Spec Exp:** Biliary Disease; Capsule Endoscopy; Pancreatic Cancer; **Hospital:** Greenwich Hosp (page 970); **Address:** Ctr GI Med Fairfield & Westchester, 500 W Putnam Ave, Ste 100, Greenwich, CT 06830; **Phone:** 203-863-2900; **Board Cert:** Internal Medicine 2008; Gastroenterology 2011; **Med School:** Mount Sinai Sch Med 1995; **Resid:** Internal Medicine, Mount Sinai Hosp 1998; **Fellow:** Gastroenterology, St. Luke's-Roosevelt Hosp 2001

Landau, Alan E MD (Ge) - **Spec Exp:** Endoscopy; Inflammatory Bowel Disease; **Hospital:** St. Vincent's Med Ctr - Bridgeport, Bridgeport Hosp; **Address:** Fairfield Co Endoscopy Ctr, 888 White Plains Rd, Ste 110, Trumbull, CT 06611; **Phone:** 203-459-4451; **Board Cert:** Internal Medicine 1988; Gastroenterology 2011; **Med School:** Boston Univ 1985; **Resid:** Internal Medicine, St Elizabeths Med Ctr 1988; **Fellow:** Gastroenterology, VA Med Ctr 1991

Latzman, Gordon MD (Ge) - **Spec Exp:** Biliary Disease; Endoscopy; Ulcerative Colitis/Crohn's; **Hospital:** St. Vincent's Med Ctr - Bridgeport, Bridgeport Hosp; **Address:** GI Health Specialists, 888 White Plains Rd, Ste 110, Trumbull, CT 06611; **Phone:** 203-459-4451; **Board Cert:** Gastroenterology 2005; **Med School:** Israel 1998; **Resid:** Internal Medicine, Mt Sinai Hosp 2001; **Fellow:** Gastroenterology, Mt Sinai Hosp 2005

Link, Richard J MD (Ge) - **Spec Exp:** Colon Cancer Screening; Gastroesophageal Reflux Disease (GERD); Inflammatory Bowel Disease; **Hospital:** Bridgeport Hosp; **Address:** Fairfield County Int Med & Gastro, 4641 Main St, Ste 1, Bridgeport, CT 06606-1827; **Phone:** 203-374-4966; **Board Cert:** Internal Medicine 1974; Gastroenterology 1989; **Med School:** UMDNJ-NJ Med Sch, Newark 1967; **Resid:** Internal Medicine, St Vincent Hosp 1970; **Fellow:** Gastroenterology, Rhode Island Hosp 1971; Gastroenterology, Bridgeport Hosp 1972

Mauer, Kenneth R MD (Ge) - **Spec Exp:** Endoscopy; Inflammatory Bowel Disease/Crohn's; Capsule Endoscopy; Colonoscopy; **Hospital:** St. Vincent's Med Ctr - Bridgeport, Bridgeport Hosp; **Address:** Gastro Assocs Fairfield Co, 425 Post Rd, Fairfield, CT 06824; **Phone:** 203-292-9000; **Board Cert:** Internal Medicine 1986; Gastroenterology 1989; **Med School:** NYU Sch Med 1983; **Resid:** Internal Medicine, Bronx Muni Hosp Ctr 1986; **Fellow:** Gastroenterology, Mount Sinai Hosp 1989

Meighan, Dennis M DO (Ge) - **Spec Exp:** Endoscopy; Biliary Disease; **Hospital:** Norwalk Hosp; **Address:** Norwalk Hosp, Div Gastroenterology, 30 Stevens St, Ste B, Med Office Bldg, Norwalk, CT 06856; **Phone:** 203-852-2278; **Board Cert:** Internal Medicine 1986; Gastroenterology 1989; **Med School:** Univ New Eng Coll Osteo Med 1982; **Resid:** Internal Medicine, Norwalk Hosp 1986; **Fellow:** Gastroenterology, Norwalk Hosp 1989

Nelson, Alan M MD (Ge) - **Spec Exp:** Swallowing Disorders; Endoscopy; Colon Cancer; **Hospital:** Bridgeport Hosp; **Address:** Fairfield Co Int Med & Gastro Assocs, 4641 Main St, Ste 1, Bridgeport, CT 06606-1827; **Phone:** 203-374-4966; **Board Cert:** Internal Medicine 1977; Gastroenterology 1979; **Med School:** Georgetown Univ 1974; **Resid:** Internal Medicine, Kings Co Hosp-SUNY Med Ctr 1976; Internal Medicine, Bridgeport Hosp 1977; **Fellow:** Gastroenterology, Yale Univ Affil Hosps 1979; **Fac Appt:** Asst Prof Med, Yale Univ

Soloway, Gregory N MD (Ge) - **Spec Exp:** Colon Cancer Screening; Barrett's Esophagus; Clostridium Difficile Disease; Endoscopic Therapies; **Hospital:** Bridgeport Hosp; **Address:** Gastroenterology Assocs, 2890 Main St Fl 2, Stratford, CT 06614; **Phone:** 203-375-1200; **Board Cert:** Gastroenterology 2004; Internal Medicine 1989; **Med School:** Cornell Univ-Weill Med Coll 1986; **Resid:** Internal Medicine, Montefiore Med Ctr 1989; **Fellow:** Gastroenterology, Montefiore Med Ctr 1993

Spivack, Julie MD (Ge) - **Spec Exp:** Colonoscopy; Gallbladder Disease; Biliary Disease; **Hospital:** St. Vincent's Med Ctr - Bridgeport, Bridgeport Hosp; **Address:** Gastro Assocs Fairfield Co, 425 Post Rd, Fairfield, CT 06824; **Phone:** 203-292-9000; **Board Cert:** Gastroenterology 2005; **Med School:** Albert Einstein Coll Med 1990; **Resid:** Internal Medicine, Beth Israel Deaconess Med Ctr 1993; **Fellow:** Gastroenterology, NY-Presby/Weill Cornell Med Ctr 1995; Gastroenterology, Meml Sloan-Kettering Cancer Ctr 1996

Taubin, Howard L MD (Ge) - **Spec Exp:** Celiac Disease; Colon Cancer Screening; Inflammatory Bowel Disease; Peptic Acid Disorders; **Hospital:** Bridgeport Hosp; **Address:** Gastroenterology Assocs, 2890 Main St Fl 2, Stratford, CT 06614; **Phone:** 203-375-1200; **Board Cert:** Internal Medicine 1972; Gastroenterology 1973; **Med School:** Univ VA Sch Med 1965; **Resid:** Internal Medicine, Montefiore Hosp 1967; Internal Medicine, Yale-New Haven Hosp 1970; **Fellow:** Gastroenterology, Yale-New Haven Hosp 1973; **Fac Appt:** Assoc Clin Prof Med, Yale Univ

Whelan, Thomas P MD (Ge) - **Spec Exp:** Food Allergy; Gastroesophageal Reflux Disease (GERD); Barrett's Esophagus; **Hospital:** Danbury Hosp; **Address:** Village Square Internal Med, 2 Elizabeth St, Bethel, CT 06801; **Phone:** 203-791-2221; **Board Cert:** Internal Medicine 1986; Gastroenterology 1989; **Med School:** Univ VT Coll Med 1983; **Resid:** Internal Medicine, Thomas Jefferson Univ Hosp 1986; **Fellow:** Gastroenterology, Temple Univ Hosp 1988

Zwas, Felice R MD (Ge) - **Spec Exp:** Gastroesophageal Reflux Disease (GERD); Barrett's Esophagus; Biliary Disease; **Hospital:** Greenwich Hosp (page 970); **Address:** Ctr GI Med Fairfield & Westchester, 500 W Putnam Ave, Ste 100, Greenwich, CT 06830; **Phone:** 203-863-2900; **Board Cert:** Internal Medicine 1983; Gastroenterology 1985; **Med School:** Columbia P&S 1980; **Resid:** Internal Medicine, NY-Presby/Columbia Univ Med Ctr 1983; **Fellow:** Gastroenterology, Beth Israel Deaconess Med Ctr 1985; **Fac Appt:** Asst Clin Prof Med, Yale Univ

Geriatric Medicine

Blagodatny, Marina L MD (Ger) - **Spec Exp:** Frail Elderly; Dementia; Cognitive Loss in Aging; Wound Healing/Care; **Hospital:** Bridgeport Hosp; **Address:** Bridgeport Hosp Ctr for Geriatrics, 95 Armory Rd, Stratford, CT 06614; **Phone:** 203-384-3388; **Board Cert:** Geriatric Medicine 2004; Hospice & Palliative Medicine 2010; **Med School:** Russia 1981; **Resid:** Internal Medicine, Brooklyn Hosp 2001; **Fellow:** Geriatric Medicine, Bellevue Med Ctr 2003

Jones, Stephen G MD (Ger) *PCP* - **Spec Exp:** Alzheimer's Disease; Dementia; **Hospital:** Greenwich Hosp (page 970), Yale-New Haven Hosp; **Address:** Greenwich Hosp, Primary Care, 5 Perryridge Rd, Greenwich, CT 06830; **Phone:** 203-863-3415; **Board Cert:** Internal Medicine 2012; Geriatric Medicine 2004; **Med School:** SUNY Stony Brook 1985; **Resid:** Internal Medicine, Stony Brook Univ Med Ctr 1989; **Fac Appt:** Assoc Clin Prof Med, Yale Univ

Geriatric Psychiatry

Dolan, Neil P MD (GerPsy) - **Spec Exp:** Cognitive Loss in Aging; Anxiety & Depression; Depression in the Elderly; **Hospital:** Bridgeport Hosp; **Address:** 267 Grant St, Bridgeport, CT 06610; **Phone:** 203-384-3897; **Board Cert:** Psychiatry 2006; Geriatric Psychiatry 2008; **Med School:** Ireland 1989; **Resid:** Psychiatry, Beth Israel Med Ctr 1995; **Fellow:** Geriatric Psychiatry, Indiana Univ Sch Med Affil Hosp 1996

Shetty, Sudhakar S MD (GerPsy) - **Spec Exp:** Depression in the Elderly; Memory Disorders; Psychiatry in Physical Illness; **Address:** Shoreline Psychiatry, 71 East Ave, Ste H, Norwalk, CT 06851; **Phone:** 203-656-1452; **Board Cert:** Psychiatry 2009; Geriatric Psychiatry 2006; **Med School:** India 1982; **Resid:** Psychiatry, St Vincents Hosp Med Ctr 1998; **Fellow:** Geriatric Psychiatry, St Vincents Hosp Med Ctr 1999

Gynecologic Oncology

Shahabi, Shohreh MD (GO) - **Spec Exp:** Hysterectomy Alternatives; Robotic Surgery; **Hospital:** Danbury Hosp; **Address:** Danbury Hosp, Gynecologic Oncology, 24 Hospital Ave, Danbury, CT 06810; **Phone:** 203-739-4900; **Board Cert:** Obstetrics & Gynecology 2014; Gynecologic Oncology 2014; **Med School:** Belgium 1992; **Resid:** Obstetrics & Gynecology, Universite Libre De Bruxelles 1997; Obstetrics & Gynecology, Yale-New Haven Hosp 2003; **Fellow:** Gynecologic Oncology, Montefiore Med Ctr 2006

Hand Surgery

Backe Jr, Henry A MD (HS) - **Spec Exp:** Upper Extremity Surgery; Upper Extremity Trauma; Carpal Tunnel Syndrome; **Hospital:** St. Vincent's Med Ctr - Bridgeport, Bridgeport Hosp; **Address:** Orthopaedic Specialty Grp, 75 Kings Highway Cutoff, Fairfield, CT 06824; **Phone:** 203-337-2600; **Board Cert:** Orthopaedic Surgery 2006; Hand Surgery 2006; **Med School:** Temple Univ 1986; **Resid:** Orthopaedic Surgery, Temple Univ Hosp 1991; **Fellow:** Hand Surgery, Hosp for Joint Diseases 1992; Joint Reconstruction, Hosp Special Surgery 1993

Crowe, John F MD (HS) - **Spec Exp:** Arthritis; Carpal Tunnel Syndrome; Rotator Cuff Surgery; **Hospital:** Greenwich Hosp (page 970); **Address:** Orthopaedic & Neurosurgery Specs, 6 Greenwich Office Park, Greenwich, CT 06831; **Phone:** 203-869-1147; **Board Cert:** Orthopaedic Surgery 1977; **Med School:** Cornell Univ-Weill Med Coll 1971; **Resid:** Surgery, St Lukes-Roosevelt Hosp 1973; Orthopaedic Surgery, Hosp Special Surgery 1976; **Fellow:** Hand Surgery, St Lukes-Roosevelt Hosp 1979

DiGiovanni, Joseph MD (HS) - **Spec Exp:** Wrist Surgery; Carpal Tunnel Syndrome; Elbow Surgery; Nerve Compression; **Hospital:** Danbury Hosp; **Address:** Danbury Orthopedics, 226 White St, Danbury, CT 06810; **Phone:** 203-797-1500 x6626; **Board Cert:** Orthopaedic Surgery 2013; **Med School:** Mount Sinai Sch Med 1994; **Resid:** Orthopaedic Surgery, Mount Sinai Med Ctr 1999; **Fellow:** Hand Surgery, NYU Hosp Joint Diseases 2000

Dowdle, John D MD (HS) - **Spec Exp:** Hand & Wrist Surgery; Elbow Surgery; **Hospital:** Stamford Hosp (page 971); **Address:** Premiere Med Grp, 1 Blachley Rd, Ste 2, Stamford, CT 06902; **Phone:** 203-325-8888; **Board Cert:** Orthopaedic Surgery 2009; Hand Surgery 2009; **Med School:** Univ Tex SW, Dallas 1988; **Resid:** Surgery, Johns Hopkins Hosp 1989; Orthopaedic Surgery, Montefiore Med Ctr 1994; **Fellow:** Hand Surgery, Roosevelt Hosp 1995

Kavookjian, Haik G MD (HS) - **Spec Exp:** Hand & Upper Extremity Surgery; **Hospital:** Stamford Hosp (page 971), Norwalk Hosp; **Address:** 555 Newfield Ave, Stamford, CT 06905; **Phone:** 203-358-0661; **Board Cert:** Orthopaedic Surgery 2008; Hand Surgery 2008; **Med School:** NY Med Coll 1985; **Resid:** Surgery, Boston Med Ctr 1987; Orthopaedic Surgery, Boston Med Ctr 1993; **Fellow:** Hand Surgery, NY-Presby/Columbia Univ Med Ctr 1994

Lunt, John MD (HS) - **Spec Exp:** Hand & Upper Extremity Surgery; Nerve Compression; Nerve Disorders/Surgery; Carpal Tunnel Syndrome; **Hospital:** Danbury Hosp; **Address:** Danbury Orthopedics, 35 Tamarack Ave, Danbury, CT 06811; **Phone:** 203-792-4263; **Board Cert:** Orthopaedic Surgery 2006; Hand Surgery 2006; **Med School:** Columbia P&S 1986; **Resid:** Orthopaedic Surgery, LIJ Med Ctr 1992; **Fellow:** Surgery, NY-Presby/Columbia Univ Med Ctr 1993

Rago, Thomas A MD (HS) - **Spec Exp:** Hand & Wrist Surgery; Upper Extremity Surgery; **Hospital:** St. Vincent's Med Ctr - Bridgeport, Bridgeport Hosp; **Address:** CT Hand & Upper Extremity Ctr, 3101 Main St, Bridgeport, CT 06606; **Phone:** 203-374-5892; **Board Cert:** Orthopaedic Surgery 2007; Hand Surgery 2007; **Med School:** Columbia P&S 1977; **Resid:** Surgery, Roosevelt Hosp 1979; Orthopaedic Surgery, Presby Hosp 1982; **Fellow:** Hand Surgery, NY-Presby/Columbia Med Ctr 1983

Hematology

Bar, Michael H MD (Hem) - **Spec Exp:** Multiple Myeloma; Leukemia & Lymphoma; Bleeding/Coagulation Disorders; Gaucher Disease; **Hospital:** Stamford Hosp (page 971); **Address:** Hematology Oncology, 34 Shelburne Rd, Stamford, CT 06902; **Phone:** 203-325-2695; **Board Cert:** Internal Medicine 1986; Medical Oncology 1989; Hematology 2010; **Med School:** Columbia P&S 1983; **Resid:** Internal Medicine, NY-Presby/Columbia Univ Med Ctr 1986; **Fellow:** Hematology & Oncology, UCSF Med Ctr 1989; **Fac Appt:** Asst Prof Med, Columbia P&S

Boyd, D. Barry MD (Hem) - **Spec Exp:** Hematologic Malignancies; Breast Cancer; Hodgkin's Lymphoma; **Hospital:** Greenwich Hosp (page 970); **Address:** Greennwich Hosp, Bendheim Cancer Ctr, 15 Valley Drive Fl 2 - Ste 200, Greenwich, CT 06831; **Phone:** 203-863-4610; **Board Cert:** Internal Medicine 1982; Medical Oncology 1987; **Med School:** Cornell Univ-Weill Med Coll 1979; **Resid:** Internal Medicine, NY-Presby/Weill Cornell Med Ctr 1982; **Fellow:** Hematology & Oncology, NY-Presby/Weill Cornell Med Ctr 1985; **Fac Appt:** Asst Clin Prof Med, Yale Univ

Duda, E Andrew MD (Hem) - **Spec Exp:** Leukemia & Lymphoma; **Hospital:** St. Vincent's Med Ctr - Bridgeport, Bridgeport Hosp; **Address:** Med Specs of Fairfield, 425 Post Rd, Fairfield, CT 06824; **Phone:** 203-255-4545; **Board Cert:** Internal Medicine 1988; Medical Oncology 1989; Hematology 2012; **Med School:** Yale Univ 1984; **Resid:** Internal Medicine, Yale-New Haven Hosp 1987; **Fellow:** Hematology & Oncology, Dana Farber Cancer Ctr 1991

Infectious Disease

Cipriani, Ralph J MD (Inf) - **Spec Exp:** Lyme Disease; Fevers of Unknown Origin; **Hospital:** Stamford Hosp (page 971), Greenwich Hosp (page 970); **Address:** PrimeCare Medical, 51 Schuyler Ave, Stamford, CT 06902; **Phone:** 203-327-1187; **Board Cert:** Infectious Disease 2011; Internal Medicine 2011; **Med School:** Albert Einstein Coll Med 1996; **Resid:** Internal Medicine, Mt Sinai Hosp 1999; **Fellow:** Infectious Disease, Mt Sinai Hosp 2001

McLeod, Gavin X MD (Inf) - **Spec Exp:** AIDS/HIV; Travel Medicine; Hospital Acquired Infections; Pneumonia; **Hospital:** Greenwich Hosp (page 970); **Address:** Greenwich Hosp, Infectious Disease, 5 Perryridge Rd, Greenwich, CT 06830; **Phone:** 203-869-8838; **Board Cert:** Internal Medicine 1988; Infectious Disease 2013; **Med School:** Univ Conn 1985; **Resid:** Internal Medicine, N Shore Univ Hosp 1988; **Fellow:** Infectious Disease, Beth Israel Deaconess Med Ctr 1992

Nee, Paul MD (Inf) - **Spec Exp:** AIDS/HIV; Travel Medicine; Bone/Joint Infections; **Hospital:** Danbury Hosp; **Address:** Danbury, Infectious Disease-WCMG, 33 Germantown Rd Fl 2, Danbury, CT 06810; **Phone:** 203-739-8310; **Board Cert:** Infectious Disease 2009; **Med School:** NY Med Coll 1994; **Resid:** Internal Medicine, Beth Israel Deaconess Hosp 1997; **Fellow:** Infectious Disease, Yale-New Haven Hosp 1999

Parry, Michael F MD (Inf) - **Spec Exp:** Antibiotic Resistance; Pneumonia; Lyme Disease; **Hospital:** Stamford Hosp (page 971), Greenwich Hosp (page 970); **Address:** 166 W Broad St, Ste 202, Stamford, CT 06902; **Phone:** 203-353-1427; **Board Cert:** Internal Medicine 1974; Infectious Disease 1978; **Med School:** Columbia P&S 1970; **Resid:** Internal Medicine, Columbia-Presby Med Ctr 1972; Internal Medicine, UCSF Med Ctr 1973; **Fellow:** Infectious Disease, Columbia-Presby Med Ctr 1976; **Fac Appt:** Clin Prof Med, Columbia P&S

Sabetta, James R MD (Inf) - **Spec Exp:** Lyme Disease; Tropical Diseases; Bone/Joint Infections; Fevers of Unknown Origin; **Hospital:** Greenwich Hosp (page 970), Stamford Hosp (page 971); **Address:** Greenwich Hosp, Main Floor, 5 Perryridge Rd, Ste 108, Greenwich, CT 06830; **Phone:** 203-869-8838; **Board Cert:** Internal Medicine 1981; Infectious Disease 1984; **Med School:** Brown Univ 1978; **Resid:** Internal Medicine, Univ NC Hosp 1979; Internal Medicine, Rhode Island Hosp 1981; **Fellow:** Infectious Disease, Yale-New Haven Hosp 1984; **Fac Appt:** Assoc Clin Prof Med, Yale Univ

Saul, Zane K MD (Inf) - **Spec Exp:** Lyme Disease; AIDS/HIV; Travel Medicine; **Hospital:** Bridgeport Hosp, Milford Hosp; **Address:** Int Med & Infectious Dis Assocs, 3241 Main St, Ste B, Stratford, CT 06614; **Phone:** 203-383-4466; **Board Cert:** Internal Medicine 2011; Infectious Disease 2000; **Med School:** Grenada 1985; **Resid:** Internal Medicine, Brooklyn Hosp 1988; **Fellow:** Infectious Disease, Hackensack Univ Med Ctr 1990

Schleiter, Gary S MD (Inf) - **Spec Exp:** Viral Infections; **Hospital:** Danbury Hosp, New Milford Hosp; **Address:** Danbury WCMG, Infectious Disease, 33 Germantown Rd Fl 2, Danbury, CT 06810; **Phone:** 203-739-8310; **Board Cert:** Internal Medicine 1983; Infectious Disease 1986; **Med School:** Wake Forest Univ 1980; **Resid:** Internal Medicine, Univ Conn Hlth Ctr 1983; **Fellow:** Infectious Disease, Univ Mass Med Ctr 1985; **Fac Appt:** Asst Clin Prof Med, Yale Univ

Yee, Arthur MD (Inf) - **Spec Exp:** Lyme Disease; Infections-Respiratory; Hospital Acquired Infections; **Hospital:** Norwalk Hosp; **Address:** Norwalk Med Grp, 40 Cross St, Ste 400, Norwalk, CT 06851; **Phone:** 203-845-4838; **Board Cert:** Internal Medicine 1986; Infectious Disease 1988; **Med School:** Univ Conn 1982; **Resid:** Internal Medicine, Columbia-Presby Med Ctr 1985; **Fellow:** Infectious Disease, Hosp Univ Penn 1988

Internal Medicine

Altbaum, Robert A MD (IM) *PCP* - **Spec Exp:** Hypertension; Asthma; Osteoporosis; **Hospital:** Norwalk Hosp; **Address:** Internal Med Assocs of Westport, 162 Kings Hwy N, Westport, CT 06880-2425; **Phone:** 203-226-0731; **Board Cert:** Internal Medicine 1978; **Med School:** Harvard Med Sch 1975; **Resid:** Internal Medicine, Mass Genl Hosp 1977; Internal Medicine, Yale-New Haven Hosp 1979

Baum, David H MD (IM) *PCP* - **Spec Exp:** Geriatric Medicine; Preventive Medicine; **Hospital:** Bridgeport Hosp, Norwalk Hosp; **Address:** Internal Med Assocs Westport, 162 Kings Hwy N, Ste 205, Westport, CT 06880; **Phone:** 203-226-0731; **Board Cert:** Internal Medicine 2004; Geriatric Medicine 2005; **Med School:** Israel 2000; **Resid:** Internal Medicine, Lenox Hill Hosp 2003; **Fellow:** Geriatric Medicine, Mt. Sinai Med Ctr 2005

Berman, Edward Roy MD (IM) - **Spec Exp:** Occupational Medicine; Geriatric Medicine; **Hospital:** Danbury Hosp; **Address:** 30 Prospect St, Ste 500, Ridgefield, CT 06877; **Phone:** 203-438-0364; **Board Cert:** Internal Medicine 1979; Occupational Medicine 1992; **Med School:** Boston Univ 1976; **Resid:** Internal Medicine, Wayne State Univ Affil Hosp 1978; Internal Medicine, Norwalk Hosp 1979

Bivona, James J MD (IM) *PCP* - **Spec Exp:** Preventive Medicine; **Hospital:** Stamford Hosp (page 971); **Address:** Stamford Primary Care, 1275 Summer St, Ste 105, Stamford, CT 06905; **Phone:** 203-325-2667; **Board Cert:** Internal Medicine 2011; **Med School:** Dominica 1997; **Resid:** Internal Medicine, Stamford Hosp 2000

Blumberg, Joel M MD (IM) *PCP* - **Spec Exp:** Preventive Cardiology; Hypertension; Non-Invasive Cardiology; Echocardiography; **Hospital:** Greenwich Hosp (page 970); **Address:** 664 W Putnam Ave, Ste 202, Greenwich, CT 06830; **Phone:** 203-661-4242; **Board Cert:** Internal Medicine 1972; Cardiovascular Disease 1974; **Med School:** NYU Sch Med 1966; **Resid:** Internal Medicine, Bellevue Hosp 1971; **Fellow:** Cardiovascular Disease, New York Hosp 1974; **Fac Appt:** Asst Clin Prof Med, Yale Univ

Costanzo, Joseph V MD (IM) *PCP* - **Spec Exp:** Preventive Medicine; **Hospital:** Stamford Hosp (page 971); **Address:** PrimeCare Med, 80 Mill River St, Ste 2400, Stamford, CT 06902; **Phone:** 203-348-9455; **Board Cert:** Internal Medicine 2010; **Med School:** Harvard Med Sch 1987; **Resid:** Internal Medicine, Jacobi Med Ctr 1990

Couture, Carolyn MD (IM) *PCP* - **Hospital:** Danbury Hosp; **Address:** Fairfield Co Primary Care, 396 Danbury Rd, Wilton, CT 06897; **Phone:** 203-276-4015; **Board Cert:** Internal Medicine 2005; **Med School:** Univ VT Coll Med 1992; **Resid:** Internal Medicine, Univ Rochester Strong Meml Hosp 1995

Dreyer, Neil P MD (IM) *PCP* - **Spec Exp:** Hypertension; Preventive Medicine; Kidney Disease; **Hospital:** Stamford Hosp (page 971); **Address:** PrimeCare Medical, 51 Schuyler Ave, Stamford, CT 06902; **Phone:** 203-327-1187; **Board Cert:** Internal Medicine 1980; Nephrology 1974; **Med School:** NYU Sch Med 1967; **Resid:** Internal Medicine, Bellevue Hosp Ctr 1970; Internal Medicine, Jacobi Med Ctr 1972; **Fellow:** Nephrology, Montefiore Med Ctr 1974; **Fac Appt:** Asst Clin Prof Med, Columbia P&S

Edelmann, Christopher M MD (IM) *PCP* - **Spec Exp:** Preventive Medicine; **Hospital:** Greenwich Hosp (page 970); **Address:** 42 Sherwood Pl, Greenwich, CT 06830; **Phone:** 203-869-0502; **Board Cert:** Internal Medicine 2009; **Med School:** Albert Einstein Coll Med 1995; **Resid:** Internal Medicine, NY-Presby/Columbia Univ Med Ctr 1998

Fennell, Gail M MD (IM) *PCP* - **Spec Exp:** Concierge Medicine; Hypertension; **Hospital:** Greenwich Hosp (page 970), Stamford Hosp (page 971); **Address:** 75 Holly Hill Ln, Greenwich, CT 06830; **Phone:** 203-413-1130; **Board Cert:** Internal Medicine 2006; **Med School:** Univ Conn 1992; **Resid:** Internal Medicine, Greenwich Hosp 1995

Fisher, Steven A MD (IM) *PCP* - **Spec Exp:** Preventive Medicine; **Hospital:** St. Vincent's Med Ctr - Bridgeport, Bridgeport Hosp; **Address:** Fairfield Co Med Grp, 15 Corporate Drive, Ste 2-1, Trumbull, CT 06611; **Phone:** 203-459-5100; **Board Cert:** Internal Medicine 1987; **Med School:** Mount Sinai Sch Med 1984; **Resid:** Internal Medicine, Montefiore Med Ctr 1987

Gamble, Sarah M DO (IM) *PCP* - **Spec Exp:** Concierge Medicine; **Hospital:** Greenwich Hosp (page 970), Stamford Hosp (page 971); **Address:** Greenwich Pure Medical, 222 Railroad Ave, Ste B, Greenwich, CT 06830; **Phone:** 203-869-2800; **Board Cert:** Internal Medicine 2009; **Med School:** Kansas City Univ of Med & Biosciences(Ostepathic) 2004; **Resid:** Internal Medicine, Westchester Med Ctr 2007

Glazer, Steven MD (IM) *PCP* - **Spec Exp:** Concierge Medicine; Preventive Medicine; **Hospital:** Norwalk Hosp, St. Vincent's Med Ctr - Bridgeport; **Address:** 128 East Ave, Norwalk, CT 06851; **Phone:** 203-852-1300; **Board Cert:** Internal Medicine 2004; **Med School:** Emory Univ 1991; **Resid:** Internal Medicine, New York Hosp/MSKCC 1995; **Fellow:** Internal Medicine, Columbia Univ Med Ctr 1997

Hasapis, Peter G MD (IM) *PCP* - **Spec Exp:** Preventive Medicine; Concierge Medicine; **Hospital:** Norwalk Hosp; **Address:** New Canaan Medical Group, 173 East Ave, New Canaan, CT 06840; **Phone:** 203-972-4218; **Board Cert:** Internal Medicine 2011; **Med School:** Cornell Univ-Weill Med Coll 1997; **Resid:** Internal Medicine, NY-Presby/Weill Cornell Med Ctr 2000

Hoffman, Pamela B MD (IM) *PCP* - **Spec Exp:** Geriatric Care; Preventive Medicine; **Hospital:** St. Vincent's Med Ctr - Bridgeport; **Address:** Jewish Home for the Elderly, 175 Jefferson St, Fairfield, CT 06825; **Phone:** 203-396-1054; **Board Cert:** Internal Medicine 1983; **Med School:** Univ VA Sch Med 1978; **Resid:** Internal Medicine, St Vincent's Hosp & Med Ctr 1981; **Fellow:** Geriatric Medicine, Jewish Inst Geriatric Care 1983

Horn, Jay A MD (IM) *PCP* - **Spec Exp:** Preventive Medicine; **Hospital:** Norwalk Hosp; **Address:** Internal Med Assocs of Westport, 162 Kings Hwy N, Fl 1, Westport, CT 06880; **Phone:** 203-226-0731; **Board Cert:** Internal Medicine 1987; **Med School:** Albert Einstein Coll Med 1984; **Resid:** Internal Medicine, Montefiore Med Ctr 1987

Israel, Shara P MD (IM) *PCP* - **Spec Exp:** Preventive Medicine; **Hospital:** Stamford Hosp (page 971); **Address:** PrimeCare Medical, 51 Schuyler Ave, Stamford, CT 06902; **Phone:** 203-327-1187; **Board Cert:** Internal Medicine 2005; **Med School:** Columbia P&S 1992; **Resid:** Internal Medicine, NY-Presby/Columbia Univ Med Ctr 1995; **Fac Appt:** Asst Prof Med, Columbia P&S

Karol, Nina S MD (IM) *PCP* - **Spec Exp:** Preventive Medicine; **Hospital:** Norwalk Hosp; **Address:** Internal Med Assocs Westport, 162 Kings Hwy N, Ste 205, Westport, CT 06880; **Phone:** 203-226-0731; **Board Cert:** Internal Medicine 2005; **Med School:** Albert Einstein Coll Med 1992; **Resid:** Internal Medicine, Mt Sinai Hosp 1993; Internal Medicine, Greenwich Hosp 1995

Klein, Neil C MD (IM) - **Spec Exp:** Inflammatory Bowel Disease/Crohn's; Ulcerative Colitis; Preventive Medicine; **Hospital:** Stamford Hosp (page 971), Norwalk Hosp; **Address:** Shoreline Medical Group, 1450 Washington Blvd, Stamford, CT 06902-2451; **Phone:** 203-327-9321; **Board Cert:** Internal Medicine 1974; Gastroenterology 1975; **Med School:** Cornell Univ-Weill Med Coll 1960; **Resid:** Internal Medicine, Presby/Weill Cornell Med Ctr 1964; **Fellow:** Gastroenterology, Presby/Weill Cornell Med Ctr 1967; **Fac Appt:** Clin Prof Med, Columbia P&S

Mayer, Deborah A MD (IM) *PCP* - **Spec Exp:** Diabetes; Hypertension; Preventive Medicine; **Hospital:** Norwalk Hosp, St. Vincent's Med Ctr - Bridgeport; **Address:** 363 Reef Rd, Ste 2E, Fairfield, CT 06824; **Phone:** 203-255-0891; **Board Cert:** Internal Medicine 1981; **Med School:** Columbia P&S 1977; **Resid:** Internal Medicine, Beth Israel Deaconess Med Ctr 1980

Mickley, Diane W MD (IM) - **Spec Exp:** Eating Disorders; **Address:** Wilkins Ctr for Eating Disorders, 7 Riversville Rd Fl 3, Greenwich, CT 06831; **Phone:** 203-531-1909; **Board Cert:** Internal Medicine 1974; **Med School:** Tufts Univ 1971; **Resid:** Internal Medicine, Barnes West County Hosp 1973; Internal Medicine, Montefiore Med Ctr 1974; **Fac Appt:** Assoc Clin Prof Med, Yale Univ

Mickley, Steven P MD (IM) *PCP* - **Spec Exp:** Cholesterol/Lipid Disorders; Cardiovascular Disease; **Hospital:** Greenwich Hosp (page 970); **Address:** Glenville Med Assocs, 7 Riversville Rd, Fl 1, Greenwich, CT 06831-3697; **Phone:** 203-531-1808; **Board Cert:** Internal Medicine 1974; **Med School:** Harvard Med Sch 1971; **Resid:** Internal Medicine, Barnes Hosp 1974; **Fellow:** Internal Medicine, U.S. Public Hlth Service 1976; **Fac Appt:** Asst Clin Prof Med, Yale Univ

Miner III, Charles MD (IM) *PCP* - **Spec Exp:** Preventive Medicine; **Hospital:** Stamford Hosp (page 971), Norwalk Hosp; **Address:** Internal Med Assocs of Darien, 1500 Post Rd Fl 1, Darien, CT 06820-4523; **Phone:** 203-276-4801; **Board Cert:** Internal Medicine 1982; **Med School:** Univ Cincinnati 1979; **Resid:** Internal Medicine, Lenox Hill Hosp 1982

Olin, Craig H MD (IM) *PCP* - **Spec Exp:** Preventive Medicine; Geriatric Medicine; Concierge Medicine; **Hospital:** Stamford Hosp (page 971), Norwalk Hosp; **Address:** Fairfield Co Personal Med, 5 High Ridge Park, Ste 104, Stamford, CT 06905; **Phone:** 203-276-4644; **Board Cert:** Internal Medicine 2006; **Med School:** NYU Sch Med 1993; **Resid:** Internal Medicine, NY-Presby/Weill Cornell Med Ctr 1996; **Fac Appt:** Asst Clin Prof Med, Columbia P&S

Osnoss, Kenneth MD (IM) *PCP* - **Spec Exp:** Asthma; Lung Disease; **Hospital:** Danbury Hosp; **Address:** Western CT Med Grp-Danbury, 79 Sand Pit Rd, Ste 102, Danbury, CT 06810-6099; **Phone:** 203-749-5700; **Board Cert:** Internal Medicine 1978; Pulmonary Disease 1980; **Med School:** Tufts Univ 1975; **Resid:** Internal Medicine, Hosp Univ Penn 1978; **Fellow:** Pulmonary Disease, Hosp Univ Penn 1980

Phillips, Steven E MD (IM) - **Spec Exp:** Lyme Disease; Tick-borne Diseases; **Hospital:** Greenwich Hosp (page 970); **Address:** 944 Danbury Rd, Wilton, CT 06897-4909; **Phone:** 203-544-0005; **Board Cert:** Internal Medicine 2006; **Med School:** SUNY Upstate Med Univ 1993; **Resid:** Internal Medicine, Greenwich Hosp 1996

Puglisi, Jeffrey S MD (IM) *PCP* - **Spec Exp:** Preventive Cardiology; Men's Health; **Hospital:** Greenwich Hosp (page 970); **Address:** Glenville Med Assocs, 7 Riversville Rd, Greenwich, CT 06831; **Phone:** 203-531-1808; **Board Cert:** Internal Medicine 2011; **Med School:** Hahnemann Univ 1998; **Resid:** Internal Medicine, Mount Sinai Med Ctr 2002

Radin, Alan M MD (IM) *PCP* - **Spec Exp:** Geriatric Medicine; Preventive Medicine; **Hospital:** Norwalk Hosp; **Address:** Prohealth Physicians-Arbor Med Grp, 195 Danbury Rd, Whitlock Bldg, Ste 210, Wilton, CT 06897-3003; **Phone:** 203-762-3353; **Board Cert:** Internal Medicine 1977; **Med School:** Penn State Coll Med 1974; **Resid:** Internal Medicine, Univ Vermont Med Ctr 1978

Rosenberg, Remi M MD (IM) *PCP* - **Spec Exp:** Preventive Medicine; **Hospital:** Stamford Hosp (page 971); **Address:** Fairfield Co Personal Med, 5 High Ridge Park, Ste 103, Stamford, CT 06905; **Phone:** 203-276-4644; **Board Cert:** Internal Medicine 2013; **Med School:** NYU Sch Med 2000; **Resid:** Internal Medicine, Boston Med Ctr 2003

Serin, Craig D MD (IM) *PCP* - **Spec Exp:** Preventive Medicine; **Hospital:** Norwalk Hosp; **Address:** Arbor Med Grp, 195 Danbury Rd, Ste 210, Wilton, CT 06897; **Phone:** 203-762-3353; **Board Cert:** Internal Medicine 2011; **Med School:** SUNY Downstate 1998; **Resid:** Internal Medicine, Jacobi Med Ctr 2001

Slogoff, Frederick B MD (IM) *PCP* - **Spec Exp:** Concierge Medicine; Cardiovascular Disease; Anxiety & Mood Disorders; **Hospital:** Stamford Hosp (page 971); **Address:** Personal Physicians of CT, 5 High Ridge Park, Ste 104, Stamford, CT 06905; **Phone:** 203-968-9500; **Board Cert:** Internal Medicine 2009; **Med School:** Mount Sinai Sch Med 1996; **Resid:** Internal Medicine, NY-Presby/Weill Cornell Med Ctr 1999; **Fac Appt:** Clin Prof Med, Columbia P&S

Smerling, Neil E MD (IM) *PCP* - **Spec Exp:** Preventive Medicine; **Hospital:** Bridgeport Hosp; **Address:** Primary Care Physicians of Fairfield, 111 Beach Rd, Fairfield, CT 06824; **Phone:** 203-259-7442; **Board Cert:** Internal Medicine 2006; **Med School:** Grenada 1988; **Resid:** Internal Medicine, New Britain Genl Hosp 1990; Internal Medicine, UConn Hlth Ctr 1991

Spano, Frank MD (IM) *PCP* - **Spec Exp:** Preventive Medicine; **Hospital:** Bridgeport Hosp, St. Vincent's Med Ctr - Bridgeport; **Address:** Fairfield County Medical Group, 15 Corporate Drive, Ste 2-1, Trumbull, CT 06611; **Phone:** 203-459-5100; **Board Cert:** Internal Medicine 1987; **Med School:** Albert Einstein Coll Med 1984; **Resid:** Internal Medicine, Jacobi Hosp 1987

Thomas, Byron S MD (IM) *PCP* - **Spec Exp:** Geriatric Care; **Hospital:** Danbury Hosp; **Address:** Danbury WCMG, Primary Care, 79 Sand Pit Rd, Ste 102, Danbury, CT 06810; **Phone:** 203-749-5700; **Board Cert:** Internal Medicine 1978; **Med School:** Univ Pittsburgh 1975; **Resid:** Internal Medicine, Mount Sinai Hosp 1978; **Fac Appt:** Asst Clin Prof Med, Yale Univ

Troy, Cathrine MD (IM) *PCP* - **Spec Exp:** Preventive Medicine; **Hospital:** Stamford Hosp (page 971), Greenwich Hosp (page 970); **Address:** Prime Care Med Assocs, 51 Schuyler Ave, Stamford, CT 06902; **Phone:** 203-327-1187; **Board Cert:** Internal Medicine 1983; **Med School:** SUNY Downstate 1980; **Resid:** Internal Medicine, Brookdale Univ Hosp Med Ctr 1983

Vadel, Shira B MD (IM) *PCP* - **Spec Exp:** Preventive Medicine; **Hospital:** Stamford Hosp (page 971); **Address:** Prime Care Med Assocs, 51 Schuyler Ave, Stamford, CT 06902; **Phone:** 203-327-1187; **Board Cert:** Internal Medicine 2010; **Med School:** Israel 1997; **Resid:** Internal Medicine, NYU Med Ctr 2000

Walsh, Francis X MD (IM) *PCP* - **Spec Exp:** Kidney Disease; Hypertension; Dialysis Care; **Hospital:** Greenwich Hosp (page 970); **Address:** Walsh-Brunetti, 31 River Rd, Ste 200, Cos Cob, CT 06807; **Phone:** 203-661-9433; **Board Cert:** Internal Medicine 1972; Nephrology 1974; **Med School:** NY Med Coll 1967; **Resid:** Internal Medicine, Greenwich Hosp 1970; **Fellow:** Nephrology, Duke Univ Med Ctr 1972; **Fac Appt:** Asst Clin Prof Med, Yale Univ

Weinshel, David MD (IM) *PCP* - **Hospital:** Danbury Hosp; **Address:** WCMG, Primary Care, 79 Sand Pit Rd, Ste 102, Danbury, CT 06810; **Phone:** 203-749-5700; **Board Cert:** Internal Medicine 1984; **Med School:** Albert Einstein Coll Med 1981; **Resid:** Internal Medicine, Danbury Hosp 1984

Zucker, Michael D MD (IM) *PCP* - **Spec Exp:** Preventive Medicine; **Hospital:** Stamford Hosp (page 971); **Address:** PrimeCare Medical, 555 Newfield Ave, Stamford, CT 06905-3330; **Phone:** 203-359-4444; **Board Cert:** Internal Medicine 1988; **Med School:** NYU Sch Med 1985; **Resid:** Internal Medicine, Stamford Hosp 1988

Interventional Cardiology

Driesman, Mitchell H MD (IC) - **Spec Exp:** Cardiac Catheterization; Clinical Trials; **Hospital:** Bridgeport Hosp; **Address:** Cardiac Specs of Fairfield, 1305 Post Rd, Fairfield, CT 06824; **Phone:** 203-292-2000; **Board Cert:** Internal Medicine 1980; Cardiovascular Disease 1983; Interventional Cardiology 2009; **Med School:** Brown Univ 1977; **Resid:** Internal Medicine, Tufts-New England Med Ctr 1980; **Fellow:** Cardiovascular Disease, Mt Sinai Hosp 1983; **Fac Appt:** Asst Clin Prof Med, Yale Univ

Fishman, Robert F MD (IC) - **Spec Exp:** Carotid Artery Stent Placement; Peripheral Vascular Disease; **Hospital:** Bridgeport Hosp; **Address:** Cardiac Specs of Fairfield, 1305 Post Rd, Fairfield, CT 06824; **Phone:** 203-292-2000; **Board Cert:** Internal Medicine 1988; Cardiovascular Disease 2011; Interventional Cardiology 2009; **Med School:** Boston Univ 1985; **Resid:** Internal Medicine, Beth Israel Deaconess Med Ctr 1988; **Fellow:** Cardiovascular Disease, Beth Israel Deaconess Med Ctr 1991

Howes, Christopher J MD (IC) - **Spec Exp:** Angiography & Stent Placement; Echocardiography; Cardiac Catheterization; **Hospital:** Greenwich Hosp (page 970), Yale-New Haven Hosp; **Address:** Cardiovascular Svcs Greenwich, 55 Holly Hill Ln, Ste 240, Greenwich, CT 06830; **Phone:** 203-863-4210; **Board Cert:** Echocardiography 2011; Cardiovascular Disease 2007; Interventional Cardiology 2009; **Med School:** Albert Einstein Coll Med 1989; **Resid:** Internal Medicine, Yale-New Haven Hosp 1992; **Fellow:** Cardiovascular Disease, Yale-New Haven Hosp 1997; **Fac Appt:** Asst Prof Med, Yale Univ

Jumper, Robert D MD (IC) - **Spec Exp:** Peripheral Vascular Disease; Nuclear Cardiology; Echocardiography; **Hospital:** St. Vincent's Med Ctr - Bridgeport, Norwalk Hosp; **Address:** Cardio Physicians Fairfield Co, 115 Technology Drive, Ste C300, Trumbull, CT 06611; **Phone:** 203-445-7093; **Board Cert:** Cardiovascular Disease 2013; Interventional Cardiology 2004; Nuclear Cardiology 2005; Echocardiography 2006; **Med School:** NY Med Coll 1996; **Resid:** Internal Medicine, Jacobi Med Ctr 2000; **Fellow:** Cardiovascular Disease, Montefiore Med Ctr 2003; Interventional Cardiology, Montefiore Med Ctr 2004

Landau, Charles MD (IC) - **Spec Exp:** Cardiac Catheterization; Angiography & Stent Placement; **Hospital:** St. Vincent's Med Ctr - Bridgeport, Bridgeport Hosp; **Address:** CT Heart & Vascular Ctr, 112 Quary Rd Fl 4 - Ste 400, Trumbull, CT 06611; **Phone:** 203-333-8800; **Board Cert:** Internal Medicine 1987; Cardiovascular Disease 2011; Interventional Cardiology 2010; **Med School:** Harvard Med Sch 1984; **Resid:** Internal Medicine, NY-Presby/Columbia Univ Med Ctr 1987; **Fellow:** Cardiovascular Disease, Boston Med Ctr 1991; Interventional Cardiology, Boston Med Ctr 1992; **Fac Appt:** Asst Clin Prof Med, Univ Conn

Mejia, Victor M MD (IC) - **Spec Exp:** Coronary Artery Disease; Peripheral Vascular Disease; **Hospital:** St. Vincent's Med Ctr - Bridgeport, Bridgeport Hosp; **Address:** CT Heart & Vascular Ctr, 112 Quary Rd Fl 4, Trumbull, CT 06611; **Phone:** 203-333-8800; **Board Cert:** Internal Medicine 2012; Cardiovascular Disease 2005; Interventional Cardiology 2006; **Med School:** Cornell Univ-Weill Med Coll 1999; **Resid:** Internal Medicine, NY-Presby/Columbia Univ Med Ctr 2002; **Fellow:** Cardiovascular Disease, Univ Hosp Penn 2005; Interventional Cardiology, Univ Hosp Penn 2006

Nero, Thomas J MD (IC) - **Spec Exp:** Sports Medicine-Cardiology; Preventive Cardiology; Echocardiography; **Hospital:** Stamford Hosp (page 971), Greenwich Hosp (page 970); **Address:** Cardio Assocs Fairfield Co, 1177 Summer St Fl 5, Stamford, CT 06905; **Phone:** 203-353-1133; **Board Cert:** Cardiovascular Disease 2011; Interventional Cardiology 2012; **Med School:** Ohio State Univ 1994; **Resid:** Internal Medicine, Beth Israel Med Ctr 1998; **Fellow:** Cardiovascular Disease, Beth Israel Med Ctr 2001; Interventional Cardiology, Beth Israel Med Ctr 2002; **Fac Appt:** Assoc Clin Prof Med, Columbia P&S

Portnay, Edward L MD (IC) - **Spec Exp:** Heart Attack; **Hospital:** Stamford Hosp (page 971), St. Vincent's Med Ctr - Bridgeport; **Address:** Cardio Assocs Fairfield Co, 117 Summer St Fl 5, Stamford, CT 06905; **Phone:** 203-353-1133; **Board Cert:** Cardiovascular Disease 2005; Interventional Cardiology 2006; **Med School:** Tufts Univ 1997; **Resid:** Internal Medicine, NYU Med Ctr 2000; **Fellow:** Cardiovascular Disease, Yale-New Haven Hosp 2004; Interventional Cardiology, Yale-New Haven Hosp 2005

Selter, Jared G MD (IC) - **Spec Exp:** Nuclear Cardiology; Peripheral Vascular Disease; Preventive Cardiology; **Hospital:** St. Vincent's Med Ctr - Bridgeport; **Address:** Cardiology Phys Fairfield Co, 115 Technology Drive, Ste C300, Trumbull, CT 06611; **Phone:** 203-445-7093; **Board Cert:** Cardiovascular Disease 2005; Interventional Cardiology 2006; Nuclear Cardiology 2005; **Med School:** Mount Sinai Sch Med 1998; **Resid:** Internal Medicine, Yale-New Haven Hosp 2001; **Fellow:** Cardiovascular Disease, Yale-New Haven Hosp 2005; Interventional Cardiology, Yale-New Haven Hosp 2006

Warshofsky, Mark MD (IC) - **Spec Exp:** Coronary Artery Disease; Heart Valve Disease; Interventional Cardiology; **Hospital:** Danbury Hosp, NY-Presby/Columbia Univ Med Ctr, NY (page 102); **Address:** Western CT Med Grp, 24 Hospital Ave, Fl 7, Danbury, CT 06810; **Phone:** 203-739-7436; **Board Cert:** Cardiovascular Disease 2007; Interventional Cardiology 2009; **Med School:** Geo Wash Univ 1990; **Resid:** Internal Medicine, Columbia-Presby Med Ctr 1993; **Fellow:** Cardiovascular Disease, Columbia-Presby Med Ctr 1996; Interventional Cardiology, Columbia-Presby Med Ctr 1998; **Fac Appt:** Asst Prof Med, Columbia P&S

Wasserman, Hal S MD (IC) - **Spec Exp:** Acute Coronary Syndromes; Heart Valve Disease; Coronary Artery Disease; Heart Attack; **Hospital:** Danbury Hosp, NY-Presby/Columbia Univ Med Ctr, NY (page 102); **Address:** Western CT Med Grp, 24 Hospital Ave Fl 7, Danbury, CT 06810; **Phone:** 203-739-7600; **Board Cert:** Internal Medicine 1985; Cardiovascular Disease 1987; Interventional Cardiology 2009; **Med School:** Columbia P&S 1982; **Resid:** Internal Medicine, NY Presby/Columbia Univ Med Ctr 1985; **Fellow:** Cardiovascular Disease, NY Presby/Columbia Univ Med Ctr 1987; Interventional Cardiology, NY Presby/Columbia Univ Med Ctr 1988; **Fac Appt:** Assoc Clin Prof Med, Columbia P&S

Maternal & Fetal Medicine

Bobby, Paul D MD (MF) - **Spec Exp:** Pregnancy-High Risk; Prenatal Diagnosis; **Hospital:** Stamford Hosp (page 971); **Address:** Stamford Hosp, Dept Maternal/Fetal Med, 30 Shelburne Rd, Whittingham Pavilion, Stamford, CT 06902; **Phone:** 203-276-7172; **Board Cert:** Obstetrics & Gynecology 2013; Maternal & Fetal Medicine 2013; **Med School:** Boston Univ 1990; **Resid:** Obstetrics & Gynecology, NYU Langone Med Ctr 1994; **Fellow:** Maternal & Fetal Medicine, Montefiore Med Ctr 1996

Bond, Annette L MD (MF) - **Spec Exp:** Pregnancy-High Risk; Multiple Gestation; Prenatal Diagnosis; Hypertension in Pregnancy; **Hospital:** Greenwich Hosp (page 970); **Address:** Greenwich Perinatology Svcs, 5 Perryridge Rd, Ste 223, Greenwich, CT 06830; **Phone:** 203-863-3674; **Board Cert:** Obstetrics & Gynecology 2013; Maternal & Fetal Medicine 2013; **Med School:** Harvard Med Sch 1983; **Resid:** Obstetrics & Gynecology, NY-Presby/Weill Cornell Med Ctr 1987; **Fellow:** Maternal & Fetal Medicine, NY-Presby/Weill Cornell Med Ctr 1989

Dunston-Boone, Gina A MD (MF) - **Spec Exp:** Amniocentesis; Multiple Gestation; Diabetes in Pregnancy; **Hospital:** Bridgeport Hosp, Yale-New Haven Hosp; **Address:** Park Ave Perinatal Specs, 267 Grant St Fl 5, Bridgeport, CT 06610; **Phone:** 203-384-3544; **Board Cert:** Obstetrics & Gynecology 2013; Maternal & Fetal Medicine 2013; **Med School:** Tufts Univ 1985; **Resid:** Obstetrics & Gynecology, NY-Presby/Weill Cornell Med Ctr 1992; **Fellow:** Maternal & Fetal Medicine, Thos Jefferson Univ Hosp 1995

Kim, Matthew J MD (MF) - **Spec Exp:** Fetal Ultrasound; Fetal Echocardiography; **Hospital:** Danbury Hosp; **Address:** Danbury, Maternal & Fetal Med-WCMG, 24 Hospital Ave Fl 2, Danbury, CT 06810; **Phone:** 203-739-7981; **Board Cert:** Obstetrics & Gynecology 2013; Maternal & Fetal Medicine 2013; **Med School:** Baylor Coll Med 1995; **Resid:** Obstetrics & Gynecology, Parkland Hlth & Hosp Sys 1999; **Fellow:** Maternal & Fetal Medicine, UCSD Med Ctr 2002

Kleinman, Gary Eleazar MD (MF) - **Spec Exp:** Pregnancy-High Risk; Genetic Disorders; **Hospital:** Bridgeport Hosp, Yale-New Haven Hosp; **Address:** Park Ave Perinatal Specs, Bridgeport, CT 06610-2805; **Phone:** 203-384-3544; **Board Cert:** Obstetrics & Gynecology 1984; Maternal & Fetal Medicine 1985; Clinical Genetics 2010; **Med School:** Creighton Univ 1977; **Resid:** Obstetrics & Gynecology, Georgetown Univ Hosp 1981; **Fellow:** Maternal & Fetal Medicine, UCLA Medical Center 1983; Clinical Genetics, LAC Harbor-UCLA Med Ctr 1992

Laifer, Steven A MD (MF) - **Spec Exp:** Prenatal Diagnosis; Pregnancy-High Risk; **Hospital:** Bridgeport Hosp, Yale-New Haven Hosp; **Address:** Park Ave Perinatal Specs, 267 Grant St Fl 5, Bridgeport, CT 06610; **Phone:** 203-384-3544; **Board Cert:** Obstetrics & Gynecology 2013; Maternal & Fetal Medicine 2013; **Med School:** SUNY Downstate 1982; **Resid:** Obstetrics & Gynecology, Johns Hopkins Hosp 1988; **Fellow:** Maternal & Fetal Medicine, Magee Womens Hosp 1991; **Fac Appt:** Asst Clin Prof ObG, Yale Univ

Shevell, Tracy MD (MF) - **Spec Exp:** Pregnancy-High Risk; Prenatal Diagnosis; **Hospital:** Stamford Hosp (page 971); **Address:** Stamford Hosp, Dept Maternal Fetal Med, 30 Shelburne Rd, Whittingham Pavilion, Stamford, CT 06904; **Phone:** 203-276-7060; **Board Cert:** Obstetrics & Gynecology 2013; Maternal & Fetal Medicine 2013; **Med School:** Albert Einstein Coll Med 1997; **Resid:** Obstetrics & Gynecology, Mt Sinai Med Ctr 2002; **Fellow:** Maternal & Fetal Medicine, NY-Presby-Columbia Univ Med Ctr 2004

Stiller, Robert J MD (MF) - **Spec Exp:** Prenatal Diagnosis; Ultrasound; Pregnancy-High Risk; Infectious Disease in Pregnancy; **Hospital:** Bridgeport Hosp, Yale-New Haven Hosp; **Address:** Park Ave Perinatal Specs, 267 Grant St Fl 5, Bridgeport, CT 06610; **Phone:** 203-384-3544; **Board Cert:** Obstetrics & Gynecology 2013; Maternal & Fetal Medicine 2013; **Med School:** UMDNJ-Rutgers Med Sch 1979; **Resid:** Obstetrics & Gynecology, Univ Conn Med Ctr 1983; **Fellow:** Maternal & Fetal Medicine, Pennsylvania Hosp-UPHS 1986; **Fac Appt:** Assoc Clin Prof ObG, Yale Univ

Medical Oncology

Angevine, Anne H MD (Onc) - **Spec Exp:** Leukemia; Lymphoma; **Hospital:** Stamford Hosp (page 971); **Address:** Bennett Cancer Ctr, 34 Shelburne Rd, Stamford, CT 06902; **Phone:** 203-325-2695; **Board Cert:** Internal Medicine 2013; Medical Oncology 2007; Hematology 2088; **Med School:** Columbia P&S 2000; **Resid:** Internal Medicine, Brigham & Women's Hosp 2003; **Fellow:** Hematology & Oncology, NY-Presby/Columbia Univ Med Ctr 2007; **Fac Appt:** Asst Clin Prof Onc, Columbia P&S

Cohenuram, Michael K MD (Onc) - **Spec Exp:** Solid Tumors; Hematologic Malignancies; Hematology; **Hospital:** Danbury Hosp, New Milford Hosp; **Address:** WCMG, Med Oncology, 95 Locust Ave, Strook Bldg - Fl 1, Danbury, CT 06810; **Phone:** 203-739-7029; **Board Cert:** Medical Oncology 2008; Hematology 2009; **Med School:** Mount Sinai Sch Med 2000; **Resid:** Internal Medicine, Rhode Island Hosp 2003; **Fellow:** Hematology & Oncology, Yale-New Haven Hosp 2008; **Fac Appt:** Asst Clin Prof Med, Univ VT Coll Med

Cooper, Robert B MD (Onc) - **Spec Exp:** Breast Cancer; Lymphoma; Colon & Rectal Cancer; Urologic Cancer; **Hospital:** Danbury Hosp; **Address:** Danbury Hosp, Hematology/Oncology, 95 Locust Ave, Strook Bldg Fl 1, Danbury, CT 06810; **Phone:** 203-739-7029; **Board Cert:** Internal Medicine 1974; Medical Oncology 1981; **Med School:** Univ Pittsburgh 1971; **Resid:** Internal Medicine, Pennsylvania Hosp 1974; **Fellow:** Medical Oncology, Unic Colorado Med Ctr 1978; **Fac Appt:** Asst Clin Prof Med, Yale Univ

Delprete, Salvatore A MD (Onc) - **Spec Exp:** Lung Cancer; Ovarian Cancer; Melanoma; Colon Cancer; **Hospital:** Stamford Hosp (page 971); **Address:** Bennett Cancer Ctr, 34 Shelburne Rd, Stamford, CT 06902-3658; **Phone:** 203-325-2695; **Board Cert:** Internal Medicine 1981; Medical Oncology 1985; Hematology 1986; **Med School:** SUNY Buffalo 1978; **Resid:** Internal Medicine, Dartmouth-Hitchcock Med Ctr 1981; **Fellow:** Pathology, Dartmouth-Hitchcock Med Ctr 1982; Hematology & Oncology, Dartmouth-Hitchcock Med Ctr 1984

Drucker, Beverly J MD/PhD (Onc) - **Spec Exp:** Breast Cancer; Head & Neck Cancer; Colon & Rectal Cancer; Clinical Trials; **Hospital:** Greenwich Hosp (page 970); **Address:** Hem Onc Assocs Greenwich, 77 Lafayette Pl, Ste 200, Greenwich, CT 06830; **Phone:** 203-863-3737; **Board Cert:** Medical Oncology 2009; **Med School:** Columbia P&S 1994; **Resid:** Internal Medicine, NY-Presby/Columbia Univ Med Ctr 1997; **Fellow:** Medical Oncology, Johns Hopkins Hosp 1999

Fischbach, Neal A MD (Onc) - **Spec Exp:** Breast Cancer; Lung Cancer; Colon Cancer; **Hospital:** Bridgeport Hosp, St. Vincent's Med Ctr - Bridgeport; **Address:** Yale New Haven Smilow Fairfield, 111 Beach Rd Fl 3, Fairfield, CT 06824; **Phone:** 203-255-2766; **Board Cert:** Medical Oncology 2014; **Med School:** Harvard Med Sch 1995; **Resid:** Internal Medicine, UCSF Med Ctr 1998; **Fellow:** Hematology & Oncology, UCSF Med Ctr 2002

Folman, Robert S MD (Onc) - **Spec Exp:** Breast Cancer; Lung Cancer; Colon & Rectal Cancer; Genitourinary Cancer; **Hospital:** Bridgeport Hosp, St. Vincent's Med Ctr - Bridgeport; **Address:** Yale New Haven Smilow Fairfield, 5520 Park Ave, Ste 203, Trumbull, CT 66111351; **Phone:** 203-502-8400; **Board Cert:** Internal Medicine 1975; Medical Oncology 1977; **Med School:** SUNY Buffalo 1972; **Resid:** Internal Medicine, Buffalo Gen Hosp 1975; **Fellow:** Medical Oncology, Meml Sloan Kettering Cancer Ctr 1977; **Fac Appt:** Asst Prof Med, Yale Univ

Frank, Richard C MD (Onc) - **Spec Exp:** Leukemia; Lymphoma; **Hospital:** Norwalk Hosp; **Address:** Norwalk Hosp, Oncology Div, 24 Stevens St, Whittingham Cancer Ctr, Norwalk, CT 06856; **Phone:** 203-845-4811; **Board Cert:** Medical Oncology 2005; Hematology 2008; **Med School:** SUNY Stony Brook 1985; **Resid:** Internal Medicine, NY-Presby/Columbia Univ Med Ctr 1992; **Fellow:** Hematology & Oncology, Meml Sloan Kettering Cancer Ctr 1996

Hollister Jr, Dickerman MD (Onc) - **Spec Exp:** Breast Cancer; Lung Cancer; Colon Cancer; Leukemia & Lymphoma; **Hospital:** Greenwich Hosp (page 970); **Address:** Hem Onc Assocs Greenwich, 77 Lafayette Pl, Ste 200, Greenwich, CT 06830; **Phone:** 203-863-3737; **Board Cert:** Internal Medicine 1978; Hematology 1980; Medical Oncology 1981; **Med School:** Univ VA Sch Med 1975; **Resid:** Internal Medicine, NY-Presby/Weill Cornell Med Ctr 1978; **Fellow:** Hematology & Oncology, NY-Presby/Weill Cornell Med Ctr 1981; **Fac Appt:** Asst Clin Prof Med, Yale Univ

Kloss, Robert MD (Onc) - **Spec Exp:** Breast Cancer; Colon Cancer; Lung Cancer; **Hospital:** Danbury Hosp, New Milford Hosp; **Address:** Danbury WCMG, Hem/Onc, 95 Locust Ave Stroock Bldg Fl 1, Danbury, CT 06810-6010; **Phone:** 203-739-7029; **Board Cert:** Internal Medicine 1979; Medical Oncology 1981; Hospice & Palliative Medicine 2008; **Med School:** Jefferson Med Coll 1976; **Resid:** Internal Medicine, SUNY Buffalo Affil Hosp 1979; **Fellow:** Hematology & Oncology, NY-Presby/Columbia Univ Med Ctr 1981

Lee, Merlin Sung MD (Onc) - **Spec Exp:** Breast Cancer; Bleeding/Coagulation Disorders; Leukemia; **Hospital:** Greenwich Hosp (page 970); **Address:** Hem Onc Assocs Greenwich, 77 Lafayette Pl, Ste 200, Greenwich, CT 06830; **Phone:** 203-863-3737; **Board Cert:** Hematology 2012; Medical Oncology 2012; **Med School:** NY Med Coll 1994; **Resid:** Internal Medicine, NY-Presby/Columbia Univ Med Ctr 1997; **Fellow:** Hematology & Oncology, NYU Med Ctr 2001

Lo, K.M. Steve MD (Onc) - **Spec Exp:** Breast Cancer; Lymphoma; **Hospital:** Stamford Hosp (page 971); **Address:** Bennett Cancer Ctr, 34 Shelburne Rd, Stamford, CT 06902; **Phone:** 203-325-2695; **Board Cert:** Internal Medicine 1989; Medical Oncology 2011; Hematology 2012; **Med School:** Harvard Med Sch 1985; **Resid:** Internal Medicine, Brigham & Womens Hosp 1988; **Fellow:** Hematology & Oncology, Dana-Farber Cancer Inst 1992; **Fac Appt:** Asst Prof Med, Columbia P&S

Malefatto, Jerry P MD (Onc) - **Spec Exp:** Breast Cancer; Colon Cancer; Lymphoma; **Hospital:** Bridgeport Hosp, St. Vincent's Med Ctr - Bridgeport; **Address:** Yale New Haven Smilow Fairfield, 5520 Park Ave, Ste 203, Trumbull, CT 06611; **Phone:** 203-502-8400; **Board Cert:** Internal Medicine 1979; Medical Oncology 1983; **Med School:** Univ Conn 1976; **Resid:** Internal Medicine, UC Irvine/VA Med Ctr 1979; **Fellow:** Hematology & Oncology, UC Irvine/VA Med Ctr 1983

Tepler, Isidore MD (Onc) - **Spec Exp:** Breast Cancer; **Hospital:** Stamford Hosp (page 971); **Address:** Bennett Cancer Ctr, 34 Shelburne Rd, Stamford, CT 06902-3658; **Phone:** 203-325-2695; **Board Cert:** Internal Medicine 1984; Hematology 1986; Medical Oncology 1989; **Med School:** Harvard Med Sch 1980; **Resid:** Internal Medicine, Mass Genl Hosp 1983; **Fellow:** Hematology, Brigham & Women's Hosp 1986; Hematology & Oncology, Dana-Farber Canc Inst 1989

Weinstein, Paul L MD (Onc) - **Spec Exp:** Breast Cancer; Lung Cancer; Colon Cancer; **Hospital:** Stamford Hosp (page 971); **Address:** Bennett Cancer Ctr, 34 Shelburne Rd, Stamford, CT 06902-3628; **Phone:** 203-325-2695; **Board Cert:** Internal Medicine 1973; Medical Oncology 1977; Hematology 1978; **Med School:** Ros Franklin Univ/Chicago Med Sch 1970; **Resid:** Internal Medicine, Montefiore Med Ctr 1973; **Fellow:** Hematology & Oncology, Montefiore Med Ctr 1977; **Fac Appt:** Assoc Clin Prof Med, Columbia P&S

Zelkowitz, Richard S MD (Onc) - **Spec Exp:** Breast Cancer; **Hospital:** Norwalk Hosp; **Address:** Norwalk Hosp, Oncology Div, 24 Stevens St, Whittingham Cancer Ctr, Norwalk, CT 06856; **Phone:** 203-845-4811; **Board Cert:** Internal Medicine 1986; Hematology 1988; Medical Oncology 1989; **Med School:** NY Med Coll 1983; **Resid:** Internal Medicine, Westchester Co Med Ctr 1986; **Fellow:** Hematology & Oncology, Brown Univ Hosps 1989

Neonatal-Perinatal Medicine

Herzlinger, Robert A MD (NP) - **Spec Exp:** Neonatology; Prematurity/Low Birth Weight Infants; **Hospital:** Bridgeport Hosp, Yale-New Haven Hosp; **Address:** Bridgeport Hosp, 267 Grant St, Ste 6, Bridgeport, CT 06610-2870; **Phone:** 203-384-3486; **Board Cert:** Pediatrics 1974; Neonatal-Perinatal Medicine 1977; **Med School:** NY Med Coll 1969; **Resid:** Pediatrics, Westchester Co Med Ctr 1971; Pediatrics, Columbia-Presby Med Ctr 1972; **Fellow:** Neonatal-Perinatal Medicine, Columbia-Presby Med Ctr 1973; Neonatal-Perinatal Medicine, Montefiore Med Ctr 1976; **Fac Appt:** Assoc Clin Prof Ped, Yale Univ

Rakos, Gerald B MD (NP) - **Spec Exp:** Neonatal Care; Prematurity/Low Birth Weight Infants; **Hospital:** Stamford Hosp (page 971); **Address:** Stamford Hosp, NICU, 30 Shelburne Rd, Box 9317, Stamford, CT 06904; **Phone:** 203-276-7085; **Board Cert:** Pediatrics 1985; Neonatal-Perinatal Medicine 1985; **Med School:** SUNY Upstate Med Univ 1980; **Resid:** Pediatrics, UMass Meml Med Ctr 1983; **Fellow:** Neonatology, Montefiore Med Ctr 1985; **Fac Appt:** Asst Clin Prof Ped, Columbia P&S

Theofanidis, Stylianos N MD (NP) - **Spec Exp:** Prematurity/Low Birth Weight Infants; Lung Disease in Newborns; **Hospital:** Greenwich Hosp (page 970); **Address:** Greenwich Hosp, Neonatology Dept, 5 Perryridge Rd, Greenwich, CT 06830; **Phone:** 203-863-3515; **Board Cert:** Neonatal-Perinatal Medicine 2011; **Med School:** Greece 1980; **Resid:** Pediatrics, St Lukes-Roosevelt Hosp 1985; **Fellow:** Neonatal-Perinatal Medicine, NY-Presby/Weill Cornell Med Ctr 1987

Nephrology

Brown, Eric Y MD (Nep) - **Spec Exp:** Kidney Disease; Hypertension; Glomerulonephritis; **Hospital:** Stamford Hosp (page 971); **Address:** Stamford Hosp, Dept Nephrology, 30 Commerce Rd, Stamford, CT 06902-4550; **Phone:** 203-324-7666; **Board Cert:** Internal Medicine 1988; Nephrology 2010; **Med School:** Emory Univ 1985; **Resid:** Internal Medicine, Johns Hopkins Hosp 1988; **Fellow:** Nephrology, Yale-New Haven Hosp 1990; **Fac Appt:** Asst Prof Med, Columbia P&S

Chan, Brenda S MD (Nep) - **Spec Exp:** Dialysis Care; Kidney Failure-Chronic; Lupus Nephritis; Glomerulonephritis; **Hospital:** Stamford Hosp (page 971), Greenwich Hosp (page 970); **Address:** Stamford Hosp, Nephrology Div, 30 Commerce Rd, Stamford, CT 06902; **Phone:** 203-324-7666; **Board Cert:** Nephrology 2007; **Med School:** Mount Sinai Sch Med 1990; **Resid:** Internal Medicine, Montefiore Med Ctr 1993; **Fellow:** Nephrology, Montefiore Med Ctr 1996

Feintzeig, Irwin D MD (Nep) - **Spec Exp:** Kidney Disease; Hypertension; Dialysis Care; **Hospital:** Bridgeport Hosp, St. Vincent's Med Ctr - Bridgeport; **Address:** Nephrology Assocs, 900 Madison Ave, Ste 209, Bridgeport, CT 06606-5534; **Phone:** 203-335-0195; **Board Cert:** Internal Medicine 1982; Nephrology 1984; **Med School:** Univ Chicago-Pritzker Sch Med 1979; **Resid:** Internal Medicine, Temple Univ Hosp 1982; **Fellow:** Nephrology, Boston Univ Med Ctr 1985; **Fac Appt:** Asst Clin Prof Med, Yale Univ

Fogel, Mitchell A MD (Nep) - **Spec Exp:** Kidney Disease-Chronic; Glomerulonephritis; Dialysis Care; **Hospital:** St. Vincent's Med Ctr - Bridgeport, Bridgeport Hosp; **Address:** Nephrology Assocs, 900 Madison Ave, Ste 209, Bridgeport, CT 06606; **Phone:** 203-335-0195; **Board Cert:** Internal Medicine 1986; Nephrology 1988; **Med School:** Univ Pennsylvania 1982; **Resid:** Internal Medicine, Boston Univ Med Ctr 1985; **Fellow:** Nephrology, Boston Univ Med Ctr 1988; **Fac Appt:** Med

Hines, William H MD (Nep) - **Spec Exp:** Dialysis Care; Hypertension; Kidney Disease; **Hospital:** Stamford Hosp (page 971), Greenwich Hosp (page 970); **Address:** Stamford Hosp, Div Nephrology, 30 Commerce Rd, Stamford, CT 06902-4550; **Phone:** 203-324-7666; **Board Cert:** Internal Medicine 1984; Nephrology 1986; **Med School:** Cornell Univ-Weill Med Coll 1981; **Resid:** Internal Medicine, Hosp U Penn 1984; **Fellow:** Nephrology, Hosp U Penn 1988; **Fac Appt:** Assoc Clin Prof Med, Columbia P&S

Hunt, William A MD (Nep) - **Spec Exp:** Hypertension; Kidney Disease; **Hospital:** Bridgeport Hosp, St. Vincent's Med Ctr - Bridgeport; **Address:** Nephrology Assocs, 900 Madison Ave, Ste 209, Bridgeport, CT 06606-5534; **Phone:** 203-335-0195; **Board Cert:** Internal Medicine 1984; Nephrology 1986; **Med School:** Yale Univ 1981; **Resid:** Internal Medicine, Univ Hosps Cleveland 1984

Neurological Surgery

Apostolides, Paul J MD (NS) - **Spec Exp:** Minimally Invasive Spinal Surgery; Spinal Surgery; **Hospital:** Greenwich Hosp (page 970), Stamford Hosp (page 971); **Address:** Ortho & Neurosurg Specs, 6 Greenwich Office Park, Greenwich, CT 06831; **Phone:** 203-869-1145; **Board Cert:** Neurological Surgery 2013; **Med School:** Univ Mass Sch Med 1991; **Resid:** Surgery, Maricopa Med Ctr 1992; Neurological Surgery, Barrow Neuro Inst 1998; **Fellow:** Spine Surgery, Barrow Neuro Inst 1997

Camel, Mark H MD (NS) - **Spec Exp:** Brain Tumors; Spinal Surgery; Minimally Invasive Spinal Surgery; **Hospital:** Greenwich Hosp (page 970), Stamford Hosp (page 971); **Address:** Ortho & Neurosurg Specs, 6 Greenwich Office Park, Greenwich, CT 06831; **Phone:** 203-869-1145 x616; **Board Cert:** Neurological Surgery 1990; **Med School:** Washington Univ, St Louis 1981; **Resid:** Neurological Surgery, Barnes Jewish Hosp 1986; **Fellow:** Neurological Surgery, Barnes Jewish Hosp 1987; **Fac Appt:** Asst Clin Prof NS, Cornell Univ-Weill Med Coll

Fiore, Amory J MD (NS) - **Spec Exp:** Minimally Invasive Spinal Surgery; Brain Tumors; Scoliosis; **Hospital:** Greenwich Hosp (page 970), Stamford Hosp (page 971); **Address:** Ortho & Neurosurg Specs, 6 Greenwich Office Park, Greenwich, CT 06831; **Phone:** 203-869-1145; **Board Cert:** Neurological Surgery 2006; **Med School:** Columbia P&S 1995; **Resid:** Neurological Surgery, NY-Presby/Columbia Univ Med Ctr 2001; **Fellow:** Spine Surgery, Emory Clinic 2002

Lipow, Kenneth I MD (NS) - **Spec Exp:** Spinal Surgery; Brain Tumors; Minimally Invasive Spinal Surgery; **Hospital:** Bridgeport Hosp, St. Vincent's Med Ctr - Bridgeport; **Address:** CT Neurosurgical Specs, 267 Grant St Fl 8, Bridgeport, CT 06610; **Phone:** 203-384-4500; **Board Cert:** Neurological Surgery 1989; **Med School:** Albert Einstein Coll Med 1978; **Resid:** Surgery, Montefiore Med Ctr 1979; Neurological Surgery, Montefiore Med Ctr 1984

Mintz, Abraham MD (NS) - **Spec Exp:** Spinal Surgery; **Hospital:** St. Vincent's Med Ctr - Bridgeport, Bridgeport Hosp; **Address:** 5520 Park Ave, rm 210, Trumbull, CT 06611; **Phone:** 203-372-6460; **Board Cert:** Neurological Surgery 1992; **Med School:** Mexico 1981; **Resid:** Surgery, Mercy Catholic Med Ctr 1983; Neurological Surgery, Jackson Meml Hosp 1989

Sanderson, Scott P MD (NS) - **Spec Exp:** Spinal Tumors; Cerebrovascular Malformations; Spinal Cord Injury; **Hospital:** Danbury Hosp, Norwalk Hosp; **Address:** Neurological Assocs SW CT, 148 East Ave, Ste 3D, Norwalk, CT 06851; **Phone:** 203-853-0003; **Board Cert:** Neurological Surgery 2010; **Med School:** NYU Sch Med 1999; **Resid:** Neurological Surgery, NYU Med Ctr 2005; **Fellow:** Spine Surgery, NYU Med Ctr 2003; **Fac Appt:** Asst Clin Prof NS, NYU Sch Med

Shahid, Syed J MD (NS) - **Spec Exp:** Brain Tumors; Spinal Surgery; Spinal Tumors; **Hospital:** Danbury Hosp, Norwalk Hosp; **Address:** Neurosurgical Assocs-SW CT, 148 East Ave, Ste 3D, Norwalk, CT 6851; **Phone:** 203-853-0003; **Board Cert:** Neurological Surgery 1983; **Med School:** Pakistan 1972; **Resid:** Surgery, Kings Co Hosp Ctr 1976; Neurology, NY Presby Hosp 1977; **Fellow:** Neurological Surgery, Kings Co Hosp Ctr 1980

Shear, Perry A MD (NS) - **Spec Exp:** Spinal Surgery; Pituitary Tumors; Cerebrovascular Surgery; **Hospital:** Bridgeport Hosp, St. Vincent's Med Ctr - Bridgeport; **Address:** Orthopaedic Specialty Grp, 75 Kings Hwy Cutoff, Ste 100, Fairfield, CT 06824; **Phone:** 203-337-2600; **Board Cert:** Neurological Surgery 1996; **Med School:** Univ Toronto 1984; **Resid:** Surgery, Toronto Genl Hosp 1985; Neurological Surgery, Ottawa Civic Hosp 1991

Simon, Scott L MD (NS) - **Spec Exp:** Spinal Surgery; Scoliosis; Stereotactic Radiosurgery; Minimally Invasive Spinal Surgery; **Hospital:** Stamford Hosp (page 971), Greenwich Hosp (page 970); **Address:** Ortho & Neurosurg Specs, 6 Greenwich Office Park, Greenwich, CT 06831; **Phone:** 203-869-1145; **Board Cert:** Neurological Surgery 2009; **Med School:** Rutgers R W Johnson Med Sch 1998; **Resid:** Surgery, Hosp Univ Penn 1999; Neurological Surgery, Hosp Univ Penn 2005; **Fellow:** Spine Surgery, Shriners Hosp Chldn 2006

Zimmerman, Gary A MD (NS) - **Spec Exp:** Spinal Surgery; Cerebrovascular Surgery; Brain Tumors; **Hospital:** Bridgeport Hosp, St. Vincent's Med Ctr - Bridgeport; **Address:** CT Neurosurgical Specs, 267 Grant St Fl 8, Bridgeport, CT 06610-2805; **Phone:** 203-384-4500; **Board Cert:** Neurological Surgery 2011; **Med School:** SUNY Downstate 1990; **Resid:** Neurological Surgery, NY-Presby/Weill Cornell Med Ctr 1996; **Fellow:** Cerebrovascular Disease, Univ Hosp 1997

Neurology

Butler, James B MD (N) - **Spec Exp:** Headache; Migraine; Huntington's Disease; Multiple Sclerosis; **Hospital:** Bridgeport Hosp, Griffin Hosp; **Address:** Neurological Specs, 4 Corporate Drive, Ste 192, Shelton, CT 06484; **Phone:** 203-924-8664; **Board Cert:** Internal Medicine 1982; Neurology 1987; **Med School:** Belgium 1979; **Resid:** Internal Medicine, Hosp St Raphael 1982; Neurology, Yale-New Haven Hosp 1985

Cuzzone, Louis J MD (N) - **Spec Exp:** Migraine; Electromyography; **Hospital:** Norwalk Hosp; **Address:** Neurology Assocs of Norwalk, 637 West Ave, Ste 200, Norwalk, CT 06850; **Phone:** 203-853-5000; **Board Cert:** Neurology 1980; **Med School:** Albert Einstein Coll Med 1975; **Resid:** Neurology, Montefiore Med Ctr 1979; **Fellow:** Electromyography, NYU Med Ctr 1980

Gross, Jeffrey L MD (N) - **Spec Exp:** Multiple Sclerosis; **Hospital:** St. Vincent's Med Ctr - Bridgeport, Milford Hosp; **Address:** Assoc Neurologists of Southern CT, 75 Kings Highway Cutoff Fl 5, Fairfield, CT 06824; **Phone:** 203-333-1133; **Board Cert:** Neurology 1985; **Med School:** Case West Res Univ 1978; **Resid:** Internal Medicine, Hosp Univ Penn 1980; Neurology, Hosp Univ Penn 1983; **Fellow:** Neuromuscular Disease, Hosp Univ Penn 1984

Litchman, Charisse D MD (N) - **Spec Exp:** Headache; Multiple Sclerosis; **Hospital:** Stamford Hosp (page 971); **Address:** Coastal Headache & Neurology Ctr, 1250 Summer St, Ste 202, Stamford, CT 06905; **Phone:** 203-969-7662; **Board Cert:** Neurology 1993; Headache Medicine 2008; **Med School:** Yale Univ 1988; **Resid:** Neurology, Yale New Haven Hosp 1989; Neurology, New York Hosp 1992; **Fac Appt:** Asst Clin Prof N, Columbia P&S

McAllister, Peter J MD (N) - **Spec Exp:** Headache; **Hospital:** St. Vincent's Med Ctr - Bridgeport, Bridgeport Hosp; **Address:** New England Inst for Neurology & Headache, 30 Buxton Farm Rd, Ste 230, Stamford, CT 06905; **Phone:** 203-914-1900; **Board Cert:** Neurology 2007; **Med School:** Univ Conn 1991; **Resid:** Internal Medicine, Med Coll VA Affil Hosp 1992; Neurology, Med Coll VA Affil Hosp 1995; **Fellow:** Neuromuscular Disease, Med Coll VA Affil Hosp 1996

Nahm, Frederick K MD/PhD (N) - **Spec Exp:** Cerebrovascular Disease; Stroke; **Hospital:** Greenwich Hosp (page 970); **Address:** NeuroCare Health, 49 Lake Ave, Ste LL3, Greenwich, CT 06830; **Phone:** 203-661-9383; **Board Cert:** Neurology 2014; **Med School:** Univ Mich Med Sch 1996; **Resid:** Neurology, UCSF Med Ctr 1997; Neurology, Beth Israel Deaconess Med Ctr 2000; **Fellow:** Clinical Neurophysiology, Mass Genl Hosp 2001

Resor, Louise D MD (N) - **Hospital:** Stamford Hosp (page 971); **Address:** Fairfield Co Neurology, 166 W Broad St, Ste 203, Stamford, CT 06902; **Phone:** 203-276-4464; **Board Cert:** Neurology 1979; **Med School:** Washington Univ, St Louis 1974; **Resid:** Neurology, NY-Presby/Columbia Univ Med Ctr 1978; **Fellow:** Neurology, NY-Presby/Columbia Univ Med Ctr 1979

Rusk, Alice H MD (N) - **Spec Exp:** Movement Disorders; Parkinson's Disease; Dystonia; **Hospital:** Greenwich Hosp (page 970), Stamford Hosp (page 971); **Address:** Greenwich Neurology, 25 Valley Drive Fl 2, Greenwich, CT 06830; **Phone:** 203-869-6446; **Board Cert:** Neurology 2006; **Med School:** Univ Conn 1991; **Resid:** Neurology, NY Hosp-Cornell Med Ctr 1995; **Fellow:** Clinical Neurophysiology, NY-Presby/Columbia Univ Med Ctr 1996

Story, Daryl R MD (N) - **Spec Exp:** Stroke; Vascular Neurology; **Hospital:** Norwalk Hosp; **Address:** Neurology Assocs of Norwalk, 637 West Ave, Ste 200, Norwalk, CT 06850; **Phone:** 203-853-5000; **Board Cert:** Neurology 2012; Vascular Neurology 2008; **Med School:** NY Med Coll 1997; **Resid:** Neurology, Yale-New Haven Hosp 2001; **Fellow:** Stroke, Yale-New Haven Hosp 2002

Wirz, Diane MD (N) - **Spec Exp:** Headache; Migraine; **Hospital:** Danbury Hosp; **Address:** Associated Neurologists, 69 Sand Pit Rd, Ste 300, Danbury, CT 06810; **Phone:** 203-748-2551; **Board Cert:** Internal Medicine 1982; Neurology 1986; Headache Medicine 2008; **Med School:** Albany Med Coll 1979; **Resid:** Internal Medicine, Danbury Hosp 1982; Neurology, Univ Conn Hlth Ctr 1985

Neuroradiology

Rosovsky, Mark A MD (NRad) - **Spec Exp:** MRI; Cardiac CT Angiography; **Hospital:** Bridgeport Hosp, St. Vincent's Med Ctr - Bridgeport; **Address:** Advanced Radiology Cons, 3 Enterprise Drive, Ste 220, Shelton, CT 06484; **Phone:** 203-452-2244; **Board Cert:** Diagnostic Radiology 1994; Neuroradiology 2007; **Med School:** SUNY Downstate 1989; **Resid:** Radiology, Beth Israel Med Ctr 1994; **Fellow:** Neuroradiology, NYU Langone Med Ctr 1996

Sullivan, Scott J MD (NRad) - **Spec Exp:** MRI; Aneurysm; **Hospital:** Greenwich Hosp (page 970); **Address:** Greenwich Hosp-Dept Radiology, 5 Perryridge Rd, Greenwich, CT 06830; **Phone:** 203-863-3960; **Board Cert:** Diagnostic Radiology 1996; Neuroradiology 2004; **Med School:** Georgetown Univ 1991; **Resid:** Radiology, Yale-New Haven Hosp 1995; **Fellow:** Neuroradiology, Yale-New Haven Hosp 1996

Nuclear Medicine

Johns, William D MD (NuM) - **Spec Exp:** PET Imaging; **Hospital:** Danbury Hosp; **Address:** Danbury Hosp, Nuclear Med, 24 Hospital Ave, Danbury, CT 06810; **Phone:** 203-739-7222; **Board Cert:** Internal Medicine 1986; Nuclear Medicine 1988; **Med School:** Univ Conn 1983; **Resid:** Internal Medicine, Danbury Hosp 1986; Nuclear Medicine, Brigham & Womens Hosp 1988

Obstetrics & Gynecology

Ayoub, Thomas V MD (ObG) - **Spec Exp:** Menopause Problems; Hormonal Disorders; **Hospital:** Norwalk Hosp; **Address:** Women's Hlth Care New England, 761 Main Ave, Ste 100, Norwalk, CT 06851; **Phone:** 203-644-1100; **Board Cert:** Obstetrics & Gynecology 2013; **Med School:** NYU Sch Med 1980; **Resid:** Obstetrics & Gynecology, Bellevue Hosp 1984

Berger, Robin MD (ObG) - **Spec Exp:** Gynecology Only; **Hospital:** Bridgeport Hosp; **Address:** Women's Healthcare of Trumbull, 5520 Park Ave, Ste 302, Trumbull, CT 06611; **Phone:** 203-374-1018; **Board Cert:** Obstetrics & Gynecology 2013; **Med School:** SUNY Downstate 1983; **Resid:** Obstetrics & Gynecology, Brookdale Hosp 1987

Besser, Gary S MD (ObG) - **Spec Exp:** Laparoscopic Surgery-Complex; Uro-Gynecology; Pelvic Surgery; Robotic Surgery; **Hospital:** Stamford Hosp (page 971), Greenwich Hosp (page 970); **Address:** Obstetrics & Gynecology Assocs, 190 W Brand St, Ste G-401, Whittingham Pavilion, Stamford, CT 06902-3661; **Phone:** 203-325-4321; **Board Cert:** Obstetrics & Gynecology 2013; **Med School:** SUNY Downstate 1982; **Resid:** Obstetrics & Gynecology, Stamford Hosp 1986; **Fac Appt:** Assoc Prof ObG, Columbia P&S

Blair, Emily E DO (ObG) - **Spec Exp:** Pregnancy-High Risk; **Hospital:** Bridgeport Hosp; **Address:** OB/GYN of Fairfield County, 1735 Post Rd, Ste 2A, Fairfield, CT 06824; **Phone:** 203-256-3990; **Board Cert:** Obstetrics & Gynecology 2013; **Med School:** Univ Osteo Med & Hlth Sci, Des Moines 1986; **Resid:** Obstetrics & Gynecology, Bridgeport Hosp 1990; **Fac Appt:** Assoc Prof ObG, Univ Conn

Cahill, Patrick J DO (ObG) - **Spec Exp:** Robotic Surgery; Uterine Fibroids; Endometriosis; **Hospital:** Stamford Hosp (page 971); **Address:** Coastal Ob/Gyn, 999 Summer St, Ste 401, Stamford, CT 06905; **Phone:** 203-353-9099; **Board Cert:** Obstetrics & Gynecology 2014; **Med School:** NY Coll Osteo Med 1996; **Resid:** Obstetrics & Gynecology, Stamford Hosp 2000

Cuteri, Joseph A MD (ObG) - **Spec Exp:** Pregnancy-High Risk; Colposcopy; Ultrasound; **Hospital:** Bridgeport Hosp, St. Vincent's Med Ctr - Bridgeport; **Address:** Shelton OB/GYN, 4 Corporate Drive, Ste 286, Shelton, CT 06484; **Phone:** 203-929-9000; **Board Cert:** Obstetrics & Gynecology 2013; **Med School:** Mexico 1984; **Resid:** Obstetrics & Gynecology, Brooklyn Hosp 1987; Obstetrics & Gynecology, Bridgeport Hosp 1989; **Fac Appt:** Asst Clin Prof ObG, Yale Univ

Deal, Robert Campbell MD (ObG) *PCP* - **Spec Exp:** Laparoscopic Surgery; Menopause Problems; Robotic Surgery; **Hospital:** Bridgeport Hosp; **Address:** Women's Hlth Care, 115 Technology Drive, Ste A100, Trumbull, CT 06611; **Phone:** 203-880-5556; **Board Cert:** Obstetrics & Gynecology 2013; **Med School:** Georgetown Univ 1990; **Resid:** Obstetrics & Gynecology, Bridgeport Hosp 1994; **Fac Appt:** Asst Clin Prof ObG, Yale Univ

Donovan, Leslie A MD (ObG) - **Spec Exp:** Adolescent Gynecology; Menopause Problems; Sexually Transmitted Diseases; Gynecology Only; **Hospital:** Greenwich Hosp (page 970); **Address:** Brookside Gynecology, 159 W Putnam Ave Fl 2, Greenwich, CT 06830; **Phone:** 203-869-7080; **Board Cert:** Obstetrics & Gynecology 2013; **Med School:** Univ Mass Sch Med 1993; **Resid:** Obstetrics & Gynecology, Maricopa Med Ctr 1997

Ferrucci, Leonard MD (ObG) - **Spec Exp:** Menstrual Disorders; Pregnancy; Endometriosis; **Hospital:** Stamford Hosp (page 971); **Address:** Ferrucci, Ferrucci & Morris, 833 Summer St, Ste 1B, Stamford, CT 06901; **Phone:** 203-325-4665; **Board Cert:** Obstetrics & Gynecology 2013; **Med School:** NY Med Coll 1987; **Resid:** Obstetrics & Gynecology, Stamford Hosp 1991

Ferrucci, Vito MD (ObG) - **Hospital:** Stamford Hosp (page 971); **Address:** Ferrucci, Ferrucci & Morris, 833 Summer St, Ste 1B, Stamford, CT 06901; **Phone:** 203-325-4665; **Board Cert:** Obstetrics & Gynecology 2013; **Med School:** NY Med Coll 1985; **Resid:** Obstetrics & Gynecology, Stamford Hosp 1989

Filor, Caroline F MD (ObG) - **Spec Exp:** Robotic Surgery; Minimally Invasive Surgery; Pain-Pelvic; Endometriosis; **Hospital:** Greenwich Hosp (page 970); **Address:** Brookside Gynecology, 159 W Putnam Ave Fl 2, Greenwich, CT 06830; **Phone:** 203-869-7080; **Board Cert:** Obstetrics & Gynecology 2013; **Med School:** NY Med Coll 1998; **Resid:** Obstetrics & Gynecology, Univ Conn Hlth Ctr 2000; Obstetrics & Gynecology, RWJ Univ Hosp 2002

Garrett, Leila J MD (ObG) - **Spec Exp:** Menopause Problems; Pap Smear Abnormalities; Sexually Transmitted Diseases; Adolescent Gynecology; **Hospital:** Greenwich Hosp (page 970); **Address:** Greenwich Gynecology, 1 Perryridge Rd, Greenwich, CT 06830; **Phone:** 203-869-8353; **Board Cert:** Obstetrics & Gynecology 2013; **Med School:** Univ Rochester 1990; **Resid:** Obstetrics & Gynecology, Univ VT Coll Med Affil Hosp 1994

Geer-Yan, Lisa MD (ObG) *PCP* - **Spec Exp:** Menstrual Disorders; Prenatal Diagnosis; Women's Health; **Hospital:** Bridgeport Hosp, St. Vincent's Med Ctr - Bridgeport; **Address:** Fairfield Women's Health Center, 140 Sherman St Fl 5, Fairfield, CT 06824; **Phone:** 203-658-8291; **Board Cert:** Obstetrics & Gynecology 2013; **Med School:** SUNY Upstate Med Univ 2001; **Resid:** Obstetrics & Gynecology, Thos Jefferson Univ Hosp 2005

Ghofrany, Shieva L MD (ObG) - **Spec Exp:** Menopause Problems; Women's Health over age 40; **Hospital:** Stamford Hosp (page 971); **Address:** Coastal OB & GYN, 999 Summer St, Ste 401, Stamford, CT 06905; **Phone:** 203-353-9099; **Board Cert:** Obstetrics & Gynecology 2013; **Med School:** Israel 1999; **Resid:** Obstetrics & Gynecology, Stamford Hosp 2003

Hagberg, Donna J MD (ObG) - **Spec Exp:** Gynecology Only; **Hospital:** Greenwich Hosp (page 970); **Address:** 31 River Rd, Ste 102, Cos Cob, CT 06807; **Phone:** 203-742-1150; **Board Cert:** Obstetrics & Gynecology 2013; **Med School:** Univ Rochester 1989; **Resid:** Internal Medicine, Yale-New Haven Hosp 1990; Obstetrics & Gynecology, Yale-New Haven Hosp 1993

Hines, Brian J MD (ObG) - **Spec Exp:** Uro-Gynecology; Incontinence; Pelvic Organ Prolapse Repair; **Hospital:** Stamford Hosp (page 971), St. Vincent's Med Ctr - Bridgeport; **Address:** 1351 Washington Blvd, Ste 201, Stamford, CT 06902; **Phone:** 203-276-4524; **Board Cert:** Obstetrics & Gynecology 2013; **Med School:** Boston Univ 1996; **Resid:** Obstetrics & Gynecology, Mt Sinai Hosp 2000; **Fellow:** Uro-Gynecology, NYU Med Ctr 2002

Jacobson, Edward MD (ObG) - **Spec Exp:** Gynecology Only; Hormonal Disorders; Laparoscopic Surgery; Menopause Problems; **Hospital:** Greenwich Hosp (page 970); **Address:** Greenwich Gynecology, 1 Perryridge Rd, Greenwich, CT 06830; **Phone:** 203-869-8353; **Board Cert:** Obstetrics & Gynecology 1981; **Med School:** NY Med Coll 1975; **Resid:** Obstetrics & Gynecology, NY-Presby/Weill Cornell Med Ctr 1979

Kerr, Alicia H MD (ObG) - **Spec Exp:** Pregnancy-High Risk; **Hospital:** Norwalk Hosp; **Address:** Women's Healthcare of New England, 761 Main Ave B Bldg - Ste 100, Norwalk, CT 6851; **Phone:** 203-644-1100; **Board Cert:** Obstetrics & Gynecology 2013; **Med School:** Ohio State Univ 1997; **Resid:** Obstetrics & Gynecology, Stamford Hosp 2001

Komarynsky, Irene I MD (ObG) - **Spec Exp:** Maternal & Fetal Medicine; Pregnancy-High Risk; Prenatal Diagnosis; **Hospital:** Stamford Hosp (page 971); **Address:** OB GYN Cons, 166 W Broad St, Ste 301, Stamford, CT 06902; **Phone:** 203-325-9920; **Board Cert:** Obstetrics & Gynecology 2013; **Med School:** Univ Chicago-Pritzker Sch Med 1979; **Resid:** Obstetrics & Gynecology, Hosp Univ Penn - UPHS 1983; **Fellow:** Maternal & Fetal Medicine, Univ IL Med Ctr 1985

Rivera, Jeanette MD (ObG) - **Spec Exp:** Uro-Gynecology; Pelvic Reconstruction; Pelvic Organ Prolapse Repair; **Hospital:** Danbury Hosp; **Address:** Urology Assocs of Danbury, 51-53 Kenosia Ave, Danbury, CT 06810; **Phone:** 203-702-2320; **Board Cert:** Obstetrics & Gynecology 2013; Female Pelvic Medicine & Reconstuctive Surgery 2013; **Med School:** Univ Conn 2000; **Resid:** Obstetrics & Gynecology, NYU Med Ctr 2004; **Fellow:** Uro-Gynecology, NYU Med Ctr 2007

Rohr, Michele M MD (ObG) - **Spec Exp:** Pelvic Reconstruction; Pap Smear Abnormalities; Laparoscopic Surgery; Vulvar & Vaginal Disorders; **Hospital:** Greenwich Hosp (page 970); **Address:** Brookside Gynecology, 159 W Putnam Ave Fl 2, Greenwich, CT 06830; **Phone:** 203-869-7080; **Board Cert:** Obstetrics & Gynecology 2013; **Med School:** Washington Univ, St Louis 1996; **Resid:** Obstetrics & Gynecology, Univ Chicago Univ Med Ctr 2000

Samuelson, Robert MD (ObG) - **Spec Exp:** Minimally Invasive Surgery; Robotic Surgery; **Hospital:** Danbury Hosp; **Address:** Danbury, Ob/Gyn-WCMG, 24 Hospital Ave, Danbury, CT 06810; **Phone:** 203-739-4900; **Board Cert:** Obstetrics & Gynecology 2013; **Med School:** Grenada 1985; **Resid:** Obstetrics & Gynecology, Hartford Hosp 1988; **Fellow:** Pelvic Surgery, Lahey Clinic 2004

Schechter, Michael D MD (ObG) - **Spec Exp:** Pregnancy-High Risk; HPV-Human Papilloma Virus; Uterine Fibroids; **Hospital:** Greenwich Hosp (page 970); **Address:** Putnam Gynecology & Obstetrics-Greenwich, 55 Holly Hill Ln, Ste 130, Greenwich, CT 06830; **Phone:** 203-622-0303; **Board Cert:** Obstetrics & Gynecology 2013; **Med School:** NYU Sch Med 1988; **Resid:** Internal Medicine, St Lukes-Roosevelt Hosp 1989; Obstetrics & Gynecology, St Lukes-Roosevelt Hosp 1992

Szeto, Marjorie MD (ObG) - **Spec Exp:** Pregnancy-High Risk; Premature Labor; Prenatal Diagnosis; **Hospital:** Norwalk Hosp; **Address:** Avery Ctr for Ob/Gyn, 12 Avery Pl, Westport, CT 06880; **Phone:** 203-227-5125; **Board Cert:** Obstetrics & Gynecology 2013; **Med School:** NYU Sch Med 1985; **Resid:** Obstetrics & Gynecology, Beth Israel Med Ctr 1989

Torbey, Marina C MD (ObG) - **Spec Exp:** Laparoscopic Surgery; Pregnancy-High Risk; **Hospital:** Bridgeport Hosp; **Address:** Women's Healthcare of Trumbull, 5520 Park Ave, Ste 302, Trumbull, CT 06611; **Phone:** 203-374-1018; **Board Cert:** Obstetrics & Gynecology 2013; **Med School:** Univ Kansas 1985; **Resid:** Obstetrics & Gynecology, Montefiore-Weiler Med Ctr 1989; **Fac Appt:** Asst Prof ObG, Albert Einstein Coll Med

Turk, Russell F MD (ObG) - **Spec Exp:** Laparoscopic Surgery; Hysteroscopic Surgery; Vulvar & Vaginal Disorders; Pregnancy-High Risk; **Hospital:** Stamford Hosp (page 971); **Address:** Riverside Ob/Gyn, 1200 E Putnam Ave, Riverside, CT 06878; **Phone:** 203-637-3337; **Board Cert:** Obstetrics & Gynecology 2013; **Med School:** Cornell Univ-Weill Med Coll 1990; **Resid:** Obstetrics & Gynecology, Albert Einstein Coll Med 1994

Ugol, Jay H MD (ObG) - **Spec Exp:** Pregnancy; Endometriosis; Uterine Fibroids; **Hospital:** Norwalk Hosp; **Address:** Women's Hlth Care of New England, 761 Main Ave, Ste 100, Norwalk, CT 06851; **Phone:** 203-644-1100; **Board Cert:** Obstetrics & Gynecology 2013; **Med School:** Georgetown Univ 1982; **Resid:** Obstetrics & Gynecology, Univ Colorado Hlth Sci Ctr 1986

Violi, Caterina MD (ObG) - **Spec Exp:** Endometriosis; Pregnancy-High Risk; Laparoscopic Surgery-Complex; Menopause Problems; **Hospital:** Greenwich Hosp (page 970); **Address:** OB GYN for women by women, 2 1/2 Dearfield Drive, Ste 101, Greenwich, CT 06831; **Phone:** 203-861-9586; **Board Cert:** Obstetrics & Gynecology 2013; **Med School:** Univ Rochester 1994; **Resid:** Obstetrics & Gynecology, Winthrop Univ Hosp 1998

Weinstein, David B MD (ObG) - **Spec Exp:** Pregnancy-High Risk; **Hospital:** Stamford Hosp (page 971); **Address:** Stamford Hosp, 190 W Broad St, Ste G-401, Whittingham Pavilion, Stamford, CT 06902; **Phone:** 203-325-4321; **Board Cert:** Obstetrics & Gynecology 2013; **Med School:** Univ Hlth Scis, Chicago Med Sch 1969; **Resid:** Obstetrics & Gynecology, NY-Presby/Weill Cornell Med Ctr 1974

Ophthalmology

Altman, Bruce S MD (Oph) - **Spec Exp:** Glaucoma; **Hospital:** Danbury Hosp; **Address:** Danbury Eye Phys & Surgeons, 69 Sand Pit Rd, Ste 101, Danbury, CT 06810; **Phone:** 203-791-2020; **Board Cert:** Ophthalmology 2013; **Med School:** Univ Pennsylvania 1986; **Resid:** Ophthalmology, Hahnemann Hosp 1991; **Fellow:** Glaucoma, Barnes-Jewish W Co Hosp 1992; Research, Scheie Eye Inst 1988

Conway Jr, Joseph L MD (Oph) - **Spec Exp:** Oculoplastic Surgery; Dry Eye Syndrome; Tearing Disorders; **Hospital:** Greenwich Hosp (page 970); **Address:** Greenwich Ophthalmology Assocs, 2046 W Main St, Ste 2, Stamford, CT 06902; **Phone:** 203-869-3082; **Board Cert:** Ophthalmology 2006; **Med School:** Penn State Coll Med 1998; **Resid:** Orthopaedic Surgery, Penn State Hershey Med Ctr 2000; Ophthalmology, NYU/Manhattan Eye Ear & Throat Hosp 2003; **Fellow:** Oculoplastic Surgery, NY-Presby/Weill Cornell Med Ctr 2004

Daccache, Armand MD (Oph) - **Spec Exp:** Retina Disorders; Macular Degeneration; Diabetic Eye Disease/Retinopathy; **Hospital:** Danbury Hosp; **Address:** Danbury Eye Phys & Surgeons, 69 Sand Pit Rd, Ste 101, Danbury, CT 06810; **Phone:** 203-791-2020; **Board Cert:** Ophthalmology 2014; **Med School:** Lebanon 1996; **Resid:** Ophthalmology, Georgetown Univ Hosp 2002; **Fellow:** Retina, LSU Interim Public Hosp 2003; Retina, Univ Virginia Hlth Sys 2004

DeBroff, Brian M MD (Oph) - **Spec Exp:** Cataract Surgery; Cataract-Pediatric; Anterior Segment Surgery; **Hospital:** Bridgeport Hosp, Yale-New Haven Hosp; **Address:** Eye Surgery Assocs, 495 Hawley Ln, Stratford, CT 06614; **Phone:** 203-375-5819; **Board Cert:** Ophthalmology 2005; **Med School:** Tufts Univ 1989; **Resid:** Internal Medicine, UPMC Mercy Hosp 1990; Ophthalmology, Univ Pittsburgh/E & E Inst 1993; **Fellow:** Anterior Segment - External Disease, Gimbel Eye Ctr 1994; **Fac Appt:** Assoc Clin Prof Oph, Yale Univ

Doctor, Leslie C MD (Oph) - **Spec Exp:** Cataract Surgery; Anterior Segment Surgery; Corneal Disease; **Hospital:** Norwalk Hosp; **Address:** Doctor & Assocs, 129 Kings Hwy N, Westport, CT 06880; **Phone:** 203-227-4113; **Board Cert:** Ophthalmology 2008; **Med School:** Ohio State Univ 1989; **Resid:** Internal Medicine, Riverside Methodist Hosp 1990; Ophthalmology, OH State Univ Med Ctr 1993; **Fellow:** Cornea & Ext Eye Disease, OH State Univ Med Ctr 1994

Driesman, Shelley K MD (Oph) - **Spec Exp:** Cataract Surgery; Contact Lenses; Glaucoma; Laser Surgery; **Hospital:** Bridgeport Hosp; **Address:** Ophthalmic Surgeons-Greater Bridgeport, 2371 Black Rock Tpke, Fairfield, CT 06825; **Phone:** 203-371-0141; **Board Cert:** Ophthalmology 1989; **Med School:** Brown Univ 1980; **Resid:** Ophthalmology, Lenox Hill Hosp 1984

Finlay, Alexis E MD (Oph) - **Spec Exp:** Refractive Surgery; Cataract Surgery; Corneal Disease & Surgery; Lens Implant; **Hospital:** Greenwich Hosp (page 970); **Address:** Ridgefield Eye Physicians, 38 B Grove St, Lower Level, Ridgefield, CT 06877; **Phone:** 203-403-3375; **Board Cert:** Ophthalmology 1989; **Med School:** Hahnemann Univ 1981; **Resid:** Ophthalmology, NY Eye and Ear Infirmary 1985; **Fellow:** Ophthalmic Pathology, Johns Hopkins Hosp 1986

Gewirtz, Joan T MD (Oph) - **Spec Exp:** Cataract Surgery; Glaucoma; Dry Eye Syndrome; **Hospital:** Stamford Hosp (page 971); **Address:** Stamford Eye Doctor, 70 Mill River St, Ste LL3, Stamford, CT 06902; **Phone:** 203-348-0868; **Board Cert:** Ophthalmology 2010; **Med School:** SUNY Downstate 1980; **Resid:** Surgery, Bellevue Hosp 1981; Ophthalmology, NYU Hosp 1983; **Fellow:** Ophthalmology, Lenox Hill Hosp 1985

Gladstein, Gina F MD (Oph) - **Spec Exp:** Glaucoma; Cataract Surgery; Lens Implant; **Hospital:** Greenwich Hosp (page 970); **Address:** Greenwich Ophthalmology Assocs, 2046 W Main St, Ste 2, Stamford, CT 06902; **Phone:** 203-869-3082; **Board Cert:** Ophthalmology 1989; **Med School:** Albert Einstein Coll Med 1983; **Resid:** Ophthalmology, Manhattan EE&T Hosp 1987; **Fellow:** Glaucoma, Manhattan EE&T Hosp 1988

Kaplan, Jeffrey N MD (Oph) - **Spec Exp:** Corneal Disease; Cataract Surgery; Lens Implant; **Hospital:** Bridgeport Hosp, St. Vincent's Med Ctr - Bridgeport; **Address:** Eye Grp of Connecticut, 4699 Main St, Ste 106, Bridgeport, CT 06606; **Phone:** 203-374-8182; **Board Cert:** Ophthalmology 1987; **Med School:** SUNY Stony Brook 1981; **Resid:** Ophthalmology, SUNY Downstate Med Ctr 1985; **Fellow:** Cornea, Dubroff Eye Ctr 1986

Mandava, Suresh MD (Oph) - **Spec Exp:** LASIK-Refractive Surgery; Cataract Surgery; Cornea Transplant; Cornea & External Eye Disease; **Hospital:** Greenwich Hosp (page 970); **Address:** Greenwich Ophthalmology Assocs, 2046 W Main St, Ste 2, Stamford, CT 06902; **Phone:** 203-869-3082; **Board Cert:** Ophthalmology 2009; **Med School:** Yale Univ 1993; **Resid:** Ophthalmology, Manhattan EE&T Hosp 1997; **Fellow:** Cornea & Refractive Surgery, Univ Minnesota Med Ctr 1998

Manjoney, Delia M MD (Oph) - **Spec Exp:** Cataract Surgery; Glaucoma; Eyelid Cosmetic Surgery; **Hospital:** St. Vincent's Med Ctr - Bridgeport; **Address:** 2720 Main St Fl 3, Bridgeport, CT 06606; **Phone:** 203-576-6500; **Board Cert:** Pediatrics 1982; Ophthalmology 1988; **Med School:** Univ VT Coll Med 1977; **Resid:** Pediatrics, Parkland Hosp/Chldns Med Ctr 1980; Ophthalmology, NY-Presby/Columbia Univ Med Ctr/Harkness 1986

Mathias, Stephen Audley MD (Oph) - **Spec Exp:** Pediatric Ophthalmology; Eye Muscle Disorders; **Hospital:** Danbury Hosp; **Address:** 69 Sand Pit Rd, Ste 101, Danbury Eye Physicians, Danbury, CT 06810-4005; **Phone:** 203-791-2020; **Board Cert:** Ophthalmology 1987; **Med School:** Univ Cincinnati 1982; **Resid:** Ophthalmology, Columbia Presby Med Ctr 1986; **Fellow:** Pediatric Ophthalmology, Columbia Presby Med Ctr 1987

Musto, Anthony MD (Oph) - **Spec Exp:** Cataract Surgery-Lens Implant; Eyelid Surgery; Diabetic Eye Disease/Retinopathy; **Hospital:** Bridgeport Hosp; **Address:** Eye Surgery Assocs, 495 Hawley Ln, Stratford, CT 06614; **Phone:** 203-375-5819; **Board Cert:** Ophthalmology 1975; **Med School:** Georgetown Univ 1968; **Resid:** Ophthalmology, USPHS Hosp 1971; Ophthalmology, Manhattan EE&T Infirm 1973; **Fac Appt:** Asst Clin Prof Oph, Yale Univ

Ostriker, Glenn E MD (Oph) - **Spec Exp:** Cataract Surgery; Glaucoma; **Hospital:** Stamford Hosp (page 971), Bellevue Hosp Ctr; **Address:** 71 Strawberry Hill Ave, Ste 116, Stamford, CT 06902; **Phone:** 203-348-6300; **Board Cert:** Ophthalmology 1987; **Med School:** NYU Sch Med 1982; **Resid:** Ophthalmology, NYU Med Ctr 1986; **Fellow:** Neurophysiology, NYU Med Ctr 1983; **Fac Appt:** Assoc Clin Prof Oph, NYU Sch Med

Paul, Matthew D MD (Oph) - **Spec Exp:** Cataract Surgery; **Hospital:** Danbury Hosp; **Address:** Danbury Eye Phys & Surgeons, 69 Sand Pit Rd, Ste 101, Danbury, CT 06810; **Phone:** 203-791-2020; **Board Cert:** Ophthalmology 1985; **Med School:** Columbia P&S 1980; **Resid:** Ophthalmology, NY-Presby/Columbia Univ Med Ctr 1984

Pinke, James R MD (Oph) - **Spec Exp:** Cataract Surgery; Glaucoma; Lens Implant; **Hospital:** Griffin Hosp; **Address:** Pinke Eye Ctr, 9 Cots St, Shelton, CT 06484-3866; **Phone:** 203-924-8800; **Board Cert:** Ophthalmology 1983; **Med School:** Tufts Univ 1978; **Resid:** Internal Medicine, Faulkner Hosp 1979; Ophthalmology, Tufts Med Ctr 1982

Piro, Philip A MD (Oph) - **Spec Exp:** Retinal Disorders; Retina/Vitreous Consultation; Retina/Vitreous Surgery; **Hospital:** Stamford Hosp (page 971), St. Vincent's Med Ctr - Bridgeport; **Address:** Retina Assocs of CT, 70 Mill River St, Ste UL3, Stamford, CT 06902; **Phone:** 203-325-4481; **Board Cert:** Ophthalmology 1986; **Med School:** Columbia P&S 1978; **Resid:** Ophthalmology, Johns Hopkins Hosp 1982; **Fellow:** Retina, LAC-USC Med Ctr 1983; Vitreoretinal Surgery, Wills Eye Ctr 1984

Potter, William S MD (Oph) - **Spec Exp:** Pediatric Ophthalmology; Strabismus-Adult & Pediatric; Lens Implant; Amblyopia; **Hospital:** Greenwich Hosp (page 970), Stamford Hosp (page 971); **Address:** Greenwich Ophthalmology Assocs, 4 Dearfield Drive, Ste G, Greenwich, CT 06831; **Phone:** 203-869-3082; **Board Cert:** Ophthalmology 1991; **Med School:** NY Med Coll 1985; **Resid:** Ophthalmology, NY E&E Infirmary 1989; **Fellow:** Pediatric Ophthalmology, Thos Jefferson Univ Hosp 1990

Rabinowitz, Stephen M MD (Oph) - **Spec Exp:** Cataract Surgery; Glaucoma; Dry Eye Syndrome; Lens Implant; **Hospital:** Bridgeport Hosp; **Address:** Ophthalmic Surgeons-Greater Bridgeport, 2371 Black Rock Tpke, Fairfield, CT 06825; **Phone:** 203-371-0141; **Board Cert:** Ophthalmology 1990; **Med School:** NYU Sch Med 1984; **Resid:** Internal Medicine, Bronx Muni Hosp 1985; Ophthalmology, Lenox Hill Hosp 1988; **Fellow:** Cornea & Ext Eye Disease, Bascom Palmer Eye Inst 1989

Reppucci, Vincent S MD (Oph) - **Spec Exp:** Retina/Vitreous Surgery; Diabetic Eye Disease; Macular Disease/Degeneration; Retina/Vitreous Consultation; **Hospital:** Danbury Hosp, New York Eye & Ear Infirm of Mt Sinai; **Address:** 65 North St, Danbury, CT 06810; **Phone:** 203-792-6291; **Board Cert:** Ophthalmology 1989; **Med School:** Albert Einstein Coll Med 1983; **Resid:** Ophthalmology, NY-Presby/Columbia Univ Med Ctr 1987; **Fellow:** Retina/Vitreous Surgery, NY-Presby/Weill Cornell Med Ctr 1988; **Fac Appt:** Assoc Prof Oph, Cornell Univ-Weill Med Coll

Robbins, Kim P MD (Oph) - **Spec Exp:** Cataract Surgery; Glaucoma; **Hospital:** Bridgeport Hosp; **Address:** Robbins Eye Ctr, 4695 Main St, Bridgeport, CT 06606; **Phone:** 203-371-5800; **Board Cert:** Ophthalmology 1985; **Med School:** NY Med Coll 1978; **Resid:** Internal Medicine, Stamford Hosp 1980; Ophthalmology, St Vincents Hosp 1983

Scartozzi, Richard MD (Oph) - **Spec Exp:** Macular Degeneration; Diabetic Eye Disease/Retinopathy; Retinal Detachment; Uveitis; **Hospital:** Danbury Hosp, Yale-New Haven Hosp; **Address:** Danbury Eye Physicians & Surgeons, 69 Sand Pit Rd, Ste 101, Danbury, CT 06810; **Phone:** 203-791-2020; **Board Cert:** Ophthalmology 2007; **Med School:** Johns Hopkins Univ 2002; **Resid:** Ophthalmology, Wills Eye Hosp 2006; **Fellow:** Retina/Vitreous Surgery, LAC-USC Med Ctr 2008

Siderides, Elizabeth MD (Oph) - **Spec Exp:** Cataract Surgery; Retinal Disorders; Retina/Vitreous Surgery; **Hospital:** Stamford Hosp (page 971); **Address:** Stamford Ophthalmology, 1351 Washington Blvd, Ste 101, Stamford, CT 06902-2453; **Phone:** 203-327-5808; **Board Cert:** Ophthalmology 1991; **Med School:** Columbia P&S 1985; **Resid:** Internal Medicine, St Luke's Hosp 1986; Ophthalmology, NYU Langone Med Ctr 1989; **Fellow:** Medical Retina, NYU Langone Med Ctr 1991

Tsong, Jerry W MD (Oph) - **Spec Exp:** Retinal Disorders; **Hospital:** Greenwich Hosp (page 970); **Address:** Greenwich Ophthalmology Assocs, 2046 W Main St, Ste 2, Stamford, CT 06902; **Phone:** 203-869-3082; **Board Cert:** Ophthalmology 2007; **Med School:** Harvard Med Sch 2002; **Resid:** Internal Medicine, Mt Sinai Med Ctr 2003; Ophthalmology, G Washington Univ Med Ctr 2006; **Fellow:** Retina, Doheny Eye Inst 2007

Vietorisz, Esteban C MD (Oph) - **Spec Exp:** Cornea & External Eye Disease; Cataract Surgery; Glaucoma; **Hospital:** Stamford Hosp (page 971); **Address:** Stamford Ophthalmology, 1351 Washington Blvd, Ste 101, Stamford, CT 06902; **Phone:** 203-327-5808; **Board Cert:** Ophthalmology 2008; **Med School:** Cornell Univ-Weill Med Coll 1991; **Resid:** Internal Medicine, Winthrop Univ Hosp 1992; Ophthalmology, NY-Presby/Weill Cornell Med Ctr 1995; **Fellow:** Cornea, Duke Univ Eye Ctr 1996

Wasserman, Eric L MD (Oph) - **Spec Exp:** Cataract Surgery; Anterior Segment Surgery; **Hospital:** Stamford Hosp (page 971); **Address:** Eye Care Ctr-Stamford, 1275 Summer St, Ste 200, Stamford, CT 06905; **Phone:** 203-978-0800; **Board Cert:** Ophthalmology 1988; **Med School:** NY Med Coll 1979; **Resid:** Internal Medicine, Danbury Hosp 1980; Ophthalmology, NY Med Coll Affil Hosp 1983; **Fellow:** Anterior Segment - External Disease, John H Sheets Eye Fdn 1984

Weber, Richard B MD (Oph) - **Spec Exp:** Retinal Disorders; **Hospital:** Stamford Hosp (page 971), Greenwich Hosp (page 970); **Address:** 1275 Summer St, Ste 103, Stamford, CT 06905; **Phone:** 203-353-1857; **Board Cert:** Internal Medicine 1979; Ophthalmology 1985; **Med School:** Albert Einstein Coll Med 1976; **Resid:** Internal Medicine, Jacobi Med Ctr 1979; Ophthalmology, Mass Eye & Ear Infirmary 1984; **Fellow:** Retina, Mass Eye & Ear Infirmary 1985

Orthopaedic Surgery

Awad, John N MD (OrS) - **Spec Exp:** Osteoporosis Spine- Kyphoplasty; Spinal Tumors; **Hospital:** Bridgeport Hosp, St. Vincent's Med Ctr - Bridgeport; **Address:** Orthopaedic Specialty Grp, 75 Kings Hwy Cutoff Fl 2, Fairfield, CT 06824; **Phone:** 203-337-2600; **Board Cert:** Orthopaedic Surgery 2007; **Med School:** Rutgers R W Johnson Med Sch 1999; **Resid:** Orthopaedic Surgery, Johns Hopkins Hosp 2004; **Fellow:** Spine Surgery, New York Univ Med Ctr 2005

Bindelglass, David F MD (OrS) - **Spec Exp:** Arthritis; Minimally Invasive Surgery; Hip Replacement; Knee Replacement; **Hospital:** Bridgeport Hosp, St. Vincent's Med Ctr - Bridgeport; **Address:** Orthopaedic Specialty Grp, 75 Kings Hwy Cutoff Fl 2, Fairfield, CT 06824; **Phone:** 203-337-2600; **Board Cert:** Orthopaedic Surgery 2005; **Med School:** Columbia P&S 1985; **Resid:** Surgery, Beth Israel Hosp 1987; Orthopaedic Surgery, NY-Presby/Columbia Univ Med Ctr 1990; **Fellow:** Joint Replacement Surgery, Kerlan-Jobe Ortho Clin 1991

Bomback, David Aaron MD (OrS) - **Spec Exp:** Scoliosis; **Hospital:** Danbury Hosp; **Address:** CT Neck & Back Specialists, 20 Germantown Rd, Ste 2, Danbury, CT 06810; **Phone:** 203-744-9700; **Board Cert:** Orthopaedic Surgery 2007; **Med School:** Columbia P&S 1999; **Resid:** Orthopaedic Surgery, Yale-New Haven Hosp 2004; **Fellow:** Spine Surgery, Hosp Special Surgery 2005

Boone, Peter S MD (OrS) - **Spec Exp:** Sports Medicine; Knee Replacement; Hip Replacement; **Hospital:** St. Vincent's Med Ctr - Bridgeport, Bridgeport Hosp; **Address:** Orthopaedic & Sports Med Ctr, 888 White Plains Rd, Ste 106, Trumbull, CT 06611; **Phone:** 203-268-2882; **Board Cert:** Orthopaedic Surgery 2005; **Med School:** Univ Pennsylvania 1985; **Resid:** Orthopaedic Surgery, UMDNJ Med Sch Affil Hosp 1991; **Fellow:** Joint Replacement Surgery, IN Univ Med Ctr 1992; **Fac Appt:** Asst Clin Prof OrS, Quinnipiac Univ-Netter Sch Med

Brand, Michael MD (OrS) - **Spec Exp:** Sports Medicine; Arthroscopic Surgery-Knee; Shoulder & Knee Surgery; Reconstructive Surgery; **Hospital:** Danbury Hosp; **Address:** Danbury Orthopedics, 73 Sand Pit Rd, Ste 204, Danbury, CT 06810; **Phone:** 203-797-1500; **Board Cert:** Orthopaedic Surgery 2014; **Med School:** Univ Rochester 1984; **Resid:** Surgery, St Lukes-Roosevelt Hosp 1986; Orthopaedic Surgery, Mass Genl Hosp 1989; **Fellow:** Sports Medicine, Kaiser Permanente Med Ctr 1991

Brittis, Dante A MD (OrS) - **Spec Exp:** Sports Medicine; Shoulder & Knee Surgery; Joint Replacement; **Hospital:** Bridgeport Hosp, St. Vincent's Med Ctr - Bridgeport; **Address:** Orthopaedic Specialty Grp, 75 Kings Hwy Cutoff Fl 2, Fairfield, CT 06824; **Phone:** 203-337-2600; **Board Cert:** Orthopaedic Surgery 2008; **Med School:** NY Med Coll 1987; **Resid:** Orthopaedic Surgery, NY-Presby/Columbia Univ Med Ctr 1993; **Fellow:** Sports Medicine, Lenox Hill Hosp 1994

Brown, David B MD (OrS) - **Spec Exp:** Spinal Surgery; Shoulder Surgery; Sports Injuries; **Hospital:** Bridgeport Hosp, St. Vincent's Med Ctr - Bridgeport; **Address:** Orthocare Specialists, 4747 Main St, Bridgeport, CT 06606-1804; **Phone:** 203-372-0649; **Board Cert:** Orthopaedic Surgery 2007; **Med School:** St Louis Univ 1974; **Resid:** Surgery, NYU Med Ctr 1977; Orthopaedic Surgery, Long Island Jewish Med Ctr 1982

Clain, Michael R MD (OrS) - **Spec Exp:** Foot & Ankle Surgery; **Hospital:** Greenwich Hosp (page 970); **Address:** Ortho & Neurosurg Specs, Greenwich Office Park Bldg 6, 40 Valley Dr, Greenwich, CT 06831; **Phone:** 203-869-1145; **Board Cert:** Orthopaedic Surgery 2014; **Med School:** Columbia P&S 1984; **Resid:** Surgery, Mt Sinai Med Ctr 1985; Orthopaedic Surgery, Lenox Hill Hosp 1990; **Fellow:** Foot & Ankle Surgery, Baylor Coll Med 1991

Cunningham, James G MD (OrS) - **Spec Exp:** Arthroscopic Surgery; Shoulder Surgery; Knee Injuries/ACL; Sports Medicine; **Hospital:** Greenwich Hosp (page 970); **Address:** Ortho & Neurosurg Specs, Greenwich Office Park Bldg 6, 40 Valley Drive, Greenwich, CT 06831; **Phone:** 203-869-1145; **Board Cert:** Orthopaedic Surgery 2012; Orthopaedic Sports Medicine 2007; **Med School:** NYU Sch Med 1983; **Resid:** Surgery, Mt Sinai Med Ctr 1984; Orthopaedic Surgery, Mt Sinai Med Ctr 1988; **Fellow:** Sports Medicine, New England Baptist Hosp 1989

D'Amico, Joseph M MD (OrS) - **Spec Exp:** Knee Replacement; Hip Replacement; Sports Medicine; **Hospital:** Stamford Hosp (page 971), Greenwich Hosp (page 970); **Address:** Orthopaedic Assocs Stamford, 1281 E Main St Fl 4, Stamford, CT 06902; **Phone:** 203-325-4087; **Board Cert:** Orthopaedic Surgery 2014; **Med School:** E Tenn State Univ 1982; **Resid:** Surgery, Georgetown Univ Affil Hosp 1984; Orthopaedic Surgery, St Luke's-Roosevelt Hosp 1988

Deluca, Jeffrey V MD (OrS) - **Spec Exp:** Shoulder & Elbow Surgery; Knee Replacement; Sports Medicine; **Hospital:** Norwalk Hosp; **Address:** Coastal Orthopaedics, 761 Main St, Ste 115, Norwalk, CT 06851-2439; **Phone:** 203-845-2200; **Board Cert:** Orthopaedic Surgery 2005; **Med School:** Temple Univ 1984; **Resid:** Surgery, Yale-New Haven Hosp 1986; Orthopaedic Surgery, Eastern VA Med Sch Affil Hosp 1991; **Fellow:** Orthopaedic Trauma, Boston Med Ctr 1987; Orthopaedic Sports Medicine, Washington Ortho & Knee Clin 1992

Ennis Jr, Francis A MD (OrS) - **Spec Exp:** Hip & Knee Replacement; Arthroscopic Surgery; Arthritis-Hip & Knee; **Hospital:** Greenwich Hosp (page 970); **Address:** Ortho & Neurosurg Specs, Greenwich Office Park Bldg 6, 40 Valley Drive, Greenwich, CT 06831; **Phone:** 203-869-1145; **Board Cert:** Orthopaedic Surgery 2007; **Med School:** Duke Univ 1999; **Resid:** Orthopaedic Surgery, Yale-New Haven Hosp 2004; **Fellow:** Reconstructive Surgery, New England Baptist Hosp 2005

FitzGibbons, James J MD (OrS) - **Spec Exp:** Arthroscopic Surgery; Joint Replacement; Sports Medicine; **Hospital:** St. Vincent's Med Ctr - Bridgeport; **Address:** Orthopaedic Specialty Grp, 75 Kings Hwy Cutoff Fl 2, Fairfield, CT 06824-5340; **Phone:** 203-337-2600; **Board Cert:** Orthopaedic Surgery 2011; **Med School:** Loyola Univ-Stritch Sch Med 1992; **Resid:** Orthopaedic Surgery, Northwestern Meml Hosp 1997; **Fellow:** Orthopaedic Sports Medicine, Mass Genl Hosp 1998

Henshaw, D. Ross MD (OrS) - **Spec Exp:** Shoulder Surgery; Knee Surgery; Hip Surgery; Arthroscopic Surgery; **Hospital:** Danbury Hosp; **Address:** Danbury Orthopaedics, 73 Sand Pit Rd, Ste 204, Danbury, CT 06810; **Phone:** 203-797-1500 x9604; **Board Cert:** Orthopaedic Surgery 2007; Orthopaedic Sports Medicine 2008; **Med School:** Columbia P&S 1998; **Resid:** Orthopaedic Surgery, NY-Presby/Columbia Univ Med Ctr 2003; **Fellow:** Sports Medicine & Shoulder Surgery, Hosp Special Surgery 2005

Hermele, Herbert I MD (OrS) - **Hospital:** Bridgeport Hosp, St. Vincent's Med Ctr - Bridgeport; **Address:** Orthopaedic Specialty Grp, 75 Kings Hwy Cutoff Fl 2, Fairfield, CT 06824-5340; **Phone:** 203-337-2600; **Board Cert:** Orthopaedic Surgery 1975; **Med School:** Albert Einstein Coll Med 1969; **Resid:** Orthopaedic Surgery, Albert Einstein Affil Hosps 1975

Hindman, Steven MD (OrS) - **Spec Exp:** Sports Injuries; Hand Surgery; Fractures; Arthroscopic Surgery; **Hospital:** Greenwich Hosp (page 970); **Address:** Ortho & Neurosurg Specs, Greenwich Office Park Bldg 6, 40 Valley Drive, Greenwich, CT 06831-5151; **Phone:** 203-869-1145; **Board Cert:** Orthopaedic Surgery 2010; **Med School:** Albert Einstein Coll Med 1982; **Resid:** Orthopaedic Surgery, Montefiore Med Ctr 1987

Hughes, Peter W MD (OrS) - **Spec Exp:** Hip Replacement; Knee Replacement; **Hospital:** Stamford Hosp (page 971); **Address:** Ortho Assocs Stamford, 1281 E Main St Fl 4, Stamford, CT 06902; **Phone:** 203-325-4087; **Board Cert:** Orthopaedic Surgery 1978; **Med School:** NY Med Coll 1972; **Resid:** Surgery, St Vincent's Hosp 1973; Orthopaedic Surgery, Metropolitan Hosp Ctr 1977; **Fellow:** Hip Surgery, Hosp for Special Surg 1978

Kavanagh, Brian F MD (OrS) - **Spec Exp:** Hip Replacement; Knee Replacement; Joint Replacement; **Hospital:** Greenwich Hosp (page 970); **Address:** Ortho & Neurosurgery Specs, 6 Greenwich Office Park, Greenwich, CT 06831; **Phone:** 203-869-1145; **Board Cert:** Orthopaedic Surgery 2007; **Med School:** Univ Conn 1979; **Resid:** Orthopaedic Surgery, Mayo Clinic 1984; **Fac Appt:** Asst Clin Prof OrS, Yale Univ

Kramer, David Lawrence MD (OrS) - **Spec Exp:** Spinal Surgery; Trauma; **Hospital:** Danbury Hosp; **Address:** CT Neck & Back Specialists, 20 Germantown Rd, Ste 2, Danbury, CT 06810; **Phone:** 203-744-9700; **Board Cert:** Orthopaedic Surgery 2009; **Med School:** Dartmouth Med Sch 1989; **Resid:** Orthopaedic Surgery, Mass Genl Hosp 1994; Orthopaedic Surgery, Beth Israel Deaconess Med Ctr 1994; **Fellow:** Reconstructive Surgery, Inselspital-Maurice E Muller 1995; Spine Surgery, Thomas Jefferson Univ Hosp 1996

Lynch, Michael M MD (OrS) - **Spec Exp:** Pediatric Sports Medicine; Sports Medicine; Arthroscopic Surgery-Shoulder; Rotator Cuff Surgery; **Hospital:** Norwalk Hosp; **Address:** Coastal Orthopaedics, 761 Main St, Ste 115, Norwalk, CT 06851-4646; **Phone:** 203-845-2200; **Board Cert:** Orthopaedic Surgery 2005; **Med School:** Dartmouth Med Sch 1984; **Resid:** Surgery, Beth Israel Deaconess Med Ctr 1986; Orthopaedic Surgery, Mass Genl Hosp 1990; **Fellow:** Pediatric Orthopaedic Surgery, Chldns Hosp 1991; Sports Medicine, Union Meml Hosp 1992

Miller, Seth R MD (OrS) - **Spec Exp:** Shoulder Surgery; Rotator Cuff Surgery; Shoulder Replacement; Arthroscopic Surgery-Shoulder; **Hospital:** Greenwich Hosp (page 970); **Address:** Orthopaedic & Neurosurgery Specialists, 6 Greenwich Office Park, Greenwich, CT 06831; **Phone:** 203-869-1145; **Board Cert:** Orthopaedic Surgery 2012; **Med School:** Mount Sinai Sch Med 1982; **Resid:** Surgery, Mt Sinai Hosp 1985; Orthopaedic Surgery, Columbia-Presby Med Ctr 1988; **Fellow:** Shoulder Surgery, Columbia-Presby Med Ctr 1989; **Fac Appt:** Asst Clin Prof S, NYU Sch Med

Nocek, David P MD (OrS) - **Spec Exp:** Hip & Knee Replacement; Shoulder Injuries; **Hospital:** Greenwich Hosp (page 970); **Address:** Orthopaedic & Neurosurg Specs, 6 Greenwich Office Park Fl 3, Greenwich, CT 06631; **Phone:** 203-869-1145; **Board Cert:** Orthopaedic Surgery 2009; **Med School:** NY Med Coll 1981; **Resid:** Orthopaedic Surgery, St Lukes Hosp 1986

Polifroni, Nicholas V MD (OrS) - **Spec Exp:** Sports Medicine; Joint Replacement; **Hospital:** Norwalk Hosp, St. Vincent's Med Ctr - Bridgeport; **Address:** Coastal Orthopaedics, 761 Main St, Ste 115, Norwalk, CT 06851; **Phone:** 203-845-2200; **Board Cert:** Orthopaedic Surgery 1984; **Med School:** NY Med Coll 1977; **Resid:** Surgery, Temple Univ Hosp 1978; Orthopaedic Surgery, Lenox Hill Hosp 1982

Sethi, Paul M MD (OrS) - **Spec Exp:** Sports Medicine; Knee Injuries; Shoulder Injuries; Elbow Surgery; **Hospital:** Greenwich Hosp (page 970); **Address:** ONS, Sports Med, 6 Greenwich Office Park, Greenwich, CT 06831; **Phone:** 203-869-1145; **Board Cert:** Orthopaedic Surgery 2005; Orthopaedic Sports Medicine 2007; **Med School:** Mount Sinai Sch Med 1997; **Resid:** Orthopaedic Surgery, Yale-New Haven Hosp 2002; **Fellow:** Sports Medicine, Kerlan Jobe Ortho Clinic 2003; Arthroscopic Surgery, Kerlan Jobe Ortho Clinic 2004

Spak, James I MD (OrS) - **Spec Exp:** Sports Medicine; Fractures; Trauma; **Hospital:** St. Vincent's Med Ctr - Bridgeport, Bridgeport Hosp; **Address:** Orthopaedic & Sports Med Ctr, 888 White Plains Rd, Ste 105, Trumbull, CT 06611; **Phone:** 203-268-2882; **Board Cert:** Orthopaedic Surgery 2011; Orthopaedic Sports Medicine 2010; **Med School:** Harvard Med Sch 1992; **Resid:** Orthopaedic Surgery, Brigham & Women's Hosp 1998; **Fellow:** Sports Medicine, Tahoe Fracture & Ortho Cl 1999

Stovell, Peter B MD (OrS) - **Spec Exp:** Joint Replacement; Sports Medicine; **Hospital:** Norwalk Hosp; **Address:** Coastal Orthopaedics, 761 Main St, Ste 115, Norwalk, CT 06851-5726; **Phone:** 203-845-2200; **Board Cert:** Orthopaedic Surgery 1976; **Med School:** Columbia P&S 1968; **Resid:** Surgery, St Luke's-Roosevelt Hosp Ctr 1970; Orthopaedic Surgery, Hosp for Special Surg 1975

Troy, Allen I MD (OrS) - **Spec Exp:** Foot & Ankle Surgery; Ankle Reconstruction; **Hospital:** Stamford Hosp (page 971); **Address:** Orthopaedic Assocs Stamford, 1281 E Main St Fl 4, Stamford, CT 06905; **Phone:** 203-325-4087; **Board Cert:** Orthopaedic Surgery 2010; **Med School:** SUNY Downstate 1979; **Resid:** Surgery, Bellevue Hosp Ctr 1980; Orthopaedic Surgery, NYU Langone Med Ctr 1984; **Fellow:** Foot & Ankle Surgery, NYU Hosp For Joint Diseases 1985

Vadasdi, Katherine B MD (OrS) - **Spec Exp:** Sports Medicine; Sports Medicine-Women; Shoulder & Elbow Surgery; **Hospital:** Greenwich Hosp (page 970); **Address:** Orthopaedic & Neurosurgery Specialists, 6 Greenwich Office Park, 10 Valley Drive, Greenwich, CT 06831; **Phone:** 203-869-1145; **Board Cert:** Orthopaedic Surgery 2011; **Med School:** Dartmouth Med Sch 2003; **Resid:** Orthopaedic Surgery, Hosp Special Surgery 2008; **Fellow:** Orthopaedic Sports Medicine, NY-Presby/Columbia Univ Med Ctr 2010

Wilchinsky, Mark E MD (OrS) - **Spec Exp:** Arthroscopic Surgery; Joint Replacement; **Hospital:** St. Vincent's Med Ctr - Bridgeport, Griffin Hosp; **Address:** Orthopaedic & Sports Med Ctr, 888 White Plains Rd, Ste 105, Trumbull, CT 6611; **Phone:** 203-268-2882; **Board Cert:** Orthopaedic Surgery 2007; **Med School:** Tulane Univ 1979; **Resid:** Orthopaedic Surgery, Univ Mass Med Ctr 1984; **Fac Appt:** Asst Prof OrS, Univ Mass Sch Med

Otolaryngology

Aferzon, Mark MD (Oto) - **Spec Exp:** Allergy; Nasal & Sinus Disorders; Snoring/Sleep Apnea; Thyroid & Parathyroid Surgery; **Hospital:** Griffin Hosp; **Address:** 2 Ivy Brook Road, Ste 110, Shelton, CT 06484; **Phone:** 203-954-0019; **Board Cert:** Otolaryngology 2013; **Med School:** Brown Univ 1997; **Resid:** Surgery, SUNY Upstate Hlth Sci Ctr 1999; Otolaryngology, Geisinger Med Ctr 2002

Bard, Michael C MD (Oto) - **Spec Exp:** Head & Neck Surgery; Sleep Disorders/Apnea; Sinus Disorders/Surgery; **Hospital:** Danbury Hosp; **Address:** Advanced Specialty Care, 107 Newtown Rd, Ste 2A, Danbury, CT 6810; **Phone:** 203-830-4700; **Board Cert:** Otolaryngology 1993; **Med School:** Mount Sinai Sch Med 1987; **Resid:** Otolaryngology, Mayo Clin 1992; **Fellow:** Head and Neck Surgery, Inst Laryngology & Otology 1993

Bianchi, Mark S MD (Oto) - **Spec Exp:** Sleep Disorders; Sinus Disorders/Surgery; Hearing Loss; Balance Disorders; **Hospital:** Bridgeport Hosp, Yale-New Haven Hosp; **Address:** Yale Otolaryngology, 2874 Main St, Stratford, CT 06615; **Phone:** 203-459-8330; **Board Cert:** Otolaryngology 1997; Sleep Medicine 2012; **Med School:** Yale Univ 1991; **Resid:** Otolaryngology, Yale-New Haven Hosp 1996; **Fac Appt:** Asst Prof Oto, Yale Univ

Bramwit, Steven A MD (Oto) - **Spec Exp:** Head & Neck Surgery; Nasal & Sinus Disorders; **Hospital:** Stamford Hosp (page 971), Greenwich Hosp (page 970); **Address:** Stamford ENT-Head & Neck Surg, 166 W Broad St, Ste 304, Stamford, CT 06902; **Phone:** 203-348-7797; **Board Cert:** Otolaryngology 2012; **Med School:** Columbia P&S 1995; **Resid:** Surgery, NY-Presby/Columbia Univ Med Ctr 1997; Otolaryngology, NY-Presby/Columbia Univ Med Ctr 2001

Brauer, Richard J MD (Oto) - **Spec Exp:** Head & Neck Surgery; Thyroid Cancer; **Hospital:** Greenwich Hosp (page 970); **Address:** Assocs of Otolaryngology, 49 Lake Ave, Ste 205, Greenwich, CT 06830; **Phone:** 203-869-0177; **Board Cert:** Otolaryngology 1981; **Med School:** Hahnemann Univ 1976; **Resid:** Surgery, Beth Israel Med Ctr 1977; Otolaryngology, Bellevue Hosp Ctr 1981; **Fellow:** Head and Neck Surgery, Montefiore Med Ctr 1982

Breda, Stephen D MD (Oto) - **Spec Exp:** Head & Neck Surgery; **Hospital:** St. Vincent's Med Ctr - Bridgeport; **Address:** 4695 Main St, Ste 1, Bridgeport, CT 06606; **Phone:** 203-371-5166; **Board Cert:** Otolaryngology 1988; **Med School:** NYU Sch Med 1983; **Resid:** Surgery, NYU Med Ctr 1985; Otolaryngology, NYU Med Ctr 1988; **Fellow:** Head and Neck Surgery, NYU Med Ctr 1988

Chervin, Bradford S MD (Oto) - **Spec Exp:** Nasal & Sinus Disorders; Swallowing Disorders; Hearing Disorders; **Hospital:** Bridgeport Hosp, Norwalk Hosp; **Address:** ENT, Allergy & Facial Plastic Surg Specs, 2600 Post Rd, Southport, CT 06890; **Phone:** 203-256-3338; **Board Cert:** Otolaryngology 2000; **Med School:** Geo Wash Univ 1993; **Resid:** Surgery, Univ of TN Coll of Med Affil Hosp 1995; Otolaryngology, Univ of TN Coll of Med Affil Hosp 1999

Feldman, Steven M MD (Oto) - **Spec Exp:** Throat Disorders; Hearing Disorders; Snoring/Sleep Apnea; **Hospital:** Greenwich Hosp (page 970); **Address:** 4 Dearfield Drive, Ste 104, Greenwich, CT 06831; **Phone:** 203-629-5500; **Board Cert:** Otolaryngology 1998; **Med School:** Albert Einstein Coll Med 1992; **Resid:** Surgery, Montefiore Med Ctr 1993; Orthopaedic Surgery, Montefiore Med Ctr 1997

Gordon, Neil A MD (Oto) - **Spec Exp:** Cosmetic Surgery-Face; Facial Rejuvenation; Rhinoplasty; Facial Plastic & Reconstructive Surgery; **Hospital:** Norwalk Hosp, Yale-New Haven Hosp; **Address:** Split Rock Surgical Assocs, 539 Danbury Rd, Wilton, CT 06897; **Phone:** 203-834-7700; **Board Cert:** Otolaryngology 1996; Facial Plastic & Reconstr Surgery 1999; **Med School:** Albert Einstein Coll Med 1990; **Resid:** Surgery, Yale-New Haven Hosp 1991; Otolaryngology, Yale New Haven Hosp 1995; **Fellow:** Facial Plastic Surgery, Tulane Univ Med Ctr 1996; **Fac Appt:** Asst Clin Prof PlS, Yale Univ

Klarsfeld, Jay MD (Oto) - **Spec Exp:** Sinus Disorders; Thyroid & Parathyroid Surgery; **Hospital:** Danbury Hosp, New Milford Hosp; **Address:** Advanced Specialty Care, 107 Newtown Rd, Ste 2A, Danbury, CT 6810; **Phone:** 203-830-4700; **Board Cert:** Otolaryngology 1986; **Med School:** Mount Sinai Sch Med 1981; **Resid:** Surgery, Mount Sinai Med Ctr 1983; Otolaryngology, Mount Sinai Med Ctr 1986

Klenoff, Bruce H MD (Oto) - **Spec Exp:** Ear Disorders/Surgery; Sinus Disorders/Surgery; Pediatric Otolaryngology; **Hospital:** Stamford Hosp (page 971); **Address:** Tully Hlth Ctr, 32 Strawberry Hill Ct, Fl 4 - Ste 4, Stamford, CT 06902; **Phone:** 203-353-0000; **Board Cert:** Otolaryngology 1976; **Med School:** Tufts Univ 1969; **Resid:** Surgery, St Elizabeth's Med Ctr 1973; Otolaryngology, Mass Eye & Ear Infirm 1976

Klenoff, Jason R MD (Oto) - **Spec Exp:** Head & Neck Surgery; Head & Neck Tumors; Airway Disorders; **Hospital:** Stamford Hosp (page 971); **Address:** Ear, Nose & Throat Ctr, 32 Strawberry Hill Ct Fl 4 - Ste 4, Stamford, CT 06902; **Phone:** 203-353-0000; **Board Cert:** Otolaryngology 2005; **Med School:** Yale Univ 1998; **Resid:** Otolaryngology, Yale-New Haven Hosp 2003

Lane, Edward M MD (Oto) - **Spec Exp:** Gastroesophageal Reflux Disease (GERD); Endoscopic Sinus Surgery; Parathyroid Disorders; Nasal Reconstruction; **Hospital:** Bridgeport Hosp, St. Vincent's Med Ctr - Bridgeport; **Address:** 4675 Main St, Bridgeport, CT 06606-1813; **Phone:** 203-372-0009; **Board Cert:** Otolaryngology 1982; **Med School:** Columbia P&S 1977; **Resid:** Surgery, St Lukes Roosevelt Hosp 1979; Otolaryngology, Columbia-Presby Hosp 1982; **Fellow:** Head and Neck Surgery, UnivTexas MD Anderson Cancer Ctr 1983

Levin, Richard A MD/DMD (Oto) - **Spec Exp:** Sinus Disorders; Hearing Disorders; Facial Plastic & Reconstructive Surgery; **Hospital:** St. Vincent's Med Ctr - Bridgeport, Yale-New Haven Hosp; **Address:** Levin & Fliegleman, 1305 Post Rd, Ste 302, Fairfield, CT 06824; **Phone:** 203-259-4700; **Board Cert:** Otolaryngology 1993; **Med School:** Tufts Univ 1987; **Resid:** Otolaryngology, Mount Sinai Hosp 1993

Levine, Steven B MD (Oto) - **Spec Exp:** Sinus Disorders; Snoring/Sleep Apnea; Hearing & Balance Disorders; Rhinosinusitis; **Hospital:** Bridgeport Hosp, Yale-New Haven Hosp; **Address:** ENT and Allergy Assocs, 160 Hawley Ln, Ste 202, Trumbull, CT 06611; **Phone:** 203-380-3707; **Board Cert:** Otolaryngology 1986; **Med School:** Univ Rochester 1981; **Resid:** Surgery, Hosp Univ Penn 1983; Otolaryngology, Hosp Univ Penn 1986; **Fellow:** Otolaryngology, NY Presby/Cornell Med Ctr 1986; **Fac Appt:** Asst Clin Prof S, Yale Univ

Parker, Andrew J MD (Oto) - **Spec Exp:** Hearing Loss; Sinus Disorders; Voice Disorders; Snoring/Sleep Apnea; **Hospital:** Norwalk Hosp; **Address:** Parker Ear, Nose & Throat, 148 East Ave, Ste 2-I, Norwalk, CT 06851; **Phone:** 203-866-8121; **Board Cert:** Otolaryngology 2012; **Med School:** Rutgers R W Johnson Med Sch 1995; **Resid:** Surgery, Beth Israel Med Ctr 1997; Otolaryngology, NY Eye & Ear Infirm 2001

Pearl, Adam W MD (Oto) - **Spec Exp:** Head & Neck Surgery; Swallowing Disorders; Voice Disorders; Hearing Loss; **Hospital:** Bridgeport Hosp, St. Vincent's Med Ctr - Bridgeport; **Address:** CT ENT Med & Surgical Specs, 15 Corporate Drive, Ste 2-8, Trumbull, CT 06611; **Phone:** 203-452-7081; **Board Cert:** Otolaryngology 2013; **Med School:** Mount Sinai Sch Med 1996; **Resid:** Surgery, Mount Sinai Med Ctr 1998; Otolaryngology, Mount Sinai Med Ctr 2002

Salzer, Stephen J MD (Oto) - **Spec Exp:** Thyroid & Parathyroid Surgery; Pediatric Otolaryngology; Sinus Disorders/Surgery; Thyroid Cancer; **Hospital:** Greenwich Hosp (page 970), Stamford Hosp (page 971); **Address:** Greenwich ENT, Head & Neck Surg, 49 Lake Ave Fl 1, Greenwich, CT 06830-4519; **Phone:** 203-869-2030; **Board Cert:** Otolaryngology 1995; **Med School:** Johns Hopkins Univ 1989; **Resid:** Surgery, Yale-New Haven Hosp 1990; Otolaryngology, Yale-New Haven Hosp 1994; **Fellow:** Laryngology, Laennec Hosp 1995

Pain Medicine

Bennett, Steven J DO (PM) - **Spec Exp:** Pain-Chronic; Pain-Cancer; Reflex Sympathetic Dystrophy (RSD); **Hospital:** Greenwich Hosp (page 970); **Address:** Northeast Medical Group, 15 Valley Drive, Greenwich, CT 06831; **Phone:** 203-863-3448; **Board Cert:** Pain Medicine 2005; **Med School:** NY Coll Osteo Med 1997; **Resid:** Internal Medicine, Lenox Hill Hosp 2000; **Fellow:** Pain Medicine, Meml Sloan Kettering Cancer Ctr 2004

Boolbol, Robert J MD (PM) - **Spec Exp:** Pain-Back; Pain-Spine; Pain-Musculoskeletal; Pain-Interventional Techniques; **Hospital:** Bridgeport Hosp, Hartford Hosp; **Address:** Pain & Spine Specs of CT, 5520 Park Ave, Ste 303, Trumball, CT 06611; **Phone:** 203-373-7330; **Board Cert:** Anesthesiology 1994; Pain Medicine 2014; **Med School:** NY Med Coll 1989; **Resid:** Surgery, Lenox Hill Hosp 1990; Anesthesiology, Univ Chicago Hosp 1993; **Fellow:** Pain Medicine, Univ Chicago Hosp 2002

Pathology

Altmeyer, Vicki L MD (Path) - **Spec Exp:** Cytopathology; Surgical Pathology; **Hospital:** Greenwich Hosp (page 970); **Address:** Greenwich Hosp, Dept Pathology, 5 Perryridge Rd, Greenwich, CT 06830-6177; **Phone:** 203-863-3061; **Board Cert:** Anatomic & Clinical Pathology 1981; Cytopathology 1993; **Med School:** Washington Univ, St Louis 1977; **Resid:** Anatomic & Clinical Pathology, Baylor Affil Hosp 1981

Babkowski, Robert C MD (Path) - **Spec Exp:** Breast Pathology; Gastrointestinal Pathology; Gynecologic Pathology; **Hospital:** Stamford Hosp (page 971); **Address:** Stamford Hosp, Pathology Dept, 30 Shelburne Rd, Stamford, CT 06902; **Phone:** 203-276-7420; **Board Cert:** Anatomic & Clinical Pathology 1996; Cytopathology 1996; **Med School:** Univ Rochester 1990; **Resid:** Anatomic & Clinical Pathology, Univ Rochester/Strong Meml Hosp 1995; **Fellow:** Cytopathology, UT MD Anderson Cancer Ctr 1996

Baer, Raymond A MD (Path) - **Spec Exp:** Hematopathology; **Hospital:** Stamford Hosp (page 971); **Address:** Stamford Pathology Grp, 30 Shelburne Rd, Stamford, CT 06902; **Phone:** 203-276-7420; **Board Cert:** Clinical Pathology 1994; Anatomic Pathology 1999; Hematology 1995; **Med School:** NY Med Coll 1989; **Resid:** Pathology, Westchester Co Med Ctr 1994; **Fellow:** Hematology, Beth Israel Deaconess Med Ctr 1995

Pinto, Marguerite Monteiro MD (Path) - **Spec Exp:** Gynecologic Pathology; Breast Pathology; **Hospital:** Bridgeport Hosp; **Address:** Bridgeport Hosp, Yale Pathology, 267 Grant St, Fl 2, Bridgeport, CT 06610; **Phone:** 203-384-3157; **Board Cert:** Pathology 1975; Cytopathology 1989; **Med School:** India 1970; **Resid:** Pathology, Bridgeport Hosp 1975; Anatomic & Clinical Pathology, Chldns Hosp 1976; **Fac Appt:** Asst Prof Path, Yale Univ

Xu, Bo MD/PhD (Path) - **Spec Exp:** Gastrointestinal Pathology; Gynecologic Pathology; Urologic Pathology; **Hospital:** Stamford Hosp (page 971); **Address:** Stamford Hosp, Dept Pathology, 30 Shelburne Rd, Stamford, CT 06902; **Phone:** 203-276-7420; **Board Cert:** Anatomic & Clinical Pathology 2002; Cytopathology 2002; **Med School:** China 1987; **Resid:** Anatomic & Clinical Pathology, New England Med Ctr 2000; **Fellow:** Cytopathology, UT MD Anderson Canc Ctr 2001

Pediatric Allergy & Immunology

Burstein, Ora MD (PA&I) - **Spec Exp:** Asthma & Allergy; Food Allergy; **Hospital:** Stamford Hosp (page 971); **Address:** Allergy & Asthma Ctr Stamford, 22 Fifth St Fl 3, Stamford, CT 06905; **Phone:** 203-978-0072; **Board Cert:** Allergy & Immunology 2005; **Med School:** Tufts Univ 1984; **Resid:** Pediatrics, Montefiore Med Ctr-Moses Campus 1987; **Fellow:** Allergy & Immunology, Montefiore Med Ctr-Moses Campus 1989

Lester, Mitchell R MD (PA&I) - **Spec Exp:** Pediatric Allergy & Immunology; Asthma & Allergy; Food Allergy; **Hospital:** Norwalk Hosp, Greenwich Hosp (page 970); **Address:** Fairfield Co Allergy, Asthma & Immunology, 148 East Ave, Ste 3G, Norwalk, CT 06851; **Phone:** 203-838-4034; **Board Cert:** Pediatrics 1987; Allergy & Immunology 2013; **Med School:** Brown Univ 1983; **Resid:** Pediatrics, Rhode Island Hosp 1987; **Fellow:** Allergy & Immunology, Natl Jewish Hlth Ctr 1994

Pediatric Cardiology

Berkwits, Kieve M MD (PCd) - **Spec Exp:** Congenital Heart Disease; **Hospital:** Bridgeport Hosp, St. Vincent's Med Ctr - Bridgeport; **Address:** 5520 Park Ave, Ste 102, Trumbull, CT 06611; **Phone:** 203-384-3783; **Board Cert:** Pediatrics 1986; Pediatric Cardiology 2010; **Med School:** Mexico 1979; **Resid:** Pediatrics, Beth Israel Med Ctr 1983; **Fellow:** Pediatric Cardiology, NY Hosp/Cornell Med Ctr 1985; **Fac Appt:** Assoc Clin Prof Ped, Yale Univ

Snyder, Michael S MD (PCd) - **Spec Exp:** Echocardiography; Fetal Echocardiography; **Hospital:** Morgan Stanley Chldns Hosp of NY-Presby, NY (page 102), Stamford Hosp (page 971); **Address:** 1500 Boston Post Rd Fl 2, Darien, CT 06820; **Phone:** 203-662-0313; **Board Cert:** Pediatrics 1984; Pediatric Cardiology 1985; **Med School:** Cornell Univ-Weill Med Coll 1979; **Resid:** Internal Medicine, NY Hosp 1980; Pediatrics, NY-Presby/Weill Cornell Med Ctr 1982; **Fellow:** Pediatric Cardiology, NY-Presby/Weill Cornell Med Ctr 1984; **Fac Appt:** Assoc Prof Ped, Columbia P&S

Pediatric Gastroenterology

Ekong, Udeme D MD (PGe) - **Spec Exp:** Liver Disease; Transplant Medicine-Liver; Neonatal Cholestasis; Nutrition; **Hospital:** Yale-New Haven Hosp, Greenwich Hosp (page 970); **Address:** Pediatric Specialty Ctr, 5 Perryridge Rd Fl 2, Greenwich, CT 06830; **Phone:** 203-785-4081; **Board Cert:** Pediatrics 2008; Pediatric Transplant Hepatology 2006; Pediatric Gastroenterology 2013; **Med School:** Nigeria 1992; **Resid:** Pediatrics, Lincoln Med & Mental Hlth Ctr 2001; **Fellow:** Pediatric Gastroenterology, NY-Presby/Columbia Univ Med Ctr 2004; Transplant Hepatology, Chldns Meml Hosp 2006; **Fac Appt:** Assoc Prof Ped, Yale Univ

Glassman, Mark S MD (PGe) - **Spec Exp:** Inflammatory Bowel Disease/Crohn's; Gastroesophageal Reflux Disease (GERD); Diarrheal Diseases; Food Allergy; **Hospital:** Norwalk Hosp, Stamford Hosp (page 971); **Address:** 148 East Ave, Ste 2N, Norwalk, CT 06851; **Phone:** 203-853-7170; **Board Cert:** Pediatrics 1983; Pediatric Gastroenterology 2012; **Med School:** SUNY Buffalo 1978; **Resid:** Pediatrics, Yale-New Haven Hosp 1981; **Fellow:** Gastroenterology & Nutrition, Chldns Hosp 1983; **Fac Appt:** Prof Ped, NY Med Coll

Pediatric Pulmonology

Dworkin, Gregory MD (PPul) - **Spec Exp:** Asthma; Chronic Lung Disease; **Hospital:** Danbury Hosp; **Address:** Children's Health & Wellness Ctr, 79 Sand Pit Rd, Ste 201, Danbury, CT 06810; **Phone:** 203-790-5437; **Board Cert:** Pediatrics 1987; **Med School:** Albany Med Coll 1982; **Resid:** Pediatrics, Mount Sinai Med Ctr 1986; **Fellow:** Pediatric Pulmonology, Mount Sinai Med Ctr 1989; **Fac Appt:** Asst Clin Prof Ped, NY Med Coll

Hen Jr, Jacob MD (PPul) - **Spec Exp:** Asthma; Critical Care; **Hospital:** Bridgeport Hosp, Yale-New Haven Hosp; **Address:** Yale-New Haven Hosp, Dept Peds, 5520 Park Ave Fl 1 - Ste 102, Trumbull, CT 06611; **Phone:** 203-384-3711; **Board Cert:** Pediatrics 1980; Pediatric Pulmonology 2013; **Med School:** UMDNJ-NJ Med Sch, Newark 1975; **Resid:** Pediatrics, UMDNJ-Univ Hosp 1978; **Fellow:** Pediatric Pulmonology, Yale-New Haven Hosp 1981; **Fac Appt:** Assoc Clin Prof Ped, Yale Univ

Sadeghi, Hossein MD (PPul) - **Spec Exp:** Asthma; Cystic Fibrosis; Bronchoscopy; Bronchitis; **Hospital:** Stamford Hosp (page 971), Greenwich Hosp (page 970); **Address:** 32 Strawberry Hill Ct, Ste 11, Stamford, CT 06902; **Phone:** 203-276-5949; **Board Cert:** Pediatrics 2010; Pediatric Pulmonology 2013; Sleep Medicine 2013; **Med School:** Australia 1990; **Resid:** Pediatrics, Royal Chldns Hosp 1992; Pediatrics, VCU Med Ctr 1995; **Fellow:** Pediatric Pulmonology, NY Med Coll Affil Hosp 1998

Pediatrics

Alon, Jamie MD (Ped) *PCP* - **Spec Exp:** Adolescent Medicine; Eating Disorders; **Hospital:** Danbury Hosp; **Address:** Pediatric Assocs-Western CT, 41 Germantown Rd, Danbury, CT 6810; **Phone:** 203-744-1680; **Board Cert:** Pediatrics 2009; **Med School:** Cornell Univ-Weill Med Coll 1998; **Resid:** Pediatrics, NY-Presby/Weill Cornell Med Ctr 2001

Beckman, Karen E MD (Ped) *PCP* - **Hospital:** Greenwich Hosp (page 970), Stamford Hosp (page 971); **Address:** Riverside Pediatrics, 35 River Rd, Ste 2, Cos Cob, CT 06807; **Phone:** 203-629-5800; **Board Cert:** Pediatrics 2007; **Med School:** Tufts Univ 1997; **Resid:** Pediatrics, NYU Langone Med Ctr 2000; **Fac Appt:** Asst Clin Prof Ped, Columbia P&S

Chessin, Robert D MD (Ped) *PCP* - **Spec Exp:** Learning Disorders; Developmental Disorders; ADD/ADHD; Autism; **Hospital:** Bridgeport Hosp, St. Vincent's Med Ctr - Bridgeport; **Address:** Pediatric Hlthcare Assocs, 4699 Main St, Ste 215, Bridgeport, CT 06606-1830; **Phone:** 203-452-8322; **Board Cert:** Pediatrics 1978; **Med School:** Johns Hopkins Univ 1973; **Resid:** Pediatrics, Duke Univ Med Ctr 1976; **Fac Appt:** Assoc Clin Prof Ped, Yale Univ

Cohen, Bruce W MD (Ped) *PCP* - **Spec Exp:** Neonatal Care; Pediatric Gastroenterology; **Hospital:** Danbury Hosp; **Address:** Pediatric Assocs-Western CT, 41 Germantown Rd, Ste 201, Danbury, CT 68104000; **Phone:** 203-744-1680; **Board Cert:** Pediatrics 2010; **Med School:** UMDNJ-NJ Med Sch, Newark 1992; **Resid:** Pediatrics, N Shore Univ Hosp 1995

Cohen, Elin R MD (Ped) *PCP* - **Spec Exp:** Developmental & Behavioral Disorders; Asthma; **Hospital:** Bridgeport Hosp, St. Vincent's Med Ctr - Bridgeport; **Address:** Black Rock Peds, 1817 Black Rock Tpke, Ste 206, Fairfield, CT 06825; **Phone:** 203-337-5333; **Board Cert:** Pediatrics 2012; **Med School:** Albert Einstein Coll Med 1993; **Resid:** Pediatrics, Montefiore Med Ctr 1996; **Fellow:** Developmental-Behavioral Pediatrics, Yale-New Haven Hosp 1999

Ferguson, Kevin MD (Ped) *PCP* - **Spec Exp:** Asthma; Obesity; Weight Management; **Hospital:** Danbury Hosp; **Address:** Pediatric Assocs-Western CT, 41 Germantown Rd, Ste 201, Danbury, CT 6810; **Phone:** 203-744-1680; **Board Cert:** Pediatrics 2009; **Med School:** Jefferson Med Coll 1998; **Resid:** Pediatrics, N Shore Univ Hosp 2001

Freedman, Richard M MD (Ped) *PCP* - **Spec Exp:** Neonatology; **Hospital:** Bridgeport Hosp, Yale-New Haven Hosp; **Address:** Ped Hlthcare Assocs, 4699 Main St, Ste 215, Bridgeport, CT 06606-1830; **Phone:** 203-452-8322; **Board Cert:** Pediatrics 1979; Neonatal-Perinatal Medicine 1981; **Med School:** Boston Univ 1975; **Resid:** Pediatrics, Yale-New Haven Hosp 1979; **Fellow:** Neonatology, Yale-New Haven Hosp 1981; **Fac Appt:** Assoc Clin Prof Ped, Yale Univ

Gropper, David MD (Ped) *PCP* - **Spec Exp:** Allergy; Infectious Disease; **Hospital:** Danbury Hosp; **Address:** Pediatric Assocs-Western CT, 41 Germantown Rd, Ste 201, Danbury, CT 6810; **Phone:** 203-744-1680; **Board Cert:** Pediatrics 2011; **Med School:** SUNY Downstate 1986; **Resid:** Pediatrics, Montefiore Med Ctr 1989

Hedrick, David A MD (Ped) *PCP* - **Hospital:** Greenwich Hosp (page 970); **Address:** Children's Med Grp-Greenwich, 42 Sherwood Pl, Greenwich, CT 06830; **Phone:** 203-661-2440; **Board Cert:** Pediatrics 2010; **Med School:** Med Coll VA 1976; **Resid:** Pediatrics, Chldns Hosp 1979

Juan, Paul E MD (Ped) *PCP* - **Spec Exp:** Developmental Disorders; Asthma; **Hospital:** Greenwich Hosp (page 970); **Address:** Valley Pediatrics of Greenwich, 25 Valley Drive Fl 2, Greenwich, CT 06831; **Phone:** 203-622-4301; **Board Cert:** Pediatrics 2008; **Med School:** NY Med Coll 1990; **Resid:** Pediatrics, Med Coll Virginia Affil Hosp 1993

Klenk, Rosemary E MD (Ped) *PCP* - **Spec Exp:** ADD/ADHD; Eating Disorders; **Hospital:** Stamford Hosp (page 971); **Address:** New England Pediatrics, 183 Cherry St, New Canaan, CT 06840; **Phone:** 203-972-5232; **Board Cert:** Pediatrics 2010; **Med School:** Cornell Univ-Weill Med Coll 1980; **Resid:** Pediatrics, NY-Presby/Columbia Univ Med Ctr 1983

Korval, Arnold B MD (Ped) *PCP* - **Hospital:** Greenwich Hosp (page 970), Stamford Hosp (page 971); **Address:** Greenwich Pediatric Assocs, 8 W End Ave, Old Greenwich, CT 06870-1642; **Phone:** 203-637-0186; **Board Cert:** Pediatrics 2009; **Med School:** St Louis Univ 1974; **Resid:** Pediatrics, Chldn's Hosp 1978

Magner, Joan A MD (Ped) *PCP* - **Hospital:** Danbury Hosp; **Address:** Ctr Pediatric Med, 107 Newtown Rd, Ste 1D, Danbury, CT 06810; **Phone:** 203-790-0822; **Board Cert:** Pediatrics 1986; **Med School:** Univ Hawaii JA Burns Sch Med 1980; **Resid:** Pediatrics, Chldns Hosp 1984

Marks, Laura MD (Ped) *PCP* - **Spec Exp:** Nutrition; Immune Deficiencies-Primary; **Hospital:** Norwalk Hosp; **Address:** Willows Pediatric Grp, 1563 Post Rd E, Westport, CT 06880; **Phone:** 203-319-3939 x1227; **Board Cert:** Pediatrics 2010; **Med School:** Yale Univ 1992; **Resid:** Pediatrics, Mass Genl Hosp 1993; Pediatrics, Yale-New Haven Hosp 1995

Mini, Katherine N MD (Ped) *PCP* - **Hospital:** Greenwich Hosp (page 970); **Address:** Chldns Med Grp, 42 Sherwood Pl, Greenwich, CT 06830-5633; **Phone:** 203-661-2440; **Board Cert:** Pediatrics 2012; **Med School:** Albert Einstein Coll Med 1994; **Resid:** Pediatrics, Yale-New Haven Hosp 1997

Mongillo, Nicholas P MD (Ped) *PCP* - **Spec Exp:** AIDS/HIV; Sports Medicine; ADD/ADHD; Behavioral Disorders; **Hospital:** Bridgeport Hosp, Yale-New Haven Hosp; **Address:** Pediatric Care Assocs, 25 Constitution Blvd S, Shelton, CT 06484; **Phone:** 203-924-7334; **Board Cert:** Pediatrics 2013; **Med School:** Grenada 1987; **Resid:** Pediatrics, Bridgeport Hosp 1990

Morelli, Alan H MD (Ped) *PCP* - **Hospital:** Stamford Hosp (page 971), Yale-New Haven Hosp; **Address:** New England Pediatrics, 166 W Broad St, Ste 103, Stamford, CT 06902; **Phone:** 203-323-1770; **Board Cert:** Pediatrics 2010; **Med School:** NY Med Coll 1982; **Resid:** Pediatrics, Yale-New Haven Hosp 1985

Perlman, Fern L MD (Ped) *PCP* - **Hospital:** Norwalk Hosp; **Address:** Bay Street Pediatrics, 20 Bay St, Westport, CT 06880; **Phone:** 203-227-3674; **Board Cert:** Pediatrics 2010; **Med School:** NY Med Coll 1975; **Resid:** Pediatrics, Lenox Hill Hosp 1978

Quinn, Kathryn J MD (Ped) *PCP* - **Spec Exp:** Infectious Disease; Preventive Medicine; **Hospital:** Bridgeport Hosp, Yale-New Haven Hosp; **Address:** Black Rock Pediatrics, 1817 Black Rock Tpke, Ste 206, Fairfield, CT 06825; **Phone:** 203-337-5333; **Board Cert:** Pediatrics 2014; **Med School:** Cornell Univ-Weill Med Coll 1996; **Resid:** Pediatrics, NY-Presby/Weill Cornell Med Ctr 1999; **Fellow:** Pediatric Infectious Disease, Boston Med Ctr 2002

Rascoff, Henry M MD (Ped) *PCP* - **Spec Exp:** Preventive Medicine; **Hospital:** Greenwich Hosp (page 970), Stamford Hosp (page 971); **Address:** Riverside Pediatrics, 35 River Rd, Ste 2, Cos Cob, CT 06807; **Phone:** 203-629-5800; **Board Cert:** Pediatrics 2012; **Med School:** Albert Einstein Coll Med 2001; **Resid:** Pediatrics, Mount Sinai Med Ctr 2004

Rothschild, Rachel MD (Ped) *PCP* - **Spec Exp:** Developmental Disorders; ADD/ADHD; **Hospital:** Danbury Hosp; **Address:** Pediatric Assocs-Western CT, 41 Germantown Rd, Ste 201, Danbury, CT 6810; **Phone:** 203-744-1680; **Board Cert:** Pediatrics 2007; **Med School:** Yale Univ 1997; **Resid:** Pediatrics, NY-Presby/Weill Cornell Med Ctr 2000

Schiz, Steven L MD (Ped) *PCP* - **Hospital:** Greenwich Hosp (page 970); **Address:** Children's Med Grp-Greenwich, 42 Sherwood Pl, Greenwich, CT 06830; **Phone:** 203-661-2440; **Board Cert:** Pediatrics 2009; **Med School:** Columbia P&S 1980; **Resid:** Pediatrics, Children's Hosp 1983

Sollinger, Jonathan E MD (Ped) *PCP* - **Spec Exp:** ADD/ADHD; Developmental & Behavioral Disorders; **Hospital:** Norwalk Hosp; **Address:** Willows Pediatric Grp, 1563 Post Rd E, Westport, CT 06880; **Phone:** 203-319-3939 x1228; **Board Cert:** Pediatrics 2010; **Med School:** Univ Conn 1999; **Resid:** Pediatrics, Montefiore Med Ctr 2002; **Fac Appt:** Asst Clin Prof Ped, Quinnipiac Univ-Netter Sch Med

Storch-Smith, Lori MD (Ped) *PCP* - **Spec Exp:** Preventive Medicine; **Hospital:** Norwalk Hosp; **Address:** Bay Street Pediatrics, 20 Bay St, Westport, CT 06880; **Phone:** 203-227-3674; **Board Cert:** Pediatrics 2014; **Med School:** Geo Wash Univ 1996; **Resid:** Pediatrics, Yale-New Haven Hosp 1999

Physical Medicine & Rehabilitation

Aaronson, Beth MD (PMR) - **Spec Exp:** Acupuncture; Neurologic Rehabilitation; Cancer Rehabilitation; Lymphedema; **Hospital:** Danbury Hosp; **Address:** Danbury WCMG, Phys Med & Rehab, 33 Germantown Rd Fl 1, Danbury, CT 06810; **Phone:** 203-794-5605; **Board Cert:** Physical Medicine & Rehabilitation 2005; **Med School:** SUNY Stony Brook 1990; **Resid:** Physical Medicine & Rehabilitation, NY-Presby/Columbia Univ Med Ctr 1994

Freedman, Janet E MD (PMR) - **Spec Exp:** Acupuncture; Lymphedema; Spasticity Management; **Hospital:** Greenwich Hosp (page 970); **Address:** Greenwich Hosp, Phys Med & Rehab, 5 Perryridge Rd, rm 3-3101, Greenwich, CT 06830; **Phone:** 203-863-4290; **Board Cert:** Physical Medicine & Rehabilitation 1988; **Med School:** Univ Wisc 1983; **Resid:** Physical Medicine & Rehabilitation, NYU Rusk Inst 1986; **Fac Appt:** Assoc Prof PMR, NY Med Coll

Grant, Linda F MD (PMR) - **Spec Exp:** Lymphedema; Acupuncture; **Hospital:** Greenwich Hosp (page 970); **Address:** Greenwich Hosp, Physical Med & Rehab, 5 Perryridge Rd, rm 3-3107, Greenwich, CT 06830; **Phone:** 203-863-4290; **Board Cert:** Physical Medicine & Rehabilitation 1990; **Med School:** UMDNJ-Rutgers Med Sch 1985; **Resid:** Physical Medicine & Rehabilitation, NYU Med Ctr 1989

Heftler, Jeffrey M MD (PMR) - **Spec Exp:** Pain Management; Spinal Rehabilitation; Pain-Interventional Techniques; Sports Injuries; **Hospital:** Greenwich Hosp (page 970); **Address:** Orthopaedic & Neurosurg Specs, 6 Greenwich Office Park, Greenwich, CT 06831; **Phone:** 203-869-1145; **Board Cert:** Physical Medicine & Rehabilitation 2012; Pain Medicine 2014; **Med School:** Rutgers R W Johnson Med Sch 1997; **Resid:** Physical Medicine & Rehabilitation, Thos Jefferson Univ Med Ctr 2001; **Fellow:** Sports Medicine, Beth Israel Med Ctr 2002

Richter, Edwin MD (PMR) - **Spec Exp:** Neuro-Rehabilitation; Brain Injury Rehabilitation; Amputee Rehabilitation; Lymphedema; **Hospital:** Stamford Hosp (page 971); **Address:** 166 W Broad St, Ste 305, Stamford, CT 06902; **Phone:** 203-316-0610; **Board Cert:** Physical Medicine & Rehabilitation 1992; **Med School:** NYU Sch Med 1987; **Resid:** Physical Medicine & Rehabilitation, NYU Med Ctr 1991; **Fac Appt:** Asst Clin Prof PMR, NYU Sch Med

Snowball, Halina M MD (PMR) - **Spec Exp:** Pain Management; Acupuncture; Sports Injuries; **Hospital:** Greenwich Hosp (page 970); **Address:** Pain Management, 2015 W Main St, Ste 100, Stamford, CT 06902; **Phone:** 203-863-4588; **Board Cert:** Physical Medicine & Rehabilitation 1990; **Med School:** Univ Fla Coll Med 1985; **Resid:** Physical Medicine & Rehabilitation, Stanford Univ Med Ctr 1989

Plastic Surgery

Attkiss, Keith J MD (PlS) - **Spec Exp:** Breast Cosmetic & Reconstructive Surgery; Liposuction & Body Contouring; **Hospital:** Greenwich Hosp (page 970); **Address:** 2 1/2 Dearfield Drive, Ste 203, Greenwich, CT 06831; **Phone:** 203-862-2700; **Board Cert:** Plastic Surgery 2011; **Med School:** Columbia P&S 1992; **Resid:** Surgery, UC Davis Med Ctr 1997; **Fellow:** Hand & Microvascular Surgery, Buncke Clin 1998; Plastic/Reconstructive Surgery, Yale-New Haven Hosp 2000

Gewirtz, Harold S MD (PlS) - **Spec Exp:** Cosmetic Surgery-Face; Breast Cosmetic & Reconstructive Surgery; Liposuction & Body Contouring; **Hospital:** Stamford Hosp (page 971), Greenwich Hosp (page 970); **Address:** 70 Mill River St, Stamford, CT 06902; **Phone:** 203-325-1381; **Board Cert:** Plastic Surgery 1984; **Med School:** Johns Hopkins Univ 1975; **Resid:** Surgery, UCLA Med Ctr 1980; **Fellow:** Plastic Surgery, NYU Langone Med Ctr 1982; **Fac Appt:** Assoc Clin Prof PlS, Columbia P&S

Goldenberg, David M MD (PlS) - **Spec Exp:** Cosmetic Surgery; Breast Reconstruction; Wound Healing/Care; **Hospital:** Danbury Hosp; **Address:** Advanced Specialty Care, 107 Newtown Rd, Ste 2C, Danbury, CT 6810; **Phone:** 203-791-9661; **Board Cert:** Plastic Surgery 1990; **Med School:** NY Med Coll 1982; **Resid:** Surgery, Montefiore Med Ctr 1986; **Fellow:** Plastic Surgery, Montefiore Med Ctr 1988; **Fac Appt:** Prof S, NY Med Coll

Islam, Sohel MD (PlS) - **Spec Exp:** Hand Surgery; **Hospital:** Danbury Hosp; **Address:** Advanced Specialty Care, Plastic Surgery, 107 Newtown Rd, Ste 2C, Danbury, CT 6810; **Phone:** 203-791-9661; **Board Cert:** Hand Surgery 2011; Plastic Surgery 2011; **Med School:** Cornell Univ-Weill Med Coll 1991; **Resid:** Surgery, St Lukes-Roosevelt Hosp Ctr 1996; Plastic Surgery, Med Coll VA Hosps 1999; **Fellow:** Hand Surgery, Yale-New Haven Hosp 2000

Newman, Fredric A MD (PlS) - **Spec Exp:** Breast Augmentation; Eyelid Surgery; Abdominoplasty; Liposuction; **Hospital:** Greenwich Hosp (page 970), Norwalk Hosp; **Address:** Aesthetic Surgery Ctr, 722 Post Rd, Ste 200, Darien, CT 06820; **Phone:** 203-656-9999; **Board Cert:** Plastic Surgery 1985; **Med School:** SUNY Downstate 1974; **Resid:** Surgery, Beth Israel Med Ctr 1977; Surgery, SUNY Downstate 1979; **Fellow:** Plastic/Reconstructive Surgery, NYU Med Ctr 1981; Plastic Surgery, Jackson Meml Hosp 1982; **Fac Appt:** Asst Prof PlS, NY Med Coll

O'Connell, Joseph B MD (PlS) - **Spec Exp:** Liposuction & Body Contouring; Cosmetic Surgery-Face; Cosmetic Surgery-Breast; **Hospital:** Bridgeport Hosp; **Address:** Plastic Surgery of Southern CT, 208 Post Rd W, Westport, CT 06880; **Phone:** 203-454-0044; **Board Cert:** Plastic Surgery 2007; **Med School:** Cornell Univ-Weill Med Coll 1981; **Resid:** Surgery, St Francis Hosp 1983; Surgery, St Vincents Med Ctr 1986; **Fellow:** Plastic Surgery, New York Hosp 1988

Passaretti, David MD (PlS) - **Spec Exp:** Cosmetic Surgery-Face; Breast Cosmetic & Reconstructive Surgery; Body Contouring After Weight Loss; **Hospital:** Greenwich Hosp (page 970), Stamford Hosp (page 971); **Address:** 722 Post Rd, Ste 200, Darien, CT 06820; **Phone:** 203-656-9999; **Board Cert:** Plastic Surgery 2005; **Med School:** Tufts Univ 1997; **Resid:** Plastic Surgery, Univ Hosps 2003; **Fellow:** Plastic/Reconstructive Surgery, Mass Genl Hosp 2005

Raskin, Elsa M MD (PlS) - **Spec Exp:** Eyelid Cosmetic & Reconstructive Surgery; Cosmetic Surgery-Face; Cosmetic Surgery-Breast; **Hospital:** Greenwich Hosp (page 970), Lenox Hill Hosp; **Address:** 2 1/2 Dearfield Drive, Ste 102, Greenwich, CT 06831-5335; **Phone:** 203-861-6620; **Board Cert:** Plastic Surgery 2012; **Med School:** Switzerland 1987; **Resid:** Ophthalmology, NY Eye & Ear Infirm 1995; Surgery, NYU Med Ctr 1999; **Fellow:** Plastic Surgery, Univ Pittsburgh Med Ctr 1996; Plastic/Reconstructive Surgery, NY Presby Hosp 2001

Rosenstock, Arthur Richard MD (PlS) - **Spec Exp:** Cosmetic Surgery-Face; Cosmetic Surgery-Breast; **Hospital:** Stamford Hosp (page 971); **Address:** 1290 Summer St, Ste 3100, Stamford, CT 06905-5326; **Phone:** 203-359-1959; **Board Cert:** Plastic Surgery 1985; **Med School:** Belgium 1976; **Resid:** Surgery, Westchester Co Med Ctr 1981; **Fellow:** Plastic/Reconstructive Surgery, VA Commonwealth Univ Med Ctr 1983

Sofer, Alfred MD (PlS) - **Spec Exp:** Cosmetic Surgery; Plastic & Reconstructive Surgery; Breast Reconstruction; **Hospital:** Norwalk Hosp, St. Vincent's Med Ctr - Bridgeport; **Address:** Plastic Surgery Ctr of Fairfield, 33 Miller St, Fairfield, CT 06824; **Phone:** 203-336-9862; **Board Cert:** Plastic Surgery 2007; **Med School:** Albany Med Coll 1993; **Resid:** Surgery, Westchester MedCenter 1998; Plastic/Reconstructive Surgery, Med Univ of SC Med Ctr 1999; **Fellow:** Microvascular Surgery, Kleinert Inst 2000

Psychiatry

Abrams, Linus S MD (Psyc) - **Spec Exp:** Psychopharmacology; Psychotherapy; Adolescent Psychiatry; **Address:** 4 Dearfield Drive, Ste 107, Greenwich, CT 06831; **Phone:** 203-861-2654; **Board Cert:** Psychiatry 2005; **Med School:** NY Med Coll 1988; **Resid:** Psychiatry, Overlook Hosp 1989; Psychiatry, Beth Israel Deaconess Med Ctr 1992

Goldberg, Joseph F MD (Psyc) - **Spec Exp:** Bipolar/Mood Disorders; Psychopharmacology; Anxiety & Depression; Cognitive Psychotherapy; **Hospital:** Mt Sinai Hosp, Silver Hill Hosp; **Address:** 128 East Avenue, Norwalk, CT 06851; **Phone:** 203-854-9607; **Board Cert:** Psychiatry 2009; **Med School:** Northwestern Univ 1992; **Resid:** Psychiatry, Payne Whitney Clin 1996; **Fellow:** Psychosomatic Medicine, Payne Whitney Clin 1998; **Fac Appt:** Clin Prof Psyc, Mount Sinai-Icahn Sch of Med

Hart, Sidney H MD (Psyc) - **Spec Exp:** Anxiety Disorders; Mood Disorders; Psychotherapy; **Hospital:** Greenwich Hosp (page 970); **Address:** 282 Railroad Ave, Fl 2, Greenwich, CT 06830; **Phone:** 203-622-1722; **Board Cert:** Psychiatry 1973; **Med School:** Albert Einstein Coll Med 1964; **Resid:** Psychiatry, Bronx Municipal Hosp 1971; **Fellow:** Liaison Psychiatry, Montefiore Hosp Med Ctr 1973

Kalman, Arlene Diane MD (Psyc) - **Spec Exp:** Child & Adolescent Psychiatry; **Hospital:** Danbury Hosp; **Address:** 54 Arrowhead Rd, Brookfield, CT 06804; **Phone:** 203-775-6100; **Board Cert:** Psychiatry 1985; **Med School:** SUNY Downstate 1980; **Resid:** Psychiatry, Bronx Muni Hosp Ctr 1983; **Fellow:** Child & Adolescent Psychiatry, Bronx Muni Hosp Ctr 1985

Lorefice, Laurence S MD (Psyc) - **Spec Exp:** Depression; Bipolar/Mood Disorders; Obsessive-Compulsive Disorder; Anxiety Disorders; **Address:** 1445 E Putnam Ave, Old Greenwich, CT 06870; **Phone:** 203-637-4006; **Board Cert:** Psychiatry 1979; **Med School:** Univ Pennsylvania 1975; **Resid:** Psychiatry, Mass Genl Hosp 1978; **Fellow:** Community Psychiatry, Mass Genl Hosp 1979

Morgan, Charles J MD (Psyc) - **Spec Exp:** Alcohol Abuse; Mood Disorders; Substance Abuse; **Hospital:** Bridgeport Hosp; **Address:** Northeast Medical Group, 226 Mill Hill Ave Fl 3, Bridgeport, CT 06610; **Phone:** 203-384-3897; **Board Cert:** Psychiatry 1990; **Med School:** Cornell Univ-Weill Med Coll 1983; **Resid:** Psychiatry, Yale-New Haven Hosp 1987; **Fac Appt:** Asst Clin Prof Psyc, Yale Univ

Mueller, F. Carl MD (Psyc) - **Spec Exp:** Anxiety & Depression; Obsessive-Compulsive Disorder; Psychopharmacology; **Hospital:** Stamford Hosp (page 971); **Address:** 999 Summer St, Ste 200, Stamford, CT 06905-5513; **Phone:** 203-357-7773; **Board Cert:** Psychiatry 1987; **Med School:** Univ Conn 1982; **Resid:** Psychiatry, Yale-New Haven Hosp 1985; **Fellow:** Psychiatry, Yale-New Haven Hosp 1986; **Fac Appt:** Asst Clin Prof Psyc, Yale Univ

Pollack, Joshua C MD (Psyc) - **Spec Exp:** Geriatric Psychiatry; Depression; **Hospital:** Greenwich Hosp (page 970); **Address:** Ctr for Healthy Aging, 5 Perryridge Rd, Greenwich, CT 06830; **Phone:** 203-863-3543; **Board Cert:** Psychiatry 2004; Geriatric Psychiatry 2006; **Med School:** Israel 1998; **Resid:** Psychiatry, Albert Einstein Coll Med Affil Hosp 2002; **Fellow:** Geriatric Psychiatry, Albert Einstein Coll Med Affil Hosp 2004

Schechter, Justin O MD (Psyc) - **Spec Exp:** Anxiety Disorders; Mood Disorders; Eating Disorders; Pregnancy & Mood Disorders; **Hospital:** Stamford Hosp (page 971); **Address:** 22 5th St Fl 3, Stamford, CT 06905; **Phone:** 203-323-7760; **Board Cert:** Psychiatry 1986; Forensic Psychiatry 2008; **Med School:** SUNY Stony Brook 1981; **Resid:** Psychiatry, Yale-New Haven Hosp 1985; **Fac Appt:** Asst Clin Prof Psyc, Yale Univ

Shapiro, Bruce MD (Psyc) - **Spec Exp:** Forensic Psychiatry; Psychopharmacology; Anxiety & Depression; Bipolar/Mood Disorders; **Hospital:** Stamford Hosp (page 971); **Address:** 666 Glenbrook Rd, River Suite, Stamford, CT 06906; **Phone:** 203-327-4144; **Board Cert:** Psychiatry 1976; **Med School:** NY Med Coll 1972; **Resid:** Psychiatry, Metropolitan Hosp Ctr 1976; **Fac Appt:** Clin Prof Psyc, Columbia P&S

Smith, Joann M MD (Psyc) - **Spec Exp:** Mood Disorders; Anxiety Disorders; Depression; Women's Health-Mental Health; **Hospital:** St. Vincent's Med Ctr - Bridgeport; **Address:** 1261 Post Rd, Ste 200-A, Fairfield, CT 06824; **Phone:** 203-255-0770; **Board Cert:** Psychiatry 1980; **Med School:** SUNY Upstate Med Univ 1974; **Resid:** Internal Medicine, Washington Hosp Ctr 1975; Psychiatry, Georgetown Univ Hosp 1979

Tamerin, John S MD (Psyc) - **Spec Exp:** Psychotherapy; Bipolar/Mood Disorders; Depression; Alcohol Abuse; **Hospital:** NY-Presby/Weill Cornell Med Ctr, NY (page 102), Greenwich Hosp (page 970); **Address:** 27 Stag Ln, Greenwich, CT 06831-3137; **Phone:** 203-661-8282; **Board Cert:** Psychiatry 1970; **Med School:** NYU Sch Med 1963; **Resid:** Psychiatry, Yale-New Haven Hosp 1965; Psychiatry, Mt Sinai Med Ctr 1967; **Fellow:** Child Psychiatry, Natl Rehab Hosp 1969; **Fac Appt:** Assoc Clin Prof Psyc, Cornell Univ-Weill Med Coll

Waynik, Mark MD (Psyc) - **Spec Exp:** Psychotherapy; Psychopharmacology; Forensic Psychiatry; **Hospital:** St. Vincent's Med Ctr - Bridgeport; **Address:** The Waynik Group, 52 Beach Rd, Ste 104, Fairfield, CT 06824; **Phone:** 203-254-2000; **Board Cert:** Psychiatry 1987; **Med School:** Mexico 1979; **Resid:** Psychiatry, Inst Living 1984

Pulmonary Disease

Berman, Lewis MD (Pul) - **Spec Exp:** Interstitial Lung Disease; Cystic Fibrosis; Emphysema; Critical Care; **Hospital:** Norwalk Hosp; **Address:** Norwalk Hosp-Dept Pulmonary Med, 34 Maple St, Norwalk, CT 06856; **Phone:** 203-852-2486; **Board Cert:** Internal Medicine 2004; Critical Care Medicine 2005; Pulmonary Disease 2004; Clinical Informatics 2014; **Med School:** Albert Einstein Coll Med 1987; **Resid:** Internal Medicine, UPMC/St Margaret Hosp 1990; **Fellow:** Pulmonary Critical Care Medicine, Yale-New Haven Hosp 1994

Bernstein, Michael A MD (Pul) - **Spec Exp:** Sleep Medicine; Pneumonia; Cystic Fibrosis; **Hospital:** Stamford Hosp (page 971); **Address:** Pulmonary Assocs Stamford, 190 W Broad St, Stamford, CT 06902; **Phone:** 203-348-2437; **Board Cert:** Internal Medicine 2007; Pulmonary Disease 2009; Critical Care Medicine 2010; Hospice & Palliative Medicine 2012; **Med School:** Duke Univ 2003; **Resid:** Internal Medicine & Pediatrics, Mount Sinai Med Ctr 2007; **Fellow:** Pulmonary Critical Care Medicine, Mount Sinai Med Ctr 2010

Brown, Robert B MD (Pul) - **Spec Exp:** Cystic Fibrosis; Chronic Obstructive Lung Disease (COPD); Critical Care; **Hospital:** St. Vincent's Med Ctr - Bridgeport; **Address:** 2800 Main St, Bridgeport, CT 06606; **Phone:** 203-576-5711; **Board Cert:** Internal Medicine 1981; Pulmonary Disease 1984; Critical Care Medicine 2007; **Med School:** SUNY Downstate 1978; **Resid:** Internal Medicine, Westchester Med Ctr 1981; **Fellow:** Pulmonary Disease, NY Med Coll Affil Hosp 1984; **Fac Appt:** Asst Prof Med, NY Med Coll

Chronakos, John MD (Pul) - **Spec Exp:** Sleep Disorders; Critical Care Medicine; **Hospital:** Danbury Hosp; **Address:** Danbury WCMG, Pulmonary & Sleep, 33 Germantown Rd Fl 2, Danbury, CT 06810; **Phone:** 203-739-7070; **Board Cert:** Internal Medicine 2011; Pulmonary Disease 2013; Critical Care Medicine 2005; Sleep Medicine 2011; **Med School:** NYU Sch Med 1998; **Resid:** Internal Medicine, NYU Langone Med Ctr 2001; **Fellow:** Pulmonary Critical Care Medicine, Mount Sinai Med Ctr 2004

Fine, Jonathan MD (Pul) - **Spec Exp:** Asthma; **Hospital:** Norwalk Hosp; **Address:** Norwalk Hosp, Div of Pulmonology, 34 Maple St Fl 3, Norwalk, CT 06856; **Phone:** 203-852-2392; **Board Cert:** Internal Medicine 1984; Pulmonary Disease 1986; Critical Care Medicine 2011; **Med School:** Yale Univ 1981; **Resid:** Internal Medicine, Yale-New Haven Hosp 1984; **Fellow:** Pulmonary Disease, Yale-New Haven Hosp 1985; Pulmonary Critical Care Medicine, UCSF Med Ctr 1988

Krinsley, James S MD (Pul) - **Spec Exp:** Asthma; Emphysema; Critical Care; **Hospital:** Stamford Hosp (page 971); **Address:** Pulmonary Assocs Stamford, 190 W Broad St, Stamford, CT 06902; **Phone:** 203-348-2437; **Board Cert:** Internal Medicine 1983; Pulmonary Disease 1986; Critical Care Medicine 2009; **Med School:** Cornell Univ-Weill Med Coll 1980; **Resid:** Internal Medicine, NYU/VA Med Ctr 1983; **Fellow:** Pulmonary Disease, Yale-New Haven Hosp 1986; **Fac Appt:** Clin Prof Med, Columbia P&S

Kurtz, Caroline P MD (Pul) - **Spec Exp:** Asthma; Cystic Fibrosis; Chronic Obstructive Lung Disease (COPD); **Hospital:** Norwalk Hosp; **Address:** 30 Stevens St, Ste C, Norwalk, CT 06850; **Phone:** 203-855-3888; **Board Cert:** Internal Medicine 1988; Pulmonary Disease 2010; Critical Care Medicine 2012; **Med School:** NYU Sch Med 1984; **Resid:** Internal Medicine, Mt Sinai Hosp 1987; **Fellow:** Pulmonary Critical Care Medicine, Mt Sinai Hosp 1990; Critical Care Medicine, Norwalk Hosp 1991

Marino, A. Michael MD (Pul) - **Spec Exp:** Asthma; Bronchitis; Emphysema; Lung Cancer; **Hospital:** Greenwich Hosp (page 970); **Address:** 5 Perryridge Rd, Greenwich, CT 06830; **Phone:** 203-661-5379; **Board Cert:** Internal Medicine 1972; Pulmonary Disease 1972; **Med School:** Georgetown Univ 1964; **Resid:** Internal Medicine, VA Med Ctr 1967; **Fellow:** Pulmonary Disease, VA Med Ctr 1969; **Fac Appt:** Assoc Clin Prof Med, Yale Univ

McCalley, Stuart W MD (Pul) - **Spec Exp:** Sleep Disorders; Chronic Obstructive Lung Disease (COPD); Asthma; Cystic Fibrosis; **Hospital:** Greenwich Hosp (page 970), Stamford Hosp (page 971); **Address:** Greenwich Medical Grp, 75 Holly Hill Ln, Greenwich, CT 06830; **Phone:** 203-869-6960; **Board Cert:** Internal Medicine 1972; Pulmonary Disease 1974; **Med School:** Case West Res Univ 1969; **Resid:** Internal Medicine, Univ Conn Hlth Ctr 1971; Internal Medicine, Univ Vermont Med Ctr 1972; **Fellow:** Pulmonary Disease, A Einstein Med Sch Affil Hosp 1974

Oelberg, David Alan MD (Pul) - **Spec Exp:** Sleep Disorders; **Hospital:** Danbury Hosp, New Milford Hosp; **Address:** WCMG, Pulmonology/Sleep Med, 33 Germantown Rd Fl 2, Danbury, CT 06810; **Phone:** 203-739-8330; **Board Cert:** Internal Medicine 2013; Pulmonary Disease 2006; Critical Care Medicine 2007; Sleep Medicine 2011; **Med School:** Canada 1990; **Resid:** Internal Medicine, Jewish Genl Hosp 1993; **Fellow:** Pulmonary Critical Care Medicine, Mass Genl Hosp 1998

Roca, Dominic J MD/PhD (Pul) - **Spec Exp:** Sleep Disorders; Allergy; **Hospital:** Stamford Hosp (page 971); **Address:** Pulmonary Assocs Stamford, 190 W Broad St, Stamford, CT 06902; **Phone:** 203-348-2437; **Board Cert:** Allergy & Immunology 2008; Pulmonary Disease 2006; Critical Care Medicine 2007; Sleep Medicine 2009; **Med School:** SUNY Downstate 1991; **Resid:** Internal Medicine, NYU Med Ctr 1994; **Fellow:** Allergy & Immunology, Boston Med Ctr 1999; Psychosomatic Medicine, Beth Israel Deaconess Med Ctr 1999; **Fac Appt:** Asst Clin Prof Med, Columbia P&S

Rudolph, Daniel J MD (Pul) - **Spec Exp:** Asthma; Pneumonia; **Hospital:** Bridgeport Hosp; **Address:** Pulmonary & Internal Med Assocs, 15 Corporate Drive, Trumbull, CT 06611; **Phone:** 203-261-3980; **Board Cert:** Internal Medicine 1985; Pulmonary Disease 1988; **Med School:** NYU Sch Med 1982; **Resid:** Internal Medicine, SUNY Stony Brook Med Ctr 1985; **Fellow:** Pulmonary Disease, Montefiore Med Ctr 1988

Sachs, Paul MD (Pul) - **Spec Exp:** Pulmonary Rehabilitation; Asthma; Chronic Obstructive Lung Disease (COPD); **Hospital:** Stamford Hosp (page 971); **Address:** Pulmonary Assocs Stamford, 190 W Broad St, Stamford, CT 06902-3633; **Phone:** 203-348-2437; **Board Cert:** Internal Medicine 1985; Pulmonary Disease 1988; Critical Care Medicine 2009; **Med School:** NYU Sch Med 1982; **Resid:** Internal Medicine, NY Hosp 1985; **Fellow:** Pulmonary Disease, Montefiore Med Ctr 1988; **Fac Appt:** Assoc Clin Prof Med, Columbia P&S

Turetsky, Arthur S MD (Pul) - **Spec Exp:** Sleep Medicine; Asthma; Chronic Obstructive Lung Disease (COPD); Tuberculosis; **Hospital:** Bridgeport Hosp; **Address:** Pulmonary & Internal Med Assocs, 15 Corporate Drive, Trumbull, CT 6611; **Phone:** 203-261-3980; **Board Cert:** Internal Medicine 1977; Pulmonary Disease 1980; Sleep Medicine 2009; **Med School:** Albert Einstein Coll Med 1974; **Resid:** Internal Medicine, Einstein Bronx Muncipal Hosp Ctr 1977; Pulmonary Disease, Bronx Municipal Hosp 1980; **Fac Appt:** Asst Clin Prof Med, Albert Einstein Coll Med

Winter, Stephen M MD (Pul) - **Spec Exp:** Emphysema; Pneumonia; Lung Cancer; Chronic Obstructive Lung Disease (COPD); **Hospital:** Norwalk Hosp; **Address:** Norwalk Hosp, Pulmonology, 34 Maple St Fl 3, Norwalk, CT 06856; **Phone:** 203-852-2392; **Board Cert:** Internal Medicine 1984; Pulmonary Disease 1986; Critical Care Medicine 2007; **Med School:** Cornell Univ-Weill Med Coll 1981; **Resid:** Internal Medicine, NY-Presby/Weill Cornell Med Ctr 1984; **Fellow:** Pulmonary Critical Care Medicine, Yale-New Haven Hosp 1987; **Fac Appt:** Clin Prof Med, Yale Univ

Radiation Oncology

Dowling, Sean W MD (RadRO) - **Spec Exp:** Breast Cancer; Gynecologic Cancer; **Hospital:** Stamford Hosp (page 971); **Address:** Stamford Hosp, Dept Radiation Oncology, 34 Shelburne Rd, Stamford, CT 06902; **Phone:** 203-276-7886; **Board Cert:** Internal Medicine 1986; Radiation Oncology 1990; **Med School:** Yale Univ 1983; **Resid:** Internal Medicine, Yale-New Haven Hosp 1986; Radiation Oncology, Yale-New Haven Hosp 1989

Fang, Deborah X MD (RadRO) - **Spec Exp:** Breast Cancer; Gastrointestinal Cancer; **Hospital:** St. Vincent's Med Ctr - Bridgeport; **Address:** St Vincents Med Ctr, Rad Oncology Dept, 2800 Main St, Bridgeport, CT 06606; **Phone:** 203-576-5085; **Board Cert:** Radiation Oncology 2011; **Med School:** China 1987; **Resid:** Radiation Oncology, Mount Sinai Med Ctr 2001

Iannuzzi, Christopher M MD (RadRO) - **Spec Exp:** Breast Cancer; Pancreatic Cancer; Head & Neck Cancer; Prostate Cancer; **Hospital:** St. Vincent's Med Ctr - Bridgeport; **Address:** St Vincents Med Ctr, Rad Oncology Dept, 2800 Main St, Bridgeport, CT 06606; **Phone:** 203-576-5085; **Board Cert:** Radiation Oncology 2011; **Med School:** Mount Sinai Sch Med 1996; **Resid:** Radiation Oncology, Mount Sinai Med Ctr 2001

Masino, Frank A MD (RadRO) - **Spec Exp:** Breast Cancer; Prostate Cancer; Brachytherapy; Stereotactic Radiosurgery; **Hospital:** Stamford Hosp (page 971); **Address:** Stamford Hosp, Radiation Oncology, 34 Shelburne Rd, Stamford, CT 06902; **Phone:** 203-276-7886; **Board Cert:** Therapeutic Radiology 1982; **Med School:** Albert Einstein Coll Med 1978; **Resid:** Therapeutic Radiology, Yale-New Haven Hosp 1982

Narayana, Ashwatha MD (RadRO) - **Spec Exp:** Brain Tumors; Brain Tumors-Metastatic; Stereotactic Radiosurgery; **Hospital:** Greenwich Hosp (page 970); **Address:** Greenwich Cancer Ctr, Radiation Oncology, 77 Lafayette Pl, Ste 240, Greenwich, CT 06830; **Phone:** 203-863-3773; **Board Cert:** Radiation Oncology 2010; **Med School:** India 1989; **Resid:** Radiation Oncology, Loyola Univ Med Ctr 1998; **Fellow:** Radiation Oncology, Johns Hopkins Hosp 1993; Radiation Oncology, Memorial Med Ctr 1993

Pathare, Pradip M MD (RadRO) - **Spec Exp:** Breast Cancer; Prostate Cancer; Head & Neck Cancer; Brain Tumors; **Hospital:** Norwalk Hosp; **Address:** Whittingham Cancer Ctr, 24 Stevens St, Norwalk, CT 06856; **Phone:** 203-852-2719; **Board Cert:** Radiology 1980; Therapeutic Radiology 1981; **Med School:** India 1975; **Resid:** Radiology, Misericordia/Lincoln Hosp 1979; Therapeutic Radiology, Yale-New Haven Hosp 1981; **Fac Appt:** Assoc Clin Prof RadRO, Yale Univ

Sanghavi, Seema MD (RadRO) - **Spec Exp:** Breast Cancer; **Hospital:** Danbury Hosp; **Address:** Danbury Hosp, Radiation Oncology, 24 Hospital Ave, Danbury, CT 06810; **Phone:** 203-739-7190; **Board Cert:** Radiation Oncology 2011; **Med School:** Northwestern Univ 1995; **Resid:** Radiation Oncology, Univ WI Hosp & Clins 2001

Spera, John A MD (RadRO) - **Spec Exp:** Breast Cancer; Prostate Cancer; Intensity Modulated Radiotherapy (IMRT); **Hospital:** Danbury Hosp; **Address:** Danbury Hosp, Dept Radiation Oncology, 24 Hospital Ave, Danbury, CT 06810-6099; **Phone:** 203-739-7190; **Board Cert:** Radiation Oncology 1987; **Med School:** Georgetown Univ 1979; **Resid:** Surgery, Hosp Univ Penn 1981; Urology, Hosp Univ Penn 1983; **Fellow:** Radiation Oncology, Hosp Univ Penn 1987

Reproductive Endocrinology

Chacho, Karol J MD (RE) - **Spec Exp:** Endometriosis; Infertility; Menopause Problems; Infertility-IVF; **Hospital:** Bridgeport Hosp, St. Vincent's Med Ctr - Bridgeport; **Address:** 4699 Main St, Ste 210, Bridgeport, CT 06606-1830; **Phone:** 203-372-5282; **Board Cert:** Obstetrics & Gynecology 2013; Reproductive Endocrinology/Infertility 2013; **Med School:** Loyola Univ-Stritch Sch Med 1978; **Resid:** Obstetrics & Gynecology, Michael Reese Hosp Med Ctr 1982; **Fellow:** Reproductive Endocrinology, Michael Reese Hosp Med Ctr 1984

Doyle, Michael B MD (RE) - **Spec Exp:** Infertility-IVF; Endometriosis; Hysteroscopic Surgery; Uterine Fibroids; **Hospital:** Norwalk Hosp, St. Vincent's Med Ctr - Bridgeport; **Address:** 4920 Main St, Ste 301, Bridgeport, CT 06606-1300; **Phone:** 203-373-1200; **Board Cert:** Obstetrics & Gynecology 2013; **Med School:** UCSF 1985; **Resid:** Obstetrics & Gynecology, Hosp Univ Penn 1989; **Fellow:** Reproductive Endocrinology, Yale-New Haven Hosp 1991

Ginsburg, Frances W MD (RE) - **Spec Exp:** Infertility-IVF; Endometriosis; Menstrual Disorders; **Hospital:** Stamford Hosp (page 971); **Address:** Stamford Hosp, Advanced Obstetrics and Gynocology, 166 W Broad St, Ste 403, Stamford, CT 06902; **Phone:** 203-276-7559; **Board Cert:** Obstetrics & Gynecology 2013; Reproductive Endocrinology 2013; **Med School:** NYU Sch Med 1980; **Resid:** Obstetrics & Gynecology, Bellevue Hosp Ctr 1984; **Fellow:** Reproductive Endocrinology, Bellevue Hosp Ctr 1986; **Fac Appt:** Asst Clin Prof ObG, Columbia P&S

Hurwitz, Joshua M MD (RE) - **Spec Exp:** Infertility-IVF; Hormonal Disorders; Endometriosis; **Hospital:** Danbury Hosp; **Address:** RMACT, 10 Glover Ave, Norwalk, CT 6850; **Phone:** 203-750-7400; **Board Cert:** Obstetrics & Gynecology 2013; Reproductive Endocrinology/Infertility 2013; **Med School:** Jefferson Med Coll 1999; **Resid:** Obstetrics & Gynecology, Thomas Jefferson Univ Hosp 2003; **Fellow:** Reproductive Endocrinology, Montefiore Med Ctr 2006; **Fac Appt:** Asst Prof ObG, Albert Einstein Coll Med

Leondires, Mark Peter MD (RE) - **Spec Exp:** Endometriosis; Polycystic Ovarian Syndrome; Asherman's Syndrome; Infertility-IVF; **Hospital:** Norwalk Hosp, Stamford Hosp (page 971); **Address:** RMACT, 10 Glover Ave, Norwalk, CT 06850; **Phone:** 203-750-7400; **Board Cert:** Obstetrics & Gynecology 2013; Reproductive Endocrinology 2013; **Med School:** Univ VT Coll Med 1991; **Resid:** Obstetrics & Gynecology, Maine Med Ctr 1995; **Fellow:** Reproductive Endocrinology/Infertility, Magee Women's Hosp 1996; Reproductive Endocrinology, Natl Inst Hlth-Clin Ctr 1999

Levi, Andrew Joseph MD (RE) - **Spec Exp:** Infertility-IVF; Preimplantation Genetic Diagnosis; Miscarriage-Recurrent; Fertility Preservation; **Hospital:** Bridgeport Hosp; **Address:** Park Ave Fertility & Reproductive Med, 5520 Park Ave, Ste 103, Trumbull, CT 06611; **Phone:** 203-372-6700; **Board Cert:** Obstetrics & Gynecology 2013; Reproductive Endocrinology/Infertility 2013; **Med School:** Univ Rochester 1995; **Resid:** Obstetrics & Gynecology, Georgetown Univ Hosp 1999; **Fellow:** Reproductive Endocrinology/Infertility, Natl Inst Hlth 2002; **Fac Appt:** Asst Clin Prof ObG, Yale Univ

Murdock, Cynthia MD (RE) - **Spec Exp:** Infertility-IVF; Reproductive Surgery; **Hospital:** Danbury Hosp; **Address:** RMACT, 10 Glover Ave, Norwalk, CT 06850; **Phone:** 203-750-7400; **Board Cert:** Obstetrics & Gynecology 2013; Reproductive Endocrinology/Infertility 2013; **Med School:** Creighton Univ 1995; **Resid:** Obstetrics & Gynecology, Creighton Univ Med Ctr 1999; **Fellow:** Reproductive Endocrinology, Natl Inst Hlth-Clin Ctr 2003

Richlin, Spencer S MD (RE) - **Spec Exp:** Infertility-IVF; Reproductive Surgery; Fertility Preservation; **Hospital:** Norwalk Hosp, Stamford Hosp (page 971); **Address:** RMACT, 10 Glover Ave, Norwalk, CT 06850-1202; **Phone:** 203-750-7400; **Board Cert:** Obstetrics & Gynecology 2013; Reproductive Endocrinology/Infertility 2013; **Med School:** USC-Keck Sch Med 1994; **Resid:** Obstetrics & Gynecology, Stamford Hosp 1999; **Fellow:** Reproductive Endocrinology, Emory Univ Hosp 2002

Williams, Shaun C MD (RE) - **Spec Exp:** Infertility-IVF; Reproductive Surgery; Fertility Preservation; **Hospital:** St. Vincent's Med Ctr - Bridgeport, Bridgeport Hosp; **Address:** RMACT, 115 Technology Drive, Ste C200, Trumbull, CT 06611; **Phone:** 203-880-5340; **Board Cert:** Obstetrics & Gynecology 2013; Reproductive Endocrinology/Infertility 2013; **Med School:** Baylor Coll Med 1995; **Resid:** Obstetrics & Gynecology, Univ Texas SW Med Ctr 1999; **Fellow:** Reproductive Endocrinology, Jones Inst for Repro Endocrinology 2002

Witt, Barry R MD (RE) - **Spec Exp:** Infertility-IVF; Endometriosis; Laparoscopic Surgery; Pregnancy Loss-Recurrent; **Hospital:** Greenwich Hosp (page 970); **Address:** Greenwich Fertility Ctr, 55 Holly Hill Ln, Ste 270, Greenwich, CT 06830; **Phone:** 203-863-2990; **Board Cert:** Obstetrics & Gynecology 2013; Reproductive Endocrinology 2013; **Med School:** NY Med Coll 1984; **Resid:** Obstetrics & Gynecology, Montefiore Med Ctr 1988; **Fellow:** Reproductive Endocrinology, Tulane Med Ctr 1990; **Fac Appt:** Assoc Prof ObG, NYU Sch Med

Rheumatology

Danehower, Richard L MD (Rhu) - **Spec Exp:** Rheumatoid Arthritis; Temporal Arteritis; Psoriatic Arthritis; Osteoarthritis; **Hospital:** Greenwich Hosp (page 970); **Address:** 49 Lake Ave, Ste 102, Greenwich, CT 06830-4501; **Phone:** 203-869-5715; **Board Cert:** Internal Medicine 1971; Rheumatology 1974; **Med School:** Univ Pennsylvania 1965; **Resid:** Internal Medicine, Univ Michigan Med Ctr 1969; **Fellow:** Rheumatology, Univ Michigan Med Ctr 1970; **Fac Appt:** Asst Clin Prof Med, Yale Univ

Gladstein, Geoffrey S MD (Rhu) - **Spec Exp:** Arthritis; Antiphospholipid Syndrome (APS); Chronic Fatigue Syndrome; Lupus/SLE; **Hospital:** Bridgeport Hosp; **Address:** PriMed Arthritis & Rheumatism Assocs, 5520 Park Ave, Ste 101, Trumbull, CT 06611; **Phone:** 203-371-5873; **Board Cert:** Internal Medicine 1976; Rheumatology 1978; **Med School:** Geo Wash Univ 1973; **Resid:** Internal Medicine, Albany Med Ctr 1976; **Fellow:** Rheumatology, Albany Med Ctr 1978

Karp, Sharon Wolfsohn MD (Rhu) - **Spec Exp:** Lupus/SLE in Women; Rheumatoid Arthritis; Psoriatic Arthritis; Fibromyalgia; **Hospital:** Stamford Hosp (page 971); **Address:** Westchester Health Shoreline Med Group, 1450 Washington Blvd, Stamford, CT 06902; **Phone:** 203-327-9321; **Board Cert:** Internal Medicine 1987; Rheumatology 1988; **Med School:** Brown Univ 1983; **Resid:** Internal Medicine, Stamford Hosp 1986; **Fellow:** Rheumatology, NYU Med Ctr 1988; **Fac Appt:** Assoc Clin Prof Med, Columbia P&S

Miller, Kenneth A MD (Rhu) - **Spec Exp:** Rheumatoid Arthritis; Osteoporosis; Vasculitis; Lupus/SLE; **Hospital:** Danbury Hosp, New Milford Hosp; **Address:** 33 Hospital Ave, Danbury, CT 06810-5954; **Phone:** 203-794-0599; **Board Cert:** Internal Medicine 1978; Rheumatology 1980; **Med School:** Rush Med Coll 1975; **Resid:** Internal Medicine, GW Univ Hosp 1978; **Fellow:** Rheumatology, Worcester City Hosp 1980

Nascimento, Joao M MD (Rhu) - **Spec Exp:** Rheumatoid Arthritis; Lupus/SLE; Psoriatic Arthritis; **Hospital:** St. Vincent's Med Ctr - Bridgeport, Bridgeport Hosp; **Address:** 3203 Main St, Bridgeport, CT 06606-4225; **Phone:** 203-371-0009; **Board Cert:** Internal Medicine 1989; Rheumatology 2012; **Med School:** Portugal 1984; **Resid:** Internal Medicine, Bridgeport Hosp 1989; **Fellow:** Rheumatology, Brown Univ Med Ctr 1991

Novack, Stuart N MD (Rhu) - **Spec Exp:** Lupus/SLE; Osteoarthritis; Rheumatoid Arthritis; Vasculitis; **Hospital:** Norwalk Hosp; **Address:** Norwalk Med Grp, 40 Cross St Fl 4, Norwalk, CT 06851; **Phone:** 203-845-4830; **Board Cert:** Internal Medicine 1971; Rheumatology 1972; **Med School:** SUNY Hlth Sci Ctr 1966; **Resid:** Internal Medicine, Maimonides Med Ctr 1968; Internal Medicine, UCLA Med Ctr 1969; **Fellow:** Rheumatology, UCLA Med Ctr 1970; **Fac Appt:** Assoc Clin Prof Med, Yale Univ

Rose, Roberta MD (Rhu) - **Spec Exp:** Lupus/SLE; Psoriatic Arthritis; Rheumatoid Arthritis; **Hospital:** Norwalk Hosp; **Address:** Norwalk Med Grp, Rheumatology Dept, 40 Cross St Fl 4, Norwalk, CT 06851; **Phone:** 203-845-4829; **Board Cert:** Internal Medicine 1984; Rheumatology 1988; **Med School:** UCSF 1981; **Resid:** Internal Medicine, Mount Sinai Med Ctr 1984; **Fellow:** Rheumatology, NYU Med Ctr 1987

Spiegel, Michael MD (Rhu) - **Hospital:** Danbury Hosp; **Address:** 33 Germantown Rd Fl 1, Danbury, CT 06810; **Phone:** 203-794-5600; **Board Cert:** Internal Medicine 1987; Rheumatology 2010; **Med School:** SUNY Downstate 1984; **Resid:** Internal Medicine, St. Francis Med Ctr 1987; **Fellow:** Rheumatology, Roger Williams Hosp 1988

Vietorisz, Tomas J MD (Rhu) - **Spec Exp:** Rheumatoid Arthritis; **Hospital:** Stamford Hosp (page 971); **Address:** PrimeCare Med Grp, 1351 Washington Blvd, Ste 402, Stamford, CT 06902; **Phone:** 203-348-9455; **Board Cert:** Internal Medicine 2011; Rheumatology 2000; **Med School:** Mount Sinai Sch Med 1988; **Resid:** Internal Medicine, Univ Pittsburgh Med Ctr 1991; **Fellow:** Rheumatology, Boston Med Ctr 1993

Surgery

Capasse, Jeanne S MD (S) - **Spec Exp:** Breast Surgery; **Hospital:** Norwalk Hosp; **Address:** Surgical Breast Care of Connecticut, 148 East Ave, Ste 2L, Norwalk, CT 06851; **Phone:** 203-846-8885; **Board Cert:** Surgery 2002; **Med School:** Cornell Univ-Weill Med Coll 1987; **Resid:** Surgery, St Lukes-Roosevelt Hosp Ctr 1992

Choi, Laura Hargie MD (S) - **Spec Exp:** Laparoscopic Surgery; Obesity/Bariatric Surgery; **Hospital:** Danbury Hosp; **Address:** Ctr Weight Loss Surgery, 111 Osborne St, Ste 209, Danbury, CT 06810; **Phone:** 203-739-7131; **Board Cert:** Surgery 2004; **Med School:** NYU Sch Med 1998; **Resid:** Surgery, St Lukes-Roosevelt Hosp 2003

Demestihas, Anthy MD (S) - **Spec Exp:** Breast Surgery; Trauma; Laparoscopic Surgery; **Hospital:** St. Vincent's Med Ctr - Bridgeport; **Address:** 2660 Main St, Ste 110, Southport, CT 06606; **Phone:** 203-332-4744; **Board Cert:** Surgery 2013; **Med School:** Mexico 1986; **Resid:** Surgery, St Vincents Med Ctr 1989; Surgery, Westchester Med Ctr 1992

Dong, Xiang D MD (S) - **Spec Exp:** Gastrointestinal Cancer; Rectal Cancer; Sarcoma; Melanoma; **Hospital:** Stamford Hosp (page 971); **Address:** Fairfield Co Surgical Specialists, 1351 Washington Blvd Fl 6 - Ste 601, Stamford, CT 06902; **Phone:** 203-276-5959; **Board Cert:** Surgery 2012; **Med School:** Duke Univ 1999; **Resid:** Surgery, Drexel Univ Coll Med Affil Hosp 2005; **Fellow:** Surgical Oncology, Univ Pittsburgh Med Ctr 2007

Dwyer, Kevin M MD (S) - **Spec Exp:** Trauma; **Hospital:** Stamford Hosp (page 971); **Address:** Fairfield Co Surgical Specialists, 1351 Washington Blvd Fl 6 - Ste 601, Stamford, CT 06902; **Phone:** 203-276-5959; **Board Cert:** Surgery 2011; Surgical Critical Care 2006; **Med School:** Georgetown Univ 1984; **Resid:** Surgery, Army Med Ctr 1991; **Fellow:** Trauma/Critical Care, Inova Fairfax Hosp 1995; Trauma/Critical Care, Univ MD Med Ctr 1996

Floch, Neil R MD (S) - **Spec Exp:** Obesity/Bariatric Surgery; Laparoscopic Surgery; **Hospital:** Norwalk Hosp, St. Vincent's Med Ctr - Bridgeport; **Address:** Fairfield Co Bariatrics & Surgical Specs, 148 East Ave, Ste 3A, Norwalk, CT 06851; **Phone:** 203-899-0744; **Board Cert:** Surgery 2008; **Med School:** Boston Univ 1992; **Resid:** Surgery, Beth Israel Med Ctr 1997; **Fellow:** Laparoscopic Surgery, Mayo Clinic 1998

Garvey, Richard J MD (S) - **Spec Exp:** Biliary Surgery; Breast Surgery; Laparoscopic Abdominal Surgery; Thyroid & Parathyroid Surgery; **Hospital:** Bridgeport Hosp; **Address:** Genl Surgeons of Greater Bridgeport, 310 Mill Hill Ave, Bridgeport, CT 06610-2863; **Phone:** 203-366-3211; **Board Cert:** Surgery 2009; **Med School:** Georgetown Univ 1974; **Resid:** Surgery, Boston Univ Med Ctr 1980

Kenler, Andrew S MD (S) - **Spec Exp:** Breast Surgery; Hernia; Laparoscopic Abdominal Surgery; Thyroid Surgery; **Hospital:** Bridgeport Hosp; **Address:** Park Avenue Surgical Assocs, 5520 Park Ave, Ste 207, Trumbull, CT 06611; **Phone:** 203-373-9015; **Board Cert:** Surgery 2006; **Med School:** Cornell Univ-Weill Med Coll 1988; **Resid:** Orthopaedic Surgery, Mass Genl Hosp 1991; Surgery, New England Deaconess Hosp 1995; **Fellow:** Nutrition & Metabolism, New England Deaconess Hosp 1993; **Fac Appt:** Asst Clin Prof S, Yale Univ

Miller, Kevin D MD (S) - **Spec Exp:** Hepatobiliary Surgery; **Hospital:** Stamford Hosp (page 971); **Address:** Fairfield Co Surgical Specialists, 1351 Washington Blvd Fl 6 - Ste 601, Stamford, CT 06902; **Phone:** 203-276-5959; **Board Cert:** Surgery 2010; **Med School:** Columbia P&S 1994; **Resid:** Surgery, Beth Israel Deaconess Hosp 1999

Pass, Helen A MD (S) - **Spec Exp:** Breast Cancer; Breast Disease; Nipple Sparing Mastectomy; **Hospital:** Stamford Hosp (page 971); **Address:** Women's Breast Ctr, Fairfield Co Surgical Specialists, 32 Strawberry Hill Ct, Stamford, CT 06902; **Phone:** 203-276-4255; **Board Cert:** Surgery 2003; **Med School:** Univ Mich Med Sch 1987; **Resid:** Surgery, Univ Texas Affil Hosp 1989; Surgery, MedStar Georgetown Univ Hosp 1994; **Fellow:** Surgical Oncology, NCI/NIH 1992

Passeri, Daniel J MD (S) - **Spec Exp:** Cancer Surgery; Laparoscopic Surgery; **Hospital:** St. Vincent's Med Ctr - Bridgeport, Bridgeport Hosp; **Address:** 888 White Plains Rd Fl 2 - Ste 206, Trumbull, CT 06611-4552; **Phone:** 203-459-2666; **Board Cert:** Surgery 2011; **Med School:** Yale Univ 1975; **Resid:** Surgery, Yale-New Haven Hosp 1980

Petrotos, Athanassios MD (S) - **Spec Exp:** Laparoscopic Surgery; Gallbladder Surgery; **Hospital:** Greenwich Hosp (page 970); **Address:** Surgical Specialists of Greenwich, 5 Perryridge Rd Fl 3 - Ste 3-2200, Greenwich, CT 6830; **Phone:** 203-863-4300; **Board Cert:** Surgery 2013; **Med School:** Greece 1991; **Resid:** Surgery, St Lukes-Roosevelt Hosp Ctr 2001

Staradub, Valerie MD (S) - **Spec Exp:** Breast Cancer & Surgery; **Hospital:** Danbury Hosp; **Address:** Breast Ctr/Western CT Medical Grp, 111 Osborne St, Ste 123, Danbury, CT 06810; **Phone:** 203-739-7040; **Board Cert:** Surgery 2008; **Med School:** Tufts Univ 1993; **Resid:** Surgery, MUSC 1999; **Fellow:** Breast Surgery, Lynn Sage Comprehensive Breast Ctr 2000

Ward, Barbara A MD (S) - **Spec Exp:** Breast Cancer; Breast Surgery; Breast Disease; **Hospital:** Greenwich Hosp (page 970); **Address:** Northeast Med Grp, Breast Care Svcs, 77 Lafayette Pl, Ste 302, Greenwich, CT 06830; **Phone:** 203-863-4250; **Board Cert:** Surgery 2011; **Med School:** Temple Univ 1983; **Resid:** Surgery, Yale-New Haven Hosp 1985; Surgery, Yale-New Haven Hosp 1990; **Fellow:** Surgical Oncology, Natl Cancer Inst 1987

Thoracic & Cardiac Surgery

Coady, Michael A MD (T&CS) - **Spec Exp:** Thoracic Aortic Surgery; Heart Valve Surgery; Aneurysm-Thoracic Aortic; **Hospital:** Stamford Hosp (page 971); **Address:** Tully Ctr, Heart & Vascular Inst, 32 Strawberry Hill Ct Fl 4, Stamford, CT 06904; **Phone:** 203-276-4415; **Board Cert:** Surgery 2010; Thoracic & Cardiac Surgery 20; **Med School:** Geo Wash Univ 1993; **Resid:** Surgery, Yale-New Haven Hosp 2000; **Fellow:** Cardiothoracic Surgery, Stanford Univ Hosp & Clin 2003

DiMeo, Albert C MD (T&CS) - **Spec Exp:** Coronary Artery Surgery; Heart Valve Surgery; Robotic Surgery; **Hospital:** St. Vincent's Med Ctr - Bridgeport; **Address:** St Vincent's Medical Ctr, Dept Cardiothoracic Surgery, 2800 Main St, Bridgeport, CT 06606; **Phone:** 203-576-5708; **Board Cert:** Surgery 2004; Thoracic Surgery 2006; **Med School:** Univ Pennsylvania 1998; **Resid:** Surgery, NY Presby Hosp 2002; **Fellow:** Thoracic Surgery, NY Presby Hosp 2004

Ebright, Michael I MD (T&CS) - **Spec Exp:** Lung Cancer; Esophageal Cancer; **Hospital:** Stamford Hosp (page 971); **Address:** Stamford Hosp, 166 W Broad St, Ste 104, Stamford, CT 06902; **Phone:** 203-276-4404; **Board Cert:** Surgery 2005; Thoracic Surgery 2009; **Med School:** NYU Sch Med 1997; **Resid:** Surgery, Univ MD Med Ctr 2004; Cardiothoracic Surgery, Univ MD Med Ctr 2006; **Fellow:** Thoracic Surgery, Meml Sloan Kettering Cancer Ctr 2007; **Fac Appt:** Asst Prof TS, Boston Univ

Feng, William C MD (T&CS) - **Spec Exp:** Cardiovascular Surgery; **Hospital:** Stamford Hosp (page 971); **Address:** Stamford Hosp, Heart & Vascular Inst, 32 Strawberry Hill Ct Fl 4, Stamford, CT 06902; **Phone:** 203-276-4415; **Board Cert:** Thoracic Surgery 2010; **Med School:** Brown Univ 1982; **Resid:** Surgery, UAB Hosp 1987; **Fellow:** Cardiothoracic Surgery, Rhode Island Hosp 1989

Lettera, James V MD (T&CS) - **Spec Exp:** Esophageal Surgery; Aneurysm-Aortic; Vascular Surgery; Peripheral Vascular Disease; **Hospital:** Bridgeport Hosp, St. Vincent's Med Ctr - Bridgeport; **Address:** CT Vascular & Thoracic Surgical Assocs, 501 Kings Hwy E, Ste 112, Fairfield, CT 06825; **Phone:** 203-382-1900; **Board Cert:** Thoracic Surgery 2014; **Med School:** Georgetown Univ 1977; **Resid:** Surgery, St Vincent's Hosp Med Ctr 1982; Thoracic Surgery, Jackson Meml Hosp 1984

Squitieri, Rafael P MD (T&CS) - **Spec Exp:** Robotic Surgery; Aneurysm-Aortic; Maze Procedure for Atrial Fibrillation; Heart Valve Surgery; **Hospital:** St. Vincent's Med Ctr - Bridgeport; **Address:** St Vincent's Medical Ctr, Dept Cardiothoracic Surgery, 2800 Main St, Bridgeport, CT 06606; **Phone:** 203-576-5708; **Board Cert:** Thoracic Surgery 2013; **Med School:** Mount Sinai Sch Med 1993; **Resid:** Surgery, Morristown Meml Hosp 1998; **Fellow:** Thoracic Surgery, Mt Sinai Med Ctr 2001

Waters, Paul F MD (T&CS) - **Spec Exp:** Lung Cancer; Esophageal Surgery; Thoracic Cancers; Esophageal Cancer; **Hospital:** Greenwich Hosp (page 970); **Address:** 77 Lafayette Pl, Ste 302, Greenwich, CT 06830; **Phone:** 203-863-4341; **Board Cert:** Surgery 2004; **Med School:** Univ Toronto 1974; **Resid:** Surgery, Univ Toronto Med Ctr 1979; Thoracic Surgery, Univ Toronto Med Ctr 1980; **Fellow:** Esophageal Surgery, Univ Chicago Hosps 1981

Urology

Hennessy, William T MD (U) - **Spec Exp:** Pediatric Urology; Urologic Cancer; **Hospital:** Danbury Hosp; **Address:** Urology Assocs of Danbury, 51-53 Kenosia Ave, Danbury, CT 6810; **Phone:** 203-748-0330; **Board Cert:** Urology 1982; **Med School:** Georgetown Univ 1976; **Resid:** Urology, Hosp Univ Penn 1980; **Fellow:** Pediatric Urology, Chldns Hosp 1982; Urologic Oncology, Meml Sloan-Kettering Cancer Ctr 1982

Muldoon, Lawrence D MD (U) - **Spec Exp:** Bladder Cancer; Kidney Cancer; Kidney Stones; Prostate Disease; **Hospital:** St. Vincent's Med Ctr - Bridgeport, Bridgeport Hosp; **Address:** Greater Bridgeport Urology, 425 Post Rd Fl 2, Fairfield, CT 06824; **Phone:** 203-254-1576; **Board Cert:** Urology 2012; **Med School:** Northwestern Univ 1984; **Resid:** Surgery, Univ Hosps 1987; Urology, Univ Hosps 1990

Nurzia, Michael J MD (U) - **Spec Exp:** Prostate Cancer; Prostate Disease; Bladder Cancer; Kidney Stones; **Hospital:** Stamford Hosp (page 971), Greenwich Hosp (page 970); **Address:** 166 W Broad St, Ste 404, Stamford, CT 06902; **Phone:** 203-356-9391 x10; **Board Cert:** Urology 2007; **Med School:** Mount Sinai Sch Med 1999; **Resid:** Urology, UMDNJ-RW Johnson Med Ctr 2005

Ranta, Jeffrey A MD (U) - **Spec Exp:** Prostate Cancer; Bladder Cancer; Kidney Stones; **Hospital:** Greenwich Hosp (page 970); **Address:** Greenwich Urological Assocs, 49 Lake Ave, Ste 201, Greenwich, CT 06830; **Phone:** 203-869-1285; **Board Cert:** Urology 2014; **Med School:** Georgetown Univ 1979; **Resid:** Surgery, Georgetown Univ Hosp 1981; Urology, Lahey Clin 1984

Santarosa, Richard P MD (U) - **Spec Exp:** Prostate Cancer; Prostate Disease; Bladder Cancer; Minimally Invasive Urologic Surgery; **Hospital:** Stamford Hosp (page 971), Greenwich Hosp (page 970); **Address:** 166 W Broad St, Ste 404, Stamford, CT 06902; **Phone:** 203-356-9391 x11; **Board Cert:** Urology 2007; **Med School:** Univ Rochester 1989; **Resid:** Surgery, Columbia-Presby Med Ctr 1991; Urology, Columbia-Presby Med Ctr 1995; **Fellow:** Neurourology, Columbia-Presby Med Ctr 1996

Serels, Scott R MD (U) - **Spec Exp:** Urology-Female; Pelvic Organ Prolapse Repair; Incontinence-Male & Female; Voiding Dysfunction; **Hospital:** Norwalk Hosp; **Address:** Urology Assocs of Norwalk, 12 Elmcrest Terr, Norwalk, CT 06850; **Phone:** 203-853-4200; **Board Cert:** Urology 2013; Female Pelvic Medicine & Reconstuctive Surgery 2013; **Med School:** NYU Sch Med 1992; **Resid:** Urology, Montefiore Med Ctr 1998; **Fellow:** Female Pelvic Medicine & Reconstuctive Surgery, Cleveland Clinic 1999

Viner, Nicholas A MD (U) - **Spec Exp:** Prostate Cancer; Kidney Stones; Bladder Cancer; Vasectomy; **Hospital:** Bridgeport Hosp, St. Vincent's Med Ctr - Bridgeport; **Address:** Urological Assocs of Bridgeport, 160 Hawley Ln, Ste 002, Trumbull, CT 66116058; **Phone:** 203-375-3456; **Board Cert:** Urology 1977; **Med School:** Vanderbilt Univ 1968; **Resid:** Surgery, Greenwich Hosp 1970; Urology, Vanderbilt Univ Hosp 1974

Vascular & Interventional Radiology

Hodges, Laura J MD (VIR) - **Spec Exp:** Uterine Fibroid Embolization; **Hospital:** Greenwich Hosp (page 970); **Address:** Greenwich Hospital, Dept Radiology, 5 Perryridge Rd, Greenwich, CT 06830; **Phone:** 203-863-3042; **Board Cert:** Diagnostic Radiology 1999; Vascular & Interventional Radiology 2012; **Med School:** Albert Einstein Coll Med 1994; **Resid:** Diagnostic Radiology, Yale-New Haven Hosp 1999; **Fellow:** Vascular & Interventional Radiology, NY-Presby/Cornell Med Ctr 2000

Sandhu, Fatejeet MD (VIR) - **Spec Exp:** Interventional Radiology; **Hospital:** Danbury Hosp; **Address:** Danbury Radiology Assocs, 24 Hospital Ave, Danbury, CT 06810; **Phone:** 203-739-7532; **Board Cert:** Diagnostic Radiology 1991; Vascular & Interventional Radiology 2006; **Med School:** Emory Univ 1986; **Resid:** Diagnostic Radiology, UCSF Med Ctr 1991; **Fellow:** Body Imaging, UCSF Med Ctr 1992; Interventional Radiology, Emory Univ Hosp 1993

Strauss, Edward B MD (VIR) - **Spec Exp:** Aneurysm-Abdominal Aortic; Thrombolytic Therapy; **Hospital:** Norwalk Hosp; **Address:** Norwalk Hosp, Radiology, 34 Maple St, Norwalk, CT 06856-3894; **Phone:** 203-852-2715; **Board Cert:** Diagnostic Radiology 1983; Nuclear Radiology 1984; Vascular & Interventional Radiology 2005; **Med School:** Yale Univ 1979; **Resid:** Diagnostic Radiology, Yale-New Haven Hosp 1983; **Fellow:** Nuclear Medicine, Yale-New Haven Hosp 1984; Vascular & Interventional Radiology, Yale-New Haven Hosp 1985

Vascular Surgery

Dietzek, Alan M MD (VascS) - **Spec Exp:** Aneurysm-Aortic; Minimally Invasive Vascular Surgery; Arterial Bypass Surgery-Leg; Carotid Artery Surgery; **Hospital:** Danbury Hosp; **Address:** 41 Germantown Rd, Ste 101, Danbury, CT 06810; **Phone:** 203-794-5680; **Board Cert:** Vascular Surgery 2009; **Med School:** Loyola Univ-Stritch Sch Med 1983; **Resid:** Surgery, LI Jewish Med Ctr 1988; **Fellow:** Vascular Surgery, Montefiore Med Ctr 1990; **Fac Appt:** Clin Prof S, Univ VT Coll Med

Gagne, Paul J MD (VascS) - **Spec Exp:** Endovascular Surgery; Aneurysm-Abdominal Aortic; Carotid Artery Surgery; Vein Disorders; **Hospital:** Norwalk Hosp, Greenwich Hosp (page 970); **Address:** Southern CT Vascular Ctr, 85 Old Kings Hwy N, Darien, CT 06820; **Phone:** 203-299-1699; **Board Cert:** Vascular Surgery 2005; **Med School:** NYU Sch Med 1986; **Resid:** Surgery, NYU Med Ctr 1991; **Fellow:** Peripheral Vascular Surgery, UAMS Med Ctr 1995

Huribal, Marsel MD (VascS) - **Spec Exp:** Endovascular Surgery; Aneurysm-Aortic; Vein Disorders; **Hospital:** Bridgeport Hosp, St. Vincent's Med Ctr - Bridgeport; **Address:** Southern CT Vascular Ctr, 495 Hawley Ln, Ste 2A, Stratford, CT 06614; **Phone:** 203-375-2861; **Board Cert:** Vascular Surgery 2008; **Med School:** Amer Univ Caribbean 1987; **Resid:** Surgery, Bridgeport Hosp 1994; **Fellow:** Vascular Surgery, Millard Filmore Hosp 1996; **Fac Appt:** Asst Clin Prof VascS, Yale Univ

Marsan, Ben U MD (VascS) - **Spec Exp:** Peripheral Vascular Disease; Vein Disorders; Aneurysm-Aortic; Endovascular Surgery; **Hospital:** Norwalk Hosp, Bridgeport Hosp; **Address:** Southern CT Vascular Ctr, 495 Hawley Ln, Ste 2A, Stratford, CT 06614; **Phone:** 203-375-2861; **Board Cert:** Vascular Surgery 2009; **Med School:** Oregon Hlth & Sci Univ 1989; **Resid:** Surgery, Flushing Hosp 1995; **Fellow:** Vascular Surgery, SUNY Buffalo Affil Hosp 1997

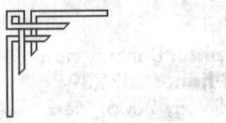

The Best in American Medicine
www.CastleConnolly.com

SECTION FOUR

Centers of Excellence

Addiction Psychiatry

PSYCHIATRY

NYU Langone's psychiatry team is dedicated to improving the health and well-being of patients by delivering peerless psychiatric services and care. NYU Langone is home to some of the nation's most respected clinical psychiatrists and psychologists, with specialties in psychoanalysis, psychopharmacology, behavioral therapy, child psychiatry, geriatric psychiatry and neuropsychiatry. We specialize in the following areas:

Child and Adolescent Psychiatry

Since 1997, the Child Study Center has treated thousands of children from around the world at its Faculty Group Practices in Manhattan and satellite clinical campuses in New Jersey and Long Island. Through its website, www.AboutOurKids.org, and through professional education programs, parents and practitioners are provided with the tools and knowledge needed to promote children's mental health. We specialize in Anxiety and Mood Disorders, Attention Deficit Hyperactivity and Behavior Disorders, Autism, Asperger's Syndrome and Communication Disorders, Learning Disorders, Tics and Tourette Disorder and more.

Adult Inpatient Services

The inpatient services unit combines comprehensive diagnostic assessment and treatment, including psychopharmacology, neuropsychology, psychotherapies and ECT.

Adult Outpatient Psychiatry

The outpatient psychiatry program provides expert treatment to individuals suffering from a broad range of mental disorders and emotional problems, including anxiety, depression (including treatment-resistant depression), manic-depression, reproductive psychiatry, attention-deficit hyperactivity disorder, eating disorders and schizophrenia.

Post-Traumatic Stress Disorder

We offer assessment and treatment of PTSD for victims of sexual and physical assault, natural disasters, terrorism and combat trauma. Treatment includes cognitive behavioral therapy and strategies for the prevention of insomnia, stress, anxiety and depression. Our Steven and Alexandra Cohen Military Family Clinic provides compassionate mental healthcare for veterans and their extended family members. The Steven and Alexandra Cohen Veterans Center is dedicated to improving diagnosis and treatment of PTSD and TBI through research.

Memory Impairment

The Pearl S. Barlow Center for Memory Evaluation and Treatment specializes in treating patients with memory impairments caused by neurological, psychological and physical ailments, as well as memory issues resulting from medication side effects, anxiety, depression and the effects of normal aging from illnesses like Alzheimer's disease.

Adolescent Medicine

HASSENFELD CHILDREN'S HOSPITAL

Hassenfeld Children's Hospital (HCH) is a full-service specialty children's hospital encompassing all children's health services at NYU Langone Medical Center. At HCH, newborns, children, adolescents and young adults receive the most comprehensive and advanced care possible from a team of pediatricians and pediatric specialists across more than 30 medical and surgical disciplines. With more than 150 full-time pediatric specialists, as well as pediatric nurses, child life specialists and social workers, Hassenfeld Children's Hospital is uniquely equipped to provide innovative pediatric subspecialty care in a highly personalized manner.

Child- and Family-Centered Care

Integral to the care we provide is a myriad of support services for children and their families. We recognize that the best outcomes are achieved when the child's family is actively involved in every step of care. For that reason, our trained specialists address the needs of not just the patient, but of parents and siblings through ongoing education and communication.

Our pediatric specialties include:

Anesthesiology

Cardiology

Cardiothoracic Surgery

Child and Adolescent Psychiatry
and Psychology/Child Study Center

Critical Care

Dermatology

Developmental and Behavioral Pediatrics

Emergency Medicine

Endocrinology

Epilepsy

Gastroenterology

Genetics

Hematology/Oncology

Infectious Diseases

Neonatology

Nephrology

Neurosurgery

Neurology

Ophthalmology

Orthopaedic Surgery

Otolaryngology

Pathology

Pulmonology

Radiology

Reconstructive and Plastic Surgery

Rehabilitation

Rheumatology

Surgery

Urology

Arthritis and
Orthopaedic Surgery

ORTHOPAEDIC SURGERY

The **Department of Orthopaedic Surgery** at NYU Langone Medical Center continues to be recognized as a national leader, **ranked #4 nationwide in *U.S. News & World Report's* 2014-2015 "Best Hospitals" survey.** Expert physicians combine extensive experience with cutting-edge research and technology to address bone and joint problems that affect a patient's ability to function. The department provides care at NYU Langone's premier outpatient facility, the Center for Musculoskeletal Care, as well as at the Hospital for Joint Diseases, our internationally-renowned inpatient musculoskeletal hospital. The clinical expertise of our world-class orthopaedic surgeons represents the full range of subspecialty areas including Adult Reconstructive, Sports Medicine and Primary Care Sports Medicine, Spine, Shoulder & Elbow, Foot & Ankle, Hand Surgery, Trauma & Fracture, Orthopaedic Oncology, and Pediatric Orthopaedics; additional areas of focus include minimally-invasive surgery and robotic-assisted joint replacement.

The department also features a number of specialized orthopaedic patient care centers:

Joint Replacement Center physicians are experts in knee, hip and shoulder replacements, complex joint revisions, and minimally invasive surgeries, conducting 3,000+ procedures annually.

The Hip Center evaluates and treats developmental, traumatic, and degenerative hip disorders and specializes in the cutting-edge, minimally invasive anterior total hip replacement technique.

The Joint Preservation and Arthritis Center is dedicated to operative and non-operative treatment of joint problems, aiming to reduce symptoms, restore function and delay the onset of degenerative arthritis and potential need for an eventual joint replacement.

The Spine Center specializes in spine disorders, including lower back and neck pain, scoliosis, osteoporosis and complex spine problems. The Center performs minimally invasive spinal fusions and was one of the first in the country to successfully perform artificial disc implantation.

The Bone Healing Center evaluates and treats problem fractures and are leaders in technologies and procedures to help patients facing a long and difficult recovery from complex fracture reconstruction or fracture healing problems.

Harkness Center for Dance Injuries offers many subsidized and free services for dancers, including clinics staffed by orthopaedists and dance physical therapists. The Center also offers state-of-the-art rehabilitation technology and free injury prevention screenings and lectures.

The Diabetes Foot and Ankle Center focuses on the prevention and recurrence of foot and ankle problems associated with complications of diabetes.

The Orthopaedic Immediate Care Center ("i-Care"), New York City's only walk-in orthopaedic clinic, uses state-of-the-art diagnostic equipment to evaluate and treat adults with hand and foot injuries, hip, arm or leg fractures, dislocation or joint injury, sprains, and bone or joint infection.

The Occupational and Industrial Orthopaedic Center (OIOC) provides clinical, educational, research and consulting services in the prevention and treatment of musculoskeletal injuries and disorders that arise from work or the work environment.

550 First Avenue (*at 31st Street*)
New York, NY 10016
www.nyulangone.org
Physician Referral: **888-7-NYU-MED** (*888-769-8633*)

RHEUMATOLOGY

Rheumatologists at NYU Langone Medical Center are dedicated to the diagnosis and treatment of patients with rheumatic illnesses, particularly autoimmune diseases. *U.S. News and World Report* **has repeatedly recognized the Division of Rheumatology as one of the best in the country, ranking #6 nationwide in the 2014-2015 "Best Hospitals" survey.** The division provides care at NYU Langone's premier outpatient facility, the Center for Musculoskeletal Care; the internationally-renowned, inpatient Hospital for Joint Diseases; and at the medical center's Tisch Hospital.

Arthritis and Autoimmunity: We offer a comprehensive program for the prevention, diagnosis and treatment of all rheumatologic conditions. Patients also have access to complete rheumatologic evaluations, orthopaedic and neurological consultative services, and participation in clinical trials using the most advanced interventional therapies, highly sophisticated diagnostic testing, and complementary medicine.

Behçet's Syndrome: We have the largest North American Behçet's Center for research and the evaluation and treatment of patients with Behçet's Syndrome, a disease that involves inflammation of the blood vessels.

Biological Treatment: Biological treatments for inflammatory arthritis, rheumatoid arthritis, lupus, psoriatic arthritis, vasculitis, and osteoporosis are administered by the Medical Center's infusion centers.

Lupus: The Center for Lupus Care and Research is devoted to the treatment and research of patients with this autoimmune disease. Patients have access to world renowned specialists in lupus, lupus and pregnancy, and related sub-specialties.

Osteoporosis: We offer comprehensive care for the prevention, evaluation and treatment of osteoporosis, including state-of-the art bone densitometers, a range of advanced drug therapies, and programs in balance training and exercise.

Psoriatic Arthritis: Patients at the Psoriatic Arthritis Center, a collaborative effort with the Department of Dermatology, are seen by both a rheumatologist and dermatologist who specialize in psoriasis and psoriatic arthritis.

We are also leaders in rheumatology research, focusing on the study of drugs, drug delivery systems and protocols, and the roles genes play in the development and treatment of rheumatic diseases, positioning us at the forefront of basic science and translational research, personalized medicine and the genetics of rheumatic diseases. The Peter D. Seligman Center for Advanced Therapeutics, renowned for breakthrough research in arthritis and Systematic Lupus Erythematosus, conducts clinical studies using a wide variety of newly developed therapies.

The Best in American Medicine
www.CastleConnolly.com

Breast Disease

NYU Langone Medical Center
550 First Avenue, New York, NY 10016
www.nyulangone.org

Laura and Isaac Perlmutter Cancer Center
160 East 34th Street, New York, NY 10016

**The Stephen D. Hassenfeld Children's Center
for Cancer and Blood Disorders**
160 East 32nd Street, New York, NY 10016

LAURA AND ISAAC PERLMUTTER CANCER CENTER

Formerly NYU Cancer Institute, the Laura and Isaac Perlmutter Cancer Center is an NCI-designated cancer center providing personalized patient care that is compassionate and state-of-the-art. The doctors and researchers work together to develop innovative therapies for patients. The Center is world-renowned for excellence in cancer-focused research, personalized care, education and community outreach. Its mission is to discover the origins of human cancer and to use that knowledge to eradicate the personal and societal burden of cancer in our community, the nation and the world. For more information about our expert physicians, call 1.888.769.8633.

Patient-Focused Setting
The Center and its multidisciplinary team of experts provide access to the latest treatment options and clinical trials, along with a variety of programs in cancer risk reduction/prevention, screening, diagnostics, genetic counseling and supportive services. In addition, the Center emphasizes the importance of a holistic approach involving integrative care, psychosocial support, survivorship, supportive oncology, and palliative care. In addition to our principal outpatient facility at 160 East 34th Street, services are also available at our Ambulatory Care Center on 38th Street in Manhattan; Rego Park, NY; and Lake Success, NY.

Renowned Expertise
Laura and Isaac Perlmutter Cancer Center brings together experts from a variety of disciplines to create collaborative research endeavors and clinical care teams. Our teams are highly skilled in minimally invasive techniques along with video-assisted and robotic surgery. We have created special programs to treat diseases such as breast cancer, brain cancer, melanoma, GI cancer, prostate cancer, hematologic malignancies, sarcoma, and lung cancer. We also continue to focus on translational programs in cancer healthcare disparities; molecularly targeted as well as immune- and stem-cell-based therapies; and the cell signaling pathways involved in cancer.

A Translational Approach
Our scientists and researchers excel in uncovering how cancer develops at the molecular level, and how we can harness that knowledge to reduce the risk of cancer and treat the disease.

Stephen D. Hassenfeld Children's Center for Cancer and Blood Disorders
As part of Hassenfeld Children's Hospital, the center is a leading pediatric outpatient facility for the treatment of childhood cancers and blood diseases. Its unique interdisciplinary and family-centered approach combines the most advanced medical treatments with psychosocial and emotional support services for young patients and their families.

Cancer Care

Where Life Continues

CALVARY HOSPITAL
1740 Eastchester Road
Bronx, NY 10461
Tel: (718) 518-2000
www.calvaryhospital.org

PALLIATIVE CARE INSTITUTE
Calvary's Teaching and Research Arm

The mission of the Palliative Care Institute (PCI), which was founded in 1985, is to transmit, through research and education, Calvary's competence in the care of patients with advanced disease. To date, we have welcomed healthcare professionals from more than 30 countries.

Each year, we train more than 800 medical students, residents, and fellows in palliative care. This includes formalized palliative care observership rotations for residency and fellowship programs throughout the New York area, including New York Medical College, Memorial Sloan Kettering Cancer Center, Mount Sinai School of Medicine, and State University of New York Health Science Center at Brooklyn.

A Model for Excellent Care

Calvary earned a reputation for skillful and compassionate control of patients' symptoms long before palliative and hospice care became popular disciplines.

In 2005, the National Cancer Institute designated Calvary an "international center for training in palliative care" and an alliance was formed between the NCI, Calvary Hospital, and the Middle East Cancer Consortium. Through this alliance, physicians and nurses from Israel, Jordan, Cyprus, Turkey, Egypt, and the Palestinian Authority are sent to Calvary to learn palliative care and increase access to palliative care throughout the Middle East.

Wound Care

The PCI directs Calvary Hospital's Center for Curative and Palliative Wound Care, dedicated to the treatment of complex, intractable wounds related to diabetes, cancer, peripheral vascular disease, and other disorders. For more information about our outstanding wound care services, call (718) 518-2577.

Research Initiatives

The PCI conducts research focusing on wound care, the psychological and emotional impact of terminal illness on patients and families, pain management, and ethical issues concerning end-of-life care.

> *For more information about*
> *Calvary's Palliative Care Institute,*
> *please call (718) 518-2147.*

John Theurer Cancer Center
at Hackensack University Medical Center

92 Second Street, Hackensack, NJ, 07601 • 551-996-5900
www.jtcancercenter.org

AT JOHN THEURER CANCER CENTER, our mission is your life. We are ranked among the top 50 cancer centers in the nation and number one in New Jersey due to our strength in oncology and promise to the patient community to provide the best possible patient outcomes through access to new medications and technology. Our patients challenge us each year to be better and we are undertaking more personalized treatment approaches to ensure that their individual needs are met. Prevention, treatment, and research advances continue to grow exponentially. We are not only keeping up with the change of pace, we are at the forefront of providing tomorrow's treatment today by:

- ✦ Taking multidisciplinary care to a new level with teams of disease-specific experts under one roof
- ✦ Delivering personalized medicine focused on novel therapies, participatory treatment, predictive measures and preventive care
- ✦ Advancing research through biomarker-driven clinical trials and translational research
- ✦ Providing holistic care that includes a wide range of complementary services important to the wellbeing of our patients that can be easily integrated into their care
- ✦ Creating a comforting environment in a new high-tech, high-touch building

We believe our model is the next step towards the future of patient care, changing the cancer care experience one patient at a time.

Innovative Care in a Patient-Centered Environment
At our center, we believe in treating the whole human. It is important to lead a healthy lifestyle during and after treatment. To this extent, we offer complimentary yoga classes, fitness classes, interactive nutrition classes in the Cooking Studio, art workshops, and a patient resource librarian to help patients find credible health information online.

Specialized Practices for Cancer
We are comprised of 14 specialized divisions and Radiation Oncology experts. Division chiefs are supported by medical, research, nursing, nutrition, and psychosocial support for more advanced, focused care.

- ✦ Blood and Marrow Stem Cell Transplantation
- ✦ Breast Oncology Division
- ✦ Gastrointestinal Oncology Division
- ✦ Geriatric Oncology Division
- ✦ Gynecologic Oncology Division
- ✦ Head and Neck Oncology Division
- ✦ Leukemia Division
- ✦ Lymphoma Division
- ✦ Multiple Myeloma Division
- ✦ Neurological Oncology Division
- ✦ Radiation Oncology Department
- ✦ Skin & Sarcoma Division
- ✦ Thoracic Oncology Division
- ✦ Urologic Oncology Division

Extraordinary Means Cutting Edge Research
Innovation is the backbone of John Theurer Cancer Center. Our doctors currently participate in over 280 bio-marker driven clinical trials to bring novel therapies to the patients of the center which is essentially, the ability to receive tomorrow's treatments today. Our dedicated Drug Discovery and Phase I Unit works closely with industry, the National Cancer Institute-National Institutes of Health (NCI-NIH) and other academic institutions to expand the Phase I portfolio for our patients.

For more information about the Regional Cancer Center, call 877-HOLY-NAME. Please mention "Castle Connolly Guide."

Holy Name Medical Center
Regional Cancer Center

718 Teaneck Road
Teaneck, NJ 07666
877-HOLY-NAME
(465-9626)
holyname.org

Holy Name Medical Center's Regional Cancer Center offers leading-edge diagnosis, staging and treatment services for people with cancer. Holy Name's outstanding team of board-certified specialists cares for patients in an environment that promotes personalized service and ready access to multiple disciplines. The Regional Cancer Center is accredited by the American College of Radiology, the American Society for Radiation Oncology, and the American College of Surgeons Commission on Cancer as a Comprehensive Community Cancer Program— accreditations that ensure access to a broad spectrum of services, and high-quality patient care, safety and technical standards.

A TEAM APPROACH

Individualized treatment plans are formulated not by a single physician, but with input from medical, radiation and surgical oncologists, pathologists and radiologists; specially trained and certified oncology nurses; and other medical specialists who render care in both outpatient and inpatient settings. State-of-the-art noninvasive technologies, including fusion PET/CT, high-resolution CT, PET, MRI, breast MRI, extremity MRI and low-dose mammography, produce exquisitely detailed images for diagnostic and treatment planning purposes.

PATIENT-CENTERED CARE

Holy Name simplifies the logistics associated with cancer therapy with ready access to services and physicians, minimal waiting, and easy parking. Oncology patients needing emergency care related to their diagnosis are admitted directly to the specialized nursing unit, without the delays associated with first visiting the Emergency Care Center.

The Regional Cancer Center features a one-stop concept with the full range of services located in a single convenient setting. Patients can arrange a consultation with their oncologist, receive radiation treatment or chemotherapy, have imaging procedures, biopsies and other tests, and receive physical rehabilitation. They can meet with the Center's oncology-certified dietitian, take part in a support group or seek the assistance of a social worker. Genetic counselors are available to work with patients and their family members.

Accurate diagnosis and staging + Targeted, precision therapy = Fewer complications, minimal side effects and improved outcomes

- PET and fusion PET/CT
- High-resolution CT and MRI
- Breast MRI
- SPECT imaging
- Low-dose digital mammography
- Robotic-assisted surgery
- Intensity-modulated radiation therapy (IMRT)
- Image-guided radiation therapy (IGRT)
- CT-guided prone breast radiation therapy
- Stereotactic body radiotherapy (SBRT)
- High-dose brachytherapy for prostate
- Stereotactic radiosurgery
- Microsphere embolization for liver
- Radiofrequency ablation
- Clinical research trials
- Supportive care, nutrition and pharmacy services, physical rehabilitation, palliative services, and home care
- Genetic counseling

Cymbrowitz Pavilion
6300 Eighth Avenue, Brooklyn, NY 11220
Phone: 718.765.2500 • Fax: 718.765.2574
Gilbert Rivera Pavilion
745 64th Street, Brooklyn, NY 11220
Phone: 718.765.2500

www.maimonidesmed.org/cancer

Maimonides Cancer Center campus consists of the Lena Cymbrowitz and Gilbert Rivera pavilions. They offer fully integrated, multimodal approach to cancer care that includes prevention, education, screening, diagnostics, treatment, palliative care, clinical research, dietary advice as well as psychological and social services. It receives funding from NIH and the Komen Foundation and is fully accredited with commendation by the Commission on Cance.

Lena Cymbrowitz Pavilion

Radiation Oncology: has the equipment, board certified physicians and medical physicists to provide every patient with state-of-the-art, evidence-based care, with attention to individual needs. Treatments include intensity modulated radiation, image guided radiation, chemoradiation and brachytherapy, all given in an airy, life-affirming environment.

Medical Oncology: provides comprehensive diagnosis; oral drug therapies; intravenous chemotherapy infusions; biological and hormonal therapies; therapies to decrease the side effects of chemotherapy; and pain treatment and supprtive care.

Pediatric Oncology: created with a particular sensitivity to the comfort and needs of children and their families. Provides the most advanced care and symptom control. The Maimonides Child Life Program provides emotional support during treatment

Surgical Oncology: provides minor surgical procedures, as well as innovative surgical techniques such as sentinel node mapping and biopsy, skin/tissue-sparing mastectomy, and nerve-sparing prostatectomy.

Research Center: conducts basic science and genetic research, as well as clinical trials that offer appropriately screened patients, who wish to volunteer, new therapies and medications.

Gilbert Rivera Pavilion

Houses the Maimonides Breast Center in a spa-like, life-affirming environment. The Center provides digital mammography, sonography, computerized interpretation, digital stereotactic biopsies, breast-specific gamma imaging, and treatment plans tailored to each patient. It has a 3T MRI scanner and a genetics counselor is also on-site. The Center is designated a Breast Imaging Center of Excellence by the American College of Radiology and is also accredited by the National Program for Breast Centers.

This year the Cancer Center was designated as "High Performing" by U.S. News & World Report. Our physicians emphasize multimodal care, which means that multiple methods of treatment are available to patients, sometimes simultaneously. Every week, physicians from radiology, surgery, pathology, radiation oncology, and medical oncology meet to discuss patient treatment at our multidisciplinary meetings. The patient's needs, as well as the disease, are considered from many perspectives.

**Maimonides
Medical Center**

1521 Jarrett Place
Bronx, New York 10461
718-862-8840
www.montefiore.org/cancer

Montefiore Einstein Center for Cancer Care

Montefiore Einstein Center for Cancer Care provides the most advanced treatments spanning all modalities for common and rare cancers, while remaining committed to treating the whole person, not just the disease. Ranked regionally and recognized as "high performing" by *U.S. News & World Report* in 2014–2015, the Center utilizes the latest diagnostic and imaging tools, advanced surgical approaches, innovative radiation therapy, and novel medical therapies to deliver world-class care to patients.

The Center for Cancer Care is expanding its reach through its partnership with White Plains Hospital to broaden its offerings to patients in Westchester County. To help detect cancer early, the Center offers low-dose computed tomography (CT) lung cancer screening for those at high risk of lung cancer, and recently launched a colon screening program.

The Center is one of four programs nationwide offering regional therapy for melanoma, sarcoma and peritoneal tumors, as well as isolated hepatic perfusion. It is also one of only a handful of programs on the East Coast using targeted immunotherapies that isolate tumors and protect healthy tissue, and one of just two programs in New York State offering high-dose interleukin-2 therapy for advanced-stage melanoma.

To meet the needs of the region's pediatric population, the Center has partnered with specialists at Children's Hospital at Montefiore (CHAM) to develop robust treatment programs for sickle cell disease, sarcomas, brain tumors and leukemia. CHAM's Blood and Marrow Transplant Program was recently designated a National Marrow Donor Program Transplant Center for Pediatrics.

The Center offers expertise in pain and palliative care, in both inpatient and outpatient settings, to improve patients' ability to tolerate treatments and improve their quality of life. In addition, the Center has added focused expertise in rehabilitative medicine to help reduce side effects and other issues related to cancer treatment. To further demonstrate its commitment to patients' overall well-being, the Center has added a full-time psychiatrist and psychological social worker to its team. Through the Caregiver Support Center, Montefiore provides specialized training and instruction that allows family and friends of cancer patients to assist with their care.

Demonstrating further excellence in care, the Center's Breast Cancer Program was recently granted a three-year/full accreditation designation by the National Accreditation Program for Breast Centers.

The Center for Cancer Care's diverse research portfolio includes more than 200 basic, translational and clinical studies that span the full spectrum of cancer care. These include a National Institutes of Health–funded study of inhaled chemotherapy for tobacco-related lung cancer; trials studying the use of magnetic resonance imaging (MRI)–guided high-intensity ultrasound to destroy bone tumors; a study on the efficacy of a novel nanomedicine for the treatment of advanced-stage lung cancer and other tumors; a National Cancer Institute–funded national study on the benefits of using a unique, targeted therapy following the resection of advanced-stage, pancreatic neuroendocrine tumors. Other ongoing research efforts focus on the use of viral therapies for colon cancer, pain management for sickle cell disease, and improved survival of patients with osteosarcoma.

⊣ NewYork-Presbyterian

Affiliated with Columbia University College of Physicians and Surgeons and Weill Cornell Medical College

A Comprehensive Cancer
Center Designated by the
National Cancer Institute

Herbert Irving Comprehensive
Cancer Center
NewYork-Presbyterian/
Columbia University Medical Center
161 Fort Washington Avenue
New York, NY 10032

Sandra and Edward Meyer Cancer Center at
Weill Cornell Medical College/
Ronald P. Stanton Clinical Cancer Program at
NewYork-Presbyterian/
Weill Cornell Medical Center
525 East 68th Street, New York, NY 10065

1-877-NYP-WELL (1-877-697-9355)   www.nyp.org/cancer

NewYork-Presbyterian Cancer Centers

Innovative cancer treatments. Personalized, compassionate care. Evidence-based medicine. These are the hallmarks of the cancer care available at NewYork-Presbyterian Hospital, where cutting-edge treatment goes beyond state-of-the-art. We treat some 7,500 people who are newly diagnosed with cancer each year.

NewYork-Presbyterian is affiliated with two of the country's top cancer centers: the National Cancer Institute-designated Herbert Irving Comprehensive Cancer Center (one of only three comprehensive NCI-designated cancer centers in New York State) and the Sandra and Edward Meyer Cancer Center at Weill Cornell Medical College/ Ronald P. Stanton Clinical Cancer Program at NewYork-Presbyterian/ Weill Cornell Medical Center. Through a multidisciplinary team approach, we combine the expertise and talents of all of the individuals responsible for a patient's care—surgical, medical, and radiation oncologists, specialized oncology nurses, social workers, and nutritionists— to deliver seamless care in a supportive and healing environment.

Our team cares for patients with the following cancers:
- AIDS-related cancers
- Bladder cancer
- Brain and other nervous system cancers
- Breast cancer
- Colorectal, pancreatic, and other digestive cancers
- Eye cancer
- Gynecologic cancers (ovarian, cervical, endometrial)
- Head and neck cancers (oral, oropharyngeal, laryngeal)
- Kidney cancer
- Lymphomas (Hodgkin's and non-Hodgkin's)
- Leukemia and Myelodysplastic Syndromes
- Liver cancer
- Mesothelioma
- Multiple Myeloma and Amyloidosis
- Pediatric cancers
- Prostate cancer
- Sarcoma
- Thoracic cancers (lung, esophageal, chest wall)

Research underlies everything we do, and sets academic medical centers such as ours apart from other cancer treatment centers. Our scientists and clinical investigators are leading more than 500 clinical trials assessing new cancer management approaches in thousands of patients.

Specialized Cancer Care Includes:

- State-of-the-art tumor genomic analysis available to inform personalized cancer care

- Surgical procedures for breast cancer that result in superior cosmetic outcomes, and evaluation of novel anticancer drugs for women with advanced disease

- Robotic surgery for prostate and gynecologic cancers

- Video-assisted thoracoscopy and lung-sparing surgery for some lung cancers

- Interventional endoscopy and laparoscopic surgery for colorectal and other cancers

- Targeted approaches to brain cancer treatment, including convection-enhanced chemotherapy and stereotactic radiosurgery

- Bone marrow and stem cell transplantation for hematologic cancers

- Combination chemotherapy, targeted anticancer agents, novel drugs available through clinical trials, and highly targeted radiation therapy

NYU Langone Medical Center
550 First Avenue, New York, NY 10016
www.nyulangone.org

Laura and Isaac Perlmutter Cancer Center
160 East 34th Street, New York, NY 10016

**The Stephen D. Hassenfeld Children's Center
for Cancer and Blood Disorders**
160 East 32nd Street, New York, NY 10016

LAURA AND ISAAC PERLMUTTER CANCER CENTER

Formerly NYU Cancer Institute, the Laura and Isaac Perlmutter Cancer Center is an NCI-designated cancer center providing personalized patient care that is compassionate and state-of-the-art. The doctors and researchers work together to develop innovative therapies for patients. The Center is world-renowned for excellence in cancer-focused research, personalized care, education and community outreach. Its mission is to discover the origins of human cancer and to use that knowledge to eradicate the personal and societal burden of cancer in our community, the nation and the world. For more information about our expert physicians, call 1.888.769.8633.

Patient-Focused Setting
The Center and its multidisciplinary team of experts provide access to the latest treatment options and clinical trials, along with a variety of programs in cancer risk reduction/prevention, screening, diagnostics, genetic counseling and supportive services. In addition, the Center emphasizes the importance of a holistic approach involving integrative care, psychosocial support, survivorship, supportive oncology, and palliative care. In addition to our principal outpatient facility at 160 East 34th Street, services are also available at our Ambulatory Care Center on 38th Street in Manhattan; Rego Park, NY; and Lake Success, NY.

Renowned Expertise
Laura and Isaac Perlmutter Cancer Center brings together experts from a variety of disciplines to create collaborative research endeavors and clinical care teams. Our teams are highly skilled in minimally invasive techniques along with video-assisted and robotic surgery. We have created special programs to treat diseases such as breast cancer, brain cancer, melanoma, GI cancer, prostate cancer, hematologic malignancies, sarcoma, and lung cancer. We also continue to focus on translational programs in cancer healthcare disparities; molecularly targeted as well as immune- and stem-cell-based therapies; and the cell signaling pathways involved in cancer.

A Translational Approach
Our scientists and researchers excel in uncovering how cancer develops at the molecular level, and how we can harness that knowledge to reduce the risk of cancer and treat the disease.

Stephen D. Hassenfeld Children's Center for Cancer and Blood Disorders
As part of Hassenfeld Children's Hospital, the center is a leading pediatric outpatient facility for the treatment of childhood cancers and blood diseases. Its unique interdisciplinary and family-centered approach combines the most advanced medical treatments with psychosocial and emotional support services for young patients and their families.

STAMFORD HOSPITAL
Bennett Cancer Center

StamfordHospital.org/cancer

Bennett Cancer Center

Stamford Hospital's Carl & Dorothy Bennett Cancer Center provides compassionate, patient-centered care from diagnosis through post treatment. We are accredited as an Academic Comprehensive Cancer Program and received the outstanding Achievement Award from the American College of Surgeons Commission on Cancer. A multidisciplinary team of physicians, oncology nurses, nurse navigators and radiation therapists, offers advanced surgical, medical and technological services in a warm, caring environment.

Expertise Combined with Comfort
Our physicians' skill, knowledge and expertise are equaled only by their compassion in dealing with our patients. They are represented on the consulting staff of Memorial Sloan-Kettering Cancer Center and teaching faculty of Columbia University College of Physicians and Surgeons. They are also active participants in national research groups. The Center is involved with more clinical trials than any other area hospital.

Genetic Counseling
We offer the only full-time cancer genetic counselor in Fairfield County, ensuring timely delivery of genetic counseling services and superior interaction with other specialists, as well as the most current information in both genetics and oncology.

Treatment Beyond the Disease
We provide chemotherapy and immunotherapy in an outpatient setting, where patients can be treated in private suites with a home-like ambiance or a group room in the company of others. Cancer cases are reviewed by a multidisciplinary team of physicians and staff. This offers patients the benefit of different specialists combining their expertise.

Our Integrative Medicine Program and other support services including the *Transitions: Choices in Recovery* post-treatment survivorship program, offer a wide range of complementary therapies along with stress management, individual, family and group therapy.

Technology that Doesn't Forget Humanity
We are the only hospital in Fairfield and Westchester Counties to offer CyberKnife™ stereoatactic radiosurgery to treat tumors with pinpoint accuracy. Additional technology includes a large bore CT scan for treatment planning and linear accelerator machines with both Intensity Modulated Radiation Therapy and Image-Guided Radiation Therapy. Our diagnostic imaging services include a 64-slice CT scan, ultrasound, nuclear medicine, PET CT and MRI.

Academic and Clinical Affiliations
Stamford Hospital is an affiliate of the New York–Presbyterian Healthcare System and a major teaching affiliate of the Columbia University College of Physicians & Surgeons.

Accreditation
The Joint Commission

Beds
305

Sponsorship
Voluntary, Not-for-Profit

For a Physician Referral or more information, please call 1.877.233.9355 or visit StamfordHospital.org /doctor.

Stamford Hospital
30 Shelburne Road
Stamford, CT 06902
203.276.1000

StamfordHospital.org

Trinitas Regional Medical Center

TRINITAS COMPREHENSIVE CANCER CENTER

225 WILLIAMSON STREET | ELIZABETH, NEW JERSEY 07207
PH 908.994.8000 | WWW.TRINITASCANCERCENTER.ORG

TRINITAS CONTINUES ITS AGGRESSIVE PURSUIT OF EXCELLENCE IN CANCER CARE

As just one of eight healthcare facilities in New Jersey to receive the American College of Surgeons National Accreditation Program for Breast Centers (NAPBC), Trinitas Regional Medical Center has been recognized for its voluntary commitment to providing the best in breast cancer diagnosis and treatment and its compliance with established NAPBC standards. Both the Diagnostic Imaging Center and the Trinitas Comprehensive Cancer Center have received this accreditation for cancer diagnosis and cancer care services.

"When the Trinitas Comprehensive Cancer Center opened its doors in 2005, it did so with the commitment to providing superior, compassionate care to those who use our many services," explains Barry Levinson, MD, Medical Director of the center. "We approach each patient with the utmost of care and direct our attention to giving them not only the best care and treatment but also the best quality of life as they survive cancer. The NAPBC accreditation underscores that commitment and encourages us to maintain the very highest standards for our patients."

Located on the main campus of Trinitas Regional Medical Center in Elizabeth, the Center is the home of the most advanced technology available to cancer patients, including the first Trilogy Linear Accelerator for radiation therapy in New Jersey. The Center is also the site of the state's first AccuBoost breast cancer treatment, and the first RapidArc radiotherapy procedure.

A major quality initiative at the Cancer Center involves a system-wide evaluation of the benefits, risks and efficient management of the increasing number of oral oncology drugs that have become available. These drugs offer a more convenient and less invasive treatment option, but they require a new model for patient education, monitoring, communications and support. Trinitas is well ahead of this curve with the development of in-depth 14-step program that features safeguards, intensive follow-up and a comprehensive system of checks and balances.

Support services include: nutrition/dietician services, genetic counseling, fatigue management, complementary therapies and services, social work, lymphedema management, Look Good – Feel Better, Made for Me boutique, art therapy, pet therapy and pain management.

Trinitas was awarded Comprehensive Cancer Program status by the American College of Surgeons' Commission on Cancer. Further, we are an approved Member of the prestigious Radiation Therapy Oncology Group. Our clinical research program gives many patients access to new treatment approaches that might not otherwise be available.

In 2013, Trinitas joined the Philadelphia-based Jefferson Kimmel Cancer Center Network, bringing Jefferson's many treatment studies to the region.

THE VALLEY HOSPITAL
An affiliate of the NewYork-Presbyterian Healthcare System

223 North Van Dien Avenue, Ridgewood, NJ 07450
Phone: 201-447-8000 • www.ValleyHealth.com
www.Facebook.com/ValleyHospital • www.Twitter.com/ValleyHospital

The Daniel & Gloria Blumenthal Cancer Center
Our cancer care experts focus on delivering today's most promising therapies with compassion and dignity. Our multidisciplinary team of board-certified medical, surgical, and radiation oncologists; specialty physicians; Magnet-recognized oncology nurses; and award-winning allied health professionals is dedicated to providing personalized care that meets every person's unique needs and expectations. Our growing clinical and translational research programs offer patients access to new therapies and innovative protocols that are unavailable at other area hospitals. Our outreach educational programs and cancer screenings strive to prevent cancer and/or detect it at an early, treatable stage. Our cancer program has earned six Disease-Specific Care Certifications for healthcare quality from the Joint Commission for colorectal cancer, lung cancer, breast cancer, pancreatic cancer, prostate cancer, and uterine-ovarian cancer, more than any other hospital in the country.

Diagnostic Imaging and Testing
Our state-of-the-art capabilities help physicians detect, stage, and monitor cancer. Our technology includes low-dose CT scanning, MRI, PET scanning, endoscopic ultrasound, endobronchial ultrasound, and digital mammography.

Powerful Therapies
Our Radiation Oncology Department and specialized centers provide all of the latest advanced modalities of radiation therapy to treat numerous cancers. Our Centers of Excellence include our Breast Center, Gamma Knife Center, Lung Cancer Center, Institute for Brain and Spine Surgery, Melanoma and Skin Cancer Center, and Urologic Oncology Center. Our surgical oncologists and other surgical specialists use the robotic daVinci surgical system, laparoscopic techniques, and other minimally invasive options to offer patients gentler procedures with quicker recoveries. Our ambulatory Medical Infusion Center provides a comfortable site for receiving outpatient chemotherapy and other infusion therapies. Our hyperthermic intraperitoneal chemotherapy (HIPEC) program is the only one in New Jersey and one of the largest in the metropolitan area.

Patient- and Family-Centered Care
At The Valley Hospital, we espouse patient- and family-centered care, which recognizes the impact a diagnosis of cancer can have on the entire family and offers services, education, and guidance for all. Our holistic nursing care and integrative medicine therapies support healing of the mind, body and spirit. Support services, such as nutrition counseling, genetic counseling, social work services, pastoral care, psychosocial counseling, rehabilitation therapy, support groups, home care, and educational programs assist patients during and after cancer care and help to improve their quality of life

A Dedication to Research
Our oncology research program endeavors to find answers to the complex questions of how cancer develops, how it behaves, why it mutates, and how it can be stopped or controlled. We are currently undergoing clicnical trials in the areas of brain cancer, breast cancer, gastrointestinal cancer, gynecologic cancer, lung cancer and multiple myeloma.

Cancer Care that is accredited by the American College of Surgeons Commission on Cancer and the American College of Radiology

■ Infusion Center and chemotherapy, including NJ's only hyperthermic intraperitoneal chemotherapy program

■ Image-guided TomoTherapy

■ Intensity-modulated radiation therapy

■ Gamma Knife Center

■ Stereotactic body radiotherapy

■ High-dose-rate after-loading brachytherapy

■ Advanced Gastrointestinal Surgery, Barrett's Esophagus, Breast, Lung, Melanoma and Skin Cancer, and Urologic Oncology Centers

■ Surgical, gynecologic, urologic, and thoracic oncologists

■ Single-port video-assisted thoracic surgery (VATS)

■ Minimally invasive breast oncoplastics surgery

■ Cancer genetics

■ Integrative healing services

■ Holistic nursing care

■ Home care and hospice

The Valley Hospital Daniel & Gloria Blumenthal Cancer Center, 201-634-5707; www.ValleyFightsCancer.com

White Plains Hospital
CANCER PROGRAM
2-4 Longview Avenue, White Plains, NY 10601 (914) 681-2700 www.wphospital.org

As the leading cancer facility in the region, the Cancer Program at White Plains Hospital provides patients with the best and most comprehensive care available in an easily accessible setting. Highly specialized clinicians and advanced technology focus on the diagnosis, care and treatment of many types of cancer including breast, prostate, lung, colorectal, pancreatic, gynecologic, thyroid and blood cancers, among others.

The hospital's Breast Program is accredited by the National Accreditation Program for Breast Centers (NAPBC) of the American College of Surgeons. Initially accredited in 1993, the Cancer Program again earned another three-year accreditation with commendation in 2013 from the American College of Surgeons Commission on Cancer, as well as their Outstanding Achievement Award, a recognition given to only 79 other cancer programs in the United States.

DISTINCTIVE FEATURES

· **Radiology and Women's Imaging** at several locations, including three specifically dedicated to the radiological needs of women- the Breast Imaging Center at the hospital's main campus, the hospital's Imaging Center at New Rochelle and the Women's Imaging Center in Rye Brook, NY

· **Surgery** including advanced thoracic, colorectal, gynecological, minimally invasive and robotic surgery, oncoplastic techniques and nipple-sparing mastectomy.

· **Medical Oncology** utilizing the most advanced technologies and specifically targeted treatments for maximal efficacy and minimization of toxicity.

· **Radiation Oncology** at the Dickstein Cancer Treatment Center using state-of-the-art therapy and expertise from physicians trained at the finest teaching hospitals in the United States.

· **Clinical Navigators** to explain treatments, procedures and side effects and provide assistance with physical, psycho-social and financial services, clinical trials and support resources.

· **Cancer Genetics Program** providing guidance on the nature and consequences of various inherited disorders, the probabilities of developing and transmitting the disorders to offspring, methods of early detection, disease management and coping strategies.

· **Research Studies and Expansive Clinical Trials** offering additional options for patients who may not respond to established treatment protocols.

·**Survivorship Program** dedicated to offering a multitude of services and resources both within the Hospital and in the community from the time of diagnosis of cancer, through treatment and beyond.

White Plains Hospital

For more than 120 years, White Plains Hospital has provided advanced, exceptional health care to the people of Westchester County and surrounding areas. Nearly 200,000 patients visit the Hospital each year for a variety of services including emergency care, internal medicine, maternity and high-risk obstetrics, minimally invasive surgery, orthopedics, oncology and cardiac care, among others.

The Hospital's capabilities for diagnosis and treatment, including state-of-the-art radiology and laboratory services, are second to none and rival those found at many nearby academic medical centers. These resources are combined with highly individualized care provided by the Hospital's more than 900 affiliated physicians and surgeons, many of whom have trained at the finest medical institutions in the country; and the more than 700 Magnet®- designated nurses with advanced training who provide skilled, compassionate care to their patients, every day.

Cancer Care at Winthrop

General Overview

Winthrop-University Hospital's Cancer Care Program is a regional leader in clinical cancer care, offering a full complement of world-class inpatient and outpatient services for adults and children with cancer. Certified by the national Commission on Cancer, Winthrop's expert multidisciplinary staff of highly trained professionals utilizes high-tech diagnostics in order to provide a broad spectrum of world-class care options that focus on prevention, leading-edge treatment and support services — all tailored to meet the unique, personal needs of each patient — with a deep sense of compassion.

Approaching care from a curative perspective, Winthrop's cancer specialists seek to maximize benefits for patients, while minimizing potential harm from treatment. They collaborate closely through regular, multidisciplinary treatment-planning conferences to secure the most appropriate treatment for each patient following a definitive diagnosis, and to ensure that National Comprehensive Cancer Network guidelines are followed.

Specialty programs and services include:

- A comprehensive Lung Cancer Program, including one of the region's first lung cancer screening programs, utilizing low dose CT scans.
- The largest outpatient Pediatric Oncology Program in Nassau County
- Cutting-edge gynecologic oncology services
- Robotic and minimally invasive treatments for pancreatic cancer
- Multidisciplinary, highly proficient urologic cancer services
- A state-of-the-art multidisciplinary Breast Health Center, recently reaccredited by the National Accreditation Program for Breast Centers (NAPBC), a program administered by the American College of Surgeons, and named as one of the 2014 America's Best Breast Centers by WomenCertified, Inc.
- Radiation Therapy: Consistently recognized, this year Winthrop's Radiation Therapy Department earned a three-year term of accreditation from the American College of Radiology, representing the highest level of quality and safety
- High-level surgical oncology, utilizing the latest robotic technology and techniques
- A new, modern Outpatient Infusion Center and Inpatient Oncology/Hematology Unit
- An exceptionally accurate Pathology Department that utilizes advanced cytogenetic and molecular pathology techniques
- Minimally invasive treatment for gastrointestinal and lung cancers
- Neuro-oncology and neurosurgical services, which specialize in the medical and surgical management of brain, spine and central nervous system tumors

CyberKnife®

Last year, Winthrop-University Hospital treated over 2,100 cancer patients with CyberKnife®, a Stereotactic Body Radiation therapy, making it one of the busiest CyberKnife centers in the world. In the latest step to provide the residents of Manhattan and the entire tri-state region with greater access to Winthrop's leading edge CyberKnife services, Winthrop has opened New York City's first (and only) CyberKnife facility. CyberKnife is a high-tech computer controlled robotic technology with cruise missile-like precision that delivers highly targeted beams of radiation to tumors while sparing healthy tissue, providing hope to patients with tumors and lesions previously considered inoperable or which are not amenable to treatment with conventional radiation due to damaging side effects. CyberKnife is effective for treating a range of cancers including prostate, breast, lung and other cancers.

Cancer Navigator Program

Winthrop's Cancer Navigator Program, the first of its kind on LI, offers individualized assistance to patients, families and caregivers, helping them to move seamlessly through the many diagnostic tests, procedures, physician visits and treatments they face after learning they have cancer. Cancer Navigators are nurses and physician assistants who specialize in the care of people with cancer. Services include reducing or eliminating barriers to care, and paving the way for early and timely screenings and diagnostic tests; educating patients about treatment options; identifying and assisting with accessing financial, legal and community support services; connecting patients and families to support groups; and facilitating access to research trials.

Cancer Center for Kids (CCFK)

Winthrop's Cancer Center for Kids (CCFK) meets the complex challenges of children's cancers and blood disorders with a relentless spirit and dedication to improving the lives of patients and their families. The CCFK is Nassau County's largest outpatient for treating children with cancer and blood disorders. Skilled and compassionate professionals embody the principles of patient and family-centered care. They not only provide comprehensive, sensitive care, but also help families endure some very tough times with support from the moment of diagnosis through intense treatments and long-term follow-up.

Research

As an academic institution, Winthrop is the site of some of the most current clinical trials and research into cancer, ensuring that patients have access to the latest therapies. The Hospital's cancer specialists and researchers are involved in rigorous basic and clinical studies of a wide variety of cancers, including lung cancer, childhood cancers, blood cancers, breast, colorectal and gynecological cancers.

Cardiac Electrophysiology

CARDIAC AND VASCULAR INSTITUTE

The Cardiac and Vascular Institute (CVI) at NYU Langone Medical Center continues to advance new techniques for repairing heart valves, curing heart rhythm disorders, and treating aortic diseases and congestive heart failure. We care for both adults and children. CVI is consistently ranked among the leading heart and heart surgery centers in *U.S. News & World Report's annual 'Best Hospitals'* rankings.

Cardiac Catheterization CVI offers superior catheter-based diagnosis and evaluation of cardiac health. Our laboratory provides a full range of procedures to evaluate, diagnose, and provide treatment options for coronary artery disease and valve conditions, including transcatheter aortic valve replacement (TAVR).

Cardiac Rehabilitation and Prevention The Joan and Joel Smilow Cardiopulmonary Rehabilitation and Prevention Center provides individualized treatment plans through NYU Langone's Rusk Rehabilitation, in a state-of-the-art and comfortable facility.

Cardiac Surgery NYU Langone is a nationally recognized leader in advanced surgical treatments for adult and congenital heart disease. We have world-renowned expertise in minimally invasive mitral valve repair, aortic valve replacement and aortic aneurysm repair, as well as specializing in high-risk and elderly patients.

Cardiology The Leon H. Charney Division of Cardiology is a leader in cardiovascular patient care, biomedical research, and education. We are advancing the field of cardiovascular medicine through a variety of innovative collaborations.

Congenital Heart Disease The pediatric and adult congenital cardiac program treats patients of all ages with inherited and acquired cardiac defects. We have a highly experienced team of specialists in pediatric and adult cardiology, pediatric interventional cardiology, congenital cardiac surgery, neonatal and pediatric cardiac intensive care, pediatric cardiac anesthesiology, nursing, and extracorporeal perfusion.

Heart Failure A multidisciplinary team offers the most advanced care for heart failure including echocardiograms, pacemaker and defibrillator implantations, open heart surgeries, remote monitoring of pulmonary artery pressure, and left ventricular assist devices.

Nuclear Cardiology/Stress The Nuclear Cardiology/Stress Laboratory performs a range of tests that assist cardiologists in the assessment and diagnosis of heart disease.

Vascular Surgery We offer diagnostic and treatment for patients with conditions ranging from arterial aneurysms to deep vein thrombosis, as well as carotid stenosis and limb salvage including minimally invasive vein surgery, endovascular aortic surgery, thoracic aneurysm correction and abdominal aneurysm interventions.

Cardiovascular Disease

HEART & VASCULAR HOSPITAL
HackensackUMC

30 Prospect Avenue, Hackensack, NJ 07601 • 551-996-2000
www.HackensackUMC.org

Opened in 2011, Heart & Vascular Hospital at HackensackUMC is one of America's most comprehensive cardiac and vascular care centers, providing a full-range of state-of-the-art invasive and noninvasive services. This "hospital within a hospital" treats all types of cardiac and vascular diseases performed by a world-class team of nurse practitioners, Magnet®-award winning nurses, technicians, specialized personnel, and more than 140 cardiologists, cardiac surgeons, vascular surgeons, and neuro-interventionalists who provide the highest quality of care.

The Heart & Vascular Hospital offers a Cardiac Rehabilitation and Wellness Center as well as designated floors for post-operative patients and specialty areas, including: Neurology/Stroke Recovery, Congestive Heart Failure, Cardiac ICU, Cardiac Surgery ICU, Cardiac Stepdown Unit, and Same Day Admission Rooms/Recovery.

AWARD-WINNING CARE

The Heart & Vascular Hospital has received the following prestigious awards and accolades:

- Ranked nationally #32 out of more than 700 hospitals in Cardiology & Heart Surgery by *U.S. News & World Report* in 2014-15
- Designation as an Accredited Chest Pain Center from the Society of Chest Pain Centers
- Healthgrades Five-Star Recipient for Treatment of Heart Failure for 12 Years in a Row
- 2014 *Becker's Hospital Review*'s 100 Hospitals With Great Heart Programs
- Received full accreditation with PCI from the Society of Cardiovascular Patient Care (SCPC) for a Full Cycle IV Accreditation – the only hospital in Bergen County to do so.

AWARD-WINNING SERVICES AND PROGRAMS

Hybrid Surgery – The Hybrid Operating Room is one of only a handful of interventional suites in the nation where open or minimally invasive surgical procedures and catheterization can be performed simultaneously.

TAVR – Shortly after it opened, the Hybrid OR was the scene of a procedure that marks a milestone in heart surgery—the transcatheter aortic valve replacement (TAVR). HackensackUMC was the first hospital in northern New Jersey to perform this procedure, and the first in the state to perform this groundbreaking minimally invasive heart valve replacement procedure via transapical delivery.

Stereotaxis Lab – The Heart & Vascular Hospital's Stereotaxis Lab - Northern New Jersey's first - shortens procedures, speeds recovery time, reduces exposure to radiation and helps more patients avoid invasive open heart surgical procedures.

Biplane Angiographic Unit – Our Biplane Angiographic Unit uses a fluoroscopic X-ray machine that images the body's circulatory dynamics from multiple angles to produce virtually unlimited views, which is crucial in obtaining views of critical procedures to treat strokes, aneurysms and brain tumors.

Focus on Patients – The Cardiac Wellness & Rehabilitation program at our Heart & Vascular Hospital is an important resource for area physicians, many of whom refer patients who are at high risk for heart disease or are recovering from heart attacks, cardiac bypass or other cardiovascular procedures.

SPECIFIC PROGRAMS OF EXCELLENCE

In addition to its award-winning cardiovascular care, the Heart & Vascular Hospital is proud to offer the following specific programs of excellence, which distinguish our medical center from the rest:

- Heart Failure Program; Cardiovascular Disease Prevention; Critical Care Medicine; Transcatheter Vascular Surgery Repair; Transcatheter Aortic Valve Replacement; Transcatheter repairs of mitral valve; Minimally Invasive Mitral Valve Repair; and Thoracic Aortic Surgery.

To learn more about our award-winning care at the Heart & Vascular Hospital at HackensackUMC, visit HackensackUMC.org.

For more information about Cardiovascular Services
or for a physician referral, call 877-HOLY-NAME.
Please mention "Castle Connolly Guide."

Holy Name Medical Center
Cardiovascular Services

718 Teaneck Road
Teaneck, NJ 07666
877-HOLY-NAME
(465-9626)
holyname.org

THE HOLY NAME HEALING TRADITION

Holy Name Medical Center's multidisciplinary team of experts provides accurate diagnosis and gender-specific care for the best cardiac outcomes. Our goal is to detect and treat cardiac disease before it becomes life-threatening, and to provide services along a continuum, so that every patient receives the right care at the right time. Prevention initiatives, leading-edge technology, progressive treatments and multi-phase cardiac rehabilitation services—Holy Name puts it all together to reduce risk factors and keep hearts healthy.

FROM DIAGNOSIS TO REHABILITATION

Holy Name's multidisciplinary cardiac team provides optimal quality of care with experts from all aspects of cardiovascular disease management: board-certified cardiologists and interventional cardiologists, neurologists and emergency medicine physicians, specialized registered nurses and exercise physiologists, registered and certified diagnostic technologists, rehabilitation specialists, and a specially trained support staff.

Holy Name is a leader in the newer, through-the-wrist cardiac catheterization. Patients who undergo radial catheterization experience fewer bleeding complications, less pain, quicker recovery and improved outcomes overall.

Most diagnostic tests and many treatment procedures can be accomplished on an outpatient basis, without an overnight stay in the Medical Center. For patients who require hospitalization with specialized care and monitoring following a medical event, the inpatient continuum of care at Holy Name features award-winning intensive care, intermediate care and telemetry units.

A Recognized Expert in Early Intervention

The Joint Commission "Top Performer on Key Quality Measures" in four areas, including heart attack and heart failure

NJ Department of Health High-Performing Hospital in four out of four measures, including heart attack and heart failure

The Joint Commission Advanced Certification—Primary Stroke Center

NJ Department of Health Inpatient Quality Indicators find stroke mortality rate significantly below state rate

Beacon Award for Critical Care Excellence awarded to Intensive Care Unit (ICU) and Telemetry Unit, gold and silver status respectively, by the American Association of Critical-Care Nurses

American Heart Association/American Stroke Association Gold Plus Achievement Award

www.maimonidesmed.org/cardiac

Cardiac Care
Maimonides has been a pioneer in cardiac care for over 100 years. The Heart & Vascular Center offers diagnostic studies and therapeutic treatments, procedures and surgeries. It has been ranked by the Centers for Medicare and Medicaid Services among the few hospitals which have achieved excellent ratings in both heart attack and heart failure patient outcomes.

Cardiology
Headed by Jacob Shani, MD, Cardiology is among the most published and respected in the field. Its many achievements include having led the historic BHAT trials which explored the efficacy of beta blockers. In addition, our Electrophysiology Lab has a superb record of achievement in diagnosing and treating arrhythmias, and our Congestive Heart Failure (CHF) Program is among the most effective in the nation.

Interventional Cardiology
Led by Robert Frankel, MD, numerous therapeutic devices have been developed and implemented here. Close collaboration with the Department of Emergency Medicine ensures that chest pain patients are evaluated immediately and that interventional procedures are used to stop heart attacks in progress. Interventional cardiology at Maimonides is currently ranked #1 in New York State for patient outcomes.

Cardiothoracic Surgery
Cardiothoracic Surgery at Maimonides has an illustrious history, setting a national standard for advances in heart surgery. Under the direction of Greg Ribakove, MD, minimally invasive and heart and valve surgeries, as well as advanced procedures such as LVAD Destination Therapy and TAVR, are offered in state-of-the-art facilities, including a hybrid OR. In collaboration with Electrophysiology, Cardiothoracic Surgery has established an Atrial Fibrillation Center of Excellence.

Historic Moments
- In 1967, the first successful human heart transplant in the nation was performed at Maimonides.
- The intra-aortic balloon pump was developed here in 1970.
- Surgical techniques protecting the spine during cardiothoracic surgery were perfected here in 1982.
- Revolutionary cardiac catheterization devices were invented here in 1992 and 1997.
- Maimonides was the first hospital in the US to implement fully automatic external cardiac defibrillators in 2001.

The latest report from the Centers for Medicare and Medicaid Services indicates that Maimonides Medical Center achieved better-than-expected results in all three categories measured – heart attack, heart failure and pneumonia – a distinction shared by only 26 other hospitals in the U.S.

**Maimonides
Medical Center**

111 East 210th Street
Bronx, New York 10467
718-920-7000
www.montefiore.org/heart

Montefiore Einstein Center for Heart and Vascular Care

The Montefiore Einstein Center for Heart and Vascular Care's proud tradition of innovation and clinical excellence has made it a national leader in adult and pediatric cardiology and cardiovascular surgery. The expertise of its physicians and surgeons spans the full spectrum of cardiovascular care—from novel therapies and interventional treatments to intricate, lifesaving procedures.

The Center's Heart Valve Repair Program offers cutting-edge treatments for complex valve conditions, including the butterfly procedure for mitral valve regurgitation and transcatheter aortic valve replacement (TAVR) for patients with severe aortic stenosis and at high risk for surgery. The Center's risk-adjusted operative mortality rate for mitral valve repair is among the best in the nation. Montefiore is one of only 13 centers nationwide offering the Perceval S Sutureless Heart Valve, which reduces patient risk by significantly reducing bypass time.

Through the Center's Heart Failure Program, adults and pediatric patients receive advanced medical and surgical interventions—including ventricular assist devices (VADs) and heart transplantation. In 2013, the Center performed 22 heart transplants (14 adult and eight pediatric) and implanted 34 VADs. Its one-year survival rate continues to be among the best in the nation, at 97 percent for adults and 100 percent for children. The New York State Department of Health has recognized the Center as a leader among the state's transplant/heart failure programs in achieving appropriate treatment measures and low mortality rates.

In the area of cardiac interventions, the Center possesses an exceptionally low mortality rate and an expanded team that includes renowned electrocardiologists, electrophysiologists and structural interventionalists.

The Center performed more than 9,000 cardiac procedures in 2013 and once again earned the Society of Thoracic Surgeons' prestigious "three-star" ranking for its commitment to surgical excellence, placing Montefiore among the nation's top open-heart surgery programs.

The Center is a leader in basic, translational and clinical research and is supported by more than $10 million in grants, including funding through the National Institutes of Health/National Heart, Lung, and Blood Institute's Cardiothoracic Surgical Trials Network for the 10th consecutive year. The Center is participating in prominent trials exploring the use of stem cells in heart failure patients. Through the LARIAT® trial, a nonsurgical method of treating atrial fibrillation, the Center is providing atrial fibrillation patients with additional options for preventing stroke. Montefiore's Goal to Reduce Readmissions at Montefiore (GRRAM) program exemplifies its commitment to reducing readmission. Within three months of implementing GRRAM, heart patient readmission rates dropped 5 percent. Montefiore is also one of 15 hospitals nationwide chosen to pioneer the American College of Cardiology's Patient Navigator Program to further reduce heart failure.

NEW YORK METHODIST HOSPITAL

THE INSTITUTE FOR CARDIOLOGY AND CARDIAC SURGERY

New York Methodist Hospital
506 Sixth Street, Brooklyn, N.Y. 11215
Phone 866 84-HEART (866 844-3278)
http://www.nym.org

SPECIALISTS AND MEDICAL SERVICES

The Institute brings together a panel of specialists and a range of services in all areas related to cardiac disease. These services, which range from screening and diagnostic procedures to emergency and ongoing treatment for heart attacks and chronic heart disease, are provided at the Hospital's specialized laboratories and clinical units, on both an inpatient and outpatient basis. New York Methodist houses state-of-the-art diagnostic and surgical facilities, including three cardiac catheterization laboratories and the New York Methodist-Cornell Heart Center which houses the most modern cardiac surgery suite in the area. The Institute's staff of physicians includes specialists in all areas of cardiology, electrophysiology, interventional cardiology and cardiac surgery.

PROGRAMS OFFERED

The programs and services offered by the Institute include consultative services, a chest pain emergency center (located in the Emergency Department), diagnostic evaluation (including cardiac MRI) and medical treatment for heart disease, interventional cardiology procedures (angioplasty and stents), electrophysiology (pacemakers, implantable defibrillators, ablation, etc.) and cardiac surgery.

* * *

Referrals to the specialists or to cardiac programs and services can be made through an individual's primary care physician or requested directly through the Institute's referral service. More information (and on-line physician referral) is available at the Hospital's website, http://www.nym.org.

THE NEW YORK METHODIST-CORNELL HEART CENTER

The New YorkMethodist-Cornell Heart Center is one of only three programs approved to perform cardiac surgery in Brooklyn. It is staffed by physicians from the prestigious Weill Cornell Medical Center of NewYork-Presbyterian Hospital.

Procedures performed at the Center include coronary bypass surgery, off-pump bypass surgery, valve replacement and repair, thoracic aneurysm repair, minimally invasive cardiac surgery and bloodless heart surgery.

Advanced treatments offered include mini-mitral heart valve repair, thoracic, endovascular valve heart repair, extracorporeal membrane oxygenation (ECMO), transcatheter aortic valve replacement (TAVR), laser lead extraction, the Lariat procedure, hybrid ablation, and a number of other procedures offered only at world-class hospitals for the treatment of heart disease.

⊣ NewYork-Presbyterian

Affiliated with Columbia University College of Physicians and Surgeons and Weill Cornell Medical College

NewYork-Presbyterian Hospital
Columbia University Medical Center
622 West 168th Street
New York, NY 10032

NewYork-Presbyterian Hospital
Weill Cornell Medical Center
525 East 68th Street
New York, NY 10065

1-877-NYP-WELL (1-877-697-9355)   www.nyp.org/heart

NewYork-Presbyterian Heart

In 2014-2015, NewYork-Presbyterian Hospital's heart and heart surgery program was ranked 3rd in the nation in the annual "Best Hospitals" survey conducted by *U.S. News & World Report*™. NewYork-Presbyterian has leading clinical programs for patients with coronary artery disease and a wide range of other heart disorders, with particular expertise in the management of:

- Aortic aneurysms, acute dissections, and trauma, with rapid diagnosis and effective medical and surgical interventions.

- Heart failure, through a robust mechanical circulatory support program. Patients come from all over the world for the placement of ventricular assist devices to be used long-term or as a bridge to transplantation. NewYork-Presbyterian Hospital/Columbia University Medical Center is one of the world's leading institutions for heart transplantation and one of the few centers offering patients a total artificial heart.

- Adults with congenital heart disorders, featuring echo-cardiography, interventional cardiac catheterization, interventional electrophysiology, and surgery. Our adult congenital heart surgeons are among the world's best for complex congenital heart surgery and cardiac transplantation. Related care is provided by specialists in high-risk pregnancy, genetics, fetal echocardiography, GI and liver disease, pulmonary medicine, and hematology.

- Cardiac rhythm abnormalities: Our experienced electro-physiologists diagnose and treat atrial fibrillation and other arrhythmias using pacemakers, implantable cardioverter defibrillators, ablation, and novel approaches to restoring normal heart rhythm.

- Valve disorders, using minimally invasive surgical approaches whenever possible. NewYork-Presbyterian Hospital doctors pioneered transcatheter aortic valve replacement (TAVR), and continue to perform more TAVR procedures than any other center in the country. Our investigators led the PARTNER Trial, which showed that TAVR is as effective as conventional open-heart surgery for reducing mortality among high-risk patients with aortic stenosis. We are also participating in the EVEREST II clinical trial, which is evaluating a new device to repair mitral valve leakage.

- Heart disorders in the elderly: NewYork-Presbyterian's surgeons have earned a reputation for performing heart surgery on the very elderly (over age 80), achieving excellent outcomes.

- Cardiac rehabilitation: NewYork-Presbyterian's Cardiac Health Center provides personalized exercise training, nutritional education, and stress management for patients who have had heart surgery and those recovering from other heart ailments.

A Reputation for Excellence

At NewYork-Presbyterian Hospital, the optimal care of patients with heart disease is achieved by combining an experienced team of clinicians with the latest advances in technology. Basic science and clinical research efforts are aimed at developing more effective ways to prevent, diagnose, and treat cardiac disorders. NewYork-Presbyterian Hospital features renowned cardiac care programs in the following areas:

- Cardiac diagnostics
- Electrophysiology
- Clinical cardiology
- Interventional cardiology
- Cardiac assist devices
- Cardiothoracic surgery, including transplantation
- Mitral valve repair

NewYork-Presbyterian, patients who require surgery may receive treatment using a robotic approach, delivered using the Siemens Artis zeego® medical imaging system. This system provides surgeons with exceptional visualization of blood vessels.

CARDIAC AND VASCULAR INSTITUTE
550 First Avenue *(at 31st Street)*
New York, NY 10016
www.nyulangone.org
Physician Referral: **888-7-NYU-MED** *(888-769-8633)*

CARDIAC AND VASCULAR INSTITUTE

The Cardiac and Vascular Institute (CVI) at NYU Langone Medical Center continues to advance new techniques for repairing heart valves, curing heart rhythm disorders, and treating aortic diseases and congestive heart failure. We care for both adults and children. CVI is consistently ranked among the leading heart and heart surgery centers in *U.S. News & World Report's annual 'Best Hospitals'* rankings.

Cardiac Catheterization CVI offers superior catheter-based diagnosis and evaluation of cardiac health. Our laboratory provides a full range of procedures to evaluate, diagnose, and provide treatment options for coronary artery disease and valve conditions, including transcatheter aortic valve replacement (TAVR).

Cardiac Rehabilitation and Prevention The Joan and Joel Smilow Cardiopulmonary Rehabilitation and Prevention Center provides individualized treatment plans through NYU Langone's Rusk Rehabilitation, in a state-of-the-art and comfortable facility.

Cardiac Surgery NYU Langone is a nationally recognized leader in advanced surgical treatments for adult and congenital heart disease. We have world-renowned expertise in minimally invasive mitral valve repair, aortic valve replacement and aortic aneurysm repair, as well as specializing in high-risk and elderly patients.

Cardiology The Leon H. Charney Division of Cardiology is a leader in cardiovascular patient care, biomedical research, and education. We are advancing the field of cardiovascular medicine through a variety of innovative collaborations.

Congenital Heart Disease The pediatric and adult congenital cardiac program treats patients of all ages with inherited and acquired cardiac defects. We have a highly experienced team of specialists in pediatric and adult cardiology, pediatric interventional cardiology, congenital cardiac surgery, neonatal and pediatric cardiac intensive care, pediatric cardiac anesthesiology, nursing, and extracorporeal perfusion.

Heart Failure A multidisciplinary team offers the most advanced care for heart failure including echocardiograms, pacemaker and defibrillator implantations, open heart surgeries, remote monitoring of pulmonary artery pressure, and left ventricular assist devices.

Nuclear Cardiology/Stress The Nuclear Cardiology/Stress Laboratory performs a range of tests that assist cardiologists in the assessment and diagnosis of heart disease.

Vascular Surgery We offer diagnostic and treatment for patients with conditions ranging from arterial aneurysms to deep vein thrombosis, as well as carotid stenosis and limb salvage including minimally invasive vein surgery, endovascular aortic surgery, thoracic aneurysm correction and abdominal aneurysm interventions.

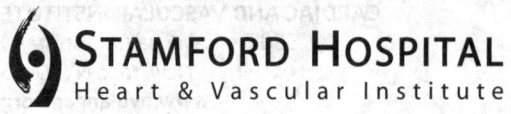

STAMFORD HOSPITAL
Heart & Vascular Institute

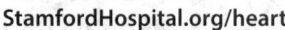 StamfordHospital.org/heart

Heart and Vascular Institute

Stamford Hospital's Heart and Vascular Institute is the only comprehensive cardiovascular program to include open heart surgery and elective and primary angioplasty in lower Fairfield County. We offer the finest cardiac services, including cardiovascular screening, diagnostic services, advanced cardiac non-surgical and surgical treatment, cardiac rehabilitation and integrative services and wellness programs.

Nationally Recognized Critical Care Unit

Stamford Hospital's Critical Care Unit has been recognized as one of the best in the country and earned the prestigious, national Codman Award, from the Joint Commission, for development of a life-saving protocol.

Cardiac Catheterization

Our two state-of-the-art Cardiac Catheterization Labs enable diagnosis and treatment of heart conditions and emergency angioplasty to open blocked coronary arteries during heart attacks. Emergency and elective angioplasty are performed for the treatment of acute myocardial infarction (heart attack) and coronary blockages.

Electrophysiology Program

We have the most comprehensive Electrophysiology Program (EP) in lower Fairfield County. We diagnose and treat electrical rhythm disorders of the heart, and offer state-of-the-art diagnostic testing. We are equipped to perform the most complex EP procedures including atrial fibrillation. A new bi-plane lab (imaging which shows two dimensions instead of a flat, one dimensional view), opens in the winter of 2014, the only one of its kind in the area.

Open Heart Surgery

Our expert team is equipped to handle any emergent and non-emergent surgical issue including CABG, valve repairs and replacements and aneurysms using state-of-the-art surgical techniques.

Cardiac Rehabilitation

Located at the Tully Health Center, we help patients with heart disease recover faster and return to full, productive lives. Together with medical and surgical treatment, cardiac rehab includes exercise, education, counseling and behavioral change strategies that lead to a healthier life.

Integrative Cardiology and Wellness Programs

Offered through our Center for Integrative Medicine and Wellness, this program offers multiple lifestyle techniques to complement and support the treatment of heart disease.

Academic and Clinical Affiliations

Stamford Hospital is an affiliate of the New York–Presbyterian Healthcare System and a major teaching affiliate of the Columbia University College of Physicians & Surgeons.

Accreditation
The Joint Commission

Beds
305

Sponsorship
Voluntary,
Not-for-Profit

For a Physician Referral or more information, please call 1.877.233.9355 or visit StamfordHospital.org /doctor.

Stamford Hospital
30 Shelburne Road
Stamford, CT 06902
203.276.1000

StamfordHospital.org

St. Francis Hospital, The Heart Center®

Catholic Health Services
At the heart of health

100 Port Washington Blvd.
Roslyn, New York 11576
www.stfrancisheartcenter.com
(516) 562-6000
1-888-HEARTNY

A Leader in Cardiac Care

St. Francis Hospital, The Heart Center® is New York State's only specialty designated cardiac center and is one of the busiest heart centers in the nation. Located in Roslyn, New York, on Long Island's North Shore, St. Francis is ranked among the top 10 hospitals in the United States for cardiology and heart surgery by *U.S. News & World Report*. It is the eighth consecutive year that *U.S. News* has named St. Francis one of the best hospitals in America. In 2014-15, the Hospital was also nationally ranked in gastroenterology and GI surgery; geriatrics; orthopedics; and neurology and neurosurgery.

St. Francis Hospital:

• Has a highly experienced team of physicians and surgeons with one of the largest volumes in the nation for cardiac surgery, interventional cardiology, and arrhythmia procedures

• Offers innovative approaches to cardiac surgery, including minimally invasive procedures and off-pump coronary artery bypass surgery, designed to minimize trauma and reduce surgical complications

• Performs one of the region's highest volumes of catheter-based techniques to correct congenital heart defects such as atrial septal defects (ASDs), ventricular septal defects (VSDs), and patent foramen ovale (PFO)

• Operates a nationally recognized Arrhythmia and Pacemaker Center staffed with electrophysiologists with over a decade of experience in radiofrequency ablation, a permanent cure for certain arrhythmias, including atrial fibrillation

• Maintains a high volume center for the implantation of cardiac pacemakers and defibrillators

• Offers a world-class program in cardiac imaging that fully integrates all technologies, including advanced methods in cardiac MRI, coronary CT angiography, PET/CT and three-dimensional echocardiography

• Has earned the Magnet designation for excellence in nursing services, an honor achieved by only 7 percent of hospitals in the U.S.

• The Hospital is a premier center for national clinical trials such as Medtronic CoreValve Trials, St. Jude Portico Trial, Abbott EVALVE Mitraclip®, COAPT- Mitraclip® Trial for coronary calcification, carotid stent trials such as Gore Scaffold, and the St. Jude Leadless Pacemaker trial. St. Francis is also conducting studies using a full range of state-of-the-art cardiac imaging modalities to examine the underlying mechanisms of heart disease.

• St. Francis is also a pioneer in transaortic valve replacement (TAVR), a new, minimally invasive procedure that channels a tube called a catheter containing a prosthetic valve through the femoral artery to reach the heart. The procedure is typically used for patients who are too elderly or ill for open-heart surgery.

St. Francis Hospital has outstanding patient satisfaction ratings, and is top-ranked for patients saying they would recommend the Hospital to family and friends.

"Our large cardiac caseload and our growing research program put us in an excellent position to introduce new techniques that can benefit thousands of people in need each year."

–Alan D. Guerci, M.D.
President and
Chief Executive Officer
Catholic Health Services
of Long Island

WINTHROP
University Hospital
Your Health Means Everything.

259 First Street, Mineola, NY 11501
1-866-WINTHROP• www.winthrop.org

CARDIAC CARE AT WINTHROP

Thoracic Aortic Vascular Treatment Center

In 2013, Winthrop was among an elite group of institutions nationwide invited to participate in the third phase of a prestigious research study using a minimally invasive procedure to treat patients with severe aortic heart valve stenosis – a chronic condition in which the aortic valve does not open properly, hindering the flow of blood from the heart to the rest of the body. Called PARTNER 2/Sapien 3, the trial continues the work of the PARTNER trial, the pivotal study which demonstrated the safety and effectiveness of the Edwards Sapien valve in transcatheter aortic valve replacement, or TAVR, a procedure that enables patients with a severe aortic stenosis to receive a new heart valve without undergoing open-heart surgery. Thanks to a smaller, improved valve, the third generation of the study makes the procedure accessible to an even larger segment of the population who previously wouldn't have been eligible. In early 2012, Winthrop had become one of only approximately 70 centers in the United States to offer TAVR.

The Pacemaker/Arrhythmia Center

The Pacemaker/Arrhythmia Center at Winthrop is a state-of-the-art facility that offers leading-edge services with highly skilled clinical cardiac electrophysiologists who specialize in the entire range of heart rhythm diagnostic and therapeutic procedures. The Center offers both inpatient and outpatient services.
In 2014, Winthrop opened its newest state-of-the-art electrophysiology lab, designed with input from a multidisciplinary team of Winthrop cardiologists, nurses, technicians, and anesthesiologists, configured for all electrophysiology procedures to treat patients with cardiac arrhythmias (heart rhythm disorders).

Hypertrophic Cardiomyopathy Treatment Center

Winthrop-University Hospital's Hypertrophic Cardiomyopathy (HCM) Treatment Center — one of the nation's handful of comprehensive resources for HCM and the only one on Long Island — treats hundreds of patients and families from the tri-state area and beyond, offering expert, specialized services that address all facets of the disease. The HCM Center is recognized as a national Center of Excellence by the National Hypertrophic Cardiomyopathy Association.

The Women's Cardiovascular Wellness and Prevention Center

Winthrop's Women's Cardiovascular Wellness and Prevention Center is a comprehensive prevention, treatment and recovery program designed for women with cardiovascular disease or at risk for such. The Center provides a full complement of cardiac and wellness services including fitness referrals, patient education, medical screening and counseling.

Center for Adult Congenital Heart Disease

Due to medical breakthroughs and progress in treatment, children born with congenital heart defects are living longer and reaching adulthood. Currently, there are more than one million adults in the United States living with repaired heart defects. As this number continues to rise, it has become apparent that a majority of these initial repairs were not "cures," but rather palliations that require life-long follow up. As they grow older, this unique population requires care for routine conditions of adulthood (such as pregnancy) and should be monitored for traditional risk factors like obesity, hypertension, diabetes and coronary artery disease. To address this growing population, Winthrop has created the Center for Adult Congenital Heart Disease, consisting of a multidisciplinary team providing patients with the expertise of pediatric cardiologists while offering a comprehensive range of services to handle adult cardiac issues. The Center is supervised by a Board Certified specialist, one of only a handful in the region. Each treatment plan is tailored to the patient, and may consist of echocardiography, arrhythmia monitoring, advanced cardiac imaging, cardiac CT and diagnostic catheterizations. If the patient is pregnant, the team works closely with Winthrop's Division of Maternal-Fetal Medicine and Winthrop's world renowned high risk obstetricians to provide them with the very best care.

Winthrop-University Hospital offers a unique and comprehensive multifaceted approach to the prevention and treatment of cardiovascular disease. Comprised of several Centers of Excellence, the cardiovascular specialists of Winthrop-University Hospital bring each patient a focused and individualized level of care not accessible elsewhere.

Winthrop's highly skilled and experienced cardiologists, cardiothoracic surgeons, specialized nurses, physician assistants, cardiology fellows and cardiovascular technologists provide patients and their primary care physicians with a wide range of sophisticated services; including access to consistently outstanding interventional cardiology, cardiac surgery, state-of-the-art computerized diagnostic cardiac catheterization procedures and expert drug-eluting stent placement - as well as innovative electrophysiology used to evaluate and treat all types of heart-rhythm disturbances with the latest generation of implantable electronic devices and pacemakers.

The Best in American Medicine
www.CastleConnolly.com

Child & Adolescent Psychiatry

550 First Avenue *(at 31st Street)*
New York, NY 10016

nyulmc.org/hassenfeld-childrens
Hassenfeld Children's Hospital Access Line: **855-NYU-KIDS**

HASSENFELD CHILDREN'S HOSPITAL

Hassenfeld Children's Hospital (HCH) is a full-service specialty children's hospital encompassing all children's health services at NYU Langone Medical Center. At HCH, newborns, children, adolescents and young adults receive the most comprehensive and advanced care possible from a team of pediatricians and pediatric specialists across more than 30 medical and surgical disciplines. With more than 150 full-time pediatric specialists, as well as pediatric nurses, child life specialists and social workers, Hassenfeld Children's Hospital is uniquely equipped to provide innovative pediatric subspecialty care in a highly personalized manner.

Child- and Family-Centered Care

Integral to the care we provide is a myriad of support services for children and their families. We recognize that the best outcomes are achieved when the child's family is actively involved in every step of care. For that reason, our trained specialists address the needs of not just the patient, but of parents and siblings through ongoing education and communication.

Our pediatric specialties include:

Anesthesiology

Cardiology

Cardiothoracic Surgery

Child and Adolescent Psychiatry
   and Psychology/Child Study Center

Critical Care

Dermatology

Developmental and Behavioral Pediatrics

Emergency Medicine

Endocrinology

Epilepsy

Gastroenterology

Genetics

Hematology/Oncology

Infectious Diseases

Neonatology

Nephrology

Neurosurgery

Neurology

Ophthalmology

Orthopaedic Surgery

Otolaryngology

Pathology

Pulmonology

Radiology

Reconstructive and Plastic Surgery

Rehabilitation

Rheumatology

Surgery

Urology

Child Neurology

NEUROLOGY & NEUROSURGERY

NYU Langone Medical Center's Departments of Neurology and Neurosurgery continue to be ranked among the nation's top 10 in the 2014-2015 *U.S. News & World Report's* annual survey of "Best Hospitals." Adult and pediatric patients travel from around the world to consult our renowned specialists for their expertise in the care, treatment, and research of neurological diseases and disorders of the brain, spine, and nervous system. These conditions range from headaches and migraines, nerve and muscle problems, pain, autism, movement disorders, and Alzheimer's disease to stroke, vascular disorders, epilepsy, multiple sclerosis and brain tumors. NYU Langone is home to one of the largest epilepsy centers in the United States, as well as the largest multiple sclerosis program in New York and the first primary stroke center established in New York City.

Neurological Expertise

We treat familial **dysautonomia** and other inherited or acquired autonomic nervous system diseases.

Our multidisciplinary team in the **Center for Cognitive Neurology** offers compassionate, expert care for diseases that affect cognition, such as Alzheimer's and dementia.

A collaborative effort between the Departments of Neurology, Orthopaedic Surgery, and Rehabilitation, the **Concussion Center** provides expert evaluation and seamless, multidisciplinary treatment.

Our Level 4 **Comprehensive Epilepsy Center** offers the most advanced medical and surgical options as well as world-renowned physicians.

Our **Multiple Sclerosis Comprehensive Care Center** provides state-of-the-art diagnostic evaluations and multidisciplinary follow-up care and management.

With one of the largest **neuro-ophthalmology** teams in the world, we offer expert care for individuals with nervous system disorders affecting vision.

Our experienced **neurogenetics** team provides comprehensive diagnosis and treatment of rare, progressive, and often debilitating inherited diseases of the nervous system.

Our specialized **Parkinson's and Movement Disorders Center** features a multidisciplinary team and a community-based support program that is a national model for improving patients' quality of life through fitness, education, and socialization.

Our **Comprehensive Stroke Care Center** provides rapid diagnosis and intervention as well as expert rehabilitation.

Our **pediatric neurology** team cares for children with developmental concerns and delays, such as failing to meet age-related milestones, and neurological conditions such as seizures, cerebral palsy, and epilepsy.

Neurosurgical Expertise

Our multidisciplinary **Brain Tumor Center** is one of the nation's leading programs, specializing in malignant and benign brain and spinal cord tumors, including skull base tumors.

The **Center for Cerebrovascular Disease** is world-renowned for treating brain aneurysms, giant intracranial aneurysms, brain vascular malformations and cavernomas, and stroke.

Our faculty include experts in the surgical treatment of primary **hyperhidrosis** (excessive sweating), including Endoscopic Thoracic Sympathectomy.

We offer the latest in **neuromodulation**, including deep brain stimulation (DBS) and peripheral nerve stimulation (PNS) for Parkinson's, essential tremor, and other conditions.

Our **Center for Advanced Radiosurgery** treats deep-seated tumors, vascular malformations, and other diseases using the Gamma Knife.

The **Spine and Peripheral Nerve Center** provides treatment for degenerative spinal diseases, spinal tumors, spinal trauma and spinal infections.

Our **pediatric neurosurgery** team treats children with brain and spinal tumors, epilepsy, hydrocephalus, pediatric spine disorders, and other congenital and developmental conditions.

Diabetes Management/ Wound Care

Diabetes and Obesity Institute at Winthrop

The facts are staggering – patients with diabetes are three times more likely to be admitted to the hospital during an emergency room visit for an unrelated condition; two out of three patients admitted to a hospital from the Emergency Room for any reason have diabetes, and many of these people don't even know that they have it. Diabetes can complicate every type of illness, surgery or medical procedure – including childbirth. So it is imperative that patients are diagnosed and treated by professionals who understand this disease.

Every healthcare professional at Winthrop-University Hospital has not only been trained to provide education to patients with diabetes, but to follow evidence-based protocols to help manage their care and prevent complications.

Joint Commission's Gold Seal of Approval™

In recognition of Winthrop's outstanding care for patients with diabetes, the Hospital has been recognized as the **first and only** teaching hospital in New York State to earn The Joint Commission's Gold Seal of Approval™ for its advanced inpatient diabetes care by demonstrating compliance with The Joint Commission's national standards for healthcare quality and safety in disease-specific care.

The care of patients with diabetes at Winthrop is closely coordinated by a multidisciplinary team of certified diabetes educators, physicians, nurses and other health professionals. By identifying patients with diabetes upon admission into the Hospital and implementing specific evidence-based protocols, Winthrop has successfully reduced complications while enhancing patient outcomes. Additionally, through an initiative designed to reduce the prevalence of hypoglycemia (low blood sugar) among inpatients, Winthrop recently reduced its hypoglycemia rate to 0.3 percent, as compared with the national hospital average of 6.0 percent.

National Accolades

Over the years, Winthrop's outstanding diabetes care has been recognized by *U.S. News & World Report* including most recently, when the Children's Medical Center was named to *U.S. News & World Report*'s 2014/2015 Best Children's Hospitals rankings for demonstrating excellence in pediatric diabetes & endocrinology. In fact, Winthrop's Division of Pediatric Diabetes and Endocrinology placed among the top 20 programs in the country (# 19).

Thirty-Five Years of Service

This year, Winthrop-University Hospital's Diabetes Education Center is celebrating 35 years of service to the community. Since opening its doors in 1979, the Diabetes Education Center has helped improve the lives of countless individuals living with diabetes through its highly regarded educational and support programs. A pioneer in the field of diabetes education, the Diabetes Education Center was the first outpatient education program in New York State accredited by the national American Diabetes Association. Today, the Center continues to equip adults and children with the knowledge and tools necessary to manage diabetes as well as to provide lifestyle programs designed to prevent diabetes.

Collaborations to Provide Quality Diabetes Care

As the regional leader in diabetes, Winthrop's Diabetes and Obesity Institute helps to ensure patients receive consistent, high quality care from the Hospital's primary care providers. In 2012, clinicians from several Hospital-affiliated primary care practices and the Winthrop Endocrinology faculty practice achieved recognition by The National Committee for Quality Assurance's (NCQA) Diabetes Recognition Program (DRP). Recognition by the NCQA's DRP identifies physicians who are well educated in diabetes management and consistently treat patients according to the best available scientific evidence. The DRP Program measures cover areas including A1C, blood pressure and cholesterol; eye examinations; foot examinations and kidney assessments; and smoking cessation advice or treatment.

A Commitment to Research

In early 2015, Winthrop-University Hospital will open its brand new, 95,000-square foot Research and Academic Center. This new building is a physical embodiment of Winthrop's commitment to research, medical education and clinical care and a tangible demonstration of the Hospital's position as the regional leader in diabetes and obesity care. It will be an epicenter of wellness care, research and medical study for Nassau County and the region as Winthrop takes on the tough job of confronting how personal habits, nutrition and the destructive forces of obesity are threatening the future and driving up the costs of healthcare.

The facility will greatly enhance Winthrop's bench to bedside research mission, making discoveries more accessible and more quickly available for patients. It will also enable Winthrop to better support its current distinguished scientists. The Center will include core laboratories, a clinical trial center and pediatric and adult endocrinology faculty clinical practices. It will also house the adult medical weight management program that complements Winthrop's surgical weight management program, and will provide space for the Healthy Kids program for families of children who are overweight.

Emergency Services

For more information about the Emergency Care Center
or for a physician referral, call 877-HOLY-NAME.
Please mention "Castle Connolly Guide."

718 Teaneck Road
Teaneck, NJ 07666
877-HOLY-NAME
(465-9626)
holyname.org

Holy Name Medical Center
Emergency Care Center

Holy Name Medical Center's George P. Pitkin MD Emergency Care Center is an ultramodern facility that combines an experienced, specialized staff with today's best practices in health care and the highest industry standards for a superior care experience. Accommodating more than 55,000 visits per year, Holy Name's emergency division offers a physical space engineered for efficiency, comfort and privacy, and a care delivery system focused on quality, safety and patient satisfaction.

The Center is staffed by board-certified emergency medicine physicians, physician assistants, nurse practitioners and registered nurses with certification in emergency nursing. In the Pediatric Fast Track, on-site board-certified pediatricians and specialized pediatric nurses provide safe, compassionate care, private rooms and a kid-friendly atmosphere to ensure that a visit to Holy Name's ER is as positive an experience as possible.

Holy Name's Emergency Care Center is able to manage mass casualty situations and has special accommodations and procedures in place for decontamination and radiation detection.

EMERGENCY RESPONDERS IN THE COMMUNITY

Holy Name Medical Center (HNMC) provides pre–Medical Center life support services to our surrounding communities. The first Medical Center–based Basic Life Support (BLS) provider in Bergen County, HNMC also supplies Mobile Intensive Care Units staffed by emergency medical technicians and paramedics trained in CPR, cardiac life support, trauma life support, incident command, HAZMAT and CBRNE (chemical, biological, radiological, nuclear and explosive) response.

Holy Name is the only hospital in the area bringing the Hybrid Ambulance to the community, combining advanced life support (ALS) and basic life support (BLS) in a single mobile intensive care unit. The Medical Center's Special Operations unit provides support to mass-gathering events, patient rescue and all-terrain transport, and EMS branch communications. To further its commitment to the community it serves, Holy Name EMS professionals also offer emergency medical training for first responders, EMTs, paramedics and other emergency service personnel.

Awards and Accreditations

- Top Performer on Key Quality Measures— from The Joint Commission for excellence in heart attack, heart failure, pneumonia and surgical care
- Magnet Recognition—from the American Nurses Credentialing Center for excellence in patient care
- High-Performing Hospital—from NJ Department of Health for providing "the correct care" for heart attack, heart failure, pneumonia and surgical patients
- Beacon Award for Critical Care Excellence® —from the American Association of Critical-Care Nurses (AACN)
- Primary Stroke Care Certification—from The Joint Commission for excellence in stroke patient care
- Gold Plus Achievement Award—from The American Heart Association/ American Stroke Association
- Hospital Safety Score "A"—from The Leapfrog Group

Endocrinology,
Diabetes & Metabolism

Clinical Diabetes Center at Montefiore

Montefiore's Clinical Diabetes Center provides comprehensive care for adults and children with type 1 and type 2 diabetes and other endocrine diseases. The Center's work is closely aligned with Albert Einstein College of Medicine's National Institutes of Health–funded Diabetes Research Center, providing translational research opportunities in association with its clinical mission. Diabetes affects more than 14 percent of the Bronx population—one of the highest rates in the nation. Montefiore's commitment to reducing this statistic and improving the health of those who reside in the communities that we serve has led to unrivaled investments in educational programs, research and outreach.

The Center employs a large staff of board-certified endocrinologists supported by a team of dedicated diabetes nurse practitioners, many of whom are also certified diabetes educators. Together they emphasize early intervention and ongoing care in both the inpatient and outpatient settings. This includes all of Montefiore's hospital campuses and 22 integrated primary care clinics in the Bronx, Westchester County and surrounding areas.

Through its nationally-recognized diabetes self-management program, the **Proactive Managed Information System for Education in Diabetes (PROMISED®),** the Center is teaching patients how to improve their health through diet and medication, use their insulin pumps and monitor their glucose. PROMISED® has twice been recognized by the American Diabetes Association for exemplary performance and has consistently surpassed national standards.

The Center's **Diabetes Disease Management Program** is composed of a multidisciplinary team that provides education and works with primary care physicians to coordinate care for those dealing with related health issues, such as wounds and kidney failure. Telephone monitoring, when needed, helps patients keep their diabetes under control.

Children's Hospital at Montefiore (CHAM) is home to one of only a handful of American Diabetes Association–recognized pediatric endocrinology programs in New York. The program offers a diabetes care team that includes endocrinologists, certified diabetes educators, nurse practitioners, psychologists, social workers and nutritionists to support both the patient and the child's family. The program also holds weekly support groups and several educational family-oriented activities throughout the year to support and educate members of the community. The Department's diabetes specialists supplement superior clinical care with advances born out of pioneering research. A prominent example is the Program's National Institutes of Health–funded work to develop an artificial pancreas that provides automated glucose measurement and insulin delivery.

INTERNAL MEDICINE

Internal medicine physicians at NYU Langone Medical Center are dedicated to treating the whole patient, and not just their disease. Our team addresses both the physical and psychological aspects of health and disease through clear communication and a fully integrated regimen of care. We specialize in the following areas:

Primary and Specialized Healthcare

General Internal Medicine offers a multidisciplinary medical approach to treating illnesses involving the heart, lungs, gastrointestinal tract, joints, bones, muscles, endocrine organs and kidneys. A wide range of laboratory, imaging and advanced diagnostic testing, ranging from throat cultures to the complex mapping of the electrical surface of the heart, is available on-site or by referral. Comprehensive women's healthcare and men's healthcare is also available. We offer a variety of convenient office locations in Manhattan and the surrounding metropolitan area.

Geriatrics

Our geriatric specialists provide comprehensive and multidisciplinary care, consultation and follow-up for elderly patients ranging from prevention and healthy aging to the treatment and care of chronic conditions including dementia, functional impairment and degenerative disorders.

The Best in American Medicine
www.CastleConnolly.com

Family Medicine

INTERNAL MEDICINE

Internal medicine physicians at NYU Langone Medical Center are dedicated to treating the whole patient, and not just their disease. Our team addresses both the physical and psychological aspects of health and disease through clear communication and a fully integrated regimen of care. We specialize in the following areas:

Primary and Specialized Healthcare

General Internal Medicine offers a multidisciplinary medical approach to treating illnesses involving the heart, lungs, gastrointestinal tract, joints, bones, muscles, endocrine organs and kidneys. A wide range of laboratory, imaging and advanced diagnostic testing, ranging from throat cultures to the complex mapping of the electrical surface of the heart, is available on-site or by referral. Comprehensive women's healthcare and men's healthcare is also available. We offer a variety of convenient office locations in Manhattan and the surrounding metropolitan area.

Geriatrics

Our geriatric specialists provide comprehensive and multidisciplinary care, consultation and follow-up for elderly patients ranging from prevention and healthy aging to the treatment and care of chronic conditions including dementia, functional impairment and degenerative disorders.

Gastroenterology

NEW YORK METHODIST HOSPITAL

THE INSTITUTE FOR DIGESTIVE AND LIVER DISORDERS

New York Methodist Hospital
506 Sixth Street, Brooklyn, N.Y. 11215
Phone 866 DIGEST-1 (866 344-3781)
http://www.nym.org

SPECIALISTS AND MEDICAL SERVICES

The Institute's panel of physician specialists includes gastroenterologists, hepatologists, surgeons, laparoscopic surgeons, radiologists, medical and radiation oncologists and pathologists. Nutritionists and psychologists are also members of the team. The latest advances in the diagnosis and treatment of the gastrointestinal tract and the liver are available. These include endoscopic ultrasound, pediatric and adult capsule endoscopy and advanced laparoscopic surgery. In addition, the Endoscopy Suite at New York Methodist Hospital enables physicians to perform highly advanced diagnostic and treatment procedures that can detect and determine disorders of the gastrointestinal tract and bile ducts as well as perform the non-surgical removal of bile duct gallstones.

PROGRAMS OFFERED

Among the programs and services offered by the Institute are a Barrett's esophagus program, colorectal cancer program, heartburn (GERD) program, chronic Hepatitis B & C program, liver transplantation evaluation program, ulcer program, bowel disorders program and pediatric gastroenterology program. Gallbladder and pancreatic conditions are also treated.

* * *

Referrals to the Institute's specialists, programs and services can be made through an individual's primary care physician or requested directly through the Institute's telephone referral service. More information (and on-line physician referral) is available at the Hospital's website, http://www.nym.org.

THE PEDIATRIC GASTROENTEROLOGY PROGRAM

Problems commonly seen by physicians affiliated with the program include regurgitation, colic, constipation, diarrhea, recurrent abdominal pain, jaundice, blood in the stool, failure to thrive and formula intolerances. Children with these disorders present a special challenge because, along with the medical treatment that they receive, they need special care to ensure that their normal growth and development is not disrupted.

Special procedures that can be used to evaluate and diagnose pediatric gastrointestinal disorders include upper and lower endoscopies, liver biopsies and suction rectal biopsies. These procedures are performed by board certified specials in pediatric gastroenterology.

550 First Avenue *(at 31st Street)*
New York, NY 10016
www.nyulangone.org
Physician Referral: **888-7-NYU-MED** *(888-769-8633)*

GASTROENTEROLOGY

NYU Langone Medical Center is dedicated to the diagnosis and treatment of patients with diseases of the gastrointestinal tract. Physicians draw on their extensive knowledge and experience in the diagnosis and management of inflammatory bowel disease, peptic ulcer disease, esophageal disorders, gastrointestinal cancer, and liver, biliary and pancreatic diseases. Laser, laparoscopic, endoscopic, and other minimally invasive options are available, and we specialize in the following areas:

Colorectal Cancer
The Medical Center offers the most advanced screening options available for the diagnosis of colon cancer. Additionally, physicians continue to investigate colorectal cancer in special populations such as women, veterans, immigrants, minorities and patients with HIV, and offer the use of standard and virtual colonoscopy for the detection of colorectal polyps and cancer.

Esophageal Diseases
The Esophageal Disease Center offers patients state-of-the-art diagnosis and treatment of esophageal disorders. The Center focuses on gastroesophageal reflux disease, esophageal motility disorders, Barrett's esophagus, adenocarcinoma of the esophagus and swallowing disorders. It also offers diagnostic studies on esophageal manometry, impedance testing for swallowing, pH catheter and impedance testing for reflux and BRAVO capsule pH testing, as well as such therapies as Barrett's ablation and esophageal dilations.

Gastrointestinal Cancers
Our Perlmutter Cancer Center physicians treat patients with all types of gastrointestinal cancers, including those of the esophagus, stomach, colon/rectum, small intestine, liver, pancreas, gallbladder, and biliary tract. They also treat individuals with complex recurring disease, including those originally treated elsewhere. Patients have the opportunity to participate in numerous clinical trials.

Complex Treatments and Diagnosis
Our physicians are highly experienced in the use of enteroscopy and capsule endoscopy for the diagnosis of gastrointestinal bleeding of unknown origin. They have special interest in the diagnosis and treatment of patients with complex pancreatic-biliary disease through the use of ERCP and endoscopic ultrasound.

Liver Lesions and Adrenal Tumors
Our team treats liver lesions with painless radiofrequency ablation and are highly skilled in laproscopic adrenalectomies.

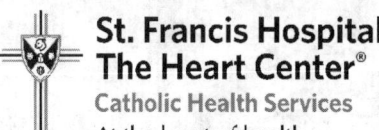

St. Francis Hospital, The Heart Center®
Catholic Health Services
At the heart of health

100 Port Washington Blvd.
Roslyn, New York 11576
www.stfrancisheartcenter.com
(516) 562-6000
1-888-HEARTNY

Gastrointestinal and Surgical Services

In a sign of its expanding strengths in non-cardiac care, in 2014-15 St. Francis Hospital was ranked 16th in the nation for the treatment of gastrointestinal disorders and GI surgery by *U.S. News & World Report* and the top hospital on Long Island in this specialty. This specialty has proven to be a pillar of St. Francis' excellent general medical and surgical care, and will continue to be a significant part of the hospital's future.

Innovative Diagnostic Procedures

The physicians in the Department of Gastroenterology at St. Francis Hospital have the skill and expertise to diagnose and treat all forms of gastrointestinal illnesses and employ essential state-of-the-art technologies to diagnose and treat the most difficult of digestive disorders. Headed by Anthony J. Celifarco, M.D., the department provides all forms of endoscopic and non-endoscopic studies on an in-patient or out-patient basis, in addition to consultative services. Procedures offered include colonoscopy, not only for routine colon cancer screening, but also to help diagnose causes of bleeding, diarrhea or constipation. Upper endoscopy is utilized to evaluate causes of abdominal pain, bleeding, weight loss, and difficulties swallowing. The department also performs endoscopic ultrasound (for diagnosis of lesions of the esophagus, stomach, and pancreas that may not be seen on standard endoscopic procedures of the GI tract), endoscopic dilation, stent placement for obstructive lesions, and enteroscopy including Balloon Enteroscopy to help visualize and treat disorders of the small intestine. One of the latest technologies, Capsule Endoscopy, can take images of the entire small intestine to find obscure causes of gastrointestinal bleeding, and help find evidence of undiagnosed disorders such as Crohn's disease. Recently, the Department of Gastroenterology acquired state-of-the-art, high-definition endoscopic equipment. Our center also performs fecal transplantations for treatment of severe Clostridium difficile colitis. In addition, the department now utilizes a carbon dioxide insufflation technique which minimizes discomfort with standard Endoscopic procedures compared to old technology. Acquiring this equipment further demonstrates the department's commitment to remain at the forefront of gastrointestinal endoscopy.

State-of-the-Art Minimally Invasive Surgical Oncology

Chairman of Surgery, Gary R. Gecelter, M.D., a renowned expert in minimally invasive surgery and surgical oncology, and his colleagues specialize in gastrointestinal surgical oncology, particularly colon, esophageal, and pancreatic cancer. Dr. Gecelter oversees the hospital's growing non-cardiac surgical program and has pioneered numerous laparoscopic techniques and is responsible for the development of flexible laparoscopy, which has led to single incision laparoscopic surgery and applies techniques used in gastroenterology. This has aided in allowing the minimally invasive resection of large abdominal tumors and even resection of esophageal cancers without having to make large chest and abdominal incisions. His team is in the forefront of integrating laparoscopy and endoscopy, particularly in the treatment of conditions such as achalasia as well as the surgical management of solid tumors of the GI tract.

St. Francis Hospital Gastroenterology Department conditions treated:

- Gastroesophageal reflux
- Peptic ulcer disease
- Biliary tract disease
- Disease of the pancreas including pancreatitis and pancreatic cancer
- Liver disease including cirrhosis and hepatitis
- Esophageal varices
- Fecal transplantations for treatment of severe Clostridium difficile disease
- Inflammatory bowel disease including ulcerative colitis and Crohn's disease
- Irritable bowel syndrome
- Colon cancer screening
- GI complications from cardiac surgery
- Celiac disease

Key treatments: Colonoscopy

Colon cancer, the third most common cancer, is a preventable condition. By using colonoscopy we are able to remove polyps and prevent the disease from occurring.

Gastrointestinal Bleeding

This condition is diagnosed using Gastroscopy, Capsule Endoscopy, Balloon Enteroscopy and Colonoscopy, and frequently can be treated without requiring surgery.

Inflammatory Bowel Disease

This disease is diagnosed based on history, physical examination, laboratory tests, colonoscopy, and capsule endoscopy. Patients are then treated with dietary measures and, if necessary, medication.

Geriatric Medicine

www.maimonidesmed.org/geriatrics

Maimonides serves one of the oldest populations in New York City, with one quarter of our patients over the age of 75. The Geriatrics Program at Maimonides is fully equipped to meet the special needs of this growing segment of the population. Directed by Barbara Paris, MD, the program encompasses inpatient and outpatient services, featuring the Acute Care for Elderly (ACE) Unit and the Safe at Home program. The staff is focused on the continuity, coordination, quality and dignity of care provided.

Patient Evaluation
ACE Unit services focus on acute medical care and account for the complex needs of hospitalized elderly patients. Special attention is given to the assessment of memory loss and understanding the underlying causes of geriatric syndromes that result in falls, incontinence and frailty. Psychosocial issues affecting elderly patients, such as loneliness and end-of-life care, are also addressed.

Wound Care and Hyperbaric Center
Elderly patients can often have wounds that do not heal easily, which is why we have a dedicated wound care team available. Individualized wound treatment is dependent upon the type and severity of the wound. Treatments include conventional and advanced wound dressings, antibiotic therapy, protective footwear, and hyperbaric oxygen therapy.

Safe at Home Program
The Safe at Home program actively manages the care of the frail elderly to keep them in their homes and within their communities. The program is designed to identify patients aged 75 years and older who are at high risk during the transitional period from hospital to home; provide them with coordinated comprehensive care after the transition from hospital to home; actively engage family caregivers and community support networks; increase patient satisfaction with their care during this transitional period; and reduce re-hospitalizations, emergency room visits, and nursing home placements.

Outpatient Geriatric Services
Our geriatric team offers comprehensive assessment and primary care services throughout Southern Brooklyn.

Maimonides Medical Center has been commended for outstanding services by a number of independent rating organizations. This year, the Geriatrics Program was designated as "High Performing" by U.S. News & World Report.

**Maimonides
Medical Center**

INTERNAL MEDICINE

Internal medicine physicians at NYU Langone Medical Center are dedicated to treating the whole patient, and not just their disease. Our team addresses both the physical and psychological aspects of health and disease through clear communication and a fully integrated regimen of care. We specialize in the following areas:

Primary and Specialized Healthcare

General Internal Medicine offers a multidisciplinary medical approach to treating illnesses involving the heart, lungs, gastrointestinal tract, joints, bones, muscles, endocrine organs and kidneys. A wide range of laboratory, imaging and advanced diagnostic testing, ranging from throat cultures to the complex mapping of the electrical surface of the heart, is available on-site or by referral. Comprehensive women's healthcare and men's healthcare is also available. We offer a variety of convenient office locations in Manhattan and the surrounding metropolitan area.

Geriatrics

Our geriatric specialists provide comprehensive and multidisciplinary care, consultation and follow-up for elderly patients ranging from prevention and healthy aging to the treatment and care of chronic conditions including dementia, functional impairment and degenerative disorders.

The Best in American Medicine
www.CastleConnolly.com

Gynecologic Oncology

NYU Langone Medical Center
550 First Avenue, New York, NY 10016
www.nyulangone.org

Laura and Isaac Perlmutter Cancer Center
160 East 34th Street, New York, NY 10016

**The Stephen D. Hassenfeld Children's Center
for Cancer and Blood Disorders**
160 East 32nd Street, New York, NY 10016

LAURA AND ISAAC PERLMUTTER CANCER CENTER

Formerly NYU Cancer Institute, the Laura and Isaac Perlmutter Cancer Center is an NCI-designated cancer center providing personalized patient care that is compassionate and state-of-the-art. The doctors and researchers work together to develop innovative therapies for patients. The Center is world-renowned for excellence in cancer-focused research, personalized care, education and community outreach. Its mission is to discover the origins of human cancer and to use that knowledge to eradicate the personal and societal burden of cancer in our community, the nation and the world. For more information about our expert physicians, call 1.888.769.8633.

Patient-Focused Setting
The Center and its multidisciplinary team of experts provide access to the latest treatment options and clinical trials, along with a variety of programs in cancer risk reduction/prevention, screening, diagnostics, genetic counseling and supportive services. In addition, the Center emphasizes the importance of a holistic approach involving integrative care, psychosocial support, survivorship, supportive oncology, and palliative care. In addition to our principal outpatient facility at 160 East 34th Street, services are also available at our Ambulatory Care Center on 38th Street in Manhattan; Rego Park, NY; and Lake Success, NY.

Renowned Expertise
Laura and Isaac Perlmutter Cancer Center brings together experts from a variety of disciplines to create collaborative research endeavors and clinical care teams. Our teams are highly skilled in minimally invasive techniques along with video-assisted and robotic surgery. We have created special programs to treat diseases such as breast cancer, brain cancer, melanoma, GI cancer, prostate cancer, hematologic malignancies, sarcoma, and lung cancer. We also continue to focus on translational programs in cancer healthcare disparities; molecularly targeted as well as immune- and stem-cell-based therapies; and the cell signaling pathways involved in cancer.

A Translational Approach
Our scientists and researchers excel in uncovering how cancer develops at the molecular level, and how we can harness that knowledge to reduce the risk of cancer and treat the disease.

Stephen D. Hassenfeld Children's Center for Cancer and Blood Disorders
As part of Hassenfeld Children's Hospital, the center is a leading pediatric outpatient facility for the treatment of childhood cancers and blood diseases. Its unique interdisciplinary and family-centered approach combines the most advanced medical treatments with psychosocial and emotional support services for young patients and their families.

Hematology

NYU Langone Medical Center
550 First Avenue, New York, NY 10016
www.nyulangone.org

Laura and Isaac Perlmutter Cancer Center
160 East 34th Street, New York, NY 10016

The Stephen D. Hassenfeld Children's Center
for Cancer and Blood Disorders
160 East 32nd Street, New York, NY 10016

LAURA AND ISAAC PERLMUTTER CANCER CENTER

Formerly NYU Cancer Institute, the Laura and Isaac Perlmutter Cancer Center is an NCI-designated cancer center providing personalized patient care that is compassionate and state-of-the-art. The doctors and researchers work together to develop innovative therapies for patients. The Center is world-renowned for excellence in cancer-focused research, personalized care, education and community outreach. Its mission is to discover the origins of human cancer and to use that knowledge to eradicate the personal and societal burden of cancer in our community, the nation and the world. For more information about our expert physicians, call 1.888.769.8633.

Patient-Focused Setting
The Center and its multidisciplinary team of experts provide access to the latest treatment options and clinical trials, along with a variety of programs in cancer risk reduction/prevention, screening, diagnostics, genetic counseling and supportive services. In addition, the Center emphasizes the importance of a holistic approach involving integrative care, psychosocial support, survivorship, supportive oncology, and palliative care. In addition to our principal outpatient facility at 160 East 34th Street, services are also available at our Ambulatory Care Center on 38th Street in Manhattan; Rego Park, NY; and Lake Success, NY.

Renowned Expertise
Laura and Isaac Perlmutter Cancer Center brings together experts from a variety of disciplines to create collaborative research endeavors and clinical care teams. Our teams are highly skilled in minimally invasive techniques along with video-assisted and robotic surgery. We have created special programs to treat diseases such as breast cancer, brain cancer, melanoma, GI cancer, prostate cancer, hematologic malignancies, sarcoma, and lung cancer. We also continue to focus on translational programs in cancer healthcare disparities; molecularly targeted as well as immune- and stem-cell-based therapies; and the cell signaling pathways involved in cancer.

A Translational Approach
Our scientists and researchers excel in uncovering how cancer develops at the molecular level, and how we can harness that knowledge to reduce the risk of cancer and treat the disease.

Stephen D. Hassenfeld Children's Center for Cancer and Blood Disorders
As part of Hassenfeld Children's Hospital, the center is a leading pediatric outpatient facility for the treatment of childhood cancers and blood diseases. Its unique interdisciplinary and family-centered approach combines the most advanced medical treatments with psychosocial and emotional support services for young patients and their families.

Home Health Care

Where Life Continues

CALVARY HOSPITAL
1740 Eastchester Road
Bronx, NY 10461
Tel: (718) 518-2000
www.calvaryhospital.org

CALVARY@HOME
HOME CARE AND HOSPICE

Calvary@Home, the umbrella for our Home Care and Hospice program, brings compassionate care to patients who can be cared for at home. Our inter-disciplinary team includes physicians, nurses, aides, social workers, spiritual care providers, volunteers, bereavement support workers, and other providers as needed. In 2013, The Joint Commission gave Calvary@ Home a Gold Seal of Approval™. Calvary received a 2012 Circle of Life Award® for innovative palliative and end-of-life care. Calvary@Home cares for more than 2,400 patients and families each year.

Certified Home Health Agency

Established in 1985, serves patients with all acute, chronic or life-limiting illnesses in their private home or nursing facility where they live. We provide a full range of specialized home healthcare experts to support patients and families. Home care patients approaching the end of life have access to palliative care services such as pain and symptom management, assistance with advance care planning, and psychosocial support. We strive to ensure continuity of care by assigning a core group of caregivers to each patient. Our community health nurses work with the patient's personal physicians to deliver appropriate care. Our home care services are available in Manhattan, the Bronx, Queens, Brooklyn, Staten Island as well as Westchester, Rockland, Putnam, and Nassau counties.

Hospice

Established in 1998, Calvary Hospice brings comprehensive care to people at home with all end-stage illnesses in their private home or nursing facility where they reside. Calvary assembles a core group of permanent staff to care for each patient, creating continuity of service for patients and families. Patients who require short-stay inpatient care can be admitted to Calvary in a seamless process. In addition to nurses, physicians and aides, Calvary social workers, spiritual counselors, and volunteers also make home visits to ensure that physical, psychosocial, emotional and spiritual needs are met. We provide bereavement services for 13 months for families. Staffing exceeds national recommendations.

Our hospice services are available in Manhattan, the Bronx, Queens, Brooklyn, as well as Nassau, Westchester and Rockland counties. Calvary Hospice has contracts with more than 25 nursing facilities in: Manhattan, the Bronx, Queens, Brooklyn, as well as Nassau, Westchester and Rockland Counties. Calvary Hospice offers short-term inpatient care at The Dawn Greene Home at Mary Manning Walsh Home on the Upper East Side of Manhattan.

For information about Calvary@Home, please call 718-518-2465.

Internal Medicine

550 First Avenue *(at 31st Street)*
New York, NY 10016

www.nyulangone.org

Physician Referral: **888-7-NYU-MED** *(888-769-8633)*

INTERNAL MEDICINE

Internal medicine physicians at NYU Langone Medical Center are dedicated to treating the whole patient, and not just their disease. Our team addresses both the physical and psychological aspects of health and disease through clear communication and a fully integrated regimen of care. We specialize in the following areas:

Primary and Specialized Healthcare

General Internal Medicine offers a multidisciplinary medical approach to treating illnesses involving the heart, lungs, gastrointestinal tract, joints, bones, muscles, endocrine organs and kidneys. A wide range of laboratory, imaging and advanced diagnostic testing, ranging from throat cultures to the complex mapping of the electrical surface of the heart, is available on-site or by referral. Comprehensive women's healthcare and men's healthcare is also available. We offer a variety of convenient office locations in Manhattan and the surrounding metropolitan area.

Geriatrics

Our geriatric specialists provide comprehensive and multidisciplinary care, consultation and follow-up for elderly patients ranging from prevention and healthy aging to the treatment and care of chronic conditions including dementia, functional impairment and degenerative disorders.

Interventional Cardiology

For more information about the Interventional Institute or for a physician referral, call 877-HOLY-NAME. Please mention "Castle Connolly Guide."

Holy Name Medical Center
Interventional Institute

718 Teaneck Road
Teaneck, NJ 07666
877-HOLY-NAME
(465-9626)
holyname.org

A REVOLUTIONARY, NONSURGICAL APPROACH

The Interventional Institute at Holy Name Medical Center offers innovative, nonsurgical treatment options for a broad spectrum of illnesses, from vascular conditions and gynecologic health problems to osteoporosis and cancer.

A dynamic field whose treatment techniques are adaptable to many different medical problems, interventional radiology is a rapidly growing medical specialty devoted to advancing patient care through minimally invasive, targeted treatments that are performed with the assistance of imaging guidance.

Under the leadership of John H. Rundback, MD, an internationally recognized specialist in the field of interventional radiology (IR), board-certified interventionalist physicians insert narrow catheters and miniature instruments through tiny incisions, and navigate them directly to the treatment site. Often performed on an outpatient basis, IR carries fewer risks than surgery, with less discomfort and faster recovery. Most important, treatment results are comparable to those of conventional approaches.

TREAT A WIDE VARIETY OF MEDICAL PROBLEMS

This revolutionary branch of medicine can shrink uterine fibroid tumors that once necessitated a hysterectomy, clear a life-threatening blood clot in a deep leg vein, eliminate leg pain and amputation risk from plaque buildup in the peripheral arteries, resolve unsightly varicose veins, stabilize painful spine fractures due to osteoporosis, and deliver chemotherapy directly to cancer cells.

Services of the Interventional Institute at Holy Name Medical Center:

- Peripheral artery disease (PAD) treatment
- Wound healing/revascularization
- Chemoembolization and transcatheter chemoembolization
- Radiofrequency ablation (RFA)
- Ablation of nonresectable lung cancers
- Uterine fibroid embolization
- Fallopian tube recanalization
- Pelvic congestion syndrome
- Deep vein thrombosis (DVT) treatment
- Endovenous laser treatment for varicose veins
- Kyphoplasty and vertebroplasty for osteoporosis
- Microsphere radioembolization

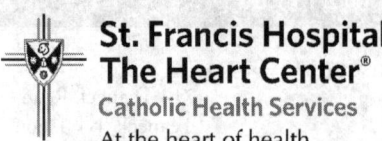

St. Francis Hospital, The Heart Center®
Catholic Health Services
At the heart of health

100 Port Washington Blvd.
Roslyn, New York 11576
www.stfrancisheartcenter.com
(516) 562-6000
1-888-HEARTNY

Noninvasive Cardiac Imaging

Using the latest in noninvasive cardiac imaging technology, St. Francis Hospital's physicians can evaluate blood flow, heart muscle strength, anatomy, and coronary artery blockages, allowing them to more effectively guide a patient's course of treatment.

Among the most recent advances in St. Francis Hospital's range of services are:

Coronary CT Angiography

St. Francis Hospital was the first hospital on Long Island to offer Multidetector Computed Tomography (MDCT) for noninvasive coronary artery imaging. Now, with more advanced technology and personalized design of imaging protocols for each individual, St. Francis can minimize radiation exposure for every patient and obtain high quality studies in patients who were previously ineligible for the test, due to rapid or irregular pulse rates

Cardiac MRI

The only center on Long Island with a dedicated Cardiac MRI program and world-class expertise in cardiac MRI, St. Francis Hospital uses MRI to evaluate heart anatomy, function, blood flow, scarring, and inflammation using advanced techniques on state-of-the-art scanners. Cardiac MRI allows physicians to evaluate effects of heart attack and coronary artery blockages and non-coronary causes of heart failure to determine whether or not patients will benefit from heart surgery or other therapies. World-renowned cardiac MRI authority Nathaniel Reichek, M.D., leads St. Francis Hospital's clinical and research applications of cardiac MRI.

Three-Dimensional Echocardiography

St. Francis Hospital is an internationally recognized leader in three dimensional echocardiography for quantifying the effects of heart disease. By creating three-dimensional reconstructions of the heart and blood flow within it, this technology provides diagnostic information which surpasses that available with conventional echocardiography in many patients and enables cardiac surgeons to plan and perform optimal repairs of malfunctioning heart valves. It also allows cardiac surgeons and interventional cardiologists to perform minimally invasive transarterial aortic valve replacements with optimal results.

Nuclear Imaging

Conventional nuclear imaging involves the injection of nuclear isotopes and imaging by a gamma camera that circles the patient's body, improving the accuracy of stress testing. St. Francis Hospital offers the latest advances in nuclear cardiology, such as positron emission tomography of the heart with CT attenuation correction (PET/CT). The nuclear cardiology laboratory at St. Francis Hospital is also a leader in developing new types of computer analysis to improve the value of all forms of cardiac nuclear imaging, and was among the first facilities in the U.S. to receive accreditation from The Intersocietal Commission for the Accreditation of Nuclear Medicine Laboratories.

Noninvasive Imaging at St. Francis Hospital include:

- Multidetector computed tomographic coronary angiography
- Cardiac MRI
- SPECT/CT nuclear Imaging
- Cardiac PET/CT imaging
- Transesophageal echocardiography
- Three-dimensional echocardiography
- Stress testing with nuclear, echocardiographic or MRI imaging.

The St. Francis Cardiac Imaging Program also supports the Hospital's nationally recognized programs in surgical and interventional cardiology, performing monitoring transesophageal echocardiography during surgical and transarterial valve replacements, catheter treatment of leaky heart valves and minimally invasive treatment to prevent stroke due to cardiac blood clots in atrial fibrillation.

In addition, St. Francis Hospital uses its leading-edge noninvasive imaging technology in its research programs on cardiovascular disease. Drawing on its depth of experience with various imaging modalities, the Hospital has launched a multidisciplinary effort at its Cardiac Research Institute to improve methods for the diagnosis and treatment of cardiac disease. Past research efforts at the Hospital include The St. Francis Heart Study – a pioneering effort and the largest study of CT calcium scoring to be conducted at any single center – which first demonstrated the value of CT calcium scoring for atherosclerotic plaque detection as a tool in cardiac risk evaluation.

The Best in American Medicine
www.CastleConnolly.com

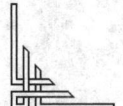

Maternal & Fetal Medicine

For more information about Women's and
Children's Health, call 877-HOLY-NAME.
Please mention "Castle Connolly Guide."

Holy Name Medical Center
Women's and Children's Health

718 Teaneck Road
Teaneck, NJ 07666
877-HOLY-NAME
(465-9626)
holyname.org

WOMEN'S AND CHILDREN'S HEALTH DISTINGUISHED FOR SERVICE EXCELLENCE

Consistently recognized for service excellence, Holy Name Medical Center's Women's and Children's Health service features superior medical care with a family-centered focus. At the core of Women's and Children's Health is the Medical Center's staff of specialized physicians and mother-baby nurses, whose expertise fosters the highly positive patient and family experience traditionally associated with Holy Name.

A COMPREHENSIVE PROGRAM OF CARE, EDUCATION AND SUPPORT

Holy Name's beautifully designed BirthPlace offers hotel-like accommodations and amenities, supported by advanced monitoring and infant care technology. The BirthPlace is equipped to address emergencies and cesarean sections with round-the-clock anesthesia coverage, and has an intermediate level II special care nursery with board-certified obstetricians, pediatricians, neonatologists and high-risk specialists available 24/7.

Board-certified perinatologists in Maternal-Fetal Medicine work as consultants with obstetricians to treat women who anticipate or are experiencing a complicated or high-risk pregnancy. They advocate a personalized, hands-on approach to patient care, meeting with the patient at every appointment. The medical team includes perinatal sonographers with advanced training and expertise in perinatal ultrasound, and genetic counselors with extensive training in high-risk pregnancy care.

- Private LDRP suites
- On-unit cesarean-section rooms
- Dedicated nursing staff for labor and delivery, postpartum, and special care nursery
- 24-hour access to board-certified anesthesiologists, obstetrician/gynecologists, pediatricians and neonatologists
- Intermediate level II special care nursery
- Maternal-fetal medicine program and perinatal high-risk services
- Genetic counseling
- Central fetal monitoring and maternal monitoring
- Education classes, support groups and infant care hotline
- State-of-the-art electronic security system
- Participant in National Cord Blood Stem Cell Program (umbilical cord blood storage for future lifesaving interventions)

Minimally Invasive Surgery

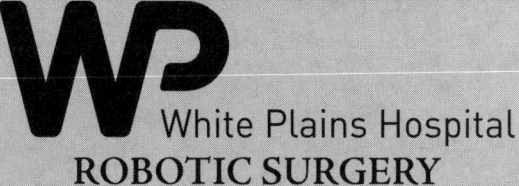

White Plains Hospital
ROBOTIC SURGERY

41 East Post Road, White Plains, NY 10601 Tel: (914) 681-0600 www.wphospital.org

White Plains Hospital is a regional leader in minimally invasive surgery. The Hospital's team of highly accomplished surgical experts performs more laparoscopic and robotic surgeries than any other hospital in Westchester County.

Minimally invasive surgery at White Plains Hospital encompasses laparoscopic and robotic procedures including:
- Robotic prostatectomy
- Gynecological surgery for benign and cancerous conditions including single-site robotic procedure
- Laparoscopic gall bladder removal and appendectomy
- Colorectal surgery
- Thoracic surgery procedures for esophagus and lungs including VATS (video-assisted thoracic surgery)
- Bariatric surgery
- Sports injury treatment including arthroscopy

Benefits of minimally invasive surgery for patients include less scarring, shorter time in the hospital and faster recovery time.

ROBOTIC SURGERY EXPERTISE

White Plains Hospital was the first community hospital in the Westchester and southern Connecticut region to acquire the da Vinci® robotic surgical system, which allows surgeons to perform complex procedures endoscopically through tiny access ports. Robotic surgery provides patients with less scarring, shorter hospital stays, quicker recovery times, and a more cosmetically pleasing alternative to traditional open surgeries. At White Plains Hospital, the da Vinci robot is used for:

- **Prostate Cancer Surgery**
- **Gynecological Surgery**
- **Thoracic Surgery**
- **Trans Oral Robotic Surgery (TORS)**
- **Colorectal Surgery**
- **General Surgery**

These procedures are performed in a newly completed state-of-the-art operating room specifically designed for robotic and other minimally invasive surgeries featuring the most sophisticated technology available, including the latest version of the da Vinci surgical system.

White Plains Hospital

For more than 120 years, White Plains Hospital has provided advanced, exceptional health care to the people of Westchester County and surrounding areas. Nearly 200,000 patients visit the Hospital each year for a variety of services including emergency care, internal medicine, maternity and high-risk obstetrics, minimally invasive surgery, orthopedics, oncology and cardiac care, among others.

The Hospital's capabilities for diagnosis and treatment, including state-of-the-art radiology and laboratory services, are second to none and rival those found at many nearby academic medical centers. These resources are combined with highly individualized care provided by the Hospital's more than 900 affiliated physicians and surgeons, many of whom have trained at the finest medical institutions in the country; and the more than 700 Magnet®- designated nurses with advanced training who provide skilled, compassionate care to their patients, every day.

Neurological Surgery

3316 Rochambeau Avenue
Bronx, New York 10467
718-920-7476
www.montefiore.org/neurosurgery

Neurological Surgery at Montefiore

Montefiore's Department of Neurological Surgery combines state-of-the-art technology with highly experienced specialists to provide exceptional care for children and adults. The Department's neurosurgeons are expert in all aspects of neurosurgery and employ the full spectrum of diagnostic and treatment modalities, including the use of intraoperative computed tomography (CT) scanners and minimally-invasive treatment approaches, such as endovascular coiling, stereotactic-guided radiosurgery and microneurosurgery.

The Department's Neurovascular Program is helping to improve the outcomes of patients with disorders related to the blood vessels of the brain—including stroke, carotid artery disease, intracranial aneurysms and arteriovenous malformations. This unique program brings neurosurgeons, neurologists and interventional radiologists together to review cases and administer treatment. The neurovascular team includes two neurosurgeons who are fellowship-trained in both neurosurgery and neurointerventional procedures. Montefiore's leading-edge program streamlines care and minimizes the risk associated with open surgery by using catheter-based approaches when appropriate.

Working in collaboration with plastic and reconstructive surgeons, otolaryngologists and other specialists from Children's Hospital at Montefiore (CHAM), the Department's pediatric neurosurgeons perform complex craniofacial reconstructions for children with rare facial tumors, traumatic injuries and birth defects—such as craniosyntosis, Apert syndrome and Crouzon syndrome. The craniofacial team uses advanced 3D technology to plan reconstructions, ensuring the best outcomes possible for these children. The team's commitment to surgical excellence has resulted in re-operative rates of less than 5 percent—substantially lower than the national average—and "return to OR" and relapse rates of less than 1 percent.

CHAM's pediatric neurosurgeons are developing new techniques for safeguarding the nervous system using neurophysiological mapping and monitoring during surgeries to remove tumors. They also specialize in alleviating the painful side effects of hydrocephalus treatment and repairing Chiari malformations.

The Department's neurosurgeons are involved in clinical research aimed at improving wound closure following spine surgery; the use of chemotherapy for the treatment of malignant brain tumors; understanding the genetics of medulloblastomas, glioblastomas and other cancers of the brain; and the use of special imaging techniques to enhance the treatment of patients with hydrocephalus.

⌐ NewYork-Presbyterian

Affiliated with Columbia University College of Physicians and Surgeons and Weill Cornell Medical College

NewYork-Presbyterian Hospital
Columbia University Medical Center
622 West 168th Street
New York, NY 10032

NewYork-Presbyterian Hospital
Weill Cornell Medical Center
525 East 68th Street
New York, NY 10065

1-877-NYP-WELL (1-877-697-9355)   www.nyp.org/neuro

NewYork-Presbyterian Neuroscience

In 2014–2015, NewYork-Presbyterian's neurology and neurosurgery program was ranked 2nd in the nation in the annual "Best Hospitals" survey conducted by *U.S. News & World Report*™. Our Neuroscience Centers offer innovative treatments to improve the quality of life of patients with neurological disorders, including:

- **Stroke/cerebrovascular disorders:** Four Stroke Centers are among the few NYS-designated primary stroke centers. Advanced medical and surgical techniques are used to diagnose and treat stroke, arteriovenous malformations, aneurysms, and carotid stenosis. 24/7 physician coverage and state-of-the-art brain monitoring in our Neuro-ICUs minimize damage and maximize the chance for a full recovery.

- **Pediatric neurology/neurosurgery:** Specialists are sensitive to the special needs of children with epilepsy, brain tumors, stroke, craniofacial disorders, vascular anomalies, and movement disorders.

- **Brain and spine tumors:** Translational research programs aim to understand the biology of these diseases and develop innovative therapies personalized for each patient.

- **Neuro-immune disorders:** Expert care is provided to patients with multiple sclerosis, neurosarcoidosis, and neuromyelitis optica.

- **Neuro-muscular disorders:** Our multidisciplinary team cares for people with neuromuscular diseases such as ALS (Lou Gehrig's Disease), Guillain-Barre syndrome, muscular dystrophy, myasthenia gravis, myopathy, and neuropathy.

- **Movement disorders:** NewYork-Presbyterian treats one of the world's largest populations of patients with movement disorders, especially Parkinson's disease. Researchers assess new drugs, imaging techniques, surgical therapies (such as deep brain stimulation), and gene therapy.

- **Memory disorders:** Our programs feature advanced care for patients with Alzheimer's disease or other memory disorders and their families, as well as clinical and laboratory research to better understand these disorders, with the goal of treating them sooner and more effectively.

- **Headaches:** Our headache specialists include neurological professionals with special training in the evaluation and treatment of chronic headaches and facial pain.

- **Sleep Disorders:** Sleep specialists at NewYork-Presbyterian provide comprehensive evaluation of sleep disorders and customize treatments. Special centers are available for children with sleep disorders.

Highlights:

- Neuro-oncologists are devising innovative approaches to bypass the blood-brain barrier and deliver chemotherapy directly to brain tumors.

- NewYork-Presbyterian is participating in the NIH-funded NeuroNEXT (Network for Excellence in Neuroscience Clinical Trials), a national effort to accelerate the development of therapies for people with neurological diseases, and is one of 25 regional stroke centers across the country funded by the NIH Stroke Trials Network (StrokeNet).

- Neurologists, neurosurgeons, and radiologists collaborated to show that intensive medical therapy is more effective than stenting for preventing a second stroke.

- Investigators devised a computer model of dementia spread to predict future disease pattern years before they occur in a patient.

- Researchers demonstrated that two genes associated with ALS work in tandem to support long-term survival of motor neurons.

550 First Avenue *(at 31st Street)*
New York, NY 10016

www.nyulangone.org

Physician Referral: **888-7-NYU-MED** *(888-769-8633)*

NEUROLOGY & NEUROSURGERY

NYU Langone Medical Center's Departments of Neurology and Neurosurgery continue to be ranked among the nation's top 10 in the 2014-2015 *U.S. News & World Report's* annual survey of "Best Hospitals." Adult and pediatric patients travel from around the world to consult our renowned specialists for their expertise in the care, treatment, and research of neurological diseases and disorders of the brain, spine, and nervous system. These conditions range from headaches and migraines, nerve and muscle problems, pain, autism, movement disorders, and Alzheimer's disease to stroke, vascular disorders, epilepsy, multiple sclerosis and brain tumors. NYU Langone is home to one of the largest epilepsy centers in the United States, as well as the largest multiple sclerosis program in New York and the first primary stroke center established in New York City.

Neurological Expertise

We treat familial **dysautonomia** and other inherited or acquired autonomic nervous system diseases.

Our multidisciplinary team in the **Center for Cognitive Neurology** offers compassionate, expert care for diseases that affect cognition, such as Alzheimer's and dementia.

A collaborative effort between the Departments of Neurology, Orthopaedic Surgery, and Rehabilitation, the **Concussion Center** provides expert evaluation and seamless, multidisciplinary treatment.

Our Level 4 **Comprehensive Epilepsy Center** offers the most advanced medical and surgical options as well as world-renowned physicians.

Our **Multiple Sclerosis Comprehensive Care Center** provides state-of-the-art diagnostic evaluations and multidisciplinary follow-up care and management.

With one of the largest **neuro-ophthalmology** teams in the world, we offer expert care for individuals with nervous system disorders affecting vision.

Our experienced **neurogenetics** team provides comprehensive diagnosis and treatment of rare, progressive, and often debilitating inherited diseases of the nervous system.

Our specialized **Parkinson's and Movement Disorders Center** features a multidisciplinary team and a community-based support program that is a national model for improving patients' quality of life through fitness, education, and socialization.

Our **Comprehensive Stroke Care Center** provides rapid diagnosis and intervention as well as expert rehabilitation.

Our **pediatric neurology** team cares for children with developmental concerns and delays, such as failing to meet age-related milestones, and neurological conditions such as seizures, cerebral palsy, and epilepsy.

Neurosurgical Expertise

Our multidisciplinary **Brain Tumor Center** is one of the nation's leading programs, specializing in malignant and benign brain and spinal cord tumors, including skull base tumors.

The **Center for Cerebrovascular Disease** is world-renowned for treating brain aneurysms, giant intracranial aneurysms, brain vascular malformations and cavernomas, and stroke.

Our faculty include experts in the surgical treatment of primary **hyperhidrosis** (excessive sweating), including Endoscopic Thoracic Sympathectomy.

We offer the latest in **neuromodulation**, including deep brain stimulation (DBS) and peripheral nerve stimulation (PNS) for Parkinson's, essential tremor, and other conditions.

Our **Center for Advanced Radiosurgery** treats deep-seated tumors, vascular malformations, and other diseases using the Gamma Knife.

The **Spine and Peripheral Nerve Center** provides treatment for degenerative spinal diseases, spinal tumors, spinal trauma and spinal infections.

Our **pediatric neurosurgery** team treats children with brain and spinal tumors, epilepsy, hydrocephalus, pediatric spine disorders, and other congenital and developmental conditions.

Neurology

111 East 210th Street
Bronx, New York 10467
718-920-4656
www.montefiore.org/neurology

Neurology at Montefiore

Montefiore's Department of Neurology offers exceptional care for the full spectrum of neurologic conditions for patients within the New York metropolitan area, Westchester County, southern Connecticut, northern New Jersey as well as nationally and internationally. The Department includes multidisciplinary programs in aging and dementia, adult and pediatric epilepsy, autism and communication disorders, Rett syndrome, headache, sleep-wake disorders, stroke, neuro-oncology, neuromuscular diseases, movement disorders, multiple sclerosis and allied disorders, neurological critical care and interventional neuroradiology and general neurology. Our partnership with Albert Einstein College of Medicine fosters an extraordinary degree of interdisciplinary biomedical scholarship and innovative "bench-to-bedside" initiatives.

- Our Headache Center offers an interdisciplinary approach to treating migraine, tension, cluster and chronic headaches, with plans under way to create an interdisciplinary infusion center.

- The nation's first accredited Sleep-Wake Disorders Center treats the full range of sleep problems associated with pediatric and adult neurological conditions. The Center is also focused on the emerging field of circadian rhythms, a timely topic as more traffic and other workplace-related accidents involving shift workers arise, and the creation of a Center for Shift Workers is planned for the future.

- We treat the broad spectrum of aging disorders that go well beyond Alzheimer's disease to involve the spectrum of degenerative dementias. Our researchers are studying whether neurodegenerative diseases begin during early development, and why certain cells are vulnerable to premature death. Our pioneering work is predicated upon advances in stem cell biology and epigenetics. The synergy between our neurology and geriatrics specialties, with programs in Aging and Dementia, Gait and Frailty, and Healthy Aging, culminates in a practice combining all aging-related specialties under one roof—the Center for the Aging Brain.

- Montefiore's premier pediatric neurology program addresses epilepsy, neuromuscular diseases and communication disorders. Montefiore's Autism and Neurodevelopmental Disorders Center is known for its sophisticated care and research relating to the autism spectrum and other pediatric communication disorders. We also house one of the nation's most comprehensive Rett syndrome programs.

- The Comprehensive Epilepsy Center, featuring pediatric and adult epilepsy monitoring units, diagnoses and develops treatment plans for all forms of epilepsy, including those requiring surgical management.

- We are known for our strength in adult and pediatric neuromuscular disorders. Our Muscular Dystrophy Clinic specializes in peripheral nerve, neuromuscular junction and primary muscle disorders, including a variety of inflammatory and immune-mediated disorders. Since launching our Myasthenia Gravis Clinic, the Department has expanded its offerings to include outpatient treatments, including infusion therapy for refractory cases.

- The Stern Stroke Center is expanding its treatment of stroke, through a state-of-the-art unit, a new telemedicine program and a neurological intensive care unit linked to a step-down unit. The Center provides advanced care and research related to cerebrovascular diseases and neurological intensive care, which is helping to define vascular risk factors in underserved populations and establishing links between stroke, dementia, headache, and metabolic and immunological disorders.

- We also house comprehensive programs in adult and pediatric neuro-oncology, including metastatic disease affecting the brain and paraneoplastic syndromes, multiple sclerosis, general neurology and emerging areas of neuroimmunology incorporating multiple allied neurological disciplines.

NEW YORK METHODIST HOSPITAL

THE INSTITUTE FOR NEUROSCIENCES

New York Methodist Hospital
506 Sixth Street, Brooklyn, N.Y. 11215
Phone: 866 DO-NEURO (866 366-3876)
http://www.nym.org

SPECIALISTS AND MEDICAL SERVICES

The Institute for Neurosciences at New York Methodist Hospital brings together a unique group of specialists and medical services, offering diagnosis and treatment of a broad range of neurological conditions, ranging from frequent headaches to Parkinson's disease to epilepsy.

The Institute's panel of physician specialists includes neurologists, neurosurgeons, psychiatrists, endocrinologists, neuroradiologists, radiation oncologists, physiatrists, geriatricians, psychologists and rehabilitation therapists.

All diagnostic and therapeutic procedures are performed at New York Methodist Hospital or at individual physicians' offices. State-of-the-art equipment to perform computed tomography (CT), magnetic resonance imaging (MRI), and magnetic resonance angiography (MRA) is located in the Hospital's Radiology Department. In addition, equipment and specialists trained to perform neurological diagnostic tests, such as electroencephalography (EEG), electromyography (EMG), and evoked potential examinations are available on the main campus.

The Institute also has a satellite office in Staten Island, located at 1 Harvey Avenue. It can be reached by calling 718 494-4360.

PROGRAMS OFFERED

Special programs and services offered by the Institute include an Alzheimer's disease/memory center, a neuropathy program, pediatric and adult epilepsy programs that offer diagnosis via video EEG, a Parkinson's disease and other movement disorders program, a pituitary program, a multiple sclerosis center, a neuro-oncology service, inpatient and outpatient psychiatry programs, rehabilitation services and a New York State–designated Stroke Center. Neurosurgeons on the Institute's panel perform highly sophisticated procedures, including deep brain stimulation surgery, vascular neurosurgery, skull base surgery and spinal surgery. A stereotactic radiosurgery service is also available at the Hospital's regional radiation oncology center.

***

Referrals to the Institute, its programs and physicians can be made through an individual's primary care physician or requested directly through the Institute's telephone referral service. More information (and on-line physician referral) is available at the Hospital's website, http://www.nym.org.

NYM's CENTER FOR PARKINSON'S DISEASE AND OTHER MOVEMENT DISORDERS

NYM's Center for Parkinson's Disease and Other Movement Disorders is the only such medical center–based program in the New York City area. The Center simplifies the diagnostic and treatment process for patients by consolidating all services.

Treatment for Parkinson's may include medication, surgery and/or specialized therapies. Some patients may be candidates for deep brain stimulation, a neurosurgical procedure that can have dramatic results. NYM is the only Hospital in Brooklyn where this surgery is performed.

The Center has a patient care coordinator to help patients with appointments, treatment regimens, transportation and coordination with insurance companies. For more information, call 718 246-8820.

NEUROLOGY & NEUROSURGERY

NYU Langone Medical Center's Departments of Neurology and Neurosurgery continue to be ranked among the nation's top 10 in the 2014-2015 *U.S. News & World Report's* annual survey of "Best Hospitals." Adult and pediatric patients travel from around the world to consult our renowned specialists for their expertise in the care, treatment, and research of neurological diseases and disorders of the brain, spine, and nervous system. These conditions range from headaches and migraines, nerve and muscle problems, pain, autism, movement disorders, and Alzheimer's disease to stroke, vascular disorders, epilepsy, multiple sclerosis and brain tumors. NYU Langone is home to one of the largest epilepsy centers in the United States, as well as the largest multiple sclerosis program in New York and the first primary stroke center established in New York City.

Neurological Expertise

We treat familial **dysautonomia** and other inherited or acquired autonomic nervous system diseases.

Our multidisciplinary team in the **Center for Cognitive Neurology** offers compassionate, expert care for diseases that affect cognition, such as Alzheimer's and dementia.

A collaborative effort between the Departments of Neurology, Orthopaedic Surgery, and Rehabilitation, the **Concussion Center** provides expert evaluation and seamless, multidisciplinary treatment.

Our Level 4 **Comprehensive Epilepsy Center** offers the most advanced medical and surgical options as well as world-renowned physicians.

Our **Multiple Sclerosis Comprehensive Care Center** provides state-of-the-art diagnostic evaluations and multidisciplinary follow-up care and management.

With one of the largest **neuro-ophthalmology** teams in the world, we offer expert care for individuals with nervous system disorders affecting vision.

Our experienced **neurogenetics** team provides comprehensive diagnosis and treatment of rare, progressive, and often debilitating inherited diseases of the nervous system.

Our specialized **Parkinson's and Movement Disorders Center** features a multidisciplinary team and a community-based support program that is a national model for improving patients' quality of life through fitness, education, and socialization.

Our **Comprehensive Stroke Care Center** provides rapid diagnosis and intervention as well as expert rehabilitation.

Our **pediatric neurology** team cares for children with developmental concerns and delays, such as failing to meet age-related milestones, and neurological conditions such as seizures, cerebral palsy, and epilepsy.

Neurosurgical Expertise

Our multidisciplinary **Brain Tumor Center** is one of the nation's leading programs, specializing in malignant and benign brain and spinal cord tumors, including skull base tumors.

The **Center for Cerebrovascular Disease** is world-renowned for treating brain aneurysms, giant intracranial aneurysms, brain vascular malformations and cavernomas, and stroke.

Our faculty include experts in the surgical treatment of primary **hyperhidrosis** (excessive sweating), including Endoscopic Thoracic Sympathectomy.

We offer the latest in **neuromodulation**, including deep brain stimulation (DBS) and peripheral nerve stimulation (PNS) for Parkinson's, essential tremor, and other conditions.

Our **Center for Advanced Radiosurgery** treats deep-seated tumors, vascular malformations, and other diseases using the Gamma Knife.

The **Spine and Peripheral Nerve Center** provides treatment for degenerative spinal diseases, spinal tumors, spinal trauma and spinal infections.

Our **pediatric neurosurgery** team treats children with brain and spinal tumors, epilepsy, hydrocephalus, pediatric spine disorders, and other congenital and developmental conditions.

Neuroradiology

550 First Avenue *(at 31st Street)*
New York, NY 10016

www.nyulangone.org

Physician Referral: **888-7-NYU-MED** *(888-769-8633)*

NEUROLOGY & NEUROSURGERY

NYU Langone Medical Center's Departments of Neurology and Neurosurgery continue to be ranked among the nation's top 10 in the 2014-2015 *U.S. News & World Report's* annual survey of "Best Hospitals." Adult and pediatric patients travel from around the world to consult our renowned specialists for their expertise in the care, treatment, and research of neurological diseases and disorders of the brain, spine, and nervous system. These conditions range from headaches and migraines, nerve and muscle problems, pain, autism, movement disorders, and Alzheimer's disease to stroke, vascular disorders, epilepsy, multiple sclerosis and brain tumors. NYU Langone is home to one of the largest epilepsy centers in the United States, as well as the largest multiple sclerosis program in New York and the first primary stroke center established in New York City.

Neurological Expertise

We treat familial **dysautonomia** and other inherited or acquired autonomic nervous system diseases.

Our multidisciplinary team in the **Center for Cognitive Neurology** offers compassionate, expert care for diseases that affect cognition, such as Alzheimer's and dementia.

A collaborative effort between the Departments of Neurology, Orthopaedic Surgery, and Rehabilitation, the **Concussion Center** provides expert evaluation and seamless, multidisciplinary treatment.

Our Level 4 **Comprehensive Epilepsy Center** offers the most advanced medical and surgical options as well as world-renowned physicians.

Our **Multiple Sclerosis Comprehensive Care Center** provides state-of-the-art diagnostic evaluations and multidisciplinary follow-up care and management.

With one of the largest **neuro-ophthalmology** teams in the world, we offer expert care for individuals with nervous system disorders affecting vision.

Our experienced **neurogenetics** team provides comprehensive diagnosis and treatment of rare, progressive, and often debilitating inherited diseases of the nervous system.

Our specialized **Parkinson's and Movement Disorders Center** features a multidisciplinary team and a community-based support program that is a national model for improving patients' quality of life through fitness, education, and socialization.

Our **Comprehensive Stroke Care Center** provides rapid diagnosis and intervention as well as expert rehabilitation.

Our **pediatric neurology** team cares for children with developmental concerns and delays, such as failing to meet age-related milestones, and neurological conditions such as seizures, cerebral palsy, and epilepsy.

Neurosurgical Expertise

Our multidisciplinary **Brain Tumor Center** is one of the nation's leading programs, specializing in malignant and benign brain and spinal cord tumors, including skull base tumors.

The **Center for Cerebrovascular Disease** is world-renowned for treating brain aneurysms, giant intracranial aneurysms, brain vascular malformations and cavernomas, and stroke.

Our faculty include experts in the surgical treatment of primary **hyperhidrosis** (excessive sweating), including Endoscopic Thoracic Sympathectomy.

We offer the latest in **neuromodulation**, including deep brain stimulation (DBS) and peripheral nerve stimulation (PNS) for Parkinson's, essential tremor, and other conditions.

Our **Center for Advanced Radiosurgery** treats deep-seated tumors, vascular malformations, and other diseases using the Gamma Knife.

The **Spine and Peripheral Nerve Center** provides treatment for degenerative spinal diseases, spinal tumors, spinal trauma and spinal infections.

Our **pediatric neurosurgery** team treats children with brain and spinal tumors, epilepsy, hydrocephalus, pediatric spine disorders, and other congenital and developmental conditions.

Obstetrics & Gynecology

STELLA & JOSEPH PAYSON BIRTHING CENTER

4802 Tenth Avenue
Brooklyn, New York 11219
Phone: 718.283.7048 • Fax: 718.283.7167

www.maimonidesmed.org/obgyn

The Stella and Joseph Payson Birthing Center features private suites with hardwood floors and a home-like environment. At the same time, physician coverage is provided 24/7 in our advanced Neonatal Intensive Care Unit. Our obstetricians and midwives have found that most families appreciate having the best of both worlds available to them.

Maimonides provides other unique services to its maternity patients. The largest doula program in the metropolitan area can be found at Maimonides. These fully-trained childbirth assistants are available to patients before, during and after delivery at no cost to families. And the maternity units utilize an electronic patient record that sets industry standards for patient safety and hospital efficiency.

This combination of family-centered services and advanced technology continues to have enormous appeal to the women we serve — over 8,500 of them last year alone. Our highly trained staff includes the finest nurses, physicians, midwives and specialists to ensure the safety and comfort of our patients. Several physicians specialize in high-risk pregnancy, including the Chair of Obstetrics & Gynecology, Howard Minkoff, MD.

Women who give birth at Maimonides also have a variety of other services available to them, including:

- A Perinatal Testing Center, directed by Shoshana Haberman, MD, offering amniocentesis, 3-D ultrasound, fetal echo-cardiograms and other diagnostic exams.

- Neonatologists on-site around-the-clock. The Norma Sutton Center for Neonatology adjoins the Payson Birthing Center and provides the most sophisticated care in a family-friendly environment.

In recognition of its excellence in obstetrics and pediatrics, Maimonides was designated a Regional Perinatal Center by the New York State Department of Health. More babies are delivered at Maimonides than at any other single-campus hospital in New York State.

**Maimonides
Medical Center**

Ophthalmology

3400 Bainbridge Avenue
Bronx, NY 10467
718-920-2020
www.montefiore.org/eyes

Ophthalmology and Visual Sciences

Montefiore's Department of Ophthalmology and Visual Sciences provides exceptional care for patients with all forms of ophthalmologic conditions. In addition to its specialty programs in neuro-ophthalmology, retina, refractive surgery (LASIK), oculoplastic surgery, uveitis, cornea and glaucoma, the Department provides a full range of surgical and general ophthalmologic services for children and adults.

The Department is the largest academic ophthalmologic program in New York and among the largest in the nation, with over 100 exam rooms, more than 30 full-time faculty members and annual patient appointments exceeding 160,000. The Department performs roughly 5,000 major surgeries annually. It provides care at eight sites throughout the Bronx and Westchester County.

Meeting the vision needs of the region's vast pediatric population is a particular focus of the Department, which has six pediatric specialists who diagnose and treat patients with common conditions such as refractive error or clogged tear ducts, as well as urgent or uncommon conditions, including ocular cancers, retinopathy of prematurity, pediatric cataracts and glaucoma, genetic conditions and malformations. Few of the nation's ophthalmology programs possess an equal depth and volume of pediatric experience.

The Bronx has a disproportionately high rate of diabetic blindness and glaucoma among adults. The Department offers strong treatment programs that emphasize early diagnosis and intervention with extensive screening and outreach efforts, including tele-ophthalmology-equipped mobile units. An estimated one in four of those screened require follow-up treatment for eye conditions. The Department also offers community health screenings in the Bronx and in parts of Queens, including Flushing, a neighborhood with a predominately Asian population.

Montefiore's ophthalmologists use the most advanced technology and treatment approaches when caring for patients with vision conditions. For example, one of our physician-scientists developed the Trabectome (NeoMedix), a surgical device used to extract the meshwork tissue in glaucoma cases.

Research is a crucial component of the Department's mission, and its faculty members are widely respected for their pioneering efforts. Dr. Barrett Katz was recently named an honoree by the Fight for Sight Foundation.

The Department is the recipient of a fully unrestricted annual grant from the Research to Prevent Blindness Foundation. The Department was recently awarded a competitive R01 grant from the National Institutes of Health (NIH) for work on developing retinal progenitor and stem cells, which could lead to treatments for macular degeneration and diabetic eye disease. The Department's current research portfolio includes nine NIH grants, and focuses on ocular stem cells, information transfer between retinal cells and brain cells, resistance to retinal ischemia and cataractogenesis, and surgical technique and instrument development.

Orthopaedic Surgery

Orthopaedics at Montefiore

The Department of Orthopaedic Surgery at Montefiore offers state-of-the-art treatments for adults and children with a wide range of musculoskeletal problems. The Department has more than 30 fellowship-trained orthopaedic surgeons and podiatrists, who are expert in adult reconstruction and joint replacement surgery, foot and ankle surgery, spine surgery, sports medicine and shoulder surgery, musculoskeletal tumor surgery, trauma surgery and pediatric orthopaedic surgery. They are supported by a multidisciplinary team of physical therapists, rheumatologists, physiatrists, nurse practitioners and social workers, who together provide seamless care from diagnosis to post-surgery rehabilitation.

Earning a national ranking in pediatric orthopaedics and a high-performing designation in adult orthopaedics from *U.S. News & World Report,* the Department draws upon the latest technology and research to achieve exceptional outcomes, while its physicians have contributed to advancements in a wide range of surgeries. The Department offers arthroscopy for all joints and is at the forefront of using adductor canal blocks to eliminate post-operative pain.

The Department's Center for Joint Replacement Surgery conducts nearly 2,000 procedures annually—making it one of the most active programs in the region. The Center specializes in complex joint replacement procedures, including anterior and posterior hip replacement and minimally-invasive knee replacement, and has particular expertise treating elderly patients or those with preexisting medical conditions.

The Department is developing one of the **strongest divisions of orthopaedic sarcoma surgery** in the nation, with orthopaedic surgeons who are specially trained in orthopaedic oncology. In collaboration with Montefiore Einstein Center for Cancer Care, these surgeons provide highly-specialized treatment for adults and children with bone tumors, as well as soft-tissue sarcoma reconstruction and metastatic cancer treatment. Procedures available at Montefiore include osteoarticular allograft bone replacement, tumor endoprostheses and allograft prosthetic composites.

Pediatric orthopaedic surgeons at Children's Hospital at Montefiore (CHAM) are pioneers in the minimally-invasive approach to treating scoliosis in children. Using just three small incisions, CHAM surgeons preserve the spinal muscles and nerves while achieving corrections that are on par with traditional open procedures. They are at the forefront of using pedicle screws to treat spinal deformities and achieve accurate placement rates between 90 and 93 percent on computed tomography scans, among the highest success rates reported.

The Department is actively researching the genetic causes of osteoarthritis; the relationship between diabetes and bone disease, particularly osteoporosis, and the immune system's response to wear debris from polyethylene and metal-on-metal joint prostheses.

THE INSTITUTE FOR ORTHOPEDIC MEDICINE AND SURGERY

New York Methodist Hospital
506 Sixth Street, Brooklyn, N.Y. 11215
Phone: 866 ORTHO-11 (866 678-4611)
http://www.nym.org.

SPECIALISTS AND MEDICAL SERVICES

The Institute for Orthopedic Medicine and Surgery at New York Methodist Hospital brings together a unique team of specialists, facilities and medical services to provide comprehensive treatment of a broad range of orthopedic disorders.

The Institute's panel of physicians includes specialists in adult and pediatric orthopedic surgery, emergency medicine, rheumatology, podiatric medicine and surgery, endocrinology, sports medicine, pain management, orthopedic oncology and neurosurgery. Other important health care team members include physical and occupational therapists. All diagnostic and therapeutic procedures are performed at New York Methodist Hospital or in the offices of the referred physicians.

PROGRAMS OFFERED

In addition to emergency orthopedic services, programs offered through the Institute include joint replacement, arthroscopic knee surgery and cartilage restoration, medical treatments for arthritis, the geriatric hip fracture program, medical and surgical treatment for hand and shoulder injuries and degenerative conditions, spine surgery, physical therapy and pain management. Podiatric physicians specialize in all foot disorders, including reconstructive foot surgery. In addition, the Institute offers complementary medicine services including chiropractic care, acupuncture and medical massage.

* * *

Referrals to the Institute, its programs and physicians can be made through an individual's primary care physician or requested directly through the Institute's telephone referral service. More information (and on-line physician referral) is available at the Hospital's website, http://www.nym.org.

THE COMPREHENSIVE BACK AND NECK PAIN CENTER

NYM's Comprehensive Back and Neck Pain Center is dedicated to providing patients with the best clinical treatment for disorders of the back and neck. Diagnosis and treatment are centrally coordinated, so that patients avoid duplication of screening and testing procedures, if they need to see more than one specialist.

The Center focuses on conservative treatment, most commonly medication and/or rehabilitation (physical or occupational) therapy. Many other modalities are also available. If surgery is recommended, minimally invasive procedures may be applicable. Treatment decisions are made with consideration for the nature and severity of the condition, as well as the patient's lifestyle and preferences. For information or to make an appointment, call 718 369-BACK (2225).

550 First Avenue *(at 31st Street)*
New York, NY 10016
www.nyulangone.org
Physician Referral: **888-7-NYU-MED** *(888-769-8633)*

ORTHOPAEDIC SURGERY

The **Department of Orthopaedic Surgery** at NYU Langone Medical Center continues to be recognized as a national leader, **ranked #4 nationwide in *U.S. News & World Report's* 2014-2015 "Best Hospitals" survey.** Expert physicians combine extensive experience with cutting-edge research and technology to address bone and joint problems that affect a patient's ability to function. The department provides care at NYU Langone's premier outpatient facility, the Center for Musculoskeletal Care, as well as at the Hospital for Joint Diseases, our internationally-renowned inpatient musculoskeletal hospital. The clinical expertise of our world-class ortho-paedic surgeons represents the full range of subspecialty areas including Adult Reconstructive, Sports Medicine and Primary Care Sports Medicine, Spine, Shoulder & Elbow, Foot & Ankle, Hand Surgery, Trauma & Fracture, Orthopaedic Oncology, and Pediatric Orthopaedics; additional areas of focus include minimally-invasive surgery and robotic-assisted joint replacement.

The department also features a number of specialized orthopaedic patient care centers:

Joint Replacement Center physicians are experts in knee, hip and shoulder replacements, complex joint revisions, and minimally invasive surgeries, conducting 3,000+ procedures annually.

The Hip Center evaluates and treats developmental, traumatic, and degenerative hip disorders and specializes in the cutting-edge, minimally invasive anterior total hip replacement technique.

The Joint Preservation and Arthritis Center is dedicated to operative and non-operative treatment of joint problems, aiming to reduce symptoms, restore function and delay the onset of degenerative arthritis and potential need for an eventual joint replacement.

The Spine Center specializes in spine disorders, including lower back and neck pain, scoliosis, osteoporosis and complex spine problems. The Center performs minimally invasive spinal fusions and was one of the first in the country to successfully perform artificial disc implantation.

The Bone Healing Center evaluates and treats problem fractures and are leaders in technologies and procedures to help patients facing a long and difficult recovery from complex fracture reconstruction or fracture healing problems.

Harkness Center for Dance Injuries offers many subsidized and free services for dancers, including clinics staffed by orthopaedists and dance physical therapists. The Center also offers state-of-the-art rehabilitation technology and free injury prevention screenings and lectures.

The Diabetes Foot and Ankle Center focuses on the prevention and recurrence of foot and ankle problems associated with complications of diabetes.

The Orthopaedic Immediate Care Center ("i-Care"), New York City's only walk-in orthopaedic clinic, uses state-of-the-art diagnostic equipment to evaluate and treat adults with hand and foot injuries, hip, arm or leg fractures, dislocation or joint injury, sprains, and bone or joint infection.

The Occupational and Industrial Orthopaedic Center (OIOC) provides clinical, educational, research and consulting services in the prevention and treatment of musculoskeletal injuries and disorders that arise from work or the work environment.

STAMFORD HOSPITAL
Orthopedic & Spine Institute

Orthopedic and Spine Institute

Stamford Hospital was the first in the region to earn the Joint Commission certification for our Total Hip and Total Knee Replacement programs in addition to our Spine Fusion Program. We were awarded the Gold Seal of Approval™ for complying with the highest national standards for safety and quality of care. Our healthcare team earned this distinction by undergoing a lengthy process of professional review, including on-site evaluations.

Total Joint Replacement

We provide comprehensive orthopedic services, including prevention, assessment, treatment and rehabilitation. Our fellowship-trained surgeons routinely perform total hip and knee replacements, as well as minimally invasive joint replacements and hip fracture surgeries using leading-edge technology to improve patient care and outcomes.

Spine Center

Experts in total spine care, from acute neck and back pain to spinal instability and deformity, we provide relief to those who may have previously tried non-surgical options. We perform more complex spine surgeries than any other hospital in the region. We also offer minimally invasive spine surgery. A team of dedicated orthopedic and neurosurgeons, nurses, anesthesiologists, physical therapists and pain-management specialists, are experienced in treating the most challenging spinal conditions.

Sports Medicine

No matter your age or level of play, amateur or seasoned professional, we can help you stay in the game. We combine hands-on evaluation and appropriate diagnostic testing to determine the best plan of care. We provide the latest surgical techniques and are experienced in performing a wide variety of advanced procedures. Our surgeons are fellowship-trained in sports medicine from some of the top programs in the country.

Chelsea Piers Connecticut

Stamford Hospital's Orthopedic and Spine Institute at Chelsea Piers CT, offers: a comprehensive *Concussion Program* complete with a multidisciplinary team of providers who work collaboratively on prevention, education, diagnosis and treatment plans. *Sports Nutrition Services*, integrative medicine, pain management, radiology, sports medicine, spine and general orthopedic care. A state-of-the-art *Motion Analysis Program* provides patients with motion and biomechanical analysis. *Athletes in the Arts* is an approach to care which gives athletes and performing artists access to experts in training and injury treatment to excel in their sport or art.

Academic and Clinical Affiliations

Stamford Hospital is an affiliate of the New York–Presbyterian Healthcare System and a major teaching affiliate of the Columbia University College of Physicians & Surgeons.

Accreditation

The Joint Commission

Beds

305

Sponsorship

Voluntary, Not-for-Profit

For a Physician Referral or more information, please call 1.877.233.9355 or visit StamfordHospital.org /doctor.

Stamford Hospital
30 Shelburne Road
Stamford, CT 06902
203.276.1000

StamfordHospital.org

WINTHROP
University Hospital

Your Health Means Everything.®

259 First Street, Mineola, NY 11501
Tel: 1-866-WINTHROP • www.winthrop.org

Department of Orthopaedic Surgery

Winthrop-University Hospital is committed to being a leading center of excellence for orthopaedic surgery on Long Island.

Dedicated to a highly individualized, multidisciplinary team approach to address the musculoskeletal needs of each patient as a whole person, Winthrop's orthopaedic surgeons address a full range of orthopaedic conditions, using both surgical and non-surgical procedures to relieve pain, discomfort, and maximize each patient's mobility.

The Winthrop Orthopaedic Surgery team is comprised of specialists who address several specialty areas of orthopaedics including: pediatric orthopaedics, hand and upper extremity surgery, minimally invasive surgery, arthroscopy, sports medicine, trauma and fracture repair, arthritis treatment, joint replacement and reconstruction surgery, spine surgery, and podiatry.

This combination of advanced treatment options and specialists in virtually every area of adult and pediatric orthopaedic medicine places Winthrop's program at the forefront of orthopaedic care on Long Island.

Robotic Orthopaedic Surgery
A leader in total joint replacement, Winthrop continues to reach new frontiers in total hip replacement surgery, total knee replacements and joint replacement revision surgery. The joint replacement team also specializes in performing minimally-invasive, bone-sparing, and tissue-conserving total hip replacements. The department also offers robotically assisted total knee replacement – a highly accurate approach to knee replacement surgery only offered at Winthrop.

Sports Medicine
Winthrop's comprehensive Sports Medicine Center features orthopaedic surgeons who focus on every joint in the body – from ankles and wrists to knees and hips – for both adults and children. Physicians work with patients individually to attain the highest levels of achievement despite any injury they may have. The Team also works with local schools to help athletes who have sustained injuries to get back in the game as quickly and safely as possible.

Hand Injuries
The hand service treats children and adults with a variety of bone and soft tissue conditions of the hand and upper extremity. Some of the more common conditions include carpal tunnel syndrome, tennis elbow, and trigger finger. The department also specializes in the treatment of deformities, re-implantations, metabolic bone disease, complex fractures, and sports-related injuries.

Foot and Ankle Treatment
Winthrop's foot and ankle team specializes in a wide range of treatments, which can range from bracing and physical therapy to surgical procedures such as bunion surgery, ankle arthroscopy, complex ligament and tendon reconstructions, total ankle replacements, and osteochondral grafting procedures.

Pediatric Care
Children's growth plates are delicate and are especially prone to fracture. Because many childhood fractures involve growth plates, it is vital for children to be evaluated quickly when a fracture occurs in order to determine the best course of treatment and avoid growth deformity. Winthrop's Division of Pediatric Orthopaedic Surgery treats pediatric patients from newborn to young adulthood.

Pediatric Cardiology

HASSENFELD CHILDREN'S HOSPITAL

Hassenfeld Children's Hospital (HCH) is a full-service specialty children's hospital encompassing all children's health services at NYU Langone Medical Center. At HCH, newborns, children, adolescents and young adults receive the most comprehensive and advanced care possible from a team of pediatricians and pediatric specialists across more than 30 medical and surgical disciplines. With more than 150 full-time pediatric specialists, as well as pediatric nurses, child life specialists and social workers, Hassenfeld Children's Hospital is uniquely equipped to provide innovative pediatric subspecialty care in a highly personalized manner.

Child- and Family-Centered Care

Integral to the care we provide is a myriad of support services for children and their families. We recognize that the best outcomes are achieved when the child's family is actively involved in every step of care. For that reason, our trained specialists address the needs of not just the patient, but of parents and siblings through ongoing education and communication.

Our pediatric specialties include:

Anesthesiology

Cardiology

Cardiothoracic Surgery

Child and Adolescent Psychiatry
  and Psychology/Child Study Center

Critical Care

Dermatology

Developmental and Behavioral Pediatrics

Emergency Medicine

Endocrinology

Epilepsy

Gastroenterology

Genetics

Hematology/Oncology

Infectious Diseases

Neonatology

Nephrology

Neurosurgery

Neurology

Ophthalmology

Orthopaedic Surgery

Otolaryngology

Pathology

Pulmonology

Radiology

Reconstructive and Plastic Surgery

Rehabilitation

Rheumatology

Surgery

Urology

Pediatric Emergency Medicine

HASSENFELD CHILDREN'S HOSPITAL

Hassenfeld Children's Hospital (HCH) is a full-service specialty children's hospital encompassing all children's health services at NYU Langone Medical Center. At HCH, newborns, children, adolescents and young adults receive the most comprehensive and advanced care possible from a team of pediatricians and pediatric specialists across more than 30 medical and surgical disciplines. With more than 150 full-time pediatric specialists, as well as pediatric nurses, child life specialists and social workers, Hassenfeld Children's Hospital is uniquely equipped to provide innovative pediatric subspecialty care in a highly personalized manner.

Child- and Family-Centered Care

Integral to the care we provide is a myriad of support services for children and their families. We recognize that the best outcomes are achieved when the child's family is actively involved in every step of care. For that reason, our trained specialists address the needs of not just the patient, but of parents and siblings through ongoing education and communication.

Our pediatric specialties include:

Anesthesiology

Cardiology

Cardiothoracic Surgery

Child and Adolescent Psychiatry
  and Psychology/Child Study Center

Critical Care

Dermatology

Developmental and Behavioral Pediatrics

Emergency Medicine

Endocrinology

Epilepsy

Gastroenterology

Genetics

Hematology/Oncology

Infectious Diseases

Neonatology

Nephrology

Neurosurgery

Neurology

Ophthalmology

Orthopaedic Surgery

Otolaryngology

Pathology

Pulmonology

Radiology

Reconstructive and Plastic Surgery

Rehabilitation

Rheumatology

Surgery

Urology

Pediatric Endocrinology

HASSENFELD CHILDREN'S HOSPITAL

Hassenfeld Children's Hospital (HCH) is a full-service specialty children's hospital encompassing all children's health services at NYU Langone Medical Center. At HCH, newborns, children, adolescents and young adults receive the most comprehensive and advanced care possible from a team of pediatricians and pediatric specialists across more than 30 medical and surgical disciplines. With more than 150 full-time pediatric specialists, as well as pediatric nurses, child life specialists and social workers, Hassenfeld Children's Hospital is uniquely equipped to provide innovative pediatric subspecialty care in a highly personalized manner.

Child- and Family-Centered Care

Integral to the care we provide is a myriad of support services for children and their families. We recognize that the best outcomes are achieved when the child's family is actively involved in every step of care. For that reason, our trained specialists address the needs of not just the patient, but of parents and siblings through ongoing education and communication.

Our pediatric specialties include:

Anesthesiology

Cardiology

Cardiothoracic Surgery

Child and Adolescent Psychiatry
    and Psychology/Child Study Center

Critical Care

Dermatology

Developmental and Behavioral Pediatrics

Emergency Medicine

Endocrinology

Epilepsy

Gastroenterology

Genetics

Hematology/Oncology

Infectious Diseases

Neonatology

Nephrology

Neurosurgery

Neurology

Ophthalmology

Orthopaedic Surgery

Otolaryngology

Pathology

Pulmonology

Radiology

Reconstructive and Plastic Surgery

Rehabilitation

Rheumatology

Surgery

Urology

Pediatric Gastroenterology

550 First Avenue *(at 31st Street)*
New York, NY 10016

nyulmc.org/hassenfeld-childrens

Hassenfeld Children's Hospital Access Line: **855-NYU-KIDS**

HASSENFELD CHILDREN'S HOSPITAL

Hassenfeld Children's Hospital (HCH) is a full-service specialty children's hospital encompassing all children's health services at NYU Langone Medical Center. At HCH, newborns, children, adolescents and young adults receive the most comprehensive and advanced care possible from a team of pediatricians and pediatric specialists across more than 30 medical and surgical disciplines. With more than 150 full-time pediatric specialists, as well as pediatric nurses, child life specialists and social workers, Hassenfeld Children's Hospital is uniquely equipped to provide innovative pediatric subspecialty care in a highly personalized manner.

Child- and Family-Centered Care

Integral to the care we provide is a myriad of support services for children and their families. We recognize that the best outcomes are achieved when the child's family is actively involved in every step of care. For that reason, our trained specialists address the needs of not just the patient, but of parents and siblings through ongoing education and communication.

Our pediatric specialties include:

Anesthesiology

Cardiology

Cardiothoracic Surgery

Child and Adolescent Psychiatry
  and Psychology/Child Study Center

Critical Care

Dermatology

Developmental and Behavioral Pediatrics

Emergency Medicine

Endocrinology

Epilepsy

Gastroenterology

Genetics

Hematology/Oncology

Infectious Diseases

Neonatology

Nephrology

Neurosurgery

Neurology

Ophthalmology

Orthopaedic Surgery

Otolaryngology

Pathology

Pulmonology

Radiology

Reconstructive and Plastic Surgery

Rehabilitation

Rheumatology

Surgery

Urology

Pediatric Hematology-Oncology

NYU Langone Medical Center
550 First Avenue, New York, NY 10016
www.nyulangone.org

Laura and Isaac Perlmutter Cancer Center
160 East 34th Street, New York, NY 10016

**The Stephen D. Hassenfeld Children's Center
for Cancer and Blood Disorders**
160 East 32nd Street, New York, NY 10016

LAURA AND ISAAC PERLMUTTER CANCER CENTER

Formerly NYU Cancer Institute, the Laura and Isaac Perlmutter Cancer Center is an NCI-designated cancer center providing personalized patient care that is compassionate and state-of-the-art. The doctors and researchers work together to develop innovative therapies for patients. The Center is world-renowned for excellence in cancer-focused research, personalized care, education and community outreach. Its mission is to discover the origins of human cancer and to use that knowledge to eradicate the personal and societal burden of cancer in our community, the nation and the world. For more information about our expert physicians, call 1.888.769.8633.

Patient-Focused Setting
The Center and its multidisciplinary team of experts provide access to the latest treatment options and clinical trials, along with a variety of programs in cancer risk reduction/prevention, screening, diagnostics, genetic counseling and supportive services. In addition, the Center emphasizes the importance of a holistic approach involving integrative care, psychosocial support, survivorship, supportive oncology, and palliative care. In addition to our principal outpatient facility at 160 East 34th Street, services are also available at our Ambulatory Care Center on 38th Street in Manhattan; Rego Park, NY; and Lake Success, NY.

Renowned Expertise
Laura and Isaac Perlmutter Cancer Center brings together experts from a variety of disciplines to create collaborative research endeavors and clinical care teams. Our teams are highly skilled in minimally invasive techniques along with video-assisted and robotic surgery. We have created special programs to treat diseases such as breast cancer, brain cancer, melanoma, GI cancer, prostate cancer, hematologic malignancies, sarcoma, and lung cancer. We also continue to focus on translational programs in cancer healthcare disparities; molecularly targeted as well as immune- and stem-cell-based therapies; and the cell signaling pathways involved in cancer.

A Translational Approach
Our scientists and researchers excel in uncovering how cancer develops at the molecular level, and how we can harness that knowledge to reduce the risk of cancer and treat the disease.

Stephen D. Hassenfeld Children's Center for Cancer and Blood Disorders
As part of Hassenfeld Children's Hospital, the center is a leading pediatric outpatient facility for the treatment of childhood cancers and blood diseases. Its unique interdisciplinary and family-centered approach combines the most advanced medical treatments with psychosocial and emotional support services for young patients and their families.

HASSENFELD CHILDREN'S HOSPITAL

Hassenfeld Children's Hospital (HCH) is a full-service specialty children's hospital encompassing all children's health services at NYU Langone Medical Center. At HCH, newborns, children, adolescents and young adults receive the most comprehensive and advanced care possible from a team of pediatricians and pediatric specialists across more than 30 medical and surgical disciplines. With more than 150 full-time pediatric specialists, as well as pediatric nurses, child life specialists and social workers, Hassenfeld Children's Hospital is uniquely equipped to provide innovative pediatric subspecialty care in a highly personalized manner.

Child- and Family-Centered Care

Integral to the care we provide is a myriad of support services for children and their families. We recognize that the best outcomes are achieved when the child's family is actively involved in every step of care. For that reason, our trained specialists address the needs of not just the patient, but of parents and siblings through ongoing education and communication.

Our pediatric specialties include:

Anesthesiology

Cardiology

Cardiothoracic Surgery

Child and Adolescent Psychiatry
  and Psychology/Child Study Center

Critical Care

Dermatology

Developmental and Behavioral Pediatrics

Emergency Medicine

Endocrinology

Epilepsy

Gastroenterology

Genetics

Hematology/Oncology

Infectious Diseases

Neonatology

Nephrology

Neurosurgery

Neurology

Ophthalmology

Orthopaedic Surgery

Otolaryngology

Pathology

Pulmonology

Radiology

Reconstructive and Plastic Surgery

Rehabilitation

Rheumatology

Surgery

Urology

The Best in American Medicine
www.CastleConnolly.com

Pediatric Infectious Disease

550 First Avenue *(at 31st Street)*
New York, NY 10016

nyulmc.org/hassenfeld-childrens

Hassenfeld Children's Hospital Access Line: **855-NYU-KIDS**

HASSENFELD CHILDREN'S HOSPITAL

Hassenfeld Children's Hospital (HCH) is a full-service specialty children's hospital encompassing all children's health services at NYU Langone Medical Center. At HCH, newborns, children, adolescents and young adults receive the most comprehensive and advanced care possible from a team of pediatricians and pediatric specialists across more than 30 medical and surgical disciplines. With more than 150 full-time pediatric specialists, as well as pediatric nurses, child life specialists and social workers, Hassenfeld Children's Hospital is uniquely equipped to provide innovative pediatric subspecialty care in a highly personalized manner.

Child- and Family-Centered Care

Integral to the care we provide is a myriad of support services for children and their families. We recognize that the best outcomes are achieved when the child's family is actively involved in every step of care. For that reason, our trained specialists address the needs of not just the patient, but of parents and siblings through ongoing education and communication.

Our pediatric specialties include:

Anesthesiology

Cardiology

Cardiothoracic Surgery

Child and Adolescent Psychiatry
  and Psychology/Child Study Center

Critical Care

Dermatology

Developmental and Behavioral Pediatrics

Emergency Medicine

Endocrinology

Epilepsy

Gastroenterology

Genetics

Hematology/Oncology

Infectious Diseases

Neonatology

Nephrology

Neurosurgery

Neurology

Ophthalmology

Orthopaedic Surgery

Otolaryngology

Pathology

Pulmonology

Radiology

Reconstructive and Plastic Surgery

Rehabilitation

Rheumatology

Surgery

Urology

Pediatric Nephrology

550 First Avenue (*at 31st Street*)
New York, NY 10016

nyulmc.org/hassenfeld-childrens

Hassenfeld Children's Hospital Access Line: **855-NYU-KIDS**

HASSENFELD CHILDREN'S HOSPITAL

Hassenfeld Children's Hospital (HCH) is a full-service specialty children's hospital encompassing all children's health services at NYU Langone Medical Center. At HCH, newborns, children, adolescents and young adults receive the most comprehensive and advanced care possible from a team of pediatricians and pediatric specialists across more than 30 medical and surgical disciplines. With more than 150 full-time pediatric specialists, as well as pediatric nurses, child life specialists and social workers, Hassenfeld Children's Hospital is uniquely equipped to provide innovative pediatric subspecialty care in a highly personalized manner.

Child- and Family-Centered Care

Integral to the care we provide is a myriad of support services for children and their families. We recognize that the best outcomes are achieved when the child's family is actively involved in every step of care. For that reason, our trained specialists address the needs of not just the patient, but of parents and siblings through ongoing education and communication.

Our pediatric specialties include:

Anesthesiology

Cardiology

Cardiothoracic Surgery

Child and Adolescent Psychiatry
and Psychology/Child Study Center

Critical Care

Dermatology

Developmental and Behavioral Pediatrics

Emergency Medicine

Endocrinology

Epilepsy

Gastroenterology

Genetics

Hematology/Oncology

Infectious Diseases

Neonatology

Nephrology

Neurosurgery

Neurology

Ophthalmology

Orthopaedic Surgery

Otolaryngology

Pathology

Pulmonology

Radiology

Reconstructive and Plastic Surgery

Rehabilitation

Rheumatology

Surgery

Urology

Pediatric Rheumatology

550 First Avenue *(at 31st Street)*
New York, NY 10016

nyulmc.org/hassenfeld-childrens

Hassenfeld Children's Hospital Access Line: **855-NYU-KIDS**

HASSENFELD CHILDREN'S HOSPITAL

Hassenfeld Children's Hospital (HCH) is a full-service specialty children's hospital encompassing all children's health services at NYU Langone Medical Center. At HCH, newborns, children, adolescents and young adults receive the most comprehensive and advanced care possible from a team of pediatricians and pediatric specialists across more than 30 medical and surgical disciplines. With more than 150 full-time pediatric specialists, as well as pediatric nurses, child life specialists and social workers, Hassenfeld Children's Hospital is uniquely equipped to provide innovative pediatric subspecialty care in a highly personalized manner.

Child- and Family-Centered Care

Integral to the care we provide is a myriad of support services for children and their families. We recognize that the best outcomes are achieved when the child's family is actively involved in every step of care. For that reason, our trained specialists address the needs of not just the patient, but of parents and siblings through ongoing education and communication.

Our pediatric specialties include:

Anesthesiology

Cardiology

Cardiothoracic Surgery

Child and Adolescent Psychiatry
  and Psychology/Child Study Center

Critical Care

Dermatology

Developmental and Behavioral Pediatrics

Emergency Medicine

Endocrinology

Epilepsy

Gastroenterology

Genetics

Hematology/Oncology

Infectious Diseases

Neonatology

Nephrology

Neurosurgery

Neurology

Ophthalmology

Orthopaedic Surgery

Otolaryngology

Pathology

Pulmonology

Radiology

Reconstructive and Plastic Surgery

Rehabilitation

Rheumatology

Surgery

Urology

Pediatric Surgery

HASSENFELD CHILDREN'S HOSPITAL

Hassenfeld Children's Hospital (HCH) is a full-service specialty children's hospital encompassing all children's health services at NYU Langone Medical Center. At HCH, newborns, children, adolescents and young adults receive the most comprehensive and advanced care possible from a team of pediatricians and pediatric specialists across more than 30 medical and surgical disciplines. With more than 150 full-time pediatric specialists, as well as pediatric nurses, child life specialists and social workers, Hassenfeld Children's Hospital is uniquely equipped to provide innovative pediatric subspecialty care in a highly personalized manner.

Child- and Family-Centered Care

Integral to the care we provide is a myriad of support services for children and their families. We recognize that the best outcomes are achieved when the child's family is actively involved in every step of care. For that reason, our trained specialists address the needs of not just the patient, but of parents and siblings through ongoing education and communication.

Our pediatric specialties include:

Anesthesiology

Cardiology

Cardiothoracic Surgery

Child and Adolescent Psychiatry
   and Psychology/Child Study Center

Critical Care

Dermatology

Developmental and Behavioral Pediatrics

Emergency Medicine

Endocrinology

Epilepsy

Gastroenterology

Genetics

Hematology/Oncology

Infectious Diseases

Neonatology

Nephrology

Neurosurgery

Neurology

Ophthalmology

Orthopaedic Surgery

Otolaryngology

Pathology

Pulmonology

Radiology

Reconstructive and Plastic Surgery

Rehabilitation

Rheumatology

Surgery

Urology

Pediatrics

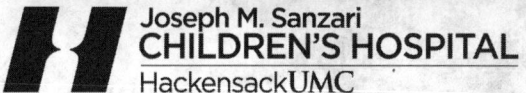

Joseph M. Sanzari
CHILDREN'S HOSPITAL
HackensackUMC

30 Prospect Avenue, Hackensack, NJ 07601 • 551-996-5300
www.HackensackUMC.org

The Joseph M. Sanzari Children's Hospital at HackensackUMC is a state-designated children's hospital and an award-winning facility that has been recognized as one of the top-ranked children's hospitals in New Jersey and in the country. It ranked 44th among the Best Children's Hospitals for Neurology and Neurosurgery in the 2014-15 Best Children's Hospitals rankings by *U.S. News & World Report* — the first hospital in New Jersey to be ranked in any Best Children's Hospitals specialty, and the only hospital in the state to be ranked in Neurology and Neurosurgery.

FACILITY:

As a state-designated children's hospital, The Joseph M. Sanzari Children's Hospital provides comprehensive patient- and family-centered medical and surgical pediatric care in more than 30 specialties, all integrated within a state-of-the-art child-focused facility. The facility offers 24-hour access to leading physicians, nurses, staff and a Pediatric Emergency/Trauma Department. It features a modern facility with children's play and family kitchen areas, and private inpatient rooms with computers, internet access, and flat-screen plasma televisions. Parents are encouraged to take part in their children's treatment and hospitalization and are welcome to stay overnight. The Joseph M. Sanzari Children's Hospital is housed with the Donna A. Sanzari Women's Hospital in the Sarkis and Siran Gabrellian Women's and Children's Pavilion; which was designed with The Deirdre Imus Environmental Health Center, and was included on the Green Guide's list of Top 10 Green Hospitals in the U.S.

SPECIALTIES:

Adolescent medicine, audiology, cardiology, child abuse and neglect, child and adolescent psychiatry, child life, clinical and laboratory immunology, critical care medicine, dermatology, developmental, Pediatric Emergency Department, endocrinology, epilepsy monitoring, gastroenterology, general pediatrics, genetics, hematology-oncology, infectious disease, neonatal-perinatal medicine, nephrology, neurodevelopmental disabilities, neuro oncology, otolaryngology, orthopaedic surgery, pain and palliative medicine, pediatric neurology, pediatric sleep, pediatric surgery, pulmonology, radiology, rehabilitation medicine, rheumatology, social work, and transplant.

SPECIALIZED PROGRAMS:

Audrey Hepburn Children's House; Community CPR and First Aid Training; David Center for Pain and Palliative Care; Sarkis & Siran Gabrellian Child Care and Learning Center; Healthy Futures; Institute for Child Development; Institute for Pediatric Cancer and Blood Disorders; JUDY Center for Down Syndrome; MOLLY Center for Children with Diabetes; SIDS Center of New Jersey; and the Steven and Richard Bader Immunological Institute.

- In 2002, HackensackUMC dedicated the world's first Audrey Hepburn Children's House, a state-designated Regional Diagnostic Center for Child Abuse and Neglect serving Bergen, Passaic, Hudson, Morris, Sussex and Warren counties.

- Our Pediatric Emergency Department is open 24 hours a day, seven days a week, and we provide care for children ranging in age from infancy through the age of 21 years.

- The Institute for Pediatric Cancer and Blood Disorders is home to the Blood and Marrow Transplant Program—the only stem cell transplant program in the state of New Jersey. The institute is also home to Cure and Beyond—the only comprehensive program dedication to childhood cancer survivors in the state.

For more information on any of the services offered at HackensackUMC, please call 551-996-5300, or visit HackensackUMC.org.

Sponsored Page

The Children's Hospital at Montefiore

3415 Bainbridge Avenue
Bronx, New York 10467
718-741-2450
www.cham.org

Pediatric Services

Children's Hospital at Montefiore (CHAM) unites leading pediatric specialists with the latest technology and research to deliver exceptional care to children in the Bronx, Westchester County and beyond. CHAM's nationally-recognized divisions and programs include the following capabilities:

- The Division of Gastroenterology and Nutrition expertly manages patients with both life-threatening and common gastrointestinal disorders. The Division is a leader in the care of patients with short bowel syndrome, inflammatory bowel disease and liver disease, with outstanding outcomes for patients requiring liver transplant.

- The Division of Hematology and Oncology offers the area's only comprehensive Sickle Cell Program, providing the latest treatment advances and screening methods for sickle cell complications, including bone marrow transplant to cure sickle cell anemia. The Division delivers exceptional care for patients with leukemia, lymphoma and neuroblastoma, and is one of the nation's leading centers for treating brain tumors and bone cancer.

- The Pediatric Heart Center is a leader in treating patients with common and rare heart conditions. The Center excels in the use of mechanical assist devices as a bridge to transplant and in cardiac ablation procedures to treat patients with cardiac arrhythmias.

- The Division of Neonatology boasts the only designated regional perinatal center serving the Bronx, achieving exceptional outcomes in the care of preterm and critically-ill term neonates.

- The Division of Pediatric Critical Care provides multidisciplinary care for children with life-threatening medical and surgical conditions. The recently expanded, state-of-the-art, 26-bed Pediatric Critical Care Unit is one of the largest and busiest in New York.

- The Division of Endocrinology and Diabetes provides exceptional care for children with endocrine disorders, thyroid disease and diabetes. Recognized by the American Diabetes Association, the Diabetes Care Team provides in-depth evaluation, treatment and counseling for patients with diabetes and their families.

- The Ira Greifer Children's Kidney Center is at the forefront of pediatric nephrology, urology and transplant medicine.

- The Division of Respiratory and Sleep Medicine is the only full-service sleep laboratory dedicated exclusively to children in the New York metropolitan area.

- The Division of Orthopaedics is revolutionizing scoliosis treatment through an innovative combination of advanced imaging technologies, minimally-invasive surgery and bloodless techniques, resulting in reduced post-operative pain, hospital stays and recovery times.

- CHAM's Emergency Department is staffed by collaborative teams of pediatric general and subspecialty surgeons with expertise in pediatric urology, ear/nose/throat, neurosurgery, plastic surgery and ophthalmology.

CHAM has an acclaimed pediatric residency training program and outstanding fellowship programs in every subspecialty.

Because CHAM is the pediatric hospital for Albert Einstein College of Medicine, research conducted by CHAM faculty has led to new therapies, safer processes and better outcomes for children throughout the world.

NewYork-Presbyterian

Affiliated with Columbia University College of Physicians and Surgeons and Weill Cornell Medical College

NewYork-Presbyterian
Morgan Stanley Children's Hospital

3959 Broadway
New York, NY 10032

NewYork-Presbyterian
Phyllis and David Komansky
Center for Children's Health

525 East 68th Street
New York, NY 10065

1-800-245-KIDS (1-800-245-5437) www.nyp.org/kids

Accreditation: The Joint Commission

Overview

The pediatric services of NewYork-Presbyterian Hospital are comprised of NewYork-Presbyterian/Morgan Stanley Children's Hospital, which is affiliated with Columbia University College of Physicians and Surgeons, and NewYork-Presbyterian/Phyllis and David Komansky Center for Children's Health, which is affiliated with Weill Cornell Medical College. Together, they serve as one of the nation's premier centers for comprehensive pediatric care. Skilled and experienced physicians, surgeons, nurses and other pediatric healthcare professionals manage some of the most complex medical conditions of children at every stage of development. Their expertise includes general pediatric care and the full range of medical and surgical subspecialties:

- Adolescent Medicine
- Allergy and Immunology
- Anesthesiology
- Blood Disorders
- Blood and Marrow Transplantation
- Cancer
- Cardiology and Cardiac Surgery
- Craniofacial and Plastic Surgery
- Critical Care
- Dermatology
- Digestive Disease
- Ear, Nose and Throat
- Emergency Department, including specialized units for burns and trauma injuries
- Endocrinology, Diabetes and Metabolism
- Epilepsy
- Genetics
- Infectious Diseases
- Kidney Disease
- Liver Disease
- Lung Disease
- Neonatal Medicine
- Neurology and Neurological Surgery
- Nutrition
- Obesity and Bariatric Surgery
- Ophthalmology
- Oral and Maxillofacial Surgery and Pediatric Dentistry
- Organ Transplantation
- Orthopaedic Surgery
- Pain Medicine
- Pediatric Surgery
- Pregnancy and Newborn Services
- Primary Care/General Pediatrics
- Psychiatry
- Radiology
- Rheumatology
- Urology

Highlights at a Glance:

- A national leader in pediatric open-heart surgery with one of the largest pediatric heart transplant programs in the nation.
- A pediatric kidney transplant program, which includes a Living Donor Program and leading edge therapies to help reduce the side effects of anti-rejection drugs.
- Pediatric cardiac surgeons at the forefront of ventricular assist devices for infants and small children as a bridge to recovery or transplantation.
- One of three Level 1-designated Regional Pediatric Trauma Centers in New York State and the only one in New York City.
- A New York State Department of Health-designated Regional Perinatal Center of Expertise for the care of women with high-risk pregnancies.
- One of the largest Type 1 diabetes programs in New York State.
- Outstanding neonatal intensive care programs setting standards of care nationwide for extremely ill newborns.
- The only program in the New York tri-state area that has active programs in both liver and small bowel transplantation.

HASSENFELD CHILDREN'S HOSPITAL

Hassenfeld Children's Hospital (HCH) is a full-service specialty children's hospital encompassing all children's health services at NYU Langone Medical Center. At HCH, newborns, children, adolescents and young adults receive the most comprehensive and advanced care possible from a team of pediatricians and pediatric specialists across more than 30 medical and surgical disciplines. With more than 150 full-time pediatric specialists, as well as pediatric nurses, child life specialists and social workers, Hassenfeld Children's Hospital is uniquely equipped to provide innovative pediatric subspecialty care in a highly personalized manner.

Child- and Family-Centered Care

Integral to the care we provide is a myriad of support services for children and their families. We recognize that the best outcomes are achieved when the child's family is actively involved in every step of care. For that reason, our trained specialists address the needs of not just the patient, but of parents and siblings through ongoing education and communication.

Our pediatric specialties include:

Anesthesiology

Cardiology

Cardiothoracic Surgery

Child and Adolescent Psychiatry
and Psychology/Child Study Center

Critical Care

Dermatology

Developmental and Behavioral Pediatrics

Emergency Medicine

Endocrinology

Epilepsy

Gastroenterology

Genetics

Hematology/Oncology

Infectious Diseases

Neonatology

Nephrology

Neurosurgery

Neurology

Ophthalmology

Orthopaedic Surgery

Otolaryngology

Pathology

Pulmonology

Radiology

Reconstructive and Plastic Surgery

Rehabilitation

Rheumatology

Surgery

Urology

Physical Medicine & Rehabilitation

Rusk Rehabilitation
550 First Avenue (*at 31st Street*)
New York, NY 10016
www.nyulangone.org
Physician Referral: **888-7-NYU-MED** (888-769-8633)

RUSK REHABILITATION

Rusk Rehabilitation at NYU Langone Medical Center has been ranked the best rehabilitation program in New York and among the top ten in the country by *U.S. News & World Report* for 25 consecutive years. Rusk is internationally renowned for the treatment of adults and children with disabilities, providing the full continuum of inpatient and outpatient rehabilitation care at multiple, state-of-the-art NYU Langone facilities and across all specialties: physical, occupational, speech/swallowing and vocational therapy, psychology, music and recreational therapy, nutrition, nursing, and social work.

CARF-Accredited Brain Injury Rehabilitation Program is tailored for patients who have medical, physical, cognitive, and behavioral changes as a result of a brain injury or neurological illness.

The Concussion Center provides seamless, multidisciplinary care for individuals with concussions, including specialized rehabilitation care provided by the Rusk team.

Rusk's CARF-Accredited Stroke Program offers an interdisciplinary team with specialized training in the medical, nursing or therapeutic care and treatment of stroke patients.

The Pediatric Rehabilitation team is particularly skilled in treating the multiple challenges of children with developmental disorders as well as children with traumatic brain injuries, brain tumors, oncologic diagnoses (such as bone tumors or musculoskeletal disease), stroke or cerebrovascular conditions, viral infections or inflammatory diseases, and rheumatic disease. Rusk's Inpatient Pediatric Rehabilitation Program is accredited by the Commission on Accreditation of Rehabilitation Facilities (CARF).

The Spinal Cord Injury Program offers a comprehensive, patient-centered array of specialized and innovative clinical and educational programs to optimize quality of life.

The Amputee Program provides specialized limb deficiency rehabilitation to patients who have undergone amputations.

The Joan and Joel Smilow Cardiac and Pulmonary Rehabilitation & Prevention Center offers a model of transitional care for patients with cardiac and lung conditions.

Orthopaedic/Musculoskeletal Rehabilitation is offered for patients with back, neck, hip, elbow and shoulder disorders, arthritis-related joint pain, conditions affecting the bones, tendon, ligaments and muscles, and for pre- and post-surgical patients.

Sports Injury Rehabilitation addresses the needs of patients with sports-related conditions, including post-operative rehabilitation for patients who require orthopaedic surgery.

Vestibular Rehabilitation addresses the evaluation and treatment of patients suffering from dizziness and imbalance.

The Women's Health Program addresses issues that uniquely affect women, including pelvic floor muscle dysfunction/pain, urinary incontinence, cancer rehabilitation and lymphedema, and prenatal and postpartum musculoskeletal conditions.

Chest Physical Therapy cares for individuals with lung congestion, secretion retention or areas of lung collapse.

The Outpatient Rehabilitation Psychology Service provides care to patients with neurological and medical conditions.

Speech-Language Pathology & Swallowing is dedicated to patients with communication disorders due to neurological problems as well as diagnosis and management of swallowing and feeding disorders.

Vocational Services provides disabled individuals with the competencies needed to return to school or work and to lead a productive life.

Psychiatry

111 East 210th Street
Bronx, New York 10467
718-920-6215
www.montefiore.org/psychiatry

Psychiatry and Behavioral Sciences at Montefiore

The Department of Psychiatry and Behavioral Sciences at Montefiore provides high-quality, compassionate care for adults and children with complicated medical and neuropsychiatric conditions, including anxiety and depression, obsessive-compulsive disorder, bipolar disorder and schizophrenia.

- In collaboration with experts at Children's Hospital at Montefiore, the Department excels in the diagnosis and treatment of autism spectrum disorders (ASD). The Department's Dialectical Behavior Therapy Program is a model for other mental health programs and addresses the critical needs of at-risk adolescents suffering from anxiety, depression or suicidal thoughts.

- Through the Bronx Accountable Healthcare Network Health Home, the Department provides accountable case management to a large number of patients with severe mental illness and other related medical disorders, and is piloting a Health and Recovery Plan for many of these individuals. The Department received national attention for a text messaging program to improve compliance for substance abuse patients. In addition, an innovative welfare-to-work program for substance abusers helps nearly 400 people obtain employment annually.

- The Department offers cognitive behavioral and family therapy to patients, as well as a Caregiver Support Center for individuals who care for a friend or loved one on an ongoing basis.

- Home to one of the nation's first child behavioral consultation teams, the Department has led the way in creating a fellowship program in child/adolescent psychosomatic medicine. For four decades, the Department has hosted the Annual Chief Residents Tarrytown Leadership Meeting—the premier training experience for incoming chief residents—as well as the popular Clinical Neurology for Psychiatrists and Psychiatry for Psychiatrists board review courses.

- This year, Albert Einstein College of Medicine's Division of Substance Abuse has joined with the Department, making it the largest substance abuse treatment program in the nation. The Department also expanded both its Alcohol and Substance Dependency Program and primary care services on Montefiore's Moses Campus.

- The Department added two large outpatient behavioral care clinics in the Bronx and now provides psychiatric consultative services at Westchester County's White Plains Hospital. In addition, we have a 22-bed comprehensive state-of-the-art inpatient unit on the Moses Campus, and a 33-bed adult unit on our Wakefield Campus.

- The Department was awarded a four-year, $5 million grant from the New York City Administration for Children's Services to provide in-home, multisystemic therapy for families in the Bronx. We also provide specialized prevention services to victims of child abuse through a contract with the Administration for Children and Families, and established the nation's first federally-funded marriage education program.

- Research efforts include studies of intranasal oxytocin for autism symptoms in Prader-Willi syndrome; vasopressin 1a antagonists to improve social cognition in high-functioning adults with ASD; the use of trichuris suis ova (whipworm) to treat inflammatory mechanisms and autism symptoms in childhood ASD; lurasidone to treat disruptive behaviors in childhood ASD; cariprazine to treat resistant depression; and brexpiprazole to treat post-traumatic stress disorder.

Pulmonary Disease

THE INSTITUTE FOR ASTHMA AND OTHER LUNG DISEASES

New York Methodist Hospital
506 Sixth Street, Brooklyn, N.Y. 11215
Phone: 866 ASK-LUNG (866 275-5864)
http://www.nym.org

SPECIALISTS AND MEDICAL SERVICES

The Institute for Asthma and Other Lung Diseases brings together a unique group of specialists and medical services to offer comprehensive diagnosis and treatment of a broad range of lung conditions. The Institute's panel of physician specialists includes both pediatric and adult pulmonologists and allergists. A larger constellation of physicians—medical oncologists, radiologists, radiation oncologists and surgeons—is available as needed. For diagnostic purposes, state-of-the-art specialty facilities—including the interventional bronchoscopy suite, the pulmonary function laboratory, the Pulmonary Hypertension Center and the Sleep Disorders Center—are conveniently located on the Hospital campus. These facilities are used to diagnose and treat a variety of lung disorders and are staffed by registered respiratory therapists, board-certified pulmonary function technologists and exercise physiologists.

PROGRAMS OFFERED

In addition to the treatment of pediatric and adult asthma, physicians affiliated with the Institute diagnose and care for patients with chronic obstructive lung disease (COPD), interstitial lung disease, infectious lung disease, pulmonary hypertension and lung cancer. Highly sophisticated interventional pulmonary services and advanced thoracic surgery procedures are performed at the Hospital.

★★★

Referrals to the Institute, its programs and physicians can be made through an individual's primary care physician or requested directly through the Institute's telephone referral service. More information (and on-line physician referral) is available at the Hospital's website, http://www.nym.org.

COMPREHENSIVE LUNG CANCER CENTER

New York Methodist Hospital's Comprehensive Lung Cancer Center coordinates and consolidates all services related to the treatment of lung cancer. One of the advantages NYM offers patients is a range of minimally invasive screening, diagnostic and treatment techniques, including the Fred L. Mazzilli Free Lung Cancer Screening Program that uses low dose computed tomography.

Treatment options include surgery (both robotic and traditional), radiation and medical oncology, but even patients who are not eligible for surgery, radiation or chemotherapy may benefit from specialized interventional pulmonology treatments.

550 First Avenue *(at 31st Street)*
New York, NY 10016
www.nyulangone.org
Physician Referral: **888-7-NYU-MED** *(888-769-8633)*

INTERNAL MEDICINE

Internal medicine physicians at NYU Langone Medical Center are dedicated to treating the whole patient, and not just their disease. Our team addresses both the physical and psychological aspects of health and disease through clear communication and a fully integrated regimen of care. We specialize in the following areas:

Primary and Specialized Healthcare

General Internal Medicine offers a multidisciplinary medical approach to treating illnesses involving the heart, lungs, gastrointestinal tract, joints, bones, muscles, endocrine organs and kidneys. A wide range of laboratory, imaging and advanced diagnostic testing, ranging from throat cultures to the complex mapping of the electrical surface of the heart, is available on-site or by referral. Comprehensive women's healthcare and men's healthcare is also available. We offer a variety of convenient office locations in Manhattan and the surrounding metropolitan area.

Geriatrics

Our geriatric specialists provide comprehensive and multidisciplinary care, consultation and follow-up for elderly patients ranging from prevention and healthy aging to the treatment and care of chronic conditions including dementia, functional impairment and degenerative disorders.

The Best in American Medicine
www.CastleConnolly.com

Rheumatology

Sleep Disorders

STAMFORD HOSPITAL
Center for Sleep Medicine

Center for Sleep Medicine

Stamford Hospital's Center for Sleep Medicine is Accredited by the American Academy of Sleep Medicine. All of our physicians are highly skilled in diagnosing and treating sleep disorders including: snoring, sleep apnea, insomnia, narcolepsy and restless legs syndrome.

In addition, The Center includes three of Fairfield County's few board-certified sleep specialists trained in pediatric sleep medicine, providing special expertise in the treatment of sleep problems in infancy through teenage years.

Personalized Care

We are one of the state's larger sleep centers, and are able to schedule appointments and sleep studies faster than most facilities.

Located in The Hospital, all rooms are private with their own bath with shower. Each hotel-like room is furnished with a queen-size bed, reclining chair and cable television. Our rooms are large enough to accommodate a caregiver, especially important for pediatric patients.

Sleep Study

Some patients require an overnight sleep study. This non-invasive test monitors heart activity, breathing, oxygenation, position, limb movement, snoring and brain activity. Sleep studies can be performed at home or in the hospital. Hospital studies provide more detailed information to the doctor. Sleep studies are scheduled according to the patient's clinical needs and insurance requirements.

Treatment Options

There are numerous treatment options available at the Center for Sleep Medicine—behavior modification, medication and in some instances custom made medical devices. Regardless of your sleep disorder, our physicians are experts in their field and will work with you to achieve a good night's sleep.

Academic and Clinical Affiliations

Stamford Hospital is an affiliate of the New York–Presbyterian Healthcare System and a major teaching affiliate of the Columbia University College of Physicians & Surgeons.

Accreditation

The Joint Commission

Beds

305

Sponsorship

Voluntary, Not-for-Profit

For a Physician Referral or more information, please call 1.877.233.9355 or visit StamfordHospital.org /doctor.

Stamford Hospital
30 Shelburne Road
Stamford, CT 06902
203.276.1000

StamfordHospital.org

Trinitas Regional Medical Center

COMPREHENSIVE SLEEP DISORDERS CENTER

210 WILLIAMSON STREET | ELIZABETH, NEW JERSEY 07207
PH 908.994.8694 | WWW.NJSLEEPDISORDERSCENTER.COM

Sleep Disorders Center

TRINITAS
COMPREHENSIVE

(908) 994-8694
210 Williamson Street
Elizabeth, NJ 07207

Accredited by The American Academy of Sleep Medicine

Getting a good night's sleep is an essential part of healthy living, but for the millions of Americans who suffer from sleep disorders, getting enough rest can be difficult, if not impossible. Left untreated, sleep disorders can have harmful, even life-threatening effects on health, well-being and safety.

The Comprehensive Sleep Disorders Center at Trinitas Regional Medical Center provides a monitored, fully attended diagnostic sleep study designed to rule out physical, non-stress related symptoms that may prevent restful sleep. The medical director is board certified in Internal Medicine, Critical Care, Sleep Medicine and Pulmonary Medicine. A team of trained sleep specialists supervises each study and coordinates follow-up care with the patient's physician. These professionals can quickly diagnose any sleep problem and, working closely with each patient's primary physician, provide expert treatment and follow-up.

Located within the main campus of Trinitas Regional Medical Center, the state-of-the-art Comprehensive Sleep Disorders Center is designed to diagnose sleep disorders, including insomnia, sleep apnea, restless leg syndrome, snoring and narcolepsy, among others. The private, comfortable testing is performed in home-like suites with soft designer sheets, pillows and a private shower. Studies are provided for adults and children as young as 18 months. Daytime studies are available to meet patient needs.

In 2010, a second sleep center was unveiled in Homewood Suites by Hilton, Cranford. The site is the first hotel-based sleep center in New Jersey.

Both locations offer state-of-the-art diagnostic sleep studies performed by specially trained sleep pulmonologists, registered polysomnographers and licensed, credentialed respiratory therapists.

The Trinitas Comprehensive Sleep Disorders Center is a fully staffed center accredited by The American Academy of Sleep Medicine - the "gold standard" accrediting body for sleep centers - offering the benefits of two distinct locations. With one location on the campus of Trinitas Regional Medical Center, a comprehensive, state-of-the-art medical facility and the other at a nearby nationally known hotel chain, patients who have sleep studies performed at Trinitas receive the high level of attention or treatment that is simply not possible to receive at a neighborhood sleep center.

The Best in American Medicine
www.CastleConnolly.com

Sports Medicine

Stroke Care

Maimonides
Medical Center

JAFFE STROKE CENTER

4802 Tenth Avenue
Brooklyn, New York 11219
Phone: 718.283.7670 • Fax: 718.635.7223

www.maimonidesmed.org/stroke

The Jaffe Stroke Center is ranked among the top 5% in the nation.

After the onset of stroke symptoms, there is a three-hour window of opportunity for the administration of a clot-busting drug. With highly specialized training, experts at certified stroke centers can administer that drug to appropriate patients.

Dr. Steven Rudolph, the Director of the Jaffe Stroke Center, has been selected as investigator in two clinical trials for the newest medical stroke therapies. This distinction is bestowed only on the most respected clinicians in that specialty.

Dr. Razvan Buciuc, Director of Interventional Neuroradiology, can insert a special instrument into a blood vessel, thread it up to the brain, and remove a stroke-causing blood clot. This procedure can greatly reduce stroke damage.

In addition, Maimonides has a multidisciplinary team of stroke experts that includes physicians and nurses from the Department of Emergency Medicine, providing the vital first response in combating stroke. The ER at Maimonides is equipped with telemedicine, an interactive system which allows consultation with a stroke neurologist in real time, when the doctor is at a remote location.

The Jaffe Stroke Center at Maimonides was awarded the Gold Plus Award for excellence in performance from the American Stroke Association's "Get With the Guidelines" Program. In addition, we have been named to the "Target: Stroke" Honor Roll.

**Maimonides
Medical Center**

Surgery

111 East 210th Street
Bronx, New York 10467
718-920-4800
www.montefiore.org/surgery

Surgery at Montefiore

Montefiore's Department of Surgery is at the forefront of innovation and offers the latest technology and treatments to ensure optimal outcomes for its adult and pediatric patients. The Department's five surgical divisions—breast, general, pediatric, transplant, and plastic and reconstructive—are led by renowned surgeons who possess an impressive breadth of experience and expertise.

The Department emphasizes the use of minimally-invasive surgical approaches as often as possible. Procedures such as single-incision laparoscopic sleeve gastrectomy and Lap Band®, transanal minimally-invasive surgery and endoscopic microsurgery, robotic-assisted liver resection and natural orifice transluminal endoscopic surgery are reducing the time that patients spend in the operating room and in their subsequent recovery.

Montefiore's clinical reputation and exceptional surgical outcomes have made it a magnet for referrals. In 2013, the Department performed 10,619 surgical procedures–an increase of more than 25 percent since 2009. It is also recognized by the American College of Surgeons' National Surgical Quality Improvement Program for exemplary outcomes in several categories, including overall morbidity and mortality.

The **Division of General Surgery** is a national leader in the use of cutting-edge cancer treatments, including hyperthermic intraperitoneal chemotherapy, isolated limb perfusion (for sarcoma or melanoma) and liver perfusion.

The **Division of Breast Surgery** is accredited by the National Accreditation Program for Breast Centers and is widely recognized for its personalized approach to care. It offers a host of surgical and reconstructive options for the treatment of patients with breast cancer and other breast disorders.

Montefiore's **Bariatric Surgery Program** is designated as a Center of Excellence in Bariatric Surgery by the American College of Surgeons. The Program has expanded its services to include young adults between the ages of 18 and 21. To date, the Program has performed more than 2,400 bariatric procedures.

The **Division of Plastic and Reconstructive Surgery's** commitment to excellence has placed it at the forefront of craniofacial, pediatric plastic and reconstructive, breast and microsurgery. This year, the Division will build upon its expertise with the addition of a hand specialist.

The **Division of Transplant Surgery** performed its first pediatric living-donor liver transplant this year, continuing its tradition of innovation. In 2013, the Division performed more than 300 solid organ transplants in adults and children, with one-year outcomes in heart, liver and kidney transplant, exceeding state and national averages.

Center for Surgical Weight Loss

At Stamford Hospital's Center for Surgical Weight Loss, patients benefit from a comprehensive program led by a team of weight management specialists. Our highly skilled on-site team consists of certified bariatric surgeons, medical specialists, registered nurses and dietitian, psychologist, and exercise physiologist who provide patients with individualized, patient-centered care.

Surgical Procedures

Grounded in the Center's philosophy of providing high-quality individualized care, patients have numerous options for bariatric surgery: gastric bypass, sleeve gastrectomy and gastric banding, all of which are performed through thumb-nail sized incisions. These laparoscopic procedures result in less pain and scarring, fewer complications and a quicker recovery. Bariatric surgery has been demonstrated to not only reduce weight, but to have profound benefits on metabolic illnesses associated with obesity, such as diabetes and high cholesterol.

Surgical Preparatory Program

Preparing for surgery is a multi-faceted endeavor. The surgical preparatory program includes medical and psychological evaluation, optimization of existing medical conditions prior to surgery, and patient education and counseling in both the individual and group setting.

Patient Care

Patients are cared for by an interprofessional team at all points of care beginning with the first office consultation, extending to in-hospital follow-up by the bariatric team, and then further extending to lifelong follow-up to monitor progress and provide support.

Non-surgical Options for Weight Loss

For those individuals interested in a non-surgical approach to weight loss, the Center offers multiple treatment modalities including dietary counseling, behavior modification, medications and meal replacements.

Academic and Clinical Affiliations

Stamford Hospital is an affiliate of the New York–Presbyterian Healthcare System and a major teaching affiliate of the Columbia University College of Physicians & Surgeons.

Accreditation

The Joint Commission

Beds

305

Sponsorship

Voluntary, Not-for-Profit

For a Physician Referral or more information, please call 1.877.233.9355 or visit StamfordHospital.org /doctor.

Stamford Hospital
30 Shelburne Road
Stamford, CT 06902
203.276.1000

StamfordHospital.org

The Best in American Medicine
www.CastleConnolly.com

Transplantation

:: Barnabas Health

95 Old Short Hills Road • West Orange, New Jersey 07052
1.888.724.7123 • barnabashealth.org

TRANSPLANT SERVICES

Our **Heart Transplant** program is the third largest in the nation with survival rates that consistently meet or exceed national benchmarks. The center is at the forefront of improving the quality of life for transplant candidates and recipients, as well as increasing access to transplant. Our unique work in establishing successful protocols for discontinuing steroid medications for immunosuppression is improving the medical management and survival rates for transplant recipients worldwide. The center is also part of groundbreaking research that is exploring innovating methods for preserving donor organs for transplant. Because the VAD program is totally integrated with heart failure and transplant services, patients are thoroughly and continually evaluated for all treatment options. The heart transplant center's experience has made it a principal site for clinical research trials of the latest generation of mechanical assist devices and a regional VAD transplantation training site. With virtually all FDA-approved and investigational implantable devices available, patients receive the device that meets their individual needs.
To learn more, call 1-888-724-7123.

Barnabas Health Renal and Pancreas Transplant Division offers compassionate and comprehensive care for adult and pediatric kidney patients. Our centers offer a full range of services from treatment of kidney stones and urinary tract infections through kidney failure, and kidney transplantation in adults and children. Our facilities are equipped for diagnosis and treatment of a full spectrum of kidney disorders, including kidney and pancreas transplant. Our pediatric program includes the first complete pediatric nephrology service in New Jersey, and our pre-natal program includes counseling for fetal renal anomalies and genetic diseases diagnosed intra-utero. Our renal transplant program is one of the largest in the United States. Additionally, the program includes New Jersey's first and only Living Donor Institute, designed to promote living donation as the best transplant option for patients with chronic kidney disease who are either on or approaching dialysis.
To learn more, call 1-888-409-4707 or 973-322-5938 .

Montefiore
Inspired Medicine

111 East 210th Street
Bronx, New York 10467
Heart: 718-920-6515
Liver: 888-795-4837
Kidney: 877-287-3536
www.montefiore.org/transplant

Montefiore Einstein Center for Transplantation

The Montefiore Einstein Center for Transplantation is one of the nation's busiest multi-organ transplant centers. Our physicians perform heart, liver, kidney and pancreas transplants in adults and children, in addition to providing innovative surgical procedures, such as living-donor liver transplantation, split liver transplants, dual kidney transplants and combined kidney-pancreas transplantation for select patients.

Specializing in organ failure management to evaluate and facilitate transplantation, the Center provides multidisciplinary management of liver cancer, a major complication of chronic liver disease, in partnership with Montefiore Einstein Center for Cancer Care. Despite long waiting times in the Northeast for donor organs, the Center utilizes every available strategy to shorten wait times and maintain patient health, while they await a donor organ, which is crucial to achieving successful outcomes in transplantation.

The Center has a broad range of transplant specialists dedicated to caring for patients pre- and post-transplantation, including a full psychosocial team, financial counselors, nutritionists, pharmacists, nurse practitioners and physical therapists. In 2013, the Center performed nearly 180 solid organ transplants, including 32 liver transplants, 124 kidney transplants and 22 heart transplants. The Center has consistently achieved superior outcomes, many times surpassing national benchmarks.

The Center works closely with a full-time organ donor liaison to promote living and deceased donor transplantation in the local community. One of the Center's major areas of focus includes identifying strategies to overcome social, economic and linguistic barriers to transplantation that are prevalent in the organ failure population. The Center's Helping Hands program provides transplant patients with assistance during each stage of the transplantation process.

Our commitment to advancing research in the field has led to a dynamic partnership with the Marion Bessin Liver Research Center at Albert Einstein College of Medicine. Investigators at the Bessin Center work with the clinical transplant team to promote pioneering work in the area of liver disease. These efforts include a trial studying the use of the extracorporeal liver-assist device (ELAD) to support patients with acute liver failure who are at a high risk of death without transplant. Other research focuses on novel therapeutic agents for hepatitis C and the use of systemic therapy—combining chemotherapy and radioembolization—to treat patients with liver tumors.

Vascular Surgery

The Best in American Medicine
www.CastleConnolly.com

Vascular Surgery

⊣⊢ NewYork-Presbyterian

Affiliated with Columbia University College of Physicians and Surgeons and Weill Cornell Medical College

NewYork-Presbyterian/
Columbia University Medical Center
622 West 168th Street
New York, NY 10032

NewYork-Presbyterian/
Weill Cornell Medical Center
525 East 68th Street
New York, NY 10065

1-877-NYP-WELL (1-877-697-9355)   www.nyp.org/vascular

NewYork-Presbyterian Vascular Program

Vascular disease can affect people of all ages and requires a wide range of expertise for appropriate and effective therapies. NewYork-Presbyterian Hospital Vascular Services, encompassing Vascular Surgery, Interventional Cardiology, Interventional Radiology and Interventional Neuro Radiology at two premiere facilities offers a comprehensive program for the prevention, diagnosis and treatment of diverse problems relating to arteries and veins throughout the body, including the aorta, abdomen, kidneys, legs and neck.

The Vascular Program brings together medical and surgical experts of two internationally renowned academic medical centers—NewYork-Presbyterian/Columbia University Medical Center and NewYork-Presbyterian/Weill Cornell Medical Center—who have vast experience in the treatment of even the most unusual vascular conditions.

Patients benefit from the Vascular Programs' proven innovative programs, cutting-edge technologies, and ground-breaking research.

- Innovative therapy for the management of arterial, aortic, carotid and complex lower extremity disease;
- Minimally invasive treatments of venous disease;
- Rigorous screenings and integrated care for patients at risk for life-threatening vascular diseases such as strokes, aortic aneurysms and dissections;
- Increased awareness, management and treatment of blood clots (DVT);
- Cutting-edge technology to manage complex arterial and venous disease including:
  - State-of-the-art robotic Siemens Artis zeego® medical imaging system;
  - Non-invasive diagnostic technologies, including CT scans, ultrasounds, MRI and MRA;
- Participation in in ground-breaking trials for management of vascular disease;
- Advances in the latest drug therapies;
- Programs that emphasize prevention measures and risk reduction.

Comprehensive Services Include:

- Comprehensive Abdominal Aortic Aneurysm Program to detect and treat one of the leading causes of of death.

- Treatment of Thoracic and Abdominal Aneurysms through surgical and minimally invasive repair.

- Amputation Prevention Program for treating vascular blockages leading to difficulty walking or the loss of a leg.

- Dedicated Vein Program providing the full spectrum of minimally invasive treatments for vein disease, from the most serious forms of vein disease to cosmetic vein issues.

- Carotid and Stroke Program to reduce the risk of stroke through managing controllable factors, and incorporating healthy lifestyle changes.

- Dedicated Wound Healing Program offering multiple therapy options for management of patients with chronic lower extremity wounds.

Women's Health

Sponsored Page

The Best in American Medicine
www.CastleConnolly.com

Wound Care

CALVARY HOSPITAL
1740 Eastchester Road
Bronx, NY 10461
Tel: (718) 518-2000
www.calvaryhospital.org

CALVARY
HOSPITAL
Where Life Continues

CENTER FOR CURATIVE AND PALLIATIVE WOUND CARE

Founded in 1899, Calvary Hospital is the nation's only acute care specialty hospital dedicated to caring for inpatients with advanced cancer. We serve people of all faith traditions in a restraint-free environment that offers 24/7 visiting hours and extensive bereavement support for families and friends. In addition to inpatient care, we offer outpatient care, home care, hospice, and wound care. All Calvary care is guided by our core values of compassion, respect for the dignity of every patient, and non-abandonment of patients and families.

Calvary Wound Care: A Proud Tradition
In the course of caring for people with advanced cancer, Calvary has developed outstanding expertise in the care of complex and chronic wounds. We extend this care to people in the community through our outpatient clinic. In 2004, we established the Center for Curative and Palliative Wound Care, where we treat patients with chronic wounds secondary to diabetes, neuropathy, chronic venous insufficiency, immobility, lymphedema, peripheral vascular disease, cancer, and other inflammatory or hematological disorders that can cause wounds. Since its inception, Calvary's Wound Care Center has recorded more than 42,000 patient visits.

A Personalized Approach
Our personalized approach to wound management goes beyond established curative protocols to address the larger goals of patient care, by seeking to enhance quality of life for patients and families. We strive to relieve the suffering of patients when wounds do not respond to standard interventions, or when demands of treatment are beyond their tolerance or stamina.

The Center for Curative and Palliative Wound Care offers treatment options for chronic wounds such as:

Venous Ulcers	Diabetic Foot Ulcers	Arterial Ulcers
Pressure Ulcers	Inflammatory Wounds	Vasculitic Ulcers
Lymphedema	Sickle Cell Ulcers	Fungating Tumors
Post-op Wounds	Wound Infection	Wounds from Radiation or Chemotherapy

Wound care personnel are available to consult with nursing homes and long-term care facilities on request. Specially trained visiting nurses and therapists provide expert wound care services for patients at home.

We are a community resource for Bronx residents, where the prevalence of Type 2 Diabetes is the highest in New York and among the highest in the country.

Support for Families
Family members often serve as caregivers. Our physicians and nurses strive to build a foundation of trust and open communication with patients and families. We teach family members to clean wounds and change dressings, and we are always available to answer questions or offer guidance about wound care.

Research is integral to the mission of the Center, which is now pursuing a number of protocols focusing on novel treatments for wounds related to diabetes and other disorders.

For information or to refer a patient to the Wound Care Center, please call (718) 518-2577.

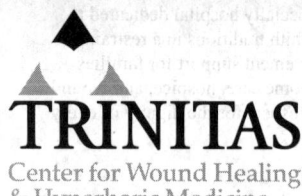

SECTION FIVE

Appendices

The Best in American Medicine
www.CastleConnolly.com

Appendix A:
Medical Boards

Intro to ABMS and Osteopathic Specialties

The following pages contain descriptions of the "official" medical specialties, approved by the American Board of Medical Specialists (for M.D.s) or by the American Osteopathic Association (for D.O.s). These are important because they are the only specialties recognized by the official governing boards. There may be physicians who call themselves one kind of specialist or another, but they may not be certified by the "official" boards. There are, in fact, over 100 such "self-designated" boards, some simply groups of physicians interested in a given area of medicine with no qualifications for membership to other groups with very specific qualifications for membership.

It is important for the medical consumer to seek out physicians certified by the ABMS or AOA to assure their doctor has had the appropriate training and passed the board certification exam.

ABMS

The ABMS is an organization of ABMS approved medical specialty boards. The mission of the ABMS is to maintain and improve the quality of medical care by assisting the Member Boards in their efforts to develop and utilize professional and educational standards for the evaluation and certification of physician specialists. The intent of certification of physicians is to provide assurance to the public that a physician specialist certified by a Member Board of the ABMS has successfully completed an approved educational program and evaluation process which includes an examination designed to assess the knowledge, skills, and experience required to provide quality patient care in that specialty. The ABMS serves to coordinate the activities of its Member Boards and to provide information to the public, the government, the profession and its Members concerning issues involving specialization and certification in medicine.

Following is a list of the addresses of the various medical specialty boards approved by the ABMS. Note that there are 24 board organizations for 25 medical specialties. Psychiatry and Neurology share the same board.

Appendix A: Medical Boards

To find out if a physician is certified, consumers can call the individual boards which may charge a fee for the information, or they can contact the ABMS at 866-275-2267 (no fee) or www.abms.org.

American Board of Allergy and Immunology
111 South Independence Mall East
Suite 701
Philadelphia, PA 19106
(215) 592-9466, (866) 264-5568

General Certification in Allergy and Immunology. Certifications awarded since 1989 are valid for 10 years. For those certified prior to 1989 there is no recertification requirement.

American Board of Anesthesiology
4208 Six Forks Rd, Ste 1500
Raleigh, NC 27609-5735
(866) 999-7501

General Certification in Anesthesiology; with Special and Added Qualifications in Critical Care Medicine, Hospice & Palliative Medicine, Pain Medicine and Pediatric Anesthesiology. Certifications awarded since 2000 are valid for 10 years.

American Board of Colon and Rectal Surgery
20600 Eureka Road, Suite 600
Taylor, MI 48180
(734) 282-9400

General Certification in Colon and Rectal Surgery. Certifications awarded since 1990 are valid for 10 years.

American Board of Dermatology
Henry Ford Health System
1 Ford Place
Detroit, MI 48202-3450
(313) 874-1088

General Certification in Dermatology; with Special Qualifications in Dermatopathology, and Pediatric Dermatology. Certifications awarded since 1991 are valid for 10 years.

American Board of Emergency Medicine

3000 Coolidge Road
East Lansing, MI 48823-6319
(517) 332-4800

General Certification in Emergency Medicine; with Special and Added Qualifications in Critical Care Medicine, Emergency Medical Services, Hospice & Palliative Medicine, Medical Toxicology, Pediatric Emergency Medicine, Sports Medicine and Undersea and Hyperbaric Medicine. Certifications awarded since 1980 are valid for 10 years.

American Board of Family Practice

1648 McGrathiana Parkway, Suite 550
Lexington, KY 40511
(859) 269-5626, (888) 995-5700

General Certification in Family Practice; with Added Qualifications in Adolescent Medicine, Geriatric Medicine, Hospice & Palliative Medicine, Sleep Medicine and Sports Medicine. Certifications awarded since 1970 are valid for 7 years.

American Board of Internal Medicine

510 Walnut Street, Suite 1700
Philadelphia, PA 19106-3699
(215) 446-3500, (800) 441-ABIM

General Certification in Internal Medicine; with Special Qualifications in Cardiovascular Disease, Endocrinology, Diabetes and Metabolism, Gastroenterology, Hematology, Infectious Disease, Medical Oncology, Nephrology, Pulmonary Disease, and Rheumatology; and Added Qualifications in Adolescent Medicine, Advanced Heart Failure & Transplant Cardiology, Clinical Cardiac Electrophysiology, Critical Care Medicine, Geriatric Medicine, Hospice & Palliative Medicine, Interventional Cardiology, Sleep Medicine, Sports Medicine and Transplant Hepatology. Certifications awarded since 1990 are valid for 10 years.

American Board of Medical Genetics

9650 Rockville Pike
Bethesda, MD 20814-3998
(301) 634-7315

General Certification in Clinical Genetics (MD), Clinical Biochemical Genetics, Clinical Cytogenetics and Clinical Molecular Genetics; with Added Qualifications in Medical Biochemical Genetics, Molecular Genetic Pathology. Certifications awarded since 2002 are valid for 2 years.

Appendix A: Medical Boards

American Board of Neurological Surgery
245 Amity Road, Suite 208
Woodbridge, CT 06525
(203) 397-2267

General Certification in Neurological Surgery. Certifications awarded since 1999 are valid for 10 years.

American Board of Nuclear Medicine
4555 Forest Park Boulevard, Suite 119
St. Louis, MO 63108
(314) 367-2225

General Certification in Nuclear Medicine. Certifications awarded since 1992 are valid for 10 years.

American Board of Obstetrics and Gynecology
2915 Vine Street
Dallas, TX 75204
(214) 871-1619

General Certification in Obstetrics and Gynecology; with Special Qualifications in Gynecologic Oncology, Maternal and Fetal Medicine, Reproductive Endocrinology/Infertility; and Added Qualifications in Female Pelvic Medicine & Reconstructive Surgery, Hospice & Palliative Medicine and Critical Care Medicine. Certifications awarded since 1986 are valid for 6 years.

American Board of Ophthalmology
111 Presidential Boulevard, Suite 241
Bala Cynwyd, PA 19004-1075
(610) 664-1175

General certification in Ophthalmology. Certifications awarded since 1992 are valid for 10 years. For those certified prior to 1992 there is no recertification requirement.

American Board of Orthopaedic Surgery
400 Silver Cedar Court
Chapel Hill, NC 27514
(919) 929-7103

General Certification in Orthopaedic Surgery; with Added Qualification in Hand Surgery and Orthopaedic Sports Medicine. Certifications awarded since 1986 are valid for 10 years.

American Board of Otolaryngology
5615 Kirby Drive, Suite 600
Houston, TX 77005
(713) 850-0399

General Certification in Otolaryngology; with Added Qualifications in Neurotology, Pediatric Otolaryngology, Plastic Surgery within the Head and Neck and Sleep Medicine. Certifications awarded since 2002 are valid for 10 years.

American Board of Pathology
4830 Kennedy Boulevard
Suite 690
Tampa, FL 33609
(813) 286-2444

General Certification in Anatomic and Clinical Pathology, Anatomic Pathology and Clinical Pathology; with Special Qualifications in Blood Banking/Transfusion Medicine, Chemical Pathology, Dermatopathology, Forensic Pathology, Hematology, Medical Microbiology, Molecular Genetic Pathology, Neuropathology and Pediatric Pathology; and Added Qualifications in Clinical Informatics and Cytopathology. Certifications awarded since 1997 are valid for 10 years.

American Board of Pediatrics
111 Silver Cedar Court
Chapel Hill, NC 27514-1651
(919) 929-0461

General Certification in Pediatrics; with Special Qualifications in Adolescent Medicine, Developmental-Behavioral Pediatrics, Neonatal-Perinatal Medicine, Pediatric Cardiology, Pediatric Critical Care Medicine, Pediatric Emergency Medicine, Pediatric Endocrinology, Pediatric Gastroenterology, Pediatric Hematology-Oncology, Pediatric Infectious Diseases, Pediatric Nephrology, Pediatric Pulmonology, and Pediatric Rheumatology; and Added Qualifications in Child Abuse Pediatrics, Hospice & Palliative Medicine, Medical Toxicology, Neurodevelopmental Disabilities, Pediatric Transplant Hepatology, Sleep Medicine and Sports Medicine. Certifications awarded since 1988 valid for 7 years.

Appendix A: Medical Boards

American Board of Physical Medicine and Rehabilitation
3015 Allegro Park Lane, S.W.
Rochester, MN 55902-4139
(507) 282-1776

General Certification in Physical Medicine and Rehabilitation; with Special
Qualifications in Pain Medicine, Pediatric Rehabilitation Medicine, and Spinal Cord
Injury Medicine; and Added Qualifications in Brain Injury Medicine, Hospice &
Palliative Medicine, Neuromuscular Medicine and Sports Medicine. Certifications
awarded since 1993 are valid for 10 years.

American Board of Plastic Surgery
Seven Penn Center, Suite 400
1635 Market Street
Philadelphia, PA 19103-2204
(215) 587-9322

General Certification in Plastic Surgery; with Added Qualifications in Hand Surgery and
Head & Neck Surgery. Certifications awarded since 1995 are valid for 10-years.

American Board of Preventive Medicine
111 W. Jackson, Suite 1110
Chicago, IL 60604
(312) 939-ABPM [2276]

General Certification in Aerospace Medicine, Occupational Medicine and Public Health
and General Preventive Medicine; with Added Qualifications in Clinical Informatics,
Medical Toxicology and Undersea and Hyperbaric Medicine. Certifications awarded since
1997 are valid for 10 years.

American Board of Psychiatry and Neurology
2150 E. Lake Cook Road, Suite 900
Buffalo Grove, IL 60089
(847) 229-6500

General Certification in Psychiatry, Neurology and Neurology with Special Qualification
in Child Neurology; with Special Qualifications in Child and Adolescent Psychiatry,
Epilepsy, Hospice & Palliative Medicine, Pain Medicine and Sleep Medicine; and Added
Qualifications in Addiction Psychiatry, Brain Injury Medicine, Clinical Neurophysiology,
Epilepsy, Forensic Psychiatry, Geriatric Psychiatry, Hospice & Palliative Medicine,
Neurodevelopmental Disabilities, Psychosomatic Medicine and Vascular Neurology.
Certifications awarded since 1994 are valid for 10 years.

American Board of Radiology

5441 E. Williams Circle

Tucson, AZ 85711

(520) 790-2900

General Certification in Diagnostic Radiology, Medical Physics or Radiation Oncology; with Special Competency in Nuclear Radiology; and Added Qualifications in Hospice & Palliative Medicine, Neuroradiology, Pediatric Radiology and Vascular and Interventional Radiology. Radiological Physics is a non-clinical certification. Certificates are valid for 10 years.

American Board of Surgery

1617 John F. Kennedy Boulevard, Suite 860

Philadelphia, PA 19103-1847

(215) 568-4000

General Certification in Surgery and Vascular Surgery; with Special Qualifications in Pediatric Surgery and Surgery of the Hand; and Added Qualifications in Complex General Surgical Oncology, Hospice & Palliative Medicine and Surgical Critical Care. Certifications awarded since 1976 are valid for 10 years.

American Board of Thoracic Surgery

633 North St. Clair Street, Suite 2320

Chicago, IL 60611

(312) 202-5900

General Certification in Thoracic and Cardiac Surgery; and Added Qualifications in Congenital Cardiac Surgery. Certifications awarded since 1976 are valid for 10 years.

American Board of Urology

600 Peter Jefferson Parkway, Suite 150

Charlottesville, VA 22911

(434) 979-0059

General Certification in Urology; and Added Qualifications in Pediatric Urology. Certifications awarded as of 1985 are valid for 10 years.

Osteopathic

The American Osteopathic Association (AOA) is a member association representing more than 78,000 osteopathic physicians (D.O.s). The AOA serves as the primary certifying body for D.O.s, and is the accrediting agency for all osetopathic medical colleges and healthcare facilities. The AOA's mission is to advance the philosophy and practice of osteopathic medicine by promoting excellence in education, research, and the delivery of quality, cost-effective healthcare within a distinct, unified profession.

American Osteopathic Association
142 E Ontario Street
Chicago, IL 60611

Consumers may call the American Osteopathic Association at (800) 621-1773 or visit the website, www.osteopathic.org, for general certification information.

American Osteopathic Board of Anesthesiology

General certification in Anesthesiology; with Added Qualifications in Critical Care Medicine, and Pain Management. Certifications awarded since 2004 are valid for 10 years. For those certified prior to 2004 there is no recertification requirement.

American Osteopathic Board of Dermatology

General certification in Dermatology; with Added Qualifications in Dermatopathology and Mohs'-Micrographic Surgery. Certifications awarded since 2004 are valid for 10 years.

American Osteopathic Board of Emergency Medicine

General certification in Emergency Medicine; with Added Qualifications in Emergency Medical Services, Medical Toxicology, and Sports Medicine. Certifications awarded since 1994 are valid for 10 years.

American Osteopathic Board of Family Physicians

General certification in Family Practice and Osteopathic Manipulative Treatment (OMT); with Added Qualifications in Geriatric Medicine, Hospice & Palliative Medicine, Sleep Medicine, Sports Medicine and Undersea & Hyperbaric Medicine. Certifications awarded since March 1,1997 are valid for 8 years.

American Osteopathic Board of Internal Medicine

General certification in Internal Medicine; with Special Qualifications in Allergy/Immunology, Cardiology, Endocrinology, Gastroenterology, Hematology, Infectious Disease, Nephrology, Oncology, Pulmonary Disease, Rheumatology; with Added Qualifications in Addiction Medicine, Critical Care Medicine, Clinical Cardiac Electrophysiology, Hospice & Palliative Medicine, Geriatric Medicine, Interventional Cardiology, Sleep Medicine, Sports Medicine and Undersea & Hyperbaric Medicine. Certifications awarded since 1993 are valid for 10 years.

American Osteopathic Board of Neurology and Psychiatry

General certification in Neurology and Psychiatry; with Special Qualifications in Child/Adolescent Psychiatry and Child/Adolescent Neurology; with Added Qualifications in Addiction Medicine, Geriatric Psychiatry, Hospice & Palliative Medicine, Neurophysiology, and Sleep Medicine. Certifications awarded since 1995 are valid for 10 years.

American Osteopathic Board of Neuromusculoskeletal Medicine

General certification in Neuromusculoskelatal Medicine & Osteopathic Manipulative Medicine; with Added qualifications in Sports Medicine.

American Osteopathic Board of Nuclear Medicine

General certification in Nuclear Medicine. Certifications awarded since 1995 are valid for 10 years. This certification is no longer issued.

American Osteopathic Board of Obstetrics and Gynecology

General certification in Obstetrics and Gynecology; with Special Qualifications in Gynecologic Oncology; Maternal and Fetal Medicine and Reproductive Endocrinology. Certifications awarded since June 2002 are valid for 6 years.

American Osteopathic Board of Ophthalmology and Otolaryngology - Head & Neck Surgery

General certification in Ophthalmology, Otolaryngology, Facial Plastic Surgery and Otolaryngology/Facial Plastic Surgery; with Added Qualifications in Otolaryngic Allergy and Sleep Medicine. Certifications awarded in Ophthalmology since 2000 are valid for 10 years. For those certified prior to 2000 there is no recertification requirement. Certifications awarded in Otolaryngology and/or Otolaryngology/Facial Plastic Surgery since 2002 are valid for 10 years.

American Osteopathic Board of Orthopaedic Surgery

General certification in Orthopaedic Surgery; with Added Qualifications in Hand Surgery. Certifications awarded since 1994 are valid for 10 years.

American Osteopathic Board of Pathology

General certification in Laboratory Medicine, Anatomic Pathology and Anatomic Pathology and Laboratory Medicine; with Special Qualifications in Forensic Pathology; and with Added Qualifications in Dermatopathology. Certifications awarded since 1995 are valid for 10 years.

American Osteopathic Board of Pediatrics

General certification in Pediatrics with Special Qualifications in Adolescent and Young Adult Medicine, Neonatology, Pediatric Allergy/Immunology and Pediatric Endocrinology; with Added Qualifications in Sports Medicine. Certifications awarded since 1995 are valid for 7 years.

American Osteopathic Board of Physical Medicine and Rehabilitation Medicine

General certification in Physical Medicine and Rehabilitation; with Added Qualifications in Hospice & Palliative Medicine and Sports Medicine. Certifications awarded since 2004 are valid
for 10 years.

American Osteopathic Board of Preventive Medicine

General certification in Preventive Medicine/Aerospace Medicine, Preventive Medicine/Occupational-Environmental Medicine and Preventive Medicine/Public Health; with Added Qualifications in Undersea & Hyperbaric Medicine. Certifications awarded since 1994 are valid for 10 years.

American Osteopathic Board of Proctology

General certification in Proctology. Certifications awarded since 2004 are valid for 10 years.

American Osteopathic Board of Radiology

General certification in Diagnostic Radiology and Radiation Oncology; with Added Qualifications in Angiography & Interventional Radiology, Neuroradiology, Pediatric Radiology and Vascular & Interventional Radiology. Certifications awarded since 2002 are valid for 10 years.

American Osteopathic Board of Surgery

General certification in General Vascular Surgery, Surgery, Neurological Surgery, Plastic and Reconstructive Surgery, Thoracic Cardiovascular Surgery, Urological Surgery; with Added Qualifications in Surgical Critical Care. Certifications awarded since 1997 are valid for 10 years.

Appendix B:
Self-Designated Medical Specialties

This list of self-designated medical specialty groups was obtained from the American Board of Medical Specialties. However, it is important to point out that these groups are not recognized by the ABMS, the governing board for the recognized twenty-four medical specialty boards (listed in Appendix A).

The organizations listed below range from highly organized groups that are attempting to formalize training and certification in their field to informal groups interested in a particular aspect of medicine.

If you wish to obtain information from any of these groups you will have to do some detective work. Because so many are informal, the location, phone and mailing addresses change frequently, depending upon the person who is functioning as secretary or administrator.

The best way to track down one of these groups is to consult the doctor listings to find a doctor who has expressed a special interest in that field, and call his or her office. You might also call a nearby academic health center in the area to see if they have a faculty or staff member known to be involved in that particular medical interest. If that fails, take the same approach with your community hospital.

A

Abdominal Surgeons

Acupuncture Medicine

Addiction Medicine

Addictionology

Adolescent Psychiatry

Aesthetic Plastic Surgery

Alcoholism and Other Drug
          Dependencies (AMSAODD)

Algology (Chronic Pain)

Alternative Medicine

Ambulatory Anesthesia

Ambulatory Foot Surgery

Anesthesia

Arthroscopic Surgery

Arthroscopy (Board of North America)

B

Bariatric Medicine

Bionic Psychology

Bloodless Medicine & Surgery

C

Chelation Therapy

Chemical Dependence

Clinical Chemistry

Clinical Ecology

Clinical Medicine and Surgery

Clinical Neurology

Clinical Neurophysiology

Clinical Neurosurgery

Clinical Nutrition

Clinical Orthopaedic Surgery

Clinical Pharmacology

Clinical Polysomnography

Clinical Psychiatry

Clinical Psychology

Clinical Toxicology

Cosmetic Plastic Surgery

Cosmetic Surgery

Council of Non-Board Certified Physicians

Critical Care in Medicine & Surgery

D

Disability Analysis

Disability Evaluating Physicians

E

Electrodiagnostic Medicine

Electroencephalography

Electromyography & Electrodiagnosis

Environmental Medicine

Epidemiology (College)

Eye Surgery

F

Facial Cosmetic Surgery

Facial Plastic & Reconstructive Surgery

Family Practice, Certification

Forensic Examiners

Forensic Psychiatry

Forensic Toxicology

H

Hand Surgery

Head, Facial & Neck Pain & TMJ Orthopaedics

Health Physics

Homeopathic Physicians

Homeotherapeutics

Hypnotic Anesthesiology, National Board for

I

Independent Medical Examiners

Industrial Medicine & Surgery

Insurance Medicine

International Cosmetic & Plastic
          Facial Reconstructive Standards

Interventional Radiology

L

Laser Surgery
Law in Medicine
Longevity Medicine/Surgery

M

Malpractice Physicians
Maxillofacial Surgeons
Medical Accreditation (American Federation for)
Medical Hypnosis
Medical Laboratory Immunology
Medical-Legal Analysis of Medicine & Surgery
Medical Legal & Workers
    Comp. Medicine & Surgery
Medical-Legal Consultants
Medical Management
Medical Microbiology
Medical Preventics (Academy)
Medical Psychotherapists
Medical Toxicology
Microbiology (Medical Microbiology)
Military Medicine
Mohs' Micrographic Surgery &
    Cutaneous Oncology

N

Neuroimaging
Neurologic & Orthopaedic Dental
    Medicine and Surgery
Neurological & Orthopaedic Medicine
Neurological & Orthopaedic Surgery
Neurological Microsurgery
Neurology
Neuromuscular Thermography
Neuro-Orthopaedic Dental Medicine
Neuro-Orthopaedic Electrodiagnosis
Neuro-Orthopaedic Laser Surgery
Neuro-Orthopaedic Psychiatry
Neuro-Orthopaedic Thoracic Medicine
Neurorehabilitation
Nutrition

O

Orthopaedic Medicine
Orthopaedic Microneurosurgery
Otorhinolaryngology

P

Pain Management (American Academy of)
Pain Management Specialties
Pain Medicine
Palliative Medicine
Percutaneous Diskectomy
Plastic Esthetic Surgeons
Prison Medicine
Professional Disability Consultants
Psychiatric Medicine
Psychiatry (American National Board of)
Psychoanalysis (American Examining
    Board in)
Psychological Medicine (International)

Q

Quality Assurance & Utilization Review

R

Radiology & Medical Imaging
Rheumatologic Surgery
Rheumatological & Reconstructive Medicine
Ringside Medicine & Surgery

S

Skin Specialists
Sleep Medicine (Polysomnography)
Spinal Cord Injury
Spinal Surgery
Sports Medicine
Sports Medicine/Surgery

T

Toxicology
Trauma Surgery
Traumatologic Medicine & Surgery
Tropical Medicine

U

Ultrasound Technology
Urologic Allied Health Professionals
Urological Surgery

W

Weight Reduction Medicine

APPENDIX C:
Hospital Listings

The following is an alphabetical listing of all hospitals that have at least one Castle Connolly Top Doctor in this guide. Institutions listed in **Bold** are profiled in this Guide in association with Castle Connolly's Partnership for Excellence program. The abbreviations as they appear in the listings are in italics below. Due to the many changes taking place in the hospital industry, the names on this list may have changed subsequent to publication of this guide.

Bayonne Medical Center   (201) 858-5000
Bayonne Med Ctr
29 E 29th St   Bayonne, NJ 07002   HUDSON

Bayshore Community Hospital   (732) 739-5900
Bayshore Community Hosp
727 N Beers St   Holmdel, NJ 07733   MONMOUTH

Bellevue Hospital Center   (212) 562-1000
Bellevue Hosp Ctr
462 First Avenue   New York, NY 10016   NEW YORK

Bergen Regional Medical Center   (201) 967-4000
Bergen Regl Med Ctr
230 East Ridgewood Avenue   Paramus, NJ 07652   BERGEN

Blythedale Children's Hospital   (914) 592-7555
Blythedale Children's Hosp
95 Bradhurst Avenue   Valhalla, NY 10595   WESTCHESTER

Bridgeport Hospital   (203) 384-3000
Bridgeport Hosp
267 Grant St   Bridgeport, CT 06610   FAIRFIELD

Bronx Lebanon Hospital Center   (718) 590-1800
Bronx Lebanon Hosp Ctr
1276 Fulton Ave   Bronx, NY 10457   BRONX

Bronx Psychiatric Center   (718) 931-0600
Bronx Psych Ctr
1500 Waters Place   Bronx, NY 10461   BRONX

Brookdale University Hospital Medical Center   (718) 240-5000
Brookdale Univ Hosp Med Ctr
One Brookdale Plaza   Brooklyn, NY 11212   KINGS

Brookhaven Memorial Hospital & Medical Center   (631) 654-7100
Brookhaven Meml Hosp & Med Ctr
101 Hospital Road   Patchogue, NY 11772   SUFFOLK

Brooklyn Hospital Center   (718) 250-8000
Brooklyn Hosp Ctr
121 DeKalb Avenue   Brooklyn, NY 11201   KINGS

Burke Rehabilitation Hospital   (914) 597-2500
Burke Rehab Hosp
785 Mamaroneck Avenue   White Plains, NY 10605   WESTCHESTER

Capital Health Medical Center - Hopewell   (609) 303-4000
Capital Health Med Ctr - Hopewell
One Capital Way   Pennington, NJ 08534   MERCER

Capital Health Regional Medical Center   (609) 394-6000
Capital Health Regl Med Ctr
750 Brunswick Avenue   Trenton, NJ 08638-4174   MERCER

CentraState Medical Center   (732) 431-2000
CentraState Med Ctr
901 West Main Street   Freehold, NJ 07728   MONMOUTH

Children's Hospital at Montefiore   (718) 741-2426
Chldns Hosp at Montefiore
3415 Bainbridge Ave   Bronx, NY 10467   BRONX

Children's Hospital of NJ at Newark   (973) 926-7000
Chldns Hosp NJ at Newark
201 Lyons Ave   Newark, NJ 07112   ESSEX

Children's Hospital of Philadelphia   (215) 590-1000
Chldns Hosp of Philadelphia
34th St & Civic Center Blvd   Philadelphia, PA 19104   PHILADELPHIA

Children's Specialized Hospital   (908) 233-3720
Children's Specialized Hosp
150 New Providence Rd   Mountainside, NJ 07092   UNION

Children's Specialized Hospital-Toms River   (732) 914-1100
Children's Specialized Hosp-Toms River
94 Stevens Rd   Toms River, NJ 08755   OCEAN

Chilton Medical Center   (973) 831-5000
Chilton Med Ctr
97 West Parkway   Pompton Plains, NJ 07444   MORRIS

Christ Hospital - Jersey City   (201) 795-8200
Christ Hosp - Jersey City
176 Palisade Avenue   Jersey City, NJ 07306   HUDSON

Clara Maass Medical Center   (973) 450-2000
Clara Maass Med Ctr
One Clara Maass Drive   Belleville, NJ 07109   ESSEX

Columbus Hospital LTACH   (973) 268-1400
Columbus Hosp
495 N 13th Street   Newark, NJ 07107   ESSEX

Community Medical Center - Toms River   (732) 557-8000
Comm Med Ctr - Toms River
99 Highway 37 W   Toms River, NJ 08755   OCEAN

Coney Island Hospital   (718) 616-3000
Coney Island Hosp
2601 Ocean Parkway   Brooklyn, NY 11235   KINGS

Danbury Hospital   (203) 739-7000
Danbury Hosp
24 Hospital Avenue   Danbury, CT 06810   FAIRFIELD

Doylestown Hospital   (215) 345-2200
Doylestown Hosp
595 W State St   Doylestown, PA 18901-2554   BUCKS

Eastern Long Island Hospital   (631) 477-1000
Eastern Long Island Hosp
201 Manor Place   Greenport, NY 11944   SUFFOLK

Elmhurst Hospital Center   (718) 334-4000
Elmhurst Hosp Ctr
79-01 Broadway   Elmhurst, NY 11373   QUEENS

Englewood Hospital & Medical Center   (201) 894-3000
Englewood Hosp & Med Ctr
350 Engle Street   Englewood, NJ 07631   BERGEN

Flushing Hospital Medical Center   (718) 670-5000
Flushing Hosp Med Ctr
4500 Parsons Blvd   Flushing, NY 11355   QUEENS

Forest Hills Hospital   (718) 830-4000
Forest Hills Hosp
102-01 66th Rd   Forest Hills, NY 11375   QUEENS

Four Winds Hospital   (914) 763-8151
Four Winds Hosp
800 Cross River Road   Katonah, NY 10536   WESTCHESTER

Franklin Hospital   (516) 256-6000
Franklin Hosp
900 Franklin Avenue   Valley Stream, NY 11580   NASSAU

Glen Cove Hospital   (516) 674-7300
Glen Cove Hosp
101 St Andrew's Ln   Glen Cove, NY 11542   NASSAU

Good Samaritan Hospital Medical Center - West Islip   (631) 376-4444
Good Samaritan Hosp Med Ctr - West Islip
1000 Montauk Highway   West Islip, NY 11795   SUFFOLK

Good Samaritan Regional Medical Center   (845) 368-5000
Good Samaritan Regional Med Ctr
255 Lafayette Ave   Suffern, NY 10901   ROCKLAND

Goryeb Children's Hospital   (973) 971-6700
Goryeb Children's Hosp
100 Madison Ave   Morristown, NJ 07960   MORRIS

Gracie Square Hospital   (212) 988-4400
Gracie Square Hosp
420 E 76th St   New York, NY 10021   NEW YORK

Greenwich Hospital   (203) 863-3000
Greenwich Hosp
5 Perryridge Rd   Greenwich, CT 06830   FAIRFIELD

Griffin Hospital   (203) 735-7421
Griffin Hosp
130 Division St   Derby, CT 06418-1377   NEW HAVEN

Hackensack University Medical Center   (551) 996-2000
Hackensack Univ Med Ctr
30 Prospect Avenue   Hackensack, NJ 07601   BERGEN

Hackensack University Medical Center-Mountainside   (973) 429-6000
Hackensack UMC-Mountainside
1 Bay Ave   Montclair, NJ 07042   ESSEX

Hackensack University Medical Center-Pascack Valley   (201) 880-2700
Hackensack UMC-Pascack Valley
250 Old Hook Rd   Westwood, NJ 07657   BERGEN

Hackettstown Regional Medical Center   (908) 852-5100
Hackettstown Reg Med Ctr
651 Willow Grove St   Hackettstown, NJ 07840   WARREN

Harlem Hospital Center   (212) 939-1000
Harlem Hosp Ctr
506 Lenox Avenue   New York, NY 10037   NEW YORK

Hartford Hospital   (860) 545-5000
Hartford Hosp
80 Seymour St   Hartford, CT 06102-5037   HARTFORD

Helen Hayes Hospital   (845) 786-4000
Helen Hayes Hosp
51-55 Route 9W N   West Haverstraw, NY 10993   ROCKLAND

Hoboken University Medical Center   (201) 418-1000
Hoboken Univ Med Ctr - Hoboken
308 Willow Ave   Hoboken, NJ 07030   HUDSON

Holy Name Medical Center   (201) 833-3000
Holy Name Med Ctr
718 Teaneck Road   Teaneck, NJ 07666-4281   BERGEN

Hospital for Special Surgery   (212) 606-1000
Hosp For Special Surgery
535 East 70th Street   New York, NY 10021   NEW YORK

Hudson Valley Hospital Center   (914) 737-9000
Hudson Valley Hosp Ctr
1980 Crompond Road   Cortlandt Manor, NY 10567   WESTCHESTER

Hunterdon Medical Center   (908) 788-6100
Hunterdon Med Ctr
2100 Wescott Dr   Flemington, NJ 08822-4604   HUNTERDON

Huntington Hospital   (631) 351-2000
Huntington Hosp
270 Park Avenue   Huntington, NY 11743   SUFFOLK

Interfaith Medical Center   (718) 613-4000
Interfaith Med Ctr
1545 Atlantic Avenue   Brooklyn, NY 11213   KINGS

Jacobi Medical Center		(718) 918-5000
Jacobi Med Ctr		
1400 Pelham Parkway South	Bronx, NY 10461	BRONX

Jamaica Hospital Medical Center		(718) 206-6000
Jamaica Hosp Med Ctr		
8900 Van Wyck Expressway	Jamaica, NY 11418	QUEENS

James J. Peters VA Medical Center-Bronx		(718) 584-9000
James J. Peters VA Med Ctr-Bronx		
130 W Kingsbridge Rd	Bronx, NY 10468	BRONX

Jersey City Medical Center		(201) 915-2000
Jersey City Med Ctr		
355 Grand Street	Jersey City, NJ 07302	HUDSON

Jersey Shore University Medical Center		(732) 775-5500
Jersey Shore Univ Med Ctr		
1945 Route 33	Neptune, NJ 07753	MONMOUTH

JFK Medical Center - Edison		(732) 321-7000
JFK Med Ctr - Edison		
65 James St	Edison, NJ 08820	MIDDLESEX

John T Mather Memorial Hospital		(631) 473-1320
John T Mather Meml Hosp		
75 N Country Rd	Port Jefferson, NY 11777	SUFFOLK

Kessler Institute for Rehabiitation - Saddle Brook		(201) 368-6000
Kessler Inst for Rehab - Saddle Brook		
300 Market St	Saddle Brook, NJ 07663	BERGEN

Kessler Institute for Rehabilitation - Chester		(973) 252-6300
Kessler Inst for Rehab - Chester		
201 Pleasant Hill Rd	Chester, NJ 07930	MORRIS

Kessler Institute for Rehabilitation - West Orange		(973) 731-3600
Kessler Inst for Rehab - W Orange		
1199 Pleasant Valley Way	West Orange, NJ 07052-1499	ESSEX

Kings County Hospital Center		(718) 245-3131
Kings Co Hosp Ctr		
451 Clarkson Avenue	Brooklyn, NY 11203	KINGS

Kingsbrook Jewish Medical Center		(718) 604-5000
Kingsbrook Jewish Med Ctr		
585 Schenectady Avenue	Brooklyn, NY 11203	KINGS

Lawrence Hospital Center   (914) 787-1000
Lawrence Hosp Ctr
55 Palmer Avenue   Bronxville, NY 10708   WESTCHESTER

Lenox Hill Hospital   (212) 434-2000
Lenox Hill Hosp
100 East 77th Street   New York, NY 10021   NEW YORK

Lenox Hill Hospital (Manhattan Eye, Ear & Throat Hosp)   (212) 838-9200
Lenox Hill Hosp (Manh Eye, Ear & Throat Hosp)
210 East 64th Street   New York, NY 10021   NEW YORK

Lincoln Medical & Mental Health Center   (718) 579-5000
Lincoln Med & Mental Hlth Ctr
234 East 149th St   Bronx, NY 10451   BRONX

Long Island Jewish Medical Center   (718) 470-7000
Long Is Jewish Med Ctr
270-05 76th Avenue   New Hyde Park, NY 11040   NASSAU

Lutheran Medical Center - Brooklyn   (718) 630-7000
Lutheran Med Ctr - Brooklyn
150 55th Street   Brooklyn, NY 11220   KINGS

Maimonides Medical Center   (718) 283-6000
Maimonides Med Ctr
4802 Tenth Avenue   Brooklyn, NY 11219   KINGS

Massapequa General Hospital   (516) 520-6000
Massapequa Genl Hosp
750 Hicksville Road   Seaford, NY 11783   NASSAU

Meadowlands Hospital Medical Center   (201) 392-3100
Meadowlands Hosp Med Ctr
55 Meadowland Parkway   Secaucus, NJ 07094   HUDSON

MedStar Georgetown University Hospital   (202) 444-2000
MedStar Georgetown Univ Hosp
3800 Reservoir Rd NW   Washington, DC 20007   DISTRICT OF COLUMBIA

Memorial Sloan Kettering Cancer Center   (212) 639-2000
Meml Sloan Kettering Canc Ctr
1275 York Avenue   New York, NY 10021   NEW YORK

Mercy Medical Center-Rockville Centre   (516) 705-2525
Mercy Med Ctr-Rockville Centre
1000 North Village Ave   Rockville Centre, NY 11570   NASSAU

Metropolitan Hospital Center - NY   (212) 423-6262
Metropolitan Hosp Ctr - NY
1901 First Avenue   New York, NY 10029   NEW YORK

MidHudson Regional Hospital   (845) 483-5000
MidHudson Regl Hosp
241 North Rd   Poughkeepsie, NY 12601   DUTCHESS

Milford Hospital   (203) 876-4000
Milford Hosp
300 Seaside Ave   Milford, CT 06460   NEW HAVEN

Monmouth Medical Center   (732) 222-5200
Monmouth Med Ctr
300 2nd Ave   Long Branch, NJ 07740-6300   MONMOUTH

Monmouth Medical Center, Southern Campus   (732) 363-1900
Monmouth Med Ctr - South
600 River Ave   Lakewood, NJ 08701-5281   OCEAN

Montefiore Medical Center-Einstein Campus   (718) 904-2000
Montefiore Med Ctr-Einstein Campus
1825 Eastchester Road   Bronx, NY 10461   BRONX

Montefiore Medical Center-Moses Campus   (718) 920-4321
Montefiore Med Ctr-Moses Campus
111 East 210 Street   Bronx, NY 10467   BRONX

Montefiore Medical Center-Wakefield Campus   (718) 920-9000
Montefiore Med Ctr-Wakefield Campus
600 E 233rd St   Bronx, NY 10466   BRONX

Montefiore Mount Vernon Hospital   (914) 664-8000
Montefiore Mt Vernon Hosp
12 N Seventh Ave   Mount Vernon, NY 10550   WESTCHESTER

Montefiore New Rochelle Hospital   (914) 632-5000
Montefiore New Rochelle Hosp
16 Guion Pl   New Rochelle, NY 10801   WESTCHESTER

Montefiore Westchester Square   (718) 430-7300
Montefiore Westchester Sq
2475 St. Raymonds Ave   Bronx, NY 10461   BRONX

Morgan Stanley Children's Hospital of NewYork-Presbyterian, NY   (212) 305-5437
Morgan Stanley Chldns Hosp of NY-Presby, NY
3959 Broadway   New York, NY 10032   NEW YORK

Morristown Medical Center   (973) 971-5000
Morristown Med Ctr
100 Madison Avenue   Morristown, NJ 07960   MORRIS

Mount Sinai Beth Israel   (212) 420-2000
Mt Sinai Beth Israel
First Avenue at 16th Street   New York, NY 10003   NEW YORK

Mount Sinai Beth Israel-Brooklyn   (718) 252-3000
Mt Sinai Beth Israel-Brooklyn
3201 Kings Highway   Brooklyn, NY 11234   KINGS

Mount Sinai Hospital   (212) 241-6500
Mt Sinai Hosp
One Gustave L. Levy Pl   New York, NY 10029   NEW YORK

Mount Sinai Hospital of Queens   (718) 932-1000
Mt Sinai Hosp of Queens
25-10 30th Avenue   Astoria, NY 11102   QUEENS

Mount Sinai Roosevelt   (212) 523-4000
Mt Sinai Roosevelt
1000 Tenth Avenue   New York, NY 10019   NEW YORK

Mount Sinai St. Luke's   (212) 523-4000
Mt Sinai St. Luke's
1111 Amsterdam Ave   New York, NY 10025   NEW YORK

Muhlenberg Regional Medical Center   (908) 668-2000
Muhlenberg Regional Med Ctr
Park Avenue and Randolph Road   Plainfield, NJ 07061   UNION

Nassau University Medical Center   (516) 572-0123
Nassau Univ Med Ctr
2201 Hempstead Tpke   East Meadow, NY 11554   NASSAU

New Milford Hospital   (860) 210-5000
New Milford Hosp
21 Elm St   New Milford, CT 06776-2993   LITCHFIELD

New York Community Hospital   (718) 692-5300
New York Comm Hosp
2525 Kings Highway   Brooklyn, NY 11229   KINGS

New York Eye & Ear Infirmary of Mount Sinai   (212) 979-4000
New York Eye & Ear Infirm of Mt Sinai
310 E 14th St   New York, NY 10009   NEW YORK

New York Hospital Queens   (718) 670-2000
NY Hosp Queens
56-45 Main St   Flushing, NY 11355   QUEENS

New York Methodist Hospital   (718) 780-3000
New York Methodist Hosp
506 6th Street   Brooklyn, NY 11215   KINGS

New York State Psychiatric Institute   (212) 543-5000
NY State Psychiatric Inst
1051 Riverside Dr   New York, NY 10032   NEW YORK

Newark Beth Israel Medical Center   (973) 926-7000
Newark Beth Israel Med Ctr
201 Lyons Ave   Newark, NJ 07112   ESSEX

Newton Medical Center   (973) 383-2121
Newton Med Ctr
175 High St   Newton, NJ 07860-1099   SUSSEX

NewYork-Presbyterian/Columbia University Medical Center, NY   (212) 305-2500
NY-Presby/Columbia Univ Med Ctr, NY
622 W 168th St   New York, NY 10032   NEW YORK

NewYork-Presbyterian/Lower Manhattan Hospital   (212) 312-5110
NY-Presby/Lower Manhattan Hosp
170 William Street   New York, NY 10038   NEW YORK

NewYork-Presbyterian/The Allen Hospital, NY   (212) 932-4000
NY-Presby Hosp/The Allen Hosp
5141 Broadway   New York, NY 10034   NEW YORK

NewYork-Presbyterian/Weill Cornell Medical Center, NY   (212) 746-5454
NY-Presby/Weill Cornell Med Ctr, NY
525 E 68th St   New York, NY 10065   NEW YORK

NewYork-Presbyterian/Westchester Division, NY   (914) 682-9100
NY-Presby/Westchester Div, NY
21 Bloomingdale Rd   White Plains, NY 10605   WESTCHESTER

North Central Bronx Hospital   (718) 519-5000
N Central Bronx Hosp
3424 Kossuth Ave   Bronx, NY 10467   BRONX

North Shore University Hospital   (516) 562-0100
N Shore Univ Hosp
300 Community Dr   Manhasset, NY 11030   NASSAU

Northern Westchester Hospital   (914) 666-1200
Northern Westchester Hosp
400 E Main St   Mount Kisco, NY 10549   WESTCHESTER

Norwalk Hospital   (203) 852-2000
Norwalk Hosp
34 Maple Street   Norwalk, CT 06850   FAIRFIELD

Nyack Hospital   (845) 348-2000
Nyack Hosp
160 N Midland Ave   Nyack, NY 10960   ROCKLAND

NYU Hospital for Joint Diseases   (212) 598-6000
NYU Hosp For Joint Dis
301 East 17th Street   New York, NY 10003   NEW YORK

NYU Langone Medical Center   (212) 263-7300
NYU Langone Med Ctr
550 First Avenue   New York, NY 10016   NEW YORK

NYU Rusk Institute   (212) 263-6028
NYU Rusk Inst
400 East 34th Street   New York, NY 10016   NEW YORK

Ocean Medical Center   (732) 840-2200
Ocean Med Ctr
425 Jack Martin Blvd   Brick, NJ 08724   OCEAN

Orange Regional Medical Center   (845) 333-1000
Orange Regl Med Ctr
707 E Main St   Middletown, NY 10940   ORANGE

Overlook Medical Center   (908) 522-2000
Overlook Med Ctr
99 Beauvoir Ave   Summit, NJ 07902   UNION

Palisades Medical Center   (201) 854-5000
Palisades Med Ctr
7600 River Road   North Bergen, NJ 07047   HUDSON

Peconic Bay Medical Center   (631) 548-6000
Peconic Bay Med Ctr
1300 Roanoke Avenue   Riverhead, NY 11901   SUFFOLK

Phelps Memorial Hospital Center   (914) 366-3000
Phelps Meml Hosp Ctr
701 N Broadway   Sleepy Hollow, NY 10591   WESTCHESTER

Plainview Hospital   (516) 719-3000
Plainview Hosp
888 Old Country Rd   Plainview, NY 11803   NASSAU

Putnam Hospital Center   (845) 279-5711
Putnam Hosp Ctr
670 Stoneleigh Ave   Carmel, NY 10512   PUTNAM

Queens Hospital Center - Jamaica   (718) 883-3000
Queens Hosp Ctr - Jamaica
82-68 164th Street   Jamaica, NY 11432   QUEENS

Raritan Bay Medical Center - Old Bridge Division   (732) 360-1000
Raritan Bay Med Ctr - Old Bridge Div
One Hospital Plaza   Old Bridge, NJ 08857   MIDDLESEX

Raritan Bay Medical Center - Perth Amboy Division   (732) 442-3700
Raritan Bay Med Ctr - Perth Amboy
530 New Brunswick Avenue   Perth Amboy, NJ 08861-3654   MIDDLESEX

Richmond University Medical Center   (718) 818-1234
Richmond Univ Med Ctr
355 Bard Ave   Staten Island, NY 10310-1699   RICHMOND

Riverview Medical Center   (732) 741-2700
Riverview Med Ctr
1 Riverview Plaza   Red Bank, NJ 07701   MONMOUTH

Robert Wood Johnson University Hospital - Hamilton   (609) 586-7900
Robert Wood Johnson Univ Hosp Hamilton
1 Hamilton Health Pl   Hamilton, NJ 08690-3599   MERCER

Robert Wood Johnson University Hospital - New Brunswick   (732) 828-3000
Robert Wood Johnson Univ Hosp - New Brunswick
1 Robert Wood Johnson Pl   New Brunswick, NJ 08903-2601   MIDDLESEX

Robert Wood Johnson University Hospital - Somerset   (908) 685-2200
Robert Wood Johnson Univ Hosp - Somerset
110 Rehill Ave   Somerville, NJ 08876   SOMERSET

Robert Wood Johnson University Hospital at Rahway   (732) 381-4200
Robert Wood Johnson Univ Hosp at Rahway
865 Stone St   Rahway, NJ 07065   UNION

Rockefeller University Hospital   (212) 327-8000
Rockefeller Univ Hosp
1230 York Avenue   New York, NY 10021   NEW YORK

Rockland Psychiatric Center		(845) 359-1000
Rockland Psych Ctr		
140 Old Orangeburg Rd	Orangeburg, NY 10962-1196	ROCKLAND
Saint Barnabas Medical Center		(973) 322-5000
St. Barnabas Med Ctr		
94 Old Short Hills Rd	Livingston, NJ 07039-5672	ESSEX
Saint Joseph's Medical Center - Yonkers		(914) 378-7000
Saint Joseph's Med Ctr - Yonkers		
127 South Broadway	Yonkers, NY 10701	WESTCHESTER
Saint Michael's Medical Center		(973) 877-5000
Saint Michael's Med Ctr		
111 Central Avenue	Newark, NJ 07102	ESSEX
St. Vincent's Hospital-Westchester		(914) 967-6500
St. Vincent's Hosp-Westchester		
275 North Street	Harrison, NY 10528	WESTCHESTER
Silver Hill Hospital		(203) 966-3561
Silver Hill Hosp		
208 Valley Rd	New Canaan, CT 06840-3899	FAIRFIELD
South Nassau Communities Hospital		(516) 632-3000
South Nassau Comm Hosp		
1 Healthy Way	Oceanside, NY 11572	NASSAU
Southampton Hospital		(631) 726-8200
Southampton Hosp		
240 Meeting House Ln	Southampton, NY 11968	SUFFOLK
Southern Ocean Medical Center		(609) 597-6011
Southern Ocean Med Ctr		
1140 Rte 72 W	Manahawkin, NJ 08050-2499	OCEAN
Southside Hospital		(631) 968-3000
Southside Hosp		
301 E Main St	Bay Shore, NY 11706	SUFFOLK
St. Barnabas Hospital - Bronx		(718) 960-9000
St. Barnabas Hosp - Bronx		
4422 Third Avenue	Bronx, NY 10457	BRONX
St. Catherine of Siena Medical Center		(631) 862-3000
St. Catherine of Siena Med Ctr		
50 Rt 25A	Smithtown, NY 11787	SUFFOLK

St. Charles Hospital (631) 474-6000
St. Charles Hosp
200 Belle Terre Rd   Port Jefferson, NY 11777   SUFFOLK

St. Clare's Hospital - Boonton Township (973) 316-1800
St. Clare's Hosp - Boonton Township
130 Powerville Rd   Boonton Township, NJ 07005   MORRIS

St. Clare's Hospital-Denville (973) 625-6000
St. Clare's Hosp-Denville
25 Pocono Road   Denville, NJ 07834   MORRIS

St. Clare's Hospital-Dover (973) 625-6000
St. Clare's Hosp-Dover
400 W Blackwell St   Dover, NJ 07801   MORRIS

St. Clare's Hospital-Sussex (973) 702-2600
St. Clare's Hosp-Sussex
20 Walnut St   Sussex, NJ 07461   SUSSEX

St. Francis Hospital - The Heart Center (516) 562-6000
St. Francis Hosp - The Heart Ctr
100 Port Washington Boulevard   Roslyn, NY 11576   NASSAU

St. Francis Medical Center - Trenton (609) 599-5000
St. Francis Med Ctr - Trenton
601 Hamilton Avenue   Trenton, NJ 08629   MERCER

St. John's Episcopal Hospital - Queens (718) 869-7000
St. John's Episcopal Hosp - Queens
327 Beach 19th Street   Far Rockaway, NY 11691   QUEENS

St. John's Riverside Hospital-Andrus Pavilion (914) 964-4444
St. John's Riverside Hosp-Andrus Pavil
967 N Broadway   Yonkers, NY 10701   WESTCHESTER

St. John's Riverside Hospital-Dobbs Ferry Pavilion (914) 693-0700
St. John's Riverside Hosp-Dobbs Ferry Pavil
128 Ashford Ave   Dobbs Ferry, NY 10522   WESTCHESTER

St. Joseph's Hospital-Nassau (516) 579-6000
St. Joseph's Hosp-Nassau
4295 Hempstead Turnpike   Bethpage, NY 11714   NASSAU

St. Joseph's Regional Medical Center - Paterson (973) 754-2000
St. Joseph's Regl Med Ctr - Paterson
703 Main St   Paterson, NJ 07503   PASSAIC

St. Joseph's Wayne Hospital   (973) 942-6900
St. Joseph's Wayne Hosp
224 Hamburg Turnpike   Wayne, NJ 07470   PASSAIC

St. Lawrence Rehabilitation Center   (609) 896-9500
St. Lawrence Rehab Ctr
2381 Lawrenceville Rd   Lawrenceville, NJ 08648   MERCER

St. Luke's Cornwall Hospital-Cornwall Campus   (845) 534-7711
St. Luke's Cornwall Hosp-Cornwall Campus
19 Laurel Ave   Cornwall, NY 12518   ORANGE

St. Mary Medical Center - Langhorne, PA   (215) 750-2000
St. Mary Med Ctr -Langhorne, PA
1201 Langhorne-Newtown Rd   Langhorne, PA 19047   BUCKS

St. Mary's Hospital - Passaic   (973) 365-4300
St. Mary's Hosp - Passaic
350 Boulevard   Passaic, NJ 07055   PASSAIC

St. Peter's University Hospital   (732) 745-8600
St. Peter's Univ Hosp
254 Easton Ave   New Brunswick, NJ 08901-1780   MIDDLESEX

St. Vincent's Medical Center - Bridgeport   (203) 576-6000
St. Vincent's Med Ctr - Bridgeport
2800 Main St   Bridgeport, CT 06606   FAIRFIELD

Stamford Hospital   (203) 276-1000
Stamford Hosp
30 Shelburne Rd   Stamford, CT 06902   FAIRFIELD

Staten Island University Hospital - North   (718) 226-9000
Staten Island Univ Hosp - North
475 Seaview Avenue   Staten Island, NY 10305   RICHMOND

Staten Island University Hospital - South   (718) 226-2000
Staten Island Univ Hosp - South
375 Seguine Avenue   Staten Island, NY 10309   RICHMOND

Steven and Alexandra Cohen Children's Medical Center of New York   (718) 470-3000
Steven & Alexandra Cohen Chldn's Med Ctr of NY
269-01 76th Ave   New Hyde Park, NY 11040   NASSAU

Stony Brook University Hospital   (631) 444-4000
Stony Brook Univ Hosp
101 Nicolls Rd   Stony Brook, NY 11794-8410   SUFFOLK

Summit Oaks Hospital   (908) 522-7000
Summit Oaks Hosp
19 Prospect St   Summit, NJ 07902   UNION

SUNY Downstate Medical Center (University Hospital of Brooklyn)   (718) 270-1000
SUNY Downstate Med Ctr (Univ Hosp Brooklyn)
450 Clarkson Ave   Brooklyn, NY 11203   KINGS

Syosset Hospital   (516) 496-6500
Syosset Hosp
221 Jericho Tpke   Syosset, NY 11791-4536   NASSAU

Trinitas Regional Medical Center   (908) 994-5000
Trinitas Regl Med Ctr
225 Williamson St   Elizabeth, NJ 07207   UNION

Rutgers University Behavioral Health   (732) 235-5500
Rutgers Univ Behavioral Hlth
671 Hoes Lane West   Piscataway, NJ 08854-5635   MIDDLESEX

University Hospital-Newark   (973) 972-4300
Univ Hosp-Newark
150 Bergen St   Newark, NJ 07103-2406   ESSEX

University Medical Center of Princeton at Plainsboro   (609) 853-7000
Univ Med Ctr Princeton at Plainsboro
One Plainsboro Rd   Plainsboro, NJ 08536   MIDDLESEX

VA Hudson Valley Medical Center-Montrose   (914) 737-4400
VA Hudson Valley Med Ctr-Montrose
622 Albany Post Rd   Montrose, NY 10548   WESTCHESTER

VA Medical Center-Brooklyn   (718) 836-6600
VA Med Ctr-Brooklyn
800 Poly Pl   Bay Ridge, NY 11209   KINGS

VA Medical Center-New York   (212) 686-7500
VA Med Ctr-New York
423 E 23rd St   New York, NY 10010   NEW YORK

Valley Hospital   (201) 447-8000
Valley Hosp
223 N Van Dien Ave   Ridgewood, NJ 07450-2736   BERGEN

Vassar Brothers Medical Center   (845) 454-8500
Vassar Bros Med Ctr
45 Reade Pl   Poughkeepsie, NY 12601-3990   DUTCHESS

Westchester Medical Center   (914) 493-7000
Westchester Med Ctr
100 Woods Rd   Valhalla, NY 10595   WESTCHESTER

White Plains Hospital   (914) 681-0600
White Plains Hosp
Davis Ave at E Post Rd   White Plains, NY 10601   WESTCHESTER

Winthrop University Hospital   (516) 663-0333
Winthrop Univ Hosp
259 1st St   Mineola, NY 11501   NASSAU

Woodhull Medical & Mental Health Center   (718) 963-8000
Woodhull Med & Mental Hlth Ctr
760 Broadway   Brooklyn, NY 11206   KINGS

Wyckoff Heights Medical Center   (718) 963-7272
Wyckoff Heights Med Ctr
374 Stockholm Street   Brooklyn, NY 11237   KINGS

Yale-New Haven Hospital   (203) 688-4242
Yale-New Haven Hosp
20 York St   New Haven, CT 06510   NEW HAVEN

Zucker Hillside Hospital   (718) 470-8100
Zucker Hillside Hosp
75-59 263rd St   Glen Oaks, NY 11004   QUEENS

The Best in American Medicine
www.CastleConnolly.com

Appendix D:
Selected Resources

AMERICAN AMBULANCE ASSOCIATION (AAA)

The American Ambulance Association represents emergency and non-emergency medical transportation providers, advocating high quality pre-hospital care and keeping these providers aware of legislation and news that may affect them.

8400 Westpark Drive
Second Floor
McLean, VA 22102

800-523-4447
703-610-9018
fax 703-610-0210
www.the-aaa.org/

AMERICA'S HEALTH INSURANCE PLANS (AHIP)

America's Health Insurance Plans is a national trade association representing nearly 1,300 member companies providing health benefits to more than 200 million Americans.

601 Pennsylvania Ave, NW
South Building Suite 500
Washington, DC 20004

202-778-3200
fax: 202-331-7487
www.ahip.org/

AMERICAN BOARD OF MEDICAL SPECIALTIES (ABMS)

The ABMS is the authoritative body for the recognition of medical specialties, coordinating 24 medical specialty boards (including 25 medical specialties) and providing information on the board certification of doctors.

353 North Clark St Ste 1400
Chicago, IL 60654

312-436-2600
fax 312-436-2700
www.abms.org

AMERICAN HOSPITAL ASSOCIATION (AHA)

A national health advocacy organization, the AHA represents hospitals and healthcare networks in legislative and regulatory matters. In 1973 the AHA adopted the Patient Bill of Rights to help patients understand their rights and responsibilities.

155 N Wacker Drive
Chicago, IL 60606

800-424-4301 or 312-422-3000
fax 312-422-4796
www.aha.org/

800 10th Street, NW
Two CityCenter, Ste 400
Washington, DC 20001

800-424-4301 or 202-638-1100
fax 202-626-3245

AMERICAN MEDICAL ASSOCIATION (AMA)

The AMA is an association that maintains information on physicians practicing throughout the nation. Healthcare consumers can use their database to check the location, licensing, education and specialty of many doctors in the United States.

330 N. Wabash Ave
Chicago, IL 60611

800-621-8335
www.ama-assn.org/

CENTER FOR MEDICAL CONSUMERS
Provides volume and outcome data on certain medical procedures performed in New York state.

239 Thompson St.   212-674-7105
New York, NY 10012   fax 212-674-7100

CenterForMedicalConsumers@gmail.com   www.medicalconsumers.org

CENTERS FOR DISEASE CONTROL AND PREVENTION (CDC)
Part of the Department of Health and Human Services, the CDC's mission is to prevent and manage diseases and illnesses. Its website contains information on a range of illnesses and the research being pursued to manage them. It also provides free faxed reports on disease risk and prevention in various parts of the world.

Public Inquiries/MASO   1-800-CDC-INFO
Mailstop E11
1600 Clifton Road
Atlanta, GA 30333

toll free number for international travelers 877 FYI-TRIP or 404-639-3534
fax information service for international travelers 888-232-3299
www.cdc.gov/netinfo.htm

THE CENTERWATCH CLINICAL TRIALS LISTING SERVICE
Profiles centers conducting clinical research by therapeutic area and geographic region, including more than 41,000 international industry and government-sponsored clinical trials and new FDA approved drug therapies, as well as 5,200 clinical trials that are actively recruiting patients.

10 Winthrop Square, Fl 5   617-948-5100
Boston, MA 02110   fax 617-948-5101
                                                    www.centerwatch.com

HEALTH CARE CHOICES
Provides information on volume and outcomes of certain medical procedures performed in hospitals in various states throughout the country.

21-10 Borden Avenue   (718) 784-5696
Long Island City, NY 11101   http://healthcarechoicesny.org

INTERNATIONAL ASSOCIATION FOR MEDICAL ASSISTANCE TO TRAVELLERS (IAMAT)
IAMAT is a non-profit organization that disseminates information on health and sanitary conditions worldwide. Membership is free but donations are appreciated. Members will receive a membership card making them eligible to access English speaking physicians all over the world. The organization also provides information on immunization requirements, malaria, and other tropical diseases, and sanitary and climactic conditions around the world. For information, send request in writing.

1623 Military Road #279   716-754-4883
Niagra Falls, NY 14304-1745   www.iamat.org

JOINT COMMISSION ON ACCREDITATION OF HEALTHCARE ORGANIZATIONS
The Joint Commission (JCAHO) is an independent, not-for-profit organization, which evaluates the quality and safety of care for nearly 17,000 health care organizations. To maintain and earn accreditation, organizations must have an extensive on-site review by a team of JCAHO health care professionals, at least once every three years. JCAHO is governed by a board that includes physicians, nurses, and consumers. JCAHO sets the standards by which health care quality is measured in America and around the world.

One Renaissance Boulevard   630-792-5800
Oakbrook Terrace, IL 60181   fax 630-792-5005
                                                    www.jointcommission.org

MEDIC ALERT FOUNDATION

The Medic Alert Foundation (a non-profit organization) provides an "ID tag" engraved with personal medical facts, as well as a 24-hour emergency response center which can release additional personal medical details. Membership is $45/year and members need to purchase the "ID tag" which sells for as low as $35.

2323 Colorado Avenue	888-633-4298
Turlock, CA 95382	Fax 209-669-2450
	www.medicalert.org

MEDLINE

One Medline Place	1-800-MEDLINE (800-633-5463)
Mundelein, IL 60060	fax 1-800-351-1512
	www.medline.com

A medical database including millions of medical references and abstracts from thousands of scientific and medical journals.

THE NATIONAL CANCER INSTITUTE (NCI)

Part of the NIH, the NCI sponsors cancer clinical trials at more than 100 sites in the United States. Trials are carried out in major medical research centers, such as teaching hospitals, as well as in community hospitals, specialized medical clinics and even in doctors' offices.

Clinical Studies Support Center (CSSC)	800-4-CANCER (800-422-6237)
9609 Medical Center Drive	www.nci.nih.gov
GB 9609 MSC 9760	www.cancer.gov
Bethesda, MD 20892	cancergovstaff@mail.nih.gov

NATIONAL CENTER FOR COMPLEMENTARY AND ALTERNATIVE MEDICINE CLEARINGHOUSE (NCCAMC)

The NCCAMC facilitates the evaluation of alternative medical treatment modalities to help determine their effectiveness and bring alternative medicine into mainstream medicine. This agency does not provide referrals.

9000 Rockville Pike	888-644-6226
Bethesda, MD 20892	fax 866-464-3616
	www.nccam.nih.gov
	info@nccam.nih.gov

NATIONAL CONSUMERS LEAGUE (NCL)

NCL is a private, nonprofit consumer advocacy organization. NCL strives to investigate, educate, and advocate on a variety of issues including healthcare. Membership is $35 annually, but individuals can also write to the organization for a list of publications that non-members can purchase.

1701 K Street, NW, Suite 1200	202-835-3323
Washington, DC 20006	fax 202-835-0747
	www.nclnet.org
	info@nclnet.org

THE NATIONAL INSTITUTES OF HEALTH (NIH)

An organization operated by the U.S. government, the NIH operates its own hospital at which the care provided is usually related to clinical studies its researchers are undertaking. Information about the Warren G. Magnuson Clinical Center is also available.

Patient Recruitment Referral Center	800-411-1222 or 301-496-4000
9000 Rockville Pike	www.nih.gov
Bethesda, MD 20892	www.clinicaltrials.gov
	nihinfo@od.nih.gov

NATIONAL INSURANCE INFORMATION INSTITUTE

The National Insurance Information Institute Helpline advises consumers on how to choose an insurance company or broker. It also offers an analysis of life insurance and assists in insurance complaints.

110 William Street
New York, NY 10038

800-942-4242 or 212-346-5500
www.iii.org

THE PATIENT ADVOCATE FOUNDATION

A national non-profit organization that provides consultation, referrals and case management to patients to ensure that they are not denied access to healthcare, insurance coverage, employment and public assistance programs during an illness. In particular, the organization maintains comprehensive information on cancer treatment options that are available to consumers through a separate website: www.oncology.com.

421 Butler Farm Rd
Hampton, VA 23666

800-532-5274
fax 757-873-8999
www.patientadvocate.org/
help@patientadvocate.org

PERSONS UNITED LIMITING SUBSTANDARDS AND ERRORS IN HEALTHCARE (P.U.L.S.E.)

A support group for the survivors of medical malpractice and substandard healthcare, this nonprofit group also advocates patient education and patient-doctor communication.

PO Box 353
Wantagh, NY 11793-0353

800-96-pulse (800-967-8573) or
516-579-4711
fax: 516-520-8105
www.PULSEamerica.org
www.PULSEofNY.org
pulse516@aol.com

PUBLIC CITIZEN'S HEALTH AND RESEARCH GROUP

A non-profit organization, the Public Citizen's Group acts as a watchdog agency by advocating accountability and the open use of doctors' disciplinary backgrounds.

1600 20th Street NW
Washington, DC 20009

202-588-1000
www.citizen.org/hrg/

VERITAS MEDICINE

An organization that allows individuals to perform confidential, personalized searches of their clinical trials database and to access information on new treatment and drug options. The text is submitted by Harvard-affiliated doctors.

11 Cambridge Center
Cambridge, MA 02142

617-234-1500

Appendix E:
State Agencies

While there is a wealth of information available through these state agencies, much of it is not user-friendly. Complicated contractual agreements and other legal documents contain information that might prove to be valuable, providing a consumer can locate it and then review it with some understanding. Often a department will suggest that a consumer visit the office for guidance in reviewing the documents. However, some of these agencies provide useful information on doctors, hospitals, and HMOs. They may also offer statistical reports and consumer-oriented studies.

CONNECTICUT

DOCTORS

Department of Public Health State of Connecticut
Practitioner Licensing and Investigations Section
410 Capitol Avenue, MS#12MQA
P.O. Box 340308
Hartford, CT 06134-0308
(860) 509-8000
www.dph.state.ct.us
Attn: Physician renewal of verification

Department of Public Health State of Connecticut
Legal Office
410 Capitol Avenue, MS#12LEG
P.O. Box 340308
Hartford, CT 06134-0308
(860) 509-7600

HOSPITALS

Department of Public Health State of Connecticut
Facilities Licensing and Investigations Section
410 Capitol Avenue, MS#12HSR
P.O. Box 340308
Hartford, CT 06134-0308
(860) 509-7400

Appendix E

HMOs

Department of Insurance (Location address)
153 Market Street, 7th Floor
Hartford, CT 06103-0816
(860) 297-3800

Department of Insurance (Mailing address)
P.O. Box 816
Hartford, CT 06142-0816
(860) 297-3800

www.ct.gov/cid/site/default.asp

Office of Health Care Access
410 Capitol Avenue, MS#13HCA
P.O. Box 340308
Hartford, CT 06134-0308
800-797-9688

TDD 860-418-7001

www.ct.gov/ohca/site/default.asp

NEW JERSEY

DOCTORS

New Jersey State Board of Medical Examiners (Location address)
140 East Front Street, 2nd Floor
Trenton, NJ 08608
(609) 826-7100

New Jersey State Board of Medical Examiners (Mailing address)
P.O. Box 183
Trenton, NJ 08625-0360

http://www.state.nj.us/lps/ca/bme/index.html
bme@dca.lps.state.nj.us

HOSPITALS

Department of Health
Division of Health Facilities Evaluation and Licensing
P.O. Box 360
120 S Stockton Street
Trenton, NJ 08625-0360
(609) 292-7837

http://www.nj.gov/health/

HMOs

Department of Health
Division of Health Facilities Evaluation and Licensing
P.O. Box 360
120 S Stockton Street
Trenton, NJ 08625-0360
(609) 292-7837

Department of Health
Office of Managed Care
20 West State St, 11th Fl
P.O. Box 325
Trenton, NJ 08625
(609) 292-5427

http://www.state.nj.us/dobi/managed.htm

Department of Banking & Insurance (Location address)
Division of Insurance, Life and Health Division
Managed Healthcare Bureau
20 West State St
P.O. Box 325
Trenton, NJ 08625
(609) 292-7272

http://www.state.nj.us/dobi/

Department of Banking & Insurance (Mailing address)
Division of Insurance, Life and Health Division
Managed Healthcare Bureau
20 West State St
P.O. Box 325
Trenton, NJ 08625
(609) 292-7272

Office of Managed Care Hotline: 1-888-393-1062
Office of managed Care Fax: (609) 633-0807
Consumer Protection Services Main Line: (609) 292-7272

NEW YORK

DOCTORS

New York State Department of Health
Office of Professional Medical Conduct
433 River Street, Suite 303
Troy, NY 12180
(518) 402-0836
www.health.state.ny.us
opmc@health.state.ny.us

New York State Education Department
Division of Professional Licensing Services
State Education Building - 2nd floor
89 Washington Avenue
Albany, NY 12234
(518) 474-3817
http://www.op.nysed.gov/home.html

op4info@mail.nysed.gov

Appendix E

Hospitals

Office of Health Systems Management
Corning Tower, Fl 14
Empire State Plaza
Albany, NY 12237
(518) 474-7028

New York State Department of Health
Bureau of Biometrics
Corning Tower, Room 2348
Empire State Plaza
Albany, NY 12237
(518) 474-3189

HMOs

New York State Insurance Department
Health Bureau
99 Washington Ave.
Albany, NY 12257
(518) 474-6272

New York State Insurance Department
Life Policy Bureau
1 Commerce Plaza, Suite 1910
Albany, NY 12257
(518) 474-4552

New York State Department of Health
Office of Managed Care
Corning Tower, Room 1911
Albany, NY 12237
(518) 473-4178

New York State Department of Health
Records Access Office
Corning Tower, Room 2364
Empire State Plaza
Albany, NY 12237
(518) 486-9144

Appendix F:
Sources of Quality Data on Hospitals

U.S. NEWS AND WORLD REPORT

U.S. News & World Report, www.usnews.com/health, has been the nation's leading source of information on hospital rankings since 1990. The Best Hospitals rankings evaluate medical centers on their competence in high-stakes situations. Their annual feature on Best Hospitals has become the standard in the field where rankings are concerned and is heavily anticipated and utilized by consumers and members of the health care profession.

WWW.WHYNOTTHEBEST.ORG

WhyNotTheBest.org was created and is maintained by The Commonwealth Fund, a private foundation working toward a high performance health system. It is a free resource for health care professionals and consumers interested in tracking performance on various measures of health care quality. It enables organizations to compare their performance against that of peer organizations, against a range of benchmarks and over a given period of time. Case studies and improvement tools spotlight successful improvement strategies of the nation's top performers. A regional map shows performance at the county, state and national levels. This site also includes process-of-care measures, patient satisfaction measures, readmission rates, mortality rates and average reimbursement rates. All of these performance measures are publicly reported on the Centers for Medicare and Medicaid Services website, Hospital Compare, and include data from nearly all U.S. hospitals.

THE LEAPFROG GROUP

The Leapfrog Group, http://www.leapfroggroup.org/cp, started in 1998 by a group of large employers. The Leapfrog Hospital Survey compares hospitals' performance on the national standards of safety, quality and efficiency - areas of healthcare that are most relevant to consumers. Hospitals that participate in The Leapfrog Hospital Survey achieve hospital-wide improvements that translate into saving millions of lives and cutting costs for hospitals and consumers. Leapfrog's survey results are later used to inform key employees on purchasing strategies.

HOSPITAL COMPARE

The Hospital Compare website was created through the efforts of the Centers for Medicare & Medicaid Services (CMS), an agency of the U.S. Department of Health and Human Services (DHHS), along with the Hospital Quality Alliance (HQA). The HQA was established to promote reporting on hospital quality of care. The HQA consists of organizations that represent consumers, hospitals, doctors and nurses, employers, accrediting organizations and Federal agencies. The information on this website can be used by patients requiring hospital care. This information helps the consumer and health care providers to compare the quality of care provided in participating hospitals. This information not only helps one to make good decisions about health care, but also encourages hospitals to improve the quality of the care that they provide to their communities. This website can be found at: www.medicare.gov/hospitalcompare

SECTION SIX

Indices

The Best in American Medicine
www.CastleConnolly.com

Subject Index

A

Academic Medical Center 14, 21-22, 71

Alternative medicine 43-45, 51

Alternative therapy 40, 45

American Board of Medical Specialties (ABMS) 4, 14, 16, 18, 41, 75, 77, 81, 82

American Board of Radiology 17, 19

American Medical Association (AMA) 32, 33, 51, 53

American Medical News 25

B

Bachelor of Medicine 8

Baseline tests 32, 34

Board certification 12, 17-19, 23, 41, 53, 73-75, 79, 81

Board eligibility 19

C

Capitation 60, 63, 64

Chiropractors 8

Chronic condition 51

Clinical trials 39-40, 45-46

Community hospitals 12, 21-22

Compendium of Certified Medical Specialists 16

Continuing Medical Education (CME) 18

Credentialing 14, 20

Cultural sensitivity 26

Health Maintenance Organization (HMO) 60-61, 63, 65

Hippocratic Oath xi

Hospital appointment 15, 20-21

Hospital referral services 7

I

Indemnity insurance 14, 32

IPA 60, 62-63

J

J.D. Power and Associates 66

L

LEXIS/NEXIS 54, 58

Licensed nurse practitioners 24

Licensure 14, 17, 24

Louis Harris Associates 66

Lupus 4, 6

Lyme disease 4, 6, 23

M

Malpractice insurance 21

Managed care 4, 6, 20, 32-33, 42, 51, 60-66

Medical history 34-35

Medical records 30, 35, 48, 52-53

Medical school faculty appointment 22

Medical schools 16-17, 21-22, 26

R

S

T

U

W

The Best in American Medicine
www.CastleConnolly.com

Specialty & Special Expertise Index

This index lists the areas that the physicians listed in the Guide have identified as their "special expertise." They are specific elements of disease, procedures, techniques and treatments for which these physicians are best known and are referred patients. Each doctor's medical specialty is also included.

Spec	Name	St	Pg

A

Abdominal Imaging

Spec	Name	St	Pg
DR	Lubat, E	NJ	753
DR	Megibow, A	NY	159
DR	Newhouse, J	NY	160
DR	Prince, M	NY	161
DR	Swirsky, M	NY	669
DR	Toth, P	NJ	753
DR	Wolf, E	NY	415

Abdominal Wall Reconstruction

Spec	Name	St	Pg
PlS	Spector, J	NY	338
PS	Weinberg, G	NY	436
S	Mandel, M	NJ	965

Abdominoplasty

Spec	Name	St	Pg
PlS	Feinberg, J	NY	591
PlS	Friedman, D	NY	333
PlS	Gallagher, P	NY	591
PlS	Gardner, J	NJ	961
PlS	Godfrey, P	NY	333
PlS	Goldstein, R	NY	439
PlS	Gotkin, R	NY	333
PlS	Kolker, A	NY	335
PlS	Lesesne, C	NY	335
PlS	Matarasso, A	NY	335
PlS	Newman, F	CT	1022
PlS	Newman, S	NY	716
PlS	Perrotti, J	NY	336
PlS	Perry, A	NJ	942

Abuse/Neglect

Spec	Name	St	Pg
AM	Johnson, R	NJ	804
AM	Steever, J	NY	121
Ger	Jacobs, L	NY	419
Ger	Lachs, M	NY	181

Acanthamoeba Keratitis

Spec	Name	St	Pg
Oph	Auran, J	NY	253

Achalasia

Spec	Name	St	Pg
Ge	Lambroza, A	NY	174

Spec	Name	St	Pg
S	Pryor, A	NY	648

Acne

Spec	Name	St	Pg
D	Alexis, A	NY	146
D	Almeida, L	NJ	906
D	Aprile, G	NY	548
D	Aranoff, S	NY	146
D	Berson, D	NY	147
D	Blank, E	NJ	837
D	Bruckstein, R	NY	548
D	Davis, J	NY	148
D	Deitz, M	NY	457
D	Demar, L	NY	148
D	Dietz, S	CT	980
D	Dolitsky, C	NY	548
D	Eisenberg, R	NJ	950
D	Falcon, R	NY	548
D	Feldman, P	NY	457
D	Fox, A	NJ	936
D	Fried, S	NJ	751
D	Giardina-Beckett, M	NJ	751
D	Goldberg, N	NY	665
D	Hefter, H	NY	548
D	Hisler, B	NY	549
D	Huh, J	NY	625
D	Lerman, J	NY	413
D	Lukash, B	NY	666
D	Maier, H	NJ	926
D	McAleer, P	CT	981
D	Notaro, A	NY	625
D	Rosen, D	NY	414
D	Rozanski, R	NJ	808
D	Scherl, S	NJ	751
D	Schweiger, E	NY	154
D	Seidenberg, R	NY	154
D	Sweeney, E	NJ	752
D	Tanzer, F	NJ	926
D	Tom, J	NY	625
D	Waldorf, D	NY	610
D	Walther, R	NY	155
D	Wattenberg, D	NY	156
D	Wechsler, A	NY	156
D	Wexler, P	NY	156
D	Whitman, G	CT	981
Ped	Panzner, E	NJ	961

Acne & Rosacea

Spec	Name	St	Pg
D	Baldwin, H	NY	456
D	Danziger, S	NY	457
D	Felderman, L	NY	148
D	Gold, J	NJ	926
D	Goldwasser, J	NY	665
D	Gribetz, C	NY	149
D	Liftin, A	NJ	808
D	Treiber, R	NY	667
D	Zeichner, J	NY	156

Acoustic Neuroma

Spec	Name	St	Pg
NS	Davis, R	NY	634
NS	Gutin, P	NY	230
NS	Jafar, J	NY	231
NS	Post, K	NY	232
Oto	Chandrasekhar, S	NY	287
Oto	Feghali, J	NY	430
Oto	Kohan, D	NY	290
Oto	Kwartler, J	NJ	959
Oto	Linstrom, C	NY	292
Oto	Roland, J	NY	293
Oto	Selesnick, S	NY	294
Oto	Storper, I	NY	295

Acupuncture

Spec	Name	St	Pg
IM	Ades, J	NY	680
IM	Ehrlich, M	NY	200
IM	Gazzara, P	NY	524
IM	Lu, B	NY	466
IM	Merrell, W	NY	205
N	Lazar, M	NJ	871
N	Padela, M	NJ	928
PM	Agin, C	NY	580
PM	Kahn, S	NY	298
PM	Lu, G	NY	706
PM	Moqtaderi, F	NY	299
PM	Ngeow, J	NY	299
PMR	Aaronson, B	CT	1020
PMR	Agri, R	NJ	855
PMR	Averill, A	NJ	786
PMR	Dillard, J	NY	327
PMR	Freedman, J	CT	1021
PMR	Grant, L	CT	1021
PMR	Ma, D	NY	328

Specialty & Special Expertise Index

Spec	Name	St	Pg
PMR	Rosenberg, C	NY	644
PMR	Snowball, H	CT	1021
Rhu	Lichtbroun, A	NJ	882
Rhu	Meed, S	NY	371

Acute Coronary Syndromes

Spec	Name	St	Pg
Cv	Besser, L	NY	521
Cv	Dangas, G	NY	126
Cv	Kim, S	NJ	746
Cv	Menegus, M	NY	411
IC	Krishnan, P	NY	209
IC	Mehran, R	NY	209
IC	Wasserman, H	CT	996

ADD/ADHD

Spec	Name	St	Pg
ChAP	Abright, A	NY	136
ChAP	Becker, I	NY	136
ChAP	Boorady, R	NY	136
ChAP	Burkes, L	NY	137
ChAP	Cammarata, S	NJ	806
ChAP	Carlson, G	NY	623
ChAP	Coffey, B	NY	137
ChAP	Cohen, L	NY	661
ChAP	Fink, C	NY	661
ChAP	Gandhi, L	NY	623
ChAP	Greenberg, R	NJ	949
ChAP	Greenhill, L	NY	661
ChAP	Hirsch, G	NY	137
ChAP	Holzer, B	NY	455
ChAP	Kafantaris, V	NY	501
ChAP	Koplewicz, H	NY	137
ChAP	Kotler, L	NJ	749
ChAP	Liaw, K	NY	138
ChAP	Lustbader, A	CT	979
ChAP	Newcorn, J	NY	138
ChAP	Pincus, E	NJ	749
ChAP	Samanich, J	CT	979
ChAP	Shampain, L	NJ	863
ChAP	Shatkin, J	NY	139
ChAP	Silva, R	NY	662
ChAP	Silverman, A	NY	663
ChAP	Turecki, S	NY	139
ChiN	Andriola, M	NY	624
ChiN	De Carlo, R	NY	522
ChiN	Grossman, E	NJ	905
ChiN	Heilbroner, P	NJ	749
ChiN	Jacobson, R	NY	663
ChiN	Kutscher, M	NY	663
ChiN	Molofsky, W	NY	141
ChiN	Pavlakis, S	NY	456
ChiN	Traeger, E	NJ	949
FMed	Gottesfeld, P	NY	671

Spec	Name	St	Pg
N	Kurlan, R	NJ	956
Ped	Berkowitz, I	NJ	785
Ped	Buchalter, M	NJ	785
Ped	Chessin, R	CT	1018
Ped	Cowan, S	NY	713
Ped	Feldman, S	NY	485
Ped	Green, A	NY	588
Ped	Kanter, A	NJ	785
Ped	Kaplan, M	NY	643
Ped	Klenk, R	CT	1019
Ped	Levinson, W	NY	713
Ped	Marcus, R	NY	826
Ped	McCarton, C	NY	323
Ped	Milanaik, R	NY	588
Ped	Mongillo, N	CT	1020
Ped	Murphy, R	NJ	895
Ped	Quinn, J	NY	643
Ped	Rothschild, R	CT	1020
Ped	Smoller, A	NJ	896
Ped	Sollinger, J	CT	1020
Psyc	Adler, L	NY	341
Psyc	Budman, C	NY	593
Psyc	Cohen, A	NY	343
Psyc	Faber, M	NJ	828
Psyc	Fennelly, B	NJ	919
Psyc	Gurland, F	NJ	789
Psyc	Kaplan, G	NJ	962
Psyc	Kowallis, G	NY	347
Psyc	Kranzler, E	NY	347
Psyc	Kremberg, M	NY	347
Psyc	Miller, D	NJ	962
Psyc	Moraille, P	NJ	842
Psyc	Oberfield, R	NY	349
Psyc	Pfeffer, C	NY	349
Psyc	Rosenthal, J	NY	350
Psyc	Silver, B	NJ	962
Psyc	Wachtel, A	NY	353
Psyc	Zornitzer, M	NJ	828

ADD/PTSD

Spec	Name	St	Pg
Psyc	Manevitz, A	NY	347

Addiction Medicine

Spec	Name	St	Pg
FMed	Stancliff, S	NY	168

Addiction Psychiatry

Spec	Name	St	Pg
AdP	Bisaga, A	NY	654
AdP	Collins, E	CT	973
AdP	Cooperman, S	CT	973
AdP	Finkelstein, M	NJ	903
AdP	Frances, R	NY	119
AdP	Galanter, I	NY	119

Spec	Name	St	Pg
AdP	Kleber, H	NY	119
AdP	Levin, F	NY	119
AdP	Paul, E	NY	119
AdP	Perkel, C	NY	119
AdP	Rosenberg, K	NY	119
AdP	Scimeca, M	NY	119
AdP	Stelwagon, J	NY	120
AdP	Weiss, C	NY	120
AdP	Westreich, L	NJ	804
AdP	Williams, J	NJ	861
Psyc	Bogen, S	NY	717
Psyc	Hindin, L	NJ	828
Psyc	Kalash, G	NY	513
Psyc	Selzer, J	NY	594
Psyc	Zaidi, S	NJ	789
Psyc	Zimberg, S	NY	354

Addiction/Substance Abuse

Spec	Name	St	Pg
AdP	Collins, E	CT	973
AdP	Cooperman, S	CT	973
AdP	Finkelstein, M	NJ	903
AdP	Frances, R	NY	119
AdP	Levin, F	NY	119
AdP	Perkel, C	NY	119
AdP	Rosenberg, K	NY	119
AdP	Scimeca, M	NY	119
AdP	Stelwagon, J	NY	120
AdP	Westreich, L	NJ	804
AdP	Williams, J	NJ	861
IM	Altholz, J	NY	681
IM	Gazzara, P	NY	524
IM	Salsitz, E	NY	206
IM	Selwyn, P	NY	422
IM	Simon, L	NY	632
Psyc	Behr, R	NY	593
Psyc	Goldman, N	NY	345
Psyc	Gurevich, M	NY	594
Psyc	Heisman, A	NY	487
Psyc	Moore, J	NY	348
Psyc	Osei-Tutu, J	NY	440
Psyc	Rosenthal, R	NY	350
Psyc	Rosner, R	NY	350
Psyc	Ross, S	NY	351
Psyc	Schneider, S	NJ	856
Psyc	Schroeder, K	NY	617
Psyc	Selzer, J	NY	594
Psyc	Spitz, H	NY	352
Psyc	Stone, M	NY	353

Addison's Disease

Spec	Name	St	Pg
EDM	Goldenberg, A	NY	627
EDM	Maclaren, N	NY	164

Specialty & Special Expertise Index

Specialty & Special Expertise Index

Spec	Name	St	Pg
PO	Merer, D	NY	710
PO	Modi, V	NY	315
PO	Respler, D	NJ	782
PO	Smith, L	NY	586
PO	Traquina, D	NJ	878
PO	Ward, R	NY	315
PPul	Lee, H	NY	484
Pul	Gordon, R	NY	595

Airway Reconstruction

Spec	Name	St	Pg
Oto	Genden, E	NY	288
PO	Bent, J	NY	435
PO	Modi, V	NY	315

Alcohol Abuse

Spec	Name	St	Pg
AdP	Bisaga, A	NY	654
AdP	Collins, E	CT	973
AdP	Finkelstein, M	NJ	903
AdP	Galanter, I	NY	119
AdP	Levin, F	NY	119
AdP	Paul, E	NY	119
AdP	Perkel, C	NY	119
AdP	Scimeca, M	NY	119
AdP	Weiss, C	NY	120
AdP	Westreich, L	NJ	804
AdP	Williams, J	NJ	861
Psyc	Kaufmann, C	NY	718
Psyc	Morgan, C	CT	1023
Psyc	Ross, S	NY	351
Psyc	Tamerin, J	CT	1024

Allergic Aspergillosis

Spec	Name	St	Pg
A&I	Ricketti, A	NJ	847

Allergic Fungal Sinusitis

Spec	Name	St	Pg
Oto	Jacobs, J	NY	289

Allergic Rhinitis

Spec	Name	St	Pg
A&I	Bassett, C	NY	121
A&I	Canfield, S	NY	122
A&I	Chang, C	NJ	741
A&I	Geller, D	NJ	741
A&I	Hirsch, A	NJ	903
A&I	Lindner, P	CT	974
A&I	Mayer, D	NY	621
A&I	Mechanic, L	NY	654
A&I	Vassallo, M	NY	452
PA&I	Herzog, R	NY	303
Ped	Kushner, S	NJ	785

Allergy

Spec	Name	St	Pg
A&I	Guida, L	NY	621
A&I	LeBenger, K	NJ	948
A&I	Lubitz, A	NY	122
A&I	Markovics, S	NY	539
A&I	Perin, P	NJ	742
A&I	Picone, F	NJ	887
A&I	Santilli, J	CT	974
A&I	Schulhafer, E	NJ	935
A&I	Tolston, E	NY	123
A&I	Weinstock, G	NY	540
Oto	Aferzon, M	CT	1014
Oto	Nass, R	NY	292
PA&I	Barisciano, L	NJ	915
PA&I	Colenda, M	NJ	779
PA&I	Fagin, J	NY	581
Ped	Gropper, D	CT	1019
Ped	Handler, R	NJ	917
Ped	Panzner, E	NJ	961
Ped	Rabinowitz, A	NJ	786
PPul	Atlas, A	NJ	916
PPul	Dimaio, M	NY	316
PPul	Kaplan, E	NJ	783
Pul	Elamir, M	NJ	842
Pul	Roca, D	CT	1025

Allergy & Immunology

Spec	Name	St	Pg
A&I	Applebaum, E	NJ	903
A&I	Backman, K	CT	973
A&I	Bassett, C	NY	121
A&I	Bell, J	CT	973
A&I	Bernstein, L	NY	409
A&I	Bielory, L	NJ	948
A&I	Bloom, K	CT	973
A&I	Blum, J	NJ	861
A&I	Blume, J	NJ	741
A&I	Bosso, J	NY	609
A&I	Boxer, M	NY	538
A&I	Brown, D	NJ	948
A&I	Buchbinder, E	NY	122
A&I	Burton, D	NY	122
A&I	Canfield, S	NY	122
A&I	Caucino, J	NJ	935
A&I	Chandler, M	NY	122
A&I	Chang, C	NJ	741
A&I	Chernack, W	NJ	903
A&I	Corn, B	NY	122
A&I	Corriel, R	NY	539
A&I	Cunningham-Rundles, C	NY	122
A&I	Deener, A	NY	654
A&I	Edwards, B	NY	539

Spec	Name	St	Pg
A&I	Falk, T	NJ	741
A&I	Fonacier, L	NY	539
A&I	Fox, J	NJ	935
A&I	Frieri, M	NY	539
A&I	From, S	NJ	741
A&I	Geller, D	NJ	741
A&I	Geraci-Ciardullo, K	NY	654
A&I	Goldman, N	NY	654
A&I	Goldstein, S	NY	539
A&I	Goodman, A	NJ	948
A&I	Goodstein, C	NJ	741
A&I	Greeley, N	NY	451
A&I	Gross, G	NJ	887
A&I	Grubman, S	NY	122
A&I	Guida, L	NY	621
A&I	Harish, Z	NJ	741
A&I	Hemmers, P	CT	974
A&I	Hirsch, A	NJ	903
A&I	Joks, R	NY	451
A&I	Jyonouchi, H	NJ	861
A&I	Kanumury, S	NJ	903
A&I	Kaufman, A	NY	409
A&I	Kesarwala, H	NJ	861
A&I	Klein, N	NY	451
A&I	Klein, R	NJ	925
A&I	Krol, K	NJ	935
A&I	Lang, P	NY	539
A&I	LeBenger, K	NJ	948
A&I	Lee, R	CT	974
A&I	Lehach, J	NY	409
A&I	Leibner, D	NJ	861
A&I	Lindner, P	CT	974
A&I	Litchman, M	CT	974
A&I	LoGalbo, P	NY	609
A&I	Lubitz, A	NY	122
A&I	Lusman, P	NY	621
A&I	Maccia, C	NJ	948
A&I	Maloney, P	NY	654
A&I	Manvar, D	NY	451
A&I	Markovics, S	NY	539
A&I	Matczuk, A	CT	974
A&I	Mayer, D	NY	621
A&I	Mazza, D	NY	123
A&I	Mechanic, L	NY	654
A&I	Menchell, D	NY	500
A&I	Mendelson, J	NJ	948
A&I	Michelis, M	NJ	742
A&I	Minikes, N	NJ	742
A&I	Mumneh, N	NJ	862
A&I	Novick, B	NY	539
A&I	Osleeb, C	NY	655
A&I	Pedinoff, A	NJ	935
A&I	Perin, P	NJ	742

Specialty & Special Expertise Index

Spec	Name	St	Pg
A&I	Perlman, D	NJ	804
A&I	Picone, F	NJ	887
A&I	Pollowitz, J	NY	655
A&I	Rao, Y	NY	521
A&I	Richheimer, M	NY	621
A&I	Ricketti, A	NJ	847
A&I	Rosenstreich, D	NY	409
A&I	Rubinstein, A	NY	410
A&I	Santilli, J	CT	974
A&I	Satnick, S	NY	621
A&I	Schulhafer, E	NJ	935
A&I	Selvaggi, T	NJ	742
A&I	Shepherd, G	NY	123
A&I	Sher, E	NJ	887
A&I	Sicklick, M	NY	540
A&I	Silverman, B	NY	451
A&I	Skripak, J	NJ	742
A&I	Slankard, M	NY	123
A&I	Southern, D	NJ	935
A&I	Sproviero, J	CT	974
A&I	Tolston, E	NY	123
A&I	Tuerk-Mendelsohn, L	NY	655
A&I	Vassallo, M	NY	452
A&I	Veksler-Offengenden, I	CT	974
A&I	Weinstock, G	NY	540
A&I	Weiss, S	NJ	804
A&I	Wertheim, D	NY	540
IM	Cunningham-Rundles, W	NY	
200			

Alzheimer's Disease

FMed	Eisenstat, S	NJ	951
Ger	Bradley, S	NY	180
Ger	Brown, M	NJ	838
Ger	Callahan, E	NY	180
Ger	Chang, C	NY	180
Ger	Chavez, L	NJ	758
Ger	Devons, C	NY	677
Ger	Gohel, R	NJ	889
Ger	Jones, S	CT	988
Ger	Katz, T	NJ	758
Ger	Khimani, K	NJ	953
Ger	Korc-Grodzicki, B	NY	181
Ger	Leipzig, R	NY	181
Ger	Morrison, R	NY	181
Ger	Pantagis, S	NJ	758
Ger	Parulekar, M	NJ	758
Ger	Redling, T	NJ	811
Ger	Schor, J	NJ	811
Ger	Solomon, R	NJ	953
Ger	Vigario, J	NJ	867
Ger	Wolf-Klein, G	NY	556

Spec	Name	St	Pg
GerPsy	Amin, R	NY	462
GerPsy	Cohen, C	NY	462
GerPsy	Devanand, D	NY	182
GerPsy	Kennedy, G	NY	419
GerPsy	Reisberg, B	NY	182
GerPsy	Serby, M	NY	182
IM	Bharathan, T	NY	465
IM	Levey, R	NY	466
IM	Sherman, F	NY	467
IM	Taubman, L	NY	560
N	Caporaso, G	NY	693
N	Coohill, L	NJ	956
N	Crystal, H	NY	472
N	Galvin, J	NY	237
N	Gordon, M	NY	568
N	Gross, E	NY	693
N	Kay, A	NY	473
N	Keilson, M	NY	473
N	Kososky, C	NJ	852
N	Levin, K	NJ	770
N	Marder, K	NY	239
N	Marks, S	NY	694
N	Mayeux, R	NY	240
N	Relkin, N	NY	241
N	Silbert, P	NJ	893
Psyc	Feinberg, T	NY	344

Amblyopia

Oph	Gallin, P	NY	258
Oph	Mulvey, L	NJ	852
Oph	Potter, W	CT	1009
Oph	Rubin, S	NY	574

Amniocentesis

MF	Dunston-Boone, G	CT	997
MF	Genc, M	NJ	891
MF	Grunebaum, A	NY	211
MF	Hutson, J	NY	211
MF	Rebarber, A	NY	212
MF	Smith, L	NJ	815

Amputee Rehabilitation

PMR	Frieden, R	NY	327
PMR	Guarracini, M	NY	616
PMR	Pechman, K	NY	715
PMR	Richter, E	CT	1021

Amyloid Heart Disease

Cv	Steingart, R	NY	135
Cv	Zucker, M	NJ	806

Amyloidosis

Hem	Vesole, D	NJ	760
Rhu	Cohen, D	NY	598

Amyloidosis/Joint Disease

Rhu	Gorevic, P	NY	370

Amyotrophic Lateral Sclerosis (ALS)

N	Belsh, J	NJ	871
N	Lange, D	NY	238
N	MacGowan, D	NY	239
N	Mitsumoto, H	NY	240
N	Schanzer, B	NJ	956
N	Sivak, M	NY	242
N	Stuebgen, J	NY	242
PMR	Bach, J	NJ	826

Anal Cancer

CRS	Gorfine, S	NY	143
CRS	Temple, L	NY	145
Onc	Goldberg, A	NY	215

Anal Disorders & Reconstruction

CRS	Brandeis, S	NY	143
CRS	Gorfine, S	NY	143
CRS	Lacqua, F	NY	522

Anaphylaxis

PA&I	Wang, J	NY	303

Anemia

Hem	Diaz, M	NY	189
Hem	Dosik, H	NY	463
Hem	Green, D	NY	190
Hem	Karp, G	NJ	867
Hem	Meyer, R	NY	191
Hem	Raphael, B	NY	192
Hem	Soff, G	NY	192
Nep	Tartini, A	NJ	768
Ped	Festa, R	NY	643
Ped	Harlow, P	NJ	785
Ped	Saraiya, N	NJ	961
PHO	Sadanandan, S	NY	483
PHO	Viswanathan, K	NY	483

Anemia in Chronic Kidney Disease

Nep	DeFabritus, A	NY	226

Specialty & Special Expertise Index

Spec	Name	St	Pg

Anemia-Aplastic

Hem	Araten, D	NY	189
Hem	Castro-Malaspina, H	NY	189
Hem	Isola, L	NY	190
Hem	Liu, D	NY	679
Hem	Schuster, M	NY	630

Anemia-Cancer Related

| Hem | Wisch, N | NY | 193 |

Anemias & Red Blood Cell Disorders

| Onc | Bernhardt, B | NY | 687 |

Aneurysm

NRad	Sullivan, S	CT	1003
NS	Steinberger, A	NJ	769
S	Drascher, G	NJ	943
S	Vitale, G	NY	601
T&CS	Seinfeld, F	NJ	857
VascS	Ascher, E	NY	495
VascS	Deitch, J	NY	533
VascS	Maldonado, T	NY	404
VascS	Mateo, R	NY	732
VascS	Simonian, G	NJ	799
VascS	Teodorescu, V	NY	405

Aneurysm-Abdominal & Thoracic Aortic

VascS	Cayne, N	NY	403
VascS	Char, D	NJ	798
VascS	Lee, A	NY	517
VascS	Lipsitz, E	NY	445
VascS	Morrissey, N	NY	405
VascS	Napolitano, M	NJ	799
VascS	Suggs, W	NY	732

Aneurysm-Abdominal Aortic

VascS	Adelman, M	NY	402
VascS	Babu, S	NY	731
VascS	D'Ayala, M	NY	495
VascS	Faries, P	NY	403
VascS	Faust, G	NY	606
VascS	Gagne, P	CT	1033
VascS	Green, R	NY	403
VascS	Grossi, R	NY	404
VascS	Jacobowitz, G	NY	404
VascS	Kagan, P	NJ	798
VascS	McKinsey, J	NY	405
VascS	Purtill, W	NY	606
VascS	Rockman, C	NY	405

VascS	Sales, C	NJ	966
VascS	Todd, G	NY	406
VIR	Strauss, E	CT	1033

Aneurysm-Aortic

T&CS	DeAnda, A	NY	386
T&CS	Girardi, L	NY	387
T&CS	Lettera, J	CT	1031
T&CS	Loulmet, D	NY	388
T&CS	Michler, R	NY	444
T&CS	Pogo, G	NY	602
T&CS	Spielvogel, D	NY	728
T&CS	Squitieri, R	CT	1031
T&CS	Taylor, J	NY	649
VascS	Benvenisty, A	NY	402
VascS	Bernik, T	NY	403
VascS	Brener, B	NJ	833
VascS	Carroccio, A	NY	403
VascS	Dietzek, A	CT	1033
VascS	Ellozy, S	NY	403
VascS	Fishman, E	NY	731
VascS	Geuder, J	NJ	798
VascS	Giangola, G	NY	403
VascS	Goldman, K	NJ	884
VascS	Harrington, E	NY	404
VascS	Harrington, M	NY	404
VascS	Huribal, M	CT	1033
VascS	Landis, G	NY	606
VascS	Laskowski, I	NY	732
VascS	Marin, M	NY	404
VascS	Marsan, B	CT	1033
VascS	McGovern, P	NJ	843
VascS	Patel, A	NJ	922
VascS	Rhee, R	NY	495
VascS	Rodino, W	NY	533
VascS	Schneider, D	NY	405
VascS	Stein, J	NY	405
VascS	Tassiopoulos, A	NY	650
VascS	Wolodiger, F	NJ	799
VIR	Choudhri, A	NJ	857

Aneurysm-Cerebral

NRad	Berenstein, A	NY	243
NRad	Gobin, Y	NY	243
NRad	Keller, I	NJ	872
NRad	Meyers, P	NY	244
NRad	Tenner, M	NY	695
NS	Bederson, J	NY	229
NS	Benitez, R	NJ	911
NS	Brisman, J	NY	566
NS	Flamm, E	NY	425
NS	Holtzman, R	NY	567

NS	Jafar, J	NY	231
NS	Langer, D	NY	231
NS	Moore, F	NJ	769
NS	Murali, R	NY	692
NS	Nosko, M	NJ	870
NS	Riina, H	NY	232
NS	Solomon, R	NY	233
NS	Stieg, P	NY	233
NS	Woo, H	NY	635

Aneurysm-Thoracic Aortic

T&CS	Abrol, S	NY	493
T&CS	Coady, M	CT	1031
T&CS	Hartman, A	NY	649
T&CS	Klein, J	NJ	795
T&CS	Stelzer, P	NY	390
T&CS	Tranbaugh, R	NY	391

Angina

Cv	Lucariello, R	NY	411
Cv	Rothman, H	NJ	748
Cv	Schulman, I	NY	133
Cv	Siskind, S	NY	501
Cv	Sklaroff, H	NY	134
Cv	Tartaglia, J	NY	660

Angiography & Stent Placement

IC	Howes, C	CT	995
IC	Landau, C	CT	995
IC	Wilentz, J	NY	210

Angiography-Coronary

Cv	Pappas, T	NY	544
Cv	Zaloom, R	NY	455
IC	Abittan, M	NY	561
IC	Moses, J	NY	209
IC	Syed, T	NJ	763

Angioplasty

Cv	Coppola, J	NY	126
Cv	Green, S	NY	543
Cv	Klapholz, M	NJ	805
Cv	Landers, D	NJ	746
Cv	Lowell, B	NJ	904
Cv	Sherman, W	NY	134
IC	Brogno, D	NY	611
IC	Shanahan, A	NJ	850
VascS	Manno, J	NJ	798
VIR	Crystal, K	NY	605
VIR	Rundback, J	NJ	798
VIR	Sperling, D	NY	401

33333333333

222222222
222222

Specialty & Special Expertise Index

Spec	Name	St	Pg
Angioplasty & Restenosis			
IC	Feit, F	NY	208

Spec	Name	St	Pg
Angioplasty & Stent Placement			
Cv	Dangas, G	NY	126
Cv	Jauhar, R	NY	543
Cv	Kim, S	NJ	746
Cv	Kosinski, E	CT	977
Cv	Shamoon, F	NJ	806
Cv	Stoupakis, G	NJ	748
Cv	Stroh, J	NJ	936
IC	Angeli, S	NJ	763
IC	Borgen, E	NY	467
IC	Brener, S	NY	467
IC	Frankel, R	NY	467
IC	Kaplan, B	NY	561
IC	Kodali, S	NY	209
IC	Lawson, W	NY	633
IC	Malpeso, J	NY	525
IC	Miller, K	NJ	814
IC	Moreno, P	NY	209
IC	Moses, J	NY	209
IC	Ong, L	NY	633
IC	Papadakos, S	NY	507
IC	Rachofsky, E	NJ	939
IC	Shani, J	NY	468
IC	Sharma, S	NY	210
IC	Stone, G	NY	210
IC	Syed, T	NJ	763
IC	Torre, S	NJ	814

Spec	Name	St	Pg
Angioplasty & Stent Replacement			
Cv	Copen, D	CT	976

Spec	Name	St	Pg
Angiosarcoma			
S	Bernik, S	NY	377

Spec	Name	St	Pg
Ankle Reconstruction			
OrS	Angel, M	NY	575
OrS	Levine, D	NY	277
OrS	Troy, A	CT	1013

Spec	Name	St	Pg
Ankle Replacement & Revision			
OrS	Ellis, S	NY	272
OrS	Greisberg, J	NY	274
OrS	O'Malley, M	NY	280
OrS	Sands, A	NY	283

Spec	Name	St	Pg
Ankylosing Spondylitis			
Rhu	Goodman, S	NY	370

Spec	Name	St	Pg
Anorectal Disorders			
CRS	Arnell, T	NY	143
CRS	Bernstein, M	NY	143
CRS	Brandeis, S	NY	143
CRS	Chessin, D	NY	143
CRS	Eisenstat, T	NJ	863
CRS	Greenwald, M	NY	547
CRS	Khaitov, S	NY	144
CRS	Lee, S	NY	144
CRS	Moseson, M	NY	547
CRS	Moskowitz, R	NJ	905
CRS	Procaccino, J	NY	547
CRS	Smithy, W	NY	624
CRS	Tarantino, D	NJ	807

Spec	Name	St	Pg
Anorectal Malformations			
PS	Velcek, F	NY	319

Spec	Name	St	Pg
Anterior Segment Surgery			
Oph	Cioffi, G	NY	255
Oph	DeBroff, B	CT	1007
Oph	Delerme, M	NY	256
Oph	DeLuca, J	NJ	774
Oph	Doctor, L	CT	1007
Oph	Dodick, J	NY	256
Oph	Hirshfield, G	NY	511
Oph	Sherman, S	NY	478
Oph	Wasserman, E	CT	1010

Spec	Name	St	Pg
Anterior Segment Trauma/Reconstruction			
Oph	Florakis, G	NY	257

Spec	Name	St	Pg
Antibiotic Resistance			
Inf	Birch, T	NJ	761
Inf	Chapnick, E	NY	464
Inf	Epstein, M	NY	558
Inf	Kesh, S	NY	679
Inf	McManus, E	NJ	908
Inf	Parry, M	CT	990
Inf	Spicehandler, D	NY	680
Inf	Weisholtz, S	NJ	762
PInf	Slavin, K	NJ	782

Spec	Name	St	Pg
Antiphospholipid Syndrome (APS)			
Rhu	Belmont, H	NY	368

Spec	Name	St	Pg
Rhu	Furie, R	NY	598
Rhu	Gladstein, G	CT	1028
Rhu	Salmon, J	NY	372

Spec	Name	St	Pg
Anxiety			
ChAP	Rabinowitz, I	NY	662

Spec	Name	St	Pg
Anxiety & Depression			
AdP	Galanter, I	NY	119
ChAP	Holzer, B	NY	455
ChAP	Lipschitz, D	CT	979
ChAP	Lustbader, A	CT	979
ChAP	Pincus, E	NJ	749
ChAP	Silverman, A	NY	663
FMed	Levy, A	NY	168
FMed	Ziering, T	NJ	937
GerPsy	Dolan, N	CT	988
GerPsy	Lantz, M	NY	182
IM	Flanzman, S	NJ	762
Psyc	Aronoff, M	NY	341
Psyc	Berkowitz, H	NY	487
Psyc	Bogen, S	NY	717
Psyc	Brodie, J	NY	342
Psyc	Bronheim, H	NY	343
Psyc	Chung, H	NY	343
Psyc	Drooker, M	NY	344
Psyc	Goldberg, J	NY	487
Psyc	Goldberg, J	CT	1023
Psyc	Goldstein, S	NY	345
Psyc	Heisman, A	NY	487
Psyc	Kahn, J	NY	718
Psyc	Kranzler, E	NY	347
Psyc	Levy, M	NY	617
Psyc	Mellman, L	NY	348
Psyc	Moore, J	NY	348
Psyc	Mueller, F	CT	1023
Psyc	Muskin, P	NY	349
Psyc	Osei-Tutu, J	NY	440
Psyc	Papp, L	NY	349
Psyc	Pfeffer, C	NY	349
Psyc	Sacks, M	NY	351
Psyc	Sadock, V	NY	351
Psyc	Samuels, S	NJ	789
Psyc	Schwartz, B	NY	440
Psyc	Shapiro, B	CT	1023
Psyc	Sofair, J	NJ	962
Psyc	Spitz, H	NY	352
Psyc	Tancredi, L	NY	353
Psyc	Tolchin, J	NY	353
Psyc	Wallack, J	NY	354
Psyc	Zornitzer, M	NJ	828

Specialty & Special Expertise Index

Specialty & Special Expertise Index

Spec	Name	St	Pg	Spec	Name	St	Pg	Spec	Name	St	Pg
A&I	Pedinoff, A	NJ	935	Ped	Juan, P	CT	1019	Pul	Bergman, M	NY	488
A&I	Perin, P	NJ	742	Ped	Kaplan, M	NY	643	Pul	Bernardini, D	NY	645
A&I	Perlman, D	NJ	804	Ped	Kotin, N	NY	322	Pul	Bernstein, C	NY	488
A&I	Picone, F	NJ	887	Ped	Kushner, S	NJ	785	Pul	Bevelaqua, F	NY	355
A&I	Pollowitz, J	NY	655	Ped	Levitzky, S	NY	322	Pul	Binder, R	NY	720
A&I	Richheimer, M	NY	621	Ped	Murphy, R	NJ	895	Pul	Blair, L	NY	355
A&I	Rubinstein, A	NY	410	Ped	Panzner, E	NJ	961	Pul	Blum, A	NY	594
A&I	Satnick, S	NY	621	Ped	Poon, E	NY	324	Pul	Bondi, E	NY	488
A&I	Schulhafer, E	NJ	935	Ped	Puder, D	NY	616	Pul	Brauntuch, G	NJ	790
A&I	Sicklick, M	NY	540	Ped	Saraiya, N	NJ	961	Pul	Breidbart, D	NY	595
A&I	Slankard, M	NY	123	Ped	Schechter, M	NY	437	Pul	Brill, J	NY	720
A&I	Tolston, E	NY	123	Ped	Zoltan, I	NY	438	Pul	Bromberg, A	NJ	790
A&I	Tuerk-Mendelsohn, L	NY	655	PPul	Aguila, H	NJ	825	Pul	Casino, J	NY	720
A&I	Vassallo, M	NY	452	PPul	Amin, N	NY	710	Pul	Castellano, M	NY	530
A&I	Weinstock, G	NY	540	PPul	Atlas, A	NJ	916	Pul	Cerrone, F	NJ	963
A&I	Weiss, S	NJ	804	PPul	Bieler, H	NJ	916	Pul	Chadha, J	NY	513
FMed	Firshein, R	NY	167	PPul	Bisberg, D	NJ	825	Pul	Cohen, M	NY	595
FMed	Ibelli, V	NY	610	PPul	Boyer, J	NY	710	Pul	De Matteo, R	NY	720
FMed	Karatoprak, O	NJ	755	PPul	Chan, S	NY	529	Pul	Delorenzo, L	NY	720
IM	Altbaum, R	CT	991	PPul	Constantinescu, A	NY	316	Pul	Dimango, E	NY	356
IM	Carosella, C	NY	681	PPul	Dimaio, M	NY	316	Pul	Donath, J	NY	595
IM	Cusumano, S	NY	559	PPul	Dozor, A	NY	710	Pul	Eden, E	NY	356
IM	Ernst, J	NY	422	PPul	Dworkin, G	CT	1018	Pul	Elamir, M	NJ	842
IM	Feuer, M	NY	201	PPul	Giusti, R	NY	484	Pul	Fein, A	NY	595
IM	Fortunato, F	NJ	813	PPul	Hen, J	CT	1018	Pul	Fiel, S	NJ	919
IM	Horovitz, L	NY	203	PPul	Kanengiser, S	NJ	783	Pul	Fine, J	CT	1024
IM	Jawetz, H	NJ	927	PPul	Kattan, M	NY	316	Pul	Fishman, D	NY	356
IM	Kapoor, S	NY	683	PPul	Kottler, W	NJ	825	Pul	Garay, S	NY	356
IM	Kozel, J	NJ	839	PPul	Krishnan, S	NY	710	Pul	Gelbman, B	NY	356
IM	Melman, M	NY	683	PPul	Lamm, C	NY	316	Pul	Goldberg, J	NJ	881
IM	Minkowitz, S	NY	205	PPul	Lee, D	NJ	783	Pul	Goldblatt, K	NJ	881
IM	Osnoss, K	CT	993	PPul	Lee, H	NY	484	Pul	Gordon, R	NY	595
IM	Simon, T	NY	467	PPul	Lowenthal, D	NY	711	Pul	Greenberg, M	NJ	829
IM	Spero, M	NY	207	PPul	Marcus, M	NY	484	Pul	Gulrajani, R	NY	488
IM	Wolff, E	NY	561	PPul	Montalvo Stanton, E	NJ	825	Pul	Hammer, A	NY	488
IM	Zupnick, H	NY	561	PPul	Nachajon, R	NJ	930	Pul	Karetzky, M	NY	440
PA&I	Barisciano, L	NJ	915	PPul	Narula, P	NY	484	Pul	Klapper, P	NY	440
PA&I	Ehrlich, P	NY	302	PPul	Ngai, P	NJ	783	Pul	Klares, S	NY	721
PA&I	Fagin, J	NY	581	PPul	Pirzada, M	NY	586	Pul	Kolodny, E	NY	357
PA&I	Fost, A	NJ	822	PPul	Quittell, L	NY	711	Pul	Krinsley, J	CT	1025
PCCM	Greenwald, B	NY	306	PPul	Sadeghi, H	CT	1018	Pul	Kurtz, C	CT	1025
Ped	Baiser, D	NJ	854	PPul	Schaeffer, J	NY	586	Pul	Leeman, B	NY	595
Ped	Berkowitz, I	NJ	785	PPul	Ting, A	NY	316	Pul	Lehrman, S	NY	721
Ped	Buchalter, M	NJ	785	PPul	Vicencio, A	NY	316	Pul	Levine, S	NJ	790
Ped	Chernobilsky, L	NY	642	Pul	Abott, M	NY	487	Pul	Libby, D	NY	357
Ped	Chianese, M	NY	587	Pul	Acquista, A	NY	354	Pul	Mandel, M	NY	721
Ped	Cohen, E	CT	1019	Pul	Adams, F	NY	354	Pul	Maniatis, T	NY	530
Ped	Corbo, E	NJ	960	Pul	Aldrich, T	NY	440	Pul	Marino, A	CT	1025
Ped	Ferguson, K	CT	1019	Pul	Altus, J	NY	594	Pul	Martins, P	NY	530
Ped	Goldstein, S	NY	512	Pul	Amoruso, R	NJ	931	Pul	McCalley, S	CT	1025
Ped	Green, A	NY	588	Pul	Appel, D	NY	440	Pul	Meixler, S	NY	721
Ped	Gruenwald, L	NJ	826	Pul	Barasch, J	NJ	789	Pul	Melillo, N	NJ	881
Ped	Handler, R	NJ	917	Pul	Baskin, M	NY	355	Pul	Mermelstein, S	NY	596

Specialty & Special Expertise Index

Spec	Name	St	Pg
T&CS	Elmann, E	NJ	795
T&CS	Fernandez, H	NY	649
T&CS	Hoffman, D	NY	388
T&CS	Michler, R	NY	444

Atrial Septal Defect

PCd	Levchuck, S	NY	582
PCd	Love, B	NY	305
PCd	Sommer, R	NY	305

Autism

ChAP	Cohen, L	NY	661
ChAP	Grice, D	NY	137
ChAP	Shatkin, J	NY	139
ChAP	Silva, R	NY	662
ChiN	Atluru, V	NY	545
ChiN	Jacobson, R	NY	663
ChiN	Kairam, R	NY	140
ChiN	Kaufman, D	NY	140
ChiN	Kosofsky, B	NY	140
ChiN	Kutscher, M	NY	663
ChiN	McAbee, G	NJ	837
ChiN	Sousa, R	NJ	749
ChiN	Traeger, E	NJ	949
FMed	Morrow, R	NY	416
Ped	Adesman, A	NY	587
Ped	Chessin, R	CT	1018
Ped	Colyer-Aversa, L	NJ	826
Ped	Cowan, S	NY	713
Ped	Cross, J	NY	320
Ped	Kanter, A	NJ	785
Ped	Levinson, W	NY	713
Ped	McCarton, C	NY	323
Ped	Smoller, A	NJ	896
Psyc	Cohen, A	NY	343
Psyc	Di Buono, M	NY	530
Psyc	Hollander, E	NY	346
Psyc	Moraille, P	NJ	842

Autism & Developmental Disorders

ChAP	Samanich, J	CT	979
ChiN	De Carlo, R	NY	522

Autoimmune Disease

A&I	Selvaggi, T	NJ	742
A&I	Sproviero, J	CT	974
N	Miller, A	NY	240
PRhu	Imundo, L	NY	317
PRhu	Starr, A	NY	317
Rhu	Chung, J	NJ	792

Spec	Name	St	Pg
Rhu	Efthimiou, P	NY	491
Rhu	Gorevic, P	NY	370
Rhu	Guma, M	NJ	792
Rhu	Parrish, E	NY	372
Rhu	Solomon, G	NY	373
Rhu	Sonpal, G	NY	514

Autoimmune Disease in Pregnancy

ObG	Mack, L	NY	571

Autoimmune Disorders

Rhu	Belostotsky, O	NY	369
Rhu	Lahita, R	NJ	830
Rhu	Marmur, R	NY	724

Autoimmune Liver Disease

Ge	Brown, R	NY	169

Autoimmune Ocular Disorders

A&I	Bielory, L	NJ	948

Autoimmune Rheumatic Disorders

Rhu	Mayer, E	NY	371
Rhu	Viennas, S	NY	514

B

Back & Neck Pain

N	Klebanoff, L	NY	238

Balance Disorders

N	Padela, M	NJ	928
N	Roberts, J	NY	241
N	Rosenberg, M	NJ	872
N	Salgado, M	NY	474
Oto	Bianchi, M	CT	1014
Oto	Garay, K	NJ	840
Oto	Gordon, M	NY	578
Oto	Hammerschlag, P	NY	289
Oto	Hoffman, R	NY	289
Oto	Kates, M	NY	705
Oto	Kwartler, J	NJ	959
Oto	Meiteles, L	NY	705
Oto	Snyder, G	NY	579
Oto	Storper, I	NY	295

Barrett's Esophagus

Ge	Basuk, P	NY	169
Ge	Cohen, J	NY	170
Ge	Finegold, J	NY	673
Ge	Genn, D	NY	674
Ge	Gerdes, H	NY	171
Ge	Gress, F	NY	172
Ge	Haber, G	NY	172
Ge	Lambroza, A	NY	174
Ge	Lax, J	NY	174
Ge	Lightdale, C	NY	175
Ge	McKinley, M	NY	554
Ge	Pais, S	NY	675
Ge	Poneros, J	NY	177
Ge	Roston, A	NY	676
Ge	Soloway, G	CT	987
Ge	Whelan, T	CT	987
Ge	Zwas, F	CT	988
T&CS	Donington, J	NY	386

Behavioral Disorders

AM	Clark-Hamilton, J	NJ	903
AM	Johnson, R	NJ	804
AM	Soren, K	NY	121
ChAP	Holzer, B	NY	455
ChAP	Newcorn, J	NY	138
ChAP	Perry, R	NY	138
ChAP	Shatkin, J	NY	139
ChiN	Kairam, R	NY	140
N	Herman, M	NJ	871
Ped	Cross, J	NY	320
Ped	Gruenwald, L	NJ	826
Ped	Handler, R	NJ	917
Ped	Hankin, D	NY	588
Ped	Igel, G	NY	437
Ped	Mongillo, N	CT	1020
Ped	Namerow, D	NJ	786
Ped	Zimmerman, S	NY	326

Behavioral Neurology

N	Bodis-Wollner, I	NY	472
N	Devinsky, O	NY	236
N	Etienne, M	NY	613
N	Marshall, R	NY	239

Behavioral Problems & Dementia

GerPsy	Reisberg, B	NY	182

Behcet's Syndrome

Rhu	Ali, Y	NY	368

Specialty & Special Expertise Index

Specialty & Special Expertise Index

Spec	Name	St	Pg	Spec	Name	St	Pg	Spec	Name	St	Pg
Hem	Boyd, D	CT	989	Onc	Klein, P	NY	217	Onc	Sparano, J	NY	424
Hem	Goldenberg, A	NY	190	Onc	Kloss, R	CT	999	Onc	Speyer, J	NY	223
Hem	Karp, G	NJ	867	Onc	Kruger, B	NY	218	Onc	Strauss, B	NY	634
Hem	Moskovits, T	NY	191	Onc	Krutchik, A	NJ	765	Onc	Tepler, I	CT	999
Hem	Vogel, J	NY	192	Onc	Kudelka, A	NY	634	Onc	Tomao, F	NY	564
Onc	Abramowitz, A	NY	508	Onc	Lebowicz, J	NY	469	Onc	Toomey, K	NJ	940
Onc	Adler, K	NJ	909	Onc	Lee, M	CT	999	Onc	Toppmeyer, D	NJ	869
Onc	Akhund, B	NY	633	Onc	Leitner, S	NJ	815	Onc	Vahdat, L	NY	224
Onc	Arena, F	NY	563	Onc	Lerma, P	NJ	850	Onc	Vinciguerra, V	NY	565
Onc	Astrow, A	NY	468	Onc	Lichter, S	NY	469	Onc	Vogl, S	NY	424
Onc	Attas, L	NJ	764	Onc	Ligresti, L	NJ	765	Onc	Waintraub, S	NJ	766
Onc	Baselga, J	NY	213	Onc	Lo, K	CT	999	Onc	Walsh, C	NJ	891
Onc	Benisovich, V	NY	508	Onc	Lonberg, M	NY	612	Onc	Wasserheit, C	NY	689
Onc	Buchholtz, M	NY	633	Onc	Malamud, S	NY	218	Onc	Wax, M	NJ	955
Onc	Budman, D	NY	563	Onc	Malefatto, J	CT	999	Onc	Weinstein, P	CT	1000
Onc	Camacho, F	NY	423	Onc	Marino, J	NY	564	Onc	Weiselberg, L	NY	565
Onc	Citron, M	NY	563	Onc	Meyers, M	NY	218	Onc	Yi, P	NJ	851
Onc	Cohen, S	NY	214	Onc	Michaelson, R	NJ	816	Onc	Zelkowitz, R	CT	1000
Onc	Condemi, G	NJ	765	Onc	Mills, N	NY	688	Path	Bleiweiss, I	NY	300
Onc	Cooper, R	CT	998	Onc	Moore, A	NY	219	Path	Hoda, S	NY	301
Onc	Cortes, E	NY	508	Onc	Nissenblatt, M	NJ	869	Path	Sanchez, M	NJ	779
Onc	DaCosta, N	NY	634	Onc	Norton, L	NY	219	Path	Tornos, C	NY	640
Onc	Dickler, M	NY	214	Onc	Offit, K	NY	220	RadRO	Adams, M	NY	531
Onc	Dosik, D	NY	469	Onc	Oratz, R	NY	220	RadRO	Ashamalla, H	NY	489
Onc	Drucker, B	CT	998	Onc	Oster, M	NY	220	RadRO	Baumann, J	NJ	881
Onc	Fang, B	NJ	939	Onc	Ostrow, S	NY	634	RadRO	Bosworth, J	NY	596
Onc	Farber, C	NJ	909	Onc	Papish, S	NJ	910	RadRO	Chadha, M	NY	360
Onc	Feldman, S	NY	687	Onc	Pascal, M	NJ	766	RadRO	Cole, R	NJ	931
Onc	Fischbach, N	CT	998	Onc	Pasmantier, M	NY	220	RadRO	Diamond, E	NY	596
Onc	Fitzgerald, D	NJ	891	Onc	Phillips, E	NY	688	RadRO	Dowling, S	CT	1026
Onc	Folman, R	CT	999	Onc	Provenzano, A	NY	688	RadRO	Dubin, D	NJ	791
Onc	Forlenza, T	NY	525	Onc	Puccio, C	NY	688	RadRO	Ennis, R	NY	361
Onc	Fornier, M	NY	215	Onc	Radovich, D	NJ	816	RadRO	Evans, A	NY	361
Onc	Forte, F	NJ	765	Onc	Rakowski, T	NJ	766	RadRO	Fang, D	CT	1026
Onc	Fuks, J	NY	423	Onc	Ramirez, M	NY	424	RadRO	Fass, D	NY	722
Onc	Gaynor, M	NY	215	Onc	Raptis, G	NY	564	RadRO	Formenti, S	NY	361
Onc	Goldberg, A	NY	215	Onc	Ratner, L	NY	221	RadRO	Gejerman, G	NJ	791
Onc	Goldberg, J	NY	688	Onc	Reichman, B	NY	221	RadRO	Gliedman, P	NY	490
Onc	Grace, W	NY	216	Onc	Rivera, Y	NJ	766	RadRO	Grann, A	NJ	829
Onc	Greenberg, H	NY	508	Onc	Robson, M	NY	222	RadRO	Haffty, B	NJ	882
Onc	Greenberg, S	NJ	891	Onc	Rosen, N	NY	689	RadRO	Iannuzzi, C	CT	1026
Onc	Guerin, B	NJ	954	Onc	Sadan, S	NY	689	RadRO	Kalnicki, S	NY	441
Onc	Halaas, J	NY	688	Onc	Salwitz, J	NJ	939	RadRO	Lee, L	NY	597
Onc	Hershman, D	NY	216	Onc	Saponara, E	NY	689	RadRO	Marienberg, E	NY	597
Onc	Hindenburg, A	NY	563	Onc	Sara, G	NY	222	RadRO	Masino, F	CT	1026
Onc	Hirschman, R	NY	216	Onc	Schleider, M	NJ	766	RadRO	McCormick, B	NY	362
Onc	Hirshaut, Y	NY	216	Onc	Schneider, R	NY	689	RadRO	McKenna, M	NJ	856
Onc	Holland, J	NY	216	Onc	Schwartz, P	NY	564	RadRO	Moorthy, C	NY	722
Onc	Hollister, D	CT	999	Onc	Sharon, D	NJ	891	RadRO	Mullen, E	NY	597
Onc	Hudis, C	NY	217	Onc	Shum, K	NY	509	RadRO	Nori, D	NY	362
Onc	Kane, M	NJ	910	Onc	Sierocki, J	NJ	850	RadRO	Park, T	NY	646
Onc	Kappel, B	NY	564	Onc	Sklarin, N	NY	223	RadRO	Pathare, P	CT	1026
Onc	Klafter, R	NY	217	Onc	Smith, J	NY	223	RadRO	Rosenbaum, A	NY	363

Specialty & Special Expertise Index

Spec	Name	St	Pg
RadRO	Rosenbluth, B	NJ	791
RadRO	Sanghavi, S	CT	1027
RadRO	Schwartz, D	NY	490
RadRO	Soffen, E	NJ	882
RadRO	Spera, J	CT	1027
RadRO	Stevens, R	NY	722
RadRO	Tinger, A	NY	722
RadRO	Wagman, R	NJ	829
RadRO	Wong, J	NJ	920
S	Alfonso, A	NY	491
S	Ashikari, A	NY	725
S	Benowitz, J	NY	600
S	Bernstein, M	NY	492
S	Blackwood, M	NJ	831
S	Bloom, N	NY	377
S	Boolbol, S	NY	377
S	Busch-Devereaux, E	NY	647
S	Cahan, A	NY	726
S	Cassell, L	NY	378
S	Cohen, B	NY	648
S	Conte, C	NY	600
S	Datta, R	NY	600
S	Diehl, W	NJ	921
S	DiGioia, J	NJ	964
S	Dultz, R	NJ	856
S	El-Tamer, M	NY	378
S	Estabrook, A	NY	379
S	Feldman, S	NY	379
S	Frost, J	NJ	964
S	Goldfarb, A	NY	379
S	Gordon, M	NY	726
S	Heerdt, A	NY	379
S	Johnson Miller, D	NJ	898
S	Joseph, P	NY	618
S	Kaleya, R	NY	492
S	Kearney, T	NJ	883
S	Lanfranchi, A	NJ	944
S	Lemercier, M	NY	726
S	Maheshwari, V	NJ	831
S	Manolas, P	NY	515
S	Mills, C	NY	381
S	Morrow, M	NY	382
S	Nowak, E	NY	382
S	O'Hea, B	NY	648
S	Pace, B	NY	515
S	Pahuja, M	NY	531
S	Pass, H	CT	1030
S	Rosenberg, V	NY	383
S	Roses, D	NY	383
S	Sas, N	NY	443
S	Schnabel, F	NY	383
S	Schwartzman, A	NY	493
S	Sclafani, L	NY	648

Spec	Name	St	Pg
S	Shapiro, R	NY	383
S	Siegel, B	NY	515
S	Simmons, R	NY	383
S	Sung, K	NY	515
S	Tartter, P	NY	384
S	Van Zee, K	NY	384
S	Ward, B	CT	1031
S	Zeitlin, A	NY	515

Breast Cancer & Surgery

Spec	Name	St	Pg
PlS	Chen, C	NY	331
PlS	Levine, J	NY	335
S	Adamo, A	NY	599
S	Arthur, K	NY	725
S	Asarian, A	NY	456
S	Axelrod, D	NY	376
S	Bernik, S	NY	377
S	Elliott, N	NJ	831
S	Goldfarb, M	NJ	898
S	Halpern, D	NY	600
S	Hertz, M	NJ	831
S	Lewis, T	NY	492
S	Lozner, J	NJ	965
S	Mandel, M	NJ	965
S	Montgomery, L	NY	443
S	Port, E	NY	382
S	Sacco, M	NJ	965
S	Staradub, V	CT	1030
S	Sultan, R	NJ	842
S	Swistel, A	NY	384
S	Weltz, C	NY	385

Breast Cancer Genetics

Spec	Name	St	Pg
ObG	Krause, C	NY	250

Breast Cancer in Elderly

Spec	Name	St	Pg
Onc	Rosenbluth, R	NJ	766
S	Tartter, P	NY	384

Breast Cancer-High Risk Women

Spec	Name	St	Pg
S	Blackwood, M	NJ	831
S	Estabrook, A	NY	379
S	Fou, A	NY	726
S	Johnson Miller, D	NJ	898
S	Schnabel, F	NY	383

Breast Cancer-Male

Spec	Name	St	Pg
S	Port, E	NY	382

Breast Cancer-Novel Therapies

Spec	Name	St	Pg
Onc	Vahdat, L	NY	224

Breast Cosmetic & Reconstructive Surgery

Spec	Name	St	Pg
PlS	Alizadeh, K	NY	590
PlS	Ascherman, J	NY	331
PlS	Attkiss, K	CT	1021
PlS	Chen, C	NY	331
PlS	Cherofsky, A	NY	530
PlS	Cozzone, J	NJ	787
PlS	Fiorillo, M	NY	616
PlS	Gardner, J	NJ	961
PlS	Garfein, E	NY	439
PlS	Gewirtz, H	CT	1021
PlS	Glasberg, S	NY	333
PlS	Godfrey, P	NY	333
PlS	Herbstman, R	NJ	880
PlS	Hetzler, P	NJ	896
PlS	Hirmand, H	NY	334
PlS	Karp, N	NY	334
PlS	Kilgo, M	NY	592
PlS	Koch, R	NY	716
PlS	Levine, J	NY	335
PlS	Lukash, F	NY	592
PlS	Otterburn, D	NY	336
PlS	Passaretti, D	CT	1022
PlS	Rose, M	NJ	897
PlS	Schulman, N	NY	337
PlS	Schwartz, M	NY	337
PlS	Sherman, J	NY	338
PlS	Silberman, M	NY	592
PlS	Spector, J	NY	338
PlS	Vickery, C	NY	340
PlS	Weinstein, L	NJ	919
PlS	Weiss, P	NY	340
PlS	Wey, P	NJ	880
PlS	Zaccaria, A	NJ	897
PlS	Zapiach, L	NJ	788
PlS	Zevon, S	NY	340

Breast Disease

Spec	Name	St	Pg
ObG	Segarra, P	NY	637
S	Ashikari, A	NY	725
S	Auguste, L	NY	599
S	Benowitz, J	NY	600
S	Bernik, S	NY	377
S	Budd, D	NJ	932
S	Cioroiu, M	NY	378
S	DiGioia, J	NJ	964
S	Fleischer, L	NY	618
S	Fou, A	NY	726

Specialty & Special Expertise Index

Spec	Name	St	Pg
S	Huston, J	NJ	831
S	Kimmelstiel, F	NY	380
S	Pass, H	CT	1030
S	Sacco, M	NJ	965
S	Siegel, B	NY	515
S	Ward, B	CT	1031

Breast Feeding Problems

Spec	Name	St	Pg
NP	Hand, I	NY	509
PGe	Jelin, A	NY	482

Breast Imaging

Spec	Name	St	Pg
DR	Berson, B	NY	157
DR	Bobroff, L	NY	610
DR	Calem-Grunat, J	NJ	752
DR	Chu, R	NJ	752
DR	Dershaw, D	NY	157
DR	Feigin, K	NY	158
DR	Goldfischer, M	NJ	752
DR	Greer, J	NJ	937
DR	Gross, J	NJ	752
DR	Grosso-Rivas, S	NJ	950
DR	Herman, Z	NY	158
DR	Levy, L	NJ	753
DR	Levy, M	NY	159
DR	Lisi-DeMartino, V	NY	668
DR	LoRusso, D	NY	668
DR	Morris, E	NY	159
DR	Novick, M	NY	160
DR	Raia, C	NY	522
DR	Sanders, L	NJ	809
DR	Sonnenblick, E	NY	161
DR	Staeger-Hirsch, C	NY	669
DR	Yang, R	NJ	937

Breast MRI

Spec	Name	St	Pg
DR	Levy, L	NJ	753
DR	Morris, E	NY	159
DR	Rosenfeld, S	NY	161
DR	Sonnenblick, E	NY	161

Breast Pathology

Spec	Name	St	Pg
Path	Babkowski, R	CT	1016
Path	Barnard, N	NJ	876
Path	Bleiweiss, I	NY	300
Path	Cohen, J	NY	300
Path	Pinto, M	CT	1017

Breast Reconstruction

Spec	Name	St	Pg
PlS	Ablaza, V	NJ	827
PlS	Addona, T	NY	589

Spec	Name	St	Pg
PlS	Ahn, C	NY	330
PlS	Allen, R	NY	331
PlS	Ashinoff, R	NJ	896
PlS	Breitbart, A	NY	590
PlS	Breslow, G	NJ	787
PlS	Chidyllo, S	NJ	896
PlS	Choi, M	NY	332
PlS	Colon, F	NJ	918
PlS	Cordeiro, P	NY	332
PlS	Dayan, J	NY	332
PlS	Disa, J	NY	332
PlS	Drimmer, M	NJ	855
PlS	Friedman, D	NY	333
PlS	Goldenberg, D	CT	1021
PlS	Grant, R	NY	334
PlS	Hoffman, L	NY	334
PlS	Hyans, P	NJ	962
PlS	Israeli, R	NY	591
PlS	Kessler, M	NY	591
PlS	Kolker, A	NY	335
PlS	Leipziger, L	NY	592
PlS	Mehrara, B	NY	336
PlS	Palaia, D	NY	716
PlS	Ponamgi, S	NJ	788
PlS	Rafizadeh, F	NJ	919
PlS	Razaboni, R	NY	336
PlS	Rosen, A	NJ	828
PlS	Sabry, M	NY	337
PlS	Smith, M	NY	338
PlS	Sofer, A	CT	1022
PlS	Starker, I	NJ	919
PlS	Sultan, M	NY	339
PlS	Talmor, M	NY	339
PlS	Ting, J	NY	340
PlS	Winters, R	NJ	788
S	Benowitz, J	NY	600

Breast Reconstruction & Augmentation

Spec	Name	St	Pg
PlS	DiGregorio, V	NY	590
PlS	Dudick, S	NJ	896
PlS	Gayle, L	NY	333
PlS	Glicksman, C	NJ	896
PlS	LoVerme, P	NJ	828
PlS	Newman, S	NY	716
PlS	Reiffel, R	NY	716
PlS	Schaffner, A	NY	337
PlS	Shafer, D	NY	338

Breast Surgery

Spec	Name	St	Pg
PlS	Broumand, S	NY	331
PlS	Goldstein, R	NY	439

Spec	Name	St	Pg
PlS	Rosenberg, M	NY	717
PlS	Suzman, M	NY	717
PlS	Tepper, H	NJ	962
S	Agarwal, N	NY	442
S	Blackwood, M	NJ	831
S	Boolbol, S	NY	377
S	Busch-Devereaux, E	NY	647
S	Cahan, A	NY	726
S	Capasse, J	CT	1029
S	Cassell, L	NY	378
S	Charny, C	NY	726
S	Chung-Loy, H	NJ	882
S	Colaco, R	NJ	964
S	Dasmahapatra, K	NJ	882
S	Demestihas, A	CT	1029
S	Dresner, L	NY	492
S	Dultz, R	NJ	856
S	Estabrook, A	NY	379
S	Feigenbaum, H	NJ	932
S	Feldman, S	NY	379
S	Fletcher, H	NJ	831
S	Garvey, R	CT	1030
S	Genato, R	NY	492
S	Goldfarb, A	NY	379
S	Grieco, M	NY	600
S	Hornyak, S	NY	531
S	Huston, J	NJ	831
S	Kenler, A	CT	1030
S	Khalife, M	NY	601
S	Kurtz, L	NY	601
S	Lanfranchi, A	NJ	944
S	Licata, J	NJ	794
S	Lozner, J	NJ	965
S	Manasseh, D	NY	492
S	McManus, S	NJ	883
S	Mills, C	NY	381
S	Pace, B	NY	515
S	Raniolo, R	NY	727
S	Sclafani, L	NY	648
S	Simmons, R	NY	383
S	Sussman, B	NJ	794
S	Wallack, M	NY	384
S	Ward, B	CT	1031

Breathing Disorders

Spec	Name	St	Pg
NP	Kaur, H	NJ	870
NP	Rai, B	NJ	816
NP	Raziuddin, K	NJ	767
NP	Steele, A	NY	565
NP	Sun, S	NJ	816
PPul	Loughlin, G	NY	316
PPul	Pirzada, M	NY	586

Specialty & Special Expertise Index

Spec	Name	St	Pg
PPul	Turcios, N	NJ	941
Pul	Altus, J	NY	594

Bronchiectasis

Pul	Dimango, E	NY	356
Pul	Fiel, S	NJ	919

Bronchiolitis Obliterans

| Pul | Stover-Pepe, D | NY | 360 |

Bronchitis

IM	Feuer, M	NY	201
Ped	Kotin, N	NY	322
PPul	Sadeghi, H	CT	1018
Pul	Bergman, M	NY	488
Pul	Blair, L	NY	355
Pul	Cohen, M	NY	595
Pul	Kolodny, E	NY	357
Pul	Marino, A	CT	1025
Pul	Stein, S	NY	360

Bronchoscopy

IM	Horovitz, L	NY	203
PPul	Krishnan, S	NY	710
PPul	Nachajon, R	NJ	930
PPul	Needleman, J	NY	484
PPul	Sadeghi, H	CT	1018
PPul	Ting, A	NY	316
PPul	Vicencio, A	NY	316
Pul	Addrizzo-Harris, D	NY	355
Pul	Bures, S	NY	720
Pul	DiCosmo, B	NY	720
Pul	Fishman, D	NY	356
Pul	Maxfield, R	NY	358
Pul	Powell, C	NY	359
Pul	Simon, C	NJ	791

Brugada Syndrome

| Cv | Kerstein, J | NY | 454 |

Burn Care

PlS	Greenstein, B	NY	439
PlS	Liebling, R	NY	439
PlS	Simpson, R	NY	592
S	Bessey, P	NY	377
S	Petrone, S	NJ	831
S	Shapiro, M	NY	648
S	Yurt, R	NY	385

Burns-Reconstructive Plastic

Surgery

PlS	Davenport, T	NY	590
PlS	Drimmer, M	NJ	855
PlS	Greenstein, B	NY	439
PlS	Rose, E	NY	337

C

Calcium Disorders

EDM	Bergman, D	NY	162
EDM	Brickman, A	NY	458
EDM	Das, S	NY	523
EDM	Goldman, J	NY	459
EDM	Hellerman, J	NY	670
EDM	Jacobs, T	NY	164
EDM	Rich, G	CT	984
EDM	Seltzer, T	NY	165
EDM	Silverberg, S	NY	166
EDM	Spiler, I	NJ	865
EDM	Warman, J	NY	459
EDM	Weinerman, S	NY	459
PEn	Agarwal, C	NY	707
PEn	Carey, D	NY	583

Cancer Detection & Staging

NuM	Agress, H	NJ	772
NuM	Friedman, K	NY	245

Cancer Genetics

CG	Bialer, M	NY	546
CG	Chung, W	NY	141
CG	Gilbert, F	NY	456
Onc	Offit, K	NY	220
Onc	Provenzano, A	NY	688
Onc	Robson, M	NY	222
Onc	Walsh, C	NJ	891

Cancer Imaging

| DR | Som, P | NY | 161 |

Cancer Immune Therapy

| Onc | Brentjens, R | NY | 214 |

Cancer in the Elderly

Ger	Korc-Grodzicki, B	NY	181
Ger	Tank, L	NJ	759

Cancer Prevention

IM	Nelson, D	NY	205
Onc	Vinciguerra, V	NY	565
Onc	Weiselberg, L	NY	565

Cancer Reconstruction

Oto	Mazzara, C	NJ	875
PlS	Baker, D	NY	331
PlS	Cordeiro, P	NY	332
PlS	Disa, J	NY	332
PlS	Kilgo, M	NY	592
PlS	Mehrara, B	NY	336
S	Swistel, A	NY	384

Cancer Rehabilitation

PMR	Aaronson, B	CT	1020
PMR	Lachmann, E	NY	328
PMR	Stubblefield, M	NY	330

Cancer Risk Assessment

Onc	Rosenbluth, R	NJ	766
Onc	Smith, J	NY	223

Cancer Surgery

CRS	Sullivan, J	NY	547
CRS	Weiser, M	NY	145
PS	Bhattacharyya, N	NJ	930
PS	La Quaglia, M	NY	318
PS	Stringel, G	NY	711
S	Allendorf, J	NY	599
S	Bloom, N	NY	377
S	Chamberlain, R	NJ	831
S	Chorost, M	NY	600
S	Conte, C	NY	600
S	Dasmahapatra, K	NJ	882
S	Goydos, J	NJ	882
S	Halpern, D	NY	600
S	Jordan, L	NJ	883
S	Kaufman, H	NJ	883
S	Kemeny, M	NY	515
S	Kimmelstiel, F	NY	380
S	Maheshwari, V	NJ	831
S	Mandel, M	NJ	965
S	McManus, S	NJ	883
S	Passeri, D	CT	1030
S	Rajpal, S	NY	493
S	Shapiro, R	NY	383
S	Talamini, M	NY	648
S	Whitman, E	NJ	921

Cancer Survivors-Late Effects of

Specialty & Special Expertise Index

Spec	Name	St	Pg
CE	Turitto, G	NY	452
CE	Whang, W	NY	125
CE	Wilbur, S	NY	452
CE	Winslow, R	CT	975
CE	Winters, S	NJ	904
CE	Zaim, S	NJ	743
Cv	Slater, W	NY	134
PCd	Leichter, D	NJ	959
PCd	Pass, R	NY	432

Cardiac Imaging

Spec	Name	St	Pg
Cv	Jauhar, R	NY	543
Cv	Kabalkin, C	NY	454
Cv	Keller, A	CT	977
Cv	Kronzon, I	NY	129
Cv	Pappas, T	NY	544
DR	Haramati, L	NY	414
DR	Spindola-Franco, H	NY	415
IC	Weiss, M	NY	686
PCd	Fish, B	NY	706

Cardiac MRI

Spec	Name	St	Pg
Cv	Heitner, J	NY	453
DR	Wolff, S	NY	161

Cardiac Rehabilitation

Spec	Name	St	Pg
Cv	Stein, R	NY	135
PMR	Whiteson, J	NY	330

Cardiac Stress Testing

Spec	Name	St	Pg
Cv	Cappucci, R	NY	656
Cv	Chesner, M	NY	541
Cv	Erlebacher, J	NJ	745
Cv	Gleckel, L	NY	542
Cv	Levine, E	NY	659
Cv	Lewis, B	NY	130
Cv	Phillips, M	NY	412
Cv	Zaloom, R	NY	455

Cardiac Surgery

Spec	Name	St	Pg
T&CS	Abrol, S	NY	493
T&CS	Batsides, G	NJ	944
T&CS	D'Alessandro, D	NY	443
T&CS	Esposito, R	NY	601
T&CS	Girardi, L	NY	387
T&CS	Isom, O	NY	388
T&CS	McCullough, J	NJ	795
T&CS	Neibart, R	NJ	898
T&CS	Saunders, C	NJ	832
T&CS	Schubach, S	NY	603
T&CS	Stewart, A	NY	391

Spec	Name	St	Pg
Cardiac Surgery-Adult			
T&CS	Bilfinger, T	NY	649
T&CS	Brown, J	NJ	921
T&CS	Goldenberg, B	NJ	832
T&CS	Krieger, K	NY	388

Spec	Name	St	Pg
Cardiac Surgery-Adult & Pediatric			
T&CS	Chai, P	NY	386
T&CS	Crooke, G	NY	493

Spec	Name	St	Pg
Cardiac Surgery-High Risk			
T&CS	Fernandez, H	NY	649

Spec	Name	St	Pg
Cardiac Tumors, Myxomas			
T&CS	Grossi, E	NY	388

Spec	Name	St	Pg
Cardiac Tumors/Cancer			
Cv	Shindler, D	NJ	863
T&CS	Donington, J	NY	386

Cardiomyopathy

Spec	Name	St	Pg
Cv	Goldschmidt, H	NJ	745
Cv	Jorde, U	NY	411
Cv	Kalman, J	NY	543
Cv	Latif, F	NY	130
Cv	Maurer, M	NY	130
Cv	Skopicki, H	NY	623
PCd	Schiff, R	NY	582

Cardiothoracic Surgery

Spec	Name	St	Pg
T&CS	Bains, M	NY	386
T&CS	DeAnda, A	NY	386
T&CS	Heim, J	NJ	883
T&CS	Lang, S	NY	516
T&CS	Merav, A	NY	728

Cardiovascular Disease

Spec	Name	St	Pg
Cv	Adibi, B	NJ	743
Cv	Akinboboye, O	NY	500
Cv	Altmann, D	NJ	862
Cv	Altschul, L	NY	622
Cv	Andersen, H	NY	125
Cv	Andrews, P	NJ	744
Cv	Anto, M	NY	541
Cv	Augenbraun, C	CT	975
Cv	Bareket, Y	NJ	744
Cv	Beniaminovitz, A	NY	609
Cv	Berdoff, R	NY	125
Cv	Berkowitz, W	NJ	744

Spec	Name	St	Pg
Cv	Besser, L	NY	521
Cv	Bhansali, R	NY	541
Cv	Blake, J	NY	125
Cv	Blick, M	NJ	904
Cv	Bloom, G	CT	976
Cv	Blum, M	NJ	904
Cv	Blumenthal, D	NY	126
Cv	Bogin, M	NY	521
Cv	Borek, M	NY	622
Cv	Borer, J	NY	452
Cv	Breen, W	NY	541
Cv	Campagna, R	NY	126
Cv	Cappucci, R	NY	656
Cv	Carabello, B	NY	126
Cv	Casale, L	CT	976
Cv	Catanese, J	NY	656
Cv	Cemaletin, N	NY	126
Cv	Channamsetty, V	CT	976
Cv	Charney, R	NY	656
Cv	Charnoff, J	NY	452
Cv	Chen, T	NY	541
Cv	Chengot, M	NY	622
Cv	Chesner, M	NY	541
Cv	Choi, J	CT	976
Cv	Cocke, T	NJ	744
Cv	Cohen, M	NY	410
Cv	Cohen, M	NY	126
Cv	Cole, W	NY	126
Cv	Conroy, D	NJ	744
Cv	Cooper, J	NY	656
Cv	Copen, D	CT	976
Cv	Coppola, J	NY	126
Cv	Costin, A	NJ	847
Cv	Cramer, M	NY	541
Cv	Criscito, M	NJ	805
Cv	Cruz, M	NJ	837
Cv	Cusack, E	CT	976
Cv	Cziner, D	NY	656
Cv	D'Agostino, R	NY	541
Cv	Dangas, G	NY	126
Cv	Daniels, J	NJ	887
Cv	Dardashti, O	NJ	744
Cv	DeLuca, A	NY	656
Cv	Dervan, J	NY	622
Cv	Deutsch, A	NY	127
Cv	Devereux, R	NY	127
Cv	Dilmanian, H	NY	453
Cv	DiVagno, L	NJ	744
Cv	Dresdale, R	NY	542
Cv	Drusin, R	NY	127
Cv	Dubois, N	NY	127
Cv	Dutta, T	NY	127
Cv	Eichman, G	NJ	744

Specialty & Special Expertise Index

Spec	Name	St	Pg
Cv	Perry-Bottinger, L	NY	660
Cv	Phillips, M	NY	412
Cv	Pilchik, R	NY	660
Cv	Pinney, S	NY	132
Cv	Pollack, B	CT	978
Cv	Poon, M	NY	132
Cv	Post, M	NY	132
Cv	Prabhu, H	NY	454
Cv	Price, T	NY	660
Cv	Pucillo, A	NY	660
Cv	Pumill, R	NJ	747
Cv	Qadir, S	NY	455
Cv	Radwaner, B	NY	132
Cv	Ragno, P	NY	544
Cv	Raska, K	NJ	904
Cv	Reichstein, R	NY	132
Cv	Reison, D	NJ	747
Cv	Rentrop, K	NY	132
Cv	Robbins, M	NY	500
Cv	Rogal, G	NJ	806
Cv	Romanello, P	NY	132
Cv	Ronen, A	CT	978
Cv	Rosenbaum, M	NY	133
Cv	Rossakis, C	NJ	747
Cv	Roth, R	NY	609
Cv	Rothman, H	NJ	748
Cv	Rozanski, A	NY	133
Cv	Ruiz, C	NY	133
Cv	Rutkovsky, E	NY	544
Cv	Rydzinski, M	NY	501
Cv	Sachs, R	NJ	949
Cv	Sagar, Y	NJ	748
Cv	Sahar, D	NY	412
Cv	Salerno, W	NJ	748
Cv	Salimi, M	NJ	925
Cv	Saroff, A	NJ	806
Cv	Saulino, P	NJ	936
Cv	Schanzer, R	NJ	862
Cv	Schiffer, M	NY	133
Cv	Schmierer, J	CT	978
Cv	Schreiber, C	NY	544
Cv	Schulman, I	NY	133
Cv	Schulze, P	NY	133
Cv	Schuster, E	CT	978
Cv	Schwartz, A	NY	133
Cv	Schwartz, C	NY	521
Cv	Schwartz, W	NY	133
Cv	Segal, R	NY	134
Cv	Seinfeld, D	NY	134
Cv	Shamoon, F	NJ	806
Cv	Shayani, S	NY	544
Cv	Sheikh, S	NY	660
Cv	Shell, R	NJ	862

Spec	Name	St	Pg
Cv	Sheris, S	NJ	949
Cv	Sherman, W	NY	134
Cv	Shimony, R	NY	134
Cv	Shindler, D	NJ	863
Cv	Shlofmitz, R	NY	544
Cv	Siegal, M	NY	134
Cv	Siegel, S	NY	134
Cv	Siepser, S	NJ	925
Cv	Silver, M	NY	660
Cv	Silverman, R	NY	412
Cv	Siskind, S	NY	501
Cv	Sklaroff, H	NY	134
Cv	Skopicki, H	NY	623
Cv	Slama, R	NJ	949
Cv	Slater, W	NY	134
Cv	Sokol, S	NY	545
Cv	Sotsky, G	NJ	748
Cv	Southren, D	NY	609
Cv	Spadaro, L	NY	545
Cv	Spiegel, A	NY	135
Cv	Stein, R	NY	135
Cv	Steinbaum, S	NY	135
Cv	Steingart, R	NY	135
Cv	Stoupakis, G	NJ	748
Cv	Stroh, J	NJ	936
Cv	Taikowski, R	CT	978
Cv	Tarkin, H	NY	660
Cv	Tartaglia, J	NY	660
Cv	Taub, C	NY	412
Cv	Teichholz, L	NJ	748
Cv	Tenenbaum, J	NY	135
Cv	Tenet, W	NY	545
Cv	Traube, C	NY	455
Cv	Tyberg, T	NY	135
Cv	Unger, A	NY	135
Cv	Variale, P	NY	135
Cv	Vazzana, T	NY	522
Cv	Wallach, R	NY	661
Cv	Wangenheim, P	NJ	806
Cv	Weg, I	NY	545
Cv	Wein, P	NY	455
Cv	Weinberg, M	NY	623
Cv	Weintraub, H	NY	136
Cv	Weisenseel, A	NY	136
Cv	Weiss, E	NJ	925
Cv	Weissman, R	NY	661
Cv	Wild, D	NJ	748
Cv	Williams, M	NJ	748
Cv	Winter, S	NY	522
Cv	Wolk, M	NY	136
Cv	Yadegar, D	NY	136
Cv	Yuen, J	NY	661
Cv	Zaloom, R	NY	455

Spec	Name	St	Pg
Cv	Zarich, S	CT	979
Cv	Zimmerman, F	NY	661
Cv	Zucker, M	NJ	806
IM	Gambarin, B	NY	465
IM	Kennish, A	NY	203
IM	Legato, M	NY	204
IM	Mickley, S	CT	993
IM	Mutterperl, M	NJ	839
IM	Sherman, F	NY	467
IM	Slogoff, F	CT	994
IM	Zaremski, B	NY	208

Cardiovascular Imaging

Cv	Kunkes, S	CT	977
Cv	Poon, M	NY	132
DR	Wolff, S	NY	161

Cardiovascular Surgery

T&CS	Feng, W	CT	1031
T&CS	Seinfeld, F	NJ	857

Career Related Problems

Psyc	Borbely, A	NY	342

Caribbean Health Care

FMed	Krotowski, M	NY	459

Carotid Artery Disease

Cv	Olin, J	NY	131
IC	Wilentz, J	NY	210
VascS	Choi, H	NY	618
VascS	Deitch, J	NY	533
VascS	Faust, G	NY	606
VascS	Harrington, M	NY	404
VascS	Purtill, W	NY	606
VascS	Rhee, R	NY	495
VascS	Rodino, W	NY	533
VascS	Tassiopoulos, A	NY	650

Carotid Artery Stent Placement

IC	Fishman, R	CT	995
IC	Petrossian, G	NY	562
NRad	Tenner, M	NY	695
NS	Solomon, R	NY	233
VIR	Hamet, M	NY	731
VIR	Scheiner, J	NY	532

Carotid Artery Surgery

NS	Langer, D	NY	231
NS	Quest, D	NY	232

Specialty & Special Expertise Index

Spec	Name	St	Pg
Oph	Kelly, S	NY	260
Oph	Klapper, D	NY	260
Oph	Koplin, R	NY	260
Oph	Kramer, P	NY	527
Oph	Kristan, R	NJ	893
Oph	Lebowitz, M	NY	477
Oph	Leib, M	NY	261
Oph	Liebmann, J	NY	261
Oph	Lippman, J	NY	699
Oph	Liva, D	NJ	774
Oph	Mackool, R	NY	511
Oph	Magramm, I	NY	261
Oph	Malik, S	NY	573
Oph	Mandava, S	CT	1008
Oph	Mandelbaum, S	NY	261
Oph	Manjoney, D	CT	1008
Oph	Marks, A	NY	573
Oph	Martin, J	NY	637
Oph	Matossian, C	NJ	852
Oph	Mayers, M	NY	428
Oph	McKee, H	NY	699
Oph	Merhige, K	NY	262
Oph	Merriam, J	NY	262
Oph	Mignone, B	NY	699
Oph	Mitchell, J	NY	262
Oph	Moazed, K	NY	262
Oph	Moskowitz, C	NY	262
Oph	Natale, B	NJ	957
Oph	Nattis, R	NY	637
Oph	Nauheim, R	NY	574
Oph	Nelson, D	NY	574
Oph	Newton, M	NY	263
Oph	Nightingale, J	NY	263
Oph	O'Malley, G	NY	637
Oph	Obstbaum, S	NY	263
Oph	Odrich, M	NY	429
Oph	Ostriker, G	CT	1009
Oph	Paul, M	CT	1009
Oph	Perry, H	NY	574
Oph	Pinke, J	CT	1009
Oph	Pinke, R	NJ	913
Oph	Prince, A	NY	264
Oph	Prywes, A	NY	574
Oph	Rabinowitz, S	CT	1009
Oph	Reich, R	NY	477
Oph	Ritterband, D	NY	264
Oph	Robbins, K	CT	1009
Oph	Romanelli, J	NY	638
Oph	Rosenbaum, P	NY	429
Oph	Rosenberg, M	NJ	774
Oph	Rosenthal, K	NY	574
Oph	Rothberg, C	NY	638
Oph	Rubin, L	NY	574

Spec	Name	St	Pg
Oph	Safran, S	NJ	853
Oph	Santamaria, J	NJ	874
Oph	Schrier, A	NY	265
Oph	Sciortino, P	NY	477
Oph	Seedor, J	NY	265
Oph	Seidman, M	NY	478
Oph	Sherman, S	NY	266
Oph	Shulman, J	NY	266
Oph	Siderides, E	CT	1010
Oph	Smith, E	NY	478
Oph	Solomon, J	NY	266
Oph	Sperber, L	NY	267
Oph	Stabile, J	NJ	774
Oph	Starr, M	NY	267
Oph	Stein, A	NY	478
Oph	Stein, M	NY	700
Oph	Sturm, R	NY	575
Oph	Suh, L	NY	267
Oph	Talansky, M	NJ	894
Oph	Tello, C	NY	267
Oph	Tostanoski, J	NY	701
Oph	Trivedi, G	NY	701
Oph	Vietorisz, E	CT	1010
Oph	Vogel, M	NJ	929
Oph	Wasserman, E	CT	1010
Oph	Weinstein, J	NY	575
Oph	Weiss, M	NY	268
Oph	Whitmore, W	NY	268
Oph	Wolf, K	NY	429
Oph	Zaidman, G	NY	701
Oph	Zellner, J	NY	478
Oph	Zerykier, A	NY	527
Oph	Zweibel, L	NY	638
Oph	Zweifach, P	NY	269

Cataract Surgery-Lens Implant

Spec	Name	St	Pg
Oph	Ackerman, J	NY	475
Oph	Berke, S	NY	572
Oph	Buxton, D	NY	254
Oph	Dodick, J	NY	256
Oph	Fishman, A	NY	510
Oph	Giliberti, O	NJ	929
Oph	Glatt, H	NJ	819
Oph	Musto, A	CT	1008
Oph	Rosenberg, M	NJ	774
Oph	Salz, A	NJ	940
Oph	Starr, C	NY	267
Oph	Wong, R	NJ	853
Oph	Zabin, S	NY	701

Cataract-Pediatric

Spec	Name	St	Pg
Oph	DeBroff, B	CT	1007

Spec	Name	St	Pg
Oph	Hall, L	NY	259
Oph	Medow, N	NY	428

Catheter Ablation

Spec	Name	St	Pg
CE	Biviano, A	NY	123
CE	Iwai, S	NY	655
CE	Krumerman, A	NY	410
CE	Lerman, B	NY	124
CE	Markowitz, S	NY	124
CE	Mittal, S	NJ	742
CE	Palma, E	NY	410
CE	Steinberg, J	NJ	743
CE	Whang, W	NY	125
CE	Winters, S	NJ	904

Celiac Disease

Spec	Name	St	Pg
Ge	Avezzano, E	NJ	756
Ge	Cooper, R	NY	170
Ge	Gettenberg, G	NY	460
Ge	Green, P	NY	172
Ge	Rubin, M	NY	177
Ge	Taubin, H	CT	987
Ge	Turtel, P	NJ	889
Ge	Zinkin, N	NY	629
PGe	Benkov, K	NY	308
PGe	Berezin, S	NY	708
PGe	Jeshion, W	NJ	781
PGe	Kazlow, P	NY	308
PGe	Koniaris, S	NJ	877
PGe	Lavine, J	NY	308
PGe	Levy, J	NY	308
PGe	Pettei, M	NY	584
PGe	Rosh, J	NJ	916
PGe	Sockolow, R	NY	309
PGe	Sunaryo, F	NJ	824

Central Nervous System Cancer

Spec	Name	St	Pg
RadRO	Garg, M	NY	441
RadRO	Ingenito, A	NJ	791
RadRO	Ryu, S	NY	646

Cerebral Palsy

Spec	Name	St	Pg
ChiN	Bennett, H	NJ	905
ChiN	Desouza, T	NJ	905
ChiN	Smith, R	NY	546
ChiN	Wells, J	NY	141
OrS	Godfried, D	NY	576
OrS	Otsuka, N	NY	280
OrS	Strongwater, A	NJ	929
PMR	Armento, M	NJ	961
PMR	Diamond, M	NJ	961

Specialty & Special Expertise Index

Spec	Name	St	Pg
ChAP	Lipschitz, D	CT	979
ChAP	Lomonaco, S	NY	662
ChAP	Lustbader, A	CT	979
ChAP	Moreau, D	NY	138
ChAP	Newcorn, J	NY	138
ChAP	Perry, R	NY	138
ChAP	Pincus, E	NJ	749
ChAP	Poll, J	CT	979
ChAP	Rabinowitz, I	NY	662
ChAP	Ravitz, A	NY	138
ChAP	Rosenfeld, A	CT	979
ChAP	Rubinstein, B	NY	662
ChAP	Rynn, M	NY	138
ChAP	Samanich, J	CT	979
ChAP	Schreiber, K	NY	662
ChAP	Seaver, R	NY	662
ChAP	Shampain, L	NJ	863
ChAP	Shatkin, J	NY	139
ChAP	Silva, R	NY	662
ChAP	Silverman, A	NY	663
ChAP	Slater, J	NY	663
ChAP	Spencer, E	NY	139
ChAP	Turecki, S	NY	139
ChAP	Walker, A	NY	663
ChAP	Walkup, J	NY	139
ChAP	Walsh, P	NY	139
ChAP	Weisbrot, D	NY	623
ChAP	Williams, D	NY	545
Psyc	Ferran, E	NY	344
Psyc	Kalman, A	CT	1023
Psyc	Katus, E	NY	594
Psyc	Lew, A	NY	718
Psyc	Oberfield, R	NY	349
Psyc	Pfeffer, C	NY	349
Psyc	Raff, A	NY	719
Psyc	Sawyer, D	NY	351
Psyc	Silver, B	NJ	962
Psyc	Tolchin, J	NY	353

Child Abuse

Spec	Name	St	Pg
Ped	Ajl, S	NY	485
Ped	Bienstock, J	NJ	785
Ped	Brown, J	NY	320
Ped	Cahill, L	NY	436
Ped	Laraque, D	NY	485
Ped	McHugh, M	NY	323
Ped	Quinn, L	NY	643
PS	Cooper, A	NY	318

Child Development

Spec	Name	St	Pg
Ped	Cohen, M	NY	320
Ped	Cross, J	NY	320

Spec	Name	St	Pg
Ped	Levitzky, S	NY	322

Child Neurology

Spec	Name	St	Pg
ChiN	Akman, C	NY	139
ChiN	Allen, J	NY	139
ChiN	Alshansky, A	NY	663
ChiN	Andriola, M	NY	624
ChiN	Aron, A	NY	139
ChiN	Atluru, V	NY	545
ChiN	Barabas, R	NJ	887
ChiN	Bennett, H	NJ	905
ChiN	Bergtraum, M	NY	546
ChiN	Cantor, L	NY	663
ChiN	Chiriboga-Klein, C	NY	140
ChiN	Cope, J	NJ	749
ChiN	De Carlo, R	NY	522
ChiN	De Vivo, D	NY	140
ChiN	Desouza, T	NJ	905
ChiN	Engel, M	NY	140
ChiN	Fryer, R	NY	140
ChiN	Goldberg, R	NJ	807
ChiN	Gould, R	NY	546
ChiN	Grossman, E	NJ	905
ChiN	Hasson, H	NY	455
ChiN	Heilbroner, P	NJ	749
ChiN	Jacobson, R	NY	663
ChiN	Kairam, R	NY	140
ChiN	Kang, H	NY	663
ChiN	Kaufman, D	NY	140
ChiN	Khakoo, Y	NY	140
ChiN	Kosofsky, B	NY	140
ChiN	Kutscher, M	NY	663
ChiN	LaJoie, J	NY	546
ChiN	Lazar, L	NJ	905
ChiN	Maytal, J	NY	546
ChiN	McAbee, G	NJ	837
ChiN	Miles, D	NY	141
ChiN	Molofsky, W	NY	141
ChiN	Moshe, S	NY	412
ChiN	Pak, J	NJ	807
ChiN	Pavlakis, S	NY	456
ChiN	Riviello, J	NY	141
ChiN	Roseman, B	NY	664
ChiN	Schubert, R	NY	456
ChiN	Sherbany, A	NY	609
ChiN	Shinnar, S	NY	413
ChiN	Smith, R	NY	546
ChiN	Sousa, R	NJ	749
ChiN	Sweeney, T	NY	664
ChiN	Sy-Kho, R	NY	546
ChiN	Traeger, E	NJ	949
ChiN	Wells, J	NY	141

Spec	Name	St	Pg
ChiN	Wolf, S	NY	141
ChiN	Wollack, J	NJ	863
N	Kadakia, S	NY	568

Child Psychiatry

Spec	Name	St	Pg
ChAP	Carlson, G	NY	623
ChAP	Shampain, L	NJ	863
Psyc	Faber, M	NJ	828
Psyc	Fennelly, B	NJ	919

Chinese Community Health

Spec	Name	St	Pg
IM	Liu, G	NY	204
IM	Lu, B	NY	466
Ped	Wu, J	NY	486

Choanal Atresia

Spec	Name	St	Pg
PO	Ward, R	NY	315

Cholesteatoma

Spec	Name	St	Pg
Oto	Feghali, J	NY	430
Oto	Kwartler, J	NJ	959
Oto	Linstrom, C	NY	292
Oto	Selesnick, S	NY	294
PO	Grunstein, E	NY	315

Cholesterol/Lipid Disorders

Spec	Name	St	Pg
Cv	Augenbraun, C	CT	975
Cv	Blum, M	NJ	904
Cv	Charnoff, J	NY	452
Cv	Chesner, M	NY	541
Cv	Cohen, M	NY	126
Cv	Cole, W	NY	126
Cv	Conroy, D	NJ	744
Cv	Criscito, M	NJ	805
Cv	Cziner, D	NY	656
Cv	D'Agostino, R	NY	541
Cv	DeLuca, A	NY	656
Cv	Dervan, J	NY	622
Cv	Deutsch, A	NY	127
Cv	DiVagno, L	NJ	744
Cv	Drusin, R	NY	127
Cv	Dutta, T	NY	127
Cv	Engel, D	NY	127
Cv	Fass, A	NY	656
Cv	Gleckel, L	NY	542
Cv	Goldberg, S	NY	542
Cv	Goodman, D	NY	128
Cv	Goodman, M	NY	542
Cv	Green, J	CT	976
Cv	Green, S	NY	543
Cv	Inra, L	NY	129

Specialty & Special Expertise Index

Spec	Name	St	Pg
Pul	Dimango, E	NY	356
Pul	Fein, A	NY	595
Pul	Fiel, S	NJ	919
Pul	Fishman, D	NY	356
Pul	Garay, S	NY	356
Pul	Gelbman, B	NY	356
Pul	Glassman, A	NJ	790
Pul	Klapper, P	NY	440
Pul	Kurtz, C	CT	1025
Pul	Leeman, B	NY	595
Pul	Levine, S	NJ	790
Pul	Libby, D	NY	357
Pul	Lowy, J	NY	358
Pul	Mandel, M	NY	721
Pul	Maniatis, T	NY	530
Pul	McCalley, S	CT	1025
Pul	Melillo, N	NJ	881
Pul	Mermelstein, S	NY	596
Pul	Miarrostami, R	NY	489
Pul	Multz, A	NY	358
Pul	O'Donnell, T	NJ	920
Pul	Raskin, J	NY	359
Pul	Sachs, P	CT	1025
Pul	Saleh, A	NY	489
Pul	Sasso, L	NY	531
Pul	Shah, S	NJ	829
Pul	Sklarek, H	NY	646
Pul	Smith, P	NY	489
Pul	Sukumaran, M	NY	360
Pul	Sussman, R	NJ	963
Pul	Thomashow, B	NY	360
Pul	Thurm, C	NY	514
Pul	Turetsky, A	CT	1026
Pul	Winter, S	CT	1026
Pul	Wurm, E	NY	722
Pul	Yip, C	NY	360
Pul	Zimmerman, M	NJ	963

Churg-Strauss Vasculitis

A&I	Boxer, M	NY	538

Ciliary Dyskinesia

PPul	Turcios, N	NJ	941

Cleft Palate/Lip

Oto	Vastola, A	NY	480
PlS	Ascherman, J	NY	331
PlS	Dagum, A	NY	644
PlS	Dudick, S	NJ	896
PlS	Olson, R	NJ	942
PlS	Ruotolo, R	NY	592
PlS	Sabry, M	NY	337

Spec	Name	St	Pg
PlS	Silver, L	NY	338
PlS	Smith, M	NY	338
PlS	Staffenberg, D	NY	339
PlS	Taub, P	NY	339
PO	Bernstein, J	NY	709
PO	Grunstein, E	NY	315
PO	Haddad, J	NY	315
PO	Modi, V	NY	315
PO	Ward, R	NY	315

Clinical Genetics

CG	Adams, D	NJ	905
CG	Anyane-Yeboa, K	NY	141
CG	Bialer, M	NY	546
CG	Chung, W	NY	141
CG	Cunniff, C	NY	142
CG	Davis, J	NY	142
CG	Desnick, R	NY	142
CG	Desposito, F	NJ	807
CG	Fox, J	NY	547
CG	Gilbert, F	NY	456
CG	Kronn, D	NY	664
CG	Lichter-Konecki, U	NY	142
CG	Marion, R	NY	413
CG	McGovern, M	NY	624
CG	Mehta, L	NY	142
CG	Ostrer, H	NY	413
CG	Pappas, J	NY	142
CG	Pedro, H	NJ	749
CG	Santolaya, J	NJ	887
CG	Sklower Brooks, S	NJ	863
CG	Wasserstein, M	NY	142

Clinical Neurophysiology

N	Abou-Fayssal, N	NY	472
N	Buckner, C	NY	472
N	Carniciu, S	NY	693
N	Charles, J	NJ	839
N	Dousmanis, A	NY	693
N	Etienne, M	NY	613
N	Kozicrynska, E	NY	473
N	Laban-Grant, O	NY	693
N	Szabo, A	NY	694
N	Tolunsky, E	NY	694

Clinical Trials

ChAP	Kafantaris, V	NY	501
ChAP	Rynn, M	NY	138
ChiN	Shinnar, S	NY	413
Cv	Heiman, M	CT	977
D	Khorasani, H	NY	151
EDM	Brillon, D	NY	163

Spec	Name	St	Pg
GO	Smith, H	NY	420
Hem	Jurcic, J	NY	190
Hem	Solomon, W	NY	463
Hem	Staszewski, H	NY	557
IC	Driesman, M	CT	995
Inf	Horowitz, H	NY	195
Inf	Landesman, S	NY	464
Inf	Telzak, E	NY	421
N	DeAngelis, L	NY	235
N	Lipton, R	NY	426
N	Mitsumoto, H	NY	240
Onc	Bajorin, D	NY	213
Onc	Beltran, H	NY	213
Onc	Chapman, P	NY	214
Onc	Dickler, M	NY	214
Onc	Drucker, B	CT	998
Onc	Hershman, D	NY	216
Onc	Holcombe, R	NY	216
Onc	Horwitz, S	NY	217
Onc	Krug, L	NY	218
Onc	O'Connor, O	NY	219
Onc	Radovich, D	NJ	816
Onc	Raza, A	NY	221
Onc	Rizvi, N	NY	221
Onc	Scher, H	NY	222
Onc	Vahdat, L	NY	224
Onc	Wolchok, J	NY	224
Oto	Shin, E	NY	295
PHO	Cheung, N	NY	310
PHO	Glade Bender, J	NY	310
PInf	Neu, N	NY	313
Psyc	Goldstein, S	NY	345
Psyc	Mann, J	NY	348
S	Montgomery, L	NY	443
T&CS	Pass, H	NY	389
U	Ghavamian, R	NY	444
U	Shabsigh, R	NY	398

Clostridium Difficile Disease

Ge	Brandt, L	NY	417
Ge	Soloway, G	CT	987

Clubfoot/Foot Deformities in Children

OrS	Hyman, J	NY	276
OrS	Nelson, J	NY	703
OrS	Vitale, M	NY	285

Coagulation/Bleeding Disorders

Hem	Karp, G	NJ	867
Hem	Lederman, C	NY	679

Specialty & Special Expertise Index

Spec	Name	St	Pg
CRS	Gallina, G	NJ	750
CRS	Gilder, M	NJ	807
CRS	Gorfine, S	NY	143
CRS	Greenwald, M	NY	547
CRS	Groff, W	NJ	950
CRS	Guillem, J	NY	143
CRS	Helbraun, M	NJ	750
CRS	Khaitov, S	NY	144
CRS	Krakovitz, E	NY	664
CRS	Ky, A	NY	144
CRS	Lacqua, F	NY	522
CRS	Lee, S	NY	144
CRS	Leiboff, A	NY	624
CRS	Littlejohn, C	CT	979
CRS	Martz, J	NY	144
CRS	McClane, J	CT	980
CRS	Milsom, J	NY	144
CRS	Moseson, M	NY	547
CRS	Moskowitz, R	NJ	905
CRS	Nizin, J	NJ	750
CRS	Orringer, R	NJ	807
CRS	Pappas, D	NY	547
CRS	Penzer, J	NY	144
CRS	Procaccino, J	NY	547
CRS	Rezac, C	NJ	863
CRS	Rivadeneira, D	NY	547
CRS	Rothberg, R	NJ	807
CRS	Smithy, W	NY	624
CRS	Sonoda, T	NY	144
CRS	Steinhagen, R	NY	145
CRS	Sullivan, J	NY	547
CRS	Tarantino, D	NJ	807
CRS	Temple, L	NY	145
CRS	Thornton, S	CT	980
CRS	Tiszenkel, H	NY	501
CRS	Waxenbaum, S	NJ	750
CRS	Weiser, M	NY	145
CRS	Whelan, R	NY	145
CRS	White, R	NJ	750
CRS	Wishner, J	NY	664
CRS	Zinkin, L	NJ	864
PS	Bodenstein, L	NY	317
S	Agarwal, N	NY	442
S	Feteiha, M	NJ	964
S	Messina, A	NY	727
S	Rolandelli, R	NJ	921
S	Slater, G	NY	384
S	Vine, A	NY	384

Colon Cancer

Spec	Name	St	Pg
CRS	Eisenstat, T	NJ	863
CRS	Lacqua, F	NY	522
CRS	Nizin, J	NJ	750
CRS	Waxenbaum, S	NJ	750
CRS	Zinkin, L	NJ	864
Ge	Bonheim, N	CT	985
Ge	Caccese, W	NY	553
Ge	Cantor, M	NY	169
Ge	Farber, C	NY	553
Ge	Finegold, J	NY	673
Ge	Frager, J	NY	417
Ge	Goldblum, L	NY	554
Ge	Goldfarb, J	NJ	756
Ge	Gupta, J	NY	460
Ge	Harrison, A	NY	629
Ge	Kairam, I	NY	173
Ge	Kressner, M	NY	675
Ge	Landau, S	NY	675
Ge	Milman, P	NY	555
Ge	Nelson, A	CT	987
Ge	Rosner, B	NJ	848
Ge	Rubin, K	NJ	757
Ge	Schneider, L	NY	178
Ge	Taffet, S	NY	676
Ge	Vogelman, A	NY	504
Ge	Waye, J	NY	179
Ge	Weiss, R	NY	180
Ge	Zingler, B	NJ	758
Ge	Zucker, I	NJ	758
Hem	Vogel, J	NY	192
Onc	Benisovich, V	NY	508
Onc	Condemi, G	NJ	765
Onc	Delprete, S	CT	998
Onc	Dosik, D	NY	469
Onc	Fang, B	NJ	939
Onc	Fischbach, N	CT	998
Onc	Fitzgerald, D	NJ	891
Onc	Friscia, P	NY	525
Onc	Fuks, J	NY	423
Onc	Greenberg, H	NY	508
Onc	Hirschman, R	NY	216
Onc	Hirshaut, Y	NY	216
Onc	Hollister, D	CT	999
Onc	Kane, M	NJ	910
Onc	Kappel, B	NY	564
Onc	Kemeny, N	NY	217
Onc	Kloss, R	CT	999
Onc	Malefatto, J	CT	999
Onc	Marino, J	NY	564
Onc	Nissenblatt, M	NJ	869
Onc	Rakowski, T	NJ	766
Onc	Rivera, Y	NJ	766
Onc	Salwitz, J	NJ	939
Onc	Schleider, M	NJ	766
Onc	Schwartz, P	NY	564
Onc	Shum, K	NY	509
Onc	Siegel, A	NY	223
Onc	Strauss, B	NY	634
Onc	Weinstein, P	CT	1000
Onc	Yi, P	NJ	851
Path	Klimstra, D	NY	301
S	Diehl, W	NJ	921
S	Gordon, M	NY	726
S	Michelassi, F	NY	381
S	Pachter, H	NY	382
S	Salky, B	NY	383

Colon Cancer Screening

Spec	Name	St	Pg
CRS	Gallina, G	NJ	750
Ge	Accurso, C	NJ	937
Ge	Augello, S	NY	503
Ge	Baiocco, P	NY	168
Ge	Bartolomeo, R	NY	553
Ge	Bernstein, B	NY	169
Ge	Cerulli, M	NY	553
Ge	Cooper, R	NY	170
Ge	Dalena, J	NJ	907
Ge	Fiske, S	NJ	810
Ge	Freiman, H	NY	171
Ge	Geders, J	NY	673
Ge	Genn, D	NY	674
Ge	Gettenberg, G	NY	460
Ge	Goldberg, M	NY	171
Ge	Khokhar, A	NY	629
Ge	Krumholz, M	NY	174
Ge	Link, R	CT	987
Ge	Markowitz, A	NY	176
Ge	Nussbaum, M	NY	504
Ge	Robbins, D	NY	177
Ge	Robilotti, J	NY	177
Ge	Schneebaum, C	NY	178
Ge	Schwartz, G	NY	555
Ge	Soloway, G	CT	987
Ge	Taubin, H	CT	987
Ge	Torman, J	NY	676
Ge	Zimbalist, E	NY	462

Colon Polyps & Cancer

Spec	Name	St	Pg
Ge	Klein, W	NJ	756
Ge	Meirowitz, R	NJ	848
Ge	Turtel, P	NJ	889

Colon Surgery

Spec	Name	St	Pg
S	Adler, H	NY	491
S	Feigenbaum, H	NJ	932
S	Frost, J	NJ	964
S	Schwartzman, A	NY	493

Specialty & Special Expertise Index

Specialty & Special Expertise Index

Specialty & Special Expertise Index

Spec	Name	St	Pg
Oph	Tostanoski, J	NY	701

Corneal Disease-Pediatric

Spec	Name	St	Pg
Oph	Medow, N	NY	428
Oph	Zaidman, G	NY	701

Corneal Ring Implants

Spec	Name	St	Pg
Oph	Fox, M	NY	257
Oph	Goldstein, M	NY	259
Oph	Sperber, L	NY	267

Coronary Angioplasty/Stents

Spec	Name	St	Pg
CE	Cohen, M	NY	655
Cv	Adibi, B	NJ	743
Cv	Eichman, G	NJ	744
Cv	Landers, D	NJ	746
Cv	Pappas, T	NY	544
Cv	Perry-Bottinger, L	NY	660
Cv	Pucillo, A	NY	660
Cv	Wangenheim, P	NJ	806
IC	Attubato, M	NY	208
IC	Brogno, D	NY	611
IC	Hjemdahl-Monsen, C	NY	685
IC	Kaid, K	NJ	814
IC	Messinger, D	NY	686
IC	Parikh, M	NY	209
IC	Petrossian, G	NY	562
IC	Slater, J	NY	210
IC	Zisfein, J	NY	562

Coronary Artery Disease

Spec	Name	St	Pg
Cv	Akinboboye, O	NY	500
Cv	Altmann, D	NJ	862
Cv	Anto, M	NY	541
Cv	Berdoff, R	NY	125
Cv	Berkowitz, W	NJ	744
Cv	Besser, L	NY	521
Cv	Blumenthal, D	NY	126
Cv	Borer, J	NY	452
Cv	Campagna, R	NY	126
Cv	Catanese, J	NY	656
Cv	Charney, R	NY	656
Cv	Charnoff, J	NY	452
Cv	Choi, J	CT	976
Cv	Cohen, M	NY	126
Cv	Cole, W	NY	126
Cv	Cooper, J	NY	656
Cv	Copen, D	CT	976
Cv	Cramer, M	NY	541
Cv	Cziner, D	NY	656
Cv	Dardashti, O	NJ	744

Spec	Name	St	Pg
Cv	DeLuca, A	NY	656
Cv	Drusin, R	NY	127
Cv	Dubois, N	NY	127
Cv	Dutta, T	NY	127
Cv	Eisenberg, S	NJ	745
Cv	Fass, A	NY	656
Cv	Feld, M	NY	657
Cv	Fisch, A	NJ	904
Cv	Forman, R	NY	410
Cv	Franklin, K	NY	127
Cv	Friedman, H	NY	453
Cv	Frishman, W	NY	657
Cv	Fuchs, R	NY	128
Cv	Fuster, V	NY	128
Cv	Ganem, A	NY	657
Cv	Gitler, B	NY	657
Cv	Goldberg, H	NY	128
Cv	Golduber, G	NY	500
Cv	Goodman, M	NY	542
Cv	Hecht, A	NY	129
Cv	Hollander, G	NY	454
Cv	Hollywood, J	NJ	745
Cv	Hsueh, J	NY	500
Cv	Inra, L	NY	129
Cv	Issa, E	NJ	746
Cv	Kalischer, A	NJ	949
Cv	Kamen, M	NY	129
Cv	Kanarek, S	NJ	746
Cv	Katechis, D	NJ	746
Cv	Katz, E	NY	129
Cv	Keller, P	NY	411
Cv	Keltz, T	NY	658
Cv	Kerstein, J	NY	454
Cv	Kirtane, S	NY	500
Cv	Kosinski, E	CT	977
Cv	Kostis, J	NJ	862
Cv	Landzberg, J	NJ	747
Cv	Lense, L	NY	622
Cv	Lituchy, A	NY	543
Cv	Marshalko, S	CT	977
Cv	Masciello, M	NY	623
Cv	Masri, B	NY	130
Cv	Matilsky, M	NY	623
Cv	Matos, M	NY	659
Cv	Meller, J	NY	131
Cv	Michaelson, S	CT	978
Cv	Miller, D	NY	131
Cv	Mintz, G	NY	544
Cv	Monrad, E	NY	412
Cv	Moskovits, N	NY	454
Cv	Nash, I	NY	131
Cv	Nicosia, T	NY	544
Cv	Paley, A	NY	659

Spec	Name	St	Pg
Cv	Patel, S	NJ	747
Cv	Poon, M	NY	132
Cv	Post, M	NY	132
Cv	Pumill, R	NJ	747
Cv	Qadir, S	NY	455
Cv	Rogal, G	NJ	806
Cv	Romanello, P	NY	132
Cv	Sahar, D	NY	412
Cv	Schiffer, M	NY	133
Cv	Schreiber, C	NY	544
Cv	Schwartz, W	NY	133
Cv	Shamoon, F	NJ	806
Cv	Shayani, S	NY	544
Cv	Shell, R	NJ	862
Cv	Shimony, R	NY	134
Cv	Siegal, M	NY	134
Cv	Siepser, S	NJ	925
Cv	Silver, M	NY	660
Cv	Stein, R	NY	135
Cv	Tenenbaum, J	NY	135
Cv	Tenet, W	NY	545
Cv	Tyberg, T	NY	135
Cv	Unger, A	NY	135
Cv	Varriale, P	NY	135
Cv	Weg, I	NY	545
Cv	Wein, P	NY	455
Cv	Weisenseel, A	NY	136
Cv	Weiss, E	NJ	925
Cv	Weissman, R	NY	661
Cv	Williams, M	NJ	748
Cv	Wolk, M	NY	136
Cv	Yuen, J	NY	661
IC	Angeli, S	NJ	763
IC	Gray, W	NY	208
IC	Innerfield, M	NY	612
IC	Marmur, J	NY	468
IC	Mejia, V	CT	996
IC	Rachofsky, E	NJ	939
IC	Stone, G	NY	210
IC	Syed, T	NJ	763
IC	Warshofsky, M	CT	996
IC	Wasserman, H	CT	996
IC	Weinberger, J	NY	210
IC	Weiss, M	NY	686
IM	Kennish, A	NY	203
IM	Lauricella, J	NJ	762
IM	Lipton, M	NY	204

Coronary Artery Disease-Complex

Spec	Name	St	Pg
IC	Brogno, D	NY	611
IC	Wilentz, J	NY	210

Specialty & Special Expertise Index

Specialty & Special Expertise Index

Specialty & Special Expertise Index

Spec	Name	St	Pg
IM	Zupnick, H	NY	561
Pul	Baram, D	NY	645
Pul	Benoff, B	NJ	790
Pul	Blum, A	NY	594
Pul	Chadha, J	NY	513
Pul	Chronakos, J	CT	1024
Pul	Fein, A	NY	595
Pul	George, L	NY	488
Pul	Mehrishi, S	NY	513
Pul	Multz, A	NY	358
Pul	Newmark, I	NY	596
Pul	Pastores, S	NY	359
Pul	Seelagy, M	NJ	856
Pul	Walser, L	NY	646
Pul	Wohlberg, G	NY	646
Pul	Wyner, P	NY	596
Pul	Zimmerman, M	NJ	963

Crohn's Disease

CRS	Sonoda, T	NY	144
CRS	Steinhagen, R	NY	145
Ge	Auerbach, M	NY	672
Ge	Field, B	NY	673
Ge	Finkelstein, W	NJ	810
Ge	Harrison, A	NY	629
Ge	Khan, A	NJ	952
Ge	Kornbluth, A	NY	174
Ge	Lebovics, E	NY	675
Ge	Lustbader, I	NY	175
Ge	Magun, A	NY	175
Ge	Marion, J	NY	175
Ge	Scherl, E	NY	178
Ge	Stein, D	NY	418
Ge	Talansky, A	NY	555
Ge	Zinkin, N	NY	629
PGe	Breglio, K	NY	482
PGe	Chawla, A	NY	641
PGe	Farhath, S	NJ	854
PGe	Levine, J	NY	308
PGe	Sockolow, R	NY	309
PGe	Spivak, W	NY	309
PGe	Tyshkov, M	NJ	960
S	Michelassi, F	NY	381
S	Rolandelli, R	NJ	921

Cryoglobulinemia

Rhu	Gorevic, P	NY	370

CT Body Scan

DR	Cohen, S	CT	982
DR	Grosso-Rivas, S	NJ	950
DR	Laks, M	NY	414

Spec	Name	St	Pg
DR	Megibow, A	NY	159
DR	Moses, S	NJ	809
DR	Mullen, D	CT	983
DR	Neistadt, L	NY	160

CT Scan

DR	Chaim, J	NY	157
DR	Cohen, B	NY	157
DR	Donahue, J	CT	982
DR	Ehrlich, C	CT	982
DR	Fey, C	CT	982
DR	Ford, R	NJ	847
DR	Fuqua, J	NY	158
DR	Geller, M	NY	610
DR	Goodman, K	NY	549
DR	Hertz, M	NY	668
DR	Kirshy, D	NY	626
DR	Lee, R	CT	982
DR	Miller, T	NY	159
DR	Mollin, J	NY	502
DR	Rifkin, M	NY	550
DR	Rozenblit, A	NY	414
DR	Sherman, S	NY	550
DR	Som, P	NY	161
DR	Swirsky, M	NY	669
DR	Yoon, S	NY	550
NuM	Agress, H	NJ	772
NuM	Freeman, L	NY	427
NuM	Gerard, P	NY	695
NuM	Scharf, S	NY	246

Cultural Psychiatry

Psyc	Ferran, E	NY	344

Cutaneous Lymphoma

D	Belsito, D	NY	146
D	Grossman, K	NJ	888
D	Grossman, M	NY	665
D	Katz, S	NY	151
D	Myskowski, P	NY	152
D	Ramsay, D	NY	153
Path	Magro, C	NY	301

Cutaneous T-cell Lymphoma

Hem	Hymes, K	NY	190
Onc	Horwitz, S	NY	217

Cystic Fibrosis

A&I	Guida, L	NY	621
PPul	Amin, N	NY	710
PPul	Atlas, A	NJ	916

Spec	Name	St	Pg
PPul	Bieler, H	NJ	916
PPul	Bisberg, D	NJ	825
PPul	Boyer, J	NY	710
PPul	Constantinescu, A	NY	316
PPul	Dimaio, M	NY	316
PPul	Dozor, A	NY	710
PPul	Giusti, R	NY	484
PPul	Kaplan, E	NJ	783
PPul	Kass, L	NY	710
PPul	Kattan, M	NY	316
PPul	Kier, C	NY	642
PPul	Kottler, W	NJ	825
PPul	Krishnan, S	NY	710
PPul	Lamm, C	NY	316
PPul	Lowenthal, D	NY	711
PPul	Montalvo Stanton, E	NJ	825
PPul	Nachajon, R	NJ	930
PPul	Needleman, J	NY	484
PPul	Pirzada, M	NY	586
PPul	Quittell, L	NY	711
PPul	Sadeghi, H	CT	1018
PPul	Ting, A	NY	316
PPul	Turcios, N	NJ	941
Pul	Berman, L	CT	1024
Pul	Bernstein, M	CT	1024
Pul	Brown, R	CT	1024
Pul	Dimango, E	NY	356
Pul	Fiel, N	NJ	919
Pul	Kurtz, C	CT	1025
Pul	McCalley, S	CT	1025
Pul	Padilla, M	NY	358
Pul	Wohlberg, G	NY	646

Cystic Fibrosis Infection

PInf	Saiman, L	NY	314

Cytopathology

Path	Altmeyer, V	CT	1016
Path	Hoda, S	NY	301

D

Dance Medicine

OrS	Hamilton, W	NY	275
OrS	Padgett, D	NY	280

Dance/Ballet Injuries

OrS	Rose, D	NY	282
SM	Metzl, J	NY	375

Specialty & Special Expertise Index

Specialty & Special Expertise Index

Specialty & Special Expertise Index

Diabetes & Heart Disease

Diabetes in Minority Populations

Diabetes in Pregnancy

Diabetes Ketoacidosis

Diabetic Eye Disease

Diabetic Eye Disease/Retinopathy

Diabetic Kidney Disease

Specialty & Special Expertise Index

Specialty & Special Expertise Index

Specialty & Special Expertise Index

Spec	Name	St	Pg
HS	Miller, J	NJ	908
HS	Raskin, K	NY	188
HS	Rosenwasser, M	NY	188
OrS	Compito, C	NY	271
OrS	Craig, E	NY	272
OrS	Cuomo, F	NY	272
OrS	Kayal, R	NJ	776
OrS	Khabie, V	NY	703
OrS	McCann, P	NY	279
OrS	Sethi, P	CT	1013
OrS	Sgaglione, N	NY	577
SM	Altchek, D	NY	374
SM	Seneviratne, A	NY	376

Electrical Status Epilepticus Of Sleep

ChiN	Riviello, J	NY	141
ChiN	Shinnar, S	NY	413

Electroconvulsive Therapy (ECT)

GerPsy	Greenberg, R	NY	462
Psyc	Bailine, S	NY	593
Psyc	Fox, H	NY	344
Psyc	Kellner, C	NY	346
Psyc	Samuels, S	NJ	789

Electrodiagnosis

N	Carniciu, S	NY	693
N	French, J	NY	236
N	Heublum, M	NY	237
N	Ober, D	NY	613
N	Olarte, M	NY	241
N	Rosenkilde, C	NY	694
N	Schaul, N	NY	569
PMR	Brief, R	NY	616
PMR	Brown, D	NJ	879
PMR	Cole, J	NJ	827
PMR	Diamond, M	NJ	961
PMR	Feinberg, J	NY	327
PMR	Filippone, M	NJ	841
PMR	Mulford, G	NJ	918
PMR	Pechman, K	NY	715
PMR	Robinson, M	NY	616
PMR	Slaten, W	NY	616
PMR	Weiss, L	NY	589

Electrolyte Disorders

Nep	Shein, L	NY	471
Nep	Sherman, R	NJ	870
Nep	Weisstuch, J	NY	228
PNep	Trachtman, H	NY	314

Electromyography

Spec	Name	St	Pg
N	Alweiss, G	NJ	770
N	Citak, K	NJ	770
N	Cuzzone, L	CT	1002
N	Herskovitz, S	NY	426
N	Kelemen, J	NY	569
N	Knep, S	NJ	928
N	Lange, D	NY	238
N	Maccabee, P	NY	473
N	MacGowan, D	NY	239
N	Ragone, P	NY	569
N	Rapoport, S	NY	241
N	Sander, H	NY	242
N	Van Engel, D	NJ	771
N	Van Slooten, D	NJ	771
N	Witte, A	NJ	852
PMR	Brown, A	NY	326
PMR	Brown, D	NJ	879
PMR	Cole, J	NJ	827
PMR	Filippone, M	NJ	841
PMR	Klecz, R	NJ	918
PMR	Ma, D	NY	328
PMR	Root, B	NY	589
PMR	Rosenberg, C	NY	644
PMR	Vallarino, R	NY	512
PMR	Weiss, L	NY	589

Electrophysiologic Testing

Cv	Lafferty, J	NY	521

Emphysema

IM	Ernst, J	NY	422
IM	Feuer, M	NY	201
IM	Horovitz, L	NY	203
IM	Kapoor, S	NY	683
IM	Minkowitz, S	NY	205
IM	Spero, M	NY	207
Pul	Abott, M	NY	487
Pul	Baskin, M	NY	355
Pul	Berman, L	CT	1024
Pul	Bernstein, C	NY	488
Pul	Bromberg, A	NJ	790
Pul	Castellano, M	NY	530
Pul	Chadha, J	NY	513
Pul	Cohen, M	NY	595
Pul	De Matteo, R	NY	720
Pul	Delorenzo, L	NY	720
Pul	Eden, E	NY	356
Pul	Goldblatt, K	NJ	881
Pul	Gordon, R	NY	595
Pul	Greenberg, M	NJ	829
Pul	Klapholz, A	NY	357

Spec	Name	St	Pg
Pul	Klapper, P	NY	440
Pul	Kolodny, E	NY	357
Pul	Krinsley, J	CT	1025
Pul	Marino, A	CT	1025
Pul	Martins, P	NY	530
Pul	Meixler, S	NY	721
Pul	Miarrostami, R	NY	489
Pul	Nath, S	NY	513
Pul	Niederman, M	NY	596
Pul	Schreiber, M	NY	721
Pul	Silverman, J	NY	514
Pul	Stein, S	NY	360
Pul	Steinberg, H	NY	596
Pul	Volcovici, G	NY	722
Pul	Winter, S	CT	1026
Pul	Wyner, P	NY	596
Pul	Yip, C	NY	360
T&CS	Glassman, L	NY	602
T&CS	Hyman, K	NY	602
T&CS	Kline, G	NJ	795

Emphysema & Asthma

Pul	Casper, T	NY	440
Pul	Glaser, M	NY	646
Pul	Lee, M	NY	357
Pul	Maxfield, R	NY	358
Pul	Thomashow, B	NY	360

Emphysema-Lung Volume Reduction

T&CS	Ginsburg, M	NY	387
T&CS	Sonett, J	NY	390

Emphysema/Alpha-1 Antitrypsin Deficiency

Pul	Eden, E	NY	356

Encopresis (fecal soiling)

PGe	Daum, F	NY	583

Endocarditis

Inf	Hartman, B	NY	195
Inf	Krieger, R	NJ	908
Inf	Yancovitz, S	NY	198

Endocrine Cancers

S	Lee, J	NY	381

Endocrine Disorders

CG	Mehta, L	NY	142

Specialty & Special Expertise Index

Spec	Name	St	Pg
ObG	Filor, C	CT	1005
ObG	Goldman, G	NY	248
ObG	Hayworth, S	NY	696
ObG	Levey, J	NJ	940
ObG	Levey, K	NY	250
ObG	Luciani, R	NJ	818
ObG	Sarabanchong, V	NY	510
ObG	Ugol, J	CT	1007
ObG	Violi, C	CT	1007
RE	Chacho, K	CT	1027
RE	David, S	NY	364
RE	Doyle, M	CT	1027
RE	Fateh, M	NY	364
RE	Ginsburg, F	CT	1027
RE	Hurwitz, J	CT	1027
RE	Klein, J	NY	723
RE	Leondires, M	CT	1027
RE	Lesorgen, P	NJ	791
RE	Matera, C	NY	365
RE	Mukherjee, T	NY	366
RE	Stangel, J	NY	723
RE	Witt, B	CT	1028
RE	Zinaman, M	NY	441

Endoscopic Sinus Surgery

Spec	Name	St	Pg
Oto	Bennett, G	NY	286
Oto	Branovan, D	NY	480
Oto	Close, L	NY	287
Oto	Drake, W	NJ	959
Oto	Edelstein, D	NY	288
Oto	Fleming, G	NJ	914
Oto	Fried, M	NY	431
Oto	Gold, S	NY	288
Oto	Henick, D	NJ	777
Oto	Huo, J	NY	512
Oto	Jacobs, J	NY	289
Oto	Josephson, J	NY	290
Oto	Krevitt, L	NY	291
Oto	Lagmay, V	NY	480
Oto	Lane, E	CT	1015
Oto	Lawson, W	NY	291
Oto	Markowitz, A	NY	292
Oto	Moisa, I	NY	579
Oto	Perlman, P	NY	579
Oto	Pincus, R	NY	293
Oto	Rosner, L	NY	579
Oto	Ryback, H	NY	705
Oto	Schaefer, S	NY	294
Oto	Shapiro, B	NY	705
Oto	Smith, J	NY	431
Oto	Snyder, G	NY	579
Oto	Soletic, R	NY	579

Endoscopic Surgery

Spec	Name	St	Pg
NS	Souweidane, M	NY	233
PS	Muensterer, O	NY	435
S	Herron, D	NY	379
S	Jordan, L	NJ	883

Endoscopic Therapies

Spec	Name	St	Pg
Ge	Burns, B	CT	986
Ge	Carr-Locke, D	NY	169
Ge	Miller, L	NY	554
Ge	Pittman, R	NJ	757
Ge	Soloway, G	CT	987

Endoscopic Ultrasound

Spec	Name	St	Pg
Ge	Ben-Menachem, T	NJ	952
Ge	Gerdes, H	NY	171
Ge	Gress, F	NY	172
Ge	Haber, G	NY	172
Ge	Hertan, H	NY	418
Ge	Ho, S	NY	418
Ge	Kim, M	NY	173
Ge	Lightdale, C	NY	175
Ge	Pochapin, M	NY	177
S	Yiengpruksawan, A	NJ	794

Endoscopy

Spec	Name	St	Pg
Ge	Abelow, A	NY	417
Ge	Abemayor, E	NY	672
Ge	Accurso, C	NJ	937
Ge	Ackert, J	NY	168
Ge	Afridi, S	NJ	848
Ge	Avezzano, E	NJ	756
Ge	Baiocco, P	NY	168
Ge	Barrison, A	NJ	952
Ge	Barro, J	CT	985
Ge	Ben-Menachem, T	NJ	952
Ge	Blumstein, M	NY	553
Ge	Buscaglia, J	NY	628
Ge	Caccese, W	NY	553
Ge	Chang, P	NY	169
Ge	Cohen, S	NY	170
Ge	Dalena, J	NJ	907
Ge	Dettmer, R	CT	986
Ge	Dieterich, D	NY	170
Ge	Erber, W	NY	460
Ge	Fath, R	NY	673
Ge	Ferran, E	NY	170
Ge	Fochios, S	NY	171
Ge	Foong, A	NY	171
Ge	Frager, J	NY	417
Ge	Frank, M	NY	171

Spec	Name	St	Pg
Ge	Gerdes, H	NY	171
Ge	Glanzman, B	NY	628
Ge	Goldberg, M	NY	171
Ge	Goldblatt, R	NY	674
Ge	Goldblum, L	NY	554
Ge	Goldin, H	NY	172
Ge	Green, P	NY	172
Ge	Greenwald, D	NY	417
Ge	Haber, G	NY	172
Ge	Ho, S	NY	418
Ge	Iswara, K	NY	461
Ge	Janec, E	NY	173
Ge	Katz, S	NY	554
Ge	Kim, M	NY	173
Ge	Knapp, A	NY	174
Ge	Kummer, B	NY	174
Ge	Kurtz, R	NY	174
Ge	Landau, A	CT	986
Ge	Latzman, G	CT	986
Ge	Lazar, R	NY	629
Ge	Leb, A	NY	461
Ge	Lebwohl, O	NY	175
Ge	Lewis, B	NY	175
Ge	Liss, M	NY	675
Ge	Ludwig, S	NJ	889
Ge	Magun, A	NY	175
Ge	Maizel, B	NY	461
Ge	Marsh, F	NY	176
Ge	Martin, C	NY	675
Ge	Mauer, K	CT	987
Ge	May, L	NY	611
Ge	Meighan, D	CT	987
Ge	Milano, A	NY	176
Ge	Miller, L	NY	554
Ge	Milman, P	NY	555
Ge	Miskovitz, P	NY	176
Ge	Nelson, A	CT	987
Ge	Nikias, G	NJ	757
Ge	Panella, V	NJ	757
Ge	Plumser, A	NJ	866
Ge	Rahmin, M	NJ	757
Ge	Rand, J	NY	504
Ge	Robbins, D	NY	177
Ge	Roth, J	NJ	757
Ge	Rubin, K	NJ	757
Ge	Schneebaum, C	NY	178
Ge	Shapiro, N	NY	676
Ge	Sherman, A	NY	178
Ge	Shike, M	NY	178
Ge	Sohn, W	NY	461
Ge	Solny, M	NY	179
Ge	Spira, R	NJ	811
Ge	Stein, L	NJ	907

Specialty & Special Expertise Index

Specialty & Special Expertise Index

Spec	Name	St	Pg
NP	Hiatt, I	NJ	870
NP	Holzman, I	NY	225
Pul	Prager, K	NY	359

Ethnic Skin Disorders

Spec	Name	St	Pg
D	Alexis, A	NY	146
D	Shieh, S	NY	154

Ewing's Sarcoma

Onc	Tap, W	NY	224
Path	Antonescu, C	NY	300
PHO	Granowetter, L	NY	311

Exercise Physiology

PCd	Schiller, M	NY	432
PPul	Needleman, J	NY	484
Pul	Malovany, R	NJ	790

Exfoliate Erythroderma

| D | Bagel, J | NJ | 847 |

Eye Allergy

| A&I | Bielory, L | NJ | 948 |

Eye Disorders-Congenital

| Oph | Derespinis, P | NY | 527 |
| Oph | Wagner, R | NJ | 820 |

Eye Infections

Oph	Aharon, R	NY	510
Oph	Eichenbaum, J	NY	256
Oph	Koplin, R	NY	260
Oph	Mayers, M	NY	428
Oph	Newton, M	NY	263
Oph	Samson, C	NY	265
Oph	Starr, M	NY	267

Eye Muscle Disorders

Oph	Campolattaro, B	NY	254
Oph	Derespinis, P	NY	527
Oph	Hall, L	NY	259
Oph	Horowitz, M	NY	699
Oph	Katz, B	NY	428
Oph	Lederman, M	NY	699
Oph	Mathias, S	CT	1008
Oph	Steele, M	NY	267
Oph	Wang, F	NY	267
Oph	Winterkorn, J	NY	511
Oph	Wisnicki, H	NY	268

Eye Muscle Disorders-Child & Adult

| Oph | Ceisler, E | NY | 255 |

Eye Trauma

| Oph | Koplin, R | NY | 260 |
| Oph | Zarbin, M | NJ | 820 |

Eye Tumors/Cancer

Oph	Abramson, D	NY	253
Oph	Finger, P	NY	257
Oph	Friedman, A	NY	258
Oph	Heinemann, M	NY	259
Oph	Marr, B	NY	262
Oph	Rodriguez-Sains, R	NY	264
Oph	Rosenbaum, P	NY	429
RadRO	McCormick, B	NY	362
RadRO	Rotman, M	NY	490

Eyelid Cancer & Reconstruction

| Oph | Della Rocca, R | NY | 256 |

Eyelid Cosmetic & Reconstructive Surgery

Oph	Bortz, J	NY	698
Oph	Gordon, J	NY	699
Oph	Kristan, R	NJ	893
Oph	Lisman, R	NY	261
Oph	Rodgers, I	NY	264
Oph	Rodriguez-Sains, R	NY	264
Oph	Schlessinger, D	NY	574
PlS	Raskin, E	CT	1022

Eyelid Cosmetic Surgery

Oph	Ackerman, J	NY	475
Oph	Goldberg, L	NY	573
Oph	Manjoney, D	CT	1008
Oph	Marks, A	NY	573
Oph	Schneck, G	NY	638

Eyelid Surgery

Oph	Dweck, M	NY	476
Oph	Musto, A	CT	1008
Oph	Schwarcz, R	NY	265
Oph	Wasserman, B	NJ	853
Oto	Mazzara, C	NJ	875
Oto	Pastorek, N	NY	292
PlS	Anton, J	NY	644
PlS	Broumand, S	NY	331
PlS	Cutolo, L	NY	530

PlS	DiGregorio, V	NY	590
PlS	Imber, G	NY	334
PlS	Kleinman, A	NY	716
PlS	Newman, F	CT	1022
PlS	Perry, A	NJ	942
PlS	Rosen, A	NJ	828
PlS	Simpson, R	NY	592
PlS	Tabbal, N	NY	339

Eyelid Surgery/Blepharoplasty

Oph	Schlessinger, D	NY	574
Oto	Jacono, A	NY	578
Oto	Slupchynskyj, O	NY	295
PlS	Hirmand, H	NY	334
PlS	Spinelli, H	NY	339

Eyelid Tumors/Cancer

Oph	Della Rocca, R	NY	256
Oph	Elahi, E	NY	257
Oph	Kazim, M	NY	260
Oph	Milite, J	NJ	874
Oph	Rodriguez-Sains, R	NY	264

Eyelid/Tear Duct Disorders

Oph	Angrist, R	NJ	940
Oph	Perry, H	NY	574
Oph	Rodgers, I	NY	264

Eyelid/Tear Duct Reconstruction

| Oph | Lisman, R | NY | 261 |
| Oph | Moazed, K | NY | 262 |

F

Fabry's Disease

| CG | Wasserstein, M | NY | 142 |

Facial Deformities/Reconstruction

| PlS | LaBruna, A | NY | 335 |

Facial Nerve Disorders

Oto	Kay, S	NJ	875
Oto	Lalwani, A	NY	291
Oto	Li, C	NY	291
Oto	Miller, P	NY	292
Oto	Roland, J	NY	293

Specialty & Special Expertise Index

Spec	Name	St	Pg
Facial Paralysis			
Oto	Costantino, P	NY	288
Facial Paralysis Reconstruction			
PlS	Baker, D	NY	331
PlS	Rose, E	NY	337
Facial Plastic & Reconstructive Surgery			
Oto	Carniol, P	NJ	959
Oto	Constantinides, M	NY	287
Oto	Gordon, N	CT	1015
Oto	Horn, C	NY	289
Oto	Levin, R	CT	1015
Oto	Mazzara, C	NJ	875
Oto	Pincus, R	NY	293
Oto	Portnoy, W	NY	293
Oto	Presti, P	NJ	959
Oto	Rizk, S	NY	293
Oto	Shohet, M	NY	295
Oto	Slupchynskyj, O	NY	295
Oto	Snyder, G	NY	579
Oto	Turk, J	NY	580
Oto	Westreich, R	NY	296
Oto	White, W	NY	296
PlS	Alizadeh, K	NY	590
PlS	Cordeiro, P	NY	332
PlS	LaBruna, A	NY	335
PlS	Levine, J	NY	335
PlS	Marotta, J	NY	644
PlS	Monasebian, D	NY	336
PlS	Otterburn, D	NY	336
PlS	Rodriguez, E	NY	336
PlS	Roth, D	NY	717
PlS	Shafer, D	NY	338
PlS	Sherman, J	NY	338
PlS	Suzman, M	NY	717
Facial Plastic Surgery			
Oph	Elahi, E	NY	257
Oto	Milgrim, L	NJ	778
Oto	Rosen, A	NJ	778
Oto	Scott, J	NY	705
Oto	Shikowitz, M	NY	579
Oto	Shugar, J	NY	295
PlS	Perrotti, J	NY	336
PlS	Schaffner, A	NY	337
Facial Rejuvenation			
D	Colbert, D	NY	147
D	Cooper, L	NJ	906

Spec	Name	St	Pg
D	Dolitsky, C	NY	548
D	Evans, L	NY	665
D	Felderman, L	NY	148
D	Foitl, D	NY	148
D	Gendler, E	NY	149
D	Gordon, M	NY	149
D	Green, M	NY	149
D	Grodberg, M	NJ	751
D	Grossman, M	NY	150
D	Hale, E	NY	150
D	Haven, L	CT	980
D	Karen, J	NY	150
D	Katz, B	NY	150
D	Levit, E	NY	457
D	Liftin, A	NJ	808
D	Narins, R	NY	667
D	Paltzik, R	NY	549
D	Polis, L	NY	153
D	Rokhsar, C	NY	154
D	Schultz, N	NY	154
D	Schweiger, E	NY	154
D	Sklar, J	NY	549
D	Treiber, R	NY	667
D	Wexler, P	NY	156
Oto	Constantinides, M	NY	287
Oto	Gordon, N	CT	1015
Oto	Sclafani, A	NY	294
PlS	D'Amico, R	NJ	787
PlS	Diktaban, T	NY	332
PlS	Figlia, P	NJ	931
PlS	Forley, B	NY	332
PlS	Funt, D	NY	591
PlS	Gallagher, P	NY	591
PlS	Ganchi, P	NJ	931
PlS	Herbstman, R	NJ	880
PlS	Hirmand, H	NY	334
PlS	Hoffman, L	NY	334
PlS	Leach, T	NJ	855
PlS	Lipson, D	NJ	787
PlS	Pyo, D	NJ	919
PlS	Rafizadeh, F	NJ	919
PlS	Sasson, H	NY	592
PlS	Silberman, M	NY	592
PlS	Weinstein, L	NJ	919
Facial Surgery-Chin & Lip			
Oto	Slupchynskyj, O	NY	295
PlS	Zide, B	NY	340
Failure to Thrive			
PGe	McFarlane-Ferreira, Y	NY	482

Spec	Name	St	Pg
Falls in the Elderly			
Ger	Karp, A	NY	181
Ger	Malik, R	NY	419
Ger	Pantagis, S	NJ	758
Ger	Vaughan, M	NY	677
Ger	Wolf-Klein, G	NY	556
Family & Couples Therapy			
Psyc	Aronoff, M	NY	341
Psyc	Spitz, H	NY	352
Family Medicine			
FMed	Acosta, R	CT	984
FMed	Annabi, I	NY	671
FMed	Aponte, A	NY	627
FMed	Apuzzo, T	NY	671
FMed	Arcati, A	NY	552
FMed	Arcati, R	NY	552
FMed	Baltus, M	NY	627
FMed	Bauchman, G	NY	167
FMed	Beauchamp, D	NJ	755
FMed	Bello, M	NJ	755
FMed	Bernardo, S	NJ	888
FMed	Biagiotti, W	NY	416
FMed	Calman, N	NY	167
FMed	Capio, M	NJ	906
FMed	Capobianco, L	NY	552
FMed	Carniciu, S	NY	671
FMed	Cassotta, J	NJ	755
FMed	Catanese, V	NJ	889
FMed	Cigno, T	CT	984
FMed	Cirello, R	NJ	809
FMed	Coloka-Kump, R	NY	416
FMed	Cordero, E	NY	416
FMed	Corson, R	NJ	937
FMed	Delaney, B	NY	416
FMed	Di Scala, R	NY	503
FMed	Duchen, D	CT	984
FMed	Duggan, M	NY	416
FMed	Ebarb, R	NY	627
FMed	Edelstein, M	NY	552
FMed	Eisenstat, S	NJ	951
FMed	Elmaleh, R	NY	167
FMed	Falkoff, A	CT	984
FMed	Farrell, M	CT	984
FMed	Filiberto, C	CT	985
FMed	Firshein, R	NY	167
FMed	Fisher, G	NY	503
FMed	Fishkin, M	NY	627
FMed	Franzetti, C	NY	416
FMed	Frisoli, A	NJ	937
FMed	Giugliano, J	NY	627

Specialty & Special Expertise Index

Spec	Name	St	Pg
PCd	Parness, I	NY	305
PCd	Presti, S	NY	305
PCd	Ramaswamy, P	NY	481
PCd	Schiff, R	NY	582
PCd	Shapir, Y	NY	582
PCd	Shenoy, R	NY	432
PCd	Snyder, M	CT	1017
PCd	Tozzi, R	NJ	780
PCd	Vallone, A	NY	582

Fetal Surgery

MF	Al-Khan, A	NJ	764
MF	Chavez, M	NY	562

Fetal Therapy

CG	Santolaya, J	NJ	887
MF	Berkowitz, R	NY	210
MF	Eddleman, K	NY	211
MF	Rebarber, A	NY	212
MF	Terrone, D	NJ	815
MF	Vintzileos, A	NY	562

Fetal Ultrasound

MF	Kim, M	CT	997

Fetal Ultrasound/Obstetrical Imaging

MF	Al-Khan, A	NJ	764
MF	Lescale, K	NY	686
ObG	Dar, P	NY	427

Fetal Urology

Ped Uro	Connor, J	NJ	917
Ped Uro	Shapiro, E	NY	319

Fevers of Unknown Origin

IM	Fried, R	NY	201
IM	Lewin, S	NY	204
Inf	Cipriani, R	CT	990
Inf	Cunha, B	NY	558
Inf	Horowitz, H	NY	195
Inf	Sabetta, J	CT	990
Inf	Sensakovic, J	NJ	868
Inf	Smith, L	NJ	813
Inf	Youssef-Bessler, M	NJ	813
PInf	Arlievsky, N	NY	615
PInf	Boscamp, J	NJ	782
PInf	Larsen, J	NY	313
PInf	Rubin, L	NY	585
PInf	Sood, S	NY	585

Fibromuscular Dysplasia

N	Tuhrim, S	NY	243

Fibromyalgia

FMed	Podell, R	NJ	951
PM	Moqtaderi, F	NY	299
Rhu	Foto, F	NY	724
Rhu	Horowitz, M	NY	370
Rhu	Karp, S	CT	1028
Rhu	Lichtbroun, A	NJ	882
Rhu	Lipstein-Kresch, E	NY	598
Rhu	Meed, S	NY	371
Rhu	Pasik, D	NJ	920
Rhu	Patel, J	NY	491
Rhu	Salem, N	NJ	793
Rhu	Solitar, B	NY	373

Fine Needle Aspiration Biopsy

Path	Bhattacharyya, P	NJ	779

Fluid/Electrolyte Balance

Nep	Garrick, R	NY	691
Nep	Mailloux, L	NY	566

Food & Drug Allergy

A&I	Buchbinder, E	NY	122
A&I	Burton, D	NY	122
A&I	From, S	NJ	741
A&I	Kanumury, S	NJ	903
A&I	Lindner, P	CT	974
A&I	Shepherd, G	NY	123
A&I	Veksler-Offengenden, I	CT	974
PA&I	Pien, G	NJ	959
Rhu	Belostotsky, O	NY	369

Food Allergy

A&I	Applebaum, E	NJ	903
A&I	Backman, K	CT	973
A&I	Bassett, C	NY	121
A&I	Bernstein, L	NY	409
A&I	Bloom, K	CT	973
A&I	Blume, J	NJ	741
A&I	Bosso, J	NY	609
A&I	Corn, B	NY	122
A&I	Corriel, R	NY	539
A&I	Edwards, B	NY	539
A&I	Fox, J	NJ	935
A&I	Frieri, M	NY	539
A&I	Geller, D	NJ	741
A&I	Geraci-Ciardullo, K	NY	654
A&I	Grubman, S	NY	122

Spec	Name	St	Pg
A&I	Hemmers, P	CT	974
A&I	Jyonouchi, H	NJ	861
A&I	Kesarwala, H	NJ	861
A&I	Klein, N	NY	451
A&I	Klein, R	NJ	925
A&I	Krol, K	NJ	935
A&I	Lang, P	NY	539
A&I	LoGalbo, P	NY	609
A&I	Maloney, P	NY	654
A&I	Mayer, D	NY	621
A&I	Mendelson, J	NJ	948
A&I	Minikes, N	NJ	742
A&I	Novick, B	NY	539
A&I	Pollowitz, J	NY	655
A&I	Silverman, B	NY	451
A&I	Skripak, J	NJ	742
A&I	Slankard, M	NY	123
A&I	Southern, D	NJ	935
A&I	Tuerk-Mendelsohn, L	NY	655
Ge	Whelan, T	CT	987
PA&I	Barisciano, L	NJ	915
PA&I	Burstein, O	CT	1017
PA&I	Ehrlich, P	NY	302
PA&I	Herzog, R	NY	303
PA&I	Lester, M	CT	1017
PA&I	Sampson, H	NY	303
PA&I	Sicherer, S	NY	303
PA&I	Wang, J	NY	303
PGe	Birnbaum, A	NY	708
PGe	Chehade, M	NY	308
PGe	Glassman, M	CT	1018

Food Allergy & Eczema

A&I	Mumneh, N	NJ	862

Foot & Ankle Deformities

OrS	Berberian, W	NJ	775
OrS	Hoisington, S	NY	702
OrS	Kulsakdinun, C	NY	430

Foot & Ankle Surgery

HS	Ark, J	NJ	849
OrS	Bauman, P	NY	269
OrS	Buschmann, W	NY	702
OrS	Butler, M	NJ	941
OrS	Clain, M	CT	1011
OrS	Deland, J	NY	272
OrS	Elliott, A	NY	272
OrS	Ellis, S	NY	272
OrS	Hoisington, S	NY	702
OrS	Holder, J	NY	702
OrS	Hubbard, C	NY	276

Specialty & Special Expertise Index

Spec	Name	St	Pg
Gallbladder Disease			
Ge	Cooper, R	NY	170
Ge	Janec, E	NY	173
Ge	Spivack, J	CT	987
Ge	Stein, J	NY	179
Gallbladder Surgery			
S	Ahlborn, T	NJ	793
S	Colaco, R	NJ	964
S	Divino, C	NY	378
S	Kurtz, L	NY	601
S	Mandel, M	NJ	965
S	Petrotos, A	CT	1030
S	Schwartzman, A	NY	493
S	Sultan, R	NJ	842
Gastric & Esophageal Disorders			
Ge	Heier, S	NY	674
Gastroenterology			
Ge	Abelow, A	NY	417
Ge	Abemayor, E	NY	672
Ge	Accurso, C	NJ	937
Ge	Ackert, J	NY	168
Ge	Afridi, S	NJ	848
Ge	Antonelle, R	NY	672
Ge	Auerbach, M	NY	672
Ge	Augello, S	NY	503
Ge	Avezzano, E	NJ	756
Ge	Bains, Y	NJ	810
Ge	Baiocco, P	NY	168
Ge	Barenberg, D	CT	985
Ge	Barrison, A	NJ	952
Ge	Barro, J	CT	985
Ge	Bartolomeo, R	NY	553
Ge	Basuk, P	NY	169
Ge	Bednarek, K	NY	169
Ge	Ben-Menachem, T	NJ	952
Ge	Bernstein, B	NY	169
Ge	Bernstein, D	NY	553
Ge	Binns, J	NJ	889
Ge	Bleicher, R	NJ	926
Ge	Blumstein, M	NY	553
Ge	Bonheim, N	CT	985
Ge	Borcich, A	NY	169
Ge	Brandt, L	NY	417
Ge	Broussard, C	NJ	756
Ge	Brown, R	NY	169
Ge	Bruckstein, A	NY	523
Ge	Burns, B	CT	986
Ge	Buscaglia, J	NY	628

Spec	Name	St	Pg
Ge	Byfield, F	NY	672
Ge	Caccese, W	NY	553
Ge	Cantor, M	NY	169
Ge	Carr-Locke, D	NY	169
Ge	Cerulli, M	NY	553
Ge	Chang, P	NY	169
Ge	Chapman, M	NY	170
Ge	Chinitz, M	NY	672
Ge	Close, G	NY	673
Ge	Cohen, J	NY	170
Ge	Cohen, S	NY	170
Ge	Cohn, W	NY	628
Ge	Connor, B	NY	170
Ge	Cooper, R	NY	170
Ge	Dalena, J	NJ	907
Ge	De Antonio, J	NJ	848
Ge	DeLillo, A	NJ	756
Ge	Dettmer, R	CT	986
Ge	DeVito, B	NY	553
Ge	Dieterich, D	NY	170
Ge	Duva, J	NY	628
Ge	Dworkin, B	NY	673
Ge	Ehrlich, J	NY	673
Ge	Erber, W	NY	460
Ge	Eskreis, D	NY	553
Ge	Esposito, S	NY	504
Ge	Farber, C	NY	553
Ge	Farkas, J	NJ	926
Ge	Fath, R	NY	673
Ge	Faust, M	NY	170
Ge	Fazio, R	NY	523
Ge	Feit, D	NJ	952
Ge	Ferges, M	NJ	938
Ge	Ferran, E	NY	170
Ge	Field, B	NY	673
Ge	Fiest, T	NJ	889
Ge	Finegold, J	NY	673
Ge	Finkelstein, W	NJ	810
Ge	Fiske, S	NJ	810
Ge	Fochios, S	NY	171
Ge	Foong, A	NY	171
Ge	Frager, J	NY	417
Ge	Frank, M	NY	171
Ge	Freiman, H	NY	171
Ge	Fried, H	NJ	756
Ge	Friedlander, C	NY	171
Ge	Friedrich, I	NJ	756
Ge	Gaglio, P	NY	417
Ge	Gamss, J	NY	460
Ge	Geders, J	NY	673
Ge	Gendler, S	NY	673
Ge	Genn, D	NY	674
Ge	Gerdes, H	NY	171

Spec	Name	St	Pg
Ge	Gerson, C	NY	171
Ge	Gettenberg, G	NY	460
Ge	Glanzman, B	NY	628
Ge	Goldberg, M	NY	171
Ge	Goldblatt, R	NY	674
Ge	Goldblum, L	NY	554
Ge	Goldenberg, D	NJ	952
Ge	Goldfarb, J	NJ	756
Ge	Goldin, H	NY	172
Ge	Gould, P	NY	554
Ge	Green, P	NY	172
Ge	Greenberg, R	NY	554
Ge	Greenwald, D	NY	417
Ge	Grendell, J	NY	554
Ge	Gress, F	NY	172
Ge	Grossman, E	CT	986
Ge	Gruss, C	CT	986
Ge	Gupta, J	NY	460
Ge	Gupta, S	NY	417
Ge	Gutwein, I	NY	418
Ge	Haber, G	NY	172
Ge	Hahn, J	NJ	838
Ge	Hale, W	CT	986
Ge	Hammerman, H	NY	172
Ge	Harary, A	NY	172
Ge	Harooni, R	NY	504
Ge	Harrison, A	NY	629
Ge	Heier, S	NY	674
Ge	Hertan, H	NY	418
Ge	Hillman, D	NY	674
Ge	Ho, S	NY	418
Ge	Hodes, S	NJ	866
Ge	Iswara, K	NY	461
Ge	Itzkowitz, S	NY	172
Ge	Jacobson, I	NY	172
Ge	Jaffe, A	NY	674
Ge	Jaffin, B	NY	173
Ge	Janec, E	NY	173
Ge	Kahaleh, M	NY	173
Ge	Kahn, O	NY	674
Ge	Kairam, I	NY	173
Ge	Kapel, R	CT	986
Ge	Katz, H	NY	674
Ge	Katz, S	NY	554
Ge	Kavaler, L	NY	173
Ge	Kenny, R	NJ	810
Ge	Kerner, M	NJ	952
Ge	Khaghan, N	CT	986
Ge	Khan, A	NJ	952
Ge	Khodadadian, S	NY	173
Ge	Khokhar, A	NY	629
Ge	Kim, M	NY	173
Ge	Kim-Schluger, H	NY	173

Specialty & Special Expertise Index

Spec	Name	St	Pg
Ge	Dalena, J	NJ	907
Ge	Duva, J	NY	628
Ge	Ehrlich, J	NY	673
Ge	Farber, C	NY	553
Ge	Fazio, R	NY	523
Ge	Fiske, S	NJ	810
Ge	Freiman, H	NY	171
Ge	Friedrich, I	NJ	756
Ge	Genn, D	NY	674
Ge	Gettenberg, G	NY	460
Ge	Glanzman, B	NY	628
Ge	Goldenberg, D	NJ	952
Ge	Gould, P	NY	554
Ge	Greenwald, D	NY	417
Ge	Gruss, C	CT	986
Ge	Harary, A	NY	172
Ge	Harrison, A	NY	629
Ge	Jaffe, A	NY	674
Ge	Kahn, O	NY	674
Ge	Kerner, M	NJ	952
Ge	Klein, W	NJ	756
Ge	Kozicky, O	NY	674
Ge	Lambroza, A	NY	174
Ge	Lax, J	NY	174
Ge	Link, R	CT	987
Ge	Ludwig, S	NJ	889
Ge	Markowitz, D	NY	176
Ge	Mayer, I	NY	461
Ge	McKinley, M	NY	554
Ge	Meirowitz, R	NJ	848
Ge	Milman, P	NY	555
Ge	Mogan, G	NJ	810
Ge	Pitchumoni, C	NJ	866
Ge	Rieber, J	NY	177
Ge	Robilotti, J	NY	177
Ge	Romeu, J	NY	177
Ge	Rosner, B	NJ	848
Ge	Roston, A	NY	676
Ge	Rubin, K	NJ	757
Ge	Rubinoff, M	NJ	757
Ge	Sable, R	NY	418
Ge	Samach, M	NJ	907
Ge	Schmerin, M	NY	178
Ge	Schneider, L	NY	178
Ge	Schwartz, G	NY	555
Ge	Solny, M	NY	179
Ge	Sorra, T	NY	461
Ge	Starpoli, A	NY	179
Ge	Stein, L	NJ	907
Ge	Tempera, P	NJ	953
Ge	Traube, M	NY	179
Ge	Vogelman, A	NY	504
Ge	Weiss, R	NY	180

Spec	Name	St	Pg
Ge	Whelan, T	CT	987
Ge	Zingler, B	NJ	758
Ge	Zucker, I	NJ	758
Ge	Zwas, F	CT	988
NP	Katzenstein, M	NY	612
Oto	Lane, E	CT	1015
PGe	Benkov, K	NY	308
PGe	Berezin, S	NY	708
PGe	Breglio, K	NY	482
PGe	Chawla, A	NY	641
PGe	Glassman, M	CT	1018
PGe	Gold, D	NY	641
PGe	Halata, M	NY	708
PGe	Jelin, A	NY	482
PGe	Levy, J	NY	308
PGe	Markowitz, J	NY	584
PGe	Rabinowitz, S	NY	482
PGe	Schwarz, S	NY	482
PGe	Sunaryo, F	NJ	824
PGe	Weinstein, T	NY	584
PGe	Wetzler, G	NY	483
PPul	Marcus, M	NY	484
PS	Friedman, D	NJ	784
S	Borao, F	NJ	898
S	Carter, M	NJ	921
S	Pryor, A	NY	648
S	Salky, B	NY	383
S	Vine, A	NY	384
T&CS	Lee, P	NY	516

Gastrointestinal Cancer

Spec	Name	St	Pg
CRS	Pappas, D	NY	547
CRS	Sullivan, J	NY	547
Ge	Cohen, J	NY	170
Ge	Erber, W	NY	460
Ge	Gerdes, H	NY	171
Ge	Gettenberg, G	NY	460
Ge	Kim, M	NY	173
Ge	Kurtz, R	NY	174
Ge	Lebwohl, O	NY	175
Ge	Lightdale, C	NY	175
Ge	Mahal, P	NJ	952
Ge	Markowitz, A	NY	176
Ge	Robbins, D	NY	177
Ge	Romeu, J	NY	177
Ge	Sgouros, A	NY	676
Ge	Shike, M	NY	178
Ge	Wang, T	NY	179
Ge	Weissman, G	NY	555
Hem	Gruenstein, S	NY	190
Hem	Wisch, N	NY	193
Onc	Caron, P	NY	687

Spec	Name	St	Pg
Onc	Casper, E	NY	687
Onc	Cortes, E	NY	508
Onc	Fine, R	NY	215
Onc	Goldberg, J	NY	688
Onc	Grossbard, M	NY	216
Onc	Holcombe, R	NY	216
Onc	Jennis, A	NJ	765
Onc	Kelsen, D	NY	217
Onc	Kozuch, P	NY	218
Onc	Lebowicz, J	NY	469
Onc	Lichter, S	NY	469
Onc	Malamud, S	NY	218
Onc	Mehrotra, B	NY	564
Onc	Moriarty, D	NJ	955
Onc	Oster, M	NY	220
Onc	Provenzano, A	NY	688
Onc	Radovich, D	NJ	816
Onc	Ruggiero, J	NY	222
Onc	Sadan, S	NY	689
Onc	Saponara, E	NY	689
Onc	Sara, G	NY	222
Onc	Sharon, D	NJ	891
Onc	Siegel, A	NY	223
Onc	Stoopler, M	NY	224
Onc	Vinciguerra, V	NY	565
Path	Crawford, J	NY	580
RadRO	Fang, D	CT	1026
RadRO	Goodman, K	NY	361
RadRO	Hu, K	NY	361
RadRO	Wagman, R	NJ	829
S	Allen, P	NY	376
S	Berman, R	NY	377
S	Brower, S	NY	378
S	Chorost, M	NY	600
S	Datta, R	NY	600
S	Diehl, W	NJ	921
S	Dong, X	CT	1029
S	Karpeh, M	NY	380
S	Labow, D	NY	381
S	Libutti, S	NY	443
S	Lieberman, M	NY	381
S	Maheshwari, V	NJ	831
S	McCain, D	NJ	794
S	Michelassi, F	NY	381
S	Newman, E	NY	382
S	Paty, P	NY	382
S	Schwartz, M	NY	383
S	Talamini, M	NY	648
VIR	Weintraub, J	NY	402

Gastrointestinal Cancer & Rare

Specialty & Special Expertise Index

Specialty & Special Expertise Index

Specialty & Special Expertise Index

Specialty & Special Expertise Index

Spec	Name	St	Pg
ObG	Yarberry-Allen, P	NY	252

Gynecomastia

Spec	Name	St	Pg
EDM	Carlson, H	NY	626
PlS	Jacobs, E	NY	334

H

Hair & Nail Disorders

Spec	Name	St	Pg
D	Goldwasser, J	NY	665
D	Kopec, A	NJ	837

Hair Loss

Spec	Name	St	Pg
D	Bernstein, R	NY	146
D	Davis, J	NY	148
D	Oestreicher, M	CT	981

Hair Loss in Women

Spec	Name	St	Pg
D	Bernstein, R	NY	146

Hair Problems in Cancer Therapy

Spec	Name	St	Pg
D	Lacouture, M	NY	151

Hair Removal-Laser

Spec	Name	St	Pg
D	Brauner, G	NJ	750
D	Grodberg, M	NJ	751
D	Rosen, D	NY	414
D	Vogel, L	NY	155

Hair Restoration/Transplant

Spec	Name	St	Pg
D	Avram, M	NY	146
D	Bernstein, R	NY	146
D	Orentreich, D	NY	152
D	Unger, W	NY	155
D	Weiss, D	NJ	752
PlS	DiBernardo, B	NJ	827
PlS	Verga, M	NY	340

Hair Transplant-Robotic Surgery

Spec	Name	St	Pg
D	Bernstein, R	NY	146

Hand & Microvascular Surgery

Spec	Name	St	Pg
PlS	Chiu, D	NY	331

Hand & Upper Extremity

Surgery

Spec	Name	St	Pg
HS	Carlson, M	NY	186
HS	Catalano, L	NY	186
HS	Choueka, J	NY	463
HS	Ende, L	NJ	907
HS	Gluck, R	NY	556
HS	Hotchkiss, R	NY	187
HS	Ilan, D	NY	678
HS	Kavookjian, H	CT	989
HS	Kulick, R	NY	420
HS	Lunt, J	CT	989
HS	Magill, R	NY	678
HS	Pianka, G	NY	678
HS	Schefer, A	NY	678
HS	Shuren, N	NY	611
HS	Strauch, R	NY	188
HS	Tan, V	NJ	812
HS	Wang, E	NY	630
HS	Wolfe, S	NY	188
OrS	Lee, S	NY	277
OrS	Taitsman, J	NJ	854
OrS	Willis, A	NJ	914

Hand & Upper Extremity Tumors

Spec	Name	St	Pg
HS	Athanasian, E	NY	186

Hand & Wrist Injuries

Spec	Name	St	Pg
OrS	Altman, W	NJ	775
OrS	Grenis, M	NJ	853

Hand & Wrist Surgery

Spec	Name	St	Pg
HS	Beldner, S	NY	186
HS	Caligiuri, D	NY	505
HS	Dowdle, J	CT	989
HS	Fragner, P	NY	678
HS	Gilbert, R	NY	187
HS	Glickel, S	NY	187
HS	Paksima, N	NY	505
HS	Pianka, G	NY	678
HS	Rago, T	CT	989
HS	Stein, P	NY	557
OrS	Green, S	NY	274
OrS	Sampson, S	NY	639

Hand Injuries

Spec	Name	St	Pg
HS	Lenzo, S	NY	187

Hand Reconstruction

Spec	Name	St	Pg
HS	King, W	NY	187
HS	Lane, L	NY	556

Spec	Name	St	Pg
OrS	Hausman, M	NY	275
PlS	Kasabian, A	NY	591

Hand Surgery

Spec	Name	St	Pg
HS	Ark, J	NJ	849
HS	Ark, J	NJ	849
HS	Athanasian, E	NY	186
HS	Backe, H	CT	988
HS	Barron, O	NY	186
HS	Beldner, S	NY	186
HS	Boretz, R	NJ	938
HS	Botwinick, N	NY	186
HS	Caligiuri, D	NY	505
HS	Carlson, M	NY	186
HS	Catalano, L	NY	186
HS	Choueka, J	NY	463
HS	Coyle, M	NJ	938
HS	Crowe, J	CT	989
HS	Daluiski, A	NY	187
HS	DiGiovanni, J	CT	989
HS	Dowdle, J	CT	989
HS	Ende, L	NJ	907
HS	Fakharzadeh, F	NJ	759
HS	Fragner, P	NY	678
HS	Gilbert, R	NY	187
HS	Glickel, S	NY	187
HS	Gluck, R	NY	556
HS	Gurland, M	NJ	759
HS	Hotchkiss, R	NY	187
HS	Hurst, L	NY	630
HS	Ilan, D	NY	678
HS	Kamler, K	NY	505
HS	Kavookjian, H	CT	989
HS	Kim, R	NJ	759
HS	King, W	NY	187
HS	Kulick, R	NY	420
HS	Lane, L	NY	556
HS	Lee, S	NY	187
HS	Lenzo, S	NY	187
HS	Lisser, S	NJ	890
HS	Lunt, J	CT	989
HS	Magill, R	NY	678
HS	Melone, C	NY	188
HS	Miller, J	NJ	908
HS	Miller-Breslow, A	NJ	760
HS	Paksima, N	NY	505
HS	Pianka, G	NY	678
HS	Polatsch, D	NY	188
HS	Pruzansky, M	NY	188
HS	Rago, T	CT	989
HS	Raskin, K	NY	188
HS	Rettig, M	NY	188

Specialty & Special Expertise Index

Specialty & Special Expertise Index

Specialty & Special Expertise Index

Spec	Name	St	Pg
Onc	Lowenthal, D	NJ	955
Onc	Phillips, E	NY	688
Onc	Saponara, E	NY	689
Onc	Shypula, G	NJ	869

Hematology-Benign

Hem	Lederman, C	NY	679
Hem	Wolf, D	NY	193

Hematopathology

Path	Baer, R	CT	1016
Path	Orazi, A	NY	301

Hemochromatosis

IM	Cardiello, G	NJ	838

Hemolytic Uremic Syndrome

PNep	Benchimol, C	NY	314
PNep	Saland, J	NY	314
PNep	Trachtman, H	NY	314

Hemophilia

PHO	Diamond, S	NJ	781
PHO	Giardina, P	NY	310
PHO	Halpern, S	NJ	781

Hemorrhoids

CRS	Bernstein, M	NY	143
CRS	Brandeis, S	NY	143
CRS	Eisenstat, T	NJ	863
CRS	Gorfine, S	NY	143
CRS	Khaitov, S	NY	144
CRS	Krakovitz, E	NY	664
CRS	Penzer, J	NY	144
CRS	Waxenbaum, S	NJ	750
CRS	White, R	NJ	750
Ge	Foong, A	NY	171

Hepatobiliary Cancer

S	Melvin, W	NY	443

Hepatitis

FMed	Sadovsky, R	NY	460
Ge	Bernstein, D	NY	553
Ge	Brown, R	NY	169
Ge	Bruckstein, A	NY	523
Ge	Cantor, M	NY	169
Ge	Dieterich, D	NY	170
Ge	Feit, D	NJ	952
Ge	Freiman, H	NY	171

Spec	Name	St	Pg
Ge	Goldfarb, J	NJ	756
Ge	Gupta, J	NY	460
Ge	Gupta, S	NY	417
Ge	Gutwein, I	NY	418
Ge	Iswara, K	NY	461
Ge	Kimball, A	NY	173
Ge	Kotler, D	NY	174
Ge	Magun, A	NY	175
Ge	Margulis, S	NJ	757
Ge	May, L	NY	611
Ge	Miskovitz, P	NY	176
Ge	Nikias, G	NJ	757
Ge	Rahmin, M	NJ	757
Ge	Rubinoff, M	NJ	757
Ge	Schiano, T	NY	178
Ge	Sherman, A	NY	178
Ge	Sorra, T	NY	461
Ge	Stein, L	NJ	907
Ge	Wayne, P	NY	676
Ge	Wickremesinghe, P	NY	524
Ge	Zingler, B	NJ	758
Ge	Zinkin, N	NY	629
Ge	Zucker, I	NJ	758
Inf	Flood, M	NY	194
Inf	McMeeking, A	NY	196
Inf	Smith, L	NJ	813
Inf	Smith, S	NJ	813
PGe	Lobritto, S	NY	309
PGe	Rabinowitz, S	NY	482
PInf	Gershon, A	NY	313

Hepatitis B & C

Ge	Cerulli, M	NY	553
Ge	Gaglio, P	NY	417
Ge	Goldberg, M	NY	171
Ge	Kenny, R	NJ	810
Ge	Khokhar, A	NY	629
Ge	Lebovics, E	NY	675
Ge	Min, A	NY	176
Ge	Sable, R	NY	418
Ge	Stein, D	NY	418
Ge	Tobias, H	NY	179
Ge	Wolf, D	NY	676
Inf	Kocher, J	NJ	761
Inf	Nahass, R	NJ	938

Hepatitis C

Ge	Bonheim, N	CT	985
Ge	Borcich, A	NY	169
Ge	Geders, J	NY	673
Ge	Jacobson, I	NY	172
Ge	Kairam, I	NY	173

Spec	Name	St	Pg
Ge	Kim-Schluger, H	NY	173
Ge	Ludwig, S	NJ	889
Ge	Lustbader, I	NY	175
Ge	Panella, V	NJ	757
Ge	Pitchumoni, C	NJ	866
Ge	Samach, M	NJ	907
Ge	Zimbalist, E	NY	462
Inf	Roland, R	NJ	953
Inf	Slim, J	NJ	812

Hepatobiliary Surgery

S	Allendorf, J	NY	599
S	Attiyeh, F	NY	376
S	Bellemare, S	NY	442
S	Bellemare, S	NY	442
S	Coppa, G	NY	600
S	Emond, J	NY	379
S	Gumbs, A	NJ	964
S	Jarnagin, W	NY	380
S	Kinkhabwala, M	NY	442
S	Lieberman, M	NY	381
S	Miller, K	CT	1030
S	Schwartz, M	NY	383
S	Teperman, L	NY	384

Hereditary Angioedema

A&I	Fox, J	NJ	935
A&I	Mumneh, N	NJ	862
A&I	Southern, D	NJ	935

Hereditary Cancer

CG	Ostrer, H	NY	413
Ge	Itzkowitz, S	NY	172
Ge	Markowitz, A	NY	176
Onc	Nissenblatt, M	NJ	869
Onc	Toppmeyer, D	NJ	869

Hernia

CRS	Krakovitz, E	NY	664
PS	Lee, T	NY	642
PS	Midulla, P	NY	318
PS	Scriven, R	NY	642
PS	Velcek, F	NY	319
S	Adler, H	NY	491
S	Amory, S	NY	376
S	Auguste, L	NY	599
S	Barie, P	NY	377
S	Bernstein, M	NY	492
S	Borriello, R	NY	492
S	Budd, D	NJ	932
S	Carter, M	NJ	921

Specialty & Special Expertise Index

Spec	Name	St	Pg
S	Charny, C	NY	726
S	Chefitz, A	NY	726
S	Colaco, R	NJ	964
S	Divino, C	NY	378
S	Fleischer, L	NY	618
S	Geller, P	NY	379
S	Genato, R	NY	492
S	Grieco, M	NY	600
S	Halpern, D	NY	600
S	Hofstetter, S	NY	380
S	Jacob, B	NY	380
S	Jordan, L	NJ	883
S	Katz, L	NY	380
S	Kenler, A	CT	1030
S	Kimmelstiel, F	NY	380
S	Kurtz, L	NY	601
S	Lau, H	NY	726
S	Leitman, I	NY	381
S	Nitzberg, R	NJ	965
S	Nowak, E	NY	382
S	Pomp, A	NY	382
S	Raniolo, R	NY	727
S	Reiner, D	NY	601
S	Reiner, M	NY	382
S	Sas, N	NY	443
S	Slater, G	NY	384
S	Zoland, M	NY	385

Hernia-Sports

Spec	Name	St	Pg
S	Zoland, M	NY	385

Herpetic Neuralgia (Shingles)

Spec	Name	St	Pg
PM	Moqtaderi, F	NY	299

Hiccups-Chronic

Spec	Name	St	Pg
Pul	Stein, S	NY	360

Hip & Knee Reconstruction

Spec	Name	St	Pg
OrS	Bostrom, M	NY	270
OrS	Meislin, R	NY	279
OrS	Rieber, M	NJ	821
OrS	Simonson, B	NY	578

Hip & Knee Replacement

Spec	Name	St	Pg
OrS	Bavaro, N	NY	701
OrS	Dowling, W	NJ	913
OrS	Drucker, D	NY	527
OrS	Ennis, F	CT	1012
OrS	Harwin, S	NY	275
OrS	Innella, R	NJ	958
OrS	Mendes, J	NJ	821

Spec	Name	St	Pg
OrS	Miyasaka, K	NY	279
OrS	Morgan, D	NY	479
OrS	Nocek, D	CT	1013
OrS	Padgett, D	NY	280
OrS	Parks, M	NY	280
OrS	Rieber, M	NJ	821
OrS	Rodriguez, J	NY	282
OrS	Salzer, R	NJ	777
OrS	Sarokhan, A	NJ	958
OrS	Simonson, B	NY	578
OrS	Stuchin, S	NY	284
OrS	Taffet, B	NJ	914
OrS	Zelicof, S	NY	704

Hip & Knee Replacement in Bone Tumors

Spec	Name	St	Pg
OrS	Healey, J	NY	275

Hip & Knee Surgery

Spec	Name	St	Pg
OrS	Gurtowski, J	NY	639
OrS	Kayal, R	NJ	776
OrS	Nercessian, O	NY	280

Hip Disorders & Dysplasia

Spec	Name	St	Pg
OrS	Kiernan, H	NY	276

Hip Disorders-Pediatric

Spec	Name	St	Pg
OrS	Rieger, M	NJ	913
OrS	Roye, D	NY	282

Hip Replacement

Spec	Name	St	Pg
OrS	Alexiades, M	NY	269
OrS	Asnis, S	NY	575
OrS	Bindelglass, D	CT	1010
OrS	Boone, P	CT	1011
OrS	Bronson, M	NY	270
OrS	Burak, C	NY	701
OrS	Cobelli, N	NY	429
OrS	Cornell, C	NY	271
OrS	D'Amico, J	CT	1011
OrS	Gutowski, W	NJ	853
OrS	Hartzband, M	NJ	776
OrS	Hughes, P	CT	1012
OrS	Kavanagh, B	CT	1012
OrS	Macaulay, W	NY	278
OrS	Mani, J	NY	478
OrS	Mc Inerney, V	NJ	929
OrS	Pellicci, P	NY	281
OrS	Rich, D	NY	577
OrS	Salvati, E	NY	282
OrS	Sculco, T	NY	284

Spec	Name	St	Pg
OrS	Seebacher, J	NY	703
OrS	Seideman, B	NY	577
OrS	Small, R	NY	704
OrS	Su, E	NY	284
OrS	Touliopoulos, S	NY	511
OrS	Walsh, R	NY	479
OrS	Windsor, R	NY	286

Hip Replacement & Revision

Spec	Name	St	Pg
OrS	Austin, K	NY	614
OrS	Bostrom, M	NY	270
OrS	Buly, R	NY	271
OrS	Mayman, D	NY	278
OrS	Meere, P	NY	279
OrS	Moucha, C	NY	279
OrS	Nercessian, O	NY	280
OrS	Ranawat, A	NY	281
OrS	Westrich, G	NY	285

Hip Replacement-Young Adults

Spec	Name	St	Pg
OrS	Mayman, D	NY	278
OrS	Pellicci, P	NY	281

Hip Resurfacing

Spec	Name	St	Pg
OrS	Bharam, S	NY	270
OrS	Dowling, W	NJ	913
OrS	Stuchin, S	NY	284
OrS	Su, E	NY	284
OrS	Taffet, B	NJ	914

Hip Surgery

Spec	Name	St	Pg
OrS	Adler, E	NY	269
OrS	Bavaro, N	NY	701
OrS	Bharam, S	NY	270
OrS	Figgie, M	NY	273
OrS	Henshaw, D	CT	1012
OrS	Kelly, B	NY	276
OrS	Kipnis, J	NY	576
OrS	Rose, D	NY	282
OrS	Sink, E	NY	284

Hirsutism (Excessive Body Hair)

Spec	Name	St	Pg
EDM	Balkin, M	NY	626

HIV

Spec	Name	St	Pg
Inf	Berkey, P	NY	679
Inf	Fernando, R	NY	631
Inf	Flood, M	NY	194
Inf	Klein, N	NY	558
Inf	Lederman, J	NY	679
Inf	Nahass, R	NJ	938

Specialty & Special Expertise Index

Spec	Name	St	Pg
Plnf	Arlievsky, N	NY	615

HIV & Blood Transfusions
Inf	Wallach, F	NY	198

HIV & Hepatitis Co-Infection
Ge	Borcich, A	NY	169
Inf	McGowan, J	NY	558

HIV in Adolescents
AM	Rudy, B	NY	121

HIV in Pregnancy
Inf	McGowan, J	NY	558

HIV Psychiatry
Psyc	Goldenberg, D	NY	345

HIV Related Kidney Disease
Nep	Singhal, P	NY	566
Nep	Winston, J	NY	228

HIV Retinitis
Oph	El Baba, F	NY	637

HIV-Related Skin Disorders
D	Roth, J	NY	154

HIV/AIDS
Inf	Glesby, M	NY	194

Hives
A&I	Bell, J	CT	973
A&I	Blum, J	NJ	861
A&I	Buchbinder, E	NY	122
A&I	Harish, Z	NJ	741
A&I	Lusman, P	NY	621
A&I	Mechanic, L	NY	654
A&I	Novick, B	NY	539
A&I	Pollowitz, J	NY	655
A&I	Vassallo, M	NY	452
A&I	Weinstock, G	NY	540

Hodgkin's Disease Consultation
Onc	Offit, K	NY	220

Hodgkin's Lymphoma
Hem	Boyd, D	CT	989

Hem	Isola, L	NY	190
Hem	Kolitz, J	NY	557
Onc	Coleman, M	NY	214
Onc	Decter, J	NY	214
Onc	Goy, A	NJ	765
Onc	Horwitz, S	NY	217
Onc	Moskowitz, C	NY	219
Onc	O'Connor, O	NY	219
Onc	Portlock, C	NY	221
Onc	Straus, D	NY	224
PHO	Halpern, S	NJ	781
PHO	Trippett, T	NY	312
RadRO	Yahalom, J	NY	363

Hormonal Disorders
EDM	Goldenberg, A	NY	627
EDM	Wexler, C	NY	627
ObG	Ayoub, T	CT	1004
ObG	Jacobson, E	CT	1005
RE	Hurwitz, J	CT	1027
RE	Stein, D	NY	367

Hospice & Palliative Medicine
H & PM	Chai, E	NY	193
H & PM	Edwards, W	NY	193
H & PM	Glare, P	NY	193
H & PM	Hallarman, L	NY	630
H & PM	Pan, C	NY	506
H & PM	Popp, B	NY	464
H & PM	Tickoo, R	NY	193

Hospital Acquired Infections
Inf	Cicogna, C	NJ	761
Inf	Corpuz, M	NY	421
Inf	Hammer, G	NY	195
Inf	Kesh, S	NY	679
Inf	Louie, E	NY	195
Inf	McLeod, G	CT	990
Inf	Mullen, M	NY	196
Inf	Nash, B	NY	631
Inf	Press, R	NY	197
Inf	Scully, B	NY	197
Inf	Simberkoff, M	NY	197
Inf	Slim, J	NJ	812
Inf	Vielemeyer, O	NY	198

Inf	Yee, A	CT	991
Plnf	Arlievsky, N	NY	615
Plnf	Litman, N	NY	434

House Calls
IM	Mulvehill, J	NY	205
IM	Primas, R	NY	206

HPV-Human Papilloma Virus
GO	Einstein, M	NY	419
GO	Zakashansky, K	NY	186
ObG	Gruss, L	NY	248
ObG	Levey, J	NJ	940
ObG	Levine, R	NY	250
ObG	Ponterio, J	NY	527
ObG	Schechter, M	CT	1006
ObG	Steer, R	NJ	912
Plnf	Herold, B	NY	434

HPV-Human Papillomavirus
ObG	Sarabanchong, V	NY	510

Huntington's Disease
N	Butler, J	CT	1002
N	Louis, E	CT	239
N	Marder, K	NY	239

Hydrocephalus
NS	Cardoso, E	NY	471
NS	Feldstein, N	NY	230
NS	McKhann, G	NY	231
NS	Mittler, M	NY	567
NS	Rekate, H	NY	567

Hydrocephalus-Adult
NS	Goodman, R	NY	230

Hydronephrosis
Ped Uro	Koo, H	NJ	785
Ped Uro	Wasnick, R	NY	642

Hyperbaric Medicine
S	Yurt, R	NY	385

Hyperhidrosis-Palmar
T&CS	Gorenstein, L	NY	387
T&CS	Keller, S	NY	444

Hyperhidrosis/Axillary

Specialty & Special Expertise Index

Spec	Name	St	Pg
Curettage			
D	Vine, J	NJ	864
Hypertension			
Cv	Akinboboye, O	NY	500
Cv	Anto, M	NY	541
Cv	Augenbraun, C	CT	975
Cv	Berkowitz, W	NJ	744
Cv	Blake, J	NY	125
Cv	Cohen, M	NY	126
Cv	Cole, W	NY	126
Cv	Conroy, D	NJ	744
Cv	Cooper, J	NY	656
Cv	Criscito, M	NJ	805
Cv	D'Agostino, R	NY	541
Cv	Deutsch, A	NY	127
Cv	Dilmanian, H	NY	453
Cv	DiVagno, L	NJ	744
Cv	Dubois, N	NY	127
Cv	Engel, D	NY	127
Cv	Fass, A	NY	656
Cv	Friedman, H	NY	453
Cv	Frishman, W	NY	657
Cv	Gelles, J	NY	453
Cv	Gleckel, L	NY	542
Cv	Green, J	CT	976
Cv	Inra, L	NY	129
Cv	Kamen, M	NY	129
Cv	Kerwin, T	NY	500
Cv	Kostis, J	NJ	862
Cv	Kulkarni, R	NJ	936
Cv	Lense, L	NY	622
Cv	Lucariello, R	NY	411
Cv	Masri, B	NY	130
Cv	Matilsky, M	NY	623
Cv	Mellow, E	NY	131
Cv	Mermelstein, E	NJ	862
Cv	Miller, D	NY	131
Cv	Mintz, G	NY	544
Cv	Mondrow, D	NJ	862
Cv	Mueller, R	NY	131
Cv	Pumill, R	NJ	747
Cv	Raska, K	NJ	904
Cv	Reichstein, R	NY	132
Cv	Romanello, P	NY	132
Cv	Schanzer, R	NJ	862
Cv	Schuster, E	CT	978
Cv	Siegel, S	NY	134
Cv	Siepser, S	NJ	925
Cv	Silver, M	NY	660
Cv	Sklaroff, H	NY	134
Cv	Stroh, J	NJ	936
Cv	Traube, C	NY	455
Cv	Unger, A	NY	135
Cv	Wein, P	NY	455
Cv	Weintraub, H	NY	136
Cv	Weiss, E	NJ	925
Cv	Williams, M	NJ	748
Cv	Wolk, M	NY	136
Cv	Zimmerman, F	NY	661
FMed	Catanese, V	NJ	889
FMed	Eisenstat, S	NJ	951
FMed	Fisher, G	NY	503
FMed	Ibelli, V	NY	610
FMed	Krotowski, M	NY	459
FMed	Levy, A	NY	168
FMed	Molnar, T	NY	503
FMed	Moynihan, B	NY	552
FMed	Roth, A	NY	503
Ger	Bullock, R	NJ	867
Ger	Villongco, R	NJ	759
IM	Altbaum, R	CT	991
IM	Alterman, L	NJ	954
IM	Bell, K	NJ	938
IM	Blum, D	NY	506
IM	Blumberg, J	CT	991
IM	Brewer, M	NY	506
IM	Butt, A	NY	465
IM	Cardiello, G	NJ	838
IM	Carosella, C	NY	681
IM	Case, D	NY	199
IM	Constantiner, A	NY	200
IM	Cusumano, S	NY	559
IM	Dhalla, S	NY	200
IM	Ditchek, A	NY	465
IM	Dreyer, N	CT	992
IM	Fazio, N	NY	682
IM	Federbush, R	NY	559
IM	Federman, A	NY	200
IM	Feldman, J	NJ	954
IM	Fennell, G	CT	992
IM	Greaney, E	NY	202
IM	Gribbon, J	NJ	813
IM	Kaiser, S	NY	466
IM	Logan, B	NY	205
IM	Mann, S	NY	205
IM	Masterson, R	NJ	891
IM	Mayer, D	CT	993
IM	Melman, M	NY	683
IM	Minkowitz, S	NY	205
IM	Mutterperl, M	NJ	839
IM	Pecker, M	NY	206
IM	Randazzo, J	NJ	908
IM	Rie, J	NY	684
IM	Rosch, E	NY	684
IM	Rubenstein, J	NY	560
IM	Rucker, S	NY	560
IM	Scaduto, P	NJ	908
IM	Sherman, I	NY	206
IM	Solomon, G	NY	207
IM	Soltren, R	NY	684
IM	Tal, K	NY	467
IM	Teffera, F	NY	422
IM	Underberg, J	NY	207
IM	Volpe, A	NJ	763
IM	Walsh, F	CT	994
IM	Weinstein, M	NY	561
IM	Witt, M	NY	208
IM	Zeale, P	NY	208
Nep	Adler, S	NY	690
Nep	Ames, R	NY	226
Nep	August, P	NY	226
Nep	Balsam, L	NY	565
Nep	Blumenfeld, J	NY	226
Nep	Brown, E	CT	1000
Nep	Buzzeo, L	NY	690
Nep	Byrd, L	NJ	910
Nep	Charytan, C	NY	509
Nep	Chou, S	NY	469
Nep	Coco, M	NY	424
Nep	Covit, A	NJ	870
Nep	Croll, J	NY	424
Nep	DeFabritus, A	NY	226
Nep	DeVita, M	NY	226
Nep	Fein, D	NJ	768
Nep	Feintzeig, I	CT	1001
Nep	Fine, P	NJ	910
Nep	Galler, M	NY	509
Nep	Gardenswartz, M	NY	226
Nep	Garrick, R	NY	691
Nep	Goldstein, C	NJ	955
Nep	Gorkin, J	NY	424
Nep	Grasso, M	NJ	817
Nep	Haratz, A	NJ	892
Nep	Hines, W	CT	1001
Nep	Hunt, W	CT	1001
Nep	Kabis, S	NJ	940
Nep	Kim, T	NY	227
Nep	Kleiner, M	NY	526
Nep	Kozin, A	NY	612
Nep	Kozlowski, J	NJ	768
Nep	Levin, D	NJ	768
Nep	Lipner, H	NY	470
Nep	Liu, D	NY	227
Nep	Lynn, R	NY	425
Nep	Mailloux, L	NY	566
Nep	Manning, E	NJ	892
Nep	Mattana, J	NY	566

Specialty & Special Expertise Index

Specialty & Special Expertise Index

Specialty & Special Expertise Index

Spec	Name	St	Pg
CRS	Lee, S	NY	144
CRS	McClane, J	CT	980
CRS	Moskowitz, R	NJ	905
CRS	Nizin, J	NJ	750
CRS	Penzer, J	NY	144
CRS	Rezac, C	NJ	863
CRS	Rivadeneira, D	NY	547
CRS	Sonoda, T	NY	144
CRS	Tarantino, D	NJ	807
CRS	Zinkin, L	NJ	864
Ge	Abemayor, E	NY	672
Ge	Bains, Y	NJ	810
Ge	Baiocco, P	NY	168
Ge	Bartolomeo, R	NY	553
Ge	Bleicher, R	NJ	926
Ge	Blumstein, M	NY	553
Ge	Bonheim, N	CT	985
Ge	Brandt, L	NY	417
Ge	Burns, B	CT	986
Ge	Cerulli, M	NY	553
Ge	Chinitz, M	NY	672
Ge	Dalena, J	NJ	907
Ge	DeLillo, A	NJ	756
Ge	Dworkin, B	NY	673
Ge	Finkelstein, W	NJ	810
Ge	Friedrich, I	NJ	756
Ge	Goldblatt, R	NY	674
Ge	Greenberg, R	NY	554
Ge	Grossman, E	CT	986
Ge	Gruss, C	CT	986
Ge	Itzkowitz, S	NY	172
Ge	Jacobson, I	NY	172
Ge	Jaffin, B	NY	173
Ge	Kahn, O	NY	674
Ge	Katz, S	NY	554
Ge	Kerner, M	NJ	952
Ge	Kornbluth, A	NY	174
Ge	Kressner, M	NY	675
Ge	Landau, A	CT	986
Ge	Landau, S	NY	675
Ge	Link, R	CT	987
Ge	Liss, M	NY	675
Ge	Ludwig, S	NJ	889
Ge	Maizel, B	NY	461
Ge	Margulis, S	NJ	757
Ge	Meirowitz, R	NJ	848
Ge	Milman, P	NY	555
Ge	Mogan, G	NJ	810
Ge	Nagler, J	NY	176
Ge	Nussbaum, M	NY	504
Ge	Panella, V	NJ	757
Ge	Ramgopal, M	NY	504
Ge	Rieber, J	NY	177

Spec	Name	St	Pg
Ge	Roston, A	NY	676
Ge	Roth, J	NJ	757
Ge	Rubin, K	NJ	757
Ge	Rubin, M	NY	177
Ge	Sable, R	NY	418
Ge	Salik, J	NY	178
Ge	Scherl, E	NY	178
Ge	Sgouros, A	NY	676
Ge	Shapiro, N	NY	676
Ge	Spielberg, A	NY	629
Ge	Spinnell, M	NJ	758
Ge	Spira, R	NJ	811
Ge	Taffet, S	NY	676
Ge	Taubin, H	CT	987
Ge	Turtel, P	NJ	889
Ge	Weissman, G	NY	555
Ge	Zimbalist, E	NY	462
PGe	Berezin, S	NY	708
PGe	Chawla, A	NY	641
PGe	Halata, M	NY	708
PGe	Kazlow, P	NY	308
PGe	Koniaris, S	NJ	877
PGe	Levine, J	NY	308
PGe	McFarlane-Ferreira, Y	NY	482
PGe	Mencin, A	NY	309
PGe	Moustafellos, E	NJ	781
PGe	Rabinowitz, S	NY	482
PGe	Schwarz, S	NY	482
PGe	Sunaryo, F	NJ	824
S	Rolandelli, R	NJ	921
S	Slater, G	NY	384

Inflammatory Bowel Disease/Crohn's

Spec	Name	St	Pg
CRS	Khaitov, S	NY	144
CRS	Milsom, J	NY	144
CRS	Procaccino, J	NY	547
Ge	Chapman, M	NY	170
Ge	Erber, W	NY	460
Ge	Finegold, J	NY	673
Ge	Frank, M	NY	171
Ge	Goldenberg, D	NJ	952
Ge	Goldin, H	NY	172
Ge	Gutwein, I	NY	418
Ge	Kenny, R	NJ	810
Ge	Kimball, A	NY	173
Ge	Mauer, K	CT	987
Ge	Mayer, I	NY	461
Ge	Milano, A	NY	176
Ge	Ullman, T	NY	179
Ge	Weg, A	NY	504
Ge	Wickremesinghe, P	NY	524

Spec	Name	St	Pg
IM	Klein, N	CT	993
PGe	Benkov, K	NY	308
PGe	Birnbaum, A	NY	708
PGe	Glassman, M	CT	1018
PGe	Jeshion, W	NJ	781
PGe	Kessler, B	NY	641
PGe	Levy, J	NY	308
PGe	Markowitz, J	NY	584
PGe	Rosh, J	NJ	916
PGe	Thompson, J	NY	433
PGe	Weinstein, T	NY	584
PGe	Wetzler, G	NY	483
PS	Dolgin, S	NY	586

Inflammatory Muscle Disease

Spec	Name	St	Pg
Rhu	Guma, M	NJ	792

Inherited Disorders

Spec	Name	St	Pg
CG	Adams, D	NJ	905
CG	Pedro, H	NJ	749

Inherited Metabolic Disorders

Spec	Name	St	Pg
CG	Desnick, R	NY	142
CG	Lichter-Konecki, U	NY	142

Insect Allergies

Spec	Name	St	Pg
A&I	Bell, J	CT	973
A&I	Chernack, W	NJ	903
A&I	Geraci-Ciardullo, K	NY	654
A&I	Goldman, N	NY	654
A&I	Krol, K	NJ	935
A&I	Lang, P	NY	539
A&I	Leibner, D	NJ	861
A&I	Shepherd, G	NY	123
A&I	Sher, E	NJ	887
A&I	Sicklick, M	NY	540

Integrative Medicine

Spec	Name	St	Pg
FMed	Firshein, R	NY	167
IM	Merrell, W	NY	205

Intensity Modulated Radiotherapy (IMRT)

Spec	Name	St	Pg
RadRO	Chadha, M	NY	360
RadRO	Chao, K	NY	361
RadRO	Cooper, J	NY	489
RadRO	Haas, J	NY	597
RadRO	Katz, A	NY	514
RadRO	Lee, N	NY	362
RadRO	Potters, L	NY	597
RadRO	Rosenbaum, A	NY	363

Specialty & Special Expertise Index

Spec	Name	St	Pg
RadRO	Sherr, D	NY	490
RadRO	Spera, J	CT	1027
RadRO	Stock, R	NY	363

Internal Medicine

Spec	Name	St	Pg
IM	Abdoo, R	NY	680
IM	Abenavoli, T	NY	680
IM	Ades, J	NY	680
IM	Alpert, B	NY	681
IM	Altbaum, R	CT	991
IM	Alterman, L	NJ	954
IM	Altholz, J	NY	681
IM	Amin, M	NY	506
IM	Amsterdam, A	NY	198
IM	Andersen, M	NY	681
IM	Aronne, L	NY	198
IM	Aversa, A	NY	681
IM	Babbar, R	NY	198
IM	Balot, B	NY	631
IM	Barley, C	NY	198
IM	Baskin, D	NY	198
IM	Baum, D	CT	991
IM	Behm, D	NY	465
IM	Bell, K	NJ	938
IM	Bennett, S	NY	681
IM	Beran, N	NY	681
IM	Berbari, N	NY	559
IM	Berger, J	NY	559
IM	Berman, E	CT	991
IM	Beyda, A	NY	506
IM	Bharathan, T	NY	465
IM	Bivona, J	CT	991
IM	Blum, D	NY	506
IM	Blumberg, J	CT	991
IM	Bonaventura, L	NJ	938
IM	Boxer, W	NY	198
IM	Bregman, Z	NY	199
IM	Brewer, M	NY	506
IM	Brunnquell, S	NJ	762
IM	Bruno, P	NY	199
IM	Bush, M	NY	199
IM	Butt, A	NY	465
IM	Cacciola, T	NJ	762
IM	Cardiello, G	NJ	838
IM	Carosella, C	NY	681
IM	Carson, J	NJ	868
IM	Case, D	NY	199
IM	Cassidy, B	NJ	869
IM	Catanzaro, D	NJ	939
IM	Charap, M	NY	199
IM	Charap, P	NY	199
IM	Chrisanderson, D	NJ	813

Spec	Name	St	Pg
IM	Cohen, B	NY	465
IM	Cohen, R	NY	199
IM	Cohen, R	NY	199
IM	Cohn, S	NY	199
IM	Colangelo, D	NY	681
IM	Collum, R	NJ	908
IM	Condo, D	NJ	839
IM	Constantiner, A	NY	200
IM	Corapi, M	NY	559
IM	Corazza, D	NJ	849
IM	Costanzo, J	CT	991
IM	Couture, C	CT	991
IM	Covey, A	NY	631
IM	Croen, K	NY	681
IM	Cunningham-Rundles, W	NY	NY 200
IM	Cusumano, S	NY	559
IM	D'Ascanio, A	NY	681
IM	De Giacomo, F	NJ	927
IM	Dechiario, A	NY	200
IM	Dedousis, J	NJ	839
IM	DeMartin, R	NJ	890
IM	Dennett, R	NY	682
IM	DeSilva, D	NJ	869
IM	Dhalla, S	NY	200
IM	DiGiacomo, W	NJ	954
IM	Ditchek, A	NY	465
IM	Dolinsky, J	NY	200
IM	Dreyer, N	CT	992
IM	Edelmann, C	CT	992
IM	Edelson, D	NY	559
IM	Ehrlich, M	NY	200
IM	Ellis, E	NY	465
IM	Engelhardt, M	NY	682
IM	Ennis, D	NY	682
IM	Ernst, J	NY	422
IM	Etingin, O	NY	200
IM	Fafalak, R	NY	200
IM	Fazio, N	NY	682
IM	Federbush, R	NY	559
IM	Federman, A	NY	200
IM	Feldman, J	NJ	954
IM	Feltheimer, S	NY	201
IM	Fennell, G	CT	992
IM	Fenster, M	NY	682
IM	Ferrante, M	NJ	939
IM	Ferrara, L	NY	611
IM	Feuer, M	NY	201
IM	Fiedler, R	NY	201
IM	Fiorentino, T	NY	682
IM	Fisher, L	NY	201
IM	Fisher, S	CT	992
IM	Flanzman, S	NJ	762

Spec	Name	St	Pg
IM	Fojas, A	NY	422
IM	Fortunato, F	NJ	813
IM	Fried, R	NY	201
IM	Friedling, S	NY	631
IM	Friedman, J	NY	201
IM	Fukilman, O	NY	507
IM	Gafanovich, M	NY	201
IM	Gajdos, R	NJ	927
IM	Galland, L	NY	201
IM	Gambarin, B	NY	465
IM	Gamble, S	CT	992
IM	Gazzara, P	NY	524
IM	Gelbard, S	NY	201
IM	Gelberg, B	NY	559
IM	German, H	NY	631
IM	Giangola, J	NJ	762
IM	Glassman, C	NY	611
IM	Glaubiger, C	NJ	762
IM	Glazer, S	CT	992
IM	Glickstein, S	NY	682
IM	Glowacki, J	NJ	890
IM	Gold, J	NJ	927
IM	Golden, F	NY	202
IM	Goldin, D	NY	202
IM	Goldman, J	NY	682
IM	Goldstein, P	NY	202
IM	Goodgold, A	NJ	954
IM	Goodman, M	NY	559
IM	Gorski, L	NY	560
IM	Gottridge, J	NY	560
IM	Granet, K	NJ	890
IM	Greaney, E	NY	202
IM	Gribbon, J	NJ	813
IM	Gross, J	NY	682
IM	Grunzweig, M	NY	465
IM	Haber, S	NY	202
IM	Hallal, E	NY	631
IM	Halperin, I	NY	202
IM	Handelsman, R	NY	611
IM	Harman, J	NJ	849
IM	Hart, C	NY	202
IM	Hasapis, P	CT	992
IM	Hauptman, A	NY	202
IM	Herzog, D	NY	682
IM	Hoffman, E	NY	202
IM	Hoffman, P	CT	992
IM	Hopkins, A	NY	683
IM	Horbar, G	NY	203
IM	Horn, J	CT	992
IM	Horovitz, L	NY	203
IM	Hotchkiss, E	NY	560
IM	Hsuih, T	NY	466
IM	Hundert, M	NY	507

Specialty & Special Expertise Index

Spec	Name	St	Pg	Spec	Name	St	Pg	Spec	Name	St	Pg
IM	Hyman, J	NY	466	IM	Messana, I	NY	507	IM	Scibetta, M	NJ	763
IM	Israel, S	CT	992	IM	Mickley, D	CT	993	IM	Selwyn, P	NY	422
IM	Jacobowitz, M	NY	683	IM	Mickley, S	CT	993	IM	Serin, C	CT	994
IM	Jawetz, H	NJ	927	IM	Miguel, E	NJ	763	IM	Sherman, F	NY	467
IM	Joseph, J	NY	507	IM	Miner, C	CT	993	IM	Sherman, I	NY	206
IM	Joy, M	NY	466	IM	Minkowitz, S	NY	205	IM	Siegel, M	NY	207
IM	Kaiser, S	NY	466	IM	Morledge, L	NY	205	IM	Silva, W	NJ	909
IM	Kaminsky, D	NY	203	IM	Morrison, D	NY	684	IM	Silverman, D	NY	207
IM	Kapoor, S	NY	683	IM	Mulvehill, J	NY	205	IM	Silvershein, D	NY	207
IM	Karmen, C	NY	683	IM	Murray, S	NJ	850	IM	Simon, L	NY	632
IM	Karol, N	CT	993	IM	Mutterperl, M	NJ	839	IM	Simon, T	NY	467
IM	Katzenelenbogen, M	NY	466	IM	Neiman, D	NJ	939	IM	Singer, M	NY	632
IM	Kennedy, J	NY	203	IM	Nelson, D	NY	205	IM	Slogoff, F	CT	994
IM	Kennish, A	NY	203	IM	Newitz, D	NY	560	IM	Smerling, N	CT	994
IM	Kent, J	NY	203	IM	Olichney, J	NY	206	IM	Smith, S	NY	207
IM	Klein, N	CT	993	IM	Olin, C	CT	993	IM	Solomon, G	NY	207
IM	Klein, W	NY	560	IM	Oppenheimer, J	NY	632	IM	Soltren, R	NY	684
IM	Knoepflmacher, P	NY	203	IM	Orsher, S	NY	206	IM	Somogyi, A	NY	507
IM	Kozel, J	NJ	839	IM	Osnoss, K	CT	993	IM	Spano, F	CT	994
IM	Krieger, S	NY	683	IM	Pappas, S	NY	684	IM	Spero, M	NY	207
IM	Kubersky, S	NY	683	IM	Pasquale, J	NY	507	IM	Stallone, J	NY	632
IM	Kurth, R	NY	203	IM	Pecker, M	NY	206	IM	Starke, C	NY	684
IM	Kushner, E	NJ	762	IM	Pelavin, M	NJ	763	IM	Storch, K	NJ	909
IM	Lalli, C	NY	632	IM	Peterson, S	NY	466	IM	Strange, T	NY	524
IM	Lamm, S	NY	203	IM	Phillips, S	CT	993	IM	Swiderski, D	NY	422
IM	Lan, V	NJ	762	IM	Pomerantz, D	NY	684	IM	Tal, A	NY	467
IM	Lauricella, J	NJ	762	IM	Porder, J	NY	206	IM	Tang, D	NY	684
IM	Lechner, M	NY	683	IM	Primas, R	NY	206	IM	Taubman, L	NY	560
IM	Legato, M	NY	204	IM	Puglisi, J	CT	993	IM	Tay, S	NY	207
IM	Leonard, M	NY	204	IM	Radin, A	CT	994	IM	Teffera, F	NY	422
IM	Leong, P	NY	560	IM	Randazzo, J	NJ	908	IM	Thomas, B	CT	994
IM	Levey, R	NY	466	IM	Raska, A	NJ	908	IM	Timpone, L	NY	561
IM	Lewin, M	NY	204	IM	Ratner, I	NY	467	IM	Troy, C	CT	994
IM	Lewin, N	NY	204	IM	Ridge, G	NY	684	IM	Turro, J	NY	685
IM	Lewin, S	NY	204	IM	Rie, J	NY	684	IM	Underberg, J	NY	207
IM	Liguori, M	NY	204	IM	Rieger, J	NY	206	IM	Vadel, S	CT	994
IM	Lipton, M	NY	204	IM	Romano, R	NY	632	IM	Valinoti, A	NJ	763
IM	Liu, G	NY	204	IM	Rommer, J	NJ	813	IM	Vega, A	NY	207
IM	Lodge, H	NY	205	IM	Rosch, E	NY	684	IM	Volpe, A	NJ	763
IM	Lodish, G	NY	683	IM	Rosen, N	NY	206	IM	Walfish, J	NY	467
IM	Logan, B	NY	205	IM	Rosenberg, R	CT	994	IM	Walsh, F	CT	994
IM	Lu, B	NY	466	IM	Rubenstein, J	NY	560	IM	Warshafsky, S	NY	685
IM	Maglaras, N	NJ	954	IM	Rucker, S	NY	560	IM	Wasserman, K	NJ	763
IM	Malik, A	NY	466	IM	Russo, J	NJ	814	IM	Wein, M	NY	685
IM	Mann, S	NY	205	IM	Salsitz, E	NY	206	IM	Weinshel, D	CT	995
IM	Margulis, S	NY	683	IM	Saltzman-Gabelman, L	NY	684	IM	Weinstein, J	NY	207
IM	Masterson, R	NJ	891	IM	Sanchez-Catanese, B	NJ	939	IM	Weinstein, M	NY	561
IM	Mastrangelo, R	NY	507	IM	Sander, N	NY	422	IM	Weiss, D	NY	632
IM	Mayer, D	CT	993	IM	Scaduto, P	NJ	908	IM	Wertheim, W	NY	632
IM	Mehta, V	NY	466	IM	Schaeffer, M	NJ	850	IM	Witt, M	NY	208
IM	Meller, J	NY	205	IM	Schaer, T	NJ	869	IM	Wolfe, M	NY	685
IM	Melman, M	NY	683	IM	Schneider, S	NY	206	IM	Wolff, E	NY	561
IM	Merrell, W	NY	205	IM	Schuster, J	NJ	763	IM	Wolfson, R	NY	685

Specialty & Special Expertise Index

Spec	Name	St	Pg	Spec	Name	St	Pg	Spec	Name	St	Pg
IM	Yaffe, B	NY	208	Cv	Greenberg, M	NY	411	IC	Lux, M	NJ	954
IM	Yamane, M	NJ	850	Cv	Hall, J	NJ	936	IC	Malpeso, J	NY	525
IM	Zaremski, B	NY	208	Cv	Jacowitz, J	NJ	746	IC	Marmur, J	NY	468
IM	Zarowitz, W	NY	685	Cv	Jauhar, R	NY	543	IC	Mehran, R	NY	209
IM	Zeale, P	NY	208	Cv	Jeremias, A	NY	622	IC	Mejia, V	CT	996
IM	Ziecheck, W	NY	208	Cv	Julie, E	NJ	925	IC	Messinger, D	NY	686
IM	Zucker, M	CT	995	Cv	Kim, S	NJ	746	IC	Mich, R	NJ	954
IM	Zupnick, H	NY	561	Cv	Klapholz, M	NJ	805	IC	Miller, K	NJ	814
				Cv	Koss, J	NY	543	IC	Moreno, P	NY	209
International Health				Cv	Landers, D	NJ	746	IC	Moses, J	NY	209
Inf	Allegra, D	NJ	908	Cv	Lituchy, A	NY	543	IC	Nero, T	CT	996
PrM	Cahill, J	NY	340	Cv	Lowell, B	NJ	904	IC	Ong, L	NY	633
				Cv	Matican, J	NJ	747	IC	Papadakos, S	NY	507
Interstitial Cystitis				Cv	Meizlish, J	CT	978	IC	Parikh, M	NY	209
ObG	Tyagi, R	NY	252	Cv	Menegus, M	NY	411	IC	Petrossian, G	NY	562
U	Marks, J	NY	396	Cv	Pappas, T	NY	544	IC	Portnay, E	CT	996
U	Moldwin, R	NY	605	Cv	Radwaner, B	NY	132	IC	Rachofsky, E	NJ	939
				Cv	Reison, D	NJ	747	IC	Selter, J	CT	996
Interstitial Lung Disease				Cv	Rossakis, C	NJ	747	IC	Shanahan, A	NJ	850
Pul	Addrizzo-Harris, D	NY	355	Cv	Ruiz, C	NY	133	IC	Shani, J	NY	468
Pul	Arcasoy, S	NY	355	Cv	Shamoon, F	NJ	806	IC	Sharma, S	NY	210
Pul	Berman, L	CT	1024	Cv	Sherman, W	NY	134	IC	Slater, J	NY	210
Pul	Binder, R	NY	720	Cv	Shlofmitz, R	NY	544	IC	Stone, G	NY	210
Pul	Fishman, D	NY	356	Cv	Stoupakis, G	NJ	748	IC	Syed, T	NJ	763
Pul	Glaser, M	NY	646	Cv	Vazzana, T	NY	522	IC	Torre, S	NJ	814
Pul	Lederer, D	NY	357	Cv	Wangenheim, P	NJ	806	IC	Warshofsky, M	CT	996
Pul	Libby, D	NY	357	IC	Abittan, M	NY	561	IC	Warshofsky, M	CT	996
Pul	Maniatis, T	NY	530	IC	Angeli, S	NJ	763	IC	Wasserman, H	CT	996
Pul	O'Donnell, T	NJ	920	IC	Attubato, M	NY	208	IC	Weinberger, J	NY	210
Pul	Posner, D	NY	359	IC	Berke, A	NY	561	IC	Weiss, M	NY	686
Pul	Saleh, A	NY	489	IC	Borgen, E	NY	467	IC	Wilentz, J	NY	210
Pul	Sasso, L	NY	531	IC	Brener, S	NY	467	IC	Zisfein, J	NY	562
Pul	Sklarek, H	NY	646	IC	Brogno, D	NY	611	PCd	Biancaniello, T	NY	640
Pul	Stover-Pepe, D	NY	360	IC	Cohen, M	NJ	814	PCd	Donnelly, C	NJ	915
Pul	Thomashow, B	NY	360	IC	Driesman, M	CT	995	PCd	Hsu, D	NY	432
Pul	Thurm, C	NY	514	IC	Feit, F	NY	208	PCd	Levchuck, S	NY	582
Pul	Wurm, E	NY	722	IC	Fishman, R	CT	995	PCd	Love, B	NY	305
				IC	Frankel, R	NY	467	PCd	Messina, J	NJ	780
Interventional Cardiology				IC	Friedman, M	NY	468	PCd	Vincent, J	NY	306
Cv	Altmann, D	NJ	862	IC	Goldstein, J	NJ	814	T&CS	Williams, M	NY	391
Cv	Andrews, P	NJ	744	IC	Gray, W	NY	208				
Cv	Blum, M	NJ	904	IC	Hjemdahl-Monsen, C	NY	685	**Interventional Endoscopy**			
Cv	Charney, R	NY	656	IC	Howes, C	CT	995	Ge	Vignesh, S	NY	462
Cv	Chengot, M	NY	622	IC	Innerfield, M	NY	612				
Cv	Cocke, T	NJ	744	IC	Jumper, R	CT	995	**Interventional Neuroradiology**			
Cv	Dervan, J	NY	622	IC	Kaid, K	NJ	814	DR	Schlesinger, S	NJ	864
Cv	Ezratty, A	NY	542	IC	Kalapatapu, K	NY	685	NRad	Berenstein, A	NY	243
Cv	Feit, A	NY	453	IC	Kaplan, B	NY	561	NRad	Fiorella, D	NY	635
Cv	Goldweit, R	NJ	745	IC	Kodali, S	NY	209	NRad	Gobin, Y	NY	243
Cv	Goyal, N	NJ	925	IC	Krishnan, P	NY	209	NRad	Keller, I	NJ	872
Cv	Green, S	NY	543	IC	Landau, C	CT	995	NRad	Meyers, P	NY	244
				IC	Lawson, W	NY	633	NRad	Ortiz, O	NY	570
				IC	Leon, M	NY	209				

Specialty & Special Expertise Index

Spec	Name	St	Pg
PRhu	Gottlieb, B	NY	586
PRhu	Haines, K	NJ	783
PRhu	Ilowite, N	NY	435
PRhu	Imundo, L	NY	317
PRhu	Kimura, Y	NJ	783
PRhu	Lazarus, H	NY	317
PRhu	Li, S	NJ	784
PRhu	Starr, A	NY	317
PRhu	Weiss, J	NJ	784

K

Kawasaki Disease

Spec	Name	St	Pg
PCd	Bierman, F	NY	706
PCd	Cooper, R	NY	581
PCd	Flynn, P	NY	304
PCd	Gewitz, M	NY	707
PCd	Issenberg, H	NY	707
PCd	Presti, S	NY	305
PCd	Romano, A	NY	582
PCd	Verma, R	NJ	823
PInf	Rubin, L	NY	585
PRhu	Imundo, L	NY	317

Keratoconus

Spec	Name	St	Pg
Oph	Asbell, P	NY	253
Oph	Cykiert, R	NY	256
Oph	Florakis, G	NY	257
Oph	Goldstein, M	NY	259
Oph	Hatsis, A	NY	573
Oph	Hersh, P	NJ	774
Oph	Udell, I	NY	575

Kidney Cancer

Spec	Name	St	Pg
DR	Akin, O	NY	156
Onc	Bradley, T	NY	563
Onc	Chachoua, A	NY	214
Onc	Feldman, D	NY	215
Onc	Gelmann, E	NY	215
Onc	Motzer, R	NY	219
Onc	Tagawa, S	NY	224
PHO	Steinherz, P	NY	312
U	Ahmed, M	NJ	795
U	Badani, K	NY	391
U	Benson, M	NY	392
U	Berman, S	NY	392
U	Catanese, A	NJ	944
U	Coleman, J	NY	392
U	Colon, I	NY	494

Spec	Name	St	Pg
U	Del Pizzo, J	NY	393
U	Dinlenc, C	NY	393
U	Droller, M	NY	393
U	Frey, H	NJ	796
U	Grasso, M	NY	394
U	Huang, W	NY	394
U	Karanikolas, N	NY	532
U	Kavoussi, L	NY	604
U	Kirschenbaum, A	NY	395
U	McKiernan, J	NY	396
U	Muldoon, L	CT	1032
U	Munver, R	NJ	797
U	Palese, M	NY	396
U	Provet, J	NY	397
U	Russo, P	NY	397
U	Saada, S	NY	494
U	Savatta, D	NJ	833
U	Sawczuk, I	NJ	797
U	Sogani, P	NY	398
U	Stifelman, M	NY	399
U	Taneja, S	NY	399
U	Weiss, R	NJ	884
VIR	Solomon, S	NY	401
VIR	Thornton, R	NY	402

Kidney Cancer-Cryosurgery

Spec	Name	St	Pg
U	Katz, A	NY	604
U	Rosenberg, G	NJ	797

Kidney Disease

Spec	Name	St	Pg
Ger	Dharmarajan, T	NY	419
Ger	Russell, R	NY	419
IM	Constantiner, A	NY	200
IM	Dreyer, N	CT	992
IM	Rucker, S	NY	560
IM	Walsh, F	CT	994
Nep	Ames, R	NY	226
Nep	August, P	NY	226
Nep	Bourla, S	NY	566
Nep	Brown, E	CT	1000
Nep	Buzzeo, L	NY	690
Nep	Chou, S	NY	469
Nep	Coco, M	NY	424
Nep	Fein, D	NJ	768
Nep	Feintzeig, I	CT	1001
Nep	Galler, M	NY	509
Nep	Grasso, M	NJ	817
Nep	Haratz, A	NJ	892
Nep	Hines, W	CT	1001
Nep	Hunt, W	CT	1001
Nep	Klein, M	NY	691
Nep	Kleiner, M	NY	526

Spec	Name	St	Pg
Nep	Lipner, H	NY	470
Nep	Manning, E	NJ	892
Nep	McAnally, J	NJ	955
Nep	Michelis, M	NY	227
Nep	Neelakantappa, K	NY	470
Nep	Pattner, A	NJ	768
Nep	Reda, D	NY	691
Nep	Rigolosi, R	NJ	768
Nep	Salifu, M	NY	470
Nep	Saltzman, M	NY	691
Nep	Sudhakar, T	NJ	851
Nep	Tartini, A	NJ	768
Nep	Thomsen, S	NJ	839
Nep	Yoo, J	NY	425
Nep	Zenenberg, R	NJ	911
PNep	Corey, H	NJ	916
PNep	Ettinger, L	NJ	782
PNep	Saland, J	NY	314
PNep	Vyas, S	NJ	824
PNep	Weiss, L	NJ	878

Kidney Disease in Pregnancy

Spec	Name	St	Pg
Nep	Kabis, S	NJ	940

Kidney Disease-Acute

Spec	Name	St	Pg
Nep	Delano, B	NY	470

Kidney Disease-Chronic

Spec	Name	St	Pg
IM	Alterman, L	NJ	954
IM	Feldman, J	NJ	954
Nep	DeFabritus, A	NY	226
Nep	DeVita, M	NY	226
Nep	Fogel, M	CT	1001
Nep	Garrick, R	NY	691
Nep	Pannone, J	NY	470
Nep	Radhakrishnan, J	NY	227
Nep	Uday, K	NY	425
Nep	Winston, J	NY	228
PNep	Hotchkiss, H	NY	314
PNep	Kaskel, F	NY	434
PNep	Lin, F	NY	314
PNep	Reidy, K	NY	435
PNep	Samsonov, D	NY	709

Kidney Disease-Geriatric

Spec	Name	St	Pg
Nep	Swidler, M	NY	228

Kidney Disease-Pediatric & Adult

Spec	Name	St	Pg
Nep	Rosen, M	NY	691

Specialty & Special Expertise Index

Specialty & Special Expertise Index

Spec	Name	St	Pg
OrS	Scuderi, G	NY	283
OrS	Warren, R	NY	285
OrS	Windsor, R	NY	286
OrS	Youm, T	NY	286
SM	Cavaliere, G	NY	725
SM	Sclafani, M	NJ	898

Knee Ligament Reconstruction

Spec	Name	St	Pg
OrS	Pidoriano, A	NY	703
SM	Gehrmann, R	NJ	830
SM	Noy, R	NY	375

Knee Meniscal Repair

Spec	Name	St	Pg
OrS	Levy, I	NY	430

Knee Reconstruction

Spec	Name	St	Pg
OrS	Cushner, F	NY	272
OrS	Decter, E	NJ	820
OrS	Gallick, G	NJ	958
OrS	Scuderi, G	NY	283
OrS	Zambetti, G	NY	286

Knee Reconstruction & Revision

Spec	Name	St	Pg
OrS	Moucha, C	NY	279

Knee Replacement

Spec	Name	St	Pg
OrS	Alexiades, M	NY	269
OrS	Asnis, S	NY	575
OrS	Austin, K	NY	614
OrS	Bindelglass, D	CT	1010
OrS	Boone, P	CT	1011
OrS	Bronson, M	NY	270
OrS	Buly, R	NY	271
OrS	Cobelli, N	NY	429
OrS	Cornell, C	NY	271
OrS	D'Amico, J	CT	1011
OrS	Deluca, J	CT	1011
OrS	Edelson, C	NY	702
OrS	Fealy, S	NY	273
OrS	Gutowski, W	NJ	853
OrS	Haas, S	NY	275
OrS	Hartzband, M	NJ	776
OrS	Hughes, P	CT	1012
OrS	Kavanagh, B	CT	1012
OrS	Kelly, M	NJ	776
OrS	Lent, D	NY	703
OrS	Macaulay, W	NY	278
OrS	Mani, J	NY	478
OrS	Marx, R	NY	278
OrS	Mc Inerney, V	NJ	929
OrS	Menezes, P	NY	479

Spec	Name	St	Pg
OrS	Pearle, A	NY	281
OrS	Pellicci, P	NY	281
OrS	Rich, D	NY	577
OrS	Rosa, R	NJ	821
OrS	Salvati, E	NY	282
OrS	Scott, W	NY	283
OrS	Scuderi, G	NY	283
OrS	Sculco, T	NY	284
OrS	Seebacher, J	NY	703
OrS	Seideman, B	NY	577
OrS	Shapiro, J	NY	577
OrS	Small, R	NY	704
OrS	Touliopoulos, S	NY	511
OrS	Walsh, R	NY	479
OrS	Windsor, R	NY	286
OrS	Yasgur, D	NY	704
SM	Delfico, A	NJ	793
SM	Luks, H	NY	725

Knee Replacement & Revision

Spec	Name	St	Pg
OrS	Bostrom, M	NY	270
OrS	Mayman, D	NY	278
OrS	Meere, P	NY	279
OrS	Moucha, C	NY	279
OrS	Ranawat, A	NY	281
OrS	Westrich, G	NY	285

Knee Surgery

Spec	Name	St	Pg
OrS	Adler, E	NY	269
OrS	Allen, A	NY	269
OrS	Bauman, P	NY	269
OrS	Bavaro, N	NY	701
OrS	Berman, M	NJ	775
OrS	Bosco, J	NY	270
OrS	Burak, C	NY	701
OrS	D'Agostino, R	NY	576
OrS	Divaris, N	NY	638
OrS	Doidge, R	NJ	776
OrS	Figgie, M	NY	273
OrS	Glashow, J	NY	274
OrS	Grossman, R	NJ	894
OrS	Haas, S	NY	275
OrS	Henshaw, D	CT	1012
OrS	Kelly, M	NJ	776
OrS	Khabie, V	NY	703
OrS	Kipnis, J	NY	576
OrS	Lent, D	NY	703
OrS	Longobardi, R	NJ	776
OrS	Lubliner, J	NY	278
OrS	McIlveen, S	NJ	777
OrS	Montgomery, K	NJ	913
OrS	Rosa, R	NJ	821

Spec	Name	St	Pg
OrS	Rozbruch, J	NY	282
OrS	Rubin, C	NY	615
OrS	Salzer, R	NJ	777
OrS	Schwartz, E	NY	511
OrS	Scott, W	NY	283
OrS	Shapiro, J	NY	577
OrS	Turtel, A	NY	285
OrS	Weinstein, R	NY	704
SM	Altchek, D	NY	374
SM	Berezin, M	NY	618
SM	Hershman, E	NY	374
SM	Jazrawi, L	NY	374
SM	Roth, N	NY	375
SM	Seneviratne, A	NY	376
SM	Williams, R	NY	376

Knee-Patella Problems

Spec	Name	St	Pg
OrS	Gladstone, J	NY	274

Knee-Patella Problems Consult

Spec	Name	St	Pg
OrS	Grelsamer, R	NY	274

L

Lacrimal Gland Disorders

Spec	Name	St	Pg
Oph	Gallin, P	NY	258
Oph	Lauer, S	NY	260

Langerhans Cell Histiocytoma

Spec	Name	St	Pg
PHO	Tugal, O	NY	709

Laparoscopic Abdominal Surgery

Spec	Name	St	Pg
S	Borao, F	NJ	898
S	Garvey, R	CT	1030
S	Grieco, M	NY	600
S	Hofstetter, S	NY	380
S	Katz, L	NY	380
S	Kenler, A	CT	1030
S	Pomp, A	NY	382
S	Salky, B	NY	383
S	Schmidt, H	NJ	794
S	Vine, A	NY	384
S	Zeitlin, A	NY	515

Laparoscopic Cholecystectomy

Spec	Name	St	Pg
S	Carter, M	NJ	921
S	Grieco, M	NY	600

Specialty & Special Expertise Index

Specialty & Special Expertise Index

Specialty & Special Expertise Index

Spec	Name	St	Pg
Oph	Santamaria, J	NJ	874
Oph	Sciortino, P	NY	477
Oph	Shulman, J	NY	266
Oph	Sperber, L	NY	267
Oph	Stabile, J	NJ	774
Oph	Starr, C	NY	267
Oph	Talansky, M	NJ	894
Oph	Wasserman, B	NJ	853
Oph	Wong, R	NJ	853
Oph	Zweibel, L	NY	638

Lead Poisoning

PEn	Noto, R	NY	707

Learning Disorders

AM	Lopez, R	NY	120
ChiN	De Carlo, R	NY	522
ChiN	Kaufman, D	NY	140
ChiN	Traeger, E	NJ	949
ChiN	Wells, J	NY	141
Ped	Acker, P	NY	712
Ped	Chessin, R	CT	1018
Ped	Cross, J	NY	320
Ped	McCarton, C	NY	323
Ped	Smoller, A	NJ	896
Psyc	Wachtel, A	NY	353

Lens Implant

Oph	Finlay, A	CT	1008
Oph	Gladstein, G	CT	1008
Oph	Goldberg, D	NJ	893
Oph	Kaplan, J	CT	1008
Oph	Pinke, J	CT	1009
Oph	Potter, W	CT	1009
Oph	Rabinowitz, S	CT	1009

Lens Implants-Multifocal

Oph	Dieck, W	NY	698
Oph	Mackool, R	NY	511
Oph	Malik, S	NY	573

Leukemia

Hem	Cook, P	NY	463
Hem	Jakubowski, A	NY	190
Hem	Jurcic, J	NY	190
Hem	Mears, J	NY	191
Hem	Meyer, R	NY	191
Hem	Niesvizky, R	NY	191
Hem	Ossias, A	NY	191
Hem	Rai, K	NY	557
Hem	Strair, R	NJ	868

Spec	Name	St	Pg
Hem	Tallman, M	NY	192
Hem	Troy, K	NY	192
Hem	Wisch, N	NY	193
IM	Halperin, I	NY	202
Onc	Angevine, A	CT	998
Onc	Berman, E	NY	213
Onc	Brentjens, R	NY	214
Onc	Frank, R	CT	999
Onc	Gabrilove, J	NY	215
Onc	Goldberg, S	NJ	765
Onc	Klafter, R	NY	217
Onc	Lee, M	CT	999
Onc	Ostrow, S	NY	634
Onc	Phillips, E	NY	688
Onc	Raza, A	NY	221
Onc	Roboz, G	NY	222
Onc	Seiter, K	NY	689
PHO	Garvin, J	NY	310
PHO	Guarini, L	NY	483
PHO	Kernan, N	NY	311
PHO	Kulpa, J	NY	483
PHO	Marcus, J	NY	311
PHO	Prockop, S	NY	312
PHO	Redner, A	NY	584
PHO	Sundaram, R	NY	483
PHO	Trippett, T	NY	312
PHO	Weiner, M	NY	312

Leukemia & Lymphoma

Hem	Allen, S	NY	557
Hem	Amorosi, E	NY	189
Hem	Bar, M	CT	989
Hem	Diuguid, D	NY	189
Hem	Dosik, H	NY	463
Hem	Duda, E	CT	990
Hem	Hymes, K	NY	190
Hem	Kolitz, J	NY	557
Hem	Landau, L	NY	420
Hem	Liu, D	NY	679
Hem	Raphael, B	NY	192
Hem	Savage, D	NY	192
Hem	Vogel, J	NY	192
Onc	Abramowitz, A	NY	508
Onc	Coleman, M	NY	214
Onc	Conti, J	NJ	815
Onc	Decter, J	NY	214
Onc	Farber, C	NJ	909
Onc	Grossbard, M	NY	216
Onc	Halaas, J	NY	688
Onc	Hollister, D	CT	999
Onc	Lowenthal, D	NJ	955
Onc	Rosenbluth, R	NJ	766

Spec	Name	St	Pg
Onc	Salwitz, J	NJ	939
Onc	Silverman, L	NY	223
Path	Bhattacharyya, P	NJ	779
PHO	Aledo, A	NY	309
PHO	Bekele, W	NJ	824
PHO	Cairo, M	NY	708
PHO	Carroll, W	NY	310
PHO	Dasgupta, I	NY	433
PHO	Gillio, A	NJ	781
PHO	Halpern, S	NJ	781
PHO	Harris, M	NJ	781
PHO	Sandoval, C	NY	709
PHO	Steinherz, P	NY	312
PHO	Tugal, O	NY	709
PHO	Weinblatt, M	NY	585
PHO	Wistinghausen, B	NY	312

Leukemia-Acute Lymphoblastic

Hem	Lamanna, N	NY	191

Leukemia-Chronic Lymphocytic

Hem	Lamanna, N	NY	191
Onc	Bernhardt, B	NY	687
Onc	Brentjens, R	NY	214

Leukemia-Myeloid

Hem	Lamanna, N	NY	191

Liaison Psychiatry

Psyc	Heisman, A	NY	487
Psyc	Kalash, G	NY	513
Psyc	Shapiro, P	NY	352
Psyc	Vivek, S	NY	513

Ligament Reconstruction

HS	Lee, S	NY	187
HS	Lisser, S	NJ	890
OrS	Hannafin, J	NY	275
OrS	Hubbard, C	NY	276
SM	Hershman, E	NY	374
SM	Levy, A	NJ	830

Limb Deformities

OrS	Feldman, D	NY	273
OrS	Fragomen, A	NY	273
OrS	Rozbruch, S	NY	282
OrS	Sabharwal, S	NJ	821
OrS	Widmann, R	NY	286

Specialty & Special Expertise Index

Spec	Name	St	Pg
Limb Lengthening			
OrS	Egol, K	NY	272
OrS	Fragomen, A	NY	273
OrS	Rozbruch, S	NY	282
OrS	Widmann, R	NY	286
Limb Lengthening (Ilizarov Procedure)			
OrS	Sabharwal, S	NJ	821
OrS	Vitale, M	NY	285
Limb Salvage			
VascS	Choi, H	NY	618
Limb Sparing Surgery			
OrS	Benevenia, J	NJ	820
OrS	Boland, P	NY	270
OrS	Kenan, S	NY	576
OrS	Patterson, F	NJ	821
VascS	Ascher, E	NY	495
VascS	Harrington, M	NY	404
VascS	Lantis, J	NY	404
VascS	Lipsitz, E	NY	445
VascS	Manno, J	NJ	798
VascS	Marin, M	NY	404
VascS	Mendes, D	NY	405
Limb Surgery/Reconstruction			
HS	Athanasian, E	NY	186
OrS	Rozbruch, S	NY	282
PlS	Elkwood, A	NJ	896
Liposuction			
D	Bank, D	NY	664
D	Kenet, B	NY	151
D	Narins, R	NY	667
D	Orentreich, D	NY	152
D	Sobel, H	NY	155
D	Wexler, P	NY	156
PlS	Anton, J	NY	644
PlS	Beran, S	NY	715
PlS	Boss, W	NJ	787
PlS	Breitbart, A	NY	590
PlS	Cutolo, L	NY	530
PlS	Leach, T	NJ	855
PlS	Matarasso, A	NY	335
PlS	Newman, F	CT	1022
PlS	Perry, A	NJ	942
PlS	Schulman, M	NY	337

Spec	Name	St	Pg
Liposuction & Body Contouring			
PlS	Ablaza, V	NJ	827
PlS	Alizadeh, K	NY	590
PlS	Aston, S	NY	331
PlS	Attkiss, K	CT	1021
PlS	Broumand, S	NY	331
PlS	Cherofsky, A	NY	530
PlS	Choi, M	NY	332
PlS	Colen, H	NY	332
PlS	Cozzone, J	NJ	787
PlS	D'Amico, R	NJ	787
PlS	Diktaban, T	NY	332
PlS	Friedman, D	NY	333
PlS	Gayle, L	NY	333
PlS	Gewirtz, H	CT	1021
PlS	Glasberg, S	NY	333
PlS	Godfrey, P	NY	333
PlS	Gotkin, R	NY	333
PlS	Greenwald, J	NY	716
PlS	Herbstman, R	NJ	880
PlS	Hetzler, P	NJ	896
PlS	Hoffman, L	NY	334
PlS	Hyans, P	NJ	962
PlS	Karp, N	NY	334
PlS	Lange, D	NJ	918
PlS	Leipziger, L	NY	592
PlS	LoVerme, P	NJ	828
PlS	Nini, K	NJ	880
PlS	O'Connell, J	CT	1022
PlS	Perrotti, J	NY	336
PlS	Romita, M	NY	336
PlS	Rosen, A	NJ	828
PlS	Rosenberg, M	NY	717
PlS	Schwartz, M	NY	337
PlS	Shafer, D	NY	338
PlS	Sherman, J	NY	338
PlS	Simpson, R	NY	592
PlS	Skolnik, R	NY	338
PlS	Sternschein, M	NJ	788
PlS	Sultan, M	NY	339
PlS	Swift, R	NY	339
PlS	Verga, M	NY	340
PlS	Weinstein, L	NJ	919
PlS	Wells, S	NY	340
PlS	Wey, P	NJ	880
PlS	Zeitels, J	NJ	962
PlS	Zevon, S	NY	340
PlS	Zubowski, R	NJ	788
Liver & Biliary Cancer			
S	Alden, D	NY	376
S	Emond, J	NY	379

Spec	Name	St	Pg
S	Newman, E	NY	382
Liver & Biliary Disease			
Ge	Antonelle, R	NY	672
Ge	Miskovitz, P	NY	176
Ge	Tobias, H	NY	179
Liver & Biliary Surgery			
S	Chabot, J	NY	378
S	Chamberlain, R	NJ	831
S	Gannon, C	NJ	857
S	Kinkhabwala, M	NY	442
S	Melvin, W	NY	443
S	Yiengpruksawan, A	NJ	794
Liver Cancer			
Onc	Grace, W	NY	216
Onc	Holcombe, R	NY	216
Onc	Kemeny, N	NY	217
Onc	O'Reilly, E	NY	220
Onc	Siegel, A	NY	223
PS	La Quaglia, M	NY	318
S	Allen, P	NY	376
S	Berman, R	NY	377
S	Brower, S	NY	378
S	DeMatteo, R	NY	378
S	Emond, J	NY	379
S	Gannon, C	NJ	857
S	Hiotis, S	NY	379
S	Jarnagin, W	NY	380
S	Karpeh, M	NY	380
S	Kemeny, M	NY	515
S	Labow, D	NY	381
S	Schwartz, M	NY	383
S	Teperman, L	NY	384
VIR	Brown, K	NY	399
VIR	Cynamon, J	NY	445
VIR	Nosher, J	NJ	884
VIR	Solomon, S	NY	401
VIR	Thornton, R	NY	402
Liver Disease			
Ge	Afridi, S	NJ	848
Ge	Augello, S	NY	503
Ge	Bains, Y	NJ	810
Ge	Bernstein, D	NY	553
Ge	Bleicher, R	NJ	926
Ge	Borcich, A	NY	169
Ge	Brown, R	NY	169
Ge	Cantor, M	NY	169
Ge	Chinitz, M	NY	672

Specialty & Special Expertise Index

Spec	Name	St	Pg
DR	Novick, M	NY	160
DR	Port, A	NY	550
DR	Raia, C	NY	522
DR	Riccio, G	CT	983
DR	Rosenfeld, S	NY	161
DR	Swirsky, M	NY	669

Mammography-Digital

Spec	Name	St	Pg
DR	LoRusso, D	NY	668

Marfan's Syndrome

Spec	Name	St	Pg
CG	Bialer, M	NY	546
CG	Davis, J	NY	142
CG	Marion, R	NY	413
Cv	Devereux, R	NY	127
PCd	Flynn, P	NY	304
PCd	Gelb, B	NY	304
PCd	Romano, A	NY	582
T&CS	Girardi, L	NY	387

Marital/Family/Sex Therapy

Spec	Name	St	Pg
Psyc	Manevitz, A	NY	347
Psyc	Sadock, V	NY	351

Maternal & Fetal Medicine

Spec	Name	St	Pg
MF	Al-Khan, A	NJ	764
MF	Alvarez, M	NJ	764
MF	Apuzzio, J	NJ	814
MF	Benito, C	NJ	909
MF	Berck, D	NY	686
MF	Berkowitz, R	NY	210
MF	Bernasko, J	NY	633
MF	Bianco, A	NY	210
MF	Bobby, P	CT	997
MF	Bond, A	CT	997
MF	Brustman, L	NY	211
MF	Bush, J	NY	468
MF	Cape, A	NY	686
MF	Chandra, P	NY	468
MF	Chavez, M	NY	562
MF	Chazotte, C	NY	422
MF	Cole, D	NY	211
MF	D'Alton, M	NY	211
MF	Dayal, A	NY	423
MF	Devine, P	NY	686
MF	Dunston-Boone, G	CT	997
MF	Eddleman, K	NY	211
MF	Eglinton, G	NY	507
MF	Einstein, F	NY	423
MF	Frieden, F	NJ	764
MF	Gallousis, F	NY	686

Spec	Name	St	Pg
MF	Genc, M	NJ	891
MF	Gimovsky, M	NJ	815
MF	Gonzalez, D	NJ	891
MF	Grunebaum, A	NY	211
MF	Henderson, C	NY	423
MF	Hutson, J	NY	211
MF	Inglis, S	NY	508
MF	Kalish, R	NY	211
MF	Kim, M	CT	997
MF	Kleinman, G	CT	997
MF	Laifer, S	CT	997
MF	Lashley, S	NJ	909
MF	Lescale, K	NY	686
MF	Meirowitz, N	NY	562
MF	Patrick, S	NY	211
MF	Principe, D	NJ	764
MF	Rebarber, A	NY	212
MF	Rochelson, B	NY	562
MF	Roman, A	NY	212
MF	Rosenn, B	NY	212
MF	Saltzman, D	NY	212
MF	Saphier, C	NJ	764
MF	Shevell, T	CT	997
MF	Sicuranza, G	NY	562
MF	Simpson, L	NY	212
MF	Skupski, D	NY	508
MF	Smith, L	NJ	815
MF	Stiller, R	CT	998
MF	Stone, J	NY	212
MF	Terrone, D	NJ	815
MF	Vintzileos, A	NY	562
MF	Vohra, N	NY	563
MF	Wapner, R	NY	212
MF	Warren, W	NJ	815
MF	Wolf, E	NJ	815
MF	Zelop, C	NJ	764
ObG	Komarynsky, I	CT	1006
ObG	Ordorica, S	NY	250

Maxillofacial & Craniofacial Surgery

Spec	Name	St	Pg
PlS	Staffenberg, D	NY	339

Maxillofacial Surgery

Spec	Name	St	Pg
PlS	Rodriguez, E	NY	336
PlS	Taub, P	NY	339

Maze Procedure for Atrial Fibrillation

Spec	Name	St	Pg
T&CS	Argenziano, M	NY	385
T&CS	Puskas, J	NY	390
T&CS	Robinson, N	NY	602

Spec	Name	St	Pg
T&CS	Squitieri, R	CT	1031

Mechanical Assist Devices

Spec	Name	St	Pg
T&CS	Camacho, M	NJ	832
T&CS	D'Alessandro, D	NY	443
T&CS	Goldstein, D	NY	444

Mediastinal Tumors

Spec	Name	St	Pg
Onc	Kris, M	NY	218
T&CS	Crawford, B	NY	386
T&CS	Keller, S	NY	444
T&CS	Kline, G	NJ	795
T&CS	Park, B	NY	389
T&CS	Shaw, J	NY	493
T&CS	Weiser, T	NY	728

Medical Oncology

Spec	Name	St	Pg
Onc	Abramowitz, A	NY	508
Onc	Adler, K	NJ	909
Onc	Aghajanian, C	NY	213
Onc	Ahmed, T	NY	687
Onc	Aisner, J	NJ	869
Onc	Akhund, B	NY	633
Onc	Angevine, A	CT	998
Onc	Arena, F	NY	563
Onc	Astrow, A	NY	468
Onc	Attas, L	NJ	764
Onc	Bajorin, D	NY	213
Onc	Baselga, J	NY	213
Onc	Bashevkin, M	NY	468
Onc	Belenkov, E	NY	213
Onc	Beltran, H	NY	213
Onc	Benisovich, V	NY	508
Onc	Berman, E	NY	213
Onc	Bernhardt, B	NY	687
Onc	Bosl, G	NY	213
Onc	Bradley, T	NY	563
Onc	Brentjens, R	NY	214
Onc	Bruckner, H	NY	423
Onc	Brunckhorst, K	NY	214
Onc	Buchholtz, M	NY	633
Onc	Budman, D	NY	563
Onc	Camacho, F	NY	423
Onc	Caron, P	NY	687
Onc	Caruso, R	NY	633
Onc	Casper, E	NY	687
Onc	Chachoua, A	NY	214
Onc	Chapman, P	NY	214
Onc	Citron, M	NY	563
Onc	Cohen, S	NY	214
Onc	Cohenuram, M	CT	998
Onc	Coleman, M	NY	214

Specialty & Special Expertise Index

Spec	Name	St	Pg	Spec	Name	St	Pg	Spec	Name	St	Pg
Onc	Condemi, G	NJ	765	Onc	Hindenburg, A	NY	563	Onc	Norton, L	NY	219
Onc	Conti, J	NJ	815	Onc	Hirschman, R	NY	216	Onc	O'Connor, O	NY	219
Onc	Cooper, R	CT	998	Onc	Hirshaut, Y	NY	216	Onc	O'Reilly, E	NY	220
Onc	Cortes, E	NY	508	Onc	Holcombe, R	NY	216	Onc	Odaimi, M	NY	525
Onc	D'Olimpio, J	NY	563	Onc	Holland, J	NY	216	Onc	Offit, K	NY	220
Onc	DaCosta, N	NY	634	Onc	Hollister, D	CT	999	Onc	Oh, W	NY	220
Onc	Daly, J	NY	508	Onc	Horwitz, S	NY	217	Onc	Oratz, R	NY	220
Onc	Decter, J	NY	214	Onc	Hudis, C	NY	217	Onc	Oster, M	NY	220
Onc	Delprete, S	CT	998	Onc	Ilson, D	NY	217	Onc	Ostrow, S	NY	634
Onc	Dickler, M	NY	214	Onc	Jagannath, S	NY	217	Onc	Papish, S	NJ	910
Onc	DiPaola, R	NJ	869	Onc	Jennis, A	NJ	765	Onc	Pascal, M	NJ	766
Onc	Dosik, D	NY	469	Onc	Kane, M	NJ	910	Onc	Pasmantier, M	NY	220
Onc	Drucker, B	CT	998	Onc	Kappel, B	NY	564	Onc	Pavlick, A	NY	220
Onc	Fang, B	NJ	939	Onc	Kelsen, D	NY	217	Onc	Pecora, A	NJ	766
Onc	Farber, C	NJ	909	Onc	Kemeny, N	NY	217	Onc	Perez-Soler, R	NY	423
Onc	Feldman, D	NY	215	Onc	Kessler, L	NY	564	Onc	Pfister, D	NY	221
Onc	Feldman, S	NY	687	Onc	Klafter, R	NY	217	Onc	Phillips, E	NY	688
Onc	Fialk, M	NY	687	Onc	Klein, P	NY	217	Onc	Pieczara, B	NJ	766
Onc	Fine, H	NY	215	Onc	Kloss, R	CT	999	Onc	Pietanza, M	NY	221
Onc	Fine, R	NY	215	Onc	Kozuch, P	NY	218	Onc	Portlock, C	NY	221
Onc	Fiore, J	NY	634	Onc	Kris, M	NY	218	Onc	Posner, M	NY	221
Onc	Fischbach, N	CT	998	Onc	Krug, L	NY	218	Onc	Provenzano, A	NY	688
Onc	Fitzgerald, D	NJ	891	Onc	Kruger, B	NY	218	Onc	Puccio, C	NY	688
Onc	Flaherty, B	NY	469	Onc	Krutchik, A	NJ	765	Onc	Radovich, D	NJ	816
Onc	Folman, R	CT	999	Onc	Kudelka, A	NY	634	Onc	Raff, J	NY	688
Onc	Forlenza, T	NY	525	Onc	Lebowicz, J	NY	469	Onc	Rakowski, T	NJ	766
Onc	Fornier, M	NY	215	Onc	Lee, M	CT	999	Onc	Ramirez, M	NY	424
Onc	Forte, F	NJ	765	Onc	Leitner, S	NJ	815	Onc	Raptis, G	NY	564
Onc	Frank, M	NJ	909	Onc	Lerma, P	NJ	850	Onc	Ratner, L	NY	221
Onc	Frank, R	CT	999	Onc	Lichter, S	NY	469	Onc	Raza, A	NY	221
Onc	Friscia, P	NY	525	Onc	Ligresti, L	NJ	765	Onc	Reichman, B	NY	221
Onc	Fuks, J	NY	423	Onc	Lippman, A	NJ	816	Onc	Rivera, Y	NJ	766
Onc	Gabrilove, J	NY	215	Onc	Lo, K	CT	999	Onc	Rizvi, N	NY	221
Onc	Gaynor, M	NY	215	Onc	Lonberg, M	NY	612	Onc	Roboz, G	NY	222
Onc	Gelmann, E	NY	215	Onc	Lowenthal, D	NJ	955	Onc	Robson, M	NY	222
Onc	Gold, J	NY	687	Onc	Maki, R	NY	218	Onc	Rosen, N	NY	689
Onc	Goldberg, A	NY	215	Onc	Malamud, S	NY	218	Onc	Rosenbluth, R	NJ	766
Onc	Goldberg, J	NY	688	Onc	Malefatto, J	CT	999	Onc	Ruggiero, J	NY	222
Onc	Goldberg, R	NY	612	Onc	Marino, J	NY	564	Onc	Sabbatini, P	NY	222
Onc	Goldberg, S	NJ	765	Onc	Mazumder, A	NY	218	Onc	Sadan, S	NY	689
Onc	Goy, A	NJ	765	Onc	Mehrotra, B	NY	564	Onc	Sagorin, C	NJ	816
Onc	Grace, W	NY	216	Onc	Mellacheruvu, S	NY	688	Onc	Saltz, L	NY	222
Onc	Greenberg, H	NY	508	Onc	Meyers, M	NY	218	Onc	Salwitz, J	NJ	939
Onc	Greenberg, S	NJ	891	Onc	Michaelson, R	NJ	816	Onc	Saponara, E	NY	689
Onc	Grossbard, M	NY	216	Onc	Mills, N	NY	688	Onc	Sara, G	NY	222
Onc	Grossman, B	NJ	850	Onc	Moore, A	NY	219	Onc	Schaebler, D	NJ	850
Onc	Guerin, B	NJ	954	Onc	Moriarty, D	NJ	955	Onc	Scher, H	NY	222
Onc	Gurubhagavatula, S	NJ	909	Onc	Morris, M	NY	219	Onc	Schleider, M	NJ	766
Onc	Halaas, J	NY	688	Onc	Moskowitz, C	NY	219	Onc	Schneider, J	NY	564
Onc	Hamilton, A	NJ	939	Onc	Motzer, R	NY	219	Onc	Schneider, R	NY	689
Onc	Harper, H	NJ	765	Onc	Muggia, F	NY	219	Onc	Schwartz, P	NY	564
Onc	Hassoun, H	NY	216	Onc	Nanus, D	NY	219	Onc	Scoppetuolo, M	NJ	816
Onc	Hershman, D	NY	216	Onc	Nissenblatt, M	NJ	869	Onc	Seiter, K	NY	689

Specialty & Special Expertise Index

Spec	Name	St	Pg
PlS	Herbstman, R	NJ	880
PO	Bent, J	NY	435
PS	Bethel, C	NJ	826
PS	Bhattacharyya, N	NJ	930
PS	Gallucci, J	NJ	879
PS	Hong, A	NY	586
PS	Kuenzler, K	NJ	784
PS	Lee, T	NY	642
PS	Midulla, P	NY	318
PS	Muensterer, O	NY	435
PS	Scriven, R	NY	642
PS	Spigland, N	NY	318
PS	Stringel, G	NY	711
PS	Tomita, S	NY	319
PS	Zitsman, J	NY	711
RE	O'Shaughnessy, A	NJ	856
RE	Schattman, G	NY	367
S	Benowitz, J	NY	600
S	Brathwaite, C	NY	600
S	Brower, S	NY	378
S	Coppa, G	NY	600
S	Fahey, T	NY	379
S	Feldman, S	NY	379
S	Feteiha, M	NJ	964
S	Fou, A	NY	726
S	Gumbs, A	NJ	964
S	Inabnet, W	NY	380
S	Kaul, A	NY	726
S	Khalife, M	NY	601
S	McGinty, J	NY	381
S	Melvin, W	NY	443
S	Pachter, H	NY	382
S	Pereira, S	NJ	794
S	Shah, P	NY	383
S	Talamini, M	NY	648
S	Trooskin, S	NJ	883
S	Weber, K	NY	727
S	Yiengpruksawan, A	NJ	794
S	Zarnegar, R	NY	385
S	Zoland, M	NY	385
T&CS	Crawford, B	NY	386
T&CS	Fontana, G	NY	387
T&CS	Lazzaro, R	NY	388
T&CS	Rizk, N	NY	390
T&CS	Saunders, C	NJ	832
T&CS	Scheinerman, S	NY	602
T&CS	Schubach, S	NY	603
T&CS	Swistel, D	NY	391
T&CS	Weiser, T	NY	728
U	Ahmed, M	NJ	795
U	Basralian, K	NJ	796
U	Birns, D	NY	392
U	Coleman, J	NY	392

Spec	Name	St	Pg
U	Eshghi, A	NY	729
U	Gershbaum, M	NY	603
U	Ghavamian, R	NY	444
U	Glassman, C	NY	729
U	Grunberger, I	NY	494
U	Lerner, S	NY	729
U	Owens, G	NY	730
U	Raboy, A	NY	532
U	Riechers, R	NY	730
U	Rosenberg, G	NJ	797
U	Saidi, J	NJ	833
U	Sandhaus, J	NY	516
U	Weinberg, J	NY	730
VascS	Carroccio, A	NY	403
VascS	Elias, S	NJ	798
VascS	Mateo, R	NY	732
VascS	Suggs, W	NY	732

Minimally Invasive Surgery-Pediatric

Spec	Name	St	Pg
Ped Uro	Casale, P	NY	319
Ped Uro	Poppas, D	NY	319
Ped Uro	Stock, J	NJ	826

Minimally Invasive Thoracic Surgery

Spec	Name	St	Pg
T&CS	Berman, S	NY	727
T&CS	Goldenberg, B	NJ	832
T&CS	Gorenstein, L	NY	387
T&CS	Harris, L	NY	493
T&CS	Hyman, K	NY	602
T&CS	Jones, D	NY	388
T&CS	Lee, P	NY	516
T&CS	Merav, A	NY	728
T&CS	Shaw, J	NY	493
T&CS	Sonett, J	NY	390
T&CS	Widmann, M	NJ	922
T&CS	Zairis, I	NJ	795

Minimally Invasive Urologic Surgery

Spec	Name	St	Pg
U	Badani, K	NY	391
U	Berman, S	NY	392
U	Boczko, J	NY	728
U	DeTorres, W	NJ	796
U	Esposito, M	NJ	796
U	Gupta, M	NY	394
U	Hall, S	NY	394
U	Santarosa, R	CT	1032
U	Stifelman, M	NY	399

Minimally Invasive Vascular

Spec	Name	St	Pg
	Surgery		
VascS	Benvenisty, A	NY	402
VascS	Brener, B	NJ	833
VascS	Dietzek, A	CT	1033
VascS	Goyal, A	NY	731
VascS	Jacobowitz, G	NY	404
VascS	Kabnick, L	NY	404
VascS	Rhee, R	NY	495
VascS	Schneider, D	NY	405
VascS	Todd, G	NY	406

Miscarriage-Recurrent

Spec	Name	St	Pg
ObG	Friedman, L	NY	248
ObG	Young, B	NY	252
RE	David, S	NY	364
RE	Drews, M	NJ	943
RE	Levi, A	CT	1027
RE	Matera, C	NY	365
RE	Stangel, J	NY	723

Mitral Valve Disease

Spec	Name	St	Pg
Cv	D'Agostino, R	NY	541
Cv	Teichholz, L	NJ	748
IM	Kennish, A	NY	203

Mitral Valve Minimally Invasive Surgery

Spec	Name	St	Pg
T&CS	Esposito, R	NY	601

Mitral Valve Prolapse

Spec	Name	St	Pg
Cv	Andersen, H	NY	125
Cv	Kobren, S	NY	543
Cv	Marshalko, S	CT	977
Cv	Zarich, S	CT	979

Mitral Valve Surgery

Spec	Name	St	Pg
IC	Gray, W	NY	208
T&CS	Adams, D	NY	385
T&CS	DeRose, J	NY	443
T&CS	Fontana, G	NY	387
T&CS	Galloway, A	NY	387
T&CS	Grossi, E	NY	388
T&CS	Naka, Y	NY	389
T&CS	Smith, C	NY	390

Mohs Surgery

Spec	Name	St	Pg
D	Albom, M	NY	145
D	Amin, S	NY	146
D	Ashinoff, R	NJ	750
D	Becker, D	NY	146

Specialty & Special Expertise Index

Specialty & Special Expertise Index

Spec	Name	St	Pg
MF	Dunston-Boone, G	CT	997
MF	Hutson, J	NY	211
MF	Rebarber, A	NY	212
MF	Simpson, L	NY	212
MF	Skupski, D	NY	508
MF	Wapner, R	NY	212
MF	Wolf, E	NJ	815
NP	Chhabra, R	NJ	767
ObG	Evans, M	NY	247
ObG	Kessler, A	NY	249
ObG	Klein, V	NY	571
ObG	Leiter, G	NY	250
ObG	Steer, R	NJ	912

Multiple Myeloma

Spec	Name	St	Pg
Hem	Allen, S	NY	557
Hem	Bar, M	CT	989
Hem	Dosik, H	NY	463
Hem	Isola, L	NY	190
Hem	Kolitz, J	NY	557
Hem	Liu, D	NY	679
Hem	Mears, J	NY	191
Hem	Niesvizky, R	NY	191
Hem	Raphael, B	NY	192
Hem	Strair, R	NJ	868
Hem	Topilow, A	NJ	890
Hem	Troy, K	NY	192
Hem	Vesole, D	NJ	760
Onc	Coleman, M	NY	214
Onc	Decter, J	NY	214
Onc	Farber, C	NJ	909
Onc	Grossbard, M	NY	216
Onc	Hamilton, A	NJ	939
Onc	Hassoun, H	NY	216
Onc	Jagannath, S	NY	217
Onc	Mazumder, A	NY	218
Onc	Silverman, L	NY	223
Onc	Straus, D	NY	224
RadRO	Yahalom, J	NY	363

Multiple Sclerosis

Spec	Name	St	Pg
N	Abou-Fayssal, N	NY	472
N	Ahluwalia, B	NY	692
N	Anselmi, G	NJ	839
N	Apatoff, B	NY	234
N	Appelbaum, J	NY	509
N	Blady, D	NJ	817
N	Blanck, R	NY	568
N	Britton, C	NY	235
N	Butler, J	CT	1002
N	Caporaso, G	NY	693
N	Chodosh, E	NJ	928

Spec	Name	St	Pg
N	Cohen, D	NY	635
N	Coll, R	NY	235
N	Cook, S	NJ	817
N	Coyle, P	NY	635
N	Duncan, D	NJ	770
N	Freddo, L	NY	426
N	Galetta, S	NY	236
N	Gilson, N	NY	892
N	Gordon, M	NY	568
N	Gottesman, M	NY	568
N	Gross, J	CT	1002
N	Litchman, C	CT	1003
N	Lublin, F	NY	239
N	Miller, A	NY	240
N	Nealon, N	NY	240
N	Newman, S	NY	569
N	Padela, M	NJ	928
N	Petito, F	NY	241
N	Sadeghi, H	NJ	839
N	Sadiq, S	NY	241
N	Schanzer, B	NJ	956
N	Snyder, D	NY	242
N	Swerdlow, M	NY	427
N	Tuchman, A	NY	243
N	Vas, G	NY	474
N	Willner, J	NJ	771
NS	Przybylski, G	NJ	871
PMR	O'Dell, M	NY	328
PMR	Stein, A	NY	589

Multiple Sclerosis/Visual Disorders

Spec	Name	St	Pg
N	Balcer, L	NY	234

Muscular Dystrophy

Spec	Name	St	Pg
ChiN	De Vivo, D	NY	140

Musculoskeletal Cancer

Spec	Name	St	Pg
OrS	Benevenia, J	NJ	820
OrS	Rapp, T	NY	281

Musculoskeletal Disorders

Spec	Name	St	Pg
OrS	Scher, D	NY	283
PMR	Gifford, I	NY	486
PMR	Gribbin, D	NJ	855
PMR	Inwald, G	NY	438
PMR	Kim, H	NY	327
PMR	Klecz, R	NJ	918
PMR	Ma, D	NY	328
PMR	Pechman, K	NY	715
PMR	Pici, R	NY	715

Spec	Name	St	Pg
PMR	Randolph, A	NY	715
PMR	Sheth, P	NY	329
PMR	Vallarino, R	NY	512
PMR	Zimmerman, J	NJ	787
Rhu	Chung, J	NJ	792
Rhu	Samuels, J	NY	372

Musculoskeletal Disorders in HIV/AIDS

Spec	Name	St	Pg
Rhu	Parrish, E	NY	372

Musculoskeletal Imaging

Spec	Name	St	Pg
DR	Adler, R	NY	156
DR	Choi, M	NY	502
DR	Desai, K	CT	982
DR	Epstein, R	NJ	864
DR	Ernberg, L	CT	982
DR	Gould, E	NY	626
DR	Haramati, N	NY	414
DR	Jacobs, M	NY	159
DR	Krinsky, G	NJ	752
DR	Lerman, J	NY	458
DR	Lubat, E	NJ	753
DR	Luchs, J	NY	550
DR	Math, K	NY	159
DR	Mintz, D	NY	159
DR	Moses, S	NJ	809
DR	Pavlov, H	NY	160
DR	Pfaff, H	NY	160
DR	Potter, H	NY	160
DR	Recht, M	NY	161
DR	Rosenberg, Z	NY	161
DR	Schweitzer, M	NY	626
PMR	Malanga, G	NJ	961
VIR	Saboeiro, G	NY	401

Musculoskeletal Infections

Spec	Name	St	Pg
OrS	Bostrom, M	NY	270

Musculoskeletal Injuries

Spec	Name	St	Pg
OrS	McClelland, S	NY	279
OrS	Yang, E	NY	511
PMR	Weinberg, J	NY	529
SM	Maharam, L	NY	375
SM	Rice, S	NJ	898

Musculoskeletal Tumors

Spec	Name	St	Pg
DR	Desai, K	CT	982
DR	Panicek, D	NY	160
OrS	Geller, D	NY	429
OrS	Hoang, B	NY	430

Spec	Name	St	Pg
OrS	Patterson, F	NJ	821

Musculoskeletal Ultrasound

Rhu	Samuels, J	NY	372

Myasthenia Gravis

FMed	Gross, H	NJ	755
N	Belsh, J	NJ	871
N	Goldstein, J	NY	237
N	Kula, R	NY	569
N	Olarte, M	NY	241
N	Ruderman, M	NJ	818
N	Sivak, M	NY	242
N	Swerdlow, M	NY	427
N	Willner, J	NJ	771
Oph	Mindel, J	NY	262

Mycobacterial Infections

Inf	Weinstein, M	NJ	868
Pul	Donath, J	NY	595

Mycosis Fungoides

D	Garzon, M	NY	148
D	Ramsay, D	NY	153
Hem	Hymes, K	NY	190

Myelodysplastic Syndromes

Hem	Castro-Malaspina, H	NY	189
Hem	Jurcic, J	NY	190
Hem	Kolitz, J	NY	557
Hem	Schuster, M	NY	630
Onc	Decter, J	NY	214
Onc	Gabrilove, J	NY	215
Onc	Goldberg, S	NJ	765
Onc	Hindenburg, A	NY	563
Onc	Pecora, A	NJ	766
Onc	Raza, A	NY	221
Onc	Roboz, G	NY	222
Onc	Seiter, K	NY	689
Onc	Silverman, L	NY	223
PHO	Prockop, S	NY	312

Myeloproliferative Diseases

Onc	Hamilton, A	NJ	939

Myeloproliferative Disorders

Hem	Fruchtman, S	NY	189
IM	Halperin, I	NY	202
Onc	Adler, K	NJ	909
Onc	Gabrilove, J	NY	215

Spec	Name	St	Pg
Onc	Roboz, G	NY	222

N

Nail Diseases

D	Brademas, M	NY	147

Nail Problems in Cancer Therapy

D	Lacouture, M	NY	151

Narcolepsy

Pul	Krieger, A	NY	357

Nasal & Sinus Disorders

A&I	Leibner, D	NJ	861
Oto	Aferzon, M	CT	1014
Oto	Bramwit, S	CT	1014
Oto	Chervin, B	CT	1014
Oto	Draizin, D	NY	578
Oto	Garay, K	NJ	840
Oto	Josephson, J	NY	290
Oto	Katz, H	NJ	778
Oto	Park, S	NY	431
Oto	Scherl, M	NJ	778
Oto	Schneider, K	NY	294
Oto	Scioscia, K	NY	579
Oto	Shugar, J	NY	295
Oto	Slavit, D	NY	295
Oto	Stewart, M	NY	295
Oto	Zbar, L	NJ	822

Nasal & Sinus Surgery

Oto	Blitzer, A	NY	287
Oto	Henick, D	NJ	777
Oto	Komisar, A	NY	290
Oto	Krespi, Y	NY	290
Oto	Scaccia, F	NJ	894
Oto	Setzen, M	NY	579
Oto	Westreich, R	NY	296
Oto	Yankelowitz, S	NY	431

Nasal Allergy

A&I	Backman, K	CT	973
A&I	Lusman, P	NY	621
A&I	Menchell, D	NY	500
A&I	Sher, E	NJ	887

Spec	Name	St	Pg

Nasal Reconstruction

Oto	Edelstein, D	NY	288
Oto	Lane, E	CT	1015
Oto	Tobias, G	NJ	778
PlS	Godfrey, N	NY	333

Nasal Surgery

Oto	Gargano, R	NY	639
Oto	Goldstein, S	NY	431
Oto	Guida, R	NY	288
Oto	Nass, R	NY	292
Oto	Rizk, S	NY	293
PlS	Godfrey, N	NY	333
PlS	Gold, A	NY	591
PlS	Goldstein, R	NY	439
PlS	Rosenblatt, W	NY	337
PlS	Schulman, N	NY	337

Nasopharyngeal Cancer

RadRO	Lee, N	NY	362

Natural Orifice Surgery (NOTES)

S	Bessler, M	NY	377

Neck Masses

PO	April, M	NY	315
PO	Dolitsky, J	NY	315

Necrotizing Enterocolitis

NP	Holzman, I	NY	225
NP	La Gamma, E	NY	690
PS	Coren, C	NY	586
PS	Scriven, R	NY	642

Neonatal & Infant Cardiac Surgery

T&CS	Bacha, E	NY	386

Neonatal Cardiology

PCd	Gewitz, M	NY	707

Neonatal Care

NP	Polin, R	NY	225
NP	Rakos, G	CT	1000
NP	Roth, P	NY	525
NP	Schanler, R	NY	565
NP	Skolnick, L	NJ	910
NP	Sokal, M	NY	469
NP	Stafford, J	NY	690

Specialty & Special Expertise Index

Spec	Name	St	Pg
Oph	Sibony, P	NY	638
Oph	Slamovits, T	NY	429
Oph	Smith, E	NY	478
Oph	Turbin, R	NJ	820
Oph	Unterricht, S	NY	478
Oph	Warren, F	NY	268
Oph	Weinberg, M	NJ	775
Oph	Winterkorn, J	NY	511
Oph	Zweifach, P	NY	269

Neuro-Otology

Spec	Name	St	Pg
N	Roberts, J	NY	241
N	Rosenberg, M	NJ	872
Oto	Roland, J	NY	293
Oto	Shah, D	NJ	894

Neuro-Pathology

Spec	Name	St	Pg
N	Belsh, J	NJ	871
Path	Rosenblum, M	NY	301
Path	Zagzag, D	NY	302

Neuro-Psychiatry

Spec	Name	St	Pg
ChAP	Rubinstein, B	NY	662
ChAP	Weisbrot, D	NY	623
ChAP	Williams, D	NY	545
GerPsy	Greenberg, R	NY	462
Psyc	Brodie, J	NY	342
Psyc	Budman, C	NY	593
Psyc	Gupta, A	NY	593
Psyc	Nass, J	NY	645
Psyc	Preter, M	NY	350
Psyc	Silver, J	NY	352

Neuro-Rehabilitation

Spec	Name	St	Pg
N	Azhar, S	NY	472
N	Fellus, J	NJ	911
PMR	Averill, A	NJ	786
PMR	Levin, S	NY	438
PMR	Richter, E	CT	1021
PMR	Whiteson, J	NY	330

Neuro-Urology

Spec	Name	St	Pg
U	Chaikin, D	NJ	922
U	Cooper, K	NY	392
U	Te, A	NY	399

Neuroblastoma

Spec	Name	St	Pg
PHO	Cheung, N	NY	310
PHO	Gardner, S	NY	310
PHO	Glade Bender, J	NY	310
PHO	Kramer, K	NY	311

Spec	Name	St	Pg
PHO	Kushner, B	NY	311
PHO	Modak, S	NY	311
PHO	Wolfe, L	NY	585
PS	La Quaglia, M	NY	318

Neurodegenerative Disorders

Spec	Name	St	Pg
N	Bressman, S	NY	234
N	Duncan, D	NJ	770

Neurodevelopmental Disabilities

Spec	Name	St	Pg
ChiN	Engel, M	NY	140
ChiN	Sherbany, A	NY	609
ChiN	Sweeney, T	NY	664
NP	Campbell, D	NY	424
Ped	Yalamanchi, K	NJ	879

Neuroendocrine Disorders

Spec	Name	St	Pg
PEn	Oberfield, S	NY	307

Neuroendocrine Tumors

Spec	Name	St	Pg
Onc	Kelsen, D	NY	217
Onc	Pietanza, M	NY	221
Onc	Ratner, L	NY	221
Onc	Saltz, L	NY	222
S	Johnson Miller, D	NJ	898
S	Libutti, S	NY	443

Neuroendocrinology

Spec	Name	St	Pg
EDM	Hodak, S	NY	164
EDM	Kleinberg, D	NY	164
EDM	Wardlaw, S	NY	166

Neurofibromatosis

Spec	Name	St	Pg
CG	Bialer, M	NY	546
CG	Davis, J	NY	142
ChiN	Allen, J	NY	139
ChiN	Aron, A	NY	139
ChiN	Sousa, R	NJ	749

Neurogenetics

Spec	Name	St	Pg
ChiN	Barabas, R	NJ	887

Neurogenic Bladder

Spec	Name	St	Pg
Ped Uro	Franco, I	NY	711
U	Fleischmann, N	NY	729
U	Vapnek, J	NY	399

Neurologic Complications-

Spec	Name	St	Pg
HIV/Infections			
N	Britton, C	NY	235

Neurologic Critical Care

Spec	Name	St	Pg
N	Boniece, I	NY	234
PCCM	Conway, E	NY	306

Neurologic Rehabilitation

Spec	Name	St	Pg
PMR	Aaronson, B	CT	1020
PMR	Ahn, J	NY	326
PMR	Gifford, I	NY	486
PMR	Stein, J	NY	330

Neurological Imaging

Spec	Name	St	Pg
N	Jamieson, D	NY	237
NuM	Strashun, A	NY	474

Neurological Surgery

Spec	Name	St	Pg
NS	Anderson, R	NY	228
NS	Angevine, P	NY	229
NS	Apostolides, P	CT	1001
NS	Arginteanu, M	NJ	769
NS	Bederson, J	NY	229
NS	Benitez, R	NJ	911
NS	Benzil, D	NY	692
NS	Beyerl, B	NJ	911
NS	Bilsky, M	NY	229
NS	Boockvar, J	NY	229
NS	Brisman, J	NY	566
NS	Brown, J	NY	566
NS	Bruce, J	NY	229
NS	Camel, M	CT	1001
NS	Cardoso, E	NY	471
NS	Carpenter, D	NJ	769
NS	Choudhri, T	NY	229
NS	Clemente, R	NJ	817
NS	Cohen, A	NY	471
NS	Davis, R	NY	634
NS	De Lotbiniere, A	NY	692
NS	Degen, J	NY	613
NS	Di Giacinto, G	NY	229
NS	Doyle, W	NY	229
NS	Eisenberg, M	NY	566
NS	Elowitz, E	NY	230
NS	Feldstein, N	NY	230
NS	Fiore, A	CT	1001
NS	Flamm, E	NY	425
NS	Frempong-Boadu, A	NY	230
NS	Fried, A	NJ	769
NS	Friedlander, M	NJ	955
NS	Ghatan, S	NY	230

Specialty & Special Expertise Index

Specialty & Special Expertise Index

Spec	Name	St	Pg
ObG	Friedman, A	NJ	873
ObG	Friedman, F	NY	248
ObG	Friedman, L	NY	248
ObG	Friedman, R	NY	427
ObG	Gannon, J	NY	696
ObG	Garrett, L	CT	1005
ObG	Geer-Yan, L	CT	1005
ObG	Gentilesco, M	NY	636
ObG	Ghofrany, S	CT	1005
ObG	Giuffrida, R	NY	696
ObG	Gluck, I	NJ	912
ObG	Goldman, G	NY	248
ObG	Goldstein, S	NY	248
ObG	Goldstein, S	NJ	893
ObG	Grano, V	NY	696
ObG	Grecco, D	NY	696
ObG	Greene, M	NY	248
ObG	Gruss, L	NY	248
ObG	Gubernick, M	NY	248
ObG	Hagberg, D	CT	1005
ObG	Haratz-Rubinstein, N	NY	475
ObG	Hardart, A	NY	249
ObG	Harris, D	NY	249
ObG	Haselkorn, J	NY	571
ObG	Hayworth, S	NY	696
ObG	Hines, B	CT	1005
ObG	Hirsch, L	NY	249
ObG	Hirt, P	NY	636
ObG	Hockstein, S	NY	249
ObG	Holland, C	NY	249
ObG	Hostin, H	NY	614
ObG	Hurst, W	NJ	772
ObG	Hyman, M	NJ	957
ObG	Jacob, J	NY	571
ObG	Jacobson, E	CT	1005
ObG	Karamitsos, H	NY	249
ObG	Keller, A	NY	696
ObG	Kent, J	NY	249
ObG	Kerr, A	CT	1006
ObG	Kessler, A	NY	249
ObG	Kim, J	NY	249
ObG	Klein, V	NY	571
ObG	Komarynsky, I	CT	1006
ObG	Kramer, M	NY	636
ObG	Krause, C	NY	250
ObG	Krim, E	NY	571
ObG	Lee, D	NY	636
ObG	Leiter, G	NY	250
ObG	Leong, M	NY	571
ObG	Levey, J	NJ	940
ObG	Levey, K	NY	250
ObG	Levine, R	NY	250
ObG	Levy, J	NY	428
ObG	Lind, L	NY	571
ObG	Luciani, R	NJ	818
ObG	Mack, L	NY	571
ObG	Maher, J	NY	475
ObG	Malley, S	NY	696
ObG	Margulis, E	NJ	957
ObG	Martens, M	NJ	893
ObG	Masson, J	NJ	840
ObG	McGovern, C	NY	696
ObG	Meacham, K	NY	696
ObG	Melnick, H	NY	250
ObG	Mendelowitz, L	NY	697
ObG	Meyer, M	NJ	773
ObG	Michel, K	NY	250
ObG	Mieszerski, L	NY	697
ObG	Miller, L	NJ	773
ObG	Minkoff, H	NY	475
ObG	Mohr, R	NJ	912
ObG	Moritz, J	NY	250
ObG	Nelson, W	NY	697
ObG	Nimaroff, M	NY	571
ObG	Ordorica, S	NY	250
ObG	Ott, A	NY	636
ObG	Pali, R	NY	428
ObG	Phillips, R	NY	250
ObG	Ponterio, J	NY	527
ObG	Postell, S	NY	475
ObG	Quartell, A	NJ	818
ObG	Rathauser, R	NJ	873
ObG	Regard, M	NY	697
ObG	Reilly, J	NY	527
ObG	Reizis, I	NY	475
ObG	Rezvani, F	NJ	773
ObG	Rivera, J	CT	1006
ObG	Rodke, G	NY	251
ObG	Rohr, M	CT	1006
ObG	Rothenberg, S	NY	251
ObG	Rubenstein, A	NJ	773
ObG	Russell, S	NY	251
ObG	Rutenberg, K	NY	251
ObG	Sadarangani, B	NY	251
ObG	Salzman, R	NY	571
ObG	Samuelson, R	CT	1006
ObG	San Roman, G	NY	636
ObG	Sanderson, R	NJ	940
ObG	Sandler, B	NY	251
ObG	Sarabanchong, V	NY	510
ObG	Sassoon, R	NY	251
ObG	Schechter, M	CT	1006
ObG	Scher, J	NY	251
ObG	Schulze, R	NJ	773
ObG	Schwartz, J	NY	251
ObG	Schweizer, W	NY	252
ObG	Segarra, P	NY	637
ObG	Seigel, M	NJ	893
ObG	Silverman, F	NY	252
ObG	Simon, B	NY	697
ObG	Smilen, S	NY	252
ObG	Soffer, J	NJ	957
ObG	Steer, R	NJ	912
ObG	Sullum, S	NY	252
ObG	Szeto, M	CT	1006
ObG	Toles, A	NY	572
ObG	Torbey, M	CT	1006
ObG	Turk, R	CT	1006
ObG	Tyagi, R	NY	252
ObG	Ugol, J	CT	1007
ObG	Ullman, J	NY	697
ObG	Uy, V	NJ	840
ObG	Vasudeva, K	NY	572
ObG	Violi, C	CT	1007
ObG	Wallis, J	NJ	912
ObG	Waterstone, M	NY	252
ObG	Weinstein, D	CT	1007
ObG	Wysoki, R	NY	697
ObG	Yale, S	NY	252
ObG	Yarberry-Allen, P	NY	252
ObG	Young, B	NY	252

Occupational Dermatology

Spec	Name	St	Pg
D	Cohen, D	NY	147
D	Cohen, S	NY	413

Occupational Disease & Injury

Spec	Name	St	Pg
OM	Mendelsohn, S	NY	572

Occupational Lung Disease

Spec	Name	St	Pg
OM	Kipen, H	NJ	873
Pul	Maxfield, R	NY	358

Occupational Medicine

Spec	Name	St	Pg
IM	Altholz, J	NY	681
IM	Berman, E	CT	991
IM	Pappas, S	NY	684
IM	Schneider, S	NY	206
IM	Zarowitz, W	NY	685
OM	Gochfeld, M	NJ	873
OM	Kipen, H	NJ	873
OM	Landrigan, P	NY	253
OM	Mendelsohn, S	NY	572
OM	Wilkenfeld, M	NY	572

Ocular Ultrasound

Spec	Name	St	Pg
Oph	Fisher, Y	NY	257

Specialty & Special Expertise Index

Spec	Name	St	Pg	Spec	Name	St	Pg	Spec	Name	St	Pg
Oph	Glatt, H	NJ	819	Oph	Magramm, I	NY	261	Oph	Pinke, J	CT	1009
Oph	Goldberg, D	NJ	893	Oph	Maher, E	NY	261	Oph	Pinke, R	NJ	913
Oph	Goldberg, L	NY	573	Oph	Malik, S	NY	573	Oph	Piro, P	CT	1009
Oph	Goldstein, M	NY	259	Oph	Mandava, S	CT	1008	Oph	Pizzarello, L	NY	637
Oph	Gordon, J	NY	699	Oph	Mandel, E	NY	261	Oph	Potter, W	CT	1009
Oph	Grabowski, W	NJ	874	Oph	Mandelbaum, S	NY	261	Oph	Prenner, J	NJ	874
Oph	Grasso, C	NY	510	Oph	Manjoney, D	CT	1008	Oph	Prince, A	NY	264
Oph	Grayson, D	NY	259	Oph	Marks, A	NY	573	Oph	Prywes, A	NY	574
Oph	Greenbaum, A	NY	699	Oph	Marr, B	NY	262	Oph	Raab, E	NY	264
Oph	Greenberg, S	NY	699	Oph	Martin, J	NY	637	Oph	Rabinowitz, S	CT	1009
Oph	Guillory, S	NY	259	Oph	Mathias, S	CT	1008	Oph	Ray, A	NY	700
Oph	Haight, D	NY	259	Oph	Matossian, C	NJ	852	Oph	Reich, R	NY	477
Oph	Hall, L	NY	259	Oph	Mayers, M	NY	428	Oph	Relland, M	NY	264
Oph	Haller, M	NY	510	Oph	McKee, H	NY	699	Oph	Reppucci, V	CT	1009
Oph	Harmon, G	NY	259	Oph	Medow, N	NY	428	Oph	Ritch, R	NY	264
Oph	Hatsis, A	NY	573	Oph	Melton, R	NY	262	Oph	Ritterband, D	NY	264
Oph	Heinemann, M	NY	259	Oph	Merhige, K	NY	262	Oph	Robbins, K	CT	1009
Oph	Hersh, P	NJ	774	Oph	Merriam, J	NY	262	Oph	Rodgers, I	NY	264
Oph	Hirshfield, G	NY	511	Oph	Metz, D	NY	477	Oph	Rodriguez-Sains, R	NY	264
Oph	Horowitz, J	NY	259	Oph	Mignone, B	NY	699	Oph	Romanelli, J	NY	638
Oph	Horowitz, M	NY	699	Oph	Milite, J	NJ	874	Oph	Rosenbaum, P	NY	429
Oph	Hufnagel, T	NY	573	Oph	Mindel, J	NY	262	Oph	Rosenberg, M	NJ	774
Oph	Hyman, G	NY	476	Oph	Mitchell, J	NY	262	Oph	Rosenthal, J	NY	264
Oph	Jabs, D	NY	260	Oph	Moazed, K	NY	262	Oph	Rosenthal, K	NY	574
Oph	Kaplan, J	CT	1008	Oph	Mogil, L	NY	477	Oph	Rothberg, C	NY	638
Oph	Kasper, W	NY	573	Oph	Morello, R	NY	700	Oph	Rubin, L	NY	574
Oph	Katz, B	NY	428	Oph	Morgan, C	NJ	913	Oph	Rubin, S	NY	574
Oph	Katz, S	NY	428	Oph	Moskowitz, B	NY	262	Oph	Rudick, A	NY	265
Oph	Kaufmann, C	NY	511	Oph	Moskowitz, C	NY	262	Oph	Sachs, R	NJ	913
Oph	Kazam, E	NJ	913	Oph	Most, R	NY	700	Oph	Saffra, N	NY	477
Oph	Kazim, M	NY	260	Oph	Muchnick, R	NY	263	Oph	Safran, S	NJ	853
Oph	Kelly, S	NY	260	Oph	Muldoon, T	NY	263	Oph	Salz, A	NJ	940
Oph	Klapper, D	NY	260	Oph	Mulvey, L	NJ	852	Oph	Salzman, J	NY	700
Oph	Kodsi, S	NY	573	Oph	Musto, A	CT	1008	Oph	Samson, C	NY	265
Oph	Koplin, R	NY	260	Oph	Napolitano, J	NJ	874	Oph	Santamaria, J	NJ	874
Oph	Kramer, P	NY	527	Oph	Natale, B	NJ	957	Oph	Scartozzi, R	CT	1009
Oph	Kristan, R	NJ	893	Oph	Nattis, R	NY	637	Oph	Schiff, W	NY	265
Oph	Kupersmith, M	NY	260	Oph	Nauheim, R	NY	574	Oph	Schlessinger, D	NY	574
Oph	Langer, P	NJ	820	Oph	Nelson, D	NY	574	Oph	Schneck, G	NY	638
Oph	Lauer, S	NY	260	Oph	Newton, M	NY	263	Oph	Schrier, A	NY	265
Oph	Lazzaro, D	NY	477	Oph	Nightingale, J	NY	263	Oph	Schubert, H	NY	265
Oph	Lebowitz, M	NY	477	Oph	Norden, R	NJ	774	Oph	Schwarcz, R	NY	265
Oph	Lederman, M	NY	699	Oph	O'Malley, G	NY	637	Oph	Sciortino, P	NY	477
Oph	Lee, C	NY	260	Oph	Obstbaum, S	NY	263	Oph	Seedor, J	NY	265
Oph	Leib, M	NY	261	Oph	Odel, J	NY	263	Oph	Seidman, M	NY	478
Oph	Liebmann, J	NY	261	Oph	Odrich, M	NY	429	Oph	Serle, J	NY	265
Oph	Lippman, J	NY	699	Oph	Ostriker, G	CT	1009	Oph	Shabto, U	NY	266
Oph	Lish, A	NY	477	Oph	Paccione, J	NY	263	Oph	Sherman, S	NY	266
Oph	Lisman, R	NY	261	Oph	Packer, S	NY	574	Oph	Sherman, S	NY	478
Oph	Liva, D	NJ	774	Oph	Palu, R	NY	263	Oph	Shulman, J	NY	266
Oph	Lombardo, J	NY	477	Oph	Paul, M	CT	1009	Oph	Sibony, P	NY	638
Oph	MacKay, C	NY	261	Oph	Perry, H	NY	574	Oph	Siderides, E	CT	1010
Oph	Mackool, R	NY	511	Oph	Phillips, H	NY	700	Oph	Sidoti, P	NY	266

Osteoarthritis

Osteomyelitis

Osteonecrosis

Osteopathic Manipulation

Osteoporosis

Specialty & Special Expertise Index

Spec	Name	St	Pg	Spec	Name	St	Pg	Spec	Name	St	Pg
Oto	Jacobs, J	NY	289	Oto	Morrow, T	NJ	822	Oto	Song, C	NY	480
Oto	Jacobson, A	NY	289	Oto	Myssiorek, D	NY	292	Oto	Sperling, N	NY	528
Oto	Jacono, A	NY	578	Oto	Nass, R	NY	292	Oto	Stewart, M	NY	295
Oto	Jahn, A	NY	289	Oto	Park, S	NY	431	Oto	Stidham, K	NY	705
Oto	Jones, J	NY	289	Oto	Parker, A	CT	1016	Oto	Storper, I	NY	295
Oto	Josephson, J	NY	290	Oto	Pastorek, N	NY	292	Oto	Strome, M	NY	296
Oto	Kacker, A	NY	290	Oto	Pearl, A	CT	1016	Oto	Sulica, R	NY	296
Oto	Kanowitz, S	NJ	914	Oto	Perlman, P	NY	579	Oto	Surow, J	NJ	778
Oto	Kase, S	NY	705	Oto	Persky, M	NY	293	Oto	Taylor, H	NJ	914
Oto	Kates, M	NY	705	Oto	Pincus, R	NY	293	Oto	Teng, M	NY	296
Oto	Katz, H	NJ	778	Oto	Pitman, M	NY	293	Oto	Tobias, G	NJ	778
Oto	Kay, S	NJ	875	Oto	Pollack, G	NY	293	Oto	Turk, J	NY	580
Oto	Khosh, M	NY	290	Oto	Portnoy, W	NY	293	Oto	Urken, M	NY	296
Oto	Klarsfeld, J	CT	1015	Oto	Presti, P	NJ	959	Oto	Vambutas, A	NY	580
Oto	Klenoff, B	CT	1015	Oto	Rizk, S	NY	293	Oto	Vastola, A	NY	480
Oto	Klenoff, J	CT	1015	Oto	Roland, J	NY	293	Oto	Volpi, D	NY	296
Oto	Kohan, D	NY	290	Oto	Rosen, A	NJ	778	Oto	Waner, M	NY	296
Oto	Komisar, A	NY	290	Oto	Rosenbaum, J	NJ	875	Oto	Westreich, R	NY	296
Oto	Koufman, J	NY	290	Oto	Rosenberg, D	NY	293	Oto	White, W	NY	296
Oto	Kraus, D	NY	290	Oto	Rosner, L	NY	579	Oto	Wong, R	NY	297
Oto	Krespi, Y	NY	290	Oto	Rossos, A	NJ	894	Oto	Woo, P	NY	297
Oto	Krevitt, L	NY	291	Oto	Rothstein, S	NY	294	Oto	Yankelowitz, S	NY	431
Oto	Kuhel, W	NY	291	Oto	Ryback, H	NY	705	Oto	Youngerman, J	NY	580
Oto	Kuriloff, D	NY	291	Oto	Sacks, S	NY	294	Oto	Zahtz, G	NY	580
Oto	Kwartler, J	NJ	959	Oto	Salzer, S	CT	1016	Oto	Zalvan, C	NY	706
Oto	La Bagnara, J	NJ	930	Oto	Scaccia, F	NJ	894	Oto	Zbar, L	NJ	822
Oto	La Marca, C	NY	512	Oto	Schaefer, S	NY	294	Oto	Zelman, W	NY	580
Oto	Lachman, R	NJ	914	Oto	Schantz, S	NY	294	Oto	Zimbler, M	NY	297
Oto	Lagmay, V	NY	480	Oto	Scharf, R	NJ	959				
Oto	Lalwani, A	NY	291	Oto	Scherl, M	NJ	778	**Otology**			
Oto	Lane, E	CT	1015	Oto	Schneider, K	NY	294	Oto	Grosso, J	NY	578
Oto	Lawson, W	NY	291	Oto	Scioscia, K	NY	579	Oto	Hanson, M	NY	480
Oto	Lazar, A	NJ	941	Oto	Sclafani, A	NY	294	Oto	Kanowitz, S	NJ	914
Oto	Lebovics, R	NY	291	Oto	Scott, J	NY	705	Oto	Kay, S	NJ	875
Oto	Levin, R	CT	1015	Oto	Selesnick, S	NY	294	Oto	Litman, R	NY	640
Oto	Levine, S	CT	1015	Oto	Setzen, M	NY	579				
Oto	Li, C	NY	291	Oto	Shaari, C	NJ	778	**Otology & Neuro-Otology**			
Oto	Li, R	NJ	854	Oto	Shah, D	NJ	894	Oto	Jahn, A	NY	289
Oto	Lim, J	NY	291	Oto	Shapiro, B	NY	705	Oto	Linstrom, C	NY	292
Oto	Linstrom, C	NY	292	Oto	Shemen, L	NY	294	Oto	McMenomey, S	NY	292
Oto	Lipinsky, E	NY	639	Oto	Shikowitz, M	NY	579	Oto	Meiteles, L	NY	705
Oto	Litman, R	NY	640	Oto	Shin, E	NY	295	Oto	Stidham, K	NY	705
Oto	Low, R	NJ	778	Oto	Shohet, M	NY	295				
Oto	Lustig, L	NY	292	Oto	Shugar, J	NY	295	**Otosclerosis**			
Oto	Markowitz, A	NY	292	Oto	Siglock, T	NY	705	Oto	Gordon, M	NY	578
Oto	Mazzara, C	NJ	875	Oto	Singh, B	NY	295	Oto	Sperling, N	NY	528
Oto	McMenomey, S	NY	292	Oto	Sinnreich, A	NY	528				
Oto	Meiteles, L	NY	705	Oto	Slavit, D	NY	295	**Ovarian Cancer**			
Oto	Milgrim, L	NJ	778	Oto	Slupchynskyj, O	NY	295	GO	Abu-Rustum, N	NY	183
Oto	Miller, A	NJ	875	Oto	Smith, J	NY	431	GO	Barakat, R	NY	183
Oto	Miller, P	NY	292	Oto	Smith, R	NY	431	GO	Brown, C	NY	183
Oto	Mittleman, M	NY	512	Oto	Snyder, G	NY	579				
Oto	Moisa, I	NY	579	Oto	Soletic, R	NY	579				

Specialty & Special Expertise Index

Spec	Name	St	Pg
GO	Caputo, T	NY	183
GO	Chi, D	NY	184
GO	Chuang, L	NY	677
GO	Curtin, J	NY	184
GO	Denehy, T	NJ	812
GO	Dottino, P	NY	184
GO	Goldberg, G	NY	420
GO	Holcomb, K	NY	184
GO	Koulos, J	NY	184
GO	Lovecchio, J	NY	556
GO	Maiman, M	NY	524
GO	Menzin, A	NY	556
GO	Nagarsheth, N	NY	185
GO	Rodriguez, L	NJ	867
GO	Smith, H	NY	420
GO	Tedjarati, S	NY	678
GO	Wallach, R	NY	185
GO	Wright, J	NY	185
ObG	Banks, J	NJ	912
Onc	Aghajanian, C	NY	213
Onc	Astrow, A	NY	468
Onc	Delprete, S	CT	998
Onc	Farber, C	NJ	909
Onc	Halaas, J	NY	688
Onc	Pasmantier, M	NY	220
Onc	Sabbatini, P	NY	222
Onc	Speyer, J	NY	223
Onc	Spriggs, D	NY	223
Onc	Strauss, B	NY	634
Path	Ellenson, L	NY	300
Path	Tornos, C	NY	640

Ovarian Cancer Genetics

Spec	Name	St	Pg
ObG	Krause, C	NY	250

Ovarian Cancer-Advanced

Spec	Name	St	Pg
GO	Burke, W	NY	183

Ovarian Cancer-Early Detection

Spec	Name	St	Pg
GO	Fishman, D	NY	184

Ovarian Failure

Spec	Name	St	Pg
RE	Chang, P	NY	364

Ovarian Masses in Children/Adolescents

Spec	Name	St	Pg
ObG	Regard, M	NY	697
PS	Dolgin, S	NY	586

Overscheduled Children

Spec	Name	St	Pg
ChAP	Rosenfeld, A	CT	979

Overuse Injuries

Spec	Name	St	Pg
SM	Halpern, B	NY	374

P

Pacemakers

Spec	Name	St	Pg
CE	Beldner, S	NY	540
CE	Bernstein, N	NY	123
CE	Biviano, A	NY	123
CE	Chinitz, L	NY	123
CE	Chiravuri, M	CT	975
CE	Cohen, M	NY	655
CE	Costeas, C	NJ	805
CE	Fan, R	NY	621
CE	Ferrick, K	NY	410
CE	Gomes, J	NY	124
CE	Gross, J	NY	410
CE	Ivanov, A	NJ	935
CE	Levine, J	NY	540
CE	Love, C	NY	124
CE	Matos, J	NY	125
CE	Rashba, E	NY	621
CE	Ruffo, S	NJ	743
CE	Shukla, G	NJ	743
CE	Slotwiner, D	NY	540
CE	Suri, R	NY	125
CE	Turitto, G	NY	452
CE	Winslow, R	CT	975
Cv	Chen, T	NY	541
Cv	Erlebacher, J	NJ	745
Cv	Feld, M	NY	657
Cv	Fisher, L	CT	976
Cv	Goldschmidt, H	NJ	745
Cv	Sagar, Y	NJ	748
Cv	Varriale, P	NY	135
IC	Kaid, K	NJ	814
IC	Zisfein, J	NY	562
T&CS	Goldenberg, B	NJ	832
T&CS	Heim, J	NJ	883
T&CS	Hoffman, D	NY	388

Pacemakers/Defibrillators

Spec	Name	St	Pg
CE	Correia, J	NJ	805
CE	Garan, H	NY	124
CE	Iwai, S	NY	655
CE	Jadonath, R	NY	540
CE	Markowitz, S	NY	124
CE	McPherson, C	CT	975
CE	Preminger, M	NJ	743
CE	Roelke, M	NJ	805
CE	Rubin, D	NY	655
CE	Sauberman, R	NJ	805
CE	Whang, W	NY	125
CE	Wilbur, S	NY	452
CE	Winters, S	NJ	904
Cv	Goodman, M	NY	542
Cv	Tarkin, H	NY	660

Paget's Disease of Bone

Spec	Name	St	Pg
EDM	Bockman, R	NY	162
EDM	Siris, E	NY	166
EDM	Weinerman, S	NY	459

Pain Management

Spec	Name	St	Pg
H & PM	Edwards, W	NY	193
H & PM	Pan, C	NY	506
H & PM	Popp, B	NY	464
IM	Bharathan, T	NY	465
N	Carver, A	NY	235
N	Citak, K	NJ	770
N	Freddo, L	NY	426
N	Grenell, S	NY	426
N	Lazar, M	NJ	871
N	Mauskop, A	NY	239
N	Sparr, S	NY	427
NS	Di Giacinto, G	NY	229
Ped	Rosenblatt, J	NJ	826
PM	Patel, N	NY	615
PM	Reyfman, L	NY	481
PM	Silverman, R	NJ	779
PMR	Agri, R	NJ	855
PMR	Cole, J	NJ	827
PMR	Dillard, J	NY	327
PMR	Filippone, M	NJ	841
PMR	Gribbin, D	NJ	855
PMR	Heftler, J	CT	1021
PMR	Inwald, G	NY	438
PMR	Lee, A	NY	328
PMR	Liss, H	NJ	787
PMR	Pechman, K	NY	715
PMR	Rho, D	NY	329
PMR	Root, B	NY	589
PMR	Snowball, H	CT	1021
PMR	Stein, P	NY	486
PMR	Valenza, J	NJ	918
PMR	Zimmerman, J	NJ	787
SM	Vaidya, S	NY	725

Specialty & Special Expertise Index

Specialty & Special Expertise Index

Specialty & Special Expertise Index

Spec	Name	St	Pg
ObG	Krause, C	NY	250
ObG	Levine, R	NY	250
ObG	Mack, L	NY	571
ObG	Rohr, M	CT	1006

Paragangliomas

Spec	Name	St	Pg
Oto	Myssiorek, D	NY	292

Paraneoplastic Syndromes

Spec	Name	St	Pg
N	Posner, J	NY	241

Parasitic Infections

Spec	Name	St	Pg
Ge	Connor, B	NY	170
Inf	Hartman, B	NY	195
Inf	Murray, H	NY	196
Inf	Weiss, L	NY	421
PrM	Cahill, J	NY	340

Parathyroid Cancer

Spec	Name	St	Pg
EDM	Haber, R	NY	163
Oto	Kuhel, W	NY	291
Oto	Shemen, L	NY	294

Parathyroid Disorders

Spec	Name	St	Pg
EDM	Agrin, R	NJ	865
EDM	Bockman, R	NY	162
EDM	Haber, R	NY	163
EDM	Hoffman, R	NY	523
EDM	Shane, E	NY	166
EDM	Silverberg, S	NY	166
Oto	Lane, E	CT	1015

Parathyroid Surgery

Spec	Name	St	Pg
S	Mendoza, E	NY	515
S	Shapiro, M	NJ	832

Parenting Issues

Spec	Name	St	Pg
AM	Alderman, E	NY	409
AM	Lopez, R	NY	120
AM	Marks, A	NY	120
AM	Zolkowski-Wynne, J	CT	973
ChAP	Lustbader, A	CT	979
ChAP	Turecki, S	NY	139
Ped	Berkowitz, I	NJ	785
Ped	Trachtenberg, J	NY	325

Parkinson's Disease

Spec	Name	St	Pg
GerPsy	Serby, M	NY	182
N	Blady, D	NJ	817
N	Bodis-Wollner, I	NY	472
N	Bressman, S	NY	234
N	Cohen, J	NY	426
N	Dickoff, D	NY	693
N	Fahn, S	NY	236
N	Foo, S	NY	236
N	Gendelman, S	NY	237
N	Gilson, N	NJ	892
N	Golbe, L	NJ	871
N	Goldstein, J	NY	237
N	Gross, E	NY	693
N	Herbstein, D	NY	237
N	Kay, A	NY	473
N	Kessler, J	NY	569
N	Knep, S	NJ	928
N	Levin, K	NJ	770
N	Levy, L	NY	569
N	Morris, J	NY	694
N	Oh, Y	NJ	872
N	Olanow, C	NY	240
N	Padela, M	NJ	928
N	Rabin, A	NJ	771
N	Rusk, A	CT	1003
N	Sachs, S	NJ	956
N	Sadeghi, H	NJ	839
N	Sage, J	NJ	872
N	Salgado, M	NY	474
N	Silbert, P	NJ	893
N	Sobol, N	NY	474
N	Vester, J	NJ	852
N	Waters, C	NY	243
N	Witte, A	NJ	852
NS	Zonenshayn, M	NY	472

Parkinson's Disease/Movement Disorders

Spec	Name	St	Pg
N	Louis, E	CT	239
NS	Goodman, R	NY	230

Parkinson's Disease/Visual Disorders

Spec	Name	St	Pg
N	Balcer, L	NY	234

Parotid Gland Surgery

Spec	Name	St	Pg
Oto	Huo, J	NY	512

Parotid Gland Tumors

Spec	Name	St	Pg
Oto	Shah, D	NJ	894

Paroxysmal Nocturnal Hemoglobinuria

Spec	Name	St	Pg
Hem	Aledort, L	NY	189

Spec	Name	St	Pg
Hem	Araten, D	NY	189

Patent Foramen Ovale(PFO) Closure

Spec	Name	St	Pg
PCd	Love, B	NY	305

Pathology

Spec	Name	St	Pg
Path	Altmeyer, V	CT	1016
Path	Antonescu, C	NY	300
Path	Babkowski, R	CT	1016
Path	Baer, R	CT	1016
Path	Barnard, N	NJ	876
Path	Bhattacharyya, P	NJ	779
Path	Bleiweiss, I	NY	300
Path	Borczuk, A	NY	300
Path	Cohen, J	NY	300
Path	Crawford, J	NY	580
Path	Ellenson, L	NY	300
Path	Esposito, M	NY	581
Path	Harpaz, N	NY	300
Path	Heller, D	NJ	822
Path	Hoda, S	NY	301
Path	Jessurun, J	NY	301
Path	Kahn, L	NY	581
Path	Klimstra, D	NY	301
Path	Lara, J	NJ	822
Path	Magro, C	NY	301
Path	Melamed, J	NY	301
Path	Olsen, D	NJ	779
Path	Orazi, A	NY	301
Path	Pinto, M	CT	1017
Path	Reuter, V	NY	301
Path	Rosenblum, M	NY	301
Path	Sanchez, M	NJ	779
Path	Soslow, R	NY	302
Path	Thung, S	NY	302
Path	Tornos, C	NY	640
Path	Travis, W	NY	302
Path	Vigorita, V	NY	481
Path	Wang, B	NY	302
Path	Wenig, B	NY	302
Path	Xu, B	CT	1017
Path	Zagzag, D	NY	302

Pediatric & Adolescent Gynecology Only

Spec	Name	St	Pg
ObG	Regard, M	NY	697

Pediatric & Adult Otolaryngology

Spec	Name	St	Pg
Oto	Li, R	NJ	854

Specialty & Special Expertise Index

Specialty & Special Expertise Index

Specialty & Special Expertise Index

Spec	Name	St	Pg
OrS	Roye, D	NY	282
OrS	Sabharwal, S	NJ	821
OrS	Scher, D	NY	283
OrS	Simon, S	NY	284
OrS	Sink, E	NY	284
OrS	Strongwater, A	NJ	929
OrS	Widmann, R	NY	286

Pediatric Otolaryngology

Spec	Name	St	Pg
Oto	Godin, D	NY	288
Oto	Grosso, J	NY	578
Oto	Jones, J	NY	289
Oto	Kase, S	NY	705
Oto	Klenoff, B	CT	1015
Oto	La Bagnara, J	NJ	930
Oto	Litman, R	NY	640
Oto	Rossos, A	NJ	894
Oto	Salzer, S	CT	1016
Oto	Surow, J	NJ	778
Oto	Vambutas, A	NY	580
Oto	Vastola, A	NY	480
Oto	Yankelowitz, S	NY	431
Oto	Youngerman, J	NY	580
Oto	Zahtz, G	NY	580
PO	April, M	NY	315
PO	Bent, J	NY	435
PO	Bernstein, J	NY	709
PO	De Serres, L	NY	710
PO	Dolitsky, J	NY	315
PO	Goldsmith, A	NY	484
PO	Grunstein, E	NY	315
PO	Haddad, J	NY	315
PO	Keller, J	NY	710
PO	Mendelsohn, M	NY	585
PO	Merer, D	NY	710
PO	Modi, V	NY	315
PO	Quraishi, H	NJ	782
PO	Respler, D	NJ	782
PO	Rosenfeld, R	NY	484
PO	Rothschild, M	NY	315
PO	Samadi, S	NJ	783
PO	Smith, L	NY	586
PO	Tavill, M	NJ	895
PO	Traquina, D	NJ	878
PO	Ward, R	NY	315

Pediatric Pathology

Spec	Name	St	Pg
Path	Heller, D	NJ	822

Pediatric Plastic Surgery

Spec	Name	St	Pg
PlS	Borah, G	NJ	880
PlS	Cherofsky, A	NY	530
PlS	Duboys, E	NY	644
PlS	Khoury, F	NY	716
PlS	Kim, T	NY	335
PlS	Lukash, F	NY	592
PlS	Ruotolo, R	NY	592
PlS	Silver, L	NY	338
PlS	Staffenberg, D	NY	339
PlS	Taub, P	NY	339
PS	Bhattacharyya, N	NJ	930

Pediatric Pulmonology

Spec	Name	St	Pg
PPul	Aguila, H	NJ	825
PPul	Amin, N	NY	710
PPul	Arens, R	NY	435
PPul	Atlas, A	NJ	916
PPul	Bieler, H	NJ	916
PPul	Bisberg, D	NJ	825
PPul	Boyer, J	NY	710
PPul	Chan, S	NY	529
PPul	Constantinescu, A	NY	316
PPul	Dimaio, M	NY	316
PPul	Dozor, A	NY	710
PPul	Dworkin, G	CT	1018
PPul	Giusti, R	NY	484
PPul	Hen, J	CT	1018
PPul	Kanengiser, S	NJ	783
PPul	Kaplan, E	NJ	783
PPul	Kass, L	NY	710
PPul	Kattan, M	NY	316
PPul	Kier, C	NY	642
PPul	Kohn, G	NJ	960
PPul	Kottler, W	NJ	825
PPul	Krishnan, S	NY	710
PPul	Lamm, C	NY	316
PPul	Lee, D	NJ	783
PPul	Lee, H	NY	484
PPul	Loughlin, G	NY	316
PPul	Lowenthal, D	NY	711
PPul	Marcus, M	NY	484
PPul	Mikkilineni, S	NJ	825
PPul	Montalvo Stanton, E	NJ	825
PPul	Nachajon, R	NJ	930
PPul	Narula, P	NY	484
PPul	Needleman, J	NY	484
PPul	Ngai, P	NJ	783
PPul	Pirzada, M	NY	586
PPul	Quittell, L	NY	711
PPul	Sadeghi, H	CT	1018
PPul	Schaeffer, J	NY	586
PPul	Ting, A	NY	316
PPul	Turcios, N	NJ	941
PPul	Vicencio, A	NY	316

Pediatric Radiology

Spec	Name	St	Pg
DR	Abramson, S	NY	156
DR	Amodio, J	NY	458
DR	Brill, P	NY	157
DR	Fefferman, N	NY	158
DR	Liebling, M	NJ	753
DR	Murphy, R	NJ	906
DR	Rosenfeld, D	NJ	864
DR	Ruzal-Shapiro, C	NY	161
DR	Underberg-Davis, S	NJ	865
NRad	Roychowdhury, S	NJ	872
RadRO	Moorthy, C	NY	722

Pediatric Rehabilitation

Spec	Name	St	Pg
Ped	Yalamanchi, K	NJ	879
PMR	Armento, M	NJ	961
PMR	Fantasia, M	NJ	879
PMR	Gifford, I	NY	486
PMR	Gold, J	NY	327
PMR	Kim, H	NY	327

Pediatric Rheumatology

Spec	Name	St	Pg
PRhu	Adams, A	NY	317
PRhu	Chalom, E	NJ	825
PRhu	Chao, C	NY	711
PRhu	Eichenfield, A	NY	317
PRhu	Gottlieb, B	NY	586
PRhu	Haines, K	NJ	783
PRhu	Ilowite, N	NY	435
PRhu	Imundo, L	NY	317
PRhu	Kimura, Y	NJ	783
PRhu	Lazarus, H	NY	317
PRhu	Lehman, T	NY	317
PRhu	Li, S	NJ	784
PRhu	Moorthy, L	NJ	878
PRhu	Starr, A	NY	317
PRhu	Weiss, J	NJ	784

Pediatric Sports Medicine

Spec	Name	St	Pg
OrS	Cristofaro, R	NY	702
OrS	Fond, J	NY	614
OrS	Lynch, M	CT	1012
OrS	Nelson, J	NY	703
Ped	Chianese, M	NY	587
SM	Rosen, J	NY	514
SM	Shifrin, S	NY	725

Pediatric Surgery

Spec	Name	St	Pg
PS	Alexander, F	NJ	784
PS	Bergman, K	NJ	960
PS	Bethel, C	NJ	826

Spec	Name	St	Pg
PS	Bhattacharyya, N	NJ	930
PS	Bodenstein, L	NY	317
PS	Cooper, A	NY	318
PS	Coren, C	NY	586
PS	Dolgin, S	NY	586
PS	Friedman, D	NJ	784
PS	Gallucci, J	NJ	879
PS	Gandhi, R	NJ	784
PS	Ginsburg, H	NY	318
PS	Hong, A	NY	586
PS	Jan, D	NY	435
PS	Kuenzler, K	NJ	784
PS	La Quaglia, M	NY	318
PS	Lee, T	NY	642
PS	McBride, W	NY	711
PS	Middlesworth, W	NY	318
PS	Midulla, P	NY	318
PS	Muensterer, O	NY	435
PS	Quaegebeur, J	NY	318
PS	Scriven, R	NY	642
PS	Spigland, N	NY	318
PS	Statter, M	NY	436
PS	Stringel, G	NY	711
PS	Stylianos, S	NY	318
PS	Tomita, S	NY	319
PS	Velcek, F	NY	319
PS	Weinberg, G	NY	436
PS	Zitsman, J	NY	711

Pediatric Thoracic Surgery

Spec	Name	St	Pg
PS	Spigland, N	NY	318

Pediatric Urology

Spec	Name	St	Pg
Ped Uro	Barone, J	NJ	941
Ped Uro	Casale, P	NY	319
Ped Uro	Connor, J	NJ	917
Ped Uro	Fleisher, M	NJ	879
Ped Uro	Franco, I	NY	711
Ped Uro	Friedman, S	NY	485
Ped Uro	Gitlin, J	NY	587
Ped Uro	Hensle, T	NJ	784
Ped Uro	Hensle, T	NJ	784
Ped Uro	Horowitz, M	NY	529
Ped Uro	Hyun, G	NY	319
Ped Uro	Koo, H	NJ	785
Ped Uro	Poppas, D	NY	319
Ped Uro	Reda, E	NY	712
Ped Uro	Schlussel, R	NY	319
Ped Uro	Shapiro, E	NY	319
Ped Uro	Stock, J	NJ	826
Ped Uro	Vates, T	NJ	879
Ped Uro	Wasnick, R	NY	642

Spec	Name	St	Pg
PS	Ginsburg, H	NY	318
U	Glassman, C	NY	729
U	Hanna, M	NY	604
U	Hennessy, W	CT	1032
U	Ring, K	NJ	965

Pediatrics

Spec	Name	St	Pg
Ped	Abularrage, J	NY	512
Ped	Acker, P	NY	712
Ped	Adesman, A	NY	587
Ped	Ajl, S	NY	485
Ped	Allendorf, D	NY	320
Ped	Alon, J	CT	1018
Ped	Altman, R	NY	712
Ped	Amer, J	NY	587
Ped	Andrade, J	NY	436
Ped	Angello, T	NY	712
Ped	Arnstein, E	NY	436
Ped	Arpadi, S	NY	320
Ped	Ashton, J	NJ	917
Ped	Avvocato, G	NY	712
Ped	Ayyanathan, K	NJ	960
Ped	Bailey, M	NY	712
Ped	Baiser, D	NJ	854
Ped	Baker, A	NJ	841
Ped	Balk, S	NY	436
Ped	Barsh, E	NY	712
Ped	Baskind, L	NY	712
Ped	Bastawros, M	NY	529
Ped	Beckman, K	CT	1018
Ped	Belamarich, P	NY	436
Ped	Berkowitz, I	NJ	785
Ped	Berkowitz, N	NY	712
Ped	Berman, M	NY	713
Ped	Bernstein, W	NY	615
Ped	Bienstock, J	NJ	785
Ped	Bloomfield, D	NY	436
Ped	Bodner, S	NY	320
Ped	Boim, M	NJ	854
Ped	Bomback, F	NY	713
Ped	Bookner, S	NY	713
Ped	Brovender, B	NY	320
Ped	Brown, J	NY	320
Ped	Buchalter, M	NJ	785
Ped	Bulmash, M	NY	485
Ped	Burstin, H	NY	320
Ped	Cahill, L	NY	436
Ped	Chambers, H	NY	437
Ped	Chernobilsky, L	NY	642
Ped	Chessin, R	CT	1018
Ped	Chianese, M	NY	587
Ped	Cohen, B	CT	1018

Spec	Name	St	Pg
Ped	Cohen, D	NY	615
Ped	Cohen, E	CT	1019
Ped	Cohen, M	NY	320
Ped	Collins, M	NY	713
Ped	Colyer-Aversa, L	NJ	826
Ped	Cooper, S	NY	587
Ped	Corbo, E	NJ	960
Ped	Coven, B	NY	713
Ped	Cowan, S	NY	713
Ped	Cross, J	NY	320
Ped	Cusumano, B	NY	643
Ped	Davis, K	NJ	961
Ped	Diamant, E	NY	616
Ped	Duchnowska, A	NY	529
Ped	Edelstein, G	NY	321
Ped	Eisenberg, A	NY	713
Ped	Esteban-Cruciani, N	NY	437
Ped	Feldman, S	NY	485
Ped	Ferguson, K	CT	1019
Ped	Ferrier, G	NY	321
Ped	Festa, R	NY	643
Ped	Frank, M	NY	321
Ped	Freedman, R	CT	1019
Ped	Freilich, S	NY	321
Ped	Friedman, E	NY	587
Ped	Gerberg, L	NY	587
Ped	Glaser, A	NY	485
Ped	Goldstein, J	NY	321
Ped	Goldstein, S	NY	512
Ped	Gotfried, F	NJ	917
Ped	Gould, E	NY	587
Ped	Green, A	NY	588
Ped	Grijnsztein, J	NY	588
Ped	Gropper, D	CT	1019
Ped	Gruenwald, L	NJ	826
Ped	Haber, P	NY	437
Ped	Handler, R	NJ	917
Ped	Hankin, D	NY	588
Ped	Harlow, P	NJ	785
Ped	Hartz, C	NY	713
Ped	Hedrick, D	CT	1019
Ped	Hes, D	NY	321
Ped	Hiltebeitel, C	NY	321
Ped	Hirschman, A	NY	437
Ped	Ho, S	NY	321
Ped	Igel, G	NY	437
Ped	Inamdar, S	NY	321
Ped	Jackson, R	NY	485
Ped	Juan, P	CT	1019
Ped	Kahn, M	NY	322
Ped	Kanter, A	NJ	785
Ped	Kaplan, M	NY	643
Ped	Karlsrud, K	NY	322

Specialty & Special Expertise Index

Castle Connolly *Top Doctors: New York Metro Area* 18th Edition

Specialty & Special Expertise Index

Specialty & Special Expertise Index

Spec	Name	St	Pg
VascS	Bernik, T	NY	403
VascS	D'Ayala, M	NY	495
VascS	Faries, P	NY	403
VascS	Faust, G	NY	606
VascS	Harrington, M	NY	404
VascS	Imegwu, O	NJ	944
VascS	Landis, G	NY	606
VascS	Laskowski, I	NY	732
VascS	Lee, A	NY	517
VascS	Lipsitz, E	NY	445
VascS	Marin, M	NY	404
VascS	Marsan, B	CT	1033
VascS	Menezes, N	NY	495
VascS	Pollina, R	NY	650
VascS	Rhee, R	NY	495
VascS	Rockman, C	NY	405
VascS	Rodino, W	NY	533
VascS	Sales, C	NJ	966
VascS	Schneider, D	NY	405
VascS	Tassiopoulos, A	NY	650
VascS	Teodorescu, V	NY	405
VascS	Yang, P	NY	406
VIR	Cynamon, J	NY	445
VIR	Rundback, J	NJ	798

Peritoneal Carcinomatosis

GO	Wallach, R	NY	185

Peritoneal Mucinous Carcinomatosis

CRS	Guillem, J	NY	143

Personality Disorders

Psyc	Barbuto, J	NY	342
Psyc	Bauman, J	NY	717
Psyc	Caligor, E	NY	343
Psyc	Caligor, E	NY	343
Psyc	Gelfand, J	NY	439
Psyc	Karasu, T	NY	346
Psyc	Preter, M	NY	350
Psyc	Rosenfeld, D	NJ	789
Psyc	Sacks, M	NY	351
Psyc	Samberg, E	NY	351
Psyc	Schneider, S	NJ	856
Psyc	Siever, L	NY	352
Psyc	Stone, M	NY	353

Personality Disorders-Borderline

Psyc	Aronson, T	NY	645
Psyc	Dulit, R	NY	718

Spec	Name	St	Pg

Pervasive Development Disorders

ChAP	Perry, R	NY	138
ChAP	Shampain, L	NJ	863

PET Imaging

DR	Bobroff, L	NY	610
DR	Cohen, B	NY	157
DR	Kirshy, D	NY	626
DR	Neistadt, L	NY	160
DR	Sherman, S	NY	550
NuM	Agress, H	NJ	772
NuM	Carrasquillo, J	NY	245
NuM	Freeman, L	NY	427
NuM	Friedman, K	NY	245
NuM	Gerard, P	NY	695
NuM	Ghesani, M	NY	245
NuM	Goldsmith, S	NY	245
NuM	Johns, W	CT	1004
NuM	Palestro, C	NY	570
NuM	Pandit-Taskar, N	NY	246

PET Imaging-Brain

NuM	Strashun, A	NY	474

Peyronie's Disease

U	Mellinger, B	NY	604
U	Sadeghi-Nejad, H	NJ	797

Phenylketonuria (PKU)

CG	Wasserstein, M	NY	142

Pheochromocytoma

Nep	Byrd, L	NJ	910
Nep	Ruddy, M	NJ	851
S	Fahey, T	NY	379

Photodynamic Therapy

D	Alexiades-Armenakas, M	NY	145
D	Gmyrek, R	NY	149
D	Scherl, S	NJ	751

Phototherapy

D	Andrews, A	NJ	750
D	Greenspan, A	NY	149
D	Soter, N	NY	155

Phyllodes Tumors

S	Bernik, S	NY	377

Spec	Name	St	Pg

Physical Medicine & Rehabilitation

PMR	Aaronson, B	CT	1020
PMR	Agri, R	NJ	855
PMR	Ahn, J	NY	326
PMR	Armento, M	NJ	961
PMR	Averill, A	NJ	786
PMR	Bach, J	NJ	826
PMR	Beer, J	NY	589
PMR	Birnbaum, H	NY	326
PMR	Brief, R	NY	616
PMR	Brown, A	NY	326
PMR	Brown, D	NJ	879
PMR	Bryce, T	NY	326
PMR	Cole, J	NJ	827
PMR	Dauhajre, R	NY	512
PMR	Diamond, M	NJ	961
PMR	Dillard, J	NY	327
PMR	Fantasia, M	NJ	879
PMR	Feinberg, J	NY	327
PMR	Filippone, M	NJ	841
PMR	Flanagan, S	NY	327
PMR	Francis, K	NJ	827
PMR	Freedman, J	CT	1021
PMR	Frieden, R	NY	327
PMR	Gifford, I	NY	486
PMR	Gold, J	NY	327
PMR	Gotlin, R	NY	327
PMR	Grant, L	CT	1021
PMR	Greenwald, B	NJ	880
PMR	Gribbin, D	NJ	855
PMR	Gross, S	NY	715
PMR	Guarracini, M	NY	616
PMR	Harris, P	NY	486
PMR	Heftler, J	CT	1021
PMR	Herrera, J	NY	327
PMR	Inwald, G	NY	438
PMR	John, S	NY	644
PMR	Kim, H	NY	327
PMR	Kirshblum, S	NJ	827
PMR	Klecz, R	NJ	918
PMR	Lachmann, E	NY	328
PMR	Lee, A	NY	328
PMR	Levin, S	NY	438
PMR	Lipetz, J	NY	589
PMR	Liss, D	NJ	787
PMR	Liss, H	NJ	787
PMR	Lutz, C	NY	328
PMR	Lutz, G	NY	328
PMR	Ma, D	NY	328
PMR	Malanga, G	NJ	961
PMR	Moldover, J	NY	328
PMR	Mulford, G	NJ	918

Specialty & Special Expertise Index

Spec	Name	St	Pg
PMR	Neely, M	NY	328
PMR	O'Dell, M	NY	328
PMR	Pak, K	NY	329
PMR	Pechman, K	NY	715
PMR	Pici, R	NY	715
PMR	Pipia, P	NY	486
PMR	Ragnarsson, K	NY	329
PMR	Randolph, A	NY	715
PMR	Rashbaum, I	NY	329
PMR	Reid, M	NY	329
PMR	Rho, D	NY	329
PMR	Richter, E	CT	1021
PMR	Robinson, M	NY	616
PMR	Root, M	NY	589
PMR	Rosenberg, C	NY	644
PMR	Ross, M	NY	486
PMR	Sheth, P	NY	329
PMR	Shumko, J	NJ	827
PMR	Simotas, A	NY	329
PMR	Slaten, W	NY	616
PMR	Snowball, H	CT	1021
PMR	Solomon, J	NY	329
PMR	Stein, A	NY	589
PMR	Stein, J	NY	330
PMR	Stein, P	NY	486
PMR	Stubblefield, M	NY	330
PMR	Thomas, D	NY	330
PMR	Thomas, M	NY	438
PMR	Vad, V	NY	330
PMR	Valenza, J	NJ	918
PMR	Vallarino, R	NY	512
PMR	Varlotta, G	NY	330
PMR	Weinberg, J	NY	529
PMR	Weiner, K	NY	529
PMR	Weiss, L	NY	589
PMR	Whiteson, J	NY	330
PMR	Zimmerman, J	NJ	787

Pigmented Lesions

Spec	Name	St	Pg
D	Rosenberg, B	NY	667

Pituitary Disorders

Spec	Name	St	Pg
EDM	Baranetsky, N	NJ	809
EDM	Benaviv-Meskin, D	CT	983
EDM	Bitton, R	NY	551
EDM	Brand, H	NY	626
EDM	Carlson, H	NY	626
EDM	Cobin, R	NJ	754
EDM	Friedman, S	NY	551
EDM	Gelato, M	NY	627
EDM	Goldman, M	NJ	754
EDM	Gordon, J	NY	551

Spec	Name	St	Pg
EDM	Jacobs, T	NY	164
EDM	Kleinberg, D	NY	164
EDM	Levine, A	NY	164
EDM	Maman, A	NJ	865
EDM	Margulies, P	NY	551
EDM	Martorella, A	NY	165
EDM	Park, P	NY	459
EDM	Rosenthal, D	NY	552
EDM	Rosman, L	NY	502
EDM	Selinger, S	NJ	951
EDM	Spiler, I	NJ	865
EDM	Wardlaw, S	NY	166
EDM	Warman, J	NY	459
EDM	Wehmann, R	NJ	754
NRad	Khandji, A	NY	244
PEn	Kohn, B	NY	306

Pituitary Tumors

Spec	Name	St	Pg
NS	Bruce, J	NY	229
NS	Cardoso, E	NY	471
NS	De Lotbiniere, A	NY	692
NS	Eisenberg, M	NY	566
NS	Murali, R	NY	692
NS	Nosko, M	NJ	870
NS	Post, K	NY	232
NS	Schwartz, A	NY	471
NS	Schwartz, T	NY	232
NS	Shear, P	CT	1002
Onc	Fine, R	NY	215
Oto	Shikowitz, M	NY	579

Plastic & Reconstructive Surgery

Spec	Name	St	Pg
PlS	Chin, S	NY	715
PlS	Israeli, R	NY	591
PlS	Kasabian, A	NY	591
PlS	Sofer, A	CT	1022

Plastic Surgery

Spec	Name	St	Pg
PlS	Ablaza, V	NJ	827
PlS	Addona, T	NY	589
PlS	Ahn, C	NY	330
PlS	Alizadeh, K	NY	590
PlS	Allen, R	NY	331
PlS	Anton, J	NY	644
PlS	Ascherman, J	NY	331
PlS	Ashinoff, R	NJ	896
PlS	Aston, S	NY	331
PlS	Attkiss, K	CT	1021
PlS	Baker, D	NY	331
PlS	Beran, S	NY	715
PlS	Borah, G	NJ	880
PlS	Boss, W	NJ	787

Spec	Name	St	Pg
PlS	Breitbart, A	NY	590
PlS	Breslow, G	NJ	787
PlS	Bromley, G	NY	331
PlS	Broumand, S	NY	331
PlS	Chen, C	NY	331
PlS	Cherofsky, A	NY	530
PlS	Chidyllo, S	NJ	896
PlS	Chin, S	NY	715
PlS	Chiu, D	NY	331
PlS	Choi, M	NY	332
PlS	Colen, H	NY	332
PlS	Colon, F	NJ	918
PlS	Cordeiro, P	NY	332
PlS	Cozzone, J	NJ	787
PlS	Cutolo, L	NY	530
PlS	D'Amico, R	NJ	787
PlS	Dagum, A	NY	644
PlS	Davenport, T	NY	590
PlS	Dayan, J	NY	332
PlS	DeVita, G	NY	590
PlS	DiBernardo, B	NJ	827
PlS	DiGregorio, V	NY	590
PlS	Diktaban, T	NY	332
PlS	Disa, J	NY	332
PlS	Drimmer, M	NJ	855
PlS	Dubner, S	NY	590
PlS	Duboys, E	NY	644
PlS	Dudick, S	NJ	896
PlS	Elkowitz, M	NY	590
PlS	Elkwood, A	NJ	896
PlS	Feinberg, J	NY	591
PlS	Figlia, P	NJ	931
PlS	Fiorillo, M	NY	616
PlS	Forley, B	NY	332
PlS	Foster, C	NY	332
PlS	Freund, R	NY	333
PlS	Friedman, D	NY	333
PlS	Funt, D	NY	591
PlS	Gallagher, P	NY	591
PlS	Ganchi, P	NJ	931
PlS	Gardner, J	NJ	961
PlS	Garfein, E	NY	439
PlS	Gayle, L	NY	333
PlS	Gewirtz, H	CT	1021
PlS	Glasberg, S	NY	333
PlS	Glicksman, C	NJ	896
PlS	Godfrey, N	NY	333
PlS	Godfrey, P	NY	333
PlS	Gold, A	NY	591
PlS	Goldenberg, D	CT	1021
PlS	Goldstein, R	NY	439
PlS	Gotkin, R	NY	333
PlS	Granick, M	NJ	827

Specialty & Special Expertise Index

Spec	Name	St	Pg
PlS	Grant, R	NY	334
PlS	Greenstein, B	NY	439
PlS	Greenwald, J	NY	716
PlS	Groeger, W	NY	591
PlS	Herbstman, R	NJ	880
PlS	Hetzler, P	NJ	896
PlS	Hidalgo, D	NY	334
PlS	Hirmand, H	NY	334
PlS	Hoffman, L	NY	334
PlS	Hunter, J	NY	334
PlS	Hyans, P	NJ	962
PlS	Imber, G	NY	334
PlS	Islam, S	CT	1022
PlS	Israeli, R	NY	591
PlS	Jacobs, E	NY	334
PlS	Karp, N	NY	334
PlS	Kasabian, A	NY	591
PlS	Kaufman, M	NJ	880
PlS	Kessler, M	NY	591
PlS	Khoury, F	NY	716
PlS	Kilgo, M	NY	592
PlS	Kim, T	NY	335
PlS	Kleinman, A	NY	716
PlS	Koch, R	NY	716
PlS	Kolker, A	NY	335
PlS	LaBruna, A	NY	335
PlS	Lange, D	NJ	918
PlS	Leach, T	NJ	855
PlS	Leipziger, L	NY	592
PlS	Lesesne, C	NY	335
PlS	Levine, J	NY	335
PlS	Levine, J	NY	335
PlS	Liebling, R	NY	439
PlS	Lipson, D	NJ	787
PlS	LoVerme, P	NJ	828
PlS	Lukash, F	NY	592
PlS	Marotta, J	NY	644
PlS	Matarasso, A	NY	335
PlS	Mehrara, B	NY	336
PlS	Monasebian, D	NY	336
PlS	Newman, F	CT	1022
PlS	Newman, S	NY	716
PlS	Nini, K	NJ	880
PlS	O'Connell, J	CT	1022
PlS	Olson, R	NJ	942
PlS	Otterburn, D	NY	336
PlS	Palaia, D	NY	716
PlS	Passaretti, D	CT	1022
PlS	Perrotti, J	NY	336
PlS	Perry, A	NJ	942
PlS	Pfeifer, T	NY	336
PlS	Pisarenko, V	NY	716
PlS	Ponamgi, S	NJ	788

Spec	Name	St	Pg
PlS	Pyo, D	NJ	919
PlS	Rafizadeh, F	NJ	919
PlS	Raskin, E	CT	1022
PlS	Razaboni, R	NY	336
PlS	Reiffel, R	NY	716
PlS	Rodriguez, E	NY	336
PlS	Romita, M	NY	336
PlS	Rose, E	NY	337
PlS	Rose, M	NJ	897
PlS	Rosen, A	NJ	828
PlS	Rosenberg, M	NY	717
PlS	Rosenblatt, W	NY	337
PlS	Rosenstock, A	CT	1022
PlS	Roth, D	NY	717
PlS	Ruotolo, R	NY	592
PlS	Sabry, M	NY	337
PlS	Samra, S	NJ	897
PlS	Sasson, H	NY	592
PlS	Schaffner, A	NY	337
PlS	Schulman, M	NY	337
PlS	Schulman, N	NY	337
PlS	Schwartz, M	NY	337
PlS	Shafer, D	NY	338
PlS	Sharma, S	NY	338
PlS	Sherman, J	NY	338
PlS	Silberman, M	NY	592
PlS	Silich, R	NY	338
PlS	Silver, L	NY	338
PlS	Simpson, R	NY	592
PlS	Skolnik, R	NY	338
PlS	Smith, M	NY	338
PlS	Smotrich, G	NJ	855
PlS	Sofer, A	CT	1022
PlS	Spector, J	NY	338
PlS	Spinelli, H	NY	339
PlS	Staffenberg, D	NY	339
PlS	Starker, I	NJ	919
PlS	Sternschein, M	NJ	788
PlS	Sultan, M	NY	339
PlS	Suzman, M	NY	717
PlS	Swift, R	NY	339
PlS	Tabbal, N	NY	339
PlS	Talmor, M	NY	339
PlS	Taub, P	NY	339
PlS	Tepper, H	NJ	962
PlS	Thorne, C	NY	339
PlS	Ting, J	NY	340
PlS	Verga, M	NY	340
PlS	Vickery, C	NY	340
PlS	Weinstein, L	NJ	919
PlS	Weiss, P	NY	340
PlS	Wells, S	NY	340
PlS	Wey, P	NJ	880

Spec	Name	St	Pg
PlS	Winters, R	NJ	788
PlS	Zaccaria, A	NJ	897
PlS	Zapiach, L	NJ	788
PlS	Zeitels, J	NJ	962
PlS	Zevon, S	NY	340
PlS	Zide, B	NY	340
PlS	Zubowski, R	NJ	788

Platelet Disorders

Hem	Aledort, L	NY	189
Hem	Billett, H	NY	420
Hem	Green, D	NY	190
Hem	Vogel, J	NY	192
PHO	Bussel, J	NY	309
PHO	Parker, R	NY	641

Pneumococcal Infections

PInf	Prince, A	NY	313

Pneumonia

CCM	Siegel, R	NY	413
Inf	Cunha, B	NY	558
Inf	McLeod, G	CT	990
Inf	Parry, M	CT	990
Ped	Corbo, E	NJ	960
Ped	Quinn, L	NY	643
PPul	Kanengiser, S	NJ	783
PPul	Kohn, G	NJ	960
Pul	Baskin, M	NY	355
Pul	Bergman, M	NY	488
Pul	Bernstein, M	CT	1024
Pul	Bondi, E	NY	488
Pul	Fein, A	NY	595
Pul	Leeman, B	NY	595
Pul	Levine, S	NJ	790
Pul	Nash, T	NY	358
Pul	Niederman, M	NY	596
Pul	Rudolph, D	CT	1025
Pul	Winter, S	CT	1026

Poison Control

PrM	Crane, M	NY	341
PrM	Hoffman, R	NY	341

Polycystic Kidney Disease

Nep	Blumenfeld, J	NY	226
Nep	Gardenswartz, M	NY	226
Nep	Winchester, J	NY	228
PNep	Goilav, B	NY	434
PNep	Kaskel, F	NY	434

Specialty & Special Expertise Index

Specialty & Special Expertise Index

Specialty & Special Expertise Index

Spec	Name	St	Pg
Cv	Meizlish, J	CT	978
Cv	Meller, J	NY	131
Cv	Mercando, A	NY	659
Cv	Mintz, G	NY	544
Cv	Moskovits, N	NY	454
Cv	Nash, I	NY	131
Cv	Neeson, F	CT	978
Cv	Neuberg, G	NY	412
Cv	O'Brien, F	NY	131
Cv	Paiusco, A	NY	454
Cv	Phillips, M	NY	412
Cv	Radwaner, B	NY	132
Cv	Raska, K	NJ	904
Cv	Reichstein, R	NY	132
Cv	Ronen, A	CT	978
Cv	Saroff, A	NJ	806
Cv	Schiffer, M	NY	133
Cv	Seinfeld, D	NY	134
Cv	Siegel, S	NY	134
Cv	Slama, R	NJ	949
Cv	Southren, D	NY	609
Cv	Spadaro, L	NY	545
Cv	Spiegel, A	NY	135
Cv	Stein, R	NY	135
Cv	Steinbaum, S	NY	135
Cv	Unger, A	NY	135
Cv	Wein, P	NY	455
Cv	Weintraub, H	NY	136
Cv	Weisenseel, A	NY	136
Cv	Weiss, E	NJ	925
Cv	Winter, S	NY	522
Cv	Zimmerman, F	NY	661
FMed	Annabi, I	NY	671
FMed	Rednor, J	NJ	848
IC	Abittan, M	NY	561
IC	Innerfield, M	NY	612
IC	Lawson, W	NY	633
IC	Nero, T	CT	996
IC	Selter, J	CT	996
IM	Blumberg, J	CT	991
IM	Case, D	NY	199
IM	Kennish, A	NY	203
IM	Lipton, M	NY	204
IM	Porder, J	NY	206
IM	Puglisi, J	CT	993
IM	Sherman, I	NY	206
IM	Underberg, J	NY	207
IM	Warshafsky, S	NY	685
IM	Zaremski, B	NY	208
PCd	Langsner, A	NY	304

Preventive Medicine

AM	Blaustein, S	NJ	925

Spec	Name	St	Pg
AM	Brill, S	NJ	861
AM	Imbornone, P	NJ	741
Cv	Rothman, H	NJ	748
FMed	Acosta, R	CT	984
FMed	Annabi, I	NY	671
FMed	Aponte, A	NY	627
FMed	Cassotta, J	NJ	755
FMed	Coloka-Kump, R	NY	416
FMed	Duchen, D	CT	984
FMed	Edelstein, M	NY	552
FMed	Falkoff, A	CT	984
FMed	Filiberto, C	CT	985
FMed	Fisher, G	NY	503
FMed	Gottesfeld, P	NY	671
FMed	Greenblatt, L	NY	628
FMed	Herbert, J	CT	985
FMed	Lyon, V	NY	168
FMed	Mallozzi, A	CT	985
FMed	McConnell, J	NJ	755
FMed	Miller, L	CT	985
FMed	Morrow, R	NY	416
FMed	Pollak, J	NJ	838
FMed	Sadovsky, R	NY	460
FMed	Steckel, R	NJ	937
FMed	Sutton, I	NY	672
FMed	Vincent, M	NY	460
Ger	Adelman, R	NY	180
Ger	Arunachalam, M	NJ	811
Ger	Baccash, E	NY	462
Ger	Banc, T	NY	676
Ger	Brody, S	NY	504
Ger	Callahan, E	NY	180
Ger	Chun, A	NY	180
Ger	Dharmarajan, T	NY	419
Ger	Feher, L	NY	181
Ger	Fields, S	NY	629
Ger	Finkelstein, M	NY	181
Ger	Fogel, J	NY	181
Ger	Gohel, R	NJ	889
Ger	Guzik, H	NY	555
Ger	Karp, A	NY	181
Ger	Korc-Grodzicki, B	NY	181
Ger	Lanman, G	NY	555
Ger	Martimucci, W	NY	677
Ger	Paris, B	NY	462
Ger	Russell, R	NY	419
Ger	Seminara, D	NY	524
IM	Balot, B	NY	631
IM	Baskin, D	NY	198
IM	Baum, D	CT	991
IM	Beyda, A	NY	506
IM	Bivona, J	CT	991
IM	Brewer, M	NY	506

Spec	Name	St	Pg
IM	Bush, M	NY	199
IM	Cacciola, T	NJ	762
IM	Charap, P	NY	199
IM	Cohen, B	NY	465
IM	Cohen, R	NY	199
IM	Cohen, R	NY	199
IM	Costanzo, J	CT	991
IM	Dechiario, A	NY	200
IM	Dhalla, S	NY	200
IM	Dolinsky, J	NY	200
IM	Dreyer, N	CT	992
IM	Edelmann, C	CT	992
IM	Ehrlich, M	NY	200
IM	Ellis, E	NY	465
IM	Etingin, O	NY	200
IM	Federman, A	NY	200
IM	Feltheimer, S	NY	201
IM	Fisher, L	NY	201
IM	Fisher, S	CT	992
IM	Fojas, A	NY	422
IM	Friedling, S	NY	631
IM	Friedman, J	NY	201
IM	Fukilman, O	NY	507
IM	Gelbard, S	NY	201
IM	Gelberg, B	NY	559
IM	German, H	NY	631
IM	Glassman, C	NY	611
IM	Glazer, S	CT	992
IM	Glowacki, J	NJ	890
IM	Goldstein, P	NY	202
IM	Gorski, L	NY	560
IM	Greaney, E	NY	202
IM	Grunzweig, M	NY	465
IM	Handelsman, R	NY	611
IM	Hasapis, P	CT	992
IM	Hauptman, A	NY	202
IM	Herzog, D	NY	682
IM	Hoffman, P	CT	992
IM	Hopkins, A	NY	683
IM	Horbar, G	NY	203
IM	Horn, J	CT	992
IM	Hsuih, T	NY	466
IM	Israel, S	CT	992
IM	Kaiser, S	NY	466
IM	Kapoor, S	NY	683
IM	Karmen, C	NY	683
IM	Karol, N	CT	993
IM	Kennedy, J	NY	203
IM	Klein, N	CT	993
IM	Kurth, R	NY	203
IM	Lamm, S	NY	203
IM	Lewin, M	NY	204
IM	Lewin, N	NY	204

Specialty & Special Expertise Index

Specialty & Special Expertise Index

Spec	Name	St	Pg
Prostate Cancer-MR Spectroscopy (MRSI)			
DR	Hricak, H	NY	158
Prostate Cancer/Robotic Surgery			
U	Agarwal, S	NJ	795
U	Badani, K	NY	391
U	Benson, M	NY	392
U	Boczko, J	NY	728
U	Eastham, J	NY	393
U	Esposito, M	NJ	796
U	Gershbaum, M	NY	603
U	Ghavamian, R	NY	444
U	Karanikolas, N	NY	532
U	Lanteri, V	NJ	797
U	Lerner, S	NY	729
U	Samadi, D	NY	397
U	Sawczuk, I	NJ	797
U	Scherr, D	NY	397
U	Tewari, A	NY	399
U	Trauzzi, S	NY	730
Prostate Disease			
U	Axelrod, S	NY	728
U	Boczko, S	NY	392
U	DeTorres, W	NJ	796
U	Fine, E	NY	393
U	Giella, J	NY	618
U	Glassman, C	NY	729
U	Gribetz, M	NY	394
U	Harris, S	NY	604
U	Kaminetsky, J	NY	394
U	Kaplan, S	NY	395
U	Katz, H	NJ	842
U	Katz, J	NJ	832
U	Lessing, J	NY	532
U	Litvin, Y	NJ	899
U	Loo, M	NY	395
U	Lowe, F	NY	395
U	Lumerman, J	NY	604
U	Margolis, E	NJ	797
U	McGovern, T	NY	396
U	Meisenberg, G	NY	494
U	Muldoon, L	CT	1032
U	Nurzia, M	CT	1032
U	Owens, G	NY	730
U	Peng, B	NY	397
U	Provet, J	NY	397
U	Raboy, A	NY	532
U	Roberts, L	NY	730
U	Rosenthal, S	NY	494

Spec	Name	St	Pg
U	Rotolo, J	NJ	899
U	Sadeghi-Nejad, H	NJ	797
U	Samadi, D	NY	397
U	Santarosa, R	CT	1032
U	Schrager, A	NY	730
U	Sunshine, R	NY	605
U	Tarasuk, A	NY	516
U	Trauzzi, S	NY	730
U	Ziegelbaum, M	NY	605
Proton Beam Therapy			
RadRO	Hug, E	NJ	943
PRP (Platelet Rich Plasma)			
OrS	Morgan, D	NY	479
Prune Belly Syndrome			
Ped Uro	Franco, I	NY	711
Pseudomotor Cerebri			
N	Lepore, F	NJ	871
Pseudoxanthoma Elasticum			
Oph	Fuchs, W	NY	258
Psoriasis			
D	Alexis, A	NY	146
D	Almeida, L	NJ	906
D	Bagel, J	NJ	847
D	Belsito, D	NY	146
D	Buchness, M	NY	147
D	Cohen, S	NY	413
D	Deitz, M	NY	457
D	Drugge, R	CT	980
D	Falcon, R	NY	548
D	Feldman, P	NY	457
D	Fox, A	NJ	936
D	Fried, S	NJ	751
D	Goldenberg, G	NY	149
D	Grossman, K	NJ	888
D	Grossman, M	NY	665
D	Hatcher, V	NY	150
D	Hisler, B	NY	549
D	Katz, S	NY	151
D	Lebwohl, M	NY	151
D	Lukash, B	NY	666
D	McAleer, P	CT	981
D	Morel, K	NY	152
D	Notaro, A	NY	625
D	Pesce, J	CT	981
D	Possick, P	NJ	751

Spec	Name	St	Pg
D	Shupack, J	NY	155
D	Skrokov, R	NY	625
D	Soter, N	NY	155
D	Sturza, J	NY	667
D	Waldorf, D	NY	610
D	Walther, R	NY	155
Psoriasis/Eczema			
D	Danziger, S	NY	457
D	Orlow, S	NY	153
Psoriatic Arthritis			
Rhu	Adlersberg, J	NY	368
Rhu	Aizer, J	NY	368
Rhu	Barone, R	NY	723
Rhu	Berger, J	NY	723
Rhu	Danehower, R	CT	1028
Rhu	Efthimiou, P	NY	491
Rhu	Goodman, S	NY	370
Rhu	Karp, S	CT	1028
Rhu	Lee, S	NY	370
Rhu	Marchetta, P	NY	371
Rhu	Marmur, R	NY	724
Rhu	Mitnick, H	NY	371
Rhu	Nascimento, J	CT	1029
Rhu	Rose, R	CT	1029
Rhu	Schwartzfarb, L	NY	372
Rhu	Solomon, G	NY	373
Rhu	Wasser, K	NJ	897
Rhu	Yegudin-Ash, J	NY	724
Psychiatry			
Psyc	Abrams, L	CT	1022
Psyc	Addonizio, G	NY	717
Psyc	Adler, L	NY	341
Psyc	Alper, K	NY	341
Psyc	Appelbaum, P	NY	341
Psyc	Arkow, S	NY	341
Psyc	Aronoff, M	NY	341
Psyc	Aronson, T	NY	645
Psyc	Attia, E	NY	341
Psyc	Badikian, A	NY	717
Psyc	Bailine, S	NY	593
Psyc	Barbuto, J	NY	342
Psyc	Basch, S	NY	342
Psyc	Bauman, J	NY	717
Psyc	Behr, R	NY	593
Psyc	Benjamin, J	NY	593
Psyc	Berkowitz, H	NY	487
Psyc	Berman, S	NY	593
Psyc	Bhatt, A	NY	593
Psyc	Bialer, P	NY	342

Specialty & Special Expertise Index

Spec	Name	St	Pg	Spec	Name	St	Pg	Spec	Name	St	Pg
Psyc	Blatter, B	NY	342	Psyc	Gupta, A	NY	593	Psyc	Mendelowitz, A	NY	513
Psyc	Bogen, S	NY	717	Psyc	Gurevich, M	NY	594	Psyc	Menza, M	NJ	881
Psyc	Bone, S	NY	342	Psyc	Gurland, F	NJ	789	Psyc	Meyers, B	NY	719
Psyc	Borbely, A	NY	342	Psyc	Harlam, D	NY	718	Psyc	Michels, R	NY	348
Psyc	Breindel, D	NY	717	Psyc	Hart, S	CT	1023	Psyc	Miller, D	NJ	962
Psyc	Breitbart, W	NY	342	Psyc	Heiman, P	NY	439	Psyc	Milone, R	NY	719
Psyc	Brenner, R	NY	593	Psyc	Heisman, A	NY	487	Psyc	Moore, J	NY	348
Psyc	Brodie, J	NY	342	Psyc	Heller, S	NY	346	Psyc	Moraille, P	NJ	842
Psyc	Bronheim, H	NY	343	Psyc	Hindin, L	NJ	828	Psyc	Morgan, C	CT	1023
Psyc	Brown, R	NY	343	Psyc	Hoffman, J	NY	346	Psyc	Mueller, F	CT	1023
Psyc	Budman, C	NY	593	Psyc	Hollander, E	NY	346	Psyc	Muskin, P	NY	349
Psyc	Bukberg, J	NY	343	Psyc	Jacoby, J	NJ	841	Psyc	Narula, A	NJ	789
Psyc	Bulgarelli, C	NY	343	Psyc	Jones, F	NJ	880	Psyc	Nass, J	NY	645
Psyc	Cabaniss, D	NY	343	Psyc	Kahn, D	NY	346	Psyc	Neschis, R	NY	719
Psyc	Caligor, E	NY	343	Psyc	Kahn, J	NY	718	Psyc	Nininger, J	NY	349
Psyc	Caracci, G	NJ	828	Psyc	Kalash, G	NY	513	Psyc	Nucci, A	NJ	828
Psyc	Cherry, S	NY	343	Psyc	Kalinich, L	NY	346	Psyc	Nunes, E	NY	349
Psyc	Chertoff, H	NJ	788	Psyc	Kalman, A	CT	1023	Psyc	Oberfield, R	NY	349
Psyc	Chung, H	NY	343	Psyc	Kaplan, G	NJ	962	Psyc	Olds, D	NY	349
Psyc	Cohen, A	NY	343	Psyc	Karasu, S	NY	346	Psyc	Opler, L	NY	719
Psyc	Coira, D	NJ	788	Psyc	Karasu, T	NY	346	Psyc	Osei-Tutu, J	NY	440
Psyc	Colah, J	NY	487	Psyc	Katus, E	NY	594	Psyc	Papp, L	NY	349
Psyc	Coplan, J	NY	487	Psyc	Katz, J	NY	594	Psyc	Pawel, M	NY	349
Psyc	Crasta, J	NY	593	Psyc	Kaufmann, C	NY	718	Psyc	Perlman, B	NY	719
Psyc	Di Buono, M	NY	530	Psyc	Kellner, C	NY	346	Psyc	Perry, B	NY	719
Psyc	Donnellan, J	NJ	942	Psyc	Klagsbrun, S	NY	718	Psyc	Pfeffer, C	NY	349
Psyc	Douglas, C	NY	344	Psyc	Kocsis, J	NY	346	Psyc	Pines, J	NY	350
Psyc	Drooker, M	NY	344	Psyc	Koreen, A	NY	645	Psyc	Pollack, J	CT	1023
Psyc	Dulit, R	NY	718	Psyc	Kowallis, G	NY	347	Psyc	Preter, M	NY	350
Psyc	Eitan, N	NY	487	Psyc	Kranzler, E	NY	347	Psyc	Preven, D	NY	350
Psyc	Faber, M	NJ	828	Psyc	Kremberg, M	NY	347	Psyc	Raff, A	NY	719
Psyc	Fallon, B	NY	344	Psyc	Krueger, R	NY	347	Psyc	Rajput, A	NY	513
Psyc	Farkas, E	NJ	788	Psyc	Kurani, D	NJ	841	Psyc	Rees, E	NY	350
Psyc	Feinberg, T	NY	344	Psyc	Lebinger, M	NY	439	Psyc	Richardson, W	NJ	962
Psyc	Fennelly, B	NJ	919	Psyc	Lee, K	NY	645	Psyc	Rochford, J	NJ	942
Psyc	Ferran, E	NY	344	Psyc	Leifer, M	NJ	855	Psyc	Roose, S	NY	350
Psyc	Finkel, J	NY	344	Psyc	Levin, A	NY	718	Psyc	Rosen, A	NY	350
Psyc	First, M	NY	344	Psyc	Levitan, S	NY	347	Psyc	Rosen, B	NY	645
Psyc	Fox, H	NY	344	Psyc	Levy, M	NY	617	Psyc	Rosenfeld, D	NJ	789
Psyc	Friedman, R	NY	345	Psyc	Lew, A	NY	718	Psyc	Rosenthal, J	NY	350
Psyc	Fyer, M	NY	345	Psyc	Liang, V	NY	594	Psyc	Rosenthal, R	NY	350
Psyc	Gabel, R	NY	718	Psyc	Lindenmayer, J	NY	347	Psyc	Rosner, R	NY	350
Psyc	Gelfand, J	NY	439	Psyc	Lipton, B	NY	347	Psyc	Ross, S	NY	351
Psyc	Gewolb, E	NJ	841	Psyc	Lorefice, L	CT	1023	Psyc	Roth, A	NY	351
Psyc	Ginsberg, D	NY	345	Psyc	Malaspina, D	NY	347	Psyc	Rubin, K	NJ	897
Psyc	Goff, D	NY	345	Psyc	Manevitz, A	NY	347	Psyc	Rubinstein, M	NY	351
Psyc	Goldberg, J	NY	487	Psyc	Mann, J	NY	348	Psyc	Russakoff, L	NY	719
Psyc	Goldberg, J	CT	1023	Psyc	Marin, D	NY	348	Psyc	Sacks, M	NY	351
Psyc	Goldenberg, D	NY	345	Psyc	Markowitz, J	NY	348	Psyc	Sadock, V	NY	351
Psyc	Goldman, N	NY	345	Psyc	Massie, M	NY	348	Psyc	Samberg, E	NY	351
Psyc	Goldstein, S	NY	345	Psyc	McGrath, P	NY	348	Psyc	Sami, S	NY	594
Psyc	Goodman, W	NY	345	Psyc	McMullen, R	NY	348	Psyc	Samuels, S	NJ	789
Psyc	Gorman, L	NY	345	Psyc	Mellman, L	NY	348	Psyc	Sawyer, D	NY	351

Specialty & Special Expertise Index

Spec	Name	St	Pg	Spec	Name	St	Pg	Spec	Name	St	Pg
NP	Perl, H	NJ	767	Pul	Dimango, E	NY	356	Pul	Maniatis, T	NY	530
Ped	Kotin, N	NY	322	Pul	Donath, J	NY	595	Pul	Marino, A	CT	1025
Ped	Suda, A	NJ	918	Pul	Eden, E	NY	356	Pul	Martins, P	NY	530
Pul	Abott, M	NY	487	Pul	Elamir, M	NJ	842	Pul	Maxfield, R	NY	358
Pul	Acquista, A	NY	354	Pul	Engler, M	NJ	790	Pul	McCalley, S	CT	1025
Pul	Adams, F	NY	354	Pul	Fein, A	NY	595	Pul	Mehrishi, S	NY	513
Pul	Addrizzo-Harris, D	NY	355	Pul	Feinsilver, S	NY	595	Pul	Meixler, S	NY	721
Pul	Aldrich, T	NY	440	Pul	Fiel, S	NJ	919	Pul	Melillo, N	NJ	881
Pul	Altus, J	NY	594	Pul	Fine, J	CT	1024	Pul	Menitove, S	NY	617
Pul	Amin, H	NY	488	Pul	Fishman, D	NY	356	Pul	Mermelstein, S	NY	596
Pul	Amoruso, R	NJ	931	Pul	Frimer, R	NY	720	Pul	Miarrostami, R	NY	489
Pul	Appel, D	NY	440	Pul	Garay, S	NY	356	Pul	Miller, R	NY	358
Pul	Arcasoy, S	NY	355	Pul	Gelbman, B	NY	356	Pul	Miller, R	NJ	829
Pul	Arno, L	NJ	942	Pul	George, L	NY	488	Pul	Mina, B	NY	358
Pul	Baram, D	NY	645	Pul	Gerhard, H	NJ	943	Pul	Multz, A	NY	358
Pul	Barasch, J	NJ	789	Pul	Glaser, M	NY	646	Pul	Nash, T	NY	358
Pul	Baskin, M	NY	355	Pul	Glassman, A	NJ	790	Pul	Nath, S	NY	513
Pul	Basner, R	NY	355	Pul	Goldberg, J	NJ	881	Pul	Nelson, J	NY	358
Pul	Benoff, B	NJ	790	Pul	Goldblatt, K	NJ	881	Pul	Newmark, I	NY	596
Pul	Benton, M	NJ	919	Pul	Gordon, R	NY	595	Pul	Niederman, M	NY	596
Pul	Bergman, M	NY	488	Pul	Goss, D	NJ	790	Pul	Novitch, R	NY	721
Pul	Berman, L	CT	1024	Pul	Greenberg, H	NY	595	Pul	O'Donnell, T	NJ	920
Pul	Bernardini, D	NY	645	Pul	Greenberg, M	NJ	829	Pul	Oelberg, D	CT	1025
Pul	Bernstein, C	NY	488	Pul	Grizzanti, J	NJ	931	Pul	Padilla, M	NY	358
Pul	Bernstein, M	CT	1024	Pul	Gulrajani, R	NY	488	Pul	Pastores, S	NY	359
Pul	Bevelaqua, F	NY	355	Pul	Hammer, A	NY	488	Pul	Pechman, P	NY	721
Pul	Binder, R	NY	720	Pul	Harangozo, A	NJ	881	Pul	Pellicone, J	NY	617
Pul	Blair, L	NY	355	Pul	Harris, L	NY	617	Pul	Polkow, M	NJ	791
Pul	Blum, A	NY	594	Pul	Hodes, D	NY	617	Pul	Posner, D	NY	359
Pul	Bondi, E	NY	488	Pul	Hwang, C	NJ	963	Pul	Powell, C	NY	359
Pul	Brauntuch, G	NJ	790	Pul	Kaplan, R	NY	357	Pul	Prager, K	NY	359
Pul	Breidbart, D	NY	595	Pul	Karetzky, M	NY	440	Pul	Prezant, D	NY	441
Pul	Brill, J	NY	720	Pul	Kassapidis, S	NY	513	Pul	Raskin, J	NY	359
Pul	Bromberg, A	NJ	790	Pul	Klapholz, A	NY	357	Pul	Roca, D	CT	1025
Pul	Brown, R	CT	1024	Pul	Klapper, P	NY	440	Pul	Rudolph, D	CT	1025
Pul	Bures, S	NY	720	Pul	Klares, S	NY	721	Pul	Sachs, P	CT	1025
Pul	Burschtin, O	NY	355	Pul	Kolodny, E	NY	357	Pul	Safirstein, B	NJ	829
Pul	Casino, J	NY	720	Pul	Krieger, A	NY	357	Pul	Saleh, A	NY	489
Pul	Casper, T	NY	440	Pul	Krinsley, J	CT	1025	Pul	Sanders, A	NY	359
Pul	Castellano, M	NY	530	Pul	Kupfer, Y	NY	489	Pul	Sasso, L	NY	531
Pul	Cerrone, F	NJ	963	Pul	Kurtz, C	CT	1025	Pul	Schluger, N	NY	359
Pul	Chadha, J	NY	513	Pul	Lederer, D	NY	357	Pul	Schreiber, M	NY	721
Pul	Chang, B	NY	617	Pul	Lee, M	NY	357	Pul	Schulster, R	NY	596
Pul	Chronakos, J	CT	1024	Pul	Leeman, B	NY	595	Pul	Schultz, B	NY	359
Pul	Cohen, M	NY	595	Pul	Lehrman, G	NY	721	Pul	Seelagy, M	NJ	856
Pul	Davis, G	NJ	897	Pul	Lehrman, S	NY	721	Pul	Sender, J	NY	441
Pul	De Matteo, R	NY	720	Pul	Lessnau, K	NY	357	Pul	Shah, S	NJ	829
Pul	Delorenzo, L	NY	720	Pul	Levine, S	NJ	790	Pul	Sherling, B	NY	722
Pul	Demetis, S	NY	488	Pul	Libby, D	NY	357	Pul	Silverman, J	NY	514
Pul	DePalo, L	NY	355	Pul	Lombardo, G	NY	489	Pul	Simon, C	NJ	791
Pul	DiCosmo, B	NY	720	Pul	Lowy, J	NY	358	Pul	Sklarek, H	NY	646
Pul	DiFabrizio, L	NY	356	Pul	Malovany, R	NJ	790	Pul	Smith, P	NY	489
Pul	DiMango, A	NY	356	Pul	Mandel, M	NY	721	Pul	Sotolongo, A	NJ	881

Specialty & Special Expertise Index

Spec	Name	St	Pg
Pul	Steiger, D	NY	360
Pul	Stein, S	NY	360
Pul	Steinberg, H	NY	596
Pul	Stover-Pepe, D	NY	360
Pul	Sukumaran, M	NY	360
Pul	Sussman, R	NJ	963
Pul	Thomashow, B	NY	360
Pul	Thurm, C	NY	514
Pul	Turetsky, A	CT	1026
Pul	Volcovici, G	NY	722
Pul	Walser, L	NY	646
Pul	Winter, S	CT	1026
Pul	Wohlberg, G	NY	646
Pul	Wurm, E	NY	722
Pul	Wyner, P	NY	596
Pul	Yip, C	NY	360
Pul	Zimmerman, M	NJ	963

Pulmonary Disease/Immunocompromised

Pul	Stover-Pepe, D	NY	360

Pulmonary Embolism

DR	Ginsberg, M	NY	158
DR	Naidich, D	NY	160
Pul	Arcasoy, S	NY	355

Pulmonary Fibrosis

Pul	Adams, F	NY	354
Pul	Bernardini, D	NY	645
Pul	DiCosmo, B	NY	720
Pul	Hammer, A	NY	488
Pul	Lederer, D	NY	357
Pul	Lowy, J	NY	358
Pul	Polkow, M	NJ	791
Pul	Posner, D	NY	359
Pul	Sussman, R	NJ	963
Pul	Thurm, C	NY	514

Pulmonary Hypertension

Cv	Dresdale, R	NY	542
Cv	Horn, E	NY	129
Cv	Klapholz, M	NJ	805
Cv	Pinney, S	NY	132
Cv	Poon, M	NY	132
Cv	Zucker, M	NJ	806
PCd	Krishnan, U	NY	304
Pul	Demetis, S	NY	488
Pul	George, L	NY	488
Pul	Glaser, M	NY	646
Pul	Krieger, A	NY	357

Spec	Name	St	Pg
Pul	Padilla, M	NY	358
Pul	Shah, S	NJ	829
Pul	Steiger, D	NY	360
Pul	Steinberg, H	NY	596

Pulmonary Infections

PPul	Lee, D	NJ	783
Pul	Stover-Pepe, D	NY	360

Pulmonary Pathology

Path	Borczuk, A	NY	300
Path	Travis, W	NY	302

Pulmonary Rehabilitation

PMR	Whiteson, J	NY	330
Pul	Novitch, R	NY	721
Pul	Raskin, J	NY	359
Pul	Sachs, P	CT	1025
Pul	Silverman, J	NY	514

Pyeloplasty

Ped Uro	Schlussel, R	NY	319

R

Radiation Oncology

RadRO	Adams, M	NY	531
RadRO	Ashamalla, H	NY	489
RadRO	Baumann, J	NJ	881
RadRO	Bodner, W	NY	441
RadRO	Bosworth, J	NY	596
RadRO	Braver, J	NJ	943
RadRO	Chadha, M	NY	360
RadRO	Chao, K	NY	361
RadRO	Choi, J	NY	722
RadRO	Cohen, R	NY	361
RadRO	Cole, R	NJ	931
RadRO	Cooper, J	NY	489
RadRO	Diamond, E	NY	596
RadRO	Donahue, B	NY	490
RadRO	Dowling, S	CT	1026
RadRO	Dubin, D	NJ	791
RadRO	Ennis, R	NY	361
RadRO	Evans, A	NY	361
RadRO	Fang, D	CT	1026
RadRO	Fass, D	NY	722
RadRO	Formenti, S	NY	361
RadRO	Garg, M	NY	441
RadRO	Gejerman, G	NJ	791

Spec	Name	St	Pg
RadRO	Gewanter, R	NY	597
RadRO	Ghaly, M	NY	597
RadRO	Gliedman, P	NY	490
RadRO	Goodman, K	NY	361
RadRO	Grann, A	NJ	829
RadRO	Haas, J	NY	597
RadRO	Haffty, B	NJ	882
RadRO	Harrison, L	NY	361
RadRO	Hu, K	NY	361
RadRO	Hug, E	NJ	943
RadRO	Iannuzzi, C	CT	1026
RadRO	Ingenito, A	NJ	791
RadRO	Isaacson, S	NY	362
RadRO	Kalnicki, S	NY	441
RadRO	Katz, A	NY	514
RadRO	Knisely, J	NY	597
RadRO	Lee, H	NY	722
RadRO	Lee, L	NY	597
RadRO	Lee, N	NY	362
RadRO	Lipsztein, R	NY	514
RadRO	Lymberis, S	NY	362
RadRO	Macher, M	NJ	882
RadRO	Marienberg, E	NY	597
RadRO	Masino, F	CT	1026
RadRO	McCormick, B	NY	362
RadRO	McKenna, M	NJ	856
RadRO	Moorthy, C	NY	722
RadRO	Mullen, E	NY	597
RadRO	Narayana, A	CT	1026
RadRO	Ng, J	NY	362
RadRO	Nori, D	NY	362
RadRO	Parashar, B	NY	362
RadRO	Park, T	NY	646
RadRO	Pathare, P	CT	1026
RadRO	Pollack, J	NY	362
RadRO	Potters, L	NY	597
RadRO	Rosenbaum, A	NY	363
RadRO	Rosenbluth, B	NJ	791
RadRO	Rotman, M	NY	490
RadRO	Ryu, S	NY	646
RadRO	Sanghavi, S	CT	1027
RadRO	Schiff, P	NY	363
RadRO	Schwartz, D	NY	490
RadRO	Schwartz, L	NJ	963
RadRO	Sherr, D	NY	490
RadRO	Soffen, E	NJ	882
RadRO	Spera, J	CT	1027
RadRO	Stevens, R	NY	722
RadRO	Stock, R	NY	363
RadRO	Tinger, A	NY	722
RadRO	Vialotti, C	NJ	791
RadRO	Wagman, R	NJ	829
RadRO	Wolden, S	NY	363

www.castleconnolly.com

1395

Specialty & Special Expertise Index

Specialty & Special Expertise Index

Rheumatologic Diseases of the Lung

Rheumatology

Specialty & Special Expertise Index

Spec	Name	St	Pg
Rhu	Russell, L	NY	372
Rhu	Salem, N	NJ	793
Rhu	Salmon, J	NY	372
Rhu	Samuels, J	NY	372
Rhu	Scarpa, N	NJ	842
Rhu	Schiff, C	NY	491
Rhu	Schwartzfarb, L	NY	372
Rhu	Silverman, J	NY	373
Rhu	Simon, J	NJ	830
Rhu	Sloane, L	NY	724
Rhu	Smiles, S	NY	373
Rhu	Solitar, B	NY	373
Rhu	Solomon, G	NY	373
Rhu	Sonpal, G	NY	514
Rhu	Spiegel, M	CT	1029
Rhu	Spiera, H	NY	373
Rhu	Spiera, R	NY	373
Rhu	Stern, R	NY	373
Rhu	Sullivan, C	NY	514
Rhu	Sullivan, J	NY	599
Rhu	Tiger, L	NY	599
Rhu	Viennas, S	NY	514
Rhu	Vietorisz, T	CT	1029
Rhu	Wallis, S	NY	724
Rhu	Wasser, K	NJ	897
Rhu	Weinstein, J	NY	442
Rhu	Whitman, H	NY	373
Rhu	Worth, D	NJ	964
Rhu	Yee, A	NY	374
Rhu	Yegudin-Ash, J	NY	724
Rhu	Zalkowitz, A	NJ	793

Rhinitis

Spec	Name	St	Pg
A&I	Applebaum, E	NJ	903
A&I	Blum, J	NJ	861
A&I	Buchbinder, E	NY	122
A&I	Burton, D	NY	122
A&I	Corn, B	NY	122
A&I	Corriel, R	NY	539
A&I	Frieri, M	NY	539
A&I	Goodman, A	NJ	948
A&I	Goodstein, C	NJ	741
A&I	Maccia, C	NJ	948
A&I	Markovics, S	NY	539
A&I	Pedinoff, A	NJ	935
A&I	Tolston, E	NY	123
A&I	Veksler-Offengenden, I	CT	974
Oto	Kanowitz, S	NJ	914
PA&I	Fagin, J	NY	581
PA&I	Torre, A	NJ	823
PO	Quraishi, H	NJ	782

Rhinoplasty

Spec	Name	St	Pg
Oto	Brunner, E	NJ	854
Oto	Cece, J	NJ	930
Oto	Constantinides, M	NY	287
Oto	Edelstein, D	NY	288
Oto	Gordon, N	CT	1015
Oto	Guida, R	NY	288
Oto	Jacono, A	NY	578
Oto	Khosh, M	NY	290
Oto	Mazzara, C	NJ	875
Oto	Miller, P	NY	292
Oto	Morrow, T	NJ	822
Oto	Pastorek, N	NY	292
Oto	Portnoy, W	NY	293
Oto	Rosner, L	NY	579
Oto	Scaccia, F	NJ	894
Oto	Sclafani, A	NY	294
Oto	Setzen, M	NY	579
Oto	Shikowitz, M	NY	579
Oto	Slupchynskyj, O	NY	295
Oto	Tobias, G	NJ	778
Oto	Westreich, R	NY	296
Oto	Zimbler, M	NY	297
PlS	Aston, S	NY	331
PlS	DeVita, G	NY	590
PlS	Diktaban, T	NY	332
PlS	Godfrey, N	NY	333
PlS	Greenwald, J	NY	716
PlS	Hidalgo, D	NY	334
PlS	Jacobs, E	NY	334
PlS	Kaufman, M	NJ	880
PlS	Lesesne, C	NY	335
PlS	Lukash, F	NY	592
PlS	Matarasso, A	NY	335
PlS	Palaia, D	NY	716
PlS	Perry, A	NJ	942
PlS	Rosenblatt, W	NY	337
PlS	Suzman, M	NY	717
PlS	Tabbal, N	NY	339
PlS	Winters, R	NJ	788

Rhinoplasty Revision

Spec	Name	St	Pg
Oto	Constantinides, M	NY	287
Oto	Josephson, J	NY	290
Oto	Portnoy, W	NY	293
Oto	Rizk, S	NY	293
Oto	Rosenberg, D	NY	293
Oto	Tobias, G	NJ	778
PlS	DeVita, G	NY	590
PlS	DiGregorio, V	NY	590
PlS	Foster, C	NY	332
PlS	Freund, R	NY	333

Spec	Name	St	Pg
PlS	Kaufman, M	NJ	880
PlS	LaBruna, A	NY	335

Rhinosinusitis

Spec	Name	St	Pg
Oto	Levine, S	CT	1015
Oto	Shin, E	NY	295

Rhinosinusitis & Asthma

Spec	Name	St	Pg
A&I	Shepherd, G	NY	123

Robotic Assisted Laparoscopic Surgery

Spec	Name	St	Pg
RE	Kofinas, G	NY	490
RE	Schattman, G	NY	367

Robotic Cardiac Surgery

Spec	Name	St	Pg
T&CS	Argenziano, M	NY	385
T&CS	DeRose, J	NY	443
T&CS	Elmann, E	NJ	795
T&CS	Loulmet, D	NY	388
T&CS	Patel, N	NY	389
T&CS	Smith, C	NY	390

Robotic Surgery

Spec	Name	St	Pg
CRS	Gallina, G	NJ	750
CRS	Ky, A	NY	144
CRS	Sullivan, J	NY	547
GO	Anderson, P	NJ	811
GO	Barakat, R	NY	183
GO	Burke, W	NY	183
GO	Denehy, T	NJ	812
GO	Goldman, N	NJ	759
GO	Gretz, H	NY	677
GO	Holcomb, K	NY	184
GO	Menzin, A	NY	556
GO	Rahaman, J	NY	185
GO	Rodriguez, L	NJ	867
GO	Shahabi, S	CT	988
GO	Taylor, R	NJ	812
GO	Vaidya, A	NJ	759
GO	Zakashansky, K	NY	186
ObG	Ascher-Walsh, C	NY	246
ObG	Besser, G	CT	1004
ObG	Burns, E	NY	695
ObG	Cahill, P	CT	1004
ObG	Crane, S	NJ	818
ObG	Deal, R	CT	1004
ObG	Englert, C	NJ	772
ObG	Filor, C	CT	1005
ObG	Grecco, D	NY	696
ObG	Keller, A	NY	696

Specialty & Special Expertise Index

Specialty & Special Expertise Index

Spec	Name	St	Pg
Pul	Gulrajani, R	NY	488
Pul	Lee, M	NY	357
Pul	Miller, R	NJ	829
Pul	Padilla, M	NY	358
Pul	Polkow, M	NJ	791
Pul	Posner, D	NY	359
Pul	Safirstein, B	NJ	829
Pul	Sender, J	NY	441
Pul	Silverman, J	NY	514
Pul	Smith, P	NY	489
Pul	Wurm, E	NY	722
Rhu	Agus, B	NY	368
Rhu	Yee, A	NY	374

Sarcoma

Spec	Name	St	Pg
Onc	Pavlick, A	NY	220
Onc	Scoppetuolo, M	NJ	816
Onc	Tap, W	NY	224
OrS	Geller, D	NY	429
OrS	Healey, J	NY	275
OrS	Hoang, B	NY	430
OrS	Rapp, T	NY	281
Oto	Kraus, D	NY	290
PHO	Glade Bender, J	NY	310
PHO	Gorlick, R	NY	433
PHO	Meyers, P	NY	311
PHO	Wistinghausen, B	NY	312
RadRO	Hug, E	NJ	943
S	Bloom, N	NY	377
S	Dong, X	CT	1029
S	Whitman, E	NJ	921

Sarcoma-Soft Tissue

Spec	Name	St	Pg
Onc	Casper, E	NY	687
Onc	Maki, R	NY	218
Onc	Tap, W	NY	224
OrS	Benevenia, J	NJ	820
OrS	Geller, D	NY	429
OrS	Healey, J	NY	275
OrS	Wittig, J	NJ	777
Path	Antonescu, C	NY	300
PHO	Granowetter, L	NY	311
PHO	Wexler, L	NY	312
RadRO	Wolden, S	NY	363
S	August, D	NJ	882
S	Berman, R	NY	377
S	Brady, M	NY	377
S	Goydos, J	NJ	882
S	Rosenberg, V	NY	383
S	Singer, S	NY	384

Sarcomas

Spec	Name	St	Pg
S	McCain, D	NJ	794

Scar Revision

Spec	Name	St	Pg
D	Rapaport, J	NJ	751

Schizophrenia

Spec	Name	St	Pg
GerPsy	Cohen, C	NY	462
Psyc	Benjamin, J	NY	593
Psyc	Goff, D	NY	345
Psyc	Harlam, D	NY	718
Psyc	Kahn, D	NY	346
Psyc	Kaufmann, C	NY	718
Psyc	Lindenmayer, J	NY	347
Psyc	Mendelowitz, A	NY	513
Psyc	Schwartz, B	NY	440
Psyc	Sullivan, T	NY	530

Sciatica

Spec	Name	St	Pg
PM	Epstein, L	NY	297
PM	Lefkowitz, M	NY	481
PM	Waldman, S	NY	299

Scleroderma

Spec	Name	St	Pg
D	Franks, A	NY	148
PRhu	Haines, K	NJ	783
PRhu	Lehman, T	NY	317
PRhu	Li, S	NJ	784
Rhu	Marcus, R	NJ	793
Rhu	Spiera, H	NY	373
Rhu	Spiera, R	NY	373
Rhu	Whitman, H	NY	373
Rhu	Yegudin-Ash, J	NY	724

Sclerotherapy

Spec	Name	St	Pg
D	Mermelstein, H	NY	666
VascS	Chaudhry, S	NY	606
VascS	Chideckel, N	NY	403

Scoliosis

Spec	Name	St	Pg
NS	Angevine, P	NY	229
NS	Fiore, A	CT	1001
NS	Jenkins, A	NY	231
NS	Simon, S	CT	1002
OrS	Bendo, J	NY	270
OrS	Bomback, D	CT	1010
OrS	Cammisa, F	NY	271
OrS	Casden, A	NY	271
OrS	Emami, A	NJ	929
OrS	Errico, T	NY	273

Spec	Name	St	Pg
OrS	Feldman, D	NY	273
OrS	Godfried, D	NY	576
OrS	Goldstein, J	NY	274
OrS	Huang, R	NY	276
OrS	Hyman, J	NY	276
OrS	Lewis, R	NY	639
OrS	Lonner, B	NY	278
OrS	Mauri, T	NY	577
OrS	McCance, S	NY	279
OrS	Merola, A	NY	479
OrS	Neuwirth, M	NY	280
OrS	Olsewski, J	NY	430
OrS	Rawlins, B	NY	281
OrS	Rieger, K	NJ	913
OrS	Rieger, M	NJ	913
OrS	Roye, D	NY	282
OrS	Schwab, F	NY	283
OrS	Spivak, J	NY	284
OrS	Tindel, N	NY	284
OrS	Vitale, M	NY	285
OrS	Widmann, R	NY	286

Seizure Disorders

Spec	Name	St	Pg
ChiN	Aron, A	NY	139
ChiN	Molofsky, W	NY	141
N	Bronster, D	NY	235
N	Dousmanis, A	NY	693
N	Ettinger, A	NY	568
N	Jutkowitz, R	NY	526
N	Oh, Y	NJ	872

Sentinel Node Surgery

Spec	Name	St	Pg
S	Blackwood, M	NJ	831
S	Boolbol, S	NY	377
S	Cohen, B	NY	648
S	Goldfarb, A	NY	379
S	Montgomery, L	NY	443
S	Nowak, E	NY	382
S	O'Hea, B	NY	648
S	Port, E	NY	382
S	Tartter, P	NY	384

Sepsis

Spec	Name	St	Pg
Pul	Davis, G	NJ	897
Pul	Multz, A	NY	358
Pul	Pastores, S	NY	359

Sepsis & Septic Shock

Spec	Name	St	Pg
PCCM	Goltzman, C	NY	707
PCCM	Greenwald, B	NY	306
PCCM	Ushay, H	NY	432

Specialty & Special Expertise Index

Specialty & Special Expertise Index

Spec	Name	St	Pg
HS	Magill, R	NY	678
HS	Wang, E	NY	630
OrS	Abrams, J	NJ	853
OrS	Adler, E	NY	269
OrS	Berman, M	NJ	775
OrS	Bosco, J	NY	270
OrS	Brown, D	CT	1011
OrS	Compito, C	NY	271
OrS	Cunningham, J	CT	1011
OrS	Cuomo, F	NY	272
OrS	D'Agostino, R	NY	576
OrS	Dines, D	NY	576
OrS	Doidge, R	NJ	776
OrS	Glashow, J	NY	274
OrS	Henshaw, D	CT	1012
OrS	Karas, E	NY	702
OrS	Khabie, V	NY	703
OrS	Kipnis, J	NY	576
OrS	Levitz, C	NY	576
OrS	Longobardi, R	NJ	776
OrS	Lubliner, J	NY	278
OrS	Marx, R	NY	278
OrS	McCann, P	NY	279
OrS	McIlveen, S	NJ	777
OrS	Miller, S	CT	1013
OrS	Montgomery, K	NJ	913
OrS	Morgan, D	NY	479
OrS	Rieber, M	NJ	821
OrS	Rozbruch, J	NY	282
OrS	Schwartz, E	NY	511
OrS	Sgaglione, N	NY	577
OrS	Tabershaw, R	NY	639
OrS	Ticker, J	NY	578
OrS	Turtel, A	NY	285
OrS	Warren, R	NY	285
OrS	Weinstein, R	NY	704
OrS	Zambetti, G	NY	286
SM	Altchek, D	NY	374
SM	Cleeman, E	NY	374
SM	Levy, A	NJ	830
SM	Rodeo, S	NY	375
SM	Roth, N	NY	375
SM	Seneviratne, A	NY	376
SM	Wickiewicz, T	NY	376

Sickle Cell Disease

Spec	Name	St	Pg
Hem	Billett, H	NY	420
Hem	Solomon, W	NY	463
Ped	Saraiya, N	NJ	961
PHO	Diamond, S	NJ	781
PHO	Drachtman, R	NJ	877
PHO	Flug, F	NJ	781

Spec	Name	St	Pg
PHO	Giardina, P	NY	310
PHO	Kulpa, J	NY	483
PHO	Moulton, T	NY	434
PHO	Sabatino, D	NY	585
PHO	Sadanandan, S	NY	483
PHO	Sheth, S	NY	312
PHO	Sundaram, R	NY	483
PHO	Viswanathan, K	NY	483
PHO	Weinblatt, M	NY	585

Sickle Cell Disease-Lung

Spec	Name	St	Pg
Pul	Aldrich, T	NY	440

Sinus Disorders

Spec	Name	St	Pg
A&I	Applebaum, E	NJ	903
A&I	Backman, K	CT	973
A&I	Bassett, C	NY	121
A&I	Bernstein, L	NY	409
A&I	Brown, D	NJ	948
A&I	Chandler, M	NY	122
A&I	Chang, C	NJ	741
A&I	Chernack, W	NJ	903
A&I	Corriel, R	NY	539
A&I	Edwards, B	NY	539
A&I	Geller, D	NJ	741
A&I	Geraci-Ciardullo, K	NY	654
A&I	Goodman, A	NJ	948
A&I	Gross, G	NJ	887
A&I	Kaufman, A	NY	409
A&I	Lusman, P	NY	621
A&I	Markovics, S	NY	539
A&I	Mazza, D	NY	123
A&I	Menchell, D	NY	500
A&I	Novick, B	NY	539
A&I	Picone, F	NJ	887
A&I	Richheimer, M	NY	621
A&I	Schulhafer, E	NJ	935
A&I	Slankard, M	NY	123
A&I	Weiss, S	NJ	804
Oto	Green, R	NY	288
Oto	Kase, S	NY	705
Oto	Klarsfeld, J	CT	1015
Oto	Lazar, A	NJ	941
Oto	Levin, R	CT	1015
Oto	Levine, S	CT	1015
Oto	Lim, J	NY	291
Oto	Moisa, I	NY	579
Oto	Parker, A	CT	1016
Oto	Pincus, R	NY	293
Oto	Rosen, A	NJ	778
Oto	Rossos, A	NJ	894
Oto	Sinnreich, A	NY	528

Spec	Name	St	Pg
Oto	Surow, J	NJ	778
Oto	Volpi, D	NY	296
PO	April, M	NY	315
PO	De Serres, L	NY	710
PO	Haddad, J	NY	315
PO	Mendelsohn, M	NY	585
PO	Merer, D	NY	710
PO	Respler, D	NJ	782
PO	Rothschild, M	NY	315
PO	Traquina, D	NJ	878

Sinus Disorders/Surgery

Spec	Name	St	Pg
Oto	Bard, M	CT	1014
Oto	Bianchi, M	CT	1014
Oto	Branovan, D	NY	480
Oto	Close, L	NY	287
Oto	Fried, M	NY	431
Oto	Godin, D	NY	288
Oto	Gold, S	NY	288
Oto	Jacobs, J	NY	289
Oto	Jones, J	NY	289
Oto	Kates, M	NY	705
Oto	Klenoff, B	CT	1015
Oto	Lawson, W	NY	291
Oto	Low, R	NJ	778
Oto	Markowitz, A	NY	292
Oto	Nass, R	NY	292
Oto	Sacks, S	NY	294
Oto	Salzer, S	CT	1016
Oto	Schaefer, S	NY	294
Oto	Scharf, R	NJ	959
Oto	Scioscia, K	NY	579
Oto	Shaari, C	NJ	778
Oto	Shohet, M	NY	295
Oto	Zahtz, G	NY	580
Oto	Zelman, W	NY	580
PO	Bent, J	NY	435
PO	Rosenfeld, R	NY	484
PO	Ward, R	NY	315

Sinus Surgery

Spec	Name	St	Pg
Oto	Bennett, G	NY	286
Oto	Cece, J	NJ	930
Oto	Chaudhry, M	NY	480
Oto	Fox, M	NY	704
Oto	Goldstein, S	NY	431
Oto	Ho, B	NJ	777
Oto	Kacker, A	NY	290
Oto	Kay, S	NJ	875
Oto	Litman, R	NY	640
Oto	Mittleman, M	NY	512
Oto	Siglock, T	NY	705

Specialty & Special Expertise Index

Spec	Name	St	Pg
Oto	Taylor, H	NJ	914

Sinus Surgery-Revision

Spec	Name	St	Pg
Oto	Bennett, G	NY	286
Oto	Jacobs, J	NY	289

Sinus Tumors

Spec	Name	St	Pg
Oto	Har-El, G	NY	289
Oto	Schaefer, S	NY	294

Sinusitis

Spec	Name	St	Pg
A&I	Bell, J	CT	973
A&I	Boxer, M	NY	538
A&I	Caucino, J	NJ	935
A&I	Goldman, N	NY	654
A&I	Goodstein, C	NJ	741
A&I	Hirsch, A	NJ	903
A&I	Kanumury, S	NJ	903
A&I	Mayer, D	NY	621
A&I	Rosenstreich, D	NY	409
A&I	Santilli, J	CT	974
A&I	Tolston, E	NY	123
IM	Lu, B	NY	466
Oto	Bennett, G	NY	286
Oto	Edelman, B	NJ	875
PA&I	Fost, A	NJ	822
PA&I	Herzog, R	NY	303
PA&I	Torre, A	NJ	823
PO	Keller, J	NY	710
PO	Samadi, S	NJ	783

Sjogren's Syndrome

Spec	Name	St	Pg
Rhu	Carsons, S	NY	598
Rhu	Kramer, N	NJ	964
Rhu	Lichtbroun, A	NJ	882
Rhu	Marchetta, P	NY	371
Rhu	Rackoff, P	NY	372
Rhu	Rosenstein, E	NJ	964
Rhu	Spiera, R	NY	373

Skin Allergies

Spec	Name	St	Pg
A&I	Bassett, C	NY	121
A&I	Fonacier, L	NY	539
A&I	From, S	NJ	741
A&I	Richheimer, M	NY	621
A&I	Vassallo, M	NY	452

Skin Cancer

Spec	Name	St	Pg
D	Albom, M	NY	145
D	Almeida, L	NJ	906
D	Amin, S	NY	146
D	Andrews, A	NJ	750
D	Aranoff, S	NY	146
D	Basuk, P	NY	624
D	Becker, D	NY	146
D	Berkowitz, E	NY	146
D	Berkowitz, R	NY	664
D	Berry, R	NY	456
D	Berson, D	NY	147
D	Bronin, A	NY	665
D	Bruckstein, R	NY	548
D	Buchness, M	NY	147
D	Burke, K	NY	147
D	Clark, R	NY	624
D	Clark, S	NY	147
D	Connolly, A	NJ	808
D	Connors, R	CT	980
D	Cooper, L	NJ	906
D	Davis, I	NY	665
D	Demar, L	NY	148
D	Demento, F	NY	548
D	Dolitsky, C	NY	548
D	Drugge, R	CT	980
D	Eisenberg, R	NJ	950
D	Falcon, R	NY	548
D	Felderman, L	NY	148
D	Fishman, M	NJ	751
D	Foitl, D	NY	148
D	Fox, J	NY	501
D	Frankel, D	NY	457
D	Fried, S	NJ	751
D	Geronemus, R	NY	149
D	Gold, J	NJ	926
D	Goldberg, D	NY	149
D	Goldenberg, G	NY	149
D	Greenspan, A	NY	149
D	Grossman, K	NJ	888
D	Hale, E	NY	150
D	Halpern, A	NY	150
D	Hisler, B	NY	549
D	Hochman, H	NY	150
D	Howanitz, N	NY	665
D	Huh, J	NY	625
D	Jacobs, M	NY	150
D	Kaporis, A	NY	666
D	Karen, J	NY	150
D	Khorasani, H	NY	151
D	Klar, T	NY	666
D	Kline, M	NY	151
D	Kolenik, S	CT	980
D	Kriegel, D	NY	151
D	Lebwohl, M	NY	151
D	Lederman, J	NY	522
D	Levy, R	NY	666
D	Lombardo, P	NY	152
D	Lukash, B	NY	666
D	Machler, B	NJ	906
D	Mackler, K	NY	666
D	Maiocco, K	CT	980
D	Marghoob, A	NY	625
D	Marmur, E	NY	152
D	Mayer, F	CT	981
D	Morman, M	NJ	751
D	Moynihan, G	NY	625
D	Myskowski, P	NY	152
D	Naidorf, E	CT	981
D	Nehal, K	NY	152
D	Notaro, A	NY	625
D	Notterman, R	NJ	847
D	Oestreicher, M	CT	981
D	Orbuch, P	NY	152
D	Oshman, R	CT	981
D	Ostad, A	NY	153
D	Pereira, F	NY	502
D	Pesce, J	CT	981
D	Podwal, M	NY	153
D	Possick, P	NJ	751
D	Prioleau, P	NY	153
D	Pruzan-Clain, D	CT	981
D	Prystowsky, J	NY	153
D	Ramsay, D	NY	153
D	Ratner, D	NY	153
D	Rigel, D	NY	153
D	Rokhsar, C	NY	154
D	Rosen, D	NY	414
D	Roth, J	NY	154
D	Safai, B	NY	154
D	Sarnoff, D	NY	549
D	Schliftman, A	NY	667
D	Schwartz, R	NJ	808
D	Shapiro, M	NY	458
D	Shelton, R	NY	154
D	Shieh, S	NY	154
D	Sibrack, L	CT	981
D	Siegel, D	NY	625
D	Silverman, M	NY	549
D	Simon, S	NY	458
D	Skrokov, R	NY	625
D	Sweeney, E	NJ	752
D	Tanenbaum, D	NY	155
D	Waldorf, D	NY	610
D	Walther, R	NY	155
D	Weinberger, G	NJ	950
D	Wong, A	NY	625
D	Wrone, D	NJ	864
D	Zeltser, R	NY	667
D	Zirvi, M	NJ	950

Specialty & Special Expertise Index

Spec	Name	St	Pg
D	Zweibel, S	NY	667
Onc	Pavlick, A	NY	220
Oto	Carniol, P	NJ	959
PlS	Bromley, G	NY	331
PlS	Granick, M	NJ	827
PlS	Groeger, W	NY	591
PlS	Hetzler, P	NJ	896
PlS	Karp, N	NY	334
PlS	Lesesne, C	NY	335
PlS	Roth, D	NY	717
RadRO	Cooper, J	NY	489
RadRO	Tinger, A	NY	722
S	Goydos, J	NJ	882

Skin Cancer & Moles

Spec	Name	St	Pg
D	Bagel, J	NJ	847
D	Danziger, S	NY	457
D	Katz, S	NY	151
D	Krant, J	NY	151
D	Rosenberg, B	NY	667
D	Treiber, R	NY	667

Skin Cancer Reconstruction

Spec	Name	St	Pg
PlS	Bromley, G	NY	331
PlS	Drimmer, M	NJ	855

Skin Cancer-Head & Neck

Spec	Name	St	Pg
Onc	Posner, M	NY	221
Oto	White, W	NY	296

Skin Diseases

Spec	Name	St	Pg
FMed	Moynihan, B	NY	552
FMed	Sutton, I	NY	672
IM	Fazio, N	NY	682

Skin Diseases in Transplants/Cancer

Spec	Name	St	Pg
D	Grossman, M	NY	665

Skin Diseases-Immunologic

Spec	Name	St	Pg
D	Liteplo, R	NY	414

Skin Infections

Spec	Name	St	Pg
D	Buchness, M	NY	147
D	Rudikoff, D	NY	414

Skin Laser Surgery

Spec	Name	St	Pg
D	Alexiades-Armenakas, M	NY	145
D	Amin, S	NY	146

Spec	Name	St	Pg
D	Avram, M	NY	146
D	Bank, D	NY	664
D	Basuk, P	NY	624
D	Biro, D	NY	457
D	Brancaccio, R	NY	457
D	Brauner, G	NJ	750
D	Bruckstein, R	NY	548
D	Clark, S	NY	147
D	De Pietro, W	NY	548
D	Downie, J	NJ	808
D	Evans, L	NY	665
D	Green, M	NY	149
D	Grossman, M	NY	150
D	Hochman, H	NY	150
D	Levine, L	NY	549
D	Levy, R	NY	666
D	Lipper, G	CT	980
D	McAleer, P	CT	981
D	Milgraum, S	NJ	864
D	Ostad, A	NY	153
D	Polis, L	NY	153
D	Rapaport, J	NJ	751
D	Rokhsar, C	NY	154
D	Rosenberg, B	NY	667
D	Safai, B	NY	154
D	Sarnoff, D	NY	549
D	Schachne, J	NY	667
D	Schliftman, A	NY	667
D	Schultz, N	NY	154
D	Shelton, R	NY	154
D	Siegel, E	NJ	808
D	Silverman, M	NY	549
D	Sobel, H	NY	155
D	Sturza, J	NY	667
D	Waldorf, H	NY	610
D	Wattenberg, D	NY	156
D	Wechsler, A	NY	156
D	Weiss, D	NJ	752
D	Whitman, G	CT	981
D	Wrone, D	NJ	864
D	Zweibel, S	NY	667
Oto	Brunner, E	NJ	854
Oto	Guida, R	NY	288

Skin Laser Surgery-Resurfacing

Spec	Name	St	Pg
D	Gmyrek, R	NY	149
D	Schweiger, E	NY	154

Skin Problems in Cancer Therapy

Spec	Name	St	Pg
D	Lacouture, M	NY	151

Skin/Soft Tissue Infections

Spec	Name	St	Pg
Inf	Aufiero, P	NJ	849
Inf	Brause, B	NY	193
Inf	Scheer, M	NY	559
Inf	Smith, P	NY	197
Inf	Soroko, T	NJ	813

Skull Base Surgery

Spec	Name	St	Pg
NS	Arginteanu, M	NJ	769
NS	Bruce, J	NY	229
NS	Davis, R	NY	634
NS	Eisenberg, M	NY	566
NS	Murali, R	NY	692
NS	Schulder, M	NY	567
NS	Schwartz, A	NY	471
Oto	Frank, D	NY	578
Oto	Lalwani, A	NY	291
Oto	Meiteles, L	NY	705

Skull Base Tumors

Spec	Name	St	Pg
NS	Bilsky, M	NY	229
NS	Golfinos, J	NY	230
NS	Jafar, J	NY	231
NS	Sen, C	NY	232
NS	Tabar, V	NY	233
Oto	Costantino, P	NY	288
Oto	Har-El, G	NY	289
Oto	Kraus, D	NY	290
Oto	Persky, M	NY	293
RadRO	Hug, E	NJ	943
RadRO	Knisely, J	NY	597
S	Shah, J	NY	383

Sleep & Snoring Disorders

Spec	Name	St	Pg
Oto	Youngerman, J	NY	580
Pul	Kupfer, Y	NY	489
Pul	Lombardo, G	NY	489
Pul	Sotolongo, A	NJ	881

Sleep Apnea

Spec	Name	St	Pg
Oto	Josephson, J	NY	290
Oto	Krevitt, L	NY	291
Oto	Rossos, A	NJ	894
Oto	Scharf, R	NJ	959
PO	April, M	NY	315
PO	Bernstein, J	NY	709
PO	Goldsmith, A	NY	484
PO	Samadi, S	NJ	783
PPul	Lee, H	NY	484
PPul	Marcus, M	NY	484
Pul	Garay, S	NY	356

Specialty & Special Expertise Index

Spec	Name	St	Pg
Special Needs-Parental Therapy			
Psyc	Dulit, R	NY	718
Spina Bifida			
CG	Marion, R	NY	413
NS	Harter, D	NY	230
PMR	Armento, M	NJ	961
PMR	Gold, J	NY	327
Spinal Access Surgery			
VascS	Nalbandian, M	NY	405
Spinal Cord Disorders			
N	Levine, D	NY	238
NS	Cardoso, E	NY	471
Spinal Cord Injury			
NRad	Lu, S	NJ	893
NS	Heary, R	NJ	817
NS	Sanderson, S	CT	1002
OrS	Hecht, A	NY	275
OrS	Huang, R	NY	276
PMR	Ahn, J	NY	326
PMR	Bryce, T	NY	326
PMR	Kirshblum, S	NJ	827
PMR	Ragnarsson, K	NY	329
PMR	Root, B	NY	589
PMR	Stein, A	NY	589
PMR	Valenza, J	NJ	918
Spinal Cord Injury & Colonic Motility			
Ge	Korsten, M	NY	418
Spinal Cord Injury-Pediatric			
PMR	Armento, M	NJ	961
PMR	Fantasia, M	NJ	879
Spinal Cord Tumors			
NS	Bilsky, M	NY	229
NS	Frempong-Boadu, A	NY	230
NS	Kaiser, M	NY	231
NS	Kornel, E	NY	692
NS	Moore, F	NJ	769
NS	Przybylski, G	NJ	871
NS	Snow, R	NY	232
NS	Steinberger, A	NJ	769
PHO	Levy, A	NY	433

Spec	Name	St	Pg
Spinal Deformity			
NS	Angevine, P	NY	229
NS	Arginteanu, M	NJ	769
NS	Heary, R	NJ	817
OrS	Bitan, F	NY	270
OrS	Dowling, T	NY	639
OrS	Girardi, F	NY	274
OrS	Kim, Y	NY	277
OrS	Kuflik, P	NY	277
OrS	Lonner, B	NY	278
OrS	Neuwirth, M	NY	280
OrS	Sama, A	NY	283
OrS	Schwab, F	NY	283
Spinal Disc Replacement			
NS	Davis, R	NY	634
NS	Elowitz, E	NY	230
NS	Hartl, R	NY	231
NS	Kaiser, M	NY	231
NS	Leon, S	NY	635
OrS	Bendo, J	NY	270
OrS	Cammisa, F	NY	271
OrS	Casden, A	NY	271
OrS	Dwyer, J	NJ	941
OrS	Emami, A	NJ	929
OrS	Girardi, F	NY	274
OrS	Goldstein, J	NY	274
OrS	Huang, R	NY	276
OrS	Kuflik, P	NY	277
OrS	Lombardi, J	NJ	874
OrS	Mauri, T	NY	577
OrS	Qureshi, S	NY	281
Spinal Disorders			
N	Haimovic, I	NY	568
N	Neophytides, A	NY	240
N	Smallberg, G	NY	242
N	Swerdlow, M	NY	427
N	Van Engel, D	NJ	771
N	Weinberg, H	NY	243
NS	Schwartz, A	NY	471
OrS	Mendes, J	NJ	821
OrS	Reich, S	NJ	875
Spinal Disorders-Degenerative			
NS	Choudhri, T	NY	229
NS	Elowitz, E	NY	230
NS	Leon, S	NY	635
NS	Onesti, S	NY	567
NS	Oppenheim, J	NY	613
OrS	Bitan, F	NY	270

Spec	Name	St	Pg
OrS	Farmer, J	NY	273
OrS	Implicito, D	NJ	776
OrS	Sama, A	NY	283
Spinal Imaging			
DR	Rokhsar, M	NJ	950
NRad	Aluri-Vallabhaneni, B	NJ	928
Spinal Imaging & Intervention			
NRad	Knopp, E	NY	244
VIR	Shams, J	NY	401
Spinal Muscular Atrophy (SMA)			
ChiN	De Vivo, D	NY	140
Spinal Reconstructive Surgery			
NS	Arginteanu, M	NJ	769
NS	Carpenter, D	NJ	769
NS	Frempong-Boadu, A	NY	230
NS	Frempong-Boadu, A	NY	230
OrS	Bendo, J	NY	270
OrS	Dwyer, J	NJ	941
OrS	Olsewski, J	NY	430
OrS	Tindel, N	NY	284
Spinal Rehabilitation			
PMR	Beer, J	NY	589
PMR	Feinberg, J	NY	327
PMR	Heftler, J	CT	1021
PMR	Lee, A	NY	328
PMR	Lipetz, J	NY	589
PMR	Lutz, G	NY	328
PMR	Moldover, J	NY	328
PMR	Neely, M	NY	328
PMR	Root, B	NY	589
PMR	Simotas, A	NY	329
PMR	Solomon, J	NY	329
PMR	Varlotta, G	NY	330
Spinal Surgery			
NS	Angevine, P	NY	229
NS	Apostolides, P	CT	1001
NS	Arginteanu, M	NJ	769
NS	Bilsky, M	NY	229
NS	Camel, M	CT	1001
NS	Carpenter, D	NJ	769
NS	Choudhri, T	NY	229
NS	Di Giacinto, G	NY	229
NS	Elowitz, E	NY	230
NS	Friedlander, M	NJ	955
NS	Heary, R	NJ	817

Specialty & Special Expertise Index

Specialty & Special Expertise Index

Spec	Name	St	Pg
S	Bank, M	NY	599
S	Barie, P	NY	377
S	Bellemare, S	NY	442
S	Benowitz, J	NY	600
S	Berman, R	NY	377
S	Bernik, S	NY	377
S	Bernstein, M	NY	492
S	Bessey, P	NY	377
S	Bessler, M	NY	377
S	Blackwood, M	NJ	831
S	Bloom, N	NY	377
S	Boolbol, S	NY	377
S	Borao, F	NJ	898
S	Borriello, R	NY	492
S	Brady, M	NY	377
S	Brathwaite, C	NY	600
S	Brower, S	NY	378
S	Budd, D	NJ	932
S	Busch-Devereaux, E	NY	647
S	Cahan, A	NY	726
S	Capasse, J	CT	1029
S	Carter, M	NJ	921
S	Cassell, L	NY	378
S	Chabot, J	NY	378
S	Chamberlain, R	NJ	831
S	Charny, C	NY	726
S	Chefitz, A	NY	726
S	Choi, L	CT	1029
S	Chorost, M	NY	600
S	Chung-Loy, H	NJ	882
S	Cioroiu, M	NY	378
S	Cohen, B	NY	648
S	Coit, D	NY	378
S	Colaco, R	NJ	964
S	Conte, C	NY	600
S	Coppa, G	NY	600
S	Cosgrove, J	NY	648
S	D'Anna, J	NY	531
S	Dakin, G	NY	378
S	Dasmahapatra, K	NJ	882
S	Datta, R	NY	600
S	DeMatteo, R	NY	378
S	Demestihas, A	CT	1029
S	Diehl, W	NJ	921
S	Diflo, T	NY	726
S	DiGioia, J	NJ	964
S	Divino, C	NY	378
S	Dong, X	CT	1029
S	Drascher, G	NJ	943
S	Dresner, L	NY	492
S	Dultz, R	NJ	856
S	Dwyer, K	CT	1030
S	El-Tamer, M	NY	378

Spec	Name	St	Pg
S	Elliott, N	NJ	831
S	Emond, J	NY	379
S	Estabrook, A	NY	379
S	Fahey, T	NY	379
S	Fahoum, B	NY	492
S	Feigenbaum, H	NJ	932
S	Feldman, S	NY	379
S	Feteiha, M	NJ	964
S	Fleischer, L	NY	618
S	Fletcher, H	NJ	831
S	Floch, N	CT	1030
S	Fou, A	NY	726
S	Fried, K	NJ	794
S	Frost, J	NJ	964
S	Gannon, C	NJ	857
S	Garvey, R	CT	1030
S	Gecelter, G	NY	600
S	Geller, P	NY	379
S	Genato, R	NY	492
S	Goldfarb, A	NY	379
S	Goldfarb, M	NJ	898
S	Gordon, M	NY	726
S	Gorecki, P	NY	492
S	Goydos, J	NJ	882
S	Greenstein, S	NY	442
S	Grieco, M	NY	600
S	Gumbs, A	NJ	964
S	Halpern, D	NY	600
S	Harris, M	NJ	794
S	Heerdt, A	NY	379
S	Herron, D	NY	379
S	Hertz, M	NJ	831
S	Hiotis, S	NY	379
S	Hofstetter, S	NY	380
S	Hornyak, S	NY	531
S	Huston, J	NJ	831
S	Inabnet, W	NY	380
S	Jacob, B	NY	380
S	Jarnagin, W	NY	380
S	Johnson Miller, D	NJ	898
S	Jordan, L	NJ	883
S	Joseph, P	NY	618
S	Kaleya, R	NY	492
S	Kapur, S	NY	380
S	Karpeh, M	NY	380
S	Kato, T	NY	380
S	Katz, L	NY	380
S	Kaufman, H	NJ	883
S	Kaul, A	NY	726
S	Kearney, T	NJ	883
S	Kemeny, M	NY	515
S	Kenler, A	CT	1030
S	Kennedy, T	NY	442

Spec	Name	St	Pg
S	Khalife, M	NY	601
S	Kimmelstiel, F	NY	380
S	Kini, S	NY	381
S	Kinkhabwala, M	NY	442
S	Kurtz, L	NY	601
S	Labow, D	NY	381
S	Lanfranchi, A	NJ	944
S	Lau, H	NY	726
S	Lee, J	NY	381
S	Leitman, I	NY	381
S	Lemercier, M	NY	726
S	Lewis, T	NY	492
S	Libutti, S	NY	443
S	Licata, J	NJ	794
S	Lieberman, M	NY	381
S	Lois, W	NY	492
S	Lozner, J	NJ	965
S	Lutchman, G	NY	531
S	Maffucci, L	NY	727
S	Maheshwari, V	NJ	831
S	Manasseh, D	NY	492
S	Mandel, M	NJ	965
S	Manolas, P	NY	515
S	Mansouri, H	NY	601
S	McCain, D	NJ	794
S	McGinty, J	NY	381
S	McManus, S	NJ	883
S	Melvin, W	NY	443
S	Mendoza, E	NY	515
S	Messina, A	NY	727
S	Michelassi, F	NY	381
S	Miller, K	CT	1030
S	Mills, C	NY	381
S	Molmenti, E	NY	601
S	Montgomery, L	NY	443
S	Morrow, M	NY	382
S	Newman, E	NY	382
S	Nitzberg, R	NJ	965
S	Nowak, E	NY	382
S	O'Hea, B	NY	648
S	Pace, B	NY	515
S	Pachter, H	NY	382
S	Pahuja, M	NY	531
S	Pass, H	CT	1030
S	Passeri, D	CT	1030
S	Paty, P	NY	382
S	Pereira, S	NJ	794
S	Petrone, S	NJ	831
S	Petrotos, A	CT	1030
S	Pomp, A	NY	382
S	Poole, J	NJ	794
S	Port, E	NY	382
S	Pryor, A	NY	648

Specialty & Special Expertise Index

Spec	Name	St	Pg
S	Rajdeo, H	NY	727
S	Rajpal, S	NY	493
S	Raniolo, R	NY	727
S	Ratner, L	NY	382
S	Reiner, D	NY	601
S	Reiner, M	NY	382
S	Rolandelli, R	NJ	921
S	Rosenberg, V	NY	383
S	Roses, D	NY	383
S	Sacco, M	NJ	965
S	Salky, B	NY	383
S	Sas, N	NY	443
S	Schmidt, H	NJ	794
S	Schnabel, F	NY	383
S	Schwartz, M	NY	383
S	Schwartzman, A	NY	493
S	Sclafani, L	NY	648
S	Shack, R	NJ	831
S	Shah, J	NY	383
S	Shah, P	NY	383
S	Shamamian, P	NY	443
S	Shapiro, M	NY	648
S	Shapiro, M	NJ	832
S	Shapiro, R	NY	383
S	Siegel, B	NY	515
S	Simmons, R	NY	383
S	Singer, S	NY	384
S	Slater, G	NY	384
S	Staradub, V	CT	1030
S	Starker, P	NJ	965
S	Strutin, M	NJ	921
S	Sultan, R	NJ	842
S	Sung, K	NY	515
S	Sussman, B	NJ	794
S	Swistel, A	NY	384
S	Talamini, M	NY	648
S	Tartter, P	NY	384
S	Teperman, L	NY	384
S	Trooskin, S	NJ	883
S	Van Zee, K	NY	384
S	Vine, A	NY	384
S	Vitale, G	NY	601
S	Wallack, M	NY	384
S	Ward, B	CT	1031
S	Ward, D	NJ	921
S	Weber, K	NY	727
S	Wedderburn, R	NY	384
S	Weltz, C	NY	385
S	Whitman, E	NJ	921
S	Yang, H	NJ	794
S	Yiengpruksawan, A	NJ	794
S	Yurt, R	NY	385
S	Zarnegar, R	NY	385

Spec	Name	St	Pg
S	Zeitlin, A	NY	515
S	Zingale, R	NY	648
S	Zoland, M	NY	385

Surgical Pathology

Spec	Name	St	Pg
Path	Altmeyer, V	CT	1016
Path	Barnard, N	NJ	876
Path	Hoda, S	NY	301
Path	Vigorita, V	NY	481

Swallowing Disorders

Spec	Name	St	Pg
Ge	Hammerman, H	NY	172
Ge	Harary, A	NY	172
Ge	Lambroza, A	NY	174
Ge	Nelson, A	CT	987
Ge	Torman, J	NY	676
Ge	Traube, M	NY	179
Oto	Amin, M	NY	286
Oto	Aviv, J	NY	286
Oto	Blitzer, A	NY	287
Oto	Chervin, B	CT	1014
Oto	Lim, J	NY	291
Oto	Pearl, A	CT	1016
Oto	Pitman, M	NY	293
Oto	Rothstein, S	NY	294
Oto	Strome, M	NY	296
Oto	Zalvan, C	NY	706
PO	Rothschild, M	NY	315
PPul	Loughlin, G	NY	316

Syncope

Spec	Name	St	Pg
CE	Correia, J	NJ	805
CE	Jadonath, R	NY	540
CE	McPherson, C	CT	975
CE	Mittal, S	NJ	742
CE	Rashba, E	NY	621
CE	Sauberman, R	NJ	805
CE	Winters, S	NJ	904
Cv	Sklaroff, H	NY	134
PCd	Kaplovitz, H	NY	481
PCd	Kurer, C	NJ	876
PCd	Vallone, A	NY	582
PCd	Walsh, C	NY	432

Syringomyelia & Spinal Cord Diseases

Spec	Name	St	Pg
N	Kula, R	NY	569

T

T cell Immune Therapy

Spec	Name	St	Pg
Onc	Brentjens, R	NY	214

Tattoo Removal

Spec	Name	St	Pg
D	Milgraum, S	NJ	864
D	Scherl, S	NJ	751

Tear Duct Problems

Spec	Name	St	Pg
Oph	Campolattaro, B	NY	254
Oph	Dweck, M	NY	476
Oph	Lederman, M	NY	699
Oph	Most, R	NY	700

Tearing Disorders

Spec	Name	St	Pg
Oph	Conway, J	CT	1007

Telemedicine

Spec	Name	St	Pg
S	Goldfarb, M	NJ	898

Temperamentally Difficult Child

Spec	Name	St	Pg
ChAP	Turecki, S	NY	139

Temporal Arteritis

Spec	Name	St	Pg
Oph	Mindel, J	NY	262
Rhu	Danehower, R	CT	1028

Tendon Surgery

Spec	Name	St	Pg
HS	Kulick, R	NY	420
HS	Lee, S	NY	187
OrS	Berberian, W	NJ	775

Testicular Cancer

Spec	Name	St	Pg
Onc	Bajorin, D	NY	213
Onc	Bosl, G	NY	213
Onc	Feldman, D	NY	215
Onc	Motzer, R	NY	219
Onc	Nanus, D	NY	219
Onc	Oh, W	NY	220
Path	Reuter, V	NY	301
U	Choudhury, M	NY	729
U	Herr, H	NY	394
U	Karanikolas, N	NY	532
U	McKiernan, J	NY	396
U	Scherr, D	NY	397
U	Schlegel, P	NY	398
U	Sheinfeld, J	NY	398
U	Weiss, R	NJ	884

Specialty & Special Expertise Index

Specialty & Special Expertise Index

Spec	Name	St	Pg
DR	Henschke, C	NY	158
DR	Khan, A	NY	550
DR	Lefkovitz, Z	NY	668
DR	Lubat, E	NJ	753
DR	Spindola-Franco, H	NY	415
DR	Toth, P	NJ	753
DR	Yankelevitz, D	NY	162

Thoracic Surgery

Spec	Name	St	Pg
PS	Alexander, F	NJ	784
PS	Gallucci, J	NJ	879
T&CS	Berman, S	NY	727
T&CS	Ginsburg, M	NY	387
T&CS	Gorenstein, L	NY	387
T&CS	Lazzaro, R	NY	388
T&CS	Lazzaro, R	NY	388

Throat Cancer

Spec	Name	St	Pg
Oto	Teng, M	NY	296

Throat Disorders

Spec	Name	St	Pg
Oto	Benson, B	NJ	777
Oto	Feldman, S	CT	1015
Oto	Green, R	NY	288
Oto	Taylor, H	NJ	914
Oto	Vastola, A	NY	480
PO	Quraishi, H	NJ	782
S	Mendoza, E	NY	515

Thromboembolic Disorders

Spec	Name	St	Pg
Pul	Steiger, D	NY	360

Thrombolytic Therapy

Spec	Name	St	Pg
VIR	Strauss, E	CT	1033

Thrombotic Disorders

Spec	Name	St	Pg
Hem	Billett, H	NY	420
Hem	Soff, G	NY	192

Thymoma

Spec	Name	St	Pg
Onc	Aisner, J	NJ	869
Onc	Kris, M	NY	218
Onc	Rizvi, N	NY	221

Thyroid & Parathyroid Cancer & Surgery

Spec	Name	St	Pg
Oto	Caruana, S	NY	287
Oto	Drake, W	NJ	959
Oto	Genden, E	NY	288
Oto	Shaari, C	NJ	778

Spec	Name	St	Pg
Oto	Smith, J	NY	431
Oto	Urken, M	NY	296
S	Lee, J	NY	381
S	Weber, K	NY	727

Thyroid & Parathyroid Imaging

Spec	Name	St	Pg
NuM	Palestro, C	NY	570
NuM	Scharf, S	NY	246

Thyroid & Parathyroid Surgery

Spec	Name	St	Pg
Oto	Aferzon, M	CT	1014
Oto	Frank, D	NY	578
Oto	Godin, D	NY	288
Oto	Har-El, G	NY	289
Oto	Ho, B	NJ	777
Oto	Klarsfeld, J	CT	1015
Oto	Komisar, A	NY	290
Oto	Kraus, D	NY	290
Oto	Krevitt, L	NY	291
Oto	La Bagnara, J	NJ	930
Oto	Lagmay, V	NY	480
Oto	Myssiorek, D	NY	292
Oto	Rosenbaum, J	NJ	875
Oto	Sacks, S	NY	294
Oto	Salzer, S	CT	1016
Oto	Shah, D	NJ	894
Oto	Smith, R	NY	431
S	Auguste, L	NY	599
S	Chabot, J	NY	378
S	Garvey, R	CT	1030
S	Rajdeo, H	NY	727
S	Roses, D	NY	383
S	Shapiro, R	NY	383

Thyroid Cancer

Spec	Name	St	Pg
EDM	Cohen, N	NY	523
EDM	Davies, T	NY	163
EDM	Fagin, J	NY	163
EDM	Fish, S	NY	163
EDM	Haber, R	NY	163
EDM	Hodak, S	NY	164
EDM	Mechanick, J	NY	165
EDM	Sabra, M	NY	165
EDM	Tuttle, R	NY	166
NuM	Goldfarb, C	NY	245
NuM	Goldsmith, S	NY	245
NuM	Palestro, C	NY	570
NuM	Pandit-Taskar, N	NY	246
Onc	Pfister, D	NY	221
Onc	Posner, M	NY	221
Oto	Boyle, J	NY	287
Oto	Brauer, R	CT	1014

Spec	Name	St	Pg
Oto	Krespi, Y	NY	290
Oto	Kuhel, W	NY	291
Oto	Persky, M	NY	293
Oto	Salzer, S	CT	1016
Oto	Schantz, S	NY	294
Oto	Shemen, L	NY	294
Oto	Singh, B	NY	295
Oto	Wong, R	NY	297
Path	Sanchez, M	NJ	779
RadRO	Lee, N	NY	362
S	Alfonso, A	NY	491
S	Gannon, C	NJ	857
S	Shah, J	NY	383
S	Trooskin, S	NJ	883

Thyroid Cancer & Surgery

Spec	Name	St	Pg
Oto	Inouye, M	NJ	777
Oto	Kuriloff, D	NY	291

Thyroid Disorders

Spec	Name	St	Pg
EDM	Agrin, R	NJ	865
EDM	Arden-Cordone, M	CT	983
EDM	Balkin, M	NY	626
EDM	Baranetsky, N	NJ	809
EDM	Benaviv-Meskin, D	CT	983
EDM	Bergman, D	NY	162
EDM	Berkowitz, R	NJ	926
EDM	Bhatt, A	NY	550
EDM	Bitton, R	NY	551
EDM	Bleich, D	NJ	809
EDM	Bloomgarden, D	NY	669
EDM	Blum, C	NY	162
EDM	Blum, D	NY	669
EDM	Brand, H	NY	626
EDM	Brickman, A	NY	458
EDM	Brillon, D	NY	163
EDM	Bucholtz, H	NJ	865
EDM	Cam, J	NJ	837
EDM	Carlson, H	NY	626
EDM	Cobin, R	NJ	754
EDM	Cohen, C	NY	415
EDM	Cohen, N	NY	523
EDM	Das, S	NY	523
EDM	Daud-Ahmad, S	NJ	754
EDM	Friedman, S	NY	551
EDM	Fuhrman, R	NJ	951
EDM	Gelato, M	NY	627
EDM	Gewirtz, G	NJ	809
EDM	Giegerich, E	NY	458
EDM	Gioia, L	NY	627
EDM	Goldberg-Berman, J	CT	983
EDM	Goldenberg, A	NY	627

Specialty & Special Expertise Index

Spec	Name	St	Pg
EDM	Goldman, J	NY	459
EDM	Goldman, M	NJ	754
EDM	Gordon, J	NY	551
EDM	Grajower, M	NY	415
EDM	Greene, L	NY	163
EDM	Greenfield, M	NY	551
EDM	Greenwald, B	NY	669
EDM	Guzman, R	NY	415
EDM	Haber, R	NY	163
EDM	Hellerman, J	NY	670
EDM	Hoffman, R	NY	523
EDM	Hupart, K	NY	551
EDM	Jacobs, T	NY	164
EDM	Kantor, A	NY	670
EDM	Klyde, B	NY	164
EDM	Leibowitz, J	NY	670
EDM	Levy, C	NY	164
EDM	Lomasky, S	NY	551
EDM	Maclaren, N	NY	164
EDM	Maman, A	NJ	865
EDM	Margulies, P	NY	551
EDM	Martorella, A	NY	165
EDM	McConnell, R	NY	165
EDM	Mechanick, J	NY	165
EDM	Nassberg, B	NJ	888
EDM	Park, P	NY	459
EDM	Peck, V	NY	165
EDM	Poretsky, L	NY	165
EDM	Rennert, N	CT	983
EDM	Resta, C	NY	459
EDM	Rosa, J	CT	984
EDM	Rosenbaum, R	NJ	951
EDM	Rosenthal, D	NY	552
EDM	Rosman, L	NY	502
EDM	Rothman, J	NY	523
EDM	Selinger, S	NJ	951
EDM	Seltzer, T	NY	165
EDM	Seplowitz, A	NY	166
EDM	Shapiro, L	NY	552
EDM	Sherry, S	NJ	926
EDM	Silverberg, A	NY	459
EDM	Silverman, M	NJ	951
EDM	Spiler, I	NJ	865
EDM	Surks, M	NY	415
EDM	Tibaldi, J	NY	503
EDM	Tohme, J	NJ	754
EDM	Warman, J	NY	459
EDM	Wehmann, R	NJ	754
EDM	Wexler, C	NY	627
EDM	Wiesen, M	NJ	754
EDM	Zonszein, J	NY	416
EDM	Zweig, S	NY	167
FMed	Sadovsky, R	NY	460

Spec	Name	St	Pg
IM	Fiedler, R	NY	201
IM	Joy, M	NY	466
NuM	Goldfarb, C	NY	245
NuM	Goldsmith, S	NY	245
NuM	Strashun, A	NY	474
Oto	Inouye, M	NJ	777
Oto	Kuriloff, D	NY	291
Oto	Teng, M	NY	296
Path	Cohen, J	NY	300
Ped	Siegal, E	NY	616
PEn	Agarwal, C	NY	707
PEn	Agdere, L	NY	482
PEn	Avruskin, T	NY	482
PEn	Carey, D	NY	583
PEn	Cerame, B	NJ	915
PEn	Chin, D	NJ	915
PEn	DiMartino-Nardi, J	NY	707
PEn	Frank, G	NY	583
PEn	Heptulla, R	NY	433
PEn	Kohn, B	NY	306
PEn	Noto, R	NY	707
PEn	Novogroder, M	NJ	780
PEn	Rapaport, R	NY	307
PEn	Speiser, P	NY	583
PEn	Torrado-Jule, C	NY	528
PEn	Wilson, T	NY	640

Thyroid Disorders in Pregnancy

EDM	Davies, T	NY	163

Thyroid Eye Disease

Oph	Kazim, M	NY	260
Oph	Langer, P	NJ	820
Oph	Milite, J	NJ	874
Oph	Schneck, G	NY	638

Thyroid Surgery

Oto	Carew, J	NY	287
Oto	Fox, M	NY	704
Oto	Huo, J	NY	512
Oto	Moisa, I	NY	579
Oto	Scott, J	NY	705
Oto	Shin, E	NY	295
Oto	Slavit, D	NY	295
S	Inabnet, W	NY	380
S	Kenler, A	CT	1030
S	Sultan, R	NJ	842

Thyroid Ultrasound

DR	Bobroff, L	NY	610
DR	Fried, K	NY	158

Spec	Name	St	Pg
EDM	McConnell, R	NY	165

Tick-borne Diseases

IM	Phillips, S	CT	993
Inf	Berkey, P	NY	679
Inf	Horowitz, H	NY	195
Inf	Nadelman, R	NY	680
Inf	Raffalli, J	NY	680
PInf	Li, K	NY	709
PInf	Saiman, L	NY	314

Tongue Cancer

Oto	Teng, M	NY	296

Tonsil/Adenoid Disorders

PO	Dolitsky, J	NY	315
PO	Modi, V	NY	315
PO	Samadi, S	NJ	783
PO	Smith, L	NY	586

Tourette's Syndrome

ChAP	Coffey, B	NY	137
ChAP	Gabbay, V	NY	137
ChAP	Grice, D	NY	137
ChAP	Hirsch, G	NY	137
ChiN	Bennett, H	NJ	905
ChiN	Desouza, T	NJ	905
ChiN	Grossman, E	NJ	905
ChiN	Schubert, R	NY	456
N	Kurlan, R	NJ	956
N	Levy, L	NY	569
N	Selman, J	NY	427
Ped	Adesman, A	NY	587
Psyc	Budman, C	NY	593
Psyc	Goodman, W	NY	345

Toxicology

Nep	Winchester, J	NY	228
Oph	Eichenbaum, J	NY	256

Tracheal Surgery

T&CS	Glassman, L	NY	602

Transesophageal Echocardiogram (TEE)

Cv	Ganem, A	NY	657
Cv	Latif, F	NY	130
Cv	Schwartz, C	NY	521

Specialty & Special Expertise Index

Specialty & Special Expertise Index

Specialty & Special Expertise Index

Spec	Name	St	Pg	Spec	Name	St	Pg	Spec	Name	St	Pg
U	Karanikolas, N	NY	532	U	Ranta, J	CT	1032	U	Trauzzi, S	NY	730
U	Katz, A	NY	604	U	Reckler, J	NY	397	U	Vapnek, J	NY	399
U	Katz, H	NJ	842	U	Richards, S	NJ	884	U	Vasselli, A	NJ	857
U	Katz, J	NJ	832	U	Richstone, L	NY	605	U	Viner, N	CT	1032
U	Katz, S	NJ	796	U	Riechers, R	NY	730	U	Vukasin, A	NJ	857
U	Kavaler, E	NY	395	U	Ring, K	NJ	965	U	Wainstein, S	NY	494
U	Kavoussi, L	NY	604	U	Roberts, L	NY	730	U	Waltzer, W	NY	649
U	Kaynan, A	NJ	922	U	Rose, J	NJ	899	U	Wasserman, G	NJ	798
U	Kerns, J	NJ	796	U	Rosenberg, G	NJ	797	U	Weinberg, J	NY	730
U	Kirschenbaum, A	NY	395	U	Rosenthal, S	NY	494	U	Weiner, D	NY	399
U	Klein, G	NY	395	U	Rossman, B	NJ	857	U	Weiss, R	NJ	884
U	Lanteri, V	NJ	797	U	Rotolo, J	NJ	899	U	Werner, M	NY	731
U	Laudone, V	NY	395	U	Russo, P	NY	397	U	Young, G	NY	399
U	Layne, J	NY	604	U	Saada, S	NY	494	U	Ziegelbaum, M	NY	605
U	Lehrhoff, B	NJ	965	U	Sadeghi-Nejad, H	NJ	797				
U	Lepor, H	NY	395	U	Saidi, J	NJ	833	**Urology-Female**			
U	Lerner, S	NY	729	U	Samadi, D	NY	397	ObG	Tyagi, R	NY	252
U	Lessing, J	NY	532	U	Sandhaus, J	NY	516	U	Biggs, G	NY	728
U	Levine, M	NY	604	U	Sandhu, J	NY	397	U	Breslin, D	NY	729
U	Levine, S	NJ	932	U	Santarosa, R	CT	1032	U	Chaikin, D	NJ	922
U	Lieberman, E	NY	604	U	Savatta, D	NJ	833	U	Cooper, K	NY	392
U	Linsenmeyer, T	NJ	833	U	Savino, M	NY	532	U	Dillon, R	NY	393
U	Litvin, Y	NJ	899	U	Sawczuk, I	NJ	797	U	Fleischmann, N	NY	729
U	Lizza, E	NY	395	U	Scardino, P	NY	397	U	Gribetz, M	NY	394
U	Loo, M	NY	395	U	Scherr, D	NY	397	U	Kavaler, E	NY	395
U	Lowe, F	NY	395	U	Schiff, H	NY	398	U	Miller, M	NJ	965
U	Lumerman, J	NY	604	U	Schiff, J	NY	398	U	Nitti, V	NY	396
U	Mackey, T	NJ	797	U	Schlegel, P	NY	398	U	Roberts, L	NY	730
U	Margolis, E	NJ	797	U	Schoenberg, M	NY	444	U	Schrager, A	NY	730
U	Marks, J	NY	396	U	Schrager, A	NY	730	U	Serels, S	CT	1032
U	Matthews, G	NY	729	U	Seidman, B	NJ	965	U	Shafizadeh, F	NY	516
U	McGovern, T	NY	396	U	Serels, S	CT	1032	U	Siegel, A	NJ	797
U	McKiernan, J	NY	396	U	Shabsigh, R	NY	398	U	Vukasin, A	NJ	857
U	Meisenberg, G	NY	494	U	Shafizadeh, F	NY	516	U	Young, G	NY	399
U	Mellinger, B	NY	604	U	Sharaby, J	NY	494				
U	Miller, M	NJ	965	U	Sheinfeld, J	NY	398	**Urticaria**			
U	Mills, C	NY	649	U	Shemtov, M	NY	398	A&I	Blum, J	NJ	861
U	Moldwin, R	NY	605	U	Shepard, B	NY	605	A&I	Burton, D	NY	122
U	Muldoon, L	CT	1032	U	Shulman, Y	NJ	842	A&I	Fox, J	NJ	935
U	Mulhall, J	NY	396	U	Siegel, A	NJ	797	A&I	From, S	NJ	741
U	Munver, R	NJ	797	U	Siegel, J	NY	730	A&I	Goodstein, C	NJ	741
U	Nagler, H	NY	396	U	Silver, D	NY	494	A&I	Guida, L	NY	621
U	Nitti, V	NY	396	U	Sogani, P	NY	398	A&I	Harish, Z	NJ	741
U	Nobert, C	NY	396	U	Spears, T	NY	649	A&I	Kaufman, A	NY	409
U	Nogueira, M	NY	730	U	Steigman, E	NJ	842	A&I	Klein, R	NJ	925
U	Nurzia, M	CT	1032	U	Stein, M	NY	398	A&I	Lee, R	CT	974
U	Owens, G	NY	730	U	Stifelman, M	NY	399	A&I	Maccia, C	NJ	948
U	Palese, M	NY	396	U	Sunshine, R	NY	605	A&I	Mendelson, J	NJ	948
U	Paul, E	NY	605	U	Taneja, S	NY	399	A&I	Perlman, D	NJ	804
U	Peng, B	NY	397	U	Tarasuk, A	NY	516	A&I	Rosenstreich, D	NY	409
U	Phillips, J	NY	730	U	Te, A	NY	399	A&I	Satnick, S	NY	621
U	Provet, J	NY	397	U	Tewari, A	NY	399	A&I	Shepherd, G	NY	123
U	Raboy, A	NY	532	U	Tillem, S	NY	516				

Specialty & Special Expertise Index

Specialty & Special Expertise Index

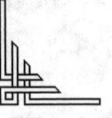

The Best in American Medicine
www.CastleConnolly.com

Alphabetical Listing of Doctors

Name	Specialty	Pg
A		
Aaronson, Beth (CT)	PMR	1020
Abdoo, Robert (NY)	IM	680
Abelow, Arthur (NY)	Ge	417
Abemayor, Elie (NY)	Ge	672
Abenavoli, Tancredi (NY)	IM	680
Abir, Farshad (NJ)	CRS	950
Abittan, Meyer (NY)	IC	561
Ablaza, Valerie (NJ)	PlS	827
Abott, Michael (NY)	Pul	487
Abou-Fayssal, Nada (NY)	N	472
Abramowitz, Avram (NY)	Onc	508
Abrams, Jeffrey (NJ)	OrS	853
Abrams, Linus (CT)	Psyc	1022
Abramson, David (NY)	Oph	253
Abramson, Sara (NY)	DR	156
Abright, A. Reese (NY)	ChAP	136
Abrol, Sunil (NY)	T&CS	493
Abu-Rustum, Nadeem (NY)	GO	183
Abularrage, Joseph (NY)	Ped	512
Accacha, Siham (NY)	PEn	583
Accardi, Frank (NY)	Oph	253
Accurso, Charles (NJ)	Ge	937
Acker, Peter (NY)	Ped	712
Ackerman, Jacob (NY)	Oph	475
Ackert, John (NY)	Ge	168
Acosta, Rodrigo (CT)	FMed	984
Acquista, Angelo (NY)	Pul	354
Adamo, Alfred (NY)	S	599
Adams, Alexa (NY)	PRhu	317
Adams, Darius (NJ)	CG	905
Adams, David (NY)	T&CS	385
Adams, Francis (NY)	Pul	354
Adams, Marc (NY)	RadRO	531
Addis, Michael (NJ)	VascS	966
Addona, Tommaso (NY)	PlS	589
Addonizio, Gerard (NY)	Psyc	717
Addonizio, Linda (NY)	PCd	303
Addrizzo-Harris, Doreen (NY)	Pul	355
Adelman, Mark (NY)	VascS	402
Adelman, Ronald (NY)	Ger	180
Ades, Joseph (NY)	IM	680
Adesman, Andrew (NY)	Ped	587
Adibi, Baback (NJ)	Cv	743
Adler, Edward (NY)	OrS	269
Adler, Harry (NY)	S	491
Adler, Kenneth (NJ)	Onc	909
Adler, Lenard (NY)	Psyc	341
Adler, Ronald (NY)	DR	156
Adler, Stephen (NY)	Nep	690
Adlersberg, Jay (NY)	Rhu	368
Advincula, Arnold (NY)	ObG	246
Aferzon, Mark (CT)	Oto	1014
Afridi, Shariq (NJ)	Ge	848
Agarwal, Chhavi (NY)	PEn	707
Agarwal, Kishan (NJ)	PCd	876
Agarwal, Nanakram (NY)	S	442
Agarwal, Sanjeev (NY)	PM	481
Agarwal, Saurabh (NJ)	U	795
Agdere, Levon (NY)	PEn	482
Aghajanian, Carol (NY)	Onc	213
Agin, Carole (NY)	PM	580
Agress, Harry (NJ)	NuM	772
Agri, Robyn (NJ)	PMR	855
Agrin, Richard (NJ)	EDM	865
Aguila, Helen (NJ)	PPul	825
Agus, Bertrand (NY)	Rhu	368
Aharon, Raphael (NY)	Oph	510
Ahlborn, Thomas (NJ)	S	793
Ahluwalia, Brij (NY)	N	692
Ahmad, Christopher (NY)	OrS	269
Ahmed, Mutahar (NJ)	U	795
Ahmed, Tauseef (NY)	Onc	687
Ahmed Hosny, M Amr (NY)	PM	297

Alphabetical Listing of Doctors

Name	Specialty	Pg	Name	Specialty	Pg
Ahn, Christina (NY)	PlS	330	Alshansky, Anna (NY)	ChiN	663
Ahn, Jung (NY)	PMR	326	Altbaum, Robert (CT)	IM	991
Aisenberg, Javier (NJ)	PEn	780	Altchek, David (NY)	SM	374
Aisner, Joseph (NJ)	Onc	869	Alterman, Lloyd (NJ)	IM	954
Aizer, Juliet (NY)	Rhu	368	Altholz, Jeffrey (NY)	IM	681
Ajl, Stephen (NY)	Ped	485	Altman, Bruce (CT)	Oph	1007
Akhund, Birjis (NY)	Onc	633	Altman, Robin (NY)	Ped	712
Akin, Oguz (NY)	DR	156	Altman, Wayne (NJ)	OrS	775
Akinboboye, Olakunle (NY)	Cv	500	Altmann, Dory (NJ)	Cv	862
Akman, Cigdem (NY)	ChiN	139	Altmann, Karen (NY)	PCd	303
Al-Aswad, Lama (NY)	Oph	253	Altmeyer, Vicki (CT)	Path	1016
Al-Khan, Abdulla (NJ)	MF	764	Altorki, Nasser (NY)	T&CS	385
Albert, Arthur (NJ)	VIR	798	Altschul, Larry (NY)	Cv	622
Alberta, Francis (NJ)	SM	793	Altus, Jonathan (NY)	Pul	594
Albom, Michael (NY)	D	145	Aluri-Vallabhaneni, Bhanu (NJ)	NRad	928
Alden, Dmitri (NY)	S	376	Alvarez, Manuel (NJ)	MF	764
Alderman, Elizabeth (NY)	AM	409	Alweiss, Gary (NJ)	N	770
Aldrich, Thomas (NY)	Pul	440	Amaral, Terry (NY)	OrS	575
Aledo, Alexander (NY)	PHO	309	Ambinder, Jeffrey (NY)	Hem	679
Aledort, Louis (NY)	Hem	189	Amer, Jeffrey (NY)	Ped	587
Alexander, Frederick (NJ)	PS	784	Ames, Richard (NY)	Nep	226
Alexiades, Michael (NY)	OrS	269	Amin, Hossam (NY)	Pul	488
Alexiades-Armenakas, Macrene (NY)	D	145	Amin, Mahendra (NY)	IM	506
Alexis, Andrew (NY)	D	146	Amin, Milan (NY)	Oto	286
Alfonso, Antonio (NY)	S	491	Amin, Nikhil (NY)	PPul	710
Ali, Yousaf (NY)	Rhu	368	Amin, Ravindra (NY)	GerPsy	462
Alizadeh, Kaveh (NY)	PlS	590	Amin, Snehal (NY)	D	146
Allegra, Donald (NJ)	Inf	908	Amis, E Stephen (NY)	DR	414
Allen, Answorth (NY)	OrS	269	Amodio, John (NY)	DR	458
Allen, Jeffrey (NY)	ChiN	139	Amorosi, Edward (NY)	Hem	189
Allen, Peter (NY)	S	376	Amoruso, Robert (NJ)	Pul	931
Allen, Robert (NY)	PlS	331	Amory, Spencer (NY)	S	376
Allen, Steven (NY)	Hem	557	Amsterdam, Alison (NY)	IM	198
Allendorf, Dennis (NY)	Ped	320	Andaz, Shahriyour (NY)	T&CS	601
Allendorf, John (NY)	S	599	Andersen, Holly (NY)	Cv	125
Almeida, Laila (NJ)	D	906	Andersen, Margaret (NY)	IM	681
Alon, Jamie (CT)	Ped	1018	Anderson, Lisa (NY)	GO	183
Alper, Kenneth (NY)	Psyc	341	Anderson, Patrick (NJ)	GO	811
Alpert, Barbara (NY)	IM	681	Anderson, Richard (NY)	NS	228

Name	Specialty	Pg	Name	Specialty	Pg
Andrade, Joseph (NY)	Ped	436	Araten, David (NY)	Hem	189
Andrei, Valeriu (NJ)	S	830	Arcasoy, Selim (NY)	Pul	355
Andrews, Alan (NJ)	D	750	Arcati, Anthony (NY)	FMed	552
Andrews, Paul (NJ)	Cv	744	Arcati, Robert (NY)	FMed	552
Andriola, Mary (NY)	ChiN	624	Arden, Martha (NY)	AM	538
Andronaco, Raymond (NJ)	U	796	Arden-Cordone, Mary (CT)	EDM	983
Anene, Okechukwu (NJ)	PCCM	877	Arena, Francis (NY)	Onc	563
Angel, Michael (NY)	OrS	575	Arens, Raanan (NY)	PPul	435
Angeli, Stephen (NJ)	IC	763	Argenziano, Michael (NY)	T&CS	385
Angello, Thomas (NY)	Ped	712	Argilla, Michael (NY)	PCd	303
Angevine, Anne (CT)	Onc	998	Arginteanu, Marc (NJ)	NS	769
Angevine, Peter (NY)	NS	229	Aries, Philip (NY)	Oph	637
Angioletti, Louis (NJ)	Oph	773	Ark, Jon (NJ)	HS	849
Angioletti, Louis (NY)	Oph	253	Arkow, Stan (NY)	Psyc	341
Angrist, Richard (NJ)	Oph	940	Arlievsky, Nina (NY)	PInf	615
Anhalt, Henry (NJ)	PEn	960	Armbruster, Robert (NY)	ObG	695
Annabi, Iyad (NY)	FMed	671	Armenakas, Noel (NY)	U	391
Anselmi, Gregory (NJ)	N	839	Armento, Michael (NJ)	PMR	961
Anto, Maliakal (NY)	Cv	541	Arnell, Tracey (NY)	CRS	143
Anton, John (NY)	PlS	644	Arno, Louis (NJ)	Pul	942
Antonelle, Robert (NY)	Ge	672	Arnold, Thomas (NY)	VascS	650
Antonescu, Cristina (NY)	Path	300	Arnon, Rica (NY)	PCd	304
Anyane-Yeboa, Kwame (NY)	CG	141	Arnouk, Issam (NY)	ObG	474
Apatoff, Brian (NY)	N	234	Arnstein, Ellis (NY)	Ped	436
Apfel, Howard (NJ)	PCd	780	Aron, Alan (NY)	ChiN	139
Aponte, Alex (NY)	FMed	627	Aronne, Louis (NY)	IM	198
Apostolides, Paul (CT)	NS	1001	Aronoff, Michael (NY)	Psyc	341
Appel, David (NY)	Pul	440	Aronson, Thomas (NY)	Psyc	645
Appel, Gerald (NY)	Nep	226	Arpadi, Stephen (NY)	Ped	320
Appelbaum, Jeffrey (NY)	N	509	Arthur, Karen (NY)	S	725
Appelbaum, Paul (NY)	Psyc	341	Arunachalam, Muthu (NJ)	Ger	811
Applbaum, Yaakov (NJ)	NRad	852	Arvan, Glenn (NY)	OrS	638
Applebaum, Eric (NJ)	A&I	903	Arvanitis, Michael (NJ)	CRS	888
April, Max (NY)	PO	315	Asarian, Armand (NY)	S	456
Aprile, Georgette (NY)	D	548	Asbell, Penny (NY)	Oph	253
Apuzzio, Joseph (NJ)	MF	814	Ascher, Enrico (NY)	VascS	495
Apuzzo, Thomas (NY)	FMed	671	Ascher-Walsh, Charles (NY)	ObG	246
Arams, Ronald (NJ)	DR	752	Ascherman, Jeffrey (NY)	PlS	331
Aranoff, Shera (NY)	D	146	Ashamalla, Hani (NY)	RadRO	489

Alphabetical Listing of Doctors

Name	Specialty	Pg	Name	Specialty	Pg
Ashany, Dalit (NY)	Rhu	368	Awad, John (CT)	OrS	1010
Ashikari, Andrew (NY)	S	725	Axelrod, Deborah (NY)	S	376
Ashinoff, Robin (NJ)	D	750	Axelrod, Sheldon (NY)	U	728
Ashinoff, Russell (NJ)	PlS	896	Ayoub, Thomas (CT)	ObG	1004
Ashley, Richard (NY)	U	603	Ayyanathan, Karpukarasi (NJ)	Ped	960
Ashton, Julie (NJ)	Ped	917	Azhar, Salman (NY)	N	472
Asnis, Deborah (NY)	Inf	506			
Asnis, Stanley (NY)	OrS	575			
Asprinio, David (NY)	OrS	701	**B**		
Aston, Sherrell (NY)	PlS	331			
Astrow, Alan (NY)	Onc	468	Babbar, Rajeev (NY)	IM	198
Athanasian, Edward (NY)	HS	186	Babitz, Lisa (NY)	Ger	180
Atlas, Arthur (NJ)	PPul	916	Babkowski, Robert (CT)	Path	1016
Atlas, Mark (NY)	PHO	584	Babu, Sateesh (NY)	VascS	731
Atluru, Vijaya (NY)	ChiN	545	Bacall, Charles (NY)	ObG	246
Attas, Lewis (NJ)	Onc	764	Baccash, Emil (NY)	Ger	462
Attia, Evelyn (NY)	Psyc	341	Bach, John (NJ)	PMR	826
Attiyeh, Fadi (NY)	S	376	Bacha, Emile (NY)	T&CS	386
Attkiss, Keith (CT)	PlS	1021	Bachmann, Gloria (NJ)	ObG	873
Attubato, Michael (NY)	IC	208	Backe, Henry (CT)	HS	988
Auerbach, Mitchell (NY)	Ge	672	Backman, Kenneth (CT)	A&I	973
Aufiero, Patrick (NJ)	Inf	849	Badani, Ketan (NY)	U	391
Augello, Sabino (NY)	Ge	503	Bade, Harry (NJ)	OrS	894
Augenbraun, Charles (CT)	Cv	975	Badikian, Arthur (NY)	Psyc	717
Augenbraun, Michael (NY)	Inf	464	Baer, Raymond (CT)	Path	1016
August, David (NJ)	S	882	Bagel, Jerry (NJ)	D	847
August, Phyllis (NY)	Nep	226	Bailey, Michele (NY)	Ped	712
Auguste, Louis (NY)	S	599	Bailine, Samuel (NY)	Psyc	593
Auran, James (NY)	Oph	253	Bains, Manjit (NY)	T&CS	386
Austin, John (NY)	DR	157	Bains, Yatinder (NJ)	Ge	810
Austin, Kenneth (NY)	OrS	614	Baiocco, Peter (NY)	Ge	168
Averill, Allison (NJ)	PMR	786	Baiser, Dennis (NJ)	Ped	854
Aversa, Alphonse (NY)	IM	681	Bajakian, Danielle (NY)	VascS	402
Avezzano, Eric (NJ)	Ge	756	Bajorin, Dean (NY)	Onc	213
Aviv, Jonathan (NY)	Oto	286	Baker, Azzam (NJ)	Ped	841
Avram, Marc (NY)	D	146	Baker, Daniel (NY)	PlS	331
Avruskin, Theodore (NY)	PEn	482	Baker, David (NY)	ObG	636
Avvento, Louis (NY)	Hem	630	Bakshi, Sanjay (NY)	PM	297
Avvocato, Gloria (NY)	Ped	712	Balcer, Laura (NY)	N	234
			Baldwin, Hilary (NY)	D	456

Name	Specialty	Pg	Name	Specialty	Pg
Balk, Sophie (NY)	Ped	436	Barron, Otis (NY)	HS	186
Balkin, Michael (NY)	EDM	626	Barsh, Elliot (NY)	Ped	712
Balot, Barry (NY)	IM	631	Bartell, Abraham (NY)	ChAP	136
Balsam, Leah (NY)	Nep	565	Bartolomeo, Robert (NY)	Ge	553
Baltus, Michele (NY)	FMed	627	Basch, Samuel (NY)	Psyc	342
Banc, Tobe (NY)	Ger	676	Baselga, Jose (NY)	Onc	213
Bangaru, Babu (NY)	PGe	308	Bashevkin, Michael (NY)	Onc	468
Bank, David (NY)	D	664	Baskin, David (NY)	IM	198
Bank, Matthew (NY)	S	599	Baskin, Martin (NY)	Pul	355
Banks, Judy (NJ)	ObG	912	Baskind, Lawrence (NY)	Ped	712
Bansal, Rajendra (NY)	Oph	254	Basner, Robert (NY)	Pul	355
Bansil, Shalini (NJ)	N	956	Basralian, Kevin (NJ)	U	796
Banzon, Manuel (NJ)	ObG	840	Bass, Anne (NY)	Rhu	368
Baorto, Elizabeth (NJ)	PInf	916	Bassett, Clifford (NY)	A&I	121
Bar, Michael (CT)	Hem	989	Bastawros, Mary (NY)	Ped	529
Bar-Chama, Natan (NY)	U	391	Basuk, Pamela (NY)	D	624
Barabas, Ronald (NJ)	ChiN	887	Basuk, Paul (NY)	Ge	169
Barakat, Richard (NY)	GO	183	Batsides, George (NJ)	T&CS	944
Baram, Daniel (NY)	Pul	645	Bauchman, Gail (NY)	FMed	167
Baranetsky, Nicholas (NJ)	EDM	809	Baum, David (CT)	IM	991
Barasch, Jeffrey (NJ)	Pul	789	Baum, Richard (NJ)	U	796
Barazani, Lance (NY)	D	548	Bauman, Jonathan (NY)	Psyc	717
Barbuto, Joseph (NY)	Psyc	342	Bauman, Phillip (NY)	OrS	269
Bard, Michael (CT)	Oto	1014	Baumann, John (NJ)	RadRO	881
Bareket, Yaron (NJ)	Cv	744	Bavaro, Nicholas (NY)	OrS	701
Barenberg, David (CT)	Ge	985	Bazil, Carl (NY)	N	234
Barie, Philip (NY)	S	377	Beauchamp, Donald (NJ)	FMed	755
Barile, Gaetano (NY)	Oph	254	Becker, David (NY)	D	146
Barisciano, Lisa (NJ)	PA&I	915	Becker, Ina (NY)	ChAP	136
Barker, Barbara (NY)	Oph	254	Beckman, Karen (CT)	Ped	1018
Barley, Christopher (NY)	IM	198	Bederson, Joshua (NY)	NS	229
Barmakian, Joseph (NJ)	OrS	958	Bednarek, Karl (NY)	Ge	169
Barnard, Nicola (NJ)	Path	876	Beer, Jeffry (NY)	PMR	589
Barone, Clement (NY)	DR	157	Behm, Dutsi (NY)	IM	465
Barone, Joseph (NJ)	Ped Uro	941	Behr, Raymond (NY)	Psyc	593
Barone, Richard (NY)	Rhu	723	Beim, Robert (NJ)	ObG	957
Barrett, Leonard (NY)	T&CS	601	Bekele, Wondwessen (NJ)	PHO	824
Barrison, Adam (NJ)	Ge	952	Belamarich, Peter (NY)	Ped	436
Barro, Jennifer (CT)	Ge	985	Beldner, Steven (NY)	HS	186

Alphabetical Listing of Doctors

Name	Specialty	Pg	Name	Specialty	Pg
Beldner, Stuart (NY)	CE	540	Bent, John (NY)	PO	435
Belenkov, Elliot (NY)	Onc	213	Benton, Marc (NJ)	Pul	919
Belilos, Elise (NY)	Rhu	598	Benvenisty, Alan (NY)	VascS	402
Bell, David (NY)	AM	120	Benzil, Deborah (NY)	NS	692
Bell, Jonathan (CT)	A&I	973	Beran, Nancy (NY)	IM	681
Bell, Kevin (NJ)	IM	938	Beran, Samuel (NY)	PlS	715
Bellemare, Sarah (NY)	S	442	Berbari, Nicholas (NY)	IM	559
Bello, Mary (NJ)	FMed	755	Berberian, Wayne (NJ)	OrS	775
Belmont, H. Michael (NY)	Rhu	368	Berck, David (NY)	MF	686
Belok, Lennart (NY)	N	234	Berdoff, Russell (NY)	Cv	125
Belostotsky, Olga (NY)	Rhu	369	Berenstein, Alejandro (NY)	NRad	243
Belsh, Jerry (NJ)	N	871	Berezin, Marc (NY)	SM	618
Belsito, Donald (NY)	D	146	Berezin, Stuart (NY)	PGe	708
Beltran, Himisha (NY)	Onc	213	Berger, Bernard (NY)	D	624
Ben-Menachem, Tamir (NJ)	Ge	952	Berger, Jack (NY)	Rhu	723
Benaviv-Meskin, Danielle (CT)	EDM	983	Berger, Jeffrey (NY)	IM	559
Benchimol, Corinne (NY)	PNep	314	Berger, Judith (NY)	Inf	421
Bendo, John (NY)	OrS	270	Berger, Robin (CT)	ObG	1004
Benedetto, Dominick (NJ)	Oph	840	Berger, Scott (NY)	NRad	695
Benedetto-Anzai, Maria (NY)	ObG	246	Bergh, Paul (NJ)	RE	920
Benedict, Leonard (NY)	ObG	570	Bergman, Donald (NY)	EDM	162
Benedicto, Milagros (NY)	ObG	510	Bergman, Kerry (NJ)	PS	960
Benevenia, Joseph (NJ)	OrS	820	Bergman, Michael (NY)	Pul	488
Beniaminovitz, Ainat (NY)	Cv	609	Bergtraum, Marcia (NY)	ChiN	546
Benisovich, Vladimir (NY)	Onc	508	Berke, Andrew (NY)	IC	561
Benitez, Ronald (NJ)	NS	911	Berke, Stanley (NY)	Oph	572
Benito, Carlos (NJ)	MF	909	Berkey, Peter (NY)	Inf	679
Benjamin, Jeffrey (NY)	N	472	Berkowitz, Eric (NY)	D	146
Benjamin, John (NY)	Psyc	593	Berkowitz, Howard (NY)	Psyc	487
Benkov, Keith (NY)	PGe	308	Berkowitz, Irwin (NJ)	Ped	785
Bennett, Garrett (NY)	Oto	286	Berkowitz, Leonard (NY)	Inf	464
Bennett, Harvey (NJ)	ChiN	905	Berkowitz, Norman (NY)	Ped	712
Bennett, Rachel (NY)	RE	723	Berkowitz, Rhonda (NY)	D	664
Bennett, Stanford (NY)	IM	681	Berkowitz, Richard (NY)	MF	210
Bennett, Steven (CT)	PM	1016	Berkowitz, Richard (NJ)	EDM	926
Benoff, Brian (NJ)	Pul	790	Berkowitz, Walter (NJ)	Cv	744
Benowitz, Joel (NY)	S	600	Berkwits, Kieve (CT)	PCd	1017
Benson, Brian (NJ)	Oto	777	Berlin, Scott (NY)	ObG	636
Benson, Mitchell (NY)	U	392	Berman, Alvin (NY)	ObG	246

Alphabetical Listing of Doctors

Name	Specialty	Pg	Name	Specialty	Pg
Biser, Seth (NY)	Oph	697	Blumberg, Joel (CT)	IM	991
Bitan, Fabien (NY)	OrS	270	Blume, Jessica (NJ)	A&I	741
Bitton, Rachelle (NY)	EDM	551	Blume, Ralph (NY)	Rhu	369
Biviano, Angelo (NY)	CE	123	Blumenfeld, Jon (NY)	Nep	226
Bivona, James (CT)	IM	991	Blumenthal, David (NY)	Cv	126
Blackwood, M. Michele (NJ)	S	831	Blumstein, Meyer (NY)	Ge	553
Blady, David (NJ)	N	817	Bobby, Paul (CT)	MF	997
Blagodatny, Marina (CT)	Ger	988	Bobroff, Lewis (NY)	DR	610
Blair, Bryan (NY)	U	728	Bochner, Bernard (NY)	U	392
Blair, Emily (CT)	ObG	1004	Bochner, Ronnie (NJ)	ObG	873
Blair, Lester (NY)	Pul	355	Bockman, Richard (NY)	EDM	162
Blaivas, Jerry (NY)	U	392	Boczko, Judd (NY)	U	728
Blake, James (NY)	Cv	125	Boczko, Stanley (NY)	U	392
Blanck, Richard (NY)	N	568	Bodenstein, Lawrence (NY)	PS	317
Blank, Ellen (NJ)	D	837	Bodis-Wollner, Ivan (NY)	N	472
Blank, Stephanie (NY)	GO	183	Bodner, Staci (NY)	Ped	320
Blatter, Brett (NY)	Psyc	342	Bodner, William (NY)	RadRO	441
Blaufox, Andrew (NY)	PCd	581	Bogen, Steven (NY)	Psyc	717
Blaustein, Silvia (NJ)	AM	925	Bogin, Marc (NY)	Cv	521
Blei, Francine (NY)	PHO	309	Boim, Marilynn (NJ)	Ped	854
Bleich, David (NJ)	EDM	809	Boland, Patrick (NY)	OrS	270
Bleicher, Robert (NJ)	Ge	926	Bomback, David (CT)	OrS	1010
Bleiweiss, Ira (NY)	Path	300	Bomback, Fredric (NY)	Ped	713
Blick, Michael (NJ)	Cv	904	Bonagura, Vincent (NY)	PA&I	581
Blitzer, Andrew (NY)	Oto	287	Bonaventura, Lisa (NJ)	IM	938
Blondo, Dennis (NJ)	Oph	873	Bond, Annette (CT)	MF	997
Bloom, Gregory (CT)	Cv	976	Bondi, Elliott (NY)	Pul	488
Bloom, Katherine (CT)	A&I	973	Bone, Stanley (NY)	Psyc	342
Bloom, Norman (NY)	S	377	Bonheim, Nelson (CT)	Ge	985
Bloomfield, Diane (NY)	Ped	436	Boniece, Irene (NY)	N	234
Bloomgarden, David (NY)	EDM	669	Bonilla, Mary Ann (NJ)	PHO	930
Bloomgarden, Zachary (NY)	EDM	162	Boniuk, Vivien (NY)	Oph	572
Blum, Alan (NY)	Pul	594	Boockvar, John (NY)	NS	229
Blum, Conrad (NY)	EDM	162	Bookner, Scott (NY)	Ped	713
Blum, Daniel (NY)	IM	506	Boolbol, Robert (CT)	PM	1016
Blum, David (NY)	EDM	669	Boolbol, Susan (NY)	S	377
Blum, Jay (NJ)	A&I	861	Boone, Peter (CT)	OrS	1011
Blum, Mark (NJ)	Cv	904	Boorady, Roy (NY)	ChAP	136
Blumberg, Isabel (NY)	ObG	247	Boorjian, Peter (NJ)	U	832

Name	Specialty	Pg	Name	Specialty	Pg
Borah, Gregory (NJ)	PlS	880	Brand, Michael (CT)	OrS	1011
Borao, Frank (NJ)	S	898	Brandeis, Steven (NY)	CRS	143
Borbely, Antal (NY)	Psyc	342	Brandt, Fredric (NY)	D	147
Borcich, Anthony (NY)	Ge	169	Brandt, Lawrence (NY)	Ge	417
Borczuk, Alain (NY)	Path	300	Brannagan, Thomas (NY)	N	234
Borek, Mark (NY)	Cv	622	Branovan, Daniel (NY)	Oto	480
Borer, Jeffrey (NY)	Cv	452	Brathwaite, Collin (NY)	S	600
Boretz, Robert (NJ)	HS	938	Brauer, Richard (CT)	Oto	1014
Borg, Morton (NY)	PCd	304	Brauner, Gary (NJ)	D	750
Borgen, Elliot (NY)	IC	467	Braunstein, Richard (NY)	Oph	254
Borkowsky, William (NY)	PInf	313	Brauntuch, Glenn (NJ)	Pul	790
Boro, Alexis (NY)	N	426	Brause, Barry (NY)	Inf	193
Borriello, Raffaele (NY)	S	492	Braver, Joel (NJ)	RadRO	943
Bortz, John (NY)	Oph	698	Brecher, Rubin (NY)	Oph	476
Boruchoff, Susan (NJ)	Inf	868	Breda, Stephen (CT)	Oto	1014
Boscamp, Jeffrey (NJ)	PInf	782	Breen, William (NY)	Cv	541
Bosco, Joseph (NY)	OrS	270	Breglio, Keith (NY)	PGe	482
Bosl, George (NY)	Onc	213	Bregman, Zachary (NY)	IM	199
Boss, William (NJ)	PlS	787	Breidbart, David (NY)	Pul	595
Bosso, John (NY)	A&I	609	Breindel, David (NY)	Psyc	717
Bostrom, Mathias (NY)	OrS	270	Breitbart, Arnold (NY)	PlS	590
Bosworth, Jay (NY)	RadRO	596	Breitbart, William (NY)	Psyc	342
Botwin, Clifford (NJ)	OrS	958	Brener, Bruce (NJ)	VascS	833
Botwinick, Nelson (NY)	HS	186	Brener, Sorin (NY)	IC	467
Bourla, Steven (NY)	Nep	566	Brenner, Dennis (NJ)	PEn	823
Boxer, Harriet (NY)	NP	565	Brenner, Ronald (NY)	Psyc	593
Boxer, Mitchell (NY)	A&I	538	Brenner, Steven (NY)	RE	598
Boxer, William (NY)	IM	198	Brentjens, Renier (NY)	Onc	214
Boyd, D. Barry (CT)	Hem	989	Breslin, David (NY)	U	729
Boyer, Joseph (NY)	PPul	710	Breslow, Gary (NJ)	PlS	787
Boyle, Jay (NY)	Oto	287	Bressman, Susan (NY)	N	234
Brademas, Mary Ellen (NY)	D	147	Brett, Elise (NY)	EDM	162
Bradley, Sara (NY)	Ger	180	Brewer, Marlon (NY)	IM	506
Bradley, Thomas (NY)	Onc	563	Brick, David (NY)	PCd	304
Brady, Mary (NY)	S	377	Brickman, Alan (NY)	EDM	458
Bram, Harris (NJ)	PM	895	Brickner, Gary (NJ)	ObG	852
Bramwit, Steven (CT)	Oto	1014	Brief, Rochelle (NY)	PMR	616
Brancaccio, Ronald (NY)	D	457	Brightman, Rebecca (NY)	ObG	247
Brand, Howard (NY)	EDM	626	Brill, Joseph (NY)	Pul	720

Alphabetical Listing of Doctors

Name	Specialty	Pg	Name	Specialty	Pg
Brill, Paula (NY)	DR	157	Brown, Marc (NY)	DR	157
Brill, Susan (NJ)	AM	861	Brown, Mitchell (NJ)	Ger	838
Brillon, David (NY)	EDM	163	Brown, Richard (NY)	Psyc	343
Briner, William (NY)	SM	599	Brown, Robert (CT)	Pul	1024
Brisman, Jonathan (NY)	NS	566	Brown, Robert (NY)	Ge	169
Brisson, Paul (NY)	OrS	270	Bruce, Jeffrey (NY)	NS	229
Brittis, Dante (CT)	OrS	1011	Bruckner, Howard (NY)	Onc	423
Britton, Carolyn (NY)	N	235	Bruckstein, Alex (NY)	Ge	523
Brodherson, Michael (NY)	U	392	Bruckstein, Robert (NY)	D	548
Brodie, Jonathan (NY)	Psyc	342	Brumberg, Heather (NY)	NP	689
Brodman, Richard (NJ)	Rhu	963	Brunckhorst, Keith (NY)	Onc	214
Brody, Samuel (NY)	Ger	504	Brunner, Eugenie (NJ)	Oto	854
Brogno, David (NY)	IC	611	Brunnquell, Stephen (NJ)	IM	762
Bromberg, Assia (NJ)	Pul	790	Bruno, Anthony (NY)	U	603
Bromberg, Beth (NY)	Oph	698	Bruno, Peter (NY)	IM	199
Bromley, Gary (NY)	PlS	331	Brustein, Harris (NY)	Oph	698
Bronheim, Harold (NY)	Psyc	343	Brustman, Lois (NY)	MF	211
Bronin, Andrew (NY)	D	665	Bryce, Thomas (NY)	PMR	326
Bronson, Michael (NY)	OrS	270	Buchalter, Maury (NJ)	Ped	785
Bronson, Richard (NY)	RE	646	Buchbinder, Ellen (NY)	A&I	122
Bronster, David (NY)	N	235	Buchholtz, Michael (NY)	Onc	633
Broumand, Stafford (NY)	PlS	331	Buchness, Mary Ruth (NY)	D	147
Broussard, Crystal (NJ)	Ge	756	Bucholtz, Harvey (NJ)	EDM	865
Brovender, Bruce (NY)	Ped	320	Buckner, Cary (NY)	N	472
Brower, Steven (NY)	S	378	Budd, Daniel (NJ)	S	932
Brown, Andrew (NY)	PMR	326	Budin, Joel (NJ)	DR	752
Brown, Andrew (NJ)	Oph	773	Budman, Cathy (NY)	Psyc	593
Brown, Arthur (NY)	Inf	194	Budman, Daniel (NY)	Onc	563
Brown, Carol (NY)	GO	183	Bukberg, Judith (NY)	Psyc	343
Brown, Christopher (NJ)	Oph	773	Bukberg, Phillip (NY)	EDM	163
Brown, David (CT)	OrS	1011	Bulgarelli, Christopher (NY)	Psyc	343
Brown, David (NJ)	PMR	879	Bullock, Richard (NJ)	Ger	867
Brown, David (NJ)	A&I	948	Bulmash, Max (NY)	Ped	485
Brown, Eric (CT)	Nep	1000	Buly, Robert (NY)	OrS	271
Brown, Jeffrey (NY)	NS	566	Burack, Lauren (NY)	D	665
Brown, Jessica (NY)	RE	363	Burak, Corey (NY)	OrS	701
Brown, Jocelyn (NY)	Ped	320	Burak, George (NY)	OrS	701
Brown, John (NJ)	T&CS	921	Bures, Sergio (NY)	Pul	720
Brown, Karen (NY)	VIR	399	Burke, Karen (NY)	D	147

Alphabetical Listing of Doctors

Name	Specialty	Pg
Burke, Patricia (NJ)	Oph	773
Burke, William (NY)	GO	183
Burkes, Lynn (NY)	ChAP	137
Burns, Bryan (CT)	Ge	986
Burns, Elisa (NY)	ObG	695
Burns, Les (NJ)	ObG	928
Burns, Mark (NY)	Rhu	723
Burns, Paul (NY)	PM	615
Burschtin, Omar (NY)	Pul	355
Burstein, Ora (CT)	PA&I	1017
Burstin, Harris (NY)	Ped	320
Burton, Daniel (NY)	A&I	122
Buscaglia, Jonathan (NY)	Ge	628
Busch-Devereaux, Erna (NY)	S	647
Buschmann, William (NY)	OrS	702
Bush, Jacqueline (NY)	MF	468
Bush, Michael (NY)	IM	199
Busillo, Christopher (NY)	Inf	194
Bussel, James (NY)	PHO	309
Bussell, Stuart (CT)	CRS	979
Buterman, Irving (NY)	ObG	247
Butler, David (NJ)	ObG	772
Butler, James (CT)	N	1002
Butler, Mark (NJ)	OrS	941
Butt, Ahmar (NY)	IM	465
Buxton, Douglas (NY)	Oph	254
Buyon, Jill (NY)	Rhu	369
Buzzeo, Louis (NY)	Nep	690
Byfield, Floyd (NY)	Ge	672
Byrd, Lawrence (NJ)	Nep	910

C

Name	Specialty	Pg
Cabaniss, Deborah (NY)	Psyc	343
Caccavale, Robert (NJ)	T&CS	944
Caccese, William (NY)	Ge	553
Cacciola, Thomas (NJ)	IM	762
Cahan, Anthony (NY)	S	726
Cahill, James (NJ)	OrS	775

Name	Specialty	Pg
Cahill, John (NY)	PrM	340
Cahill, Linda (NY)	Ped	436
Cahill, Patrick (CT)	ObG	1004
Cairo, Mitchell (NY)	PHO	708
Calem-Grunat, Jaclyn (NJ)	DR	752
Calhoun, Sean (NJ)	VIR	922
Caligiuri, Daniel (NY)	HS	505
Caligor, Eve (NY)	Psyc	343
Callahan, Eileen (NY)	Ger	180
Callahan, Lisa (NY)	SM	374
Calman, Neil (NY)	FMed	167
Cam, Jenny Rose (NJ)	EDM	837
Camacho, Fernando (NY)	Onc	423
Camacho, Margarita (NJ)	T&CS	832
Camel, Mark (CT)	NS	1001
Cammarata, Sandra (NJ)	ChAP	806
Cammisa, Frank (NY)	OrS	271
Campagna, Robert (NY)	Cv	126
Campbell, Deborah (NY)	NP	424
Campolattaro, Brian (NY)	Oph	254
Canfield, Stephen (NY)	A&I	122
Cangemi, Francis (NJ)	Oph	819
Cannarozzi, Nicholas (NJ)	Rhu	830
Cantor, Liliah (NY)	ChiN	663
Cantor, Michael (NY)	Ge	169
Capasse, Jeanne (CT)	S	1029
Cape, Alison (NY)	MF	686
Capio, Mario (NJ)	FMed	906
Caplivski, Daniel (NY)	Inf	194
Capobianco, Luigi (NY)	FMed	552
Caporaso, Gregg (NY)	N	693
Capozzi, James (NY)	OrS	575
Cappucci, Roger (NY)	Cv	656
Caprio, Martha (NY)	NP	225
Caputo, Anthony (NJ)	Oph	819
Caputo, Thomas (NY)	GO	183
Carabello, Blase (NY)	Cv	126
Caracci, Giovanni (NJ)	Psyc	828
Cardiello, Gary (NJ)	IM	838

Alphabetical Listing of Doctors

Name	Specialty	Pg	Name	Specialty	Pg
Cardoso, Erico (NY)	NS	471	Castellano, Michael (NY)	Pul	530
Carew, John (NY)	Oto	287	Castro-Magana, Mariano (NY)	PEn	583
Carey, Dennis (NY)	PEn	583	Castro-Malaspina, Hugo (NY)	Hem	189
Carlin, Elizabeth (NJ)	NP	767	Catalano, Louis (NY)	HS	186
Carlson, Gabrielle (NY)	ChAP	623	Catallozzi, Marina (NY)	AM	120
Carlson, Harold (NY)	EDM	626	Catanese, Anthony (NJ)	U	944
Carlson, Michelle (NY)	HS	186	Catanese, James (NY)	Cv	656
Carmine, Linda (NY)	AM	538	Catanese, Vincent (NJ)	FMed	889
Carney, Alexander (NJ)	Rhu	856	Catanzaro, Donna (NJ)	IM	939
Carniciu, Sanda (NY)	N	693	Caucino, Julie (NJ)	A&I	935
Carniciu, Stere (NY)	FMed	671	Cavaliere, Gregg (NY)	SM	725
Carniol, Paul (NJ)	Oto	959	Cavallaro, Barbara (NJ)	ObG	772
Caron, Philip (NY)	Onc	687	Cayne, Neal (NY)	VascS	403
Carosella, Christine (NY)	IM	681	Cece, John (NJ)	Oto	930
Carpenter, Duncan (NJ)	NS	769	Ceisler, Emily (NY)	Oph	255
Carr-Locke, David (NY)	Ge	169	Cemaletin, Nevber (NY)	Cv	126
Carrasquillo, Jorge (NY)	NuM	245	Censullo, Michael (NJ)	VIR	884
Carroccio, Alfio (NY)	VascS	403	Cerame, Barbara (NJ)	PEn	915
Carroll, William (NY)	PHO	310	Cerrone, Federico (NJ)	Pul	963
Carson, Jeffrey (NJ)	IM	868	Cerulli, Maurice (NY)	Ge	553
Carsons, Steven (NY)	Rhu	598	Cervia, Joseph (NY)	Inf	558
Carter, Mitchel (NJ)	S	921	Chabot, John (NY)	S	378
Caruana, Salvatore (NY)	Oto	287	Chacho, Karol (CT)	RE	1027
Carucci, John (NY)	D	147	Chachoua, Abraham (NY)	Onc	214
Caruso, Rocco (NY)	Onc	633	Chadha, Jang (NY)	Pul	513
Carver, Alan (NY)	N	235	Chadha, Manjeet (NY)	RadRO	360
Casale, Linda (CT)	Cv	976	Chai, Emily (NY)	H & PM	193
Casale, Pasquale (NY)	Ped Uro	319	Chai, Paul (NY)	T&CS	386
Casden, Andrew (NY)	OrS	271	Chaiken, Barry (NY)	Oph	255
Case, David (NY)	IM	199	Chaikin, David (NJ)	U	922
Casino, Joseph (NY)	Pul	720	Chaim, Joshua (NY)	DR	157
Casper, Daniel (NY)	Oph	254	Chalal, Jeffrey (NJ)	DR	888
Casper, Ephraim (NY)	Onc	687	Chalas, Eva (NY)	GO	556
Casper, Theodore (NY)	Pul	440	Chalom, Elizabeth (NJ)	PRhu	825
Cassell, Lauren (NY)	S	378	Chamberlain, Ronald (NJ)	S	831
Cassidy, Brian (NJ)	IM	869	Chambers, Hazel (NY)	Ped	437
Casson, Ira (NY)	N	509	Chan, Brenda (CT)	Nep	1000
Cassotta, Joseph (NJ)	FMed	755	Chan, Siu-Pun (NY)	PPul	529
Castellano, Bartolomeo (NY)	Oto	528	Chandler, Michael (NY)	A&I	122

Name	Specialty	Pg	Name	Specialty	Pg
Chandra, Prasanta (NY)	MF	468	Chen, Timothy (NY)	Cv	541
Chandrasekhar, Sujana (NY)	Oto	287	Chengot, Mathew (NY)	Cv	622
Chang, Benjamin (NY)	Pul	617	Chern, Relly (NY)	Oph	255
Chang, Christine (NY)	Ger	180	Chernack, William (NJ)	A&I	903
Chang, Cindy (NJ)	A&I	741	Chernobilsky, Lev (NY)	Ped	642
Chang, Peter (NY)	Ge	169	Cherofsky, Alan (NY)	PlS	530
Chang, Peter (NY)	RE	364	Cherry, Sabrina (NY)	Psyc	343
Chang, Stanley (NY)	Oph	255	Chertoff, Harvey (NJ)	Psyc	788
Channamsetty, Venu (CT)	Cv	976	Chervin, Bradford (CT)	Oto	1014
Chao, Chun (NY)	PRhu	711	Chesner, Michael (NY)	Cv	541
Chao, K.S. Clifford (NY)	RadRO	361	Chess, Jeremy (NY)	Oph	428
Chapman, Cary (NY)	OrS	271	Chessin, David (NY)	CRS	143
Chapman, Kenneth (NY)	PM	297	Chessin, Robert (CT)	Ped	1018
Chapman, Mark (NY)	Ge	170	Cheung, Nai-Kong (NY)	PHO	310
Chapman, Paul (NY)	Onc	214	Chhabra, Rakesh (NJ)	NP	767
Chapnick, Edward (NY)	Inf	464	Chi, Dennis (NY)	GO	184
Char, Daniel (NJ)	VascS	798	Chianese, Maurice (NY)	Ped	587
Charap, Mitchell (NY)	IM	199	Chideckel, Norman (NY)	VascS	403
Charap, Peter (NY)	IM	199	Chidyllo, Stephen (NJ)	PlS	896
Charles, Howard (NY)	Oph	698	Chin, Daisy (NJ)	PEn	915
Charles, James (NJ)	N	839	Chin, Jean (NY)	ObG	247
Charles, Norman (NY)	Oph	255	Chin, Patrick (NJ)	Oph	774
Charney, Jonathan (NY)	N	235	Chin, Simon (NY)	PlS	715
Charney, Richard (NY)	Cv	656	Chinitz, Larry (NY)	CE	123
Charnoff, Judah (NY)	Cv	452	Chinitz, Marvin (NY)	Ge	672
Charny, Caleb (NY)	S	726	Chinn, Bertram (NJ)	CRS	950
Charytan, Chaim (NY)	Nep	509	Chiravuri, Murali (CT)	CE	975
Chase, Mark (NJ)	OrS	820	Chiriboga-Klein, Claudia (NY)	ChiN	140
Chaudhry, M. Rashid (NY)	Oto	480	Chiu, David (NY)	PlS	331
Chaudhry, Saqib (NY)	VascS	606	Chodosh, Eliot (NJ)	N	928
Chavez, Laura (NJ)	Ger	758	Choi, H (NY)	VascS	618
Chavez, Martin (NY)	MF	562	Choi, Janet (NY)	RE	364
Chawla, Anupama (NY)	PGe	641	Choi, Joonun (CT)	Cv	976
Chazotte, Cynthia (NY)	MF	422	Choi, Julie (NY)	RadRO	722
Chefitz, Allen (NY)	S	726	Choi, Laura (CT)	S	1029
Chehade, Mirna (NY)	PGe	308	Choi, Mark (NY)	DR	502
Chen, Constance (NY)	PlS	331	Choi, Mihye (NY)	PlS	332
Chen, Lucy (NJ)	Oph	912	Cholst, Ina (NY)	RE	364
Chen, Serena (NJ)	RE	829	Chorost, Mitchell (NY)	S	600

Alphabetical Listing of Doctors

Name	Specialty	Pg	Name	Specialty	Pg
Chou, Shyan-Yih (NY)	Nep	469	Cofsky, Richard (NY)	Inf	464
Choudhri, Ajay (NJ)	VIR	857	Cohall, Alwyn (NY)	AM	120
Choudhri, Tanvir (NY)	NS	229	Cohen, Alice (NJ)	Hem	812
Choudhury, Muhammad (NY)	U	729 ·	Cohen, Anders (NY)	NS	471
Choueka, Jack (NY)	HS	463	Cohen, Arnold (NY)	Psyc	343
Chrisanderson, Donna (NJ)	IM	813	Cohen, Barry (NY)	IM	465
Chronakos, John (CT)	Pul	1024	Cohen, Barry (NJ)	Nep	851
Chu, Regina (NJ)	DR	752	Cohen, Ben (NY)	Oph	255
Chuang, Linus (NY)	GO	677	Cohen, Bradley (NY)	S	648
Chuck, Roy (NY)	Oph	428	Cohen, Bruce (CT)	Ped	1018
Chun, Audrey (NY)	Ger	180	Cohen, Burton (NY)	DR	157
Chun, Thomas (NJ)	U	796	Cohen, Carl (NY)	GerPsy	462
Chung, Henry (NY)	Psyc	343	Cohen, Charmian (NY)	EDM	415
Chung, Jeff (NJ)	Rhu	792	Cohen, Daniel (NY)	Rhu	598
Chung, Wendy (NY)	CG	141	Cohen, Daniel (NY)	N	635
Chung-Loy, Harold (NJ)	S	882	Cohen, Daniel (NY)	Ped	615
Ciccone, Patrick (NJ)	U	832	Cohen, David (NY)	Nep	226
Cicogna, Cristina (NJ)	Inf	761	Cohen, David (NY)	D	147
Cigno, Thomas (CT)	FMed	984	Cohen, Elin (CT)	Ped	1019
Cioffi, George (NY)	Oph	255	Cohen, Jean-Marc (NY)	Path	300
Cioroiu, Michael (NY)	S	378	Cohen, Jeffrey (NY)	N	235
Cipriani, Ralph (CT)	Inf	990	Cohen, Joel (NY)	N	426
Cirello, Richard (NJ)	FMed	809	Cohen, Jonathan (NY)	Ge	170
Citak, Kenneth (NJ)	N	770	Cohen, Lee (NY)	ChAP	661
Citron, Marc (NY)	Onc	563	Cohen, Leeber (NY)	Oph	255
Clain, Michael (CT)	OrS	1011	Cohen, Marc (NJ)	IC	814
Clark, Richard (NY)	D	624	Cohen, Martin (NY)	CE	655
Clark, Sheryl (NY)	D	147	Cohen, Martin (NY)	Cv	410
Clark-Hamilton, Jill (NJ)	AM	903	Cohen, Michael (NY)	Pul	595
Cleeman, Edmond (NY)	SM	374	Cohen, Michael (NY)	Cv	126
Clemente, Roderick (NJ)	NS	817	Cohen, Michel (NY)	Ped	320
Close, Georgia (NY)	Ge	673	Cohen, Neil (NY)	EDM	523
Close, Lanny (NY)	Oto	287	Cohen, Richard (NY)	IM	199
Coady, Michael (CT)	T&CS	1031	Cohen, Richard (NY)	RadRO	361
Cobelli, Neil (NY)	OrS	429	Cohen, Robert (NY)	IM	199
Cobin, Rhoda (NJ)	EDM	754	Cohen, Seth (NY)	Ge	170
Cocke, Thomas (NJ)	Cv	744	Cohen, Seymour (NY)	Onc	214
Coco, Maria (NY)	Nep	424	Cohen, Steven (NY)	D	413
Coffey, Barbara (NY)	ChAP	137	Cohen, Steven (NJ)	Oph	819

Alphabetical Listing of Doctors

Name	Specialty	Pg	Name	Specialty	Pg
Cohen, Steven (CT)	DR	982	Connors, Richard (CT)	D	980
Cohenuram, Michael (CT)	Onc	998	Conroy, Daniel (NJ)	Cv	744
Cohn, Symra (NY)	IM	199	Constad, William (NJ)	Oph	840
Cohn, William (NY)	Ge	628	Constantiner, Arturo (NY)	IM	200
Coira, Diego (NJ)	Psyc	788	Constantinescu, Andrei (NY)	PPul	316
Coit, Daniel (NY)	S	378	Constantinides, Minas (NY)	Oto	287
Colaco, Rodolfo (NJ)	S	964	Conte, Charles (NY)	S	600
Colah, Jessy (NY)	Psyc	487	Conti, John (NJ)	Onc	815
Colangelo, Daniel (NY)	IM	681	Conway, Edward (NY)	PCCM	306
Colbert, David (NY)	D	147	Conway, Joseph (CT)	Oph	1007
Cole, David (NY)	MF	211	Coohill, Lisa (NJ)	N	956
Cole, Jeffrey (NJ)	PMR	827	Cook, Perry (NY)	Hem	463
Cole, Robert (NJ)	RadRO	931	Cook, Stuart (NJ)	N	817
Cole, William (NY)	Cv	126	Cook-Bolden, Fran (NY)	D	148
Coleman, Donald (NY)	Oph	256	Cooper, Arthur (NY)	PS	318
Coleman, Jonathan (NY)	U	392	Cooper, Jay (NY)	RadRO	489
Coleman, Morton (NY)	Onc	214	Cooper, Jerome (NY)	Cv	656
Colen, Helen (NY)	PlS	332	Cooper, Kimberly (NY)	U	392
Colenda, Maryann (NJ)	PA&I	779	Cooper, Lauren (NJ)	D	906
Coll, Raymond (NY)	N	235	Cooper, Robert (CT)	Onc	998
Collins, Adriane (NY)	Inf	631	Cooper, Robert (NY)	Ge	170
Collins, Eric (CT)	AdP	973	Cooper, Rubin (NY)	PCd	581
Collins, Margaret (NY)	Ped	713	Cooper, Seymour (NY)	Ped	587
Collum, Robert (NJ)	IM	908	Cooper, Stanley (NY)	VIR	605
Coloka-Kump, Rodika (NY)	FMed	416	Cooperman, Alan (NJ)	ObG	818
Colon, Francisco (NJ)	PlS	918	Cooperman, Sheila (CT)	AdP	973
Colon, Ivan (NY)	U	494	Cope, Jennifer (NJ)	ChiN	749
Colton, Marc (NJ)	U	922	Copen, David (CT)	Cv	976
Colyer-Aversa, Lori (NJ)	Ped	826	Coplan, Jeremy (NY)	Psyc	487
Compito, Catherine (NY)	OrS	271	Coppa, Gene (NY)	S	600
Compito, Gerard (NJ)	DR	847	Copperman, Alan (NY)	RE	364
Comrie, Millicent (NY)	ObG	475	Coppola, John (NY)	Cv	126
Condemi, Giuseppe (NJ)	Onc	765	Corapi, Mark (NY)	IM	559
Condo, Dominick (NJ)	IM	839	Corazza, Douglas (NJ)	IM	849
Confino, Joel (NJ)	Oph	957	Corbo, Emanuel (NJ)	Ped	960
Connolly, Adrian (NJ)	D	808	Cordasco, Frank (NY)	OrS	271
Connolly, Mark (NJ)	T&CS	932	Cordeiro, Peter (NY)	PlS	332
Connor, Bradley (NY)	Ge	170	Cordero, Evelyn (NY)	FMed	416
Connor, John (NJ)	Ped Uro	917	Coren, Charles (NY)	PS	586

Alphabetical Listing of Doctors

Name	Specialty	Pg	Name	Specialty	Pg
Corey, Howard (NJ)	PNep	916	Croll, James (NY)	Nep	424
Corn, Beth (NY)	A&I	122	Crooke, Gregory (NY)	T&CS	493
Cornell, Charles (NY)	OrS	271	Cross, Jennifer (NY)	Ped	320
Corpuz, Marilou (NY)	Inf	421	Crowe, David (NY)	PCd	706
Correia, Joaquim (NJ)	CE	805	Crowe, John (CT)	HS	989
Corriel, Robert (NY)	A&I	539	Cruz, Merle (NJ)	Cv	837
Corson, Richard (NJ)	FMed	937	Crystal, Howard (NY)	N	472
Cortes, Engracio (NY)	Onc	508	Crystal, Kenneth (NY)	VIR	605
Cosgrove, John (NY)	S	648	Culligan, Patrick (NJ)	ObG	912
Cosman, Felicia (NY)	EDM	610	Cunha, Burke (NY)	Inf	558
Cossari, Alfred (NY)	Oph	637	Cunniff, Christopher (NY)	CG	142
Costantino, Peter (NY)	Oto	288	Cunningham, James (CT)	OrS	1011
Costanzo, Joseph (CT)	IM	991	Cunningham-Rundles, Charlotte (NY)		A&I
Costeas, Constantinos (NJ)	CE	805	122		
Costin, Andrew (NJ)	Cv	847	Cunningham-Rundles, Ward (NY)	IM	200
Coupey, Susan (NY)	AM	409	Cuomo, Frances (NY)	OrS	272
Couture, Carolyn (CT)	IM	991	Curtin, John (NY)	GO	184
Coven, Barbara (NY)	Ped	713	Cusack, Evelyn (CT)	Cv	976
Coven, Roger (NJ)	ObG	772	Cushner, Fred (NY)	OrS	272
Covey, Alexander (NY)	IM	631	Cushner, Michael (NY)	OrS	702
Covey, Anne (NY)	VIR	400	Cusumano, Barbara (NY)	Ped	643
Covit, Andrew (NJ)	Nep	870	Cusumano, Stephen (NY)	IM	559
Cowan, Stephen (NY)	Ped	713	Cuteri, Joseph (CT)	ObG	1004
Cox, Kathryn (NY)	ObG	247	Cutolo, Louis (NY)	PlS	530
Coyle, Michael (NJ)	HS	938	Cuzzone, Louis (CT)	N	1002
Coyle, Patricia (NY)	N	635	Cykiert, Robert (NY)	Oph	256
Cozzone, John (NJ)	PlS	787	Cynamon, Jacob (NY)	VIR	445
Cracchiolo, Bernadette (NJ)	GO	811	Cziner, David (NY)	Cv	656
Craig, Edward (NY)	OrS	272			
Cramer, Marvin (NY)	Cv	541			
Crane, Michael (NY)	PrM	341	**D**		
Crane, Richard (NY)	Rhu	369	D'Agostini, Robert (NJ)	OrS	941
Crane, Stephen (NJ)	ObG	818	D'Agostino, Richard (NY)	OrS	576
Crasta, Jovita (NY)	Psyc	593	D'Agostino, Ronald (NY)	Cv	541
Crawford, Bernard (NY)	T&CS	386	D'Alessandro, David (NY)	T&CS	443
Crawford, James (NY)	Path	580	D'Alton, Mary (NY)	MF	211
Criscito, Mario (NJ)	Cv	805	D'Amico, Donald (NY)	Oph	256
Cristofaro, Robert (NY)	OrS	702	D'Amico, Joseph (CT)	OrS	1011
Croen, Kenneth (NY)	IM	681	D'Amico, Richard (NJ)	PlS	787

Name	Specialty	Pg	Name	Specialty	Pg
D'Anna, John (NY)	S	531	Davis, Jessica (NY)	CG	142
D'Ascanio, Alfredo (NY)	IM	681	Davis, Joyce (NY)	D	148
D'Aversa, Gerard (NY)	Oph	572	Davis, Kenneth (NJ)	Ped	961
D'Ayala, Marcus (NY)	VascS	495	Davis, Nicole (NJ)	ObG	873
D'Esposito, Robert (NY)	U	603	Davis, Owen (NY)	RE	364
D'Olimpio, James (NY)	Onc	563	Davis, Raphael (NY)	NS	634
Dabney, Lisa (NY)	ObG	247	Davis, William (NY)	SM	618
Daccache, Armand (CT)	Oph	1007	Dayal, Ashlesha (NY)	MF	423
DaCosta, Noshir (NY)	Onc	634	Dayan, Alan (NY)	Oph	256
Dagum, Alexander (NY)	PlS	644	Dayan, Joseph (NY)	PlS	332
Dakin, Gregory (NY)	S	378	De Antonio, Joseph (NJ)	Ge	848
Daknis, Charles (NJ)	PM	895	De Carlo, Regina (NY)	ChiN	522
Dalena, John (NJ)	Ge	907	De Giacomo, Frank (NJ)	IM	927
Daluiski, Aaron (NY)	HS	187	De Lotbiniere, Alain (NY)	NS	692
Daly, Jane (NY)	Onc	508	De Matteo, Robert (NY)	Pul	720
Damien, Miguel (NJ)	RE	897	De Pietro, William (NY)	D	548
Danehower, Richard (CT)	Rhu	1028	De Serres, Lianne (NY)	PO	710
Dangas, George (NY)	Cv	126	De Vivo, Darryl (NY)	ChiN	140
Daniels, Jeffrey (NJ)	Cv	887	Deal, Robert (CT)	ObG	1004
Danziger, Stephen (NY)	D	457	DeAnda, Abelardo (NY)	T&CS	386
Dar, Pe'er (NY)	ObG	427	DeAngelis, Lisa (NY)	N	235
Daras, Michael (NY)	N	235	DeBroff, Brian (CT)	Oph	1007
Dardashti, Omid (NJ)	Cv	744	Dechiario, Alan (NY)	IM	200
Das, Seshadri (NY)	EDM	523	Decter, Edward (NJ)	OrS	820
Dasgupta, Indira (NY)	PHO	433	Decter, Julian (NY)	Onc	214
Dasmahapatra, Kumar (NJ)	S	882	Dedousis, John (NJ)	IM	839
Datta, Rajiv (NY)	S	600	Deener, Avi (NY)	A&I	654
Datta, Samyadev (NJ)	PM	778	DeFabritus, Albert (NY)	Nep	226
Daud-Ahmad, Sameera (NJ)	EDM	754	Degen, Jeffrey (NY)	NS	613
Dauhajre, Richard (NY)	PMR	512	Deitch, Jonathan (NY)	VascS	533
Daum, Fredric (NY)	PGe	583	Deitz, Marcia (NY)	D	457
Davenport, Deborah (NY)	ObG	636	Del Pizzo, Joseph (NY)	U	393
Davenport, Thomas (NY)	PlS	590	Del Rio, Marcela (NY)	PNep	434
David, Sami (NY)	RE	364	DeLacure, Mark (NY)	Oto	288
Davidson, Dennis (NY)	NP	634	Deland, Jonathan (NY)	OrS	272
Davidson, Lawrence (NJ)	Oph	819	Delaney, Brian (NY)	FMed	416
Davies, Terry (NY)	EDM	163	Delaney, Veronica (NY)	Nep	691
Davis, George (NJ)	Pul	897	Delano, Barbara (NY)	Nep	470
Davis, Ira (NY)	D	665	DeLeo, Vincent (NY)	D	148

Alphabetical Listing of Doctors

Name	Specialty	Pg	Name	Specialty	Pg
Delerme, Milton (NY)	Oph	256	DeVito, Bethany (NY)	Ge	553
Delfico, Anthony (NJ)	SM	793	Devons, Cathryn (NY)	Ger	677
DeLillo, Anthony (NJ)	Ge	756	Dhalla, Satish (NY)	IM	200
Della Rocca, Robert (NY)	Oph	256	Dharmarajan, Thiruvinvamvalai (NY)		Ger
Delorenzo, Lawrence (NY)	Pul	720	419		
Delprete, Salvatore (CT)	Onc	998	Dhruvakumar, Sandhya (CT)	CE	975
DeLuca, Albert (NY)	Cv	656	Di Buono, Mark (NY)	Psyc	530
Deluca, Jeffrey (CT)	OrS	1011	Di Giacinto, George (NY)	NS	229
DeLuca, Joseph (NJ)	Oph	774	Di Leo, Frank (NY)	Oph	637
Demar, Leon (NY)	D	148	Di Scala, Reno (NY)	FMed	503
DeMartin, Robert (NJ)	IM	890	Diamant, Esther (NY)	Ped	616
DeMatteo, Ronald (NY)	S	378	Diamond, Ezriel (NY)	RadRO	596
Demento, Frank (NY)	D	548	Diamond, Martin (NJ)	PMR	961
Demestihas, Anthy (CT)	S	1029	Diamond, Sharon (NY)	ObG	247
Demetis, Spiro (NY)	Pul	488	Diamond, Steven (NJ)	PHO	781
Denehy, Thad (NJ)	GO	812	Diaz, Michael (NY)	Hem	189
Dennett, Ronald (NY)	IM	682	DiBernardo, Barry (NJ)	PlS	827
Denny, Donald (NJ)	VIR	884	Dickler, Maura (NY)	Onc	214
DePalo, Louis (NY)	Pul	355	Dickoff, David (NY)	N	693
Derespinis, Patrick (NY)	Oph	527	DiCosmo, Bruno (NY)	Pul	720
DeRose, Joseph (NY)	T&CS	443	Dieck, William (NY)	Oph	698
Dershaw, D. David (NY)	DR	157	Diehl, William (NJ)	S	921
Dervan, John (NY)	Cv	622	Dieterich, Douglas (NY)	Ge	170
Desai, Amita (NJ)	Inf	761	Dietz, Stephanie (CT)	D	980
Desai, Kapil (CT)	DR	982	Dietzek, Alan (CT)	VascS	1033
DeSilva, Derrick (NJ)	IM	869	DiFabrizio, Larry (NY)	Pul	356
Desnick, Robert (NY)	CG	142	Diflo, Thomas (NY)	S	726
Desouza, Trevor (NJ)	ChiN	905	DiGiacomo, William (NJ)	IM	954
Desposito, Franklin (NJ)	CG	807	DiGioia, Julia (NJ)	S	964
DeTorres, Wayne (NJ)	U	796	DiGiovanni, Joseph (CT)	HS	989
Dettmer, Robert (CT)	Ge	986	DiGregorio, Vincent (NY)	PlS	590
Deutsch, Adam (NY)	Cv	127	Diktaban, Theodore (NY)	PlS	332
Deutsch, James (NY)	Oph	476	Dillard, James (NY)	PMR	327
Devanand, Davangere (NY)	GerPsy	182	Dillon, Robert (NY)	U	393
Devereux, Richard (NY)	Cv	127	Dilmanian, Hajir (NY)	Cv	453
Devine, Patricia (NY)	MF	686	Dimaio, Mary (NY)	PPul	316
Devinsky, Orrin (NY)	N	236	DiMango, Angela (NY)	Pul	356
DeVita, Gregory (NY)	PlS	590	Dimango, Emily (NY)	Pul	356
DeVita, Maria (NY)	Nep	226	DiMartino-Nardi, Joan (NY)	PEn	707

Name	Specialty	Pg	Name	Specialty	Pg
DiMeo, Albert (CT)	T&CS	1031	Dowdle, John (CT)	HS	989
Dines, David (NY)	OrS	576	Dower, Samuel (NJ)	EDM	809
Dines, Joshua (NY)	OrS	576	Dowling, Sean (CT)	RadRO	1026
Dinkin, Marc (NY)	N	236	Dowling, Thomas (NY)	OrS	639
Dinlenc, Caner (NY)	U	393	Dowling, William (NJ)	OrS	913
DiPaola, Robert (NJ)	Onc	869	Downey, Robert (NY)	T&CS	387
Disa, Joseph (NY)	PlS	332	Downie, Jeanine (NJ)	D	808
Distefano, Michael (NJ)	OrS	775	Doyle, Michael (CT)	RE	1027
Ditchek, Alan (NY)	IM	465	Doyle, Werner (NY)	NS	229
Diuguid, David (NY)	Hem	189	Dozor, Allen (NY)	PPul	710
DiVagno, Leonardo (NJ)	Cv	744	Drachtman, Richard (NJ)	PHO	877
Divaris, Nicholas (NY)	OrS	638	Draizin, Dennis (NY)	Oto	578
Divgi, Chaitanya (NY)	NuM	245	Drake, William (NJ)	Oto	959
Divino, Celia (NY)	S	378	Drascher, Gary (NJ)	S	943
Diwan, Sudhir (NY)	PM	297	Dreifuss, Ronald (NY)	VIR	400
Dobrenis, Andrea (NY)	ObG	247	Dresdale, Robert (NY)	Cv	542
Doctor, Leslie (CT)	Oph	1007	Dresner, Lisa (NY)	S	492
Dodick, Jack (NY)	Oph	256	Drews, Michael (NJ)	RE	943
Doidge, Robert (NJ)	OrS	776	Drexler, Ellen (NY)	N	472
Dolan, Neil (CT)	GerPsy	988	Dreyer, Neil (CT)	IM	992
Dolgin, Stephen (NY)	PS	586	Dreyfuss, Patricia (NJ)	ObG	912
Dolinsky, Jason (NY)	IM	200	Driesman, Mitchell (CT)	IC	995
Dolitsky, Charisse (NY)	D	548	Driesman, Shelley (CT)	Oph	1008
Dolitsky, Jay (NY)	PO	315	Drillings, Gary (NJ)	OrS	929
Donahue, Bernadine (NY)	RadRO	490	Drimmer, Marc (NJ)	PlS	855
Donahue, John (CT)	DR	982	Droller, Michael (NY)	U	393
Donath, Joseph (NY)	Pul	595	Drooker, Martin (NY)	Psyc	344
Dong, Xiang (CT)	S	1029	Drucker, Beverly (CT)	Onc	998
Donington, Jessica (NY)	T&CS	386	Drucker, David (NY)	OrS	527
Donnellan, Joseph (NJ)	Psyc	942	Drugge, Rhett (CT)	D	980
Donnelly, Christine (NJ)	PCd	915	Drusin, Ronald (NY)	Cv	127
Donovan, Leslie (CT)	ObG	1005	Drzala, Mark (NJ)	OrS	958
Dor, Nathan (NY)	ObG	475	Dubin, David (NJ)	RadRO	791
Dosik, David (NY)	Onc	469	Dubner, Sanford (NY)	PlS	590
Dosik, Harvey (NY)	Hem	463	Dubois, Nicholas (NY)	Cv	127
Dottino, Peter (NY)	GO	184	Duboys, Elliot (NY)	PlS	644
Douglas, Carolyn (NY)	Psyc	344	Duchen, Douglas (CT)	FMed	984
Douros, Stella (NY)	Oph	476	Duchnowska, Alicja (NY)	Ped	529
Dousmanis, Athanasios (NY)	N	693	Duda, E Andrew (CT)	Hem	990

Alphabetical Listing of Doctors

Name	Specialty	Pg	Name	Specialty	Pg
Dudick, Stephen (NJ)	PlS	896	Efthimiou, Petros (NY)	Rhu	491
Duggan, Mary (NY)	FMed	416	Eglinton, Gary (NY)	MF	507
Dulit, Rebecca (NY)	Psyc	718	Egol, Kenneth (NY)	OrS	272
Dultz, Rachel (NJ)	S	856	Ehrlich, Conrad (CT)	DR	982
Duncan, David (NJ)	N	770	Ehrlich, James (NY)	Ge	673
Dunkel, Ira (NY)	PHO	310	Ehrlich, Martin (NY)	IM	200
Dunston-Boone, Gina (CT)	MF	997	Ehrlich, Paul (NY)	PA&I	302
Durante, Anthony (NY)	Oto	578	Eichenbaum, Joseph (NY)	Oph	256
Dutta, Timothy (NY)	Cv	127	Eichenfield, Andrew (NY)	PRhu	317
Duva, Joseph (NY)	Ge	628	Eichler, Joel (NJ)	Oph	819
Dweck, Alyssa (NY)	ObG	695	Eichman, Gerard (NJ)	Cv	744
Dweck, Monica (NY)	Oph	476	Eilen, Bonnie (NY)	ObG	695
Dworkin, Brad (NY)	Ge	673	Einstein, Francine (NY)	MF	423
Dworkin, Gregory (CT)	PPul	1018	Einstein, Mark (NY)	GO	419
Dwyer, James (NJ)	OrS	941	Eisenberg, Amy (NY)	Ped	713
Dwyer, Kevin (CT)	S	1030	Eisenberg, Mark (NY)	NS	566
Dyme, Joshua (NJ)	PCd	780	Eisenberg, Richard (NJ)	D	950
			Eisenberg, Sheldon (NJ)	Cv	745
			Eisenstat, Steven (NJ)	FMed	951
			Eisenstat, Theodore (NJ)	CRS	863

E

Name	Specialty	Pg	Name	Specialty	Pg
Eastham, James (NY)	U	393	Eitan, Noam (NY)	Psyc	487
Ebani, Jack (NJ)	U	898	Ekong, Udeme (CT)	PGe	1017
Ebarb, Raymond (NY)	FMed	627	El Baba, Fadi (NY)	Oph	637
Ebright, Michael (CT)	T&CS	1031	El-Sadr, Wafaa (NY)	Inf	194
Eddleman, Keith (NY)	MF	211	El-Tamer, Mahmoud (NY)	S	378
Edelman, Bruce (NJ)	Oto	875	Elahi, Ebrahim (NY)	Oph	257
Edelman, Robert (NY)	U	603	Elamir, Mazhar (NJ)	Pul	842
Edelmann, Christopher (CT)	IM	992	Elias, Steven (NJ)	VascS	798
Edelson, Charles (NY)	OrS	702	Elkind, Barry (NJ)	Cv	837
Edelson, David (NY)	IM	559	Elkind, Mitchell (NY)	N	236
Edelstein, Barbara (NY)	DR	157	Elkowitz, Marc (NY)	PlS	590
Edelstein, David (NY)	Oto	288	Elkwood, Andrew (NJ)	PlS	896
Edelstein, Gary (NY)	Ped	321	Ellenson, Lora (NY)	Path	300
Edelstein, Martin (NY)	FMed	552	Elliott, Andrew (NY)	OrS	272
Eden, Edward (NY)	Pul	356	Elliott, Nancy (NJ)	S	831
Edgar, Ellen (NY)	N	510	Ellis, Earl (NY)	IM	465
Edwards, Bruce (NY)	A&I	539	Ellis, Scott (NY)	OrS	272
Edwards, Wendy (NY)	H & PM	193	Ellozy, Sharif (NY)	VascS	403
Effron, Charles (NJ)	N	770	Elmaleh, Rebecca (NY)	FMed	167

Alphabetical Listing of Doctors

Name	Specialty	Pg
Elmann, Elie (NJ)	T&CS	795
Elowitz, Eric (NY)	NS	230
Emami, Arash (NJ)	OrS	929
Emond, Jean (NY)	S	379
Ende, Leigh (NJ)	HS	907
Eng, Margaret (NJ)	Inf	890
Engel, David (NY)	Cv	127
Engel, Harry (NY)	Oph	257
Engel, J. Mark (NJ)	Oph	874
Engel, Lenore (NY)	ChAP	455
Engel, Murray (NY)	ChiN	140
Engelhardt, Martin (NY)	IM	682
Engler, Mitchell (NJ)	Pul	790
Englert, Christopher (NJ)	ObG	772
Ennis, David (NY)	IM	682
Ennis, Francis (CT)	OrS	1012
Ennis, Ronald (NY)	RadRO	361
Epstein, Lawrence (NY)	PM	297
Epstein, Marcia (NY)	Inf	558
Epstein, Robert (NJ)	DR	864
Erber, William (NY)	Ge	460
Erlebacher, Jay (NJ)	Cv	745
Ernberg, Lauren (CT)	DR	982
Ernst, Jerome (NY)	IM	422
Errico, Thomas (NY)	OrS	273
Escher, Jeffrey (NY)	Ger	677
Esformes, Ira (NJ)	OrS	776
Eshghi, A Majid (NY)	U	729
Eskreis, David (NY)	Ge	553
Esposito, Donna (NY)	Oph	257
Esposito, Michael (NY)	Path	581
Esposito, Michael (NJ)	U	796
Esposito, Rick (NY)	T&CS	601
Esposito, Stephen (NY)	Ge	504
Estabrook, Alison (NY)	S	379
Esteban-Cruciani, Nora (NY)	Ped	437
Etienne, Mill (NY)	N	613
Etingin, Orli (NY)	IM	200
Ettinger, Alan (NY)	N	568

Name	Specialty	Pg
Ettinger, Leigh (NJ)	PNep	782
Evans, Andrew (NY)	RadRO	361
Evans, Lydia (NY)	D	665
Evans, Mark (NY)	ObG	247
Ezratty, Ari (NY)	Cv	542

F

Name	Specialty	Pg
Faber, Mark (NJ)	Psyc	828
Fader, Andrew (NY)	Ger	677
Fafalak, Robert (NY)	IM	200
Fagin, James (NY)	PA&I	581
Fagin, James (NY)	EDM	163
Fahey, Thomas (NY)	S	379
Fahn, Stanley (NY)	N	236
Fahoum, Bashar (NY)	S	492
Fakharzadeh, Frederick (NJ)	HS	759
Falco, Thomas (NY)	Cv	622
Falcon, Ronald (NY)	D	548
Falk, Theodore (NJ)	A&I	741
Falkoff, Alan (CT)	FMed	984
Faller, Jason (NY)	Rhu	369
Fallon, Brian (NY)	Psyc	344
Fan, Roger (NY)	CE	621
Fang, Bruno (NJ)	Onc	939
Fang, Deborah (CT)	RadRO	1026
Fantasia, Michele (NJ)	PMR	879
Farber, Bruce (NY)	Inf	558
Farber, Charles (NY)	Ge	553
Farber, Charles (NJ)	Onc	909
Farhath, Sabeena (NJ)	PGe	854
Faries, Peter (NY)	VascS	403
Farkas, Edward (NJ)	Psyc	788
Farkas, John (NJ)	Ge	926
Farmer, James (NY)	OrS	273
Farrell, Matthew (CT)	FMed	984
Farrell, Robert (NY)	U	516
Farrer, William (NJ)	Inf	953
Fass, Arthur (NY)	Cv	656

Alphabetical Listing of Doctors

Name	Specialty	Pg	Name	Specialty	Pg
Fass, Daniel (NY)	RadRO	722	Feldman, Saul (NY)	Ped	485
Fastenberg, David (NY)	Oph	572	Feldman, Sheldon (NY)	S	379
Fateh, Majid (NY)	RE	364	Feldman, Steven (CT)	Oto	1015
Fath, Robert (NY)	Ge	673	Feldman, Stuart (NY)	Onc	687
Faust, Glenn (NY)	VascS	606	Feldman, Tatyana (NJ)	Hem	760
Faust, Michael (NY)	Ge	170	Feldstein, Neil (NY)	NS	230
Faust, Michael (NJ)	ObG	772	Fellman, Damon (NJ)	N	770
Fazio, Nelson (NY)	IM	682	Fellus, Jonathan (NJ)	N	911
Fazio, Richard (NY)	Ge	523	Felsenstein, Jerome (NY)	D	665
Fealy, Stephen (NY)	OrS	273	Feltheimer, Seth (NY)	IM	201
Federbush, Richard (NY)	IM	559	Feng, William (CT)	T&CS	1031
Federman, Alex (NY)	IM	200	Fennell, Gail (CT)	IM	992
Fefferman, Nancy (NY)	DR	158	Fennelly, Bryan (NJ)	Psyc	919
Feghali, Joseph (NY)	Oto	430	Fennoy, Ilene (NY)	PEn	306
Feher, Laszlo (NY)	Ger	181	Fenster, Mitchell (NY)	IM	682
Feigenbaum, Howard (NJ)	S	932	Ferges, Mitchell (NJ)	Ge	938
Feigenblum, David (NJ)	CE	742	Ferguson, Kevin (CT)	Ped	1019
Feigin, Kimberly (NY)	DR	158	Fern, Craig (NY)	Oph	698
Fein, Alan (NY)	Pul	595	Fernandes, John (NJ)	PCd	823
Fein, Deborah (NJ)	Nep	768	Fernandez, Harold (NY)	T&CS	649
Fein, Frederick (NY)	Cv	542	Fernandez, Jacinto (NJ)	ObG	772
Feinberg, Joseph (NY)	PMR	327	Fernando, Rajeev (NY)	Inf	631
Feinberg, Joseph (NY)	PlS	591	Fernbach, Barry (NJ)	Hem	760
Feinberg, Todd (NY)	Psyc	344	Ferran, Elena (NY)	Ge	170
Feingold, Daniel (NY)	CRS	143	Ferran, Ernesto (NY)	Psyc	344
Feinsilver, Steven (NY)	Pul	595	Ferrante, Maurice (NJ)	IM	939
Feinstein, Neil (NY)	Oph	476	Ferrara, Lisa (NY)	IM	611
Feinstein, Ronald (NY)	AM	538	Ferrick, Kevin (NY)	CE	410
Feintzeig, Irwin (CT)	Nep	1001	Ferrier, Genevieve (NY)	Ped	321
Feit, Alan (NY)	Cv	453	Ferro, John (NY)	N	613
Feit, David (NJ)	Ge	952	Ferrone, Philip (NY)	Oph	573
Feit, Frederick (NY)	IC	208	Ferrucci, Leonard (CT)	ObG	1005
Feld, Michael (NY)	Cv	657	Ferrucci, Vito (CT)	ObG	1005
Felderman, Lenora (NY)	D	148	Festa, Robert (NY)	Ped	643
Feldman, Darren (NY)	Onc	215	Feteiha, Muhammad (NJ)	S	964
Feldman, David (NJ)	SM	920	Feuer, Martin (NY)	IM	201
Feldman, David (NY)	OrS	273	Fey, Christopher (CT)	DR	982
Feldman, Jeffrey (NJ)	IM	954	Fialk, Mark (NY)	Onc	687
Feldman, Philip (NY)	D	457	Fiedler, Robert (NY)	IM	201

Name	Specialty	Pg	Name	Specialty	Pg
Fiel, Stanley (NJ)	Pul	919	Fisher, George (NY)	FMed	503
Field, Barry (NY)	Ge	673	Fisher, Laura (NY)	IM	201
Fields, Suzanne (NY)	Ger	629	Fisher, Lawrence (CT)	Cv	976
Fields, Theodore (NY)	Rhu	369	Fisher, Margaret (NJ)	PInf	895
Fiest, Thomas (NJ)	Ge	889	Fisher, Martin (NY)	AM	538
Figgie, Mark (NY)	OrS	273	Fisher, Steven (CT)	IM	992
Figlia, Paul (NJ)	PlS	931	Fisher, Yale (NY)	Oph	257
Filiberto, Cosmo (CT)	FMed	985	Fishkin, Michael (NY)	FMed	627
Filippone, Mark (NJ)	PMR	841	Fishman, Allen (NY)	Oph	510
Filor, Caroline (CT)	ObG	1005	Fishman, David (NY)	GO	184
Fine, Eugene (NY)	U	393	Fishman, Donald (NY)	Pul	356
Fine, Howard (NY)	Onc	215	Fishman, Eric (NY)	VascS	731
Fine, Jonathan (CT)	Pul	1024	Fishman, Miriam (NJ)	D	751
Fine, Paul (NJ)	Nep	910	Fishman, Robert (CT)	IC	995
Fine, Robert (NY)	Onc	215	Fisk, Marc (NJ)	Cv	805
Finegold, Jonathan (NY)	Ge	673	Fiske, Steven (NJ)	Ge	810
Finger, Paul (NY)	Oph	257	Fitzgerald, Denis (NJ)	Onc	891
Fink, Candida (NY)	ChAP	661	FitzGibbons, James (CT)	OrS	1012
Fink, Matthew (NY)	N	236	Fitzpatrick, Maurice (NJ)	NRad	872
Finkel, Jay (NY)	Psyc	344	Flaherty, Brian (NY)	Onc	469
Finkelstein, Mario (NJ)	AdP	903	Flamm, Eugene (NY)	NS	425
Finkelstein, Martin (NY)	Ger	181	Flanagan, Steven (NY)	PMR	327
Finkelstein, Warren (NJ)	Ge	810	Flanzman, Susan (NJ)	IM	762
Finlay, Alexis (CT)	Oph	1008	Flatow, Evan (NY)	OrS	273
Fiore, Amory (CT)	NS	1001	Fleischer, Lee (NY)	S	618
Fiore, John (NY)	Onc	634	Fleischer, Marian (NY)	CRS	456
Fiorella, David (NY)	NRad	635	Fleischman, Jay (NY)	Oph	698
Fiorentino, Thomas (NY)	IM	682	Fleischmann, Nicole (NY)	U	729
Fiorillo, Michael (NY)	PlS	616	Fleisher, Michael (NJ)	Ped Uro	879
Firshein, Richard (NY)	FMed	167	Fleming, Gregory (NJ)	Oto	914
First, Michael (NY)	Psyc	344	Fletcher, H. Stephen (NJ)	S	831
Fisch, Arthur (NJ)	Cv	904	Flisser, Eric (NY)	RE	364
Fisch, Harry (NY)	U	393	Floch, Neil (CT)	S	1030
Fischbach, Neal (CT)	Onc	998	Flood, Mary (NY)	Inf	194
Fischer, Harry (NY)	Rhu	369	Florakis, George (NY)	Oph	257
Fish, Bernard (NY)	PCd	706	Flores, Raja (NY)	T&CS	387
Fish, Stephanie (NY)	EDM	163	Florio, Philip (NY)	ObG	696
Fishbach, Mitchell (NY)	Cv	657	Flug, Frances (NJ)	PHO	781
Fishbane-Mayer, Jill (NY)	ObG	248	Flynn, Maryirene (NY)	OrS	527

Alphabetical Listing of Doctors

Name	Specialty	Pg	Name	Specialty	Pg
Flynn, Patrick (NY)	PCd	304	Fox, Stuart (NJ)	N	911
Foca, Marc (NY)	PInf	313	Fracchia, John (NY)	U	393
Fochios, Steven (NY)	Ge	171	Frager, Joseph (NY)	Ge	417
Fogel, Joyce (NY)	Ger	181	Fragner, Paul (NY)	HS	678
Fogel, Mitchell (CT)	Nep	1001	Fragomen, Austin (NY)	OrS	273
Foitl, Daniel (NY)	D	148	Frances, Richard (NY)	AdP	119
Fojas, Antonio (NY)	IM	422	Francis, Kathleen (NJ)	PMR	827
Foley, Carmel (NY)	ChAP	545	Francis, Michelle (NY)	ObG	248
Folman, Robert (CT)	Onc	999	Franck, Jeanne (NY)	D	548
Fomberstein, Barry (NY)	Rhu	441	Franco, Israel (NY)	Ped Uro	711
Fonacier, Luz (NY)	A&I	539	Frank, Douglas (NY)	Oto	578
Fond, Jason (NY)	OrS	614	Frank, Graeme (NY)	PEn	583
Fong, Raymond (NY)	Oph	257	Frank, Martin (NJ)	Onc	909
Fontana, Gregory (NY)	T&CS	387	Frank, Maura (NY)	Ped	321
Foo, Sun-Hoo (NY)	N	236	Frank, Michael (NY)	Ge	171
Foong, Anthony (NY)	Ge	171	Frank, Richard (CT)	Onc	999
Ford, Robert (NJ)	DR	847	Frankel, David (NY)	D	457
Forlenza, Thomas (NY)	Onc	525	Frankel, Robert (NY)	IC	467
Forley, Bryan (NY)	PlS	332	Franklin, Kenneth (NY)	Cv	127
Forman, Mark (NJ)	T&CS	832	Franks, Andrew (NY)	D	148
Forman, Robert (NY)	Cv	410	Franzetti, Carl (NY)	FMed	416
Forman, Scott (NY)	Oph	698	Frattarola, Michael (NJ)	ObG	957
Formenti, Silvia (NY)	RadRO	361	Freddo, Lorenza (NY)	N	426
Fornari, Victor (NY)	ChAP	501	Freedman, Gordon (NY)	PM	298
Fornier, Monica (NY)	Onc	215	Freedman, Janet (CT)	PMR	1021
Forte, Francis (NJ)	Onc	765	Freedman, Jeffrey (NY)	Oph	476
Fortunato, Franklin (NJ)	IM	813	Freedman, Richard (CT)	Ped	1019
Fost, Arthur (NJ)	PA&I	822	Freeman, Leonard (NY)	NuM	427
Foster, Craig (NY)	PlS	332	Freilich, Stephanie (NY)	Ped	321
Foto, Frank (NY)	Rhu	724	Freiman, Hal (NY)	Ge	171
Fou, Adora (NY)	S	726	Frempong-Boadu, Anthony (NY)	NS	230
Fox, Alissa (NJ)	D	936	French, Jacqueline (NY)	N	236
Fox, Herbert (NY)	Psyc	344	Freund, Robert (NY)	PlS	333
Fox, James (NJ)	A&I	935	Frey, Howard (NJ)	U	796
Fox, Joshua (NY)	D	501	Fried, Arno (NJ)	NS	769
Fox, Joyce (NY)	CG	547	Fried, Harry (NJ)	Ge	756
Fox, Mark (NY)	Oto	704	Fried, Karen (NY)	DR	158
Fox, Martin (NY)	Oph	257	Fried, Kenneth (NJ)	S	794
Fox, Sarah (NY)	ChAP	137	Fried, Marvin (NY)	Oto	431

Name	Specialty	Pg	Name	Specialty	Pg
Fried, Richard (NY)	IM	201	Fuchs, Richard (NY)	Cv	128
Fried, Sharon (NJ)	D	751	Fuchs, Wayne (NY)	Oph	258
Frieden, Faith (NJ)	MF	764	Fuhrman, Robert (NJ)	EDM	951
Frieden, Richard (NY)	PMR	327	Fukilman, Oscar (NY)	IM	507
Friedlander, Charles (NY)	Ge	171	Fuks, Joachim (NY)	Onc	423
Friedlander, Devin (NJ)	N	940	Funt, David (NY)	PlS	591
Friedlander, Marvin (NJ)	NS	955	Fuqua, James (NY)	DR	158
Friedling, Steven (NY)	IM	631	Furie, Richard (NY)	Rhu	598
Friedman, Adie (NY)	VIR	400	Fuster, Valentin (NY)	Cv	128
Friedman, Alan (NJ)	ObG	873	Fyer, Minna (NY)	Psyc	345
Friedman, Alan (NY)	Oph	258			
Friedman, David (NJ)	PS	784			
Friedman, David (NY)	PlS	333			
Friedman, Deborah (NY)	PCd	707			
Friedman, Eugene (NY)	Ped	587	**G**		
Friedman, Frederick (NY)	ObG	248			
Friedman, Howard (NY)	Cv	453	Gabbay, Vilma (NY)	ChAP	137
Friedman, Jeffrey (NY)	IM	201	Gabel, Richard (NY)	Psyc	718
Friedman, Kent (NY)	NuM	245	Gabelman, Gary (NY)	Cv	657
Friedman, Lynn (NY)	ObG	248	Gabrilove, Janice (NY)	Onc	215
Friedman, Michael (NY)	IC	468	Gafanovich, Marina (NY)	IM	201
Friedman, Richard (NY)	Psyc	345	Gaffney, Joseph (NJ)	PCd	876
Friedman, Robert (NY)	Oph	258	Gaglio, Paul (NY)	Ge	417
Friedman, Ronit (NY)	ObG	427	Gagne, Paul (CT)	VascS	1033
Friedman, Sanford (NY)	Cv	127	Gainey, Patrick (NJ)	N	892
Friedman, Seth (NY)	EDM	551	Gajdos, Robert (NJ)	IM	927
Friedman, Steven (NY)	Ped Uro	485	Galanter, I Marc (NY)	AdP	119
Friedrich, Ivan (NJ)	Ge	756	Galetta, Steven (NY)	N	236
Frieri, Marianne (NY)	A&I	539	Gallagher, Mary (NY)	PEn	306
Frimer, Richard (NY)	Pul	720	Gallagher, Pamela (NY)	PlS	591
Friscia, Philip (NY)	Onc	525	Galland, Leo (NY)	IM	201
Frishman, William (NY)	Cv	657	Galler, Marilyn (NY)	Nep	509
Frisoli, Anthony (NJ)	FMed	937	Gallick, Gregory (NJ)	OrS	958
Frohman, Larry (NJ)	Oph	819	Gallin, Pamela (NY)	Oph	258
From, Stuart (NJ)	A&I	741	Gallina, Gregory (NJ)	CRS	750
Fromer, Mark (NY)	Oph	258	Gallousis, Francene (NY)	MF	686
Frost, James (NJ)	S	964	Galloway, Aubrey (NY)	T&CS	387
Fruchtman, Steven (NY)	Hem	189	Gallucci, John (NJ)	PS	879
Fryer, Robert (NY)	ChiN	140	Galvin, James (NY)	N	237
			Gambarin, Boris (NY)	IM	465
			Gamble, Sarah (CT)	IM	992
			Gamss, Jeffrey (NY)	Ge	460

Alphabetical Listing of Doctors

Name	Specialty	Pg	Name	Specialty	Pg
Ganchi, Parham (NJ)	PlS	931	Gelbard, Sandra (NY)	IM	201
Gandhi, Lajpat (NY)	ChAP	623	Gelberg, Burt (NY)	IM	559
Gandhi, Rajinder (NJ)	PS	784	Gelbfish, Gary (NY)	VascS	495
Ganem, Amanda (NY)	Cv	657	Gelbfish, Joseph (NY)	Cv	453
Gannon, Christopher (NJ)	S	857	Gelbman, Brian (NY)	Pul	356
Gannon, Jennifer (NY)	ObG	696	Gelfand, Janice (NY)	Psyc	439
Garan, Hasan (NY)	CE	124	Geller, Bradley (NJ)	Oph	774
Garay, Kenneth (NJ)	Oto	840	Geller, David (NY)	OrS	429
Garay, Stuart (NY)	Pul	356	Geller, Debora (NJ)	A&I	741
Garcia, Mario (NY)	Cv	411	Geller, Eric (NJ)	N	818
Gardenswartz, Mark (NY)	Nep	226	Geller, Mark (NY)	DR	610
Gardin, Julius (NJ)	Cv	745	Geller, Peter (NY)	S	379
Gardner, James (NJ)	PlS	961	Gelles, Jeremiah (NY)	Cv	453
Gardner, Sharon (NY)	PHO	310	Gelmann, Edward (NY)	Onc	215
Garfein, Evan (NY)	PlS	439	Geltzeiler, Jules (NJ)	U	899
Garfinkel, Matthew (NJ)	OrS	874	Genato, Romulo (NY)	S	492
Garg, Madhur (NY)	RadRO	441	Genc, Mehmet (NJ)	MF	891
Gargano, Robert (NY)	Oto	639	Gendelman, Seymour (NY)	N	237
Gargiulo, Juan (NY)	PM	640	Genden, Eric (NY)	Oto	288
Garner, Bruce (NY)	Rhu	491	Gendler, Ellen (NY)	D	149
Garner, Steven (NY)	DR	458	Gendler, Seth (NY)	Ge	673
Garrett, Leila (CT)	ObG	1005	Genn, David (NY)	Ge	674
Garrick, Renee (NY)	Nep	691	Gennace, Ronald (NJ)	OrS	776
Garvey, Michael (NY)	Nep	227	Gentile, Ronald (NY)	Oph	258
Garvey, Richard (CT)	S	1030	Gentilesco, Michael (NY)	ObG	636
Garvin, James (NY)	PHO	310	George, Liziamma (NY)	Pul	488
Garzon, Maria (NY)	D	148	Geraci-Ciardullo, Kira (NY)	A&I	654
Gass, Alan (NY)	Cv	657	Gerard, Perry (NY)	NuM	695
Gayle, Lloyd (NY)	PlS	333	Gerberg, Lynda (NY)	Ped	587
Gaynor, Mitchell (NY)	Onc	215	Gerdes, Hans (NY)	Ge	171
Gazzara, Paul (NY)	IM	524	Gerhard, Harvey (NJ)	Pul	943
Gecelter, Gary (NY)	S	600	German, Harold (NY)	IM	631
Geders, Jane (NY)	Ge	673	Geronemus, Roy (NY)	D	149
Geer-Yan, Lisa (CT)	ObG	1005	Gershbaum, Meyer (NY)	U	603
Gehrmann, Robin (NJ)	SM	830	Gershon, Anne (NY)	PInf	313
Gejerman, Glen (NJ)	RadRO	791	Gerson, Charles (NY)	Ge	171
Gekowski, Kathleen (NJ)	Inf	849	Getrajdman, George (NY)	VIR	400
Gelato, Marie (NY)	EDM	627	Gettenberg, Gary (NY)	Ge	460
Gelb, Bruce (NY)	PCd	304	Geuder, James (NJ)	VascS	798

Alphabetical Listing of Doctors

Name	Specialty	Pg	Name	Specialty	Pg
Gliklich, Jerry (NY)	Cv	128	Goldberg, Robert (NY)	Onc	612
Glowacki, Jan (NJ)	IM	890	Goldberg, Roy (NY)	Ger	419
Gluck, Ian (NJ)	ObG	912	Goldberg, Steven (NY)	Cv	542
Gluck, Robert (NY)	HS	556	Goldberg, Stuart (NJ)	Onc	765
Gmyrek, Robyn (NY)	D	149	Goldberg-Berman, Judith (CT)	EDM	983
Gobin, Y. Pierre (NY)	NRad	243	Goldblatt, Kenneth (NJ)	Pul	881
Gochfeld, Michael (NJ)	OM	873	Goldblatt, Robert (NY)	Ge	674
Godfrey, Norman (NY)	PlS	333	Goldblum, Lester (NY)	Ge	554
Godfrey, Philip (NY)	PlS	333	Golden, Brian (NY)	Rhu	370
Godfried, David (NY)	OrS	576	Golden, Flavia (NY)	IM	202
Godin, David (NY)	Oto	288	Goldenberg, Alan (NY)	EDM	627
Goff, Donald (NY)	Psyc	345	Goldenberg, Alec (NY)	Hem	190
Gohel, Rekha (NJ)	Ger	889	Goldenberg, Bruce (NJ)	T&CS	832
Goilav, Beatrice (NY)	PNep	434	Goldenberg, David (CT)	PlS	1021
Goland, Robin (NY)	EDM	163	Goldenberg, David (NJ)	Ge	952
Golbe, Lawrence (NJ)	N	871	Goldenberg, David (NY)	Psyc	345
Gold, Alan (NY)	PlS	591	Goldenberg, Gary (NY)	D	149
Gold, David (NY)	PGe	641	Goldfarb, Alisan (NY)	S	379
Gold, Jeffrey (NJ)	IM	927	Goldfarb, C. Richard (NY)	NuM	245
Gold, Joan (NY)	PMR	327	Goldfarb, Joel (NJ)	Ge	756
Gold, Jonathan (NJ)	D	926	Goldfarb, Michael (NJ)	S	898
Gold, Julie (NY)	Onc	687	Goldfischer, Mindy (NJ)	DR	752
Gold, Marji (NY)	FMed	416	Goldin, Daniel (NY)	IM	202
Gold, Scott (NY)	Oto	288	Goldin, Howard (NY)	Ge	172
Goldberg, Arthur (NY)	Onc	215	Goldman, Gary (NY)	ObG	248
Goldberg, Daniel (NJ)	Oph	893	Goldman, Jack (NY)	IM	682
Goldberg, David (NY)	D	149	Goldman, Joel (NY)	EDM	459
Goldberg, Gary (NY)	GO	420	Goldman, Kenneth (NJ)	VascS	884
Goldberg, Harvey (NY)	Cv	128	Goldman, Martin (NY)	Cv	128
Goldberg, Jeffrey (NY)	Psyc	487	Goldman, Michael (NJ)	EDM	754
Goldberg, Jonathan (NY)	Onc	688	Goldman, Neil (NY)	Psyc	345
Goldberg, Jory (NJ)	Pul	881	Goldman, Neil (NY)	A&I	654
Goldberg, Joseph (CT)	Psyc	1023	Goldman, Noah (NJ)	GO	759
Goldberg, Leslie (NY)	Oph	573	Goldschmidt, Howard (NJ)	Cv	745
Goldberg, Marc (NJ)	Rhu	931	Goldsmith, Ari (NY)	PO	484
Goldberg, Myron (NY)	Ge	171	Goldsmith, Stanley (NY)	NuM	245
Goldberg, Neil (NY)	D	665	Goldstein, Carl (NJ)	Nep	955
Goldberg, Nieca (NY)	Cv	128	Goldstein, Daniel (NY)	T&CS	444
Goldberg, Rina (NJ)	ChiN	807	Goldstein, Jeffrey (NY)	OrS	274

Alphabetical Listing of Doctors

Name	Specialty	Pg	Name	Specialty	Pg
Grann, Alison (NJ)	RadRO	829	Greenblatt, Louis (NY)	FMed	628
Grano, Vanessa (NY)	ObG	696	Greene, Jeffrey (NY)	Inf	194
Granowetter, Linda (NY)	PHO	311	Greene, Loren (NY)	EDM	163
Grant, Arthur (NY)	N	473	Greene, Miriam (NY)	ObG	248
Grant, John (NY)	NS	567	Greenfield, Martin (NY)	EDM	551
Grant, Linda (CT)	PMR	1021	Greengart, Alvin (NY)	Cv	453
Grant, Robert (NY)	PlS	334	Greenhill, Laurence (NY)	ChAP	661
Grasso, Cono (NY)	Oph	510	Greenman, James (NJ)	Inf	953
Grasso, Michael (NJ)	Nep	817	Greenspan, Alan (NY)	D	149
Grasso, Michael (NY)	U	394	Greenstein, Bruce (NY)	PlS	439
Graver, L. Michael (NY)	T&CS	515	Greenstein, Stuart (NY)	S	442
Gray, William (NY)	IC	208	Greenwald, Blaine (NY)	GerPsy	505
Grayson, Douglas (NY)	Oph	259	Greenwald, Bonnie (NY)	EDM	669
Grazi, Richard (NY)	RE	490	Greenwald, Brian (NJ)	PMR	880
Greaney, Edward (NY)	IM	202	Greenwald, Bruce (NY)	PCCM	306
Grecco, Dominic (NY)	ObG	696	Greenwald, David (NY)	Ge	417
Greeley, Norman (NY)	A&I	451	Greenwald, Joshua (NY)	PlS	716
Green, Abraham (NY)	Ped	588	Greenwald, Marc (NY)	CRS	547
Green, David (NY)	Hem	190	Greer, Jeannete (NJ)	DR	937
Green, Jeffrey (CT)	Cv	976	Greif, Richard (NY)	Cv	658
Green, Mark (NY)	N	237	Greisberg, Justin (NY)	OrS	274
Green, Michele (NY)	D	149	Greisman, Stewart (NY)	Rhu	370
Green, Peter (NY)	Ge	172	Grelsamer, Ronald (NY)	OrS	274
Green, Richard (NY)	VascS	403	Grendell, James (NY)	Ge	554
Green, Robert (NY)	Oto	288	Grenell, Steven (NY)	N	426
Green, Stephen (NY)	Cv	543	Grenis, Michael (NJ)	OrS	853
Green, Steven (NY)	OrS	274	Gress, Frank (NY)	Ge	172
Green, Stuart (NY)	Rhu	491	Gretz, Herbert (NY)	GO	677
Greenbaum, Allen (NY)	Oph	699	Gribbin, Dorota (NJ)	PMR	855
Greenberg, Harly (NY)	Pul	595	Gribbon, John (NJ)	IM	813
Greenberg, Howard (NY)	Onc	508	Gribetz, Carin (NY)	D	149
Greenberg, Mark (NY)	Cv	411	Gribetz, Michael (NY)	U	394
Greenberg, Martin (NJ)	Pul	829	Grice, Dorothy (NY)	ChAP	137
Greenberg, Robert (NY)	GerPsy	462	Grieco, Michael (NY)	S	600
Greenberg, Ronald (NY)	Ge	554	Grifo, James (NY)	RE	365
Greenberg, Rosalie (NJ)	ChAP	949	Grijnsztein, Jacob (NY)	Ped	588
Greenberg, Steven (NY)	Oph	699	Grimshaw, Robert (NY)	Ger	677
Greenberg, Susan (NJ)	Onc	891	Grizzanti, Joseph (NJ)	Pul	931
Greenberg, Yisachar (NY)	CE	452	Grodberg, Michele (NJ)	D	751

Name	Specialty	Pg	Name	Specialty	Pg
Grodman, Richard (NY)	Cv	521	Guarini, Ludovico (NY)	PHO	483
Groeger, William (NY)	PlS	591	Guarracini, Mary (NY)	PMR	616
Groff, Walter (NJ)	CRS	950	Gubernick, Martin (NY)	ObG	248
Gropper, David (CT)	Ped	1019	Gudavalli, Madhu (NY)	NP	469
Gross, Dennis (NY)	D	150	Guerin, Bonni (NJ)	Onc	954
Gross, Elliott (NY)	N	693	Guida, Louis (NY)	A&I	621
Gross, Gary (NJ)	A&I	887	Guida, Robert (NY)	Oto	288
Gross, Harvey (NJ)	FMed	755	Guillem, Jose (NY)	CRS	143
Gross, Jay (NY)	CE	410	Guillory, Samuel (NY)	Oph	259
Gross, Jeffrey (CT)	N	1002	Gulrajani, Ramesh (NY)	Pul	488
Gross, Jeffrey (NY)	IM	682	Guma, Michael (NJ)	Rhu	792
Gross, Joshua (NJ)	DR	752	Gumbs, Andrew (NJ)	S	964
Gross, Stacy (NY)	PMR	715	Gumprecht, Jeffrey (NY)	Inf	194
Grossbard, Michael (NY)	Onc	216	Gundy, Edward (NY)	OrS	702
Grossi, Eugene (NY)	T&CS	388	Gupta, Adarsh (NY)	Psyc	593
Grossi, Robert (NY)	VascS	404	Gupta, Jagdish (NY)	Ge	460
Grossman, Bernard (NJ)	Onc	850	Gupta, Mantu (NY)	U	394
Grossman, Edward (CT)	Ge	986	Gupta, Sanjeev (NY)	Ge	417
Grossman, Elliot (NJ)	ChiN	905	Gurevich, Michael (NY)	Psyc	594
Grossman, Kenneth (NJ)	D	888	Gurland, Frances (NJ)	Psyc	789
Grossman, Marc (NY)	D	665	Gurland, Mark (NJ)	HS	759
Grossman, Melanie (NY)	D	150	Gurtowski, James (NY)	OrS	639
Grossman, Robert (NJ)	OrS	894	Gurubhagavatula, Sarada (NJ)	Onc	909
Grossman, Susan (NY)	Nep	526	Gusmorino, Paul (NY)	PM	298
Grosso, John (NY)	Oto	578	Gutin, Philip (NY)	NS	230
Grosso-Rivas, Sue Jane (NJ)	DR	950	Gutowski, W. Thomas (NJ)	OrS	853
Grubb, William (NJ)	PM	876	Gutwein, Isadore (NY)	Ge	418
Gruber, Michael (NY)	N	237	Guzik, Howard (NY)	Ger	555
Grubman, Samuel (NY)	A&I	122	Guzman, Rodolfo (NY)	EDM	415
Gruenstein, Steven (NY)	Hem	190			
Gruenwald, Laurence (NJ)	Ped	826			
Grunberger, Ivan (NY)	U	494	**H**		
Grunebaum, Amos (NY)	MF	211			
Grunfeld, Lawrence (NY)	RE	365	Haas, Jonathan (NY)	RadRO	597
Grunstein, Eli (NY)	PO	315	Haas, Steven (NY)	OrS	275
Grunzweig, Milton (NY)	IM	465	Haber, Gregory (NY)	Ge	172
Gruss, Claudia (CT)	Ge	986	Haber, Patricia (NY)	Ped	437
Gruss, Leslie (NY)	ObG	248	Haber, Richard (NY)	EDM	163
Guardarramas, Gabriel (NY)	FMed	167	Haber, Stuart (NY)	IM	202
			Habib, Ramez (NY)	Oto	480

Alphabetical Listing of Doctors

Name	Specialty	Pg	Name	Specialty	Pg
Haddad, Joseph (NY)	PO	315	Hand, Ivan (NY)	NP	509
Haffty, Bruce (NJ)	RadRO	882	Handelsman, Richard (NY)	IM	611
Hagberg, Donna (CT)	ObG	1005	Handler, Robert (NJ)	Ped	917
Hagopian, George (NY)	GO	505	Hankin, Dorie (NY)	Ped	588
Hahn, John (NJ)	Ge	838	Hanley, Gerard (NY)	Cv	453
Haight, David (NY)	Oph	259	Hanna, Moneer (NY)	U	604
Haimovic, Itzhak (NY)	N	568	Hannafin, Jo (NY)	OrS	275
Haines, Kathleen (NJ)	PRhu	783	Hanon, Samuel (NY)	CE	124
Halaas, Jeffrey (NY)	Onc	688	Hanson, Matthew (NY)	Oto	480
Halata, Michael (NY)	PGe	708	Har-El, Gady (NY)	Oto	289
Hale, Elizabeth (NY)	D	150	Haramati, Linda (NY)	DR	414
Hale, James (NJ)	OrS	776	Haramati, Nogah (NY)	DR	414
Hale, William (CT)	Ge	986	Harangozo, Andrea (NJ)	Pul	881
Hall, Jason (NJ)	Cv	936	Harary, Albert (NY)	Ge	172
Hall, Lisabeth (NY)	Oph	259	Haratz, Alan (NJ)	Nep	892
Hall, Simon (NY)	U	394	Haratz-Rubinstein, Natan (NY)	ObG	475
Hallal, Edward (NY)	IM	631	Hardart, Anne (NY)	ObG	249
Hallarman, Lynn (NY)	H & PM	630	Harden, Cynthia (NY)	N	568
Haller, Melvin (NY)	Oph	510	Harish, Ziv (NJ)	A&I	741
Halperin, Ira (NY)	IM	202	Harlam, Dean (NY)	Psyc	718
Halperin, John (NJ)	N	956	Harlow, Paul (NJ)	Ped	785
Halperin, Jonathan (NY)	Cv	128	Harman, John (NJ)	IM	849
Halpern, Allan (NY)	D	150	Harmon, Gregory (NY)	Oph	259
Halpern, Brian (NY)	SM	374	Harnick, David (NY)	CE	124
Halpern, David (NY)	S	600	Harooni, Robert (NY)	Ge	504
Halpern, Neil (NY)	CCM	145	Harpaz, Noam (NY)	Path	300
Halpern, Steven (NJ)	PHO	781	Harper, Harry (NJ)	Onc	765
Hamburger, Max (NY)	Rhu	647	Harrington, Elizabeth (NY)	VascS	404
Hamet, Marc (NY)	VIR	731	Harrington, Martin (NY)	VascS	404
Hametz, Irwin (NJ)	D	888	Harris, Dena (NY)	ObG	249
Hamilton, Audrey (NJ)	Onc	939	Harris, Leon (NY)	Pul	617
Hamilton, William (NY)	OrS	275	Harris, Loren (NY)	T&CS	493
Hammel, Jay (NY)	DR	549	Harris, Michael (NJ)	S	794
Hammer, Arthur (NY)	Pul	488	Harris, Michael (NJ)	PHO	781
Hammer, Glenn (NY)	Inf	195	Harris, Philip (NY)	PMR	486
Hammer, Scott (NY)	Inf	195	Harris, Steven (NY)	U	604
Hammerman, Hillel (NY)	Ge	172	Harrison, Aaron (NY)	Ge	629
Hammerschlag, Paul (NY)	Oto	289	Harrison, Louis (NY)	RadRO	361
Hamroff, Glenn (NY)	Cv	658	Hart, Catherine (NY)	IM	202

Name	Specialty	Pg	Name	Specialty	Pg
Hart, Douglas (NY)	Cv	658	Heldman, Jay (NJ)	D	751
Hart, Sidney (CT)	Psyc	1023	Helfet, David (NY)	OrS	276
Harter, David (NY)	NS	230	Helfgott, David (NY)	Inf	195
Hartl, Roger (NY)	NS	231	Heller, Debra (NJ)	Path	822
Hartman, Alan (NY)	T&CS	649	Heller, Paul (NJ)	GO	907
Hartman, Barry (NY)	Inf	195	Heller, Stanley (NY)	Psyc	346
Hartz, Cindi (NY)	Ped	713	Hellerman, James (NY)	EDM	670
Hartzband, Mark (NJ)	OrS	776	Hemmers, Philip (CT)	A&I	974
Harwin, Steven (NY)	OrS	275	Hen, Jacob (CT)	PPul	1018
Hasapis, Peter (CT)	IM	992	Henderson, Cassandra (NY)	MF	423
Haselkorn, Joan (NY)	ObG	571	Henick, David (NJ)	Oto	777
Hasson, Henry (NY)	ChiN	455	Hennessy, William (CT)	U	1032
Hassoun, Hani (NY)	Onc	216	Henschke, Claudia (NY)	DR	158
Hatcher, Virgil (NY)	D	150	Henshaw, D. Ross (CT)	OrS	1012
Hatsis, Alexander (NY)	Oph	573	Hensle, Terry (NJ)	Ped Uro	784
Hauptman, Allen (NY)	IM	202	Heptulla, Rubina (NY)	PEn	433
Hausman, Michael (NY)	OrS	275	Herbert, Joshua (CT)	FMed	985
Haven, Lynne (CT)	D	980	Herbstein, Diego (NY)	N	237
Havens, Jennifer (NY)	ChAP	137	Herbstman, Robert (NJ)	PlS	880
Hayes, Leslie (NY)	AM	451	Herman, David (NJ)	Inf	938
Hayworth, Scott (NY)	ObG	696	Herman, Martin (NJ)	N	871
Healey, John (NY)	OrS	275	Herman, Zeva (NY)	DR	158
Heary, Robert (NJ)	NS	817	Hermele, Herbert (CT)	OrS	1012
Hecht, Alan (NY)	Cv	129	Herold, Betsy (NY)	PInf	434
Hecht, Andrew (NY)	OrS	275	Herr, Harry (NY)	U	394
Hedrick, David (CT)	Ped	1019	Herrera, Joseph (NY)	PMR	327
Heerdt, Alexandra (NY)	S	379	Herron, Daniel (NY)	S	379
Hefter, Harold (NY)	D	548	Hersh, Peter (NJ)	Oph	774
Heftler, Jeffrey (CT)	PMR	1021	Hershman, Dawn (NY)	Onc	216
Hegyi, Thomas (NJ)	NP	870	Hershman, Elliott (NY)	SM	374
Heier, Stephen (NY)	Ge	674	Hershman, Ronnie (NY)	Cv	543
Heilbroner, Peter (NJ)	ChiN	749	Herskovitz, Steven (NY)	N	426
Heim, John (NJ)	T&CS	883	Hertan, Hilary (NY)	Ge	418
Heiman, Mark (CT)	Cv	977	Hertz, Marc (NY)	DR	668
Heiman, Peter (NY)	Psyc	439	Hertz, Marcie (NJ)	S	831
Heinemann, Murk (NY)	Oph	259	Hertz, Steven (NJ)	VascS	833
Heisman, Alexander (NY)	Psyc	487	Herzlinger, Robert (CT)	NP	1000
Heitner, John (NY)	Cv	453	Herzog, David (NY)	IM	682
Helbraun, Mark (NJ)	CRS	750	Herzog, Ronit (NY)	PA&I	303

Alphabetical Listing of Doctors

Name	Specialty	Pg	Name	Specialty	Pg
Hes, Dyan (NY)	Ped	321	Hodges, Laura (CT)	VIR	1032
Hetzler, Peter (NJ)	PlS	896	Hodosh, Richard (NJ)	NS	955
Heublum, Michael (NY)	N	237	Hoffman, Darryl (NY)	T&CS	388
Hiatt, I Mark (NJ)	NP	870	Hoffman, Eileen (NY)	IM	202
Hibbard, Claire (NY)	DR	668	Hoffman, Janet (NY)	DR	550
Hicks, Patricia (NJ)	PA&I	779	Hoffman, Joel (NY)	Psyc	346
Hidalgo, David (NY)	PlS	334	Hoffman, Lloyd (NY)	PlS	334
Hiesiger, Emile (NY)	N	237	Hoffman, Pamela (CT)	IM	992
Hillman, Deborah (NY)	Ge	674	Hoffman, Richard (NY)	EDM	523
Hiltebeitel, Carolyn (NY)	Ped	321	Hoffman, Robert (NY)	PrM	341
Hindenburg, Alexander (NY)	Onc	563	Hoffman, Ronald (NY)	Oto	289
Hindin, Lee (NJ)	Psyc	828	Hofstetter, Steven (NY)	S	380
Hindman, Steven (CT)	OrS	1012	Hoisington, Samuel (NY)	OrS	702
Hines, Brian (CT)	ObG	1005	Holcomb, Kevin (NY)	GO	184
Hines, William (CT)	Nep	1001	Holcombe, Randall (NY)	Onc	216
Hiotis, Spiros (NY)	S	379	Holder, Jonathan (NY)	OrS	702
Hirmand, Haideh (NY)	PlS	334	Holland, Claudia (NY)	ObG	249
Hirsch, Andrew (NJ)	A&I	903	Holland, Elbridge (NJ)	FMed	906
Hirsch, Bruce (NY)	Inf	558	Holland, James (NY)	Onc	216
Hirsch, Glenn (NY)	ChAP	137	Hollander, Eric (NY)	Psyc	346
Hirsch, Lissa (NY)	ObG	249	Hollander, Gerald (NY)	Cv	454
Hirschman, Alan (NY)	Ped	437	Holliday, Roy (NY)	DR	158
Hirschman, Richard (NY)	Onc	216	Hollister, Dickerman (CT)	Onc	999
Hirshaut, Yashar (NY)	Onc	216	Hollywood, Jacqueline (NJ)	Cv	745
Hirshfield, Gary (NY)	Oph	511	Holodny, Andrei (NY)	NRad	243
Hirt, Paula (NY)	ObG	636	Holtzman, Robert (NY)	NS	567
Hisler, Barbara (NY)	D	549	Holzberg, Norman (NJ)	Oto	821
Hjemdahl-Monsen, Craig (NY)	IC	685	Holzer, Barry (NY)	ChAP	455
Ho, Bryan (NJ)	Oto	777	Holzman, Ian (NY)	NP	225
Ho, Sammy (NY)	Ge	418	Hon, Man (NY)	VIR	606
Ho, Sharon (NY)	Ped	321	Hong, Andrew (NY)	PS	586
Hoang, Bang (NY)	OrS	430	Honig, Stephen (NY)	Rhu	370
Hochman, Herbert (NY)	D	150	Hopkins, Arthur (NY)	IM	683
Hockstein, Steven (NY)	ObG	249	Horbar, Gary (NY)	IM	203
Hoda, Syed (NY)	Path	301	Horn, Corinne (NY)	Oto	289
Hodak, Steven (NY)	EDM	164	Horn, Evelyn (NY)	Cv	129
Hodes, David (NY)	Pul	617	Horn, Jay (CT)	IM	992
Hodes, Steven (NJ)	Ge	866	Horner, Neil (NJ)	NRad	957
Hodges, David (NJ)	Cv	745	Hornyak, Stephen (NY)	S	531

Name	Specialty	Pg
Horovitz, Len (NY)	IM	203
Horowitz, Harold (NY)	Inf	195
Horowitz, Jason (NY)	Oph	259
Horowitz, Marc (NY)	Oph	699
Horowitz, Mark (NY)	Ped Uro	529
Horowitz, Mark (NY)	FMed	167
Horowitz, Mark (NY)	Rhu	370
Horowitz, Steven (CT)	Cv	977
Horwitz, Steven (NY)	Onc	217
Hostin, Helen (NY)	ObG	614
Hotchkiss, Edward (NY)	IM	560
Hotchkiss, Hilary (NY)	PNep	314
Hotchkiss, Robert (NY)	HS	187
Housman, Arno (NY)	U	729
Howanitz, Nancy (NY)	D	665
Howes, Christopher (CT)	IC	995
Hricak, Hedvig (NY)	DR	158
Hsu, Daphne (NY)	PCd	432
Hsueh, John (NY)	Cv	500
Hsuih, Terence (NY)	IM	466
Hu, Kenneth (NY)	RadRO	361
Huang, Russel (NY)	OrS	276
Huang, William (NY)	U	394
Hubbard, Christopher (NY)	OrS	276
Hudis, Clifford (NY)	Onc	217
Hufnagel, Thierry (NY)	Oph	573
Hug, Eugen (NJ)	RadRO	943
Hughes, Peter (CT)	OrS	1012
Huh, Julie (NY)	D	625
Hundert, Michael (NY)	IM	507
Hunt, William (CT)	Nep	1001
Hunter, John (NY)	PIS	334
Huo, Jerry (NY)	Oto	512
Hupart, Kenneth (NY)	EDM	551
Huribal, Marsel (CT)	VascS	1033
Hurst, Lawrence (NY)	HS	630
Hurst, Wendy (NJ)	ObG	772
Hurwitz, Diana (NY)	D	666
Hurwitz, Joshua (CT)	RE	1027

Name	Specialty	Pg
Huston, Jan (NJ)	S	831
Hutson, J. Milton (NY)	MF	211
Hwang, Cheng-hong (NJ)	Pul	963
Hyans, Peter (NJ)	PIS	962
Hyler, Irene (NY)	ChAP	662
Hyman, George (NY)	Oph	476
Hyman, Jeffrey (NY)	IM	466
Hyman, Joshua (NY)	OrS	276
Hyman, Kevin (NY)	T&CS	602
Hyman, Martin (NJ)	ObG	957
Hymes, Kenneth (NY)	Hem	190
Hyun, Grace (NY)	Ped Uro	319

I

Name	Specialty	Pg
Iannuzzi, Christopher (CT)	RadRO	1026
Ibelli, Vincent (NY)	FMed	610
Igel, Gerard (NY)	Ped	437
Ilan, Doron (NY)	HS	678
Ilowite, Norman (NY)	PRhu	435
Ilson, David (NY)	Onc	217
Imber, Gerald (NY)	PIS	334
Imbornone, Peter (NJ)	AM	741
Imegwu, Obi (NJ)	VascS	944
Implicito, Dante (NJ)	OrS	776
Imundo, Lisa (NY)	PRhu	317
Inabnet, William (NY)	S	380
Inamdar, Sarla (NY)	Ped	321
Ingenito, Anthony (NJ)	RadRO	791
Inglis, Steven (NY)	MF	508
Ingrassia, Joseph (NY)	FMed	610
Innella, Robin (NJ)	OrS	958
Innerfield, Michael (NY)	IC	612
Inouye, Masayuki (NJ)	Oto	777
Inra, Lawrence (NY)	Cv	129
Inwald, Gary (NY)	PMR	438
Iorio, Richard (NY)	OrS	276
Ipp, Lisa (NY)	AM	120
Isaacson, Steven (NY)	RadRO	362

Alphabetical Listing of Doctors

Name	Specialty	Pg	Name	Specialty	Pg
Islam, Sohel (CT)	PlS	1022	Jafar, Jafar (NY)	NS	231
Isola, Luis (NY)	Hem	190	Jaffe, Alan (NY)	Ge	674
Isom, O. Wayne (NY)	T&CS	388	Jaffin, Barry (NY)	Ge	173
Israel, Alan (NJ)	Hem	760	Jagannath, Sundar (NY)	Onc	217
Israel, Jessica (NJ)	Ger	889	Jahn, Anthony (NY)	Oto	289
Israel, Shara (CT)	IM	992	Jahre, Caren (NY)	NRad	244
Israeli, Ron (NY)	PlS	591	Jaile-Marti, Jesus (NY)	NP	690
Issa, Ebrahim (NJ)	Cv	746	Jain, Subhash (NY)	PM	298
Issenberg, Henry (NY)	PCd	707	Jakubowski, Ann (NY)	Hem	190
Istrico, Richard (NY)	FMed	503	Jamieson, Dara (NY)	N	237
Iswara, Kadirawelpillai (NY)	Ge	461	Jan, Dominique (NY)	PS	435
Itzkowitz, Steven (NY)	Ge	172	Janec, Eileen (NY)	Ge	173
Ivanov, Alexander (NJ)	CE	935	Jarnagin, William (NY)	S	380
Iwai, Sei (NY)	CE	655	Jauhar, Rajiv (NY)	Cv	543
			Javit, Daniel (NY)	VIR	400
			Jawetz, Harold (NJ)	IM	927

J

Name	Specialty	Pg	Name	Specialty	Pg
			Jayaram, Nadubeethi (NY)	OrS	528
Jabs, Douglas (NY)	Oph	260	Jazrawi, Laith (NY)	SM	374
Jackson, Rosemary (NY)	Ped	485	Jelin, Abraham (NY)	PGe	482
Jacob, Brian (NY)	S	380	Jenkins, Arthur (NY)	NS	231
Jacob, Jessica (NY)	ObG	571	Jennis, Andrew (NJ)	Onc	765
Jacobowitz, Glenn (NY)	VascS	404	Jeremias, Allen (NY)	Cv	622
Jacobowitz, Marilyn (NY)	IM	683	Jeshion, Wendy (NJ)	PGe	781
Jacobs, Elliot (NY)	PlS	334	Jessurun, Jose (NY)	Path	301
Jacobs, Jonathan (NY)	Inf	195	John, Sylvia (NY)	PMR	644
Jacobs, Joseph (NY)	Oto	289	Johns, William (CT)	NuM	1004
Jacobs, Laurie (NY)	Ger	419	Johnson, Alan (NY)	NRad	570
Jacobs, Michael (NY)	D	150	Johnson, Diane (NY)	Inf	558
Jacobs, Morton (NY)	DR	159	Johnson, Robert (NJ)	AM	804
Jacobs, Thomas (NY)	EDM	164	Johnson, Sabrina (NY)	FMed	628
Jacobson, Adam (NY)	Oto	289	Johnson Miller, Denise (NJ)	S	898
Jacobson, Edward (CT)	ObG	1005	Joks, Rauno (NY)	A&I	451
Jacobson, Ira (NY)	Ge	172	Jones, David (NY)	T&CS	388
Jacobson, Marc (NY)	AM	538	Jones, Frank (NJ)	Psyc	880
Jacobson, Ronald (NY)	ChiN	663	Jones, Jacqueline (NY)	Oto	289
Jacoby, Jacob (NJ)	Psyc	841	Jones, Stephen (CT)	Ger	988
Jacono, Andrew (NY)	Oto	578	Jonna, Siva (NJ)	PCCM	877
Jacowitz, Joel (NJ)	Cv	746	Jordan, Barry (NY)	N	693
Jadonath, Ram (NY)	CE	540	Jordan, Lawrence (NJ)	S	883

Name	Specialty	Pg	Name	Specialty	Pg
Jorde, Ulrich (NY)	Cv	411	Kalinich, Lila (NY)	Psyc	346
Joseph, John (NY)	IM	507	Kalischer, Alan (NJ)	Cv	949
Joseph, Patricia (NY)	S	618	Kalish, Robin (NY)	MF	211
Joseph, Rosy (NJ)	Nep	768	Kalman, Arlene (CT)	Psyc	1023
Josephson, Jordan (NY)	Oto	290	Kalman, Jill (NY)	Cv	543
Joy, Mark (NY)	IM	466	Kalnicki, Shalom (NY)	RadRO	441
Juan, Paul (CT)	Ped	1019	Kamalakar, Peri (NJ)	PHO	824
Julie, Edward (NJ)	Cv	925	Kamen, Mazen (NY)	Cv	129
Jumper, Robert (CT)	IC	995	Kaminetsky, Jed (NY)	U	394
Jurcic, Joseph (NY)	Hem	190	Kaminsky, Donald (NY)	IM	203
Jutkowitz, Robert (NY)	N	526	Kamler, Kenneth (NY)	HS	505
Jyonouchi, Harumi (NJ)	A&I	861	Kanarek, Steven (NJ)	Cv	746
			Kane, Michael (NJ)	Onc	910
			Kanengiser, Steven (NJ)	PPul	783
			Kang, Harriet (NY)	ChiN	663

K

Name	Specialty	Pg	Name	Specialty	Pg
Kabalkin, Chaim (NY)	Cv	454	Kang, Pritpal (NY)	Cv	454
Kabis, Suzanne (NJ)	Nep	940	Kanner, Ronald (NY)	N	568
Kabnick, Lowell (NY)	VascS	404	Kanowitz, Seth (NJ)	Oto	914
Kacker, Ashutosh (NY)	Oto	290	Kanter, Alan (NJ)	Ped	785
Kadakia, Satish (NY)	N	568	Kantor, Alan (NY)	EDM	670
Kafantaris, Vivian (NY)	ChAP	501	Kanumury, Sunita (NJ)	A&I	903
Kagan, Peter (NJ)	VascS	798	Kapel, Robert (CT)	Ge	986
Kahaleh, Michel (NY)	Ge	173	Kaplan, Barry (NY)	IC	561
Kahn, David (NY)	Psyc	346	Kaplan, Ellen (NJ)	PPul	783
Kahn, Jeffrey (NY)	Psyc	718	Kaplan, Gabriel (NJ)	Psyc	962
Kahn, Leonard (NY)	Path	581	Kaplan, Jeffrey (CT)	Oph	1008
Kahn, Max (NY)	Ped	322	Kaplan, Jonathan (NY)	EDM	551
Kahn, Oren (NY)	Ge	674	Kaplan, Kenneth (NY)	Cv	658
Kahn, Stuart (NY)	PM	298	Kaplan, Martin (NY)	Ped	643
Kaid, Khalil (NJ)	IC	814	Kaplan, Matthew (NY)	PNep	483
Kairam, Indira (NY)	Ge	173	Kaplan, Rana (NY)	Pul	357
Kairam, Ram (NY)	ChiN	140	Kaplan, Ronald (NY)	PM	298
Kaiser, Michael (NY)	NS	231	Kaplan, Sherri (NY)	D	666
Kaiser, Paul (NJ)	N	851	Kaplan, Steven (NY)	U	395
Kaiser, Stephen (NY)	IM	466	Kaplovitz, Harry (NY)	PCd	481
Kalapatapu, Kumar (NY)	IC	685	Kapoor, Satish (NY)	IM	683
Kalash, Glenn (NY)	Psyc	513	Kaporis, Athena (NY)	D	666
Kaleya, Ronald (NY)	S	492	Kappel, Bruce (NY)	Onc	564
Kalikow, Kevin (NY)	ChAP	662	Kapur, Sandip (NY)	S	380

Alphabetical Listing of Doctors

Name	Specialty	Pg	Name	Specialty	Pg
Karamitsos, Harry (NY)	ObG	249	Katz, Jeffrey (NJ)	U	832
Karanikolas, Nicholas (NY)	U	532	Katz, Lester (NY)	S	380
Karas, Evan (NY)	OrS	702	Katz, Seymour (NY)	Ge	554
Karasu, Sylvia (NY)	Psyc	346	Katz, Steven (NJ)	U	796
Karasu, T Byram (NY)	Psyc	346	Katz, Steven (NY)	Oph	428
Karatoprak, Ohan (NJ)	FMed	755	Katz, Stuart (NY)	Cv	129
Karen, Julie (NY)	D	150	Katz, Susan (NY)	D	151
Karetzky, Monroe (NY)	Pul	440	Katz, Terri (NJ)	Ger	758
Karlsrud, Katherine (NY)	Ped	322	Katzenelenbogen, Moshe (NY)	IM	466
Karmen, Carol (NY)	IM	683	Katzenstein, Martin (NY)	NP	612
Karol, Nina (CT)	IM	993	Kaufman, Alan (NY)	A&I	409
Karp, Adam (NY)	Ger	181	Kaufman, Andrew (NJ)	PM	822
Karp, George (NJ)	Hem	867	Kaufman, David (NY)	ChiN	140
Karp, Nolan (NY)	PlS	334	Kaufman, David (NY)	Cv	411
Karp, Sharon (CT)	Rhu	1028	Kaufman, David (NY)	N	426
Karpeh, Martin (NY)	S	380	Kaufman, Howard (NJ)	S	883
Kasabian, Armen (NY)	PlS	591	Kaufman, Matthew (NJ)	PlS	880
Kase, Jordan (NY)	NP	690	Kaufmann, Charles (NY)	Psyc	718
Kase, Steven (NY)	Oto	705	Kaufmann, Cheryl (NY)	Oph	511
Kaskel, Frederick (NY)	PNep	434	Kaul, Ashutosh (NY)	S	726
Kasper, William (NY)	Oph	573	Kaur, Harpreet (NJ)	NP	870
Kass, Lewis (NY)	PPul	710	Kauvar, Arielle (NY)	D	151
Kassapidis, Sotirios (NY)	Pul	513	Kavaler, Elizabeth (NY)	U	395
Kassotis, John (NY)	CE	452	Kavaler, Leon (NY)	Ge	173
Katechis, Dennis (NJ)	Cv	746	Kavanagh, Brian (CT)	OrS	1012
Kates, Matthew (NY)	Oto	705	Kavookjian, Haik (CT)	HS	989
Kato, Tomoaki (NY)	S	380	Kavoussi, Louis (NY)	U	604
Kattan, Meyer (NY)	PPul	316	Kay, Arthur (NY)	N	473
Katus, Eli (NY)	Psyc	594	Kay, Richard (NY)	Cv	658
Katz, Aaron (NY)	U	604	Kay, Scott (NJ)	Oto	875
Katz, Alan (NY)	RadRO	514	Kayal, Robert (NJ)	OrS	776
Katz, Andrea (NJ)	Ped	942	Kaynan, Ayal (NJ)	U	922
Katz, Barrett (NY)	Oph	428	Kazam, Ezra (NJ)	Oph	913
Katz, Bruce (NY)	D	150	Kazim, Michael (NY)	Oph	260
Katz, Edward (NY)	Cv	129	Kazlow, Philip (NY)	PGe	308
Katz, Harry (NJ)	Oto	778	Kearney, Thomas (NJ)	S	883
Katz, Henry (NY)	Ge	674	Keating, Richard (NY)	Cv	658
Katz, Herbert (NJ)	U	842	Keefe, David (NY)	RE	365
Katz, Jack (NY)	Psyc	594	Keilson, Marshall (NY)	N	473

Alphabetical Listing of Doctors

Name	Specialty	Pg	Name	Specialty	Pg
Keiser, Harold (NY)	Rhu	442	Kesarwala, Hemant (NJ)	A&I	861
Keith, Marie (NY)	Ped	322	Kesh, Sandra (NY)	Inf	679
Kelemen, John (NY)	N	569	Kessler, Alan (NY)	ObG	249
Keller, Adina (NY)	ObG	696	Kessler, Bradley (NY)	PGe	641
Keller, Andrew (CT)	Cv	977	Kessler, George (NY)	FMed	167
Keller, Irwin (NJ)	NRad	872	Kessler, Jeffrey (NY)	N	569
Keller, Jeffrey (NY)	PO	710	Kessler, Leonard (NY)	Onc	564
Keller, Marla (NY)	Inf	421	Kessler, Martin (NY)	PlS	591
Keller, Peter (NY)	Cv	411	Kessler, William (NJ)	Hem	953
Keller, Steven (NY)	T&CS	444	Khabie, Victor (NY)	OrS	703
Kellner, Charles (NY)	Psyc	346	Khaghan, Neda (CT)	Ge	986
Kelly, Anna (NY)	NRad	244	Khaitov, Sergey (NY)	CRS	144
Kelly, Bryan (NY)	OrS	276	Khakoo, Yasmin (NY)	ChiN	140
Kelly, Michael (NJ)	OrS	776	Khalife, Michael (NY)	S	601
Kelly, Stephen (NY)	Oph	260	Khan, Amber (NJ)	Ge	952
Kelsen, David (NY)	Onc	217	Khan, Arfa (NY)	DR	550
Keltz, Martin (NY)	RE	365	Khandji, Alexander (NY)	NRad	244
Keltz, Theodore (NY)	Cv	658	Khilnani, Neil (NY)	VIR	400
Kemeny, M. Margaret (NY)	S	515	Khimani, Karim (NJ)	Ger	953
Kemeny, Nancy (NY)	Onc	217	Khodadadian, Shawn (NY)	Ge	173
Kenan, Samuel (NY)	OrS	576	Khokhar, Asim (NY)	Ge	629
Kenet, Barney (NY)	D	151	Kholwadwala, Dipak (NY)	PCd	581
Kenigsberg, Daniel (NY)	RE	647	Khorasani, Hooman (NY)	D	151
Kenler, Andrew (CT)	S	1030	Khosh, Maurice (NY)	Oto	290
Kennedy, Gary (NY)	GerPsy	419	Khoury, F. Frederic (NY)	PlS	716
Kennedy, James (NY)	IM	203	Khoury, Paul (NY)	DR	668
Kennedy, Timothy (NY)	S	442	Khulpateea, Neekianund (NY)	GO	463
Kennish, Arthur (NY)	IM	203	Kier, Catherine (NY)	PPul	642
Kenny, Raymond (NJ)	Ge	810	Kiernan, Howard (NY)	OrS	276
Kent, Jennifer (NY)	IM	203	Kilgo, Matthew (NY)	PlS	592
Kent, Joan (NY)	ObG	249	Kim, Heakyung (NY)	PMR	327
Kepecs, Gilbert (NJ)	Rhu	792	Kim, Joyce (NY)	ObG	249
Kernan, Nancy (NY)	PHO	311	Kim, Matthew (CT)	MF	997
Kerner, Michael (NJ)	Ge	952	Kim, Michelle (NY)	Ge	173
Kerns, John (NJ)	U	796	Kim, Richard (NJ)	HS	759
Kerr, Alicia (CT)	ObG	1006	Kim, Steve (NJ)	Cv	746
Kerr, Leslie (NY)	Rhu	370	Kim, Tae Ho (NY)	PlS	335
Kerstein, Joshua (NY)	Cv	454	Kim, Tonia (NY)	Nep	227
Kerwin, Todd (NY)	Cv	500	Kim, Yongjung (NY)	OrS	277

Alphabetical Listing of Doctors

Name	Specialty	Pg	Name	Specialty	Pg
Kim-Schluger, Hyung (NY)	Ge	173	Klein, Victor (NY)	ObG	571
Kimball, Annetta (NY)	Ge	173	Klein, Walter (NJ)	Ge	756
Kimmelstiel, Fred (NY)	S	380	Klein, William (NY)	IM	560
Kimura, Yukiko (NJ)	PRhu	783	Kleinbaum, Jerry (NY)	EDM	670
King, Michael (CT)	DR	982	Kleinberg, David (NY)	EDM	164
King, William (NY)	HS	187	Kleiner, Morton (NY)	Nep	526
Kini, Subhash (NY)	S	381	Kleinman, Andrew (NY)	PlS	716
Kinkhabwala, Milan (NY)	S	442	Kleinman, Gary (CT)	MF	997
Kipen, Howard (NJ)	OM	873	Kleinman, Paul (NY)	OrS	430
Kipnis, James (NY)	OrS	576	Klenk, Rosemary (CT)	Ped	1019
Kirchoff, Kathryn (NY)	N	426	Klenoff, Bruce (CT)	Oto	1015
Kirschenbaum, Alexander (NY)	U	395	Klenoff, Jason (CT)	Oto	1015
Kirshblum, Steven (NJ)	PMR	827	Kligfield, Paul (NY)	Cv	129
Kirshy, David (NY)	DR	626	Kligler, Benjamin (NY)	FMed	167
Kirtane, Sanjay (NY)	Cv	500	Klimstra, David (NY)	Path	301
Kizelshteyn, Grigory (NY)	PM	706	Kline, Gary (NJ)	T&CS	795
Klafter, Robert (NY)	Onc	217	Kline, Mitchell (NY)	D	151
Klagsbrun, Samuel (NY)	Psyc	718	Klion, Mark (NY)	OrS	277
Klapholz, Ari (NY)	Pul	357	Klos, Andrzej (NJ)	Ped	841
Klapholz, Marc (NJ)	Cv	805	Kloss, Robert (CT)	Onc	999
Klapper, Daniel (NY)	Oph	260	Klyde, Barry (NY)	EDM	164
Klapper, Philip (NY)	Pul	440	Knackmuhs, Gary (NJ)	Inf	761
Klar, Tobi (NY)	D	666	Knapp, Albert (NY)	Ge	174
Klares, Scott (NY)	Pul	721	Knep, Stanley (NJ)	N	928
Klarsfeld, Jay (CT)	Oto	1015	Knightly, John (NJ)	NS	911
Klebanoff, Louise (NY)	N	238	Knisely, Jonathan (NY)	RadRO	597
Kleber, Herbert (NY)	AdP	119	Knoepflmacher, Paul (NY)	IM	203
Klecz, Robert (NJ)	PMR	918	Knopp, Edmond (NY)	NRad	244
Klein, George (NY)	U	395	Kobren, Steven (NY)	Cv	543
Klein, James (NJ)	T&CS	795	Koch, Robert (NY)	PlS	716
Klein, Janice (NY)	NP	225	Kocher, Jeffrey (NJ)	Inf	761
Klein, Jeffrey (NY)	RE	723	Kocsis, James (NY)	Psyc	346
Klein, Michael (NY)	Nep	691	Kodali, Susheel (NY)	IC	209
Klein, Natalie (NY)	Inf	558	Kodsi, Sylvia (NY)	Oph	573
Klein, Neil (CT)	IM	993	Kofinas, George (NY)	RE	490
Klein, Norman (NY)	A&I	451	Kohan, Darius (NY)	Oto	290
Klein, Patricia (NJ)	N	770	Kohn, Brenda (NY)	PEn	306
Klein, Paula (NY)	Onc	217	Kohn, Gary (NJ)	PPul	960
Klein, Robert (NJ)	A&I	925	Kolbovsky, Iosif (NY)	Nep	691

Alphabetical Listing of Doctors

Name	Specialty	Pg	Name	Specialty	Pg
Kolenik, Steven (CT)	D	980	Kowallis, George (NY)	Psyc	347
Kolitz, Jonathan (NY)	Hem	557	Kozel, Joseph (NJ)	IM	839
Kolker, Adam (NY)	PlS	335	Kozicky, Orest (NY)	Ge	674
Kolker, Dov (NY)	OrS	478	Kozin, Arthur (NY)	Nep	612
Kolodny, Erwin (NY)	Pul	357	Koziorynska, Ewa (NY)	N	473
Kolsky, Neil (NJ)	Ped	785	Kozlowski, Jeffrey (NJ)	Nep	768
Komarynsky, Irene (CT)	ObG	1006	Kozuch, Peter (NY)	Onc	218
Komisar, Arnold (NY)	Oto	290	Krakovitz, Evan (NY)	CRS	664
Kon, Shulamite (NY)	Ped	322	Kramer, David (CT)	OrS	1012
Kondziolka, Douglas (NY)	NS	231	Kramer, Kim (NY)	PHO	311
Koniaris, Soula (NJ)	PGe	877	Kramer, Mitchell (NY)	ObG	636
Konka, Sudarsanam (NY)	Cv	454	Kramer, Neil (NJ)	Rhu	964
Koo, Harry (NJ)	Ped Uro	785	Kramer, Philip (NY)	Oph	527
Kopec, Anna (NJ)	D	837	Krant, Jessica (NY)	D	151
Kopelman, Rima (NJ)	Rhu	792	Kranzler, Elliot (NY)	Psyc	347
Koplewicz, Harold (NY)	ChAP	137	Kranzler, L. Stephan (NY)	N	693
Koplin, Richard (NY)	Oph	260	Krasikov, Tatiana (NJ)	Cv	746
Koppel, Barbara (NY)	N	238	Kraus, Dennis (NY)	Oto	290
Koppel, Jeremy (NY)	GerPsy	505	Krause, Cynthia (NY)	ObG	250
Korc-Grodzicki, Beatriz (NY)	Ger	181	Kraushaar, Barry (NY)	SM	618
Koreen, Amy (NY)	Psyc	645	Kreitzer, Joel (NY)	PM	298
Kornbluth, Arthur (NY)	Ge	174	Kreitzer, Paula (NY)	PEn	583
Kornel, Ezriel (NY)	NS	692	Kremberg, M Roy (NY)	Psyc	347
Korosi, Anthony (NY)	Nep	691	Kremen, Neil (NY)	GerPsy	505
Korsten, Mark (NY)	Ge	418	Krespi, Yosef (NY)	Oto	290
Korval, Arnold (CT)	Ped	1019	Kressner, Michael (NY)	Ge	675
Kosinski, Edward (CT)	Cv	977	Krevitt, Lane (NY)	Oto	291
Kosofsky, Barry (NY)	ChiN	140	Kriegel, David (NY)	D	151
Kososky, Charles (NJ)	N	852	Krieger, Ana (NY)	Pul	357
Koss, Jerome (NY)	Cv	543	Krieger, Karl (NY)	T&CS	388
Kostis, John (NJ)	Cv	862	Krieger, Richard (NJ)	Inf	908
Kotin, Neal (NY)	Ped	322	Krieger, Sharon (NY)	IM	683
Kotkes, Herschel (NY)	PM	298	Krilov, Leonard (NY)	PInf	585
Kotler, Donald (NY)	Ge	174	Krim, Eileen (NY)	ObG	571
Kotler, Lisa (NJ)	ChAP	749	Krinsky, Glenn (NJ)	DR	752
Kottler, William (NJ)	PPul	825	Krinsley, James (CT)	Pul	1025
Kottmeier, Stephen (NY)	OrS	639	Kris, Mark (NY)	Onc	218
Koufman, Jamie (NY)	Oto	290	Krishnan, Prakash (NY)	IC	209
Koulos, John (NY)	GO	184	Krishnan, Sankaran (NY)	PPul	710

Alphabetical Listing of Doctors

Name	Specialty	Pg
Krishnan, Usha (NY)	PCd	304
Kristal, Leonard (NY)	D	625
Kristan, Ronald (NJ)	Oph	893
Krol, Kristine (NJ)	A&I	935
Kron, Leo (NY)	ChAP	138
Kronn, David (NY)	CG	664
Kronzon, Itzhak (NY)	Cv	129
Krotowski, Mark (NY)	FMed	459
Krueger, Richard (NY)	Psyc	347
Krug, Lee (NY)	Onc	218
Kruger, Bernard (NY)	Onc	218
Krumerman, Andrew (NY)	CE	410
Krumholz, Michael (NY)	Ge	174
Krutchik, Allan (NJ)	Onc	765
Kubersky, Steven (NY)	IM	683
Kudelka, Andrzej (NY)	Onc	634
Kuenzler, Keith (NJ)	PS	784
Kuflik, Paul (NY)	OrS	277
Kuhel, William (NY)	Oto	291
Kula, Roger (NY)	N	569
Kulick, Roy (NY)	HS	420
Kulkarni, Rachana (NJ)	Cv	936
Kulpa, Jolanta (NY)	PHO	483
Kulsakdinun, Chaiyaporn (NY)	OrS	430
Kumar, Mark (NJ)	VascS	966
Kummer, Bart (NY)	Ge	174
Kunkes, Steven (CT)	Cv	977
Kuo, Jonathann (NY)	PM	299
Kupersmith, Andrew (NY)	Cv	658
Kupersmith, Mark (NY)	Oph	260
Kupfer, Yizhak (NY)	Pul	489
Kurani, Devendra (NJ)	Psyc	841
Kurer, Cheryl (NJ)	PCd	876
Kurfist, Lee (NY)	Ped	643
Kuriloff, Daniel (NY)	Oto	291
Kurlan, Roger (NJ)	N	956
Kurth, Rebecca (NY)	IM	203
Kurtz, Caroline (CT)	Pul	1025
Kurtz, Lewis (NY)	S	601
Kurtz, Robert (NY)	Ge	174
Kurucz, Oliver (NY)	Rhu	617
Kushner, Brian (NY)	PHO	311
Kushner, Evan (NJ)	IM	762
Kushner, Susan (NJ)	Ped	785
Kutcher, Rosalyn (NY)	DR	668
Kutnick, Richard (NY)	Cv	130
Kutscher, Martin (NY)	ChiN	663
Kuzniecky, Ruben (NY)	N	238
Kwartler, Jed (NJ)	Oto	959
Ky, Alex (NY)	CRS	144

L

Name	Specialty	Pg
La Bagnara, James (NJ)	Oto	930
La Gamma, Edmund (NY)	NP	690
La Marca, Charles (NY)	Oto	512
La Quaglia, Michael (NY)	PS	318
Laban-Grant, Olgica (NY)	N	693
Labar, Douglas (NY)	N	238
Labow, Daniel (NY)	S	381
LaBruna, Anthony (NY)	PlS	335
Lachman, Reid (NJ)	Oto	914
Lachmann, Elisabeth (NY)	PMR	328
Lachs, Mark (NY)	Ger	181
Lacouture, Mario (NY)	D	151
Lacqua, Frank (NY)	CRS	522
Lafaro, Rocco (NY)	T&CS	727
Lafferty, James (NY)	Cv	521
Lagmay, Victor (NY)	Oto	480
Lahita, Robert (NJ)	Rhu	830
Laifer, Steven (CT)	MF	997
Laitman, Robert (NY)	Nep	425
LaJoie, Josiane (NY)	ChiN	546
Laks, Mitchell (NY)	DR	414
Lallas, Thomas (NY)	GO	184
Lalli, Corradino (NY)	IM	632
Lalwani, Anil (NY)	Oto	291
Lamanna, Nicole (NY)	Hem	191

Alphabetical Listing of Doctors

Name	Specialty	Pg	Name	Specialty	Pg
Lederman, Josiane (NY)	D	522	Lehrman, Stuart (NY)	Pul	721
Lederman, Martin (NY)	Oph	699	Leib, Martin (NY)	Oph	261
Lee, Alexander (NY)	PMR	328	Leibner, Donald (NJ)	A&I	861
Lee, Andy (NY)	VascS	517	Leiboff, Arnold (NY)	CRS	624
Lee, April (NY)	AM	521	Leibowitz, Evan (NJ)	Rhu	792
Lee, Carol (NY)	Oph	260	Leibowitz, Jonas (NY)	EDM	670
Lee, Donna (NJ)	PPul	783	Leichter, Donald (NJ)	PCd	959
Lee, Douglas (NY)	ObG	636	Leifer, Bennett (NJ)	Ger	758
Lee, Francis (NY)	OrS	277	Leifer, Marvin (NJ)	Psyc	855
Lee, Haesoon (NY)	PPul	484	Leipsner, George (NJ)	FMed	755
Lee, Henry (NY)	RadRO	722	Leipzig, Rosanne (NY)	Ger	181
Lee, Huey-Jen (NJ)	DR	808	Leipziger, Lyle (NY)	PlS	592
Lee, James (NY)	S	381	Leiter, Gila (NY)	ObG	250
Lee, Kwang (NY)	Psyc	645	Leitman, I. Michael (NY)	S	381
Lee, Leonard (NJ)	T&CS	883	Leitner, Stuart (NJ)	Onc	815
Lee, Lucille (NY)	RadRO	597	Lemercier, Maud (NY)	S	726
Lee, Marjorie (NY)	Pul	357	Lenci, Margaret (NY)	Rhu	724
Lee, Merlin (CT)	Onc	999	Lense, Lloyd (NY)	Cv	622
Lee, Nancy (NY)	RadRO	362	Lent, David (NY)	OrS	703
Lee, Nellie (NJ)	Cv	747	Lenzo, Salvatore (NY)	HS	187
Lee, Paul (NY)	T&CS	516	Leon, Martin (NY)	IC	209
Lee, Richard (CT)	A&I	974	Leon, Steven (NY)	NS	635
Lee, Ronald (CT)	DR	982	Leonard, Daniel (NY)	Cv	659
Lee, Sang (NY)	CRS	144	Leonard, John (NY)	Hem	191
Lee, Sang (NY)	Ge	675	Leonard, Michael (NY)	IM	204
Lee, Sicy (NY)	Rhu	370	Leondires, Mark (CT)	RE	1027
Lee, Steve (NY)	HS	187	Leong, Mary (NY)	ObG	571
Lee, Steven (NY)	OrS	277	Leong, Pauline (NY)	IM	560
Lee, Thomas (NY)	NS	692	Lepor, Herbert (NY)	U	395
Lee, Thomas (NY)	PS	642	Lepore, Frederick (NJ)	N	871
Leeman, Benjamin (NY)	Pul	595	Lerma, Pauline (NJ)	Onc	850
Lefkovitz, Zvi (NY)	DR	668	Lerman, Bruce (NY)	CE	124
Lefkowitz, Mathew (NY)	PM	481	Lerman, Jay (NY)	D	413
Lefton, Daniel (NY)	NRad	244	Lerman, Jay (NY)	DR	458
Legato, Marianne (NY)	IM	204	Lerner, Chester (NY)	Inf	195
Lehach, Joan (NY)	A&I	409	Lerner, Elliot (NJ)	NRad	771
Lehman, Thomas (NY)	PRhu	317	Lerner, Seth (NY)	U	729
Lehrhoff, Bernard (NJ)	U	965	Lerner, William (NJ)	Hem	890
Lehrman, Gary (NY)	Pul	721	Lescale, Keith (NY)	MF	686

Name	Specialty	Pg	Name	Specialty	Pg
Lesesne, Carroll (NY)	PIS	335	Levine, William (NY)	SM	375
Leslie, Denise (NY)	DR	668	Levinson, William (NY)	Ped	713
Lesorgen, Philip (NJ)	RE	791	Levit, Eyal (NY)	D	457
Lesser, Robert (NY)	Rhu	491	Levitan, Stephan (NY)	Psyc	347
Lessing, Jeffrey (NY)	U	532	Levitt, Jacob (NY)	D	152
Lessnau, Klaus-Dieter (NY)	Pul	357	Levitt, Miriam (NY)	Ped	714
Lester, Mitchell (CT)	PA&I	1017	Levitz, Craig (NY)	OrS	576
Lettera, James (CT)	T&CS	1031	Levitzky, Susan (NY)	Ped	322
Levchuck, Sean (NY)	PCd	582	Levy, Adam (NY)	PHO	433
Levey, James (NJ)	ObG	940	Levy, Albert (NY)	FMed	168
Levey, Kenneth (NY)	ObG	250	Levy, Andrew (NJ)	SM	830
Levey, Robert (NY)	IM	466	Levy, Carol (NY)	EDM	164
Levi, Andrew (CT)	RE	1027	Levy, Daniel (NJ)	DR	808
Levin, Alexander (NJ)	PM	876	Levy, I Martin (NY)	OrS	430
Levin, Andrew (NY)	Psyc	718	Levy, Joseph (NY)	PGe	308
Levin, David (NJ)	Nep	768	Levy, Judith (NY)	ObG	428
Levin, Frances (NY)	AdP	119	Levy, Kirk (NJ)	N	770
Levin, Kenneth (NJ)	N	770	Levy, Lauren (NJ)	DR	753
Levin, Richard (CT)	Oto	1015	Levy, Lewis (NY)	N	569
Levin, Sheryl (NY)	PMR	438	Levy, Michael (NY)	Psyc	617
Levine, Alice (NY)	EDM	164	Levy, Miriam (NY)	DR	159
Levine, David (NY)	N	238	Levy, Ross (NY)	D	666
Levine, David (NY)	OrS	277	Lew, Arthur (NY)	Psyc	718
Levine, Evan (NY)	Cv	659	Lewin, Margaret (NY)	IM	204
Levine, Jamie (NY)	PIS	335	Lewin, Neal (NY)	IM	204
Levine, Jeremiah (NY)	PGe	308	Lewin, Sharon (NY)	IM	204
Levine, Joseph (NY)	CE	540	Lewis, Benjamin (NY)	Cv	130
Levine, Joshua (NY)	PIS	335	Lewis, Blair (NY)	Ge	175
Levine, Laurie (NY)	D	549	Lewis, Owen (NY)	ChAP	138
Levine, Martin (NJ)	FMed	838	Lewis, Ronald (NY)	OrS	639
Levine, Michael (NY)	U	604	Lewis, Theophilus (NY)	S	492
Levine, Mitchell (NY)	NS	567	Lewko, Michael (NJ)	Rhu	932
Levine, Randy (NY)	Hem	191	Li, Chun-Lun (NY)	Oto	291
Levine, Richard (NY)	ObG	250	Li, Karl (NY)	PInf	709
Levine, Robert (NJ)	Ge	756	Li, Ronald (NJ)	Oto	854
Levine, Selwyn (NJ)	Pul	790	Li, Suzanne (NJ)	PRhu	784
Levine, Seth (NJ)	U	932	Liakeas, George (NY)	FMed	168
Levine, Steven (CT)	Oto	1015	Liang, Vera (NY)	Psyc	594
Levine, Steven (NY)	N	473	Liaw, Karen (NY)	ChAP	138

Alphabetical Listing of Doctors

Name	Specialty	Pg	Name	Specialty	Pg
Libby, Daniel (NY)	Pul	357	Lipsitz, Evan (NY)	VascS	445
Libutti, Steven (NY)	S	443	Lipson, David (NJ)	PlS	787
Licata, Joseph (NJ)	S	794	Lipstein-Kresch, Esther (NY)	Rhu	598
Licata, Joseph (NY)	Ped	322	Lipsztein, Roberto (NY)	RadRO	514
Licciardi, Frederick (NY)	RE	365	Lipton, Brian (NY)	Psyc	347
Lichtbroun, Alan (NJ)	Rhu	882	Lipton, Jeffrey (NY)	PHO	584
Lichter, Stephen (NY)	Onc	469	Lipton, Mark (NY)	IM	204
Lichter-Konecki, Uta (NY)	CG	142	Lipton, Richard (NY)	N	426
Lichtstein, Elliott (NJ)	Cv	747	Lis, Eric (NY)	NRad	244
Lieb, Mark (NY)	Cv	659	Lish, Adam (NY)	Oph	477
Lieberman, Elliott (NY)	U	604	Lisi-DeMartino, Virna (NY)	DR	668
Lieberman, Kenneth (NJ)	PNep	782	Lisman, Richard (NY)	Oph	261
Lieberman, Michael (NY)	S	381	Liss, Donald (NJ)	PMR	787
Liebling, Melissa (NJ)	DR	753	Liss, Howard (NJ)	PMR	787
Liebling, Ralph (NY)	PlS	439	Liss, Mark (NY)	Ge	675
Liebmann, Jeffrey (NY)	Oph	261	Lisser, Steven (NJ)	HS	890
Lieman, Harry (NY)	RE	723	Litchman, Charisse (CT)	N	1003
Liftin, Alan (NJ)	D	808	Litchman, Mark (CT)	A&I	974
Lightdale, Charles (NY)	Ge	175	Liteplo, Ronald (NY)	D	414
Ligresti, Louise (NJ)	Onc	765	Litman, Nathan (NY)	PInf	434
Liguori, Michael (NY)	IM	204	Litman, Richard (NY)	Oto	640
Lijtmaer, Hugo (NJ)	N	771	Litman, Steven (NY)	PM	640
Lim, Jessica (NY)	Oto	291	Littlejohn, Charles (CT)	CRS	979
Lin, Fangming (NY)	PNep	314	Lituchy, Andrew (NY)	Cv	543
Lind, Lawrence (NY)	ObG	571	Litvin, Y. Samuel (NJ)	U	899
Lindenmayer, Jean-Pierre (NY)	Psyc	347	Liu, David (NY)	Nep	227
Lindner, Paul (CT)	A&I	974	Liu, DeLong (NY)	Hem	679
Link, Richard (CT)	Ge	987	Liu, George (NY)	IM	204
Linsenmeyer, Todd (NJ)	U	833	Liva, Douglas (NJ)	Oph	774
Linstrom, Christopher (NY)	Oto	292	Lizza, Eli (NY)	U	395
Lipetz, Jason (NY)	PMR	589	Lo, K.M. Steve (CT)	Onc	999
Lipinsky, Edward (NY)	Oto	639	Lobritto, Steven (NY)	PGe	309
Lipner, Henry (NY)	Nep	470	Lodge, Henry (NY)	IM	205
Lipow, Kenneth (CT)	NS	1001	Lodish, Galya (NY)	IM	683
Lipper, Graeme (CT)	D	980	Lodish, Stephanie (NJ)	Ped	917
Lippman, Alan (NJ)	Onc	816	LoGalbo, Peter (NY)	A&I	609
Lippman, Jay (NY)	Oph	699	Logan, Bruce (NY)	IM	205
Lipschitz, Deborah (CT)	ChAP	979	Lois, William (NY)	S	492
Lipschitz, Robin (NY)	Rhu	371	Lomasky, Steven (NY)	EDM	551

Name	Specialty	Pg	Name	Specialty	Pg
Lombardi, Joseph (NJ)	OrS	874	Lubat, Edward (NJ)	DR	753
Lombardo, Gerard (NY)	Pul	489	Lubell, Harry (NY)	Ped	714
Lombardo, James (NY)	Oph	477	Lubitz, Arthur (NY)	A&I	122
Lombardo, Peter (NY)	D	152	Lublin, Fred (NY)	N	239
Lomnitz, David (CT)	Cv	977	Lubliner, Jerry (NY)	OrS	278
Lomonaco, Salvatore (NY)	ChAP	662	Lucak, Susan (NY)	Ge	175
Lonberg, Mathew (NY)	Onc	612	Lucariello, Richard (NY)	Cv	411
London, Ronald (NY)	Ped	714	Luchs, Jonathan (NY)	DR	550
Longobardi, Raphael (NJ)	OrS	776	Luciani, Richard (NJ)	ObG	818
Lonner, Baron (NY)	OrS	278	Luciano, Daniel (NY)	N	239
Loo, Marcus (NY)	U	395	Ludwig, Shelly (NJ)	Ge	889
Lookstein, Robert (NY)	VIR	400	Lukash, Barbara (NY)	D	666
Lopez, Clark (NY)	FMed	460	Lukash, Frederick (NY)	PlS	592
Lopez, Ralph (NY)	AM	120	Luks, Howard (NY)	SM	725
Lorber, Daniel (NY)	EDM	502	Lumerman, Jeffrey (NY)	U	604
Lorefice, Laurence (CT)	Psyc	1023	Lunt, John (CT)	HS	989
Loren, Gary (NJ)	PM	854	Lusman, Paul (NY)	A&I	621
Loria, Jeffrey (NY)	Ge	175	Lustbader, Andrew (CT)	ChAP	979
Lorich, Dean (NY)	OrS	278	Lustbader, Ian (NY)	Ge	175
LoRusso, Diane (NY)	DR	668	Lustig, Lawrence (NY)	Oto	292
Lottick, Adam (CT)	CE	975	Lutchman, Gordon (NY)	S	531
Loughlin, Gerald (NY)	PPul	316	Lutz, Christopher (NY)	PMR	328
Louie, Eddie (NY)	Inf	195	Lutz, Gregory (NY)	PMR	328
Louis, Elan (CT)	N	239	Lutzker, Letty (NJ)	NuM	818
Loulmet, Didier (NY)	T&CS	388	Lux, Michael (NJ)	IC	954
Love, Barry (NY)	PCd	305	Luxenberg, Douglas (NY)	PCd	582
Love, Charles (NY)	CE	124	Lyden, John (NY)	OrS	278
Lovecchio, John (NY)	GO	556	Lydic, Michael (NY)	RE	647
LoVerme, Paul (NJ)	PlS	828	Lyman, Neil (NJ)	Nep	910
Low, Ronald (NJ)	Oto	778	Lymberis, Stella (NY)	RadRO	362
Lowe, Franklin (NY)	U	395	Lynch, Michael (CT)	OrS	1012
Lowell, Barry (NJ)	Cv	904	Lynn, Robert (NY)	Nep	425
Lowenthal, Dennis (NJ)	Onc	955	Lyon, Claudia (NY)	FMed	460
Lowenthal, Diana (NY)	PPul	711	Lyon, Valerie (NY)	FMed	168
Lowy, Joseph (NY)	Pul	358			
Lozner, Jerrold (NJ)	S	965			
Lu, Bing (NY)	IM	466	**M**		
Lu, Gabriel (NY)	PM	706	Ma, Dong (NY)	PMR	328
Lu, Stanley (NJ)	NRad	893	Macaulay, William (NY)	OrS	278

Name	Specialty	Pg	Name	Specialty	Pg
Maccabee, Paul (NY)	N	473	Malaspina, Dolores (NY)	Psyc	347
Maccia, Clement (NJ)	A&I	948	Maldonado, Thomas (NY)	VascS	404
MacGowan, Daniel (NY)	N	239	Malefatto, Jerry (CT)	Onc	999
Macher, Mark (NJ)	RadRO	882	Malik, Asim (NY)	IM	466
Machler, Brian (NJ)	D	906	Malik, Rubina (NY)	Ger	419
Macina, Lucy (NY)	Ger	556	Malik, Sajid (NY)	Oph	573
Mack, Laurence (NY)	ObG	571	Malits, Bella (NY)	PM	706
MacKay, Cynthia (NY)	Oph	261	Malley, Susan (NY)	ObG	696
MacKenzie, C Ronald (NY)	Rhu	371	Mallozzi, Angelo (CT)	FMed	985
Mackessy, Richard (NJ)	OrS	958	Mally, Pradeep (NY)	NP	225
Mackey, Timothy (NJ)	U	797	Maloney, Patrick (NY)	A&I	654
Mackler, Karen (NY)	D	666	Malovany, Robert (NJ)	Pul	790
Mackool, Richard (NY)	Oph	511	Malpeso, James (NY)	IC	525
Maclaren, Noel (NY)	EDM	164	Maman, Arie (NJ)	EDM	865
Maddalo, Anthony (NY)	OrS	703	Manasseh, Donna-Marie (NY)	S	492
Maddineni, Shekher (NY)	VIR	731	Mancini, Donna (NY)	Cv	130
Maffucci, Leonard (NY)	S	727	Mandava, Suresh (CT)	Oph	1008
Maggio, William (NJ)	NS	892	Mandel, Eric (NY)	Oph	261
Magid, Steven (NY)	Rhu	371	Mandel, Marc (NJ)	S	965
Magill, Richard (NY)	HS	678	Mandel, Michael (NY)	Pul	721
Maglaras, Nicholas (NJ)	IM	954	Mandel, Steven (NY)	N	239
Magner, Joan (CT)	Ped	1019	Mandelbaum, Sidney (NY)	Oph	261
Magramm, Irene (NY)	Oph	261	Manevitz, Alan (NY)	Psyc	347
Magro, Cynthia (NY)	Path	301	Manginello, Frank (NJ)	NP	767
Magun, Arthur (NY)	Ge	175	Mani, John (NY)	OrS	478
Mahal, Pradeep (NJ)	Ge	952	Mani, Susan (CT)	Cv	977
Mahalingam, Banu (NJ)	Cv	847	Maniatis, Theodore (NY)	Pul	530
Maharam, Lewis (NY)	SM	375	Maniscalco, Anthony (NY)	N	473
Maher, Elizabeth (NY)	Oph	261	Manjoney, Delia (CT)	Oph	1008
Maher, John (NY)	ObG	475	Mankes, Seth (NY)	DR	626
Maheshwari, Vivek (NJ)	S	831	Mann, J. John (NY)	Psyc	348
Maier, Herbert (NJ)	D	926	Mann, Ronald (NY)	OrS	703
Mailloux, Lionel (NY)	Nep	566	Mann, Samuel (NY)	IM	205
Maiman, Mitchell (NY)	GO	524	Manners, Richard (NY)	Ped	643
Maiocco, Kenneth (CT)	D	980	Manning, Eric (NJ)	Nep	892
Maizel, Barry (NY)	Ge	461	Manno, Joseph (NJ)	VascS	798
Maki, Robert (NY)	Onc	218	Manolas, Panagiotis (NY)	S	515
Malamud, Stephen (NY)	Onc	218	Mansouri, Hormoz (NY)	S	601
Malanga, Gerard (NJ)	PMR	961	Manvar, Dolly (NY)	A&I	451

Alphabetical Listing of Doctors

Name	Specialty	Pg	Name	Specialty	Pg
Matos, Jeffrey (NY)	CE	125	McClelland, Shearwood (NY)	OrS	279
Matos, Marshall (NY)	Cv	659	McClung, John (NY)	Cv	659
Matossian, Cynthia (NJ)	Oph	852	McConnell, Julie (NJ)	FMed	755
Matta, Raymond (NY)	Cv	130	McConnell, Rachel (NY)	RE	366
Mattana, Joseph (NY)	Nep	566	McConnell, Robert (NY)	EDM	165
Mattes, Leonard (NY)	Cv	130	McCormick, Beryl (NY)	RadRO	362
Matthews, Gerald (NY)	U	729	McCormick, Paul (NY)	NS	231
Mauer, Kenneth (CT)	Ge	987	McCullough, Jock (NJ)	T&CS	795
Maurer, Mathew (NY)	Cv	130	McFarlane-Ferreira, Yvonne (NY)	PGe	482
Mauri, Thomas (NY)	OrS	577	McGinn, Joseph (NY)	T&CS	532
Mauskop, Alexander (NY)	N	239	McGinty, James (NY)	S	381
Maxfield, Roger (NY)	Pul	358	McGovern, Catherine (NY)	ObG	696
May, Louis (NY)	Ge	611	McGovern, Margaret (NY)	CG	624
Mayer, Daniel (NY)	A&I	621	McGovern, Patrick (NJ)	VascS	843
Mayer, Deborah (CT)	IM	993	McGovern, Peter (NJ)	RE	792
Mayer, Elizabeth (NY)	Rhu	371	McGovern, Thomas (NY)	U	396
Mayer, Fern (CT)	D	981	McGowan, Joseph (NY)	Inf	558
Mayer, Ira (NY)	Ge	461	McGrath, Patrick (NY)	Psyc	348
Mayers, Marguerite (NY)	Ped	437	McHugh, Margaret (NY)	Ped	323
Mayers, Martin (NY)	Oph	428	McIlveen, Stephen (NJ)	OrS	777
Mayeux, Richard (NY)	N	240	McKee, Heather (NY)	Oph	699
Mayman, David (NY)	OrS	278	McKenna, Michael (NJ)	RadRO	856
Maytal, Joseph (NY)	ChiN	546	McKhann, Guy (NY)	NS	231
Mazumder, Amitabha (NY)	Onc	218	McKiernan, James (NY)	U	396
Mazza, David (NY)	A&I	123	McKinley, Matthew (NY)	Ge	554
Mazzara, Carl (NJ)	Oto	875	McKinney, James (NJ)	N	871
Mazzola, Catherine (NJ)	NS	911	McKinsey, James (NY)	VascS	405
Mc Inerney, Vincent (NJ)	OrS	929	McLaughlin, Mark (NJ)	NS	851
McAbee, Gary (NJ)	ChiN	837	McLeod, Gavin (CT)	Inf	990
McAleer, Patricia (CT)	D	981	McMahon, Donna-Marie (NY)	Ped	643
McAllister, Peter (CT)	N	1003	McManus, Edward (NJ)	Inf	908
McAnally, James (NJ)	Nep	955	McManus, Susan (NJ)	S	883
McBride, Whitney (NY)	PS	711	McMeeking, Alexander (NY)	Inf	196
McCain, Donald (NJ)	S	794	McMenomey, Sean (NY)	Oto	292
McCalley, Stuart (CT)	Pul	1025	McMullen, Robert (NY)	Psyc	348
McCance, Sean (NY)	OrS	279	McPherson, Craig (CT)	CE	975
McCann, Peter (NY)	OrS	279	Meacham, Kevin (NY)	ObG	696
McCarton, Cecelia (NY)	Ped	323	Mears, John (NY)	Hem	191
McClane, James (CT)	CRS	980	Mechanic, Laura (NY)	A&I	654

Alphabetical Listing of Doctors

Name	Specialty	Pg	Name	Specialty	Pg
Mechanick, Jeffrey (NY)	EDM	165	Melville, Gordon (NJ)	DR	937
Medici, Mark (NY)	OrS	614	Melvin, W. Scott (NY)	S	443
Medina, Emma (NY)	Cv	659	Menchell, David (NY)	A&I	500
Medow, Norman (NY)	Oph	428	Mencin, Ali (NY)	PGe	309
Meed, Steven (NY)	Rhu	371	Mendelowitz, Alan (NY)	Psyc	513
Meere, Patrick (NY)	OrS	279	Mendelowitz, Lawrence (NY)	ObG	697
Megibow, Alec (NY)	DR	159	Mendelsohn, Michael (NY)	PO	585
Mehran, Roxana (NY)	IC	209	Mendelsohn, Sara (NY)	OM	572
Mehrara, Babak (NY)	PlS	336	Mendelson, Joel (NJ)	A&I	948
Mehrishi, Sandeep (NY)	Pul	513	Mendes, Donna (NY)	VascS	405
Mehrotra, Bhoomi (NY)	Onc	564	Mendes, John (NJ)	OrS	821
Mehta, Davendra (NY)	CE	125	Mendoza, Ernesto (NY)	S	515
Mehta, Hasit (NY)	NRad	695	Mendoza, Francis (NY)	OrS	279
Mehta, Lakshmi (NY)	CG	142	Mendoza, Glenn (NY)	NP	612
Mehta, Rajeev (NJ)	NP	870	Menegus, Mark (NY)	Cv	411
Mehta, Viplov (NY)	IM	466	Menezes, Nelson (NY)	VascS	495
Meighan, Dennis (CT)	Ge	987	Menezes, Placido (NY)	OrS	479
Meirowitz, Natalie (NY)	MF	562	Menitove, Stephen (NY)	Pul	617
Meirowitz, Robert (NJ)	Ge	848	Menza, Matthew (NJ)	Psyc	881
Meisenberg, Gene (NY)	U	494	Menzin, Andrew (NY)	GO	556
Meisler, Susan (NY)	Ped	714	Merav, Avraham (NY)	T&CS	728
Meislin, Robert (NY)	OrS	279	Mercando, Anthony (NY)	Cv	659
Meiteles, Lawrence (NY)	Oto	705	Meredith, Gary (NY)	Rhu	598
Meixler, Steven (NY)	Pul	721	Merer, David (NY)	PO	710
Meizlish, Jay (CT)	Cv	978	Merhige, Kenneth (NY)	Oph	262
Mejia, Victor (CT)	IC	996	Merker, Edward (NY)	FMed	671
Melamed, Jonathan (NY)	Path	301	Mermelstein, Erwin (NJ)	Cv	862
Melillo, Nicholas (NJ)	Pul	881	Mermelstein, Harold (NY)	D	666
Mellacheruvu, Smitha (NY)	Onc	688	Mermelstein, Steve (NY)	Pul	596
Meller, Jennifer (NY)	IM	205	Merola, Andrew (NY)	OrS	479
Meller, Jose (NY)	Cv	131	Merrell, Woodson (NY)	IM	205
Mellinger, Brett (NY)	U	604	Merriam, John (NY)	Oph	262
Mellman, Lisa (NY)	Psyc	348	Mesad, Salah (NY)	N	526
Mellow, Ellen (NY)	Cv	131	Messana, Ida (NY)	IM	507
Melman, Martin (NY)	IM	683	Messina, Amanda (NY)	S	727
Melnick, Hugh (NY)	ObG	250	Messina, John (NJ)	PCd	780
Melone, Charles (NY)	HS	188	Messinger, David (NY)	IC	686
Melton, Roberta (NY)	Oph	262	Metz, Dennis (NY)	Oph	477
Meltzer, Alan (NJ)	Ped	917	Metz, John (NJ)	FMed	865

Alphabetical Listing of Doctors

Name	Specialty	Pg	Name	Specialty	Pg
Metzger, Scott (NJ)	PM	895	Miller, David (NJ)	Psyc	962
Metzl, Jordan (NY)	SM	375	Miller, Dennis (NY)	Inf	196
Meyer, David (NY)	T&CS	602	Miller, Jane (NJ)	RE	792
Meyer, Dodi (NY)	Ped	323	Miller, Jeffrey (NJ)	HS	908
Meyer, Monica (NJ)	ObG	773	Miller, Kenneth (CT)	Rhu	1028
Meyer, Richard (NY)	Hem	191	Miller, Kenneth (NJ)	IC	814
Meyers, Barnett (NY)	Psyc	719	Miller, Kevin (CT)	S	1030
Meyers, Marleen (NY)	Onc	218	Miller, Larry (NY)	Ge	554
Meyers, Paul (NY)	PHO	311	Miller, Leslie (CT)	FMed	985
Meyers, Philip (NY)	NRad	244	Miller, Lisa Ann (NJ)	ObG	773
Miarrostami, Rameen (NY)	Pul	489	Miller, Mark (NJ)	U	965
Mich, Robert (NJ)	IC	954	Miller, Philip (NY)	Oto	292
Michaelson, Richard (NJ)	Onc	816	Miller, Rachel (NY)	Pul	358
Michaelson, Stephen (CT)	Cv	978	Miller, Richard (NJ)	Pul	829
Michel, Ketly (NY)	ObG	250	Miller, Seth (CT)	OrS	1013
Michelassi, Fabrizio (NY)	S	381	Miller, Seth (NY)	Ge	554
Michelis, Mary Ann (NJ)	A&I	742	Miller, Theodore (NY)	DR	159
Michelis, Michael (NY)	Nep	227	Miller-Breslow, Anne (NJ)	HS	760
Michels, Robert (NY)	Psyc	348	Mills, Carl (NY)	U	649
Michler, Robert (NY)	T&CS	444	Mills, Christopher (NY)	S	381
Mickley, Diane (CT)	IM	993	Mills, Nancy (NY)	Onc	688
Mickley, Steven (CT)	IM	993	Milman, Perry (NY)	Ge	555
Middlesworth, William (NY)	PS	318	Milone, Richard (NY)	Psyc	719
Middleton, John (NJ)	Inf	868	Milsom, Jeffrey (NY)	CRS	144
Midulla, Peter (NY)	PS	318	Milstein, David (NY)	NuM	427
Mieszerski, Laura (NY)	ObG	697	Mims, Timothy (NY)	PM	615
Mignone, Biagio (NY)	Oph	699	Min, Albert (NY)	Ge	176
Miguel, Eduardo (NJ)	IM	763	Mina, Bushra (NY)	Pul	358
Mikkilineni, Sushmita (NJ)	PPul	825	Mindel, Joel (NY)	Oph	262
Milanaik, Ruth (NY)	Ped	588	Miner, Charles (CT)	IM	993
Milano, Andrew (NY)	Ge	176	Mini, Katherine (CT)	Ped	1019
Miles, Daniel (NY)	ChiN	141	Minikes, Neil (NJ)	A&I	742
Milgraum, Sandy (NJ)	D	864	Minkoff, Howard (NY)	ObG	475
Milgrim, Laurence (NJ)	Oto	778	Minkowitz, Susan (NY)	IM	205
Milite, James (NJ)	Oph	874	Mintz, Abraham (CT)	NS	1002
Miller, Aaron (NY)	N	240	Mintz, Douglas (NY)	DR	159
Miller, Andrew (NJ)	Oto	875	Mintz, Guy (NY)	Cv	544
Miller, Daniel (NY)	FMed	671	Mirante, Rosanna (NY)	Ped	323
Miller, David (NY)	Cv	131	Miskovitz, Paul (NY)	Ge	176

Alphabetical Listing of Doctors

Name	Specialty	Pg	Name	Specialty	Pg
Mitchell, John (NY)	Oph	262	Moorthy, Chitti (NY)	RadRO	722
Mitnick, Hal (NY)	Rhu	371	Moorthy, Lakshmi (NJ)	PRhu	878
Mitnick, Julie (NY)	DR	159	Moqtaderi, Farideh (NY)	PM	299
Mitsumoto, Hiroshi (NY)	N	240	Moraille, Pascale (NJ)	Psyc	842
Mittal, Suneet (NJ)	CE	742	Moreau, Donna (NY)	ChAP	138
Mittleman, Myles (NY)	Oto	512	Morel, Kimberly (NY)	D	152
Mittler, Mark (NY)	NS	567	Morelli, Alan (CT)	Ped	1020
Miyasaka, Kenji (NY)	OrS	279	Morello, Robert (NY)	Oph	700
Mizrachi-Jonisch, Ayelet (NY)	D	666	Moreno, Pedro (NY)	IC	209
Moazed, Kambiz (NY)	Oph	262	Moreta, Henry (NY)	N	635
Modak, Shakeel (NY)	PHO	311	Morgan, Charles (CT)	Psyc	1023
Modi, Vikash (NY)	PO	315	Morgan, Charles (NJ)	Oph	913
Mogan, Glen (NJ)	Ge	810	Morgan, Daniel (NY)	OrS	479
Mogil, Laurey (NY)	Oph	477	Moriarty, Daniel (NJ)	Onc	955
Mohr, JP (NY)	N	240	Moritz, Jacques (NY)	ObG	250
Mohr, Robert (NJ)	ObG	912	Morledge, Louis (NY)	IM	205
Moisa, Idel (NY)	Oto	579	Morman, Manuel (NJ)	D	751
Moldover, Jonathan (NY)	PMR	328	Morris, Elizabeth (NY)	DR	159
Moldwin, Robert (NY)	U	605	Morris, James (NY)	N	694
Mollin, Joel (NY)	DR	502	Morris, Michael (NY)	Onc	219
Molmenti, Ernesto (NY)	S	601	Morrison, Donna (NY)	IM	684
Molnar, Thomas (NY)	FMed	503	Morrison, R. Sean (NY)	Ger	181
Molofsky, Walter (NY)	ChiN	141	Morrison, Susan (NJ)	PA&I	822
Monahan, Marianne (NY)	Nep	691	Morrissey, Nicholas (NY)	VascS	405
Monasebian, Douglas (NY)	PlS	336	Morrow, Monica (NY)	S	382
Mondrow, Daniel (NJ)	Cv	862	Morrow, Robert (NY)	FMed	416
Mone, Suzanne (NJ)	PCd	915	Morrow, Todd (NJ)	Oto	822
Mongillo, Nicholas (CT)	Ped	1020	Mosca, Ralph (NY)	T&CS	389
Monrad, E. Scott (NY)	Cv	412	Moses, Jeffrey (NY)	IC	209
Montalvo Stanton, Evelyn (NJ)	PPul	825	Moses, Stuart (NJ)	DR	809
Montero, Carlos (NY)	OrS	577	Moseson, Michael (NY)	CRS	547
Montgomery, Kenneth (NJ)	OrS	913	Moshe, Solomon (NY)	ChiN	412
Montgomery, Leslie (NY)	S	443	Moskovits, Norbert (NY)	Cv	454
Monti, Louis (NY)	Ped	323	Moskovits, Tibor (NY)	Hem	191
Montoya-Iraheta, Carlos (NY)	PCd	582	Moskowitz, Bruce (NY)	Oph	262
Moore, Anne (NY)	Onc	219	Moskowitz, Craig (NY)	Onc	219
Moore, Frank (NJ)	NS	769	Moskowitz, Craig (NY)	Oph	262
Moore, Joanne (NY)	Psyc	348	Moskowitz, Richard (NJ)	CRS	905
Moorjani, Harish (NY)	Inf	680	Most, Richard (NY)	Oph	700

Alphabetical Listing of Doctors

Name	Specialty	Pg	Name	Specialty	Pg
Motiwala, Rajeev (NY)	N	240	Myssiorek, David (NY)	Oto	292
Motzer, Robert (NY)	Onc	219			
Moucha, Calin (NY)	OrS	279			
Moulton, Thomas (NY)	PHO	434			
Moussa, Ghias (NJ)	Cv	837	**N**		
Moustafellos, Elaine (NJ)	PGe	781	Nachajon, Roberto (NJ)	PPul	930
Moynihan, Brian (NY)	FMed	552	Nachman, Sharon (NY)	PInf	641
Moynihan, Gavan (NY)	D	625	Nackenson, Marcia (NY)	AM	654
Muchnick, Richard (NY)	Oph	263	Nadelman, Robert (NY)	Inf	680
Mueller, F. Carl (CT)	Psyc	1023	Nagarsheth, Nimesh (NY)	GO	185
Mueller, Richard (NY)	Cv	131	Nagler, Harris (NY)	U	396
Muensterer, Oliver (NY)	PS	435	Nagler, Jerry (NY)	Ge	176
Muggia, Franco (NY)	Onc	219	Nahass, Ronald (NJ)	Inf	938
Mukherjee, Tanmoy (NY)	RE	366	Nahm, Frederick (CT)	N	1003
Muldoon, Lawrence (CT)	U	1032	Naidich, David (NY)	DR	160
Muldoon, Thomas (NY)	Oph	263	Naidich, Thomas (NY)	NRad	244
Mulford, Gregory (NJ)	PMR	918	Naidorf, Ellen (CT)	D	981
Mulgaonkar, Shamkant (NJ)	Nep	817	Najarian, James (NJ)	Nep	910
Mulhall, John (NY)	U	396	Najjar, Sessine (NJ)	Inf	927
Mullen, David (CT)	DR	983	Najjar, Souhel (NY)	N	526
Mullen, Edward (NY)	RadRO	597	Naka, Yoshifumi (NY)	T&CS	389
Mullen, Michael (NY)	Inf	196	Nalbandian, Matthew (NY)	VascS	405
Multz, Alan (NY)	Pul	358	Namerow, David (NJ)	Ped	786
Mulvehill, Joseph (NY)	IM	205	Nanus, David (NY)	Onc	219
Mulvey, Lauri (NJ)	Oph	852	Napolitano, Joseph (NJ)	Oph	874
Mumneh, Nayla (NJ)	A&I	862	Napolitano, Massimo (NJ)	VascS	799
Munver, Ravi (NJ)	U	797	Narayana, Ashwatha (CT)	RadRO	1026
Muraca, Glenn (NY)	FMed	503	Narins, Rhoda (NY)	D	667
Murali, Raj (NY)	NS	692	Narula, Amarjot (NJ)	Psyc	789
Murdock, Cynthia (CT)	RE	1028	Narula, Pramod (NY)	PPul	484
Murphy, Ramon (NY)	Ped	323	Nascimento, Joao (CT)	Rhu	1029
Murphy, Robert (NJ)	Ped	895	Nash, Bernard (NY)	Inf	631
Murphy, Robyn (NJ)	DR	906	Nash, Ira (NY)	Cv	131
Murray, Henry (NY)	Inf	196	Nash, Thomas (NY)	IM	358
Murray, Simon (NJ)	IM	850	Nass, Jack (NY)	Psyc	645
Muskin, Philip (NY)	Psyc	349	Nass, Richard (NY)	Oto	292
Musto, Anthony (CT)	Oph	1008	Nassberg, Barton (NJ)	EDM	888
Mutterperl, Mitchell (NJ)	IM	839	Natale, Benjamin (NJ)	Oph	957
Myskowski, Patricia (NY)	D	152	Nath, Sunil (NY)	Pul	513
			Nattis, Richard (NY)	Oph	637

Name	Specialty	Pg	Name	Specialty	Pg
Nauheim, Richard (NY)	Oph	574	Newman, Scott (NY)	PlS	716
Neal, Wendy (NJ)	AM	804	Newman, Stephen (NY)	N	569
Nealon, Nancy (NY)	N	240	Newman-Cedar, Meryl (NY)	Ped	323
Nee, Paul (CT)	Inf	990	Newmark, Ian (NY)	Pul	596
Needleman, Joshua (NY)	PPul	484	Newton, Michael (NY)	Oph	263
Neelakantappa, Kotresha (NY)	Nep	470	Ng, John (NY)	RadRO	362
Neely, Michael (NY)	PMR	328	Ngai, Pakkay (NJ)	PPul	783
Neeson, Francis (CT)	Cv	978	Ngeow, Jeffrey (NY)	PM	299
Nehal, Kishwer (NY)	D	152	Nguyen, Khanh (NY)	T&CS	389
Neibart, Eric (NY)	Inf	196	Nicholas, Stephen (NY)	OrS	280
Neibart, Richard (NJ)	T&CS	898	Nickerson, Katherine (NY)	Rhu	372
Neiman, Deborah (NJ)	IM	939	Nicosia, Thomas (NY)	Cv	544
Neistadt, L Daniel (NY)	DR	160	Niederman, Michael (NY)	Pul	596
Nelson, Alan (CT)	Ge	987	Niesvizky, Ruben (NY)	Hem	191
Nelson, David (NY)	Oph	574	Nightingale, Jeffrey (NY)	Oph	263
Nelson, Deena (NY)	IM	205	Nikias, George (NJ)	Ge	757
Nelson, John (NY)	Hem	679	Nimaroff, Michael (NY)	ObG	571
Nelson, John (NY)	OrS	703	Nini, Kevin (NJ)	PlS	880
Nelson, Judith (NY)	Pul	358	Nininger, James (NY)	Psyc	349
Nelson, William (NY)	ObG	697	Nisonson, Barton (NY)	SM	375
Neophytides, Andreas (NY)	N	240	Nissenblatt, Michael (NJ)	Onc	869
Nepola, Neil (NY)	FMed	523	Nitti, Victor (NY)	U	396
Nercessian, Ohannes (NY)	OrS	280	Nitzberg, Richard (NJ)	S	965
Nero, Thomas (CT)	IC	996	Nizin, Joel (NJ)	CRS	750
Nerwen, Clifford (NY)	Ped	588	Nobert, Craig (NY)	U	396
Neschis, Ronald (NY)	Psyc	719	Nocek, David (CT)	OrS	1013
Neu, Natalie (NY)	PInf	313	Nogueira, Mark (NY)	U	730
Neuberg, Gerald (NY)	Cv	412	Nolan, Sheila (NY)	PInf	709
Neugarten, Joel (NY)	Nep	425	Norden, Richard (NJ)	Oph	774
Neuwirth, Michael (NY)	OrS	280	Nori, Dattatreyudu (NY)	RadRO	362
Nevin, Marie (NJ)	EDM	906	Norton, Larry (NY)	Onc	219
New, Maria (NY)	PEn	307	Nosher, John (NJ)	VIR	884
Newburger, Amy (NY)	D	667	Noskin, Olga (NJ)	N	771
Newcorn, Jeffrey (NY)	ChAP	138	Nosko, Michael (NJ)	NS	870
Newhouse, Jeffrey (NY)	DR	160	Notar-Francesco, Vincent (NY)	Ge	461
Newitz, Deborah (NY)	IM	560	Notaro, Antoinette (NY)	D	625
Newman, Elliot (NY)	S	382	Noto, Richard (NY)	PEn	707
Newman, Fredric (CT)	PlS	1022	Notterman, Robyn (NJ)	D	847
Newman, Lawrence (NY)	N	240	Nouri, Shahin (NY)	N	473

Alphabetical Listing of Doctors

Name	Specialty	Pg	Name	Specialty	Pg
Novack, Stuart (CT)	Rhu	1029	Odel, Jeffrey (NY)	Oph	263
Novick, Brian (NY)	A&I	539	Odrich, Marc (NY)	Oph	429
Novick, Mark (NY)	DR	160	Oeffinger, Kevin (NY)	Ped	323
Novitch, Richard (NY)	Pul	721	Oelberg, David (CT)	Pul	1025
Novogroder, Michael (NJ)	PEn	780	Oestreicher, Mark (CT)	D	981
Nowak, Eugene (NY)	S	382	Offit, Kenneth (NY)	Onc	220
Nowak-Wegrzyn, Anna (NY)	PA&I	303	Oghia, Hady (NY)	Ped	485
Nowakowski, Francis (NY)	VIR	400	Oh, William (NY)	Onc	220
Noy, Ron (NY)	SM	375	Oh, Youn (NJ)	N	872
Noyes, Nicole (NY)	RE	366	Oh, Young (NY)	OrS	703
Nucci, Annamaria (NJ)	Psyc	828	Oko, Piotr (NJ)	Ped	841
Nucci-Sack, Anne (NY)	AM	121	Olanow, C Warren (NY)	N	240
Nunes, Edward (NY)	Psyc	349	Olarte, Marcelo (NY)	N	241
Nurzia, Michael (CT)	U	1032	Olds, David (NY)	Psyc	349
Nussbaum, Michel (NY)	Ge	504	Olichney, John (NY)	IM	206
			Olin, Craig (CT)	IM	993
			Olin, Jeffrey (NY)	Cv	131
			Olsen, Drew (NJ)	Path	779

O

Name	Specialty	Pg	Name	Specialty	Pg
O'Brien, Daryl (NJ)	Ped	786	Olsewski, John (NY)	OrS	430
O'Brien, Francis (NY)	Cv	131	Olson, Robert (NJ)	PlS	942
O'Connell, Joseph (CT)	PlS	1022	Onesti, Stephen (NY)	NS	567
O'Connor, Brian (NJ)	PCd	823	Ong, Lawrence (NY)	IC	633
O'Connor, Owen (NY)	Onc	219	Opler, Lewis (NY)	Psyc	719
O'Dell, Michael (NY)	PMR	328	Oppedisano, Carlyn (NY)	Ped	437
O'Donnell, Timothy (NJ)	Pul	920	Oppenheim, Jeffrey (NY)	NS	613
O'Hagan Sotsky, Carol (NJ)	Inf	761	Oppenheim, Jennifer (NY)	Ped	485
O'Hea, Brian (NY)	S	648	Oppenheimer, Ellen (NJ)	PEn	823
O'Leary, Patrick (NY)	OrS	280	Oppenheimer, John (NY)	IM	632
O'Malley, Grace (NY)	Oph	637	Oratz, Ruth (NY)	Onc	220
O'Malley, Martin (NY)	OrS	280	Orazi, Attilio (NY)	Path	301
O'Regan, Simon (CT)	FMed	985	Orbe, Jessica (NY)	Ped	323
O'Reilly, Eileen (NY)	Onc	220	Orbuch, Philip (NY)	D	152
O'Reilly, Richard (NY)	PHO	312	Ordorica, Steven (NY)	ObG	250
O'Shaughnessy, Althea (NJ)	RE	856	Orentreich, David (NY)	D	152
Ober, David (NY)	N	613	Oribe, Emilio (NY)	N	510
Oberfield, Richard (NY)	Psyc	349	Orlow, Seth (NY)	D	153
Oberfield, Sharon (NY)	PEn	307	Orringer, Robert (NJ)	CRS	807
Obstbaum, Stephen (NY)	Oph	263	Orsher, Stuart (NY)	IM	206
Odaimi, Marcel (NY)	Onc	525	Orsini, William (NJ)	D	888

Alphabetical Listing of Doctors

Name	Specialty	Pg	Name	Specialty	Pg
Parnes, Eliezer (NY)	Nep	470	Pechman, Karen (NY)	PMR	715
Parness, Ira (NY)	PCd	305	Pechman, Paul (NY)	Pul	721
Parrish, Edward (NY)	Rhu	372	Peck, Valerie (NY)	EDM	165
Parry, Michael (CT)	Inf	990	Pecker, Mark (NY)	IM	206
Parulekar, Manisha (NJ)	Ger	758	Pecora, Andrew (NJ)	Onc	766
Pascal, Mark (NJ)	Onc	766	Pedinoff, Andrew (NJ)	A&I	935
Pasik, Deborah (NJ)	Rhu	920	Pedro, Helio (NJ)	CG	749
Pasmantier, Mark (NY)	Onc	220	Pegler, Cynthia (NY)	AM	121
Pasquale, Jack (NY)	IM	507	Pelavin, Martin (NJ)	IM	763
Pasquariello, Palmo (NY)	Ped	324	Pellicci, Paul (NY)	OrS	281
Pass, Harvey (NY)	T&CS	389	Pellicone, John (NY)	Pul	617
Pass, Helen (CT)	S	1030	Pena, Joseph (NY)	RE	647
Pass, Robert (NY)	PCd	432	Peng, Benjamin (NY)	U	397
Passaretti, David (CT)	PlS	1022	Penzer, Jason (NY)	CRS	144
Passeri, Daniel (CT)	S	1030	Pepe, John (NY)	Nep	526
Pastore, Doris (NY)	AM	121	Pereira, Frederick (NY)	D	502
Pastorek, Norman (NY)	Oto	292	Pereira, Stephen (NJ)	S	794
Pastores, Stephen (NY)	Pul	359	Perelstein, Eduardo (NY)	PNep	314
Patchell, Roy (NJ)	N	852	Perez-Soler, Roman (NY)	Onc	423
Patel, Amit (NJ)	VascS	922	Perin, Noel (NY)	NS	232
Patel, Jitendra (NY)	Rhu	491	Perin, Patrick (NJ)	A&I	742
Patel, Neil (NY)	PM	615	Perkel, Charles (NY)	AdP	119
Patel, Nirav (NY)	T&CS	389	Perl, Harold (NJ)	NP	767
Patel, Sanjeev (NJ)	Cv	747	Perlman, Barry (NY)	Psyc	719
Pathare, Pradip (CT)	RadRO	1026	Perlman, David (NY)	Inf	196
Patrick, Sharon (NY)	MF	211	Perlman, Donald (NJ)	A&I	804
Patterson, Francis (NJ)	OrS	821	Perlman, Fern (CT)	Ped	1020
Pattner, Austin (NJ)	Nep	768	Perlman, Jeffrey (NY)	NP	225
Paty, Philip (NY)	S	382	Perlman, Philip (NY)	Oto	579
Paul, Edward (NY)	AdP	119	Perron, Reed (NJ)	N	771
Paul, Elliot (NY)	U	605	Perrotti, John (NY)	PlS	336
Paul, Matthew (CT)	Oph	1009	Perry, Arthur (NJ)	PlS	942
Pavlakis, Steven (NY)	ChiN	456	Perry, Bradford (NY)	Psyc	719
Pavlick, Anna (NY)	Onc	220	Perry, Henry (NY)	Oph	574
Pavlov, Helene (NY)	DR	160	Perry, Richard (NY)	ChAP	138
Pawel, Michael (NY)	Psyc	349	Perry-Bottinger, Lynne (NY)	Cv	660
Pearl, Adam (CT)	Oto	1016	Persky, Mark (NY)	Oto	293
Pearl, Michael (NY)	GO	630	Pesce, Joseph (CT)	D	981
Pearle, Andrew (NY)	OrS	281	Peterson, Monte (NY)	Ger	182

Name	Specialty	Pg	Name	Specialty	Pg
Peterson, Stephen (NY)	IM	466	Pinsky, Steven (NY)	PM	580
Peterson, Thomas (NJ)	NS	769	Pinto, Marguerite (CT)	Path	1017
Petito, Frank (NY)	N	241	Pipia, Paul (NY)	PMR	486
Petrone, Sylvia (NJ)	S	831	Piro, Philip (CT)	Oph	1009
Petrossian, George (NY)	IC	562	Pirzada, Melodi (NY)	PPul	586
Petrotos, Athanassios (CT)	S	1030	Pisarenko, Vadim (NY)	PlS	716
Pettei, Michael (NY)	PGe	584	Piskun, Andrew (NJ)	OrS	875
Peyster, Robert (NY)	NRad	635	Pitchumoni, Capecomorin (NJ)	Ge	866
Pfaff, H Charles (NY)	DR	160	Pitman, Michael (NY)	Oto	293
Pfeffer, Cynthia (NY)	Psyc	349	Pittaro, Denise (CT)	DR	983
Pfeifer, Samantha (NY)	RE	366	Pittaro, Michael (CT)	CE	975
Pfeifer, Tracy (NY)	PlS	336	Pittman, Robert (NJ)	Ge	757
Pfister, David (NY)	Onc	221	Piwoz, Julia (NJ)	PInf	782
Philipp, Claire (NJ)	Hem	867	Pizzarello, Louis (NY)	Oph	637
Phillips, Elizabeth (NY)	Onc	688	Plancher, Kevin (NY)	OrS	281
Phillips, Howard (NY)	Oph	700	Planer, Benjamin (NJ)	NP	767
Phillips, John (NY)	U	730	Plumser, Allan (NJ)	Ge	866
Phillips, Malcolm (NY)	Cv	412	Pochapin, Mark (NY)	Ge	177
Phillips, Robin (NY)	ObG	250	Podell, Richard (NJ)	FMed	951
Phillips, Steven (CT)	IM	993	Podwal, Mark (NY)	D	153
Pianka, George (NY)	HS	678	Pogo, Gustave (NY)	T&CS	602
Picciano, Anne (NJ)	FMed	866	Polatsch, Daniel (NY)	HS	188
Piccione, Paul (NY)	Ge	461	Polifroni, Nicholas (CT)	OrS	1013
Piccirilli, Dora (NY)	FMed	671	Polin, Richard (NY)	NP	225
Pici, Ralph (NY)	PMR	715	Polis, Laurie (NY)	D	153
Picone, Frank (NJ)	A&I	887	Politsky, Jeffrey (NJ)	N	956
Pidoriano, Arthur (NY)	OrS	703	Polkow, Melvin (NJ)	Pul	791
Pieczara, Beata (NJ)	Onc	766	Poll, Joan (CT)	ChAP	979
Pien, Gary (NJ)	PA&I	959	Pollack, Brian (CT)	Cv	978
Pierce, Sean (NJ)	NRad	771	Pollack, Geoffrey (NY)	Oto	293
Pietanza, Maria (NY)	Onc	221	Pollack, Jed (NY)	RadRO	362
Pilchik, Robert (NY)	Cv	660	Pollack, Joshua (CT)	Psyc	1023
Pile-Spellman, John (NY)	NRad	570	Pollack, Shoshannah (NJ)	D	926
Pincus, Emile (NJ)	ChAP	749	Pollak, Joseph (NJ)	FMed	838
Pincus, Robert (NY)	Oto	293	Pollina, Robert (NY)	VascS	650
Pines, Jeffrey (NY)	Psyc	350	Pollock, Alan (NY)	Inf	196
Pinke, James (CT)	Oph	1009	Pollock, Jeffrey (NJ)	N	956
Pinke, Robert (NJ)	Oph	913	Pollock, Roger (NJ)	OrS	777
Pinney, Sean (NY)	Cv	132	Pollowitz, James (NY)	A&I	655

Alphabetical Listing of Doctors

Name	Specialty	Pg	Name		Pg
Polsky, Bruce (NY)	Inf	196	Prabhu, H. Sudhakar (NY)	Cv	454
Pomerantz, Daniel (NY)	IM	684	Prager, Kenneth (NY)	Pul	359
Pomp, Alfons (NY)	S	382	Prakash, Anaka (NJ)	Ge	838
Ponamgi, Suri (NJ)	PlS	788	Preis, Oded (NY)	Ped	486
Poneros, John (NY)	Ge	177	Preminger, Mark (NJ)	CE	743
Ponterio, Jane (NY)	ObG	527	Prenner, Jonathan (NJ)	Oph	874
Pontoriero, Michael (NJ)	T&CS	932	Press, Robert (NY)	Inf	197
Poole, John (NJ)	S	794	Presti, Paul (NJ)	Oto	959
Poon, Eric (NY)	Ped	324	Presti, Salvatore (NY)	PCd	305
Poon, Michael (NY)	Cv	132	Preter, Maurice (NY)	Psyc	350
Poplausky, Maurice (NY)	DR	668	Pretto, Zorayda (NY)	EDM	670
Popp, Beth (NY)	H & PM	464	Preven, David (NY)	Psyc	350
Poppas, Dix (NY)	Ped Uro	319	Prezant, David (NY)	Pul	441
Popper, Laura (NY)	Ped	324	Prezioso, Paula (NY)	Ped	324
Porder, Joseph (NY)	IM	206	Price, Andrew (NY)	OrS	281
Poretsky, Leonid (NY)	EDM	165	Price, Thomas (NY)	Cv	660
Porges, Andrew (NY)	Rhu	599	Primas, Ronald (NY)	IM	206
Port, Abraham (NY)	DR	550	Prince, Alice (NY)	PInf	313
Port, Elisa (NY)	S	382	Prince, Andrew (NY)	Oph	264
Port, Jeffrey (NY)	T&CS	390	Prince, Martin (NY)	DR	161
Portlock, Carol (NY)	Onc	221	Principe, David (NJ)	MF	764
Portnay, Edward (CT)	IC	996	Prine, Linda (NY)	FMed	168
Portnoy, William (NY)	Oto	293	Prioleau, Philip (NY)	D	153
Porwancher, Richard (NJ)	Inf	849	Procaccino, John (NY)	CRS	547
Posada, Roberto (NY)	PInf	313	Prockop, Susan (NY)	PHO	312
Posner, David (NY)	Pul	359	Proskin, Wendy (NY)	Ped	714
Posner, Jerome (NY)	N	241	Provenzano, Anthony (NY)	Onc	688
Posner, Marshall (NY)	Onc	221	Provet, John (NY)	U	397
Possick, Paul (NJ)	D	751	Pruzan-Clain, Debra (CT)	D	981
Post, Kalmon (NY)	NS	232	Pruzansky, Mark (NY)	HS	188
Post, Martin (NY)	Cv	132	Pryor, Aurora (NY)	S	648
Postell, Scott (NY)	ObG	475	Prystowsky, Janet (NY)	D	153
Pothuri, Bhavana (NY)	GO	185	Prywes, Arnold (NY)	Oph	574
Potter, Hollis (NY)	DR	160	Przybylski, Gregory (NJ)	NS	871
Potter, William (CT)	Oph	1009	Puccio, Carmelo (NY)	Onc	688
Potters, Louis (NY)	RadRO	597	Pucillo, Anthony (NY)	Cv	660
Powell, Charles (NY)	Pul	359	Puder, Douglas (NY)	Ped	616
Powell, Jeffrey (NY)	EDM	670	Puglisi, Jeffrey (CT)	IM	993
Poynor, Elizabeth (NY)	GO	185	Pujol-Morato, Fernando (NY)	Inf	464

Alphabetical Listing of Doctors

Name	Specialty	Pg	Name	Specialty	Pg
Rashba, Eric (NY)	CE	621	Reidy, Kimberly (NY)	PNep	435
Rashbaum, Ira (NY)	PMR	329	Reiffel, Robert (NY)	PlS	716
Raska, Anna (NJ)	IM	908	Reilly, James (NY)	ObG	527
Raska, Karel (NJ)	Cv	904	Reilly, John (NY)	OrS	528
Raskin, Elsa (CT)	PlS	1022	Reiner, Dan (NY)	S	601
Raskin, Jonathan (NY)	Pul	359	Reiner, Mark (NY)	S	382
Raskin, Keith (NY)	HS	188	Reinitz, Elizabeth (NY)	Rhu	724
Rathauser, Robert (NJ)	ObG	873	Reisberg, Barry (NY)	GerPsy	182
Ratner, Desiree (NY)	D	153	Reisner, Michelle (NJ)	Ger	838
Ratner, Ina (NY)	IM	467	Reison, Dennis (NJ)	Cv	747
Ratner, Lloyd (NY)	S	382	Reizis, Igal (NY)	ObG	475
Ratner, Lynn (NY)	Onc	221	Rekate, Harold (NY)	NS	567
Raucher, Harold (NY)	Ped	324	Relkin, Norman (NY)	N	241
Ravitz, Alan (NY)	ChAP	138	Relland, Maureen (NY)	Oph	264
Rawlins, Bernard (NY)	OrS	281	Remy, Prospere (NY)	Ge	418
Ray, Audell (NY)	Oph	700	Rennert, Nancy (CT)	EDM	983
Rayfield, Elliot (NY)	EDM	165	Rentrop, K. Peter (NY)	Cv	132
Raymond, Gerald (NJ)	Ped	855	Repice, Michael (NY)	Rhu	647
Raza, Azra (NY)	Onc	221	Reppucci, Vincent (CT)	Oph	1009
Razaboni, Rosa (NY)	PlS	336	Resmovits, Marvin (NY)	Ped	588
Raziuddin, Khaja (NJ)	NP	767	Resor, Louise (CT)	N	1003
Rebarber, Andrei (NY)	MF	212	Respler, Don (NJ)	PO	782
Recht, Michael (NY)	DR	161	Resta, Christine (NY)	EDM	459
Rechter, Lesley (NY)	FMed	552	Rettig, Michael (NY)	HS	188
Reckler, Jon (NY)	U	397	Reuter, Victor (NY)	Path	301
Reda, Dominick (NY)	Nep	691	Reyfman, Leonid (NY)	PM	481
Reda, Edward (NY)	Ped Uro	712	Rezac, Craig (NJ)	CRS	863
Reddy, Mallikarjuna (NY)	FMed	503	Rezvani, Fred (NJ)	ObG	773
Redling, Theresa (NJ)	Ger	811	Rhee, Robert (NY)	VascS	495
Redner, Arlene (NY)	PHO	584	Rho, Dae (NY)	PMR	329
Rednor, Jeffrey (NJ)	FMed	848	Ribakove, Greg (NY)	T&CS	493
Rees, Ellen (NY)	Psyc	350	Riccio, Gioia (CT)	DR	983
Regard, Monique (NY)	ObG	697	Rice, Stephen (NJ)	SM	898
Reich, Raymond (NY)	Oph	477	Rich, Daniel (NY)	OrS	577
Reich, Steven (NJ)	OrS	875	Rich, Glenn (CT)	EDM	984
Reicher, Oscar (NJ)	OrS	929	Richards, Steven (NJ)	U	884
Reichman, Bonnie (NY)	Onc	221	Richardson, William (NJ)	Psyc	962
Reichstein, Robert (NY)	Cv	132	Richel, Peter (NY)	Ped	714
Reid, Malcolm (NY)	PMR	329	Richheimer, Michael (NY)	A&I	621

Alphabetical Listing of Doctors

Name	Specialty	Pg	Name	Specialty	Pg
Richlin, Spencer (CT)	RE	1028	Robinson, Michael (NY)	PMR	616
Richman, Daniel (NY)	PM	299	Robinson, Newell (NY)	T&CS	602
Richstone, Lee (NY)	U	605	Roboz, Gail (NY)	Onc	222
Richter, Edwin (CT)	PMR	1021	Robson, Mark (NY)	Onc	222
Ricketti, Anthony (NJ)	A&I	847	Roca, Dominic (CT)	Pul	1025
Ridge, Gerald (NY)	IM	684	Rochelson, Burton (NY)	MF	562
Rie, Jonathan (NY)	IM	684	Rochford, Joseph (NJ)	Psyc	942
Rieber, Jonathan (NY)	Ge	177	Rockman, Caron (NY)	VascS	405
Rieber, Michael (NJ)	OrS	821	Rodeo, Scott (NY)	SM	375
Riechers, Roger (NY)	U	730	Rodgers, I. Rand (NY)	Oph	264
Rieder, Jessica (NY)	AM	409	Rodino, William (NY)	VascS	533
Rieger, Jill (NY)	IM	206	Rodke, Gae (NY)	ObG	251
Rieger, Kenneth (NJ)	OrS	913	Rodriguez, Eduardo (NY)	PlS	336
Rieger, Mark (NJ)	OrS	913	Rodriguez, Jose (NY)	OrS	282
Rifkin, Matthew (NY)	DR	550	Rodriguez, Lorna (NJ)	GO	867
Rigel, Darrell (NY)	D	153	Rodriguez-Sains, Rene (NY)	Oph	264
Rigolosi, Robert (NJ)	Nep	768	Roelke, Marc (NJ)	CE	805
Riina, Howard (NY)	NS	232	Rogal, Gary (NJ)	Cv	806
Ring, Kenneth (NJ)	U	965	Rogers, David (NY)	VIR	516
Ritch, Robert (NY)	Oph	264	Rohr, Michele (CT)	ObG	1006
Ritter, Jill (NJ)	Rhu	830	Rokhsar, Cameron (NY)	D	154
Ritterband, David (NY)	Oph	264	Rokhsar, Michael (NJ)	DR	950
Rivadeneira, David (NY)	CRS	547	Rokito, Andrew (NY)	SM	375
Rivera, Jeanette (CT)	ObG	1006	Roland, J. Thomas (NY)	Oto	293
Rivera, Yadyra (NJ)	Onc	766	Roland, Robert (NJ)	Inf	953
Riviello, James (NY)	ChiN	141	Rolandelli, Rolando (NJ)	S	921
Rizk, Nabil (NY)	T&CS	390	Romagnoli, Mario (NY)	Inf	197
Rizk, Samieh (NY)	Oto	293	Roman, Ashley (NY)	MF	212
Rizvi, Naiyer (NY)	Onc	221	Romanelli, John (NY)	Oph	638
Robbins, David (NY)	Ge	177	Romanello, Paul (NY)	Cv	132
Robbins, John (NY)	NS	692	Romano, Alicia (NY)	PEn	708
Robbins, Kim (CT)	Oph	1009	Romano, Angela (NY)	PCd	582
Robbins, Michael (NY)	Cv	500	Romano, John (NY)	D	154
Robbins, Noah (NY)	Inf	421	Romano, Rosario (NY)	IM	632
Roberti, M. Isabel (NJ)	PNep	824	Romeu, Jose (NY)	Ge	177
Roberts, J Kirk (NY)	N	241	Romita, Mauro (NY)	PlS	336
Roberts, Larry (NY)	U	730	Rommer, James (NJ)	IM	813
Roberts, Matthew (NY)	OrS	282	Ronen, Alon (CT)	Cv	978
Robilotti, James (NY)	Ge	177	Roose, Steven (NY)	Psyc	350

Name	Specialty	Pg	Name	Specialty	Pg
Root, Barry (NY)	PMR	589	Rosenberg, Michael (NY)	PInf	434
Rosa, Joseph (CT)	EDM	984	Rosenberg, Michael (NJ)	N	872
Rosa, Richard (NJ)	OrS	821	Rosenberg, Remi (CT)	IM	994
Rosch, Elliott (NY)	IM	684	Rosenberg, Vladimiro (NY)	S	383
Rose, Donald (NY)	OrS	282	Rosenberg, Zehava (NY)	DR	161
Rose, Elliott (NY)	PlS	337	Rosenblatt, Joshua (NJ)	Ped	826
Rose, Howard (NY)	OrS	282	Rosenblatt, William (NY)	PlS	337
Rose, John (NJ)	U	899	Rosenblum, Bruce (NJ)	NS	892
Rose, Michael (NJ)	PlS	897	Rosenblum, Marc (NY)	Path	301
Rose, Roberta (CT)	Rhu	1029	Rosenbluth, Benjamin (NJ)	RadRO	791
Rosell, Frank (NY)	T&CS	532	Rosenbluth, Richard (NJ)	Onc	766
Rosello, Lori (NY)	Ped	324	Rosenfeld, Alvin (CT)	ChAP	979
Roseman, Bruce (NY)	ChiN	664	Rosenfeld, David (NJ)	Psyc	789
Rosemarin, Jack (NY)	Ge	675	Rosenfeld, David (NJ)	DR	864
Rosen, Allen (NJ)	PlS	828	Rosenfeld, Richard (NY)	PO	484
Rosen, Arie (NJ)	Oto	778	Rosenfeld, Stanley (NY)	DR	161
Rosen, Arnold (NY)	Psyc	350	Rosenfeld, Suzanne (NY)	Ped	324
Rosen, Bruce (NY)	Psyc	645	Rosenfeld, Walter (NJ)	AM	903
Rosen, Douglas (NY)	D	414	Rosenkilde, Carl (NY)	N	694
Rosen, Evelyn (NY)	GerPsy	462	Rosenn, Barak (NY)	MF	212
Rosen, Jeffrey (NY)	SM	514	Rosenstein, Elliot (NJ)	Rhu	964
Rosen, Michael (NY)	Nep	691	Rosenstein, Roger (NJ)	HS	760
Rosen, Nedra (NY)	IM	206	Rosenstock, Arthur (CT)	PlS	1022
Rosen, Norman (NY)	Onc	689	Rosenstreich, David (NY)	A&I	409
Rosen, Robert (NY)	VIR	401	Rosenthal, David (NY)	EDM	552
Rosenbaum, Alfred (NY)	RadRO	363	Rosenthal, Jeanne (NY)	Oph	264
Rosenbaum, Jeffrey (NJ)	Oto	875	Rosenthal, Jesse (NY)	Psyc	350
Rosenbaum, Marlon (NY)	Cv	133	Rosenthal, Kenneth (NY)	Oph	574
Rosenbaum, Michael (NY)	Ped	324	Rosenthal, Richard (NY)	Psyc	350
Rosenbaum, Pearl (NY)	Oph	429	Rosenthal, Sheldon (NY)	U	494
Rosenbaum, Robert (NJ)	EDM	951	Rosenwaks, Zev (NY)	RE	366
Rosenberg, Benjamin (NY)	D	667	Rosenwasser, Melvin (NY)	HS	188
Rosenberg, Craig (NY)	PMR	644	Roses, Daniel (NY)	S	383
Rosenberg, David (NY)	Oto	293	Rosewater, Karen (NY)	AM	121
Rosenberg, Gene (NJ)	U	797	Rosh, Joel (NJ)	PGe	916
Rosenberg, Howard (NY)	Inf	197	Rosman, Lawrence (NY)	EDM	502
Rosenberg, Kenneth (NY)	AdP	119	Rosner, Bruce (NJ)	Ge	848
Rosenberg, Michael (NY)	PlS	717	Rosner, Louis (NY)	Oto	579
Rosenberg, Michael (NJ)	Oph	774	Rosner, Richard (NY)	Psyc	350

Name	Specialty	Pg	Name	Specialty	Pg
Rosner, Saran (NY)	NS	692	Rubin, Cheryl (NY)	OrS	615
Rosovsky, Mark (CT)	NRad	1003	Rubin, David (NY)	CE	655
Ross, Jody (NY)	Ped	714	Rubin, David (NY)	Inf	506
Ross, Marc (NY)	PMR	486	Rubin, Kenneth (NJ)	Psyc	897
Ross, Stephen (NY)	Psyc	351	Rubin, Kenneth (NJ)	Ge	757
Rossakis, Constantine (NJ)	Cv	747	Rubin, Laurence (NY)	Oph	574
Rossi, Dennis (NY)	DR	550	Rubin, Lorry (NY)	PInf	585
Rossman, Barry (NJ)	U	857	Rubin, Marc (NJ)	Ge	849
Rossos, Apostolos (NJ)	Oto	894	Rubin, Moshe (NY)	Ge	177
Roston, Alfred (NY)	Ge	676	Rubin, Steven (NY)	Oph	574
Roth, Alan (NY)	FMed	503	Rubinoff, Mitchell (NJ)	Ge	757
Roth, Andrew (NY)	Psyc	351	Rubinstein, Arye (NY)	A&I	410
Roth, Douglas (NY)	PlS	717	Rubinstein, Boris (NY)	ChAP	662
Roth, Jeffrey (NY)	D	154	Rubinstein, Morton (NY)	Psyc	351
Roth, Joseph (NJ)	Ge	757	Rucker, Steve (NY)	IM	560
Roth, Neil (NY)	SM	375	Ruddy, Michael (NJ)	Nep	851
Roth, Patrick (NJ)	NS	769	Ruderman, Marvin (NJ)	N	818
Roth, Philip (NY)	NP	525	Rudick, Albert (NY)	Oph	265
Roth, Richard (NY)	Cv	609	Rudikoff, Donald (NY)	D	414
Rothberg, Charles (NY)	Oph	638	Rudin, Eric (NY)	EDM	670
Rothberg, Robert (NJ)	CRS	807	Rudman, Michael (NJ)	PM	914
Rothenberg, Susan (NY)	ObG	251	Rudolph, Daniel (CT)	Pul	1025
Rothman, Howard (NJ)	Cv	748	Rudolph, Steven (NY)	N	474
Rothman, Jeffrey (NY)	EDM	523	Rudy, Bret (NY)	AM	121
Rothschild, Michael (NY)	PO	315	Ruffo, Scott (NJ)	CE	743
Rothschild, Rachel (CT)	Ped	1020	Ruggiero, Joseph (NY)	Onc	222
Rothstein, Stephen (NY)	Oto	294	Ruiz, Carlos (NY)	Cv	133
Rotman, Marvin (NY)	RadRO	490	Rundback, John (NJ)	VIR	798
Rotolo, James (NJ)	U	899	Ruoff, Michael (NY)	Ge	177
Rowley, Scott (NJ)	Hem	760	Ruotolo, Charles (NY)	OrS	577
Roychowdhury, Sudipta (NJ)	NRad	872	Ruotolo, Rachel (NY)	PlS	592
Roye, David (NY)	OrS	282	Rusch, Valerie (NY)	T&CS	390
Rozanski, Alan (NY)	Cv	133	Rush, Thomas (NY)	Inf	680
Rozanski, Reuben (NJ)	D	808	Rusk, Alice (CT)	N	1003
Rozbruch, Jacob (NY)	OrS	282	Russakoff, L. Mark (NY)	Psyc	719
Rozbruch, S. Robert (NY)	OrS	282	Russell, Linda (NY)	Rhu	372
Rozenblit, Alla (NY)	DR	414	Russell, Robin (NY)	Ger	419
Rubenstein, Andrew (NJ)	ObG	773	Russell, Shereen (NY)	ObG	251
Rubenstein, Jack (NY)	IM	560	Russo, John (NJ)	IM	814

Alphabetical Listing of Doctors

Name	Specialty	Pg	Name	Specialty	Pg
Russo, Paul (NY)	U	397	Sadovsky, Richard (NY)	FMed	460
Rutenberg, Kathryn (NY)	ObG	251	Saenger, Paul (NY)	PEn	708
Rutkovsky, Edward (NY)	Cv	544	Safai, Bijan (NY)	D	154
Rutkovsky, Lisa (NY)	PCd	512	Safdieh, Joseph (NY)	N	241
Ruzal-Shapiro, Carrie (NY)	DR	161	Saffra, Norman (NY)	Oph	477
Ryback, Hyman (NY)	Oto	705	Safirstein, Benjamin (NJ)	Pul	829
Rydzinski, Mayer (NY)	Cv	501	Safran, Steven (NJ)	Oph	853
Rynn, Moira (NY)	ChAP	138	Sagar, Yogesh (NJ)	Cv	748
Ryu, Samuel (NY)	RadRO	646	Sage, Jacob (NJ)	N	872
			Sagorin, Charles (NJ)	Onc	816
			Saha, Prantik (NY)	Ped	325
			Sahar, David (NY)	Cv	412

S

Name	Specialty	Pg	Name	Specialty	Pg
Saada, Simon (NY)	U	494	Saidi, James (NJ)	U	833
Saal, Stuart (NY)	Nep	227	Saiman, Lisa (NY)	PInf	314
Sabatino, Dominick (NY)	PHO	585	Saland, Jeffrey (NY)	PNep	314
Sabbatini, Paul (NY)	Onc	222	Salazer, Thomas (NJ)	Nep	768
Sabetta, James (CT)	Inf	990	Saleh, Anthony (NY)	Pul	489
Sabharwal, Sanjeev (NJ)	OrS	821	Salem, Noel (NJ)	Rhu	793
Sable, Robert (NY)	Ge	418	Salerno, William (NJ)	Cv	748
Sabnani, Indu (NJ)	Hem	812	Sales, Clifford (NJ)	VascS	966
Saboeiro, Gregory (NY)	VIR	401	Salgado, Miran (NY)	N	474
Sabra, Mona (NY)	EDM	165	Salifu, Moro (NY)	Nep	470
Sabry, M. Zakir (NY)	PIS	337	Salik, Erez (CT)	DR	983
Sacco, Margaret (NJ)	S	965	Salik, James (NY)	Ge	178
Sachs, Paul (CT)	Pul	1025	Salimi, Mostafa (NJ)	Cv	925
Sachs, R. Gregory (NJ)	Cv	949	Salky, Barry (NY)	S	383
Sachs, Ronald (NJ)	Oph	913	Salmon, Jane (NY)	Rhu	372
Sachs, Stephen (NJ)	N	956	Salsitz, Edwin (NY)	IM	206
Sacker, Ira (NY)	Ped	324	Saltz, Leonard (NY)	Onc	222
Sacks, Michael (NY)	Psyc	351	Saltzman, Daniel (NY)	MF	212
Sacks, Steven (NY)	Oto	294	Saltzman, Martin (NY)	Nep	691
Sadan, Sara (NY)	Onc	689	Saltzman-Gabelman, Lori (NY)	IM	684
Sadanandan, Swayam (NY)	PHO	483	Salvati, Eduardo (NY)	OrS	282
Sadarangani, Balvinder (NY)	ObG	251	Salwitz, James (NJ)	Onc	939
Sadeghi, Hooshang (NJ)	N	839	Salz, Alan (NJ)	Oph	940
Sadeghi, Hossein (CT)	PPul	1018	Salzer, Richard (NJ)	OrS	777
Sadeghi-Nejad, Hossein (NJ)	U	797	Salzer, Stephen (CT)	Oto	1016
Sadiq, Saud (NY)	N	241	Salzman, Jacqueline (NY)	Oph	700
Sadock, Virginia (NY)	Psyc	351	Salzman, Ronnie (NY)	ObG	571

Name	Specialty	Pg	Name	Specialty	Pg
Sama, Andrew (NY)	OrS	283	Santilli, John (CT)	A&I	974
Samach, Michael (NJ)	Ge	907	Santolaya, Joaquin (NJ)	CG	887
Samadi, David (NY)	U	397	Saphier, Carl (NJ)	MF	764
Samadi, Sharyar (NJ)	PO	783	Saponara, Eduardo (NY)	Onc	689
Samanich, John (CT)	ChAP	979	Sara, Gabriel (NY)	Onc	222
Samberg, Eslee (NY)	Psyc	351	Sarabanchong, Voravut (NY)	ObG	510
Sami, Sherif (NY)	Psyc	594	Saraiya, Narendra (NJ)	Ped	961
Sampson, Hugh (NY)	PA&I	303	Sarnoff, Deborah (NY)	D	549
Sampson, Steven (NY)	OrS	639	Saroff, Alan (NJ)	Cv	806
Samra, Said (NJ)	PlS	897	Sarokhan, Alan (NJ)	OrS	958
Samson, C. Michael (NY)	Oph	265	Sas, Norman (NY)	S	443
Samsonov, Dmitry (NY)	PNep	709	Sasso, Louis (NY)	Pul	531
Samuels, Jonathan (NY)	Rhu	372	Sasson, Homayoun (NY)	PlS	592
Samuels, Steven (NJ)	Psyc	789	Sassoon, Robert (NY)	ObG	251
Samuelson, Robert (CT)	ObG	1006	Satnick, Steven (NY)	A&I	621
San Roman, Gerardo (NY)	ObG	636	Sauberman, Roy (NJ)	CE	805
Sanchez, Miguel (NJ)	Path	779	Sauer, Mark (NY)	RE	366
Sanchez-Catanese, Betty (NJ)	IM	939	Saul, Zane (CT)	Inf	990
Sander, Howard (NY)	N	242	Saulino, Patrick (NJ)	Cv	936
Sander, Norbert (NY)	IM	422	Saunders, Craig (NJ)	T&CS	832
Sanders, Abraham (NY)	Pul	359	Savage, David (NY)	Hem	192
Sanders, Leslie (NJ)	AM	948	Savatsky, Gary (NJ)	SM	793
Sanders, Linda (NJ)	DR	809	Savatta, Domenico (NJ)	U	833
Sanderson, Rhonda (NJ)	ObG	940	Savino, Michael (NY)	U	532
Sanderson, Scott (CT)	NS	1002	Savino, Robert (CT)	EDM	984
Sandhaus, Jeffrey (NY)	U	516	Sawczuk, Ihor (NJ)	U	797
Sandhu, Fatejeet (CT)	VIR	1033	Sawyer, David (NY)	Psyc	351
Sandhu, Harvinder (NY)	OrS	283	Scaccia, Frank (NJ)	Oto	894
Sandhu, Jaspreet (NY)	U	397	Scaduto, Philip (NJ)	IM	908
Sandler, Benjamin (NY)	ObG	251	Scardino, Peter (NY)	U	397
Sandoval, Claudio (NY)	PHO	709	Scarpa, Nicholas (NJ)	Rhu	842
Sands, Andrew (NY)	OrS	283	Scartozzi, Richard (CT)	Oph	1009
Sanelli, Pina (NY)	NRad	570	Schachne, Jeffrey (NY)	D	667
Sanford, Marie (NY)	Ped	325	Schaebler, David (NJ)	Onc	850
Sanger, Joseph (NY)	NuM	246	Schaefer, Steven (NY)	Oto	294
Sanghavi, Seema (CT)	RadRO	1027	Schaeffer, Janis (NY)	PPul	586
Sangiorgio, Maria (NY)	N	694	Schaeffer, Mark (NJ)	IM	850
Santamaria, Jaime (NJ)	Oph	874	Schaer, Teresa (NJ)	IM	869
Santarosa, Richard (CT)	U	1032	Schaffner, Adam (NY)	PlS	337

Alphabetical Listing of Doctors

Name	Specialty	Pg	Name	Specialty	Pg
Schanler, Richard (NY)	NP	565	Schleider, Michael (NJ)	Onc	766
Schantz, Stimson (NY)	Oto	294	Schleifer, Steven (NJ)	Psyc	828
Schanzer, Bernard (NJ)	N	956	Schleiter, Gary (CT)	Inf	990
Schanzer, Robert (NJ)	Cv	862	Schlesinger, Scott (NJ)	DR	864
Scharf, Richard (NJ)	Oto	959	Schlessinger, David (NY)	Oph	574
Scharf, Robert (NY)	Psyc	351	Schliftman, Alan (NY)	D	667
Scharf, Stephen (NY)	NuM	246	Schluger, Neil (NY)	Pul	359
Schattman, Glenn (NY)	RE	367	Schlussel, Richard (NY)	Ped Uro	319
Schaul, Neil (NY)	N	569	Schmerin, Michael (NY)	Ge	178
Schechter, Justin (CT)	Psyc	1023	Schmidt, Hans (NJ)	S	794
Schechter, Michael (CT)	ObG	1006	Schmidt-Sarosi, Cecilia (NY)	RE	367
Schechter, Miriam (NY)	Ped	437	Schmierer, Jeffrey (CT)	Cv	978
Scheer, Max (NY)	Inf	559	Schnabel, Freya (NY)	S	383
Schefer, Alan (NY)	HS	678	Schneck, Gideon (NY)	Oph	638
Schein, Jonah (NY)	Psyc	351	Schneebaum, Cary (NY)	Ge	178
Scheiner, Jonathan (NY)	VIR	532	Schneider, Darren (NY)	VascS	405
Scheinerman, Samuel Jacob (NY)	T&CS	602	Schneider, Jeffrey (NY)	Onc	564
Scher, David (NY)	OrS	283	Schneider, Kenneth (NY)	Oto	294
Scher, Howard (NY)	Onc	222	Schneider, Lewis (NY)	Ge	178
Scher, Jonathan (NY)	ObG	251	Schneider, Marcie (CT)	AM	973
Scherer, Susan (NJ)	Ped	917	Schneider, Robert (NY)	Onc	689
Scherl, Ellen (NY)	Ge	178	Schneider, Samuel (NJ)	Psyc	856
Scherl, Michael (NJ)	Oto	778	Schneider, Stephen (NJ)	EDM	865
Scherl, Sharon (NJ)	D	751	Schneider, Steven (NY)	IM	206
Scherr, Douglas (NY)	U	397	Schob, Clifford (NJ)	OrS	821
Schiano, Thomas (NY)	Ge	178	Schoenberg, Mark (NY)	U	444
Schiff, Carl (NY)	Rhu	491	Schonfeld, Steven (NJ)	NRad	872
Schiff, Howard (NY)	U	398	Schor, Joshua (NJ)	Ger	811
Schiff, Jonathan (NY)	U	398	Schottenstein, Douglas (NY)	PM	299
Schiff, Peter (NY)	RadRO	363	Schrager, Alan (NY)	U	730
Schiff, Russell (NY)	PCd	582	Schreiber, Carl (NY)	Cv	544
Schiff, William (NY)	Oph	265	Schreiber, Klaus (NY)	ChAP	662
Schiffer, Mark (NY)	Cv	133	Schreiber, Michael (NY)	Pul	721
Schiller, Myles (NY)	PCd	432	Schrier, Amilia (NY)	Oph	265
Schiller, Robert (NY)	FMed	168	Schroeder, Karl (NY)	Psyc	617
Schiowitz, Emanuel (NY)	FMed	460	Schubach, Scott (NY)	T&CS	603
Schiz, Steven (CT)	Ped	1020	Schubert, Hermann (NY)	Oph	265
Schlam, Everett (NJ)	FMed	810	Schubert, Romaine (NY)	ChiN	456
Schlegel, Peter (NY)	U	398	Schulder, Michael (NY)	NS	567

Alphabetical Listing of Doctors

Name	Specialty	Pg	Name	Specialty	Pg
Schulhafer, Edwin (NJ)	A&I	935	Schweitzer, Mark (NY)	DR	626
Schulman, Ira (NY)	Cv	133	Schweizer, William (NY)	ObG	252
Schulman, Matthew (NY)	PlS	337	Schwinn, Hans (NY)	FMed	628
Schulman, Norman (NY)	PlS	337	Scibetta, Maria (NJ)	IM	763
Schulster, Rita (NY)	Pul	596	Scigliano, Eileen (NY)	Hem	192
Schultz, Barbara (NY)	Pul	359	Scimeca, Michael (NY)	AdP	119
Schultz, Neal (NY)	D	154	Sciortino, Patrick (NY)	Oph	477
Schulze, Paul (NY)	Cv	133	Scioscia, Kenneth (NY)	Oto	579
Schulze, Ruth (NJ)	ObG	773	Sclafani, Anthony (NY)	Oto	294
Schuss, Steven (NJ)	Ped	786	Sclafani, Lisa (NY)	S	648
Schuster, Edward (CT)	Cv	978	Sclafani, Michael (NJ)	SM	898
Schuster, Joseph (NJ)	IM	763	Scofield, Lisa (NJ)	Ped	930
Schuster, Michael (NY)	Hem	630	Scoppetuolo, Michael (NJ)	Onc	816
Schwab, Frank (NY)	OrS	283	Scott, John (NY)	Oto	705
Schwarcz, Robert (NY)	Oph	265	Scott, Richard (NJ)	RE	943
Schwartz, Allan (NY)	Cv	133	Scott, W Norman (NY)	OrS	283
Schwartz, Amit (NY)	NS	471	Scriven, Richard (NY)	PS	642
Schwartz, Bruce (NY)	Psyc	440	Scuderi, Giles (NY)	OrS	283
Schwartz, Charles (NY)	Cv	521	Sculco, Thomas (NY)	OrS	284
Schwartz, David (NY)	RadRO	490	Scully, Brian (NY)	Inf	197
Schwartz, Evan (NY)	OrS	511	Seaman, Cheryl (NY)	Psyc	352
Schwartz, Gary (NY)	Ge	555	Seaver, Robert (NY)	ChAP	662
Schwartz, Jeffrey (NY)	OrS	283	Seebacher, J Robert (NY)	OrS	703
Schwartz, Joel (NY)	NRad	614	Seedor, John (NY)	Oph	265
Schwartz, Joseph (NJ)	EDM	754	Seelagy, Marc (NJ)	Pul	856
Schwartz, Judith (NY)	ObG	251	Segal, Robert (NY)	Cv	134
Schwartz, Lawrence (NY)	DR	161	Segal-Maurer, Sorana (NY)	Inf	506
Schwartz, Louis (NJ)	RadRO	963	Segarra, Pedro (NY)	ObG	637
Schwartz, Mark (NY)	PlS	337	Seideman, Bruce (NY)	OrS	577
Schwartz, Michael (NY)	Psyc	645	Seiden, Howard (NY)	PCd	305
Schwartz, Myron (NY)	S	383	Seidenberg, Roy (NY)	D	154
Schwartz, Paula (NY)	Onc	564	Seidman, Barry (NJ)	U	965
Schwartz, Robert (NJ)	D	808	Seidman, Mitchell (NY)	Oph	478
Schwartz, Theodore (NY)	NS	232	Seigel, Mark (NJ)	ObG	893
Schwartz, William (NY)	Cv	133	Seigel, Warren (NY)	AM	451
Schwartzfarb, Lanny (NY)	Rhu	372	Seinfeld, David (NY)	Cv	134
Schwartzman, Alexander (NY)	S	493	Seinfeld, Fredric (NJ)	T&CS	857
Schwarz, Steven (NY)	PGe	482	Seiter, Karen (NY)	Onc	689
Schweiger, Eric (NY)	D	154	Selesnick, Samuel (NY)	Oto	294

Alphabetical Listing of Doctors

Name	Specialty	Pg	Name	Specialty	Pg
Seliger, Glenn (NY)	N	614	Shamamian, Peter (NY)	S	443
Selinger, Sharon (NJ)	EDM	951	Shamoon, Fayez (NJ)	Cv	806
Selman, Jay (NY)	N	427	Shamoon, Harry (NY)	EDM	415
Selter, Jared (CT)	IC	996	Shampain, Lawrence (NJ)	ChAP	863
Seltzer, Terry (NY)	EDM	165	Shams, Joseph (NY)	VIR	401
Selvaggi, Thomas (NJ)	A&I	742	Shanahan, Andrew (NJ)	IC	850
Selwyn, Peter (NY)	IM	422	Shane, Elizabeth (NY)	EDM	166
Selzer, Jeffrey (NY)	Psyc	594	Shani, Jacob (NY)	IC	468
Seminara, Donna (NY)	Ger	524	Shapir, Yehuda (NY)	PCd	582
Sen, Chandranath (NY)	NS	232	Shapiro, Barry (NY)	Oto	705
Sender, Joel (NY)	Pul	441	Shapiro, Bruce (CT)	Psyc	1023
Seneviratne, Aruna (NY)	SM	376	Shapiro, Ellen (NY)	Ped Uro	319
Sensakovic, John (NJ)	Inf	868	Shapiro, Jeffrey (NY)	OrS	577
Seplowitz, Alan (NY)	EDM	166	Shapiro, Kenneth (NY)	Nep	613
Serby, Michael (NY)	GerPsy	182	Shapiro, Lawrence (NY)	EDM	552
Serels, Scott (CT)	U	1032	Shapiro, Marc (NY)	S	648
Sergiou, Harry (NY)	Ped	486	Shapiro, Mark (NJ)	DR	753
Serin, Craig (CT)	IM	994	Shapiro, Michael (NJ)	S	832
Serle, Janet (NY)	Oph	265	Shapiro, Michael (NY)	D	458
Serur, Eli (NY)	GO	463	Shapiro, Neil (NY)	Ge	676
Sethi, Paul (CT)	OrS	1013	Shapiro, Peter (NY)	Psyc	352
Sett, Suvro (NY)	T&CS	728	Shapiro, Richard (NY)	S	383
Setton, Avi (NY)	NRad	570	Shapiro, Warren (NY)	Nep	470
Setzen, Michael (NY)	Oto	579	Sharaby, Jacob (NY)	U	494
Sgaglione, Nicholas (NY)	OrS	577	Sharan, Alok (NY)	OrS	430
Sgouros, Anthony (NY)	Ge	676	Sharma, Samin (NY)	IC	210
Shaari, Christopher (NJ)	Oto	778	Sharma, Sheel (NY)	PlS	338
Shabsigh, Ridwan (NY)	U	398	Sharon, David (NJ)	Onc	891
Shabto, Uri (NY)	Oph	266	Sharpe, Arleen (NY)	FMed	671
Shack, Robert (NJ)	S	831	Shatkin, Jess (NY)	ChAP	139
Shafer, David (NY)	PlS	338	Shaw, Jason (NY)	T&CS	493
Shafizadeh, Farshad (NY)	U	516	Shaw, Ronda (NY)	Psyc	352
Shah, Darsit (NJ)	Oto	894	Shaw-Brachfeld, Jennifer (NJ)	Ped	918
Shah, Jatin (NY)	S	383	Shayani, Steven (NY)	Cv	544
Shah, Paresh (NY)	S	383	Shear, Perry (CT)	NS	1002
Shah, Pritesh (NJ)	Psyc	789	Shebairo, Raymond (NY)	OrS	577
Shah, Smita (NJ)	Pul	829	Sheikh, Shahid (NY)	Cv	660
Shahabi, Shohreh (CT)	GO	988	Shein, Leon (NY)	Nep	471
Shahid, Syed (CT)	NS	1002	Sheinart, Kara (NY)	N	242

Name	Specialty	Pg	Name	Specialty	Pg
Sheinfeld, Joel (NY)	U	398	Shindler, Daniel (NJ)	Cv	863
Shell, Roger (NJ)	Cv	862	Shinnar, Shlomo (NY)	ChiN	413
Shelmet, John (NJ)	EDM	848	Shlofmitz, Richard (NY)	Cv	544
Shelton, Ronald (NY)	D	154	Shohet, Michael (NY)	Oto	295
Shemen, Larry (NY)	Oto	294	Shugar, Joel (NY)	Oto	295
Shemtov, M Mendel (NY)	U	398	Shukla, Gunjan (NJ)	CE	743
Shenoy, Rajesh (NY)	PCd	432	Shulman, Julius (NY)	Oph	266
Shepard, Barry (NY)	U	605	Shulman, Melanie (NY)	N	242
Shepard, Richard (NY)	FMed	168	Shulman, Yale (NJ)	U	842
Shepherd, Gillian (NY)	A&I	123	Shum, Kee (NY)	Onc	509
Sher, Ellen (NJ)	A&I	887	Shumko, John (NJ)	PMR	827
Sherbany, Ariel (NY)	ChiN	609	Shupack, Jerome (NY)	D	155
Sheris, Steven (NJ)	Cv	949	Shuren, Neal (NY)	HS	611
Sherling, Bruce (NY)	Pul	722	Shypula, Gregory (NJ)	Onc	869
Sherman, Alex (NY)	Ge	178	Sibony, Patrick (NY)	Oph	638
Sherman, Frederic (NY)	IM	467	Sibrack, Laurence (CT)	D	981
Sherman, Howard (NY)	Ge	418	Sicherer, Scott (NY)	PA&I	303
Sherman, Iris (NY)	IM	206	Sicklick, Marc (NY)	A&I	540
Sherman, John (NY)	PlS	338	Sicuranza, Genevieve (NY)	MF	562
Sherman, Richard (NJ)	Nep	870	Siderides, Elizabeth (CT)	Oph	1010
Sherman, Scott (NY)	DR	550	Sidoti, Paul (NY)	Oph	266
Sherman, Spencer (NY)	Oph	266	Siegal, Elliot (NY)	Ped	616
Sherman, Steven (NY)	Oph	478	Siegal, Michael (NY)	Cv	134
Sherman, Warren (NY)	Cv	134	Siegel, Abby (NY)	Onc	223
Sherr, David (NY)	RadRO	490	Siegel, Andrew (NJ)	U	797
Sherry, Stephen (NJ)	EDM	926	Siegel, Beth (NY)	S	515
Sheth, Parag (NY)	PMR	329	Siegel, Daniel (NY)	D	625
Sheth, Sujit (NY)	PHO	312	Siegel, David (NY)	VIR	606
Shetty, Sudhakar (CT)	GerPsy	988	Siegel, Eric (NJ)	D	808
Shevell, Tracy (CT)	MF	997	Siegel, Judy (NY)	U	730
Shieh, Sherry (NY)	D	154	Siegel, Marc (NY)	IM	207
Shifrin, Seth (NY)	SM	725	Siegel, Robert (NY)	CCM	413
Shike, Moshe (NY)	Ge	178	Siegel, Stephen (NY)	Cv	134
Shikowitz, Mark (NY)	Oto	579	Siegler, Eugenia (NY)	Ger	182
Shim-Chang, Helen (NY)	D	155	Siepser, Stuart (NJ)	Cv	925
Shimony, Rony (NY)	Cv	134	Sierocki, John (NJ)	Onc	850
Shin, Edward (NY)	Oto	295	Siever, Larry (NY)	Psyc	352
Shin, Helen (NJ)	D	751	Siglock, Timothy (NY)	Oto	705
Shinbach, Kent (NY)	Psyc	352	Silberman, Mark Illan (NY)	PlS	592

Alphabetical Listing of Doctors

Name	Specialty	Pg	Name	Specialty	Pg
Silbert, Glenn (NJ)	Oph	774	Simonian, Gregory (NJ)	VascS	799
Silbert, Paul (NJ)	N	893	Simons, Grant (NJ)	CE	743
Silberzweig, James (NY)	VIR	401	Simonson, Barry (NY)	OrS	578
Silich, Robert (NY)	PIS	338	Simotas, Alexander (NY)	PMR	329
Silva, Raul (NY)	ChAP	662	Simpson, David (NY)	N	242
Silva, Waldemar (NJ)	IM	909	Simpson, Lynn (NY)	MF	212
Silver, Bennett (NJ)	Psyc	962	Simpson, Roger (NY)	PIS	592
Silver, David (NY)	U	494	Singer, Lewis (NY)	PCCM	432
Silver, Jonathan (NY)	Psyc	352	Singer, Mark (NY)	IM	632
Silver, Lester (NY)	PIS	338	Singer, Samuel (NY)	S	384
Silver, Michael (NY)	Cv	660	Singh, Anup (NJ)	PNep	878
Silverberg, Arnold (NY)	EDM	459	Singh, Avtar (NY)	N	694
Silverberg, Nanette (NY)	D	155	Singh, Bhuvanesh (NY)	Oto	295
Silverberg, Shonni (NY)	EDM	166	Singhal, Pravin (NY)	Nep	566
Silverman, Amy (NY)	ChAP	663	Sink, Ernest (NY)	OrS	284
Silverman, Bernard (NY)	A&I	451	Sinnreich, Abraham (NY)	Oto	528
Silverman, David (NY)	IM	207	Sippel, Kimberly (NY)	Oph	266
Silverman, Frank (NY)	ObG	252	Sipzner, Robert (NJ)	Nep	817
Silverman, Jill (NY)	Rhu	373	Siris, Ethel (NY)	EDM	166
Silverman, Joel (NY)	Pul	514	Siskind, Steven (NY)	Cv	501
Silverman, Lawrence (NJ)	PEn	915	Sisti, Michael (NY)	NS	232
Silverman, Lewis (NY)	Onc	223	Sivak, Mark (NY)	N	242
Silverman, Mark (NY)	D	549	Sivitz, Jennifer (NJ)	PEn	824
Silverman, Mitchell (NJ)	EDM	951	Sklar, Charles (NY)	PEn	307
Silverman, Robert (NJ)	PM	779	Sklar, Jeffrey (NY)	D	549
Silverman, Ronald (NY)	N	694	Sklarek, Howard (NY)	Pul	646
Silverman, Rubin (NY)	Cv	412	Sklarin, Nancy (NY)	Onc	223
Silvershein, Daniel (NY)	IM	207	Sklaroff, Herschel (NY)	Cv	134
Simberkoff, Michael (NY)	Inf	197	Sklower, Jay (NJ)	FMed	838
Similon, Philippe (NY)	Ped	325	Sklower Brooks, Susan (NJ)	CG	863
Simmons, Rache (NY)	S	383	Skolnick, Lawrence (NJ)	NP	910
Simon, Beth (NY)	ObG	697	Skolnik, Richard (NY)	PIS	338
Simon, Clifford (NJ)	Pul	791	Skopicki, Hal (NY)	Cv	623
Simon, Jonathan (NJ)	Rhu	830	Skripak, Justin (NJ)	A&I	742
Simon, Lloyd (NY)	IM	632	Skripkus, Aldona (NJ)	Ped	841
Simon, Scott (CT)	NS	1002	Skrokov, Robert (NY)	D	625
Simon, Sheldon (NY)	OrS	284	Skupski, Daniel (NY)	MF	508
Simon, Steven (NY)	D	458	Slakter, Jason (NY)	Oph	266
Simon, Todd (NY)	IM	467	Slama, Robert (NJ)	Cv	949

Name	Specialty	Pg	Name	Specialty	Pg
Slamovits, Thomas (NY)	Oph	429	Smithy, William (NY)	CRS	624
Slankard, Marjorie (NY)	A&I	123	Smoller, Alison (NJ)	Ped	896
Slaten, Warren (NY)	PMR	616	Smotkin, David (NY)	GO	420
Slater, Gary (NY)	S	384	Smotrich, Gary (NJ)	PlS	855
Slater, James (NY)	IC	210	Snepar, Richard (NJ)	Inf	868
Slater, Jonathan (NY)	ChAP	663	Snow, Robert (NY)	NS	232
Slater, William (NY)	Cv	134	Snowball, Halina (CT)	PMR	1021
Slavin, Kevin (NJ)	PInf	782	Snyder, Barbara (NJ)	AM	861
Slavit, David (NY)	Oto	295	Snyder, David (NY)	N	242
Slim, Jihad (NJ)	Inf	812	Snyder, Gary (NY)	Oto	579
Sloane, Lori (NY)	Rhu	724	Snyder, Michael (CT)	PCd	1017
Slogoff, Frederick (CT)	IM	994	Snyder, Stephen (NY)	Psyc	352
Slotwiner, David (NY)	CE	540	Soave, Rosemary (NY)	Inf	197
Slovin, Susan (NY)	Onc	223	Sobel, Howard (NY)	D	155
Slupchynskyj, Oleh (NY)	Oto	295	Sobol, Norman (NY)	N	474
Small, Eric (NY)	SM	725	Sockolow, Robbyn (NY)	PGe	309
Small, Robert (NY)	OrS	704	Sofair, Jane (NJ)	Psyc	962
Small, Steven (NY)	OrS	704	Sofer, Alfred (CT)	PlS	1022
Smallberg, Gerald (NY)	N	242	Soff, Gerald (NY)	Hem	192
Smerling, Neil (CT)	IM	994	Soffen, Edward (NJ)	RadRO	882
Smilen, Scott (NY)	ObG	252	Soffer, Jeffrey (NJ)	ObG	957
Smiles, Stephen (NY)	Rhu	373	Sofocleous, Constantinos (NY)	VIR	401
Smith, Craig (NY)	T&CS	390	Softness, Barney (NY)	Ped	325
Smith, Edward (NY)	Oph	478	Sogani, Pramod (NY)	U	398
Smith, Harriet (NY)	GO	420	Sohn, Won (NY)	Ge	461
Smith, Joann (CT)	Psyc	1024	Soifer, Todd (NY)	OrS	479
Smith, Jonathan (NY)	Oto	431	Sokal, Myron (NY)	NP	469
Smith, Julia (NY)	Onc	223	Sokol, Sergio (NY)	Cv	545
Smith, Lee (NY)	PO	586	Soletic, Raymond (NY)	Oto	579
Smith, Leon (NJ)	MF	815	Solitar, Bruce (NY)	Rhu	373
Smith, Leon (NJ)	Inf	813	Sollinger, Jonathan (CT)	Ped	1020
Smith, Mark (NY)	PlS	338	Solny, Meyer (NY)	Ge	179
Smith, Paul (NY)	Inf	197	Solomon, Gary (NY)	Rhu	373
Smith, Peter (NJ)	VIR	843	Solomon, Gregory (NY)	IM	207
Smith, Peter (NY)	Pul	489	Solomon, Ira (NY)	Oph	700
Smith, Richard (NY)	Oto	431	Solomon, Jennifer (NY)	PMR	329
Smith, Robin (NY)	ChiN	546	Solomon, Joel (NY)	Oph	266
Smith, Sharon (NY)	IM	207	Solomon, Robert (NY)	NS	233
Smith, Stephen (NJ)	Inf	813	Solomon, Robert (NJ)	Ger	953

Alphabetical Listing of Doctors

Name	Specialty	Pg	Name	Specialty	Pg
Solomon, Sherry (NY)	Oph	700	Spears, Thomas (NY)	U	649
Solomon, Stephen (NY)	VIR	401	Spector, Jason (NY)	PlS	338
Solomon, William (NY)	Hem	463	Speiser, Phyllis (NY)	PEn	583
Soloway, Bruce (NY)	FMed	417	Spektor, Vadim (NJ)	DR	809
Soloway, Gregory (CT)	Ge	987	Spencer, Elizabeth Kay (NY)	ChAP	139
Solowiejczyk, David (NJ)	PCd	780	Spencer, Eric (NY)	OrS	704
Soltren, Rafael (NY)	IM	684	Spera, John (CT)	RadRO	1027
Som, Peter (NY)	DR	161	Sperber, Laurence (NY)	Oph	267
Sommer, Robert (NY)	PCd	305	Sperber, Steven (NJ)	Inf	761
Somogyi, Anthony (NY)	IM	507	Sperling, David (NY)	VIR	401
Sonett, Joshua (NY)	T&CS	390	Sperling, Neil (NY)	Oto	528
Song, Christopher (NY)	Oto	480	Spero, Marc (NY)	IM	207
Sonnenblick, Emily (NY)	DR	161	Speyer, James (NY)	Onc	223
Sonoda, Toyooki (NY)	CRS	144	Spicehandler, Debra (NY)	Inf	680
Sonoda, Yukio (NY)	GO	185	Spiegel, Alan (NY)	Cv	135
Sonpal, Girish (NY)	Rhu	514	Spiegel, Michael (CT)	Rhu	1029
Sood, Sunil (NY)	PInf	585	Spielberg, Alan (NY)	Ge	629
Sorbera, Carmine (NY)	CE	655	Spielman, Joel (NJ)	OrS	914
Soren, Karen (NY)	AM	121	Spielvogel, David (NY)	T&CS	728
Soriano, John (NJ)	Ge	907	Spiera, Harry (NY)	Rhu	373
Soroko, Theresa (NJ)	Inf	813	Spiera, Robert (NY)	Rhu	373
Sorra, Toomas (NY)	Ge	461	Spigland, Nitsana (NY)	PS	318
Soskel, Neil (NY)	FMed	552	Spiler, Ira (NJ)	EDM	865
Soslow, Robert (NY)	Path	302	Spindola-Franco, Hugo (NY)	DR	415
Sosulski, Richard (NY)	Ped	644	Spinelli, Henry (NY)	PlS	339
Soter, Nicholas (NY)	D	155	Spinnell, Mitchell (NJ)	Ge	758
Sotolongo, Anays (NJ)	Pul	881	Spinowitz, Bruce (NY)	Nep	509
Sotsky, Gerald (NJ)	Cv	748	Spira, Robert (NJ)	Ge	811
Sousa, Rolando (NJ)	ChiN	749	Spitalewitz, Samuel (NY)	Nep	471
Southern, D (NJ)	A&I	935	Spitz, Henry (NY)	Psyc	352
Southren, David (NY)	Cv	609	Spivack, Julie (CT)	Ge	987
Souweidane, Mark (NY)	NS	233	Spivak, Jeffrey (NY)	OrS	284
Spadaro, Louise (NY)	Cv	545	Spivak, William (NY)	PGe	309
Spaide, Richard (NY)	Oph	266	Splain, Shepard (NY)	OrS	479
Spak, James (CT)	OrS	1013	Spriggs, David (NY)	Onc	223
Spandorfer, Steven (NY)	RE	367	Sproviero, Joseph (CT)	A&I	974
Spano, Frank (CT)	IM	994	Squitieri, Rafael (CT)	T&CS	1031
Sparano, Joseph (NY)	Onc	424	Staats, Peter (NJ)	PM	895
Sparr, Steven (NY)	N	427	Stabile, John (NJ)	Oph	774

Name	Specialty	Pg	Name	Specialty	Pg
Staeger-Hirsch, Christine (NY)	DR	669	Stein, Mitchell (NY)	Oph	700
Staffenberg, David (NY)	PlS	339	Stein, Perry (NY)	PMR	486
Stafford, John (NY)	NP	690	Stein, Peter (NY)	HS	557
Stallone, James (NY)	IM	632	Stein, Randy (NY)	EDM	670
Stam, Lawrence (NY)	Nep	471	Stein, Richard (NY)	Cv	135
Stambuk, Hilda (NY)	NRad	245	Stein, Ruth (NY)	Ped	438
Stancliff, Sharon (NY)	FMed	168	Stein, Sidney (NY)	Pul	360
Stanford, Paulette (NJ)	AM	804	Stein, Stefan (NY)	Psyc	352
Stangel, John (NY)	RE	723	Steinbaum, Suzanne (NY)	Cv	135
Staradub, Valerie (CT)	S	1030	Steinberg, Harry (NY)	Pul	596
Starc, Thomas (NY)	PCd	305	Steinberg, Jonathan (NJ)	CE	743
Starke, Charles (NY)	IM	684	Steinberg, L Gary (NY)	PCd	305
Starker, Isaac (NJ)	PlS	919	Steinberger, Alfred (NJ)	NS	769
Starker, Paul (NJ)	S	965	Steingart, Richard (NY)	Cv	135
Starkman, Harold (NJ)	PEn	916	Steinhagen, Randolph (NY)	CRS	145
Starpoli, Anthony (NY)	Ge	179	Steinherz, Laurel (NY)	PCd	306
Starr, Amy (NY)	PRhu	317	Steinherz, Peter (NY)	PHO	312
Starr, Christopher (NY)	Oph	267	Stelwagon, Jennifer (NY)	AdP	120
Starr, Michael (NY)	Oph	267	Stelzer, Paul (NY)	T&CS	390
Staszewski, Harry (NY)	Hem	557	Stern, Harvey (NY)	DR	415
Statter, Mindy (NY)	PS	436	Stern, Leonard (NY)	Nep	227
Steckel, Rebecca (NJ)	FMed	937	Stern, Marla (NY)	Ped	325
Steele, Andrew (NY)	NP	565	Stern, Richard (NY)	Rhu	373
Steele, Mark (NY)	Oph	267	Sternschein, Michael (NJ)	PlS	788
Steer, Robert (NJ)	ObG	912	Stevens, Randy (NY)	RadRO	722
Steever, John (NY)	AM	121	Stewart, Allan (NY)	T&CS	391
Steiger, David (NY)	Pul	360	Stewart, Michael (NY)	Oto	295
Steigman, Elliot (NJ)	U	842	Stidham, Katrina (NY)	Oto	705
Stein, Adam (NY)	PMR	589	Stieg, Philip (NY)	NS	233
Stein, Alan (NY)	Inf	465	Stifelman, Michael (NY)	U	399
Stein, Arnold (NY)	Oph	478	Stiller, Robert (CT)	MF	998
Stein, Barry (NY)	Ped	325	Stilwell, Anne (NY)	PM	528
Stein, Daniel (NY)	RE	367	Stock, Jeffrey (NJ)	Ped Uro	826
Stein, David (NY)	Ge	418	Stock, Richard (NY)	RadRO	363
Stein, Jeffrey (NY)	Ge	179	Stollman, Yacov (NY)	Ge	461
Stein, Jeffrey (NY)	VascS	405	Stone, Gregg (NY)	IC	210
Stein, Joel (NY)	PMR	330	Stone, Joanne (NY)	MF	212
Stein, Lawrence (NJ)	Ge	907	Stone, Michael (NY)	Psyc	353
Stein, Mark (NY)	U	398	Stoopler, Mark (NY)	Onc	224

Alphabetical Listing of Doctors

Name	Specialty	Pg	Name	Specialty	Pg
Storch, Kenneth (NJ)	IM	909	Sullivan, James (NY)	Rhu	599
Storch-Smith, Lori (CT)	Ped	1020	Sullivan, Scott (CT)	NRad	1003
Storper, Ian (NY)	Oto	295	Sullivan, Timothy (NY)	Psyc	530
Story, Daryl (CT)	N	1003	Sullum, Stanford (NY)	ObG	252
Stoupakis, George (NJ)	Cv	748	Sultan, Khalid (NY)	RE	367
Stovell, Peter (CT)	OrS	1013	Sultan, Mark (NY)	PlS	339
Stover-Pepe, Diane (NY)	Pul	360	Sultan, Ronald (NJ)	S	842
Strain, James (NY)	Psyc	353	Sun, Shyan (NJ)	NP	816
Strair, Roger (NJ)	Hem	868	Sunaryo, Francis (NJ)	PGe	824
Strange, Theodore (NY)	IM	524	Sundaram, Revathy (NY)	PHO	483
Strashun, Arnold (NY)	NuM	474	Sundaresan, Narayan (NY)	NS	233
Strassberg, Barbara (NY)	Ped	438	Sung, Kap-Jae (NY)	S	515
Strauch, Robert (NY)	HS	188	Sunku, Bhanu (NY)	PGe	708
Straus, David (NY)	Onc	224	Sunshine, Robert (NY)	U	605
Strauss, Barry (NY)	Onc	634	Suri, Ranjit (NY)	CE	125
Strauss, Edward (CT)	VIR	1033	Surks, Martin (NY)	EDM	415
Stringel, Gustavo (NY)	PS	711	Surow, Jason (NJ)	Oto	778
Stroh, Jack (NJ)	Cv	936	Susman, Jonathan (NY)	VIR	402
Strome, Marshall (NY)	Oto	296	Sussman, Barry (NJ)	S	794
Strongwater, Allan (NJ)	OrS	929	Sussman, Norman (NY)	Psyc	353
Strongwater, Richard (NY)	FMed	672	Sussman, Robert (NJ)	Pul	963
Strutin, Millard (NJ)	S	921	Sutton, Ira (NY)	FMed	672
Stubblefield, Michael (NY)	PMR	330	Suzman, Michael (NY)	PlS	717
Stuchin, Steven (NY)	OrS	284	Svitra, Paul (NY)	Oph	575
Stuebgen, Joerg-Patrick (NY)	N	242	Swedler, Jane (NY)	AM	538
Sturm, Richard (NY)	Oph	575	Swee, David (NJ)	FMed	866
Sturza, Jeffrey (NY)	D	667	Sweeney, Eugene (NJ)	D	752
Stylianos, Steven (NY)	PS	318	Sweeney, Tanya-Marie (NY)	ChiN	664
Su, Edwin (NY)	OrS	284	Swerdlow, Michael (NY)	N	427
Suda, Anjuli (NJ)	Ped	918	Swiderski, Deborah (NY)	IM	422
Sudhakar, Telechery (NJ)	Nep	851	Swidler, Mark (NY)	Nep	228
Sugarman, Lynn (NJ)	Ped	786	Swift, Richard (NY)	PlS	339
Suggs, William (NY)	VascS	732	Swiller, Hillel (NY)	Psyc	353
Suh, Leejee (NY)	Oph	267	Swirsky, Michael (NY)	DR	669
Sukumaran, Muthiah (NY)	Pul	360	Swistel, Alexander (NY)	S	384
Sulica, Radu (NY)	Oto	296	Swistel, Daniel (NY)	T&CS	391
Sullivan, Catherine (NY)	Rhu	514	Sy-Kho, Rosemarie (NY)	ChiN	546
Sullivan, Christina (NY)	Ped	438	Syed, Tariqshah (NJ)	IC	763
Sullivan, James (NY)	CRS	547	Szabo, Albert (NY)	N	694

Name	Specialty	Pg	Name	Specialty	Pg
Szeto, Marjorie (CT)	ObG	1006	Tassiopoulos, Apostolos (NY)	VascS	650
			Taub, Cynthia (NY)	Cv	412
			Taub, Peter (NY)	PlS	339
T			Taubin, Howard (CT)	Ge	987
Tabachnick, John (NJ)	FMed	951	Taubman, Lowell (NY)	IM	560
Tabar, Viviane (NY)	NS	233	Tavill, Michael (NJ)	PO	895
Tabbal, Nicolas (NY)	PlS	339	Tay, Steven (NY)	IM	207
Tabershaw, Richard (NY)	OrS	639	Taylor, Howard (NJ)	Oto	914
Taffet, Berton (NJ)	OrS	914	Taylor, James (NY)	T&CS	649
Taffet, Sanford (NY)	Ge	676	Taylor, Noel (NY)	Psyc	353
Tagawa, Scott (NY)	Onc	224	Taylor, Robert (NJ)	GO	812
Taikowski, Richard (CT)	Cv	978	Te, Alexis (NY)	U	399
Taitsman, James (NJ)	OrS	854	Tedjarati, Sean (NY)	GO	678
Tal, Avraham (NY)	IM	467	Teffera, Fassil (NY)	IM	422
Talamini, Mark (NY)	S	648	Tehrany, Armin (NY)	OrS	284
Talansky, Arthur (NY)	Ge	555	Teichholz, Louis (NJ)	Cv	748
Talansky, Marvin (NJ)	Oph	894	Tello, Celso (NY)	Oph	267
Tallia, Alfred (NJ)	FMed	866	Telzak, Edward (NY)	Inf	421
Tallman, Martin (NY)	Hem	192	Tempera, Patrick (NJ)	Ge	953
Talmor, Mia (NY)	PlS	339	Temple, Larissa (NY)	CRS	145
Tamerin, John (CT)	Psyc	1024	Tenenbaum, Joseph (NY)	Cv	135
Tamler, Ronald (NY)	EDM	166	Tenet, William (NY)	Cv	545
Tan, Reynaldo (NY)	Nep	471	Teng, Marita (NY)	Oto	296
Tan, Virak (NJ)	HS	812	Tenner, Michael (NY)	NRad	695
Tancredi, Laurence (NY)	Psyc	353	Teodorescu, Victoria (NY)	VascS	405
Taneja, Samir (NY)	U	399	Teperman, Lewis (NY)	S	384
Tanenbaum, Diane (NY)	D	155	Tepler, Isidore (CT)	Onc	999
Tang, David (NY)	IM	684	Tepler, Melvin (NY)	OrS	479
Tank, Lisa (NJ)	Ger	759	Teplitz, Glenn (NY)	HS	557
Tantawi, Mohamed (NJ)	Ped	786	Tepper, Howard (NJ)	PlS	962
Tanzer, Floyd (NJ)	D	926	Terjanian, Terenig (NY)	Onc	525
Tap, William (NY)	Onc	224	Terraciano, Anthony (NY)	Oph	429
Tarantino, Debra (NJ)	CRS	807	Terrone, Dom (NJ)	MF	815
Tarasuk, Albert (NY)	U	516	Teusink, J. Paul (NY)	Psyc	353
Tarkin, Howard (NY)	Cv	660	Tewari, Ashutosh (NY)	U	399
Tartaglia, Joseph (NY)	Cv	660	Theofanidis, Stylianos (CT)	NP	1000
Tartell, Jay (NY)	DR	502	Thomas, Byron (CT)	IM	994
Tartini, Albert (NJ)	Nep	768	Thomas, David (NY)	PMR	330
Tartter, Paul (NY)	S	384	Thomas, Mark (NY)	PMR	438

Alphabetical Listing of Doctors

Name	Specialty	Pg	Name	Specialty	Pg
Thomas, Vinoo (NY)	PM	299	Torbey, Marina (CT)	ObG	1006
Thomashow, Byron (NY)	Pul	360	Torman, Julie (NY)	Ge	676
Thompson, John (NY)	PGe	433	Tornos, Carmen (NY)	Path	640
Thomsen, Stephen (NJ)	Nep	839	Torrado-Jule, Carmen (NY)	PEn	528
Thorne, Charles (NY)	PlS	339	Torre, Arthur (NJ)	PA&I	823
Thornton, Raymond (NY)	VIR	402	Torre, Sabino (NJ)	IC	814
Thornton, Scott (CT)	CRS	980	Tortolani, Anthony (NY)	T&CS	494
Thung, Swan (NY)	Path	302	Tortoriello, Drew (NY)	RE	367
Thurm, Craig (NY)	Pul	514	Tostanoski, Jean (NY)	Oph	701
Tibaldi, Joseph (NY)	EDM	503	Toth, Patrick (NJ)	DR	753
Ticker, Jonathan (NY)	OrS	578	Touliopoulos, Steven (NY)	OrS	511
Tickoo, Roma (NY)	H & PM	193	Tozzi, Robert (NJ)	PCd	780
Tierney, Peter (NJ)	FMed	866	Trachtenberg, Jennifer (NY)	Ped	325
Tiger, Louis (NY)	Rhu	599	Trachtman, Howard (NY)	PNep	314
Tillem, Steven (NY)	U	516	Tracz, Michal (NY)	Nep	613
Timpone, Leonard (NY)	IM	561	Traeger, Eveline (NJ)	ChiN	949
Tindel, Nathaniel (NY)	OrS	284	Traister, Michael (NY)	Ped	325
Tindel-Kahn, Lori (NY)	Oph	700	Tranbaugh, Robert (NY)	T&CS	391
Ting, Andrew (NY)	PPul	316	Traquina, Diana (NJ)	PO	878
Ting, Jess (NY)	PlS	340	Traube, Charles (NY)	Cv	455
Tinger, Alfred (NY)	RadRO	722	Traube, Morris (NY)	Ge	179
Tiszenkel, Howard (NY)	CRS	501	Trauzzi, Stephen (NY)	U ·	730
Tiwari, Ram (NY)	Oph	429	Travis, William (NY)	Path	302
Tobias, Daniel (NJ)	GO	907	Treiber, Ruth (NY)	D	667
Tobias, Geoffrey (NJ)	Oto	778	Treiser, Susan (NJ)	RE	943
Tobias, Hillel (NY)	Ge	179	Trilling, Jeffrey (NY)	FMed	628
Todd, George (NY)	VascS	406	Trippett, Tanya (NY)	PHO	312
Tohme, Jack (NJ)	EDM	754	Trivedi, Gaurang (NY)	Oph	701
Tolchin, Joan (NY)	Psyc	353	Trooskin, Stanley (NJ)	S	883
Toles, Allen (NY)	ObG	572	Troy, Allen (CT)	OrS	1013
Tolston, Evelyn (NY)	A&I	123	Troy, Cathrine (CT)	IM	994
Tolunsky, Eugene (NY)	N	694	Troy, Kevin (NY)	Hem	192
Tom, Jack (NY)	D	625	Tsiouris, Simon (NJ)	Inf	761
Tomao, Frank (NY)	Onc	564	Tsong, Jerry (CT)	Oph	1010
Tomita, Sandra (NY)	PS	319	Tuchman, Alan (NY)	N	243
Toomey, Kathleen (NJ)	Onc	940	Tuckman, David (NY)	HS	557
Topilow, Arthur (NJ)	Hem	890	Tuerk-Mendelsohn, Lois (NY)	A&I	655
Topilow, Harvey (NJ)	Oph	775	Tugal, Oya (NY)	PHO	709
Toppmeyer, Deborah (NJ)	Onc	869	Tuhrim, Stanley (NY)	N	243

Name	Specialty	Pg
Tulla, Carlos (NY)	VIR	731
Turbin, Roger (NJ)	Oph	820
Turcios, Nelson (NJ)	PPul	941
Turecki, Stanley (NY)	ChAP	139
Turetsky, Arthur (CT)	Pul	1026
Turitto, Gioia (NY)	CE	452
Turk, Jon (NY)	Oto	580
Turk, Russell (CT)	ObG	1006
Turner, Ira (NY)	N	569
Turow, Victor (NY)	Ped	589
Turro, James (NY)	IM	685
Turtel, Andrew (NY)	OrS	285
Turtel, Lawrence (NJ)	Oph	894
Turtel, Penny (NJ)	Ge	889
Tuttle, R. Michael (NY)	EDM	166
Tyagi, Renuka (NY)	ObG	252
Tyberg, Theodore (NY)	Cv	135
Tyshkov, Michael (NJ)	PGe	960

U

Name	Specialty	Pg
Uday, Kalpana (NY)	Nep	425
Udell, Ira (NY)	Oph	575
Ugol, Jay (CT)	ObG	1007
Uhm, Kyudong (NJ)	Onc	927
Ullman, Joel (NY)	ObG	697
Ullman, Thomas (NY)	Ge	179
Umakanthan, Suganthini (NJ)	Ger	811
Underberg, James (NY)	IM	207
Underberg-Davis, Sharon (NJ)	DR	865
Unger, Allen (NY)	Cv	135
Unger, Walter (NY)	D	155
Unis, George (NY)	OrS	285
Unterricht, Sam (NY)	Oph	478
Urban, William (NY)	OrS	479
Uribarri, Jaime (NY)	Nep	228
Urken, Mark (NY)	Oto	296
Ushay, H Michael (NY)	PCCM	432
Uy, Vena (NJ)	ObG	840

V

Name	Specialty	Pg
Vad, Vijay (NY)	PMR	330
Vadasdi, Katherine (CT)	OrS	1013
Vadel, Shira (CT)	IM	994
Vahdat, Linda (NY)	Onc	224
Vaidya, Ami (NJ)	GO	759
Vaidya, Sudhir (NY)	SM	725
Vaillancourt, Philippe (NY)	PM	640
Valenza, Joseph (NJ)	PMR	918
Valinoti, Anne Marie (NJ)	IM	763
Vallarino, Ramon (NY)	PMR	512
Vallone, Ambrose (NY)	PCd	582
Vambutas, Andrea (NY)	Oto	580
Van Besien, Koen (NY)	Hem	192
Van Engel, Daniel (NJ)	N	771
van Gilder, Max (NY)	Ped	325
Van Slooten, David (NJ)	N	771
Van Zee, Kimberly (NY)	S	384
Vangvanichyakorn, Kamtorn (NJ)	NP	816
Vapnek, Jonathan (NY)	U	399
Vargas-Rodriguez, Ileana (NY)	PEn	307
Varlotta, Gerard (NY)	PMR	330
Varriale, Philip (NY)	Cv	135
Vas, George (NY)	N	474
Vassallo, Milo (NY)	A&I	452
Vasselli, Anthony (NJ)	U	857
Vastola, A Paul (NY)	Oto	480
Vasudeva, Kusum (NY)	ObG	572
Vates, Thomas (NJ)	Ped Uro	879
Vaughan, Margaret (NY)	Ger	677
Vazzana, Thomas (NY)	Cv	522
Vega, Aida (NY)	IM	207
Veksler-Offengenden, Irena (CT)	A&I	974
Velcek, Francisca (NY)	PS	319
Verga, Michele (NY)	PIS	340
Verma, Rajiv (NJ)	PCd	823
Versfelt, Mary (NY)	Ped	714
Vesole, David (NJ)	Hem	760

Alphabetical Listing of Doctors

Name	Specialty	Pg	Name	Specialty	Pg
Vester, John (NJ)	N	852	Volpi, David (NY)	Oto	296
Vialotti, Charles (NJ)	RadRO	791	Vukasin, Alexander (NJ)	U	857
Vicencio, Alfin (NY)	PPul	316	Vyas, Shefali (NJ)	PNep	824
Vickery, Carlin (NY)	PlS	340			
Vielemeyer, Ole (NY)	Inf	198			
Viennas, Stelios (NY)	Rhu	514			
Vietorisz, Esteban (CT)	Oph	1010	W		
Vietorisz, Tomas (CT)	Rhu	1029	Wachtel, Alan (NY)	Psyc	353
Vigario, Jose (NJ)	Ger	867	Wager, Marc (NY)	Ped	714
Vignesh, Shivakumar (NY)	Ge	462	Wager, Steven (NY)	Psyc	354
Vigorita, Vincent (NY)	Path	481	Wagle, Sharad (NJ)	Psyc	789
Villafranca, Manuel (NJ)	Psyc	963	Wagman, Raquel (NJ)	RadRO	829
Villongco, Raymond (NJ)	Ger	759	Wagner, Claudia (NJ)	FMed	952
Vincent, Julie (NY)	PCd	306	Wagner, Ira (NY)	CCM	145
Vincent, Miriam (NY)	FMed	460	Wagner, Rudolph (NJ)	Oph	820
Vinciguerra, Vincent (NY)	Onc	565	Wainstein, Sasha (NY)	U	494
Vine, Anthony (NY)	S	384	Waintraub, Stanley (NJ)	Onc	766
Vine, John (NJ)	D	864	Walczyk, John (NY)	D	549
Viner, Nicholas (CT)	U	1032	Wald, Leonard (NY)	DR	669
Vingan, Roy (NJ)	NS	770	Waldman, Seth (NY)	PM	299
Vintzileos, Anthony (NY)	MF	562	Waldorf, Donald (NY)	D	610
Violi, Caterina (CT)	ObG	1007	Waldorf, Heidi (NY)	D	610
Visconti, Ernest (NY)	Ped	529	Walfish, Jacob (NY)	IM	467
Viswanathan, Kusum (NY)	PHO	483	Walker, Audrey (NY)	ChAP	663
Viswanathan, Ramaswamy (NY)	Psyc	487	Walkup, John (NY)	ChAP	139
Vitale, Gerard (NY)	S	601	Wallach, Elizabeth (NY)	PEn	307
Vitale, Michael (NY)	OrS	285	Wallach, Frances (NY)	Inf	198
Vitting, Kevin (NJ)	Nep	928	Wallach, Robert (NY)	GO	185
Vivek, Seeth (NY)	Psyc	513	Wallach, Ronald (NY)	Cv	661
Voellmicke, Kurt (NY)	OrS	704	Wallack, Joel (NY)	Psyc	354
Vogel, James (NY)	Hem	192	Wallack, Marc (NY)	S	384
Vogel, Louis (NY)	D	155	Wallis, Joseph (NJ)	ObG	912
Vogel, Mitchell (NJ)	Oph	929	Wallis, Susan (NY)	Rhu	724
Vogelman, Arthur (NY)	Ge	504	Walser, Lawrence (NY)	Pul	646
Vogiatzi, Maria (NY)	PEn	307	Walsh, B. Timothy (NY)	Psyc	354
Vogl, Steven (NY)	Onc	424	Walsh, Christina (NJ)	Onc	891
Vohra, Nidhi (NY)	MF	563	Walsh, Christine (NY)	PCd	432
Volcovici, Guido (NY)	Pul	722	Walsh, Francis (CT)	IM	994
Volpe, Anthony (NJ)	IM	763	Walsh, Joseph (NY)	Oph	267
			Walsh, Peter (NY)	ChAP	139

Name	Specialty	Pg	Name	Specialty	Pg
Walsh, Raymond (NY)	OrS	479	Waye, Jerome (NY)	Ge	179
Walther, Robert (NY)	D	155	Wayne, Peter (NY)	Ge	676
Waltzer, Wayne (NY)	U	649	Waynik, Mark (CT)	Psyc	1024
Waner, Milton (NY)	Oto	296	Weber, Kaare (NY)	S	727
Wang, Beverly (NY)	Path	302	Weber, Pamela (NY)	Oph	638
Wang, Edward (NY)	HS	630	Weber, Richard (CT)	Oph	1010
Wang, Frederick (NY)	Oph	267	Wechsler, Amy (NY)	D	156
Wang, John (NY)	Nep	228	Wedderburn, Raymond (NY)	S	384
Wang, Julie (NY)	PA&I	303	Weg, Arnold (NY)	Ge	504
Wang, Timothy (NY)	Ge	179	Weg, Ira (NY)	Cv	545
Wangenheim, Paul (NJ)	Cv	806	Wehmann, Robert (NJ)	EDM	754
Wapner, Ronald (NY)	MF	212	Wei, Fong (NJ)	Nep	851
Ward, Barbara (CT)	S	1031	Weill, Terry (NY)	Psyc	354
Ward, David (NJ)	S	921	Wein, Michael (NY)	IM	685
Ward, Robert (NY)	PO	315	Wein, Paul (NY)	Cv	455
Wardlaw, Sharon (NY)	EDM	166	Weinberg, Gerard (NY)	PS	436
Warman, Jacob (NY)	EDM	459	Weinberg, Harold (NY)	N	243
Warner, Robert (NY)	D	156	Weinberg, Jeffrey (NY)	PMR	529
Warren, Floyd (NY)	Oph	268	Weinberg, Jerry (NY)	U	730
Warren, Michelle (NY)	RE	367	Weinberg, Marc (NY)	Cv	623
Warren, Russell (NY)	OrS	285	Weinberg, Martin (NJ)	Oph	775
Warren, Wendy (NJ)	MF	815	Weinberger, George (NJ)	D	950
Warshafsky, Stephen (NY)	IM	685	Weinberger, Jesse (NY)	N	243
Warshofsky, Mark (CT)	IC	996	Weinberger, Judah (NY)	IC	210
Wasnick, Robert (NY)	Ped Uro	642	Weinberger, Michael (NY)	PM	300
Wasser, Kenneth (NJ)	Rhu	897	Weinberger, Sylvain (NY)	Ped	326
Wasserheit, Carolyn (NY)	Onc	689	Weinblatt, Mark (NY)	PHO	585
Wasserman, Barry (NJ)	Oph	853	Weiner, David (NY)	U	399
Wasserman, Eric (CT)	Oph	1010	Weiner, Howard (NY)	NS	233
Wasserman, Gary (NJ)	U	798	Weiner, Kevin (NY)	PMR	529
Wasserman, Hal (CT)	IC	996	Weiner, Lon (NY)	OrS	285
Wasserman, Kenneth (NJ)	IM	763	Weiner, Michael (NY)	PHO	312
Wasserstein, Melissa (NY)	CG	142	Weiner, Richard (NY)	Ped	438
Waters, Cheryl (NY)	N	243	Weinerman, Stuart (NY)	EDM	459
Waters, Paul (CT)	T&CS	1031	Weinfeld, Steven (NY)	OrS	285
Waterstone, Melissa (NY)	ObG	252	Weingarten, Phyllis (NY)	Oph	614
Wattenberg, Debra (NY)	D	156	Weingarten-Arams, Jacqueline (NY)	PCCM	433
Wax, Michael (NJ)	Onc	955	Weinshel, David (CT)	IM	995
Waxenbaum, Steven (NJ)	CRS	750	Weinstein, David (CT)	ObG	1007

Alphabetical Listing of Doctors

Name	Specialty	Pg	Name	Specialty	Pg
Weinstein, Jay (NY)	IM	207	Weiss, Robert (NJ)	U	884
Weinstein, Joseph (NY)	Oph	575	Weiss, Steven (NJ)	A&I	804
Weinstein, Joshua (NY)	Rhu	442	Weissbrot, Jay (NY)	Ped	715
Weinstein, Larry (NJ)	PlS	919	Weissman, Gary (NY)	Ge	555
Weinstein, Mark (NY)	IM	561	Weissman, Ronald (NY)	Cv	661
Weinstein, Melvin (NJ)	Inf	868	Weisstuch, Joseph (NY)	Nep	228
Weinstein, Paul (CT)	Onc	1000	Weiswasser, Jonathan (NJ)	VascS	899
Weinstein, Richard (NY)	OrS	704	Weizman, Howard (NJ)	Nep	769
Weinstein, Samuel (NY)	T&CS	444	Wells, John (NY)	ChiN	141
Weinstein, Toba (NY)	PGe	584	Wells, Scott (NY)	PlS	340
Weinstock, Gary (NY)	A&I	540	Welsh, Howard (NY)	Psyc	354
Weintraub, Howard (NY)	Cv	136	Welshinger, Marie (NJ)	GO	867
Weintraub, Joshua (NY)	VIR	402	Weltz, Christina (NY)	S	385
Weintraub, Michael (NY)	N	694	Wenig, Bruce (NY)	Path	302
Weisbrot, Deborah (NY)	ChAP	623	Werner, Michael (NY)	U	731
Weiselberg, Lora (NY)	Onc	565	Wertheim, David (NY)	A&I	540
Weisenseel, Arthur (NY)	Cv	136	Wertheim, Iris (NY)	GO	678
Weiser, Kenneth (NY)	EDM	671	Wertheim, William (NY)	IM	632
Weiser, Martin (NY)	CRS	145	Weseley, Peter (NY)	Oph	268
Weiser, Robert (NY)	VascS	495	Westcott, Mark (NY)	VIR	402
Weiser, Todd (NY)	T&CS	728	Westreich, Laurence (NJ)	AdP	804
Weisholtz, Steven (NJ)	Inf	762	Westreich, Richard (NY)	Oto	296
Weiss, Carol (NY)	AdP	120	Westrich, Geoffrey (NY)	OrS	285
Weiss, Christopher (NJ)	Ped	786	Wetzler, Graciela (NY)	PGe	483
Weiss, Darryl (NJ)	D	752	Wexler, Craig (NY)	EDM	627
Weiss, Deborah (NY)	IM	632	Wexler, Leonard (NY)	PHO	312
Weiss, E Michael (NJ)	Cv	925	Wexler, Patricia (NY)	D	156
Weiss, Gabriella (NJ)	Inf	927	Wey, Philip (NJ)	PlS	880
Weiss, Jennifer (NJ)	PRhu	784	Whang, William (NY)	CE	125
Weiss, Jona (NY)	Ped	326	Whelan, Richard (NY)	CRS	145
Weiss, Jonathan (NY)	DR	669	Whelan, Thomas (CT)	Ge	987
Weiss, Louis (NY)	Inf	421	White, Ronald (NJ)	CRS	750
Weiss, Lyn (NY)	PMR	589	White, William (NY)	Oto	296
Weiss, Lynne (NJ)	PNep	878	Whiteson, Jonathan (NY)	PMR	330
Weiss, Melvin (NY)	IC	686	Whitley-Williams, Patricia (NJ)	PInf	878
Weiss, Michael (NY)	Oph	268	Whitman, Eric (NJ)	S	921
Weiss, Paul (NY)	PlS	340	Whitman, Gail (CT)	D	981
Weiss, Rita (NY)	Onc	565	Whitman, Hendricks (NY)	Rhu	373
Weiss, Robert (NY)	Ge	180	Whitmore, Wayne (NY)	Oph	268

Name	Specialty	Pg	Name	Specialty	Pg
Whyte, Dilys (NY)	PNep	642	Wisoff, Jeffrey (NY)	NS	233
Wickiewicz, Thomas (NY)	SM	376	Wisotsky, David (NJ)	Ped	786
Wickremesinghe, Prasanna (NY)	Ge	524	Wistinghausen, Birte (NY)	PHO	312
Widmann, Mark (NJ)	T&CS	922	Witt, Barry (CT)	RE	1028
Widmann, Roger (NY)	OrS	286	Witt, Marvin (NY)	IM	208
Wiesen, Mark (NJ)	EDM	754	Witte, Arnold (NJ)	N	852
Wilbur, Sabrina (NY)	CE	452	Wittig, James (NJ)	OrS	777
Wilchinsky, Mark (CT)	OrS	1014	Wiznia, Andrew (NY)	PA&I	431
Wild, David (NJ)	Cv	748	Wohlberg, Gary (NY)	Pul	646
Wilentz, James (NY)	IC	210	Wolchok, Jedd (NY)	Onc	224
Wilkenfeld, Marc (NY)	OM	572	Wolden, Suzanne (NY)	RadRO	363
Wilkin, Daniel (NJ)	FMed	755	Wolf, David (NY)	Ge	676
Williams, Ann (CT)	FMed	985	Wolf, David (NY)	Hem	193
Williams, Daniel (NY)	ChAP	545	Wolf, Edward (NJ)	MF	815
Williams, Gail (NY)	Nep	228	Wolf, Ellen (NY)	DR	415
Williams, Jill (NJ)	AdP	861	Wolf, Kenneth (NY)	Oph	429
Williams, Marcus (NJ)	Cv	748	Wolf, Steven (NY)	ChiN	141
Williams, Mathew (NY)	T&CS	391	Wolf-Klein, Gisele (NY)	Ger	556
Williams, Riley (NY)	SM	376	Wolfe, Lawrence (NY)	PHO	585
Williams, Shaun (CT)	RE	1028	Wolfe, Mary (NY)	IM	685
Willis, Andrew (NJ)	OrS	914	Wolfe, Scott (NY)	HS	188
Willner, Joseph (NJ)	N	771	Wolff, Edward (NY)	IM	561
Wilson, Thomas (NY)	PEn	640	Wolff, Steven (NY)	DR	161
Winchester, James (NY)	Nep	228	Wolfson, Robert (NY)	IM	685
Windsor, Russell (NY)	OrS	286	Wolk, Michael (NY)	Cv	136
Winfree, Christopher (NY)	NS	233	Wollack, Jan (NJ)	ChiN	863
Winslow, Robert (CT)	CE	975	Wolodiger, Fred (NJ)	VascS	799
Winston, Jonathan (NY)	Nep	228	Wong, Anthony (NY)	D	625
Winter, Robin (NJ)	FMed	866	Wong, Austin (NJ)	PCd	780
Winter, Stephen (CT)	Pul	1026	Wong, James (NJ)	RadRO	920
Winter, Steven (NY)	Cv	522	Wong, Raymond (NY)	Oph	268
Winterkorn, Jacqueline (NY)	Oph	511	Wong, Richard (NJ)	Oph	853
Winters, Richard (NY)	Psyc	354	Wong, Richard (NY)	Oto	297
Winters, Richard (NJ)	PlS	788	Woo, Henry (NY)	NS	635
Winters, Stephen (NJ)	CE	904	Woo, Peak (NY)	Oto	297
Wirz, Diane (CT)	N	1003	Wormser, Gary (NY)	Inf	680
Wisch, Nathaniel (NY)	Hem	193	Worth, David (NJ)	Rhu	964
Wishner, Jerald (NY)	CRS	664	Wright, Jason (NY)	GO	185
Wisnicki, H. Jay (NY)	Oph	268	Wrone, David (NJ)	D	864

Alphabetical Listing of Doctors

Name	Specialty	Pg	Name	Specialty	Pg
Wu, Jason (NY)	Ped	486	Yeh, Timothy (NJ)	PCCM	823
Wurm, Emanuel (NY)	Pul	722	Yellin, Joseph (NY)	N	474
Wurzel, Carol (NY)	Ped	715	Yi, Peter (NJ)	Onc	851
Wyner, Perry (NY)	Pul	596	Yiengpruksawan, Anusak (NJ)	S	794
Wysoki, Randee (NY)	ObG	697	Yip, Chun (NY)	Pul	360
Wyszynski, Bernard (NY)	Psyc	440	Yoo, Jinil (NY)	Nep	425
			Yoon, Sydney (NY)	DR	550
			Yorke, Eric (NJ)	Ped	942
X			Youm, Thomas (NY)	OrS	286
Xu, Bo (CT)	Path	1017	Youner, Craig (NY)	DR	502
Xu, Weizhen (NJ)	PEn	877	Young, Bruce (NY)	ObG	252
			Young, George (NY)	U	399
			Young, Joshua (NY)	Oph	269
			Young, Saryna (NY)	D	667
Y			Youngerman, Jay (NY)	Oto	580
Yablon, Steven (NY)	Nep	613	Youssef-Bessler, Manal (NJ)	Inf	813
Yablonsky, Thaddeus (NJ)	VIR	922	Yu, Yi-Hao (CT)	EDM	984
Yadegar, Daniel (NY)	Cv	136	Yudin, Howard (NY)	FMed	672
Yaffe, Bruce (NY)	IM	208	Yuen, Jeannette (NY)	Cv	661
Yagoda, Arnold (NY)	Oph	268	Yurt, Roger (NY)	S	385
Yahalom, Joachim (NY)	RadRO	363			
Yaker, Michael (NY)	Ped	326			
Yalamanchi, Krishan (NJ)	Ped	879	**Z**		
Yale, Suzanne (NY)	ObG	252			
Yamada, Yoshiya (NY)	RadRO	363	Zabin, Steven (NY)	Oph	701
Yamane, Michael (NJ)	IM	850	Zaccaria, Alan (NJ)	PlS	897
Yancovitz, Stanley (NY)	Inf	198	Zaffer, Imran (NY)	Ge	629
Yang, Edward (NY)	OrS	511	Zagzag, David (NY)	Path	302
Yang, Hee (NJ)	S	794	Zahtz, Gerald (NY)	Oto	580
Yang, Paul (NY)	VascS	406	Zaidi, Syed (NJ)	Psyc	789
Yang, Roger (NJ)	DR	937	Zaidman, Gerald (NY)	Oph	701
Yang, S Steven (NY)	HS	189	Zaim, Sina (NJ)	CE	743
Yankelevitz, David (NY)	DR	162	Zairis, Ignatios (NJ)	T&CS	795
Yankelowitz, Stanley (NY)	Oto	431	Zakashansky, Konstantin (NY)	GO	186
Yannuzzi, Lawrence (NY)	Oph	268	Zalkowitz, Alan (NJ)	Rhu	793
Yarberry-Allen, Patricia (NY)	ObG	252	Zaloom, Robert (NY)	Cv	455
Yasgur, David (NY)	OrS	704	Zalvan, Craig (NY)	Oto	706
Yee, Arthur (CT)	Inf	991	Zambetti, George (NY)	OrS	286
Yee, Arthur (NY)	Rhu	374	Zapiach, Luis (NJ)	PlS	788
Yegudin-Ash, Julia (NY)	Rhu	724	Zapolanski, Alex (NJ)	T&CS	795

Name	Specialty	Pg	Name	Specialty	Pg
Zarbin, Marco (NJ)	Oph	820	Zingale, Robert (NY)	S	648
Zaremski, Benjamin (NY)	IM	208	Zingler, Barry (NJ)	Ge	758
Zarich, Stuart (CT)	Cv	979	Zinkin, Lewis (NJ)	CRS	864
Zarnegar, Rasa (NY)	S	385	Zinkin, Noah (NY)	Ge	629
Zarowitz, William (NY)	IM	685	Zirvi, Monib (NJ)	D	950
Zauber, N Peter (NJ)	Hem	812	Zisfein, Jerome (NY)	IC	562
Zbar, Lloyd (NJ)	Oto	822	Zitsman, Jeffrey (NY)	PS	711
Zeale, Peter (NY)	IM	208	Zlatanic, Jusuf (NY)	Ge	180
Zeichner, Joshua (NY)	D	156	Zoland, Mark (NY)	S	385
Zeitels, Jerrold (NJ)	PlS	962	Zolkind, Neil (NY)	Psyc	719
Zeitlin, Alan (NY)	S	515	Zolkowski-Wynne, Joanna (CT)	AM	973
Zelazny, Daniel (NY)	SM	725	Zoltan, Irving (NY)	Ped	438
Zelefsky, Michael (NY)	RadRO	363	Zonenshayn, Martin (NY)	NS	472
Zelenetz, Andrew (NY)	Onc	224	Zonszein, Joel (NY)	EDM	416
Zelicof, Steven (NY)	OrS	704	Zornitzer, Michael (NJ)	Psyc	828
Zelkowitz, Richard (CT)	Onc	1000	Zou, Shengping (NY)	PM	300
Zellner, James (NY)	Oph	478	Zubowski, Robert (NJ)	PlS	788
Zelman, Warren (NY)	Oto	580	Zucker, Ira (NJ)	Ge	758
Zelop, Carolyn (NJ)	MF	764	Zucker, Mark (NJ)	Cv	806
Zeltser, Ross (NY)	D	667	Zucker, Michael (CT)	IM	995
Zeltsman, Vadim (NY)	T&CS	603	Zuckerman, Joseph (NY)	OrS	286
Zenenberg, Robert (NJ)	Nep	911	Zupnick, Henry (NY)	IM	561
Zerykier, Abraham (NY)	Oph	527	Zwas, Felice (CT)	Ge	988
Zevon, Scott (NY)	PlS	340	Zweibel, Lawrence (NY)	Oph	638
Zide, Barry (NY)	PlS	340	Zweibel, Stuart (NY)	D	667
Ziecheck, Wendy (NY)	IM	208	Zweifach, Philip (NY)	Oph	269
Ziegelbaum, Michael (NY)	U	605	Zweig, Susan (NY)	EDM	167
Ziering, Thomas (NJ)	FMed	937			
Zimbalist, Eliot (NY)	Ge	462			
Zimberg, Sheldon (NY)	Psyc	354			
Zimbler, Marc (NY)	Oto	297			
Zimmerman, Franklin (NY)	Cv	661			
Zimmerman, Gary (CT)	NS	1002			
Zimmerman, Jerald (NJ)	PMR	787			
Zimmerman, Marc (NY)	Onc	612			
Zimmerman, Mark (NJ)	Pul	963			
Zimmerman, Robert (NY)	NRad	245			
Zimmerman, Sol (NY)	Ped	326			
Zinaman, Michael (NY)	RE	441			

The Best in American Medicine
www.CastleConnolly.com

Acknowledgments

The publishers would like to thank the entire staff for their many hours and days of intense and precise work on this guide in order to further its goal of assisting consumers in making the best healthcare choices.

Castle Connolly Executive Management:

Chairman	John K. Castle
President & CEO	John J. Connolly, Ed.D.
Vice President, Chief Medical & Research Officer	Jean Morgan, M.D.
Vice President, Chief Strategy & Operations Officer	William Liss-Levinson, Ph.D.

Vice President, Advertising	Mark McGinty
Senior Research & Healthcare Associate	Maryann Hynd, RN

Research Coordinators

Terysia Browne	Cheri-Ann Parris
Najette Clarke	Zachary Preneta
Catherine Hoffman-Freiria	Maria Salvador
Nadina Horril	Mariadiep Vu
Yuliya Nagdimova	

Book Layout, Database Management	Russell Hodgson
Office Manager	Magda Spyridakis
Director of Client Relations & Research Operations	Nicki Hughes
Manager, Client Relations	Adam Akmal-Gonzalez

We also would like to extend our gratitude to the American Board of Medical Specialties (ABMS) for allowing us to use excerpts, especially the descriptions of medical specialties and subspecialties, from the text of their publication "Which Medical Specialist for You?"

Other Publications from Castle Connolly Medical Ltd.:
America's Top Doctors® and *America's Top Doctors*® *for Cancer*
Order online at http://www.castleconnolly.com/books

Corporate Membership for Corporations & Organizations

This service enables an employer to assist employees in identifying Top Doctors to care for themselves and their families. It is a low-cost, non-intrusive service that will result in better care and, ultimately, lower healthcare costs. For as low as a few dollars per year, employees can have complete access to the Castle Connolly website and database of Top Doctors who were nominated by their peers and screened by the Castle Connolly physician-led research team.

Instead of simply choosing a doctor's name from the phone book or a plan directory, the employee can compare physician names to the Castle Connolly database of 40,000 plus Top Doctors and select from among the best doctors in the country. This will result in overall better care, lower costs and improved morale. Once an employee logs on to the Castle Connolly database, valuable background information is available on every Top Doctor such as: medical school, board certifications, fellowships, hospital affiliations, residencies and much more, to allow them to make the best informed decision they can make when selecting a doctor.

Top Doctors can have an enormous impact. For patients and their families, the value of receiving first-class medical care is great but unquantifiable – it is measured in quality and even length of life. Employers, however, can see the results in their bottom line. Faulty diagnoses and improper treatment take a toll in productivity and ripple out into higher workplace costs. No company should have to "make do" for weeks or months without a key employee or executive, when a Top Doctor may have solved the patient's problem quickly and efficiently. The effort to identify the best doctors from ordinary ones is justified by the money saved on incorrect treatments, unnecessary surgery and days lost from work.

The Corporate Membership is suited for employers of varying sizes and can also be of great value to professional, social, civic, fraternal and religious associations. Castle Connolly may also be able to adapt and tailor the presentation of the database to meet the specific corporate client's needs.

New Movers Program

The Castle Connolly New Movers Program is designed to alleviate that concern, or even fear, as well as the time-consuming struggle to identify the right – and best – doctors and hospitals in one's new community or region. The service can be provided on a family basis (those living in the household) or for a single client. The service includes identifying primary care physicians, including Pediatricians, OB/GYN's, Internists and Family Practitioners as well as other specialists that may be needed: for example, Ophthalmologists, Allergists, Endocrinologists, Surgeons or others as required.

Perhaps nothing is more challenging to a family that has relocated to a new community than finding appropriate healthcare resources, especially physicians. While they can turn to recommendations from new neighbors and friends, or select names from the phone book or a plan directory, that is hardly adequate, especially if there are special healthcare needs in the family.

A Castle Connolly Health Advisor will identify two or three recommendations for up to six different medical specialties. If, for some reason the client wishes to change doctors within two months, Castle Connolly will identify new physicians in the same specialty. After the selection process occurs, the Health Advisor will make an introductory phone call to the physician's office. This typically facilitates faster appointments.

Healthcare Solutions

Castle Connolly's Healthcare Solutions is designed to help your employees and their loved ones navigate through the healthcare system with less stress, faster service and better outcomes. It is a high touch service with a hands-on health advocate to serve as a guide and dedicated healthcare champion 24 hours a day, 7 days a week, 365 days a year. Why have your most valued employees, your most critical asset, spend their time -- and possibly company time –coping with difficult and complex medical issues they may know little about, when Castle Connolly's Healthcare Solutions professionals can resolve them quickly and expertly. With one phone call, your employees will gain priority access to a global network of best-in-class medical professionals, Castle Connolly Top Doctors™, and higher quality patient resources. Our professional staff coordinates the entire process to provide consistency and support during their time of need.

Services include, but are not limited to, the following:

» Identifying top physicians and hospitals (nationally)

» Identifying reputable non-physician providers, such as Dieticians, Physical and Occupational Therapists, etc.

» Facilitating second opinions

» Defining complex medical terminology and situations

» Providing a list of tailored questions to discuss with your medical team

» Conducting medical research on your health condition

» Navigating the healthcare system

» Assisting with medical record retrieval and/or arranging a medical record review

» Identifying and assisting with eldercare issues

» Coordinating a hospital transfer

» Arranging medical transport or evacuation for travelers

» Coordinating with the employers' other vendors for continuity of care

Healthcare Solutions can be made available to your organization as a specific number of cases during the course of the year with the option to obtain more, or as a yearly retainer. Organizations may opt to make this service available for all of their employees, or to select groups such as high level executives or partners.

For further information on Healthcare Solutions, Corporate Membership, New Movers, and Doctor-Patient Advisor Program, please contact:

William Liss-Levinson, Ph.D.
Vice President, Chief Strategy &
Operations Officer.

Castle Connolly Medical Ltd.
42 West 24th Street, 2nd Floor
New York, NY 10010

212.367.8400 ext. 114
bliss-levinson@castleconnolly.com

Strategic Relationships

Castle Connolly Medical Ltd. has a number of strategic relationships that may be of interest to consumers and physicians.

Everyday Health, Inc. comprises some of the nation's leading online health information resources. With over 25 comprehensive health websites including www.EverydayHealth.com, www.Carepages.com, PDRHealth.com and www.WhatToExpect.com, information and knowledge is accessible on a wide range of health topics such as lifestyle offerings in pregnancy, diet and fitness to in-depth medical content for condition prevention and management.

MedPage Today is a trusted and reliable source for clinical and policy coverage that directly affects the lives and practices of health care professionals. Physicians and other healthcare professionals may also receive Continuing Medical Education (CME) credits at no cost for participating in MedPage Today hosted educational activities.

MedPage Today and Castle Connolly have partnered together to deliver breaking medical news, information related to clinical guidelines updates and implementation, clinical research studies and other medical breakthrough topics widely reported in the consumer media to Castle Connolly Top Doctors in a co-branded, daily e-newsletter. A team of experienced medical editors and writers at MedPage Today create the articles, and clinical content is reviewed and approved by a team of physicians under the direction of the Office of CME of the Perelman School of Medicine at the University of Pennsylvania.

For more information, please contact our Manager of Client Relations, Adam Akmal-Gonzalez, at (212) 367-8400 Ext. 123.

♥ sharecare

Sharecare is an interactive, social Q&A platform designed to greatly simplify the search for quality healthcare information and help consumers live their healthiest life. Sharecare has enlisted the nation's leading health experts, care providers, organizations, and brands to join the health and wellness conversation and empowering users with high-quality, relevant answers to their health questions from multiple expert perspectives and with interactive health and wellness tools to take action on what they've learned.

The website was launched in 2010 by Jeff Arnold, founder of WebMD, and Emmy–award winning host, Dr. Mehmet Oz, in partnership with Harpo Studios, Sony Pictures Television and Discovery Communications.

Castle Connolly teamed up with Sharecare in 2011. Dr. John Connolly, President and CEO of CCML, is one of the featured experts on Sharecare for healthcare choice questions. Find out more at www.sharecare.com

where consumers become patients

Vitals (www.vitals.com), an innovative online doctor review and comparison service from MDx Medical Inc., is the comprehensive source for vital information, peer evaluations and patient feedback on more than 700,000 doctors nationwide. Drawing upon prestigious information repositories, cutting-edge search and comparison technologies, and a robust patient feedback mechanism, Vitals has organized key information to help patients make an informed choice in their search for the right doctor. Castle Connolly and Vitals have a branding relationship in which those physicians who are Castle Connolly Top Doctors™ and appear on Vitals web sites have an icon indicating their status and recognition as a Castle Connolly Top Doctor.

In 2012, Castle Connolly will begin displaying insurance plans that are accepted by all physicians listed as Castle Connolly Top Doctors. An appointment scheduling feature will also appear on our site for those physicians who wish to participate in this feature. Additional information can be found at www.vitals.com.

LIFESTREAM MD

Castle Connolly Medical Ltd. has a strategic relationship with Castle Connolly LifeStream MD to provide a unique health advisory service designed for families and executives, especially those who travel regularly or may have more than one residence.

Each client is assigned a Castle Connolly LifeStream MD physician who is available to them by phone 24/7/365. A client call from anywhere in the world is answered promptly and the client is connected with their Castle Connolly LifeStream MD physician advisor.

The Castle Connolly LifeStream MD physician acts as a health manager assisting in navigation of an increasingly complex health care environment. The Castle Connolly LifeStream MD physician does not replace the member's primary physician or specialists, but provides additional independent counsel and services that provide security to our members either at home or while traveling.

In the United States, the Castle Connolly LifeStream MD physician will use the Castle Connolly database of Top Doctors to assure that the client is cared for in the best medical facilities by the top doctors. Assistance in securing timely appointments with specialists and records transfers is facilitated as needed. Outside of the United States, Castle Connolly LifeStream MD has an affiliation with International SOS, the world's largest and leading provider of travel medical assistance to assure the LifeStream MD member is cared for by the best doctors and hospitals available in that region or, if necessary, is transported to a place where that care is available.

For more information, please visit www.lifestreammd.com.

EMPOWERED DOCTOR

Empowered Doctor is a media, news and marketing service. Empowered Doctor produces syndicated consumer health reports. Its video and text news stories appear on major media websites, including CBS. Empowered Doctor also provides marketing services to hospitals, clinics and individual physicians by generating visibility in online search and social media. Empowered Doctor's clients benefit from the company's efficient methodologies for generating new patient referrals.

For more information call 888-333-1027 or visit www.empowereddoctor.com

DrScore.com
PATIENTS SPEAK, DOCTORS LISTEN

Founded by Steven Feldman, M.D., DrScore.com is an interactive online survey site where patients can rate their physicians, as well as find a physician based on their service level preference.

The mission of DrScore.com is to improve medical care by giving patients a forum for rating their physician and by giving doctors an affordable, objective, non-intrusive means of documenting the quality of care that they provide. Visitors on Castle Connolly's website who are searching for "top doctors" have the option to also rate these and other physicians they have been to as patients, as well as to see if these physicians have been rated previously by other consumers on DrScore.com. Visitors to DrScore.com will be able to see if their doctors and/or other doctors are Castle Connolly "top doctors."

For more information, visit www.drscore.com.

grandparents.com®
it's great to be grand.

Grandparents.com is dedicated to enhancing the lives of America's 70 million grandparents by fostering family connections, via child- and grandparent-friendly activities, travel ideas, compelling lifestyle features, expert advice, gift ideas, recipes, and more. Visitors have access to a range of tools, including groups, discussions, a homepage blog, photo sharing, and a Facebook page and Twitter feeds. Through the Grandparents.com Grand Deals page members can receive discounts and incentives they can use every day, in categories like gifts, clothes, and vitamins, plus exclusive opportunities to save on hotels, cruises, auto rentals, theme park trips, theatrical productions, and insurance. Grandparents can share their membership benefits with four extended family and household members. In 2010, Grandparents.com was ranked as the No. 3 website for seniors, boomers, and grandparents, following the U.S. Government and AARP. Castle Connolly provides access to its Top Doctors' database, its Doctor-Patient Advisor and New Movers programs for Grandparents.com members.

ConsumerMedical™ ⟴

Your GPS for Healthcare™

ConsumerMedical was started in 1996 to offer high-quality, high-impact employee benefit programs to help employees and their dependents, and has been a pioneer in Medical Decision Support® services. CMR addresses all medical conditions at any point within the continuum of care, by providing personalized, evidence-based medical research, information, access to genuine, in-person second opinions and support services to employees who face serious, complicated, and chronic illness, or would like to become well-informed healthcare consumers.

Leveraging a state-of-the-art integrated model of web, phone, and print-based services, CMR enables employees to fully understand and evaluate their options so they can make the most informed medical decisions possible with their doctors. The company is privately held and currently provides services to more than 750,000 Americans, achieving extremely high levels of user and customer satisfaction, improved clinical quality outcomes, and generated excellent ROI.

Castle Connolly and CMR are working together to provide Castle Connolly's various corporate services to CMR client companies and their employees.

For more information, please visit: www.consumermedical.com.

Castle Connolly Private Health Partners, LLC (CCPHP) is a national network of the finest and most exceptional physicians offering a unique opportunity to work among the very best in concierge medicine focused on uncompromised quality. CCPHP partners with top physicians in a joint ownership arrangement to adopt, deploy and support a patient membership practice model promoting high quality healthcare. By leveraging a proven, proprietary conversion methodology and a successful service strategy, CCPHP supports both physicians and patients in a retainer-based medical practice so that they can enjoy the advantages of unrushed and patient-centered care.

The CCPHP concierge medicine model offers patients who value greater attention to their health increased care, connectivity and convenience to their primary physician. Among the amenities and enhancements are extended office visits, same-day or next-day scheduling, collaborative health planning, coordinated primary and specialist physician care, health coaching and wellness programs, enhanced, personalized follow-up and periodic check-ins, reduced use of specialty and ED care, 24/7 availability, telemedicine / virtual visits and house calls (in some practices).

Among the advantages that physicians see from partnership with CCPHP are enhancing relationship with, and ability to serve, each patient, reducing administrative burdens, reducing office expenses, maintaining ownership and control of practice, offering flexibility in programs appropriate for physician's and patients' preferences, and Increasing long term stability in their practice outlook.

Through its partner physicians, CCPHP presents a unique, customizable concierge practice model and on-going support providing tangible patient benefits that have been documented in recent medical studies and experience surveys. Such benefits include stronger physician-patient relationships, improved health status, improved confidence and ability to self-manage their health through dynamic health coaching and other robust tools, and reduced use of specialty and emergency care.

For more information, please contact Jerry Stanley at jstanley@ccphp.net.

National Physician of the Year Awards

Castle Connolly Medical Ltd. proudly hosted its ninth annual ***National Physician of the Year Awards*** on March 31, 2014 at The Pierre Hotel in New York City. It was a spectacular evening which allowed us to recognize both the outstanding honorees and the excellence of the many thousands of physicians throughout the nation.

The Genesis of the National Physician of the Year Award.

Each year we receive thousands of nominations from physicians and the medical leadership of major medical centers, specialty hospitals, teaching hospitals and regional and community medical centers across the United States as an integral part of our research, screening and selection process to identify ***America's Top Doctors***®. The selected physicians, while spread across all fifty states and involved in more than 70 medical specialties and subspecialties, all share one distinguishing professional attribute: an unwavering dedication to their patients and to medicine as a whole. Each and every one of these outstanding medical professionals is a symbol of the clinical excellence that characterizes American medicine. In honor of these exemplary physicians, Castle Connolly Medical Ltd. has created the ***National Physician of the Year Awards*** to recognize the thousands of excellent, dedicated physicians across the United States. Our Medical Advisory Board selected the honorees from the hundreds nominated in a special nomination process conducted months before the event.

The honorees, Drs. Susan B. Bressman, Catherine R. deVries, and Michael S. Saag, are superb examples of excellence in clinical medical practice. In addition to these awards for Clinical Excellence, Castle Connolly Medical Ltd. honored Drs. Victor Fazio and Hagop M. Kantarjian for their lifetime achievement in medicine. Dr. Mehmet and Lisa Oz, founders of HealthCorps and exemplary recipients for the ninth National Health Leadership Award.

Each honoree received a beautiful and distinctive porcelain figurine created by the Boehm Porcelain Company exclusively for the National Physician of the Year Awards. The award features a golden caduceus, the symbol of the medical community, surrounded by a golden laurel wreath. Laurel wreaths were used by the ancients to crown and honor their leaders.

The caduceus and laurel rest upon a column accented by the signature Castle Connolly logo. By combining the caduceus and the laurel wreaths, the award embodies the excellence in medical achievement that the National Physician of the Year Awards celebrates each year.

2014 National Physician of the Year Awards Honorees

"Top Doctors Make a Difference™"

For Clinical Excellence

Susan B. Bressman, MD.
Alan and Joan Mirken Chair
Departments of Neurology, Mount Sinai Beth Israel, Mount Sinai St. Luke's
and Mount Sinai Roosevelt
Professor of Neurology, Icahn School of Medicine, Mount Sinai

Catherine R. deVries, M.D.
Professor of Surgery, University of Utah
Director, University of Utah Center for Global Surgery
University of Utah Health Care and Primary Children's Hospital

Michael S. Saag, M.D.
Professor of Medicine
and director of the UAB Center for AIDS Research (CFAR)
University of Alabama at Birmingham

For Lifetime Achievement

Victor Fazio, M.D.
Chairman Emeritus
Digestive Disease Institute
Department of Colorectal Surgery
Cleveland Clinic

Hagop M. Kantarjian, M.D.
Department Chair, Department of Leukemia,
Division of Cancer Medicine
Research Chair, Department of Leukemia,
Division of Cancer Medicine
The University of Texas MD Anderson Cancer Center

National Health Leadership

Dr. Mehmet Oz
Host: The Dr. Oz Show, best-selling author, Founder of HealthCorps

Lisa Oz
Host: The Lisa Oz Show, best-selling author, Founder of HealthCorps

2013 National Physician of the Year Awards Honorees

"Top Doctors Make a Difference™"

For Clinical Excellence

Gopal Badlani, M.D.
Professor and Vice Chair for Clinical Affairs
Department of Urology
Wake Forest Baptist Medical Center

Jo A. Hannafin, M.D., Ph.D.
Hospital for Special Surgry
Professor of Orthopaedic Surgery
Weill Cornell Medical College

Jerry A. Shields, M.D.
Professor of Ophthalmology
Thomas Jefferson University
Director, Oncology Service
Wills Eye Institute

For Lifetime Achievement

Michael R. Harrison, M.D.
Professor Emeritus of Surgery, Pediatrics,
Obstetrics, Gynecology & Reproductive Sciences
Founding Director, Fetal Treatment Center
University of California, San Francisco

Sterling Williams, M.S., M.D., Ph.D.
Clinical Professor of Obstetrics & Gynecology
George Washington University Medical School
Vice President of Education
American College of Obstetricians & Gynecologists

National Health Leadership

Dawn Halfaker
President and CEO
Halfaker and Associated, LLC
President, Board of Directors, Wounded Warrior Project

2012 National Physician of the Year Awards Honorees

"Top Doctors Make a Difference™"

For Clinical Excellence

Richard Edelson, M.D.
Aaron B. and Marguerite Lerner Professor
Chairman of the Department of Dermatology
Yale School of Medicine.

Susan Mackinnon, M.D.
Chief of Plastic and Reconstructive Surgery
Washington University School of Medicine

John M. Morton, M.D., M.P.H., F.A.C.S.
Associate Professor of Surgery
Stanford University
Chief of Minimally Invasive Surgery,
Director of Bariatric Surgery and Surgical Quality

For Lifetime Achievement

Robert L. Brent, M.D., Ph.D., D.Sc.
Distinguished Professor of Pediatrics, Radiology and Pathology
Louis and Bess Stein Professor of Pediatrics at the Jefferson Medical College
and the Nemours/Alfred I. DuPont Hospital for Children

John G. Clarkson, M.D.
Dean Emeritus and Professor of Ophthalmology
Anne Bates Leach Eye Hospital/Bascom Palmer Eye Institute
Department of Ophthalmology
Miller School of Medicine at the University of Miami

National Health Leadership

Marlo Thomas
National Outreach Director
St. Jude Children's Research Hospital

2011 National Physician of the Year Awards Honorees

"Doctors Make a Difference"

For Clinical Excellence

Armando E. Giuliano, M.D., FACS, FRCSED
Chief of Science and Medicine
John Wayne Cancer Institute at Saint John's Health Center,
Santa Monica, CA

O. Wayne Isom, M.D.
Chairman of the Dept. of Cardiothoracic Surgery
New York Presbyterian-Weill Cornell Medical College

David W. Kennedy, M.D.
Otorhinolaryngology Professor at the
University of Pennsylvania

For Lifetime Achievement

George P. Canellos, M.D.
Served as Founding Chief of Medical Oncology at
Dana-Farber Cancer Institute;

Matthew D. Davis, M.D.
University of Wisconsin Medical Center
Chair, UW Opthalmology

National Health Leadership

Evelyn H. Lauder
Chairman of The Breast Cancer Research Foundation®

2010

Clinical Excellence
John B. Buse, M.D., Ph.D.
Director of the Diabetes Care Center, Professor, Chief of the Division of
Endocrinology and Executive Associate Dean for Clinical Research,
University of North Carolina School of Medicine, Chapel Hill

Larry Norton, M.D.
Deputy Physician-in-Chief, Memorial Hospital, Memorial Sloan-Kettering
Cancer Center, for Breast Cancer Programs
Medical Director of the MSKCC's Breast and Imaging Center, Evelyn H.
Lauder Breast Center

Ching-Hon Pui, M.D.
Department Chair of Oncology, St. Jude Children's Research Hospital
Medical Director of the St. Jude International Outreach China Program,
holder of the Fahad Nassar Al-Rashid Chair of Leukemia Research

Lifetime Achievement
Basil I Hirschowitz, M.D.
Director, Gastroenterology Division, The University of Alabama
Receipient of the Kettering Medal from the General Motors Cancer
Foundation; Friedenwald Medal of the AGA; the Schindler Medal and the
Crystal Award for lifetime contributions to Endoscopy by the ASGE;
honorary doctorate of Gothenburg University; honorary fellow of the Royal
Society of Medicine

Leonard Apt, M.D.
Professor of Ophthalmology Emeritus; Director Emeritus and Founder of
the Division of Pediatric Opthalmology and Strabismus, and Co-Director of
UCLA's Center for Child Blindness

National Health Leadership
Alexandra Reeve Givens and Matthew Reeve
Trustees, The Christopher & Dana Reeve Foundation

2009

Clinical Excellence
Carol R. Bradford, M.D.,
Professor and Chair
Department of Otolaryngology
University of Michigan Medical System

Diane E. Meier, M.D.,
Director, Center to Advance Palliative Care
Mount Sinai School of Medicine

Judd W. Moul, M.D.,
Chief of Urology
Duke University Medical Center

Lifetime Achievement
Emil J. Freireich, M.D., D. Sc. (Hon.),
Ruth Harriet Ainsworth Chair, Distinguished Teaching Professor
Director, Special Medical Education Programs
Director, Adult Leukemia Research Program
The University of Texas M.D. Anderson Cancer Center

Thomas E. Starzl, M.D., Ph.D.
Professor of Surgery, Emeritus
Distinguished Service Professor
University of Pittsburgh Medical Center

National Health Leadership
Page Morton Black
Chairman of the Board, Parkinson's Disease Foundation

****

2008

Clinical Excellence
Robert W. Carlson, M.D.
Medical Oncology
Stanford University Medical Center

Stanley Chang, M.D.
Ophthalmology
New York-Presbyterian Hospital

L. Dade Lunsford, M.D.
Neurological Surgery
University of Pittsburgh Medical Center

Lifetime Achievement
Jacqueline A. Noonan, M.D.
Pediatric Cardiology
University of Kentucky Medical Center

Robert W. Schrier, M.D.
Nephrology
University of Colorado Health Sciences Center

National Health Leadership
Suzanne and Robert Wright
Vice-Chair of the Board, General Electric Company
Co-founders of Autism Speaks™

****

2007

Clinical Excellence
Delos M. Cosgrove, M.D.
Chairman, Board of Governors
CEO and President
The Cleveland Clinic

Joseph G. McCarthy, M.D.
Lawrence D. Bell Professor of Plastic Surgery
Director, The Institute of Reconstructive Plastic Surgery
NYU Medical Center

Patrick C. Walsh, M.D.
University Distinguished Service Professor and Director of Urology
The James Buchanan Brady Urological Institute
The Johns Hopkins Hospital

Lifetime Achievement
Maria Delivoria-Papadopoulos, M.D.
Director, The Neonatal Intensive Care Unit
St. Christopher's Hospital for Children;
Professor of Pediatrics, Physiology and Obstetrics/Gynecology
Drexel University College of Medicine

National Health Leadership
The Honorable Nancy G. Brinker
Founder of Susan G. Komen for the Cure
Former U.S. Ambassador to Hungary

****

2006

Clinical Excellence
Bart Barlogie, M.D., Ph.D.
Director, Myeloma Institute for Research Therapy
University of Arkansas for Medical Services

Marilyn J. Bull, M.D.
Morris Green Professor of Pediatrics
Riley Hospital for Children

Michael J. Zinner, M.D.
Moseley Professor of Surgery
Harvard Medical School
Surgeon-in-Chief, Brigham & Women's Hospital

Lifetime Achievement
Michael E. DeBakey, M.D.
Chancellor Emeritus, Baylor College of Medicine

National Health Leadership
Princess Yasmin Aga Khan
Honorary Vice Chair
Alzheimer's Association

Castle Connolly maintains Facebook, Twitter, LinkedIn and Sharecare accounts in an effort to keep consumers informed of the latest news not only regarding Castle Connolly Medical Ltd., its Top Doctors and Top Hospitals, but also reports on various health observances and events. A live Twitter feed can also be found on the homepage of www.castleconnolly.com.

Consumers who use our print guides, online database or refer to our regional magazine features can find up-to-date information about Castle Connolly, healthcare and medical news by logging onto these social networking sites:

www.facebook.com/TopDoctors

Blog - Ask America's Top Doctors™
www.castleconnolly.com/blog

www.twitter.com/CastleConnolly

http://linkd.in/mP4Lmb (case sensitive)

Do you have a story about a Castle Connolly Top Doctor or Top Hospital that you want to share? If so, please email a link to the article to:

Diep Vu
Senior Research Associate & Social Media Coordinator
mvu@castleconnolly.com

Doctor-Patient Advisor for Individual Consumers

Doctor-Patient Advisor is a Castle Connolly Medical Ltd. service providing one-on-one consultations with a physician or nurse practitioner to individuals who have serious or complex medical problems or to anyone who feels he/she needs assistance finding the right physician for any purpose. Each client will receive personalized assistance in identifying the appropriate specialists for his/her condition, utilizing the Castle Connolly Medical Ltd. database of physicians and hospitals, as well as individual searches, to locate the best resources to meet the client's needs.

Fee: $375. For further information call (212) 367-8400 x 116.

Premium Membership to www.CastleConnolly.com

Reap the benefits of membership with Castle Connolly. Gain access to ALL online top doctor listings and get discounts on book purchases from our extensive catalog.

• Search among more than 40,000 Castle Connolly Top Doctor listings
• Search among select hospitals and centers of excellence
• Receive a 30% discount on all book purchases

Membership Levels:
• Monthly - $1.99
• One year - $24.95
• Two years - $34.95

For more information visit: www.CastleConnolly.com/membership

Other Products From Castle Connolly

Castle Connolly Guides
Titles Include:
- *America's Top Doctors*®
- *America's Top Doctors*® *for Cancer*

And Many More

To order other Castle Connolly guides at a 15% discount please visit

http://www.CastleConnolly.com/books

When ordering use discount code: **NY18DOM**

Castle Connolly's Top Doctors Available Online
- Free Access to 20 -25% of Castle Connolly's Top Doctors
- Purchase Access to the entire database of more than 40,000 doctor profiles

http://www.castleconnolly.com/membership

Customer Feedback

We appreciate your comments regarding our guides. Please email us at info@castleconnolly.com

The Best in American Medicine
www.CastleConnolly.com

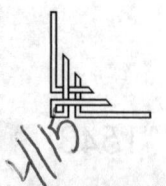